INCOME-RELATED BENEFITS: THE LEGISLATION

1999 EDITION

Commentary By

Penny Wood, LL.B., M.Sc.
Solicitor, Part-Time Chairman,
Social Security Appeal Tribunals

Consultant Editor and
Original Commentary By

John Mesher, B.A., B.C.L., LL.M.
Barrister, Professor Associate of Law,
University of Sheffield

LONDON
SWEET & MAXWELL
1999

Published in 1999 by
Sweet & Maxwell Limited of
100 Avenue Road,
London NW3 3PF.
Computerset by Wyvern 21 Ltd, Bristol.
Printed in England
Clays Ltd, St Ives plc.

No natural forests were destroyed to make this product.
Only farmed timber was used and re-planted.

A catalogue record for this book is
available from the British Library

A CIP catalogue record for this book is available from the British Library

ISBN 0 421 702 508 ✓

FOREWORD TO THE 1999 EDITION

No-one working in the field of means tested benefits could manage without "*Mesher*". It conveniently and comprehensively gathers in one place all the statutory material and comments upon it authoritatively and lucidly.

By the end of November 1999, all the provisions of the Social Security Act 1998, and regulations made pursuant to it, will have been brought into effect in respect of all benefits. Until that time some benefits will be governed by the old procedures and some by the new. I wish everyone the best of good fortune in navigating this transitional period. Calm blue seas will, I hope, lie beyond it.

Meanwhile this book will continue to provide the mainstay that all practitioners have come to expect of it. I extend a warm welcome to this edition.

His Honour Judge Michael Harris
President of the ITS/TAS

July 1999

PREFACE

During the course of 1999 the new system of decision-making and appeals heralded by the Social Security Act 1998 will be brought into force on a phased basis. The stated policy intention is to improve the processes for decisions and appeals; the chosen measures include simplifying the arrangements for first-tier decision-making by having all decisions taken in the name of the Secretary of State (thus abolishing the independent status of adjudication officers), replacing the concept of review with provisions for "revising" and "superseding" decisions, reducing the time limit for appeal to one month, and allowing tribunals to consist of one, two or three members, depending on the nature of the appeal. In addition, the Independent Tribunal Service is to be replaced by a new agency called the Appeals Service and the functions of the five separate tribunals (society security appeal tribunals, disability appeal tribunals, medical appeal tribunals, child support appeal tribunals and vaccine damage tribunals) are to be transferred to a single unified appeal tribunal. Although some of the changes made by the 1998 Act are already in force (most notably that for appeals lodged on or after May 21, 1998 tribunals are restricted to considering only the circumstances existing at the date of the decision under appeal and that a SSAT may consist of one, two or three members), the decision was taken to implement the main adjudication and appeal changes at different times for different benefits. The transitional and savings provisions for each benefit will be set out in a series of commencement orders. For the benefits covered by this book the new arrangements will take effect from October 5, 1999 for family credit and disability working allowance, October 18, 1999 for jobseeker's allowance and November 29, 1999 for income support and social fund payments (see reg. 1(2) of the Social Security and Child Support (Decisions and Appeals) Regulations 1999 (S.I. 1999 No. 991)).

This means that the legislation relating to the new provisions for decisions and appeals will appear in the 1999 Supplement to this book, since the pattern of previous editions has been followed of adopting "up-rating day" (April 12, 1999) as the cut-off point for inclusion of statutory materials. However, where possible a note has been included in the annotations to indicate the main provisions of the Administration Act and the Adjudication Regulations that will be affected by the changes. For the moment the annotations throughout the book continue to refer to "AOs" and "SSATs" but these should be read as references to the "Secretary of State" and "appeal tribunals" respectively when the Social Security Act 1998 comes fully into effect. In addition, the 1999 Supplement will contain the legislation relating to the introduction of working families tax credit and disabled person's tax credit due to replace family credit and disability working allowance on October 5, 1999. Readers should also note that a new set of regulations governing appeals to the Social Security Commissioners came into force on June 1, 1999 (see the Social Security Commissioners (Procedure) Regulations 1999 (S.I. 1999 No. 1495)).

No doubt due to the fact that the focus has been on bringing the new decision-making and appeals system into operation, the changes to the substantive legislation covered by this book have been fewer than usual this year. There have, however, been various, largely beneficial, amendments, for example, those necessitated by the continuing development of the Government's various "New Deal" programmes, the introduction of a disregard of payments received under so-called "creditor insurance" policies, and changes in the rules for offsetting of child care expenses in family credit and disability working allowance to allow charges that will be incurred during the period of an award, as well as

vii

those that are being incurred at the date of claim, to be taken into account. Note also the Government's acceptance (following *CIS 3283/1997*) that a share in jointly-owned property should be given its true market value, rather than a deemed value by reference to the value of the property as a whole (see the notes to reg. 52 of the Income Support Regulations). In addition, there have been some developments in the wake of the 1998 Act, see, for example, the substitution of a new reg. 37A of the Claims and Payments Regulations allowing for the suspension of payment of benefit pending the outcome of a test case and the continuing transfer of SSAT work to a chairman sitting alone, culminating in all appeals heard by a SSAT being dealt with by a one person tribunal from October 1, 1999 (see President's Circulars Nos 14, 16 and 17). Perhaps, however, some of the more important developments this year have been in the case-law arena. For example, the provisions affecting school ancillary workers and students continue to be fertile areas of challenge, as does the "all work test" and other issues associated with assessing a person's incapacity for work, although the stream of Commissioners' decisions on the latter has reduced to a steady trickle. The first decisions on the contentious late claim provisions in reg. 19 of the Claims and Payments Regulations are also beginning to emerge. But the most startling development has undoubtedly been in relation to the habitual residence test and in particular the Government's response to the ECJ's decision's in *Swaddling v. Adjudication Officer* (see the notes to reg. 21(3) of the Income Support Regulations).

The main objective of this book remains unaltered. Its purpose is to bring together the legislation, both Acts of Parliament and regulations, governing cases which could come before an appeal tribunal in income support, income-based JSA, family credit and social fund (maternity and funeral expenses and cold weather payments) appeals and on certain aspects of disability working allowance claims. In addition, Social Fund Directions given by the Secretary of State and Circulars to appeal tribunals issued by the President of the Independent Tribunal Service (ITS) (to become the Appeals Service) are included. The book does not deal with all the income-related benefits contained in the Social Security Contributions and Benefits Act 1992. Housing benefit and council tax benefit are excluded. The legislation on these benefits, with a full commentary, can be found in Findlay, Poynter, Stagg and Ward, *CPAG's Housing Benefit and Council Tax Benefit: the legislation.*

The book similarly continues to be structured in broadly the same way as earlier editions. It is divided into eight parts: I. Benefits Acts; II. Income Support; III. Jobseeker's Allowance; IV. Family Credit; V. Disability Working Allowance; VI. The Social Fund; VII. Adjudication and Administration; and VIII. President's Circulars. Parts II to VI contain no Acts of Parliament. The Social Security Contributions and Benefits Act 1992 in Part I deals with entitlement to income support, family credit, disability working allowance and the social fund and the Jobseekers Act does the same in relation to jobseeker's allowance. The sections of the Child Support Act 1991 dealing with reduced benefit directions (which can be applied to income support, income-based JSA, family credit or disability working allowance) and deductions from income support or income-based JSA as a contribution towards child maintenance are also included in Part I. Parts VII and VIII contain the Social Security Administration Act 1992, the Social Security (Consequential Provisions) Act 1992 (which has provisions on the effects of the consolidation process in 1992), those parts of the Social Security Act 1998 that have so far come into force, the regulations on claims, payments and adjudication and the President's Circulars.

The text of all the legislation is set out as amended and in force on April 13, 1999 (although it has also been possible to include the Income Support (General) (Standard Interest Rate Amendment) (No. 5) Regulations 1999 (S.I. 1999 No. 1411) (in force June 20, 1999). All of the text has amendments and definitions noted. Under the "AMENDMENT" heading at the end of each section, regulation or Schedule is a numbered note referring to any amending provision with the date on which the amendment came into force. Where a provision contains a reference to a statute as it existed before the 1992 consolidation a note in square brackets immediately follows it showing the location of the reference in the consolidating legislation. The Contributions and Benefits Act is abbreviated as "SSCBA" and the Administration Act as "SSAA". See section 2(4) of the Consequential Provisions Act for the meaning of such references from July 1, 1992 (the date on which the consolidating legislation came into force) onwards. The old legislation of course remains relevant in relation to periods before July 1, 1992. After each section of the consolidating legislation is a "DERIVATION" heading showing which part of the old legislation has gone into the new provision. There are also Tables of Destinations near the front of the book showing in broad outline where provisions of the Social Security Act 1975 and the Social Security Act 1986 can be found in the consolidating legislation. It is hoped that this gives enough information for readers to continue to be able to work backwards and forwards between the old and the new legislation (when this is still necessary).

Apart from the updating, rewriting and correcting process and the incorporation of material contained in the 1998 Supplement, decisions of the courts and the Social Security Commissioners given up to about the end of June 1999 have been taken into account.

I continue to enjoy the generous consultative support and assistance of John Mesher, for which I am extremely grateful. But I should stress that I remain solely responsible for the contents of this edition (as I have been for the previous five editions), and in particular for any views expressed. CPAG's support and co-operation, in particular through their former legal officer (now consultant solicitor), David Thomas, Peter Ridpath in their publications department, and Martin Barnes, their Director, has also continued unabated. In addition I want to thank Les Allamby, Simon Cox, Carolyn George, Beth Lakhani, Chris Orr, Simon Osborne, Earl Piggott-Smith, Richard Poynter, Mary Shirley, Djuna Thurley, Jill Walker and those at Sweet and Maxwell who have been involved in the production of this book, for their assistance. I am also particularly grateful to those Social Security Commissioners and others who have sent me copies of decisions. As always, essential parts of the book result from information and cooperation from both DSS and ITS officials. Their help is particularly vital in ensuring that the book is as up to date as possible. However, all the comments in the book are made in a personal capacity and are in no way "official" or endorsed by the Independent Tribunal Service. Nor do the views expressed necessarily coincide with those of CPAG.

I warmly welcome comments from readers pointing out errors, omissions or the need for clarification. These should be sent to me c/o Sweet and Maxwell, 100 Avenue Road, London NW3 3PF.

This is the last year that this book will appear in this form. In 2000 it is planned to amalgamate this book with *Bonner, Non-Means Tested Benefits: the Legislation* and *Rowland, Medical Appeals Tribunals: the Legislation* to form a new three volume publication covering the main areas of the new Appeals Service's jurisdiction (apart from child support). Apart from an enforced weeding out of some of the older historical sections in the annotations, this should also provide the opportunity, long overdue, for the book's size (and weight) to be reduced. In the meantime, however, I hope that, despite its bulk, this book will continue to be of practical assistance both to those who advise claimants and to those who adjudicate on their claims and appeals.

Penny Wood

CONTENTS

PART I
BENEFITS ACTS

PART II
INCOME SUPPORT

Contents

PART III
JOBSEEKER'S ALLOWANCE

S.I. No.

PART IV
FAMILY CREDIT

S.I. No.

Contents

PART V
DISABILITY WORKING ALLOWANCE

S.I. No.

PART VI
THE SOCIAL FUND

S.I. No.

Contents

PART VII
ADJUDICATION AND ADMINISTRATION

PART VIII
PRESIDENT'S CIRCULARS

SOURCES OF INFORMATION

This book cannot provide a general introduction to the law and inevitably some familiarity with the system has been assumed. It may though help readers who are not already experts to have some information about the kinds of sources referred to in the notes and on sources of information about up-to-date developments.

Commissioners' decisions

There are many references to decisions of the Social Security Commissioners, who decide appeals from Social Security Appeal Tribunals (under the Social Security Act 1998 to become "appeal tribunals"). Their decisions are binding on tribunals and on the adjudication officers (under the 1998 Act the Secretary of State) who make the initial decisions within the DSS. Each decision has a file number within the Commissioners' office (*e.g. CIS 1/1988:* "C" for Commissioner, "IS" for income support). Some decisions are "starred" and certain of these are circulated amongst other Commissioners to be considered for reporting. If the Chief Social Security Commissioner decides that a decision is to be reported, it receives a new reference (*e.g. R(IS) 1/90:* "R" for report). Copies of reported decisions can be inspected at local offices of the Benefits Agency and copies should also be available at main tribunal venues. They have ceased to be published by the Stationery Office and for the moment copies are being produced by the Central Adjudication Service.

Starred and other unreported decisions are available for consultation at the Commissioners' offices in London and Edinburgh, and on subscription. They are also becoming increasingly available on the Internet (http://www.hywels.demon.co.uk/commrs/decns.htm).

Although the Chief Commissioner has directed that so far as possible the authorities should refer to reported decisions only, the legal position is that all decisions of individual Commissioners have equal authority. A decision of a Tribunal of Commissioners binds individual Commissioners, unless there are compelling reasons for not following it. A tribunal or adjudication officer must follow a decision of a Tribunal of Commissioners in preference to a decision of an individual Commissioner. If decisions of individual Commissioners conflict, then prima facie a reported decision has more weight than an unreported one. This is because a decision will not be reported unless it commands the assent of a majority of Commissioners. However, a tribunal or adjudication officer is free to follow whichever decision is considered correct and there is no obligation to prefer a later decision to an earlier one. See *R(I) 12/75* (an industrial injuries case) for the statement of these principles.

There are also references in the text to a number of decisions of Northern Ireland Commissioners. Although such decisions are not binding they are of persuasive authority in Great Britain.

Commissioners' decisions, including unreported decisions and those awaiting publication, are noted and commented on in the *Journal of Social Security Law* and in CPAG's *Welfare Rights Bulletin*. Summaries also appear in the *Adviser* and are sometimes published in the *Law Society's Gazette*.

Decisions of the courts

Decisions of the courts bind the Social Security Commissioners and all below them in the system. However, it has been confirmed in *CSBO v. Leary*, appendix to *R(SB) 6/85*, that Divisional Court decisions on appeal from SBATs under the statutory right of appeal before 1980 do not bind the Commissioners. Divisional Court decisions on judicial review of the Commissioners do bind them (*Commock v. Chief Adjudication Officer*, appendix to *R(SB) 6/90*). See also *CIS 16992/1996, CIS 2809/1997* and *CFC 1580/1997* in the notes to section 24 of the Administration Act which further discusses the extent to which Commissioners are bound by decisions of the High Court (or in Scotland, the Outer House of the Court of Session). Decisions of the Court of Appeal of Northern Ireland are not binding on Commissioners in Great Britain but are persuasive; *R(SB) 1/90* holds that identically worded provisions operating in both Northern Ireland and Great Britain are to be interpreted uniformly. Decisions of the Court of Session are binding.

Social security cases are not always well reported. Where possible references have been given to the ordinary series of law reports. Some older cases are only reported in a former HMSO publication *Decisions of the courts relating to supplementary benefits and family income supplements legislation*. This is often called "the Little Yellow Book". Decisions are given a number, *e.g.* SB 24. Although the coverage is full before 1980, more recent decisions are not included. Cases are increasingly available on the Internet.

Once again court decisions will be noted and commented on in the *Journal of Social Security Law* and CPAG's *Welfare Rights Bulletin*.

Official guidance

A 13 volume Adjudication Officer's Guide, published by the Stationery Office, contains guidance on entitlements across a wide range of benefits from the Chief Adjudication Officer. Volumes 4 to 7 cover jobseeker's allowance and income support and Volume 8 covers family credit and disability working allowance. The Adjudication Officer's Guide is published on the Internet (http://www.cas.gov.uk). Note that the Central Adjudication Service is being wound down as the changes in decision-making and appeals introduced by the Social Security Act 1998 are phased in. Guidance will no longer be in the format of the Adjudication Officer's Guide. A new Decision-maker's Guide is currently being developed.

The Income Support Guide (eight volumes) contains procedural instructions and there are other guides on specific subjects, for example, the Benefits Agency Guide on income support for 16/17 year-olds. The Social Fund Guide contains guidance from the Secretary of State and the binding directions which are reproduced in this book.

Unofficial guidance

There is a large number of guides. CPAG's own *Welfare Benefits Handbook* (now in two volumes) published annually each spring, is unrivalled as a practical and comprehensive introduction from the claimant's viewpoint. See also the *Disability Rights Handbook*, published annually by Disability Alliance.

TABLE OF DESTINATIONS

Social Security Act 1986

1986 Act	Contributions and Benefits Act 1992 Administration Act 1992
s.20	SSCBA, ss.123 124, 125, 129, 137
	SSAA, s.72
s.21	SSCBA, ss.124, 128, 129
s.22	SSCBA, ss.134, 135, 136
s.23	SSCBA, ss.126
s.23A	SSCBA, s.127
s.24	SSAA, s.106
s.24A	SSAA, s.107
s.24B	SSAA, s.108
s.26	SSAA, s.105
s.27	SSAA, s.74
s.27A	SSAA, s.126
s.32	SSCBA, ss.138, 140
	SSAA, s.64
s.33	SSCBA, ss.138, 139, 140
s.34	SSAA, s.66
s.35	SSAA, s.65
s.51	SSAA, s.5
s.51B	SSAA, s.7
s.53	SSAA, s.71
s.64A	SSAA, s.159
s.64B	SSAA, s.160
s.84(1)	SSCBA, s.137(1)
	SSAA, s.191

TABLE OF DESTINATIONS

Social Security Act 1975

1975 Act	Administration Act 1992
s.97	ss.38, 39, 41, 52
s.98	s.20
s.99	s.21
s.100	s.22
s.100A	s.30
s.100B	s.31
s.100C	s.32
s.100D	s.33
s.101	ss.23, 34
s.102	s.36
s.103	s.37
s.104	ss.25, 26, 27, 28, 29, 69
s.114	s.58
s.115	s.59
s.115A	s.53
s.115B	s.56
s.115C	s.54
s.116	s.57
s.117	s.60
s.119	s.61
s.160	s.124
s.165A	s.1
s.165B	s.2
s.165D	s.68
Sched. 10	Sched. 2
Sched. 13	Sched. 3

TABLE OF CASES

Table of Cases

Table of Cases

Table of Cases

Table of Cases

Table of Cases

TABLE OF SOCIAL SECURITY COMMISSIONER'S DECISIONS

Table of Social Security Commissioner's Decisions

Table of Social Security Commissioner's Decisions

Table of Social Security Commissioner's Decisions

TABLE OF CIRCULARS

PART I

BENEFITS ACTS

Social Security Contributions and Benefits Act 1992

(1992 c. 4)

SECTIONS REPRODUCED

PART VII

INCOME-RELATED BENEFITS

General

PART VIII

THE SOCIAL FUND

PART XIII

GENERAL

Interpretation

Part VII

Income-related Benefits

General

Income-related benefits

123.—(1) Prescribed schemes shall provide for the following benefits (in this Act referred to as "income-related benefits")—

(a) income support;
(b) family credit;
(c) disability working allowance;
(d) housing benefit; and
[¹(e) council tax benefit.]
(2) The Secretary of State shall make copies of schemes prescribed under subsection (1)(a), (b) or (c) above available for public inspection at local offices of the Department of Social Security at all reasonable hours without payment. [*Subss. (3) to (6) omitted as applying only to housing benefit and council tax benefit.*]

DERIVATION

Social Security Act 1986, s.20(1) and (2).

AMENDMENT

1. Local Government Finance Act 1992, Sched. 9, para. 1(1) (April 1, 1993).

Income support

Income support

124.—(1) A person in Great Britain is entitled to income support if—

[¹(a) he is of or over the age of 16;]
(b) he has no income or his income does not exceed the applicable amount;
(c) he is not engaged in remunerative work and, if he is a member of a married or unmarried couple, the other member is not so engaged; [¹. . .]
[¹(d) except in such circumstances as may be prescribed, he is not receiving relevant education;
(e) he falls within a prescribed category of person; and
(f) he is not entitled to a jobseeker's allowance and, if he is a member of a married or unmarried couple, the other member of the couple is not entitled to an income-based jobseeker's allowance.]
(2) [². . .].
(3) [². . .].

4

(4) Subject to subsection (5) below, where a person is entitled to income support, then—

(a) if he has no income, the amount shall be the applicable amount; and

(b) if he has income, the amount shall be the difference between his income and the applicable amount.

(5) Where a person is entitled to income support for a period to which this subsection applies, the amount payable for that period shall be calculated in such manner as may be prescribed.

(6) Subsection (5) above applies—

(a) to a period of less than a week which is the whole period for which income support is payable; and

(b) to any other period of less than a week for which it is payable.

DERIVATION

Subs. (1): Social Security Act 1986, s.20(3).
Subs. (2): 1986 Act, s.20(4N).
Subs. (3): 1986 Act, s.20(4).
Subss. (4) to (6): 1986 Act, s.21(1) to (1B).

AMENDMENTS

1. Jobseekers Act 1995, Sched. 2, para. 30 (October 7, 1996).
2. Jobseekers Act 1995, Sched. 3 (October 7, 1996).

DEFINITIONS

"Great Britain"—see s.172(a).
"income-based jobseeker's allowance"—see s.137(1) and Jobseekers Act, s.35(1).
"married couple"—see s.137(1).
"prescribed"—*ibid*.
"unmarried couple"—*ibid*.

GENERAL NOTE

Subsection (1)

Here the general conditions of entitlement to income support are set out. Note the amendments made on October 7, 1996 as a consequence of the introduction of jobseeker's allowance (JSA) (see below). All of the conditions must be satisfied for there to be entitlement to income support (*CIS 166/1994*). There is also a capital test under s.134(1).

If there is entitlement under this subsection, the amount of income support is laid down in subss. (4) to (6).

There is no contributions test or requirement of citizenship (but see para. 17 of Sched. 7 to the Income Support (General) Regulations on persons from abroad). However, although a person qualifies if he is in Great Britain, an habitual residence condition was introduced on August 1, 1994. See the additional definition of "person from abroad" in reg. 21(3) of the Income Support (General) Regulations, and the notes to that definition. Reg. 4 of the Income Support Regulations allows an award to continue for a short period of temporary absence from Great Britain, but otherwise income support cannot be paid to a person outside Great Britain. See *CIS 863/1994* and *CIS 564/1994* which hold that income support is not a social security benefit within Art. 4(1) of E.C. Regulation 1408/71. Although income support has been listed by the U.K. government as included in the new category of "special non-contributory benefits" to which Regulation 1408/71 applies from June 1, 1992 (see Arts. 4(2a) and Annex IIa), such benefits cannot be "exported" (*i.e* paid where the claimant is in another Member State) (Art. 10a). Article 10a provides for the granting of such benefits "exclusively in the territory of the Member State in which [the person] reside[s], in accordance with the legislation of that State". ("Resides" means "habitually resides": Art. 1(h)). It was argued in *Perry v. Chief Adjudication Officer, The Times*, October 20, 1998, also to be reported as *R(IS) 4/99*, (the appeal against the decision in *CIS 863/1994*) that Art. 10a conferred a positive right to income support on the claimant because of his habitual residence in the U.K., and that he remained entitled to income support by virtue of that right, even during periods of temporary absence. But the Court of Appeal rejected this argument. The language of Art. 10a made it clear that special non-contributory benefits

5

were to be granted in accordance with the domestic law of the Member State. Presence in Great Britain was a requirement of the U.K.'s legislation (subject to the exceptions in reg. 4 of the Income Support Regulations) and this was not incompatible with Art. 10a. The Court of Appeal also agreed with the Commissioner that the claimant could not rely on Art. 2(4) of E.C. Regulation 1247/92 (the Regulation which introduced the June 1992 amendment) to export an entitlement to income support in respect of periods before June 1, 1992.

Paragraph (a)

From October 7, 1996 the minimum age for income support is again 16 (as it was until September 1988 before most 16- and 17-year-olds were excluded). But to be entitled a person must fall within a prescribed category (para. (e)). See reg. 4ZA of and Sched. 1B to the Income Support Regulations for these categories. Note that a person aged 16 to 18 in relevant education is still only entitled to income support in certain circumstances (para. (d) and reg. 13 of the Income Support Regulations).

The reduction in the lower age limit is a consequence of the replacement from October 7, 1996 of income support by income-based JSA for people who are required to be available for work as a condition of receiving benefit. To be entitled to income-based JSA a person must in general be at least 18 (Jobseekers Act, s.3(1)(f)(i)), although there are exceptions which are similar, but not identical, to those that used to operate for income support (see the 1996 edition for reg. 13A of and Sched. 1A to the Income Support Regulations and the further escape under s.125; these provisions were revoked on October 7, 1996). Entitlement to JSA excludes entitlement to income support (para. (f)).

Paragraph (b)

The person's income (which includes the income of the claimant's family) must be less than the applicable amount (effectively the figure set for the family's requirements under s.135).

CIS 166/1994 confirms that the conditions in subs. (1) are cumulative. The fact that the claimant was not working in his business and so para. (c) did not apply, did not mean that income from that business could not potentially disentitle him under para. (b). See the notes to reg. 30 of the Income Support Regulations.

Paragraph (c)

The introduction of the condition in para. (c) marked an important change from the supplementary benefit rules. If either the claimant or his partner is in remunerative work (defined in regs. 5 and 6 of the Income Support Regulations) there is no entitlement to income support. For supplementary benefit, this condition was only applied to the claimant. The transitional protection announced on April 28, 1988 (see p. 198 of the 1988 edition) has remained on an extra-statutory basis.

Note that from October 7, 1996 the limit for remunerative work in the case of a partner is 24 hours or more a week (Income Support Regulations, reg. 5(1A)). It remains 16 or more for the claimant.

Paragraph (d)

See regs. 12 and 13 of the Income Support Regulations.

Paragraph (e)

From October 7, 1996 only certain categories of people are entitled to income support. See reg. 4ZA of and Sched. 1A to the Income Support Regulations for these categories. They are similar to those groups who formerly were exempt from the requirement to be available for work for the purposes of income support (see Sched. 1 to the Income Support Regulations which was revoked on October 7, 1996), but there are some differences.

Paragraph (f)

Entitlement to JSA excludes entitlement to income support (any "top-up" to a person's contribution-based JSA will be by way of income-based JSA, not income support); if the claimant is a member of a couple, he will also not qualify for income support if his partner is entitled to income-based JSA. But although entitlement to income support and JSA is mutually exclusive, some people may be eligible for either, *i.e.* those who fall into a prescribed category for income support but who also satisfy the labour market conditions for JSA. See the notes to reg. 4ZA of the Income Support Regulations for discussion of the position of such claimants and of the fact that the raising of the limit for remunerative work for partners to 24 hours a week from October 7, 1996 may create a "better-off" problem for some claimants.

Subsection (4)

This provision sets out the basic means test calculation for income support. Providing that the conditions of entitlement imposed by subs. (1) and the capital test under s.134(1) are satisfied, the claimant's income is set against his applicable amount, calculated according to regs. 17 to 22 of the Income Support (General) Regulations. The difference is the amount of benefit. The claimant's income includes that of the other members of his family (s.136(1)).

Subsections (5) and (6)

These provisions allow regulations to deal with entitlement for part-weeks. See regs. 73 to 77 of the Income Support (General) Regulations.

Severe hardship cases

125.[¹ . . .]

AMENDMENT

1. Jobseekers Act 1995, Sched. 3 (October 7, 1996).

Trade disputes

126.—(1) This section applies to a person, other than a child or a person of a prescribed description—

(a) who [² is prevented from being entitled to a jobseeker's allowance by section 14 of the Jobseekers Act 1995 (trade disputes)]; or

(b) who would be so [² prevented] if otherwise entitled to that benefit,

except during any period shown by the person to be a period of incapacity for work [¹ . . .] or to be within the maternity period.

(2) In subsection (1) above "the maternity period" means the period commencing at the beginning of the 6th week before the expected week of confinement and ending at the end of the 7th week after the week in which confinement takes place.

(3) For the purposes of calculating income support—

(a) so long as this section applies to a person who is not a member of a family, the applicable amount shall be disregarded;

(b) so long as it applies to a person who is a member of a family but is not a member of a married or unmarried couple, the portion of the applicable amount which is included in respect of him shall be disregarded;

(c) so long as it applies to one of the members of a married or unmarried couple—

(i) if the applicable amount consists only of an amount in respect of them, it shall be reduced to one half; and

(ii) if it includes other amounts, the portion of it which is included in respect of them shall be reduced to one-half and any further portion of it which is included in respect of the member of the couple to whom this section applies shall be disregarded;

(d) so long as it applies to both members of a married or unmarried couple—

(i) if neither of them is responsible for a child or person of a prescribed description who is a member of the same household, the applicable amount shall be disregarded; and

(ii) in any other case, the portion of the applicable amount which is included in respect of them and any further portion of it which is included in respect of either of them shall be disregarded.

(4) Where a reduction under subsection (3)(c) above would not produce a sum which is a multiple of 5p, the reduction shall be to the nearest lower sum which is such a multiple.

(5) Where this section applies to a person for any period, then, except so far as regulations provide otherwise—

    (a) in calculating the entitlement to income support of that person or a member of his family the following shall be treated as his income and shall not be disregarded—

        (i) any payment which he or a member of his family receives or is entitled to obtain by reason of the person to whom this section applies being without employment for that period; and

        (ii) without prejudice to the generality of sub-paragraph (i) above, any amount which becomes or would on an application duly made become available to him in that period by way of repayment of income tax deducted from his emoluments in pursuance of section 203 of the Income and Corporation Taxes Act 1988; and

    (b) any payment by way of income support for that period or any part of it which apart from this paragraph would be made to him, or to a person whose applicable amount is aggregated with his—

        (i) shall not be made if the weekly rate of payment is equal to or less than the relevant sum; or

        (ii) if it is more than the relevant sum, shall be at a weekly rate equal to the difference.

(6) In respect of any period less than a week, subsection (5) above shall have effect subject to such modifications as may be prescribed.

(7) Subject to subsection (8) below, the "relevant sum" for the purposes of subsection (5) above shall be [³£27.50].

(8) If an order under section 150 of the Administration Act (annual up-rating) has the effect of increasing payments of income support, from the time when the order comes into force there shall be substituted, in subsection (5)(b) above, for the references to the sum for the time being mentioned in it references to a sum arrived at by—

    (a) increasing that sum by the percentage by which the personal allowance under paragraph 1(1) of Part I of Schedule 2 to the Income Support (General) Regulations 1987 for a single person aged not less than 25 has been increased by the order; and

    (b) if the sum so increased is not a multiple of 50p, disregarding the remainder if it is 25p and, if it is not, rounding it up or down to the nearest 50p,

and the order shall state the substituted sum.

DERIVATION

  Social Security Act 1986, s.23.

AMENDMENTS

  1. Social Security (Incapacity for Work) Act 1994, Sched. 1, para. 31 (April 13, 1995).
  2. Jobseekers Act 1995, Sched. 2, para. 31 (October 7, 1996).
  3. Social Security Benefits Up-rating Order 1999 (S.I. 1999 No. 264), art. 20 (April 12, 1999).

DEFINITIONS

  "child"—see s.137(1).
  "family"—*ibid.*
  "married couple"—*ibid.*
  "prescribed"—*ibid.*
  "the Administration Act"—see s.174.
  "unmarried couple"—see s.137(1).

GENERAL NOTE

  The trade dispute rule, long an important part of the supplementary benefit scheme, was considerably simplified in the income support rules, although most of the stringency remains.

Subsection (1)

The rule applies to anyone other than a child or young person (Income Support (General) Regulations, reg. 14) who is disentitled to JSA, or would be disentitled, under s.14 of the Jobseekers Act. Thus the income support rule depends directly on the JSA rule, and the income support question need not be finally decided until the JSA question is resolved (Adjudication Regulations, reg. 56).

The rule does not apply when the person involved is incapable of work. There is no trade dispute disqualification for incapacity benefit. The rule also does not apply in the maternity period, defined in subs. (2).

If the rule applies there are consequences for the way in which applicable amounts are calculated. This is dealt with in subs. (3). There are also consequences for the way in which income is calculated. This is dealt with in subs. (5) and in a number of regulations. The most immediate effect is that the person is treated as in remunerative work for the seven days following the first day of the stoppage of work or the day on which the claimant withdrew his labour (Income Support Regulations, reg. 5(4)). The result is that neither the person nor his partner can be entitled to income support at all for those days (s.124(1)(c)).

Subsection (3)

This provision sets out the effect on the applicable amount if the claimant is not excluded by the conditions of entitlement.

(a) A single claimant with no child or young person in the household is to have no applicable amount, and so cannot be entitled to any benefit. There is the possibility of a crisis loan under the social fund but only for expenses which result from a disaster or for items for cooking or heating (including fireguards) (Social Fund Direction, 17(a) and (f)).

(b) For a single claimant with a child or young person in the household, the "portion of the applicable amount included in respect of" the claimant is disregarded. It is clear that the personal allowance for the claimant is taken out, and so is any premium payable on account of the claimant's disability or age or because she is a carer. Arguably the family premium and the lone parent element of the family premium are not included "in respect of" the claimant and so remain, but the *Adjudication Officer's Guide* only accepts this in the case of the basic family premium (see para. 37639).

(c) For a couple where the trade dispute rule applies to only one of them, if they have no premiums on top of their personal allowance, that allowance is reduced by a half. This is a different rule from supplementary benefit, which would have left the other partner with the appropriate personal allowance for a single claimant. If there are any premiums, then the rule in para. (b) applies. Thus any premium payable solely for the person involved in the dispute (*e.g.* a carer premium) is taken out, but according to para. 37642 of the *Adjudication Officer's Guide* such a premium will be included in full if it is for the person not involved in the dispute. Any premium paid for the couple (*e.g.* a pensioner premium) is reduced by half. But para. 37642 accepts that the family premium is payable in full. It is easier to argue for the retention of the family premium here, since that would be paid to the remaining partner if the partner involved in the trade dispute disappeared. Obviously, the lone parent premium is not applicable because the couple remain a couple.

(d) For a couple where the trade dispute rule applies to both of them, the applicable amount is nil if there is no child or young person in the household. If there is a child or young person, then the family premium and any premium paid for that person's disability is allowed on top of the personal allowance for that person.

Note that housing costs are payable, provided that at least one member of the family (e.g. a child or young person) is not involved in the dispute. The housing costs are treated as the responsibility of the member or members not involved in the dispute (Income Support Regulations, Sched. 3, para. 2(2)).

Subsection (5)

If the trade dispute rule applies, the normal rules about income are modified. Under para. (a) any payment which a member of the family receives or is entitled to obtain by reason of the person involved in the trade dispute being without employment must be taken into account. In *R(SB) 29/85* a loan from a local authority Social Work Department (the Scottish equivalent of a Social Services Department) to meet arrears of hire purchase repayments was held to be capable of being such a payment. The claimant had not been in arrears before the dispute and the loan was to be repaid on his return to work. But on the facts it was a payment of capital, not income. Now reg. 41(3) of the Income Support (General) Regulations secures that in trade dispute cases payments under ss.17 or 24 of the Children Act 1989 or ss.12, 24 or 26 of the Social Work (Scotland) Act 1968 (now the Children (Scotland) Act 1995) (payments to families to prevent children being taken into care, etc.)

are treated as income, not capital. Nor does the disregard of such income in para. 28 of Sched. 9 to the Income Support (General) Regulations apply in trade dispute cases. Other categories of income normally disregarded but counted here are income in kind (para. 21) and charitable or voluntary payments (para. 15). Holiday pay paid more than four weeks after the termination of employment (normally capital) is earnings (reg. 35(1)(d)).

The other main category under para. (a) is income tax refunds paid or due. The effect of reg. 48(2) is that in trade dispute cases refunds do not count as capital. The assumption is then that they count as income, but this does not seem to be provided for expressly.

Under para. (b) there is the final automatic deduction of the "relevant sum." This is the sum specified in subs. (6). as increased in future years under subs. (7). The sum was increased to £27.50 in April 1999. The relevant sum is often called "assumed strike pay," but is deducted regardless of whether the person involved is entitled to strike pay, a member of a union, or even on strike.

The "compensation" for this rule is that any payment from a trade union up to the amount of £27.50 is disregarded (Sched. 9, para. 34).

The cumulative result of these income rules, plus the reductions in applicable amounts, is that even married strikers will often receive very little benefit indeed. Their only resort is the social fund for crisis loans in disasters or for items for cooking or heating (including fireguards) (Social Fund Direction, 17(a) and (f)).

Effect of return to work

127. If a person returns to work with the same employer after a period during which section 126 above applies to him, and whether or not his return is before the end of any stoppage of work in relation to which he is or would be [¹ prevented from being entitled to a jobseeker's allowance]—

   (a) that section shall cease to apply to him at the commencement of the day on which he returns to work; and
   (b) until the end of the period of 15 days beginning with that day section 124(1) above shall have effect in relation to him as if the following paragraph were substituted for paragraph (c)—
   "(c) in the case of a member of a married or unmarried couple, the other member is not engaged in remunerative work; and"; and
   (c) any sum paid by way of income support for that period of 15 days to him or, where he is a member of a married or unmarried couple, to the other member of that couple, shall be recoverable in the prescribed manner from the person to whom it was paid or from any prescribed person or, where the person to whom it was paid is a member of a married or unmarried couple, from the other member of the couple.

DERIVATION

Social Security Act 1986, s.23A.

AMENDMENT

1. Jobseekers Act 1995, Sched. 2, para. 32 (October 7, 1996).

DEFINITIONS

"married couple"—see s.137(1).
"prescribed"—*ibid.*
"unmarried couple"—*ibid.*

GENERAL NOTE

This section allows income support to be paid for the first 15 days following a return to work from a trade dispute. Normally the work would exclude entitlement to benefit under s.124(1)(c) regardless of whether any wages were payable or not. The rules about the relevant sum and income tax refunds under s.126 do not apply, but the other adjustments to the income rules do apply. Applicable amounts are calculated in the ordinary way. Note that any advance of earnings or loan made by the employer counts as earnings (Income Support (General) Regulations, reg. 48(5) and (6)). In addition, any payment of benefit under this section is recoverable under subs. (c) and Part VIII of the Payments Regulations.

Family credit

Family credit

128.—(1) Subject to regulations under section 5(1)(a) of the Administration Act, a person in Great Britain is entitled to family credit if, when the claim for it is made or is treated as made—

(a) his income—
    (i) does not exceed the amount which is the applicable amount at such date as may be prescribed; or
    (ii) exceeds it, but only by such an amount that there is an amount remaining if the deduction for which subsection (2)(b) below provides is made;

(b) he or, if he is a member of a married or unmarried couple, he or the other member of the couple, is engaged and normally engaged in remunerative work;

(c) except in such circumstances as may be prescribed, neither he nor any member of his family is entitled to a disability working allowance; and

(d) he or, if he is a member of a married or unmarried couple, he or the other member, is responsible for a member of the same household who is a child or a person of a prescribed description.

(2) Where a person is entitled to family credit, then—

(a) if his income does not exceed the amount which is the applicable amount at the date prescribed under subsection (1)(a)(i) above, the amount of the family credit shall be the amount which is the appropriate maximum family credit in his case; and

(b) if his income exceeds the amount which is the applicable amount at that date, the amount of the family credit shall be what remains after the deduction from the appropriate maximum family credit of a prescribed percentage of the excess of his income over the applicable amount.

(3) Family credit shall be payable for a period of 26 weeks or such other period as may be prescribed and, subject to regulations, an award of family credit and the rate at which it is payable shall not be affected by any change of circumstances during that period or by any order under section 150 of the Administration Act.

(4) Regulations may provide that an award of family credit shall terminate—

(a) if a person who was a member of the family at the date of the claim becomes a member of another family and some member of that family is entitled to family credit; or

(b) if income support [1, an income-based jobseeker's allowance] or a disability working allowance becomes payable in respect of a person who was a member of the family at the date of the claim for family credit.

(5) Regulations shall prescribed the manner in which the appropriate maximum family credit is to be determined in any case.

(6) The provisions of this Act relating to family credit apply in relation to persons employed by or under the Crown as they apply in relation to persons employed otherwise than by or under the Crown.

DERIVATION

Subs. (1): Social Security Act 1986, s.20(5) and (5A).
Subs. (2): 1986 Act, s.21(2) and (3).
Subs. (3): 1986 Act, s.20(6).

Subs. (4): 1986 Act, s.20(10).
Subs. (5): 1986 Act, s.21(6)(a).
Subs. (6): 1986 Act, s.79(3).

AMENDMENT

1. Jobseekers Act 1995, Sched. 2, para. 33 (October 7, 1996).

DEFINITIONS

"child"—see s.137(1).
"family"—*ibid.*
"Great Britain"—see s.172(1).
"income-based jobseeker's allowance"—see s.137(1) and Jobseekers Act, s.35(1).
"married couple"—see s.137(1).
"prescribed"—*ibid.*
"the Administration Act"—see s.174.
"unmarried couple"—see s.137(1).

GENERAL NOTE

Note that family credit is due to be replaced by working families tax credit from October 5, 1999. See the 1999 Supplement to this book for details of the new scheme.

Subsection (1)
Here the general conditions of entitlement to family credit are set out, apart from the capital test under s.134(1). The conditions must be met at the date of claim. Satisfaction at a later date will not do (but note reg. 13(6) of the Claims and Payments Regulations which from October 1994 allows claims for family credit to be made up to three days in advance).

As for income support and income-based JSA, the claimant must be in Great Britain, but here reg. 3 of the Family Credit (General) Regulations deems a person to be present or not present in certain circumstances. Family credit is a "family benefit" within Art. 4(1)(h) of E.C. Regulation 1408/71 and is not excluded from the scope of the Regulation as a form of social assistance under Art. 4(4) (*Hughes v. Chief Adjudication Officer* Case C-78/91 [1992] E.C.R. I-4839). Under Art. 73 the family of a person employed in a Member State is entitled to family benefits in that State although resident in another Member State. Thus, Mrs Hughes, who lived in the Republic of Ireland, could claim family credit in Northern Ireland because her husband worked there. With effect from June 1, 1992, the U.K. took advantage of amendments to Regulation 1408/71 introduced by E.C. Regulation 1247/92 to name family credit, (among other benefits) as a "special non-contributory benefit", to be confined exclusively to U.K. territory. However, the DSS have accepted that family credit is still payable to people in Mrs Hughes' position. This is apparently because family credit is a family benefit within Art. 4(1) and so this overrides the fact that it has been named as a "special non-contributory benefit". Thus the residence rule for family credit still does not apply in these circumstances.

The most important condition is that the claimant or, if she has a partner, she or her partner is in remunerative work and normally engaged in remunerative work. See reg. 4 of the Family Credit Regulations. Although the minimum hours to qualify were reduced from 24 to 16 for both income support and family credit in April 1992, the methods of calculating the hours differ. Also, a claimant may be excluded from income support (and now income-based JSA) by work, but fail to be entitled to family credit because the work is not normal (note reg. 6(27) and (28) of the Claims and Payments Regulations). On the other hand, the increased income support limit for remunerative work in the case of a partner (24 hours a week from October 7, 1996; the same limit applies for income-based JSA) may give the couple the choice of which benefit to claim. Another reason for not qualifying for family credit might be a failure to meet the condition in para. (d), that the claimant (or partner) is responsible for a child or "person of a prescribed description" in the household. A "person of a prescribed description" is a person aged 16 to 18 who is still in full time secondary-level education (Family Credit Regulations, reg. 6) (a "young person"). If an adult is treated as responsible for a child or young person under reg. 7, she is then treated as in the same household by reg. 8. (For people in remunerative work without children, note the earnings top-up scheme that has been piloted in eight areas of the country since October 1996: see the note at the beginning of the Family Credit Regulations.) Para. (c) spells out that if any member of the family is entitled to disability working allowance at the date of claim for family credit, then there can be no entitlement to family credit.

Reg. 52 of the Family Credit Regulations lifts this condition where a claim for family credit is made within 42 days before the expiry of an award of disability working allowance for a period running on from the end of that award. See s.134(2) for the prevention of overlaps of entitlement.

If paras. (b) to (d) are met, then under para. (a) there is a test of the family's income against the applicable amount (see s.135 and Family Credit Regulations, reg. 47). It is crucial to the family credit scheme that the test is to be applied at the date of claim, although in principle evidence coming to light after that date may be relevant (*CFC 14/1991*). Satisfaction of the income test a few weeks later is not in itself any good. A fresh claim has to be made. If the income is less than the applicable amount, the maximum family credit is payable under subs. (2)(a). If the income exceeds the applicable amount, then the amount of benefit, if any, is calculated under subs. (2)(b).

For an example of the importance of the date of claim see *CFC 11141/1995*. The claimant, who worked as a domestic assistant, claimed family credit on December 13, 1994. Her husband commenced "agency work" two weeks beforehand and was paid for that work on December 4 and 11, 1994. He did no more work after December 8, 1994. The AO awarded family credit from November 29, 1994 (the date the claimant's husband started work), taking account of her husband's earnings. The Commissioner found that there was no evidence to show that when the award was made the backdating of the claim had ever been considered by an officer acting on behalf of the Secretary of State as required by what was then reg. 19(3) of the Claims and Payments Regulations (now see reg. 19(6); note also *CSIS 61/1992* in the notes to reg. 19(6)–(7)). The consequence was that the date of claim was December 13, 1994, at which date the claimant's husband was not in employment and had no earnings to be taken into account.

Note that there is no age limit (upper or lower) for a claimant of family credit, although in practice the requirements of remunerative work for at least 16 hours a week and responsibility for a child or young person will exclude almost all under-16s.

A person under 16 cannot be one of a married or unmarried couple (*CFC 7/1992*).

Subsection (2)

Under para. (a) where the family's income does not exceed the applicable amount (Family Credit Regulations, reg. 47) the maximum family credit (reg. 46) is payable.

Under para. (b) where the family's income exceeds the applicable amount, then the maximum credit is reduced by 70 per cent. of the excess (reg. 48). Providing that what is left of the maximum credit is more than 49p (Claims and Payments Regulations, reg. 27(2)), that amount is the benefit payable. If the maximum credit is eroded completely, there is no entitlement under subs. (1)(a)(ii).

Subsection (3)

The normal length of an award of family credit is 26 weeks. The 1987 Transitional Regulations allowed different periods to be fixed in the early months following the start of the scheme in April 1988. Once an award is made it will not be affected by a change in circumstances (although see subs. (4) and regs. 49, 49A, 51 and 51A of the Family Credit Regulations) or by the annual uprating of benefits under s.150 of the Administration Act during the currency of the award. An award may be reviewed if it was made in ignorance of or under a mistake as to a material fact (as in *R(FIS) 1/89*) or for error of law (Administration Act, s.25(1)(a) and (2), formerly s.104(1)(a) and (1A) of the Social Security Act 1975). There can be no review for an actual or anticipated change of circumstances (Administration Act, s.25(1)(b) and (bb), and formerly s.104(1)(b) and (bb) of the 1975 Act).

Subsection (4)

See reg. 50 of the Family Credit Regulations.

Subsection (5)

See reg. 46 of the Family Credit Regulations.

Disability working allowance

Disability working allowance

129.—(1) A person in Great Britain who has attained the age of 16 and [²qualifies under subsection (2) or (2A) below] is entitled to a disability working allowance if, when the claim for it is made or is treated as made—

(a) he is engaged and normally engaged in remunerative work;

    (b) he has a physical or mental disability which puts him at a disadvantage in getting a job;

    (c) his income—

        (i) does not exceed the amount which is the applicable amount at such date as may be prescribed; or

        (ii) exceeds it, but only by such an amount that there is an amount remaining if the deduction for which subsection (5)(b) below provides is made; and

    (d) except in such circumstances as may be prescribed, neither he nor, if he has a family, any member of it, is entitled to family credit.

    (2) Subject to subsection (4) below, a person qualifies under this subsection if—

    (a) for one or more of the 56 days immediately preceding the date when the claim for a disability working allowance is made or is treated as made there was payable to him one or more of the following—

        [³(i) the higher rate of short-term incapacity benefit or long-term incapacity benefit;]

        (ii) a severe disablement allowance;

        (iii) income support [⁴, an income-based jobseeker's allowance], housing benefit or [¹council tax benefit],

      or a corresponding benefit under any enactment having effect in Northern Ireland;

    (b) when the claim for a disability working allowance is made or is treated as made there was payable to him one or more of the following—

        (i) an attendance allowance;

        (ii) a disability living allowance;

        (iii) an increase of disablement pension under section 104 above;

        (iv) an analogous pension increase under a war pension scheme or an industrial injuries scheme,

      or a corresponding benefit under any enactment having effect in Northern Ireland; or

    (c) when the claim for a disability working allowance is made or is treated as made, he has an invalid carriage or other vehicle provided by the Secretary of State under section 5(2)(a) of the National Health Service Act 1977 and Schedule 2 to that Act or under section 46 of the National Health Service (Scotland) Act 1978 or provided under Article 30(1) of the Health and Personal Social Services (Northern Ireland) Order 1972.

    [²(2A) A person qualifies under this subsection if—

    (a) on one or more of the 56 days immediately preceding the date when the claim for a disability working allowance is made or is treated as made he was engaged in training for work and

    (b) a relevant benefit was payable to him for one or more of the 56 days immediately preceding—

        (i) the first day of training for work falling within the 56 days mentioned in paragraph (a) above or

        (ii) an earlier day of training for work which formed part of the same period of training for work as that day.

    (2B) For the purposes of subsection (2A) above—

    (a) the following are relevant benefits—

        (i) the higher rate of short-term incapacity benefit

        (ii) long-term incapacity benefit

        (iii) a severe disablement allowance,

      or a corresponding benefit under any enactment having effect in Northern Ireland;

    (b) "training for work" means training for work in pursuance of arrangements made under section 2(1) of the Employment and Training Act

1973 or section 2(3) of the Enterprise and New Towns (Scotland) Act 1990 or training of such other description as may be prescribed; and

(c) a period of training for work means a series of consecutive days of training for work, there being disregarded for this purpose such days as may be prescribed.]

(3) For the purposes of subsection (1) above a person has a disability which puts him at a disadvantage in getting a job only if he satisfies prescribed conditions or prescribed circumstances exist in relation to him.

(4) If the only benefit mentioned in paragraph (*a*) of subsection (2) above which is payable to a person as there mentioned is—

(a) a benefit mentioned in sub-paragraph (iii) of that paragraph; or

(b) a corresponding benefit under any enactment having effect in Northern Ireland,

he only qualifies under that subsection in prescribed circumstances.

(5) Where a person is entitled to a disability working allowance, then—

(a) if his income does not exceed the amount which is the applicable amount at the date prescribed under subsection (1)(c)(i) above, the amount of the disability working allowance shall be the amount which is the appropriate maximum disability working allowance in his case; and

(b) if his income exceeds that amount, the amount of the disability working allowance shall be what remains after the deduction from the appropriate maximum disability working allowance of a prescribed percentage of the excess of his income over that amount.

(6) A disability working allowance shall be payable for a period of 26 weeks or such other period as may be prescribed and, subject to regulations, an award of a disability working allowance and the rate at which it is payable shall not be affected by any change of circumstances during that period or by any order under section 150 of the Administration Act.

(7) Regulations may provide that an award of a disability working allowance to a person shall terminate if—

(a) a disability working allowance becomes payable in respect of some other person who was a member of his family at the date of his claim for a disability working allowance; or

(b) income support [⁴, an income-based jobseeker's allowance] or family credit becomes payable in respect of a person who was a member of the family at that date.

(8) Regulations shall prescribe the manner in which the appropriate maximum disability working allowance is to be determined in any case.

(9) The provisions of this Act relating to disability working allowance apply in relation to persons employed by or under the Crown as they apply in relation to persons employed otherwise than by or under the Crown.

DERIVATION

Subs. (1): Social Security Act 1986, s.20(6A) and (6D).
Subss. (2) and (3): 1986 Act, s.20(6B) and (6C).
Subs. (4): 1986 Act, s.20(6E).
Subs. (5): 1986 Act, s.21(3A) and (3B).
Subs. (6): 1986 Act, s.20(6F).
Subs. (7): 1986 Act, s.27B(4).
Subs. (8): 1986 Act, s.21(6)(aa).
Subs. (9): 1986 Act, s.79(3).

AMENDMENTS

1. Local Government Finance Act 1992, Sched. 9, para. 2 (April 1, 1993).
2. Social Security (Incapacity for Work) Act 1994, s.10 (April 13, 1995).

3. Social Security (Incapacity for Work) Act 1994, Sched. 1, para. 32 (April 13, 1995).
4. Jobseekers Act 1995, Sched. 2, para. 34 (October 7, 1996).

DEFINITIONS

"family"—see s.137(1).
"Great Britain"—see s.172(1).
"income-based jobseeker's allowance"—see s.137(1) and Jobseekers Act, s.35(1).
"industrial injuries scheme"—see s.137(1).
"prescribed"—*ibid.*
"the Administration Act"—see s.174.
"war pension scheme"—see s.137(1).

GENERAL NOTE

Note that disability working allowance is due to be replaced by disabled person's tax credit from October 5, 1999. See the 1999 Supplement to this book for details of the new scheme.

Disability working allowance was introduced by the Disability Living Allowance and Disability Working Allowance Act 1991 with effect from April 6, 1992. That Act amended the Social Security Act 1975 and the Social Security Act 1986. This section of the 1992 Act consolidates the amendments to ss.20 and 21 of the 1986 Act.

See the General Note at the beginning of the Disability Working Allowance (General) Regulations for the background and general structure of the benefit.

Subsection (1)

This provision sets out the general conditions of entitlement to disability working allowance, apart from the capital test under s.134(1). All of these conditions have to be satisfied at the date of claim. However, the adjudication rules for disability working allowance appear to make the choice of the exact date of claim slightly less crucial than in family credit. A claimant may within three months of an AO's decision denying entitlement apply for a review on any ground (Administration Act, s.30(1) and Adjudication Regulations, reg. 25(1)). "Any ground" would seem to include a change of circumstances such that the conditions of s.129(1) are satisfied after the date of claim. Any fresh claim made within this three month period is treated as an application for review (Administration Act, s.30(13)). But note that an award of benefit made on such a deemed review can only take effect from the date of the fresh claim (Adjudication Regulations, reg. 66(1)).

General conditions

The claimant must be present in Great Britain. See reg. 5 of the Disability Working Allowance (General) Regulations, which is very similar to reg. 3 of the Family Credit (General) Regulations. Disability working allowance has been named by the U.K. with effect from June 1, 1992, as a benefit which is for the purposes of E.C. Regulation 1408/71 exclusively confined to U.K. territory. But see the notes to s. 128(1) and s. 1(2) of the Jobseekers Act.

Secondly, the claimant must be at least 16. Presumably it was considered that since the test of responsibility for a child or young person is not part of the disability working allowance scheme, a different rule to that for family credit was necessary. Then the claimant must satisfy one of the four alternative qualifications in subss. (2) or (2A) and all four of the conditions in subs. (1)(a) to (d).

Remunerative work

On para. (a), see reg. 6 of the Disability Working Allowance Regulations. As for family credit, work for less than 16 hours a week does not come within the definition of remunerative work. A claimant may fail to be entitled to disability working allowance because of not being "normally engaged" in remunerative work, but be excluded from income support or income-based JSA by work of at least 16 hours in particular weeks (note that from October 7, 1996 the income support limit for remunerative work in the case of a partner is 24 hours a week; the same limit applies for income-based JSA; note also reg. 6(27) and (28) of the Claims and Payments Regulations). One effect of this test is that a claim made in advance of starting work will fail, although from October 1994 reg. 13(6) of the Claims and Payments Regulations allows claims for disability working allowance to be made up to three days in advance. (Reg. 13B of the Claims and Payments Regulations only allowed advance initial claims at the beginning of the scheme in March and April 1992.) There is also political commitment to giving priority to claims from those who have just started work

(Mr. N. Scott, Standing Committee E, col. 190, January 17, 1991), so that there is as little delay as possible in getting benefit to someone in these circumstances.

Physical or mental disability

On para. (b), what amounts to a physical or mental disability which puts the claimant at a disadvantage in getting a job is to be defined in regulations (subs. (3)). Reg. 3 of and Sched. 1 to the Disability Working Allowance Regulations prescribe a long list of alternative conditions. See the notes to Sched. 1 for the details. On an initial claim a claimant's declaration that he has such a disability is conclusive, unless either the claim or other evidence before the AO indicates that he does not (Administration Act, s.11(2) and Disability Working Allowance Regulations, reg. 4). On a repeat claim, one of the qualifying conditions must be met directly.

The question whether the claimant satisfies this condition is a "disability question." Any appeal from an AO's decision on a disability question is to a disability appeal tribunal (DAT) and not to a SSAT (Adjudication Regulations, reg. 27). Indeed, if an appeal on disability working allowance raises a disability question along with other questions, the whole appeal goes to a DAT. If in the course of an appeal to a SSAT a disability question first arises, the SSAT cannot deal with it (Administration Act, s.36(2)). See the notes to that subsection for what follows in such circumstances.

Income

Under para. (c), the income of the claimant and any family is set against the applicable amount (prescribed in reg. 52 of the Disability Working Allowance Regulations). If income is less than the applicable amount, sub-para. (i) is met. If income exceeds the applicable amount, the same calculation is made under subs. (5)(b) as for family credit; 70 per cent. of the excess is deducted from the maximum disability working allowance. If some amount remains, sub-para. (ii) is met, but benefit of less than 50p is not payable (Claims and Payments Regulations, reg. 27(2)).

Non-entitlement to family credit

In general, under para. (d), if any member of a family is entitled to family credit no member of the family can be entitled to disability working allowance. Since the test under subs.(1) is applied at the date of claim, reg. 57 of the Disability Working Allowance Regulations lifts this condition when a claim for disability working allowance is made within 28 days before the expiry of a family credit award for a period running on from the end of that award.

Subsections (2), (2A) and (2B)

In addition to satisfying the conditions of subs. (1) the claimant must also at the date of claim fall into one of the four categories set out here. In all cases the equivalent Northern Ireland benefits count equally with the British benefits.

Under subs. (2)(a), either higher rate short-term incapacity benefit, long-term incapacity benefit (or invalidity benefit: reg. 18(1) of the Disability Working Allowance and Income Support (General) Amendment Regulations 1995, p.1054), severe disablement allowance or income support, income-based JSA, housing benefit or council tax benefit with the higher pensioner (on the ground of disability) or disability premium (subs. (4) and Disability Working Allowance Regulations, reg. 7) must have been payable for at least one day in the 56 days before the date of claim. All the conditions of entitlement and payability must be met. This condition operates normally on an initial claim. If it is satisfied on the initial claim then on any repeat claim (*i.e.* one made up to eight weeks after the expiry of the previous award) it is treated as still satisfied (Administration Act, s.11(3)).

Under subs. (2)(b), either attendance allowance, disability living allowance or constant attendance allowance under an industrial injuries scheme or a war pension scheme must be payable at the date of claim. The test is applied to initial and repeat claims. For claims made before April 6, 1992, mobility allowance is substituted for disability living allowance in s.20(6B)(b)(ii) of the Social Security Act 1986 (Disability Living Allowance and Disability Working Allowance Act 1991, s.6(5) and Social Security (Consequential Provisions) Act 1992, Sched. 4, para. 21).

Under subs. (2)(c), the claimant must have some kind of invalid carriage or vehicle provided under the legislation listed.

Under subss. (2A) and (2B), the claimant must have been undergoing training for work (see below) for at least one day in the eight weeks before the date of claim. In addition, he must have been getting higher rate short-term incapacity benefit, long-term incapacity benefit (or invalidity benefit: reg. 18(2) of the Disability Working Allowance and Income Support (General) Amendment Regulations 1995, p.1054), or severe disablement allowance within the eight weeks before his first day of training for work started. This can be an earlier day which counts as part of the same period of training for work. "Training for work" means training arranged under s.2(1) of the Employment and Training Act 1973 or, in Scotland, s.2(3) of the Enterprise and New Towns (Scotland) Act 1990 (subs. (2B)(b)), or a course which a person attends for at least 16 hours a week and the main purpose of which is to teach occupational or vocational skills (reg. 7A of the Disability Working Allowance Regulations). Reg. 7B of the Disability Working Allowance Regulations lists the days that are disregarded under subs. (2B)(c).

Subsection (3)
See note to subs. (1)(b). The conditions and circumstances are prescribed in the Disability Working Allowance Regulations, reg. 3 and Sched. 1.

Subsection (4)
See note to subs. (2)(a).

Subsection (5)
Under para. (a), where the family's income does not exceed the applicable amount (Disability Working Allowance Regulations, reg. 52) the maximum allowance (reg. 51) is payable.
Under para. (b), where the family's income exceeds the applicable amount, then the maximum allowance is reduced by 70 per cent. of the excess (reg. 53). Providing that what is left of the maximum allowance is more than 49p (Claims and Payments Regulations, reg. 27(2)), that amount is the benefit payable. If the maximum allowance is eroded completely, there is no entitlement under subs. (1)(c)(ii).

Subsection (6)
The normal length of an award of disability working allowance is 26 weeks, the same as for family credit. Once an award is made, it and the rate of payment will not generally be affected by a change in circumstances (although see subs. (7), s.30(5)(b) of the Administration Act and regs. 54 to 56A of the Disability Working Allowance Regulations) or by the annual uprating of benefits under s. 150 of the Administration Act during the currency of the award. The process of appeal against an AO's decision has to start with an application within three months to review the decision "on any ground" (Administration Act, s.30(1)), but where an award has been made, this subsection seems to require that it is only the position as at the date of claim which can be considered. An application for an "ordinary" review can only be made later than three months after notice of the AO's decision (Administration Act, s.30(5) and Adjudication Regulations, reg. 25(1)). Potential grounds of review include ignorance of or mistake as to a material fact (as in *R(FIS) 1/89* for family credit) and error of law (Administration Act, s.30(5)(a) and (c)). Advance awards under reg. 13B or 13C of the Claims and Payments Regulations can be reviewed if the conditions of entitlement are not satisfied at the start date of the award (s.30(5)(d)). Section 30(5)(b) allows regulations to prescribe situations in which there can be review for change of circumstances, which this subsection also allows. The only regulations made directly under this power are regs. 56 and 56A of the Disability Working Allowance Regulations. Reg. 54 (death of claimant) is made under s.5 of the Administration Act (formerly s.51 of the 1986 Act) and reg. 55 is made under subs. (7) of this section.

Subsection (7)
See reg. 55 of the Disability Working Allowance Regulations.

Subsection (8)
See reg. 51 of the Disability Working Allowance Regulations.

General

Exclusions from benefit

134.—(1) No person shall be entitled to an income-related benefit if his capital or a prescribed part of it exceeds the prescribed amount.
(2) Except in prescribed circumstances the entitlement of one member of a family to any one income-related benefit excludes entitlement to that benefit for any other member for the same period.
(3) [¹ . . .]
(4) Where the amount of any income-related benefit would be less than a prescribed amount, it shall not be payable except in prescribed circumstances.

DERIVATION

Subs. (1): Social Security Act 1986, s.22(6).
Subs. (2): 1986 Act, s.20(9).
Subs. (4): 1986 Act, s.21(7).

AMENDMENT

1. Local Government Finance Act 1992, Sched. 9, para. 7 (April 1, 1993).

DEFINITIONS

"family"—see s.137(1).
"prescribed"—*ibid.*

GENERAL NOTE

Subsection (1)
The capital limit for income support and family credit was raised to £8,000 from £6,000 in April 1990 (Income Support (General) Regulations, reg. 45 and Family Credit (General) Regulations, reg. 28). From April 8, 1996 the capital limit for income support was further raised to £16,000 for claimants living permanently in residential care or nursing homes (including those with preserved rights), residential accommodation or Polish resettlement homes (Income Support Regulations, regs. 45(b) and 53(1B)). The limit for disability working allowance was set at £16,000, the same as for housing benefit, after a response from the Social Security Advisory Committee and pressure during the progress of the Disability Living Allowance and Disability Working Allowance Act 1991 through the House of Lords (Disability Working Allowance (General) Regulations, reg. 31). The basis for the difference is that the disabled may need to save up for expensive equipment or unexpected outlays.

Since the capital rule operates as an exclusion to benefit it is arguable that the burden of proof that a claimant's capital exceeds the limit is on the AO. The Tribunal of Commissioners in *CIS 417/ 1992* (to be reported as *R(IS) 5/98*) treat satisfaction of the capital rule as part of what the claimant has to prove in showing entitlement to income support. However, the contrary argument was not put to the Tribunal. But once it has been shown that the claimant possesses an item of capital, it is for him to prove that one of the disregards in Sched. 10 applies (*CIS 240/1992*). Similarly, if it has been established that the claimant is the legal owner of a property, the burden is on him to show that the beneficial ownership does not follow the legal ownership (*CIS 30/1993*).

Subsection (4)
See regs. 26(4) and 27(2) of the Claims and Payments Regulations.

The applicable amount

135.—(1) The applicable amount, in relation to any income-related benefit, shall be such amount or the aggregate of such amounts as may be prescribed in relation to that benefit.

(2) The power to prescribe applicable amounts conferred by subsection (1) above includes power to prescribe nil as an applicable amount.

[¹(3) In prescribing, for the purposes of income support, amounts under subsection (1) above in respect of accommodation in any area for qualifying persons in cases where prescribed conditions are fulfilled, the Secretary of State shall take into account information provided by local authorities or other prescribed bodies or persons with respect to the amounts which they have agreed to pay for the provision of accommodation in relevant premises in that area.

(4) In subsection (3) above—
"accommodation" includes any board or care;
"local authority"—

      (a) in relation to areas in England and Wales, has the same meaning as it has in Part III of the National Assistance Act 1948; and

    (b) in relation to areas in Scotland, has the meaning given by section
        1(2) of the Social Work (Scotland) Act 1968;
"qualifying person" means any person who falls within—
    (a) subsection (1) of section 26A of the National Assistance Act 1948
        (which is inserted by the National Health Service and Community
        Care Act 1990 and relates to persons ordinarily resident in residen-
        tial care or nursing homes immediately before the commencement
        of that section); or
    (b) subsection (1) of section 86A of the Social Work (Scotland) Act
        1968 (the corresponding provision for Scotland),
    or who would fall within either of those subsections apart from any
    regulations under subsection (3) of the section in question;
"relevant premises"—
    (a) in relation to areas in England and Wales, has the meaning given
        by section 26A(2) of the National Assistance Act 1948; and
    (b) in relation to areas in Scotland, has the meaning given section
        86A(2) of the Social Work (Scotland) Act 1968.]

(5) In relation to income support, housing benefit and [²council tax benefit],
the applicable amount for a severely disabled person shall include an amount
in respect of his being a severely disabled person.

(6) Regulations may specify circumstances in which persons are to be treated
as being or as not being severely disabled.

DERIVATION

    Social Security Act 1986, s.22(1) to (4).

AMENDMENTS

    1. To be omitted until s.9 of the Social Security Act 1990 is brought into force: Social Security
(Consequential Provisions) Act 1992, s.6 and Sched. 4, Part I.
    2. Local Government Finance Act 1992, Sched. 9, para. 8 (April 1, 1993).

DEFINITION

    "prescribed"—see s.137(1).

GENERAL NOTE

Subsection (1)
    See reg. 47 of the Family Credit (General) Regulations, regs. 17 to 22 of and Sched. 2 to the
Income Support (General) Regulations and reg. 52 of the Disability Working Allowance (General)
Regulations.
    CIS 683/1993 confirms that a claimant's applicable amount can only consist of elements specified
in the relevant regulations. It cannot be increased by the amount of maintenance (or insurance
premiums) the claimant is required to pay.

Subsection (2)
    See reg. 21 of and Sched. 7 to the Income Support Regulations.

Subsections (3) and (4)
    The predecessors of these subsections were inserted into s.22 of the 1986 Act by s.9 of the Social
Security Act 1990 and are closely bound up with the Government's community care reforms. Those
reforms under the National Health Service and Community Care Act 1990 were intended to come
into force in April 1991, but after the passage of the Social Security Act 1990, it was announced
that they would not come into effect until April 1993. These amendments have not yet come into
force (see Social Security (Consequential Provisions) Act 1992, Sched. 4, paras. 1 and 4).

Subsections (5) and (6)

See para. 13 of Sched. 2 to the Income Support (General) Regulations. A provision requiring the payment of a community care addition to income support to very severely disabled people was put into the 1986 Act when it was going through the House of Lords. Although the Government did not wish to have this requirement in the legislation it did not seek to remove its spirit when the Bill returned to the House of Commons. But it put in its own amendments which have now become subss. (5) and (6).

In *CIS 372/1990* the Commissioner held that s.22(4) of the 1986 Act (the predecessor of subs. (6)) did not authorise the making of regulations prescribing conditions to be satisfied before a person counts as severely disabled other than conditions relating to the extent of that person's disablement. Otherwise, the mandatory provision of s.22(3) (the predecessor of subs. (5)) would be undermined. He therefore went on to hold that heads (ii) and (iii) of para. 13(2)(a) of Sched. 2, on the severe disability premium, were not validly part of the General Regulations. This was because they referred to the presence of a non-dependant in the claimant's household and to the receipt of invalid care allowance by another person, and not to the claimant's disability.

On appeal, the majority of the Court of Appeal took the opposite view, that s.22(4) gave the Secretary of State power to specify financial and domestic conditions as part of the circumstances in which a person was or was not to be treated as severely disabled (*Chief Adjudication Officer v. Foster* [1992] Q.B. 31, [1991] 3 All E.R. 846). Therefore the provisions were valid. Lord Donaldson M.R. dissented trenchantly, saying that if s.22(4) allowed regulations to specify conditions not relating to the severity of disability this would "emasculate the imperative contained in subsection (3) and indeed . . . render it otiose."

The House of Lords ([1993] A.C. 754, [1993] 1 All E.R. 705) also held the provisions to be valid. Lord Bridge agreed that subs. (3) (now subs. (5)) required the applicable amount for a severely disabled person to include some amount in respect of being such a person. But subs. (4) (now subs. (6)) was a deeming provision which allowed the Secretary of State to define who was to be treated as severely disabled. He could do this by reference to circumstances which either related to the degree of disability or affected the extent of need for income support arising from the disability. If the only power intended to be given by subs. (4) was a power to define the degree of disability which qualified as severe, the language used was totally inappropriate for that purpose (especially compared with the precise code for determining the degree of disability which qualified someone for severe disablement allowance).

Lord Bridge would have reached this conclusion without looking at the Parliamentary history of the subsections in Hansard, but following *Pepper v. Hart* [1993] A.C. 593, [1992] 3 W.L.R. 1032 this could be consulted. The statements of Ministers in both Houses of Parliament on the government amendments made clear that it was intended to use the regulation-making power to prescribe that the severe disability premium should only be applicable where the person was receiving the higher rate of attendance allowance, was living in a household with no other adult able to care for him and had no-one eligible for invalid care allowance in respect of him. Therefore, the ambiguity in the regulation-making power was to be resolved so as to authorise that use of the power.

The House of Lords' decision settled the scope of subss. (5) and (6). See the notes to para. 13 of Sched. 2 to the Income Support (General) Regulations for the conditions for the severe disability premium. On the powers of the Social Security Commissioners, SSATs and AOs to determine the validity or otherwise of regulations, see the notes to ss.21 and 23 of the Administration Act.

Income and capital

136.—(1) Where a person claiming an income-related benefit is a member of a family, the income and capital of any member of that family shall, except in prescribed circumstances, be treated as the income and capital of that person.

(2) Regulations may provide that capital not exceeding the amount prescribed under section 134(1) above but exceeding a prescribed lower amount shall be treated, to a prescribed extent, as if it were income of a prescribed amount.

(3) Income and capital shall be calculated or estimated in such manner as may be prescribed.

(4) A person's income in respect of a week shall be calculated in accordance with prescribed rules; and the rules may provide for the calculation to be made by reference to an average over a period (which need not include the week concerned).

(5) Circumstances may be prescribed in which—
(a) a person is treated as possessing capital or income which he does not possess;
(b) capital or income which a person does possess is to be disregarded;
(c) income is to be treated as capital;
(d) capital is to be treated as income.

DERIVATION

Subs. (1): Social Security Act 1986, s.22(5).
Subss. (2) to (5): 1986 Act, s.22(7) to (9).

DEFINITIONS

"family"—see s.137(1).
"prescribed"—*ibid.*

GENERAL NOTE

Subsection (1)
The general rule for income support, family credit and disability working allowance is that all of the family's (as defined in s.137(1)) income and capital should be aggregated together and treated as the claimant's. See reg. 23(1) of the Income Support (General) Regulations, reg. 10(1) of the Family Credit (General) Regulations and reg. 12(1) of the Disability Working Allowance (General) Regulations. The main exceptions are for children and young persons (see regs. 44 and 47 of the Income Support Regulations, regs. 27 and 30 of the Family Credit Regulations and regs. 30 and 33 of the Disability Working Allowance Regulations).

Subsection (2)
Reg. 53 of the Income Support Regulations and reg. 36 of the Family Credit Regulations provide for an income to be assumed to be produced from capital between £3,000 and £8,000. For those income support claimants for whom the capital limit was raised to £16,000 on April 8, 1996 (see regs. 45(b) and 53(1B) of the Income Support Regulations), the tariff income rule only applies to capital over £10,000. Although the capital limit for disability working allowance is also £16,000, reg. 40 of the Disability Working Allowance Regulations provides for income to be assumed from capital between £3,000 and £16,000.

Subsections (3) to (5)
Large parts of the regulations deal with the matters covered by these subsections.

Interpretation of Part VII and supplementary provisions

137.—(1) In this Part of this Act, unless the context otherwise requires—
[¹"billing authority" has the same meaning as in Part I of the Local Government Finance Act 1992;]
"child" means a person under the age of 16;
[¹ ...]
"dwelling" means any residential accommodation, whether or not consisting of the whole or part of a building and whether or not comprising separate and self-contained premises;
"family" means—
(a) a married or unmarried couple;
(b) a married or unmarried couple and a member of the same household for whom one of them is or both are responsible and who is a child or a person of a prescribed description;
(c) except in prescribed circumstances, a person who is not a member of a married or unmarried couple and a member of the same household for whom that person is responsible and who is a child or a person of a prescribed description;

[²"income-based jobseeker's allowance" has the same meaning as in the Job-seekers Act 1995;]

"industrial injuries scheme" means a scheme made under Schedule 8 to this Act or section 159 of the 1975 Act or under the Old Cases Act;

[¹"levying authority" has the same meaning as in Part II of the Local Government Finance Act 1992;]

"married couple" means a man and woman who are married to each other and are members of the same household;

[¹ ...]

"prescribed" means specified in or determined in accordance with regulations;

"unmarried couple" means a man and woman who are not married to each other but are living together as husband and wife otherwise than in pre-scribed circumstances;

"war pension scheme" means a scheme under which war pensions (as defined in section 25 of the Social Security Act 1989) are provided;

"week", in relation to [¹council tax benefit], means a period of seven days beginning with a Monday.

(2) Regulations may make provision for the purposes of this Part of this Act—

  (a) as to circumstances in which a person is to be treated as being or not being in Great Britain;

  (b) continuing a person's entitlement to benefit during periods of temporary absence from Great Britain;

  (c) as to what is or is not to be treated as remunerative work or as employment;

[²(d) as to circumstances in which a person is or is not to be treated as engaged or normally engaged in remunerative work;]

  (e) as to what is or is not to be treated as relevant education;

  (f) as to circumstances in which a person is or is not to be treated as receiving relevant education;

  (g) specifying the descriptions of pension increases under war pension schemes or industrial injuries schemes that are analogous to the benefits mentioned in section 129(2)(b)(i) to (iii) above;

  (h) as to circumstances in which a person is or is not to be treated as occupying a dwelling as his home;

  (i) for treating any person who is liable to make payments in respect of a dwelling as if he were not so liable;

  (j) for treating any person who is not liable to make payments in respect of a dwelling as if he were so liable;

  (k) for treating as included in a dwelling any land used for the purposes of the dwelling;

  (l) as to circumstances in which persons are to be treated as being or not being members of the same household;

  (m) as to circumstances in which one person is to be treated as responsible or not responsible for another.

DERIVATION

Subs. (1): Social Security Act, ss. 20(11) and 84(1).
Subs. (2): 1986 Act, s. 20(12).

AMENDMENTS

1. Local Government Finance Act 1992, Sched. 9, para. 9 (April 1, 1993).
2. Jobseekers Act 1995, Sched. 2, para. 35 (October 7, 1996).

"the 1975 Act"—see s. 174.
"the Old Cases Act"—*ibid.*

GENERAL NOTE

Subsection (1)

These definitions are important throughout the income support, family credit and disability working allowance schemes.

"*child.*" Note the restricted definition which gives rise to the need to define "young persons" in regulations, to cater for the over-15s.

"*dwelling.*" See the notes to the definition of "dwelling occupied as the home" in reg. 2(1) of the Income Support (General) Regulations.

"*family.*" The definition effectively covers couples with or without children and single claimants with children. It may be that some contexts in the regulations require that single claimants without children are also included where a "family" is referred to.

Under para. (a), see the later definitions of married couple and unmarried couple.

Para. (b) covers couples and any child or young person (see reg. 14 of the Income Support Regulations, reg. 6 of the Family Credit (General) Regulations and reg. 8 of the Disability Working Allowance (General) Regulations) in the household for whom one of the couple is responsible. On the general test of membership of the household and children, see *England v. Secretary of State for Social Services* [1982] 3 F.L.R. 222, *R(FIS) 4/83* and *R(SB) 14/87*. See also the notes under "married couple" and "unmarried couple". There are deeming rules in reg. 16 of the Income Support Regulations, regs. 8 and 9 of the Family Credit Regulations and regs. 9 and 10 of the Disability Working Allowance Regulations.

Para. (c) covers a single claimant who is responsible for a child in the same household.

"*income-based jobseeker's allowance.*" See ss. 35(1) and 1(4) of the Jobseekers Act.

"*married couple.*" The crucial question here is whether the couple are members of the same household. In *Santos v. Santos* [1972] 2 All E.R. 246 at 255 it was said that "household" refers to "people held together by a particular kind of tie". No doubt the approach taken in *R(SB) 13/82, R(SB) 4/83* and *CSB 463/1986* would apply here, subject to the deeming regulations mentioned above. The basic point of these and other decisions is that a house can contain a number of households. According to *R(SB) 4/83*, the concept of a household is a matter of commonsense and common experience. If a person in practice has exclusive occupation of separate accommodation from another person they do not live in the same household. In *CSB 463/1986* two claimants physically shared one room in a house as well as other facilities, but otherwise lived separately. They were in separate households. Thus a husband and wife can maintain separate households under the same roof. If the couple have decided to live apart in the same house, there can be separate households even if the husband is still maintaining the wife (*CIS 72/1994*). In *CIS 671/1992* the claimant and his wife shared a room in a home for the mentally ill. Both suffered from senile dementia and they did not understand that they were husband and wife. It is held that there must be some communality, something that can be identified as a domestic establishment. Mere presence in the same room did not turn them into a household. It is a question of fact in each case. In *CIS 81/1993* the same Commissioner similarly concludes that a husband and wife (who were not mentally incapacitated) were not members of the same household where they lived in separate rooms in a nursing home, were billed separately and had only limited contact with each other.

In *CIS 671/1992* the Commissioner also considers whether the claimant and his wife could be said to be members of some other household (the home as a whole). He refers to the decision of the House of Lords in *Simmons v. Pizzey* [1979] A.C. 37 (occupants of a woman's refuge not a single household), and concludes that all the residents of the home were not one household.

These decisions are followed in *CIS 4935/1997*, which also concerned a married couple who shared a double room in a residential home (for which they were billed separately). The room was furnished with their own furniture and they had a kettle and a toaster to make breakfast, although they ate their main meals in the communal dining room. They spent much of their time together and were able to wash and dress themselves, apart from needing assistance to get out of the bath. They had entered the home because it was becoming difficult to cope on their own and so they needed someone else to undertake the organisation of their domestic and personal activities. The Commissioner agrees with *CIS 671/1992* that for there to be a "household" there had to be a domestic establishment. This meant two or more people living together as a unit and enjoying a reasonable level of independence and self-sufficiency. If the degree of independence and self-sufficiency fell below a certain level, there was no longer a domestic establishment and therefore no longer a household. The point at which this occurred was a matter for the common sense of the tribunal. The tribunal had correctly concluded in this case that the claimants were not members of the same household.

Although a person cannot simultaneously have two households he can spend, for example, six months of the year in one household and six in another (*CIS 11304/1995*).

A person under 16 cannot be a member of a married or unmarried couple (*CFC 7/1992*).

"unmarried couple." The meaning and effect of this definition raises one of the most contentious issues in the whole of the law of social security—the cohabitation rule. The term "cohabitation" is now replaced by "living together as husband and wife," which is thought to be more neutral. The "rule" arises from the facts that the applicable amount for a couple is less than that for two single claimants and that a claimant is excluded from entitlement to income support if her partner is in remunerative work. The principle of aggregation between husband and wife is itself controversial, but while it remains, so it is argued, a couple living together as husband and wife must be treated in the same way. This is despite the fact that the legal position of such a couple in many other respects is different from that of a married couple.

While the law remains as it is, it is crucial to identify when a couple are living together as husband and wife. The first point to note is that the income support scheme recognises other ways of living together and has specific rules for determining the entitlement of claimants who live in someone else's household or have someone else living in their household. Webster J. put this very well in *Robson v. Secretary of State for Social Services* [1982] 3 F.L.R. 232, 236, when he said that "the legislation provides for three different situations: two persons who are living together being husband and wife is the first; two persons living together as husband and wife is the second; and two persons living together not as husband and wife is the third. It seems to me that where the facts show that there are two persons living together not being husband and wife, then both the second and third situations must be considered." Thus to show that a couple are living together is only the first step, not the final one, as so often happens in practice (see also, *e.g. Crake v SBC, Butterworth v. SBC* [1982] 1 All E.R. 498, 502, SB 38).

There have been a number of Commissioner's decisions on a similar rule in widow's benefit (the test is held to be the same in *R(SB) 17/81* and *R(G) 3/81* and the same principles will apply for the income-related benefits), but the position reached is fairly vague. Early attempts to obtain a judicial definition of "cohabitation" were unsuccessful ("for my part it is so well-known that nothing I could say about it could possibly assist in its interpretation hereafter," Lord Widgery C. J. in *R. v. S.W. London A.T., ex p. Barnett*, SB 4). The examination of three main matters is required in deciding if a woman is cohabiting with a man as his wife: "(1) their relationship in relation to sex: (2) their relationship in relation to money: (3) their general relationship. Although all three are as a rule relevant, no single one of them is necessarily conclusive" (*R(G) 3/71*). In *CIS 87/1993*, however, the Commissioner expresses the view that it is the parties' general relationship that is most important (see below).

In response to criticisms about the operation of the cohabitation rule the Supplementary Benefits Commission produced published guidelines. The last formulation in summary form was in the 1984 edition of the *Supplementary Benefits Handbook*. A previous form of these guidelines had been approved as "an admirable signpost; the approach cannot be faulted" (Woolf J. in *Crake v SBC, Butterworth v. SBC, supra*) and were found to correspond to the *R(G) 3/71* test in *R(SB) 17/81*. The Handbook said (para. 2.13) that the main criteria are:

"1. Members of the same household

The couple must be living in the same household and neither partner will usually have any other home where they normally live. This implies that the couple live together, apart from absences necessary for employment, visits to relatives, etc.

2. Stability

Living together as husband and wife clearly implies more than an occasional or very brief association. When a couple first live together, it may be clear from the start that the relationship is similar to that of husband and wife (for example, if the woman has taken the man's name and borne his child), but in cases where at the outset the nature of the relationship is less clear it may be right not to regard the couple as living together as husband and wife until it is apparent that a stable relationship has been formed.

3. Financial support

In most husband and wife relationships one would expect to find financial support of one party by the other, or sharing of household expenses, but the absence of any such arrangement does not of itself prove that a couple are not living together.

4. Sexual relationship

Similarly, a sexual relationship is a normal part of a marriage and therefore of living together as husband and wife. But its absence at any particular time does not necessarily prove that a couple are not living as husband and wife.

5. Children

When a couple are caring for a child of their union, there is a strong presumption that they are living together as husband and wife.

6. Public acknowledgment

Whether the couple have represented themselves to other people as husband and wife is relevant. However, many couples living together do not wish to pretend that they are actually married. The fact that they retain their identity publicly as unmarried people does not mean that they cannot be regarded as living together as husband and wife.''

The Handbook was wrong to claim that these guidelines had been approved by courts and a Commissioner, for there had been changes in form. The most important, in the paragraph on ''sexual relationship,'' are devastatingly set out by the Commissioner in *R(SB) 35/85*. It was the 1979 version which was approved in *Crake* and *Butterworth* and in *R(SB) 17/81* and which referred to a sexual relationship as an important as well as a normal part of marriage and also noted that the presence of a sexual relationship did not necessarily prove that a couple were living as husband and wife. The 1982 edition added a new sentence ''However, if a couple have never had such a relationship it is most unlikely that they should be regarded as living together as husband and wife.'' The 1983 edition ''watered down'' that sentence to suggesting that ''it may be wrong'' to regard the couple as living together as husband and wife in such circumstances. In the 1984 edition this final sentence disappeared altogether, along with the suggestion that the presence of a sexual relationship does not necessarily prove that a couple are living as husband and wife. In the meantime, the law has remained exactly the same. However, it is correct to stress that there is no single way by which the issue can be decided in every case. For the criteria tend not to help in making the basic distinction between couples living together as husband and wife and those living together in other ways. As *CIS 87/1993* emphasises, it is important to consider *why* the couple are living together.

The issues are now dealt with in Part 15 of the AOG, where the issues are discussed quite fully and with reference to a range of decisions. It is notable that in para. 15026 a sexual relationship is now described as an important part of marriage, and the presence of a sexual relationship is said not to be conclusive in itself of living together as husband and wife.

Household

Being members of the same household is obviously necessary. The approach to the meaning of ''household'' in the definition of ''householder'' for supplementary benefit purposes (see the notes on ''married couple'') may be relevant. In *R(SB) 30/83* the Commissioner holds that the issue is not decided on a week-by-week basis. So where the woman was absent during University terms living in a rented bedsitter, the couple were living together throughout. This principle was implicitly applied in *R(SB) 8/85*. The claimant lived with a Mr. G, whose employment brought him to the area and was said to go back to his wife at weekends. The Commissioner holds that a person can only be a member of one couple, and so of one household, at a time. This appears to leave open, to be determined according to the circumstances, whether Mr. G was living with the claimant for five days a week and with his wife for two days, or with only one of them. *CIS 11304/1995* explicitly states that there can be two households in these circumstances. Mr. K lived with his wife in Zimbabwe for six months of the year and with the claimant in England for the other half of the year. Although Mr. K could not simultaneously have two households, he could spend six months of the year in one household and six in another. If a person maintains and from time to time lives in the same house as his lawful spouse there is an initial presumption that they form a married couple.

In *R(SB) 19/85* the claimant had been living together with (another) Mr. G as his wife in Manchester. She did not move with him to London because there was no place available in a London hospital for her to have dialysis on a kidney machine. Although *R(SB) 30/83* holds that the relationship can continue despite temporary absences, the Commissioner holds that the situation here was different. Effectively, the claimant and Mr. G had ceased to live together in the same accommodation. At the time, reg. 2(2) of the Supplementary Benefit (Aggregation) Regulations, deeming a couple still to be members of the same household through temporary absences, only applied to married couples, not as later also to unmarried couples. Now see reg. 16(1) of the Income Support Regulations.

Stability
The stability of a relationship is only of great weight if the relationship is one like husband and wife. There is no reason why a stable landlady-lodger relationship or flat-sharing relationship should not last for many years (see, for example, *CP 8001/1995*). However, it is sometimes suggested that an element of permanency in a relationship may differentiate it from, say, an employer-housekeeper relationship (*e.g. Campbell v. Secretary of State for Social Services* [1983] 4 F.L.R. 138, where the "housekeeper" had sold her furniture and intended to apply for a joint local authority tenancy with the man). This forward-looking approach does make sense. But, as *CP 8001/1995* points out, even if an arrangement has become an established and settled one after some years, it does not follow that it has been on the same footing since the couple first started living together.

Financial support
The approach to financial support seems to make almost any arrangement point the same way, except a very clearly fixed commercial rate. If the man pays a lot, he is supporting the woman. If he pays very little, this shows that the relationship is more than a commercial one. This makes it very difficult for parties who are friends, or where the man pays what he can afford, where the proper conclusion may merely be that the two people share a household.

Sexual relationship
There has been an attempt to decrease reliance on the existence of a sexual relationship, partly in response to criticism of "sex snoopers" and methods of investigation. Officers are now instructed not to initiate questions about sexual relationships and not to seek to inspect sleeping arrangements, but to note statements and evidence presented by the claimant. However, if a rule is to distinguish people living together as husband and wife from people living together in some other way it seems impossible not to give great significance to the nature of the sexual relationship. By playing down its importance, either as being present or absent, the Handbook inevitably shifted the test closer to one which simply tested whether the couple were living together in one household. The Commissioner in *CIS 87/1993* considers that where there has never been a sexual relationship, strong alternative grounds are needed to reach the conclusion that the relationship is akin to that of husband and wife. In his view, the instruction to DSS officers not to ask about the physical aspects of the relationship is inappropriate in an inquisitorial system, and if the information is not volunteered, such questions may have to be asked. But care will need to be taken to prevent any such investigation becoming over-intrusive.
In *CSB 150/1985* the Commissioner held that an unmarried couple who refrained on principle from any sexual relationship could not be described as living together as husband and wife. The claimant and his fiancee lived in the same house, but were Mormons. That religion forbids sexual relationships before marriage.

Children and public acknowledgment
The shared care of children, especially children of the couple, and public acknowledgment are obviously important factors. In *R(G) 1/79* the adoption of the same name on the electoral register was decisive. Other elements might be whether the couple visit relatives or friends, or go on holiday, together.

What these points come to is that the so-called "objective facts" of a relationship may be capable of being interpreted either way. This, then, leaves the authorities in a difficulty, although it is clear that the burden of proof (where relevant: see *CIS 317/1994* below) is on the DSS, at least when the rule operates as a disqualification. In two decisions the Divisional Court has stressed the importance of looking at the intention of the parties in explaining the "objective facts." In *Butterworth v. SBC, supra,* the claimant was disabled following a serious accident, and invited the man, whom she had known for five years, to move into her house, since she was then on her own. The man had his own bedroom, with a lock on the door. He did the cooking and household tasks, and they lived as one household. Woolf J. says:
"If the only reason that [the man] went to that house temporarily was to look after Mrs. Butterworth in her state of illness and, albeit, while doing so, acted in the same way as an attentive husband would behave towards his wife who suffered an illness, this does not amount to living together as husband and wife because it was not the intention of the parties that there should be such a relationship. Looked at without knowing the reason for the man going to live

there, it would appear that they were living together as husband and wife, but when the reason was known that would explain those circumstances.''

In *Robson's* case (above), the parties were both seriously disabled, needing wheelchairs and invalid cars. They had been friends for a long time before they were widowed. They moved together into a two-bedroom maisonette at their social worker's suggestion. They lived as one household. As so often the SBAT assumed that this was conclusive, and this was an error of law. In order to provide guidance to tribunals, Webster J. says that often it is only possible to decide into which category a relationship falls by considering the objective facts,

"because usually the intention of the parties is either unascertainable, or, if ascertainable, is not to be regarded as reliable. But if it is established to the satisfaction of the tribunal that the two persons concerned did not intend to live together as husband and wife and still do not intend to do so, in my judgment it would be a very strong case indeed sufficient to justify a decision that they are, or ought to be treated as if they are, husband and wife.''

Although subsequent Divisional Court decisions (*e.g. Kaur v. Secretary of State for Social Services* [1982] 3 F.L.R. 237) have not referred to intention as a factor, it has not been rejected either. However, in *R(SB) 17/81* the Commissioner says that Webster J.'s words are of no real assistance to tribunals. For, he says, it is "the conduct of the person concerned to which regard has to be paid", *i.e.* "what he or she does or says at the relevant time." If *R(SB) 17/81* is taken as deciding that only the "objective facts" as identified by the Handbook criteria are relevant, and that the intention of the parties is not relevant, it need not be followed as being inconsistent with persuasive decisions of the Divisional Court. If *R(SB) 17/81* is taken as a reminder of the difficulties of establishing intention it is in line with those decisions, although evidence of intention should not be as limited as suggested. On the facts of *R(SB) 17/81* the couple shared a sexual relationship and one household, but said that there was nothing permanent about the relationship. The Commissioner points out that the fact that they did not intend to marry did not mean that they did not intend to live together as though they were married.

It is the second view of *R(SB) 17/81* which seems to have been applied in recent Commissioners' decisions, although AOs commonly rely on the first view in submissions to tribunals. *CSSB 145/1983* is a decision on facts reminiscent of *Robson's* case. Two disabled people living in a sheltered housing scheme moved into one flat to share living expenses and provide mutual support. At the beginning the Housing Association running the flats did not have the funds to divide the one bedroom. There was no sexual relationship. The SSAT had decided that the situation was no different from that of a married couple where one partner had a serious disability. The Commissioner holds this to be a wrong approach. A sharing of expenses and mutual support can arise between people of the same sex, or between brother and sister, and does not in itself amount to living together as husband and wife.

In *R(SB) 35/85* the claimant was a widow in her seventies. She had taken over the tenancy of her bungalow in 1976, on the death of her brother, with whom she had lived for some years. In 1974, Mr. W, who needed care and help, had moved into the household. By August 1984, he was a widower. The claimant did the cooking and there was a sharing of household expenses. The Commissioner holds that the SSAT, in finding the claimant and Mr W to be living together as husband and wife, had failed to see that the existence of a common household was only one ingredient in the decision. He adopts as helpful guidance the approach of Woolf J. in *Butterworth's* case that it is impossible to categorise all the kinds of explanation of why two people were sharing a household which would mean that the two were not living together as husband and wife.

In *CIS 87/1993* the claimant maintained that the only relationship between him and Mrs B, with whom he was living, was that of patient and carer. The Commissioner decides that the SSAT had failed to consider their general relationship and *why* they were living together. He expresses reservations about the "criteria" relied upon by AOs in cohabitation cases. He points out that Woolf J. in *Crake* and *Butterworth* considered it wrong to refer to them as "criteria" and preferred the description "admirable signposts". There was nothing in *R(SB) 17/81* to suggest that only these admirable signposts had to be considered. In the Commissioner's view, the admirable signposts failed to emphasise the significance of the parties' "general relationship". It was arguable that it was the parties' general relationship that was of paramount importance and that their sexual and their financial relationship were only relevant for the light they threw upon the general relationship.

The importance of looking at the totality of the parties' relationship and of not simply using the criteria as items on a checklist to be ticked off one by one is emphasised in *CP 8001/1995*. The claimant was a widow who had taken in a lodger. He paid her rent and a contribution towards expenses, but they did not pool resources, even though she had a right to draw cheques on his bank account. As time passed, they became friends, watched TV and ate together and went on holiday together in a group of friends. There was no sexual relationship, but on occasion they went halves on a twin-bedded room when staying in a hotel. The Commissioner decides that even though there were elements in the arrangement which matched those found in a normal marriage, it was equally akin to that of a brother and sister living in the same household, and that the totality of the evidence did not add up to a husband and wife relationship.

Burden of proof

In *CIS 317/1994* the Commissioner decides that the question of onus of proof did not arise where the question of whether the claimant was living together as husband and wife with her alleged partner fell to be determined on an *initial* claim for income support. What had to be considered was all the relevant facts. He pointed to the duty on the claimant to provide such information as may be required to decide the claim (see reg. 7(1) of the Claims and Payments Regulations). The Commissioner also considered that although living together as husband and wife operated as a disqualification for widow's benefit it did not do so for income support. But, with respect, this distinction seems more apparent than real. Even though cohabitation is not an automatic bar in all cases, if the claimant's alleged partner is in remunerative work, or has income or capital which disentitles them to income support, or has himself already claimed income support, the effect of a living together decision will be to disqualify the claimant from income support. Thus it is suggested that the burden of proof (on the AO) may come into play in marginal cases (if the claimant otherwise satisfies the conditions of entitlement to income support), even on initial claims. If benefit is stopped on a review on the grounds of alleged cohabitation, the burden of proof will be on the AO. However, as pointed out above, it is often not so much the facts that may be in issue as the interpretation of those facts. Here the intention of the parties and the reason why they are living together may be the deciding factors (and see *CIS 87/1993* above).

Part VIII

The Social Fund

Payments out of the social fund

138.—[¹(1) There may be made out of the social fund, in accordance with this Part of this Act—
    (a) payments of prescribed amounts, whether in respect of prescribed items or otherwise, to meet, in prescribed circumstances, maternity expenses and funeral expenses; and
    (b) payments by way of community care grant, crisis loan or budgeting loan to meet other needs in accordance with directions given or guidance issued by the Secretary of State.]
(2) Payments may also be made out of that fund, in accordance with this Part of this Act, of a prescribed amount or a number of prescribed amounts to prescribed descriptions of persons, in prescribed circumstances, to meet expenses for heating which appear to the Secretary of State to have been or to be likely to be incurred in cold weather.
(3) The power to make a payment out of the social fund such as is mentioned in subsection (1)(b) above may be exercised by making a payment to a third party with a view to the third party providing, or arranging for the provision of, goods or services for the applicant.
(4) In this section "prescribed" means specified in or determined in accordance with regulations.
    [¹(5) In this Part—
    "budgeting loan" means a loan awarded in circumstances specified in directions issued by the Secretary of State for the purpose of defraying an intermittent expense;
    "community care grant" means a grant awarded in circumstances so specified for the purpose of meeting a need for community care;
    "crisis loan" means a loan awarded in circumstances so specified for the purpose of meeting an immediate short term need;
and any reference in this subsection to meeting a need or defraying an expense includes a reference to helping to meet the need or to defray the expense.]

DERIVATIONS

Subss. (1) and (2): Social Security Act 1986, s.32(2) and (2A).
Subs. (3): 1986 Act, s.33(1A).
Subs. (4): 1986 Act, s.84(1).

AMENDMENT

1. Social Security Act 1998, s.70 (April 5, 1999).

GENERAL NOTE

This book cannot contain any real discussion of the general social fund scheme. It is concerned with claims which can lead to an appeal to a SSAT. Since such appeals only lie from decisions of AOs, the decisions of social fund officers (SFOs) cannot be appealed to a SSAT. A system of review is set out in s.66 of the Administration Act. If an applicant insists on appealing to a SSAT against a decision of a SFO, a SSAT chairman may dispose of the purported appeal as outside the SSAT's jurisdiction (Adjudication Regulations, reg. 3(7)). Only the payments for maternity and funeral expenses under subs. (1)(a) and for cold weather under subs. (2) are dealt with by AOs and SSATs. Only the sections relating to these payments have substantial comments. But the primary legislation relating to the social fund is included, since it will be of use to many readers. In the later Social Fund section are the regulations on the review process and the general directions issued by the Secretary of State under s.140(2) to (4) (formerly ss.32(2)(b), 33(10) and (10A) of the Social Security Act 1986), which are binding on SFOs.

Note that under the Social Security Act 1998 SFOs will be replaced by "appropriate officers" who will take decisions on behalf of the Secretary of State (see s.36 of the 1998 Act). The separate system of social fund reviews will continue (see s.38 of the Act). The new system for decision-making and appeals under the 1998 Act is due to take effect for the social fund on November 29, 1999.

Subsection (1)(a)

Subsection (1)(a) is re-enacted by s.70(1)(a) of the 1998 Act with effect from April 5, 1999. This part of the social fund scheme was originally brought into operation in April 1987 to enable payments to be made for maternity and funeral expenses. These are made under the ordinary system of adjudication and under regulations required to be made by subs. (1)(a). They are not subject to any budget. See the Social Fund Maternity and Funeral Expenses (General) Regulations 1987. The death grant and the maternity grant, formerly payable under the Social Security Act 1975, were abolished (1986 Act, ss.38 and 41) and the provisions for maternity and funeral expenses under the supplementary benefit regulations were removed in April 1987 (General Regulations, regs. 13 to 15).

Subs. (1)(*a*) does little more than provide the framework for the detailed entitlement set out in the General Regulations. See s.78(4) of the Administration Act on the recovery of funeral payments from the estate of the deceased.

New restrictions on payments for funeral expenses were introduced on June 5, 1995 and there was further clarification and tightening-up of the rules on April 7, 1997 (see regs. 7 and 7A of the General Regulations and the notes to those regulations). Note also the changes introduced on November 17, 1997.

The argument that maternity (or funeral expenses) that do not qualify under subs. (1)(a) can come within subs. (1)(b) was rejected in *R. v. Social Fund Inspector, ex parte Harper*, High Court, February 7, 1997. Harrison J. held that subss. (1)(a) and (b) provided mutually exclusive methods of meeting particular needs and that maternity and funeral expenses were only intended to be met to the extent laid down in the General Regulations.

Subsection (1)(b)

The previous form of this subsection gave the discretion ("may") to make payments to meet "other needs" (other than for maternity and funeral expenses (*R. v. Social Fund Inspector, ex parte Harper*), see the note to subs. (1)(a)). The wording of the new form, inserted by s.70 of the Social Security Act 1998, is more specific, referring explicitly to the three types of payment from the discretionary social fund (see the definitions in subs. (5)). Under the previous system an application was made to the social fund as a whole (although it was possible to specify the category of payment sought). An applicant will now have to complete an application form for the type of payment that he wishes to obtain. If the person applies for a crisis loan this can be treated as an application for a community care grant and vice versa (see s.140(4)(aa) and Social Fund Direction 49). However, there is no provision for an application for a budgeting loan to be considered under any other category.

Subsection (1)(b) also contains the general power for the Secretary of State to give directions and guidance, which are given particular statutory force under s.140(2) and (5) of this Act and s.66(7), (9) and (10) of the Administration Act. There are more specific powers in s.140(2) to (4) and s.66(8) and s.168(5) of the Administration Act. The Secretary of State's directions are set out in Part VI of this book.

In *R. v. Social Fund Officer and Secretary of State for Social Security, ex parte Stitt* it was argued that the predecessor of subs. (1)(b) did not empower the Secretary of State to give directions which limited the categories of need which could be met from the social fund. The applicant and his wife already had three children when they had triplets. The applicant was then on an Employment Training course. He applied for a community care grant to assist with the care of the triplets. The application was rejected because direction 29 (by reference to direction 12(h)) excluded payments for domestic assistance. The Divisional Court (*The Times*, February 23, 1990, *The Independent*, February 23, 1990) held that the Secretary of State had power to give "such directions as can reasonably be regarded as being necessary for the proper 'control and management' of the Social Fund so as to enable that fund to meet the needs of applicants which cannot be met out of their own resources" (see s.167(2) of the Administration Act, formerly s.32(5) of the 1986 Act). This power covered directions defining needs. The Court of Appeal (*The Times*, July 4, 1990) agreed that the directions were validly made, but Butler-Sloss L.J. and Sir Patrick Connor found the power in ss.32(1)(b) and 33(10) of the 1986 Act (now this subsection and s.140(2)) rather than in s.32(5). All the judges expressed their surprise (at the least) at the scope of the unsupervised powers to give directions.

In *R. v. Secretary of State for Social Security, ex parte Healey* (and the associated actions in *Smith* and *Stitt II*), *The Independent*, April 18, 1991, *The Times*, April 22, 1991, the Divisional Court accepts that the Court of Appeal's decision means that the Secretary of State has power to define the categories of need to be met. The power is not limited to excluding needs which can be met by some body or person other than the social fund. The Secretary of State must not act irrationally in exercising the power, but this does not prevent him excluding needs which may not be met elsewhere. The Court of Appeal ([1991] 4 Admin. L.R. 713) confirms this decision and rejects the argument that a court may quash directions if it finds them merely unreasonable, rather than irrational.

Subsection (2)

Although the predecessor of this subsection was in force from April 1988, the regulations which it required were not in place until November 7, 1988 (Social Fund Cold Weather Payments (General) Regulations 1988). The form of the scheme, as embodied in the 1988 Regulations, has been amended several times. The current form does not require a separate claim to be made for a severe weather payment. As for maternity and funeral expenses, the decisions are made by AOs, with appeals to a SSAT, and are not subject to any budget.

Note also the Social Fund Winter Fuel Payment Regulations 1998 under which all pensioner households received a one-off payment in the winter of 1998 towards their fuel bills. A similar payment was made in 1999. It has been announced that the scheme will be continued for the winter of 1999/2000, when the payment for people in receipt of income support will increase from £50 to £100.

Awards by social fund officers

139.—(1) The questions whether a payment such as is mentioned in section 138(1)(b) is to be awarded and how much it is to be shall be determined by a social fund officer.

(2) A social fund officer may determine that an award shall be payable in specified instalments at specified times.

(3) [¹ . . .].

(4) An award [²of a crisis loan or a budgeting loan] shall be repayable upon such terms and conditions as before the award is paid the Secretary of State notifies to the person by or on behalf of whom the application for it was made.

(5) Payment of an award shall be made to the applicant unless the social fund officer determines otherwise.

Subss. (1) to (4): Social Security Act 1986 Act, s.33(2) to (4A).
Subs. (5): 1986, s.33(11).

AMENDMENTS

1. Social Security Act 1998, Sched. 7, para. 72(3) (April 5, 1999).
2. Social Security Act 1998, Sched. 7, para. 72(4) (April 5, 1999).

GENERAL NOTE

Subsection (1)
   This provision secures that decisions on payments from the general social fund are made by social fund officers, so that there is no appeal to a SSAT.
   Note that under the Social Security Act 1998 SFOs will be replaced by "appropriate officers" who will take decisions on behalf of the Secretary of State (see s.36 of the 1998 Act). The separate system of social fund reviews will continue (see s.38 of the Act). The changes are due to take effect for the social fund on November 29, 1999.

Subsection (4)
   The Social Fund Directions specify what categories of need may be met by grants and which by loans. S.78 of the Administration Act is concerned with the mechanism of recovering loans. See the notes to s.78 and also the Social Fund (Recovery by Deductions from Benefits) Regulations 1988 in Part VI.

Principles of determination

   140.—(1) In determining whether to make an award [¹ of a community care grant or a crisis loan] to the applicant or the amount or value to be awarded a social fund officer shall have regard, subject to subsection (2) below, to all the circumstances of the case and, in particular—
   (a) the nature, extent and urgency of the need;
   (b) the existence of resources from which the need may be met;
   (c) the possibility that some other person or body may wholly or partly meet it;
   (d) where the payment is repayable, the likelihood of repayment and the time within which repayment is likely;
   (e) any relevant allocation under section 168(1) to (4) of the Administration Act.
   [¹ (1A) Subject to subsection (2) below, in determining whether to make an award of a budgeting loan to the applicant, or the amount or value to be awarded, an appropriate officer shall have regard to—
   (a) such of the applicant's personal circumstances as are of a description specified in directions issued by the Secretary of State; and
   (b) the criteria specified in paragraphs (b) to (e) of subsection (1) above;
but where the criterion mentioned in paragraph (a) above would preclude the award of such a loan, the appropriate officer shall have regard instead to such other criterion as may be specified in directions so issued.]
   (2) A social fund officer shall determine any question in accordance with any general directions issued by the Secretary of State and in determining any question shall take account of any general guidance issued by him.
   (3) Without prejudice to the generality of subsection (2) above, the Secretary of State may issue directions under that subsection for the purpose of securing that a social fund officer or group of social fund officers shall not in any specified period make awards of any specified description which in the aggregate exceed the amount, or a specified portion of the amount, allocated to that officer

or group of officers under section 168(1) to (4) for payments under awards of that description in that period.

(4) Without prejudice to the generality of subsection (2) above, the power to issue general directions conferred on the Secretary of State by that subsection includes power to direct—

   (a) that in circumstances specified in the direction a social fund officer shall not determine an application and, without prejudice to the generality of this paragraph, that a social fund officer shall not determine an application which is made before the end of a specified period after the making of an application by the same person for a payment such as is mentioned in section 138(1)(b) above to meet the same need and without there having been any relevant change of circumstances since the previous application;

[¹(aa) that in circumstances specified in the direction an application for an award of a community care grant may be treated as an application for an award of a crisis loan, and vice versa;]

   (b) that for a category of need specified in the direction a social fund officer shall not award less than an amount specified in the direction;

   (c) that for a category of need specified in the direction a social fund officer shall not award more than an amount so specified;

   (d) that payments to meet a category of need specified in the direction shall in all cases or in no case be made by instalments;

   (e) [¹ . . .]

   (f) that a payment such as is mentioned in section 138(1)(b) above shall only be awarded to a person if either—

      (i) he is in receipt of a benefit which is specified in the direction and the circumstances are such as are so specified; or

      (ii) in a case where the conditions specified in subparagraph (i) above are not satisfied, the circumstances are such as are specified in the direction;

and the power to issue general guidance conferred on him by that subsection includes power to give social fund officers guidance as to any matter to which directions under that subsection may relate.

(5) In determining a question a social fund officer shall take account (subject to any directions or guidance issued by the Secretary of State under this section) of any guidance issued by the social fund officer nominated for his area under section 64 of the Administration Act.

DERIVATIONS

   Subss. (1) to (4): Social Security Act 1986, s.33(9) to (10A).
   Subs. (5): 1986 Act, s.32(11).

AMENDMENT

   1. Social Security Act 1998, s.71 (April 5, 1999).

GENERAL NOTE

Subsection (1)

The effect of subs. (1) is that the social fund officer (SFO) must have regard to the five statutory factors in every case, as well as all the circumstances of the particular case.

Note that from April 5, 1999 subs. (1) only applies to community care grants and crisis loans. For the principles of determination for budgeting loans from April 5, 1999, see subs. (1A).

However, subs. (1) (and subs. (1A)) is subject to subs. (2), which requires the SFO to follow directions given by the Secretary of State and to take account of guidance. Taking account seems to mean the same as having regard, so that Secretary of State's guidance can effectively be added to the list in subs. (1). See *R. v. Social Fund Inspector ex parte Taylor, The Times,* January 20,

1998, in which Dyson J. holds that the effect of the guidance in para. 3002 of the *Social Fund Guide* (to consider the listed questions "in order") was that an SFI was required, when deciding an application for a community care grant, to assess the need and determine its priority before taking budget considerations into account. This was the case even though subs. (1) itself does not lay down a fixed order of consideration. The effect of subs. (5) is to add guidance given by area SFOs to the list, providing that that guidance is not contrary to the Secretary of State's directions or guidance. But directions are overriding, provided that they are within the Secretary of State's statutory power, and so take precedence to the subs. (1) factors.

The requirement to have regard to the budget allocated to the local office (para. (e)) is of particular interest, since it is the budget which is responsible for many of the novel, if not unique, features of the Social Fund. In subs. (1) the state of the budget is just one factor to be taken into account and is given no overriding status. The Social Fund Directions did not originally deal with the budget. Paras. 2016 and 2054 of the Social Fund Manual (containing the guidance) said that a payment was not to be made if it would result in the local office budget being exceeded. In *R. v. Social Fund Inspector and Secretary of State for Social Security, ex parte Roberts, The Times*, February 23, 1990, *The Independent* February 23, 1990, the Divisional Court struck down these, and some other, paragraphs as unlawful. They adopted the language of direction when there was no power to do so. Now see subs. (3).

Subsection (1A)

This provides that from April 5, 1999 decisions on budgeting loans are to be made according to the principles in subs. (1)(b) to (e) and taking into account those of the applicant's personal circumstances that are specified in the Secretary of State's directions. The other criteria in subs. (1) ("all the circumstances of the case" and "the nature, extent and urgency of the need") thus no longer apply to budgeting loans. But note that subs. (1A), like subs. (1), is subject to subs. (2) (see the note to subs. (1)). If no loan would be awarded on the basis of the specified personal circumstances, regard is to be had to other criteria as laid down in the directions. See Social Fund Directions 50 to 53 for the details (note also Directions 8 to 10). The intention is to speed up and simplify decision-making on budgeting loans, by basing it on weighted criteria set out in the directions, rather than the SFO's discretion.

Note that references to "appropriate officer" in subs. (1A) are to be read as references to "social fund officer" until para. 73 of Sched. 7 to the Social Security Act 1998 comes into force (Social Security Act 1998 (Commencement No. 6) Order 1999 (S.I. 1999 No. 1055), art. 3(2)). Para. 73 of Sched. 7 substitutes "appropriate officer" for "social fund officer" throughout s.140.

Subsection (2)

A SFO must follow directions issued by the Secretary of State and must take account of guidance. The directions and guidance were originally published in the *Social Fund Manual*. They were then contained in Volumes 1 and 2 of the *Social Fund Officer's Guide*, produced by the Benefits Agency late in 1991, reissued as the *Social Fund Guide* in 1993. A new version of the *Social Fund Guide* was issued on April 1, 1995, volume 1 containing guidance on the budget and community care grants, and volume 2 on loans, trade disputes and reviews. The Secretary of State's directions were in volume 2. A further new form of the *Social Fund Guide* (now in one volume) was published in May 1999.

See the note to subs. (1) for the interaction of subss.(1) and (2). See subs. (5) for guidance by area SFOs.

Subsection (3)

The predecessor of subs. (3) (s.33(10ZA) of the 1986 Act) was introduced from July 13, 1990. Its intention was described by the Minister for Social Security as follows (H.C. Hansard, March 28, 1990, Vol. 170, col. 580).

"[It] is essential to the successful operation of the fund that its resources are managed so as not to exceed the amounts allocated for payments. Under the present legislation, it would be possible to issue directions on matters relating to the control of the budget. I have already mentioned the power that we are taking in respect of directions for the management and control of local budgets. The additional power that we are taking under the new clause will reinforce the effect of those directions by giving the Secretary of State explicit power to issue directions requiring social fund officers to keep within their allocations.

Such directions will, therefore, preclude a social fund officer, or a group of social fund officers, from making any award that would result in the sums allocated to that officer or group of officers being exceeded. This must be right if the scheme is to operate within the strict monetary limits, as Parliament originally intended, and as was recognised by the court."

It is clear that subs. (3) authorises such directions, which could anyway have been made under the general power of subs. (2). Directions were issued in September 1990 (see Part VI).

An extra £12.3 million was put into the 1990–91 budget to make up for the extra expenditure incurred as a result of the judgment in *Roberts* before the new directions were issued.

Subsection (4)

This provision lists some matters on which the Secretary of State may issue directions, without prejudicing the generality of subs. (2).

Subsection (5)

Under s.64(3) of the Administration Act the Secretary of State may nominate a SFO for an area who is to issue guidance to SFOs in the area about matters specified by the Secretary of State. Direction 41 requires the Area SFO to review and revise planned levels of expenditure and priorities each month.

PART XIII

GENERAL

Interpretation

Application of Act in relation to territorial waters

172. In this Act—
(a) any reference to Great Britain includes a reference to the territorial waters of the United Kingdom adjacent to Great Britain;
(b) any reference to the United Kingdom includes a reference to the territorial waters of the United Kingdom.

DERIVATION

Social Security Act 1986, s.84(4).

Age

173. For the purposes of this Act a person—
(a) is over or under a particular age if he has or, as the case may be, has not attained that age; and
(b) is between two particular ages if he has attained the first but not the second;
and in Scotland (as in England and Wales) the time at which a person attains a particular age expressed in years is the commencement of the relevant anniversary of the date of his birth.

DERIVATION

Social Security Act 1975, Sched. 20.

References to Acts

174. In this Act—
"the 1975 Act" means the Social Security Act 1975;
"the 1986 Act" means the Social Security Act 1986;
"the Administration Act" means the Social Security Administration Act 1992;
"the Consequential Provisions Act" means the Social Security (Consequential Provisions) Act 1992;

"the Northern Ireland Contributions and Benefits Act" means the Social Security Contributions and Benefits (Northern Ireland) Act 1992;
"the Old Cases Act" means the Industrial Injuries and Diseases (Old Cases) Act 1975; and
"the Pensions Act" means the Social Security Pensions Act 1975.

Subordinate legislation

Regulations, orders and schemes

175.—(1) Subject to [²subsection (1A) below], regulations and orders under this Act shall be made by the Secretary of State.

[²(1a) Subsection (1) above has effect subject to—
(a) any provision of Part I or VI of this Act providing for regulations or an order to be made by the Treasury or by the Commissioners of Inland Revenue, and
(b) section 145(5) above.]

(2) Powers under this Act to make regulations, orders or schemes shall be exercisable by statutory instrument.

(3) Except in the case of an order under section 145(3) above and in so far as this Act otherwise provides, any power under this Act to make regulations or an order may be exercised—
(a) either in relation to all cases to which the power extends, or in relation to those cases subject to specified exceptions, or in relation to any specified cases or classes of case;
(b) so as to make, as respects the cases in relation to which it is exercised—
  (i) the full provision to which the power extends or any less provision (whether by way of exception or otherwise),
  (ii) the same provision for all cases in relation to which the power is exercised, or different provision for different cases or different classes of case or different provision as respects the same case or class of case for different purposes of this Act;
  (iii) any such provision either unconditionally or subject to any specified condition;
and where such a power is expressed to be exercisable for alternative purposes it may be exercised in relation to the same case for any or all of those purposes; and powers to make regulations or an order for the purposes of any one provision of this Act are without prejudice to powers to make regulations or an order for the purposes of any other provision.

(4) Without prejudice to any specific provision in this Act, any power conferred by this Act to make regulations or an order (other than the power conferred in section 145(3) above) includes power to make thereby such incidental, supplementary, consequential or transitional provision as appears to the [²person making the regulations or order] to be expedient for the purposes of the regulations or order.

(5) Without prejudice to any specific provisions in this Act, a power conferred by any provision of this Act except—
(a) sections 30, 47(6), [¹25B(2)(a)] and 145(3) above and paragraph 3(9) of Schedule 7 to this Act;
(b) section 122(1) above in relation to the definition of "payments by way of occupational or personal pension"; and
(c) Part XI,
to make regulations or an order includes power to provide for a person to exercise a discretion in dealing with any matter.

(6) [*Omitted as relating only to housing benefit and community charge benefit.*]

(7) Any power of the Secretary of State under any provision of this Act, except the provisions mentioned in subsection (5)(a) and (b) above and Part IX, to make any regulations or order, where the power is not expressed to be exercisable with the consent of the Treasury, shall if the Treasury so direct be exercisable only in conjunction with them.

(8) and (9) [*Omitted as relating only to ss.116 to 120.*]

(10) Any reference in this section or section 176 below to an order or regulations under this Act includes a reference to an order or regulations made under any provision of an enactment passed after this Act and directed to be construed as one with this Act; but this subsection applies only so far as a contrary intention is not expressed in the enactment so passed, and without prejudice to the generality of any such direction.

DERIVATION

Social Security Act 1986, ss. 83(1) and 84(1).

AMENDMENTS

1. Social Security (Incapacity for Work) Act 1994, Sched. 1, para. 36 (April 13, 1995).
2. Social Security Contributions (Transfer of Functions, etc.) Act 1999, s.2 and Sched. 3, para. 29 (April 1, 1999).

Parliamentary control

176.—(1) and (2) [*Omitted as not applying to income-related benefits.*]

(3) A statutory instrument—

(a) which contains (whether alone or with other provisions) any order, regulations or scheme made under this Act by the Secretary of State, [¹the Treasury or the Commissioners of Inland Revenue,] other than an order under section 145(3) above; and

(b) which is not subject to any requirement that a draft of the instrument shall be laid before and approved by a resolution of each House of Parliament,

shall be subject to annulment in pursuance of a resolution of either House of Parliament.

DERIVATION

Social Security Act 1986, s.83(4).

AMENDMENT

1. Social Security Contributions (Transfer of Functions, etc.) Act 1999, s.2 and Sched. 3, para. 30 (April 1, 1999).

Short title, commencement and extent

177.—(1) This Act may be cited as the Social Security Contributions and Benefits Act 1992.

(2) This Act is to be read, where appropriate, with the Administration Act and the Consequential Provisions Act.

(3) The enactments consolidated by this Act are repealed, in consequence of the consolidation, by the Consequential Provisions Act.

(4) Except as provided in Schedule 4 to the Consequential Provisions Act, this Act shall come into force on 1st July 1992.

(5) The following provisions extend to Northern Ireland—
 section 16 and Schedule 2;
 section 116(2); and
 this section.

(6) Except as provided by this section, this Act does not extend to Northern Ireland.

DEFINITIONS

 "the Administration Act"—see s. 174.
 "the Consequential Provisions Act"—*ibid.*

Jobseekers Act 1995

(1995 c.18)

SECTIONS REPRODUCED

PART I

THE JOBSEEKER'S ALLOWANCE

Entitlement

Miscellaneous

PART II

BACK TO WORK SCHEMES

PART III

MISCELLANEOUS AND SUPPLEMENTAL

SCHEDULE

GENERAL NOTE

From October 7, 1996 a new benefit, jobseeker's allowance (JSA), replaced unemployment benefit and income support for those claimants who are required to be available for employment as a condition of receiving benefit. Income support remains for those who are not required to be available for work (*e.g.* lone parents, people aged 60 or over and those incapable of work). Following the pattern of recent social security legislation, the Jobseekers Act contains only the bare bones of the scheme; the detail is in the Jobseeker's Allowance Regulations. The Jobseeker's Allowance (Transitional Provisions) Regulations contain the transitional provisions for existing claimants.

The introduction of JSA represented a fundamental overhaul of the benefits system for unemployed people; it constituted "the biggest administrative shake-up in Britain's public benefit system since the welfare state began" (*Financial Times*, August 21, 1996). Under JSA it remains an essential condition of entitlement to benefit that the unemployment must be involuntary but there is yet further emphasis on the requirement for claimants to be taking positive steps to rejoin the labour market and on the importance of training, in particular for 16 and 17-year-olds. The White Paper (Cm. 2687 (1994)) described JSA as a "modern benefit designed specifically to help meet the needs of unemployed people and get them back into jobs". Certainly the emphasis of the scheme is on the latter, the compulsory "jobseeker's agreement", the tighter benefit sanctions and the power to use jobseeker's directions to "improve the claimant's prospects of being employed" being particular examples.

Another of the government's aims in introducing JSA was to rationalise the previous dual system of benefits for the unemployed. But while JSA is a single benefit it has two distinct elements, contribution-based JSA (which broadly replaces unemployment benefit) and income-based JSA (which is now the means-tested benefit for unemployed people instead of income support). Although there are some central common conditions (see s. 1 of the Act), there are also separate rules of entitlement for each component (see ss. 2 and 3 of the Act). This book concentrates on the provisions relating to income-based JSA and also deals with the common conditions. See *Bonner et al. Non-Means-Tested Benefits: the Legislation (Bonner)* for the provisions specific to contribution-based JSA and the common conditions.

Among the consequences of the amalgamation of unemployment benefit and income support for the unemployed is the fact that the rate of benefit (not including the premiums and housing costs elements of income-based JSA) is now the same for both contribution-based and income-based JSA. The model adopted is that of income support, so that contribution-based JSA is payable at a different rate depending on the claimant's age, with a lower rate for those under 25 (an approach which does not fit easily with the insurance-based concept of a contributory benefit). In addition, JSA is to be a weekly benefit (unlike unemployment benefit which was a daily benefit) and there will normally be a three-day waiting period for both types of JSA (which previously only applied to unemployment benefit). Note also that there are no longer any differences between the rules governing availability for, and actively seeking, work for the two elements of the benefit. All claims will be dealt with at a JobCentre (although 16 and 17-year-olds also have to register with the Careers Service), and as one might expect with a single benefit, there is just one claim form.

The introduction of JSA thus involved many changes in the benefit system for unemployed people, in terms both of the rules governing entitlement and of administrative practices. But three major changes should be highlighted. First, all claimants are required to enter into a jobseeker's agreement as a condition of entitlement to benefit. Secondly, contribution-based JSA is only payable for a maximum of six months (but note the transitional protection for some claimants up to April 1997). Thirdly, where a sanction is imposed for voluntary unemployment, a failure to comply with the labour market conditions, etc., there is no automatic entitlement to a reduced rate of benefit. A reduced rate of income-based JSA will only be payable in certain cases of hardship. In addition, the sanction will "eat into" the person's entitlement to contribution-based JSA (see further *Bonner*).

In relation to income-based JSA, the means test is broadly the same as that for income support and many of the other rules mirror those that apply to income support. Where there are differences, these are noted at the appropriate places in the commentary. One important change that was made to the income support rules alongside the introduction of JSA is that from October 7, 1996, in the case of a claimant's partner, remunerative work is defined as 24 (not 16) hours a week. This also applies to income-based JSA.

Note also the power in s. 29 to pilot new regulations and the back to work bonus scheme introduced by s. 26. See the notes to those sections.

Part I

The Jobseeker's Allowance

Entitlement

The jobseeker's allowance

1.—(1) An allowance, to be known as a jobseeker's allowance, shall be payable in accordance with the provisions of this Act.

(2) Subject to the provisions of this Act, a claimant is entitled to a jobseeker's allowance if he—

(a) is available for employment;

(b) has entered into a jobseeker's agreement which remains in force;

(c) is actively seeking employment;

(d) satisfies either—

    (i) the conditions set out in section 2; or

    (ii) the conditions set out in section 3;

(e) is not engaged in remunerative work;

(f) is capable of work;

(g) is not receiving relevant education;

(h) is under pensionable age; and

(i) is in Great Britain.

(3) A jobseeker's allowance is payable in respect of a week.

(4) In this Act—

"a contribution-based jobseeker's allowance" means a jobseeker's allowance entitlement to which is based on the claimant's satisfying conditions which include those set out in section 2; and

"an income-based jobseeker's allowance" means a jobseeker's allowance entitlement to which is based on the claimant's satisfying conditions which include those set out in section 3.

"capable of work"—see s. 35(2) and Sched. 1, para. 2.
"claimant"—see s. 35(1).
"employment"—see ss. 35(1), 7(8) and JSA Regs., reg. 3 and 4.
"entitled"—see s. 35(1).
"Great Britain"—*ibid.*
"jobseeker's agreement"—*ibid.*
"pensionable age"—*ibid.* JSA Regs., reg. 3.
"relevant education"—see s. 35(2), Sched. 1, para. 14 and JSA Regs., reg. 54.
"remunerative work"—see s. 35(2), Sched. 1, para. 1 and JSA Regs., reg. 51.
"week"—see s. 35(1).

GENERAL NOTE

Subsection (2)

Here the general conditions of entitlement to jobseeker's allowance are set out. In addition, the claimant has to meet the conditions in s. 2 in order to qualify for contribution-based JSA and/or those in s. 3 for income-based JSA. Section 2 is not reproduced (see *Bonner*), but note that one of the conditions for contribution-based JSA (as well as income-based JSA: see s. 3(1)(b)) is that the claimant is not entitled to income support (any "top-up" to his contribution-based JSA will be by means of income-based JSA). See also the corresponding amendment to s. 124(1)(f) of the Contributions and Benefits Act. The idea is that entitlement to JSA and income support should be mutually exclusive, although some people may be eligible for either if they fulfill the conditions of entitlement for both benefits. Income support is now only available to people who fall into certain groups (see reg. 4ZA of and Sched. 1B to the Income Support Regulations). See the notes to reg. 4ZA for discussion of the position of claimants who may be able to claim either JSA or income support and of the fact that the 24-hour limit for remunerative work for partners under JSA (the same limit applies to income support from October 7, 1996) may lead to a "better-off" problem for some claimants.

There is also a capital rule under s. 13(1) for income-based JSA.

The conditions in paras. (a) to (c) (the "labour market" conditions) are amplified in ss. 6 to 11 and regs. 5–22 and 31–45 of the JSA Regulations. It is a central requirement for entitlement to JSA that the claimant has entered into a jobseeker's agreement which remains in force (para. (c); see the notes to s. 9). Reg. 34 of the JSA Regulations treats a person as having satisfied this condition in certain circumstances. Under para. (e), see reg. 51 of the JSA Regulations for the meaning of remunerative work. Note the specific requirement in para. (f) that the claimant must be capable of work. See para. 2 of Sched. 1 which provides that the tests for determining whether a person is capable or incapable of work in ss. 171A to 171G of the Contributions and Benefits Act 1992 (see *Bonner*) apply to JSA. So if an AO decides, for example in connection with a claim for incapacity benefit, that a person is not incapable of work, he will be treated as satisfying para. (f). But note reg. 55 of the JSA Regulations which allows a person to remain in receipt of JSA whilst incapable of work for up to two weeks (subject to a limit of two such periods in any 12 months).

Under para. (g) the person must not be receiving relevant education (defined in reg. 54 of the JSA Regulations). (A 16- to 18-year-old who is in relevant education *may* be able to claim income support: see reg. 13 of the Income Support Regulations; and in that case may also be able to claim income-based JSA: see the notes to reg. 54). Full-time students (defined in reg. 1(3) of the JSA Regulations) are generally excluded from JSA by being treated as not available for work, except for student couples with a child who can claim, but only in the summer vacation (reg. 15(a) of the JSA Regulations), and note reg. 14(1)(a) and (k) (participation in an approved employment-related course or Venture Trust programme). See reg. 4ZA of the Income Support Regulations for those full-time students who can claim income support.

JSA is not available to those who have reached pensionable age (para. (b)). See reg. 3 of the JSA Regulations for the definition of "pensionable age".

A person qualifies if he is in Great Britain (para. (i)) (but note the habitual residence condition for income-based JSA, see below). Reg. 50 of the JSA Regulations allows a person to be treated as in Great Britain during a short period of temporary absence of up to 4 or 8 weeks in certain circumstances, but not otherwise. However, for people exercising Community rights, E.C. Regulation 1408/71 will enable contribution-based JSA to be "exported" (*i.e.* paid where the claimant resides in another Member State) for up to three months, as was the case for unemployment benefit (see Arts. 4(1)(g) and 69). The position of income-based JSA under Regulation 1408/71 is unclear but arguably is different from income support (see *CIS 863/1994* and *CIS 564/1994* which hold that as a general social benefit income support does not fall within Art. 4(1) of Regulation 1408/ 71). The U.K. Government has added income-based JSA to the list of "special non-contributory benefits" to which Regulation 1408/71 applies from June 1, 1992 (see Art. 4(2a) and Annex IIa), which category also includes income support. Under Art. 10a such benefits cannot be exported to another Member State. Yet arguably, income-based JSA comes within Article 4(1)(g) (and thus *is* exportable under Art. 69), as it is not a general benefit but is specifically designed to provide protection against unemployment, and the fact that it is based on financial need should not prevent this. See *Hughes v. Chief Adjudication Officer*, Case C-78/91, [1992] E.C.R. I-4839 in which the ECJ held that family credit was a social security benefit within Art. 4(1)(h) ("family benefits") and was not excluded from the scope of the Regulation as a form of social assistance under Art. 4(4). Note also other cases such as *Piscitello*, Case 139/82, [1983] E.C.R. 1427 and *Giletti*, Joined Cases 379–381/85 and 93/86, [1987] E.C.R. 955 which held that allowances paid to supplement a social security benefit within Art. 4(1) and which conferred a legal entitlement were covered by Art. 4(1) and the fact that they were income-related was irrelevant. (Income-based JSA can of course be paid either on its own or as a "top-up" to contribution-based JSA.)

Note that in *CDLA 913/1994* (which concerned the exportability of disability living allowance) the Government argued that benefits listed in Annex IIa fell exclusively within the category of special non-contributory benefits under Art. 4(2a) and not within the category of social security benefits under Article 4(1). It maintained that the new category of special non-contributory benefits was intended to deal with the difficulty of classifying benefits as between social security and social assistance and (where relevant) to alter the position of exportability as regards these benefits. The claimant contended that the purpose of Arts. 4(2a) and 10a was to add to the benefits which were covered by Regulation 1408/71, not to take away any protection enjoyed under Art. 4(1) before these provisions were introduced. The Commissioner in *CDLA 913/1994* referred to the ECJ the question whether the effect of Arts. 4(2a) and 10a was to remove from the scope of Art. 4(1) a benefit which prior to June 1, 1992 would have fallen within it. In *Snares v. Adjudication Officer*, Case C-20/96, [1977] E.C.R. I-6057 (also to be reported as *R(DLA) 5/99*) the ECJ ruled that disability living allowance fell exclusively within Arts. 4(2)(a) and 10a, so a person who was awarded it after June 1, 1992 could not export it to another Member State.

Although there is no requirement of citizenship, for income-based JSA the treatment of "people from abroad" mirrors that of income support and the rules include the importing of the "habitual residence" test (see reg. 85(4) of and para. 14 of Sched. 5 to the JSA Regulations).

Subsection (3)

JSA is paid on a weekly basis, like income support, but unlike unemployment benefit which was a daily benefit. Note the provisions in regs. 150 to 155 of the JSA Regulations for calculating payment of JSA for part-weeks.

The income-based conditions

3.—(1) The conditions referred to in section 1(2)(d)(ii) are that the claimant—
(a) has an income which does not exceed the applicable amount (determined in accordance with regulations under section 4) or has no income;
(b) is not entitled to income support;
(c) is not a member of a family one of whose members is entitled to income support;
(d) is not a member of a family one of whose members is entitled to an income-based jobseeker's allowance;
(e) is not a member of a married or unmarried couple the other member of which is engaged in remunerative work; and
(f) is a person—
    (i) who has reached the age of 18; or
    (ii) in respect of whom a direction under section 16 is in force; or
    (iii) who has, in prescribed circumstances to be taken into account for a prescribed period, reached the age of 16 but not the age of 18.
(2) Regulations may provide for one or both of the following conditions to be included in the income-based conditions, in the case of a person to whom subsection (1)(f)(ii) or (iii) applies—
(a) a condition that the claimant must register for employment;

(b) a condition that the claimant must register for training.

(3) In subsection (1)(f)(iii) ''period'' includes—

(a) a period of a determinate length;

(b) a period defined by reference to the happening of a future event; and

(c) a period of a determinate length but subject to earlier determination upon the happening of a future event.

(4) Regulations under subsection (2) may, in particular, make provision by reference to persons designated by the Secretary of State for the purpose of the regulations.

DEFINITIONS

"claimant"—see s. 35(1).
"employment"—*ibid.*, JSA Regs., reg. 4.
"family"—see s. 35(1).
"income-based conditions"—*ibid.*
"income-based jobseeker's allowance"—see s. 1(4).
"married couple"—see s. 35(1).
"prescribed"—*ibid.*
"training"—*ibid.*
"unmarried couple"—*ibid.*

GENERAL NOTE

Subsection (1)

This contains the further conditions for entitlement to income-based JSA in addition to those in s. 1 and the capital rule under s. 13(1).

Under para. (a), the person's income (which includes the income of his family: s. 13(2) and reg. 88(1) of the JSA Regulations) must be less than the applicable amount (effectively the figure set for the family's requirements under s. 4(5)). He must in general be at least 18 (para. (f)(i)), except if he comes within certain categories (para. (f)(iii)), or the Secretary of State has directed that he will otherwise suffer severe hardship (para. (f)(ii) and s. 16). (See regs. 57–68 of the JSA Regulations for those 16- and 17-year-olds who are entitled to income-based JSA and the conditions of their eligibility.) If the person is a member of a couple, his partner must not be engaged in remunerative work (in the case of a partner remunerative work is work of 24 hours or more a week: reg. 51(1)(b) of the JSA Regulations) (para. (e)). Paras. (b) and (c) confirm that income-based JSA is not payable if the claimant, or any member of his family, is entitled to income support. See the corresponding amendment to s. 124(1) of the Contributions and Benefits Act as regards the conditions of entitlement to income support. In addition, para. (d) excludes entitlement if another member of the family is entitled to income-based JSA.

Subsection (2)

See reg. 62 of the JSA Regulatiions.

Amount payable by way of jobseeker's allowance

4.—(1) In the case of a contribution-based jobseeker's allowance, the amount payable in respect of a claimant (''his personal rate'') shall be calculated by—

(a) determining the age-related amount applicable to him; and

(b) making prescribed deductions in respect of earnings and pension payments.

(2) The age-related amount applicable to a claimant, for the purposes of subsection (1)(a), shall be determined in accordance with regulations.

(3) In the case of an income-based jobseeker's allowance, the amount payable shall be—

(a) if a claimant has no income, the applicable amount;

(b) if a claimant has an income, the amount by which the applicable amount exceeds his income.

(4) Except in prescribed circumstances, a jobseeker's allowance shall not be

payable where the amount otherwise payable would be less than a prescribed minimum.

(5) The applicable amount shall be such amount or the aggregate of such amounts as may be determined in accordance with regulations.

(6) Where a claimant satisfies both the contribution-based conditions and the income-based conditions but has no income, the amount payable shall be—

    (a) the applicable amount, if that is greater than his personal rate; and

    (b) his personal rate, if it is not.

(7) Where the amount payable to a claimant to whom subsection (6) applies is the applicable amount, the amount payable to him by way of a jobseeker's allowance shall be taken to consist of two elements—

    (a) one being an amount equal to his personal rate; and

    (b) the other being an amount equal to the excess of the applicable amount over his personal rate.

(8) Where a claimant satisfies both the contribution-based conditions and the income-based conditions and has an income, the amount payable shall be—

    (a) the amount by which the applicable amount exceeds his income, if the amount of that excess is greater than his personal rate; and

    (b) his personal rate, if it is not.

(9) Where the amount payable to a claimant to whom subsection (8) applies is the amount by which the applicable amount exceeds his income, the amount payable to him by way of a jobseeker's allowance shall be taken to consist of two elements—

    (a) one being an amount equal to his personal rate; and

    (b) the other being an amount equal to the amount by which the difference between the applicable amount and his income exceeds his personal rate.

(10) The element of a jobseeker's allowance mentioned in subsection (7)(a) and that mentioned in subsection (9)(a) shall be treated, for the purpose of identifying the source of the allowance, as attributable to the claimant's entitlement to a contribution-based jobseeker's allowance.

(11) The element of a jobseeker's allowance mentioned in subsection (7)(b) and that mentioned in subsection (9)(b) shall be treated, for the purpose of identifying the source of the allowance, as attributable to the claimant's entitlement to an income-based jobseeker's allowance.

(12) Regulations under subsection (5) may provide that, in prescribed cases, an applicable amount is to be nil.

DEFINITIONS

    "claimant"—see s. 35(1).
    "contribution-based conditions"—*ibid.*
    "contribution-based jobseeker's allowance"—see s. 1(4).
    "earnings"—see s. 35(3).
    "income-based conditions"—see s. 35(1).
    "income-based jobseeker's allowance"—see s. 1(4).
    "pension payments"—see s. 35(1).
    "prescribed"—*ibid.*

GENERAL NOTE

This section is concerned with the amount of a jobseeker's allowance. The various rules it contains arise out of the fact that JSA is a single benefit with two different elements: contribution-based JSA and income-based JSA. Thus, for example, when both components are payable it is necessary to identify each element for accounting purposes, contribution-based JSA being payable out of the National Insurance Fund and income-based JSA out of general taxation (see subss. (7), (9), (10) and (11)), and because of the 182-day limit on entitlement for contribution-based JSA (see s. 5(1) in *Bonner*). Subs. (1) provides the basic framework for the calculation of the amount payable by way of contribution-based JSA (the "personal rate") and subs. (3) does the same for income-based

JSA (by setting the person's income, if any, against his applicable amount). If the claimant satisfies the conditions of entitlement for both contribution-based and income-based JSA and his personal rate is either greater than his applicable amount if he has no income, or is greater than his applicable amount minus his income, the amount of JSA payable will be the personal rate (subss. (6)(b) and (8)(b)). This reflects the fact that contribution-based JSA, although subject to increased (when compared with unemployment benefit) reduction in respect of the *claimant's* own earnings and pension payments (see the notes to subs. (1) in *Bonner*), still falls considerably short of being a totally means-tested benefit.

For further details of this section in relation to contribution-based JSA see *Bonner*. The rest of this note deals only with those provisions that are specific to income-based JSA.

Subsection (3)

This provision sets out the basic means test calculation for income-based JSA. Provided that the conditions of entitlement imposed by ss. 1 and 3 and the capital test under s. 13(1) are satisfied, the claimant's income is set against his applicable amount, calculated according to regs. 82 to 87 of the JSA Regulations. The difference is the amount of benefit. The claimant's income includes that of the other members of his family (s. 13(2)).

Subsection (4)

See reg. 87A of the JSA Regulations.

Subsection (5)

See regs. 82 to 87 of and Scheds. 1 to 5 to the JSA Regulations. These adopt the income support model, although there are some changes to the premiums to reflect the fact that JSA is not payable to people over pensionable age.

Subsection (12)

See reg. 85 of and Sched. 5 to the JSA Regulations.

Jobseeking

Availability for employment

6.—(1) For the purposes of this Act, a person is available for employment if he is willing and able to take up immediately any employed earner's employment.

(2) Subsection (1) is subject to such provisions as may be made by regulations; and those regulations may, in particular, provide that a person—

(a) may restrict his availability for employment in any week in such ways as may be prescribed; or

(b) may restrict his availability for employment in any week in such circumstances as may be prescribed (for example, on grounds of conscience, religious conviction or physical or mental condition or because he is caring for another person) and in such ways as may be prescribed.

(3) The following are examples of restrictions for which provision may be made by the regulations—

(a) restrictions on the nature of the employment for which a person is available;

(b) restrictions on the periods for which he is available;

(c) restrictions on the terms or conditions of employment for which he is available;

(d) restrictions on the locality or localities within which he is available.

(4) Regulations may prescribe circumstances in which, for the purposes of this Act, a person is or is not to be treated as available for employment.

(5) Regulations under subsection (4) may, in particular, provide for a person who is available for employment—

(a) only in his usual occupation,

(b) only at a level of remuneration not lower than that which he is accustomed to receive, or

    (c) only in his usual occupation and at a level of remuneration not lower
        than that which he is accustomed to receive,
to be treated, for a permitted period, as available for employment.

    (6) Where it has been determined ("the first determination") that a person
is to be treated, for the purposes of this Act, as available for employment in
any week, the question whether he is available for employment in that week
may be subsequently determined on a review of the first determination.

    (7) In this section "permitted period", in relation to any person, means such
period as may be determined in accordance with the regulations made under
subsection (4).

    (8) Regulations under subsection (4) may prescribe, in relation to permitted
periods—

    (a) the day on which any such period is to be regarded as having begun in
        any case;
    (b) the shortest and longest periods which may be determined in any case;
    (c) factors which an adjudication officer may take into account in determin-
        ing the period in any case.

    (9) For the purposes of this section "employed earner's employment" has
the same meaning as in the Benefits Act.

DEFINITIONS

    "adjudication officer"—see s. 35(1).
    "Benefits Act"—*ibid.*
    "employed earner's employment"—SSCBA, ss. 2(1), 122(1).
    "employment"—see s. 35(1) and JSA Regs, reg. 4.
    "prescribed"—see s. 35(1).
    "regulations"—*ibid.*
    "week"—*ibid.*, JSA Regs., reg. 4.

GENERAL NOTE

    This section and ss. 7 to 11 expand on the "labour market conditions" for entitlement to JSA
in s. 1(a) to (c). However, much of the key detail remains in the regulations made under these
sections (see Part II of the JSA Regulations). Note that regulations made under ss. 6 and 7 are
subject to the affirmative procedure (s. 37(1)(c)).

Subsection (1)
    It is a basic requirement for entitlement to JSA (as it was for unemployment benefit and income
support for unemployed people) that the person be "available for employment" (s. 1(2)(a)). This
subsection encapsulates the unemployment benefit case law principle that to be available the person
must be willing and able to accept at once any offer of suitable employment (*R(U)1/53, Shaukat
Ali v. CAO*, reported as Appendix to *R(U) 1/85*, and *R(U) 2/90*). (See *Bonner* for further details of
the unemployment benefit case law.) A person is able to take up employment immediately even if
he first has to obtain clearance in respect of any job, where that clearance is more or less a formality
and normally a telephone call would suffice (*CSU 182/1997*, which concerned a former Inland
Revenue employee who had taken early retirement and so was subject to the "Rules on the acceptance of outside appointments by Crown Servants").
    Note that the claimant must be available for employed earner's employment (as defined in the
Contributions and Benefits Act, ss. 2(1) and 122 (subs. (9)); availability for self-employment is not
sufficient (although taking steps to establish oneself as self-employed can suffice for the condition
of actively seeking employment in some circumstances: see s. 7(8) and reg. 20 of the JSA Regulations; see also regs. 18(3)(i) and 19(1)(r)). The claimant must also normally be available for a
minimum of 40 hours a week (reg. 6(1) of the JSA Regulations, for the exceptions see regs. 13
and 17(2)), but be willing to accept employment of less than 40 hours a week (reg. 6(2)). "Week"
means "benefit week" (reg. 4 of the JSA Regulations).
    Regs. 7, 8, 13 and 16 of the JSA Regulations allow for various restrictions to be imposed on
availability and reg. 5 of the JSA Regulations relaxes the requirement of *immediate* availability for
certain groups. See the notes to those regulations for discussion of these provisions. Note in particular that under reg. 13(3) a claimant can restrict his availability in the light of his physical or mental

condition without having to show that he still has reasonable prospects of finding employment. A person's jobseeker's agreement (see s. 9 and reg. 31 of the JSA Regulations) will set out the details of his availability and any agreed restrictions.

Regs. 14 and 15 of the JSA Regulations provide for people in certain circumstances to be treated as available/not available for employment respectively and reg. 17 deals with those who have been laid off or kept on short-time (see the notes to those regulations).

Note that where there is an unresolved question as to an existing claimant's availability for work (or active search for work), JSA will not be paid until the AO's decision is made, subject to the possibility of a hardship payment (see regs. 141(5) and 142(3) of the JSA Regulations); this differs from the position under unemployment benefit (see the former reg. 12A of the Unemployment, Sickness and Invalidity Benefit Regulations in the 1996 edition of *Bonner*). See reg. 37(1A) of the Claims and Payments Regulations which allows payment of JSA to be suspended in such circumstances. This contrasts with the position where an AO is unable to decide immediately whether a benefit sanction under s. 19 should be imposed. In that case the AO is to proceed on the assumption that the question will be answered in the claimant's favour (see reg. 56A(3) of the Adjudication Regulations; paras. (5)–(7) of reg. 56A apply where it is subsequently decided that a sanction should be imposed).

Subsections (2), (3), (4), (5), (7) and (8)
See regs. 5 to 17 of the JSA Regulations.

Subsection (6)
This allows for a person's actual availability for employment to be determined on review where he has previously been treated as available.

Actively seeking employment

7.—(1) For the purposes of this Act, a person is actively seeking employment in any week if he takes in that week such steps as he can reasonably be expected to have to take in order to have the best prospects of securing employment.

(2) Regulations may make provision—
   (a) with respect to steps which it is reasonable, for the purposes of subsection (1), for a person to be expected to have to take in any week;
   (b) as to circumstances (for example, his skills, qualifications, abilities and physical or mental limitations) which, in particular, are to be taken into account in determining whether, in relation to any steps taken by a person, the requirements of subsection (1) are satisfied in any week.

(3) Regulations may make provision for acts of a person which would otherwise be relevant for purposes of this section to be disregarded in such circumstances (including circumstances constituted by, or connected with, his behaviour or appearance) as may be prescribed.

(4) Regulations may prescribe circumstances in which, for the purposes of this Act, a person is to be treated as actively seeking employment.

(5) Regulations under subsection (4) may, in particular, provide for a person who is actively seeking employment—
   (a) only in his usual occupation;
   (b) only at a level of remuneration not lower than that which he is accustomed to receive; or
   (c) only in his usual occupation and at a level of remuneration not lower than that which he is accustomed to receive,
to be treated, for the permitted period determined in his case for the purposes of section 6(5), as actively seeking employment during that period.

(6) Regulations may provide for this section, and any regulations made under it, to have effect in relation to a person who has reached the age of 16 but not the age of 18 as if "employment" included "training".

(7) Where it has been determined ("the first determination") that a person is to be treated, for the purposes of this Act, as actively seeking employment

in any week, the question whether he is actively seeking employment in that week may subsequently be determined on a review of the first determination.

(8) For the purposes of this section—

"employment" means employed earner's employment or, in prescribed circumstances—

(a) self-employed earner's employment; or

(b) employed earner's employment and self-employed earner's employment; and

"employed earner's employment" and "self-employed earner's employment" have the same meaning as in the Benefits Act.

DEFINITIONS

"Benefits Act"—see s. 35(1).
"employed earner's employment"—see SSCBA, ss. 2(1), 122(1).
"prescribed"—see s. 35(1).
"regulations"—*ibid.*
"self-employed earner's employment"—SSCBA, ss. 2(1), 122(1).
"training"—see s. 35(1), JSA Regs., regs. 65(6) and 57(1).
"week"—see s. 35(1), JSA Regs., reg. 4.

GENERAL NOTE

This section concerns the second of the "labour market" conditions of entitlement to JSA, that of "actively seeking employment". See s. 6 for the requirement to be available for employment and ss. 9 to 11 on the jobseeker's agreement. For the detail of the rules relating to actively seeking employment see regs. 18–22 of the JSA Regulations. Regulations made under s. 7 are subject to the affirmative procedure (s. 37(1)(c)).

Subsections (1) and (2)

Subs. (1) contains the definition of "actively seeking employment". It is based on the test previously in reg. 12B(1) of the Unemployment, Sickness and Invalidity Benefit Regulations (see the 1996 edition of *Bonner*), except that "best prospects of securing employment" has replaced "best prospects of receiving offers of employment". The intention presumably is to reinforce the positive role that the claimant himself is required to play in finding work. "Employment" is defined in subs. (8); for the purpose of the "actively seeking" rule it can include self-employment, as well as work as an employee, in certain circumstances (see regs. 18(3)(i), 19(1)(r) and 20(2) of the JSA Regulations).

Subs. (2) allows for regulations to specify in more detail the conditions a person has to meet in order to satisfy the actively seeking employment test. See reg. 18 of the JSA Regulations. Note that under reg. 18(1) a person will normally be expected to take more than one step on one occasion during a week ("week" means "benefit week", regs. 4 and 1(3)), unless that one step is all that is reasonable for him to do that week. The steps a claimant has to take will be set out in his jobseeker's agreement (see s. 9 and reg. 31 of the JSA Regulations).

There are further regulation-making powers in subss. (3) to (6) (see the notes to those subsections).

Note that where there is an unresolved question as to whether an existing claimant is actively seeking employment, the position is the same as in relation to availability for work. JSA will not be paid until the AO's decision is made, subject to the possibility of a hardship payment (see regs. 141(5) and 142(3) of the JSA Regulations) (this is similar to the position under the previous benefit regime for unemployed people, except that hardship payments under JSA are more restricted). See reg. 37(1A) of the Claims and Payments Regulations which allows payment of JSA to be suspended in such circumstances. This contrasts with the position where an AO is unable to decide immediately whether a benefit sanction under s. 19 should be imposed. In that case the AO is to proceed on the assumption that the question will be answered in the claimant's favour (see reg. 56A(3) of the Adjudication Regulations; paras. (5)–(7) of reg. 56A apply where it is subsequently decided that a sanction should be imposed).

Subsection (3)

This has been described as a "remarkable" provision (see N. Wikeley, "The Jobseekers Act 1995: What the Unemployed Need is a Good Haircut" (1996) 25 I.L.J. 71–76). It enables steps that a claimant has taken to comply with the actively seeking employment test to be disregarded in prescribed circumstances (with the result that he might then not satisfy the test, and so not be entitled to JSA). Such circumstances include (but are not limited to) those relating to his behaviour or appearance. This regulation-making power was considered necessary to deal with a claimant who "behaves or presents himself in such a way as deliberately to reduce or extinguish his chance of receiving offers of employment" (DSS's *Notes on Clauses* to the Jobseekers Bill). If confined to such deliberate undermining of job opportunities the power is less controversial. The concern, however, is with the potential width of the provision, especially when taken in conjunction with an employment officer's power to issue a jobseeker's direction "to improve the claimant's prospects of being employed" (s. 19(10)(b)(ii)) and to impose a sanction of two (or four, for a further breach within 12 months) weeks' loss of benefit for non-compliance (s. 19(2) and (5)(a), reg. 69 of the JSA Regulations). Note that this new power is in addition to s. 19(6)(c) (carried over from unemployment benefit) under which a person can be sanctioned for not availing himself, without good cause, of a particular job opportunity (see *R(U) 28/55*, in which a man who went for a job interview as a parcel porter in a "dirty and unshaven state" was disqualified from unemployment benefit). The purpose of this provision, however, is to seek to exert more control over a person's jobseeking behaviour in general.

The use to which the regulation made under this power (reg. 18(4) of the JSA Regulation) will be put remains to be seen. Paras. (a) and (b) of reg. 18(4) are relatively straightforward (although the phrase "spoiled the application" in para. (b) may lead to some problems of interpretation; the context would seem to suggest that it is deliberate rather than accidental "spoiling" of a job application that is the intended target). But para. (c) will involve more subjective decision-making. Moreover, the risk of applying the rule in a discriminatory fashion on the grounds of race or sex (*e.g. viz-à-viz* men with long hair) will need to be borne in mind (see N. Wikeley, cited above). Note that all three sub-paras. do not apply if the circumstances were "due to reasons beyond [the claimant's] control".

Subsections (4) and (5)
See regs. 19 to 22 of the JSA Regulations. Note that under subs. (4) there is no power to make regulations to treat a person as *not* actively seeking employment (compare s. 6(4) in relation to availability for employment).

Subsection (6)
See reg. 65 of the JSA Regulations.

Subsection (7)
This allows for the question whether a person was actually actively seeking employment in any week ("week" means "benefit week", regs. 4 and 1(3)) to be determined on review where he has previously been treated as actively seeking work. See s. 6(6) for the equivalent provision in relation to availability for work.

Subsection (9)
See the note to subss. (1) and (2) above.

Attendance, information and evidence

8.—(1) Regulations may make provision for requiring a claimant—
(a) to attend at such place and at such time as the Secretary of State may specify; and
(b) to provide information and such evidence as may be prescribed as to his circumstances, his availability for employment and the extent to which he is actively seeking employment.
(2) Regulations under subsection (1) may, in particular—
(a) prescribe circumstances in which entitlement to a jobseeker's allowance is to cease in the case of a claimant who fails to comply with any regulations made under that subsection;
(b) provide for entitlement to cease at such time (after he last attended in compliance with requirements of the kind mentioned in subsection (1)(a)) as may be determined in accordance with any such regulations;
(c) provide for entitlement not to cease if the claimant shows, within a pre-

scribed period of his failure to comply, that he had good cause for that failure; and

(d) prescribe—

    (i) matters which are, or are not, to be taken into account in determining whether a person has, or does not have, good cause for failing to comply with any such regulations; and

    (ii) circumstances in which a person is, or is not, to be regarded as having, or not having, good cause for failing to comply with any such regulations.

DEFINITIONS

"claimant"—see s. 35(1).
"employment"—*ibid.*, JSA Regs., reg. 4.
"prescribed"—see s. 35(1).
"regulations"—*ibid.*

GENERAL NOTE

This provision enables claimants to be directed to attend at a JobCentre to "sign on" so that their availability for work and the steps they are taking to find work can be checked. See regs. 23–30 of the JSA Regulations.

The jobseeker's agreement

9.—(1) An agreement which is entered into by a claimant and an employment officer and which complies with the prescribed requirements in force at the time when the agreement is made is referred to in this Act as "a jobseeker's agreement".

(2) A jobseeker's agreement shall have effect only for the purposes of section 1.

(3) A jobseeker's agreement shall be in writing and be signed by both parties.

(4) A copy of the agreement shall be given to the claimant.

(5) An employment officer shall not enter into a jobseeker's agreement with a claimant unless, in the officer's opinion, the conditions mentioned in section 1(2)(a) and (c) would be satisfied with respect to the claimant if he were to comply with, or be treated as complying with, the proposed agreement.

(6) The employment officer may, and if asked to do so by the claimant shall forthwith, refer a proposed jobseeker's agreement to an adjudication officer for him to determine—

(a) whether, if the claimant concerned were to comply with the proposed agreement, he would satisfy—

    (i) the condition mentioned in section 1(2)(a), or

    (ii) the condition mentioned in section 1(2)(c); and

(b) whether it is reasonable to expect the claimant to have to comply with the proposed agreement.

(7) An adjudication officer to whom a reference is made under subsection (6)—

(a) shall, so far as practicable, dispose of it in accordance with this section before the end of the period of 14 days from the date of the reference;

(b) may give such directions, with respect to the terms on which the employment officer is to enter into a jobseeker's agreement with the claimant, as the adjudication officer considers appropriate;

(c) may direct that, if such conditions as he considers appropriate are satisfied, the proposed jobseeker's agreement is to be treated (if entered into) as having effect on such date, before it would otherwise have effect, as may be specified in the direction.

(8) Regulations may provide—

(a) for such matters as may be prescribed to be taken into account by an adjudication officer in giving a direction under subsection (7)(c); and

(b) for such persons as may be prescribed to be notified of—

(i) any determination of an adjudication officer under this section;

(ii) any direction given by an adjudication officer under this section.

(9) Any determination of an adjudication officer under this section shall be binding.

(10) Regulations may provide that, in prescribed circumstances, a claimant is to be treated as having satisfied the condition mentioned in section 1(2)(b).

(11) Regulations may provide that, in prescribed circumstances, a jobseeker's agreement is to be treated as having effect on a date, to be determined in accordance with the regulations, before it would otherwise have effect.

(12) Except in such circumstances as may be prescribed, a jobseeker's agreement entered into by a claimant shall cease to have effect on the coming to an end of an award of a jobseeker's allowance made to him.

(13) In this section and section 10 "employment officer" means an officer of the Secretary of State or such other person as may be designated for the purposes of this section by an order made by the Secretary of State.

DEFINITIONS

"adjudication officer"—see reg. 35(1).
"claimant"—*ibid.*
"prescribed"—*ibid.*
"regulations"—*ibid.*

GENERAL NOTE

It is a central requirement for entitlement to JSA that a claimant has entered into a "jobseeker's agreement" that remains in force (s. 1(2)(b)). Since benefit will not be paid until this condition is met, the word "agreement" seems something of a misnomer. Note also subs. (2) which states that a jobseeker's agreement is only to have effect for the purposes of satisfying the conditions of entitlement to JSA and thus does not give rise to any wider rights or duties. See reg. 34 of the JSA Regulations (made under subs. (10)) for when a jobseeker's agreement will be treated as having been made.

A jobseeker's agreement is an agreement entered into by the claimant and an employment officer (defined in subs. (13)) which satisfies "prescribed requirements" (subs. (1)). See reg. 31 of the JSA Regulations for what a jobseeker's agreement has to contain. A jobseeker's agreement must be in writing and signed by both parties (subs. (3)) and a copy must be given to the claimant (subs. (4)).

The basic purpose of the jobseeker's agreement is to set out what the claimant has to do in order to satisfy the conditions of availability for, and actively seeking, work and to enable the action that the claimant takes in pursuance of those requirements to be monitored and, if necessary, re-directed. Thus subs. (5) provides that an employment officer can only enter into a jobseeker's agreement if he is satisfied that by complying with its terms the claimant will qualify as available for, and actively seeking, work. If there is disagreement between the claimant and the employment officer over the terms of the agreement, the employment officer may, and if asked to do so by the claimant must immediately, refer the matter to an AO (subs. (6)). If an agreement is referred to an AO, the claimant should consider applying for a hardship payment (see regs. 141(2) and 142(2) of the JSA Regulations) because he will not be paid JSA until the issue is resolved.

The AO will decide whether the proposed terms would enable the claimant to satisfy the conditions of availability for, and actively seeking, work (subs. (6)(a)). But he will also consider whether it is reasonable for the claimant to have to comply with those terms (subs. (6)(b)). Thus, *e.g.*, the AO may decide that the claimant can further restrict his hours of availability or take less steps than the employment officer is proposing and still satisfy s. 1(2)(a) and (c). Under subs. (7) the AO can give directions as to the terms on which the employment officer is to enter into the agreement and may also direct that the agreement, if entered into, is to be backdated.

See reg. 32 of the JSA Regulations (made under subs. (8)(a)) for circumstances that the AO must take into account when deciding whether to backdate the agreement (the list is not exhaustive). The import of reg. 32 is that if the AO considers that the claimant's proposals or actions have been reasonable the jobseeker's agreement is likely to be backdated, either to the date of claim, or perhaps to a later date (if *e.g.* paras. (c) or (d) of reg. 32 apply, and the date that the claimant was prepared to enter into the agreement was later than the date of claim). The consequence is that the claimant will be paid arrears of JSA from that date. The fact that a jobseeker's agreement that is referred to an AO under subs. (5) is not, once it is agreed, automatically backdated to the date of claim (compare the position where there is no such reference, see reg. 35 of the JSA Regulations) means that by not reaching an agreement with the employment officer a claimant risks a possible loss of benefit. This raises the issue of whether it may be better for a claimant to initially agree the terms of his jobseeker's agreement with the employment officer and then apply to vary its conditions under s. 10. (There is no time restriction on applications to vary under s. 10 nor do any grounds, such as change of circumstances, have to be shown.) But the claimant would have to comply with the terms of the agreement until the variation was agreed, since otherwise he would risk his benefit being suspended (see reg. 37(1A) of the Claims and Payments Regulations) if there was doubt as to whether he satisfied the conditions of availability for, and/or actively seeking, work.

Note subs. (7)(a) which requires the AO to deal with the reference within 14 days, as far as practicable (a similar rule to that for AO decisions under s. 21(1) of the Administration Act). The claimant will be notified of the AO's decision (subs. (8)(b); reg. 33 of the JSA Regulations); presumably this will be done in writing, although there is no requirement to that effect. The AO's determination is binding (subs. (9)), but will be subject to review and appeal under s. 11.

Note that there is no time limit within which the claimant is required to sign the agreement after he has been notified of the AO's decision (compare the position where an AO, or a SSAT, makes a decision or direction in relation to the variation of a jobseeker's agreement: see s. 10(6)(c) and reg. 38 of the JSA Regulations and s. 11(5) and reg. 43), but as the claimant will have been without benefit unless he was eligible for a hardship payment under regs. 141(2) or 142(2), clearly he would be advised to sign the agreement as soon as possible in order to be paid JSA. If the claimant disagrees with the AO's decision and applies for a review under s. 11, and possibly subsequently appeals against the review decision, he will not be eligible for a hardship payment during the review and appeal process unless he comes within reg. 140(1) and so reg. 141(4) applies (although arrears will be paid if the outcome is in the claimant's favour *and* the jobseeker's agreement is backdated, see above). See the notes to regs. 140–142. As an alternative, a claimant could consider signing the jobseeker's agreement and then applying to vary its terms under s. 10, see above.

If a jobseeker's agreement is not referred to an AO, that is, if the claimant and the employment officer can agree what it should contain, it will be automatically backdated to the date of claim (subs. (11); reg. 35 of the JSA Regulations).

A jobseeker's agreement will usually come to an end at the same time as the JSA claim itself. But reg. 36 (made under subs. (12)) provides for a jobseeker's agreement to continue in specified circumstances.

See s. 10 and regs. 37–40 of the JSA Regulations on the rules for variation of a jobseeker's agreement and s. 11 and regs. 41–45 for the procedure for challenging AOs' directions and determinations in relation to jobseekers' agreements.

Variation of jobseeker's agreement

10.—(1) A jobseeker's agreement may be varied, in the prescribed manner, by agreement between the claimant and any employment officer.

(2) Any agreement to vary a jobseeker's agreement shall be in writing and be signed by both parties.

(3) A copy of the agreement, as varied, shall be given to the claimant.

(4) An employment officer shall not agree to a variation of a jobseeker's agreement, unless, in the officer's opinion, the conditions mentioned in section 1(2)(a) and (c) would continue to be satisfied with respect to the claimant if he were to comply with, or be treated as complying with, the agreement as proposed to be varied.

(5) The employment officer may, and if asked to do so by the claimant shall forthwith, refer a proposed variation of a jobseeker's agreement to an adjudication officer for him to determine—

    (a) whether, if the claimant concerned were to comply with the agreement as proposed to be varied, he would satisfy—

        (i) the condition mentioned in section 1(2)(a), or

        (ii) the condition mentioned in section 1(2)(c); and

(b) whether it is reasonable to expect the claimant to have to comply with the agreement as proposed to be varied.

(6) An adjudication officer to whom a reference is made under subsection (5)—

(a) shall, so far as practicable, dispose of it in accordance with this section before the end of the period of 14 days from the date of the reference;

(b) shall give such directions as he considers appropriate as to—

(i) whether the jobseeker's agreement should be varied, and

(ii) if so, the terms on which the claimant and the employment officer are to enter into an agreement to vary it;

(c) may bring the jobseeker's agreement to an end where the claimant fails, within a prescribed period, to comply with a direction given under paragraph (b)(ii);

(d) may direct that, if—

(i) the jobseeker's agreement is varied, and

(ii) such conditions as he considers appropriate are satisfied,

the agreement as varied is to be treated as having effect on such date, before it would otherwise have effect, as may be specified in the direction.

(7) Regulations may provide—

(a) for such matters as may be prescribed to be taken into account by an adjudication officer in giving a direction under subsection (6)(b) or (d); and

(b) for such persons as may be prescribed to be notified of—

(i) any determination of an adjudication officer under this section;

(ii) any direction given by an adjudication officer under this section.

(8) Any determination of an adjudication officer under this section shall be binding.

DEFINITIONS

"adjudication officer"—see s. 35(1).
"claimant"—*ibid.*
"employment officer"—see s. 9(13).
"jobseeker's agreement"—see ss. 35(1), 9(1).
"prescribed"—see s. 35(1).
"regulations"—*ibid.*

GENERAL NOTE

This provides for the variation of jobseekers' agreements. See also regs. 37–40 of the JSA Regs which have been made under this section. Clearly an agreement will need altering over time *e.g.* due to the fact that the claimant's "permitted period" (see reg. 16 of the JSA Regulations) has come to an end, or to reflect changes in the claimant's circumstances or in the labour market.

Variation of an agreement requires the agreement of both the claimant and the employment officer (subs. (1)). Either party can propose a change (reg. 37 of the JSA Regulations). The change must be in writing and signed by both parties (subs. (2)) and a copy of the varied agreement must be given to the claimant (subs. (3)). There is no time restriction on applications to vary under s. 10 nor do any grounds, such as change of circumstances, have to be shown.

Subs. (4) and (5) reproduce the provisions in s. 9(5) and (6) so that an employment officer can only agree to a variation if he considers that under the new terms the claimant will continue to qualify as available for, and actively seeking, work, and he can, and if the claimant requests must immediately, refer a proposed variation to an AO for decision. Until the change has been agreed, or adjudicated upon by the AO, the existing terms of the claimant's jobseeker's agreement will remain in force (see para. 26955 of the *AOG*).

The AO will deal with the reference in the same way as if an original agreement had been referred (subs. (6)). However, if the claimant fails to sign the varied agreement within 21 days of the issue of the AO's direction as to the varied terms, the AO can bring the jobseeker's agreement to an end (subs. (10)(c) and reg. 38 of the JSA Regulations), with the result that the claimant will no longer be entitled to JSA (s. 1(2)(b)), unless he is in one of the groups who can qualify for a hardship payment under reg. 141(4) of the JSA Regulations (see reg. 140(1) for such groups).

Note also reg. 39 (made under subs. (7)(a)) which requires the AO to give preference to the claimant's wishes if he considers that both the claimant's and the employment officer's proposals satisfy subs. (5). The AO can backdate the varied agreement (subs. (6)(d)). The only guidance on backdating is in reg. 39. If the AO has accepted the claimant's proposals for variation, whether in preference to those of the employment officer or otherwise, the variation is likely to be backdated. The claimant will be notified of the AO's decision (subs. (7)(b); reg. 40 of the JSA Regulations); presumably this will be done in writing, although there is no requirement to that effect. The AO's determination on a variation is binding (subs. (8)), but will be subject to review and appeal under s. 11.

See s. 11 and regs. 41–45 for the procedure for challenging AOs' directions and determinations in relation to the variation of jobseekers' agreements.

Jobseeker's agreement: reviews and appeals

11.—(1) Any determination of, or direction given by, an adjudication officer under section 9 or 10 may be reviewed (by a different adjudication officer) on the application of the claimant or of an employment officer.

(2) Regulations may make provision with respect to the procedure to be followed on a review under this section.

(3) The claimant may appeal to a social security appeal tribunal against any determination of, or direction given by, an adjudication officer on a review under this section.

(4) A social security appeal tribunal determining an appeal under this section may give a direction of a kind which an adjudication officer may give under section 9(7)(b) or (c) or (as the case may be) section 10(6)(b) or (d).

(5) Where a social security appeal tribunal gives a direction under subsection (4) of a kind which may be given by an adjudication officer under section 10(6)(b)(ii), an adjudication officer may bring the jobseeker's agreement to an end if the claimant fails to comply with the direction within a prescribed period.

(6) An appropriate person may, on the ground that it was erroneous in point of law, appeal to a Commissioner against the decision of a social security appeal tribunal on an appeal under this section.

(7) Any of the following is an appropriate person for the purposes of subsection (6)—

(a) the claimant;

(b) an adjudication officer;

(c) in prescribed circumstances, a trade union;

(d) in prescribed circumstances, any other association which exists to promote the interests and welfare of its members.

(8) Subsection (7) to (10) of section 23 of the Administration Act (appeals to Commissioners) shall apply in relation to appeals under this section as they apply in relation to appeals under that section.

(9) In this section "Commissioner" has the same meaning as in the Administration Act.

DEFINITIONS

"adjudication officer"—see s. 35(1).
"Administration Act"—*ibid.*
"claimant"—*ibid.*
"jobseeker's agreement"—*ibid.*, s. 9(1).
"regulations"—see s. 35(1).

GENERAL NOTE

Subsections (1) to (3)

A determination or direction given by an AO in relation to a jobseeker's agreement, or its variation, cannot be appealed directly to a SSAT. A claimant must first ask for the direction or determination to be reviewed; the review will be carried out by a different AO (subs. (1)). An employment officer can also ask for such a review (subs. (1)). If still dissatisfied, the claimant (but not the employment officer) can then appeal against the review decision to a SSAT (subs. (3)).

See reg. 41 of the JSA Regulations on the procedure for reviews. The application has to be in writing, with its grounds, and be made within three months of the date on which the claimant was notified of the determination or direction. Reg. 41(3) deals with postal delays. The claimant will be notified of the review decision and of his right of appeal to a SSAT (reg. 41(5)).

Reg. 42 of the JSA Regulations provides for specified regulations of the Adjudication Regulations (subject to certain modifications) to apply to appeals to SSATs under this section. The usual three months' time limit for appeals applies; appeals are normally to be submitted to the JobCentre where the claimant signs on.

Subsections (4) and (5)

Subs. (4) expressly provides that a SSAT hearing an appeal under s. 11 has the same power as the AO to give directions as to the terms of the jobseeker's agreement, including whether the agreement should be backdated, although this should follow from general principles. If the appeal concerns a proposed variation of a jobseeker's agreement and the claimant fails to comply with the tribunal's direction as to the terms of the varied agreement, the AO (not the SSAT) has power to bring the jobseeker's agreement to an end within 21 days of the date the tribunal's direction was issued (reg. 43 of the JSA Regulations).

Subsections (6) to (9)

The claimant or the AO can appeal against a SSAT's decision made under this section on the ground of error of law (subs. (6) and (7)(a) and (b)). So can a trade union or other associations in certain circumstances (subs. (7)(c) and (d) and reg. 45 of the JSA Regulations). Subs. (8) applies s. 23(7)–(10) of the Administration Act to appeals under this section. Those provisions are concerned with applications for leave to appeal to a Commissioner and the Commissioner's powers on finding a tribunal decision to be wrong in law. In addition the Social Security Commissioners Procedure Regulations 1987 (S.I. 1987 No. 214) are applied, with certain exceptions, by reg. 44 of the JSA Regulations.

Income and capital

Income and capital: general

12.—(1) In relation to a claim for a jobseeker's allowance, the income and capital of a person shall be calculated or estimated in such manner as may be prescribed.

(2) A person's income in respect of a week shall be calculated in accordance with prescribed rules.

(3) The rules may provide for the calculation to be made by reference to an average over a period (which need not include the week concerned).

(4) Circumstances may be prescribed in which—

(a) a person is treated as possessing capital or income which he does not possess;

(b) capital or income which a person does possess is to be disregarded;

(c) income is to be treated as capital;

(d) capital is to be treated as income.

DEFINITIONS

"prescribed"—see s. 35(1).
"week"—*ibid.*

This section is very similar to subss. (3) to (5) of s. 136 of the Contributions and Benefits Act and contains extensive powers to prescribe how a claimant's capital and income is to be calculated for the purposes of JSA. See Part VIII of and Scheds. 6, 7 and 8 to the JSA Regulations.

See also s. 13.

Income and capital: income-based jobseeker's allowance

13.—(1) No person shall be entitled to an income-based jobseeker's allowance if his capital, or a prescribed part of it, exceeds the prescribed amount.

(2) Where a person claiming an income-based jobseeker's allowance is a member of a family, the income and capital of any member of that family shall, except in prescribed circumstances, be treated as the income and capital of the claimant.

(3) Regulations may provide that capital not exceeding the amount prescribed under subsection (1), but exceeding a prescribed lower amount, shall be treated, to a prescribed extent, as if it were income of a prescribed amount.

DEFINITIONS

"claimant"—see s. 35(1).
"family"—*ibid.*
"income-based jobseeker's allowance"—see s. 1(4).
"prescribed"—see s. 35(1).
"regulations"—*ibid.*

GENERAL NOTE

The provisions in this section mirror those in ss. 134(1) and 136(1) and (2) of the Contributions and Benefits Act.

Subsection (1)

Like income support, the capital limit for income-based JSA is £8,000, except where the claimant lives permanently in a residential care or nursing home, residential accommodation or a Polish resettlement home when it is £16,000 (JSA Regulations, regs. 107 and 116(1B)).

See the note to s. 134(1) of the Contributions and Benefits Act.

Subsection (2)

The general rule for income-based JSA (as for income support) is that all of the family's (as defined in s. 35(1)) income and capital is aggregated together and treated as the claimant's (see reg. 88(1) of the JSA Regulations). The main exceptions are for children and young persons (see regs. 106 and 109 of the JSA Regulations).

Subsectopm (3)

This enables a similar "tariff income" rule to the one that operates for income support to be applied to income-based JSA. Reg. 116 of the JSA Regulations provides for an income to be assumed to be produced from capital between £3,000 and £8,000 (£10,000 and £16,000 in the case of claimants living permanently in residential care or nursing homes, etc.).

Trade disputes

Trade disputes

14.—(1) Where—

(a) there is a stoppage of work which causes a person not to be employed on any day; and

(b) the stoppage is due to a trade dispute at his place of work,

that person is not entitled to a jobseeker's allowance for the week which includes that day unless he proves that he is not directly interested in the dispute.

(2) A person who withdraws his labour on any day in furtherance of a trade dispute, but to whom subsection (1) does not apply, is not entitled to a jobseeker's allowance for the week which includes that day.

(3) If a person who is prevented by subsection (1) from being entitled to a jobseeker's allowance proves that during the stoppage—

(a) he became bona fide employed elsewhere;

(b) his employment was terminated by reason of redundancy within the meaning of [¹section 139(1) of the Employment Rights Act 1996];

(c) he bona fide resumed employment with his employer but subsequently left for a reason other than the trade dispute,

subsection (1) shall be taken to have ceased to apply to him on the occurrence of the event referred to in paragraph (a) or (b) or (as the case may be) the first event referred to in paragraph (c).

(4) In this section "place of work", in relation to any person, means the premises or place at which he was employed.

(5) Where separate branches of work which are commonly carried on as separate businesses in separate premises or at separate places are in any case carried on in separate departments on the same premises or at the same place, each of those departments shall, for the purposes of subsection (4), be deemed to be separate premises or (as the case may be) a separate place.

AMENDMENT

1. Employment Rights Act 1996, Sched. 1, para. 67(2) (August 22, 1996).

DEFINITIONS

"employment"—see s. 35(1) and JSA Regs., regs. 3 and 4.
"entitled"—see s. 35(1).
"trade dispute"—*ibid.*
"week"—*ibid.*

GENERAL NOTE

This section denies JSA to *claimants* affected by or involved in trade disputes. If the person involved in the dispute is a member of a couple, his partner can claim JSA (provided that she is not also involved in a trade dispute). But unless the partner was already entitled to income-based JSA, there will be no entitlement to this for the seven days following the first day of the stoppage of work or the day on which the person first withdrew his labour because he will be treated as in remunerative work for those days (JSA Regulations, reg. 52(2) and s. 3(1)(e)). Where the partner of an income-based JSA claimant is involved in a trade dispute, see further s. 15.

The rules under this section are broadly the same as those in the former s. 27 of the Contributions and Benefits Act which disqualified claimants from unemployment benefit. First, a claimant will not be entitled to JSA for any week during which he was unemployed on any day as a result of a stoppage of work due to a trade dispute at his place of work (see subss. (4) and (5)), unless he had no direct interest in the dispute (subs. (1)), or unless subs. (3) applies. Secondly, a claimant, not caught by subs. (1), who has withdrawn his labour in furtherance of a trade dispute on any day will not be entitled to JSA throughout that week (subs. (2)). Note that where the rules bite, disentitlement is for a whole week (because JSA is a weekly benefit; under unemployment benefit the disqualification was applied on a daily basis). The fact that a claimant involved in a trade dispute is not *entitled* to JSA means that weeks caught by s. 14 do not eat into the 26 weeks' entitlement for contribution-based JSA. See also reg. 47(3)(e) (jobseeking periods).

See *Bonner* for detailed discussion of the case law on the trade dispute disqualification under unemployment benefit which will remain relevant to the interpretation of this section.

Effect on other claimants

15.—(1) Except in prescribed circumstances, subsection (2) applies in relation to a claimant for an income-based jobseeker's allowance where a member of his family ("A") is, or would be, prevented by section 14 from being entitled to a jobseeker's allowance.

(2) For the purposes of calculating the claimant's entitlement to an income-based jobseeker's allowance—

(a) any portion of the applicable amount which is included in respect of A shall be disregarded for the period for which this subsection applies to the claimant;

(b) where the claimant and A are a married or unmarried couple, any portion of the applicable amount which is included in respect of them shall be reduced to one half for the period for which this subsection applies to the claimant;

(c) except so far as regulations provide otherwise, there shall be treated as the claimant's income—

   (i) any amount which becomes, or would on an application duly made become, available to A in relation to that period by way of repayment of income tax deducted from A's emoluments in pursuance of section 203 of the Income and Corporation Taxes Act 1988 (PAYE); and

   (ii) any other payment which the claimant or any member of his family receives or is entitled to obtain because A is without employment for that period; and

(d) any payment by way of a jobseeker's allowance for that period or any part of it which apart from this paragraph would be made to the claimant—

   (i) shall not be made, if the weekly rate of payment ("the rate") would be equal to or less than the prescribed sum; and

   (ii) shall be at a weekly rate equal to the difference between the rate and the prescribed sum, if the rate would be more than the prescribed sum.

(3) Where a reduction under subsection (2)(b) would not produce a sum which is a multiple of 5p, the reduction shall be to the nearest lower sum which is such a multiple.

(4) Where A returns to work with the same employer after a period during which subsection (2) applied to the claimant (whether or not his return is before the end of any stoppage of work in relation to which he is, or would be, prevented from being entitled to a jobseeker's allowance), subsection (2) shall cease to apply to the claimant at the commencement of the day on which A returns to work.

(5) In relation to any period of less than a week, subsection (2) shall have effect subject to such modifications as may be prescribed.

(6) Subsections (7) to (9) apply where an order made under section 150 of the Administration Act (annual up-rating of benefits) has the effect of increasing the sum prescribed in regulations made under section 4(5) as the personal allowance for a single person aged not less than 25 ("the personal allowance").

(7) For the sum prescribed in regulations made under subsection (2)(d) there shall be substituted, from the time when the order comes into force, a sum arrived at by increasing the prescribed sum by the percentage by which the personal allowance has been increased by the order.

(8) If the sum arrived at under subsection (7), is not a multiple of 50p—

(a) any remainder of 25p or less shall be disregarded;

(b) any remainder of more than 25p shall be rounded up to the nearest 50p.

(9) The order shall state the sum substituted for the sum prescribed in regulations made under subsection (2)(d).

(10) Nothing in subsection (7) prevents the making of further regulations under subsection (2)(d) varying the prescribed sum.

<small>DEFINITIONS</small>

"applicable amount"—see s. 35(1).
"the Administration Act"—*ibid.*

58

"claimant"—*ibid.*
"employment"—*ibid.*, JSA Regs., reg. 3 and 4.
"family"—see s. 35(1).
"income-based jobseeker's allowance"—*ibid.*, s. 1(4).
"married couple"—see s. 35(1).
"prescribed"—*ibid.*
"unmarried couple"—*ibid.*

GENERAL NOTE

Subsection (1)

This provision applies where the partner of an income-based JSA claimant is involved in a trade dispute. Although subs. (1) refers to a member of the claimant's family, the effect of reg. 171(b)(i) of the JSA Regulations is that subs. (2) can only apply to the claimant's partner. Note that benefit will not be affected if the claimant's partner is incapable of work or within the "maternity period" (six weeks before and seven weeks after confinement) (reg. 171(b)(ii) of the JSA Regulations). If the *claimant* is involved in a trade dispute see s. 14.

Note also reg. 52(2) of the JSA Regulations which treats a partner as in remunerative work for the seven days following the first day of the stoppage of work or the first day on which the partner withdrew his labour if the claimant was not entitled to income-based JSA when the partner became involved in the dispute. The result is to disentitle the claimant for those days (s. 3(1)(e)). The partner is not treated as in remunerative work outside this period (reg. 53(g)).

Subsection (2)

This follows the rules for income support in s. 126(3)(c) and (5) of the Contributions and Benefits Act. See the notes to s. 126. The basic principle is that where the claimant's partner is involved in a trade dispute, no benefit is payable in respect of him (paras. (a) and (b)). The "prescribed sum" for the purposes of para. (d) is £27.50 from April 12, 1999 (reg. 172 of the JSA Regulations).

Subsection (4)

Subs. (2) ceases to apply from the day the claimant's partner returns to work.

Persons under 18

Severe hardship

16.—(1) If it appears to the Secretary of State—
(a) that a person—
    (i) has reached the age of 16 but not the age of 18,
    (ii) is not entitled to a jobseeker's allowance or to income support, and
    (iii) is registered for training but is not being provided with any training, and
(b) that severe hardship will result to him unless a jobseeker's allowance is paid to him,
the Secretary of State may direct that this section is to apply to him.
(2) A direction may be given so as to have effect for a specified period.
(3) The Secretary of State may revoke a direction if—
(a) it appears to him that there has been a change of circumstances as a result of which failure to receive a jobseeker's allowance need no longer result in severe hardship to the person concerned;
(b) it appears to him that the person concerned has—
    (i) failed to pursue an opportunity of obtaining training; or
    (ii) rejected an offer of training,
and has not shown good cause for doing so; or
(c) he is satisfied that it was given in ignorance of some material fact or was based on a mistake as to some material fact and considers that, but for that ignorance or mistake, he would not have given the direction.
(4) In this section "period" includes—
(a) a period of a determinate length;

(b) a period defined by reference to the happening of a future event; and
(c) a period of a determinate length but subject to earlier determination upon the happening of a future event.

DEFINITION

"training"—see s. 35(1), JSA Regs., reg. 57(1).

GENERAL NOTE

Subsections (1) and (2)
This provision is similar to the former s. 125 of the Contributions and Benefits Act (revoked on October 7, 1996) which dealt with income support severe hardship directions.

Subs. (1) requires that the person under 18 is not entitled to income support or JSA, so the person must fall outside the categories covered in regs. 59 to 61 of the JSA Regulations and not be eligible for income support under reg. 4ZA of and Sched. 1B to the Income Support Regulations. (He must also not be entitled to contribution-based JSA, but this is very unlikely in the case of a person under 18.) The other main conditions are that the person is registered for, but not receiving, training and that severe hardship will (not may) result if JSA is not paid. The question of whether these conditions are satisfied is for the Secretary of State, and even if they are, there is a discretion whether or not to allow benefit. There is no right of appeal to an appeal tribunal from the Secretary of State's decision.

To claim JSA on the grounds of severe hardship, the person should first register for work and training with the Careers Service where he will be given a ES9 referral form to take to the JobCentre (but see reg. 62 of the JSA Regulations for the exceptions to this rule). Staff are instructed that all 16- and 17-year-old claimants should be allowed to make an application for JSA and should not be turned away by the JobCentre. An initial check will be made to see if the young person is eligible for JSA as of right (see regs. 59 to 61 of the JSA Regulations). If not, and the application on the grounds of severe hardship fails at this stage, it will automatically be referred to the Severe Hardship Claims Unit for consideration. The Employment Service has produced detailed guidance on JSA for 16- and 17-year-olds (*Employment Service Guidance, JSA for 16 and 17 year olds*). Chapter 7, which deals with the severe hardship interview, states that the young person should be informed of the need to contact parents, whether or not the young person is living with them, or a third party, in order to verify the information he or she has given. The young person's consent to do this is required, but refusal of permission without good reason may mean that there will not be enough evidence on which to make a direction (although all such potential "nil" decisions still have to go to the Severe Hardship Claims Unit). At the same time no "undue pressure" is to be placed on the young person to give permission. This could be difficult to implement in practice. However, the guidance also states (more flexibly) that evidence from a responsible third party (*e.g.* a relative, social worker or voluntary worker), either in person, by telephone or in writing, may mean that contact with the young person's parents is not necessary.

A direction may be made for a definite period (subs. (2)) (usually eight weeks, but this can be varied according to the circumstances), it can be renewed and it may be revoked if any of the conditions in subs. (3) apply. If a direction is made the AO must consider all the other conditions of entitlement.

Note that the three-day waiting period for JSA does not apply if a s. 16 direction has been made (reg. 46(1) of the JSA Regulations).

Subsection (3)
Once a direction is made under this section the claimant satisfies s. 3(1)(f)(ii). If the claimant ceases to satisfy the other conditions of entitlement, entitlement will cease. The Secretary of State has a general discretion to revoke a direction whenever there is a change of circumstances which means that severe hardship no longer need follow from non-payment of JSA (para. (a)). This emphasises the strictness of the test under subs. (1). If severe hardship will not definitely follow from the non-payment of JSA, subs. (1) cannot operate. It appears that the revocation of the direction may be retrospective from the date of the change of circumstances, and if there was a failure to disclose facts constituting the change the overpayment is recoverable under s. 71A of the Administration Act. A direction may also be revoked if it was originally given in ignorance of or under a mistake as to a material fact which would have altered the decision on the inevitability of severe hardship (para. (c)). If there was misrepresentation of or failure to disclose that material fact, recovery under s. 71A may arise.

In addition, para. (b) allows for revocation of a direction where the person has failed to pursue or refused a training opportunity without good cause ("good cause" for these purposes is not defined, so the existing case law on its meaning will be relevant).

Note that in such a case the sanctions provided for in s. 19(5) do not apply (s. 20(2)). The young person's "offence" will be dealt with by revocation of the direction, if this is considered appropriate, or by reduction of his JSA under reg. 63(1)(b), if this applies. If a direction is revoked the young person can apply for another severe hardship direction to be made but it seems that it will be subject to a 40% reduction (20% if the young person is pregnant or seriously ill) of the appropriate personal allowance under para. 1 of Sched. 1 to the JSA Regulations for the first two weeks (s. 17(3)(a) and reg. 63(1)(a)). See the notes to s. 17 and reg. 63.

Note that the sanctions in s. 19(5) also do not apply if a young person who is the subject of a severe hardship direction commits the lesser "misdemeanour" of failing to complete a training course without good cause (s. 20(2)). Instead his JSA will be reduced in accordance with s. 17 and reg. 63 of the JSA Regulations, if applicable. But note that the sanctions in s. 19(6) do apply.

Reduced payments

17.—(1) Regulations may provide for the amount of an income-based jobseeker's allowance payable to any young person to whom this section applies to be reduced—

(a) in such circumstances,

(b) by such a percentage, and

(c) for such a period,

as may be prescribed.

(2) This section applies to any young person in respect of whom—

(a) a direction is in force under section 16; and

(b) either of the conditions mentioned in subsection (3) is satisfied.

(3) The conditions are that—

(a) the young person was previously entitled to an income-based jobseeker's allowance and that entitlement ceased by virtue of the revocation of a direction under section 16;

(b) he has failed to complete a course of training and no certificate has been issued to him under subsection (4) with respect to that failure.

(4) Where a young person who has failed to complete a course of training—

(a) claims that there was good cause for the failure; and

(b) applies to the Secretary of State for a certificate under this subsection.

the Secretary of State shall, if he is satisfied that there was good cause for the failure, issue a certificate to that effect and give a copy of it to the young person.

(5) In this section "young person" means a person who has reached the age of 16 but not the age of 18.

GENERAL NOTE

Under this section regulations can provide for JSA that is being paid because a severe hardship is in force to be paid at a reduced rate. See reg. 63 of the JSA Regulations which has been made under this section. Note that although subs. (3)(a) refers to revocation of a s. 16 direction generally, it is only where a direction has been revoked under s. 16(3)(b) that a reduction will be applied under reg. 63 (see reg. 63(1)(a)).

Note that under para. (4) it is the Secretary of State who will decide whether the young person had good cause for failing to complete the training and issue (or not) a certificate to that effect. Para. (4) thus takes the question of whether there was good cause for the failure out of the jurisdiction of the adjudicating authorities, although it seems that the formal decision to actually impose a sanction under reg. 63 will still be taken by an AO. See reg. 63A(8) of the Adjudication Regulations in relation to reviews where a sanction has been imposed under reg. 63 of the JSA Regulations but the Secretary of State then issues a good cause certificate under s. 17(4).

Note also that if a young person who is the subject of a severe hardship direction fails to pursue or refuses a training opportunity without good cause (so that the direction is liable to be revoked under s. 16(3)(b)), or fails to complete a training course without good cause, the sanctions provided for in s. 19(5) do not apply (s. 20(2)). The young person's "offence" will be dealt with under s. 16, or this section and reg. 63 of the JSA Regulations, as appropriate. See the notes to reg. 63.

Denial of jobseeker's allowance

Circumstances in which a jobseeker's allowance is not payable

19.—(1) Even though the conditions for entitlement to a jobseeker's allowance are satisfied with respect to a person, the allowance shall not be payable in any of the circumstances mentioned in subsection (5) or (6).

(2) If the circumstances are any of those mentioned in subsection (5), the period for which the allowance is not to be payable shall be such period (of at least one week but not more than 26 weeks) as may be prescribed.

(3) If the circumstances are any of those mentioned in subsection (6), the period for which the allowance is not to be payable shall be such period (of at least one week but not more than 26 weeks) as may be determined by the adjudication officer.

(4) Regulations may prescribe—

(a) circumstances which an adjudication officer is to take into account, and

(b) circumstances which he is not to take into account,

in determining a period under subsection (3).

(5) The circumstances referred to in subsection (1) and (2) are that the claimant—

(a) has, without good cause, refused or failed to carry out any jobseeker's direction which was reasonable, having regard to his circumstances;

(b) has, without good cause—

(i) neglected to avail himself of a reasonable opportunity of a place on a training scheme or employment programme;

(ii) after a place on such a scheme or programme has been notified to him by an employment officer as vacant or about to become vacant, refused or failed to apply for it or to accept it when offered to him;

(iii) given up a place on such a scheme or programme; or

(iv) failed to attend such a scheme or programme on which he has been given a place; or

(c) has lost his place on such a scheme or programme through misconduct.

(6) The circumstances referred to in subsections (1) and (3) are that the claimant—

(a) has lost his employment as an employed earner through misconduct;

(b) has voluntarily left such employment without just cause;

(c) has, without good cause, after a situation in any employment has been notified to him by an employment officer as vacant or about to become vacant, refused or failed to apply for it or to accept it when offered to him; or

(d) has, without good cause, neglected to avail himself of a reasonable opportunity of employment.

(7) In such circumstances as may be prescribed, including in particular where he has been dismissed by his employer by reason of redundancy within the meaning of [¹section 139(1) of the Employment Rights Act 1996] after volunteering or agreeing to be so dismissed, a person who might otherwise be regarded as having left his employment voluntarily is to be treated as not having left voluntarily.

(8) Regulations may—

(a) prescribe matters which are, or are not, to be taken into account in determining whether a person—

(i) has, or does not have, good cause for any act or omission; or

(ii) has, or does not have, just cause for any act or omission; or

(b) prescribe circumstances in which a person—

> (i) is, or is not, to be regarded as having, or not having, good cause for any act or omission; or
>
> (ii) is, or is not, to be regarded as having, or not having, just cause for any act or omission.

(9) Subject to any regulations under subsection (8), in determining whether a person has, or does not have, good cause or (as the case may be) just cause for any act or omission, any matter relating to the level of remuneration in the employment in question shall be disregarded.

(10) In this section—

(a) "employment officer" means an officer of the Secretary of State or such other person as may be designated for the purposes of this section by an order made by the Secretary of State;

(b) "jobseeker's direction" means a direction in writing given by an employment officer with a view to achieving one or both of the following—

> (i) assisting the claimant to find employment;
>
> (ii) improving the claimant's prospects of being employed; and

(c) "training scheme" and "employment programme" have such meaning as may be prescribed.

AMENDMENT

1. Employment Rights Act 1996, Sched. 1, para. 67(2) (August 22, 1996).

DEFINITIONS

"adjudication officer"—see s. 35(1).
"claimant"—*ibid.*
"employment"—see s. 35(1) and JSA Regs., reg. 75(4) and (5).
"employment programme"—see JSA Regs., reg. 75(1).
"prescribed"—see s. 35(1).
"regulations"—*ibid.*
"training scheme"—see JSA Regs., reg. 75(1).
"week"—see JSA Regs., reg. 75(2) and (3).

GENERAL NOTE

Even if a person satisfies the conditions of entitlement for JSA it will not be paid to him if any of the circumstances in subss. (5) or (6) apply (subs. (1)). This section thus continues the sanctions for "voluntary unemployment" that existed under previous benefit regimes for unemployed people. However, there are some important differences from this section's immediate predecessor, s. 28 of the Contributions and Benefits Act.

First, there are now two different types of sanction: a fixed sanction of two weeks, or four in the case of a second sanction within 12 months (reg. 69 of the JSA Regulations), for the lesser misdemeanours covered by subs. (5) (failure to comply with a jobseeker's direction and loss or refusal of a training scheme or employment programme opportunity (subs. (2)); and a discretionary sanction of between one and 26 weeks for the loss or refusal of employment in the situations dealt with in subs. (6) (subs. (3)). It will be noted that only subs. (3) refers to an adjudication officer deciding whether a sanction is to be imposed, but the effect of s. 20(1)(d) of the Administration Act is that decisions on both types of sanction will be taken by AOs.

Secondly, there is power to prescribe (i) circumstances to be taken into account in deciding the length of the discretionary sanction (subs. (4), see reg. 70; previously this was a matter entirely for the discretion of the adjudicating authorities); (ii) factors to be considered when deciding whether a claimant has either "good cause" or "just cause" in relation to the offences covered by this section and circumstances that will or will not constitute good or just cause (subs. (8)) (the power in s. 28(5) of the Contributions and Benefits Act only related to "good cause"); in fact no regulations have yet been made under the power in subs. (8)(a)(ii), but see regs. 72 and 73 which are concerned with good cause for the purposes of subs. (5)(a), (6)(c) and (d) and subs. (5)(b) respectively; note also subs. (9). See also the power in subs. (7) and reg. 71 which has been made under that subsection.

Thirdly, it should be noted that, unlike disqualification under s. 28 of the Contributions and Benefits Act, the effect of subs. (1) is not to disentitle a claimant from JSA if a sanction is imposed, but to provide that JSA is not payable. The result is that any sanction eats into the person's entitlement to contribution-based JSA (see further *Bonner*). On the other hand, full housing benefit and council tax benefit will continue to be payable (see reg. 2(3A) of the Housing Benefit Regulations 1987 and the Council Tax Benefit Regulations 1992 respectively) to claimants who would otherwise be getting income-based JSA. Claimants awarded hardship payments will also be entitled to full housing/council tax benefit because hardship payments count as payments of income-based JSA.

Another major difference from the position before October 7, 1996 is that if a sanction is imposed under this section no payment of JSA will be made, unless the person qualifies for a hardship payment. Compare reg. 22 of the Income Support Regulations (now revoked) which *inter alia* allowed for income support to be paid subject to a "voluntary unemployment deduction" in cases of disqualification or potential disqualification from unemployment benefit. See regs. 140–146 of the JSA Regulations made under s. 20(4)–(6) and the notes to those regulations for when hardship payments (*i.e.* income-based JSA at a reduced rate) will be made. Note that hardship payments will not be payable for the first 14 days except to certain "vulnerable" groups; the effect of this rule is that a claimant who suffers a fixed two-week penalty under subs. (5) may not be eligible for any JSA during the period of the sanction, however severe his hardship. Furthermore, in the case of a "New Deal sanction" (see the notes to reg. 69) hardship payments will not be available at all (even if the fixed sanction is for a four-week period), except to claimants in one of the vulnerable groups (see regs. 140(4A) and 140A)). There is the possibility of a Social Fund crisis loan for expenses that result from a disaster, etc., (see the note to s.20(4)–(6)).

Note also that under JSA any sanction under s. 19 does not commence until the AO's decision is made (unlike unemployment benefit where the claimant was suspended from unemployment benefit when a question of disqualification arose). See reg. 56A(3) of the Adjudication Regulations which provides that if an AO is unable to decide immediately whether a sanction should be imposed under s. 19, the claim is to be determined on the assumption that the question will be answered in the claimant's favour. Reg. 56A(5)–(7) apply where it is subsequently decided that a sanction should be imposed.

See also the other provisions in s. 20(1)–3) that provide exceptions from the operation of s. 19.

Finally note reg. 74A of the JSA Regulations which provides that even though a sanction under s. 19 has been imposed, a claimant will still be paid income-based JSA if he is getting a training allowance but not doing Work Based Training for Young People (in Scotland "Skillseekers"), the new name for Youth Training, etc. See reg. 170 which exempts such a claimant from having to satisfy the labour market conditions.

Subsection (2)

See reg. 69 of the JSA Regulations. Note that in both subs. (2) and reg. 69 "week" means benefit week (reg. 75(3)). For the definition of "benefit week" see reg. 1(3). Elsewhere in s. 19 (and Part V of the Regulations) "week" means a period of seven days (with one exception, see reg. 75(2)).

Subsections (3) and (4)

For the "offences" covered by subs. (6) the length of the penalty remains within the discretion of the adjudicating authorities, subject to reg. 70 which has been made under subs. (4). The maximum period for which a sanction can be imposed continues to be 26 weeks ("week" means seven days, reg. 75(2) of the JSA Regulations). As JSA is a weekly benefit the minimum period of a sanction is one week (the minimum disqualification under unemployment benefit was one day). But as *Bonner* points out, this does not mean that a sanction can only be imposed in terms of whole weeks (see regs. 150–155 of the JSA Regulations which provides for payment of JSA for part-weeks; reg. 152(1)(c) specifically refers to the situation where a s. 19 sanction is imposed).

Reg. 70 provides that in deciding the length of the sanction under subs. (6) an AO must weigh up all the circumstances. It then deals with factors that are to be taken into account in four particular situations (some of which reflect the position previously reached in unemployment benefit case law, see *Bonner*). Note reg. 70(c) which allows the rate of pay and the hours of work to be considered in deciding the period of sanction where a person has left employment of 16 hours or less a week, although under subs. (9) the level of pay is to be discounted in deciding the prior issue of whether a person had just cause for leaving the employment in question. The national minimum wage in force from April 1, 1999 (broadly £3.60 for those aged 22 or over; £3.00 for those aged 18–21) and the Working Time Regulations 1998 (S.I. 1998 No. 1833) will be relevant to the issues under reg. 70(c). See the note to subs. (9) below as to the effect of the National Minimum Wage Act 1998 on the rule in that provision. It is important to emphasise that paras. (a) to (d) of reg. 70 are only examples of factors to be taken into account in certain specified situations. This does not mean that such factors may not be relevant in other circumstances, nor does reg. 70 limit in any way the issues for consideration when deciding the length of a sanction under subs. (6). The principle developed under unemployment benefit law that the discretion as to the period of disqualification (now the period of sanction) is to be exercised judicially and sensibly, taking account of all the circumstances *(R(U) 8/74 (T))* will continue to apply; the first question will of course continue to be whether the circumstances merit the imposition of a sanction at all (see the notes to subs. (6)). See *Bonner* for further discussion of the existing case law on determining the period of sanction. It will be an error of law for a SSAT not to indicate that it has considered the period of sanction and the issues it has taken into account in that regard *(R(U) 4/87;* see also *R(U) 3/79).*

Where an AO has chosen to rely on the procedure in reg. 56A of the Adjudication Regulations in relation to whether a sanction should be imposed under subs. (6) and a decision to impose a sanction is subsequently made, the effect of reg. 56A(6)(a) and (7) is that the sanction will normally operate from the beginning of the next benefit week. If however, the AO makes an immediate decision or refers the question to a tribunal for decision, the legislation does not lay down when the sanction is to start (for subs. (5) sanctions see reg. 69). Presumably the approach that was taken in unemployment benefit case law will continue to apply, broadly that the sanction should begin from the day following the loss of employment, etc., or the first day of the benefit week following its imposition if JSA has been in payment, or at the end of any period during which the claimant is treated as in remunerative work under reg. 52(3) of the JSA Regulations because he has received a compensation payment (see further *Bonner* and paras. 39037–45 of the *Adjudication Officer's Guide).* If a sanction has begun, or been imposed but not yet begun, and a person then finds a job or undertakes training for a short time but claims JSA again before the sanction has expired, it again seems likely that the unemployment benefit position will apply, that is, he will not be entitled to JSA (other than possibly a hardship payment) until the end of the sanction period, even though the loss of the employment or training itself would not be grounds for sanction (see *CU 64/1994* (which refers to *R(U) 13/64)* and para. 39032 *AOG).*

Subsection (5)

This subsection sets out the situations in which a fixed sanction of two weeks, or four in the case of a second sanction within 12 months (see reg. 69 of the JSA Regulations), may be imposed. Note that a "New Deal sanction" will only be for four weeks if imposed within 12 months of a previous New Deal sanction (or possibly a Project Work sanction): see further the notes to reg. 69. For the predecessors of this provision see s. 28(1)(d)–(g) of the Contributions and Benefits Act and reg. 21A of the Income Support Regulations.

Failure to carry out a jobseeker's direction

Para. (a) applies where a claimant has, without good cause, refused or failed to carry out a reasonable jobseeker's direction. Jobseekers' directions are issued by employment officers (defined in subs. (10)(a)), and so are not appealable as such. But the decision as to whether a sanction should be imposed for non-compliance will be taken by an AO (s. 20(1)(d) of the Administration Act), which will thus generate the usual rights of appeal to a tribunal (and beyond). According to subs. (10)(b) the object of a jobseeker's direction is to help the claimant to find employment and/or improve his chances of being employed. The *Adjudication Officer's Guide* gives as examples of a jobseeker's direction an instruction to apply for a particular vacancy, make a speculative approach to an employer, *e.g.* by sending a CV, attend a course on job search skills or join a job club (para. 39633). Thus the effect of a jobseeker's direction can be to turn voluntary training schemes or other employment initiatives into compulsory ones.

A jobseeker's direction must be "reasonable", be for the purpose set out in subs. (10)(b) and take account of the claimant's individual circumstances. In addition, a sanction will not be applied if the claimant had "good cause" for not complying with the direction. See reg. 72 of the JSA Regulations, made under subs. (8), which sets out some circumstances which will constitute good cause (see paras. (4) and (5) of reg. 72) and some which will not (see paras. (6) and (7)), together with a number of factors to be taken into account when considering whether there was good cause for non-compliance (see para. (2)). The list in reg. 72(2) is not exhaustive and the existing case law on good cause will continue to be relevant. There may often be some overlap between the issue of whether the jobseeker's direction was reasonable and whether the claimant had good cause for non-compliance (as there was in the past in the case law concerning good cause between the questions of whether a job was suitable in the particular circumstances of the claimant and whether he had good cause to refuse it *(cf. R(U) 20/60, R(U) 5/71* and *R(U) 2/77)).* In *Crewe v. Social Security Commissioner* [1982] 2 All E.R. 745, 751 Slade L.J. suggested that good cause meant "reasonable cause" and involved a lower burden than showing "just cause", which required the balancing of individual interests against the interests of all the contributors to the National Insurance Fund. See further *Bonner*.

One question that arises is the use of jobseekers' directions to require claimants to take part-time work. Reg. 72(5A) exempts a person from sanction under subs. (6)(c) or (d) for refusing work of less than 24 hours a week, or of less than 16 hours a week if he has been allowed to restrict his availability to less than 24 hours a week. However, there is no such exemption for not complying with a direction under subs. (5)(a) requiring him to apply for a job for less than 24/16 hours. But it would seem a nonsense for an employment officer to be able to direct a person to apply for such a job when he is statutorily deemed to have good cause for refusing to do so. This is not, however, the view taken in the *Adjudication Officer's Guide* (see para. 39651).

Note the statement in the *Adjudication Officer's Guide* that if a claimant after an initial refusal changes his mind and carries out a jobseeker's direction and can still achieve something by doing this para. (a) does not apply and that if a sanction has already been applied the decision to impose it should be reviewed (see paras. 39640–2).

Training scheme or employment programme "offences"

Para. (b) penalises a claimant who without good cause neglects to avail himself of, gives up, or fails to attend a training scheme or employment programme place (sub-paras. (i), (iii) and (iv)), or refuses or fails to apply for or accept such a place that has been notified to him by an employment officer (sub-para. (ii)). Para. (c) applies where a person has lost a training scheme or employment programme place through misconduct. The classic description of "misconduct" as conduct that is "blameworthy, reprehensible and wrong" (*R(U) 2/77*) will presumably be relevant here (see further *Bonner*). "Training scheme" and "employment programme" for the purposes of s. 19 and Part V of the JSA Regulations are defined in reg. 75(1). The form of reg. 75 introduced on January 5, 1988 distinguishes between the three employment programmes and the one training scheme that make up the "New Deal Options" for 18–24 year-olds (see reg. 75(1)(a)(ii) and (b)(ii)) and the other employment programmes and training schemes that count for the purposes of s. 19. Reg. 75(1)(a)(i) lists these employment programmes; training scheme in reg. 75(1)(b)(i) means Work Based Training for Young People (in Scotland "Skillseekers") which is the new name for training focussed on 16/17 year-olds (replacing Youth Training, Modern Apprenticeships, National Traineeships and other provision). In some areas of the country a claimant may also have been required to take part in a pilot scheme (see s. 29) called Project Work and could have been sanctioned for refusing to do so without good cause. However, Project Work was abolished in May 1998. (For a discussion of the conditions in the JSA (Pilot Scheme) Regulations 1996 (S.I. 1996 No. 1307) for the imposition of a Project Work sanction see *CJSA 5600/1997*). Note also the separate provision in reg. 75(1)(b)(iii), introduced on June 1, 1998, which concerns claimants aged 25 or over who are being treated as available for work under reg. 17A of the JSA Regulations while attending a full-time employment-related course (see the notes to reg. 17A). A claimant aged 25 or over cannot be required to go on such a course. However, if he is treated as available for employment under reg. 17A while attending such a course, he can be sanctioned for failing to attend, or giving up, the course without good cause or losing his place through misconduct. It is also possible for an employment officer to issue a jobseeker's direction requiring a claimant to attend a "non-compulsory" scheme; if the claimant fails to comply without good cause he could be liable to sanction under para. (a). For further details of training schemes and employment programmes see CPAG's *Welfare Benefits Handbook* (1999/2000 ed.), and for updated information see CPAG's *Welfare Rights Bulletin*. For a brief summary of the New Deal see the note to reg. 75.

For para. (b)(ii) to apply the claimant must have been notified of the training scheme or employment programme place by an employment officer (defined in subs. (10)(a)). This is not required in the case of the other sub-paragraphs in para. (b). "Notified" is not defined but presumably the notification must include sufficient details of the training scheme or employment programme place to enable the claimant to be able to apply for it (see *R(U) 32/52*). See also *CSU 7/1995* in the note to subs. (6)(c).

Sub-paras. (ii) and (iv) refer to "failure" to apply for or accept or to attend a training scheme or employment programme place. Since these do not simply say that the claimant does not attend, it may be arguable that the notion of "failure" imports a requirement of a breach of some obligation (see *R(SB) 21/82*). This was the view taken in *CIS 292/1994* in relation to 'failure to attend" a course in reg. 21A(3)(e) of the Income Support Regulations, although the actual decision was based on the fact that the course was not a "relevant course" for the purposes of reg. 21A. Clearly in those circumstances attendance on the course was not reasonably to be expected. However, in *CSIS 38/1994* the Commissioner rejects this approach. He states that in *R(SB) 21/82*, which concerned "failure to disclose" in relation to overpayment of benefit, there was quite clearly a legal (see, in particular, reg. 32(1) of the Claims and Payments Regulations), and a moral, duty to make disclosure.

But there was no breach of any moral or legal obligation by a claimant failing to attend a course. However, the Commissioner did accept that "failure" to attend in reg. 21A(3)(e) was not the same as simple non-attendance. "Failure" indicated some default or lapse by the claimant. Thus, for example, if the claimant turned up for the course on time but all the places were allocated before he reached the head of the queue, this would not constitute a failure to attend. In that case the claimant was late because he had been kept waiting by the Job Centre where he had gone to make an enquiry at 9.30 a.m. (the time the course was due to start). The Commissioner does not decide whether this amounted to a "failure" to attend but remits the case to a new tribunal for further investigation of the facts. However, the meaning of "failure" may be of less significance in relation to the "offences" in sub-paras. (ii) and (iv) because of the general exemption from sanction under para. (b) if the claimant shows good cause for the failure to attend, etc. (there was no such exemption under reg. 21A).

Sub-para. (iv) does not specify whether the failure to attend refers to the whole scheme or programme or whether failing to attend part of it will suffice to bring that sub-paragraph into play (compare reg. 21A(3)(e) of the Income Support Regulations, see the 1996 edition of this book). The view taken in the *Adjudication Officer's Guide* is that an *unauthorised* (emphasis added) absence of one day will constitute a failure to attend and that a claimant will have failed to attend even if he intends to go back to the scheme or programme (para. 39743). Thus if the absence is authorised (presumably by the person running the scheme or programme) this should not trigger the application of sub-para. (iv). An absence of a very short period may be ignored on the *de minimis* principle.

Note the statement in the *Adjudication Officer's Guide* that if a claimant after an initial refusal changes his mind and applies for a training scheme or employment programme place before it has been filled, sub-para. (ii) does not apply and that if a sanction has already been applied the decision to impose it should be reviewed (see paras. 39401–2).

Under sub-para. (iii) a person has not given up a training scheme or employment programme if he has been dismissed from it (confirmed in *AOG*, para. 39742). Para. (c) will only apply if the dismissal was due to the claimant's misconduct.

See also reg. 73 which lists a number of circumstances that will constitute good cause under para. (b), but these are "without prejudice to any other circumstances in which a person may be regarded as having good cause" for the purposes of para. (b). The existing case law on good cause will therefore continue to be relevant (see further the note to para. (5)(a)).

Where a decision to apply a sanction is made under subs. (5), it begins on the first day of the following benefit week (reg. 69 of the JSA Regulations). It will last for four weeks if the decision to impose it is made within 12 months of a previous fixed sanction (the 12 months runs from the start of the earlier sanction); otherwise two weeks. But note that a "New Deal sanction" will only be for four weeks if it is incurred within 12 months of a previous New Deal sanction (or possibly a Project Work sanction): see further the notes to reg. 69. The claimant may be eligible for a hardship payment under regs. 141(6) or 142(5) of the JSA Regulations (see the notes to those regulations). But note that eligibility for hardship payments is limited to those in the "vulnerable groups" (see reg. 140(1)) in the case of New Deal sanctions (see regs. 140(4A) and 140A).

Subsection (6)

This is concerned with the loss or refusal of employment (whereas subs. (5) deals with non-compliance with jobseekers' directions and loss or refusal of training scheme or employment programme places). If the conditions of any of the paragraphs are met, a sanction of between one and 26 weeks will be applied (subs. (3), see the notes to that subsection), although a claimant may be eligible for a hardship payment under regs. 141(6) or 142(5) of the JSA Regulations (see the notes to those regulations).

The provisions in subs. (6) are substantially the same as those that formerly led to disqualification from unemployment benefit under s. 28(1)(a)–(c) of the Contributions and Benefits Act. See *Bonner* for discussion of the existing case law on these provisions.

Under paras. (b) and (d), note s. 20(3) and reg. 74 of the JSA Regulations on trial periods. On volunteering for redundancy and voluntarily leaving see subs. (7) and reg. 71.

There is an exemption from sanction under paras. (c) and (d) if the claimant can show good cause for the refusal or failure to apply for or accept the notified employment, or the neglect to avail. See reg. 72, made under subs. (8), which sets out some circumstances which will constitute good cause (see paras. (4) and (5) of reg. 72) and some which will not (see paras. (6) and (7)), together with a number of factors to be taken into account when considering whether there was good cause under paras. (c) and (d) (see para. (2) of reg. 72; the list in reg. 72(2) is not exhaustive). Note in addition reg. 72(8) and (9) in relation to good cause under para. (d). Subject to reg. 72, however, the existing case law on "good cause" will remain relevant (see further the note to para. (5)(a)). Note also subs. (9).

On the meaning of "accept a situation in any employment" in para. (6)(c) see *CSU 7/1995*. The claimant was offered the job of a lampshade maker at a wage of £79 per week, having been informed of the vacancy by the Employment Service. But she changed her mind and did not start the job because the wage was too low to meet her commitments. The SSAT decided that since she did accept the offer of employment, s. 28(1)(b) of the Contributions and Benefits Act (whose terms were substantially similar to para. (6)(c)) did not operate to disqualify her from receiving unemployment benefit. However, the Commissioner held that although normally acceptance of an offer of a situation would be tantamount to accepting the situation it could not have been intended that it would be possible to defeat the operation of s. 28(1)(b) by an acceptance in theory but a repudiation in practice. The claimant had not "accepted the situation" within the meaning of s. 28(1)(b).

See also *CJSA 4179/1997* in which the claimant was offered a "trial" as a part-time car washer. The tribunal dealt with the case under para. (c) but the Commissioner expressed doubt as to whether the "trial" was an offer of a "situation in any employment". The tribunal should have investigated what the trial involved. If para. (c) did not apply, para. (d) should then have been considered.

Note reg. 56A of the Adjudication Regulations where the *AO* is unable to decide immediately whether a sanction should be imposed under this subsection.

Subsection (7)

See the notes in *Bonner* and reg. 71 of the JSA Regulations.

Subsection (8)

See regs. 72 and 73 of the JSA Regulations which are concerned with good cause for the purposes of subss. (5)(a), (6)(c) and (d) and subs. (5)(b) respectively. So far, no regulations have been made on the meaning of just cause.

Subsection (9)

Unlike its predecessor, s. 28(5), this applies where just cause, as well as good cause, is in issue. But see reg. 70(c) and various provisions in reg. 72 of the JSA Regulations.

Note also that from April 1, 1999 there is a national minimum wage for most workers (broadly £3.60 per hour for those aged 22 or over; £3.00 per hour for those aged 18 to 21). It is suggested that as a consequence of the national minimum wage legislation subs. (9) should not prevent a claimant from being able to show, *e.g.* just cause for leaving voluntarily, if his employer refuses to pay him at his appropriate minimum rate, or, *e.g.* good cause for refusing employment, if the proposed rate of pay is not at least at the minimum wage level that applies to him. This is on the basis that the rule in subs. (9) should not be applied in a way that runs contrary to the National Minimum Wage Act 1998.

Exemptions from section 19

20.—(1) Nothing in section 19, or in regulations under that section, shall be taken to prevent payment of a jobseeker's allowance merely because the claimant refuses to seek or accept employment in a situation which is vacant in consequence of a stoppage of work due to a trade dispute.

(2) Section 19 does not apply, in the circumstances mentioned in subsection (5) of that section, if—

  (a) a direction is in force under section 16 with respect to the claimant; and

  (b) he has acted in such a way as to risk—

    (i) having that direction revoked under subsection (3)(b) of section 16; or

    (ii) having the amount of his jobseeker's allowance reduced by virtue of section 17, because he has failed to complete a course of training.

(3) Regulations shall make provision for the purpose of enabling any person of a prescribed description to accept any employed earner's employment without falling within section 19(6)(b) or (d) should he leave that employment voluntarily and without just cause at any time during a trial period.

(4) In such circumstances as may be prescribed, an income-based jobseeker's

allowance shall be payable to a claimant even though section 19 prevents payment of a jobseeker's allowance to him.

(5) A jobseeker's allowance shall be payable by virtue of subsection (4) only if the claimant has complied with such requirements as to the provision of information as may be prescribed for the purposes of this subsection.

(6) Regulatiions under subsection (4) may, in particular, provide for a jobseeker's allowance payable by virtue of that subsection to be—

(a) payable at a prescribed rate;

(b) payable for a prescribed period (which may differ from the period fixed under section 19(2) or (3)).

(7) In subsection (3), "trial period" has such meaning as may be prescribed.

(8) Regulations may make provision for determining, for the purposes of this section, the day on which a person's employment is to be regarded as commencing.

DEFINITIONS

"claimant"—see s. 35(1).
"employment"—*ibid.*, JSA Regs., reg. 4.
"income-based jobseeker's allowance"—see s. 1(4).
"prescribed"—see s. 35(1).
"regulations"—*ibid.*
"trade dispute"—*ibid.*
"training"—*ibid.*
"trial period"—JSA Regs., reg. 74(4).

GENERAL NOTE

Subss. (1)–(3) provide for exemptions from the sanctions in s. 19 and subss. (4)–(6) allow for hardship payments where JSA is not payable because of the application of s. 19.

Subsection (1)

This maintains the traditional "neutral" approach to trade disputes taken in social security law. A claimant is not required to be a strike-breaker and so will not be sanctioned for refusing work that is vacant because of a trade dispute.

Subsection (2)

If a young person who is the subject of a severe hardship direction fails to pursue or refuses a training opportunity without good cause or fails to complete a training course without good cause, s. 19(5) does not apply. The young person's "offence" will be dealt with by revocation of the direction under s. 16(3) or reduction in his JSA under s. 17 as appropriate. See reg. 63 of the JSA Regulations.

Subsection (3)

This subsection, combined with reg. 74 of the JSA Regulations, enables a person to take a job and then leave it within a trial period without falling foul of s. 19(6)(b) or (d). It is not necessary for the employment to have been undertaken on a trial basis. The person must not have worked, been self-employed, a full-time student (defined in reg. 1(3)) or in relevant education (see reg. 54) for 13 weeks before the start of the job (reg. 74(1)). Certain activities do not count for this purpose (see reg. 74(2) and (3)). The protection applies if the person leaves the employment voluntarily without just cause at any time after the beginning of the fifth week (see *R(U) 1/92*) and by the end of the twelfth week (reg. 74(4)). "Week" means a period of seven days (reg. 75(2)) and weeks in which the person works (see *Suffolk County Council v. Secretary of State for the Environment and Alcock* [1985] I.R.L.R. 24, [1984] I.C.R. 882) for less than 16 hours are disregarded (reg. 74(4)). This rule will not apply if the person does not leave voluntarily (*e.g.* he is dismissed); if the person had just cause for leaving the employment he will not need to rely on this rule.

Subsections (4) to (6)

In the past a claimant suspended or disqualified from unemployment benefit under s. 28(1) of the Contributions and Benefits Act, or who would have been so disqualified if otherwise entitled, could (if eligible) receive reduced payments of income support (see reg. 22 of the Income Support Regulations (now revoked) in the 1996 edition of this book; see also reg. 21A (also now revoked) which provided for claimants' income support to be reduced in the case of failure to attend certain compulsory courses). Under the new scheme, however, there is no automatic entitlement to reduced income-based JSA where a sanction is imposed under s. 19. Benefit will only be paid if a claimant can show that he, or a member of his household, will suffer hardship as a result of the sanction. If a "hardship payment" is made, it will be subject to a 40 per cent or 20 per cent reduction of the appropriate personal allowance for a single claimant and will not be payable for the first two weeks, except to certain claimants (*i.e.* those who come within one of the "vulnerable" groups listed in reg. 140(1)). In the case of a "New Deal" sanction (see the notes to reg. 69) hardship payments will not be available at all (even if the sanction is for four weeks), except to claimants in one of the vulnerable groups (see regs. 140(4A) and 140A(1)). For a claimant who is not in one of the vulnerable groups there is the possibility of a crisis loan from the Social Fund during the period of a New Deal sanction, but only for expenses arising out of a disaster or for items for cooking or heating (including fireguards) (see Social Fund Direction 17(d) and (f)). In the case of a non-New Deal sanction a claimant who is not getting hardship payments will only have access to a crisis loan for expenses resulting from a disaster or for items for cooking or heating for 14 days starting on the first day of the benefit week following the end of the sanction (Social Fund Direction 17(c) and (f)). (See Direction 18(2) for crisis loans for a partner's living expenses in such a case.) Because JSA is paid fortnightly in arrears, if, for example, such a sanction is for two weeks, this will mirror the period when the effect of the sanction is actually felt. This restricted access to crisis loans does not apply to claimants in one of the vulnerable groups who have been awarded hardship payments (Direction 17(e)).

Note that where a s. 19 sanction is imposed, the effect is that JSA is not *payable* (see s. 19(1)). *Entitlement* to JSA continues during the period of the sanction. It thus eats into the 182-day maximum period of entitlement for contribution-based JSA: see s. 5 in *Bonner*. On the other hand, full housing benefit and council tax benefit will continue to be payable (see reg. 2(3A) of the Housing Benefit Regulations 1987 and the Council Tax Benefit Regulations 1992 respectively), for claimants who would otherwise be getting income-based JSA. Claimants awarded hardship payments will also be entitled to full housing/council tax benefit because hardship payments count as payments of income-based JSA.

See regs. 140–146 of the JSA Regulations for the rules governing hardship payments and the notes to those regulations. Under subs. (5) see reg. 144.

Miscellaneous

Supplementary provisions

21. Further provisions in relation to a jobseeker's allowance are set out in Schedule 1.

Recovery of sums in respect of maintenance

23.—(1) Regulations may make provision for the court to have power to make a recovery order against any person where an award of income-based jobseeker's allowance has been made to that person's spouse.

(2) In this section "recovery order" means an order requiring the person against whom it is made to make payments to the Secretary of State or to such other person or persons as the court may determine.

(3) Regulations under this section may make provision for the transfer by the Secretary of State of the right to receive payments under, and to exercise rights in relation to, a recovery order.

(4) Regulations made under this section may, in particular, include provision—

(a) as to the matters to which the court is, or is not, to have regard in determining any application under the regulations; and

(b) as to the enforcement of recovery orders.

(5) In this section, ''the court'' means—

(a) in relation to England and Wales, a magistrates' court; and

(b) in relation to Scotland, the sheriff.

DEFINITIONS

''income-based jobseeker's allowance''—see s. 1(4).
''regulations''—see s. 35(1).

GENERAL NOTE

This section is concerned with the enforcement of a person's liability to maintain his spouse
where an award of jobseeker's allowance has been made to that spouse (compare ss. 106 and 107
of the Administration Act in relation to income support). It is not known how often these powers
to recover spousal maintenance are in fact used since the child support maintenance system introduced by the Child Support Act 1991 has been in operation.

PART II

BACK TO WORK SCHEMES

The back to work bonus

26.—(1) Regulations may make provision for the payment, in prescribed circumstances, of sums to or in respect of persons who are or have been entitled
to a jobseeker's allowance or to income support.

(2) A sum payable under the regulations shall be known as ''a back to work
bonus''.

(3) Subject to section 617 of the Income and Corporation Taxes Act 1988
(which, as amended by paragraph 16 of Schedule 2, provides for a back to work
bonus not to be taxable), a back to work bonus shall be treated for all purposes
as payable by way of a jobseeker's allowance or (as the case may be) income
support.

(4) The regulations may, in particular, provide for—

(a) a back to work bonus to be payable only on the occurrence of a prescribed event;

(b) a bonus not to be payable unless a claim is made before the end of the
prescribed period;

(c) the amount of a bonus (subject to any maximum prescribed by virtue of
paragraph (g)) to be determined in accordance with the regulations;

(d) enabling amounts to be calculated by reference to periods of entitlement
to a jobseeker's allowance and periods of entitlement to income support;

(e) treating a bonus as payable wholly by way of income support or wholly
by way of a jobseeker's allowance, in a case where amounts have been
calculated in accordance with provision made by virtue of paragraph (d);

(f) keeping persons who may be entitled to a bonus informed of the amounts
calculated in accordance with any provision of the regulations made by
virtue of paragraph (c);

(g) the amount of a bonus not to exceed a prescribed maximum;

(h) a bonus not to be payable if the amount of the bonus which would otherwise be payable is less than the prescribed minimum;

(i) prescribed periods to be disregarded for prescribed purposes;

(j) a bonus which has been paid to a person to be treated, in prescribed circumstances and for prescribed purposes, as income or capital of his or of any other member of his family;

(k) treating the whole or a prescribed part of an amount which has accrued towards a person's bonus—
  (i) as not having accrued towards his bonus; but
  (ii) as having accrued towards the bonus of another person;

(l) the whole or a prescribed part of a back to work bonus to be payable, in such circumstances as may be prescribed, to such person, other than the person who is or had been entitled to a jobseeker's allowance or to income support, as may be determined in accordance with the regulations.

DEFINITIONS

"prescribed"—see s. 35(1).
"regulations"—*ibid.*

GENERAL NOTE

See the Social Security (Back to Work Bonus) (No. 2) Regulations 1996.

Pilot schemes

29.—(1) Any regulations to which this subsection applies may be made so as to have effect for a specified period not exceeding 12 months.

(2) Any regulations which, by virtue of subsection (1), are to have effect for a limited period are referred to in this section as "a pilot scheme".

(3) A pilot scheme may provide that its provisions are to apply only in relation to—

(a) one or more specified areas or localities;

(b) one or more specified classes of person;

(c) persons selected—
  (i) by reference to prescribed criteria; or
  (ii) on a sampling basis.

(4) A pilot scheme may make consequential or transitional provision with respect to the cessation of the scheme on the expiry of the specified period.

(5) A pilot scheme ("the previous scheme") may be replaced by a further pilot scheme making the same, or similar, provision (apart from the specified period) to that made by the previous scheme.

(6) Subject to subsection (8), subsection (1) applies to—

(a) regulations made under this Act, other than—
  (i) regulations made under section 4(2) or (5) which have the effect of reducing any age-related amount or applicable amount; or
  (ii) regulations made under section 27;

(b) regulations made under the Administration Act, so far as they relate to a jobseeker's allowance;

(c) regulations made under Part VII of the Benefits Act (income-related benefits), other than any mentioned in subsection (7); and

(d) regulations made under the Administration Act, so far as they relate to income-related benefits payable under Part VII of the Benefits Act.

(7) The regulations referred to in subsection (6)(c) are—

(a) regulations under section 128(5) of the Benefits Act which have the effect of reducing the appropriate maximum family credit;

(b) regulations under section 129(8) of that Act which have the effect of reducing the appropriate maximum disability working allowance;

(c) regulations under section 130(4) of that Act which have the effect of reducing the appropriate maximum housing benefit;

(d) regulations under section 131(10)(a) of that Act which have the effect of reducing the appropriate maximum council tax benefit; and

(e) regulations reducing any of the sums prescribed under section 135(1) of that Act.

(8) Subsection (1) applies only if the regulations are made with a view to ascertaining whether their provisions will, or will be likely to, encourage persons to obtain or remain in work or will, or will be likely to, facilitate the obtaining by persons of work or their remaining in work.

DEFINITIONS

"the Administration Act"—see s. 35(1).
"the Benefits Act"—*ibid.*
"regulations"—*ibid.*

GENERAL NOTE

This important provision contains a new power to "pilot" changes in regulations across particular geographical areas and/or specified categories of claimants for a period of up to 12 months (this period can be extended: see subs. (5)). The power can only be exercised in relation to the types of regulations listed in subs. (6) and with a view to assessing whether the proposed changes are likely to encourage or help people to find or remain in work (subs. (8)). Regulations made under this section are subject to the affirmative resolution procedure (s. 37(1)(c)).

The early indications are that this power will be used on a fairly regular basis. See also the Earnings Top-up Scheme referred to in the notes at the beginning of the Family Credit Regulations.

PART III

MISCELLANEOUS AND SUPPLEMENTAL

Termination of awards

31.—(1) Regulations may make provision allowing, in prescribed circumstances, an award of income support to be brought to an end by an adjudication officer where the person to whom it was made, or where he is a member of a married or unmarried couple his partner, will be entitled to a jobseeker's allowance if the award is brought to an end.

(2) Regulations may make provision allowing, in prescribed circumstances, an award of a jobseeker's allowance to be brought to an end by an adjudication officer where the person to whom it was made, or where he is a member of a married or unmarried couple his partner, will be entitled to income support if the award is brought to an end.

(3) In this section "partner" means the other member of the couple concerned.

DEFINITIONS

"adjudication officer"—see s. 35(1).
"married couple"—*ibid.*
"unmarried couple"—*ibid.*

See reg. 56B of the Adjudication Regulations.

Interpretation

35.—(1) In this Act—

"adjudication officer" means an adjudication officer appointed under section 38 of the Administration Act;

"the Administration Act" means the Social Security Administration Act 1992;

"applicable amount" means the applicable amount determined in accordance with regulations under section 4;

"benefit year" has the meaning given by section 2(4);

"the Benefits Act" means the Social Security Contributions and Benefits Act 1992;

"child" means a person under the age 16;

"claimant" means a person who claims a jobseeker's allowance;

"continental shelf operations" has the same meaning as in section 120 of the Benefits Act;

"contribution-based conditions" means the conditions set out in section 2;

"contribution-based jobseeker's allowance" has the meaning given in section 1(4);

"employed earner" has the meaning prescribed for the purposes of this Act;

"employment", except in section 7, has the meaning prescribed for the purposes of this Act;

"entitled", in relation to a jobseeker's allowance, is to be construed in accordance with—

(a) the provisions of this Act relating to entitlement; and

(b) sections 1 and 68 of the Administration Act;

"family" means—

(a) a married or unmarried couple;

(b) a married or unmarried couple and a member of the same household for whom one of them is, or both are, responsible and who is a child or a person of a prescribed description;

(c) except in prescribed circumstances, a person who is not a member of a married or unmarried couple and a member of the same household for whom that person is responsible and who is a child or a person of a prescribed description;

"Great Britain" includes the territorial waters of the United Kingdom adjacent to Great Britain;

"income-based conditions" means the conditions set out in section 3;

"income-based jobseeker's allowance" has the meaning given in section 1(4);

"jobseeker's agreement" has the meaning given by section 9(1);

"jobseeking period" has the meaning prescribed for the purposes of this Act;

"married couple" means a man and woman who are married to each other and are members of the same household;

"occupational pension scheme" has the same meaning as it has in the Pension Schemes Act 1993 by virtue of section 1 of that Act;

"pensionable age" has the meaning prescribed for the purposes of this Act;

"pension payments" means—

(a) periodical payments made in relation to a person, under a personal pension scheme or, in connection with the coming to an end of an employment of his, under an occupational pension scheme or a public service pension scheme; and

(b) such other payments as may be prescribed;

"personal pension scheme" means—

(a) a personal pension scheme as defined by section 1 of the Pension Schemes Act 1993;

(b) a contract or trust scheme approved under Chapter III of Part XIV of the Income and Corporation Taxes Act 1988; and

(c) a personal pension scheme approved under Chapter IV of that Part of that Act;

"prescribed" [[1], except in section 27 (and in section 36 so far as relating to regulations under section 27),] means specified in or determined in accordance with regulations;

"public service pension scheme" has the same meaning as it has in the Pension Schemes Act 1993 by virtue of section 1 of that Act;

"regulations" [[1], except in section 27 (and in section 36 so far as relating to regulations under section 27),] means regulations made by the Secretary of State;

"tax year" means the 12 months beginning with 6th April in any year;

"trade dispute" means any dispute between employers and employees, or between employees and employees, which is connected with the employment or non-employment or the terms of employment or the conditions of employment of any persons, whether employees in the employment of the employer with whom the dispute arises, or not;

"training" has the meaning prescribed for the purposes of this Act and, in relation to prescribed provisions of this Act, if regulations so provide, includes assistance to find training or employment, or to improve a person's prospects of being employed, of such a kind as may be prescribed;

"unmarried couple" means a man and woman who are not married to each other but are living together as husband and wife otherwise than in prescribed circumstances;

"week" means a period of 7 days beginning with a Sunday or such other period of 7 days as may be prescribed;

"work" has the meaning prescribed for the purposes of this Act;

"year", except in the expression "benefit year", means a tax year.

(2) The expressions "capable of work", "linked period", "relevant education" and "remunerative work" are to be read with paragraphs 2, 3, 14 and 1 of Schedule 1.

(3) Subject to any regulations made for the purposes of this subsection, "earnings" is to be construed for the purposes of this Act in accordance with section 3 of the Benefits Act and paragraph 6 of Schedule 1 to this Act.

AMENDMENT

1. Social Security Contributions (Transfer of Functions, etc.) Act 1999, s.2 and Sched. 3, para. 62 (April 1, 1999).

GENERAL NOTE

In addition to the above definitions there are further important definitions in the JSA Regulations, some of which relate to the whole of the Regulations (see regs. 1(3) and 3) and some of which only apply to specified Parts.

"*child*". The restriction to a person under 16 gives rise to the need to define "young person" in the JSA Regulations to cater for the over-15s (see regs. 57(1) and 76(1)).

"*employed earner*". See reg. 3 of the JSA Regulations.

"*employment*". See s. 7(8) and regs. 3 and 4 of the JSA Regulations.

"*family*". The definition is the same as in s. 137(1) of the Contributions and Benefits Act. See the notes to that definition. For "person of a prescribed description" see reg. 76(1) of the JSA Regulations.

"*married couple*". The definition is the same as in s. 137(1) of the Contributions and Benefits Act. See the notes to that definition.

"*occupational pension scheme*". The definition in the Pension Schemes Act, s. 1 is set out in the note to "*occupational pension*" in reg. 2(1) of the Income Support Regulations.

"*pensionable age*". See reg. 3 of the JSA Regulations.

"*personal pension scheme*". Under para. (a), the definition in the Pension Schemes Act, s.1 is set out in the note to "*personal pension scheme*" in reg. 2(1) of the Income Support Regulations.

"*public service pension scheme*". The meaning in s. 1 of the Pension Schemes Act is "an occupational pension scheme established by or under an enactment or the Royal prerogative or a Royal charter, being a scheme (a) all the particulars of which are set out in, or in a legislative instrument made under, an enactment, Royal warrant or charter, or (b) which cannot come into force, or be amended, without the scheme or amendment being approved by a Minister of the Crown or government department, and includes any occupational pension scheme established, with the concurrence of the Treasury, by or with the approval of any Minister of the Crown and any occupational pension scheme prescribed by regulations made by the Secretary of State and the Treasury jointly as being a scheme which ought in their opinion to be treated as a public service pension scheme for the purposes of this Act".

"*unmarried couple*". The definition is the same as in s. 137(1) of the Contributions and Benefits Act. See the notes to that definition.

Regulations and orders

36.—(1) Any power under this Act to make regulations or orders, other than an order under section 9(13) or 19(10)(a), shall be exercisable by statutory instrument.

(2) Any such power may be exercised—

(a) either in relation to all cases to which it extends, or in relation to those cases subject to specified exceptions, or in relation to any specified cases or classes of case;

(b) so as to make, as respects the cases in relation to which it is exercised—

    (i) the full provision to which the power extends or any less provision (whether by way of exception or otherwise),

    (ii) the same provision for all cases in relation to which it is exercised, or different provision for different cases or different classes of case or different provision as respects the same case or class of case for different purposes of this Act,

    (iii) any such provision either unconditionally or subject to any specified condition.

(3) Where any such power is expressed to be exercisable for alternative purposes it may be exercised in relation to the same case for any or all of those purposes.

(4) Any such power includes power—

(a) to make such incidental, supplemental, consequential or transitional provision as appears to the Secretary of State [¹, or (in the case of regulations made by the Treasury) to the Treasury,] to be expedient; and

(b) to provide for a person to exercise a discretion in dealing with any matter.

(5) Any power to make regulations or an order for the purposes of any provision of this Act is without prejudice to any power to make regulations or an order for the purposes of any other provision.

AMENDMENT

1. Social Security Contributions (Transfer of Functions, etc.) Act 1999, s.2 and Sched. 3, para. 63 (April 1, 1999).

DEFINITION

"regulations"—see s. 35(1).

GENERAL NOTE

See s. 37 for the regulations which require approval by affirmative resolution.

Parliamentary control

37.—(1) Subsection (2) applies in relation to the following regulations (whether made alone or with other regulations)—
- (a) regulations made under, or by virtue of, any provision of this Act other than—
  - (i) section 6, 7, 26, 29 or 40;
  - (ii) paragraph (b) of the definition of "pension payments" in section 35(1), or
  - (iii) paragraph 17 of Schedule 1,
  before the date on which jobseeker's allowances first become payable;
- (b) the first regulations to be made under section 26;
- (c) regulations made under section 6, 7, 29, paragraph (b) of the definition of "pension payments" in section 35(1) or paragraph 17 of Schedule 1.

(2) No regulations to which this subsection applies shall be made unless a draft of the statutory instrument containing the regulations has been laid before Parliament and approved by a resolution of each House.

(3) Any other statutory instrument made under this Act, other than one made under section 41(2), shall be subject to annulment in pursuance of a resolution of either House of Parliament.

DEFINITIONS

"pension payments"—see s. 35(1).
"regulations"—*ibid.*

GENERAL NOTE

Note in particular that regulations governing availability for, and actively seeking, employment and pilot schemes have to be approved by affirmative resolution (subs. (1)(c)).

Transitional provisions

40.—(1) The Secretary of State may by regulations make such transitional provision, consequential provision or savings as he considers necessary or expedient for the purposes of or in connection with—
- (a) the coming into force of any provision of this Act; or
- (b) the operation of any enactment repealed or amended by any such provision during any period when the repeal or amendment is not wholly in force;

(2) Regulations under this section may in particular make provision—
- (a) for the termination or cancellation of awards of unemployment benefit or income support;
- (b) for a person whose award of unemployment benefit or income support has been terminated or cancelled under regulations made by virtue of paragraph (a) to be treated as having been awarded a jobseeker's allowance (a "transitional allowance")—
  - (i) of such a kind,
  - (ii) for such period,

(iii) of such an amount, and

(iv) subject to such conditions,

as may be determined in accordance with the regulations;

(c) for a person's continuing entitlement to a transitional allowance to be determined by reference to such provision as may be made by the regulations;

(d) for the termination of an award of a transitional allowance;

(e) for the review of an award of a transitional allowance;

(f) for a contribution-based jobseeker's allowance not to be payable for a prescribed period where a person is disqualified for receiving unemployment benefit;

(g) that days which were days of unemployment for the purposes of entitlement to unemployment benefit, and such other days as may be prescribed, are to be treated as having been days during which a person was, or would have been, entitled to a jobseeker's allowance;

(h) that days which were days of entitlement to unemployment benefit, and such other days as may be prescribed, are to be treated as having been days of entitlement to a contribution-based jobseeker's allowance;

(i) that the rate of a contribution-based transitional allowance is to be calculated by reference to the rate of unemployment benefit paid or payable.

DEFINITIONS

"contribution-based jobseeker's allowance"—see s. 1(4).
"prescribed"—see s. 35(1).
"regulations"—*ibid.*

GENERAL NOTE

See the Jobseeker's Allowance (Transitional Provisions) Regulations 1996 (S.I. 1996 No. 2657) which are consolidating regulations that replaced the Jobseeker's Allowance (Transitional Provisions) Regulations 1995 (S.I. 1995 No. 3276), as amended, from November 4, 1996.

Short title, commencement, extent etc.

41.—(1) This Act may be cited as the Jobseekers Act 1995.

(2) Section 39 and this section (apart from subsections (4) and (5)) come into force on the passing of this Act, but otherwise the provisions of this Act come into force on such day as the Secretary of State may by order appoint.

(3) Different days may be appointed for different purposes.

(4) Schedule 2 makes consequential amendments.

(5) The repeals set out in Schedule 3 shall have effect.

(6) Apart from this section, section 39 and paragraphs 11 to 16, 28, 67 and 68 of Schedule 2, this Act does not extend to Northern Ireland.

SCHEDULE 1   **Section 21**

SUPPLEMENTARY PROVISIONS

Remunerative work

1.—(1) For the purposes of this Act, "remunerative work" has such meaning as may be prescribed.

(2) Regulations may prescribe circumstances in which, for the purposes of this Act—

(a) a person who is not engaged in remunerative work is to be treated as engaged in remunerative work; or

(b) a person who is engaged in remunerative work is to be treated as not engaged in remunerative work.

Capacity for work

2.—(1) The question whether a person is capable or incapable of work shall be determined, for the purposes of this Act, in accordance with the provisions of Part XIIA of the Benefits Act.

(2) References in Part XIIA of the Benefits Act to the purposes of that Act shall be construed, where those provisions have effect for the purposes of this Act by virtue of sub-paragraph (1), as references to the purposes of this Act.

(3) Section 171B of the Benefits Act (incapacity for work: the own occupation test) shall have effect, as applied by sub-paragraph (1) for the purposes of this Act, as if for the references in subsections (3) and (4)(a) to any purpose of the Benefits Act there were substituted references to any purpose of this Act.

Linking periods

3. Regulations may provide—

(a) for jobseeking periods which are separated by not more than a prescribed number of weeks to be treated, for purposes of this Act, as one jobseeking period;

(b) for prescribed periods ("linked periods") to be linked, for purposes of this Act, to any jobseeking period.

Waiting days

4. Except in prescribed circumstances, a person is not entitled to a jobseeker's allowance in respect of a prescribed number of days at the beginning of a jobseeking period.

Periods of less than a week

5. Regulations may make provision in relation to—

(a) entitlement to a jobseeker's allowance, or

(b) the amount payable by way of such an allowance,

in respect of any period of less than a week.

Employment protection sums

6.—(1) In relation to any contribution-based jobseeker's allowance, regulations may make provision—

(a) for any employment protection sum to be treated as earnings payable by such person, to such person and for such period as may be determined in accordance with the regulations; and

(b) for any such period, so far as it is not a period of employment, to be treated as a period of employment.

(2) In this paragraph "employment protection sum" means—

(a) any sum, or a prescribed part of any sum—

    (i) payable, in respect of arrears of pay, under an order for reinstatement or re-engagement made under [¹the Employment Rights Act 1996];

    (ii) payable, by way of pay, under an order made under that Act for the continuation of a contract of employment;

    (iii) payable, by way of remuneration, under a protective award made under section 189 of the Trade Union and Labour Relations (Consolidation) Act 1992; and

(b) any prescribed sum which the regulations provide is to be treated as related to any sum within paragraph (a).

Pension payments

7. Regulations may make provision, for the purposes of any provision of, or made under, this Act—

(a) for such sums by way of pension payments to be disregarded for prescribed purposes;

(b) as to the week in which any pension payments are to be treated as having begun;

(c) for treating, in a case where—

    (i) a lump sum is paid to a person in connection with a former employment of his or arrangements are made for a lump sum to be so paid; or

    (ii) benefits of any description are made available to a person in connection with a former employment of his or arrangements are made for them to be made so available; or

    (iii) pension payments to a person are assigned, reduced or postponed or are made otherwise than weekly,

such payments as being made to that person by way of weekly pension payments as are specified in or determined under the regulations;

(d) for the method of determining whether pension payments are made to a person for any week and their amount.

Exemptions

8. Regulations may prescribe circumstances in which a person may be entitled to an income-based jobseeker's allowance without—

(a) being available for employment;

(b) having entered into a jobseeker's agreement; or

(c) actively seeking employment.

9. Regulations may provide—

(a) for an income-based jobseeker's allowance to which a person is entitled by virtue of regulations under paragraph 8 to be payable at a prescribed rate;

(b) for it to be payable for a prescribed period.

Claims yet to be determined and suspended payments

10.—(1) In such circumstances as may be prescribed, a claimant may be treated as being entitled to an income-based jobseeker's allowance before his claim for a jobseeker's allowance has been determined.

(2) In such circumstances as may be prescribed, an income-based jobseeker's allowance shall be payable to a claimant even though payment to him of a jobseeker's allowance has been suspended by virtue of regulations under [² section 5(1)(n) or (nn)] of the Administration Act.

(3) A jobseeker's allowance shall be payable by virtue of sub-paragraph (1) or (2) only if the claimant has complied with such requirements as to the provision of information as may be prescribed for the purposes of this paragraph.

(4) Regulations may make provision for a jobseeker's allowance payable by virtue of sub-paragraph (1) or (2) to be—

(a) payable at a prescribd rate;

(b) payable for a prescribed period;

(c) treated as being a contribution-based jobseeker's allowance for the purposes of section 5 of this Act.

(5) Regulations may make provision—

(a) for the recovery, by prescribed means and in prescribed circumstances, of the whole or part of any amount paid by virtue of sub-paragraph (1) or (2);

(b) for the whole or part of any amount paid by virtue of sub-paragraph (1) to be treated, if an award is made on the claim referred to there, as having been paid on account of the jobseeker's allowance awarded;

(c) for the whole or part of any amount paid by virtue of sub-paragraph (2) to be treated, if the suspension referred to there is lifted, as having been paid on account of the suspended allowance.

Presence in and absence from Great Britain

11.—(1) Regulations may provide that in prescribed circumstances a claimant who is not in Great Britain may nevertheless be entitled to a contribution-based jobseeker's allowance.

(2) Regulations may make provision for the purposes of this Act as to the circumstances in which a person is to be treated as being or not being in Great Britain.

Households

12. Regulations may make provision for the purposes of this Act as to the circumstances in which persons are to be treated as being or not being members of the same household.

Responsibility for another person

13. Regulations may make provision for the purposes of this Act as to the circumstances in which one person is to be treated as responsible or not responsible for another.

Relevant education

14. Regulations may make provision for the purposes of this Act—

(a) as to what is or is not to be treated as relevant education; and

(b) as to the circumstances in which a person is or is not to be treated as receiving relevant education.

Calculation of periods

15. Regulations may make provision for calculating periods for any purpose of this Act.

Employment on ships etc.

16.—(1) Regulations may modify any provision of this Act in its application to any person who is, has been, or is to be—

(a) employed on board any ship, vessel, hovercraft or aircraft,

(b) outside Great Britain at any prescribed time or in any prescribed circumstances, or

(c) in prescribed employment in connection with continental shelf operations,

so far as that provision relates to a contribution-based jobseeker's allowance.

(2) The regulations may in particular provide—

(a) for any such provision to apply even though it would not otherwise apply;

(b) for any such provision not to apply even though it would otherwise apply;

(c) for the taking of evidence, in a country or territory outside Great Britain, by a British consular official or other prescribed person;

(d) for enabling payment of the whole, or any part of a contribution-based jobseeker's allowance to be paid to such of the claimant's dependants as may be prescribed.

Additional conditions

17. Regulations may require additional conditions to be satisfied with respect to the payment of a jobseeker's allowance to any person who is, has been, or is to be, in employment which falls within a prescribed description.

Benefits Act purposes

18. Regulations may provide for—

(a) a jobseeker's allowance;

(b) a contribution-based jobseeker's allowance; or

(c) an income-based jobseeker's allowance,

to be treated, for prescribed purposes of the Benefits Act, as a benefit, or a benefit of a prescribed description.

AMENDMENTS

1. Employment Rights Act 1996, Sched. 1, para. 67(3) (August 22, 1996).

2. Social Security Act 1998, Sched. 6, para. 5(2) (May 21, 1998). This amendment applies from May 21, 1998 until s.21(2)(d) of the 1998 Act comes into force.

DEFINITIONS

"the Benefits Act"—see s. 35(1).
"contribution-based jobseeker's allowance"—see s. 1(4).
"employment"—see s. 35(1).
"Great Britain"—*ibid.*
"income-based jobseeker's allowance"—see s. 1(4).
"jobseeker's agreement"—see s. 35(1).
"jobseeking period"—*ibid.*
"pension payments"—*ibid.*
"prescribed"—*ibid.*
"regulations"—*ibid.*
"week"—*ibid.*

Asylum and Immigration Act 1996

(1996 c. 49)

SECTION REPRODUCED

11. Saving for social security regulation.

SCHEDULE REPRODUCED

Schedule 1, Part I.

GENERAL NOTE

Section 11 of this Act was introduced in response to the Court of Appeal's decision in *R. v. Secretary of State for Social Security, ex parte Joint Council for the Welfare of Immigrants and another* [1996] 4 All E.R. 385. This had challenged the validity of the Social Security (Persons from Abroad) Miscellaneous Amendments Regulations 1996 (S.I. 1996 No. 30) in so far as they drastically curtail the benefit entitlement of asylum seekers. The Court of Appeal (by a majority) held that the regulations were indeed *ultra vires* as (*per* Simon Brown L.J.) they were so "uncompromisingly draconian in effect . . . Parliament cannot have intended a significant number of genuine asylum seekers to be impaled on the horns of so intolerable a dilemma: the need either to abandon their claims to refugee status or alternatively to maintain them as best they can but in a state of utter destitution".

Section 11(1) specifically authorises the making of regulations to exclude asylum seekers from benefits, while s. 11(4) and para. 2 of Sched. 1 reinstate the invalid parts of the 1996 Regulations with effect from July 24, 1996. Note also para. 6 of Sched. 1 which concerns asylum seekers who are excluded from benefit by the reinstatement effected by para. 2.

For discussion of these provisions see the notes to reg. 70 of the Income Support Regulations and see reg. 12(1) of the Social Security (Persons from Abroad) Miscellaneous Amendments Regulations 1996 (p. 498).

On s. 11(2) see reg. 21ZA of the Income Support Regulations.

Saving for social security regulations

11.—(1) Notwithstanding any enactment or rule of law, regulations may exclude any person who has made a claim for asylum from entitlement to any of the following benefits, namely—

(a) income support, housing benefit and council tax benefit under the Social Security Contributions and Benefits Act 1992;

(b) income support and housing benefit under the Social Security Contributions and Benefits (Northern Ireland) Act 1992; and

(c) jobseeker's allowance under the Jobseekers Act 1995 or the Jobseekers (Northern Ireland) Order 1995.

(2) Regulations may provide that, where such a person who is so excluded is subsequently recorded by the Secretary of State as a refugee within the meaning of the Convention—

(a) that person may, within a prescribed period, claim the whole or any prescribed proportion of any income support, housing benefit or council tax benefit to which he would have been entitled had he been recorded as a refugee immediately after he made the claim for asylum; and

[Subss. (2)(b) and (3) are omitted as not relevant to the benefits covered by this book]

(4) Schedule 1 to this Act—

(a) Part I of which modifies the Social Security (Persons from Abroad) Miscellaneous Amendments Regulations 1996; and

(b) Part II of which modifies the Social Security (Persons from Abroad) (Miscellaneous Amendments) Regulations (Northern Ireland) 1996,

shall have effect.

(5) The Jobseeker's Allowance (Amendment) Regulations 1996 shall have effect as if they had been made on the day on which this Act is passed.

(6) In this section—

"claim for asylum" and "the Convention" have the same meanings as in the 1993 Act;

"prescribed" means prescribed by regulations;

"regulations"—

(a) in relation to income support, housing benefit or council tax benefit under the Social Security Contributions and Benefits Act 1992, means regulations under that Act or the Social Security Administration Act 1992;

(b) in relation to income support or housing benefit under the Social Security Contributions and Benefits (Northern Ireland) Act 1992, means regulations under that Act or the Social Security Administration (Northern Ireland) Act 1992;

(c) in relation to jobseeker's allowance under the Jobseekers Act 1995, means regulations under that Act or the Social Security Administration Act 1992;

(d) in relation to jobseeker's allowance under the Jobseekers (Northern Ireland) Order 1995, means regulations under that Order or the Social Security Administration (Northern Ireland) Act 1992.

DEFINITIONS

"claim for asylum"—see the Asylum and Immigration Appeals Act 1993.
"the Convention"—*ibid.*

SCHEDULE 1

MODIFICATIONS OF SOCIAL SECURITY REGULATIONS

PART I

SOCIAL SECURITY (PERSONS FROM AROAD) MISCELLANEOUS AMENDMENTS REGULATIONS 1996

Preliminary

1. In this Part of this Schedule—
(a) 'the 1996 Regulations" means the Social Security (Persons from Abroad) Miscellaneous Amendments Regulations 1996; and
(b) expressions which are used in the 1996 Regulations have the same meanings as in those Regulations.

Income Support

2. In regulation 8 of the 1996 Regulations (amendment of the Income Support Regulations)—
(a) paragraph (2) so far as relating to the sub-paragraph added to regulation 21(3) of the Income Support Regulations as sub-paragraph (j); and
(b) paragraph (3)(c) and (d),
shall have effect as if the 1996 Regulations had been made, and had come into force, on the day on which this Act is passed.

[Paras. 3 and 4 are omitted as not relevant to the benefits covered by this book]

General

5. Regulation 12(1) of the 1996 Regulations (saving) shall have effect as if after the words "shall continue to have effect" there were inserted the words "(both as regards him and as regards persons who are members of his family at the coming into force of these Regulations)".

6.—(1) Subject to sub-paragraph (2) below, any person who is excluded from entitlement to income support, housing benefit or council tax benefit by any of the provisions which are modified by the preceding provisions of this Part of this Schedule—
(a) shall not be entitled to the benefit for any period beginning on or after the day on which this Act is passed; and
(b) shall not be entitled to the benefit for any period beginning on or after 5th February

1996 except on a claim made before the day on which this Act is passed, or an application made before that day for the review of a decision.

(2) Nothing in this paragraph shall apply in any case where a person is entitled to the benefit in question either—

(a) by virtue of regulation 12(1) of the 1996 Regulations (saving); or

(b) by virtue of regulations making such provision as is mentioned in section 11(2) of this Act.

PART II

SOCIAL SECURITY (PERSONS FROM ABROAD) (MISCELLANEOUS AMENDMENTS) REGULATIONS (NORTHERN IRELAND) 1996

Preliminary

7. In this Part of this Schedule "the 1996 Regulations" means the Social Security (Persons from Abroad) (Miscellaneous Amendments) Regulations (Northern Ireland) 1996.

Income support

8. In regulation 4 of the 1996 Regulations (amendment of the Income Support (General) Regulations)—

(a) paragraph (2) so far as relating to the paragraph added to regulation 21(3) of the Income Support (General) Regulations (Northern Ireland) 1987 as paragraph (j); and

(b) paragraph (3)(b),

shall have effect as if the 1996 Regulations had been made, and had come into operation, on the day on which this Act is passed.

[Para. 9 is omitted as not relevant to the benefits covered by this book].

General

10. Regulation 11(1) of the 1996 Regulations (saving) shall have effect as if after the words "shall have effect" there were inserted the words "(both as regards him and as regards persons who are members of his family at the coming into operation of these Regulations)".

11.—(1) Subject to sub-paragraph (2) below, any person who is excluded from entitlement to income support or housing benefit by any of the provisions which are modified by the preceding provisions of this Part of this Schedule—

(a) shall not be entitled to the benefit for any period beginning on or after the day on which this Act is passed; and

(b) shall not be entitled to the benefit for any period beginning on or after 5th February 1996 except on a claim made before the day on which this Act is passed, or an application made before that day for the review of a decision.

(2) Nothing in this paragraph shall apply in any case where a person is entitled to the benefit in question either—

(a) by virtue of regulation 11(1) of the 1996 Regulations (saving); or

(b) by virtue of regulations making such provision as is mentioned in section 11(2) of this Act.

Child Support Act 1991

(1991 c. 48)

GENERAL NOTE

This book does not deal directly with the system of child support maintenance, not least because appeals from decisions of child support officers (CSOs) go to child support appeal tribunals, rather than SSATs. For a full treatment, see Jacobs and Douglas, *Child Support Legislation*. Note that the procedures for determining claims and appeals are due to change fundamentaly when the Social Security Act 1998 comes into force. For child support the implementation date is June 1, 1999. Decision-making will be transferred to the Secretary of State and appeals will go to a unified appeal tribunal. See the 1999 Supplement to this book for further details of the new system for decision-making and appeals.

The child support legislation provides for income-related benefits to be reduced where a parent on benefit fails to co-operate in the process of assessing maintenance from an absent parent. Note that family credit and disability working allowance are due to be replaced by working families tax credit and disabled person's tax credit from October 5, 1999. It is understood that people in receipt of these credits will not be required to apply for a maintenance assessment to be made. See the 1999 Supplement for further details.

In addition, where an absent parent is on income support or income-based JSA, a deduction can be made from his income support or income-based JSA as a contribution towards child maintenance. (The deduction can also be made from the absent parent's contribution-based JSA if he would be entitled to income-based JSA at the same rate but for the fact that he is getting contribution-based JSA: Claims and Payments Regulations 1987, Sched. 9, para. 1(1), definition of "specified benefit", and para. 1(2)). In addition, deductions for arrears of child support maintenance can be made from contribution-based JSA (even where there would be no entitlement to income-based JSA) in certain circumstances: see para. 7B of Sched. 9.)

Those parts of the child support legislation relevant to the reduction and the deduction are included in this book.

Note s. 10 of the Child Support Act 1995 which from April 1997 provides for income support and income-based JSA claimants receiving child maintenance to build up a "child maintenance bonus". See the Social Security (Child Maintenance Bonus) Regulations 1996.

Applications by those receiving benefit

6.—(1) Where income support, [¹ an income-based jobseeker's allowance,] family credit or any other benefit of a prescribed kind is claimed by or in respect of, or paid to or in respect of, the parent of a qualifying child she shall, if—

(a) she is a person with care of the child; and

(b) she is required to do so by the Secretary of State,
authorise the Secretary of State to take action under the Act to recover child support maintenance from the absent parent.

(2) The Secretary of State shall not require a person ("the parent") to give him the authorisation mentioned in subsection (1) if he considers that there are reasonable grounds for believing that—

(a) if the parent were to be required to give that authorisation; or

(b) if she were to give it.

there would be a risk of her, or of any child living with her, suffering harm or undue distress as a result.

(3) Subsection (2) shall not apply if the parent requests the Secretary of State to disregard it.

(4) The authorisation mentioned in subsection (1) shall extend to all children of the absent parent in relation to whom the parent first mentioned in subsection (1) is a person with care.

(5) That authorisation shall be given, without unreasonable delay, by completing and returning to the Secretary of State an application—

(a) for the making of a maintenance assessment with respect to the qualifying child or qualifying children; and

(b) for the Secretary of State to take action under this Act to recover, on her behalf, the amount of child support maintenance so assessed.

(6) Such an application shall be made on a form (''a maintenance application form'') provided by the Secretary of State.

(7) A maintenance application form shall indicate in general terms the effect of completing and returning it.

(8) Subsection (1) has effect regardless of whether any of the benefits mentioned there is payable with respect to any qualifying child.

(9) A person who is under a duty imposed by subsection (1) shall, so far as she reasonably can, comply with such regulations as may be made by the Secretary of State with a view to the Secretary of State or the child support officer being provided with the information which is required to enable—

(a) the absent parent to be traced;

(b) the amount of child support maintenance payable by the absent parent to be assessed; and

(c) that amount to be recovered from the absent parent.

(10) The obligation to provide information which is imposed by subsection (9)—

(a) shall not apply in such circumstances as may be prescribed; and

(b) may, in such circumstances as may be prescribed, be waived by the Secretary of State.

(11) A person with care who has authorised the Secretary of State under subsection (1) but who subsequently ceases to fall within that subsection may request the Secretary of State to cease acting under this section.

(12) It shall be the duty of the Secretary of State to comply with any request made under subsection (11) (but subject to any regulations made under subsection (13)).

(13) The Secretary of State may by regulations make such incidental or transitional provision as he thinks appropriate with respect to cases in which he is requested under subsection (11) to cease to act under this section.

(14) The fact that a maintenance assessment is in force with respect to a person with care shall not prevent the making of a new maintenance assessment with respect to her in response to an application under this section.

AMENDMENT

1. Jobseekers Act 1995, Sched. 2, para. 20(2) (October 7, 1996).

DEFINITIONS

''absent parent''—see Child Support Act 1991, s.54
''child support maintenance''—*ibid.*
''qualifying child''—*ibid.*

Disability working allowance is prescribed as a benefit to which s. 6 applies along with income support, income-based JSA and family credit (Child Support (Maintenance Assessment Procedure) Regulations 1992, reg. 34). Note that family credit and disability working allowance are due to be replaced by working families tax credit and disabled person's tax credit from October 5, 1999. It is understood that people in receipt of these credits will not be required to apply for a maintenance assessment to be made. See the 1999 Supplement to this book for further details.

A parent who has claimed, or is being paid ("paid" means "actually paid", not "lawfully paid": *Secretary of State for Social Security v. Harmon, Carter and Cocks, The Times*, June 10, 1998, CA, also to be reported as *R(CS) 4/99*) one of these benefits and who has care of a qualifying child has general obligations to authorise the Secretary of State to take action against the absent parent (subs. (1)) and to provide the necessary information (subs. (9)). The Child Support (Information, Evidence and Disclosure) Regulations 1992 prescribe the information required. However, those obligations depend on the Secretary of State having under subs. (1)(b) required the parent to give authorisation. In exercising his discretion as to whether to require authorisation, the Secretary of State is not in breach of his obligation to consider the welfare of any child under s.2 of the 1991 Act if he does not first seek the views of the absent parent (*R(CS) 1/98*); see also *R. v. Secretary of State for Social Security, ex p. Lloyd* [1995] 1 F.L.R. 856). Subsection (2) provides that a requirement to give authorisation is not to be made if the Secretary of State considers that there are reasonable grounds for believing that there is a risk of harm or undue distress to the parent with care or any children living with her from compliance. There is no provision for appeal from the Secretary of State's decision to require the parent to authorise action, but there could be a challenge through judicial review. *CCS 17/ 1994* confirms that once the parent with care has authorised the Secretary of State to take action under subs. (1), the CSO to whom the application is referred for determination has no option but to deal with it. (This determination will usually involve an assessment being made.) If the parent considers that she has been misled by the Secretary of State, her remedy is against the Secretary of State, not the adjudicating authorities who have no jurisdiction in the matter. The Secretary of State must cease acting at the request of the parent if she has stopped getting a relevant benefit, or she is no longer the parent with care of the child (subss. (11) and (12); see *CCS 4725/1995*). In other circumstances the Secretary of State could also decide under subs. (2) that the parent is no longer required to give authorisation and cease acting at her request.

Note that subs. (9)(a) refers to providing information to enable the absent parent to be *traced* (the relevant regulation made under this power is reg. 3(1)(e) of the Child Support (Information, Evidence and Disclosure) Regulations). In *CCS 15221/1996* the parent with care had given particulars of the absent parent, but when he did not accept paternity she refused to give further details of their relationship or to undergo DNA testing or to consent to it for her child. The Commissioner holds that the obligation to provide information to allow the absent parent to be traced did not require the parent with care to submit herself or her child to scientific tests. "Tracing" related to the whereabouts of an alleged parent and not to the determination of parentage (which was generally a matter for the courts). The consequence was that there was no jurisdiction to make a reduced benefit direction in these circumstances.

If, once the obligations under subss. (1) and (9) have arisen, the Secretary of State considers that the parent has failed to comply he must serve a notice on the parent that he intends to refer the case to a CSO to take action under s. 46 and must then wait for two weeks (until October 7, 1996 the period required was six weeks) before making the reference (Maintenance Assessment Procedure Regulations, reg. 35). If within that time the parent with care states in writing why there is a risk of harm or undue distress to her or any children living with her, the notice period continues to be six weeks. Note the transitional protection for cases where the failure to comply arose before October 7, 1996 in reg. 25(2) of the Child Support (Miscellaneous Amendments) Regulations 1996, (p. 572). Once the relevant period has expired, the CSO may then consider making a reduced benefit direction. See CCS 1037/1995 in the note to s. 46. The parent has a right of appeal under s. 46(7) to a child support appeal tribunal against a CSO's decision to give a reduced benefit direction.

Note that under the Social Security Act 1998 child support officers are to be abolished and all decision-making is to be transferred to the Secretary of State. Appeals will go to a unified appeal tribunal. For child support the implementation date for the new system of decision-making and appeals is June 1, 1999. The time limits and the procedure in reg. 35 of the Maintenance Assessment Procedure Regulations are also due to change on that date. See the 1999 Supplement to this book for further details.

Special cases

Contribution to maintenance by deduction from benefit

43.—(1) This section applies where—
(a) by virtue of paragraph 5(4) of Schedule 1, an absent parent is taken for the purposes of that Schedule to have no assessable income; and
(b) such conditions as may be prescribed for the purposes of this section are satisfied.

(2) The power of the Secretary of State to make regulations under [¹section 5 of the Social Security Administration Act 1992 by virtue of subsection (1)(p),] (deductions from benefits) may be exercised in relation to cases to which this section applies with a view to securing that—
(a) payments of prescribed amounts are made with respect to qualifying children in place of payments of child support maintenance; and
(b) arrears of child support maintenance are recovered.

AMENDMENT

1. Social Security (Consequential Provisions) Act 1992, Sched. 2, para. 113 (July 1, 1992).

GENERAL NOTE

This section, Sched. 1, para. 5(4) and regs. 13 and 28 and Scheds. 4 and 5 of the Child Support (Maintenance Assessments and Special Cases) Regulations 1992 have been reproduced for the assistance of SSATs hearing appeals against the deduction of £5.20 from the income support or income-based JSA of absent parents as a contribution towards the maintenance of their children. The deduction was increased to an amount equal to 10 per cent of the personal allowance for a single claimant aged not less than 25 with effect from April 8, 1996 (previously it was 5 per cent). If the full £5.20 cannot be deducted because other deductions are being made which have a higher priority, £2.60 can be deducted (see paras. 7A(4), 8(1) and 9 of Sched. 9 to the Claims and Payments Regulations). Note that contributions for child maintenance have the lowest priority of the deductions covered by Sched. 9. The conditions referred to in subs. (1)(b) are set out in reg. 28(1) of and Sched. 4 to the Maintenance Assessments and Special Cases Regulations. Any appeal concerning whether an absent parent is exempt from these deductions has to go to a child support appeal tribunal. The issues before a SSAT will be mainly whether there are other deductions that have a higher priority and whether there is sufficient income support in payment for the deduction to be made. Under the Social Security Act 1998 the functions of SSATs and CSATs (together with those of disability appeal, medical appeal and vaccine damage tribunals) are to be transferred to unified appeal tribunals. The implementation date for the changes depends on the benefit being claimed. The commencement date for child support is June 1, 1999 but the new system is not due to take effect for JSA until October 18, 1999 and November 29, 1999 for income support. See the 1999 Supplement to this book for further details.

Note *CCS 16904/1996* in which the Commissioner conducts a detailed analysis of the legislation on deductions in place of child support maintenance. He states that at first sight it is difficult to see where the liability to make payments in place of child support maintenance comes from. However, he considers that this "hole" in the legislation is filled by the general duty to maintain a child under s.1 of the Act. This requires the payment of such "maintentance" (not just child support maintenance) as determined in accordance with the provisions of the Act. Thus if a CSO decides s.43 applies, the absent parent will have an unfulfilled responsibility to maintain. That responsibility is sufficient to give rise to a liability on the absent parent to make payment and a corresponding entitlement of the parent with care to receive the amounts deducted by the Secretary of State (see reg. 35 of and para. 7A of Sched. 9 to the Claims and Payments Regulations). The absent parent in that case had contended that the CSO had failed to consider whether the condition in reg. 28(1)(c) of the Maintenance Assessments and Special Cases Regulations was satisfied (*i.e.* that he was not in receipt of certain benefits) and that this failure rendered the decision to make deductions in place of child support maintenance void and of no effect. Although the Commissioner was satisfied on the evidence that the CSO's decision was legally flawed in this respect, that flaw did not render the decision of no effect because the defect could be cured by a tribunal (see by way of analogy *CSIS 8/1995*).

Miscellaneous and supplemental

Failure to comply with obligations imposed by section 6

46.—(1) This section applies where any person ("the parent")—
  (a) fails to comply with a requirement imposed on her by the Secretary of State under section 6(1); or
  (b) fails to comply with any regulation made under section 6(9).

(2) A child support officer may serve written notice on the parent requiring her, before the end of the specified period, either to comply or to give him her reasons for failing to do so.

(3) When the specified period has expired, the child support officer shall consider whether, having regard to any reasons given by the parent, there are reasonable grounds for believing that, if she were to be required to comply, there would be a risk of her or of any children living with her suffering harm or undue distress as a result of complying.

(4) If the child support officer considers that there are such reasonable grounds, he shall—
  (a) take no further action under this section in relation to the failure in question; and
  (b) notify the parent, in writing, accordingly.

(5) If the child support officer considers that there are no such reasonable grounds, he may[¹, except in prescribed circumstances,] give a reduced benefit direction with respect to the parent.

(6) Where the child support officer gives a reduced benefit direction he shall send a copy of it to the parent.

(7) Any person who is aggrieved by a decision of a child support officer to give a reduced benefit direction may appeal to a child support appeal tribunal against that decision.

(8) Sections 20(2) to (4) and 21 shall apply in relation to appeals under subsection (7) as they apply in relation to appeals under section 20.

(9) A reduced benefit direction shall take effect on such date as may be specified in the direction.

(10) Reasons given in response to a notice under subsection (2) may be given in writing or orally.

(11) In this section—
"comply" means to comply with the requirement or with the regulation in question; and "complied" and "complying" shall be construed accordingly;
"reduced benefit direction" means a direction, binding on the adjudication officer, that the amount payable by way of any relevant benefit to, or in respect of, the parent concerned be reduced by such amount, and for such period, as may be prescribed;
"relevant benefit" means income support, [² an income-based jobseeker's allowance,] family credit or any other benefit of a kind prescribed for the purposes of section 6; and
"specified", in relation to any notice served under this section, means specified in the notice; and the period to be specified shall be determined in accordance with regulations made by the Secretary of State

AMENDMENTS

1. Child Support Act 1995, Sched. 3, para. 12 (October 1, 1995).
2. Jobseekers Act 1995, Sched. 2, para. 20(4) (October 7, 1996).

(1991 c. 48, s.46)

GENERAL NOTE

Note that under the Social Security Act 1998 child support officers are to be abolished and all decision-making is to be transferred to the Secretary of State. Appeals will go to a unified appeal tribunal. For child support the implementation date for the new system of decision-making and appeals is June 1, 1999. There are also amendments to Part IX of the Maintenance Assessment Procedure Regulations from that date; note in particular that the time limits and procedure in reg. 35 will change. For details of these changes see the 1999 Supplement to this book.

Note also that family credit and disability working allowance are due to be replaced by working families tax credit and disabled person's tax credit on October 5, 1999. It is understood that people in receipt of these credits will not be required to apply for a maintenance assessment to be made. See the 1999 Supplement for further details.

For the CSO to act under s.46 the parent must have failed to comply with the obligations under s.6(1) or (9). The written notice under subs. (2) to comply or give reasons must give 14 days to do so (Maintenance Assessment Procedure Regulations, reg. 35(3)).

If the parent complies, s.46 ceases to apply. If she does not, the CSO must consider whether there are reasonable grounds for believing that there would be a risk of harm or undue distress to her or any children living with her from compliance. (On risk of harm or undue distress see *CCS 1037/1995, CCS 6096/1995, CCS 7003/1995* and *CCS 12609/1996*.) If not, he may give a reduced benefit direction (subs. (5)). Reg. 35A of the Maintenance Assessment Procedure Regulations provides that from January 22, 1996 a reduced benefit direction will not be issued if the parent's (or any partner's) income support or income-based JSA includes a disability, higher pensioner or disabled child premium, or, where family credit or disability working allowance is in payment, an amount equal to the disability or disabled child premium is included in the calculation of the parent's exempt income. *CCS 1037/1995* confirms that the discretion in subs. (5) means that there are two stages to the CSO's considerations. Even if in the CSO's view there is no risk of harm or undue distress, he then has to go on to decide whether or not to issue a reduced benefit direction. In exercising that discretion he must, in accordance with s. 2 of the 1991 Act, "have regard to the welfare of any child likely to be affected by his decision". Thus he should look to see if there is some exceptional or special factor that suggests that the welfare of a child would be adversely affected by a reduced benefit direction. The Commissioner gives as examples of such special factors the age or state of health of the child or parent. These are now covered, to some extent at least, by reg. 35A, but it may be that there are other relevant factors, depending on the circumstances of the particular case.

Any appeal against the CSO's decision to issue a reduced benefit direction has to be to a child support appeal tribunal (subs. (7)). *CCS 15109/1996* rejects the argument that a CSAT could only consider the evidence available to the CSO at the time of issuing the direction. The Commissioner referred to the CSO's discretion as to whether to impose a direction and pointed out that there was no limitation on the grounds on which an appeal could be made under subs. (7). The normal principles therefore applied, so that in deciding whether the direction should have been made the CSAT could take account of any evidence available to it at the date of its hearing. The Commissioner also dismissed the argument that once the time for making representations under subs. (2) had expired and a direction had been made, the direction could only be challenged by way of an application for review under reg. 42 of the Maintenance Assessment Procedure Regulations, pointing to the fact that the right of appeal under subs. (7) did not arise until a direction had been made. Furthermore, a parent with care was "a person aggrieved" for the purpose of subs. (7), even though she had not made any response to the notice under subs. (2).

The direction is, under subs. (11), binding on the AO and requires the amount of income support, income-based JSA, family credit or disability working allowance payable to or in respect of the parent to be reduced. See the Maintenance Assessment Procedure Regulations for the amount of the reduction, its length and the complicated provisions for its suspension, ending or extension. At April 1999 benefit rates the reduction is £20.56 per week; it lasts for three years.

The intention seems to be that the giving of the direction will be a change of circumstances requiring a review by the AO of any existing award of benefit under s.25(1)(b) or 30(5)(b) of the Administration Act. See reg. 51A of the Family Credit (General) Regulations and reg. 56A of the Disability Working Allowance (General) Regulations for provisions allowing review of awards of family credit and disability working allowance when certain action is taken in relation to reduced benefit directions. Any appeal about such reviews or the resulting revised decisions must go to a SSAT, but the issues will be mainly arithmetical.

SCHEDULE 1

Section 11

MAINTENANCE ASSESSMENTS

PART I

CALCULATION OF CHILD SUPPORT MAINTENANCE

Assessable income

5.—(4) Where income support [¹, an income-based jobseeker's allowance] or any other benefit of a prescribed kind is paid to or in respect of a parent who is an absent parent or a person with care that parent shall, for the purposes of this Schedule, be taken to have no assessable income.

[The rest of the Schedule has not been reproduced.]

AMENDMENT

1. Jobseekers Act 1995, Sched. 2, para. 20(7) (October 7, 1996).

Child Support Act 1995

(1995 c. 34)

SECTION REPRODUCED

10. The child maintenance bonus

The child maintenance bonus

10.—(1) The Secretary of State may by regulations make provision for the payment, in prescribed circumstances, of sums to persons—
   (a) who are or have been in receipt of child maintenance; and
   (b) to or in respect of whom income support or a jobseeker's allowance is or has been paid.
   (2) A sum payable under the regulations shall be known as "a child maintenance bonus".
   (3) A child maintenance bonus shall be treated for all purposes as payable by way of income support or (as the case may be) a jobseeker's allowance.
   (4) Subsection (3) is subject to section 617 of the Income and Corporation Taxes Act 1988 (which, as amended by paragraph 1 of Schedule 3, provides for a child maintenance bonus not to be taxable).
   (5) The regulations may, in particular, provide for—
   (a) a child maintenance bonus to be payable only on the occurrence of a prescribed event;
   (b) a bonus not to be payable unless a claim is made before the end of the prescribed period;
   (c) the amount of a bonus (subject to any maximum prescribed by virtue of paragraph (f)) to be determined in accordance with the regulations;
   (d) enabling amounts to be calculated by reference to periods of entitlement to income support and periods of entitlement to a jobseeker's allowance;
   (e) treating a bonus as payable wholly by way of a jobseeker's allowance

or wholly by way of income support, in a case where amounts have been calculated in accordance with provision made by virtue of paragraph (d);

(f) the amount of a bonus not to exceed a prescribed maximum;

(g) a bonus not to be payable if the amount of the bonus which would otherwise be payable is less than the prescribed minimum;

(h) prescribed periods to be disregarded for prescribed purposes;

(i) a bonus which has been paid to a person to be treated, in prescribed circumstances and for prescribed purposes, as income or capital of hers or of any other member of her family;

(j) treating the whole or a prescribed part of an amount which has accrued towards a person's bonus—

    (i) as not having accrued towards her bonus; but

    (ii) as having accrued towards the bonus of another person.

(6) The Secretary of State may by regulations provide—

(a) for the whole or a prescribed part of a child maintenance bonus to be paid in such circumstances as may be prescribed to such person, other than the person who is or had been in receipt of child maintenance, as may be determined in accordance with the regulations;

(b) for any payments of a prescribed kind which have been collected by the Secretary of State, and retained by him, to be treated for the purposes of this section as having been received by the appropriate person as payments of child maintenance.

(7) In this section—

"appropriate person" has such meaning as may be prescribed;

"child" means a person under the age of 16;

"child maintenance" has such meaning as may be prescribed;

"family" means—

    (a) a married or unmarried couple;

    (b) a married or unmarried couple and a member of the same household for whom one of them is, or both are, responsible and who is a child or a person of a prescribed description;

    (c) except in prescribed circumstances, a person who is not a member of a married or unmarried couple amd a member of the same household for whom that person is resonsible and who is a child or a person of a prescribed description;

"married couple" means a man and woman who are married to each other and are members of the same household; and

"unmarried couple" means a man and woman who are not married to each other but are living together as husband and wife otherwise than in prescribed circumstances.

(8) For the purposes of this section, the Secretary of State may by regulations make provision as to the circumstances in which—

(a) persons are to be treated as being or not being members of the same household;

(b) one person is to be treated as responsible or not responsible for another.

GENERAL NOTE

See the Social Security (Child Maintenance Bonus) Regulations 1996.

PART II

INCOME SUPPORT

Income Support (General) Regulations 1987

(S.I. 1987 No. 1967)

Chapter VII

Liable relatives

Chapter VIIA

Child support

Chapter VIII

Students

Part VI

Applicable Amounts and Assessment of Income and Capital in Urgent Cases

Part VII

Calculation of Income Support for Part-Weeks

PART I

GENERAL

Citation and commencement

1. These Regulations may be cited as the Income Support (General) Regulations 1987 and shall come into force on 11th April 1988.

Interpretation

2.—(1) In these Regulations, unless the context otherwise requires
"the Act" means the Social Security Act 1986;
"attendance allowance" means:—

(a) an attendance allowance under section 35 of the Social Security Act [SSCBA, s.64];

(b) an increase of disablement pension under section 61 or 63 of that Act [SSCBA, s.104 or 105];

(c) a payment under regulations made in exercise of the power conferred by section 159(3)(b) of that Act;

(d) an increase of an allowance which is payable in respect of constant attendance under section 5 of the Industrial Injuries and Diseases (Old Cases) Act 1975;

(e) a payment by virtue of articles 14, 15, 16, 43 or 44 of the Personal Injuries (Civilians) Scheme 1983 or any analogous payment; or

(f) any payment based on need for attendance which is paid as part of a war disablement pension;

[26"the benefit Acts" means the Contributions and Benefits Act and the Jobseekers Act 1955;]

"benefit week" has the meaning prescribed in paragraph 4 of Schedule 7 to the Social Security (Claims and Payments) Regulations 1987 [4and for the purposes of calculating any payment of income and of regulation 74(2)(a) "benefit week" shall also mean the period of 7 days ending on the day before the first day of the first benefit week following the date of claim or the last day on which income support is paid if it is in payment for less than a week;]

[6"board and lodging accommodation" means—

(a) accommodation provided to a person or, if he is a member of a family, to him or any other member of his family, for a charge which is inclusive of the provision of that accommodation and at least some cooked or prepared meals which both are cooked or prepared (by a

person other than the person to whom the accommodation is provided or a member of his family) and are consumed in that accommodation or associated premises; or
(b) accommodation provided to a person in a hotel, guest house, lodging house or some similar establishment,

except accommodation provided by a close relative of his or of any other member of his family, or other than on a commercial basis;]
[³¹"the Children Order" means the Children (Northern Ireland) Order 1995;]
"claimant" means a person claiming income support;
"close relative" means a parent, parent-in-law, son, son-in-law, daughter, daughter-in-law, step-parent, step-son, step-daughter, brother, sister, or the spouse of any of the preceding persons or, if that person is one of an unmarried couple, the other member of that couple;
[¹⁹"community charge benefit" means community charge benefits under Part VII of the Contributions and Benefits Act as originally enacted;]
"concessionary payment" means a payment made under arrangements made by the Secretary of State with the consent of the Treasury which is charged either to the National Insurance Fund or to a Departmental Expenditure Vote to which payments of benefit under the Act, the Social Security Act or the Child Benefit Act 1975 are charged;
[¹⁹"the Contributions and Benefits Act" means the Social Security Contributions and Benefits Act 1992;]
"co-ownership scheme" means a scheme under which a dwelling is let by a housing association and the tenant, or his personal representative, will, under the terms of the tenancy agreement or of the agreement under which he became a member of the association, be entitled, on his ceasing to be a member and subject to any condition stated in either agreement, to a sum calculated by reference directly or indirectly to the value of the dwelling;
"couple" means a married or an unmarried couple;
"course of study" means any full-time course of study or sandwich course whether or not a grant is made for attending it;
"Crown tenant" means a person who occupies a dwelling under a tenancy or licence where the interest of the landlord belongs to Her Majesty in right of the Crown or to a government department or is held in trust for Her Majesty for the purposes of a government department, except (in the case of an interest belonging to Her Majesty in right of the Crown) where the interest is under the management of the Crown Estate Commissioners;
[²²"date of claim" means the date on which the claimant makes, or is treated as making, a claim for income support for the purposes of regulation 6 of the Social Security (Claims and Payments) Regulations 1987;]
[¹⁵"disability living allowance" means a disability living allowance under section 37ZA of the Social Security Act [SSCBA, s.71];
"disability working allowance" means a disability working allowance under section 20 of the Act [SSCBA, s.129];]
"dwelling occupied as the home" means the dwelling together with any garage, garden and outbuildings, normally occupied by the claimant as his home including any premises not so occupied which it is impracticable or unreasonable to sell separately, in particular, in Scotland, any croft land on which the dwelling is situated;
"earnings" has the meaning prescribed in regulation 35 or, as the case may be, 37;
[²⁸"earnings top-up" means the allowance paid by the Secretary of State under the Earnings Top-up Scheme;]
[²⁸"the Earnings Top-up Scheme" means the Earnings Top-up Scheme 1996;]

"employed earner" shall be construed in accordance with section 2(1)(a) of the Social Security Act [SSCBA, s.2(1)*a*];

[[4]"employment" except for the purposes of section 20(3)(d) of the Act [SSCBA, s.124(1)(d)], includes any trade, business, profession, office or vocation;]

"housing association" has the meaning assigned to it by section 1(1) of the Housing Associations Act 1985;

[[30]"housing benefit expenditure" means expenditure in respect of which housing benefit is payable as specified in regulation 10(1) of the Housing Benefit (General) Regulations 1987 but does not include any such expenditure in respect of which an amount is applicable under regulation 17(1)(e) or 18(1)(f) (housing costs);]

[[27]"immigration authorities" in regulation 21(3) (special cases) means an adjudicator, an immigration officer or an immigration appeal tribunal appointed for the purposes of the Immigration Act 1971 and in addition means the Secretary of State;]

"invalid carriage or other vehicle" means a vehicle propelled by petrol engine or by electric power supplied for use on the road and to be controlled by the occupant;

[[14]"last day of the course" has the meaning prescribed in regulation 61 for the purposes of the definition of "period of study";]

"liable relative" has the meaning prescribed in regulation 54;

"lone parent" means a person who has no partner and who is responsible for, and a member of the same household as, a child or young person;

"long tenancy" means a tenancy granted for a term of years certain exceeding twenty one years, whether or not the tenancy is, or may become, terminable before the end of that term by notice given by or to the tenant or by re-entry, forfeiture (or, in Scotland, irritancy) or otherwise and includes a lease for a term fixed by law under a grant with a covenant or obligation for perpetual renewal unless it is a lease by sub-demise from one which is not a long tenancy;

[[6]"lower rate" where it relates to rates of tax has the same meaning as in the Income and Corporation Taxes Act 1988 by virtue of section 832(1) of that Act;]

[[22]"maternity leave" means a period during which a woman is absent from work because she is pregnant or has given birth to a child, and at the end of which she has a right to return to work either under the terms of her contract of employment or under Part III of the Employment Protection (Consolidation) Act 1978;]

"mobility allowance" means an allowance under section 37A of the Social Security Act;

"mobility supplement" means any supplement under article 26A of the Naval, Military and Air Forces etc (Disablement and Death) Service Pensions Order 1983 including such a supplement by virtue of any other scheme or order or under Article 25A of the Personal Injuries (Civilians) Scheme 1983;

"net earnings" means such earnings as are calculated in accordance with regulation 36

"net profit" means such profit as is calculated in accordance with regulation 38;

"non-dependant" has the meaning prescribed in regulation 3;

"non-dependant deduction" means a deduction that is to be made under regulation 17(*e*) and paragraph 11 of Schedule 3;

"nursing home" has the meaning prescribed in regulation 19(3);

"occupational pension" means any pension or other periodical payment under an occupational pension scheme but does not include any discretionary payment out of a fund established for relieving hardship in particular cases;

"partner" means where a claimant—

(a) is a member of a married or an unmarried couple, the other member of that couple;

(b) is married polygamously to two or more members of his household, any such member;

"payment" includes a part of a payment;

[[23]"pay period" means the period in respect of which a claimant is, or expects to be, normally paid by his employer, being a week, a fortnight, four weeks, a month or other shorter or longer period as the case may be;]

[[25]"pension fund holder" means with respect to a personal pension scheme or retirement annuity contract, the trustees, managers or scheme administrators, as the case may be, of the scheme or contract concerned;]

[[10]"period of study" means the period beginning with the start of the course of study and ending with the last day of the course or such earlier date as the student abandons it or is dismissed from it; but any period of attendance by the student at his educational establishment in connection with the course which is outside the period of the course shall be treated as part of the period of study;]

[[22]"personal pension scheme" has the same meaning as in [[25] section 1 of the Pension Schemes Act 1993] and, in the case of a self-employed earner, includes a scheme approved by the Inland Revenue under Chapter IV of Part XIV of the Income and Corporation Taxes Act 1988;]

"policy of life insurance" means any instrument by which the payment of money is assured on death (except death by accident only) or the happening of any contingency dependent on human life, or any instrument evidencing a contract which is subject to payment of premiums for a term dependent on human life;

[[5]"polygamous marriage" means any marriage during the subsistence of which a party to it is married to more than one person and the ceremony of marriage took place under the law of a country which permits polygamy;]

[[18]"preserved right" means a preserved right for the purposes of regulation 19;]

[[16]"qualifying person" means a person in respect of whom payment has been made from the Fund [[21]or the Eileen Trust];]

[[26]. . .]

"relative" means close relative, grand-parent, grand-child, uncle, aunt, nephew or niece;

"relevant enactment" has the meaning prescribed in regulation 16(8)(a);

"remunerative work" has the meaning prescribed in regulation 5;

[[4]"residential accommodation" except in [[8] regulation 19 and Schedule 3B] has the meaning prescribed in regulation 21(3);]

[[18]"residential allowance" means the weekly amount determined in accordance with paragraph 2A of Schedule 2;]

"residential care home" has the meaning prescribed in regulation 19(3);

[[25]"retirement annuity contract" means a contract or trust scheme approved under Chapter III of Part XIV of the Income and Corporation Taxes Act 1988;]

"self-employed earner" shall be construed in accordance with section 2(1)(b) of the Social Security Act [SSCBA, s.2(1)(b)];

"single claimant" means a claimant who neither has a partner nor is a lone parent;

"Social Security Act" means the Social Security Act 1975;

"student" has the meaning prescribed in regulation 61;

"supplementary benefit" means a supplementary pension or allowance under section 1 or 4 of the Supplementary Benefits Act 1976;

"terminal date" in respect of a claimant means the terminal date in his case for the purpose of regulation 7 of the Child Benefit (General) Regulations 1976;

[²¹"the Eileen Trust" means the charitable trust of that name established on 29th March 1993 out of funds provided by the Secretary of State for the benefit of persons eligible for payment in accordance with its provisions;]

[¹⁶"the Fund" means moneys made available from time to time by the Secretary of State for the benefit of persons eligible for payment in accordance with the provisions of a scheme established by him on 24th April 1992 or, in Scotland, on 10th April 1992;]

[²⁰"the Independent Living (Extension) Fund" means the Trust of that name established by a deed dated 25th February 1993 and made between the Secretary of State for Social Security of the one part and Robin Glover Wendt and John Fletcher Shepherd of the other part;]

[²"the Independent Living Fund" means the charitable trust established out of funds provided by the Secretary of State for the purpose of providing financial assistance to those persons incapacitated by or otherwise suffering from very severe disablement who are in need of such assistance to enable them to live independently;]

[²⁰"the Independent Living (1993) Fund" means the Trust of that name established by a deed dated 25th February 1993 and made between the Secretary of State for Social Security of the one part and Robin Glover Wendt and John Shepherd of the other part;]

[²⁰"the Independent Living Funds" means the Independent Living Fund, the Independent Living (Extension) Fund and the Independent Living (1993) Fund;]

[⁹"the Macfarlane (Special Payments) Trust" means the trust of that name, established on 29th January 1990 partly out of funds provided by the Secretary of State, for the benefit of certain persons suffering from haemophilia;]

[¹³"the Macfarlane (Special Payments) (No.2) Trust" means the trust of that name, established on 3rd May 1991 partly out of funds provided by the Secretary of State, for the benefit of certain persons suffering from haemophilia and other beneficiaries;]

[¹"the Macfarlane Trust" means the charitable trust, established partly out of funds provided by the Secretary of State to the Haemophilia Society, for the relief of poverty or distress among those suffering from haemophilia;]

"training allowance" means an allowance (whether by way of periodical grants or otherwise) payable—.

   (a) out of public funds by a Government department or by or on behalf of the [¹² Secretary of State for Employment] [¹¹, Scottish Enterprise or Highlands and Islands Enterprise];

   (b) to a person for his maintenance or in respect of a member of his family; and

   (c) for the period, or part of the period, during which he is following a course of training or instruction provided by, or in pursuance of arrangements made with, that department or approved by that department in relation to him or so provided or approved by or on behalf of [¹²the Secretary of State for Employment] [¹¹, Scottish Enterprise or Highlands and Islands Enterprise],

   but it does not include an allowance paid by any Government department to or in respect of a person by reason of the fact that he is following a course of full-time education [⁷, other than under arrangements

made under section 2 of the Employment and Training Act 1973,] or
is training as a teacher;
[²⁴"voluntary organisation" means a body, other than a public or local authority, the activities of which are carried on otherwise than for profit;]
[¹⁹"water charges" means—
   (a) as respects England and Wales, any water and sewerage charges
       under Chapter 1 of Part V of the Water Act 1991;
   (b) as respects Scotland, any water and sewerage charges under Sched-
       ule 11 to the Local Government Finance Act 1992;
   in so far as such charges are in respect of the dwelling which a person
   occupies as his home.]
[³²"welfare to work beneficiary" means a person—
   (a) to whom regulation 13A(1) of the Social Security (Incapacity for
       Work) (General) Regulations 1995 applies; and
   (b) who again becomes incapable of work for the purposes of Part XIIA
       of the Contributions and Benefits Act 1992;]
[²³"year of assessment" has the meaning prescribed in section 832(1) of the
Income and Corporation Taxes Act 1988;]
"young person" has the meaning prescribed in regulation 14,
[³"youth training scheme [¹² or youth training]" means—
   (a) arrangements made under section 2 of the Employment and Training
       Act 1973 (functions of the Secretary of State); or
   (b) arrangements made by the Secretary of State for persons enlisted in
       Her Majesty's forces for any special term of service specified
       in regulations made under section 2 of the Armed Forces Act 1966
       (power of Defence Council to make regulations as to engagement
       of persons in regular forces),
   for purposes which include the training of persons who, at the beginning
   of their training, are under the age of 18.]
(2) In these Regulations, unless the context otherwise requires, a reference—
(a) to a numbered Part is to the Part of these Regulations bearing that
    number;
(b) to a numbered regulation or Schedule is to the regulation in or Schedule
    to these Regulations bearing that number;
(c) in a regulation or Schedule to a numbered paragraph is to the paragraph
    in that regulation or Schedule bearing that number;
(d) in a paragraph to a lettered or numbered sub-paragraph is to the sub-
    paragraph in that paragraph bearing that letter or number.
(3) Unless the context requires otherwise, any reference to the claimant's
family or, as the case may be, to being a member of his family, shall be construed for the purposes of these Regulations as if it included in relation to a
polygamous marriage a reference to any partner and any child or young person
who is treated as the responsibility of the claimant or his partner, where that
child or young person is a member of the claimant's household.
[²⁹(4) For the purposes of these Regulations references to "benefit under the
benefit Acts" shall be construed as including a reference to earnings top-up.]

AMENDMENTS

1 Income Support (General) Amendment Regulations 1988 (S.I. 1988 No. 663), reg. 2 (April 11, 1988).
2. Family Credit and Income Support (General) Amendment Regulations 1988 (S.I. 1988 No. 999), reg. 4 (June 9, 1988).
3. Income Support (General) Amendment No.3 Regulations 1988 (S.I. 1988 No. 1228), reg. 2 (August 29, 1988).
4. Income Support (General) Amendment No.4 Regulations 1988 (S.I. 1988 No. 1445), reg. 2 (September 12, 1988).

5. Income Support (General) Amendment No.5 Regulations 1988 (S.I. 1988 No. 2022), reg. 2(*b*) (December 12, 1988).

6. Income Support (General) Amendment No.5 Regulations 1988 (S.I. 1988 No. 2022), reg. 2(*a*) (April 10, 1989).

7. Income Support (General) Amendment No. 2 Regulations 1989 (S.I. 1989 No. 1323), reg. 2 (August 21, 1989).

8. Income Support (General) Amendment Regulations 1989 (S.I. 1989 No. 534), Sched. 1 para. 1, (October 9, 1989).

9. Income-related Benefits Schemes Amendment Regulations 1990 (S.I. 1990 No. 127), reg. 3 (January 31, 1990).

10. Social Security Benefits (Student Loans and Miscellaneous Amendments) Regulations 1990 (S.I. 1990 No. 1549), reg. 5(2) (September 1, 1990)

11. Enterprise (Scotland) Consequential Amendments Order 1991 (S.I. 1991 No. 387), art. 9 (April 1, 1991).

12. Income Support (General) Amendment Regulations 1991 (S.I. 1991 No. 236), reg. 2 (April 8, 1991).

13. Income-related Benefits Schemes and Social Security (Recoupment) Amendment Regulations 1991 (S.I. 1991 No. 1175), reg. 5 (May 11, 1991).

14. Income Support (General) Amendment No. 4 Regulations 1991 (S.I. 1991 No. 1559), reg. 2 (August 5, 1991).

15. Disability Living Allowance and Disability Working Allowance (Consequential Provisions) Regulations 1991 (S.I. 1991 No. 2742), reg. 11(2) (April 6, 1992).

16. Income-related Benefits Schemes and Social Security (Recoupment) Amendment Regulations 1992 (S.I. 1992 No. 1101), reg. 6(2) (May 7, 1992).

17. Income-related Benefits Schemes (Miscellaneous Amendments) (No.3) Regulations 1992 (S.I. 1992 No. 2155), reg. 12 (October 5, 1992).

18. Social Security Benefits (Amendments Consequential Upon the Introduction of Community Care) Regulations 1992 (S.I. 1992 No. 3147), reg. 2(1) (April 1, 1993).

19. Income-related Benefits Schemes (Miscellaneous Amendments) Regulations 1993 (S.I. 1993 No. 315), reg. 3 (April 12, 1993).

20. Social Security Benefits (Miscellaneous Amendments) (No. 2) Regulations 1993 (S.I. 1993 No. 963), reg. 2 (April 22, 1993).

21. Income-related Benefits Schemes and Social Security (Recoupment) Amendment Regulations 1993 (S.I. 1993 No. 1249), reg. 4 (May 14, 1993).

22. Income-related Benefits Schemes (Miscellaneous Amendments) (No. 4) Regulations 1993 (S.I. 1993 No. 2119), reg. 2 (October 4, 1993).

23. Income-related Benefits Schemes (Miscellaneous Amendments) (No. 5) Regulations 1994 (S.I. 1994 No. 2139), reg. 22 (October 3, 1994).

24. Income-related Benefits Schemes (Miscellaneous Amendments) Regulations 1995 (S.I. 1995 No. 516), reg. 17 (April 10, 1995).

25. Income-related Benefits Schemes and Social Security (Claims and Payments) (Miscellaneous Amendments) Regulations 1995 (S.I. 1995 No. 2303), reg. 6(2) (October 2, 1995).

26. Income Support (General) (Jobseeker's Allowance Consequential Amendments) Regulations 1996 (S.I. 1996 No. 206), reg. 2 (October 7, 1996).

27. Income-related Benefits Schemes and Social Fund (Miscellaneous Amendments) Regulations 1996 (S.I. 1996 No. 1944), reg. 6(2) (October 7, 1996).

28. Income-related Benefits Schemes and Social Fund (Miscellaneous Amendments) Regulations 1996 (S.I. 1996 No. 1944), reg. 13 and Sched., para. 1 (October 7, 1996).

29. Income-related Benefits Schemes and Social Fund (Miscellaneous Amendments) Regulations 1996 (S.I. 1996 No. 1944), reg. 13 and Sched., para. 2 (October 7, 1996).

30. Income-related Benefits and Jobseeker's Allowance (Miscellaneous Amendments) Regulations 1997 (S.I. 1997 No. 65), reg. 4(1) (April 7, 1997).

31. Social Security (Miscellaneous Amendments) Regulations 1998 (S.I. 1998 No. 563), reg. 5(1) and (2)(e) (April 6, 1998).

32. Social Security (Welfare to Work) Regulations 1998 (S.I. 1998 No. 2231), reg. 13(2) (October 5, 1998).

Definitions

"dwelling"—see 1986 Act, s.84(1) (SSCBA, s.137(1)).
"family"—see 1986 Act, s.20(11) (SSCBA, s.137(1)).
"married couple"—*ibid.*

"occupational pension scheme"—see 1986 Act, s.84(1) (PSA, s. 1).
"unmarried couple"—see 1986 Act, s.20(11) (SSCBA, s.137(1)).

General Note

The significance of most of these definitions is mentioned in the notes to the regulations in which they occur. A few points are noted here.

"*Board and lodging accommodation*." Now that since April 1989, there are no special calculations of benefit for claimants in board and lodging accommodation (as opposed to residential care or nursing homes), the definition is of less significance than in the past. Either the accommodation must be in some establishment like a hotel or lodging house or the charge must include the provision of some cooked or prepared meals in the accommodation or associated premises. The requirement in para. (a) that a charge is made for the accommodation has logically to be considered before the exclusion of non-commercial arrangements. In *CSB 1163/1988* the claimant moved with her two children into a house owned by the Jesus Fellowship Church (Baptist), where 17 other people also lived. Meals were provided. The terms of her occupation were that she should put all her income into a "common purse." A basic charge to cover food, accommodation and running costs was set, but any excess of the claimant's income was regarded as a donation to the Church. The Commissioner holds that the claimant was not a boarder because she did not pay a "charge." She was one of a joint community of persons, all sharing their income and outgoings. See also *R. v. Sheffield Housing Benefits Review Board, ex parte Smith, Rugby Borough Council Housing Benefits Review Board, ex parte Harrison and Daventry District Council Housing Benefits Review Board, ex parte Bodden*, below. Some family arrangements may be of this kind. Similarly, if a person makes a contribution of whatever he can afford week by week to the household expenses, this is probably not a charge. On the other hand, a fixed, but low, amount may require the non-commercial basis exception to be examined. Recent cases on the meaning of "board" in the Rent Acts (*e.g. Otter v. Norman* [1988] 2 All E. R. 897, HL) indicate that merely providing the ingredients will not amount to preparing a meal. This was specifically decided in the supplementary benefit context in *CSB 950/1987*. The argument that getting a packet of cornflakes out of a cupboard constituted preparation was rejected.

If this primary definition is met there is an exclusion either if the accommodation is provided by a close relative (see definition below) of the claimant or any member of his family (see s.137(1)) or if it is provided on other than a commercial basis. Provision by a limited company, of which a close relative of the resident is a director or a shareholder, is not provision by a close relative *(R(SB) 9/89)*. In this case the company was formed well before the resident went into the home. It might be different if the company was a mere facade or had been formed for a fraudulent or improper purpose. In *R(IS) 2/91* the claimant became a resident in a nursing home of which his daughter was the sole proprietor. He was actually cared for by the staff employed by his daughter. Nonetheless, his accommodation and meals were "provided" by his daughter. "Provided" means "made available."

What is a commercial basis is unclear, although the Adjudication Officer's Guide suggests that the phrase should be interpreted broadly, not simply that a profit has to be made (para. 29049). If the charge and the arrangements are as one would expect in a commercial relationship it can clearly be argued that the basis is commercial. The AOG considers that if the intention is to cover the cost of food plus a reasonable amount for accommodation, the arrangement should also be regarded as commercial. This approach is confirmed by *CSB 1163/1988* (above), where the SSAT had decided that "commercial basis" contained an element of profit. The Commissioner holds that this was an error of law and that the phrase means a basis that is intended to be more or less self-financing and not provided as part of a quasi "family" setting. On the facts, the lack of the intention to make a profit by the Church did not prevent the basis being commercial, but the "community" nature of the arrangement did. It was probable that if the claimant paid no income in for at least a short time, she would not have been asked to leave. In *R. v. Sheffield Housing Benefits Review Board, ex parte Smith, Rugby Borough Council Housing Benefits Review Board, ex parte Harrison and Daventry District Council Housing Benefits Review Board, ex parte Bodden, The Times*, December 28, 1994, (housing benefit cases which also concerned the Jesus Fellowship Church) Blackburne J. reaches a similar conclusion. In deciding whether an arrangement was on a commercial basis, it was necessary to look at the arrangement as a whole. It was not correct only to consider the amount payable for the accommodation and to ignore the other terms of the agreement. As far as family arrangements are concerned, all the circumstances must be considered. If money has been spent adapting accommodation to a disabled person's needs, this may be relevant. It is not the case, as is often argued by AOs, that if a person enters into an arrangement with a friend or a non-close relative it is automatically non-commercial. In *CIS 195/1991* (confirmed in *CSIS 28/1992*, and *CSIS 40/1992*, to be reported as *R(IS) 17/94*, and in *CIS 529/1994*) whether a family arrangement was on a commercial basis is held to be entirely a question of fact for the SSAT, which has to consider whether it is similar to that which might have been arranged with a paying lodger (see the notes to reg. 3).

"*close relative.*" The words "brother" and "sister" include half-brothers and half-sisters *(R(SB) 22/87)*. The same decision confirms that if a child is adopted it becomes the child of its adoptive parents and ceases to have any legal relationship with its natural parents or brothers or sisters. It is legal relationships which are referred to in the definition of "close relative."

"*couple.*" "Married couple" and "unmarried couple" are defined in s.137(1) of the Contributions and Benefits Act (1986 Act, s.20(11)).

"*date of claim.*" See the notes to reg. 6 of the Social Security (Claims and Payments) Regulations.

"*dwelling occupied as the home.*" "Home" is no longer defined, but the present definition contains many similarities to that of "home" in the old Supplementary Benefit (Requirements) Regulations and (Resources) Regulations. Instead of referring to accommodation, it refers to a dwelling, but since the definition of "dwelling" in s.137(1) of the Contributions and Benefits Act (1986 Act, s.84(1)) refers to residential accommodation, there is probably not much difference. The s.137(1) definition does specify that a dwelling can be the whole or part of a building and need not comprise separate and self-contained premises. The dwelling must be normally occupied as the home by the claimant. There is no reference here to the claimant's family, but presumably if the claimant has a family within s.137(1) of the Contributions and Benefits Act (1986 Act, s.20(11)), the family's home will normally be his home, but see *CIS 81/1991* below.

It is probably the case that the reference to "the dwelling" means that only one dwelling at a time can meet the definition. However, it is not entirely clear that the normal rule that the singular includes the plural is excluded, and it is thought necessary to include several deeming rules on housing costs in para. 3 of Sched. 3. *R(SB) 30/83* decided that two completely separate units could not constitute one home. *R(SB) 10/89* held that two units about 600 yards apart, neither of which on their own could accommodate the assessment unit were one home. The Commissioner relied on some Rent Act cases on when something is let as a separate dwelling (in particular, *Langford Property Co. Ltd. v. Goldrich* [1949] 1 K.B. 511). In *CIS 299/1992* it was held that a bungalow and an adjoining caravan constituted one dwelling. In *CIS 81/1991* the claimant lived in one house and members of his family slept in another. The second house did not come within the definition in reg. 2(1) as it was not occupied by the *claimant* as his home. The Commissioner distinguishes *R(SB) 10/89* on the grounds that it was decided in relation to the significantly different definition of "home" in the Supplementary Benefit Regulations, which referred to ". . . the accommodation . . . normally occupied by the assessment unit . . .". He also holds that the reference in the definition of dwelling in s.137(1) (1986 Act, s.84(1)) to "separate and self-contained premises" does not mean that a dwelling can be spread over separate buildings. This decision may be correct where only members of the claimant's family live in the other property. However, where a claimant occupies two physically separate properties, both may still constitute the dwelling normally occupied by the claimant as his home depending on all the circumstances.

Para. 3 of Sched. 3 allows payments to be made for two homes in limited circumstances. It also appears that accommodation cannot be normally occupied until some person has actually moved in *(R(SB) 27/84, R(SB) 7/86)*, given the special rule created in para. 3(7) for periods before anyone moves in. In an unstarred decision, *CIS 4/1990*, the Commissioner doubts the existence of a rule that occupation requires residence. The same point was made in the supplementary benefit context in *CSB 524/1985* (not quoted by the Commissioner) and *CSSB 34/1987*. While it is right that the word used in the legislation is "occupy" and not "reside," it must also be noted that the definition requires not simply occupation, but occupation as the home. This point was the basis of *R(SB) 7/86*, also not mentioned in *CIS 4/1990*. It may be that the issue of what is sufficient to amount to occupation is one of fact in each set of circumstances.

The definition extends to any garden or outbuildings which are occupied as part of the home (like the toilet and coalstore in outbuildings in *R(SB) 13/84* or the "development land" in *R(SB) 27/84* which might have been part of the garden). *CIS 427/1991* holds that the line between a garden and other land occupied with a dwelling is to be drawn according to the view of the ordinary man in the street.

If a building or a garden is occupied as part of the home it does not matter that they could be sold separately. This only comes into play when some buildings or land are not so occupied. Then those premises still count as part of the home if it is impracticable or unreasonable to sell them separately. A potential limit to this extension is exposed by *CSB 965/1986*, where the claimant was a tenant of a council house and owned a half-share in a small-holding two fields away. The small-holding was clearly not occupied as part of the home. The Commissioner holds that the extension could not apply since the home could not be sold and therefore the question of separate sale could not arise. This decision seems dubious, especially since the definition refers by way of example to croft land in Scotland, where the crofter is often only a tenant. But perhaps *CSB 965/1986* can be supported on the basis that if the small-holding was the only premises actually owned by the claimant it could not be unreasonable or impracticable to sell it separately. In *CIS 427/1991* the Commissioner holds that *R(SB) 13/84* was wrong in suggesting that property outside Scotland which is comparable to croft land is to be treated on the same principles. In considering reasonableness and practicability all the circumstances must be considered, including the use to which the premises are put, any profit made from them, etc. *(R(SB) 13/84* and *R(SB) 27/84)*. In *CIS 427/1991* the state of health of the claimant's wife was a factor of which account could be taken in assessing whether it was unreasonable to sell land held with the home but not occupied as the home (she was a manic depressive who needed the adjoining fields for therapeutic walking). Medical evidence as to the therapeutic benefit would obviously be highly desirable in these circumstances.

CIS 616/1992 holds that the common parts of a block of flats (*e.g.* the entrance hall or staircases) do not come within the definition. It is not impracticable or unreasonable to sell such areas separately but quite simply impossible to do so.

"*the Earnings Top-up Scheme*". This is a pilot project which is to run for three years from October 1996 in eight areas of the country (in four of those areas the allowance is paid at a higher rate). Its purpose is to assist single people and couples in low-paid work who do *not* have dependent children but otherwise it is broadly similar to family credit. The scheme is governed by the Earnings Top-up Rules 1996, not by regulations. Note para. (4). The Government will decide whether to provide this or a similar scheme on a statutory basis depending on the effectiveness of the pilot project in encouraging people to take up low-paid work.

"*employed earner.*" The meaning in s.2(1)(*a*) of the Contributions and Benefits Act (1975 Act, s.2(1)(*a*)) is "a person who is gainfully employed in Great Britain either under a contract of service, or in an office (including elective office) with emoluments chargeable to income tax under Schedule E."

"*occupational pension*". Section 1 of the Pension Schemes Act 1993 defines an "occupational pension scheme" as "any scheme or arrangement which is comprised in one or more instruments or agreements and which has, or is capable of having, effect in relation to one or more descriptions or categories of employments so as to provide benefits, in the form of pensions or otherwise, payable on termination of service, or on death or retirement, to or in respect of earners with qualifying service in an employment of any such description or category".

"*personal pension scheme*". The meaning in s.1 of the Pension Schemes Act 1993 is "any scheme or arrangement which is comprised in one or more instruments or agreements and which has, or is capable of having, effect so as to provide benefits, in the form of pensions or otherwise, payable on death or retirement to or in respect of employed earners who have made arrangements with the trustees or managers of the scheme for them to become members of it".

"*self-employed earner.*" The meaning in s.2(1)(b) of the Contributions and Benefits Act (1975 Act, s.2(1)(b)) is "a person who is gainfully employed in Great Britain otherwise than in employed earner's employment (whether or not he is also employed in such employment)."

"*training allowance*". *CIS 858/1994* holds that payments from the European Social Fund can fall within this definition. As part of his part-time course the claimant went on a two-week placement in Brussels and Strasbourg, for which funds were provided by the European Social Fund. The Commissioner decided that this meant that he was in receipt of a training allowance and so could continue to be paid income support during his absence abroad (under reg. 4(2)(c)(i) and para. 11 of Sched. 1 in force at that time; see the 1996 edition of this book). The payment from the European Social Fund was out of "public funds" administered in the U.K. by the Department of Employment and so could be said to be made "by or on behalf of the Secretary of State for Employment"; the Secretary of State would also have to have been satisfied that the course, or at least the placement, came within the ambit of the European Social Fund and so could be said to have "approved" the course.

"*welfare to work beneficiary*". Under reg. 13A(1) of the Social Security (Incapacity for Work) (General) Regulations 1995 a person is a "welfare to work beneficiary" if (i) he has ceased to be entitled to a benefit (other than statutory sick pay) on or after October 5, 1998 which he was getting on the grounds of incapacity for work ("benefit" for this purpose includes incapacity benefit, severe disablement allowance, income support paid on the basis of incapacity for work, or any of the income support, income-based JSA, housing benefit or council tax benefit disability premiums awarded on that ground, or national insurance credits for incapacity for work: reg. 13A(4) of the Incapacity for Work Regulations); (ii) he had been incapable of work for more than 28 weeks (his "previous period of incapacity for work") when his benefit entitlement stopped (it is not necessary for the person to have been in receipt of benefit for the whole of the period); (iii) the previous period of incapacity for work ended 28 weeks or more after the end of any earlier "linking term" (see below) (reg. 13A(3)(b)); (iv) he started a training course for which he receives a training allowance under s.2(1) of the Employment and Training Act 1973 or s.2(3) of the Enterprise and New Towns (Scotland) Act 1990 or work for which he is paid or expects to be paid within a week (*i.e.* any period of seven days: reg. 2(1) of the Incapacity for Work Regulations) of benefit entitlement ending (exempt work under reg. 17 of the Incapacity for Work Regulations does not count but otherwise "work" is not further defined); and (v) *either* notified the Secretary of State (verbally or in writing) that he had started work or training within a month (i.e. a calendar month: Interpretation Act 1978, Sched. 1) of benefit ceasing *or* successfully appealed against a decision that he was capable of work under the "own occupation test" or the "all work test" (see the notes to para. 7(a) of Sched. 1B for a summary of these tests) and the resulting period of incapacity for work was more than 28 weeks. Note that if the previous period of incapacity for work stopped because the person was found capable of work (other than a capacity decision made solely because the person started work), and any appeal was unsuccessful, the intention is that reg. 13A(1) will not apply (reg. 13A(3)(a)). Nor will it do so, it seems, if the person's previous period of incapacity ended because he was treated as capable of work under reg. 7 or 8 of the Incapacity for Work Regulations for failing without good cause to return the all work test questionnaire or attend for a medical examination, even in that case in the event of a successful appeal.

If the person satisfies these conditions, he counts as a "welfare to work beneficiary" for 52 weeks starting on the first day after the end of his previous period of incapacity for work (the "linking term"). This is a fixed period and it is irrelevant whether the person stops work or training or if there are any further days of incapacity in that period. The effect is to provide a 52-week linking rule between periods of incapacity for work for the purpose of access to the disability and higher pensioner premiums and payment of housing costs (see the new paras. 10(4) and 12(1A) inserted into Sched. 2 and the new paras. 7(10) and 14(10) inserted into Sched. 3 with effect from October 5, 1998 and the notes to those paragraphs). In addition, if a welfare to work beneficiary becomes incapable of work and reclaims benefit within the linked term, he will be treated as incapable of work for up to 91 days if (i) during his previous period of incapacity for work he passed the all work test or was exempt from the test under reg. 10 of the Incapacity for Work Regulations (severe conditions) (note this will not apply if the person was treated as incapable of work under reg. 27 of those Regulations (exceptional circumstances)) and (ii) he submits medical evidence of his incapacity for work. The 91 days need not be consecutive but must fall within the 52-week linking period or the first 13 weeks after the end of that period. After 91 days the person will have to satisfy the normal rules for incapacity for work.

Once the 52-week linking period expires, a person can requalify as a welfare to work beneficiary if he meets the requirements for this, including the fact that at least 28 weeks have passed since the end of the previous linking term. Note that days of incapacity within that linking term can count towards satisfying the condition of 28 weeks incapacity (under the normal eight week linking rule: see s.30(1)(c) of the Contributions and Benefits Act).

"*year of assessment*". The meaning in s.832(1) of the Income and Corporation Taxes Act 1988 is "with reference to any tax year, the year for which such tax was granted by any Act granting income tax." A tax year is the 12 months beginning with April 6 in any year.

Paragraph (3)
Note that special provision is only made for polygamous marriages. If the claimant is not married, the ordinary living together as husband and wife rules apply (Contributions and Benefits Act, s.137(1); 1986 Act, s.20(11)).

Paragraph (4)
See the note to the definition of "the Earnings Top-up Scheme".

[¹Disapplication of section 1(1A) of the Administration Act

2A. Section 1(1A) of the Administration Act (requirement to state national insurance number) shall not apply—
  (a) to a child or young person in respect of whom income support is claimed;
  (b) to a partner in respect of whom a claim for income support is made or treated as made before [² 5th October 1998].]

AMENDMENTS

1. Social Security (National Insurance Number Information: Exemption) Regulations 1997 (S.I. 1997 No. 2676), reg. 10 (December 1, 1997).

2. Social Security (National Insurance Number Information: Exemption) (No. 2) Regulations 1997 (S.I. 1997 No. 2814), reg. 2 (December 1, 1997).

"child"—see SSCBA, s. 137(1).
"partner"—see reg. 2(1).
"young person"—see reg. 14.

GENERAL NOTE

Subs. (1A), together wth subss. (1B) and (1C), was inserted into s. 1 of the Administration Act by s. 19 of the Social Security Administration (Fraud) Act 1997 and came into force on December 1, 1997. The effect of these provisions is that where s. 1(1)(a) of the Administration Act (no entitlement to benefit unless a claim for it is made) applies, *i.e.* generally, there will also be no entitlement to benefit unless the claimant provides a national insurance (NI) number, together with information or evidence to show that it is his, *or* provides evidence or information to enable his NI number to be traced, *or* applies for a NI number and provides sufficient information or evidence for one to be allocated to him. A P45 or P60 form will be evidence of a person's NI number but these may not always be available; other evidence which shows the person's number should also be sufficient. This requirement for an NI number applies to both the claimant and any person for whom he is claiming, except in prescribed circumstances (subss. (1A) and (1C)). The effect of reg. 2A is that any child or young person included in the income support claim is exempt; so too is any partner for income support claims made, or treated as made, before October 5, 1998 but not where income support is claimed on or after that date.

Definition of non-dependant

3.—(1) In these Regulations, "non-dependant" means any person, except someone [³ to whom paragraph (2), (2A) or (2B) applies], who normally resides with a claimant [⁴or with whom a claimant normally resides.]
[³(2) This paragraph applies to—
(a) any member of the claimant's family;
(b) a child or young person who is living with the claimant but who is not a member of his household by virtue of regulation 16 (circumstances in which a person is to be treated as being or not being a member of the household);
(c) a person who lives with the claimant in order to care for him or for the claimant's partner and who is engaged for that purpose by a charitable or [⁵voluntary organisation] which makes a charge to the claimant or the claimant's partner for the care provided by that person;
(d) the partner of a person to whom sub-paragraph (c) applies.
(2A) This paragraph applies to a person, other than a close relative of the claimant or the claimant's partner,—
(a) who is liable to make payments on a commercial basis to the claimant or the claimant's partner in respect of his occupation of the claimant's dwelling;
(b) to whom the claimant or the claimant's partner is liable to make payments on a commercial basis in respect of his occupation of that person's dwelling;
(c) who is a member of the household of a person to whom sub-paragraph (a) or (b) applies.
(2B) Subject to paragraph (2C), this paragraph applies to—
(a) a person who jointly occupies the claimant's dwelling and who is either—
(i) a co-owner of that dwelling with the claimant or the claimant's partner (whether or not there are other co-owners); or

(ii) jointly liable with the claimant or the claimant's partner to make payments to a landlord in respect of his occupation of that dwelling;
(b) a partner of a person whom sub-paragraph (a) applies.

(2C) Where a person is a close relative of the claimant or the claimant's partner, paragraph (2B) shall apply to him only if the claimant's, or the claimant's partner's, co-ownership, or joint liability to make payments to a landlord in respect of his occupation, of the dwelling arose either before 11th April 1988, or, if later, on or before the date upon which the claimant or the claimant's partner first occupied the dwelling in question.]

(3) [². . .].

(4) For the purposes of this regulation a person resides with another only if they share any accommodation except a bathroom, a lavatory or a communal area [¹ but not if each person is separately liable to make payments in respect of his occupation of the dwelling to the landlord].

(5) In this regulation "communal area" means any area (other than rooms) of common access (including halls and passageways) and rooms of common use in sheltered accommodation.

AMENDMENTS

1. Income Support (General) Amendment Regulations 1989 (S.I. 1989 No. 534), reg. 2 (April 10, 1989).
2. Income Support (General) Amendment Regulations 1989 (S.I. 1989 No. 534), Sched. 1, para. 2 (October 9, 1989).
3. Income Support (General) Amendment No. 6 Regulations 1991 (S.I. 1991 No. 2334), reg. 2 (November 11, 1991).
4. Income-related Benefits Schemes (Miscellaneous Amendments) (No. 6) Regulations 1994 (S.I. 1994 No. 3061), reg. 2(2) (December 2, 1994).
5. Income-related Benefits Schemes (Miscellaneous Amendments) Regulations 1995 (S.I. 1995 No. 516), reg. 18 (April 10, 1995).

DEFINITIONS

"child"—see 1986 Act, s.20(11) (SSCBA, s.137(1)).
"claimant"—see reg. 2(1).
"dwelling"—see 1986 Act, s.84(1) (SSCBA, s.137(1)).
"family"—*ibid.*
"local authority"—see 1986 Act, s.84(1).
"partner"—see reg. 2(1).
"voluntary organisation"—*ibid.*
"young person"—*ibid.*, reg. 14.

GENERAL NOTE

Paragraph (1)
The definition of "non-dependant" is important for a number of purposes, particularly deductions from housing costs and qualification for the severe disability premium. Its use for different purposes causes difficulties. What might be a sensible test for determining when a contribution towards accommodation costs ought to be assumed from an independent person who shares the claimant's accommodation might be less sensible in determining a severely disabled person's financial needs.

A person who normally resides with the claimant, or with whom the claimant normally resides, (*Chief Adjudication Officer and Another v. Bate* [1996] 2 All E.R. 790, HL), unless within the important exceptions in paras. (2) to (2C), is a non-dependant.

The December 1994 amendment to para. (1) was the government's immediate (within 48 hours) response to the Court of Appeal's decision in *Bate v. Chief Adjudication Officer and Secretary of State for Social Security* on November 30, 1994 (*The Times*, December 12, 1994). Ms Bate was a severely disabled person who lived in her parents' home. The Court of Appeal decided that because her parents were the "householders", in the sense that it was they who jointly occupied the home as tenants, they did not normally reside with *her*, but she normally resided with *them*. Thus they did not come within the definition of non-dependant at all. The Court recognised that this construction did not fit easily with the amendment to reg. 3(2)(d) on April 10, 1989 (now recast in para. (2A)), but did not consider that the meaning of the initial regulation could be determined by later amendments. The April 1989 amendment simply showed that the draftsman had assumed that "residing with the claimant" had the meaning which the Court had rejected. However, the House of Lords disagreed, holding that "resides with" meant no more than that the claimant and the other person lived in the same dwelling. It was not limited to the situation where it was the *claimant's* household or dwelling.

The December 2, 1994 regulations (S.I. 1994 No. 3061) were introduced without first being referred to the Social Security Advisory Committee. Section 173(1)(a) of the Administration Act permits this if the Secretary of State considers it inexpedient to refer proposed regulations by reason of urgency. The failure to refer these proposed regulations was challenged by Ms Bate (see Welfare Rights Bulletin 125). It was argued that the Court of Appeal had decided that it was Parliament's intention that people in Ms Bate's position should be entitled to a severe disability premium (and therefore it intended that financial provision should be made for this) and so the Secretary of State could not say that it was urgent that payment of the premium should stop. In addition, the Secretary of State should not be allowed to sidestep the consultation procedure, which Parliament clearly considered important, in this way. (See the comment of Hobhouse L.J. in *Chief Adjudication Officer v. Palfrey and Others* (Court of Appeal, February 8, 1995) that one reason at least for the consultation procedure is the "remarkable latitude" given to the maker of regulations in the Social Security Acts.) But leave to bring judicial review was refused both by the High Court and the Court of Appeal.

Paras. (4) and (5) provide a partial definition of "resides with." In its original form, para. (4) put forward only one necessary, but not on its own sufficient, condition about sharing accommodation. But the general test of para. (1) still had to be satisfied. On "sharing of accommodation" see *CSIS 185/1995* in the note to para. (4). The post-April 1989 form of para. (4) specifically excludes from the definition a situation where co-residents are separately liable to make payments to a landlord. Such a person is already paying for accommodation costs. "Landlord" does not require there to be a tenancy; licensees can come within the exclusion (*CSIS 43/1992*).

Outside this exclusion the arrangement must still come within the general meaning of "residing with" and be the normal situation to come within the definition in para. (1). In *CSIS 100/1993* the claimant's daughter sometimes stayed in her mother's home and used that address for official correspondence. The Commissioner says that where correspondence is sent is a possible indicator that the daughter normally resided with the claimant, but equally, having regard to the other places the daughter stayed, it could be that she had no "fixed abode" (and thus did not normally reside with the claimant). This is further expanded on in *CIS 14850/1996* where the Commissioner states that for a person to be "normally resident" it was necessary for him to have lived in the house concerned, if not permanently, for a sufficient length of time for it to be regarded as his usual abode. The question of normal residence was a practical one to be determined in the light of common sense (see *CSIS 76/1991*). It would be relevant to consider why the residence started, its duration, the relationship, if any, between the people concerned, including its history; the reason why the residence had been taken up and whether it had lasted longer than its original purpose; and whether there was any alternative residence the person could take up. In that case a woman who was previously unknown to the claimant but who may have been his daughter came to live with him on the breakdown of her marriage. The matrimonial proceedings were protracted and she was also waiting for a council house. When the claimant applied for his income support to be reviewed to include a severe disability premium she had been living in his house for nine months. The Commissioner considered that since they had not previously known each other normal residence might take longer to establish and even longer if they were not in fact close relatives. If "the daughter" was waiting for alternative accommodation her residence could be quite lengthy without necessarily becoming normal. Questions such as what steps she had taken to find other accommodation, or with regard to her former matrimonial home, would also need to be investigated.

Paragraphs (2) to (2C)

These provisions except those who would otherwise count as non-dependants from coming within that category. The exceptions have been through a convoluted series of forms, whose meaning has been a matter of great controversy. The convolutions are traced in previous editions, and great care must be taken in identifying what form of the regulation is in effect at particular dates which may be relevant to outstanding claims and appeals. See *CIS 20034/1997* for a useful summary of the position in relation to each of the periods from October 9, 1989 for a severely disabled claimant living with his family. The House of Lords in *Foster v. Chief Adjudication Officer* [1993] A.C. 754; [1993] 1 All E.R. 705 holds that the amendment made on October 9, 1989 (to add the conditions now substantially contained in para. (2B)(a)(i) and (ii)) was not *ultra vires* on the ground of irrationality.

Note that regs. 4 to 6 of the Income Support (General) Amendment No. 6 Regulations 1991 provide transitional protection for claimants who were entitled to the severe disability premium before October 21, 1991, by virtue of the pre-November 1991 form of reg. 3 (see p.488).

In *CSIS 28/1992* and *CSIS 40/1992* (to be reported as *R(IS) 17/94*), a Tribunal of Commissioners states that SSATs, when considering, for example, a claimant's right to a severe disability premium, should deal with the position from the date of claim down to the date when the issues are finally decided (preferring the approach of *CIS 391/1992* and *CIS 417/1992* (T) (to be reported as *R(IS) 5/98*) to that of *CIS 649/1992*, where the Commissioner held that an adjudicating authority should only consider the position as at the date from which benefit is sought). *CIS 649/1992* is also inconsistent with, for example, *CIS 654/1991*, to be reported as *R(IS) 3/93*, (see the notes to reg. 23(2) of the Adjudication Regulations). But in relation to appeals lodged on or after May 21, 1998, note the effect of s.22(8) of the Administration Act inserted by para. 3 of Sched. 6 to the Social Security Act 1998 where there is a change of circumstances after the date of the AO's decision: see the notes to s.22(8). In addition, *R(IS) 17/94* dealt with an argument that once a claimant had acquired a right to a severe disability premium, its removal by subsequent amendment of reg. 3(2) was prevented by s. 16(1)(c) of the Interpretation Act (protection of acquired rights). Section 16 applies unless the contrary intention appears. The Commissioners hold that the words "shall come into force in relation to a particular claimant" in reg. 1(1) of S.I. 1989 No. 534 (the regulations at issue) indicated that the regulations were intended to apply to existing claimants. A claim made after the regulations came into force would be subject to them without the need for these words. Thus they were clearly intended to provide for existing claimants.

Paragraph (2)

These four categories excluded from the definition of non-dependant have been in the regulation since 1988 and are relatively straightforward. They cover those who are not sufficiently independent of the claimant to be a non-dependant.

(a) A member of the family. This, by reference to s.137(1) of the Contributions and Benefits Act (1986 Act, s.20(11)), covers children and 16–18 year-olds treated as in full time secondary level education as well as partners, but only if members of the same household.

(b) Children who are not members of the family under the operation of the special rules in reg. 16.

(c) and (d) Certain carers provided at a charge by charities or voluntary bodies, plus the carer's partner.

Paragraph (2A)

This is a recasting in November 1991 of the previous para. (2)(d) to (db). The difference is that a close relative (defined in reg. 2(1)) of the claimant or his partner does not come within para. (2A). Thus, for instance, the parents of a severely disabled person may no longer come within para. (2A). If they are not to be non-dependants from November 1991, they must come within paras. (2B) and (2C). Outside the close relative exception, the effect of para. (2A) now is that where the relationship between the claimant (or the claimant's partner) and the other person (or a member of that person's household) is a commercial one, that person is not a non-dependant. No further contribution to accommodation costs is therefore appropriate.

There must be a legal liability (as distinct from a moral or ethical obligation (*CIS 754/1991*)) to make payments for accommodation, *i.e.* rent or a board and lodging charge, on a commercial basis. The first question is whether there is a liability to pay. It has been held on the pre-November 1991 version of para. (2A) that a severely disabled claimant living with, for example, his parents can be their licensee and therefore liable to pay for his accommodation in the sense that if no payment is made the licence could terminate (*CIS 195/1991, CIS 754/1991*). In deciding whether such a liability exists there would need to be findings as to the terms on which a claimant lives in his parents' home, the amount and regularity of the payments and the use made of the claimant's contributions. If the payments go towards rent or a mortgage that would be a stronger case than if they are used for the claimant's own personal needs (*CIS 754/1991*), but they need not be applied directly to accommodation costs. If the claimant's contributions go into a general fund used for household costs (including accommodation) that will suffice (*CSIS 28/1992* and *CSIS 40/1992*, to be reported as *R(IS)17/94*). It will then be necessary to conclude on the basis of the relevant findings whether there was an intention to create legal relations. Such an intention can be inferred from a course of conduct (see Scarman L.J. in *Horrocks v. Forray* [1976] 1 W.L.R. 230 at 239). *CIS 754/1991* holds that this might not be too difficult to infer where an adult member of the family is making regular payments in respect of his occupation. It may be easier to infer where the parents depend on the claimant's contributions because of their own financial circumstances. In his directions to the new SSAT in *CIS 754/1991* the Commissioner concludes:

"In essence there should be what I might call a broad approach to satisfaction of the condition keeping in mind that the AO has throughout accepted that in [*CIS 195/1991*] it was right to conclude that the claimant [had a liability to make payments in respect of his occupation]. I should have thought that the facts in many of the cases are likely to be essentially indistinguish-able from those in [*CIS/195/1991*].''

The facts in *CIS/195/1991* were that the claimant's parents took £20 per week from his benefit. The rest of the money was used for his own needs. The SSAT found that the claimant lived in his parents' house as a licensee and paid them £20 in respect of his occupation of it.

But what of the situation where there can be no contractual liability because one of the parties lacks the capacity to make a contract? In *CIS 195/1991* the claimant was held to be capable of incurring a liability to make payment, despite his mental disability. Under English law the contract was voidable because of his mental disability, not void. However, in Scottish law an "incapax" is not capable of making any personal contract. *CSIS 28/1992* and *CSIS 40/1992* (to be reported as *R(IS) 17/94*) hold that first Scottish cases SSATs must first consider whether a claimant is so mentally incapacitated as to be incapax. But if this is the case, the doctrine of recompense may well apply to establish a liability on the incapax, so that the result is similar in practical terms to that in *CIS 195/1991* (see 1993 Supplement for fuller discussion of *CSIS 28/1992* and *CSIS 40/1992*). The doctrine of recompense is also considered in *CSIS 641/1995*, although on the particular facts of that case (see the summary in the 1998 Supplement to this book) it did not apply. In *CIS 754/1991* the Commissioner expresses the *obiter* view that where a person has no contractual capacity at all, the doctrine of restitution does not seem available to assist claimants in England in the way that recompense can in Scotland. Thus in English cases for mentally disabled claimants it will generally be necessary for there to be a finding of sufficient contractual capacity. On the facts of both *CIS 195/1991* and *CIS 754/1991* the capacity required does not seem to be of a very high order. The claimant in *CIS 754/1991* was found to have sufficient contractual capacity despite having Downs syndrome and needing an appointee to act for her in social security matters.

Since October 1, 1990, the liability to pay has had to be on a commercial basis. The words "commercial basis" govern the nature of the liability, not just the quality of the payments made (*CSIS 28/1992* and *CSIS 40/1992*, to be reported as *R(IS)17/94*). For a discussion of "commercial basis" see *CSB 1163/1988* and the notes to the definition of "board and lodging accommodation" in reg. 2(1). In *CIS 195/1991* (approved in *CSIS 28/1992* and *CSIS 40/1992*) the Commissioner held that the question of whether an arrangement is on a commercial basis was entirely one of fact for the SSAT. What has to be considered is whether the arrangement is the sort that might have been entered into if the parents had taken in a lodger, instead of, in *CIS 195/1991*, their physically and mentally handicapped son. This approach was also expressly approved by another Tribunal of Commissioners in *CIS 529/1994*. The claimant, who was severely disabled, lived with her parents and paid them £25 per week. The Commissioners emphasise that *CIS 195/1991* had only considered that a commercial arrangement in a family situation was unlikely, not that it was impossible or even improbable. They also confirm that a profit element is not necessary, nor was it relevant whether the family depended financially on the payments or whether they would take any action if the claimant did not pay (although these last two factors were relevant to the question of whether there was a liability to make payments, see *CIS 754/1991*). The Commissioners rejected the AO's contention that in considering the adequacy of the claimant's payments a deduction should be made for the value of the care provided by the parents, pointing out that reg. 3 referred to payments in respect of the *occupation* of the dwelling.

Although there might still be some scope for structuring an informal relationship to get within para. (2A), the requirement of a commercial basis (since October 1, 1990) and the exclusion of close relatives (from November 11, 1991) provide quite a stringent control. Note the transitional protection in regs. 4 to 6 of the Income Support (General) Amendment No. 6 Regulations 1991 (see p. 488) for claimants entitled to the severe disability premium before October 21, 1991.

SSATs faced with sorting out severe disability premium entitlement, in particular for the periods October 9, 1989 to September 30, 1990 and October 1, 1990 to November 10, 1991, will need to pay particular regard to the Commissioners' decisions discussed above. There is a useful summary of the position in relation to each of the periods from October 9, 1989 in *CIS 20034/1997*.

Paragraphs (2B) to (2C)

These provisions replace the previous para. (2)(c) on joint occupiers, and impose a considerably stricter test. The biggest change in November 1991 was to exclude joint occupiers who are close relatives (see reg. 2(1)) from the operation of para. (2B) except in restricted circumstances. This is done by para. (2C). If the close relative met the conditions of para. (2B) either before April 11, 1988, or as soon as the claimant or partner moved to the current home, then advantage can be taken of para. (2B). The aim is to exclude arrangements made within a family (in the non-income support sense) designed to take advantage of the definition of a non-dependant. The thinking is that if the arrangement was the basis on which the occupation of the home by the claimant started it is likely to be a genuine one. Existing claimants excluded by this rule may particularly benefit from the transitional protection mentioned above. *CIS 80/1994* rejects the argument that para. (2C) is invalid on the ground that it operates retrospectively. The Commissioner states that para. (2C) imposes a new condition of future eligibility (though with reference to past events). Thus it does not take away any vested right or create any new obligation in regard to events that have already passed.

In *CIS 650/1993* the claimant had been a joint tenant of her home with her husband. When he died in 1990 she became the sole tenant. Later her sister came to live with her and they became joint tenants. The Commissioner rejects the claimant's contention that the previous joint liability of the claimant and her husband meant that para. (2C) was satisfied. In the context of reg. 3, para. (2C) only referred to the joint liability of the claimant and the person currently residing with her and not to any other joint liability.

In *CIS 216/1997* the claimant who was in receipt of the severe disability premium gave up the tenancy of her local authority home (with effect from January 22, 1995) and went to live with her daughter and her family. She moved to her daughter's home on January 16, 1995 and became a joint tenant with her of that home on January 23, 1995. During the week from January 16 to 22, the claimant was moving her belongings from her old home to her new, although she slept at her daughter's home from January 16. The Commissioner decides that the claimant was to be regarded as having "first occupied" her new home when she first normally resided there. It was clear from the evidence that arrangements for the joint tenancy had been made with the local authority before the claimant moved in with her daughter. The move and the creation of the joint tenancy were inextricably linked. In his view the claimant did not finally become an occupier of her new home until January 23, 1995 and so para. (2C) applied.

The rest of para. (2B) is based on the provisions in force from October 1989. First, there must be joint occupation of the claimant's home. In *CIS 180/1989* the claimant was a single woman in receipt of attendance allowance, severe disablement allowance and income support. She lived with her parents, who owned the house. The Commissioner held that "jointly occupies" is not to be given a technical meaning, but its ordinary meaning. The phrase applies where "persons who normally reside together jointly occupy the premises in the sense of equality of access and use as distinct from a situation where restrictions are imposed in relation to those matters." It did not matter, under the legislation in force at the relevant time, that the claimant did not have any proprietary interest in the house. *CIS 180/1989* (approved by the Tribunal of Commissioners in *CSIS 28/1992* and *CSIS 40/1992*, to be reported as *R(IS)17/94*) has governed the position, particularly in severe disability premium cases, for the period before October 9, 1989, when amendments to impose the extra conditions now substantially contained in para. (2B)(a)(i) and (ii) were made. Indeed, it has been usual for AOs to concede that for the period before October 9, 1989, parents or other family members are not non-dependants.

It might be objected that the approach of *CIS 180/1989* expanded the exception on joint occupation so far that it excluded everyone who would be caught by the primary definition of a non-dependant. This is not so. People can reside together, but without the equality of access and use stressed by the Commissioner. The House of Lords in the *Foster* case, where it was conceded that the claimant's parents were joint occupiers up to October 9, 1989, expressed similar doubts that the exception, if widely construed, might eat up the rule, but did not reach any authoritative conclusion. In a decision on the equivalent housing benefit provision (*Fullwood v. Chesterfield Borough Council, The Times,* June 15, 1993) the Court of Appeal specifically rejected the basis of *CIS 180/1989*, holding that "jointly occupies" is a technical legal phrase, meaning "occupies by right jointly with one or more persons". Thus, joint occupation entails either a joint tenancy or joint liability to make payments under an agreement for occupation. This decision strictly only related to housing benefit, but both the Court of Appeal and the House of Lords in *Bate* (see above) accepted that the phrase should be given the same meaning for the purposes of income support. It connoted a legal relationship and not merely factual co-residence.

From October 9, 1989, it has been specifically provided that one of two extra conditions must be satisfied. One is that the claimant (or partner) is a co-owner of the home with the other person (or partner). This is unchanged since October 9, 1989. The other condition is that there is joint liability to make payments in respect of the occupation of the home to a landlord. This was changed in November 1991 from the October 9, 1989 form to specify that the payments must be to a landlord. The result is broadly to confirm the outcome of *CIS 299/1990* (discussed in the 1991 edition), and to remove the problem of interpretation addressed in that decision. These conditions narrowed the scope of para. (2B) considerably. Where there is separate, rather than joint, liability a person is deemed not to be residing with the claimant (para. (4)).

Paragraph (3)

The revocation removes the special rule for boarders and hostel-dwellers.

Paragraph (4)

The original form of para. (4) merely meant that if accommodation other than bathroom, lavatory or a communal area was not shared, one person was not "residing with" another. It did not mean that the person was "residing with" the other just because such accommodation was shared. The general test of para. (1) still has to be satisfied. See *CSIS 100/1993* and *CIS 14850/1996* above. Para. (4) now also excludes from the definition of non-dependant a person who is separately liable to make payments to the landlord. See *CSIS 43/1992* above. Joint tenants and co-owners (other than close relatives of the claimant or partner) are excluded by para. (2B)(a).

CSIS 185/1995 holds that a person does not share a kitchen with another if it is not used physically by him but only by a third party to prepare food on his behalf. The Commissioner also points out that the issue is whether there is a "sharing of *accommodation*". So deciding whether the claimant shared a room simply because some of her clothes were stored there, would depend on what use, if any, the claimant made of the room, by considering what was stored there, in what, and to what extent, if any, the claimant herself went in and out of the room to deal with her property.

[¹Permitted period

3A.—(1) For the purposes of regulation 17(6), [². . .], paragraph 7(6) of Schedule 3A, paragraph 6(3) of Schedule 3B and paragraphs 4 and 6 of Schedule 8 (applicable amounts, mortgage interest, protected sums and earnings to be disregarded), where a claimant has ceased to be entitled to income support—

    (a) because he or his partner becomes engaged in remunerative work the permitted period, [³. . .] shall be 12 weeks; or

    (b) for any other reason, the permitted period shall be eight weeks.

(2)[³. . .].

(3)[³. . .].

AMENDMENTS

1. Income Support (General) Amendment No. 3 Regulations 1989 (S.I. 1989 No. 1678), reg. 2 (October 9, 1989).

2. Social Security (Income Support, Claims and Payments and Adjudication) Amendment Regulations 1995 (S.I. 1995 No. 2927), reg. 4 (December 12, 1995).

3. Income Support (General) (Jobseeker's Allowance Consequential Amendments) Regulations 1996 (S.I. 1996 No. 206), reg. 3 (October 7, 1996).

GENERAL NOTE

Reg. 3A provides a definition of the maximum permitted period of break in entitlement for the application of the various provisions set out in para. (1).

The omission of paras. (2) and (3) is a consequence of the introduction of jobseeker's allowance on October 7, 1996.

PART II

CONDITIONS OF ENTITLEMENT

[¹Prescribed categories of person

4ZA.—(1) Subject to the following provisions of this regulation, a person to whom any paragraph of Schedule 1B applies falls within a prescribed category of person for the purposes of section 124(1)(e) of the Contributions and Benefits Act (entitlement to income support).

(2) Paragraph (1) does not apply to a student during the period of study.

(3) A student during the period of study falls within a prescribed category of person for the purposes of section 124(1)(e) of the Contributions and Benefits Act only if—

(a) regulation 70(3)(a) applies to him; or

(b) paragraph 1, 2, 10, 11, 12, or 18 of Schedule 1B applies to him; or

(c) any other paragraph of Schedule 1B applies to him and he has a partner who is also a student, and either he or his partner is treated as responsible for a child or young person, but this provision shall apply only for the period of the summer vacation appropriate to his course.]

[²(4) A person who falls within a prescribed category in Schedule 1B for the purposes of this regulation for any day in a benefit week, shall fall within that category for the whole of that week.]

AMENDMENTS

1. Income Support (General) (Jobseeker's Allowance Consequential Amendments) Regulations 1996 (S.I. 1996 No. 206), reg. 4 (October 7, 1996).

2. Income-related Benefits and Jobseeker's Allowance (Amendment) (No. 2) Regulations 1997 (S.I. 1997 No. 2197), reg. 5(2) (October 6, 1997).

DEFINITIONS

"child"—see SSCBA, s.137(1).
"benefit week"—see reg. 2(1).
"partner"—*ibid*.
"period of study"—*ibid*.
"student"—see reg. 61.
"young person"—see reg. 14.

GENERAL NOTE

Paragraph (1)

As a consequence of the introduction of JSA on October 7, 1996, the income support scheme has had to undergo a fundamental restructuring. Income support is no longer available to people who are claiming benefit because they are unemployed. People who have to be available for, and actively seeking, work as a condition of receiving benefit now have to claim JSA. Since October 7, 1996, in order to qualify for income support a person has to fall within a "prescribed category" (see SSCBA s.124(1)(e)). These categories are set out in the new Sched. 1B. The categories in Sched. 1B broadly resemble most of those in the former Sched. 1 (people not required to be available for employment) which was revoked on October 7, 1996, but there are some differences. See the notes to Sched. 1B. For the position of students, see paras. (2) and (3).

Sched. 1B provides an exhaustive list of the circumstances in which a person will be entitled to income support. There is no category of analogous circumstances or provision for a reduced rate of benefit on the ground of hardship for people who do not come within these categories (compare the former reg. 8(3), see the 1996 edition of this book). Moreover, the provision for hardship payments under JSA is considerably restricted (see regs. 140–146 of the JSA Regulations and the notes to those regulations). For the very limited provision for urgent cases outside the normal scope of the income support rules see reg. 70.

Note that entitlement to income support and JSA is mutually exclusive, although some people may be eligible for either. Section 124(1)(f) of the Contributions and Benefits Act provides that entitlement to JSA excludes entitlement to income support (any "top-up" to a person's contribution-based JSA will be by way of income-based JSA). Similarly, a person will not be entitled to JSA (contribution- or income-based) if he is entitled to income support (ss.2(1)(d) and 3(1)(b) of the Jobseekers Act). However, there is nothing to prevent a person who qualifies for income support claiming JSA if he also fulfils the conditions of entitlement for JSA. But in most circumstances it will be better for him to claim income support so as to avoid the risk of being "sanctioned" for not complying with the labour market conditions. If the claimant is a member of a couple he will not be entitled to income support if his partner is claiming *income-based* JSA (SSCBA s.124(1)(f)). If his partner is claiming *contribution-based* JSA he will be able to claim income support if he is eligible for this, or his partner can claim income-based JSA. If the claimant is incapable of work it will be better for him to claim income support in order to qualify for the disability premium under para. 12(1)(b) of Sched. 2 after serving the appropriate waiting period. If the only basis for qualifying for the premium is incapacity for work for 364 days (or 196 days if he is terminally ill), his partner will not be able to get a JSA disability premium for him (see para. 14 of Sched. 1 to the JSA Regulations). Moreover, note the "better-off" problem that has been created for some claimants as a result of the raising of the limit for remunerative work for partners to 24 hours a week from October 7, 1996 (see Income Support Regulations, reg. 5(1A), JSA Regulations reg. 51(1)(b)). The consequence of this rule change is that if the claimant's partner is working between 16 and 24 hours a week the couple may have to consider whether they will gain more by claiming family credit (or disability working allowance or, in certain areas of the country, earnings top-up): see further the notes to reg. 4 of the Family Credit Regulations. Note reg. 6(27) and (28) of the Claims and Payments Regulations. Note also that family credit and disability working allowance are due to be replaced by working families tax credit and disabled person's tax credit from October 5, 1999. See the 1999 Supplement to this book for further details.

Paragraphs (2) and (3)
The effect of paras. (2) and (3) is to exclude most students (defined in reg. 61) from entitlement to income support from the beginning of their course to the end (see the definition of period of study in reg. 2(1)). A student will only be entitled during his period of study if he is a "person from abroad" entitled to urgent cases payments because he is temporarily without funds (para. (3)(a)), or a lone parent, a single foster parent, a student who qualifies for the disability or severe disability premium, or who has been incapable of work for 28 weeks (two or more periods separated by not more than eight weeks count as continuous), or who is disabled and entitled under para. 11 of Sched. 1B, or deaf, or a refugee learning English (para. (3)(b)). Student couples with a child who fall within any of the other paragraphs in Sched. 1B may claim but only in the summer vacation (para. (3)(c)).

Note the transitional protection in reg. 8 of the Income-related Benefits Schemes and Social Fund (Miscellaneous Amendments) Regulations 1996 (S.I. 1996 No. 1944) (p. 501) for students who counted as part-time on July 31, 1996 under the definition in reg. 61 that applied before October 7, 1996. They can continue to get income support until the part-time course that they were undertaking on July 31, 1996 ends, or they abandon or are dismissed from it, as long as they were continuously entitled to income support from July 31 to October 7, 1996, fall within one of the categories in Sched. 1B (apart from those listed in para. (3)(b)), satisfy the other conditions of entitlement for income support and were not entitled to JSA in the benefit week after the week which includes October 7, 1996. This rule ceases to apply if there is a break in entitlement to income support of more than 12 weeks.

Paragraph (4)
This confirms that if a person satisfies any of the paragraphs in Sched. 1B on any day in a benefit week, he is treated as doing so for the whole of that week.

Temporary absence from Great Britain

4.—(1) Where a claimant is entitled to income support for a period immediately preceding a period of temporary absence from Great Britain, his entitlement to income support [² shall continue only—
   (a) in the circumstances specified in paragraph (2), during the first 4 weeks of that period of temporary absence; and
   (b) in the circumstances specified in paragraph (3), during the first 8 weeks of that period.]

(2) The circumstances in which a claimant's entitlement to income support is to continue during the first four weeks of a temporary absence from Great Britain are that—
   (a) the period of absence is unlikely to exceed 52 weeks; and
   (b) while absent from Great Britain, the claimant continues to satisfy the other conditions of entitlement to income support; and
   (c) any one of the following conditions apply—
      (i) the claimant falls within one or more of the prescribed categories of person listed in Schedule 1B other than paragraphs 7, 15, 20, 21, 24, 25, 26 or 27 of that Schedule; or
      (ii) the claimant falls within paragraph 7 of Schedule 1B (persons incapable of work) and his absence from Great Britain is for the sole purpose of receiving treatment from an appropriately qualified person for the incapacity by reason of which he satisfies the conditions of that paragraph; or]

(iii) he is in Northern Ireland; or

(iv) he is a member of a couple and he and his partner are both absent from Great Britain, and a premium referred to in paragraphs 9, [⁵9A,] 10, 11 or 13 of Schedule 2 (applicable amounts) is applicable in respect of his partner; [¹ or

[³(v) on the day on which the absence began he had satisfied the provisions of [⁴ paragraph 7 of Schedule 1B] (persons incapable of work) for a continuous period of not less than—

(aa) 196 days in the case of a claimant who is terminally ill within the meaning of section 30B(4) of the Contributions and Benefits Act, or who is entitled to the highest rate of the care component of disability living allowance; or

(bb) 364 days in any other case,

and for this purpose any two or more separate periods separated by a break of not more than 56 days shall be treated as one continuous period.]]

[²(3) The circumstances in which a claimant's entitlement to income support is to continue during the first 8 weeks of a temporary absence from Great Britain are that—

(a) the period of absence is unlikely to exceed 52 weeks; and

(b) the claimant continues to satisfy the other conditions of entitlement to income support; and

(c) the claimant is, or the claimant and any other member of his family are, accompanying a member of the claimant's family who is a child or young person solely in connection with arrangements made for the treatment of that child or young person for a disease or bodily or mental disablement; and

(d) those arrangements relate to treatment—

(i) outside Great Britain;

(ii) during the period whilst the claimant is, or the claimant and any member of his family are, temporarily absent from Great Britain; and

(iii) by, or under the supervision of, a person appropriately qualified to carry out that treatment.

(4) In paragraphs (2) and (3) "appropriately qualified" means qualified to provide medical treatment, physiotherapy or a form of treatment which is similar to, or related to, either of those forms of treatment.]

AMENDMENTS

1. Income Support (General) Amendment Regulations 1988 (S.I. 1988 No. 663), reg. 3 (April 11, 1988).

2. Income Support (General) Amendment Regulations 1990 (S.I. 1990 No. 547), reg. 3 (April 9, 1990).

3. Disability Working Allowance and Income Support (General) Amendment Regulations 1995 (S.I. 1995 No. 482), reg. 5 (April 13, 1995).

4. Income Support (General) (Jobseeker's Allowance Consequential Amendments) Regulations 1996 (S.I. 1996 No. 206), reg. 5 (October 7, 1996).

5. Income-related Benefits Schemes and Social Fund (Miscellaneous Amendments) Regulatiojns 1996 (S.I. 1996 No. 1944), reg. 6(3) (October 7, 1996).

DEFINITIONS

"claimant"—see reg. 2(1).
"couple"—*ibid.*
"disability living allowance"—*ibid.*
"partner"—*ibid.*

GENERAL NOTE

This provision takes over from reg. 3 of the old Conditions of Entitlement Regulations a limited right to benefit during the claimant's absence from Great Britain (normally excluded by s.124(1) of the Contributions and Benefits Act; 1986 Act, s.20(3)); see *Perry v. Chief Adjudication Officer, The Times*, October 20, 1998, also to be reported as *R(IS) 4/99*, in the note to s.124(1)). Great Britain means England, Scotland and Wales. If it is the claimant's partner who is temporarily absent, see Sched. 7, para. 11.

Paragraph (1)

The absence must be temporary, on the meaning of which see *Chief Adjudication Officer v. Ahmed & Others, The Times*, April 6, 1994 (Court of Appeal). In *R. v. Social Security Commissioner, ex parte Akbar, The Times*, November 6, 1991, Hodgson J. had decided that temporary meant "not permanent". The Court of Appeal in *Ahmed* says that this is wrong, although the decision in *Akbar* itself was correct. However, the Court does agree with Hodgson J. that an absence can be temporary, even though the intended date for return remains uncertain. Thus *R(S) 1/85* should not be followed on this point. The Court of Appeal holds that the decision as to whether a person is temporarily absent is one of fact for the adjudicating authority concerned. Relevant factors include the claimant's intention (although this is not decisive) and the length of the absence. If a person initially has the intention of not returning or an intention to stay for some fixed period which goes beyond the temporary (*e.g.* a matter of years), the absence is not temporary from the outset. In practice, the 52–week period referred to in paras. (2)(a) and (3)(a) is likely to be the most important test.

The claimant must have been entitled to income support immediately before the temporary absence. Since the reference is to entitlement, it does not seem that income support must actually have been received. But a claim must have been made for that period before entitlement can arise (Administration Act, s.1).

If the conditions set out in para. (2) are met, entitlement at the rate which would have been payable if the claimant had remained in Great Britain, can continue for the first four weeks of the temporary absence. If the conditions of para. (3) are met, entitlement can continue for the first eight weeks of absence. When calculating periods of absence from Great Britain the day of leaving and the day of return are both days on which the person is in Great Britain (see para. 22718 of the *Adjudication Officer's Guide* and *R(S)1/66*).

If the claimant does not satisfy the conditions for continuing entitlement or the four or eight weeks are exhausted, any partner remaining in Great Britain may claim. If the absence is temporary, the couple ought on principle to remain members of the same household (although the effect of reg. 16(3)(d) is obscure).

Paragraph (2)

Sub-paras. (a) and (b) are self-explanatory. It is important that all the other conditions of entitlement must continue to be satisfied. The five conditions in sub-para. (c) are alternatives.

Head (i) covers claimants eligible for income support, apart from by reason of incapacity for work (but see (ii) and (v)), secondary education, trade disputes or being a person from abroad.

Some of the conditions which lead to eligibility for income support will obviously continue during absence abroad (*e.g.* pregnancy) but others may not (*e.g.* temporarily looking after children, if the children are left behind). Since the October 1993 change in the test of responsibility for a child, a lone parent who goes abroad temporarily without her children should continue to be eligible for income support under para. 1 of Sched. 1B. This is because reg. 15(1) now makes receipt of child benefit the primary test of responsibility. Child benefit can continue to be paid while a claimant is temporarily absent from Great Britain for up to eight weeks. Only if no claim for child benefit has been made is the person with whom the child usually lives treated as responsible under reg. 15(2)(a). The matter has to be tested week by week (*CIS 49/1991*). See the 1993 edition for the potential problems for lone parents absent abroad prior to October 4, 1993.

Head (ii) covers incapacity for work, but only subject to these conditions (as applied to incapacity benefit by reg. 2(1) of the Social Security (Persons Abroad) Regulations 1975). See *R(S) 2/86* and *R(S) 1/90* for the conditions and head (v). Para. (4) defines when the person providing treatment is appropriately qualified.

Head (iii) is self explanatory.

Head (iv) refers to the pensioner and disability premiums, but only applies to couples who are both abroad. It requires the premium to be "applicable". It is clearly arguable that "applicable" means "ought to be applied", so that entitlement to the premium, even if it is not actually in payment, will do.

Head (v) allows those incapable of work for at least 52 weeks, or 28 weeks if they are terminally ill (*i.e.* expected to die from a progressive disease within six months) or entitled to the highest rate care component of disability living allowance, to use the regulation free of the conditions of head (ii). Two or more periods of incapacity count as one continuous period unless there is a break of more than eight weeks. Before April 13, 1995 the minimum period was 28 weeks for all claimants, but it has been increased for most claimants in line with the changes following the introduction of incapacity benefit. For the details of incapacity benefit see *Bonner, Non-Means Tested Benefits: the Legislation*. Note reg. 8(1) of the Income-related Benefits Schemes and Social Security (Claims and Payments) (Miscellaneous Amendments) Regulations 1995 (p. 498), which provides that in deciding whether a claimant can satisfy head (v) on or after October 2, 1995, a period of incapacity immediately before April 13, 1995 can count towards the 52 (or 28) weeks, provided it is linked to, or part of, the current period. See also the transitional provision in reg. 27(2) of the Income Support (General) (Jobseeker's Allowance Consequential Amendments) Regulations 1996 (p. 499) in relation to the October 1996 changes to income support that are a consequence of the introduction of JSA.

Paragraph (3)

The conditions in heads (a) and (b) are the same as in para. (2)(a) and (b). Then the effect of heads (c) and (d) is that where the claimant is accompanying a child or young person in their family abroad for that child or young person to receive treatment, entitlement can continue for eight weeks. The claimant's absence must be solely for that purpose. The treatment must be for a medical condition and be carried out by an appropriately qualified person within the meaning of para. (4). There seems to be no reason why a claimant accompanying a child should be more deserving than a claimant going abroad for treatment for himself.

Persons treated as engaged in remunerative work

5.—(1) Subject to the following provisions of this regulation, for the purposes of section 20(3)(c) of the Act [SSCBA, s.124(1)(c)] (conditions of entitlement to income support), remunerative work is work in which a person is engaged, or, where his hours of work fluctuate, he is engaged on average, for [⁶not less than 16 hours] a week being work for which payment is made or which is done in expectation of payment.

[⁹ (1A) In the case of any partner of the claimant paragraph (1) shall have effect as though for the words "16 hours" there were substituted the words "24 hours".]

(2) [⁸Subject to paragraph (3B),] the number of hours for which a person is engaged in work shall be determined—

   (a) where no recognisable cycle has been established in respect of a person's work, by reference to the number of hours or, where those hours are likely to fluctuate, the average of the hours, which he is expected to work in a week;

   (b) where the number of hours for which he is engaged fluctuate, by reference to the average of hours worked over—

      (i) if there is a recognisable cycle of work, the period of one complete cycle (including, where the cycle involves periods in which the person does no work, those periods but disregarding any other absences);

      (ii) in any other case, the period of five weeks immediately before the date of claim or the date of review, or such other length of time as may, in the particular case, enable the person's average hours of work to be determined more accurately.

(3) A person shall be treated as engaged in remunerative work during any period for which he is absent from work referred to in paragraph (1) if the absence is either without good cause or by reason of a recognised, customary or other holiday.

[⁷(3A) A person shall not be treated as engaged in remunerative work on any day on which the person is on maternity leave or is absent from work because he is ill.]

[⁸(3B) Where for the purpose of paragraph (2)(b)(i), a person's recognisable cycle of work at a school, other educational establishment or other place of employment is one year and includes periods of school holidays or similar vacations during which he does not work, those periods and any other periods not forming part of such holidays or vacations during which he is not required to work shall be disregarded in establishing the average hours for which he is engaged in work.]

(4) A person who makes a claim and to whom or whose partner section 23 of the Act [SSCBA, s.126] (trade disputes) applies [¹or applied] shall, for the period of seven days following the date on which the stoppage of work due to a trade dispute at his or his partner's place of work commenced or, if there is no stoppage, the date on which he or his partner first withdrew his labour in furtherance of a trade dispute, be treated as engaged in remunerative work.

(5) A person who was, or was treated as being, engaged in remunerative work and in respect of that work earnings to which [⁴regulation 35(1)(b) to (d) and (i)] (earnings of employed earners) applies are [³paid] shall be treated as engaged in remunerative work for the period for which those earnings are taken into account in accordance with Part V.

[²(6) For the purposes of this regulation, in determining the number of hours in which a person is engaged or treated as engaged in remunerative work, no account shall be taken of any hours in which the person is engaged in an employment or a scheme to which paragraph (*a*) to [⁷paragraph (k)] of regulation 6 (persons not treated as engaged in remunerative work) applies.]

[⁵(7) For the purposes of paragraphs (1) and (2), in determining the number of hours for which a person is engaged in work, that number shall include any time allowed to that person by his employer for a meal or for refreshment, but only where that person is, or expects to be, paid earnings in respect of that time.]

AMENDMENTS

1. Income Support (General) Amendment Regulations 1988 (S.I. 1988 No. 663), reg. 4 (April 11, 1988).
2. Income Support (General) Amendment No. 4 Regulations 1988 (S.I. 1988 No. 1445), reg. 3 (September 9, 1988).
3. Income Support (General) Amendment No. 5 Regulations 1988 (S.I. 1988 No. 2022), reg. 3 (December 12, 1988).
4. Income Support (General) Amendment No. 2 Regulations 1989 (S.I. 1989 No. 1323), reg. 3 (October 9, 1989).
5. Income Support (General) Amendment Regulations 1990 (S.I. 1990 No. 547), reg. 4 (April 9, 1990).
6. Income Support (General) Amendment No. 4 Regulations 1991 (S.I. 1991 No. 1559), reg. 3 (April 7, 1992).
7. Income-related Benefits Schemes (Miscellaneous Amendments) (No. 4) Regulations 1993 (S.I. 1993 No. 2119), reg. 3 (October 4, 1993).
8. Income-related Benefits Schemes (Miscellaneous Amendments) Regulations 1995 (S.I. 1995 No. 516), reg. 19 (April 10, 1995).
9. Income-related Benefits Schemes and Social Fund (Miscellaneous Amendments) Regulations 1996 (S.I. 1996 No. 1944), reg. 6(4) (October 7, 1996).

DEFINITIONS

"the Act"—see reg. 2(1).
"date of claim"—*ibid.*
"maternity leave"—*ibid.*
"partner"—*ibid.*

GENERAL NOTE

One of the most significant departures in income support, as compared to supplementary benefit, was the reduction of the limit for remunerative work to 24 hours per week and the application of the test to both the claimant and his partner. Then, from April 1992, the limit was reduced again to 16 hours, which excludes a significant number of part-time workers. Important transitional protection for existing claimants was provided in regs. 22 to 24 of the Income Support (General) Amendment No. 4 Regulations 1991 (see p.486). As part of the same package, the qualification for family credit (and disability working allowance) was reduced to 16 hours per week, but not everyone has children or is disabled.

From October 7, 1996, another important change was made alongside the introduction of JSA. In the case of a partner the limit for remunerative work is now 24 hours or more a week (para. (1A)). It remains 16 or more for the claimant (and for non-dependants: see para. 18 of Sched. 3, and for a child or young person whose earnings are not disregarded: see para. 15 of Sched. 8). The same rules apply for JSA. One consequence of this change is the creation of a "better-off" problem for some claimants. If the clamaint's partner is working between 16 and 24 hours a week they may need to consider whether they will gain more by claiming family credit (or disability working allowance, or earnings top-up in certain areas of the country): see further the notes to reg. 4 of the Family Credit Regulations. Note reg. 6(27) and (28) of the Claims and Payments Regulations. Note also that in October 1999 family credit and disability working allowance are to be replaced by working families' tax credit and disabled person's tax credit respectively: see the 1999 Supplement to this book for further details.

Because income support is normally paid in arrears, the disentitlement applies immediately a person starts remunerative work, regardless of whether wages have been paid or when they will be paid. This situation is specifically mentioned in the Social Fund Guide as one in which a crisis loan might be payable if no other resources are available. The details of the test are therefore important. Note the exceptions in reg. 6, brought in by para. (6).

Paragraph (1)

First note that the test is in terms of work, not employment. Therefore, the precise categorisation of the activities carried out may not be crucial. This is illustrated in two family credit decisions (remunerative work is a qualification for family credit). In *CFC 7/1989* the claimant's husband was working in connection with Moral Re-Armament, a Christian charity, for about 38 hours a week. He received payment by persuading individuals to covenant income to him. He was not employed by Moral Re-Armament or the covenantors, nor did he contract with them on a self-employed basis. But this did not matter, because what he did was undoubtedly work and he was paid for it. In *R(FC) 2/90* both the claimant and her husband were officers of the Salvation Army. It was accepted, following the decision of the Court of Appeal in *Rogers* v. *Booth* [1937] 2 All E.R. 751, that the relationship of officers to the Salvation Army is spiritual, not contractual. Nevertheless, the onerous duties of officers were "work."

Remunerative

Work is remunerative if payment is made for it, or it is done in the expectation of payment. There is a significant difference from the common law test (on which see *R(FIS) 1/83*), because the mere hope of or desire for payment is not the same as expectation (although note that in *CIS 85/1997* the Commissioner comments that he did not see any fundamental distinction between "hope of" and "expectation of" payment). Thus in *CFC 3/1989*, the claimant's husband, who regarded himself as a self-employed writer, but who had not sold any manuscripts and did not anticipate any sales in the next six months, was not in remunerative work. The Commissioner puts forward a rule of thumb, not a binding principle, that for work to be done in the expectation of payment some payment must be expected within 26 weeks of the relevant date. This was based partly on the length of a family credit award, but there clearly should be one dividing line between the income support and family credit systems. In *R(IS) 1/93* the Commissioner holds that the guiding principle on when there is an expectation of payment should be common sense and an appreciation of the realities of the situation. The claimant, another writer, had sent several works to publishers, but had had negligible success in selling anything. She was working "on spec," with only the hope of payment, not an expectation. In *Kevin Smith v. Chief Adjudication Officer* (CA, October 11, 1994) the claimant's partner, who was in receipt of an enterprise allowance, wished to establish herself as an agent for pop groups and spent a lot of time building up contacts in the pop music world. The Court of Appeal, having said that the question is really one of fact, distinguishes between work done to set up a business, which is not done in expectation of payment, and work carried out once the business is established, which it would be reasonable to infer was done in expectation of payment. On the facts of that case the claimant's partner was not engaged in remunerative work. On the other side of the line, see *CIS 434/1994* in which a person who had started an estate agent's business and was working without pay until the business became profitable was held to be in remunerative work.

In *CIS 929/1995* the two or three hours a freelance musician spent practising each day did not count as hours of work for the purposes of reg. 5(1).

In *CIS 815/1992* the claimant's wife worked in a general shop owned by the two of them. For several months she had worked without pay and had no expectation of receiving any in the future because the business was making a loss. The Commissioner holds that the SSAT had been correct in concluding that on the facts she was not in remunerative work. This decision was upheld by the Court of Appeal in *Chief Adjudication Officer v. Ellis* (February 15, 1995). In *Ellis* the Court gives some general guidance on the questions to be considered when deciding whether a person is in remunerative work. In particular, the Court draws a distinction between a person providing a service (such as the claimant carrying on a translation agency in *Perrot v. SBC* [1980] 3 All E.R. 110 where the unprofitability of her business was irrelevant) and the position of a retail shop. The Court points out that the price paid for goods sold in a shop is not payment for the work of the salesman, but the price of the goods sold. Thus simply carrying on a retail business did not necessarily mean that a person was in remunerative work (so *CSIS 39/1994* should not be followed on this point). But if the person was not expecting to make any money the question had to be asked why the shop was being kept open. In this case the answer was clear. The claimant's wife was carrying on the business in the hope of disposing of the goodwill. She was not in remunerative work.

In *R(IS) 5/95* the claimant who was both a director and an employee of a small limited company had also worked for some months without pay, due to financial difficulties. The Commissioner states that it was necessary to consider in relation to each week whether he was working in his capacity as an employee or a director (although the functions of a director of a small private company were quite slight (*R(U) 1/93*, para. 5)). If this work had been done as an employee it was only remunerative if any payment expected was in that capacity (although reg. 42(6) (notional earnings) would also need to be considered). Moreover expectation of payment meant payment for current work. It may be that this is not the case for the self-employed, although the Court of Appeal in *Ellis* states that the question of whether work is done in expectation of payment is to be decided at the time the work is done, not at the end of the year or other accounting period.

The payment must be in return for the work *(R(FIS) 1/86)*, but need not derive from an employer. Thus the payments by covenantors in *CFC 7/1989* (see above) counted. So too did the payments from the Salvation Army in *R(FC) 2/90*, although they were not paid under contract and were aimed at providing for the officers' actual needs. There was a distinction from the maintenance grant paid to a student. Provision for actual needs went beyond mere maintenance. A grant is not in return for work *(R(FIS) 1/86)*, so that students and trainees *(R(FIS) 1/83)* will still not be said to be in remunerative work. The argument that enterprise allowance is paid in return for work was rejected by the Court of Appeal in *Kevin Smith v. Chief Adjudication Officer* (above). The Court holds that it is a payment to enable people to establish themselves in business, not for work. This conclusion was indicated both by the terms of the enterprise allowance scheme and reg. 37(1). If receipt of enterprise allowance by itself meant that a person had to be treated as engaged in remunerative work, the inclusion in reg. 37(1) of enterprise allowance as earnings was unnecessary since the calculation stage envisaged by reg. 37 would never be reached.

A payment in kind will count in the same way as a payment in cash. In *CFC 33/1993* the provision of rent-free accommodation and the payment of gas and electricity bills meant that the claimant's work was done for payment.

Hours of work

If the engagement is for a regular 16 hours or more (24 hours in the case of a partner: para. (1A)), para. (1) seems to be satisfied directly. But para. (1) is silent on what is the appropriate period to look at when determining whether a person is engaged in work for 16 (or 24) hours or more a week. This causes certain difficulties (see below). If the hours fluctuate, averaging must be carried out. Para. (2) says how. Note *R(IS) 8/95* (below) which states that the claimant's hours of work are not fixed at the date of the claim but should be considered week by week.

Engaged in work

It is hours during which the person is engaged in work and is paid (or at least expects payment) which are crucial. The calculation is usually relatively easy for employees. Thus in *CIS 3/1989* the claimant's paid one hour lunch break did not count towards the limit. He was not "engaged in" work for that hour. The precise result is reversed from April 1990, by para. (7), but the principle might apply in other situations. *R(FC) 1/92* suggests that where the nature of the job requires a person to work beyond the contractually specified hours, the longer hours count. But it is not clear just how this translates from the old family credit provision to income support. For the self-employed the test is not of hours costed and charged to a client, but of hours of activities which are essential to the undertaking *(R(FIS) 6/85)*. Thus time spent in preparation, research, doing estimates and accounts, travel for the purposes of the undertaking, keeping a shop open, etc., must all count. But activities carried on merely in the hope, rather than expectation, of payment are not remunerative. The actual hours of work must be considered. In *CIS 815/1992*, although the shop in which the claimant's wife worked was open from 8.30am to 6.30pm Monday to Friday, she only spent three hours a day in it. The rest of the time she was in her home (which was in the same premises), ready to go into the shop if the shop bell rang. The Commissioner expresses the view (without finally deciding the point) that on the particular facts of that case (a small shop with little stock and fewer customers) the hours "on call" may not be hours of work. The decision in *CIS 815/1992* was upheld by the Court of Appeal in *Chief Adjudication Officer v. Ellis* (see above), but the Court of Appeal does not deal with this particular point. But in *CIS 85/1997* the same Commissioner decides that the time spent by a self-employed minicab driver waiting at the cab office for potential customers (which he was not obliged to do) was work done in expectation of payment. This seems somewhat dubious, in that it was not essential to his work for him to spend that time there. However, the decision was upheld by the Court of Appeal (*Kazantzis v. Chief Adjudication Officer, The Times*, June 30, 1999). In *R(IS) 12/95* all the hours that a share fisherman was at sea (including those that he was not on watch or was sleeping) counted. The Commissioner referred to *Suffolk County Council v. Secretary of State for the Environment and another* [1984] I.C.R. 882 in which the House of Lords had distinguished between a regular fireman required to remain in the station while on duty and a retained fireman free to do as he pleases until called upon. The claimant could not do as he pleased during his rest period. He had to stay on the trawler and could be summoned to assist if, for example, there was a storm. In the *Suffolk* case the House of Lords held that a retained fireman's waiting time could not be taken into account in calculating his contractual hours of employment. The claimant in *CIS 85/1997* had attempted to rely on this decision but the Commissioner points out that the circumstances were not analogous. The issue under para. (1) is not whether the claimant was employed during his waiting time but whether he was "at work" during that time.

CIS 514/1990 holds that although recipients of enterprise allowance must undertake to work for at least 36 hours a week in their business, that does not mean that they must automatically be treated as doing so for benefit purposes (see *Kevin Smith v. Chief Adjudication Officer* above on whether enterprise allowance is paid in return for work).

Paragraph (2)
Para. (2) is exceptionally difficult to make sense of. Comprehensive restructuring of reg. 5, as has been carried out on the equivalent family credit provision, is required. The opening words of para. (2) suggest a mechanism for determining the hours worked in all cases, but sub-paras. (a) and (b) only apply in restricted circumstances (confirmed in *CJSA 3816/1997*). In particular, a person who works for a regular number of contracted hours seems to fall outside para. (2) and inside para. (1). The difficulties in operating para. (2) are compounded by the fact that reg. 5 makes no provision as to the period over which a claimant is to be considered to be engaged in work for the number of hours calculated under it (see below under *Term-time workers*).

Sub-paragraph (a)
Sub-para. (a) can only apply where no recognisable cycle has been established. An obvious situation is where a person has just started work. But if a person works a contractually-set number of hours, with no overtime, is this a case where there is no "cycle" at all (so that sub-para. (*a*) applies) or is it an immediately recognisable cycle (so that para. (1) applies)? The Commissioner's definition in *CIS 493/1993* of a "cycle" as a "recurrent round" which contains within it a complete description of the work done, the end of one cycle being the beginning of another, is helpful but does not answer this kind of question. In *R(IS) 8/95* the Commissioner emphasises that sub-para. (a) refers to where no recognised cycle has been *established*. Thus it applies not only when employment has just begun, but also when evidence of past hours of work does not reflect the current position (*e.g.* where there has been a change of hours), so that what has to be considered is what is likely to happen in the future (see below).

CIS 11228/1995 concerned a school bus driver who had worked 20 hours a week during term times since December 1993. He had no written contract of employment and was paid only for each journey he made. His claim for income support for the Easter holidays in 1995 was refused on the ground that he had a recognisable cycle of work over a year and that applying paras. (2)(b)(i) and (3B) he was in remunerative work. But the Commissioner decides that no recognisable cycle of work had been established by April 1995. In *R(IS) 15/94* (see below) it had been held that a yearly cycle had been established after about 18 months. But the school receptionist with whom that case was concerned had a written contract of employment setting out the future pattern of her work. In this case, in the absence of any document dealing with the claimant's terms and conditions of employment, any cycle could only be discerned by looking at the actual past pattern of work. In the

Commissioner's view, where there had only been 15 months of work, this was not enough on its own to establish the essential element of recurrence in any yearly cycle. The claim therefore had to be considered under the forward-looking approach of sub-para. (a). It should be treated as made for a definite period (the Easter school holidays), during which time the claimant was expected to do no work. Accordingly, he was not engaged in remunerative work for this period.

If sub-para. (a) does apply, the test is of the number of hours the person is expected to work, or be paid for a meal-break (para. (7)). Could this test go beyond contracted hours of work? If the hours are likely to fluctuate, an average is to be taken. There is no provision for the period over which the average is to be calculated, so that presumably whatever period is most appropriate to the circumstances must be chosen. (See *CIS 11228/1995* above and *R(IS) 8/95* below). It seems that only hours of actual work should count in the averaging *(R(FIS) 2/ 82* and see *R(IS) 7/96* in which the Commissioner held that the notional hours attributable to the claimant's six weeks' paid holiday were not to be included in the total number of hours worked during the cycle under sub-para. (b)(i). He points out that para. (1) defines remunerative work as work "in (not *for*) which a person is engaged"). On the effect of para. (3) see *R(IS) 15/94, CIS 14661/1996, CIS 521/1994, CJSA 3816/1997, CIS 1118/1997, CIS 3216/1997 and CJSA 3218/1997* in the discussion under *"Term-time only workers"*.

Sub-paragraph (b)

Sub-para. (b) can only apply if the hours worked do fluctuate. There is enormous difficulty in some cases in determining the period over which fluctuation should be tested. For example, school ancillary workers may have contracts for absolutely regular hours during term-time, with no work required during school holidays. It is arguable that this is not an example of fluctuating hours, but of periods of work for non-fluctuating hours followed by periods of no work. The person would then be engaged in work for the regular number of hours in term-time and not so engaged outside term-time. But this has not been the approach taken by the Commissioners (see below under *"Term-time only workers"*). Note also para. (3B) (see below).

Sub-para. (b)(ii) applies if the hours fluctuate but there is no recognisable cycle, in which case an average is taken, normally over the five weeks before the week of claim. An alternative period should only be used if it can be demonstrated that it will produce a more accurate average *(R(FIS) 1/81* and *R(FIS) 2/83)*, but not, for example, because there is no evidence of the hours worked in one of those weeks *(R(IS) 12/95)*.

R(IS) 8/95 contains a useful analysis of how the various rules in para. (2) can operate. The claimant who had been working a regular 37-hour week went onto a period of short time, working one week on and one week off. There was the possibility that he could be called in on non-working weeks. The claimant therefore argued that his claim should be considered on a week by week basis under para. (2)(a). However, this was rejected by the Commissioner, who decided that the claim was to be treated as made for an indefinite period under reg. 17(1) of the Claims and Payments Regulations (see the notes to reg. 17) and then went on to consider how para. (2) applied in this situation. In his view, para. (2)(a) looked forward and was directed to the situation where there was no (or insufficient) evidence of recent working hours on which to decide the working hours for the week in question. Para. (2)(b) applied where there was such evidence, and that evidence showed a fluctuation of hours. The point at which the test shifted from a forward-looking one under sub-para. (a) to a backward-looking one under sub-para. (b) depended on the circumstances. A claimant's hours of work had to be considered week by week throughout the period in issue and were not fixed at the date of claim. The result was that sub-para. (a) applied at the beginning of the claim when it was expected that the claimant's hours would fluctuate; the appropriate period for averaging the hours at that time was two weeks. When there had been two two-week cycles of one week on and one week off sub-para. (b)(i) came into play. When later the recognisable cycle was broken because the claimant had less weeks off, sub-para. (b)(ii) applied. On any test the minimum hours that the claimant was working were more than 16 a week and so he was engaged in remunerative work throughout the period.

Term-time only workers

There have been quite a number of decisions on the application of para. (2) to school ancillary workers. It has generally been assumed (contrary to the interpretation suggested above) that, unless a recognised cycle has not been established so that sub-para. (a) applies (for an example see *CIS 11228/1995* above), school ancillary workers who only work during term-time are covered by sub-para. (b)(i). See, for example, *CIS 261/1990, R(IS) 15/94* and *R(IS) 7/96*. In *CIS 261/1990* (unstarred), it was assumed that sub-para. (b) applies in such circumstances but the contrary argument was not put and the actual decision was on another ground. In *R(IS) 7/96* the claimant worked 20 hours a week during term-time (38 weeks) and was paid for an additional six weeks holiday.

During the remaining eight weeks of the year she neither worked nor was paid. The Commissioner decides that over the academic year her hours fluctuated and so she came within sub-para. (b)(i). He follows *R(IS) 15/94* (and *CIS 261/1990*) in holding that in the case of a school ancillary worker the appropriate cycle is one year. But in *R(IS) 7/96*, unlike *R(IS) 15/94*, the claimant's hours did not fluctuate during term-time. The Commissioner in *R(IS) 7/96* does not seem to have considered the possibility that sub-para. (b) might not apply at all in these circumstances. In *R(IS) 15/94* the claimant was a school receptionist whose contractual hours of work were 22 hours per week during 'term-time only' but her actual hours of work fluctuated each week. She was not paid during the school holidays, although she did work on occasional days during the holidays when asked to do so. The Commissioner applies sub-para. (b)(i), holding that the recognisable cycle was a yearly one and that the school holidays were included in the cycle as "periods in which the person does no work" (disagreeing with *CIS 261/1990*). A similar approach to averaging the hours worked over the cycle was taken in *R(IS) 7/96* (see the 1997 edition of this book for further details of these decisions). This approach worked to the claimant's advantage in establishing entitlement to income support, but it was a disadvantage in family credit terms. The policy intention apparently was that benefit entitlement should be based on the average hours worked during term-time and so para. (3B) was introduced (see below).

It is important to note that in all three of these decisions the claimants' contracts of employment continued throughout the year; they did not have a separate one for each term. The argument against the application of sub-para. (b) will be much stronger if the person's contract terminates at the end of each period of work. See *CU 121/1994* which concerned a lecturer whose appointment was for Hilary Term 1994 to Trinity Term 1995 inclusive, but whom the college stated was employed during term-time only. She was paid for the hours she taught, plus a retainer of £200 in each of the first two terms. She was free to take other employment during the vacations. The Commissioner accepts that on the facts her contract terminated at the end of each term. He followed *R(U) 7/68* which held that "terminated" in reg. 7(1)(h) of the Social Security (Unemployment, Sickness and Invalidity Benefit) Regulations 1983 did not mean "finally discharged without any intention of resuming the relationship of employer and employee on the next available opportunity", but had its natural and ordinary meaning in that as soon as the contract terminated so did the employment.

Clearly whether or not there is a continuing contract of employment will depend on the facts in each case. If a person's contract does terminate at the end of each term, she should be able to claim income support (or JSA) during the school holidays (see the *Adjudication Officer's Guide*, para. 25195). In these circumstances she is not engaged in work outside term-time and so sub-para. (b) (and para. (3B)) does not apply at all, and the case has to be determined under the primary rule in para. (1). The same should apply to other employees who have periods of work interspersed with periods of no work (and no continuing contract of employment), for example, seasonal workers.

However, on the basis of some (but not all, see *CSJSA 395/1998* below) of the recent authorities, even if a school ancillary or similar worker's contract of employment subsists throughout the year, she will be eligible for income support (or more probably JSA) during the school holidays. But the routes taken by the Commissioners have varied and often conflict, at least to some degree. Note that some of the decisions discussed below relate to periods before the introduction of para. (3B) in April 1995.

CIS 14661/1996 exposed the effect of para. (3) in these circumstances (but see *CIS 1118/1997, CIS 3216/1997 and CJSA 3218/1997* below, in which the Commissioner considers that his decision in *CIS 14661/1996* was wrongly decided on the legislation as it existed before the introduction of para. (3B)). In *CIS 14661/1996* the claimant was a catering assistant at a University who worked during term-time only. Her claim for income support for the period of the 1992 Christmas vacation was refused on the ground that she was absent from work by reason of a recognised, customary or other holiday. The Commissioner refers to *C.W.U. 7/48* and *C.W.U. 8/48* (both unemployment bene-fit cases but the same rules for deciding whether the absence was by reason of a recognised or customary holiday applied: see *R(SB) 7/84*) which had held that there was a distinction between the position of school ancillary staff and teachers and had recognised that holidays of a length appropri-ate to one class were inappropriate to the other (see also *R(U) 17/62* in relation to university staff). Although working patterns had changed, in the Commissioner's view, this distinction remained. School canteen assistants, for example, did not work during school holidays and were paid at a low hourly rate which was often linked to that of other local authority workers who expected to work for many more weeks each year. Teachers, on the other hand, were paid a professional salary and often had to carry out a substantial amount of work in the holidays. It was not unreasonable to regard teachers as "on holiday" during those parts of the school holidays when they were not actually working, but it was simply unrealistic to regard a catering assistant as being on holiday for 16 weeks in any year. The result was that apart from the Christmas period which on the facts was a holiday for the claimant, she was not to be treated as in remunerative work under para. (3) for the remainder of the vacation as this was a period of lay-off imposed by the employer and not holiday. *CIS 14661/1996* has been followed in *CJSA 3816/1997* and a similar view was taken in *CIS 521/ 1994*. It therefore seems to be accepted that dicta in *R(IS) 15/94* and *R(IS) 7/96* to the effect that the whole of the school holidays are "recognised, customary or other" holidays for school ancillary workers are wrong (*C.W.U. 7/48, C.W.U. 8/48* and *R(U) 17/62* were not referreed to in those cases).

CIS 521/1994 concerned an assistant in a school who worked for 40 weeks a year and who was refused income support for the 1993 summer holiday. The Commissioner considered that since the claimant was not "at work" during the summer break, it was first necessary to decide whether she was to be treated as engaged in remunerative work under para. (3). It was only if a person was to be so treated during the week or weeks for which income support was claimed that it was necessary to consider para. (2). Having regard to the nature of the claimant's contract of employment, it was clear that the summer break was not a period of holiday in relation to the claimant herself. Thus para. (3) did not apply and she was not to be regarded as in remunerative work during the school summer holidays.

The Commissioner's approach in *CIS 521/1994* is a little surprising and does not seem to be consistent with his own decision in *R(IS) 15/94*. See para. 14 of *R(IS) 15/94* in which he held that para. (3) did *not* come into play until it had first been established under the terms of paras. (1) and (2) that the work from which the claimant was absent was normally carried on for at least 16 hours a week.

CIS 521/1994 is not followed in *CJSA 3816/1997*, which concerned the similar (although not identical) provisions in the JSA Regulations (regs. 51 and 52; reg. 51(1) is the equivalent of para. (1) and reg. 51(2) the equivalent of paras. (2) and (3B), although note that, unlike para. (3B) which only applies for the purposes of para. (2)(b)(i), reg. 51(2)(c) contains a separate rule which is not dependent on whether or not the person's hours fluctuate). The claimant in *CJSA 3816/1997* was a laboratory assistant at a school who worked for 42 weeks a year. She made a claim for JSA in respect of the half-term holiday in February 1997. The Commissioner holds that reg. 51(1) did not operate independently from the remainder of the regulation. In the situations covered by reg. 51(2), that paragraph had to be considered and applied in order to apply reg. 51(1). The Commissioner further held that where reg. 52(1) (the equivalent of para. (3)) applied, there was no need to refer (again) to the calculation provisions of reg. 51(2), since the effect of reg. 52(1) would be to treat the person as in remunerative work. This approach to the order in which the various rules in regs. 51 and 52 are to be applied is consistent with *R(IS) 15/94* and it is suggested that it is to be preferred to that of the Commissioner in *CIS 521/1994* (and see *CIS 1118/1997, CIS 3216/1997 and CJSA 3218/1997* which agrees with the criticism made in *CJSA 3816/1997* of *CIS 521/1994*).

However, the Commissioner in *CJSA 3816/1997* did agree with *CIS 521/1994* and *CIS 14661/ 1996* that for the person to be deemed to be engaged in remunerative work by reason of a holiday, the holiday had to be one that was for the claimant herself "a recognised, customary or other holiday" and not just a holiday in the general sense.

The Commissioner in *CJSA 3816/1997* then went on to consider how the rule in reg. 51(2)(c) (the equivalent of para. (3B)) was to be applied. He pointed out that reg. 51(2)(c) was concerned with the calculation of hours of work but did not (as para. (3B) does not) state the period over which the claimant was to be regarded as being engaged in work for those hours. However, the fact that reg. 52(1) deemed a person to be engaged in remunerative work while "on holiday" indicated that a person was not to be considered as engaged in work throughout the whole of the yearly cycle. Thus the most sensible interpretation seemed to be that the claimant was not to be regarded as engaged in remunerative work for any period during which (i) she did no work and (ii) she was not treated as being in remunerative work under reg. 52(1). Further, as the calculation was performed in weeks and reg. 1(3) of the JSA Regulations defined "week" as a period of seven days, the periods for which the claimant was not engaged in remunerative work were any periods of seven days in which she did no work at all.

In *CIS 1118/1997, CIS 3216/1997* and *CJSA 3218/1997* the Commissioner agrees with *CJSA 3816/1997* that reg. 5 (as is the case under the equivalent JSA Regulations) makes no provision as to the period over which a claimant is to be considered to be engaged in work for the hours calculated under paras. (1) and (2). But in his view, where the number of hours had to be averaged over a period that included periods of no work, the resulting decision as to whether the person was, or was not, in renumerative work, applied to the whole period (subject to the exception in para. (3A)), including the periods of no work. He considered that this followed from *R(IS) 8/95* in which the Commissioner had assumed that the claimant was to be treated as engaged in remunerative work throughout the whole two week cycle and in his view that decision was to be preferred to *CIS 521/1994* and his own decision in *CIS 14661/1996*. However, although he considered that *CIS 521/1994* and *CIS 14661/1996* had been wrongly decided on the form of reg. 5 as it existed at the time material to those cases, para. (3B) had since been introduced to reverse the effect of *R(IS) 15/94* by excluding school holidays in calculating a person's hours of work. It followed that a decision that a person was engaged in remunerative work because of the number of hours worked during term-time would thus only apply during the term-time periods. Therefore, unless para. (3) or (5) applied, a person to whom para. (3B) applied, was not to be regarded as engaged in remunerative work during school holidays. This was effectively the conclusion reached in *CJSA 3816/1997*, although by a different path, and in the Commissioner's view the approach in *CJSA 3816/1997* to the JSA equivalent of para. (3B) was again inconsistent with *R(IS) 8/95*. The Commissioner also points out that the consequence of his approach was that para. (3) would not apply to days of actual holiday falling within the school holidays or other periods of non-work as it only came into play in respect of holidays within a period of remunerative employment *(R(IS) 15/94)*. In his view, such days of holiday should therefore be ignored.

The Commissioner in *CIS 1118/1998, CIS 3216/1997* and *CJSA 3218/1997* also dealt with the issue of pay received during the school holidays. The claimant in *CIS 3216/1997* and *CJSA 3218/1997* worked for approximately 20 hours during term-time and was paid on a monthly basis depending on the hours that he had worked that month. He had no entitlement to paid holidays. The Commissioner points out that since he was not in remunerative work during the school holidays (including the half-term holidays) but his employment had not terminated, the effect of para. 1(b) of Sched. 8 was that all his earnings fell to be disregarded (he had no entitlement to holiday pay or retainer so the exceptions to the rule in para. 1(b) did not apply).

The claimant's wife in *CIS 1118/1997* had two contracts of employment. Under the first she worked for 23 hours a week during term-time. She was paid for 44 weeks of the year made up of 38 term-time weeks, four weeks annual leave and two weeks "statutory" holidays. Her salary was paid in 12 equal monthly instalments. Under the second, she worked for $6\frac{1}{4}$ hours a week during term-time and was paid weekly. In addition, she was paid four weeks annual leave, two weeks "statutory" holidays and a retainer for eight weeks. The Commissioner decides that there was no income to be taken into account under the first contract as it was not possible to identify any particular period of 6 weeks as being a holiday for the claimant's wife (note the effect of para. (5) if it had been possible to identify a particular period or periods in the school holidays as a holiday for the claimant herself). In addition, the only payment from her second employment that counted was the retainer as this employment was part-time (see para. 2 of Sched. 8). In the Commissioner's view, this employment had to be viewed separately for the purpose of applying the rules in Sched. 8, although it might have been necessary to aggregate the hours of her two jobs if all the earnings under the first contract had not been disregarded under para. 1 of that Schedule.

However, in *CSJSA 395/1998* (and a number of other cases heard at the same time) the Commissioner disagrees that a person was only to be taken as engaged in remunerative work during that part of the cycle of work that had been taken into account in establishing her average hours of work. In his view, the cycle referred to in reg. 51(2)(c) of the JSA Regulations (the equivalent of para. (3B)) was not broken by school holidays or similar vacations. To decide otherwise would mean that it would lose its character as a cycle of work in the course of a year. The fact that periods in which no work was done were to be taken out for the purpose of calculating hours of work did not have the consequence that those periods became independent of the cycle of work and subject to the deeming provisions in reg. 52.

The Commissioner in *CSJSA 395/1998* points out that his interpretation results in there being no anomaly between workers referred to in reg. 51(2)(c) (para. (3B)) and other short-time workers covered by reg. 51(2)(b)(i) (para. (2)(b)(i)). But the way the legislation is drafted would seem to indicate that these two groups are to be treated differently; this is particularly the case in JSA where the rule covering school ancillary and similar workers operates independently (see the note to reg. 51 of the JSA Regulations). Moreover, the substance of the rules for these two groups *is* different: for workers within para. (2)(b)(i) periods of no-work are included in averaging the hours of work over the cycle but for school ancillary and similar workers such periods are excluded. Furthermore, the effect of the decision in *CSJSA 395/1998* is to equate the cycle of work with the period for which the person is to be regarded as engaged in remunerative work but it is suggested that this is not what reg. 5 achieves. Reg. 5 is concerned with calculating a person's hours of work but is silent as to the period over which the result of that calculation is to apply. It is suggested that the relevance of a recognisable cycle of work for the purposes of paras. (2)(b)(i) and (3B) (reg. 51(2)(i) and (2)(c) of the JSA Regulations) is that the length of the cycle provides the period (subject to certain inclusions/exclusions) over which the hours of work are to be averaged. If the result of the averaging is that a person's hours of work are 16 (or 24 in the case of a partner) or more, reg. 5 (regs. 51 and 52 of the

JSA Regulations) does not have the consequence that the person is to be regarded as engaged in remunerative work throughout the whole cycle (see *CJSA 3816/1997*).

It would certainly seem right that the decision as to whether the person is, or is not, in remunerative work should apply to all the periods within the cycle that have been included in the averaging. But does it necessarily follow that a person will not count as in remunerative work during periods that have been excluded (unless para. (3) or (5) apply)? Although the approach taken in *CIS 1118/1997, CIS 3216/1997 and CJSA 3218/1997* is attractively straightforward, it is suggested that it does not pay sufficient attention to the fact that for para. (3B) to apply there has to be a yearly cycle of work. It is therefore suggested that where periods during the cycle have been excluded under para. (3B) in calculating the hours of work, such periods *do* have to be looked at separately for the very reason that they have been excluded from the calculation. The other provisions of reg. 5, in particular para. (3), need to be considered in relation to these periods and so following *CIS 14661/1996* and *CJSA 3816/1997* school ancillary workers should not be regarded as in remunerative work during school holidays, unless it is a period of holiday in relation to them. It is suggested that this approach avoids having to ignore days of actual holiday during the periods of no-work (which is a consequence of the decision in *CIS 1118/1997, CIS 3216/1997 and CJSA 3218/1997)*, although note that if no particular part of the school holidays can be identified as a holiday for the claimant, the claimant will not be disentitled for any part of the school holidays, even if her pay includes an element of holiday pay (see *R(IS) 7/96* and *CIS 14661/1996)*. It is also respectfully suggested that the fact that certain periods in the cycle are considered separately does not "break the cycle of work" for these purposes to any further extent than has already been effected by excluding those periods when averaging the hours of work.

Thus the recent caselaw in this area is somewhat confusing and contradictory. Note that the AO has been granted leave to appeal to the Court of Appeal in *CIS 1118/1997, CIS 3216/1997 and CJSA 3218/1997* and that the claimants in *CSJSA 395/1998* and *CSJSA 390/1998* (together with *CSJSA 23/1999* in which the Commissioner applied his decision in *CSJSA 395/1998)* have been given leave to appeal to the Court of Session. It is to be hoped that both Courts adopt a similar approach so that the position in relation to these workers is finally clarified.

Self-employment

In the case of a self-employed worker who has periods of work interspersed with periods of no work the position is less clear. Para. (1) does not state what is the appropriate period to look at when determining whether a person is engaged in remunerative work. Each case will therefore depend to some extent on its own facts. If, for example, a person carries on a business for six months of the year and does no work in connection with that business for the rest of the year, it must be arguable that the period to be looked at is the six months when his business is dormant and that during that time he is not engaged in work. This is the approach taken in the *Adjudication Officer's Guide*, paras. 25151–2. However, this is not the conclusion reached by the Commissioner in *CIS 493/1993*. The claimant ran a guest house with a six-month season and did a minimal amount of work during the closed season. The claimant had argued that there were two cycles, or periods, one in which he worked more than 16 hours every week and the second during which he was not engaged in work at all. The Commissioner states that the first question was whether there was a recognisable cycle, and the second was whether the claimant's hours fluctuated within that cycle. The basis of this approach seems to have been that para. (2) is to be used to determine the number of hours for which a person is engaged in work. But para. (2) does not provide a rule for deciding the number of hours worked per week in all cases. It applies in the circumstances described in the opening words of sub-paras. (a) and (b) *(R(IS) 8/95)*. It is suggested that the first question is what is the appropriate period for deciding whether a claimant is engaged in remunerative work, which will depend on the facts of each case, before going on to consider whether the particular circumstances referred to in para. (2) apply. Note that para. (3B) would not seem to apply to the self-employed (see below).

Paragraph (3)

A person is deemed to be in remunerative work, and so excluded from entitlement under s.124(1)(c) of the Contributions and Benefits Act (1986 Act, s.20(3)(c)), in these circumstances. Para. (3) does not come into play until it has been established under the terms of paras. (1) (2) and (3B) (as appropriate) that the work from which the person is absent is normally carried on for at least 16 hours a week (24 in the case of a partner from October 1996) *(R(IS) 15/94, CIS 1118/1997, CIS 3216/1997 and CJSA 3218/1997*, although *CIS 521/1994* is to the contrary).

Absence for any kind of holiday, not just recognised or customary holidays (on which see *R(SB) 7/84)*, comes under para. (3). However, as *CIS 14661/1996* emphasises, a distinction must be drawn between holidays and periods of non-working imposed by the employer. What has to be considered is whether the holidays in issue are holidays in relation to the claimant. For discussion of the position of school ancillary and similar workers see under *"Term-time only workers"*. If a contract of employment comes to an end on the completion of a period of work the following period cannot be a holiday *(R(U) 2/87)* or a period of absence from work. The category of absence without good cause is an open one. Absence due to incapacity for work through illness or disability will obviously be for a good cause. Such absence is now specifically covered by para. (3A).

Paragraph (3A)
This confirms that a person who is away sick or a woman on maternity leave is not treated as in remunerative work. The effect is that there is no automatic exclusion from entitlement under s.124(1)(c) of the Contributions and Benefits Act (1986 Act, s.20 (3)(c)) but any pay will be taken into account as income (regs. 35(2) and 40(4); note the disregards in paras. 1, 4 and 4A of Sched. 9). The definition of maternity leave in reg. 2(1) means that a woman counts as on maternity leave only if she has either a statutory or a contractual right to return to work. Prior to October 4, 1993, the same result could be achieved by treating such absences as for a good cause (see para. (3)). This will continue to be the case for absence due to paternity leave or other leave (*e.g.* compassionate leave).

Paragraph (3B)
This provides that if a person has an annual cycle of work which includes periods of no work, for example, school holidays, such periods are ignored in averaging hours of work. This rule was introduced in response to the approach taken by *R(IS) 15/94* and *R(IS) 7/96* to the calculation of school ancillary workers' hours of work (see above). A similar rule was introduced for family credit and disability working allowance (and housing and council tax benefit) at the same time. The effect of para. (3B) is to make it easier for workers like school ancillary workers to qualify for family credit (or from October 1996 earnings top-up if they live in an area of the country where this is being piloted), but not income support. However, see the discussion under the heading "Term-time only workers" as regards claims for income support (or JSA) from such workers during the school holidays.
The wording of para. (3B) seems to indicate that it only applies to employees, and not the self-employed. Note that this paragraph will not apply if a recognisable cycle of work has not yet been established (see *CIS 11228/1995* above). Note also that in *CJSA 3816/1997* (which concerned the similar provision in the JSA Regulations, reg. 51(2)(c)) the Commissioner considered that for this rule to apply the person must do no work in the holidays. *CIS 11228/1995* also holds that the meaning of "other place of employment" is not limited by the preceding words, so that para. (3B) applies to *any* place of employment, including schools and other educational establishments.

Paragraph (4)
See the notes to s.126 of the Contributions and Benefits Act (1986 Act, s.23).

Paragraph (5)
Where income payments in lieu of notice or remuneration are paid or (within four weeks of termination) holiday pay, the person is treated as in remunerative work for the period covered. See regs. 29 and 31.

Paragraph (7)
Paid meal or refreshment breaks count in the calculation of the hours for which a person is engaged in work.

Persons not treated as engaged in remunerative work

6. A person shall not be treated as engaged in [² remunerative work in so far as—]
[³(a) he is mentally or physically disabled, and by reason of that disability—
    (i) his earnings are reduced to 75 per cent. or less of what a person without that disability and working the same number of hours would reasonably be expected to earn in that employment or in comparable employment in that area; or

(ii) his number of hours of work are 75 per cent. or less of what a person without that disability would reasonably be expected to undertake in that employment or in comparable employment in that area.]

(b) he is engaged in child minding in his home;

(c) he is engaged by a charity or [⁷voluntary organisation [⁸- -],] or is a volunteer where the only payment received by him or due to be paid to him, is a payment which is to be disregarded under regulation 40(2) and paragraph 2 of Schedule 9 (sums to be disregarded in the calculation of income other than earnings);

(d) he is engaged on a scheme for which a training allowance is being paid; [⁴ ...]

(e) subject to regulation 5(4) [² and (5)] (persons treated as engaged in remunerative work) he is a person to whom section 23 of the Act [SSCBA, s.126] (trade disputes) applies [¹ or in respect of whom section 20(3) of the Act [SSCBA, s.124(1)] (conditions of entitlement to income support) has effect as modified by section 23A(b) of the Act [SSCBA, s.127(b)] (effect of return to work)]; [⁴ ...]

[⁹(f) he is a person to whom paragraph 4 of Schedule 1B applies;]

[⁶(g) he is in employment, and—

(i) lives in, or is temporarily absent from, a residential care home, a nursing home or residential accommodation, and either

(ii) his, or his partner's, applicable amount falls to be calculated in accordance with Part I of Schedule 4 (applicable amounts of persons in residential care and nursing homes) or, as the case may be, paragraphs 9, 10 to 10D, 13, 16 or 18 of Schedule 7 (applicable amounts in special cases), or

(iii) he or his partner satisfies the conditions specified in paragraph 2A(2) of Part I of Schedule 2 (conditions for entitlement to a residential allowance);]

[⁴(h) he is engaged in any one of the employments mentioned in heads (a) to (d) of sub-paragraph (1) of paragraph 7 of Schedule 8 (which relates to persons serving as firemen, in coastal rescue activities etc); [⁵ ...]

(j) he is performing his duties as a councillor, and for this purpose "councillor" has the same meaning as in paragraph 2(6) of Schedule 8 to the Social Security Act 1989;][⁵ or

(k) he is engaged in caring for a person who is accommodated with him by virtue of arrangements made under any of the provisions referred to in paragraph 26 [⁷or in accordance with paragraph 27] of Schedule 9 (sums to be disregarded in the calculation of income other than earnings) and is in receipt of any payment specified in [⁷those paragraphs].]

AMENDMENTS

1. Income Support (General) Amendment Regulations 1988 (S.I. 1988 No. 663), reg. 5 (April 11, 1988).

2. Income Support (General) Amendment No. 4 Regulations 1988 (S.I. 1988 No. 1445), reg. 4 (September 12, 1988).

3. Income Support (General) Amendment No. 4 Regulations 1991 (S.I. 1991 No. 1559), reg. 4 (October 7, 1991).

4. Income Support (General) Amendment Regulations 1992 (S.I. 1992 No. 468), reg. 2 (April 6, 1992).

5. Income-related Benefits Schemes (Miscellaneous Amendments) (No. 3) Regulations 1992 (S.I. 1992 No. 2155), reg. 13 (October 5, 1992).

6. Social Security Benefits (Miscellaneous Amendments) Regulations 1993 (S.I. 1993 No. 518), reg. 5 (April 1, 1993).

7. Income-related Benefits Schemes (Miscellaneous Amendments) (No. 5) Regulations 1994 (S.I. 1994 No. 2139), reg. 23 (October 3, 1994).

8. Income-related Benefits Schemes (Miscellaneous Amendments) Regulations 1995 (S.I. 1995 No. 516), reg. 20 (April 10, 1995).

9. Income Support (General) (Jobseeker's Allowance Consequential Amendments) Regulations 1996 (S.I. 1996 No. 206), reg. 6 (October 7, 1996).

DEFINITIONS

"the Act"—see reg. 2(1).
"remunerative work"—*ibid.*
"training allowance"—*ibid.*
"voluntary organisation"—*ibid.*

GENERAL NOTE

These categories must be deemed not to be in remunerative work for the time engaged in these activities, although the "not" could be better placed. The effect is that there is not an automatic exclusion from entitlement under s.124(1)(c) of the Contributions and Benefits Act (1986 Act, s.20(3)(c)). Any earnings from employment must still be taken into account as income. Most of the categories are self-explanatory.

The previous form of para. (a) made the test for the disabled a 75 per cent. reduction in earning capacity. The new form splits the test into two alternatives. The first, in sub-para. (i), compares the claimant's earnings with what a non-disabled person doing the same job for the same hours would earn. The second, in sub-para. (ii), compares the hours worked with what a non-disabled person would do in the same job. In either case, if the claimant falls below 75 per cent. of the comparison level he is deemed not to be engaged in remunerative work.

It was thought that most of those assisted by the old form of para. (a) would continue to be assisted by the new form, but there is a saving provision in regs. 22 to 24 of the Income Support (General) Amendment No. 4 Regulations 1991 (see p. 485) for those who lost out.

Para. (b) deems a person who is childminding in her own home not to be in remunerative work. However, there is no specific provision in Sched. 1B to enable childminders to qualify for income support. If a claimant who is a childminder does not come within any other paragraph of Sched. 1B, it may be possible to argue that para. 3 applies (looking after a child whose parent is temporarily absent from home). This would be along the lines that a parent who is out at work is absent from home on a temporary basis. Para. 3 does not seem to require that the person should be looking after the child all the time; as long as this is done on a regular basis this should suffice.

Under para. (c), para. 2 of Sched. 9 refers to payments solely of expenses to volunteers or people working for charitable or voluntary bodies. A volunteer is someone who without any legal obligation performs a service for another person without expectation of payment (*R(1S)12/92*).

Under para. (d), training allowances are most commonly paid to people on Work Based Training for Young People (in Scotland "Skillseekers"), which has replaced Youth Training, Modern Apprenticeships, etc.

Under para. (e), reg. 5(4) deems those in trade disputes to be in remunerative work for the first seven days of stoppage and reg. 5(5) deems those who have received holiday pay or payments in lieu of notice or remuneration to be in remunerative work for the period covered.

Para. (g) deems residents in residential care or nursing homes (defined in reg. 19(3)) or residential accommodation (defined in reg. 21(3)), or who are only temporaily absent from such accommodation, not to be engaged in remunerative work. The reference to Sched. 7 is to the paragraphs dealing with people who are in residential accommodation or who are temporarily in any of the three types of accommodation.

Under para. (j), the definition of "councillor" is—

"(a) in relation to England and Wales, a member of a London borough council, a county council, a district council, a parish or community council, the Common Council of the City of London or the Council of the Isles of Scilly; and

(b) in relation to Scotland, a member of a regional, islands or district council."

Under para. (k) foster-parents who receive statutory payments for fostering, or people receiving payments for providing temporary care in their home, are deemed not to be in remunerative work by reason of those payments.

Meaning of employment

7.—[¹. . .]

AMENDMENT

1. Income Support (General) (Jobseeker's Allowance Consequential Amendments) Regulations 1996 (S.I. 1996 No. 206), reg. 28 and Sched. 3 (October 7, 1996).

Persons not required to be available for employment

8.—[¹ . . .]

AMENDMENT

1. Income Support (General) (Jobseeker's Allowance Consequential Amendments) Regulations 1996 (S.I. 1996 No. 206), reg. 28 and Sched. 3 (October 7, 1996).

Persons treated as available for employment

9.—[¹ . . .]

AMENDMENT

1. Income Support (General) (Jobseeker's Allowance Consequential Amendments) Regulations 1996 (S.I. 1996 No. 206), reg. 28 and Sched. 3 (October 7, 1996).

Circumstances in which claimants are not to be treated as available for employment

10.—[¹ . . .]

AMENDMENT

1. Income Support (General) (Jobseeker's Allowance Consequential Amendments) Regulations 1996 (S.I. 1996 No. 206), reg. 28 and Sched. 3 (October 7, 1996).

[¹Actively seeking employment

10A.—[² . . .].]

AMENDMENTS

1. Income Support (General) Amendment No. 2 Regulations 1989 (S.I. 1989 No. 1323), reg. 6 (October 9, 1989).
2. Income Support (General) (Jobseeker's Allowance Consequential Amendments) Regulations 1996 (S.I. 1996 No. 206), reg. 28 and Sched. 3 (October 7, 1996).

Registration for employment

11.—[¹ . . .]

AMENDMENT

1. Income Support (General) (Jobseeker's Allowance Consequential Amendments) Regulations 1996 (S.I. 1996 No. 206), reg. 28 and Sched. 3 (October 7, 1996).

[¹Relevant Education

12.—(1) For the purposes of these Regulations a child or young person is to be treated as receiving relevant education if, and only if—
(a) he is not receiving advanced education; but
(b) he is receiving full-time education for the purposes of section 2 of the

Child Benefit Act 1975 [SSCBA, s.142] (meaning of child) or, as the case may be, he is treated as a child for the purposes of that section.

(2) For the purposes of this regulation "receiving advanced education" means participating in any course (whether full-time or part-time)—

(a) leading to a postgraduate degree or comparable qualification, a first degree or comparable qualification, a diploma of higher education, a higher national diploma, [²a higher national diploma or higher national certificate of either the Business & [³Technology] Education Council] or the Scottish Vocational Education Council or a teaching qualification; or

(b) any other course which is a course of a standard above ordinary national diploma, [²a national diploma or national certificate of either the Business & [³Technology] Education Council or the Scottish Vocational Education Council], a general certificate of education (advanced level), a Scottish certificate of education [²(higher level)] or a Scottish certificate of sixth year studies.]

AMENDMENTS

1. Income Support (General) Amendment Regulations 1990 (S.I. 1990 No. 547), reg. 5 (April 9, 1990).

2. Income-related Benefits Schemes (Miscellaneous Amendments) (No. 3) Regulations 1992 (S.I. 1992 No. 2155), reg. 14 (October 5, 1992).

3. Income-related Benefits Schemes (Miscellaneous Amendments) (No. 4) Regulations 1993 (S.I. 1993 No. 2119), reg. 4 (October 4, 1993).

DEFINITIONS

"child"—see 1986 Act, s.20(11) (SSCBA, s.137(1)).
"young person"—see regs. 2(1) and 14.

GENERAL NOTE

The general rule under s.124(1)(d) of the Contributions and Benefits Act is that if a claimant is receiving relevant education he is not entitled to income support. Reg. 12 provides an exhaustive test of when a person is to be treated as receiving relevant education. The 1990 formulation is a tidying-up. Note that only a child or young person can qualify and that relevant education does not include a course of advanced education. There is a reference over to the child benefit legislation and the reg. 12 question is one which under reg. 56 of the Adjudication Regulations need not be determined immediately by the income support AO (reg. 56(3)(b)). The AO can proceed on the assumption that the child benefit decision will be adverse to the claimant in the income support sense, if it has not already been determined.

See on the child benefit test, regs. 5, 6, 7, 7A, 7B, 7C and 7D of the Child Benefit (General) Regulations 1976 in Bonner *et al.*, *Non-Means Tested Benefits: the Legislation*. The effect used to be contained in reg. 10 of the old Supplementary Benefit (Conditions of Entitlement) Regulations (see 1987 edition of this book). Contact hours of at least 12 per week are required. See *R(F) 1/93* in which the Commissioner held that supervised study (in reg. 5 of the Child Benefit Regulations) "would normally be understood to import the presence or close proximity of a teacher or tutor". Relevant education continues through temporary interruptions, like school holidays. When a person ceases actually to receive relevant education he is treated as doing so (unless he is in remunerative work of 24 hours or more a week and in certain other circumstances) until the next terminal date after he reaches compulsory school leaving age, or after he leaves relevant education if he stays on beyond compulsory school leaving age, or until he reaches 19 if this is earlier. The terminal dates are the first Monday in January, the first Monday after Easter Monday, or the first Monday in September. For England and Wales (but not Scotland) there is now a single school leaving date: the last Friday in June in the school year in which the child's 16th birthday falls (see the Education (School Leaving Date) Order (S.I. 1997 No. 1970)). Thus in 1999 children in England and Wales who reach 16 before September 1, 1999 can leave school on Friday, June 25, 1999; their terminal date will be Monday, September 6, 1999 and they count as being in relevant education until the Sunday after that date (unless the exceptions apply). For a child who stays on beyond compulsory school leaving age the three terminal dates are still applicable. There is also the possibility of a person remaining a "child" for an extension period of 12 weeks beyond the terminal date (or 16 weeks if the terminal date is the first Monday in September) if he is under 18, registered for work or training, not in remunerative work of 24 hours or more a week, not in receipt of income support/income-based JSA in his own right and not on Work Based Training for Young People (which has replaced Youth Training and other training provision for 16/17 year-olds). In England and Wales for a child whose school leaving date is June 25, 1999 the extension period will be September 13, 1999 to January 2, 2000.

Note that reg. 13 allows certain claimants to receive income support though in relevant education.

Circumstances in which persons in relevant education may be entitled to income support

13.—(1) Notwithstanding that a person is to be treated as receiving relevant education under regulation 12 (relevant education) he shall, if paragraph (2) applies to him and he satisfies the other conditions of entitlement to income support, be entitled to income support.

(2) This paragraph applies to [³a person aged 16 or over but under 19 (hereinafter referred to as an eligible person)] who—

(a) is the parent of a child for whom he is treated as responsible under regulation 15 (circumstances in which a person is to be treated as responsible or not responsible for another) and who is treated as a member of his household under regulation 16 (circumstances in which a person is to be treated as being or not being a member of the household); or

(b) is severely mentally or physically handicapped and because of that he would be unlikely, even if he were available for employment, to obtain employment within the next 12 months; or

(c) has no parent nor any person acting in the place of his parents; or

[¹(d) of necessity has to live away from his [² parents and any] person acting in the place of his parents because—

(i) he is estranged from his [² parents and that person]; or

(ii) he is in physical or moral danger; or

(iii) there is a serious risk to his physical or mental health;] or

[⁴(dd) has ceased to live in accommodation provided for him by a local authority under Part III of the Children Act 1989 (local authority support for children and families) and is of necessity living away from his parents and any person acting in place of his parents;]

(e) is living away from his parents and any person acting in the place of his parents in a case where his parents are or, as the case may be, that person is unable financially to support him and—

(i) chronically sick or mentally or physically disabled; or

(ii) detained in custody pending trial or sentence upon conviction or under a sentence imposed by a court; or

(iii) prohibited from entering or re-entering Great Britain; or

(f) [⁶...]

(g) [⁶...]

[⁶(h) is a person to whom paragraph 18 of Schedule 1B (refugees) applies.]

(3) In this regulation—

[⁵(a) any reference to a person acting in the place of an eligible person's parents includes—

(i) for the purposes of paragraph (2)(c), (d) and (dd), a reference to a local authority or voluntary organisation where the eligible person is being looked after by them under a relevant enactment or where the eligible person is placed by the local authority or voluntary organisation with another person, that other person whether or not a payment is made to him;

137

     (ii) for the purposes of paragraph (2)(e), the person with whom the person is so placed;]
- (b) "chronically sick or mentally disabled" means, in relation to a person to whom that expression refers, a person—
  - (i) in respect of whom the condition specified in paragraph 12(1) of Schedule 2 (additional condition for the higher pensioner and disability premiums) is satisfied; or
  - (ii) in respect of whom an amount under article 26 of the Naval, Military and Air Forces etc. (Disablement and Death) Services Pension Order 1983 (provision of expenses in respect of appropriate aids for disabled living) is payable in respect of the cost of providing a vehicle, or maintaining a vehicle to a disabled person; or
  - (iii) who is substantially and permanently disabled.

AMENDMENTS

1. Family Credit and Income Support (General) Amendment Regulations 1989 (S.I. 1989 No. 1034), reg. 4 (July 10, 1989).
2. Income Support (General) Amendment Regulations 1991 (S.I. 1991 No. 236), reg. 5 (April 8, 1991).
3. Income Support (General) Amendment No. 4 Regulations 1991 (S.I. 1991 No. 1559), reg. 6 (August 5, 1991).
4. Income Support (General) Amendment Regulations 1992 (S.I. 1992 No. 468), reg. 3 (April 6, 1992).
5. Income Support (General) Amendment Regulations 1992 (S.I. 1992 No. 468), Sched., para. 2 (April 6, 1992).
6. Income Support (General) (Jobseeker's Allowance Consequential Amendments) Regulations 1996 (S.I. 1996 No. 206), reg. 7 (October 7, 1996).

DEFINITIONS

"child"—see 1986 Act, s.20(11) (SSCBA, s.137(1)).
"local authority"—see 1986 Act, s.84(1).
"relevant enactment"—see reg. 2(1), reg. 16(8)(a).

GENERAL NOTE

In the circumstances set out in para. (2) a claimant, if he satisfies the other conditions of entitlement, is entitled to income support although in relevant education. The regulation can only benefit someone aged from 16 to 18 inclusive. If a claimant satisfies any of para. (2)(a) to (e), he will be eligible for income support under para. 15 of Sched. 1B. If he comes within para. (2)(h), he will qualify under para. 18.

Paragraph (2)
Sub-para. (a). A person of at least 16 who is the parent of a child who is in the same household can claim although in relevant education.
Sub-para. (b). Severe mental or physical handicap has no special meaning. Qualification for one of the higher levels of the care component of disability living allowance would certainly do, although the *Adjudication Officer's Guide* requires medical evidence to be provided in support of the claim (paras. 25308–25311). See *CIS 632/1994*.
Sub-para. (c). A parent presumably means a natural parent or an adoptive parent. A person acting in place of parents may include some informal relationships, for example, where a child's parents have died and the child is brought up by another member of the family, but see the decisions referred to below. If a person is claiming child benefit in respect of a pupil, this would be a strong factor. However, a sponsor under the Immigration Act 1971 is not a person acting in place of parents. A sponsor's duties are restricted to the maintenance and accommodation of the dependant without recourse to public funds and there is no responsibility for other aspects of the dependant's life (*R(IS) 9/94*).
Para. (3)(a)(i) specifically includes for this purpose local authorities and voluntary organisations who are looking after children (what used to be known as having them in care) under a relevant

enactment (defined in reg. 16(8)(a)), and foster parents with whom the pupil has been placed by *the* local authority or voluntary organisation. Since head (i) refers to pupils placed by "the", not "a", local authority or voluntary organisation, it would seem that head (i) only applies where the pupil is being looked after by the local authority or voluntary organisation under a relevant enactment. In *CIS 447/1994* the claimant was estranged from his parents. A local authority social worker gave him a list of approved accommodation and he went to lodge at an address on the list. The Commissioner decides that "placed" in the second limb of para. (3)(a)(i) referred to placement under the Children Act. But even if it did not, in the Commissioner's view, providing the claimant with a list of approved accommodation did not constitute "placing" him (even in a non-technical sense) with another person. This did not mean that the second limb was redundant. Its purpose was to make clear that where a claimant had been placed with a person by a local authority, it was estrangement, etc., from that person, not from the local authority, that was relevant. *CIS 11766/1996* concerned the position of a claimant who had continued to live with his ex-foster parents after his care order had ended. The Commissioner follows the approach of *CSB 325/1985* and holds that ex-foster parents cease to be acting in place of parents when their fostering contract comes to an end.

Sub-para. (d). See sub-para. (c) above for the meaning of parent and of person acting in place of a parent. The 1991 amendment to the effect that the pupil must be living away from parents *and* substitutes (and see head (i) on estrangement) was described by the DSS as technical. However, this was a change of substance. The previous form referred to living away from or estrangement from parents *or* substitutes. When the Conditions of Entitlement Regulations were in this form, *CSB 677/1983* decided that the pupil qualified if estranged from his parents even though he was not estranged from a person acting in their place. Now the pupil has to be living away from or estranged from both. See sub-para. (dd) on pupils leaving care.

Head (i). Estrangement has "connotations of emotional disharmony" *(R(SB) 2/87)* and it seems that it can exist although financial support is being provided. The 1989 form of sub-para. (d) is an attempt to provide a test of "genuine estrangement." It is in some respects stricter than the previous form because in addition to showing estrangement, the person in relevant education must also show that as a result, at least partly, of that he has of necessity to live away from his parents and any substitute. It is obviously a matter of judgment when estrangement is serious enough to necessitate that the young person leaves home. There is perhaps some widening in the addition of two extra categories which may lead to a need to leave home.

CIS 11441/1995 decides that estrangement from a local authority can exist. The claimant, aged 16, was in the care of a local authority but because of her violent and aggressive behaviour in a community home it had been decided that she should live in rented accommodation by herself. She was given help to find suitable accommodation and the authority met her liability for council tax and because income support had been refused provided her with a payment equivalent to her income support entitlement. Her rent was met through housing benefit. The care order remained in place as the claimant wished it to continue for "emotional" reasons. The Commissioner decides that sub-para. (dd) did not apply because the local authority were continuing to provide the claimant with accommodation by supervising and assisting in the arrangements for her rented accommodation (see s.23(2)(f) of the Children Act 1989). But sub-para. (d) did apply. The claimant was "living away" from the local authority because she was living away from the people who represented the authority, *i.e.* the community home (the terms of reg. 13 were clearly intended to reverse *R(SB) 2/87* which had held that it was not possible for a person to live away from a local authority). Further it was "necessary" for her to do this because it had been accepted that it was not possible for the claimant to live in a community home or with foster parents. Moreover she was "estranged" from the local authority because she was estranged from the community home where the local authority had placed her. The fact that she continued to have some contact with and received some assistance from the local authority did not alter the fact of the estrangement.

Head (ii). Under head (ii), the meaning of "physical or moral danger" is again a matter of judgment. It is not a term of art with an established meaning. Obvious points are that a person can be in danger from himself or from others and that a danger can exist before any harm has actually occurred (see *Kelly v. Monklands District Council* 1986 S.L.T. 169 on the phrase "at risk of sexual or financial exploitation" in the Code of Guidance on Homelessness). Nor is the danger specified to be immediate, but the test will no doubt be whether the danger is sufficient to necessitate living away from parents or their substitute. The danger does not have to emanate from the pupil's parents. In *R(IS) 9/94* the claimant's parents were in a refugee camp in Ethiopia, having fled there after civil war broke out in Somalia. It is held that he had to live away from his parents in view of the situation in Somalia, as otherwise he was in physical or moral danger; in addition, there was a serious risk to his physical or mental health under head (iii).

Head (iii). Under head (iii) there is an echo of the "serious risk to health" test of reg. 30 of the

Supplementary Benefit (Single Payments) Regulations. There was there some dispute about how closely a SSAT had to define the seriousness of the risk (compare *R(SB) 5/81* and *CSB 11/81* with *R(SB) 3/82* and *R(SB) 8/82*). The nature of the risk must no doubt be identified (as the danger must be under head (ii)) and some reason given why it is serious enough to necessitate living away from parents or their substitute. See *R(IS) 9/94* in the notes to head (ii).

See the transitional protection in reg. 13 of the Family Credit and Income Support (General) Amendment Regulations 1989.

Sub-para. (dd). This provision protects the entitlement of pupils leaving local authority care who need to live away from their parents and any substitute without the necessity of proving estrangement or moral danger or one of the other conditions in sub-para. (d). See the note to sub-para. (c) for the meaning of parent and person acting in place of a parent.

Sub-para. (e). Here the pupil must be living away from both parents and persons acting in place of parents, and they must be unable to provide financial support. The reason for this inability must be one of those listed. See para. (3)(b) for the definition of chronically sick or mentally or physically disabled. See the note to sub-para. (c) for the meaning of parent and person acting in place of a parent.

Head (iii). In *R(IS) 9/94* the claimant's parents who were in a refugee camp in Ethiopia had no leave to enter the U.K. at the date of the AO's decision. Under s.3 of the Immigration Act 1971 (subject to certain exceptions) all persons who are not British citizens require leave to enter the U.K. The claimant's parents were thus prohibited from entering Great Britain.

Sub-para. (h). This is a special case of refugees.

Paragraph (3)

The previous form of sub-para. (a) (see the Supplement to the 1991 edition) remains in force in Scotland. The new form was introduced on April 6, 1992, as a consequence of the Children Act 1989.

See the note to para. (2)(c).

[¹Persons under 18 years

13A.—[². . .],]

AMENDMENTS

1. Income Support (General) Amendment No. 3 Regulations 1988 (S.I. 1988 No. 1228), reg. 4 (September 12, 1988).
2. Income Support (General) (Jobseeker's Allowance Consequential Amendments) Regulations 1996 (S.I. 1996 No. 206), reg. 28 and Sched. 3 (October 7, 1996).

PART III

MEMBERSHIP OF THE FAMILY

Persons of a prescribed description

14.—(1) Subject to paragraph (2), a person of a prescribed description for the purposes of section 20(11) of the Act [SSCBA, s.137(1)] as it applies to income support (definition of the family) and section 23(1) [¹and (3)] of the Act [SSCBA, s.126(1) and (3)] is a person aged 16 or over but under 19 who is treated as a child for the purposes of section 2 of the Child Benefit Act 1975 [SSCBA, s.142] (meaning of child), and in these Regulations such a person is referred to as a "young person".

(2) Paragraph (1) shall not apply to [²a person who is receiving advanced education within the meaning of regulation 12(2) (relevant education) or to] a person who is entitled to income support or would, but for section 20(9) of the Act [SSCBA, s.134(2)] (provision against dual entitlement of members of family), be so entitled.

AMENDMENTS

1. Income Support (General) Amendment No. 4 Regulations 1988 (S.I. 1988 No. 1445), reg. 5 (September 12, 1988).
2. Income Support (General) Amendment Regulation 1990 (S.I. 1990 No. 547), reg. 6 (April 9, 1990).

DEFINITION

"the Act"—see reg. 2(1).

GENERAL NOTE

For the circumstances in which a person of 16 to 18 is treated as a child for child benefit purposes, see reg. 12. If such a person is receiving advanced education or could be entitled to income support in their own right (see reg. 13), that person does not come within reg. 14.

Circumstances in which a person is to be treated as responsible or not responsible for another

15.—[¹(1) Subject to the following provisions of this regulation, a person is to be treated as responsible for a child or young person for whom he is receiving child benefit.

(1A) In a case where a child ("the first child") is in receipt of child benefit in respect of another child ("the second child"), the person treated as responsible for the first child in accordance with the provisions of this regulation shall also be treated as responsible for the second child.

(2) In the case of a child or young person in respect of whom no person is receiving child benefit, the person who shall be treated as responsible for that child or young person shall be—

(a) except where sub-paragraph (b) applies, the person with whom the child or young person usually lives; or

(b) where only one claim for child benefit has been made in respect of the child or young person, the person who made that claim.]

(3) Where regulation 16(6) (circumstances in which a person is to be treated as being or not being a member of the household) applies in respect of a child or young person, that child or young person shall be treated as the responsibility of the claimant for that part of the week for which he is under that regulation treated as being a member of the claimant's household.

(4) Except where paragraph (3) applies, for the purposes of these Regulations a child or young person shall be treated as the responsibility of only one person in any benefit week and any person other than the one treated as responsible for the child or young person under this regulation shall be treated as not so responsible.

AMENDMENT

1. Income-related Benefits Schemes (Miscellaneous Amendments) (No. 4) Regulations 1993 (S.I. 1993 No. 2119), reg. 5 (October 4, 1993).

DEFINITIONS

"benefit week"—see reg. 2(1).
"child"—see 1986 Act, s.20(11) (SSCBA, s.137(1)).
"claimant"—see reg. 2(1).
"young person"—*ibid.*, reg. 14.

Paragraph (1)

The definition of family in s.137(1) of the Contributions and Benefits Act (1986 Act, s.20(11)) refers to a person being responsible for a child or young person (on which see reg. 14). Reg. 15 now makes the test of responsibility receipt of child benefit. Up to October 4, 1993, the test was "primary responsibility", and receipt of child benefit was only relevant in cases of doubt. See the notes to reg. 15 in the 1993 edition and *Whelan v. Chief Adjudication Officer, The Independent,* November 14, 1994. The Court of Appeal confirmed that the question of who had "primary responsibility" for a child had to be assessed on a week to week basis. On the facts, the claimant had primary responsibility for the children in the three weeks in the summer when they stayed with her.

The test for family credit and disability working allowance is still whether the child normally lives with the adult and receipt of child benefit only becomes relevant where this is unclear. The different rules may therefore make it possible in certain cases for one person to claim income support and another family credit or disability working allowance for the same child at the same time.

Paragraph (1A)

If a child (B) for whom a person (A) is responsible gets child benefit for another child (C), (A) is also treated as responsible for (C).

Paragraph (2)

If no one is receiving child benefit for the child, then if one claim only has been made, the person who made that claim is responsible. Otherwise the person responsible is the person with whom the child usually lives. (See the notes to reg. 7 of the Family Credit (General) Regulations on "living with".) Since para. (4) refers to consideration of responsibility on the basis of benefit weeks, the test of where a child usually lives should be applied week by week and not on some kind of overall assessment on a long-term basis (*CIS 49/1991*). In the vast majority of cases, however, the question of who is responsible for a child for the purposes of income support will now be determined by who is receiving child benefit. The rules for child benefit include methods of establishing priorities between claimants, and a child benefit claimant can agree that someone with lower priority should be paid it.

Paragraphs (3) and (4)

Para. (4) provides that only one person can be treated as responsible for a child in any one benefit week. There is no provision for dividing up income support where a child spends time in different households. The only exceptions are under para. (3), which allows a person to be treated as responsible for a child for the part of the week in which he is in the household, but only where the child is being looked after by a local authority or is in custody (reg. 16(6)). The result of the new test is that if someone else is in receipt of child benefit for a child in any one benefit week, an income support claimant cannot be treated as responsible for that child even if the child spends most of, or even all, his time with the claimant. This may provide for even greater administrative simplicity than the previous test of primary responsibility but at a cost of a lack of justice in certain situations. However, it may be possible, because of the different rules for family credit and disability working allowance, for one person to claim income support and another family credit or disability working allowance for the same child at the same time.

Circumstances in which a person is to be treated as being or not being a member of the household

16.—(1) Subject to paragraphs (2) and (5), the claimant and any partner and, where the claimant or his partner is treated as responsible under regulation 15 (circumstances in which a person is to be treated as responsible or not responsible for another) for a child or young person, that child or young person and any child of that child or young person shall be treated as members of the same household [¹notwithstanding that any of them] [⁷is temporarily living away from the other members of his family].

[⁷(2) Paragraph (1) shall not apply to a person who is living away from the other members of his family where—

(a) that person does not intend to resume living with the other members of his family; or

(b) his absence from the other members of his family is likely to exceed 52 weeks, unless there are exceptional circumstances (for example the person is in hospital or otherwise has no control over the length of his absence), and the absence is unlikely to be substantially more than 52 weeks.]

(3) Paragraph (1) shall not apply in respect of any member of a couple or of a polygamous marriage where—

(a) one, both or all of them are patients detained in a hospital provided under section 4 of the National Health Service Act 1977 (special hospitals) or section 90(1) of the Mental Health (Scotland) Act 1984 (provision of hospitals for patients requiring special security); or

[⁹(b) one, both or all of them are—

(i) detained in custody pending trial or sentence upon conviction or under a sentence imposed by a court; or

(ii) on temporary release in accordance with the provisions of the Prison Act 1952 or the Prisons (Scotland) Act 1989;]

(c) [⁶...]

(d) the claimant is abroad and does not satisfy the conditions of regulation 4 (temporary absence from Britain); or

(e) one of them is permanently in residential accommodation or in a residential care or a residential nursing home.

(4) A child or young person shall not be treated as a member of the claimant's household where he is—

[⁵(a) placed with the claimant or his partner by a local authority under section 23(2)(a) of the Children Act 1989 or by a voluntary organisation under section 59(1)(a) of that Act; or

(b) placed with the claimant or his partner prior to adoption; or]

(c) placed for adoption with the claimant or his partner pursuant to a decision under the Adoption Agencies Regulations 1983 or the Adoption Agencies (Scotland) Regulations 1984.

(5) Subject to paragraph (6), paragraph (1) shall not apply to a child or young person who is not living with the claimant [¹and who]—

(a) [⁴in a case which does not fall within sub-paragraph (aa),] has been continuously absent from Great Britain for a period of more than four weeks commencing—

(i) [⁸ subject to paragraph (5A),] where he went abroad before the date of claim for income support, with that date;

(ii) in any other case, [⁴on the day which immediately follows the day] on which he went abroad; or

[⁴(aa) where regulation 4(3) or paragraph 11A or 12A of Schedule 7 (temporary absence abroad for the treatment of a child or young person) applies, has been continuously absent from Great Britain for a period of more than eight weeks, that period of eight weeks commencing—

(i) [⁸ subject to paragraph (5A),] where he went abroad before the date of the claim for income support, on the date of that claim;

(ii) in any other case, on the day which immediately follows the day on which he went abroad; or]

(b) has been an in-patient or in [¹accommodation provided under any of the provisions referred to in [²any of sub-paragraphs (a) to (d) [³(excluding heads (i) and (ii)] of sub-paragraph (d)) of the definition of residential accommodation] in regulation 21(3)] for a continuous period of more than 12 weeks commencing—

(i) [⁸ subject to paragraph (5A),] where he became an in-patient or, as the case may be, entered that accommodation, before the date of the claim for income support, with that date; or

  (ii) in any other case, with the date on which he became an in-patient or entered that accommodation,

and, in either case, has not been in regular contact with either the claimant or any member of the claimant's household; or

[5(c) is being looked after by a local authority under a relevant enactment; or

  (d) has been placed with a person other than the claimant prior to adoption; or]

  (e) has been placed for adoption pursuant to a decision under the Adoption Agencies Regulations 1983 or the Adoption Agencies (Scotland) Regulations 1984; or

  (f) is detained in custody pending trial or sentence upon conviction or under a sentence imposed by a court.

[8(5A) Sub-paragraphs (a)(i), (aa)(i) and (b)(i) of paragraph (5) shall not apply in a case where immediately before the date of claim for income support the claimant was entitled to an income-based jobseeker's allowance.]

(6) A child or young person to whom any of the circumstances mentioned in sub-paragraphs (c) or (f) of paragraph (5) applies shall be treated as being a member of the claimant's household only for that part of any benefit week where that child or young person lives with the claimant.

(7) Where a child or young person for the purposes of attending the educational establishment at which he is receiving relevant education is living with the claimant or his partner and neither one is treated as responsible for that child or young person that child or young person shall be treated as being a member of the household of the person treated as responsible for him and shall not be treated as a member of the claimant's household.

(8) In this regulation—

[5(a) "relevant enactment" means the Army Act 1955, the Social Work (Scotland) Act 1968, the Matrimonial Causes Act 1973, the Adoption (Scotland) Act 1978, the Family Law Act 1986 and the Children Act 1989;]

  (b) "voluntary organisation" has the meaning assigned to it in the [5Children Act 1989] or, in Scotland, the Social Work (Scotland) Act 1968.

AMENDMENTS

  1. Income Support (General) Amendment Regulations 1988 (S.I. 1988 No. 663), reg. 8 (April 11, 1988).
  2. Income Support (General) Amendment Regulations 1989 (S.I. 1989 No. 534), reg. 3 (April 10, 1989).
  3. Income Support (General) Amendment Regulations 1989 (S.I. 1989 No. 534), Sched. 1, para. 3 (October 9, 1989).
  4. Income Support (General) Amendment Regulations 1990 (S.I. 1990 No. 547), reg. 7 (April 9, 1990).
  5. Income Support (General) Amendment Regulations 1992 (S.I. 1992 No. 468), Sched., para. 3 (April 6, 1992). *Note:* The previous form (see the 1991 edition) of sub-paras. (4)(a) and (b), (5)(c) and (d) and (8)(a) and (b) remains in force in Scotland. The new form was introduced on April 6, 1992, as a consequence of the Children Act 1989.
  6. Social Security Benefits (Amendments Consequential Upon the Introduction of Community Care) Regulations 1992 (S.I. 1992 No. 3147), Sched. 1, para. 1 (April 1, 1993).
  7. Income-related Benefits Schemes (Miscellaneous Amendments) (No. 4) Regulations 1993 (S.I. 1993 No. 2119), reg. 6 (October 4, 1993).
  8. Income Support (General) (Jobseeker's Allowance Consequential Amendments) Regulations 1996 (S.I. 1996 No. 206), reg. 8 (October 7, 1996).
  9. Income-related Benefits Schemes and Social Fund (Miscellaneous Amendments) Regulations 1996 (S.I. 1996 No. 1944), reg. 6(5) (October 7, 1996).

"child"—see 1986 Act, s.20(11) (SSCBA, s.137(1)).
"claimant"—see reg. 2(1).
"couple"—*ibid.*
"date of claim"—*ibid.*
"dwelling occupied as the home"—*ibid.*
"local authority"—see 1986 Act, s.84(1).
"nursing home"—see reg. 2(1), reg. 19(3).
"partner"—see reg. 2(1).
"polygamous marriage"—*ibid.*
"residential accommodation"—*ibid.*, reg. 21(3).
"residential care home"—*ibid.*, reg. 19(3).
"young person"—*ibid.*, reg. 14.

GENERAL NOTE

Paragraph (1)

This provision does two things. The first is to provide that a claimant and partner are deemed to be members of the same household, notwithstanding that they are temporarily apart. Before October 4, 1993, the deeming applied notwithstanding one partner's absence from the dwelling occupied as the home (see below). Since a partner is one of a married or unmarried couple and it is an essential part of the definition of both kinds of couple that the parties should be members of the same household, para. (1) cannot subvert the general meaning of household referred to in the notes to s.137(1) of the Contributions and Benefits Act (see *CIS 671/1992*). Para. (1) must only mean that because one partner is temporarily living elsewhere this does not in itself mean that membership of the same household ceases. This means that the exceptions in para. (3) perhaps do not achieve much, but probably indicate that those circumstances do terminate membership of the household.

The other thing done by para. (1) is to deem that where an adult is responsible for a child or young person under reg. 15, the child or young person is to be treated as in the same household as the adult, notwithstanding that one of them is temporarily living elsewhere (again, before October 4, 1993, the test was absence from the home). This deeming is more significant. There are exceptions in paras. (4) and (5).

Thus the test under para. (1) is now one of absence from other members of the family, rather than from the home. *CIS 209/1989* held that the old form of para. (1) only applied if there was a dwelling which could be regarded as the home of both partners. This is no longer required, but it is still necessary for the family to have previously lived as members of the same household. (See notes to s.137(1) of the Contributions and Benefits Act under *"married couple"* on the meaning of household.) The Commissioner in *CIS 508/1992* seems to have accepted that the home need not have been in this country; how this applies to the new test of absence from other members of the family is not entirely clear. Temporarily is not defined and each case will need to be decided on its particular facts. However, adjudicating authorities still need to investigate whether either of the conditions in para. (2) applies. Note in particular *CIS 13805/1996* in the note to para. (2).

Paragraph (2)

Para. (1) does not apply where the person living away does not intend to resume living together with the other members of the family or is likely to be away for more than 52 weeks (or longer in exceptional circumstances, provided it is not substantially longer). When either of these conditions applies membership of the same household immediately ceases.

In *CIS 13805/1996* the Commissioner points out that the "not" in para. (2)(a) relates to "intend" rather than "resume". This was significant because it was possible for a person to have no intention one way or the other. For example, where a couple had agreed to live apart for a couple of months, and neither had an intention to resume living with the other, but equally neither had an intention not to do so, para. (2)(a) could apply. This interpretation was further supported by the fact that once an intention not to resume living together had been formed, a separation was no longer temporary and so para. (1) ceased to apply in any event; thus para. (2)(a) would serve no function (other perhaps than to provide a partial definition of "temporary") if it was read as only operating when there was an intention not to resume living together. The facts in *CIS 13805/1996* were that the claimant's husband was in Pakistan. He had applied for permission to enter the U.K. but it had not yet been granted. They intended to resume living together, as long as permission was granted for the claimant's husband to join her. The Commissioner states that the question therefore was whether such intention counted for the purposes of para. (2)(a). *CIS 508/1992* and *CIS 484/1993* had held in relation to para. 4(8) of the former Sched. 3 (now para. 3(10)) that the intention to return must not be a contingent one. In the Commissioner's view the same interpretation applied for the purposes of para. (2)(a), since there was no material distinction between that provision and para. (2)(a). Thus para. (2)(a) applied because the claimant's intention to resume living in the same household as her husband was not an unqualified one. Therefore the fact that the claimant's husband was in remunerative work did not bar her from entitlement to income support.

Paragraph (3)

Para. (1) does not apply in these circumstances, as between partners and polygamous marriages. The intention seems to be that the members of the couple or marriage cease to be partners in these circumstances, but para. (3) does not exactly say so. Under sub-para. (b) a person required to live in a bail hostel is not "detained in custody" pending trial (*R(IS) 17/93*); see Sched. 7, para. 9 as to how his applicable amount is calculated if he is a member of a couple. However, once a person has been charged, he is detained in custody pending trial, even if subsequently no trial takes place (*R(IS) 1/94*). In *Chief Adjudication Officer v. Carr, The Times*, June 2, 1994, the Court of Appeal upheld the decision in *CIS 561/1992* that a person on home leave while serving a prison sentence was not "detained in custody" during the leave period. The definition of "prisoner" in reg. 21(3) was amended with effect from April 10, 1995, so as to include periods of temporary release, and sub-para. (b) has now been similarly amended with effect from October 7, 1996.

Paragraph (4)

Children or young persons are not to be members of the household of their foster-parents or the people they are placed with for adoption. They therefore cannot be a member of the family.

Paragraph (5)

Para. (1) does not apply to a child or young person who is not living with the claimant when one of heads (a) to (f) applies. Again, the intention seems to be that in these circumstances the child or young person is to be treated as not a member of the household, but para. (5) does not expressly say so. It may be that the general test of membership of the household is relevant.

See para. (8) for the meaning of "relevant enactment."

Paragraph (6)

This provision provides a limited exception to para. (5), allowing a claimant to receive benefit for children or young persons being looked after by a local authority or in custody for the days on which they are in the claimant's home.

Paragraph (7)

This is a special rule where children live away from home while at school.

PART IV

APPLICABLE AMOUNTS

Applicable amounts

17. Subject to regulations [⁸ 18 to 22A] and 70 (applicable amounts in other cases and reductions in applicable amounts and urgent cases), a claimant's weekly applicable amount shall be the aggregate of such of the following amounts as may apply in his case:

    (a) an amount in respect of himself or, if he is a member of a couple, an amount in respect of both of them, determined in accordance with paragraph 1(1), (2) or (3), as the case may be, of Schedule 2;

    (b) an amount determined in accordance with paragraph 2 of Schedule 2 in respect of any child or young person who is a member of his family, except a child or young person whose capital, if calculated in accordance with Part V in like manner as for the claimant, [⁷except as provided in regulation 44(1) (modifications in respect of children and young persons)], would exceed £3,000;

[⁶(bb) an amount in respect of himself, or where the claimant is a member of a family, an amount in respect of any member of the family aged 16 or over, determined in accordance with paragraph 2A of Schedule 2 (residential allowance);]

(c) if he is a member of a family of which at least one member is a child or young person, an amount determined in accordance with Part II of Schedule 2 (family premium);

(d) the amount of any premiums which may be applicable to him, determined in accordance with Parts III and IV of Schedule 2 (premiums);

(e) any amounts determined in accordance with Schedule 3 (housing costs) which may be applicable to him in respect of mortgage interest payments or such other housing costs as are prescribed in that Schedule.

[¹(f) any amounts determined in accordance with [²paragraphs (2) to (7)].

[²(g) the amount of the protected sum which may be applicable to him determined in accordance with Schedule 3A [³or, as the case may be, 3B].]

(2) Where—

(a) a claimant has throughout the period beginning on 11th April 1988 and ending immediately before the coming into force of paragraphs 25 to 28 of Schedule 10 (capital to be disregarded) failed to satisfy the capital condition in section 22(6) of the Act (no entitlement to benefit if capital exceeds prescribed amount); and

(b) as a consequence he is not entitled to any transitional addition, special transitional addition or personal expenses addition under Part II of the Transitional Regulations; and

(c) had those paragraphs been in force on 11th April 1988 he would have satisfied that condition and been entitled to any such addition,

the amount applicable under this paragraph shall, subject to paragraph (3) be equal to the amount of any transitional addition, special transitional addition and personal expenses addition to which he would be entitled under Part II of the Transitional Regulations had he been entitled to any such addition in the week commencing 11th April 1988.

(3) For the purposes of paragraph (2), in determining a claimant's total benefit income in his second benefit week for the purpose of calculating the amount of any transitional addition to which he would have been entitled, no account shall be taken of any payment referred to in paragraph (1)(j) of regulation 9 of the Transitional Regulations (total benefit income) which is made in respect of that week to compensate for the loss of entitlement to income support.

(4) Subject to paragraph (6), where—

(a) the claimant or any member of his family was temporarily absent from his home in the claimant's first or second benefit week (or both), because he was—

(i) a patient; or

(ii) outside Great Britain for the purpose of receiving treatment for any disease or bodily or mental disablement or for the purpose of accompanying a child or young person who is outside Great Britain for the purpose of receiving such treatment; or

(iii) in a residential care or nursing home or in accommodation provided under any of the provisions referred to in any of subparagraphs (*a*) to (d) of the definition of residential accommodation in regulation 21(3) (special cases); or

(iv) in the care of a local authority under a relevant enactment; or

(v) staying with a person who was contributing to his maintenance; and

(b) as a result—

(i) in the claimant's first benefit week his requirements for the purpose of calculating his entitlement to supplementary benefit were increased or reduced or he was not entitled to that benefit; or

(ii) in the claimant's second benefit week his applicable amount was increased or reduced or he was not entitled to income support; and

(c) the period during which his requirements were, or his applicable amount was, increased or reduced, or he was not entitled to benefit, or any one or more of those circumstances existed, did not exceed eight weeks,

the amount applicable under this paragraph (4) shall be equal to the amount determined under paragraph (5).

(5) The amount for the purposes of paragraph (4) shall be an amount equal to the difference between—

(a) the amount that his total benefit income in his first benefit week would have been had he been entitled in respect of that week to supplementary benefit calculated on the basis that he or any member of his family had not been absent from the home; and, if less,

(b) the amount of his total benefit income in the first complete week after the period of temporary absence ends; but for the purpose of calculating his total benefit income in that week—

(i) no account shall be taken of any payment referred to in paragraph (1)(j) of regulation 9 of the Transitional Regulations which is made in respect of that week to compensate for the loss (in whole or in part) of entitlement to income support; and

(ii) if the period of temporary absence ends after the coming into force of paragraph (4), the amount of income support to be taken into account shall, notwithstanding regulation 9(6) of the Transitional Regulations, be calculated as if that paragraph were not in force.

(6) The amount under paragraph (4) shall cease to be applicable to a claimant if he ceases to be entitled to income support for a period exceeding [⁴the permitted period determined in accordance with regulation 3A (permitted period)].

[⁴(6A) For the purposes of paragraph (6), where a claimant has ceased to be entitled to income support because he or his partner is participating in arrangements for training made under section 2 of the Employment and Training Act 1973 [⁵or section 2 of the Enterprise and New Towns (Scotland) Act 1990] or attending a course at an employment rehabilitation centre established under that section [⁵of the 1993 Act], he shall be treated as if he had been entitled to income support for the period during which he or his partner is participating in such arrangements or attending such a course.]

(7) In this Regulation—

"first benefit week" and "second benefit week" have the meanings given to those expressions in regulations 2(1) of the Transitional Regulations and shall also include the week which would have been the claimant's "first benefit week" or, as the case may be, "second benefit week" had he been entitled to supplementary benefit or, as the case may be, income support in that week;

"total benefit income" has, subject to paragraphs (3) and (5)(b), the same meaning as in regulation 9 of the Transitional Regulations;

"Transitional Regulations" means the Income Support (Transitional Regulations 1987.]

AMENDMENTS

1. Income Support (General) Amendment No. 2 Regulations 1988 (S.I. 1988 No. 910), reg. 2 (May 30, 1988).
2. Income Support (General) Amendment No. 4 Regulations 1988 (S.I. 1988 No. 1445), Sched. 1, para. 11 (April 10, 1989).
3. Income Support (General) Amendment Regulations 1989 (S.I. 1989 No. 534), Sched. 1, para. 17 (October 9, 1989).

4. Income Support (General) Amendment No. 3 Regulations 1989 (S.I. 1989 No. 1678), reg. 4 (October 9, 1989).

5. Enterprise (Scotland) Consequential Amendments Order 1991 (S.I. 1991 No. 387), arts. 2 and 9 (April 1, 1991).

6. Social Security Benefits (Amendments Consequential Upon the Introduction of Community Care) Regulations 1992 (S.I. 1992 No. 3147), reg. 2(1) (April 1, 1993).

7. Income-related Benefits Schemes (Miscellaneous Amendments) (No. 4) Regulations 1993 (S.I. 1993 No. 2119), reg. 7 (October 4, 1993).

8. Income Support (General) (Jobseeker's Allowance Consequential Amendments) Regulations 1996 (S.I. 1996 No. 206), reg. 9 (October 7, 1996).

DEFINITIONS

"child"—see 1986 Act, s.20(11) (SSCBA, s.137(1)).
"claimant"—see reg. 2(1).
"couple"—*ibid.*
"family"—see 1986 Act, s.20(11) (SSCBA, s.137(1)).
"young person"—see reg. 2(1), reg. 14.

GENERAL NOTE

Reg. 17 sets out the categories which go towards the total applicable amount, which is then set against the claimant's income to determine entitlement.

The categories cover first a personal allowance for the claimant, as a single person or a member of a couple. The amount of the allowance is specified in Sched. 2. A personal allowance (again specified in Sched. 2) is also added for each child or young person who is a member of the family (defined in s.137 of the Contributions and Benefits Act; 1986 Act, s.20(11)). If the child's or young person's own capital exceeds £3,000, then no personal allowance is included for that child. In that case, any income of the child is not treated as the claimant's (reg. 44(5)). The capital of a child or young person is never treated as the claimant's (reg. 47). There is a specific residential allowance for new residents (from April 1993) in residential care and nursing homes. See para. 2A of Sched. 2. And see reg. 19 for the treatment of existing residents.

The second main category covers premiums. If a member of the claimant's family is a child or young person, the family premium is included (see Part II of Sched. 2). The other premiums are in Parts III and IV of Sched. 2.

The third category covers housing costs, set out in Sched. 3. Note reg. 56(1)(a) of the Adjudication Regulations.

The fourth category, in sub-paras. (f) and (g), covers transitional protection for a number of groups. Sub-para. (f) first deals with those assisted by paras. 25 to 28 of Sched. 10 on disregarded capital, which were inserted from May 30, 1988. The details are in paras. (2) and (3). Sub-para. (f) secondly deals with groups who lost out on the ordinary transitional protection because of temporary absence from home around April 11, 1988. Here the details are in paras. (4) to (6). Sub-para. (g) applies Scheds. 3A and 3B, giving transitional protection to certain claimants in board and lodging accommodation on the change in the income support system on April 10, 1989, and to hostel-dwellers and operators on the changes in October 1989. See the notes to Sched. 3A and 3B.

Paragraphs (2) and (3)

These provisions apply where a person was continuously excluded from entitlement to income support by the capital rule before the additional disregards were added with effect from May 30, 1988. If the person would have satisfied the capital rule on April 11, 1988, if those disregards had been in the regulations and would have been entitled to some transitional protection, then the amount of that protection is applicable from May 30, 1988. There is no statutory provision for filling the gap between April 11 and May 30, but extra-statutory payments were made. The effect of para. (3) is that in doing the calculations of total benefit income in the second benefit week around April 11, any extra-statutory payment is to be ignored.

Paragraphs (4) to (6A)

Where the calculation of total benefit income in either the first or second benefit week is affected by a person's temporary absence from home (for one of the reasons set out in para. (4)(a)), then the calculation can be done as if the person was still at home. The absence must not exceed eight (or sometimes 12) weeks (para. (4)(c)) and the addition applied will cease if there is a subsequent break in entitlement of more than eight (or sometimes 12) weeks (para. (6)).

There are special rules for particular categories in regs. 18 to 22A, in particular for residents in residential care and nursing homes.

Polygamous marriages

18.—[¹(1) Subject to paragraph (2) and regulations] [⁸19 to 22A] and 70 (applicable amounts in other cases and reductions in applicable amounts and urgent cases), where a claimant is a member of a polygamous marriage his weekly applicable amount shall be the aggregate of such of the following amounts as may apply in his case:

    (a) the highest amount applicable to him and one of his partners determined in accordance with paragraph 1(3) of Schedule 2 as if he and that partner were a couple;

    (b) an amount equal to the differences between the amounts specified in [⁸sub-paragraph (3)(d)][⁴and (1)(e)] of paragraph 1 of Schedule 2 in respect of each of his other partners;

    (c) an amount determined in accordance with paragraph 2 of Schedule 2 (applicable amounts) in respect of any child or young person for whom he or a partner of his is responsible and who is a member of the same household except a child or young person whose capital, if calculated in accordance with Part V in like manner as for the claimant, [⁷except as provided in regulation 44(1) (modifications in respect of children and young persons)], would exceed £3,000;

[⁶(cc) an amount, whether in respect of the claimant or any member of his household aged 16 or over, determined in accordance with paragraph 2A of Schedule 2 (residential allowance);]

    (d) if he or another partner of the polygamous marriage is responsible for a child or young person who is a member of the same household, the amount specified in Part II of Schedule 2 (family premiums);

    (e) the amount of any premiums which may be applicable to him determined in accordance with Parts III and IV of Schedule 2 (premiums);

    (f) any amounts determined in accordance with Schedule 3 (housing costs) which may be applicable to him in respect of mortgage interest payments or such other housing costs as are prescribed in that Schedule.

[²(g) any amount determined in accordance with regulation 17(1)(f) (applicable amounts);]

[³(h) the amount of the protected sum which may be applicable to him determined in accordance with Schedule 3A [⁵or, as the case may be, 3B].]

[¹(2) In the case of a partner who is aged less than 18, the amount which applies in respect of that partner shall be nil unless—

    (a) that partner is treated as responsible for a child, or

[⁸(b) that partner is a person who—

      (i) had he not been a member of a polygamous marriage would have qualified for income support under regulation 4ZA; or

      (ii) satisfies the requirements of section 3(1)(f)(iii) of the Jobseekers Act 1995 (prescribed circumstances for persons aged 16 but less than 18); or

      (iii) is the subject of a direction under section 16 of the Jobseekers Act 1995 (persons under 18: severe hardship).]

AMENDMENTS

1. Income Support (General) Amendment No. 3 Regulations 1988 (S.I. 1988 No. 1228), reg. 5 (September 9, 1988).
2. Income Support (General) Amendment No. 4 Regulations 1988 (S.I. 1988 No. 1445), reg. 6 (September 9, 1988).

3. Income Support (General) Amendment No. 4 Regulations 1988 (S.I. 1988 No. 1445), Sched. 1, para. 12 (April 10, 1989).

4. Family Credit and Income Support (General) Amendment Regulations 1989 (S.I. 1989 No. 1034), reg. 5 (July 10, 1989).

5. Income Support (General) Amendment Regulations 1989 (S.I. 1989 No. 534), Sched. 1, para. 17 (October 9, 1989).

6. Social Security Benefits (Amendments Consequential Upon the Introduction of Community Care) Regulations 1992 (S.I. 1992 No. 3147), reg. 2(1) (April 1, 1993).

7. Income-related Benefits Schemes (Miscellaneous Amendments) (No. 4) Regulations 1993 (S.I. 1993 No. 2119) reg. 8 (October 4, 1993).

8. Income Support (General) (Jobseeker's Allowance Consequential Amendments) Regulations 1996 (S.I. 1996 No. 206), reg. 10 (October 7, 1996).

DEFINITIONS

"the Act"—see reg. 2(1).
"child"—see 1986 Act, s.20(11) (SSCBA, s.137(1)).
"claimant"—see reg. 2(1).
"couple"—*ibid.*
"partner"—*ibid.*
"polygamous marriage"—*ibid.*
"young person"—*ibid.*, reg. 14.

GENERAL NOTE

Reg. 18 contains special rules for polygamous marriages, but not for other kinds of relationships. There the ordinary living together as husband and wife rule in s.137(1) of the Contributions and Benefits Act (1986 Act, s.20(11)) applies.

Applicable amounts for persons in residential care and nursing homes

19.—[¹[⁶(1) Subject to [¹²regulation 22A] (reduction of applicable amounts) where a claimant has a preserved right and either—
- (a) lives in a residential care or nursing home; or
- (b) is a member of a family and he and the members of his family live in such a home,]

his weekly applicable amount shall, except in a case to which regulation 21 (applicable amounts in special cases) or Part II of Schedule 4 (persons to whom regulation 19 does not apply) applies, be calculated in accordance with Part I of that Schedule.]

[⁵(1ZA) A person to whom paragraph (1) applies shall be treated as not being severely disabled.]

[⁶(1ZB) In this regulation a person has a preserved right, subject to paragraphs (1ZE) and (1ZF), where—
- (a) on 31st March 1993, he was living in a residential care home or a nursing home, and—
  - (i) was entitled to income support for the benefit week in which that day fell and his applicable amount was calculated in accordance with Part I of Schedule 4; or
  - (ii) was not in that week entitled to income support because he was able to meet the cost of the accommodation from other sources available to him, but subsequently becomes entitled to income support; or
  - [¹⁰(iii) was not in that week entitled to income support, but was residing with his partner as a member of a couple on the relevant date where the partner was a person to whom head (i) or (ii) applies; or]
- (b) he would have been living in a residential care home or nursing home on 31st March 1993 but for an absence which, including that day, does not exceed—

151

(i) except in a case to which head (ii) applies—
- (aa) where the person was before his absence a temporary resident in the home, 4 weeks, or
- (bb) where the person was before his absence a permanent resident in the home, 13 weeks; or

(ii) where throughout the period of absence the person was a patient, 52 weeks,

and the provisions of sub-paragraph (a) would have applied to him but for that absence.

(1ZC) Subject to paragraphs (1ZD), (1ZE) and (1ZF), a person also has a preserved right where—
- (a) on 31st March 1993 he was living in a residential care home or nursing home within the meaning of paragraph (3) as then in force, and was entitled to income support but his applicable amount was not calculated in accordance with Part I of Schedule 4 because he was a person to whom paragraph 14 of Schedule 4 applied (accommodation provided by a close relative); and
- (b) after 31st March 1993, either—
    - (i) he moved from the home in which he was residing on that date to another residential care home or nursing home, or
    - (ii) the ownership of the home changed,

    and in the home to which he moved, or as the case may be, following the change of ownership, the accommodation and meals (if any) are provided for him by a person other than a close relative of his [⁸or of any member] of his family, and are provided on a commercial basis.

(1ZD) Where a person has a preserved right under paragraph (1ZC), that right shall commence on the first full day of residence in the residential care home or nursing home to which he moved, or as the case may be, the day after the ownership of the [⁹home] changed.

(1ZE) [¹⁰In England and Wales,] a person does not have a preserved right by virtue of paragraph (1ZB) (a)(ii) or (1ZC) where the residential care home in which he was living provided both board and personal care for less than 4 persons.

[¹⁰(1ZEA) Where, in Scotland, a person would have had a preserved right by virtue of paragraph (1ZB)(a)(ii) or (1ZC) but for the provisions of paragraph (1ZE) as it originally had effect, that person shall be treated from the date this regulation has effect in respect of him as though the first two paragraphs referred to continued to have effect in his case.]

(1ZF) Paragraphs (1ZB) and (1ZC) shall cease to apply to a person who has a preserved right where he is absent from a residential care home or nursing home and that absence exceeds a period of—
- (a) except in a case to which sub-paragraph (b) applies—
    - (i) 4 weeks, where the person was before his absence a temporary resident in the home; or
    - (ii) 13 weeks, where the person was before his absence a permanent resident in the home; or
- (b) 52 weeks where throughout the period of absence the person was a patient.

(1ZG)—
- (a) A person who acquired a preserved right under paragraph (1ZB) or (1ZC) shall cease to have that right where either—
    - (i) he moves from the home he resided in, or would but for an absence specified in paragraph (1ZB)(b) have resided in, on 31st March 1993 to another residential care home or nursing home, or
    - (ii) the ownership of that home changes;

    and in the home to which he moves, or as the case may be, following

the change of ownership, the accommodation and meals (if any) are provided for him by a close relative of his, [⁸or of any member] of his
family, [⁸or are provided] otherwise than on a commercial basis;
(b) a preserved right acquired under paragraph (1ZB) or (1ZC) which ceased
to apply to a person in accordance with sub-paragraph (a) shall, notwithstanding that paragraph, revive and again apply in his case where—
  (i) he moves from the home mentioned in sub-paragraph (a)(i) to
another residential care home or nursing home, or
  (ii) the ownership of that home changes, or in the case of a home mentioned in sub-paragraph (a)(ii), changes again,
and in the home to which he moves, or as the case may be, following
the change or further change of ownership, the accommodation and meals
(if any) are provided for him otherwise than by a close relative of his,
[⁸or of any member] of his family, and are provided on a commercial
basis.

(1ZH) For the purposes of paragraphs (1ZB) and (1ZF) a person is a permanent resident in a residential care home or nursing home where the home is his
principal place of abode, and a temporary resident where it is not.

(1ZJ) For the avoidance of doubt, the expression "residential care home" in
paragraphs (1ZB) and (1ZE) has the meaning it bore on 31st March 1993.]

[⁸(1ZK) Where a person—
(a) formerly had a preserved right by virtue of paragraph (1ZB); and
(b) on 1st April 1993 was living in a home which was exempt from registration under Part I of the Registered Homes Act 1984 pursuant to section
1(4)(a) of that Act (exemption from registration in respect of certain
homes) because one or more of the residents were treated as relatives
pursuant to section 19(4) of that Act; and
(c) is living in that home on 4th October 1993; and
(d) between 1st April 1993 and 4th October 1993 he has not been absent
from that home, or has been absent from it for a period not exceeding
13 weeks;
then subject to paragraph (1ZL) that person shall be treated for the purposes of
this regulation as though he had a preserved right on and after 4th October
1993.

(1ZL) Paragraph (1ZK) shall cease to apply to a person who is treated as
though he had a preserved right where he is absent from a residential care home
or nursing home and that absence exceeds a period of—
(a) except in a case to which sub-paragraph (b) applies, 13 weeks; or
(b) 52 weeks where throughout the period of absence the person was a
patient.]

[⁹(1ZM) Where a person is treated in accordance with paragraph (1ZK) as
having a preserved right, paragraph (1ZG) shall apply to that person as if he
had acquired a preserved right under paragraph (1ZB).]

[¹⁰(1ZN) Where a person—
(a) on 31st March 1993 was a member of a couple and his partner acquired
a preserved right under paragraph (1ZB)(a)(i);
(b) before 3rd October 1994 ceased to be a member of a couple; and
(c) between 31st March 1993 and 3rd October 1994 has been living in a
residential care home or a nursing home,
he shall be treated for the purposes of this regulation as having a preserved
right from 3rd October 1994.

(1ZO) Subject to paragraph (1ZG), where a person would have been living
in a residential care home or nursing home on 31st March 1993 but for an
absence which, including that day, does not exceed—
(a) where the person was before his absence a temporary resident in the
home, 4 weeks; or

(b) where the person was before his absence a permanent resident in the home, 13 weeks; or

(c) where throughout the period of absence the person was a patient, 52 weeks,

and the provisions of paragraph (1ZN) would have applied to him but for that absence, he shall be treated as having a preserved right from 3rd October 1994.

(1ZP) Where a person is treated as having a preserved right in accordance with paragraphs (1ZK), (1ZN) or (1ZO) above, paragraph (1ZG) shall apply to that person as if he had acquired a preserved right under paragraph (1ZB).

(1ZQ) Where a person to whom paragraph (IZO) refers is absent from a residential care home or nursing home in the period from 31st March 1993 to 3rd October 1994 for a period which exceeds a period to which paragraph (1ZO) refers and which is appropriate in his case, he shall cease to be treated as having a preserved right.]

[[11](1ZR) A person who acquired a preserved right under paragraph (1ZB) or (1ZC) shall cease to have that right if—

(a) he resides in a home which falls within sub-paragraph (c) of the definition of "residential care home" in paragraph (3) (homes run by the Abbeyfield Society) and which is not registered or deemed to be registered under any of the enactments referred to in sub-paragraph (a) or (e) of that definition;

(b) he requires personal care, including assistance with bodily functions, and that residential care home does not provide such care; and

(c) he, or a person on his behalf, contracts with another person or body to provide that care,

but that preserved right shall revive if any of the conditions specified in sub-paragraphs (a) to (c) above ceases to apply and that person would, but for this provision, have retained that right.]

[[1](1A) For the purposes of paragraph (1)(b) [[4]and Schedule 4] a claimant and the members of his family are to be taken as living in a residential care home or nursing home even during periods when one or more members of the family are temporarily absent from the home but only if the claimant or his partner is living in the home during any such period.]

(2) Where—

(a) a claimant immediately before 27th July 1987 was in receipt of supplementary benefit as a boarder in a residential care home which was not required to register under Part I of the Registered Homes Act 1984 because section 1(4) of that Act (registration) applied to it; and

(b) immediately before 11th April 1988 his appropriate amount fell to be determined, by virtue of regulation 3 of the Supplementary Benefit (Requirements and Resources) Amendment Regulations 1987 (transitional provisions), in accordance with paragraph 1 of Schedule 1A to the Supplementary Benefit Requirements Regulations 1983 (maximum amounts for residential care homes) or would have been so determined but for his temporary absence from the home,

his weekly applicable amount shall be calculated in accordance with Part I of Schedule 4 (applicable amounts of persons in residential care homes or nursing homes) as if the home was a residential care home within the meaning of this regulation if, and for so long as, the claimant remains resident in the same home apart from any temporary absence, and the home continues to provide accommodation with board and personal care for the claimant by reason of his old age, disablement, past or present dependence on alcohol or drugs or past or present mental disorder.

(3) In this regulation and Schedule 4—

"nursing home" means—

(a) premises which are a nursing home or mental nursing home within the meaning of the Registered Homes Act 1984 and which are either registered under Part II of that Act or exempt from registration under section 37 thereof (power to exempt Christian Science Homes); or

(b) any premises used or intended to be used for the reception of such persons or the provision of such nursing or services as is mentioned in any paragraph of subsection (1) of section 21 or section 22(1) of the Registered Homes Act 1984 (meaning of nursing home or mental nursing home) or, in Scotland, as are mentioned in section 10(2) of the Nursing Homes Registration (Scotland) Act 1938 (interpretation) and which are maintained or controlled by a body instituted by special Act of Parliament or incorporated by Royal Charter;

(c) in Scotland,

(i) premises which are a nursing home within the meaning of section 10 of the Nursing Homes Registration (Scotland) Act 1938 which are either registered under that Act or exempt from registration under section 6 or 7 thereof (general power to exempt homes and power to exempt Christian Science Homes); or

(ii) premises which are a private hospital within the meaning of section 12 of the Mental Health (Scotland) Act 1984 (private hospitals), and which are registered under that Act,;

"residential care home" means an establishment—

[¹(a) which is required to be registered under Part I of the Registered Homes Act 1984 and is so registered [⁷, or is deemed to be registered under section 2(3) of the Registered Homes (Amendment) Act 1991 (which refers to the registration of small homes where the application for registration has not been determined)]; or]

(b) [⁷ ...]

(c) run by the Abbeyfield Society including all bodies corporate or incorporate which are affiliated to that Society; or

(d) [²which provides residential accommodation with both board and personal care and is] managed or provided by a body incorporated by Royal Charter or constituted by Act of Parliament other than a local social services authority; or

(e) in Scotland, which is a home registered under section 61 of the Social Work (Scotland) Act 1968 or is an establishment provided by [⁷a housing association registered with Scottish Homes established by the Housing (Scotland) Act 1988] which provides care equivalent to that given in residential accommodation provided under Part IV of the Social Work (Scotland) Act [⁸1968; or]

[⁸(f) which is exempt from registration under Part I of the Registered Homes Act 1984 pursuant to section 1(4)(a) of that Act (exemption from registration in respect of certain homes) because one or more of the residents are treated as relatives pursuant to section 19(4) of that Act;]

[²and in paragraphs (b) and (d) of this definition "personal care" means personal care for persons in need of personal care by reason of [³old] age, disablement, past or present dependence on alcohol or drugs, or past or present mental disorder.]

"temporary absence" means—

(a) [¹in paragraph (2) or] in the case of a person who is over pensionable age, 52 weeks;

(b) in any other case, 13 weeks.

(4) In Schedule 4 the expressions "old age", "mental disorder", "mental handicap", "drug or alcohol dependence" and "disablement" have the same

meanings as those expressions have for the purposes of the Registered Homes Act 1984 and Regulations made thereunder.

[[4](5) Notwithstanding the foregoing paragraphs of this regulation, where—

(a) a person has been registered under the Registered Homes Act 1984 in respect of premises which have been carried on as a residential care home or, as the case may be, a nursing home, and that person has ceased to carry on such a home; and

(b) an application for registration under that Act has been made by another person and that application has not been determined or abandoned,

the applicable amount of a person resident in those premises shall be determined under Schedule 4 as if the most recent registration under the Registered Homes Act 1984 in respect of those premises continued until the day on which the application is determined or abandoned.]

AMENDMENTS

1. Income Support (General) Amendment Regulations 1988 (S.I. 1988 No. 663), reg. 9 (April 11, 1988).
2. Income Support (General) Amendment No. 4 Regulations 1988 (S.I. 1988 No. 1445), reg. 7 (September 9, 1988).
3. Income Support (General) Amendment No. 5 Regulations 1988 (S.I. 1988 No. 2022), reg. 4 (December 12, 1988).
4. Income Support (General) Amendment No. 3 Regulations 1989 (S.I. 1989 No. 1678), reg. 5 (October 9, 1989).
5. Income Support (General) Amendment (No. 3) Regulations 1991 (S.I. 1991 No. 1033), reg. 2 (May 20, 1991).
6. Social Security Benefits (Amendments Consequential Upon the Introduction of Community Care) Regulations 1992 (S.I. 1992 No. 3147), reg. 3 (April 1, 1993).
7. Social Security Benefits (Amendments Consequential Upon the Introduction of Community Care) Regulations 1992 (S.I. 1992 No. 3147), Sched. 1, para. 2 (April 1, 1993).
8. Income-related Benefits Schemes (Miscellanous Amendments) (No. 4) Regulations 1993 (S.I. 1993 No. 2119), reg. 9 (October 4, 1993).
9. Income-related Benefits Schemes (Miscellanous Amendments) Regulations 1994 (S.I. 1994 No. 527), reg. 2 (April 11, 1994).
10. Income-related Benefits Schemes (Miscellaneous Amendments) (No. 5) Regulations 1994 (S.I. 1994 No. 2139), reg. 24 (October 3, 1994).
11. Income-related Benefits Schemes (Miscellaneous Amendments) Regulations 1996 (S.I. 1996 No. 462), reg. 2 (April 8, 1996).
12. Income Support (General) (Jobseeker's Allowance Consequential Amendments) Regulations 1996 (S.I. 1996 No. 206), reg. 11 (October 7, 1996).

DEFINITIONS

"benefit week"—see reg. 2(1).
"claimant"—*ibid.*
"close relative"—*ibid.* "family"—see 1986 Act, s.20(11) (SSCBA, s.137(1)).
"partner"—see reg. 2(1).
"relative"—*ibid.*
"remunerative work"—*ibid.*
"supplementary benefit"—*ibid.*

GENERAL NOTE

Note the increased upper and lower capital limits for people living permanently in residential care and nursing homes from April 1996 (regs. 45(b) and 53(1A), see the note to reg. 53).

A new system of income support for new residents of residential care and nursing homes was introduced from April 1, 1993. The system is described in the notes to para. 2A of Sched. 2. Essentially, new residents receive the ordinary income support entitlement plus a fixed residential allowance towards the cost of accommodation. It is then for the local authority to deal with the cost of the care provided in the home. But the existing system is maintained in force under reg. 19 and Sched. 4 for most of those who were resident in, or only temporarily absent from, homes on March 31, 1993. *CIS 101/1994* concerned a residential care home which operated a "care and cluster" system. In January 1993 the claimant moved into one of the "clusters". He still spent the majority of his time in the main house but slept and had breakfast in the "cluster". The Commissioner decides that the claimant was not "living" in a residential care home on March 31, 1993 and had no preserved right. "Living" should be given its ordinary, everyday meaning. The claimant's move into the "cluster" was a deliberate and planned step in the process of preparing him for living in the outside community. It was not a case, for example, of him simply sleeping there because there was no room in the main home. See also *R(IS) 2/92* and *CIS 579/1992*.

Access to the existing system depends on the claimant having a "preserved right" (para.(1)). "Preserved right" is defined in paras. (1ZB) to (1ZQ).

Para. (1ZB) deals with most cases. Para. (1ZC) covers cases where the accommodation is provided by close relatives. The basic rule in para. (1ZB) applies to those resident in a residential care home (as defined on March 31, 1993: para. (1ZJ)) or nursing home on that date. Therefore, residential care homes with less than four residents are covered if they met the conditions in head (b) of the definition in reg. 19(3) as at March 31, 1993. However, in England and Wales (but now not Scotland) there is different treatment of those entitled to income support on March 31, 1993 (para. (1ZB)(a)(i)) and those who were not entitled to income support on that date because they were self-financing (para. (1ZB)(a)(ii)), or qualify for a preserved right under para. (1ZC). A person does not have a preserved right under paras. (1ZB)(a)(ii) or (1ZC) if resident in a residential care home with less than four residents (para. (1ZE)). The thinking is that it would be too difficult to check, possibly several years after April 1993, that such a home met the condition under the old reg. 19(3). Where a resident was entitled to income support on March 31, 1993, a check would necessarily have been made. In Scotland, homes with less than four residents were not exempt from the requirement to register before April 1993 and so this rationale does not apply. The effect of para. (1ZEA) is to extend preserved rights to claimants in Scotland who were self-financing residents on March 31, 1993, or who qualify for a preserved right under para. (1ZC), irrespective of the size of the home.

Under para. (1ZB)(a)(iii), from October 3, 1994, a claimant's partner also has a preserved right where the couple were resident in a residential care or nursing home on March 31, 1993, and the claimant fell within para. (1ZB)(a)(i) or (ii). This will protect the partner's position if, for example, the claimant dies. Para. (1ZN) provides that this applies to a partner of a resident entitled to income support on March 31, 1993 who ceased to be a member of a couple before October 3, 1994, and who has continued to live in a residential care or nursing home up to October 3, 1994; certain absences are ignored (paras. (1ZO) and (1ZQ)), and this preserved right can be lost (and revive) in accordance with para. (1ZG) (para. (1ZP)).

Due to the change in the definition of residential care home in para. (3) from April 1993, residents of small homes that remained exempt from registration (see below) could have a preserved right by virtue of para. (1ZB), but not be paid income support in accordance with Part I of Sched. 4 after April 1993. From October 4, 1993, the definition of residential care home has been expanded to include those small homes not required to register because one or more residents are treated as relatives for registration purposes (category (f): see below); residents of such homes have a preserved right from October 4, 1993 and will be entitled to income support under Part I of Sched. 4, if they satisfy the conditions of para. (1ZK). This preserved right can be lost (and revive) in accordance with para. (1ZG) (para. (1ZM)). A resident of such a home who was self-financing on March 31, 1993 would not have a preserved right because of para. (1ZE).

If the person is temporarily absent from a home on March 31, 1933, there may still be a preserved right under the conditions of para. (1ZB)(b).

Under para. (1ZC) if a resident would have qualified for a preserved right under para. (1ZB) if the accommodation had not been provided by a close relative, there is a preserved right when that situation changes or there is a move to another home which qualifies.

Paras. (1ZF), (1ZG), (1ZL), (1ZM), (1ZP), (1ZQ) and (1ZR) define when a preserved right ceases to exist. Under paras. (1ZF), (1ZL) and (1ZQ) the preserved right is lost (and cannot revive) if one of the prescribed kinds of absence occurs. The absence has to be from any residential care or nursing home so that the preserved right can survive any number of moves. Each period of absence must be considered separately. There are no linking rules. Under paras. (1ZG), (1ZM) and (1ZP) the preserved right is lost temporarily if accommodation becomes provided by a close relative or on a non-commercial basis, but can revive. Para. (1ZR) deals with residents of Abbeyfield Homes. The preserved right is lost temporarily if the person needs personal care which the Home does not provide and outside arrangements have been made for the provision of such care (sub-paras. (b) and (c)). This does not apply if the Home is registered (sub-para. (a)). The intention is to enable such residents to claim ordinary income support and housing benefit so that they have more dispos-able income to pay for the care (any attendance allowance would then be disregarded: Sched. 9, para. 9). The preserved right will revive if any of the conditions in sub-paras. (a) to (c) cease to apply.

If a claimant qualifies under para. (1), income support is calculated much as before the new system was introduced. The main rules are in Sched. 4.

Part II of Sched. 4 lists people in homes who do not fall under reg. 19. They then have to be considered as ordinary claimants. There are also some special categories in reg. 21 and Sched. 7.

Where a person is temporarily absent from a residential care or nursing home, para. 16 of Sched. 7 allows a retaining fee to be paid in certain circumstances. In *CIS 5415/1995* the claimant went to stay in another residential care home for a four week trial period, during which time he was liable to pay a retaining fee to his original home. The Commissioner rejects the AO's contention that the operation of para. 16 is limited to where the claimant is absent from that *type* of accommoda-tion, rather than a particular home. She also dismisses the argument that the words "except in a case to which regulation 21 . . . applies" in para. (1) meant that regs. 19 and 21 (and thus Scheds. 4 and 7) could not apply at the same time. In her view the fact that under col. (2) of para. 16 the claimant's applicable amount could be increased to take account of a retaining fee calculated in accordance with para. 1(1)(a) of Sched. 4 showed that this was not the case. However, these argu-ments were accepted by the Commissioner in *CSIS 833/1995*. He also points out that para. 16 of Sched. 7 applies where, but for the person's temporary absence from his normal accommodation, his applicable amount would be calculated in accordance with reg. 19. The claimant was entitled to income support under reg. 19 and Sched. 4 in respect of the home in which she was temporarily residing and thus was not entitled in addition to payment of a retaining fee for the home in which she normally lived under para. 16. The Commissioner in *CIS 5415/1995* seems to have dealt with this point by accepting the submission that in these circumstances a claimant's applicable amount fell to be calculated by reference to two separate provisions and there was nothing to prevent regs. 19 and 21 applying at the same time. (As events turned out the claimant in *CSIS 833/1995* was later awarded the retainer fee because it was accepted that benefit under reg. 19 and Sched. 4 had been wrongly paid for her period in the temporary home. This does not however affect the Commis-sioner's reasoning). There is thus a conflict between these decisions and SSATs will have to decide which interpretation they prefer.

Meaning of nursing home and residential care home
"Nursing home" and "residential care home" are defined in para. (3).

Nursing home In England and Wales, if the home is not run by a body set up by special Act of Parliament or Royal Charter (para. (b)), the home must not only come within the category of nursing home in the Registered Homes Act 1984, but actually be registered under that Act (para. (a)). Para. (c) applies the same rule through the Scottish legislation. See para. (5) for changes in the registered proprietor.

Residential care home The definition has been somewhat simplified from April 1993, since the Registered Homes (Amendment) Act 1991 requires the registration of homes with less than four residents (but see category (f) below). Now under para. (a) the basic test is registration by the local authority. The local authority will apply the criteria of board and personal care at that stage. A small home can be deemed to be registered while waiting for registration.

Categories (c) and (d) do not require registration. Under (c) all Abbeyfield Homes are included whether or not they provide board and personal care and whether or not they meet the conditions for registration (*R(SB) 11/91*). There is no special category for Abbeyfield Homes under the new system (Sched. 2, para. 2A).

In category (d), a decision is necessary on whether board and personal care is provided. By analogy with cases on the Rent Acts (see *Otter v. Norman* [1988] 2 All E. R. 897 for a discussion), "board" requires the provision of some prepared food or drink which goes beyond the trivial. It does not require any particular standard of substantiality, but a cup of cocoa, say, would not do on its own. "Personal care" is only defined to the extent of limiting the reasons why it has to be provided. The *Adjudication Officer's Guide* (para. 29041) suggests that "personal care" means "all that the proprietors must do to preserve and promote the health, safety and well being of the resid-ents. [It] is broadly the same as the care which might be provided by a competent carer, which includes washing, bathing, dressing, toiletry needs, administration of medicines and when a resident falls sick, the kind of attention someone would receive from a carer under the guidance of a GP, a nurse, or any other member of the primary health care service." This is helpful, but should not be seen to imply that a particular level of personal care must be provided. If something beyond the trivial which counts as personal care is provided, then personal care is provided, even though much more care would be desirable.

Category (f) has been added from October 4, 1993 to include small homes not required to register because one or more residents are *treated* as relatives for the purposes of Part I of the Registered Homes Act 1984. Under s.1(4)(a), as amended by the Registered Homes (Amendment) Act 1991, and s.19(4) of the 1984 Act, homes with less than four residents are not required to register where the only residents are those who run the home, employees, their relatives or people who are treated as relatives because they have lived there for at least five years. Thus homes which are not required to register because the residents are genuine relatives are not covered by category (f). Residents of homes in category (f) will be entitled to income support under Part I of Sched. 4 from October 4, 1993 if they satisfy the conditions of para. (1ZK) (see above).

The consequence if a home fails to get into either of the definitions is that a resident does not qualify under para. (1) and may also not qualify for a residential allowance under para. 2A of Sched. 2, so being restricted to the ordinary allowances and premiums plus housing benefit.

There are other important definitions dealt with below under para. (4).

Once the category of home is settled, paras.(1) and (1A) deal with the residence of the claimant and his family (if any).

Para. (1ZA) secures that a person who qualifies under para. (1) does not qualify for the severe disability premium. The person's care needs are deemed to be taken care of by the residential care or nursing home.

Paragraph (2)

This provision continues the transitional protection formerly given by reg. 3 of the Supplementary Benefit (Requirements and Resources) Amendment Regulations 1987, dating from July 27, 1987. For receipt of supplementary benefit as a boarder, see *R(SB) 12/87* and *CSB 29/1986*.

Paragraph (4)

"Mental disorder" is defined in s.55 of the Registered Homes Act 1984 as "mental illness, arrested or incomplete development of mind, psychopathic disorder, and any other disorder or disability of mind." "Mental handicap" is defined in reg. 1(2) of the Residential Care Homes Regulations 1984 as "a state of arrested or incomplete development of mind which includes impairment of intelligence and social functioning." Thus, "mental disorder" can include "mental handicap." Senility is not a mental handicap, but it can amount to a mental disorder *(R(SB) 17/88)*.

"Disablement" is defined in s.20(1) of the 1984 Act as meaning that the person concerned is "blind, deaf or dumb or substantially and permanently handicapped by illness, injury or congenital deformity or any other disability prescribed by the Secretary of State."

Paragraph (5)

This provision allows the definition to be met through gaps in registration when proprietors change.

Applicable amounts for persons in board and lodging accommodation and hostels

20.—[¹. . .]

AMENDMENT

1. Income Support (General) Amendment Regulations 1989 (S.I. 1989 No. 534), Sched. 1, para. 4 (October 9, 1989).

GENERAL NOTE

As from October 1989, most hostel-dwellers, unless their accommodation comes within the amended definition of residential accommodation in reg. 21(3), are entitled to the ordinary income support personal allowances and premiums and to housing benefit for their accommodation. See Sched. 3B for transitional protection from October 1989 and April 1990.

Boarders had already been transferred to a similar system from April 1989. Their transitional protection is under Sched. 3A.

Special cases

21.—(1) Subject to [²¹regulation 21ZA (treatment of refugees) and][¹⁹regulation 22A] (reductions in applicable amounts) in the case of a person to whom any paragraph in column (1) of Schedule 7 applies (applicable amounts in special cases), the amount included in the claimant's weekly amount in respect of him shall be the amount prescribed in the corresponding paragraph in column (2) of that Schedule; but no amount shall be included in respect of a child or young person if the capital of that child or young person calculated in accordance with Part V in like manner as for the claimant, [¹³except as provided in regulation 44(1) (modifications in respect of children and young persons)], would exceed £3,000.

[⁶(1A) Except where the amount prescribed in Schedule 7 in respect of a person to whom paragraph (1) applies includes an amount applicable under regulation 17(1)(d) or 18(1)(e), a person to whom paragraph (1) applies shall be treated as not being severely disabled.]

(2) In Schedule 7, for the purposes of paragraph 1, 2, 3 or 18 (patients), where a person has been a patient for two or more distinct periods separated by one or more intervals each not exceeding 28 days, he shall be treated as having been a patient continuously for a period equal in duration to the total of those distinct periods.

(3) [¹⁸Subject to paragraph (3F),] in Schedule 7—

''person from abroad'' means a person, who—

   (a) has a limited leave as defined in section 33(1) of the Immigration Act 1971 (hereinafter referred to as ''the 1971 Act'') to enter or remain in the United Kingdom which was given in accordance with any provision of the immigration rules (as defined in that section) which refers to there being, or to there needing to be, no recourse to public funds or to there being no charge on public funds during that limited leave; but this sub-paragraph shall not apply to a person who is a national of a Member State, a state which is a signatory to the European Convention on Social and Medical Assistance (done in Paris on 11th December 1953), [⁵a state which is a signatory to the Council of Europe Social Charter (signed in Turin on 18th October 1961),] [²⁰. . .] [³, unless, in the case of a national of a state which is a signatory of that European Convention, he has made an application for the conditions of his leave to remain in the United Kingdom to be varied, and that application has not been determined or an appeal from that application is pending under Part II of the 1971 Act (appeals);] or

   (b) having a limited leave (as defined in section 33(1) of the 1971 Act) to enter or remain in the United Kingdom, has remained without further leave under that Act beyond the time limited by the leave; or

   (c) is the subject of a deportation order being an order under section 5(1) of the 1971 Act (deportation) requiring him to leave and prohibiting him from entering the United Kingdom; or

   (d) is adjudged by the immigration authorities to be an illegal entrant (as defined in section 33(1) of the 1971 Act) who has not subsequently been given leave under that Act to enter or remain in the United Kingdom; or

   (e) has been allowed temporary admission to the United Kingdom by virtue of paragraph 21 of Schedule 2 to the 1971 Act; or

  (f) has been allowed temporary admission to the United Kingdom by the Secretary of State outside any provision of the 1971 Act; or

  (g) has not had his immigration status determined by the Secretary of State; [¹¹or

  (h) is a national of a member State and is required by the Secretary of State to leave the United Kingdom;] [¹⁷or

  (i) has been given leave to enter, or remain in, the United Kingdom by the Secretary of State upon an undertaking given by another person or persons in writing in pursuance of immigration rules within the meaning of the Immigration Act 1971, to be responsible for his maintenance and accommodation; and he has not been resident in the United Kingdom for a period of at least 5 years beginning from the date of entry or the date on which the undertaking was given in respect of him, whichever date is the later; or

  (j) while he is a person to whom any of the definitions in sub-paragraphs (a) to (i) applies in his case, submits a claim to the Secretary of State, which is not finally determined, for asylum under the Convention;]

[¹⁴"person from abroad" also means a claimant who is not habitually resident in the United Kingdom, [²⁰ the Channel Islands, the Isle of Man or the Republic of Ireland], but for this purpose, no claimant shall be treated as not habitually resident in the United Kingdom who is—

  (a) a worker for the purposes of Council Regulation (EEC) No. 1612/68 or (EEC) No. 1251/70 or a person with a right to reside in the United Kingdom pursuant to Council Directive No. 68/360/EEC or No. 73/148/EEC; or

  (b) a refugee within the definition in Article 1 of the Convention relating to the Status of Refugees done at Geneva on 28th July 1951, as extended by Article 1(2) of the Protocol relating to the Status of Refugees done at New York on 31st January 1967; or

  (c) a person who has been granted exceptional leave [²⁴ to enter the United Kingdom by an immigration officer within the meaning of the Immigration Act 1971, or] to remain in the United Kingdom by the Secretary of State.]

"patient" means a person (other than a prisoner) who is regarded as receiving free in-patient treatment within the meaning of the Social Security (Hospital In-Patients) Regulations 1975;

[¹⁶"prisoner" means a person who—

  (a) is detained in custody pending trial or sentence upon conviction or under a sentence imposed by a court; or

  (b) is on temporary release in accordance with the provisions of the Prison Act 1952 or the Prisons (Scotland) Act 1989,

other than a person [²³ who is detained in hospital under the provisions of the Mental Health Act 1983, or, in Scotland, under the provisions of the Mental Health (Scotland) Act 1984 or the Criminal Procedure (Scotland) Act 1995;]]

[⁹"residential accommodation" means, subject to the following provisions of this regulation, accommodation provided by a local authority in a home owned or managed by that or another local authority—

  (a) under sections 21 to 24 [¹⁶...] of the National Assistance Act 1948 (provision of accommodation); or

  (b) in Scotland, under section 13B or 59 of the Social Work (Scotland) Act 1968 (provision of residential and other establishments) [¹⁵...]; or

  (c) under section 7 of the Mental Health (Scotland) Act 1984 (functions of local authorities), where the accommodation is provided for a person whose stay in that accommodation has become other than temporary.]

[[7](3A) Where on or after 12th August 1991 a person is in, or only temporarily absent from, residential accommodation within the meaning of paragraph (3) and that accommodation subsequently becomes a residential care home within the meaning of regulation 19 (applicable amounts for persons in residential care and nursing homes) that person shall continue to be treated as being in residential accommodation within the meaning of paragraph (3) if, and for so long as, he remains in the same accommodation [[22]. . .].]

[[10](3B) In a case where on 31st March 1993 a person was in or was temporarily absent from accommodation provided under section 26 of the National Assistance Act 1948, the definition of "residential accommodation" in paragraph (3) shall have effect in relation to that case as if for the words "provided by a local authority in a home owned or managed by that or another authority" there were substituted the words "provided in accordance with arrangements made by a local authority", and for the words in sub-paragraph (a) "under sections 21 to 24 [[16]. . .]" there were substituted the words "under section 26".

(3C) In a case where on 31st March 1993 a person was in or was temporarily absent from accommodation provided by a local authority under section 21 of the National Assistance Act 1948, the definition of "residential accommodation" in paragraph (3) shall have effect in relation to that case as if, after the words "by that or another [[12]local] authority" there were inserted the words "or provided in accordance with arrangements made by a local authority".]

[[15](3D) In Scotland, in a case where on the 31st March 1993 a person was in or was temporarily absent from accommodation provided under section 13B in a private or voluntary sector home, section 59(2)(c) of the Social Work (Scotland) Act 1968 or section 7 of the Mental Health (Scotland) Act 1984 in a voluntary or private sector home, the definition of "residential accommodation" in paragraph (3) shall have effect in that case as if—

(a) for the words "provided by a local authority in a home owned or man-aged by that or another local authority" there were substituted the words "provided in accordance with arrangements made by a local authority"; and

(b) for the words in sub-paragraph (b) "under section 13B or 59" there were substituted the words "under section 13B or 59(2)(c)";

and for the purpose of this paragraph the definition of "residential accommoda-tion" above shall continue to have effect as though the words "other than in premises registered under section 61 of that Act (registration) and which are used for the rehabilitation of alcoholics or drug addicts." were retained at the end of sub-paragraph (b) of the definition.

(3E) In Scotland, in a case where on 31st March 1993 a person was in or was temporarily absent from accommodation the provision of which was secured by a local authority under section 13B in a home owned or managed by that or another local authority, section 59(2)(a) or (b) of the Social Work (Scotland) Act 1968, or section 7 of the Mental Health (Scotland) Act 1984 in a home owned or managed by that or another local authority, the definition of "residen-tial accommodation" in paragraph (3) shall have effect in relation to that case as if, after the words "by that or another local authority" there were inserted the words "or provided in accordance with arrangements made by a local authority".]

[[18](3F) In paragraph (3) "person from abroad" does not include any person in Great Britain who left the territory of Montserrat after 1st November 1995 because of the effect on that territory of a volcanic eruption.]

(4) A person who would, but for this paragraph, be in residential accommodation within the meaning of paragraph (3) shall not be treated as being in residential accommodation if he is a person—

(a) who is under the age of 18 and in the care of a local authority under Part II or III of the Social Work (Scotland) Act 1968 (promotion of social welfare of children in need of care), or

(b) [¹⁶. . .]

(c) for whom board is not provided.]

[⁸(4A) [⁹In paragraph (4), sub-paragraph (c)] shall apply only to accommodation—

(a) where no cooked or prepared food is made available to the claimant in consequence solely of his paying the charge for the accommodation or any other charge which he is required to pay as a condition of occupying the accommodation, or both of those charges, or

(b) where such food is actually made available for his consumption on payment of a further charge or charges.]

[¹⁰(4B) In the case of a person who on 31st March 1993 was either in or only temporarily absent from, residential accommodation within the meaning of regulation 21(3) as then in force, paragraph (4) shall apply as if sub-paragraph (c) was omitted.]

(5) A claimant to whom paragraph 19 of Schedule 7 (disability premium) applies shall be entitled to income support for the period in respect of which that paragraph applies to him notwithstanding that his partner was also entitled to income support for that same period.

AMENDMENTS

1. Income Support (General) Amendment No. 4 Regulations 1988 (S.I. 1988 No. 1445), Sched. 1, para. 1 (April 10, 1989).

2. Income Support (General) Amendment Regulations 1989 (S.I. 1989 No. 534), Sched. 1, para. 5 (October 9, 1989).

3. Income Support (General) Amendment Regulations 1990 (S.I. 1990 No. 547), reg. 8 (April 9, 1990).

4. Income Support (General and Transitional) Amendment Regulations 1990 (S.I. 1990 No. 2324), reg. 2 (December 17, 1990).

5. Income Support (General) Amendment Regulations 1991 (S.I. 1991 No. 236), reg. 7 (April 8, 1991).

6. Income Support (General) Amendment (No. 3) Regulations 1991 (S.I. 1991 No. 1033), reg. 2 (May 20, 1991).

7. Income Support (General) Amendment (No. 5) Regulations 1991 (S.I. 1991 No. 1656), reg. 2 (August 12, 1991).

8. Income-related Benefits Schemes (Miscellaneous Amendments) (No. 3) Regulations 1992 (S.I. 1992 No. 2155), reg. 15 (October 5, 1992).

9. Social Security Benefits (Amendments Consequential Upon the Introduction of Community Care) Regulations 1992 (S.I. 1992 No. 3147), Sched. 1, para. 3 (April 1, 1993).

10. Social Security Benefits (Miscellaneous Amendments) Regulations 1993 (S.I. 1993 No. 518), reg. 5 (April 1, 1993).

11. Income-related Benefits Schemes (Miscellaneous Amendments) Regulations 1993 (S.I. 1993 No. 315), reg. 4 (April 12, 1993).

12. Income-related Benefits Schemes (Miscellaneous Amendments) (No. 4) Regulations 1993 (S.I. 1993 No. 2119), reg. 10 (October 4, 1993).

13. Income-related Benefits Schemes (Miscellaneous Amendments) Regulations 1994 (S.I. 1994 No. 527), reg. 3 (April 11, 1994).

14. Income-related Benefits Schemes (Miscellaneous Amendments) (No. 3) Regulations 1994 (S.I. 1994 No. 1807), reg. 4(1) (August 1, 1994).

15. Income-related Benefits Schemes (Miscellaneous Amendments) (No. 5) Regulations 1994 (S.I. 1994 No. 2139), reg. 25 (October 3, 1994).

16. Income-related Benefits Schemes (Miscellaneous Amendments) Regulations 1995 (S.I. 1995 No. 516), reg. 21 (April 10, 1995).

17. Social Security (Persons from Abroad) Miscellaneous Amendments Regulations 1996 (S.I. 1996 No. 30), reg. 8(2) (February 5, 1996).

18. Income-related Benefits (Montserrat) Regulations 1996 (S.I. 1996 No. 2006), reg. 4 (August 28, 1996).

19. Income Support (General) (Jobseeker's Allowance Consequential Amendments) Regulations 1996 (S.I. 1996 No. 206), reg. 12 (October 7, 1996).

20. Income-related Benefits Schemes and Social Fund (Miscellaneous Amendments) Regulations 1996 (S.I. 1996 No. 1944), reg. 6(6) (October 7, 1996).

21. Income Support and Social Security (Claims and Payments) (Miscellaneous Amendments) Regulations 1996 (S.I. 1996 No. 2431), reg. 2 (October 15, 1996).

22. Income Support (General) Amendment (No. 3) Regulations 1996 (S.I. 1996 No. 2614), reg. 2 (November 8, 1996).

23. Social Security (Miscellaneous Amendments) Regulations 1998 (S.I. 1998 No. 563), reg. 8(1) and (2)(c)(i) (April 6, 1998).

24. Social Security (Miscellaneous Amendments) Regulations 1998 (S.I. 1998 No. 563), reg. 18(3) and (4)(c) (April 6, 1998).

DEFINITIONS

"child"—see 1986 Act, s.20(11) (SSCBA, s.137(1)).
"claimant"—see reg. 2(1).
"local authority"—*ibid.*
"residential care home"—*ibid.*, reg. 19(3).
"young person"—*ibid.*, reg. 14.

GENERAL NOTE

Paragraph (1)
Applicable amounts in special cases are to be as prescribed in Sched. 7. It is confirmed that the rule in reg. 17(b), disallowing a personal allowance for a child or young person who has capital of more than £3,000, applies to Sched. 7.

On para. 16 of Sched. 7 see *CIS 5415/1995* and *CSIS 833/1995* in the notes to reg. 19.

Under para. 6 of Sched. 7 a person "without accommodation" is only entitled to a personal allowance for himself (or the allowance for a couple, if he is a member of a couple). In *CIS 16772/1996* the claimant had lived in his car for approximately two weeks. He was refused a disability premium as part of his income support. The Commissioner decides that a car could not be regarded as accommodation in the context of para. 6. He approved of the following description of accommodation in para. 29503 of the *Adjudication Officer's Guide*: "An effective shelter from the elements which is capable of being heated; and in which the occupants can sit, lie down, cook and eat; and which is reasonably suited for continuous occupation". While there is force in the Commissioner's reasoning in relation to a car, his (*obiter*) view that an ordinary tent or touring caravan may not constitute accommodation is more surprising (particularly in the light of the AO's concession to the contrary). It is suggested that the AO's distinction between a car as a means of transport and a tent (or caravan) as a means of shelter is correct. In this connection, note also para. 17(1)(f) of Schedule 3 under which payments in respect of a tent count as allowable housing costs (without any restriction as to the kind of tent).

Paragraph (1A)
This provision secures that, except where the particular paragraph of Sched. 7 expressly allows the payment of a premium, a person whose entitlement falls under Sched. 7 does not qualify for the severe disability premium.

Paragraph (2)
This provision supplies a linking rule for hospital patients (see para. (3)) who come out of hospital for short periods.

Paragraph (3)
This paragraph contains some important definitions for Sched. 7, which are also referred to in other parts of the Regulations.

"Person from abroad"
With the new sub-paras. (i) and (j) introduced on February 5, 1996 and the additional definition of "person from abroad" inserted into para. (3) from August 1, 1994, there are effectively ten categories:

(1) those present in the U.K. with limited leave subject to the condition that there is no recourse to public funds;
(2) overstayers;
(3) those subject to a deportation order;
(4) illegal entrants;
(5) those allowed temporary admission to the U.K.;
(6) those whose immigration status has not been determined;
(7) EU nationals who are required to leave the U.K.;
(8) those subject to a sponsorship undertaking;
(9) those falling within (1) to (8) who apply for asylum;
(10) those who are not habitually resident in the U.K., the Channel Islands, the Isle of Man or the Republic of Ireland, subject to the exceptions in (a), (b) or (c) of that part of the definition.

Note para. (3F). A person who left Montserrat after November 1, 1995 because of the effects of volcanic eruption does not count as a person from abroad. It does not seem to be necessary for the person to have come directly to Great Britain from Montserrat.
See para. 17 of Sched. 7 for the special rules for persons from abroad.

(1) For this category (sub-para. (a)) to apply the person must need leave to enter or remain in the U.K. In *R(SB) 11/88* it was held that it was for a SSAT to decide for supplementary benefit purposes whether a person was a patrial and so did not need leave to enter the country. The claimant had mistakenly been granted limited leave in 1982, and the immigration authorities did not in fact lift immigration controls until 1985. Although a SSAT should approach the Home Office for information if an issue of patriality arises and the person does not have a certificate of entitlement, it was not bound to apply the decision of the immigration authorities from 1982. *R(SB) 2/85* and *R(SB) 25/85*, giving conclusive effect to the decisions of the immigration authorities on the terms of leave, are held to be confined to situations where it is clear that leave is required for entry. A proper statement of the terms of leave should be obtained from the Home Office (*CSSB 137/1982*). These principles should also apply to income support.
  Sub-para. (a) cannot apply to nationals of EU Member States or to nationals of so-called "convention countries". The convention countries, apart from those which have joined the E.U., are Iceland, Malta, Norway and Turkey. The exception for nationals of these countries who are applying to vary their leave only affects Maltese and Turkish citizens as Iceland and Norway are part of the European Economic Area (see below). The 1991 amendment brought in signatories to the European Social Charter. This now only affects Cyprus, as Austria has joined the E.U.
(2) Some people who do not fall into sub-para. (a) may be given limited leave to be present in the U.K. with no conditions about public funds and thus may fall into para. (b) if they remain beyond the time limited by their leave. This cannot apply to nationals of the Republic of Ireland, the Isle of Man or the Channel Islands, who have freedom of travel within the U.K. (Immigration Act 1971, s.1(3)).
  In the past there was doubt as to whether E.U. nationals could have limited leave within this category (see *R v. Pieck* [1981] Q.B. 571) and for that reason sub-para. (h) was added from April 1993. Note also that on July 20, 1994 s. 7(1) of the Immigration Act 1988 was brought into force, which expressly provides that a person exercising Community rights does not require leave to enter or remain in the U.K.
(3) A British citizen cannot be deported, nor can some citizens of the Commonwealth and the Republic of Ireland (Immigration Act 1971, s.7(1)).
(4) Under sub-para. (d) the judgment of the immigration authorities on the person's status as an illegal entrant has to be accepted by the AO and SSAT.
(5) Sub-paras. (e) and (f) cover all forms of temporary admission. An asylum seeker, unless he is detained, will be granted temporary admission pending investigation of his claim for asylum (see *CIS 3108/1997*).
(6) Sub-para. (g) covers those whose immigration status has not been determined by the immigration authorities. This must be subject to the principles of *R(SB) 11/88*.
(7) *Sub-para. (h)*. Nationals of the European Economic Area (EEA) States who are exercising Community rights of freedom of movement may enter or remain in the U.K. without requiring leave under the Immigration Act 1971. The EEA comprises E.U. Member States (Austria, Belgium, Denmark, Finland, France, Germany, Greece, Republic of Ireland, Italy, Luxembourg, The Netherlands, Portugal, Spain, Sweden and the U.K.) plus Norway, Liechtenstein and Iceland (nationals of the EEA States have rights of free movement within the EEA from January 1, 1994 under the Agreement establishing the EEA). The position of EEA nationals exercising

Community rights is now set out in the Immigration (European Economic Area) Order 1994 (S.I. 1994 No. 1895) (the I (EEA) Order), in force from July 20, 1994. Broadly, those exercising Community rights include workers within the meaning of article 48 of the E.C. Treaty (which therefore includes some work seekers, see *Antonissen* below), self-employed people, providers or recipients of services within the meaning of article 60 of the Treaty, plus others whose right of residence is subject to the condition that they are self-financing, including students and retired people, Such a person counts as a "qualified person" (article 6 of the I(EEA) Order) who has a right of residence under article 4 of the Order. Under the I(EEA) Order EEA nationals who cease to be qualified persons are treated as if they required leave to enter or remain and can be removed from the U.K. They have a right of appeal under the Immigration Act 1971.

A person may cease to be a quailified person if, for example, he has not found employment after a certain length of time, or he is here in a non-economic capacity and he claims income support. The question of an E.U. national's right to remain in the U.K. for an *unlimited* period for the purpose of seeking employment was considered by the ECJ in *R v. Immigration Appeal Tribunal ex parte Antonissen* [1991] E.C.R. 1–745. The Court held that the six months allowed under para. 143 of the then current Statement of Changes in Immigration Rules (HC 169) during which a person should obtain work did not "appear in principle to be insufficient". However, the Court also said that if a person showed he had "genuine chances" of finding employment he could not be required to leave the host Member State. In *R v. Secretary of State for Home Department ex parte Vitale and Do Amaral* [1995] All E.R. (E.C.) 946, [1955] 3 C.M.L.R. 605, Judge J held that the limitations on the rights of free movement approved by the ECJ in *Antonissen* remained effective, despite article 8a(1) of the E.C. Treaty, inserted by the Treaty of the European Union from November 1, 1993. Article 8a(1) provides that every E.U. citizen has "the right to move and reside freely within the territory of the Member States, subject to the limitations and conditions laid down in this Treaty and by the measures adopted to give it effect". On appeal the Court of Appeal ([1996] All E.R. 461]) confirmed that article 8a did not create an unqualified right of every E.U. citizen to reside in any Member State as and when they may wish. (For further discussion of *Vitale and Do Amaral* and of *Castelli and Tristan-Garcia v. Westminister City Council* [1996] H.L.R. 616, see the 1997 edition of this book. In *Castelli* the Court of Appeal held that the fact that an EEA national had ceased to be a qualified person did not mean that he was not lawfully present here.)

"Required to leave". Since 1993 the Home Office has sent letters to those who have not found work after six months requiring them to leave. Similar letters are sent to those here in a non-economic capacity who have been claiming income support. These letters refer to the Secretary of State's view that the person is not lawfully resident under E.C. law and state that the person should make arrangements to leave the U.K. This "requirement" to leave is not enforced but has in the past resulted in the withdrawal of income support under sub-para. (h).

But in *CIS 472/1994* decided on May 4, 1995, the Commissioner held that the Home Office letter did not *require* a person to leave within the meaning of sub-para. (h). This was because the form of words used fell short of the necessary degree of compulsion or insistence for there to be such a "requirement". They were words of "advice" that the person should make arrangements to leave, but no more. The same conclusion was reached by Popplewell J. in *R v. Oxford SSAT ex p. Wolke* (High Court, April 30, 1996). The facts in *Wolke* were similar, except that the terms of the Home Office letter had by that stage been amended to include an additional statement that if the person did not leave the U.K. on a voluntary basis then in the present circumstances steps would not be taken to enforce departure. Further, Miss Wolke's letter was sent after the I(EEA) Order had come into force (unlike the letter in *CIS 472/1994*).

The AO appealed to the Court of Appeal against the decisions in *CIS 472/1994* and *Wolke*. The Court of Appeal ([1996] All E.R. (E.C.) 850) allowed the appeal by a majority, holding that the Home Office letter was a requirement to leave within sub-para. (h), so that both claimants were "persons from abroad" and not entitled to income support. However, the claimants' appeals were allowed by the House of Lords, Lord Slynn dissenting (*Remelien v. Secretary of State for Social Security and Another, Chief Adjudication Officer v. Wolke* [1998] 1 All E.R. 129, also to be reported as *R(IS) 13/98*). Lord Hoffmann, who gave judgment for the majority, said that a requirement to leave would only arise when a deportation order or an order for removal under article 15(2) of the I(EEA) Order had been made (after any appeals had run their course). The Home Office letter did not amount to such a requirement, since there was no legal obligation to leave. Lord Hoffmann pointed to the fact that sub-para. (h) had been added to para. (3) following the ECJ's decision in *Antonissen*. The Court's answer in *Antonissen* had referred to a right of appeal. But there was no effective right of appeal against the Home Office's letter. It was accepted that there was no appeal to an immigration adjudicator against the letter; in addition Lord Hoffman disagreed with Judge J.'s view in *Vitale and Do Amaral* that the Home

Office's letter could be judicially reviewed or appealed to a SSAT (in relation to the latter he said that the judge appeared not to have taken account of s.22(3)(a) of the Administration Act). Lord Hoffman also rejected the argument that on his construction sub-para. (h) was superfluous because orders for removal under article 15(2) of the I(EEA) Order could fall within sub-para. (c). In his view there was a distinction between a deportation order (which required a person not merely to leave but also not to return) and a power of "removal" (which permitted return in certain circumstances). The fact that a decision to remove was *treated* as a deportation order for the purposes of appeal only emphasised that the removal was not a deportation order.

The result is that receipt of a Home Office letter requiring the claimant to leave will not trigger the operation of sub-para. (h) and thus will have no effect on the claimant's entitlement to income support.

(8) Sub-para. (i) covers sponsored immigrants who claim income support on or after February 5, 1996. It only applies for five years from the date of entry into the U.K. or the undertaking, whichever is the later (or until the person becomes a British citizen). A formal written undertaking must have been required under the Immigration Act 1971; those who have entered the U.K. with the support of an informal arrangement do not fall within sub-para. (i). If the sponsor(s) has/have died, the person will be entitled to urgent cases payments of income support (see reg. 70(3)(c)).

Note the transitional protection in reg. 12(2) of the Social Security (Persons from Abroad) Miscellaneous Amendments Regulations 1996 (see p. 498) for sponsored immigrants entitled to income support before February 5, 1996.

(9) Sub-para. (j), in force from February 5, 1996, covers people who fall within sub-paras. (a) – (i) who apply for asylum. It applies until their asylum application is finally determined. See reg. 70(3) – (3B) for those asylum seekers who are entitled to urgent cases payments and note the transitional protection in reg. 12(1) of the Social Security (Persons From Abroad) Miscellaneous Amendments Regulations 1996 (see p. 498). On June 21, 1996 the Court of Appeal held (by a majority) that these Regulations were *ultra vires* insofar as they amended previous regulations to deny income support, housing benefit and council tax benefit to asylum seekers, but the defects were cured and the Regulations made valid by the Asylum and Immigration Act 1996 with effect from July 24, 1996. See further the notes to reg. 70(3) – (3B).

(10) This additional definition of "person from abroad" introduces an "habitual residence" test for income support from August 1, 1994. A similar rule was introduced for housing benefit and council tax benefit at the same time. The test also applies for income-based JSA. The provision has been the subject of various challenges (see under "*Swaddling*" and "*Validity of the habitual residence test*") and the question of the meaning of habitual residence in this context is currently before the House of Lords (see under *CIS 2326/1995 (Nessa)*).

Note: The government announced on June 14, 1999 that, following a Departmental review and taking account of the ECJ's decision in *Swaddling* (see below), the habitual residence test was to be reformed. The DSS Press Release stated that the Government had accepted that the ECJ's judgment had "made it clear that people returning to the U.K. from an E.U. member state and re-establishing their ties here should be treated as habitually resident immediately upon their return. However, we believe it would be wrong to limit this important principle to people returning from a member state of the E.U. and have issued guidance to staff administering the test advising them to extend the effect of the judgment to people returning from any country overseas and re-establishing their ties here." It does seem somewhat strange that the Government has decided to proceed by way of guidance in this instance, since this interpretation of habitual residence clearly does involve a change in domestic law as it currently stands. Moreover, the Government *is* planning to legislate to implement another proposed change, namely to treat as habitually resident people who are brought here from an area of civil unrest or who are deported to the U.K. Note that it is also proposed to reduce the period when habitual residence enquiries are made to two years, and to introduce the use of a standard proforma to facilitate information gathering and decision making on cases involving the application of the habitual residence test.

It should also be noted that the House of Lord's judgment in *Nessa* (see below under *CIS 2326/1995*) is currently awaited. The claimant in that case had come to the U.K. for the first time and so would not fall into the "re-establishing ties" category.

The notes below therefore need to be read bearing in mind that the law (and practice) in this area is currently in a state of flux and may well be subject to substantial change in the near future. See the 1999 Supplement to this book for further developments.

Background to the introduction of the habitual residence test

Part of the Government's justification for this significant and controversial change in the conditions of entitlement for income support was its concern about the potential growth of "benefit tourism", particularly with the expansion of the EEA. No evidence, however, was produced to indicate that this is a widespread problem. Although the intended target of the rule is EEA nationals, others, for example U.K. citizens, particularly those from ethnic minorities, with family ties in other countries who have spent time living and working in those countries, or U.K. nationals returning after working abroad for a prolonged period, may experience difficulties in satisfying the test. The Social Security Advisory Committee's recommendation (Cm. 2609/1994) that an habitual residence condition should not be imposed without research being undertaken to quantify the perceived problem and the potential effects of the proposed test was not accepted. The Committee also made other recommendations were the proposals to be implemented, some of which are reflected in the regulation's final form.

The test

All claimants, including U.K. nationals and nationals of other EEA States, are subject to the test, unless they fall within one of the exempted groups (see below). The test applies to all new and repeat claims for income support from August 1, 1994. Existing claimants were not affected (see reg. 4(2) of the Income-related Benefits Schemes (Miscellaneous Amendments) (No. 3) Regulations 1994 (p. 494)). The requirement only applies to the claimant, not a partner or dependant. *R(IS)6/96* confirms that since this rule operates as an exclusion from benefit, the burden of proof is on the AO. This would seem to be correct, although it is not the view of the Commissioner in *CIS 12294/1996*. But his approach is based on the principle that in matters of evidence the burden is on the person seeking to establish the particular proposition being contended. In practical terms, clearly it will be very useful for a claimant to present evidence that goes towards establishing that he is habitually resident.

The basic rule is that a claimant who is not habitually resident in any part of the Common Travel Area (CTA) of the U.K., the Channel Islands, the Isle of Man and the Republic of Ireland is defined as a "person from abroad" and will not be entitled to ordinary income support. (Note that a "person from abroad" who qualifies for income support under reg. 70(3) (urgent cases) will be entitled to this even if they do not satisfy the habitual residence test.) However, certain groups are treated as habitually resident (sub-paras. (a) to (c)) and these are considered first.

Who is exempt?

Sub-para. (a)

A person who is a "worker" for the purposes of E.C. Regulations 1612/68 or 1251/70, or who has a right of residence under E.C. Directives 68/360 or 73/148, is exempt. These Regulations and Directives apply to all EEA nationals, including U.K. nationals who are exercising Community rights: *R v. Immigration Appeal Tribunal and Surinder Singh, ex parte Secretary of State for the Home Department*, ECJ Case C-370/90, [1992] 3 All E.R. 798. Community rights include the right to move in order to work, or to seek work (Art. 48 of the Treaty of Rome). A U.K. National who has moved to another EEA country to work and then returns to the U.K. in order to seek work is thus exercising his right to freedom of movement, and this is so whether or not he claims income support/income-based JSA (contrary to the assertion frequently made by AOs); exemption from the habitual residence test will, however, depend on whether he counts as a worker (see below) or can otherwise satisfy or be treated as satisfying the habitual residence test. But note that as a result of the ECJ's decision in *Swaddling*, such a person may count as habitually resident immediately on his return (see below). Obviously in most cases a person who is a worker or work seeker will now have to claim income-based JSA rather than income support (unless, for example, he is incapable of work).

E.C. Regulations 1612/68 and 1251/70
Regulation 1612/68 provides for freedom of movement for workers and their families.

The main question is what is meant by "worker" in this context. "Worker" is not defined in Regulation 1612/68 (or in the E.C. Treaty). However, the word is to be interpreted broadly and as a matter of Community, not national, law (*Levin* [1982] E.C.R. 1035). A person's motives for working in another Member State are not relevant (*Bettray* [1989] E.C.R 1621). "Worker" includes those who work part-time or whose pay is below subsistence level, provided that they are pursuing an activity that is "genuine and effective" and not on such a small scale as to be "marginal and ancillary" (*Levin*, and *Kempf* [1986] E.C.R. 1741). If the work is very limited *and* only on an irregular or occasional basis, this may indicate that it is a marginal and ancillary activity (*Raulin* [1992] E.C.R. 1–1027). But if it can be described as an economic activity (*Levin*), as opposed to, for example, a hobby, this should count as work, even if it is for only a few hours a week. In *CIS 12909/1996* an au pair who had worked for five weeks (being paid £35 for a 13 hour week, plus free board and lodging) was held to be a worker.

Thus if the person has genuinely worked, even for a very short period, they can count as a worker. There seems to be no reason why this should not include work done during a previous stay in the U.K. (even if on this occasion the person has not yet obtained employment). And see further the question referred to the ECJ by the Commissioner in *Swaddling* (below), although this was not answered by the Court. It was accepted by the Advocate General in *Scrivner* [1985] E.C.R. 1027 that if a worker becomes unemployed or incapable of work, they remain a worker for the purposes of Regulation 1612/68. (The ECJ itself did not comment on the point because the national court had accepted that Mr Scrivner still had the status of worker and so no question on this issue was put to the ECJ.) Mr Scrivner had worked in Belgium but had given up his job for personal reasons and then registered as in search of work. The ECJ held that he was entitled to the Belgian "minimex" (a benefit which provided a "minimum means of subsistence"), as this was a social advantage within Article 7(2) of Regulation 1612/68 which could not be denied to migrant workers. However, the DSS took the view that an unemployed worker does not retain worker status. In *CIS 4521/1996* (to be reported as *R(IS) 3/97*), the AO submitted that the ECJ's judgments in *Lair* [1988] E.C.R. 3161 and *Raulin* meant that immediately on ceasing employment a person lost the status of worker and became merely a work seeker. But this is rejected by the Commissioner. He points out that *Lair* had held that worker status was retained by a person who had voluntarily given up work in order to take up vocational training which was linked to the previous job. In *Raulin* it was decided that if the training had no link with the previous occupation, worker status was only retained in the case of a migrant worker who was involuntarily unemployed. But those cases were dealing with situations where people could be said to have taken themselves out of the labour market by undertaking full-time studies. The ECJ recognised that nevertheless those concerned could be regarded as retaining the status of worker under certain conditions. Those cases did not deal at all with the situation where a person ceased voluntarily or involuntarily to be in an employment relationship but remained in the labour market, *e.g.* by making genuine efforts to find work. In such circumstances a person did not immediately lose the status of "worker" for the purposes of Regulation 1612/68. However the claimant in *R(IS) 3/97* had never been employed in the U.K., so the Commissioner did not actually have to directly decide whether sub-para. (a) applied in these circumstances.

But the question did directly arise in *CIS 12909/1996*. The claimant was a French national who after coming to the U.K. had worked as an au pair with a family (being paid £35 for a 13-hour week, with free board and lodging) for about five weeks before she claimed income support on July 31, 1995. It was accepted that the claimant had been a "worker" for the purposes of Regulation 1612/68 before she claimed income support. But the AO contended that if a person left employment voluntarily the status of worker was lost. The Commissioner concludes, having regard in particular to para. 29 of the ECJ's judgment in *Lair*, that a person who had left employment but remained in the labour market retained the status of worker for the purposes of Regulation 1612/68. It did not in itself matter whether the previous employment was left voluntarily or involuntarily. The issue was whether the circumstances of the leaving, and in particular the person's intentions and actions at the time, indicated whether or not the person was still in the labour market. The claimant in this case had continued to seek work after her employment had ended; she thus continued to be a "worker" and so was to be treated as habitually resident under sub-para. (a). *CIS 12909/1996* is followed in *CIS 16410/1996*.

R(IS) 3/97 also deals with the position of a person seeking work who has not previously worked in the U.K. The claimant was a national of the Republic of Ireland. In 1991 he went to France where he worked as an agricultural labourer. In October 1994 he came to the U.K., registered as unemployed and claimed income support. The Commissioner holds that it was plain from the ECJ's judgment in *Lebon* [1987] E.C.R. 2811 that a person who was simply a work seeker, that is, who had moved from one Member State to another to seek employment, was not a worker for the purposes of Regulation 1612/68. In *Lebon* the ECJ decided that the right to equal treatment as regards social and tax advantages (which would include income support) in Article 7(2) of Regulation 1612/68 only applied to workers and not to those who moved to seek employment. The ECJ stated that people who moved in order to seek employment only enjoyed equal treatment as regards access to such employment in accordance with Article 48 of the Treaty and Articles 2 and 5 of Regulation 1612/68. Moreover, as the ECJ had ruled in *Raulin*, in deciding whether a person was a worker for the purposes of Regulation 1612/68, account could only be taken of occupational activities pursued in the host State but not activities pursued elsewhere in the Community. Thus, as the claimant had never worked in the U.K., he was not a worker for the purposes of Regulation 1612/68. However, this does not entirely deal with the argument that sub-para. (a) does not say "worker in the U.K. for the purposes of Regulation 1612/68'' (*cf* "person with a right to reside in the United Kingdom"). The ECJ's judgment in *Raulin* inevitably did not decide this point, since the argument is based on the wording of sub-para. (a) itself, not on the Community meaning of worker.

Regulation 1251/70, *inter alia*, grants a right of residence after termination of employment to certain retired or incapacitated workers. For this to apply, a worker must have reached pension age when he stopped work, been employed in the host State for the last 12 months and lived there for more than three years, or ceased work due to a permanent incapacity and lived in the host State for more than two years (if the incapacity resulted from an accident at work or occupational disease entitling him to benefit there is no residence condition). If his spouse is a national there are no required periods of employment or residence (article 2). However, as the Commissioner in *CIS 12909/1996* points out, the test under sub-para. (a) is not whether the claimant has a right to remain in the U.K. under Regulation 1251/70. It is whether the claimant counts as a worker for the purposes of that Regulation. Article 1 of Regulation 1251/70 states that the provisions of the Regulation apply to "nationals of a Member State who have worked as employed persons in the territory of another Member State" and to their families. Thus the Commissioner in *CIS 12909/1996* thought it possible (although he did not express a firm conclusion on the point) that a national of a Member State who had worked as an employed person in the U.K. could be "a worker for the purposes of Regulation 1251/70". This was especially in view of Article 4(2), which treats periods of involuntary unemployment (and absences due to illness or accident) as periods of employment for the purposes of Article 2 (and see also para. 34 of the ECJ's judgment in *Lair*). If this is the case, this would be a less onerous test than under Regulation 1612/68. *R(IS) 3/97* confirms that only employment in the host State in question is relevant to the assessment of whether someone is a worker for the purposes of Regulation 1251/70.

E.C. Directives 68/360 and 73/148

People who have a right to reside under E.C. Directives 68/360 or 73/148 are also treated as habitually resident. (The I(EEA) Order implements, *inter alia*, Directives 68/360 and 73/148.) Directive 68/360 covers workers and members of their families who come within Regulations 1612/68 or 1251/70. Members of the worker's family who have a right to "install" themselves with the worker are his spouse, their children who are under the age of 21 or dependent, and their ascendant relatives who are dependent (Article 10(1) of Regulation 1612/68). In addition, Article 10(2) provides that Member States shall "facilitate the admission of" other members of a worker's family who are either dependent or who were living under his roof in the previous country. It is not clear whether the latter also have a right of residence for these purposes (see Wyatt and Dashwood, *European Community Law* (3rd ed.), pp. 246 and 282).

Directive 68/360 is concerned with the issue of residence permits, but the right to reside does not derive from the permit but from Community law itself (*Royer* [1976] E.C.R. 497, *Echternach* [1989] E.C.R. 723, *Raulin, Roux* [1991] E.C.R. 1–273; and see *CIS 16410/1996* below). Thus workers who satisfy the conditions for obtaining (or retaining) a residence permit are covered, even if they have not applied for one. Residence permits are issued on the basis of confirmation from the employer of the worker's employment. They are for five years unless the employment is expected to last less than one year; where the expected period of the worker's employment is more than three months but less than a year a permit *may* be (but is not automatically: *CIS 16410/1996*) limited to this period. A worker whose employment is not expected to last more than three months has a right of residence without a residence permit for the expected duration of the employment. Seasonal workers, and frontier workers (*i.e.* those who return to another Member State at least once a week) also have a right of residence without a residence permit. A residence permit does not end if the worker becomes involuntarily unemployed or temporarily incapable of work. It would seem to follow that it *may* be withdrawn if the person becomes *voluntarily* unemployed but clearly all the circumstances would need to be taken into account. Presumably such a decision should be taken by the Home Office. A residence permit may also be withdrawn if the person leaves the U.K. for more than six months (unless this is for military service).

It should be remembered, as *CIS 16410/1996* points out (and see *Royer*, etc., above), that a worker's right of residence derives directly from article 48 of the Treaty and not from the Directive, which does not of itself impose any conditions on that right. As the Commissioner in *CIS 16410/1996* states, a right of residence under Directive 68/360 will thus primarily be of relevance for someone who was not a worker, for example, a member of a worker's family. Similarly *CIS 4521/1995*, to be reported as *R(IS) 3/97*, confirms that Directive 68/630 does not provide a right of residence for work seekers. The right of EEA Nationals to stay in other Member States for the purpose of seeking employment derives not from that Directive but from Article 48(3) of the Treaty of Rome and (probably) Regulation 1612/68 (see the ECJ's judgment in *Antonissen*, paras. 8–15).

Directive 73/148, which is very similar to Directive 68/360, covers the self-employed and those who are providing or receiving services, and their families. It also applies to EEA nationals who are seeking self-employment, or to provide or receive services. As in the case of Directive 68/360, the permit does not create the right to reside which derives from the Treaty itself, but only confirms it. Residence permits for the self-employed are to be granted for at least five years; for providers or recipients of services they may be limited to the duration of the service. A permit is not to be withdrawn because the person is temporarily incapable of work. Services are those that are normally paid for, and include industrial, commercial, craft and professional activities (Article 60 of the Treaty). The ECJ has held that tourism, medical treatment and education are covered (*Luisi* [1984] E.C.R. 377). The Directive does not, for example, specify the level of service, or impose any qualifying period, in order for a right of residence to be granted. Thus its application could be quite wide.

Note that sub-para. (a) does not refer to E.C. Directive 75/34 under which those who have retired from self-employment because of old age or incapacity have a right to reside; the rules are similar to those that apply to retired workers under Regulation 1251/70. It is not clear why this directive has not been included.

Sub-paras. (b) and (c)

Refugees and people who have been granted exceptional leave to enter, or to remain in, the U.K. are treated as habitually resident (note that before April 6, 1998 sub-para. (c) only referred to those who had been granted exceptional leave to *remain* in (not to enter) the U.K.)

In *CIS 564/1994*, heard together with *CIS 7250/1995*, the Commissioner confirms that a person counts as a refugee entitled to the protection of the 1951 Convention from the time he fulfills the criteria contained in the definition in the Convention. It is not necessary for his status as a refugee to have been recognised by the Home Office, since such recognition does not make the person a refugee but merely declares him to be one.

Meaning of habitual residence

Note that following the ECJ's decision in Swaddling (see below), the Government has issued guidance that people returning from any country overseas to re-establish ties here should be treated as habitually resident immediately on their return. See further the beginning of this note. Note also that the House of Lords' judgment in Nessa (see CIS 2326/1995 below) is currently awaited. The notes below on the requirement of an appreciable period in order to establish habitual residence therefore need to be modified for those who fall into the category of "returning to re-establish ties" in the U.K. However, in the view of the fact that the House of Lords' judgment in Nessa is not yet available, the existing notes analysing the habitual residence test as it has so far been applied for the purposes of income support/income-based JSA have been retained in this edition. See the 1999 Supplement to this book for further developments.

"Habitual residence" is not defined in the regulation and therefore the words must be given their natural and ordinary meaning (see *Shah v. Barnet London Borough Council* [1983] 2 A.C. 309, [1983] 1 All E.R. 226, *Re J (A Minor)* [1990] 2 A.C. 562, *R(IS) 6/96* and *CIS 2326/1995*). Whether a person is habitually resident is a question of fact to be decided by reference to all the circumstances in each case (*Re J*). Habitual residence is not the same as domicile (*R(U)8/88*). It is possible to be habitually resident in more than one country (although it is unusual); it is also possible to be habitually resident in none. A person does not have to be continually present in a country in order to be habitually resident. There is no time limit after which habitual residence is established, but the longer the length of stay the more likely the person is to be habitually resident. On the other hand, a person may be habitually resident shortly after arriving in a country depending on the circumstances. For people who are "re-establishing ties" in the U.K., see *Swaddling* (below) and the recent guidance on the application of the habitual residence test referred to at the beginning of this note. Originally the practice was that if a person stated on their income support claim form that they had not entered the U.K. within the last five years habitual residence would be assumed. The SSAC had recommended that the trigger point for generating inquiries into habitual residence should be reduced to two years. This has now been accepted by the Government (see the beginning of this note).

The concept of habitual residence occurs in European law, in particular in E.C. Regulation 1408/71 dealing with social security for migrant workers, and has been considered in several Commissioners' decisions on unemployment benefit (see *R(U) 7/85, R(U) 4/86, CU 285/1985* and in particular *R(U) 8/88* which has appendices summarising these decisions together with references to the relevant European provisions and case law). However, it is important to remember that the context of this case law is that of returning workers claiming to have retained their "habitual residence" while working elsewhere, in order to qualify for unemployment benefit. It is thus mainly concerned with looking at the past. In *Di Paolo v. Office National de L'Emploi* [1977] E.C.R. 315 the ECJ stated that account had to be taken of factors such as the nature of a person's occupation, the reasons for moving to another State to work and the length of residence before the person moved. The Court also held that stable employment could outweigh other factors in determining habitual residence. But as the Commissioner in *CIS 2326/1995* points out, that decision was concerned with the particular context of Article 71(1)(b)(ii) of Regulation 1408/71 (the exception to the general rule that an unemployed person should receive unemployment benefit from the State where he was last employed) and the ECJ was not suggesting that the factors mentioned were the only ones to be taken into account in determining habitual residence. In his view *Di Paolo* should not be used to illustrate the meaning of habitual residence except with great caution. Furthermore, as the SSAC's report said, the case law's emphasis on the length and stability of employment does not take account of the fact that part-time or temporary work, or short fixed-term contracts, may be the only available option for many people coming to the U.K. In addition, where availability is not a condition for receiving benefit, as is now the case for income support, employment related factors may be of little assistance in determining whether a person is habitually resident. Note, however, that the ECJ in *Swaddling* apparently adopts a similar approach to the meaning of "residence" (*i.e.* habitual residence: see Article 1(h) of Regulation 1408/71) for the purpose of Article 10a, as it had laid down in *Di Paolo* (although the emphasis on stable employment is much reduced). But it seems questionable whether the approach used to determine whether habitual residence has been *retained* during an absence is necessarily appropriate when the issue is whether habitual residence has been *(re-) established*.

The concept of habitual residence also occurs in certain areas of U.K. law, *e.g.* tax, family and child support law. Here it has sometimes been equated to "ordinarily resident". See, for example *Kapur v. Kapur* [1984] F.L.R. 920, a case on the meaning of habitual residence in the Domicile and Matrimonial Proceedings Act 1973, which holds that there is no real distinction between "ordinary" and "habitual" residence. Bush J. in *Kapur* refers to the House of Lords' decision in *Shah* (which concerned the interpretation of "ordinarily resident" in the Education Act 1962) where ordinary residence was held to include habitual residence. Lord Scarman states that the words "ordinarily resident" were to be given their natural and ordinary meaning which was "habitually and normally resident, apart from temporary or occasional absences of long or short duration". Habitually meant that the residence had to be adopted voluntarily and for a settled purpose (see *IRC v. Lysaght* [1928] A.C. 234). In the light of the House of Lords' decision in *Shah* Bush J. declined to follow *Cruse v. Chittum* [1974] 2 All E.R. 940 which had held that habitual residence was something more than ordinary residence. In *Shah* Lord Scarman points out that a settled purpose could be for a limited period; there was no need to intend to stay indefinitely. Such a purpose could include education, employment, health, family or "merely love of the place". Thus in *CA 35/1992* a woman, who had gone to Malta for health reasons, intending to return within 18 months, was held to be ordinarily resident there. The fact that a person has a restricted right to stay in the U.K. does not prevent him from being habitually resident (*Shah* and *Kapur*), and see *R(IS) 6/96*, where the Commissioner states that the test focuses on the fact and nature of the residence and not on the legal right of abode. Thus an asylum seeker may become habitually resident before his status as a refugee is recognised by the Home Office (*CIS 564/1994*). The residence must, however, be lawful (*Shah*). It is clear from these cases that habitual residence can be acquired quite quickly. In the domestic context, as the law currently stands, it probably cannot be acquired in a single day (*Macrae v. Macrae* [1949] 2 All E.R. 34, which held that habitual residence could be gained as easily as it is lost, is of doubtful authority in the light of *Re J*, see below), but certainly where there is a settled purpose a short period may suffice, depending on the circumstances. But for people who are "re-establishing ties" in the U.K., see *Swaddling* (below) and the recent guidance on the application of the habitual residence test referred to at the beginning of this note. Note also that the House of Lords' judgment in *Nessa* which should clarify the position is currently awaited.

The SSAC expressed regret that the chosen test was not ordinary residence as this was the test for family credit and disability working allowance and one with which U.K. adjudicators were more familiar. They understood that the DSS's view was that habitual residence implied "a stronger, more regular physical presence in the country and association with it" than ordinary residence did. But they considered that the difference between the two was one of emphasis and they were unable to find any uniquely distinguishing factor.

The test in the context of income support

Two important Commissioners' decisions, *R(IS) 6/96* and *CIS 2326/1995*, have considered the meaning of habitually resident in the context of income support. Note that the claimant in *CIS 2326/*

1995 (Nessa) appealed to the Court of Appeal but her appeal was dismissed by a majority: see below. A further appeal was made to the House of Lords which was heard on May 11, 1999. At the time of writing the judgment was not available. Its meaning has also been considered by the ECJ in relation to people who are covered by Regulation 1408/71 (*Swaddling v. Adjudication Officer*, Case C-90/97, ECJ, February 25, 1999, *The Times*, March 4, 1999, also to be reported as *R(IS) 6/99*). As a consequence, the current position is that there is a difference in the test, namely in relation to the requirement for an appreciable period, in the domestic and European context (but note the Government's recently-issued guidance to staff administering the test advising them to extend the effect of the ECJ's judgment in *Swaddling* to people returning from *any* country overseas and re-establishing ties here). It is to be hoped that the House of Lords' judgment in *Nessa* will resolve this unsatisfactory situation.

R(IS) 6/96

In *R(IS) 6/96* the claimant was a British National who had been born in Burma and lived there all her life until she came to the U.K. in June 1992. Her husband and children remained in Burma. She obtained employment in July 1992 but was made redundant in May 1994. She then claimed income support. In July 1994 she returned to Burma as her husband was thought to be terminally ill. She returned on August 20, 1994 and claimed income support on August 31. Her claim was refused on the grounds that she was not habitually resident in the U.K. The Commissioner allowed her appeal because on the facts she had clearly become habitually resident in the U.K. by July 1994 and this was not affected by her temporary absence for a month. See Lord Scarman in *Shah* who refers to temporary or occasional absences of long or short duration not affecting ordinary residence and the ECJ's judgment in *Di Paolo* where the Court takes a similar view in relation to habitual residence. See also *CIS 14591/1996* below.

However, the Commissioner also gives general guidance on the principles to be adopted in applying the habitual resident test for the purposes of income support. He emphasises that the facts of each case had to be considered and that it was not possible to provide a complete definition of habitual residence or to list all the relevant factors. It was for the adjudicating authorities to be satisfied that a claimant was not habitually resident, rather than for the claimant to prove his habitual residence (although a tribunal should try to decide the issue by further investigation of the facts rather then relying on the burden of proof). To be resident a person had to be seen to be making a "genuine home for the time being" here but it need not be his only home or a permanent one. (Actual residence in two places is perfectly possible: *CIS 16410/1996*.) In deciding whether the person had become habitually resident, the most important factors were the length, continuity and general nature of the actual residence. An appreciable period of time, together with a settled intention, were necessary to establish habitual residence. What counted as an "appreciable period of time" depended on the facts of each case. It should be a period which showed "a settled and viable pattern of living here as a resident". Thus the practicality of a person's arrangements for residence had to be considered. In determining whether the plans were viable, the possibility of claiming income support had to be left out of account (although this did not mean that there must be no conceivable circumstances in which a person might need to resort to income support). The Commissioner recognised that since habitual residence could be abandoned in a day (see *Re J*), there could be a period when the claimant was not habitually resident anywhere.

The Commissioner's approach in *R(IS) 6/96* was largely based on Lord Brandon's comments in *Re J*, which was a child abduction case. Lord Brandon stated *inter alia* that whether a person was habitually resident was a question of fact to be decided by reference to all the circumstances of any particular case and that an appreciable period of time and a settled intention were necessary to establish habitual residence. Since the question the House of Lords was deciding was whether J had *ceased* to be habitually resident in Western Australia (which Lord Brandon held could happen in a single day if a person left with a settled intention not to return but to take up long-term residence elsewhere), the point that "an appreciable period of time and a settled intention" were needed to establish habitual residence was technically *obiter*. However, Lord Brandon's comments are clearly strong dicta and have been adopted in a large number of subsequent family law cases (see *CIS 2326/1995*). The Commissioner in *R(IS) 6/96* did not consider that there was any inconsistency between the approach taken in *Re J* and what was said by Lord Scarman in *Shah* and the ECJ in *Di Paolo*. All emphasised that the correct approach was a factual and practical one, taking into account all the individual's circumstances. In his view, however, where habitual residence may differ from ordinary residence was in the need for there to be an appreciable period of actual residence before a person became habitually resident.

CIS 2326/1995

In *CIS 2326/1995* the claimant came to the U.K. in August 1994 when aged 55. She had previously lived all her life in Bangladesh. Her father-in-law in whose house she had been living had died and she had come to the U.K. for the emotional support of her late husband's brother and his family. Her husband had lived and worked in the U.K. until his death in 1975 and she had a right of abode here. She claimed income support in September 1994.

The Commissioner holds that when the habitual residence test was introduced into the income support scheme the intention was to use the same legal concept as was already in use in other contexts. In his view the Child Support Commissioner in *R(CS) 5/96* was not suggesting that habitual residence had a different meaning in different statutory contexts, but merely that the significance of factors may vary in different circumstances. He therefore decided *R(IS) 6/96* had been right to hold, following *Re J*, that for a person to be habitually resident an appreciable period of residence as well as a settled intention had to be shown. However, he does not agree with all the reasoning in *R(IS) 6/96* and he adds two important qualifications.

The first concerned the examples given in *R(IS) 6/96* of what might amount to an appreciable period in certain circumstances. Because of the danger of examples being read as minimum or normal periods, he did not think that any periods should be mentioned. There was no minimum period necessary to establish habitual residence (see *Cameron v. Cameron* 1996 S.L.T. 306). Even Lord Brandon's statement that a person could not become habitually resident in a single day had to be read in its context, that of "a sharp-edged leaving of the country of existing habitual residence with the intention to take up long-term residence in another country". The context and all the circumstances had to be considered in each case. Thus, *e.g.* if a person lived in different countries for part of each year, he could simultaneously be habitually resident in both. Moreover, periods spent in the U.K. prior to the date of the latest arrival here could be relevant in assessing what was an appreciable period under the *Re J* principle. The appreciable period did not need to be continuous and periods spent in this country while the person was still habitually resident in another country could count as part of the appreciable period to be taken into account after the actual arrival, as long as they were connected with the settled intention to reside here. Thus visits for the purpose of making arrangements to live here could count, but not those that were merely holidays or to see relatives.

The second qualification was that the viability of a person's residence in the U.K., either generally or with or without assistance from public funds, was only one relevant factor among others, to be given the appropriate weight according to the circumstances. In his view *R(IS) 6/96* should not be read as imposing an additional condition that only residence without resort to income support or public assistance was relevant to the *Re J* test. See also *CIS 14591/1996* and *CIS 16097/1996* which agree with *CIS 2326/1995* that the question of whether the residence is viable in the U.K. without recourse to public funds is only one factor, and not by itself decisive.

The Commissioner in *CIS 2326/1995* did not consider that *Shah* supported the conclusion that, for the purposes of applying the ordinary residence test, evidence of past residence on an established and settled basis was always necessary. (The students in *Shah* had already been resident for three years because in order to be eligible for local authority grants they had to show three years' ordinary residence.) But he did consider that a habit took time to establish and that residence only changed its quality at the point at which it became habitual. Thus he rejected the argument that once sufficient time had elapsed for the residence to become habitual that showed that it had been habitual from the outset. However, he did state that subsequent conduct could act as confirmation that a claimant's intentions were settled from the outset. He also points out that the ECJ did not decide in *Di Paolo* that a person's habitual residence was where he had his habitual centre of interests. The location of a person's centre of interests might be one relevant factor in determining habitual residence but the two concepts were not synonymous.

The claimant in *CIS 2326/1995* appealed to the Court of Appeal but her appeal was dismissed (*Nessa v. Chief Adjudication Officer* [1998] 2 All E.R. 728). The Court of Appeal (by a majority) followed *Re J* and held that in order to establish habitual residence it was necessary for a claimant not only to have been in the U.K. voluntarily, and for settled purposes, but also to have fulfilled those conditions for an appreciable period of time. However, the appreciable period need not be particularly long. The dissenting judge (Thorpe L.J.) considered that Lord Brandon's comments in *Re J* were clearly *obiter* and that an appreciable period was not an essential ingredient of habitual residence. In his view the adjective "habitual" ensured that "the connection [to the country] is not transitory or temporary but enduring and the necessary durability can be judged prospectively in exceptional cases". Leave to appeal to the House of Lords was granted and the appeal was heard on May 11, 1999. At the time of writing the House of Lords' judgment was not yet available.

In *CIS 15927/1996*, however, the Commissioner takes the view that a significant period of time had to elapse between the commencement of residence here and its becoming habitual. The length of time depended on the circumstances but it would normally require residence (*i.e.* setting up a home: see *R(IS) 6/96*, para. 19) of at least some months. The Commissioner repeats his view, first expressed in *R(CS) 5/96*, that "habitual" had to be interpreted in the context of the legislation at issue and that its meaning in other jurisdictions was not of much assistance. But this comment has to be read in the light of the Court of Appeal's judgment in *Nessa*, in which the majority followed Lord Brandon in *Re J*. Certainly his overall approach would seem to require longer periods of residence to establish habitual residence than would follow from the Court of Appeal's approach in *Nessa* and that of the Commissioners in *CIS 2326/1995* and *R(IS) 6/96*.

Settled intention and appreciable period—the test following R(IS) 6/96 and CIS 2326/1995

Thus it is clear that whether a person is habitually resident in the U.K. (more technically in the CTA) is a question of fact to be decided by reference to all the circumstances of the particular case (recently emphasised by the Court of Appeal in *Re M (A Minor) (Habitual Residence), The Times*, January 3, 1996). Habitual residence can continue during absences of long or short duration. It is for the tribunal to be satisfied that the claimant is not habitually resident (*CIS 2326/1995*). Some of the relevant factors will include the length of time in the U.K., the reason for coming (or returning) here, the claimant's intentions, the location of his possessions and family, where he has previously worked, the length and purpose of any absence from the U.K., etc. The intention to reside here does not need to be permanent or indefinite but can be for a limited period (*e.g.*, for the purposes of education as in *Shah*; see also *Cameron v. Cameron* quoted in *CIS 2326/1995* where the Court of Appeal said that the settled intention necessary under *Re J* was an intention to reside here for an appreciable period). But if the claimant's intention is conditional, *e.g.* on benefit being awarded, this is not a settled intention to stay (*CIS 12703/1996*). The question to be asked is whether "in all the circumstances, including the settledness of the person's intentions as to residence, the residence has continued for a sufficient period for it to be said to be habitual" (*CIS* 2326/1995). There is no minimum appreciable period and in some circumstances it will be quite short. See, *e.g. Re F (A Minor) (Child Abduction)* [1992] 1 F.L.R. 548 where one month was accepted as sufficient. In *Re B (Minors) (Abduction) (No. 2)* [1993] 1 F.L.R. 993, Waite J., after referring to the assumption of habitual residence requiring an appreciable period of time and a settled intention, states that ". . . Logic would suggest that provided the purpose was settled, the period of habitation need not be long". So if the settled intention is very strong, the appreciable period may shrink. It may be that if the claimant is returning to a country where he has lived before, habitual residence can be acquired more quickly (in this connection note the DSS's view in para. 11 of its original memorandum to SSAC (Cm 2609) that ". . . In some circumstances, for instance returning U.K. nationals, it will be possible to become habitually resident from the moment of entry"). And now see the recently-issued guidance following *Swaddling* (below) that people returning to the U.K. from overseas to "re-establish ties" should be treated as immediately habitually resident. Equally, if the claimant has come to the U.K., *e.g.* because he needs to be near relatives due to failing health and has severed all ties with his previous country, it is difficult to see why such a person should not become habitually resident at a very early stage. It may be that it was these kinds of situations that the Commissioner in *CIS 2326/1995* had in mind when he said that subsequent conduct could act as confirmation of a claimant's stated intentions and help to show that they were settled from the outset. But in those circumstances it does not seem to be the quality of the residence that has changed, only the evidence about it.

One other point should be made. The Commissioner's dilution in *CIS 2326/1995* of the statement in *R(IS) 6/96* that for the residence to count the claimant's plans for living in the U.K. had to be "viable", in the sense of viable without resort to income support, is to be welcomed. Such a requirement, if that was what it was intended to be, could have the effect of preventing some people (*e.g.* those who are unable to work because of age or ill-health) from ever becoming habitually resident because they could never bridge the viability gap. It also carries with it the danger of imposing a condition that a person be self-supporting (at least for a time), when the chosen test is that of habitual residence rather than "without recourse to public funds". It seems to add a substantial gloss to the *Re J* test. The Commissioner in *CIS 2326/1995* considered that viability might be relevant in assessing whether a person's intentions were truly settled. That seems less controversial, but for the reasons already stated, whether the person's need to resort to public funds should enter into the consideration, is highly questionable.

R(IS) 6/96 and *CIS 2326/1995* (as confirmed by the Court of Appeal in *Nessa*) clarified some of these points in relation to the habitual residence test (and raised some new issues). They emphasised the need for adjudicating authorities to thoroughly investigate all the circumstances of each case. The test remains subjective and will continue to require adjudicating authorities to balance many often competing factors. As SSAC commented in para. 34 of its report on the proposal to introduce the habitual residence rule (Cm 2609): "The basic difficulty of an habitual residence test [is that] . . . it allows for the construction of a case for or against the claimant in almost every circumstance''. There will thus continue to be much room for argument and no doubt frequent appeals against adverse AOs' decisions.

Note that a person can remain habitually resident during periods of even comparatively lengthy absence. See, for example, *CIS 1459/1996*. In June 1993 the claimant and his wife came to the U.K. with the intention of living here permanently. But in October 1994 they returned to India to be with their daughter-in-law until she could obtain entry clearance. This was finally granted after some 13 months. The claimant's claim for income support made on his return to the U.K. in November 1995 was refused on the ground that he was not habitually resident. However, the Commissioner decides that the claimant had become habitually resident before he went to India in October 1994 and had remained so throughout the period of his absence. He had retained a settled intention to live in the U.K. permanently and his absence was always intended to be temporary.

Swaddling

The claimant was a British national who until he was 23 had lived and worked in the U.K. From 1980 to 1994 for the majority of the time he worked in France. In late 1994 he was made redundant. After failing to find further employment in France, he returned to the U.K. in January 1995 to live with his brother and in order to obtain work here. His claim for income support made on January 9, 1995 was refused on the ground that he was not habitually resident in the U.K. The Commissioner held that the appropriate appreciable period in all the circumstances was eight weeks from the date of his return to the U.K. Under the terms of purely domestic law the claimant was thus not entitled to income support for the period January 9 to March 3, 1995. The Commissioner rejected an argument put forward by the claimant that under Art. 10a(2) of E.C. Regulation 1408/71 he could rely on his period of residence in France to satisfy the habitual residence condition. The Commissioner decided that Art. 10a(2) did not assist the claimant since the habitual residence test did not make entitlement to income support subject to *completion* of a period of employment, self-employment or residence (note that in Regulation 1408/71 ''residence'' means ''habitual residence'': Art 1(h)) but went to whether habitual residence had been established initially.

But the Commissioner did refer to the ECJ the question whether the application of a habitual residence test (involving the requirement of an appreciable period of residence) to a person who had exercised his right to freedom of movement and had worked and been habitually resident in another Member State and then returned to the U.K. to seek work infringed Art. 48 of the Treaty of Rome. It was contended on behalf of the claimant that the test had the effect of deterring a person from exercising his Community rights since he had been made worse off by its application than if he had worked throughout in the U.K. For the A.O. it was submitted that the principle in Art. 48 did not extend to conditions for acquiring entitlement to a non-contributory benefit like income support.

However the ECJ (Case C-90/97, *The Times*, March 4, 1999, also to be reported as *R(IS)6/99*) did not answer the question as to whether there had been an infringement of Art. 48 since it considered that the case could be dealt with under Regulation 1408/71. It was accepted that Mr Swaddling was a person covered by Regulation 1408/71 (as an employed person he had been subject to both the British and French social security schemes). Art. 10a(1) provides that a person to whom the Regulation applies is to be granted certain special non-contributory benefits (which include income support) in the territory of the Member State in which he resides. ''Reside'' means ''habitually reside'': Art. 1(h). The Court stated that in deciding where a person habitually resided, account had to be taken in particular of his family situation; the reasons which had led him to move; the length and continuity of his residence; the fact (where this was the case) that he was in stable employment; and his intention as it appeared from all the circumstances. However, the Court also held that the length of residence in the Member State in which payment of benefit was sought could not be regarded as an intrinsic element of the concept of residence within the meaning of Art. 10a.

The result of the ECJ's judgment would thus seem to be that a person covered by Regulation 1408/71 can be habitually resident in a Member State for the purposes of Art. 10a on the day of arrival if the circumstances as a whole, including the other factors referred to by the Court, lead to that conclusion. The Community meaning of ''habitually resident'' therefore differs from the interpretation that currently applies in a domestic context (although this may change once the House of Lords have given their decision in *Nessa*). The ECJ's interpretation also seems to be inherently discriminatory, since it will normally be easier for returning nationals to show that they are re-establishing ties with their country of origin than it will be for, *e.g.*, other EEA nationals. One question that arises is to whom does the ECJ's judgment apply? Clearly it covers returning British nationals who come within the scope of Regulation 1408/71 and, as already indicated, it is difficult to see how non-British EEA nationals in a similar position could be excluded without breaching Art. 7 of Regulation 1612/68. However, the guidance issued to AOs (AM(AOG) 109) extends the effect of the ECJ's judgment to an income support/income-based JSA claimant of *any* nationality who was previously resident in the CTA, moved to live in another country and has returned to resume the previous residence. AOs are advised to take account of the length and continuity of the previous residence in the CTA and "whether the claimant has sufficient links with the previous residence to be regarded as picking up the pieces of their old life". The Government's desire to avoid discrimination in the application of the test is to be applauded but the legal basis for the interpretation adopted by the guidance is not entirely clear.

Habitual residence and "down to the date of decision"

If a person fails the habitual residence test this does not mean to say that he cannot satisfy it at a subsequent date, particularly if further information is produced or there is a change in circumstances, or simply due to passage of time. *CIS 11481/1995* and *CIS 17208/1996* confirm that the principle that a tribunal should consider the position from the date of claim down to the date of its decision applied in the context of habitual residence. Depending on the length of time before the tribunal hearing, a SSAT may, therefore, have found that sufficient time had elapsed for the residence to have become habitual at some point between the date of the AO's decision and the tribunal hearing. But note that in relation to appeals brought on or after May 21, 1998 (the date the Social Security Act 1998 received the Royal Assent), a tribunal will only be able to consider the position up to the date of the AO's decision (see the new subs. (8) inserted into s.22 of the Administration Act by para. 3 of Sched. 6 to the 1998 Act which applies until s.12(8)(b) of the Act is brought into force). Thus a claimant will have to submit a fresh claim (or claims) as time elapses (and appeal as necessary), in order for any changes in his circumstances to be considered, or simply because he has been here longer. See President's Circular No. 15 which helpfully points out that this does not necessarily render irrelevant evidence which comes into existence after the AO's decision. A tribunal will still be able to take this into account if it throws further light on circumstances that did obtain at the time of the decision. This may be particularly germane in some habitual residence cases. Note that s.22(8) has no effect on the period of any award made by a tribunal hearing an appeal lodged on or after May 21, 1998. Any such award of income support (or income-based JSA) will normally be for an indefinite period (see reg. 17 of the Claims and Payments Regulations).

Validity of the habitual residence test

In *R v. Secretary of State for Social Security ex parte Sarwar, Getachew and Urbanek* (High Court, April 11, 1995) the habitual residence rule was challenged on two grounds: first, that the regulation introducing the test was *ultra vires*, and secondly that the test was unlawful under European law.

On the first point, it was contended that because s.124(1) of the Contributions and Benefits Act states that "a person in Great Britain is entitled to income support ...", it was not within the Secretary of State's regulation-making powers to qualify this simple presence test by introducing the further requirement of habitual residence. The change was not limited to a class of claimants, but created a universal test of habitual residence (subject only to very limited exceptions) and thus was inconsistent with the primary legislation. It was significant that the regulation had not been made under s.137(2)(a) (circumstances in which a person is to be treated as being or not being in Great Britain), but under s.135(2) (power to prescribe nil applicable amount). If the new regulation had purported to treat anyone who was not habitually resident as not being in Great Britain, the fact that the test was being amended on a universal basis would have been more obvious. But prescribing a nil applicable amount for all claimants who are not habitually resident (subject to the limited exceptions) had the same effect. Indeed this was the intended effect (see the Secretary of State's statement in response to the SSAC's report on this proposed change: "These regulations will introduce a test of habitual residence into the Income Support, Housing Benefit and Council Tax Benefit schemes" (para. 2)).

However, the High Court rejected this argument and held that the provision was valid. The Court stated that Parliament had only intended that physical presence in Great Britain should be a necessary, but not a sufficient, condition for eligibility. If the test could have been introduced directly under s.137(2)(a), the Court saw no reason why this could not be done indirectly under s.135(1) and (2). This seems unsatisfactory and does not deal with the main argument. The Court's reasoning that s.137(2)(a) would be otiose if Parliament intended that every person physically present in Great Britain would be eligible for income support misses the point. It was not being argued that the Secretary of State did not have power to treat people as not being in Great Britain, but that he did not have power to introduce a universal test of habitual residence without amending the primary legislation.

The Court also held that the new test was not contrary to European law. Article 6 of the E.C. Treaty prohibits any discrimination on the grounds of nationality within the scope of the operation of the Treaty. Article 48 provides for freedom of movement for workers. Article 48(3) states that this includes the right to, *inter alia*, move freely within Member States to accept offers of employment actually made, stay in a Member State for the purpose of employment and remain there after the employment has ended (subject to the conditions set out in the implementing regulations). It was argued that the provision indirectly discriminates in favour of Irish nationals against other EEA nationals because Irish nationals are more likely to be habitually resident in Ireland and thus exempt from the test. The Court was prepared to accept that this could be discriminatory. But this did not assist the applicants because in *Lebon* the ECJ had decided that the right to equal treatment as regards social and tax advantages in Article 7(2) of Regulation 1612/68 only applied to workers, not work seekers. Although *Lebon* was decided under Regulation 1612/68, not the Treaty, this was immaterial as a Regulation could not detract from rights under the Treaty, although it might add to them. Since the applicants, as work seekers, had no right under Article 48 to income support, the issue as to whether the alleged discrimination was in favour of U.K. and Irish nationals, or just U.K. nationals, was irrelevant (see *Humbel* [1988] E.C.R. 5365). The rights of free movement and residence were not co-extensive with the right to maintenance (*Brown* [1988] E.C.R. 3205, *Raulin* [1992] E.C.R. 1027).

Article 8a (inserted by the Treaty of European Union) provides for the right to move and reside freely within the Member States, subject to the conditions in the Treaty and the implementing legislation. The question whether Article 8a confers additional rights (or is merely declaratory) and whether it is of direct effect had already been referred to the ECJ in *R v. Secretary of State for the Home Department ex parte Adams* [1995] All E.R. (EC) 177 (which reference has since been discontinued). But even if Article 8a did create a new right of residence, it was qualified by the last part of the provision, and so subject to the ECJ's decision in *Lebon*.

This decision was appealed to the Court of Appeal but the appeal was dismissed (*R v. Secretary of State for Social Security, ex parte Sarwar and ex parte Getachew* [1997] 3 C.M.L.R. 647), although Millett L.J. held that the similar housing benefit rule was *ultra vires*.

However, note that in *Sala v. Freistaat Bayern*, Case C-85/96, ECJ, May 12, 1998, the ECJ held a EEA national lawfully resident in the host Member State, could rely on Art. 6 in all situations which fell within the *material* scope of Community law. Thus she had the right not to be discriminated against on nationality grounds in relation to benefits covered by Regulations 1408/71 and/or 1612/68, even if she did not fall within the personal scope of those Regulations. This decision would seem to throw the Court's approach in *Sarwar* into question.

Mr Getachew had also challenged decisions to refuse him an urgent cases payment under reg. 70(3) and an interim payment. His claim that reg. 70(3)(g) could apply was rejected (see the notes to reg. 70(3) in the 1995 edition). Sub-para. (g), together with other sub-paras. of reg. 70(3), was revoked on February 5, 1996. Note also the changes to reg. 2(1) of the Payments Regulations restricting entitlement to interim payments from February 5, 1996.

See also *Swaddling* discussed above.

"Patient"

Reg. 2(2) of the Hospital In-Patients Regulations requires that the person is or has been maintained free of charge while undergoing treatment in a NHS hospital or a similar institution. There have been amendments in November 1987 and November 1992 so that in all cases a person is to be regarded as maintained free of charge unless the accommodation and services are provided under s.65 of the National Health Service Act 1987 (or the Scottish equivalent) or para. 14 of Sched. 2 to the National Health Service and Community Care Act 1990, which relate only to fee-paying patients in NHS and Trust hospitals. In *CS 249/1989* and *CIS 371/1990* (to be reported as *R(IS) 7/92*) the Commissioners regretfully apply the unambiguous effect of the 1987 amendment, which means that even where considerable contributions to maintenance are made, the person is still treated as a patient, with the consequent reduction in income support specified in Sched. 7. However, *CS 249/1989* states that this only applies if the person is actually in hospital 24 hours a day. But the Commissioner in *CIS 192/1991* disagrees, holding that the deeming applies despite the person's absence from the hospital during each period of 24 hours. In her view *R(S) 4/84* was not authority for holding that anything less than 24 hours' actual presence in a hospital took the person outside the provisions of reg. 2(2). In fact, as *CDLA 11099/1995* points out, *R(S) 4/84* is positive authority to the contrary. In *R(S) 4/84* the claimant spent every night in hospital receiving treatment but attended a college during the day. The Commissioner held that she satisfied the condition of undergoing treatment as an in-patient but that she was not maintained free of charge by the hospital because she had to maintain herself during the day. It was for that reason that the claimant succeeded in *R(S) 4/84*. The effect of the 1987 amendment to the "full-out" words in reg. 2(2) had been to deem the condition of being maintained free of charge to be satisfied if a person was undergoing treatment as an in-patient (except in the case of a private patient in a NHS hospital). *R(S) 4/84* had clearly accepted that the claimant's treatment overnight as an in-patient was sufficient for the purposes of reg. 2(2).

In *R(IS) 8/96* the Commissioner approaches the issue in a different way. In relation to whether a person counts as a patient if he is absent from hospital during the day, however, the result is the same as in *CIS 192/1991*. In *R(IS) 8/96* the claimant had been in hospital between April and September 1993 but had had various periods of home leave and could go out during the day. The Commissioner holds, following *CIS 131/49* (reported), *R(S) 8/51* and *R(S) 9/52*, that in deciding whether a person was an in-patient, the circumstances existing at the beginning of a day were to be treated as continuing throughout that day. Thus a day on which a person was admitted, or returned, to hospital was not a day on which a person was to be treated as an in-patient, but a day on which a person was discharged from, or left, hospital did count as such a day. The rule in *R(S) 1/66* (disqualification only for days throughout which a person was absent from Great Britain) did not apply in this context. The provision at issue in that case employed a different phrase "for any period *during* which" (which the Commissioner had decided meant "throughout"), whereas reg. 2(2) merely referred to any period "for which" the person receives free in-patient treatment.

However, in *CSS 617/1997* the Commissioner considered that the approach in *R(S) 1/66* did apply for the benefit at issue in that case (severe disablement allowance (SDA)). The claimant came home from hospital on a Friday morning and returned on the following Monday evening. The AO decided that he was only entitled to the full rate of SDA for three days (Saturday to Monday). The Commissioner points out that the claimant remained entitled to SDA while in hospital, albeit that it was paid at the reduced personal expenses rate; the question therefore was for what period that partial suspension of *payment* was lifted. One of the powers under which the Hospital In-Patients Regulations were made was s.82(6) SSA 1975 [s.113(2) SSCBA]. That power authorised regulations to suspend payment of benefit to a person *during* any period in which he was undergoing treatment as an in-patient. Applying the approach in *R(S) 1/66*, the Commissioner concluded that there was only authority to suspend payment of benefit in this case for days throughout which the claimant was an in-patient, with the consequence that he was entitled to the full rate of SDA for all four days at home. The Commissioner expressed the view, however, that the effect of the Hospital In-patient Regulations might be different where the question was one of basic entitlement to benefit. It is not clear that this attempt to reconcile the various conflicting decisions on this issue works, since, for example, entitlement to income support may well continue while a person is an in-patient, although the rate of payment will be reduced in accordance with the rules in Sched. 7. The current guidance to AOs in relation to income support/income-based JSA is that the circumstances that exist at the start of the day should be treated as continuing throughout the day (see the *Adjudication Officer's Guide*, paras. 29372–4).

In *White v. Chief Adjudication Officer, The Times*, August 2, 1993, the Health Authority had made an agreement with a nursing home under which the home agreed to reserve 18 places for people nominated by the Health Authority in return for a grant. The claimant who had been in hospital for some years was transferred to the nursing home under this arrangement. The Court of Appeal agreed with *CIS 371/1990* (to be reported as *R(IS) 7/92*) that the definition of "hospital" in s.128 of the National Health Service Act 1977 applied. In s.128 "hospital" includes "any institution for the reception and treatment of persons suffering from illness", and "illness" is defined to include mental disorder and "any injury or disability requiring medical or dental treatment or nursing". The claimant was mentally ill and required appropriate nursing. The nursing home had agreed to maintain appropriate staffing, including qualified mental nurses. Medication was dispensed (although not prescribed) by the nursing home. Thus the home was a hospital within the meaning of the Hospital In-Patient Regulations. It was not maintained under the National Health Service Act 1977, but the claimant was receiving treatment there pursuant to arrangements made by the Health Authority on behalf of the Secretary of State under the 1977 Act which was enough to bring the hospital within reg. 2(2)(b). The claimant was therefore not entitled to income support as his income exceeded his reduced applicable amount as a hospital in-patient. Note that reg. 2(2) of the Hospital In-Patient Regulations was amended on November 16, 1992. It is not clear whether such an arrangement will still fall within the terms of reg. 2(2) as amended.

See also *Botchett v. Chief Adjudication Officer, The Times*, May 8, 1996 (also to be reported as *R(IS) 10/96*. The claimant had severe learning disabilities and was resident in a registered nursing home. The nursing home had been part of a hospital but in 1991 was transferred to a trust which was funded by the health authority. The Court of Appeal held that the claimant's disability came within the definition of mental disorder, the care and assistance she received from nursing as opposed to domestic staff was to be regarded as "medical or other treatment" within reg. 2(2) and that the home was a "similar institution" to a hospital. She was therefore a "patient" for the purposes of income support.

However, in *CDLA 7980/1995* (which concerned the almost identical provision to reg. 2(2) in reg. 8(1) of the Social Security (Disability Living Allowance) Regulations 1991) the Commissioner points out that to bring the definition into play the medical or other treatment has to be provided "in a hospital or similar institution". In that case the claimant, who had severe learning difficulties and was an epileptic, left long-term hospital accommodation and went to live in a privately-rented house with five other tenants. Staff employed by Stockport Health Trust provided 24-hour care for the tenants but medication was prescribed by their individual GPs. The rent and other outgoings of the house were met from the tenants' benefits and the tenants were free to come and go as they wished. Having noted that paras. (a) and (c) of the definition of "hospital" in s.128 of the National Health Service Act 1977 begin with the words "any institution", the Commissioner holds that used in connection with the word "hospital", those words connoted "some sort of formal body or structure which controls all aspects of the treatment or care that is provided including the premises in which that treatment or care is carried out. They mean more than just a building in which care and treatment takes place". There was no institution in that sense on the facts of this case. The treatment and care took place in a house let to the six occupants who were responsible for the rent and other outgoings. The fact that their money and affairs were managed on their behalf did not mean that they ceased to be responsible for the cost of accommodation, food, etc. ordered in their names. Leave to appeal against this decision was granted by the Commissioner but the appeal did not proceed.

"Prisoner"

A person is detained in custody pending trial once he has been charged. It does not matter that in fact no trial takes place because the proceedings are discontinued. For the period he was in custody he was a prisoner *(R(IS) 1/94)*. However, a person required to live in a bail hostel is not detained in custody pending trial *(R(IS) 17/93)*; see Sched. 7, para. 9 as to how his applicable amount is calculated if he is a member of a couple.

Sub-para. (b) of the definition has been added to reverse the effect of *Chief Adjudication Officer v. Carr, The Times*, June 2, 1994, also to be reported as *R(IS) 20/95*, (which was the appeal from *CIS 561/1992*). A majority of the Court of Appeal had upheld the Commissioner's decision that a person serving a prison sentence who was released for a period of home leave was not a prisoner during that leave period. A person on temporary release will now continue to count as a prisoner and will not be eligible for income support. A person on income support with whom the prisoner stays while released on temporary licence can apply for a community care grant for his living expenses (see Social Fund Direction 4(a)(iv)).

Only people detained in custody awaiting trial or sentence have a limited entitlement to income support (see Sched. 7, para. 8(b)).

"Residential accommodation"

This definition applies where the person's stay is more than temporary and controls the application of the so-called "Part III rate" under para. 13 of Sched. 7. Note that para. (4) excludes from the definition under-18s in care in Scotland (sub-para. (a)), and accommodation where board is not provided (sub-para. (c)). The effect of sub-para. (c) is that residents of some types of local authority hostels are not shifted onto ordinary income support and housing benefit with other hostel-dwellers. If board is available, residents remain entitled to the "Part III rate" under para. 13 of Sched. 7. See the notes to the definition of "residential care home" in reg. 19 for "board". Para. (4A) in effect provides that board is available where any cooked or prepared food is provided in return for an inclusive charge. The intention is that if residents buy their own food or meals when they want them they are not restricted to the Part III rate.

Section 21(1) of the National Assistance Act 1948 obliges a local authority to provide accommodation for local residents "who by reason of age, illness, disability or other circumstances are in need of care and attention which is not otherwise available to them" (note that with effect from April, 1, 1993, s.21 only covers cases of illness and disability: see s.42 of, and Scheds. 9 and 10 to, the National Health Service and Community Care Act 1990). In *CA 2985/1997* the tribunal erred in law for not investigating whether the local authority had power to act under s. 21(1), since this had been put directly in issue by the claimant. The claimant contended that accommodation was "otherwise available". The Commissioner refers to *R. v. Sefton MBC, ex parte Help the Aged and Charlotte Blanchard* [1997] 4 All E.R. 532 which had clearly established that accommodation was "not otherwise available" if the claimant did not have the means to pay for it. Subject to this, in his view it was a question of fact in each case. A key aspect, apart from means, would be whether the claimant or some other appropriate person was capable of organising the accommodation (see Department of Health Circular (LAC (98) 19)).

See also *CSIS 453/1995* which concerned s.59 of the Social Work (Scotland) Act 1968. The

Commissioner concludes on the facts that the claimant's accommodation had not been secured by the local authority within s.59(2)(c) and that accordingly she was entitled to income support at the residential care home rate.

Note the increased upper and lower capital limits for most people living permanently in residential accommodation from April 1996 (regs. 45(b) and 53(1A), see the note to reg. 53; note reg. 53(4)).

Paragraph (3A)

Local authorities have duties to provide accommodation under the statutes mentioned in the definition of residential accommodation in para. (3), either in their own homes or by meeting the costs of independent homes. Residents then make a contribution to the costs. By agreement between the Government and local authorities the minimum weekly charge has been set at 80 per cent. of the basic rate of retirement pension. The resident can qualify for the ordinary rates of income support.

The Government was concerned that some local authorities had transferred their own homes to independent bodies (or were planning to do so) and required residents who did not wish to move to sign undertakings to arrange their own accommodation. If this had the effect of absolving the local authority from their duty to provide accommodation, the costs would be transferred from the local authorities to the income support budget. There was concern that the long-term welfare of existing residents was at risk if the local authority's responsibility was removed. Thus para. (3A) was introduced to provide that if residential accommodation became a residential care home after August 11, 1991, existing residents continue to be treated as if they were still in residential accommodation. There were originally two conditions to this. The first was that the person stays in the same accommodation. This condition remains. (There may be scope for manipulation here.) The second condition was that the local authority remained under a duty to provide or arrange for accommodation for the person. (This requirement has been removed with effect from November 8, 1996, see below). At the same time as reg. 21 was amended the Secretary of State issued Directions under the National Assistance Act 1948 and the National Health Service Act 1977 that in these circumstances of transfer the local authority remains under a duty. *CIS 298/1992* and *CIS 641/1992* decide that para. (3A) did effect a material change in the law and was not (as the AO had argued) merely declaratory. In both cases the claimants were resident in "Part III" homes for the elderly, the management of which was transferred by the local authority to a voluntary organisation before August 12, 1991. The residents were given the option of staying in the same home or moving to another home still run by the local authority. Both claimants stayed in their current home. The Commissioner holds that the evidence showed that the agreement between the local authority and the voluntary organisation in both cases did not come within s.26 of the National Assistance Act 1948. Thus the claimants were entitled to income support at the residential care home rate. The general approach of *CIS 298/1992* and *CIS 641/1992* is followed by the Commissioner in *CA 60/1993* (to be reported as *R(A) 1/95*), but he also points out that in deciding whether an arrangement is made under s.26 of the 1948 Act, s.26(2) is of central importance. Section 26(2) required that the arrangement provide for payments by the local authority to the voluntary organisation. This was because the essence of a s.26 arrangement was that the accommodation was provided in fulfilment of the local authority's duty under s.21(1) and so under s.26(3) the person concerned was under no liability to pay the voluntary organisation for the accommodation, but was obliged to refund the local authority for the payments made to the voluntary organisation (the obligation was subject to reduction on the grounds of the person's inability to pay). Thus if the residents were liable to make payments for their accommodation to the voluntary organisation a necessary characteristic of a s.26 arrangement was missing and the continued provision of accommodation was not pursuant to Part III of the 1948 Act. The Commissioner's decision in *CIS 298/1992* and *CIS 641/1992* was confirmed by the Court of Appeal in *Chief Adjudication Officer v. Harris* and *Chief Adjudication Officer v. Gibbon* (April 15, 1994, unreported). The Court of Appeal has also upheld the decision in *CA 60/1993* in *Chief Adjudication Officer v. Steane, The Times*, December 19, 1995. The CAO appealed to the House of Lords in both cases but the appeals were dismissed (*Chief Adjudication Officer and another v. Quinn (on behalf of Jane Harris, deceased), Same v. Gibbon* and *Same v. Steane* [1996] 4 All E.R. 72, also to be reported as *R(A) 3/96*). The House of Lords held that none of the arrangements had been made under s.26 because there was no provision for the local authority to make payments to the voluntary organisations concerned in accordance with s.26(2).

Following the House of Lords' judgment in *Quinn (Harris), Gibbon* and *Steane*, para. (3A) has been amended with effect from November 8, 1996 (despite the fact that Lord Slynn did consider that it had effected a change in the law; the transfers in *Harris, Gibbon* and *Steane* had all taken place *before* para. (3A) was introduced in August 1991). It is now no longer a condition that for the rule in para. (3A) to apply the local authority has to remain under a duty to provide or arrange for accommodation for the person concerned.

Paragraphs (3B) to (3E)

The intention of these paragraphs is that where a local authority accepted responsibility for accommodating a person prior to April 1, 1993, they remain responsible for them.

[¹Treatment of refugees

21ZA.—(1) Where a person has submitted a claim for asylum and is notified that he has been recorded by the Secretary of State as a refugee within the definition in Article 1 of the Convention relating to the Status of Refugees done at Geneva on 28th July 1951 as extended by Article 1(2) of the Protocol relating to the Status of Refugees done at New York on 31st January 1967 he shall cease to be a person from abroad for the purposes of regulation 21 (special cases) and Schedule 7 (applicable amounts in special cases) from the date he is so recorded.

(2) Except in the case of a refugee to whom paragraph (3) refers, a refugee to whom paragraph (1) applies, who claims income support within 28 days of receiving the notification referred to in that paragraph, shall have his claim for income support for whichever of the periods referred to in paragraph (4) applies in his case determined as if he had been an asylum seeker for the purposes of regulation 70 (urgent cases) in respect of any such period.

(3) A refugee to whom paragraph (1) applies, who was notified that he had been recorded as a refugee in the period from 24th July 1996 to 15th October 1996 and who claims income support within 28 days of the later date, shall have his claim for income support for whichever of the periods referred to in paragraph (4) applies in his case determined as if he had been an asylum seeker for the purposes of regulation 70 in respect of any such period.

(4) The periods to which this paragraph refers are—

(a) in the case of a claimant who made a claim for asylum upon arrival in the United Kingdom, the period from the date on which his claim for asylum was first refused by the Secretary of State or 5th February 1996 if that is later, to the date he is recorded by the Secretary of State as a refugee;

(b) in the case of a claimant whose claim for asylum is made other than on arrival in the United Kingdom, the period from the date of that claim, or 5th February 1996 if that is later, to the date he is recorded by the Secretary of State as a refugee.

(5) Any income support, which has otherwise been paid to the claimant or any partner of his in respect of any part of the period of an award to which paragraph (2) or (3) applies, shall be offset against any award due to the claimant by virtue of that paragraph except to the extent that the benefit paid to that partner was due in respect of a period during which he was not a partner of the claimant.]

1. Income Support and Social Security (Claims and Payments) (Miscellaneous Amendments) Regulations 1996 (S.I. 1996 No. 2431), reg. 3 (October 15, 1996).

DEFINITIONS

"claimant"—see reg. 2(1).
"partner"—*ibid.*

GENERAL NOTE

The effect of this provision is to allow asylum seekers whose refugee status is recognised by the Home Office to claim urgent cases payments of income support retrospectively for the period they were denied benefit as an asylum seeker. (The normal time limits for claims do not apply: Claims and Payments Regulations, reg. 19(8)). This concession was introduced during the passage through Parliament of the Asylum and Immigration Act 1996 (see s.11(2)). Section 11(4) of and para. 2 of Sched. 1 to that Act reinstate those parts of the Social Security (Persons from Abroad) Miscellaneous Amendments Regulations 1996 that had been struck down as *ultra vires* by the Court of Appeal in *R v. Secretary of State for Social Security, ex parte Joint Council for the Welfare of Immigrants and Another* [1996] 4 All E.R. 385 (see the notes to reg. 70(3A)–(3B)). The Act came into force on July 24, 1996. From that date, unless the transitional protection in reg. 12(1) of the 1996 Regulations applies, an asylum seeker is only entitled to urgent cases payments if he has claimed asylum "on arrival" (or within three months of an "upheaval direction" being made); and entitlement only lasts until the first decision is recorded on his asylum claim (or if that occurred before February 5, 1996 and an appeal was pending on that date, or submitted within the time limits for appeal, until that appeal is determined).

Note that in *CIS 564/1994*, heard together with *CIS 7250/1995*, the Commissioner rejects the claimant's argument that once her status as a refugee had been recognised by the Home Office she was retrospectively entitled to income support at the full rate from the date she first applied for asylum and was awarded urgent cases payments. See further the notes to reg. 70(3A)–(3B).

Paragraph (1)
This merely confirms that an asylum seeker ceases to count as a "person from abroad" on the date that the Secretary of State's recognition of his refugee status is recorded. From that date he can qualify for full income support/income-based JSA under the normal rules. Refugees are treated as satisfying the habitual residence test (reg. 21(3), additional definition of "person from abroad", sub-para. (b), JSA Regulations, reg. 85(4), second definition of "person from abroad", sub-para. (b)).

Paragraphs (2)–(5)
If the person claims income support within 28 days of being notified that his status as a refugee has been recorded by the Secretary of State (or by November 12, 1996 if he received the notification between July 24 and October 15, 1996: para. (3)), urgent cases payments can be awarded for the period from the date of the claim for asylum, or the first refusal of the asylum claim if the asylum claim was made "on arrival", to the date his status as a refugee was recorded. But no payment will be made under these provisions for any period before February 5, 1996. Any income support that has already been paid to the claimant (or any partner) for this period will be offset. But this does not apply for any part of the period that the partner was not the claimant's partner. In the case of a couple, the claim must be made by the person who is the refugee but if they are both refugees, either of them can claim (reg. 4(3C) of the Claims and Payments Regulations).

Note that any income support awarded under this provision is ignored as income (para. 57 of Sched. 9); it is also disregarded as capital but only for 52 weeks from the date of receipt (para. 49 of Sched. 10). There are similar disregards for any housing benefit or council tax benefit awarded under parallel provisions in the Housing Benefit and Council Tax Benefit Regulations (see paras 5 and 52 of Sched. 9 and paras 48 and 47 of Sched. 10 respectively).

[¹Reductions in applicable amounts in certain cases of failure to attend courses

21A.—[². . .].]

AMENDMENTS

1. Income Support (General and Transitional) Amendment Regulations 1990 (S.I. 1990 No. 2324), reg. 3 (December 17, 1990).
2. Income Support (General) (Jobseeker's Allowance Consequential Amendments) Regulations 1996 (S.I. 1996 No. 206), reg. 28 and Sched. 3 (October 7, 1996).

Reductions in applicable amounts in certain cases of actual or notional unemployment benefit disqualification

22.—[¹. . .]

AMENDMENT

1. Income Support (General) (Jobseeker's Allowance Consequential Amendments) Regulations 1996 (S.I. 1996 No. 206), reg. 28 and Sched. 3 (October 7, 1996).

[¹Reduction in applicable amount where the claimant is appealing against a decision that he is not incapable of work

22A.—(1) Subject to paragraph (3), where a claimant falls within paragraph 25 of Schedule 1B (persons appealing against a decision that they are not incapable of work under the all work test), and none of the other paragraphs of that Schedule applies to him, his applicable amount shall be reduced by a sum equivalent to 20 per cent. of the following amount—

(a) in the case of a person to whom regulation 17 or 18 or paragraphs 6, 9 to 12, 16, 17(c)(i) or (d)(i) of Schedule 7 applies—

 (i) where he is a single claimant aged less than 18 or a member of a couple or a polygamous marriage where all the members, in either case, are less than 18, the amount specified in paragraph 1(1)(a), (b) or (c), as the case may be, of Schedule 2 (applicable amounts);

 (ii) where he is a single claimant aged not less than 18 but less than 25 or a member of a couple or a polygamous marriage where one member is aged not less than 18 but less than 25 and the other member, or in the case of a polygamous marriage each other member, is a person under 18 who—

 (aa) does not qualify for income support under regulation 4ZA, or who would not so qualify if he were to make a claim; and

 (bb) does not satisfy the requirements of section 3(1)(f)(iii) of the Jobseekers Act 1995 (prescribed circumstances for persons aged 16 but less than 18); and

 (cc) is not the subject of a direction under section 16 of the Jobseekers Act 1995 (persons under 18: severe hardship),

 the amount specified in paragraph 1(1)(d) of that Schedule;

 (iii) where he is a single claimant aged not less than 25 or a member of a couple or a polygamous marriage (other than a member of a couple or a polygamous marriage to whom head (ii) of this sub-paragraph applies) at least one of whom is aged not less than 18, the amount specified in paragraph 1(1)(e) of that Schedule;

(b) in the case of a person to whom regulation 19 applies (applicable amounts for people in residential care and nursing homes), the amount allowed for personal expenses for him specified in paragraph 13 of Schedule 4.

(2) A reduction under paragraph (1) shall, if it is not a multiple of 5p, be rounded to the nearest such multiple or, if it is a multiple of 2.5p but not of 5p, to the next lower multiple of 5p.

(3) Paragraph (1) shall not apply to a claimant who is appealing against a decision that he is not incapable of work under the all work test where that decision was made on the first application of the test to the claimant, and the claimant was, immediately prior to 13th April 1995, either—

(a) in receipt of invalidity pension under Part II of the Contributions and Benefits Act as then in force, or severe disablement allowance; or

(b) incapable of work in accordance with paragraph 5 of Schedule 1 as in force on 12th April 1995 and had been so for a continuous period of 28 weeks.]

<small>AMENDMENT</small>

1. Income Support (General) (Jobseeker's Allowance Consequential Amendments) Regulations 1996 (S.I. 1996 No. 206), reg. 13 (October 7, 1996).

Paras. (1) and (2) of this regulation replace the provisions formerly in regs. 8(2A) and 22 (now revoked). Para. (3) repeats the transitional protection in reg. 19(5) of the Disability Working Allowance and Income Support (General) Amendment Regulations 1995 (see p. 495).

The regulation applies where a claimant is appealing against a decision that he is fit for work on the basis of the "all work test" and so is eligible for income support under para. 25 of Sched. 1B (and does not qualify under any of the other paragraphs in Sched. 1B). See the notes to para. 7 of Sched. 1B for a summary of the all work test and when it applies. A claimant will be eligible for income support under para. 25 until the appeal is determined (which should mean the final determination of the appeal, *e.g.* if it is taken to the Social Security Commissioner). However, his income support will be reduced by 20 per cent of the appropriate personal allowance for a single claimant of his age (para. (1)). (If the appeal is successful the reduction will be repaid). But full income support will be paid where the claimant has appealed after failing his first all work test if he had been incapable of work for 28 weeks or in receipt of invalidity benefit or severe disablement allowance immediately before April 13, 1995 (para. (3)). Note also reg. 27(3) of the Income Support (General) (Jobseeker's Allowance Consequential Amendments) Regulations 1996 which provides that the reduction under para. (1) does not apply to people who are covered by reg. 19(5) of the Disability Working Allowance and Income Support (General) Amendment Regulations 1995 as orignally made (see the notes to reg. 19(5) and (6) of those Regulations).

Unless para. (3) (or the transitional protection in reg. 27(3)) applies, in order to receive full benefit the person will have to sign on as available for work and claim JSA while waiting for his appeal to be decided. The *Adjudication Officer's Guide* accepts that the fact that a person has been available for employment should not prejudice the appeal about incapacity (para. 18339). See further the notes to para. 25 of Sched. 1B.

PART V

INCOME AND CAPITAL

Chapter I

General

Calculation of income and capital of members of claimant's family and of a polygamous marriage

23.—(1) [¹Subject to paragraphs (2) and (4) and to regulation 44 (modifications in respect of children and young persons), the income and capital of a claimant's partner and] the income of a child or young person which by virtue of section 22(5) of the Act [SSCBA, s.136(1) is to be treated as income and capital of the claimant, shall be calculated in accordance with the following provisions of this Part in like manner as for the claimant; and any reference to the "claimant" shall, except where the context otherwise requires, be construed, for the purposes of this Part, as if it were a reference to his partner or that child or young person.

(2) Regulations 36(2) and 38(2), so far as they relate to paragraphs 1 to 10 of Schedule 8 (earnings to be disregarded) and regulation 41(1) (capital treated as income) shall not apply to a child or young person.

(3) [¹Subject to paragraph (5)] where a claimant or the partner of a claimant is married polygamously to two or more members of his household—

(a) the claimant shall be treated as possessing capital and income belonging to each such member and the income of any child or young person who is one of that member's family; and

(b) the income and capital of that member or, as the case may be, the income of that child or young person shall be calculated in accordance with the

185

following provisions of this Part in like manner as for the claimant or, as the case may be, as for any child or young person who is a member of his family.

[¹(4) Where at least one member of a couple is aged less than 18 and the applicable amount of the couple falls to be determined under [²paragraphs 1(3)(b), (c), (f) or (g)] of Schedule 2 (applicable amounts), the income of the claimant's partner shall not be treated as the income of the claimant to the extent that—

(a) in the case of a couple where both members are aged less than 18, the amount specified in paragraph 1(3)(a) of that Schedule exceeds the amount specified in [²paragraph 1(3)(c)] of that Schedule; and

(b) in the case of a couple where only one member is aged less than 18, the amount specified in paragraph 1(3)(d) of that Schedule exceeds the amount which applies in that case which is specified in [²paragraph 1(3)(f) or (g)] of that Schedule.

(5) Where a member of a polygamous marriage is a partner aged less than 18 and the amount which applies in respect of him under regulation 18(2) (polygamous marriages) is nil, the claimant shall not be treated as possessing the income of that partner to the extent that an amount in respect of him would have been included in the applicable amount if he had fallen within the circumstances set out in regulation 18(2)(a) or (b).]

AMENDMENTS

1. Income Support (General) Amendment No. 3 Regulations 1988 (S.I. 1988 No. 1228), reg. 6 (September 12, 1988).
2. Income Support (General) (Jobseeker's Allowance Consequential Amendments) Regulations 1996 (S.I. 1996 No. 206), reg. 14 (October 7, 1996).

DEFINITIONS

"child"—see 1986 Act, s.20(11) (SSCBA, s.137(1)).
"claimant"—see reg. 2(1).
"family"—see 1986 Act, s.20(11) (SSCBA, s.137(1)).
"partner"—see reg. 2(1).
"polygamous marriage"—*ibid.*
"young person"—*ibid.*, reg. 14.

GENERAL NOTE

Resources are to be either capital or income. There is nothing in between. The distinction between capital and income is one which has given a good deal of trouble in the past, and in many other legal contexts. There is no attempt at any general definition in the Regulations, although see regs. 35, 41 and 48. The approach tends to be that around the borderlines a decision can go either way, and it is only if a decision is completely unreasonable that it embodies an error of law *(R. v. W. London SBAT, ex parte Taylor* [1975] 2 All E. R. 790). But ultimately the question is one of law (see *Lillystone v. SBC* [1982] 3 F.L.R. 52 (C.A.))

So far as general principle goes it has been said that the "essential feature of receipts by way of income is that they display an element of periodic recurrence. Income cannot include ad hoc receipts." (Bridge J. in *R. v. Supplementary Benefits Commission, ex parte Singer* [1973] 1 W. L. R. 713). This links the notion of recurrence (which may only be expected in the future) with the notion of a period to which the income is linked. Similar notions are applied by the Commissioner in *R(SB) 29/85* where the issue was the proper treatment of a £15 loan made to a striking miner by a local authority Social Work Department to meet arrears on hire purchase agreements. The Commissioner holds that this was a capital payment, since it was a "one-off" advance and there was no evidence that it was one of a series of payments. Earlier he had referred to income payments normally bearing a readily identifiable relationship with a period. However, periodic recurrence alone is not enough. The nature of the obligation (if any) under which a payment is made must be looked at. A capital payment may be made by instalments. Then in general each instalment is a capital payment, so that reg. 41 is necessary. The general rule is supported by the Court of Appeal in *Lillystone v. SBC* where the purchase price of a house was to be paid in monthly instalments over 10 years. It was agreed that each £70 instalment, when it was paid, was capital, not income.

In *R(SB) 2/83* the Tribunal of Commissioners says "In most cases capital resources arise out of income resources. They represent savings out of past earnings. However, before they undergo the metamorphosis from income to capital all relevant debts, including, in particular, tax liabilities, are first deducted." In *R(SB) 35/83* the Commissioner holds that accumulated earnings will not become capital until all relevant liabilities are deducted. Since the "relevant liabilities" seems to mean the deductions appropriate under the benefit legislation, presumably it is only the categories mentioned in reg. 36(3), if not already deducted, which can be considered, plus, it seems, expenses necessarily incurred in obtaining the earnings *(R(FC) 1/90* and *R(IS) 16/93*—see the note to reg. 36(3)). *CIS 563/1991* decides that such expenses are not deductible in the case of income other than earnings (see the note to reg. 40(1)). There is no provision for deducting amounts which are to be used for ordinary current expenditure *(CIS 654/1991*, to be reported as *R(IS) 3/93)*. *R(IS) 3/93* also confirms that a payment does not metamorphose into capital until the end of the period to which it is attributed as income. Thus, for example, payment of a month's salary, attributable for a forward period of a month from the date it was due to be paid, would retain its character as income until the end of that period.

This principle should apply to other forms of income as it does to earnings. Thus if, for instance, arrears of a social security benefit are paid, then any amount of those arrears left after the end of the period to which the benefit is properly attributed as income comes into the category of capital. *R(SB) 4/89*, holding arrears of special hardship allowance to be income, did not deal with this point.

Paragraph (1)

This provision contains the basic rule on the aggregation of resources. The income and capital of the claimant's partner is treated as the claimant's. Note that the definition of partner refers on to married and unmarried couples, defined in s.137(1) of the Contributions and Benefits Act (1986 Act, s.20(11)) (and see para. (3) for polygamous marriages). It is an essential part of the definition of both kinds of couple that the parties should be members of the same household, so that reg. 16 may also be relevant. There are special rules for couples where at least one member is under 18 (paras (4) and (5)).

Only the income of a child or young person in the claimant's household is aggregated with the claimant's (confirmed in reg. 47). If a child or young person has capital over £3,000 there is no personal allowance for that child (reg. 17(b)) and any income of the child is not aggregated (reg. 44(5)). The word "claimant" in the following regulations includes those whose income or capital is aggregated.

Paragraph (2)

Where a child or young person has earnings, the normal disregards in paras 1 to 10 of Sched. 8, which in particular include the £5, £10 and £15 disregards, do not apply, but the rest do. The effect of para. 14 of Sched. 8 is that most earnings are disregarded. Reg. 41(1) on capital payable by instalments does not apply to children or young persons because there is special provision, referring to the £3,000 limit, in reg. 44(1).

Paragraph (4)

This paragraph applies where a couple receives less than the ordinary couple's rate of personal allowance because of the ineligibility of one partner who is under 18 (this is the effect of the reference to para. 1(3)(b), (c), (f) and (g) of Sched. 2). The income of the ineligible partner is not treated as the claimant's except to the extent that it exceeds the difference between the reduced rate of personal allowance and the ordinary rate. The aggregation of capital is not affected.

Paragraph (5)

This makes similar provision for polygamous marriages.

[¹ Income of participants in the self-employment route of the Employment Option of the New Deal

23A. Chapters II, III, IV, V, VII and VIIA of this Part and regulations 62 to 66A, 68 and 69 shall not apply to any income which is to be calculated in accordance with Chapter IVA of this Part (participants in the self-employment route of the Employment Option of the New Deal).]

ecurity (Miscellaneous Amendments) (No. 4) Regulations 1998 (S.I. 1998 No. 1174),
ne 1, 1998).

/OTE

Regulation 23A takes any gross receipts from trading while on the self-employment route of the
Employment Option of the New Deal for 18 to 24-year-olds out of the categories of earnings,
self-employed earnings and income other than earnings for the purposes of any claim for income
support. The rules for liable relative payments, payments of child support maintenance and student
income (except reg. 67) also do not apply. Any such receipts may only be taken into account in
accordance with regs. 39A to 39D.

For a brief summary of the self-employment route of the Employment Option, see the note to
reg. 75(1) of the JSA Regulations.

Treatment of charitable or voluntary payments

24.—[¹. . .]

AMENDMENT

1. Income Support (General) Amendment No. 5 Regulations 1988 (S.I. 1988 No. 2022), reg.5
(December 12, 1988).

Liable relative payments

25. Regulations 29 to 44, 46 to 52 and Chapter VIII of this Part shall not
apply to any payment which is to be calculated in accordance with Chapter VII
thereof (liable relatives).

[¹Child support

25A. Regulations 29, 31, 32, 40 and 42 and Chapter VII of this Part shall not
apply to any payment which is to be calculated in accordance with chapter VIIA
of this Part (child support).]

AMENDMENT

1. Social Security (Miscellaneous Provisions) Amendment Regulations 1993 (S.I. 1993 No. 846),
reg. 2 (April 19, 1993).

GENERAL NOTE

Reg. 25A takes payments of child support maintenance, paid under an assessment carried out in
accordance with the Child Support Acts 1991–1995, out of the categories of income other than
earnings and of liable relative payments. They may only be taken into account for income support
purposes in accordance with regs. 60A to 60D.

Calculation of income and capital of students

26. The provisions of Chapters II to VI of this Part (income and capital) shall
have effect in relation to students and their partners subject to the modifications
set out in Chapter VIII thereof (students).

DEFINITIONS

"partner"—see reg. 2(1).
"student"—*ibid.*, reg. 61.

[¹Rounding of fractions

27. Where any calculation under this Part results in a fraction of a penny that fraction shall, if it would be to the claimant's advantage, be treated as a penny, otherwise it shall be disregarded.]

AMENDMENT

1. Income Support (General) Amendment Regulations 1988 (S.I. 1988 No. 663), reg. 13 (April 11, 1988).

Chapter II

Income

Calculation of income

28.—(1) For the purposes of section 20(3) of the Act [SSCBA, s.124(1)] (conditions of entitlement to income support), the income of a claimant shall be calculated on a weekly basis—
  (a) by determining in accordance with this Part, other than Chapter VI, the weekly amount of his income; and
  (b) by adding to that amount the weekly income calculated under regulation 53 (calculation of tariff income from capital).
  [¹(2) For the purposes of paragraph (1) "income" includes capital treated as income under regulations 41 (capital treated as income) and income which a claimant is treated as possessing under regulation 42 (notional income).]

AMENDMENT

1. Income Support (General) Amendment No. 4 Regulations 1991 (S.I. 1991 No. 1559), reg. 7 (October 7, 1991).

DEFINITIONS

"the Act"—see reg. 2(1).
"claimant"—*ibid.*

GENERAL NOTE

Reg. 28 simply confirms that all resources which would come under the description of income, including resources specifically treated as earnings or income, are to be taken into account in the income calculation.

Calculation of earnings derived from employed earner's employment and income other than earnings

29.—(1) [¹. . .] Earnings derived from employment as an employed earner and income which does not consist of earnings shall be taken into account over a period determined in accordance with the following paragraphs and at a weekly amount determined in accordance with regulation 32 (calculation of weekly amount of income).
  (2) Subject to [⁴the following provisions of this regulation], the period over which a payment is to be taken into account shall be—
  (a) in a case where it is payable in respect of a period, a period equal to the length of that period;
  (b) in any other case, a period equal to such number of weeks as is equal to the number obtained (and any fraction shall be treated as a corresponding

fraction of a week) by dividing the net earnings, or in the case of income which does not consist of earnings, the amount of that income [³less any amount paid by way of tax on that income which is disregarded under paragraph 1 of Schedule 9 (income other than earnings to be disregarded)] by the amount of income support which would be payable had the payment not been made plus an amount equal to the total of the sums which would fall to be disregarded from that payment under Schedule 8 [³(earnings to be disregarded) or, as the case may be, any paragraph of Schedule 9 other than paragraph 1 of that Schedule,] as is appropriate in the claimant's case;

and that period shall begin on the date on which the payment is treated as paid under regulation 31 (date on which income is treated as paid).

[⁴(2A) The period over which a Career Development Loan, which is paid pursuant to section 2 of the Employment and Training Act 1973, shall be taken into account shall be the period of education and training intended to be supported by that loan.

(2B) Where grant income as defined in Chapter VIII of this Part has been paid to a person who ceases to be a student before the end of the period in respect of which that income is payable and, as a consequence, the whole or part of that income falls to be repaid by that person, that income shall be taken into account over the period beginning on the date on which that income is treated as paid under regulation 31 and ending—

(a) on the date on which repayment is made in full; or

[⁵(aa) where the grant is paid in instalments, on the day before the next instalment would have been paid had the claimant remained a student; or]

(b) on the last date of the academic term or vacation during which that person ceased to be a student,

whichever shall first occur.]

(3) Where earnings not of the same kind are derived from the same source and the periods in respect of which those earnings would, but for this paragraph, fall to be taken into account—

(a) overlap, wholly or partly, those earnings shall be taken into account over a period equal to the aggregate length of those periods;

(b) and that period shall begin with the earliest date on which any part of those earnings would otherwise be treated as paid under regulation 31 (date on which income is treated as paid).

[²(4) In a case to which paragraph (3) applies, earnings under regulation 35 (earnings of employed earners) shall be taken into account in the following order of priority—

(a) earnings normally derived from the employment;

(b) any payment to which paragraph (1)(b) or (c) of that regulation applies;

(c) any payment to which paragraph (1)(i) of that regulation applies;

(d) any payment to which paragraph (1)(d) of that regulation applies.]

[¹(4A) Where earnings to which regulation 35(1)(b) to (d) (earnings of employed earners) applies are paid in respect of part of a day, those earnings shall be taken into account over a period equal to a day.]

[²(4B) Where earnings to which regulation 35(1)(i)(i) applies (earnings of employed earners) are paid in respect of or on the termination of any employment which is not part-time employment, the period over which they are to be taken into account shall be—

(a) a period equal to such number of weeks as is equal to the number (less any fraction of a whole number) obtained by dividing the net earnings by the maximum weekly amount which, on the date on which the payment of earnings is made, is specified in paragraph 8(1)(c) of Schedule 14 to the Employment Protection (Consolidation) Act 1978; or

(b) a period equal to the length of the specified period,
whichever is the shorter, and that period shall begin on the date on which the payment is treated as paid under regulation 31 (date on which income is treated as paid).

(4C) Any earnings to which regulation 35(1)(i)(ii) applies which are paid in respect of or on the termination of part-time employment, shall be taken into account over a period equal to one week.

(4D) In this regulation—

(a) "part-time employment" means employment in which a person is not to be treated as engaged in remunerative work under regulation 5 or 6 (persons treated, or not treated, as engaged in remunerative work);

(b) "specified period" means a period equal to—

(i) the period of notice which is applicable to a person, or would have been applicable if it had not been waived; less

(ii) any part of that period during which the person has continued to work in the employment in question or in respect of which he has received a payment to which regulation 35(1)(c) applies,

and for the purposes of this definition "period of notice" means the period of notice of termination of employment to which a person is entitled by statute or by contract, whichever is the longer, or, if he is not entitled to such notice, the period of notice which is customary in the employment in question.]

(5) For the purposes of this regulation the claimant's earnings and income which does not consist of earnings shall be calculated in accordance with Chapters III and V respectively of this Part.

AMENDMENTS

1. Income Support (General) Amendment No. 5 Regulations 1988 (S.I. 1988 No.2022), reg. 7 (December 12, 1988).

2. Income Support (General) Amendment No. 2 Regulations 1989 (S.I. 1989 No. 1323), reg. 9 (October 9, 1989).

3. Income Support (General) Amendment Regulations 1990 (S.I. 1990 No. 547), reg. 10 (April 9, 1990).

4. Income-related Benefits and Jobseeker's Allowance (Miscellaneous Amendments) Regulations 1997 (S.I. 1997 No. 65), reg. 5 (April 7, 1997).

5. Social Security (Miscellaneous Amendments) Regulations 1998 (S.I. 1998 No. 563), reg. 12 (April 6, 1998).

DEFINITIONS

"claimant"—see reg. 2(1), reg. 23(1).
"employed earner"—see reg. 2(1).
"grant income"—see reg. 61.
"student"—see regs. 2(1), 61.

GENERAL NOTE

Paragraphs (1) and (2)
This regulation applies to the earnings of employees and income other than earnings. Thus it covers other social security benefits. Earnings from self-employment are dealt with in reg. 30. It defines the period over which income is to be taken into account and the date on which that period starts. The general rule is set out in para. (2). The first part (familiar from reg. 9(2)(a) of the old Resources Regulations) is that where a payment is in respect of a period it is to be taken into account for an equal period. A fortnight's unemployment benefit is to be taken into account for a fortnight (*R(SB) 17/82*), a month's salary for a month, an annual covenant for a year (*R(SB) 25/86*, but see Chapter VIII for students). There will be problems in determining the period in respect of which a payment is made in some cases. For instance, is holiday pay

191

in terms of days, to be attributed to each of the seven days in a week (as done in *R(SB) 11/ 85* and *CSB 1004/1988*), or is it in terms of weeks, so that only five days' worth is attributed to each week? If a supply teacher works for a varying number of days in each month, being paid at the end of the month, is that payment in respect of the month or in respect of the number of days worked? Much will turn on the precise contractual situation and the terms used by the parties, as confirmed by *CIS 654/1991* (to be reported as *R(IS) 3/93*). Decisions on the former reg. 7(1)(g) of the Social Security (Unemployment, Sickness and Invalidity Benefit) Regulations 1983 (like *R(U) 3/84*) may be helpful.

The question in relation to supply teachers was specifically considered in *CIS 242/1989* (to be reported as *R(IS) 10/95*). The claimant had worked as a supply teacher for five days in the month of June. She was paid for work done in a month at the end of the following month. The Commissioner accepts that the claimant's contract with the local education authority was on a daily basis (see *R(U) 2/87*). But he rejected her argument that the period for which payment was made was five days. He holds that since she was employed on a daily basis, she was in fact paid for five different periods in June. Para. (2)(a) clearly only envisaged payment in respect of a single period, since neither para. (2) nor reg. 32(1) could operate satisfactorily if a single payment could be in respect of two or more periods. Thus the payment for the days worked in a particular month had to be attributed to the period of a month. *CIS 242/1989* is followed with some reluctance in *CIS 167/1992*. The result of this approach is that the period is determined by the employer's administrative arrangements for payment, rather than the terms of the employment. But it is surely arguable that the period in respect of which the payment was payable was one day. The terms of the claimant's employment were that she was paid £42.23 per session (*i.e.* day). The Commissioner's approach equates the period in respect of which a payment is *payable* with the period for which payment is *due to be made*, which is not necessarily the same. Moreover, the Commissioner does not seem to have taken account of the fact that "payment" can include part of a payment (see reg. 2(1)). Thus some of the operational difficulties referred to by the Commissioner could be overcome by dividing the claimant's monthly payment by the number of days worked in that month and attributing this on a daily basis. However, this does not deal with the point that all the payments would be due on one day. If the payments were due before the date of the claim, reg. 31(1)(a) would apply to attribute them all to that day; if they were paid during a claim see reg. 32(5) and reg. 31(1)(b). See also para. 13 of Sched. 8.

Para. (2A) relates to Career Development Loans.

Para. (2B), in force from April 7, 1997, concerns the situation where a person is due to repay part or all of a student grant because he leaves or is dismissed from his course before it finishes. The grant income (defined in reg. 61) will be taken into account from the date it is treated as paid under reg. 31 until full repayment has been made, or, where the grant is paid in instalments, the day before the next instalment would be due, or the last day of the term or vacation in which the person ceases to be a student, whichever is earlier. See reg. 32(6A) for calculation of the weekly amount to be taken into account and note reg. 40(3B). Para. (2B) thus confirms the effect of the decision in *CIS 5185/1995*. The claimant who had been a full-time student left his course and claimed income support on January 10, 1994. The education authority did not inform him of the amount of the grant he had to repay until March 20, 1994. The Commissioner holds that the claimant was not entitled to income support because until the grant was repaid it was income that remained available to the claimant and had to be taken into account (see *R. v. Bolton SBAT, ex parte Fordham* [1981] 1 All E.R. 50 and *CSB 1408/ 1988*) and it exceeded his applicable amount. Moreover, once the claimant had ceased to be a student, the disregards in reg. 62 did not apply (but now see reg. 32(6A)). The Commissioner rejects the argument that the grant income could be disregarded under the principle in *Barclays Bank v. Quistclose Investments Ltd* [1970] A.C. 567. That principle did not apply because the education authority retained no beneficial interest in the grant. They merely reserved the right to demand repayment of a sum calculated in accordance with how much of the relevant term had expired when the claimant ceased to be a student.

However, in *CIS 12263/1996* the Commissioner took the view that as soon as a student had abandoned his course and an obligation to repay the balance of his grant to the education authority arose, he held the money on constructive trust for the authority. Thus in assessing the claimant's entitlement to income support the repayable balance of the grant was not to be taken into account as his income. The Commissioner in *CIS 12263/1996* considered that the *Quistclose* case was concerned with a "purpose trust" (*i.e.* where a grant or loan was impressed with a particular purpose from the beginning), whereas in this situation a constructive trust had arisen because the grant had been paid on the condition that the claimant continued to be a student. He also distinguished the Court of Appeal's decision in *Fordham* on the ground that in that case there had been uncertainty as to the obligation to repay (there was none here). Moreover, an alternative approach was that once the balance of the grant became repayable it could no longer be regarded as the claimant's income at all (see para. 9(7) of *R(SB) 20/83*).

Leave to appeal against the decision in *CIS 5185/1995* was granted by the Court of Appeal but the appeal was not pursued for financial reasons. However, an appeal was brought by the AO against the decision in *CIS 12263/1996* (*Chief Adjudication Officer v. Leeves*, November 6, 1998, CA, to be reported as *R(IS) 5/99*). It was conceded on behalf of the claimant that there was no constructive trust in these circumstances, since no proprietary right had been retained by the education authority, nor had any fiduciary obligation been created. However, the Court of Appeal held that money that the claimant was under a "certain and immediate liability" to repay did not amount to income. Thus once the claimant had received a request for immediate repayment of a specified sum from the local education authority the grant ceased to count as his income (although it fell to be treated as such until that time, even though he had abandoned his course). The Court distinguished its decision in *Fordham* as the liability to repay in that case had been uncertain.

Thus in relation to periods before April 7, 1997, the repayable balance of a grant will not count as a claimant's income from the date that the liability to repay has "crystallised" (*Leeves*). As regards periods after April 6, 1997, para. (2B) will apply. However, it is suggested that this is subject to the preliminary question of whether the repayable grant counts as the claimant's income at all. If it does not do so because there is a "certain and immediate" liability to repay, it is arguable that para. (2B) will not (or will cease to) apply. This is because neither para. (2B), nor reg. 40(3B) or reg. 32(6A), would seem to have the effect of deeming the grant to be income but simply provide for the period over which the grant is to be taken into account *if* it does count as income, and the method of calculating that income. Compare the wording of reg. 40(3A) (treatment of student loans where a claimant has ceased to be a student): this requires "a sum equal to the weekly amount" to be taken into account as income.

Where para. (2B) is applicable (for example, where repayment is not required immediately, or the amount of the repayment has not been calculated), note that the disregards for grant income in reg. 62 will apply (reg. 32(6A)); see also reg. 40(3B).

Any grant or covenant income or student loan left over at the end of the person's course is disregarded as income (see para. 61 of Sched. 9).

Note the special rules set out in paras. (4B) to (4D) for calculating the period over which compensation payments (see reg. 35(1)(i) and (3)) are to be taken into account.

If the payment is not in respect of a period then there is a mechanical rule in para. (2)(b) spreading it at the rate of income support which would otherwise be payable, taking account of any disregards.

Once the period is fixed, it begins on the date specified in reg. 31.

Paragraphs (3) and (4)

Para. (3) establishes an exception in the case of earnings only, to the rule about the date from which a payment is to be taken into account. It is to deal mainly with the situation on the termination of employment when a claimant may be entitled to regular earnings, week in hand payments, pay in lieu of notice or compensation for breach of contract and holiday pay. The effect is that each payment which is not disregarded (Sched. 8, paras. 1 to 3) is to be taken into account for the appropriate period, and the periods are to be put together consecutively. Then the aggregate period starts on the earliest date which would be fixed for any of the periods under reg. 31. Note that para. (3) only applies where the earnings are of different kinds, and derive from the same source. Thus it would not apply to payments from different employers.

Para. (4) deals with the order in which payments in lieu of notice, compensation payments and holiday pay are to be taken into account in conjunction with ordinary earnings.

Paragraph (4A)

Earnings paid in respect of a part of a day are taken into account for a day.

Paragraph (4B)

This provision defines the length of the period for which a payment of compensation on the termination of full-time employment is to be taken into account. The line between full-time and part-time is drawn by para. (4D)(a) and reg. 35(3)(c). What is a payment of compensation is defined in reg. 35(3)(*a*). There are two alternative periods, whichever is the shorter being applied. The first is obtained by dividing the amount of the payment by the maximum weekly sum specified at the relevant time for the purposes of calculating statutory redundancy payments and the basic award for unfair dismissal. From April 1, 1989, the sum was £172, from April 1, 1990, it was £184, from April 1, 1991, it was £198, from April 1, 1992 (not increased in

193

1993 or 1994), it was £205, from September 27, 1995 (not increased in 1996 or 1997) it was £210 and from April 1, 1998 it has been £220. This calculation will give an advantage to lower paid workers, for whom the period may be shorter than the number of weeks' wages represented by the payment. The second alternative is the "specified period," defined in para. (4D)(b) as the period of notice to which the person was legally entitled (or customarily entitled for civil servants with no contractual entitlement) less any period worked out or already covered by a payment in lieu of notice. This secures that if a person receives a payment which is larger than would be required to make up for the uncovered period of notice, he is not affected beyond the legal notice period.

Although the end of para. (4B) provides that the payment is to be treated as paid on the date fixed by reg. 31, this result may well be displaced by the operation of paras. (3) and (4).

Paragraph (4C)
Where a payment of compensation is made on the termination of part-time employment (para. (4D)(a) and reg. 35(3)(c)) it is to be taken into account for one week. See also reg. 32(7).

Calculation of earnings of self-employed earners

30.—(1) Except where paragraph (2) applies, where a claimant's income consists of earnings from employment as a self-employed earner the weekly amount of his earnings shall be determined by reference to his average weekly earnings from that employment—

(a) over a period of [¹one year]; or
(b) where the claimant has recently become engaged in that employment or there has been a change which is likely to affect the normal pattern of business, over such other period [¹. . .] as may, in any particular case, enable the weekly amount of his earnings to be determined more accurately.

(2) Where the claimant's earnings consist of royalties or sums paid periodically for or in respect of any copyright those earnings shall be taken into account over a period equal to such number of weeks as is equal to the number obtained (and any fraction shall be treated as a corresponding fraction of a week) by dividing the earnings by the amount of income support which would be payable had the payment not been made plus an amount equal to the total of the sums which would fall to be disregarded from the payment under Schedule 8 (earnings to be disregarded) as is appropriate in the claimant's case.

(3) For the purposes of this regulation the claimant's earnings shall be calculated in accordance with Chapter IV of this Part.

AMENDMENT

1. Income-related Benefits Schemes (Miscellaneous Amendments) (No. 4) Regulations 1993 (S.I. 1993 No. 2119), reg. 11 (October 4, 1993).

DEFINITIONS

"claimant"—see reg. 2(1), reg. 23(1).
"self-employed earner"—see reg. 2(1).

GENERAL NOTE

Reg. 30 applies to earnings from self-employment. A person is a self-employed earner if he is in "gainful employment", other than employed earner's employment (SSCBA, s. 2(1)(b), imported by reg. 2(1)). In *CIS 166/1994* the claimant was a self-employed builder, whose work had dried up, although he had not ceased trading. The Commissioner points out that a person can be in gainful employment, even though he is not working or receiving any money from the employment (see e.g., *Vandyk v. Minister of Pensions and National Insurance* [1955] 1 Q.B. 29). Whether the claimant was in gainful employment depended on his current and prospective activities and intentions. The Commissioner endorsed a detailed list of factors put forward by the AO for determining this. He also held that *R(FC) 2/90* which decided that the question whether a person was employed, or

194

self-employed, for the purposes of income support or family credit, was for decision by the adjudicating authorities, not the Secretary of State, had not been affected by the 1992 consolidating legislation.

Thus it is for the adjudicating authorities to decide whether particular earnings are self-employed earnings falling within reg. 30, without being bound by the way they have been treated for contribution purposes (*CIS 14409/1996*). This was despite s. 2(3) of the Contributions and Benefits Act 1992 (person treated as an employed earner in relation to a particular employment to be so treated for all contribution and benefit purposes). If the adjudicating authorities took a different view from the Secretary of State it was a matter for her what action she took in order to ensure compliance with s. 2(3). The claimant in *CIS 14409/1996* was an actor. Although his general status was that of a self-employed earner, his gross receipts for the previous year included earnings from radio and television engagements from which Class 1 national insurance contributions as a employed earner had been deducted. The SSAT decided that because the majority of his earnings were as a self-employed earner all his earnings fell to be calculated under reg. 30. The Commissioner holds that this was plainly wrong (see s. 2 of the 1992 Act and *Fall v. Hitchen* [1973] 1 W.L.R. 286) and that what the tribunal should have addressed was the question of the nature of these particular earnings. On the facts the claimant was quite clearly carrying out his broadcasting work as a person in business on his own account (see *Market Investigations v. Ministry of Social Security* [1969] 2 Q.B. 173). Thus the AO had been correct to treat the earnings from the radio and television contracts as self-employed earnings.

Note that if the self-employment has ceased, earnings from that self-employment (other than royalty or copyright payments) are ignored (para. 3 of Sched. 8).

The earnings (calculated under regs. 37 to 39) are generally to be averaged over a period of one year. Contrary to what was said in earlier editions, it does not seem necessary that the period immediately precedes the benefit week in question. Any one year period—normally the last year for which accounts are available—will do. The alternative period under para. (1)(b) can only be chosen if there has been a change likely to affect the normal pattern of business or if the self-employment has recently started. In *CIS 166/1994* the Commissioner accepts that where such a change had produced, or was likely to produce, a substantial reduction in the claimant's earnings, it was appropriate for the period to start from the date of the change (with the likely result that no earnings fell to be taken into account). See also *CIS 14409/1996*. Note also the more general exception hidden in reg. 38(10), which allows the amount of any item of income or expenditure to be calculated over a different period if that will produce a more accurate figure.

Para. (2) supplies a special rule for payments of royalties or for copyright, which are to be spread in the same way as income of an employee not in respect of a period (reg. 29(2)(b)).

Note that the profit simply derived from a capital asset is not earnings, which must be derived from some employment or occupation. See *R(U) 3/77*.

Date on which income is treated as paid

31.—(1) Except where paragraph (2) applies, a payment of income to which regulation 29 (calculation of earnings derived from employed earner's employment and income other than earnings) applies shall be treated as paid—

> (a) in the case of a payment which is due to be paid before the first benefit week pursuant to the claim, on the date on which it is due to be paid;
>
> (b) in any other case, on the first day of the benefit week in which it is due to be paid or the first succeeding benefit week in which it is practicable to take it into account.

(2) Income support, [⁴jobseeker's allowance], [²maternity allowance,] [³short-term or long term incapacity benefit], or severe disablement allowance [³. . .],shall be treated as paid on the day of the benefit week in respect of which [¹it is payable].

AMENDMENTS

1. Income Support (General) Amendment Regulations 1988 (S.I. 1988 No. 663), reg. 14 (April 11, 1988).

2. Income Support (General) Amendment No. 4 Regulations 1988 (S.I. 1988 No. 1445), reg. 8 (September 12, 1988).

3. Disability Working Allowance and Income Support (General) Amendment Regulations 1995 (S.I. 1995 No. 482), reg. 10 (April 13, 1995).
4. Income Support (General) (Jobseeker's Allowance Consequential Amendments) Regulations 1996 (S.I. 1996 No. 206), reg. 15 (October 7, 1996).

DEFINITIONS

"benefit week"—see reg. 2(1).

GENERAL NOTE

Paragraph (1)
This provision applies to determine when the period of attribution of earnings from employment and income other than the benefits specified in para. (2) (fixed in reg. 29) begins. The crucial date is that on which the payment is due to be paid. This date may well be different from the date of actual payment. Legal obligations must be considered, *e.g.* the terms of a contract of employment *(R(SB) 33/83)*. If a claimant's contract of employment is terminated without due notice any deferred holiday pay and wages withheld under week-in-hand arrangements are due immediately. So are any agreed payments in lieu of notice *(R(SB) 22/84* and *R(SB) 11/85)*. Note the operation of regs. 29(3) and (4) when different kinds of earnings are received for overlapping periods.

In *CIS 590/1993* the claimant had been dismissed from her employment in April 1991 because she was pregnant. In June 1992 she was awarded compensation by an industrial tribunal under the Sex Discrimination Act 1975 which included one month's loss of earnings. The tribunal had deducted the income support paid to the claimant for the month after her dismissal. It is held that the loss of earnings element of the award was to be taken into account as earnings under reg. 35 (see the notes to reg. 35). For the purpose of reg. 31(1), the date on which it was due to be paid was the date when the lost earnings were due to be paid, not when the award was made. This was because the award was to be regarded as a payment in lieu of remuneration and the purpose of the sex discrimination legislation was to put the claimant in the position she would have been if the employer had not acted unlawfully. If the payment was treated as due at the date of the award this could produce unfairness. The result was that the earnings were to be attributed to a period of one month in April/May 1991 and she was to be treated as in remunerative work for that period. However, the income support that had been paid to the claimant for that period was not recoverable as there had been no failure to disclose or misrepresentation. It had in any event been recouped.

If the payment is due before the first week pursuant to the claim (on which see Sched. 7 to the Claims and Payments Regulations), it is treated as paid on the date it is due. This date then starts the period under reg. 29. In other cases the payment is treated as paid on the first day of the benefit week in which it is due (or the next week if the main rule is impracticable).

Paragraph (2)
It seems that the effect of para. (2) is that all these benefits are treated as paid on a daily basis. A proportion of the weekly rate is treated as paid for each day covered by the entitlement. This should avoid overlaps of the kind revealed in *R(SB) 15/82*. See regs. 75(b) and 32(4).

Calculation of weekly amount of income

32.—(1) For the purposes of regulation 29 (calculation of earnings derived from employed earner's employment and income other than earnings), subject to [³paragraphs (2) to (7)][¹. . .], where the period in respect of which a payment is made—
  (a) does not exceed a week, the weekly amount shall be the amount of that payment;
  (b) exceeds a week, the weekly amount shall be determined—
      (i) in a case where that period is a month, by multiplying the amount of the payment by 12 and dividing the product by 52;
      (ii) in a case where that period is three months, by multiplying the amount of the payment by 4 and dividing the product by 52;
      (iii) in a case where that period is a year by dividing the amount of the payment by 52;
      (iv) in any other case by multiplying the amount of the payment by 7

and dividing the product by the number equal to the number of days in the period in respect of which it is made.

(2) Where a payment for a period not exceeding a week is treated under regulation 31(1)(a) (date on which income is treated as paid) as paid before the first benefit week and a part is to be taken into account for some days only in that week (the relevant days), the amount to be taken into account for the relevant days shall be calculated by multiplying the amount of the payment by the number equal to the number of relevant days and dividing the product by the number of days in the period in respect of which it is made.

(3) Where a payment is in respect of a period equal to or in excess of a week and a part thereof is to be taken into account for some days only in a benefit week (the relevant days), the amount to be taken into account for the relevant days shall, except where paragraph (4) applies, be calculated by multiplying the amount of the payment by the number equal to the number of relevant days and dividing the product by the number of days in the period in respect of which it is made.

(4) In the case of a payment of—

(a) [⁵. . .] [²maternity allowance], [⁴short-term or long-term incapacity benefit], or severe disablement allowance [⁴. . .], the amount to be taken into account for the relevant days shall be the amount of benefit [¹payable] in respect of those days;

(b) income support [⁵or jobseeker's allowance], the amount to be taken into account for the relevant days shall be calculated by multiplying the weekly amount of the benefit by the number of relevant days and dividing the product by seven.

(5) Except in the case of a payment which it has not been practicable to treat under regulation 31(1)(b) as paid on the first day of the benefit week in which it is due to be paid, where a payment of income from a particular source is or has been paid regularly and that payment falls to be taken into account in the same benefit week as a payment of the same kind and from the same source, the amount of that income to be taken into account in any one benefit week shall not exceed the weekly amount determined under paragraph (1)(a) or (b), as the case may be, of the payment which under regulation 31(1)(b) (date on which income is treated as paid) is treated as paid first.

(6) Where the amount of the claimant's income fluctuates and has changed more than once, or a claimant's regular pattern of work is such that he does not work every week, the foregoing paragraphs may be modified so that the weekly amount of his income is determined by reference to his average weekly income—

(a) if there is a recognisable cycle of work, over the period of one complete cycle (including, where the cycle involves periods in which the claimant does no work, those periods but disregarding any other absences);

(b) in any other case, over a period of five weeks or such other period as may, in the particular case, enable the claimant's average weekly income to be determined more accurately.

[⁶(6A) Where income is taken into account under paragraph (2B) of regulation 29 over the period specified in that paragraph, the amount of that income to be taken into account in respect of any week in that period shall be an amount equal to the amount of that income which would have been taken into account under regulation 62 had the person to whom that income was paid not ceased to be a student.]

[³(7) Where any payment of earnings is taken into account under paragraph (4C) of regulation 29 (calculation of earnings derived from employed earner's employment and income other than earnings), over the period specified in that paragraph, the amount to be taken into account shall be equal to the amount of the payment.]

AMENDMENTS

1. Income Support (General) Amendment Regulations 1988 (S.I. 1988 No. 663), reg. 15 (April 11, 1988).
2. Income Support (General) Amendment Regulations 1988 (S.I. 1988 No. 1445), reg. 8 (September 12, 1988).
3. Income Support (General) Amendment No. 2 Regulations 1989 (S.I. 1989 No. 1323), reg. 10 (October 9, 1989).
4. Disability Working Allowance and Income Support (General) Amendment Regulations 1995 (S.I. 1995 No. 482), reg. 11 (April 13, 1995).
5. Income Support (General) (Jobseeker's Allowance Consequential Amendments) Regulations 1996 (S.I. 1996 No. 206), reg. 16 (October 7, 1996).
6. Income-related Benefits and Jobseeker's Allowance (Miscellaneous Amendments) Regulations 1997 (S.I. 1997 No. 65), reg. 6 (April 7, 1997).

DEFINITIONS

"benefit week"—see reg. 2(1).
"claimant"—*ibid.*, reg. 23(1).
"student"—see regs. 2(1), 61.

GENERAL NOTE

Paragraph (1)
This provision gives a straightforward method of converting payments to be taken into account for various periods to a weekly equivalent. Reg. 75 deals with the calculation for part-weeks of entitlement.

Paragraphs (2) to (4)
These provisions establish the rules where the period for which a payment is to be taken into account under regs. 29 and 31 does not coincide with a benefit week and some odd days ("the relevant days") come into a benefit week.

Paragraph (5)
There are two different rules, according to whether two payments from the same regular source fall into the same benefit week because of the rules of attribution or because of the operation of reg. 31(1)(b). The general rule is the first one, under which the maximum amount to be taken into account in the benefit week is the weekly amount of the payment due first. The *Adjudication Officer's Guide* (para. 30081) gives an example of how this could arise. A claimant has been receiving statutory sick pay from his employer every two weeks. He receives a payment for two weeks on November 15. This is attributed to the period November 15 to November 28 inclusive. The claimant is to return to work on December 2 and receives a final payment of two weeks' sick pay on November 26. The AO treats this as paid on November 22 for the period November 22 to December 5. For the income support benefit week from November 22 to November 28 the amount of sick pay to be taken into account is limited to the weekly amount of the payment made on November 15. There is an exception to this rule in that if the first payment was due to be paid before the date of claim it is to be disregarded (Sched. 8, para. 13 and Sched. 9, para. 35). Then there will no longer be an overlap. The second rule applies where under reg. 31(1)(b) it has not been practicable to take a payment into account in the benefit week in which it was due to be paid. The payment then is taken into account in the first practicable benefit week. In this situation both payments can be taken into account in the same week, although each payment can have the appropriate disregard applied (Sched. 8, para. 10 and Sched. 9, para. 37). The disregards in para. 13 of Sched. 8 and para. 35 of Sched. 9 (see above) may also apply.

Paragraph (6)
This paragraph is oddly placed because it only allows the preceding paragraphs to be modified, not any of the other regulations on the calculation or attribution of income.

Paragraph (6A)
Reg. 29(2B) deals with the period over which a student grant is to be taken into account in the case of a person who has left or been dismissed from his course before it finishes and so has to repay part or all of his grant. Para. (6A) provides that where reg. 29(2B) applies, the weekly amount of the income to be taken into account is to be calculated in accordance with reg. 62. This means that the grant income

will be apportioned over the period of study (*i.e.* from the beginning of the academic ye
before the summer vacation), except for those elements which are apportioned over 52 w
disregards in reg. 62(2) and (2A) will apply. See further reg. 62 and the notes to that re
also reg. 40(3B) which provides that the amount of the grant income to be taken into ac
calculated on the basis that none of it has been repaid. But note *Chief Adjudication Off*
(November 6, 1998, CA, to be reported as *R(IS) 5/99*) in the notes to reg. 29(2B) and
discussed in those notes as to when reg. 29(2B) applies.

Any grant or covenant income or student loan left over at the end of the person's course is
disregarded as income (see para. 61 of Sched. 9).

Paragraph (7)
Where a payment of compensation (reg. 35(3)(a)) is made on the termination of part-time employment (reg. 29(4D)(e) and reg. 35(3)(c)) it is taken into account for a week (reg. 29(4C)). This
provision confirms that the whole payment is taken into account for that week.

Weekly amount of charitable or voluntary payment

33.—(1) [¹. . .]

AMENDMENT

1. Income Support (General) Amendment No. 5 Regulations 1988 (S.I. 1988 No. 2022), reg. 8
(December 12, 1988).

Incomplete weeks of benefit

34. [¹. . .]

AMENDMENT

1. Income Support (General) Amendment Regulations 1988 (S.I. 1988 No. 663), reg. 16 (April
11. 1988).

Chapter III

Employed Earners

Earnings of employed earners

35.—(1) [²Subject to paragraphs (2) and (3),] "earnings" means in the case
of employment as an employed earner, any remuneration or profit derived from
that employment and includes—
  (a) any bonus or commission;
  (b) any payment in lieu of remuneration except any periodic sum paid to a
      claimant on account of the termination of his employment by reason of
      redundancy;
  (c) any payment in lieu of notice [². . .];
  (d) any holiday pay except any payable more than four weeks after the ter-
      mination or interruption of employment but this exception shall not apply
      to a claimant to whom [¹section 23 of the Act [SSCBA, s.126] (trade
      disputes) applies or in respect of whom section 20(3) of the Act [SSCBA,
      s.124(1)] (conditions of entitlement to income support) has effect as
      modified by section 23A(*b*) of the Act [SSCBA, s.127(b)] (effect to
      return to work)];
  (e) any payment by way of a retainer;
  (f) any payment made by the claimant's employer in respect of expenses
      not wholly, exclusively and necessarily incurred in the performance of
      the duties of the employment, including any payment made by the claim-
      ant's employer in respect of—

(i) travelling expenses incurred by the claimant between his home and place of employment;

(ii) expenses incurred by the claimant under arrangements made for the care of a member of his family owing to the claimant's absence from home;

(g) any award of compensation made under section 68(2) or 71(2)(a) of the Employment Protection (Consolidation) Act 1978 (remedies for unfair dismissal and compensation);

(h) any such sum as is referred to in section 18(2) of the Social Security (Miscellaneous Provisions) Act 1977 (certain sums to be earnings for social security purposes).

[²(i) where—

(i) a payment of compensation is made in respect of employment which is not part-time employment and that payment is not less than the maximum weekly amount, the amount of the compensation less the deductible remainder, where that is applicable;

(ii) a payment of compensation is made in respect of employment which is part-time, the amount of the compensation.]

[²(1A) For the purposes of paragraph (1)(i)(i) the "deductible remainder"—

(a) applies in cases where dividing the amount of compensation by the maximum weekly amount produces a whole number plus a fraction; and

(b) is equal to the difference between—

(i) the amount of the compensation; and

(ii) the product of the maximum weekly amount multiplied by the whole number.]

(2) "Earnings" shall not include—

(a) any payment in kind;

(b) any remuneration paid by or on behalf of an employer to the claimant [⁴in respect of a period throughout which the claimant is on maternity leave or is absent from work because he is ill]];

(c) any payment in respect of expenses wholly, exclusively and necessarily incurred in the performance of the duties of the employment;

(d) any occupational pension.

[⁵(e) any lump sum payment made under the Iron and Steel Re-adaptation Benefits Scheme].

[²(3) In this regulation—

(a) "compensation" means any payment made in respect of or on the termination of employment in a case where a person has not received or received only part of a payment in lieu of notice due or which would have been due to him had he not waived his right to receive it, other than—

(i) any payment specified in paragraph (1)(a) to (h);

(ii) any payment specified in paragraph (2)(a) to [⁵(e)];

(iii) any redundancy payment within the meaning of section 81(1) of the Employment Protection (Consolidation) Act 1978, and

(iv) any refund of contributions to which that person was entitled under an occupational pension scheme within the meaning of section 66(1) of the Social Security Pensions Act 1975;

[³(v) any compensation payable by virtue of section 173 or section 178(3) or (4) of the Education Reform Act 1988;]

(b) "maximum weekly amount" means the maximum weekly amount which, on the date on which the payment of compensation is made, is specified in paragraph 8(1)(c) of Schedule 14 to the Employment Protection (Consolidation) Act 1978;

(c) "part-time employment" means employment in which a person is not

to be treated as engaged in remunerative work under regulation 5 or 6
(persons treated, or not treated, as engaged in remunerative work).]

AMENDMENTS

1. Income Support (General) Amendment Regulations 1988 (S.I. 1988 No. 663), reg. 17 (April
11, 1988).
2. Income Support (General) Amendment No. 2 Regulations 1989 (S.I. 1989 No. 1323), reg. 11
(October 9, 1989).
3. Education (Inner London Education Authority) (Transitional and Supplementary Provisions)
(No. 2) Order 1990 (S.I. 1990 No. 774), art. 2 (April 1, 1990).
4. Income-related Benefits Schemes (Miscellaneous Amendments) (No. 4) Regulations 1993 (S.I.
1993 No. 2119), reg. 12 (October 4, 1993).
5. Social Security (Miscellaneous Amendments) Regulations 1997 (S.I. 1997 No. 454), reg. 7
(April 7, 1997).

DEFINITIONS

"the Act"—see reg. 2(1).
"claimant"—*ibid.*, reg. 23(1).
"employed earner"—see reg. 2(1).
"family"—see 1986 Act, s.20(11) (SSCBA, s.137(1)).
"maternity leave"—see reg. 2(1).
"occupational pension"—see reg. 2(1).

GENERAL NOTE

Reg. 35 applies to earnings from employment as an employed earner. See the definition in reg.
2(1). The category of office-holder includes holders of elective office, such as local councillors.
Some payments made to councillors (*e.g.* for travelling expenses and subsistence allowances: *CIS
89/1989*) will be excluded under para. (2)(*c*), but attendance allowances, which are not paid to meet
specific expenses, count as earnings (*R(IS) 6/92*). *CIS 77/1993* decides that basic allowances are
also earnings, but applies the disregard in para. (2)(c), reg. 40(4) and Sched. 9, para. 3. The purpose
of the basic allowance is to compensate the councillor for his time and to cover the expenses incurred
in the execution of his duties. The expenses may, as in that case, absorb the total allowance. The
Commissioner points out that since March 18, 1992, basic allowances had been disregarded for the
purposes of the former reg. 7(1)(g)(i) of the Social Security (Unemployment, Sickness and Invalidity
Benefit) Regulations 1983. The allowance was therefore treated differently on depending on whether
unemployment benefit or income support was claimed. However, its treatment under JSA is the
same as for income support. See also the notes to reg. 36(3).

Paragraph (1)
This paragraph first provides a general definition of earnings from employment as an employee—
any remuneration or profit derived from that employment—and then deems certain payments to be
earnings. Para. (2) provides a number of exceptions and Sched. 8 lists items which would otherwise
count as earnings which are to be disregarded. In particular under paras. 1 to 3 final earnings due
on the termination or interruption of employment are disregarded.
The general test covers straightforward wages or salary, but can extend to other remuneration
derived from employment. According to *R(SB) 21/86*, these are wide words, which mean "having
their origin in." Thus if it had been necessary to decide whether a compensatory award for unfair
dismissal by an Industrial Tribunal was derived from employment, the Commissioner would have
held that it did. *R(SB) 21/86* is followed in *CIS 590/1993*, which concerned the loss of earnings
element in a compensation award for sex discrimination. Payments to a NCB employee in lieu of
concessionary coal constituted remuneration derived from employment (*R(SB) 2/86*). Tips and gratuities would be an example of payments from third parties which are nonetheless derived from
employment (see Williams, *Social Security Taxation*, paras. 4.21 to 4.22 for discussion of the income
tax cases).
The particular categories in sub-paras. (a) to (i) are deemed to be earnings, whether they would
in general count as earnings or not (*R(SB) 21/86*). Only a few categories require comment.
Sub-para. (b). A payment in lieu of remuneration will in its nature be an income payment. Capital
payments (*e.g.* for the loss of the job itself) are excluded. *R(SB) 21/86* held that a compensatory
award for unfair dismissal made by an Industrial Tribunal was a payment in lieu of remuneration,

to be taken into account for the number of weeks specified in the award. Such an award is now expressly included in sub-para. (g), but if it can also fall into (b) it will lead to complete disentitlement to income support under reg. 5(5), regardless of the weekly amount of the award. In *CIS 590/1993* the claimant's award of compensation under the Sex Discrimination Act included amounts for injured feelings, the loss of a tax rebate and one month's loss of earnings. It was accepted that the first two items counted as capital. The Commissioner follows *R(SB) 21/86* and holds that the loss of earnings element fell to be treated as earnings under sub-para. (b). There was no reason for drawing a distinction between a compensatory award for unfair dismissal and that part of a sex discrimination award that was for loss of earnings. The fact that only the former was referred to in sub-para. (g) did not imply that the loss of earnings elements in sex (or race) discrimination awards (or indeed awards made by county courts for breach of employment contracts) were excluded from para. (1), since the categories listed in sub-paras. (a) to (i) were only included as examples. See the notes to reg. 31(1) as to when the earnings were treated as due to be paid.

Sub-para. (*c*). This sub-paragraph is now confined to payments in lieu of notice, whether full or partial. Presumably, it covers payments expressly in lieu of notice (see *CIS 400/1994*). "Global" payments will fall under sub-para. (i). If earnings under this sub-paragraph are received, entitlement is excluded under reg. 5(5) for the period covered.

Sub-para. (*d*). Holiday pay which is payable (*i.e.* due to be paid, not received or paid: *R(SB) 15/82, R(SB) 33/83, R(SB) 11/85*) within four weeks of termination or interruption of employment counts as earnings. In cases of termination holiday pay will be due immediately, unless the contract of employment expressly provides otherwise. Therefore, whenever it is paid (and presumably it cannot count until it is actually paid) it will count as earnings to be taken into account for the benefit week in which it was due to be paid. Then s.74 of the Administration Act (1986 Act, s.27) might come into play. If employment is merely interrupted it is more likely that holiday pay will not be payable immediately. Earnings received under this sub-paragraph lead to disentitlement under reg. 5(5).

Holiday pay outside this sub-paragraph is capital (reg. 48(3)).

CIS 894/1994 holds that for a payment to be holiday pay there has to be entitlement to holidays under the contract of employment. The claimant worked on a North Sea oil rig. His contract of employment provided that there was no entitlement to holidays but that he would accrue 42 hours vacation pay per quarter. He could ask for this pay at any time and payment would be made at the end of the quarter. On the termination of his employment he was paid 100 days accrued vacation pay. The Commissioner decides that the vacation pay was not holiday pay in the ordinary sense of the word. It had nothing to do with the taking of holidays but was in reality compensation for the fact that there was no holiday entitlement. The consequence was that it fell to be disregarded under para. 1(a)(ii) of Sched. 8.

Sub-para. (*e*). *R(IS) 9/95* decides that a guarantee payment under s.12 of the Employment Protection (Consolidation) Act 1978 is a payment by way of a retainer.

Sub-para. (*f*). The conditions here are in line with those under which expenses are deductible from earnings for income tax purposes. Payment for all items beyond those solely necessary for *the performance of* the duties of the employment are caught. It is not enough if the expenses are incurred in order to enable the person to perform those duties (*Smith v. Abbott* [1994] 1 All ER 673). The express mention of the expenses of travel to and from work and of looking after a family member merely spells this out. (On child care expenses see *Jackson and Cresswell v. Chief Adjudication Officer* Joined Cases C-63/91 and C-64/91 [1992] ECR I-4737 and *CFC 19/1990 (Meyers)*, to be reported as *R(FC) 2/98*, in the notes to reg. 36(3)). The reimbursement of a local councillor's home telephone expenses in *CIS 38/1989* is an example. On the evidence, the expenses were necessarily incurred, but not wholly or exclusively, in the performance of his duties as a councillor. On other evidence, such expenses could be apportioned between personal and employment purposes (*cf. R(FC) 1/91, CFC 26/1989* and *R(FIS) 13/91* on reg. 38(3)). See also *CFC 836/1995* in the notes to reg. 38(11) on apportionment of expenses between earnings as an employee and from self-employment. There is helpful guidance in *R(FIS) 4/85*.

CIS 89/1989 holds that travel and subsistence allowances paid to a local councillor, which included travel from home to the place of employment, were for necessary etc. expenses, because a councillor's home is also a place of employment. *R(IS) 6/92* confirms this result, because under s.174(1) of the Local Government Act 1972 payments of travelling and subsistence allowances can only be made where the expenses have been necessarily incurred for the performance of any duty as a councillor. Therefore, such a payment must fall outside sub-para. (f) and within para. (2)(c). In *CIS 77/1993* it was accepted that a local councillor's expenses (*e.g.* the use of his home and telephone) could lead to the whole of his basic allowance being disregarded (see above). The approach taken in the *Adjudication Officer's Guide* applies these decisions (see paras. 31072–5). See also the notes to reg. 36(3).

Sub-para. (*g*). If awards of compensation can only come under this sub-paragraph and not (b) they do not lead to complete disentitlement, but the amount must be considered.

Sub-para. (*h*). The sums referred to in s.18(2) of the 1977 Act are maternity pay under s.40 of the Employment Protection (Consolidation) Act 1978, arrears of pay under s.122(3)(a); arrears of pay under an order for reinstatement or re-engagement; a sum payable under an award for the continuation of a contract; and remuneration under a protective award.

Sub-para. (*i*). There was a significant change in 1989 in the treatment of lump sum payments made on the termination of employment, which was designed to simplify decision-making. It was along similar lines to the change in the UB rules, but introduced several differences. In *CIS 400/ 1994* the Commissioner drew attention to the different ways that termination payments at the end of a period of employment were treated by the income support and unemployment benefit legislation. In particular, the definition of "compensation" was not the same (*e.g.*, for unemployment benefit purposes "compensation" could include payments in lieu of notice; for income support it cannot). For the position under JSA, see reg. 98(1)(b) and (3) of the JSA Regulations.

There are separate provisions depending whether it is full-time or part-time employment which is terminated. The dividing line is defined in para. (6)(c) and reg. 29(4D)(a) by adopting the test of remunerative work in regs. 5 and 6.

Full-time employment. This new category of earnings is added to the list while sub-para. (c) is restricted to payments in lieu of notice and not payments of compensation for loss of employment. For full-timers sub-para. (i) applies to a payment of "compensation" which equals or exceeds the "maximum weekly amount".

"Compensation" is defined in para. (3)(a). First, the person must not have received a payment in lieu of all the notice to which he was legally entitled. If this has happened, no other payment can be "compensation" within sub-para. (i) (confirmed in *CIS 400/1994*). Second, all the payments already counted as earnings by para. (1)(a) to (h) or excluded from that category by para. (2), statutory redundancy payments and refunds of pension contributions are excluded. Other payments made in respect of or on the termination of employment count as compensation. It does not particularly matter what the employer calls the payment, providing that it is connected to the termination (*cf. R(U) 4/92* and *R(U) 5/92*), so that merely calling the payment a capital payment (*e.g.* for loss of the job as a capital asset) does not take it outside sub-para. (i). The main categories will be payments from employers which are not precisely categorised (*e.g.* the ubiquitous "*ex gratia*" payment) and payments made in settlement of claims for unfair or wrongful dismissal (providing that a payment in lieu of full notice has not already been paid). But a payment solely in relation to racial discrimination during employment is not within the definition (*CU 88/1991*).

The "maximum weekly amount" is defined in para. (3)(b) and is the amount specified at the relevant time as the maximum to be used in calculating the basic award for unfair dismissal and redundancy payments. The figure in effect from April 1, 1989, was £172, from April 1, 1990, was £184, from April 1, 1991, was £198, from April 1, 1992 (not increased in 1993 or 1994) was £205, from September 27, 1995 (not increased in 1996 or 1997) was £210 and from April 1, 1998 is £220.

If a payment is "compensation" then its amount has to be divided by the maximum weekly amount. If this division produces a whole number plus a fraction the portion of the amount of the compensation representing that fraction is ignored as earnings. It is the "deductible remainder" (para. (1B)). But it appears to be capital (reg. 48(11)). The payment less any deductible remainder is taken into account as income for the same number of weeks as the whole number (reg. 29(4B)(a)). However, the rigid application of this rule could result in the payment being taken into account for longer than the claimant's notice period. Therefore, under reg. 29(4B)(b) the payment is to be taken into account for a period equal to the person's notice entitlement (less any days of notice worked or covered by a payment in lieu of notice) if this is shorter. This is the "specified period" (reg. 29(4D)(b).

The date on which this period is to start is defined by reg. 31 (reg. 29(4B)). Often this will be the date of termination, but it may be later, *e.g.* where there is a settlement of an unfair dismissal claim. But see *CIS 590/1993* referred to above and in the notes to reg. 31(1). If there is an identifiable loss of earnings element in the settlement, such a payment may come within para (1)(a) to (h) (and thus fall outside the definition of "compensation") and be due to be paid on the date when the lost earnings, etc., were due to be paid. Note the effect of reg. 29(3) and (4).

Where the payment is small, less in total than the "maximum weekly amount," these provisions do not apply and the payment is treated as capital (reg. 48(11)).

Part-time employment. For part-time employment the whole payment of "compensation" is to be taken into account in one week (reg. 35(1)(i)(ii) and reg. 29(4C)), generally the week in which it is due to be paid (reg. 31).

Paragraph (2)

These amounts—payments in kind, sick or maternity pay, reimbursement of necessary expenses and occupational pensions—are not earnings, but do count as other income (reg. 40(4)). It is apparently intended that lump sum payments covered by sub-para. (e) should count as capital (as their nature would indicate), although reg. 40(4) has not also been amended. Note that income in kind is disregarded (Sched. 9, para. 21) and so are payments of necessary expenses (Sched. 9, para. 3). There is no provision for the disregard of ill-health payments or occupational pensions (confirmed in *CIS 6/1989*). If a person is remunerated by payments in kind, there is the possibility of notional earnings being attributed to the person under reg. 42(6).

See the notes to para. (1)(f) for what are necessary, etc., expenses. In a decision on the equivalent provision in the Family Credit (General) Regulations (reg. 19(2)), the Commissioner suggested that its effect is that expenditure by the employee on necessary etc. expenses is to be deducted from the amount of his earnings (*CFC 2/1989*). This does not seem to be consistent with the pattern of reg. 35, which is otherwise concerned with payments to the employee, and is rejected in *R(FC) 1/90*, *R(IS) 16/93* and *CIS 77/1993*. See the notes to reg. 19(2) of the Family Credit Regulations for full discussion of the point. The payment can be by way of reimbursement to the employee for expenses initially met by him (*CIS 77/1993*). But the application of the principle of *Parsons v. Hogg* to the meaning of 'gross earnings' in reg. 36 will, it seems, permit the deduction from earnings of necessary, etc., expenses incurred by the employee. See the notes to reg. 36(3).

CIS 4317/1997 has highlighted an anomaly in the legislation that results from sick or maternity pay not being treated as earnings. The claimant stopped work in September 1996 because of illness. He was paid four weeks' statutory and contractual sick pay on October 31, 1996 and his contract of employment was terminated on the same day. He claimed income support on November 1 but was treated as having income for four weeks from October 31 under regs. 29(1) and (2) and 31(1). The Commissioner confirmed that this was correct. Although final earnings were disregarded under para. 1 of Sched. 8, there was no equivalent disregard in Sched. 9 (or elsewhere) to enable final payments of sick pay to be ignored. He rejected the argument that reg. 29(2) was *ultra vires*. This argument was renewed before the Court of Appeal but was dismissed (*Owens v. Chief Adjudication Officer*, April 29, 1999). The claimant had contended that the power in s.136(5)(a) (person can be treated as possessing income or capital which he does not possess) did not apply where the person in fact possessed the income; it therefore did not authorise a provision treating income received by the claimant at one time as available to him at another time. In addition, reg. 29(2) was outside the power in s.136(3) (income to be calculated or estimated in prescribed manner). It was contended that simply shifting income from one period to another was neither "calculation" not "estimation". But the Court of Appeal held that reg. 29(2) was within the power in s.136(5)(a). A deeming provision by its very nature had the effect of treating a fact or state of affairs as existing for a stated purpose when that fact or state of affairs did not in truth exist. Section 136(5)(a) was sufficiently widely framed to authorize a provision that spread or apportioned income to a stated period. The Court also rejected the contention that reg. 29(2) was *ultra vires* on the ground of irrationality. However, the Court of Appeal (like the Commissioner and the SSAT) expressed disquiet at the anomalous result arising from the different treatment of sick pay and final earnings and voiced the hope that the operation of the regulations in these circumstances would be reconsidered.

Calculation of net earnings of employed earners

36.—(1) For the purposes of regulation 29 (calculation of earnings of employed earners) the earnings of a claimant derived from employment as an employed earner to be taken into account shall, subject to paragraph (2), be his net earnings.

(2) There shall be disregarded from a claimant's net earnings, any sum specified in paragraphs 1 to 13 of Schedule 8.

(3) For the purposes of paragraph (1) net earnings shall be calculated by taking into account the gross earnings of the claimant from that employment less—

(a) any amount deducted from those earnings by way of—
    (i) income tax;
    (ii) primary Class 1 contributions under the Social Security Act; and
(b) one-half of any sum paid by the claimant [[1]in respect of a pay period] by way of a contribution towards an occupational or personal pension scheme.

AMENDMENT

1. Income-related Benefits Schemes (Miscellaneous Amendments) (No. 5) Regulations 1994 (S.I. 1994 No. 2139), reg. 26 (October 3, 1994).

DEFINITIONS

"claimant"—see reg. 2(1), reg. 23(1).
"employed earner"—see reg. 2(1).
"occupational pension scheme"—see 1986 Act, s.84(1). (PSA, s.1).
"pay period"–see reg. 2(1).
"personal pension scheme"—*ibid.*
"Social Security Act"—*ibid.*

GENERAL NOTE

Paragraph (1)
Earnings defined in reg. 35 are to be converted to net earnings before being taken into account. This is to be done according to para. (3).

Paragraph (2)
After the conversion to net earnings has been carried out, the amounts specified in paras. 1 to 13 of Sched. 8 are to be disregarded. The disregards of paras. 1 to 10 do not apply to children or young persons, but under reg. 44(6) paras. 14 and 15 do apply, which leads to the earnings of children or young persons being disregarded in most cases.

Paragraph (3)
Only this limited list of deductions for payments made by the employee may be made from gross earnings. Nothing is to be deducted for travel costs, child care expenses or meals at work. This leads to a much simpler calculation than under supplementary benefit. The compensation was an increase in the basic disregard from its previous £4 to £5. *R(FC) 1/90* holds that if the employee makes contributions to both an occupational and a personal pension scheme, half of both contributions can be deducted.

There is, however, some doubt about the meaning of "gross earnings." In *R(FC) 1/90* the Commissioner refers to the principle adopted by the Court of Appeal in *Parsons v. Hogg* [1985] 2 All E. R. 897, appendix to *R(FIS) 4/85*, and by the Commissioner in *R(FIS) 4/85*, that "earnings," even associated with the word "gross," in the Family Income Supplements (General) Regulations 1980 meant not the remuneration actually received, but the receipts after payment of expenses wholly and necessarily incurred in the course of winning those receipts. He applies this principle to the equivalent provision to reg. 36 in the Family Credit (General) Regulations (reg. 20) and holds that expenses necessarily wholly and exclusively incurred by the employee in the performance of the duties of employment are to be deducted from the gross receipts to produce a figure of gross earnings. The same Commissioner applies the principle to income other than earnings in *CIS 25/1989*, but this has not been followed in *CIS 563/1991* (see the note to reg. 40(1)). In *R(FC) 1/90*, the claimant's expenditure on work equipment might be deducted, but not child-care expenses (*R(FIS) 2/88*).

The wording of reg. 36 is not the same as was considered in *Parsons v. Hogg*, so that there was some doubt about the application of the principle. In *R(IS) 6/92* the Commissioner held that an attendance allowance paid to a local councillor had to be taken into account as earnings, subject only to the £5 disregard, although the councillor incurred necessary, etc., expenses on such things as stationery and telephone calls. However, the Commissioner referred only to reg. 35 and not to reg. 36 or any of the decisions cited in the previous paragraph. In *CIS 77/1993*, which concerned a local councillor's basic allowance, the same Commissioner considered that *Parsons v. Hogg* did not apply, but decided that the allowance fell within reg. 35(2)(c). However, the application of *Parsons v. Hogg* does produce a result where only resources actually available to the person are counted. It is also the approach taken in para. 31015 of the *Adjudication Officer's Guide*. *R(IS) 16/93* has now expressly decided that the principle of *Parsons v. Hogg* applies to reg. 36. This has been followed in *CIS 507/1994*. *Parsons v. Hogg* has also been applied to "gross earnings" in para. 1(3) of Sched. 1 to the Child Support (Maintenance Assessments and Special Cases) Regulations 1992 (S.I. 1992 No. 1815) in *R(CS) 2/96*. *CCS 318/1995* decided that an armed forces "local overseas allowance" could be deducted on the ground that it covered the special expenses of working abroad, whereas a lodgings allowance for those stationed in the UK was not allowable (*CCS 5352/1995*). Rent allowances for police officers would seem not to be a deductible expense (*CCS 2320/1997*, *CCS 10/1994* and *CCS 12598/1996*, although *CCS 12769/1996* is to the contrary).

In calculating the amount of necessary, etc., expenses to be deducted the principle established in *R(FC) 1/91*, *CFC 26/1989* and *R(IS) 13/91* should be applied. That is that if items have a dual private and work use, and that use can be apportioned on a time basis, the appropriate proportion should be deducted. See the note to reg. 38(3). See also *CFC 836/1995* in the notes to reg. 38(11) on apportionment of expenses between two employments.

In *R(IS) 10/91*, a challenge to the inability to deduct child-care expenses from earnings as being discriminatory and therefore contrary to EC Directive 79/7 was rejected. On appeal, the Court of Appeal referred the question whether supplementary benefit and/or income support fall within art. 3 of the Directive to the European Court of Justice (*Cresswell v. Chief Adjudication Officer, Jackson v. Chief Adjudication Officer*, December 21, 1990).

A similar question in relation to housing benefit had been referred by the Divisional Court in *R. v. Secretary of State for Social Security, ex parte Smithson* (June 26, 1990). The Advocate General's opinion in *Smithson* (delivered on November 20, 1991) was that the provisions on higher pensioner premium were part of the statutory scheme protecting against the risks of invalidity and old age, so that they came within art. 3. The ECJ (February 4, 1992) (Case 243/90) disagreed, finding that the higher pensioner premium was an inseparable part of the whole scheme of housing benefit, which was intended to compensate for the fact that the beneficiary's income was insufficient to meet housing costs and not to provide protection against one of the risks specified in art. 3(1) (*e.g.* sickness, invalidity, old age). Although criteria concerning protection against old age and sickness were part of the criteria for determining the level against which the beneficiary's income was tested, that did not affect the purpose of the whole scheme.

Once that decision had been made, the ECJ's decision in *Cresswell and Jackson* (July 16, 1992) [1992] ECR I-4737, [1993] 3 All ER 265, also reported as Appendix 2 to *R(IS) 10/91*, followed fairly inevitably. Benefits such as supplementary benefit and income support could be granted in a variety of personal situations to persons whose means are insufficient to meet their needs as defined by statute. Therefore they did not come within article 3(1) of the Directive. In the particular cases the claimants' theoretical needs were set independently of any consideration of any of the risks specified in art. 3(1). Nor did the fact that the conditions of entitlement to a benefit affected a single parent's ability to take up access to vocational training or part-time employment bring that benefit within EC Directive 76/207 on equal treatment for men and women as regards access to employment, vocational training and promotion, and working conditions. Benefit schemes only come within Directive 76/207 if their subject matter is access to employment, etc., or working conditions.

These decisions seem to rule out challenges to the income support scheme under either Directive, as accepted in *CIS 8/1990* and *CIS 375/1990*. But note that the position may well be different under JSA.

However, the possibility of a challenge to the family credit scheme under Directive 76/207 remained. Family credit similarly did not, until October 4, 1994, permit the offsetting of any child care expenses against earnings. See regs. 13(1)(c) and 13A of the Family Credit Regulations and regs. 15(1)(c) and 15A of the Disability Working Allowance Regulations for the limited disregard of child care costs that has now been introduced for these benefits. In *CFC 19/1990* (*Meyers*), to be reported as *R(FC) 2/98*, the claimant argued that the previous family credit rule was discriminatory and in breach of Directive 76/207. The contention was that since the main purpose of family credit is to supplement the income of low-paid workers, family credit is directly concerned with access to employment and/or working conditions. The Commissioner referred the question as to whether family credit was covered by Directive 76/207 to the ECJ. On July 13, 1995 the ECJ (*Meyers v. Adjudication Officer*, Case C-116/94, [1995] All E.R.(EC) 705) held that family credit is concerned with both access to employment and working conditions and so fell within the scope of Directive 76/207. The case then went back to the Commissioner for him to consider whether the family credit rules did indirectly discriminate against women and, if so, whether this was objectively justifiable. The Commissioner accepted that the absence of a child care costs disregard had a disparate impact on women but found that this discrimination was objectively justified and so the family credit rules were compatible with Directive 76/207. See further the notes to reg. 13A of the Family Credit Regulations.

In addition, there may be a possibility of challenge under art. 7 of E.C. Regulation 1612/68 on social and tax advantages. In *O'Flynn v. Chief Adjudication Officer* (July 29, 1992) the Court of Appeal accepted that a social fund funeral payment is a social advantage within the Regulation. See the notes to reg. 7(1) of the Social Fund Maternity and Funeral Expenses Regulations.

Chapter IV

Self-Employed Earners

Earnings of self-employed earners

37.—(1) Subject to paragraph (2), "earnings", in the case of employment as a self-employed earner, means the gross receipts of the employment and shall include any allowance paid under section 2 of the Employment and Training Act 1973 [¹or section 2 of the Enterprise and New Towns (Scotland) Act 1990] to the claimant for the purpose of assisting him in carrying on his business.

[²(2) "Earnings" shall not include—

  (a) where a claimant is involved in providing board and lodging accommodation for which a charge is payable, any payment by way of such a charge;

[³(b) any payment to which paragraph 26 or 27 of Schedule 9 refers (payments in respect of a person accommodated with the claimant under an arrangement made by a local authority or voluntary organisation and payments made to the claimant by a health authority, local authority or voluntary organisation in respect of persons temporarily in the claimant's care).]]

AMENDMENTS

1. Enterprise (Scotland) Consequential Amendments Order 1991 (S.I. 1991 No. 387), art. 2 (April 1, 1991).

2. Income-related Benefits Schemes (Miscellaneous Amendments) (No. 3) Regulations 1992 (S.I. 1992 No. 2155), reg. 16 (October 5, 1992).

3. Income-related Benefits Schemes (Miscellaneous Amendments) (No. 5) Regulations 1994 (S.I. 1994 No. 2139), reg. 27 (October 3, 1994).

DEFINITIONS

  "board and lodging accommodation"—see reg. 2(1).
  "claimant"—see reg. 2(1), reg. 23(1).
  "self-employed earner"—see reg. 2(1).
  "voluntary organisation—*ibid.*

GENERAL NOTE

Paragraph (1)

The starting point for the self-employed is the figure of gross receipts, including Business Start-up Allowance (previously enterprise allowance), to be reduced to net profits under reg. 38.

In *CFC 4/1991*, the claimant's husband had recently started a construction business. He received a loan of £5,500 from a relative and made part repayment of £4,000 not long afterwards. The AO and the SSAT treated the loan as part of the "gross receipts" of the self-employment. The repayment could not be deducted from the gross receipts because of reg. 22(5)(a) of the Family Credit (General) Regulations (the equivalent of reg. 38(5)(a) below). The result was that the net profit so calculated took the claimant above family credit level. The Commissioner found that the loan was a capital receipt, but concluded that the words of reg. 21(1) of the Family Credit Regulations (the equivalent of reg. 37(1)) were unambiguous and included capital receipts. On appeal under the name of *Kostanczwk*, an order of the Registrar of the Court of Appeal (dated August 21, 1992) allowed the appeal by consent and directed that capital receipts not generated by a claimant's business do not form part of the gross receipts of that employment for the purposes of reg. 21 of the Family Credit Regulations. As *CFC 3/1992* (to be reported as *R(FC) 1/97*) confirmed, since that direction was contained in an Order made by consent and without argument it was not binding on anyone other than the parties to the Order and the tribunal to whom the direction was made. But as the decision in *CFC 4/1991* had been set aside by the Court of Appeal, *CFC 24/1989* remained at that time the only authoritative Commissioner's decision on the point. In *CFC 24/1989* it was held that a grant of £900 from the Prince's Youth Business Trust to assist in the setting up of a business was not part of the gross receipts. The Commissioner focuses on the bizarre consequences if a capital receipt has to count as part of the gross receipts, when capital expenditure cannot be deducted from the gross receipts. The approach of *CFC 24/1989* was to be preferred as a matter of principle. In *CFC 23/1991* a legacy used to keep the claimant's business afloat was not a receipt of the business. The argument that since reg. 37 is placed within the income section of the regulations, gross receipts must mean "revenue receipts" and exclude loans or receipts from the sale of capital assets, etc., did seem to be a convincing one. This has now been confirmed by *CFC 3/1992*. In a comprehensive decision the Commissioner holds that neither a loan for business purposes nor the proceeds of sale of capital assets (in that case a car and a computer printer) form part of the gross receipts of the employment for the purposes of reg. 21 of the Family Credit Regulations (the equivalent of reg. 37). See also *CFC 2298/1995* in the note to s.69 of the Administration Act which holds that a consent order is not a "determination . . . of a Commissioner or the court" within s.69, nor did an AO's decision fall to be reviewed "in consequence of" it because it was not binding in other cases.

Paragraph (2)

   CIS 55/1989 decided that the predecessor of sub-para. (a), which referred to a claimant "employed" in providing board and lodging accommodation, applied whenever the claimant made a charge for providing the accommodation. It was not necessary for the claimant to provide it by way of business. The substitution of the word "involved" reinforces this conclusion. The payments received count as income under reg. 40(4), but subject to disregards.

   Sub-para. (b) applies to payments to foster-parents and to people for providing temporary care in their home. Those payments are disregarded as income other than earnings under paras. 26 and 27 of Sched. 9. Sub-para. (b) ensures that they are not treated as earnings. See also reg. 6(k).

Calculation of net profit of self-employed earners

   38.—(1) For the purposes of regulation 30 (calculation of earnings of self-employed earners), the earnings of a claimant to be taken into account shall be—
   (a) in the case of a self-employed earner who is engaged in employment on his own account, the net profit derived from that employment;
   (b) in the case of a self-employed earner whose employment is carried on in partnership or is that of a share fisherman within the meaning of the Social Security (Mariners' Benefits) Regulations 1975, his share of the net profit derived from that employment less—
      (i) an amount in respect of income tax and of social security contributions payable under the Social Security Act [SSCBA] calculated in accordance with regulation 39 (deduction of tax and contributions for self-employed earners); and
      (ii) [¹one half of any premium paid [²in the period that is relevant under regulation 30] in respect of a retirement annuity contract or a personal pension scheme].

   (2) There shall be disregarded from a claimant's net profit any sum, where applicable, specified in paragraphs 1 to 13 of Schedule 8.

   (3) For the purposes of paragraph (1)(a) the net profit of the employment shall, except where paragraph (9) applies, be calculated by taking into account the earnings of the employment over the period determined under regulation 30 (calculation of earnings of self-employed earners) less—
   (a) subject to paragraphs (5) to (7), any expenses wholly and exclusively defrayed in that period for the purposes of that employment;
   (b) an amount in respect of—
      (i) income tax; and
      (ii) social security contributions payable under the Social Security Act [SSCBA],
      calculated in accordance with regulation 39 (deduction of tax and contributions for self-employed earners); and
   (c) [¹one half of any premium paid[²in the period that is relevant under regulation 30] in respect of a retirement annuity contract or a personal pension scheme].

(4) For the purposes of paragraph (1)(b), the net profit of the employment shall be calculated by taking into account the earnings of the employment over the period determined under regulation 30 less, subject to paragraphs (5) to (7), any expenses wholly and exclusively defrayed in that period for the purposes of that employment.

(5) Subject to paragraph (6), no deduction shall be made under paragraph (3)(a) or (4) in respect of—

(a) any capital expenditure;

(b) the depreciation of any capital asset;

(c) any sum employed or intended to be employed in the setting up or expansion of the employment;

(d) any loss incurred before the beginning of the period determined under regulation 30 (calculation of earnings of self-employed earners);

(e) the repayment of capital on any loan taken out for the purposes of the employment;

(f) any expenses incurred in providing business entertainment.

(6) A deduction shall be made under paragraph (3)(a) or (4) in respect of the repayment of capital on any loan used for—

(a) the replacement in the course of business of equipment or machinery; and

(b) the repair of an existing business asset except to the extent that any sum is payable under an insurance policy for its repair.

(7) An adjudication officer shall refuse to make a deduction in respect of any expenses under paragraph (3)(a) or (4) where he is not satisfied that the expense has been defrayed or, having regard to the nature of the expense and its amount, that it has been reasonably incurred.

(8) For the avoidance of doubt—

(a) a deduction shall not be made under paragraph (3)(a) or (4) in respect of any sum unless it has been expended for the purposes of the business;

(b) a deduction shall be made thereunder in respect of—

(i) the excess of any VAT paid over VAT received in the period determined under regulation 30 (calculation of earnings of self-employed earners);

(ii) any income expended in the repair of an existing asset except to the extent that any sum is payable under an insurance policy for its repair;

(iii) any payment of interest on a loan taken out for the purposes of the employment.

(9) Where a claimant is engaged in employment as a child minder the net profit of the employment shall be one-third of the earnings of that employment, less—

(a) an amount in respect of—

(i) income tax; and

(ii) social security contributions payable under the Social Security Act [SSCBA],

calculated in accordance with regulation 39 (deduction of tax and contributions for self-employed); and

(b) [¹one half of any premium paid in respect of a retirement annuity contract or personal pension scheme].

(10) Notwithstanding regulation 30 (calculation of earnings of self-employed earners) and the foregoing paragraphs, an adjudication officer may assess any item of a claimant's income or expenditure over a period other than that determined under regulation 30 as may, in the particular case, enable the weekly amount of that item of income or expenditure to be determined more accurately.

(11) For the avoidance of doubt where a claimant is engaged in employment as a self-employed earner and he is also engaged in one or more other employ-

ments as a self-employed or employed earner any loss incurred in any one of his employments shall not be offset against his earnings in any other of his employments.

(12)[³- - -].

AMENDMENTS

1. Income-related Benefits Schemes (Miscellaneous Amendments) (No. 4) Regulations 1993 (S.I. 1993 No. 2119), reg. 13 (October 4, 1993).
2. Income-related Benefits Schemes (Miscellaneous Amendments) (No. 5) Regulations 1994 (S.I. 1994 No. 2139), reg. 28 (October 3, 1994).
3. Income-related Benefits Schemes and Social Security (Claims and Payments) (Miscellaneous Amendments) Regulations 1995 (S.I. 1995 No. 2303), reg. 6(3) (October 2, 1995).

DEFINITIONS

"claimant"—see reg. 2(1), reg. 23(1).
"personal pension scheme"—see reg 2(1).
"retirement annuity contract"—*ibid.*
"self-employed earner"—*ibid.*
"Social Security Act"—*ibid.*

GENERAL NOTE

The structure is as follows.
(1) General rule
(2) Disregards
(3) Net profit of sole traders
(4) Net profit of partners and share fishermen
(5) Deductions are not allowed
(6) Deductions allowed
(7) Tests for (3), (4) and (6)
(8) Tests for (3), (4) and (6)
(9) Child minders
(10) Period of calculation to be adjusted
(11) Two employments

Paragraph (1)
This provision sets up two categories—
  (a) those in employment on their own account ("sole traders") and
  (b) partners and share fishermen.
For both, the earnings to be taken into account under reg. 30 are to be net profits. Under (b) the deductions for income tax, social security contributions and personal pension or retirement annuity (see reg. 2(1)) premiums are put under para. (1). For (a), these appear in para. (3).

Paragraph (2)
See the notes to reg. 36(2).

Paragraph (3)
For sole traders apart from child minders (para. (9)) the starting point in calculating net profit under para. (1) is earnings, *i.e.* gross receipts (see notes to reg. 37(1) on the meaning of gross receipts). From that are deducted expenses. Any expenses wholly and exclusively defrayed may be deducted providing that they are reasonably incurred (para. (7)) and the rules of paras. (5) and (6) are applied. The expenses must have been actually defrayed, so that unpaid liabilities cannot be deducted (*CIS 212/1989*).
There has been considerable doubt about whether the cost of items which have a dual use, for business and private purposes, can be apportioned. *The Adjudication Officer's Guide* originally suggested that the cost of telephone calls, units of gas or electricity consumption and petrol could be apportioned (because consumption can be identified as for business or private purposes), but not, for instance, standing charges or road fund tax or insurance for a car. In a series of appeals heard together, the Commissioner convincingly demolished this approach (*R(FC) 1/91, CFC 26/1989* and *R(IS) 13/91*). He holds that where expenses can be apportioned on a time basis, this can identify

the amount wholly and exclusively defrayed on business expenses. There remain some expenses, like the cost of lunches for clients, which are not capable of apportionment. The Commissioner also holds that the apportionment made by the Inspector of Taxes is cogent evidence of the amounts wholly and exclusively incurred for the purposes of the business, which should be accepted in the absence of evidence to the contrary. The *Adjudication Officer's Guide* was subsequently amended to reflect this decision. Now see para. 31029. See also *CFC 836/1995* in the note to para. (11).

The standard deductions for tax and social security contributions (see reg. 39) and personal pension or retirement annuity (see reg. 2(1)) premiums are made.

Paragraph (4)
For partners and share fishermen the calculation is effectively the same apart from the standard deductions already in para. (1)(b).

Paragraph (5)
No deductions are allowed for these items, many of which will appear in profit and loss accounts. But see para. (6) for exceptions to (e).

Paragraph (6)
Deductions can be made for the repayment of capital on loans for these repairs or replacements. The interest on such a loan will be an allowable expense under the general test (and see para. (8)(b)(iii)).

Paragraph (7)
This provision confirms that an expense must have been actually paid out (*CIS 212/1988*), and imposes a general test of reasonableness.

Paragraph (8)
The test of business purpose merely confirms the general requirement under paras. (3) and (4). It is useful to have the categories in (b) expressly confirmed.

Paragraph (9)
For child-minders the simple rule of taking profit as one third of gross receipts is used. The standard deductions are then made. Child-minders who work at home are treated as not in remunerative work (reg. 6(b)). See the note to reg. 6(b).

Paragraph (10)
This provision gives a very general power to average items over different periods from that set in reg. 30, where the basic rule is to take the previous one year.

Paragraph (11)
R(FC) 1/93 applies the principle that a loss in one employment cannot be set off against a profit or earnings in another separate employment. The claimant ran a sub-post office and a shop in the same premises. The Commissioner decides that carrying out the office of sub-postmistress was employment as an employed earner, while running the shop was employment as a self-employed earner. The loss made by the shop could not be set off against the claimant's earnings as a sub-postmistress. *CFC 836/1995* concerned similar facts. However, the Commissioner went on to consider the apportionment of expenses between the two employments. Applying by analogy *R(FC) 1/91* (apportionment of expenses between business and personal use), he held that expenses which were not solely attributable to the shop could be apportioned between the shop and the claimant's husband's employment as a sub-postmaster. The basis of the apportionment in that case was 75 per cent to the post office and 25 per cent to the shop, since the primary reason most customers visited the premises was for the post office services. Thus 75 per cent of the expenses relating to the general running of the premises and the two activities and the repayments on a loan to acquire the post office and shop could be deducted from the earnings as a sub-postmaster, as the Commissioner accepted that these had been wholly, exclusively and necessarily incurred in the performance of the duties of sub-postmaster (see *R(FC) 1/90*, applying *Parsons v. Hogg*).

Deduction of tax and contributions for self-employed earners

39.—(1) The amount to be deducted in respect of income tax under regulation 38(1)(b)(i), (3)(b)(i) or (9)(a)(i) (calculation of net profit of self-employed earners) shall be calculated on the basis of the amount of chargeable income and as if that income were assessable to income tax at ['the lower rate or, as the case may be, the lower rate and the basic rate of tax] less only the personal relief to which the claimant is entitled under sections 8(1) and (2) and 14(1)(a) and (2) of the Income and Corporation Taxes Act 1970 (personal relief) as is appropriate to his circumstances; but, if the period determined under regulation 30 (calculation of earnings of self-employed earners) is less than a year, ['the earnings to which the lower rate [³. . .] of tax is to be applied and] the amount of the personal relief deductible under this paragraph shall be calculated on a pro rata basis.

(2) The amount to be deducted in respect of social security contributions under regulation 38(1)(b)(i), (3)(b)(ii) or (9)(a)(ii) shall be the total of—

[²(a) the amount of Class 2 contributions payable under section 11(1) or, as the case may be, 11(3) of the Contributions and Benefits Act at the rate applicable at the date of claim except where the claimant's chargeable income is less than the amount specified in section 11(4) of that Act (small earnings exception) for the tax year in which the date of claim falls; but if the assessment period is less than a year, the amount specified for that tax year shall be reduced pro rata; and

(b) the amount of Class 4 contributions (if any) which would be payable under section 15 of that Act (Class 4 contributions recoverable under the Income Tax Acts) at the percentage rate applicable at the date of claim on so much of the chargeable income as exceeds the lower limit but does not exceed the upper limit of profits and gains applicable for the tax year in which the date of claim falls; but if the assessment period is less than a year, those limits shall be reduced pro rata.]

(3) In this regulation "chargeable income" means—

(a) except where sub-paragraph (b) applies, the earnings derived from the employment less any expenses deducted under paragraph (3)(a) or, as the case may be, (4) of regulation 38;

(b) in the case of employment as a child minder, one-third of the earnings of that employment.

AMENDMENTS

1. Income-related Benefits Schemes (Miscellaneous Amendments) (No. 3) Regulations 1992 (S.I. 1992 No. 2155), reg. 17 (October 5, 1992).
2. Income-related Benefits Schemes (Miscellaneous Amendments) (No. 4) Regulations 1993 (S.I. 1993 No. 2119), reg. 14 (October 4, 1993).
3. Income-related Benefits Schemes (Miscellaneous Amendments) (No. 5) Regulations 1994 (S.I. 1994 No. 2139), reg. 29 (October 3, 1994).

DEFINITIONS

"claimant"—see reg. 2(1), reg. 23(1).
"date of claim"—see reg. 2(1).
"lower rate"—see reg. 2(1).
"Social Security Act"—*ibid.*

GENERAL NOTE

Paragraph (1)
The deduction for income tax from the amount of earnings calculated under reg. 38 is to be made by applying the lower and basic rates of tax (*i.e.* currently 10 and 23 per cent. respectively) and the personal relief as a single or married person. This figure may well be higher than the actual tax payable. The references to the Income and Corporation Taxes Act 1970 need to be up-dated to the consolidating 1988 Act.

Paragraph (2)

Deductions are made for the Class 2 and Class 4 Social Security contributions payable on the amount calculated under reg. 38.

[¹ Chapter IVA

Participants in the Self-Employment Route of the Employment Option of the New Deal

Interpretation

39A. In this Chapter—

"self-employment route" means that part of the Employment Option of the New Deal which is specified in regulation 75(1)(a)(ii)(aa)(ii) of the Jobseeker's Allowance Regulations 1996;

"special account" means, where a person was carrying on a commercial activity in respect of which assistance is received under the self-employment route, the account into which the gross receipts from that activity were payable during the period in respect of which such assistance was received.]

AMENDMENT

1. Social Security (Miscellaneous Amendments) (No. 4) Regulations 1998 (S.I. 1998 No. 1174), reg. 6(3) (June 1, 1998).

GENERAL NOTE

Regulations 39A to 39D are the same in substance as regs. 102A to 102D of the JSA Regulations (apart from necessary differences in cross-references). They apply to the income from "test-trading" of people who have taken part in the self-employment route of the Employment Option of the New Deal for 18 to 24-year-olds. See the notes to reg. 102C of the JSA Regulations. For a brief summary of the self-employment route of the Employment Option see the note to reg. 75(1) of the JSA Regulations.

See also reg. 23A, the effect of which is that the normal rules for the treatment of income do not apply to receipts from trading while on the self-employment route; such receipts are only to be taken into account as income in accordance with regs. 39A to 39D.

Note also the disregards in para. 64 of Sched. 9 and para. 6(3) and (4) and para. 52 of Sched. 10.

[¹ Treatment of gross receipts of participants in the self-employment route of the Employment Option of the New Deal

39B. The gross receipts of a commercial activity carried on by a person in respect of which assistance is received under the self-employment route, shall be taken into account in accordance with the following provisions of this Chapter.]

AMENDMENT

1. Social Security (Miscellaneous Amendments) (No. 4) Regulations 1998 (S.I. 1998 No. 1174), reg. 6(3) (June 1, 1998).

GENERAL NOTE

See the note to reg. 39A.

[¹ Calculation of income of participants is the self-employment route of the Employment Option of the New Deal

39C.—(1) The income of a person who has received assistance under the

213

self-employment route shall be calculated by taking into account the whole of the monies in the special account at the end of the last day upon which such assistance was received and deducting from those monies—

    (a) an amount in respect of income tax calculated in accordance with regulation 39D (deduction in respect of tax for participants in the self-employment route of the Employment Option of the New Deal); and

    (b) any sum to which paragraph (4) refers.

(2) Income calculated pursuant to paragraph (1) shall be apportioned equally over a period which starts on the date the income is treated as paid under paragraph (3) and is equal in length to the period beginning with the day upon which assistance was first received under the self-employment route and ending on the last day upon which such assistance was received.

(3) Income calculated pursuant to paragraph (1) shall be treated as paid—

    (a) in the case where it is due to be paid before the first benefit week in respect of which the participant or his partner first claims income support following the last day upon which assistance was received under the self-employment route, on the day in the week in which it is due to be paid which corresponds to the first day of the benefit week;

    (b) in any other case, on the first day of the benefit week in which it is due to be paid.

(4) This paragraph refers, where applicable in each benefit week in respect of which income calculated pursuant to paragraph (1) is taken into account pursuant to paragraphs (2) and (3), to the sums which would have been disregarded under paragraphs 4 to 6B and 9 of Schedule 8 had the income been earnings.]

AMENDMENT

    1. Social Security (Miscellaneous Amendments) (No. 4) Regulations 1998 (S.I. 1998 No. 1174), reg. 6(3) (June 1, 1998).

GENERAL NOTE

    See the note to reg. 39A.

[¹ Deduction in respect of tax for participants in the self-employment route of the Employment Option of the New Deal

39D.—(1) The amount to be deducted in respect of income tax under regulation 39C(1)(a) (calculation of income of participants in the self-employment route of the Employment Option of the New Deal) in respect of the period determined under regulation 39C(2) shall be calculated as if—

    (a) the chargeable income is the only income chargeable to tax:

    (b) the personal reliefs which are applicable to the person receiving assistance under the self-employment route by virtue of sections 257(1), 257A(1) and 259 of the Income and Corporation Taxes Act 1988 (personal reliefs) are allowable against that income; and

    (c) the rate at which the chargeable income less the personal relief is assessable to income tax is the lower rate of tax or, as the case may be, the lower rate and the basic rate of tax.

(2) For the purpose of paragraph (1), the lower rate of tax to be applied and the amount of the personal relief deductible shall, where the period determined under regulation 39C(2) is less than a year, be calculated on a pro rata basis.

(3) In this regulation, "chargeable income" means the monies in the special account at the end of the last day upon which assistance was received under the self-employment route.]

AMENDMENT

1. Social Security (Miscellaneous Amendments) (No. 4) Regulations 1998 (S.I. 1998 No. 1174), reg. 6(3) (June 1, 1998).

GENERAL NOTE

See the note to reg. 39A.

Chapter V

Other Income

Calculation of income other than earnings

40.—(1) For the purposes of regulation 29 (calculation of income other than earnings) the income of a claimant which does not consist of earnings to be taken into account shall, subject to [⁶paragraphs (2) to (3B)], be his gross income and any capital treated as income under regulations [¹...] 41 and 44 ([¹...] capital treated as income and modifications in respect of children and young persons).

(2) There shall be disregarded from the calculation of a claimant's gross income under paragraph (1), any sum, where applicable, specified in Schedule 9.

(3) Where the payment of any benefit under the benefit Acts is subject to any deduction by way of recovery the amount to be taken into account under paragraph (1) shall be the gross amount payable.

[²(3A) Where a loan is made to a person pursuant to arrangements made under section 1 of the Education (Student Loans) Act 1990 [³ or article 3 of the Education (Student Loans) (Northern Ireland) Order 1990] and that person ceases to be a student before the end of the academic year in respect of which the loan is payable or, as the case may be, before the end of his course, a sum equal to the weekly amount apportionable under paragraph (2) of regulation 66A shall be taken into account under paragraph (1) for each [⁵ benefit week], in the period over which the loan fell to be apportioned, following the date on which that person ceases to be a student; but in determining the weekly amount apportionable under paragraph (2) of regulation 66A so much of that paragraph as provides for a disregard shall not have effect.]

[⁴(3B) In the case of income to which regulation 29(2B) applies (calculation of income of former students), the amount of income to be taken into account for the purposes of paragraph (1) shall be the amount of that income calculated in accordance with regulation 32(6A) and on the basis that none of that income has been repaid.]

(4) For the avoidance of doubt there shall be included as income to be taken into account under paragraph (1) any payment to which regulation 35(2) or 37(2) (payments not earnings) applies.

AMENDMENTS

1. Income Support (General) Amendment No. 5 Regulations 1988 (S.I. 1988 No. 2022), reg. 9 (December 12, 1988).
2. Social Security Benefits (Student Loans and Miscellaneous Amendments) Regulations 1990 (S.I. 1990 No. 1549), reg. 5(4) (September 1, 1990).
3. Income Support (General) Amendment Regulations 1991 (S.I. 1991 No. 236), reg. 9 (March 13, 1991).
4. Income-related Benefits and Jobseeker's Allowance (Miscellaneous Amendments) Regulations 1997 (S.I. 1997 No. 65), reg. 7 (April 7, 1997).
5. Income-related Benefits and Jobseeker's Allowance (Amendment) (No. 2) Regulations 1997 (S.I. 1997 No. 2197), reg. 5(3) (October 6, 1997).

6. Social Security (Miscellaneous Amendments) Regulations 1998 (S.I. 1998 No. 563), reg. 13(1)(a) (April 6, 1998).

Definitions

"benefit Acts"—see reg. 2(1).
"benefit week"—*ibid.*
"claimant"—see reg. 2(1), reg. 23(1).
"student"—see reg. 2(1), reg. 61.

General Note

Paragraph (1)
This paragraph mainly confirms that all forms of income other than earnings fall into this category, and provides that the gross amount is to be taken into account. The first point is that the income must of course be the claimant's (or his partner's or children's). Money that a claimant is under a "certain and immediate liability" to repay does not amount to income (see *Chief Adjudication Officer v. Leeves* (November 6, 1998, CA, to be reported as *R(IS) 5/99*) in the notes to reg. 29(2B)). Secondly, the amount of the gross income has to be calculated. *CIS 25/1989* holds that, applying the principle of *Parsons v. Hogg* [1985] 2 All E.R. 897, appendix to *R(FIS) 4/85*, expenditure necessary to produce the income is to be deducted to produce a figure of gross income. The claimant was entitled to £21.60 per month sickness benefit from the Ideal Benefit Society only while he continued to pay £60 annual payment to the Society. The monthly equivalent (£5) was to be deducted from the £21.60. However, in *CIS 563/1991* the Commissioner disagrees with *CIS 25/1989* and holds that gross income in para. (1) means without any deduction of the expenses incurred in gaining that income, except to the extent expressly allowed by Sched. 9. He considers that the various provisions in Sched. 9 relating to deduction of expenses incurred by the claimant would not be necessary if "gross income" meant income after deducting the expenses of obtaining it. In his view *CIS 25/1989*, in applying *Parsons v. Hogg* in this context, had not paid sufficient regard to the fact that that case was concerned with earnings of employed earners and involved different statutory provisions. The phrase "gross income" was an equivocal one, as indicated by the Court of Appeal's decision in *Parsons v. Hogg*, and the statutory context had to be considered. The principle of *Parsons v. Hogg* had been applied to earnings in *R(FC) 1/90* and *R(IS) 16/93*, (but apparently not to attendance and basic allowances paid to councillors, which are counted as earnings, in *R(IS) 6/92* and *CIS 77/1993*). The Commissioner in *CIS 563/1991* considered that the statutory context of earnings of employed earners and income other than earnings was sufficiently different not to necessitate a uniform approach to the deduction of expenses, and so did not find it necessary to question the correctness of those decisions. The Commissioner acknowledges that the Tribunal of Commissioners in para. 37 of *CIS 85/1992* (formerly to be reported as *R(IS) 5/98* but now to be reported as *R(IS) 26/95*) assumed that the rental income that was to be taken into account should be net of expenses. However, in his view, they were not expressing a firm conclusion on this question, but simply deciding that the same amount should be treated as capital under reg. 48(4) as would have been taken into account as income. (See the note to reg. 48(4) as to how income treated as capital is to be attributed.) The meaning of "gross income" was not dealt with by the Court of Appeal in *Chief Adjudication Officer v. Palfrey and Others, The Times*, February 17, 1995 (which is the appeal from *CIS 85/1992* and other decisions). The approach adopted by the Commissioner in *CIS 563/1991* is cogently argued and is to be preferred to that of *CIS 25/1989*. He adopts the same conclusion in *CIS 82/1993* which was heard at the same time. See the notes to reg. 36(3) on the application of *Parsons v. Hogg* to the meaning of "gross earnings".
Certain kinds of income are disregarded under Sched. 9 (para. (2)). There is now no special rule for charitable or voluntary payments. Note reg. 48 on income treated as capital.
The major form of such income for income support claimants will be from other social security benefits. All benefits of an income nature (presumably benefits like disablement gratuity and widow's payment continue to be treated as capital although there is now no classification in the regulations (*cf. R(SB) 4/89*)) count in full as income unless disregarded under Sched. 9. Benefits disregarded include housing benefit (para. 5), mobility allowance, the mobility component of disability living allowance or mobility supplement (paras. 6 and 8), attendance allowance or the care component of disability living allowance, except for residents of residential care and nursing homes (paras. 9 and 9A), social fund payments (para. 31) and council tax benefit (para. 52). Benefits which count as income are income whether they are paid on time or in the form of arrears (*R(SB) 4/89*). Then reg. 31 defines the date on which the income is treated as paid. The fact that there is a partial disregard of some kinds of benefit arrears as capital in para. 7 of Sched. 10 does not affect this conclusion. This is because the conclusion, and *R(SB) 4/89*,

must be subject to the principle of *R(SB) 2/83* and *R(SB) 35/83* that at some point accumulated income turns into capital. The sensible approach would be that if any amount of income is still possessed after the end of the period to which it is properly attributed as income under regs. 29 and 31, then it becomes capital, subject to the deduction of relevant liabilities under *R(SB) 2/83* and *R(SB) 35/83*. See *CIS 654/ 1991*, to be reported as *R(IS)3/93*. Thus there is still something for para. 7 of Sched. 10 to bite on.

Paragraph (2)
This paragraph authorises the disregards in Sched. 9. See *CIS 563/1991* discussed in the note to para. 22 of Sched. 9 and *CIS 82/1993* and *CIS 13059/1996* in the notes to paras. 19 and 30 where more than one disregard applies. *CIS 683/1993* confirms that income can only be disregarded to the extent allowed for by Sched. 9. Therefore, no deduction could be made for the maintenance payments made by the claimant, whether under a court order or otherwise, or for his insurance premiums, in calculating his income.

Paragraph (3)
If deductions are made from social security benefits for recovery of overpayments or social fund loans the gross amount of benefit is used in the calculation of income support.

Paragraph (3A)
If a student ceases to be a student in the middle of a period for which a student loan is attributed under reg. 66A, the balance of the loan is treated as income under para. (3A) but the £10 disregard under reg. 66A(2) no longer applies.
Note para. 61 of Sched. 9 under which any part of a student loan left over at the end of a course is ignored.

Paragraph (3B)
See the notes to regs. 29(2B) and 32(6A). But note *Chief Adjudication Officer v. Leeves* (November 6, 1998, CA, to be reported as *R(IS) 5/99*) and the argument discussed in the notes to reg. 29(2B) as to when that provision applies.
Note also para. 61 of Sched. 9 under which any grant or covenant income or student loan left over at the end of the person's course is disregarded.

Paragraph (4)
These amounts, which do not count as earnings, do count as other income. However, note the disregards in paras. 1, 3, 4, 4A, 18, 20, 21, 26 and 27 of Sched. 9.

Capital treated as income

41.—(1) Any capital payable by instalments which are outstanding on the first day in respect of which income support is payable or the date of the determination of the claim, whichever is earlier, or, in the case of a review, the date of any subsequent review shall, if the aggregate of the instalments outstanding and the amount of the claimant's capital otherwise calculated in accordance with Chapter VI of this Part exceeds [⁵£8,000][⁷ or, in a case where regulation 45(b) applies, £16,000], be treated as income.

(2) Any payment received under an annuity shall be treated as income.

(3) In the case of a person to whom section 23 of the Act [SSCBA, s.126] (trade disputes) applies [¹or in respect of whom section 20(3) of the Act [SSCBA, s.124(1)] (conditions of entitlement to income support) has effect as modified by section 23A(b) of the Act [SSCBA, s.127(b)] (effect of return to work)], any payment under [⁶section 17 or 24 of the Children Act 1989] [³or, as the case may be, section 12, 24 or 26 of the Social Work (Scotland) Act 1968 (local authorities' duty to promote welfare of children and powers to grant financial assistance to persons in, or formerly in, their care) shall be treated as income].

[²(4) In the case of a person to whom section 20(3) of the Act [SSCBA, s.124(1)] (conditions of entitlement to income support) has effect as modified by section 23A(b) of that Act [SSCBA, s.127(b)] (effect of return to work), any amount by way of repayment of income tax deducted from his emoluments in pursuance of section 203 of the Income and Corporation Taxes Act 1988, shall be treated as income.]

[[4](5) Any earnings to the extent that they are not a payment of income shall be treated as income.]

[[7](6) Any Career Development Loan paid pursuant to section 2 of the Employment and Training Act 1973 shall be treated as income.]

AMENDMENTS

1. Income Support (General) Amendment Regulations 1988 (S.I. 1988 No. 663), reg. 18 (April 11, 1988).
2. Income Support (General) Amendment No. 4 Regulations 1988 (S.I. 1988 No. 1445), reg. 9 (September 12, 1988).
3. Family Credit and Income Support (General) Amendment Regulations 1989 (S.I. 1989 No. 104), reg. 7 (July 10, 1989).
4. Income Support (General) Amendment No. 2 Regulations 1989 (S.I. 1989 No. 1323), reg. 13 (October 9, 1989).
5. Income-related Benefits (Miscellaneous Amendments) Regulations 1990 (S.I. 1990 No. 671), reg. 5 (April 9, 1990).
6. Income Support (General) Amendment Regulations 1992 (S.I. 1992 No. 468), Sched., para. 4 (April 6, 1992).
7. Income-related Benefits and Jobseeker's Allowance (Miscellaneous Amendments) Regulations 1997 (S.I. 1997 No. 65), reg. 3 (April 7, 1997).

DEFINITIONS

"the Act"—see reg. 2(1).
"claimant"—*ibid.*

GENERAL NOTE

Paragraph (1)
The value of the right to receive any outstanding instalments of capital payable by instalments is disregarded (Sched. 10, para. 16). See the notes to reg. 23 on the line between capital and income. Normally each instalment, when it is paid, would add to the claimant's capital (*Lillystone v. SBC* [1982] 3 F.L.R. 52). The literal effect of para. (1) is that if the amount of the instalments outstanding plus the claimant's (including partner's: reg. 23) other capital comes to more than £8,000 (£16,000 in the case of claimants living permanently in residential care or nursing homes (including those with preserved rights), residential accommodation or Polish resettlement homes: regs. 45(b) and 53(1B)), the whole amount outstanding is to be treated as income. What para. (1) does not say is what this means. A capital sum cannot simply be treated as income. The common sense rule would be that each instalment, when paid, was treated as a payment of income (as suggested in paras. 33531 and 33536 of the *Adjudication Officer's Guide*), but this is not expressed in para. (1). For an example of where the rule in para. (1) applied see *R(IS) 7/98* in the notes to para. 15 of Sched. 10.

Paragraph (2)
The value of the right to receive income under an annuity is disregarded as capital (Sched. 10, para. 11). The income under some "home income" schemes is disregarded under para. 17 of Sched. 9.

Paragraph (3)
R(SB) 29/85 decided that some payments under this legislation were capital. In trade dispute cases, all payments count as income.

Paragraph (4)
In trade dispute cases repayments of PAYE tax, normally capital, are to be treated as income.

Paragraph (5)
This seems merely to confirm that sums which are defined as earnings in reg. 35 which might under the general law be categorised as capital are income.

Paragraph (6)

This treats Career Development Loans, which are provided in order to help adults pay for vocational education or training, as income. However, the income will be disregarded under para. 59 of Sched. 9, except any part of the loan that was applied for and has been paid to meet the cost of food, ordinary clothing or footwear (defined in para. 59(2)), household fuel, rent for which housing benefit is payable, housing costs met by income support, home charges met under reg. 19 for people with preserved rights, council tax or water charges during the period of training or education. On "ordinary clothing or footwear" see paras. 33665–6 of the *Adjudication Officer's Guide*. In addition, any part of the loan left over at the end of the course is ignored (para. 60 of Sched. 9).

For treatment of career development loans before these rules were introduced on April 7, 1997, see *CIS 507/1997*.

Notional income

42.—(1) A claimant shall be treated as possessing income of which he has deprived himself for the purpose of securing entitlement to income support or increasing the amount of that benefit.

(2) Except in the case of—

(a) a discretionary trust;

(b) a trust derived from a payment made in consequence of a personal injury;

[[23](c) jobseeker's allowance; or]

[[25](d) child benefit to which paragraph (2D) refers;]

[[8](e) family credit;

(f) disability working allowance,]

[[20](g) a personal pension scheme or retirement annuity contract where the claimant is aged under 60,]

[[24](h) earnings top-up,] [[26] or

(i) any sum to which paragraph 44(a) or 45(a) of Schedule 10 (disregard of compensation for personal injuries which is administered by the Court) refers,] [[30] or

(j) rehabilitation allowance made under section 2 of the Employment and Training Act 1973],

income which would become available to the claimant upon application being made but which has not been acquired by him shall be treated as possessed by him but only from the date on which [[1]it could be expected to be acquired were an application made.]

[[20](2A) Where a person, aged not less than 60, is a member of, or a person deriving entitlement to a pension under, a personal pension scheme, or is a party to, or a person deriving entitlement to a pension under, a retirement annuity contract, and—

(a) in the case of a personal pension scheme, he fails to purchase an annuity with the funds available in that scheme where—

(i) he defers, in whole or in part, the payment of any income which would have been payable to him by his pension fund holder;

(ii) he fails to take any necessary action to secure that the whole of any income which would be payable to him by his pension fund holder upon his applying for it, is so paid; or

(iii) income withdrawal is not available to him under that scheme; or

(b) in the case of a retirement annuity contract, he fails to purchase an annuity with the funds available under that contract,

the amount of any income foregone shall be treated as possessed by him, but only from the date on which it could be expected to be acquired were an application for it to be made.

(2B) The amount of any income foregone in a case to which either head (2A)(a)(i) or (ii) applies shall be the maximum amount of income which may be withdrawn from the fund and shall be determined by the adjudication officer who shall take account of information provided by the pension fund holder in accordance with regulation 7(5) of the Social Security (Claims and Payments) Regulations 1987.

(2C) The amount of any income foregone in a case to which either head (2A)(a)(iii) or sub-paragraph (2A)(b) applies shall be the income that the claimant could have received without purchasing an annuity had the funds held under the relevant personal pension scheme or retirement annuity contract been held under a personal pension scheme where income withdrawal was available and shall be determined in the manner specified in paragraph (2B).]

[25(2D) This paragraph refers to child benefit payable in accordance with regulation 2(1)(a)(ii) of the Child Benefit and Social Security (Fixing and Adjustment of Rates) Regulations 1976 (weekly rate for only, elder or eldest child of a lone parent) but only to the extent that it exceeds the amount specified in regulation 2(1)(a)(i) of those Regulations.]

(3) Except in the case of a discretionary trust, or a trust derived from a payment made in consequence of a personal injury, any income which is due to be paid to the claimant but—

  (a) has not been paid to him;
  (b) is not a payment prescribed in regulation 9 or 10 of the Social Security (Payments on Account, Overpayment and Recovery) Regulations 1987 (duplication and prescribed payments or maintenance payments) and not made on or before the date prescribed in relation to it,

shall [10except for any amount to which paragraph (3A) or (3B) applies] be treated as possessed by the claimant.

[10(3A) This paragraph applies to an amount which is due to be paid to the claimant under an occupational pension scheme but which is not paid because the trustees or managers of the scheme have suspended or ceased payments [13. . .] due to an insufficiency of resources.

(3B) This paragraph applies to any amount by which a payment made to the claimant from an occupational pension scheme falls short of the payment to which he was due under the scheme where the shortfall arises because the trustees or managers of the scheme have insufficient resources available to meet in full the scheme's liabilities [13. . .].]

[2(4) [32 Any payment of income, other than a payment of income specified in paragraph (4ZA)], made—

  (a) to a third party in respect of a single claimant or in respect of a member of the family (but not a member of the third party's family) shall be treated—
    (i) in a case where the payment is derived from a payment of any benefit under the benefit Acts, a war disablement pension [21, war widow's pension or a pension payable to a person as a widow under the Naval, Military and Air Forces Etc. (Disablement and Death) Service Pensions Order 1983 insofar as that Order is made under the Naval and Marine Pay and Pensions Act 1865 [22or the Pensions and Yeomanry Pay Act 1884], or is made only under section 12(1) of the Social Security (Miscellaneous Provisions) Act 1977 and any power of Her Majesty otherwise than under an enactment to make provision about pensions for or in respect of persons who have been disabled or have died in consequence of service as members of the armed forces of the Crown,] as possessed by that single claimant, if it is paid to him, or by that member, if it is paid to any member of that family;
    (ii) in any other case, as possessed by that single claimant or by that member to the extent that it is used for the food, ordinary clothing or footwear, household fuel, rent or rates for which housing benefit is payable, [16or] [7. . .] any housing costs to the extent that they are met under regulations 17(1)(e) or 18(1)(f) (housing costs) [16. . .]

[⁴...] [³...] [⁴...], of that single claimant or, as the case may be, of any member of that family[⁷, or is used for any [¹²council tax] or water charges for which that claimant or member is liable];

(b) to a single claimant or a member of the family in respect of a third party (but not in respect of another member of that family) shall be treated as possessed by that single claimant or, as the case may be, that member of the family to the extent that it is kept or used by him or used by or on behalf of any member of the family;

but, except where sub-paragraph (a)(i) applies and in the case of a person to whom section 23 of the Act [SSCBA, s.126] (trade disputes) applies, this paragraph shall not apply to any payment in kind.]

[³² (4ZA) Paragraph (4) shall not apply in respect of a payment of income made—

(a) under the Macfarlane Trust, the Macfarlane (Special Payments) Trust, the Macfarlane (Special Payments) (No. 2) Trust, the Fund, the Eileen Trust or the Independent Living Funds;

(b) pursuant to section 19(1)(a) of the Coal Industry Act 1994 (concessionary coal); or

(c) pursuant to section 2 of the Employment and Training Act 1973 in respect of a person's participation—

(i) in an employment programme specified in regulations 75(1)(a)(ii) of the Jobseeker's Allowance Regulations 1996;

(ii) in a training scheme specified in regulation 75(1)(b)(ii) of those Regulations; or

(iii) in a qualifying course within the meaning specified in regulation 17A(7) of those Regulations.]

[¹⁶(4A) Where the claimant lives in a residential care home or a nursing home, or is temporarily absent from such a home, any payment made by a person other than the claimant or a member of his family in respect of some or all of the cost of maintaining the claimant or a member of his family in that home shall be treated as possessed by the claimant or by that member of his family.]

(5) Where a claimant's earnings are not ascertainable at the time of the determination of the claim or of any subsequent review the adjudication officer shall treat the claimant as possessing such earnings as is reasonable in the circumstances of the case having regard to the number of hours worked and the earnings paid for comparable employment in the area.

(6) Where—

(a) a claimant performs a service for another person; and

(b) that person makes no payment of earnings or pays less than that paid for a comparable employment in the area,

the adjudication officer shall treat the claimant as possessing such earnings (if any) as is reasonable for that employment unless the claimant satisfies him that the means of that person are insufficient for him to pay or to pay more for the service; but this paragraph shall not apply to a claimant who is engaged by a charitable or [¹⁹voluntary organisation] or is a volunteer if the adjudication officer is satisfied [¹⁹in any of those cases] that it is reasonable for him to provide his services free of charge [²⁹or in a case where the service is performed in connection with the claimant's participation in an employment or training programme in accordance with regulation 19(1)(q) of the Jobseeker's Allowance Regulations 1996].

(7) Where a claimant is treated as possessing any income under any of [³¹ paragraphs (1) to (4A)] the foregoing provisions of this Part shall apply for the purposes of calculating the amount of that income as if a payment had actually been made and as if it were actual income which he does possess.

(8) Where a claimant is treated as possessing any earnings under paragraph (5) or (6) the foregoing provisions of this Part shall apply for the purposes of

calculating the amount of those earnings as if a payment had actually been made and as if they were actual earnings which he does possess except that paragraph (3) of regulation 36 (calculation of net earnings of employed earners) shall not apply and his net earnings shall be calculated by taking into account the earnings which he is treated as possessing, less—

(a) an amount in respect of income tax equivalent to an amount calculated by applying to those earnings [¹¹the lower rate or, as the case may be, the lower rate and the basic rate of tax] in the year of assessment less only the personal relief to which the claimant is entitled under sections 8(1) and (2) and 14(1)(a) and (2) of the Income and Corporation Taxes Act 1970 (personal relief) as is appropriate to his circumstances; but, if the period over which those earnings are to be taken into account is less than a year, [¹¹the earnings to which the lower rate [¹⁸. . .] of tax is to be applied and] the amount of the personal relief deductible under this paragraph shall be calculated on a pro rata basis;

[¹⁶(b) where the weekly amount of those earnings equals or exceeds the lower earnings limit, an amount representing primary Class 1 contributions under the Contributions and Benefits Act, calculated by applying to those earnings the initial and main primary percentages in accordance with sections 8(1) (a) and (b) of that Act; and]

(c) one-half of any sum payable by the claimant [¹⁷in respect of a pay period] by way of a contribution towards an occupational or personal pension scheme.

[¹⁰(8A) In paragraphs (3A) and (3B) the expression "resources" has the same meaning as in the Social Security Pensions Act 1975 by virtue of section 66(1) of that Act.]

[²(9) In paragraph (4) the expression "ordinary clothing or footwear" means clothing or footwear for normal daily use, but does not include school uniforms, or clothing or footwear used solely for sporting activities.]

AMENDMENTS

1. Income Support (General) Amendment Regulations 1988 (S.I. 1988 No. 663), reg. 19 (April 11, 1988).
2. Income Support (General) Amendment (No. 4) Regulations 1988 (S.I. 1988 No. 1445), reg. 10 (September 12, 1988).
3. Income Support (General) Amendment (No. 4) Regulations 1988 (S.I. 1988 No. 1445), Sched. 1, para. 4 (April 10, 1989).
4. Income Support (General) Amendment Regulations 1989 (S.I. 1989 No. 534), Sched. 1, para. 7 (October 9, 1989).
5. Income-related Benefits Schemes Amendment Regulations 1990 (S.I. 1990 No. 127), reg. 3 (January 31, 1990).
6. Income-related Benefits Schemes and Social Security (Recoupment) Amendment Regulations 1991 (S.I. 1991 No.1175), reg. 5 (May 11, 1991).
7. Income Support (General) Amendment No. 4 Regulations 1991 (S.I. 1991 No. 1559), reg. 8 (October 7, 1991).
8. Income Support (General) Amendment Regulations 1992 (S.I. 1992 No. 468), reg. 4 (April 6, 1992).
9. Income-related Benefits Schemes and Social Security (Recoupment) Amendment Regulations 1992 (S.I. 1992 No. 1101), reg. 6 (May 7, 1992).
10. Income Support (General) Amendment (No. 2) Regulations 1992 (S.I. 1992 No. 1198), reg. 2 (May 22, 1992).
11. Income-related Benefits Schemes (Miscellaneous Amendments) (No. 3) Regulations 1992 (S.I. 1992 No. 2155), reg. 18 (October 5, 1992).
12. Income-related Benefits Schemes (Miscellaneous Amendments) Regulations 1993 (S.I. 1993 No. 315), Sched., para. 2 (April 1, 1993).
13. Income-related Benefits Schemes (Miscellaneous Amendments) Regulations 1993 (S.I. 1993 No. 315), reg. 6 (April 12, 1993).

14. Social Security Benefits (Miscellaneous Amendments) (No. 2) Regulations 1993 (S.I. 1993 No. 963), reg. 2(3) (April 22, 1993).

15. Income-related Benefits Schemes and Social Security (Recoupement) Amendment Regulations 1993 (S.I. 1993 No. 1249), reg. 4(3) (May 14, 1993).

16. Income-related Benefits Schemes (Miscellaneous Amendments) Regulations 1994 (S.I. 1994 No. 527), reg. 4 (April 11, 1994).

17. Income-related Benefits Schemes (Miscellaneous Amendments) (No. 5) Regulations 1994 (S.I. 1994 No. 2139), reg. 26 (October 3, 1994).

18. Income-related Benefits Schemes (Miscellaneous Amendments) (No. 5) Regulations 1994 (S.I. 1994 No. 2139), reg. 29 (October 3, 1994).

19. Income-related Benefits Schemes (Miscellaneous Amendments) Regulations 1995 (S.I. 1995 No. 516), reg. 22 (April 10, 1995).

20. Income-related Benefits Schemes and Social Security (Claims and Payments) (Miscellaneous Amendments) Regulations 1995 (S.I. 1995 No. 2303), reg. 6(4) (October 2, 1995).

21. Income-related Benefits Schemes Amendment (No. 2) Regulations 1995 (S.I. 1995 No. 2792), reg. 6(2) (October 28, 1995).

22. Income-related Benefits Schemes (Widows' etc. Pensions Disregards) Amendment Regulations 1995 (S.I. 1995 No. 3282), reg. 2 (December 20, 1995).

23. Income Support (General) (Jobseeker's Allowance Consequential Amendments) Regulations 1996 (S.I. 1996 No. 206), reg. 17 (October 7, 1996).

24. Income-related Benefits Schemes and Social Fund (Miscellaneous Amendments) Regulations 1996 (S.I. 1996 No. 1944), reg. 13 and Sched., para. 3 (October 7, 1996).

25. Child Benefit, Child Support and Social Security (Miscellaneous Amendments) Regulations 1996 (S.I. 1996 No. 1803), reg. 37 (April 7, 1997).

26. Income-related Benefits and Jobseeker's Allowance (Amendment) (No. 2) Regulations 1997 (S.I. 1997 No. 2197), reg. 5(4) (October 6, 1997).

27. Income-related Benefits and Jobseeker's Allowance (Amendment) (No. 2) Regulations 1997 (S.I. 1997 No. 2197), reg. 7(3) and (4)(e) (October 6, 1997).

28. Social Security Amendment (New Deal) Regulations 1997 (S.I. 1997 No. 2863), reg. 17(1) and (2)(e) (January 5, 1998).

29. Social Security Amendment (New Deal) Regulations 1997 (S.I. 1997 No. 2863), reg. 17(3) and (4)(e) (January 5, 1998).

30. Social Security (Miscellaneous Amendments) Regulations 1998 (S.I. 1998 No. 563), reg. 6(1) and (2)(e) (April 6, 1998).

31. Social Security (Miscellaneous Amendments) Regulations 1998 (S.I. 1998 No. 563), reg. 13(1)(b) (April 6, 1998).

32. Social Security Amendment (New Deal) (No. 2) Regulations 1998 (S.I. 1998 No. 2117), reg. 2(2) (September 24, 1998).

DEFINITIONS

"the Act"—see reg. 2(1).
"benefit Acts"—see reg. 2(1).
"claimant"—see reg. 2(1), reg. 23(1).
"earnings"—see reg. 2(1).
"earnings top-up"—*ibid.*
"family"—see 1986 Act, s.20(11) (SSCBA, s.137(1)).
"lower rate"—see reg. 2(1).
"occupational pension scheme"—see 1986 Act, s.84(1) (PSA, s.1).
"pay period"—see reg. 2(1).
"pension fund holder"—*ibid.*
"personal pension scheme"—*ibid.*
"retirement annuity contract"—*ibid.*
"single claimant"—*ibid.*
"Social Security Act"—*ibid.*
"the Eileen Trust"—*ibid.*
"the Fund"—*ibid.*
"the Independent Living Funds"—*ibid.*
"the Macfarlane (Special Payments) Trust"—*ibid.*
"the Macfarlane (Special Payments) (No. 2) Trust"—*ibid.*
"the Macfarlane Trust"—*ibid.*
"voluntary organisation"—*ibid.*

"war widow's pension"—*ibid.*
"water charges"—see reg. 2(1).
"year of assessment"—*ibid.*

GENERAL NOTE

The structure is as follows.
(1) Deprivation of income
(2)–(2D) Income available on application
(3) Income due
(3A) and (3B) Income from occupational pension schemes not paid
(4)–(4A) Third parties
(5) Earnings not ascertainable
(6) Underpaid services
(7) Calculation
(8) Deductions
(8A) and (9) Definitions

Paragraph (1)
See notes to reg. 51(1). A social security benefit is "income" which a claimant may be treated as still possessing under para. (1) (*CSIS 57/1992*). But a refusal to take up an offer of employment would not be a deprivation of income (see *CCS 7967/1995* decided under the child support legislation).

Note that the corresponding regulation under JSA (reg. 105(1) of the JSA Regulations) applies if a person has deprived himself of income in order to secure entitlement to or increase the amount of JSA *or income support*. That avoids the question that might otherwise have arisen on a claimant transferring from income support to JSA as to whether a deprivation which had only been for the purposes of income support could be caught by reg. 105(1). But para. (1) has not been similarly amended.

Paragraphs (2) to (2D)
See notes to reg. 51(2). There are some extra excluded categories here. The fact that a number of social security benefits are excluded suggests that social security benefits generally are caught by the rule. It is not at all clear that such benefits "would become available upon application being made" if an award has not already been made. Stages of the gathering of evidence and a decision by the AO are necessary before a claimant becomes entitled to payment. The words "would become" may be broad enough to cover that process, but that could only be the case where entitlement is straightforward. See *CIS 16271/1996*. The income available to be acquired by the claimant must be for his own benefit (and not, for example, rent under a sub-lease that had to be paid straight over to the head landlord) (*CIS 15052/1996*).

The new form of para. (2)(d) and the insertion of para. (2D) from April 7, 1997 reflect the simultaneous changes made to child benefit whereby instead of the increase to child benefit for the eldest or only child of a lone parent (commonly referred to as one parent benefit) there is (for the time being) to be a separate composite rate of child benefit for such a child. See the amendments to reg. 2 of the Child Benefit and Social Security (Fixing and Adjustment of Rates) Regulations 1976 (S.I. 1976 No. 1267) effected by reg. 5 of the Child Benefit, Child Support and Social Security (Miscellaneous Amendments) Regulations 1996 (S.I. 1996 No. 1803) in *Bonner*. Note that under para. (2D) it is only the additional amount of child benefit for a lone parent that is excluded from the rule in para. (2). See also the abolition of the lone parent premium in favour of a higher rate of family premium for lone parents in Sched. 2. These changes are part of the previous Government's explicit policy of "narrow[ing] the existing gap between benefits which go to lone parents and those which go to couples" (see the DSS's note to the Social Security Advisory Committee appended to the Committee's report on the changes, Cm. 3296), the first step of which was not to increase one parent benefit (and the lone parent premium for means-tested benefits) in April 1996. The same approach has been adopted by the present Government. It abolished the lone parent rate of child benefit for new claims from July 6, 1998 (see s.72 of the Social Security Act 1998), although there is some protection for existing recipients and for lone parents who were getting income support or income-based JSA and who make a claim for the lone parent rate of child benefit on starting work. In addition, from April 6, 1998 the rate of the family premium for new lone parents and for lone parents making a new claim (subject to a 12-week linking rule) has been the same as for couples (see para. 3 of Sched. 2, but note the protection for existing lone parents). As "compensation" for these cuts, child benefit for the eldest child was increased by £2.50 (in addition to the annual up-rating increase) in April 1999 and the personal allowance in means-tested benefits for a child in the lowest age band was increased by £2.50 in November 1998. These increases applied to *all* claimants with children but were intended to offset to some extent the loss of the additional benefit for lone parents.

The exclusion of family credit from April 1992, is intended, in conjunction with regs. 22 to 24 of the Income Support (General) Amendment No. 4 Regulations 1991, to allow claimants a choice of which method of support they prefer on the change in the minimum working hours for family credit from 24 to 16. Income support may be claimed to top up family credit, but there is no penalty for not claiming family credit. There is similar protection on the introduction of disability working allowance. See also para. (2)(h) in relation to earnings top-up. On earnings top-up, see the note at the beginning of the Family Credit Regulations.

Under para. 2(g) income available on request from a personal pension scheme or under a retirement annuity contract is exempt from the notional income rules until a person reaches 60. If after 60 the person fails to purchase an annuity with the money available from, and (if this is an option) does not draw the income from, such a pension fund, he will be assumed to have an amount of income determined in accordance with paras. (2B) or (2C) (para. (2A)). No notional capital will be assumed (see reg. 51(2)(d)) and any actual capital is disregarded (see Sched. 10, para. 23A). See also the amendments to regs. 7 and 32 of the Claims and Payments Regulations. Note that para. (2A) only applies to existing claimants from the date their income support is reviewed following provision of the relevant information about their pension fund, or October 1, 1998, if that is sooner; for new claims it has effect from the date of the claim (reg. 1(5) of the amending regulations).

On para. (2)(i), see the notes to paras. 44 and 45 of Sched. 10.

The purpose of para. (2)(j) is to enable a claimant who is on a full-time rehabilitation course and so eligible for rehabilitation allowance from the DfEE to choose whether to claim the allowance or remain on income support. Rehabilitation courses are designed to assist people who have been incapable of work for a prolonged period to return to the labour market. If a person claims the allowance he is treated as capable of work and so would cease to be entitled to income support on the ground of incapacity for work (although he could claim JSA).

Paragraph (3)

To start with the exclusion in sub-para. (b), the 1987 Payments Regulations were revoked and replaced by the 1988 Regulations set out in this book. The reference to regs. 9 and 10 can be taken (under the Interpretation Act 1978) to be a reference to regs. 8 and 9 of the 1988 Regulations. This excludes almost all social security benefits from the operation of this paragraph (although abandoning entitlement might be a deprivation of income under para. (1)). The other exclusions are of income due, but not paid, under discretionary trusts and trusts of personal injury compensation, and entitlements under occupational pension schemes covered by paras. (3A) and (3B).

Outside these exclusions if income is due, *i.e.* legally due, it is to be treated as possessed by the claimant, and as income. The value of a debt would normally be a capital asset. Note that there is no discretion. An example would be of wages legally due but not paid, or payments on termination of employment due but not paid. However, the income that is due to be paid must be payable to the claimant for his own benefit (and not, for example, rent under a sub-lease that has to be paid straight over to the head landlord) (*CIS 15052/1996*).

See reg. 70(2)(b) (urgent cases) for the possibility of payment when notional income is attributed under para. (3).

Paragraphs (3A) and (3B)

Where a payment due from an occupational pension scheme is either not made or is not made in full because of a deficiency in the scheme's resources (defined in para. (8A)) the amount not paid does not fall within para. (3). The original form of the provisions applied only where the scheme stopped making payments to members of the scheme. The amendment puts beyond doubt that if payments to relatives or dependants of members are stopped, para. (3) does not apply.

Paragraph (4) and (4ZA)

See the notes to reg. 51(3) and (3A) and *CFC 13585/1996* in the note to reg. 26(3) of the Family Credit Regulations.

In *CJSA 3411/1998* the claimant was on a one year residential training course. He was in receipt of an adult education bursary, part of which was paid directly to the college. The Commissioner decides that no notional income was to be attributed to the claimant under reg. 105(10)(a)(ii) of the JSA Regulations (the equivalent of sub-para. (a)(ii)). Of the listed items only "food" was covered by the payment to the college (the power supplies used in the college did not constitute "household fuel"). But this was not caught by reg. 105(10)(a)(ii) as the food provided by the

225

college was a "payment in kind". These words referred to any payment to, or income of, the claimant in kind as well as any payment to the third party in kind.

Paragraph (4A)

Any payment made by a third party towards the cost of a claimant and his family's residential care or nursing home fees counts as the claimant's income. However, under paras. 15, 15A, 30, 30A and 64 of Sched. 9 certain "top-up" payments to people in residential care and nursing homes are disregarded. "Person" in para. (4A) will include a local authority (Sched. 1 to the Interpretation Act 1978).

Paragraph (5)

This is a very general discretion. The AO (or SSAT) must have regard to the number of hours worked and the going rate locally for comparable employment in deciding what is reasonable, but is not prevented from considering all relevant circumstances (*R(SB) 25/83, R(SB) 15/86, R(SB) 6/88*).

Paragraph (6)

This provision has been tightened up in a number of respects in comparison with its supplementary benefit predecessor. If the two conditions in sub-paras. (a) and (b) are met there is no discretion whether or not to apply para. (6), unless the claimant comes within one of the specific exceptions. It appears that for sub-para. (a) any unpaid or underpaid service will do, subject to the exclusion of volunteers or workers for charities or voluntary organisations where it is reasonable for the person to make no charge or people on an employment programme or training scheme for at least three days in a week who are not being paid a training allowance (see below). In *R(SB) 3/92* on the old law the Commissioner held that the rule applied where a mother provided services to her disabled adult son out of love and affection. On appeal in *Sharrock v. Chief Adjudication Officer* (March 26, 1991; appendix to *R(SB) 3/92*) the Court of Appeal agreed that such relationships came within the old provision, providing that the service provided was of a character for which an employer would be prepared to pay. In *CIS 93/1991* the Commissioner holds that the principle of *Sharrock* applies to reg. 42(6), which thus covers services provided within informal family relationships without any contract. Under supplementary benefit there was no proviso exempting volunteers etc. at the time. Now unpaid carers can be defined as volunteers (*CIS 93/1991*), so that there is a discretion not to apply the rule (see below). In *CIS 422/1992* (which again concerned Mrs Sharrock), the Commissioner held that she was a volunteer and that it was reasonable for her to provide her services free. The evidence was that her son made a substantial contribution to the household expenses. If she were to charge for her services the whole basis of the arrangement between them would have to change, which could have a deleterious effect on their relationship. (However, the part of the son's contribution that was not in respect of *his* living and accommodation costs could not be disregarded under para. 18 of Sched. 9.) It is difficult to see how in most cases it can be unreasonable for carers to look after a relative without payment. This is acknowledged by para. 31199 of the *Adjudication Officer's Guide* which also lists factors to be considered in cases of doubt which are broadly in line with those suggested in *CIS 93/1991* (see below).

Under sub-para. (b) the "employer" must either make no payment or pay less than is paid for comparable employment in the area. Since the amount of notional earnings is set according to what is reasonable for that comparable employment, it seems that some comparable employment must exist in all cases.

Some of the points made in *R(SB) 13/86* on the old law will still apply to para. (6). It must be necessary to identify the employer for whom the services were provided. "Person" includes a company or other corporate employer (Interpretation Act 1978). Thus in *R(IS) 5/95* where the claimant, who was an employee and director of a small company, was working unpaid because of the company's financial difficulties, it was necessary to consider whether para. (6) applied.

Particulars of the services provided and any payments made must be ascertained. See *CIS 701/ 1994* on the factors to consider when assessing comparable employment (the claimant in that case was again a carer) and the amount of notional earnings.

It was suggested in earlier editions that although payments of earnings in kind are disregarded in the calculation of income (reg. 35(2)(a) and Sched. 9, para. 21), payments in kind should be considered in testing whether a claimant is paid at all or is paid less than the rate for comparable employment. However, *CIS 11482/1995* decides that this is not correct. The claimant's wife worked as a shop assistant for 12 hours a week for which she was paid £5 in cash and took goods to the value of £36 from the shelves. The Commissioner, after deciding that earnings in para. (6) meant earnings as defined in regs. 35 or 37 (see reg. 2(1)), holds that since earnings in kind were ignored when considering whether any payment at all of earnings had been made, this must also be the case when deciding whether a person was paid less than the rate for comparable employment. Thus in considering whether the claimant's wife was paid less than the rate for comparable employment, the £36 that she received in goods was to be left out of account. But to avoid unfair double counting it was necessary to deduct any cash payments in the calculation of her notional earnings under para. (6). This was permissible because para. (6) allowed the amount of earnings which would be paid for comparable employment to be adjusted where circumstances made it reasonable. However, it would not be "reasonable" to deduct the earnings in kind because that did not involve a double counting as the actual value of the earnings in kind was disregarded.

The claimant can then escape if he proves (on the balance of probabilities) that the person to whom he has provided the services has insufficient means to pay more. This could well cause difficulties for claimants reluctant to make embarrassing enquiries. But there is an interest in preventing employers from economising at the expense of the income support budget. The Court of Appeal in *Sharrock v. Chief Adjudication Officer* suggests that "means" refers simply to monetary resources and is a matter of broad judgment. No automatic test of ignoring certain benefits or regarding an income above income support level as available should be adopted. In *CIS 93/1991*, the claimant looked after his elderly and severely disabled father, but declined to give any information about the father's means. The Commissioner confirms that in such circumstances the basic rule of para. (6) must be applied, but subject to the proviso on volunteers.

The proviso firstly allows volunteers or those engaged by charities or voluntary organisations not to have any notional earnings if it is reasonable for them to provide their services free of charge. Volunteer in this context means someone who without any legal obligation performs a service for another person without expectation of payment (*R(IS) 12/92*). Thus, it would seem that if any payment is made to the claimant, the proviso cannot apply. The Commissioner in *CIS 93/1991* holds that the means of the "employer" is a factor here, but other factors are relevant too. It may be more reasonable for close relatives to provide services free of charge than for others to do so. The basis on which the arrangement was made, the expectations of the family members concerned, the housing arrangements and the reason why the carer gave up any paid work might need to be considered. Anomalies like the loss of invalid care allowance if the carer accepted payment should be considered. So should the question of what alternatives would be available if the relative ceased to provide the care. If there was no realistic alternative to the relative continuing to provide the care and the person would not agree to make any payment, that would point to it being reasonable for the claimant to provide the services free of charge (*CIS 701/1994*). In *CIS 93/1991* the SSAT went wrong in not properly considering their discretion under the proviso and concentrating on the legitimate inference that the "employer" could afford to pay the going rate. In *CIS 701/1994* the Commissioner expresses the view that if a person had substantial resources that were genuinely surplus to requirements, that would be different from the situation, for example, of a person saving towards the costs of future residential care. It should be noted that the test is whether it is reasonable for the person to provide his services free of charge, rather than whether it is reasonable for payment not to be made for the service, although this is a factor (*CIS 147/1993*). If the claimant was receiving training while, or by doing, the work, this may be relevant (*R(IS) 12/92*).

In *CIS 93/1991* the Commissioner points out that the aim of the rule is clearly to prevent an employer who has the means to pay the going rate profiting at the expense of the public purse. If, therefore, a claimant volunteers to undertake painting work (as in *CIS 147/1993*), which otherwise would have remained undone, there is no element of financial profit to the employer in the claimant doing the work. If, however, the employer would have paid the claimant if he had not said he did not wish to be paid, it may be concluded that it was not reasonable for the claimant to offer his services free of charge.

The proviso also covers the situation where a person is on an employment programme or training scheme for three or more days in any benefit week and is not paid a training allowance. This may occur, for example, if the person is on a "taster" of a New Deal option (see further the notes to reg. 19(1)(q) of the JSA Regulations). The proviso ensures that a person who is on such a programme or scheme will not be treated as possessing notional earnings by virtue of providing a service for which he is not being paid. (For income support purposes this proviso will usually only be relevant to the claimant's partner rather than the claimant himself). Presumably if the programme or scheme is for less than three days, notional earnings may have to be considered but only if all the conditions for the application of para. (6) are met.

Paragraphs (7) to (8)

If notional income counts it is to be calculated as though it was actual income. Notional deductions are to be made from earnings to get a net figure.

Paragraph (9)
The examples given in para. 33666 of the *Adjudication Officer's Guide* suggest that wellington boots are not for "normal daily use", nor are special shoes needed because of a disability (as these are not worn by people in general on a daily basis).

Notional earnings of seasonal workers

43. [¹. . .].

AMENDMENT

1. Income Support (General) Amendment No. 2 Regulations 1989 (S.I. 1989 No. 1323), reg. 14 (October 9, 1989).

GENERAL NOTE

When the special rules for seasonal workers were removed from the unemployment benefit scheme this was consequently also done for income support.

Modifications in respect of children and young persons

44.—(1) Any capital of a child or young person payable by instalments which are outstanding on the first day in respect of which income support is payable or at the date of the determination of the claim, whichever is earlier, or, in the case of a review, the date of any subsequent review shall, if the aggregate of the instalments outstanding and the amount of that child's or young person's other capital calculated in accordance with Chapter VI of this Part in like manner as for the claimant [². . .] would exceed £3000, be treated as income.

(2) In the case of a child or young person who is residing at an educational establishment at which he is receiving relevant education—
   (a) any payment made to the educational establishment, in respect of that child's or young person's maintenance, by or on behalf of a person who is not a member of the family or by a member of the family out of funds contributed for that purpose by a person who is not a member of the family, shall be treated as income of that child or young person but it shall only be taken into account over periods during which that child or young person is present at that educational establishment; and
   (b) if a payment has been so made, for any period in a benefit week in term-time during which that child or young person returns home, he shall be treated as possessing an amount of income in that week calculated by multiplying the amount of personal allowance and disabled child premium, if any, applicable in respect of that child or young person by the number equal to the number of days in that week in which he was present at his educational establishment and dividing the product by seven; but this sub-paragraph shall not apply where the educational establishment is provided under section 8 of the Education Act 1944 (duty of local authority to secure primary and secondary schools) by a local education authority or where the payment is made under section 49 or 50 of the Education (Scotland) Act 1980 (power of education authority to assist persons).

(3) Where a child or young person—
   (a) is resident at an educational establishment and he is wholly or partly maintained at that establishment by a local education authority under section 8 of the Education Act 1944; or
   (b) is maintained at an educational establishment under section 49 or 50 of the Education (Scotland) Act 1980,
he shall for each day he is present at that establishment be treated as possessing

an amount of income equal to the sum obtained by dividing the amount of personal allowance and disabled child premium, if any, applicable in respect of him by seven.

(4) Where the income of a child or young person who is a member of the claimant's family calculated in accordance with [² Chapters I to V] of this Part exceeds the amount of the personal allowance and disabled child premium, if any, applicable in respect of that child or young person, the excess shall not be treated as income of the claimant.

(5) Where the capital of a child or young person if calculated in accordance with Chapter VI of this Part in like manner as for the claimant, [²except as provided in paragraph (1)], would exceed £3,000, any income of that child or young person shall not be treated as income of the claimant.

(6) In calculating the net earnings or net profit of a child or young person there shall be disregarded, (in addition to any sum which falls to be disregarded under paragraphs 11 to 13), any sum specified in paragraphs 14 and 15 of Schedule 8 (earnings to be disregarded).

(7) Any income of a child or young person which is to be disregarded under Schedule 9 (income other than earnings to be disregarded) shall be disregarded in such manner as to produce the result most favourable to the claimant.

(8) Where a child or young person is treated as possessing any income under paragraphs (2) and (3) the foregoing provisions of this Part shall apply for the purposes of calculating that income as if a payment had actually been made and as if it were actual income which he does possess.

[¹(9) For the purposes of this regulation, a child or young person shall not be treated as present at his educational establishment on any day if on that day he spends the night with the claimant or a member of his household.]

AMENDMENTS

1. Income Support (General) Amendment Regulations 1988 (S.I. 1988 No. 663), reg. 20 (April 11, 1988).
2. Income-related Benefits Schemes (Miscellaneous Amendments) (No. 4) Regulations 1993 (S.I. 1993 No. 2119), reg. 15 (October 4, 1993).

DEFINITIONS

"child"—see 1986 Act, s.20(11) (SSCBA, s.137(1)).
"claimant"—see reg. 2(1), reg. 23(1).
"family"—see 1986 Act, s.20(11) (SSCBA, s.137(1)).
"young person"—see reg. 2(1), reg. 14.

GENERAL NOTE

Paragraph (1)
See the notes to reg. 41(1) for the general test. If a child or young person has capital of more than £3,000, no personal allowance is included for him (reg. 17(b)) and his income is disregarded (para. (5)).

Paragraph (2)
If a child or young person is at a boarding school, payments made to the school for maintenance by, or from funds contributed to by, someone outside the family (as defined in s.137(1) of the Contributions and Benefits Act; 1986 Act, s.20(11)) are subject to these special rules. See para. (9).

Paragraph (3)
Children and young persons at maintained boarding schools are treated as possessing an income sufficient to wipe out their personal allowance and disabled child premium (if applicable). See para. (9).
CIS 164/1994 follows *CIS 656/1995* and confirms that children can be "resident" at a school even if they come home at half-term and during the school holidays and could do so at weekends.

The local education authority had accepted responsibility for the children's tuition and boarding fees and so they were "maintained" by the local authority within para. (3)(a), even though strictly speaking s. 8 of the Education Act 1994 was concerned with the maintenance of schools by local education authorities, not children in schools. The claimant's appeal against this decision was dismissed by the Court of Appeal (*Barton v. Chief Adjudication Officer and Secretary of State for Social Security*, May 16, 1996, to be reported as *R(IS) 11/96*).

Paragraph (4)
If a child's or young person's income exceeds his personal allowance, plus any disabled child premium, the excess is disregarded.

Paragraph (5)
If a child or young person has capital over £3,000, their income does not count as the claimant's. There is no personal allowance for the child or young person, but the rest of the family's benefit is not affected by that person's income.

Paragraph (6)
This paragraph brings in the disregard of the earnings of most children and young persons.

Paragraph (7)
The disregards in Sched.9 are to be applied in the most favourable way.

Paragraph (8)
Income under paras. (2) and (3) is to be calculated as if it was actual income.

Chapter VI

Capital

Capital limit

[¹**45.** For the purposes of section 134(1) of the Contributions and Benefits Act as it applies to income support (no entitlement to benefit if capital exceeds prescribed amount)—
  (a) except where paragraph (b) applies, the prescribed amount is £8,000;
  (b) where the circumstances prescribed in regulation 53(1B) apply in the claimant's case, the prescribed amount is £16,000.]

AMENDMENT

1. Income-related Benefits Schemes (Miscellaneous Amendments) Regulations 1996 (S.I. 1996 No. 462), reg. 12(1) (April 8, 1996).

DEFINITION

"claimant"—see reg. 2(1), reg. 23(1).

GENERAL NOTE

Under s.134(1) of the Contributions and Benefits Act there is no entitlement to income support if the claimant's capital exceeds the prescribed amount. £8,000 has been prescribed since April 9, 1990 and this remains the same for most claimants. However, from April 8, 1996 the upper limit is raised to £16,000 for claimants living permanently in residential care or nursing homes (including those with preserved rights), residential accommodation or Polish resettlement homes (para. (b)). In addition, the tariff income rule only applies to capital over £10,000 for these claimants. See the notes to reg. 53. The capital of a claimant's partner is aggregated with the claimant's (reg. 23(1)), but not that of children or young persons (reg. 47).

In *CIS 127/1993* the Commissioner raises the question of where the burden of proof lies when considering whether the capital rule is satisfied. The Tribunal of Commissioners in *CIS 417/1992* (to be reported as *R(IS) 5/98*) treat this as part of what the claimant has to prove in showing entitlement to income support. However, the argument that the capital rule operates as an exception to the conditions of basic entitlement does not appear to have been put. See sidenote to s.134 which is entitled "Exclusions from benefit". But once it has been shown that the claimant possesses an item of capital, it is for him to prove that one of the disregards in Sched. 10 applies (*CIS 240/1992*). Similarly, once it has been established that the claimant is the legal owner of a property, the burden is on her to show that she does not have any or all of the beneficial interest (*CIS 30/1993*).

Calculation of capital

46.—(1) For the purposes of Part II of the Act [SSCBA, Part VII] as it applies to income support, the capital of a claimant to be taken into account shall, subject to paragraph (2), be the whole of his capital calculated in accordance with this Part and any income treated as capital under [¹regulation 48 (income treated as capital)].

(2) There shall be disregarded from the calculation of a claimant's capital under paragraph (1) any capital, where applicable, specified in Schedule 10.

AMENDMENT

1. Income Support (General) Amendment No. 5 Regulations 1988 (S.I. 1988 No. 2022), reg. 10 (December 12, 1988).

DEFINITIONS

"the Act"—see reg. 2(1).
"claimant"—*ibid.*, reg. 23(1).

GENERAL NOTE

All the claimant's (and partner's) capital, both actual and notional, counts towards the £8,000 (or £16,000: see reg. 45(b)) limit, subject to the disregards in Sched.10. In *CIS 600/1995* the Commissioner considers that claimants should be advised by the Benefits Agency of the existence of the disregards so that they can take advantage of them (the claimant had received a criminal injuries compensation award so that the trust disregard in para. 12 of Sched. 10 could be relevant).

There is a good deal of law on actual capital.

The first condition is of course that the capital resource is the claimant's or his partner's. This is not as simple as it sounds. In *CIS 634/1992* the claimant was made bankrupt on November 29, 1990. However, his trustee in bankruptcy was not appointed until April 1991. Between November 29 and December 28, 1990, when he claimed income support the claimant divested himself of most of his capital. Under the Insolvency Act 1986 (subject to certain exceptions) a bankrupt's property does not vest in his trustee in bankruptcy on the making of a bankruptcy order, but only when the trustee is appointed. The appointment does not have retrospective effect. It is held that since he had failed to give a satisfactory account of how he had disposed of his capital he was to be treated as still possessing it (*R(SB) 38/85* referred to in the notes to reg. 51(1)). Thus the claimant was not entitled to income support prior to the appointment of the trustee in bankruptcy because until then he possessed actual capital over the income support limit.

Note that money that a claimant is under a "certain and immediate liability" to repay will not count as his capital (see *Chief Adjudication Officer v. Leeves*, November 6, 1998, CA, to be reported as *R(IS) 5/99*, below).

Beneficial ownership
The mere fact that an asset or a bank or building society account is in the claimant's name alone does not mean that it belongs to the claimant. It is the "beneficial ownership" which matters. The claimant may hold the asset under a trust which means that he cannot simply treat the asset as his, but must treat it as if it belonged to the beneficiary or beneficiaries under the trust. It is they who are "beneficially entitled." A trustee may also be a beneficiary, in which case the rule in reg. 52 may come into play, or may have no beneficial interest at all.

An example of the first situation is *R(IS) 2/93*. The claimant had a building society account in her sole name, which she had had since before her marriage. Her husband deposited the bulk of the money in it, including his salary. On their separation, the AO and the SSAT treated the entire amount in the account as part of the claimant's capital. The Commissioner holds that she was not solely beneficially entitled to the money so that reg. 52 had to operate. There is helpful guidance on the limited circumstances in which the "presumption of advancement" (*i.e.* that when a husband puts an asset into his wife's name he intends to make an outright gift of it) will operate in modern circumstances. In *CIS 553/1991* where a house was in the husband's sole name it is held that its valuation should take into account the wife's statutory right of occupation under the Matrimonial Homes Act 1967. See also *CIS 461/1994*, to be reported as *R(IS) 1/97*, in the note to para. 5 of Sched. 10. In most cases of spouses, in whoever's name the asset is, there will be some degree of joint ownership. But if an asset is in the sole name of one, arguably the other should not be treated as having a half share under reg. 52 until it has been established that s/he does own at least part of it.

There have been several examples of the second situation, where the claimant has no beneficial interest at all. In *R(SB) 49/83* the claimant had bought a house, but said that this was on behalf of his son, who was paying off the loan. The Commissioner held that if this could be established, the claimant would hold the house on a resulting trust for his son. It would not then be part of his capital resources. See *CSB 200/1985* (applying *Cowcher v. Cowcher* [1972] 1 W. L. R. 425) for the position where another person provides part of the money. In *R(SB) 53/83* the claimant's son had paid him £2,850 to be used for a holiday in India. The claimant died without taking the holiday or declaring the existence of the money to the DHSS. The Commissioner, applying the principle of *Barclays Bank Ltd. v. Quistclose Investments Ltd.* [1970] A. C. 567, held that there was a trust to return the money to the son if the primary purpose of the loan was not carried out. Since the Commissioner held that there had been no overpayment while the claimant was alive, this must mean that the claimant held the money on trust to use it for the specified purpose or to return it. It was not part of the claimant's resources. This is an important decision, which overtakes some of the reasoning of *R(SB) 14/81* (see below). The actual decision in *R(SB) 53/83* was reversed (by consent) by the Court of Appeal, because the Commissioner had differed from the appeal tribunal on a point of pure fact. *R(SB) 1/85* holds that this does not affect its authority on the issue of principle. In *R(SB) 1/85*, the claimant's mother-in-law had some years previously provided the money for the purchase of the lease of a holiday chalet for the use of the claimant's mentally handicapped son, Keith. The lease was in the claimant's name and its current value was probably about £5,000. The AO's initial statement of the facts was that the mother-in-law had bought the chalet in the claimant's name. The Commissioner holds that this would give rise to a presumption of a resulting trust in her favour, so that the claimant would have no beneficial interest in the chalet—nothing he could sell. The presumption could be rebutted if in fact the mother-in-law had made an outright gift to the claimant, or to Keith. In the second case the claimant again would have no beneficial interest. In the first, he would be caught, for even if he had said that he intended to use the chalet purely for Keith, he had not made the necessary written declaration of trust (Law of Property Act 1925, s.53). Another possibility was that the mother-in-law had made a gift to the claimant subject to an express (but unwritten) trust in favour of Keith, when again the claimant clearly would not be the beneficial owner. This is a very instructive decision, which will give valuable guidance in sorting out many family-type arrangements. *CIS 30/1993* also sets out helpful guidance on the points to consider when deciding whether a resulting trust has been created. The claimant had purchased her flat with the proceeds of sale of her previous home. She had bought that home as a sitting tenant with the aid of a loan, the repayments on which had been made by her children. The Commissioner states that the children's contributions indicated a resulting trust in their favour in the beneficial interest in the house in proportion to their and the claimant's contributions to the purchase price. If the claimant had, as a sitting tenant, received a discount on the price, that would be treated as a contribution. The resulting trust would transfer to the flat on the sale of the house. However, the presumption of a resulting trust created by the children's contributions could be rebutted by proof of the purchasers' true intentions, *e.g.* that an outright gift was, or different beneficial interests under the trust than those created by the presumption were, intended.

The *Quistclose* principle was re-affirmed in *R(SB) 12/86*, where £2,000 was lent to the claimant on condition that she did not touch the capital amount, but only took the interest, and repaid the £2,000 on demand. The £2,000 was not part of her capital, never having been at her disposal. The Commissioner in *CSB 975/1985* was prepared to apply the principle to a loan on mortgage from a Building Society for property renovation. But it would have to be found that the loan was made for no other purpose and was to be recoverable by the Building Society if for any reason the renovations could not be carried out. However, *CIS 5185/1995* decides that it does not apply to a student grant which the claimant became liable to repay to the education authority when he left his course early (for the treatment of student grants in these circumstances now see reg. 29(2B) but note the argument discussed in the notes to reg. 29(2B) as to when that provision applies). The Commissioner holds that the grant was income that remained available to him until it was repaid to the authority (see *R v. Bolton SBAT, ex parte Fordham* [1981] 1 All E.R. 50 and *CSB 1408/1988*). It could not be disregarded under the *Quistclose* principle because the education authority

232

retained no beneficial interest in the grant. The authority merely reserved the right to demand repayment of a sum calculated according to the unexpired balance of the relevant term when the person ceased to be a student. But in *CIS 12263/1996* the Commissioner took the view that as soon as a student had abandoned his course and an obligation to repay the balance of his grant to the education authority arose, he held the money on constructive trust for the authority. The Commissioner in *CIS 12263/1996* considered that the *Quistclose* case was concerned with a "purpose trust" (*i.e.* where a grant or loan was impressed with a particular purpose from the beginning), whereas in this situation a constructive trust had arisen because the grant been paid on the condition that the claimant continued to be a student. An appeal was brought against this decision by the AO (*Chief Adjudication Officer v. Leeves*, November 6, 1998, CA, to be reported as *R(IS) 5/99*). It was conceded on behalf of the claimant that there was no constructive trust in these circumstances, since no proprietary right had been retained by the education authority, nor had any fiduciary obligation been created. However, the Court of Appeal held that money that the claimant was under a "certain and immediate liability" to repay did not amount to income. Thus once the claimant had received a request for immediate repayment of a specified sum from the local education authority the grant ceased to count as his income (although it fell to be treated as such until that time, even though he had abandoned his course). The Court distinguished its decision in *Fordham* as the liability to repay in that case had been uncertain. The same principle will apply to capital that the claimant is under an obligation to repay. Once the liability to repay has "crystallised" (*Leeves*), it will cease to be part of the claimant's resources.

The dangers and difficulties of *Quistclose* are further pointed out in *CSB 1137/1985*, particularly where family transactions are concerned. If a gift or loan is made with a particular motive, the whole sum becomes part of the recipient's resources. The intention to impose a trust must appear expressly (as in *R(SB) 12/86*) or by implication from the circumstances. Perhaps it is easier to prove (*e.g.* by contemporaneous documents) such an intention in business transactions. Often such evidence will be lacking in domestic situations, but the issue is one of proof, as is shown in *R(IS) 1/ 90*. There, the claimant established a Building Society account in his own name which was to be used solely to finance his son's medical education. He executed no documents about the account. It was argued that there was sufficient evidence of a declaration of trust over the account, but the Commissioner holds that the claimant had not unequivocally renounced his beneficial interest in the sum in the account. Although he had earmarked the money for the son's education, the situation was like an uncompleted gift and there was insufficient evidence of a declaration of trust. There is a thin line between an outright gift or loan, and one subject to an implied trust. In *CIS 69/1994* where the claimant had transferred her flat to her daughter partly on the condition that her daughter looked after her, it is held that the gift failed when this condition was not fulfilled and the daughter held the flat on trust for her mother. An appeal against this decision was dismissed by the Court of Appeal (*Ellis v. Chief Adjudication Officer, The Times*, May 14, 1997). The claimant had argued that the condition was void for uncertainty but this was rejected by the Court.

The furthest extension so far of the *Quistclose* principle is in *CFC 21/1989*. The claimant's father paid her each month an amount to meet her mortgage obligation to a building society. The Commissioner accepts that the money was impressed with a trust that it should be used only for that purpose and did not form part of her capital. The extension is that the purpose was to meet expenditure on an item which could be covered by income support.

For the position under Scots law see *CSIS 701/1997*. The claimant agreed that he would pay his former wife (from whom he was separated) £22,250, representing a share of his pension. When he claimed income support, the claimant had £15,500 in his bank account which he said he was holding for his wife. The Commissioner decides that the £15,500 was not subject to a trust. This was because there had been no delivery of the subject of the trust, nor any satisfactory equivalent to delivery, "so as to achieve irrevocable divestiture of the truster and investiture of the trustee in the trust estate", as required by Scots law (see *Clark Taylor & Co. Ltd v. Quality Site Development (Edinburgh) Ltd.* 1981 S.C. 11). There was no separate bank account and had been no clear indication to the claimant's wife that the money was held on trust for her. In addition, the Requirements of Writing (Scotland) Act 1995 required the trust to be proved in writing and the signature of the grantor. This had not been done here. The Commissioner also decided that the money could not be regarded as matrimonial property for the purposes of the Family Law (Scotland) Act 1995, since the claimant's severance package (which was being used to pay his wife) only came into existence after the parties ceased to cohabit and thus did not satisfy the definition of matrimonial property in s.10(3) and (4) of the Act. It was also clear that the claimant was not holding the sum as his wife's agent as there was no evidence of her consent to this. Finally, there was no "incumbrance" within the meaning of reg. 49(a)(ii) preventing the claimant disposing of the money. The consequence was that the £15,500 counted as the claimant's capital. (*Note*: as (1999) 6 *J.S.S.L.* D41 points out, the outcome of this case is in fact unlikely to have been different if the principles of trust law in England

and Wales had been applied. However, capital that a claimant is under a "certain and immediate liability" to repay will not count as his capital (see *Leeves* above).)

See also the doctrine of secret trusts, under which a person who receives property under an intestacy when the deceased refrained from making a will in reliance on that person's promise to carry out his expressed intentions, holds the property on trust to carry out those intentions *(CSB 989/1985)*.

Another example of the legal owner having nothing to sell is *R(SB) 23/85*. The claimant's wife in a home-made and legally ineffective deed of gift purported to give an uninhabitable property to her son. He, as intended, carried out the works to make it habitable. The Commissioner holds that although a court will not normally "complete" such an "uncompleted gift" in favour of someone who has not given valuable consideration, one of the situations in which a transfer of the property will be ordered is where the intended recipient is induced to believe that he has or will have an interest in the property and acts on that belief to his detriment. Thus in the meantime the claimant's wife held the property merely as a "bare trustee" and could not lawfully transfer it to anyone but the son. There is discussion of what kind of action might give rise to the right to complete the gift in *R(SB) 7/87*. See also *CIS 807/1991* on proprietary estoppel.

Choses in action

There is also a remarkable range of interests in property which do have a present market value and so are actual capital resources. These are usually things in action (or choses in action), rights to sue for something. Debts, even where they are not due to be paid for some time, are things in action which can be sold. A good example is *R(SB) 31/83* where the claimant in selling a house allowed the purchaser a mortgage of £4,000, to be redeemed in six months. The debt conferred a right to sue and had to be valued at what could be obtained on the open market. Similarly, a life interest in a trust fund is a present asset which can be sold and has a market value *(R(SB) 2/84, R(SB) 43/84, R(SB) 15/86 and R(SB) 13/87)*. The practical effect is reversed by para. 13 of Sched. 10. An action for breach of fiduciary duty against an attorney appointed under the Enduring Powers of Attorney Act 1985 who had used the claimant's capital to repay her own debts also constitutes actual capital; so too would a claim against the attorney for misapplication of capital on the ground that she had made gifts outside the circumstances sanctioned by s. 3(5) of the 1985 Act (this allows an attorney to make gifts (to herself or others) "provided that the value of each such gift is not unreasonable having regard to all the circumstances and in particular the size of the donor's estate") *(CIS 12403/1996)*.

Bank or building society accounts

A more direct way of holding capital is in a bank or building society account. In *CSB 296/1985* the claimant's solicitor received £12,000 damages on behalf of the claimant and placed the money on deposit, presumably in the solicitor's client account. The Commissioner held that the £12,000 was an actual resource of the claimant, on the basis that there was no difference in principle between monies being held by a solicitor on behalf of a client and monies held by a bank or building society on behalf of a customer. This decision was upheld by the Court of Appeal in *Thomas v. Chief Adjudication Officer* (reported as *R(SB) 17/87*). Russell L. J. says "the possession of this money by the solicitors as the agent for the claimant was, in every sense of the term, possession by the claimant." This seems to involve valuing the amount of money directly, not as a technical chose in action. However, the importance of the legal relationship between a bank and a customer being one of debtor and creditor was revealed in *CSB 598/1987*. A large cheque was paid into the claimant's wife's bank account on October 9, 1987. The amount was credited to her account on that date, but the cheque was not cleared until October 15. The bank's paying-in slips reserved the bank's right to "postpone payment of cheques drawn against uncleared effects which may have been credited to the account." The effect was that the bank did not accept the relationship of debtor and creditor on the mere paying in of a cheque. Thus the amount did not become part of the claimant's actual resources until October 15. A person who deliberately refrains from paying in a cheque may be fixed with notional capital under reg. 51.

In *CIS 600/1995* the Commissioner confirms that money in a building society or bank (or solicitor's client) account is an actual resource in the form of a chose in action. It is not, as the SSAT had decided, held in trust. If the money is in an account from which it can be withdrawn at any time, its value is the credit balance (less any penalties for early withdrawal, etc.). But if the money cannot be withdrawn for a specified term the value will be less (although the notional capital rules may come into play in respect of the difference in value: *CIS 494/1990*).

Interests in trusts

The nature of interests in capital under trusts gives rise to several problems. It is clear that a person may have an absolute vested interest under a trust, although payment is deferred, *e.g.* until the age of 21. This was the case in *R(SB) 26/86*, where the resource was held to be the person's share of the fund. However, an interest may be contingent on reaching a particular age. This appears to have been one of the assumptions on which the Court of Appeal decided the unsatisfactory case of *Peters v. Chief Adjudication Officer, R(SB) 3/89*. It was conceded that sums were held on trust to be paid over to each of three sisters on attaining the age of 18, with the power to advance up to 50 per cent. of the capital before then. In the end, the Court of Appeal accepted the valuation of half of the full value for each sister under 18. The precise finding may depend on the supplementary benefit rule on discretionary trusts, which has not been translated into the income support legislation. But some statements about the general market value of such interests are made. May L. J. says "in an appropriate market a discretionary entitlement of up to 50 per cent. now and at least 50 per cent. in, say, six months in a given case, or three to four years in another, could well be said to have a value greater than 50 per cent. of the capital value of the trust."

This clearly supports the view that a contingent interest has a market value and so is actual capital. Although often a potential benefit under a discretionary trust will have no market value, a discretion to advance capital before the contingency happens may affect the value of the contingent interest. In some circumstances also a purely discretionary trust may produce a capital asset, as where the claimant is the only real beneficiary under a "spendthrift" trust (*R(SB) 25/83*, especially para. 18). In the family law context, the courts are prepared to look at the realities of what a person is likely to receive under a discretionary trust in assessing financial resources under s.25 of the Matrimonial Causes Act 1973 (*Browne v. Browne* [1989] 1 F.L.R. 291 and *J. v. J. (C. intervening)* [1989] 1 F. L. R. 453). The income support law is not so flexible, but it is certain that all interests which can be sold or borrowed against should be considered.

Realisation of assets

R(SB) 18/83 stresses that there are more ways of realising assets than sale. In particular, assets can be charged to secure a loan which can be used to meet requirements. In that case the asset was a minority shareholding in a family company. The Commissioner says that only a person prepared to lend money without security would do so in such circumstances. The articles of association of the company provided that if a shareholder wanted to sell shares they were to be offered to the existing shareholders at the fair value fixed by the auditors. The Commissioner holds that the regulations do not require assets to be valued at a figure higher than anything the person would realise on them, *i.e.* the auditor's fair value. This is in line with the purpose of the capital cut-off that a claimant can draw on resources until they fall below the limit.

This approach to valuation can usefully deal with unrealisable assets. See the notes to reg. 49. However, it is no part of the definition of capital that it should be immediately realisable, although its market value may be affected by such factors. It thus remains possible (especially in circumstances like those imposed by reg. 52 below) for a claimant to be fixed with a large amount of capital which is not available to him. If this takes the claimant over the £8,000 (or £16,000: see reg. 45(b)) limit, a crisis loan may be appropriate while the claimant attempts to realise the asset or raise a commercial loan (*Social Fund Guide*, para. 4717–8).

Deduction of liabilities

The general rule is that the whole of a capital resource is to be taken into account. Liabilities are not to be deducted from the value (*R(SB) 2/83*). Otherwise, it is only if a debt is secured on the capital asset that it can be deducted, at the stage specifically required by reg. 49 or 50 (*R(IS) 21/93*). See the notes to reg. 49.

Disregard of capital of child or young person

47. The capital of a child or young person who is a member of the claimant's family shall not be treated as capital of the claimant.

Definitions

"child"—see 1986 Act, s.20(11) (SSCBA, s.137(1)).
"claimant"—see reg. 2(1), reg. 23(1).
"family"—see 1986 Act, s.20(11) (SSCBA, s.137(1)).
"young person"—see reg. 2(1), reg. 14.

The capital of a child or young person is not aggregated with the claimant's. But if that person's capital is over £3,000 there is no personal allowance for that person (reg. 17(b)) and any income is not aggregated with the claimant's either (reg. 44(5)).

Income treated as capital

48.—(1) Any [². . .] bounty derived from employment to which paragraph 7 of Schedule 8 applies [²and paid at intervals of at least one year] shall be treated as capital.

(2) Except in the case of an amount to which section 23(5)(a)(ii) of the Act [SSCBA, s.126(5)(a)(ii)] (refund of tax in trade disputes cases) [²or regulation 41(4) (capital treated as income)] applies, any amount by way of a refund of income tax deducted from profits or emoluments chargeable to income tax under Schedule D or E shall be treated as capital.

(3) Any holiday pay which is not earnings under regulation 35(1)(d) (earnings of employed earners) shall be treated as capital.

(4) Except any income derived from capital disregarded under paragraph 1, 2, 4, 6, [³12 or 25 to 28] of Schedule 10, any income derived from capital shall be treated as capital but only from the date it is normally due to be credited to the claimant's account.

(5) Subject to paragraph (6), in the case of employment as an employed earner, any advance of earnings or any loan made by the claimant's employer shall be treated as capital.

[¹(6) Paragraph (5) shall not apply to a person to whom section 23 of the Act [SSCBA, s.126] (trade disputes) applies or in respect of whom section 20(3) of the Act [SSCBA, s.124(1)] (conditions of entitlement to income support) has effect as modified by section 23A(b) [SSCBA, s.127(*b*)] (effect of return to work).]

(7) Any payment under section 30 of the Prison Act 1952 (payments for discharged prisoners) or allowance under section 17 of the Prisons (Scotland) Act 1952 (allowances to prisoners on discharge) shall be treated as capital.

[¹¹(8) Any payment made by a local authority, which represents arrears of payments under—

(a) paragraph 15 of Schedule 1 to the Children Act 1989 (power of a local authority to make contributions to a person with whom a child lives as a result of a residence order); or

(b) section 34(6) or as the case may be, section 50 of the Children Act 1975 (payments towards maintenance for children),

shall be treated as capital.

(8A) Any payment made by an authority, as defined in Article 2 of the Children Order which represents arrears of payments under Article 15 of, and paragraph 17 of Schedule 1 to, that Order (contribution by an authority to child's maintenance), shall be treated as capital.]

[³(9) Any charitable or voluntary payment which is not made or not due to be made at regular intervals, other than one to which paragraph (10) applies, shall be treated as capital.

(10) This paragraph applies to a payment—

(a) which is made to a person to whom section 23 of the Act [SSCBA, s.126] (trade disputes) applies or in respect of whom section 20(3) of the Act [SSCBA, s.124(1)] (conditions of entitlement to income support) has effect as modified by section 23A(b) of the Act [SSCBA, s.127(b)] (effect of return to work) or to a member of the family of such a person;

(b) to which regulation 44(2) (modification in respect of children and young persons) applies; or

(c) which is made under the Macfarlane Trust[⁵, or the Macfarlane (Special Payments) Trust][⁶, the Macfarlane (Special Payments) (No. 2) Trust] [⁸, the Fund][¹⁰, the Eileen Trust] or [⁹ the Independent Living Funds].]

[⁴(11) Any compensation within the meaning of regulation 35(3) (earnings of employed earners) which is made in respect of employment which is not part-time employment within the meaning of that regulation, to the extent that it is not earnings by virtue of regulation 35(1)(i)(i) shall be treated as capital.]

AMENDMENTS

1. Income Support (General) Amendment Regulations 1988 (S.I. 1988 No. 663), reg. 21 (April 11, 1988).
2. Income Support (General) Amendment No. 4 Regulations 1988 (S.I. 1988 No. 1445), reg. 11 (September 12, 1988).
3. Income Support (General) Amendment No. 5 Regulations 1988 (S.I. 1988 No. 2022), reg. 11 (December 12, 1988).
4. Income Support (General) Amendment No. 2 Regulations 1989 (S.I. 1989 No. 1323), reg. 15 (October 9, 1989).
5. Income-related Benefits Schemes Amendment Regulations 1990 (S.I. 1990 No. 127), reg. 33 (January 31, 1990).
6. Income-related Benefits Schemes and Social Security (Recoupment) Amendment Regulations 1991 (S.I. 1991 No. 1175), reg. 5 (May 11, 1991).
7. Income Support (General) Amendment Regulations 1992 (S.I. 1992 No. 468), Sched., para. 5 (April 6, 1992).
8. Income-related Benefits Schemes and Social Security (Recoupment) Amendment Regulations 1992 (S.I. 1992 No. 1101), reg. 6 (May 7, 1992).
9. Social Security Benefits (Miscellaneous Amendments) (No. 2) Regulations 1993 (S.I. 1993 No. 963), reg. 2(3) (April 22, 1993).
10. Income-related Benefits Schemes and Social Security (Recoupment) Amendment Regulations 1993 (S.I. 1993 No. 1249), reg. 4(3) (May 14, 1993).
11. Social Security (Miscellaneous Amendments) Regulations 1998 (S.I. 1998 No. 563), reg. 14(1) (April 6, 1998).

DEFINITIONS

"the Act"—see reg. 2(1).
"child"—see 1986 Act, s.20(11) (SSCBA, s.137(1)).
"the Children Order"—see reg. 2(1).
"claimant"—see 1986 Act, s.20(11), (SSCBA, s.137(1)), reg. 23(1).
"employed earner"—see reg. 2(1).
"family"—see 1986 Act, s.20(11) (SSCBA, s.137(1)).
"local authority"—see 1986 Act, s.84(1).
"the Eileen Trust"—see reg. 2(1).
"the Fund"—*ibid.*
"the Independent Living Funds"—*ibid.*
"the Macfarlane (Special Payments) Trust"—*ibid.*
"the Macfarlane (Special Payments) (No. 2) Trust"—*ibid.*
"the Macfarlane Trust"—*ibid.*

GENERAL NOTE

Most of these categories deemed to be capital are self-explanatory. They are then disregarded as income (Sched. 9, para. 32).

Paragraph (4)
The general rule is that the income from capital is not to be treated as income, but is added to the capital when it is credited. The excepted cases are premises and business assets plus trusts of personal injury compensation. Note that paras. 44 and 45 of Sched. 10 have not been added to the list of excepted cases. Thus payments to a claimant from funds held in court that derive from damages for personal injury or compensation for the death of a parent will count as capital, whatever the nature of those payments. The words "income derived from capital" would seem wide enough

237

to cover payments of income that are made to the claimant from such funds. Such payments may also fall under para. 12 of Sched. 10 (see *CIS 368/1994* in the note to para. 12). But in such a case, following *CIS 563/1991* (see below), the disregard in para. 44 or 45 should take precedence and the payments count as capital. Thus if the payments do not take the claimant's capital over £3,000 (£10,000 for claimants permanently in residential care), they should not affect the claimant's income support.

The income must be derived from some capital asset of the claimant (*CIS 25/1989*). A twelve month assured shorthold tenancy is not a capital asset and income from the subletting of rooms is not "derived from" the tenancy (*CIS 82/1993*).

The income covered by this provision is disregarded as income (Sched. 9, para. 22), but remember that capital over £3,000 (or £10,000 for claimants permanently in residential care) is deemed to produce a tariff income under reg. 53.

In *CIS 563/1991* the Commissioner considers that the effect of para. (4) is to treat a payment of income as capital for the same length of time as it would have been taken into account as income. So, for example, a payment of a month's rent from a property let out to tenants counts as capital for a month from the date that the claimant is due to receive it. After that, reg. 48(4) ceases to have effect. Money spent during that month cannot form part of the claimant's actual capital at the end of the month (subject to the possible effect of the notional capital rule in reg. 51(1)). Although saved-up income only metamorphoses into capital after deducting all relevant debts (see the notes to reg. 23), the Commissioner considers that where para. (4) has effected a statutory metamorphosis, any unspent money at the end of the period covered by para. (4) continues to count as capital; it does not change into income and then immediately back into capital. Thus any outstanding debts will only reduce the amount of the capital if they are secured on the capital itself (reg. 49(a)(ii)). *CIS 563/1991* also deals with the situation where more than one disregard in Sched. 10 could apply. If a property was disregarded under para. 26 (taking steps to dispose of premises) the rental income from it would count as income and would only be ignored to the extent allowed for by para. 22(2) of Sched. 9. But if the property was let by the claimant and the para. 5 disregard also applied (as was possible under the form of para. 5 in force before October 2, 1995: see the 1995 edition of this work) the rental income would count as capital. The Commissioner concludes that considering reg. 48(4) and para. 22 of Sched. 9 together, the primary rule was that income derived from capital was to be treated as capital. The disregard in para. 5 therefore took precedence, and the rental income counted as capital, even during periods when the property could also be disregarded under one or more of the provisions listed in para. 22 and para. (4). Note that under the new form of para. 5 a property let to tenants by the claimant is no longer disregarded (see the note to para. 5); the rent will still generally count as capital under the normal rule in para. (4) (unless one of the exceptions applies).

Paragraphs (8) and (8A)

These paragraphs provide that arrears of payments made by local authorities in Great Britain (para. (8)) and authorities in Northern Ireland (para. (8A)) towards the maintenance of children are treated as capital. Current payments above the level of the personal allowance applicable for the child plus any disabled child premium are ignored as income (para. 25(1)(b)–(d) of Sched. 9).

Paragraphs (9) and (10)

Regs. 24 and 33 on charitable or voluntary payments were revoked from December 1988. See the notes to para. 15 of Sched. 9 for the meaning of "charitable" and "voluntary." The general rule in para. (9) is that such payments not made or due to be made at regular intervals are to be treated as capital. This rule does not apply to the three kinds of payments set out in para. (10). However, there is nothing to say how such payments are to be treated. Presumably they must be treated as capital or income according to general legal principles (on which see the notes to reg. 23). Similarly, there is nothing expressly to say how payments which are made or due to be made regularly are to be treated, but no doubt they will usually have the character of income.

Paragraph (11)

The elements of compensation on the termination of full-time employment which do not count as earnings under reg. 35(1)(i) are payments of less than the "maximum weekly amount" and "deductible remainders" (see notes to reg. 35).

Calculation of capital in the United Kingdom

49. Capital which a claimant possesses in the United Kingdom shall be calculated—

(a) except in a case to which sub-paragraph (b) applies, at its current market or surrender value, less —
   (i) where there would be expenses attributable to sale, 10 per cent.; and
   (ii) the amount of any incumbrance secured on it;
(b) in the case of a National Savings Certificate—
   (i) if purchased from an issue the sale of which ceased before 1st July last preceding the first day on which income support is payable or the date of the determination of the claim, whichever is the earlier, or in the case of a review, the date of any subsequent review, at the price which it would have realised on that 1st July had it been purchased on the last day of that issue;
   (ii) in any other case, at its purchase price.

DEFINITION

"claimant"—see reg. 2(1), reg. 23(1).

GENERAL NOTE

The general rule is that the market value of the asset is to be taken. The surrender value will be taken if appropriate (although the surrender value of life insurance policies and of annuities is totally disregarded (Sched. 10, paras. 15 and 11)). The value at this stage does not take account of any incumbrances secured on the assets, since those come in under para. (a)(ii) (*R(IS) 21/93*). In *R(SB) 57/83* and *R(SB) 6/84* the test taken is the price that would be commanded between a willing buyer and a willing seller at a particular date. In *R(SB) 6/84* it is stressed that in the case of a house it is vital to know the nature and extent of the interest being valued. Also, since what is required is a current market value, the Commissioner holds that an estate agent's figure for a quick sale was closer to the proper approach than the District Valuer's figure for a sale within three months. All the circumstances must be taken into account in making the valuation. In *CIS 553/1991* it is held that in valuing a former matrimonial home the wife's statutory right of occupation under the Matrimonial Homes Act 1967 has to be taken into account. Similarly, if personal possessions are being valued, it is what the possessions could be sold for which counts, not simply what was paid for them (*CIS 494/1990*). Sometimes a detailed valuation is not necessary, such as where the value of an asset is on any basis clearly over the £8,000 (or £16,000: see reg. 45(b)) limit (*CSIS 40/1989*).

It is accepted that the test of the willing buyer and the willing seller is the starting point for the valuation of shares (*R(SB) 57/83*, *R(SB) 12/89* and *R(IS) 2/90*). The latter case emphasises that in the income support context the value must be determined on the basis of a very quick sale, so that the hypothetical willing seller would be at a corresponding disadvantage. In the case of private companies there is often a provision in the articles of association that a shareholder wishing to sell must first offer the shares to other shareholders at a "fair value" fixed by the auditors (this was the case in *R(SB) 18/83* and *R(IS) 2/90*). Then the value of the shares ought not to be higher than the fair value, but for income support purposes may well be less. The possible complications are set out in *CSB 488/1982* (quoted with approval in *R(SB) 12/89* and *R(IS) 2/90*). In *R(IS) 8/92* it is suggested that the market value is what a purchaser would pay for the shares subject to the same restriction. Whether the shareholding gives a minority, equal or controlling interest is particularly significant. All the circumstances of the share structure of the company must be considered. For instance, in *R(SB) 12/89* shares could only be sold with the consent of the directors, which it was indicated would not be forthcoming. It seems to be agreed that valuation according to Inland Revenue methods is not appropriate (*R(SB) 18/83* and *R(IS) 2/90*), although it is suggested in *R(SB) 12/89* that the Inland Revenue Shares Valuation Division might be able to assist SSATs. It is not known if this is so. What is absolutely clear is that the total value of the company's shareholding cannot simply be divided in proportion to the claimant's holding *(R(SB) 18/83)*. However, in the case of shares in companies quoted on the London Stock Exchange the Inland Revenue method of valuation should be used (*R(IS) 18/95*). This involves looking at all the transactions relating to the relevant share during the previous day, taking the lowest figure and adding to this a quarter of the difference between the lowest and the highest figure. The Commissioner considered that AOs could use the valuation quoted in newspapers (which is the mean between the best bid and best offer price at the close of business the previous day) to obtain approximate valuations. However, where a completely accurate valuation was essential, the Inland Revenue method would need to be adopted.

The proper approach to valuation can usefully deal with unrealisable assets. Sometimes their market value will be nil (*e.g.* a potential interest under a discretionary trust: *R(SB) 25/83)*; sometimes it will be very heavily discounted. However, if the asset will be realisable after a time, it may have a current value. The claimant may be able to sell an option to purchase the asset in the future (see *R(IS) 8/92)* or borrow, using the asset as security. But the valuation must reflect the fact that the asset is not immediately realisable. In *R(IS) 4/96* the claimant had on his divorce transferred his interest in the former matrimonial home to his wife in return for a charge on the property which could only be enforced if she died, remarried or cohabited for more than six months. The claimant's former wife was 46 and in good health. A discount had to be applied to the present day value of the charge to reflect the fact that it might not be realisable for as long as 40 years or more; consequently it was unlikely to be worth more than £3,000. It should similarly be remembered that if, exceptionally, personal possessions are being taken into account (*e.g.* they have been bought to secure benefit), their value is not what was paid for them, but what could be obtained for them if sold as second-hand (*CIS 494/1990*). As the Tribunal of Commissioners in *R(SB) 45/83* point out, the market value (in this case of an interest in an entire trust fund) must reflect the outlay the purchaser would expect to incur in obtaining transfer of the assets and the profit he would expect as an inducement to purchase. If there might be some legal difficulty in obtaining the underlying asset (as there might have been in *R(SB) 21/83* and in *CIS 654/1993* (to be reported as *R(IS) 13/95*) where shares were held in the names of the claimant's children) this must be taken into account.

The general rule is that the whole of a capital resource is to be taken into account. Liabilities are not to be deducted from the value (*R(SB) 2/83*). Otherwise, it is only where a debt is secured on the capital asset that it is deducted under para. (a)(ii). The standard case would be a house that is mortgaged. The amount of capital outstanding would be deducted from the market value of the house. In *R(SB) 14/81* (see Sched. 10, para. 8) the claimant had been lent £5,000 for work on his bungalow, which was mortgaged to secure the debt. He had £3,430 left. Although he was obliged to make monthly repayments this liability could not be deducted from the £3,430, for the debt was not secured on the money. However, the principle of *R(SB) 53/83* (see the notes to reg. 46) would make the money not part of the claimant's resources. In *R(SB) 18/83* the Commissioner says that personal property such as shares (or money) can be charged by a contract for valuable consideration (*e.g.* a loan) without any writing or the handing over of any title documents. But this is not the case in Scots law (*R(SB) 5/88*). In *R(IS) 18/95* the claimant's brokers had a lien on his shares for the cost of acquisition and their commission which fell to be offset against the value of the shares. *CIS 368/1993* concerned money held under a solicitor's undertaking. £40,000 of the proceeds of sale of the claimant's house was retained by his solicitors in pursuance of an undertaking to his bank given because of a previous charge on the property. The Commissioner decides that the undertaking was an incumbrance within para. (a)(ii). It was the equivalent of a pledge or lien and was secured on the proceeds of sale. Thus the £40,000 did not count as part of the claimant's resources. In *CIS 69/1994* the claimant transferred her flat to her daughter on the understanding that the daughter would care for her in the flat and pay off the mortgage. The daughter complied with the second condition, but evicted her mother from the flat. The Commissioner decides that the gift of the flat to the daughter had been subject to the condition that she looked after her mother. As that condition had not been fulfilled, the gift failed and the daughter held the property on trust for the claimant. In valuing the claimant's interest under para. (a), the mortgage was to be deducted because the daughter was to be treated as subrogated to the rights of the mortgagee. In addition, the costs of the litigation to recover the property from the daughter also fell to be deducted. The claimant appealed against this decision to the Court of Appeal but her appeal was dismissed (*Ellis v. Chief Adjudication Officer, The Times*, May 14, 1997).

The first deduction to be made under para. (a) is a standard 10 per cent. if there would be any expenses attributable to sale, as there almost always will be. The second is the amount of any incumbrance secured on the asset. There is particularly full and helpful guidance on the nature of incumbrances on real property and the evidence which should be examined in *R(IS) 21/93*, and see above. In *CSIS 701/1997* the Commissioner points out that the word "incumbrance" is unknown to the law of Scotland, but goes on to interpret para. (a)(ii) as meaning that there must be something attached to the capital in question that prevents the claimant from disposing of it.

Calculation of capital outside the United Kingdom

50. Capital which a claimant possesses in a country outside the United Kingdom shall be calculated—

    (a) in a case in which there is no prohibition in that country against the transfer to the United Kingdom of an amount equal to its current market or surrender value in that country, at that value;

(b) in a case where there is such a prohibition, at the price which it would realise if sold in the United Kingdom to a willing buyer,

less, where there would be expenses attributable to sale, 10 per cent. and the amount of any incumbrance secured on it.

"claimant"—see reg. 2(1), reg. 23(1).

GENERAL NOTE

There had been problems under supplementary benefit in valuing overseas assets. Now the standard rules about the deduction of 10 per cent. for sale expenses and the deduction of the amount of any incumbrance secured on the asset apply. But then there are two separate situations. Under para. (a), if there is no prohibition in the country where the asset is located against transferring to the U.K. an amount of money equal to the asset's value in that country, the market value there is the test. If there are merely restrictions or delays in transfer this does not seem to come within para. (a). If there is such a prohibition, under para. (b) the value is the market value in the U.K.

Notional capital

51.—(1) A claimant shall be treated as possessing capital of which he has deprived himself for the purpose of securing entitlement to income support or increasing the amount of that benefit [⁶ except—

(a) where that capital is derived from a payment made in consequence of any personal injury and is placed on trust for the benefit of the claimant; or

(b) to the extent that the capital which he is treated as possessing is reduced in accordance with regulation 51A (diminishing notional capital rule)] [¹⁵or

(c) any sum to which paragraph 44(a) or 45(a) of Schedule 10 (disregard of compensation for personal injuries which is administered by the Court) refers].

(2) Except in the case of—

(a) a discretionary trust;

(b) a trust derived from a payment made in consequence of a personal injury; or

(c) any loan which would be obtainable if secured against capital disregarded under Schedule 10, [¹³ or

(d) a personal pension scheme or retirement annuity contract,] [¹⁵ or

(e) any sum to which paragraph 44(a) or 45(a) of Schedule 10 (disregard of compensation for personal injuries which is administered by the Court) refers,]

any capital which would become available to the claimant upon application being made but which has not been acquired by him shall be treated as possessed by him but only from the date on which [¹ it could be expected to be acquired were an application made.]

[²(3) [¹⁷ Any payment of capital, other than a payment of capital specified in paragraph (3A)], made—

(a) to a third party in respect of a single claimant or in respect of a member of the family (but not a member of the third party's family) shall be treated—

(i) in a case where that payment is derived from a payment of any benefit under the benefit Acts, a war disablement pension [¹⁴, war widow's pension or a pension payable to a person as a widow under the Naval, Military and Air Forces Etc. (Disablement and Death)

Service Pensions Order 1983 in so far as that Order is made under the Naval and Marine Pay and Pensions Act 1865 or the Pensions and Yeomanry Pay Act 1884, or is made only under section 12(1) of the Social Security (Miscellaneous Provisions) Act 1977 and any power of Her Majesty otherwise than under an enactment to make provision about pensions for or in respect of persons who have been disabled or who have died in consequence of service as members of the armed forces of the Crown,] as possessed by that single claimant, if it is paid to him, or by that member if it is paid to any member of the family;

    (ii) in any other case, as possessed by that single claimant or by that member to the extent that it is used for the food, ordinary clothing or footwear, household fuel, rent or rates for which housing benefit is payable, [⁸. . .] any housing costs to the extent that they are met under regulation 17(1)(e) and 18(1)(f) (housing costs) or accommodation charge to the extent that it is met under regulation 19 [⁴. . .] (persons in residential care or nursing homes [³. . .] [⁴. . .]), of that single claimant or, as the case may be, of any member of that family[⁸, or is used for any [¹⁰council tax] or water charges for which that claimant or member is liable];

(b) to a single claimant or a member of the family in respect of a third party (but not in respect of another member of the family) shall be treated as possessed by that single claimant or, as the case may be, that member of the family to the extent that it is kept or used by him or used by or on behalf of any member of the family.]

[¹⁷ (3A) Paragraph (3) shall not apply in respect of a payment of capital made—

(a) under the Macfarlane Trust, the Macfarlane (Special Payments) Trust, the Macfarlane (Special Payments) (No. 2) Trust, the Fund, the Eileen Trust or the Independent Living Funds;

(b) pursuant to section 2 of the Employment and Training Act 1973 in respect of a person's participation—

    (i) in an employment programme specified in regulation 75(1)(a)(ii) of the Jobseeker's Allowance Regulations 1996;

    (ii) in a training scheme specified in regulation 75(1)(b)(ii) of those Regulations; or

    (iii) in a qualifying course within the meaning specified in regulation 17A(7) of those Regulations.]

(4) Where a claimant stands in relation to a company in a position analogous to that of a sole owner or partner in the business of that company, he shall be treated as if he were such sole owner or partner and in such a case—

(a) the value of his holding in that company shall, notwithstanding regulation 46 (calculation of capital), be disregarded; and

(b) he shall, subject to paragraph (5), be treated as possessing an amount of capital equal to the value or, as the case may be, his share of the value of the capital of that company and the foregoing provisions of this Chapter shall apply for the purposes of calculating that amount as if it were actual capital which he does possess.

(5) For so long as the claimant undertakes activities in the course of the business of the company, the amount which he is treated as possessing under paragraph (4) shall be disregarded.

(6) Where a claimant is treated as possessing capital under any of paragraphs (1) to (4), the foregoing provisions of this Chapter shall apply for the purposes of calculating its amount as if it were actual capital which he does possess.

[¹(7) For the avoidance of doubt a claimant is to be treated as possessing capital under paragraph (1) only if the capital of which he has deprived himself is actual capital.]

[²(8) In paragraph (3) the expression "ordinary clothing or footwear" means clothing or footwear for normal daily use, but does not include school uniforms, or clothing or footwear used solely for sporting activities].

AMENDMENTS

1. Income Support (General) Amendment Regulations 1988 (S.I. 1988 No. 663), reg. 22 (April 11, 1988).

2. Income Support (General) Amendment No. 4 Regulations 1988 (S.I. 1988 No. 1445), reg. 12 (September 12, 1988).

3. Income Support (General) Amendment No. 4 Regulations (S.I. 1988 No. 1445), Sched. 1, para. 4 (April 10, 1989).

4. Income Support (General) Amendment Regulations 1989 (S.I. 1989 No. 534), Sched. 1, para. 7 (October 9, 1989).

5. Income-related Benefits Schemes Amendment Regulations 1990 (S.I. 1990 No. 127), reg. 3 (January 31, 1990).

6. Income Support (General) Amendment No. 3 Regulations 1990 (S.I. 1990 No. 1776), reg. 5 (October 1, 1990).

7. Income-related Benefits Schemes and Social Security (Recoupment) Amendment Regulations 1991 (S.I. 1991 No. 1175), reg. 5 (May 11, 1991).

8. Income Support (General) Amendment No. 4 Regulations 1991 (S.I. 1991 No. 1559), reg. 8 (August 5, 1991).

9. Income-related Benefits Schemes and Social Security (Recoupment) Amendment Regulations 1992 (S.I. 1992 No. 1101), reg. 6 (May 7, 1992).

10. Income-related Benefits Schemes (Miscellaneous Amendments) Regulations 1993 (S.I. 1993 No. 315), Sched., para. 3 (April 1, 1993).

11. Social Security Benefits (Miscellaneous Amendments) (No. 2) Regulations 1993 (S.I. 1993 No. 963), reg. 2(3) (April 22, 1993).

12. Income-related Benefits Schemes and Social Security (Recoupment) Amendment Regulations 1993 (S.I. 1993 No. 1249), reg. 4(3) (May 14, 1993).

13. Income-related Benefits Schemes and Social Security (Claims and Payments) (Miscellaneous Amendments) Regulations 1995 (S.I. 1995 No. 2303), reg. 6(5) (October 2, 1995).

14. Income-related Benefits and Jobseeker's Allowance (Miscellaneous Amendments) Regulations 1997 (S.I. 1997 No. 65), reg. 9 (April 7, 1997).

15. Income-related Benefits and Jobseeker's Allowance (Amendment) (No. 2) Regulations 1997 (S.I. 1997 No. 2197), reg. 5(4) (October 6, 1997).

16. Social Security Amendment (New Deal) Regulations 1997 (S.I. 1997 No. 2863), reg. 17(5) and (6)(e) (January 5, 1998).

17. Social Security Amendment (New Deal) (No. 2) Regulations 1998 (S.I. 1998 No. 2117), reg. 3(2) and (3)(c) (September 24, 1998).

DEFINITIONS

"the benefit Acts"—see reg. 2(1).
"claimant"—see reg. 2(1), reg. 23(1).
"family"—see 1986 Act, s.20(11) (SSCBA, s.137(1)).
"personal pension scheme"—see reg. 2(1).
"retirement annuity contract"—*ibid.*
"the Eileen Trust"—*ibid.*
"the Fund"—*ibid.*
"the Independent Living Funds"—see reg. 2(1).
"the Macfarlane (Special Payments) Trust"—*ibid.*
"the Macfarlane (Special Payments) (No. 2) Trust"—*ibid.*
"the Macfarlane Trust"—*ibid.*
"water charges"—see reg. 2(1).

GENERAL NOTE

Paragraph (1)
In order for para. (1) to apply, only two elements must be proved by the AO—that the person

has deprived himself of actual capital (see para. (7)) and that his purpose was to secure entitlement to or increase the amount of income support. It is clear that the principles applied to these questions for supplementary benefit purposes are to be applied to para. (1) *(CIS 24/1988, CIS 40/1989* and *R(IS) 1/91*, although the first decision is in error in failing to note the crucial difference identified in the next sentence). There is now no discretion (the regulation says "shall," not "may"). This was thought to give rise to the problems mentioned at the end of this note. These problems led to the insertion of reg. 51(A), applying a diminishing capital rule. Capital subject to that rule is excluded from reg. 51(1) by sub-para. (b). *R(IS) 1/91* overturned the previous understanding of the effect of reg. 51(1) and is discussed at the end of this note and in the note to reg. 51A. Sub-para. (a) excludes the operation of reg. 51(1) where money derived from compensation for personal injury is placed on trust for the claimant. Sub-para. (c) does the same in respect of funds held in court on behalf of a person that derive from damages for personal injury to that person. See also the note to para. 12 of Sched. 10.

Deprivation

Here the onus of proof is complicated by the relationship with the claimant's actual capital. Once it is shown that a person did possess, or received, an asset, the burden shifts to him to show that it has ceased to be a part of his actual capital, to be valued under reg. 49 *(R(SB) 38/85)*. Therefore, para. (1) can only come into play after these two stages have been passed, with the second stage depending on the claimant. If he cannot satisfactorily account for the way in which an asset or a sum of money which he says he no longer has was disposed of, the proper conclusion is that it remains a part of his actual capital. In *CIS 634/1992* the claimant was made bankrupt on November 29, 1990. Between November 29 and December 28, 1990, when he claimed income support the claimant divested himself of most of his capital. His trustee in bankruptcy was not appointed until April 1991. Under the Insolvency Act 1986 (subject to certain exceptions) a bankrupt's property does not vest in his trustee on the making of a bankruptcy order but only when the trustee is appointed. However, s. 284 of the Insolvency Act 1986 makes any disposal of property or payment by a bankrupt between the presentation of a bankruptcy petition and the vesting of his estate in his trustee void (except with the consent or later ratification of the court). The claimant could not therefore in law deprive himself of any resources from November 29, onwards and reg. 51(1) could not apply. However, since he had failed to give a satisfactory account of how he had disposed of his capital, he was to be treated as still possessing it *(R(SB) 38/85)*. Thus he was not entitled to income support prior to the appointment of the trustee in bankruptcy because until then he possessed actual capital over the income support limit.

"Deprive" is an ordinary English word and is not to be given any special legal definition *(R(SB) 38/85, R(SB) 40/85)*. The result is that a person deprives himself of a resource if he ceases to possess it, regardless of the reason for doing so or the fact that he receives some other resource in return. This is the clear assumption in *R(SB) 38/85* and is expressly decided in *R(SB) 40/85*. That decision holds that the approach in the *S Manual* (para. 6042—set out on p. 177 of the second edition of this book), that a person had not deprived himself of a resource if he spent money or changed it into another form which is still available to him, was wrong. The effect is to put the main emphasis on the purpose of the deprivation. *CIS 494/1990* appears to adopt a different principle. The issue was the treatment of the use of capital to buy a vehicle, for the purpose of securing entitlement to benefit. The value of such a personal possession is not disregarded under para. 10 of Sched. 10. The Commissioner points out that the value of the vehicle will be considerably less than the purchase price, and appears to treat only this "depreciation" as notional capital under s.51(1). It seems that the Commissioner is not saying that the use of the capital to buy a personal possession is not a deprivation (which would be directly contrary to *R(SB) 40/85*) because he considers that the amount of notional capital will increase as the actual value of the possession decreases over time. But he suggests no reason why the full amount of the purchase price, rather than merely the depreciation, is not to be the amount of notional capital under reg. 51(1). These points were not necessary to the decision in the case, but were part of the guidance to a new tribunal, and it is suggested that they should be regarded with caution. See also under *Diminishing capital*, below.

It is arguable that a person cannot deprive himself of something which he has never possessed, but it may be that a deliberate failure to acquire an asset is also a deprivation. In *CSB 598/1987* it is suggested that a deliberate failure to pay a cheque into a bank account could be a deprivation. See also *CIS 1586/1997* which states that a sale at a known undervalue and the release of a debtor from a debt were capable of amounting to deprivation.

If the claimant's attorney appointed under the Enduring Powers of Attorney Act 1985 repays a loan or makes gifts of the claimant's capital this may amount to deprivation by the claimant, since the attorney is the agent of the claimant *(CIS 12403/1991)*. In that case there was a question as to whether the loan was the responsibility of the claimant or the attorney and whether the gifts were allowable under s. 3(5) of the 1985 Act which permits the making of gifts "provided that the value of each such gift is not unreasonable having regard to all the circumstances and in particular the size of the donor's estate". The Commissioner states that the new tribunal would have to consider whether the payments were properly made; if not, there would be a claim against the attorney which would constitute actual capital; if they were properly made the question of deprivation would have to be considered.

Purpose

Here the AO must show that the person's purpose is one of those mentioned in para. (1). There is unlikely to be direct evidence of purpose (although there might be contemporary letters or documents), so that primary facts must be found from which an inference as to purpose can be drawn (*CSB 200/1985, R(SB) 40/85*).

The view put forward in *CSB 28/81*, that the test is of the person's predominant purpose, is rejected in *R(SB) 38/85* and *R(SB) 40/85*. In *R(SB) 38/85* it was suggested that it was enough that a subsidiary purpose was to obtain supplementary benefit. In *R(SB) 40/85* the Commissioner says that this must be a "significant operative purpose." If the obtaining of benefit was a foreseeable consequence of the transaction then, in the absence of other evidence, it could be concluded that this was the person's purpose. This would exclude some cases caught by the width of the approach to deprivation, *e.g.* where a resource is converted into another form in which it is still taken into account. For then there would be no effect on eligibility for benefit. But beyond that situation there remain great difficulties. The Commissioners mention a number of relevant factors, *e.g.* whether the deprivation was a gift or in return for a service, the personal circumstances of the person (*e.g.* age, state of health, employment prospects, needs), whether a creditor was pressing for repayment of a loan. It must be an issue of fact when these other factors indicate that the reasonably foreseeable consequence of obtaining benefit was not a significant operative factor. The length of time since the disposal of the capital may be relevant (*CIS 264/1989*). Where the claimant had been warned about the consequences of a transaction by the local DSS office (*i.e.* that reg. 51(1) would be applied) and still went ahead, this showed that he could not have as any part of his purpose securing of entitlement, or continued entitlement, to income support (*CIS 621/1991*). In effect, the test seems to be whether the person would have carried out the transaction at the same time if there had been no effect on eligibility for benefit. The onus of proof on the AO may come into play in marginal cases.

A number of recent decisions have firmed up the principles to be applied. *CIS 124/1990* holds that it must be proved that the person actually knew of the capital limit rule, otherwise the necessary deliberate intention to obtain benefit could not have been present. It is not enough that the person ought to have known of the rule. The crunch comes, and the resolution with the approach in *R(SB) 40/85* (where it was suggested that the existence of some limit might be said to be common knowledge), in the assessment of the evidence about the person's knowledge. The Commissioner stresses that the person's whole background must be considered, including experience of the social security system and advice which is likely to have been received from the family and elsewhere. The burden of proof is on the AO, but in some circumstances a person's assertion that they did not know of the rule will not be credible. In *CIS 124/1990* itself the claimant was illiterate and spoke and understood only Gujerati. The Commissioner says that this should put her in no better or worse situation than a literate claimant whose mother tongue was English, but that the possibility of misunderstandings in interpretation should be considered. *CIS 124/1990* is followed in *R(SB) 12/91*, where the necessity of a positive finding of fact, based on sufficient evidence, that the person knew of the capital limit is stressed. Evidence that the person had been in receipt of supplementary benefit or income support for some years was not in itself enough. But information which the person has received, together with his educational standing and other factors, will be material in deciding whether actual knowledge exists or not. *CIS 30/1993* similarly holds that it is not possible to infer actual knowledge of the capital limits simply from the claimant signing a claim form which contained that information. The claimant was partially sighted and had not completed the claim form herself but merely signed it. It was necessary for the SSAT to indicate what evidence satisfied it that the claimant did know of the capital limits.

The Commissioner in *R(SB) 9/91* stresses that a positive intention to obtain benefit must be shown to be a significant operative purpose. It is not enough for the AO merely to prove that the obtaining of benefit was a natural consequence of the transaction in question. The claimant had transferred her former home to her two daughters. Evidence was given that her sole intention was to make a gift to her daughters, as she intended to leave the property to them in her will and it was no longer of any use to her (she being permanently in need of residential nursing care). The Commissioner notes that this did not explain why the transfer was made when it was, why the proceeds of sale of the property would not have been of use to the claimant and what she thought she would live on if she gave the property away. She had been in receipt of supplementary benefit for several years. On the evidence the obtaining of benefit was a significant operative purpose. In *CIS 242/1993*, another case where the claimant had gone into residential care, the Commissioner reaches the opposite conclusion on the facts. The claimant's son had cared for his mother for 15 years. When she went into a residential care home, she gave her share of the proceeds of sale of their jointly owned home to her son to be used towards the purchase of his flat. The Commissioner accepts that she had relinquished her share in gratitude to her son and not to secure income support. In *R(IS) 13/94* the claimant's capital was in excess of the statutory limit when he purchased his council house. The deposit used up enough of his capital to bring him below the limit. It was necessary to consider whether para. (1) applied to this use of the capital since the claimant was apparently dependent on income support to meet the mortgage interest. But in *CIS 600/1995* using a criminal injuries compensation award to pay off part of a mortgage was not caught by para. (1). The SSAT had found that the claimant's purpose had been to secure his future and to reduce the burden on the DSS for his mortgage payments. This was a matter for the judgment of the tribunal.

In *CIS 109/1994* and *CIS 112/1994* the claimants had used their capital to purchase an annuity and a life insurance policy respectively. In *CIS 109/1994* the claimant was both physically and mentally frail and lived in a nursing home. The tribunal found that at the material time she had no knowledge of the income support capital and deprivation of capital rules, and entered into the transaction on her son's advice, who considered that this was the best use of her capital to enable her to stay in the nursing home. The Commissioner holds that the tribunal had not erred in concluding that she had not purchased the annuity in order to obtain income support. In *CIS 112/1994* the Commissioner decides that para. (1) did apply, but that para. 15 of Sched. 10 applied to disregard the life policy. The Commissioner also deals with "double counting" of notional and actual capital (see below). See also *R(IS) 7/98* where capital had been used to purchase an "investment bond". The Commissioner decides that the bond fell within the definition of "policy of life insurance" in reg. 2(1) and so could be disregarded under para. 15 of Sched. 10. But the claimant's intention at the time of the investment had to be considered to see whether para. (1) applied.

If capital is used to repay debts which are immediately payable then this cannot be said to be for the purpose of obtaining benefit *(R(SB) 12/91)*. (Note also that capital that a claimant is under a "certain and immediate liability" to repay should not in fact be treated as his capital: *Chief Adjudication Officer v. Leeves*, November 6, 1998, CA, to be reported as *R(IS) 5/99*.) In *R(SB) 12/91* there were doubts whether the alleged debts, to members of the family, were legally enforceable debts and whether they were owed by the claimant personally. But the fact that a debt is not legally enforceable and immediately repayable does not mean that repayment of it must be for the purpose of securing income support. It is still necessary to consider the claimant's purpose in repaying the debt *(CIS 2627/1995)*.

CIS 40/1989 provides an interesting example on its facts of the securing or increase of benefit not being a significant operative purpose. The claimant had been on supplementary benefit and then income support since 1978. Her father died intestate. The estate consisted almost entirely of a house in which the claimant's sister had lived with the father. The claimant and her sister were the sole beneficiaries of the estate. Legal proceedings had to be taken to enforce a sale of the house. In March 1988 the claimant received £38,000 net of costs, which her solicitor divided equally between the claimant, her son, her daughter and her grand-daughter. After repaying a number of debts and buying a second-hand car, the amount possessed by the claimant quickly fell below £6,000. The AO and the SSAT found that she should be treated as still possessing the amounts given to her children and grandchild. The Commissioner, having heard the claimant give evidence and be cross-examined, accepted that her purpose was to carry out her father's wishes, which were that the house should be used to provide for his grandchildren and great-grandchildren. She had originally intended to take nothing, but had been encouraged by her children to take a quarter share. She knew of the capital limit, but did not know of the effect her actions would have on her benefit entitlement. On these particular facts, the Commissioner found that para. (1) did not apply.

There may be a problem in the transfer from the corresponding supplementary benefit regulation (Resources Regulations, reg. 4(1)). Reg. 51(1) only mentions income support. What if a person deprived himself of capital in December 1987, thinking only of supplementary benefit. On a claim for income support, can he be caught by reg. 51(1)? In *CIS 259/1990* (which was to be reported as *R(IS) 8/91*, but has been withdrawn from reporting) the Commissioner accepts that the purpose must be to secure or increase income support, but held that the claimant in March 1987, knew enough about the effect of depleting her resources on her means-tested benefit for her purpose to satisfy reg. 51(1). The Commissioner found that the claimant was aware that the existing means-tested benefit was to be replaced by another means-tested benefit (although the evidential basis for this finding does not appear). There was an appeal to the Court of Appeal, but the decision was set aside by consent. In *R(IS) 14/93* the Commissioner does not accept the reliance in *CIS 259/*

1990 on the enactment of the Social Security Act 1986 well before the income support scheme came into operation. He holds that a provision of a statute has no legal existence until it comes into force. Therefore, when in that case the claimant in November/December 1987, divested himself of capital he could not have done it with the intention of obtaining income support, because at that time it did not exist. Nor can the words "income support" be taken to refer to means-tested benefits which previously went under the name of supplementary benefit. This approach has the merit of not making the result depend on the vagaries of the particular claimant's advance knowledge of the nature of the income support reforms in April 1988.

Note that the correspoinding regulation under JSA (reg. 113(1) of the JSA Regulations) applies if a person has deprived himself of capital in order to secure entitlement to or increase the amount of JSA *or income support*. That avoids the question that might otherwise have arisen on a claimant transferring from income support to JSA as to whether a deprivation which had only been for the purposes of income support could be caught by reg. 113(1). But para. (1) has not been similarly amended.

Diminishing capital

There may also be problems from the removal of discretion in the shift to income support. Under the Supplementary Benefit (Resources) Regulations this was used in particular for two purposes. One was to avoid double counting with the rule about personal possessions, now contained in para. 10 of Sched. 10. The value of personal possessions is not disregarded if they were acquired with the intention of reducing capital so as to gain entitlement to benefit. With no discretion at either end a claimant could have the market value of the possessions counted as part of his actual capital and the money he spent on them counted as notional capital under this paragraph. The Commissioner in *CIS 494/1990* avoids this problem by treating only the shortfall between the market value of the personal possessions from time to time and the purchase price (the "depreciation") as the notional capital to be imputed under reg. 51(1). However, he does not explain how reg. 51(1) should be interpreted so as not to make the whole purchase price the amount of the notional capital. It is also difficult to combine a rising level of notional capital over time, in line with the reduction in the market value of the personal possessions, with the diminishing notional capital rule under reg. 51A. Although *CIS 494/1990* satisfactorily avoids double counting, its suggestions cannot yet be confidently accepted.

In *CIS 112/1994* the Commissioner recognises the gross unfairness to a claimant if she were to be penalised twice because of the lack of discretion in para. (1). In the Commissioner's view this is not the intention of the regulation. But in that case double counting did not arise. The claimant had purchased a life insurance policy with a legacy. Although she was to be treated as still possessing the notional capital by virtue of para. (1), the actual capital (the life policy) could be disregarded under para. 15 of Sched. 10.

The second problem for which the use of discretion was useful was that it was unfair to fix a claimant with an amount of notional capital for eternity. If he had still had the capital and not been entitled to benefit, he would have had to use up the capital for living expenses. Thus the figure of notional capital could be reduced by the equivalent of the weekly benefit lost by the capital counting (*R(SB) 38/85, R(SB) 40/85*). There had seemed no possibility of such a process applying to reg. 51(1) until the decision of the Tribunal of Commissioners in *R(IS) 1/91*. The Tribunal concluded that the diminishing capital rule did apply. This is because para. (6) provides that regs. 45 to 50 apply to the calculation of notional capital as if it was actual capital. If a claimant has capital over the prescribed limit, reasonable expenditure on living and other sensible expenses (not necessarily limited to income support rates) will reduce the amount of capital until it falls below the limit. He will then be entitled to income support. The same situation is held to apply where it is notional capital, rather than actual, which is held initially. The decision is wrong in principle, because if actual capital is held, the actual amount, reduced by any expenditure, must be considered week by week. This is not a consequence of any of regs. 45 to 50 and there is no analogy with the notional reduction of notional capital. Para. (6) is primarily concerned with the calculation of the market value of assets. Nonetheless, *R(IS) 1/91* must be followed in relation to weeks before October 1, 1990.

With effect from October 1, 1990, reg. 51A provides an express diminishing notional capital rule. *R(IS) 9/92* decides that while the principles of *R(IS) 1/91* apply up to that date, they do not apply thereafter. They are superseded by the rules laid down in reg. 51A.

Paragraph (2)

It is not at all clear what sort of capital would be caught by this rule. It must be available simply on application, with no other conditions, but not amount to actual capital (*cf. R(SB) 26/86* and *R(SB) 17/87*). Examples might be money held in court which would be released on application or arrears of employer's sick pay which needed to be applied for. Note the exclusions. Although discretionary trusts are specifically excluded, a potential beneficiary would not seem to be caught by para. (2) anyway. More than an application is needed for payment to be made: the discretion has to be exercised. On sub-para. (d) see the note to reg. 42(2) to (2C). On sub-para. (e) see the notes to paras. 44 and 45 of Sched. 10.

Paragraphs (3) and (3A)

Sub-para. (a) applies where payments are made to a third party in respect of the claimant or a member of the claimant's family. If the payment is derived from a benefit listed in head (i) it counts as the claimant's. In other cases it counts as the claimant's in so far as it is actually used for food, ordinary clothing or footwear, fuel or housing or accommodation costs. Note *CJSA 3411/1998* in the note to reg. 42(4) and (4ZA).

"Ordinary clothing or footwear" is defined in para. (8). Para. 34866 of the *Adjudication Officer's Guide* suggests that wellington boots are not for "normal daily use", nor are special shoes needed because of a disability (as these are not worn by people in general on a daily basis).

If the payment is used for other items or costs it does not form part of the claimant's capital. Note that if the conditions are met, there is no discretion whether or not to apply para. (3). In this respect, as in others, *R(SB) 6/88* would be decided differently under income support.

The operation of sub-para. (b) is clear. In these circumstances the payment would not form part of the claimant's actual capital in view of the obligation to use it for a third party.

Paragraph (3) does not apply to payments from the listed Trusts and Funds nor to payments made in respect of an 18–25 year-old who is on a "New Deal" option or a person aged 25 or over who is undertaking a "qualifying course" (para. (3A)). For a brief summary of the New Deal options see the notes to reg. 75 of the JSA Regulations. On "qualifying course", see the note to reg. 17A of those Regulations. Regulation 17A allows a person aged 25 or over to be treated as available for work (see reg. 21A of the JSA Regulations for the parallel provision in relation to the active seeking of work) while attending a full-time employment-related course. This concession is part of the Government's scheme to assist that age group to find work. While taking part in a New Deal option, a person may be eligible to receive a grant of £400 (spread over six months) or be able to apply for payments from a Discretionary Fund operated by the Employment Service to cover exceptional costs; payments may also be made from the Discretionary Fund in respect of people on a "qualifying course". Such payments may be paid to the provider of the employment or training rather than to the person himself. They will not count as notional capital for the purposes of any claim for income support.

Paragraphs (4) and (5)

These two paragraphs establish an artificial method of dealing with one person companies or similar. The basic legal position is that if there is a company, the shareholders' assets are the value of the shares, not the value of the company's assets (*R(SB) 57/83*). But under para. (4), if the claimant is in a position analogous to a sole owner or partner in the business of the company (on which, see *R(IS) 8/92*), the value of his shareholding is disregarded, and he is treated as possessing a proportionate share of the capital of the company. The value is the net worth of the company's total assets taken together (*R(IS) 13/93*). The value of one particular asset within the total is not relevant in itself. However, as long as the claimant undertakes activities in the course of the business of the company, the amount produced by para. (4) is disregarded (para. (5)). Temporary interruptions in activity (*e.g.* holidays, short-term sickness) ought not to prevent para. (5) from applying. It is accepted in *R(IS) 13/93* that any activities which are more than *de minimis* satisfy para. (4).

Paragraph (6)

One of the effects of para. (6) is that the disregards in Sched. 10 can apply to notional capital. However, *CIS 30/1993* decides that the disregard in para. 26 of Sched. 10 (taking steps to dispose of premises) could not apply where the claimant had already disposed of the capital so as to trigger reg. 51(1). Reg. 51(6) did not provide any authority for altering the provisions of Sched. 10 which could only apply where their conditions were met. This is a different view from that taken in some other decisions. See the note to para. 26 of Sched. 10.

CIS 231/1991 confirms that it is not necessary for the disregard under Sched. 10 to have been applicable before the claimant deprived himself of the capital. The claimant had transferred his former home to his parents who were both over 60. When he claimed income support his parents were living in the home. The Commissioner holds that the former home fell to be disregarded under para. 4(a) of Sched. 10; the disregard in para. 4 applied to notional, as well as actual, capital.

248

Paragraph (7)

The capital of which a person has deprived himself must be actual capital. In *CIS 240/1992* and *CIS 30/1993* the Commissioner raises the question (without expressing a conclusion) as to whether para. (1) can apply when a claimant is deemed to possess an equal share in a capital asset under reg. 52. In *CIS 240/1992* the claimant had a quarter share in a property, but the effect of reg. 52 was to treat him as having a half share. The claimant's parents (his mother owned the other three-quarters of the property) then bought his share for £5,000, out of which he repaid them loans of £3,883. The Commissioner points out that as reg. 52 operated to treat the claimant as having a notional equal share in the property, his actual share should not also count, since otherwise there would be double counting. Therefore, when he sold his actual share to his parents, was there no disposal of *actual* capital at all, or no disposal to the extent that his notional share exceeded his actual share? Para. 34809 of the *Adjudication Officer's Guide* assumes that the rule in para. (1) can only apply to the claimant's actual share of the capital, even though the effect of reg. 52 is to deem him to own a larger share. But this does not entirely deal with the Commissioner's point. In fact, in *CIS 240/1992*, since the property was subject to a tenancy, even if under para. (1) the claimant was treated as still possessing his actual interest, the disregard in para. 5 of Sched. 10 (as in force at that time) would result in him having no capital. The new tribunal would also have to consider whether para. (1) applied when the claimant repaid the loans (see *R(SB) 12/91* above).

[¹Diminishing notional capital rule

51A.—(1) Where a claimant is treated as possessing capital under regulation 51(1) (notional capital), the amount which he is treated as possessing—

(a) in the case of a week that is subsequent to—
  (i) the relevant week in respect of which the conditions set out in paragraph (2) are satisfied, or
  (ii) a week which follows that relevant week and which satisfies those conditions,

shall be reduced by an amount determined under paragraph (2);

(b) in the case of a week in respect of which paragraph (1)(a) does not apply but where—
  (i) that week is a week subsequent to the relevant week, and
  (ii) that relevant week is a week in which the condition in paragraph (3) is satisfied,

shall be reduced by the amount determined under paragraph (3).

(2) This paragraph applies to a benefit week or part week where the claimant satisfies the conditions that—

(a) he is in receipt of income support; and
(b) but for regulation 51(1), he would have received an additional amount of income support in that benefit week or, as the case may be, that part week;

and in such a case, the amount of the reduction for the purposes of paragraph (1)(a) shall be equal to that additional amount.

(3) Subject to paragraph (4), for the purposes of paragraph (1)(b) the condition is that the claimant would have been entitled to income support in the relevant week, but for regulation 51(1), and in such a case the amount of the reduction shall be equal to the aggregate of—

(a) the amount of income support to which the claimant would have been entitled in the relevant week but for regulation 51(1); and for the purposes of this sub-paragraph if the relevant week is a part-week that amount shall be determined by dividing the amount of income support to which he would have been so entitled by the number equal to the number of days in the part-week and multiplying the quotient by 7;
(b) the amount of housing benefit (if any) equal to the difference between his maximum housing benefit and the amount (if any) of housing benefit which he is awarded in respect of the benefit week, within the meaning of regulation 2(1) of the Housing Benefit (General) Regulations 1987 (interpretation), which includes the last day of the relevant week;

   (c) the amount of community charge benefit (if any) equal to the difference between his maximum community charge benefit and the amount (if any) of community charge benefit which he is awarded in respect of the benefit week, within the meaning of regulation 2(1) of the Community Charge Benefits (General) Regulations 1989 (interpretation) which includes the last day of the relevant week.

[²(d) the amount of council tax benefit (if any) equal to the difference between his maximum council tax benefit and the amount (if any) of council tax benefit which he is awarded in respect of the benefit week which includes the last day of the relevant week, and for this purpose "benefit week" has the same meaning as in regulation 2(1) of the Council Tax Benefit (General) Regulations 1992 (interpretation).]

(4) The amount determined under paragraph (3) shall be re-determined under that paragraph if the claimant makes a further claim for income support and the conditions in paragraph (5) are satisfied, and in such a case—

   (a) sub-paragraphs (a), (b) and (c) of paragraph (3) shall apply as if for the words "relevant week" there were substituted the words "relevant subsequent week"; and

   (b) subject to paragraph (6), the amount as re-determined shall have effect from the first week following the relevant subsequent week in question.

(5) The conditions are that—

   (a) a further claim is made 26 or more weeks after—

      (i) the date on which the claimant made a claim for income support in respect of which he was first treated as possessing the capital in question under regulation 51(1); or

      (ii) in a case where there has been at least one re-determination in accordance with paragraph (4), the date on which he last made a claim for income support which resulted in the weekly amount being re-determined; or

      (iii) the date on which he last ceased to be in receipt of income support; whichever last occurred; and

   (b) the claimant would have been entitled to income support but for regulation 51(1).

(6) The amount as re-determined pursuant to paragraph (4) shall not have effect if it is less than the amount which applied in that case immediately before the re-determination and in such a case the higher amount shall continue to have effect.

(7) For the purpose of this regulation—

   (a) "part-week" means a period to which sub-section (1A) of section 21 of the Act [SSCBA, s.124(5)] (amount etc. of income support) applies;

   (b) "relevant week" means the benefit week or part-week in which the capital in question of which the claimant has deprived himself within the meaning of regulation 51(1)—

      (i) was first taken into account for the purpose of determining his entitlement to income support; or

      (ii) was taken into account on a subsequent occasion for the purpose of determining or re-determining his entitlement to income support on that subsequent occasion and that determination or re-determination resulted in his beginning to receive, or ceasing to receive, income support;

and where more than one benefit week or part-week is identified by reference to heads (i) and (ii) of this sub-paragraph the later or latest such benefit week or, as the case may be, the later or latest such part-week;

   (c) "relevant subsequent week" means the benefit week or part-week which includes the day on which the further claim or, if more than one further claim has been made, the last such claim was made.]

AMENDMENTS

1. Income Support (General) Amendment No. 3 Regulations 1990 (S.I. 1990 No. 1776), reg. 6 (October 1, 1990).
2. Income-related Benefits Schemes (Miscellaneous Amendments) Regulations 1993 (S.I. 1993 No. 315), Sched., para. 4 (April 1, 1993).

DEFINITIONS

"benefit week"—see reg. 2(1).
"claimant"—*ibid.*
"community charge benefit"—*ibid.*

GENERAL NOTE

See the note to reg. 51(1) for the general background. Reg. 51A provides for the reduction of the amount of notional capital fixed by reg. 51(1). If the amount of notional capital remaining is not sufficient to remove entitlement to income support altogether, it is to be treated as reducing each week by the amount by which income support would be increased if it did not exist at all (paras. (1)(a) and (2)). If the amount does remove entitlement it is to be treated as reducing each week by the amount of income support the person would receive if the notional capital had not been fixed plus the proportion of rent and council tax not met by housing benefit or council tax benefit (paras. (1)(b) and (3)). There are complicated provisions for redetermination and recalculation.

The inter-relationship of this regulation, which ties the reduction in notional capital very much to income support rates, and *R(IS) 1/91* is of considerable difficulty. The Tribunal of Commissioners' diminishing capital rule works on reasonable expenditure not necessarily limited to income support rates. Could a claimant take the benefit of this more generous rule, or had its implication from the regulations been destroyed by the introduction of this express provision? *R(IS) 9/92* holds that the second alternative is correct.

Capital jointly held

52. Except where a claimant possesses capital which is disregarded under regulation 51(4) (notional capital), where a claimant and one or more persons are beneficially entitled in possession to any capital asset they shall be treated as if each of them were entitled in possession [¹to the whole beneficial interest therein in an equal share and the foregoing provisions of this Chapter shall apply for the purposes of calculating the amount of capital which the claimant is treated as possessing as if it were actual capital which the claimant does possess.]

AMENDMENT

1. Social Security Amendment (Capital) Regulations 1998 (S.I. 1998 No. 2250), reg. 2 (October 12, 1998).

DEFINITION

"claimant"—see reg. 2(1), reg. 23(1).

GENERAL NOTE

This regulation was amended on October 12, 1998 following the decision in *CIS 15936/1996, CIS 263/1997* and *CIS 3283/1997* (see the common Appendix). In that decision the Commissioner held that the October 1995 amendment to the regulation was *ultra vires.* The October 1995 amendment had provided that the value of a claimant's actual or deemed share of jointly-owned capital was to be calculated by dividing the net value of the capital as a whole by the number of co-owners. The aim of that amendment had been to reverse the effect of the Court of Appeal's decision in *Chief Adjudication Officer v. Palfrey and others, The Times,* February 17, 1995 (see below). See the 1998 edition of this book for the October 1995 form of reg. 52. The Government decided not to appeal against the decision in *CIS 15936/1996, CIS 263/1997* and *CIS 3283/1997* but (somewhat unusually) to restore the form of the regulation that existed before October 2, 1995. A similar amendment has been made to the JSA, Family Credit, Disability Working Allowance, Housing Benefit and Council Tax Benefit Regulations.

The result, broadly, is that there is no double "deeming" under this regulation. The first "deeming" remains, *i.e.* joint owners are still deemed to have equal shares in the property, whatever the legal or equitable position (see further under *Scope of the rule*). But the second, that the value of the share was to be "deemed" by reference to the value of the property as a whole, does not. Thus instead of attributing what could be a totally artificial value to the deemed (or actual) share, it will, following *Palfrey*, have to be given its true market value. This will go some way to mitigating the worst effects of this rule in certain cases but it will still have arbitrary and unfair consequences for some claimants.

The basis of the Commissioner's decision in *CIS 15936/1996, CIS 263/1997* and *CIS 3283/1997* was that the October 1995 amendment was outside the powers in s.136(3) and (5)(a) of the Contributions and Benefits Act 1992. He held that the power in s.136(3) to provide for the calculation or estimation of capital did not allow assets to be valued in a way that had no relationship to their actual value. In addition, s.136(5)(a) did not authorise the amendment because the amendment was concerned with valuation, not the actual capital or income which a person did or did not possess.

The decision in *CIS 15936/1996, CIS 263/1997* and *CIS 3283/1997* was given on May 21, 1998. The guidance to AOs on the effect of this decision expressed the view that it could not be applied for any period before May 21, 1998 because of s.69 of the Administration Act 1992 (the "anti-test case rule"). However, it is by no means certain that s.69 is applicable in cases of *ultra vires* regulations. There is indeed provision for this in s.27(5) of the Social Security Act 1998 (which is not yet in force but will replace s.69 when the new system of decision-making and appeals comes into operation later in 1999) but s.69 is silent on the matter. Given the nature of *ultra vires* declarations, it is certainly arguable that in the absence of an express provision, s.69 does not apply in this situation.

The validity of reg. 52 was also challenged before the Tribunal of Commissioners in *CIS 391/1992 (Palfrey)* and *CIS 417/1992* (which were to be reported as *R(IS) 5/98* but now will be reported as *R(IS) 26/95*) on the ground of irrationality. But the Commissioners held, given their ruling on valuation under reg. 52, that irrationality had not been made out and that reg. 52 was validly made. The Court of Appeal in *Palfrey* did not express a view as to whether reg. 52 was invalid, as this argument only became relevant if the CAO's construction of reg. 52 was correct.

Scope of the rule

Previous editions have described this regulation as containing an extraordinary rule (a view endorsed in *CIS 408/1990*). In *CIS 807/1991* the rule is described as draconian. Shared interests in assets had caused difficult problems of valuation under supplementary benefit. The intention of reg. 52 was to provide a solution which is simple to apply, but the conceptual difficulties posed are formidable.

The intended effect of reg. 52 is that except in the case of deemed ownership of a company's assets under reg. 51(4), if the claimant has any share of the beneficial interest (*i.e.* the right to dispose of something) in an asset he is treated as having an equal share in the interest, regardless of the legal and equitable position. ("In possession" means that ownership is enjoyed at present, rather than on the happening of some event in the future.) Thus if a person has a 10 per cent. interest in a house, and another person has a 90 per cent. interest, each is treated as having a 50 per cent. interest. There are many situations in which such a division might occur. The same could apply to, say, joint bank accounts or Building Society accounts. The result can easily be, in conjunction with the rules on disregards in Sched. 10, that a claimant is fixed with capital assets which he is not legally entitled to at all, let alone able to realise immediately. Although crisis loans under the social fund may be available (Social Fund Guide, para. 4717–8), the guidance presently given is in terms of short-term support while assets are realised, which does not meet the case. Normally the claimant's "remedy" for the artificial effects of reg. 52 is to dispose of his share in the asset, when he will receive an amount appropriate to his actual legal share. But this will not always be possible. The deprivation rule in reg. 51(1) should not apply in these circumstances: see reg. 51(7) and the note to that paragraph and para. 34809 of the *Adjudication Officer's Guide*.

However, doubt as to the ambit of reg. 52 was raised as a result of the decision in *CIS 7097/1995*. The claimant's husband went to live in a nursing home on a permanent basis. In order to help finance the cost of this, £7,000 National Savings belonging to him was cashed in and paid into their joint bank account. It was never intended that this should thereby become part of the joint money in the account; it had simply been paid into the account so that the nursing home fees could be paid by direct debit. A separate tally was kept of this money which had been declared as the husband's own money for the purposes of his application to the local authority for help with the nursing home fees. The AO treated the claimant as entitled to half of the balance in the joint account (including her husband's National Savings) which when added to her other capital meant that she did not qualify for income support. However, the Commissioner holds that reg. 52 did not apply to her husband's National Savings. Reg. 52 only operated where property was held in joint beneficial ownership because it was only then that two or more people were "beneficially entitled in possession" to a given capital asset. Reg. 52 was needed because of the special nature of joint beneficial ownership and deemed a joint beneficial owner to have the equal share that he would by law have if the joint ownership was severed. But cases where property was held in undivided shares fell outside reg. 52 because under such an arrangement each co-owner was beneficially and individually entitled to his own share of the actual capital. His share was a different asset from the shares belonging to the others; and in contrast to the joint right of a joint owner was an asset which was separately disposable by him. On the facts of this case, there was clear evidence that the normal presumption of joint beneficial ownership between a husband and wife operating a joint bank account did not apply. It was obviously intended that the balance of the husband's National Savings was to remain his sole property and that it had merely been paid into the joint account for convenience. The consequence was that the claimant was entitled to income support as her capital did not include any of her husband's National Savings.

The question whether reg. 52 also applies to deem actual unequal shares in a capital asset to be equal shares was, as the Commissioner in *CIS 7097/1995* points out, expressly reserved by the Tribunal of Commissioners in *CIS 417/1992* (heard together with *CIS 391/1992 (Palfrey)*, see below) and there was no argument on the point before the Court of Appeal. But it was considered, albeit briefly, in *CIS 240/1992*. In that case the claimant and his mother were tenants in common of a property, the claimant's share being one quarter. The Commissioner accepted that a situation where a claimant had an unequal share of the beneficial interest fell within the scope of reg. 52, so that the claimant was to be treated as having a half-share in the property. See also *CIS 127/1993*. Moreover, in *CIS 15936/1996, CIS 263/1997* and *CIS 3283/1997* the Commissioner expressly dissents from any general statement in *CIS 7097/1995* that reg. 52 was confined to joint tenancies. In his view, reg. 52 applied to all kinds of co-ownership, including joint tenancies and tenancies in common.

Clearly the policy intention is that reg. 52 has effect beyond the fairly limited role of deeming a person to have an equal share of a capital asset that is in joint beneficial ownership. It may be that *CIS 7097/1995* should be restricted to its particular facts, *i.e.* where it was clearly intended that the money in question should not become part of the joint asset but had simply been paid into the joint bank account for convenience and so was not really a joint asset at all. The issue will in any event be of less significance in view of the decision in *CIS 15936/1996, CIS 263/1997* and *CIS 3283/1997* and the fact that reg. 52 has been restored to its pre-October 1995 form.

Note that reg. 52 only applies where the beneficial interest is shared. It does not apply merely because there is a separation between legal and beneficial interests, for instance where one person holds assets on trust for another. But if an interest in a trust fund is shared, then reg. 52 may apply. This was the case in *R(IS)2/93*, where a building society account in the claimant's sole name was in fact a joint asset of herself and her (separated) husband. She had to be treated as possessing half of the amount in the account, regardless of how it might be dealt with in matrimonial proceedings. But it is arguable that in the case of assets that are the subject of matrimonial dispute, reg. 52 should not apply and their value should be disregarded, until ownership is resolved. See *Welfare Rights Bulletin* 108 p.5, referring to *CIS 298/1989* (a decision given without reasons). This should apply whether or not a couple were married. See also *CIS 461/1994*, to be reported as *R(IS) 1/97*, in the note to para. 5 of Sched. 10.

Valuation under regulation 52

The restoration of reg. 52 to its original form means that it is the deemed equal share that has to be valued, *not* the proportionate share of the overall value that has to be taken (see the Court of Appeal's decision in *Chief Adjudication Officer v. Palfrey and others, The Times,* February 17, 1995 which had upheld the Tribunal of Commissioner's decisions in *CIS 391/1992* and *CIS 417/1992* (which were to be reported as *R(IS) 5/98* but now will be reported as *R(IS) 26/95*). The Tribunal of Commissioners gave detailed guidance as to the basis of a proper valuation of such a share (paras. 53 and 54 in *CIS 391/1992*). In both *CIS 391/1992* and *CIS 417/1992* ownership was shared with relatives who were unable or unwilling to sell the property or buy the claimant's interest. The Commissioners recognised, as did the Court of Appeal, that the market value in such cases may well be nil. Note *CIS 767/1993*, to be reported as *R(IS) 3/96*, which contains a useful discussion as to whether the District Valuer's opinion supplied in that case met the requirements of *CIS 391/1992*. The current AOG guidance suggests that AOs should obtain an expert opinion on the market value of a deemed share in land/premises. In a case where the other owners will not buy the share or agree to a sale of the asset as a whole, the guidance states that the valuer should not simply assume that a court would order a sale but must consider the particular circumstances and take into account legal costs, length of time to obtain possession, etc. The guidance also says that the expert would need to explain whether on the facts of the case there was any market for the deemed share and indicate how the value of the deemed share had been calculated.

See the 1995 edition for a summary of the Tribunal of Commissioners' decision and the Court of Appeal's decision in *Palfrey*. See also *CIS 413/1992* which notes the differences that arise from the law of property in Scotland. In *CIS 391/1992* and *CIS 417/1992* the Tribunal of Commissioners state that the SSAT should have exercised its inquisitorial jurisdiction to call for the documents under which the property was acquired in order to sort out the beneficial ownership. But in *CIS 127/1993* the Commissioner did not find this necessary, since it was not disputed that the house had been conveyed into the names of the claimant and her daughter, and the method of valuation was the same whether the claimant and her daughter actually had equal shares or were deemed to do so by reg. 52.

Note the increased upper and lower capital limits for people permanently in residential care from April 1996 (regs. 45(b) and 53(1A), see the note to reg. 53).

Calculation of tariff income from capital

53.—(1) [³Except where the circumstances prescribed in paragraph (1B) apply to the claimant,] where the claimant's capital calculated in accordance with this Part exceeds £3,000 it shall be treated as equivalent to a weekly income of £1 for each complete £250 in excess of £3,000 but not exceeding [²£8,000].

[³(1A) Where the circumstances prescribed in paragraph (1B) apply to the claimant and that claimant's capital calculated in accordance with this Part exceeds £10,000, it shall be treated as equivalent to a weekly income of £1 for each complete £250 in excess of £10,000 but not exceeding £16,000.

(1B) For the purposes of paragraph (1A) and regulation 45, the prescribed circumstances are that the claimant lives permanently in—

    (a) a residential care or nursing home [⁴...] and that home [⁴...] provides board and personal care for the claimant by reason of his old age, disablement, past or present dependence on alcohol or drugs or past or present mental disorder; or

    (b) an establishment run by the Abbeyfield Society including all bodies corporate or incorporate which are affiliated to that Society; or

    (c) accommodation provided under section 3 of, and Part II of the Schedule to, the Polish Resettlement Act 1947 (provision of accommodation in camps) where the claimant requires personal care [⁵ by reason of old age, disablement, past or present dependence on alcohol or drugs, past or present mental disorder or a terminal illness and the care is provided in the home].

[⁴(d) residential accommodation.]

(1C) For the purposes of paragraph (1B), a claimant shall be treated as living permanently in such home or accommodation where he is absent—

    (a) from a home or accommodation referred to in sub-paragraph [⁴(a), (b) or (d)] of paragraph (1B)—

        (i) in the case of a claimant referred to in regulation 19(2) or in the case of a person over pensionable age, for a period not exceeding 52 weeks, and

        (ii) in any other case, for a period not exceeding 13 weeks;

    (b) from accommodation referred to in sub-paragraph (c) of paragraph (1B), where the claimant, with the agreement of the manager of the accommodation, intends to return to the accommodation in due course.]

(2) Notwithstanding [³paragraphs (1) and (1A)], where any part of the excess is not a complete £250 that part shall be treated as equivalent to a weekly income of £1.

(3) For the purposes of [³paragraphs (1) and (1A)], capital includes any income treated as capital under regulations [¹ . . .] 48 and 60 ([¹ . . .] income treated as capital and liable relative payments treated as capital).

[³(4) For the purposes of this regulation, the definition of "residential accommodation" in regulation 21(3) (applicable amounts of income support in special cases) shall have effect as if, after the words "subject to the following provisions of this regulation", there were inserted "(except paragraphs (4) and (4A))."]

AMENDMENTS

1. Income Support (General) Amendment No. 5 Regulations 1988 (S.I. 1988 No. 2022), reg. 13 (December 12, 1988).
2. Income-Related Benefits (Miscellaneous Amendments) Regulations 1990 (S.I. 1990 No. 671), reg. 5 (April 9, 1990).
3. Income-related Benefits Schemes (Miscellaneous Amendments) Regulations 1996 (S.I. 1996 No. 462), reg. 12(1) (April 8, 1996).
4. Income-related Benefits and Jobseeker's Allowance (Miscellaneous Amendments) Regulations Regulations 1997 (S.I. 1997 No. 65), reg. 8 (April 7, 1997).
5. Income-related Benefits and Jobseeker's Allowance (Amendment) (No. 2) Regulations 1997 (S.I. 1997 No. 2197), reg. 7(5) and (6)(a) (October 6, 1997).

DEFINITIONS

"claimant"—see reg. 2(1), reg. 23(1).
"nursing home"—see reg. 19(3).
"residential accommodation"—see reg. 21(3).
"residential care home"—see reg. 19(3).

GENERAL NOTE

The overall capital limit under reg. 45 has been £8,000 since April 1990, but from April 8, 1996 it has been raised to £16,000 for claimants living permanently in residential care or nursing homes (including those with preserved rights), residential accommodation or Polish resettlement homes (see reg. 45(b) and para. (1B)). For these claimants the tariff income rule only applies to capital between £10,000 and £16,000 (para. (1A)).

The effect of paras. (1) and (1A) is that if the claimant and partner have capital over £3,000 (£10,000 for claimants within para. (1B)), but not over £8,000 (£16,000 for para. (1B) claimants), it is treated as producing an income of £1 per week for each complete £250 between the limits, and £1 per week for any odd amount left over. Thus if a claimant (other than one to whom para. (1B) applies) has exactly £6,000, that is treated as producing £12 per week. If he has £4,001, that is treated as producing £5 per week. The actual income from most forms of capital is disregarded under para. 22 of Sched. 9.

Paragraph (1B)
See the notes to the definitions of residential care home and nursing home in reg. 19(3) and residential accommodation in reg. 21 (note the effect of para. (4) which enables people in residential accommodation who are under 18 or not receiving board to benefit from the higher capital limits). Under sub-para. (b) all Abbeyfield Homes are included whether or not they provide board and personal care.

Paragraph (1C)
This deals with periods of temporary absence from the accommodation for claimants covered by para. (1B).

Chapter VII

Liable Relatives

Interpretation

54. In this Chapter, unless the context otherwise requires—
"claimant" includes a young claimant;
"liable relative" means—

(a) a spouse or former spouse of a claimant or of a member of the claimant's family;

(b) a parent of a child or young person who is a member of the claim- ant's family or of a young claimant;

(c) a person who has not been adjudged to be the father of a child or young person who is a member of the claimant's family or of a young claimant where that person is contributing towards the main- tenance of that child, young person or young claimant and by reason of that contribution he may reasonably be treated as the father of that child, young person or young claimant;

(d) a person liable to maintain another person by virtue of section 26(3)(c) of the Act [SSAA, s.78(6)(c)] (liability to maintain) where the latter is the claimant or a member of the claimant's family,

and, in this definition, a reference to a child's, young person's or young claimant's parent includes any person in relation to whom the child, young person or young claimant was treated as a child or a member of the family;

"payment" means a periodical payment or any other payment made by or derived from a liable relative including, except in the case of a discretion- ary trust, any payment which would be so made or derived upon applica- tion being made by the claimant but which has not been acquired by him but only from the date on which [¹it could be expected to be acquired were an application made]; but it does not include any payment—

(a) arising from a disposition of property made in contemplation of, or as a consequence of—

    (i) an agreement to separate; or

    (ii) any proceedings for judicial separation, divorce or nullity of marriage;

(b) made after the death of the liable relative;

(c) made by way of a gift but not in aggregate or otherwise exceeding £250 in the period of 52 weeks beginning with the date on which the payment, or if there is more than one such payment the first payment, is made; and, in the case of a claimant who continues to be in receipt of income support at the end of the period of 52 weeks, this provision shall continue to apply thereafter with the modification that any subsequent period of 52 weeks shall begin with the first day of the benefit week in which the first payment is made after the end of the previous period of 52 weeks;

(d) to which regulation 44(2) applies (modifications in respect of chil- dren and young persons);

(e) made—

    (i) to a third party in respect of the claimant or a member of the claimant's family; or

    (ii) to the claimant or to a member of the claimant's family in respect of a third party,

    where having regard to the purpose of the payment, the terms under which it is made and its amount it is unreasonable to take it into account;

(f) in kind;

(g) to, or in respect of, a child or young person who is to be treated as not being a member of the claimant's household under regulation 16 (circumstances in which a person is to be treated as being or not being a member of the same household);

(h) which is not a periodical payment, to the extent that any amount of that payment—

(i) has already been taken into account under this Part by virtue of a previous claim or determination; or

(ii) has been recovered under section 27(1) of the Act [SSAA, s.74(1)] (prevention of duplication of payments) or is currently being recovered; or

(iii) at the time the determination is made, has been used by the claimant except where he has deprived himself of that amount for the purpose of securing entitlement to income support or increasing the amount of that benefit;

"periodical payment" means—

(a) A payment which is made or is due to be made at regular intervals in pursuance of a court order or agreement for maintenance;

(b) in a case where the liable relative has established a pattern of making payments at regular intervals, any such payment;

(c) any payment not exceeding the amount of income support payable had that payment not been made;

(d) any payment representing a commutation of payments to which subparagraphs (a) or (b) of this definition applies whether made in arrears or in advance,

but does not include a payment due to be made before the first benefit week pursuant to the claim which is not so made;

"young claimant" means a person aged 16 or over but under 19 who makes a claim for income support.

AMENDMENT

1. Income Support (General) Amendment Regulations 1988 (S.I. 1988 No. 663), reg. 23 (April 11, 1988).

DEFINITIONS

"the Act"—see reg. 2(1).
"benefit week"—*ibid.*
"child"—see 1986 Act, s.20(11) (SSCBA, s.137(1)).
"claimant"—see reg. 2(1), reg. 23(1).
"family"—see 1986 Act, s.20(11) (SSCBA, s.137(1)).
"young person"—see reg. 2(1), reg. 14.

GENERAL NOTE

The rules for liable relative payments do not apply to payments of child support maintenance paid under an assessment carried out in accordance with the Child Support Acts 1991–1995 (reg. 25A). They are taken into account as income in accordance with regs. 60A to 60D.

"Liable relative."
Note that the definition for these purposes is not restricted to those who are obliged to maintain others under s.78(6) of the Administration Act (1986 Act, s.26(3)), but includes in particular, a former spouse and a person who may reasonably be treated as the father of a child (by reason of contributing to the maintenance of the child).

"Payment."
The general definition is very wide, including payments not yet acquired which would be made on application (*cf.* reg. 51(2)). The general category of "payment" is divided into "periodical payments" (further defined below) and "other payments." This division is important in the following regulations.
The list of exceptions is also very important—

(a) A payment arising from a disposition of property made in connection with an agreement to separate or matrimonial proceedings is not a liable relative payment (LRP). There had been great problems in construing the similar, but not identical, supplementary benefit provision,

in particular in deciding when a payment "resulted from" a disposition of property. Although the words here are "arising from," the authoritative settlement of the supplementary benefit problem in *R(SB)1/89* should apply. The claimant received a payment of £2,500 from her ex-husband pursuant to a county court order. This was a consent order made on the basis that the claimant gave up any claims against her ex-husband's houses. The Tribunal of Commissioners holds that there must be a chain of causation, however short, between the disposition and the payment, and that the prior disposition does not have to be by way of sale. Where a payment is made in discharge of a claimant's proprietary interest (or a claim to such an interest) it results from a disposition of property. Where it is made in discharge of maintenance obligations the payment stands alone and does not result from a disposition. *R(SB) 1/89* approves the result of *CSB 1160/1986* where a husband and wife had a joint building society account. On their separation they agreed to split the account and as a result the husband paid £2,500 to the wife, who was receiving supplementary benefit. It was held that the building society account was "property" and that the agreement to split it was a "disposition." The payment then resulted from a disposition of property. It was not a LRP, and had to be dealt with under the ordinary rules on resources.
(b) Payments made after the liable relative's death are not LRPs.
(c) Gifts up to £250 in 52 weeks do not count as LRPs. In view of para. (f), para. (c) must apply to gifts of money or property.
(d) Reg. 44(2) applies to payments to residential schools for a child's or young person's maintenance.
(e) Payments from liable relatives to third parties in respect of the claimant or a member of the claimant's family do not count as LRPs if it would be unreasonable for them to do so. Here much of the guidance in *R(SB) 6/88* is still relevant. This indicates that while the factors mentioned must be considered, other relevant factors may also be considered. If the payment is not a LRP, see reg. 51(3).

Similar rules apply to payments to a member of the claimant's family for a third party (and see para. (9)).
(f) Payments in kind are not LRPs. This could be an important factor in benefit planning.
(g) Payments to or in respect of a child or young person who would otherwise be a member of the claimant's household, but is treated as not being in the household by reg. 16, do not count as LRPs. See reg. 51(3).
(h) Where an "other payment" is being considered, its amount is to be reduced if any of the three categories listed apply. Category (iii) is likely to be particularly important where there is a significant gap between the date of receipt of the payment in question and the date on which the claim for income support (or presumably a question arising on review) is determined. See the notes to reg. 51(1) for the difficulties of deciding when a claimant's purpose is to secure or increase entitlement to income support.

"Periodical payment."
This definition is also very wide, as the four categories are alternatives.
Sub-paras. (a) and (b) are relatively straightforward, covering the standard cases where payments are due to be made at regular intervals or a regular pattern has been established.
The effect of sub-para. (d) is that a payment of arrears of payments under (a) and (b), or a payment in advance, also counts as a periodical payment (subject to the final exception). If, however, a regular pattern of payments has ceased to exist and there is no court order or agreement to make regular payments, such a payment cannot be a commutation of payments under sub-paras. (a) or (b) (*Bolstridge v. Chief Adjudication Officer, The Times*, May 5, 1993). It will be a matter of fact in each case by what date a regular pattern of payments ceases to exist. The facts in *Bolstridge* were that the claimant's ex-husband paid her maintenance of £40 per week on a voluntary basis up to July 31, 1986. He was then made redundant and ceased making payments. In September 1987 her ex-husband made her a payment of £10,500 "in lieu of future maintenance". In July 1988, she claimed income support. The Court of Appeal held that, in the absence of any subsisting contract or outstanding liability, it could not be said that by September 1987, there was an agreement for maintenance of any particular sum or any pattern of regular payment. Therefore, the £10,500 was not a periodical payment. It was an "other payment", to be taken into account under reg. 57. Any part of the total amount which fell outside the definition of "payment" (above) would not be taken into consideration at all. In particular, amounts which the claimant had already spent for "legitimate" purposes would be excluded under sub-para. (h)(iii) of the definition.
The intention of sub-para. (c) seems to be that relatively small payments (*i.e.* up to the amount of one week's income support) are to be treated as periodical payments.

The final exception is crucial to the working of the LRP system. If a payment was due to be made before the first benefit week, pursuant to the claim, but is paid in or after that benefit week, it is an "other payment," not a periodical payment. Thus the treatment of arrears will vary according to whether the claimant was or was not in receipt of benefit during the period to which the arrears relate (on which see *McCorquodale v. Chief Adjudication Officer*, reported as *R(SB) 1/88*).

Treatment of liable relative payments

55. [¹Subject to regulation 55A and] except where regulation 60(1) (liable relative payments to be treated as capital) applies a payment shall—
(a) to the extent that it is not a payment of income, be treated as income;
(b) be taken into account in accordance with the following provisions of this Chapter.

AMENDMENT

1. Social Security Benefits (Maintenance Payments and Consequential Amendments) Regulations 1996 (S.I. 1996 No. 940), reg. 6(2) (April 19, 1996).

DEFINITION

"payment"—see reg. 54.

GENERAL NOTE

The general rule is that if a payment falls into the definition in reg. 54, it is to be taken into account as income. It is only in the limited circumstances described in reg. 60(1) that it can be treated as capital, and therefore be much less likely to affect benefit. See also reg. 55A.

[¹Disregard of payments treated as not relevant income

55A. Where the Secretary of State treats any payment as not being relevant income for the purposes of section 74A of the Social Security Administration Act 1992 (payment of benefit where maintenance payments collected by Secretary of State), that payment shall be disregarded in calculating a claimant's income.]

AMENDMENT

1. Social Security Benefits (Maintenance Payments and Consequential Amendments) Regulations 1996 (S.I. 1996 No. 940), reg. 6(3) (April 19, 1996).

DEFINITIONS

"payment"—see reg. 54.
"relevant income"—see reg. 2(c), Social Security Benefits (Maintenance Payments and Consequential Amendments) Regulations 1996.

GENERAL NOTE

See the note to s. 74A of the Administration Act.

Period over which periodical payments are to be taken into account

56.—(1) The period over which a periodical payment is to be taken into account shall be—
(a) in a case where the payment is made at regular intervals, a period equal to the length of that interval;
(b) in a case where the payment is due to be made at regular intervals but is

not so made, such number of weeks as is equal to the number (and any fraction shall be treated as a corresponding fraction of a week) obtained by dividing the amount of that payment by the weekly amount of that periodical payment as calculated in accordance with regulation 58(4) (calculation of the weekly amount of a liable relative payment);

(c) in any other case, a period equal to a week.

(2) The period under paragraph (1) shall begin on the date on which the payment is treated as paid under regulation 59 (date on which a liable relative payment is to be treated as paid).

<small>DEFINITION</small>

"periodical payment"—see reg. 54.

<small>GENERAL NOTE</small>

If a periodical payment is actually paid at regular intervals, it is to be taken into account for the length of the interval. If it is due to be paid regularly but is not, each payment is spread at the weekly rate of proper payment. In other cases (*e.g.* some payments within sub-para. (c) of the definition of periodical payment) the payment is taken into account for a week.

The application of reg. 56 to payments under sub-para. (d) of the definition of periodical payment is not straightforward. In *Bolstridge v. Chief Adjudication Officer, The Times*, May 5, 1993, it was accepted that reg. 56(1)(b) can be given a sensible meaning only if the word "payment" in that regulation sometimes applies to the commutated payment and sometimes to the payment that was due to be made at regular intervals.

Payments are taken into account from the date on which they are treated as paid under reg. 59.

Period over which payments other than periodical payments are to be taken into account

57.—(1) Subject to paragraph (2), the number of weeks over which any payment other than a periodical payment is to be taken into account shall be equal to the number (and any fraction shall be treated as a corresponding fraction of a week) obtained by dividing that payment by—

(a) where the payment is in respect of the claimant or the claimant and any child or young person who is a member of the family, the aggregate of £2 and the amount of income support which would be payable if the payment had not been made;

[¹(b) where the payment is in respect of one, or more than one, child or young person who is a member of the family, the lesser of the amount (or the aggregate of the amounts) prescribed under Schedule 2, in respect of—

  (i) the personal allowance of the claimant and each such child or young person;

  (ii) any family [². . .] premium;

  (iii) any disabled child premium in respect of such a child; and

  (iv) any carer premium if, but only if, that premium is payable because the claimant is in receipt, or is treated as being in receipt, of invalid care allowance by reason of the fact that he is caring for such a child or young person who is severely disabled;

and the aggregate of £2 and the amount of income support which would be payable had the payment not been made.]

(2) Where a liable relative makes a periodical payment and any other payment concurrently and the weekly amount of that periodical payment, as calculated in accordance with regulation 58 (calculation of the weekly amount of a liable relative payment), is less than—

(a) in a case where the periodical payment is in respect of the claimant or the claimant and any child or young person who is a member of the

family, the aggregate of £2 and the amount of income support which
would be payable had the payment not been made; or

(b) in a case where the periodical payment is in respect of one or more than
one child or young person who is a member of the family, the aggregate
of the amount prescribed in Schedule 2 in respect of each such child or
young person and any family [². . .] premium,

that other payment shall, subject to paragraph (3), be taken into account over
a period of such number of weeks as is equal to the number obtained (and any
fraction shall be treated as a corresponding fraction of a week) by dividing that
payment by an amount equal to the extent of the difference between the amount
referred to in sub-paragraph (a) or (b), as the case may be, and the weekly
amount of the periodical payment.

(3) If—

(a) the liable relative ceases to make periodical payments, the balance (if
any) of the other payment shall be taken into account over the number
of weeks equal to the number obtained (and any fraction shall be treated
as a corresponding fraction of a week) by dividing that balance by the
amount referred to in sub-paragraph (a) or (b) of paragraph (1), as the
case may be;

(b) the amount of any subsequent periodical payment varies, the balance (if
any) of the other payment shall be taken into account over a period of
such number of weeks as is equal to the number obtained (and any
fraction shall be treated as a corresponding fraction of a week) by dividing that balance by an amount equal to the extent of the difference
between the amount referred to in sub-paragraph (a) or (b) of paragraph
(2) and the weekly amount of the subsequent periodical payment.

(4) The period under paragraph (1) or (2) shall begin on the date on which
the payment is treated as paid under regulation 59 (date on which a liable relative
payment is treated as paid) and under paragraph (3) shall begin on the first day
of the benefit week in which the cessation or variation of the periodical payment
occurred.

AMENDMENTS

1. Income Support (General) Amendment No. 3 Regulations 1990 (S.I. 1990 No. 1776), reg. 7
(October 15, 1990).
2. Child Benefit, Child Support and Social Security (Miscellaneous Amendments) Regulations
1996 (S.I. 1996 No. 1803), reg. 38 (April 7, 1997).

DEFINITIONS

"child"—see 1986 Act, s.20(11) (SSCBA, s.137(1)).
"claimant"—see reg. 2(1), reg. 23(1), reg. 54.
"family"—see 1986 Act, s.20(11) (SSCBA, s.137(1)).
"liable relative"—see reg. 54.
"payment"—*ibid.*
"periodical payment"—*ibid.*
"young person"—see reg. 2(1), reg. 14.

GENERAL NOTE

This regulation deals with payments other than periodical payments. The basic rule under para.
(1) is to spread them at the rate of income support for the people the payment is for, plus £2 if
one of them is the claimant. Since October 1990, para. (1)(b) deems more elements of the applicable
amount to be treated as for a child. Paras. (2) and (3) modify this rule where the payment is in
addition to periodical payments so as to spread the payments at the rate of the difference between

the amount of the periodical payment and the amount identified in para. (1), as long as the periodical payments continue to be made.

See reg. 58(5) for the weekly amount to be taken into account.

Calculation of the weekly amount of a liable relative payment

58.—(1) Where a periodical payment is made or is due to be made at intervals of one week, the weekly amount shall be the amount of that payment.

(2) Where a periodical payment is made or is due to be made at intervals greater than one week and those intervals are monthly, the weekly amount shall be determined by multiplying the amount of the payment by 12 and dividing the product by 52.

(3) Where a periodical payment is made or is due to be made at intervals and those intervals are neither weekly nor monthly, the weekly amount shall be determined by dividing that payment by the number equal to the number of weeks (including any part of a week) in that interval.

(4) Where a payment is made and that payment represents a commutation of periodical payments whether in arrears or in advance, the weekly amount shall be the weekly amount of the individual periodical payments so commutated, as calculated under paragraphs (1) to (3) as is appropriate.

(5) The weekly amount of a payment to which regulation 57 applies (period over which payments other than periodical payments are to be taken into account) shall be equal to the amount of the divisor used in calculating the period over which the payment or, as the case may be, the balance is to be taken into account.

DEFINITIONS

    "payment"—see reg. 54.
    "periodical payment"—*ibid.*

GENERAL NOTE

    The weekly rate of periodical payments is normally calculated by dividing the payment into weekly bits depending on the intervals between payment dates (paras. (1) to (3)). For a commutation of periodical payments, whether in arrears or in advance (which itself comes within the definition of periodical payment), the weekly rate is the appropriate one for the recurring payments.

Date on which a liable relative payment is to be treated as paid

59.—(1) A periodical payment is to be treated as paid—
  (a) in the case of a payment which is due to be made before the first benefit week pursuant to the claim, on the day in the week in which it is to be paid which corresponds to the first day of the benefit week;
  (b) in any other case, on the first day of the benefit week in which it is due to be paid unless, having regard to the manner in which income support is due to be paid in the particular case, it would be more practicable to treat it as paid on the first day of a subsequent benefit week.

(2) Subject to paragraph (3), any other payment shall be treated as paid—
  (a) in the case of a payment which is made before the first benefit week pursuant to the claim, on the day in the week in which it is paid which corresponds to the first day of the benefit week;
  (b) in any other case, on the first day of the benefit week in which it is paid unless, having regard to the manner in which income support is due to be paid in the particular case, it would be more practicable to treat it as paid on the first day of a subsequent benefit week.

(3) Any other payment paid on a date which falls within the period in respect

of which a previous payment is taken into account, not being a periodical payment, is to be treated as paid on the first day following the end of that period.

"benefit week"—see reg. 2(1).
"payment"—see reg. 54.
"periodical payment"—*ibid.*

GENERAL NOTE

Paragraph (1)
This provision effectively applies the ordinary rule for income (see reg. 31) to periodical payments. Under sub-para. (a) for the payment still to be a periodical payment it must have been paid
as well as been due before the first benefit week pursuant to the claim. Once the benefit week is
determined under para. 4 of Sched. 7 to the Claims and Payments Regulations, prior weeks can be
counted off and payments attributed to the first day of each week. Under sub-para. (b), for other
periodical payments (which can include many payments of arrears) the crucial thing is the benefit
week in which the payment is due, or, if it would be more practicable, a subsequent week. A
payment of arrears within the definition of a periodical payment may well have been due in a large
number of past weeks, for which benefit has already been paid on the assumption that no LRP had
been received. This would seem to trigger the application of s.74(1) of the Administration Act (1986
Act, s.27(1)). Para. 33834 of the *Adjudication Officer's Guide* suggests that in such circumstances
it is more practicable to take the payment into account from the next benefit week in which the
amount of benefit can be adjusted, although the *Guide* does not really face the problem of payments
of arrears. If continuing periodical payments are being made, the spreading of a payment of arrears
over future benefit weeks could lead to more than one periodical payment being taken into account
in the same benefit week. Whether this leaves the claimant better off than if recovery under s.74(1)
had been triggered depends on the levels of payment in relation to income support entitlement. It
is not at all clear that this solution is "more practicable" than spreading the payment of arrears
over the past period to which the arrears related. The latter solution, with the recovery of any
overpayment under s.74(1), may be better.

Paragraph (2)
This provision applies to all "other payments", including payments of arrears identified in the
final exception to the definition of "periodical payment". Here it is the date of actual payment,
rather than the date on which payment is due, which is crucial. Sub-para. (a) applies to payments
made before the first benefit week pursuant to the claim. Sub-para. (b) applies in all other cases,
and allows attribution to a later benefit week than that of payment if that is more practicable.
The result for payments of arrears relating to a period before entitlement to benefit, is that the
payment is treated as income to be spread at the rate identified in reg. 58 from the date of actual
payment. This reverses the result of *McCorquodale v. Chief Adjudication Officer* (reported as *R(SB)
1/88)*. If this results in one "other payment" being attributed to a benefit week to which another
"other payment" has already been attributed, the attribution of the later payment is deferred until
the first one runs out (para. (3)).

Liable relative payments to be treated as capital

60.—(1) Subject to paragraph (2), where a liable relative makes a periodical
payment concurrently with any other payment, and the weekly amount of the
periodical payment as calculated in accordance with regulation 58(1) to (4)
(calculation of the weekly amount of a liable relative payment), is equal to or
greater than the amount referred to in sub-paragraph (a) of regulation 57(2)
(period over which payments other than periodical payments are to be taken into
account) less the £2 referred to therein, or sub-paragraph (b) of that regulation,
as the case may be, the other payment shall be treated as capital.

(2) If, in any case, the liable relative ceases to make periodical payments, the
other payment to which paragraph (1) applies shall be taken into account under
paragraph (1) of regulation 57 but, notwithstanding paragraph (4) thereof, the
period over which the payment is to be taken into account shall begin on the

first day of the benefit week following the last one in which a periodical payment was taken into account.

DEFINITIONS

"benefit week"—see reg. 2(1).
"liable relative"—see reg. 54.
"payment"—*ibid.*
"periodical payment"—*ibid.*

GENERAL NOTE

If a periodical payment at least equals the income support rate for the person(s) it is for, any other payment made at the same time is treated as capital. If the liable relative later stops making the periodical payments the other payment can be tapped as income under para. (2).

[¹*Chapter VIIA*

Child Support

Interpretation

60A. In this Chapter—
"child support maintenance" means such periodical payments as are referred to in section 3(6) of the Child Support Act 1991;
"maintenance assessment" has the same meaning as in the Child Support Act 1991 by virtue of section 54 of that Act.]

AMENDMENT

1. Social Security (Miscellaneous Provisions) Amendment Regulations 1993 (S.I. 1993 No. 846), reg. 3 (April 19, 1993).

GENERAL NOTE

Section 3(6) of the Child Support Act 1991 refers to "periodical payments which are required to be paid in accordance with a maintenance assessment." A "maintenance assessment" is defined in s.54 as "an assessment of maintenance made under [the Child Support Act 1991] and, except in prescribed circumstances, includes an interim maintenance assessment."

[¹Treatment of child support maintenance

60B. [²Subject to regulation 60E,] all payments of child support maintenance shall to the extent that they are not payments of income be treated as income and shall be taken into account on a weekly basis in accordance with the following provisions of this Chapter.]

AMENDMENTS

1. Social Security (Miscellaneous Provisions) Amendment Regulations 1993 (S.I. 1993 No. 846), reg. 3 (April 19, 1993).
2. Social Security Benefits (Maintenance Payments and Consequential Amendments) Regulations 1996 (S.I. 1996 No. 940), reg. 6(4) (April 19, 1996).

DEFINITIONS

"child support maintenance"—see reg. 60A.
"payment"—see reg. 2(1).

GENERAL NOTE

Since the definition of "child support maintenance" refers to payments which are required to be made periodically, it appears that payments in commutation of periodical payments, either in advance or in arrears, will be payments of child support maintenance, providing that there is a subsisting liability under a maintenance assessment (see *Bolstridge v. Chief Adjudication Officer*, *The Times*, May 5, 1993). They then have to be treated as payments of income. See reg. 60C(5) for commutation payments. Payments made at the periodical intervals required under the maintenance assessment would be income anyway, but are to be taken into account according to the rules set out in regs. 60C and 60D.

All income under Chapter VIIA is taken into account in full in assessing entitlement to income support. There are no disregards. But see reg. 60E.

[¹Calculation of the weekly amount of payments of child support maintenance

60C.—(1) The weekly amount of child support maintenance shall be determined in accordance with the following provisions of this regulation.

(2) Where payments of child support maintenance are made weekly, the weekly amount shall be the amount of that payment.

(3) Where payments of child support maintenance are made monthly, the weekly amount shall be determined by multiplying the amount of the payment by 12 and dividing the product by 52.

(4) Where payments of child support are made at intervals and those intervals are not a week or a month, the weekly amount shall be determined by dividing that payment by the number equal to the number of weeks (including any part of a week) in that interval.

(5) Where a payment is made and that payment represents a commutation of child support maintenance the weekly amount shall be the weekly amount of the individual child support maintenance payments so commuted as calculated in accordance with paragraphs (2) to (4) as appropriate.

(6) Paragraph (2), (3) or, as the case may be, (4) shall apply to any payments made at the intervals specified in that paragraph whether or not—

  (a) the amount paid is in accordance with the maintenance assessment, and
  (b) the intervals at which the payments are made are in accordance with the intervals specified by the Secretary of State under regulation 4 of the Child Support (Collection and Enforcement) Regulations 1992].

AMENDMENT

1. Social Security (Miscellaneous Provisions) Amendment Regulations 1993 (S.I. 1993 No. 846), reg. 3 (April 19, 1993).

DEFINITIONS

  "child support maintenance"—see reg. 60A.
  "maintenance assessment"—*ibid.*
  "payment"—see reg. 2(1).

GENERAL NOTE

The Secretary of State specifies the day and interval by reference to which payments of child support maintenance are to be paid by the liable person (Child Support (Collection and Enforcement) Regulations 1992, reg. 4). Paras. (2) to (4) work easily when payments of the full amount of the maintenance assessment are made at regular intervals. Then they supply simple arithmetical rules for working out the weekly amount and reg. 60D defines when each payment is to be treated as made. If the payments are not made at regular intervals, it is not clear whether para. (4) should apply, taking the interval since the last payment to define the weekly amount, or whether the payment should be treated as a commutation of past maintenance under para. (5). If regular payments are made of less than the maintenance assessment, the effect of para. (6) is that the actual amount paid should be treated as income, not the amount properly due. If later a payment of arrears is made in a lump sum, does para. (5) apply to that payment as a commutation of child support maintenance, or does the definition of child support maintenance mean that para. (5) only applies to payments which are multiples of the payments required to be made under the maintenance assessment? It would seem that the former is intended, because there can be recovery of overpaid income support under s.74(1) of the Administration Act when arrears of child support maintenance are paid only to take account of the period between the effective date of the maintenance assessment and the date when normal periodical payments start (Social Security (Payments on account, Overpayments and Recovery) Regulations 1988, reg. 7(1)(b): see below). In practice, where the parent with care is on income support, it is likely that payments of arrears by an absent parent for periods after normal periodical payments start will be made direct to the Child Support Agency who will retain an amount equal to the income support that would not have been paid if the child support maintenance had been paid on time. But if arrangements for payment direct to the Child Support Agency have not yet been made (*e.g.* where the absent parent has only just fallen into arrears), para. (5) may apply to any payments made in these circumstances.

Para. (5) deals with payments which are commutations of child support maintenance. Although nothing is said expressly, it would seem to cover commutations both in advance or in arrears. There is little problem over payments in advance.

[¹Date on which child support maintenance is to be treated as paid

60D.—[²(1) Subject to paragraph (2),] a payment of child support maintenance is to be treated as paid—

    (a) [² subject to sub-paragraph (aa),] in the case of a payment which is due to be paid before the first benefit week pursuant to the claim, on the day in the week in which it is due to be paid which corresponds to the first day of the benefit week;

[²(aa) in the case of any amount of a payment which represents arrears of maintenance for a week prior to the first benefit week pursuant to a claim, on the day of the week in which it became due which corresponds to the first day of the benefit week;]

    (b) in any other case, on the first day of the benefit week in which [²it is due to be paid] or the first day of the first succeeding benefit week in which it is practicable to take it into account.]

[²(2) Where a payment to which paragraph (1)(b) refers is made to the Secretary of State and then transmitted to the person entitled to receive it, the payment shall be treated as paid on the first day of the benefit week in which it is transmitted or, where it is not practicable to take it into account in that week, the first day of the first succeeding benefit week in which it is practicable to take the payment into account.]

AMENDMENTS

1. Social Security (Miscellaneous Provisions) Amendment Regulations 1993 (S.I. 1993 No. 846), reg. 3 (April 19, 1993).
2. Income-related Benefits Schemes and Social Fund (Miscellaneous Amendments) Regulations 1986 (S.I. 1996 No. 1944), reg. 6(7) (October 7, 1996).

DEFINITIONS

    "benefit week"—see reg. 2(1).
    "child support maintenance"—see reg. 60A.

GENERAL NOTE

Sub-paragraphs (a) and (b) of para. (1) contain the same rule as in reg. 31(1). Para. (1)(aa) clarifies the position (possibly superfluously) where any arrears of child support maintenance are paid that were due before income support was first paid. Para. (2) sets the date when child support mainten-ance payments that are paid via the Child Support Agency are treated as paid.

[¹Disregard of payments treated as not relevant income

60E. Where the Secretary of State treats any payment of child support maintenance as not being relevant income for the purposes of section 74A of the Social Security Administration Act 1992 (payment of benefit where maintenance payments collected by Secretary of State), that payment shall be disregarded in calculating a claimant's income.]

AMENDMENT

1. Social Security Benefits (Maintenance Payments and Consequential Amendments) Regulations 1996 (S.I. 1996 No. 940), reg. 6(5) (April 19, 1996).

DEFINITIONS

"child support maintenance"—see reg. 60A.
"payment"—see reg. 2(1).
"relevant income"—see reg. 2(c), Social Security Benefits (Maintenance Payments and Consequential Amendments) Regulations 1996.

GENERAL NOTE

See the note to s. 74A of the Administration Act.

Chapter VIII

Students

Interpretation

61. In this Chapter, unless the context otherwise requires—
[⁸"college of further education" means a college of further education within the meaning of Part I of the Further and Higher Education (Scotland) Act 1992;]
[⁸"contribution" means any contribution in respect of the income [¹⁰ of a student or] of any other person which the Secretary of State or an education authority takes into account in ascertaining the amount of the student's grant, or any sums, which in determining the amount of a student's allowance or bursary in Scotland under the Further and Higher Education (Scotland) Act 1992, the Secretary of State or education authority takes into account being sums which the Secretary of State or the education authority consider that the holder of the allowance or bursary, the holder's parents and the holder's spouse can reasonably be expected to contribute towards the holder's expenses;]
[⁸"course of advanced education" means—
   (a) a course leading to a postgraduate degree or comparable qualification, a first degree or comparable qualification, a diploma of higher education or a higher national diploma; or
   (b) any other course which is of a standard above advanced GNVQ or equivalent, including a course which is of a standard above a general certificate of education (advanced level), a Scottish certificate of education (higher level) or a Scottish certificate of sixth year studies;]
"covenant income" means the income [⁸. . .] payable to a student under a Deed of Covenant by a person whose income is, or is likely to be, taken into account in assessing the student's grant or award;
"education authority" means a government department, a local education authority as defined in section 114(1) of the Education Act 1944

(interpretation), [⁸a local education authority as defined in section 123 of the Local Government (Scotland) Act 1973], an education and library board established under Article 3 of the Education and Libraries (Northern Ireland) Order 1986, any body which is a research council for the purposes of the Science and Technology Act 1965 or any analogous government department, authority, board or body, of the Channel Islands, Isle of Man or any other country outside Great Britain;

[⁸"the FEFC" means the Further Education Funding Council for England or the Further Education Funding Council for Wales;]

[⁸"full-time course of advanced education" means a course of advanced education which is taken by a person who is—

(a) attending a full-time course of study which is not funded in whole or in part by the FEFC or a full-time course of study which is not funded in whole or in part by the Secretary of State for Scotland at a college of further education or a full-time course of study which is a course of higher education and is funded in whole or in part by the Secretary of State for Scotland;

(b) undertaking a course of study which is funded in whole or in part by the FEFC if it involves more than 16 guided learning hours per week for the student in question, according to the number of guided learning hours per week for that student set out in the case of a course funded by the FEFC for England, in his learning agreement signed on behalf of the establishment which is funded by the FEFC for the delivery of that course or, in the case of a course funded by the FEFC for Wales, in a document signed on behalf of the establishment which is funded by the FEFC for the delivery of that course; or

(c) undertaking a course of study (not being higher education) which is funded in whole or in part by the Secretary of State for Scotland at a college of further education if it involves—

(i) more than 16 hours per week of classroom-based or workshop-based programmed learning under the direct guidance of teaching staff according to the number of hours set out in a document signed on behalf of the college; or

(ii) 16 hours or less per week of classroom-based or workshop-based programmed learning under the direct guidance of teaching staff and it involves additional hours using structured learning packages supported by the teaching staff where the combined total of hours exceeds 21 per week, according to the number of hours set out in a document signed on behalf of the college;]

[⁸"full-time course of study" means a full-time course of study which—

(a) is not funded in whole or in part by the FEFC or a full-time course of study which is not funded in whole or in part by the Secretary of State for Scotland at a college of further education or a full-time course of study which is a course of higher education and is funded in whole or in part by the Secretary of State for Scotland;

(b) is funded in whole or in part by the FEFC if it involves more than 16 guided learning hours per week for the student in question, according to the number of guided learning hours per week for that student set out in the case of a course funded by the FEFC for England, in his learning agreement signed on behalf of the establishment which is funded by the FEFC for the delivery of that course or, in the case of a course funded by the FEFC for Wales, in a document signed on behalf of the establishment which is funded by the FEFC for the delivery of that course; or

(c) is not higher education and is funded in whole or in part by the

Secretary of State for Scotland at a college of further education if it involves—

    (i) more than 16 hours per week of classroom-based or workshop-based programmed learning under the direct guidance of teaching staff according to the number of hours set out in a document signed on behalf of the college; or

    (ii) 16 hours or less per week of classroom-based or workshop-based programmed learning under the direct guidance of teaching staff and it involves additional hours using structured learning packages supported by the teaching staff where the combined total of hours exceeds 21 per week, according to the number of hours set out in a document signed on behalf of the college;]

"grant" means any kind of educational grant or award and includes any scholarship, studentship, exhibition, allowance or bursary [²but does not include a payment derived from funds made available by the Secretary of State for the purpose of assisting students in financial difficulties under section 100 of the Education Act 1944, [⁸ section 65 of the Further and Higher Education Act 1992] or section 73 of the Education (Scotland) Act 1980 [⁸ or section 40 of the Further and Higher Education (Scotland) Act 1992]];

"grant income" means—

    (a) any income by way of a grant;

    (b) in the case of a student other than one to whom sub-paragraph (c) refers, any contribution which has been assessed whether or not it has been paid;

    (c) in the case of a student to whom [⁹ paragraph 1, 2 10, 11 or 12 of Schedule 1B] applies (lone parent or disabled student), any contribution which has been assessed and which has been paid;

and any such contribution which is paid by way of a covenant shall be treated as part of the student's grant income;

[⁸"higher education" means higher education within the meaning of Part II of the Further and Higher Education (Scotland) Act 1992;]

[³"last day of the course" means the date on which the last day of the final academic term falls in respect of the course in which the student is enrolled;]

"period of study" means—

    (a) in the case of a course of study for one year or less, the period beginning with the start of the course [³and ending with the last day of the course];

    (b) in the case of a course of study for more than one year, in the first or, as the case may be, any subsequent year of the course, [³other than the final year of the course,] the period beginning with the start of the course or, as the case may be, that year's start and ending with either—

        (i) the day before the start of the next year of the course in a case where the student's grant is assessed at a rate appropriate to his studying throughout the year, or, if he does not have a grant, where it would have been assessed at such a rate had he had one; or

        (ii) in any other case the day before the start of the normal summer vacation appropriate to his course;

    [³(c) in the final year of a course of study of more than one year, the period beginning with that year's start and ending with the last day of the course;]

"periods of experience" has the meaning prescribed in paragraph 1(1) of Schedule 5 to the [⁸Education (Mandatory Awards) Regulations 1995];

"sandwich course" has the meaning prescribed in paragraph 1(1) of Schedule 5 to [[8] Education (Mandatory Awards) Regulations 1995];

[[8]"standard maintenance grant" means—

(a) except where paragraph (b) or (c) applies, in the case of a student attending a course of study at the University of London or an establishment within the area comprising the City of London and the Metropolitan Police District, the amount specified for the time being in paragraph 2(2)(a) of Schedule 2 to the Education (Mandatory Awards) Regulations 1995 ("the 1995 Regulations") for such a student;

(b) except where paragraph (c) applies, in the case of a student residing at his parents' home, the amount specified in paragraph 3(2) thereof;

(c) in the case of a student receiving an allowance or bursary under the Further and Higher Education (Scotland) Act 1992, the amount of money specified as "standard maintenance allowance" for the relevant year appropriate for the student set out in the Guide to Undergraduate allowances issued by the Student Awards Agency for Scotland, or its nearest equivalent in the case of a bursary as set by the local education authority;

(d) in any other case, the amount specified in paragraph 2(2) of Schedule 2 to the 1995 Regulations other than in sub-paragraph (a) or (b) thereof;]

[[4]"student" means a person, other than a person in receipt of a training allowance,] aged less than 19 who is attending a full-time course of advanced education or, as the case may be, a person aged 19 or over but under pensionable age who is attending a full-time course of study at an educational establishment; and for the purposes of this definition—

(a) a person who has started on such a course shall be treated as attending it [[7]- - -] until [[3]the last day of the course] or such earlier date as he abandons it or is dismissed from it;

(b) a person on a sandwich course shall be treated as attending a full-time course of advanced education or, as the case may be, of study;

"year" in relation to a [[8]course of study], means the period of 12 months beginning on 1st January, 1st April or 1st September according to whether the academic year of the course in question begins in the spring, the summer or the autumn respectively.

AMENDMENTS

1. Income Support (General) Amendment No. 5 Regulations 1988 (S.I. 1988 No. 2022), reg. 14 (December 12, 1988).

2. Social Security Benefits (Student Loans and Miscellaneous Amendments) Regulations 1990 (S.I. 1990 No. 1549), reg. 5(5) (September 1, 1990).

3. Income Support (General) Amendment No. 4 Regulations 1991 (S.I. 1991 No. 1559), reg. 10 (August 5, 1991).

4. Income Support (General) Amendment Regulations 1992 (S.I. 1992 No. 468), reg. 5 (April 6, 1992).

5. Income-related Benefits Schemes (Miscellaneous Amendments) (No. 3) Regulations 1992 (S.I. 1992 No. 2155), reg. 19 (October 5, 1992).

6. Income-related Benefits Schemes (Miscellaneous Amendments) (No.4) Regulations 1993 (S.I. 1993 No. 2119), reg. 16 (October 4, 1993).

7. Social Security Benefits (Miscellaneous Amendments) Regulations 1995 (S.I. 1995 No. 1742), reg. 2 (August 1, 1995).

8. Income-related Benefits Schemes and Social Fund (Miscellaneous Amendments) Regulations 1996 (S.I. 1996 No. 1944), reg. 6(8) (October 7, 1996).

9. Income-related Benefits and Jobseeker's Allowance (Amendment) (No. 2) Regulations 1997 (S.I. 1997 No. 2197), reg. 5(5) (October 6, 1997).

10. Social Security (Miscellaneous Amendments) Regulations 1998 (S.I. 1998 No. 563), reg. 4(1) and (2)(e) (April 6, 1998).

DEFINITIONS

"training allowance"—see reg. 2(1).
"course of study"—*ibid.*

GENERAL NOTE

"Grant"

R(SB) 20/83 decided that "award" included a loan. However, in *R(IS) 16/95* the Commissioner disagrees with *R(SB) 20/83*. In his view, "award", if given its everyday meaning, particularly in the context of academic grants and awards, implied an outright gift with no liability to repay. Thus the education loan received by the claimant's partner from the Norwegian Government did not fall within reg. 61, but was to be taken into account as income under reg. 40 (see *R(SB) 7/88*). Reg. 66A (concerning the student loan scheme) had been introduced simply for the removal of doubt and did not indicate that, without it, loans would not count as income.

"Grant income"

Note that in most cases a parental contribution is included whether paid or not.

Where a person is due to repay part or all of a student grant because he leaves or is dismissed from his course before it finishes, see regs. 29(2B), 32(6A) and 40(3B). But note *Chief Adjudication Officer v. Leeves* (November 6, 1998, CA, to be reported as *R(IS) 5/99*) in the notes to reg. 29(2B) and the argument discussed in those notes as to when reg. 29(2B) applies. Note also para. 61 of Sched. 9 under which any grant (or covenant income or student loan) left over at the end of a person's course is ignored.

"Student"

The definition of student here is important not just for Chapter VIII on the income of students, but also because it feeds back in through the additional definition of "period of study" in reg. 2(1) to remove most students' entitlement (see reg. 4ZA(2) and (3)). Note that those in receipt of a training allowance are excluded from the definition.

There are two categories. A person under 19 is a student if attending a full-time course of advanced education. Advanced education is defined earlier in reg. 61.

A person of 19 or over (but under pensionable age) is a student if attending a full-time course of study at an educational establishment. It does not have to be any particular level. A person of 19 cannot be in relevant education, because that only applies to children or young persons (reg. 12). The reference is to a course of study, rather than of education, as it was in the Supplementary Benefit (Conditions of Entitlement) Regulations. This probably makes little difference, although it makes it harder to argue that students pursuing degrees purely by research, with no coursework, are not "attending" a course (see *(R(SB) 26/82)*), but pursuing or following it. *R(SB) 25/87* decides that a pupil barrister is not a student because pupillage is not a course of education, but an assimilation of specific vocational skills by attending on the pupil master. Presumably, a pupil barrister would be said not to be attending a "course of study" (the phrase here) either. *CIS 50/1990* suggests that this approach is not lightly to be extended to other circumstances. The claimant was attending an intensive shorthand and typing course at a commercial Training Centre. There was little difficulty in deciding that this was a full-time course. The Commissioner holds that since there was active tuition, the claimant was engaged in study, regardless of the technical nature of the skills studied. The Centre was within the ordinary meaning of "educational establishment." In *CIS 5034/1995*, to be reported as *R(IS) 5/97*, a person attending the Bar Vocational Course at the Council of Legal Education was a student. *R(SB) 25/87* was clearly distinguishable. See also *CIS 450/1997* which decides that a Project 2000 student nurse came within the definition of "student".

On the meaning of "course", see *R(IS) 1/96*. The claimant was training to be an architect. He had obtained his degree and had to find a year's placement with a firm before undertaking a further two years' study (to be followed by a further year's practical experience) in order to complete his professional training. The Commissioner holds that he was not a student during the year "out". In the Commissioner's view, a course was a "unified sequence of study, tuition and/or practical training . . . intended to lead to one or more qualifications obtained on its completion". So if a profession required more than one qualification for which colleges did not provide a single sequence of tuition and/or experience, the person was not engaged on one continuous "course" throughout, but completed one "course" before moving onto another. Thus para (a) of the definition of student did not apply to him. Para. (b) also did not apply as the claimant was not on a "sandwich course", since any periods of outside practical experience were not "associated with" his full-time study within the meaning of the Mandatory Awards Regulations. See also *CIS 576/1994* in which the Commissioner similarly decides that the course is the whole course leading to the qualification and not a separate course each year.

"Full-time course"

The shifting of the words "full-time", as compared with the supplementary benefit definition, emphasises that it is the course which has to be full-time, rather than the claimant's hours of attendance on it (see *R(SB) 40/83*, *R(SB) 41/83*, *CSB 176/1987*). Note that the definition of student applies for the entire length of a full-time course, as confirmed by the August 1991 amendments. The definition applies unless the student abandons the course or is dismissed from it (see further below). Note *CIS 368/1992* which decided that a student who exercised the option of working in France for a year as part of her course remained a student throughout her four-year course. Her course was continuing, even if in a different form.

Thus the question whether the course is full- or part-time is clearly crucial, since the exclusion from income support does not apply to part-time students who may be eligible for benefit if they fall within any of the categories in Sched. 1B. Until October 1996 there was no definition of "full-time course", so whether or not a course was full-time depended on the particular facts. The effect of the definitions of "full-time course of study" and "full-time course of advanced education" inserted from October 7, 1996 is that in England and Wales the cut-off for a full-time course that is totally or partly funded by the Further Education Funding Council (FEFC) is 16 or more "guided learning hours" each week. The number of a person's "guided learning hours" will be set out in his learning agreement with his college. Guided learning hours are "hours when a member of staff is present to guide learning on a programme including lectures, tutorials and supervised study", as opposed to time spent in private study (*Adjudication Officer's Guide*, para. 35045). Note the different definitions that apply in Scotland. But for courses which are not so funded, whether or not a course is full-time will continue to be determined by the circumstances in each case. The educational establishment's description of the course is not conclusive but should be accepted unless challenged by pertinent evidence (*R(SB) 40/83; R(SB) 41/83*).

In *CIS 152/1994* the Commissioner recognised that recent developments in education, and in particular the advent of modular courses, have blurred the distinction between full-time and part-time courses, and that what is in essence the same course can often be accessed on either a full-time or a part-time basis. The claimant had begun a full-time course in 1992, studying 21 and three quarters hours a week. In 1993 he reduced the number of modules he was taking from seven to five, so that his hours of study became 15 a week. The Commissioner states that it is no longer sufficient just to look at the course. The overall circumstances (*e.g.* the hours of study, number of modules, length of time it would take to obtain the qualification on the basis of five as opposed to seven modules at a time, correspondence from the college, fees payable and any relevant information in the college prospectus) therefore had to be examined to ascertain whether the course the claimant was *now* attending was full or part-time. (But see *O'Connor* (below) which agrees with Hobhouse L.J. in *Webber* (below) that whether a course is full-time for the purpose of para. (a) is determined at its start, not according to later changes). See also *CSIS 62/1992* in which the claimant who was allowed to transfer to a part-time course at the end of his three year full-time course to retake a subject he had failed a number of times did not fall within the definition of student.

A similar approach was taken in *CIS 576/1994*. The claimant's modular degree course could be undertaken on a full-time or part-time basis. He attended on a full-time basis for the first year and then changed to part-time. He became full-time again for the last two terms of the third year. The Commissioner states that para. (a) of the definition of "student" did not have the effect of turning a course, attendance on which was on a part-time basis, into a full-time course. Whether a person was, or was not, attending a full-time course depended on the facts at the material time. The factors suggested in *CIS 152/1994* were relevant; whether the person had a local authority grant or student loan might also be pertinent since these were not available to part-time students (see the Mandatory Awards Regulations). The claimant was not a student when he was attending part-time.

An appeal against this decision was dismissed by the Court of Appeal (*Chief Adjudication Officer v. Webber* [1997] 4 All E.R. 274) but for differing reasons. Hobhouse L.J. stated that the definition of "course of study" presupposes that it is possible at the outset to categorise a course as full-time or part-time and that the same categorisation will apply from the start to the end of the course. But that assumption did not accord with the practice of many educational institutions. Many courses allowed students the option of attending on a full- or part-time basis at different stages of the course, as was the case in this appeal. The consequence was that the claimant had *never* been a student because the course on which he was enrolled did not require full-time attendance and so could not be described as full-time. Such an interpretation clearly has significant implications and goes considerably beyond that of the Commissioner. Evans L.J. held that the deeming provision in para. (a) of the definition could not be relied upon to confer the status of student when this did not in fact exist. In his view, if interpreted in that way the provision created "an anomalous class of people left to destitution without state support of any kind" and he would require "express words of the utmost clarity to persuade [him] that Parliament intended to produce that disgraceful result". Peter Gibson L.J.'s judgment was based on the fact that the definition of "student" at the time in question included the words "throughout any period of term or vacation within it" (which phrase was omitted from August 1, 1995 following the Court of Appeal's decision in *Clarke and Faul*, see below).

The result of these differing approaches was that the position was somewhat unclear. However in *O'Connor* (see below), the judges who were in the majority agreed with Hobhouse L.J. that the status of student was determined by the nature of the course at its beginning and distinguished their own decision from that in *Webber* on that basis. Auld L.J. stated that in Mr O'Connor's case his course was a full-time three year course, with no provision for part-time or modular or other flexible arrangements. Although he had been allowed a year's break in order to re-take exams that he had failed, this was not an option of the course when he started it. But if at its start a course could be followed full- or part-time according to the student's preference, the position was different for the reasons given by Hobhouse L.J. in *Webber*. It therefore seems that a claimant on a (modular) course which cannot be characterised as full-time at the outset because he may study full- or part-time for different periods of it will not come within the definition of "student". However, in view of the diversity of courses and the much greater flexibility in terms of learning methods, attendance and participation now offered by many higher education institutions, it is suggested that determining whether a claimant's course falls on the *Webber* or the *O'Connor* side of the line may not always be straightforward.

"Attending [a course] . . . abandons . . . or is dismissed from it"
Other aspects of the definition of "student" have also come under scrutiny in several cases.

Until July 31, 1995, para. (a) had included the words "throughout any period of term or vacation within it" after the words "treated as attending it". In *Chief Adjudication Officer and Secretary of State for Social Security v. Clarke and Faul* [1995] E.L.R. 259 the Court of Appeal decided (by a majority) that the two claimants who had been allowed to "intercalate" (that is, take time off from their course) were not students during their intercalating years. This was because there could be no period of term or vacation within a course when the student was not attending the course at all. The purpose of the regulations was that a person should count as a student for income support purposes when he would be entitled to support under the students' grants and loans systems because he was attending a course. If he took time off from his course he was not eligible for such support. Thus during such time he should not be excluded from income support. Hoffman L.J. commented that "one would . . . expect that a student's exclusion from social security benefits would be mirrored by his entitlement to an education award and a student loan. Otherwise there would be an anomalous class of people who for no obvious reason were left to destitution without state support of any kind". The purpose of the August 1995 amendment to para. (a) was to reverse the effect of this decision (confirmed in *CIS 14477/1996;* the argument that the amendment was *ultra vires* on the grounds of irrationality was rejected by both the Commissioner and the Court of Appeal in *O'Connor* (see below). The old form of para. (a) was also at issue in *Driver v. Chief Adjudication Officer* (Court of Appeal, December 12, 1996, to be reported as *R(IS) 6/97*). The claimant who was on a sandwich course claimed income support when her industrial placement ended prematurely. The Court (again by a majority) decided that the reasoning in *Clarke and Faul* did not apply and that the claimant continued to be a student throughout the period of her intended placement.

Following the amendment to para. (a) a person will count as a student during any period of temporary absence from the course. In *Clarke* the claimant had a right to resume her course at an agreed date. But what if a person's attendance on a course has ceased in circumstances in which he has no *right* to return? Could it be argued that he has "abandoned" or "been dismissed" from the course? The Commissioner in *CIS 514/1992* (which was the decision appealed against in *Clarke*) decided that a course could be abandoned temporarily, but the Court of Appeal considered that "abandon" in the context of the definition of "student" in reg. 61 meant "abandon permanently". Presumably "dismissal" similarly refers to final dismissal. But in *CIS 13986/1996* the Commissioner holds that a claimant who was not attending his course because he had failed exams and was only permitted to return if and when he successfully passed the resits a year later had been dismissed from his *original* course. If he succeeded in passing the re-sit examinations the course that he would be joining would be a *different* course.

However, *CIS 13986/1996* is not followed in *CIS 15594/1996* (which also concerned a claimant who had to resit exams after a year's interval). In the Commissioner's view, if a person was re-admitted after an interval to follow essentially the same programme, that person was returning to the same course. Moreover, such an interpretation was consistent with the Court of Appeal's reasoning in *Clarke and Faul*, whereas the approach taken in *CIS 13986/1996* undermined the distinction made by the Court between final abandonment and an abandonment that was not final (which in his view was part of the *ratio decidendi* of its decision). Since the same principles should be applied to cases of abandonment and dismissal, it followed that the construction adopted in *CIS 13986/1996* was not consistent with *Clarke and Faul*. The Commissioner also rejected the argument that the August 1995 amendment reversing *Clarke and Faul* was *ultra vires* on the ground of irrationality. See also *CIS 13276/1996* (heard at the same time as *CIS 15594/1996*) which concerned a claimant who was given a year's leave of absence from her full-time course following a car accident.

The same issues have been examined by yet another Commissioner in *CIS 14255/1996*. Again the claimant was a student who had failed exams and had to resit them a year later. The Commissioner agrees with *CIS 15594/1996* rather than *CIS 13986/1996*. He specifically deals with the fact that what was said by the Court of Appeal in *Clarke* and *Faul* about the meaning of "abandons" was not, strictly speaking, a necessary part of the decision. However, all three members of the Court had held the Commissioner's decision to be wrong and thus clearly their construction had to be followed in respect of any period before the legislation was amended. In relation to the period after August 1, 1995, the Commissioner raises the question, based on dicta in *Thomson v. Moyse* [1961] A.C. 967, that *Clarke* and *Faul* might no longer be strictly binding as the definition had been amended. But he concludes that he should follow *Clarke* and *Faul* and leave it to the Court of Appeal to say if any part of that decision should not be followed.

It should be noted that in *CIS 14255/1996* the Commissioner also considered that the approach taken by Evans L.J. in *Webber* (see above) was inconsistent with *Clarke* and *Faul*. In his view, for the approach taken by Evans L.J. to work, the interpretation adopted in *CIS 13986/1996* that there could be two (or more) separate full-time courses was a necessary ingredient. However, while this might be so if Evans L.J.'s approach is relied upon in the case of a person who is hoping to return to a full-time course, it is not necessarily so in other situations. In the case of modular courses, or in other situations where there is no obligation to resume studying on a full-time basis, clearly Evans L.J.'s approach is not incosistent with *Clarke* and *Faul* if there is no intention to return to a full-time course.

The decision in *CIS 15594/1996* was appealed to the Court of Appeal. But in *O'Connor v. Chief Adjudication Officer and another, The Times*, March 11, 1999 (also to be reported as *R(IS) 7/99*) the appeal was dismissed by a majority. Arguments were put on both the construction of para. (a) and the validity of the August 1995 amendment. On the construction argument, Auld L.J. stated that the position had been put beyond doubt by the August 1995 amendment following the decision in *Clarke* and *Faul*. The clear purpose of that amendment was to underline the deemed continuity of full-time student status even when interrupted, for whatever reason. He agreed with Hobhouse L.J. in *Webber* that commitment to a full-time course at the start was the determining factor, not what happened thereafter. On the meaning of course, he preferred the Commissioner's approach to that of *CIS 13986/1996*. On the *vires* point, although he considered that the Commissioner had applied the wrong test (the correct test being the normal *Wednesbury* one), in his view irrationality had not been made out.

It therefore seems fairly clearly established that a person whose course is full-time (as determined at its start) will count as a student until the last day of the course (subject to abandonment or dismissal), regardless of non-attendance on the course for whatever reason. Note however, that a student who has been incapable of work for 28 weeks (or who qualifies for a disability or severe disability premium) will be eligible for income support (reg. 4ZA(3)(b) and para. 10 of Sched. 1B).

Calculation of grant income

62.—(1) The amount of a student's grant income to be taken into account shall, subject to [³paragraphs (2) and (2A)], be the whole of his grant income.

(2) There shall be disregarded from the amount of a student's grant income any payment—

(a) intended to meet tuition fees or examination fees;

(b) [⁴. . .]

(c) intended to meet additional expenditure incurred by a disabled student in respect of his attendance on a course;

(d) intended to meet additional expenditure connected with term time residential study away from the student's educational establishment;

(e) on account of the student maintaining a home at a place other than that at which he resides during his course but only to the extent that his rent or rates is not met by housing benefit;

(f) on account of any other person but only if that person is residing outside of the United Kingdom and there is no applicable amount in respect of him;

(g) intended to meet the cost of books and equipment [⁴. . .] or if not so intended an amount equal to [⁵£295] towards such costs;

(h) intended to meet travel expenses incurred as a result of his attendance on the course.

[²(2A) Where in pursuance of an award a student is in receipt of a grant in respect of maintenance under regulation 17(b) of the Education (Mandatory Awards) Regulations 1991, there shall be excluded from his grant income a sum equal to the amount from time to time specified in paragraph 7(4) of Schedule 2 to those Regulations, being the amount to be disregarded in respect of travel costs in the particular circumstances of his case.]

(3) A student's grant income [¹, except any amount intended for the maintenance of dependants under [²Part 3 of Schedule 2 to the Education (Mandatory Awards) Regulations 1991] or intended for an older student under Part 4 of that Schedule,] shall be apportioned—

(a) subject to paragraph (4), in a case where it is attributable to the period of study, equally between the weeks in that period;

(b) in any other case, equally between the weeks in the period in respect of which it is payable.

[¹(3A) Any amount intended for the maintenance of dependants or for an older student under the provisions referred to in paragraph (3) shall be apportioned equally over a period of 52 weeks or, if there are 53 benefit weeks (including part-weeks) in the year, 53.]

(4) In the case of a student on a sandwich course, any periods of experience within the period of study shall be excluded and the student's grant income shall be apportioned equally between the remaining weeks in that period.

AMENDMENTS

1. Income Support (General) Amendment Regulations 1988 (S.I. 1988 No. 663), reg. 24 (April 11, 1988).

2. Income Support (General) Amendment Regulations 1992 (S.I. 1992 No. 468), reg. 5 (April 6, 1992).

3. Income-related Benefits Schemes (Miscellaneous Amendments) (No. 3) Regulations 1992 (S.I. 1992 No. 2155), reg. 20 (October 5, 1992).

4. Income-related Benefits Schemes and Social Fund (Miscellaneous Amendments) Regulations 1996 (S.I. 1996 No. 1944), reg. 6(9) (October 7, 1996).

5. Social Security (Student Amounts Amendment) Regulations 1998 (S.I. 1998 No. 1379), reg. 2 (August 31, 1998, or if the student's period of study begins between August 1, and 30, 1998, the first day of the period).

DEFINITIONS

"grant income"—see reg. 61.
"period of study"—*ibid.*
"periods of experience"—*ibid.*
"sandwich course"—*ibid.*
"student"—*ibid.*

GENERAL NOTE

A student's grant is first to be subject to the disregards listed in paras. (2) and (2A). In *CIS 91/ 1994* the claimant argued that the disregard for books in para. (2)(g) should be apportioned over 52 weeks. It would then reduce the dependants and mature student elements of her grant that were

275

taken into account in calculating her income support during the summer vacation. But the Commissioner holds that the deduction in sub-para. (g) could only be applied to the basic maintenance grant, as this was clearly the part of the grant which contained provision for books.

Para. (2A) is necessary because the standard maintenance grant no longer contains a set amount intended for travel costs. This is confirmed by *R(IS) 7/95* where the Commissioner decides that only the notional amount for travel expenses provided for in para. 7(4) of Sched. 2 to the Mandatory Awards Regulations (currently £166 for 1998/9) could be deducted from the claimant's partner's grant, not his actual, much higher, travel costs. Although para. 2(h) allowed the disregard of any sum "intended to meet travel expenses", the scheme of the Education (Mandatory Awards) Regulations made it clear that the basic grant was payable solely for maintenance. No amount was payable for travel expenses except in certain circumstances, which did not apply in this case. It was the intention of the grant-making authority, not of the student, that counted under sub-para. (h). *R(IS) 16/95* similarly holds that in the case of the disregard for tuition fees under sub-para. (a), it is the intention of the provider of the payment that has to be considered. The fact that the claimant's partner spent all his grants from the Norwegian Government on tuition fees was irrelevant.

A grant is normally apportioned over the weeks of the period of study, *i.e.* from the beginning of the academic year to the day before the summer vacation (para. (3)). The elements of the grant for mature students or dependants are apportioned over 52 weeks (para. (3A)), but only while the person remains a student. *CIS 7/1988* holds that these elements of grant would ordinarily be attributable to the same period as the maintenance grant under the Mandatory Awards Regulations. *CIS 7/1988* is followed (with some reservation) in *R(IS) 1/96*, where the Commissioner points out that under reg. 15(1) of the Mandatory Awards Regulations an award comes to an end on the expiry of the course. This supported the conclusion that in the final year the dependants and mature student elements were, like the ordinary maintenance grant, to be treated as payable for the period up to the day before the summer vacation. After that date the person was no longer a student and reg. 62 no longer applied.

In *R(IS) 15/95* the claimant claimed income support for the summer vacation at the end of the first year of her course. Her grant included a dependants allowance and a single parent's allowance. The Commissioner decides that the single parent element had to be apportioned over 52 weeks. This was because the single parent's allowance was provided for in Sched. 4 to the Mandatory Awards Regulations. The effect of Sched. 4 was to increase in certain circumstances the amount awarded under Part III of Sched. 2 for the maintenance of dependants. Sched. 4 on its own awarded nothing. Thus the single parent's allowance was in fact merely an increase of the amount intended for the maintenance of dependants and so fell to be apportioned in accord with para. (3A). Even if this was not the case, the allowance had to be apportioned equally between the weeks in the period in respect of which it was payable (para. (3)(b)). That period was 52 weeks (see paras. 12(1) and 20 of Sched. 2 to the Mandatory Awards Regulations).

Subject to reg. 62, a student's grant will be taken into account as income under reg. 40. Thus any relevant disregards in Sched. 9 will apply (*R(IS) 16/95*).

Calculation of covenant income where a contribution is assessed

63.—(1) Where a student is in receipt of income by way of a grant during a period of study and a contribution has been assessed, the amount of his covenant income to be taken into account for that period and any summer vacation immediately following shall be the whole amount of his covenant income less, subject to paragraph (3), the amount of the contribution.

(2) The weekly amount of the student's covenant income shall be determined—

    (a) by dividing the amount of income which falls to be taken into account under paragraph (1) by 52 or, if there are 53 benefit weeks (including part weeks) in the year, 53; and

    (b) by disregarding from the resulting amount, £5.

(3) For the purposes of paragraph (1), the contribution shall be treated as increased by the amount, if any, by which the amount excluded under [¹regulation 62(2)(h) (calculation of grant income) falls short of the amount for the time being specified in paragraph 7(4)(i) of Schedule 2 to the Education (Mandatory Awards) Regulations 1991 (travel expenditure).]

AMENDMENT

1. Income Support (General) Amendment Regulations 1992 (S.I. 1992 No. 468), reg. 5 (April 6, 1992).

DEFINITIONS

"benefit week"—see reg. 2(1).
"contribution"—see reg. 61.
"covenant income"—*ibid.*
"grant"—*ibid.*
"period of study"—*ibid.*
"standard maintenance grant"—*ibid.*
"student"—*ibid.*

GENERAL NOTE

Although the number of covenants have dropped away following the 1988 Budget, some existing covenants may have continued running, perhaps at inadequate levels.

If a student has a grant, with a parental contribution assessed, covenant income is only taken into account to the extent that it exceeds the assessed contribution (plus any addition under para. (3)). The definition of covenant income in reg. 61 confines it to the payment net of tax. Any excess is spread over the whole year, with a £5 per week disregard.

Covenant income where no grant income or no contribution is assessed

64.—(1) Where a student is not in receipt of income by way of a grant the amount of his covenant income shall be calculated as follows—

  (a) any sums intended for any expenditure specified in regulation 62(2)(a) to (f), (calculation of grant income) necessary as a result of his attendance on the course, shall be disregarded;

  (b) any covenant income, up to the amount of the standard maintenance grant, which is not so disregarded, shall be apportioned equally between the weeks of the period of study and there shall be disregarded from the covenant income to be so apportioned the amount which would have been disregarded under [¹regulation 62(2)(g) and (h) and (2A)] (calculation of grant income) had the student been in receipt of the standard maintenance grant;

  (c) the balance, if any, shall be divided by 52 or, if there are 53 benefit weeks (including part weeks) in the year, 53 and treated as weekly income of which £5 shall be disregarded.

(2) Where a student is in receipt of income by way of a grant and no contribution has been assessed, the amount of his covenant income shall be calculated in accordance with sub-paragraphs (a) to (c) of paragraph (1), except that—

  (a) the value of the standard maintenance grant shall be abated by the amount of his grant income less an amount equal to the amount of any sums disregarded under regulation 62(2)(a) to (f); and

  (b) the amount to be disregarded under paragraph (1)(b) shall be abated by an amount equal to the amount of any sums disregarded under [¹regulation 62(2)(g) and (h) and (2A)].

AMENDMENT

1. Income Support (General) Amendment Regulations 1992 (S.I. 1992 No. 468), reg. 5 (April 6, 1992).

"benefit week"—see reg. 2(1).
"contribution"—see reg. 61.
"covenant income"—*ibid.*
"grant"—*ibid.*
"grant income"—*ibid.*
"standard maintenance grant"—*ibid.*
"student"—*ibid.*

GENERAL NOTE

Paragraph (1)
If the student has no grant, first any sums earmarked for things listed in reg. 62(2)(a) to (f) are excluded. Then the amount of covenant income up to the rate of the standard maintenance grant (less the items specified above) is spread over the weeks of the period of study, disregarding items specified in reg. 62(2)(g) and (h) and (2A). Then any excess is spread over the whole year with a £5 p.w. disregard.

Paragraph (2)
If the student has a grant with no parental contribution, the effect is to spread the covenant income, after topping up any deficiency from the standard maintenance grant, over the whole year, as in para. (1).

Relationship with amounts to be disregarded under Schedule 9

65. No part of a student's convenant income or grant income shall be disregarded under paragraph 15 of Schedule 9 (charitable and voluntary payments) and any other income [¹to which sub-paragraph (1) of that paragraph applies shall be disregarded only to the extent that] the amount disregarded under regulation 63(2)(b) (calculation of covenant income where a contribution is assessed) or, as the case may be, 64(1)(c) (convenant income where no grant income or no contribution is assessed) is less than [²£20].

AMENDMENTS

1. Income Support (General) Amendment Regulations 1990 (S.I. 1990 No. 547), reg. 14 (April 9, 1990).
2. Income-related Benefits Schemes (Miscellaneous Amendments) Regulations 1996 (S.I. 1996 No. 462), reg. 8 (April 8, 1996).

DEFINITIONS

"covenant income"—see reg. 61.
"grant income"—*ibid.*
"student"—*ibid.*

Other amounts to be disregarded

66.—(1) For the purposes of ascertaining income [¹other than grant income, covenant income and loans treated as income in accordance with regulation 66A], any amounts intended for any expenditure specified in regulation 62(2) (calculation of grant income) necessary as a result of his attendance on the course shall be disregarded but only if, and to the extent that, the necessary expenditure exceeds or is likely to exceed the amount of the sums disregarded under regulation 62(2) [¹and (2A)], 63(3) and 64(1)(a) or(b) (calculation of grant income and convenant income) on like expenditure.

(2) Where a claim is made in respect of any period in the normal summer vacation and any income is payable under a Deed of Convenant which com-

mences or takes effect after the first day of that vacation, that income shall be disregarded.

AMENDMENT

1. Income-related Benefits Schemes (Miscellaneous Amendments) Regulations 1994 (S.I. 1994 No. 527), reg. 5 (April 11, 1994).

DEFINITIONS

"covenant income"—see reg. 61.
"grant income"—*ibid.*

GENERAL NOTE

Paragraph (2) will not be of any practical effect, because new covenants are unlikely to be made now that the tax advantages have been removed in the 1988 Budget.

[¹Treatment of student loans

66A.—(1) A loan which is made to a student pursuant to arrangements made under section 1 of the Education (Student Loans) Act 1990 [² or article 3 of the Education (Student Loans)(Northern Ireland) Order 1990] shall be treated as income.

(2) In calculating the weekly amount of the loan to be taken into account as income—

(a) except where sub-paragraph (b) applies, the loan shall be apportioned equally between the weeks in the academic year in respect of which the loan is payable;

(b) in the case of a loan which is payable in respect of the final academic year of the course or if the course is only of one academic year's duration, in respect of that year the loan shall be apportioned equally between the weeks in the period beginning with the start of the final academic year or, as the case may be, the single academic year and ending with [³the last day of the course,]

and from the weekly amount so apportioned there shall be disregarded £10.

[⁴(3) For the purposes of this regulation a student shall be treated as possessing the maximum amount of any loan referred to in paragraph (1) which he will be able to acquire in respect of an academic year by taking reasonable steps to do so.]]

AMENDMENTS

1. Social Security Benefits (Student Loans and Miscellaneous Amendments) Regulations 1990 (S.I. 1990 No. 1549), reg. 5(7) (September 1, 1990).
2. Income Support (General) Amendment Regulations 1991 (S.I. 1991 No. 236), reg. 9 (March 13, 1991).
3. Income Support (General) Amendment No. 4 Regulations 1991 (S.I. 1991 No. 1559), reg. 12 (August 5, 1991).
4. Income-related Benefits Schemes (Miscellaneous Amendments) Regulations 1996 (S.I. 1996 No. 462), reg. 9 (April 8, 1996).

GENERAL NOTE

If a student is, exceptionally, entitled to income support the amount of the maximum student loan that he would be entitled to if he applied for it is treated as income, whether he actually applies for the loan or not. The income is to be apportioned under para. (2) over the weeks covered by the loan, with a £10 disregard. Sub-para. (b) applies to a loan payable for the final, or only, year of the course and sub-para. (a) applies in other cases. Under para. (a), the loan is to be apportioned over the weeks in the academic year. Academic year is not defined but it is suggested that it means the period between September/October and June/July that the student attends his course (*i.e.* excluding the summer vacation). This interpretation would mean that a student loan is attributed to the same period as the basic maintenance grant (see reg. 62(3)), which would seem appropriate as the student loan scheme was orginally introduced as a supplement to, and gradually to replace, the maintenance grant. Note however that this is not the approach taken in the *Adjudication Officer's Guide* (para. 35252). See reg. 40(3A) for the position where a student ends the course prematurely.

See *R(IS) 16/95* referred to in the note to "grant" in reg. 61.

Disregard of contribution

67. Where the claimant or his partner is a student and [¹, for the purposes of assessing a contribution to the student's grant, the other partner's income has been taken into account, an account equal to that contribution shall be disregarded for the purposes of assessing that other partner's income.]

AMENDMENT

1. Income-related Benefits Schemes (Miscellaneous Amendments) Regulations 1996 (S.I. 1996 No. 462), reg. 10 (April 8, 1996).

DEFINITIONS

"claimant"—see reg. 2(1), reg. 23(1).
"contribution"—see reg. 61.
"grant"—*ibid.*
"partner"—see reg. 2(1).
"student"—see reg. 61.

[¹ **Further disregard of student's income**

67A. Where any part of a student's income has already been taken into account for the purposes of assessing his entitlement to a grant, the amount taken into account shall be disregarded in assessing that student's income.]

AMENDMENT

1. Social Security (Miscellaneous Amendments) Regulations 1998 (S.I. 1998 No. 563), reg. 4(3) and (4)(e) (April 6, 1998),

DEFINITIONS

"grant"—see reg. 61.
"student"—*ibid.*

Income treated as capital

68. Any amount by way of a refund of tax deducted from a student's income shall be treated as capital.

DEFINITION

"student"—see reg. 61.

Disregard of changes occurring during summer vacation

69. In calculating a student's income an adjudication officer shall disregard any change in the standard maintenance grant occurring in the recognised summer vacation appropriate to the student's course, if that vacation does not form part of his period of study, from the date on which the change occurred up to the end of that vacation.

Definitions

"period of study"—see reg. 61.
"standard maintenance grant"—*ibid.*
"student"—*ibid.*

PART VI

URGENT CASES

Urgent cases

70.—(1) In a case to which this regulation applies, a claimant's weekly applicable amount and his income and capital shall be calculated in accordance with the following provisions of this Part.

(2) Subject to paragraph (4), this regulation applies to—

(a) a claimant to whom paragraph (3) (certain persons from abroad) applies;

(b) a claimant who is treated as possessing income under regulation 42(3) (notional income);

(c) [¹. . .].

(3) This paragraph applies to a person from abroad within the meaning of regulation 21(3) (special cases) who—

(a) having, during any one period of limited leave of a kind referred to in sub-paragraph (a) of that definition (including any period as extended), supported himself without recourse to public funds other than any such recourse by reason of the previous application of this sub-paragraph, is temporarily without funds during that period of leave because remittances to him from abroad have been disrupted provided that there is a reasonable expectation that his supply of funds will be resumed;

[²(b) is an asylum seeker for the purposes of paragraph 3A;]

[³(c) is a person to whom sub-paragraph (i) of that definition (sponsored immigrant) applies and the person or persons who gave the undertaking to provide for his maintenance and accommodation has, as the case may be have, died;]

(d) [². . .];

(e) [³. . .];

(f) [³. . .];

(g) [³. . .];

(h) [³. . .];

(i) [³. . .];

(j) [³. . .].

[²(3A) For the purposes of this paragraph, a person—

[³(a) is an asylum seeker when he submits on his arrival (other than on his re-entry) in the United Kingdom from a country outside the Common Travel Area a claim for asylum to the Secretary of State that it would be contrary to the United Kingdom's obligations under the Convention for him to be removed from, or required to leave, the United Kingdom and that claim is recorded by the Secretary of State as having been made; or

(aa) becomes, while present in Great Britain, an asylum seeker when—

(i) the Secretary of State makes a declaration to the effect that the country of which he is a national is subject to such a fundamental change in circumstances that he would not normally order the return of a person to that country, and

    (ii) he submits, within a period of 3 months from the day that declaration was made, a claim for asylum to the Secretary of State under the Convention relating to the Status of Refugees, and

    (iii) his claim for asylum under that Convention is recorded by the Secretary of State as having been made; and

  (b) ceases to be an asylum seeker—

    (i) in the case of a claim for asylum which, on or after 5th February 1996, is recorded by the Secretary of State as having been determined (other than on appeal) or abandoned, on the date on which it is so recorded, or

    (ii) in the case of a claim for asylum which is recorded as determined before 5th February 1996 and in respect of which there is either an appeal pending on 5th February 1996 or an appeal is made within the time limits specified in rule 5 of the Asylum Appeals (Procedure) Rules 1993, on the date on which that appeal is determined.]

(3B) In paragraph (3A), "the Convention" means the Convention relating to the Status of Refugees done at Geneva on 28th July 1951 and the protocol to that Convention [³; and "the Common Travel Area" means the United Kingdom, the Channel Islands, the Isle of Man and the Republic of Ireland collectively.]]

(4) This regulation shall only apply to a person to whom paragraph (2)(b) [¹applies, where the income he is treated as possessing by virtue of regulation 42(3) (notional income)] is not readily available to him; and—

  (a) the amount of income support which would be payable but for this Part is less than the amount of income support payable by virtue of the provisions of this Part; and

  (b) the adjudication officer is satisfied that, unless the provisions of this Part are applied to the claimant, the claimant or his family will suffer hardship.

AMENDMENTS

1. Income Support (General) Amendment No. 2 Regulations 1989 (S.I. 1989 No. 1323), reg. 16 (October 9, 1989).

2. Income Support (General) Amendment No. 3 Regulations 1993 (S.I. 1993 No. 1679), reg. 2 (August 2, 1993).

3. Social Security (Persons from Abroad) Miscellaneous Amendments Regulations 1996 (S.I. 1996 No. 30), reg. 8(3) (February 5, 1996).

DEFINITIONS

"the 1971 Act"—see reg. 21(3).
"claimant"—see reg. 2(1).
"family"—see 1986 Act, s. 20(11) (SSCBA, s.137(1)).
"partner"—see reg. 2(1).

GENERAL NOTE

Paragraphs (1) and (2)

The provision for urgent cases outside the normal scope of the income support rules is very restricted. The two categories are certain persons from abroad (para. (3); this category is now quite limited, see below) and claimants who are treated as possessing income which is due, but has not been paid. In the last case the notional income must not be readily available and the AO must be satisfied that the claimant or his family would suffer hardship if the normal income support entitlement was not brought up to the urgent cases rate (para. (4)). Applicable amounts are adjusted under reg. 71, and income and capital rules are in reg. 72.

Paragraph (3)

The first condition is that the person comes within the definition of "person from abroad" in reg. 21(3). Generally, under Sched. 7 such a person has an applicable amount of nil (para. 17). Then if the person falls into one of sub-paras. (a) to (c) there can be entitlement on the conditions of reg. 71. A person who comes within para. (3) is eligible for income support (reg. 4ZA(1) and Sched. 1B, para. 21).

The scope of para. (3) was considerably restricted on February 5, 1996. See the 1995 edition for the previous form of para. (3) and the notes to that paragraph. There was no transitional protection for people who were receiving urgent cases payments under the sub-paragraphs that were revoked. Their entitlement to urgent cases payments therefore ceased.

The only "people from abroad" now entitled to urgent cases payments are: (i) those who have limited leave to remain in the U.K. without recourse to public funds whose funds from abroad have temporarily dried up (sub-para. (a)); (ii) certain asylum seekers (sub-para. (b) and paras. (3A)–(3B)); (iii) a sponsored immigrant (see the notes to reg. 21(3)(i)) whose sponsor(s) has/have died (sub-para. (c)). See below for the transitional protection for asylum seekers and sponsored immigrants.

Paras. (3A) to (3B)

Before February 5, 1996, asylum seekers were entitled to urgent cases payments of income support at all stages from the submission of their initial asylum application until the final decision on it was made (including any appeal or representations). The stated justification for the draconian restrictions on the right of asylum seekers to claim benefit introduced by reg. 8(3) of the Social Security (Persons from Abroad) Miscellaneous Amendments Regulations 1996 was the Government's belief that "the current benefit arrangements encourage abuses of the asylum system . . . in two major ways: the ready availability of benefits for asylum applicants provides an incentive for people to make unfounded asylum claims . . . both to prolong their stay in the U.K. and to gain access to benefits; the availability of benefits throughout the asylum process provides an incentive for failed asylum seekers to lodge and prolong unfounded appeals" (para. 11 of the DSS's Explanatory Memorandum to the Social Security Advisory Committee, Cm 3062/1996). Despite widespread and highly publicised criticisms of its proposals and SSAC's recommendation that they should be completely withdrawn, the Government pressed ahead (although certain concessions were made, particularly in relation to transitional protection for existing claimants). A challenge to the validity of the regulations was lost in the High Court on March 25, 1996. However, on June 21, 1996, the Court of Appeal (by a majority) struck down as *ultra vires* those parts of the amending regulations which denied income support, housing benefit or council tax benefit to any asylum seeker whose asylum application had not been finally determined (*R v. Secretary of State for Social Security, ex p. Joint Council for the Welfare of Immigrants and Another* [1996] 4 All E.R. 385). The Court held that the regulations were unlawful because they contravened the Asylum and Immigration Appeals Act 1993 by drastically interfering with the rights of asylum seekers under that Act. The Government's speedy response was to introduce amendments to the Asylum and Immigration Bill then going through Parliament in order to validate those parts of the regulations affected by the Court of Appeal's decision. See s. 11(1) and (4) of and Sched. 1 to the Asylum and Immigration Act 1996 in Part I of this book. The Act came into force on July 24, 1996. Para. 2(b) of Sched. 1 reinstates paras. (3A) and (3B) in their February 5, 1996 form from that date. The consequence is that asylum seekers will only be entitled to urgent cases payments on or after July 24, 1996 if they can qualify under para. (3A) or can benefit from the transitional protection in reg. 12(1) of the 1996 Regulations (see below).

Under para. (3A) the only categories of asylum seekers who are now entitled to urgent cases payments are those who apply for asylum "on arrival" (other than re-entry) in the U.K. from a country outside the Common Travel Area (see para. (3B)) and those who, while present in Great Britain, apply for asylum within three months of a declaration by the Secretary of State that the country of which they are a national is going through such a fundamental change of circumstances that they would not normally be ordered to return there (para. (3A)(a) and (aa)). In both cases the application for asylum must be officially recorded. A declaration under para. (3A)(aa)(i) was made in respect of Zaire on May 16, 1997, for three months; and in respect of Sierra Leone on July 1, 1997, again for a three month period. See below for the position of asylum seekers between February 5 and July 24, 1996.

"On arrival"

It is not entirely clear what "on arrival" in the U.K. means. (Note that there is no set procedure for applying for asylum; an application does not need to be in writing but can be made orally.) It should be noted that sub-para. (a) simply refers to "on arrival . . . in the U.K.". It does not refer to arrival *at a port* (or *immigration control*), nor are the words "on arrival" qualified by words such as "immediately" or "on the date of". Moreover the test chosen is that of arrival, rather than the more precise term of "entry" into the U.K. (for the distinction in domestic law see *R v. Naillie* [1993] A.C. 674). It could therefore be argued that a person who, for example, did not apply for asylum at the port of entry, but immediately after leaving the port went straight to the Immigration Department and made an application there, had applied for asylum "on arrival" in the U.K. However, this has not been the approach taken in the Commissioners' decisions that have so far emerged on this issue. The Commissioners have recognised the inexact nature of the term "on arrival" but have concluded that it should be interpreted narrowly in the light of the Ministerial statements made while the Asylum and Immigration Bill (now the 1996 Act) was going through Parliament. Thus in *CIS 2719/1997* the Commissioner accepts that sub-para. (a) does not specify at what stage during the process of arriving in this country (disembarkation, passing through immigration control, passing through customs or leaving the port or airport) an application for asylum has to be made. But after having regard to statements made by the Secretary of State in the House of Commons (HC Vol. 281, cols. 844 to 879) under the *Pepper v. Hart* ([1993] A.C. 593) principle, the Commissioner concludes that the application (or at least an indication of an intention to make an asylum application) had to be made while the claimant was still within the port of arrival. However, it did not necessarily have to be made before clearing immigration control (as had been held in *CIS 143/1997*; see also para. 36144 of the *Adjudication Officer's Guide*). In the Commissioner's view, the process of arrival finished when the person arriving left the port of arrival; it did not continue beyond that point. Thus to count under sub-para. (a) an asylum application had to be made before leaving the port; if for whatever reason it was not, sub-para. (a) was not satisfied.

See also *CIS 1137/1997* (heard with *CIS 2719/1997*), the particular facts of which may explain the Commissioner's choice of test for the meaning of "on arrival". In *CIS 1137/1997* the claimant and his mother were escorted through immigration control at Heathrow airport by an agent who then left them at the airport. Later that day they were taken to the office of the Refugee Arrivals Project at Terminal 2. There was no Persian speaker there and neither the claimant nor his mother spoke English. The Project staff placed the claimant and his mother in a hotel for the night and the next morning took them to the Immigration and Nationality Department at Lunar House, Croydon, where claims for asylum were made. The Commissioner directed the new tribunal, in the course of considering whether the claimant had made his asylum application "on his arrival", to make findings on whether the claimant had made contact with anyone acting in the name of the Secretary of State before he left Heathrow airport, whether that contact was recorded by that person, the locus of the Refugee Arrivals Project, whether it had any mandate from the Secretary of State to deal with asylum seekers and whether anyone from the Project contacted an immigration officer in Heathrow on the day of the claimant's arrival.

In *CIS 4117/1997* the Commissioner (who was the same Commissioner who decided *CIS 143/1997*) accepts that the relatively vague term "on his arrival" was used deliberately instead of any more precise term, in order to maintain a level of flexibility. But the degree of flexibility had to be measured in the light of Parliament's clear intention that in the ordinary case of a person arriving at a recognised port of entry with full immigration control and interpretation facilities, the person's entitlement to benefit should depend upon him making an application for asylum at that port. The statements made by the Secretary of State in the House of Commons (HC, Vol. 281, cols. 846 to 848) showed a willingness to take account of matters wholly beyond the claimant's control that might make an immediate claim for asylum impossible (*e.g.* the lack of an interpreter). But this did not extend to other matters, such as wrong advice given by an agent to the claimant. The Commissioner did not have to decide in that case whether asylum had to be claimed before the claimant cleared immigration control or left the port of entry. However, he did point to the existence of para. 6(2) of Sched. 2 to the Immigration Act 1971 (which allows an immigration officer to cancel a notice giving leave to enter within 24 hours of the conclusion of an examination under para. 2 of the Schedule), as leaving open the possibility of a person returning to an immigration officer at the port of entry and making a claim for asylum that could be treated as made "on arrival", even though he had originally passed beyond immigration control (and indeed had left the port of entry).

Thus in some circumstances "clearing immigration control" may be a more extensive concept than that of leaving the port of entry. See also the statement by the Secretary of State in the House of Commons that "People who arrive at an airport or other port of entry with no interpretation facility are told to come back and complete the formalities in a few days' time. They are then treated as if they have just arrived and were making an in-port claim although such a claim is made two or three days later. That flexibility will continue . . ." (col. 846).

CIS 3231/1997 also decides that the test is whether asylum was claimed at immigration control. The Commissioner accepts that if for some reason immigration control was not available, for example because of a strike or the lack of an appropriate interpreter, it would be sufficient if the claim for asylum was made at the first opportunity. In that case the claimant had been smuggled out of Iraq in the back of a lorry; he was sedated throughout the journey until he was put out in London. With the help of his brother he went to an immigration office in Cardiff the next day (although he did not actually claim asylum until he was interviewed by an immigration officer three days later). The tribunal decided that he had claimed asylum "on arrival" because he had done so "as soon as reasonably practicable" after entry into the U.K. However the Commissioner holds that this was not the correct test and that a person who was smuggled in and made his asylum claim a day or so later had not claimed asylum "on his arrival".

In *CIS 3231/1997* the Commissioner expressed the view that a person who had gained entry by being smuggled in or otherwise landing unofficially should not be in a better position than a person who had gone through the normal procedures. But it is difficult to see what else a person in similar circumstances to those of the claimant in *CIS 3231/1997* could do. It would certainly seem arguable that while he remained hidden in the lorry the claimant in *CIS 3231/1997* had not "arrived" in the U.K. in the sense of having made an appearance here (see the *Shorter Oxford English Dictionary* definition of "arrival"); moreover, if he was put out of the lorry (in a confused state) at a point where there were no immigration facilities he would need time to make enquiries as to where to go. Provided that this was done as soon as reasonably practicable, it is difficult to see why this does not come within the latitude that the use of the term "on arrival" was apparently intended by Parliament to achieve. Moreover, note in this connection the Commissioner's reference in *CIS 4117/1997* to Article 31 of the Geneva Convention relating to the Status of Refugees which forbids the imposition of "penalties, on account of their illegal entry or presence, on refugees who, coming directly from a territory where their life or freedom was threatened in the sense of Article 1, enter or are present in [a] territory without authorisation, provided they present themselves without delay to the authorities and show good cause for their illegal entry or presence". It is certainly arguable that the refusal of income support could amount to a "penalty" in these circumstances, and more-over, since there is acknowledged to be some ambiguity in the term "on arrival" (see *CIS 2719/1997* and *CIS 4117/1997*) that sub-para. (a) should be construed in a manner that is not inconsistent with the U.K.'s international obligations. A broad interpretation would also seem to be justified on the basis that the provision severely curtails the right of asylum seekers to claim benefit (see Dyson J. in *Vijeikis* referred to below under *"Upheaval Declarations"*).

Note that the claimants in *CIS 2719/1997*, *CIS 1137/1997* and *CIS 3231/1997* were granted leave to appeal to the Court of Appeal. However, the appeals were withdrawn; the reasons for this are not known.

Thus the result of the Commissioners' decisions that have so far emerged on the meaning of the term "on arrival" seems to be that if a person enters the country through a recognised port of entry and does not claim asylum before clearing immigration control (*CIS 143/1997* and *CIS 3231/1997*), or before leaving the port of entry (*CIS 2719/1997* and *CIS 1137/1997*), he will not come within sub-para. (a). His reasons for not claiming asylum at the port of entry (*e.g.* because he was advised not to do so by an agent) will not be relevant (*CIS 2719/1997* and *CIS 1137/1997*), unless they were wholly outside his control (*CIS 4117/1997* and *CIS 3231/1997*) (*e.g.* lack of an appropriate interpreter, or possibly his state of health: note the example given in para. 36144 of the *Adjudication Officer's Guide* of a person suffering a severe asthma attack and being unable to speak before passing through immigration control; if the person was hospitalised but went straight to the Immigration Department to make an asylum application after being discharged from hospital the *Guide* suggests that this would count as made "on arrival"). If the person does not pass through (*i.e.* clear) immigration control, *e.g.* because he does not enter the country through a recognised port or because there are no immigration facilities available at the port, it seems (see *CIS 4117/1997* and *CIS 3231/1997*) that he will be treated as making an application for asylum on arrival as long as the application is made as soon as reasonably practicable after his arrival in the country.

Note also that the arrival must be from a country outside the Common Travel Area. Presumably this refers to the country that the person originally departed from. So the fact that person's flight was via, *e.g*, the Isle of Man, or even that it was diverted there, should not mean that sub-para. (a) does not apply. But what if the person spends a few days in the Isle of Man before coming to the U.K.? Further, those who apply on "re-entry" are excluded from sub-para. (a). The purpose presum-ably is to stop people trying to get within this sub-paragraph by leaving the U.K. for a short time and then making an asylum application at the port of entry on their return. But if the person last visited the U.K., *e.g.*, some years ago or there is no connection between their departure after the last visit and their arrival on this occasion this would not seem to be a "re-entry", but a *fresh* entry into the U.K. Arguably it should just mean re-entry within the same period of leave. This seems to be accepted in the *Adjudication Officer's Guide:* see para. 36143.

Finally note that there are special rules to provide for the control of entry of foreign nationals through the Channel Tunnel under amendments that have been made to the Immigration Act 1971.

The effect of this is that British immigration control extends into the Tunnel and a person who encounters an immigration officer on the train will have passed through immigration control before he has arrived in England.

"Upheaval declarations"

The wording of para. (3A)(aa) is also not straightforward. The DSS argues that it only applies to people who are in Great Britain at the time that the Secretary of State makes the "upheaval" declaration. But it is arguable that the words "while present in Great Britain" in head (aa) are only there to draw a distinction between the situation covered by head (aa) and that dealt with by head (a), *i.e.* they are there merely to differentiate between people who apply for asylum "on arrival" in the U.K. and in-country applicants. Further, the word "when" merely introduces the conditions in sub-heads (i), (ii) and (iii) which all have to be satisfied before a person can qualify as an asylum seeker under head (aa) and is there to indicate that a person cannot become an asylum seeker until these conditions have been fulfilled; it does not however mean that it is a requirement that the person is in Great Britain "when" the declaration is made. If this was the intention this could have been made clear by placing the words "while present in Great Britain" in sub-head (i) itself, since clearly under sub-heads (ii) and (iii) the person would have to be in the country at the time. More-over, it is suggested that the approach of Dyson J. in *Vijeikis* (see below) is relevant here, *i.e.* since it is not possible to say that the *only* construction is that the words "while present in Great Britain" do require a person to be here when the declaration is made and since these provisions dramatically restrict the rights of asylum seekers to claim benefit they should be strictly construed. Finally, the policy reasons for the DSS's construction are not entirely clear. Why is it necessary for the person to be in *Great Britain* when the declaration is made? What happens if he was previously in Great Britain but was, for example, in France for a short visit on the day that the declaration was made? Why does head (aa) refer to Great Britain while head (a) refers to the U.K.—what is the position if the person is in Northern Ireland when the declaration is made but comes to Great Britain the next day? What about a person who has left their home country because of the upheaval there but has not yet arrived in Great Britain by the time the declaration is made? Why does this head not apply to a person who was absent from their home country when the fundamental change in circum-stances occurred and is not able to return there but who was not present in Great Britain at the time the Secretary of State recognised this situation. Furthermore, if the DSS's interpretation is accepted the result could be that a person who happened to be in Great Britain at the time the declaration was made but is then absent for less than three months could qualify as an asylum seeker under head (aa) but a person who arrived the day after the making of the declaration could not, even though they have remained here ever since. For these reasons it is suggested that head (aa) should be interpreted as not requiring the person to be actually present in Great Britain when the declaration is made.

Note that head (aa) only covers nationals of the country concerned (as confirmed in *R v. Secretary of State for Social Security ex parte Grant*, High Court, July 31, 1997).

"Ceases to be an asylum seeker"

The person's entitlement to urgent cases payments will end when the first decision is recorded as made on his asylum application (or his application is abandoned) if this is on or after February 5, 1996 (para. (3A)(b)(i)), or, if that decision was recorded as made before February 5, 1996 and an appeal is pending by February 5, 1996, or is submitted within the time limits for appeal, on the date that appeal is determined (para. (3A)(b)(ii)), (but see below for the position between February 5 and July 24, 1996). Sub-para. (b)(ii) will include cases where the time limit for appealing under r. 5 of the 1993 Rules has been extended. The argument that sub-para. (b) either should be construed as only applying where claims for asylum were made after February 5, 1996 or was *ultra vires* was rejected by Dyson J. in *R. v. Secretary of State for Social Security, ex p. Vijeikis, Zaheer and Okito* (High Court, July, 10, 1997); an appeal against this decision was dismissed by the Court of Appeal on March 5, 1998.

The DSS's original view was that a decision was recorded by the Immigration Department on the date it was received by the asylum applicant (see AOG Memo 3/85). Presumably this was a reference to the date of the letter conveying the decision, or the date of the interview at which the applicant was informed of the decision. The position is complicated by the fact that the right of appeal is against the immigration decision that is made as a consequence of the Secretary of State's decision on the asylum application, not the asylum decision itself. These decisions could be made simultaneously or possibly several months apart. But in practice it seems that the Benefits Agency withdrew benefit from the date it was informed of the Home Office's initial decision. This often had the consequence that an asylum seeker first learnt of the refusal of his asylum claim when his benefit stopped, although according to evidence given in *ex parte Karaoui and Abbad* since the beginning of November 1996 it has been the Home Office's practice to inform asylum seekers of the decision on their claim at the same time as notification is sent to the Benefits Agency.

R. v. Secretary of State for the Home Department ex parte Karaoui and Abbad, (High Court, March 11, 1997) decides that for sub-para. (b)(i) to apply it is only necessary for a decision to have been made and recorded. There is no requirement that the claimant has been notified of the decision (or provided with reasons for it). But a decision has not been recorded unless there is "a reliable document . . . which clearly shows when the decision was made and what the decision was". A brief endorsement by a supervisor on a memorandum proposing refusal is not sufficient. Benefit should therefore only be withdrawn when a proper record of the decision is available. See also *R v. Secretary of State for the Home Department ex p. Salem, The Times*, March 8, 1998, in which the Court of Appeal holds, by a majority, that an asylum application had been determined and recorded for the purposes of sub-para. (b)(i), even though the Home Secretary was considering fresh representations. However, Hobhouse L.J. in his dissenting judgment considered that the word "determined" imported a degree of finality and should not be reduced to the equivalent of "first refused" or "for the time being declined". Mr Salem was granted leave to appeal to the House of Lords but before his case could be heard he won his appeal against rejection of his claim for asylum and was paid arrears of income support. The House of Lords accepted that it could deal with academic appeals if a sufficiently important point was involved but declined to hear Mr Salem's appeal.

If the Home Office's decision is to accept that the person is a refugee (or to grant exceptional leave to remain), he can qualify for income support/income-based JSA under the normal rules (refugees and those with exceptional leave to enter or remain are treated as satisfying the habitual residence test: see reg. 21(3), additional definition of "person from abroad", sub-paras. (b) and (c) and the equivalent provision in reg. 85 of the JSA Regulations). *CIS 564/1994*, heard together with *CIS 7250/1995*, rejects the argument that once the claimants' status as refugees had been recognised by the Home Office they were retrospectively entitled to income support at the full rate from the date they first applied for asylum and were awarded urgent cases payments. Articles 23 and 24 of the 1951 Geneva Convention require the same treatment with respect to, *inter alia*, social security to be given to refugees as is accorded to nationals. The Commissioner accepted that the claimants counted as refugees entitled to the protection of the Convention from the time they fulfilled its criteria and that recognition of that status by the Home Office was merely declaratory. However, the Convention was not part of U.K. law and its terms could only be relied upon if there was any ambiguity in the U.K. provisions. There was no such ambiguity in reg. 21(3), under which the claimants were clearly "persons from abroad", entitled only to urgent cases payments, until the Home Office had accepted their refugee status. The Commissioner also holds that E.C. Regulation 1408/71 did not assist the claimants. The main reason for this was that neither of the claimants came within the personal scope of Regulation 1408/71, as defined in Article 2, because they were not "employed or self-employed persons who are or have been subject to the legislation of one or more Member States". A subsidiary reason was that for most of the period in issue income support did not come within the scope of Regulation 1408/71 (see *CIS 836/1994* in the notes to SSCBA, s. 124, which holds that income support was not covered by Regulation 1408/71 until its amendment by Regulation 1247/92 on June 1, 1992). The Commissioner also raises (but does not decide) the question whether if the claimants had fallen within Article 2 they could have relied on Regulation 1408/71 when they had only resided in one Member State and no question of freedom of movement was involved.

Note that from October 15, 1996 reg. 21ZA allows for retrospective payment of income support at the urgent cases rate to refugees whose status has been recognised by the Home Office (see the notes to reg. 21ZA). Refugees are exempt from the habitual residence test (reg. 21(3), additional definition of "person from abroad", sub-para. (b)).

Note that changes have also been made to the rules for non-contributory benefits which mean that from February 5, 1996, claimants whose right to be in Great Britain is "subject to any limitation or condition" will not be entitled to family credit, disablity working allowance, disability living allowance, attendance allowance, invalid care allowance or severe disablement allowance. Certain people are treated as satisfying this requirement. See the notes to reg. 3 of the Family Credit Regulations for details of this new test. Existing claimants remain entitled to these benefits until their awards are reviewed (see reg. 12(3) of the Social Security (Persons from Abroad) Miscellaneous Amendments Regulations 1996, p. 967 and the notes to reg. 3 of the Family Credit Regulations). Asylum seekers will not be entitled to these benefits if they claim them on or after February 5, 1996, which means that they will not be able to qualify for the disability, severe disability, higher pensioner or disabled child premium on the ground of receipt of the relevant disability benefit.

For asylum seekers who are not entitled to urgent cases payments, there may be the possibility of a crisis loan from the Social Fund. But this would only be available if their situation constituted a "disaster" and they could show that they were likely to be able to repay the loan. The Court of Appeal held in *R. v. Hammersmith and Fulham London Borough Council and Others ex parte M and Others, The Times*, February 19, 1997 that destitute asylum seekers could qualify for assistance under the National Assistance Act 1948, s. 21(1)(a). This should also apply to other people rendered destitute by lack of benefit, *e.g.* those who have failed the habitual residence test or sponsees who are not entitled to benefit. But note *R. v. Newham London Borough Council ex parte Gorenkin, The Times*, June 9, 1997 in which Carnwath J. holds that a local authority has no power to provide food vouchers under s. 21(1)(a) unless accommodation is also being provided. In addition, in *R. v. Secretary of State for Health, ex p. Hammersmith and Fulham London Borough Council and Others, The Times*, July 31, 1997, Laws J. held that assistance under s.21(1) had to be provided in kind and that there was no power to make cash payments in lieu of any such provision. This decision was upheld by the Court of Appeal (*The Times*, September 9, 1998).

Entitlement from February 5 to July 23, 1996

As a result of the Court of Appeal's decision in *ex parte JCWI*, asylum seekers were entitled to benefit under the old form of para. (3A) (see the 1995 edition of this book) until July 24, 1996 (it was accepted that the Court of Appeal's judgment was not a "relevant determination" within ss. 68 and 69 of the Administration Act and so the limits on backdating did not apply: see AOG Memo Vol 3/90). But unless they qualified under the new form of para. (3A) that entitlement ceased when the Asylum and Immigration Act 1996 reintroduced the parts of the 1996 Regulations that had been declared invalid by the Court of Appeal (para. 6(1)(a) of Sched. 1 to the Act); see *ex parte T* below which holds that the transitional protection for asylum seekers entitled to benefit before February 5, 1996 does not extend to those who were only entitled on or after that date. Note that a claim or application for review by a person who qualified for urgent cases payments on or after February 5, 1996 as a result of the Court of Appeal's judgment in *ex parte JCWI* had to be made before July 24, 1996 (para. 6(1)(b) of Sched. 1 to the 1996 Act). Note also reg. 21ZA, in force from October 15, 1996, which allows those whose refugee status is subsequently recognised by the Home Office to make a retrospective claim for urgent cases payments for the period they were denied benefit as an asylum seeker.

Transitional Protection

There is some transitional protection for asylum seekers entitled to benefit before February 5, 1996 (see reg. 12(1) of the Social Security (Persons from Abroad) Miscellaneous Amendments Regulations 1996, p. 498). The effect of this is that an asylum seeker who was entitled to urgent cases payments before February 5, 1996 under the previous form of para. (3A)(a) will continue to be entitled until he ceases to count as an asylum seeker under sub-para. (b) (see above). *CIS 3108/ 1997* confirms that the protection in reg. 12(1) only extends to the acqusition of asylum seeker status, not its loss.

It was suggested in the 1997 edition of this book that entitlement at some point (not necessarily immediately) before February 5, 1996 should be sufficient. However, in *R. v. Secretary of State for Social Security, ex p. Vijeikis, Zaheer and Okito* (High Court, July 10, 1997) Dyson J. held that in order to rely on the transitional protection in reg. 12(1) a claimant had to be entitled to benefit *immediately* before February 5, 1996. He reluctantly accepted that the words "those provisions of those Regulations as then in force shall continue to have effect" in reg. 12(1) (together with the words "at the coming into force of these Regulations" in the amendment to reg. 12(1) introduced by para. 5 of Sched. 1 to the Asylum and Immigration Act 1996) showed clearly that the paragraph was an ordinary saving clause which only preserved the entitlement of persons who were entitled to benefit at the time when the new rules came into force. A person who once was, but no longer is, entitled to benefit could not be described as a person in respect of whom the provisions "continue" to have effect. Moreover, the wording of reg. 12(2) and (3) showed that only those who were currently entitled to or receiving benefit at the time the new rules came into force were protected by the saving provisions in those paragraphs and it would be surprising if the phrase "before the coming into force of these Regulations" had a different meaning in para. (1) than in the other paragraphs in reg. 12. This decision was upheld by the Court of Appeal (*R. v. Secretary of State for Social Security, ex p. Vijeikis and Vijeikeine and Zaheer*, March 5, 1998).

The same conclusion was reached by the Commissioner in *CIS 16992/1996, CIS 2809/1997* and *CFC 1580/1997*. The Commissioner decides that he was not bound by Dyson J.'s decision in *Vijeikis* but in his view it was correct. In *CIS 2809/1997* the Commissioner also rejects an argument that the claimant was entitled to income support by virtue of E.C. Regulation 1408/71. The claimant had argued that he was a "worker" and a "refugee" within Article 1(a) and (d), that income support came within Article 4(2)(a), and so he was entitled to equality of treatment with nationals of the U.K. by virtue of Article 3(1). However, the Commissioner holds that because he had not exercised the right of freedom of movement within the E.U. he could derive no assistance from Regulation 1408/71, relying on *Land Nordhein-Westfalen v. Uecker* and *Jacquet v. Land Nordhein-Westfalen* (joined cases C-64/96 and C-65/96). The ECJ had held in that case that Regulation 1612/68 could not apply where there was no movement from one Member State to another and the Commissioner considered that the same reasoning applied to Regulation 1408/71. The claimant in *CIS 2809/1997* appealed to the Court of Appeal but his appeal was dismissed (*Krasniqi v. Chief Adjudication Officer and the Secretary of State for Social Security*, December 10, 1998, unreported, CA). The Court of Appeal held that Regulation 1408/71 did not apply to a matter which was wholly internal to a single Member State (see *Petit*, Case 153/91, [1992] E.C.R. I-4973).

However, it is suggested that it remains arguable that the transitional protection can continue to apply if there is a break in claim after February 5, 1996 but a further claim is made before the person ceases to count as an asylum seeker under para. (3A)(b). Reg. 12(1) only requires that the person is entitled to benefit before the coming into force of the 1996 Regulations. It does not make any reference to his entitlement being continuous after that date (compare, for example, reg. 28(1) of the Income-related Benefits Schemes (Miscellaneous Amendments) Regulations 1995 (see p. 496).

Note the amendment to reg. 12(1) made by para. 5 of Sched. 1 to the 1996 Act with effect from July 24, 1996. This enables those who are no longer members of the claimant's family (*e.g.* a separated partner or a child who is no longer a dependent) to qualify for the transitional protection in their own right. However, the person must have been a member of the claimant's family at the coming into force of the Regulations, *i.e.*, February 5, 1996 (as confirmed in *ex. p. Vijeikis, Zaheer and Okito*). It will also allow members of a couple to "swap the claimant role" without losing the transitional protection.

When the restrictions on asylum seekers' entitlement to benefit were reimposed by the Asylum and Immigration Act 1996 on July 24, 1996, the question arose as to whether the transitional protection in reg. 12(1) covered people entitled to benefit prior to July 24, 1996 as a result of the Court of Appeal's judgment in *ex parte JCWI* or only those entitled before February 5, 1996, the date the regulations originally came into force. The DSS's view was that it did not apply to the former, relying on para. 6(1)(a) of Sched. 1 to the Act. But it was certainly arguable that since reg. 12(1) refers to those entitled to benefit under para. (3A) as in force before the coming into force of the 1996 Regulations (which is July 24, 1996 in relation to para. (3A): see para. 2 of Sched. 1) and since para. 6(2) states that para. 6(1) does not apply where a person is entitled to benefit under reg. 12(1), that the former were covered. However, in *R. v. Secretary of State for Social Security ex parte T*, March 18, 1997, the Court of Appeal held that reg. 12(1) only applied to those entitled to benefit before February 5, 1996. The Act had only "modified" those provisions in the 1996 Regulations which had been declared unlawful in *ex parte JCWI*, that is, those that related to the denial of income support, housing benefit and council tax benefit. This did not apply to reg. 12(1). Ms T's claim for income support which had been made on February 20, 1996 fell under the modified provisions and so para. 6(1) of Sched. 1 excluded her entitlement to benefit from July 24, 1996.

Reg. 12(2) contains transitional protection for sponsored immigrants entitled to income support before February 5, 1996. This continues until the entitlement to income support ends. The claimant must have been entitled to income support immediately before February 5, 1996 for reg. 12(2) to apply (*CIS 16992/1996*).

Applicable amounts in urgent cases

71.—(1) For the purposes of calculating any entitlement to income support under this Part—

(a) except in a case to which [¹sub-paragraph (b), (c) or (d)] applies, a claim-ant's weekly applicable amount shall be the aggregate of—

(i) 90 per cent. of the amount applicable in respect of himself or, if he is a member of a couple or of a polygamous marriage, of the amount applicable in respect of both of them under paragraph 1(1), (2) or (3) of Schedule 2 or, as the case may be, the amount applicable in respect of them under regulation 18 (polygamous marriages); [¹²and where regulation 22A (reduction in applicable amount where the claimant is appealing against a decision that he is not incapable of work) applies, the reference in this head to 90 per cent. of the amount applicable shall be construed as a reference to 90 per cent. of the relevant amount under that regulation reduced by 20 per cent;]

(ii) the amount applicable under paragraph 2 of Schedule 2 in respect of any child or young person who is a member of his family except a child or young person whose capital, if calculated in accordance with Part V in like manner as for the claimant, [¹⁰except as provided in regulation 44(1) (modifications in respect of children and young persons)], would exceed £3,000;

(iii) the amount, if applicable, specified in [⁵Part II or III of Schedule 2 (premiums)]; and

(iv) any amounts applicable under [²regulation 17(1)(e) or, as the case may be, 18(1)(f) (housing costs]; [⁴and

(v) the amount of the protected sum which may be applicable to him determined in accordance with Schedule 3A [⁷or, as the case may be, 3B];]

[⁹(vi) the amount, if applicable, specified in paragraph 2A of Schedule 2;]

(b) where the claimant is a resident in [³. . .] [⁶. . .] a residential care home or a nursing home [⁹and has a preserved right], his weekly applicable amount shall be the aggregate of—

(i) 90 per cent. of the amount of the allowance for personal expenses prescribed in paragraph 13(a) of Schedule 4 (applicable amounts of persons in residential care and nursing homes) [⁶. . .] or, if he is a member of a couple or of a polygamous marriage, of the amount applicable in respect of both or all of them; [¹²and where regulation 22A (reduction in applicable amount where the claimant is appealing against a decision that he is not incapable of work) applies, the reference in this head to 90 per cent. of the amount shall be construed as a reference to 90 per cent. of the relevant amount under that regulation reduced by 20 per cent;]

(ii) the amount applicable under paragraph 13(b) to (e) of Schedule 4 [⁶. . .] in respect of any child or young person who is a member of his family except a child or young person whose capital, if calculated in accordance with Part V in like manner as for the claimant, [¹⁰except as provided in regulation 44(1) (modifications in respect of children and young persons)], would exceed £3,000;

(iii) the amount in respect of the weekly charge for his accommodation calculated in accordance with regulation 19 and Schedule 4 [⁶. . .] except any amount in respect of a child or young person who is a member of the family and whose capital, if calculated in accordance with Part V in like manner as for the claimant, [¹⁰except as provided in regulation 44(1) (modifications in respect of children and young persons)], would exceed £3,000;

(c) where the claimant is resident in residential accommodation, his weekly applicable amount shall be the aggregate of—

(i) [⁸98 per cent.] of the amount [⁹. . .] referred to in column (2) of paragraph 13(a) to (c) and (e) of Schedule 7 (applicable amounts in special cases) applicable to him;

(ii) the amount applicable under column (2) of paragraph 13(d) of Schedule 7, in respect of any child or young person who is a member of his family except a child or young person whose capital, if calculated in accordance with Part V in like manner as for the claimant, [¹⁰except as provided in regulation 44(1) (modifications in respect of children and young persons)], would exceed £3,000;

(iii) [⁸. . .]

[¹(d) except where sub-paragraph (b) or (c) applies, in the case of a person to whom any paragraph, other than paragraph 17, in column (1) of Schedule 7 (special cases) applies, the amount shall be 90 per cent. of the amount applicable in column 2 of that Schedule in respect of the claimant and partner (if any), plus, if applicable—

    (i) any amount in respect of a child or young person who is a member of the family except a child or young person whose capital, if calculated in accordance with Part V in like manner as for the claimant, [¹⁰except as provided in regulation 44(1) (modifications in respect of children and young persons)], would exceed £3,000;

    (ii) any premium under [⁵Part II or III of Schedule 2]; and

    [²(iii) any amounts applicable under regulation 17(1)(e) or, as the case may be, 18(1)(f)]; [⁴and

    (iv) the amount of the protected sum which may be applicable to him determined in accordance with Schedule 3A [⁷or, as the case may be, 3B].]

(2) The period for which a claimant's weekly applicable amount is to be calculated in accordance with paragraph (1) where paragraph (3) of regulation 70 (urgent cases) applies shall be—

    (a) in a case to which sub-paragraph (a) of paragraph (3) of that regulation applies, any period, or the aggregate of any periods, not exceeding 42 days during any one period of leave to which that regulation applies;

    (b) [¹¹...];

    (c) [¹¹...];

    (d) [¹¹...];

    (e) [¹¹...];

    (f) [¹¹...],

[¹(3) Where the calculation of a claimant's applicable amount under this regulation results in a fraction of a penny that fraction shall be treated as a penny.]

AMENDMENTS

1. Income Support (General) Amendment Regulations 1988 (S.I. 1988 No. 663), reg. 25 (April 11, 1988).

2. Income Support (General) Amendment No. 4 Regulations 1988 (S.I. 1988 No. 1445), reg. 15 (September 12, 1988).

3. Income Support (General) Amendment No. 4 Regulations 1988 (S.I. 1988 No. 1445), Sched. 1, para. 5 (April 10, 1989).

4. Income Support (General) Amendment No. 4 Regulations 1988 (S.I. 1988 No. 1445), Sched. 1, para. 13 (April 10, 1989).

5. Family Credit and Income Support (General) Amendment Regulations 1989 (S.I. 1989 No. 1034), reg. 9 (July 10, 1989).

6. Income Support (General) Amendment Regulations 1989 (S.I. 1989 No. 534), Sched. 1, para. 8 (October 9, 1989).

7. Income Support (General) Amendment Regulations 1989 (S.I. 1989 No. 534), Sched. 1, para. 17 (October 9, 1989).

8. Social Security Benefits (Amendments Consequential Upon the Introduction of Community Care) Regulations 1992 (S.I. 1992 No. 3147), Sched. 1, para. 4 (April 1, 1993).

9. Income-related Benefits Schemes (Miscellaneous Amendments) (No. 4) Regulations 1993 (S.I. 1993 No. 2119), reg. 17 (October 4, 1993).

10. Income-related Benefits Schemes (Miscellaneous Amendments) Regulations 1994 (S.I. 1994 No. 527), reg. 6 (April 11, 1994).

11. Social Security (Persons from Abroad) Miscellaneous Amendments Regulations 1996 (S.I. 1996 No. 30), reg. 8(4) (February 5, 1996).

12. Income Support (General) (Jobseeker's Allowance Consequential Amendments) Regulations 1996 (S.I. 1996 No. 206), reg. 18 (October 7, 1996).

DEFINITIONS

"the 1971 Act"—see reg. 21(3).
"child"—see 1986 Act, s.20(11) (SSCBA, s.137(1)).
"claimant"—see reg. 2(1).
"couple"—*ibid.*
"family"—see 1986 Act, s.20(11) (SSCBA, s.137(1)).
"nursing home"—see reg. 2(1), reg. 19(3).
"polygamous marriage"—see reg. 2(1).
"residential accommodation"—*ibid.*, reg. 21(3).
"residential care home"—*ibid.*, reg. 19(3).
"young person"—*ibid.*, reg. 14.

GENERAL NOTE

Paragraph (1)
The basic rule, with detailed variations, is that 90 per cent. of the applicable amount for the claimant and any partner is allowed, full personal allowance for children and young persons not excluded on capital grounds, (from July 1989) all premiums, and housing costs.

Paragraph (2)
Payments under reg. 70(2)(b) appear to last as long as the conditions for entitlement.
Para. (2) now only covers payments under reg. 70(3)(a); the length of payment is strictly limited. For payments under reg. 70(3)(b) see para. (3A) of that regulation. In the case of payments under reg. 70(3)(c) presumably these will continue while the conditions of entitlement are met.

Assessment of income and capital in urgent cases

72.—(1) The claimant's income shall be calculated in accordance with Part V subject to the following modifications—
[¹⁰(a) any income other than—
    (i) a payment of income or income in kind made under the Macfarlane Trust, the Macfarlane (Special Payments) Trust, the Macfarlane (Special Payments) (No. 2) Trust, the Fund, the Eileen Trust or the Independent Living Funds; or
    (ii) income to which paragraph 5, 7 (but only to the extent that a concessionary payment would be due under that paragraph for any non-payment of income support under regulation 70 of these Regulations or of jobseeker's allowance under regulation 147 of the Jobseeker's Allowance Regulations 1996 (urgent cases)), 31, 39(2), (3) or (4), 40, 52 or 57 of Schedule 9 (disregard of income other than earnings) applies,
  possessed or treated as possessed by him, shall be taken into account in full nothwithstanding any provision in that Part disregarding the whole or any part of that income;]
  (b) any income to which regulation 53 (calculation of tariff income from capital) applies shall be disregarded;
  (c) income treated as capital by virtue of [² regulation 48(1), (2), (3) and (9)] (income treated as capital) shall be taken into account as income;
  (d) in a case to which paragraph (2)(b) of regulation 70 (urgent cases) applies, any income to which regulation 42(3) (notional income) applies shall be disregarded;
  (e) [³. . .].
(2) The claimant's capital calculated in accordance with Part V, but including any capital referred to in paragraphs 3 and, to the extent that such assets as are referred to in paragraph 6 consist of liquid assets, 6 [²and, except to the extent that the arrears referred to in paragraph 7 consist of arrears of housing benefit payable under Part II of the Act or Part II of the Social Security and Housing Benefits Act 1982 [SSCBA, Part VII] [¹⁰ or any arrears of benefit due under

regulation 70 of these Regulations or regulation 147 of the Jobseeker's Allowance Regulations 1996 (urgent cases)], 7, 9(b), 19, 30 [⁹, 32 and 47 to 49] of Schedule 10] (capital to be disregarded) shall be taken into account in full and the amount of income support which would, but for this paragraph be payable under this regulation, shall be payable only to the extent that it exceeds the amount of that capital.

AMENDMENTS

1. Family Credit and Income Support (General) Amendment Regulations 1988 (S.I. 1988 No. 999), reg. 6 (June 9, 1988).
2. Income Support (General) Amendment No. 5 Regulations 1988 (S.I. 1988 No. 2022), reg. 15 (December 12, 1988).
3. Income Support (General) Amendment No. 2 Regulations 1989 (S.I. 1989 No. 1323), reg. 17 (October 9, 1989).
4. Income-related Benefits Schemes Amendment Regulations 1990 (S.I. 1990 No. 127, reg. 3 (January 31, 1990).
5. Income-related Benefits Schemes and Social Security (Recoupment) Amendment Regulations 1991 (S.I. 1991 No. 1175), reg. 5 (May 11, 1991).
6. Income-related Benefits Schemes and Social Security (Recoupment) Amendment Regulations 1992 (S.I. 1992 No. 1101), reg. 6 (May 7, 1992).
7. Social Security Benefits (Miscellaneous Amendments) (No. 2) Regulations 1993 (S.I 1993 No. 963), reg. 2(3) (April 22, 1993).
8. Income-related Benefits Schemes and Social Security (Recoupment) Amendment Regulations 1993 (S.I 1993 No. 1249), reg 4(3) (May 14, 1993).
9. Income Support and Social Security (Claims and Payments) (Miscellaneous Amendments) Regulations 1996 (S.I. 1996 No. 2431), reg. 4 (October 15, 1996).
10. Social Security (Miscellaneous Amendments) Regulations 1998 (S.I. 1998 No. 563), reg. 19(1) (April 6, 1998).

DEFINITIONS

"the Act"—see reg. 2(1).
"claimant"—*ibid.*
"concessionary payment"—*ibid.*
"the Eileen Trust"—*ibid.*
"the Fund"—*ibid.*
"the Independent Living Funds"—*ibid.*
"the Macfarlane (Special Payments) Trust"—*ibid.*
"the Macfarlane (Special Payments) (No. 2) Trust"—*ibid.*
"the Macfarlane Trust"—*ibid.*

GENERAL NOTE

Paragraph (1)
This paragraph modifies the ordinary rules on income in urgent cases. All income is to be taken into account, free of any disregards, except for income from the Macfarlane Trusts (haemophiliacs), the Fund, the Eileen Trust or the Independent Living Funds, all forms of housing benefit, council tax benefit, backdated payments of income support under reg. 21ZA and the notional income which causes the problem in cases under reg. 70(2)(b). Note the April 6, 1998 amendment which adds social fund payments and concessionary payments for the non-payment of income support under reg. 70 or income-based JSA under reg. 147 of the JSA Regulations to this list (see the note to para. (2) below). The tariff income from capital under reg. 53 is disregarded, but that is of little consequence given para. (2). Under sub-para. (c) several items of income normally treated as capital retain their status as income.

Paragraph (2)
The calculation of capital is much as normal. Categories normally disregarded which count for urgent cases purposes are the proceeds of sale of a former home, liquid assets of a business, arrears of certain benefits, certain sums deposited with Housing Associations, refunds of MIRAS

tax, training bonuses under £200, payments to compensate for loss of transitional protection and backdated payments of income support, housing benefit and council tax benefit made after recognition of refugee status. But note that the amendment of April 6, 1998 allows any arrears of income support under reg. 70 or income-based JSA under reg. 147 of the JSA Regulations to be ignored. There had been a problem that if arrears of such payments were paid the claimant could lose entitlement to further awards of urgent cases payments. This had particularly affected asylum seekers where there had been a delay in verifying information, etc.

Once the capital has been calculated a payment for urgent cases is only to be made in so far as it exceeds the amount of capital. There is no £16,000, £8,000, £10,000, £3,000, £500 or £1 exemption.

[[1]PART VII

CALCULATION OF INCOME SUPPORT FOR PART-WEEKS

Amount of income support payable

73.—(1) Subject to regulations 75 (modifications in income) and 76 (reduction in certain cases), where a claimant is entitled to income support for a period (referred to in this Part as a part-week) to which subsection (1A) of section 21 of the Act [SSCBA, s.124(5)] (amount etc. of income-related benefit) applies, the amount of income support payable shall, except where paragraph (2) applies, be calculated in accordance with the following formulae—

(a) if the claimant has no income, $\dfrac{N \times A}{7}$;

(b) if the claimant has income, $\dfrac{N \times (A - I)}{7}$ − B.

(2) Subject to regulations 75 and 76, in the case of a claimant to whom regulation 19 [[3]...] (persons in residential care or nursing homes [[3]...]) applies, where the weekly charge for the accommodation is due to be paid during a part-week to which regulation 74(1)(*a*) or (*b*) applies, the amount of income support payable shall be calculated in accordance with the following formulae—

(a) if the claimant has no income, A;

(b) if the claimant has income, (A − I) − B.

(3) In this Regulation—

"A", subject to paragraph (4), means the claimant's weekly applicable amount in the relevant week;

"B" means the amount of any income support, [[5]jobseeker's allowance], [[2]maternity allowance,] [[4]short-term or long-term incapacity benefit], or severe disablement allowance payable in respect of any day in the part-week;

"I" means his weekly income in the relevant week less B;

"N" means the number of days in the part-week;

"relevant week" means the period of 7 days determined in accordance with regulation 74.

(4) In a case to which paragraph (2) applies, a claimant's weekly applicable amount shall be—

(a) where the weekly charge for the accommodation includes all meals, the aggregate of the following amounts—

  (i) the weekly charge for the accommodation determined in accordance with paragraph 1(1)(a) of Schedule 4 [[3]...]; and

  (ii) the amount calculated in accordance with the formula—

$$\frac{(N \times P)}{7} + \frac{(N \times H)}{7} ;$$

(b) where the weekly charge for the accommodation does not include all meals, the aggregate of the following amounts—
    (i) the weekly charge for the accommodation determined in accordance with paragraph 1(1)(a) of Schedule 4 [³...] less M; and
    (ii) The amount calculated in accordance with the formula—

$$\frac{(N \times M)}{7} + \frac{(N \times P)}{7} + \frac{(N \times H)}{7} .$$

(5) In paragraph (4)—

"H" means the weekly amount determined in accordance with paragraph 1(1)(c) of Schedule 4[³...];

"M" means the amount of the increase for meals calculated on a weekly basis in accordance with paragraph 2 of Schedule 4 [³...];

"P" means the weekly amount for personal expenses determined in accordance with paragraph 13 of Schedule 4 [³...].]

AMENDMENTS

1. Income Support (General) Amendment Regulations 1988 (S.I. 1988 No. 663), reg. 27 (April 11, 1988).
2. Income Support (General) Amendment No. 4 Regulations 1988 (S.I. 1988 No. 1445), reg. 17 (September 12, 1988).
3. Income Support (General) Amendment Regulations 1989 (S.I. 1988 No. 534), Sched. 1, para. 9 (October 9, 1989).
4. Disability Working Allowance and Income Support (General) Amendment Regulations 1995 (S.I. 1995 No. 482), reg. 12 (April 13, 1995).
5. Income Support (General) (Jobseeker's Allowance Consequential Amendments) Regulations 1996 (S.I. 1996 No. 206), reg. 19 (October 7, 1996).

DEFINITIONS

"the Act"—see reg. 2(1).
"claimant"—*ibid.*

GENERAL NOTE

Although the rules set out in regs. 73 to 77 do look very complex, they set out a relatively straightforward method of calculating benefit for part-weeks. See *CIS 706/1997* for an exposition of how these rules operate.

[¹**Relevant week**

74.—(1) Where the part-week—
(a) is the whole period for which income support is payable or occurs at the beginning of the claim, the relevant week is the period of 7 days ending on the last day of that part-week; or
(b) occurs at the end of the claim, the relevant week is the period of 7 days beginning on the first day of that part-week.
(2) Where during the currency of a claim the claimant makes a claim for a relevant social security benefit within the meaning of paragraph 4 of Schedule 7 to the Social Security (Claims and Payments) Regulations 1987 and as a result his benefit week changes, for the purpose of calculating the amount of income support payable—
(a) for the part-week beginning on the day after his last complete benefit week before the date from which he makes a claim for the relevant social security benefit and ending immediately before that date, the relevant

week is the period of 7 days beginning on the day after his last complete benefit week (the first relevant week);

(b) for the part-week beginning on the date from which he makes a claim for the relevant social security benefit and ending immediately before the start of his next benefit week after the date of that claim, the relevant week is the period of 7 days ending immediately before the start of his next benefit week (the second relevant week).

(3) Where during the currency of a claim the claimant's benefit week changes at the direction of the Secretary of State under paragraph 3 of Schedule 7 to the Social Security (Claims and Payments) Regulations 1987, for the purpose of calculating the amount of income support payable for the part-week beginning on the day after his last complete benefit week before the change and ending immediately before the change, the relevant week is the period of 7 days beginning on the day after the last complete benefit week.]

AMENDMENT

1. Income Support (General) Amendment Regulations 1988 (S.I. 1988 No. 663), reg. 27 (April 11, 1988).

DEFINITIONS

"benefit week"—see reg. 2(1).
"claimant"—*ibid.*

[¹Modifications in the calculation of income

75.—For the purposes of regulation 73 (amount of income support payable for part-weeks), a claimant's income and the income of any person which the claimant is treated as possessing under section 22(5) of the Act [SSCBA, s.136(1)] or regulation 23(3) shall be calculated in accordance with Part V and, where applicable, VI subject to the following modifications—

(a) any income which is due to be paid in the relevant week shall be treated as paid on the first day of that week;

(b) any income support, [⁴jobseeker's allowance], [²maternity allowance,] [³short-term or long-term incapacity benefit], or severe disablement allowance [³. . .]payable in the relevant week but not in respect of any day in the part-week shall be disregarded;

(c) where the part-week occurs at the end of the claim, any income or any change in the amount of income of the same kind which is first payable within the relevant week but not on any day in the part-week shall be disregarded;

(d) where the part-week occurs immediately after a period in which a person was treated as engaged in remunerative work) under regulation 5(5) (persons treated as engaged in remunerative work) any earnings which are taken into account for the purposes of determining that period shall be disregarded;

(e) where regulation 74(2) (relevant week) applies, any payment of income which—
  (i) is the final payment in a series of payments of the same kind or, if there has been an interruption in such payments, the last one before the interruption;
  (ii) is payable in respect of a period not exceeding a week; and
  (iii) is due to be paid on a day which falls within both the first and second relevant weeks,
  shall be taken into account in either the first relevant week or, if it

is impracticable to take it into account in that week, in the second relevant week; but this paragraph shall not apply to a payment of income support, [⁴jobseeker's allowance], [²maternity allowance,] [³short-term or long-term incapacity benefit] or severe disablement allowance [³. . .];

(f) where regulation 74(2) applies, any payment of income which—
   (i) is the final payment in a series of payments of the same kind or, if there has been an interruption in such payments, the last one before the interruption;
   (ii) is payable in respect of a period exceeding a week but not exceeding 2 weeks; and
   (iii) is due to be paid on a day which falls within both the first and second relevant weeks,
   shall be disregarded; but this sub-paragraph shall not apply to a payment of income support, [⁴jobseeker's allowance], [²maternity allowance,] [³short-term or long term incapacity benefit], or severe disablement allowance, [³. . .]

(g) where regulation 74(2) applies, if the weekly amount of any income which is due to be paid on a day which falls within both the first and second relevant weeks is more than the weekly amount of income of the same kind due to be paid in the last complete benefit week, the excess shall be disregarded;

(h) where only part of the weekly amount of income is taken into account in the relevant week, the balance shall be disregarded.]

AMENDMENTS

1. Income Support (General) Amendment Regulations 1988 (S.I. 1988 No. 663), reg. 27 (April 11, 1988).
2. Income Support (General) Amendment No. 4 Regulations 1988 (S.I. 1988 No. 1445), reg. 17 (September 12, 1988).
3. Disability Working Allowance and Income Support (General) Amendment Regulations 1995 (S.I. 1995 No. 482), reg. 13 (April 13, 1995).
4. Income Support (General) (Jobseeker's Allowance Consequential Amendments) Regulations 1996 (S.I. 1996 No. 206), reg. 20 (October 7, 1996).

DEFINITIONS

"claimant"—see reg. 2(1).
"Social Security Act"—*ibid.*

[¹Reduction in certain cases

76.—There shall be deducted from the amount of income support which would, but for this regulation, be payable for a part-week—

(a) [² in the case of a claimant to whom regulation 22A (reduction in applicable amount where the claimant is appealing against a decision that he is not incapable of work) applies], the proportion of the relevant amount specified therein appropriate to the number of days in the part-week;

(b) where regulation 75(f) (modifications in the calculation of income) applies, one-half of the amount disregarded under regulation 75(f) less the weekly amount of any disregard under Schedule 8 or 9 appropriate to that payment.]

AMENDMENTS

1. Income Support (General) Amendment Regulations 1988 (S.I. 1988 No. 663), reg. 27 (April 11, 1988).
2. Income Support (General) (Jobseeker's Allowance Consequential Amendments) Regulations 1996 (S.I. 1996 No. 206), reg. 21 (October 7, 1996).

DEFINITION

"claimant"—see reg. 2(1).

[¹Modification of section 23(5) of the Act [SSCBA, s.126(5)]

77.—Where income support is payable for a part-week, section 23(5) of the Act [SSCBA, s.126(5)] (trade disputes) shall have effect as if the following paragraph were substituted for paragraph (b)—

"(b) any payment by way of income support for a part-week which apart from this paragraph would be made to him, or to a person whose applicable amount if aggregated with his—
  (i) shall not be made if the payment for the part-week is equal to or less than the proportion of the relevant sum appropriate to the number of days in the part-week; or
  (ii) if it is more than that proportion, shall be made at a rate equal to the difference."]

AMENDMENT

1. Income Support (General) Amendment Regulations 1988 (S.I. 1988 No. 663), reg. 27 (April 11, 1988).

DEFINITION

"the Act"—see reg. 2(1)

SCHEDULES

[¹SCHEDULE 1B   Regulation 4ZA

PRESCRIBED CATEGORIES OF PERSON

Lone parents

1. A person who is a lone parent and responsible for a child who is a member of his household.

Single persons looking after foster children

2. A single claimant or a lone parent with whom a child is placed by a local authority or voluntary organisation within the meaning of the Children Act 1989 or, in Scotland, the Social Work (Scotland) Act 1968.

Persons temporarily looking after another person

3. A person who is—

    (a) looking after a child because the parent of that child or the person who usually looks after him is ill or is temporarily absent from his home; or

    (b) looking after a member of his family who is temporarily ill.

Persons caring for another person

    4. A person (the carer)—

    (a) who is regularly and substantially engaged in caring for another person if—

        (i) the person being cared for is in receipt of attendance allowance [². . .] or the care component of disability living allowance at the highest or middle rate prescribed in accordance with section 72(3) of the Contributions and Benefits Act; or

        (ii) the person being cared for has claimed attendance allowance [². . .] but only for the period up to the date of determination of that claim, or the period of 26 weeks from the date of that claim, whichever date is the earlier; or

    [²(iia) the person being cared for has claimed attendance allowance in accordance with section 65(6)(a) of the Contributions and Benefits Act (claims in advance of entitlement), an award has been made in respect of that claim under section 65(6)(b) of that Act and, where the period for which the award is payable has begun, that person in receipt of the allowance;]

        (iii) the person being cared for has claimed entitlement to a disability living allowance but only for the period up to the date of determination of that claim, or the period of 26 weeks from the date of that claim, whichever date is the earlier; or

    [²(iiia) the person being cared for has claimed entitlement to the care component of a disability living allowance in accordance with regulation 13A of the Social Security (Claims and Payments) Regulations 1987 (advance claims and awards), an award at the highest or middle rate has been made in respect of that claim and, where the period for which the award is payable has begun, that person is in receipt of the allowance;]

    (b) who is engaged in caring for another person and who is in receipt of an invalid care allowance.

    5. A person to whom paragraph 4 applied, but only for a period of 8 weeks from the date on which that paragraph ceased to apply to him.

    6. A person who, had he previously made a claim for income support, would have fulfilled the conditions of paragraph 4, but only for a period of 8 weeks from the date on which he ceased to fulful those conditions.

Persons incapable of work

    7. A person who—

    (a) is incapable of work in accordance with the provisions of Part XIIA of the Contributions and Benefits Act and the regulations made thereunder (incapacity for work); or

    (b) is treated as incapable of work by virtue of regulations made under section 171D of that Act (persons to be treated as incapable or capable of work); or

    (c) is treated as capable of work by virtue of regulations made under section 171E(1) of that Act (disqualification etc); or

    (d) is entitled to statutory sick pay.

Disabled workers

    8. A person to whom regulation 6(a) (persons not treated as engaged in remunerative work) applies.

Persons in employment living in residential care homes, nursing homes or residential accommodation

9. A person to whom regulation 6(g) applies.

Disabled students

10. A person who is a student and—

(a) whose applicable amount includes the disability premium or severe disability premium; or

(b) who has satisfied the provisions of paragraph 7 for a continuous period of not less than 196 days, and for this purpose any two or more separate periods separated by a break of not more than 56 days shall be treated as one continuous period.

11. A person who is a student and who—

(a) immediately before 1st September 1990 was in receipt of income support by virtue of paragraph 7 of Schedule 1 as then in force; or

(b) on or after that date makes a claim for income support and at a time during the period of 18 months immediately preceding the date of that claim was in receipt of income support either by virtue of that paragraph or regulation 13(2)(b),

but this paragraph shall not apply where for a continuous period of 18 months or more the person has not been in receipt of income support.

Deaf students

12. A person who is a student in respect of whom—

(a) a supplementary requirement has been determined under paragraph 10 of Schedule 2 to the Education (Mandatory Awards) Regulations 1995; or

(b) an allowance or, as the case may be, bursary has been granted which includes a sum under paragraph (1)(d) of regulation 6 of the Students' Allowances (Scotland) Regulations 1991 or, as the case may be, the Education Authority Bursaries (Scotland) Regulations 1995 in respect of expenses incurred; or

(c) a payment has been made under section 2 of the Education Act 1962; or

(d) a supplementary requirement has been determined under paragraph 10 of Schedule 7 to the Students Awards Regulations (Northern Ireland) 1995 or a payment has been made under article 50(3) of the Education and Libraries (Northern Ireland) Order 1986,

on account of his disability by reason of deafness.

Blind persons

13. A person who is registered as blind complied by a local authority under section 29 of the National Assistance Act 1948 (welfare services) or, in Scotland, has been certified as blind and in consequence he is registered as blind in a register maintained by or on behalf of a regional or islands council, but a person who has ceased to be registered as blind on regaining his eyesight shall nevertheless be treated as so registered for a period of 28 weeks following the date on which he ceased to be so registered.

Pregnancy

14. A woman who—

(a) is incapable of work by reason of pregnancy; or

(b) is or has been pregnant but only for the period commencing 11 weeks before her expected week of confinement and ending seven weeks after the date on which her pregnancy ends.

Persons in education

15. A person to whom any provision of regulation 13(2)(a) to (e) (persons receiving relevant education who are parents, severely handicapped persons, orphans and persons estranged from their parents or guardian) applies.

Certain persons aged 50 who have not been in remunerative work for 10 years

16.—(1) Subject to sub-paragraph (2), a person who on 6th October 1996 or at any time during the eight weeks immediately preceding that date [³was in receipt of income support and] satisfied the conditions of paragraph 13 of Schedule 1 as in force on that date (persons aged not less than 50 who had not been in remunerative work during the previous 10 years).

(2) If a person to whom sub-paragraph (1) applies ceases to be entitled to income support, and subsequently makes a further claim for income support, this paragraph shall continue to apply to him only if—

(a) the further claim for income support is made within 8 weeks of the date he ceased to be so entitled; and

(b) he has not been in remunerative work since he ceased to be so entitled.

Persons aged 60 or over

17. A person aged not less than 60.

Refugees

18. A person who is a refugee within the definition in Article 1 of the Convention relating to the Status of Refugees done at Geneva on 28th July 1951 as extended by Article 1(2) of the Protocol relating to the Status of Refugees done at New York on 31st January 1967 and who—

(a) is attending for more than 15 hours a week a course for the purpose of learning English so that he may obtain employment; and

(b) on the date on which that course commenced, had been in Great Britain for not more than 12 months.

but only for a period not exceeding nine months.

Persons required to attend court

19. A person who is required to attend court as a justice of the peace, a party to any proceedings, a witness or a juror.

Persons affected by a trade dispute

20. A person to whom section 126 of the Contributions and Benefits Act (trade disputes) applies or in respect of whom section 124(1) of the Act (conditions of entitlement to income support) has effect as modified by section 127(b) of the Act (effect of return to work).

Persons from abroad

21. A person to whom regulation 70(3) (applicable amount of certain persons from abroad) applies.

Persons in custody

22. A person remanded in, or committed in, custody for trial or for sentencing.

Member of couple looking after children while other member temporarily abroad

23. A person who is a member of a couple and who is treated as responsible for a child who is a member of his household where the other member of that couple is temporarily not present in the United Kingdom.

Persons appealing against a decision that they are not incapable of work

24. A person—
(a) in respect of whom it has been determined for the purposes of section 171B of the Contributions and Benefits Act (the own occupation test) that he is not incapable of work; and
(b) whose medical practitioner continues to supply evidence of his incapacity for work in accordance with regulation 2 of the Social Security (Medical Evidence) Regulations 1976 (evidence of incapacity for work); and
(c) who has made and is pursuing an appeal against the determination that he is not so incapable,
but only for the period prior to the determination of his appeal.

25. A person—
(a) in respect of whom it has been determined for the purposes of section 171C of the Contributions and Benefits Act (the all work test) that he is not incapable of work; and
(b) who has made and is pursuing an appeal against the determination that he is not so incapable.
but only for the period prior to the determination of his appeal.

26. A person who on 6th October 1996 was not required to be available for employment by virtue of regulation 8(2) (persons appealing against decisions that they are not incapable of work) as modified by the savings provision in regulation 20(1) or (3) of the Disability Working Allowance and Income Support (General) Amendment Regulations 1995, but only for a period prior to the determination of his appeal.

27. A person who on 6th October 1996 was required to register for employment by virtue of regulation 11(2) (persons appealing against decisions that they are not incapable of work) as modified by the savings provisions in regulation 20(2) or (3) of the Disability Working Allowance and Income Support (General) Amendment Regulations 1995, but only for the period prior to the determination of his appeal.

28. A person who is engaged in training, and for this purpose "training" means training for which persons aged under 18 are eligible and for which persons aged 18 to 24 may be eligible provided in England and Wales, directly or indirectly by a Training and Enterprise Council pursuant to its arrangement with the Secretary of State (whether that arrangement is known as an Operating Agreement or by any other name) and, in Scotland, directly or indirectly by a Local Enterprise Company pursuant to its arrangement with, as the case may be, Scottish Enterprise or Highlands and Islands Enterprise (whether that arrangement is known as an Operating Contract or by any other name).

AMENDMENTS

1. Income Support (General) (Jobseeker's Allowance Consequential Amendments) Regulations 1996 (S.I. 1996 No. 206), reg. 22 and Sched. 1 (October 7, 1996).

2. Jobseeker's Allowance and Income Support (General) (Amendment) Regulations 1996 (S.I. 1996 No. 1517), reg. 33 (October 7, 1996).

3. Social Security and Child Support (Miscellaneous Amendments) Regulations 1997 (S.I. 1997 No. 827), reg. 5 (April 7, 1997).

DEFINITIONS

"attendance allowance"—see reg. 2(1).
"child"—see SSCBA, s.137(1)).
"disability living allowance"—see reg. 2(1).
"lone parent"—*ibid.*
"payment"—*ibid.*
"single claimant"—*ibid.*
"student"—*ibid.*, reg. 61.
"voluntary organisation"—see reg. 2(1).

GENERAL NOTE

As a consequence of the introduction of JSA on October 7, 1996, the income support scheme has had to undergo a fundamental restructuring. Income support is no longer available to people who are claiming benefit because they are unemployed. People who have to be available for, and actively seeking, work as a condition of receiving benefit now have to claim JSA. Since October 7, 1996, in order to qualify for income support a person has to fall within a "prescribed category" (see SSCBA, s.124(1)(e) and reg. 4ZA). Sched. 1B sets out these categories.

See the notes to reg. 4ZA for discussion of the position of claimants who may be able to claim either income support or JSA; note also that the raising of the limit for remunerative work for partners to 24 hours a week from October 7, 1996 may mean that some couples will have to decide whether they will gain more by claiming family credit (or disability working allowance or, in certain areas of the country, earnings top-up): see the notes to Family Credit Regulations, reg. 4. Family credit and disability working allowance are due to be replaced by working families tax credit and disabled person's tax credit from October 5, 1999. See the 1999 Supplement to this book for further details.

The categories in Sched. 1B broadly resemble most of those in the former Sched. 1 (people not required to be available for employment) (revoked on October 7, 1996), but there are some differences. There is no equivalent to paras. 12 (Open University students attending a residential course), 18 (discharged prisoners) or 23 (persons taking child abroad for medical treatment) of the former Sched. 1. But if people in these circumstances claim JSA they will be treated as available for work (see sub-paras. (f), (h) and (c) respectively of reg. 14(1) of the JSA Regulations). See the note to para. 28 for people in receipt of a training allowance.

Sched. 1B provides an exhaustive list of the circumstances in which a person will be entitled to income support. There is no category of analogous circumstances or provision for a reduced rate of benefit on the ground of hardship for people who do not come within these categories (compare the former reg. 8(3), see the 1996 edition of this book). Moreover, the provision for hardship payments under JSA is considerably restricted (see regs. 140–146 of the JSA Regulations and the notes to those regulations). For the very limited provision for urgent cases outside the normal scope of the income support rules, see reg. 70.

Paragraph 1
See reg. 15 for responsibility for a child and reg. 16 for membership of the household. Once a child turns into a young person (reg. 14) or ceases to be a member of the family (SSCBA, s.137(1)), a lone parent ceases to fall under para. 1.

Paragraph 2
Special provision is necessary for foster children because they are not members of the foster-parent's household (reg. 16(4)).

Paragraph 3
This covers a person who is looking after a child because his parent or the person who usually looks after him is ill or temporarily absent, or a member of the family (SSCBA, s.137(1)) who is temporarily ill.

See the note to reg. 6(b) on childminders.

Paragraphs 4–6

There is no requirement that alternative arrangements cannot be made. Under para. 4(a) the fact of being substantially and regularly engaged in providing care for someone who receives or has been awarded attendance allowance or one of the two higher care components of disability living allowance or who is waiting for a decision on entitlement is enough. In the last case, entitlement to income support under para. 4(a) lasts for up to 26 weeks from the date of the claim for attendance/disability living allowance, or until it is decided, whichever is the earlier. For invalid care purposes "substantial" is 35 hours a week. Para. 4(b) covers anyone in receipt of invalid care allowance. The effect of paras. 5 and 6 is that the carer can qualify for income support in the eight weeks after ceasing to meet the conditions in para. 4 (note the transitional provision in reg. 27(1) of the Income Support (General) (Jobseeker's Allowance Consequential Amendments) Regulations 1996 (p. 499)).

Paragraph 7

This covers people who are incapable of work. A person who is not capable of work will not be entitled to JSA (s.1(2)(f) of the Jobseekers Act). But note reg. 55 of the JSA Regulations which allows a JSA award to continue while a person is incapable of work for up to two weeks (subject to a limit of two such periods in any 12 months).

Since April 13, 1995, the framework for deciding whether a person is capable or incapable of work has been contained in Part XIIA of the Contributions and Benefits Act (ss.171A–G) and s.61A of the Administration Act. The detail is in regulations, see in particular the Social Security (Incapacity for Work) (General) Regulations 1995 (S.I. 1995 No. 311). Note regs. 19–21 which deal with adjudication. Reg. 19 provides that a decision on a person's capacity for work in connection with a claim for one benefit is conclusive for the purposes of all other benefits; reg. 20 provides that if a question of incapacity arises on a claim for any benefit, this is to be decided by an AO, even if other questions are decided by another authority (this will mean AOs and SSATs deciding incapacity questions that arise, for example, in connection with a disability premium on a housing benefit claim); and reg. 21 provides that a SSAT must sit with a medical assessor in any case that involves consideration of whether the claimant satisfies the "all work test" (see the notes to s.61A(4) of the Administration Act). Note that under the new system for decision-making and appeals coming into force for income support on November 29, 1999 (and for incapacity benefit on September 6, 1999) regs. 19–22 of the Incapacity for Work Regulations will be revoked. For the new form of reg. 19 see reg. 10 of the Social Security and Child Support (Decisions and Appeals) Regulations 1999 (S.I. 1999 No. 991). Appeals about incapacity for work will be heard by a two-person tribunal consisting of a chairman and a doctor; there will no longer be a medical assessor sitting with the tribunal in all work test cases.

See further the note to s.61A(2) of the Administration Act for a brief discussion of the nature of AO's decisions under reg. 19, particularly in relation to decisions on "credits". See also the note to s.61A(3).

Para. 7 covers four categories: those who are incapable of work (sub-para. (a)); those who are treated as incapable of work (sub-para. (b)); those who are treated as capable of work under regulations made under s. 171E(1) of the Contributions and Benefits Act (see reg. 18 of the Incapacity for Work Regulations) (sub-para. (c)); and those who are entitled to statutory sick pay (sub-para. (d)). See also paras. 24–27 which apply to claimants who are appealing against a decision that they are capable of work.

Sub-para. (a).

A person who is incapable of work under the tests for deciding incapacity for work in the 1992 Act is eligible for income support. The following is a summary of the rules for deciding incapacity for work. For further detail and the text of the legislation see *Bonner*.

There are two tests for assessing whether a person is incapable of work. For many people the "own occupation test" will apply for the first 28 weeks of incapacity; during this time the claimant has to show that "he is incapable by reason of some specific disease or bodily or mental disablement of doing work which he could reasonably be expected to do in the course of the occupation in which he was so engaged" (s. 171B(2) of the Contributions and Benefits Acts). While this test applies a claimant is likely to satisfy sub-para. (a) if he sends in medical certificates, unless an AO decides that he is capable of work in his "own occupation".

If the "own occupation test" does not apply (*e.g.* because the claimant has been unemployed for 13 or more weeks in the 21 weeks before the incapacity for work began), or after 28 weeks, the "all work test" applies. Claimants can be treated as satisfying this test until they are assessed under it, in which case they must submit, or continue to submit medical or other evidence of their incapacity in accordance with the Social Security (Medical Evidence) Regulations 1976 (reg. 28 of the Incapacity for Work Regulations). See *CSIS 65/1991* which decided that under what is now reg. 2(1)(d) of the Medical Evidence Regulations evidence of incapacity need not be in the form of medical certificates and *CS 12476/1996* which holds that that ruling and the principle established in *R(IS) 8/93* that medical certificates may be supplied on a retrospective basis applied to reg. 28. But note the exception in reg. 28 for claimants who have been found capable of work, or treated as capable of work under reg. 7 or 8 of the Incapacity for Work Regulations, in the last six months. In this case a claimant will not be treated as satisfying the all work test unless his condition has significantly worsened or he is suffering from a different condition, or, in a case where he was treated as capable of work under reg. 7, he has since returned the incapacity for work questionnaire.

Note that if a person does any work (subject to certain exceptions) he is treated as capable of work on each day of that week (but only on the actual days worked if it is the first or last week of the claim), even if he has passed the all work test or is treated as incapable of work (see regs. 16 and 17 of the Incapacity for Work Regulations). *CIB 14656/1996* decides that the domestic tasks carried out by the claimant for the benefit of her lodger and herself did not constitute work within reg. 16(2), as they fell within the exception for "domestic tasks carried out in his own home". On the evidence, the lodger was part of the "home". The Commissioner also considered it possible for "work" to be so trivial or negligible so as to be excluded on the *de minimis* principle (although not on the facts of that case). *CSIB 608/1997* confirms that the exemption for therapeutic work under reg. 17(1)(a)(i) is only applicable where the work is undertaken on the advice of a doctor; if no such advice has been given reg. 17(1)(a)(i) cannot apply. However, if such advice is given later, even if the work was not initially undertaken on the advice of a doctor, reg. 17(1)(a) may apply from that later date (*CIB 534/1998*).

There are also rules for treating a person as capable of work if he fails without good cause either to return the all work test questionnaire within the time limit, or to attend a medical examination of which at least seven days' written notice has been given (see regs. 7–9 of the Incapacity for Work Regulations).

If the all work test has not yet been applied, the provision of retrospective medical certificates should suffice to satisfy sub-para. (a) (see *R(IS) 8/93*, followed in *CIS 714/1991*, and *CS 12476/1996* above). Such backdated medical evidence could be relevant in relation to the waiting period for entitlement to a disability premium under para. 12(1)(b)(ii) of Sched. 2. Note the new limits from April 7, 1997 on backdating claims for income support in reg. 19 of the Claims and Payments Regulations.

The "all work test"

Reg. 24 of the Incapacity for Work Regulations defines the all work test as "a test of the extent of a person's incapacity, by reason of some specific disease or bodily or mental disablement, to perform the activities prescribed in the Schedule" (*i.e.* the Schedule to the Incapacity for Work Regulations). Part I of the Schedule is concerned with physical disabilities and Part II with mental disabilities. Each Part lists a number of "activities", sub-divided into "descriptors"; a claimant's capacity for work is decided by measuring his ability to perform these various activities. (Note that significant changes to the wording of some of the descriptors were introduced on January 6, 1997: see further *Bonner*). If the claimant's disabilities result in him scoring the required number of points, he will pass the all work test and medical evidence will no longer be required. Non-medical considerations, such as age, education, previous work experience and other personal factors are not relevant, nor is the person's ability to undertake actual jobs (confirmed in *CIB 14534/1996*, see below).

A claimant satisifies the test if he reaches 15 points from the physical descriptors, or 10 from the mental health descriptors, or 15 from a combination of both (see reg. 25(1) of the Incapacity for Work Regulations). Where descriptors from both the physical and mental activities apply, a score of between 6 to 9 points (inclusive) from the mental health descriptors counts as 9 and a score of less than 6 is ignored (reg. 26(1) of the Incapacity for Work Regulations). For the mental health descriptors, all the points from the various descriptors are added together, whether or not they relate to the same activity (reg. 26(4)). But in relation to the physical descriptors, only one descriptor (that with the highest score) from each activity counts; moreover in the case of the activities of "walking" and "walking up and down stairs", only the highest scoring descriptor from *either* activity is counted (reg. 26(2)–(3)). *CSIB 13/1996* confirms that there are no limits on the scoring, other than those in reg. 26 (or that arise from the wording of the Schedule itself). In *CSIB 13/1996* the claimant's vision was severely defective. The tribunal awarded him points under descriptor 2(d) (cannot walk up and down stairs without holding on) as well as under 12(d) (cannot see well enough to recognise a friend across the room). The AO contended that the proper approach was to look at the source of the claimant's difficulties. Thus where the problem was with vision and not walking, the descriptors listed in relation to vision were the only ones which could be applied. However, this is rejected by the Commissioner who holds that in the absence of any express provision precluding overlapping between the 14 activities in Part I of the Schedule (except in relation to "walking" and "walking up and down stairs"), there was no compelling reason for implying one.

Reg. 25(3) of the Incapacity for Work Regulations, introduced on Jaunary 6, 1997, makes clear that Part I descriptors can only be applied where a claimant's incapacity arises from some physical disablement or illness and Part II descriptors only if there is some specific mental illness or disablement. *CIB 14446/1996* decides that reg. 25(3) effected a material change in the law. The claimant suffered from chronic depression. One of the consequences was that she was restless and had grave difficulty sitting in a chair for longer than half an hour. The tribunal decided that descriptor 3(c) (cannot sit comfortably for more than 30 minutes without having to move from the chair) applied. The Commissioner states that before January 6, 1997, reg. 25 did not require any connection between the nature of the illness or disablement giving rise to incapacity and the points that could be scored by a claimant in relation to any of the descriptors in the Schedule. Thus there was nothing at that time to prevent an adjudicating authority applying to a claimant a physical disablement descriptor that stemmed from a mental cause. But from January 6, 1997 none of the sitting descriptors could apply to the claimant if the cause of her incapacity was mental illness or disablement.

Applying the descriptors

The Commissioners' decisions that have emerged so far on the all work test have agreed that "an overall requirement of 'reasonableness' " has to be applied when considering whether a person can undertake a specified activity, including whether he is capable of doing it most of the time. Thus "reasonable regularity" can properly be considered. If the person can only accomplish the activity occasionally this should be discounted (*CI/95(IB)*, a decision of the Northern Ireland Chief Commissioner, approved in *CSIB 17/1996, CIB 13161/1996* and *CIB 13508/1996* and *CIB 14587/1996*). As *CIB 13161/1996* and *CIB 13508/1996* put it, the question whether a person "cannot" do something depends on whether he is *normally* able to perform the stated activity as and when he is called upon to do so. This decision also states that the language of the descriptors has to be read "in a reasonably broad and not a restricted literal sense". *CIB 16150/1996* applies the same approach to the mental health descriptors. Assessments should not be based on a "snapshot" but upon the claimant's functional ability over a period of time, applying a test of reasonableness. But the mental health descriptors can only apply if they result from mental disablement; they must not be "mere matters of mood" (*CIB 14202/ 1996*, followed in *C53/98 (1B)* (a Northern Ireland decision), and reg. 24 of the Incapacity for Work Regulations) (and see reg. 25(3), introduced on January 6, 1997, referred to above).

See also *CIB 16182/1966* in which the Commissioner considered the effect of pain-killers in relation to the all work test. The claimant contended that he had only been able to perform the tests carried out by the BAMS doctor because he had taken very strong pain-killers. The Commissoner states that the fact that a claimant took pain-killers before a medical examination was not relevant if it was reasonable to expect him to take such pain-killers whenever pain affected his ability to carry out relevant tasks. If, on the other hand, it would be unwise for the claimant to take pain-killers on all such occasions, so that he sometimes had to put up with the pain and would be unable to carry out the tasks he performed for the examining doctor, it would be relevant because the medical examination would not show the real extent of the claimant's disablement.

CIB 5361/1997 confirms that when applying the physical descriptors it is necessary to work *down* from the top of each activity in the Schedule and stop as soon as a relevant descriptor is reached. The advice apparently given to the BAMS doctor in training sessions to work "from the bottom up" and tick the first appropriate descriptor was flatly contrary to reg. 26(3) of the Incapacity for Work Regulations (descriptor with the highest score in respect of each activity in Part I to count). It had therefore invalidated not only his evidence but also the SSAT's decision based upon it.

The relevance of a work context

However, *CI/95(IB), CSIB 17/1996, CIB 14587/1996, CIB 13161/1996* and *CIB 13508/1996* also hold that the ability to undertake the activity does not have to be considered in the context of a working situation (contrary to the view taken by the DSS in the *Medical Advisers' Guide to Incapacity Benefit*, paras. 960–966; note that this guidance has been replaced by the *Incapacity Benefit Handbook for Medical Services Doctors* which generally takes a less liberal line, although it does suggest, for example, the need to consider whether the claimant could carry out an action which causes moderate pain "reliably, safely and repeatedly in the workplace" (p. 89, para. 17)). This is because, as the Commissioner in *CIB 14587/1996* puts it, "these individual tests relate to the claimant's capacity to carry out ordinary functions in everyday life ... [as] a convenient means of assessing ... [whether the claimant can] ... be treated as capable or incapable of work". In his view this approach avoided the difficulty that would otherwise arise of having to decide which particular work context was applicable to the claimant in question. But there also would not seem to be any justification on the statutory wording for considering the test *simply* in a domestic context (see the Commissioner's reference in *CIB 14587/1996* to judging the claimant's abilities according to the needs of everyday living at home), since particular factors may operate in that environment which do not apply elsewhere.

Moreover, to ignore the relevance of a work environment seems a somewhat odd approach when the stated purpose of the test is to establish whether or not the person is capable of work (although it has to be said that the reality is that the test is one of disability, not incapacity for work). It also may not be one that is universally accepted—see *CIB 14332/1996* in which the Commissioner indicates that he would want to take another look at the issue, bearing in mind that the Schedule to the Incapacity for Work Regulations is headed "Disabilities which may make a person incapable of work". But if factors such as fatigue, pain and risk to health are taken into account in considering whether a person can undertake the specified activities (see below), as well as "reasonable regularity", the fact that the activities do not have to be set in a work context may not make a great deal of difference in many cases. It is noteworthy that the Commissioner in *CIB 13161/1996* and *CIB 13508/1996* did not consider that reference to a working situation to justify importing the concept of reasonable regularity was in itself wrong; in his view what was not permissible was using the notion of a work context to import a separate and additional test over and above that required by the legislation.

The effect of pain, fatigue and risk to health

Clearly factors such as pain and fatigue are relevant to the question of whether a person can carry out an activity with reasonable regularity. This is expressly acknowledged in *CIB 13161/1996* and *CIB 13508/1996* where the Commissioner states that in deciding which descriptor applied, the effect of pain and fatigue and the increasing difficulty of performing the task on a repeated basis, beyond that experienced by a fit person, had to be taken into account. The question, however, is what level of pain, etc. is required before it can be said that the claimant "cannot" do one of the specified activities. In *CIB 14587/1996* the test put forward by the Commissioner was—could the claimant bend or kneel "without at least too much discomfort" and could he repeat the exercise "within a reasonable time". *R1/62(SB)*, a Northern Ireland decision under the former sickness/invalidity bene-fit regime, held that functions which could be performed only with "substantial" pain were to be discounted. This decision is referred to in *CIB 14772/1996*, which also says that if the carrying out of a particular activity normally caused the claimant a "significant" degree of nausea or dizziness, then such nausea or dizziness should be treated as equivalent to pain.

It is suggested that discomfort caused by, for example breathlessness, will also be relevant. The distinction drawn between "pain" and "severe discomfort" in some mobility allowance/disability living allowance decisions (see *CDLA 12940/1996* for a discussion of this issue) would not seem particularly appropriate in the context of assessing whether a claimant "cannot" perform a specific activity. The question is, it is submitted, simply whether the claimant's ability to undertake that activity is sufficiently impaired for the relevant descriptor to apply. Decisions on the meaning of severe discomfort for the purposes of mobility allowance/disability living allowance may, however, be of some assistance in relation to activity 1 (walking without stopping or *severe discomfort*). In *CDLA 12940/1996* the Commissioner takes the view that discomfort described the sensation experienced from lesser levels of pain but that pain was not identical with severe discomfort. A person suffering severe pain was almost certainly suffering severe discomfort. But it did not follow that, because someone was not suffering severe pain, he was not suffering severe discomfort. Discomfort was a broader concept which could include other factors that caused uneasiness as well as pain. See also *CDLA 1389/1997*.

Note *CSIB 12/1996* in which the Commissioner stated that if there was a real risk to a person's health from carrying out an activity, particularly if this was on the basis of medical advice, the appropriate descriptor should be treated as met.

On the relevance of pain-killers in relation to the all work test, see *CIB 16182/1996* referred to under "*Applying the descriptors*".

Intermittent conditions

In *CIB 13161/1996* and *CIB 13508/1996* the Commisioner observed that by requiring the all work test to be satisfied on a day-to-day basis, the legislation largely ignored the problems of people who had "good days and bad days" and those who were rendered unemployable by serious but intermittent conditions. Where a person did suffer from an intermittent condition, the current form of the legislation did not allow an overall view to be taken over a continuous period. Thus a tribunal would need to identify all relevant individual days of incapacity (possibly on the basis of a rough and ready assessment on the best evidence available) down to the date of their decision in order to ascertain the claimant's entitlement (bearing in mind the rules on a period of incapacity for work: see SSCBA, s. 30C in *Bonner*).

However, although ss.30A to 30E of the Contributions and Benefits Act 1992, dealing with incapacity benefit, talks in terms of "days of incapacity", there is no reference in the wording of the Schedule to the Incapacity for Work Regulations itself to the descriptors being met on a daily basis; indeed activities 13 (continence) and 14 (remaining conscious without having epileptic or similar seizures during waking moments) clearly do not have to be satisfied on a daily basis. It is, for example, possible for a person who has an involuntary episode of lost or altered consciousness at least once a month to score 15 points and so pass the all work test. Yet the person may be able to function normally in between such episodes. Thus *certain* intermittent conditions may be catered for in the legislation but only if they are covered by the specific descriptors in activities 13 and 14 (in this respect note the change to activity 14 introduced on January 6, 1997). However, the fact that some intermittent conditions can lead to the all work test being satisfied, adds weight to the view that an assessment of the application of the descriptors *can* (contrary to the Commissioner's conclusion) be conducted on an overall basis to see whether the all work test is satisfied.

Furthermore, a number of other decisions have either attempted to "water down" the effect of the Commissioner's approach in *CIB 13161/1996* and *CIB 13508/1996* (see, for example, *CIB 911/1997* and *CSIB 459/1997*) or have explicitly disagreed with it (see *CIB 15231/1996* and *CSIB 684/1997*). In *CIB 15231/1996* the Commissioner states that in his view a claimant did not fail the all work test simply because he could perform the descriptors on a particular day, nor did he pass it simply because he could not perform the descriptors on that day. Although the test was to be applied on a daily basis, compliance with it was not dependent upon the circumstances prevailing on a particular day. The assessment of compliance on a particular day should be based on a claimant's functional ability over such period as the tribunal considered appropriate to enable them to get a true and fair picture of the claimant's capacity. The Commissioner pointed to the similar approach taken in relation to disability living allowance (see *R(A) 2/74*) and previously invalidity benefit (under which entitlement to benefit had also been geared to days of incapacity for work: see s.57(1)(a), SSCBA). In his view, therefore, it *was* possible for an overall view of the claimant's condition to be taken when applying the all work test. In *CSIB 648/1997* the Commissioner considered that the difficulties in applying *CIB 13161/1996* and *CIB 13508/1996*, given a tribunal's duty (at that time) to determine the appeal down to the date of its hearing (see *CIB 14430/1996, CIS 12015/1996* and *CS 12054/1996* below), meant that "the proper approach was to determine the matter on a broad and reasonable basis ... over the period that requires to be considered and determine whether there are periods when the test is satisfied so as to award points and periods when it is not". Precise consideration of the claimant's condition on a daily basis was not necessary. See also *CIB 6244/1997* (a case concerning chronic fatigue syndrome) in which the Commissioner approaches the issue by distinguishing between variable and intermittent conditions (while recognising that some conditions would involve characteristics of both).

As a result of these conflicting decisions, a Tribunal of Commissioners was convened to consider this issue (*CIB 14534/1996*). The Commissioners accept that a broad approach had to be taken when considering whether a person satisfied the all work test and that it was generally unnecessary to consider each day in isolation. In their view this was the only approach that could sensibly be applied when the AO was making what was in effect a prospective determination for an extended period. Moreover, it did not follow from the fact that incapacity benefit was a daily benefit that the all work test had to literally be satisfied in respect of each day. The Tribunal considered that the "normative approach" adopted in *R(A) 2/74* applied equally to incapacity benefit, since there was no real distinction between the requirement for attendance allowance that a claimant should satisfy the statutory conditions *throughout* a period and the stipulation in relation to incapacity benefit that entitlement arose in respect of *any day* of incapacity. The Commissioners warned adjudicating authorities not to stray too far from an arithmetical approach that had regard to what the claimant's abilities were "most of the time" (see *C1/95(IB)*). But in deciding whether a claimant "cannot" perform an activity, the frequency

of "bad" days, the length of periods of "bad" days and of intervening periods, the severity
of the claimant's disablement on both "good" and "bad" days and the unpredictability of
"bad" days were all relevant. The Tribunal concluded that this broad approach might not be
markedly different from that taken under the legislation in force before April 1995. However,
there was a difference in the case of claimants who only had short episodes of disablement,
e.g. on four or five days a month. Previously they might have been found continuously incapable
of work on the ground that there was no work that they could reasonably be expected to do.
But under the current legislation this did not apply. As had been pointed out in both *CIS 13161/
1996 and CIB 13508/1996* and in *CIB 6244/1997*, in those cases the particular days on which
the claimant was incapable of work would have to be identified. However, since AOs seldom
needed to look *back* over any substantial period and for appeals brought on or after May 21,
1998 a tribunal would only be concerned with the claimant's capacity for work at the date of
the AO's decision (see s.22(8) of the Administration Act), this might not be so onerous as had
sometimes been suggested.

"Down to the date of hearing" and the burden of proof
Case law had clearly established that a tribunal should deal with the issue of the claimant's
incapacity down to the date of its hearing (*CSIB 9/1996; CIB 14430/1996, CIS 12015/1996* and
CS 12054/1996 (Tribunal of Commissioners); *CSIB 298/1997; CIB 16092/1996* and *CIB 90/
1997*) (but note the change introduced by the Social Security Act 1998, see below). Thus even
if it concluded that the claimant was capable of work at the time the AO's decision was made,
a tribunal had to take account of any relevant change of circumstances such as a deterioration
in the claimant's health. Presumably a SSAT could also have taken account of any subsequent
improvement.
The down to the date of the decision principle applied whether the appeal was against the
refusal of an original claim (*R(S) 1/83*) or a decision on review (*CIB 14430/1996, CIS 12015/
1996* and *CS 12054/1996*: see further the notes to reg. 17(4) of the Claims and Payments
Regulations). In addition, *CSIB 298/1997* and *CIB 16092/1996* and *CIB 90/1997* confirm that
the principle applied to appeals from AOs' decisions given for credit purposes as well as review
decisions relating to an award of benefit. There was however an exception to the rule that was
exposed in *CS 12476/1996*. The Commissioner decides that where the appeal was against an
AO's decision reviewing and terminating an award of invalidity benefit, and the claimant was
found not to be incapable of work on April 12, 1995, a SSAT would not have to consider the
matter beyond that date. This was because a claimant had to be entitled to invalidity benefit
immediately before April 13, 1995 in order to transfer to a transitional award of long-term
incapacity benefit under reg. 17 of the Incapacity Benefit (Transitional) Regulations (see reg. 11
for transfer to a transitional award of short-term incapacity benefit where a person was entitled
to sickness benefit immediately before April 13, 1995). If the claimant was found to be incapable
of work on April 12, 1995, the down to the date of hearing principle would apply in the
normal way.
But in relation to appeals brought on or after May 21, 1998 (the day the Social Security Act
1998 received the Royal Assent), a tribunal will only be able to consider the position up to the
date of the AO's decision (see the new subs. (8) inserted into s.22 of the Administration Act
by para. 3 of Sched. 6 to the 1998 Act which applies until s.12(8)(b) of the Act is brought
into force). Thus a claimant will have to submit a fresh claim (or claims) as time elapses (and
appeal as necessary), in order for any changes in his circumstances to be considered. See
President's Circular No. 15 which helpfully points out that this does not necessarily render
irrelevant evidence which comes into existence after the AO's decision. A tribunal will still be
able to take this into account if it throws further light on circumstances that did obtain at the
time of the decision. Note that s.22(8) has no effect on the period of any award made by a
tribunal hearing an appeal lodged on or after May 21, 1998. Any such award of income support
will normally be for an indefinite period (see reg. 17 of the Claims and Payments Regulations).
However, see *CS 12476/1996* in which the Commissioner states that if the claimant has made
a subsequent claim which has already been determined (whether favourably or adversely), the
period to be considered by the tribunal will end on the day before the first day of that new
claim. This is based on *CM 91A/1993*, but would seem to go beyond what was said by a
Tribunal of Commissioners in *R(S) 1/83* (see para. 11 in which the Commissioners state that a
new claim will not automatically terminate the running of the old claim, although it will do so
in certain circumstances, *e.g.* if an undisputed award is made on the new claim). See also *CSIB
203/1997*.

The burden of proof and the need for a review
Another issue that has been considered by the Commissioners is where the burden of proof
lies in decisions concerning incapacity for work. Clearly where the decision under appeal is a

review decision terminating an award of benefit the burden of proof will be on the AO (*R(S) 3/90*). In *CIB 16092/1996* and *CIB 90/1997* the Commissioner concludes that an AO's decision on "credits" under reg. 19 of the Incapacity for Work Regulations will also generally be a review decision (except where the previous decision on credits was made by the Secretary of State under the pre-April 13, 1995 legislation). He points out that reg. 28 of the Incapacity for Work Regulations only treats a claimant as satisfying the all work test; it does not deem him to be incapable of work. Thus an AO will still have had to make a decision on incapacity for work. When an actual assessment under the all work test is carried out and an AO is asked to make a decision on capacity for work there will need to be a review of that decision if it is to be altered. *CIB 16092/1996 and CIB 90/1997* are followed in *CIB 6244/1997*. Note also *CIB 911/1997* (another "credits" case), in which the Commissioner states that although the burden was on the AO at the date the claimant was found not to be incapable of work, it was on the claimant to show incapacity from a later date, and see *CIB 248/1997* in which he deals with this point in further detail. (This will of course no longer be relevant under the Social Security Act 1998.)

CIB 3899/1997 considers the position where the claimant has failed the all work test having previously satisfied it. The Commissioner rejects the AO's submission that an adverse assessment under the test in itself gave grounds for review in cases involving a second (or subsequent) application of the all-work-test. In considering whether there were grounds for review, adjudicating authorities had to consider and give proper weight to the evidence on which the previous decision had been based. The SSAT in this case had simply allowed the claimant's appeal on the basis that no grounds for reviewing the decision given on the first application of the all work test had been shown. However, the Commissioner decides that the tribunal should, in accordance with the principles of natural justice, have given the AO an opportunity to put forward a case on the issue of review. As this was a "paper hearing" the tribunal should have adjourned in order to allow the AO to produce the previous all work test assessment and to make submissions to support a review. In the case of an oral hearing the Commissioner considered that it might be possible for the tribunal to hear submissions as to the grounds for review (if there was a presenting officer present and an opportunity to look at the claimant's file). However, presenting officers are rarely present at all work test appeals and the likelihood of the papers on any previous all work test assessment being available is remote. The Commissioner's ruling that a tribunal should adjourn in these circumstances will not have found favour with those trying to speed up the clearance time for appeals! It is to be hoped that now AOs have notice of this decision they will address the issue of review and include the previous papers in their submissions as a matter of course. If this is not done, it is suggested that there will be less grounds for maintaining that there has been a breach of natural justice if a tribunal proceeds to deal with the appeal, since the AO will already have had the opportunity to produce the required information.

CSIB 459/1997 confirms that where the claimant has put in contention particular descriptors, the tribunal should reach specific findings on each and not merely make a general statement to the effect that the report of the BAMS doctor is accepted. See also the statement of "best practice" in *CSIB 324/1997*: a tribunal should make findings of fact about the claimant's disability (or disabilities) and which activities are adversely affected, and then decide which descriptors apply and why, dealing in particular with any that were put in contention that have been found not to apply (para. 11). Clearly there will only be a need to set this out in detail where a full statement of the tribunal's decision is requested. But generalised findings and reasons recorded on a standard form are unlikely to be sufficient (*CIB 3983/1997*). *C46/97(IB)* (a decision of the Northern Ireland Chief Commissioner) commends the approach of *CSIB 324/1997* as the "best and safest practice" but says that it will not be necessary to follow it in all cases. One example would be where the tribunal's conclusion on a fundamental matter in reality covered all the areas in dispute (see *CIB 16572/1996*). The Chief Commissioner considered that where a claimant had previously been in receipt of incapacity benefit it would be appropriate to give reasons for departing from the earlier decision to award benefit (see *Kitchen and others v. Secretary of State for Social Services* [1993] N.L.J.R. 1370).

Inquisitorial approach and medical evidence

Several Commissioners' decisions have confirmed that in applying the all work test tribunals should adopt an inquisitorial approach. See, for example, *CIB 14442/1996* in which the Commissioner states that tribunals should not "regard the scope of their inquiries as circumscribed by the boxes claimants may or may not have ticked [on the incapacity for work questionnaire (IB50)] . . .". In *CIB 14908/1996* the SSAT is held to have erred in refusing to consider the mental health descriptors when the claimant's mental health problems were put in issue at the hearing; the fact that the Benefits Agency's doctors (two in that case) had not applied the mental health descriptors did not excuse the tribunal from doing so. But note *CIB 14202/1996* in which the Commissioner states that a SSAT should be hesitant about going into the question of possible mental disabilities unless they had been raised beforehand and there was some medical or similar evidence on the point (this is followed in *C53/98(1B)*, a decision of a Northern Ireland Commissioner). A tribunal faced with this situation may therefore wish to consider whether to adjourn in order for a Benefits Agency's doctor to carry out a full assessment (although this may not be necessary if other medical evidence is available at the hearing).

The Commissioners have also generally agreed that *all* medical (and other) evidence should be carefully evaluated, without any in-built preference being given to the Benefits Agency's doctor's report (although this approach is not universal: see *CIB 17257/1996*. By way of analogy, see *CSDLA 856/1997* which deals with the prevalence or otherwise of an EMP's report, and contrast *CDLA 8462/1995*, which was decided by the same Commissioner as *CIB 17257/1996*.) See *CIB 14722/1996* in which a Tribunal of Commissioners states that a SSAT "should not adopt the findings of the Benefits Agency Medical Service medical officer unless they are satisfied, after considering all the medical evidence, that his findings are an accurate reflection of that evidence". In accordance with general principles, a tribunal will err if it fails to explain why it prefers, *e.g.* the Benefits Agency's doctor's assessment to the claimant's own evidence or that of his doctor (see, for example *CSIB 597/1997* and *CSIB 848/1997*) or fails to make its own findings of fact after having weighed up all the evidence (see, for example *CIB 4981/1997* and *CIB 407/1998*).

In *CIB 14442/1996* the tribunal had given little weight to the G.P.'s evidence because of the leading nature of the questions asked by the claimant's representative. The Commissioner, however, did not consider that the fact that the G.P. had been asked to give yes/no answers to specific descriptors was by itself a sufficient reason for rejecting the evidence; in his view if the G.P. had thought the questions he was being asked gave an exaggerated description of the claimant's disability he could have easily said so. See also *CIB 13038/1996* in which the Commissioner holds that the tribunal were wrong to have rejected the claimant's G.P.'s evidence simply on the ground that she had only known the claimant for six months and depended heavily on what the claimant had told her. On the other hand in *CIB 14908/1996*, where a Benefits Agency's doctor had written a report without examining or even seeing the claimant, the Commissioner comments that "because such evidence can have so little weight, perhaps none at all, the practice of asking for reports on claimants from doctors who see nothing but the papers has, normally, nothing to commend it."

In *CS 2776/1997* the Commissioner suggests that when considering the all work test a tribunal will need to have regard to not only the medical evidence that weighed with the AO but the whole history of the case and any other relevant evidence. On a second (or subsequent) application of the all work test it is not generally the practice for previous IB50s and BAMS reports to be included in the papers. But a SSAT is of course entitled to ask to see these.

Note also *CIB 15325/1996* (followed in *CIB 17533/1996*) which holds that a Med 4 is not a prerequisite before the AO can make a decision as to whether the claimant satisfies the all work test (even if the claimant has been asked to obtain such a form).

CIB 16604/1996 deals with the not uncommon situation of a claimant suggesting that the tribunal can check his medical records, or write to his G.P., etc. The Commissioner set aside the tribunal's decision on the ground that there had been a breach of natural justice. The claimant should have been told that he should obtain his own evidence as the tribunal was unlikely to do so. The Commissioner suggests that a sentence to this effect could be included in the standard information sent to claimants about appeal hearings.

It should also be borne in mind that a claimant's own evidence does not necessarily need to be corroborated (*R(SB) 33/85*).

Role of the medical assessor

This is explored in *CSIB 101/1996* and *CSIB 72/1996*. The Commissioner confirms that case law on the role of assessors (see *R(I) 14/51* and *R v. Deputy Industrial Injuries Commissioner ex parte Jones* [1962] 2 All E.R. 430) applied to medical assessors. Thus the role of a medical assessor was not to supply evidence but to help the tribunal understand the evidence. By asking the medical assessor for a direct opinion on a crucial issue (was the claimant on his evidence losing control of his bowels once a week?) and relying on the answer as the basis for its decision, the tribunal had erred in law. If in the exceptional case it was necessary to ask the assessor for a direct opinion on an issue, a tribunal should not accept that opinion unless satisfied it was sound (*R(I) 14/51*). In *CSIB 72/1996* the medical assessor had also exceeded his function by giving a practical demonstration of how to put on and take off a jacket with one immobilised wrist, since clearly this was evidence rather than information or advice.

However, in *CIB 17257/1996* the Commissioner saw nothing wrong with the medical assessor's advice to a tribunal that from a medical point of view there were no further grounds for bringing the claimant within the scope of the descriptors. The tribunal relied on this advice in its decision. Much could depend on the context, but the use of a medical assessor in this way runs the risk of the assessor deciding (or appearing to decide) which descriptors apply (which is clearly for the tribunal only), rather than confining himself to giving advice on the medical questions involved in the case. It is suggested that the approach of *CSIB 101/1996* and *CSIB 72/1996* is to be preferred.

See also *CIB 17533/1996* in which the Commissioner comments on the suggestion in *R(I) 14/51* that it would usually be desirable for the Chairman to briefly summarise the effect of any advice given by the medical assesor at the end of the hearing and to allow the parties an opportunity to comment on it if they wished to do so. Although this might be good practice in certain cases, there was no legal requirement for this to be done.

On the role of the medical assessor in general, see further the notes to s.61A(4) of the Administration Act.

Note that under the new system for decision-making and appeals which is due to start for income support on November 29, 1999 (and for incapacity benefit on September 6, 1999), appeals about incapacity for work will be heard by a two-person tribunal consisting of a chairman and a doctor; there will no longer be a medical assessor sitting with the tribunal in all work test cases.

Specific activities/descriptors
Various decisions have considered the meaning of individual descriptors.

Activity 2 (stairs). The Commissioner in *CIB 13161/1996* and *CIB 13508/1996* states that the stairs are to be "of normal size, breadth and grip, not some imaginary set of steep awkward metal stairs in somewhere like a ship's engine room". *CIB 5065/1997* emphasis that all the descriptors in activity 2 relate to walking up *and* down stairs, *i.e.* in both directions consecutively. Equally a restriction in walking ability only when going *down* stairs but not up is sufficient (*CIB 15804/1996*). Safety is a relevant factor in assessing whether a claimant needs to hold on while on stairs (*CIB 17088/1996*).

Activity 3 (sitting). The chair to be considered is "an upright chair with a back, but no arms". Thus if the evidence related to sitting in other types of chair, an appropriate deduction might have to be made from the length of time the claimant was able to remain sitting before becoming so uncomfortable that she had to move from the chair (*CSIB 12/1996*). *CSIB 38/1996* decides that activity 3 only applies where the sitting itself causes the discomfort which requires the person to move from the chair. Thus if the claimant had to move from the chair after 30 minutes simply because of his need to visit the toilet, activity 3 was not relevant. But if sitting aggravated the claimant's bladder condition, then activity 3 would need to be considered. The amendment to descriptors 3(b) to (e), in effect from January 6, 1997, confirms the approach of *CSIB 38/1996* to these descriptors.

Activity 4 (standing). *CIB 1244/1997* decides that the words "the use of an aid" meant that the only aids that had to be disregarded were those that were "used", as opposed to "worn", and which were used to support the whole of the body rather than a particular limb or part of the body. Thus the claimant's ability to stand had to be assessed taking account of the benefit he derived from his corset. But if he was unable to wear it all day, or he had been advised not to, this would have to be taken into account when making an overall assessment of the claimant's ability to stand. Note that from January 6, 1997 the amendment to reg. 25(2) of the Incapacity for Work Regulations produces the same result as the Commissioner's interpretation in this case.

Activity 6 (bending and kneeling). In *CSIB 12/1996* the Commissioner considered that if a person could only straighten up by holding onto something, or with assistance, the relevant descriptor would be satisfied. Note that the effect of the amendment to descriptors 6(b) and (c) from January 6, 1997 is that these descriptors will not be satisfied if the claimant can perform the activity by a combination of bending and kneeling.

Activity 7 (manual dexterity). The Commissioners have confirmed that descriptor 7(d) (cannot use a pen or pencil) refers to using a pen or pencil for the purposes for which they are normally used. Thus if the claimant was unable to use a pen or pencil to write in a normal manner (*CIB 13161/1996* and *CIB 13508/1996*), or to write reasonably clearly and at a reasonable speed (*R(IB) 1/98* and *CSIB 17/1996*) descriptor 7(d) would apply. Merely being able to tick a box on a form and sign it was not sufficient (*R(IB 1/98*). *R(IB)1/98* also holds that the words "with either hand'' were to be implied. Thus, for example, an ambidextrous person would not satisfy descriptor 7(d) if he had sufficient use of one hand.

On descriptors 7(c) and (g) (cannot pick up a coin which is 2.5 centimetres or less in diameter), see *CDWA 3213/1997*. This concerned the similar test in para. 6 of Sched. 1 to the Disability Working Allowance Regulations. The claimant in *CDWA 3213/1997* had no thumb on his left hand and the terminal joint of his right thumb was missing. He maintained that he was only able to pick up a coin of the prescribed size by shoving it across a surface and catching it in his hand. The Commissioner holds that the tests in Sched. 1 were to be performed in the normal way and not by employing some unusual or awkward manoeuvre. The normal way of picking up coins with one hand was to use the pinch grip between the thumb and fingers. An ability to pick up with the fingers alone was irrelevant because that ability did not demonstrate the presence or absence of the pinch grip.

Activity 8 (lifting and carrying). The governing words of this activity were amended to read ''Lifting and carrying by the use of the upper body and arms (excluding all other activities specified in Part 1 of this Schedule)'' with effect from January 6, 1997. *CIS 5744/1997* holds that this did not mean that the word ''carry'' should be deprived of all effect. The tribunal should have disregarded difficulties resulting from walking but not those occurring while walking (*e.g.* the claimant's ability to maintain sufficient grip to hold the object for a time). In relation to descriptor 8(c), *CSIB 17/1996* confirms that it is a normal kettle and not a specially adapted one that has to be considered.

Activity 11 (hearing). *CIB 590/1998* decides that if a claimant cannot understand a person speaking in a normal voice on a busy street without frequent repetition, descriptor 11(e) will apply. Like the other descriptors, descriptor 11(e) had to be applied in the light of what was reasonable.

Activity 13 (continence). In *CIB 14332/1996* the Commissioner considers that a claimant may ''lose control of his bowels'' even though he does not actually mess himself. Similarly in *CSIB 101/1996* the Commissioner refers to the possibility that urgency may amount to loss of control. *CSIB 85/1996* confirms that there is a distinction between ''no voluntary control'' and ''loses control'': the former imports no voluntary control at all whereas the latter indicates that there is some control that has been lost.

In *CSIB 38/1996* the Commissioner holds that for there to be ''no voluntary control over bladder'' (descriptor 13(b)), there had to be some degree of urgency which the exercise of will could not postpone (otherwise perhaps than *de minimis*). But he then goes on to say that in deciding whether a claimant had no voluntary control, medication that the claimant took to help control his bladder had to be discounted, since control assisted by medication was not voluntary. This seems somewhat extraordinary, given that the normal practice is to take account of the effect of medication (and see reg. 18(1)(b) of the Incapacity for Work Regulations (disqualification for failure to attend for medical treatment) which indicates that the effect of medication is not to be excluded). It is therefore suggested that this decision should be viewed with caution. Of course, if the medication does not achieve the intended or expected result the relevant descriptor may well be applicable.

C2/98 (IB) (a decision of a Northern Ireland Commissioner and thus of persuasive authority) holds that a colostomy bag was a prosthesis since it was a replacement for the final part of the anus. The consequence was that a person with a *properly functioning* colostomy bag would not score any points under activity 13 as he would not have a problem with continence. The Commissioner disagrees with two other decisions, *C11/96 (IB)* (claimant fitted with an ileostomy bag had *no* voluntary control over her bowels) and *CIB 14210/1996* (no question of control could arise in respect of an organ (the claimant's bladder) that had been removed and therefore activity 13 was not applicable). The Commissioner in *C2/98(IB)* has granted leave to appeal to the Northern Ireland Court of Appeal but it is suggested that her reasoning seems more persuasive than the approach taken in the other decisions.

Activity 14 (Remaining conscious). Note the amendment to this activity in effect from January 6, 1997 which substituted the words ''without having epileptic or similar seizures during waking moments'' for the words ''other than for normal periods of sleep''. Thus decisions such as *CSIB 14/1996*, in which the Commissioner held that a distracted state due to pain might constitute ''altered consciousness'', and *CSIB 44/1997* in which he considered that involuntary or irresistible sleep might amount to ''lost consciousness'', will not be relevant after that date. It seems unlikely that such conditions would come within the description of ''similar seizures'', but it may depend on the particular circumstances. Note that *CIB 16122/1996* decides that ''similar seizures'' means those that are similar in *effect* to an epileptic seizure; it is not necessary for them to be similar in cause. The Commissioner also agrees with *CSIB 597/1997* that the only disabilities that are relevant under para. 14 in its post-January 6, 1997 form are those which are consequent upon epileptic or similar seizures.

In *C13/96 (IB)* and *C8/96 (IB)*, quoted with approval in *CIB 15231/1996*, the Northern Ireland Chief Commissioner states that "consciousness in this context means "awareness" and a person has an involuntary episode of altered consciousness when he has reached a state of mental confusion such that he is no longer properly aware of his surroundings or his condition". The claimants in all three cases suffered from vertigo; the Commissioners accepted that this could result in episodes of altered consciousness under activity 14 (at least as this was drafted up to January 6, 1997).

Note that "the day in respect to which it falls to be determined whether [the claimant] is incapable of work" in descriptors 14(d) to (f) is the day on which the AO makes his decision (*CIB 16372/1996*) or the date of any subsequent adjudication (*CSIB 597/1997*).

Part II: Mental disabilities. See *CIB 2008/1997* which discusses a number of the descriptors in activities 15, 17 and 18. On descriptor 16(b) (needs alcohol before midday), *C1/98 (IB)* (a decision of a Northern Ireland Commissioner) holds that the word "needs" imports an element of compulsion, obligation or necessity and agrees with *CIB 17254/1996* that the fact that a person desires something does not mean that he has a need for it.

Sub-para. (b)

Claimants who are treated as incapable of work are also eligible for income support. This includes those who are exempt from the all work test (see reg. 10 of the Incapacity for Work Regulations) and others who count as incapable of work in certain circumstances, *e.g.* a person in hospital (see regs. 11–15 of the Incapacity for Work Regulations). In limited circumstances a person will be treated as incapable of work even if he fails the all work test (see reg. 27 of the Incapacity for Work Regulations). On the interpretation of reg. 27(d) (major operation within three months) in its pre-January 6, 1997 form, following the decision in *R. v. Secretary of State for Social Security, ex parte Moule* (September 12, 1996, HC), see *CIS 1748/1997* (noted in the 1998 Supplement to this book).

Sub-para. (c)

This covers a person who is being treated as capable of work under reg. 18 of the Incapacity for Work Regulations (made under s.171E of the Contributions and Benefits Act). Reg. 18 provides that a person may be treated as capable of work for a period of up to six weeks if he has become incapable of work through his own misconduct (see *R(S) 2/53*), failed without good cause to have treatment (other than vaccination, inoculation or major surgery), or without good cause either behaved in a way that will retard his recovery or been absent from home without stating where he has gone.

Sub-para. (d)

A person who is entitled to statutory sick pay will be eligible for income support.

If para. 7 does not apply, an adjudicating authority should go on to consider para. 8 (*CIS 137/1992*). However, even if para. 8 applies, para. 7 should always be considered as this may be the only route to enable the claimant to qualify for a disability premium under para. 12(1)(b) of Sched. 2, or a £15 earnings disregard under para. 4 of Sched. 8.

Paragraph 8

This paragraph employs the same wording as para. 6 of the former Sched. 1. The text applies to a "person", although the heading is "Disabled workers". In *CSIS 89/1990* which concerned the pre-October 1991 form of para. 6 the Commissioner convincingly shows that the heading is not relevant to the interpretation of the provision itself, being the equivalent of a marginal or side-note in a statute. Even if the heading were to be relevant, the words in para. 6 were plain, so that it applied to a person who was not a worker. The claimant in *CSIS 89/1990* had not been economically active for some years, but this did not prevent the application of para. 6.

The post-October 1991 form of para. 6, instead of setting out its conditions directly, referred on to reg. 6(a), as para. 8 now does. Reg. 6(a) was also amended from October 1991. Before October 1991 the test under reg. 6(a) was a disabled person's reduced earning *capacity*. The post-October 1991 form of reg. 6(a), by comparing the claimant's earnings or hours of work with those of a non-disabled person, seems to require that the claimant is actually working. But what if the claimant's hours of work are nil? Reg. 6(a) itself would not be needed in such circumstances, but if a person satisfies its conditions (*i.e.* he is not incapable of work but his earnings or hours of work are less (*i.e.* nil) because of his mental or physical disability) could he not come within para. 8? Para. 8 still refers to a "person", not a "worker" and thus does not actually require that a person is economically active.

Paragraph 9

See the notes to reg. 6(g).

Paragraphs 10–12

These paragraphs cover students (defined in reg. 61) who contrary to the normal rule can claim income support (see reg. 4ZA(2) and (3)). Para. 10 applies to a student who qualifies for the disability or severe disability premium (sub-para. (a)) or who has been incapable of work for at least 28 weeks (sub-para. (b)). Two or more periods of incapacity count as one continuous period unless there is a break of more than eight weeks. For the purposes of para. 10 note the transitional provision in reg. 27(2) of the Income Support (General) (Jobseeker's Allowance Consequential Amendments) Regulations 1996 (p. 499).

Para. 11 continues to protect disabled students who no longer fell under para. 7 of the former Sched. 1 following its amendment on September 1, 1990. See *CIS 276/1989* on the pre-September 1990 form of para. 7, which held that in asking whether the student was unlikely to obtain employment within a reasonable period of time, the period started with the date of claim, not with the end of the course.

Para. 12 applies to students who are within the definition of "deaf" for one of the various grant purposes.

Paragraph 13

Only those registered as blind with the local authority can use this paragraph and the 28 weeks' period of grace on regaining sight. But other categories may be available for the unregistered.

Paragraph 15

Since October 7, 1996 the lower age limit for income support is now 16 in all cases (SSCBA s.124(1)(a)). However, the exclusion for 16–18 year olds who are receiving relevant education remains, except for those who fall within reg. 13(2). This paragraph enables young people covered by reg. 13(2)(a)–(e) to claim income support; a young person to whom reg. 13(2)(h) applies will be eligible under para. 18. See the notes to reg. 13 for the circumstances in which reg. 13(2) applies.

Paragraph 16

Para. 13 of the former Sched. 1 covered people aged not less than 50 who had not been in remunerative work for 10 years, had been exempt from the reqirement to be available during that time (or who would have been exempt had a claim for income support been made, see *CIS 613/1995* below), and had no prospect of future employment. The provision is not repeated in Sched. 1B, but under para. 16 a person who was in receipt of income support and satisfied the former para. 13 on October 6, 1996, or at any time in the previous eight weeks, will be entitled to income support (note the linking rule in sub-para. (2)). Thus a person who only falls into this category after October 6, 1996 will not qualify for income support on that ground.

Para. 13 applied if the person had been exempt from the requirement to be available for 10 years or would have been so exempt "had a claim for income support been made by or in respect of him". In *CIS 613/1995* the Commissioner decides that "in respect of him" referred to where a claim could have been made by the claimant's husband in respect of her. In that case he would have had to satisfy the conditions of entitlement. As his partner she would not have been required to be available for work. Accordingly the claimant satisfied para. 13.

In *R(SB) 5/87* it was suggested that to have no prospect of future employment, a person has to have no realistic prospects of securing employment in his working life. It is not necessary to show that the person's prospects are nil, but the test is still strict and merely poor prospects will not do.

Paragraph 22

A person required to live in a bail hostel is not "detained in custody" (*R(IS) 17/93*; note the effect of Sched. 7, para. 9, if a person in a bail hostel is a member of a couple). However, once a person has been charged, he is detained in custody pending trial, even if subsequently no trial takes place (*R(IS) 1/94*). See the notes to "prisoner" in reg. 21(3). The definition of prisoner was amended from April 10, 1995 to reverse the effect of *Chief Adjudication Officer v. Carr* (to be reported as

R(IS) 26/95) which held that a person serving a prison sentence was not "in custody" while on home leave.

Paragraph 23

Someone in this situation could not come within para. 1 because they would not be a lone parent while the absence of the partner was only temporary, but clearly deserves the same treatment in these circumstances.

Paragraphs 24–27

There was no equivalent of these paragraphs in the former Sched. 1.

Paras. 24 and 25 replace the provisions formerly in reg. 8(2) and (2A) (revoked on October 7, 1996) and cover those who are appealing against a decision that they are capable of work under the "own occupation test" (para. 24) or the "all work test" (para. 25). See the note to para. 7 for a summary of these tests and when they apply.

Under para. 24, if the claimant's own doctor continues to certify that he is incapable of work while he is pursuing an appeal against the incapacity decision, he will be eligible for income support pending the determination of the appeal. This should mean the final determination of the appeal, *e.g.* if it is taken to the Social Security Commissioner. The person does not have to have been in receipt of income support before the incapacity decision was made. If para. 24 applies full income support is payable (compare para. 25).

If the claimant is appealing against capacity for work on the basis of the all work test, there is no requirement under para. 25 for him to continue to submit medical certificates from his own doctor. This is because they are no longer required once the all work test has been applied. Again it is not necessary for the person to have been in receipt of income support before the incapacity decision was made. But if para. 25 applies, the claimant's income support is reduced by 20 per cent of the appropriate personal allowance for a single claimant of his age until the appeal is determined (reg. 22A), unless he is appealing after failing his first all work test and immediately before April 13, 1995 he had been incapable of work for 28 weeks or in receipt of invalidity benefit or severe disablement allowance (reg. 22A(3); and see the transitional protection in reg. 27(3) of the Income Support (General) (Jobseeker's Allowance Consequential Amendments) Regulations 1996 referred to in the note to reg. 22A(3)). (If the appeal is successful, the reduction will repaid.) See above for when an appeal is determined.

In order to receive full benefit, a claimant who is appealing against a failure to satisfy the all work test will have to sign on as available for work and claim JSA (unless any of the other paragraphs of Sched. 1B apply). This could place the claimant in a dilemma if he is maintaining that he is unable to work. The best course may be for him to say to the Employment Service that he has been found capable of work and that he will accept any suitable work having regard to his limitations (see reg. 13(3) of the JSA Regulations). The *Adjudication Officer's Guide* accepts that the fact that a person has been available for employment should not prejudice the appeal about incapacity (para. 18339).

Reg. 8(2) had been amended and reg. 8(2A) had been introduced on April 13, 1995 as a consequence of the introduction of the new tests for incapacity for work. There was transitional protection for claimants who were pursuing an incapacity appeal and to whom the previous form of reg. 8(2) applied on April 12, 1995 and for those who appealed against an AO's decision on incapacity made on or before April 12, 1995. In those cases the old form of reg. 8 continued to apply (reg. 20(1) and (3) of the Disability Working Allowance and Income Support (General) Amendment Regulations 1995 (see p. 495)). Para. 26 covers such a person to whom the pre-April 13, 1995 form of reg. 8(2) still applied on October 6, 1996. He will be eligible for income support (without reduction) pending the determination of his incapacity appeal. See above for when an appeal is determined.

Para. 27 provides the same result for a person to whom the pre-April 13, 1995 form of reg. 11(2) still applied on October 6, 1996. See the 1996 edition of this book for reg. 11 which was revoked on October 7, 1996.

Paragraph 28

Para. 11 of the former Sched. 1 applied to a person in receipt of a training allowance. Para. 28 only covers a person under 24 who is undergoing Work Based Training for Young People (which has replaced Youth Training and other training provision focussed on 16/17 year olds). However, under reg. 170 of the JSA Regulations a person in receipt of a training allowance (in respect of training *other* than that covered by para. 28) may qualify for income-based JSA without having to be available for, or actively seek, employment or enter into a jobseeker's agreement.

SCHEDULE 2   **Regulations 17 [³(1)] and 18**

APPLICABLE AMOUNTS

[³⁵PART I

Personal Allowances

1. The weekly amounts specified in column (2) below in respect of each person or couple specified in column (1) shall be the weekly amounts specified for the purposes of regulations 17(1) and 18(1) (applicable amounts and polygamous marriages).

Column (1)	Column (2)
Person or Couple	*Amount*
(1) Single claimant aged—	
(a) except where head (b) or (c) of this sub-paragraph applies, less than 18;	(1)(a) £30.95;
[²⁸(b) less than 18 who falls within any of the circumstances specified in paragraph 1A;]	(b) £40.70;
(c) less than 18 who satisfies the condition in paragraph 11(a);	(c) £40.70;
(d) not less than 18 but less than 25;	(d) £40.70;
(e) not less than 25.	(e) £51.40.
(2) Lone parent aged—	(2)
(a) except where head (b) or (c) of this sub-paragraph applies, less than 18;	(a) £30.95;
[²⁸(b) less than 18 who falls within any of the circumstances specified in paragraph 1A;]	(b) £40.70;
(c) less than 18 who satisfies the condition in paragraph 11(a);	(c) £40.70;
(d) not less than 18.	(d) £51.40.
[²⁸(3) Couple—	(3)
(a) where both members are aged less than 18 and—	(a) £61.35;
(i) at least one of them is treated as responsible for a child; or	
(ii) had they not been members of a couple, each would have qualified for income support under regulation 4ZA; or	
(iii) the claimant's partner satisfies the requirements of section 3(1)(f)(iii) of the Jobseekers Act 1995 (prescribed circumstances for persons aged 16 but less than 18); or	
(iv) there is in force in respect of the claimant's partner a direction under section 16 of the Jobseekers Act 1995 (persons under 18: severe hardship);	
(b) where both members are aged less than 18 and head (a) does not apply but one member of the couple falls within any of the circumstances specified in paragraph 1A;	(b) £40.70;
(c) where both members are aged less than 18 and heads (a) and (b) do not apply;	(c) £30.95;
(d) where both members are aged not less than 18;	(d) £80.65;
(e) where one member is aged not less than 18 and the other member is a person under 18 who—	(e) £80.65;
(i) qualifies for income support under regulation 4ZA, or who would so qualify if he were not a member of a couple; or	
(ii) satisfies the requirements of section 3(1)(f)(iii) of the Jobseekers Act 1995 (prescribed circumstances for persons aged 16 but less than 18); or	

Column (1)	Column (2)
Person or Couple	*Amount*
(iii) is the subject of a direction under section 16 of the Job-seekers Act 1995 (persons under 18: severe hardship);	
(f) where the claimant is aged not less than 18 but less than 25 and his partner is a person under 18 who—	(f) £40.70;
(i) would not qualify for income support under regulation 4ZA if he were not a member of a couple; and	
(ii) does not satisfy the requirements of section 3(1)(f)(iii) of the Jobseekers Act 1995 (prescribed circumstances for persons aged 16 but less than 18); and	
(iii) is not the subject of a direction under section 16 of the Jobseekers Act 1995 (persons under 18: severe hardship);	
(g) where the claimant is aged not less than 25 and his partner is a person under 18 who—	(g) £51.40.
(i) would not qualify for income support under regulation 4ZA if he were not a member of a couple; and	
(ii) does not satisfy the requirements of section 3(1)(f)(iii) of the Jobseekers Act 1995 (prescribed circumstances for persons aged 16 but less than 18); and	
(iii) is not the subject of a direction under section 16 of the Jobseekers Act 1995 (persons under 18: severe hardship).]]	

[^{28}**1A.**—(1) The circumstances referred to in paragraph 1 are that—

(a) the person has no parents nor any person acting in the place of his parents;

(b) the person—

    (i) is not living with his parents nor any person acting in the place of his parents; and

    (ii) in England and Wales, was being looked after by a local authority pursuant to a relevant enactment who placed him with some person other than a close relative of his; or in Scotland, was in the care of a local authority under a relevant enactment and whilst in that care was not living with his parents or any close relative, or was in custody in any institution to which the Prison Act 1952 or the Prisons (Scotland) Act 1989 applied immediately before he attained the age of 16;

(c) the person is in accommodation which is other than his parental home, and which is other than the home of a person acting in the place of his parents, who entered that accommodation—

    (i) as part of a programme of rehabilitation or resettlement, that programme being under the supervision of the probation service or a local authority; or

    (ii) in order to avoid physical or sexual abuse; or

    (iii) because of a mental or physical handicap or illness and needs such accommodation because of his handicap or illness;

(d) the person is living away from his parents and any person who is acting in the place of his parents in a case where his parents are or, as the case may be, that person is, unable financially to support him and his parents are, or that person is—

    (i) chronically sick or mentally or physically disabled; or

    (ii) detained in custody pending trial or sentence upon conviction or under sentence imposed by a court; of

    (iii) prohibited from entering or re-entering Great Britain; or

(e) the person of necessity has to live away from his parents and any person acting in the place of his parents because—

    (i) he is estranged from his parents and that person; or
    (ii) he is in physical or moral danger; or
    (iii) there is a serious risk to his physical or mental health.
(2) In this paragraph—
(a) "chronically sick or mentally or physically disabled" has the same meaning it has in regulation 13(3)(b) (circumstances in which persons in relevant education are to be entitled to income support);
(b) in England and Wales, any reference to a person acting in place of a person's parents includes a reference to—
    (i) where the person is being looked after by a local authority or voluntary organisation who place him with a family, a relative of his, or some other suitable person, the person with whom the person is placed, whether or not any payment is made to him in connection with the placement; or
    (ii) in any other case, any person with parental responsibility for the child, and for this purpose "parental responsibility" has the meaning it has in the Children Act 1989 by virtue of section 3 of that Act;
(c) in Scotland, any reference to a person acting in place of a person's parents includes a reference to a local authority or voluntary organisation where the person is in their care under a relevant enactment, or to a person with whom the person is boarded out by a local authority or voluntary organisation whether or not any payment is made by them.]

[³⁵**2.**[³⁰—(1)] The weekly amounts specified in column (2) below in respect of each person specified in column (1) shall [³⁰, for the relevant period specified in column (1),] be the weekly amounts specified for the purposes of regulations 17(1)(b) and 18(1)(c).

Column (1)	Column (2)
Child or Young Person	*Amount*
[³⁰Person in respect of the period— (a) beginning on that person's date of birth and ending on the day preceding the first Monday in September following that person's eleventh birthday;	(a) £20.20;
(b) beginning on the first Monday in September following that person's eleventh birthday and ending on the day preceding the first Monday in September following that person's sixteenth birthday;	(b) £25.90;
(c) beginning on the first Monday in September following the person's sixteenth birthday and ending on the day preceding that person's nineteenth birthday.]	(c) £30.95.

[³⁰(2) In column (1) of the table in paragraph (1), "the first Monday in September" means the Monday which first occurs in the month of September in any year.]

[¹⁷**2A.**—(1) The weekly amount for the purposes of regulation 17(1)(bb) and 18(1)(cc) (residential allowance) in respect of a person who satisfies the conditions specified in sub-paragraph (2) shall be—
(a) except in a case to which head (b) applies, £59.40; and
(b) where the home in which the person resides is situated within the area described in Schedule 3C (the Greater London area), £66.10.]
(2) Subject to sub-paragraphs [²⁰(3), (4) and (4A)], the conditions are—
(a) the person resides in a residential care home or a nursing home [²⁰or is regarded pursuant to sub-paragraph (4A) as residing in such a home];
[¹⁸(aa) the person both requires personal care [³¹ by reason of old age, disablement, past or present dependence on alcohol or drugs, past or present mental disorder or a terminal illness and the care is provided in the home];]
(b) he does not have a preserved right;

319

(c) he is aged 16 or over;

(d) both the person's accommodation and such meals (if any) as are provided for him are provided on a commercial basis; and

(e) no part of the weekly charge for accommodation is met by housing benefit.

(3) For the purposes of sub-paragraph (2), but subject to sub-paragraph (4), a person resides in a residential care home where the home in which he resides—

(a) is registered under Part I of the Registered Homes Act 1984 or is deemed to be so registered by virtue of section 2(3) of the Registered Homes (Amendment) Act 1991 (registration of small homes where application for registration not determined);

(b) is managed or provided by a body incorporated by Royal Charter or constituted by Act of Parliament (other than a social services authority) and provides both board and personal care for the claimant; or

(c) is in Scotland and is registered under section 61 of the Social Work (Scotland) Act 1968 or is an establishment provided by a housing association registered with Scottish Homes established by the Housing (Scotland) Act 1988 which provides care equivalent to that given in residential accommodation provided under Part IV of the Social Work (Scotland) Act 1968;

and a person resides in a nursing home where the home in which he resides is such a home for the purposes of regulation 19.

(4) A person shall not be regarded as residing in a nursing home for the purposes of sub-paragraph (2) where the home in which he resides is a hospice, and for this purpose "hospice" means a nursing home which—

(a) if situate in England and Wales, is registered under Part II of the Registered Homes Act 1984, or

(b) if situate in Scotland, is exempted from the operation of the Nursing Homes Registration (Scotland) Act 1938 by virtue of section 6 of that Act,

[²¹and whose primary function is to provide palliative care for persons resident there who are suffering from a progressive disease in its final stages].

[²⁰(4A) For the purposes of sub-paragraph (2)(a), where a person's principal place of residence is a residential care home or nursing home, and he is temporarily absent from that home, he shall be regarded as continuing to reside in that home—

(a) where he is absent because he is a patient, for the first six weeks of any such period of absence, and for this purpose—

(i) "patient" has the meaning it has in Schedule 7 by virtue of regulation 21(3), and

(ii) periods of absence separated by not more than 28 days shall be treated as a single period of absence equal in duration to all those periods; and

(b) for the first three weeks of any other period of absence.]

(5) Where—

(a) a person has been registered under the Registered Homes Act 1984 in respect of premises which have been carried on as a residential care home or, as the case may be, a nursing home, and that person has ceased to carry on such a home; and

(b) an application for registration under that Act has been made by another person and that application has not been determined or abandoned,

then any question arising for determination under this paragraph shall be determined as if the most recent registration in respect of those premises continued until the day on which the application is determined or abandoned.]

PART II

**Regulations 17[³(1)](*c*)
[³and 18(1)](*d*)**

Family Premium

3. [³²—(1)] The weekly amount for the purposes of regulations 17[³(1)](c) [³and

18(1)](*d*) in respect of a family of which at least one member is a child or young person shall be [²⁹—

(a) where the claimant is a lone parent [³² to whom the conditions in both sub-paragraphs (2) and (3) apply] and no premium is applicable under paragraph 9, 9A, 10 or 11, £15.75;

(b) in any other case,] [³⁶£13.90].

[³² (2) The first condition for the purposes of sub-paragraph (1)(a) is that the claimant—

(a) was both a lone parent and entitled to income support on 5th April 1998; or

(b) does not come within head (a) above but—

    (i) was both a lone parent and entitled to income support on any day during the period of 12 weeks ending on 5th April 1998;

    (ii) was both a lone parent and entitled to income support on any day during the period of 12 weeks commencing on 6th April 1998; and

    (iii) the last day in respect of which (i) above applied was no more than 12 weeks before the first day in respect of which (ii) above applied.

(3) The second condition for the purposes of sub-paragraph (1)(a) is that as from the appropriate date specified in sub-paragraph (4), the claimant has continued, subject to sub-paragraph (5), to be both a lone parent and entitled to income support.

(4) The appropriate date for the purposes of sub-paragraph (3) is—

(a) in a case to which sub-paragraph (2)(a) applies, 6th April 1988;

(b) in a case to which sub-paragraph (2)(b) applies, the first day in respect of which sub-paragraph (2)(b)(ii) applied.

(5) For the purposes of sub-paragraph (3), where the claimant has ceased, for any period of 12 weeks or less, to be—

(a) a lone parent; or

(b) entitled to income support; or

(c) both a lone parent and entitled to income support,

the claimant shall be treated, on again becoming both a lone parent and entitled to income support, as having continued to be both a lone parent and entitled to income support throughout that period.

(6) In determining whether the conditions in sub-paragraphs (2) and (3) apply, entitlement to an income-based jobseeker's allowance shall be treated as entitlement to income support for the purposes of any requirement that a person is entitled to income support.]

PART III   **Regulations 17[³(1)](*d*)**
                                           [³and 18(1)](*e*)

Premiums

4. Except as provided in paragraph 5, the weekly premiums specified in Part IV of this Schedule shall, for the purposes of regulations 17[³(1)](d)[³ and 18(1)](*e*), be applicable to a claimant who satisfies the condition specified in [²⁹paragraphs 9] [¹⁰ to 14ZA] in respect of that premium.

5. Subject to paragraph 6, where a claimant satisfies the conditions in respect of more than one premium in this Part of this Schedule, only one premium shall be applicable to him and, if they are different amounts, the higher or highest amount shall apply.

6.—(1) The severe disability premium to which paragraph 13 applies may be applicable in addition to [⁷any other premium which may apply under this Schedule.]

(2) [¹⁰The disabled child premium and carer premium to which paragraphs 14 and 14ZA respectively apply] may be applicable in addition to any other premium which may apply under this Schedule.

7.—[¹⁰(1) Subject to sub-paragraph (2)] for the purposes of this Part of this Schedule, once a premium is applicable to a claimant under this Part, a person shall be treated as being in receipt of any benefit—

   (a) in the case of a benefit to which the Social Security (Overlapping Benefits) Regulations 1979 applies, for any period during which, apart from the provisions of those Regulations, he would be in receipt of that benefit; and

   (b) for any period spent by a claimant in undertaking a course of training or instruction provided or approved by the [[12]Secretary of State for Employment] under section 2 of the Employment and Training Act 1973 [[11], or by Scottish Enterprise or Highlands and Islands Enterprise under section 2 of the Enterprise and New Towns (Scotland) Act 1990,] [[7]or for any period during which he is in receipt of a training allowance].

[[10](2) For the purposes of the carer premium under paragraph 14ZA, a person shall be treated as being in receipt of invalid care allowance by virtue of sub-paragraph (1)(a) only if and for so long as the person in respect of whose care the allowance has been claimed remains in receipt of attendance allowance[[15], or the care component of disability living allowance at the highest or middle rate prescribed in accordance with section 37ZB(3) of the Social Security Act [SSCBA, s.72(3)]].]

Lone Parent Premium

   8. [[29]. . .].

[Pensioner premium for persons under 75

   9. The condition is that the claimant—

   (a) is a single claimant or lone parent aged not less than 60 but less than 75; or

   (b) has a partner and is, or his partner is, aged not less than 60 but less than 75.

Pensioner premium for persons 75 and over

   9A. The condition is that the claimant—

   (a) is a single claimant or lone parent aged not less than 75 but less than 80; or

   (b) has a partner and is, or his partner is, aged not less than 75 but less than 80.]

Higher Pensioner Premium

   10.—(1) Where the claimant is a single claimant or a lone parent, the condition is that—

   (a) he is aged not less than 80; or

   (b) he is aged less than 80 but not less than 60, and

      (i) the additional condition specified in paragraph 12(1)(a) [[1]or (c)] is satisfied; or

      (ii) he was entitled to income support and the disability premium was applicable to him in respect of a benefit week within eight weeks of his 60th birthday and he has, subject to sub-paragraph (3), remained continuously entitled to income support since attaining that age.

   (2) Where the claimant has a partner, the condition is that—

   (a) he or his partner is aged not less than 80; or

   (b) he or his partner is aged less than 80 but not less than 60 and either—

      (i) the additional condition specified in paragraph 12(1)(a) [[1]or (c)] is satisfied [[16]. . .]; or

(ii) he was entitled to income support and the disability premium was applicable to him in respect of a benefit week within eight weeks of his 60th birthday and he has, subject to sub-paragraph (3), remained continuously entitled to income support since attaining that age.

(3) For the purposes of this paragraph and paragraph 12—

(a) once the higher pensioner premium is applicable to a claimant, if he then ceases, for a period of eight weeks or less, to be entitled to income support, he shall, on becoming re-entitled to income support, thereafter be treated as having been continuously entitled thereto;

(b) in so far as sub-paragraphs (1)(b)(ii) and (2)(b)(ii) are concerned, if a claimant ceases to be entitled to income support for a period not exceeding eight weeks which includes his 60th birthday, he shall, on becoming re-entitled to income support, thereafter be treated as having been continuously entitled thereto.

[³³ (4) In the case of a claimant who is a welfare to work beneficiary, references in sub-paragraphs (1)(b)(ii), (2)(b)(ii) and (3)(b) to a period of 8 weeks shall be treated as references to a period of 52 weeks.]

Disability Premium

11. The condition is that—

(a) where the claimant is a single claimant or a lone parent, he is aged less than 60 and the additional condition specified in paragraph 12 is satisfied; or

(b) where the claimant has a partner, either—

(i) the claimant is aged less than 60 and the additional condition specified in paragraph [¹12(1)(a), (b) or (c)] is satisfied by him; or

(ii) his partner is aged less than 60 and the additional condition specified in paragraph 12(1)(a) [¹or (c)] is satisfied by his partner.

Additional condition for the Higher Pensioner and Disability Premiums

12.—(1) Subject to sub-paragraph (2) and paragraph 7 the additional condition referred to in paragraphs 10 and 11 is that either—

(a) the claimant or, as the case may be, his partner—

(i) is in receipt of one or more of the following benefits: attendance allowance, [¹⁵disability living allowance, disability working allowance], mobility supplement, [²⁵long-term incapacity benefit] under [²²Part II of the Contributions and Benefits Act or severe disablement allowance under Part III of that Act] [¹but, in the case of [²⁵long-term incapacity benefit] or severe disablement allowance only where it is paid in respect of him]; or

(ii) is provided by the Secretary of State with an invalid carriage or other vehicle under section 5(2) of the National Health Service Act 1977 (other services) or, in Scotland, under section 46 of the National Health Service (Scotland) Act 1978 (provision of vehicles) or receives payments by way of grant from the Secretary of State under paragraph 2 of Schedule 2 to that 1977 Act (additional provisions as to vehicles) or, in Scotland, under that section 46; or

(iii) is registered as blind in a register compiled by a local authority under section 29 of the National Assistance Act 1948 (welfare services) or, in Scotland, has been certified as blind and in consequence he is registered as blind in a register maintained by or on behalf of a regional or islands council; or

[²⁶(b) the claimant—

(i) is entitled to statutory sick pay or [²⁷is, or is treated as, incapable of work,] in accordance with the provisions of Part XIIA of the Contributions and Benefits Act and the regulations made thereunder (incapacity for work), and

  (ii) has been so entitled or so incapable [^{27}, or has been treated as so incapable,] for a continuous period of not less than—

    (aa) 196 days in the case of a claimant who is terminally ill within the meaning of section 30B(4) of the Contributions and Benefits Act; or

    (bb) 364 days in any other case;

    and for these purposes any two or more periods of entitlement or incapacity separated by a break of not more than 56 days shall be treated as one continuous period; or]

 (*c*) the claimant or, as the case may be, his partner was in receipt of either—

  [^{15}(i) [^{25}long-term incapacity benefit] under [^{22}Part II of the Contributions and Benefits Act] when entitlement to that benefit ceased on account of the payment of a retirement pension under [^{22}that Act] and the claimant has since remained continuously entitled to income support and, if the [^{25}long-term incapacity benefit] was payable to his partner, the partner is still alive; or]

  (ii) except where paragraph 1(a), (b), (c)(ii) or (d)(ii) of Schedule 7 (patients) applies, attendance allowance [^{14}or disability living allowance but payment of benefit has been suspended in accordance with regulations made under [^{24}section 113(2) of the Contributions and Benefits Act 1992 or otherwise abated as a consequence of the claimant or his partner becoming a patient within the meaning of regulation 21(3) (special cases)],]

 and, in either case, the higher pensioner premium or disability premium has been applicable to the claimant or his partner.

[^{34} (1A) In the case of a claimant who is a welfare to work beneficiary, the reference in sub-paragraph (1)(b) to a period of 56 days shall be treated as a reference to a period of 52 weeks.]

(2) For the purposes of sub-paragraph (1)(a)(iii), a person who has ceased to be registered as blind on regaining his eyesight shall nevertheless be treated as blind and as satisfying the additional condition set out in that sub-paragraph for a period of 28 weeks following the date on which he ceased to be so registered.

(3) [^{26}. . .]

(4) For the purpose of sub-paragraph (1)(c), once the higher pensioner premium is applicable to the claimant by virtue of his satisfying the condition specified in that provision, if he then ceases, for a period of eight weeks or less, to be entitled to income support, he shall on again becoming so entitled to income support, immediately thereafter be treated as satisfying the condition in sub-paragraph (1)(c).

[^{4}(5) For the purposes of sub-paragraph (1)(b), once the disability premium is applicable to a claimant by virtue of his satisfying the additional condition specified in that provision, he shall continue to be treated as satisfying that condition for any period spent by him in undertaking a course of training provided under section 2 of the Employment and Training Act 1973 [^{7}or for any period during which he is in receipt of a training allowance].]

[^{25}(6) For the purposes of sub-paragraph (1)(a)(i) and (c)(i), a reference to a person in receipt of long-term incapacity benefit includes a person in receipt of short-term incapacity benefit at a rate equal to the long-term rate by virtue of section 30B(4)(a) of the Contributions and Benefits Act (short-term incapacity benefit for a person who is terminally ill), or who would be or would have been in receipt of short-term incapacity benefit at such a rate but for the fact that the rate of short-term incapacity benefit already payable to him is or was equal to or greater than the long-term rate.]

Severe Disability Premium

13.—(1) The condition is that the claimant is a severely disabled person.

(2) For the purposes of sub-paragraph (1), a claimant shall be treated as being a severely disabled person if, and only if—

(a) in the case of a single claimant[¹⁹, a lone parent or a claimant who is treated as having no partner in consequence of sub-paragraph (2A)]—

  (i) he is in receipt of attendance allowance [¹⁵or the care component of disability living allowance at the highest or middle rate prescribed in accordance with section 37ZB(3) of the Social Security Act [SSCBA, s.72(3)]], and

  (ii) subject to sub-paragraph (3), he has no non-dependants aged 18 or over [²³normally residing with him or with whom he is normally residing,] and

  (iii) [⁷ . . .] an invalid care allowance under section 37 of the Social Security Act [SSCBA, s.70] [⁷is not in payment to anyone] in respect of caring for him;

(b) if he has a partner—

  (i) he is in receipt of attendance allowance [¹⁵, or the care component of disability living allowance at the highest or middle rate prescribed in accordance with section 37ZB(3) of the Social Security Act [SSCBA, s.72(3)]]; and

  (ii) his partner is also in receipt of such an allowance or, if he is a member of a polygamous marriage, all the partners of that marriage are in receipt thereof; and

  (iii) subject to sub-paragraph (3), he has no non-dependants aged 18 or over [²³normally residing with him or with whom he is normally residing,]

  and either [⁷an invalid care allowance is in payment to someone] in respect of caring for only one of the couple or, in the case of a polygamous marriage, for one or more but not all the partners of the marriage, or, as the case may be, [⁷such an allowance is not in payment to anyone] in respect of caring for either member of the couple or any partner of the polygamous marriage.

[¹⁹(2A) Where a claimant has a partner who does not satisfy the condition in sub-paragraph (2)(b)(ii), and that partner is blind or is treated as blind within the meaning of paragraph 12(1)(a)(iii) and (2), that partner shall be treated for the purposes of sub-paragraph (2) as if he were not a partner of the claimant.]

(3) For the purposes of sub-paragraph (2)(a)(ii) and (2)(b)(iii) no account shall be taken of—

(a) a person receiving attendance allowance [¹⁵, or the care component of disability living allowance at the highest or middle rate prescribed in accordance with section 37ZB(3) of the Social Security Act [SSCBA, s.72(3)]]; or

(b) [²¹ . . .]

(c) subject to sub-paragraph (4), a person who joins the claimant's household for the first time in order to care for the claimant or his partner and immediately before so joining the claimant or his partner was treated as a severely disabled person; [¹⁹ or

(d) a person who is blind or is treated as blind within the meaning of paragraph 12(1)(a)(iii) and (2).]

[¹(3A)For the purposes of sub-paragraph (2)(b) a person shall be treated as being in receipt of—

(a) attendance allowance[¹⁵, or the care component of disability living allowance at the highest or middle rate prescribed in accordance with section 37ZB(3) of the Social Security Act [SSCBA, s.72(3)]] if he would, but for his being a patient for a period exceeding 28 days, be so in receipt;

(b) invalid care allowance if he would, but for the person for whom he was caring being a patient in hospital for a period exceeding 28 days, be so in receipt.]

[²²(3ZA) For the purposes of sub-paragraph (2)(a)(iii) and (2)(b), no account shall be taken of an award of invalid care allowance to the extent that payment of such an award is back-dated for a period before the date on which the award is made.]

(4) Sub-paragraph (3)(c) shall apply only for the first 12 weeks following the date on which the person to whom that provision applies first joins the claimant's household.

Disabled Child Premium

14. The condition is that a child or young person for whom the claimant or a partner of his is responsible and who is a member of the claimant's household—
  (a) has no capital or capital which, if calculated in accordance with Part V in like manner as for the claimant, [²¹except as provided in regulation 44(1) (modifications in respect of children and young persons)], would not exceed £3,000; and
  (b) is in receipt of [¹⁵disability living allowance] or is no longer in receipt of that allowance because he is a patient provided that the child or young person continues to be a member of the family; or
  (c) is blind or treated as blind within the meaning of paragraph 12(1)(a)(iii) and (2).

[¹⁰Carer premium

14ZA.—(1) [¹³Subject to sub-paragraphs (3) and (4),] the condition is that the claimant or his partner is, or both of them are, in receipt of invalid care allowance under section 37 of the Social Security Act [SSCBA, s.70].

(2) If a claimant or his partner, or both of them, would be in receipt of invalid care allowance but for the provisions of the Social Security (Overlapping Benefits) Regulations 1979, where—
  (a) the claim for that allowance was made on or after 1st October 1990, and
  (b) the person or persons in respect of whose care the allowance has been claimed remains or remain in receipt of attendance allowance[¹⁵, or the care component of disability living allowance at the highest or middle rate prescribed in accordance section 37ZB(3) of the Social Security Act [SSCBA, s.72(3)]]

he or his partner, or both of them, as the case may be, shall be treated for the purposes of sub-paragraph (1) as being in receipt of invalid care allowance.]

[¹⁴(3) Where a carer premium is awarded but the person in respect of whom it has been awarded either ceases to be in receipt of, or ceases to be treated as in receipt of, invalid care allowance, the condition for the award of the premium shall be treated as satisfied for a period of eight weeks from the date on which that person ceased to be in receipt of, or ceased to be treated as in receipt of, invalid care allowance.

(4) Where a person who has been receiving, or who has been treated as receiving invalid care allowance ceases to be in receipt of, or ceases to be treated as in receipt, of that allowance and makes a claim for income support, the condition for the award of the carer premium shall be treated as satisfied for a period of eight weeks from the date that the person was last in receipt of, or was last treated as being in receipt of, invalid care allowance.]

[³ Persons in receipt of concessionary payments

14A. For the purpose of determining whether a premium is applicable to a person [¹²under paragraphs 12 to 14ZA], any concessionary payment made to compensate that person for the non-payment of any benefit mentioned in those paragraphs shall be treated as if it were a payment of that benefit.]

[⁸Person in receipt of benefit

14B. For the purposes of this Part of this Schedule, a person shall be regarded as being in receipt of any benefit if, and only if, it is paid in respect of him and shall be so regarded only for any period in respect of which that benefit is paid.]

[³⁷PART IV

Weekly Amounts of Premiums Specified in Part III

Column (1)	Column (2)
Premium	*Amount*
15.—(1) [²⁹. . .]	(1) [²⁹. . .].
(2) Pensioner premium for persons aged under 75—	(2)
(a) where the claimant satisfies the condition in paragraph 9(a);	(a) £23.60;
(b) where the claimant satisfies the condition in paragraph 9(b).	(b) £35.95.
(2A) Pensioner premium for persons aged 75 and over—	(2A)
(a) where the claimant satisfies the condition in paragraph 9A(a);	(a) £25.90;
(b) where the claimant satisfies the condition in paragraph 9A(b).	(b) £39.20.
(3) Higher Pensioner Premium—	(3)
(a) where the claimant satisfies the condition in paragraph 10(1)(a) or (b);	(a) £30.85;
(b) where the claimant satisfies the condition in paragraph 10(2)(a) or (b).	(b) £44.65.
(4) Disability Premium—	(4)
(a) where the claimant satisfies the condition in paragraph 11(a);	(a) £21.90;
(b) where the claimant satisfies the condition in paragraph 11(b).	(b) £31.25.
(5) Severe Disability Premium—	(5)
(a) where the claimant satisfies the condition in paragraph 13(2)(a);	(a) £39.75;
(b) where the claimant satisfies the condition in paragraph 13(2)(b).	(b)
(i) if there is someone in receipt of an invalid care allowance or if he or any partner satisfies that condition only by virtue of paragraph 13(3A);	(i) £39.75;
(ii) if on-one is in receipt of such an allowance.	(ii) £79.50.
(6) Disability Child Premium—	(6) £21.90 in respect of each child or young person in respect of whom the conditions specified in paragraph 14 are satisfied.
(7) Carer Premium—	(7) £13.95 in respect of each person who satisfied the condition specified in paragraph 14ZA.]

PART V

Rounding of Fractions

16. Where income support is awarded for a period which is not a complete benefit week and the applicable amount in respect of that period results in an amount which includes a fraction of a penny that fraction shall be treated as a penny.

AMENDMENTS

1. Income Support (General) Amendment Regulations 1988 (S.I. 1988 No. 663), reg. 29 (April 11, 1988).
2. Income Support (General) Amendment No. 3 Regulations 1988 (S.I. 1988 No. 1228). reg. 9 (September 12, 1988).
3. Income Support (General) Amendment No. 4 Regulations 1988 (S.I. 1988 No. 1445), reg. 19 (September 12, 1988).
4. Income Support (General) Amendment No. 5 Regulations 1988 (S.I. 1988 No. 2022), reg. 17(*b*) (December 12, 1988).
5. Income Support (General) Amendment No. 5 Regulations 1988 (S.I. 1988 No. 2022), reg. 17(*a*) (April 10, 1989).
6. Income Support (General) Amendment Regulations 1989 (S.I. 1989 No. 534), reg. 5 (October 9, 1989).
7. Income Support (General) Amendment No. 3 Regulations 1989 (S.I. 1989 No. 1678), reg. 6 (October 9, 1989).
8. Income Support (General) Amendment Regulations 1990 (S.I. 1990 No. 547), reg. 17 (April 9, 1990).
9. Income Support (General) Amendment No. 2 Regulations 1990 (S.I. 1990 No. 1168). reg. 2 (July 2, 1990).
10. Income Support (General) Amendment No. 3 Regulations 1990 (S.I. 1990 No. 1776), reg. 8 (October 1, 1990).
11. Enterprise (Scotland) Consequential Amendments Order 1991 (S.I. 1991 No. 3870, art. 9 (April, 19910.
12. Income Support (General) Amendment Regulations 1991 (S.I. 1991 No. 236), reg. 2 (April 8, 1991).
13. Income Support (General) Amendment No. 4 Regulations 1991 (S.I. 1991 No. 236). reg. 15 (August 5, 1991).
14. Income Support (General) Amendment No. 4) Regulations 1991 (S.I. 1991 No. 1559), reg. 15 (October 7, 1991).
15. Disability Living Allowance and Disability Working Allowance (Consequential Provisions) Regulations 1991 (S.I. 1991 No. 2742), reg. 11(4) (April 6, 1992).
16. Income Support (General) Amendment Regulations 1992 (S.I. 1992 No. 468), reg. 6 (April 6, 1992).
17. Social Security Benefits (Amendments Consequential Upon the Introduction of Community Care) Regulations 1992 (S.I. 1992 No. 3147), reg. 2 (April 1, 1993).
18. Social Security Benefits (Miscellaneous Amendments) Regulations 1993 (S.I. 1993 No. 518), reg. 5 (April 1, 1993).
19. Income-related Benefits Schemes (Miscellaneous Amendments) (No. 2) Regulations 1993 (S.I. 1993 No. 1150), reg. 3 (May 25, 1993).
20. Income Support (General) Amendment (No. 2) Regulations 1993 (S.I. 1993 No. 1219), reg. 2 (May 31, 1993).
21. Income-related Benefits Schemes (Miscellaneous Amendments) (No. 4) Regulations 1993 (S.I. 1993 No. 2119), reg. 18 (October 4, 1993).
22. Income-related Benefits Schemes (Miscellaneous Amendments) (No. 5) Regulations 1994 (S.I. 1994 No. 2139), reg. 30 (October 3, 1994).
23. Income-related Benefits Schemes (Miscellaneous Amendments) (No. 6) Regulations 1994 (S.I. 1994 No. 3061), reg. 2(3) (December 2, 1994).
24. Income-related Benefits Schemes (Miscellaneous Amendments) Regulations 1995 (S.I. 1995 No. 516), reg. 24 (April 10, 1995).
25. Disability Working Allowance and Income Support (General) Amendment Regulations 1995 (S.I. 1995 No. 482), reg. 16 (April 13, 1995).

26. Disability Working Allowance and Income Support (General) Amendment Regulations 1995 (S.I. 1995 No. 482), reg. 17 (April 13, 1995).

27. Income-related Benefits Schemes and Social Security (Claims and Payments) (Miscellaneous Amendments) Regulations 1995 (S.I. 1995 No. 2303), reg. 6(8) (October 2, 1995).

28. Income Support (General) (Jobseeker's Allowance Consequential Amendments) Regulations 1996 (S.I. 1996 No. 206), reg. 23 and Sched. 2 (October 7, 1996).

29. Child Benefit, Child Support and Social Security (Miscellaneous Amendments) Regulations 1996 (S.I. 1996 No. 1803), reg. 39 (April 7, 1997).

30. Income-related Benefits and Jobseeker's Allowance (Personal Allowances for Children and Young Persons) (Amendment) Regulations 1996 (S.I. 1996 No. 2545), reg. 2 (April 7, 1997).

31. Income-related Benefits and Jobseeker's Allowance (Amendment) (No. 2) Regulations 1997 (S.I. 1997 No. 2197), reg. 7(5) and (6)(a) (October 6, 1997).

32. Social Security Amendment (Lone Parents) Regulations 1998 (S.I. 1998 No. 766), reg. 12 (April 6, 1998).

33. Social Security (Welfare to Work) Regulations 1998 (S.I. 1998 No. 2231), reg. 13(3)(a) (October 5, 1998).

34. Social Security (Welfare to Work) Regulations 1998 (S.I. 1998 No. 2231), reg. 13(3)(b) (October 5, 1998).

35. Social Security Benefits Up-rating Order 1999 (S.I. 1999 No. 264), art. 18(3) and Sched. 4 (April 12, 1999).

36. Social Security Benefits Up-rating Order 1999 (S.I. 1999 No. 264), art. 18(4)(b) (April 12, 1999).

37. Social Security Benefits Up-rating Order 1999 (S.I. 1999 No. 264), art. 18(5) and Sched. 5 (April 12, 1999).

DEFINITIONS

"attendance allowance"—see reg. 2(1).
"benefit week"—*ibid.*
"child"—see 1986 Act, s. 20(11) (SSCBA, s.137(1)).
"claimant"—see reg. 2(1).
"close relative"—*ibid.*
"couple"—*ibid.*
"disability living allowance"—*ibid.*
"disability working allowance"—*ibid.*
"family"—see 1986 Act. s.20(11) (SSCBA, s.137(1)).
"invalid carriage or other vehicle"—see reg. 2(1).
"lone parent"—*ibid.*
"mobility supplement"—*ibid.*
"non-dependent"—see reg. 3.
"nursing home"—see regs. 2(1) and 19(3).
"partner"—see reg. 2(1).
"polygamous marriage"—*ibid.*
"preserved right"—see reg. 2(1) and 19.
"residential care home"—see regs. 2(1) and 19(3).
"single claimant"—see reg. 2(1).
"Social Security Act"—*ibid.*
"welfare to work beneficiary"—*ibid.*
"young person"—*ibid.*, reg. 14.

GENERAL NOTE

The details of the personal allowances and premiums are at the heart of the income support system. Their adequacy or otherwise is crucial to the success of the scheme. The personal allowances can be looked at as a simplified version of the supplementary benefit scale rates (note that there is no long-term rate and no special rate for pensioners), but the premiums were a new departure in April 1988. Instead of an attempt, through supplementary benefit additional requirements, to tailor the level of benefit to the individual needs and circumstances of the claimant and his family, higher amounts of benefit are now targeted on fairly broad categories of claimant. In such a structure benefit may be adequate for those with routine and predictable needs (although of course there is always room for argument about the adequacy of particular rates), but it is almost impossible to make it adequate for those with unusually high needs. The Transitional Regulations protected transferring claimants to some extent, but had the effect, particularly for those with large transitional additions, of preventing any real increase in benefit for, in some cases, several years. An improvement of the structure for pensioners was introduced in October 1989 and for those caring for the disabled in October 1990.

Personal Allowances

Paragraph 1

This paragraph was amended (and para. 1A was introduced) in October 1996 as a consequence of the changes to income support following the introduction of JSA.

The lower age limit for income support is now 16 (SSCBA, s.124(1)(a)) but a person is only eligible if he falls into one of the categories prescribed by reg. 4ZA and Sched. 1B (s.124(1)(e)). (Note too that a person aged 16–18 in relevant education is still only entitled to income support in certain circumstances (s.124(1)(d) and reg. 13)). However, the age-break of 18 remains significant as regards the rate of the personal allowance (and so the immense complexity of sub-para. (3) is retained), with another very significant break at 25 for single claimants.

For couples, where both partners are aged less than 18, the lower couple rate is only paid if either a child is a member of the family, or both partners are eligible for income support, or the non-claiming partner is either eligible for JSA or the subject of a severe hardship direction under s.16 of the Jobseekers Act 1995 (sub-para. (3)(a)). If this does not apply but one member of the couple comes within para. 1A (person living away from parents and anyone acting in place of parents in specified circumstances), the personal allowance is the same as the higher rate for a single claimant under 18 (sub-para. (3)(b)), but otherwise only the equivalent of the lower rate for a single claimant under 18 is paid (sub-para. (3)(c)). Where one partner is 18 or over and the other is under 18, the higher couple rate is only paid if the partner under 18 is eligible for income support or income-based JSA or the subject of a JSA severe hardship direction (sub-para. (3)(e)). If this is not the case, the personal allowance is the same as for a single claimant (sub-para. (3)(f)), with another age-break at 25 (sub-para. (3)(g)).

The crucial age for lone parents is 18 (sub-para. (2)(d)). Lone parents of 16 and 17 are always eligible (para. 1 of Sched. 1B) but are paid at a higher rate if they fall within para. 1A (person living away from parents and any substitute in certain circumstances) or qualify for a disability premium (sub-para. (2)(b) and (c)).

Single claimants under 18 qualify for the 18–24-year-old rate if they fall within para. 1A (sub-para. (1)(b)) or qualify for a disability premium (sub-para. (1)(c)). But for single claimants there is another very significant break at the age of 25 (para. 1(1)(e)). This is connected to the absence of any distinction in the personal allowances between householders and non-householders. Instead, the assumptions are made that most single people of 25 and over are responsible for their own households and that most single people under 25 are not responsible for independent households, typically living with parents. Thus a higher rate is paid to those of 25. Both these assumptions are correct, looking at the entire age-groups involved, but clearly have no direct applicability to the needs and circumstances of individuals. Young single claimants were one of the losing groups in the 1988 reforms.

See para. 2A for the treatment of residents in residential care and nursing homes and Sched. 7 for special cases, such as hospital patients. From April 1989 there are no special rules for people in board and lodging accommodation and from October 1989 no special rules for residents in most hostels.

Paragraph 1A

This paragraph lists those categories of 16- and 17-year-olds who qualify for the higher rate of personal allowance under para. 1(1)(b), (2)(b) and (3)(b). The categories replicate those formerly in paras. 6–9A of Part II of Schedule 1A (Sched. 1A was revoked on October 7, 1996 as a consequence of the changes to income support following the introduction of JSA).

See sub-para. (2) for definitions. On heads (a), (d) and (e) of sub-para. (1), see the notes to reg. 13(2)(c), (e) and (d) respectively. Head (b) is similar to reg. 13(2)(dd) but there are some important differences in the wording. Those covered by head (c) are expected to be particularly vulnerable.

Paragraph 2

This lays down the rates of personal allowance for dependant children and young persons. From April 7, 1997, the allowance no longer increases from the 11th, 16th or 18th birthday of the child or young person concerned. It now only rises twice and the increase does not take effect until the first Monday in September after the child's 11th or 16th birthday. The Government's somewhat thin justification for these changes was that the timing of the increases was thus more closely aligned with the transition to secondary or further education. But the result is a reduction in benefit income which for some families will be considerable, depending on how soon after the first Sunday in September the relevant birthday falls. The abolition of the increase at 18 will also involve a substantial loss (£9.05 per week at April 1996 rates) if a dependent young person is continuing in non-advanced education after 18. For the Social Security Advisory Committee's report which opposed the changes see Cm. 3393/1996.

The new age bands only apply if a dependent child or young person becomes 11, 16 or 18 on or after April 7, 1997. See the transitional protection in reg. 10(1) and (2) of the Income-related Benefits and Jobseeker's Allowance (Personal Allowances for Children and Young Persons) (Amendment) Regulations 1996 (p. 502) for those reaching 11, 16 or 18 before that date; note that it is not necessary for income support to have been in payment on the relevant birthday. Note also that the changes do not affect young people receiving income support in their own right.

The same changes were made to income-based JSA from April 7, 1997 and to council tax benefit and housing benefit from April 1 and 7, 1997. They applied to family credit and disability working allowance from October 7, 1997; for these benefits the credit or allowance for the child or young person concerned will only increase from the award beginning on or after the first Tuesday in September following the relevant birthday. There is a small palliative for housing and council tax benefit, family credit and disability working allowance claimants who are eligible for the child care costs disregard in that the period for which this applies has been correspondingly extended up to the first Monday in September following the child's 11th birthday (housing and council tax benefit), and from October 7, 1997 lasts to the end of the family credit or disability working allowance award which spans that Monday.

The Government announced in March 1999 that it intends to equalise the personal allowances for children in the two lower age bands. The increase is to take effect in two stages. The current rate for a child in the lowest age band will be increased by £4.70 (to £24.90) in October 1999. From April 2000 there will be a single rate of personal allowance for children from birth to the September after their 16th birthday.

Paragraph 2A

A new structure of benefit for residents in residential care and nursing homes was introduced in April 1993. Anyone with a "preserved right" is excluded from the new system (sub-para. (2)(b)). People who were resident in a home on March 31, 1993 (apart from residents, not entitled to income support, in residential care homes in England and Wales with less than four residents) have preserved rights, which means that they can continue to receive income support under the old system of reg. 19(3) and Sched. 4. See reg. 19 (1ZB) to (1ZR) for details.

If a person is not excluded by the "preserved right" provisions, the new system was described as follows by the DSS to the Social Security Advisory Committee (Appendix 2 to Cm. 2215, para. 6).

"Under the new Community Care arrangements from April 1993 people entering residential care and nursing homes at public expense will be able to claim Income Support on a similar basis to those living in their own home. Additionally, they will be able to receive a Residential Allowance, as part of their Income Support entitlement, as a contribution towards their 'accommodation costs'. They will have their care needs assessed by the local authority who will meet any extra cost involved. In deciding the ability of an individual to contribute towards their fees in the care home, the local authority will carry out a financial assessment. This will largely follow the rules which currently apply to Income Support under regulations being prepared by the Department of Health.

Resources will be transferred to the local authorities to enable them to meet their new responsibilities. The White Paper commitment is that the Government will transfer to local authorities what it would otherwise have spent on DSS benefits, taking into account expenditure on existing cases and the continuing eligibility for benefit of new residents."

The residential allowance is set at £59.40 (£66.10 for London) for each adult resident. Outside the conditions of para. 2A there may be entitlement to ordinary income support and housing benefit, or to the "Part III" rate for "residential accommodation." There are detailed conditions in sub-para. (2).

(a) The person must be a resident in a residential care or nursing home. Through reg. 2(1), the definitions in reg. 19(3) are incorporated, subject to some special rules in para. 2A. Thus, for residential care homes, the home must be in one of the three categories specified in sub-para (3). There is no separate category for Abbeyfield Homes, so that they only qualify if registered under the 1984 Act. Under the Registered Homes (Amendment) Act 1991 residential care homes with less than four residents have to be registered. The local authority has to apply the standards of board and personal care.

From May 31, 1993, the period for which claimants who are absent from their residential care or nursing home can continue to receive a residential allowance has been extended. The previous limit was six days. Now it will continue for six weeks where the claimant is in hospital and three weeks in any other case. Periods in hospital separated by not more than 28 days count as one period. There is a transitional provision applying to claimants who had been temporarily absent from a home for more than six days on May 31, 1993: see Income Support (General) Amendment (No. 2) Regulations 1993 (S.I. 1993 No. 1219) p. 492.

(aa) This condition ensures that the person concerned requires personal care and is not simply a resident in a home which provides such care to others. The amendment made in October 1997 brings the definition of "personal care" broadly into line with that used in reg. 19(3)(d) (except that sub-para. (2)(aa) also includes a reference to personal care required by reason of terminal illness).

(b) The person must not have a preserved right (reg. 19).

(c) Under-16s are not entitled to residential allowances.

(d) On a "commercial basis": see the notes to reg. 2(1) on "board and lodging accommodation."

(e) It is a condition that housing benefit is not received for the accommodation. Generally there can be no entitlement to housing benefit if there is potential entitlement to a residential allowance. But for Royal Charter/Act of Parliament homes, where there is a care test under sub-para. (3)(b), housing benefit can be claimed as an alternative without the need to meet the care test.

Note the increased upper and lower capital limits for people living permanently in residential care or nursing homes from April 1996 (regs. 45(b) and 53(1A), see the note to reg. 53).

Premiums

Paragraph 3

The family premium is treated differently from the other premiums. It is awarded whenever there is a child or young person in the claimant's family. It is of the same amount whether there is one child or 10 in the family. It does not matter that no personal allowance is included for the child, *e.g.* because he has capital over £3,000.

Note also regs. 15(3) and 16(6), the effect of which is that if a child is being looked after by a local authority or is in custody and then returns home for part of a week the premium will be paid for the days that the child is at home.

Until April 7, 1997 the family premium was paid at one rate. However, on that date the separate lone parent premium (see the former para. 8 of Sched. 2 in the 1996 edition of this book) was abolished and the family premium became payable at two rates. The higher rate (which incorporated the former lone parent premium) was paid if the claimant was a lone parent and did not qualify for one of the pensioner or a disability premium. Thus it applied in the same circumstances in which the former lone parent premium used to apply. The lower rate was paid in any other case. This change was part of an explicit policy of reducing the additional benefit paid to lone parents (see also the similar changes that have been made to child benefit), the first stage of which in 1996 had been to freeze the rate of the lone parent premium at the April 1995 rate of £5.20. Because of the uprating increase in the "basic" family premium the additional amount for a lone parent in fact decreased in April 1997 by 25p. For the Social Security Advisory Committee's (SSAC) report on these changes see Cm. 3296 (1996).

The further change from April 6, 1998 is that the rate of the family premium for existing claimants who become lone parents and for lone parents making a new claim (subject to the 12-week linking rule, see below) is now the same as for couples. The only lone parents who qualify for the higher rate of the family premium after April 5, 1998 are those who satisfy the conditions in sub-paras. (2) and (3); in addition they must not be getting one of the pensioner or a disability premium (but if their entitlement to such a premium ceases, see below). This category is in fact more extensive than that covered by the original form of the April 1988 amendments to para. 3 (see Social Security (Lone Parents) (Amendment) Regulations 1997 (S.I. 1997 No. 1790) which were revoked by reg. 2 of the amending regulations). For SSAC's report on the changes as first proposed, see Cm. 3713 (1997). The current amending regulations were not referred to SSAC before they were made, due to "the urgency of the matter" (they were not made until March 16 and the previous amending regulations had been due to come into force on April 6, 1998), although the Government stated that SSAC would be given an opportunity to comment on them. It is noteworthy that, although originally rejected by the Government, many of SSAC's recommendations were taken into account in the amending regulations.

In order to qualify for the higher rate family premium a claimant must have been a lone parent (defined in reg. 2(1)) and either (i) entitled (see *R/(SB) 12/87*) to income support (or income-based

JSA (sub-para. (6)) on April 5, 1998, or (ii) entitled to income support (or income-based JSA) on at least one day in the 12 weeks immediately before April 6, 1998 and entitled again on at least one day no more than 12 weeks later (sub-para. (2)). Note that it is only necessary for the claimant to have been a lone parent at the relevant dates(s); there is no requirement that she must have been receiving the higher rate of the family premium. Thus if this was not payable because, for example, she was entitled to a disability premium, she will still be able to qualify for the higher rate family premium in the future if the disability premium ceases to be payable, as long as she satisfies the other conditions in sub-paras. (2) and (3). It is also not necessary for the claimant to have been entitled to income support (or income-based JSA) on April 5, 1998, as long as she was entitled to one of these benefits in the 12 weeks starting on April 6, 1998 and had been so entitled no more than 12 weeks earlier. Moreover, sub-para. (2) will also apply where income support or income-based JSA, even though not in payment at the time, is subsequently awarded for the relevant period. Thus it should cover a claimant who makes a successful backdated claim or who is awarded income support under reg. 21ZA (asylum seeker whose refugee status has been recognised) for this period.

Once a claimant satisfies sub-para. (2)(a) or (b) she will be entitled to the higher rate family premium as long as she continues to be a lone parent and entitled to income support (or income-based JSA) (sub-paras. (3) and (4)). Under sub-para. (5) a claimant will be deemed to satisfy this requirement during breaks of no more than 12 weeks when she is not a lone parent, *or* entitled to income support (or income-based JSA), *or* both. This means that it will be possible for a lone parent who moves from income support to income-based JSA (or vice versa) to retain entitlement to the higher rate family premium, as long as there is no more than a 12-week gap between entitlement to either benefit.

The higher rate of the family premium was not increased in April 1998 and so the additional amount for a lone parent then became only £4.70. The Government stated that it would be further reduced in April 1999 by an increase in the ordinary rate of the family premium of £2.50. From April 1999 the differential between the two rates has in fact dropped to £1.85 since the higher rate of the premium has remained at its April 1997 level. The Government also announced that the personal allowance for a child in the lowest age band would be increased by £2.50 in November 1998 (to £19.80p). This applied to all claimants with children in that age group but was also supposed to provide some compensation, if only in cash terms, for the loss of lone parents' additional benefit.

Note that from April 6, 1998 all lone parents (not just those who qualify for the higher rate family premium) are entitled to a £15 disregard for part-time earnings (see para. 5 of Sched. 8).

Note also that receipt of the higher rate family premium (or an overlapping pensioner or disability premium) will enable a lone parent who starts work to claim the lone parent rate of child benefit after its abolition on July 6, 1998. On the abolition of the lone parent rate of child benefit for new claimants from July 6, 1998 and the transitional protection provisions, see the Child Benefit and Social Security (Fixing and Adjustment of Rates) (Amendment) Regulations 1998 (S.I. 1998 No. 1581) in *Bonner*.

Paragraphs 4 to 7

These provisions establish the general framework for the other premiums, in paras. 9 to 14. Para. 4 provides that in each case the premium is applicable to the claimant, although often the condition relates to some other member of his family. The general rule is that only one of these premiums is applicable. If the claimant satisfies the conditions for more than one, the highest is applicable (para. 5). But a number of exceptions appear in para. 6. The severe disability premium (SDP) is allowed in addition to any other premium, as is the disabled child premium (DCP) and the carer premium (CP), rather like the "basic" family premium (see para. 3(1)(b)).

Many of the conditions for premiums are based on the receipt of other social security benefits. Para. 7(1) deals with two situations where, once a premium has been allowed, the person concerned ceases actually to receive the other benefit. It allows entitlement to the premium to continue if the person has only ceased to receive the relevant benefit because of another, overlapping, benefit or is on a government training course or in receipt of a training allowance (the main example being Work Based Training for Young People, which has replaced Youth Training and other training provision focussed on 16/17 year olds). See para. 14B on the meaning of receipt of benefit.

Under para. 7(2), the above rules do not allow the CP to continue unless the person cared for continues to receive attendance allowance or one of the two higher rates of the care component of disability living allowance.

Paragraphs 9 and 9A

These provisions, together with the increases in the higher pensioner premium under para. 15(3), implemented the Government's commitment to give increased help to needy pensioners in October

1989. The ordinary pensioner premium under para. 9 is now limited to people aged 60 to 74. Para. 9A provides a separate premium for those aged 75 to 79, with a current differential over the ordinary pensioner premium of £2.30 for a single person and £3.25 for a couple (para. 15(2A)). The effect of reg. 14(1D) of the Transitional Regulations is that these increases do not affect any transitional addition in payment.

Paragraph 10

The first qualification for the HPP is that the claimant or any partner is aged 80 or over. If this is not satisfied there are another two alternatives, providing that at least one of the claimant or any partner is aged at least 60. The first was originally that the person of 60-plus satisfies the disability test in para. 12(1)(a) or (c). From April 1992 the test may be satisfied by a partner who is under 60. The second is that the claimant was entitled to income support (or income-based JSA: reg. 32 of the Income Support (General) (Jobseeker's Allowance Consequential Amendments) Regulations 1996 (see p. 500) under which entitlement to income-based JSA counts as entitlement to income support for the purpose of satisfying any condition that the person is or has been entitled to income support) with the disability premium in the eight weeks (from October 5, 1998, 52 weeks in the case of a ''welfare to work beneficiary'' (para. (4)); see the notes to reg. 2(1) for when a person counts as a welfare to work beneficiary) before his 60th birthday and has been continuously entitled to income support (or income-based JSA) since that birthday. In the case of a couple the person who qualified for the disability premium can be the partner. Although there are linking rules in sub-para. (3), the eight-week test is most arbitrary. All sorts of things might cause a person not to be entitled to income support just before a 60th birthday (obtaining capital from the proceeds of an endowment or retirement annuity policy, for instance), which have nothing to do with future disability needs. In addition, *CIS 458/1992* decides that a premium is not applicable unless it actually forms part of the claimant's applicable amount (but see *CIS 11293/1996* in the notes to para. 12).

Sub-para. (3)(a) allows breaks of eight weeks once the HPP has been allowed. Sub-para. (3)(b) allows a break of eight weeks if it straddles the 60th birthday. From October 5, 1998, the break under sub-para. (3)(b) (but not sub-para. (3)(a)) can be up to 52 weeks in the case of a ''welfare to work beneficiary'' (sub-para. (4)). For the definition of ''welfare to work beneficiary'' see reg. 2(1) and the notes to that regulation.

The premium is £30.85 if the claimant does not have a partner, £44.65 for a couple (para. 15(3)). It thus takes precedence over the pensioner premium.

Paragraph 11

The qualification for the DP can be for the claimant personally to satisfy one of the conditions in para. 12. If it is the claimant's partner who might qualify, then only para. 12(1)(a) or (c), not (b), will do. In either case, the person qualifying must be under 60. The premium is £21.90 if the claimant does not have a partner, £31.25 for a couple (para. 15(4)).

Paragraph 12

Sub-para. (1) prescribes three alternative disablement conditions for HPP and DP. Heads (a) and (c) can be satisfied by either the claimant or his partner; head (b) can only be satisfied by the claimant. As far as possible the conditions are made to depend on decisions already taken by other authorities, so that decision-making here should be routine.

Head (a) applies to receipt of the benefits listed in head (i), provision of or grant towards an invalid carriage, or being registered blind. From April 1990, para. 14B defines receipt of benefit in terms of payment, reversing the effect of *R(SB) 12/87*. Long-term incapacity benefit requires 52 weeks of incapacity for work, and has a contribution test. (Previously invalidity pension required only 28 weeks of incapacity.) Note sub-para. (6), the effect of which is to treat a person who is terminally ill as in receipt of long-term incapacity benefit after 28 weeks. Severe disablement allowance is non-contributory, but has an additional (and tough) test of disablement. The extension to all levels of disability living allowance brought in some previously excluded claimants. See sub-para. (2) for blindness, and the notes to para. 13 of Sched. 1B.

Entitlement to HPP is affected by the discriminatory age limit for claims for long-term incapacity benefit (previously invalidity benefit) that results from the U.K.'s different pensionable ages for men and women (*i.e.* 65 for men, 60 for women; full equalisation of pensionable age will not be achieved until April, 2020) (but see *CIB 13368/1998* below where the entitlement to incapacity benefit derives from an industrial injury or a prescribed industrial disease). (As a result of the ECJ's decision in *Secretary of State for Social Security v. Thomas* [1993] E.C.R. I-1247, [1993] 4 All E.R. 556, the discriminatory age limit for initial claims for severe disablement allowance was finally changed on October 28, 1994 (see Social Security (Severe Disablement Allowance and Invalid Care Allowance) Amendment Regulations 1994 (S.I. 1994 No. 2556).) In *Secretary of State for Social Security and*

Chief Adjudication Officer v. Graham and Others (Case C-92/94, [1995] 3 C.M.L.R. 169, [1995] All E.R. (E.C.) 865) the ECJ held that the different treatment of men and women in relation to invalidity benefit was not in breach of EC Directive 79/7 on equal treatment for men and women in matters of social security. The discrimination in the rules for invalidity benefit was permitted under Article 7(1)(a) of the Directive as it was "necessarily and objectively linked" to the U.K.'s different pension ages (see *Thomas*). The Court's reasoning is scanty (compare the Advocate General's Opinion delivered on June 15, 1995). But the judgment has (for the time being at least) put an end to the argument that a discriminatory link to pensionable age for *contributory* (as opposed to non-contributory: see *Thomas*) benefits is unlawful. See the 1995 edition of this book for further details of *Graham* (and associated issues) and related European caselaw on the scope of Directive 79/7. Long-term incapacity benefit is not payable to people over pensionable age (except those who were over pensionable age before April 13, 1995 who remain eligible for up to five years over that age). The consequence of the ECJ's judgment in *Graham* is that this discrimination against women (and its effect on entitlement to HPP) remains (until the pensionable age differential is finally abolished). Note, however, that in *CIB 13368/1996* the Commissioner has held that for women who were getting invalidity benefit because of industrial injury or prescribed disease (and who were therefore deemed to satisfy the contributions conditions: see reg. 31 of the Social Security (Unemployment, Sickness and Invalidity Benefit) Regulations 1983 (S.I. 1983 No. 1598), and who transferred to transitional incapacity benefit, the discriminatory age limit is unlawful. In his view, the provision at issue (reg. 17(4) of the Social Security (Incapacity Benefit) (Transitional) Regulations 1995) fell on the *Thomas*, rather than the *Graham*, side of the line.

The current form of head (b) is a consequence of the changes associated with the introduction of incapacity benefit (which replaced sickness benefit and invalidity benefit from April 13, 1995). It is no longer linked to what is now para. 7 of Sched. 1B (see the 1994 edition for notes on the previous form of head (b)), although it employs the same criteria as heads (a), (b) and (d) of para. 7. See the notes to para. 7 of Sched. 1B. The test must now be satisfied for a continuous period of at least 52 weeks before a disability or higher pensioner premium can be awarded under head (b), unless the claimant is terminally ill when the period is 28 weeks. Two or more periods separated by not more than eight weeks (from October 5, 1998, 52 weeks in the case of a "welfare to work beneficiary" (sub-para. (1A)); see the notes to reg. 2(1) for when a person counts as a welfare to work beneficiary) count as one continuous period. A person is defined as terminally ill if he is expected to die from a progressive disease within six months. If the person has been incapable of work (or entitled to statutory sick pay) for 28 weeks by the time an AO decides he is terminally ill, head (b) will immediately apply. Before April 13, 1995 the qualifying period under head (b) was 28 weeks. There is some transitional protection, see below. In the case of a couple, head (b) can only be satisfied by the claimant.

A person is entitled to statutory sick pay from the first day of incapacity (even though it is not paid for the first three "waiting days"). Otherwise it is only days on which it is accepted that the claimant is, or is to be treated as, incapable of work in accordance with the new rules for determining incapacity for work (see the notes to para. 7 of Sched. 1B) that count. A claimant does not have to be in receipt of income support during the qualifying period, so if a person has been incapable of work for 52 weeks before claiming income support head (b) will immediately apply. Any days when the claimant is treated as capable of work under the new incapacity rules (see the notes to para. 7 of Sched. 1B) will not count, but note the linking rule. A person may be treated as capable of work for a maximum of 6 weeks under reg. 18 of the Social Security (Incapacity for Work) (General) Regulations; or indefinitely in other cases. Thus the effect of a decision to treat a claimant as capable of work may (depending on the circumstances) only result in that period not counting towards establishing entitlement to a disability or higher pensioner premium, rather than necessitate a return to square one. If the claimant has already been awarded a premium it will not be payable while he is treated as capable of work. But if this is for eight weeks or less it will apply again immediately after the break. Note also the 52-week linking rule from October 5, 1998 for a claimant who is a "welfare to work beneficiary" (see reg. 2(1) and the notes to that regulation).

Note *CIS 15611/1996* which decides that a claimant who had been entitled to a disability premium before going into prison and who continued to be incapable of work while in prison did not have to re-serve the 52 week qualifying period on his release. Although days of disqualification from incapacity benefit during a period of imprisonment did not count as days of incapacity for work under reg. 4(1)(b) of the Incapacity Benefit Regulations 1994, this only applied for the purposes of incapacity benefit. The Incapacity for Work (General) Regulations 1995 contained no such provision and so subject to the claimant providing evidence of his incapacity for work throughout his period in prison he was entitled to a disability premium when he reclaimed income support on his release.

If a claimant makes a late claim for a benefit on the grounds of incapacity for work, the days on which it is accepted that he was, or was to be treated as, incapable of work should count under head (b). It does not matter that there is no entitlement to the benefit because the claim is late. See *R(IS) 8/93* (but note the amendments to reg. 2(1) of the Social Security (Medical Evidence) Regulations 1976 (S.I. 1976 No. 615) from April 13, 1995).

There is transitional protection for claimants entitled to a disability premium on April 12, 1995 under head (b) as then in force. See reg. 19(2) to (4) of the Disability Working Allowance and Income Support (General) Amendment Regulations 1995 (p. 494). The premium will continue to be paid as long as they remain incapable of work (in accordance with the new rules, including the transitional protection). Note the linking rule. In addition, any period immediately before April 13, 1995 during which a claimant satisfied para. 5 of Sched. 1 as then in force (see the 1994 edition) counts towards the qualifying period under head (b).

Head (c) applies where receipt of some benefits specified in (a) only ceased because of age limits or going into hospital. The claimant has to remain continuously entitled to income support (or income-based JSA: reg. 32 of the Income Support (General) (Jobseeker's Allowance Consequential Amendments) Regulations 1996 (see p. 500) under which entitlement to income-based JSA counts as entitlement to income support for the purpose of satisfying any condition that the person is or has been entitled to income support) and if it is his partner who has ceased to receive long-term incapacity benefit she must still be alive. Note the linking rule in sub-para. (4). Note also sub-para. (6) in relation to incapacity benefit, the effect of which is to treat a person who is terminally ill as in receipt of long-term incapacity benefit after 28 weeks. There is transitional protection for claimants entitled to a higher pensioner premium under the old form of head (c)(i) at any time in the eight weeks before April 12, 1995 (*i.e.* those who transferred to retirement pension from invalidity benefit): see reg. 20(4) of the Disability Working Allowance and Income Support (General) Amendment Regulations 1995 (p. 495).

CIS 587/1990 exposes a gap in the legislation which has not yet been closed. The claimant transferred from invalidity benefit to retirement pension in 1982. He could not qualify under the old form of head (c) because he had not been continuously entitled to income support since the transfer. If he had delayed the transfer until after April 10, 1988, he would have qualified. The extent of his need at the relevant date (April 1990) was identical under either alternative. See sub-para. (4) for linking rules. Another gap is highlighted by *CIS 458/1992* which holds that the condition that a premium has been applicable requires that it should have been part of the claimant's applicable amount. So where a claimant had been in a residential care home he could not use head (c), because Sched. 4 has no provision for premiums. But see *CIS 11293/1996* in the notes to para. 4(6) of Sched. 3 where the Commissioner holds that housing costs were "applicable" under para. 5A(3) of the former Sched. 3 if they were potentially applicable.

Paragraph 13

The presence of this category is required by s.22(3) of the 1986 Act, now s.135(5) of the Contributions and Benefits Act. The concern which prompted the inclusion of that subsection was that a severely disabled claimant on supplementary benefit might be getting high additional requirements for a range of extra needs (*e.g.* heating, laundry, diet, wear and tear on clothes, etc.), which the ordinary disability premium would go nowhere near matching. However, the conditions for the SDP are so tight that very few will qualify. The Independent Living Fund was set up to provide further cash help to the very severely disabled, but its budget was usually fully spent part way through its financial year. The Fund was suspended in 1992. On April 1, 1993, it was replaced by two funds, the Independent Living (Extension) Fund which took over payments to existing beneficiaries and the Independent Living (1993) Fund for new applications.

First note that the SDP can only apply to the claimant, not to his partner. But since a couple has a free choice as to which of them should be the claimant (Claims and Payments Regulations, reg. 4) this should not be a problem.

If the claimant has no partner, he first must be in receipt of attendance allowance or one of the two higher rates of the care component of disability living allowance, *i.e.* he must require attention or supervision (sub-para. (2)(a)(i)). Then there must be no non-dependants of 18 or over residing with him (sub-para. (2)(a)(ii)). The addition of the words "with whom he is normally residing" from December 2, 1994 is to reverse the effect of the Court of Appeal's decision in *Bate v. Chief Adjudication Officer and Secretary of State for Social Security* on November 30, 1994 (since overturned by the House of Lords: see the notes to reg. 3). The effect of sub-para. (3) is that adults in receipt of attendance allowance or one of the two higher rates of care component of disability living allowance or who are registered as blind or treated as blind or carers for the first 12 weeks of residence do not count for this purpose. "Non-dependant" is defined in reg. 3. See the notes to that regulation for the intricacies of the definition. Care must be taken to apply the particular form of reg. 3 in force at the relevant time. The current version makes it very difficult for the parents with whom an adult claimant is living not to be regarded as non-dependants. Finally, no-one must be receiving invalid care allowance for caring for the claimant (sub-para. (2)(a)(iii)). *R(IS) 14/94* held that where arrears of ICA were awarded, it had been "in payment" for the period covered by the arrears. "In payment" in sub-para. (2)(a)(iii) did not mean timeously in payment. Thus an SDP that had been paid for the same period could be recovered under s. 74(4) of the Administration Act (s. 27(4) of the 1986 Act). This was despite the fact that the recipient of the SDP and the recipient of the ICA were different people whose requirements and resources were not aggregated for the purposes of income support. See the notes to s. 74 for a full discussion of *R(IS) 14/94*. The claimant was granted leave to appeal to the Court of Appeal, but the appeal was not proceeded with as the DSS issued internal guidance stating that such overpayments were not to be recovered. Now sub-para. (3ZA) provides that where an award of ICA is made which includes arrears, entitlement to the severe disability premium only ceases from the date the award of ICA is actually made. This should avoid any question of an overpayment of an SDP by reason of a backdated award of invalid care allowance.

If the claimant has a partner, the assumption is that the partner can care for the claimant. So there is an additional qualification that the partner is also in receipt of a qualifying allowance (sub-para. (2)(b)(ii)) or, if not, is registered as blind or treated as blind (sub-para. (2A)). There must be no eligible non-dependants in residence (see above), and at least one of the couple must not have a carer receiving invalid care allowance.

In *CIS 372/1990* and a number of associated appeals, the Commissioner held that sub-para. (2)(a)(ii) and (iii) were not validly made, since s.22(4) of the Social Security Act 1986 (now s.135(6) of the Contributions and Benefits Act) only gave power to prescribe conditions relating to a claim-ant's disability. Section 22(3) (SSSCBA, s.135(5)) requires a severely disabled person's applicable amount to include a special premium. Heads (ii) and (iii) are concerned with the presence of others in the household and the benefit entitlement of other people, which are not connected to the claim-ant's disability. This cogently argued decision was reversed by the Court of Appeal in *Chief Adjudication Officer v. Foster* [1992] Q.B. 31, [1991] 3 All E.R. 846, which held by a majority that the provisions were valid. The House of Lords confirmed this part of the Court of Appeal's decision (*Foster v. Chief Adjudication Officer* [1993] A.C. 754, [1993] 1 All E.R. 705). Therefore, the full conditions of para. 13 must be applied at all points of its history. See the notes to s.135 of the Contributions and Benefits Act for more details, and the notes to s.23 of the Administration Act for the power of the Social Security Commissioners and others to determine whether regulations have been validly made.

The premium is high, since it is in addition to DP or HPP (para. 6(1)). For a claimant without a partner it is £39.75. For a couple (where both partners have to qualify) it is £39.75 for each of them who does not have a carer with invalid care allowance (para. 15(5)).

It was argued in *R(IS) 10/94* that for periods before April 1990, (when para. 14B was introduced) where a lone parent received attendance allowance in respect of a child under 16, para. 13(2)(a)(i) was satisfied. Reg. 6(4) of the Social Security (Attendance Allowance) (No. 2) Regulations 1975 made the parent entitled to the attendance allowance in these circumstances. But if the parent, and not the child, were treated as in receipt of attendance allowance, that would mean that a child could never have satisfied the conditions of para. 14(b) on the DCP. *R(IS) 10/94* decides that in the context of para. 14(b) a child is in receipt of attendance allowance when the child satisfies the prescribed conditions and the meaning must be the same in para. 13(2)(a)(i). The introduction of para. 14B in April 1990, providing that a person is to be regarded as in receipt of any benefit only where it is paid in respect of that person was to clarify the law, not to change it. The decision in *R(IS) 10/94* was confirmed by the Court of Appeal in *Rider and Others v. Chief Adjudication Officer, The Times*, January 30, 1996. The Court held that on an overall comparison of the words "in receipt of" in paras. 13(2)(a)(i) and 14(b) (and also para. 12(1)(a)(i) in relation to the disability premium), it could be seen that the words were not to be read just as they stood but as importing the additional requirement that the attendance allowance should be payable in respect of the recipient's own needs. Para. 13 (and para. 12) was concerned only with the needs of claimants and their partners; para. 14 only with the needs of children and young persons.

Note that from November 14, 1994, entitlement to a severe disability premium has been added to the list of questions that the AO need not determine immediately (Adjudication Regulations, reg. 56(1)(b) and (3)(c)).

Paragraph 14

Since the DP applies to the claimant or partner only, and the SDP to the claimant only, separate provision has to be made for children. The child must either be receiving disability living allowance (or only not be, because of being a patient) or be registered blind or treated as blind. See para. 14B for receipt of benefit and *Rider and Others v. CAO* in the notes to para. 13. Any level of either

337

the care or the mobility component will do. The child is excluded if his capital exceeds £3,000. The premium has from April 1990 been increased to the same rate as that of the adult DP, *i.e.* £21.90 (para. 15(6)), and is paid in addition to any other premium. The range of need within this category will also be vast. A disabled child would have qualified a claimant for very large supplementary benefit additional requirements. The limit of £21.90 on top of what would be paid for the presence of any child is now somewhat more realistic for severe disabilities.

Paragraph 14ZA
The carer premium is part of the Government's shift of resources amongst the disabled. It goes to a person who is receiving invalid care allowance, or is treated as receiving it (sub-para. (2)). The amount is £13.95 for each person who qualifies. The CP may encourage the claiming of ICA, against which must be balanced the possible loss of SDP for the disabled person being cared for. See *R(IS) 14/94* above and para. 13(3ZA). Under sub-paras. (3) and (4) entitlement to the premium continues for eight weeks after ceasing to receive ICA.

Paragraph 14A
In paras. 12 to 14ZA receipt of a concessionary (*i.e.* extra-statutory) payment to compensate for non-payment of a benefit is to be equated with actual payment of that benefit.

Paragraph 14B
This important definition of receipt of benefit in terms of payment, not entitlement, reverses the effect of *R(SB) 12/87*. It makes for a further simplification of decision-making. It also ended the argument that it was the parent of a child under 16 who qualified for attendance allowance who received the benefit. See the note to para. 13.

[¹SCHEDULE 3   **Regulations 17(1)(e)
and 18(1)(f)**

HOUSING COSTS

Housing Costs

  1.—(1) Subject to the following provisions of this Schedule, the housing costs applicable to a claimant are those costs—
    (a) which he or, where he is a member of a family, he or any member of that family is, in accordance with paragraph 2, liable to meet in respect of the dwelling occupied as the home which he or any other member of his family is treated as occupying, and
    (b) which qualify under paragraphs 15 to 17.
  (2) In this Schedule—
"housing costs" means those costs to which sub-paragraph (1) refers;
"existing housing costs" means housing costs arising under an agreement entered into before 2nd October 1995, or under an agreement entered into after 1st October 1995 ("the new agreement")—
    (a) which replaces an existing agreement between the same parties in respect of the same property; and
    (b) where the existing agreement was entered into before 2nd October 1995; and
    (c) which is for a loan of the same amount as or less than the amount of the loan under the agreement it replaces, and for this purpose any amount payable [². . .] to arrange the new agreement and included in the loan shall be disregarded;
"new housing costs" means housing costs arising under an agreement entered into after 1st October 1995 other than an agreement referred to in the definition of "existing housing costs";
"standard rate" means the rate for the time being specified in paragraph 12.
  (3) For the purposes of this Schedule a disabled person is a person—
    (a) in respect of whom a disability premium, a disabled child premium, a pensioner premium for persons aged 75 or over or a higher pensioner premium is included

in his applicable amount or the applicable amount of a person living with him; or
(b) [².. .] who, had he in fact been entitled to income support, would have had included in his applicable amount a disability premium, a disabled child premium, a pensioner premium for persons aged 75 or over or a higher pensioner premium.

(4) For the purposes of sub-paragraph (3), a person shall not cease to be a disabled person on account of his being disqualified for receiving benefit or treated as capable of work by virtue of the operation of section 171E of the Contributions and Benefits Act (incapacity for work, disqualification etc.).

[⁶ **Previous entitlement to income-based jobseeker's allowance**

1A.—(1) Where a claimant or his partner was in receipt of or was treated as being in receipt of income-based jobseeker's allowance not more than 12 weeks before one of them becomes entitled to income support or, where the claimant or his partner is a person to whom paragraph 14(2) or (8) (linking rules) refers, not more than 26 weeks before becoming so entitled and—
(a) the applicable amount for that allowance included an amount in respect of housing costs under paragraph 14 or 15 of Schedule 2 to the Jobseeker's Allowance Regulations 1996; and
(b) the circumstances affecting the calculation of those housing costs remain unchanged since the last calculation of those costs,
the applicable amount in respect of housing costs for income support shall be the applicable amount in respect of those costs current when entitlement to income-based jobseeker's allowance was last determined.

(2) Where, in the period since housing costs were last calculated for income-based jobseeker's allowance, there has been a change of circumstances, other than a reduction in the amount of an outstanding loan, which increases or reduces those costs, the amount to be met under this Schedule shall, for the purposes of the claim for income support, be recalculated so as to take account of that change.]

Circumstances in which a person is liable to meet housing costs

2.—(1) A person is liable to meet housing costs where—
(a) the liability falls upon him or his partner but not where the liability is to a member of the same household as the person on whom the liability falls;
(b) because the person liable to meet the housing costs is not meeting them, the claimant has to meet those costs in order to continue to live in the dwelling occupied as the home and it is reasonable in all the circumstances to treat the claimant as liable to meet those costs;
(c) he in practice shares the housing costs with other members of the household none of whom are close relatives either of the claimant or his partner, and
(i) one or more of those members is liable to meet those costs, and
(ii) it is reasonable in the circumstances to treat him as sharing responsibility.

(2) Where any one or more, but not all, members of the claimant's family are affected by a trade dispute, the housing costs shall be treated as wholly the responsibility of those members of the family not so affected.

Circumstances in which a person is to be treated as occupying a dwelling as his home

3.—(1) Subject to the following provisions of this paragraph, a person shall be treated as occupying as his home the dwelling normally occupied as his home by himself or, if he is a member of a family, by himself and his family and he shall not be treated as occupying any other dwelling as his home.

(2) In determining whether a dwelling is the dwelling normally occupied as the claimant's home for the purposes of sub-paragraph (1) regard shall be had to any other dwell-

ing occupied by the claimant or by him and his family whether or not that other dwelling is in Great Britain.

(3) Subject to sub-paragraph (4), where a single claimant or a lone parent is a student or is on a training course and is liable to make payments (including payments of mortgage interest or, in Scotland, payments under heritable securities or, in either case, analogous payments) in respect of either (but not both) the dwelling which he occupies for the purpose of attending his course of study or his training course or, as the case may be, the dwelling which he occupies when not attending his course, he shall be treated as occupying as his home the dwelling in respect of which he is liable to make payments.

(4) A full-time student shall not be treated as occupying a dwelling as his home for any week of absence from it, other than an absence occasioned by the need to enter hospital for treatment, outside the period of study, if the main purpose of his occupation during the period of study would be to facilitate attendance on his course.

(5) Where a claimant has been required to move into temporary accommodation by reason of essential repairs being carried out to the dwelling normally occupied as his home and he is liable to make payments (including payments of mortgage interest or, in Scotland, payments under heritable securities or, in either case, analogous payments) in respect of either (but not both) the dwelling normally occupied or the temporary accommodation, he shall be treated as occupying as his home the dwelling in respect of which he is liable to make those payments.

(6) Where a person is liable to make payments in respect of two (but not more than two) dwellings, he shall be treated as occupying both dwellings as his home only—

(a) where he has left and remains absent from the former dwelling occupied as the home through fear of violence in that dwelling or by a former member of his family and it is reasonable that housing costs should be met in respect of both his former dwelling and his present dwelling occupied as the home; or

(b) in the case of a couple or a member of a polygamous marriage where a partner is a student or is on a training course and it is unavoidable that he or they should occupy two separate dwellings and reasonable that housing costs should be met in respect of both dwellings; or

(c) in the case where a person has moved into a new dwelling occupied as the home, except where sub-paragraph (5) applies, for a period not exceeding four benefit weeks if his liability to make payments in respect of two dwellings is unavoidable.

(7) Where—

(a) a person has moved into a dwelling and was liable to make payments in respect of that dwelling before moving in; and

(b) he had claimed income support before moving in and either that claim has not yet been determined or it has been determined but an amount has not been included under this Schedule and if the claim has been refused a further claim has been made within four weeks of the date on which the claimant moved into the new dwelling occupied as the home; and

(c) the delay in moving into the dwelling in respect of which there was liability to make payments before moving in was reasonable and—

    (i) that delay was necessary in order to adapt the dwelling to meet the disablement needs of the claimant or any member of his family; or

    (ii) the move was delayed pending the outcome of an application under Part VIII of the Contributions and Benefits Act for a social fund payment to met a need arising out of the move or in connection with setting up the home in the dwelling and either a member of the claimant's family is aged five or under or the claimant's applicable amount includes a premium under paragraph 9, 9A, 10, 11, 13 or 14 of Schedule 2; or

    (iii) the person became liable to make payments in respect of the dwelling while he was a patient or was in residential accommodation,

he shall be treated as occupying the dwelling as his home for any period not exceeding four weeks immediately prior to the date on which he moved into the dwelling and in respect of which he was liable to make payments.

(8) This sub-paragraph applies to a person who enters residential accommodation—

(a) for the purpose of ascertaining whether the accommodation suits his needs; and

(b) with the intention of returning to the dwelling which he normally occupies as his home should, in the event, the residential accommodation prove not to suit his needs,

and while in the accommodation, the part of the dwelling which he normally occupies as his home is not let, or as the case may be, sub-let to another person.

(9) A person to whom sub-paragraph (8) applies shall be treated as occupying the dwelling he normally occupies as his home during any period (commencing with the day he enters the accommodation) not exceeding 13 weeks in which the person is resident in the accommodation, but only in so far as the total absence from the dwelling does not exceed 52 weeks.

(10) A person, other than a person to whom sub-paragraph (11) applies, shall be treated as occupying a dwelling as his home throughout any period of absence not exceeding 13 weeks, if, and only if—

(a) he intends to return to occupy the dwelling as his home; and

(b) the part of the dwelling normally occupied by him has not been let or, as the case may be, sub-let to another person; and

(c) the period of absence is unlikely to exceed 13 weeks.

(11) This sub-paragraph applies to a person whose absence from the dwelling he normally occupies as his home is temporary and—

(a) he intends to return to occupy the dwelling as his home; and

(b) while the part of the dwelling which is normally occupied by him has not been let or, as the case may be, sub-let; and

(c) he is—

    (i) detained in custody on remand pending trial or, as a condition of bail, required to reside in a hostel approved under section 27(1) of the Probation Service Act 1993, or, as the case may be, detained pending sentence upon conviction, or

    (ii) resident in a hospital or similar institution as a patient, or

    (iii) undergoing or, as the case may be, his partner or his dependent child is undergoing, in the United Kingdom or elsewhere, medical treatment, or medically approved convalescence, in accommodation other than residential accommodation, or

    (iv) following, in the United Kingdom or elsewhere, a training course, or

    (v) undertaking medically approved care of a person residing in the United Kingdom or elsewhere, or

    (vi) undertaking the care of a child whose parent or guardian is temporarily absent from the dwelling normally occupied by that parent or guardian for the purpose of receiving medically approved care or medical treatment, or

    (vii) a person who is, whether in the United Kingdom or elsewhere, receiving medically approved care provided in accommodation other than residential accommodation, or

    (viii) a student to whom sub-paragraph (3) or (6)(b) does not apply, or

    (ix) a person other than a person to whom sub-paragraph (8) applies, who is receiving care provided in residential accommodation; or

    (x) a person to whom sub-paragraph (6)(a) does not apply and who has left the dwelling he occupies as his home through fear of violence in that dwelling [², or by a person] who was formerly a member of his family; and

(d) the period of his absence is unlikely to exceed a period of 52 weeks or, in exceptional circumstances, is unlikely substantially to exceed that period.

(12) A person to whom sub-paragraph (11) applies is to be treated as occupying the dwelling he normally occupies as his home during any period of absence not exceeding 52 weeks beginning with the first day of that absence.

(13) In this paragraph—

(a) "medically approved" means certified by a medical practitioner;

(b) "patient" means a person who is undergoing medical or other treatment as an in-patient in a hospital or similar institution;

(c) "residential accommodation" means accommodation—

    (i) provided under sections 21 to 24 and 26 of the National Assistance Act 1948 (provision of accommodation); or

    (ii) provided under sections 13B and 59 of the Social Work (Scotland) Act 1968 (provision of residential and other establishments) where board is available to the claimant; or

    (iii) which is a residential care home within the meaning of that expression in regulation 19(3) (persons in residential care or nursing homes) other than sub-paragraph (b) of that definition; or

    (iv) which is a nursing home;

(d) "training course" means such a course of training or instruction provided wholly or partly by or on behalf of or in pursuance of arrangements made with, or approved by or on behalf of, Scottish Enterprise, Highlands and Islands Enterprise, a government department or the Secretary of State.

Housing costs not met

4.—(1) No amount may be met under the provisions of this Schedule—

(a) in respect of housing benefit expenditure; or

(b) where the claimant is in accommodation which is a residential care home or a nursing home except where he is in such accommodation during a temporary absence from the dwelling he occupies as his home and in so far as they relate to temporary absences, the provisions of paragraph 3(8) to (12) apply to him during that absence.

(2) Subject to the following provisions of this paragraph, loans which, apart from this paragraph qualify under paragraph 15 shall not so qualify where the loan was incurred during the relevant period and was incurred—

(a) after 1st October 1995, or

(b) after 2nd May 1994 and the housing costs applicable to that loan were not met by virtue of the former paragraph 5A of this Schedule in any one or more of the 26 weeks preceding 2nd October 1995, or

(c) subject to sub-paragraph (3), in the 26 weeks preceding 2nd October 1995 by a person—

    (i) who was not at that time entitled to income support; and

    (ii) who becomes, or whose partner becomes entitled to income support after 1st October 1995 and that entitlement is within 26 weeks of an earlier entitlement to income support for the claimant or his partner.

(3) Sub-paragraph (2)(c) shall not apply in respect of a loan where the claimant has interest payments on that loan met without restrictions under an award of income support in respect of a period commencing before 2nd October 1995.

[²(4) The "relevant period" for the purposes of this paragraph is any period during which the person to whom the loan was made—

(a) is entitled to income support, or

(b) is living as a member of a family one of whom is entitled to income support, together with any linked period, that is to say a period falling between two such periods of entitlement to income support separated by not more than 26 weeks.]

[⁷(4A) For the purposes of sub-paragraph (4), a person shall be treated as entitled to income support during any period when he or his partner was not so entitled because—

(a) that person or his partner was participating in an employment programme specified in regulation 75(1)(a)(ii) of the Jobseeker's Allowance Regulations 1996; and

(b) in consequence of such participation that person or his partner was engaged in remunerative work or had an income in excess of the claimant's applicable amount as prescribed in Part IV.]

(5) For the purposes of sub-paragraph (4)—

(a) any week in the period of 26 weeks ending on 1st October 1995 on which there arose an entitlement to income support such as is mentioned in that sub-paragraph shall be taken into account in determining when the relevant period commences; and

(b) two or more periods of entitlement and any intervening linked periods shall together form a single relevant period.

(6) Where the loan to which sub-paragraph (2) refers has been applied—

(a) for paying off an earlier loan, and that earlier loan qualified under paragraph 15 [⁴during the relevant period]; or

[⁴(b) to finance the purchase of a property where an earlier loan, which qualified under paragraph 15 or 16 during the relevant period in respect of another property, is paid off (in whole or in part) with monies received from the sale of that property;]

then the amount of the loan to which sub-paragraph (2) applies is the amount (if any) by which the new loan exceeds the earlier loan.

(7) Notwithstanding the preceding provisions of this paragraph, housing costs shall be met in any case where a claimant satisfies any of the conditions specified in sub-paragraphs (8) to (11) below, but—

(a) those costs shall be subject to any additional limitations imposed by the sub-paragraph; and

(b) where the claimant satisfies the conditions in more than one of these sub-paragraphs, only one sub-paragraph shall apply in his case and the one that applies shall be the one most favourable to him.

(8) The conditions specified in this sub-paragraph are that—

(a) during the relevant period the claimant or a member of his family acquires an interest (''the relevant interest'') in a dwelling which he then occupies or continues to occupy, as his home; and

(b) in the week preceding the week in which the relevant interest was acquired, housing benefit was payable to the claimant or a member of his family;

so however that the amount to be met by way of [². . .] housing costs shall initially not exceed the aggregate of—

    (i) the housing benefit payable in the week mentioned at sub-paragraph (8)(b); and

    (ii) any amount included in the applicable amount of the claimant or a member of his family in accordance with regulation 17(1)(e) or 18(1)(f) in that week;

and shall be increased subsequently only to the extent that it is necessary to take account of any increase, arising after the date of the acquisition, in the standard rate or in any housing costs which qualify under paragraph 17 (other housing costs).

(9) The condition specified in this sub-paragraph is that the loan was taken out, or an existing loan increased, to acquire alternative accommodation more suited to the special needs of a disabled person than the accommodation which was occupied before the acquisition by the claimant.

(10) The conditions specified in this sub-paragraph are that—

(a) the loan commitment increased in consequence of the disposal of the dwelling occupied as the home and the acquisition of an alternative such dwelling; and

(b) the change of dwelling was made solely by reason of the need to provide separate sleeping accommodation for children of different sexes aged 10 or over who belong to the same family as the claimant.

(11) The conditions specified in this sub-paragraph are that—

(a) during the relevant period the claimant or a member of his family acquires an interest (''the relevant interest'') in a dwelling which he then occupies as his home; and

(b) in the week preceding the week in which the relevant interest was acquired, the applicable amount of the claimant or a member of his family included an amount determined by reference to paragraph 17 and did not include any amount specified in paragraph 15 or paragraph 16;

so however that the amount to be met [²by way of housing costs] shall initially not exceed the amount so determined, and shall be increased subsequently only to the extent that it is necessary to take account of any increase, arising after the date of acquisition, in the standard rate or in any housing costs which qualify under paragraph 17 (other housing costs).

(12) The following provisions of this Schedule shall have effect subject to the provisions of this paragraph.

Apportionment of housing costs

5.—(1) Where the dwelling occupied as the home is a composite hereditament and—

(a) before 1st April 1990 for the purposes of section 48(5) of the General Rate Act 1967 (reduction of rates on dwellings), it appeared to a rating authority or it was determined in pursuance of subsection (6) of section 48 of that Act that the hereditament, including the dwelling occupied as the home, was a mixed hereditament and that only a proportion of the rateable value of the hereditament was attributable to use for the purpose of a private dwelling; or

(b) in Scotland, before 1st April 1989 an assessor acting pursuant to section 45(1) of the Water (Scotland) Act 1980 (provision as to valuation roll) has apportioned the net annual value of the premises including the dwelling occupied as the home between the part occupied as a dwelling and the remainder,

the amounts applicable under this Schedule shall be such proportion of the amounts applicable in respect of the hereditament or premises as a whole as is equal to the proportion of the rateable value of the hereditament attributable to the part of the hereditament used for the purposes of a private tenancy or, in Scotland, the proportion of the net annual value of the premises apportioned to the part occupied as a dwelling house.

(2) Subject to sub-paragraph (1) and the following provisions of this paragraph, where the dwelling occupied as the home is a composite hereditament, the amount applicable under this Schedule shall be the relevant fraction of the amount which would otherwise be applicable under this Schedule in respect of the dwelling occupied as the home.

(3) For the purposes of sub-paragraph (2), the relevant fraction shall be obtained in accordance with the formula—

$$\frac{A}{A + B}$$

where—

"A" is the current market value of the claimant's interest in that part of the composite hereditament which is domestic property within the meaning of section 66 of the Act of 1988;

"B" is the current market value of the claimant's interest in that part of the composite hereditament which is not domestic property within that section.

(4) In this paragraph—

"composite hereditament" means—

(a) as respects England and Wales, any hereditament which is shown as a composite hereditament in a local non-domestic rating list;

(b) as respects Scotland, any lands and heritages entered in the valuation roll which are part residential subjects within the meaning of section 26(1) of the Act of 1987;

"local non-domestic rating list" means a list compiled and maintained under section 41(1) of the Act of 1988;

"the Act of 1987" means the Abolition of Domestic Rates Etc. (Scotland) Act 1987;

"the Act of 1988" means the Local Government Finance Act 1988.

(5) Where responsibility for expenditure which relates to housing costs met under this

Schedule is shared, the amounts applicable shall be calculated by reference to the appropriate proportion of that expenditure for which the claimant is responsible.

Existing housing costs

6.—(1) Subject to the provisions of this Schedule, the existing housing costs to be met in any particular case are—
- (a) where the claimant has been [²entitled to] income support for a continuous period of 26 weeks or more, the aggregate of—
  - (i) an amount determined in the manner set out in paragraph 10 by applying the standard rate to the eligible capital for the time being owing in connection with a loan which qualifies under paragraph 15 or 16; and
  - (ii) an amount equal to any payments which qualify under paragraph 17(1)(a) to (c);
- (b) where the claimant has been [²entitled to] income support for a continuous period of not less than 8 weeks but less than 26 weeks, an amount which is half the amount which would fall to be met by applying the provisions of sub-paragraph (a);
- (c) in any other case, nil.

[²(1A) For the purposes of sub-paragraph (1) [⁶ and subject to sub-paragraph (1B)], the eligible capital for the time being owning shall be determined on the date the existing housing costs arc first met and thereafter on each anniversary of that date.]

[⁶(1B) Where a claimant or his partner ceases to be in receipt of or treated as being in receipt of income-based jobseeker's allowance and one of them becomes entitled to income support in a case to which paragraph 1A applies, the eligible capital for the time being owing shall be recalculated on each anniversary of the date on which the housing costs were first met for whichever of the benefits concerned the claimant or his partner was first entitled.]

(2) Where immediately before 2nd October 1995 a claimant's applicable amount included a sum by way of housing costs in accordance with regulation 17(1)(e) or 18(1)(f), but the claimant had not on that date been entitled to income support for a continuous period of 26 weeks or more, the amount of the housing costs to be met in his case shall, for the balance of the 26 weeks falling after 1st October 1995, be determined in accordance with sub-paragraph (3).

(3) Subject to sub-paragraph (4), where the claimant had on 1st October 1995—
- (a) been entitled to income support for less than 16 consecutive weeks (including the benefit week in which 1st October 1995 falls), any housing costs to be met in his case shall remain at the amount they were before 2nd October 1995 until the end of the 16th consecutive week of that entitlement and shall thereafter be determined as if he had been entitled for a continuous period of 26 weeks;
- (b) been entitled for 16 consecutive weeks or more but less than 26 consecutive weeks (including the benefit week in which 1st October 1995 falls), any housing costs to be met in his case shall be determined as if he had been entitled for 26 weeks.

(4) Sub-paragraph (3) above shall apply in a particular case only for so long as the agreement in respect of which a sum by way of housing costs falls to be met immediately before 2nd October 1995 in accordance with regulation 17(1)(e) or 18(1)(f) remains in force.

Transitional Protection

7.—(1) Where the amount applicable to a claimant by way of housing costs under regulation 17(1)(e) or regulation 18(1)(f) (as the case may be) in the benefit week which includes 1st October 1995 ("the first benefit week") is greater than the amount which, in accordance with paragraphs 6 and 10, is applicable in his case in the next succeeding benefit week ("the second benefit week"), the claimant shall be entitled to have his

345

existing housing costs increased by an amount (referred to in this paragraph as "add back") determined in accordance with the following provisions of this paragraph.

(2) Where the amount to be met by way of housing costs in the first benefit week is greater than the amount to be met in the second benefit week, then the amount of the add back shall be a sum representing the difference between those amounts.

(3) Where the amount of existing housing costs, disregarding the add back, which is applicable to the claimant increases after the second benefit week, the amount of the add back shall be decreased by an amount equal to that increase, and the amount of the add back shall thereafter be the decreased amount.

(4) Any increase in the amount of the existing housing costs, disregarding the add back, shall reduce the amount of the add back in the manner specified in sub-paragraph (3), and where the amount of the add back is reduced to nil, the amount of the existing housing costs shall thereafter not include any amount by way of add back.

(5) Where a person or his partner—

(a) was entitled to income support; and

(b) had an applicable amount which included an amount by way of add back in accordance with this paragraph; and

(c) ceased to be entitled to income support for a continuous period in excess of 12 weeks,

then, on the person or his partner again becoming entitled to income support, the applicable amount of the claimant shall be determined without reference to the provisions relating to add back in sub-paragraphs (1) to (4).

(6) Where a person whose applicable amount included an amount by way of add back under this paragraph loses the right to have an amount by way of housing costs included in his applicable amount, then where that person's applicable amount again includes an amount by way of housing costs, that amount shall be determined without reference to the provisions relating to add back in sub-paragraphs (1) to (4).

(7) Where the partner of a person to whom sub-paragraph (6) applies becomes entitled to income support and—

(a) his applicable amount includes an amount by way of existing housing costs, and

(b) those housing costs are in respect of payments which were formerly met in the applicable amount of the person to whom sub-paragraph (6) applies,

then the provisions of this paragraph shall apply to the partner as they would if he had been responsible for the housing costs immediately before 2nd October 1995 [²provided the claim is made not more than 12 weeks after the last day of entitlement to housing costs relating to a claim made by the person to whom sub-paragraph (6) applies].

(8) Where in the first benefit week, a claimant's applicable amount included an amount by way of housing costs which was calculated by reference to paragraph 7(1)(b)(ii) of Schedule 3 as then in force (50 per cent. of eligible interest met) then for the purposes of this paragraph, the amount of the add back shall be determined by reference to the amount which would have been applicable on that day if 100 per cent. of the claimant's eligible interest had been met, but only from the benefit week following the final benefit week in which paragraph 7(1)(b)(ii) of Schedule 3 would, had it remained in force, have applied in the claimant's case.

(9) Where the existing housing costs of the claimant are determined by reference to two or more loans which qualify under this Schedule, then the provisions of this paragraph shall be applied separately to each of those loans and the amount of the add back (if any) shall be determined in respect of each loan.

[⁹(10) In the case of a person who is a welfare to work beneficiary, the references in sub-paragraphs (5)(c) and (7) to a period of 12 weeks shall be treated as references to a period of 52 weeks.]

New housing costs

8.—(1) Subject to the provisions of this Schedule, the new housing costs to be met in any particular case are—

(a) where the claimant has been [²entitled to] income support for a continuous period of 39 weeks or more, an amount—
  (i) determined in the manner set out in paragraph 10 by applying the standard rate to the eligible capital for the time being owing in connection with a loan which qualifies under paragraph 15 or 16; and
  (ii) equal to any payments which qualify under paragraph 17(1)(a) to (c);
(b) in any other case, nil.

[²(1A) For the purposes of sub-paragraph (1) [⁶ and subject to sub-paragraph (1B),] the eligible capital for the time being owing shall be determined on the date the new housing costs are first met and thereafter on each anniversary of that date.]

[⁶(1B) Where a claimant or his partner ceases to be in receipt of or treated as being in receipt of income-based jobseeker's allowance and one of them becomes entitled to income support in a case to which paragraph 1A applies, the eligible capital for the time being owning shall be recalculated on each anniversary of the date on which the housing costs were first met for whichever of the benefits concerned the claimant or his partner was first entitled.]

(2) This sub-paragraph applies to a claimant who at the time the claim is made—
[³(a) is a person to whom paragraph 4 or 5 of Schedule 1B (persons caring for another person) applies;]
(b) is detained in custody pending trial or sentence upon conviction; or
(c) has been refused payments under a policy of insurance on the ground that—
  (i) the claim under the policy is the outcome of a pre-existing medical condition which, under the terms of the policy, does not give rise to any payment by the insurer; or
  (ii) he was infected by the Human Immunodeficiency Virus,
and the policy was taken out to insure against the risk of being unable to maintain repayments on a loan which is secured by a mortgage or a charge over land, or (in Scotland) by a heritable security.

(3) This sub-paragraph applies subject to sub-paragraph (5) where a person claims income support because of—
(a) the death of a partner; or
(b) being abandoned by his partner,
and where the person's family includes a child.

(4) In the case of a claimant to whom sub-paragraph (2) or (3) applies, any new housing costs shall be met as though they were existing housing costs and paragraph 6 applied to them.

(5) Sub-paragraph (3) shall cease to apply to a person who subsequently becomes one of a couple.

General exclusions from paragraphs 6 and 8

9.—(1) Paragraphs 6 and 8 shall not apply where—
(a) the claimant or his partner is aged 60 or over;
(b) the housing costs are payments—
  (i) under a co-ownership agreement;
  (ii) under or relating to a tenancy or licence of a Crown tenant; or
  (iii) where the dwelling occupied as the home is a tent, in respect of the tent and the site on which it stands.
(2) In a case falling within sub-paragraph (1), the housing costs to be met are—
(a) where head (a) of sub-paragraph (1) applies, an amount—
  (i) determined in the manner set out in paragraph 10 by applying the standard rate to the eligible capital for the time being owing in connection with a loan which qualifies under paragraph 15 or 16; and
  (ii) equal to the payments which qualify under paragraph 17;
(b) where head (b) of sub-paragraph (1) applies, an amount equal to the payments which qualify under paragraph 17(1)(d) to (f).

The calculation for loans

10.—(1) The weekly amount of existing housing costs or, as the case may be, new housing costs to be met under this Schedule in respect of a loan which qualifies under paragraph 15 or 16 shall be calculated by applying the formula:—

$$\frac{(A \times B) \times C}{52}$$

where—

A = the amount of the loan which qualifies under paragraph 15 or 16;

B = the standard rate for the time being specified in respect of that loan under paragraph 12;

C = the difference between 100 per cent. and the applicable percentage of income tax within the meaning of section 369(1A) of the Income and Corporation Taxes Act 1988 (mortgage interest payable under deduction of tax) for the year of assessment in which the payment of interest becomes due.

(2) Where section 369 of the Income and Corporation Taxes Act 1988 does not apply to the interest on a loan or a part of a loan, the formula applied in sub-paragraph (1) shall have effect as if C had a value of 1.

General provisions applying to new and existing housing costs

11.—(1) [².. .].

(2) Where on or after 2nd October 1995 a person enters into a new agreement in respect of a dwelling and an agreement entered into before 2nd October 1995 ("the earlier agreement") continues in force independently of the new agreement, then—

  (a) the housing costs applicable to the new agreement shall be calculated by reference to the provisions of paragraph 8 (new housing costs);

  (b) the housing costs applicable to the earlier agreement shall be calculated by reference to the provisions of paragraph 6 (existing housing costs);

and the resulting amounts shall be aggregated.

(3) [²Sub-paragraph (2) does] not apply in the case of a claimant to whom paragraph 9 applies.

(4) Where for the time being a loan exceeds, or in a case where more than one loan is to be taken into account, the aggregate of those loans exceeds the appropriate amount specified in sub-paragraph (5), then the amount of the loan or, as the case may be, the aggregate amount of those loans, shall for the purposes of this Schedule, be the appropriate amount.

(5) Subject to the following provisions of this paragraph, the appropriate amount is £100,000.

(6) Where a person is treated under paragraph 3(6) (payments in respect of two dwellings) as occupying two dwellings as his home, then the restrictions imposed by sub-paragraph (4) shall be applied separately to the loans for each dwelling.

(7) In a case to which paragraph 5 (apportionment of housing costs) applies, the appropriate amount for the purposes of sub-paragraph (4) shall be the lower of—

  (a) a sum determined by applying the formula—

    P × Q, where—

    P = the relevant fraction for the purposes of paragraph 5, and

    Q = the amount or, as the case may be, the aggregate amount for the time being of any loan or loans which qualify under this Schedule; or

  (b) the sum for the time being specified in sub-paragraph (5).

(8) In a case to which paragraph 15(3) or 16(3) (loans which qualify in part only) applies, the appropriate amount for the purposes of sub-paragraph (4) shall be the lower of—

  (a) a sum representing for the time being the part of the loan applied for the purposes specified in paragraph 15(1) or (as the case may be) paragraph 16(1); or

(b) the sum for the time being specified in sub-paragraph (5).

(9) In the case of any loan to which paragraph 16(2)(k) (loan taken out and used for the purpose of adapting a dwelling for the special needs of a disabled person) applies the whole of the loan, to the extent that it remains unpaid, shall be disregarded in determining whether the amount for the time being specified in sub-paragraph (5) is exceeded.

[²(10) Where in any case the amount for the time being specified for the purposes of sub-paragraph (5) is exceeded and there are two or more loans to be taken into account under either or both paragraphs 15 and 16, then the amount of eligible interest in respect of each of those loans to the extent that the loans remain outstanding shall be determined as if each loan had been reduced to a sum equal to the qualifying portion of that loan.

(11) For the purposes of sub-paragraph (10), the qualifying portion of a loan shall be determined by applying the following formula—

$$R \times \frac{S}{T}$$

where—

R = the amount for the time being specified for the purposes of sub-paragraph (4);
S = the amount of the outstanding loan to be taken into account;
T = the aggregate of all outstanding loans to be taken into account under paragraphs 15 and 16.]

The standard rate

12.—(1) The standard rate is the rate of interest applicable to a loan which qualifies under this Schedule and—

(a) except where sub-paragraph (2) applies, is [¹³6.66 per cent.] per annum; or
(b) where sub-paragraph (2) applies, shall equal the actual rate of interest charged on the loan on the day the housing costs first fall to be met.

(2) This sub-paragraph applies where the actual rate of interest charged on the loan which qualifies under this Schedule is less than 5 per cent. per annum on the day the housing costs first fall to be met and ceases to apply when the actual rate of interest on that loan is 5 per cent. per annum or higher.

(3) Where in a case to which sub-paragraph (2) applies, the actual rate of interest on the loan rises to 5 per cent. per annum or higher, the standard rate applicable on that loan shall be determined in accordance with sub-paragraph (1)(a).

(4) [²...]

Excessive Housing Costs

13.—(1) Housing costs which, apart from this paragraph, fall to be met under this Schedule shall be met only to the extent specified in sub-paragraph (3) where—

(a) the dwelling occupied as the home, excluding any part which is let, is larger than is required by the claimant and his family and any child or young person to whom regulation 16(4) applies (foster children) and any other non-dependants having regard, in particular, to suitable alternative accommodation occupied by a household of the same size; or
(b) the immediate area in which the dwelling occupied as the home is located is more expensive than other areas in which suitable alternative accommodation exists; or
(c) the outgoings of the dwelling occupied as the home which are met under paragraphs 15 to 17 are higher than the outgoings of suitable alternative accommodation in the area.

(2) For the purposes of heads (a) to (c) of sub-paragraph (1), no regard shall be had to the capital value of the dwelling occupied as the home.

(3) Subject to the following provisions of this paragraph, the amount of the loan which falls to be met shall be restricted and the excess over the amounts which the claimant would need to obtain suitable alternative accommodation shall not be allowed.

(4) Where, having regard to the relevant factors, it is not reasonable to expect the claimant and his family to seek alternative cheaper accommodation, no restriction shall be made under sub-paragraph (3).

(5) In sub-paragraph (4) "the relevant factors" are—

(a) the availability of suitable accommodation and the level of housing costs in the area; and

(b) the circumstances of the family including in particular the age and state of health of its members, the employment prospects of the claimant and, where a change in accommodation is likely to result in a change of school, the effect on the education of any child or young person who is a member of his family, or any child or young person who is not treated as part of his family by virtue of regulation 16(4) (foster children).

(6) Where sub-paragraph (4) does not apply and the claimant (or other member of the family) was able to meet the financial commitments for the dwelling occupied as the home when these were entered into, no restriction shall be made under this paragraph during the first 26 weeks of any period of entitlement to income support nor during the next 26 weeks if and so long as the claimant uses his best endeavours to obtain cheaper accommodation or, as the case may be, no restriction shall be made under this paragraph on review during the 26 weeks from the date of the review nor during the next 26 weeks if and so long as the claimant uses his best endeavours.

(7) For the purposes of calculating any period of 26 weeks referred to in sub-paragraph (6), and for those purposes only, a person shall be treated as entitled to income support for any period of 12 weeks or less in respect of which he was not in receipt of income support and which fell immediately between periods in respect of which he was in receipt thereof.

(8) Any period in respect of which—

(a) income support was paid to a person, and

(b) it was subsequently determined on appeal or review that he was not entitled to income support for that period,

shall be treated for the purposes of sub-paragraph (7) as a period in respect of which he was not in receipt of income support.

(9) Heads (c) to (f) of sub-paragraph (1) of paragraph 14 shall apply to sub-paragraph (7) as they apply to paragraphs 6 and 8 but with the modification that the words "Subject to sub-paragraph (2)" were omitted and references to "the claimant" were references to the person mentioned in sub-paragraph (7).

Linking rule

14.—(1) Subject to sub-paragraph (2), for the purposes of this Schedule—

(a) a person shall be treated as being in receipt of income support during the following periods—

    (i) any period in respect of which it was subsequently held, on appeal or review, that he was entitled to income support; and

    (ii) any period of 12 weeks or less in respect of which he was not in receipt of income support and which fell immediately between periods in respect of which

        [⁴(aa) he was, or was treated as being, in receipt of income support,

        (bb) he was treated as entitled to income support for the purpose of sub-paragraph (5) or (5A), or

        (cc) (i) above applies;]

(b) a person shall be treated as not being in receipt of income support during any period other than a period to which (a)(ii) above applies in respect of which it is subsequently held on appeal or review that he was not so entitled;

(c) where—

    (i) the claimant was a member of a couple or a polygamous marriage; and

    (ii) his partner was, in respect of a past period, in receipt of income support for himself and the claimant; and

    (iii) the claimant is no longer a member of that couple or polygamous marriage; and

    (iv) the claimant made his claim for income support within twelve weeks of ceasing to be a member of that couple or polygamous marriage,

he shall be treated as having been in receipt of income support for the same period as his former partner had been or had been treated, for the purposes of this Schedule, as having been;

  (d) where the claimant's partner's applicable amount was determined in accordance with paragraph 1(1) (single claimant) or paragraph 1(2) (lone parent) of Schedule 2 (applicable amounts) in respect of a past period, provided that the claim was made within twelve weeks of the claimant and his partner becoming one of a couple or polygamous marriage, the claimant shall be treated as having been in receipt of income support for the same period as his partner had been or had been treated, for the purposes of this Schedule, as having been;

  (e) where the claimant is a member of a couple or a polygamous marriage and his partner was, in respect of a past period, in receipt of income support for himself and the claimant, and the claimant has begun to receive income support as a result of an election by the members of the couple or polygamous marriage, he shall be treated as having been in receipt of income support for the same period as his partner had been or had been treated, for the purposes of this Schedule, as having been;

[⁷(ee) where the claimant—

    (i) is a member of a couple or a polygamous marriage and the claimant's partner was, immediately before the participation by any member of that couple or polygamous marriage in an employment programme specified in regulation 75(1)(a)(ii) of the Jobseeker's Allowance Regulations 1996, in receipt of income support and his applicable amount included an amount for the couple or for the partners of the polygamous marriage; and

    (ii) has, immediately after that participation in that programme, begun to receive income support as a result of an election under regulation 4(3) of the Social Security (Claims and Payments) Regulations 1987 by the members of the couple or polygamous marriage,

the claimant shall be treated as having been in receipt of income support for the same period as his partner had been or had been treated, for the purposes of this Schedule, as having been;]

  (f) where—

    (i) the claimant was a member of a family of a person (not being a former partner) entitled to income support and at least one other member of that family was a child or young person; and

    (ii) the claimant becomes a member of another family which includes that child or young person; and

    (iii) the claimant made his claim for income support within 12 weeks of the date on which the person entitled to income support mentioned in (i) above ceased to be so entitled,

the claimant shall be treated as being in receipt of income support for the same period as that person had been or had been treated, for the purposes of this Schedule, as having been.

(2) Where a claimant, with the care of a child, has ceased to be in receipt of income support in consequence of the payment of child support maintenance under the Child Support Act 1991 and immediately before ceasing to be so in receipt an amount determined in accordance with paragraph 6(1)(a)(i) or paragraph 8(1)(a)(i) was applicable to him, then—

  (a) if the child support maintenance assessment concerned is terminated or replaced on review by a lower assessment in consequence of the coming into force on or after 18th April 1995 of regulations made under the Child Support Act 1991; or

(b) where the child support maintenance assessment concerned is an interim maintenance assessment and, in circumstances other than those referred to in head (a), it is terminated or replaced after termination by another interim maintenance assessment or by a maintenance assessment made in accordance with Part I of Schedule 1 to the Child Support Act 1991, in either case of a lower amount than the assessment concerned,

sub-paragraph (1)(a)(ii) shall apply to him as if for the words "any period of 12 weeks or less" there were substituted the words "any period of 26 weeks or less".

(3) For the purposes of this Schedule, where a claimant has ceased to be entitled to income support because he or his partner is participating in arrangements for training made under section 2 of the Employment and Training Act 1973 or attending a course at an employment rehabilitation centre established under that section, he shall be treated as if he had been in receipt of income support for the period during which he or his partner was participating in such arrangements or attending such a course.

[⁷(3ZA) For the purposes of this Schedule, a claimant who has ceased to be entitled to income support because—

(a) that claimant or his partner was participating in an employment programme specified in reglation 75(1)(a)(ii) of the Jobseeker's Allowance Regulations 1996; and

(b) in consequence of such participation the claimant or his partner was engaged in remunerative work or had an income in excess of the claimant's applicable amount as prescribed in Part IV,

shall be treated as if he had been in receipt of income support for the period during which he or his partner was participating in that programme.]

[²(3A) Where, for the purposes of sub-paragraphs [⁷(1), (3) and (3ZA)], a person is treated as being in receipt of income support, for a certain period, he shall be treated as being entitled to income support for the same period.]

[⁷(3B) For the purposes of this Schedule, in determining whether a person is entitled to or to be treated as entitled to income support, entitlement to a contribution-based jobseeker's allowance immediately before a period during which that person or his partner is participating in an employment programme specified in regulation 75(1)(a)(ii) of the Jobseeker's Allowance Regulations 1996 shall be treated as entitlement to income support for the purposes of any requirement that a person is, or has been, entitled to income support for any period of time.]

(4) For the purposes of this Schedule, sub-paragraph (5) applies where a person is not entitled to income support by reason only that he has—

(a) capital exceeding £8,000; or

(b) income exceeding the applicable amount which applies in his case, or

(c) both capital exceeding £8,000 and income exceeding the applicable amount which applies in his case.

(5) A person to whom sub-paragraph (4) applies shall be treated as entitled to income support throughout any period of not [²more] than 39 weeks which comprises only days—

(a) on which he is entitled to unemployment benefit, [³a contribution-based jobseeker's allowance,] statutory sick pay or incapacity benefit; or

(b) on which he is, although not entitled to any of the benefits mentioned in head (a) above, entitled to be credited with earnings equal to the lower earnings limit for the time being in force in accordance with [¹²regulation 8A or 8B] of the Social Security (Credits) Regulations 1975; or

(c) in respect of which the claimant is treated as being in receipt of income support.

[²(5A) Subject to sub-paragraph (5B), a person to whom sub-paragraph (4) applies and who is either a person to whom [³paragraph 4 or 5 of Schedule 1B (persons caring for another person) applies] or a lone parent shall, for the purposes of this Schedule, be treated as entitled to income support throughout any period of not more than 39 weeks following the refusal of a claim for income support made by or on behalf of that person.

(5B) Sub-paragraph (5A) shall not apply in relation to a person mentioned in that sub-paragraph who, during the period referred to in that sub-paragraph—

(a) is engaged in, or is treated as engaged in, remunerative work or whose partner is engaged in, or is treated as engaged in, remunerative work;

[³(b) is a student, other than one who would qualify for income support under regulation 4ZA(3) (prescribed categories of person);]

(c) is temporarily absent from Great Britain, other than in the circumstances specified in regulation 4(2) and (3)(c) (temporary absence from Great Britain).]

(6) In a case where—

(a) [²sub-paragraphs (5) and (5A) apply] solely by virtue of sub-paragraph (4)(b); and

(b) the claimant's income includes payments under a policy taken out to insure against the risk that the policy holder is unable to meet any loan or payment which qualifies under paragraphs 15 to 17,

[²sub-paragraphs (5) and (5A)] shall have effect as if for the words "throughout any period of not [²more] than 39 weeks" there shall be substituted the words "throughout any period that payments made in accordance with the terms of the policy".

(7) [². . .]

(8) This sub-paragraph applies—

(a) to a person who claims income support, or in respect of whom income support is claimed, and who—

(i) received payments under a policy of insurance taken out to insure against loss of employment, and those payments are exhausted; and

(ii) had a previous award of income support where the applicable amount included an amount by way of housing costs; and

(b) where the period in respect of which the previous award of income support was payable ended not more than 26 weeks before the date the claim was made.

(9) Where sub-paragraph (8) applies, in determining—

(a) for the purposes of paragraph 6(1) whether a person has been [²entitled to] income support for a continuous period of 26 weeks or more; or

(b) for the purposes of paragraph 8(1) whether a claimant has been [²entitled to] income support for a continuous period of 39 weeks or more,

any week falling between the date of the termination of the previous award and the date of the new claim shall be ignored.

[¹⁰(10) In the case of a person who is a welfare to work beneficiary, the references in sub-paragraphs (1)(a)(ii), (1)(d) and (1)(f)(iii) to a period of 12 weeks shall be treated as references to a period of 52 weeks.]

Loans on residential property

15.—(1) A loan qualifies under this paragraph where the loan was taken out to defray monies applied for any of the following purposes—

(a) acquiring an interest in the dwelling occupied as the home; or

(b) paying off another loan to the extent that the other loan would have qualified under head (a) above had the loan not been paid off.

(2) For the purposes of this paragraph, references to a loan include also a reference to money borrowed under a hire purchase agreement for any purpose specified in heads (a) and (b) of sub-paragraph (1) above.

(3) Where a loan is applied only in part for the purposes specified in heads (a) and (b) of sub-paragraph (1), only that portion of the loan which is applied for that purpose shall qualify under this paragraph.

Loans for repairs and improvements to the dwelling occupied as the home

16.—(1) A loan qualifies under this paragraph where the loan was taken out, with or without security, for the purpose of—

(a) carrying out repairs and improvements to the dwelling occupied as the home;

    (b) paying any service charge imposed to meet the cost of repairs and improvements to the dwelling occupied as the home;

    (c) paying off another loan to the extent that the other loan would have qualified under head (a) or (b) of this sub-paragraph had the loan not been paid off,

and the loan was used for that purpose, or is used for that purpose within 6 months of the date of receipt or such further period as may be reasonable in the particular circumstances of the case.

(2) In sub-paragraph (1) "repairs and improvements" means any of the following measures undertaken with a view to maintaining the fitness of the dwelling for human habitation or, where the dwelling forms part of a building, any part of the building containing that dwelling—

    (a) provision of a fixed bath, shower, wash basin, sink or lavatory, and necessary associated plumbing, including the provision of hot water not connected to a central heating system;

    (b) repairs to existing heating systems;

    (c) damp proof measures;

    (d) provision of ventilation and natural lighting;

    (e) provision of drainage facilities;

    (f) provision of facilities for preparing and cooking food;

    (g) provision of insulation of the dwelling occupied as the home;

    (h) provision of electric lighting and sockets;

    (i) provision of storage facilities for fuel or refuse;

    (j) repairs of unsafe structural defects;

    (k) adapting a dwelling for the special needs of a disabled person; or

    (l) provision of separate sleeping accommodation for children of different sexes aged 10 or over who are part of the same family as the claimant.

(3) Where a loan is applied only in part for the purposes specified in sub-paragraph (1), only that portion of the loan which is applied for that purpose shall qualify under this paragraph.

Other housing costs

17.—(1) Subject to the deduction specified in sub-paragraph (2) and the reductions applicable in sub-paragraph (5), there shall be met under this paragraph the amounts, calculated on a weekly basis, in respect of the following housing costs—

    (a) payments by way of rent or ground rent relating to a long tenancy and, in Scotland, payments by way of feu duty;

    (b) service charges;

    (c) payments by way of rentcharge within the meaning of section 1 of the Rentcharges Act 1977;

    (d) payments under a co-ownership scheme;

    (e) payments under or relating to a tenancy or licence of a Crown tenant;

    (f) where the dwelling occupied as the home is a tent, payments in respect of the tent and the site on which it stands.

(2) Subject to sub-paragraph (3), the deductions to be made from the weekly amounts to be met under this paragraph are—

    (a) where the costs are inclusive of any of the items mentioned in paragraph 5(2) of Schedule 1 to the Housing Benefit (General) Regulations 1987 (payment in respect of fuel charges), the deductions prescribed in that paragraph unless the claimant provides evidence on which the actual or approximate amount of the service charge for fuel may be estimated, in which case the estimated amount;

    (b) where the costs are inclusive of ineligible service charges within the meaning of paragraph 1 of Schedule 1 to the Housing Benefit (General) Regulations 1987 (ineligible service charges) the amounts attributable to those ineligible service charges or where that amount is not separated from or separately identified within the housing costs to be met under this paragraph, such part of the payments made in respect of those housing costs which are fairly attributable to the provision of those ineligible services having regard to the costs of comparable services;

(c) any amount for repairs and improvements, and for this purpose the expression "repairs and improvements" has the same meaning it has in paragraph 16(2).

(3) Where arrangements are made for the housing costs, which are met under this paragraph and which are normally paid for a period of 52 weeks, to be paid instead for a period of 53 weeks, or to be paid irregularly, or so that no such costs are payable or collected in certain periods, or so that the costs for different periods in the year are of different amounts, the weekly amount shall be the amount payable for the year divided by 52.

(4) Where the claimant or a member of his family—

(a) pays for reasonable repairs or redecorations to be carried out to the dwelling they occupy; and

(b) that work was not the responsibility of the claimant or any member of his family; and

(c) in consequence of that work being done, the costs which are normally met under this paragraph are waived,

then those costs shall, or a period not exceeding 8 weeks, be treated as payable.

(5) Where in England and Wales an amount calculated on a weekly basis in respect of housing costs specified in sub-paragraph (1)(e) (Crown tenants) includes water charges, that amount shall be reduced—

(a) where the amount payable in respect of water charges is known, by that amount;

(b) in any other case, by the amount which would be the likely weekly water charge had the property not been occupied by a Crown tenant.

Non-dependant deductions

18.—(1) Subject to the following provisions of this paragraph, the following deductions from the amount to be met under the preceding paragraphs of this Schedule in respect of housing costs shall be made—

[⁸(a) in respect of a non-dependent aged 18 or over who is engaged in any renumerative work, [¹¹£46.35];]

(b) in respect of a non-dependant aged 18 or over to whom head (a) does not apply, [¹¹£7.20].

(2) In the case of a non-dependant aged 18 or over to whom sub-paragraph (1)(a) applies because he is in [²remunerative] work, where the claimant satisfies the adjudication officer that the non-dependant's gross weekly income is—

(a) less than [¹¹£80.00], the deduction to be made under this paragraph shall be the deduction specified in sub-paragraph (1)(b);

(b) not less than [¹¹£80.00] but less than [¹¹£118.00], the deduction to be made under this paragraph shall be [¹¹£16.50];

(c) not less than [¹¹£118.00] but less than [¹¹£155.00], the deduction to be made under this paragraph shall be [¹¹£22.65];

[⁸(d) not less than [¹¹£155.00] but less than [¹¹£204.00], the deduction to be made under this paragraph shall be [¹¹£37.10];

(e) not less than [¹¹£204.00] but less [¹¹£255.00], the deduction to be made under this paragraph shall be [¹¹£42.25]].

(3) Only one deduction shall be made under this paragraph in respect of a couple or, as the case may be, the members of a polygamous marriage, and where, but for this sub-paragraph, the amount that would fall to be deducted in respect of one member of a couple or polygamous marriage is higher than the amount (if any) that would fall to be deducted in respect of the other, or any other, member, the higher amount shall be deducted.

(4) In applying the provisions of sub-paragraph (2) in the case of a couple or, as the case may be, a polygamous marriage, regard shall be had, for the purpose of sub-

paragraph (2), to the couple's or, as the case may be, all the members of the polygamous marriage's, joint weekly income.

(5) Where a person is a non-dependant in respect of more than one joint occupier of a dwelling (except where the joint occupiers are a couple or members of a polygamous marriage), the deduction in respect of that non-dependant shall be apportioned between the joint occupiers (the amount so apportioned being rounded to the nearest penny) having regard to the number of joint occupiers and the proportion of the housing costs in respect of the dwelling occupied as the home payable by each of them.

(6) No deduction shall be made in respect of any non-dependants occupying the dwelling occupied as the home of the claimant, if the claimant or any partner of his is—

(a) blind or treated as blind by virtue of paragraph 12 of Schedule 2 (additional condition for the higher pensioner and disability premiums); or

(b) receiving in respect of himself either—
    (i) an attendance allowance; or
    (ii) the care component of the disability living allowance.

(7) No deduction shall be made in respect of a non-dependant—

(a) if, although he resides with the claimant, it appears to the adjudication officer that the dwelling occupied as his home is normally elsewhere; or

(b) if he is in receipt of a training allowance paid in connection with a Youth Training Scheme established under section 2 of the Employment and Training Act 1973 or section 2 of the Enterprise and New Towns (Scotland) Act 1990; or

(c) if he is a full-time student during a period of study or, if he is not in remunerative work, during a recognised summer vacation appropriate to his course; or

(d) if he is aged under 25 and in receipt of income support [⁵or an income-based jobseeker's allowance]; or

(e) in respect of whom a deduction in the calculation of a rent rebate or allowance falls to be made under regulation 63 of the Housing Benefit (General) Regulations 1987 (non-dependant deductions); or

(f) to whom, but for paragraph (2C) of regulation 3 (definition of non-dependant) paragraph (2B) of that regulation would apply; or

(g) if he is not residing with the claimant because he has been a patient for a period in excess of six weeks, or is a prisoner, and for these purposes—
    (i) "patient" and "prisoner" have the meanings given in regulation 21(3) (special cases), and
    (ii) the period of six weeks shall be calculated by reference to paragraph (2) of that regulation as if that paragraph applied in his case.

(8) In the case of a non-dependant to whom sub-paragraph (2) applies because he is in [²remunerative] work, there shall be disregarded from his gross income—

(a) any attendance allowance or disability living allowance received by him;

(b) any payment made under the Macfarlane Trust, the Macfarlane (Special Payments) Trust, the Macfarlane (Special Payments) (No.2) Trust, the Fund, the Eileen Trust or the Independent Living Funds which, had his income fallen to be calculated under regulation 40 (calculation of income other than earnings), would have been disregarded under paragraph 21 of Schedule 9 (income in kind); and

(c) any payment which, had his income fallen to be calculated under regulation 40 would have been disregarded under paragraph 39 of Schedule 9 (payments made under certain trusts and certain other payments).

Rounding of fractions

19. Where any calculation made under this Schedule results in a fraction of a penny, that fraction shall be treated as a penny.]

AMENDMENTS

1. Social Security (Income Support and Claims and Payments) Amendment Regulations 1995 (S.I. 1995 No. 1613), reg. 2 and Sched. 1 (October 2, 1995).

2. Social Security (Income Support, Claims and Payments and Adjudication) Amendment Regulations 1995 (S.I. 1995 No. 2927), reg. 5 (December 12, 1995).

3. Income Support (General) (Jobseeker's Allowance Consequential Amendments) Regulations 1996 (S.I. 1996 No. 206), reg. 24 (October 7, 1996).

4. Income-related Benefits Schemes and Social Fund (Miscellaneous Amendments) Regulations 1996 (S.I. 1996 No. 1944), reg. 6(10) (October 7, 1996).

5. Social Security and Child Support (Miscellaneous Amendments) Regulations 1997 (S.I. 1997 No. 827), reg. 6 (April 7, 1997).

6. Social Security (Miscellaneous Amendments) (No. 4) Regulations 1997 (S.I. 1997 No. 2305), reg. 2 (October 22, 1997).

7. Social Security Amendment (New Deal) Regulations 1997 (S.I. 1997 No. 2863), reg. 16 (January 5, 1998).

8. Social Security (Non-Dependant Deductions) Regulations 1996 (S.I. 1996 No. 2518), reg. 4 (April 6, 1998).

9. Social Security (Welfare to Work) Regulations 1998 (S.I. 1998 No. 2231), reg. 13(4)(a) (October 5, 1998).

10. Social Security (Welfare to Work) Regulations 1998 (S.I. 1998 No. 2231), reg. 13(4)(b) (October 5, 1998).

11. Social Security Benefits Up-rating Order 1999 (S.I. 1999 No. 264), art. 18(6) (April 12, 1999).

12. Social Security Benefits (Miscellaneous Amendments) Regulations 1999 (S.I. 1999 No. 714), reg. 3 (April 5, 1999).

13. Income Support (General) (Standard Interest Rate Amendment) (No. 5) Regulations 1999 (S.I. 1999 No. 1411), reg. 2 (June 20, 1999).

DEFINITIONS

"attendance allowance"—see reg. 2(1).
"benefit week"—*ibid.*
"claimant"—*ibid.*
"close relative"—*ibid.*
"couple"—*ibid.*
"course of study"—*ibid.*
"co-ownership scheme"—*ibid.*
"Crown tenant"—*ibid.*
"disability living allowance"—*ibid.*
"dwelling occupied as the home"—*ibid.*
"family"—see SSCBA, s.137(1).
"housing benefit expenditure"—see reg. 2(1).
"lone parent"—*ibid.*
"non-dependant"—see reg. 3.
"nursing home"—see reg. 19(3).
"partner"—see reg. 2(1).
"period of study"—*ibid.*
"polygamous marriage"—*ibid.*
"remunerative work"—see reg. 5.
"residential care home"—see reg. 2(1).
"single claimant"—*ibid.*
"student"—see reg. 61.
"the Eileen Trust"—see reg. 2(1).
"the Fund"—*ibid.*
"the Independent Living Funds"—*ibid.*
"the Macfarlane (Special Payments) Trust"—*ibid.*
"the Macfarlane (Special Payments) (No.2) Trust"—*ibid.*
"the Macfarlane Trust"—*ibid.*
"training allowance"—*ibid.*
"water charges"—*ibid.*
"welfare to work beneficiary"—*ibid.*
"year of assessment"—*ibid.*

GENERAL NOTE

A new Schedule 3 came into force on October 2, 1995 which introduced major changes to the rules for payment of housing costs by income support. See the notes to Schedule 3 in the 1995 edition of this work for details of the previous rules. See also the associated changes to paras. 29 and 30 of Sched. 9, Scheds. 9 and 9A of the Claims and Payments Regulations and reg. 63 of the Adjudication Regulations. Note reg. 5(2) of the Social Security (Income Support and Claims and Payments) Amendment Regulations 1995 which preserves the operation of previous saving provisions (see p. 497).

The new rules place further substantial limits on the housing costs that will be met by income support. Since August 1993 this has been increasingly restricted. The upper ceiling for loans, first introduced on August 2, 1993, has been reduced twice and is now (since April 10, 1995) £100,000. Since May 2, 1994, interest on loans taken out or increased while a person was entitled to income support (or caught by the 26 weeks linking rule), which increased his housing costs, has not been met, subject to certain exceptions (note that from October 2, 1995 this only applies to loans taken out for house purchase and not those for repairs and improvements). These limits were in addition to those applying to tenants buying their own homes and the rules concerning excessive housing costs. All these provisions have been retained (although there is no longer a separate rule for tenants who buy their own homes, to whom para. 4(8) will now apply). However, the new restrictions signify a more fundamental change of approach to the meeting of housing costs by income support.

The main new departure is that no mortgage interest (nor some other housing costs—see below) is to be paid at all for certain periods which vary according to whether the loan or other agreement existed before October 2, 1995 (for the position of replacement loans see below). Interest will also generally be payable at a set rate rather than at the actual rate charged. Interest on arrears of interest (previously payable in limited circumstances, *e.g.* on arrears which accrued during the first 16 weeks of a claim) will not be met, nor will interest on loans for non-approved purposes for separated partners. In addition, the loans for repairs and improvements that qualify have been further restricted. There is some transitional protection for existing claimants. Note also that *all* payments of loan interest will be made directly to lenders who participate in the mortgage interest direct scheme; previously such loan interest payments were paid to claimants during the 50 per cent. period (see the amendment to para. 2 of Sched. 9A to the Claims and Payments Regulations).

These changes have been introduced as part of the Government's long-term aim of replacing state support with private insurance where possible. According to the Social Security Advisory Committee's (SSAC) report on the proposals (Cm. 2905(1995)), about 10 per cent. of all home buyers then had mortgage payment protection insurance (para. 16). The DSS's Memorandum to SSAC also referred to the need to simplify the calculation of housing costs (which were responsible for 13.1 per cent. of all income support errors in the period April to December 1994). But the Memorandum acknowledged that the introduction of a set rate of interest was also part of a clear policy that the State would not, even in the long-term, take full responsibility for borrowers' commitments (para. 36). SSAC recommended that the changes, in particular for existing borrowers, be postponed until April 1996 and made a number of other proposals to mitigate the effect of the new scheme. However, most of the recommendations were rejected. In reply to SSAC, the Government stated that the shift to private insurance for payment of mortgage interest was primarily directed at new loans (*i.e.* those taken out after October 1, 1995). In the Government's view the changes did not increase the need for mortgage insurance for existing borrowers, because most mortgage protection policies do not cover the first two months (under the new rules the waiting period for existing borrowers is eight weeks). But this ignores other important features of the new rules (such as 50 per cent only for the next 18 weeks, interest to be paid at the standard rate, etc.) which will also have a major impact on existing borrowers. The concessions made by the Government in response to the widespread criticism of the new restrictions were very limited. Where concessions were made, for example in relation to carers, this generally only resulted in the existing borrower rule being applied, rather than complete exemption from the changes.

In addition, from October 7, 1996, the effect of reg. 32 of the Income Support (General) (Jobseeker's Allowance Consequential Amendments) Regulations 1996 (see p. 500) should be noted. This provides that entitlement to income-based JSA counts as entitlement to income support for the purpose of satisfying any condition that the person is or has been entitled to income support for any period of time. It also has the same effect where the requirement is that the person is or has been treated as being in receipt of income support. This is obviously important for claimants transferring from JSA to income support. See para. 18 of Sched. 2 to the JSA Regulations where the transfer is the other way round. Note also para. 1A, introduced on October 22, 1997.

Paragraph 1—Housing costs

To be entitled to a sum for housing costs, the claimant, or another member of the family, must be liable to meet any of those costs on the home which are eligible under paras. 15–17. Para. 2 deals with when a person is "liable to meet" housing costs (which has replaced the more cumbersome "treated as responsible for the expenditure which relates to housing costs"). Whether a person is occupying a dwelling as his home is essentially a question of fact (*CIS 480/1992*).

CIS 636/1992 (confirmed by the Court of Appeal in *Brain v. Chief Adjudication Officer*, December 2, 1993) held in relation to the previous form of Sched. 3 that an amount for housing costs was limited to what the claimant was actually required to pay. Under the terms of her mortgage the claimant was not liable to pay any capital or interest so long as the amount outstanding (including accrued interest) did not exceed 75 per cent. of the value of the mortgaged property. She was not entitled to an amount for mortgage interest while she was not liable to pay it. The reasoning in that case would also seem to apply to the new form of Sched. 3, despite the differences in the wording. See also *CIS 743/1993* in the note to para. 2(a).

Note also reg. 56(1)(a) of the Adjudication Regulations which specifically provides that where a claimant's housing costs cannot be immediately determined, an AO can decide the claim on the basis of those costs that can be immediately determined.

Housing costs are limited to those specified in paras. 15–17. To be doubly sure, para. 4(1) excludes housing benefit expenditure and also provides that if a person is in a residential care or nursing home, no housing costs can usually be paid. But if the person is temporarily absent from his home, see para. 3(8)–(12) as to when housing costs for that dwelling can continue to be met although the person is in the residential care home, etc.

The categories in paras. 15–17 are the same as those listed in para. 1 of the former Sched. 3 (but note the reduced eligibility of loans for repairs and improvements: see para. 16). As far as mortgage interest, payments under a hire-purchase agreement and interest on loans for repairs and improvements are concerned, the question is no longer whether the interest is eligible, but whether the loan qualifies (see paras. 15 and 16). Presumably this is at least partly the consequence of introducing a standard rate of interest (see para. 12). It also means that the kind of situation dealt with in *R(IS) 11/95* (where the question was whether interest on a replacement loan was eligible where the original loan had been interest free—see p. 264 of the 1995 edition of this work) will no longer be an issue.

Note the restrictions on loans that will be met in paras. 4(2)–(12), 11(4)–(11) and 13.

Para. 1 contains some important definitions, notably "existing housing costs" and "new housing costs". These are needed because under the new rules no housing costs (subject to certain exceptions: see para. 9) are paid at all for certain periods. The length of the period depends on whether the housing costs are "existing" or "new" housing costs. Note the protection for existing claimants in para. 6(2)–(4), the expanded linking rules in para. 14, that certain claimants with new housing costs are treated as existing borrowers (see para. 8(2)–(5)) and the exemptions from the waiting periods in para. 9. As before, if the claimant or partner is aged at least 60, "full" housing costs are met from the beginning of the claim. Since para. 9(1)(b) only covers miscellaneous housing costs in para. 17(1)(d)–(f), this means that the waiting periods and the 50 per cent. rule apply not only to qualifying loans under paras. 15 and 16 but also to the housing costs in para. 17(1)(a)–(c).

"Existing housing costs" are those which arise under an agreement made before October 2, 1995. They also include those relating to an agreement made after October 1, 1995 if it replaces one made before October 2, 1995 and is between the same parties, in respect of the same property and for a loan of the same amount or less (excluding any arrangement fees). "New housing costs" are those that arise under an agreement made after October 1, 1995, other than one which qualifies as an existing loan (see above). Thus replacement loans, except for the limited category which count as existing loans, will be treated as new housing costs. The policy intention apparently is that the new housing costs rules should apply if a "new lending decision" is involved, for example, where the remortgage is with a new lender. The concession is mainly intended to benefit claimants whose existing lenders are prepared to let them change their mortgage because their interest rate is higher than the standard rate (see para. 12). But since any remortgage, even if it is with the same lender, will technically involve a new lending decision, this distinction seems difficult to justify. SSAC had recommended that existing borrowers who change lenders in order to pay a lower rate of interest should continue to be treated as existing borrowers (para. 60). But this was rejected by the Government on the grounds that this involved "new borrowing" which could be embarked upon in full knowledge of the income support rules. However, the effect of this approach could be to penalise such borrowers (if they had to claim income support at some future date) and thus it may act as a disincentive to their seeking to obtain a new loan on more favourable terms. Moreover, the requirement that to count as existing housing costs the new agreement has to be between the same parties could have particular implications for separating couples. As has been suggested (see Nick Wikeley, "Income Support and Mortgage Interest: the New Rules" (1995) 2 *Journal of Social Security Law* 168 at 170), it may thus be advisable where, for example, one partner is taking over the whole mortgage that was previously in joint names for the couple to seek a variation of the existing mortgage, rather than a remortgage (or possibly not to seek to formally change their mortgage agreement at all).

Note that the guidance to Adjudication Officers (*Adjudication Officer's Guide*, para. 28602) states that if two building societies merge, or one takes over the other, and existing borrowers are asked to sign new agreements, this should be treated as existing housing costs since no new borrowing has occurred. Apparently this is on the basis that in these circumstances the parties are effectively the same. But para. 28602 does not adopt the same approach where, for example, a single person becomes one of a couple and a remortgage is taken out in their joint names. In those circumstances the guidance takes the view that the new agreement is not between the same parties. Although there may be other reasons for distinguishing between these two situations (*e.g.* the remortgage may involve some alteration in the terms of the mortgage, such as a different interest rate) the distinction in terms of the test to be applied in deciding whether or not the agreement counts as existing housing costs is not immediately obvious.

If a claimant has both an existing and a new agreement, the rules for existing and new housing costs will apply respectively (para. 11(2)).

Paragraph 1A—previous entitlement to income-based JSA

The effect of this provision is that a claimant who moves from income-based JSA to income support within a linked period (normally 12 weeks but 26 weeks if para. 14(2) or (8) apply) will recieve the same amount for housing costs on any eligible loan as he did under JSA. The same will apply if it is the claimant's partner who was, or was treated as, getting income-based JSA or who becomes entitled to income support. But if there has been a change in circumstances (other than a reduction in the amount of the loan), the housing costs will be recalculated. A parallel provision has been inserted into Sched. 2 to the JSA Regulations that has the same result where the claimant moves from income support to income-based JSA. See also paras. 6(1B) and 8(1B) under which the anniversary date for the recalculation of the eligible capital in these circumstances will be the date that the claimant or his partner was first entitled to housing costs under either benefit.

Paragraph 2—liability to meet housing costs

Para. 2 is similar to the former para. 3 (although there are some differences in sub-paras. (b) and (c)). It defines when a person is "liable to meet housing costs", which has replaced the former "treated as responsible for the expenditure which relates to housing costs". Three situations are specified, to satisfy para. 1(1).

(a) Where the claimant, or any partner, has a liability for housing costs, it must not be to a member of the same household. See *R(SB) 13/82, R(SB) 4/83*, CSB 145/1984 and *CSB 463/1986*, and the notes to s.137(1) of the Contributions and Benefits Act.

Where a separated spouse or cohabitee has a joint mortgage with the former partner who has left the home, normally the liability for the mortgage will be a joint and several one (although each case will depend on the exact terms of the mortgage deed or loan agreement). This means that each party will be legally liable for the whole payment. Even if each party is liable separately for a defined share of the payment, then the claimant will in most circumstances of separation be treated as responsible for the other party's share under sub-para. (b), if the other party is not paying this. But if the claimant is only paying half the mortgage interest (even though she is jointly and severally liable), because payments for the other half are being made by someone else, the amount of her housing costs will be restricted to what she actually pays (*CIS 743/1993*, and see *CIS 636/1992* in the note to para. 1). See para. 5(5).

(b) The wording of this has been changed so that in all cases it has to be reasonable to treat the claimant as liable for the housing costs where the liable person is not meeting them; under the former para. 3(1)(b) this was not necessary where it was the person's former partner who was liable for, but not paying, the housing costs. This may not make much difference in practice, as in most cases of separated partners it will probably be reasonable to treat the claimant as liable.

An example of where the former para. 3(1)(b) was applied is *R(IS) 12/94*. The claimant lived with her daughter and grandson. Her daughter had a mortgage on their home. Following the death of her daughter the claimant applied for income support. The daughter's will left the property in trust for her son until he reached 21 (he was then aged seven). The Commissioner holds that "the person" liable can include an incorporeal person such as the estate of a deceased person. The daughter's estate was liable to pay the mortgage but was not doing so. It was reasonable to treat the claimant as liable for the mortgage interest.

In *CIS 141/1993* the claimant lived with her daughter in a home in their joint names. The daughter took out a hire purchase agreement for a central heating boiler and a cooker. The claimant reimbursed her daughter for half of the hire purchase payments. The claimant argued that she could bring herself within sub-para. (1)(b) because there was a possibility that if the payments were not made, British Gas would apply for a charging order on the home under the Charging Orders Act 1979. The Commissioner holds that for sub-para. (1)(b) to apply, there had to be an immediate threat to the continued occupation of the home, not a theoretical possibility of this in the future. On its particular facts this decision would seem to be correct (the daughter was in fact making the payments). But it is suggested that importing a requirement of an immediate threat to possession into sub-para. (1)(b) is not justified by the wording of the provision and so this decision should be restricted to its particular circumstances.

(c) Only sharing with another member of the same household will do, but see the definition of close relative. This enables sharers to get their proportionate share of housing costs. See para. 5(5).

Paragraph 3—occupying a dwelling as the home
Generally a claimant can only have one home—the one normally occupied (sub-paras. (1) and (2)), although in some circumstances two separate units of accommodation may constitute one dwelling (see notes to reg. 2(1)). *R(SB) 7/86* holds that premises cannot be "normally occupied as the home" if the claimant has never actually resided in them. Doubts expressed about this rule in *CSB 524/1985* and *CIS 4/1990* may lead to the issue being one of fact in each case.

Sub-paras. (3) and (4). These give special rules for choosing the home of students with a term-time and a vacation base.
In some circumstances payments will be made for two homes. The limit in para. 11(5) will be applied separately to each home (para. 11(6)).

Sub-para. (5). This covers moving into temporary accommodation while repairs are done. There is no limit in sub-para. (5) itself as to how long it can apply. *CIS 719/1994* rejects the AO's argument that para. 4(8) of the former Sched. 3 (now para. 3(10)) applied to restrict the operation of sub-para. (5). The claimant's house had been declared unfit for human habitation in 1989 and he had moved into rented accommodation while the repairs were carried out. These had still not been completed when he claimed income support in December 1992. The Commissioner holds that once the SSAT had found that the claimant was to be treated as occupying the house as his home by virtue of sub-para. (5) they had been right to ignore the fact that he had been absent from that home for more than 52 weeks (which was the limit for temporary absences under para. 4(8)). Para. 4(8) provided an alternative basis to the bases provided by the other sub-paragraphs for treating a claimant as occupying a dwelling as his home while temporarily absent from it. In taking this approach the Commissioner does not follow *CIS 252/1994* which had reached the opposite conclusion. It is suggested that the construction adopted in *CIS 719/1994* is to be preferred, since the former sub-paras. (3)–(8) (now sub-paras. (3)–(12)) do seem to deal with specific and distinct situations. The reasoning in *CIS 719/1994* will also apply to para. 3 which has a similar structure to that of the former para. 4. Although the wording of para. 3(10) is different from para. 4(8) it is not materially different in relation to this issue. There is also an additional argument, which supports the conclusion of *CIS 719/1994*, although not all its reasoning. Where sub-para. (5) applies, its effect is to define which dwelling a claimant is to be treated as occupying. So long as the same situation prevails, the claimant is not to be treated as absent from that dwelling. Therefore sub-paras. (10) and (11) simply do not bite in these circumstances.

Sub-para. (6). This allows payments in three cases where there is an overlap of liability. *R(SB) 7/86* decides that there must be a liability at both the "outgoing" end and the "ingoing" end. It was suggested that a legal liability at the outgoing end might not be necessary, but *CSSB 564/1987* decides that the liability in respect of the old home had to constitute a responsibility for housing expenditure within reg. 14 of the Requirements Regulations. It was argued there that the claimant was liable to make payments to her father as a licensee, but she could not be responsible under reg. 14 because the payment was to another member of the same household (differing from *CSB 865/1986*).

It is not clear how these principles might apply under the rules for income support. Para. 2 deals with liability (including in sub-para. (a) an exclusion of liability to a member of the same household), but only for housing costs. Items which count as housing costs are those which qualify under paras. 15–17 (see para. 1(1) and (2)) and do not include ordinary rent or payments as a licensee to occupy a dwelling. A straightforward application of *CSSB 564/1987* would conclude that there could be no overlap of liability if there was only an obligation to make these kinds of payments at the ingoing end. However, it is necessary to look at the problem to which sub-para. (6) is directed. This is that the "new home" would not ordinarily count as "the dwelling occupied as the home" when the claimant had not moved in, or the family more regularly lived elsewhere (reg. 2(1), sub-para. (1), *R(SB) 7/86*). Sub-para. (6) is to enable the "new home" to be treated as occupied as the home. In the circumstances it does not seem to matter that the liability in respect of the "old home" was

361

not one included as a housing cost, provided that there was a true liability. But the reference in sub-para. (6)(a) and (b) to meeting two lots of housing costs and the definition of "housing costs" in para. 1(2) raise doubts. See sub-para. (7).

Of the three cases covered, one is fear of violence in the former home or by a former member of the family. This can continue as long as reasonable. The fear of violence leading to the claimant leaving the former home has to be directed against the claimant, not caused by him (*CIS 339/1993*). The second is where one of a couple is a student or on a training course and the double expenditure is unavoidable. This can also continue as long as reasonable. The third is an unavoidable overlap of liability on moving home. What is unavoidable is a matter of fact. This can last for a maximum of four weeks.

CIS 543/1993 contains some useful guidance as to when head (a) will apply, although its particular facts were highly unusual. The claimant was a former police officer who had been convicted of conspiracy to murder but whose release was later ordered by the Home Secretary. On his release he went to live with his wife in a rented flat. They also owned a house in another part of the country which was let to tenants on an assured shorthold tenancy. The claimant had left this house through fear of violence from gangsters when he was on bail pending trial. The Commissioner points out that head (a) is not restricted to domestic violence and can apply in any case where one of the reasons for the claimant leaving the home was fear of violence in that home. It did not matter if in addition there was a fear of violence in places other than the home. But a fear of violence outside the home, even if in the vicinity of the home, would not suffice. Furthermore, the relevant leaving was the last one before the week to which head (a) might apply. Leaving in this context meant the ending of normal occupation of the home; it should be interpreted broadly as the circumstances of the departure might well be confused and distressing. Moreover, if a person had left, and was currently absent from, a home through fear of violence there, he *remained* absent for that reason, even if during an intervening period the absence was for a different reason (in this case imprisonment).

Although the claimant in this case was liable to make payments for two dwellings he did not have two lots of income support housing costs as his current accommodation was rented. The Commissioner states that in these circumstances the test in head (a) had to be interpreted as asking whether it was reasonable to meet housing costs for the former dwelling when another dwelling was currently occupied as the person's home. The question of reasonableness had to be determined at the date when the adjudicating authority was considering the issue (although what it was reasonable for the claimant to have done at the time could be relevant in deciding this question), and in the light of all the circumstances. These could include among other factors the length of absence, whether it was reasonable to expect the person to take steps to end the liability in respect of the former home (*e.g.*, whether there was a hope of resuming occupation, whether it was practicable to end the liability, his current financial situation and means of support), and the extent to which the liability was in practice being met otherwise than through income support (in this case from the tenants' rent). The conclusion might be different in relation to different weeks.

Sub-para. (7). This is an important provision allowing a person in certain circumstances to be treated as occupying a dwelling as his home for up to four weeks before moving in. This has consequences for entitlement to housing benefit and may fill in some of the gaps in sub-para. (6). The decision can only be made once the claimant has moved in. Then the claimant can be treated as occupying the dwelling for up to four weeks before the date of the move. The delay in moving while there was a liability to make payments must have been reasonable and fall into one of the three categories set out in sub-para. (7)(c). The categories cover: (i) delay necessary for adaptations for disablement needs; (ii) delay while a social fund application is determined and a member of the family is aged under six, over 59 or is disabled; and (iii) the move is from being a patient or in residential accommodation (see sub-para. (13)).

See para. 6(6) of Sched. 7 to the Claims and Payments Regulations.

Sub-paras. (8) to (12). These deal with temporary absences from home. See also the definitions in sub-para. (13). These rules were tightened up in April 1995, despite the Social Security Committee's (Cm. 2783) recommendation that the changes should not proceed, as the Government considered that the previous rules were too generous in some cases. Claimants whose absence began before April 10, 1995 remained subject to the previous temporary absence rule (52 weeks irrespective of the reason for absence: see the 1994 edition of this work) while that absence continued. See the Housing Benefit, Council Tax Benefit and Income Support (Amendments) Regulations 1995 (S.I. 1995 No. 625), reg. 7.

The primary rule is in sub-para. (10). Sub-paras. (11) and (12) deal with absences in special cases and there is a separate provision for absences due to trial periods in residential accommodation (sub-paras. (8) and (9)).

Under sub-para. (10) a person is to be treated as occupying the home during any absence of up to 13 weeks. All three heads (a) to (c) have to be satisfied (see the Northern Ireland decision *R(IS) 1/91* and *R(IS) 17/93*). *CIS 613/1997* confirms that as long as all three conditions are satisfied a claimant will be entitled to the benefit of the rule for the first 13 weeks' absence, even if in the event his absence extends beyond that period. This decision also holds that although there is a difference in wording between the previous provision (para. 4(8) of the former Sched. 3) and sub-para. (10), their effect is the same. *CIS 508/1992* and *CIS 484/1993* hold that the intention to return in head (a) must be an unqualified one. It is not enough for the intention to be contingent on the outcome of an event (such as a partner's admission into the U.K.: *CIS 508/1992*, or the obtaining of employment: *CIS 484/1993*. The same should apply to sub-para. (11) (see below). Note that there is no discretion under head (c), as there was before April 1995. If the absence is likely to exceed 13 weeks, the person is not treated as occupying the home from the outset.

Sub-paras. (11) and (12) deal with absences for particular reasons. Sub-para. (11)(c) lists those people who can be treated as occupying the home during temporary absences of up to 52 weeks. They are: people remanded in custody pending trial or sentence, and those required to live in a bail hostel; patients; people (or whose partner, or dependant child, is) undergoing medical treatment or medically approved convalescence in the U.K., or abroad (but not in residential accommodation); people providing or receiving (but not in residential accommodation) medically approved care in the U.K. or abroad; people caring for a child whose parent or guardian is temporarily away from home in order to receive medical treatment or medically approved care; people in residential accommodation, other than on a trial basis; people on a training course (defined in sub-para. (13)(d)) in the U.K. or abroad; people in fear of violence who are not covered by sub-para. (6)(a); eligible students not covered by sub-paras. (3) or (6)(b). Several of the categories refer to "medically approved" care (or convalescence: head (iii)), which is defined in sub-para. (13)(a). According to DSS guidance, some kind of corroboration from a doctor (or nurse) will do, not necessarily in the form of a medical certificate. There does not seem to be any restriction on who can provide the care.

A person in one of the categories in head (c) must also satisfy the conditions in heads (a), (b) and (d). Heads (a) and (b) are the same as heads (a) and (b) in sub-para. (10), except that the use of the word "while" in head (b) confirms that if there has been a letting, the person can satisfy sub-para. (11) when it terminates. On head (a), see *CIS 508/1992* and *CIS 484/1993* above. Under head (d) (as was the case under the pre-April 1995 rule), sub-para. (12) can apply where the absence is unlikely substantially to exceed 52 weeks and there are exceptional circumstances. Presumably a stay in hospital or other circumstances over which the person has no control (which were previously given as examples under the old rule) should qualify.

Sub-paras. (8) and (9) apply where a person has gone into residential accommodation (defined in sub-para. (13)(c)) for a trial period with the intention of returning to his own home if the accommodation proves unsuitable. If the person has entered the home for the purpose of, *e.g.*, respite care, or convalescence, the 52 weeks rule, not this one, should apply (see sub-para. (11)(ix)). There will obviously be some grey areas here; as was pointed out to SSAC in the course of their consultation on these rules, the reason given for entry into a residential home may well vary depending on who is asked. Note that, in this case, unlike absences covered by sub-paras. (10) and (11), the person does not have to intend to return home within a specified period. He will be treated as occupying his home during the first 13 weeks of the absence, starting with the day he first goes into the residential accommodation (*not* the date his absence from home begins) even if it is likely at the outset that he will be away for longer. There is no limit on the number of times sub-paras. (8) and (9) can apply, so a person will be able to try out different homes. But the 13 weeks is subject to a maximum of 52 weeks for that period of absence. So, for example, if the person has been in hospital for 40 weeks before going into a residential home for a trial period, he will only be treated as occupying his own home for a further 12 weeks.

If the reason for the absence changes, the rule governing absence for the latest reason will apply. The intention is that the absence will count from the first day the person left his own home, not the date the reason changed, except where the special rule for trial periods in residential accommodation applies.

There are no linking rules for any of these provisions (see *R v. Penwith District Council Housing Benefit Review Board ex parte Burt* (1990) 22 H.L.R. 292 on the equivalent housing benefit provisions). This means that provided the person returns to his own home for a period, he can be treated as occupying his own home for repeated 13 or 52 week absences. As the rules do not specify any length of time for which the person must return to his own home, presumably a very short period (24 hours?) will suffice.

Paragraph 4—Housing costs not met

Sub-para. (1). This provision is similar to para. 5 of the former Sched. 3. It excludes housing benefit expenditure and payment of housing costs if a person is in a residential care or nursing home. But if the person in a residential care or nursing home is only temporarily absent from his home see para. 3(8)–(12) as to when he can continue to receive housing costs for his home.

Sub-paras. (2)–(12) contain the restriction on payment of interest on loans taken out while income support (or, from October 7, 1996, income-based JSA: see reg. 32 of the Income Support (General) (Jobseeker's Allowance Consequential Amendments) Regulations 1996, p. 500) is being claimed (or a person is caught by the linking rule) which was first introduced on May 2, 1994 (see para. 5A of the former Sched. 3). It stemmed from the Government's concern about possible "upmarketing" at the expense of the benefit system, although no figures were produced as to the numbers of people said to have been exploiting income support by taking on bigger mortgages while on benefit. There may be many reasons why a claimant needs to take out or increase a loan while in receipt of income support (or income-based JSA) which have nothing to do with "upmarketing". Some, but by no means all, of these are catered for by the limited exceptions in sub-paras. (8)–(11). Furthermore, as the Social Security Advisory Committee pointed out (Cm 2537(1994)), "not only has it been Government policy to encourage home ownership, but . . . the rented sector is unable to meet the demands placed on it".

Sub-para. (2). This provision contains the basic rule. Note that the restriction now only applies to loans (or money borrowed under a hire purchase agreement) for house purchase. Before October 2, 1995 it also applied to *some* loans for repairs and improvements. (See *CIS 14141/1996* which decides that para. 5A of the former Sched. 3 was not invalid on the ground of irrationality, even though it had the unfair and absurd result of treating claimants with identical needs for housing costs differently. The Commissioner holds that para. 5A did prevent claimants with no previous housing costs for loan interest from receiving housing costs for new loans for repairs and improvements, but not claimants who had been receiving housing costs for loan interest.) Sub-para. (2) states that a loan for house purchase will not be eligible if it has been incurred during "the relevant period" (see sub-paras. (4)–(5)), and (i) after October 1, 1995, or (ii) after May 2, 1994 and the loan interest was not met under the former para. 5A in the 26 weeks before October 2, 1995, or (iii) between April 3, and October 1, 1995 when the person was not entitled to income support but he or his partner became entitled after October 1, 1995 and were entitled within the previous 26 weeks, unless interest on the loan was being met before October 2, 1995 (see sub-para. (3)). (The purpose of heads (b) and (c) of sub-para. (2) is presumably to catch loans which might otherwise escape restriction because the new Schedule is not retrospective.) But in the case of replacement loans the restriction will only apply to the extent of any increase in the amount loaned (see sub-para. (6)).

It is not entirely clear when a loan is incurred in this context. For example, if a further advance is added to a person's existing mortgage does this constitute incurring a loan, or is it merely increasing a loan that has already been incurred? (It may be that it is the former that is intended; *cf.* sub-para. (6) which catches increases in the amount borrowed in the case of replacement loans.) Will the restriction apply where the terms of an existing mortgage are varied rather than a new agreement entered into (as may happen, *e.g.*, where a couple separate and one member takes over the whole mortgage for which they were previously jointly and severally liable)? In those circumstances it would certainly seem arguable that the loan was incurred when the mortgage was first taken out, not when its terms were changed. It should also be noted that it is the date that the loan was incurred that counts, not the date that the person became liable to meet (see para. 2) the housing costs.

The restriction only applies to loans taken out by the claimant or a member of his family during the claimant's current entitlement to income support or a period of non-entitlement included in "the relevant period" by the operation of sub-para. (4). Note sub-paras. (4A) and (5). Note also reg. 32 of the Income Support (General) (Jobseeker's Allowance Consequential Amendments) Regulations 1996 (see p. 500), the effect of which is that entitlement to income-based JSA will count as entitlement to income support. Although sub-para. (2) does not specifically limit the period during which the loan will not qualify to the claimant's current claim (and any linked period), it is understood that this is the intention. Sub-para. (2) does refer to "the" (not "a") relevant period. Moreover, any other interpretation would have a draconian effect. Thus if entitlement to income support (and income-based JSA) ceases for more than 26 weeks, the claimant should be paid the full amount of his loan interest (at the standard rate: see para. 12) if he makes a further claim (subject to the waiting periods (paras. 6(1) and 8(1)) and the ceiling on loans (para. 11(5)). In addition loans taken out *before* a claimant or his partner claimed income support (or income-based JSA) are not caught (subject to the 26 week linking rule).

There are exceptions in sub-paras. (7)–(11).

Sub-paras. (4) and (5). Periods of entitlement to income support (or income-based JSA: reg. 32 of the Income Support (General) (Jobseeker's Allowance Consequential Amendments) Regulations 1996, see p. 500, assuming that this rule can be interpreted as a "requirement" that the person is, or has been, entitled to income support: see reg. 32(a)) separated by 26 weeks or less are treated as continuous for the purposes of sub-para. (2). So a loan taken out during a period of 26 weeks or less that falls between two periods of entitlement to income support (and/or income-based JSA) will be subject to the restriction. The 26 weeks is much more stringent than the normal linking rule (now 12 weeks: see para. 14(1)). There is also no provision for the restriction to cease to apply if there is a major change of circumstances (*cf.* para. 10(2)(b) in the former Sched. 3 for tenants who bought their own homes).

The effect of sub-para. (4) is that if a couple who are in receipt of income support (or income-based JSA) separate, the restriction will also apply to the partner who was not the claimant if s/he claims income support (or income-based JSA) within 26 weeks.

Note sub-para. (4A), the effect of which is that any period which the claimant or his partner spends on a New Deal option for 18–24 year-olds during which he (or his partner) is in remunerative work or has an income that is too high to qualify for income support will count as part of the relevant period. Thus even though the claimant (or his partner) may not be entitled to income support (or income-based JSA) for 26 weeks because the claimant (or his partner) is taking part in this kind of New Deal option, this will not break the running of any relevant period for the purposes of sub-para. (4). For a brief summary of the New Deal see the notes to reg. 75 of the JSA Regulations.

Sub-para. (6). This will cover the situation where a person moves, or remortgages his home, when only the increase in the amount loaned will be caught by sub-para. (2). Under head (a) the replaced loan must have been qualified under para. 15 during the relevant period (defined in sub-para. (4); note para. (4A)). The inclusion of the words "during the relevant period" from October 7, 1996 is significant, since sub-para. (2) treats a loan that would otherwise qualify under para. 15 because of its purpose as not doing so if it was incurred during the relevant period and at any of the times specified in sub-para. (2). Head (b) was also amended on October 7, 1996. The previous form (see the 1996 edition of this book) was potentially quite wide as it merely required that a previous loan (or loans: ss.6(c) and 23(1) of the Interpretation Act 1978) that was secured on another property had been wholly or partly repaid. So it seemed that the earlier loan could, for example, have been for business purposes, or one that was not eligible under sub-para. (2). But under the new form the loan that has been repaid has to be one that qualified under para. 15 or 16 during the relevant period (although there is no requirement that it was a secured loan). It does not seem to be necessary for the repaying of the earlier loan and the taking out of the new to be connected in time. See *CIS 7273/1995* which confirms that the fact that there was a gap (of over two years) between paying off the old mortgage and taking out the new larger one did not remove the claimant's entitlement to housing costs to the extent met on the original mortgage. This was a decision on para. 5A(3) of the former Sched. 3 (see the 1995 edition of this book) but the position should be the same under sub-para. (6). Under the former para. 5A(3) and (7), if the claimant (or a member of the family) received housing benefit during the gap, it seemed that interest payments could be restricted to the amount of housing benefit payable in the intervening period, even if the second home was cheaper than the first. But this will not be the case under sub-para. (6). If there is no increase (or even a decrease) in the amount of the claimant's new loan, the restriction will not apply, whether or not the claimant receives housing benefit in the intervening period. Sub-para. (8) may, however, come into play in cases where sub-para. (2) does bite and the claimant received housing benefit during the gap.

Thus the effect of sub-para. (6) would seem to be that if a couple who are in receipt of income support (or income-based JSA) separate, and the former home is sold each partner will be entitled to interest on a loan up to the previous amount (*i.e.* each would receive interest on a £30,000 loan if that was the amount of the loan they had as a couple). *CIS 11293/1995* decides that this was the position under the previous rule in para. 5A(3) of the former Sched. 3. The claimant was jointly and severally liable with her ex-husband for a mortgage of £18,000 on the home in which she lived. She was awarded housing costs on £9,000 only. She then sold that house and moved to a new home which she purchased with a mortgage of £18,000 (the old mortgage having been paid off). The Commissioner holds that she was entitled to interest on £18,000 because the "new liability" under para. 5A(3) did not exceed the "former liability". It was the claimant's legal liability that was material, not what had actually been paid as income support housing costs, and she had potentially been liable for all the interest on the original mortgage. The Commissioner disagrees with *CIS 5353/ 1995* which considered that housing costs were only "applicable" under para. 5A(3) if they had actually been met; in his view "applicable" in para. 5A(3) meant "potentially applicable". The comparison in sub-para. (6) is between the amount of the old and new *loans*, which wording would seem to achieve the same result as in *CIS 11293/1995*. But if one member of the couple buys a new property without the former matrimonial home being sold, sub-para. (2) will apply and the loan will not be eligible (unless it involved some remortgaging and so sub-para. (6)(a) applies). A new (or increased, but see the note to sub-para. (2) for discussion of when a loan is incurred) loan to buy out the other partner's share will not be met if it is taken out during the relevant period. If the couple were not in receipt of income support (or income-based JSA), the restriction will not apply if the loan for the new property, or to buy out the other partner's share, is taken out before a claim for income support (or income-based JSA), is made (subject to the 26 week linking rule).

Sub-para. (8). A person receiving housing benefit who buys a home will be paid housing costs but only up to the level of the housing benefit payable in the week before the purchase, together with any amount for housing costs that he was being paid that week. Sub-para. (8) covers tenants who buy their own homes as well as those receiving housing benefit who move into owner occupation. The more generous treatment of the former under the rules in para. 10(1) and (2) of the former Sched. 3 (see the 1995 edition of this book pp. 262 and 269–270) no longer applies. Thus there is no provision, for example, for the restriction to cease to apply if there is a major change of circumstances. There can be an increase in the restricted level equivalent to any subsequent increase in the standard rate (*not* the claimant's actual rate) or in housing costs that are eligible under para. 17. But there is no provision for subsequent reductions. So if the standard rate is later lowered or the para. 17 housing costs reduce, a claimant can continue to enjoy the partial relief from restriction due to the previous increase (*R(IS) 8/94*). If the housing costs fall below the restricted level the amount payable will be the lower figure (*R(IS) 8/94*).

No reference is made to loans under para. 16. Does this mean that if sub-para. (8) applies, no payment will be made for loans for repairs and improvements? This would seem unfair and also illogical in view of the exclusion of para. 16 loans from the restriction in sub-para. (2). It is understood that it is not the DSS's intention to preclude payment for loans for repairs and improvements taken out by people covered by sub-para. (8) (or sub-para. (11) where the same point arises). The DSS take the view that because sub-para. (2) only relates to para. 15 loans these provisions do not affect para. 16 loans at all.

Sub-para. (9). If the loan is taken out, or increased, to acquire a home to meet the needs of a disabled person, this is exempt from restriction under sub-para. (2) (although the excessive housing costs rule (para. 13) and the ceiling on loans in para. 11(5) could apply). This provision should cover people wanting to move into sheltered accommodation. Note that the new accommodation only has to be more suited to the needs of the disabled person; there is no requirement that it has been specifically adapted for that person's needs (*CIS 16250/1996*). A person counts as disabled if he qualifies for the disability, disabled child, higher pensioner or enhanced pensioner premium, or would do so if entitled to income support, including periods when he is disqualified from receiving benefit or treated as capable of work under the incapacity rules (para. 1(3) and (4)). (See the notes to para. 7 of Sched. 1B and Bonner *et al*, *Non-Means Tested Benefits: the Legislation* for more details on the incapacity for work rules.) This definition of a disabled person is quite restrictive and may exclude some people who need care even though they do not, or would not, qualify for these premiums. However, *CIS 13661/1996* confirms that it is an exhaustive definition. The disabled person does not have to be a member of the claimant's family, or to have previously lived with the claimant. However he does have to qualify as a disabled person at the time the loan is taken out (*CIS 7273/1995*).

The scope of this provision is discussed in *CIS 14551/1996*. The Commissioner points out that the fact that new accommodation is more suited to the special needs of the disabled person only has to be *a* reason for its acquisition, not the sole or predominant reason; moreover, the test is whether the new accommodation is more suited, not whether it was reasonable to acquire it. Further, the person's overall mental and physical condition had to be taken into account, not just the condition that triggered the application of the definition of "disabled person". But the person's needs had to stem from a specific disease or bodily or mental disablement to count under this paragraph. The claimant had contended that part of the reason for moving was to alleviate mental stress caused by financial worries. The Commissioner accepts that, for example, moving to smaller or more compact accommodation that is less expensive to heat, or to accommodation that is nearer to a person who can look after the claimant so as to reduce that person's travelling expenses, could come within this provision. But it was the accommodation itself that had to be more suited, not the terms of its acquisition, so moving simply in order to reduce mortgage liability, or so as to take advantage of the exemption from restriction under this provision, would not be covered.

Sub-para. (9) only applies to loans to purchase a home. A loan taken out to adapt a home to meet the needs of a disabled person will be eligible under para. 16 (see para. 16(2)(k) and note para. 11(9)).

Sub-para. (10). Increased loans taken out because of a need to move to provide separate sleeping accommodation for male and female children aged 10 or over who are members of the claimant's family are exempt (although the ceiling on loans in para. 11(5) and the excessive housing costs rule (para. 13) could apply). See *CIS 14657/1996.*

Sub-para. (11). Claimants who were only receiving para. 17 housing costs before they purchased their home will have their loan interest met up to the level of their previous housing costs. The rule is similar to that for claimants previously in receipt of housing benefit in sub-para. (8). The restricted level can be increased for subsequent increases in the standard rate or in para. 17 housing costs (see the notes to sub-para. (8)).

Paragraph 5—Apportionment of housing costs

Sub-para. (1). This allows the expenditure on premises used for mixed purposes (*e.g.* business and domestic) to be apportioned and the part attributable to a private dwelling met (subject to the limit in para. 11(7)). Where the "composite hereditament" existed before the community charge came into force the apportionment follows the rateable value of each part of the premises (sub-para. (1)). Where the composite hereditament comes into existence after the advent of the community charge, the apportionment is to follow the current market value of each part (sub-paras. (2)–(4)).

Sub-para. (5). In *CIS 743/1993* the Commissioner holds that "responsible" at the end of sub-para. (5) did not mean legally responsible (as it did elsewhere in the Schedule), but referred to the proportion of the shared responsibility that a claimant was actually paying. The claimant was jointly and severally liable with her ex-husband under the terms of the mortgage, but only paid half the mortgage interest. She was only entitled to housing costs for the amount she actually paid.

Where para. 5 applies, the effect of para. 11(7) is that the ceiling on loans is applied to the eligible part of the loan.

Paragraph 6—Existing housing costs

Note the restriction on house purchase loans incurred while entitled to income support (or income-based JSA: reg. 32 of the Income Support (General) (Jobseeker's Allowance Consequential Amendments) Regulations 1996, see p. 500), or while a person is caught by the linking rule, in para. 4(2)–(12), as well as the limits imposed under paras. 11(5) and 13.

Sub-para. (1). In the case of existing housing costs (defined in para. 1(2)), none are payable for the first eight weeks, and only 50 per cent. for the next 18 weeks (sub-para. (1)(b) and (c)). Once the claimant has been entitled to income support (and/or income-based JSA: reg. 32 of the Income Support (General) (Jobseeker's Allowance Consequential Amendments) Regulations 1996, see p. 500) for a continuous period of 26 weeks (note the linking rules in para. 14), "full" housing costs are met (see below). But the waiting periods do not apply if the claimant or partner is aged at least 60, or to housing costs that qualify under para. 17(1)(d)–(f), *i.e.*, payments under a co-ownership scheme, by a Crown tenant or in respect of a tent (para. 9). In these cases housing costs will be met from the start of the income support claim, although interest on qualifying loans will be calculated at the standard rate. *R(IS) 2/94* rejected the argument that under para. 7(1)(b)(i) of the former Sched. 3 receipt of income support on *any* claim for a continuous period of what was then 16 weeks was sufficient. The qualifying period recommenced each time a fresh claim for income support was made (subject to the linking rules—see para. 14).

There is no actual equivalent to para. 7(2) of the former Sched. 3 in the new Schedule. That provision avoided the creation of a "mortgage trap" which could have resulted from the then 50 per cent. rule (see the note to para. 7(2) in the 1995 edition of this work). Under the new rules the possibility remains that if the result of a nil or 50 per cent. figure for housing costs is that a claimant does not qualify for income support, he will never clock up the necessary weeks of entitlement to qualify for "full" housing costs under sub-para. (1)(a). Para. 14(4) to (9) will assist many claimants who could otherwise be caught in this trap, but not all. See the notes to para. 14 below.

To calculate the amount of housing costs that are payable under para. 6, for loans that qualify under paras. 15 or 16 the standard rate (see para. 12) is applied to the eligible capital owing for the time being (sub-para. (1)(a)(i)). To this are added the actual payments due for any housing costs in para. 17(1)(a)–(c) (*i.e.* ground rent, service charges and rentcharges) (sub-para. (1)(a)(ii)).

"Eligible capital" is not defined, but see paras. 4(2)–(12), 11(4)–(9) and 13 for the limits on loans that will be met. What does "eligible capital for the time being owing" mean? Does it just mean the original amount of the loan less any that has been repaid, or could it include an increase in that capital, due, for example, to capitalised interest? The terms of the claimant's mortgage may be relevant here. See, for example, *CIS 146/1993*, where the claimant's mortgage repayments were adjusted annually. Any arrears due to changes in interest rates during the year were capitalised, divided into 12 and added to the monthly instalments for the following year. The Commissioner holds that the capitalised interest was not arrears but part of the interest payable in the following year. Thus it qualified as eligible interest. But the interest on the capitalised interest was to be treated as arrears and so was not payable. A similar distinction may be relevant to the question of what is the eligible capital owing for the time being, depending on the terms of the mortgage. In *CIS 141/1993* the Commissioner confirmed that for interest to qualify as eligible interest under the former para. 7(3), any increase in the capital owing on the loan had to be for the purpose of acquiring an interest in the home. But there are important differences between para. 6(1)(a)(i) (and para. 8(1)(a)(i)) and the former para. 7(3) and so the same construction may not be appropriate. How these differences will be interpreted remains to be seen.

Note that the amount of eligible capital will be recalculated only once a year (sub-paras. (1A) and (1B)). See also reg. 63(7) of the Adjudication Regulations which provides that a review due to a reduction in eligible capital will only have effect on the next anniversary of the date the claimant's housing costs were first met. Since reg. 63(7) only applies to *reductions* in the outstanding capital, arguably a review due to any eligible increase should take effect in the normal way (despite sub-paras. (1A) and (1B)). Indeed this is the approach taken in the *Adjudication Officer's Guide* (see para. 28563).

See the notes to paras. 15 and 16 for which loans are eligible.

The formula for determining the weekly amount of loan interest payable is in para. 10. Interest is only met when the claimant is actually required to pay it (*CIS 636/1992 (Brain)* and *CIS 743/ 1993* referred to in the notes to para. 1).

Only interest is covered, not the capital element in loan repayments. There are a number of way round this deficiency. First, the lender may be prepared to accept repayments of interest only. Second, if the claimant sub-lets part of the home, the first £4 of any payments (plus £9.25, if heating is included) is disregarded (Sched. 9, para. 19). See also *CIS 13059/1996* referred to below. Contributions to living or accommodation expenses by someone who normally resides with the claimant are disregarded entirely (Sched. 9, para. 18) (but see para. 18 of this Schedule). See also para. 20 of Sched. 9 for the disregard of board and lodging payments. Payments from others to meet capital repayments (or interest not met by income support or premiums on a mortgage protection or buildings insurance policy) are disregarded (Sched. 9, para. 30). See *CIS 13059/1996* in the note to para. 30 of Sched. 9 which decides (contrary to the view expressed in *CIS 82/1993*) that the disregard in para. 30(1) can apply to payments made by a tenant (or licensee) of the claimant who lives in his home. Payments from liable relatives would not be disregarded, but if made direct to the lender might be excluded from the liable relative provisions (reg. 54). Payments from mortgage protection policies are disregarded to the extent that they cover capital repayments (or interest on a qualifying loan that is not met by income support or the premiums on a mortgage protection or buildings insurance policy) (Sched. 9, para. 29).

The cost of premiums on insurance policies connected with the loan is also not met (*R(SB) 46/ 83*).

There is no longer any provision for the payment of interest on arrears of interest. Under the old rules interest on arrears accrued during a period subject to the 50 per cent. restriction was allowed (para. 7(6) of the former Sched. 3). But there is no such provision in relation to arrears that accrue during the new waiting periods. In addition, interest that accrues on deferred interest loans is no longer covered. Interest on loans for non-approved purposes in the case of separated spouses is also no longer met (see para. 7(7) of the former Sched. 3 for the old rule). But note the transitional protection for existing claimants in regulation 3 of the Income Support (General) Amendment and Transitional Regulations 1995 (p. 497, and see note to para. 7 below).

Sub-paras. (2)–(4). Under the former Sched. 3 the 50 per cent. rule only applied for the first 16 weeks of a claim (there was no "nil" period). These sub-paragraphs contain some protection for claimants entitled to housing costs immediately before October 2, 1995 who have not yet been entitled to income support for 26 weeks on that date. If on October 1, 1995 a claimant has been entitled to income support for less than 16 weeks his housing costs will remain the same (even if the interest rate changes), until he has been entitled for 16 weeks when they will be calculated as if he had been entitled for 26 weeks (*i.e.* 100 per cent at the standard rate). If he has been entitled for 16 or more but less than 26 weeks by October 1, 1995, he will be treated as if he had been entitled for 26 weeks. This will cease to apply if the agreement under which those housing costs arise ends. (See also para. 7(8), noted below.) Since these provisions only apply where the claimant's income support included an amount for housing costs immediately before October 2, 1995 (see sub-para. (2)), they will not assist claimants who were not entitled to income support on October 1, 1995 because their income exceeded their applicable amount due to the former 50 per cent. rule. It may be possible for claimants who are unemployed or sick, lone parents or carers to rely on paras. 14(4)–(6) to treat them as entitled to income support during the 16 weeks and thus to qualify under para. 6(3)(a) in that way, but this still leaves the problem of para. 6(2), which would seem to govern the operation of para. 6(3). But note the linking rules in para. 14. So, for example, a claimant may still benefit from these provisions if he claims income support after October 1, 1995 but that claim links with a previous claim·made before October 2, 1995 which included an amount for housing costs.

Paragraph 7—Transitional protection

This paragraph is not straightforward. This at least partly stems from the fact that some of the provisions refer to "housing costs", some to "existing housing costs" and some only to qualifying loans. It contains the following detailed rules. Sub-paras. (1) and (2) provide that if a claimant's housing costs under the former Sched. 3 in the benefit week which includes October 1, 1995 ("the first benefit week") are more than the amount payable under para. 6 in the next benefit week ("the second benefit week") that amount will be increased by the difference between the amount of his housing costs in the first and second benefit weeks, called the "add back" (sub-para. (1) and (2)). Thus if no housing costs are applicable in the week including October 1, 1995, the claimant will not be entitled to any add back. As to whether an amount for housing costs is applicable in the week including October 1, 1995 see *CSIS 162/1996* below. If the claimant has more than one qualifying loan the add back will be calculated separately for each loan (sub-para. (9)). If the claimant's existing housing costs, less the add back, increase after the second benefit week, the add back will be reduced by the amount of any increase until it is reduced to nil when it will cease to apply (sub-paras. (3) and (4)). Thus, for example, increases in the standard rate under para. 12 will reduce the amount of the add back and this will not be increased again if the standard rate subsequently decreases. An allowable increase in a loan will also reduce the add back (but not if the increase in borrowing is by way of a separate loan). But as existing housing costs include not only mortgage interest but also, for example, ground rent and service charges, will any add back be reduced by increases in such costs? It is understood that this was not the intention and that sub-paras. (3) and (4) are really only meant to deal with qualifying loans (despite the reference to "existing housing costs"). Note that where there is more than one loan the reduction of the add back on one will not affect the add back on the other (see sub-para. (9)).

If entitlement to income support (and/or income-based JSA: reg. 32 of the Income Support (General) (Jobseeker's Allowance Consequential Amendments) Regulations 1996, see p. 500) ceases for more than 12 weeks (from October 5, 1998, 52 weeks where the person or his partner is a "welfare to work beneficiary" (sub-para. (10)); see the notes to reg. 2(1) for when a person counts as a welfare to work beneficiary) no add back will be payable on any new claim (sub-para. (5)). In addition, if a person ceases to be entitled to housing costs (for any length of time) the add back is lost (sub-para. (6)). But if that person's partner (or former partner?) claims income support within 12 weeks (from October 5, 1998, 52 weeks in the case of a "welfare to work beneficiary"), including existing housing costs previously met in that person's claim, the partner will have the add back (sub-para. (7)).

Sub-para. (8) provides that if in the first benefit week the claimant had not been in receipt of income support for 16 weeks and so only 50 per cent. of his eligible interest was being met under the former para. 7(1)(b)(ii), the add back will be calculated as though he was receiving 100 per cent. of his eligible interest at that time (the reference to "on that day" is presumably meant to be "in that week"). But any add back will not be paid until the date the claimant would have become entitled to 100 per cent. interest if the old rules had remained in force.

See also para. 6(2)–(4) which contains some protection for claimants entitled to housing costs before October 2, 1995 in relation to the increased waiting period for existing housing costs.

Note the important additional transitional protection for existing claimants in reg. 3 of the Income Support (General) Amendment and Transitional Regulations 1995 (p. 497). Interest on arrears of interest, on loans for non-approved purposes or for repairs and improvements that are no longer eligible that was included in a claimant's applicable amount for income support on October 1, 1995 will continue to be met for as long as the claimant continues to satisfy the conditions of para. 7(6), 7(7) or 8(1)(a) of the former Sched. 3 (see the 1995 edition of this book) and be in, or treated as in, receipt of income support (and/or, from October 7, 1996, income-based JSA: reg. 32 of the Income Support (General) (Jobseeker's Allowance Consequential Amendments) Regulations 1996, see p. 500). Note reg. 3(3) which provides that only the linking rules in para. 14(1)(a), (c) and (e) will apply in these cases. Since the effect of reg. 3(2) is to treat these three categories as eligible housing costs under para. 15 or 16, the protection in reg. 3 will operate separately from the rules for add back in para. 7 and will not be affected by them.

CSIS 162/1996 deals with the relationship between the transitional protection in para. 7 and in reg. 3 and the question whether the claimant had an applicable amount for housing costs in the week including October 1, 1995. The claimant had been in receipt of income support, including an amount for interest on a loan for repairs and improvements under para. 8 of the former Sched. 3, until September 20, 1995. He then obtained work but reclaimed income support on October 23, 1995 when his employment ended. His housing costs were calculated under para. 16 which resulted in a lower award than on his original claim. But the Commissioner holds that reg. 3 applied so that the claimant was entitled to have his housing costs met in accordance with the former para. 8. The Commissioner's reasoning was as follows. The claimant fell to be treated as in receipt of income support during the period September 20 to October 23, 1995 under the linking rule in para. 14(1)(a)(ii). Since he was to be treated as being in receipt of income support he must also be regarded as being entitled to income support. Consequently he had a "benefit week" in each of the weeks in the gap in his income support claim within the meaning of para. 4 of Sched. 7 to the Claims and Payments Regulations (see the definition of "benefit week" in reg. 2(1)) because he was sufficiently "entitled" to a social security benefit. He also had an applicable amount in those weeks because if a person is to be treated as entitled to, and in receipt of, income support in any particular week, his applicable amount can be ascertained in accordance with Part IV in the normal way. The Commissioner also considered that the transitional protection in reg. 3 applied in this case, rather than that in para. 7. This was because reg. 3 dealt with the particular situation at issue in this case, whereas para. 7 was a general provision and operated only where no specific provision applied. The result was that the claimant's income support was not subject to diminution of any "add back" which would have been the case if para. 7 had applied. Instead his housing costs would continue to be met in accordance with the former para. 8 as long as he remained in, or treated as in, receipt of income support. The AO has appealed against this decision. The appeal is due to be heard by the Court of Session on October 19 and 20, 1999.

On para. 7(6) of the former Sched. 3, which allowed interest on arrears of interest to be met in certain circumstances, note *CIS 8166/1995*. The Commissioner decides that for the former para. 7(6)(c) to apply it was not necessary for the mortgage to specifically stipulate that the liability to make payments had been deferred for at least two years. It was sufficient for the terms of the mortgage to result in there being a deferral period of at least two years.

Note also the transitional protection in relation to housing costs for claimants transferring from income support to JSA in reg. 87(4) to (6) and para. 18 of Sched. 2 to the JSA Regulations.

Paragraph 8—New housing costs

Note the restriction on house purchase loans incurred while entitled to income support (or income-based JSA: reg. 32 of the Income Support (General) (Jobseeker's Allowance Consequential Amendments) Regulations 1996, see p. 500), or while a person is caught by the linking rule, in para. 4(2)–(12) as well as the limits imposed under paras. 11(5) and 13.

Sub-para. (1). New housing costs (defined in para. 1(2)) are not met until the claimant has been entitled to income support (and/or income-based JSA: reg. 32 of the Income Support (General) (Jobseeker's Allowance Consequential Amendments) Regulations 1996, see p. 500) for 39 weeks (but see the exceptions in para. 9). The rules for calculating the amount of new housing costs that are payable are the same as for existing housing costs (see the note to para. 6(1) above). The drafting of para. 8(1)(a) could be improved. It is not clear why sub-para. (1)(a) has not adopted the same format as para. 6(1)(a). Presumably it is intended that the amounts in heads (i) and (ii) are to be aggregated but para. 8(1)(a) does not exactly say that.

Sub-paras. (2)–(5). New housing costs will be treated as existing housing costs for claimants who are eligible for income support as carers, are in custody pending trial or sentence, have been refused payment under a mortgage protection policy because of a pre-existing medical condition or HIV or who are lone parents who have claimed due to the death of, or being abandoned by, a partner (sub-paras. (2)–(4)). In the case of a lone parent this will cease to apply if she becomes a member of a couple again (sub-para. (5)). These exemptions from the 39 week waiting period seem very limited. For example, why does head (c) of para. 8(2) not extend to all those who are refused payment under a mortgage protection policy, or people who cannot obtain insurance because of their medical condition? Further, sub-para. (3) will only apply if there is a child in the family. A young person (*i.e.* aged 16–18) will not do.

"Abandoned" in sub-para. (3)(b) has so far been given a restrictive meaning by the Commissioners. In *CIS 5177/1997* the claimant's husband had failed to support her financially and had been cruel to her and the children for some months. Her solicitor wrote to him suggesting that he should leave the matrimonial home, which he did shortly afterwards. The Commissioner holds that abandonment in the context of sub-para. (3) was similar to desertion. Thus its essence was (i) physical separation and (ii) an absence of consent to it on the part of the deserted or abandoned partner. The claimant's husband could not be said to have abandoned her because she had (through her solicitor) suggested that he went and the actual separation was by agreement. In *CIS 2210/1998* the claimant's husband was sentenced to prison for three years. The Commissioner concludes that a separation forced upon the parties by the husband's imprisonment did not constitute abandonment within the meaning of sub-para. (3)(b). In his view deliberate withdrawal of both the husband's society and his financial support was required for the sub-paragraph to apply.

Paragraph 9—Exclusions from paras. 6 and 8

Claimants who are, or whose partner is, aged at least 60 are exempt from the waiting periods and have their housing costs met from the beginning of a claim (sub-paras. (1)(a) and (2)(a)). Interest on qualifying loans will be calculated at the standard rate (see para. 12). Housing costs in para. 17(1)(d)–(f), *i.e.*, payments under a co-ownership scheme, by a Crown tenant or in respect of a tent, are also met from the start of a claim for income support (sub-paras. (1)(b) and (2)(b)).

Note the restriction on house purchase loans incurred while entitled to income support (or income-based JSA: reg. 32 of the Income Support (General) (Jobseeker's Allowance Consequential Amendments) Regulations 1996, see p. 500), or while a person is caught by the linking rule, in para. 4(2)–(12) as well as the limits imposed under paras. 11(5) and 13.

Paragraph 10—Calculation for loans

This contains the formula (referred to in paras. 6(1)(a)(i) and 8(1)(a)(i)) for calculating the weekly amount of interest that will be met on a qualifying loan. Presumably "A" is only intended to refer to the amount of a loan that qualifies under para. 15 or 16 to the extent that it comprises eligible capital, although sub-para. (1) does not actually say that. See sub-para. (2) if the loan is outside the MIRAS (mortgage interest relief at source) scheme.

Paragraph 11—New and existing housing costs

Sub-para. (2). If a claimant has both an existing and a new agreement, the rules for existing and new housing costs will be applied respectively and the amounts aggregated.

Sub-paras. (4)–(11). These contain the provisions first introduced in August 1993 relating to the ceiling on loans (see the notes to para. 7(6B)–(6F) of the former Sched. 3 in the 1995 edition of this book). For SSAC's report on these changes see Cm. 2272. Sub-paras. (4) and (5) provide that there is an absolute limit on the size of loans that can be taken into account in calculating housing costs. The current limit is £100,000 (sub-para. (5)). If there is more than one loan, all qualifying loans (except any loan taken out to adapt a home for disablement needs (sub-para. (9)) are aggregated and the total amount outstanding is subject to the ceiling (sub-para. (4)). Sub-para. (10) provides that the restriction is to be applied proportionately to each loan where the total outstanding exceeds the ceiling. If a claimant qualifies for loan interest for two homes the limit is applied separately to the loans for each home (sub-para. (6)). If only a proportion of the loan is for a qualifying purpose, or the property is used for mixed purposes (*e.g.* business and domestic), the limit is applied to the proportion of the loan covered by income support (sub-paras. (7) and (8)).

If the loan was "to adapt a dwelling" for the needs of a disabled person, that loan is ignored in calculating whether the limit on loans in sub-para. (5) is exceeded (sub-para. (9)). For when a person counts as disabled see para. 1(3) and (4) and the note to para. 4(9). The disabled person does not have to be a member of the claimant's family. "Adapt a dwelling" is not defined, but this should include the building of an extension, for example. See *CIS 278/1992* and the other decisions referred to in the notes to para. 8 of the former Sched. 3 in the 1995 edition of this book on the meaning of reasonable improvements to the home to improve its fitness for occupation.

The limit on loans was £150,000 from August 2, 1993 until April 10, 1994, £125,000 from April 11, 1994 to April 9, 1995 and has been £100,000 since April 10, 1995. The rules applied to loans taken out before, as well as those taken out or increased after, these dates, but there was transitional protection for existing claimants (see reg. 4 of the Income Support (General) Amendment No. 3 Regulations 1993 (p. 493) and reg. 28 of the Income-related Benefits Schemes (Miscellaneous Amendments) Regulations 1995 (p. 496). The effect of this is that there is no limit on the existing loans of claimants entitled to income support on August 2, 1993 (or who were treated as entitled by virtue of the linking rules) while their entitlement continues; for claimants who did not qualify for this protection but who were entitled, or treated as entitled, to income support on April 11, 1994, the ceiling on their existing loans is £150,000 while they remain entitled to income support (reg. 4). There was similar transitional protection in connection with the reduction of the limit to £100,000 from April 10, 1995 (reg. 28). *CIS 12885/1996* confirms that the claimant's entitlement to income support must be continuous; the protection is lost if it ceases for even a single day. Note that reg. 5(2) of the amending regulations preserves the operation of the respective saving provisions (see the Social Security (Income Support and Claims and Payments) Amendment Regulations 1995 (p. 497)). Note also reg. 32 of the Income Support (General) (Jobseeker's Allowance Consequential Amendments) Regulations 1996 (see p. 500) under which entitlement to income-based JSA counts for the purpose of satisfying a condition that the person is entitled to income support.

The limit applies from the beginning of a claim, so that the 50 per cent. for weeks 9 to 26 in the case of existing housing costs applies to the restricted amount of a loan. The ceiling on loans is in addition to the rules on "excessive" housing costs (see para. 13) and the restriction on house purchase loans incurred while entitled to income support (or income-based JSA: reg. 32 of the Income Support (General) (Jobseeker's Allowance Consequential Amendments) Regulations 1996, see p. 500), or while a person is caught by the linking rule (see para. 4(2)–(12)). Note that the disregard in para. 29 of Sched. 9 of payments from mortgage protection policies includes any interest payment on a qualifying loan that is not met by income support; see also the disregard in para. 30(1)(b) of Sched. 9 and *CIS 13059/1996* in the note to that paragraph.

Paragraph 12—Standard rate

Interest on eligible loans is now to be paid at the standard rate. This is either the set figure in sub-para. (1)(a) (8.39 per cent from October 2, 1995; 8.00 per cent from January 28, 1996; 7.74 per cent from April 28, 1996; 7.48 per cent from June 30, 1996; 7.16 per cent from September 1, 1996; 6.89 per cent from December 22, 1996; 7.20 per cent from April 20, 1997; 7.57 per cent from September 28, 1997; 7.97 per cent from November 30, 1997; 8.34 per cent from May 31, 1998; 8.65 per cent from December 27, 1998; 8.24 per cent from February 28, 1999; 7.75 per cent from March 28, 1999; 7.39 per cent from April 25, 1999; 7.08 per cent from May 16, 1999; and 6.66 per cent from June 27, 1999) or the actual rate of interest if that is less than five per cent. on the day housing costs are first payable. In the latter case that rate will apply (ignoring any changes in it) until it reaches five per cent. when the standard rate will apply. Thus there will generally be no "gain" for those with low interest rates (indeed they may lose if their interest rate increases above the rate charged on the day housing costs first become payable without reaching the five per cent. threshold), at least until their interest rate becomes five per cent. There may then be a small gain if their rate of interest is below the current set rate but above five per cent. But there is no protection for significant "losers" (except through the transitional protection provisions—see above). This disparity in treatment is difficult to justify. As SSAC pointed out (para. 58), it is often those on lowest incomes who need to resort to lenders charging higher rates of interest in order to secure a loan (for example, because they have no, or minimal, capital to contribute towards the purchase). Thus the use of a standard rate of interest could result in greater arrears and risk of repossession. SSAC's recommendation that claimants who switched lenders in order to pay a lower rate of interest should continue to be treated as existing borrowers was, however, rejected by the Government. Remortgages taken out after October 1, 1995, in order to reduce a claimant's interest rate (or indeed for some other reason), will only count as existing borrowing if all the conditions in the definition of "existing housing costs" in para. 1(2) are satisfied.

The set figure in sub-para. (1)(a) comes from the Central Statistical Office's Financial Statistics Table 7.1L and represents a weighted average of the rates applied by the top 20 building societies (SSAC report, para. 56). The Government has stated that the trigger for change in that figure will be movements of 0.25 per cent. or more.

Paragraph 13—Excessive housing costs

This restricts the housing costs that will be met where the accommodation is too large or expensive. These limits are in addition to the ceiling on loans (para. 11(4)–(11)), and the restriction on house purchase loans incurred while the claimant is entitled to income support (or income-based JSA: reg. 32 of the Income Support (General) (Jobseeker's Allowance Consequential Amendments) Regulations 1996, see p. 500), or caught by the linking rule (para. 4(2)–(12)).

The rules are very similar to those in para. 10(3)–(7) of the former Sched. 3, but the linking rule in sub-para. (7) is 12, not eight, weeks. Note that there is no equivalent to the former para. 10(1)–(2) relating to tenants who buy their homes, as they are now covered by the stricter rules in para. 4(8). See the notes to para. 10(1)–(2) in the 1995 edition of this book for a discussion of the former provisions.

Sub-para. (1). This does not specifically provide for any deduction for the presence of a non-dependant to be made first, before deciding whether the level of housing costs is excessive (unlike the former para. 10(3)). But since sub-para. (1) refers to housing costs that fall to be met under this Schedule, this indicates that it is the amount of housing costs net of deductions (and restrictions) that is the relevant figure.

There are three sets of circumstances in which a restriction can be applied. The first is that the home is unnecessarily large for the claimant's family, including any foster children and non-dependants living in the household. An absolutely literal reading of the provision would lead to the result that it does not apply to a single claimant, who does not have a family. *CIS 104/1991* decides that the words must be read as "the claimant and his family (if any)." Any part of the home which is let is ignored in assessing the size of the accommodation against the needs of its occupants. At base is an issue of opinion about what is unnecessarily large. Some common situations caught by this provision (*e.g.* a married couple whose children have left home, or a deserted spouse) may escape under sub-para. (4) or (6).

The second set of circumstances, under head (b), is that the immediate area of the home is more expensive than other areas in which suitable alternative accommodation is available. It is not at all clear how restricted the immediate area might be, but it will probably be more limited than the area under (c). *CSB 1016/1982* suggests that the delimitation of an area is likely to be within the knowledge of SSATs. It must be possible also to identify another cheaper area (using the *CSB 1016/1982* definition) in which suitable alternative accommodation exists. The condition of suitability will limit the distance within which other areas can be sought (*R(IS) 12/91*).

Finally, under head (c), there is a restriction if the outgoings of the home are higher than for suitable alternative accommodation in the area (not the immediate area). In *CSB 1016/1982* (in relation to an earlier formulation of this rule) "area" was said to connote "something more confined, restricted and more compact than a locality or district. It might consist of dwelling houses or flats contiguous to a road or a number of roads, refer to a neighbourhood or even to a large block of flats. It is not capable of precise definition." This approach was commended for the purposes of sub-para. (1) in *CIS 34/1989* and *R(IS) 12/91*.

If sub-para. (1) applies, sub-para. (3) provides that the "amount of the loan" shall be restricted and the excess expenditure over that for a home of suitable size or expense will not be met. The purpose of the reference to "the amount of *the loan*" is not entirely clear, since sub-para. (1) applies to any housing costs met under Sched. 3, not just qualifying loans. Sub-paras. (4) and (6) contain exceptions to the operation of sub-paras. (1) and (3).

R(IS) 9/91 decides that sub-paras. (1) and (3) operate in the same way as *R(SB) 6/89* decided that the old reg. 21 of the Requirements Regulations did. The excess is not the difference between the actual expenditure and the maximum that would be allowed for a family of similar size in a home of the necessary size or in an acceptably cheaper area. The excess is the difference between the actual expenditure and the housing costs which would be incurred by the claimant in the alternative accommodation. On the facts of *R(IS) 9/91*, the net proceeds of sale of the existing home would have completely covered the cost of acquiring alternative accommodation, so that there would be no income support housing costs. Thus the entire actual expenditure was "excess".

Sub-para. (4). If it is not reasonable to expect the claimant to seek alternative cheaper accommodation, no restriction is to be made at all. It must already have been determined under sub-para. (1) that cheaper alternative accommodation which is suitable exists. All the relevant factors set out in sub-para. (5) must be considered.

Under head (a) the availability of suitable accommodation must be judged objectively (*R(SB) 7/89* and *R(IS) 10/93*). The particular circumstances of the claimant and his family are taken into account under head (b). The reference in head (a) to area is particularly obscure. Does it mean the area in which the home is situated or can it include another area in which suitable accommodation is available? In *CSB 1016/1982* it is suggested that it only governs the level of housing costs, not the availability of suitable accommodation, but it seems to be assumed in *R(SB) 7/89* that it governs both matters.

Sub-para. (5)(b) brings in all the relevant circumstances, not just those mentioned (*R(SB) 6/89, R(SB) 7/89* and *R(IS) 10/93*). One relevant factor mentioned in *CSB 1016/1982* was that the home had only just come into the claimant's occupation in matrimonial proceedings. In *CSB 617/1988* the claimant was assured by the manager of the local DSS office before she moved from a house with a mortgage of £25,000 to a house with a mortgage of £69,890 that the full interest on the new mortgage would be met by supplementary benefit. Although such an assurance could not bind the AO by creating an estoppel (*R(SB) 14/88*) it was one of the circumstances to be considered. (*CSB 617/1988* is reported as *R(SB) 14/89*, but it is the unreported version that should be referred to, as the reported decision omits the last three paragraphs which are the relevant ones here.)

Financial hardship is also a relevant factor. In *R(SB) 6/89* the invidious financial position the claimant would be put in if she were forced to sell the home in which she had lived for many years before its renovation was complete was relevant. As was the claimant's inability to find a buyer because of the stagnant housing market (*CIS 347/1992*). In that case the claimant had been advised of a price range for selling his home and would suffer financial hardship if forced to sell below that price. In *CIS 434/1992* the not uncommon problem of a negative equity was relevant. A further factor mentioned in *R(SB) 7/89* was that if the claimant sold his home, his lenders would not be prepared to lend to him again, but if the proceeds of sale were not put to purchasing another house, the capital would disentitle him from benefit. Thus rented accommodation may not be a straightforward alternative. *R(IS) 10/93* holds that the inability of the claimant to obtain suitable accommodation is a relevant factor. As in that case, that inability may stem from the fact that the claimant is unable to sell his existing home, despite making all reasonable efforts to do so.

Sub-para. (6). If the restriction is not removed completely under sub-para. (4) there can be a limited exemption here. If the claimant (or a member of the family) was able to meet the financial commitments for the home when they were first entered into, there is to be no restriction under this paragraph (but the ceiling in para. 11(5) may apply) for the first six months on income support (and/or income-based JSA: reg. 32 of the Income Support (General) (Jobseeker's Allowance Consequential Amendments) Regulations 1996, see p. 500) or from the date on which the housing costs are determined on review to be excessive. This should include a person who was a member of the family when the mortgage was taken on (*e.g.* where a couple have separated). The exemption can be extended for up to another six months so long as the claimant uses his best endeavours to obtain cheaper accommodation. What are the best endeavours is an issue of fact. *R(SB) 7/89* holds that a claimant can only be penalised for failing to use his best endeavours if he has been given some advance notice of the necessity to do so. In *R(IS) 13/92* the claimant's housing costs were restricted by the AO from the beginning of the claim to £146.85 a week, the amount appropriate to interest on a capital sum of £110,000. At the time the capital and accrued unpaid interest amounted to £696,063.44. The Commissioner agreed that a restriction under sub-paras. (1) and (3) was indicated, but on the evidence the claimant was able to meet the financial commitments for the dwelling at the time the mortgage was obtained. Therefore the absence of restriction for the first six months under sub-para. (6) was mandatory. The Commissioner did however consider that the initial improper restriction by the AO operated as a notice of the intention to restrict housing costs after the six months under *R(SB) 7/89*. The Court of Appeal in *Secretary of State for Social Security v. Julien, The Times*, April 21, 1992, confirmed the Commissioner's decision, saying that the issue is ability to meet the financial commitments, not prudence.

In *CIS 104/1991* the Commissioner takes the approach of *R(SB) 7/89* a little further. He holds that if the claimant could afford the housing commitments when he took them on there cannot be a restriction until there has been an explicit notice in an AO's decision that there may be a restriction in six months' time. The sub-para. (6) meter has to be started explicitly and it has to run for six months. In *CIS 104/1991* only two months notice was given. The claimant had to be allowed another four months and then the question of using the best endeavours to obtain cheaper accommodation had to be explored.

In *CIS 3163/1997* the claimant contended that because there would have to be a review at the end of any exemption period under sub-para. (6), this meant that on that review a new automatic 26 weeks' exemption from restriction would have to be allowed (with a possible extension for an extra 26 weeks), and so on, on a rolling basis. However, the Commissioner holds that the reference to review in sub-para. (6) was to the review which first started the sub-para. (6) clock running within any period of income support entitlement. The maximum period for the application of sub-para. (6) was thus 52 weeks from the date of that review (or from the start of entitlement if sub-para. (6) was applied immediately on the award of entitlement). To allow a new automatic 26-week period to start on any review would undermine the manifest purpose of sub-para. (6).

Sub-paras. (7) to (9). A person can now only requalify for the deferment of a restriction under sub-para. (6) if there is a break in entitlement to income support of more than 12 weeks. Note that the linking rules in para. 14(1)(c) to (f) apply.

Paragraph 14—Linking rules

These rules are particularly important for the waiting periods under paras. 6 and 8, but apply throughout the Schedule. Sub-paras. (1)–(3) largely reproduce para. 7(9), (12) and (11) respectively of the former Sched. 3, except that the linking period in sub-para. (1) is 12 (from October 5, 1998, 52 in some cases for a "welfare to work beneficiary", see below), not eight, weeks. SSAC had recommended 26 weeks because a shorter linking period could act as a disincentive to work in view of the new waiting periods.

Reg. 32 of the Income Support (General) (Jobseeker's Allowance Consequential Amendments) Regulations 1996 (see p. 500) should also be noted. This provides that entitlement to income-based

JSA counts as entitlement to income support for the purpose of satisfying any condition that the person is or has been entitled to income support for any period of time. It also has the same effect where the requirement is that the person is or has been treated as being in receipt of income support. See para. 18(1)(c) of Sched. 2 to the JSA Regulations for the converse provision under the JSA rules.

Note the new linking rules in sub-para. (1)(ee) and sub-paras. (3ZA) and (3B) introduced on January 5, 1998 as a consequence of the "New Deal". For a brief summary of the New Deal for 18–24 year-olds see the notes to reg. 75 of the JSA Regulations. The intention is that time spent on the New Deal should not put claimants at a disadvantage in terms of qualifying for housing costs. Thus under sub-para. (3ZA) a claimant is deemed to be in receipt of income support during any period that he stops getting income support because he or his partner is on a New Deal option that results in him (or his partner) being in remunerative work or having an income that is too high to qualify for income support. In addition, sub-para. (1)(ee) treats a claimant as in receipt of income support for the same period that his partner was in receipt, or treated as in receipt, of income support where the claimant is awarded income support for the couple immediately after either of them has been taking part in one of the three New Deal employment programmes and immediately before this his partner had been getting income support for the couple. See also sub-para. (3B) which treats any period of entitlement to contribution-based JSA immediately before a person or his partner took part in a New Deal employment programme as a period of entitlement to income support. Similar provisions have been inserted into Sched. 2 to the JSA Regulations (see para. 13(1)(ee) and (3A) of Sched. 2; an equivalent of sub-para. (3B) is obviously not needed).

Note in addition that from October 5, 1998 the linking rules in sub-paras. (1)(a)(ii), (1)(d) and (1)(f)(iii) (but not (1)(c)(iv)) are 52 weeks in the case of a "welfare to work beneficiary" (sub-para. (10)). See the notes to reg. 2(1) for when a person counts as a welfare to work beneficiary. This change is part of the Government's New Deal for Disabled People. The aim of the extended linking periods is that the person should not be worse off if he has to reclaim benefit within a year because he (or his partner) has again become incapable of work. For JSA there is a similar extension to the linking rules where the claimant's partner is a welfare to work beneficiary (see para. 13(12) of Sched. 2 to the JSA Regulations).

Sub-para. (3A). The waiting periods in paras. 6 and 8 talk in terms of entitlement to income support but the linking rules in sub-paras. (1)–(3ZA) refer to deemed receipt of income support. Sub-para. (3A) states that deemed receipt for the purposes of sub-paras. (1), (3) and (3ZA) counts as deemed entitlement, to confirm that these linking rules apply to the waiting periods.

Sub-paras. (4)–(9). These were new in October and December 1995 and are intended to assist claimants in satisfying the waiting periods. Note also sub-para. (3B) (see above). Sub-paras. (4), (5), (5A) and (5B) provide that a person who is not entitled to income support only because s/he has too much capital and/or income will be treated as so entitled for any period (or periods: Interpretation Act 1978, s.6) of up to 39 weeks during which s/he is entitled to unemployment benefit, contribution-based JSA, statutory sick pay or incapacity benefit (or credits), eligible for income support as a carer, a lone parent, or treated as in receipt of income support (and/or income-based JSA: reg. 32 of the Income Support (General) (Jobseeker's Allowance Consequential Amendments) Regulations 1996, see p. 500). Note that a lone parent includes a person who is responsible only for a young person (*i.e.* aged 16–18) (see reg. 2(1)). (But since such a lone parent will not be eligible for income support under para. 1 of Sched. 1B, she will have to satisfy one of the other paragraphs in Sched. 1B in order to come within para. (4).) In the case of carers and lone parents covered by sub-para. (5A) it is necessary for a claim for income support to have been made, the refusal of which fixes the start of the deemed entitlement. The absence of such a requirement in sub-para. (5) would seem to imply that it is not necessary for a claim to have been made for a person to benefit from this provision (although the use of the word "only" in sub-para. (4) could indicate otherwise). Although sub-para. (4) states that these rules apply where a person is not entitled to income support only because of excess capital and/or income, sub-para. (5B) also provides that for lone parents and carers covered by sub-para. (5A) the deemed entitlement does not apply if during the relevant period the person would not be entitled to income support because s/he (or any partner) is in remunerative work or s/he is a student (other than one who is eligible for income support) or temporarily absent from Great Britain. Is the effect of this, for example, that if a lone parent finds work after sub-para. (5A) has applied to her for, say, 20 weeks, the deemed entitlement under that sub-paragraph does not apply at all? Although the wording of sub-para. (5B) is not entirely clear, the fact that where the period of work is 12 (or from October 5, 1998, 52 in the case of a "welfare to work beneficiary", see above) weeks or less the linking rule in sub-para. (1)(a)(ii)(bb) will apply so that the period of work can count under sub-para. (5)(c) indicates that this is not the case and that sub-para. (5B) only applies to the periods when the lone parent or carer is in remunerative work, etc. (Note that because sub-para. (3A) now treats deemed receipt of income support as deemed entitlement for the purposes of sub-paras. (1), (3) and (3ZA), such a period of 12 (or 52) weeks or less can in fact count directly under sub-para. (1)(a)(ii)(bb) without having to go via the sub-para. (5)(c) route. This is relevant for JSA. Paragraph 13(6) of Sched. 2 to the JSA Regulations contains no equivalent of sub-para. (5)(c), but since such a provision is no longer needed in these circumstances the effect of these rules will be the same for both income support and JSA.) The amendments to sub-para. (1)(a)(ii) introduced on October 7, 1996 have addressed the problem raised in the 1996 edition of this book that the linking rule in that sub-paragraph might not have applied because under its pre-October 1996 form the period of deemed receipt had to fall between periods of *receipt* (or deemed receipt) of income support whereas sub-paras. (5) and (5A) treat a person as *entitled* to income support. (There was the same potential problem before October 7, 1996 for people who fell within sub-para. (5) and who, for example, worked for a period of 12 weeks or less between two periods of unemployment.) Note that this may not be too much of an issue for carers and many lone parents, for whom new housing costs are treated as existing housing costs (see para. 8(2)–(5)). But it could be if, for example, their income disqualifies them until "full" housing costs are payable. In addition, not all lone parents are covered by para. 8(3).

Note that if the only reason for non-entitlement to income support is too much income, and the person's income includes payments under a policy taken out to insure against the risk of not being able to meet eligible housing costs, s/he will treated as entitled to income support for the period that the insurance payments are made (sub-para. (6)).

Sub-paras. (8) and (9). If a claim for income support is made by, or in respect of, a person whose payments under a policy to insure against a loss of employment have stopped and who had been getting income support (and/or income-based JSA: reg. 32 of the Income Support (General) (Jobseeker's Allowance Consequential Amendments) Regulations 1996, see p. 500) including housing costs within the last 26 weeks, the weeks in between the claims are ignored for the purpose of deciding whether the claimant has been entitled to income support for either the 26 or 39 week qualifiying period.

Paragraph 15—Loans on residential property
Under the new rules the question is no longer whether the interest is eligible, but whether the loan qualifies. Thus the situation dealt with in *R(IS) 11/95* where the original loan was interest free (see the notes to para. 7(3) of the former Sched. 3 in the 1995 edition of this book) will no longer be an issue. This paragraph (and para. 16) deal with whether a loan is for a qualifying purpose. Note the restrictions on loans that will be met in paras. 4(12), 11(4)–(11) and 13.

Clearly there has to be a loan for para. 15 to apply. *CIS 14483/1996* concerned a scheme for Muslims operated by the Albaraka International Bank because the Koran prohibits the payment or charging of interest on money loaned. Under the scheme the claimant and the bank jointly purchased the property; the legal estate vested in the claimant who held it on trust for himself and the bank and the beneficial interest was divided into investment shares. The claimant agreed to purchase a number of shares from the bank each month and to pay the bank an amount of "mesne profit" each month to reflect his use of the bank's share in the property. The Commissioner holds that the mesne profit did not constitute "eligible interest" which could be met under para. 7(3) of the former Sched. 3 (see the 1995 edition of this book) because there was no loan. The agreement was not in the nature of a mortgage but was a form of co-partnership, designed specifically to prevent the payment of interest.

Sub-para. (1). The loan (or any increase in the loan, *CIS 141/1993*) must either be for the purpose of acquiring an interest in the home, or paying off another loan which was for an approved purpose. In the second situation the loan will only qualify to the extent that the old loan would have qualified. The cost of acquiring an interest in the home includes besides the purchase price expenses necessary for the purchase, *e.g.* stamp duty, legal fees (see *Adjudication Officer's Guide*, para. 28520). Loans include hire purchase agreements (sub-para. (2)). An overdraft facility is a loan for this purpose (see *CIS 6010/1995* in the notes to para. 16).

In *Guest v. Chief Adjudication Officer* (April 2, 1998, unreported, CA) it was a condition of the claimant's loan of £85,000 to purchase his home that there would be a further charge of £30,000 on the property in order that the building society could recoup some of its loss in relation to his previous mortgage. The Commissioner held that this "further advance" of £30,000 was simply a transfer of part of the claimant's liability under the earlier mortgage to his new property and that this did not represent the taking out of a loan for the purposes of para. 7(3) of Sched. 3 (as in force before October 2, 1995). In addition, it did not fall within para. 7(3)(a) (now sub-para. (1)(a)), as this did not extend to money which had to be spent on some other purpose as a result of a precondition imposed by some other person (*e.g.* the mortgagee). Para. 7(3)(b) (now sub-para. (1)(b)) also did not apply as the provision of alternative security for part of the claimant's pre-existing liability did not amount to "paying off another loan". Moreover, that liability had not been incurred for the purpose of purchasing any interest in his *present* home. The Court of Appeal dismissed the claimant's appeal, holding that no loan as such had been taken out and that the Commissioner's conclusions as to the ambit of para. 7(3) were correct. Head (b) had to be read in the light of the essential purpose of Sched. 3, which was to provide housing costs in respect of the dwelling occupied as the claimant's home (*i.e.* his present home). Although there are differences between the former para. 7(3) and sub-para. (1), the reasoning in this decision will apply equally to sub-para. (1).

"Interest" includes a "further interest". In *R(IS) 7/93*, the claimant had been living in leasehold property for some time and receiving housing costs for the interest on the loan to acquire that interest. He received a further advance to enable him to buy the freehold reversion. It is held that the loan to acquire a further interest was for a qualifying purpose, and it did not matter that he already had one interest. "An interest" in the home should include both legal and equitable interests. In *CIS 465/1994* the Commissioner holds that "acquiring an interest" covers the situation where the owner does not have a present right of possession and takes out a mortgage to buy out sitting tenants so that she can move into the property. The tenants were statutory tenants under the Rent Act 1977. The Commissioner states that the primary purpose of Sched. 3 was to help with the costs of acquiring or keeping a roof over one's head. Interest in sub-para. (1)(a) was not restricted to "an interest in land" in the Law of Property Act sense, although it did contemplate "an interest of a proprietary nature or some closely analogous right of tenure or occupancy similar to that of a true tenant". Moreover, acquiring an interest could include purchasing an interest only for the purpose of extinguishing it (see *R(1S)6/95* in the notes to para. 3 of Sched. 10 which regards a similar transaction as a sale from the tenant's point of view). The Commissioner distinguished *R(IS) 4/95* (see below) on the ground partly that the right of occupation at issue in that case was not a right of exclusive occupation.

Sub-paras. (1)(a) and (b) are not mutually exclusive, so eligible interest can be allowed under both heads.

In *R(IS) 6/94* the claimant and his wife had bought their home in joint names with the help of a mortgage. They were equitable joint tenants. The claimant was made bankrupt and a trustee in bankruptcy appointed. The trustee in bankruptcy sold the claimant's former interest in the home to the claimant's wife. She obtained a mortgage to pay for this and to discharge the original mortgage (among other things). When the claim for income support was made, interest was only allowed on an amount equal to the original loan under sub-para. (1)(b). The Commissioner points out that on the appointment of the trustee in bankruptcy the claimant's estate vested in him and the equitable joint tenancy was severed (*In re Dennis* (*a Bankrupt*) [1992] 3 W.L.R. 204). It was replaced by an equitable tenancy in common, under which the trustee and the claimant's wife held equal shares. Therefore, when buying the claimant's former interest in the home, his wife was acquiring a further interest in it and the interest on the part of the mortgage advanced for that purpose was payable under sub-para. (1)(a).

When a claimant buys a former partner's interest in the home this will constitute acquiring a further interest in a home (but note para. 4(2)–(12)). In *CIS 762/1994* the former matrimonial home was transferred to the claimant on the basis that she paid her ex-husband £5,000 and released him from all liability under the mortgage. The original mortgage had been for £43,200 but had increased to just over £52,300 because of arrears. The bank would not agree to the transfer of the house into the claimant's name unless the arrears were discharged. She therefore took out a second loan for £52,300 to discharge the original loan and the arrears. The AO only awarded housing costs on £43,200. But the Commissioner holds that the claimant was entitled to housing costs on the full amount of the second loan. That loan had been applied in part to acquire the husband's interest in the home, the consideration for which included releasing him from all liability under the mortgage, and in part to pay off the original loan of £43,200, and so the whole of it was eligible. However, if the claimant and partner still count as a couple, the acquisition by one of them of the other's interest in the home, does not come within sub-para. (1)(a). They are one entity for the purposes of income support, and any transaction between them, when together they previously owned the entire interest, does not give rise to housing costs *(R(IS) 1/95)*. *R(IS) 4/95* decides that a Class F land charge (registered by a spouse to protect his or her rights under the Matrimonial Homes Act 1983) is not "an interest in the dwelling occupied as the home", but a mere right of occupation (see *Wroth v. Tyler* [1974] Ch. 30).

R(IS) 11/94 holds that "dwelling occupied as the home" in sub-para. (1)(a) includes any dwelling intended to be occupied as the home, since most properties are acquired before they become a home. If a person acquires a site and then builds a home on it, all the costs connected with the acquisition of the site and the subsequent building work constitute "monies applied" for the purpose of "acquiring an interest" in the home. Such building costs include the value of the claimant's own labour (put in this case at £9,000) and all bank charges (including overdraft interest) necessary to enable the home to be built up to the first day of occupation. However, any interest accruing after the claimant moves into the home is not eligible. In *CIS 679/1992* a loan taken out to purchase a strip of land to extend the claimant's garden was for the purpose of acquiring an interest in what was, at the date of the claim, the dwelling occupied as the home.

CIS 297/1994 holds that the intention to make the property the home has to be formed at the date of acquisition and implemented as soon as practicable. But it would seem at least arguable that the wording of para. 15(1)(a) does not actually require this, and that if the dwelling is now occupied as the home, even if this was not the case, or the intention, at the time the interest was acquired, sub-para. (1)(a) can apply.

In *R(IS) 18/93* the land certificate of the claimant's home had been deposited with a bank as security for a company loan. When the bank threatened to call in the loan when the company was in trouble, the claimant obtained a mortgage to discharge the debt to the bank. This loan was not for a qualifying purpose. The deposit of the land certificate may have been evidence of the creation of an incumbrance on the claimant's title to the home, but the bank did not acquire an interest in the home. Therefore the mortgage loan was not to acquire the bank's interest. *CIS 336/1993* reaches a similar conclusion. It made no difference that the bank's charge had been created by way of a legal mortgage rather than deposit of the land certificate. By effecting the charge the claimant had not parted with an interest in his home. When he obtained release of the charge he did not acquire any interest.

CIS 563/1991 considered when money is being *applied* for an approved purpose. Clearly this is the case if it is spent directly on the purchase price and the legal and other expenses of the purchase. The Commissioner considers that it could also include money used for the purchase of goods or some other interest in property that then formed part of the consideration for the transfer of the interest in the home. However, it does not extend to money that has to to be spent on some other purpose as a result of a precondition imposed by some other person, *e.g.* the mortgagee (*Guest v. Chief Adjudication Officer*, April 2, 1998, unreported, CA).

Sub-para. (3). The proportion of a loan for an eligible purpose defines the proportion of the loan that qualifies under para. 15 (subject to the limit in para. 11(8)).

Paragraph 16—Loans for repairs and improvements

Sub-para. (1). Loans for the purpose of repairs or improvements to the home, or for service charges to pay for repairs or improvements, or loans to pay off such loans, are eligible (although these have been considerably restricted: see sub-para. (2)). This includes repairs or improvements to any part of the building containing the claimant's home, *e.g.* the common parts of a block of flats (see sub-para. (2)). *R(IS) 5/96* holds that the loan has to be for repairs or improvements to the home that is currently occupied. Thus the claimant was not entitled to interest on a bank loan for central heating after he moved from that home. "Repairs and improvements" are defined in sub-para. (2). The loan has to be used for the repairs, etc., within six months or some further period. If the loan is not so used, the claimant is not entitled to interest on it even during the six months or any extended period (*CIS 257/1994*). The capital amount of the loan is disregarded under para. 8(b) of Sched. 10.

CIS 6010/1995 decides that the use of an overdraft facility to finance building works could constitute a taking out of a loan for repairs and improvements. The claimant's builders required immediate payment, so she arranged an overdraft in order to pay them before her improvement grant came through. The AO refused payment of the interest on the overdraft on the ground that an overdraft facility was not a loan. The Commissioner holds that the wide ordinary meaning of "loan" as "money borrowed at interest" applied in this context and this covered the drawing of money on overdraft. There was clear evidence that the bank had agreed to grant the overdraft facility for the specific purpose of financing the building works. The Commissioner leaves open the questions whether a loan would be "taken out" where there was no advance arrangement and whether the required purpose could easily be shown in such circumstances.

Note that the overall limit on loans applies (see para. 11(4) and (5) but note the exception in para. 11(9)) as well as the general limits in para. 13. But the restriction in para. 4(2)–(12) (loans incurred while entitled to income support, or income-based JSA; reg. 32 of the Income Support (General) (Jobseeker's Allowance Consequential Amendments) Regulations 1996, see p. 500) does not apply to loans for repairs and improvements.

Sub-para. (2). There has been a considerable tightening up of the extent to which loans for repairs and improvements will be met by income support. To qualify, both repairs and improvements must now be undertaken with a view to "maintaining the fitness of the dwelling for human habitation

...", *and* be one of the listed measures. This is narrower than para. 8(3) of the former Sched. 3 under which any major repairs were covered if they were "necessary to maintain the fabric" of the home. Now for repairs to be eligible they must not only maintain the home's fitness for human habitation but also come within heads (a)–(l). The test in the former para. 8(3) (that applied to improvements only) was that of "improving ... fitness for occupation" (see *CIS 643/1993* which held that if the claimant considered that the work would improve the property this should be accepted, save in the most exceptional cases). The notion of "maintaining" is narrower than "improving" fitness. Moreover, the new criterion of human habitation seems to be an attempt to move away from the particular needs of the claimant in favour of a more "objective" standard (but see the new head (k) which necessarily will involve consideration of the needs of the disabled person concerned).

The most notable omission from the listed measures is the former head (k), "other improvements which are reasonable in the circumstances" (see the notes to para. 8(3) of the former Sched. 3 in the 1995 edition of this book as to the ambit of this provision). But the scope of several others has also been narrowed. For example, provision of heating is no longer covered, only repairs to an existing heating system under head (b) (the use of the word "system" indicates that a replacement boiler, for example, should be covered as *part* of a heating system and see *CIS 15036/1996*); head (j) seems considerably more limited than the former head (f) which referred to improvement in the structural condition of the home; and loans for facilities for storing food are no longer included (head (f)). Cupboards and a refrigerator are such facilities (*CIS 14468/1996*); the Commissioner also holds that a loan for a refrigerator would not in any event be covered by para. 16 unless it is a fixture within the home (see *CIS 363/1993*). "Provision of" has replaced "provision or improvement of" in a number of places (reflecting the change in the overall test from "improving" to "maintaining" the fitness of the home). "Provision of" would not seem to be limited to initial installation, but could cover repairs to, or replacement of, an existing facility (see *R v. Social Fund Inspector ex p. Tuckwood* (High Court, April 27, 1995). Heads (k) and (l) are new and make provision for these two specific situations. Note that a loan to which the new head (k) applies is ignored for the purposes of the ceiling on loans (para. 11(9)).

On head (l) see *CIS 14657/1996*. The Commissioner points out that the loan has to be taken out "for the purpose" of the relevant improvements. The claimant's loan could therefore fall within head (l) where his daughter was aged 10 but her brother would not reach that age for another year or so because the money was being used for something that was bound to happen in the near future. The Commissioner also decides that the cost of a survey could come within head (j) as reasonably incidental to the carrying out of the work covered by that head.

See *CIS 15036/1996* which concerned whether replacement of a central heating boiler came within para. 8(3)(h) of the former Sched. 3 ("provision of heating, including central heating"). The Commissioner decides that the installation of the new boiler was an improvement which had been undertaken with a view to "improving fitness for occupation" and so came within para. 8(3) (it was not contended that it constituted a major repair necessary to maintain the fabric of the home). The fact that the boiler had merely been replaced by its modern equivalent did not matter. The Commissioner refers to *Morcom v. Campbell-Johnson* [1956] 1 Q.B. 106 in which Denning L.J. had drawn a distinction between the provision of something new which would constitute an improvement and the replacement of something worn out, albeit with a modern equivalent, which would come within the category of repairs, not improvement. Presumably on the basis of this dictum the replacement of a boiler would also fall within head (b) as it would seem to fulfil the test of maintaining fitness for human habitaiton. The consequence for the claimant in *CIS 15036/1996* was that the element of her service charge attributable to the new boiler had to be deducted under the former para. 9(2)(c) (now para. 17(2)(c)). Note that the Commissioner has granted the claimant leave to appeal to the Court of Appeal but it is not known when the appeal will be heard.

CIS 2132/1998 also concerns service charges. The claimant had been billed for the cost of renewing a flat over one of the other flats in her block. The Commissioner decides that this did not come within any of the relevant heads in sub-para. (2). Head (g) did not apply as the roof was not part of the dwelling occupied by the claimant as her home. Head (j) was also not applicable, as there was no evidence that the roof had been renewed because of an unsafe structural defect. In addition, although a repair to a roof could, depending on its nature, be a damp-proofing measure, the renewal of a roof did not fall within head (c).

Sub-para. (3). See the note to para. 15(3).

Paragraph 17—Other housing costs

This provision lists the other miscellaneous housing costs covered by income support (sub-para. (1)(a)–(f), which are the same as para. 1(c)–(i) of the former Sched. 3 except that the list has been reordered) and contains the conditions for meeting these costs (which are virtually identical to the former para. 9, subject to some tidying-up of the wording).

Of these items, the category of "service charges" (sub-para. (1)(b)) is probably of most interest. This phrase is given no special definition. (It does not include an administration fee charged by a lender where mortgage payments are in arrears (*CIS 392/1994*).) *CIS 157/1989* suggested that it means charges in respect of a service rendered to a tenant by the landlord. The Tribunal of Commissioners in *R(IS) 3/91* and *R(IS) 4/91* decides that the category can extend to owner-occupiers as well. The essence is the determination and arranging of what would otherwise be left for the occupier to do for himself, on the basis of an arrangement which the terms of occupation of the property make binding on all those with the same interest in the property. However, things within the housing benefit definition of ineligible service charges are excluded (sub-para. (2)(b)). This list covers charges in respect of day-to-day living expenses, a number of personal services and other services "not connected with the provision of adequate accommodation" (see *CIS 1460/1995* below). Under sub-para. (2)(c) charges for the cost of repairs and improvements, as defined in para. 16(2), are also deducted. The narrowing of the scope of para. 16(2) will mean a corresponding reduction in the exclusion of service charges under sub-para. (2)(c). For interest on loans for service charges for repairs and improvement, see para. 16. If a charge includes fuel charges, deductions are also made (except for charges in respect of communal areas: para. 4 of Sched. 1 to the Housing Benefit Regulations, confirmed in *CIS 1460/1995*). The standard amounts to be deducted under sub-para. (2)(a) are (from April 1996, not increased in April 1997, 1998 or 1999): heating (apart from hot water), £9.25; hot water, £1.15; lighting, 80p; cooking, £1.15. The standard amounts can be altered on evidence of the actual or estimated charge. Note that since housing benefit expenditure is excluded generally under para. 4(1)(a), this means that no service charge, payment of which by a tenant is a condition for the occupation of the home (and therefore within the definition of rent), can count under Sched. 3.

In *R(IS) 3/91* a leaseholder's share of the cost of roof repairs was a service charge. The obligation was imposed on the claimant by the conditions of her occupation and the service was connected with the provision of adequate accommodation, so that the exclusion in sub-para. (2)(b) did not bite. But the exclusion in sub-para. (2)(c) would now apply (assuming that roof repairs would qualify under para. 16(2): see head (j)). In *R(IS) 4/91* the claimant, an owner-occupier, had to pay £93 a year to have his cess-pit emptied. The appeal had to be returned to the SSAT for further findings of fact, but it was suggested that if the service was carried out by an outside contractor engaged by the claimant, the cost would not be a service charge.

In *R(IS) 4/92* it was held that sums required to be paid by a tenant under the terms of the lease to reimburse the landlord for the cost of property insurance were a service charge within the principles set out in *R(IS) 3/91* and *R(IS) 4/91*. The Commissioner also found that the landlord's obligation to use any money paid out under the insurance policy as a result of fire on reinstatement of the property meant that the charge was connected with the provision of adequate accommodation. The Commissioner in *CSIS 4/1990* doubted that building insurance was so connected (referring to the earlier decision in *CIS 17/1988* where there was a suggestion to the contrary). The Court of Session in the *McSherry* case (which is the appeal in *CSIS 4/1990*) does not deal with this point. However, in *R(IS) 19/93* the Commissioner agrees with *R(IS) 4/92* and dissents from the suggestion in *CIS 17/1988*. The weight of authority would therefore seem to favour the interpretation taken in *R(IS) 4/92* in relation to payments by tenants to reimburse landlords for the cost of building insurance. But note the effect of para. 4(1)(a). In *R(IS) 4/92* the Commissioner made his award subject to enquiries whether the reimbursement of the landlord's insurance premiums would be included in the claimant's rent for housing benefit purposes.

In *Dunne v. Department of Health and Social Security* (September 10, 1993), the Court of Appeal in Northern Ireland decided that the building insurance premium paid by the claimant as an owner occupier was not a service charge. Although the claimant was obliged to take out such insurance under the terms of both his building lease and his mortgage, it did not fulfill the test laid down in *R(IS) 3/91* and *R(IS) 4/91*. Such a premium was to be distinguished from payment required to be made to the landlord for building insurance by occupiers of a block of flats which clearly was a service charge. In *Secretary of State for Social Security v. McSherry* (March 17, 1994) the property insurance premium at issue was mandatory under the terms of the claimant's mortgage. The Court of Session agrees with the decision in *Dunne*, holding that the omission of insurance premiums from para. 1 of the former Sched. 3 (in contrast to the express provision for routine maintenance and insurance in the supplementary benefit scheme) was deliberate. (*R(SB) 1/90* holds that although decisions of the Court of Appeal of Northern Ireland are not binding on Commissioners in Great Britain, identically worded provisions operating in both Northern Ireland and Great Britain are to be interpreted uniformly. Decisions of the Court of Session are binding.)

R(IS) 19/93 had come to a similar conclusion. The Commissioner states that the claimant's obligation to pay the insurance premium to his building society was not an obligation arising from his interest or estate in the property, but from his mortgage. It was a consequence of the claimant's financial arrangements, not his ownership of the property itself, and thus was not a service charge. In essence, the payment was no different from a house insurance premium paid under an ordinary contract between an owner/occupier and his insurance company (which had been held in *CIS 17/1988* not to constitute a service charge).

The result is that whether the obligation to pay insurance charges or to reimburse a landlord for the payment of insurance premiums constitutes a service charge depends upon it coming within the principles set out in *R(IS) 3/91* and *R(IS) 4/91*. It seems clear that payments required to be made to the landlord from occupiers of a block of flats to cover insurance for the building are a service charge, whereas a building insurance premium payable under the terms of a claimant's mortgage is not. An insurance charge of the kind concerned in *R(IS) 4/92* also constitutes a service charge. On the other hand, an obligation on the claimant to effect insurance under the terms of a lease would not qualify.

CIS 1460/1995 concerned a service charge for residents of sheltered accommodation for the elderly. The claimant lived in a self-contained bungalow and had the use of communal areas (pathways and gardens) and a communal lounge; the service charge covered the costs of broadly the maintenance of the common areas and the structure of the buildings, as well as a resident warden. The Commissioner accepts that the terms of the appendix to *R(IS) 3/91* and *R(IS) 4/91* as a whole (as opposed to the headnote) made it clear that a service charge was only to be excluded under sub-para. (2)(b) to the extent it related to matters specified as ineligible in para. 1 of Sched. 1 to the Housing Benefit Regulations; there was no overriding test of connection with the adequacy of the accommodation (see para. 1(g) of Sched. 1). Where an element of a service charge was not dealt with in sub-paras. (a)–(f) of para. 1 of Sched. 1 so that sub-para. (g) had to be considered, a common sense view had to be taken. In general, where a claimant had a right to use a communal lounge, gardens, etc., services related to those communal areas should be accepted as related to the provision of adequate accommodation. Para. 1 as a whole did contemplate that charges for communal areas could be eligible (see, for example, sub-para. (a)(ii) (laundry facilities), (iii) (children's play area) and (iv) (cleaning of communal areas)). Moreover, if service charges were thought to be excessive, the appropriate control mechanism was para. 10 (now see para. 13). On the meaning of para. 1(g) itself, although it excluded services which related purely to meeting the personal needs of residents, this did not mean that in considering whether a service was related to the provision of adequate accommodation the question of suitability for the personal needs of the residents was not relevant (see Sedley J. in *R. v. North Cornwall District Council ex parte Singer and Others* (High Court, November 26, 1993, pp. 11–12 of the transcript). Para. 1 of Sched. 1 did envisage that the personal needs of the claimant could be considered (see sub-para. (a)(iv) on window-cleaning and (c) on emergency alarm systems where the eligibility of a service charge depended on the claimant's personal circumstances). What was connected to the provision of adequate accommodation, including how far the personal needs of residents should be taken into account, was a question of fact in each case (para. 17 of the appendix to *R(IS) 3/91* and *R(IS) 4/91*). The Commissioner also deals with the meaning of ''sheltered accommodation'' (see the definition of ''communal area'' in para. 7 of Sched. 1 to the Housing Benefit Regulations which includes rooms of common use in sheltered accommmodation). He suggests that the characteristics of such accommodation were the grouping together of individual dwellings, which were offered primarily to those with some special housing need, and where some communal facilites, the employment of a warden and an emergency alarm system, were included. But accommodation could still be sheltered accommodation even without some of these features.

Paragraph 18–Non-dependent deductions

Non-dependent is defined in reg. 3. The standard deductions depend on whether the non-dependent is in remurative work or not, and the level of earnings (sub-paras. (1) and (2)). The same deduction is made for a couple as for a single person (sub-paras. (3) and (4)). Note that no deduction is made from the benefit of a claimant who (or whose partner) is blind or who is in receipt of attendance allowance or the care component of disability living allowance for himself (sub-para. (6)). Note also the list in sub-para. (7) of non-dependants for whom no deduction is made. Those covered include those getting a training allowance while on Work Based Training for Young People (which has replaced Youth Training and other training provision focussed on 16/17 year olds) (head (b)); students (head (c)); under-25s on income support or income-based JSA (head (d)); those for whom a deduction has already been made from a rent allowance or rebate (head (e)); people who would not count as non-dependents under reg. 3(2B) but for reg. 3(2C) (*e.g.* co-owners who are close relatives or their partners, where the co-ownership arose after April 11, 1988) (head (f)); patients absent from home for more than six weeks, and prisoners (head (g)).

[¹SCHEDULE 3A   **Regulations 17(1)(g),
18(1)(h) and 71(1)(a)(v)
and (d)(iv)**

PROTECTED SUM

Interpretation

1.—(1) In this Schedule—
[³"eligible housing benefit" means
    (a) for the period of 7 consecutive days beginning on 3rd April 1989, the amount
    of housing benefit to which the claimant or his partner was entitled in that
    period which relates to the board and lodging accommodation normally occu-
    pied as the home by him or, if he has a partner, by him and his partner;
    (b) for the period of 7 consecutive days beginning on 10th April 1989 or, in a
    case to which paragraph 7(7)(b) applies, for the period of 7 consecutive days
    referred to in that paragraph, the amount of the claimant's or his partner's
    maximum housing benefit determined in accordance with regulation 61 of
    the Housing Benefit (General) Regulations 1987 (maximum housing benefit)
    which relates to that accommodation;]
"first week" means the benefit week beginning on a day during the period of 7 days
    commencing on 3rd April 1989;
"income support" includes any sum payable under Part II of the Income Support
    (Transitional) Regulations 1987;
"protected sum" means the amount applicable under this Schedule [⁹or by virtue of
    regulation 87(2) of the Jobseeker's Allowance Regulations 1996] [³to a claimant
    who in the first week is living in board and lodging accommodation or who or
    whose partner is temporarily absent in that week from that accommodation];
[³"protected total" means—
    (a) the total of the claimant's applicable amount under regulation 20 (applicable
    amounts for persons in board and lodging accommodation) in the first week
    or, in a case to which paragraph 7(7) applies, if the protected person or any
    partner of his is temporarily absent from his accommodation in that week,
    the amount which would have fallen to be calculated under that regulation
    for that week as if there had been no temporary absence; and
    (b) the amount of any eligible housing benefit for the period of 7 consecutive
    days beginning 3rd April 1989;]
"relevant provisions" means—
    (a) regulation 17(1)(a) to (f) (applicable amounts);
    (b) regulation 18(1)(a) to (g) (polygamous marriages);
    (c) regulation 71(1)(a)(i) to (iv) (urgent cases);
    (d) regulation 71(1)(d)(i) to (iii);
    (e) in relation to a case to which paragraph 17(b)(ii) or (c)(i) of Schedule 7
    (persons from abroad) applies, the regulations specified in that paragraph but
    as if the reference to regulation 17(1)(g) in that paragraph were omitted; or
    (f) in relation to a case to which paragraph 17(d)(i) of that Schedule applies, the
    regulations specified in that paragraph but as if the reference to regulation 18
    were a reference to regulation 18(1)(a) to (g) only;
"second week" means the benefit week beginning on a day during the period of 7
    days commencing on 10th April 1989.
[³"third week" means the benefit week beginning on a day during the period of 7
    days commencing on 17th April 1989.]
(2) For the purposes of this Schedule—
(a) in determining a claimant's applicable amount in his first week, second week or
    any subsequent benefit week no account shall be taken of any reduction under

regulation 22 (reduction in certain cases of unemployment benefit disqualification);
(b) [²except in so far as it relates to any temporary absence to which paragraph 7(7) refers,] where a change of circumstances takes effect in the claimant's second week which, had it taken effect in the first week, would have resulted in a lesser applicable amount in respect of that week, his applicable amount in the first week shall be determined as if the change of circumstances had taken effect in that week.

Protected sum

2. [³Subject to sub-paragraph (2) and the following paragraphs] of this Schedule, where the protected total of a claimant is more than—
(a) his applicable amount in the second week determined in accordance with the relevant provisions; and
(b) any eligible housing benefit for the period [³of 7 consecutive days] beginning 10th April 1989,
the protected sum applicable to the claimant shall be an amount equal to the difference.
[³(2) Where—
(a) in the second week a claimant's income calculated in accordance with Part V or, as the case may be, VI exceeds the aggregate of his applicable amount determined in accordance with the relevant provisions and X; and
(b) the amount of income support to which he is entitled in the first week is more than the amount of housing benefit to which he would, but for this sub-paragraph, have been entitled in the period of 7 consecutive days beginning on 10th April 1989.
the protected sum applicable to the claimant shall, subject to sub-paragraph (3), be an amount equal to $X + Y + 10$ pence.
(3) Where a claimant or his partner is, or both are, entitled in the first, second and third weeks to a relevant social security benefit or to more than one such benefit and consequent upon the Social Security Benefits Up-rating Order 1989 the claimant or his partner is, or both are, entitled to an increase in any one or more of those benefits in the third week, the protected sum under sub-paragraph (2) shall be increased by an amount equal to the difference between—
(a) the amount of benefit or aggregate amount of those benefits to which the claimant or his partner is, or both are, entitled in the third week; and, if less,
(b) the amount of benefit or aggregate amount of those benefits to which the claimant or his partner is, or both are, entitled in the second week.
(4) In this paragraph—
"X" means the sum which, but for sub-paragraph (2), would be the protected sum applicable under sub-paragraph (1);
"Y" means the amount of the excess to which sub-paragraph (2)(a) refers;
"relevant social security benefit" means—
(a) child benefit;
(b) any benefit under the Social Security Act [SSCBA];
(c) war disablement pension;
(d) war widow's pension;
(e) any payment under a scheme made under the Industrial Injuries and Diseases (Old Cases) Act 1975;
(f) any concessionary payment.]

Persons not entitled to a protected sum

3. A protected sum shall not be applicable to a claimant where in the first week—
(a) he is aged under 25 and, if he is a member of a couple, his partner is also aged under 25; and

383

(b) he is required to be available for employment for the purposes of section 20(3)(d)(i) of the Act [SSCBA, s.124(1)(d)(i)]; and

(c) he was not in receipt of supplementary benefit as a boarder on November 24, 1985; and

(d) none of the conditions in paragraph 16(4) of Schedule 5 (applicable amounts of persons in board and lodging accommodation or hostels) applies to him.

[²(2) A protected sum shall not be applicable to a claimant [³unless he, or any partner of his, is entitled to housing benefit for the period of 7 consecutive days beginning 10th April 1989 or, where paragraph 7(7)(b) applies, for the period of 7 consecutive days referred to in that paragraph in respect of] the board and lodging accommodation normally occupied as the home by him, or if he has a partner, by him and his partner.

(3) Subject to paragraph 7, a protected sum shall not be applicable to a claimant where he changes or vacates his accommodation during the period of 7 consecutive days beginning 10th April 1989.]

Period of application

4. Subject to paragraph 7, the protected sum shall not be applicable to a claimant for more than—

(a) in the case of a claimant who is a member of a family and that family includes a child or young person and during the first week that family was in accommodation not provided or secured by a local authority under section 63 or 65(2) or (3)(a) of the Housing (Scotland) Act 1987, a period of 52 weeks beginning with the second week;

(b) in any other case, a period of 13 weeks beginning with the second week.

Reduction of protected sum

5.—(1) Subject to [⁸sub-paragraphs (2) to (6)], the protected sum shall be reduced by the amount of any increase, in a benefit week subsequent to the second week, in the claimant's applicable amount determined in accordance with the relevant provisions.

(2) Where regulation 22 (reduction in certain cases of unemployment benefit disqualification) [⁶or regulation 21A (reductions in certain cases of failure to attend courses)] ceases to apply to a claimant and as a result his applicable amount increases no account shall be taken of that increase.

[³(3) Where by virtue of the coming into force of regulation 5 of the Income Support (General) Amendment Regulations 1989 the claimant's applicable amount increases in his benefit week beginning on a day during the period of 7 days commencing on 9th October 1989, no account shall be taken of that increase.]

[⁵(4) Where a claimant's applicable amount increases because a child or young person mentioned in paragraph (5)(c) of regulation 16 (circumstances in which a person is treated or not treated as a member of the household) is treated as a member of the claimant's household under paragraph (6) of that regulation, the claimant's protected sum shall not be reduced by the amount of that increase unless the child or young person has been treated as a member of the household for a continuous period which exceeds 8 weeks.]

[⁷(5) Where by virtue of the coming into force of regulation 15(a), (b) or (c) of the Income Support (General) Amendment No. 4 Regulations 1991 a claimant's applicable amount increases in his benefit week beginning on a day during the period of 7 days commencing on 1st October 1991, no account shall be taken of that increase.]

[⁸(6) Where by virtue of the coming into force of regulation 3(1) and (2) of the Income-Related Benefits Amendment Regulations 1992 a claimant's applicable amount increases in his benefit week beginning on a day during the period of 7 days commencing on 5th October 1992, no account shall be taken of that increase.]

Termination of protected sum

6. Subject to paragraph 7, the protected sum shall cease to be applicable if—
(a) that amount is reduced to nil under paragraph 5; or
(b) the claimant changes or [²vacates] his accommodation; or
(c) the claimant ceases to be entitled to income support.

Protected persons

7.—(1) Subject to sub-paragraph (2), for the purposes of this paragraph a protected person is a claimant, where—
(a) in respect of the first week he is entitled to an increase under paragraph 7 of Schedule 5 (applicable amounts of persons in board and lodging accommodation or hostels) because either he or, if he is one of a couple or a member of a polygamous marriage, he or his partner satisfies any of the conditions in paragraph 8 of that Schedule; or
(b) in the first week the claimant or, if he has a partner, either he or his partner—
 (i) is in need of personal care by reason of [²old age,] mental or physical disablement, mental illness, or dependence on alcohol or drugs; and
 (ii) is receiving both board and personal care in accommodation other than a residential care home or nursing home or residential accommodation within the meaning of regulation 21(3) (special cases) [³ . . .]; and
 (iii) is in accommodation which he entered under arrangements for his personal care made by a statutory authority or a voluntary or charitable body and those arrangements are being supervised on a continuing basis by that authority or body; or
(c) he or, if he has a partner, either he or his partner but for his temporary absence from his accommodation for a period not exceeding 13 weeks, which includes the first week, would have satisfied (a) or (b) above.
(2) A claimant is not a protected person if he or, if he has a partner, he or his partner, in the first week, is temporarily living in board and lodging accommodation and that accommodation is not the accommodation normally occupied as the home.
(3) Paragraph 4 shall not apply to a protected person.
(4) Paragraph 6(b) shall not apply to a protected person if:
(a) he moves to accommodation where he satisfies conditions (i) to (iii) of sub-paragraph (1)(b); or
(b) he becomes a patient within the meaning of regulation 21(3); or
(c) on his ceasing to be a patient within the meaning of regulation 21(3), either he returns to the accommodation which he occupied immediately before he became a patient, or he moves to other accommodation where he satisfies conditions [²(i) to (iii)] of sub-paragraph (1)(b); or
(d) in a case to which sub-paragraph (6) applies, on his becoming re-entitled to income support, he is either in the accommodation which he occupied immediately before he ceased to be entitled to income support, or in accommodation where he satisfies conditions (i) to (iii) of sub-paragraph (1)(b).
[³(5) Except where sub-paragraph (7) applies, where a protected sum was applicable to a protected person immediately before he or any partner of his became a patient within the meaning of regulation 21(3) for a period of 14 weeks or less, he shall, subject to sub-paragraph (4)(c), on his or, as the case may be, his partner's easing to be a patient, be entitled to a protected sum equal to—
(a) the amount by which his protected total exceeds his applicable amount determined in accordance with the relevant provisions in the first benefit week in which his applicable amount ceases to be determined under paragraph 1 of Schedule 7 and either—

       (i) any eligible housing benefit for the period of 7 consecutive days beginning on 10th April 1989; or, if greater,

      (ii) in a case where sub-paragraph (7)(b) applied, any eligible housing benefit for the period of 7 consecutive days referred to in that sub-paragraph; or

  (b) the amount of the protected sum to which he was entitled in the immediately preceding benefit week,

whichever is the lower.

(6) Paragraph 6(c) shall not apply to a protected person who has ceased to be entitled to income support for [⁴a period not exceeding the permitted period determined in accordance with regulation 3A (permitted period)]—

  (a) if immediately before he ceased to be so entitled a protected sum was applicable to him; and

  (b) except where sub-paragraph (7) applies, if during that period the protected person becomes re-entitled, or would by virtue of this sub-paragraph be re-entitled, to income support he shall, subject to sub-paragraph (4)(d), be entitled to a protected sum equal to—

      (i) the amount by which his protected total exceeds his applicable amount determined in accordance with the relevant provisions in the first complete benefit week in which he becomes so re-entitled and either any eligible housing benefit for the period of 7 consecutive days beginning 10th April 1989 or, if greater, in a case to which sub-paragraph (7)(*b*) applied, any eligible housing benefit for the period of 7 consecutive days referred to in that sub-paragraph; or

     (ii) the amount of the protected sum to which he was previously entitled,

    whichever is the lower.

(7) Where a protected person or any partner of his is temporarily absent from his accommodation for a period not exceeding 13 weeks which includes the first or second week (or both)—

  (a) in a case where a protected sum was applicable to the protected person immediately before his or, as the case may be, his partner's return to that accommodation and the full charge was made for the accommodation during the temporary absence, on the protected person's or, as the case may be, his partner's return to that accommodation, the protected person shall be entitled to a protected sum equal to—

      (i) the amount by which his protected total exceeds his applicable amount determined in accordance with the relevant provisions in the first complete benefit week after his or, as the case may be, his partner's return to that accommodation and any eligible housing benefit for the period of 7 consecutive days beginning 10th April 1989; or

     (ii) the amount of the protected sum which was applicable to him in the immediately preceding benefit week,

    whichever is the lower;

  (b) in a case where—

      (i) a protected sum has not at any time been applicable to the protected person; or

     (ii) immediately before the protected person's or, as the case may be, his partner's return to that accommodation a protected sum was applicable but a reduced charge was made for the accommodation during the temporary absence.

the protected person on his or, as the case may be, his partner's return to that accommodation shall, subject to sub-paragraph (8), be entitled to a protected sum equal to the amount by which his protected total exceeds his applicable amount determined in accordance with the relevant provisions in the first complete benefit week after his or, as the case may be, his partner's return to that accommodation and the amount of eligible housing benefit for the period of 7 consecutive days beginning on the date determined in accordance with regulation 65 or, as the case may be, 68(2) of the Housing Benefit (General) Regulations 1987 (date on which entitlement is to commence or change of circumstances is to take effect) following that person's return to that accommodation.

(8) Where, in a case to which sub-paragraph (7)(b)(i) applies—

(a) in the first complete benefit week after the protected person's or, as the case may be, his partner's return to his accommodation the protected person's income calculated in accordance with Part V or, as the case may be, VI exceeds the aggregate of his applicable amount determined in accordance with the relevant provisions and X; and

(b) the amount of income support to which he was entitled in the first week is more than the amount of housing benefit to which he would, but for this sub-paragraph, have been entitled in the period of 7 consecutive days beginning on the date determined in accordance with regulation 65 or, as the case may be, 68(2) of the Housing Benefit (General) Regulations 1987 following the case may be, his partner's return to that accommodation.

the protected sum applicable shall, subject to sub-paragraph (9), be an amount equal to $X + Y + 10$ pence.

(9) Where the protected person or, as the case may be, his partner returns to the accommodation in the second week and he or his partner is, or both are, entitled in the first, second and third weeks to a relevant social security benefit or to more than one such benefit and consequent upon the Social Security Benefits Up-rating Order 1989 he or his partner is, or both are, entitled to an increase in any one or more of those benefits in the third week, the protected sum under sub-paragraph (8) shall be increased by an amount equal to the difference between—

(a) the amount of benefit or aggregate amount of those benefits to which the protected person or his partner is, or both are, entitled in the third week; and, if less,

(b) the amount of benefit or aggregate amount of those benefits to which the protected person or his partner is, or both are, entitled in the second week.

(10) In sub-paragraph (8)—

"X" means the sum which, but for sub-paragraph (8), would be the protected sum applicable in a case to which sub-paragraph (7)(b)(i) applies;

"Y" means the amount of the excess to which sub-paragraph (8)(*a*) refers;

"relevant social security benefit" has the same meaning as in paragraph 3(4).]]

AMENDMENTS

1. Income Support (General) Amendment No. 4 Regulations 1988 (S.I. 1988 No. 1445), Sched. 2 (April 10, 1989).

2. Income Support (General) Amendment No. 5 Regulations 1988 (S.I. 1988 No. 2022), reg. 19 (April 10, 1989).

3. Income Support (General) Amendment Regulations 1989 (S.I. 1989 No. 534), reg. 7 and Sched. 1 (April 10, 1989).

4. Income Support (General) Amendment No. 3 Regulations 1989 (S.I. 1989 No. 1678), reg. 8 (October 9, 1989).

5. Income Support (General) Amendment Regulations 1990 (S.I. 1990 No. 547), reg. 19 (April 9, 1990).

6. Income Support (General and Transitional) Amendment Regulations 1990 (S.I. 1990 No. 2324), reg. 4 (December 17, 1990).

7. Income Support (General) Amendment No. 4 Regulations 1991 (S.I. 1991 No. 1559), reg. 17 (October 1, 1991).

8. Income-related Benefits Amendment Regulations 1992 (S.I. 1992 No. 1326), reg. 3(3) (October 5, 1992).

9. Income Support (General) (Jobseeker's Allowance Consequential Amendments) Regulations 1996 (S.I. 1996 No. 206), reg. 25 (October 7, 1996).

DEFINITIONS

"the Act"—see reg. 2(1).

"benefit week"—*ibid.*
"board and lodging accommodation"—*ibid.*
"child"—see 1986 Act, s.20(11) (SSCBA, s.137(1)).
"claimant"—see reg. 2(1).
"couple"—*ibid.*
"employment"—*ibid.*
"family"—see 1986 Act, s.20(11) (SSCBA, s.137(1)).
"local authority"—see 1986 Act, s.84(1).
"partner"—see reg. 2(1).
"polygamous marriage"—*ibid.*
"young person"—*ibid.*, reg. 14.

GENERAL NOTE

Sched. 3A is made necessary by the removal from the Regulations of the special treatment of those in board and lodging accommodation. Before April 1989, such claimants received their board and lodging charge (subject to a maximum amount, and a maximum length of time for some under-25s) plus a personal allowance, but were not eligible for housing benefit. From April 1989, they receive ordinary personal allowances and premiums, but are eligible for housing benefit. Sched. 3A provides transitional protection if there is a loss of income for existing claimants, in the form of a "protected sum" to make up the difference.

R(IS) 2/92 holds that to be a protected person within para. 7(1)(a) a person must actually have been entitled to an increase of the maximum amount for boarders under para. 7 of Sched. 5 immediately before the benefit week beginning in the week from April 3, 1989.

[¹SCHEDULE 3B   **Regulations 17(1)(g),
18(1)(h) and 71(1)(a)(v)
and (d)(iv)**

PROTECTED SUM

Interpretation

1.—(1) In this Schedule—
"eligible housing benefit" means—
    (a) for the period of 7 consecutive days beginning on 2nd October 1989, the amount of housing benefit to which the claimant or his partner was entitled in that period which relates to the hostel normally occupied as the home by him or, if he has a partner, by him and his partner;
    (b) for the period of 7 consecutive days beginning on 9th October 1989 or, in a case to which paragraph 6(4) (b) applies, for the period of 7 consecutive days referred to in that paragraph, the amount of the claimant's or his partner's maximum housing benefit determined in accordance with regulation 61 of the Housing Benefit (General) Regulations 1987 (maximum housing benefit) which relates to that accommodation.
"first week" means the benefit week beginning on a day in the period of 7 days commencing on 2nd October 1989;
"hostel" means any establishment which immediately before the commencement of this Schedule was a hostel within the meaning of regulation 20(2) (applicable amounts for persons in hostels);
"income support" includes any sum payable under Part II of the Income Support (Transitional) Regulations 1987;
"March benefit week" means the benefit week beginning on a day during the period of 7 consecutive days beginning 20th March 1989;
"protected sum" means the amount applicable under this Schedule [⁷or by virtue of regulation 87(2) of the Jobseeker's Allowance Regulations 1996] to a claimant

who in the first week is living in a hostel or who or whose partner is temporarily absent in that week from that accommodation;

"protected total" means—

    (a) the total of the claimant's applicable amount under regulation 20 in the first week or, [² ...] if the claimant or any partner of his is temporarily absent from his accommodation [²for a period not exceeding 14 weeks which includes that week], the amount which would have fallen to be calculated under that regulation for that week as if there had been no temporary absence; and

    (b) the amount of any eligible housing benefit for the period of 7 consecutive days beginning 2nd October 1989;

"relevant benefit week" means the benefit week beginning on a day during that period of 7 consecutive days commencing on 9th April 1990;

"relevant provisions" means—

    (a) regulation 17(1)(a) to (f) (applicable amounts);

    (b) regulation 18(1)(a) to (g) (polygamous marriages);

    (c) regulation 71(1)(a)(i) to (iv) (urgent cases);

    (d) regulation 71(1)(d)(i) to (iii);

  [²(dd) paragraph 13 of Schedule 7 (persons in residential accommodation);]

    (e) in relation to a case to which paragraph 17(b)(ii) or (c)(i) of Schedule 7 (persons from abroad) applies, the regulations specified in that paragraph but as if the reference to regulation 17(1)(g) in that paragraph were omitted; or

    (f) in relation to a case to which paragraph 17(d)(i) of that Schedule applies, the regulations specified in that paragraph but as if the reference to regulation 18 were a reference to regulation 18(1)(a) to (g) only;

"second week" means the benefit week beginning on a day during the period of 7 consecutive days commencing on 9th October 1989.

(2) For the purposes of this Schedule—

(a) in determining a claimant's applicable amount in his first week, second week or any subsequent benefit week no account shall be taken of any reduction under regulation 22 (reduction in certain cases of unemployment benefit disqualification);

(b) except in so far as it relates to any temporary absence to which paragraph 6(4) refers, where a change of circumstances takes effect in the claimant's second week which, if it had taken effect in the first week, would have resulted in a lesser applicable amount in respect of that week, his applicable amount in the first week shall be determined as if the change of circumstances had taken effect in that week.

Protected sum

2.—(1) Subject to the following provisions of this paragraph and the following paragraphs of this Schedule, where the protected total of a claimant is more than—

(a) his applicable amount in the second week determined in accordance with the relevant provisions less the amount of any increase consequent on the coming into force of regulation 5 of the Income Support (General) Amendment Regulations 1989; and

(b) any eligible housing benefit for the period of 7 consecutive days beginning 9th October 1989,

the protected sum applicable to the claimant shall be an amount equal to the difference.

(2) Where—

(a) in the second week a claimant's income calculated in accordance with Part V or, as the case may be, VI exceeds the aggregate of his applicable amount determined in accordance with the relevant provisions and X; and

(b) the amount of income support to which he is entitled in the first week is more than the amount of housing benefit to which he would, but for this sub-paragraph, have been entitled in the period of 7 consecutive days beginning on 9th October 1989, the protected sum applicable to the claimant shall be an amount equal to $X + Y + 10$ pence.

(3) In sub-paragraph (2)—

"X" means the sum which, but for sub-paragraph (2), would be the protected sum applicable under sub-paragraph (1);

"Y" means the amount of the excess to which sub-paragraph (2)(a) refers.

(4) For the period beginning with the claimant's relevant benefit week the protected sum applicable to the claimant shall, subject to sub-paragraph (6), and the following paragraphs of this Schedule, be—

(a) the total of—

(i) the amount of the allowance for personal expenses for the claimant or, if he is a member of a family, for him and for each member of his family in the first week determined, or which, but for any temporary absence, would have been determined, in accordance with paragraph 11 of Schedule 5 as then in force;

(ii) [³subject to sub-paragraph (7)] the amount of any increase for meals in the first week determined, or which, but for any temporary absence, would have been determined, in accordance with paragraph 2 of that Schedule; and

(iii) the amount or, if he is a member of a family, the aggregate of the amounts determined in accordance with sub-paragraph (5),

less the aggregate of his applicable amount in the second week determined, or which, but for any temporary absence, would have been determined, in accordance with the relevant provisions and, where applicable, the amount of any reduction in the protected sum made by virtue of paragraph 4 in a benefit week occurring before the relevant benefit week; or

(b) the amount of the protected sum which was applicable to him in the immediately preceding benefit week,

whichever is the lower.

(5) For the purposes of sub-paragraph (4)(a), where in the first week the accommodation charge makes or, but for any temporary absence, would have made, provision or no provision for meals, as respects each person an amount shall be determined as follows—

(a) in a case where the provision is for at least three meals a day—

(i) for the claimant, £17.20;

(ii) for a member of his family aged 16 or over, £12.50;

(iii) for a member of the family aged less than 16, £6.25;

(b) except where head (c) applies, in a case where the provision is for less than three meals a day—

(i) for the claimant, £13.85;

(ii) for a member of his family aged 16 or over, £8.30;

(iii) for a member of his family aged less than 16, £4.15;

(c) in a case where the provision is for breakfast only—

(i) for the claimant, £7.05;

(ii) for a member of his family, £1.50;

(d) in a case where there is no provision for meals, for the claimant or, if he is a member of a family, for the claimant and for the members of his family for whom there is no such provision, £5.55;

(6) Where in the relevant benefit week the claimant is in, or only temporarily absent from, residential accommodation, the protected sum applicable to the claimant for the period beginning with that week shall[², subject to the following paragraphs of this Schedule,] be—

(a) equal to the difference between—

(i) the amount of the allowance for personal expenses for the claimant or, if he is a member of a family, for him and for each member of his family in the first week determined, or which, but for any temporary absence, would have been determined, in accordance with paragraph 11 of Schedule 5 as then in force; and

(ii) the amount of the allowance for personal expenses for the claimant or, if he is a member of a family, for him and for each member of his family in the second week determined, or which, but for any temporary absence would have been determined, under paragraph 13 of Schedule 7 (persons in residential accommodation),

less, where applicable, the amount of any reduction in the protected sum made by virtue of paragraph 4 in a benefit week occurring before the relevant benefit week; or

(b) the amount of the protected sum which was applicable to him in the immediately preceding benefit week,

whichever is the lower.

[³(7) In the case of a member of a family who in the first week is a child aged less than 11, the amount of any increase for meals under sub-paragraph (4)(a)(ii) shall be either—

(a) the amount of any such increase in the first week determined, or which, but for any temporary absence, would have been determined, in accordance with paragraph 2 of Schedule 5 as then in force; or

(b) £17.65,

whichever is the lower.]

Persons not entitled to a protected sum

3.—(1) Subject to paragraph 6, a protected sum shall not be applicable to a claimant where he changes or vacates his hostel during the period of 7 consecutive days beginning 9th October 1989.

(2) Except where regulation 8(2)(b) of the Housing Benefit (General) Regulations 1987 (eligible housing costs) applies, a protected sum shall not be applicable to a claimant unless he, or any partner of his, is entitled to housing benefit for the period of 7 consecutive days beginning 9th October 1989 or, where paragraph 6(4)(b) applies, for the period of 7 consecutive days referred to in that paragraph, in respect of the hostel normally occupied as the home by him, or if he has a partner, by him and his partner.

(3) A protected sum shall not be applicable to a claimant where—

(a) he has been or would, but for any temporary absence, have been in the same accommodation in both the March benefit week and the second week, and—
   (i) his applicable amount in both those weeks fell or would have fallen, but for any temporary absence, to be determined under paragraph 13(1) of Schedule 7; or
   (ii) his applicable amount in the second week fell or would have fallen, but for any temporary absence, to be determined under that paragraph and would also have fallen to be so determined in the March benefit week had his stay in that accommodation been other than temporary; or

(b) his applicable amount in the second week fell or would have fallen, but for any temporary absence, to be determined under that paragraph and would also have fallen to be so determined in the March benefit week had he been in the same accommodation in that week and had his stay in that accommodation been other than temporary[²; or

(c) his applicable amount in the first week fell or would have fallen, but for any temporary absence, to be determined under regulation 20 but would not have fallen to be so determined in the March benefit week had he been in the same accommodation in that week and had his stay in that accommodation been other than temporary.

(4) For the purposes of sub-paragraph (3), where—

(a) a claimant's applicable amount in respect of the March benefit week has been determined under paragraph 13(1) of Schedule 7 and it is subsequently determined on review that it fell to be determined under regulation 20, he shall, notwithstanding that review, be treated as if his applicable amount fell to be determined under that paragraph;

(b) a claimant has been temporarily absent from his accommodation in the March benefit week and immediately before the period of temporary absence his applicable amount was determined under paragraph 13(1) of Schedule 7, he shall be treated as if his applicable amount would have fallen to be determined under that paragraph during the period of temporary absence notwithstanding that it is subsequently determined on review that immediately before the period of temporary absence it fell to be determined under regulation 20;

(c) a claimant has entered his accommodation after the March benefit week, he shall be treated as if his applicable amount, had he been in that accommodation in the March benefit week, would not have fallen to be determined under regulation 20 in that week if the applicable amounts of other claimants in that accommodation in that week were determined otherwise than under that regulation notwithstanding that it is subsequently determined on review that they fell to be determined under regulation 20.]

Reduction of protected sum

4.—(1) Subject to [⁶sub-paragraphs (2) to (5)], the protected sum shall be reduced by the amount of any increase, in a benefit week subsequent to the second week, in the claimant's applicable amount determined in accordance with the relevant provisions.

(2) Where regulation 22 (reduction in certain cases of unemployment benefit disqualification) [⁴or regulation 21A (reductions in certain cases of failure to attend courses)] ceases to apply to a claimant and as a result his applicable amount increases no account shall be taken of that increase.

[³(3) Where a claimant's applicable amount increases because a child or young person mentioned in paragraph (5)(c) of regulation 16 (circumstances in which a person is treated or not treated as a member of the household) is treated as a member of the claimant's household under paragraph (6) of that regulation, the claimant's protected sum shall not be reduced by the amount of that increase unless the child or young person has been treated as a member of the household for a continuous period which exceeds 8 weeks.]

[⁵(4) Where by virtue of the coming into force of regulation 15(a), (b) or (c) of the Income Support (General) Amendment No. 4 Regulations 1991 a claimant's applicable amount increases in his benefit week beginning on a day during the period of 7 days commencing on 1st October 1991, no account shall be taken of that increase.]

[⁶(5) Where by virtue of the coming into force of regulation 3(1) and (2) of the Income-Related Benefits Amendment Regulations 1992 a claimant's applicable amount increases in his benefit week beginning on a day during the period of 7 days commencing on 5th October 1992, no account shall be taken of that increase.]

Termination of protected sum

5. Subject to paragraph 6, the protected sum shall cease to be applicable if—

(a) that amount is reduced to nil under paragraph 4; or
(b) the claimant changes or vacates his hostel; or
(c) the claimant ceases to be entitled to income support.

Modifications in cases of temporary absence and loss of entitlement to income support

6.—(1) Paragraph 5(b) shall not apply to a claimant if—

(a) he becomes a patient within the meaning of regulation 21(3) (special cases); or
(b) on ceasing to be a patient within the meaning of regulation 21(3), he returns to the hostel which he occupied immediately before he became a patient; or
(c) in a case to which sub-paragraph (3) applies, on his becoming re-entitled to

income support, he is in the accommodation which he occupied immediately before he ceased to be entitled to income support.

(2) Except where sub-paragraph (4) applies, where a protected sum was applicable to the claimant immediately before he or any partner of his became a patient within the meaning of regulation 21(3) for a period of 14 weeks or less, he shall, subject to sub-paragraph (1)(b), on his or, as the case may be, his partner ceasing to be a patient be entitled to a protected sum equal to—

(a) the amount by which his protected total exceeds his applicable amount determined in accordance with the relevant provisions in the first benefit week in which his applicable amount ceases to be determined under paragraph 1 of Schedule 7 and either—

    (i) any eligible housing benefit for the period of 7 consecutive days beginning on 9th October 1989; or, if greater,

    (ii) in a case where sub-paragraph (4)(b) applied, any eligible housing benefit for the period of 7 consecutive days referred to in that sub-paragraph; or

[³(aa) where the first benefit week in which his applicable amount ceases to be determined under paragraph 1 of Schedule 7 is the relevant benefit week, the amount determined under paragraph 2(4) or, as the case may be, paragraph 2(6), less any reduction under paragraph 4(1) other than a reduction which arises by virtue of his ceasing to be a patient within the meaning of regulation 21(3); or]

(b) the amount of the protested sum to which he was entitled in the immediately preceding benefit week

whichever is the lower.

(3) Paragraph 5(c) shall not apply to a claimant who has ceased to be entitled to income support for [²a period not exceeding the permitted period determined in accordance with regulation 3A (permitted period)]—

(a) if immediately before he ceased to be so entitled a protected sum was applicable to him; and

(b) except where sub-paragraph (4) applies, if during that period he becomes re-entitled, or would by virtue of this sub-paragraph be re-entitled, to income support he shall, subject to sub-paragraph (1)(c), be entitled to a protected sum equal to—

    (i) the amount by which his protected total exceeds his applicable amount determined in accordance with the relevant provisions in the first benefit week in which he becomes so re-entitled and either any eligible housing benefit for the period of 7 consecutive days beginning 9th October 1989 or, if greater, in a case to which sub-paragraph (4)(b) applied, any eligible housing benefit for the period of 7 consecutive days referred to in that sub-paragraph; or

    [³(ii) where the first benefit week in which he becomes so re-entitled is the relevant benefit week, the amount determined under paragraph 2(4) or, as the case may be, paragraph 2(6), less any reduction under paragraph 4(1) in that benefit week; or

    (iii) where the first benefit week in which he becomes so re-entitled is a week subsequent to the relevant benefit week, the amount which would have been determined under paragraph 2(4) or, as the case may be, paragraph 2(6) had he been entitled in the relevant benefit week, less any reduction under paragraph 4(1) in the benefit week in which he becomes re-entitled; or

    (iv) the amount of the protested sum to which he was previously entitled,]

whichever is the lower.

(4) Where a claimant or any partner of his temporarily absent from his accommodation for a period not exceeding 14 weeks which includes the first or second week (or both)—

(a) in a case where a protected sum was applicable to the claimant immediately before his or, as the case may be, his partner's return to that accommodation and the full charge was made for that accommodation during the temporary absence, on the claimant's or, as the case may be, his partner's return to that accommodation, the claimant shall be entitled to a protected sum equal to—

    (i) the amount by which his protected total exceeds his applicable amount determined in accordance with the relevant provisions in the first complete benefit week after his, or as the case may be, his partner's return to that accommodation and any eligible housing benefit for the period of 7 consecutive days beginning 9th October 1989; or

    (ii) the amount of the protected sum which was applicable to him in the immediately preceding benefit week,

whichever is the lower.

  (b) in a case where—

    (i) a protected sum has not at any time been applicable to the claimant; or

    (ii) immediately before the claimant's or, as the case may be, his partner's return to that accommodation a protected sum was applicable to the claimant but a reduced charge was made for the accommodation during the temporary absence,

the claimant on his or, as the case may be, his partner's, return to that accommodation shall, subject to sub-paragraph (5), be entitled to a protected sum equal to the amount by which his protected total exceeds his applicable amount determined in accordance with the relevant provisions in the first complete benefit week after his or, as the case may be, his partner's return to that accommodation and the amount of eligible housing benefit for the period of 7 consecutive days beginning on the date determined in accordance with regulation 65 or, as the case may be, 68(2) of the Housing Benefit (General) Regulations 1987 (date on which entitlement is to commence or change of circumstances is to take effect) following that person's return to that accommodation.

(5) Where, in a case to which sub-paragraph (4)(b)(i) applies—

  (a) in the first complete benefit week after the claimant's or, as the case may be, his partner's return to his accommodation the claimant's income calculated in accordance with Part V or, as the case may be, VI exceeds the aggregate of his applicable amount determined in accordance with the relevant provisions and X; and

  (b) the amount of income support to which he was entitled in the first week is more than the amount of housing benefit to which he would, but for this sub-paragraph, have been entitled in the period of 7 consecutive days beginning on the date determined in accordance with regulation 65 or, as the case may be, 68(2) of the Housing Benefit (General) Regulations 1987 following his or, as the case may be, his partner's return to that accommodation,

the protected sum applicable to the claimant shall be an amount equal to $X + Y + 10$ pence.

(6) In sub-paragraph (5)—

"X" means the sum which, but for sub-paragraph (5), would be the protected sum applicable in a case to which sub-paragraph (4)(b)(i) applies;

"Y" means the amount of the excess to which sub-paragraph (5) (a) refers.

(7) The foregoing provisions of this paragraph shall not apply to a claimant if he or, if he has a partner, he or his partner, in the first week is temporarily living in a hostel and that accommodation is not the accommodation normally occupied as the home.]

AMENDMENTS

1. Income Support (General) Amendment Regulations 1989 (S.I. 1989 No. 534), Sched. 1, para. 18 and Sched. 2 (October 9, 1989).

2. Income Support (General) Amendment No. 3 Regulations 1989 (S.I. 1989 No. 1678), reg. 9 (October 9, 1989).

3. Income Support (General) Amendment Regulations 1990 (S.I. 1990 No. 547), reg. 20 (April 9, 1990).

4. Income Support (General and Transitional) Amendment Regulations 1990 (S.I. 1990 No. 2324), reg. 5 (December 17, 1990).

5. Income Support (General) Amendment No. 4 Regulations 1991 (S.I. 1991 No. 1559), reg. 17 (October 1, 1991).

6. Income-related Benefits Amendment Regulations 1992 (S.I. 1992 No. 1326), reg. 3(4) (October 5, 1992).

7. Income Support (General) (Jobseeker's Allowance Consequential Amendments) Regulations 1996 (S.I. 1996 No. 206), reg. 25 (October 7, 1996).

GENERAL NOTE

These complex provisions provide transitional protection for those hostel-dwellers who are moved on to housing benefit in October 1989. A full description cannot be given here, but there is a helpful summary on pp.4 and 5 of *Welfare Rights Bulletin* 91 (August 1989).

The main provision is in para. 2. Sub-paras. (1) to (3) deal with the position from October 9, 1989. For claimants who are residents in or only temporarily absent from a hostel in the week before that date, their protected sum is normally the difference between their applicable amount in that week and their applicable amount plus housing benefit in the following week (para. 2(1)). If the claimant's income is too high for entitlement to income support on the ordinary rules there is a special calculation in para. 2(2). Note that the transitional protection ceases if the claimant changes or vacates his hostel or ceases to be entitled to income support (para. 5) subject to the exceptions in para. 6.

Para. 2(4) to (6) deals with protection from April 9, 1990. See *CIS 168/1990* and *CIS 340/1990* on the definition of "hostel" and *CIS 142/1991*.

[¹SCHEDULE 3C   **Regulation 2A(1)(*b*)**

THE GREATER LONDON AREA

The area described in this Schedule comprises—
(a) the Boroughs of

[²Barking and Dagenham]	Croydon
Barnet	Ealing
Bexley	Enfield
Brent	Greenwich
Bromley	Hackney
Camden	Haringey
City of Westminster	Hammersmith & Fulham
Harrow	Merton
Havering	Newham
Hillingdon	Redbridge
Hounslow	Richmond-Upon-Thames
Islington	Southwark
Kensington and Chelsea	Sutton
Kingston-Upon-Thames	Tower Hamlets
Lambeth	Waltham Forest
Lewisham	Wandsworth

(b) the City of London;
(c) in the County of Essex that part of the district of Epping Forest which comprises the parishes of Chigwell and Waltham Holy Cross;
(d) in the County of Hertfordshire, that part of the Borough of Broxbourne which lies south of Cheshunt Park, including Slipe Lane, and that part of the district of Hertsmere which comprises the former parishes of Elstree, Ridge, Shenley and South Mimms;
(e) in the County of Surrey, the Borough of Spelthorne and that part of the

Borough of Elmbridge which was formerly administered by the Old
Esher District Council.]

AMENDMENTS

1. Social Security Benefits (Amendments Consequential Upon the Introduction of Community
Care) Regulations 1992 (S.I. 1992 No. 3147), reg. 2(3) and Sched. 2 (April 1, 1993).
2. Income-related Benefits and Jobseeker's Allowance (Miscellaneous Amendments) Regulations
1997 (S.I. 1997 No. 65), reg. 10 (April 7, 1997).

SCHEDULE 4   **Regulation 19**

PART I

Applicable Amounts of Persons in Residential Care and Nursing Homes

1. Subject to sub-paragraph (2), the weekly applicable amount of a claimant to whom
regulation 19 applies shall be the aggregate of—

  (a) subject to paragraph 3, the weekly charge for the accommodation, including all
meals and services, provided for him or, if he is a member of a family, for him
and his family increased, where appropriate, in accordance with paragraph 2 but,
except in a case to which paragraph 12 applies, subject to the maximum determined in accordance with paragraph 5; and

  (b) a weekly amount for personal expenses for him and, if he is a member of a family,
for each member of his family determined in accordance with paragraph 13; and

  (c) where he is only temporarily in such accommodation any amount applicable under
[²regulation 17(1)(e) or 18(1)(f)] (housing costs) in respect of the dwelling normally occupied as the home; [²and

  (d) any amount in accordance with regulation 17(1)(f) or 18(1)(g) (applicable
amounts).]

(2) No amount shall be included in respect of any child or young person who is a
member of the claimant's family if the capital of that child or young person calculated
in accordance with Part V in like manner as for the claimant, except where otherwise
provided, would exceed £3,000.

2.—(1) Where, in addition to the weekly charge for accommodation, a separate charge
is made for the provision of heating, attention in connection with bodily functions, supervision, extra baths, laundry or a special diet needed for a medical reason, the weekly
charge for the purpose of paragraph 1(1)(a) shall be increased by the amount of that
charge.

(2) Where the weekly charge for accommodation does not include the provision of all
meals, it shall, for the purpose of paragraph 1(1)(a), be increased in respect of the claimant or, if he is a member of a family, in respect of each member of his family by the
following amount:

  (a) if the meals can be purchased within the residential care or nursing home, the
amount equal to the actual cost of the meals, calculated on a weekly basis; or

  (b) if the meals cannot be so purchased, the amount calculated on a weekly basis—

    (i) for breakfast, at a daily rate of £1.10;

    (ii) for a midday meal, at a daily rate of £1.55; and

    (iii) for an evening meal, at a daily rate of £1.55;

except that, if some or all of the meals are normally provided free of charge or at a
reduced rate, the amount shall be reduced to take account of the lower charge or
reduction.

3. Where any part of the weekly charge for the accommodation is met by housing
benefit, an amount equal to the part so met shall be deducted from the amount calculated
in accordance with paragraph 1(1)(a).

396

4. [¹. . .]

5.—(1) Subject to paragraph 12 the maximum referred to in paragraph 1(1)(a) shall be—

    (a) in the case of a single claimant, the appropriate amount in respect of that claimant specified in or determined in accordance with paragraphs 6 to 11;

[⁵(b) in the case of a claimant who is a member of a family the aggregate of the following amounts—

        (i) in respect of the claimant, the appropriate amount in respect of him specified in or determined in accordance with paragraph 6 to 11;

        (ii) in respect of each member of his family who lives in the home aged under 11, $1\frac{1}{2}$ times the amount specified in paragraph 2(a) of Schedule 2;

        (iii) in respect of each member of his family aged not less than 11 who lives in the home, an amount which would be the appropriate amount specified in or determined in accordance with paragraph 6 to 11 if the other member were the claimant.]

(2) The maximum amount in respect of a member of the family aged under 11 calculated in the manner referred to in sub-paragraph (1)(b)(i) shall be rounded to the nearest multiple of 5p by treating an odd amount of 2.5p or more as 5p and by disregarding an odd amount of less than 2.5p.

Residential care homes

[¹¹**6.**—(1) Subject to sub-paragraph (2) and paragraphs 8 to 11, where the accommodation provided for the claimant is a residential care home for persons in need of personal care by virtue of—

    (a) old age, the appropriate amount shall be £218.00 per week;

    (b) past or present mental disorder but excluding mental handicap, the appropriate amount shall be £230.00 per week;

    (c) past or present drug or alcohol dependence, the appropriate amount shall be £230.00 per week;

    (d) mental handicap, the appropriate amount shall be £262.00 per week;

    (e) physical disablement, the appropriate amount shall be—

        (i) in the case of a person to whom paragraph 8 applies, £298.00 per week, or

        (ii) in any other case £218.00 per week; or

    (f) any condition not falling within sub-paragraphs (*a*) to (*e*) above, the appropriate amount shall be £218.00 per week.]

(2) Where the claimant is over pensionable age and—

[³(a) he is registered as blind in a register compiled by a local authority under section 29 of the National Assistance Act (welfare services) or, in Scotland has been certified as blind and in consequence he is registered as blind in a register maintained by or on behalf of a regional or islands council; or]

[⁸(b) he—

        (i) is entitled to attendance allowance at the higher rate in accordance with section 65(3) of the Contributions and Benefits Act, or the care component of disability living allowance at the highest rate prescribed in accordance with section 72(3) of the Contributions and Benefits Act, or

        (ii) has made a claim for attendance allowance or disability living allowance and, in respect of that claim, a decision has been made that he satisfies the disability conditions, but he has not yet completed the qualifying period for that benefit; or]

    (c) he is in receipt of any payment based on need for attendance which is payable—

        (i) under section 61 of the Social Security Act [SSCBA, s.104], or

        (ii) by virtue of article 14 of the Naval, Military and Air Forces etc (Disablement and Death) Service Pensions Order 1983 or article 14 of the Personal Injuries (Civilians) Scheme 1983, the appropriate amount shall, except where sub-pargraph (1)(d) or (e)(i) applies, be [¹⁰£252.00] per week.

[⁸(3) In this paragraph—
(a) "the disability conditions" means—
    (i) in the case of attendance allowance, the conditions in section 64(2) and (3) of the Contributions and Benefits Act; and
    (ii) in the case of disability living allowance, the conditions in section 72(1)(b) and (c) of the Contributions and Benefits Act;
(b) "the qualifying period" means—
    (i) in the case of attendance allowance, the period specified in section 65(1)(b) of the Contributions and Benefits Act; and
    (ii) in the case of disability living allowance, the period specified in section 72(2)(a) of the Contributions and Benefits Act.]

Nursing homes

[¹¹7. Subject to paragraphs 8 to 11, where the accommodation provided for the claimant is a nursing home for persons in need of personal care by virtue of—
(a) past or present mental disorder but excluding mental handicap, the appropriate amount shall be £326.00 per week;
(b) mental handicap, the appropriate amount shall be £332.00 per week;
(c) past or present drug or alcohol dependence, the appropriate amount shall be £326.00 per week;
(d) physical disablement, the appropriate amount shall be—
    (i) in the case of a person to whom paragraph 8 applies, £367.00 per week, or
    (ii) in any other case, £325.00 per week;
(e) terminal illness, the appropriate amount shall be £325.00 per week; or
(f) any condition not falling within sub-paragraphs (a) to (e), the appropriate amount shall be £325.00 per week.]

8. For the purposes of paragraphs 6(e) and 7(d) this paragraph applies to a person under pensionable age or a person over pensionable age who, before attaining pensionable age, had become physically disabled.

9. The appropriate amount applicable to a claimant in a residential care home or nursing home shall, subject to paragraph 10, be determined—
(a) where the home is a residential care home registered under Part I of the Registered Homes Act 1984, by reference to the particulars recorded in the register kept by the relevant registration authority for the purposes of that Act; or
(b) where the home is a residential care home not so registered or a nursing home, by reference to the type of care which, taking into account the facilities and accommodation provided, the home is providing to the claimant.

10.—(1) Where more than one amount would otherwise be applicable, in accordance with paragraph 9, to a claimant in a residential care home or a nursing home, the appropriate amount in any case shall be determined in accordance with the following sub-paragraphs.

(2) Where the home is a residential care home registered under Part I of the Registered Homes Act 1984 and where the personal care that the claimant is receiving corresponds to the care received by a category of residents for whom the register indicates that the home provides accommodation, the appropriate amount shall be the amount, in paragraph 6 or 8, as the case may be, as is consistent with that personal care.

(3) Where the home is a residential care home which is so registered but where the personal care that the claimant is receiving does not correspond to the care received by a category of residents for whom the register indicates that the home provides accommodation, the appropriate amount shall be the lesser or least amount, in paragraphs 6 or 8, as the case may be, as is consistent with those categories.

(4) In any case not falling within sub-paragraph (2) or (3), the appropriate amount shall be whichever amount of the amounts applicable in accordance with paragraph 6 or 7 or 9 is, having regard to the types of personal care that the home provides, most consistent with the personal care being received by the claimant in that accommodation.

11.—[¹¹(1) Where the accommodation provided for the claimant is a residential care home or a nursing home which is, in either case, situated in the Greater London area and the actual charge for that accommodation exceeds the appropriate amount in his case by virtue of the preceding paragraphs of this Schedule, that amount shall be increased by any excess up to—

(a) in the case of a residential care home, £45.00;

(b) in the case of a nursing home, £50.00.]

(2) In sub-paragraph (1), "the Greater London area" means all those areas specified [⁸in Schedule 3C.]

Circumstances in which the maximum is not to apply

12.—(1) Where a claimant who satisfies the conditions in sub-paragraph (2) has been able to meet the charges referred to in paragraphs 1 or 2 without recourse to income support or supplementary benefit, the maximum determined in accordance with paragraph 5 shall not apply for the period of 13 weeks or, if alternative accommodation is found earlier, such lesser period following the date of claim except to the extent that the claimant is able to meet out of income disregarded for the purposes of Part V the balance of the actual charge over the maximum.

(2) The conditions for the purposes of sub-paragraph (1) are that—

(a) the claimant has lived in the same accommodation for more than 12 months; and

(b) he was able to afford the charges in respect of that accommodation when he took up residence; and

(c) having regard to the availability of suitable alternative accommodation and to the circumstances mentioned in paragraph 10(7)(b) of Schedule 3 (housing costs), it is reasonable that the maximum should not apply in order to allow him time to find altenative accommodation; and

(d) he is not a person who is being accommodated—

(i) by a housing authority under Part III of the Housing Act 1985 (housing the homeless), or

(ii) by a local authority under [⁷ section 20 of the Children Act 1989 (provision of accommodation for children: general)] or, in Scotland, section 12 of the Social Work (Scotland) Act 1968 (general welfare); and

(e) he is seeking alternative accommodation and intends to leave his present accommodation once alternative accommodation is found.

(3) Where—

(a) the claimant was a resident in a residential care home or nursing home immediately before 29 April 1985 and has continued after that date to be resident in the same accommodation, apart from any period of temporary absence; and

(b) immediately before that date, the actual charge for the claimant's accommodation was being met either wholly or partly out of the claimant's resources, or, wholly or partly out of other resources which can no longer be made available for this purpose; and

(c) since that date the local authority have not at any time accepted responsibility for the making of arrangements for the provision of such accommodation for the claimant; and

(d) the Secretary of State, in his discretion, has determined that this sub-paragraph shall have effect in the particular case of the claimant in order to avoid exceptional hardship,

the maximum amount shall be the rate specified in sub-paragraph (4) if that rate exceeds the maximum which, but for this sub-paragraph, would be determined under paragraph 5.

(4) For the purposes of sub-paragraph (3) the rate is either—

(a) the actual weekly charge for the accommodation immediately before 29 April 1985 plus £10; or

(b) the aggregate of the following amounts—

    (i) the amount estimated under regulation 9(6) of the Supplementary Benefit (Requirements) Regulations 1983 as then in force as the reasonable weekly charge for the area immediately before that date;

    (ii) £26.15; and

    (iii) if the claimant was entitled at that date to attendance allowance under section 35 of the Social Security Act at the higher rate £28.60 or, as the case may be, at the lower rate, £19.10,

whichever is the lower amount.

Personal allowances

[¹¹**13**. The allowance for personal expenses for the claimant and each member of his family referred to paragraph 1(1)(b) shall be—

(a) for the claimant £14.75; and if he has a partner, for his partner, £14.75;

(b) for a young person aged 18, £14.75;

(c) for a young person aged under 18 but over 16, £10.25;

(d) for a child aged under 16 but over 11, £8.85;

(e) for a child aged under 11, £6.05.]

PART II

Persons to Whom Regulation 19 Does Not Apply

[¹**14**. A claimant or, if he is a member of a family, the claimant and the members of his family where the accommodation and meals (if any) of the claimant or, as the case may be, the claimant and the members of his family are provided in whole or in part by a close relative of his or of any member of his family, or other than on a commercial basis.]

15. A person who is on holiday and during a period which has not continued for more than 13 weeks is absent from his home or from a hospital or similar institution in which he is normally a patient.

16. [⁹. . .]

17. [⁹. . .]

[⁶**18**. A person who is living in a residential care home within the meaning of paragraph (d) of the definition of ''residential care home'' in regulation 19(3) and who is not in receipt of personal care by reason of old age, disablement, past or present dependence on alcohol or drugs or past or present mental disorder.]

AMENDMENTS

1. Income Support (General) Amendment Regulations 1988 (S.I. 1988 No. 663), reg. 31 (April 11, 1988).

2. Income Support (General) Amendment No. 4 Regulations 1988 (S.I. 1988 No. 1445), reg. 21 (September 12, 1988).

3. Income Support (General) Amendment No. 5 Regulations 1988 (S.I. 1988 No. 2022), reg. 20 (December 12, 1988).

4. Income Support (General) Amendment Regulations 1989 (S.I. 1989 No. 534), reg. 8 (April 10, 1989).

5. Income Support (General) Amendment No. 3 Regulations 1989 (S.I. 1989 No. 1678), reg. 10 (October 9, 1989).

6. Income Support (General) Amendment No. 4 Regulations 1991 (S.I. 1991 No. 1559), reg. 18 (October 7, 1991).

7. Income Support (General) Amendment Regulations 1992 (S.I. 1992 No. 468), Sched., para. 8 (April 6, 1992) (amendment to para. 17 in respect of England and Wales only, not Scotland. For the previous form of para. 17 see the 1991 edition.)

8. Income-related Benefits Schemes (Miscellaneous Amendments) (No. 4) Regulations 1993 (S.I. 1993 No. 2119), reg. 20 (October 4, 1993).

9. Income-related Benefits and Jobseeker's Allowance (Amendment) (No. 2) Regulations 1997 (S.I. 1997 No. 2197), reg. 5(6) (October 6, 1997).

10. Social Security Benefits Up-rating Order 1999 (S.I. 1999 No. 264), art. 18(7) (April 12, 1999).

11. Social Security Benefits Up-rating Order 1999 (S.I. 1999 No. 264), art. 18(7) and Sched. 6 (April 12, 1999).

DEFINITIONS

"attendance allowance"—see reg. 2(1).
"benefit week"—*ibid.*
"child"—see 1986 Act, s.20(11) (SSCBA, s.137(1)).
"claimant"—see reg. 2(1).
"date of claim"—*ibid.*
"disability living allowance"—*ibid.*
"disablement"—see reg. 19(4).
"drug or alcohol dependence"—*ibid.*
"family"—see 1986 Act, s.20(11) (SSCBA, s.137(1)).
"local authority"—see 1986 Act, s.84(1).
"mental disorder"—see reg. 19(4).
"mental handicap"—*ibid.*
"nursing home"—see reg. 2(1), reg. 19(3).
"old age"—see reg. 19(4).
"partner"—see reg. 2(1).
"relevant enactment"—*ibid.*, reg. 16(8)(a).
"residential care home"—see reg. 2(1), reg. 19(3).
"single claimant"—see reg. 2(1).
"supplementary benefit"—*ibid.*
"temporary absence"—see reg. 19(3).
"young person"—see reg. 2(1), reg. 14.

GENERAL NOTE

The history of the supplementary benefit provisions on residential care and nursing homes had been of continuing complexity and difficulty, with terrible technical problems. Sched. 4 is still complicated, but at least the rules can be made sense of. The Government's programme for community care had significant implications for income support (for the original proposals see Chap. 9 of the White Paper *Caring for People: Community Care in the Next Decade and Beyond*). Sched. 4 now only applies to claimants who have a "preserved right" under reg. 19 to receive income support under the pre-April 1993 arrangements. New residents, excluded from Sched. 4, may only resort to ordinary income support plus the residential allowance under para. 2A of Sched. 2.

"Residential care home" and "nursing home" are defined in reg. 19(3). See the notes to that regulation.

Note the increased upper and lower capital limits for people living permanently in residential care or nursing homes from April 1996 (regs. 45(b) and 53(1A), see the note to reg. 53).

Paragraph 1
There are four elements in the applicable amount of a resident in a residential care or nursing home with a preserved right: (a) the weekly charge for accommodation, board, services, and any separate charge for items mentioned in para. 2(1), plus an amount for any extra meals under para. 2(2), all subject to the maximum set in para. 5; (b) the personal allowance under para. 13; (c) any housing costs for the claimant's old home if he is only temporarily in the residential care or nursing home; and (d) any transitional protection under reg. 17(2) to (7).

Paragraph 2
For a separate charge to be met under sub-para. (1) it must be made by the home in which the

claimant is resident. Only charges for services provided by the home, not third parties count (*CSB 754/1988,* confirmed in *Pearce v. Chief Adjudication Officer, The Times,* May 10, 1990).

Under sub-para. (2) the amounts for meals have not changed for many years.

Paragraph 3

If any part of the charge is met by housing benefit, it is deducted from the charge to be met under para. 1(1)(a).

Paragraph 5

The maximum to be met under para. 1(1)(a) is set by paras. 6 to 11 for adults and children over 10 also living in the home. For children under 11, it is one and a half times the ordinary personal allowance for a child under 11.

Paragraph 6

On the various categories, see the definitions in the notes to reg. 19(4). The Residential Care Homes Regulations 1984 require the register kept by the local authority of homes which are registered to record the number of residents in defined categories which coincide with those specified in para. 6(1)(a) to (e). Note the effect of para. 8 on para. 6(1)(e), and of para. (2) on the disabled over pensionable age. Attendance allowance and the care component of disability living allowance is not disregarded for residents in residential care or nursing homes (Sched. 9, para. 9). The maximum can be increased under para. 11 for homes in Greater London.

Paragraph 7

See the notes to reg. 19(4) for definitions, and note to para. 6 above. Nursing homes are not registered for particular categories.

Paragraph 8

In *R(SB) 16/88* the Tribunal of Commissioners raises the possibility that the differential age for men and women, created by the use of "pensionable age", might infringe EC Directive 79/7 on equal treatment, but see *Jackson and Cresswell v. Chief Adjudication Officer,* ECJ, Joined Cases C-63/91 and C-64/91 [1992] E.C.R. I-4737 in the notes to reg. 36.

Paragraph 9

For residential care homes which are registered, under sub-para. (a) the appropriate maximum is to be determined by reference to the register under the 1984 Act. This is effectively the result reached on the supplementary benefit provisions by the Tribunal of Commissioners in *R(SB) 15/88, R(SB) 16/88* and *R(SB) 17/88.* Thus, if a home is registered for only one category, that is the maximum to be applied, regardless of the care actually received by the resident. If more than one category is on the register, para. 10 applies.

For nursing homes and for unregistered residential care homes (*e.g.* before April 1993 those with less than four residents which have not registered voluntarily), the test is the type of care being provided to the claimant. This should normally produce an appropriate category (contrary to the view of the Commissioner in *CSIS 2/1991*), but para. 10 still makes reference to this class of homes. The emphasis on the care provided to the claimant is different from the rules produced on the supplementary benefit provision by the Tribunal of Commissioners in *R(SB) 12/88, R(SB) 13/88* and *R(SB) 14/88.* In *CIS 263/ 1991* the claimant suffered from osteoporosis and osteoarthritis. She was not terminally ill but received similar care to those who were. The Commissioner holds that the appropriate category is para. 7(e) because this was most consistent with the personal care she actually received. The SSAT had erred in concluding that because she was not terminally ill she could not receive this rate.

Paragraph 10

This provision only applies where the rules of para. 9 produce alternative amounts. This should only be a real possibility in the case of registered residential care homes. Here the rules are set out in sub-paras. (2) and (3). If the care which the claimant is receiving corresponds to a category for which the home is registered, that category supplies the maximum. If the care received by the claimant does not correspond to such a category, the maximum is to be the lowest of the amounts specified for the categories for which the home is registered. Note that a home can only be registered for categories corresponding to para. 6(1)(a) to (e). It cannot be registered for "any condition not falling within sub-paragraphs (a) to (e)" (sub-para. (f)).

In any other case, which should not exist, the test is what is most consistent with the personal care being received by the claimant.

Paragraph 11

This provision allows the extension of the maximum by £45.00 (residential care homes) or £50.00 (nursing homes) in the Greater London area.

Paragraph 12(1) and (2)

There is a period of grace in these circumstances in which a charge over the maximum will be met. In *CIS 515/1990*, the Commissioner held that although there was then no definition of date of claim in the Income Support Regulations, the definition of "claim for benefit" in reg. 2(1) of the Claims and Payments Regulations could be incorporated. This included at the time an application for the review of an award or decision in order to obtain any increase of benefit. Therefore, although the claimant first claimed and was awarded income support in February 1989, the 13 week period under sub-para. (1) could run from December 1989, when an application to increase the amount of income support to cover the full fees was made. This decision must be wrong in importing a definition used for very different Regulations and ignoring the natural meaning of the words "date of claim." However, there does not appear to be any other Commissioner's decision to the contrary. With effect from March 9, 1992, the definition of "claim for benefit" in the Claims and Payments Regulations has been narrowed, so as not to cover reviews aimed at increasing the amount of a benefit. "Date of claim" is now (from October 4, 1993) defined in reg. 2(1), which cross-refers to the Claims and Payments Regulations.

CIS 515/1990 also decides that the condition in sub-para. (1) of having been able to meet the home's charges without recourse to income support does not have to be met immediately before the date of claim. Sub-para. (c) was also held to be satisfied, because alternative accommodation was being sought. But since the evidence was that no suitable alternative accommodation was available, there must be doubt that it was reasonable to allow time to find alternative accommodation.

Paragraph 12(3) and (4)

This provision contains a transitional rule protecting those who were resident in residential care or nursing homes immediately before April 29, 1985, although not necessarily claimants. The rule can only apply if, in addition to meeting the conditions in sub-para. (3)(a) to (c), the Secretary of State has exercised his discretion in favour of the claimant to avoid exceptional hardship. The rule produces a choice of protected amounts, which will replace the maximum calculated under para. 5 if either is higher than that amount. The first is the actual charge immediately before April 29, 1985, plus £10. The second is the total of the three amounts listed in head (b). For the estimation of the reasonable weekly charge under the Requirements Regulations as in force immediately before April 29, 1985, see *R(SB) 12/88* which indicates that many of the estimates made by AOs could have been too low. The maximum should be fixed at the highest amount being charged for full board and lodging by establishments in the area providing a suitable standard for the needs of occupants, having disregarded charges which are way above those of the majority.

PART II

Paras. 14 to 18 prescribe the categories of resident who are not allowed to receive benefit under the special rules of reg. 19.

Paragraph 14

See the notes to the definitions of "board and lodging accommodation" and "close relative" in reg. 2(1).

Paragraphs 16 and 17

These paragraphs have been deleted with effect from October 6, 1997 as they are obsolete.

Paragraph 18

This provision is only concerned with residential care homes run by statutory bodies or bodies incorporated by Royal Charter. The form of para. (d) of the definition in reg. 19 includes such homes if they provide personal care to at least one resident. The effect then seemed to be to give all residents, whether receiving personal care or not, access to the special level of benefit. Para. 18 removes that possibility and limits access to those receiving personal care for the specified reasons.

It is not clear that the unintended effect removed by para. 18 is limited to homes within para. (d) of the definition.

SCHEDULE 7   **Regulation 21**

APPLICABLE AMOUNTS IN SPECIAL CASES

Column (1)	Column (2)
[24**Patients** **1.** Subject to paragraphs 2, 2A, 3 and 18, a person who has been a patient for a period of more than six weeks and who is—	**1.**
(a) a single claimant;	(a) £16.70 plus any amount applicable under regulation 17(1)(e), (f) or (g);
(b) a lone parent;	(b) £16.70 plus any amounts applicable to him under regulation 17(1)(b), (c), (e), (f) or (g) or under regulation 17(1)(d) because of paragraph [20. . .] 14 of Schedule 2 (applicable amounts);
(c) a member of a couple— (i) where only one of the couple is a patient or, where both members of the couple are patients but only one has been a patient for that period; (ii) where both members of the couple have been a patient for that period;	(c) (i) the amount applicable in respect of both of them under regulation 17(1) reduced by £13.35; (ii) £33.40 plus any amounts which may be applicable under regulation 17(1)(b), (c), (e), (f), or (g) or under regulation 17(1)(d) because of paragraph 14 of Schedule 2;
(d) a member of a polygamous marriage— (i) where at least one member of the polygamous marriage is not a patient or has not been a patient for more than that period; (ii) where all the members of the polygamous marriage have been patients for more than that period.	(d) (i) the applicable amount under regulation 18 (polygamous marriages) shall be reduced by £13.35 in respect of each such member who is a patient; (ii) the applicable amount shall be £16.70 in respect of each member plus any amounts applicable under regulation 18(1)(c), (d), (f), (g) or (h) or (e) because of his satisfying the condition specified in paragraph 14 of Schedule 2.
2. A single claimant who has been a patient for a continuous period of more than 52 weeks, where— (a) the following conditions are satisfied— (i) a person has been appointed to act for him under regulation 33 of the Social Security (Claims and Payments) Regulations 1987 (persons unable to act); and (ii) his income support is payable to an administrative officer of the hospital or other institution either as or at the request of the person so appointed; and (iii) a registered medical practitioner treating him certifies that all or part of his income support cannot be used by him or on his behalf; or	**2.** (a) Such amount (if any) not exceeding £13.35 as is reasonable having regard to the views of the hospital staff and the patient's relatives if available as to the amount necessary for this personal use;

404

Column (1)	Column (2)
(b) those conditions are not satisfied.	(b) £13.35.
2A. A single claimant [²² who is detained in hospital under the provisions of the Mental Health Act 1983, or, in Scotland, under the provisions of the Mental Health (Scotland) Act 1984 or the Criminal Procedure (Scotland) Act 1995,] and who immediately before his detention [²³ under any of those Acts] was a prisoner.	**2A.** £13.35.
3. Subject to paragraph 18—	**3.**
(a) a claimant who is not a patient and who is a member of a family of which another member is a child or young person who has been a patient for a period of more than 12 weeks; or	(a) The amount applicable to him under regulation 17(1) or 18 except that the amount applicable under regulation 17(1)(b) or 18(1)(c) in respect of the child or young person referred to in Column (1) of this paragraph shall be £13.35 instead of an amount determined in accordance with paragraph 2 of Schedule 2; or
(b) where the person is a member of a family and paragraph 1 applies to him and another member of the family who is a child or young person has been a patient for a period of more than 12 weeks.	(b) the amount applicable to him under paragraph 1 except that the amount applicable under regulation 17(1) (b) or 18(1)c) in respect of the child or young person referred to in Column (1) of this paragraph shall be £13.35 instead of an amount determined in accordance with paragraph 2 of Schedule 2.]
4. [⁶. . .]. **5.** [⁶. . .].	
Claimants without accommodation **6.** A claimant who is without accommodation.	**6.** The amount applicable to him under regulation 17[³(1)](a) only.
Members of religious orders **7.** A claimant who is a member of and fully maintained by religious order.	**7.** Nil.
Prisoners **8.** A person—	**8.**
(a) except where sub-paragraph (b) applies, who is a prisoner;	(a) Nil;
(b) who is detained in custody pending trial or sentence following conviction by a court.	(b) only such amount, if any, as may be applicable under regulation 17[³(1)](e).
9. A claimant who is a member of a couple and who is temporarily separated from his partner [¹⁰where—	**9.** Either—
(a) one member of the couple is—	(a) the amount applicable to him as a member of a couple under regulation 17; or
(i) not a patient but is resident in a nursing home, or	
(ii) resident in a residential care home, or	
(iii) resident in premises used for the rehabilitation of alcoholics or drug addicts, or	

Column (1)	Column (2)
(iv) resident in accommodation provided under section 3 of and Part II of the Schedule to, the Polish Resettlement Act 1947 (provision of accommodation in camps), or (v) participating in arrangements for training made under section 2 of the Employment and Training Act 1973 [¹² or section 2 of the Enterprise and New Towns (Scotland) Act 1990] or attending a course at an employment rehabilitation centre established under that section [¹² of the 1973 Act], where the course requires him to live away from the dwelling occupied as the home, or (vi) in a probation or bail hostel approved for the purpose by the Secretary of State; and (b) the other member of the couple is—	
(i) living in the dwelling occupied as the home, or (ii) a patient, or (iii) in residential accommodation, or (iv) resident in a residential care home or nursing home;]	(b) the aggregate of his applicable amount and that of his partner assessed under the provisions of these Regulations as if each of them were a single claimant, or a lone parent, whichever is the greater.

Polygamous marriages where one or more partners are temporarily separated

10. A claimant who is a member of a polygamous marriage and who is temporarily separated from a partner of his, where one of them is living in the home while the other member is—	**10.** Either—
(a) not a patient but is resident in a nursing home; or	(a) the amount applicable to the members of the polygamous marriage under regulation 18; or
(b) resident in a residential care home; or (c) [¹. . .] (d) resident in premises used for the rehabilitation of alcoholics or drug addicts; or (e) attending a course of training or instruction provided or approved by the [¹²Secretary of State for Employment] where the course requires him to live away from home; or (f) in a probation or bail hostel approved for the purpose by the Secretary of State.	(b) the aggregate of the amount applicable for the members of the polygamous marriage who remain in the home under regulation 18 and the amount applicable in respect of those members not in the home calculated as if each of them were a single claimant, or a lone parent, whichever is the greater.

[²⁴Single claimants temporarily in local authority accommodation

10A. A single claimant who is temporarily in accommodation referred to in any of sub-paragraphs (a) to (d) (excluding heads (i) and (ii) of sub-paragraph (d)) of the	**10A.** £66.75 of which £14.75 is for personal expenses plus any amounts applicable under regulation 17(1)(e), (f) or (g).

Column (1)	Column (2)
definition of residential accommodation in regulation 21(3) (special cases).	
Couples and members of polygamous marriages where one member is or all are temporarily in local authority accommodation **10B.**—(1) A claimant who is a member of a couple and temporarily separated from his partner where one of them is living in the home while the other is in accommodation referred to in any of sub-paragraphs (a) to (d) (excluding heads (i) and (ii) of sub-paragraph (d) of the definition of residential accommodation in regulation 21(3) (special cases).	**10B.**—(1) The aggregate of the amount applicable for the member who remains in the home calculated as if he were a single claimant under regulation 17(1), 19 or 21 and in respect of the other member £66.75 of which £14.75 is for personal expenses.
(2) A claimant who is a member of a polygamous marriage and who is temporarily separated from a partner of his where one is, or some are, living in the home while one is, or some are, in accommodation referred to in sub-paragraph (1).	(2) The aggregate of the amount applicable, for the members of the polygamous marriage who remain in the home, under regulation 18 and in respect of each member not in the home £66.75 of which £14.75 is for personal expenses.
(3) A claimant who is a member of a couple or a member of a polygamous marriage where both members of that couple or all the members of that marriage are in accommodation referred to in sub-paragraph (1).	(3) For each member of that couple or marriage £66.75 of which £14.75 is for personal expenses plus, if appropriate, the amount applicable under regulation 17(1)(e), (f) or (g) or 18(1)(f) or (h).
Lone parents who are in residential accommodation temporarily **10C.** A claimant who is a lone parent who has entered residential accommodation temporarily.	**10C.** £66.75 of which £14.75 is for personal expenses, plus—
	(a) in respect of each child or young person who is a member of his family, the amount in respect of him prescribed in paragraph 2(a), (b), (c) or (d) of Schedule 2 or under this Schedule as appropriate; and
	(b) any amount which would be applicable to the claimant if he were not temporarily living away from the dwelling occupied as his home, under regulation 17(1)(c), (e), (f) or (g) [[20]. . .].]
10D. [[15]. . .]	
Couples where one member is abroad. **11.** [[11]Subject to paragraph 11A] a claimant who is a member of a couple and whose partner is temporarily not present in [[3]United Kingdom].	**11.** For the first four weeks of that absence, the amount applicable to them as a couple under regulation 17, or [[9]19 or 21] as the case may be and thereafter the amount applicable to the claimant in Great Britain under regulation 17 or [[9]19 or 21] as the case may be as if the claimant were a single claimant or, as the case may be, a lone parent.

Column (1)	Column (2)
[¹¹**Couple or member of couple taking child or young person abroad for treatment** **11A.** [¹⁵—(1)] A claimant who is a member of a couple where either— (a) he or his partner is, or, (b) both he and his partner are absent from the United Kingdom [¹⁴in the circumstances specified in paragraph (2). (2) For the purposes of sub-paragraph (1), the specified circumstances are— (a) in respect of a claimant, those in regulation 4(3)(a) to (d); (b) in respect of a claimant's partner as if regulation 4(3)(a) to (d) applies to that partner.]	**11A.** For the first eight weeks of that absence, the amount applicable to the claimant under regulation 17(1), 19 or 21, as the case may be, and, thereafter, if the claimant is in Great Britain the amount applicable to him under regulation 17(1), 19 or 21, as the case may be, as if the claimant were a single claimant, or, as the case may be, a lone parent.
Polygamous marriages where any member is abroad **12.** Subject to paragraph 12A, a claimant who is a member of a polygamous marriage where— (a) he or one of his partners is, or (b) he and one or more of his partners are, or (c) two or more of his partners are, temporarily absent from the United Kingdom.	**12.** For the first four weeks of that absence, the amount applicable to the claimant under regulations 17 to 21, as the case may be, and thereafter, if the claimant is in Great Britain the amount applicable to him under regulations 18 to 21, as the case may be, as if any member of the polygamous marriage not in the United Kingdom were not a member of the marriage.
Polygamous marriage: taking child or young person abroad for treatment **12A.** [¹⁵—(1)] A claimant who is a member of a polygamous marriage where— (a) he or one of his partners is, (b) he and one or more of his partners are, or (c) two or more of his partners are, absent from the United Kingdom [¹⁴in the circumstances specified in paragraph (2). (2) For the purposes of sub-paragraph (1), the specified circumstances are— (a) in respect of a claimant, those in regulation 4(3)(a) to (d); (b) in respect of a claimant's partner or partners, as the case may be, as if regulation 4(3)(a) to (d) applied to that partner or those partners.]	**12A.** For the first 8 weeks of that absence the amount applicable to the claimant under regulations 18 to 21, as the case may be, as if any member of the polygamous marriage not in the United Kingdom were not a member of the marriage.]
[²⁴**Persons in residential accommodation.** **13.**—(1) Subject to sub-paragraph (2), a person in or only temporarily absent from residential accommodation who is— (a) a single claimant; (b) a lone parent; (c) one of a couple; (d) a child or young person;	**13.**—(1) Any amount applicable under regulation 17(1)(f) or (g) or 18(1)(g) or (h), plus— (a) £66.75 of which £14.75 is for personal expenses; (b) the amount specified in sub-paragraph (a) of this column; (c) twice the amount specified in sub-paragraph (a) of this column; (d) the appropriate amount in respect of him prescribed in paragraph 2 of Schedule 2 (applicable amounts);

Column (1)	Column (2)
(e) a member of a polygamous marriage.	(e) the amount specified in sub-paragraph (a) of this column multiplied by the number of members of the polygamous marriage in or only temporarily absent from that accommodation.
(2) A single claimant who has become a patient and whose residential accommodation was provided by and managed by a local authority.	(2) Any amount applicable under regulation 17(1)(f) or (g), plus £14.75.

Polish Resettlement

13A. [¹⁹(1)] A claimant for whom accommodation is provided under section 3 of, and Part II of the Schedule to, the Polish Resettlement Act 1947 (provision of accommodation in camps) [¹⁹where the claimant both requires personal care and is provided with it in the accommodation and—	**13A.** —(1) The aggregate of—
(a) is resident in that accommodation on 31st March 1995 or is temporarily absent on that date; or	(a) the weekly charge for the accommodation provided for him, or if he is a member of a family, for him and his family subject to the maximum determined in accordance with sub-paragraph (2); and
(b) is first provided with such accommodation and care on or after 1st April 1995; or	(b) a weekly amount for personal expenses for him or, if he is a member of a family, for him and for each member of his family determined in accordance with sub-paragraph (3) [¹⁹or, in the case of a claimant to whom sub-paragraph (1)(b) or (c) of Column (1) applies, determined in accordance with sub-paragraph (3A) below.]
(c) is re-admitted to such accommodation on or after 1st April 1995 where his absence has been other than temporary.	
(2) In this paragraph ''personal care'' means care [²¹ which a claimant requires by reason of old age, disablement, past or present dependence on alcohol or drugs, past or present mental disorder or a terminal illness.]	(2) The maximum referred to in sub-paragraph (1)(a) shall be—
	(a) in the case of a single claimant, £367.00;
	(b) in the case of a claimant who is a member of a family the aggregate of the following amounts—
	(i) in respect of the claimant, £367.00;
	(ii) in respect of each member of his family who lives in the accommodation aged under 11, $1\frac{1}{2}$ times the amount specified in paragraph 2(a) of Schedule 2;
	(iii) in respect of each member of his family aged not less than 11 who lives in the accommodation, £367.00; and
	(iv) where the claimant is a lone parent, in respect of each member of the family who does not live in the accommodation, the amount which would be applicable in respect of that member under Schedule 2.
(3) An absence is temporary for the	(3) [¹⁹Except where the claimant is a

Column (1)	Column (2)
purposes of sub-paragraph (1) where the absent resident with the agreement of the manager of the accommodation intends to return to the accommodation in due course.]	person to whom sub-paragraph (1)(b) or (c) of Column (1) refers,] the amount for personal expenses referred to in sub-paragraph (1)(b) shall be—
	(a) for the claimant, £17.35; (b) for his partner, £17.35; (c) for a young person aged 18, £15.55; (d) for a young person aged under 18 but over 16, £10.25; (e) for a child aged under 16 but over 11, £8.85; (f)for a child under 11, £6.05. [¹⁹(3A) In the case of a claimant to whom sub-paragraph (1)(b) or (c) of Column (1) applies, the amount for personal expenses referred to in sub-paragraph (1)(b) above, shall be the aggregate of the amounts which are relevant to him and which are referred to in Schedule 4 paragraph 13.]
	(4) The maximum amount in respect of a member of a family aged under 11 calculated in the manner referred to in [¹⁹sub-paragraph (2)(b)(ii)] shall be rounded to the nearest multiple of 5p by treating an odd amount of 2.5p or more as 5p and by disregarding an odd amount of less than 2.5p.]
[¹⁸**Polish resettlement: Persons temporarily absent from accommodation** **13B.** Where a claimant or his partner is temporarily absent from accommodation to which paragraph 13A applies for which the claimant is liable to pay a retaining fee, and but for that absence from that accommodation his applicable amount would be calculated in accordance with that paragraph and the absent person—	**13B.** The amount otherwise applicable to him under these Regulations may be increased to take account of the retaining fee—
(a) is a patient; or	(a) in a case to which sub-paragraph (a) of Column 1 applies— (i) where the person has been a patient for a period of 6 weeks or less, by an amount not exceeding the maximum amount referred to in paragraph 13A(2)(a); (ii) where the person has been a patient for a period of more than 6 weeks, by an amount not exceeding 80 per cent. of the normal weekly charge for that accommodation, but any such increase shall not be for a continuous period of more than 52 weeks;
(b) is a person to whom sub-paragraph (a) does not apply.	(b) in a case of a person to whom sub-paragraph (b) of Column 1 applies, by an amount not exceeding 80 per cent. of the normal weekly charge for

Column (1)	Column (2)
	that accommodation, but any such increase shall not be for a continuous period of more than 4 weeks.]
Polish resettlement **14.** [⁹. . .]	
Resettlement units **15.** [⁹. . .]	
Persons temporarily absent from a hostel, residential care or nursing home	
16. [¹⁷Where a person is temporarily absent from accommodation for which he is liable to pay a retaining fee, and but for his temporary absence from that accommodation his applicable amount would be calculated in accordance with regulation 19 (applicable amounts for persons in residential care and nursing homes), and]—	**16.** The amount otherwise applicable to him under these Regulations may be increased to take account of the retaining fee by an amount not exceeding 80 per cent. of the applicable amount referred to in paragraph 1(1)(a) of Schedule 4 (applicable amounts of persons in residential care or nursing homes) and—
(a) he is a person in accommodation referred to in [⁸any of sub-paragraphs (a) to (d) ([⁹excluding heads (i) and (ii)] of sub-paragraph (d) of the definition of residential accommodation] [¹in regulation 21(3)] (special cases) and paragraph 13 does not apply to him by reason only that his stay in that accommodation has not become other than temporary; or	(a) in a case to which sub-paragraph (a) to (b) of column 1 applies any such increase shall not be for a continuous period of more than 52 weeks;
(b) he is a person to whom paragraph 1 to 3 [³ or 18(b)(i), (b)(ii) case two, or (b)(iv) cases one and three (patients)] applies; or	(b) in a case of a person to whom only sub-paragraph (c) of column 1 applies, any such increase shall not be for a continuous period of more than four weeks.
(c) he is absent for a period of at least one week from that accommodation being accommmodation either in a residential care home or nursing home and he is not required to be available for employment.	
17. Except in relation to a person from abroad to whom regulation 70(3) applies (urgent cases)—	**17.**
(a) a person from abroad who is a single claimant;	(a) Nil;
(b) a lone parent—	(b)
(i) where he is a person from abroad;	(i) nil;
(ii) [¹⁴. . .];	(ii) [¹⁴. . .];
(c) a member of a couple	(c)
(i) where the claimant is not a person from abroad but his partner is such a person, whether or not regulation 70 applies to that partner;	(i) the amount applicable in respect of him only under regulation 17[³(1)](a) plus in respect of any child or young person who is a member of his family and who is not a person from abroad, any amounts which may be applicable to him under regulation 17[³(1)](b), (c) or (d) plus the amount applicable to him under [⁷regulation 17(1)(e), (f) and (g)] [³or as the

Column (1)	Column (2)
	case may be,] [⁹regulation 19 or 21];
(ii) where the claimant is a person from abroad but his partner is not such a person;	(ii) nil;
(iii) where the claimant and his partner are both persons from abroad;	(iii) nil;
(d) where regulation 18 (polygamous marriages) applies and—	(d)
(i) the claimant is not a person from abroad but one or more but not all of his partners are persons from abroad;	(i) the amounts determined in accordance with that regulation or [⁹regulation 19 or 21] in respect of the claimant and any partners of his and any child or young person for whom he or any partner is treated as responsible, who are not persons from abroad;
(ii) the claimant is a person from abroad, whether or not one or more of his partners are persons from abroad;	(ii) nil;
(iii) the claimant and all his partners are persons from abroad;	(iii) nil;
(e) where any amount is applicable to the claimant under regulation 17(d) because of Part III of Schedule 2 because he or his partner satisfies the conditions prescribed therein and he or his partner as the person so satisfying the condition is a person from abroad.	(e) no amount shall be applicable under regulation 17(d) because of Part III of Schedule 2.

[²⁴Persons in residential care or nursing homes who become patients

18. A claimant to whom regulation 19 (persons in residential care or nursing homes) applies immediately before he or a member of his family became a patient where—

18.

(a) he or any member of his family has been a patient for a period of six weeks or less and the claimant—

(a)

(i) continues to be liable to meet the weekly charge for the accommodation without reduction in respect of himself or that member of his family who is a patient;

(i) the amount which would be applicable under regulation 19 as if the claimant or the member of the family who is a patient were resident in the accommodation to which regulation 19 applies;

(ii) continues to be liable to meet the weekly charge for the accommodation but at a reduced rate;

(ii) the amount which would be applicable under regulation 19 having taken into account the reduced charge, as if the claimant or the member of the family who is a patient were resident in the accommodation to which regulation 19 applies;

(iii) is a single claimant and is likely to return to the accommodation, but has ceased to be liable to meet the weekly charge for that accommodation; or

(iii) the amount applicable to him (if any) under paragraph 2(2) of Schedule 4 (meal allowances) plus the amount in respect of him as an allowance for personal expenses under paragraph 13 of Schedule 4 as if he were

Column (1)	Column (2)
	residing in the accommodation to which regulation 19 applies plus any amount applicable under regulation 17(1)(f);
(iv) is a single claimant who ceases to be liable to meet the weekly charge for the accommodation, and who is unlikely to return to the accommodation;	(iv) the amount which would be applicable to him under regulation 17(1);
(b) he or his partner has been a patient for a period of more than six weeks and the patient is—	(b)
(i) a single claimant;	(i) £16.70 plus any amount applicable under regulation 17(1)(f), plus either the amount prescribed in paragraph 16 in respect of any retaining fee he is liable to pay for the accommodation or the amount applicable by virtue of regulation 17(1)(e), but not both;
(ii) a lone parent;	(ii) where one or more children or young persons remain in the accommodation, the amount applicable to the family as if regulation 19, having taken into account any reduction in charge, continued to apply to all the members of the family except that where the lone parent is the patient no amount shall be applicable in respect of him under paragraph 2(2) of Schedule 4 (meals allowances) and for the amount in respect of the allowance for personal expenses prescribed by paragraph 13 of Schedule 4, there shall be substituted the amount £16.70; —where all the children or young persons are absent from the accommodation, £16.70 plus any amounts applicable to him under regulation 17(1)(b), (c), (d) or (f) plus, if appropriate, either the amount applicable under Column (2) of paragraph 16(a) or the amount applicable by virtue of regulation 17(1)(e) (housing costs) but not both; —where one or more children or young persons are also patients and have been so for more than 12 weeks, in respect of those children and young persons remaining in the accommodation and the lone parent patient the amount specified in case one of Column (2) of sub-paragraph (b)(ii) save that the child or young person who has been a patient for more than 12 weeks

Column (1)	Column (2)
	shall be disregarded as a member of the family in assessing the amount applicable under regulation 19, and in respect of each such child or young person there shall be added the amount of £16.70;
(iii) one of a couple or polygamous marriage and one of that couple or marriage is not a patient or has been a patient or has been a patient for six weeks or less;	(iii) where the members of the family not patients remain in the accommodation, the amount applicable to the family as if regulaton 19 having taken into account any reduction in charge, continued to apply to all the members of the family except that in respect of the member of the couple or polygamous marriage who has been a patient for more than six weeks no amount shall be applicable in respect of him under paragraph 2(2) of Schedule 4 and for the amount in respect of the allowance for personal expenses prescribed by paragraph 13 of Schedule 4 there shall be substituted the amount of £16.70; —where one or more children or young persons are also patients and have been so for more than 12 weeks, in respect of those children and young persons and the member of the couple or polygamous marriage remaining in the accommodation the amount specified in case one of column (2) of sub-paragraph (b)(iii) save that the child or young person who has been a patient for more than 12 weeks shall be disregarded as a member or the family in assessing the amount applicable under regulation 19 and in respect of each such child or young person there shall be added the amount of £13.35;
(iv) one of a couple or polygamous marriage where all the members of that couple or marriage are patients and have been so for more than six weeks;	(iv) where there is no child or young person in the family £16.70 in respect of each member of the couple or polygamous marriage plus any amount applicable under regulation 17(1)(f) or 18(1)(g), plus either the amount prescribed in paragraph 16 in respect of any retaining fee for the accommodation he is liable to pay or the amount applicable by virtue of regulation 17(1)(e) or 18(1)(f), but not both; —where there is a child or young person remaining in the accommodation, the amount which would be applicable in respect of the family as if regulation 19 having

414

Column (1)	Column (2)
	taken into account any reduction in charge continued to apply to all the members of the family except that in respect of each member of the couple of polygamous marriage no amount shall be applicable in respect of him under paragraph 2(2) of Schedule 4, and for the amount in respect of the allowance for personal expenses prescribed by paragraph 13 of Schedule 4 in respect of each member there shall be substituted the amount of £16.70;
	—where there is a child or young person in the family but no child or young person remains in the accommodation, the amount applicable under paragraph 1(c) or 1(d) as is appropriate plus either the amount applicable under Column (2) of paragraph 16(a) or the amount applicable by virtue of regulation 17(1)(e) or 18(1)(f) but not both;
	—where one or more children or young persons are also patients and have been so for more than 12 weeks, in respect of those children and young persons remaining in the accommodation and the members of the couple or polygamous marriage, the amount specified in case two of Column (2) of sub-paragraph (b)(iv) save that the child or young person who has been a patient for more than 12 weeks shall be disregarded as a member of the family in assessing the amount applicable under regulation 19, and in respect of each such child or young person there shall be added the amount of £13.35;
(c) a child or young person who has been a patient for a period of more than 12 weeks.	(c) the amount applicable under regulation 19 as if that child or young person was not a member of the family plus an amount of £13.35 in respect of that child or young person.]

Claimants entitled to the disability premium for a past period

19. A claimant—	**19.** The amount only of the disability premium applicable by virtue of paragraph 11(b) of Schedule 2 as specified in paragraph 15(4)(b) of that Schedule.
(a) whose time for claiming income support has been extended under regulation 19(2) of the Social Security (Claims and Payments) Regulations 1987 (time for claiming benefit); and	
(b) whose partner was entitled to income support in respect of the period begin-	

Column (1)	Column (2)
ning with the day on which the claim-ant's claim is treated as made under [¹⁹regulation 6(3) of those Regulations] and [¹⁹ending with the day before the day] on which the claim is actually made; and (c) who satisfied the condition in para-graph 11(*b*) of Schedule 2 and the additional condition referred to in that paragraph and specified in paragraph 12(1)(b) of that Schedule in respect of that period. **Rounding of fractions** **20.** Where any calculation under this Schedule or as a result of income support being awarded for a period less than one complete benefit week results in a fraction of a penny that fraction shall be treated as a penny.	

AMENDMENTS

1. Income Support (General) Amendment Regulations 1988 (S.I. 1988 No. 663), reg. 33 (April 11, 1988).

2. Employment Act 1988, s.24(3) (May 26, 1988).

3. Income Support (General) Amendment No. 4 Regulations 1988 (S.I. 1988 No. 1445), reg. 23 (September 12, 1988).

4. Income Support (General) Amendment No. 5 Regulations 1988 (S.I. 1988 No. 2022), reg. 21 (December 12, 1988).

5. Income Support (General) Amendment No. 4 Regulations 1988 (S.I. 1988 No. 1445), Sched. 1, para. 1 (April 10, 1989).

6. Income Support (General) Amendment No. 4 Regulations 1988 (S.I. 1988 No. 1445), Sched. 1, para. 10 (April 10, 1989).

7. Income Support (General) Amendment No. 4 Regulations 1988 (S.I. 1988 No. 1445), Sched. 1, para. 15 (April 10, 1989).

8. Income Support (General) Amendment Regulations 1989 (S.I. 1989 No. 534), reg. 9 (April 10, 1989).

9. Income Support (General) Amendment Regulations 1989 (S.I. 1989 No. 534), Sched. 1, para. 13 (October 9, 1989).

10. Income Support (General) Amendment No. 3 Regulations 1989 (S.I. 1989 No. 1678), reg. 11 (October 9, 1989).

11. Income Support (General) Amendment Regulations 1990 (S.I. No. 547), reg. 21 (April 9, 1990).

12. Enterprise (Scotland) Consequential Amendments order 1991 (S.I. 1991 No. 387), art. 2 (April 1, 1991.

13. Income Support (General) Amendment Regulations 1991 (S.I. 1991 No. 236), reg. 2(1) (April 8, 1991).

14. Income Support (General) Amendment Regulations 1991 (S.I. 1991 No. 236), reg. 13 (April 8, 1991).

15. Income Support (General) Amendment No. 4 Regulations 1991 (S.I. 1991 No. 1559), reg. 19 (October 7, 1991).

16. Social Security Benefits (Amendments Consequential Upon the Introduction of Community Care) Regulations 1992 (S.I. 1992 No. 3147), Sched. 1, para. 6 (April 1, 1993).

17. Income-related Benefits Schemes (Miscellaneous Amendments) (No. 4) Regulations 1993 (S.I. 1993 No. 2119), reg. 21 (October 4, 1993).

18. Income-related Benefits Schemes (Miscellaneous Amendments) (No. 5) Regulations 1994 (S.I. 1994 No. 2139), reg. 31 (October 3, 1994).

19. Income-related Benefits Schemes (Miscellaneous Amendments) Regulations 1995 (S.I. 1995 No. 516), reg. 26 (April 10, 1995).

20. Child Benefit, Child Support and Social Security (Miscellaneous Amendments) Regulations 1996 (S.I. 1996 No. 1803), reg. 40 (April 7, 1997).

21. Income-related Benefits and Jobseeker's Allowance (Amendment) (No. 2) Regulations 1997 (S.I. 1997 No. 2197), reg. 5(7) (October 6, 1997).

22. Social Security (Miscellaneous Amendments) Regulations 1998 (S.I. 1998 No. 563), reg. 8(1) and (2)(c)(ii) (April 6, 1998).

23. Social Security (Miscellaneous Amendments) Regulations 1998 (S.I. 1998 No. 563), reg. 8(3) (April 6, 1998).

24. Social Security Benefits Up-rating Order 1999 (S.I. 1999 No. 264), art. 18(8) and Sched. 7 (April 12, 1999).

DEFINITIONS

"child"—see 1986 Act, s.20(11) (SSCBA, s.137(1)).
"claimant"—see reg. 2(1).
"couple"—*ibid.*
"family"—see 1986 Act, s.20(11) (SSCBA, s.137(1)).
"lone parent"—see reg. 2(1).
"nursing home"—see reg. 2(1), reg. 19(3).
"partner"—see reg. 2(1).
"patient"—see reg. 21(3).
"person from abroad"—*ibid.*
"polygamous marriage"—see reg. 2(1).
"prisoner"—see reg. 21(3).
"relative"—see reg. 2(1).
"residential accommodation"—see reg. 21(3).
"residential care home"—see reg. 2(1), reg. 19(3).
"single claimant"—see reg. 2(1).
"young person"—*ibid.*, reg. 14.

GENERAL NOTE

See the notes to reg. 21.

SCHEDULE 8 **Regulations 36(2), 38(2) and 44(6)**

SUMS TO BE DISREGARDED IN THE CALCULATION OF EARNINGS

1. In the case of a claimant who has been engaged in remunerative work as an employed earner ['or, had the employment been in Great Britain would have been so engaged]—
  (a) any earnings paid or due to be paid [²in respect of that employment which has terminated]—
      (i) by way of retirement but only if on retirement he is entitled to a retirement pension under the Social Security Act [SSCBA], or would be so entitled if he satisfied the contribution conditions;
      (ii) otherwise than by retirement except earnings to which regulation 35(1)(b) to (e) and [⁵(g) to (i)] applies (earnings of employed earners);
[¹⁰(b) where—
      (i) the employment has not been terminated, but
      (ii) the claimant is not engaged in remunerative work,
    any earnings in respect of that employment except earnings to which regulation 35(1)(d) and (e) applies; but this sub-paragraph shall not apply where the claimant has been suspended from his employment.]
[¹⁰**2.**—In the case of a claimant who, before the date of claim—

417

(a) has been engaged in part-time employment as an employed earner or, where the employment has been outside Great Britain, would have been so engaged had the employment been in Great Britain, and

(b) has ceased to be engaged in that employment, whether or not that employment has been terminated,

any earnings in respect of that employment except any payment to which regulation 35(1)(e) applies; but this paragraph shall not apply where the claimant has been suspended from his employment.]

3. In the case of a claimant who has been engaged in remunerative work or part-time employment as a self-employed earner [¹or, had the employment been in Great Britain, would have been so engaged] and who has ceased to be so employed, from the date of the cessation of his employment any earnings derived from that employment except earnings to which regulation 30(2) (royalties etc.) applies.

[⁴**4.**—(1) In a case to which this paragraph applies, £15; but notwithstanding regulation 23 (calculation of income and capital of members of claimant's family and of a polygamous marriage), if this paragraph applies to a claimant it shall not apply to his partner except where, and to the extent that, the earnings of the claimant which are to be disregarded under this paragraph are less than £15.

(2) This paragraph applies where the claimant's applicable amount includes, or but for his being an in-patient or in accommodation in a residential care home or nursing home or in residential accommodation would include, an amount by way of a disability premium under Schedule 2 (applicable amounts).

(3) This paragraph applies where—

(a) the claimant is a member of a couple, and—

    (i) his applicable amount would include an amount by way of the disability premium under Schedule 2 but for the higher pensioner premium under that Schedule being applicable; or

    (ii) had he not been an in-patient or in accommodation in a residential care home or nursing home or in residential accommodation his applicable amount would include the higher pensioner premium under that Schedule and had that been the case he would also satisfy the condition in (i) above; and

(b) he or his partner is under the age of 60 and at least one is engaged in part-time employment.

(4) This paragraph applies where—

(a) the claimant's applicable amount includes, or but for his being an in-patient or in accommodation in a residential care home or nursing home or in residential accommodation would include, an amount by way of the higher pensioner premium under Schedule 2; and

(b) the claimant or, if he is a member of a couple, either he or his partner has attained the age of 60; and

(c) immediately before attaining that age he or, as the case may be, he or his partner was engaged in part-time employment and the claimant was entitled by virtue of sub-paragraph (2) or (3) to a disregard of £15; and

(d) he or, as the case may be, he or his partner has continued in part-time employment.

(5) This paragraph applies where—

(a) the claimant is a member of a couple and—

    (i) his applicable amount would include an amount by way of the disability premium under Schedule 2 but for the pensioner premium for persons aged 75 and over under that Schedule being applicable; or

    (ii) had he not been an in-patient or in accommodation in a residential care home or nursing home or in residential accommodation his applicable amount would include the pensioner premium for persons aged 75 and over under that Schedule and had that been the case he would also satisfy the condition in (i) above; and

(b) he or his partner has attained the age of 75 but is under the age of 80 and the other is under the age of 60 and at least one member of the couple is engaged in part-time employment.

(6) This paragraph applies where—

(a) the claimant is a member of a couple and he or his partner has attained the age of 75 but is under the age of 80 and the other has attained the age of 60; and

(b) immediately before the younger member attained that age either member was engaged in part-time employment and the claimant was entitled by virtue of sub-paragraph (5) to a disregard of £15; and

(c) either he or his partner has continued in part-time employment.

[⁶(7) For the purposes of this paragraph—

(a) except where head (b) or (c) applies, no account shall be taken of any period not exceeding eight consecutive weeks occurring—

(i) on or after the date on which the claimant or, if he is a member of a couple, he or his partner attained the age of 60 during which either was or both were not engaged in part-time employment or the claimant was not entitled to income support; or

(ii) immediately after the date on which the claimant or his partner ceased to participate in arrangements for training made under section 2 of the Employment and Training Act 1973 [⁷or section 2 of the Enterprise and New Towns (Scotland) Act 1990] or to attend a course at an employment rehabilitation centre established under that section [⁷of the 1973 Act];

(b) in a case where the claimant has ceased to be entitled to income support because he, or if he is a member of a couple, he or his partner becomes engaged in remunerative work, no account shall be taken of any period, during which he was not entitled to income support, not exceeding the permitted period determined in accordance with regulation 3A (permitted period) occurring on or after the date on which the claimant or, as the case may be, his partner attained the age of 60;

(c) no account shall be taken of any period occurring on or after the date on which the claimant or, if he is a member of a couple, he or his partner attained the age of 60 during which the claimant was not entitled to income support because he or his partner was participating in arrangements for training made under section 2 of the Employment and Training Act 1973 [⁷or section 2 of the Enterprise and New Towns (Scotland) Act 1990] or attending a course at an employment rehabilitation centre established under that section [⁷of the 1973 Act].]]

[¹³**5.** In a case where the claimant is a lone parent and paragraph 4 does not apply, £15.]

[¹¹**6.** Where the claimant is a member of a couple—

(a) in a case to which none of paragraphs 4, 6A, 6B, 7 and 8 applies, £10; but notwithstanding regulation 23 (calculation of income and capital of members of claimant's family and of a polygamous marriage), if this paragraph applies to a claimant it shall not apply to his partner except where, and to the extent that, the earnings of the claimant which are to be disregarded under this sub-paragraph are less than £10;

(b) in a case to which one or more of paragraphs 4, 6A, 6B, 7 and 8 applies and the total amount disregarded under those paragraphs is less than £10, so much of the claimant's earnings as would not in aggregate with the amount disregarded under those paragraphs exceed £10.]

[⁹**6A.**—(1) In a case to which none of paragraphs 4 to 6 applies to the claimant, and subject to sub-paragraph (2), where the claimant's applicable amount includes an amount by way of the carer premium under Schedule 2 (applicable amounts), £15 of the earnings of the person who is, or at any time in the preceding eight weeks was, in receipt of invalid care allowance or treated in accordance with paragraph 14ZA(2) of that Schedule as being in receipt of invalid care allowance.

(2) Where the carer premium is awarded in respect of the claimant and of any partner of his, their earnings shall for the purposes of this paragraph be aggregated, but the

amount to be disregarded in accordance with paragraph (1) shall not exceed £15 of the aggregated amount.

6B. Where the carer premium is awarded in respect of a claimant who is a member of a couple and whose earnings are less than £15, but is not awarded in respect of the other member of the couple, and that other member is engaged in an employment—

(a) specified in paragraph 7(1), so much of the other member's earnings as would not when aggregated with the amount disregarded under paragraph 6A exceed £15;

(b) other than one specified in paragraph 7(1), so much of the other member's earnings from such other employment up to £5 as would not when aggregated with the amount disregarded under paragraph 6A exceed £15.]

7.—(1) In a case to which none of paragraphs [⁹4 to 6B] applies to the claimant, £15 of earnings derived from one or more employments as—

(a) a part-time fireman in a fire brigade maintained in pursuance of the Fire Services Acts 1947 to 1959;

(b) an auxiliary coastguard in respect of coast rescue activities;

(c) a person engaged part time in the manning or launching of a lifeboat;

(d) a member of any territorial or reserve force prescribed in Part I of Schedule 3 to the Social Security (Contributions) Regulations 1979;

but, notwithstanding regulation 23 (calculation of income and capital of members of claimant's family and of a polygamous marriage), if this paragraph applies to a claimant it shall not apply to his partner except to the extent specified in sub-paragraph (2).

(2) If the claimant's partner is engaged in employment—

(a) specified in sub-paragraph (1) so much of his earnings as would not in aggregate with the amount of the claimant's earnings disregarded under this paragraph exceed £15;

(b) other than one specified in sub-paragraph (1) so much of his earnings from that employment up to £5 as would not in aggregate with the claimant's earnings disregarded under this paragraph exceed £15.

8. Where the claimant is engaged in one or more employments specified in paragraph 7(1) but his earnings derived from such employments are less than £15 in any week and he is also engaged in any other part-time employment so much of his earnings from that other employment up to £5 as would not in aggregate with the amount of his earnings disregarded under paragraph 7 exceed £15.

9. In a case to which none of paragraphs 4 to 8 applies to the claimant, £5.

[¹¹**10.** Notwithstanding the foregoing provisions of this Schedule, where two or more payments of the same kind and from the same source are to be taken into account in the same benefit week, because it has not been practicable to treat the payments under regulation 31(1)(b) (date on which income treated as paid) as paid on the first day of the benefit week in which they were due to be paid, there shall be disregarded from each payment the sum that would have been disregarded if the payment had been taken into account on the date on which it was due to be paid.]

11. Any earnings derived from employment which are payable in a country outside the United Kingdom for such period during which there is a prohibition against the transfer to the United Kingdom of those earnings.

12. Where a payment of earnings is made in a currency other than sterling, any banking charge or commission payable in converting that payment into sterling.

13. Any earnings which are due to be paid before the date of claim and which would otherwise fall to be taken into account in the same benefit week as a payment of the same kind and from the same source.

14. Any earnings of a child or young person except earnings to which paragraph 15 applies.

15. [⁸In the case of earnings of a child or young person who although not receiving full-time education for the purposes of section 2 of the Child Benefit Act 1975 [SSCBA, s.142] (meaning of "child") is nonetheless treated for the purposes of these Regulations as receiving relevant education and] who is engaged in remunerative work, if—

(a) an amount by way of a disabled child premium under Schedule 2 (applicable amounts) is, or but for his accommodation in a [⁴residential care home or nursing home] would be, included in the calculation of his applicable amount and his earning capacity is not, by reason of his disability, less than 75 per cent of that which he would, but for that disability normally be expected to earn, £15;

(b) in any other case, £5.

[¹¹**15A.** In the case of a claimant who—

(a) has been engaged in employment as a member of any territorial or reserve force prescribed in Part I of Schedule 3 to the Social Security (Contributions) Regulations 1979; and

(b) by reason of that employment has failed to satisfy any of the conditions for entitlement to income support other than section 124(1)(b) of the Contributions and Benefits Act (income support in excess of the applicable amount),

any earnings from that employment paid in respect of the period in which the claimant was not entitled to income support.]

16. In this Schedule "part-time employment" means employment in which the person is not to be treated as engaged in remunerative work under regulation 5 or 6 (persons treated, or not treated, as engaged in remunerative work).

AMENDMENTS

1. Income Support (General) Amendment Regulations 1988 (S.I. 1988 No. 663). reg. 34 (April 11, 1988).

2. Income Support (General) Amendment No. 4 Regulations 1988 (S.I. 1988 No. 1445), reg. 24 (September 12, 1988).

3. Income Support (General) Amendment No. 4 Regulations 1988 (S.I. 1988 No. 1445), Sched. 1, para. 8 (April 10, 1989).

4. Income Support (General) Amendment Regulations 1989 (S.I. 1989 No. 534), reg. 10 and Sched. 1 (October 9, 1989).

5. Income Support (General) Amendment No. 2 Regulations 1989 (S.I. 1989 No. 1323), reg. 18 (October 9, 1989).

6. Income Support (General) Amendment No. 3 Regulations 1989 (S.I. 1989 No. 1678), reg. 12 (October 9, 1989).

7. Enterprise (Scotland) Consequential Amendments Order 1991 (S.I. 1991 No. 387), arts. 2 and 9 (April 1, 1991).

8. Income Support (General) Amendment Regulations 1992 (S.I.1992 No. 468), reg. 7 (April 6, 1992).

9. Income-related Benefits Schemes (Miscellaneous Amendments) Regulations 1993 (S.I. 1993 No. 315), reg. 8 (April 12, 1993).

10. Income-related Benefits Schemes (Miscellaneous Amendments) (No. 4) Regulations 1993 (S.I. 1993 No. 2119), reg. 22 (October 4, 1993).

11. Income-related Benefits Schemes and Social Fund (Miscellaneous Amendments) Regulations 1996 (S.I. 1996 No. 1944), reg. 6(11) (October 7, 1996).

12. Child Benefit, Child Support and Social Security (Miscellaneous Amendments) Regulations 1996 (S.I. 1996 No. 1803), reg. 41 (April 7, 1997).

13. Social Security Amendment (Lone Parents) Regulations 1998 (S.I. 1998 No. 766), reg. 13 (April 6, 1998).

DEFINITIONS

"benefit week"—see reg. 2(1).

"child"—see 1986 Act, s.20(11) (SSCBA, s.137(1)).

"claimant"—see reg. 2(1).

"couple"—*ibid.*

"date of claim"—*ibid.*

"employed earner"—*ibid.*

"family"—see 1986 Act, s.20(11) (SSCBA, s.137(1)).

"nursing home"—see reg. 2(1), reg. 19(3).

"partner"—see reg. 2(1).

"polygamous marriage"—*ibid.*

"remunerative work"—*ibid.*

"residential accommodation"—see reg. 2(1), reg. 21(3).

"residential care home"—see reg. 2(1), reg. 19(3).
"Social Security Act"—see reg. 2(1).
"supplementary benefit"—*ibid.*
"young person" *ibid.*, reg. 14.

GENERAL NOTE

Paras. 1 to 13 and 15A apply to adults. Paras. 14 and 15 apply to children and young persons only. Paras. 1 to 10 do not apply to children or young persons (reg. 23(2)).

Paragraph 1
This disregard is crucial to entitlement following the termination of full time employment (*i.e.* 16 hours or more per week in the case of the claimant, 24 hours or more per week for a partner: reg. 5(1) and (1A); references to the "claimant" in Part V of the Income Support Regulations include his partner (if any) or any child, unless the context otherwise requires (reg. 23(1)). The effect, under sub-para. (a)(ii), is that final payments of wages and salary are disregarded. This means that entitlement can begin immediately, unless a payment in lieu of wages or notice or holiday pay is due or a compensation payment is made. If any of these payments are made, reg. 5(5) treats the person as in full-time work for the number of weeks covered by the payments (regs. 29(3) and (4)). Once that period has ended, any money remaining counts as capital (*CIS 104/1989* and *CIS 654/1991*, to be reported as *R(IS) 3/93*). The disregard is more extensive if the employment has not terminated but the person is working less than 16 hours a week (or none at all). The old form of para. 1(b) applied the disregard if the employment had been "interrupted". In *CIS 301/1989* it was held that a shift from full-time to part-time employment with the same employer was an interruption of "the" employment. If the evidence had supported the replacement of one contract with another this would have been a termination. The new wording should cover this type of situation with less linguistic contortion. The disregard in sub-para. (b) does not apply if the person has been suspended. Payments by way of a retainer (reg. 35(1)(e)) are not disregarded under sub-para. (a)(ii) or (b). *R(IS) 9/95* decides that a guarantee payment under s. 12 of the Employment Protection (Consolidation) Act 1978 counts as a retainer.
If the person retires at pensionable age no earnings due on termination are taken into account.

Paragraph 2
There is a more extensive disregard where the person's part-time (*i.e.* less than 16 hours per week (24 hours in the case of a partner): para. 16 and reg. 5(1) and (1A)) work has stopped before the claim (provided he has not been suspended). On payments within reg. 35(1)(e) see *R(IS) 9/95* in the note to para. 1. It is not necessary for the employment to have ended. If the part-time work ends while the claimant is claiming income support, payments are taken into account as earnings in the usual way.

Paragraph 3
When a self-employed person leaves that employment, only royalties or payments for copyright count.

Paragraph 4
This provision allows a disregard of £15 between the claimant and any partner, if the claimant meets the basic conditions for a disability premium or if the conditions for the enhanced or higher pensioner premium are met, with the restrictive extra conditions of sub-paras. (3)(b) and (5)(b).

Paragraph 5
If the claimant is a lone parent the first £15 of net earnings are disregarded. Since April 6, 1998 it has not been necessary for the claimant to be receiving the lone parent rate of the family premium under para. 3(1)(a) of Sched. 2 for this disregard to apply; *all* lone parent now qualify for a disregard under this paragraph, unless they are entitled to a £15 disregard under para. 4.

Paragraph 6
From October 7, 1996 the previous £15 disregard for long-term unemployed couples aged less than 60 which applied under this paragraph has been replaced by a £10 earnings disregard that will apply to all couples. This is the same as the disregard that applies for JSA.

Paragraphs 6A and 6B
Where the carer premium is payable, the first £15 of the earnings of the carer are disregarded. If the carer does not use up the disregard, what is spare may be applied to a (non-carer) partner's

earnings under para. 6B. Only £5 may be disregarded in this way, except for the employments mentioned in para. 7(1).

Paragraph 7
Earnings from these activities attract a £15 disregard, but a couple cannot have a total disregard of more than £15.

Paragraph 9
The basic disregard of net earnings from part-time work is £5.

Paragraph 10
See notes to reg. 32(5).

Paragraph 13
Where earnings are due before the date of claim, overlaps with payments of the same kind are avoided. See notes to reg. 32(5).

Paragraphs 14 and 15
The general rule is that the earnings of children and young persons are disregarded, but where such a person has left school and is treated as in relevant education until the next terminal date, earnings from "remunerative work" do count, subject to a £5 disregard (£15 for the disabled). Note the transitional protection for Easter school leavers who were working for more than 16 hours a week, but less than 24, immediately before April 6, 1992 in reg. 10 of the Income Support (General) Amendment Regulations 1992 (see p. 491). Remunerative work for the purposes of excluding payment of child benefit in these circumstances remains 24 hours a week (regs. 1(2) and 7(3) of the Child Benefit (General) Regulations).

Paragraph 15A
This introduces a new disregard (that also applies for JSA) of earnings paid to a member of the reserve forces while attending training (and therefore not entitled to income support).

<h2 style="text-align:center">SCHEDULE 9   Regulation 40(2)</h2>

SUMS TO BE DISREGARDED IN THE CALCULATION OF INCOME OTHER THAN
EARNINGS

1. Any amount paid by way of tax on income which is taken into account under regulation 40 (calculation of income other than earnings).

2. Any payment in respect of any expenses incurred by a claimant who is—
(a) engaged by a charitable or [³²voluntary organisation]; or
(b) a volunteer,
if he otherwise derives no remuneration or profit from the employment and is not to be treated as possessing any earnings under regulation 42(6) (notional income).

3. In the case of employment as an employed earner, any payment in respect of expenses wholly, exclusively and necessarily incurred in the performance of the duties of the employment.

4. In the case of a payment of statutory sick pay under Part I of the Social Security and Housing Benefits Act 1982 or statutory maternity pay under Part V of the Act or any remuneration paid by or on behalf of an employer to the claimant who for the time being is unable to work due to illness or maternity—
(a) any amount deducted by way of primary Class 1 contributions under the Social Security Act [SSCBA];
(b) one-half of any sum paid by the claimant by way of a contribution towards an occupational or personal pension scheme.

[¹**4A.** In the case of the payment of statutory sick pay under Part II of the Social Security (Northern Ireland) Order 1982 or statutory maternity pay under Part VI of the Social Security (Northern Ireland) Order 1986—
(a) any amount deducted by way of primary Class 1 contributions under the Social Security (Northern Ireland) Act 1975;

(b) one-half of any sum paid by way of a contribution towards an occupational or personal pension scheme.]

5. Any housing benefit. [⁴¹including any amount of housing benefit to which a person is entitled by virtue of regulation 7B of the Housing Benefit (General) Regulations 1987 (entitlement of a refugee to housing benefit)].

6. Any mobility allowance [¹⁸or the mobility component of disability living allowance].

7. Any concessionary payment made to compensate for the non-payment of—

(a) any payment specified in [¹⁸paragraph 6 [⁴⁸ or 9]];

(b) income support [⁴⁸ or jobseeker's allowance].

8. Any mobility supplement or any payment intended to compensate for the non-payment of such a supplement.

[²⁵**9.** Any attendance allowance or the care component of disability living allowance, but, where the claimant's applicable amount falls to be calculated in accordance with Part I of Schedule 4 [³⁴ or paragraph 13A of Schedule 7] only to the extent that it exceeds the amount for the time being specified as the higher rate of attendance allowance for the purposes of section 64(3) of the Social Security Contributions and Benefits Act 1992 or, as the case may, be the highest rate of the care component of disability living allowance for the purposes of section 72(4)(a) of that Act.]

[²⁹**9A.** . . .]

10. Any payment to the claimant as holder of the Victoria Cross or George Cross or any analogous payment.

11. Any sum in respect of a course of study attended by a child or young person payable by virtue of regulations made under section 81 of the Education Act 1944 (assistance by means of scholarships and otherwise), or by virtue of section 2(1) of the Education Act 1962 (awards for courses of further education) or section 49 of the Education (Scotland) Act 1980 (power to assist persons to take advantage of educational facilities) [⁴³ or section 12(2)(c) of the Further and Higher Education (Scotland) Act 1992 (provision of financial assistance to students)].

12. In the case of a claimant to whom regulation 9(1) (persons treated as available for employment) applies, any sums intended for any expenditure specified in paragraph (2) of regulation 62 (calculation of grant income) necessary as a result of his attendance on his course.

[¹**13.** In the case of a claimant participating in arrangements for training made under section 2 of the Employment and Training Act 1973 [¹³or section 2 of the Enterprise and New Towns (Scotland) Act 1990] or attending a course at an employment rehabilitation centre established under that section [¹³of the 1973 Act]—

(a) any travelling expenses reimbursed to the claimant;

(b) any living away from home allowance under section 2(2)(d) [¹³of the 1973 Act or section 2(4)(c) of the 1990 Act] but only to the extent that his rent or rates payable in respect of accommodation not normally occupied by him as his home are not met by housing benefit; .

(c) any training premium,

[⁴⁴(d) any child care expenses reimbursed to the claimant in respect of his participation in an employment programme specified in regulation 75(1)(a)(ii) of the Jobseeker's Allowance Regulations 1996 or in a training scheme specified in regulation 75(1)(b)(ii) of those Regulations,]

but this paragraph, except in so far as it relates to a payment under sub-paragraph (a), [⁴⁴(b), (c) or (d)], does not apply to any part of any allowance under section 2(2)(d) [¹³of the 1973 Act or section 2(4)(c) of the 1990 Act].]

14.[³⁴ . . .]

[¹⁰**15.**—[²⁹(1) Subject to sub-paragraph (3) and paragraphs 36, 37 and 39, [³⁹£20] of any charitable payment or of any voluntary payment made or due to be made at regular intervals, except any payment to which sub-paragraph (2) or paragraph 15A applies.]

(2) Subject to [²⁹sub-paragraphs (3) and (6)] and paragraph 39, any charitable payment or voluntary payment made or due to be made at regular intervals which is intended and used for an item other than food, ordinary clothing or footwear, household fuel, rent or

rates for which housing benefit is payable, [[16]. . .] any housing costs to the extent that they are met under regulation 17(1) (e) or 18(1)(f) (housing costs) or any accommodation charges to the extent that they are met under regulation 19 (persons in residential care or nursing homes)[[30]. . .], of a single claimant or, as the case may be, of the claimant or any other member of his family[[16], or is used for any [[23]council tax] or water charges for which that claimant or member is liable].

(3) Sub-paragraphs (1) and (2) shall not apply—

(a) to a payment which is made by a person for the maintenance of any member of his family or of his former partner or of his children;

(b) in the case of a person to whom section 23 of the Act [SSCBA, s.126] (trade disputes) applies or in respect of whom section 20(3) of the Act [SSCBA, s.124(1)] (conditions of entitlement to income support) has effect as modified by section 23A(b) of the Act [SSCBA, s.127(b)] (effect of return to work).

(4) For the purposes of sub-paragraph (1) where a number of charitable or voluntary payments fall to be taken into account in any one week they shall be treated as though they were one such payment.

(5) For the purposes of sub-paragraph (2) the expression "ordinary clothing or footwear" means clothing or footwear for normal daily use, but does not include school uniforms, or clothing or footwear used solely for sporting activities.]

[[29](6) Sub-paragraph (2) shall apply to a claimant in a residential care home or nursing home only if his applicable amount falls to be calculated in accordance with regulation 19.]

[[25]**15A.**—(1) Subject to the following provisions of this paragraph, in the case of a claimant placed in a residential care home or nursing home by a local authority under section 26 of the National Assistance Act 1948, [[32]sections 13A, 13B and 59(2)(c) of the Social Work (Scotland) Act 1968 or section 7 of the Mental Health (Scotland) Act 1984] any charitable payment or voluntary payment made or due to be made at regular intervals.

(2) This paragraph shall apply only where—

(a) the claimant was placed in the residential care or nursing home by the local authority because the home was the preferred choice of the claimant, and

(b) the cost of the accommodation was in excess of what the authority would normally expect to pay having regard to the needs of the claimant assessed in accordance with section 47 of the National Health Service and Community Care Act 1990.

(3) This paragraph shall not apply in the case of a person whose applicable amount falls to be calculated under regulation 19 (persons in residential care or nursing homes with preserved rights).

(4) The amount to be disregarded under sub-paragraph (1) shall not exceed the difference between the actual cost of the accommodation provided by the local authority and the cost the authority would normally incur for a person with the particular needs of the claimant.]

[[38]**15B.**—(1) Subject to sub-paragraphs (2) and (3), where a claimant—

(a) is a person to whom regulation 19 (preserved rights to income support) or paragraph 13A, 13B, 16 or 18 of Schedule 7 (applicable amounts in special cases) applies;

(b) is not residing with his spouse; and

(c) at least 50 per cent. of any occupational pension of his [[42], or of any income from a personal pension scheme or a retirement annuity contract of his,] is being paid to, or in respect of, his spouse for that spouse's maintenance,

an amount equal to 50 per cent. of the pension[[42], pensions or income] concerned.

[[42](2) Where a claimant is entitled to pensions or income referred to in sub-paragraph (1) from more than one source, all such pensions and income to which he is entitled shall be aggregated for the purposes of that sub-paragraph.]

(3) This paragraph shall not have effect in respect of that part of any [[42]pension or

income referred to in sub-paragraph (1)] to which a spouse is legally entitled whether under a court order or not.]

[³⁵**16.** Subject to paragraphs 36 and 37, £10 of any of the following, namely—

  (a) a war disablement pension (except insofar as such a pension falls to be disregarded under paragraph 8 or 9);

  (b) a war widow's pension;

  (c) a pension payable to a person as a widow under the Naval, Military and Air Forces Etc. (Disablement and Death) Service Pensions Order 1983 insofar as that Order is made under the Naval and Marine Pay and Pensions Act 1865 [³⁷ or the Pensions and Yeomary Pay Act 1884], or is made only under section 12(1) of the Social Security (Miscellaneous Provisions) Act 1977 and any power of Her Majesty otherwise than under an enactment to make provision about pensions for or in respect of persons who have been disabled or have died in consequence of service as members of the armed forces of the Crown;

  (d) a payment made to compensate for the non-payment of such a pension as is mentioned in any of the preceding sub-paragraphs;

  (e) a pension paid by the government of a country outside Great Britain which is analogous to any of the pensions mentioned in sub-paragraphs (a) to (c) above;

  (f) a pension paid to victims of National Socialist persecution under any special provision made by the law of the Federal Republic of Germany, or any part of it, or of the Republic of Austria.]

17. Where a person receives income under an annuity purchased with a loan which satisfies the following conditions—

  (a) that the loan was made as part of a scheme under which not less than 90 per cent. of the proceeds of the loan were applied to the purchase by the person to whom it was made of an annuity ending with his life or with the life of the survivor of two or more persons (in this paragraph referred to as "the annuitants") who include the person to whom the loan was made;

  (b) that the interest on the loan is payable by the person to whom it was made or by one of the annuitants;

  (c) that at the time the loan was made the person to whom it was made or each of the annuitants had attained the age of 65;

  (d) that the loan was secured on a dwelling in Great Britain and the person to whom the loan was made or one of the annuitants owns an estate or interest in that dwelling; and

  (e) that the person to whom the loan was made or one of the annuitants occupies the accommodation on which it was secured as his home at the time the interest is paid,

the amount, calculated on a weekly basis equal to—

    [³¹(i) where, or insofar as, section 369 of the Income and Corporation Taxes Act 1988 (mortgage interest payable under deduction of tax) applies to the payments of interest on the loan, the interest which is payable after deduction of a sum equal to income tax on such payments at the applicable percentage of income tax within the meaning of section 369(1A) of that Act;]

      (ii) in any other case the interest which is payable on the loan without deduction of such a sum.

[³²**18.** Any payment made to the claimant by a person who normally resides with the claimant, which is a contribution towards that person's living and accommodation costs, except where that person is residing with the claimant in circumstances to which paragraph 19 or 20 refers.]

[³⁰**19.** Where the claimant occupies a dwelling as his home and the dwelling is also occupied by [³²another person], and there is a contractual liability to make payments to the claimant in respect of the occupation of the dwelling by that person or a member of his family—

(a) £4 of the aggregate of any payments made in respect of any one week in respect of the occupation of the dwelling by that person or a member of his family, or by that person and a member of his family; and

(b) a further [⁴⁰£9.25], where the aggregate of any such payments is inclusive of an amount for heating.]

[³⁰**20.** Where the claimant occupies a dwelling as his home and he provides in that dwelling board and lodging accommodation, an amount, in respect of each person for whom such accommodation is provided for the whole or any part of a week, equal to—

(a) where the aggregate of any payments made in respect of any one week in respect of such accommodation provided to such person does not exceed £20.00, 100 % of such payments; or

(b) where the aggregate of any such payments exceeds £20.00, £20.00 and 50 % of the excess over £20.00.]

[¹**21.**—(1) Subject to sub-paragraph (2), except where regulation 42(4)(a)(i) (notional income) applies or in the case of a person to whom section 23 of the Act [SSCBA, s.126] (trade disputes) applies and for so long as it applies, any income in kind;

(2) The exception under sub-paragraph (1) shall not apply where the income in kind is received from the Macfarlane Trust[⁸, the Macfarlane (Special Payments) Trust] [¹⁵, the Macfarlane (Special Payments) (No. 2) Trust][²¹, the Fund][²⁷, the Eileen Trust] [² or [²⁶the Independent Living Funds]].]

22.—(1) Any income derived from capital to which the claimant is or is treated under regulation 52 (capital jointly held) as beneficially entitled but, subject to sub-paragraph (2), not income derived from capital disregarded under paragraph 1, 2, 4, 6 [³12 or 25 to 28] of Schedule 10.

(2) Income derived from capital disregarded under paragraph 2 [³4 or 25 to 28] of Schedule 10 but [²⁴only to the extent of—

(a) any mortgage repayments made in respect of the dwelling or premises in the period during which that income accrued; or

(b) any council tax or water charges which the claimant is liable to pay in respect of the dwelling or premises and which are paid in the period during which that income accrued.

(3) The definition of ''water charges'' in regulation 2(1) shall apply to subparagraph (2) with the omission of the words ''in so far as such charges are in respect of the dwelling which a person occupies as his home''.]

23. Any income which is payable in a country outside the United Kingdom for such period during which there is a prohibition against the transfer to the United Kingdom of that income.

24. Where a payment of income is made in a currency other than sterling, any banking charge or commission payable in converting that payment into sterling.

25.—(1) Any payment made to the claimant in respect of a child or young person who is a member of his family—

[²⁰(a) in accordance with regulations made pursuant to section 57A of the Adoption Act 1976 or with a scheme approved by the Secretary of State under section 51 of the Adoption (Scotland) Act 1978 (schemes for payment of allowances to adopters);

[⁴⁹(b) which is a payment made by a local authority in pursuance of section 34(6) or, as the case may be, section 50 of the Children Act 1975 (contributions towards the cost of the accommodation and maintenance of a child);

(c) which is a payment made by a local authority in pursuance of section 15(1) of, and paragraph 15 of Schedule 1 to, the Children Act 1989 (local authority contribution to a child's maintenance where the child is living with a person as a result of a residence order);

(d) which is a payment made by an authority, as defined in Article 2 of the Children Order, in pursuance of Article 15 of, and paragraph 17 of Schedule 1 to, that Order (contribution by an authority to child's maintenance);]]

to the extent specifed in sub-paragraph (2).

(2) In the case of a child or young person—

(a) to whom regulation 44(5) (capital in excess of £3,000) applies, the whole payment;

(b) to whom that regulation does not apply, so much of the weekly amount of the payment as exceeds the applicable amount in respect of that child or young person and where applicable to him any amount by way of a disabled child premium.

26. Any payment made by a local authority to the claimant with whom a person is [²⁰accommodated by virtue of arrangements made under section 23(2)(a) of the Children Act 1989 (provision of accommodation and maintenance for a child whom they are looking after)] or, as the case may be, [³section 21] of the Social Work (Scotland) Act 1968 or by a voluntary organisation under [²⁰section 59(1)(a) of the 1989 Act (provision of accommodation by voluntary organisations)] or by a care authority under regulation 9 of the Boarding Out and Fostering of Children (Scotland) Regulations 1985 (provision of accommodation and maintenance for children in care).

27. [⁴⁶ Any payment made to the claimant or his partner for a person ("the person concerned"), who is not normally a member of the claimant's household but is temporarily in his care, by—

(a) a health authority;

(b) a local authority;

(c) a voluntary organisation; or

(d) the person concerned pursuant to section 26(3A) of the National Assistance Act 1948.]

28. Except in the case of a person to whom section 23 of the Act [SSCBA, s.126] (trade disputes) applies [¹or in respect of whom section 20(3) of the Act [SSCBA, s.124(1)] (conditions of entitlement to income support) has effect as modified by section 23A(b) of the Act [SSCBA, s.127(b)] (effect of return to work)], [⁶any payment made by a local authority [²⁰in accordance with section 17 or 24 of the Children Act 1989] or, as the case may be, section 12, 24 or 26 of the Social Work (Scotland) Act 1968 (local authorities' duty to promote welfare of children and powers to grant financial assistance to persons in, or formerly in, their care).]

[³³**29.**—(1) Subject to sub-paragraph (2) any payment received under an insurance policy, taken out to insure against the risk of being unable to maintain repayments on a loan which qualifies under paragraph 15 or 16 of Schedule 3 (housing costs in respect of loans to acquire an interest in a dwelling, or for repairs and improvements to the dwelling, occupied as the home) and used to meet such repayments, to the extent that it does not exceed the aggregate of—

(a) the amount, calculated on a weekly basis, of any interest on that loan which is in excess of the amount met in accordance with Schedule 3 (housing costs);

(b) the amount of any payment, calculated on a weekly basis, due on the loan attributable to the repayment of capital; and

(c) any amount due by way of premiums on—

(i) that policy, or

(ii) a policy of insurance taken out to insure against loss or damage to any building or part of a building which is occupied by the claimant as his home.

(2) This paragraph shall not apply to any payment which is treated as possessed by the claimant by virtue of regulation 42(4)(a)(ii) (notional income).

30.—(1) Except where paragraph 29 [⁵⁰or 30ZA] applies, and subject to sub-paragraph (2), any payment made to the claimant which is intended to be used and is used as a contribution towards—

(a) any payment due on a loan if secured on the dwelling occupied as the home which does not qualify under Schedule 3 (housing costs);

(b) any interest payment or charge which qualifies in accordance with paragraphs 15 to 17 of Schedule 3 to the extent that the payment or charge is not met;

   (c) any payment due on a loan which qualifies under paragraph 15 or 16 of Schedule 3 attributable to the payment of capital;

   (d) any amount due by way of premiums on—

      (i) [³⁶ an insurance policy taken out to insure against the risk of being unable to make the payments referred to in (a) to (c) above;] or

      (ii) a policy of insurance taken out to insure against loss or damage to any building or part of a building which is occupied by the claimant as his home.

   (e) his rent in respect of the dwelling occupied by him as his home but only to the extent that it is not met by housing benefit; or his accommodation charge but only to the extent that the actual charge increased, where appropriate, in accordance with paragraph 2 of Schedule 4 exceeds the amount determined in accordance with regulation 19 (residential care and nursing homes) or the amount payable by a local authority in accordance with Part III of the National Assistance Act 1948.

(2) This paragraph shall not apply to any payment which is treated as possessed by the claimant by virtue of regulation 42(4)(a)(ii) (notional income).]

[⁵⁰**30ZA.**—(1) Subject to sub-paragraph (2), any payment received under an insurance policy, other than an insurance policy referred to in paragraph 29, taken out to insure against the risk of being unable to maintain repayments under a regulated agreement as defined for the purposes of the Consumer Credit Act 1974 or under a hire-purchase agreement or a conditional sale agreement as defined for the purposes of Part III of the Hire-Purchase Act 1964.

(2) A payment referred to in sub-paragraph (1) shall only be disregarded to the extent that the payment received under that policy does not exceed the amounts, calculated on a weekly basis, which are used to—

   (a) maintain the repayments referred to in sub-paragraph (1); and

   (b) meet any amount due by way of premiums on that policy.]

[²⁹**30A.**—(1) Subject to sub-paragraphs (2) and (3), in the case of a claimant in a residential care home or nursing home, any payment, whether or not the payment is charitable or voluntary but not a payment to which paragraph 15A applies, made to the claimant which is intended to be used and is used to meet the cost of maintaining the claimant in that home.

(2) This paragraph shall not apply to a claimant for whom accommodation in a residential care home or nursing home is provided by a local authority under section 26 of the National Assistance Act 1948, or whose applicable amount falls to be calculated in accordance with regulation 19.

(3) The amount to be disregarded under this paragraph shall not exceed the difference between—

   (a) the claimant's applicable amount less any of the amounts referred to in paragraph 13 of Schedule 4 (personal allowances) which would be applicable to the claimant if his applicable amount fell to be calculated in accordance with that Schedule, and

   (b) the weekly charge for the accommodation.]

[¹⁹**31.** Any social fund payment made pursuant to Part III of the Act [SSCBA, Part VIII].]

32. Any payment of income which under regulation 48 (income treated as capital) is to be treated as capital.

33. Any payment under paragraph 2 of Schedule 6 to the Act [SSCBA, s. 148] (pensioners' Christmas bonus).

34. In the case of a person to whom section 23 of the Act [SSCBA, s.126] (trade disputes) applies and for so long as it applies, any payment up to the amount of the relevant sum within the meaning of sub-section (6) of that section made by a trade union; but, notwithstanding regulation 23 (calculation of income and capital of members of claimant's family and of a polygamous marriage) if this paragraph applies to a claimant it shall not apply to his partner except where, and to the extent that, the amount to be disregarded under this paragraph is less than the relevant sum.

35. Any payment which is due to be paid before the date of claim which would otherwise fall to be taken into account in the same benefit week as a payment of the same kind and from the same source.

36. The total of a claimant's income or, if he is a member of a family, the family's income and the income of any person which he is treated as possessing under regulation 23(3) (calculation of income and capital of members of claimant's family and of a polygamous marriage) to be disregarded under regulation 63(2)(b) and 64(1)(c) (calculation of covenant income where a contribution assessed)[11, regulation 66A(2) (treatment of student loans)] and [10paragraphs 15(1)] and 16 shall in no case exceed [39£20] per week.

37. Notwithstanding paragraph 36 where two or more payments of the same kind and from the same source are to be taken into account in the same benefit week, there shall be disregarded from each payment the sum which would otherwise fall to be disregarded under this Schedule; but this paragraph shall only apply in the case of a payment which it has not been practicable to treat under regulation 31(1)(b) (date on which income treated as paid) as paid on the first day of the benefit week in which it is due to be paid.

[1**38.** Any resettlement benefit which is paid to the claimant by virtue of regulation 3 of the Social Security (Hospital In-Patients) Amendment (No. 2) Regulations 1987.

[15**39.**—(1) Any payment made under the Macfarlane Trust, the Macfarlane (Special Payments) Trust, the Macfarlane (Special Payments) (No. 2) Trust ("the Trusts"), [21the Fund][27, the Eileen Trust] or [26the Independent Living Funds].

(2) Any payment by or on behalf of a person who is suffering or who suffered from haemophilia [21or who is or was a qualifying person], which derives from a payment made under any of the Trusts to which sub-paragraph (1) refers and which is made to or for the benefit of—

    (a) that person's partner or former partner from whom he is not, or where that person has died was not, estranged or divorced;

    (b) any child who is a member of that person's family or who was such a member and who is a member of the claimant's family; or

    (c) any young person who is a member of that person's family or who was such a member and who is a member of the claimant's family.

(3) Any payment by or on behalf of the partner or former partner of a person who is suffering or who suffered from haemophilia [21or who is or was a qualifying person] provided that the partner or former partner and that person are not, or if either of them has died were not, estranged or divorced, which derives from a payment made under any of the Trusts to which sub-paragraph (1) refers and which is made to or for the benefit of—

    (a) the person who is suffering from haemophilia [21or who is a qualifying person];

    (b) any child who is a member of that person's family or who was such a member and who is a member of the claimant's family; or

    (c) any young person who is a member of that person's family or who was such a member and who is a member of the claimant's family.

(4) Any payment by a person who is suffering from haemophilia [21or who is a qualifying person], which derives from a payment under any of the Trusts to which sub-paragraph (1) refers, where—

    (a) that person has no partner or former partner from whom he is not estranged or divorced, nor any child or young person who is or had been a member of that person's family; and

    (b) the payment is made either—

        (i) to that person's parent or step-parent, or

        (ii) where that person at the date of the payment is a child, a young person or a student who has not completed his full-time education and has no parent or step-parent, to his guardian,

but only for a period from the date of the payment until the end of two years from that person's death.

(5) Any payment out of the estate of a person who suffered from haemophilia [21or who was a qualifying person], which derives from a payment under any of the Trusts to which sub-paragraph (1) refers, where—

    (a) that person at the date of his death (the relevant date) had no partner or former partner from whom he was not estranged or divorced, nor any child or young person who was or had been a member of his family; and

(b) the payment is made either—
  (i) to that person's parent or step-parent, or
  (ii) where that person at the relevant date was a child, a young person or a student who had not completed his full-time education and had no parent or step-parent, to his guardian,

but only for a period of two years from the relevant date.

(6) In the case of a person to whom or for whose benefit a payment referred to in this paragraph is made, any income which derives from any payment of income or capital made under or deriving from any of the Trusts.]

[²¹(7) For the purposes of sub-paragraphs (2) to (6), any reference to the Trusts shall be construed as including a reference to the Fund [²⁷and the Eileen Trust].]]

[³**40.** Any payment made by the Secretary of State to compensate for the loss (in whole or in part) of entitlement to housing benefit.]

[⁴**41.** Any payment made by the Secretary of State to compensate a person who was entitled to supplementary benefit in respect of a period ending immediately before 11th April 1988 but who did not become entitled to income support in respect of a period beginning with that day.

42. Any payment made by the Secretary of State to compensate for the loss of housing benefit supplement under regulation 19 of the Supplementary Benefit (Requirements) Regulations 1983.

43. Any payment made to a juror or a witness in respect of attendance at a court other than compensation for loss of earnings or for the loss of a benefit payable under the benefit Acts.

44. [²³ . . .].]

[⁹**45.** Any community charge benefit.

46. Any payment in consequence of a reduction of a personal community charge pursuant to regulations under section 13A of the Local Government Finance Act 1988 or section 9A of the Abolition of Domestic Rates Etc (Scotland) Act 1987 (reduction of liability for personal community charges) [²³or reduction of council tax under section 13 or, as the case may be, section 80 of the Local Government Finance Act 1992 (reduction of liability for council tax).]

47. Any special war widows payment made under—

(a) the Naval and Marine Pay and Pensions (Special War Widows Payment) Order 1990 made under section 3 of the Naval and Marine Pay and Pensions Act 1865;
(b) the Royal Warrant dated 19th February 1990 amending the Schedule to the Army Pensions Warrant 1977;
(c) the Queen's Order dated 26th February 1990 made under section 2 of the Air Force (Constitution) Act 1917;
(d) the Home Guard War Widows Special Payments Regulations 1990 made under section 151 of the Reserve Forces Act 1980;
(e) the Orders dated 19th February 1990 amending Orders made on 12th December 1980 concerning the Ulster Defence Regiment made in each case under section 140 of the Reserve Forces Act 1980;

and any analogous payment made by the Secretary of State for Defence to any person who is not a person entitled under the provisions mentioned in subparagraphs (a) to (e) of this paragraph.]

[¹²**48.**—(1)Any payment or repayment made—

(a) as respects England and Wales, under regulation 3, 5 or 8 of the National Health Service (Travelling Expenses and Remission of Charges) Regulations 1988 (travelling expenses and health service supplies);
(b) as respects Scotland, under regulation 3, 5 or 8 of the National Health Service (Travelling Expenses and Remission of Charges) (Scotland) Regulations 1988 (travelling expenses and health service supplies).

(2) Any payment or repayment made by the Secretary of State for Health, the Secretary of State for Scotland or the Secretary of State for Wales which is analogous to a payment or repayment mentioned in sub-paragraph (1).

49. Any payment made under regulation 9 to 11 or 13 of the Welfare Food Regulations 1988 (payments made in place of milk tokens or the supply of vitamins).

50. Any payment made either by the Secretary of State for the Home Department or by the Secretary of State for Scotland under a scheme established to assist relatives and other persons to visit persons in custody.]

[¹⁹**51.** Any payment (other than a training allowance) made, whether by the Secretary of State or by any other person, under the Disabled Persons (Employment) Act 1944 or in accordance with arrangements made under section 2 of the Employment and Training Act 1973 to assist disabled persons to obtain or retain employment despite their disability.]

[²³**52.** Any council tax benefit] [⁴¹including any amount of council tax benefit to which a person is entitled by virtue of regulation 4D of the Council Tax Benefit (General) Regulations 1992 (entitlement of a refugee to council tax benefit)].]

[³⁰**53.** Where the claimant is in receipt of any benefit under Parts II, III or V of the Contributions and Benefits Act [³⁴or pension under the Naval, Military and Air Forces Etc. (Disablement and Death) Service Pensions Order 1983], any increase in the rate of that benefit arising under Part IV (increases for dependants) or section 106(a) (unemployability supplement) of that Act [³⁴or the rate of that pension under that Order] where the dependant in respect of whom the increase is paid is not a member of the claimant's family.]

[³¹**54.** Any supplementary pension under article 29(1A) of the Naval, Military and Air Forces etc. (Disablement and Death) Service Pensions Order 1983 (pensions to widows).

55. In the case of a pension awarded at the supplementary rate under article 27(3) of the Personal Injuries (Civilians) Scheme 1983 (pensions to widows), the sum specified in paragraph 1(c) of Schedule 4 to that Scheme.

56.—(1) Any payment which is—
   (a) made under any of the Dispensing Instruments to a widow of a person—
      (i) whose death was attributable to service in a capacity analogous to service as a member of the armed forces of the Crown; and
      (ii) whose service in such capacity terminated before 31st March 1973; and
   (b) equal to the amount specified in article 29(1A) of the Naval, Military and Air Forces etc. (Disablement and Death) Service Pensions Order 1983 (pensions to widows).

(2) In this paragraph "the Dispensing Instruments" means the Order in Council of 19th December 1881, the Royal Warrant of 27th October 1884 and the Order by His Majesty of 14th January 1922 (exceptional grants of pay, non-effective pay and allowances).]

[⁴¹**57.** Any amount of income support to which a person is entitled by virtue of regulation 21ZA above (treatment of refugees).]

[⁴²**58.** Any payment made under the Community Care (Direct Payments) Act 1996 or under section 12B of the Social Work (Scotland) Act 1968.

59.—(1) Subject to paragraph 60, any Career Development Loan paid to the claimant pursuant to section 2 of the Employment and Training Act 1973 except to the extent that the loan has been applied for and paid in respect of living expenses for the period of education and training supported by that loan and those expenses relate to any one or more of the items specified in sub-paragraph (2).

(2) The items specified for the purposes of sub-paragraph (1) are food, ordinary clothing or footwear, household fuel, rent for which housing benefit is payable, or any housing costs to the extent that they are met under regulation 17(1)(e) or 18(1)(f) (housing costs) or any accommodation charges to the extent that they are met under regulation 19 (persons in residential care or nursing homes), of the claimant or, where the claimant is

a member of a family, any other member of his family, or any council tax or water charges for which that claimant or member is liable.

(3) For the purposes of this paragraph, "ordinary clothing and footwear" means clothing or footwear for normal daily use, but does not include school uniforms, or clothing and footwear used solely for sporting activities.

60. Any Career Development Loan paid to the claimant pursuant to section 2 of the Employment and Training Act 1973 where the period of education and training supported by that loan has been completed.

61. (1) Any payment specified in sub-paragraph (2) to a claimant who was formerly a student and who has completed the course in respect of which those payments were made.

(2) The payments specified for the purposes of sub-paragraph (1) are—

(a) any grant income and covenant income as defined for the purposes of Chapter VIII of Part V;

(b) any loan made pursuant to arrangements made under section 1 of the Education (Student Loans) Act 1990 or article 3 of the Education (Student Loans) (Northern Ireland) Order 1990.]

[⁵²**62.** Any mandatory top-up payment made to a person pursuant to section 2 of the Employment and Training Act 1973 in respect of that person's participation in an employment programme specified in—

(a) regulation 75(1)(a)(ii)(aa)(ii) of the Jobseeker's Allowance Regulations 1996 (self-employment route of the Employment Option of the New Deal);

(b) regulation 75(1)(a)(ii)(bb) of those Regulations (Voluntary Sector Option of the New Deal); or

(c) regulation 75(1)(a)(ii)(cc) of those Regulations (Environment Task Force Option of the New Deal).]

[⁴⁵**63.** Any discretionary payment to meet, or to help meet, special needs made to a person pursuant to section 2 of the Employment and Training Act 1973 in respect of that person's participation in the Full-Time Education and Training Option of the New Deal as specified in regulation 75(1)(b)(ii) of the Jobseeker's Allowance Regulations 1996.]

[⁵¹**64.**—(1) Subject to sub-paragraph (2), in the case of a person who is receiving, or who has received, assistance under an employment programme specified in regulation 75(1)(a)(ii)(aa)(ii) of the Jobseeker's Allowance Regulations 1996 (self-employment route of the Employment Option of the New Deal), any payment to the person—

(a) to meet expenses wholly and necessarily incurred whilst carrying on the commercial activity;

(b) which is used or intended to be used to maintain repayments on a loan taken out by that person for the purpose of establshing or carrying on the commercial activity,

in respect of which such assistance is or was received.

(2) Sub-paragraph (1) shall apply only in respect of payments which are paid to that person from the special account as defined for the purposes of Chapter IVA of Part V.]

[⁵³**65.**—(1) Subject to sub-paragraph (2), any discretionary payment made pursuant to section 2 of the Employment and Training Act 1973 to meet, or help meet, special needs of a person who is undertaking a qualifying course within the meaning specified in regulation 17A(7) of the Jobseeker's Allowance Regulations 1996.

(2) No amount shall be disregarded pursuant to sub-paragraph (1) in respect of travel expenses incurred as a result of the student's attendance on the course where an amount in respect of those expenses had already been disregarded pursuant to regulation 66(1) (student's income to be disregarded).]

[⁵⁴**66.** Any payment made with respect to a person on account of the provision of after-care under section 117 of the Mental Health Act 1983 or section 8 of the Mental Health (Scotland) Act 1984 or the provision of accommodation or welfare services to which Parts III and IV of the National Health Service and Community Care Act 1990 refer, which falls to be treated as notional income under paragraph (4A) of regulation 42 above (payments made in respect of a person in a residential care or nursing home).]

AMENDMENTS

1. Income Support (General) Amendment Regulations 1988 (S.I. 1988 No. 663), reg. 35 (April 11, 1988).
2. Family Credit and Income Support (General) Amendment Regulations 1988 (S.I. 1988 No. 999), reg. 5 (June 9, 1988).
3. Income Support (General) Amendment No. 4 Regulations 1988 (S.I. 1988 No. 1445), reg. 25 (September 12, 1988).
4. Income Support (General) Amendment No. 5 Regulations 1988 (S.I. 1988 No. 2022), reg. 22 (December 12, 1988).
5. Income Support (General) Amendment No. 4 Regulations 1988 (S.I. 1988 No. 1445), Sched. 1, para. 9 (April 10, 1989).
6. Family Credit and Income Support (General) Amendment Regulations 1989 (S.I. 1989 No. 1034), reg. 12 (July 10, 1989).
7. Income Support (General) Amendment Regulations 1989 (S.I. 1989 No. 534), Sched. 1, para. 15 (October 9, 1989).
8. Income-related Benefits Schemes Amendment Regulations 1990 (S.I. 1990 No. 127), reg. 3 (January 31, 1990).
9. Income Support (General) Amendment Regulations 1990 (S.I. 1990 No. 547), reg. 22(e) (April 1, 1990).
10. Income Support (General) Amendment Regulations 1990 (S.I. 1990 No. 547), reg. 22 (April 1, 1990).
11. Income-related Benefits Amendment Regulations 1990 (S.I. 1990 No. 1657), reg. 5(4) (September 1, 1990).
12. Income Support (General) Amendment No. 3 Regulations 1990 (S.I. 1990 No. 1776), reg. 10 (October 1, 1990).
13. Enterprise (Scotland) Consequential Amendments Order 1991 (S.I. 1991 No. 387), arts. 2 and 9 (April 1, 1991).
14. Income Support (General) Amendment Regulations 1991 (S.I. 1991 No. 236), reg. 14 (April 8, 1991).
15. Income-related Benefits Schemes and Social Security (Recoupment) Amendment Regulations 1991 (S.I. 1991 No. 1175), reg. 5 (May 11, 1991).
16. Income Support (General) Amendment No. 4 Regulations 1991 (S.I. 1991 No. 1559), reg. 20 (October 7, 1991).
17. Social Security Benefits Up-rating (No. 2) Order 1991 (S.I. 1991 No. 2910), art. 13(13) (April 6, 1992).
18. Disability Living Allowance and Disability Working Allowance (Consequential Provisions) Regulations 1991 (S.I. 1991 No. 2742), reg. 11(6) (April 6, 1992).
19. Income Support (General) Amendment Regulations 1992 (S.I. 1992 No. 468), reg. 8 (April 6, 1992).
20. Income Support (General) Amendment Regulations 1992 (S.I. 1992 No. 468), Sched., para. 9 (April 6, 1992).
21. Income-related Benefits Schemes and Social Security (Recoupment) Amendment Regulations 1992 (S.I. 1992 No. 1101), reg. 6 (May 7, 1992).
22. Social Security Benefits (Amendments Consequential Upon the Introduction of Community Care) Regulations 1992 (S.I. 1992 No. 3147), Sched. 1, para. 7 (April 1, 1993).
23. Income-related Benefits Schemes (Miscellaneous Amendments) Regulations 1993 (S.I. 1993 No. 315), Sched., para. 5 (April 1, 1993).
24. Income-related Benefits Schemes (Miscellaneous Amendments) Regulations 1993 (S.I. 1993 No. 315), reg. 9 (council tax and council tax benefit: April 1, 1993; otherwise April 12, 1993).
25. Social Security Benefits (Miscellaneous Amendments) Regulations 1993 (S.I. 1993 No. 518), reg. 5 (April 1, 1993).
26. Social Security Benefits (Miscellaneous Amendments) (No. 2) Regulations 1993 (S.I. 1993 No. 963), reg. 2(3) (April 22, 1993).
27. Income-related Benefits Schemes and Social Security (Recoupment) Amendment Regulations 1993 (S.I. 1993 No. 1249), reg. 4(4) (May 14, 1993).
28. Income Support (General) Amendment No. 3 Regulations 1993 (S.I. 1993 No. 1679), reg. 6 (August 2, 1993).

29. Income-related Benefits Schemes (Miscellaneous Amendments) (No. 4) Regulations 1993 (S.I. 1993 No. 2119), reg. 23 (October 4, 1993).

30. Income-related Benefits Schemes (Miscellaneous Amendments) Regulations 1994 (S.I. 1994 No. 527), reg. 9 (April 11, 1994).

31. Income-related Benefits Schemes (Miscellaneous Amendments) (No. 5) Regulations 1994 (S.I. 1994 No. 2139), reg. 32 (October 3, 1994).

32. Income-related Benefits Schemes (Miscellaneous Amendments) Regulations 1995 (S.I. 1995 No. 516), reg. 27 (April 10, 1995).

33. Social Security (Income Support and Claims and Payments) Amendment Regulation 1995 (S.I. 1995 No. 1613), reg. 4 and Sched. 3 (October 2, 1995).

34. Income-related Benefits Schemes and Social Security (Claims and Payments) (Miscellaneous Amendments) Regulations 1995 (S.I. 1995 No. 2303), reg. 6(9) (October 2, 1995).

35. Income-related Benefits Schemes Amendment (No. 2) Regulations 1995 (S.I. 1995 No. 2792), reg. 6(3) (October 28, 1995).

36. Social Security (Income Support, Claims and Payments and Adjudication) Amendment Regulations 1995 (S.I. 1995 No. 2927), reg. 6 (December 12, 1995).

37. Income-related Benefits Schemes (Widows, etc. Pensions Disregards) Amendment Regulations 1995 (S.I. 1995 No. 3282), reg. 2 (December 20, 1995).

38. Income Support (General) Amendment Regulations 1996 (S.I. 1996 No. 606), reg. 2 (April 8, 1996).

39. Income-related Benefits Schemes (Miscellaneous Amendments) Regulations 1996 (S.I. 1996 No. 462), reg. 8 (April 8, 1996).

40. Social Security Benefits Up-rating Order 1996 (S.I. 1996 No. 599), reg. 18(13) (April 8, 1996).

41. Income Support and Social Security (Claims and Payments) (Miscellaneous Amendments) Regulations 1996 (S.I. 1996 No. 2431), reg. 5 (October 15, 1996).

42. Income-related Benefits and Jobseeker's Allowance (Miscellaneous Amendments) Regulations 1997 (S.I. 1997 No. 65), reg. 2(3) (April 7, 1997).

43. Income-related Benefits and Jobseeker's Allowance (Amendment) (No. 2) Regulations 1997 (S.I. 1997 No. 2197), reg. 7(7) and (8)(e) (October 6, 1997).

44. Social Security Amendment (New Deal) Regulations 1997 (S.I. 1997 No. 2863), reg. 17(7) and (8)(e) (January 5, 1998).

45. Social Security Amendment (New Deal) Regulations 1997 (S.I. 1997 No. 2863), reg. 17(9) and (10)(e) (January 5, 1998).

46. Social Security (Miscellaneous Amendments) Regulations 1998 (S.I. 1998 No. 563), reg. 7(3) and (4)(e) (April 6, 1998).

47. Social Security (Miscellaneous Amendments) Regulations 1998 (S.I. 1998 No. 563), reg. 13(1)(c) (April 6, 1998).

48. Social Security (Miscellaneous Amendments) Regulations 1998 (S.I. 1998 No. 563), reg. 15(1) (April 6, 1998).

49. Social Security (Miscellaneous Amendments) Regulations 1998 (S.I. 1998 No. 563), reg. 15(2) (April 6, 1998).

50. Social Security (Miscellaneous Amendments) (No. 3) Regulations 1998 (S.I. 1998 No. 1173), reg. 4 (June 1, 1998).

51. Social Security (Miscellaneous Amendments) (No. 4) Regulations 1998 (S.I. 1998 No. 1174), reg. 6(4) (June 1, 1998).

52. Social Security (Miscellaneous Amendments) (No. 4) Regulations 1998 (S.I. 1998 No. 1174), reg. 7(3) and (4)(e) (June 1, 1998).

53. Social Security Amendment (New Deal) (No. 2) Regulations 1998 (S.I. 1998 No. 2117), reg. 4(4) (September 24, 1998).

54. Social Security Amendment (New Deal) (No. 2) Regulations 1998 (S.I. 1998 No. 2117), reg. 6(2) (September 24, 1998).

DEFINITIONS

"the Act"—see reg. 2(1).
"attendance allowance"—*ibid.*
"the benefit Acts"—*ibid.*
"benefit week"—*ibid.*
"child"—see 1986 Act, s.20(11) (SSCBA, s.137(1)).
"the Children Order"—see reg. 2(1).
"claimant"—*ibid.*

"course of study"—*ibid.*
"disability living allowance"—*ibid.*
"dwelling occupied as the home"—*ibid.*
"employed earner"—*ibid.*
"family"—see 1986 Act, s.20(11) (SSCBA, s.137(1)).
"local authority"—see 1986 Act, s.84(1).
"mobility allowance"—see reg. 2(1).
"mobility supplement"—*ibid.*
"nursing home"—*ibid.*, reg. 19(3).
"occupational pension"—see reg. 2(1).
"occupational pension scheme"—see 1986 Act, s.84(1) (PSA, s. 1).
"payment"—see reg. 2(1).
"personal pension scheme"—*ibid.*
"primary Class 1 contribution"—*ibid.*
"qualifying person"—*ibid.*
"residential care home"—see reg. 2(1), reg. 19(3).
"retirement annuity contract"—see reg. 2(1).
"Social Security Act"—*ibid.*
"special account"—see reg. 39A.
"the Eileen Trust"—*ibid.*
"the Fund"—*ibid.*
"the Independent Living Funds"—*ibid.*
"the Macfarlane (Special Payments) Trust"—*ibid.*
"the Macfarlane (Special Payments) (No.2) Trust"—*ibid.*
"the Macfarlane Trust"—*ibid.*
"training allowance"—*ibid.*
"voluntary organisation"—*ibid.*
"young person"—*ibid.*, reg. 14.

GENERAL NOTE

Paragraph 1
There is no provision in Chapter V itself for deducting tax. So if taxable payments are treated as income under reg. 40 a disregard is needed.

Paragraph 2
A payment purely of expenses to a volunteer or someone working for a charity or a voluntary organisation is disregarded unless the person is caught by reg. 42(6) on underpaid services. A volunteer is someone who without any legal obligation performs a service for another person without expectation of payment (*R(IS) 12/92*).

Paragraph 3
Such payments are not earnings (reg. 35(2)), but are income (reg. 40(4)). See the notes to reg. 35(1)(f) for "wholly, exclusively and necessarily." *CFC 2/1989* might suggest that payments made by the employee for necessary, etc., expenses out of such income are to be deducted from that income. But that is not consistent with the scheme of the legislation and is rejected in *R(FC) 1/90*, *R(IS) 16/93* and *CIS 77/1993*. See the notes to reg. 35(2), and to reg. 19(2) of the Family Credit Regulations. However, note the effect of the application of the principle in *Parsons v. Hogg* to the meaning of "gross earnings" (see the notes to reg. 36(3)).

Paragraphs 4 and 4A
The standard deductions are to be made from contractual or statutory sick or maternity pay, which are not earnings (reg. 35(2)), but are income (reg. 40(4)).

Paragraph 5
See also paras. 40, 42, 45, 46 and 52.

Paragraph 6
Mobility allowance or the mobility component of disability living allowance is disregarded. See also paras. 7 and 8.

Paragraph 9

The general rule is that attendance allowance and the care component of disability living allowance is disregarded.

Before April 1993 attendance allowance was not disregarded as income for residents in residential care or nursing homes, on the basis that the claimant's attendance needs would be met in the home. Until April 1991 this applied to all such residents, even though their benefit was not calculated under the special provisions in Sched. 4. From April 1991 if the claimant was in one of the excluded categories in Part II of Sched. 4 (and so restricted to the ordinary benefit calculation, rather than having the home's fees met by the higher level of income support), attendance allowance was disregarded. It would be needed in those circumstances.

With the introduction of the care in the community reforms in April 1993, the system has changed. Attendance allowance and the care component of disability living allowance will normally cease to be payable after a claimant has been a resident in a residential care or nursing home for four weeks. (See *CPAG's Welfare Benefits Handbook* as to when people in residential care and nursing homes may continue to receive attendance allowance or the care component of disability living allowance without restriction.) For that four weeks, there is a disregard under para. 9 for new residents after April 1, 1993, who will not fall under Sched. 4 at all, but will be entitled to the residential allowance under para. 2A of Sched. 2. Only existing residents who have preserved rights will continue to be eligible for the higher rate of income support under Sched. 4. For such residents (and for claimants who live in Polish resettlement homes) attendance allowance and the care component of disability living allowance will only be disregarded under para. 9 in so far as it exceeds the ordinary maximum amount. It is possible for an attendance allowance to do this because of the width of the definition in reg. 2(1).

Paragraph 11

Educational maintenance allowances are disregarded in full, instead of in part, as under supplementary benefit.

Paragraph 13

These elements of training allowances are disregarded. Note sub-para. (d), under which any payment for childcare costs to a person who is or has been taking part in a New Deal option is disregarded. See the notes to reg. 75 of the JSA Regulations for a brief summary of the New Deal and paras. 62 to 65 for other disregards of certain payments made to people on New Deal options.

Paragraph 15

If charitable or voluntary payments are intended and used for items other than those listed in sub-para. (2) they are disregarded (sub-para. (2)). For claimants in residential care and nursing homes this disregard only applies if they have a preserved right (sub-para. (6)). Note the exceptions in sub-para. (3) and para. 39. Otherwise the normal disregard of regular charitable or voluntary payments is £20 (increased from £10 with effect from April 8, 1996) (sub-para. (1)). The provision assumes that such payments amount to income. For irregular payments, see reg. 48(9).

There is no special definition of "charitable" or "voluntary." The words must be applied to whoever makes the payment. In *R. v. Doncaster Borough Council, ex parte Boulton, The Times*,December 31, 1992, on the equivalent provision in housing benefit, Laws J. holds that the word "charitable" appearing in a statute providing for the distribution and calculation of legal rights must refer only to payments under a charitable trust, rather than referring to acts done for some generous motive. He finds the legislative purpose to be to allow charities to make payments to claimants knowing that they will not simply reduce the amount of benefit. That decision must be highly persuasive, but does not pre-empt the income support position.

Laws J. also takes a different view to that expressed in the 1992 edition on the meaning of "voluntary." He holds that it does not refer to a payment which is not compulsory or not legally enforceable, but to a payment for which the person making the payment gets nothing in return. It does not matter that in voluntarily undertaking the payment the person comes under an obligation. The legislative purpose would then be consistent with that for charitable payments. He then had to apply this principle to payments by the National Coal Board in lieu of concessionary coal to a miner's widow. The concessionary coal scheme and the conditions for the payment of cash in lieu, including to widows, is contained in a collective agreement which is incorporated into miners' contracts of employment. Laws J. holds that neither he nor the Housing Benefit Review Board had sufficient evidence of the particular contractual arrangements to be able to conclude that under the principle of *Beswick v. Beswick* [1968] A.C. 58 the widow could as administratrix of her husband's estate obtain specific performance of the contract to make payments to his widow. However, he was satisfied that the NCB did receive something in return for payments made under the collective agreement, in the promotion of the efficient running of the coal industry. An element of this purpose was seeing that employees, ex-employees and their spouses were properly looked after. Therefore, he finds that the payments were not voluntary and the disregard did not apply. On this point also, the *Boulton* case cannot be conclusive for income support purposes, but is cogently argued and persuasive. It has been applied to para. 15 in *R(IS) 4/94*. In *CIS 702/1991* an annuity had been purchased for the claimant under the terms of her friend's will. It was argued that the payments under the annuity were "voluntary" as in essence there was a gift of them from the friend under the will. It is held that the disregard in para. 15 did not apply since the payments under the annuity were contractual in nature. That was consistent with the decision of Laws J. in the *Boulton* case. See also *CIS 492/1992*.

If regular payments are not charitable or voluntary they count as ordinary income with no disregard.

Paragraph 15A

Where a claimant is newly placed after April 1, 1993, by a local authority in a residential care or nursing home whose fee is more expensive than would normally be met, charitable or voluntary payments may be disregarded in so far as they make up the difference. This is only so if the reason for the placement is the choice of the claimant.

Paragraph 15B

An occupational pension or income from a personal pension scheme or retirement annuity contract (see reg. 2(1) for the definitions of these terms) is normally taken into account in full. But from April 1996 residents of residential care or nursing homes who have preserved rights (or claimants in Polish resettlement homes) who are married but not living with their spouse had 50 per cent of any occupational pensions(s) ignored provided at least that amount of the pension(s) was being paid to maintain their spouse. This only applies to claimants who are married and only covered occupational, not personal, pensions. But from April 1997 this disregard has been extended to income from personal pension schemes and retirement annuity contracts.

Paragraph 16

The £10 disregard under sub-para. (a) only applies if the payment is not fully disregarded under paras. 8 or 9.

"War disablement pension" is not defined in either these Regulations or any relevant part of the Contributions and Benefits Act 1992. However, it was defined in s.84(1) of the Social Security Act 1986. When these regulations were first introduced they were made under the 1986 Act. Thus, in the absence of any other definition, the meaning in s.84(1) applies (*CIS 276/1998*; see Interpretation Act 1978, s.11). Section 84(1) defined a war disablement pension as:

"(a) any retired pay, pension or allowance granted in respect of disablement under powers conferred by or under the Air Force (Constitution) Act 1917, the Personal Injuries (Emergency Provisions) Act 1939, the Pensions (Navy, Army, Air Force and Mercantile Marine) Act 1939, the Polish Resettlement Act 1947 or Part VII or s.151 of the Reserve Forces Act 1980;

(b) without prejudice to para. (a) of this definition, any retired pay or pension to which sub-section (1) of s.365 of the Income and Corporation Taxes Act 1970 applies''.

The claimant in *CIS 276/1998* was discharged from the RAF on medical grounds and was awarded a service invaliding pension. This pension was exempt from income tax under s.315 of the Income and Corporation Taxes Act 1988 (formerly s.365 of the 1970 Act). The AO treated the pension as an occupational pension. But the Commissioner holds that the concepts of occupational pension and war disablement pension were not mutually exclusive. The claimant's pension clearly fell within para. (b) of the definition in s.84(1) and so it was also a war disablement pension. He was thus entitled to a £10 disregard under sub-para. (a).

Paragraph 17

If a person takes out one of these schemes for converting the capital value of the home into income, then so much of the annuity as goes to the mortgage interest is disregarded. The conditions are complicated. Only schemes entered by those aged at least 65 count.

Paragraph 18

The inter-relationship of this and the following two paragraphs is now much clearer. The new form of this paragraph, together with the amendment to para. 19, was introduced in April 1995, following the decision in *CIS 82/1993*. The Commissioner held that on the previous wording the dividing line between paras. 18 and 19 was not whether a payment for accommodation was made under a contractual obligation, but whether or not the payment was made by a person who normally resided with the claimant. Para. 19 only applied where the person did not normally reside with the claimant. (See the 1994 Supplement for a summary of the Commissioner's reasoning.) "Normally resides" in para. 18 had no special meaning (*cf.* reg. 3) and could include someone who was liable to make payments to the claimant for his occupation of the claimant's home. On the facts, the two "lodgers" who shared the claimant's flat, and each paid him £70 per week, did reside with him. The result was that para. 18, not para. 19, applied. "Payment" could include part of a payment (see reg. 2(1)), so the proportion of each payment that went to meeting the "lodger's" living and accommodation costs could be disregarded under para. 18 (*CIS 422/1992* followed). The evidence was that the benefit of the outgoings on the flat was shared more or less equally between the three occupants, so the Commissioner divided the rent, water rates and fuel costs by three and added to this the cost of the services provided by the claimant (*e.g.* laundry, routine repairs and replacements). This led to a much larger proportion of each payment (£47) being disregarded, than would have been the case if para. 19 applied.

The new form of para. 18, and the amendment to para. 19, have dealt with most of the difficulties exposed in *CIS 82/1993* regarding the inter-relationship of these two paragraphs. Paras. 18, 19 and 20 can now all apply where the person is residing with the claimant, so the problem identified in previous editions of this book (see the note to para. 19 in the 1994 edition) no longer exists. If para. 18 applies, payments by someone who normally resides with the claimant towards his own living and accommodation costs continue to be wholly disregarded. The new wording confirms, as decided in *CIS 422/1992* and *CIS 82/1993*, that it is only payments towards the "lodger's" living expenses that are disregarded (see above). However, para. 18 does not apply in the circumstances covered by paras. 19 and 20, so that those provisions must be looked at first. The intention is that payments from sub-tenants and licensees should fall within para. 19, not para. 18 (see below).

If the person making the payment is a non-dependant (see reg. 3), note that standard deductions are made from housing costs for the presence of a non-dependant in the household (see para. 18 of Sched. 3).

Paragraph 19

Whenever the person occupying the claimant's home has a contractual liability to make payments this paragraph will now apply. This is certainly wide enough to cover income from sub-tenants and licensees. The disregard is small. People referred to in paras. 18 and 20 are no longer excluded, but para. 18 does not apply if the circumstances come within para. 19 (see above). Although some payments could fall within both para. 19 and para. 20, it does not matter that there is no provision for choosing between them, for a claimant can simply take advantage of the more generous disregard in para. 20 when the conditions of that paragraph are met (*CIS 82/1993*).

In *CIS 82/1993* the Commissioner raised the possibility of whether the disregard in para. 30(d) (now para. 30(1)(e)) (contribution intended and used towards rent) might apply to payments by a sub-tenant or licensee of a tenant. He accepted the AO's submission that in view of the specific provisions in paras. 18, 19 and 20, para. 30(d) (now (1)(e)) did not cover such payments, but did consider that legislative clarification of the relationship between para. 30 and paras. 18, 19 and 20 would be useful. It is not clear on the wording of para. 30(1)(e) why payments from a sub-tenant or licensee should be excluded, provided that they are intended and used as a contribution towards rent not met by housing benefit. Payments may be disregarded under more than one paragraph of Sched. 9, provided this is not specifically proscribed. Para. 30(1)(e) does not refer to payments under paras. 18, 19 or 20; the only payments that are specifically excluded from para. 30 are those covered by para. 29. This approach has indeed now been taken by the Commissioner in *CIS 13059/1996*, who declines to follow *CIS 82/1993* on this point. He decides that para. 30 can apply at the same time as any of paras. 18 to 20 because paras. 18 to 20 are not concerned with the same sort of payments as para. 30. Para. 30 makes provision for disregarding payments designed to help meet certain elements of a claimant's housing expenditure, whereas this is not the specific purpose of paras. 18 to 20. See further the notes to para. 30.

In April 1994 the wording of para. 19 was tightened up so that only one disregard per week applies to payments for each licence or subtenancy. On the pre-April 1994 form a separate disregard could have applied to each payment regardless of the period covered by it (*e.g.* daily).

Paragraph 20
This disregard (and not para. 18) applies when a person provides board and lodging accommodation in his home. The post-April 1994 form makes it clear that only one disregard is allowed per week per boarder (see the notes to para. 19).

Paragraph 21
Income in kind is normally disregarded. Earnings in kind are not earnings (reg. 35(2)), but are income. There is some scope for benefit planning here, but note *CIS 11482/1995* in the notes to reg. 42(6) (notional earnings).

Paragraph 22
The general rule is that the actual income derived from capital is disregarded as income. It can go to increase the amount of capital under reg. 48(4). But income in the categories specified—premises, business assets and trusts of (but not funds held in court that derive from) personal injury compensation (see the note to reg. 48(4))—is not disregarded. Where this income is from premises whose capital value is disregarded, any mortgage repayments, water charges and council tax can be set off against it. Mortgage repayments in sub-para. (2)(a) include capital and interest, buildings insurance, and if an endowment policy is a condition of the mortgage, premiums on that policy (*CFC 13/1993*). *CIS 563/1991* deals with the situation where both a disregard in the excepted categories and a disregard under some other paragraph of Sched. 10 apply. See the notes to reg. 48(4).

Paragraph 24
In *CIS 627/1995* the Commissioner puts forward the view that since para. 24 disregards the *cost* of converting a payment into sterling, it was the *gross* sterling equivalent of the claimant's Canadian pension that had to be taken into account (*i.e.* the cost of conversion had to be added back to the net amount paid to the claimant). However, it is respectfully suggested that the purpose of para. 24 is not to disregard any banking charge or commission *as a cost*, but simply to ensure that the amount of any banking charge or commission is not included in the income taken into account. Although the wording of para. 24 could be clearer, it seems unlikely that the Commissioner's interpretation is the intended one. It is also not the approach taken in the *Adjudication Officer's Guide* (see para. 33398).

Paragraph 25
Payments to adopters are taken into account up to the level of the personal allowance applicable for the adopted child plus any disabled child premium (sub-para. (a)). Anything above that level is disregarded. The same approach is applied to payments from local authorities towards the maintenance of children by sub-paras. (b)–(d). The new form of sub-paras. (b)–(d) introduced on April 6, 1998 includes such payments from authorities in Northern Ireland (sub-para. (d)).

Paragraph 26
Payments to foster-parents are disregarded completely. Foster-children are not members of the family (reg. 16(4)).
The amendments to para. 26 introduced on April 6, 1992, as a consequence of the Children Act 1989, do not apply in Scotland.

Paragraph 27
CIS 17020/1996 concerned a local authority scheme for placing disabled people in the carers' own homes. In order to attempt to take advantage of the disregard in para. 27 the local authority sent the disabled person a bill for his care and accommodation and then paid the money to the claimant, instead of the disabled person paying the claimant directly. However, the Commissioner decides that para. 27 only applied to payments made by a local authority from its own resources. The appropriate disregard was in para. 20. He also discusses the meaning of the words "not normally a member of the claimant's household but is temporarily in his care". In his view the word "normally" referred to the period of the membership, not the manner of it. The question of whether the disabled person was temporarily in the claimant's care was one of fact, having regard to the intention of the parties and the length of the stay.

Paragraph 28
Reg. 41(3) deems all such payments in trade dispute cases to be income and not capital. Then this disregard does not apply in trade dispute cases. Outside that special situation payments under the legislation (broadly to prevent children going into care, for the Scottish legislation now see the

Children (Scotland) Act 1995; Interpretation Act, s. 17(2)(a) will apply) can be capital or income (*R(SB) 29/85*). Income is disregarded here and capital under para. 17 of Sched. 10.

Paragraph 29

Since October 1995 the proceeds of mortgage protection policies can be used to cover payments in respect of *any* interest on a loan that qualifies under paras. 15 or 16 of Sched. 3 that is not met by income support, capital repayments on a qualifying loan and any premiums on the policy and any building insurance policy. (Despite the ''or'' in head (c) the disregard presumably applies to premiums on both types of policy if premiums on both are due.) Any excess counts as income. If the loan is not a qualifying loan see para. 30. According to the *Adjudication Officer's Guide* ''capital repayments'' include not only repayments of capital on a repayment mortgage but also payments into endowment policies, personal equity plans, personal pension plans and other investment plans that have been taken out to repay a mortgage or loan (para. 33231). Note reg. 63(8) and (9) of the Adjudication Regulations which provides that certain changes in the loan interest payable will not lead to an immediate review of the amount disregarded under this paragraph.

Sub-para. (2) seems merely declaratory as the disregard only applies to payments for housing costs that are not met by income support.

Paragraph 30

Payments other than those disregarded under para. 29 or, from June 1, 1998, para. 30ZA, earmarked for these elements of housing expenditure, are ignored (para. (1)). Note that payments from liable relatives are dealt with in reg. 54. Since October 1995 the disregard extends to payments on *any* loan secured on the home that is not a qualifying loan under Sched. 3 (*e.g.* a loan for business purposes) (head (a)); any housing cost that is eligible under Sched. 3 to the extent that it is not met by income support (head (b)); capital repayments on a qualifying loan (head c)), and premiums on any buildings insurance policy and (since December 1995) any policy taken out to insure against the risk of not being able to make the payments in heads (a) to (c) (head (d)). On the meaning of capital repayments see the note to para. 29. Note reg. 63(8) and (9) of the Adjudication Regulations which provides that certain loan interest changes will not lead to an immediate review of the amount disregarded under heads (a) to (c).

CIS 13059/1996 decides (contrary to the view taken in *CIS 82/1993*, see the note to para. 19) that para. (1) can apply to payments made by a tenant (or licensee) of the claimant who lives in her home. The claimant's mortgage interest was met by income support but only to the extent of the interest on £125,000 (there was about £160,000 owing on her mortgage). There were two tenants living in her flat. The AO decided that the rent received from the tenants had to be taken into acount in calculating the claimant's income support, subject only to the disregard in para. 19. However, the Commissioner concludes that para. 30 could apply at the same time as para. 19 (or para. 18 or 20) because these paragraphs were not concerned with the same sort of payments. Paras. 18 to 20 were not intended to make specific provision for disregarding payments designed to help meet a claimant's housing costs, whereas para. 30 was so intended. Moreover, there was no reason why para. 30 should not apply to payments made under a contractual liability. The Commissioner also deals with the meaning of the phrase ''payment . . . which is intended to be used and is used as a contribution towards'' in para. (1). He rejects the argument that it was only necessary to look at the intention of the claimant. But he holds that it was possible to infer from a tenancy agreement that the tenant intended the landlord to use the rent, so far as necessary, to pay the landlord's own liabilities on the property so that the tenant could continue to occupy it. ''Intended'' in para. (1) was used in the sense of ''designed'' or ''calculated'' and it was necessary to look at the general context in which payments were made in order to ascertain the intention of the parties. The Commissioner also confirms that there was no reason why part of a payment could not be disregarded under para. 30 in addition to part being disregarded under any of paras. 18 to 20. (See reg. 2(1): ''payment'' includes part of a payment). Thus in addition to the para. 19 disregard, a further amount to cover the claimant's mortgage interest that was not met under paras. 7 and 8 of Sched. 3 as then in force could be disregarded from the rent payments.

Again, sub-para. (2) seems merely declaratory as the disregard under para. (1) only applies to elements of housing expenditure that are not met by income support.

Paragraph 30ZA

This provides for a disregard of payments received under so-called ''creditor insurance'' policies. It will apply to payments received under an insurance policy to cover, for example, hire-purchase payments or loan or similar payments. But any excess above the amount of the payment due, plus any premiums on the policy concerned, counts as income.

Paragraph 30A

Where a claimant in a residential care or nursing home does not have a preserved right under reg. 19, and whose accommodation has not been arranged by a local authority, payments towards the cost of the home's fees are disregarded. The amount ignored is the difference between the claimant's applicable amount less personal expenses and the weekly charge for the accommodation.

Paragraph 34

This is the compensation for the automatic counting of the "relevant sum" as part of the family's income under s.126(5)(b) of the Contributions and Benefits Act (1986 Act, s.23(5)(b)). From April 1999 the relevant sum is £27.50.

Paragraph 35

See notes to reg. 32(5).

Paragraph 37

See notes to reg. 32(5).

Paragraph 39

The disregard now extends to payments to haemophiliacs from the three trusts, and to non-haemophiliacs from the Fund and the Eileen Trust, and to distributions of income payments to the close family, or to a slightly wider class for the two years following such a person's death. Any payments from the Independent Living Funds are ignored.

Paragraph 47

These are the special payments to compensate pre-1973 war widows who had not benefited from amendments to the Armed Forces Pension Scheme. There was a commitment that the payments would not affect means-tested benefits. See paras. 54–56.

Paragraph 51

These are payments from certain Department of Employment special schemes for disabled people, such as the "business on own account" scheme, the "personal reader service" and the "fares to work" scheme.

Paragraph 53

Increases for dependants who are not residing with the claimant paid with certain benefits (*e.g.* retirement pension) or war pensions are disregarded. Such increases are only paid if the claimant is contributing at least that amount to the maintenance of the dependant.

Paragraphs 54–56

See para. 47. These new disregards arose from the transfer of responsibility for the payment of most pre-1973 war widows' pensions from the Ministry of Defence to the DSS from October 1994.

Paragraph 57

See the note to reg. 21ZA.

Paragraph 58

The Community Care (Direct Payments) Act 1996 allows local authorities to make cash payments in lieu of community care services to disabled people aged 18–65 (payments may continue after 65 if they began before a person's 66th birthday). Such payments are to be ignored.

Paragraphs 59–60

Career Development Loans are provided in order to help adults pay for vocational education or training. They are treated as income under reg. 41(6), but under para. 59 that income is ignored, except any part of the loan that was applied for and has been paid to meet the cost of food, ordinary clothing or footwear (defined in para. 59(2)), household fuel, rent for which housing benefit is payable, housing costs met by income support, home charges met under reg. 19 for people with preserved rights, council tax or water charges during the period of the training or education. On "ordinary clothing or footwear" see paras. 33665–6 of the *Adjudication Officer's Guide*. In addition, any part of the loan left over at the end of the course is ignored (para. 60).

For treatment of career development loans before these rules were introduced on April 7, 1997, see *CIS 507/1997*.

Paragraph 61

Any grant or covenant income or student loan left over at the end of a person's course is ignored. See regs. 29(2B), 32(6A) and 40(3B) for the position where part or all of a student's grant is repayable because he has left or is dismissed from his course before it finishes.

Paragraphs 62 and 63

These paragraphs provide that the following will be ignored: the grant of £400 (spread over six months) that is paid to a person who is getting a training allowance rather than a wage while taking part in either the Voluntary Sector or the Environment Task Force options, or who is on the self-employment route of the Employment option, of the "New Deal" for 18–24 year-olds; and any discretionary payments made to a participant on the Full-Time Education and Training option to cover exceptional costs. Note also that any payment for childcare costs made to a person on a New Deal option is also ignored (see para. 13(d)). For a brief summary of the New Deal see the notes to reg. 75 of the JSA Regulations.

Paragraph 64

(*Note*: this is a new para. 64; the previous para. 64 is now para. 66).

This disregards any payment to a person, who is on, or has left, the self-employment route of the Employment option, from his "special account" (defined in reg. 39A) if it is (i) to meet expenses wholly and necessarily incurred in his business while on the self-employment route; or (ii) used, or intended to be used, to make repayments on a loan taken out for the purposes of that business. For the treatment of a person's income from "test-trading" while on the self-employment route, see regs. 39A to 39D and the note to reg. 102C of the JSA Regulations. For a brief summary of the self-employment route of the Employment Option, see the note to reg. 75(1) of the JSA Regulations.

Paragraph 65

See the note to para. 63 of Sched. 7 to the JSA Regulations.

Paragraph 66

This is the renumbered para. 64. See the note to reg. 42(4A).

SCHEDULE 10   **Regulation 46(2)**

Capital to be Disregarded

1. The dwelling occupied as the home but, notwithstanding regulation 23 (calculation of income and capital of members of claimant's family and of a polygamous marriage), only one dwelling shall be disregarded under this paragraph.

2. Any premises acquired for occupation by the claimant which he intends to occupy [⁴as his home] within 26 weeks of the date of acquisition or such longer period as is reasonable in the circumstances to enable the claimant to obtain possession and commence occupation of the premises.

3. Any sum directly attributable to the proceeds of sale of any premises formerly occupied by the claimant as his home which is to be used for the purchase of other premises intended for such occupation within 26 weeks of the date of sale or such longer period as is reasonable in the circumstances to enable the claimant to complete the purchase.

4. Any premises occupied in whole or in part by—

(a) a partner or relative of [¹²a single claimant or any member of] the family [⁴as his home] where that person is aged 60 or over or is incapacitated;

(b) the former partner of a claimant [² . . .] as his home; but this provision shall not apply where the former partner is a person from whom the claimant is estranged or divorced.

[²⁶**5.** Any future interest in property of any kind, other than land or premises in respect of which the claimant has granted a subsisting lease or tenancy, including sub-leases or sub-tenancies.]

6.—[^{12}(1)] The assets of any business owned in whole or in part by the claimant and for the purposes of which he is engaged as a self-employed earner or, if he has ceased to be so engaged, for such period as may be reasonable in the circumstances to allow for disposal of any such asset.

[^{12}(2) The assets of any business owned in whole or in part by the claimant where—
(a) he is not engaged as a self-employed earner in that business by reason of some disease or bodily or mental disablement; but
(b) he intends to become engaged (or, as the case may be, re-engaged) as a self-employed earner in that business as soon as he recovers or is able to become engaged, or re-engaged, in that business;

for a period of 26 weeks from the date on which the claim for income support is made, or is treated as made, or, if it is unreasonable to expect him to become engaged or re-engaged in that business within that period for such longer period as is reasonable in the circumstances to enable him to become so engaged or re-engaged.]

[^{33}(3) In the case of a person who is receiving assistance under an employment programme specified in regulation 75(1)(a)(ii)(aa)(ii) of the Jobseeker's Allowance Regulations 1996 (self-employment route of the Employment Option of the New Deal), the assets acquired by that person for the purpose of establishing or carrying on the commercial activity in respect of which such assistance is being received.

(4) In the case of a person who has ceased carrying on the commercial activity in respect of which assistance was received as specified in sub-paragraph (3), the assets relating to that activity for such period as may be reasonable in the circumstances to allow for disposal of any such asset.]

7. Any arrears of, or any concessionary payment made to compensate for arrears due to the non-payment of,—
(a) any payment specified in paragraph 6, [^{16}8, 9 or 9A] of Schedule 9 (other income to be disregarded);
(b) an income-related benefit or [^{28}an income-based jobseeker's allowance,] supplementary benefit, family income supplement under the Family Income Supplements Act 1970 or housing benefit under Part II of the Social Security and Housing Benefits Act 1982;
[^{29}(c) any earnings top-up,]

but only for a period of 52 weeks from the date of the receipt of the arrears or of the concessionary payment.

8. Any sum—
(a) paid to the claimant in consequence of damage to, or loss of the home or any personal possession and intended for its repair or replacement; or
(b) acquired by the claimant (whether as a loan or otherwise) on the express condition that it is to be used for effecting essential repairs or improvements to the home,

and which is to be used for the intended purpose, for a period of 26 weeks from the date on which it was so paid or acquired or such longer period as is reasonable in the circumstances to enable the claimant to effect the repairs, replacement or improvements.

9. Any sum—
(a) deposited with a housing association as defined in section 189(1) of the Housing Act 1985 or section 338(1) of the Housing (Scotland) Act 1987 as a condition of occupying the home;
(b) which was so deposited and which is to be used for the purchase of another home, for the period of 26 weeks of such longer period as is reasonable in the circumstances to complete the purchase.

10. Any personal possessions except those which had or have been acquired by the claimant with the intention of reducing his capital in order to secure entitlement to supplementary benefit or income support or to increase the amount of that benefit.

11. The value of the right to receive any income under an annuity and the surrender value (if any) of such an annuity.

[^{12}**12.** Where the funds of a trust are derived from a payment made in consequence of any personal injury to the claimant, the value of the trust fund and the value of the right to receive any payment under that trust.]

13. The value of the right to receive any income under a life interest or from a liferent.

14. The value of the right to receive any income which is disregarded under paragraph 11 of Schedule 8 or paragraph 23 of Schedule 9 (earnings or other income to be disregarded).

15. The surrender value of any policy of life insurance.

16. Where any payment of capital falls to be made by instalments, the value of the right to receive any outstanding instalments.

17. Except in the case of a person to whom section 23 of the Act [SSCBA, s.126] (trade disputes) applies [¹or in respect of whom section 20(3) of the Act [SSCBA, s.124(1)] (conditions of entitlement to income support) has effect as modified by section 23A(b) of the Act [SSCBA, s.127(b)] (effect of return to work)], [⁶any payment made by a local authority [¹⁸in accordance with section 17 or 24 of the Children Act 1989] or, as the case may be, section 12, 24 or 26 of the Social Work (Scotland) Act 1968 (local authorities' duty to promote welfare of children and powers to grant financial assistance to persons in, or formerly in, their care).]

[¹⁷**18.** Any social fund payment made pursuant to Part III of the Act [SSCBA, Part VIII].]

19. Any refund of tax which fell to be deducted under section 26 of the Finance Act 1982 (deductions of tax from certain loan interest) on a payment of relevant loan interest for the purpose of acquiring an interest in the home or carrying out repairs or improvements in the home.

20. Any capital which under [¹¹regulation 41, 44(1) or 66A (capital treated as income, modifications in respect of children and young persons or treatment of student loans)] is to be treated as income.

21. Where a payment of capital is made in a currency other than sterling, any banking charge or commission payable in converting that payment into sterling.

[¹**22.**—[¹⁴(1) Any payment made under the Macfarlane Trust, the Macfarlane (Special Payments) Trust, the Macfarlane (Special Payments) (No. 2) Trust ("the Trusts"), [¹⁹the Fund][²³, the Eileen Trust] or [²¹the Independent Living Funds].

(2) Any payment by or on behalf of a person who is suffering or who suffered from haemophilia [¹⁹or who is or was a qualifying person], which derives from a payment made under any of the Trusts to which sub-paragraph (1) refers and which is made to or for the benefit of—

(a) that person's partner or former partner from whom he is not, or where that person has died was not, estranged or divorced;

(b) any child who is a member of that person's family or who was such a member and who is a member of the claimant's family; or

(c) any young person who is a member of that person's family or who was such a member and who is a member of the claimant's family.

(3) Any payment by or on behalf of the partner or former partner of a person who is suffering or who suffered from haemophilia [¹⁹or who is or was a qualifying person] provided that the partner or former partner and that person are not, or if either of them has died were not, estranged or divorced, which derives from a payment made under any of the Trusts to which sub-paragraph (1) refers and which is made to or for the benefit of—

(a) the person who is suffering from haemophilia [¹⁹or who is a qualifying person];

(b) any child who is a member of that person's family or who was such a member and who is a member of the claimant's family; or

(c) any young person who is a member of that person's family or who was such a member and who is a member of the claimant's family.

(4) Any payment by a person who is suffering from haemophilia [¹⁹or who is a qualifying person], which derives from a payment under any of the Trusts to which sub-paragraph (1) refers, where—

(a) that person has no partner or former partner from whom he is not estranged or

divorced, nor any child or young person who is or had been a member of that person's family; and
(b) the payment is made either—
    (i) to that person's parent or step-parent, or
    (ii) where that person at the relevant date was a child, a young person or a student who had not completed his full-time education and had no parent or step-parent, to his guardian,
but only for a period of two years from the date of the payment until the end of two years from that person's death.

(5) Any payment out of the estate of a person who suffered from haemophilia [¹⁹or who was a qualifying person], which derives from a payment under any of the Trusts to which sub-paragraph (1) refers, where—
(a) that person at the date of his death (the relevant date) had no partner or former partner from whom he was not estranged or divorced, nor any child or young person who was or had been a member of his family; and
(b) the payment is made either—
    (i) to that person's parent or step-parent, or
    (ii) where that person at the relevant date was a child, a young person or a student who had not completed his full-time education and had no parent or step-parent, to his guardian,
but only for a period of two years from the relevant date.

(6) In the case of a person to whom or for whose benefit a payment referred to in this paragraph is made, any capital resource which derives from any payment of income or capital made under or deriving from any of the Trusts.]

[¹⁹(7) For the purposes of sub-paragraphs (2) to (6), any reference to the Trusts shall be construed as including a reference to the Fund [²³and the Eileen Trust].]

23. The value of the right to receive an occupational [¹⁵or personal] pension.

[²⁶**23A.** The value of any funds held under a personal pension scheme or retirement annuity contract.]

24. The value of the right to receive any rent [²⁶except where the claimant has a reversionary interest in the property in respect of which rent is due.]]

[²**25.** Where a claimant has ceased to occupy what was formerly the dwelling occupied as the home following his estrangement or divorce from his former partner, that dwelling for a period of 26 weeks from the date on which he ceased to occupy that dwelling.

26. Any premises where the claimant is taking reasonable steps to dispose of those premises, for a period of 26 weeks from the date on which he first took such steps, or such longer period as is reasonable in the circumstances to enable him to dispose of those premises.

[⁵**27.** Any premises which the claimant intends to occupy as his home, and in respect of which he is taking steps to obtain possession and has sought legal advice or has commenced legal proceedings, with a view to obtaining possession, for a period of 26 weeks from the date on which he first sought such advice or first commenced such proceedings whichever is earlier, or such longer period as is reasonable in the circumstances to enable him to obtain possession and commence occupation of those premises.]

28. Any premises which the claimant intends to occupy as his home to which essential repairs or alterations are required in order to render them fit for such occupation, for a period of 26 weeks from the date on which the claimant first takes steps to effect those repairs or alterations, or such longer period as is reasonable in the circumstances to enable those repairs or alterations to be carried out and the claimant to commence occupation of the premises.]

[⁴**29.** Any payment in kind made by a charity [⁸or under the Macfarlane (Special Payments) Trust][¹⁹, the Macfarlane (Special Payments) (No. 2) Trust][²², the Fund or the Independent Living (1993) Fund].

30. [²⁴£200 of any payment, or, if the payment is less than £200, the whole of any payment] made under section 2 of the Employment and Training Act 1973 (functions of the Secretary of State) [¹³or section 2 of the Enterprise and New Towns (Scotland) Act 1990] as a training bonus to a person participating in arrangements for training made under that section [¹³of the 1973 Act].

31. Any payment made by the Secretary of State to compensate for the loss (in whole or in part) of entitlement of housing benefit.]

[⁵**32.** Any payment made by the Secretary of State to compensate a person who was entitled to supplementary benefit in respect of a period ending immediately before 11th April 1988 but who did not become entitled to income support in respect of a period beginning with that day.

33. Any payment made by the Secretary of State to compensate for the loss of housing benefit supplement under regulation 19 of the Supplementary Benefit (Requirements) Regulations 1983.

34. Any payment made to a juror or a witness in respect of attendance at a court other than compensation for loss of earnings or for the loss of a benefit payable under the benefit Acts.

35. [²⁰. . .].]

[⁹**36.** Any payment in consequence of a reduction of a personal community charge pursuant to regulations under section 13A of the Local Government Finance Act 1988 or section 9A of the Abolition of Domestic Rates Etc (Scotland) Act 1987 (reduction of liability for personal community charge) [²⁰or reduction of council tax under section 13 or, as the case may be, section 80 of the Local Government Finance Act 1992 (reduction of liability for council tax)] but only for a period of 52 weeks from the date of the receipt of the payment.]

[¹⁰**37.** Any grant made to the claimant in accordance with a scheme made under section 129 of the Housing Act 1988 or section 66 of the Housing (Scotland) Act 1988 (schemes for payments to assist local housing authority and local authority tenants to obtain other accommodation) which is to be used—

(a) to purchase premises intended for occupation as his home; or

(b) to carry out repairs or alterations which are required to render premises fit for occupation as his home

for a period of 26 weeks from the date on which he received such a grant or such longer period as is reasonable in the circumstances to enable the purchase, repairs or alterations to be completed and the claimant to commence occupation of those premises as his home.]

[¹²**38.**— (1) Any payment or repayment made—

(a) as respects England and Wales, under regulation 3, 5 or 8 of the National Health Service (Travelling Expenses and Remission of Charges) Regulations 1988 (travelling expenses and health service supplies);

(b) as respects Scotland, under regulation 3, 5 or 8 of the National Health Service (Travelling Expenses and Remission of Charges) (Scotland) Regulations 1988 (travelling expenses and health service supplies);

but only for a period of 52 weeks from the date of receipt of the payment or repayment.

(2) Any payment or repayment made by the Secretary of State for Health, the Secretary of State for Scotland or the Secretary of State for Wales which is analogous to a payment or repayment mentioned in sub-paragraph (1); but only for a period of 52 weeks from the date of receipt of the payment or repayment.

39. Any payment made under regulation 9 to 11 or 13 of the Welfare Food Regulations 1988 (payments made in place of milk tokens or the supply of vitamins), but only for a period of 52 weeks from the date of receipt of the payment.

40. Any payment made either by the Secretary of State for the Home Department or by the Secretary of State for Scotland under a scheme established to assist relatives and other persons to visit persons in custody, but only for a period of 52 weeks from the date of receipt of the payment.

41. Any arrears of special war widows payment which is disregarded under paragraph 47 of Schedule 9 (sums to be disregarded in the calculation of income other than earnings) [²⁵ or of any amount which is disregarded under paragraph 54, 55 or 56

447

of that Schedule], but only for a period of 52 weeks from the date of receipt of the arrears.]

[¹⁷**42.** Any payment (other than a training allowance, or a training bonus under section 2 of the Employment and Training Act 1973) made, whether by the Secretary of State or by any other person, under the Disabled Persons (Employment) Act 1944 or in accordance with arrangements made under section 2 of the Employment and Training Act 1973 to assist disabled persons to obtain or retain employment despite their disability.

43. Any payment made by a local authority under section 3 of the Disabled Persons (Employment) Act 1958 to homeworkers under the Blind Homeworkers' Scheme.]

[²⁵**44.** Any sum of capital administered on behalf of a person [³¹. . .] by the High Court under the provisions of Order 80 of the Rules of the Supreme Court, the County Court under Order 10 of the County Court Rules 1981, or the Court of Protection, where such sum derives from—

  (a) an award of damages for a personal injury to that person; or
  (b) compensation for the death of one or both parents [³¹ where the person concerned is under the age of 18].]

45. Any sum of capital administered on behalf of a person [³¹. . .] in accordance with an order made under Rule 43.15 of the Act of Sederunt (Rules of the Court of Session 1994) 1994 or under Rule 131 of the Act of Sederunt (Rules of the Court, consolidation and amendment) 1965, or under Rule 36.14 of the Ordinary Cause Rules 1993 or under Rule 128 of the Ordinary Cause Rules, where such sum derives from—

  (a) an award of damages for a personal injury to that person; or
  (b) compensation for the death of one or both parents [³¹ where the person concerned is under the age of 18].]

[²⁷**46.** Any payment to the claimant as holder of the Victoria Cross or George Cross.]

[³⁰**47.** Any amount of council tax benefit to which a person is entitled by virtue of regulation 4D of the Council Tax Benefit (General) Regulations 1992 (entitlement of a refugee to council tax benefit), but only for a period of 52 weeks from the date that such an amount is received.

48. Any amount of housing benfit to which a person is entitled by virtue of regulation 7B of the Housing Benefit (General) Regulations 1987 (entitlement of a refugee to housing benefit), but only for a period of 52 weeks from the date that such an amount is received.

49. Any amount of income support to which a person is entitled by virtue of regulation 21ZA above (treatment of refugees), but only for a period of 52 weeks from the date that such an amount is received.]

[³⁴**50.** Any mandatory top-up payment made to a person pursuant to section 2 of the Employment and Training Act 1973 in respect of that person's participation in an employment programme specified in—

  (a) regulation 75(1)(a)(ii)(aa)(ii) of the Jobseeker's Allowance Regulations 1996 (self-employment route of the Employment Option of the New Deal);
  (b) regulation 75(1)(a)(ii)(bb) of those Regulations (Voluntary Sector Option of the New Deal); or
  (c) regulation 75(1)(a)(ii)(cc) of those Regulations (Environment Task Force Option of the New Deal),

but only for a period of 52 weeks from the date of receipt of the payment.]

[³²**51.** Any discretionary payment to meet, or to help meet, special needs made to a person pursuant to section 2 of the Employment and Training Act 1973 in respect of that person's participation in the Full-Time Education and Training Option of the New Deal as specified in regulation 75(1)(b)(ii) of the Jobseeker's Allowance Regulations 1996 but only for a period of 52 weeks from the date of receipt of the payment.]

[³⁵**52.** In the case of a person who is receiving, or who has received, assistance under an employment programme specified in regulation 75(1)(a)(ii)(aa)(ii) of the Jobseeker's Allowance Regulations 1996 (self-employment route of the Employment Option of the New Deal), any sum of capital which is acquired by that person for the purpose of establishing or carrying on the commercial activity in respect of which such assistance is or was received but only for a period of 52 weeks from the date on which that sum was acquired.]

[³⁶**53.** Any discretionary payment made pursuant to section 2 of the Employment and Training Act 1973 to meet, or help meet, special needs of a person who is undertaking a qualifying course with the meaning specified in regulation 17A(7) of the Jobseeker's Allowance Regulations 1996 but only for the period of 52 weeks from the date of receipt of that payment.]

AMENDMENTS

1. Income Support (General) Amendment Regulations 1988 (S.I. 1988 No. 663), reg. 36 (April 11, 1988).
2. Income Support (General) Amendment No. 2 Regulations 1988 (S.I. 1988 No. 910), reg. 3 (May 30, 1988).
3. Family Credit and Income Support (General) Amendment Regulations 1988 (S.I. 1988 No. 999), reg. 5 (June 9, 1988).
4. Income Support (General) Amendment No. 4 Regulations 1988 (S.I. 1988 No. 1445), reg. 26 (September 12, 1988).
5. Income Support (General) Amendment No. 5 Regulations 1988 (S.I. 1988 No. 2022), reg. 23 (December 12, 1988).
6. Family Credit and Income Support (General) Amendment Regulations 1989 (S.I. 1989 No. 1034), reg. 12 (July 10, 1989).
7. Income Support (General) Amendment Regulations 1989 (S.I. 1989 No. 534), Sched. 1, para. 18 (October 9, 1989).
8. Income-related Benefits Schemes Amendment Regulations 1990 (S.I. 1990 No. 127), reg. 3 (January 31, 1990).
9. Income Support (General) Amendment Regulations 1990 (S.I. 1990 No. 547), reg. 23(*a*) (April 1, 1990).
10. Income Support (General) Amendment Regulations 1990 (S.I. 1990 No. 547), reg. 23(*b*) (April 9, 1990).
11. Social Security Benefits (Student Loans and Miscellaneous Amendments) Regulations 1990 (S.I. 1990 No. 1549), reg. 5(9) (September 1, 1990).
12. Income Support (General) Amendment No. 3 Regulations 1990 (S.I. 1990 No. 1776), reg. 11 (October 1, 1990).
13. Enterprise (Scotland) Consequential Amendments Order 1991 (S.I. 1991 No. 387), arts, 2 and 9 (April 1, 1991).
14. Income-related Benefits Schemes and Social Security (Recoupment) Amendment Regulations 1991 (S.I. 1991 No. 1175), reg. 5 (May 11, 1991).
15. Income Support (General) Amendment No. 4 Regulations 1991 (S.I. 1991 No. 1559), reg. 21 (October 7, 1991).
16. Disability Living Allowance and Disability Working Allowance (Consequential Provisions) Regulations 1991 (S.I. 1991 No. 2742), reg. 11(7) (April 6, 1992).
17. Income Support (General) Amendment Regulations 1992 (S.I. 1992 No. 468), reg. 9 (April 6, 1992).
18. Income Support (General) Amendment Regulations 1992 (S.I. 1992 No. 468), Sched., para. 10 (April 6, 1992).
19. Income-related Benefits Schemes and Social Security (Recoupment) Amendment Regulations 1992 (S.I. 1992 No. 1101), reg. 6(8) (May 7, 1992).
20. Income-related Benefits Schemes (Miscellaneous Amendments) Regulations 1993 (S.I. 1993 No. 315), Sched., para. 6 (April 1, 1993).
21. Social Security Benefits (Miscellaneous Amendments) (No. 2) Regulations 1993 (S.I. 1993 No. 963), reg. 2(3) (April 22, 1993).
22. Social Security Benefits (Miscellaneous Amendments) (No. 2) Regulations 1993 (S.I. 1993 No. 963), reg. 2(5) (April 22, 1993).
23. Income-related Benefits Schemes and Social Security (Recoupment) Amendment Regulations 1993 (S.I. 1993 No. 1249), reg. 4(5) (May 14, 1993).
24. Income-related Benefits Schemes (Miscellaneous Amendments) (No. 4) Regulations 1993 (S.I. 1993 No. 2119), reg. 24 (October 4, 1993).
25. Income-related Benefits Schemes (Miscellaneous Amendments) (No. 5) Regulations 1994 (S.I. 1994 No. 2139), reg. 33 (October 3, 1994).

26. Income-related Benefits Schemes and Social Security (Claims and Payments) (Miscellaneous Amendments) Regulations 1995 (S.I. 1995 No. 2303), reg. 6(10) (October 2, 1995).

27. Income-related Benefits Schemes (Miscellaneous Amendments) Regulations 1996 (S.I. 1996 No. 462), reg. 11(1) (April 8, 1996).

28. Income Support (General) (Jobseeker's Allowance Consequential Amendments) Regulations 1996 (S.I. 1996 No. 206), reg. 26 (October 7, 1996).

29. Income-related Benefits Schemes and Social Fund (Miscellaneous Amendments) Regulations 1996 (S.I. No. 1944), reg. 13 and Sched., para. 7 (October 7, 1996).

30. Income Support and Social Security (Claims and Payments) (Miscellaneous Amendments) Regulations 1996 (S.I. 1996 No. 2431), reg. 6 (October 15, 1996).

31. Income-related Benefits and Jobseeker's Allowance (Amendment) (No. 2) Regulations 1997 (S.I. 1997 No. 2197), reg. 7(9) and (10)(e) (October 6, 1997).

32. Social Security Amendment (New Deal) Regulations 1997 (S.I. 1997 No. 2863), reg. 17(11) and (12)(e) (January 5, 1998).

33. Social Security (Miscellaneous Amendments) (No. 4) Regulations 1998 (S.I. 1998 No. 1174), reg. 7(7) and (8)(e) (June 1, 1998).

34. Social Security (Miscellaneous Amendments) (No. 4) Regulations 1998 (S.I. 1998 No. 1174), reg. 7(9) and (10)(e) (June 1, 1998).

35. Social Security (Miscellaneous Amendments) (No. 4) Regulations 1998 (S.I. 1998 No. 1174), reg. 7(11) and (12)(e) (June 1, 1998).

36. Social Security Amendment (New Deal) (No. 2) Regulations 1998 (S.I. 1998 No. 2117), reg. 5(2) and (3)(c) (September 24, 1998).

DEFINITIONS

"the Act"—see reg. 2(1).
"the benefit Acts"—*ibid.*
"child"—see 1986 Act, s.20(11) (SSCBA, s.137(1)).
"claimant"—see reg. 2(1).
"dwelling occupied as the home"—*ibid.*
"earnings top-up"—*ibid.*
"family"—see 1986 Act, s.20(11) (SSCBA, s.137(1)).
"income-related benefit"—see 1986 Act, s.84(1).
"occupational pension"—see reg. 2(1).
"partner"—*ibid.*
"payment"—*ibid.*
"personal pension scheme"—*ibid.*
"policy of life insurance"—*ibid.*
"qualifying person"—*ibid.*
"relative"—*ibid.*
"retirement annuity contract"—*ibid.*
"self-employed earner"—*ibid.*
"supplementary benefit"—*ibid.*
"the Eileen Trust"—*ibid.*
"the Fund"—*ibid.*
"the Independent Living Funds"—*ibid.*
"the Macfarlane (Special Payments) Trust"—*ibid.*
"the Macfarlane (Special Payments) (No. 2) Trust"—*ibid.*
"the Macfarlane Trust"—*ibid.*
"training allowance"—*ibid.*
"young person"—*ibid.*, reg. 14.

GENERAL NOTE

Capital may be disregarded under more than one paragraph of Sched. 10 at the same time, or in succession. There is no provision in reg. 46(2) or Sched. 10 for establishing any order of priority if different paragraphs of Sched. 10 are applicable, so the claimant will be entitled to the benefit of the most favourable disregard (this is also the case for Sched. 9). The disregards in Sched. 10 apply to notional capital (*CIS 25/1990, CIS 81/1991, CIS 562/1992* and *CIS 30/1993*), provided that their conditions are met (*CIS 30/1993*). See the note to para. 26.

In *CIS 600/1995* the Commissioner expresses the view that claimants should be advised by the Benefits Agency of the existence of relevant disregards so that they can take advantage of them. In that case the claimant had received a criminal injuries compensation award so he could have taken steps to utilise the disregard in para. 12.

Paragraph 1

The value of the home is disregarded. Para. 3 of Sched. 3 contains rules about when a person is or is not to be treated as occupying a dwelling as his home. The fact that Sched. 10 did not originally contain paras. 25 to 28 gave rise to a number of problems (for which see p.178 of the 1988 edition). The introduction of, in particular, a disregard of the value of premises which are for sale will solve, or at least postpone, many of the problems. See reg. 17(f) and (2) to (7) for transitional protection for those excluded from income support from April 11, 1988 to May 29, 1988, and Sched. 9, para. 41 and Sched. 10, para. 32.

On the meaning of "dwelling occupied as the home", see notes to reg. 2(1). Para. 1 can apply to notional capital (*CIS 81/1991* (although it was not necessary to the decision) and *CIS 30/1993*).

Paragraph 2

The value must be disregarded for the first 26 weeks after the acquisition. Thereafter all the circumstances must be looked at in deciding what is reasonable. There must be some realistic prospect of occupation starting. Previous editions suggested that the requirement that the premises have been "acquired for occupation by the claimant" would exclude some forms of acquisition (*e.g.* inheritance). But according to para. 34546 of the *Adjudication Officer's Guide*, a person may acquire premises if he buys, is given or inherits them. "Premises" is to be given a reasonably wide meaning; thus acquiring land on which a person intends to build his home is covered by the disregard (see *CIS 8475/1995* in the note to para. 3).

The income from premises whose value is disregarded under this provision counts as income (Sched. 9, para. 22), but mortgage repayments, water charges and council tax can be set off against it.

Paragraph 3

The sum must be directly attributable to the actual (*R(IS) 4/96*) proceeds of sale of a home, and must be intended for the purchase of another home (not repairs or refurbishment: *R(SB) 14/85*; *CIS 368/1993*). *R(IS)6/95* decides that para. 3 is not restricted to circumstances where a claimant is free to sell to a third party but can apply where a statutory tenancy of a home has been surrendered to the landlord. The claimant had sold his home, albeit technically by a surrender rather than a sale, and it was irrelevant to whom he had sold it.

As well as the purchase of a home that is already erected, the disregard also covers buying land and building a house on it (*CIS 8475/1995*). In *CIS 8475/1995* the claimant decided to use the proceeds of sale of his former home to buy a plot of land and build a bungalow on it. When he made his claim for income support the sale proceeds were held on deposit. By the date of the tribunal hearing the claimant had used the majority of the proceeds to purchase and clear the land. He had about £10,000 left for materials and labour to build the bungalow. The Commissioner decides that the claimant's intended use of the proceeds of sale fell within para. 3. The words "purchase of other premises" in para. 3 were to be given a reasonably wide meaning and included the outlay of money in stages to acquire land and build a house on it. This approach was consistent with that adopted in *R(IS) 11/94* in relation to housing costs met by income support (see the notes to para. 15 of Sched. 3); the Commissioner also agrees with *CIS 767/1993* (to be reported as *R(IS) 3/96*) that the word "premises" in the first four paragraphs of this Schedule has a similar meaning (see the note to para. 4). But the disregard in para. 3 only applied to sums of money. Once the claimant had acquired the plot of land, the land and the partly-built bungalow as the work progressed, fell to be disregarded under para. 2. On the facts of this case it was reasonable for the period of the disregard under paras. 2 and 3 to be extended to 18 months from the date of the claim for income support. The Commissioner comments that in self-build cases a disregard of 12 months rather than six will normally be reasonable.

In *CIS 8475/1995* the Commissioner also makes the point that there is a difference between the wording "is to be used" in para. 3 and the tests of intended occupation in, for example, paras. 2, 27 and 28. In his view, para. 3 required an element of practical certainty as well as subjective intent. This could be shown, for example, by a binding contract for purchase which had not yet been completed, or an agreement "subject to contract" in circumstances where it seemed likely that the money would not be diverted to other purposes. On the facts of that case the Commissioner found obtaining planning permission, placing the purchase in the hands of solicitors and accepting a builder's quote to be sufficient. But a different view was taken in *CIS 685/1992* (not referred to in *CIS 8475/1995*). *CIS 685/1992* decides that it is not necessary, in order for there to be an extension of the primary 26 week period, that an intention to occupy specific premises should have been formed before the end of that period. If the proceeds of sale had not been used at the end of the 26 weeks there was a general discretion for the AO (or SSAT) to allow a longer period for the finding of another home and the completion of its purchase. However, a mere hope that the proceeds might be used at some future date for another home was not sufficient. The Commissioner declined to follow the more restricted view of para. 3 adopted in *CIS 321/1990* which decided that if sufficient negotiations were not in being at the end of the 26 week period there could be no extension.

In *CIS 222/1992* the claimant intended to use her share of the proceeds of sale of her deceased mother's house to purchase her own council house. The claimant had lived in her mother's house for a short time some 10 years before. The Commissioner rejects the argument that the claimant was entitled to the benefit of the disregard in para. 3 because she formerly occupied her mother's home as her home. He finds that the conditions for a purposive construction of para. 3 were satisfied (see Lord Diplock at p. 105 in *Jones v. Wrotham Park Settled Estates Ltd.* [1980] AC 74), and holds that para. 3 only applied where the claimant had owned the property when she had lived there.

Paragraph 4

In *CIS 767/1993*, to be reported as *R(IS) 3/96*, the Commissioner rejects a submission from the AO (said to reflect the policy intention) that para. 4 applied to disregard premises of any kind and extent. He decides that "premises" in para. 4 was to be interpreted in accordance with the definition of "dwelling occupied as the home" in reg. 2(1). The first four paragraphs of Sched. 10 were all concerned with disregarding the claimant's home or what would be the home if the claimant was in actual occupation, and thus it was entirely consistent for "premises" in paras. 2, 3 and 4 to be given a similar interpretation. Thus when the claimant went to live in a residential care home the farmhouse she jointly owned with her husband could be ignored under para. 4(b), but not the farmland which had its own access and could have been sold separately.

"Relative" is defined in reg. 2(1). "Incapacitated" is not. Para. 34429 of the *Adjudication Officer's Guide* suggests that receipt of incapacity benefit, statutory sick pay, disability working allowance (as well as more rigorous benefits like severe disablement allowance, attendance allowance and disability living allowance) or an equivalent degree of incapacity will do. Occupation by a former partner does not count if there has been estrangement or divorce, but see para. 25. Under supplementary benefit, occupation was held to connote occupation as a residence, not merely as a holiday home (*R(SB) 1/85*). Under sub-para. (b) it does not now matter that the claimant also occupies the home.

In *CIS 231/1991* the claimant had transferred his former home to his parents who were both over 60. When he claimed income support they were living in the home. The Commissioner decides that para. 4(a) applied to the former home; the disregard applied to notional, as well as actual, capital.

Paragraph 5

Before October 2, 1995 the disregard in para. 5 applied to "any reversionary interest". The new form is in response to the Court of Appeal's decision in *Chief Adjudication Officer v. Palfrey and Others, The Times*, February 17, 1995, which upheld the Tribunal of Commissioners' decision in *CIS 85/1992* (which was to have been reported as *R(IS) 5/98* but is now to be reported as *R(IS) 26/95*) that property subject to a tenancy was a reversionary interest and so was to be disregarded. The Commissioners had held that *R(SB) 3/86* (which decided that a reversionary interest was "something which does not afford any present enjoyment but carries a vested or contingent right to enjoyment in the future" and that a landlord's interest in a freehold property was not merely such an interest) was not to be followed. In *CIS 85/1992* the rented property was freehold, but *CIS 563/1991* and *CIS 615/1993* confirmed that the disregard under the previous form of para. 5 applied to leasehold property as well.

It was considered that the effect of these decisions was to create an easy loophole which could enable a claimant to have the capital value of property disregarded simply by letting it, and so the new form of para. 5 was introduced. Under the new form, the disregard applies to future interests in property but not land or premises which have been let by the claimant. A future interest in property is one that does not take effect immediately. An example would be where the claimant's entitlement only arises on the death of a person who has a life interest in the particular fund or property. Note that for the exception to operate, the lease etc., has to be granted by the claimant. So, if the tenancy was granted by someone else (*e.g.* before the claimant owned the property) the disregard should still apply.

CIS 635/1994 suggests that the disregard could also apply if the property was subject to an irrevocable licence (rather than a lease or tenancy). The Commissioner expressed doubts as to whether a freehold or leasehold interest in a property subject to a tenancy could be said to be a future interest, but considered that the way the exception was put appeaared to assume that it was. This meant that the new disregard might not be limited (as at first sight it seemed to be) to future interests in the sense of interests where there was no right at all until the future event happened. If the consequence is that the new form of para. 5 covers situations where the claimant's interest affords no present enjoyment (and is a future interest in that sense) then, leaving aside the exception, the disregard itself may not be significantly different. Indeed it could be argued that a future interest is wider than a reversionary interest as it could include not only an interest that will revert to the claimant but also one that will only take effect in the future. (Note that in *Palfrey* both the Court of Appeal and the Commissioners considered that the capital value of the element of possession involved in a tenanted property fell to be disregarded under para. 24 (in its previous form); it was the right to regain possession of the property at the end of the term which was a purely reversionary right that was covered by the old form of para. 5.)

See also *CIS 461/1994*, to be reported as *R(IS) 1/97*. The claimant on separating from his wife had agreed that she could remain in the former matrimonial home (which was in his sole name) for her lifetime. There was no written agreement. The Commissioner decides that in the circumstances an irrevocable licence had been granted or could be inferred which gave rise to a constructive trust which in turn made the wife a tenant for life for the purposes of the Settled Land Act 1925. The Commissioner decides that the test laid down in *Ashburn Anstalt v. Arnold* [1989] Ch. 1 for imposing a constructive trust, that is, that the owner of the property had so conducted himself that it would be inequitable to allow him to deny the beneficiary an interest in the property, was satisfied. The result was that the claimant's interest in the former matrimonial home was a reversionary one as it did not afford any present enjoyment. If the claimant's interest can similarly be ignored under the new form of para. 5 (see above), this decision may have potentially wide implications for separating couples.

Note also *R(IS) 4/96* which decides that a charge on a former matrimonial home which was not to be enforced until the claimant's ex-wife died, remarried or cohabited for longer than six months was not a reversionary interest but gave the claimant a secured debt payable at a future date (see *Re Fisher* [1943] Ch. 377).

See also the amendment to para. 24.

Rent from tenanted property, as and when it is received, will generally count as capital, not income (Sched. 9, para. 22), under reg. 48(4). But note the excepted cases, *e.g.*, if the property is up for sale (and so disregarded under para. 26). See the notes to reg. 48(4) and para. 22 of Sched. 9 and note *CIS 563/1991* discussed in the note to reg. 48(4).

Paragraph 6

The business assets of a self-employed person are primarily disregarded under sub-para. (1) if he is engaged in the business. Para. 34375 of the *Adjudication Officer's Guide* states that a person should be treated as engaged in a business for as long as he performs some work in it (*e.g.* checking stock), even for as little as half an hour a week. Business assets have to be distinguished from personal assets by asking if they are "part of the fund employed and risked in the business" (*R(SB) 4/85*). The income tax and accounting position are factors to be taken into account, but are not conclusive (*CFC 10/1989*). *CFC 15/1990*, to be reported as *R(FC) 2/92*, holds that the ownership by an individual of a tenanted house is not a business. Since October 2, 1995 a property that the claimant has let to tenants is no longer disregarded as a reversionary interest (see the notes to para. 5).

In *CIS 841/1994* although the claimant was only a sleeping partner, the Commissioner decides that she continued to be gainfully employed and so a self-employed earner (s. 2(1)(b) of the Contributions and Benefits Act 1992) in the farm business she owned with her son. The claimant had ceased to take an active role, having gone to live permanently in a residential care home, but she remained entitled to a share of the profits and capital and jointly and severally liable for the partnership's losses. Thus her share of the partnership assets, including the farm, fell to be disregarded under para. 6. See also *CG 19/1994* where the claimant who had become a partner in her husband's business solely for tax purposes was held to be gainfully employed in the business. But the decision in *CIS 841/1994* was appealed to the Court of Appeal, which allowed the appeal (*Chief Adjudication Officer v. Knight*, April 9, 1997). The Court held that for the disregard in para. 6 to apply, a financial commitment to a business on its own was insufficient. The claimant had to be involved or engaged in the business in some practical sense as an earner. Thus a sleeping partner in a business managed and worked exclusively by others could not benefit from para. 6.

If the claimant ceases to be engaged in the business, the value of the assets is disregarded for a period which is reasonable to allow them to be disposed of. Where the self-employed person is temporarily not engaged in the business because of illness, there is a disregard under sub-para. (2).

Sub-paras. (3) and (4) disregards any assets of a buisness carried on while a person is participating in the self-employment route of the Employment option of the New Deal for 18 to 24-year-olds, and, if the person later ceases to be engaged in that business, for a period which is reasonable to allow them to be disposed of. See also para. 52 under which any capital acquired for the purposes of such a business is ignored for 52 weeks from the date of receipt. For a brief summary of the self-employment route of the Employment option, see the note to reg. 75(1) of the JSA Regulations.

Income from capital disregarded under para. 6 is not disregarded (Sched. 9, para. 22).

Paragraph 7

Arrears of benefit which would be income when paid on the proper date retain their character as income *(R(SB) 4/89)*. However, if any money is left after the end of the period to which the benefit is attributed as income then this will be capital (see notes to reg. 40(1)). Para. 7 applies, under sub-para. (a), to mobility allowance or supplement, attendance allowance and any care or mobility component of disability living allowance, under sub-para. (b), to income support, income-based JSA, family credit, housing benefit, council tax benefit, supplementary benefit and FIS and under sub-para. (c), to earnings top-up. For these benefits there is a disregard for 52 weeks from the date of receipt. See also paras. 38 to 41 and 47 to 49.

Paragraph 8

This meets the problems in *R(SB) 14/81* and para. 8(2) of *R(SB) 14/85*. Such sums may not be part of the claimant's capital anyway (see *CSB 975/1985* and the notes to reg. 46).

R(IS) 6/95 decides that sub-para. (a) only applies where the claimant has suffered damage to, or the loss of, his property against his will, not where he has deliberately brought this about. Thus it did not cover payment received for the surrender of a statutory tenancy of the claimant's home. *CIS 368/1993* rejects the argument that money (in that case proceeds of sale of a previous home) earmarked for the renovation of the claimant's home came within sub-para. (b). The Commissioner decides that the money had not been "acquired on the express condition" that it was to be used for the renovation, but as a consequence of the sale.

Paragraph 9

Sub-para (b) gets round the problem in *R(SB) 4/87*.

Paragraph 10

The supplementary benefit exceptions to the general disregard of the value of personal possessions have been considerably narrowed. Now it is only possessions bought with the intention of reducing capital so as to gain supplementary benefit or income support which count. See the notes to reg. 51(1) for "purpose" and for possible problems of double counting with para. 10. Note that the corresponding paragraph under JSA (para. 15 of Sched. 8 to the JSA Regulations) applies if a person has bought possessions with the intention of reducing capital in order to secure entitlement to or increase the amount of JSA *or income support*. That avoids the question that might otherwise have arisen on a claimant transferring from income support to JSA as to whether possessions that had been bought only for the purpose of income support could be caught by para. 15 of Sched. 8. But para. 10 has not been similarly amended.

If the value of personal possessions does count, it is their current market value which must be included (reg. 49). See *CIS 494/1990* and *CIS 112/1994*.

Presumably anything which is not real property is a personal possession. Providing that it is an object and not a right to sue for something, like a debt. But hard lines might have to be drawn between coins and bank-notes (obviously capital) and investments like paintings, stamps, furniture (apparently disregarded). What about gold bars?

Paragraph 12

There is an unlimited disregard of the value of a trust fund deriving from payment in compensation for personal injury. This seems particularly generous compared to the treatment of other forms of capital. Note that although para. 12 refers to "personal injury to the claimant" the *Adjudication Officer's Guide* simply refers to a payment made because of a personal injury (para. 34412). Presumably this is because "claimant" (unless the context otherwise requires) includes a partner and any children for the purposes of Part V of the Regulations (see reg. 23(1)).

If there is no trust the amount of compensation counts as capital, even though it is in a solicitor's hands *(Thomas v. Chief Adjudication Officer*, reported as *(R(SB) 17/87)*; see also *CIS 600/1995* in the notes to reg. 46). If the claimant then transfers the compensation to trustees, the exception in reg. 51(1)(a) operates so that he will not be treated as having deprived himself of the capital placed on trust. Although putting money into a trust would normally count as deprivation, to do so in the case of trusts of personal injury compensation would defeat the purpose of para. 12. It is not necessary for the trust to be set up before the compensation is received as suggested in the 1993 edition. Furthermore, since para. 12 refers to funds "derived" from personal injury compensation, it is certainly arguable that the disregard should also apply even if the compensation was initially used for other purposes before being placed on trust. An example could be if the compensation was used to buy a home but this was later sold and the proceeds of sale put on trust. If the money placed on trust derived (in the sense of "originated") from personal injury compensation, there would seem to be no policy reason why the disregard in para. 12 should not apply. The purpose of the disregard is presumably to allow such compensation payments to be used for the person's disablement needs that have arisen as a result of the injury. The fact that the funds have been employed elsewhere for an intermediate period would not seem to affect this policy intention.

CIS 368/1994 decides that the disregard in para. 12 applied where the compensation was held and administereed by a combination of the Public Trustee and the Court of Protection. In the Commissioner's view, the word "trust" was used to cover the situation where the legal estate was in one person and the beneficial interest in another. It did not matter for the purposes of para. 12 whether a particular trust had been set up or whether there was in operation a statutory scheme involving, for example, the Court of Protection. The effect of this decision would seem to be that the disregard in para. 12 can apply whether the money is administered by the Court of Protection itself or held in the name of the receiver or the Public Trustee.

Now see paras. 44 and 45 which have introduced a specific disregard for funds held in court that derive from damages for personal injury or compensation for the death of a parent. See the notes to paras. 44 and 45 and note the October 1997 amendments to those paragraphs. Note also that paras. 44 and 45 have not been added to the list of exceptions in reg. 48(4). This means that payments to a claimant from funds disregarded under those paragraphs will apparently be treated as capital under the rule in reg. 48(4), even if due to their nature (*e.g.* because they are made periodically) they would otherwise count as income. See further the notes to reg. 48(4).

Note that "personal injury" includes a disease and any injuries suffered as a result of a disease (*e.g.* amputation of both legs following meningitis and septicaemia), as well as any accidental or criminal injury *(R(SB) 2/89)*.

Any payment from the trust will be income or capital depending on the nature of the payment (income from trusts disregarded under this paragraph is one of the excepted cases from the general rule in reg. 48(4) that income from capital counts as capital). But there is scope for benefit planning here, for example, if the payments are used to pay for expenses not covered by income support, *e.g.*, ineligible housing costs (see para. 30 of Sched. 9), or to purchase items that are ignored for income support, *e.g.*, personal possessions or a holiday. Note also the rules for payments to third parties in regs. 42(4) and 51(3) and for voluntary payments (see para. 15 of Sched. 9). The notional income rule in reg. 42(2) (income available on application) and the notional capital rules in reg. 51(1) (deprivation of capital) and reg. 51(2) (capital available on application) do not apply to trusts of personal injury compensation.

Paragraph 13
This reverses the result of *R(SB) 43/84*.

Paragraph 14
The provisions mentioned deal with situations where foreign income or earnings cannot be transmitted to the United Kingdom.

Paragraph 15
The surrender value of all life insurance policies is disregarded. In supplementary benefit there was a limit of £1,500.

In *R(IS) 7/98* the claimant had placed her capital in an "investment bond". This provided for a low guaranteed minimum death benefit if the investment had not been fully cashed in before death. But it also included, among other surrender options, a "monthly withdrawal plan", under which the claimant received a sum of £75.20 a month by way of partial encashment until the value of the investment was exhausted. The Commissioner decides that the bond fell within the definition of "policy of life insurance" in reg. 2(1). For this definition to apply, it was not necessary for death of the investor to be the only contingency under which money was payable (see *CIS 122/1991*), nor was the relative size of the death benefits on one hand, and the investments benefits on the other, relevant (see *Gould v. Curtis* [1913] 3 K.B. 84). The value of the bond therefore fell to be disregarded under para. 15 (even though its full investment value was obtainable on demand and so would have come within reg. 51(2) (capital available on demand), except for para. 15). However, in relation to the original decision to purchase the bond, the deprivation rule in reg. 51(1) would have to be considered (see *CIS 112/1994* (and *CIS 109/1994*) in the notes to reg. 51). Moreover, since the £75.20 monthly payments represented payments of capital by instalments, for as long as the total outstanding under the policy together with any other capital belonging to the claimant exceeded £8,000, such payments would count as income for the period they were paid under reg. 41. (See para. 16 as regards the right to receive these payments.)

Paragraph 16
See reg. 41(1) and *R(IS) 7/98* in the note to para. 15.

Paragraph 17
Although in ordinary cases the nature of such payments as capital or income depends on general principles of law *(R(SB) 29/85)*, in trade dispute cases reg. 41(3) secures that they are all treated as income. (From April 1, 1997, for the Scottish legislation see the Children (Scotland) Act 1995: Interpretation Act, s. 17(2)(a) will apply.)

Paragraph 20
This is to avoid double counting.

Paragraph 22
These funds are intended to provide extra cash help to haemophiliacs and non-haemophiliacs who have contracted HIV through blood or tissue transfusions, their families and the severely disabled. All are government-funded. The disregard extends to distributions of capital to the close family of haemophiliacs and non-haemophiliacs, or to a slightly wider class for the two years after the haemophiliac's or non-haemophiliac's death.

Paragraph 23
Accrued rights to receive an occupational or personal pension in the future are often amongst a person's most valuable assets, but they are not capable of being bought or sold, and so have no market value anyway.

Paragraph 23A
See the notes to reg. 42(2)–(2C).

Paragraph 24
This paragraph was amended on October 2, 1995 at the same time as the new form of para. 5 was introduced. See the notes to para. 5. Since the annual amount of the rent due can be used to calculate the value of a tenanted property the amendment will prevent the annual rent (and thus the capital value of the property) from being reduced to nil because of the disregard.

Paragraph 25
This paragraph applies where a claimant has ceased to be part of a couple because of estrangement or divorce and has left what was formerly the home. In these circumstances the claimant may well have an actual or deemed (see reg. 52) interest in the dwelling, but no longer be able to get within para. 1. But see the notes to reg. 52 on disputed matrimonial assets. Divorce is an easily proved event, but estrangement is a less hard edged concept. It has "connotations of emotional disharmony" *(R(SB) 2/87)*, but no doubt is to be given its ordinary, everyday meaning. Since the two people concerned must no longer be partners, there must be more than a temporary absence (and see reg. 16).
The disregard is limited to 26 weeks from the date on which the claimant left the dwelling, with no extension. In this time arrangements must be made.

Paragraph 26
This provision restores some of the effect of the similar supplementary benefit disregard. It will ease some of the problems noted on p. 178 of the 1988 edition, but not all of them. It applies if reasonable steps are being taken to dispose of premises. "Premises" in para. 26 is to be construed widely and includes land without buildings *(CIS 7319/1995* (to be reported as *R(IS) 4/97*), preferring *CSB 222/1986* to *CIS 673/1993*). See also *CIS 767/1993*, to be reported as *R(IS) 3/96*, and *CIS 8475/1995* in the notes to paras. 3 and 4. What are reasonable steps must be a question of fact. The Commissioner in *CIS 7319/1995* considers that the test is an objective one. So, if the sale price was totally unrealistic, that attempt at sale should be disregarded and the period of the disregard would not start to run until reasonable steps to dispose of the premises were *first* taken. In his view the period of the disregard must be continuous. *CIS 6908/1995* also confirms that the disregard starts when the claimant first takes steps to dispose of the premises, which may well be before a property is put on the open market. The initial disregard is for 26 weeks, but can be extended where reasonable to enable the disposal to be carried out.

456

In *CIS 562/1992* it is held that the 26 weeks does not run from the beginning of each fresh claim for income support, but from the day on which the claimant first took steps to dispose of the property. On its particular facts (it was several years since the property was first put on the market and the claimant had transferred ownership of it to his son for some time but then taken it back) this decision seems right. However, if a property is up for sale, then is genuinely taken off the market and put up for sale again later, it must be arguable that the time under para. 26 runs from the second occasion of taking steps to dispose of the property. In *CIS 6908/1995* the Commissioner accepts that the 26 weeks could run while the property was being disregarded under some other paragraph of Sched. 10. But it would often be right to extend the period to a date (at least) 26 weeks after the property had ceased to be disregarded under that other paragraph (because otherwise the effect could be to deprive a claimant of the benefit of para. 26). The Commissioner also suggests some of the factors that might be relevant in deciding whether the 26 weeks should be extended. Besides the efforts made by the claimant to dispose of the property, other factors might be the state of the housing market, the claimant's intentions as regards the proceeds of sale, the value of his interest in the property and his ability to borrow money on the strength of that interest. Each case would depend on its own facts.

CIS 30/1993 decides that this disregard cannot apply to notional capital if the claimant has already disposed of the same capital so as to trigger reg. 51(1). This is because para. 26 is only applicable where the *claimant* is taking steps to dispose of premises. The Commissioner in *CIS 30/1993* acknowledges that this view is different from that taken in some other decisions, but having reviewed these *(R(SB) 9/91*, *CIS 25/1990*, *CIS 81/1991* and *CIS 562/1992*) concludes that the only one in which this question had been central to the appeal was *CIS 25/1990* and in that case the point had not been argued in any detail. He was therefore not bound by it. *(R1/92 (IS)*, a decision of the Chief Commissioner in Northern Ireland, had come to the same conclusion as he had done.) It had been argued on behalf of the claimant that if the property was put up for sale by the actual possessor of it, para. 26 should apply. The AO had submitted, first, that the wording of para. 26 made it clear that the disregard only applied if the claimant was taking steps to dispose of the premises; second, that the purpose of the disregard in para. 26 was to allow the claimant a reasonable time to liquidate assets to provide money to live on. There could be no guarantee that the third party would allow the proceeds of sale to be used to support the claimant and thus there was no reason to delay counting the notional capital. The Commissioner holds that the words of para. 26 were plain and unambiguous and could not apply because the claimant could not be taking steps to dispose of what she had already disposed of. This seems unfair in that a claimant deemed to have notional capital may suffer an additional penalty through not being able to benefit from the disregard in para.26. But the Commissioner's conclusion is cogently argued.

Paragraph 27

In these circumstances the claimant will have an interest in the premises, but it would be unfair to count the value of the interest. The initial disregard is for 26 weeks, with an extension as reasonable.

In *CIS 240/1992* the legal advice given to the claimant was that he could not obtain possession of the premises until the end of the current tenancy. The Commissioner states that for para. 27 to apply the claimant must be taking steps to obtain possession and rejects a submission that a failure to take steps that were bound to be unsuccessful did not preclude the application of para 27. But in seeking legal advice was not the claimant taking such steps? Para. 27 does not require the claimant to have commenced legal proceedings for the disregard to apply; it is sufficient if he has sought legal advice with a view to obtaining possession. Provided that a claimant is willing to commence proceedings immediately the tenancy ends (which did not appear to be the case in *CIS 240/1992*) it is difficult to see what other steps he could take in such circumstances.

Paragraph 28

Since the value of the home is disregarded, this is a limited extension. Then the disregard is for 26 weeks, with an extension as reasonable.

Paragraph 29

Payments of earnings or other income in kind are disregarded (see regs. 35(2) and 40(4) and Sched. 9, para. 21). Most payments of capital in kind would be personal possessions (see para. 10).

Paragraph 42

These are capital payments from special Department of Employment schemes to assist disabled people, such as the "business on own account" scheme and the "personal reader service."

Paragraph 43

Start-up capital payments under the Blind Homeworkers' Scheme are disregarded, but payments of income are taken into account.

Paragraphs 44–45

These paragraphs were amended in October 1997 so that the disregard of funds held in court that derive from damages for personal injury is no longer restricted to under 18-year-olds but now applies without age limit. However, where the compensation was awarded for the death of a parent (or parents), the person concerned must be under 18 for the disregard to apply.

See para. 12 for the disregard of compensation payments for personal injury placed on trust. *CIS 368/1994* decided that the disregard in para. 12 applied to compensation for personal injury that was held and administered by the Court of Protection, since in the circumstances such an arrangement amounted to a "trust". The disregard in para. 44(a) will now apply to damages for personal injury held by the Court of Protection (and also the High Court and the County Court, and, under para. 45(a), the equivalent Scottish courts), whatever the age of the person. But note that under paras. 44(a) and 45(a) the award must be for injury to that person; this does not, however, seem to be the case in relation to the disregard under para. 12 (see para. 34412 of the *Adjudication Officer's Guide* and notes to para. 12).

Note that funds disregarded under paras. 44(a) and 45(a) are excluded from the notional income rule in reg. 42(2) (income available on application) and the notional capital rules in reg. 51(1)(c) and (2)(e) (deprivation of capital and capital available on application). Note further that paras. 44 and 45 have not been added to the list of expected cases in reg. 48(4). This means that payments to a claimant from funds disregarded under paras. 44 or 45 will apparently count as capital, whatever the nature of those payments. See further the notes to reg. 48(4).

"Personal injury" includes a disease and any injuries suffered as a result of a disease (*e.g.* amputation of both legs following meningitis and septicaemia), as well as any accidental or criminal injury (*R(SB) 2/89.*

Paragraph 49

See the note to reg. 21ZA.

Paragraphs 50 and 51

See the notes to paras. 62 and 63 of Sched. 9. Note that if these payments count as capital they will only be disregarded for 52 weeks from the date of receipt.

Paragraph 52

Any capital acquired for the purposes of a business carried on while a person is participating in the self-employment route of the Employment option of the New Deal for 18 to 24-year-olds is ignored for 52 weeks from the date of receipt. For a brief summary of the self-employment route of the Employment option, see the note to reg. 75(1) of the JSA Regulations.

Paragraph 53

See the note to para. 48 of Sched. 8 to the JSA Regulations.

Income Support (Liable Relatives) Regulations 1990

(S.I. 1990 No. 1777)

Made by the Secretary of State under s.166(1) to (3A) of the Social Security Act 1975 and ss. 24A(1), 24B(5) and 84(1) of the Social Security Act 1986

Citation, commencement and interpretation

1.—(1) These Regulations may be cited as the Income Support (Liable Relatives) Regulations 1990 and shall come into force on 15th October 1990.

(2) In these Regulations—

"the Act" means the Social Security Act 1986; and

"the Income Support Regulations" means the Income Support (General) Regulations 1987.

Prescribed amounts for the purposes of section 24A of the Act [SSAA, s.107]

2.—(1) For the purposes of section 24A of the Act [SSAA, s.107] (recovery of expenditure on income support: additional amounts and transfer of orders) the amount which may be included in the sum which the court may order the other parent to pay under section 24(4) of the Act [SSAA, s.106(2)] shall be the whole of the following amounts which are payable to or for the claimant—
  (a) any personal allowance under paragraph 2 of Part I of Schedule 2 to the Income Support Regulations for each of the children whom the other parent is liable to maintain;
  (b) any family premium under paragraph 3 of Part II of that Schedule;
  (c) any lone parent premium under paragraph 8 of Part III of that Schedule;
  (d) any disabled child premium under paragraph 14 of Part III of that Schedule in respect of a child whom the other parent is liable to maintain; and
  (e) any carer premium under paragraph 14ZA of Part III of that Schedule if, but only if, that premium is payable because the claimant is in receipt, or is treated as being in receipt, of invalid care allowance by reason of the fact that he is caring for a severely disabled child or young person whom the other parent is liable to maintain.

(2) If the court is satisfied that in addition to the amounts specified in paragraph (1) above the liable parent has the means to pay, the sum which the court may order him to pay under section 24 of the Act [SSAA, s.106] may also include all or some of the amount of any personal allowance payable to or for the claimant under paragraph 1 of Part I of Schedule 2 to the Income Support Regulations.

Notice to the Secretary of State of applications to alter etc. maintenance orders

3.—(1) For the purposes of section 24B(5) of the Act [SSAA, s.108(5)] (prescribed person in prescribed circumstances to notify the Secretary of State of application to alter etc. a maintenance order) the prescribed person is, and in paragraph (2) below that expression means,—
  (a) in England and Wales—
      (i) in relation to the High Court, where the case is proceeding in the deputy principal registry the senior registrar of that registry, and where the case is proceeding in a district registry the district registrar;
      (ii) in relation to a county court, the proper officer of that court within the meaning of Order 1, Rule 3 of the County Court Rules 1981; and
      (iii) in relation to a magistrates' court, the clerk to the justices of that court; and
  (b) in Scotland—
      (i) in relation to the Court of Session, the deputy principal clerk of session; and
      (ii) in relation to a sheriff court, the sheriff clerk.

(2) For the purposes of that subsection the prescribed circumstances are that before the final determination of the application the Secretary of State has made a written request to the prescribed person that he be notified of any such application, and has not made a written withdrawal of that request.

GENERAL NOTE

See the notes to ss.107 and 108 of the Administration Act.

Income Support (Transitional) Regulations 1987

(S.I. 1987 No. 1969)

Made by the Secretary of State under ss.84(1) and 89(1) of the Social Security Act 1986

Citation and commencement

1. These Regulations may be cited as the Income Support (Transitional) Regulations 1987 and shall come into force on 23rd November 1987.

Interpretation

2.—(1) In these Regulations, unless the context otherwise requires—
"the Act" means the Social Security Act 1986;
"adjudicating authority" means any person or body with responsibility under the Social Security Acts 1975 to 1986, and regulations made thereunder, for the determination of claims for any benefit under those Acts and questions arising in connection with a claim for, or award of, or disqualification for receiving such benefit;
"benefit week"—
  (a) in relation to supplementary benefit, has the meaning given to it in regulation 7 of the Supplementary Benefit (Determination of Questions) Regulations 1980;
  (b) in relation to income support, has the meaning given to it by paragraph 4 of Schedule 7 to the Social Security (Claims and Payments) Regulations 1987;

"domestic assistance addition" means an additional requirement under paragraph 15 of Schedule 4 to the Requirements Regulations;

"first benefit week" means the benefit week beginning on a day during the period of 7 days commencing on 4th April 1988;

"former beneficiary" means a person who, for a period immediately preceding 11th April 1988, is entitled to supplementary benefit;

"former housing benefit supplement recipient" means a person in respect of whom an amount is applicable under regulation 19 of the Requirements Regulations for a period immediately preceding 4th April 1988;

"General Regulations" means the Income Support (General) Regulations 1987;

"income support" means income support under Part II of the Act [SSCBA, Part VII];

"Requirements Regulations" means the Supplementary Benefit (Requirements) Regulations 1983;

"second benefit week" means the benefit week beginning on a day during the period of 7 days commencing on 11th April 1988;

"Social Security Act" means the Social Security Act 1975;

"patient" has the same meaning as in regulation 21(3) of the General Regulations;

"personal expenses addition" means an amount of income support payable in accordance with regulation 13 in addition to any income support to which a person may be entitled under Part II of the Act [SSCBA, Part VII];

"special transitional addition" means an amount of income support payable in accordance with regulation 15 in addition to any income support to which a person may be entitled under Part II of the Act [SSCBA, Part VII];

"supplementary benefit" means a supplementary pension or allowance under the Supplementary Benefits Act 1976;

"transitional addition" means an amount of income support payable in accordance with regulations 10 to 13 in addition to any income support to which a person may be entitled under Part II of the Act [SSCBA, Part VII];

"unemployed person" means a person who is or is required to be available for employment;

and other expressions have the same meaning as in the General Regulations.

(2) Unless the context otherwise requires, any reference in these Regulations to a numbered regulation or Part is a reference to the regulation or Part bearing that number in these Regulations, and any reference in a regulation to a numbered paragraph is a reference to the paragraph bearing that number in that regulation.

[[1](3) In these Regulations the expressions "transitional addition" and "special transitional addition" include any amount payable by virtue of regulation 87(1) of the Jobseeker's Allowance Regulations 1996.]

AMENDMENT

1. Income Support (General) (Jobseeker's Allowance Consequential Amendments) Regulations 1996 (S.I. 1996 No. 206), reg. 29(2) (October 7, 1996).

GENERAL NOTE

Paragraph (1)

"*former beneficiary*". *CIS 12016/1996* decides that in the context of reg. 4(1) a "former beneficiary" was a person who had claimed supplementary benefit and had been found by an adjudicating authority to be entitled to it. It was not possible for a person who had satisfied the conditions of entitlement to supplementary benefit immediately before April 11, 1988 but who had not claimed it, to be treated by virtue of reg. 4(1) as if he had claimed income support from the first benefit week beginning after April 11, 1988.

[¹Permitted period

2A.—(1) For the purposes of regulations 14 and 15 (reduction and termination of transitional addition and special transitional addition) where a claimant has ceased to be entitled to income support—

(a) because he or his partner becomes engaged in remunerative work the permitted period, [². . .] shall be 12 weeks; or

(b) for any other reason, the permitted period shall be eight weeks.

(2) [². . .]

(3) [². . .].

AMENDMENTS

1. Income Support (Transitional) Amendment Regulations 1989 (S.I. 1989 No. 1626), reg. 2 (October 9, 1989).
2. Income Support (General) (Jobseeker's Allowance Consequential Amendments) Regulations 1996 (S.I. 1996 No. 206), reg. 29(3) (October 7, 1996).

PART I

TRANSITIONAL ARRANGEMENTS

Claims for income support made before 11th April 1988

3.—(1) A claim for income support may be made on or after 14th March 1988 and before 11th April 1988, and a claim for supplementary benefit made during that period may be treated in addition as a claim for income support.

(2) Paragraph (1) and regulation 4 (deeming of claims for income support by former beneficiaries) shall not apply in the case of a person affected by a trade dispute (that is to say a person in respect of whom the applicable amount or a proportion of the applicable amount falls to be disregarded by virtue of section 23 of the Act [SSCBA, s.126]).

(3) Subject to the provisions of this regulation, any claim for income support made or treated as made in accordance with paragraph (1) may be determined before 11th April 1988 in accordance with the Act and Regulations made under that Act as if those provisions were in force.

(4) Any claim made or treated as made in accordance with paragraph (1) shall be treated as made for a period commencing on 11th April 1988.

(5) A decision which is given awarding income support on such a claim as is referred to in paragraph (1)—

(a) may award the benefit from 11th April 1988 if it appears probable that the conditions for entitlement to income support for the person who made that claim will be satisfied;

(b) shall be subject to the conditions for entitlement being so satisfied on the date from which the benefit is awarded;

(c) may be reviewed if any question arises as to the satisfaction of those conditions.

DEFINITIONS

"applicable amount"—see 1986 Act, s.84(1).
"the Act"—see reg. 2(1).

"income support"—*ibid.*
"supplementary benefit"—*ibid.*

Deeming of claims for income support by former beneficiaries

4.—(1) Notwithstanding the provisions of section 165A of the Social Security Act [SSAA, s.1], but subject to regulation 3(2) (persons affected by a trade dispute), in the case of a former beneficiary or a former housing benefit supplement recipient it shall not be a condition of entitlement to income support for a period commencing in the week beginning 11th April 1988 that he makes a claim for such benefit and the provisions of the Act and Regulations made thereunder shall apply, subject to the following provisions of this Part, as if a claim for that benefit had been duly made by the former beneficiary or the former housing benefit supplement recipient in respect of a period commencing on the first day of his second benefit week.

(2) Where by virtue of paragraph (1) a person's entitlement to income support falls to be determined as if a claim for it had been duly made, the claimant's entitlement in respect of a period commencing in the week beginning 11th April 1988 may nevertheless be determined at an earlier date if the claimant is entitled to supplementary benefit at the date of the determination; and any such claim shall be determined in accordance with the Act and Regulations made under that Act as if those provisions were in force.

(3) A decision which is given awarding income support on a determination made under this regulation—

(a) may award the benefit from the first day of his second benefit week if it appears probable that the conditions for entitlement to income support will be satisfied;

(b) shall be subject to the conditions for entitlement being so satisfied on the date from which the benefit is awarded;

(c) may be reviewed if any question arises as to the satisfaction of those conditions.

DEFINITIONS

"the Act"—see reg. 2(1).
"former beneficiary"—*ibid.*
"former housing benefit recipient"—*ibid.*
"income support"—*ibid.*
"second benefit week"—*ibid.*
"Social Security Act"—*ibid.*
"supplementary benefit"—*ibid.*

GENERAL NOTE

Paragraph (1)
See *CIS 12016/1996* in the note to the definition of "former beneficiary" in reg. 2(1).

[¹Payments on account of income support

4A.—(1) Where, by virtue of regulation 4 (deeming of claims by former beneficiaries), a person's entitlement to income support, for a period commencing in the week beginning 11th April 1988, falls to be determined as if a claim for it had been duly made and no determination has been made by that date, the Secretary of State may make a payment on account of income support and the amount of such payment shall be offset by the adjudicating authority in reduction of any income support, any transitional payment of income support under regulation 7 (transitional payments for former beneficiaries) and any addition under Part II, subsequently awarded.

(2) Where a payment on account has been made under paragraph (1) and the adjudicating authority determines that there is no entitlement to income support, or that the entitlement is less than the amount of the payment on account, that authority shall determine the amount of the overpayment.

(3) The amount of any overpayment determined under paragraph (2) shall be recoverable by the Secretary of State by the same procedures and subject to the same conditions as if it were recoverable under section 53(1) of the Act [SSAA, s.71] (over-payments).

(4) A payment on account under this regulation may be made by means of an instrument of payment or such other means as appears to the Secretary of State to be appropriate in the circumstances of any particular case and, notwithstanding the repeal of any enactment, may be made by an instrument of payment or book of serial orders issued for the purpose of paying supplementary benefit.]

AMENDMENT

1. Income Support (Transitional) Amendment Regulations 1988 (S.I. 1988 No. 521), reg. 2 (April 11, 1988).

DEFINITIONS

"the Act"—see reg. 2(1).
"adjudicating authority"—*ibid.*
"former beneficiary"—*ibid.*
"income support"—*ibid.*
"supplementary benefit"—*ibid.*

Questions deemed to have been determined and treatment of income

5.—(1) Where, for a period commencing on or after 11th April 1988, it appears that the entitlement of a former beneficiary to income support, or the amount of such benefit to which he is entitled, depends upon the determination of any question by an adjudicating authority and such a question has been so determined in respect of that former beneficiary's entitlement to supplementary benefit immediately before 11th April 1988, that question shall be deemed to have been so determined for the purposes of the said entitlement to income support.

(2) For the purposes of determining a claimant's entitlement to income support for a period commencing on or after 11th April 1988, any earnings paid before that date on the termination or interruption of—

(a) the claimant's employment shall be taken into account in accordance with Part V of the General Regulations (income and capital) as if that Part were in force at the date of the termination or interruption of the employment and, except in the case of a claimant who was not treated as engaged in remunerative full-time work within the meaning of regulation 9(1)(a) of the Supplementary Benefit (Conditions of Entitlement) Regulations 1981 (circumstances in which persons are to be treated as engaged in remunerative full-time work), the claimant shall be treated as being engaged in remunerative work for that part of the period (if any), falling on or after 11th April 1988, for which those earnings are to be taken into account;

(b) the employment of the partner of a former beneficiary, except where the partner was engaged in that employment for less than 30 hours per week, shall notwithstanding the revocation of the Supplementary Benefit (Resources) Regulations 1981, be taken into account in accordance with those Regulations as if they were still in force.

(3) Except in the case of earnings to which paragraph (2) applies or would, but for the exception specified in sub-paragraph (b) thereof, apply, where in the case of a former beneficiary to whom regulation 4 applies a payment of income would, but for this paragraph, fall to be treated as paid under regulation 31(1)(a) of the General Regulations (date on which income treated as paid) before the first day of the benefit week in which he is first entitled to income support, that payment shall be treated as paid on that day and any part of the payment which has been taken into account in determining the former beneficiary's entitlement to supplementary benefit shall, notwithstanding Part V of the General Regulations, be disregarded in determining his entitlement to income support.

(4) Where an adjudicating authority has determined that payment of an amount of supplementary benefit awarded to a former beneficiary for a period immediately preceding 11th April 1988 should be paid to another person or body, such determination shall be deemed to have been made for the purposes of income support to which the former beneficiary is entitled on or after 11th April 1988.

(5) For the purposes of the application of paragraph 14 of Schedule 4 to the General Regulations (applicable amounts of persons in residential care and nursing homes), or paragraph 12 of Schedule 5 to those Regulations (applicable amounts of persons in board and lodging accommodation), to a former beneficiary in respect of whom income support becomes payable for a period immediately following a period in respect of which supplementary benefit was payable, the expression ''close relative'' shall, for so long as he continues to be entitled without interruption to income support, be given the meaning assigned to it immediately before 11th April 1988 by regulation 2 of the Requirements Regulations (interpretation).

[[1](6) For the purposes of determining a claimant's entitlement to income support for a period commencing on or after 11th April 1988, regulation 43 of the General Regulations (notional earnings of seasonal workers) shall apply for the purposes of determining a person's earnings in the period of his off-season or last period of normal employment beginning before that date as if that regulation and Parts IV and V of the General Regulations (applicable amounts and income and capital) were in force throughout that period.]

AMENDMENT

1. Income Support (Transitional) Amendment Regulations 1988 (S.I. 1988 No. 521), reg. 3 (April 11, 1988).

DEFINITIONS

"adjudicating authority"—see reg. 2(1).
"benefit week"—*ibid*.
"earnings"—see General Regulations, reg. 2(1).
"former beneficiary"—see reg. 2(1).
"General Regulations"—*ibid*.
"income support"—*ibid*.
"partner"—see General Regulations, reg. 2(1).
"payment"—*ibid*.
"supplementary benefit"—see reg. 2(1).

GENERAL NOTE

CSIS 89/1990 holds that para. (1) only applies where entitlement to or the amount of income support depends on the determination of a question and the same question has already been determined for supplementary benefit. So a decision for supplementary benefit purposes to lift the requirement to be available for employment was not carried over into income support, because neither entitlement to income support nor its amount depends on that question.

Appointments for former beneficiaries unable to act

6. Where the Secretary of State has made an appointment under regulation 26 of the Supplementary Benefit (Claims and Payments) Regulations 1981 of a person to exercise any right to which a former beneficiary may be entitled under the Supplementary Benefits Act 1976 and to receive and deal on his behalf with any sums payable to that former beneficiary under or by virtue of that Act, and such appointment has not, before 11th April 1988, been revoked by the Secretary of State or terminated by the resignation of the person appointed, that appointment shall be deemed, for the purposes of income support for that former beneficiary, to be an appointment made under regulation 33 of the Social Security (Claims and Payments) Regulations 1987 (persons unable to act).

DEFINITIONS

"former beneficiary"—see reg. 2(1).
"income support"—*ibid.*

Transitional payments for former beneficiaries

7.—(1) Where a former beneficiary is entitled to income support on the first day of his second benefit week—

(a) he shall, notwithstanding the repeal or revocation of any enactment, be entitled to and be paid supplementary benefit for the period commencing on 11th April 1988 and ending with the day 6 days after the first day of his first benefit week except where that benefit week commences on 4th April 1988;

(b) if the former beneficiary is a person to whom income support is payable in arrears, he shall also be entitled to a transitional payment of income support in respect of a period of, or two consecutive periods of, 7 days determined in accordance with paragraph (2).

(2) For the purposes of paragraph (1)(b)—

(a) in the case of a former beneficiary who is an unemployed person whose supplementary benefit had been paid by means of a book of serial orders or who is not an unemployed person, the transitional payment shall be in respect of the period of 7 days commencing with the day following the last day in respect of which supplementary benefit is payable in his case;

(b) in any other case, the transitional payment shall be in respect of two consecutive periods of 7 days commencing with the day following the last day in respect of which supplementary benefit is payable in his case.

(3) The amount of the transitional payment in respect of any such period shall be equal to the amount of income support payable in arrears for the benefit week or, in the case of a claimant whose entitlement to income support is for a period of less than a benefit week the amount which would have been payable had he been entitled to income support for the benefit week, commencing in the same calendar week as the period of seven days in respect of which the transitional payment is made.

(4) The transitional payment shall be made in advance and, in a case to which paragraph (2)(b) applies, the transitional payment may be made in two instalments if it appears to the Secretary of State to be appropriate in the circumstances of the particular case.

(5) In calculating the income of a former beneficiary for the purpose of determining his entitlement to income support in respect of any day for which that benefit becomes payable to him in arrears there shall be disregarded any supplementary benefit or any transitional payment payable to him under this regulation.

(6) Where a former beneficiary is not entitled to income support on the first day of his second benefit week he shall, notwithstanding the repeal or revocation of any enactment, be entitled to and be paid supplementary benefit for the period commencing on 11th April 1988 and ending with the day 6 days after the first day of his first benefit week except where that benefit week commences on 4th April 1988.

<small>DEFINITIONS</small>

"benefit week"—see reg. 2(1).
"first benefit week"—*ibid.*
"former beneficiary"—*ibid.*
"income support"—*ibid.*
"second benefit week"—*ibid.*
"supplementary benefit"—*ibid.*
"unemployed person"—*ibid.*

[¹Transitional payments for persons claiming supplementary benefit

7A.—(1) Except where regulation 7 applies (transitional payments for former beneficiaries), where a person makes a claim for supplementary benefit in the week commencing 4th April 1988 and, but for regulation 7(1)(a) of the Supplementary Benefit (Determination of Questions) Regulations 1980 (date of commencement of entitlement), he would have been entitled to supplementary benefit for a week beginning with the day on which the claim is made, he shall, if—
    (a) he is entitled to income support on the first day of his second benefit week; and
    (b) he is a person to whom income support is payable in arrears,
be entitled to a transitional payment of income support in respect of a period of, or two consecutive periods of, 7 days determined in accordance with paragraph (2).

(2) For the purposes of paragraph (1)—
    (a) in the case of an unemployed person, the transitional payment shall be in respect of two consecutive periods of 7 days commencing with the first day of his second benefit week;
    (b) in any other case, the transitional payment shall be in respect of the period of 7 days commencing with the first day of his second benefit week.

(3) Subject to paragraph (4), the amount of the transitional payment in respect of any such period shall be equal to the amount of income support payable in arrears for the benefit week or, in the case of a claimant whose entitlement to income support is for a period of less than a benefit week, the amount which would have been payable had he been entitled to income support for the benefit week, commencing in the same calendar week as the period of seven days in respect of which the transitional payment is made.

(4) Where a person is entitled to income support for a period falling before the first day of his second benefit week, the amount of the transitional payment shall be reduced by the amount of income support payable for that period.

(5) The transitional payment shall be made in advance and, in a case to which paragraph (2)(a) applies, the transitional payment may be made in two instalments if it appears to the Secretary of State to be appropriate in the circumstances of the particular case.

(6) In calculating the income of a person entitled to a transitional payment

under this regulation for the purpose of determining his entitlement to income support in respect of any day for which income support becomes payable to him in arrears there shall be disregarded any transitional payment payable to him under this regulation.

(7) Where a person is entitled to a transitional payment under this regulation or, but for his being a person to whom income support is payable in advance, would have been so entitled, Part II shall apply to him—

(a) as if he were a former beneficiary who had been entitled to supplementary benefit in the first benefit week; and

(b) as if that benefit week began on the day on which the claim for supplementary benefit was made.

(8) Where paragraph (7) applies, the amount of supplementary benefit to which that person is, for the purposes of Part II, to be treated as entitled shall be equal to the amount which would have been payable in the first benefit week had he been entitled to supplementary benefit for that week.]

AMENDMENT

1. Income Support (Transitional) Amendment Regulations 1988 (S.I. 1988 No. 521), reg. 4 (April 11, 1988).

DEFINITIONS

"benefit week"—see reg. 2(1).
"former beneficiary"—*ibid.*
"income support"—*ibid.*
"second benefit week"—*ibid.*
"supplementary benefit"—*ibid.*
"unemployed person"—*ibid.*

Treatment for income support purposes of periods relating to supplementary benefit

8.—(1) For the purpose of determining under regulation 4(1) of the General Regulations (temporary absence from Great Britain) whether a claimant is entitled to income support during a period of absence, that provision shall be construed as though there were inserted immediately after the words "entitled to income support" the words "or supplementary benefit".

(2) For the purpose of determining under regulation 21(4)(b)(ii) of the General Regulations (special cases) whether a local authority has accepted, in relation to a former beneficiary responsibility therein referred to for a period of not less than 2 years immediately before that person attained pensionable age, that provision shall be construed as though there were inserted immediately after the words "under and by virtue of that regulation" the words "or under or by virtue of the Supplementary Benefits Act 1976".

(3) Where, in relation to supplementary benefit for a former beneficiary in respect of a period immediately before 11th April 1988, his normal requirements fell to be reduced by virtue of regulation 8 of the Requirements Regulations 1983 (actual or notional unemployment benefit disqualification), regulation 22 of the General Regulations (reduction of applicable amount in cases of voluntary unemployment) shall apply to the calculation of that former beneficiary's applicable amount on 11th April 1988 with the modification that the relevant period specified in paragraph (6) of that regulation shall be reduced by the number of whole benefit weeks corresponding to the number of such weeks immediately preceding that date during which his normal requirements had been so reduced.

(4) For the purpose of determining whether, in any case, the additional condition for higher pensioner premium or disability premium, specified in paragraph

12(1)(b) of Schedule 2 to the General Regulations (applicable amounts), is satisfied for any period before 24th October 1988, that provision shall be construed as though there were inserted therein, immediately after the reference to the Social Security Act, a reference to the Supplementary Benefits Act 1976.

(5) For the purposes of paragraph 7 of Schedule 3 to the General Regulations (housing costs), any reference to income support shall be construed as if it included a reference to supplementary benefit and in sub-paragraph (2)(a) of that paragraph references to a claimant's income and applicable amount shall be construed as if they included references to his resources and requirements determined for the purposes of entitlement to supplementary benefit.

(6) Where, in relation to supplementary benefit for a former beneficiary in respect of a period immediately before 11th April 1988, his housing requirements fell to be restricted by virtue of regulation 20 or 21 of the Requirements Regulations (special cases and restrictions where amounts are excessive)—

(a) paragraph 10 of Schedule 3 to the General Regulations (housing costs) shall apply to the calculation of that former beneficiary's applicable amount in his second benefit week with the modification that the references in paragraph 10(2)(a) and (6) of that Schedule to income support shall be construed as if they included a reference to supplementary benefit; and

(b) in computing the 8 week period referred to in paragraph 10(2)(c) of that Schedule any week falling before 11th April 1988 which is within that 8 week period and during which supplementary benefit was payable shall be treated as a week in which income support was payable.

DEFINITIONS

"applicable amount"—see 1986 Act, s.84(1).
"benefit week"—see reg. 2(1).
"former beneficiary"—*ibid.*
"General Regulations"—*ibid.*
"income support"—*ibid.*
"local authority"—see 1986 Act, s.84(1).
"Requirements Regulations"—see reg. 2(1).
"Social Security Act"—*ibid.*
"supplementary benefit"—*ibid.*

PART II

TRANSITIONAL PROTECTION

Total benefit income

9.—(1) In this Part a person's total benefit income in his first benefit week means, subject to paragraphs (2) to (5) and (7), and regulation 13(1) (special provisions for persons in residential care and nursing homes), the aggregate of the amount of any of the following benefits or payments to which he or his partner was, or both were, entitled in respect of that week—

(a) supplementary benefit;
(b) family income supplement;
(c) child benefit;
(d) any benefit under the Social Security Act;
(e) war disablement pension;
(f) war widow's pension;

(g) any payment made under a scheme made under the Industrial Injuries and Diseases (Old Cases) Act 1975;

(h) statutory maternity pay under Part V of the Act;

(i) statutory sick pay under Part I of the Social Security and Housing Benefits Act 1982;

(j) any payment made otherwise than in accordance with any of the Acts under which the benefits or payments specified in sub-paragraphs (a) to (g) are made under arrangements made by the Secretary of State with the consent of the Treasury which is charged to the National Insurance Fund or to a Departmental Expenditure Vote to which payments of any benefit or payment specified in those sub-paragraphs are charged.

(2) Where a change of circumstances takes effect in a person's second benefit week which, had it taken effect in his first benefit week, would have resulted in a lesser amount of supplementary benefit being payable in respect of that week, the amount of supplementary benefit taken into account for the purpose of calculating his total benefit income in his first benefit week shall be the amount (if any) that would have been payable had the change of circumstances taken effect in that week [¹but this paragraph shall not apply where the change of circumstances is the admission to hospital of the person in his second benefit week.]

(3) If a former beneficiary's requirements for the purpose of calculating his entitlement to supplementary benefit in his first benefit week include an amount in respect of housing requirements under Part IV of the Requirements Regulations to which he is entitled by virtue of regulation 14(4) of those Regulations (housing requirements) and, in a case to which sub-paragraph (a) of that provision applies, if in that week he has been absent from his home for 52 weeks or more, the amount of supplementary benefit taken into account for the purpose of calculating his total benefit income in that benefit week shall be reduced by the amount of those housing requirements.

(4) If, in respect of his first benefit week, a former beneficiary who is entitled to supplementary benefit in respect of that benefit week is also entitled to housing benefit in the form of a rate rebate, his total benefit income in that benefit week shall be increased by—

(a) if he is a single claimant aged under 25, £1.00;

(b) in any other case, £1.30.

(5) Where a claimant, other than one whose requirements were modified under regulation 10(2) or (3) of the Requirements Regulations (modifications of normal requirements in special cases), is—

(a) a member of a couple and either he or his partner has been in hospital immediately before 11th April 1988 for at least 6, but not more than 9, weeks; or

(b) a lone parent who immediately before that date has been in hospital for at least 6 weeks,

the amount of supplementary benefit to be taken into account for the purpose of calculating his total benefit income in his first benefit week shall be the amount (if any) that would have been payable had his requirements fallen to be determined in accordance with paragraph 2 of Schedule 3 to the Requirements Regulations (modifications in the case of patients).

(6) In this Part a person's total benefit income in relation to his second and any subsequent benefit week means, subject to paragraph (7) and regulations 11 and 13(1) (persons in residential care and nursing homes), the aggregate of the following amounts—

(a) the amount of any income support, family credit and child benefit to which he or his partner is, or both are, entitled in respect of that week;

(b) where he or his partner is, or both are, entitled in respect of that week to any benefit or payment specified in paragraph (1)(d) to (i), the amount of the weekly rate of that benefit to which he is normally entitled as increased, if appropriate, by the order made by the Secretary of State under section 63 of the Act with effect from 11th April 1988;

(c) any payment referred to in paragraph (1)(j) which he or his partner receives, or both receive, in respect of that week.

(7) The amount of any of the benefits specified in sub-paragraphs (a) to (c) of this paragraph shall, to the extent that it is disregarded for the purpose of calculating a person's resources under the Supplementary Benefit (Resources) Regulations 1981 or a person's income under the General Regulations, be disregarded for the purpose of calculating a person's total benefit income in his first, second or any subsequent benefit week—

(a) mobility allowance;
(b) mobility supplement; and
(c) attendance allowance.

(8) In this Part references to a person's income in a benefit week subsequent to his first benefit week are references to his income, and the income of any member of his family which would be treated as his under section 22(5) of the Act, calculated under Part V of the General Regulations (income and capital).

[[1](9) For the purposes of paragraph (1)(a) or (6)(a), where a claimant is a person to whom regulation 8 of the Requirements Regulations or regulation 22 of the General Regulations (reductions in certain cases of unemployment disqualification) applies, the amount of supplementary benefit or income support to be taken into account shall be the amount to which the claimant would have been entitled but for that regulation.]

AMENDMENT

1. Income Support (Transitional) Amendment Regulations 1988 (S.I. 1988 No. 521), reg. 5 (April 11, 1988).

DEFINITIONS

"the Act"—see reg. 2(1).
"benefit week"—*ibid.*
"claimant"—see General Regulations, reg. 2(1).
"couple"—*ibid.*
"family"—see 1986 Act, s.20(11) (SSCBA, s.137(1)).
"first benefit week"—see reg. 2(1).
"former beneficiary"—*ibid.*
"General Regulations"—*ibid.*
"lone parent"—see General Regulations, reg. 2(1).
"mobility allowance"—*ibid.*
"mobility supplement"—*ibid.*
"partner"—*ibid.*
"Requirements Regulations"—see reg. 2(1).
"second benefit week"—*ibid.*
"single claimant"—see General Regulations, reg. 2(1).
"Social Security Act"—see reg. 2(1).
"supplementary benefit"—*ibid.*
"war disablement pension"—see 1986 Act, s.84(1).
"war widow's pension"—*ibid.*

GENERAL NOTE

Reg. 9 does not create any right to payment of benefit in the week beginning April 4, 1988 (*CIS 6/1988*).

Transitional addition

10.—(1) Except in a case to which regulation 11 or 12 applies (special provisions for patients and persons in board and lodging accommodation and hostels) and subject to the following provisions of this Part, where—

(a) a former beneficiary was entitled to supplementary benefit in respect of his first benefit week; and

(b) either—

    (i) he is awarded income support in respect of his second benefit week; or

    (ii) he is not entitled to income support in respect of that week only because his applicable amount calculated in accordance with the General Regulations does not exceed his income; and

(c) his total benefit income in his second benefit week is less than his total benefit income in his first benefit week,

he shall be entitled to a transitional addition.

(2) Subject to regulation 12(2), 13(5) or 14 (special provision for persons in residential care or nursing homes and reduction and termination of transitional addition), and except in a case to which paragraph (3) applies, the amount of the transitional addition to which a former beneficiary is entitled under paragraph (1) shall be the difference between his total benefit income in his first and second benefit weeks.

(3) Subject to regulation 14 the amount of the transitional addition applicable to a former beneficiary who in respect of his first benefit week was entitled to a domestic assistance addition of £10 or more shall be the amount (if any) obtained by subtracting from his total benefit income in his first benefit week the amount of his domestic assistance addition, the sum determined under paragraph (4) and, where applicable, (5).

(4) The sum for the purposes of paragraph (3) shall be—

(a) in a case where in his second benefit week a severe disability premium is applicable to the former beneficiary for the purpose of calculating his applicable amount under Part IV of the General Regulations (applicable amounts), his total benefit income in his second benefit week less the amount of that premium;

(b) in any other case, his total benefit income in his second benefit week.

(5) If the amount of the former beneficiary's domestic assistance addition is less than the amount of his severe disability premium, the sum for the purposes of paragraph (3) shall be the amount of the difference between the addition and the premium.

DEFINITIONS

    "applicable amount"—see General Regulations, reg. 2(1).
    "domestic assistance addition"—see reg. 2(1).
    "first benefit week"—*ibid.*
    "former beneficiary"—*ibid.*
    "General Regulations"—*ibid.*
    "income support"—*ibid.*
    "second benefit week"—*ibid.*
    "supplementary benefit"—*ibid.*

GENERAL NOTE

    CIS 193/1989 holds that reg. 10 cannot be impugned as discriminatory under the Sex Discrimination Act 1975 because it was made under powers provided in the Social Security Act 1986, which therefore to that extent impliedly repealed the Sex Discrimination Act 1975. The discrimination complained of arises because the protection under reg. 10 is given to a former beneficiary, *i.e.* a claimant. The claimant of supplementary benefit within a couple would usually have been the man. If the woman has to claim income support in her own right, because, for example, the man dies or they separate, she is not entitled to the transitional protection.

Special provisions for patients

11.—(1) Where, immediately before 11th April 1988—

(a) a claimant was a member of a married or unmarried couple for the purposes of paragraph 3(1) of Schedule 1 to the Supplementary Benefits Act 1976 or a spouse of a polygamous marriage; and

(b) he or any partner was entitled to supplementary benefit; and

(c) he was not himself a patient but any partner of his had been a patient for a period of 52 weeks or more,

he shall, subject to regulations 12 to 14 and 16 (special cases and reduction and termination of, and persons not entitled to, transitional additions), be entitled to a transitional addition calculated in accordance with paragraph (2).

(2) Subject to regulation 14, the amount of the transitional addition to which a claimant is entitled under paragraph (1) shall be the amount (if any) obtained by subtracting from his total benefit income in his first benefit week the amount of his total benefit income in the second benefit week ['and the amount of his partner's total benefit income in his partner's second benefit week].

(3) In this regulation, references to a claimant's partner are references to the person who, immediately before 11th April 1988 was the other member of a married or unmarried couple for the purposes of paragraph 3(1) of Schedule 1 to the Supplementary Benefits Act 1976 or was a spouse to whom the former beneficiary was polygamously married.

AMENDMENT

1. Income Support (Transitional) Amendment Regulations 1988 (S.I. 1988 No. 521), reg. 6 (April 11, 1988).

DEFINITIONS

"claimant"—see General Regulations, reg. 2(1).
"first benefit week"—see reg. 2(1).
"former beneficiary"—*ibid.*
"patient"—*ibid.*, General Regulations, reg. 21(3).
"polygamous marriage"—see General Regulations, reg. 2(1).
"second benefit week"—see reg. 2(1).
"supplementary benefit"—*ibid.*

Special provisions for persons in board and lodging accommodation and hostels

12.—(1) Where a claimant is temporarily absent for ['a period of less than 13 weeks which includes his first and second benefit week (or both)] from his board and lodging accommodation or his hostel and, in the case of board and lodging accommodation was immediately before his absence entitled to an increase under regulation 9(7) of the Requirements Regulations (modifications of requirements of boarders), he shall, notwithstanding regulation 14 (reduction and termination of transitional addition), on his return to that accommodation be entitled to a transitional addition of an amount equal to the difference between—

(a) the amount that his total benefit income in his first benefit week would have been had he been entitled in respect of that week to supplementary benefit on the basis that he was in that board and lodging accommodation or hostel; and, if less,

(b) the amount of his total benefit income in the first complete benefit week in respect of which his applicable amount for the purpose of calculating his entitlement to income support is to be calculated under Schedule 5 to the General Regulations (applicable amounts for persons in board and lodging accommodation and hostels).

(2) If a claimant becomes entitled to a transitional addition under paragraph

(1) he shall cease to be entitled to any transitional addition to which he would, but for this provision, be entitled under regulation 10 (transitional addition) while not in board and lodging accommodation or a hostel.

(3) Where a claimant who is in board and lodging accommodation or a hostel and who is entitled to a transitional addition under paragraph (1) or regulation 10 (transitional addition) temporarily leaves his board and lodging accommodation or a hostel for a period of 8 weeks or less or, if he becomes a patient, for a period of 14 weeks or less and, in the case of board and lodging accommodation he is entitled to an increase under paragraph 7 of Schedule 5 to the General Regulations, any increase in his applicable amount for the purpose of calculating his entitlement to income support on his return to that accommodation shall be disregarded for the purpose of regulation 14(1) (reduction in transitional addition).

(4) Regulation 14(3) [¹and (4)] (re-entitlement to a transitional addition after periods of 8 weeks or less) shall apply to a claimant who is in board and lodging accommodation and entitled to an increase under paragraph 7 of Schedule 5 to the General Regulations, or in a hostel and who, in either case was immediately before the period of 8 weeks, entitled to a transitional addition under paragraph (1) or regulation 10 notwithstanding that the amount of the transitional addition to which he is entitled is less than £10.

AMENDMENT

1. Income Support (Transitional) Amendment Regulations 1988 (S.I. 1988 No. 521), reg. 7, (April 11, 1988).

DEFINITIONS

"applicable amount"—see 1986 Act, s.84(1).
"benefit week"—see General Regulations, reg. 2(1).
"claimant"—*ibid.*
"first benefit week"—see reg. 2(1).
"General Regulations"—*ibid.*
"income support"—*ibid.*
"patient"—*ibid.*, General Regulations, reg. 21(3).
"Requirements Regulations"—see reg. 2(1).
"second benefit week"—*ibid.*
"supplementary benefit"—*ibid.*

Special provisions for persons in residential care and nursing homes

13.—(1) For the purpose of calculating the total benefit income of a claimant who is in a residential care or nursing home, where in his first benefit week an allowance for personal expenses is applicable under regulation 9(17)(e) of the Requirements Regulations (personal expenses for boarders)—

(a) in that benefit week, the amount of that allowance shall be deducted from the amount of supplementary benefit to which he is entitled in respect of that week; and

(b) in his second benefit week, the amount in respect of personal expenses applicable in his case under paragraph 13 of Schedule 4 to the General Regulations (applicable amounts of persons in residential care or nursing homes) shall be deducted from the amount of income support to which he is entitled in respect of that week.

(2) Subject to paragraph (3) and to regulation 16 (persons not entitled to personal expenses addition), a former beneficiary to whom paragraph (1) applies shall be entitled, in addition to any transitional addition to which he may be entitled under paragraph (5) or regulation 10 (transitional addition), to a personal expenses addition of an amount equal to the difference between the amount of the allowance for personal expenses under regulation 9(17)(e)

of the Requirements Regulations referred to in paragraph (1) and, if less, the amount of the allowance for personal expenses referred to in paragraph (1)(b).

(3) The amount of the personal expenses addition under paragraph (2) [¹(6) or (8)] shall be reduced by the amount of any increase in the amount in respect of personal expenses referred to in paragraph (1)(b).

(4) Subject to paragraphs (5) and (8), a claimant who ceases to reside or, if he is a member of a family, who and whose family cease to reside, in a residential care or nursing home [¹. . .], shall cease to be entitled to any transitional addition and personal expenses addition under this Part [¹except where he ceases or, as the case may be, he and his family cease, to reside in the home in the circumstances specified in paragraph 16 or 18 of column (1) of Schedule 7 to the General Regulations (applicable amounts in special cases) and he intends or, as the case may be, they intend to return to the home].

(5) Notwithstanding regulation 14 (reduction and termination of transitional and personal expenses addition), where a claimant is temporarily absent from his residential care or nursing home for a period which includes his [¹first and second benefit week (or both)], he shall be entitled on his return to a residential care or nursing home to a transitional addition of an amount equal to the difference between—

(a) the amount that his total benefit income in his first benefit week would have been had he been entitled in respect of that week to supplementary benefit calculated on the basis that he was a boarder in that residential care or nursing home for that week; and, if less,

(b) the amount of his total benefit income in the first complete week in respect of which his applicable amount for the purpose of calculating his entitlement to income support is to be calculated in accordance with Schedule 4 to the General Regulations (applicable amounts for claimants in residential care and nursing homes).

(6) A claimant to whom paragraph (5) applies and to whom in respect of his first benefit week an allowance for personal expenses would have been applicable under regulation 9(17)(e) of the Requirements Regulations shall also be entitled to a personal expenses addition of an amount equal to the difference between the amount that his personal expenses allowance would have been in respect of his first benefit week and, if less, the amount in respect of personal expenses applicable under paragraph 13 of Schedule 4 to the General Regulations.

(7) If a claimant becomes entitled to a transitional addition under paragraph (5) he shall cease to be entitled to any transitional addition to which he would, but for this provision, be entitled under regulation 10 (transitional addition) while not in a residential care or nursing home.

(8) Notwithstanding regulation 14 (reduction and termination of transitional and personal expenses addition), where a claimant is temporarily absent from his residential care or nursing home for a period after his second benefit week (whether or not he thereby ceases to be entitled to income support), he shall be entitled on his return to a residential care or nursing home to—

[¹(a) a transitional addition equal to the amount to which he was entitled immediately before his period of temporary absence less, if his applicable amount would have increased had he not been absent, the amount of the increase; and for the purposes of this sub-paragraph, any increase in the amount of personal expenses where a personal expenses addition is in payment shall be disregarded;

(b) a personal expenses addition equal to the amount to which he was entitled immediately before his period of temporary absence less, if the amount of personal expenses applicable in his case under paragraph 13 of Schedule 4 to the General Regulations would have increased had he not been absent, the amount of that increase.]

(9) For the purposes of paragraphs (5), (8) and (10) a claimant is temporarily absent only if the period of his temporary absence does not exceed—

(a) in the case of a person who is of pensionable age, 52 weeks; or

(b) in any other case, 13 weeks.

(10) Where a claimant—

(a) was in receipt of supplementary benefit as a boarder in a residential care or nursing home within the meaning of regulation 9 of the Requirements Regulations (boarders) and immediately before 11th April 1988 his requirements fell to be determined in accordance with paragraph (17)(a) to (e) or (i) to (k) of that regulation (protected amounts); or

(b) would have satisfied the conditions in sub-paragraph (*a*) above but for his being temporarily absent from such a home,

and he ceases to be entitled to income support and a transitional addition or personal expenses addition or both, he shall notwithstanding regulation 14, if he becomes re-entitled to income support, become re-entitled to such an addition of the same amount as he would have been entitled to had he not ceased to be entitled to income support, provided that he has continued since that date to be resident in a residential care or nursing home.

(11) Where—

(a) the claimant's partner has died; and

(b) immediately before his death the partner was entitled to a transitional addition or personal expenses addition or both under this Part; and

(c) after the partner's death the claimant has continued to be a resident in the same accommodation as he and his partner occupied immediately before the partner's death,

the claimant shall be entitled to a transitional addition or personal expenses addition or both equal to one-half of the amount to which his partner was entitled immediately before his death.

AMENDMENT

1. Income Support (Transitional) Amendment Regulations 1988 (S.I. 1988 No. 521), reg. 8 (April 11, 1988).

DEFINITIONS

"benefit week"—see reg. 2(1).
"claimant"—see General Regulations, reg. 2(1).
"first benefit week"—see reg. 2(1).
"former beneficiary"—*ibid.*
"General Regulations"—*ibid.*
"income support"—*ibid.*
"nursing home"—see General Regulations, reg. 2(1), reg. 19(3).
"partner"—see General Regulations, reg. 2(1).
"personal expenses addition"—see reg. 2(1).
"Requirements Regulations'—*ibid.*
"residential care home"—see General Regulations, reg. 2(1), reg. 19(3).
"second benefit week"—see reg. 2(1).
"supplementary benefit"—*ibid.*
"transitional addition"—*ibid.*

Reduction and termination of transitional and personal expenses addition

14.—(1) The amount of a claimant's transitional addition shall be reduced—

(a) if, in respect of any benefit week subsequent to his second benefit week, he is entitled to income support as well as a transitional addition and his applicable amount under Part IV [³or VI] of the General Regulations increases, by the amount of that increase [¹but this subparagraph shall not apply to an increase to which regulation 13(3) applies (increase in personal expenses)];

(b) if, in respect of any benefit week subsequent to his second benefit week, he is entitled only to a transitional addition [¹or, as the case may be, to a transitional addition and a special transitional addition], by the amount of any increase in his income.

(c) if, in respect of any benefit week subsequent to his second benefit week, he is entitled only to a transitional addition and personal expenses addition under regulation 13(2) (special provisions for persons in residential care or nursing homes), by the amount of any increase in his income;

(d) if, in respect of any benefit week subsequent to his second benefit week he becomes entitled to income support as a result of an increase in his applicable amount under Part IV [³or VI] of the General Regulations and immediately before that increase he was entitled only to a transitional addition, by the amount of that increase less the amount by which his income exceeded his applicable amount prior to that increase;

(e) if, in respect of any benefit week subsequent to his second benefit week he ceases to be entitled to income support because his income exceeds his applicable amount, by the amount by which his income exceeds the applicable amount.

[¹(1A) Notwithstanding paragraph (1)(a) or (d) where [⁵regulation 21A or 22] of the General Regulations (reductions in applicable amounts) ceases to apply to the claimant and as a result his applicable amount increases, his transitional addition shall not be reduced by the amount of that increase.

(1B) Notwithstanding paragraph (1)(a) or (d) where a person has entered accommodation referred to in any of sub-paragraphs (a) to (d) of the definition of residential accommodation in regulation 21(3) of the General Regulations (special cases), or a residential care home or nursing home, for a period of 8 weeks or less and as a result his applicable amount increases, his transitional addition shall not be reduced by the amount of that increase.]

[²(1C) Notwithstanding paragraph (1)(b), (c) or (e) the amount of a claimant's transitional addition shall not be reduced if, and to the extent that, the increase in his income or, as the case may be, the reason his income exceeds his applicable amount, is attributable to the receipt of a training allowance.]

[⁷(1CA) Notwithstanding paragraph (1)(b), (c) or (e) the amount of a claimant's transitional addition shall not be reduced if, and to the extent that, the increase in his income or, as the case may be, the reason his income exceeds his applicable amount is attributable to the amendment made by regulation 2 of the Child Benefit and Social Security (Fixing and Adjustment of Rates) Amendment No.2 Regulations 1991.]

[⁷(1D) Notwithstanding paragraph (1)(a) or (d), the amount of a claimant's transitional addition shall not be reduced if, and to the extent that, the increase in his applicable amount is attributable to the amendments made by regulation 5(a) and (c) of the Income Support (General) Amendment Regulations 1989 and that increase in his applicable amount takes effect in his benefit week beginning on a day during the period of 7 days commencing on 9th October 1989.]

[⁷(1DA) Notwithstanding paragraph (1)(a) or (d), the amount of a claimant's transitional addition shall not be reduced if, and to the extent that, the increase in his applicable amount is attributable to the amendments made by regulation 15(a), (b) or (c) of the Income Support (General) Amendment No.4 Regulations 1991 and that increase in his applicable amount takes effect in his benefit week beginning on a day during the period of 7 days commencing on 1st October 1991.]

[⁷(1DZA) Notwithstanding paragraph (1)(a) or (d), the amount of a claimant's transitional addition shall not be reduced if, and to the extent that, the increase in his applicable amount is attributable to the amendments made by regulation 3(1) and (2) of the Income-Related Benefits Amendment Regulations 1992 and that increase in his applicable amount takes effect in his benefit week beginning on a day during the period of 7 days commencing on 5th October 1992.]

[³(1E) Notwithstanding paragraph (1)(a) or (d), where a claimant's applicable amount increases by virtue of his or his partner's participation or ceasing to participate in arrangements for training under section 2 of the Employment and Training Act 1973 [⁶or section 2 of the Enterprise and New Towns (Scotland) Act 1990] or his or his partner's attendance or ceasing to attend at a course at an employment rehabilitation centre established under that section [⁶of the 1993 Act], his transitional addition shall not be reduced by the amount of that increase.

(1F) Notwithstanding paragraph (1)(a) or (d), where—

(a) a claimant has ceased to be entitled to a transitional addition because he or his partner becomes engaged in remunerative work and immediately before he so ceased a higher pensioner premium or a disability premium was applicable to him under paragraph 10 or, as the case may be, 11 of Schedule 2 to the General Regulations (applicable amounts); and

(b) he becomes re-entitled to that addition by virtue of paragraph (3A) or (4A) or regulation 15(4) (special transitional addition),

his transitional addition shall not be reduced if the higher pensioner premium or the disability premium again becomes applicable to him to the extent that any increase in his applicable amount is attributable to that premium.]

[⁴(1G) Notwithstanding paragraph (1)(a) or (d), where a claimant's applicable amount increases because a child or young person mentioned in paragraph (5)(c) of regulation 16 of the General Regulations (circumstances in which a person is treated or not treated as a member of the household) is treated as a member of the claimant's household under paragraph (6) of that regulation, the claimant's transitional addition shall not be reduced by the amount of that increase unless the child or young person has been treated as a member of the household for a continuous period which exceeds eight weeks.]

(2) A claimant shall cease to be entitled to a transitional addition if—

(a) in the case of a claimant who is entitled to income support as well as a transitional addition—

   (i) subject to regulation 15(4) (special transitional addition), he ceases to be entitled to income support for a reason other than that his applicable amount under Part IV of the General Regulations (applicable amounts) does not exceed his income; or

   (ii) the amount of his transitional addition is reduced to nil by virtue of paragraph (1); or

(b) in the case of a claimant to whom paragraph (1)(b), (c) or (e) applies—

   (i) subject to regulation 15(4), he would no longer, if he claimed, be entitled to income support for a reason other than that his applicable amount under Part IV of the General Regulations does not exceed his income; or

   (ii) the amount of his transitional addition is reduced to nil by virtue of paragraph (1).

(3) [³Except where paragraph (3A) applies,] a claimant who either—

(a) has ceased to be entitled to income support but remained entitled to a transitional addition; or

(b) has ceased to be entitled to income support and a transitional addition,

and immediately before he so ceased was entitled to a transitional addition of £10 or more shall, [¹if he becomes re-entitled to income support not more than 8 weeks after the day on which he has ceased to be so entitled, in the benefit week in which he becomes re-entitled, be re-entitled to a transitional addition of an amount equal to the amount of the transitional addition to which he was previously entitled subject to any reduction in that amount which would have occurred under paragraph (1)(a) had he remained entitled to income support.]

[³(3A) A claimant who has ceased to be entitled to income support and a transitional addition because he or his partner has become engaged in remunerative work shall, if during the permitted period determined in accordance with regulation 2A (permitted period) beginning with the day after the day on which he ceased to be so entitled he or his partner has ceased to be engaged in that work, be re-entitled to a transitional addition of an amount equal to the amount of transitional addition to which he was previously entitled subject to any reduction in that amount which would have occurred under paragraph (1)(a) had he remained entitled to income support.]

(4) [³Except where paragraph (4A) applies,] a claimant who, was entitled only to a transitional addition of £10 or more and who has ceased to be entitled to such an addition—

   (a) for a reason other than that his income exceeds his applicable amount; or

   (b) because his income exceeds his applicable amount and the amount of his transitional addition,

shall, [¹if not more than 8 weeks after the day on which he ceased to be so entitled neither the reason in sub-paragraph (a) nor (b) applies to him, be re-entitled to a transitional addition of an amount equal to the amount by which his total benefit income in his first benefit week exceeds his total benefit income in the benefit week in which neither sub-paragraph applies to him, or the amount to which he was previously entitled, whichever is the lower.]

[³(4A) A claimant who was entitled only to a transitional addition and who has ceased to be entitled to such an addition because he or his partner became engaged in remunerative work shall, if during the permitted period determined in accordance with regulation 2A beginning with the day after the day on which he has ceased to be so entitled he or his partner ceased to be engaged in that work, be re-entitled to a transitional addition of an amount equal to the amount by which his total benefit income in his first benefit week exceeds his total benefit income in the benefit week in which he becomes re-entitled, or the amount to which he was previously entitled, whichever is the lower.]

(5) The amount of a claimant's personal expenses addition shall be reduced if, in any benefit week, he is entitled only to a personal expenses addition, by the amount of any increase in his income [²but not if, and to the extent that, the increase is attributable to the receipt of a training allowance.]

(6) A claimant shall cease to be entitled to a personal expenses addition if—

   (a) in the case of a claimant who is entitled to income support as well as a personal expenses addition—

      (i) he ceases to be entitled to income support for a reason other than that his applicable amount under Part IV of the General Regulations (applicable amounts) does not exceed his income; or

      (ii) the amount of his personal expenses addition is reduced to nil by virtue of paragraph (5) or regulation 13(3).

   (b) in the case of a claimant who is entitled only to a personal expenses addition—

      (i) he would no longer, if he claimed, be entitled to income support for a reason other than that his applicable amount under Part IV of the General Regulations does not exceed his income; or

      (ii) the amount of his personal expenses addition is reduced to nil by virtue of paragraph (5) or regulation 13(3).

AMENDMENTS

1. Income Support (Transitional) Amendment Regulations 1988 (S.I. 1988 No. 521), reg. 9 (April 11, 1988).

2. Income Support (Transitional) Amendment No. 2 Regulations 1988 (S.I. 1988 No. 670). reg. 2 (April 11, 1988).

3. Income Support (Transitional) Amendment Regulations 1989 (S.I. 1989 No. 1626), reg. 3 (October 9, 1989).

4. Income Support (Transitional) Amendment No. 2 Regulations 1989 (S.I. 1989 No. 2340), reg. 2 (December 14, 1989).

5. Income Support (General and Transitional) Amendment Regulations 1990 (S.I. 1990 No. 2324), reg. 6 (December 17, 1990).

6. Enterprise (Scotland) Consequential Amendments Order 1991 (S.I. 1991 No. 387) arts. 2 and 10 (April 1, 1991).

7. Income Support (Transitional) Amendment Regulations 1991 (S.I. 1991 No. 1600), reg. 2 (October 1, 1991).

8. Income-related Benefits Amendment Regulations 1992 (S.I. 1992 No. 1326), reg. 3(4) (October 5, 1992).

DEFINITIONS

"applicable amount"—see 1986 Act, s.84(1).
"benefit week"—see reg. 2(1).
"claimant"—see General Regulations, reg. 2(1).
"first benefit week"—see reg. 2(1).
"General Regulations"—*ibid.*
"income support"—*ibid.*
"personal expenses addition"—*ibid.*
"second benefit week"—*ibid.*
"transitional addition"—*ibid.*

GENERAL NOTE

CIS 250/1992 rejects a contention that reg. 14 and in particular para. (1)(a) was invalid. It had been argued that para. (1)(a) was irrational as it made no distinction between claimants with differing needs and had maintained the claimant's income support at the same level while other claimants had had the benefit of annual up-rating increases. The Commissioner also follows *CIS 295/1989* which held that the Transitional Regulations were not in breach of the European Convention for the Protection of Human Rights (in particular Art. 14 and Art. 1 of the First Protocol).

Paragraph (1)

Two Commissioners' decisions have held that sub-para. (a) only applies to increases in the applicable amount in relation to its amount in the "second benefit week," *i.e.* the first week of the income support scheme in April 1988. In *CSIS 30/1989* the claimant's wife went into hospital for more than six weeks, so that the claimant's applicable amount was reduced under para. 1 of Sched. 7 to the Income Support (General) Regulations. When she came out of hospital, his applicable amount was increased to its previous level. The AO treated this as an increase under para. (1) and reduced the claimant's transitional addition by the same amount. The Commissioner held that there was not an increase under para. (1) because there was no increase against the base of the second benefit week. In *R(IS) 6/93* one of the claimant's children was taken into care and his applicable amount was accordingly reduced. The child later came back to live with the claimant and the applicable amount was restored. The AO reduced his transitional addition to nil. The Commissioner applied the principle of *CSIS 30/1989* to produce the same result. At the relevant time para. (1G) was not in force and so could not affect the interpretation of para. (1). But the Commissioner considered that it might not affect the principle anyway. An appeal to the Court of Appeal in *R(IS) 6/93* upholds the Commissioner's decision (*Chief Adjudication Officer v. Dommett*, March 12, 1992, appendix to *R(IS) 6/93*). But the Court of Appeal stresses the temporary nature of the change which produced the effect on the applicable amount.

Paragraph (2)

R(IS) 1/94 holds that where a person is detained in custody pending trial and his applicable amount is reduced to nil under para. 8(b) of Sched. 7, he ceases to be entitled to a transitional addition by virtue of sub-para. (a)(i). However, this does not seem correct. Sub-para. (a)(i) applies where a claimant ceases to be entitled to income support for a reason other than his applicable amount does not exceed his income. But in *R(IS) 1/94* the claimant ceased to be entitled because his applicable amount, reduced to nil, no longer exceeded his income, also apparently nil. Reg. 16(3) removes a prisoner's entitlement to a transitional addition, but arguably that only applies during the period in custody and does not cause the entitlement to cease. In *R(IS) 1/94* the claimant's transitional addition was less than £10 and so he could not have relied on para. (3) for its restoration on his release in any event. In *R(IS) 2/95*, which concerned another prisoner, the Commissioner takes the view that what led to his ceasing to be entitled to income support *was* the fact that his applicable amount had become nil and thus could not exceed his income.

Paragraph (3)

R(IS) 2/95 decides that where a person's applicable amount has been reduced to nil under para. 8 of Sched. 7 because he is a prisoner, this means that he has ceased to be entitled to income support. This is not a case where payment is denied of an underlying entitlement but under Sched. 7, para. 8, there is no entitlement at all. However, the claimant was not entitled to restoration of his transitional addition when he was released as he did not meet the other conditions of para. (3).

Special transitional addition

15.—(1) Subject to regulation 16 (persons not entitled to transitional additions), where the amount of a claimant's domestic assistance addition in respect of his first benefit week is £10 or more and is greater than the amount (if any) of the severe disability premium for the purpose of calculating his applicable amount under Part IV of the General Regulations (applicable amounts) [¹in his second benefit week], he shall be entitled to a special transitional addition of an amount equal to the difference between his domestic assistance addition and the severe disability premium [¹(if any)].

(2) Where a claimant is not entitled to income support or a transitional addition, the amount of a special transitional addition under paragraph (1) to which he is entitled shall be reduced by the amount of any increase in his income [²but not if, and to the extent that, the increase is attributable to the receipt of a training allowance] [⁴or to the receipt of an increase in the weekly rate of child benefit which is attributable to the amendments made by regulation 2 of the Child Benefit and Social Security (Fixing and Adjustment of Rates) Amendment No. 2 Regulations 1991.]

(3) Subject to paragraph (4) a claimant shall cease to be entitled to a special transitional addition under paragraph (1) if—

   (a) he ceases to be entitled to income support for a reason other than that his applicable amount under Part IV of the General Regulations (applicable amounts) does not exceed his income; or

   (b) his applicable amount for the purposes of calculating his entitlement to income support falls to be determined under Schedule 4 to, or paragraphs 1 to 4, 13 and 18 of Schedule 7 to, the General Regulations (applicable amounts for persons in residential care and nursing homes or residential accommodation or hospital patients); [¹or

   (c) in the case of a claimant who is entitled to income support as well as a transitional addition he ceases to be entitled to income support and a transitional addition for a reason other than that his applicable amount under Part IV of the General Regulations does not exceed his income; or

   (d) in the case of a claimant who is entitled to a transitional addition and a special transitional addition he would not, if he claimed, be entitled to income support for a reason other than that his applicable amount under Part IV of the General Regulations does not exceed his income; or

   (e) he would, but for this sub-paragraph, be entitled only to a special transitional addition and he would not, if he claimed, be entitled to income support for a reason other than that his applicable amount does not exceed his income; or

(f) the amount of his special transitional addition is reduced to nil by virtue of paragraph (2).]

(4) Where a claimant ceases to be entitled to a special transitional addition—

[¹(a) by virtue of paragraph (3)(a), (c), (d) or (e) he shall be re-entitled to such an addition of the same amount as previously if, [³during the permitted period determined in accordance with regulation 2A (permitted period) beginning with the day after] the day on which he ceased to be so entitled, he becomes re-entitled to income support or a transitional addition;]

(b) by virtue of paragraph (3)(b) he shall be re-entitled to such an addition of the same amount as previously if, [³during the permitted period determined in accordance with regulation 2A (permitted period) beginning with the day after] [¹the day on which his applicable amount fell to be determined under the provisions of the General Regulations referred to in paragraph (3)(b), those provisions ceased to apply to him.]

[¹(c) by virtue of paragraph (3) (f) he shall be re-entitled to such an addition of the same amount as previously if [³during the permitted period determined in accordance with regulation 2A (permitted period) beginning with the day after] the day on which he ceased to be so entitled the reason for the cessation ceased to apply to him.]

AMENDMENTS

1. Income Support (Transitional) Amendment Regulations 1988 (S.I. 1988 No. 521), reg. 10 (April 11, 1988).
2. Income Support (Transitional) Amendment No. 2 Regulations 1988 (S.I. 1988 No. 670), reg. 2(3) (April 11, 1988).
3. Income Support (Transitional) Amendment Regulations 1989 (S.I. 1989 No. 1626), reg. 4 (October 9, 1989).
4. Income Support (Transitional) Amendment Regulations 1991 (S.I. 1991 No. 1600), reg. 3 (October 1, 1991).

DEFINITIONS

"applicable amount"—see 1986 Act, s.84(1).
"claimant"—see General Regulations, reg. 2(1).
"domestic assistance addition"—see reg. 2(1).
"General Regulations"—*ibid.*
"income support"—*ibid.*
"transitional addition"—*ibid.*

GENERAL NOTE

The amounts of special transitional additions have been up-rated annually, most recently by 2.1 per cent. from April 12, 1999 under art. 19 of the Social Security Benefits Up-rating Order 1999 (S.I. 1999 No. 264).

Paragraph (3)
R(IS) 2/95 decides that where a person's applicable amount is reduced to nil under para. 8 of Sched. 7, he has ceased to be entitled to income support. Since the reason for this was that his applicable amount (nil) no longer exceeded his income (also nil), the claimant could not bring himself within sub-para. (c). He therefore could not rely on para. (4)(a) (even if he met its other conditions) for the restoration of his special transitional addition on his release.

Persons not entitled to transitional additions

16.—(1) A person without accommodation shall not be entitled to a transitional addition, personal expenses addition or a special transitional addition.

(2) A person who is in board and lodging accommodation or a hostel shall not be entitled to a special transitional addition.

[¹(3) A prisoner within the meaning of regulation 21(3) of the General Regulations (special cases) shall not be entitled to a transitional addition, personal expenses addition or special transitional addition.]

AMENDMENT

1. Income Support (Transitional) Amendment Regulations 1988 (S.I. 1988 No. 521), reg. 11 (April 11, 1988).

DEFINITIONS

"General Regulations"—see reg. 2(1).
"personal expenses addition"—*ibid.*
"special transitional addition"—*ibid.*
"transitional addition"—*ibid.*

GENERAL NOTE

Paragraph (3)
   See *R(IS) 1/94* and *R(IS) 2/95* in the notes to regs. 14 and 15.

Income Support (Transitional) Regulations 1988

(S.I. 1988 No. 1229)

Made by the Secretary of the State under s.18(4) of the Social Security Act 1988

GENERAL NOTE

These regulations protect couples where one partner is less than 18 who were entitled to benefit on September 11, 1988. Reg. 4 allows advance decisions reviewing entitlement from September 12, 1988.

Citation, commencement and interpretation

1.—(1) These Regulations may be cited as the Income Support (Transitional) Regulations 1988 and shall come into force as follows—
   (a) regulations 1 and 4, on 5th August 1988;
   (b) regulations 2 and 3, on 12th September 1988.
   (2) In these Regulations "the General Regulations" means the Income Support (General) Regulations 1987 and unless the context otherwise requires the expressions used in these regulations shall have the same meaning as in the General Regulations.

Couples

2.—(1) This regulation applies where, on 11th September 1988—
   (a) the claimant is a member of a couple and has continued after that date to be a member of the same couple; and
   (b) the claimant is entitled to income support; and
   (c) the claimant is aged not less than 18; and
   (d) the other member of that couple is aged less than 18 and had ceased full-time education on or before 11th April 1988.
   (2) This regulation shall cease to apply where the member of the couple to whom paragraph (1)(d) above refers attains the age of 18.

(3) Where this regulation applies—

(a) the claimant's applicable amount for the purpose of determining his entitlement to income support shall be determined as if paragraph 1(3)(c) of Schedule 2 to the General Regulations (applicable amounts) applied and paragraph 1(3)(a), (b), (d), (e) and (f) of that Schedule shall not apply; and

(b) regulation 23(4) of the General Regulations (calculation of income and capital) and paragraph 1(3) of Schedule 5 to the General Regulations (applicable amounts of persons in board and lodging accommodation or hostels) shall not apply.

Polygamous marriages

3.—(1) This regulation applies where, on 11th September 1988—

(a) the claimant is a member of a polygamous marriage and has continued after that date to be a member of that polygamous marriage; and

(b) the claimant is entitled to income support; and

(c) the claimant is aged not less than 18; and

(d) at least one other member of that marriage is aged less than 18 and had ceased full-time education on or before 11th April 1988

(2) This regulation shall cease to apply where the member of the polygamous marriage to whom paragraph (1)(d) above refers has, or if there is more than one such member, those members have, attained the age of 18.

(3) Where this regulation applies the claimant's applicable amount for the purpose of determining his entitlement to income support shall be determined as if regulations 18(2) and 23(5) of the General Regulations (polygamous marriages) did not apply.

Review of awards of income support

4.—(1) This regulation shall apply to a person who will be aged less than 18 on 12th September 1988.

(2) Any decision awarding income support to a person to whom this regulation applies may be reviewed under section 104 of the Social Security Act before 12th September 1988 as if—

(a) regulations 2 and 3 of these Regulations; and

(b) any amendments to the Act and any Regulations made under the Act to come into force not later than 12th September 1988,

were already in force.

(3) Any decision given on review in accordance with paragraph (2) shall have effect as from 12th September 1988.

Family Credit and Income Support (General) Amendment Regulations 1989

(S.I. 1989 No. 1034)

Made by the Secretary of State under ss.20(3)(a) and (d), 22(1), (8) and (9) and 84(1) of the Social Security Act 1986 and s.166(1) to (3A) of the Social Security Act 1975

[In force July 10, 1989]

Transitional provision

13. Where, immediately before the coming into force of regulation 4 of these Regulations, a person was entitled to income support by virtue of paragraph (2)(d) of regulation 13 of the Income Support Regulations, notwithstanding that he was to be treated as receiving relevant education under regulation 12 of those Regulations, that paragraph shall continue to apply to him as if the substitution made by regulation 4 of these Regulations had not been made for so long as he continues to satisfy the other conditions of entitlement to income support.

GENERAL NOTE

This regulation came into force on July 10, 1989, the same date as did the amendment to reg. 13 of the Income Support (General) Regulations. Anyone entitled under the old form of reg. 13(2)(d) on July 9, 1989, continues to have their entitlement determined under that provision. If there is any break in the claimant's satisfaction of the other conditions of entitlement to income support this transitional protection is lost. There can be a break in actual receipt of benefit providing that the conditions of entitlement are still met. But these conditions will include not only those set out in s.124(1) of the Contributions and Benefits Act (1986 Act, s.20(3)), but also the requirement to make a claim imposed by s.1 of the Administration Act (1975 Act, s.165A).

Social Security Benefits (Student Loans and Miscellaneous Amendments) Regulations 1990

(S.I. 1990 No. 1549)

Made by the Secretary of State under ss.20(3)(d), (8) and (12)(d), (g) to (i), 22(8) and (9), 29(3), 31C(3) and 84(1) of the Social Security Act 1986 and ss.17(2)(a), 20(3) and 166(1) to (3A) of the Social Security Act 1975

[In force September 1, 1990]

Transitional provision

7.—(1) Where, immediately before 1st September 1990, a student was entitled to housing benefit, income support or unemployment benefit, as the case may be, the Housing Benefit Regulations, the Income Support Regulations or the Unemployment Benefit Regulations, as the case may be, shall continue to apply to him as if the amendments made by regulation 4(2) to (6) and (9) to (11), 5(2) to (5) and (7) to (9) or 6 of these Regulations had not been made but only for the period ending immediately before the date on which he is due to start or is due to resume his course of study.

(2) In paragraph (1) the expression "student" has the same meaning as in the Housing Benefit Regulations, Income Support Regulations or Unemployment Benefit Regulations, as the case may be, as in force immediately before 1st September 1990.

GENERAL NOTE

The Housing Benefit Regulations are the Housing Benefit (General) Regulations 1987, the Income Support Regulations are the Income Support (General) Regulations 1987 and the Unemployment Benefit Regulations are the Social Security (Unemployment, Sickness and Invalidity Benefit) Regulations 1983.

Income Support (General) Amendment No. 4 Regulations 1991

(S.I. 1991 No. 1559)

Made by the Secretary of State under ss.20(3)(a) and (d)(i), (12)(c) and (d)(i), 22(1), (8), (9)(a) and (b) and 84(1) of the Social Security Act 1986 and s.166(1) to (3A) of the Social Security Act 1975

[In force, in relation to the amendments to reg. 6(a) of and to para. 6 of Sched. 1 to the General Regulations, on October 7, 1991, and in relation to the amendment to reg. 5(1) of the General Regulations, on April 7, 1992]

Saving provision

22.—(1) Where this regulation applies to a person, regulation 5 of, or, as the case may be, regulation 6(a) of, and paragraph 6 of Schedule 1 to, the General Regulations shall continue to apply to him until the occurrence of one of the events specified in regulation 23 of these Regulations as if the amendments made by regulation 3 or, as the case may be, regulations 4(a) and 13(b) of these Regulations, had not been made.

(2) This regulation applies to a person—

(a) who satisfied the relevant qualifying conditions in the week immediately preceding the date on which regulation 3 or, as the case may be, regulations 4(a) and 13(b) of these Regulations came into force; and

(b) who in that week was, or whose partner was, entitled to income support.

(3) This regulation applies to a person—

(a) who satisfied the relevant qualifying condition in at least one of the eight weeks immediately preceding the date on which regulation 3 or, as the case may be, regulations 4(a) and 13(b) of these Regulations came into force, but who did not satisfy that condition in the week immediately preceding that date; and

(b) who in the week in which he satisfied that condition was, or whose partner was, entitled to income support; and

(c) who in a week commencing not more than eight weeks after the date on which he last satisfied the relevant qualifying condition, again satisfies that condition and in that week he, or his partner, is entitled to income support.

(4) This regulation applies to a person—

(a) who, or whose partner, ceased to be entitled to income support because he, or his partner, became engaged in remunerative work for a period not exceeding the permitted period determined in accordance with regulation 24 of these Regulations and that period had commenced but had not ended before the coming into force of regulation 3 or regulations 4(a) and 13(b) of these Regulations, as the case may be; and

(b) who satisfied the relevant qualifying condition in the week immediately before that period commenced; and

(c) who in the week which commences immediately after the date on which that period ends, again satisfies the relevant qualifying condition and in that week he, or his partner, is entitled to income support.

(5) This regulation applies to a person—

(a) who, or whose partner, was entitled to income support immediately before he or his partner participated in arrangements for training made under section 2 of the Employment and Training Act 1973 or section 2 of the Enterprise and New Towns (Scotland) Act 1990 or attended a course at an employment rehabilitation centre established under section 2 of the Employment and Training Act 1973 and that training or course had commenced but had not ended before the coming into force of regulation 3 or regulations 4(a) and 13(b) of these Regulations, as the case may be; and

(b) who satisfied the relevant qualifying condition in the week immediately before the commencement of the period during which he or his partner participated in that training or attended that course; and

(c) who in a week commencing not more than eight weeks after the date on which that period ends, again satisfies the relevant qualifying condition and in that week he, or his partner, is entitled to income support.

(6) For the purpose of determining whether—

(a) regulation 5 of the General Regulations continues to apply to a person as if the amendment made thereto by regulation 3 of these Regulations had not been made, the relevant qualifying condition is that he is engaged in work, or where the hours of work fluctuate, engaged on average, for at least 16 hours but less than 24 hours a week; or

(b) regulation 6(a) of, and paragraph 6 of Schedule 1 to, the General Regulations continue to apply to a person as if the amendments made thereto by regulations 4(a) and 13(b) of these Regulations had not been made, the relevant qualifying condition is that he is engaged in work, he is mentally or physically disabled and his earning capacity is, by reason of that disability, reduced to 75 per cent. or less of what he would, but for that disability, be reasonably expected to earn.

(7) In this regulation and in regulations 23 and 24 of these Regulations except where the context otherwise requires, the terms used have the same meanings as in the General Regulations.

Circumstances in which regulation 22 ceases to apply

23.—(1) Subject to paragraph (2) of this regulation, regulation 22 of these Regulations shall cease to apply to a person if—

(a) he ceases to satisfy the relevant qualifying condition; or

(b) he, or his partner, ceases to be entitled to income support,

for a period in excess of eight consecutive weeks.

(2) For the purposes of paragraph (1) of this regulation—

(a) except where sub-paragraph (b) of this paragraph applies, in a case where the person, or his partner, ceases to be entitled to income support because he, or his partner, becomes engaged in remunerative work, no account shall be taken of any period during which he, or his partner, was not entitled to income support, not exceeding the permitted period determined in accordance with regulation 24 of these Regulations;

(b) no account shall be taken of—

(i) any period during which the person, or his partner, was participating in arrangements for training made under section 2 of the Employment and Training Act 1973 or section 2 of the Enterprise and New Towns (Scotland) Act 1990 or attending a course at an employment rehabilitation centre established under section 2 of the Employment and Training Act 1973; and

(ii) a further period not exceeding eight consecutive weeks commencing immediately after the end of the period referred to in head (i) of this sub-paragraph.

Permitted period

24.—(1) For the purposes of regulations 22 and 23 of these Regulations, where a person has ceased to be entitled to income support—

(a) because he, or his partner, becomes engaged in remunerative work the permitted period, [¹. . .] shall be twelve weeks; or
(b) for any other reason, the permitted period shall be eight weeks.
(2) [¹. . .]
(3) [¹. . .].

AMENDMENT

1. Income Support (General) (Jobseeker's Allowance Consequential Amendments) Regulations 1996 (S.I. 1996 No. 206), reg. 30 (October 7, 1996).

Income Support (General) Amendment No. 6 Regulations 1991

(S.I. 1991 No. 2334)

Made by the Secretary of State under ss.22(1) and 84(1) of the Social Security Act 1986 and s.166(1) to (3A) of the Social Security Act 1975

[In force November 11, 1991]

Saving Provision in relation to Severe Disability Premium

4.—(1)The provisions of this regulation are subject to regulation 5.
(2) Where paragraph (3), (4), (5) or (6) applies to a claimant, sub-paragraph (2)(a)(ii), or, as the case may be, sub-paragraph (2)(b)(iii) of paragraph 13 of Schedule 2 to the General Regulations shall have effect as if the relevant amendment had not been made.
(3) This paragraph applies to a claimant who satisfied both the qualifying conditions in the week immediately preceding 21st October 1991.
(4) This paragraph applies to a claimant—
(a) who satisfied both the qualifying conditions in at least one of the eight weeks immediately preceding 21st October 1991, but did not satisfy either or both of those conditions in the week immediately preceding that date; and
(b) who in a week commencing not more than eight weeks after the date on which he last satisfied both the qualifying conditions, would again have satisfied both those conditions if the relevant amendment had not been made.
(5) This paragraph applies to a claimant—
(a) who ceased to be entitled to income support because he became engaged in remunerative work for a period not exceeding the permitted period determined in accordance with regulation 6 and that period had commenced but had not ended before 21st October 1991; and
(b) who satisfied both the qualifying conditions in the week ending on the day before the first day of that period commenced; and
(c) who in the week which commences on the day immediately following the day on which that period ends, would again have satisfied both the qualifying conditions if the relevent amendment had not been made.
(6) This paragraph applies to a claimant—
(a) who satisfied both the qualifying conditions immediately before he—
    (i) participated in arrangements for training made under section 2 of the Employment and Training Act 1973 or section 2 of the Enterprise and New Towns (Scotland) Act 1990; or
    (ii) attended a course at an employment rehabilitation centre established under section 2 of the Employment and Training Act 1973,
    and he had begun the training or joined the course before 21st October

1991 and was still continuing with the training or course at that date; and

(b) who in the week which commences on the day immediately following the last day he attended the training or course, would again have satisfied both the qualifying conditions if the relevant amendment had not been made.

(7) The "qualifying conditions" means the two qualifying conditions set out in paragraph (8)(a) and (b) below.

(8) For the purposes of paragraph (7)—

(a) the first qualifying condition is that the claimant—

(i) has made a claim for income support which has not been determined, but had it been determined and an award made, his applicable amount would have included severe disability premium; or

(ii) has a current award of income support and the applicable amount appropriate to that award includes severe disability premium; or

(iii) has a current award of income support and has before 21st October 1991 made an application in writing in accordance with section 104(2) of the Social Security Act requesting a review of that award, where the ground, or one of the grounds for review, is that—

(aa) he has become a co-owner with a close relative of the dwelling which he and that close relative jointly occupy as their home; or

(bb) he has become jointly liable with a close relative to make payments to a landlord in respect of the dwelling which he and that close relative jointly occupy as their home,

whether or not there are other co-owners or other persons jointly liable to make such payments and, if revised, the applicable amount appropriate to the award includes severe disability premium in respect of a period prior to that date;

(b) the second qualifying condition is that the person is—

(i) a co-owner, with a close relative, of the dwelling he and that close relative jointly occupy as their home, whether or not there are other co-owners; or

(ii) jointly liable, with a close relative, to make payments to a landlord in respect of the dwelling he and that close relative jointly occupy as their home, whether or not there are other persons jointly liable to make such payments.

[¹(9) For the purposes of paragraph (8)(b) and regulation 5(2)(b), where a person has satisfied the second qualifying condition, but his circumstances change so that he no longer satisfies it, he shall nonetheless be treated as satisfying it for so long as he is a person to whom paragraph (10) applies.

(10) This paragraph applies to a person—

(a) who was, together with a close relative of his, either a co-owner of, or jointly liable to make payments to a landlord in respect of, the dwelling which he and that close relative jointly occupied as their home; and

(b) who has since become, with that close relative or any other close relative, either—

(i) jointly liable to make payments to a landlord in respect of that dwelling or any other dwelling; or

(ii) a co-owner of that dwelling or any other dwelling,

which he and the close relative jointly occupy as their home (whether or not there are other co-owners, or other persons jointly liable to make such payments).]

AMENDMENT

1. Income-related Benefits Schemes (Miscellaneous Provisions) Amendment Regulations 1991 (S.I. 1991 No. 2695), reg. 5 (December 27, 1991).

DEFINITIONS

"claimant"—see General Regulations, reg. 2(1).
"close relative"—*ibid.*
"dwelling occupies as the home"—*ibid.*
"partner"—*ibid.*
"permitted period"—see reg. 6.
"relevant amendment"—see General Note.
"remunerative work"—see General Regulations, reg. 2(1).
"Social Security Act"—*ibid.*

GENERAL NOTE

The "relevant amendment" is the amendment to the definition of non-dependant in reg. 3 of the Income Support (General) Regulations with effect from November 11, 1991, by reg. 2 of these Regulations (reg. 1(3)). These Regulations were made on October 21, 1991, which is why that is the date used in reg. 4 to fix the transitional protection. Reg. 4 allows existing claimants to continue to receive the benefit of the severe disability premium where they previously met the new conditions for joint occupiers of the home, except that the joint occupation was with a close relative.

Reg. 5 defines when the protection of reg. 4 ceases to apply.

Circumstances in which regulation 4 ceases to apply

5.—(1) Regulation 4 shall cease to apply to a claimant, or his partner, on the relevant day and shall not apply on any day thereafter.

(2) The relevant day is the first day after a period of eight consecutive weeks throughout which—

(a) subject to paragraph (3), he is not entiled to income support; or

(b) he is unable to satisfy, or be treated as satisfying, the second qualifying condition.

(3) For the purpose of calculating a period in excess of eight weeks in paragraph (2)(a) above the following periods shall be disregarded—

(a) where the claimant, or his partner, becomes engaged in remunerative work, any period during which he, or his partner, was not entitled to income support, not exceeding the permitted period determined in accordance with regulation 6;

(b) any period during which the claimant, or his partner, was participating in arrangements for training made under section 2 of the Employment and Training Act 1973 or section 2 of the Enterprise and New Towns (Scotland) Act 1990 or attending a course at an employment rehabilitation centre established under section 2 of the Employment and Training Act 1973.

DEFINITIONS

"claimant"—see General Regulations, reg. 2(1).
"partner"—*ibid.*
"permitted period"—see reg. 6.
"qualifying condition"—see reg. 4(7).

Definition of 'permitted period' for the purposes of regulations 4 and 5

6.—(1) For the purposes of regulations 4(5) and 5(3)(a), where a claimant has ceased to be entitled to income support because he or his partner became engaged in remunerative work, [¹. . .] the permitted period shall be a period of 12 consecutive weeks.

(2) [¹. . .]
(3) [¹. . .]

AMENDMENT

1. Income Support (General) (Jobseeker's Allowance Consequential Amendments) Regulations 1996 (S.I. 1996 No. 206), reg. 31 (October 7, 1996).

DEFINITIONS

"claimant"—see General Regulations, reg. 2(1).
"partner"—*ibid.*
"relevant education"—see General Regulations, reg. 12.
"remunerative work"—see General Regulations, reg. 2(1).
"student"—*ibid.*

Income Support (General) Amendment Regulations 1992

(S.I. 1992 No. 468)

Made by the Secretary of State under ss.20(3)(a) and (d) and (12)(c), (d)(i), (f) and (k), 22(1), (8) and (9) and 84(1) of the Social Security Act 1986, s.166(1) to (3A) of the Social Security Act 1975 and s.5(1) of the Disability Living Allowance and Disability Working Allowance Act 1991

[In force April 6, 1992]

Saving provision for children and young persons working 16 or more, but less than 24, hours a week

10.—(1) Paragraph (2) below shall apply subject to paragraph (3) below where in the benefit week which in relation to a particular claimant commences on or after 7th April but before 14th April 1992, a child or young person in respect of whom a sum is brought into account in determining the claimant's applicable amount would but for this regulation—
  (a) be engaged in remunerative work by reason of the fact that the work in which he is engaged, or where his hours of work fluctuate, in which he is engaged on average, amounts to 16 or more but less than 24 hours a week, being work for which payment is made or which is done in expectation of payment; and
  (b) have earnings from that work which fall to be disregarded in accordance with regulation 44(6) of and paragraph 15 of Schedule 8 to the General Regulations.
(2) Where this paragraph applies, regulation 5(1) of the General Regulations (persons treated as engaged in remunerative work) shall have effect in relation to the child or young person mentioned in paragraph (1) above as if for the reference to 16 hours there was substitued a reference to 24 hours; so however that this paragraph shall not apply in relation to him on any day on which he is neither a child nor a young person.
(3) Paragraph (2) above shall not apply where, in relation to the particular claimant, the benefit week mentioned in paragraph (1) above is his first benefit week pursuant to the claim.
(4) In this regulation, the expression 'young person' has the same meaning as it has in the General Regulations (by virtue of regulation 14).

DEFINITIONS

"child"—see 1986 Act, s.20(11) (SSCBA, s.137(1)).
"the General Regulations"—the Income Support (General) Regulations 1987 (reg. 1(4)).

GENERAL NOTE

Normally any earnings of a child or young person who is a member of the claimant's family are completely disregarded (General Regulations, Sched. 8, para. 14). But under para. 15 of Sched. 8, as amended from April 1992, if the child or young person has ceased actually to be in relevant education and is treated as continuing in relevant education up to the next "terminal date," earnings from employment for more hours than the limit for part-time work are not completely disregarded. Before April 1992 the limit was 24 hours. On April 7, 1992, it changed to 16 hours. This provision protects the position of a claimant with a child or young person in this position who was working for less than 24 hours a week, but more than 16 hours a week, immediately before the change. The protection is short-lived, as the status of child or young person will expire when the terminal date is reached.

Introduction of disability living allowance

11.—(1) Any payment of disability living allowance made pursuant to the Social Security Act 1975 [SSCBA] which, in accordance with regulation 31 of the General Regulations is treated as paid on a day before this regulation comes into force, shall be treated for the purposes of Parts V and VI of those Regulations (which contain provisions for the calculation of income and capital)—

    (a) as a payment of mobility allowance, to the extent that it consists of mobility component; and

    (b) as a payment of attendance allowance, to the extent that it consists of care component.

(2) Where—

    (a) on or after the date this regulation comes into force a payment falls to be made and that payment includes an amount in respect both of disability living allowance and of attendance allowance, mobility allowance or both ('the former benefits'); and

    (b) payment of disability living allowance and the former benefits would but for this regulation be regarded, pursuant to regulation 29(2) of the General Regulations as being made for concurrent periods commencing on the same day,

then that regulation shall have effect as if the payment falling to be made consisted solely of disability living allowance.

(3) In this regulation—

    (a) attendance allowance means an attendance allowance under section 35 of the Social Security Act 1975 [SSCBA, s.64];

    (b) mobility allowance means an allowance under section 37A of that Act;

    (c) disability living allowance means an allowance under section 37ZA of that Act [SSCBA, s.71]; and

    (d) any reference to the day the regulation comes into force is a reference to the day determined, in the particular case, in accordance with regulation 1(2) above.

DEFINITION

"the General Regulations"—the Income Support (General) Regulations 1987 (reg. 1(4)).

Income Support (General) Amendment (No. 2) Regulations 1993

(S.I. 1993 No. 1219)

Made by the Secretary of State under ss.135(1), 137(1) and 175(1) to (5) of the Social Security Contributions and Benefits Act 1992

[In force May 31, 1993]

Transitional provisions

3. Where—

(a) on 31st May 1993 a person is temporarily absent from a home, and his absence forms part of a period which on that day exceeded 6 days, and

(b) before that day paragraph 2A of Schedule 2 to the principal Regulations as in force on 30th May 1993 applied to him,

he shall be treated for the purposes of paragraph 2A of Schedule 2 to the principal Regulations, as amended by regulation 2 above, as if his first day of absence was 31st May 1993.

GENERAL NOTE

See the notes to para. 2A of Sched. 2 to the Income Support (General) Regulations. Para. 2A of Sched. 2 was amended by reg. 2 of these Regulations on May 31, 1993.

Income Support (General) Amendment No. 3 Regulations 1993

(S.I. 1993 No. 1679)

Made by the Secretary of State under ss.135(1), 136(5)(b), 137(1) and 175(1) to (4) of the Social Security Contributions and Benefits Act 1992

[In force August 2, 1993]

2.—(4) In the case of a claimant who was entitled to income support by virtue of regulation 70 of the Income Support Regulations for the benefit week which includes 2nd August 1993, then in respect of each day after that date on which the claimant's entitlement to income support continues, regulation 70 shall continue to apply in his case as if the preceding provisions of this regulation had not been made.

GENERAL NOTE

See the notes to reg. 70(3) in the 1995 edition of this book. Reg. 70(3) was amended by reg. 2(1) to (3) of these Regulations on August 2, 1993.

Saving

4.—(1) In the case of a claimant who was entitled to income support for the benefit week which included 2nd August 1993 then, but subject to paragraph (3), in respect of each day after that date on which the claimant's entitlement to income support continues, Schedule 3 to the Income Support Regulations shall continue to apply in his case as if regulation 3 of these Regulations had not been made.

(2) Heads (c) to (f) of sub-paragraph (9) of paragraph 7 of Schedule 3 to the Income Support Regulations shall apply to paragraph (1) above as they apply to sub-paragraph (1) of paragraph 7, but with the modification that for the words "in receipt of income support", wherever they occur, there were substituted the words "entitled to income support" and that the words "Subject to sub-paragraphs (10) and (11)" were omitted.

(3) In its application to any loan taken out or increased after 2nd August 1993 Schedule 3 to the Income Support Regulations shall have effect as amended by regulation 3 of these Regulations.

(4) Paragraphs (1) and (3) above shall apply as from 11th April 1994 as if for the references to "2nd August 1993" wherever they occur there were substituted references to "11th April 1994".

GENERAL NOTE

See the notes to para. 7(6B) to (6F) of the former Sched. 3 to the Income Support (General) Regulations in the 1995 edition of this book. Para. 7 of the former Sched. 3 was amended by reg. 3 of these regulations on August 2, 1993. See also the notes to para. 11(4)–(11) of the new Sched. 3.

Income-related Benefits Schemes (Miscellaneous Amendments) (No. 3) Regulations 1994

(S.I. 1994 No. 1807)

Made by the Secretary of State under ss.131(3)(b), 135(1), 137(1) and (2)(i) and 175(1), (3) and (4) of the Social Security Contributions and Benefits Act 1992

[In force August 1, 1994]

4.—(2) The provisions of this regulation shall only apply in the case of a claimant who was entitled to income support on 31st July 1994 where a claim for income support is made or treated as made by or in respect of him after that date, and where those provisions do apply they shall apply from the first day of the period in respect of which that claim is made.

GENERAL NOTE

See the note to the amendment to reg. 21(3) of the Income Support Regulations inserted by reg. 4(1) of these regulations.

Where there is a change of circumstances a claimant may be required to fill in a new claim form for administrative purposes, but this is not necessarily a new or repeat claim. If a person is protected by this provision and there is a review of his claim (*e.g.* because of a change of circumstances) he should continue to have the benefit of that protection.

Disability Working Allowance and Income Support (General) Amendment Regulations 1995

(S.I. 1995 No. 482)

Made by the Secretary of State under ss.124(1)(d)(i) and (3), 129(2B)(b) and (c) and (8), 135(1), 137(1) and 175(1), (3) and (4) of the Social Security Contributions and Benefits Act 1992 and s.12(1) of the Social Security (Incapacity for Work) Act 1994

[In force April 13, 1995]

Transitional provisions with respect to the Income Support Regulations

19.—(1) Sickness benefit shall be a qualifying benefit for the purposes of regulation 9(2)(a)(i) of the Income Support Regulations, and for this purpose "sickness benefit" means sickness benefit under section 31 of the Social Security Contributions and Benefits Act 1992 as in force on 12th April 1995.

(2) Where the disability premium was applicable to a claimant on 12th April 1995 by virtue of paragraph 12(1)(b) of Schedule 2 to the Income Support Regulations as in force on that date, the disability premium shall continue to be applicable to that claimant for so long as paragraph 12(1)(b)(i) of that Schedule applies to him.

(3) Paragraph (2) shall not apply to a claimant to whom paragraph 12(1)(b)(i) of Schedule 2 to the Income Support Regulations has ceased to apply for a period of more than 56 continuous days.

(4) Where on 12th April 1995 paragraph 5 of Schedule 1 to the Income Support Regulations (persons incapable of work) as in force on that date applied to a claimant, but the disability premium was not applicable to him, that claimant shall be treated for the purposes of paragraph 12(1) of Schedule 2 to the Income Support Regulations as if, throughout the period that paragraph 5 of Schedule 1 had applied to him, paragraph 12(1)(b)(i) of Schedule 2 applied to him.

(5) Where an adjudication officer on or after 13th April 1995, determines that a claimant fails to satisfy the incapacity for work test, in accordance with regulations made under section 171C of the Contributions and Benefits Act (the all work test), on its first application to the claimant concerned, and the claimant, immediately prior to [[1]13th April 1995], was either—

(a) incapable of work and had been so for a continuous period of 28 weeks in circumstances to which paragraph 5 of Schedule 1 of the Income Support Regulations refers (persons incapable of work not required to be available for employment); or

(b) in receipt of invalidity benefit or severe disablement allowance,

then, in a case in which either regulations 8(2A) or 11(2A) of the Income Support Regulations applies (persons not required to be available for employment and registration for employment), notwithstanding regulation 22(1A) and (5A) of the Income Support Regulations (reductions in applicable amounts), the amount of any income support to which the claimant is entitled shall be calculated in accordance with regulation 17 of those Regulations.

[[1](6) Where—

(a) a determination of the amount of a person's benefit has been made in a case to which paragraph (5) of this regulation, as originally made, had effect; and

(b) an appeal to which regulation 8(2A) or 11(2A) of the Income Support Regulations (persons not required to be available or registered for employment) refers, remains outstanding on 2nd October 1995;

the amount of any benefit to which he is entitled shall continue to be determined under paragraph (5), as originally made, until the determination of the appeal.]

Savings with respect to the Income Support Regulations

20.—(1) Where a person was not required to be available for employment on 12th April 1995 by virtue of regulation 8(2) of the Income Support Regulations as in force on that date, that regulation shall continue to apply in that person's case as if regulation 6 of these Regulations had not been made.

(2) Where a claimant was not required to register for employment on 12th April 1995 by virtue of regulation 11(2) of the Income Support Regulations as in force on that date, that regulation shall continue to apply in that claimant's case as if regulation 8 of these Regulations had not been made.

(3) Where a claimant appeals against a decision of an adjudication officer that he is not incapable of work, and that decision was made on or before 12th April 1995, regulations 8 and 11 of the Income Support Regulations shall apply in that claimant's case as if these Regulations had not been made.

(4) Where the higher pensioner premium was applicable to a claimant on, or at any time during the 8 weeks immediately preceding, 12th April 1995 by virtue of paragraph 12(1)(c)(i) of Schedule 2 to the Income Support Regulations as in force on that date, paragraph 12 of that Schedule shall continue to apply in that claimant's case as if regulation 16 of these Regulations had not been made.

AMENDMENT

1. Income-related Benefits Schemes and Social Security (Claims and Payments) (Miscellaneous Amendments) Regulations 1995 (S.I. 1995 No. 2303), reg. 8(2) (October 2, 1995).

General Note

These transitional and saving provisions relate to some of the amendments made to the Income Support Regulations as a consequence of the introduction of incapacity benefit and the new tests for deciding incapacity for work from April 13, 1995. See the notes to reg. 22A of, and paras. 24–27 of Sched. 1B to, the Income Support Regulations.

Reg. 19(5) was amended on October 2, 1995 to make it clear that it only applied to people who had been incapable of work for 28 weeks or in receipt of invalidity benefit or severe disablement allowance immediately before April 13, 1995 (and not to people who were so incapable, etc. by the date of the adjudication officer's decision). Reg. 19(6) allows payment of full income support under the previous form of reg. 19(5) to those whose appeals are outstanding on October 2, 1995 until the appeal has been determined. This should mean the final determination of the appeal, *e.g.*, if it is taken to the Social Security Commissioner.

See the further transitional protection in reg. 27(3) of the Income Support (General) (Jobseeker's Allowance Consequential Amendments) Regulations 1996 (p. 499).

Income-related Benefits Schemes (Miscellaneous Amendments) Regulations 1995

(S.I. 1995 No. 516)

Made by the Secretary of State under ss.123(1)(a) to (c), 128(5), 129(4) and (8), 135(1), 136(3), (5)(a) and (b), 137(1), (2)(c) and (d)(i) and 175(1), (3) and (4) of the Social Security Contributions and Benefits Act 1992

[In force April 10, 1995]

Saving

28.—(1) In the case of a claimant who was entitled to income support for the benefit week which included 9th April 1995 then, but subject to paragraph (3), in respect of each day after that date on which the claimant's entitlement to income support continues, Schedule 3 to the Income Support Regulations shall continue to have effect as though regulation 25(c) of these Regulations had not been made.

(2) Heads (c) to (f) of sub-paragraph (9) of paragraph 7 of Schedule 3 to the Income Support Regulations shall apply to paragraph (1) above as they apply to sub-paragraph (1) of paragraph 7, but with the modification that for the words "in receipt of income support", wherever they appear, there were substituted the words "entitled to income support" and that the words "Subject to sub-paragraphs (10) and (11)" were omitted.

(3) In its application to any loan taken out or increased after 9th April 1995, Schedule 3 to the Income Support Regulations shall have effect as amended by regulation 25(c) of these Regulations.

DEFINITION

"claimant"—see General Regulations, reg. 2(1).

General Note

See the notes to para. 7(6B) to (6F) of the former Sched. 3 to the Income Support (General) Regulations in the 1995 edition of this book. Para. 7(6C) of the former Sched. 3 was amended by reg. 25(c) of these Regulations on April 10, 1995. See also the notes to para. 11(4)–(11) of the new Sched. 3.

Social Security (Income Support and Claims and Payments) Amendment Regulations 1995

(S.I. 1995 No. 1613)

Made by the Secretary of State under ss.135(1), 136(5)(b), 137(1) and 175(1) and (3)–(5) of the Social Security Contributions and Benefits Act 1992 and ss.5(1)(p). 15A(2), 189(1) and (4) and 191 of the Social Security Administration Act 1992

[In force October 2, 1995]

Revocations and savings

5.—(2) The revocation by paragraph (1) above and Schedule 4 to these Regulations of any provision previously amended or substituted but subject to a saving for existing beneficiaries does not affect the continued operation of those savings.

GENERAL NOTE

See the notes to paras. 11(4)–(11) of Sched. 3 to the Income Support Regulations.

Income Support (General) Amendment and Transitional Regulations 1995

(S.I. 1995 No. 2287)

Made by the Secretary of State under ss.135(1), 137(1) and 175(1) and (3) to (5) of the Social Security Contributions and Benefits Act 1992

[In force October 2, 1995]

Transitional protection

3.—(1) Where a claimant for income support whose applicable amount, in the benefit week which included 1st October 1995, included an amount in respect of the interest on a loan or part of a loan by virtue of paragraph 7(6), 7(7) or 8(1)(a) of Schedule 3 to the Income Support Regulations (housing costs) ("the former paragraphs") as then in force and that loan or part of a loan is not a qualifying loan for the purposes of paragraphs 15 and 16 of Schedule 3 to the Income Support Regulations, paragraphs (2) and (3) shall have effect in his case.

(2) A loan or part of a loan to which paragraph (1) applies shall qualify as a loan to which paragraph 15 or 16, as the case may be, of Schedule 3 to the Income Support Regulations applies, for as long as any of the former paragraphs would have continued to be satisifed had it remained in force and the claimant remains in receipt of income support or is treated as being in receipt of income support.

(3) Heads (a), (c) and (e) of sub-paragraph (1) of paragraph 14 of Schedule 3 to the Income Support Regulations shall apply to paragraph (2) above as they apply to Schedule 3, but as if the words "Subject to sub-paragraph (2)" at the beginning were omitted.

DEFINITION

"claimant"—see General Regulations, reg. 2(1).

497

GENERAL NOTE

See the note to para. 7 of Sched. 3 to the Income Support Regulations.

Income-related Benefits Schemes and Social Security (Claims and Payments) (Miscellaneous Amendments) Regulations 1995

(S.I. 1995 No. 2303)

Made by the Secretary of State under ss.123(1), 124(1)(d), 129(3), 130(2) and (4), 135(1), 136(1) and (3)–(5), 137(1) and (2)(b), (d), (h), (i) and (l) and 175(1) and (3)–(6) of the Social Security Contributions and Benefits Act 1992 and ss.5(1)(h), (i) and (o), 6(1)(h) and (i) and 189 of the Social Security Administration Act

[In force October 2, 1995]

Transitional provision with respect to the Income Support Regulations

8.—(1) In determining whether a claimant is entitled to income support on or after 2nd October 1995 and whether he satisfies the provisions of either—
  (a) regulation 4(2)(c)(v) of the Income Support Regulations (temporary absence from Great Britain); or
  (b) paragraph 7 of Schedule 1 to those Regulations (disabled students not required to be available for work);
in a case where the claimant, for a period up to and including 12th April 1995, was continuously incapable of work for the purposes of paragraph 5 of Schedule 1 to the Income Support Regulations, as it was then in force, that period of incapacity shall be treated as forming part of a subsequent period of incapacity beginning not later than 7th June 1995 to which the provisions referred to in paragraphs (a) or (b) above refer and which is continuous to the date of the determination in question.

DEFINITION

"claimant"—see General Regulations, reg. 2(1).

GENERAL NOTE

See the notes to reg. 4(2)(c)(v) of the Income Support Regulations. For para. 7 of Sched. 1 see the 1996 edition of this book.

Social Security (Persons from Abroad) Miscellaneous Amendments Regulations 1996

(S.I. 1996 No. 30)

Made by the Secretary of State under ss.64(1), 68(4)(c)(i), 70(4), 71(6), 123(1), 124(1), 128(1), 129(1), 130(1) and (2), 131(1) and (3), 135, 137(1) and (2)(a) and (i) and 175(1) and (3)–(5) of the Social Security Contributions and Benefits Act 1992 and s.5(1)(r) of the Social Security Administration Act 1992

[In force February 5, 1996]

Saving

12.—(1) Where, before the coming into force of these Regulations, a person who becomes an asylum seeker under regulation 4A(5)(a)(i) of the Council Tax Benefit Regulations, regulation 7A(5)(a)(i) of the Housing Benefit Regulations or regulation 70(3A)(a) of the Income Support Regulations, as the case may be, is entitled to benefit under any of those Regulations, those provisions of those Regulations as then in force shall continue to have effect [¹(both as regards him and as regards persons who are members of his family at the coming into force of these Regulations)] as if regulations 3(a) and (b), 7(a) and (b) or 8(2) and (3)(c), as the case may be, of these Regulations had not been made.

(2) Where, before the coming into force of these Regulations, a person in respect of whom an undertaking was given by another person or persons to be responsible for his maintenance and accommodation, claimed benefit to which he is entitled, or is receiving benefit, under the Council Tax Benefit Regulations, the Housing Benefit Regulations or the Income Support Regulations, as the case may be, those Regulations as then in force shall have effect as if regulations 3, 7 or 8, as the case may be, of these Regulations had not been made.

AMENDMENT

1. Asylum and Immigration Act 1996, Sched. 1, para. 5 (July 24, 1996).

GENERAL NOTE

See the notes to "person from abroad" in reg. 21(3) and to reg. 70 of the Income Support Regulations.

Income Support (General) (Jobseeker's Allowance Consequential Amendments) Regulations 1996

(S.I. 1996 No. 206)

Made by the Secretary of State under s.40 of the Jobseekers Act 1995 and ss. 124(1)(e), 137(1) and 175(1) to (4) of the Social Security Contributions and Benefits Act 1992.

[In force October 7, 1996]

Transitional provisions

27.—(1) Where on 6th October 1996 or at any time during the eight weeks immediately preceding that date paragraph 4(1) of Schedule 1 to the principal Regulations (persons caring for another person) as in force on that date applied to a claimant, or would have applied to him if he had made a claim for income support, the claimant shall be treated for the purposes of paragraphs 5 and 6 of Schedule 1B to the principal Regulations as if, throughout the period that paragraph 4(1) of Schedule 1 applied or would have applied to him, paragraph 4 of Schedule 1B had applied or would have applied to him.

(2) Where on 6th October 1996 paragraph 5 of Schedule 1 to the principal Regulations (persons incapable of work) as in force on that date applied to a claimant, the claimant shall be treated for the purposes of regulation 4(2)(c)(v) of and paragraph 10 of Schedule 1B to the principal Regulations as if, throughout the period that paragraph 5 of Schedule 1 applied to him, paragraph 7 of Schedule 1B had applied to him.

(3) Where—

    (a) a determination of the amount of a person's benefit has been made in a case to which regulation 19(5) of The Disability Working Allowance and Income Support (General) Amendment Regulations 1995 as originally made had effect (amendments consequential on the coming into force of the Social Security (Incapacity for Work) Act 1994: transitional provisions); and

    (b) an appeal to which regulations 8(2A) or 11(2A) of the principal Regulations as in force on 2nd October 1995 referred (persons not required to be available or registered for employment), has still to be determined,

regulation 22A(1) of the principal Regulations (reduction in applicable amount where the claimant is appealing against a decision that he is not incapable of work) shall not apply to that person.

DEFINITION

    "claimant"—see General Regulations, reg. 2(1).

GENERAL NOTE

    These transitional provisions relate to the some of the changes made to the income support scheme as a result of the introduction of JSA on October 7, 1996. On para. (3) see the notes to regs. 19 and 20 of the Disability Working Allowance and Income Support (General) Amendment Regulations 1995 on p. 494 and reg. 22A of the Income Support Regulations.

Continuity with jobseeker's allowance

    32. In determining whether a person is entitled to income support [¹or is to be treated as being in receipt of income support or whether any amount is applicable or payable—

    (a) entitlement to an income-based jobseeker's allowance shall be treated as entitlement to income support for the purposes of any requirement that a person is or has been entitled to income support for any period of time; and

    (b) a person who is treated as being in receipt of income-based jobseeker's allowance shall be treated as being in receipt of income support for the purposes of any requirement that he is or has been treated as being in receipt of income support for any period of time.]

AMENDMENT

    1. Income-related Benefits Schemes and Social Fund (Miscellaneous Amendments) Regulations 1996 (S.I. 1996 No. 1944), reg. 12 (October 7, 1996).

GENERAL NOTE

    Para. (a) of this important provision allows entitlement to income-based JSA to count as entitlement to income support for the purposes of satisfying any requirement that the person is or has been entitled to income support for any period of time. Para. (b) has the same effect where the requirement is that the person is or has been treated as being in receipt of income support. This could be relevant, for example, in relation to waiting periods or the linking rules for payment of housing costs. For the JSA provision see para. 18(1)(c) of Sched. 2 to the JSA Regulations.

Income-related Benefits Schemes and Social Fund (Miscellaneous Amendments) Regulations 1996

(S.I. 1996 No. 1944)

Made by the Secretary of State under ss. 123(1), 128(3), 129(6), 130(5), 131(3)(b), 135(1), 136(3) to (5), 137(1) and (2)(a), (d), (i) and (l) and 175(1), (3) and (4) of the Social Security Contributions and Benefits Act 1992, ss. 63, 78(2), 189(1) and (3) to (5) and 191 of the Social Security Administration Act 1992 and ss. 36(1) and 40(1) of the Jobseekers Act 1995.

[In force October 7, 1996].

Transitional provision for income support

8.—(1) This paragraph applies in the case of a person who—
(a) on 31st July 1996 is engaged in a course of education which is not a course of study, within the meaning of paragraph (4);
(b) is not a student within the meaning of regulation 61 of the Income Support Regulations as it had effect on that date;
(c) is entitled to income support in respect of that date;
(d) remains continuously entitled to that benefit from 31st July to 7th October 1996; and
(e) is not entitled to jobseeker's allowance in the benefit week which follows the benefit week which includes 7th October 1996.
(2) Subject to paragraph (3), a person to whom paragraph (1) applies who—
(a) continues to attend the course referred to in paragraph (1)(a) on 7th October 1996;
(b) falls within any of the categories of persons referred to in Schedule 1B of the Income Support Regulations (prescribed categories of persons), disregarding paragraphs 1, 2, 10, 11, 12 and 18;
(c) otherwise satisfies the conditions of entitlement to income support,
shall continue to be entitled to that benefit until the last day of the course or until he abandons or is dismissed from the course.
(3) Where a person to whom paragraph (1) applies also satisfies the conditions specified in paragraph (2)(a) to (c) in respect of an award of income support, if he then ceases, for a period of 12 weeks or less, to be entitled to income support but otherwise satisfies those conditions throughout that period, for the purposes of paragraph (2) he shall be treated, on becoming re-entitled to income support, as if he had been continuously entitled to that benefit throughout that period.
(4) In this regulation—
""course of study" means any full-time course of study or sandwich course whether or not a grant is made for attending it;";
""sandwich course" has the meaning prescribed in paragraph 1(1) of Schedule 5 to the Education (Mandatory Awards) Regulations 1995".

DEFINITION

"benefit week"—see General Regulations, reg. 2(1).

GENERAL NOTE

This provides transitional protection for certain people affected by the changes to the definitions in reg. 61 of the Income Support Regulations on October 7, 1996. See the notes to reg. 61.

Income-related Benefits and Jobseeker's Allowance (Personal Allowances for Children and Young Persons) (Amendment) Regulations 1996

(S.I. 1996 No. 2545)

Made by the Secretary of State under ss. 128(1)(a)(i) and (5), 129(1)(c)(i) and (8). 135(1). 136(3) and (4), 137(1) and 175(1), (3) and (4) of the Social Security Contributions and Benefits Act 1992 and ss. 4(5), 35(1) and 36(1), (2) and (4) of the Jobseekers Act 1995.

[In force April 7, 1997].

Transitional provisions

10.—(1) Where, in relation to a claim for income support, jobseeker's allowance, housing benefit or council tax benefit, a claimant's weekly applicable amount includes a personal allowance in respect of one or more children or young persons who are, as at the day before the appropriate date these Regulations come into force for the purpose of those benefits in accordance with regulation 1 of these Regulations (referred to in this regulation as "the appropriate date"), aged 11, 16 or 18, the provisions specified in regulation 2(7) of these Regulations shall have effect, for the period specified in paragraph (2) below, as if regulation 2 of these Regulations had not been made.

(2) The period specified for the purposes of paragraph (1) above shall be, in relation to each particular child or young person referred to in that paragraph, the period beginning on the appropriate date and ending—

(a) where that child or young person is aged 11 or 16 as at the day before the appropriate date, on 31st August 1997;

(b) where that young person is aged 18 as at the day before the appropriate date, on the day preceding the day that young person ceases to be a person of a prescribed description for the purposes of regulation 14 of the Income Support Regulations, regulation 76 of the Jobseeker's Allowance Regulations, regulation 13 of the Housing Benefit Regulations or regulation 5 of the Council Tax Benefit Regulations.

DEFINITIONS

"child"—see SSCBA, s. 137(1).
"claimant"—see General Regulations, reg. 2(1).
"young person"—see General Regulations, regs. 2(1) and 14.

GENERAL NOTE

See the notes to para. 2 of Sched. 2 to the Income Support Regulations. Para. 2 of Sched. 2 and para. 2 of Sched. 1 to the JSA Regulations were amended by reg. 2 of these Regulations on April 7, 1997.

The weekly amount for a person aged not less than 18 in sub-para. (d) of the previous form of para. 2 of Sched. 2 and para. 2 of Sched. 1 to the JSA Regulations was increased to £38.90 from April 7, 1997 (Social Security Benefits Up-rating Order 1997 (S.I. 1997 No. 543), arts. 18(4) and 24(4)). The weekly amounts in sub-paras. (a), (b) and (c) were also increased and were the same as the amounts in sub-paras. (a), (b) and (c) of the 1997 form of the respective paras.

Community Charges (Deductions from Income Support) (No. 2) Regulations 1990

(S.I. 1990 No. 545)

*Made by the Secretary of State under ss.22(3) and 146(6) and Sched. 4 para.
6 of the Local Government Finance Act 1988*

GENERAL NOTE

The first version of these Regulations (S.I. 1990 No. 107) was defective and was replaced.

The Community Charges (Deductions from Income Support) (Scotland) Regulations 1989 (S.I. 1989 No. 507) made provision for Scotland from April 10, 1989. They have been amended by S.I. 1990 No. 113 to bring them into line with these Regulations, but are not reproduced.

Citation, commencement and interpretation

1.—(1) These Regulations may be cited as the Community Charges (Deductions from Income Support) (No. 2) Regulations 1990 and shall come into force on 1st April 1990.

(2) In these Regulations, unless the context otherwise requires—

"the 1975 Act" means the Social Security Act 1975;

"the 1986 Act" means the Social Security Act 1986;

"adjudication officer" means an officer appointed in accordance with section 97(1) of the 1975 Act [SSAA, s.38];

"appropriate social security office" means an office of the Department of Social Security which is normally open to the public for the receipt of claims for income support and includes an office of the [¹Department for Education and Employment] which is normally open to the public for the receipt of claims for [¹jobseeker's allowance and income support];

"Commissioner" means the Chief or any other Social Security Commissioner appointed in accordance with section 97(3) of the 1975 Act or section 13(5) of the Social Security Act 1980 [SSAA, s.52], and includes a Tribunal of 3 Commissioners constituted in accordance with section 116 of the 1975 Act [SSAA, s.57];

[²"contribution-based jobseeker's allowance", except in a case to which paragraph (b) of the definition of income-based jobseeker's allowance applies, means a contribution-based jobseeker's allowance uner Part I of the Jobseekers Act 1995, but does not include any back to work bonus under section 26 of the Jobseekers Act which is paid as jobseeker's allowance;]

"couple" means a married or unmarried couple;

"debtor" means a person against whom a liability order has been obtained;

"5 per cent. of the personal allowance for a single claimant aged not less than 25" and

"5 per cent. of the personal allowance for a couple where both members are aged not less than 18" means, in each case, where the percentage is not a multiple of 5 pence, the sum obtained by rounding that 5 per cent. to the next higher such multiple;

"income support" means income support within the meaning of the 1986 Act [¹but does not include any back to work bonus under section 26 of the Jobseekers Act which is paid as income support;]

[²"income-based jobseeker's allowance" means—

    (a) an income-based jobseeker's allowance under Part I of the Jobseekers Act 1995; and

    (b) in a case where, if there was no entitlement to contribution-based jobseeker's allowance, there would be entitlement to income-based jobseeker's allowance at the same rate, contribution-based jobseeker's allowance;]

but does not include any back to work bonus under section 26 of the Jobseekers Act which is paid as jobseeker's allowance;]

    [[1]"Jobseekers Act" means the Jobseekers Act 1995;

    "jobseeker's allowance" means an allowance under Part I of the Jobseekers Act but does not include any back to work bonus under section 26 of that Act which is paid as jobseeker's allowance;]

    "liability order" means an order under regulation 29 of the Community Charges (Administration and Enforcement) Regulations 1989;

    "married couple" has the meaning ascribed to it in section 20(11) of the 1986 Act [SSCBA, s.137(1)];

    "payments to third parties" means direct payments to third parties in accordance with Schedule 9 to the Social Security (Claims and Payments) Regulations 1987;

    "polygamous marriage" means a marriage to which section 22B of the Social Security Act 1986 [SSCBA, s.133] refers;

    "single debtor" means a debtor who is not a member of a couple;

    "tribunal", except in relation to a Tribunal of 3 Commissioners, means a social security appeal tribunal constituted in accordance with section 97(2) to (2E) of the 1975 Act [SSAA, s.41]; and

    "unmarried couple" has the meaning ascribed to it in section 20(11) of the 1986 Act [SSCBA, s.137(1)].

(3) Unless the context otherwise requires, any reference in these Regulations to a numbered regulation or Schedule is a reference to the regulation and Schedule bearing that number in the Regulations and any reference in a regulation or Schedule to a numbered paragraph is a reference to the paragraph of that regulation or Schedule having that number.

AMENDMENTS

    1. Social Security (Jobseeker's Allowance Consequential Amendments) (Deductions) Regulations 1996 (S.I. 1996 No. 2344), reg. 6 (October 7, 1996).

    2. Social Security (Miscellaneous Amendments) Regulations 1998 (S.I. 1998 No. 563), reg. 3(1) and (2)(a) (April 1, 1998). (Note that the commencement date for this provision was amended by Social Security (Miscellaneous Amendments) (No. 2) Regulations 1998 (S.I. 1998 No. 865), reg. 2 (March 20, 1998).)

[[3]Deductions from income support or jobseeker's allowance]

    2.—(1) Where a debtor is entitled to income support [[3]or jobseeker's allowance], an authority may apply to the Secretary of State by sending an application in respect of the debtor or, where a liability order is made against a couple in respect of both of the couple, to an appropriate social security office asking the Secretary of State to deduct sums from any amount payable to the debtor, or as the case may be either of the couple by way of income support [[3]or jobseeker's allowance].

    (2) An application from an authority shall be in writing and shall contain the following particulars—

    (a) the name and address of the debtor or where the liability order is made against a couple, the names and address of both of them;

    (b) the name and place of the court which made the liability order;

    (c) the date when the liability order was made;

    (d) the total amount of the arrears specified in the liability order;

(e) the total amount which the authority wishes to have deducted from income support [³or jobseeker's allowance].

(3) Where it appears to the Secretary of State that an application from an authority gives insufficient particulars to enable the debtor to be identified he may require the authority to furnish such further particulars as may reasonably be required.

(4) Subject to paragraph (5), where the Secretary of State receives an application from an authority, he shall refer it to an adjudication officer who shall determine the following questions—

(a) whether there is sufficient entitlement to income support [³or income-based jobseeker's allowance] to enable the Secretary of State to make any deduction—

   (i) where a liability order is made against a single debtor, or a debtor who is a member of a couple, or a member of a polygamous marriage, at a rate of 5 per cent. of the personal allowance set out in Schedule 2 to the Income Support (General) Regulations 1987, [²paragraph 1(1)(e)] [³or, as the case may be, paragraph 1(1)(e) of Schedule 1 to the Jobseeker's Allowance Regulations 1996] (single claimant aged not less than 25); or

   (ii) where a liability order is made against a couple and income support [³or income-based jobseeker's allowance] is payable in respect of both of them, at a rate of 5 per cent. of the personal allowance set out in Schedule 2 to the Income Support (General) Regulations 1987, paragraph 1(3)(c) [³or, as the case may be, paragraph 1(3)(e) of Schedule 1 to the Jobseeker's Allowance Regulations 1996] (couple where both members are aged not less than 18),

and, if the amount payable by way of income support [³or income-based jobseeker's allowance] to the debtor were to be 10 pence or more after any such deduction, the adjudication officer shall determine that there is sufficient entitlement;

[³(aa) whether there is sufficient entitlement to contribution-based jobseeker's allowance to enable the Secretary of State to make any deduction, and for this purpose the adjudication officer shall determine that there is sufficient entitlement if the amount of contribution-based jobseeker's allowance payable before any deduction under these regulations is equal to or more than one-third of the age-related amount applicable to the debtor under section 4(1)(a) of the Jobseekers Act;]

(b) the priority of any sum to be deducted as against any payments to third parties where there is insufficient entitlement to income support [³or jobseeker's allowance] to meet both the deduction in respect of arrears of community charges and those payments to third parties, and the following priorities shall apply—

[¹(zi) any liability mentioned in regulation 34A of the Social Security (Claims and Payments) Regulation 1987 (mortgage interest);]

   (i) any liability mentioned in paragraph 3 of Schedule 9 (housing costs) to the Social Security (Claims and Payments) Regulations 1987;

   (ii) any liability mentioned in paragraph 5 of Schedule 9 (service charges for fuel, and rent not falling within paragraph 2(1)(a)) to those Regulations;

   (iii) any liability mentioned in paragraph 6 of Schedule 9 (fuel costs) to those Regulations;

   (iv) any liability mentioned in paragraph 7 of Schedule 9 (water charges) to those Regulations;

   (v) any liability for arrears in respect of community charges, and the adjudication officer shall determine these questions so far as is practical within 14 days of receipt of the reference.

(5) Where at the time the Secretary of State is making deductions in respect of an application from an authority he receives one or more further applications [²or one or more applications under regulation 2 of the Council Tax (Deductions from Income Support) Regulations 1993] from an authority in respect of the person from whom the deductions are being made, he shall refer those further applications to the adjudication officer in accordance with the following order of priority, namely, the one bearing the earliest date shall be referred first and each subsequent application shall be referred, one at a time and in date order, only after deductions under any earlier application have ceased.

(6) Subject to any right of appeal or review under these Regulations, the decision of the adjudication officer shall be final.

AMENDMENTS

1. Social Security (Claims and Payments) Amendment Regulation 1992 (S.I. 1992 No. 1026), reg. 7 (May 25, 1992).
2. Social Security (Claims and Payments) Amendment (No. 3) Regulations 1993 (S.I. 1993 No. 2113), reg. 5 (September 27, 1993).
3. Social Security (Jobseeker's Allowance Consequential Amendments) (Deductions) Regulations 1996 (S.I. 1996 No. 2344), reg. 7 (October 7, 1996).

DEFINITIONS

"adjudication officer"—see reg. 1(2).
"authority"—see Local Government Finance Act 1988, s.144.
"appropriate social security officer"—see reg. 1(2).
"couple"—*ibid.*
"debtor"—*ibid.*
"5 per cent. of the personal allowance for a single claimant aged not less than 25"—*ibid.*
"5 per cent. of the personal allowance for a couple where both members are aged not less than 18"—*ibid.*
"income support"—*ibid.*
"Jobseekers Act"—*ibid.*
"jobseeker's allowance"—*ibid.*
"liability order"—*ibid.*
"payments to third parties"—*ibid.*
"polygamous marriage"—*ibid.*

GENERAL NOTE

R(IS) 3/92 holds that if the Secretary of State accepts the validity (*i.e.* the form and content) of an application under para. (2), the AO or SSAT must also accept it. But where there is an issue as to whether the claimant is a "debtor" (defined in reg. 1(2)) at all, the SSAT must satisfy itself that the basic conditions for the operation of the procedure exist: namely that there *is* a subsisting liability order, properly obtained, under which there *is* outstanding a sum due of the amount sought to be deducted from income support (*CIS 11861/1996*, to be reported as *R(IS) 1/98*). In that case neither the alleged liability order nor any evidence from the local authority confirming that an amount was still due from the claimant had been produced, whereas the claimant had produced evidence which appeared to substantiate that she was in fact in credit on her community charge account. The Commissioner therefore decided that there was no jurisdiction to make any deduction from the claimant's income support in respect of the community charge.

[¹Deductions from debtor's jobseeker's allowance

2A.—(1) Where the adjudication officer has determined that there is sufficient entitlement to income-based jobseeker's allowance, the Secretary of State may deduct—

    (a) in a case to which regulation 2(4)(a)(i) applies, a sum equal to 5 per cent. of the personal allowance for a single claimant aged not less than 25; or

    (b) in a case to which regulation 2(4)(a)(ii) applies, and subject to paragraph (4), a sum equal to 5 per cent. of the personal allowance for a couple where both members are aged not less than 18,

and pay that sum to the authority towards satisfaction of any outstanding sum which is or forms part of the amount in respect of which the liability order was made.

(2) Subject to paragraph (3), where the adjudication officer has determined that there is sufficient entitlement to contribution-based jobseeker's allowance, the Secretary of State may deduct a sum equal to one-third of the age-related amount applicable to the debtor under section 4(1)(a) of the Jobseekers Act, and pay that sum to the authority towards satisfaction of any outstanding sum which is or forms part of the amount in respect of which the liability order was made.

(3) For the purposes of paragraph (2) where the sum that would otherwise fall to be deducted includes a fraction of a penny, the sum to be deducted shall be rounded down to the next whole penny.

(4) In a case to which paragraphs (1)(b) and (2) apply, deductions shall be made in accordance with paragraph (2).]

AMENDMENT

1. Social Security (Jobseeker's Allowance Consequential Amendments) (Deductions) Regulations 1996 (S.I. 1996 No. 2344), reg. 8 (October 7, 1996).

DEFINITIONS

    "adjudication officer"—see reg. 1(2).
    "authority"—see Local Government Finance Act 1988, s. 144.
    "couple"—see reg. 1(2).
    "debtor"—*ibid.*
    "5 per cent of the personal allowance for a single claimant aged not less than 25"—*ibid.*
    "5 per cent of the personal allowance for a couple where both members are aged not less than 18"—*ibid.*
    "Jobseekers Act"—*ibid.*
    "jobseeker's allowance"—*ibid.*
    "liability order"—*ibid.*

Notification of decision

3. The Secretary of State shall notify the debtor in writing of the adjudication officer's decision as soon as is practicable after he receives that decision and at the same time he shall notify the debtor of his right of appeal.

DEFINITIONS

    "adjudication officer"—see reg. 1(2).
    "debtor"—*ibid.*

Circumstances, time of making and termination of deductions

4.—(1) The Secretary of State shall make deductions from income support [¹or jobseeker's allowance] only—

(a) where the debtor is entitled to income support [¹or jobseeker's allow-
ance] throughout any benefit week and the amount to which he is
entitled is sufficient to enable him to make the deductions; and

(b) in respect of one application at a time.

(2) The Secretary of State shall make deductions from income support [¹or
jobseeker's allowance] at a time which corresponds to the payment of income
support [¹or jobseeker's allowance] to the debtor and he shall cease making
deductions when—

(a) a payment to a third party has priority;

(b) there is insufficient entitlement to income support [¹or jobseeker's allow-
ance] to enable him to make the deduction;

(c) entitlement to income support [¹or jobseeker's allowance] ceases;

(d) an authority withdraws its application for deductions to be made; or

(e) the debt in respect of which he was making the deductions is
discharged.

(3) Payments shall be made to the authority at such intervals as the Secretary
of State may decide.

AMENDMENT

1. Social Security (Jobseeker's Allowance Consequential Amendments) (Deductions) Regulations
1996 (S.I. 1996 No. 2344), reg. 9 (October 7, 1996).

DEFINITIONS

"adjudication officer"—see reg. 1(2).
"authority"—see Local Government Finance Act 1988, s.144.
"debtor"—see reg. 1(2).
"income support"—*ibid.*
"jobseeker's allowance"—*ibid.*

Appeal

5.—(1) Where the adjudication officer has decided a question under regulation
2(4), the debtor may appeal to a tribunal.

(2) Subject to paragraph (5), an appeal lies to a Commissioner from any
decision of a tribunal on the grounds that the decision of that tribunal was
erroneous in point of law and the persons who may appeal are the debtor and
the adjudication officer.

(3) If it appears to the Chief Commissioner or, in the case of his inability
to act, to such other of the Commissioners as he may have nominated to
act for that purpose, that an appeal falling to be heard by one of the
Commissioners involves a question of law of special difficulty, he may direct
that the appeal be dealt with, not by that Commissioner alone but by a
Tribunal consisting of any 3 of the Commissioners and if the decision is
not unanimous, the decision of the majority shall be the decision of the
Tribunal.

(4) Subject to paragraph (5), an appeal on a question of law lies to the Court
of Appeal from any decision of a Commissioner on a question of law and the
persons who may appeal are—

(a) the debtor;

(b) the adjudication officer; and

(c) the Secretary of State.

(5) No appeal lies—

    (a) to the Commissioner from a decision of a tribunal without the leave of the chairman of the tribunal which gave the decision or, if he refuses leave, without the leave of the Commissioner, or

    (b) to the Court of Appeal from a decision of a Commissioner, without the leave of the Commissioner who decided the case, or if he refuses, without the leave of the Court of Appeal.

    (6) Where in any case it is impracticable, or it would be likely to cause undue delay for an application for leave to appeal against a decision of a tribunal to be determined by the person who was the chairman of that tribunal, that application shall be determined by any other person qualified under section 97(2D) of the 1975 Act [SSAA, s.41(4)] to act as a chairman of tribunals.

    (7) In a case where the Chief Commissioner considers that it is impracticable, or would be likely to cause undue delay, for an application for leave to appeal to the Court of Appeal to be determined by the Commissioner who decided the case, that application shall be determined—

    (a) where the decision was a decision of an individual Commissioner, by the Chief Commissioner or a Commissioner selected by the Chief Commissioner, and

    (b) where the decision was a decision of a Tribunal of Commissioners, by a differently constituted Tribunal of Commissioners selected by the Chief Commissioner.

    (8) If the office of Chief Commissioner is vacant, or if the Chief Commissioner is unable to act, paragraph (7) shall have effect as if the expression "the Chief Commissioner" referred to such other of the Commissioners as may have been nominated to act for the purpose either by the Chief Commissioner or, if he has not made such nomination, by the Lord Chancellor.

DEFINITIONS

    "adjudication officer"—see reg. 1(2).
    "Commissioner"—*ibid.*
    "debtor"—*ibid.*
    "tribunal"—*ibid.*

Review

    6.—(1) Any decision under these Regulations of an adjudication officer, a tribunal or a Commissioner may be reviewed at any time by an adjudication officer if—

    (a) the officer is satisfied that the decision was given in ignorance of, or was based on a mistake as to, some material fact; or

    (b) there has been a relevant change of circumstances since the decision was given.

    (2) Any decision of an adjudication officer may be reviewed by an adjudication officer on the grounds that the decision was erroneous in point of law.

    (3) A question may be raised with a view to review under this regulation by means of an application in writing to an adjudication officer, stating the grounds of the application.

    (4) On receipt of any such application, the adjudication officer shall take it into consideration and, so far as is practicable, dispose of it within 14 days of its receipt.

    (5) A decision given by way of revision or a refusal to review under this regulation shall be subject to appeal in the same manner as an original decision

and regulation 5(1) and Schedule 2 shall apply with the necessary modification in relation to a decision given on review as they apply to the original decision on a question.

<small>DEFINITIONS</small>

"adjudication officer"—see reg. 1(2).
"Commissioner"—*ibid.*
"tribunal"—*ibid.*

Correction of accidental errors

7.—(1) Subject to regulation 9, accidental errors in any decision or record of a decision made under regulations 2(4), 5 and 6 and Schedule 2 may at any time be corrected by the person or tribunal by whom the decision was made or a person or tribunal of like status.

(2) A correction made to, or to the record of, a decision shall be deemed to be part of the decision or, of that record, and written notice of it shall be given as soon as practicable to every party to the proceedings.

<small>DEFINITIONS</small>

"tribunal"—see reg. 1(2).

Setting aside decisions on certain grounds

8.—(1) Subject to regulation 9, on an application made by a party to the proceedings, a decision, made under regulations 2(4), 5, 6 and Schedule 2 by an adjudication officer, a tribunal or a Commissioner ("the adjudicating authority"), together with any determination given on an application for leave to appeal to a Commissioner or the Court of Appeal against such a decision may be set aside by the adjudicating authority which gave the decision or an authority of like status, in a case where it appears just to set that decision aside on the grounds that—

   (a) a document relating to the proceedings in which the decision was given was not sent to, or was not received at an appropriate time by a party or their representative or was not received at the appropriate time by the person or tribunal who gave the decision;

   (b) in the case of an appeal to a tribunal or an oral hearing before a Commissioner a party to the proceedings in which the decision was given or the party's representative was not present at the hearing relating to the proceedings; or

   (c) the interests of justice so require.

(2) An application under this regulation shall be made in accordance with regulation 10 and Schedule 1.

(3) Where an application to set aside is made under paragraph (1) every party to the proceedings shall be sent a copy of the application and shall be afforded a reasonable opportunity of making representations on it before the application is determined.

(4) Notice in writing of a determination on an application to set aside a decision shall be given to every party to the proceedings as soon as may be practicable and the notice shall contain a statement giving the reasons for the determination.

(5) For the purpose of determining under these Regulations an application to set aside a decision, there shall be disregarded, but subject to any contrary intention, any provision in any enactment or instrument to the effect that any notice or other document required or authorised to be given or sent to any person shall be deemed to have been given or sent if it was sent to that person's last known notified address.

DEFINITIONS

"adjudication officer"—see reg. 1(2).
"Commissioner"—*ibid.*
"tribunal"—*ibid.*

Provisions common to regulations 7 and 8

9.—(1) In calculating any time specified in Schedule 1 there shall be disregarded any day falling before the day on which notice was given of a correction of a decision or the record thereof pursuant to regulation 7 or on which notice is given that a determination of a decision shall not be set aside following an application under regulation 8, as the case may be.

(2) There shall be no appeal against a correction made under regulation 7 or a refusal to make such a correction or against a determination under regulation 8.

(3) Nothing in regulation 7 or 8 shall be construed as derogating from any inherent or other power to correct errors or set aside decisions which is exercisable apart from these Regulations.

Manner of making applications or appeals and time limits

10.—(1) Any application or appeal set out in Column (1) of Schedule 1 shall be made or given by sending or delivering it to the appropriate office within the specified time.

(2) In this regulation—
(a) "appropriate office" means the office specified in Column (2) of Schedule 1 opposite the description of the relevant application or appeal listed in Column (1); and
(b) "specified time" means the time specified in Column (3) of that Schedule opposite the description of the relevant application or appeal so listed.

(3) The time specified by this regulation and Schedule 1 for the making of any application or appeal (except an application to the chairman of a tribunal for leave to appeal to a Commissioner) may be extended for special reasons, even though the time so specified may already have expired, and any application for an extension of time under this paragraph shall be made to and determined by the person to whom the application or appeal is sought to be made or, in the case of a tribunal, its chairman.

(4) An application under paragraph (3) for an extension of time (except where it is made to a Commissioner) which has been refused may not be renewed.

(5) Any application or appeal set out in Column (1) of Schedule 1 shall be in writing and shall contain—
(a) the name and address of the appellant or applicant;

511

(b) the particulars of the grounds on which the appeal or application is to be made or given; and

(c) his address for service of documents if it is different from that in sub-paragraph (a);

and in the case of an appeal to the Commissioner, but subject to paragraph 21(2) of Schedule 2, the notice of appeal shall have annexed to it a copy of the determination granting leave to appeal and a copy of the decision against which leave to appeal has been granted.

(6) Where it appears to an adjudication officer, or chairman of a tribunal, or Commissioner that an application or appeal which is made to him, or the tribunal, gives insufficient particulars to enable the question at issue to be determined, he may require, and in the case of a Commissioner, direct that the person making the application or appeal shall furnish such further particulars as may reasonably be required.

(7) The conduct and procedure in relation to any application or appeal shall be in accordance with Schedule 2.

DEFINITIONS

"adjudication officer"—see reg. 1(2).
"Commissioner"—*ibid.*
"tribunal"—*ibid.*

Manner and time for the service of notices etc.

11.—(1) Any notice or other document required or authorised to be given or sent to any person under these Regulations shall be deemed to have been given or sent if it was sent by post properly addressed and pre-paid to that party at his ordinary or last notified address.

(2) Any notice or other document required or authorised to be given to an appropriate social security office or office of the clerk to a tribunal shall be treated as having been so given or sent on the day that it is received in the appropriate social security office or office of the clerk to the tribunal.

(3) Any notice or document required to be given, sent or submitted to, or served on, a Commissioner—

(a) shall be given, sent or submitted to an office of the Social Security Commissioners;

(b) shall be deemed to have been given, sent or submitted if it was sent by post properly addressed and pre-paid to an office of the Social Security Commissioners.

DEFINITIONS

"appropriate social security office"—see reg. 1(2).
"Commissioner"—*ibid.*
"tribunal"—*ibid.*

Revocation

12. The Community Charges (Deductions from Income Support) Regulations 1990 are hereby revoked.

SCHEDULE 1 **Regulation 10(1)**

TIME LIMITS FOR MAKING APPLICATIONS OR APPEALS

Column (1)	Column (2)	Column (3)
Application or Appeal	*Appropriate Office*	*Specified time*
1. Appeal to a tribunal from an adjudication officer's decision (regulation 5).	An appropriate social security office.	3 months beginning with the date when notice in writing of the decision was given to the appellant.
2. Application to the Chairman for leave to appeal to a Commissioner from the decision of a tribunal (paragraph 16, Schedule 2).	The office of the Clerk to the tribunal.	3 months beginning with the date when a copy of the record of the decision was given to the applicant.
3. Application to— (a) an adjudication officer; (b) a tribunal; or (c) a Commissioner, to set aside decision (regulation 8).	(a) An appropriate social security office; (b) The office of the clerk to the tribunal; (c) An office of the Social Security Commissioners;	(a) and (b) 3 months beginning with the date when notice in writing of the decision was given to the applicant. (c) 30 days from the date on which notice in writing of the decision was given to the applicant by an officer of the Social Security Commissioners.
4. Application for leave to appeal to the Commissioner where the chairman has refused leave (paragraph 17, Schedule 2).	An office of the Social Security Commissioners.	42 days beginning with the date when notice in writing of the decision by the chairman to refuse leave was given to the applicant.
5. Appeal to the Commissioner (regulation 5).	An office of the Social Security Commissioners.	42 days beginningwith the date when notice in writing of the decision was given to the applicant.
6. Leave to appeal to the Court of Appeal (regulation 5(5) and Schedule 2).	An office of the Social Security Commissioners.	3 months beginning with the date when notice in writing of the decision was given to the applicant.

DEFINITIONS

   "adjudication officer"—see reg. 1(2).
   "appropriate social security office"—*ibid.*
   "Commissioner"—*ibid.*
   "tribunal"—*ibid.*

SCHEDULE 2   **Regulation 10(7)**

CONDUCT AND PROCEDURE IN RELATION TO APPEALS AND APPLICATIONS

Common provisions in connection with appeals and applications

1.—(1) Subject to the provisions of these Regulations—

(a) the procedure in connection with the consideration of any appeal, or any application in relation to questions to which these Regulations relate, shall be such as the adjudication officer, chairman of the tribunal or the Commissioner may determine;

(b) any person who by virtue of these Regulations has the right to be heard at a hearing may be accompanied and represented by another person whether having professional qualifications or not, and for the purposes of any proceedings at any hearing any such representative shall have all the rights and powers to which the person whom he represents is entitled under these Regulations.

(2) Nothing in these Regulations shall prevent a member of the Council on Tribunals in his capacity as such from being present at any oral hearing before a tribunal or a Commissioner, notwithstanding that the hearing is not in public.

2. Reasonable notice (being not less than 10 days beginning on the day on which notice is given and ending on the day before the hearing of the appeal) of the time and place of any oral hearing before the tribunal or the Commissioner shall be given to every party to the proceedings, and if such notice had not been given to a person to whom it should have been given under the provisions of this paragraph the hearing may only proceed with the consent of that person.

3. At any oral hearing any party shall be entitled to be present and be heard.

Postponements and adjournments

4.—(1) Where a person to whom notice of an oral hearing has been given wishes to apply for that hearing to be postponed he shall do so in writing to the chairman of the tribunal or the Commissioner stating his reasons for the application and the chairman or the Commissioner may grant or refuse the application as he sees fit.

(2) An oral hearing may be adjourned at any time on the application of any party to the proceedings or on the motion of the tribunal or the Commissioner.

Striking out of proceedings for want of prosecution

5.—(1) The chairman of a tribunal or the Commissioner may, subject to sub-paragraph (2), on the application of any party to the proceedings or of his own motion, strike out any appeal or application for want of prosecution.

(2) Before making an order under sub-paragraph (1) the chairman of a tribunal or the Commissioner, as the case may be, shall send notice to the person against whom it is proposed that any order should be made giving him a reasonable opportunity to show cause why such an order should not be made.

(3) The chairman of a tribunal or the Commissioner, as the case may be, may, on application by the party concerned, give leave to reinstate any application or appeal which has been struck out in accordance with sub-paragraph (1).

Application and Appeals to the Tribunal

Procedure in connection with determinations

6. For the purpose of arriving at its decision a tribunal shall, and for the purpose of discussing any question of procedure may, notwithstanding anything in these Regulations, order all persons not being members of the tribunal other than its clerk to withdraw from the sitting of the tribunal except that—

    (a) a member of the Council on Tribunals, the President of Social Security Appeal Tribunals and any full-time chairman; and

    (b) with the leave of the chairman of the tribunal, if no person having the right to be heard objects, any person mentioned in paragraph 13(1)(b) and (d) (except a person undergoing training as an adjudicating officer).

may remain present at any such sitting.

Oral hearings

7. A tribunal shall hold an oral hearing of every appeal made to them.

8. If a party to the proceedings to whom notice has been given under paragraph 2 should fail to appear at the hearing, the tribunal may, having regard to all the circumstances, including any explanation offered for the absence, proceed with the case notwithstanding his absence or give such directions with a view to the determination of the case as they think fit.

9. Any oral hearing before a tribunal shall be in public except that the hearing shall be in private where the debtor requests a private hearing, or where the chairman is satisfied in the particular circumstances of the case that intimate personal or financial circumstances may have to be disclosed, or that considerations of public security are involved.

10. Any case may with the consent of the debtor or his representative, but not otherwise, be proceeded with in the absence of any one member other than the chairman.

11. Where an oral hearing is adjourned and at the hearing after the adjournment the tribunal is differently constituted otherwise than through the operation of paragraph 10, the proceedings at that hearing shall be by way of a complete rehearing of the case.

12.—(1) The decision of the majority of the tribunal shall be the decision of the tribunal but, where the tribunal consists of an even number, the chairman shall have a second or casting vote.

    (2) The chairman of a tribunal shall—

    (a) record in writing all its decisions; and

    (b) include in the record of every decision a statement of the reasons for such decision and of their findings on questions of fact material thereto; and

    (c) if a decision is not unanimous, record a statement that one of the members dissented and the reasons given by him for so dissenting.

    (3) As soon as may be practicable after a case has been decided by a tribunal, a copy of the record of the decision made in accordance with this paragraph shall be sent to every party to the proceedings who shall also be informed of the conditions governing appeals to a Commissioner.

13.—(1) The following persons shall be entitled to be present at an oral hearing (whether or not it is in private) but shall take no part in the proceedings—

    (a) the President of Social Security Appeal Tribunals;

    (b) any person undergoing training as a chairman or other member of a tribunal, or as a clerk to a tribunal, or as an adjudication officer;

    (c) any person acting on behalf of the President of the Social Security Appeal Tribunals, the Chief Adjudication Officer appointed under section 97(1B) of the 1975 Act, or the Secretary of State, in the training or supervision of clerks to tribunals or adjudication officers or officers of the Secretary of State or in the monitoring of standards of adjudication by adjudication officers;

    (d) any regional or full-time chairman of appeal tribunals appointed under paragraph 1A of Schedule 10 to the 1975 Act; and

(e) with the leave of the chairman of the tribunal and with the consent of every party to the proceedings actually present, any other person.

(2) Nothing in sub-paragraph (1) affects the rights of any person mentioned in heads (a) and (b) at any oral hearing where he is sitting as a member of the tribunal or acting as its clerk, and nothing in this paragraph prevents the presence at an oral hearing of any witness.

14. Any person entitled to be heard at an oral hearing may address the tribunal, may give evidence, may call witnesses and may put questions directly to any other person called as a witness.

Withdrawal of Appeals

15. Any appeal to the tribunal under these Regulations may be withdrawn by the person who made the appeal—
- (a) before the hearing begins by giving written notice of intention to withdraw to the tribunal and with the consent in writing of the adjudication officer who made the decision; or
- (b) after the hearing has begun with the leave of the chairman of the tribunal at any time before the determination is made.

Application to a Chairman for leave to appeal from a tribunal to a Commissioner

16.—(1) Subject to the following provisions of this paragraph, an application to the chairman of a tribunal for leave to appeal to a Commissioner from a decision of the tribunal shall be made—
- (a) orally at the hearing after the decision is announced by the tribunal; or
- (b) as provided by regulation 10 and Schedule 1.

(2) Where an application in writing for leave to appeal is made by an adjudication officer, the clerk to the tribunal shall, as soon as may be practicable, send a copy of the application to every other party to the proceedings.

(3) The decision of the chairman on an application for leave to appeal made under sub-paragraph (1)(a) shall be recorded in the record of the proceedings of the tribunal, and an application under sub-paragraph (1)(b) shall be recorded in writing and a copy shall be sent to each party to the proceedings.

(4) A person who has made an application to the chairman of a tribunal for leave to appeal to a Commissioner may withdraw his application at any time before it is determined by giving written notice of intention to the chairman.

[Paras. 17 to 36 on appeals to the Commissioner and the Court of Appeal omitted.]

DEFINITIONS

"adjudication officer"—see reg. 1(2).
"Commissioner"—*ibid.*
"debtor"—*ibid.*
"tribunal"—*ibid.*

Fines (Deductions from Income Support) Regulations 1992

(S.I. 1992 No. 2182)

Made by the Secretary of State under ss. 24 and 30 of the Criminal Justice Act 1991.

Citation, commencement and interpretation

1.—(1) These Regulations may be cited as the Fines (Deductions from Income Support) Regulations 1992 and shall come into force on 1st October 1992.

(2) In these Regulations, unless the context otherwise requires—

"the 1971 Act" means the Vehicles (Excise) Act 1971;

"the 1973 Act" means the Powers of the Criminal Courts Act 1973;

"the 1992 Act" means the Social Security Administration Act 1992;

"adjudication officer" means an officer appointed in accordance with section 38(1) of the 1992 Act;

"application" means an application made under regulation 2 in the form and containing the information specified in regulation 3(1);

"appropriate appeal court" means, except in regulation 9(9), the appropriate court as determined in accordance with regulation 9(9) and 9(10);

"benefit week" has the meaning prescribed in regulation 2(1) of the Income Support Regulations [²or, as the case may be, regulation 1(3) of the Jobseeker's Allowance Regulations 1996;]

"the Claims and Payments Regulations" means the Social Security (Claims and Payments) Regulations 1987;

"Commissioner" means the Chief or any other Social Security Commissioner appointed in accordance with section 52(1) or (2) of the 1992 Act and includes a Tribunal of Commissioners constituted in accordance with section 57(1) of that Act;

[³"contribution-based jobseeker's allowance", except in a case to which paragraph (b) of the definition of income-based jobseeker's allowance applies, means a contribution-based jobseeker's allowance under Part I of the Jobseekers Act 1995, but does not include any back to work bonus under section 26 of the Jobseekers Act which is paid as jobseeker's allowance;]

"court" means in England and Wales a magistrates' court and in Scotland a court;

"5 per cent. of the personal allowance for a single claimant aged not less than 25" means, where the percentage is not a multiple of 5 pence, the sum obtained by rounding that 5 per cent. to the next higher such multiple;

[²"income support" means income support under Part VII of the Social Security Contributions and Benefits Act 1992, but does not include any back to work bonus under section 26 of the Jobseekers Act which is paid as income support;]

"Income Support Regulations" means the Income Support (General) Regulations 1987;

[³"income-based jobseeker's allowance" means—

(a) an income-based jobseeker's allowance under Part I of the Jobseekers Act 1995; and

(b) in a case where, if there was no entitlement to contribution-based jobseeker's allowance, there would be entitlement to income-based jobseeker's allowance at the same rate, contribution-based jobseeker's allowance,

but does include any back to work bonus under section 26 of the Jobseekers Act which is paid as jobseeker's allowance;]

[²"Jobseekers Act" means the Jobseekers Act 1995;

"jobseeker's allowance" means an allowance under Part I of the Jobseekers Act but does not include any back to work bonus under section 26 of that Act which is paid as jobseeker's allowance;]

"payments to third parties" means direct payments to third parties in accordance with Schedules 9 and 9A to the Claims and Payments Regulations, regulation 2(4) of the Community Charges (Deductions from Income Support) (No. 2) Regulations 1990 and regulation 2(4) of the Community Charges (Deductions from Income Support) (Scotland) Regulations 1989 [¹and regulation 2 of the Council Tax (Deductions from Income Support) Regulations 1993];

"personal allowance for a single claimant aged not less than 25" means the amount specified in paragraph 1(1)(e) of column 2 of Schedule 2 to the Income Support Regulations [²or, as the case may be, the amount specified in paragraph 1(1)(e) of Schedule 1 to the Jobseeker's Allowance Regulations 1996;]

"social security office" means an office of the Department of Social Security which is open to the public for the receipt of claims for income support and includes an office of the [²Department for Education and Employment] which is open to the public for the receipt of claims for [²jobseeker's allowance and income support];

"tribunal" means a social security appeal tribunal constituted in accordance with section 41 of the 1992 Act; and

(3) Unless the context otherwise requires, any reference in these Regulations to a numbered regulation, Part or Schedule bearing that number in these Regulations and any reference in a regulation or Schedule to a numbered paragraph is a reference to the paragraph of that regulation or Schedule having that number.

AMENDMENTS

1. Deductions from Income Support (Miscellaneous Amendment) Regulations 1993 (S.I. 1993 No. 495), reg. 3 (April 1, 1993).

2. Social Security (Jobseeker's Allowance Consequential Amendments) (Deductions) Regulations 1996 (S.I. 1996 No. 2344), reg. 10 (October 7, 1996).

3. Social Security (Miscellaneous Amendments) Regulations 1998 (S.I. 1998 No. 563), reg. 3(1) and (2)(d) (April 1, 1998). (Note that the commencement date for this provision was amended by Social Security (Miscellaneous Amendments) (No. 2) Regulations 1998 (S.I. 1998 No. 865), reg. 2 (March 20, 1998).)

[¹Application for deductions from income support or jobseeker's allowance]

2.—(1) Where a fine has been imposed on an offender by a court or a sum is required to be paid by a compensation order which has been made against an offender by a court and (in either case) the offender is entitled to income support [¹or jobseeker's allowance], the court may, subject to paragraph (2), apply to the Secretary of State asking him to deduct sums from any amounts payable to the offender by way of income support [¹or jobseeker's allowance], in order to secure the payment of any sum which is or forms part of the fine or compensation.

(2) Before making an application the court shall make an enquiry as to the offender's means.

AMENDMENT

1. Social Security (Jobseeker's Allowance Consequential Amendments) (Deductions) Regulations 1996 (S.I. 1996 No. 2344), reg. 11 (October 7, 1996).

DEFINITIONS

"court"—see reg. 1(2).
"income support"—*ibid.*
"jobseeker's allowance"—*ibid.*

Contents of application

3.—(1) An application shall be made in the form set out in Schedule 3, or a form to like effect, and shall contain the following information—
    (a) the name and address of the offender, and, if it is known, his date of birth;

   (b) the date when the fine was imposed or the compensation order made;

   (c) the name and address of the court imposing the fine or making the compensation order;

   (d) the amount of the fine or the amount payable by the compensation order as the case may be;

   (e) the date on which the application is made;

   (f) the date on which the court enquired into the offender's means;

   (g) whether the offender has defaulted in paying the fine, compensation order or any instalment of either.

(2) A court making an application shall serve it on the Secretary of State by sending or delivering it to a social security office.

(3) Where it appears to the Secretary of State that an application from a court gives insufficient information to enable the offender to be identified, he may require the court to furnish such further information as he may reasonably require for that purpose.

DEFINITIONS

"application"—see reg. 1(2).
"court"—*ibid.*
"social security office"—*ibid.*

[¹Reference to adjudication officer

4.—(1) Where the Secretary of State receives an application from a court in respect of an offender, he shall, subject to regulation 7(5), refer it forthwith to an adjudication officer who shall determine whether there is sufficient entitlement to income support [²or jobseeker's allowance] to enable the Secretary of State to make any deduction.

(2) The adjudication officer shall determine there is sufficient entitlement to income support [¹or income-based jobseeker's allowance] to enable the Secretary of State to make a deduction—

   (a) if the amount payable by way of income support [²or income-based jobseeker's allowance] after any deduction to be made under regulation 6 is 10 pence or more; and

   (b) if the aggregate amount payable under one or more of the following provisions, namely paragraphs 3(2)(a), 5(6), 6(2)(a), 7(3)(a) and 7(5)(a) of Schedule 9 to the Claims and Payments Regulations, [³. . .] and regulation 2 of the Council Tax (Deductions from Income Support) Regulations 1993, together with the amount to be deducted under regulation 6 does not exceed an amount equal to 3 times 5 per cent of the personal allowance for a single claimant aged not less than 25 years.

[²(2A) The adjudication officer shall determine that there is sufficient entitlement to contribution-based jobseeker's allowance to enable the Secretary of State to make a deduction if the amount of contribution-based jobseeker's allowance payable before any deduction under these regulations is equal to or more than one-third of the age-related amount applicable to the offender under section 4(1)(a) of the Jobseekers Act.]

(3) The adjudication officer shall determine whether there is sufficient entitlement to income support [²or jobseeker's allowance] to enable a deduction to be made, so far as is practicable, within 14 days of receipt of the reference from the Secretary of State.]

AMENDMENTS

   1. Deductions from Income Support (Miscellaneous Amendment) Regulations 1993 (S.I. 1993 No. 495), reg. 3 (April 1, 1993).

2. Social Security (Jobseeker's Allowance Consequential Amendments) (Deductions) Regulations 1996 (S.I. 1996 No. 2344), reg. 12 (October 7, 1996).

3. Social Security and Child Support (Miscellaneous Amendments) Regulations 1997 (S.I. 1997 No. 827), reg. 8(1) (April 7, 1997).

DEFINITIONS

"adjudication officer"—see reg. 1(2).
"application"—*ibid.*
"the Claims and Payments Regulations"—*ibid.*
"court"—*ibid.*
"5 per cent. of the personal allowance for a single claimant aged not less than 25"—*ibid.*
"income support"—*ibid.*
"Jobseekers Act"—*ibid.*
"jobseeker's allowance"—*ibid.*
"payments to third parties"—*ibid.*

Notification of decision

5. The Secretary of State shall notify the offender and the court in writing of the adjudication officer's decision so far as is practicable within 14 days from the date on which he receives that decision and at the same time he shall notify the offender of his right of appeal.

DEFINITIONS

"adjudication officer"—see reg. 1(2).
"court"—*ibid.*

[¹Deductions from offender's income support or income-based jobseeker's allowance]

6. Where the adjudication officer has determined that there is sufficient entitlement to income support [¹or income-based jobseeker's allowance] the Secretary of State may deduct a sum equal to 5 per cent. of the personal allowance for a single claimant aged not less than 25 and pay that sum to the court towards satisfaction of the fine or the sum required to be paid by compensation order.

AMENDMENT

1. Social Security (Jobseeker's Allowance Consequential Amendments) (Deductions) Regulations 1996 (S.I. 1996 No. 2344), reg. 13 (October 7, 1996).

DEFINITIONS

"adjudication officer"—see reg. 1(2).
"court"—*ibid.*
"5 per cent. of the personal allowance for a single claimant aged not less than 25"—*ibid.*

[¹Deductions from offender's contribution-based jobseeker's allowance

6A.—(1) Subject to paragraphs (2) and (3), where the adjudication officer has determined that there is sufficient entitlement to contribution-based jobseeker's allowance, the Secretary of State may deduct a sum equal to one-third of the age-related amount applicable to the offender under section 4(1)(a) of the Jobseekers Act, and pay that sum to the court towards satisfaction of the fine or the sum required to be paid by the compensation order.

(2) No deduction shall be made under this regulation where a deduction is being made from the offender's contribution-based jobseeker's allowance under

the Community Charges (Deductions from Income Support) (No. 2) Regulations 1990, the Community Charges (Deductions from Income Support) (Scotland) Regulations 1989 or the Council Tax (Deductions from Income Support) Regulations 1993.

(3) Where the sum that would otherwise fall to be deducted under this regulation includes a fraction of a penny, the sum to be deducted shall be rounded down to the next whole penny.]

AMENDMENT

1. Social Security (Jobseeker's Allowance Consequential Amendments) (Deductions) Regulations 1996 (S.I. 1996 No. 2344), reg. 14 (October 7, 1996).

DEFINITIONS

"adjudication officer"—see reg. 1(2).
"court"—*ibid.*
"Jobseekers Act"—*ibid.*

Circumstances, time of making and termination of deductions

7.—(1) The Secretary of State may make deductions from income support ['or jobseeker's allowance] under regulation 6 ['or 6A] only if—
- (a) the offender is entitled to income support ['or jobseeker's allowance] throughout any benefit week; and
- (b) no deductions are being made in respect of the offender under any other application.

(2) The Secretary of State shall not make a deduction unless—
- (a) the offender at the date of application by the court is aged not less than 18;
- (b) the offender is entitled to income support ['or jobseeker's allowance]; and
- (c) the offender has defaulted in paying the fine, compensation order or any instalment of either.

(3) The Secretary of State shall make deductions from income support ['or jobseeker's allowance] by reference to the times at which payment of income support ['or jobseeker's allowance] is made to the offender.

(4) The Secretary of State shall cease making deductions from income support ['or jobseeker's allowance] if—
- (a) there is no longer sufficient entitlement to income support ['or jobseeker's allowance] to enable him to make the deduction;
- (b) entitlement to income support ['or jobseeker's allowance] ceases;
- (c) a court withdraws its application for deductions to be made; or
- (d) the liability to make payment of the fine or under the compensation order as the case may be has ceased.

(5) Where at any time during which the Secretary of State is making deductions in respect of an application he receives one or more further applications in respect of the offender from whom the deductions are being made, he shall refer those further applications to the adjudication officer in accordance with the following order of priority, namely, the one bearing the earliest date shall be referred first and each subsequent application shall be referred, one at a time and in date order, only after deductions under any earlier application have ceased.

(6) Payments of sums deducted from income support ['or jobseeker's allowance] by the Secretary of State under these Regulations shall be made to the court at intervals of 13 weeks.

(7) Where the whole of the amount to which the application relates has been

paid, the court shall so far as is practicable give notice of that fact within 21 days to the Secretary of State.

(8) The Secretary of State shall notify the offender in writing of the total of the sums deducted by him under any application—

(a) on receipt of a written request for such information from the offender; or

(b) on the termination of deductions made under any such application.

AMENDMENT

1. Social Security (Jobseeker's Allowance Consequential Amendments) (Deductions) Regulations 1996 (S.I. 1996 No. 2344), reg. 15 (October 7, 1996).

DEFINITIONS

"adjudication officer"—see reg. 1(2).
"authority"—*ibid.*
"benefit week"—*ibid.*
"court"—*ibid.*
"income support"—*ibid.*
"jobseeker's allowance"—*ibid.*

Withdrawal of application

8. A court may withdraw an application at any time by giving notice in writing to the social security office to which the application was sent or delivered.

DEFINITIONS

"application"—see reg. 1(2).
"court"—*ibid.*
"social security office"—*ibid.*

Appeal

9.—(1) Where the adjudication officer has determined a question under regulation 4, the offender may appeal to a tribunal.

(2) Subject to paragraph (5), an appeal lies to a Commissioner from any decision of a tribunal on the grounds that the decision of that tribunal was erroneous in point of law and the persons who may appeal are the offender and the adjudication officer.

(3) If it appears to the Chief Commissioner or, in the case of his inability to act, to such other of the Commissioners, as he may have nominated to act for that purpose, that an appeal falling to be heard by one of the Commissioners involves a question of law of special difficulty, he may direct that the appeal be dealt with, not by that Commissioner alone but by a Tribunal consisting of any three of the Commissioners and if the decision is not unanimous, the decision of the majority shall be the decision of the Tribunal.

(4) Subject to paragraph (5), an appeal on a question of law lies to the appropriate appeal court from any decision of a Commissioner and the persons who may appeal are—

(a) the offender;

(b) the adjudication officer; and

(c) the Secretary of State.

(5) No appeal lies—

(a) to the Commissioner from a decision of a tribunal without the leave of the chairman of the tribunal which gave the decision or, if he refuses leave, without the leave of the Commissioner, or

(b) to the appropriate appeal court from a decision of a Commissioner, without the leave of the Commissioner who decided the case, or if he refuses, without the leave of the appropriate appeal court.

(6) Where in any case it is impracticable, or it would be likely to cause undue delay, for an application for leave to appeal against a decision of a tribunal to be determined by the person who was the chairman of that tribunal, that application shall be determined by any other person qualified under section 41(4) of the 1992 Act to act as a chairman of tribunals.

(7) In a case where the Chief Commissioner considers that it is impracticable, or would be likely to cause undue delay, for an application for leave to appeal to the appropriate appeal court to be determined by the Commissioner who decided the case, that application shall be determined—

(a) where the decision was a decision of an individual Commissioner, by the Chief Commissioner or a Commissioner selected by the Chief Commissioner, and

(b) where the decision was a decision of a Tribunal of Commissioners, by a differently constituted Tribunal of Commissioners selected by the Chief Commissioner.

(8) If the office of Chief Commissioner is vacant, or if the Chief Commissioner is unable to act, paragraph (7) shall have effect as if the expression "the Chief Commissioner" referred to such other of the Commissioners as may have been nominated to act for the purpose either by the Chief Commissioner or, if he has not made such nomination, by the Lord Chancellor.

(9) On an application to a Commissioner for leave under this regulation it shall be the duty of the Commissioner to specify as the appropriate court—

(a) the Court of Appeal if it appears to him that the relevant place is in England and Wales; and

(b) the Court of Session if it appears to him that the relevant place is in Scotland;

except that if it appears to him, having regard to the circumstances of the case and in particular to the convenience of the persons who may be parties to the proposed appeal, that he should specify a different court mentioned in paragraphs (a) and (b) above as the appropriate court, it shall be his duty to specify that court as the appropriate court.

(10) In paragraph (9)—

"the relevant place", in relation to an application for leave to appeal from a decision of a Commissioner, means the premises where the tribunal whose decision was the subject of the Commissioner's decision usually exercises its functions.

DEFINITIONS

"the 1992 Act"—see reg. 1(2).
"adjudication officer"—*ibid.*
"appropriate appeal court"—*ibid.*
"Commissioner"—*ibid.*
"tribunal"—*ibid.*

Review

10.—(1) Any decision under these Regulations of an adjudication officer, a tribunal or a Commissioner may be reviewed at any time by an adjudication officer, if—

   (a) the officer is satisfied that the decision was given in ignorance of, or was based on a mistake as to, some material fact; or

   (b) there has been a relevant change of circumstances since the decision was given.

(2) Any decision of an adjudication officer may be reviewed by an adjudication officer on the grounds that the decision was erroneous in point of law.

(3) A question may be raised with a view to review under this regulation by means of an application in writing to an adjudication officer, stating the grounds of the application.

(4) On receipt of any such application, the adjudication officer shall take it into consideration and, so far as is practicable, dispose of it within 14 days of its receipt.

(5) A decision given by way of revision or a refusal to review under this regulation shall be subject to appeal in the same manner as an original decision and regulation 9(1) and Schedule 2 shall apply with the necessary modification in relation to a decision given on review as they apply to the original decision on a question.

DEFINITIONS

    "adjudication officer"—see reg. 1(2).
    "Commissioner"—*ibid.*
    "tribunal"—*ibid.*

Correction of accidental errors

   11.—(1) Subject to regulation 13, accidental errors in any decision or record of a decision made under regulations 4, 9 and 10 and Schedule 2 may at any time be corrected by the person or tribunal by whom the decision was made or a person or tribunal of like status.

(2) A correction made to, or to the record of, a decision shall be deemed to be part of the decision, or of that record, and written notice of it shall be given as soon as practicable to every party to the proceedings.

DEFINITION

    "tribunal"—see reg. 1(2).

Setting aside decisions on certain grounds

   12.—(1) Subject to regulation 13, on an application made by a party to the proceedings, a decision, made under regulation 4, 9, 10 and Schedule 2 by an adjudication officer, a tribunal or a Commissioner ("the adjudicating authority"), together with any determination given on an application for leave to appeal to a Commissioner or the Court of Appeal against such a decision may be set aside by the adjudicating authority which gave the decision or an authority of like status, in a case where it appears just to set that decision aside on the grounds that—

   (a) a document relating to the proceedings in which the decision was given was not sent to, or was not received at an appropriate time [¹by a party to the proceedings or the party's representative] or was not received at the appropriate time by the person or tribunal who gave the decision;

   (b) in the case of an appeal to a tribunal or an oral hearing before a Commissioner a party to the proceedings in which the decision was given or the party's representative was not present at the hearing relating to the proceedings; or

   (c) the interests of justice so require.

(2) An application under this regulation shall be made in accordance with regulation 14 and Schedule 1.

(3) Where an application to set aside is made under paragraph (1) every party to the proceedings shall be sent a copy of the application and shall be afforded a reasonable opportunity of making representations on it before the application is determined.

(4) Notice in writing of a determination on an application to set aside a decision shall be given to every party to the proceedings as soon as may be practicable and the notice shall contain a statement giving the reasons for the determination.

(5) For the purpose of determining under these Regulations an application to set aside a decision, there shall be disregarded, but subject to any contrary intention, any provision in any enactment or instrument to the effect that any notice or other document required or authorised to be given or sent to any person shall be deemed to have been given or sent if it was sent to that person's last known notified address.

AMENDMENT

1. Deductions from Income Support (Miscellaneous Amendment) Regulations 1993 (S.I. 1993 No. 495), reg. 3 (April 1, 1993).

DEFINITIONS

"adjudication officer"—see reg. 1(2).
"Commissioner"—*ibid.*
"tribunal"—*ibid.*

Provisions common to regulations 11 and 12

13.—(1) In calculating any time specified in Schedule 1 there shall be disregarded any day falling before the day on which notice was given of a correction of a decision or the record there of pursuant to regulation 11 or on which notice is given that a determination of a decision shall not be set aside following an application under regulation 12, as the case may be.

(2) There shall be no appeal against a correction made under regulation 11 or a refusal to make such a correction or against a determination under regulation 12.

(3) Nothing in regulation 11 or 12 shall be construed as derogating from any inherent or other power to correct errors or set aside decisions which is exercisable apart from these Regulations.

Manner of making applications or appeals and time limits

14.—(1) Any application or appeal set out in Column (1) of Schedule 1 shall be made or given by sending or delivering it to the appropriate office within the specified time.

(2) In this regulation—
  (a) "appropriate office" means the office specified in Column (2) of Schedule 1 opposite the description of the relevant application or appeal listed in Column (1); and
  (b) "specified time" means the time specified in Column (3) of that Schedule opposite the description of the relevant application or appeal so listed.

(3) The time specified by this regulation and Schedule 1 for the making of any application or appeal (except an application to the chairman of a tribunal for leave to appeal to a Commissioner) may be extended for special reasons,

even though the time so specified may already have expired, and any application for an extension of time under this paragraph shall be made to and determined by the person to whom the application or appeal is sought to be made or, in the case of a tribunal, its chairman.

(4) An application under paragraph (3) for an extension of time (except where it is made to a Commissioner) which has been refused may not be renewed.

(5) Any application or appeal set out in Column (1) of Schedule 1 shall be in writing and shall contain—

(a) the name and address of the appellant or applicant;

(b) the particulars of the grounds on which the appeal or application is to be made or given; and

(c) his address for service of documents if it is different from that in sub-paragraph (a);

and in the case of an appeal to the Commissioner, but subject to paragraph 21(2) of Schedule 2, the notice of appeal shall have annexed to it a copy of the determination granting leave to appeal and a copy of the decision against which leave to appeal has been granted.

(6) Where it appears to an adjudication officer, chairman of a tribunal or Commissioner that an application or appeal which is made to him, or to the tribunal, gives insufficient particulars to enable the question at issue to be determined, he may require, and in the case of a Commissioner, direct that the person making the application or appeal shall furnish such further particulars as may reasonably be required.

(7) The conduct and procedure in relation to any application or appeal shall be in accordance with Schedule 2.

DEFINITIONS

"adjudication officer"—see reg. 1(2).
"Commissioner"—*ibid.*
"tribunal"—*ibid.*

Manner and time for the service of notices etc.

15.—(1) Any notice or other document required or authorised to be given or sent to any person under these Regulations shall be deemed to have been given or sent if it was sent by post properly addressed and pre-paid to [¹that person] at his ordinary or last notified address.

(2) Any notice or other document required or authorised to be given to an appropriate social security office or office of the clerk to a tribunal shall be treated as having been so given or sent on the day that it is received in the appropriate social security office or office of the clerk to the tribunal.

(3) Any notice or document required to be given, sent or submitted to, or served on, a Commissioner—

(a) shall be given, sent or submitted to an office of the Social Security Commissioners;

(b) shall be deemed to have been given, sent or submitted if it was sent by post properly addressed and pre-paid to an office of the Social Security Commissioners.

AMENDMENT

1. Deductions from Income Support (Miscellaneous Amendment) Regulations 1993 (S.I. 1993 No. 495), reg. 3 (April 1, 1993).

"Commissioner"—see reg. 1(2).
"social security office"—*ibid.*
"tribunal"—*ibid.*

[Scheds. 1 to 3 are omitted. Scheds. 1 and 2 are substantially the same as Scheds. 1 and 2 to the Community Charges (Deductions from Income Support) (No. 2) Regulations 1990. Sched. 3 sets out the form to be used under reg. 3(1)]

Council Tax (Deductions from Income Support) Regulations 1993

(S.I. 1993 No. 494)

Made by the Secretary of State under ss.14(3), 97(5), 113 and 116(1) of and Scheds. 4, paras. 1 and 6, and 8, para. 6, to the Local Government Finance Act 1992

Citation, commencement and interpretation

1.—(1) These Regulations may be cited as the Council Tax (Deductions from Income Support) Regulations 1993 and shall come into force on 1st April 1993.

(2) In these Regulations, unless the context otherwise requires—

"the Administration Act" means the Social Security Administration Act 1992;

"adjudication officer" means an officer appointed in accordance with section 38(1) of the Administration Act;

"application" means an application made under regulation 2 or regulation 3 containing the information specified in regulation 4;

"appropriate appeal court" means the appropriate court as determined in accordance with regulation 10(9) and 10(10);

"authority" means—

(a) in relation to England and Wales, a billing authority, and

(b) in relation to Scotland, a levying authority;

"benefit week" has the meaning prescribed in regulation 2(1) of the Income Support (General) Regulations 1987 [¹or, as the case may be, regulation 1(3) of the Jobseeker's Allowance Regulations 1996;]

"Claims and Payments Regulations" means the Social Security (Claims and Payments) Regulations 1987;

"Commissioner" means the Chief or any other Social Security Commissioner appointed in accordance with section 52(1) or (2) of the Administration Act, and includes a Tribunal of Commissioners constituted in accordance with section 57(1) of that Act;

[²"contribution-based jobseeker's allowance", except in a case to which paragraph (b) of the definition of income-based jobseeker's allowance applies, means a contribution-based jobseeker's allowance under Part I of the Jobseekers Act 1995, but does not include any back to work bonus under section 26 of the Jobseekers Act which is paid as jobseeker's allowance;]

"debtor"—

(a) in relation to England and Wales, has the same meaning as in paragraph 6 of Schedule 4 to the Local Government Finance Act, and

(b) in relation to Scotland, has the same meaning as in paragraph 6 of Schedule 8 to that Act;

"5 per cent. of the personal allowance for a single claimant aged not less

527

than 25'' means, where the percentage is not a multiple of 5 pence, the sum obtained by rounding that 5 per cent. to the next higher such multiple;

"income support" means income support within the meaning of the Social Security Contributions and Benefits Act 1992 [¹but does not include any back to work bonus under section 26 of the Jobseekers Act which is paid as income support;]

[²"income-based jobseeker's allowance" means—

(a) an income-based jobseeker's allowance under Part I of the Jobseekers Act 1995; and

(b) in a case where, if there was no entitlement to contribution-based jobseeker's allowance, there would be entitlement to income-based jobseeker's allowance at the same rate, contribution-based jobseeker's allowance,

but does not include any back to work bonus under section 26 of the Jobseekers Act which is paid as jobseeker's allowance;]

[¹"Jobseekers Act" means the Jobseekers Act 1995;

"jobseeker's allowance" means an allowance under Part I of the Jobseekers Act but does not include any back to work bonus under section 26 of that Act which is paid as jobseeker's allowance;]

"the Local Government Finance Act" means the Local Government Finance Act 1992;

"personal allowance for a single claimant aged not less than 25" means the amount specified in paragraph 1(1)(e) of column 2 of Schedule 2 to the Income Support (General) Regulations 1987 [¹or, as the case may be, the amount specified in paragraph 1(1)(e) of Schedule 1 to the Jobseeker's Allowance Regulations 1996;];

"social security office" means an office of the Department of Social Security which is open to the public for the receipt of claims for income support and includes an office of the [¹Department for Education and Employment] which is open to the public for the receipt of claims for [¹jobseeker's allowance and income support];

"tribunal", except in relation to a Tribunal of three Commissioners, means a social security appeal tribunal constituted in accordance with section 41 of the Administration Act.

(3) Unless the context otherwise requires, any reference in these Regulations to a numbered regulation or Schedule is a reference to the regulation or Schedule bearing that number in these Regulations and any reference in a regulation or Schedule to a numbered paragraph is a reference to the paragraph of that regulation or Schedule having that number.

AMENDMENTS

1. Social Security (Jobseeker's Allowance Consequential Amendments) (Deductions) Regulations 1996 (S.I. 1996 No. 2344), reg. 17 (October 7, 1996).

2. Social Security (Miscellaneous Amendments) Regulations 1998 (S.I. 1998 No. 563), reg. 3(1) and (2)(c) (April 1, 1998). (Note that the commencement date for this provision was amended by Social Security (Miscellaneous Amendments) (No. 2) Regulations 1998 (S.I. 1998 No. 865), reg. 2 (March 20, 1998).)

[¹Application for deductions from income support or jobseeker's allowance: England and Wales]

2. Where a liability order has been made against a debtor by a magistrates' court and the debtor is entitled to income support [¹or jobseeker's allowance] the billing authority concerned may apply to the Secretary of State asking him to deduct sums from any amounts payable to the debtor by way of income support [¹or jobseeker's allowance] in order to secure the payment of any outstanding sum which is or forms part of the amount in respect of which the liability order was made.

AMENDMENT

1. Social Security (Jobseeker's Allowance Consequential Amendments) (Deductions) Regulations 1996 (S.I. 1996 No. 2344), reg. 18 (October 7, 1996).

DEFINITIONS

"debtor"—see reg. 1(2).
"income support"—*ibid.*
"jobseeker's allowance"—*ibid.*

[²Application for deductions from income support or jobseeker's allowance: Scotland]

3.—(1) Where a levying authority has obtained a summary warrant or a decree against a debtor in respect of arrears of sums payable under paragraph 1(1) of Schedule 8 to the [¹Local Government Finance Act] and the debtor is entitled to income support [²or jobseeker's allowance], the levying authority may, without prejudice to its right to pursue any other means of recovering such arrears, apply to the Secretary of State asking him to deduct sums from any amounts payable to the debtor by way of income support [²or jobseeker's allowance] in order to secure the payment of any outstanding sum which is or forms part of the amount in respect of which the summary warrant or decree was granted.

AMENDMENTS

1. Social Security (Claims and Payments) Amendment (No. 3) Regulations 1993 (S.I. 1993 No. 2113), reg. 6 (September 27, 1993).
2. Social Security (Jobseeker's Allowance Consequential Amendments) (Deductions) Regulations 1996 (S.I. 1996 No. 2344), reg. 19 (October 7, 1996).

DEFINITIONS

"debtor"—see reg. 1(2).
"income support"—*ibid.*
"jobseeker's allowance"—*ibid.*
"Local Government Finance Act"—*ibid.*

Contents of application

4.—(1) An application shall contain the following particulars—
(a) the name and address of the debtor;
(b) the name and address of the authority making the application;
(c) the name and place of the court which made the liability order or granted the summary warrant, or decree as the case may be;
(d) the date on which the liability order was made or the summary warrant or decree granted as the case may be;
(e) the amount specified in the liability order, summary warrant or decree as the case may be;
(f) the total sum which the authority wishes to have deducted from income support [¹or jobseeker's allowance].
(2) An authority making application shall serve it on the Secretary of State by sending or delivering it to a social security office.
(3) Where it appears to the Secretary of State that an application from an

authority gives insufficient particulars to enable the debtor to be identified he may require the authority to furnish such further particulars as may reasonably be required for that purpose.

AMENDMENT

1. Social Security (Jobseeker's Allowance Consequential Amendments) (Deductions) Regulations 1996 (S.I. 1996 No. 2344), reg. 20 (October 7, 1996).

DEFINITIONS

"application"—see reg. 1(2).
"authority"—*ibid.*
"debtor"—*ibid.*
"jobseeker's allowance"—*ibid.*
"social security office"—*ibid.*

GENERAL NOTE

On regs. 2, 3 and 4 see *R(IS) 3/92* and *CIS 11861/1996*, to be reported as *R(IS) 1/98*, in the notes to reg. 2 of the Community Charges (Deductions from Income Support) (No. 2) Regulations 1990. *CIS 1725/1997* confirms that *R(IS) 1/98* applies to deductions for council tax arrears as well as those for arrears of the community charge.

Reference to adjudication officer

5.—(1) Where the Secretary of State receives an application from an authority, he shall, subject to regulation 8(4), refer it forthwith to an adjudication officer who shall determine whether there is sufficient entitlement to income support [¹or jobseeker's allowance] to enable the Secretary of State to make any deduction.

(2) The adjudication officer shall determine there is sufficient entitlement to income support [¹or income-based jobseeker's allowance] to enable the Secretary of State to make a deduction—
  (a) if the amount payable by way of income support [¹or income-based jobseeker's allowance] after any deduction to be made under regulation 7 is 10 pence or more;
  (b) if the aggregate amount payable under one or more of the following provisions, namely paragraphs 3(2)(a), 5(6), 6(2)(a), 7(3)(a), 7(5)(a) of Schedule 9 [². . .] to the Claims and Payments Regulations, together with the amount to be deducted under regulation 7, does not exceed an amount equal to 3 times 5 per cent. of the personal allowance for a single claimant aged not less than 25 years.

[¹(2A) The adjudication officer shall determine that there is sufficient entitlement to contribution-based jobseeker's allowance to enable the Secretary of State to make a deduction if the amount of contribution-based jobseeker's allowance payable before any deduction under these regulations is equal to or more than one-third of the age-related amount applicable to the debtor under section 4(1)(a) of the Jobseekers Act.]

(3) The adjudication officer shall determine whether there is sufficient entitlement to income support to [¹or jobseeker's allowance] enable a deduction to be made, so far as is practicable, within 14 days of receipt of the reference from the Secretary of State.

AMENDMENTS

1. Social Security (Jobseeker's Allowance Consequential Amendments) (Deductions) Regulations 1996 (S.I. 1996 No. 2344), reg. 21 (October 7, 1996).

2. Social Security and Child Support (Miscellaneous Amendments) Regulations 1997 (S.I. 1997 No. 827), reg. 8(2) (April 7, 1997).

DEFINITIONS

''adjudication officer''—see reg. 1(2).
''application''—*ibid.*
''authority''—*ibid.*
''Claims and Payments Regulations''—*ibid.*
''5 per cent. of the personal allowance for a single claimant aged not less than 25''—*ibid.*
''jobseeker's allowance''—*ibid.*

Notification of decision

6. The Secretary of State shall notify the debtor and the authority in writing of the adjudication officer's decision so far as is practicable within 14 days from the date on which he receives that decision and at the same time he shall notify the debtor of his right of appeal.

DEFINITIONS

''adjudication officer''—see reg. 1(2).
''authority''—*ibid.*
''debtor''—*ibid.*

[¹Deductions from debtor's income support or income-based jobseeker's allowance]

7. Where the adjudication officer has determined that there is sufficient entitlement to income support [¹or income-based jobseeker's allowance] the Secretary of State may deduct a sum equal to 5 per cent. of the personal allowance for a single claimant aged not less than 25 and pay that sum to the authority towards satisfaction of any outstanding sum which is or forms part of the amount in respect of which the liability order was made or the summary warrant or the decree was granted.

AMENDMENT

1. Social Security (Jobseeker's Allowance Consequential Amendments) (Deductions) Regulations 1996 (S.I. 1996 No. 2344), reg. 22 (October 7, 1996).

DEFINITIONS

''adjudication officer''—see reg. 1(2).
''authority''—*ibid.*
''debtor''—*ibid.*
''5 per cent. of the personal allowance for a single claimant aged not less than 25''—*ibid.*
''income support''—*ibid.*

[¹Deductions from debtor's contribution-based jobseeker's allowance

7A.—(1) Subject to paragraph (2), where the adjudication officer has determined that there is sufficient entitlement to contribution-based jobseeker's allowance, the Secretary of State may deduct a sum equal to one-third of the age-related amount applicable to the debtor under section 4(1)(a) of the Jobseekers Act, and pay that sum to the authority towards satisfaction of any outstanding sum which is or forms part of the amount in respect of which the liability order was made or the summary warrant or decree was granted.
(2) Where the sum that would otherwise fall to be deducted under this regula-

tion includes a fraction of a penny, the sum to be deducted shall be rounded down to the next whole penny.]

AMENDMENT

1. Social Security (Jobseeker's Allowance Consequential Amendments) (Deductions) Regulations 1996 (S.I. 1996 No. 2344), reg. 23 (October 7, 1996).

DEFINITIONS

"adjudication officer"—see reg. 1(2).
"authority"—*ibid.*
"debtor"—*ibid.*
"Jobseekers Act"—*ibid.*

Circumstances, time of making and termination of deductions

8.—(1) The Secretary of State may make deductions from [¹income support or jobseeker's allowance under regulation 7 or 7A] only if—
  (a) the debtor is entitled to income support [¹or jobseeker's allowance] throughout any benefit week;
  (b) no deductions are being made in respect of the debtor under any other application; and
  (c) no payments are being made under regulation 2 of the Community Charge (Deductions from Income Support) (Scotland) Regulations 1989 or regulation 2 of the Community Charge (Deductions from Income Support) (No. 2) Regulations 1990.
  (2) The Secretary of State shall make deductions from income support [¹or jobseeker's allowance] by reference to the times at which payment of income support [¹or jobseeker's allowance] is made to the debtor.
  (3) The Secretary of State shall cease making deductions from income support [¹or jobseeker's allowance] if—
  (a) there is no longer sufficient entitlement to income support [¹or jobseeker's allowance] to enable him to make the deduction;
  (b) an authority withdraws its application for deductions to be made; or
  (c) the debt in respect of which he was making deductions is discharged.
  (4) Where at any time during which the Secretary of State is making deductions in respect of an application he receives one or more further applications in respect of the debtor from whom the deductions are being made, he shall refer those further applications to the adjudication officer in accordance with the following order of priority, namely, the one bearing the earliest date shall be referred first and each subsequent application shall be referred, one at a time and in date order, only after deductions under any earlier application have ceased.
  (5) Payments of sums deducted from income support [¹or jobseeker's allowance] by the Secretary of State under these Regulations shall be made to the authority concerned, as far as is practicable, at intervals not exceeding 13 weeks.
  (6) Where the whole of the amount to which the application relates has been paid, the authority concerned shall, so far as is practicable, give notice of that fact within 21 days to the Secretary of State.
  (7) The Secretary of State shall notify the debtor in writing of the total of the sums deducted by him under any application—
  (a) on receipt of a written request for such information from the debtor; or
  (b) on the termination of deductions made under any such application.

AMENDMENT

1. Social Security (Jobseeker's Allowance Consequential Amendments) (Deductions) Regulations 1996 (S.I. 1996 No. 2344), reg. 24 (October 7, 1996).

DEFINITIONS

"adjudication officer"—see reg. 1(2).
"authority"—*ibid.*
"benefit week"—*ibid.*
"debtor"—*ibid.*
"income support"—*ibid.*
"jobseeker's allowance"—*ibid.*

[Regs. 9 to 16 and Scheds. 1 and 2 are omitted as being substantially the same as regs. 8 to 15 of and Scheds. 1 and 2 to the Fines (Deductions from Income Support) Regulations 1992, with the substitution of "debtor" and "authority" for "offender" and "court".]

Social Security (Back to Work Bonus) (No. 2) Regulations 1996

(S.I. 1996 No. 2570)

Made by the Secretary of State under ss.26, 35(1) and (3) and 36(2) to (5) of the Jobseekers Act 1995

ARRANGEMENT OF REGULATIONS

GENERAL NOTE

These regulations revoke the Social Security (Back to Work) Bonus Regulations 1996 (as amended) and re-enact their provisions, with effect from November 4, 1996.

The regulations contain the detailed (and complex) rules relating to the back to work bonus that was introduced by s. 29 of the Jobseekers Act on October 7, 1996. There are no notes or definitions after each individual regulation but the main provisions are summarised in the following paragraphs.

Most of the relevant definitions are in reg. 1, although there also needs to be some reference to the Jobseekers Act 1995.

The back to work bonus scheme (like the child maintenance bonus scheme) is part of the government's continuing programme of incentives to encourage people to move into full-time employment. The bonus is a tax-free sum of up to £1000 that can build up while a claimant (or partner) is working part-time (*i.e.* less than 16 hours (claimant), 24 hours (partner) a week) and in receipt of income support (before the age of 60) or JSA. Note that unlike the child maintenance bonus, the bonus can accrue during periods when the only entitlement is to contribution-based JSA (see reg. 1(3)).

To start accruing a bonus the person must have served a "waiting period" of 91 days during which he was entitled, or treated as entitled, to JSA or income support (reg. 6). Days before July 1, 1996 do not count (see reg. 27(1) and (3)). Thus the three "waiting days" at the beginning of a JSA claim cannot count as these are not days of entitlement (Jobseekers Act, Sched. 1, para. 4), but days on which a claimant is sanctioned under s. 19 of the Jobseekers Act can do so, as long as he continues to sign on (see reg. 3(1); note also reg. 3(2) which applies where a person is not being paid contribution-based JSA because of the amount of his pension). But apart from days covered by reg. 3(1) and (2), days when benefit is not payable are not treated as days of entitlement (reg. 3(3)). In addition, reg. 5 deems certain other days to be days of non-entitlement, including days on which hardship payments of JSA are paid because the claimant has failed to satisfy the labour market conditions, or is awaiting an AO's decision on this issue (but if the AO's decision is in the claimant's favour such days will count).

Two or more periods of entitlement can be linked if they are separated by 12 weeks or less, or a "connecting period", or two connecting periods separated by not more than 12 weeks, or a connecting period followed by a period of not more than 12 weeks, or a period of jury service (reg. 2(2)–(4)). A "connecting period" is a period of training (see reg. 1(2)) for which a training allowance (see reg. 1(2)) is payable (but not if the person is an employee), or during which the person is paid maternity allowance, or is entitled (for a maximum of two years) to incapacity benefit, severe disablement allowance or invalid care allowance, which starts within 12 weeks of income support or JSA ceasing (reg. 4(1)). In the case of a connecting period based on entitlement to incapacity benefit, severe disablement allowance or invalid care allowance, note the additional rules in reg. 4(1)(d) and (2)–(4).

After the 13 weeks waiting period the bonus builds up during a period (or periods; see the linking rules above) of entitlement to JSA or income support in which the claimant (or any partner) has earnings from part-time work (the "bonus period"). It accrues at the rate of half the amount by which the earnings reduce the income support or JSA (reg. 8(1)). In the case of contribution-based JSA this does not apply in respect of a partner's earnings (reg. 8(2)). Thus earnings in weeks in which no benefit is payable, or which are not taken into account in calculating the amount of benefit for whatever reason (even if they are subsequently taken into account in deciding that there has been a recoverable overpayment) will not count towards the bonus (see reg. 8(2) and (4)–(5)).

The maximum bonus payable is £1,000 (reg. 8(6), but note reg. 13 (single persons who become couples) and reg. 15 (single claimants who are couples)). The minimum is £5 (reg. 8(9)).

The bonus will become payable in the following situations. The first is if the person (or his partner) satisfies the "work condition", that is, his (or his partner's) entitlement to income support or JSA ceases because he (or his partner) starts or returns to work (other than a return to work for the same employer where the absence was due to a trade dispute: reg. 19(8)), or works more hours, or has increased earnings (reg. 7(2)). This will also apply if the person's entitlement to income support or JSA ceases for any other reason but the work condition is met by him or his partner within 14 days, as a result of which entitlement to benefit would have ended if it had not already done so (reg. 7(3)). The work condition has to be met before the penultimate day before the person reaches 60 (income support) or pensionable age (JSA). Note that there is no requirement that the increased hours or earnings should last for a minimum period, or that the job should be a permanent one (there may be scope for some benefit planning here). Thirdly, a bonus will be payable where a person started training (defined in reg. 1(2)) within 12 weeks of ceasing to be entitled to income support or JSA, or the end of a connecting period and within 14 days of finishing the training (and before he reaches 60 (income support) or pensionable age (JSA)) he works for 16 hours or more a week or his earnings equal or exceed the amount of the training allowance that he received (reg. 7(4)). Finally, a former member of a couple who satisfies the work condition within 14 days of the couple separating can qualify for the bonus (the separation must have occurred before the person claiming the bonus reaches 60) (reg. 7(5)). The person must claim the bonus within 12 weeks of entitlement to income support or JSA ceasing, the training ending or the separation, respectively. Note the provision for late claims (see reg. 23(6)). If a person becomes entitled to income support or JSA again within 12 weeks and before he has claimed his bonus, the effect of reg. 7(7) and (8) is that his accrued bonus will be carried over to his new claim. In this case he will not have to serve a new waiting period (see reg. 2(2) and (3)(b)(i)). But he will have to do so if a bonus is paid and he then reclaims income support or JSA (however short the break in claim) (see reg. 2(4); note also reg. 25(2)).

Note also that if a person is entitled to income support on the day before he reaches 60, or JSA on the day before he reaches pensionable age (*i.e.* 65 (man), 60 (woman)), any accrued bonus is automatically payable; it is not necessary for the work condition to be met or a claim to be made (reg. 17(1)–(3)). If his entitlement ceased 12 weeks (exactly?) before he reached 60 (income support) or pensionable age (JSA), he will qualify for a bonus if he makes a claim within 12 weeks of attaining that age, even though the work condition is not met (reg. 17(5)).

There are special rules for couples who separate, or if one partner dies, and for single people who become couples.

See regs. 22–23 for the rules governing claims for the bonus; note also reg. 26.

For a discussion of the requirements for a bonus to be payable, see *CIS 2397/1998*.

The bonus is treated as income support or income-based JSA (s. 26(3) of the Jobseekers Act), depending on which was last in payment in the bonus period (reg. 24). Thus decisions on claims will be made by an AO (Administration Act, s. 20) and on appeal by a SSAT.

Note that the bonus counts as capital for the purpose of income support, JSA, family credit and disability working allowance (reg. 21). For family credit and disability working allowance (but not income support or income-based JSA), it is disregarded for 52 weeks from the date of receipt (Family Credit Regulations, Sched. 3, para. 50, Disability Working Allowance Regulations, Sched. 4, para. 49). The same disregard applies for housing benefit, council tax benefit and earnings top-up.

Citation, commencement and interpretation

1.—(1) These Regulations may be cited as the Social Security (Back to Work Bonus) (No. 2) Regulations 1996 and shall come into force on 4th November 1996.

(2) In these Regulations—

"the Act" means the Jobseekers Act 1995;

"applicant" means the person claiming the bonus;

"benefit week"—

    (a) where the benefit is income support, has the meaning it has in the Income Support Regulations by virtue of regulation 2(1) of those Regulations;

    (b) where the benefit is a jobseeker's allowance, has the meaning it has in the Jobseeker's Allowance Regulations by virtue of regulation 1(3) of those Regulations;

"bonus" means a back to work bonus;

"bonus period" means a period beginning on the first day of entitlement to a qualifying benefit in a period of entitlement to a qualifying benefit which falls after the waiting period and ends on the last day of that period of entitlement;

"claim" means a claim made in accordance with regulation 22;

"couple" means a married or an unmarried couple;

"earnings" means, unless the context requires otherwise, any earnings which are payable within the bonus period and which—

    (a) where the qualifying benefit is income support, are net earnings or net profit within the meaning of regulation 2 of the Income Support Regulations or are treated as earnings in accordance with regulation 42(5) or (6) of the Income Support Regulations; or

    (b) where the qualifying benefit is a jobseeker's allowance, are net earnings or net profit within the meaning of regulation 1(3) of the Jobseeker's Allowance Regulations or are treated as earnings in accordance with regulation 105(12) or (13) of the Jobseeker's Allowance Regulations,

and for this purpose an amount is payable on the date it is treated as paid for the purpose of regulation 31 of the Income Support Regulations where the qualifying benefit is income support, and for the purpose of

regulation 96 of the Jobseeker's Allowance Regulations where the qualifying benefit is a jobseeker's allowance;
"employment" includes any trade, business, profession, office or vocation;
"the Income Support Regulations" means the Income Support (General)
Regulations 1987;
"the Jobseeker's Allowance Regulations" means the Jobseeker's Allowance
Regulations 1996;
"partner" means where the person—
  (a) is a member of a married or unmarried couple, the other member of
      that couple;
  (b) is married polygamously to two or more members of his household,
      any such member;
"pensionable age" has the meaning it has in section 122(1) of the Benefits
Act;
"period of entitlement to a qualifying benefit" shall be construed in accordance with regulations 2 and 3;
"polygamous marriage" means any marriage during the subsistence of which
a party to it is married to more than one person and the ceremony of
marriage took place under the law of a country which permits polygamy;
"training" means training for which a training allowance is payable;
"training allowance" means an allowance (whether by way of periodical
grants or otherwise) payable—
  (a) out of public funds by a Government department or by or on behalf
      of the Secretary of State for Education and Employment, Scottish
      Enterprise or Highlands and Islands Enterprise; and
  (b) to a person for his maintenance or in respect of a member of his
      family; and
  (c) for the period, or part of the period, during which he is following a
      course of training or instruciton provided by, or in pursuance of
      arrangements made with, that department or approved by that
      department in relation to him or so provided or approved by or on
      behalf of the Secretary of State for Education and Employment,
      Scottish Enterprise or Highlands and Islands Enterprise,
but it does not include an allowance paid by any Government department
to or in respect of a person by reason of the fact that he is following a course
of full-time education, other than under arrangements made under section
2 of the Employment and Training Act 1973 or section 2 of the Enterprise
and New Towns (Scotland) Act 1990, or is training as a teacher;
"waiting period" means the period of 91 consecutive days to which regulation 6 refers;
"week" means period of 7 days;
"work condition" has the meaning it has in regulation 7(2)(b).
(3) For the purposes of these Regulations the qualifying benefits are a jobseeker's allowance and income support.
(4) In these Regulations, unless the context otherwise requires, a reference—
  (a) to a numbered section is to the section of the Act bearing that number;
  (b) to a numbered regulation is to the regulation in these Regulations bearing
      that number;
  (c) in a regulation to a numbered paragraph is to the paragraph in that regula-
      tion bearing that number,
  (d) in a paragraph to a lettered or numbered sub-paragraph is to the sub-
      paragraph in that paragraph bearing that letter or number.

Period of entitlement to a qualifying benefit

2.—(1) A period of entitlement to a qualifying benefit comprises only days
on which a person is entitled to, or treated as entitled to, a qualifying benefit.

(2) Subject to paragraph (4), any two or more periods of entitlement to a qualifying benefit separated by an intervening period specified in paragraph (3) shall link together to form a single period of entitlement to a qualifying benefit.

(3) The intervening periods specified in this paragraph are—

(a) any connecting period for the purposes of regulation 4;

(b) any period of not more than 12 weeks falling between—
    (i) two periods of entitlement to a qualifying benefit;
    (ii) two connecting periods;
    (iii) a connecting period and a period of entitlement to a qualifying benefit;

(c) any period—
    (i) in respect of which a person is summoned for jury service and is required to attend court; and
    (ii) which immediately follows a day of entitlement to a qualifying benefit and is immediately followed by a day of entitlement to a qualifying benefit.

(4) A period of entitlement to a qualifying benefit which would, but for this paragraph, have continued shall end—

(a) where the applicant satisfies the work condition and claims a bonus, on the last day of entitlement to a qualifying benefit which precedes the day on which he first satisfies those requirements;

(b) where the applicant satisfies the condition in regulation 7(4) or (5) (requirements for a bonus) and claims a bonus, on the last day of entitlement to a qualifying benefit which precedes the day on which he first satisfies that condition;

(c) where a bonus is paid in anticipation of an applicant satisfying either of the conditions specified in regulation 7(4)(b) or the condition specified in regulation 7(5)(c), but the applicant then fails to satisfy the relevant condition, on the last day taken into account in determining the award of the qualifying benefit in respect of which the bonus is paid;

(d) where a bonus is paid in anticipation of an applicant or his partner satisfying the work condition, but the work condition is then not satisfied, on the last day taken into account in determining the award of the qualifying benefit in respect of which the bonus is paid;

(e) where the person dies, on the date of his death.

Period of entitlement to a qualifying benefit: further provisions

3.—(1) Any day falling within a period during which a jobseeker's allowance is not payable in accordance with section 19 shall be treated as a day of entitlement to a qualifying benefit only if and for so long as the claimant complies with the requirements as to attendance and the provision of information and evidence contained in regulations made in accordance with section 8(1).

(2) Any day falling within a period during which a jobseeker's allowance is not payable by virtue of section 4(1) solely because of deductions in respect of pension payments shall be treated as a day of entitlement to a qualifying benefit only if and for so long as the claimant complies with requirements as to attendance contained in regulations made in accordance with section 8(1) for the purpose of obtaining any credit in accordance with section 22(5) of the Benefits Act.

(3) Except as provided in paragraphs (1) and (2), no day falling within a period in which a person has an entitlement to a qualifying benefit but—

(a) no benefit is payable; or

(b) the weekly amount of benefits which is payable is less than 10p or in the case of a person to whom section 14 (trade disputes) applies, £5,

shall be treated as a day of entitlement to a qualifying benefit.

(4) Paragraph (5) applies in the case of a person ("the recipient") who has not been entitled to a qualifying benefit, but—

(a) was the partner of a person who has died and that person was entitled to a qualifying benefit other than a contribution-based jobseeker's allowance immediately before his death; or

(b) has separated from a partner who at the date of separation had been entitled to a qualifying benefit other than a contribution-based jobseeker's allowance; or

(c) is one of a couple whose partner has been entitled to a qualifying benefit other than a contribution-based jobseeker's allowance but where entitlement for the qualifying benefit ceased to be that of the partner and became instead that of the recipient.

(5) Where this paragraph applies and paragraph (6) is satisfied in the case of a recipient to whom paragraph (4) applies, the period of entitlement to a qualifying benefit established by the recipient's partner shall be treated as if it had also been established by the recipient.

(6) In the case of a recipient to whom paragraph (4) refers, paragraph (5) applies only where the recipient is entitled to a qualifying benefit within 12 weeks of the date on which—

(a) the partner died; or

(b) the couple separated; or

(c) in the case of a polygamous marriage, one or more members of the marriage separated; or

(d) where paragraph (4)(c) applies, the partner's entitlement to the qualifying benefit ceased.

Connecting period

4.—(1) Subject to the following provisions of this regulation, a connecting period arises where—

(a) within 12 weeks of a person ceasing to be entitled to a qualifying benefit he attends training, except where the person enters into a contract of service with the provider of the training, and lasts throughout the period of training;

(b) within 12 weeks of a person ceasing to be entitled to a qualifying benefit a maternity allowance becomes payable, and lasts throughout the period maternity allowance is payable to the person;

(c) a person ceases to be entitled to a qualifying benefit and in respect of the whole or part of the period of 12 weeks immediately following the day he ceases to be entitled, he becomes entitled ("the new entitlement") to any one of the following benfits—

(i) incapacity benefit;

(ii) severe disablement allowance; or

(iii) invalid care allowance,

and the connecting period lasts until the new entitlement ends or until the expiration of a period of 2 years from the date in respect of which the new entitlement began, whichever is the earlier;

(d) a person ceases to be entitled to one of the benefits mentioned in sub-paragraph (c) above and in respect of the whole or part of the period of 12 weeks immediately following the day he ceases to be so entitled, he becomes entitled to the same or another of those benefits, and the connecting period lasts until the end of the period of entitlement to that benefit or until the expiration of the period of 2 years from the day in respect of which the new entitlement mentioned in sub-paragraph (c) began, whichever is the earlier; or

(e) a person who is treated under paragraph (4) of regulation 3 as having established a period of entitlement to a qualifying benefit under paragraph (5) of the same regulation satisfies the preceding sub-paragraphs of this paragraph within 12 weeks of the date which applies in his case in accordance with paragraph (6) of regulation 3, and lasts throughout the period the person satisfies the preceding sub-paragraphs of this paragraph.

(2) Notwithstanding paragraph (1)(d) where two periods of incapacity for work within the meaning of section 30C(1) of the Benefits Act are separated by a period of more than 8 weeks, the second of those periods is only a connecting period where, in the weeks between the two periods of incapacity for work, the person was entitled to a qualifying benefit which ceased with the onset of the second of those periods of incapacity for work.

(3) In any relevant period, only one connecting period which arises in accordance with paragraph (1)(c) or (d) shall apply in any particular case, and for this purpose, a "relevant period" is the period which falls between periods of entitlement to a qualifying benefit.

(4) For the purposes of paragraph (1)(d) any part of the period of up to 12 weeks mentioned in that sub-paragraph in which the person was not entitled to one of the benefits to which paragraph (1)(c) refers shall be disregarded in determining the period of 2 years.

Periods of entitlement which do not qualify

5.—(1) The periods specified in ['paragraph (4)] shall be treated for the purposes of these Regulations as periods in which a person is not entitled to a qualifying benefit.

(2) Any earnings in any benefit week in a period specified in paragraph (4) shall not be taken into account in determining—
(a) whether a person has earnings from employment; or
(b) the amount of those earnings.

(3) Paragraph (2)—
(a) shall not apply where during a benefit week there are days of entitlement to a qualifying benefit; and
(b) the formula set out in regulation 8(1)(c) shall apply to any earnings in the benefit week in which those days fall, except that "N" shall represent the number of days of entitlement to the qualifying benefit.

(4) The periods specified in this paragraph are any period during which—
(a) interim payments were made to the person in accordance with regulation 2 of the Social Security (Payments on Account. Overpayments and Recovery) Regulations 1988 and in respect of which no award of a qualifying benefit was subsequently made to him;
(b) subject to ['paragraph (5)], the person's applicable amount is determined in accordance with Part VI of the Income Support Regulations (urgent cases) or with Part X of the Jobseeker's Allowance Regulations (urgent cases); or
(c) the person is entitled to a jobseeker's allowance in accordance with Part IX of the Jobseeker's Allowance Regulations (hardship) ['because]—
  (i) he fails to satisfy any one or more of the conditions specified in section 1(2)(a) to (c) (availability for and actively seeking employment); or
  (ii) subject to ['paragraph (6)], he has submitted a claim for a jobseeker's allowance but the adjudication officer has not determined whether those conditions are satisfied.

(5) ['Paragraph (4)(b)] shall not apply in the case of a person to whom—
(a) regulation 70(2)(a) of the Income Support Regulations (certain persons from abroad); or

(b) regulation 147(2)(a) of the Jobseeker's Allowance Regulations (certain persons from abroad).

applies.

(6) Paragraph (4)(c)(ii) shall not apply to any period in respect of which the claim for a jobseeker's allowance is determined by the adjudication officer in the claimant's favour.

AMENDMENT

1. Social Security (Miscellaneous Amendments) Regulations 1997 (S.I. 1997 No. 454), reg. 3(2) (April 7, 1997).

Waiting period

6.—(1) A person shall not be entitled to a bonus unless he has served or is treated as having served a waiting period.

(2) A waiting period is the period comprising the first 91 days in a period of entitlement to a qualifying benefit in which the claim for the bonus is made or which precedes a claim made in accordance with regulation 22(1)(b).

Requirements for a bonus

7.—(1) An applicant who has served, or is treated as having served, a waiting period shall be entitled to a bonus where he satisfies any one of the conditions set out in paragraphs (2) to (5).

(2) The first condition is that—
  (a) he or his partner has or had earnings of which a part only has been disregarded in determining the amount of those earnings for the purposes of a qualifying benefit;
  (b) he or his partner takes up or returns to or increases the number of hours in which in any week he or his partner is engaged in employment or the earnings from an employment in which he or his partner is engaged are increased ("the work condition"), and—
    (i) that employment results; or
    (ii) those earnings result; or
    (iii) the increase in the number of hours and an increase in earnings together result, in entitlement to a qualifying benefit (other than a partner's entitlement to a contribution-based jobseeker's allowance) in respect of himself, and where he has a partner, his family, ceasing;
  (c) he claims the bonus before the end of a period of 12 weeks immediately following the day in respect of which entitlement to the qualifying benefit ceased as mentioned in sub-paragraph (b); and
  (d) in a case where the qualifying benefit to which the applicant was entitled—
    (i) was income support, he has not attained the day before the age of 60; or
    (ii) was a jobseeker's allowance, he has not attained the day before pensionable age,
    at the time the work condition was satisfied.

(3) The second condition is that—
  (a) within 14 days of his ceasing to be entitled to a qualifying benefit he or his partner satisfy the work condition;
  (b) had the work condition been satisfied on the day he was last entitled to a qualifying benefit, that entitlement would as a consequence have ceased;

(c) he satisfies the requirements of paragraph (2)(a) and (d); and

(d) he claims the bonus within 12 weeks of his ceasing to be entitled to a qualifying benfit.

(4) The third condition is that—

(a) within 12 weeks of ceasing to be entitled to a qualifying benefit or within 12 weeks of a connecting period ceasing, the applicant commences training;

(b) within 14 days of the day he last attended training—

    (i) he takes up or returns to or increases the number of hours in which he is engaged in employment, or where his hours of work fluctuate, is engaged on average, for not less than 16 hours per week; or

    (ii) he takes up employment, or increases his earnings from his existing employment, as a result of which weekly earnings equal or exceed the amount of the training allowance payable to him in the last week of training;

(c) he claims the bouns before the end of the period of 12 weeks immediately following the day on which the training ceased;

(d) he satisfies the requirements specified in paragraph (2)(a); and

(e) in a case where the qualifying benefit to which a person was entitled—

    (i) was income support, he satisfied the requirements specified in paragraph (4)(b) before he attained the age of 60;

    (ii) was a jobseeker's allowance, he satisfied the requirements specified in paragraph (4)(b) before he attained pensionable age.

(5) The fourth condition is that—

(a) the applicant is formerly one of a couple, or of a polygamous marriage, who have separated and the separation took place before the person attained the age of 60;

(b) at the date of separation, either the applicant or his partner was entitled to a qualifying benefit;

(c) within 14 days of the separation—

    (i) he takes up or returns to or increases the number of hours in which he is engaged in employment, or where his hours of work fluctuate, is engaged on average, for not less than 16 hours per week; or

    (ii) he takes up employment or increases his earnings from his existing employment, as a result of which his weekly earnings, had he been entitled to a qualifying benefit on the day of separation, equalled or exceeded the amount that would have been the applicable amount or the age-related amount in his case;

(d) he satisfies the requirements specified in paragraph (2)(a); and

(e) he claims the bonus within 12 weeks of the day on which the separation occurred.

(6) For the purpose of determining whether any of the above conditions are satisfied, any change of circumstance other than those specified in the preceding provisions of this regulation which occurred at the same time as a change specified in those provisions and which would of itself have resulted in a loss of entitlement to a qualifying benefit shall be disregarded.

(7) Subject to paragraph (8) a person—

(a) who—

    (i) becomes entitled to, or whose partner becomes entitled to, a qualifying benefit within 12 weeks of the day in respect of which his last previous entitlement to a qualifying benefit ceased; and

    (ii) has not made, and whose partner has not made, a claim for a bonus before the day in respect of which the most recent entitlement to a qualifying benefit first arose,

shall be treated as not satisfying the requirements of paragraph (2)(c) or

Social Security (Back to Work Bonus) (No. 2) Regulations 1996

(3)(d) for the period of 12 weeks following the day in respect of which the last previous entitlement to a qualifying benefit ceased;

(b) who—

    (i) becomes entitled to, or whose partner becomes entitled to, a qualifying benefit before the end of the period of 12 weeks immediately following the day on which training ceased; and

    (ii) has not made, and whose partner has not made, a claim for a bonus before the day in respect of which the most recent entitlement to a qualifying benefit arose,

shall be treated as not satisfying the requirements of paragraph (4)(c) for the period of 12 weeks following the day on which training ceased;

(c) who—

    (i) becomes entitled to, or whose partner becomes entitled to, a qualifying benefit before the end of the period of 12 weeks following the day on which the separation occurred; and

    (ii) has not made, and whose partner has not made, a claim for a bonus before the day in respect of which the most recent entitlement to a qualifying benefit arose,

shall be treated as not satisfying the requirements of paragraph (5)(e) for the period of 12 weeks following the day on which the separation occurred.

(8) Notwithstanding the provisions of paragraph (7) a person shall be able to claim a bonus where he satisfies the work condition or either of the requirements specified in paragraph (4)(b) or the requirements specified in paragraph (5)(c) following the day in respect of which the most recent period of entitlement to a qualifying benefit arose.

Amount payable

8.—(1) Subject to the following provisions of these Regulations, the amount of the bonus payable to an applicant shall be the aggregate of—

(a) half the amount of that part of the applicant's earnings in any benefit week falling either wholly or partly within the bonus period, but which are not disregarded in accordance with regulation 36(2) or 38(2) of, and paragraphs 4 to 9 of Schedule 8 to, the Income Support Regulations or, as the case may be, regulation 99(2) or 101(2) of, and paragraphs 5 to 11 of Schedule 6 to, the Jobseeker's Allowance Regulations;

(b) where the person is one of a couple or a member of a polygamous marriage, half the amount of the partner's earning which are not disregarded in accordance with the provisions mentioned in sub-paragraph (a); and

(c) where earnings are payable to the applicant or his partner in a benefit week falling either partly or wholly within the bonus period which includes a part week of entitlement to a qualifying benefit in accordance with Part VII of the Income Support Regulations or Part XI of the Jobseeker's Allowance Regulations which falls within the bonus period, half the amount calculated by applying the formula—

$$\frac{G}{7} \times N$$

where—

    G is the earnings of the applicant and his partner, in the relevant benefit weeks which are not disregarded in accordance with the provisions mentioned in sub-paragraph (a) or (b); and

    N is the number of days in the part-week.

(2) Earnings for any benefit week in respect of which the person is entitled to a qualifying benefit but no benefit is payable or the applicable amount is Nil, shall be disregarded for the purposes of determining the amount of any bonus payable in his case.

(3) Paragraph (1)(b) shall not apply where the qualifying benefit to which the applicant is entitled is a contribution-based jobseeker's allowance.

(4) Where—
  (a) within the bonus period, a person or his partner has earnings in any benefit week, but the person fails to disclose those earnings or discloses earnings which are less than the amount of those earnings;
  (b) as a result of the failure to disclose those earnings a qualifying benefit is paid at a higher rate than it would have been had the earnings been disclosed;
  (c) those earnings are taken into account, or fully taken into account, on a review of the decision awarding the qualifying benefit; and
  (d) as a result of the review an overpayment of benefit arises,
then those earnings which were not disclosed shall be disregarded in determining the amount of the bonus.

(5) Except in a case to which paragraph (4) applies, where—
  (a) in the bonus period, a person or his partner has earnings in any benefit week;
  (b) the adjudication officer is satisfied that the whole or part of those earnings were not taken into account in determining the amount of any qualifying benefit payable, whether because of a misrepresentation, official error or otherwise; and
  (c) had those earnings been fully taken into account, the amount of the qualifying benefit would have been less than the amount in fact paid,
then those earnings in so far as they were not fully taken into account shall be disregarded in determining the amount of the bonus.

(6) Except in a case to which regulation 13 (single persons who become couples) or 15(5)(a) (single claimants who are couples) applies, the maximum sum payable by way of a bonus to an applicant in respect of a bonus period is £1,000.

(7) In the case of a couple who separate, any earnings paid to either of them after the maximum sum specified in paragraph (6) has been reached but before the date of the separation, shall be disregarded in calculating the amount of any bonus payable on a claim made by either of them or if they are one of a couple the other member of that couple after the date of separation.

(8) Where one or more members of a polygamous marriage separate, any earnings paid to any of them after the maximum sum specified in paragraph (6) has been reached but before the date of separation, shall be disregarded in calculating the amount of any bonus payable on a claim made by any person who is or was a member of that marriage after the date of separation or, if they become one of a couple, by the other member of that couple.

(9) Where the amount of the bonus which would, but for this paragraph, be payable to an applicant is less than £5, the bonus shall not be payable.

(10) Where the amount of a bonus would, but for this paragraph, include a fraction of a penny, that fraction shall be disregarded if it is less than a half penny and shall otherwise be treated as a penny.

(11) Subject to paragraphs (6) to (10), the amount of the bonus payable shall be the whole of the amount calculated in accordance with this regulation.

(12) In paragraph (5), ''official error'' means a mistake made or something done or omitted to be done by an officer of the Department of Social Security or the Department for Education and Employment acting as such where the person claiming the qualifying benefit or any person acting on his behalf has not caused, or materially contributed to, that mistake or omission.

(13) In this regulation "part-week" means an entitlement to a qualifying benefit in respect of any period of less than a week.

Secretary of State to issue estimates

9.—(1) Where it appears to the Secretary of State that a person who is in receipt of a qualifying benefit, or the partner of such a person, has served, or is treated as having served, the waiting period and that, were the conditions of regulation 7 also to be satisfied, a bonus may be payable to that person, he shall, within a year of the waiting period having been served, provide the person claiming the qualifying benefit with a written statement of the amount he estimates may be payable by way of a bonus in his particular case, and shall provide further such statements at intervals of not more than one year as appears to him to be appropriate in the circumstances of the case.

(2) The issue by the Secretary of State of a statement under paragraph (1) shall not be binding upon the adjudication officer when he makes his determination on a claim for a bonus as to—

   (a) whether the applicant satisfies the conditions of entitlement to the bonus; and

   (b) the amount, if any, payable where a bonus is awarded.

Couples who separate

10.—(1) In the case of a couple who separate and at the date of separation one member of the couple has days of entitlement to a qualifying benefit other than a contribution-based jobseeker's allowance which count towards the waiting period, those days of entitlement which count, up to a maximum of 91 days, shall count towards a waiting period for the other member of the couple in a case where he is entitled to a qualifying benefit within 12 weeks of the date of separation, and shall be treated as days on which the other member of the couple was entitled to a qualifying benefit.

(2) Where one or more members of a polygamous marriage separate and at the date of separation any one of them has days of entitlement to a qualifying benefit other than a contribution-based jobseeker's allowance which count towards the waiting period, those days of entitlement which count, up to a maximum of 91 days, shall count towards a waiting period of any person who is or was a member of that marriage, where he is entitled to a qualifying benefit within 12 weeks of the date of separation, and shall be treated as days on which any person who is or was a member of that marriage was entitled to a qualifying benefit.

(3) Where—

   (a) a person is treated in accordance with paragraph (1) or (2) as having days on which he was entitled to a qualifying benefit;

   (b) within 12 weeks of the date of separation the person becomes a partner of another person ("the new partner"); and

   (c) those days of entitlement are greater in number than the days of entitlement to a qualifying benefit (if any) which otherwise accrued to the new partner on the date the person becomes his partner,

then the number of waiting days the new partner is required to serve in accordance with regulation 6(2) when he makes a claim for a qualifying benefit for the couple shall be reduced by a number equal to the number by which the days which count under paragraph (1) or (2) exceed the days of entitlement to a qualifying benefit which had otherwise accrued to the new partner on the date the partner referred to in paragraph (1) or (2) becomes his partner.

Couples who separate where the partner has earnings

11.—(1) This regulation applies where—
    (a) a person who is in receipt of a qualifying benefit other than a contribution-based jobseeker's allowance has a partner;
    (b) the partner has earnings; and
    (c) he and the partner separate ("the separated partner").

(2) From the date of separation, any part of the bonus which, in accordance with regulation 8(1)(b) accrued by virtue of the separated partner's earnings shall, except to the extent specified in paragraph (4) or where paragraph (6) applies, accrue to that partner or in accordance with paragraph (5) (partners who form a new relationship) and not to the other member of the couple.

(3) The amount which shall accrue to the separated partner in accordance with paragraph (2) (referred to in this regulation as "the accrued bonus") shall be the aggregate of the weekly amounts determined in accordance with the formula—

$$\frac{A}{B} \times C$$

where—
    A is the earnings of the separated partner in the benefit week in question in respect of which he has earnings in that part of the bonus period which falls before the date of separation;
    B is the total of the earnings of both members of the couple, or in the case of a polygamous marriage, all the members of the marriage, in that week in that part of the bonus period which falls before the date of separation; and
    C is the amount of the bonus calculated in respect of that week which would have been payable had it been payable on the day before the couple, or some or all of the members of a polygamous marriage, separated in respect of the earnings of both, or, as the case may be, all of them.

(4) In paragraph (3), no account shall be taken at A and B of the earnings of a partner which were taken into account for the purposes of a qualifying benefit before the person became a member of a couple; and the amount of the bonus payable in respect of those earnings shall continue to be determined in accordance with regulation 8.

(5) Where the separated partner becomes the partner of another recipient ("the new partner") of a qualifying benefit within 12 weeks of the date of separation, then the new partner shall have the same rights to the accrued bonus as the person who was formerly the partner would have had on the day before the separation had the bonus been payable on that day.

(6) Where the conditions for entitlement to a bonus, other than the need to make a claim, are fulfilled before the date of separation, but the claim for the bonus is made after the date of separation, the bonus shall be payable to the person entitled to the qualifying benefit before those conditions were fulfilled and no part of it shall be payable to the separated partner.

Couples who separate where the separated partner has attained the age of 60

12.—(1) This regulation applies where—
    (a) a person in receipt of a qualifying benefit has a partner;

(b) the partner has earnings;

(c) before a claim for a bonus based wholly or partly on those earnings is made, he and his partner separate ("the separated partner"); and

(d) the separated partner—
    (i) has attained the age of 60 at the date of separation; or
    (ii) does so within 12 weeks of the date of separation and does not claim a qualifying benefit before attaining that age.

(2) From the date of separation or, if later, the date the person attained the age of 60, any part of the bonus which, in accordance with regulation 8(1)(b), accrued by virtue of the separated partner's earnings shall, except where paragraph (8) applies, accrue to the separated partner or in accordance with paragraph (7) (partners who form new relationships) and not to the other member of the couple, or in the case of a polygamous marriage, the other members of the marriage.

(3) The amount which accrued to the separated partner in accordance with paragraph (2) or (6) shall be determined in accordance with the formula specified in paragraph (3) and in accordance with paragraph (4) of regulation 11.

(4) It is a condition of entitlement to the bonus that the separated partner—
    (a) except where sub-paragraph (b) applies, makes a claim for a bonus within 12 weeks of the date of separation; or
    (b) where at the date of separation the separated partner is within 12 weeks of attaining the age of 60, makes a claim for a bonus within 12 weeks of attaining that age.

(5) A separated partner who makes a claim in accordance with paragraph (4) shall not be required to serve the period of waiting days specified in regulation 6.

(6) In the case of a person who—
    (a) is a separated partner;
    (b) claims income support within 12 weeks of the date of separation;
    (c) at the date of separation had attained the age of 60; and
    (d) before the date of separation had earnings which were taken into account in determining the amount of the couple's earnings, or in the case of a polygamous marriage, the earnings of the members of that marriage, for the purpose of a qualifying benefit,
any part of the bonus which in accordance with regulation 8(1)(b) accrued by virtue of the separated partner's earnings shall accrue to the separated partner and shall be payable to him if the claim for income support is determined in his favour.

(7) Where the separated partner becomes the partner of another recipient ("the new partner") of a qualifying benefit within 12 weeks of the date of separation, then the new partner shall have the same rights to the accrued bonus as the person who was formerly the partner would have had on the day before the separation had the bonus been payable on that day.

(8) Where the conditions for entitlemnent to a bonus, other than the need to make a claim, are fulfilled before the date of separation, but the claim for the bonus is made after the date of separation, the bonus shall be payable to the person entitled to the qualifying benefit before those conditions were fulfilled and no part of it shall be payable to the separated partner.

Single persons who become couples

13.—(1) This regulation applies where two persons form a couple and within the period of 12 weeks immediately before they do so—
    (a) both had entitlement to a qualifying benefit; and
    (b) both were within their bonus period.

(2) In the case of a couple to whom this regulation applies, other than a couple to whom paragraph (5) applies, the amount of the bonus shall be—

(a) except where sub-paragraph (b) applies and subject to the limit imposed by regulation 8(6), the aggregate of the bonuses which have accrued to each member of the couple before the day they became a couple, together with any amount which accrued to the person making the claim by reference to his earnings and those of his partner after they became a couple; or

(b) where the aggregate of the bonuses which had accrued to each member of the couple before the day they became a couple exceeds £1,000, the aggregate amount.

(3) For the avoidance of doubt, in the case of a couple to whom paragraph (2)(b) applies, the amount of the bonus shall not increase by reference to any earnings payable to either member of the couple after they became a couple.

(4) This regulation applies to members of a polygamous marriage as it applies to a couple but as if references to a couple were references [¹. . .] to the members of the polygamous marriage and references to each member of the couple were references to two or more members of the polygamous marriage.

(5) Where both members of the couple are entitled to a contribution-based jobseeker's allowance, bonuses accrued to each of them, whether or not the bonuses accrued before they became a couple, shall not be aggregated.

AMENDMENT

1. Social Security (Miscellaneous Amendments) Regulations 1997 (S.I. 1997 No. 454), reg. 3(3) (April 7, 1997).

Single persons who become couples: further provisions

14.—(1) This regulation applies where two persons become a couple and—

(a) within the period of 12 weeks immediately before they do so only one of the two has a previous entitlement to a qualifying benefit and either—
    (i) is within his bonus period; or
    (ii) is serving his waiting period; and

(b) the other member makes a claim for a qualifying benefit, other than a contribution-based jobseeker's allowance.

(2) The number of days the person mentioned in paragraph (1)(a) has served of the waiting period referred to in regulation 6 shall be deducted from the number of days of the waiting period the other member of the couple is required to serve.

(3) Any bonus which has accrued to the person mentioned in paragraph (1)(a) shall be treated as the bonus of the claimant and not that person.

Single claimants who are couples

15.—(1) Where—

(a) two persons are living together as a married or unmarried couple;

(b) each of those persons was in receipt of a qualifying benefit during the whole or part of the time they were a couple; and

(c) had they declared they were a couple, either—
    (i) no qualifying benefit would have been payable to them; or
    (ii) a qualifying benefit would have been payable to only one member of the couple,

the provisions of these Regulations shall have effect subject to paragraphs (3) to (5).

(2) Where—

(a) three or more persons who are living together are members of a polygamous marriage,

(b) two or more of those persons were in receipt of a qualifying benefit during the whole or part of the time they lived together and were members of a polygamous marriage; and

(c) had they declared that they were members of a polygamous marriage, either,

(i) no qualifying benefit would have been payable to them; or

(ii) a qualifying benefit would have been payable to only one or some of the members of the polygamous marriage,

the provisions of these Regulations shall also have effect subject to the following paragraphs.

(3) In a case where in any benefit week no benefit would have been payable, any earnings received in that benefit week shall be disregarded in determining the amount of the bonus.

(4) In a case where a qualifying benefit is or would have been payable to one member of the couple or polygamous marriage, any earnings which were taken into account in the separate awards of the qualifying benefit to each member of the couple or polygamous marriage shall, subject to paragraph (5), be taken into account in accordance with regulation 8.

(5) Where at the time the persons mentioned in paragraph (1)(a) or (2)(a) first become a married or unmarried couple or members of a polygamous marriage, the amount of any bonus, determined in accordance with the preceding provisions of this regulation and regulation 8—

(a) would be £1,000 or more, the amount of the bonus shall be the higher amount and shall not be increased further by reference to any earnings accruing since that time; or

(b) was less than £1,000, earnings accruing since that time shall be taken into account in accordance with regulation 8, but not so as to increase the amount of the bonus payable to more than £1,000.

Couples both of whom are entitled to a qualifying benefit

16.—(1) Where—

(a) one member of a couple is entitled to a contribution-based jobseeker's allowance; and

(b) the other member of the couple is entitled to an income-based jobseeker's allowance or to income support; or

(c) one member of a polygamous marriage is entitled to a contribution-based jobseeker's allowance; and

(d) another member of the polygamous marriage is entitled to an income-based jobseeker's allowance,

any bonus which accrues in respect of the earnings of the person entitled to a contribution-based jobseeker's allowance shall accrue to the bonus of the person who within the bonus period was last entitled to an income-based jobseeker's allowance or to income support.

(2) Where—

(a) two persons become a couple;

(b) neither member of the couple has served his waiting period;

(c) both members of the couple have, at the time they become a couple, a current period of entitlement to a qualifying benefit, or had a period of entitlement to a qualifying benefit within 12 weeks of the day after they became a couple;

(d) one member of the couple has fewer days of entitlenment to a qualifying benefit (represented by ''A'') in that period than the other member (represented by ''B'');

(e) the person entitled to the qualifying benefit after they became a couple is the person with the fewer days of entitlement; and

    (f) the qualifying benefit to which he is entitled is not a contribution-based jobseeker's allowance,

then the number of waiting days the person is required to serve in accordance with regulation 6(2) shall be reduced by a number equal to the number by which B exceeds A.

Persons attaining pensionable age

17.—(1) Where—
    (a) the qualifying benefit is income support and the person entitled to the qualifying benefit has attained the day immediately preceding his 60th birthday; or
    (b) the qualifying benefit is a jobseeker's allowance and the person entitled to the qualifying benefit has attained the day immediately preceding pensionable age,

and in either case the person is within the bonus period, he shall, notwithstanding that the requirement specified in paragraph (2) is not satisfied in his case, be entitled to a bonus.

    (2) The requirement specified in this paragraph is that entitlement to the bonus has not arisen because—
    (a) the person has not claimed the bonus;
    (b) the work condition is not satisfied; or
    (c) the person has not claimed the bonus and the work condition is not satisfied.

    (3) In the case of a person who is entitled to a bonus in accordance with paragraph (1), the bonus period and the period of entitlement to a qualifying benefit shall end on the day he attained the age of 60 or, as the case may be, pensionable age.

    (4) Where a person who ceases to be entitled to a jobseeker's allowance after attaining the age of 60 becomes entitled to income support within 12 weeks of ceasing to be entitled to a jobseeker's allowance, or after an intervening period as provided for in regulation 2, he shall be entitled to a bonus in accordance with paragraph (1)(a) on the day he claims income support, and notwithstanding paragraph (3) his bonus period shall be treated as ending on the day he claims income support.

    (5) Where, 12 weeks before attaining—
    (a) the age of 60, the person ceased to be entitled to income support; or
    (b) pensionable age, the person ceased to be entitled to a jobseeker's allowance,

but failed to satisfy any one of the conditions specified in regulation 7, he shall, if he makes a claim for a bonus in the period of 12 weeks after he attains that age, be entitled to the bonus notwithstanding his failure to satisfy any of those conditions.

    (6) Where a person to whom paragraph (5) applies becomes entitled to income support within the period of 12 weeks after he attains the age of 60, or, as the case may be, pensionable age, or after an intervening period as provided for in regulation 2, he shall be entitled to a bonus notwithstanding his failure to satisfy any one of the conditions specified in regulation 7.

    (7) The amount of any bonus to which a person may be entitled in accordance with this regulation shall be calculated in accordance with regulation 8.

Death

18.—(1) Subject to paragraph (4), where—
  (a) a person dies;
  (b) the person leaves behind a partner;

(c) immediately before his death, the person was entitled to a qualifying benefit; and

(d) immediately before his death the person would have been entitled to a bonus but for his failure to make a claim for it and satisfy the work condition,

paragraphs (2), (5) and (6) shall apply.

(2) Where the partner of a deceased person becomes entitled to a qualifying benefit for a period commencing within 12 weeks of the person's death then—

(a) any waiting period served by the deceased person shall be treated as having been served by the partner; and

(b) any amount which accrued towards his bonus shall be treated as having accrued towards the partner's bonus.

(3) Where at the date of death a person had been entitled to a qualifying benefit for less than 91 consecutive days, then those days count towards any waiting period which the partner is required to serve under regulation 6 [¹where that partner becomes entitled to a qualifying benefit no more than 12 weeks after the date of death].

(4) This regulation does not apply where the qualifying benefit the deceased person was entitled to was a contribution-based jobseeker's allowance.

(5) Where the deceased person referred to in paragraph (2) was a member of a polygamous marriage—

(a) any waiting period accruing under paragraph (2)(a) shall accrue to each of the deceased's partners;

(b) any amount accrued towards the deceased person's bonus shall accrue towards each partner's bonus in accordance with the formula—

$$\frac{D \times F}{E} \times \frac{1}{X}$$

where—

D is the amount of the deceased person's earnings during his bonus period;

E is the total earnings of all members of the marriage in the deceased person's bonus period;

F is the amount of the bonus which would have been payable on the day before the death of the deceased had he been entitled to the bonus on that day; and

X is the number of surviving partners of the marriage.

(6) In the case of a partner who had earnings in the deceased partner's bonus period, which are included in the value "E" in paragraph (5), any amount of bonus which accrued to that partner in accordance with that paragraph shall be increased by an amount equal to the value of half those earnings.

AMENDMENT

1. Social Security (Miscellaneous Amendments) Regulations 1997 (S.I. 1997 No. 454), reg. 3(4) (April 7, 1997).

Trade disputes

19.—(1) The provisions of paragraphs (2) and (4) are subject to paragraph (6).

(2) Where—

(a) the qualifying benefit is a jobseeker's allowance;

(b) the partner of the person claiming the benefit is not employed on any day because of a stoppage of work; and

(c) that stoppage is due to a trade dispute at the partner's place of work,

any earnings of the partner during the stoppage shall be disregarded in determining the amount of the bonus unless he proves he is not directly interested in the dispute.

(3) In paragraph (2), "place of work" has the meaning it has in section 14 by virtue of sub-section (4) of that section.

(4) Where—

(a) the qualifying benefit is income support;

(b) the person claiming the benefit, or his partner, is not employed on any day because of a stoppage of work; and

(c) that stoppage is due to a trade dispute at his place of employment,

any earnings of that person or his partner, as the case may be, during the stoppage shall be disregarded in determining the amount of the bonus unless he proves he is not directly interested in the dispute.

(5) In paragraph (4), "place of employment" and "trade dispute" have the meanings they have in the Benefits Act by virtue of section 27(3) of that Act.

(6) Where in any benefit week the partner referred to in paragraph (2)(b) or, as the case may be, the partner or the person claiming the benefit referred to in paragraph (4)(b) is within her maternity pay period or is incapable of work, this regulation shall not apply in respect of [¹that partner's or that person's earnings] for that benefit week.

(7) In paragraph (6) "maternity pay period" has the meaning it has in the Benefits Act by virtue of section 165(1) of that Act.

(8) Where the person claiming the benefit referred to in paragraph (2)(a) or (4)(a) or his partner, as the case may be, is again employed at the place of employment where the stoppage of work occurred, that employment shall not satisfy the work condition and no bonus shall be payable in consequence of it.

AMENDMENT

1. Social Security (Miscellaneous Amendments) Regulations 1997 (S.I. 1997 No, 454), reg. 3(5) (April 7, 1997).

Share fishermen

20. In their application to share fishermen who are entitled to a contribution-based jobseeker's allowance, these Regulations shall have effect as if references to earnings were references to earnings earned in any benefit week within the bonus period, whether or not they were payable in that benefit week.

Bonus to be treated as capital for certain purposes

21. Any bonus paid to an applicant shall be treated as capital of his for the purposes of—

(a) housing benefit;

(b) council tax benefit;

(c) family credit;

(d) disability working allowance;

(e) income support;

(f) a jobseeker's allowance.

Claiming a bonus

22.—(1) A claim for a bonus shall be made in writing on a form approved for the purpose by the Secretary of State and shall be made—

(a) subject to paragraph (7), not earlier than the beginning of the benefit week which precedes the benefit week in which an award of a qualifying benefit comes to an end; and

(b) subject to regulation 23(5), not later than the end of the period of 12 weeks immediately following—

    (i) in the case of a person who satisfies the 3rd condition in regulation 7, the last day on which he was engaged in training;

    (ii) in the case of a person to whom the 4th condition specified in regulation 7 applies (couples who separate, the date of separation;

    (iii) in the case of a person to whom regulation 12 applies (couples who separate where the separated partner has attained the age of 60), the date of separation;

    (iv) in the case of a person who has attained pensionable age or, where the qualifying benefit is income support the age of 60, the date he attained that age;

    (v) in any other case, the date on which entitlement to a qualifying benefit ceased on satisfaction of the work condition.

(2) A claim for a bonus shall be delivered or sent to an office of the Department of Social Security or of the Department for Education and Employment.

(3) If a claim is defective at the date when it is received, the Secretary of State may refer the claim to the person making it and if the form is received properly completed within one month, or such longer period as the Secretary of State may consider reasonable, from the date on which it is so referred, the Secretary of State may treat the claim as if it had been duly made in the first instance.

(4) A claim which is made on the form approved for the time being is, for the purposes of paragraph (3), properly completed if it is completed by the applicant in accordance with instructions on the form and defective if it is not.

(5) An applicant shall furnish such certificates, documents, information and evidence in connection with the claim, or any question arising out of it, as may be required by the Secretary of State and shall do so within one month of being required to do so or such longer period as the Secretary of State may consider reasonable.

(6) In the case of a person who has served or is treated as having served a waiting period in accordance with regulation 6(1) (waiting period) and is a member of a couple in respect of whom income support or an income-based jobseeker's allowance is payable, the claim for the bonus shall be made by the member of the couple entitled to the benefit.

(7) A person who has an employment to take up, or whose earnings from or the hours of employment will increase, within 14 days of completing his training or the date of separation and that employment satisfies the requirements of regulation 7(4)(b) or (5)(c) may make a claim for a bonus—

(a) in the case of a person who satisfies all the other requirements of the 3rd condition specified in regulation 7, up to 14 days before the day following the last day of attendance on the course;

(b) in the case of a person who satifies all the other conditions of the 4th condition specified in regulation 7, up to 13 days before the day on which he complies with the condition, but not before the day after the separation.

Claims: further provisions

23.—(1) A person who has made a claim may amend it at any time by notice in writing received at an appropriate office before a determination has been made on a claim, and any claim so amended may be treated as if it had been so amended in the first instance.

(2) A person who has made a claim may withdraw it at any time before a determination has been made on it, by notice to the appropriate office, and any such notice of withdrawal shall have effect when it is received.

(3) The date on which the claim is made shall be—

(a) in the case of a claim which meets the requirements of regulation 22(1), the date on which it is received at the appropriate office; or

(b) in the case of a claim treated under regulation 22(3) as having been duly made, the date on which the claim was received in an appropriate office in the first place.

(4) In this regulation, the "appropriate office" means an office of the Department of Social Security or the Department for Education and Employment.

(5) In the case of a person who—

(a) ceases to be entitled to a qualifying benefit; and

(b) again becomes entitled to a qualifying benefit in the same period of entitlement to a qualifying benefit,

for the reference to 12 weeks in regulation 22(1)(b) there shall be substituted a reference to a period equal to the period falling between the last day of entitlement to a qualifying benefit mentioned at sub-paragraph (a) and the first day of entitlement to a qualifying benefit mentioned at sub-paragraph (b).

(6) Where the applicant proves there was good cause throughout the period from the expiry of the 12 weeks specified in regulation 22(1), for failure to claim the bonus within the specified time, the time for claiming the bonus shall be extended to the date on which the claim is made or to a period of 12 months, whichever is the shorter period.

Payment of bonus

24. A bonus calculated by reference to earnings payable during periods of entitlement to income support and to a jobseeker's allowance shall be treated as payable—

(a) wholly by way of a jobseeker's allowance, where the qualifying benefit last in payment in the bonus period was a jobseeker's allowance; or

(b) wholly by way of income support, where the qualifying benefit last in payment in the bonus period was income support.

Award of bonus

25.—(1) Where the adjudication officer is satisfied that a person satisfies, or will satisfy, the work condition or either of the requirements specified in regulation 7(4)(b) or the requirements specified in regulation 7(5)(c) he may award a bonus in advance of the condition or requirement being met.

(2) If, having been awarded a bonus in advance in accordance with paragraph (1), the person fails to satisfy the conditions, he shall not be entitled to any further bonus until he has served a further waiting period in accordance with regulation 6 (waiting period).

Payments on death

26.—(1) Where a person satisfies the requirements for entitlement to a bonus other than the need to make a claim, but dies within 12 weeks of the last day of entitlement to a qualifying benefit, the Secretary of State may appoint such person as he may think fit to claim a bonus in place of the deceased person.

(2) Where the conditions specified in paragraph (3) are satisfied, a claim may be made by the person appointed for a back to work bonus to which the deceased person would have been entitled if he had claimed it in accordance with regulation 22 (claiming a bonus).

(3) Subject to the following provisions of this regulation, the following conditions are specified for the purposes of paragraph (2)—

(a) the application to the Secretary of State to be appointed a fit person to make a claim shall be made within 6 months of the date of death;

(b) the claim shall be made in writing within 6 months of the date the appointment was made.

(4) Subject to paragraphs (5) and (6), the Secretary of State may, in exceptional circumstances, extend the period for making an application or a claim to such longer period as he considers appropriate in the particular case.

(5) Where the period is extended in accordance with paragraph (4), the period specified in paragraph (3)(a) or (b) shall be shortened by a corresponding period.

(6) The Secretary of State shall not extend the period of claim in accordance with paragraph (4) for more than 12 months from the date of death, but in calculating that period any period between the date when an application for a person to be appointed to make a claim is made and the date when the Secretary of State makes the appointment shall be disregarded.

(7) A claim made in accordance with paragraph (2) shall be treated, for the purposes of these Regulations, as if made on the date of the deceased's death.

Transitional matters

27.—(1) For the purposes of determining whether a person satisfies the requirements of regulation 6 (waiting period), days on or after 1st July 1996 but before 7th October 1996 in respect of which a person was entitled to unemployment benefit shall be treated as days of entitlement to a contribution-based jobseeker's allowance, and shall include those Sundays, or the day substituted for Sunday by regulations made under the former section 25A(1)(e) of the Benefits Act, which fall only between days of entitlement to unemployment benefit.

(2) Where in accordance with transitional provisions made under section 40 the rules as to the calculation of earnings which apply in the case of a person entitled to a jobseeker's allowance are those which applied before 7th October 1996 to that person in respect of an entitlement to unemployment benefit, then—

(a) any day of entitlement to a jobseeker's allowance including any day on which the person would be entitled to a jobseeker's allowance if the day were not a Sunday or, as mentioned in paragraph (1), the day substituted for Sunday, shall count towards the waiting period specified in regulation 6; but

(b) any earnings of that person or his partner calculated in accordance with those rules shall be disregarded in determining the amount of any bonus payable to him.

(3) Any period of entitlement to income support which falls before 1st July 1996 shall not count for the purposes of regulation 6 (waiting period).

(4) No bonus period shall commence before 7th October 1996.

Revocations

28. The Social Security (Back to Work Bonus) Regulations 1996, the Social Security (Back to Work Bonus) (Amendment) Regulations 1996 and regulation 4 of the Social Security and Child Support (Jobseeker's Allowance) (Miscellaneous Amendments) Regulations 1996 are hereby revoked.

Child Support (Maintenance Assessment Procedure) Regulations 1992

(S.I. 1992 No. 1813)

Made by the Secretary of State under various provisions of the Child Support Act 1991

REGULATIONS REPRODUCED

PART I

GENERAL

GENERAL NOTE

Note that under the Social Security Act 1998 child support officers and adjudication officers are to be abolished and all decision-making is to be transferred to the Secretary of State. Appeals will go to a unified appeal tribunal. For child support the implementation date for the new system of decision-making and appeals is June 1, 1999. There are also amendments to Part IX of the Maintenance Assessment Procedure Regulations from that date; note in particular that the time limits and procedure in reg. 35 will change. For details of these changes see the 1999 Supplement to this book.

Note also that family credit and disability working allowance are due to be replaced by working families tax credit and disabled person's tax credit on October 5, 1999. It is understood that people in receipt of these credits will not be required to apply for a maintenance assessment to be made. See the 1999 Supplement for further details.

Only the regulations necessary to understand how a reduced benefit direction operates are reproduced. There are no notes or definitions after each individual regulation. Most relevant definitions are in reg. 1, although there also needs to be some reference to the Child Support Act 1991.

Once a reduced benefit direction is given by a CSO it is binding on the AO (Child Support Act 1991, s. 46(11)). The AO must then apply the reduction in making any initial decision on a claim for income support, income-based JSA, family credit or disability working allowance and review any existing award on a relevant change of circumstances. See reg. 51A of the Family Credit (General) Regulations and reg. 56A of the Disability Working Allowance (General) Regulations for the authority to review those benefits. For income support, or income-based JSA, the power in s. 25(1)(b) of the Administration Act appears to be sufficient.

Reg. 36 specifies that the reduction is to be of a fixed amount for a fixed period. There is no discretion to alter either element whatever the circumstances. Where a reduced benefit direction is given on or after October 7, 1996, the reduction is by 40 per cent. of the income support personal allowance for a single claimant aged not less than 25 and will last for three years (reg. 36(2)). The previous level of reduction (20 per cent. of such personal allowance for the first 26, and 10 per cent. for the following 52, weeks) continued to apply in relation to directions given before October 7, 1996, as did the other provisions in regs. 36 and 47 that were amended or revoked on that date (see reg. 25(3) and (4) of the Child Support (Miscellaneous Amendments) Regulations 1996 (p. 572). Thus, for example, if a reduced benefit direction given before October 7, 1996 had been in operation for the full period, no further direction could be issued in relation to the children covered by the direction (see the former reg. 36(9) in the 1996 edition of this book). This will apply even if the parent makes a further claim for benefit. See below for the position where a direction is given on or after October 7, 1996.

From April 1999 the amount of the reduction is £20.56 per week. This amount is subject to reg. 37, under which a reduction will be adjusted so as not to reduce the amount of income-related benefit below a minimum amount. The minimum is 10p for income support and income-based JSA and 50p for family credit and disability working allowance. A direction is suspended where income support or income-based JSA is payable under the special rules applying to hospital patients or persons in residential accommodation or residential care or nursing homes (regs. 40 and 40ZA).

Reg. 40A which provided for directions made after January 22, 1996 to be suspended if certain other deductions were already being made from the claimant's, or any partner's, income support or, from October 28, 1996, income-based JSA (see the amendments to reg. 40A made by reg. 6(3) of the Social Security and Child Support (Jobseeker's Allowance) (Miscellaneous Amendments) Regulations 1996 (S.I. 1996 No. 2538)) was revoked on January 13, 1997. See the 1996 edition of this book for reg. 40A and the related reg. 49A (which was revoked at the same time), and note the transitional protection in reg. 16(3) of the Child Support (Miscellaneous Amendments) (No. 2) Regulations 1996 (p. 573) where a direction was suspended under reg. 40A on January 13, 1997.

From January 22, 1996 a direction will not be given if the parent's, or any partner's, income support or income-based JSA includes a disability, higher pensioner or disabled child premium, or, where family credit or disability working allowance is in payment, an amount equal to the disability or disabled child premium is included in the calculation of the parent's exempt income (reg. 35A).

If the parent complies with her obligations under s. 6 of the Child Support Act 1991 (presumably to be determined by a CSO) the direction ceases to be in force (reg. 41). If she gives additional reasons for not complying, a CSO may review and lift the requirement to comply, in which case the direction ceases to be in force (reg. 42). If all of the relevant benefits cease to be payable the direction is suspended (reg. 38). The balance of the reduction period is applied if benefit becomes payable again within 52 weeks. The same applies if the sole qualifying child ceases to be a child or to be qualifying (reg. 48).

Reg. 36(9) used to provide that once a reduced benefit direction had been in operation for the full period, another direction could not be given in relation to the children covered by the direction. This provision has been revoked from October 7, 1996. Presumably the purpose is to allow another direction to be issued if the previous one has expired and the parent still fails to comply. Whether there is power under s. 46 of the Child Support Act 1991 to issue such repeated reduced benefit directions is not entirely clear. If an *additional* qualifying child appears a further direction may be given (reg. 47).

PART I

GENERAL

Citation, commencement and interpretation

1.—(1) These Regulations may be cited as the Child Support (Maintenance Assessment Procedure) Regulations 1992 and shall come into force on 5th April 1993.

(2) In these Regulations, unless the context otherwise requires—

"the Act" means the Child Support Act 1991;

"applicable amount"[², except in regulation 40ZA,] is to be construed in accordance with Part IV of the Income Support Regulations;

"applicable amounts Schedule" means Schedule 2 to the Income Support Regulations;

"award period" means a period in respect of which an award of family credit or disability working allowance is made;

"balance of the reduction period" means, in relation to a direction that is or has been in force, the portion of the period specified in a direction in respect of which no reduction of relevant benefit has been made;

"benefit week", in relation to income support, has the same meaning as in the Income Support Regulations, [² in relation to jobseeker's allowance has the same meaning as in the Jobseeker's Allowance Regulations,] and, in relation to family credit and disability working allowance, is to be construed in accordance with the Social Security (Claims and Payments) Regulations 1987;

"direction" means reduced benefit direction;

"disability working allowance" has the same meaning as in the Social Security Contributions and Benefits Act 1992;

[*definitions omitted as not relating to reduced benefit directions*]

"Income Support Regulations" means the Income Support (General) Regulations 1987;

[²"the Jobseeker's Allowance Regulations" means the Jobseeker's Allowance Regulations 1996;]

[*definitions omitted as not relating to reduced benefit directions*]

"obligation imposed by section 6 of the Act" is to be construed in accordance with section 46(1) of the Act;

"parent with care" means a person who, in respect or the same child or children, is both a parent and a person with care;

"the parent concerned" means the parent with respect to whom a direction is given;

[*definition omitted as not relating to reduced benefit directions*]

"relevant benefit" means income support, [²income-based jobseeker's allowance,] family credit or disability working allowance;

[*definition omitted as not relating to reduced benefit directions*]

(3) In these Regulations, references to a direction as being "in operation", "suspended", or "in force" shall be construed as follows—

a direction is "in operation" if, by virtue of that direction, relevant benefit is currently being reduced;

a direction is "suspended" if [¹. . .]—

(a) after that direction has been given, relevant benefit ceases to be payable, or becomes payable at one of the rates indicated in regulation 40(3) [²or, as the case may be, regulation 40ZA(4)]; [¹. . .]

(b) at the time that the direction is given, relevant benefit is payable at one of the rates indicated in regulation 40(3)[²or, as the case may be, regulation 40ZA(4)], [¹or]

[¹(c) at the time that the direction is given one or more of the deductions set out in regulation 40A is being made from the income support [²or income-based jobseeker's allowance] payable to or in respect of the parent concerned,]

and these Regulations provide for relevant benefit payable from a later date to be reduced by virtue of the same direction;

a direction is "in force" if it is either in operation or is suspended,

and cognate terms shall be construed accordingly.

(4) The provisions of Schedule 1 shall have effect to supplement the meaning of "child" in section 55 of the Act.

[*Paras. (5) to (9) not reproduced*]

AMENDMENTS

1. Child Support (Miscellaneous Amendments) (No. 2) Regulations 1995 (S.I. 1995 No. 3261), reg. 15 (January 22, 1996).
2. Social Security and Child Support (Jobseeker's Allowance) (Consequential Amendments) Regulations 1996 (S.I. 1996 No. 1345), reg. 5(2) (October 7, 1996).

PART IX

REDUCED BENEFIT DIRECTIONS

Prescription of disability working allowance for the purposes of section 6 of the Act

34. Disability working allowance shall be a benefit of a prescribed kind for the purposes of section 6 of the Act.

Periods for compliance with obligations imposed by section 6 of the Act

35.—(1) Where the Secretary of State considers that a parent has failed to comply with an obligation imposed by section 6 of the Act he shall serve written notice on that parent that, unless she complies with that obligation, he intends to refer the case to a child support officer to take action under section 46 of the Act if the child support officer considers such action to be appropriate.

[¹(2) The Secretary of State shall not refer a case to a child support officer prior to the expiry of a period of—

    (a) 2 weeks from the date he serves notice under paragraph (1) on the parent in question; or
    (b) 6 weeks from that date, where, before the expiry of 2 weeks from service of that notice, he has received from the parent in question in writing her reasons why she believes that if she were to be required to comply with an obligation imposed by section 6 of the Act, there would be a risk, as a result of that compliance, of her or any child or children living with her suffering harm or undue distress,

and the notice shall contain a statement setting out the provisions of sub-paragraphs (a) and (b).]

(3) Where [¹a] child support officer serves written notice on a parent under section 46(2) of the Act, the period to be specified in that notice shall be 14 days.

AMENDMENT

1. Child Support (Miscellaneous Amendments) Regulations 1996 (S.I. 1996 No. 1945), reg. 13 (October 7, 1996).

[¹Circumstances in which a reduced benefit direction shall not be given

35A. A child support officer shall not after 22nd January 1996 give a reduced benefit direction where—

    (a) income support is paid to or in respect of the parent in question and the applicable amount of the claimant for income support includes one or more of the amounts set out in paragraph 15(3), (4) or (6) of Part IV of Schedule 2 to the Income Support (General) Regulations 1987; or

[²(aa) income-based jobseeker's allowance is paid to or in respect of the parent in question and the applicable amount of the claimant for income-based jobseeker's allowance includes one or more of the amounts set out in paragraph 20(4), (5) or (7) of Schedule 1 to the Jobseeker's Allowance Regulations; or]

(b) an amount equal to one or more of the amounts specified in sub-paragraph (a) is included, by virtue of regulation 9 of the Maintenance Assessments and Special Cases Regulations, in the exempt income of the parent in question and family credit or disability working allowance is paid to or in respect of that parent.]

AMENDMENTS

1. Child Support (Miscellaneous Amendments) (No. 2) Regulations 1995 (S.I. 1995 No. 3261), reg. 37 (January 22, 1996).

2. Social Security and Child Support (Jobseeker's Allowance) (Consequential Amendments) Regulations 1996 (S.I. 1996 No. 1345), reg. 5(5) (October 7, 1996).

Amount of and period of reduction of relevant benefit under a reduced benefit direction

36.—(1) The reduction in the amount payable by way of a relevant benefit to, or in respect of, the parent concerned and the period of such reduction by virtue of a direction shall be determined in accordance with paragraphs (2) to (9).

(2) Subject to paragraph (6) and regulations 37, 38(7) [², 40 and 40ZA], there shall be a reduction for a period of [³156 weeks] from the day specified in the direction under the provisions of section 46(9) of the Act in respect of each such week equal to

[³$0.4 \times B$]

where B is an amount equal to the weekly amount, in relation to the week in question, specified in column (2) of paragraph 1(1)(e) of the applicable amounts Schedule.

(3)[³. . .].

(4) [¹Subject to paragraphs [³(4A),] (5), (5A) and (5B)], a direction shall come into operation on the first day of the second benefit week following the review, carried out by the adjudication officer in consequence of the direction, of the relevant benefit that is payable.

[³(4A) Subject to paragraphs (5), (5A) and (5B), where a reduced benefit direction ("the subsequent direction") is made on a day when a reduced benefit direction ("the earlier direction") is in force in respect of the same parent, the subsequent direction shall come into operation on the day immediately following the day on which the earlier direction ceased to be in force.]

(5) Where the relevant benefit is income support and the provisions of regulation 26(2) of the Social Security (Claims and Payments) Regulations 1987 (deferment of payment of different amount of income support) apply, a direction shall come into operation on such later date as may be determined by the Secretary of State in accordance with those provisions.

[¹(5A) Where the relevant benefit is family credit or disability working allowance and, at the time a direction is given, a lump sum payment has already been made under the provisions of regulation 27(1A) of the Social Security (Claims and Payments) Regulations 1987 (payment of family credit or disability working allowance by lump sum) the direction shall, subject to paragraph (5B), come into operation on the first day of any benefit week which immediately follows the period in respect of which the lump sum payment was made, or the first day of any benefit week which immediately follows 18th April 1995 if later.

(5B) Where the period in respect of which the lump sum payment was made is not immediately followed by a benefit week, but family credit or disability working allowance again becomes payable, or income support [²or income-based jobseeker's allowance] becomes payable, during a period of 52 weeks from the date the direction was given, the direction shall come into operation on the first day of the second benefit week which immediately follows the expiry of a period of 14 days from service of the notice specified in paragraph (5C).

(5C) Where paragraph (5B) applies, the parent to or in respect of whom family credit or disability working allowance has again become payable, or income support [²or income-based jobseeker's allowance] has become payable, shall be notified in writing by a child support officer that the amount of family credit, disability working allowance [², income support or income-based job-seeker's allowance] paid to or in respect of her will be reduced in accordance with the provisions of paragraph (5B) if she continues to fail to comply with the obligations imposed by section 6 of the Act.

(5D) Where—

(a) family credit or disability working allowance has been paid by lump sum under the provisions of regulation 27(1A) of the Social Security (Claims and Payments) Regulations 1987 (whether or not a benefit week immediately follows the period in respect of which the lump sum payment was made); and

(b) where income support [²or income-based jobseeker's allowance] becomes payable to or in respect of a parent to or in respect of whom family credit or disability working allowance was payable at the time the direction referred to in paragraph (5A) was made, income support [²or, as the case may be, income-based jobseeker's allowance] shall become a relevant benefit for the purposes of that direction and the amount payable by way of income support [²or, as the case may be, income-based jobseeker's allowance] shall be reduced in accordance with that direction.

(5E) In circumstances to which paragraph (5A) or (5B) applies, where no relevant benefit has become payable during a period of 52 weeks from the date on which a direction was given, it shall lapse.]

[³(6) Where the benefit payable is income support or income-based jobseekers allowance and there is a change in the benefit week whilst a direction is in operation, the period of the reduction specified in paragraph (2) shall be a period greater than 155 weeks but less than 156 weeks and ending on the last day of the last benefit week falling entirely within the period of 156 weeks specified in that paragraph.]

(7) Where the weekly amount specified in column (2) of paragraph 1(1)(e) of the applicable amounts Schedule changes on a day when a direction is in operation, the amount of the reduction of the relevant benefit shall be changed—

(a) where the benefit is income support, [²or income-based jobseeker's allowance], the first day of the first benefit week to commence for the parent concerned on or after the day that weekly amount changes;

(b) where the benefit is family credit or disability working allowance, from the first day of the next award period of that benefit for the parent concerned commencing on or after the day that weekly amount changes.

(8) Only one direction in relation to a parent shall be in force at any one time.

(9) [³...]

AMENDMENTS

1. Child Support and Income Support (Amendment) Regulations 1995 (S.I. 1995 No. 1045), reg. 38 (April 18, 1995).
2. Social Security and Child Support (Jobseeker's Allowance) (Consequential Amendments) Regulations 1996 (S.I. 1996 No. 1345), reg. 5(6) (October 7, 1996).
3. Child Support (Miscellaneous Amendments) Regulations 1996 (S.I. 1996 No. 1945), reg. 14 (October 7, 1996).

Modification of reduction under a reduced benefit direction to preserve minimum entitlement to relevant benefit

37. Where in respect of any benefit week the amount of the relevant benefit that would be payable after it has been reduced following a direction would, but for this regulation, be nil or less than the minimum amount of that benefit that is payable as determined—

  (a) in the case of income support, by regulation 26(4) of the Social Security (Claims and Payments) Regulations 1987;

[¹(aa) in the case of income-based jobseeker's allowance, by regulation [²87A of the Jobseeker's Allowance Regulations 1996;]]

  (b) in the case of family credit and disability working allowance, by regulation 27(2) [² of the Social Security (Claims and Payments) Regulations 1987],

the amount of that reduction shall be decreased to such extent as to raise the amount of that benefit to the minimum amount that is payable.

AMENDMENTS

1. Social Security and Child Support (Jobseeker's Allowance) (Consequential Amendments) Regulations 1996 (S.I. 1996 No. 1345), reg. 5(7) (October 7, 1996).
2. Social Security and Child Support (Jobseeker's Allowance) (Miscellaneous Amendments) Regulations 1996 (S.I. 1996 No. 2538), reg. 6(2) (October 28, 1996).

Suspension of a reduced benefit direction when relevant benefit ceases to be payable

38.—(1) Where relevant benefit ceases to be payable to, or in respect of, the parent concerned at a time when a direction is in operation, that direction shall, subject to paragraph (2), be suspended for a period of 52 weeks from the date the relevant benefit has ceased to be payable.

(2) Where a direction has been suspended for a period of 52 weeks and no relevant benefit is payable at the end of the period, it shall cease to be in force.

(3) Where a direction is suspended and relevant benefit again becomes payable to or in respect of the parent concerned, the amount payable by way of that benefit shall, subject to regulation 40, [¹40ZA,] 41 and 42, be reduced in accordance with that direction for the balance of the reduction period.

(4) The amount or, as the case may be, amounts of the reduction to be made during the balance of the reduction period shall be determined in accordance with regulation 36(2) [².. .].

(5) No reduction in the amount of benefit under paragraph (3) shall be made before the expiry of a period of 14 days from service of the notice specified in paragraph (6), and the provisions of regulation 36(4) shall apply as to the date when the direction again comes into operation.

(6) Where relevant benefit again becomes payable to or in respect of a parent with respect to whom a direction is suspended she shall be notified in writing by a child support officer that the amount of relevant benefit paid to or in respect

of her will again be reduced, in accordance with the provisions of paragraph (3), if she continues to fail to comply with the obligations imposed by section 6 of the Act.

(7) Where a direction has ceased to be in force by virtue of the provisions of paragraph (2), a further direction in respect of the same parent given on account of that parent's failure to comply with the obligations imposed by section 6 of the Act in relation to one or more of the same qualifying children shall, unless it also ceases to be in force by virtue of the provisions of paragraph (2), be in operation for the balance of the reduction period relating to the direction that has ceased to be in force, and the provisions of paragraph (4) shall apply to it.

AMENDMENTS

1. Social Security and Child Support (Jobseeker's Allowance) (Consequential Amendments) Regulations 1996 (S.I. 1996 No. 1345), reg. 5(8) (October 7, 1996).
2. Child Support (Miscellaneous Amendments) Regulations 1996 (S.I. 1996 No. 1945), reg. 15 (October 7, 1996).

Reduced benefit direction where family credit or disability working allowance is payable and income support becomes payable

39.—(1) Where a direction is in operation in respect of a parent to whom or in respect of whom family credit or disability working allowance is payable, and income support [¹ or income-based jobseeker's allowance] becomes payable to or in respect of that parent, income support [¹or, as the case may be, income-based jobseeker's allowance] shall become a relevant benefit for the purposes of that direction, and the amount payable by way of income support [¹or, as the case may be, income-based jobseeker's allowance] shall be reduced in accordance with that direction for the balance of the reduction period.

(2) The amount or, as the case may be, the amounts of the reduction to be made during the balance of the reduction period shall be determined in accordance with regulation 36(2) [². . .].

AMENDMENTS

1. Social Security and Child Support (Jobseeker's Allowance) (Consequential Amendments) Regulations 1996 (S.I. 1996 No. 1345), reg. 5(9) (October 7, 1996).
2. Child Support (Miscellaneous Amendments) Regulations 1996 (S.I. 1996 No. 1945), reg. 16 (October 7, 1996).

Suspension of a reduced benefit direction when a modified applicable amount is payable

40.—(1) Where a direction is given or is in operation at a time when income support is payable to or in respect of the parent concerned but her applicable amount falls to be calculated under the provisions mentioned in paragraph (3), that direction shall be suspended for so long as the applicable amount falls to be calculated under the provisions mentioned in that paragraph, or 52 weeks, whichever period is the shorter.

[²(1A) Where a direction is given or is in operation at a time when income support is payable to or in respect of the parent concerned, but her applicable amount includes a residential allowance under regulation 17 of, and paragraph 2A of Schedule 2 to, the Income Support Regulations (applicable amounts for those in residential care or nursing homes), that direction shall be suspended for as long as her applicable amount includes a residential allowance under regulation 17 and paragraph 2A of Schedule 2, or 52 weeks, whichever period is the shorter.]

(2) Where a case falls within paragraph (1) [² or (1A)] and a direction has been suspended for a period of 52 weeks, it shall cease to be in force.

(3) The provisions of paragraph (1) shall apply where the applicable amount in relation to the parent concerned falls to be calculated under—

(a) regulation 19 of and Schedule 4 to the Income Support Regulations (applicable amounts for persons resident in residential care and nursing homes);

(b) regulation 21 of and paragraphs 1 to 3 of Schedule 7 to the Income Support Regulations (patients);

(c) regulation 21 of and paragraphs 10B, 10C [¹. . .] and 13 of Schedule 7 to the Income Support Regulations (persons in residential accommodation).

AMENDMENTS

1. Child Support (Miscellaneous Amendments) Regulations 1993 (S.I. 1993 No. 913), reg. 13 (April 5, 1993).
2. Child Support and Income Support (Amendment) Regulations 1995 (S.I. 1995 No. 1045), reg. 39 (April 18, 1995).

[¹Suspension of a reduced benefit direction in the case of modified applicable amounts in jobseeker's allowance

40ZA.—(1) Where a direction is given or is in operation at a time when income-based jobseeker's allowance is payable to or in respect of the parent concerned but her applicable amount falls to be calculated under the provisions mentioned in paragraph (4), that direction shall be suspended for so long as the applicable amount falls to be calculated under those provisions, or 52 weeks, whichever period is the shorter.

(2) Where a direction is given or is in operation at a time when income-based jobseeker's allowance is payable to or in respect of the parent concerned, but her applicable amount includes a residential allowance under regulation 83(c) of and paragraph 3 of Schedule 1 to the Jobseeker's Allowance Regulations (persons in residential care or nursing homes), that direction shall be suspended for as long as her applicable amount includes such a residential allowance, or 52 weeks, whichever period is the shorter.

(3) Where a case falls within paragraph (1) or (2) and a direction has been suspended for a period of 52 weeks, it shall cease to be in force.

(4) The provisions of paragraph (1) shall apply where the applicable amount in relation to the parent concerned falls to be calculated under—

(a) regulation 85 of and paragraph 1 or 2 of Schedule 5 to the Jobseeker's Allowance Regulations (patients);

(b) regulation 85 of and paragraph 8, 9 or 15 of Schedule 5 to the Jobseeker's Allowance Regulations (persons in residential accommodation); or

(c) regulation 86 of and Schedule 4 to the Jobseeker's Allowance Regulations (applicable amounts for persons in residential care and nursing homes).]

AMENDMENT

1. Social Security and Child Support (Jobseeker's Allowance) (Consequential Amendments) Regulations 1996 (S.I. 1996 No. 1345), reg. 5(10) (October 7, 1996).

[¹Suspension of a reduced benefit direction where certain deductions are being made from income support

40A.—[². . .]]

AMENDMENTS

1. Child Support (Miscellaneous Amendments) (No. 2) Regulations 1995 (S.I. 1995 No. 3261), reg. 38 (January 22, 1996).
2. Child Support (Miscellaneous Amendments) (No. 2) Regulations 1996 (S.I. 1996 No. 3196), reg. 9 (January 13, 1997).

Termination of a reduced benefit direction following compliance with obligations imposed by section 6 of the Act

41.—(1) Where a parent with care with respect to whom a direction is in force complies with the obligations imposed by section 6 of the Act, that direction shall cease to be in force on the date determined in accordance with paragraph (2) or (3), as the case may be.

(2) Where the direction is in operation, it shall cease to be in force on the last day of the benefit week during the course of which the parent concerned complied with the obligations imposed by section 6 of the Act.

(3) Where the direction is suspended, it shall cease to be in force on the date on which the parent concerned complied with the obligations imposed by section 6 of the Act.

Review of a reduced benefit direction

42.—(1) Where a parent with care with respect to whom a direction is in force [¹or some other person] gives the Secretary of State reasons—
   (a) additional to any reasons given by [¹the parent with care] in response to the notice served on her under section 46(2) of the Act for having failed to comply with the obligations imposed by section 6 of the Act; or
   (b) as to why [¹the parent with care] should no longer be required to comply with the obligations imposed by section 6 of the Act,
the Secretary of State shall refer the matter to a child officer who shall conduct a review of the direction (''a review'') to determine whether the direction is to continue or is to cease to be in force.

(2) Where a parent with care with respect to whom a direction is in force [¹or some other person] gives a child support officer reasons of the kind mentioned in paragraph (1), a child support officer shall conduct a review to determine whether the direction is to continue or is to cease to be in force.

[¹(2A) Where a direction is in force and the Secretary of State becomes aware that a question arises as to whether the welfare of a child is likely to be affected by the direction continuing in force, he shall refer the matter to a child support office who shall conduct a review to determine whether the direction is to continue or is to cease to be in force.

(2B) Where a direction is in force and a child support officer becomes aware that a question arises as to whether the welfare of a child is likely to be affected by the direction continuing to be in force a child support officer shall conduct a review to determine whether the direction is to continue or is to cease to be in force.]

(3) A review shall not be carried out by the child support officer who gave the direction with respect to the parent concerned.

(4) Where the child support officer who is conducting a review considers that the parent concerned is no longer to be required to comply with the obligations imposed by section 6 of the Act, the direction shall cease to be in force on the date determined in accordance with paragraph (5) or (6), as the case may be.

(5) Where the direction is in operation, it shall cease to be in force on the last day of the benefit week during the course of which [¹the reasons specified in paragraph (1) were given] [² or the Secretary of State or a child support officer becomes aware of a question of a kind mentioned in paragraph (2A) or (2B)].

(6) Where the direction is suspended, it shall cease to be in force on the date on which [¹the reasons specified in paragraph (1) were given].

(7) [¹ . . .]

(8) A child support officer shall on completing a review immediately notify the parent concerned of his decision, so far as that is reasonably practicable, and shall give the reasons for his decision in writing.

[¹(9) A parent with care who is aggrieved by a decision of a child support officer following a review may appeal to a child support appeal tribunal against that decision.

(10) Sections 20(2) to (4) and 21 of the Act shall apply in relation to appeals under paragraph (9) as they apply in relation to appeals under section 20 of the Act.

(11) A notification under paragraph (8) shall include information as to the provision of paragraph (9) and (10).]

AMENDMENT

1. Child Support (Miscellaneous Amendments) Regulations 1993 (S.I. 1993 No. 913), reg. 14 (April 5, 1993).
2. Child Support and Income Support (Amendment) Regulations 1995 (S.I. 1995 No. 1045), reg. 40 (April 18, 1995).

Termination of a reduced benefit direction where a maintenance assessment is made following an application by a child under section 7 of the Act

43. Where a qualifying child of a parent with respect to whom a direction is in force applies for a maintenance assessment to be made with respect to him under section 7 of the Act, and an assessment is made in response to that application in respect of all of the qualifying children in relation to whom the parent concerned failed to comply with the obligations imposed by section 6 of the Act, that direction shall cease to be in force from the date determined in accordance with regulation 45.

Termination of a reduced benefit direction where a maintenance assessment is made following an application by an absent parent under section 4 of the Act

44. Where—
  (a) an absent parent applies for a maintenance assessment to be made under section 4 of the Act with respect to all of his qualifying children in relation to whom the other parent of those children is a person with care;
  (b) a direction is in force with respect to that other parent following her failure to comply with the obligations imposed by section 6 of the Act in relation to those qualifying children; and
  (c) an assessment is made in response to that application by the absent parent for a maintenance assessment,
that direction shall cease to be in force on the date determined in accordance with regulation 45.

Date from which a reduced benefit direction ceases to be in force following a termination under regulation 43 or 44

45.—(1) The date a direction ceases to be in force under the provisions of regulation 43 or 44 shall be determined in accordance with paragraphs (2) and (3).

(2) Where the direction is in operation, it shall cease to be in force on the last day of the benefit week during the course of which the Secretary of State is supplied with the information that enables a child support officer to make the assessment.

(3) Where the direction is suspended, it shall cease to be in force on the date on which the Secretary of State is supplied with the information that enables a child support officer to make the assessment.

Cancellation of a reduced benefit direction in cases of error

46. Where a child support officer is satisfied that a direction was given as a result of an error on the part of the Secretary of State or a child support officer, or though not given as a result of such an error has not subsequently ceased to be in force as a result of such an error, the child support officer shall cancel the direction and it shall be treated as not having been given, or as having ceased to be in force on the date it would have ceased to be in force if that error had not been made, as the case may be.

Reduced benefit directions where there is an additional qualifying child

47.—(1) Where a direction is in operation or would be in operation but for the provisions of regulation 40 [¹or 40ZA] and a child support officer gives a further direction with respect to the same parent on account of that parent failing to comply with the obligations imposed by section 6 of the Act in relation to an additional qualifying child of whom she is a person with care, the earlier direction shall cease to be in force on the last day of the benefit week preceding the benefit week on the first day of which, in accordance with the provisions of regulation 36(4), the further direction comes into operation, or would come into operation but for the provisions of regulation 40 [¹or 40ZA].

(2) Where a further direction comes into operation in a case falling within paragraph (1), the provisions of regulation 36 shall apply to it.

[²(3) Where—

(a) a direction (''the earlier direction'') has ceased to be in force by virtue of regulation 38(2); and

(b) a child support officer gives a direction (''the further direction'') with respect to the same parent on account of that parent's failure to comply with the obligations imposed by section 6 of the Act in relation to an additional qualifying child,

as long as that further direction remains in force, no additional direction shall be brought into force with respect to that parent on account of her failure to comply with the obligations imposed by section 6 of the Act in relation to one or more children in relation to whom the earlier direction was given.]

(4) Where a case falls within paragraph (1) or (3) and the further direction, but for the provisions of this paragraph would cease to be in force by virtue of the provisions of regulation 41 or 42, but the earlier direction would not have ceased to be in force by virtue of the provisions of those regulations, the later direction shall continue in force for a period (''the extended period'') calculated in accordance with the provisions of paragraph (5) and the reduction of relevant benefit [²for the extended period shall be determined in accordance with regulation 36(2).]

(5) The extended period for the purposes of paragraph (4) shall be
[²(156–F–S) weeks]
where—
F is the number of weeks for which the earlier direction was in operation;
and
S is the number of weeks for which the later direction has been in operation.
(6) [². . .]
(7) [². . .]
(8) In this regulation "an additional qualifying child" means a qualifying
child of whom the parent concerned is a person with care and who was either
not such a qualifying child at the time the earlier direction was given or had
not been born at the time the earlier direction was given.

AMENDMENTS

1. Social Security and Child Support (Jobseeker's Allowance) (Consequential Amendments)
Regulations 1996 (S.I. 1996 No. 1345), reg. 5(11) (October 7, 1996).
2. Child Support (Miscellaneous Amendments) Regulations 1996 (S.I. 1996 No. 1945), reg. 17
(October 7, 1996).

Suspension and termination of a reduced benefit direction where the sole qualifying child ceases to be a child or where the parent concerned ceases to be a person with care

48.—(1) Where, whilst a direction is in operation—
(a) there is, in relation to that direction, only one qualifying child, and that
child ceases to be a child within the meaning of the Act; or
(b) the parent concerned ceases to be a person with care,
the direction shall be suspended from the last day of the benefit week during
the course of which the child ceases to be a child within the meaning of
the Act, or the parent concerned ceases to be a person with care, as the case
may be.
(2) Where, under the provisions of paragraph (1), a direction has been suspended for a period of 52 weeks and no relevant benefit is payable at that time,
it shall cease to be in force.
(3) If during the period specified in paragraph (1) the former child again
becomes a child within the meaning of the Act or the parent concerned again
becomes a person with care and relevant benefit is payable to or in respect of
that parent, a reduction in the amount of that benefit shall be made in accordance
with the provisions of paragraphs (3) to (7) of regulation 38.

Notice of termination of a reduced benefit direction

49.—(1) Where a direction ceases to be in force under the provisions of
regulations 41 to 44 or 46 to 48, or is suspended under the provisions of regulation 48, a child support officer shall serve notice of such termination or suspension, as the case may be, on the adjudication officer and shall specify the date
on which the direction ceases to be in force or is suspended, as the case may
be.
(2) Any notice served under paragraph (1) shall set out the reasons why the
direction has ceased to be in force or has been suspended.
(3) The parent concerned shall be served with a copy of any notice served
under paragraph (1).

[¹Notice of termination of suspension of a reduced benefit direction

49A.—[². . .]]

AMENDMENTS

1. Child Support (Miscellaneous Amendments) (No. 2) Regulations 1995 (S.I. 1995 No. 3261), reg. 39 (January 22, 1996).
2. Child Support (Miscellaneous Amendments) (No. 2) Regulations 1996 (S.I. 1996 No. 3196), reg. 9 (January 13, 1997).

Rounding provisions

50. Where any calculation made under this Part of these Regulations results in a fraction of a penny, that fraction shall be treated as a penny if it exceeds one half, and shall otherwise be disregarded.

Child Support (Maintenance Assessments and Special Cases) Regulations 1992

(S.I. 1992 No. 1815)

Made by the Secretary of State under various provisions of the Child Support Act 1991

REGULATIONS REPRODUCED

PART II

CALCULATION OR ESTIMATION OF CHILD SUPPORT MAINTENANCE

13. The minimum amount

PART III

SPECIAL CASES

28. Amount payable where absent parent is in receipt of income support or other prescribed benefit.

GENERAL NOTE

See the note to s. 43 of the Child Support Act 1991.

PART II

The minimum amount

13.—(1) Subject to regulation 26, for the purposes of paragraph 7(1) of Schedule 1 to the Act the minimum amount shall be [¹ 2 multiplied by] 5 per centum of the amount specified in paragraph 1(1)(e) of the relevant Schedule (income support personal allowance for single claimant aged not less than 25).

(2) Where [¹ the 5 per centum amount] calculated under paragraph (1) results in a sum other than a multiple of 5 pence, it shall be treated as the sum which is the next higher multiple of 5 pence.

AMENDMENT

1. Child Support (Maintenance Assessments and Special Cases) and Social Security (Claims and Payments) (Amendment Regulations 1996 (S.I. 1996 No. 481), reg. 2 (April 8, 1996).

PART III

Amount payable where absent parent is in receipt of income support or other prescribed benefit

28.—(1) Where the condition specified in section 43(1)(a) of the Act is satisfied in relation to an absent parent (assessable income to be nil where income support [³, income-based jobseeker's allowance] or other prescribed benefit is paid), the prescribed conditions for the purposes of section 43(1)(b) of the Act are that—

(a) the absent parent is aged 18 or over;

(b) he does not satisfy the conditions in paragraph [⁴3(1)(a) or (b)] of the relevant Schedule (income support family premium) [¹and does not have day to day care of any child (whether or not a relevant child)]; and

(c) [¹his income does not include] one or more of the payments or awards specified in Schedule 4 (other than by reason of a provision preventing receipt of overlapping benefits or by reason of a failure to satisfy the relevant contribution conditions).

(2) For the purposes of section 43(2)(a) of the Act, the prescribed amount shall be equal to the minimum amount prescribed in regulation 13(1) for the purposes of paragraph 7(1) of Schedule 1 to the Act.

[¹[²(3) Subject to paragraph (4), where—

(a) an absent parent is liable under section 43 of the Act and this regulation to make payments in place of payments of child support maintenance with respect to two or more qualifying children in relation to whom there is more than one parent with care; or

(b) that absent parent and his partner (within the meaning of regulation 2(1) of the Social Security (Claims and Payments) Regulations 1987) are both liable to make such payments,

the prescribed amount mentioned in paragraph (2) shall be apportioned between the persons with care in the same ratio as the maintenance requirements of the qualifying child or children in relation to each of those persons with care bear to each other.]

(4) If, in making the apportionment required by paragraph (3), the effect of the application of regulation 2(2) would be such that the aggregate amount payable would be different from the amount prescribed in paragraph (2) the Secretary of State shall adjust the apportionment so as to eliminate that difference; and that adjustment shall be varied from time to time so as to secure that, taking one week with another and so far as is practicable, each person with care receives the amount which she would have received if no adjustment had been made under this paragraph.

(5) The provisions of Schedule 5 shall have effect in relation to cases to which section 43 of the Act and this regulation apply.]

AMENDMENTS

1. Child Support (Miscellaneous Amendments) Regulations 1993 (S.I. 1993 No. 913), reg. 26 (April 5, 1993).

2. Child Support (Maintenance Assessment and Special Cases) Amendment Regulations 1993 (S.I. 1993 No. 925), reg. 2(2) (April 26, 1993).
3. Social Security and Child Support (Jobseeker's Allowance) (Consequential Amendments) Regulations 1996 (S.I. 1996 No. 1345), reg. 6(3) (October 7, 1996).
4. Child Support (Miscellaneous Amendments) Regulations 1998 (S.I. 1998 No. 58), reg. 55 (April 6, 1998).

SCHEDULE 4   **Regulation 26(1)(b)(i)**

CASES WHERE CHILD SUPPORT MAINTENANCE IS NOT TO BE PAYABLE

The payments and awards specified for the purposes of regulation 26(1)(b)(i) are—
  (a) the following payments under the Contribution and Benefits Act—
    [²(i) incapacity benefit under section 30A;
    (ii) long-term incapacity benefit for widows under section 40;
    (iii) long-term incapacity benefit for widowers under section 41;]
    (iv) maternity allowance under section 35;
    (v) [² . . .];
    (vi) attendance allowance under section 64;
    (vii) severe disablement allowance under section 68;
    (viii) invalid care allowance under section 70;
    (ix) disability living allowance under section 71;
    (x) disablement benefit under section 103;
    (xi) disability working allowance under section 129;
    (xii) statutory sick pay within the meaning of section 151;
    (xiii) statutory maternity pay within the meaning of section 164;
  (b) awards in respect of disablement made under (or under provisions analogous to)—
    (i) the War Pensions (Coastguards) Scheme 1944 (S.I. 1944 No. 500);
    (ii) the War Pensions (Naval Auxiliary Personnel) Scheme 1964 (S.I. 1964 No. 1985);
    (iii) the Pensions (Polish Forces) Scheme 1964 (S.I. 1964 No. 2007);
    (iv) the War Pensions (Mercantile Marine) Scheme 1964 (S.I. 1964 No. 2058);
    (v) the Royal Warrant of 21st December 1964 (service in the Home Guard before 1945) (Cmnd. 2563);
    (vi) the Order by Her Majesty of 22nd December 1964 concerning pensions and other grants in respect of disablement or death due to service in the Home Guard after 27th April 1952 (Cmnd. 2564);
    (vii) the Order by Her Majesty (Ulster Defence Regiment) of 4th January 1971 (Cmnd. 4567);
    (viii) the Personal Injuries (Civilians) Scheme 1983 (S.I. 1983 No. 686);
    (ix) the Naval, Military and Air Forces Etc. (Disablement and Death) Service Pensions Order 1983 (S.I. 1983 No. 883); and
  (c) payments from [¹the Independent Living (1993) Fund or the Independent Living (Extension) Fund].

AMENDMENTS

1. Child Support (Miscellaneous Amendments) Regulations 1993 (S.I. 1993 No. 913), reg. 34 (April 5, 1993).
2. Child Support and Income Support (Amendment) Regulations 1995 (S.I. 1995 No. 1045), reg. 58 (April 13, 1995).

[¹SCHEDULE 5   **Regulation 28(5)**

PROVISIONS APPLYING TO CASES TO WHICH SECTION 43 OF THE ACT AND
REGULATION 28 APPLY

1. In this Schedule—
[²(a)] "relevant decision" means a decision of a child support officer given under section 43 of the Act (contribution to maintenance by deduction from benefit) and
regulation 28[²; and
  (b) "relevant person" has the same meaning as in regulation 1(2) of the Maintenance
  Assessment Procedure Regulations.]
[³**2.** A relevant decision may be reviewed by a child support officer, either on application by a relevant person or of his own motion—
  (a) if it appears to him that the absent parent has at some time after that decision was
  given satisfied the conditions prescribed by regulation 28(1) or, as the case may
  be, no longer satisfies those conditions; or
  (b) if it appears to him that the relevant decision was wrong in law or was made in
  ignorance of, or based on a mistake as to, a material fact.]
3. A relevant decision [³ made on or before 18th April 1994] shall be reviewed by a
child support officer[³ after] it has been in force for 52 weeks.
[³**3A.** A relevant decision made after 18th April 1994 shall be reviewed by a child
support officer after it has been in force for 104 weeks.]
4.—(1) Before conducting a review under paragraph 6 the child support officer
shall—
  (a) give 14 days' notice of the proposed review to the relevant persons [² . . .]; and
  (b) invite representations, either in person or in writing, from the relevant persons on
  any matter relating to the review and set out the provisions of sub-paragraphs (2)
  to (4) in relation to such representations.
  (2) Subject to sub-paragraph (3), where the child support officer conducting the review
does not, within 14 days of the date on which notice of the review was given, receive a
request from a relevant person to make representations in person, or receives such a
request and arranges for an appointment for such representations to be made but that
appointment is not kept, he may complete the review in the absence of such representations from that person.
  (3) Where the child support of officer conducting the review is satisfied that there was
good reason for failure to keep an appointment, he shall provide for a further opportunity
for the making of representations by the relevant person concerned before he completes
the review.
  (4) Where the child support officer conducting the review does not receive written
representations from a relevant person within 14 days of the date on which notice of the
review was given, he may complete the review in the absence of written representations
from that person.
5. After completing a review under paragraph 2, 3 or 6, the child support officer shall
notify all relevant persons of the result of the review and—
  (a) in the case of a review under paragraph 2 or 3, of the right to apply for a further
  review under paragraph (6); and
  (b) in the case of a review under [²paragraph 6], of the right of appeal under section
  20 of the Act as applied by paragraph 8.
6. Where a child support officer has made a decision under regulation 28 or paragraph
2 or 3, any relevant person may apply to the Secretary of State for a review of that
decision and, subject to the modifications set out in paragraph 7, the provisions of section
18(5) to (7) of the Act shall apply to such a review.
7. The modifications to the provisions of section 18(5) to (7) of the Act referred to in
paragraph 6 are—

(a) any reference in those provisions to a maintenance assessment shall be read as a reference to a relevant decision; and

(b) subsection 6 shall apply as if the reference to the cancellation of an assessment was omitted.

[²7A. If, on a review under paragraph 2, 3, or 6, the relevant decision is revised ("the revised decision") the revised decision shall have effect—

(a) if the revised decision is that no payments such as are mentioned in section 43 of the Act are to be made, from the date on which the event giving rise to the review occurred: or

(b) if the revised decision is that such payments are to be made, from the date on which the revised decision is given.]

8. The provisions of section 20 of the Act (appeals) shall apply in relation to a review or a refusal to review under paragraph 6.

9. The provisions of paragraphs (1) and (2) of regulation 5 of the Child Support (Collection and Enforcement) Regulations 1992 shall apply to the transmission of payments in place of child support maintenance under section 43 of the Act and regulation 28 as they apply to the transmission of payments of child support maintenance.]

AMENDMENTS

1. Child Support (Miscellaneous Amendments) Regulations 1993 (S.I. 1993 No. 913), reg. 26(3) and Sched. (April 5, 1993).
2. Child Support (Maintenance Assessment and Special Cases) Amendment Regulations 1993 (S.I. 1993 No. 925), reg. 2(3) (April 26, 1993).
3. Child Support and Income Support (Amendment) Regulations 1995 (S.I. 1995 No. 1045), reg. 59 (April 18, 1995).

Child Support (Miscellaneous Amendments) Regulations 1996

(S.I. 1996 No. 1945)

Made by the Secretary of State under ss.14(1), 21(2), 32(1), 42(3), 46(11), 47(1) and (2), 51, 52(4) and 54 of, and paras. 5(1) and (2), 6, 8 and 11 of Sched. 1 to, the Child Support Act 1991.

[In force October 7, 1996]

Transitional provisions

25.—(1) *Omitted.*

(2) The provisions of regulation 35 of the Maintenance Assessment Procedure Regulations in force prior to 7th October 1996 shall continue to apply to any case where the failure to comply referred to in paragraph (1) of that regulation arose prior to that date.

(3) The provisions of regulation 36 of the Maintenance Assessment Procedure Regulations in force prior to 7th October 1996 shall [¹ apply with the amendments made by regulation 5(6) of the Social Security and Child Support (Jobseeker's Allowance) (Consequential Amendments) Regulations 1996] to a parent in respect of whom a reduced benefit direction was given prior to that date.

(4) The provisions of regulation 47 of the Maintenance Assessment Procedure Regulations in force prior to 7th October 1996 shall [¹ apply with the amendments made by regulation 5(11) of the Social Security and Child Support (Jobseeker's Allowance) (Consequential Amendments) Regulations 1996] to any reduced benefit direction made prior to that date, and in relation to an earlier direction referred to in paragraph (4) of that regulation, which was in force prior

to that date, whether or not the further direction referred to in that paragraph was made after that date.

(5) *Omitted.*

AMENDMENT

1. Social Security and Child Support (Jobseeker's Allowance) (Transitional Provisions) (Amendment) Regulations 1996 (S.I. 1996 No. 2378), reg. 3 (October 6, 1996).

Child Support (Miscellaneous Amendments) (No. 2) Regulations 1996

(S.I. 1996 No. 3196)

Made by the Secretary of State under various provisions of the Child Support Act 1991.

[In force January 13, 1997]

Transitional provision

16.—(1) *Omitted.*

(2) *Omitted.*

(3) The provisions of regulations 40A and 49A of the Maintenance Assessment Procedure Regulations in force prior to 13th January 1997 shall continue to apply to a reduced benefit direction which at that date is suspended under the provisions of regulation 40A.

Social Security (Child Maintenance Bonus) Regulations 1996

(S.I. 1996 No. 3195)

Made by the Secretary of State under ss.10 and 26(1) to (3) of the Child Support Act 1995, ss.5(1)(p), 6(1)(q), 71(8), 78(2), 189(1), (3) and (4) and 191 of the Social Security Administration Act 1992 and ss.136 (5)(b), 137(1) and 175(1) and (3) of the Social Security Contributions and Benefits Act 1992.

GENERAL NOTE

These regulations contain the details of the child maintenance bonus scheme introduced by s. 10 of the Child Support Act 1995. There are no notes or definitions after each individual regulation but the following paragraphs contain a brief summary of the main provisions. Most of the relevant definitions are in reg. 1, although there also needs to be some reference to the Child Support Acts 1991 and 1995 (by s. 27(2) of the 1995 Act expressions in that Act have the same meaning as in the 1991 Act).

From April 7, 1997 a person who has a qualifying child (*i.e.* a child, one or both of whose parents are absent parents: see Child Support Act 1991, s. 3(1)) living with her, and who is receiving, or (from April 1, 1998) is due ro receive, child maintenance while she (or her partner) is entitled (whether or not benefit is payable: regs. 1(7) and 4) to income support or income-based JSA, will be able to build up a child maintenance bonus (reg. 4(1)). This is known as the "bonus period". A bonus period can only start on or after April 7, 1997. Note that although the definition of "qualifying benefit" in reg. 1(4) refers to income support and "jobseeker's allowance", the effect of reg. 2(1) is that a bonus can only accrue while the person is entitled to income-based JSA. Note also that for the purpose of accumulating the bonus, days on which entitlement to income support/income-based JSA is at the urgent cases rate because the claimant is treated as possessing income which is due but has not been paid, do not count (reg. 4(9)).

Two or more bonus periods separated by one "connected period" (but not more than one: reg.

4(5)) can link to form one period (reg. 4(2)). A "connected period" is a period of 12 weeks or less, or two years or less throughout which incapacity benefit, severe disablement allowance or invalid care allowance is payable to the person claiming the bonus, or a period throughout which maternity allowance is payable to that person (reg. 4(3)).

Child maintenance includes maintenance paid under an agreement (whether enforceable or not) or a court order (but not spousal maintenance), and deductions from benefit as a contribution towards child maintenance, as well as child support maintenance (reg. 1(2)). Note that from April 1, 1998 this includes maintenance, etc., that is payable as well as that which is paid.

For the definition of "child" see s. 55 of the 1991 Act which is in effect the same as for the purposes of child benefit (see s. 142 of the Contributions and Benefits Act and the notes to reg. 12 of the Income Support Regulations). A qualifying child will be treated as living with the person claiming the bonus during any temporary absence of not more than 12 weeks (reg. 4(6)).

The amount of the bonus will be £5 for each benefit week in which at least £5 child maintenance was due (or the amount due for that week if less than £5), or the total amount of child maintenance paid in the bonus period, or £1,000, whichever is the lowest (reg. 5). It is not taxable.

The bonus will be payable when the person's (or her partner's) entitlement to income support or income-based JSA ceases because she (or her partner) starts or returns to work (other than a return to work for the same employer where the absence was due to a trade dispute: reg. 3(2)), or works more hours, or has increased earnings (this is referred to as "the work condition") (reg. 3(1)(c) and (d)). From April 1, 1998 the work condition must normally be met within 14 days of the end of the person's bonus period (reg. 3(1)(f)(iii) (under the previous form of reg. 3(1)(f) the limit was 14 days of the person ceasing to be entitled to income support/income-based JSA; thus it was possible, for example, for a person whose bonus period had ended because a child had ceased to be a qualifying child but who had remained in receipt of income support/income-based JSA to claim a bonus some considerable time after her bonus period had ended). But if the absent parent dies, ceases to be habitually resident in the U.K. or is found not to be the parent of the qualifying child(ren), the time limit for satisfying the work condition is 12 weeks from the earliest date on which any of these events occurs; or if the person cares for only one child and that child dies, the time limit is 12 months from the date of death (reg. 3(1)(f)(i) and (ii)). A bonus will also be payable if entitlement to income support or income-based JSA ceased for any other reason but the work condition is met within the time limits in reg. 3(1)(f) (reg. 3(1A)). The work condition has to be satisfied before the penultimate day before the person's 60th birthday (or his 65th birthday if a man and the qualifying benefit was income-based JSA) (reg. 3(1)(e)). See reg. 8 for the special rules that apply to a person who has reached this age, or is approaching it. Apart from people covered by reg. 8(1) and (2), a claim for the bonus has to be made, usually within 28 days of income support/income-based JSA ceasing (regs. 3(1)(a) and 8(5)). For the rules governing claims see regs. 10–11; note also reg. 13.

In the case of a couple, the person entitled to the bonus is the person with care of the child and to whom child maintenance is payable; where this applies to both members of the couple, each of them will qualify for a bonus (reg. 9(1) and (2)). If a couple separate, they both count for the purpose of the bonus period as entitled to income support/income-based JSA on the days benefit was being paid to them as a couple (reg. 9(5)).

If a person with care of a qualifying child dies, accrued bonus can be passed on to the new person caring for the child if the conditions in reg. 7 are met.

The bonus is treated as income support or income-based JSA (s. 10(3) of the Child Support Act 1995), depending on which was last in payment in the bonus period (reg. 12). Thus decisions on claims will be made by an AO (Administration Act, s. 20) and on appeal by a SSAT.

The bonus counts as capital for the purpose of income support, income-based JSA, family credit and disability working allowance (reg. 14). For family credit and disability working allowance (but not income support or income-based JSA), it is disregarded for 52 weeks from the date of receipt (Family Credit Regulations, Sched. 3, para. 51 and Disability Working Allowance Regulations, Sched. 4, para. 50). This also applies for housing benefit, council tax benefit and earnings top-up.

Citation, commencement and interpretation

1.—(1) These Regulations may be cited as the Social Security (Child Maintenance Bonus) Regulations 1996 and shall come into force on 7th April 1997.

(2) In these Regulations—

"the Act" means the Child Support Act 1995;

"applicant", except where regulation 8 (retirement) applies, means the person claiming the bonus;

"appropriate office" means an office of the Department of Social Security or the Department for Education and Employment;

"benefit week"—

(a) where the relevant benefit is income support, has the meaning it has in the Income Support (General) Regulations 1987 by virtue of regulation 2(1) of those Regulations; or

(b) where the relevant benefit is a jobseeker's allowance, has the meaning it has in the Jobseeker's Allowance Regulations 1996 by virtue of regulation 1(3) of those Regulations;

"bonus" means a child maintenance bonus;

"bonus period" comprises the days specified in regulation 4;

[²"child maintenance" means maintenance in any of the following forms—

(a) child support maintenance paid or payable;

(b) maintenance paid or payable by an absent parent to a person with care of a qualifying child, under an agreement (whether enforceable or not) between them, or by virtue of an order of a court; or

(c) maintenance deducted from any benefit payable to an absent parent who is liable to maintain a qualifying child,

which, as the case may be, is paid, payable or deducted on or after 1st April 1998, but does not include any maintenance paid or payable in respect of a former partner];

"couple" means a married or an unmarried couple;

"income-based jobseeker's allowance" has the same meaning as in the Jobseekers Act by virtue of section 1(4) of that Act;

"the Jobseekers Act" means the Jobseekers Act 1995;

"jobseeker's allowance" means an income-based Jobseeker's allowance'

"partner" means where a person, whether an applicant or otherwise,—

(a) is a member of a married or unmarried couple, the other member of that couple;

(b) is married polygamously to two or more members of his household, any such member; or

(c) is a member of a marriage to which section 133(1)(b) of the Social Security Contributions and Benefits Act 1992 (polygamous marriages) refers and the other party to the marriage has one or more additional spouses, the other party;

"work condition" means the condition specified at regulation 3(1)(c).

(3) Expressions used in these Regulations and in the Child Support Act 1991 have the same meaning in these Regulations as they have in that Act.

(4) For the purposes of the Regulations, the qualifying benefits are a jobseeker's allowance and income support.

(5) In these Regulations, where—

(a) a payment is made in any benefit week by an absent parent to a person with care;

(b) the absent parent pays both child maintenance and maintenance for the person with care; and

(c) there is no evidence as to which form of maintenance that payment is intended to represent,

the first £5 of any such payment or, where the amount of payment is less than £5, that amount shall be treated as if it was a payment of child maintenance.

(6) For the purposes of these Regulations, child maintenance is treated as payable where it is paid under an agreement which is not enforceable.

(7) Where a person is entitled to a qualify benefit on any day but no qualifying benefit is payable to her in respect of that day, that person shall be treated for the purposes of these Regulations [¹ other than regulation 4 (bonus period)] as not entitled to a qualifying benefit for that day.

(8) In these Regulations, unless the context otherwise requires, a reference—

(a) to a numbered section is to the section of the Act bearing that number;
(b) to a numbered regulation is to the regulation in these Regulations bearing that number;
(c) in a regulation to a numbered paragraph is to the paragraph in that regulation bearing that number;
(d) in a paragraph to a lettered or numbered sub-paragraph is to the sub-paragraph in that paragraph bearing that letter or number.

AMENDMENTS

1. Social Security (Miscellaneous Amendment) Regulations 1977 (S.I. 1997 No. 454), reg. 8(2) (April 6, 1997).
2. Social Security (Miscellaneous Amendments) Regulations 1998 (S.I. 1998 No. 563), reg. 2(2) (April 1, 1998). (Note that the commencement date for this provision was amended by Social Security (Miscellaneous Amendments) (No. 2) Regulations 1998 (S.I. 1998 No. 865), reg. 2 (March 20, 1998).)

Application of the Regulations

2.—(1) Subject to paragraph (2), these Regulations apply only in a case where on or after 7th April 1997 an absent parent has paid child maintenance in respect of a qualifying child and that maintenance has been—
(a) taken into account in determining the amount of a qualifying benefit payable to the person with care or the partner of that person; or
(b) retained by the Secretary of State in accordance with section 74A(3) of the Social Security Administration Act 1992 (payable of benefit where maintenance payments are collected by the Secretary of State).

(2) Regulation 6 (Secretary of State to issue estimates) applies also where a child maintenance assessment has been made but no maintenance has been paid.

(3) No day falling before 7th April 1997 shall be taken into account in determining whether any condition specified in these Regulations is satisfied or whether any period specified in these Regulations commenced.

Entitlement to a bonus

3.—(1) An applicant is entitled to a bonus where—
(a) she has claimed a bonus in accordance with regulation 10 (claiming a bonus);
(b) the claim related to days falling within a bonus period;
(c) except where paragraph (2) applies, she satisfies the work condition, that is to say, she or her partner takes up or returns to work or increases the number of hours in which in any week she or her partner is engaged in employment or the earnings from an employment in which she or her partner are engaged is increased;
(d) as a result of satisfying the work condition any entitlement to a qualifying benefit in respect of herself and, where she has a partner, her family ceases;
(e) in a case where the qualifying benefit which ceased—
    (i) was income support, the person with care has not reached the day before her 60th birthday;
    (ii) was a jobseeker's allowance, the person with care has not reached the day before she attains pensionable age,
    at the time the work condition is satisfied; and
[²(f) the work condition is satisfied within the period of—
    (i) in a case where an applicant with care cares for one child only and that child dies, 12 months immediately following the date of death;
    (ii) in a case where the absent parent has—

      (aa) died;

      (bb) ceased to be habitually resident in the United Kingdom; or

      (cc) has been found not to be the parent of the qualifying child or children,

      12 weeks immediately following the first date on which any of those events occurs;

    (iii) in any other case, 14 days immediately following the day on which the bonus period applying to the applicant comes to an end.]

[¹(1A) In the case of an applicant who satisfies the requirements of paragraph (1)(f) but whose entitlement, or whose partner's entitlement, to a qualifying benefit ceased otherwise than as a result of satisfying the work condition, for sub-paragrph (d) of paragraph (1) there shall be substituted the following sub-paragraph—

      "(d) had the work condition been satisfied on the day she, or her partner, was last entitled to a qualifying benefit, that entitlement would as a consequence have ceased."]

(2) A person who is absent from work because of a trade dispute at her place of work and returns to work with the employer she worked for before the dispute began, does not thereby satisfy the requirements of paragraph (1)(c).

(3) In paragraph (2), "place of work", in relation to any person, means the premises at which she was employed.

(4) An applicant is also entitled to a bonus where she satisfies the requirements specified in regulation 8 (retirement).

1. Social Security (Miscellaneous Amendments) Regulations 1997 (S.I. 1997 No. 454), reg. 8(3) (April 6, 1997).

2. Social Security (Miscellaneous Amendments) Regulations 1998 (S.I. 1998 No. 563), reg. 2(3) (April 1, 1998). (Note that the commencement date for this provision was amended by Social Security (Miscellaneous Amendments) (No. 2) Regulations 1998 (S.I. 1998 No. 865), reg. 2 (March 20, 1998).)

Bonus period

4.—(1) A bonus period comprises only days falling on or after 7th April 1997 [¹, other than days to which paragraph (9) applies,] on which—

  (a) the applicant or, where the applicant has a partner, her partner is entitled to, or is treated as entitled to a qualifying benefit whether it is payable or not;

  (b) the applicant has residing with her a qualifying child; and

  (c) child maintenance is either—

      [²(i) paid or payable to the applicant; or]

     (ii) retained by the Secretary of State in accordance with section 74A(3) of the Social Security Administration Act 1992.

(2) Any two or more bonus periods separated by any one connected period shall be treated as one bonus period.

(3) For the purposes of these Regulations, "a connected period" is—

  (a) any period of not more than 12 weeks falling between two bonus periods to which paragraph (1) refers;

  (b) any period of not more than 12 weeks throughout which—

      (i) [¹. . .]

     (ii) the applicant ceases to be entitled to a qualifying benefit on becoming one of a couple and the couple fail to satisfy the conditions of entitlement to a qualifying benefit; or

  (c) any period throughout which maternity allowance is payable to the applicant; or

(d) any period of not more than 2 years throughout which incapacity benefit, severe disablement allowance or invalid care allowance is payable to the applicant.

(4) In calculating any period for the purposes of paragraph(3) no regard shall be had to any day which falls before 7th April 1997.

(5) Bonus periods separated by two or more connected periods shall not link to form a single bonus period but shall instead remain separate bonus periods.

(6) Where a qualifying child is temporarily absent for a period not exceeding 12 weeks from the home he shares with the applicant, the applicant shall be treated as satisfying the requirements of paragraph (1)(b) throughout that absence.

(7) A bonus period which would, but for this paragraph, have continued shall end—

(a) where the applicant or, where the applicant has a partner, her partner, satisfies the work condition and claims a bonus, on the last day of entitlement to a qualifying benefit to which any award made on that claim applies; or

[¹(b) on the date of death of a person with a care of a qualifying child to whom child maintenance is payable.

(8) In paragraphs (1)(c)(i) and (9) "claimant"—

(a) where the qualifying benefit is income support, means a person who claims income support; and

(b) where the qualifying benefit is a jobseeker's allowance, means a person who claims a jobseeker's allowance.

(9) This paragraph applies to days on which the claimant is a person to whom—

(a) regulation 70 of the Income Support (General) Regulations 1987 (urgent cases) applies other than by virtue of paragraph (2)(a) of that regulation (certain persons from abroad), or

(b) regulation 147 of the Jobseeker's Allowance Regulations 1996 applies other than by virtue of paragraph (2)(a) of that regulation.]

AMENDMENTS

1. Social Security (Miscellaneous Amendments) Regulations 1997 (S.I. 1997 No. 454), reg. 8(4) (April 6, 1997).

2. Social Security (Miscellaneous Amendments) Regulations 1998 (S.I. 1998 No. 563), reg. 2(4) (April 1, 1998). (Note that the commencement date for this provision was amended by Social Security (Miscellaneous Amendments) (No. 2) Regulations 1998 (S.I. 1998 No. 865), reg. 2 (March 20, 1998).)

Amount payable

5.—(1) The amount of the bonus shall be—

(a) subject to the following provisions of this regulation, a sum representing the aggregate of—

   (i) £5 for each benefit week in the bonus period in which the amount of child maintenance payable was not less than £5; and

   (ii) where in any benefit week in the bonus period the amount of child maintenance payable was less than £5, the amount that was payable;

(b) the amount of the child maintenance paid in the bonus period; or

(c) £1,000,

whichever amount is the least.

(2) [¹...]

(3) So much of any child maintenance paid in excess of the amount either—

(a) declared for the purposes of determining the amount of qualifying benefit payable to the applicant or her partner; or

(b) retained by the Secretary of State in accordance with section 74A(3) of
the Social Security Administration Act 1992,
shall be disregarded in determining the amount payable under paragraph (1).
(4) [¹. . .]
(5) Where but for this paragraph the amount of bonus payable in accordance
with paragraph (1) would be less than £5, the amount of the bonus shall be Nil.

AMENDMENT

1. Social Security (Miscellaneous Amendments) Regulations 1997 (S.I. 1997 No. 454), reg. 8(5)
(April 6, 1997).

Secretary of State to issue estimates

6.—(1) Where it appears to the Secretary of State that a person [¹ with care],
or the partner of such a person, may satisfy the requirments of regulation 3
(entitlement to a bonus) he may issue to [¹ that person] a written statement of
the amount he estimates may be payable by way of a bonus in his particular
case, and may provide such further statements as appear appropriate in the circumstance, stating the amount he estimates may be payable.
(2) The issue by the Secretary of State of a statement under paragraph (1)
shall not be binding on the adjudication officer when he makes his determination
on a claim for a bonus as to—
(a) whether the applicant satisfies the conditions of entitlements to the bonus;
and
(b) the amount, in any, payable where the bonus is awarded.

AMENDMENT

1. Social Security (Miscellaneous Amendments) Regulations 1997 (S.I. 1997 No. 454), reg. 8(6)
(April 6, 1997).

Death of a person with care of a child

7.—(1) In a case where—
(a) the person (A) with care of a [¹ qualifying child to whom child maintenance is payable dies];
(b) on the date of her death, the person (A) was entitled or, where she has a
partner, her partner was entitled to a qualifying benefit or had been so
entitled within the 12 weeks ending on the date of her death;
(c) after the death, another person (B), who is a close relative of the person
(A) and who was not before the death a person with the care of the child,
become the person with care; and
(d) that other person was entitled or, where the other person has a partner,
the other person or her partner was entitled to a qualifying benefit on the
day the person (A) died or becomes entitled to a qualifying benefit within
12 weeks of the day on which the person (A) was last entitled to a
qualifying benefit,
then any weeks forming part of the bonus period of the person (A) which was
current at the date of her death or within 12 weeks of the date on which she
died shall be treated as part of the bonus period of the person (B) to the extent
that those weeks are not otherwise a part of her bonus period.
(2) In this Regulation, "close relevant" means a parent, parent-in-law, son,
son-in-law, daughter, daughter-in-law, step-parent, step-son, step-daughter,
brother, sister, or the spouse of any of the proceeding persons or, if that person
is one of an unmarried couple, the other member of that couple.

AMENDMENT

1. Social Security (Miscellaneous Amendments) Regulations 1997 (S.I. 1997 No. 454), reg. 8(7) (April 6, 1997).

Retirement

8.—(1) In a case where the person with care of the child in respect of whom child maintenance is payable (the applicant) or the applicant's partner, either—

(a) is entitled to income support on the day before the applicant attains the age of 60; or

(b) is entitled to a jobseeker's allowance on the day before the applicant attains pensionable age,

the bonus period shall end on the day before the applicant attains 60 or, as the case may be, pensionable age and a bonus shall become payable to the applicant whether or not a claim is made for it.

(2) Where an applicant who ceases to be entitled to a jobseeker's allowance after attaining the age of 60 without satisfying the condition in paragraph (1)(b) above, becomes entitled to income support within—

(a) a period of 12 weeks of him ceasing to be entitled to a jobseeker's allowance; or

(b) the duration of any connected period to which regulations 4(3) applies which immediately follows such an entitlement and which applies in his case,

he shall be entitled to the bonus as though paragraph (1) were satisfied in his case and his bonus period shall be treated as though it ended on the day he becomes entitled to income support.

(3) No day which falls after the day the bonus period ends in accordance with paragraph (1) or (4) or is treated as ending in accordance with paragraph (2), shall form part of that or any other bonus period.

(4) Paragraph (5) shall apply where—

(a) the applicant or the applicant's partner—

(i) ceased to be entitled to income support in the 12 weeks preceding the date of the applicant attaining the age of 60;

(ii) ceased to be entitled to a jobseeker's allowance in the 12 weeks preceding the date of the applicant attaining pensionable age; and

(b) the person who ceased to be so entitled failed to satisfy the requirements of regulations 3(1)(c) to (f).

(5) Where this paragraph applies—

(a) the bonus period shall end on the day entitlement to the qualifying benefit ceased; and

(b) a bonus shall become payable to the applicant, but only where a claim is made for it in accordance with regulation 10 (claiming a bonus).

(6) In this regulation, ''applicant'' includes, where no claim is made, a person who would have been an applicant had a claim for a bonus been required.

Couples

9.—(1) In the case of a couple, the person entitled to the bonus is the person who has the care of the child and to whom child maintenance is payable in respect of that child.

(2) Where each member of a couple has both the care of a child aand child maintenance is payable in respect of the child for whom they have care, each of them may qualify for a bonus in accordance with these Regulations where a qualifying benefit ceases to be payable to either of them because one them,

whether or not the person to whom the benefit was payable, satisfies the work condition.

(3) A member of a couple to whom paragraph (2) applies shall not qualify for a bonus unless she claims it in accordance with regulation 10 (claiming a bonus).

(4) Subject to paragraph (5), these Regulations shall apply to both members of a couple who separate as if they had never been one of a couple.

(5) In the case of a couple who separate any entitlement to a qualifying benefit of one member of the couple during the time they were a couple shall be treated as the entitlement of both members of the couple for the purpose only of determining whether any day falls within a bonus period.

Claiming a bonus

10.—(1) A claim for a bonus shall be made in writing on a form approved for the purpose by the Secretary of State and shall be made—
  (a) not earlier than the beginning of the benefit week which precedes the benefit week in which an award of a qualifying benefit come to an end; and
  (b) except in a case to which sub-paragraph [². . .] (d) applies, not later than 28 days after the day the qualifying benefit [¹. . .] ceases; or
  [¹(c) [². . .]]
  (d) in the case of a person to whom regulation 8(4) refers, not later than 28 days after the day the applicant attains the age of 60 or, as the case may be, pensionable age.

(2) A claim for a bonus shall be delivered or sent to an appropriate office.

(3) If a claim is defective at the time it is received, the Secretary of State may refer the claim to the person making it and if the form is received properly completed within one month, or such longer period as the Secretary of State may consider reasonable, from the date on which it is so referred, the Secretary of State may treat the claim as if it had been duly made in the first instance.

(4) A claim which is made on the form approved form the time being is, for the purposes of paragraph (3), properly completed if it is completed in accordance with instructions on the form and defective if it is not.

(5) A person who claims a bonus shall furnish such certificates, documents, information and evidence in connection with the claim, or any questions arising out of it, as may be required by the Secretary of State and shall do so within one month of being required to do so or such longer period as the Secretary of State may consider reasonable.

(6) Where a person who has attained the age of 60 but has not attained pensionable age for the purposes of a jobseeker's allowance ceases to be entitled to a jobseeker's allowance and becomes instead entitled to income support, regulation 8 (retirement) and this regulation shall apply in his case as if he attained the age of 60 on the day he first became entitled to income support.

AMENDMENTS

1. Social Security (Miscellaneous Amendments) Regulations 1997 (S.I. 1997 No. 454), reg. 8(8) (April 6, 1997).
2. Social Security (Miscellaneous Amendments) Regulations 1998 (S.I. 1998 No. 563), reg. 2(5) (April 1, 1998). (Note that the commencement date for this provision was amended by Social Security (Miscellaneous Amendments) (No. 2) Regulations 1998 (S.I. 1998 No. 865), reg. 2 (March 20, 1998).)

Claims: further provisions

11.—(1) A person who has made a claim may amend it at any time by notice in writing received at an appropriate office before a determination has been made on the claim, and any claim so amended may be treated as if it had been so amended in the first instance.

(2) A person who has made a claim may withdraw it at any time before a determination has been made on it, by notice to an appropriate office and any such notice of withdrawal shall have effect when it is received.

(3) The date on which the claim is made shall be—
  (a) in the case of a claim which meets the requirements of regulation 10(1), the date on which it is received at an appropriate office; or
  (b) in the case of a claim treated under regulation 10(3) as having been duly made, the date on which the claim was received in an appropriate office in the first place.

(4) Where the applicant proves there was good cause throughout the period from the expiry of the 28 days specified in regulation 10(1), for failure to claim the bonus within the specified time, the time for claiming the bonus shall be extended to the date on which the claim is made or to a period of 6 months, whichever is the shorter period.

Payment of bonus

12. A bonus calculated by reference to child maintenance paid during periods of entitlement to a jobseeker's allowance and to income support shall be treated as payable—
  (a) wholly by way of a jobseeker's allowance, where the qualifying benefit last in payment in the bonus period was a jobseeker's allowance; or
  (b) wholly by way of income support, where the qualifying benefit last in payment in the bonus period was income support.

Payments on death

13.—(1) Where a person satisfies the requirements for entitlement to a bonus other than the need to make a claim, but dies within 28 days of the last day of entitlement to a qualifying benefit, the Secretary of State may appoint such person as he may think fit to claim a bonus in place of the deceased person.

(2) Where the conditions specified in paragraph (3) are satisfied, a claim may be made by the person appointed for the purpose of claiming a bonus to which the deceased person would have been entitled if he had claimed it in accordance with regulation 10 (claiming a bonus).

(3) Subject to the following provisions of this regulation, the following conditions are specified for the purposes of paragraph (2)—
  (a) the application to the Secretary of State to be appointed a fit person to make a claim shall be made within 6 months of the date of death; and
  (b) the claim shall be made in writing within 6 months of the date the appointment was made.

(4) Subject to paragraphs (5) and (6), the Secretary of State may, in exceptional circumstances, extend the period for making an application or a claim to such longer period as he considers appropriate in the particular case.

(5) Where the period is extended in accordance with paragraph (4), the period specified in paragraph (3)(a) or (b) shall be shortended by a corresponding period.

(6) The Secretary of State shall not extend the period for making an

application or a claim in accordance with paragraph (4) for more than 12 months from the date of death, but in calculating that period any period between the date when an application for a person to be appointed to make a claim is made and the date when the Secretary of State makes the appointment shall be disregarded.

(7) A claim made in accordance with paragraph (2) shall be treated, for the purposes of these Regulations, as if made on the date of the deceased's death.

Bonus to be treated as capital for certain purposes

14. Any bonus paid to an applicant shall be treated as capital of hers for the purposes of—
   (a) housing benefit;
   (b) council tax benefit;
   (c) family credit;
   (d) disability working allowance;
   (e) income support;
   (f) a jobseeker's allowance.

PART III

JOBSEEKER'S ALLOWANCE

Jobseeker's Allowance Regulations 1996

(S.I. 1996 No. 207)

Part IV

Young Persons

Part V

Sanctions

Part VI

Membership of the Family

Part VII

Amounts

Part VIII

Income and Capital

Chapter I

General

Chapter VII

Liable Relatives

Chapter VIII

Child support

Chapter IX

Full-time students

PART IX

HARDSHIP

PART I

GENERAL

Citation, commencement and interpretation

1.—(1) These Regulations may be cited as the Jobseeker's Allowance Regulations 1996.

(2) These Regulations shall come into force on 7th October 1996.

(3) In these Regulations—

"the Act" means the Jobseekers Act 1995;

"attendance allowance" means—

    (a) an attendance allowance under section 64 of the Benefits Act;

    (b) an increase of disablement pension under section 104 or 105 of the Benefits Act (increases where constant attendance needed and for exceptionally severe disablement);

    (c) a payment under regulations made in accordance with section 111 of, and paragraph 7(2) of Schedule 8 to, the Benefits Act (payments for constant attendance in workmen's compensation cases);

    (d) an increase in allowance which is payable in respect of constant attendance under section 111 of, and paragraph 4 of Schedule 8 to, the Benefits Act (industrial diseases benefit schemes);

    (e) a payment by virtue of article 14, 15, 16, 43 or 44 of the Personal Injuries (Civilians) Scheme 1983 or any analogous payment;

    (f) any payment based on the need for attendance which is paid as an addition to a war disablement pension;

"benefit week" means a period of 7 days ending on the day which corresponds with the day of the week specified in a notice given or sent to the claimant in accordance with regulation 23 (attendance) [3 requiring him to provide a signed declaration as referred to in regulation 24(6) or, in the case of a claimant who is not normally required to attend in person, on the day which corresponds with the day of the week specified by the Secretary of State in accordance with regulation 24(10) for the provision of a signed declaration,] except—

    [4 (a) where—

        (i) the Secretary of State requires attendance otherwise than at regular two weekly intervals, or in the case of a claimant who is paid benefit in accordance with Part III, other than regulation 20A, of the Claims and Payments Regulations at the time he provides a signed declaration as referred to in regulation 24(6), the "benefit week" ends on such day as the Secretary of State may specify in a notice in writing given or sent to the claimant;

        (ii) in accordance with an award of income support that includes the relevant day, the "benefit week" ends on a Saturday, the "benefit week" shall end on a Saturday, or on such other day as the Secretary of State may specify in a notice in writing given or sent to the claimant; or

        (iii) in accordance with an award of unemployment benefit that includes the relevant day, the claimant is paid benefit in respect of a period of seven days ending on the week-day specified in a written notice given to him by the Secretary of State for the purpose of his claiming unemployment benefit, and that day is a Saturday, the "benefit week" shall end on a Saturday or on such other day as the Secretary of State may specify in a notice in writing given or sent to the claimant;]

    [3 (aa) where the Secretary of State has set a day for payment of a jobseeker's allowance in respect of a claim, but no notice has yet been given or sent to the claimant in accordance with regulation 23, the "benefit week" means a period of 7 days ending on the day which has been set;]

    (b) for the purpose of calculating any payment of income in accordance with Part VIII, "benefit week" also means the period of 7 days ending on the day before the first day of the benefit week following the date of claim or, as the case may be, the last day on which a jobseeker's allowance is paid if it is in payment for [4 less than a week,

and in this definition "relevant day" has the meaning it has in the Jobseeker's Allowance (Transitional Provisions) Regulations 1995.]

"board and lodging accommodation" means—

(a) accommodation provided to a person or, if he is a member of a
family, to him or any other member of his family, for a charge which
is inclusive of the provision of that accommodation and at least some
cooked or prepared meals which both are cooked or prepared (by a
person other than the person to whom the accommodation is provided or a member of his family) and are consumed in that accommodation or associated premises; or

(b) accommodation provided to a person in a hotel, guest house, lodging
house or some similar establishment,

except accommodation provided by a close relative of his or of any other
member of his family, or other than on a commercial basis;

[7"the Children Order" means the Children (Northern Ireland) Order 1995;]

"Claims and Payments Regulations" means the Social Security (Claims and
Payments) Regulations 1987;

"close relative" means, except in Parts II [4 ...] and V, a parent, parent-in-
law, son, son-in-law, daughter, daughter-in-law, step-parent, step-son,
step-daughter, brother, sister, or the spouse of any of the preceding
persons or, if that person is one of an unmarried couple, the other
member of that couple;

"college of further education" means a college of further education within
the meaning of Part I of the Further and Higher Education (Scotland)
Act 1992;

"concessionary payment" means a payment made under arrangements made
by the Secretary of State with the consent of the Treasury which is
charged either to the National Insurance Fund or to a Departmental
Expenditure Vote to which payments of benefit under the Act or the
Benefits Act are charged;

"co-ownership scheme" means a scheme under which a dwelling is let by a
housing association and the tenant, or his personal representative, will,
under the terms of the tenancy agreement or of the agreement under
which he became a member of the association, be entitled, on his ceasing
to be a member and subject of any condition stated in either agreement,
to a sum calculated by reference directly or indirectly to the value of the
dwelling;

"couple" means a married or an unmarried couple;

"course of advanced education" means—

(a) a course leading to a postgraduate degree or comparable qualification, a first degree or comparable qualification, a diploma of higher
education or a higher national diploma; or

(b) any other course which is of a standard above advanced GNVQ or
equivalent, including a course which is of a standard above a general
certificate of education (advanced level), a Scottish certificate of
education (higher level) or a Scottish certificate of sixth year studies;

"course of study" means any course of study, including a course of advanced
education and an employment-related course, whether or not it is a sandwich course and whether or not a grant is made for attending or undertaking it and for the purposes of this definition a person who has started a
course of study shall be treated as attending or undertaking it, as the case
may be, until the last day of the course or such earlier date as he abandoned it or is dismissed from it;

"Crown tenant" means a person who occupies a dwelling under a tenancy
or licence where the interest of the landlord belongs to Her Majesty in
right of the Crown or to a government department or is held in trust for

Her Majesty for the purposes of a government department, except (in the case of an interest belonging to Her Majesty in right of the Crown) where the interest is under the management of the Crown Estate Commissioners;

"date of claim" the date on which the claimant makes, or is treated as making, a claim for a jobseeker's allowance for the purposes of regulation 6 of the Claims and Payments Regulations;

"disability living allowance" means a disability living allowance under section 71 of the Benefits Act;

"disability working allowance" means a disability working allowance under section 129 of the Benefits Act;

"dwelling occupied as the home" means the dwelling together with any garage, garden and outbuildings, normally occupied by the claimant as his home including any premises not so occupied which it is impracticable or unreasonable to sell separately, in particular, in Scotland, any croft land on which the dwelling is situated;

"earnings" has the meaning specified, in the case of an employed earner, in regulation 98, or in the case of a self-employed earner, in regulation 100;

[⁴"earnings top-up" means the allowance paid by the Secretary of State under the Earnings Top-up Scheme;]

[⁴"the Earnings Top-up Scheme" means the Earnings Top-up Scheme 1996 as amended from time to time;]

"the Eileen Trust" means the charitable trust of that name established on 29th March 1993 out of funds provided by the Secretary of State for the benefit of persons eligible for payment in accordance with its provisions;

"employment-related course" means a course the purpose of which is to assist persons to acquire or enhance skills required for employment, for seeking employment or for a particular occupation;

"the FEFC" means the Further Education Funding Council for England or the Further Education Funding Council for Wales;

"full-time course of advanced education" means a course of advanced education which is taken by a person who is—

   (a) attending a full-time course of study which is not funded in whole or in part by the FEFC or a full-time course of study [¹ . . .] which is not funded in whole or in part by the Secretary of State for Scotland at a college of further education [¹ or a full-time course of study which is a course of higher education and is funded in whole or in part by the Secretary of State for Scotland;]

   (b) undertaking a course of study which is funded in whole or in part by the FEFC if it involves more than 16 guided learning hours per week for the student in question, according to the number of guided learning hours per week for that student set out in the case of a course funded by the FEFC for England, in his learning agreement signed on behalf of the establishment which is funded by the FEFC for the delivery of that course or, in the case of a course funded by the FEFC for Wales, in a document signed on behalf of the establishment which is funded by the FEFC for the delivery of that course; or

   (c) undertaking a course of study (not being higher education) which is funded in whole or in part by the Secretary of State for Scotland at a college of further education if it involves—

      (i) more than 16 hours per week of classroom-based or workshop-based programmed learning under the direct guidance of teaching staff according to the number of hours set out in a document signed on behalf of the college; or

      (ii) 16 hours or less per week of classroom-based or workshop-based programmed learning under the direct guidance of teaching staff and it involves additional hours using structured learning packages supported by the teaching staff where the combined total of hours exceeds 21 per week, according to the number of hours set out in a document signed on behalf of the college;

"full-time student" means a person, other than a person in receipt of a training allowance, who is—

(a) aged less than 19 and undertaking a full-time course of advanced education or

(b) aged 19 or over but under pensionable age and—

    (i) attending a full-time course of study which is not funded in whole or in part by the FEFC or a full-time course of study [[1] ...] which is not funded in whole or in part by the Secretary of State for Scotland at a college of further education [[1] or a full-time course of study which is a course of higher education and is funded in whole or in part by the Secretary of State for Scotland;]

    (ii) undertaking a course of study which is funded in whole or in part by the FEFC if it involves more than 16 guided learning hours per week for the student in question, according to the number of guided learning hours per week for that student set out, in the case of a course funded by the FEFC for England, in his learning agreement signed on behalf of the establishment which is funded by the FEFC for the delivery of that course or, in the case of a course funded by the FEFC for Wales, in a document signed on behalf of the establishment which is funded by the FEFC for the delivery of that course; or

    (iii) undertaking a course of study (not being higher education) which is funded in whole or in part by the Secretary of State for Scotland at a college of further education if it involves—

        (aa) more than 16 hours per week of classroom-based or workshop-based programmed learning under the direct guidance of teaching staff according to the number of hours set out in a document signed on behalf of the college; or

        (bb) 16 hours or less per week of classroom or workshop based programmed learning under the direct guidance of teaching staff and it involves additional hours using structured learning packages supported by the teaching staff where the combined total of hours exceeds 21 per week, according to the number of hours set out in a document signed on behalf of the college;

"the Fund" means moneys made available from time to time by the Secretary of State for the benefit of persons eligible for payment in accordance with the provisions of a scheme established by him on 24th April 1992 or, in Scotland, on 10th April 1992;

"higher education" means higher education within the meaning of Part II of the Further and Higher Education (Scotland) Act 1992;

"housing association" has the meaning assigned to it by section 1(1) of the Housing Associations Act 1985;

[[5]"housing benefit expenditure" means expenditure in respect of which housing benefit is payable as specified in regulation 10(1) of the Housing Benefit (General) Regulations 1987 but does not include any such expenditure in respect of which an amount is applicable under regulation 83(f) or 84(1)(g) (housing costs);]

"Income Support Regulations" means the Income Support (General) Regulations 1987;

"the Independent Living (Extension) Fund" means the Trust of that name established by a deed dated 25th February 1993 and made between the

Secretary of State for Social Security of the one part and Robin Glover Wendt and John Fletcher Shepherd of the other part;

"the Independent Living Fund" means the charitable trust established out of funds provided by the Secretary of State for the purpose of providing financial assistance to those persons incapacitated by or otherwise suffering from very severe disablement who are in need of such assistance to enable them to live independently;

"the Independent Living (1993) Fund" means the Trust of that name established by a deed dated 25th February 1993 and made between the Secretary of State for Social Security of the one part and Robin Glover Wendt and John Fletcher Shepherd of the other part;

"the Independent Living Funds" means the Independent Living Fund, the Independent Living (Extension) Fund and the Independent Living (1993) Fund;

"invalid carriage or other vehicle" means a vehicle propelled by a petrol engine or by electric power supplied for use on the road and to be controlled by the occupant;

"jobseeking period" means the period described in regulation 47 [8except where otherwise provided];

"last day of the course" has the meaning prescribed in regulation 130 for the purposes of the definition of "period of study" in this paragraph;

"liable relative" has the meaning prescribed in regulation 117;

"lone parent" means a person who has no partner and who is responsible for, and a member of the same household as, a child or young person;

"long tenancy" means a tenancy granted for a term of years certain exceeding twenty one years, whether or not the tenancy is, or may become, terminable before the end of that term by notice given by or to the tenant or by re-entry, forfeiture (or, in Scotland, irritancy) or otherwise and includes a lease for a term fixed by law under a grant with a covenant or obligation for perpetual renewal unless it is a lease by sub-demise from one which is not a long tenancy;

"lower rate" where it relates to rates of tax has the same meaning as in the Income and Corporation Taxes Act 1988 by virtue of section 832(1) of that Act;

"the Macfarlane (Special Payments) Trust" means the trust of that name, established on 29th January 1990 partly out of funds provided by the Secretary of State for the benefit of certain persons suffering from haemophilia;

"the Macfarlane (Special Payments) (No.2) Trust" means the trust of that name, established on 2nd May 1991 partly out of funds provided by the Secretary of State, for the benefit of certain persons suffering from haemophilia and other beneficiaries;

"the Macfarlane Trust" means the charitable trust, established partly out of funds provided by the Secretary of State to the Haemophilia Society, for the relief of poverty or distress among those suffering from haemophilia;

"making a claim" includes treated as making a claim;

"maternity leave" means a period during which a woman is absent from work because she is pregnant or has given birth to a child, and at the end of which she has a right to return to work either under the terms of her contract of employment or under Part III of the Employment Protection (Consolidation) Act 1978;

"mobility supplement" means any supplement under article 26A of the Naval, Military and Air Forces etc (Disablement and Death) Service Pensions Order 1983 including such a supplement by virtue of any other scheme or order or under article 25A of the Personal Injuries (Civilians) Scheme 1983;

"net earnings" means such earnings as are calculated in accordance with regulation 99;

"net profit" means such profit as is calculated in accordance with regulation 101;

"non-dependant" has the meaning prescribed in regulation 2;

"non-dependant deduction" means a deduction that is to be made under regulation 83(f) and paragraph 17 of Schedule 2;

"nursing home" means—

 (a) premises which are a nursing home or mental nursing home within the meaning of the Registered Homes Act 1984 and which are either registered under Part II of that Act or exempt from registration under section 37 thereof (power to exempt Christian Science Homes); or

 (b) any premises used or intended to be used for the reception of such persons or the provision of such nursing or services as is mentioned in any paragraph of subsection (1) of section 21 or section 22(1) of the Registered Homes Act 1984 (meaning of nursing home or mental nursing home) or, in Scotland, as are mentioned in section 10(2) of the Nursing Homes Registration (Scotland) Act 1938 (interpretation) and which are maintained or controlled by a body instituted by special Act of Parliament or incorporated by Royal Charter;

 (c) in Scotland,

  (i) premises which are a nursing home within the meaning of section 10 of the Nursing Homes Registration (Scotland) Act 1938 which are either registered under that Act or exempt from registration under section 6 or 7 thereof (general power to exempt homes and power to exempt Christian Science Homes); or

  (ii) premises which are a private hospital within the meaning of section 12 of the Mental Health (Scotland) Act 1984 (private hospitals), and which are registered under that Act;

"occupational pension" means any pension or other periodical payment under an occupational pension scheme but does not include any discretionary payment out of a fund established for relieving hardship in particular cases;

"partner" means where a claimant—

 (a) is a member of a married or an unmarried couple, the other member of that couple;

 (b) is married polygamously to two or more members of his household, any such member;

"part-time student" means a person who is attending or undertaking a course of study and who is not a full-time student;

"payment" includes a part of a payment;

"pay period" means the period in respect of which a claimant is, or expects to be, normally paid by his employer, being a week, a fortnight, four weeks, a month or other longer or shorter period as the case may be;

"period of study" except in Parts II, IV and V means—

 (a) in the case of a course of study for one year or less, the period beginning with the start of the course and ending with the last day of the course;

 (b) in the case of a course of study for more than one year, in the first or, as the case may be, any subsequent year of the course, other than the final year of the course, the period beginning with the start of the course or, as the case may be, that year's start and ending with either—

  (i) the day before the start of the next year of the course in a case where the student's grant is assessed at a rate appropriate to his study throughout the year, or, if he does not have a grant, where it would have been assessed at such a rate had he had one; or

    (ii) in any other case the day before the start of the normal summer vacation appropriate to his course;

  (c) in the final year of a course of study of more than one year, the period beginning with that year's start and ending with the last day of the course;

"policy of life insurance" means any instrument by which the payment of money is assured on death (except death by accident only) or the happening of any contingency dependent on human life, or any instrument evidencing a contract which is subject to payment of premiums for a term dependent on human life;

"polygamous marriage" means any marriage during the subsistence of which a party to it is married to more than one person and the ceremony of marriage took place under the law of a country which permits polygamy;

"preserved rights" means preserved rights for the purposes of regulation 86;

"qualifying person" means a person in respect of whom payment has been made from the Fund or the Eileen Trust;

"relative" means close relative, grand-parent, grand-child, uncle, aunt, nephew or niece;

"relevant enactment" has the meaning prescribed in [² regulation 78(9)(a)];

"remunerative work" has the meaning prescribed in regulation 51(1);

"residential accommodation" has the meaning prescribed in regulation 85(4);

"residential allowance" means the weekly amount determined in accordance with paragraph 3 of Schedule 1;

"residential care home" means an establishment—

  (a) which is required to be registered under Part I of the Registered Homes Act 1984 and is so registered, or is deemed to be registered under section 2(3) of the Registered Homes (Amendment) Act 1991 (which refers to the registration of small homes where the application for registration has not been determined); or

  (b) run by the Abbeyfield Society including all bodies corporate or incorporate which are affiliated to that Society; or

  (c) which provides residential accommodation with both board and personal care and is managed or provided by a body incorporated by Royal Charter or constituted by Act of Parliament other than a local social services authority; or

  (d) in Scotland, which is a home registered under section 61 of the Social Work (Scotland) Act 1968 or is an establishment provided by a housing association registered with Scottish Homes established by the Housing (Scotland) Act 1988 which provides care equivalent to that given in residential accommodation provided under Part IV of the Social Work (Scotland) Act 1968; or

  (e) which is exempt from registration under Part I of the Registered Homes Act 1984 pursuant to section 1(4)(a) of that Act (exemption from registration in respect of certain homes) because one or more of the residents are treated as relatives pursuant to section 19(4) of that Act;

and in paragraph (c) of this definition "personal care" means personal care for persons in need of personal care by reason of disablement, past or present dependence on alcohol or drugs, or past or present mental disorder;

"sandwich course" has the meaning prescribed in paragraph 1(1) of Schedule 5 to the Education (Mandatory Awards) Regulations 1994 and any person on a sandwich course shall be treated as attending or undertaking a course of advanced education or, as the case may be, attending or undertaking a course of study;

"self-employed earner" has the meaning it has in Part I of the Benefits Act by virtue of section 2(1)(b) of that Act;

"single claimant" means a claimant who neither has a partner nor is a lone parent;

"terminal date" in respect of a claimant means the terminal date in his case for the purposes of regulation 7 of the Child Benefit (General) Regulations 1976;

"training allowance" means an allowance (whether by way of periodical grants or otherwise) payable—

(a) out of public funds by a Government department or by or on behalf of the Secretary of State for Education and Employment, Scottish Enterprise or Highlands and Islands Enterprise; and

(b) to a person for his maintenance or in respect of a member of his family; and

(c) for the period, or part of the period, during which he is following a course of training or instruction provided by, or in pursuance of arrangements made with, that department or approved by that department in relation to him or so provided or approved by or on behalf of the Secretary of State for Education and Employment, Scottish Enterprise or Highlands and Islands Enterprise,

but it does not include an allowance paid by any Government department to or in respect of a person by reason of the fact that he is following a course of full-time education, other than under arrangements made under section 2 of the Employment and Training Act 1973 [³ or section 2 of the Enterprise and New Towns (Scotland) Act 1990,] or is training as a teacher;

"voluntary organisation" means a body, other than a public or local authority, the activities of which are carried on otherwise than for profit;

"war disablement pension" means a pension payable to a person in respect of disablement—

(a) under the Naval, Military and Air Forces Etc (Disablement and Death) Service Pensions Order 1983 and any order re-enacting the provisions of that order;

(b) under the Personal Injuries (Civilians) Scheme 1983, and any subsequent scheme made under the Personal Injuries (Emergency Provisions) Act 1939;

(c) under any scheme made under the Pensions (Navy, Army, Air Force and Mercantile Marine) Act 1939 or the Polish Resettlement Act 1947 applying the provisions of any such order as is referred to in paragraph (a);

(d) under the order made under section 1(5) of the Ulster Defence Regiment Act 1969 concerning pensions and other grants in respect of disablement or death due to service in the Ulster Defence Regiment;

(e) under the order in council of 19 December 1881, the Royal Warrant of 27 October 1884, or the order by His Majesty of 14 January 1922 (exceptional grants of pay, non-effective pay and allowances);

(f) paid by the Overseas Development Administration and which is analogous to any of the pensions mentioned in the preceding paragraphs;

"war widow's pension" means a pension payable to a woman as a widow under any of the enactments mentioned in the definition of "war disablement pension" in respect of the death or disablement of any person;

"water charges" means—

(a) as respects England and Wales, any water and sewerage charges under Chapter 1 of Part V of the Water Industry Act 1991;

(b) as respects Scotland, any water and sewerage charges under Schedule 11 to the Local Government Finance Act 1992;

in so far as such charges are in respect of the dwelling which a person occupies as his home;

"week" in [⁶ the definitions of "full-time course of advanced education" and of "full-time student" and] [³ Parts III, VI, VII, VIII, IX, X, XI, XII and XIII] means a period of 7 days;

[⁹"welfare to work beneficiary" means a person—

(a) to whom regulation 13A(1) of the Social Security (Incapacity for Work) (General) Regulations 1995 applies; and

(b) who again becomes incapable of work for the purposes of Part XIIA of the Contributions and Benefits Act 1992;]

"year of assessment" has the meaning prescribed in section 832(1) of the Income and Corporation Taxes Act 1988;

"young person" except in Part IV has the meaning prescribed in regulation 76.

(4) In these Regulations, unless the context otherwise requires, a reference—

(a) to a numbered section is to the section of the Act bearing that number;

(b) to a numbered Part is to the Part of these Regulations bearing that number;

(c) to a numbered regulation or Schedule is to the regulation in or Schedule to these Regulations bearing that number;

(d) in a regulation or Schedule to a numbered paragraph is to the paragraph in that regulation or Schedule bearing that number;

(e) in a paragraph to a lettered or numbered sub-paragraph is to the sub-paragraph in that paragraph bearing that letter or number.

(5) Unless the context requires otherwise, any reference to the claimant's family or, as the case may be, to a member of his family, shall be construed for the purposes of these Regulations as if it included in relation to a polygamous marriage a reference to any partner and to any child or young person who is treated as the responsibility of the claimant or his partner, where that child or young person is a member of the claimant's household.

AMENDMENTS

1. Jobseeker's Allowance (Amendment) Regulations 1996 (S.I. 1996 No. 1516), reg. 2 (October 7, 1996).

2. Jobseeker's Allowance (Amendment) Regulations 1996 (S.I. 1996 No. 1516), reg. 20 and Sched. (October 7, 1996).

3. Jobseeker's Allowance and Income Support (General) (Amendment) Regulations 1996 (S.I. 1996 No. 1517), reg. 2 (October 7, 1996).

4. Social Security and Child Support (Jobseeker's Allowance) (Miscellaneous Amendments) Regulations 1996 (S.I. 1996 No. 2538), reg. 2(2) (October 28, 1996).

5. Income-related Benefits and Jobseeker's Allowance (Miscellaneous Amendments) Regulations 1997 (S.I. 1997 No. 65), reg. 4(2) (April 7, 1997).

6. Social Security (Miscellaneous Amendments) Regulations 1997 (S.I. 1997 No. 454), reg. 2(2) (April 7, 1997).

7. Social Security (Miscellaneous Amendments) Regulations 1998 (S.I. 1998 No. 563), reg. 5(1) and (2)(f) (April 6, 1998).

8. Social Security Amendment (New Deal) Regulations 1998 (S.I. 1998 No. 1274), reg. 2 (June 1, 1998).

9. Social Security (Welfare to Work) Regulations 1998 (S.I. 1998 No. 2231), reg. 14(2) (October 5, 1998).

DEFINITIONS

"Benefits Act"—see Jobseekers Act s. 35(1).
"child"—*ibid.*
"claimant"—*ibid.*
"family"—*ibid.*
"married couple"—*ibid.*
"occupational pension scheme"—*ibid.*
"unmarried couple"—*ibid.*

GENERAL NOTE

See the notes to reg. 2(1) of the Income Support Regulations for points on some of these definitions, namely, "board and lodging accommodation", "close relative", "dwelling occupied as the home", "the Earnings Top-up Scheme", "occupational pension", "self-employed earner", "training allowance", "welfare to work beneficiary" and "year of assessment". Otherwise, the significance of particular definitions is dealt with in the notes to the regulations in which they occur.

Note the additional definitions in reg. 3 and the definitions in reg. 4 for the purposes of Part II (jobseeking), Part IV (young persons), Part V (sanctions) and various sections of the Jobseekers Act.

Definition of non-dependant

2.—(1) In these Regulations, "non-dependant" means any person, except a person to whom paragraph (2), (3) or (4) applies, who normally resides with the claimant or with whom the claimant normally resides.

(2) This paragraph applies to—

(a) any member of the claimant's family;

(b) a child or young person who is living with the claimant but who is not a member of his household by virtue of regulation 78 (circumstances in which a person is to be treated as being or not being a member of the household);

(c) a person who lives with the claimant in order to care for him or for the claimant's partner and who is engaged for that purpose by a charitable or voluntary organisation (other than a public or local authority) which makes a charge to the claimant or the claimant's partner for the care provided by that person;

(d) the partner of a person to whom sub-paragraph (c) applies.

(3) This paragraph applies to a person, other than a close relative of the claimant or the claimant's partner,—

(a) who is liable to make payments on a commercial basis to the claimant or the claimant's partner in respect of his occupation of the claimant's dwelling;

(b) to whom the claimant or the claimant's partner is liable to make payments on a commercial basis in respect of his occupation of that person's dwelling;

(c) who is a member of the household of a person to whom sub-paragraph (a) or (b) applies.

(4) Subject to paragraph (5), this paragraph applies to—

(a) a person who jointly occupies the claimant's dwelling and who is either—

(i) a co-owner of that dwelling with the claimant or the claimant's partner (whether or not there are other co-owners); or

(ii) jointly liable with the claimant or the claimant's partner to make payments to a landlord in respect of his occupation of that dwelling; or

(b) a partner of a person to whom sub-paragraph (a) applies.

(5) Where a person is a close relative of the claimant or the claimant's partner,

paragraph (4) shall apply to him only if the claimant's, or the claimant's partner's, co-ownership, or joint liability to make payments to a landlord in respect of his occupation, of the dwelling arose either before 11th April 1988, or, if later, on or before the date upon which the claimant or the claimant's partner first occupied the dwelling in question.

(6) For the purposes of this regulation a person resides with another only if they share any accommodation except a bathroom, a lavatory or a communal area but not if each person is separately liable to make payments in respect of his occupation of the dwelling to the landlord.

(7) In this regulation "communal area" means any area (other than rooms) of common access (including halls and passageways) and rooms of common use in sheltered accommodation.

DEFINITIONS

"child"—see Jobseekers Act, s. 35(1).
"claimant"—*ibid.*
"close relative"—see reg. 1(3).
"family"—see s. 35(1).
"partner"—see reg. 1(3).
"voluntary organisation"—*ibid.*

GENERAL NOTE

See the notes to reg. 3 of the Income Support Regulations.

[¹Disapplication of section 1(1A) of the Administration Act

2A. Section 1(1A) of the Administration Act (requirement to state national insurance number) shall not apply—
  (a) to a child or young person in respect of whom jobseeker's allowance is claimed;
  (b) to any claim for jobseeker's allowance made or treated as made before 5th October 1998].

AMENDMENT

1. Social Security (National Insurance Number Information: Exemption) Regulations 1997 (S.I. 1997 No. 2676), reg. 12 (December 1, 1997).

DEFINITIONS

"child"—see Jobseekers Act, s. 35(1).
"young person"—see reg. 76.

GENERAL NOTE

See the notes to s. 1(1A)–(1C) of the Administration Act and reg. 2A of the Income Support Regulations. Note that in the case of jobseeker's allowance, unlike income support, the requirement to have, or apply for, a national insurance number as a condition of entitlement to benefit does not apply to any claim made or treated as made before October 5, 1998 (para. (b)).

Meanings of certain expressions used in the Jobseekers Act 1995

3. For the purposes of the Act and of these Regulations—
  "employed earner" has the meaning it has in Part I of the Benefits Act by virtue of section 2(1)(a) of that Act;
  [¹"employment", except as provided in regulations 4 and 75, includes any trade, business, profession, office or vocation;]

"pensionable age" has the meaning it has in Parts I to VI of the Benefits Act by virtue of section 122(1) of that Act.

AMENDMENT

1. Social Security Amendment (New Deal) Regulations 1997 (S.I. 1997 No. 2863), reg. 2 (January 5, 1998).

DEFINITION

"the Benefits Act"—see Jobseekers Act, s. 35(1).

GENERAL NOTE

"*employed earner*". See the note to reg. 2(1) of the Income Support Regulations.

"*employment*". From January 5, 1998 this definition and the definition of "employment" in reg. 4 have been amended as a consequence of the introduction of the "New Deal" for 18–24 year-olds. For a brief summary of the New Deal see the notes to reg. 75. The amendments remove Part V of these Regulations and s. 19 of the Jobseekers Act from the list of provisions in reg. 4 in which employment only refers to work as an employee and does not include self-employment (unless otherwise stated), employment for the purposes of Part V and s. 19 now being defined in reg. 75. This provides that employment for the purposes of those provisions refers to work as an employee, *except* work in which a person is employed while on the Employment, Voluntary Sector or Environment Task Force options of the New Deal (reg. 75(4)). But note that this does not apply to s. 19(9) in which "employment" simply means employed earner's employment (reg. 75(5)). These amendments are needed because people on the Employment option will, and on the Voluntary Sector and Environment Task Force options may, be employees and thus would otherwise potentially be liable to sanctions of up to 26 weeks under s. 19(6) of the Act for refusing or losing, etc. their place on the option. The intention is that the fixed term sanctions of two or four weeks will apply to all people taking part in the New Deal, regardless of whether they are employed or in receipt of an allowance. See further the notes to reg. 69.

Note also the definition of employment in s. 7(8) of the Act for the purposes of regs. 18 to 22.

"*pensionable age*". Pensionable age is 65 for men and for women born after April 5, 1955, and 60 for women born before April 6, 1950 (Pensions Act, 1995, s. 126 and Sched. 4, Part I). Women born between April 6, 1950 and April 5, 1955 will reach pensionable age at a date between their 60th and 65th birthday (the exact days are set out in Part I of Sched. 4 to the Pensions Act 1995).

PART II

JOBSEEKING

Chapter I

Interpretation

Interpretation of Parts II, IV and V

4. In Parts II, IV and V and, as provided below, the Act—
"appropriate office" means the office of the Department for Education and Employment which the claimant is required to attend in accordance with a notice under regulation 23, or any other place which he is so required to attend;
"caring responsibilities" means responsibility for caring for a child or for an elderly person or for a person whose physical or mental condition requires him to be cared for, who is either in the same household or a close relative;
"casual employment" means employment from which the employee can be

released without his giving any notice [³except where otherwise provided];

"close relative" means [¹, except in Part IV,] a spouse or other member of an unmarried couple, parent, step-parent, grandparent, parent-in-law, son, step-son, son-in-law, daughter, step-daughter, daughter-in-law, brother, sister, grandchild or the spouse of any of the preceding persons or, if that person is one of an unmarried couple, the other member of that couple;

"elderly person" means a person of over pensionable age;

"employment" in sections 1, 3, 6, 8, 14 [² . . .] and 20 and paragraph 8 of Schedule 1 to the Act and in [²Parts II and IV] means employed earner's employment except where otherwise provided;

"employment officer" means a person who is an employment officer for the purposes of sections 9 and 10;

[³"examination" in relation to a qualifying course means an examination which is specified as an examination related to the qualifying course in a document signed on behalf of the establishment at which the qualifying course is being undertaken;

"made a claim for a jobseeker's allowance" includes treated as having made a claim for the allowance and treated as having an award of the allowance in accordance with regulation 5, 6 or 7 of the Jobseeker's Allowance (Transitional Provisions) Regulations 1996;]

"Outward Bound course" means any course or programme for personal development which is made available to persons who are not in employment by the charitable trust known as the Outward Bound Trust Limited;

"part-time member of a fire brigade" means a person who is a part-time member of a fire brigade maintained in pursuance of the Fire Services Acts 1947–1959;

"pattern of availability" has the meaning given in regulation 7;

"period of study" means the period beginning with the start of the course of study and ending with the last day of the course or such earlier date as the student abandons it or is dismissed from it; but any period of attendance by the student at his educational establishment, or any period of study undertaken by the student, in connection with the course which occurs before or after the period of the course shall be treated as part of the period of study;

"a person who is kept on short-time" means a person whose hours of employment have been reduced owing to temporary adverse industrial conditions;

"a person who is laid off" means a person whose employment has been suspended owing to temporary adverse industrial conditions;

[³"qualifying course" has the meaning given in regulation 17A;

"term-time" in relation to a qualifying course means the period specified as term-time in relation to a person to whom regulation 17A(2) applies in a document signed on behalf of the establishment at which the qualifying course is being undertaken;

"vacation" in relation to a qualifying course means any period falling within the period of study, which is not term-time;]

"voluntary work" means work for an organisation the activities of which are carried on otherwise than for profit, or work other than for a member of the claimant's family, where no payment is received by the claimant or the only payment due to be made to him by virtue of being so engaged is a payment in respect of any expenses reasonably incurred by him in the course of being so engaged;

"week" in sections 6 and 7 and in Parts II and IV means benefit week except where provided otherwise in Parts II and IV;

"work camp" means any place in Great Britain where people come together under the auspices of a charity, a local authority or a voluntary organisation to provide a service of benefit to the community or the environment.

AMENDMENTS

1. Social Security and Child Support (Jobseeker's Allowance) (Miscellaneous Amendments) Regulations 1996 (S.I. 1996 No. 2538), reg. 2(3) (October 28, 1996).
2. Social Security Amendment (New Deal) Regulations 1997 (S.I. 1997 No. 2863), reg. 3 (January 5, 1998).
3. Social Security Amendment (New Deal) Regulations 1998 (S.I. 1998 No. 1274), reg. 3 (June 1, 1998).

DEFINITIONS

"benefit week"—see reg. 1(3).
"child"—see Jobseekers Act, s. 35(1).
"couple"—see reg. 1(3).
"course of study"—*ibid.*
"payment"—*ibid.*
"pensionable age"—see reg. 3.
"voluntary organisation"—see reg. 1(3).

GENERAL NOTE

"*close relative*". See the note to reg. 2(1) of the Income Support Regulations.
"*employment*". See the note to the definition of "employment" in reg. 3.

Chapter II

Availability for employment

Exceptions to requirement to be available immediately: carers, voluntary workers, persons providing a service and persons under an obligation to provide notice

5.—(1) In order to be regarded as available for employment, a person who has caring responsibilities or who is engaged in voluntary work is not required to be able to take up employment immediately, providing he is willing and able to take up employment on being given 48 hours' notice.

(2) In order to be regarded as available for employment, a person who is engaged, whether by contract or otherwise, in providing a service with or without remuneration, other than a person who has caring responsibilities or who is engaged in voluntary work, is not required to be able to take up employment immediately, providing he is willing and able to take up employment on being given 24 hours' notice.

(3) In order to be regarded as available for employment, a person who is in employed earner's employment and is not engaged in remunerative work and who is required by section 49 of the Employment Protection (Consolidation) Act 1978 to give notice to terminate his contract is not required to be able to take up employment immediately, providing he is willing and able to take up employment immediately he is able to do so in accordance with his statutory obligations.

(4) Where in accordance with regulation 7, 13 or 17 a person is only available for employment at certain times, he is not required to be able to take up employment at a time at which he is not available, but he must be willing and able to take up employment immediately he is available.

(5) Where in accordance with paragraph (1) or (2) a person is not required to be able to take up employment immediately, the 48 hour and 24 hour periods referred to in those paragraphs include periods when in accordance with regulation 7 or 13 he is not available.

DEFINITIONS

"caring responsibilities"—see reg. 4.
"employment"—*ibid.*
"voluntary work"—*ibid.*
"remunerative work"—see regs. 1(3) and 51(1).

GENERAL NOTE

This regulation contains the exceptions to the rule in s. 6(1) of the Jobseekers Act that a person must be willing and able to take up employed earner's employment *immediately*. Apart from the provisions in paras. (1)–(3) allowing certain groups to be available only on notice, para. (4) makes clear that the condition of immediate availability does not operate during periods when the claimant is not required to be available for employment under regs. 7, 13 and 17 (see the notes to those regulations), provided that he can take up employment as soon as he is available. See also reg. 72(5)(b).

Paragraph (1)
A claimant who has "caring responsibilities" or who is doing "voluntary work" (both defined in reg. 4) only has to be available on 48 hours' notice. "Caring responsibilities" means that the person is looking after a member of the same household or a close relative (defined in reg. 4) who is a child, of or over pensionable age, or who needs caring for because of his physical or mental condition. See also reg. 13(4) which allows a claimant with caring responsibilities to restrict his availability to accommodate those responsibilities provided he is available for at least 16 hours a week and still has a reasonable chance of finding work despite the restriction. "Voluntary work" is work done for an organisation that does not carry on its activities for profit, or other than for a member of the claimant's family, for which no payment, or only payment of reasonable expenses, is made (reg. 4). See reg. 12 where the voluntary work coincides with the person's accepted pattern of availability.
Note that under para. (5) the 48 hours includes periods when the person is not available in accordance with reg. 7 or 13. Thus, for example, if a carer who under the terms of her jobseeker's agreement only has to be available on Thursdays and Fridays receives a job offer on Saturday, the 48 hours' notice will run from that day. But para. (4) will enable her to satisfy the availability condition until Thursday because of her permitted pattern of availability, provided that she is willing and able to take up the job on Thursday.
Under para. (1) the person has to be able to take up employment "on being given 48 hours' notice". In *CIS 142/1993* the Commissioner decided that the same phrase (except that the required notice was only 24 hours) in reg. 12(1) of the Unemployment, Sickness and Invalidity Benefit Regulations 1983 meant that the notice should only start to run when the claimant would receive notification of the job (in that case by a telephone call from his parents in the evening as he was doing voluntary work during the day). See also para. 26236 of the *Adjudication Officer's Guide.*

Paragraph (2)
A claimant who is providing a service, other than as a carer or volunteer and so does not come within para. (1), only has to be available on 24 hours' notice. For when the notice starts to run, see *CIS 142/1993* above. The 24 hours includes periods when the person is not available in accordance with reg. 7 or 13 (para. (5)). But note the effect of para. (4) (see the note to para. (1) above).
The service does not have to be for payment or provided under a contract. *CU 96/1994* held that "service" in reg. 12(1) of the Unemployment, Sickness and Invalidity Benefit Regulations (the predecessor of this provision) could include an act to help a family member. Taking a child to school was not a service (it was simply fulfilling a parental duty) but taking his wife to college could be. It should be noted that reg. 12(1) contained an additional requirement that in the circumstances it was not reasonable to require the claimant to be available at less than 24 hours' notice. There is no such limitation in para. (2).

Paragraph (3)

This covers a claimant who is working for less than 16 hours a week who is required to give notice to terminate his employment (the minimum statutory notice is one week after a month's continuous employment: s. 86 of the Employment Rights Act 1996 which has replaced s. 49 of the Employment Protection (Consolidation) Act 1978). In such a case the person only has to be available to take up employment as soon as he can do so "in accordance with his statutory obligations". Note the effect of para. (4), if relevant (see the note to para. (1)).

Paragraph (4)

This states that a person who is only available for work at certain times in accordance with reg. 7, 13 or 17 (see the notes to those provisions) is not required to be able to take up employment during his periods of non-availability, provided he can do so as soon as he is available. The provision is necessary to ensure that the requirement to be *immediately* available does not have the effect of overriding any such permitted pattern of availability.

Employment of at least 40 hours per week

6.—(1) In order to be regarded as available for employment, a person must be willing and able to take up employment of at least 40 hours per week, unless he has restricted his availability in accordance with paragraph (3) or (4) of regulation 13 or paragraph (2) of regulation 17 or two or more of those provisions.

(2) In order to be regarded as available for employment, a person must be willing and able to take up employment of less than 40 hours per week but not for a greater number of hours per week than the number for which he is available in accordance with paragraph (3) or (4) of regulation 13 or paragraph (2) of regulation 17 or two or more of those provisions.

DEFINITIONS

"employment"—see reg. 4.
"week"—*ibid.*

GENERAL NOTE

The normal rule under JSA is that to be regarded as available for work a person must be willing and able to take up employment for at least 40 hours a week but also be prepared to work for less than 40 hours a week. Note the exceptions in regs. 13(3) and (4) and 17(2) (see the notes to those regulations). "Week" means "benefit week" (reg. 4; for "benefit week" see reg. 1(3)).

Thus the effect of para. (2) is that a claimant may be required to take a part-time job. But note the limit on the operation of this paragraph that results from reg. 72(5A). This exempts a person from sanction under s. 19(6)(c) or (d) if he has refused work of less than 24 hours a week, or of less than 16 hours a week if he has been allowed to restrict his availability to less than 24 hours a week. It is not necessary under reg. 72(5A) for the number of hours to be the specific reason for refusing the job. Thus even if the reason for the refusal of a job for less than 24/16 hours a week is, *e.g.* the hourly rate of pay, the claimant will still be able to rely on reg. 72(5A). However, note that reg. 72(5A) does not apply for the purposes of s. 19(5)(a) (jobseeker's directions) (contrast reg. 72(5)). For further discussion see the note to reg. 72(5A).

Note that although a person normally has to be available for at least 40 hours a week this does not necessarily mean that he has to be available every day of the week. Reg. 7(2) allows for a "pattern of availability" to be agreed (which will be recorded in the claimant's jobseeker's agreement under reg. 31), provided that this does not "considerably reduce" the claimant's prospects of securing employment.

Restriction of hours for which a person is available to 40 hours per week

7.—(1) Except as provided in regulation 13 and in regulation 17(2), a person may not restrict the total number of hours for which he is available for employment to less than 40 hours in any week.

(2) A person may restrict the total number of hours for which he is available for employment in any week to 40 hours or more providing
    (a) the times at which he is available to take up employment (his ''pattern of availability'') are such as to afford him reasonable prospects of securing employment;
    (b) his pattern of availability is recorded in his jobseeker's agreement and any variations in that pattern are recorded in a varied agreement and
    (c) his prospects of securing employment are not reduced considerably by the restriction imposed by his pattern of availability.

(3) A person who has restricted the total number of hours for which he is available in accordance with paragraph (2) and who is not available for employment, and is not to be treated as available for employment in accordance with regulation 14, for one day or more in a week in accordance with his pattern of availability shall not be regarded as available for employment even if he was available for employment for a total of 40 hours or more during that week.

DEFINITIONS

    ''employment''—see reg. 4.
    ''week''—*ibid.*

GENERAL NOTE

This is a general provision concerning restrictions on hours of work. See also reg. 8 relating to other restrictions on availability, reg. 13 which deals with limits on availability in particular circumstances, and reg. 17 for people on short-time.

Paragraph (1)
This simply confirms (see reg. 6(1)) that a person must be available for work for at least 40 hours a week (''week'' means ''benefit week'', *i.e.* normally the seven days ending on the day the claimant signs on: regs. 4 and 1(3)), unless regs. 13 and/or 17(2) apply.

Paragraph (2)
Paragraph (2) allows a claimant to limit his hours of availability to ''40 or more'' a week (''week'' means ''benefit week'' (regs. 4 and 1(3)), provided that the times he is available (and any variation) are set out in his jobseeker's agreement (see reg. 31) (sub-para. (b)), still allow him a reasonable prospect of finding employment (sub-para. (a)) and do not ''considerably reduce'' that prospect (sub-para. (c)). Thus under sub-para. (c) some reduction in the claimant's chances of finding employment is permitted, but not a considerable reduction. Note that under this paragraph there is no reference to restrictions imposed under other provisions; thus only the limits on the claimant's hours will need to be considered in deciding whether the ''reasonable prospects'' test is satisfied under this rule. But if the claimant is also placing other restrictions on his availability, *e.g.* as regards the nature of the work or the rate of pay he will accept, he will have to show that he can satisfy the reasonable prospects test having regard to all his restrictions (see reg. 8 and/or 13(2)).
Reg. 10(1)(a) to (d) contains a non-exhaustive list of the factors to be considered when deciding whether a person still has a reasonable chance of finding work despite the restrictions he wishes to impose under this rule; the burden of proof is on the claimant (reg. (10(2)).
The restriction allowed by para. (2) is to ''40 hours or more'' a week. It may therefore be arguable that by agreeing a pattern of availability, a claimant can avoid the condition in reg. 6(2) that he must be prepared to accept work of less than 40 hours. (There is no indication in the wording of para. (2) that it is subject to reg. 6(2).) On the other hand, the words ''or more'' may simply indicate that a claimant does not have to restrict his hours to 40 exactly, but can choose some higher limit.
A claimant does not have to be available on days and at times outside his permitted pattern of availability (reg. 5(4)). But note para. (3) whose purpose is to ensure that any such pattern, once agreed, is adhered to. If the claimant is not available for work for one or more of the days in a week on which he has agreed to be available (and such a day is not covered by reg. 14 (deemed availability)), he will be treated as not available for work for the whole of that benefit week, even if he is available for a total of at least 40 hours at other times in that week.
CJSA 1279/1998 illustrates the harsh way in which para. (3) can operate in certain situations. The claimant went on holiday for a week starting on a Saturday and stated that he would not be

available for employment during that time. His benefit week ran from Wednesday to Tuesday. The effect of para. (3) in these circumstances was that he was not available for employment for two weeks (not just one). The Commissioner took the view that because the claimant did not fall within para. (1), he must come within para. (2). However, this seems to ignore the fact that para. (2) refers to a person who has *restricted* his availability in any week to 40 hours or more. If a person is available for 40 hours a week and has not placed any restriction on the days and hours that he will work it is suggested that para. (2) (and consequently para. (3)) do not apply to him. *The Adjudication Officer's Guide* (para. 26233) takes the view that if such a person goes away and is not available for one (or more) days in a benefit week he *is* restricting his availability. (But is this a case of *restricted* availability or of *non*-availability for the day(s) of absence?) In order to avoid being caught by para. (3) para. 26233 states that the person would have to comply with the conditions in para. (2) (including arranging for the changes to his availability to be recorded in a varied jobseeker's agreement) and ensure that he was available during the agreed times. This may be a way round the rule in para. (3) for some claimants. Note that a claimant who goes on holiday and remains available for work can be exempt from the actively seeking work condition; this can apply for a maximum of two weeks in any 12 months (see reg. 19(1)(p)).

Other restrictions on availability

8. Subject to regulations 6, 7 and 9, any person may restrict his availability for employment by placing restrictions on the nature of the employment for which he is available, the terms or conditions of employment for which he is available (including the rate of remuneration) and the locality or localities within which he is available, providing he can show that he has reasonable prospects of securing employment notwithstanding those restrictions and any restrictions on his availability in accordance with regulations 7(2), 13(2), (3), (4) or 17(2).

DEFINITIONS

"employment"—see reg. 4.

GENERAL NOTE

This is a general provision which allows a person to place restrictions on the nature, the terms and conditions (including the rate of pay but note reg. 9) and the location of the work he is available for, as long as he can show that he still has a reasonable chance of finding work despite those restrictions and any other restrictions permitted under regs. 7(2) (hours of work), 13(2) (religious or conscientious objection), 13(3) (disability), 13(4) (caring responsibilities) or 17(2) (person on short-time). However, in so far as any restrictions allowed under this regulation relate to hours of work or rate of pay they are also subject to the rules in regs. 6–7 and 9 respectively.

See reg. 10(1) which sets out a non-exhaustive list of the factors to be considered when deciding whether a person still has a reasonable chance of finding work despite the limits that he wishes to impose under this rule, and reg. 10(2) which restates that the burden of proof in relation to that issue is on the claimant.

A preliminary question that may arise is whether the claimant is actually imposing any restrictions on his availability. This is for the AO to establish (as para. 26467 of the *Adjudication Officer's Guide* accepts; the same paragraph also states that "restrictions are the conditions claimants insist on, not their preference or desires"). It may therefore be necessary for a tribunal to investigate the reasons for the claimant's statements and whether he intended them to be restrictions he was imposing on his availability (see *CSIS 13/1991*). If the practice suggested in para. 26468 of the *AOG* is followed (i.e. that the claimant should be advised of the possible consequences of placing restrictions on his availability and that evidence of those restrictions should be up to date), this should not usually be an issue.

Note also reg. 16 which may allow a claimant to restrict his availability to his usual occupation and/or rate of pay for up to 13 weeks.

No restrictions on pay after six months

9. After the expiry of the six month period beginning with the date of claim, a person may not restrict his availability for employment by placing restrictions on the level of remuneration in employment for which he is available.

DEFINITIONS

"date of claim"—see reg. 1(3).
"employment"—see reg. 4.

GENERAL NOTE

This contains a specific rule in relation to restrictions on the rate of pay that a claimant is prepared to accept. Such restrictions can only be imposed for six months from the date of claim (defined in reg. 1(3)). But see the note to reg. 13(3).

For the rules as to a claimant's "permitted period" (if any), see reg. 16. Note that under reg. 16(1)(b) a claimant may be able to limit his availability to work at his usual rate of pay but only for a maximum of 13 weeks from the date of claim.

Reasonable prospects of employment

10.—(1) For the purpose of regulations 7 and 8 and paragraphs (2) and (4) of regulation 13, in deciding whether a person has reasonable prospects of securing employment, regard shall be had, in particular, to the following matters—
(a) his skills, qualifications and experience;
(b) the type and number of vacancies within daily travelling distance from his home;
(c) the length of time for which he has been unemployed;
(d) the job applications which he has made and their outcome;
(e) if he wishes to place restrictions on the nature of the employment for which he is available, whether he is willing to move home to take up employment.
(2) It shall be for the claimant to show that he has reasonable prospects of securing employment if he wishes to restrict his availability in accordance with regulation 7 or 8 or paragraph (2) or (4) of regulation 13.

DEFINITIONS

"employment"—see reg. 4.

GENERAL NOTE

Whether a claimant will be allowed to impose restrictions on his availability for work under regs. 7 (hours of work), 8 (other restrictions), 13(2) (religious or conscientious objection) and 13(4) (carer) depends on him being able to show that he still has "reasonable prospects of securing employment" despite the restrictions. Note that this condition does not apply in the case of restrictions under reg. 13(3) (disability). Para. (2) confirms that it is for the claimant to show that he has reasonable prospects of finding employment, given the restrictions he wishes to impose.

Para. (1) lists some particular factors to be considered in deciding this question but all the available evidence should be taken into account. Para. 26485 of the *Adjudication Officer's Guide* makes clear that the decision should not be based simply on the number of vacancies fitting the claimant's restrictions that have been notified to the JobCentre. Any evidence from the claimant, together with any information from other sources (which should be noted by the AO on the papers: para. 26486, *AOG*) should be considered.

Note that para.(1)(e) only applies where the claimant wishes to limit the type of work for which he is available (which may arise under reg. 8 or 13(2)). A claimant's willingness to move home is only a factor to be taken into account under this sub-paragraph, not a requirement.

Part-time students

11.—(1) If in any week a person is a part-time student and
(a) he falls within paragraph (2)
(b) he has restricted the total number of hours for which he is available in accordance with regulation 7(2), [¹ 13(3) or (4)] or 17(2); and

    (c) the hours of his course of study fall in whole or in part within his pattern of availability,

in determining whether he is available for employment no matter relating to his course of study shall be relevant providing he is willing and able to re-arrange the hours of his course in order to take up employment at times falling within his pattern of availability, to take up such employment immediately or, if he falls within paragraph (1), (2) or (3) of regulation 5, at the time specified in that paragraph and providing he complies with the requirements of regulation 6.

  (2) A person falls within this paragraph if

    (a) for a continuous period of not less than 3 months falling immediately before the date on which he first attended the course of study he was in receipt of jobseeker's allowance or incapacity benefit or was on a course of training or he was in receipt of income support and he fell within paragraph 7 of Schedule 1B to the Income Support Regulations or

    (b) during the period of 6 months falling immediately before the date on which he first attended the course of study he was

        (i) for a period, or periods in the aggregate, of not less than 3 months in receipt of jobseeker's allowance or incapacity benefit or on a course of training or he was in receipt of income support and he fell within paragraph 7 of Schedule 1B to the Income Support Regulations and

      (ii) after the period referred to in (i), or in the case of periods in the aggregate, after the first such period and throughout the remainder of the 6 months for which that sub-paragraph did not apply to him, engaged in remunerative work or other work the emoluments of which are such as to disentitle him from receipt of jobseeker's allowance or incapacity benefit or from receipt of income support which would have been payable because he fell within paragraph 7 of Schedule 1B to the Income Support Regulations

and the period of 3 months referred to in sub-paragraph (i) or, as the case may be, the period of 6 months referred to in sub-paragraph (ii), fell wholly after the terminal date.

  (3) In this regulation, "training" means training for which persons aged under 18 are eligible and for which persons aged 18 to 24 may be eligible provided in England and Wales directly or indirectly by a Training and Enterprise Council pursuant to its arrangement with the Secretary of State (whether that arrangement is known as an Operating Agreement or by any other name) and, in Scotland, directly or indirectly by a Local Enterprise Company pursuant to its arrangement with, as the case may be, Scottish Enterprise or Highlands and Islands Enterprise (whether that arrangement is known as an Operating Contract or by any other name).

AMENDMENT

  1. Jobseeker's Allowance and Income Support (General) (Amendment) Regulations 1996 (S.I. 1996 No. 1517), reg. 3 (October 7, 1996).

DEFINITIONS

    "course of study"—see reg. 1(3).
    "employment"—see reg. 4.
    "part-time student"—see reg. 1(3).
    "pattern of availability"—see regs. 4 and 7(2)(a).
    "terminal date"—see reg. 1(3).

GENERAL NOTE

  The effect of this provision, broadly, is to disregard a part-time student's course of study when deciding whether he is available for employment, as long as he is prepared and able to re-arrange the hours of his course in order to take up employment, to start work immediately, or on notice if reg. 5(1), (2) or (3) applies, and he complies with reg. 6. However, it only applies to part-time students who satisfy the conditions in para. (2) and who have restricted the hours they are available under regs. 7(2), 13(3) or (4) or 17(2). Note that if a part-time student's hours of study fall completely outside the times he has agreed to be available for work he will not need to rely on this provision as his availability will not be affected.

A part-time student is a person who is undertaking a course of study who is not a full-time student (reg. 1(3)). See reg. 1(3) for the definitions of "full-time student" and "course of study" and the notes to reg. 130. Note the transitional protection in reg. 15 of the Jobseeker's Allowance (Transitional Provisions) Regulations 1996 (replacing reg. 13 of the 1995 Regulations) for part-time students who were entitled to income support on July 31, 1996 under the "21 hour rule" in the former reg. 9(1)(c) of the Income Support Regulations (see the 1996 edition of this book.)

This regulation does not apply to a person in relevant education (defined in reg. 54(1) and (2), see the notes to reg. 54) because such a person is excluded from JSA (s. 1(2)(g) of the Jobseekers Act). But note that under reg. 54(3) a young person (*i.e* under 19: reg. 76) who is a part-time student on a course other than one of advanced education or of a kind within para. (b) of the definition of full-time student in reg. 1(3) and who satisfies para. (2) of this regulation does not count as in relevant education (and will not do so after he finishes or leaves his part-time course (reg. 54(4))). Thus para. (1) may apply to such a young person.

A part-time student (except a person whose course does not conflict with his permitted pattern of availability) who does not satisfy the conditions in this regulation will probably not be treated as available unless he is prepared to abandon his course in order to take up employment. But note that a pilot scheme ("Workskill") (see the notes to s. 29 of the Jobseekers Act) was introduced in some areas from April 1997 (and further extended in September 1997) to allow claimants to study full- or part-time without having to be available for work. See also reg. 17A, in force from June 1, 1998, under which a claimant aged 25 or over may be able to attend a full-time employment-related course while continuing to receive JSA.

Paragraph (2)

The main condition (sub-para. (a)) is that for the whole three months immediately before the course the claimant was either in receipt of JSA, incapacity benefit or income support while sick or on Work Based Training for Young People (which has replaced Youth Training and other training focused on 16/17 year olds) (see the definition of training in para. (3); *AOG*, paras. 39726–8). Receipt of benefit means entitlement to benefit, whether benefit is actually in payment or not (*R(SB) 12/87*). The intention is that the claimant should be primarily unemployed and not simply wishing to continue to study on benefit. A person who leaves school in the summer will not be entitled to JSA until the first Monday in September (see reg. 54(2)) and thus will not have had three months on benefit in time to start a course before January.

The three months (or the six months in sub-para. (b), see below) cannot begin until after the "terminal date", that is, after the person has ceased to be treated as in relevant education. If the claimant starts (say in September) a course whose contact hours are below 12, so as to be outside the definition of relevant education (see the notes to reg. 54), and after three months on benefit increases the hours, it may be difficult to decide when the claimant first attended "the" course. The official view in the previous edition of the *Adjudication Officer's Guide* (para. 25529) (in relation to the 21-hour rule in the former reg. 9 of the Income Support Regulations, see the 1996 edition of this book) was that a mere change in hours did not mean that a new course was starting, so that the three months' benefit would have been at the wrong time, but that if the subjects taken had changed there would have been a new course.

Under sub-para. (b) a claimant can mix receipt of a relevant benefit, Work Based Training and work over the six months, provided that the relevant benefit and the Work Based Training add up to at least three months.

Volunteers

12. If in any week a person is engaged in voluntary work and

(a) he has restricted the total number of hours for which he is available in accordance with regulation 7(2), [¹13(3) or (4)] or 17(2) and

(b) the hours in which he is engaged in voluntary work fall in whole or in part within his pattern of availability

in determining whether he is available for employment no matter relating to his voluntary work shall be relevant providing he is willing and able to re-arrange the hours in which he is engaged in voluntary work in order to take up employment on being given 48 hours' notice at times falling within his pattern of availability and providing he complies with the requirements of regulation 6.

AMENDMENT

1. Jobseeker's Allowance and Income Support (General) (Amendment) Regulations 1996 (S.I. 1996 No. 1517), reg. 4 (October 7, 1996).

DEFINITIONS

"employment"—see reg. 4
"pattern of availability"—*ibid.* and reg. 7(2)(a).
"voluntary work"—see reg. 4.

GENERAL NOTE

If a person has restricted his hours of availability under regs. 7(2), 13(3) or (4) or 17(2), any voluntary work (defined in reg. 4) that he does which coincides with the times he has agreed to be available for work will be disregarded when deciding whether he is available for work, as long as he is prepared and able, on 48 hours' notice, to re-arrange his voluntary work in order to take up employment and he complies with reg. 6. If a person's voluntary work falls outside his permitted pattern of availability this regulation does not apply as his availability will not be affected.

See also reg. 5(1) under which a person doing voluntary work only has to be available on 48 hours' notice.

Additional restrictions on availability for certain groups

13.—(1) In any week a person may restrict his availability for employment in the following ways, if the circumstances set out apply.

(2) Subject to regulations 6, 7 and 9, a person may impose restrictions on the nature of the employment for which he is available by reason of a sincerely held religious belief, or a sincerely held conscientious objection providing he can show that he has reasonable prospects of employment notwithstanding those restrictions and any restrictions on his availability in accordance with regulation 7(2), 8, paragraph (3) or (4) of this regulation or regulation 17(1) or (2).

(3) A person may restrict his availability in any way providing the restrictions are reasonable in the light of his physical or mental condition.

(4) A person with caring responsibilities may restrict the total number of hours for which he is available for employment to less than 40 hours in any week providing

(a) in that week he is available for employment for as many hours as his caring responsibilities allow and for the specific hours that those responsibilities allow and

(b) he has reasonable prospects of securing employment notwithstanding that restriction and

(c) he is available for employment of at least 16 hours in that week.

(5) In deciding whether a person satisfies the conditions in paragraph (4)(a), regard shall be had, in particular, to the following matters—

(a) the particular hours and days spent in caring;

(b) whether the caring responsibilities are shared with another person;

(c) the age and physical and mental condition of the person being cared for.

DEFINITIONS

"caring responsibilities"—see reg. 4.
"employment"—*ibid.*
"week"—*ibid.*

Regs. 7 and 8 are general provisions relating to restrictions on availability, whereas this important regulation allows limits to be placed on availability in three particular sets of circumstances. A person may be able to take advantage of more than one of its provisions at any one time, as they are not exclusive, but they are each subject to their own conditions. See also the rules in reg. 17 for people on short-time which may apply in addition to these provisions.

Paragraph (2)
A person can restrict the *nature* of the work he is available for on the grounds of a sincere religious belief or conscientious objection, as long as he still has a reasonable chance of finding employment despite that restriction and any other restrictions allowed under regs. 7(2), 8, paras. (3) or (4) or reg. 17(1) or (2). Para. (2) is expressly made subject to regs. 6, 7 and 9, confirming that limits as regards hours of work or rate of pay have to comply with the terms of those regulations. The claimant may also be able to rely on the provisions in regs. 7(2) or 8 (or paras. (3) or (4) of reg. 17 if applicable) to place other restrictions on his availability.

See reg. 10(1) which sets out a non-exhaustive list of the factors to be considered when deciding whether a person still has a reasonable chance of finding work despite the limits that he wishes to impose under this rule, and reg. 10(2) which restates that the burden of proof in relation to that issue is on the claimant.

Paragraph (3)
This provision is potentially quite wide. It permits *any* restrictions on availability that are reasonable because of the claimant's physical or mental condition.

Unlike restrictions allowed under regs. 7(2), 8, or paras. (2) or (4) the claimant does not have to show under this rule that he still has reasonable prospects of finding work despite the restrictions. In the case of restrictions on availability imposed under reg. 7(2) or para. (4) the claimant only has to show that he has a reasonable chance of finding employment despite the limits on his hours permitted under the respective provision. But under reg. 8 and para. (2) restrictions that have been allowed under other provisions, including this paragraph, have to be taken into account in deciding whether the person still has reasonable prospects of finding work. The consequence seems to be that restrictions under this paragraph will be subject to the reasonable prospects test if combined with other restrictions under reg. 8 or para. (2), despite the clear wording of this paragraph. However, a person with physical or mental disabilities may well wish to impose limits on, *e.g.*, the nature or the location of the work for which he is available but only *because of* those disabilities. If that is the case the correct approach would seem to be for the claim to be considered under this paragraph alone rather than under a combination of *e.g.* this paragraph and reg. 8. The approach taken by the *Adjudication Officer's Guide* is to distinguish between restrictions that are connected with the claimant's disability and those that are not (para. 26449).

Note also that para. (3) is not made subject to any other provisions. Thus, for example, although restrictions on the rate of pay may only be imposed for six months under reg. 9, the DfEE apparently accepts that restrictions under para. (3) can include limits on the rate of pay the claimant will accept *after* six months, as long as the restriction is reasonable in the light of his condition, *e.g.* because of additional transport costs (see *Welfare Rights Bulletin* 138, p. 4).

Paragraphs (4) and (5)
A person with caring responsibilities can limit the hours he is available, provided that he is available for as long as those responsibilities allow, which must be for a minimum of 16 hours a week ("week" means "benefit week" (regs. 4 and 1(3))), and he still has a reasonable chance of finding employment despite *this* restriction. Note that under this rule there is no reference to restrictions imposed under other provisions; thus if the person's availability is also limited under para. (3) that will not be relevant here. However, if in addition the person wishes to impose restrictions that are not connected with his caring responsibilities, *e.g.* as to the nature of the work he will accept, he will have to show that he can satisfy the reasonable prospects test having regard to all his restrictions (see reg. 8 and/or para. (2)).

"Caring responsibilities" means that the person is looking after a member of the same household or a close relative (defined in reg. 4) who is a child, of or over pensionable age or who needs caring for because of his physical or mental condition. In deciding the extent to which the caring responsibilities do restrict the person's availability, regard is to be had to the factors in para. (5) (not an exhaustive list).

See reg. 10(1)(a) to (d) which contains a non-exhaustive list of the factors to be considered when deciding whether a person still has a reasonable chance of finding work despite the restrictions he wishes to impose under this rule; the burden of proof is on the claimant (reg. 10(2)).

See also reg. 5(1) under which a carer only has to be available for employment on 48 hours' notice.

Note that a person who is a carer may qualify for income support as an alternative to JSA (see para. 4 of Sched. 1B to the Income Support Regulations).

Circumstances in which a person is to be treated as available

14.—(1) A person, other than one [² to whom regulation 15(a), (b) or (c) applies,] shall be treated as available for employment in the following circumstances for as long as those circumstances apply, subject to any maximum period specified in this paragraph—

  (a) notwithstanding regulation 15(a), if he is participating as a full-time student in an employment-related course where participation by him has been approved before the course started by an employment officer, for a maximum of 2 weeks and one such course in any period of 12 months;

  (b) if he is attending a residential work camp, for a maximum of 2 weeks and one such occasion in any period of 12 months;

  (c) if he is temporarily absent from Great Britain because he is taking a member of his family who is a child or young person abroad for treatment, for a maximum of 8 weeks;

  (d) if he is engaged in the manning or launching of a lifeboat or in the performance of duty as a part-time member of a fire brigade or engaged during an emergency in duties for the benefit of others;

  (e) if he is a member of a couple and is looking after a member of his family who is a child while the other member is temporarily absent from the United Kingdom, for a maximum of 8 weeks;

  (f) if he is following an Open University course and is attending, as a requirement of that course, a residential course, for a maximum of one week per course;

  (g) if he is temporarily looking after a child full-time because the person who normally looks after the child is ill or temporarily absent from home or the person is looking after a member of the family who is ill, for a maximum of 8 weeks;

  (h) if he has been discharged from detention in a prison, remand centre or youth custody institution, for one week commencing with the date of his discharge;

[²(i) if the period beginning on the date of claim and ending on the day before the beginning of the first week after the date of claim is less than 7 days and the circumstances in paragraph (2A) apply, for any part of that period when he is not treated as available for employment under any other provision of this regulation;]

[¹(j) if the award is terminated other than on the last day of a week, for the period beginning with the beginning of the week in which the award is terminated and ending on the day on which the award is terminated;]

  (k) notwithstanding regulation 15(a), if he is participating in a programme provided by the Venture Trust in pursuance of an arrangement made by the Secretary of State for the Home Department with the Trust, for a maximum of 4 weeks and one such programme in any period of 12 months;

  (l) if he is treated as capable of work in accordance with regulation 55, for the period determined in accordance with that regulation;

  (m) if he is temporarily absent from Great Britain to attend an interview for employment and has given notice to an employment officer, in writing if so required by the employment officer, that he will be so absent for a maximum of one week;

(n) if he is a member of a couple and he and his partner are both absent from Great Britain and a premium referred to in paragraph 10, 11, 12, 13 or 15 of Schedule 1 (applicable amounts) is applicable in respect of his partner, for a maximum of 4 weeks.

(2) A person, other than one to whom regulation 15 applies, shall be treated as available for employment in the following circumstances—

(a) if there is a death or serious illness of a close relative or close friend of his;

(b) if there is a domestic emergency affecting him or a close relative or close friend of his;

(c) if there is a funeral of a close relative or close friend of his;

(d) if he has caring responsibilities and the person being cared for has died;

for the time required to deal with the emergency or other circumstance and for a maximum of one week on the occurrence of any of the circumstances set out in sub-paragraphs (a) to (d), or any combination of those circumstances, and on no more than 4 such periods in any period of 12 months.

[² (2A) A person shall be treated as available for employment under paragraph (1)(i) only if—

(a) where a pattern of availability is recorded in his jobseeker's agreement, or where he has restricted the hours for which he is available in accordance with regulations 13(3) or (4) or 17(2) and that restriction has been agreed with an employment officer, he is available for employment during such of the period referred to in paragraph (1)(i) as he is not treated as available for employment under any other provision of this regulation, in accordance with—

(i) his pattern of availability or, as the case may be, the hours to which he has restricted his availability in accordance with regulations 13(3) or (4) or 17(2), and

(ii) any other restrictions he has placed on his availability for employment which will apply in the first week after the date of claim, provided those restrictions have been agreed with an employment officer, and

(iii) if he falls within regulation 5, that regulation;

(b) where no pattern of availability is recorded in his jobseeker's agreement, he is available for employment during such of the period referred to in paragraph (1)(i) as he is not treated as available for employment under any other provision of this regulation—

(i) in accordance with any restrictions he has placed on his availability for employment which will apply in the first week after the date of claim, provided those restrictions have been agreed with an employment officer, and

(ii) for 8 hours on each day falling within that period on which he is not treated as available for employment to any extent under any other provision of this regulation, and

(iii) if he falls within regulation 5, in accordance with that regulation.]

(3) If any of the circumstances set out in paragraph (1), except those in sub-paragraphs (i) and (j), or any of those set out in paragraph (2) apply to a person for part of a week, he shall for the purposes of regulation 7(1) be treated as available for 8 hours on any day on which those circumstances applied subject to the maximum specified in paragraph (1) or (2), unless he has restricted the total number of hours for which he is available in a week in accordance with regulation 7(2), [¹ 13(4)] or 17(2). If he has so restricted the total number of hours for which he is available, he shall, for the purposes of regulation [¹ 7(1), 13(4) or 17(2)], be treated as available for the number of hours for which he

would be available on that day in accordance with his pattern of availability recorded in his jobseeker's agreement, if any of the circumstances set out in paragraph (1) except those in sub-paragraphs (i) and (j) or any of those set out in paragraph (2) applied on that day, subject to the maximum specified in paragraph (1) or (2).

(4) In paragraph (1)(c), "treatment" means treatment for a disease or bodily or mental disablement by or under the supervision of a person qualified to provide medical treatment, physiotherapy or a form of treatment which is similar to, or related to, either of those forms of treatment.

(5) For the purposes of paragraph (1)(d),

  (a) a person is engaged in duties for the benefit of others while—

    (i) providing assistance to any person whose life may be endangered or who may be exposed to the risk of serious bodily injury or whose health may be seriously impaired,

    (ii) protecting property of substantial value from imminent risk of serious damage or destruction, or

    (iii) assisting in measures being taken to prevent a serious threat to the health of the people,

as a member of a group of persons organised wholly or partly for the purpose of providing such assistance or, as the case may be, protection;

  (b) events which may give rise to an emergency include—

    (i) a fire, a flood or an explosion,

    (ii) a natural catastrophe,

    (iii) a railway or other transport accident,

    (iv) a cave or mountain accident,

    (v) an accident at sea,

    (vi) a person being reported missing and the organisation of a search for that person.

(6) In paragraph (1), except in sub-paragraphs (i) and (j), and in paragraph (2), "week" means any period of 7 consecutive days.

AMENDMENTS

1. Jobseeker's Allowance and Income Support (General) (Amendment) Regulations 1996 (S.I. 1996 No. 1517), reg. 5 (October 7, 1996).
2. Social Security (Jobseeker's Allowance and Mariners' Benefits) (Miscellaneous Amendments) Regulations 1997 (S.I. 1997 No. 563), reg. 2 (March 11, 1997).

DEFINITIONS

"capable of work"—see Jobseekers Act, s. 35(2), Sched. 1, para. 2.
"child"—see Jobseekers Act, s.35(1).
"close relative" see reg. 4.
"couple"—see reg. 1(3).
"date of claim"—*ibid.*
"employment"—see reg. 4.
"employment officer"—*ibid.*
"employment-related course"—see reg. 1(3).
"family"—see Jobseekers Act, s. 35(1).
"full-time student"—see reg. 1(3).
"Great Britain"—see Jobseekers Act, s. 35(1).
"partner" – see reg. 1(3).
"part-time member of a fire brigade"—see reg. 4.
"week" (in paras. (1)(i), (j), (3))—see reg. 4.
"work camp"—*ibid.*
"young person"—see regs. 1(3), 76.

GENERAL NOTE

Paras. (1) and (2) of this regulation set out various situations in which a person will be treated as available for employment. See reg. 19 for the rules which deem a person to be actively seeking employment in the same circumstances (reg. 19 also contains some additional categories). For when a jobseeker's agreement will be treated as having been made, see reg. 34; note in particular para. (c).

If a person comes within reg. 15(a), (b) or (c) (people who are deemed not available) this regulation cannot apply to him, except if he is a full-time student on an approved employment-related course when he will be deemed to be available for up to two weeks (para. (1)(a)), or on a Venture Trust programme when the period of deemed availability is up to four weeks (para. (1)(k)); this is limited to one course per 12 months in either case.

Note para. (1)(i) (see also para. (2A)) and (j) under which a person can be treated as available for periods at the beginning and end of his claim for JSA respectively and para. (1)(l) which applies for the period that a person is treated as capable of work under reg. 55.

On para. (1)(h) see *Chief Adjudication Officer v. Carr, The Times*, June 2, 1994 (also to be reported as *R(IS) 20/95*). A person has not been "discharged" while on a period of temporary release, since he is only "discharged" at the end of his sentence.

Para. (3) deals with the position where para. (1) (except sub-paras. (i) and (j)) and para. (2) apply for part-weeks ("week" in para. (1) (except in sub-paras. (i) and (j)) and para. (2) means a period of seven days (para. (6)). Paras. (4) to (6) contain various definitions.

Note s. 6(6) of the Jobseekers Act (see the note to that subsection).

See also reg. 16 which deems a claimant to be available during his "permitted period" (if any) and reg. 17 under which claimants who are laid off or kept on short-time can be treated as available; there is a limit of 13 weeks under both regulations. In addition, from June 1, 1998, reg. 17A allows a claimant aged 25 or over to be treated as available for work while attending a full-time employment-related course. See further the notes to that regulation.

Note that where there is an unresolved question as to an existing claimant's availability for work JSA will not be paid until the AO's decision is made, subject to the possibility of a hardship payment (see regs. 141(5) and 142(3)). See reg. 37(1A) of the Claims and Payments Regulations which allows payments of JSA to be suspended in such circumstances.

Circumstances in which a person is not to be regarded as available

15. A person shall not be regarded as available for employment in the following circumstances—

(a) if he is a full-time student during the period of study unless he has a partner who is also a full-time student, if either he or his partner is treated as responsible for a child or a young person, but this exception shall apply only for the period of the summer vacation appropriate to his course and providing he is available for employment in accordance with the provisions of this Chapter or unless he is treated as available in accordance with regulation 14(1)(a) or 14(1)(k);

(b) if he is a prisoner on temporary release in accordance with the provisions of the Prison Act 1952 or rules made under section 39(6) of the Prisons (Scotland) Act 1989;

[¹(bb) if the period beginning on the date of claim and ending on the day before the beginning of the first week after the date of claim is less than 7 days, for that period, unless he is treated as available for employment for that period in accordance with regulation 14;]

(c) if she is in receipt of maternity allowance or maternity pay in accordance with section 35 or sections 164–171 respectively of the Benefits Act.

AMENDMENT

1. Social Security (Jobseeker's Allowance and Mariners' Benefits) (Miscellaneous Amendments) Regulations 1997 (S.I. 1997 No. 563), reg. 3 (March 11, 1997).

DEFINITIONS

"child"—see Jobseekers Act, s. 35(1).
"employment"—see reg. 4.
"full-time student"—see reg. 1(3).
"partner"—*ibid.*
"period of study"—see reg. 4.
"young person"—see regs. 1(3), 76.

GENERAL NOTE

This provision deems certain claimants not to be available for work, and thus not entitled to JSA, even though they might otherwise satisfy the availability condition.

Para. (a) excludes full-time students (defined in reg. 1(3)) during their period of study (defined in reg. 4) from JSA, except student couples with a child who may claim but only in the summer vacation and providing the claimant is available for work. In addition (notwithstanding para. (a)) all full-time students (including those who are members of a student couple) will be treated as available for work for up to two weeks while on an approved employment-related course (reg. 14(1)(a)) or for up to four weeks if on a Venture Trust programme (reg. 14(1)(k)); this is limited to one course per 12 months in either case. Note the definition of period of study for the purposes of the availability rules in reg. 4. See the notes to reg. 130 for discussion of the definition of full-time student.

Note also reg. 17A, in force from June 1, 1998, under which a claimant aged 25 or over may be treated as available for work while attending a full-time employment-related course, notwithstanding para. (a). See further the notes to that regulation.

The other groups covered by reg. 15 are prisoners on temporary release (para. (b)), women receiving maternity allowance or statutory maternity pay (para. (c)) and people who are not treated as available for work at the beginning of their claim (para. (bb)).

Further circumstances in which a person is to be treated as available: permitted period

16.—(1) A person who is available for employment
(a) only in his usual occupation:
(b) only at a level of remuneration not lower than that which he is accustomed to receive, or
(c) only in his usual occupation and at a level of remuneration not lower than that which he is accustomed to receive
may be treated for a permitted period as available for employment in that period.

(2) Whether a person should be treated as available for a permitted period and if so, the length of that permitted period shall be determined having regard to the following factors—
(a) the person's usual occupation and any relevant skills or qualifications which he has;
(b) the length of any period during which he has undergone training relevant to that occupation;
(c) the length of the period during which he has been employed in that occupation and the period since he was so employed;
(d) the availability and location of employment in that occupation.

(3) A permitted period shall be for a minimum of one week and a maximum of 13 weeks and shall start on the date of claim and in this paragraph "week" means any period of 7 consecutive days.

DEFINITIONS

"date of claim"—see reg. 1(3).
"employment"—see reg. 4.

GENERAL NOTE

The effect of this regulation is to allow some claimants a "permitted period" during which they are only required to be available for employment in their usual occupation, or at their usual rate of pay, or in which both these conditions apply (para. (1)). The permitted period will last for between one and 13 weeks ("week" means a period of seven days) starting from the date of claim (para. (3)). Whether a claimant will be granted a permitted period depends on the factors listed in para. (2). If one is allowed, this will be recorded in his jobseeker's agreement (reg. 31(f)).

Whether a claimant has a usual occupation will be a question of fact. His previous work history will obviously be relevant. The *Adjudication Officer's Guide* suggests that if a claimant has recently started a new occupation this may be regarded as his usual occupation after as little as two or three weeks' employment if he intends to follow that occupation in the future (paras. 26403–4). The *Guide* further suggests that a claimant may have more than one usual occupation if he regularly follows more than one occupation (para. 26406).

A person who has been laid off or kept on short-time for 13 weeks will not be allowed a permitted period; if he ceases to be laid off or on short-time within 13 weeks and becomes fully unemployed he may be granted a permitted period but it will end at the latest 13 weeks after the date of his JSA claim (see reg. 17(4)).

See the corresponding rule in relation to the actively seeking employment condition in reg. 20.

Laid off and short-time workers

17.—(1) A person who is laid off shall be treated as available for employment providing he is willing and able to resume immediately the employment from which he has been laid off and to take up immediately any casual employment which is within daily travelling distance of his home or, if he falls within paragraph (1) or (2) of regulation 5, at the time specified in that regulation.

(2)—[¹(a)] A person who is kept on short-time shall be treated as available for employment, providing he is willing and able to resume immediately the employment in which he is being kept on short-time and to take up immediately any casual employment which is within daily travelling distance of his home or, if he falls within paragraph (1) or (2) of regulation 5, at the time specified in that regulation in the hours in which he is not working short-time but the total number of hours for which he works and is available for casual employment must be at least 40 in any week [¹unless paragraph (b) or (c) applies.

  (b) The total number of hours for which a person kept on short-time works and is available for casual employment may be less than 40 in any week if that person has imposed restrictions on his availability which are reasonable in the light of his physical or mental condition;

  (c) The total number of hours for which a person kept on short-time works and is available for casual employment may be less than 40 in any week if he has caring responsibilities providing the total number of hours for which he works and is available for casual employment is as many as his caring responsibilities allow and for the specific hours those responsibilities allow and is at least 16 in any week;]

(3) A person shall not be treated as available for employment in accordance with this regulation for more than 13 weeks, starting with the day after the day he was laid off or first kept on short-time.

(4) A person who is laid off or kept on short-time may not be treated as available for employment for a permitted period in accordance with regulation 16, unless he ceases to be laid off or kept on short-time within 13 weeks of the day on which he was laid off or first kept on short time, in which case he may be treated as available for employment for a permitted period ending a maximum of 13 weeks after the date of claim.

(5) In paragraphs (3) and (4), "week" means any period of 7 consecutive days.

AMENDMENT

1. Jobseeker's Allowance and Income Support (General) (Amendment) Regulations 1996 (S.I. 1996 No. 1517), reg. 6 (October 7, 1996).

DEFINITIONS

"caring responsibilities"—see reg. 4.
"casual employment"—*ibid.*
"date of claim"—see reg. 1(3).
"employment"—see reg. 4.
"a person who is kept on short-time"—*ibid.*
"a person who is laid off"—*ibid.*
"week" (in para. (2))—*ibid.*

GENERAL NOTE

This regulation allows claimants who are laid off or kept on short-time (both defined in reg. 4) to be treated as available for work for up to 13 weeks, provided that they are available for casual work (defined in reg. 4) within daily travelling distance of their home as well as remaining available for their own employment.

See the corresponding rule in relation to the actively seeking condition in reg. 21.

[¹Further circumstances in which a person is to be treated as available: full-time students participating in a qualifying course

17A.—(1) A person to whom paragraph (2) applies shall, notwithstanding regulation 15(a), be treated as available for employment in accordance with paragraph (3).

(2) This paragraph applies to a person—

(a) who is aged 25 years or over; and

(b) [²subject to paragraph (2A),] who has made a claim for a jobseeker's allowance and has been receiving benefit within a jobseeking period for not less than 2 years as at the date he started, or is due to start, the qualifying course and for the purposes of this paragraph the linking provision set out in regulation 48 shall apply.

[²(2A) A person who has been receiving benefit in accordance with paragraph (b) of the definition of "receiving benefit" in paragraph (7) shall, for the purposes of paragraph (2)(b), be treated as having received benefit within a jobseeking period.]

(3) Subject to paragraph (4), where an employment officer has determined, having regard to the factors specified in paragraph (5), that a person to whom paragraph (2) applies may undertake a qualifying course, that person shall be treated as available for employment in any week in which he is undertaking the qualifying course as a full-time student and—

(a) which falls wholly or partly in term-time, providing he—

   (i) provides evidence, as often as may be required by an employment officer, within 5 days of being so required by the employment officer, consisting of a document signed by him and on behalf of the establishment at which he is undertaking the qualifying course, confirming that he is attending the establishment when required to attend, in such form as may be required by the employment officer; and

   (ii) provides evidence, as often as may be required by an employment officer, within 5 days of being so required by the employment officer, consisting of a document signed by him and on behalf of the establishment at which he is undertaking the qualifying course, confirming that he is making satisfactory progress on the course, in such form as may be required by the employment officer;

(b) in which he is taking examinations relating to the qualifying course; or

(c) which falls wholly in a vacation from the qualifying course, if he is willing and able to take up immediately any casual employment.

(4) In a case where the combined duration of—

(a) any qualifying course, other than one falling within paragraph (6), which a person to whom paragraph (2) applies has previously undertaken in respect of which he was, for any part of such qualifying course, treated as available for employment in accordance with paragraph (3); and

(b) the qualifying course which he is currently undertaking

is more than 1 year, the person shall only be treated as available for employment in accordance with paragraph (3) if he has been receiving benefit within a job-seeking period for not less than 2 years since the last day of the most recent such qualifying course in respect of which he was, for any part, treated as available in accordance with paragraph (3), and for the purposes of this paragraph the linking provision set out in regulation 48 shall apply.

(5) The factors which an employment officer must take into account when determining whether a person may undertake a qualifying course are—

(a) the skills, qualifications and abilities of that person;

(b) whether the course would assist him to acquire new skills and qualifications;

(c) whether he would have to give up a course of study in order to undertake this course;

(d) any needs arising from his physical or mental condition;

(e) the time which has elapsed since he was last engaged in employment as an employed earner or as a self-employed earner;

(f) his work experience;

(g) the number of jobs in the labour market and, if relevant, the local labour market, which require the skills and qualifications which he would acquire on the course; and

(h) any evidence about whether this course or this type of course has facilitated the obtaining by persons of work.

(6) A qualifying course falls within this paragraph if the person had good cause for any act or omission for the purposes of section 19(5)(b) in relation to that course.

(7) In this regulation—

"benefit" means income support, unemployment benefit or a jobseeker's allowance and "receiving benefit" means [²receiving—

(a) benefit which that person has claimed and received as an unemployed person or in accordance with Part I of the Act; or

(b) income support which that person has claimed and received as an asylum seeker pursuant to regulation 70(3A) of the Income Support Regulations but only to the extent that—

(i) any periods in respect of which he was in receipt of income support as an asylum seeker pursuant to regulation 70(3A) of the Income Support Regulations link with the jobseeking period which includes the date on which he started, or is due to start, the qualifying course and for this purpose, such periods shall link where they are separated by a period of 12 weeks or less in respect of which he was not in receipt of income support; and

(ii) he is, at the date he started, or is due to start, the qualifying course, a person to whom paragraph (7A) applies;]

"casual employment" means employment from which the employee can be released without his giving any notice or, if he is required to give notice, employment from which he can be released before the end of the vacation;

"duration" in relation to a qualifying course means the period beginning with the start of the course and ending with the last day of the course;

"jobseeking period" means the period described in regulation 47 and any period treated as a jobseeking period pursuant to regulation 47A;

"last day" in relation to a qualifying course means the date on which the last day of the course falls, or the date on which the final examination relating to that course is completed, whichever is the later;
"qualifying course" means a course which—
(a) is an employment-related course;
(b) lasts no more than 12 consecutive months; and
(c) except where it falls within paragraph (8), is either—
    (i) a course of a description falling within Schedule 2 to the Further and Higher Education Act 1992; or
    (ii) a programme of learning falling within section 6 of the Further and Higher Education (Scotland) Act 1992.

[²(7A) Subject to paragraph (7B), this paragraph shall apply in the case of a person—
(a) who—
    (i) is a refugee within the definition of Article 1 of the Convention relating to the Status of Refugees done at Geneva on 28th July 1951, as extended by Article 1(2) of the Protocol relating to the Status of Refugees done at New York on 31st January 1967; or
    (ii) has been granted exceptional leave—
        (aa) to enter the United Kingdom by an immigration officer appointed for the purposes of the Immigration Act 1971; or
        (bb) to remain in the United Kingdom by the Secretary of State; and
(b) who was in receipt of income support as an asylum seeker pursuant to regulation 70(3A) of the Income Support Regulations at any time during the period of 12 weeks immediately preceding the beginning of the job-seeking period which includes the date on which he started, or is due to start, the qualifying course.

(7B) Paragraph (7A) shall include a person who has been recorded as a refugee by the Secretary of State within the definition in sub-paragraph (a) of that paragraph and whose claim for income support was determined in accordance with regulation 21ZA(2) or (3) of the Income Support Regulations (treatment of refugees).]

(8) A course or a programme of learning which is of a standard above that of a course or programme of learning falling within paragraph (c) of the definition of "qualifying course" falls within this paragraph if an employment officer so determines in a particular case.]

AMENDMENTS

1. Social Security Amendment (New Deal) Regulations 1998 (S.I. 1998 No. 1274), reg. 4 (June 1, 1998).
2. Jobseeker's Allowance Amendment (New Deal) Regulations 1998 (S.I. 1998 No. 2874), reg. 2 (November 24, 1998).

DEFINITIONS

"course of study"—see reg. 1(3).
"employed earner"—see reg. 3, SSCBA, s. 2(1)(a).
"employment"—see reg. 4.
"employment officer"—*ibid.*
"employment-related course"—see reg. 1(3).
"examination"—see reg. 4.
"full-time student"—see reg. 1(3).
"made a claim for jobseeker's allowance"—see reg. 4.
"self-employed earner"—see reg. 1(3), SSCBA, s. 2(1)(b).
"term-time"—see reg. 4.
"vacation"—*ibid.*
"week"—ibid.

This provision allows claimants aged 25 and over to study full-time for up to a year on an employment-related course while continuing to receive JSA. (A pilot scheme, "Workskill", had been operating in some areas to enable claimants to undertake full- or part-time employment-related training or study since April 1997; further areas were included in the scheme from September 1997.)

To be eligible, the claimant must be aged 25 or over, have been receiving JSA (or a combination of JSA, unemployment benefit or income support as an unemployed person (see the definitions of "benefit" and "receiving benefit" in para. (7)) for at least two years (including any linking periods: see reg. 48) at the time the course starts, and be undertaking a "qualifying course" (para. (2)). (Note the amendments made in November 1998 to enable refugees or people with exceptional leave to enter or remain in the U.K. to count periods in receipt of income support as asylum seekers (including periods for which they have been awarded income support retrospectively under reg. 21ZA of the Income Support Regulations) towards the two years, provided such periods link with (*i.e.* are within 12 weeks of) the current jobseeking period.) A "qualifying course" is an employment-related course (defined in reg. 1(3)), which lasts for no more than 12 consecutive months, and which is at the level of a course or programme of learning within Sched. 2 to the Further and Higher Education Act 1992 or s. 6 of the Further and Higher Education (Scotland) Act 1992 (para. (7)); in certain cases the course may be at a higher level (para. (8)). The course has to be approved by an employment officer, who must take into account the factors listed in para. (5) (para. (3)). Note also paras. (4) and (6).

If these conditions are met, the claimant will be treated as available for work in any week (i) that falls wholly or partly in term-time, as long as he meets certain requirements relating to evidence of attendance and satisfactory progress on the course; (ii) in which he is taking examinations relating to the course; or (iii) which falls wholly in a vacation, as long as he is available for casual employment (defined in para. (7)) (para. (3)). See reg. 21A for the corresponding rule in relation to the actively seeking work condition.

However, the other conditions of entitlement for JSA will still apply. Thus, for example, a claimant could be sanctioned for refusing or failing to apply for or accept a notified job without good cause or for not complying with a jobseeker's direction. But note reg. 72(3A) which contains some additional grounds of good cause for a claimant on a qualifying course who refuses to apply for, etc., a notified job vacancy or neglects to avail himself of a reasonable opportunity of employment.

A claimant cannot be required to go on a qualifying course. But once he has started on such a course he can be sanctioned for two (or four) weeks if he fails to attend without good cause, gives up his place without good cause, or loses it through misconduct. See reg. 75(1)(b)(iii), and note the additional circumstances that will constitute good cause in reg. 73(2B)(b); note also reg. 73(4) and (2B)(a).

Chapter III

Actively seeking employment

Steps to be taken by persons actively seeking employment

18.—(1) For the purposes of section 7(1) (actively seeking employment) a person shall be expected to have to take more than one step on one occasion in any week unless taking one step on one occasion is all that it is reasonable for that person to do in that week.

(2) Steps which it is reasonable for a person to be expected to have to take in any week include—

    (a) oral or written applications (or both) for employment made to persons—

        (i) who have advertised the availability of employment; or

        (ii) who appear to be in a position to offer employment;

    (b) seeking information on the availability of employment from—

        (i) advertisements;

        (ii) persons who have placed advertisements which indicate the availability of employment;

        (iii) employment agencies and employment businesses;

        (iv) employers;

(c) registration with an employment agency or employment business;

(d) appointment of a third party to assist the person in question in finding employment;

(e) seeking specialist advice, following referral by an employment officer, on how to improve the prospects of securing employment having regard to that person's needs and in particular in relation to any mental or physical limitations of that person;

(f) drawing up a curriculum vitae;

(g) seeking a reference or testimonial from a previous employer;

(h) drawing up a list of employers who may be able to offer employment to him with a view to seeking information from them on the availability of employment;

(i) seeking information about employers who may be able to offer employment to him;

(j) seeking information on an occupation with a view to securing employment in that occupation.

(3) In determining whether, in relation to any steps taken by a person, the requirements of section 7(1) are satisfied in any week, regard shall be had to all the circumstances of the case, including—

(a) his skills, qualifications and abilities;

(b) his physical or mental limitations;

(c) the time which has elapsed since he was last in employment and his work experience;

(d) the steps which he has taken in previous weeks and the effectiveness of those steps in improving his prospects of securing employment;

(e) the availability and location of vacancies in employment;

(f) any time during which he was—

    (i) engaged in the manning or launching of a lifeboat or in the performance of duty as a part-time member of a fire brigade or engaged during an emergency in duties for the benefit of others,

    (ii) attending an Outward Bound course,

    (iii) in the case of a blind person, participating in a course of training in the use of guide dogs,

    (iv) participating in training in the use of aids to overcome any physical or mental limitations of his in order to improve his prospects of securing employment,

    (v) engaged in duties as a member of any territorial or reserve force prescribed in Part I of Schedule 3 to the Social Security (Contributions) Regulations 1979,

    (vi) participating as a part-time student in an employment-related course,

    (vii) participating for less than 3 days in an employment or training programme for which a training allowance is not payable;

(g) any time during which he was engaged in voluntary work and the extent to which it may have improved his prospects of securing employment;

(h) whether he is treated as available for employment under regulation 14;

(i) whether he has applied for, or accepted, a place on, or participated in, a course or programme the cost of which is met in whole or in part out of central funds or by the European Community and the purpose of which is to assist persons to select, train for, obtain or retain employed earner's employment or self-employed earner's employment; and

(j) where he had no living accommodation in that week the fact that he had no such accommodation and the steps which he needed to take and has in fact taken to seek such accommodation.

(4) Any act of a person which would otherwise be relevant for purposes of section 7 shall be disregarded in the following circumstances—

(a) where, in taking the act, he acted in a violent or abusive manner,

(b) where the act comprised the completion of an application for employment and he spoiled the application,

(c) where by his behaviour or appearance he otherwise undermined his prospects of securing the employment in question,

unless those circumstances were due to reasons beyond his control.

(5) In this regulation—

"employment agency" and "employment business" mean an employment agency or (as the case may be) employment business within the meaning of the Employment Agencies Act 1973;

"employment or training programme" means a course or programme the person's participation in which is attributable to arrangements made by the Secretary of State under section 2 of the Employment and Training Act 1973 for the purpose of assisting persons to select, train for, obtain or retain employed earner's employment.

DEFINITIONS

"employment"—see regs. 3, 4.
"employment officer"—see reg. 4.
"employment-related course"—see reg. 1(3).
"engaged during an emergency in duties for the benefit of others"—see reg. 22.
"Outward Bound course"—see reg. 4.
"part-time member of a fire brigade"—see reg. 4.
"part-time student"—see reg. 1(3).
"training allowance"—*ibid*.
"voluntary work"—see reg. 4.
"week"—*ibid*.

GENERAL NOTE

It is a condition of entitlement to JSA that a person is actively seeking employment (s.1(2)(b) of the Jobseekers Act). The test of actively seeking employment under s. 7(1) of the Act is that a person is taking in any week "such steps as he can reasonably be expected to have to take in order to have the best prospects of securing employment". This regulation expands on that test. Note that for the purposes of the actively seeking rule employment can include self-employment, as well as work as an employee in certain circumstances (see regs. 18(3)(i), 19(1)(r) and 20(2)). See also regs. 19 to 22 under which a person is treated as actively seeking employment in certain circumstances.

Paragraph (1)

This contains the general rule that in order to satisfy the actively seeking employment test, a person will be expected to take more than one "step" on one occasion in any week ("week" means "benefit week", regs. 4 and 1(3)) unless taking that step on that occasion was all that it was reasonable for him to do that week. Thus it would seem that a claimant must take a minimum of one step a week, unless he can be treated as actively seeking employment in that week (see regs. 19–22). Details of the steps a claimant has agreed to take will be set out in his jobseeker's agreement (reg. 31(e)).

The Adjudication Officer's Guide gives as examples of what counts as separate steps: reading the situations vacant pages in a newspaper or magazine, checking the advertisements displayed in the JobCentre, registering with an employment agency, writing to an employer or applying for a particular vacancy. Thus, writing to three employers, or applying for three vacancies on the same day, amounts to three steps to find employment (para. 26611).

Paragraphs (2) and (3)

Para. (2) gives examples of what might constitute a "step" and para. (3) lists factors to be taken into account when deciding whether the steps taken by a person in any week satisfy the actively seeking employment rule. It is important to note that neither list is exhaustive. Further, as para. 26620 of the *Adjudication Officer's Guide* recognises, the type of work that a person is looking for will be relevant when deciding which steps will give him the best chance of finding employment. Moreover, the steps that a claimant has taken in previous weeks will often affect what he can reasonably be expected to do in a subsequent week, *e.g.* if he has already written to employers about vacancies and is waiting for a reply (see paras. 26644–46 of the *AOG*).

Note the definitions in para. (5), and on "engaged during an emergency in duties for the benefit of others" in para. (3)(f)(i), see reg. 22.

Paragraph (4)
See the notes to s. 7(3) of the Jobseekers Act.

[¹Actively seeking employment in the period at the beginning of a claim

18A.—(1) Paragraph (2) applies in any case where the period beginning on the date of claim and ending on the day before the beginning of the first week after the date of claim is less than 7 days.

(2) Where this paragraph applies, a person is actively seeking employment in the period referred to in paragraph (1) if he takes in that period such steps as he can reasonably be expected to have to take in order to have the best prospects of securing employment and in determining whether a person has taken such steps—

    (a) the steps which it is reasonable for him to be expected to have to take include those referred to in regulation 18(2); and

    (b) regard shall be had to all the circumstances of the case, including those matters referred to in regulation 18(3).]

AMENDMENT

1. Social Security (Jobseeker's Allowance and Mariners' Benefits) (Miscellaneous Amendments) Regulations 1997 (S.I. 1997 No. 563), reg. 4 (March 11, 1997).

DEFINITIONS

"employment"—see regs. 3, 4.

Circumstances in which a person is to be treated as actively seeking employment

19.—(1) A person shall be treated as actively seeking employment in the following circumstances, subject to paragraph (2) and to any maximum period specified in this paragraph—

    (a) in any week during which he is participating for not less than 3 days as a full-time student in an employment-related course where participation by him has been approved before the course started by an employment officer, for a maximum of 2 weeks and one such course in any period of 12 months;

    (b) in any week during which he is attending for not less than 3 days a residential work camp, for a maximum of 2 weeks and one such occasion in any period of 12 months;

    (c) in any week during which he is temporarily absent from Great Britain for not less than 3 days because he is taking a member of his family who is a child or young person abroad for treatment, for a maximum of 8 weeks;

    (d) in any week during which he is engaged for not less than 3 days in the manning or launching of a lifeboat or in the performance of duty as a part-time member of a fire brigade or engaged during an emergency in duties for the benefit of others;

    (e) if he is a member of a couple, in any week during which he is for not less than 3 days looking after a member of his family who is a child while the other member is temporarily absent from the United Kingdom, for a maximum of 8 weeks;

    (f) if he is following an Open University course, in any week during which he is attending for not less than 3 days, as a requirement of that course, a residential course, for a maximum of one week per course;

    (g) in any week during which he is for not less than 3 days temporarily looking after a child full-time because the person who normally looks after the child is ill or temporarily absent from home or the person is looking after a member of the family who is ill, for a maximum of 8 weeks;

    (h) in the first week after the date of claim if he is treated as available for employment to any extent in that week under regulation 14(1)(h);

    (i) [² . . .]

[¹ (j) [if the award is terminated other than on the last day of a week, for the period beginning with the beginning of the week in which the award is terminated and ending on the day on which the award is terminated;]

    (k) in any week during which he is participating for not less than 3 days in a programme provided by the Venture Trust in pursuance of an arrangement made by the Secretary of State for the Home Department with the Trust, for a maximum of 4 weeks and one such programme in any period of 12 months;

    (l) in any week during which he is for not less than 3 days treated as capable of work in accordance with regulation 55;

    (m) in any week during which he is temporarily absent from Great Britain for not less than 3 days in order to attend an interview for employment and has given notice to an employment officer, in writing if so required by the employment officer, that he will be so absent, for a maximum of 1 week;

    (n) if he is a member of a couple, in any week during which he and his partner are both absent from Great Britain for not less than 3 days and in which a premium referred to in paragraph 10, 11, 12, 13 or 15 of Schedule 1 (applicable amounts) is applicable in respect of his partner, for a maximum of 4 weeks;

    (o) in any week during which he is treated as available for employment on not less than 3 days under regulation 14(2):

    (p) in any week in respect of which he has given notice to an employment officer, in writing if so required by the employment officer, that—

        (i) he does not intend to be actively seeking employment, but

        (ii) he does intend to reside at a place other than his usual place of residence for at least one day;

    (q) in any week during which he is participating for not less than 3 days in an employment or training programme for which a training allowance is not payable;

[³(r) in any week, being part of a single period not exceeding 8 weeks falling within a period of continuous entitlement to a jobseeker's allowance, during which he is taking active steps to establish himself in self-employed earner's employment under any scheme for assisting persons to become so employed—

        (i) where, in Wales, his participation under the scheme is attributable to arrangements made by the Secretary of State under section 2 of the Employment and Training Act 1973,

        (ii) where, in Scotland, the scheme—

            (aa) is established by virtue of arrangements made by Scottish Enterprise or Highlands and Islands Enterprise under section 2(3) of the Enterprise and New Towns (Scotland) Act 1990 or

            (bb) is directly or indirectly provided by, or with financial assistance from, the Secretary of State,

(iii) where, in England, the scheme is directly or indirectly provided by, or with financial assistance from, the Secretary of State, the Urban Regeneration Agency, an urban development corporation or a housing action trust,

and the single period referred to above shall begin with the week in which he is accepted on a place under the scheme.]

(2) In any period of 12 months a person shall be treated as actively seeking employment under paragraph (1)(p) only for the number of weeks specified in one of the following subparagraphs—

(a) a maximum of 2 weeks; or

(b) a maximum of 3 weeks during which he is attending for at least 3 days in each such week an Outward Bound course; or

(c) if he is a blind person, a maximum of 6 weeks during which, apart from a period of no more than 2 weeks, he participates for a maximum period of 4 weeks in a course of training in the use of guide dogs of which at least 3 days in each such week is spent in that training.

(3) In this regulation—

"employment or training programme" means a course or programme the person's participation in which is attributable to arrangements made by the Secretary of State under section 2 of the Employment and Training Act 1973 for the purpose of assisting persons to select, train for, obtain or retain employment;

"housing action trust" means a corporation established by an order of the Secretary of State pursuant to section 62(1) of the Housing Act 1988;

"treatment" means treatment for a disease or bodily or mental disablement by or under the supervision of a person qualified to provide medical treatment, physiotherapy or a form of treatment which is similar to, or related to, either of those forms of treatment;

"urban development corporation" means a corporation established by an order of the Secretary of State pursuant to section 135(1) of the Local Government, Planning and Land Act 1980;

"Urban Regeneration Agency" means the agency referred to in section 158(1) of the Leasehold Reform, Housing and Urban Development Act 1993;

AMENDMENTS

1. Jobseeker's Allowance and Income Support (General) (Amendment) Regulations 1996 (S.I. 1996 No. 1517), reg. 7 (October 7, 1996).

2. Social Security (Jobseeker's Allowance and Mariners' Benefits) (Miscellaneous Amendments) Regulations 1997 (S.I. 1997 No. 563), reg. 5 (March 11, 1997).

3. Social Security Amendment (New Deal) Regulations 1998 (S.I. 1998 No. 1274), reg. 5 (June 1, 1998).

DEFINITIONS

"capable of work"—see Jobseekers Act, s. 35(2), Sched. 1, para. 2.
"child"—see Jobseekers Act, s.35(1).
"couple"—see reg. 1(3).
"date of claim"—*ibid.*
"employment"—see reg. 4.
"employment officer"—*ibid.*
"employment-related course"—see reg. 1(3).
"engaged during an emergency in duties for the benefit of others"—see reg. 22.
"family"—see Jobseekers Act, s. 35(1).
"full-time student"—see reg. 1(3).
"Great Britain"—see Jobseekers Act, s. 35(1).
"partner"—see reg. 1(3).

"part-time member of a fire brigade"—see reg. 4.
"self-employed earner's employment"—see Jobseekers Act 1995, s. 7(8), SSCBA, ss. 2(1), 122(1).
"training allowance"—see reg. 1(3).
"week"—see reg. 4
"work camp"—*ibid.*
"young person"—see regs. 1(3), 76.

GENERAL NOTE

Para. (1) lists a variety of circumstances in which a person will be treated as actively seeking employment if the conditions of the relevant sub-paragraph are satisfied. Sub-paras. (a)–(n) and (o) match the situations covered by reg. 14(1)(a)–(n) (except reg. 14(1)(i)) and 14(2) (treated as available for work) respectively. For when a jobseeker's agreement will be treated as having been made, see reg. 34; note in particular reg. 34(c).

See reg. 18A and para. (1)(j) under which a person can be treated as actively seeking employment for periods at the beginning and end respectively of his claim for JSA, and para. (1)(l) which applies for the period that a person is treated as capable of work under reg. 55.

For the definition of "treatment" in para. (1)(c), see para. (3) and on "engaged during an emergency in duties for the benefit of others" in para. (1)(d), see reg. 22.

Sub-para. (p) enables a person to be treated as actively seeking employment for the relevant period specified in para. (2)(a), (b) or (c) if he has given notice (in writing if required) that in that week he does not intend to be actively seeking employment, and intends to be away from home for at least one day. Thus sub-para. (p) and para. (2)(a) will allow a claimant to take up to two weeks' holiday but he must remain available for employment in that period (see *CJSA 1279/1998* in the notes to reg. 7). The weeks in para. (2)(a), (b) or (c) do not have to be consecutive but this rule can apply only once in any 12 months period.

Sub-para. (q) covers people on an employment or training programme (defined in para. (3)) for which a training allowance (defined in reg. 1(3)) is not paid and sub-para. (r) applies to people who are on a scheme with a view to establishing themselves in self-employment. See the definitions in para. (3). One example of when sub-para. (q) may apply is where an 18–25 year-old is on a "New Deal taster" (see the notes to reg. 75(1)). He will not be paid a training allowance while sampling a New Deal option but will continue to receive JSA. During the Gateway period of the New Deal a claimant has to continue to satisfy the labour market conditions. If the taster lasts three days or more in any benefit week he can be treated as actively seeking work under sub-para. (q), although he will still have to remain available for work. See reg. 105(13) which ensures that a claimant undertaking a programme or scheme within sub-para. (q) is not treated as possessing notional earnings on the basis that he is providing a service for which he is not being paid. Any actual earnings that are received will be taken into account in the normal way.

Note s. 7(7) of the Jobseekers Act (see the note to that subsection).

See also reg. 20 which deems a claimant to be actively seeking employment during his "permitted period" (if any) and reg. 21 under which claimants who are laid off or kept on short-time can be treated as actively seeking work. In addition, from June 1, 1998, reg. 21A deems a claimant who is treated as available for work under reg. 17A while attending a full-time employment-related course to be actively seeking employment. Note the condition in reg. 21A(c) for this rule to apply in the vacation. See further the notes to reg. 17A.

Note that where there is an unresolved question as to whether an existing claimant is actively seeking employment JSA will not be paid until the AO's decision is made, subject to the possibility of a hardship payment (see regs. 141(5) and 142(3)). See reg. 37(1A) of the Claims and Payments Regulations which allows payments of JSA to be suspended in such circumstances.

Further circumstances in which a person is to be treated as actively seeking employment: permitted period

20.—(1) A person to whom paragraph (2) does not apply shall be treated as actively seeking employment in any week during any permitted period determined in his case in accordance with regulation 16, if he is actively seeking employment in that week—

(a) only in his usual occupation,

(b) only at a level of remuneration not lower than that which he is accustomed to receive, or

(c) only in his usual occupation and at a level of remuneration not lower than that which he is accustomed to receive.

(2) A person to whom this paragraph applies shall be treated as actively seeking employment in any week during any permitted period determined in his case in accordance with regulation 16, if he is actively seeking employment, self-employed earner's employment, or employment and self-employed earner's employment in that week—

(a) only in his usual occupation,
(b) only at a level of remuneration not lower than that which he is accustomed to receive, or
(c) only in his usual occupation and at a level of remuneration not lower than that which he is accustomed to receive.

(3) Paragraph (2) applies to a person who has, at any time during the period of 12 months immediately preceding the date of claim, been engaged in his usual occupation in self-employed earner's employment.

DEFINITIONS

"employment"—see regs. 3, 4.
"employed earner's employment" see Jobseekers Act, s. 7(8), SSCBA, ss. 2(1), 122(1).
"self-employed earner's employment"—ibid.
"week"—see reg. 4.

GENERAL NOTE

Paragraph (1)
This paragraph treats a person as actively seeking employment during his "permitted period" (if any). See reg. 16 and the notes to that regulation.

Paragraphs (2) and (3)
If a person has been self-employed in his normal occupation at any time within the 12 months before he claimed JSA, he will be treated as actively seeking employment during any permitted period under reg. 16 (see the notes to reg. 16), even though he is only looking for self-employment, employment, or both, in his normal occupation and/or at his normal rate of pay. Thus these paragraphs allow a person who has previously been self-employed to seek only self-employment during his permitted period, but he will still have to be available for work as an employed earner during that time. The maximum length of a permitted period is 13 weeks.

Further circumstances in which a person is to be treated as actively seeking employment: laid off and short-time workers

21. A person who has restricted his availability for employment in accordance with regulation 17(1) or, as the case may be, regulation 17(2), shall in any week in which he has so restricted his availability for not less than 3 days be treated as actively seeking employment in that week if he takes such steps as he can reasonably be expected to have to take in order to have the best prospects of securing employment for which he is available under regulation 17.

DEFINITIONS

"employment"—see reg. 4.
"week"—ibid.

GENERAL NOTE

This treats a person who has been laid off or kept on short-time as actively seeking employment during any week that his availability is restricted under reg. 17 for three or more days, as long as he is able to resume the employment from which he has been laid off or put on short time immediately and is taking reasonable steps to find casual work within daily travelling distance of his home.

See reg. 17 and the notes to that regulation for the rules for workers who have been laid off or put on short time. The maximum time for which a person can restrict his availability under reg. 17 is 13 weeks.

[¹Further circumstances in which a qualifying person is to be treated as actively seeking employment: full-time students participating in a qualifying course

21A. A person who is treated as available for employment in accordance with regulation 17A(3) shall be treated as actively seeking employment in any week—

  (a) which, in relation to the qualifying course, falls wholly or partly in term-time;
  (b) in which he is taking examinations relating to the qualifying course; or
  (c) which falls wholly in a vacation from the qualifying course, if in that week he takes such steps as he can reasonably be expected to have to take in order to have the best prospects of securing employment for which he is available under regulation 17A(3)(c).]

AMENDMENT

  1. Social Security Amendment (New Deal) Regulations 1998 (S.I. 1998 No. 1274), reg. 6 (June 1, 1998).

DEFINITIONS

  "employment"—see reg. 4.
  "examination"—*ibid.*
  "qualifying course"—*ibid.*, reg., 17A(7).
  "term-time"—see reg. 4.
  "vacation"—*ibid.*
  "week"—*ibid.*

GENERAL NOTE

  Under this rule a claimant who is deemed to be available for employment while undertaking a full-time employment-related course is treated as actively seeking employment. Note that for this to apply in the vacation the claimant must be taking reasonable steps to find casual employment (para. (c)). See the notes to reg. 17A for when a claimant will be treated as available for work while on such a full-time course.

Interpretation of certain expressions for the purposes of regulations 18(3)(f)(i) and 19(1)(d)

22. For the purposes of regulations 18(3)(f)(i) and 19(1)(d)—
  (a) a person is engaged in duties for the benefit of others while—
    (i) providing assistance to any person whose life may be endangered or who may be exposed to the risk of serious bodily injury or whose health may be seriously impaired,
    (ii) protecting property of substantial value from imminent risk of serious damage or destruction, or
    (iii) assisting in measures being taken to prevent a serious threat to the health of the people,
    as a member of a group of persons organised wholly or partly for the purpose of providing such assistance or, as the case may be, protection;
  (b) events which may give rise to an emergency include—
    (i) a fire, a flood or an explosion,

    (ii) a natural catastrophe,
    (iii) a railway or other transport accident,
    (iv) a cave or mountain accident,
    (v) an accident at sea,
    (vi) a person being reported missing and the organisation of a search for that person.

GENERAL NOTE

The conditions in this regulation are quite restrictive, although the list in para. (b) is not exhaustive. See *CU 113/1991.*

Chapter IV

Attendance, Information and Evidence

Attendance

23. A claimant shall attend at such place and at such time as the Secretary of State may specify by a notice in writing given or sent to the claimant.

GENERAL NOTE

A claimant is required to attend at the place and time (which must include the day: *CJSA 4775/ 1997*) notified to him in writing, in order to make declarations of availability for and active seeking of work and to provide other information required by reg. 24. This is known as his "signing on" day and is usually once a fortnight, although a person may be required to attend more frequently, *e.g.* if there is some query as to the validity of his claim.
For the penalty for non-compliance with this regulation see regs. 25–30.

Provision of information and evidence

24.—(1) A claimant shall provide such information as to his circumstances, his availability for employment and the extent to which he is actively seeking employment as may be required by the Secretary of State in order to determine the entitlement of the claimant to a jobseeker's allowance, whether that allowance is payable to him and, if so, in what amount.

(2) A claimant shall furnish such other information in connection with the claim, or any question arising out of it, as may be required by the Secretary of State.

(3) Where—
    (a) a jobseeker's allowance may be claimed by either member of a couple, or
    (b) entitlement to a jobseeker's allowance or whether that allowance is payable and, if so, in what amount, is or may be affected by the circumstances of either member of a couple or any member of a polygamous marriage,
the Secretary of State may require the member of the couple other than the claimant to certify in writing whether he agrees to the claimant's making the claim, or that he, or any member of a polygamous marriage, confirms the information given about his circumstances.

(4) A claimant shall furnish such certificates, documents and other evidence as may be required by the Secretary of State for the determination of the claim.

(5) A claimant shall furnish such certificates, documents and other evidence affecting his continuing entitlement to a jobseeker's allowance, whether that allowance is payable to him and, if so, in what amount as the Secretary of State may require.

(6) A claimant shall, if the Secretary of State requires him to do so, provide a signed declaration to the effect that—

[¹ (a) since making a claim for a jobseeker's allowance or since he last provided a declaration in accordance with this paragraph he has either been available for employment or satisfied the circumstances to be treated as available for employment, save as he has otherwise notified the Secretary of State,]

(b) since making a claim for a jobseeker's allowance or since he last provided a declaration in accordance with this paragraph he has either been actively seeking employment to the extent necessary to give him his best prospects of securing employment or he has satisfied the circumstances to be treated as actively seeking employment, save as he has otherwise notified the Secretary of State, and

(c) since making a claim for a jobseeker's allowance or since he last provided a declaration in accordance with this paragraph there has been no change to his circumstances which might affect his entitlement to a jobseeker's allowance or the [¹ . . .] amount of such an allowance, save as he has notified the Secretary of State.

(7) A claimant shall notify the Secretary of State—

(a) of any change of circumstances which has occurred which he might reasonably be expected to know might affect his entitlement to a jobseeker's allowance or the payability or amount of such an allowance; and

(b) of any such change of circumstances which he is aware is likely so to occur,

and shall do so as soon as reasonably practicable after its occurrence or, as the case may be, after he becomes so aware, by giving notice in writing (unless the Secretary of State determines in any particular case to accept notice given otherwise than in writing) to the appropriate office.

(8) Where, pursuant to paragraph (1) or (2), a claimant is required to provide information he shall do so when he attends in accordance with a notice under regulation 23, if so required by the Secretary of State, or within such period as the Secretary of State may require.

(9) Where, pursuant to paragraph (4) or (5), a claimant is required to provide certificates, documents or other evidence he shall do so within seven days of being so required or such longer period as the Secretary of State may consider reasonable.

(10) Where, pursuant to paragraph (6), a claimant is required to provide a signed declaration he shall provide it on the day on which he is required to attend in accordance with a notice under regulation 23 or on such other day as the Secretary of State may require.

AMENDMENT

1. Jobseeker's Allowance and Income Support (General) (Amendment) Regulations 1996 (S.I. 1996 No. 1517), reg. 8 (October 7, 1996).

DEFINITIONS

"appropriate office"—see reg. 4.
"couple"—see reg. 1(3).
"polygamous marriage—*ibid.*

GENERAL NOTE

This regulation sets out a claimant's obligations in relation to providing information and other evidence in connection with his claim for JSA. Note the time limit in para. (9) for the provision of documents, etc. under paras. (4) and (5).

See para. (6) as regards the declaration normally required when "signing on". For the penalty for not providing the declaration in para. (6) in accordance with para. (10) see regs. 25–27 and 29.

The obligation in para. (7) to report changes of circumstances can be relevant to the recoverability of an overpayment under s. 71 of the Administration Act. See also para. (6)(c). Although para. (7) requires notice generally to be given in writing, the Secretary of State can accept notification otherwise than in writing. Oral disclosures have always counted as disclosure under s. 71 (*R(SB) 40/84*). Note the reference in para. (7) to reporting changes of circumstances that are likely to occur, as well as those that have taken place (compare reg. 32(1) of the Claims and Payments Regulations which does not apply to JSA). Failure to disclose such potential future changes will not of course be relevant to s. 71, since until the material event has occurred there will be no question of an overpayment.

Entitlement ceasing on a failure to comply

25.—(1) Subject to regulation 27, entitlement to a jobseeker's allowance shall cease in the following circumstances—
  (a) if the claimant fails to attend on the day specified in a notice under regulation 23, other than a notice requiring attendance under an employment programme or a training scheme;
  (b) if—
    [[1](i) the claimant attends on the day specified in a notice under regulation 23 but fails to attend at the time specified in that notice (other than a notice requiring attendance under an employment programme or a training scheme), and the Secretary of State has informed the claimant in writing that a failure to attend, on the next occasion on which he is required to attend, at the time specified in such a notice may result in his entitlement to a jobseeker's allowance ceasing, and]
    (ii) he fails to attend at the time specified in such a notice on the next occasion;
  (c) if the claimant was required to provide a signed declaration as referred to in regulation 24(6) and he fails to provide it on the day on which he ought to do so in accordance with regulation 24(10).
  (2) In this regulation, "an employment programme" and "a training scheme" have the meaning given in regulation 75.

AMENDMENT

1. Jobseeker's Allowance (Amendment) Regulations 1999 (S.I. 1999 No. 530), reg. 2 (March 25, 1999).

DEFINITIONS

  "an employment programme"—see reg. 75.
  "a training scheme"—*ibid.*

GENERAL NOTE

Para. (1) provides for a person's JSA to cease if he fails to attend on the *day* he is required to do so under reg. 23 (sub-para. (a)), or at the *time* he is required to, but in this case only if this is the second time he has failed to attend at the specified time and he was advised in writing that a failure to attend on the next occasion at the specified time could result in his entitlement to JSA ceasing (sub-para. (b)), or if he fails to provide a declaration as to availability, etc. in accordance with reg. 24(6) on the due date under reg. 24(10) (sub-para. (c)). In all cases, there is an automatic escape if the claimant shows good cause for his failure if he does so within the next five working days (defined in reg. 27(2)) after the day he failed to comply (reg. 27). See reg. 30 for the circumstances in which a claimant will be treated as having good cause for failing to comply with a notice to attend under reg. 23. If reg. 30 does not apply, see reg. 28 for examples of the factors to be taken into account in deciding whether a claimant had good cause for failing to comply with such a notice. But clearly an AO will have to take into account all the circumstances when deciding good cause. Regulation 29 gives examples (again the list is not exhaustive) of the factors to be considered where the question is whether the claimant had good cause for failing to provide a declaration as to availability etc. on the due date. Reg. 29(a) will clearly be relevant where a person has been allowed to "sign on" by post. Reg. 26 deals with when a claimant's entitlement to JSA is to stop if reg. 25 applies.

The new form of sub-para. (b)(i) was introduced on March 25, 1999 following the decision in *CJSA 4775/1997*. In that case the Commissioner held that before entitlement could cease under sub-para. (a) for failure to attend on the specified day, the same procedure had to be followed (*i.e.* a warning letter was required) as in the case of a failure to attend at the specified time under sub-para. (b). The Commissioner's reasoning was that the words "at such time" in reg. 23 clearly included the day on which attendance was to take place, there being no separate reference in reg. 23 to the specified day. Thus "time" in sub-para. (b)(i) also encompassed the specified day, otherwise the word "time" would mean different things in regs. 23 and 25. The AO had argued that this approach rendered sub-para. (a) redundant. But the Commissioner considered that since reg. 25 imposed a penalty, the interpretation to be adopted was the one that avoided the penalty (see *e.g.* Plowman J. in *HPC Productions Limited* [1962] 2 W.L.R. 51 at 66). Moreover, because the old form of sub-para. (b)(i) did not, unlike sub-para. (a), exclude notices requiring attendance on an employment programme or training scheme, the result was a greater penalty for a claimant who attended on the correct day but at the wrong time than for a claimant who failed to attend on the day at all. The Commissioner concluded that the only way to make sense of reg. 25 was to regard sub-para. (a) as an example of sub-para. (b).

The new form of sub-para. (b)(i) specifically excludes notices requiring attendance at an employment programme or training scheme and is intended to make clear that sub-paras. (a) and (b) are concerned with different situations. Under sub-para. (a) a person's JSA will cease (without warning) if he fails to attend on the correct day and does not show good cause for his failure within the next five working days. Entitlement can start again if the person makes a further claim for JSA but he will normally lose benefit for the intervening period (generally from the day after he last "signed on": see reg. 26), unless any of the rules for backdating apply (see reg. 19(4)–(7) of the Claims and Payments Regulations). Note in addition the circumstances listed in reg. 6(4B) of the Claims and Payments Regulations in which the new claim will be treated as made on the day after the previous JSA award ended. But under sub-para. (b) entitlement cannot cease unless a written warning has been given. The person can reclaim JSA on the day of his second failure to attend on time but under reg. 6(4C) of the Claims and Payments Regulations the claim is treated as made on the following day. In those circumstances it seems that the person will only lose one day's benefit (presumably because reg. 26(b) will apply).

Despite the fact that para. (1) refers to a claimant's entitlement to JSA ceasing, it will still be necessary for there to be a decision by an AO reviewing the claimant's award of JSA under s.25 of the Administration Act, although clearly para. (1) will provide grounds for such a review (presumably under s.25(1)(b)). See *CSIS 137/1994* in the notes to reg. 17(4) of the Claims and Payments Regulations which holds that reg. 17(4) does not provide a separate and independent jurisdiction for conducting reviews but acts as a trigger for the operation of the normal review procedures. Thus on an appeal a SSAT will need to consider whether the conditions for the termination of the claimant's entitlement to JSA under para. (1) are met, including whether there was good cause for the claimant's failure to attend, etc. This issue may present itself not only directly in the context of an appeal against a decision under reg. 25 but perhaps more commonly where the claimant is appealing against a refusal to backdate a fresh claim for JSA, made after a previous claim has been "closed" under reg. 25. In such circumstances there is rarely any evidence of an AO's decision terminating the previous claim. Clearly if the original claim has not been validly terminated the question of backdating the subsequent claim will probably become irrelevant (subject to there being any complicating factors). In the absence of an AO's decision on this question, a SSAT may consider it appropriate to deal with the issue of whether the original claim had been validly terminated as a question first arising in the course of the appeal (see s.36 of the Administration Act).

Note reg. 37AA(3) and (3A) under which payment of a person's JSA can be withheld where a person fails to comply with a notice to attend or to provide a declaration on the due date.

Time at which entitlement is to cease

26. Entitlement to a jobseeker's allowance shall cease in accordance with regulation 25 on whichever is the earlier of—

    (a) the day after the last day in respect of which the claimant has provided information or evidence which [[2] shows that he continues to be entitled] to a jobseeker's allowance,

(b) if [¹regulation 25(1)(a) or (b)] applies, the day on which he was required to attend, and

(c) if [¹regulation 25(1)(c)] applies, the day on which he ought to have provided the signed declaration,

provided that it shall not cease earlier than the day after he last attended in compliance with a notice under regulation 23.

AMENDMENTS

1. Jobseeker's Allowance (Amendment) Regulations 1996 (S.I. 1996 No. 1516), reg. 8 and Sched. (October 7, 1996).
2. Jobseeker's Allowance and Income Support (General) (Amendment) Regulations 1996 (S.I. 1996 No. 1517), reg. 9 (October 7, 1996).

GENERAL NOTE

Where reg. 25 applies, the claimant's entitlement to JSA will cease either from the day he failed to attend or provide the declaration or, if earlier (as will usually be the case), from the day after he last provided information showing his entitlement to JSA. But it will not stop earlier than the day after he last actually attended the JobCentre. The effect of this is that if a person misses his "signing-on" day and does not attend again until a fortnight later, he may lose benefit for four weeks, unless any of the rules for backdating claims (see reg. 19(4)–(7) of the Claims and Payments Regulations) apply. Note in addition the circumstances listed in reg. 6(4B) of the Claims and Payments Regulations in which a new claim will be treated as made on the day after the previous JSA award ended. Where entitlement has ceased under reg. 25(1)(b) and the person makes a fresh claim for JSA on the day of his second failure to attend on time, that claim will be treated as made on the following day (reg. 6(4C) of the Claims and Payments Regulations). In those circumstances it seems that the person will only lose one day's benefit (presumably because reg. 26(b) will apply).

See reg. 37AA(3) and (3A) under which payment of a person's JSA can be withheld where a person fails to comply with a notice to attend or to provide a declaration on the due date.

Where entitlement is not to cease

27.—(1) Entitlement to a jobseeker's allowance shall not cease if the claimant shows, before the end of the fifth working day after the day on which he failed to comply with a notice under regulation 23 or to provide a signed declaration in accordance with regulation 24, that he had good cause for the failure.

(2) In this regulation, "working day" means any day on which the appropriate office is not closed.

DEFINITION

"appropriate office"—see reg. 4.

GENERAL NOTE

See the notes to reg. 25.

Matters to be taken into account in determining whether a claimant has good cause for failing to comply with a notice under regulation 23

28.—(1) Subject to regulation 30, in determining, for the purposes of regulation 27, whether a claimant has good cause for failing to comply with a notice under regulation 23 the matters which are to be taken into account shall include the following—

(a) whether the claimant misunderstood the requirement on him due to any learning, language or literacy difficulties of the claimant or any misleading information given to the claimant by an employment officer;

(b) whether the claimant was attending a medical or dental appointment, or accompanying a person for whom the claimant has caring responsibilities to such an appointment, and whether it would have been unreasonable, in the circumstances, to rearrange the appointment;

(c) any difficulty with the claimant's normal mode of transport and whether there was any reasonable available alternative;

(d) the established customs and practices of the religion, if any, to which the claimant belongs;

(e) whether the claimant was attending an interview for employment.

(2) In this regulation, "employment" means employed earner's employment except in relation to a claimant to whom regulation 20(2) applies and for the duration only of any permitted period determined in his case in accordance with regulation 16, in which case, for the duration of that period, it means employed earner's employment or self-employed earner's employment.

DEFINITIONS

"caring responsibilities"—see reg. 4.
"employed earner's employment"—see regs. 3, 4, SSCBA, s. 2(1).
"employment officer"—see reg. 4.
"self-employed earner's employment"—see regs. 1(3), 3, SSCBA, s. 2(1).

GENERAL NOTE

See the notes to reg. 25.

Matters to be taken into account in determining whether a claimant has good cause for failing to provide a signed declaration

29. In determining, for the purposes of regulation 27, whether a claimant has good cause for failing to comply with a requirement to provide a signed declaration, as referred to in regulation 24(6), on the day on which he ought to do so the matters which are to be taken into account shall include the following—

(a) whether there were adverse postal conditions;

(b) whether the claimant misunderstood the requirement on him due to any learning, language or literacy difficulties of the claimant or any misleading information given to the claimant by an employment officer.

DEFINITION

"employment officer"—see reg. 4.

GENERAL NOTE

See the notes to reg. 25.

Circumstances in which a claimant is to be regarded as having good cause for failing to comply with a notice under regulation 23

30. For the purposes of regulation 27, a claimant is to be regarded as having good cause for failing to comply with a notice under regulation 23—

(a) where, if regulation 5(1) applies in his case, he was required to attend at a time less than 48 hours from receipt by him of the notice;

(b) where, if regulation 5(2) applies in his case, he was required to attend at a time less than 24 hours from receipt by him of the notice;

(c) where he was, in accordance with regulation 14(1)(a)–(g), (k)–(n) or 14(2), treated as available for employment on the day on which he failed to attend;

(d) where the day on which he failed to attend falls in a week in which he was, in accordance with regulation 19(1)(p) and 19(2), treated as actively seeking employment.

DEFINITIONS

"employment"—see reg. 4.
"week"—*ibid.*

GENERAL NOTE

See the notes to reg. 25.

Chapter V

Jobseeker's Agreement

Contents of jobseeker's agreement

31. The prescribed requirements for a jobseeker's agreement are that it shall contain the following information—
  (a) the claimant's name;
  (b) where the hours for which the claimant is available for employment are restricted in accordance with regulation 7, the total number of hours for which he is available and any pattern of availability;
  (c) any restrictions on the claimant's availability for employment including restrictions on the location or type of employment, in accordance with regulations 5, 8, 13 and 17;
  (d) a description of the type of employment which the claimant is seeking;
  (e) the action which the claimant will take—
      (i) to seek employment; and
      (ii) to improve his prospects of finding employment;
  (f) the dates of the start and of the finish of any permitted period in his case for the purposes of sections 6(5) and 7(5);
  (g) a statement of the claimant's right—
      (i) to have a proposed jobseeker's agreement referred to an adjudication officer;
      (ii) to seek a review of any determination of, or direction given by, an adjudication officer; and
      (iii) to appeal to a social security appeal tribunal against any determination of, or direction given by, an adjudication officer on a review.
  (h) the date of the agreement.

DEFINITIONS

"employment"—see regs. 3, 4.
"pattern of availability"—see regs. 4, 7.

GENERAL NOTE

It is a central requirement for entitlement to JSA that the claimant has entered into a jobseeker's agreement which remains in force (s. 1(2)(b) of the Jobseekers Act). Jobseekers' agreements are dealt with in ss. 9–11 of the Act. See the notes to those sections for the main discussion of the regulations in this Chapter, but there are also some annotations to individual regulations, see below.

Reg. 31 sets out what a jobseeker's agreement is required to contain (see s. 9(1) of the Act). A jobseeker's agreement will be on Form ES3.

Back-dating of a jobseeker's agreement by an adjudication officer

32. In giving a direction under section 9(7)(c), the adjudication officer shall take into account all relevant matters including—

(a) where the claimant refused to accept the agreement proposed by the employment officer, whether he was reasonable in so refusing;

(b) where the claimant has signified to the employment officer or to the adjudication officer that the claimant is prepared to accept an agreement which differs from the agreement proposed by the employment officer, whether the terms of the agreement which he is prepared to accept are reasonable;

(c) where the claimant has signified to the employment officer or to the adjudication officer that the claimant is prepared to accept the agreement proposed by the employment officer, that fact;

(d) the date on which, in all the circumstances, he considers that the claimant was first prepared to enter into an agreement which the adjudication officer considers reasonable; and

(e) where the date on which the claimant first had an opportunity to sign a jobseeker's agreement was later than the date on which he made a claim, that fact.

DEFINITION

"employment officer"—see reg. 4.

GENERAL NOTE

See the notes to s. 9 of the Jobseekers Act.

Notification of determinations and directions under section 9

33. The claimant shall be notified of—

(a) any determination of the adjudication officer under section 9;

(b) any direction given by the adjudication officer under section 9.

GENERAL NOTE

See the notes to s. 9 of the Jobseekers Act.

Jobseeker's agreement treated as having been made

34. A claimant is to be treated as having satisfied the condition mentioned in section 1(2)(b)—

(a) where he is permitted to make a claim for a jobseeker's allowance without attending at an office of the Department for Education and Employment or of the Department of Social Security, for the period beginning with the date of claim and ending on the date on which he has an interview with an employment officer for the purpose of drawing up a jobseeker's agreement;

(b) where, after the date of claim, the claim is terminated before he has an interview with an employment officer for the purpose of drawing up a jobseeker's agreement;

(c) as long as he is treated as available for employment in accordance with regulation 14 where the circumstances set out in that regulation arise after the date of claim and before he has an interview with an employment officer for the purpose of drawing up a jobseeker's agreement;

(d) as long as there are circumstances not peculiar to the claimant which make impracticable or unduly difficult the normal operation of the provisions governing, or the practice relating to, the claiming, awarding or payment of jobseeker's allowance.

[¹(e) where the claimant was in receipt of a training allowance and was, in

641

accordance with regulation 170, entitled to an income-based jobseeker's allowance without being available for employment, having entered into a jobseeker's agreement or actively seeking employment, for the period beginning with the date on which regulation 170 ceased to apply to him and ending on the date on which he has an interview with an employment officer for the purpose of drawing up a jobseeker's agreement.]

AMENDMENT

1. Jobseeker's Allowance (Amendment) Regulations 1996 (S.I. 1996 No. 1516), reg. 3 (October 7, 1996).

DEFINITIONS

"date of claim"—see reg. 1(3).
"employment"—see regs. 3, 4.
"employment officer"—see reg. 4.
"training allowance"—see reg. 1(3).

GENERAL NOTE

This regulation treats a jobseeker's agreement as having been made in the following circumstances:
(a) where a person is allowed to claim by post, in which case he will be treated as having signed a jobseeker's agreement from the date of claim to the date of his interview with an employment officer to draw up an agreement. The normal rule is that a claim for JSA has to be made in person at the JobCentre (reg. 4(6)(a) of the Claims and Payments Regulations);
(b) where a claim ends before the interview with an employment officer to draw up a jobseeker's agreement;
(c) while the claimant is deemed to be available under any of the rules in reg. 14 if the circumstances arose after the date of claim and before the interview with an employment officer to draw up a jobseeker's agreement;
(d) where there are operational difficulties in relation to the claiming, awarding or payment of JSA (*e.g.* a strike by the Employment Service staff);
(e) where the claimant was in receipt of a training allowance and entitled to income-based JSA under reg. 170 without satisfying the labour market conditions, from the date that that situation ceased to apply to the date of his interview with an employment officer to draw up a jobseeker's agreement.

Automatic back-dating of jobseeker's agreement

35. Where a jobseeker's agreement is signed on a date later than the date of claim and there is no reference of that agreement to an adjudication officer under section 9(6), the agreement shall be treated as having effect on the date of claim.

DEFINITION

"date of claim"—see reg. 1(3).

GENERAL NOTE

See the notes to s. 9 of the Jobseekers Act.

Jobseeker's agreement to remain in effect

36. A jobseeker's agreement entered into by a claimant shall not cease to have effect on the coming to an end of an award of a jobseeker's allowance made to him—

(a) where a further claim for a jobseeker's allowance is made within a period not exceeding 14 days; or

[¹ (b) in respect of any part of a period of suspension, where—

    (i) the Secretary of State has directed under regulation 37(1A) of the Claims and Payments Regulations that payment under an award be suspended for a definite or indefinite period on the ground that a question arises whether the conditions for entitlement to that allowance are or were fulfilled or the award ought to be revised,

    (ii) subsequently that suspension expires or is cancelled in respect of a part only of the period for which it has been in force, and

    (iii) it is then determined that the award should be revised to the effect that there was no entitlement to the allowance in respect of all or any part of the period between the start of the period over which the award has been suspended and the date when the suspension expires or is cancelled; or]

(c) for as long as the claimant satisfies the conditions of entitlement to national insurance credits, other than any condition relating to the existence of a jobseeker's agreement, in accordance with the Social Security (Credits) Regulations 1975.

AMENDMENT

1. Jobseeker's Allowance and Income Support (General) (Amendment) Regulations 1996 (S.I. 1996 No. 1517), reg. 10 (October 7, 1996).

GENERAL NOTE

The normal position will be that a jobseeker's agreement will come to an end when the claim to JSA stops. This regulation sets out three situations where this will not be the case. Note the 14 day linking rule in para. (a).

Variation of jobseeker's agreement

37. The prescribed manner for varying a jobseeker's agreement shall be in writing and signed by both parties in accordance with section 10(2) on the proposal of the claimant or the employment officer.

DEFINITION

"employment officer"—see reg. 4.

GENERAL NOTE

See the notes to s. 10 of the Jobseekers Act.

Direction to vary agreement: time for compliance

38. The prescribed period for the purposes of section 10(6)(c) shall be the period of 21 days beginning with the date on which the direction was issued.

GENERAL NOTE

See the notes to s. 10 of the Jobseekers Act.

Variation of agreement: matters to be taken into account

39. In giving a direction under section 10(6)(b) or (d) an adjudication officer shall take into account the preference of the claimant if he considers that both the claimant's proposals and those of the employment officer satisfy the requirements of section 10(5).

"employment officer"—see reg. 4.

GENERAL NOTE

See the notes to s. 10 of the Jobseekers Act.

Notification of determinations and directions under section 10

40. The claimant shall be notified of—
(a) any determination of the adjudication officer under section 10;
(b) any direction of the adjudication officer under section 10.

GENERAL NOTE

See the notes to s. 10 of the Jobseekers Act.

Procedure for reviews

41.—(1) This regulation applies to an application for a review under section 11.
(2) An application for a review to which this regulation applies shall—
(a) be made in writing,
(b) set out the grounds for the application, and
(c) be made to an appropriate office within the period of 3 months beginning with the date on which the determination or direction was notified to the claimant.
(3) Where a claimant submits an application for a review by post which would have arrived in the appropriate office in the ordinary course of the post within the period prescribed by paragraph (2)(c) but is delayed by postal disruption caused by industrial action whether within the postal service or elsewhere, that period shall expire on the day the application is received at the appropriate office if that day does not fall within the period prescribed by paragraph (2)(c).
(4) The adjudication officer shall proceed to deal with any question arising on a review to which this regulation applies in accordance with sections 9 and 10 and regulations 31 to 39.
(5) The claimant shall be notified of any determination of, or direction given by, an adjudication officer on a review to which this regulation applies and shall be notified of his right to appeal to a social security appeal tribunal against any such determination or direction under section 11(3).
(6) Accidental errors in, or in the record of, any determination of, or direction given by, an adjudication officer on a review to which this regulation applies may be corrected by the adjudication officer who made the determination, or gave the direction, or by another adjudication officer.
(7) A correction made to, or to the record of, a determination or direction shall be deemed to be part of the determination or direction or of that record and the claimant and the employment officer shall be notified of it in writing as soon as practicable.

DEFINITIONS

"appropriate office"—see reg. 4.
"employment officer"—*ibid.*

See the notes to s. 11 of the Jobseekers Act.

Appeals to Social Security Appeal Tribunal

42. Parts I and II and in Part III in regulation 22(1) to (3) and 23 and 24 of the Social Security (Adjudication) Regulations 1995 shall apply in relation to appeals to the social security appeals tribunal under section 11(3) as they apply to appeals to that tribunal under the Social Security Administration Act 1992 with the following modifications—
   (a) in regulation 6(2), the addition of the words "or section 11(3) of the Jobseekers Act 1995 (c.18)" after the words "Administration Act";
   (b) in Schedule 2, after entry 11, the addition of—
      (i) in column 1, the words "Appeal to an appeal tribunal against any determination of, or direction given by, an adjudication officer on a review under section 11 of the Jobseekers Act 1995";
      (ii) in column 2, the words—"the office of the Department for Education and Employment which the claimant is required to attend in accordance with a notice under regulation 23 of the Jobseeker's Allowance Regulations 1996 [¹(S.I. 1996/207)], or any other place which he is so required to attend";
      (iii) in column 3, the words "3 months beginning with the date when notice in writing of the determination or direction was given to the claimant".

AMENDMENT

1. Social Security (Miscellaneous Amendments) Regulations 1997 (S.I. 1997 No. 454), reg. 2(3) (April 7, 1997).

GENERAL NOTE

See the notes to s. 11 of the Jobseekers Act.

Direction of Social Security Appeal Tribunal: time limit for compliance

43. The prescribed period for the purposes of section 11(5) shall be the period of 21 days beginning with the date on which the direction was issued.

GENERAL NOTE

See the notes to s. 11 of the Jobseekers Act.

Appeals to the Commissioner

44. The Social Security Commissioners Procedure Regulations 1987, except regulations 8, 12(2), 23, 28, 31(5), (6), (7) and (8), 32 and 33, shall apply in relation to appeals to the Commissioner under section 11(6) as they apply in relation to appeals under section 23 of the Administration Act.

See the notes to s. 11 of the Jobseekers Act.

Appropriate person

45. A trade union or other association which exists to promote the interests and welfare of its members shall be an appropriate person for the purposes of section 11(6) where—
  (a) the claimant is a member of the union or of the association, as the case may be, at the time of the appeal and was so immediately before the question at issue arose; or
  (b) the question at issue is a question as to or in connection with entitlement of a deceased person who was at the time of his death a member of the union or of the association, as the case may be.

GENERAL NOTE

See the notes to s. 11 of the Jobseekers Act.

PART III

OTHER CONDITIONS OF ENTITLEMENT

Waiting days

46.—(1) Paragraph 4 of Schedule 1 to the Act shall not apply in a case where—
  (a) a person's entitlement to a jobseeker's allowance commences within 12 weeks of an entitlement of his to income support, incapacity benefit or invalid care allowance coming to an end; or
  (b) a claim for a jobseeker's allowance falls to be determined by reference to section 3(1)(f)(ii) (persons under the age of 18).
  (2) In the case of a person to whom paragraph 4 of Schedule 1 to the Act applies, the number of days is 3.

DEFINITION

"the Act"—see reg. 1(3).

GENERAL NOTE

There are no "waiting days" for income support. However, para. 4 of Sched. 1 to the Jobseekers Act and para. (2) import the unemployment benefit rule (see SSCBA, s. 25(3)) that at the beginning of a jobseeking period (see reg. 47) there is no entitlement to JSA for three days (subject to the exceptions in para. (1)). This rule applies to both contribution-based and income-based JSA. As JSA is a weekly benefit, Saturday and Sunday count as waiting days. The number of waiting days was to have been increased to seven from April 1999 but this change has been postponed; the Government stated that the proposal would be further considered as part of its Comprehensive Spending Review. For the Social Security Advisory Committee's report on this proposed change (which in the Committee's view "would add unacceptably to the hardship experienced by unemployed people and their families"), see Cm. 3829 (1998).

Note the linking rules for jobseeking periods in reg. 48. See also reg. 56B(4) of the Adjudication Regulations which provides that where a person is in receipt of income support and either he or his partner claims and is awarded JSA and as a consequence his income support terminates the waiting days rule does not apply.

A sanction imposed under s. 19 of the Act (see Part V of these Regulations) will not begin until after any waiting days have been served. But a claimant who is entitled to income-based JSA will qualify for maximum housing benefit and/or council tax benefit during any waiting days (see reg. 2(3A)(b) of the Housing Benefit Regulations 1987 and the Council Tax Benefit Regulations 1992 respectively).

Paragraph (1)
Waiting days do not apply where the person has been entitled to income support, incapacity benefit or invalid care allowance within the last 12 weeks (sub-para. (a)) or is under 18 and the subject of a severe hardship direction under s. 16 of the Jobseekers Act (sub-para. (b)).

Jobseeking period

47.—(1) For the purposes of the Act, but subject to paragraphs (2) and (3), the "jobseeking period" means any period throughout which the claimant satisfies or is treated as satisfying the conditions specified in paragraphs (a) to (c) and (e) to (i) of subsection (2) of section 1 (conditions of entitlement to a jobseeker's allowance).

(2) Any period in which—

(a) a claimant does not satisfy any of the requirements in section 1(2)(a) to (c), and

(b) a jobseeker's allowance is payable to him in accordance with Part IX (Hardship),

shall, for the purposes of paragraph (1), be treated as a period in which the claimant satisfies the conditions specified in paragraphs (a) to (c) of subsection (2) of section 1.

[¹ (2A) Any period in which a claimant is entitled to a jobseeker's allowance in accordance with regulation 11(3) of the Jobseeker's Allowance (Transitional Provisions) Regulations 1995 shall, for the purposes of paragraph (1), be treated as a period in which he satisfies the conditions specified in paragraphs (a) to (c) and (e) to (i) of subsection (2) of section 1.]

(3) The following periods shall not be, or be part of, a jobseeking period—

(a) any period in respect of which no claim for a jobseeker's allowance has been made or treated as made;

(b) such period as falls before the day on which a claim for a jobseeker's allowance is made or treated as made [². . .];

(c) where a claim for a jobseeker's allowance has been made or treated as made but no entitlement to benefit arises in respect of a period before the date of claim by virtue of section 1(2) of the Administration Act (limits for backdating entitlement), that period;

(d) where—

(i) a claimant satisfies the conditions specified in paragraphs (a) to (c) and (e) to (i) of subsection (2) of section 1; and

(ii) entitlement to a jobseeker's allowance ceases in accordance with regulation 25 (entitlement ceasing on a failure to comply),

the period beginning with the date in respect of which, in accordance with regulation 26, entitlement ceases and ending with the day before the date in respect of which the claimant again becomes entitled to a jobseeker's allowance; or

(e) any week in which a claimant is not entitled to a jobseeker's allowance in accordance with section 14 (trade disputes).

(4) [*Omitted as not relating to income-based jobseeker's allowance.*]

AMENDMENTS

1. Social Security and Child Support (Jobseeker's Allowance) (Miscellaneous Amendments) Regulations 1996 (S.I. 1996 No. 2538), reg. 2(4) (October 28, 1996).

2. Social Security Benefits (Miscellaneous Amendments) Regulations 1999 (S.I. 1999 No. 714), reg. 2(1) (April 5, 1999).

DEFINITIONS

"the Act"—see reg. 1(3).
"claimant"—see Jobseekers Act, s. 35(1).
"contribution-based jobseeker's allowance"—see Jobseekers Act, s. 1(4).
"week"—see reg. 1(3).

GENERAL NOTE

A jobseeking period is simply the period during which the claimant meets, or is treated as meeting, the conditions of entitlement to JSA in s. 1(2)(a)–(c) and (e)–(i) of the Jobseekers Act (*i.e.* the basic conditions of entitlement for JSA other than those that relate specifically to contribution-based or income-based JSA). Thus it is similar to the former unemployment benefit concept of a "period of interruption of employment". "Waiting days" (see para. 4 of Sched. 1 to the Act and reg. 46) are part of a jobseeking period. For the purposes of the definition in para. (1), para. (2) treats a claimant who does not satisfy the labour market conditions in s. 1(2) (a)–(c) but who is in receipt of a hardship payment as satisfying those conditions. Note also para. (2A); reg. 11(3) of the 1995 Transitional Regulations is now reg. 13(3) of the Jobseeker's Allowance (Transitional) Regulations 1996. In addition, reg. 49 provides that certain other days for people over 60 but under pensionable age will count as part of a jobseeking period.

However, the following do not count as part of a jobseeking period: (i) any period for which no JSA claim has been made or treated as made; (ii) any period which is before the day on which a claim is made or treated as made (note that where the time for claiming is extended under reg. 19 of the Claims and Payments Regulations the claim is treated as made at the beginning of the period for which the claim is deemed to be in time (reg. 6(3) of those Regulations); the April 1999 amendment to para. (3)(b) has simply deleted an obsolete reference to good cause for late claims); (iii) any period for which there is no entitlement to benefit by virtue of s.1(2) of the Administration Act; (iv) any days on which the claimant is not entitled to JSA under reg. 25 (failing without good cause to attend, etc.); (v) any week (defined in reg. 1(3)) in which the claimant is not entitled to JSA because he is involved in a trade dispute (para. (3)).

See reg. 48 for the linking rules for jobseeking periods and note reg. 47A.

[¹ Jobseeking periods: periods of interruption of employment

[³47A.—(1)] For the purposes of section 2(4)(b)(i) and for determining any waiting days—

[²(za) where a linked period commenced before 7th October 1996 [³ . . .], any days of unemployment which form part of a period of interruption of employment where the last day of unemployment in that period of interruption of employment was no more than 8 weeks before the date upon which that linked period commenced;]

(a) where a jobseeking period or a linked period commences on 7th October 1996, any period of interruption of employment ending within the 8 weeks preceding that date; or

(b) where a jobseeking period or a linked period commences after 7th October 1996, any period of interruption of employment ending within the 12 weeks preceding the day the jobseeking period or linked period commenced,

shall be treated as a jobseeking period [²and, for the purposes of paragraph (za), a day shall be treated as being, or not being, a day of unemployment in accordance with section 25A of the Social Security Contributions and Benefits Act 1992 and with any regulations made under that section, as in force on 6th October 1996].]

[³(2) In paragraph (1) "period of interruption of employment" in relation to a period prior to 7th October 1996 has the same meaning as it had in the Benefits

Act by virtue of section 25A of that Act (determination of days for which unemployment benefit is payable) as in force on 6th October 1996.]

AMENDMENTS

1. Social Security and Child Support (Jobseeker's Allowance) (Miscellaneous Amendments) Regulations 1996 (S.I. 1996 No. 2538), reg. 2(5) (October 28, 1996).
2. Jobseeker's Allowance (Amendment) (No. 2) Regulations 1997 (S.I. 1997 No. 2677), reg. 2 (December 1, 1997).
3. Social Security (Miscellaneous Amendments) Regulations 1998 (S.I. 1998 No. 563), reg. 16 (April 1, 1998).

DEFINITION

"jobseeking period "— see reg. 47.

Linking periods

48.—(1) For the purposes of the Act, two or more jobseeking periods shall be treated as one jobseeking period where they are separated by a period comprising only—

    (a) any period of not more than 12 weeks;

    (b) a linked period;

    (c) any period of not more than 12 weeks falling between—

        (i) any two linked periods; or

        (ii) a jobseeking period and a linked period;

[¹ (d) a period in respect of which the claimant is summoned for jury service and is required to attend court.]

(2) Linked periods for the purposes of the Act are any of the following periods—

    (a) to the extent specified in paragraph (3), any period throughout which the claimant is entitled to an invalid care allowance under section 70 of the Benefits Act;

    (b) any period throughout which the claimant is incapable of work, or is treated as incapable of work, in accordance with Part XIIA of the Benefits Act;

    (c) any period throughout which the claimant was entitled to a maternity allowance under section 35 of the Benefits Act;

    (d) any period throughout which the claimant was engaged in training for which a training allowance is payable.

[² (e) a period which includes 6th October [³ 1996] during which the claimant attends court in response to a summons for jury service and which was immediately preceded by a period of entitlement to unemployment benefit.]

[⁴(f) any period throughout which the claimant was participating—

        (i) in the Employment Option of the New Deal as specified in regulation 75(1)(a)(ii)(aa);

        (ii) either in the Voluntary Sector Option of the New Deal as specified in regulation 75(1)(a)(ii)(bb) or in the Environment Task Force Option of the New Deal as specified in regulation 75(1)(a)(ii)(cc) and was not entitled to a jobseeker's allowance because, as a consequence of his participation in either of those options, the claimant was engaged in remunerative work or failed to satisfy the condition specified either in section 2(1)(c) or in section 3(1)(a).]

(2A) [*Omitted as not relating to income-based jobseeker's allowance.*]

(3) A period of entitlement to invalid care allowance shall be a linked period only where it enables the claimant to satisfy contribution conditions for entitle-

ment to a contribution-based jobseeker's allowance which he would otherwise be unable to satisfy.

1. Jobseeker's Allowance and Income Support (General) (Amendment) Regulations 1996 (S.I. 1996 No. 1517), reg. 15 (October 7, 1996).
2. Social Security and Child Support (Jobseeker's Allowance) (Miscellaneous Amendments) Regulations 1996 (S.I. 1996 No. 2538), reg. 2(6) (October 28, 1996).
3. Social Security (Miscellaneous Amendments) Regulations 1997 (S.I. 1997 No. 454), reg. 2(4) (April 7, 1997).
4. Social Security Amendment (New Deal) Regulations 1997 (S.I. 1997 No. 2863), reg. 4 (January 5, 1998).

DEFINITIONS

"the Act"—see reg. 1(3).
"the Benefits Act"—*ibid.*
"claimant"—see Jobseekers Act, s. 35(1).
"remunerative work"—see reg. 51(1).
"training allowance"—see reg. 1(3).
"week"—*ibid.*

GENERAL NOTE

For the meaning of "jobseeking period" see reg. 47. This regulation provides for jobseeking periods to be linked (and so treated as one period) in certain situations. The linking rules are important in deciding, for example, whether a claimant has to serve the "waiting days" (see para. 4 of Sched. 1 to the Jobseekers Act 1995 and reg. 46) if he reclaims JSA (contribution- or income-based) after a break in claim. Moreover, if two or more jobseeking periods are linked, the claimant has to satisfy the contribution conditions at the beginning of the first period, not the current period, for the purposes of contribution-based JSA (see further *Bonner*).

Paragraph (1)
Two or more jobseeking periods are treated as linked if they are separated by a period of no more than 12 weeks, a "linked period", a period of no more than 12 weeks and a linked period, a period of no more than 12 weeks between two linked periods, or a period during which the claimant is on jury service.

Paragraph (2)
A "linked period" is any period during which the claimant is incapable, or is treated as incapable, of work, or getting maternity allowance, or undertaking training for which a training allowance is payable, or getting invalid care allowance (but in this case only if this enables a claimant to qualify for contribution-based JSA who would not otherwise do so, see para. (3)), or (from October 28, 1996) any period which includes October 6, 1996 when the claimant was on jury service and immediately before that was entitled to unemployment benefit (sub-paras. (a)–(e)).
The new sub-para. (f), in force from January 5, 1998, adds to this list any period which the claimant spends on the New Deal Employment option, or on the Voluntary Sector or Environment Task Force options during which he is in remunerative work or his earnings are too high to qualify for contribution-based JSA or his income is too high to qualify for income-based JSA. Many claimants who participate in the New Deal will be paid a training allowance and so are already covered by sub-para. (d). However, the intention is that all claimants who take part in the New Deal should be treated in the same way for the purpose of the linking rules and that claimants should not be any worse off if they have to reclaim JSA after participating in the New Deal. Thus sub-para. (f) has been introduced to ensure that any period during which a claimant is engaged in employment while on a New Deal option will count as a linked period. For a brief summary of the New Deal for 18–24 year-olds see the notes to reg. 75.

Note also reg. 47A and reg. 3(3) and (4) of the Jobseeker's Allowance (Transitional) Regulations 1996.

Persons approaching retirement and the jobseeking period

49.—(1) The provisions of this regulation apply only to days which fall—

(a) after 6th October 1996; and

(b) within a tax year in which the claimant has attained the age of 60 but is under pensionable age;

and in respect of which a jobseeker's allowance is not payable because the decision of the determining authority is that the claimant—

(i) has exhausted his entitlement to a contribution-based jobseeker's allowance; or

(ii) fails to satisfy one or both the contribution conditions specified in section 2(1)(a) and (b); or

(iii) is entitled to a contribution-based jobseeker's allowance but the amount payable is reduced to Nil by virtue of deductions made in accordance with regulation 81 for pension payments.

[¹ (2) For the purposes of paragraph (1) of regulation 47 (jobseeking period) but subject to paragraphs (3) and (4), any days to which paragraph (1) applies and in respect of which the person does not satisfy or is not treated in accordance with regulation 14, 16, 17, 19, 20, 21 or 34 as satisfying the conditions specified in paragraphs (a) to (c) of subsection (2) of section (1) (conditions of entitlement to a jobseeker's allowance), shall be days on which the person is treated as satisfying the condition in paragraphs (a) to (c) and (e) to (i) of subsection (2) of section (1).]

(3) Where a person—

(a) [¹ . . .]

(b) is employed as an employed earner or a self-employed earner for a period of more than 12 weeks,

then no day which falls within or follows that period shall be days on which the person is treated as satisfying those conditions so however that this paragraph shall not prevent paragraph (2) from again applying to a person who makes a claim for a jobseeker's allowance after that period.

(4) Any day which is, for the purposes of section 30C of the Benefits Act, a day of incapacity for work falling within a period of incapacity for work shall not be a day on which the person is treated as satisfying the conditions referred to in paragraph (2).

AMENDMENT

1. Jobseeker's Allowance and Income Support (General) (Amendment) Regulations 1996 (S.I. 1996 No. 1517), reg. 16 (October 7, 1996).

DEFINITIONS

"the Benefits Act"—see Jobseekers Act, s.35(1).
"claimant"—*ibid.*
"contribution-based jobseeker's allowance"—see Jobseekers Act, s. 1(4).
"pensionable age"—see reg. 3.

Persons temporarily absent from Great Britain

50.—(1) For the purposes of the Act, a claimant shall be treated as being in Great Britain during any period of temporary absence from Great Britain—

(a) not exceeding 4 weeks in the circumstances specified in paragraphs (2), (3) and (4);

(b) not exceeding 8 weeks in the circumstances specified in paragraph (5).

(2) The circumstances specified in this paragraph are that—

(a) the claimant is in Northern Ireland and satisfies the conditions of entitlement to a jobseeker's allowance; and

(b) immediately preceding the period of absence from Great Britain the claimant was entitled to a jobseeker's allowance; and

(c) the period of absence is unlikely to exceed 52 weeks.

(3) The circumstances specified in this paragraph are that—

(a) immediately preceding the period of absence from Great Britain the claimant was entitled to a jobseeker's allowance; and

(b) the period of absence is unlikely to exceed 52 weeks; and

(c) while absent from Great Britain, the claimant continues to satisfy, or be treated as satisfying, the other conditions of entitlement to a jobseeker's allowance; and

(d) is one of a couple, both of whom are absent from Great Britain, where a premium referred to in paragraphs 10, 11, 12, 13 or 15 of Schedule 1 (applicable amounts) is applicable in respect of the claimant's partner.

(4) The circumstances of this paragraph are that—

(a) while absent from Great Britain the person is in receipt of a training allowance; and

(b) regulation 170 (person in receipt of training allowance) applies in his case; and

(c) immediately preceding his absence from Great Britain, he was entitled to a jobseeker's allowance.

(5) The circumstances specified in this paragraph are that—

(a) immediately preceding the period of absence from Great Britain, the claimant was entitled to a jobseeker's allowance; and

(b) the period of absence is unlikely to exceed 52 weeks; and

(c) the claimant continues to satisfy or be treated as satisfying the other conditions of entitlement to a jobseeker's allowance; and

(d) the claimant is, or the claimant and any other member of his family are, accompanying a member of the claimant's family who is a child or young person solely in connection with arrangements made for the treatment of that child or young person for a disease or bodily or mental disablement; and

(e) those arrangements relate to treatment—

    (i) outside Great Britain;

    (ii) during the period whilst the claimant is, or the claimant and any member of his family are, temporarily absent from Great Britain; and

    (iii) by, or under the supervision of, a person appropriately qualified to carry out that treatment.

(6) A person shall also be treated, for the purposes of the Act, as being in Great Britain during any period of temporary absence from Great Britain where—

(a) the absence is for the purpose of attending an interview for employment; and

(b) the absence is for 7 consecutive days or less; and

(c) notice of the proposed absence is given to the employment officer before departure, and is given in writing if so required by the officer; and

(d) on his return to Great Britain the person satisfies the employment officer that he attended for the interview in accordance with his notice.

(7) In this regulation—

"appropriately qualified" means qualified to provide medical treatment, physiotherapy or a form of treatment which is similar to, or related to, either of those forms of treatment;

"employment officer" means a person who is an employment officer for the purposes of sections 9 and 10.

DEFINITIONS

"the Act"—see reg. 1(3).
"child"—see Jobseekers Act, s. 35(1).
"claimant"—*ibid.*
"couple"—see reg. 1(3).
"employment"—see reg. 3.
"entitled"—see Jobseekers Act, s. 35(1).
"family"—*ibid.*
"Great Britain"—*ibid.*
"partner"—see reg. 1(3).
"training allowance"—*ibid.*
"week"—*ibid.*
"young person"—*ibid,* reg. 76.

GENERAL NOTE

It is a condition of entitlement to JSA that a person is in Great Britain (s. 1(2)(i) of the Jobseekers Act). This provision treats a person as being in Great Britain for a short period of temporary absence of up to four weeks if he satisfies the conditions in paras. (2), (3) or (4) or up to eight weeks if para. (5) applies. Paras. (2), (3) and (5) cover the same situations as those in heads (iii) and (iv) of para. (2)(c) and para. (3) of reg. 4 of the Income Support Regulations (see the notes to reg. 4). Note also the separate provision in para. (6) for absence for the purpose of attending an employment interview. On "temporary absence" see the notes to reg. 4 of the Income Support Regulations.

The effect of E.C. Regulation 1408/71 on this rule should, however, be noted. Under the co-ordination provisions of Regulation 1408/71 it is clear that contribution-based JSA can be "exported" (*i.e.* paid where the claimant resides in another EEA country) for three months while a claimant looks for work in that country (see the notes to reg. 21(3), definition of "person from abroad", for those countries which are members of the EEA). But the question arises whether this could also apply to income-based JSA. The government has included income-based JSA in the list of "special non-contributory benefits" to which Regulation 1408/71 applies from June 1, 1992 (see Arts. 4(2a) and Annex IIa). Such benefits cannot be exported (Art. 10a). But since both the contribution-based and the income-based elements of JSA are subject to the condition that the claimant is unemployed and so clearly relate to the risk covered by Art. 4(1)(g) of Regulation 1408/71, it would seem that entitlement to income-based JSA should also be exportable (for up to three months). However, see *Snares v. Adjudication Officer* Case C-20/96 [1997] E.C.R. I-6057, in the notes to s.1 of the Jobseekers Act. In that case the ECJ ruled that disability living allowance (also listed in Annex IIa) fell exclusively within Arts. 4(2)(a) and 10a, so a person who was awarded it after June 1, 1992 could not export it to another EEA country.

Remunerative work

51.—(1) For the purposes of the Act "remunerative work" means—
(a) in the case of the claimant, work in which he is engaged or, where his hours of work fluctuate, is engaged on average, for not less than 16 hours per week; and
(b) in the case of any partner of the claimant, work in which he is engaged or, where his hours of work fluctuate, is engaged on average, for not less than 24 hours per week; [¹ and
(c) in the case of a non-dependant, or of a child or young person to whom paragraph 18 of Schedule 6 refers, work in which he is engaged or, where his hours of work fluctuate, is engaged on average, for not less than 16 hours per week,]
and for those purposes, [³ "work" is work] for which payment is made or which is done in expectation of payment.

(2) For the purposes of paragraph (1), the number of hours in which the claimant or his partner is engaged in work shall be determined—

    (a) where no recognisable cycle has been established in respect of a person's work, by reference to the number of hours or, where those hours are likely to fluctuate, the average of the hours, which he is expected to work in a week;

    (b) where the number of hours for which he is engaged fluctuate, by reference to the average of hours worked over—

        (i) if there is a recognisable cycle of work, and sub-paragraph (c) does not apply, the period of one complete cycle (including, where the cycle involves periods in which the person does not work, those periods but disregarding any other absences);

        (ii) in any other case, the period of five weeks immediately before the date of claim or the date of review, or such other length of time as may, in the particular case, enable the person's average hours of work to be determined more accurately;

    (c) where the person works at a school or other educational establishment or at some other place of employment and the cycle of work consists of one year but with school holidays or similar vacations during which he does no work, by disregarding those periods and any other periods in which he is not required to work.

(3) In determining in accordance with this regulation the number of hours for which a person is engaged in remunerative work—

    (a) that number shall include any time allowed to that person by his employer for a meal or for refreshments, but only where the person is, or expects to be, paid earnings in respect of that time;

    (b) no account shall be taken of any hours in which the person is engaged in an employment or scheme to which any one of paragraphs (a) to (h) of regulation 53 (person treated as not engaged in remunerative work) applies;

    (c) no account shall be taken of any hours in which the person is engaged otherwise than in an employment as an earner in caring for—

        (i) a person who is in receipt of attendance allowance [1 ...] or the care component of disability living allowance at the highest or middle rate; or

        (ii) a person who has claimed an attendance allowance [1 ...] or a disability living allowance, but only for the period beginning with the date of claim and ending on the date the claim is determined or, if earlier, on the expiration of the period of 26 weeks from the date of claim; or

        (iii) another person [2 and] is in receipt of an invalid care allowance under Section 70 of the [1Benefits Act; or

        (iv) a person who has claimed either attendance allowance or disability living allowance and has an award of attendance allowance or the care component of disability living allowance at one of the two higher rates prescribed under section 72(4) of the Benefits Act for a period commencing after the date on which that claim was made.]

(4) In the case of a person to whom regulation 22 of the Income Support (General) Amendment No. 4 Regulations 1991 would have applied had he been entitled to income support and not a jobseeker's allowance, paragraph (1)(a) shall have effect as if for the reference to 16 hours there was substituted a reference to 24 hours.

(5) In determining for the purposes of paragraph (4) whether regulation 22 of the 1991 Regulations applies, regulations 23 and 24 of those Regulations shall have effect as if the references to income support included also a reference to income-based jobseeker's allowance.

(S.I. 1996 No. 207, reg. 51)

AMENDMENTS

1. Jobseekers's Allowance (Amendment) Regulations 1996 (S.I. 1996 No. 1516), reg. 9 (October 7, 1996).
2. Jobseekers's Allowance (Amendment) Regulations 1996 (S.I. 1996 No. 1516), reg. 20 and Sched. (October 7, 1996).
3. Social Security (Miscellaneous Amendments) Regulations 1997 (S.I. 1997 No. 454), reg. 2(5) (April 7, 1997).

DEFINITIONS

"the Act"—see reg. 1(3)
"attendance allowance"—*ibid.*
"the Benefits Act"—see Jobseekers Act, s.35(1).
"child"—*ibid.*
"claimant"—*ibid.*
"date of claim"—see reg. 1(3).
"disability living allowance"—*ibid.*
"earnings"—*ibid.*
"employment"—see reg. 3.
"partner"—see reg. 1(3).
"payment"—*ibid.*
"week"—*ibid.*
"young person"—*ibid.*, reg. 76.

GENERAL NOTE

A person who is in remunerative work is not entitled to JSA (s. 1(2)(e) of the Jobseekers Act). This applies to both contribution-based and income-based JSA. For income-based JSA there is also no entitlement if a person is a member of a couple whose partner is engaged in remunerative work (s. 3(1)(e) of the Jobseekers Act).

Para. (1) contains the basic rule. Remunerative work is work for 16 hours or more on average a week in the case of the claimant (sub-para. (a)), or a non-dependent (see reg. 2) or a child or young person who has left school and is treated as in relevant education until the next terminal date (sub-para. (c)). (Whether a non-dependent or such a child or young person is in remunerative work is relevant to income-based JSA: see para. 17 of Sched. 2 (non-dependent deductions from housing costs) and para. 18 of Sched. 6 (earnings of a child or young person not disregarded).) But in the case of a partner remunerative work is 24 hours or more a week (sub-para. (b)). Work is remunerative if payment is made for it, or it is done in the expectation of payment. See further the notes to reg. 5 of the Income Support Regulations.

Para. (2) is similar to reg. 5(2) and (3B) and para. (3)(a) and (b) to reg. 5(7) and (6) respectively of the Income Support Regulations. On para. (3)(c) see the note to reg. 53 below. Like reg. 5(2) of the Income Support Regulations, the opening words of para. (2) suggest a mechanism for determining the hours worked in all cases but sub-paras. (a), (b) and (c) do not cover all situations. In particular, a person who works for a regular number of contracted hours seems to fall outside para. (2) and inside para. (1).

There is great difficulty in applying the rules in this regulation (and reg. 52) in some cases. One example of this is school ancillary workers who work a regular number of hours during term-time but who do not work in the school holidays. See the discussion of this issue in the notes to reg. 5. The issue of whether school ancillary workers can claim benefit during the school holidays has been brought sharply into focus by the importing of the income support rules on remunerative work into both income-based and contribution-based JSA (previously some of these workers were able to claim unemployment benefit during school holiday periods). The structure of the JSA Regulations is not the same as the Income Support Regulations—in particular the JSA Regulations spread the rules for determining whether a person is, or is to be treated as, in remunerative work over two regulations; in addition, the rule in para. (2) (c) does not only apply where the person's hours of work fluctuate but operates independently (compare reg. 5(3B) of the Income Support Regulations, which only applies for the purposes of reg. 5(2)(b)(i)). But it is suggested that this does not materially affect the application of the rules for determining whether such "term-time only" workers are engaged in remunerative work during the school holidays; and see *CJSA 3816/1997.*

Paragraphs (4) and (5)

Regs. 22 to 24 of the Income Support (General) Amendment No. 4 Regulations 1991 (S.I. 1991 No. 1559) (see p. 486) provided transitional protection for existing income support claimants when the limit for remunerative work for income support was reduced from 24 to 16 hours per week in April 1992. The effect of paras. (4) and (5) is to continue that protection for claimants on the transfer to jobseeker's allowance.

Persons treated as engaged in remunerative work

52.—(1) Except in the case of a person on maternity leave or absent from work through illness, a person shall be treated as engaged in remunerative work during any period for which he is absent from work referred to in regulation 51(1) (remunerative work) where the absence is either without good cause or by reason of a recognised, customary or other holiday.

(2) For the purposes of an income-based jobseeker's allowance, the partner of a claimant shall be treated as engaged in remunerative work where—

    (a) the partner is or was involved in a trade dispute; and

    (b) had the partner claimed a jobseeker's allowance, section 14 (trade disputes) would have applied in his case; and

    (c) the claimant was not entitled to an income-based jobseeker's allowance when the partner became involved in the trade dispute;

and shall be so treated for a period of 7 days beginning on the date the stoppage of work at the partner's place of employment commenced, or if there was no stoppage of work, the date on which the partner first withdrew his labour in furtherance of the trade dispute.

(3) A person who was, or was treated as being, engaged in remunerative work and in respect of that work earnings to which [¹ regulation 98(1)(b) and (c)] (earnings of employed earners) applies are paid, shall be treated as engaged in remunerative work for the period for which those earnings are taken into account in accordance with Part VIII.

AMENDMENT

    1. Jobseekers's Allowance (Amendment) Regulations 1996 (S.I. 1996 No. 1516), reg. 20 and Sched. (October 7, 1996).

DEFINITIONS

    "maternity leave"—see reg. 1(3).
    "partner"—*ibid*.
    "remunerative work"—see reg. 51(1).
    "trade dispute"—see Jobseekers Act, s. 35(1).

GENERAL NOTE

    This provision deems people to be in remunerative work in certain circumstances.

Paragraph (1)

    See reg. 5(3) and (3A) of the Income Support Regulations and the notes to those paragraphs. See also the discussion under the heading "Term-time only workers" in the notes to reg. 5.

Paragraph (2)

    See the notes to s. 15 of the Jobseekers Act.

Paragraph (3)

    Where a person was in remunerative work and any "compensation payment" (defined in reg. 98(3)) or (within four weeks of termination or interruption of employment) holiday pay is paid, the person is treated as in remunerative work for the period covered by the payment (see regs. 94(2) and (6) to (9) for this period; note reg. 94(3) and (4) where both kinds of payment are made).

Persons treated as not engaged in remunerative work

53. A person shall be treated as not engaged in remunerative work in so far as—

  (a) he is engaged by a charity or a voluntary organisation or is a volunteer where the only payment received by him or due to be paid to him is a payment which is to be disregarded under regulation 103(2) and paragraph 2 of Schedule 7 (sums to be disregarded in the calculation of income other than earnings);

  (b) he is engaged on a scheme for which a training allowance is being paid;

  (c) he is in employment and—

    (i) lives in, or is temporarily absent from, a residential care home, a nursing home or residential accommodation, and either

    (ii) his, or his partner's, applicable amount falls to be calculated in accordance with Schedule 4 (applicable amounts of persons in residential care or nursing homes), or, as the case may be, paragraphs 5 to 9 or 15 to 17 of Schedule 5 (applicable amounts in special cases), or

    (iii) he or his partner satisfies the conditions specified in paragraph 3(2) of Part I of Schedule 1 (conditions of entitlement to a residential allowance);

  (d) he is engaged in employment as—

    (i) a part-time member of a fire brigade maintained in pursuance of the Fire Services Acts 1947 to 1959;

    (ii) an auxiliary coastguard in respect of coastal rescue activities;

    (iii) a person engaged part-time in the manning or launching of a lifeboat;

    (iv) a member of any territorial or reserve force prescribed in Part I of Schedule 3 to the Social Security (Contributions) Regulations 1979;

  (e) he is performing his duties as a councillor, and for this purpose "councillor" has the same meaning as in section 171F(2) of the Benefits Act;

  (f) he is engaged in caring for a person who is accommodated with him by virtue of arrangements made under any of the provisions referred to in paragraph 27 or 28 of Schedule 7 (sums to be disregarded in the calculation of income other than earnings), and is in receipt of any payment specified in that paragraph;

  (g) he is—

    (i) the partner of the claimant; and

    (ii) involved in a trade dispute; and

    (iii) not a person to whom regulation 52(2) applies,

and had he claimed a jobseeker's allowance, section 14 (trade disputes) would have applied in his case;

  (h) he is mentally or physically disabled, and by reason of that disability—

    (i) his earnings are reduced to 75 per cent. or less of what a person without that disability and working the same number of hours would reasonably be expected to earn in that employment or in comparable employment in the area; or

    (ii) his number of hours [¹of] work are 75 per cent. or less of what a person without that disability would reasonably be expected to undertake in that employment or in comparable employment in the area.

AMENDMENT

1. Jobseekers's Allowance (Amendment) Regulations 1996 (S.I. 1996 No. 1516), reg. 20 and Sched. (October 7, 1996).

DEFINITIONS

"the Benefits Act"—see Jobseekers Act, s.35(1).
"earnings"—see reg. 1(3).
"employment"—see reg. 3.
"partner"—see reg. 1(3).
"remunerative work"—see reg. 51(1).
"residential accommodation"—see reg. 1(3).
"residential allowance"—*ibid.*
"residential care home"—*ibid.*
"nursing home"—*ibid.*
"trade dispute"—see Jobseekers Act, s. 35(1).
"training allowance"—see reg. 1(3).
"voluntary organisation"—*ibid.*

GENERAL NOTE

See the notes to reg. 6 of the Income Support Regulations. Except for (g), the categories are the same as in paras. (a), (c), (d) and (g) to (k) of reg. 6. On (g), see the notes to s. 15 of the Jobseekers Act.

Unlike income support (see reg. 6(f)), carers are not covered by reg. 53. Instead, unless they are "employed as an earner", no account is taken of the hours they spend in caring in deciding whether they are engaged in remunerative work (see reg. 52(3)(c)).

There is no equivalent to reg. 6(b). So a childminder working 16 or more hours a week (or 24 if she is the partner of a claimant) may count as in remunerative work.

Relevant education

54.—(1) Only full-time education which is undertaken by a child or young person and which is not a course of advanced education shall be treated as relevant education for the purposes of the Act.

(2) A child or young person who is receiving full-time education for the purposes of section 142 of the Benefits Act (meaning of child) or who is treated as a child for the purposes of that section shall be treated as receiving full-time education.

(3) A young person who—
  (a) is a part-time student; and
  (b) before he became a part-time student fulfilled the requirements specified for a person falling within paragraph (2) of regulation 11 (part-time students); and
  (c) is undertaking a course of study, other than a course of advanced education or a course of study of a kind specified in head (i), (ii) or (iii) of the definition of "full-time student" in regulation 1(3),
shall not be treated as receiving relevant education.

(4) A young person to whom paragraph (3) applied and who has completed or terminated his course of part-time study shall not be treated as receiving relevant education.

[¹(5) A young person who is participating in the Full-Time Education and Training Option of the New Deal as specified in regulation 75(1)(b)(ii) shall not be treated as receiving relevant education.]

AMENDMENT

1. Social Security Amendment (New Deal) Regulations 1997 (S.I. 1997 No. 2863), reg. 5 (January 5, 1998).

DEFINITIONS

"the Benefits Act"—see Jobseekers Act, s.35(1).
"child"—*ibid.*

"course of advanced education"—see reg. 1(3).
"course of study"—*ibid.*
"part-time student"—*ibid.*
"young person"—*ibid*, reg. 76.

GENERAL NOTE

Paragraphs (1) and (2)
    Under s. 1(2)(g) of the Jobseekers Act a person is excluded from JSA if he is in relevant education (except if he is in a category who can claim income support while in relevant education (see regs. 57(2) and (4)(a) and reg. 61(1)(c)). Paras. (1) and (2) provide an exhaustive test of when a person is to be treated as receiving relevant education.
    Note that only a child or young person (that is, a person aged under 19: see reg. 76) can qualify and that relevant education does not include a course of advanced education (defined in reg. 1(3)). There is a reference over to the child benefit legislation and the reg. 54 question is one which under reg. 56A of the Adjudication Regulations need not be determined immediately by the JSA AO (reg. 56A(2)(b)). The AO can proceed on the assumption that the child benefit decision will be adverse to the claimant in the JSA sense, if it has not already been determined.
    See on the child benefit test, regs. 5, 6, 7, 7A, 7B, 7C and 7D of the Child Benefit (General) Regulations 1976 in *Bonner, Non-Means-Tested Benefits: the Legislation.* Contact hours of at least 12 per week are required. See *R(F) 1/93* in which the Commissioner held that supervised study (in reg. 5 of the Child Benefit Regulations) "would normally be understood to import the presence or close proximity of a teacher or tutor". Relevant education continues through temporary interruptions, like school holidays. When a person ceases actually to receive relevant education he is treated as doing so (unless he is in remunerative work of 24 hours or more a week and in certain other circumstances) until the next terminal date after he reaches compulsory school leaving age, or after he leaves relevant education if he stays on beyond compulsory school leaving age, or until he reaches 19 if this is earlier. The terminal dates are the first Monday in January, the first Monday after Easter Monday, or the first Monday in September. For England and Wales (but not Scotland) there is now a single school leaving date: the last Friday in June in the school year in which the child's 16th birthday falls (see the Education (School Leaving Date) Order 1997 (S.I. 1997 No. 1970)). Thus in 1999 children in England and Wales who reach 16 before September 1, 1999 can leave school on Friday, June 25, 1999; their terminal date will be Monday, September 6, 1999 and they count as being in relevant education until the Sunday after that date (unless the exceptions apply). For a child who stays on beyond compulsory school leaving age the three terminal dates are still applicable. There is also the possibility of a person remaining a "child" for an extension period of 12 weeks beyond the terminal date (or 16 weeks if the terminal date is the first Monday in September) if he is under 18, registered for work or training, not in remunerative work of 24 hours or more a week, not in receipt of income support/income-based JSA in his own right and not on Work Based Training for Young People (which has replaced Youth Training and other training provision for 16/17 year-olds). In England and Wales for a child whose school leaving date is June 25, 1999, the extension period will be September 13, 1999 to January 2, 2000.
    Note that some claimants may be able to receive income support though in relevant education (see reg. 13 of the Income Support Regulations), in which case they may also be eligible for JSA (see above). It will normally be better for most young people to claim income support in these circumstances, so as to avoid the risk of being sanctioned for not complying with the JSA labour market conditions.

Paragraphs (3) and (4)
    Under para. (3) a 16– to 18-year-old who is a part-time student (see the definitions of full-time and part-time student in reg. 1(3)) undertaking a course other than one of advanced education or of a kind within para. (b) of the definition of "full-time student" in reg. 1(3) who satisfies the conditions in sub-para (b) does not count as in relevant education (and will not so count after he finishes or leaves his part-time course (para. (4)). The conditions in para. (3)(b) are that for the three months before he started his course he was in receipt of JSA or incapacity benefit or income support while sick or on Work Based Training for Young People (which has replaced Youth Training and other training provision focused on 16/17 year-olds) or in the six months before the course was in receipt of any of these benefits or on Work Based Training for a total of three months and for the remainder of the time was in remunerative work (see reg. 51) or earning too much to be entitled to benefit (in both cases the three and the six months must be after the young person has ceased to be in relevant education).

See reg. 11 which may enable such a part-time student to be accepted as available for work even though his hours of study coincide with the times he is required to be available for employment.

Paragraph (5)

See the notes to reg. 75 for a brief summary of the New Deal for 18–24 year-olds. This provision ensures that a young person (*i.e.* aged under 19) who is on the Full-Time Education and Training option is not treated as in relevant education. Note that reg. 56A(2)(b) of the Adjudication Regulations has not been amended to include this paragraph, so it seems that if any question arises under this paragraph the reg. 56A procedure will not be available and the JSA AO will have to decide the question. This should not however cause any difficulty as presumably it will be relatively easy for the JSA AO to ascertain whether or not a young person is taking part in this New Deal option.

Short periods of sickness

55.—(1) Subject to the following provisions of this regulation, a person who—

    (a) [¹ has been awarded a jobseeker's allowance] or is a person to whom any of the circumstances mentioned in section 19(5) or (6) apply; and

    (b) proves to the satisfaction of the adjudication officer that he is unable to work on account of some specific disease or disablement; and

    (c) but for his disease or disablement, [¹ would satisfy] the requirements for entitlement to a jobseeker's allowance other than those specified in section 1(2)(a), (c) and (f) (available for and actively seeking employment, and capable of work),

shall be treated for a period of not more than 2 weeks as capable of work, except where the claimant states in writing that for the period of his disease or disablement he proposes to claim or has claimed incapacity benefit, severe disablement allowance or income support.

(2) The evidence which is required for the purposes of paragraph (1)(b) is a declaration made by the claimant in writing, in a form approved for the purposes by the Secretary of State, that he has been unfit for work from a date or for a period specified in the declaration.

(3) The preceding provisions of this regulation shall not apply to a claimant on more than two occasions in any one jobseeking period or where a jobseeking period exceeds 12 months, in each successive 12 months within that period and for the purposes of calculating any period of 12 months, the first 12 months in the jobseeking period commences on the first day of the jobseeking period.

(4) The preceding provisions of this regulation shall not apply to any person where the first day in respect of which he is unable to work falls within 8 weeks of—

    (a) an entitlement of his to incapacity benefit, severe disablement allowance or statutory sick pay; or

    (b) an entitlement to income support where the person claiming a jobseeker's allowance satisfied the requirements for a disability premium by virtue of paragraph 12(1)(b) of Schedule 2 to the Income Support Regulations.

AMENDMENT

1. Jobseeker's Allowance and Income Support (General) (Amendment) Regulations 1996 (S.I. 1996 No. 1517), reg. 17 (October 7, 1996).

DEFINITIONS

    "adjudication officer"—see Jobseekers Act, s. 35(1).
    "capable of work"—see Jobseekers Act, s. 35(2) and Sched. 1, para. 2.
    "claimant"—see Jobseekers Act, s. 35(1).
    "jobseeking period"—see regs. 1(3) and 47(1)–(3).

GENERAL NOTE

Para. (1) allows a JSA award to continue while a person is incapable of work for up to two weeks (subject to a limit of two such periods in any 12 months (para. (3)) by treating him as capable of work for that period. This does not apply if the person was entitled to incapacity benefit, severe disablement allowance, statutory sick pay or income support with a disability premium on the grounds of his incapacity for work in the eight weeks before the first day that he became unfit for work. Presumably the intention is to avoid a claimant having to chop and change between benefits where his period of incapacity is only likely to be short. However, a person can still choose to claim an incapacity benefit in these circumstances if he wishes to do so.

PART IV

YOUNG PERSONS

Interpretation of Part IV

57.—(1) In this Part—

"the Careers Service" means a person of any description with whom the Secretary of State has made an arrangement under section 10(1) of the Employment and Training Act 1973 and any person to whom he has given a direction under section 10(2) of that Act;

"child benefit extension period" means

(a) in the case of a person who ceases to be treated as a child by virtue of section 142(1)(a) of the Benefits Act (meaning of child) or regulation 7 of the Child Benefit (General) Regulations 1976 (circumstances in which a person who has ceased to receive full-time education is to continue to be treated as a child)

   (i) on or after the first Monday in September, but before the first Monday in January of the following year, the period ending with the last day of the week which falls immediately before the week which includes the first Monday in January in that year;

   (ii) on or after the first Monday in January but before the Monday following Easter Monday in that year, the period ending with the last day of the week which falls 12 weeks after the week which includes the first Monday in January in that year;

   (iii) at any other time of the year, the period ending with the last day of the week which falls 12 weeks after the week which includes the Monday following Easter Monday in that year;

(b) in the case of a person who was not treated as a child by virtue of section 142(1)(a) of the Benefits Act immediately before he was 16 and who has not been treated as a child by virtue of Regulation 7 of the Child Benefit (General) Regulations 1976 (interruption of full-time education), the period ending with the date determined in accordance with sub-paragraph (i), (ii) or (iii) of paragraph (a) as if he had ceased full-time education on the first date on which education ceased to be compulsory for a person of his age in England and Wales or, if he is resident in Scotland, in Scotland;

and in this sub-paragraph "week" means a period of 7 days beginning with a Monday and "year" means a period of 12 months beginning on 1st January;

"chronically sick or mentally or physically disabled" has the same meaning as in regulation 13(3)(b) of the Income Support Regulations (circumstances in which persons in relevant education may be entitled to income support);

"full-time education" has the same meaning as in regulation 1 of the Child
Benefit (General) Regulations 1976;

"suitable training" means training which is suitable for that young person in
vocationally relevant respects, namely his personal capacity, aptitude, his
preference, the preference of the training provider, the level of approved
qualification aimed at, duration of the training, proximity and prompt
availability of the training;

"training" in sections 3, 16 and 17 and in this Part except in regulation 65
read with section 7 and except in the phrase "suitable training", means
training for which persons aged under 18 are eligible and for which
persons aged 18 to 24 may be eligible provided in England and Wales,
directly or indirectly by a Training and Enterprise Council [³, or a Chamber of Commerce, Training and Enterprise, under its contractual arrangement with the Secretary of State] and, in Scotland, directly or indirectly
by a Local Enterprise Company pursuant to its arrangement with, as the
case may be, Scottish Enterprise or Highlands and Islands Enterprise
(whether that arrangement is known as an Operating Contract or by any
other name);

"treatment" means treatment for a disease or bodily or mental disablement
by or under the supervision of a person qualified to provide medical
treatment, physiotherapy or a form of treatment which is similar to, or
related to, either of those forms of treatment;

[¹"young person" means a person who has reached the age of 16 but not the
age of 18 and who does not satisfy the conditions in section 2 or whose
entitlement to a contribution-based jobseeker's allowance has ceased as
a result of sub-section (1) of section 5.]

(2) A young person falls within this paragraph if he is

(a) a member of a married couple where the other member of that couple
   (i) has reached the age of 18 or
   (ii) is a young person who has registered for employment and training
     in accordance with regulation 62 or
   (iii) is a young person to whom paragraph (4) applies;

(b) a person who has no parent nor any person acting in the place of his
parents;

(c) a person who—
   (i) is not living with his parents nor any person acting in the place of
     his parents; and
   (ii) immediately before he attained the age of 16 was
     (aa) [² in England and Wales] being looked after by a local authority
       pursuant to a relevant enactment which placed him with some
       person other than a close relative of his [² . . .]
     (bb) in custody in any institution to which the Prison Act 1952
       applies or under [² the Prisons (Scotland) Act 1989; or]
    [²(cc) in Scotland, in the care of a local authority under a relevant
       enactment and whilst in that care was not living with his parents
       or any close relative.]

(d) a person who is in accommodation which is other than his parental home
and which is other than the home of a person acting in the place of his
parents, who entered that accommodation—
   (i) as part of a programme of rehabilitation or resettlement, that pro-
     gramme being under the supervision of the probation service or a
     local authority; or
   (ii) in order to avoid physical or sexual abuse; or
   (iii) because of a mental or physical handicap or illness and he needs
     such accommodation because of his handicap or illness;

(e) a person who is living away from his parents and any person who is acting in the place of his parents in a case where his parents are or, as the case may be, that person is, unable financially to support him and his parents are, or that person is—

    (i) chronically sick or mentally or physically disabled; or

    (ii) detained in custody pending trial or sentence upon conviction or under a sentence imposed by a court; or

    (iii) prohibited from entering or re-entering Great Britain;

(f) a person who of necessity has to live away from his parents and any person acting in the place of his parents because—

    (i) he is estranged from his parents and that person; or

    (ii) he is in physical or moral danger; or

    (iii) there is a serious risk to his physical or mental health.

[² (3)(a) In England and Wales, any reference in this regulation to a person acting in place of a person's parents includes a reference to—

    (i) where the person is being looked after by a local authority or voluntary organisation which places him with a family, a relative of his, or some other suitable person, the person with whom the person is placed, whether or not any payment is made to him in connection with the placement; or

    (ii) in any other case, any person with parental responsibility for the child, and for this purpose "parental responsibility" has the meaning it has in the Children Act 1989 by virtue of section 3 of that Act; and

(b) in Scotland, any reference in this regulation to a person acting in place of a person's parents includes a reference to a local authority or voluntary organisation where the person is in its care under a relevant enactment, or to a person with whom the person is boarded out by a local authority or voluntary organisation whether or not any payment is made by it.]

(4) This paragraph applies to

(a) a person who falls under any of the following paragraphs of Schedule 1B to the Income Support Regulations

Paragraph 1	(lone parents)
Paragraph 2	(single person looking after foster children)
Paragraph 3	(persons temporarily looking after another person)
Paragraph 4	(persons caring for another person)
Paragraph 10	(disabled students)
Paragraph 11	
Paragraph 12	
Paragraph 13	(blind persons)
Paragraph 14	(pregnancy)
Paragraph 15	(persons in education)
Paragraph 18	(refugees)
Paragraph 21	(persons from abroad)
Paragraph 23	(member of couple looking after children while other member temporarily abroad)
Paragraph 28	(persons in receipt of a training allowance);

(b) a person who is a member of a couple and is treated as responsible for a child who is a member of his household;

(c) a person who is laid off or kept on short-time, who is available for employment in accordance with section 6 and Chapter II of Part II read with regulation 64 and who has not been laid off or kept on short-time for more than 13 weeks;

(d) a person who is temporarily absent from Great Britain because he is taking a member of his family who is a child or young person abroad for treatment, and who is treated as being in Great Britain in accordance

with regulation 50(1)(b) or whose entitlement to income support is to
continue in accordance with regulation 4(3) of the Income Support Regulations and who is not claiming a jobseeker's allowance or income
support;

(e) a person who is incapable of work and training by reason of some disease
or bodily or mental disablement if, in the opinion of a medical practitioner, that incapacity is unlikely to end within 12 months because of
the severity of that disease or disablement.

AMENDMENTS

1. Jobseekers's Allowance (Amendment) Regulations 1996 (S.I. 1996 No. 1516), reg. 4 (October
7, 1996).
2. Jobseeker's Allowance and Income Support (General) (Amendment) Regulations 1996 (S.I.
1996 No. 1517), reg. 11 (October 7, 1996).
3. Jobseeker's Allowance (Amendment) (No. 2) Regulations 1998 (S.I. 1998 No. 1698), reg. 2
(August 4, 1998).

DEFINITIONS

"the Benefits Act"—see Jobseekers Act, s.35(1).
"child"—*ibid*.
"close relative"—see reg. 4.
"couple"—see reg. 1(3).
"employment"—see reg. 4.
"married couple"—see Jobseekers Act, s. 35(1).
"a person who is kept on short-time"—see reg. 4.
"a person who is laid off "—*ibid*.
"relative"—see reg. 1(3).
"voluntary organisation"—*ibid*.

GENERAL NOTE

Subsection (1)
"*young person*". To be entitled to income-based JSA, a person must in general be 18 (s.
3(1)(f)(i) of the Jobseekers Act). This Part of the Regulations deals with the exceptions to this
general exclusion (see s. 3(1)(f)(ii) and (iii) of the Jobseekers Act). The lower age limit does
not apply to contribution-based JSA, although in practice people below 18 will be unlikely to
satisfy the contribution conditions (see s. 2(1) of the Jobseekers Act). If a 16- or 17-year-old
does qualify for contribution-based JSA, he does not count as a young person for the purposes
of this Part.
The categories of 16- and 17-year-olds who under regs. 58–61 are entitled to income-based
JSA are similar (but not identical) to those who qualified for income support before October 7,
1996. (16- and 17-year-olds who are entitled to benefit while in relevant education can still
claim income support under reg. 13 of the Income Support Regulations, see para. 15 of Sched.
1B to those Regulations.) In *some* cases (see reg. 61), a 16- or 17-year-old who is eligible for
income-based JSA will also be eligible for income support. Because of the stricter benefit
regime associated with JSA, it will usually be better for such a young person to claim income
support. If the claimant does not come within one of the prescribed circumstances for JSA there
is still the possibility of a severe hardship direction being made by the Secretary of State under
s. 16 of the Jobseekers Act, which then exempts the young person from the lower age limit
(see s. 3(1)(f)(ii)).
It is important to remember that satisfying an exception only gets the young person past the age
condition for income-based JSA. All the other conditions of entitlement (see ss. 1 and 3 of the
Jobseekers Act) must be met. In order to meet the labour market conditions the young person will
have to (i) register for work and training with the Careers Service (defined in reg. 57(1)), or in
certain circumstances with the Employment Service, (reg. 62); (ii) be available for work, although
if he has not been "sanctioned" for a training-related "offence" or refusing a job opportunity or
voluntary unemployment or losing a job through misconduct, laid off or put on short-time or
accepted an offer to enlist in the armed forces within the next eight weeks, he can restrict his
availability to employment where the employer provides "suitable training" (defined in reg. 57(1))

(reg. 64); (iii) actively seek work and training (reg. 65); and (iv) enter into a jobseeker's agreement (reg. 66).

Subsections (2) to (4)
    See the notes to regs. 58–61.

Young persons to whom section 3(1)(f)(iii) applies

58. For the period specified in relation to him, a young person to whom regulation 59, 60 or 61 applies shall be regarded as a person within prescribed circumstances for the purposes of section 3(1)(f)(iii) of the Act (conditions of entitlement for certain persons under the age of 18).

DEFINITION

    "young person"—see reg. 57(1).

GENERAL NOTE

    This regulation, together with regs. 59, 60 and 61, prescribes the circumstances in which, and the periods for which, 16- and 17-year-olds can be exempted from the lower age limit of 18 imposed by s. 3(1)(f)(i) of the Jobseekers Act. See the notes to regs. 59, 60 and 61.

Young persons in the child benefit extension period

59.—(1) For the period specified in paragraph (2), this regulation applies to a young person who falls within paragraph (2) of regulation 57.
    (2) The period in the case of any person falling within paragraph (1) is the child benefit extension period, except where regulation 61(1)(d) or (e) applies.

DEFINITIONS

    "child benefit extension period"—see reg. 57(1).
    "young person"—*ibid.*

GENERAL NOTE

    A 16- or 17-year-old who comes within any of the categories in reg. 57(2) is exempt from the ordinary lower age limit for income-based JSA imposed by s. 3(1)(f)(i) of the Jobseekers Act until the end of the child benefit extension period, unless reg. 61(1)(d) or (e) applies (see below). See reg. 57(1) for the definition of the "child benefit extension period" and the notes to reg. 54. Note that reg. 59 only gets the young person past the age condition for income-based JSA. All the other conditions of entitlement must be met (see the note to the definition of "young person" in reg. 57(1)).
    The categories in reg. 57(2) are broadly the same as those in the former Part II of Sched. 1A to the Income Support Regulations (revoked on October 7, 1996) (16- or 17-year-old exempt from the age test for income support during the child benefit extension period). Note, however, the slightly different conditions in reg. 57(2)(a)(ii) (the young person must have registered for employment *and* training), and in reg. 57(4)(c) and (d).
    Reg. 61(1)(d) and (e) apply to a young person who is otherwise eligible for JSA who either cannot register with the Careers Service because of an emergency there (head (d)) or would suffer hardship because of the extra time it would take for him to register at the Careers Service (head (e)). If the young person registers at the Employment Service instead he will be exempt from the lower age limit for the period allowed in reg. 61(2)(c) or (d) (normally two weeks if reg. 61(1)(d) applies or 5 days in the case of reg. 61(1)(e)).
    See also regs. 60 and 61.

Young persons at the end of the child benefit extension period

60.—(1) For the period specified in relation to him in paragraph (2), this regulation applies to a young person who is—

(a) a person who has ceased to live in accommodation provided for him by a local authority under Part III of the Children Act 1989 (local authority support for children and families) and is of necessity living away from his parents and any person acting in place of his parents;

(b) a person who has been discharged from any institution to which the Prison Act 1952 applies or from custody under the Criminal Procedure (Scotland) Act 1975 after the child benefit extension period and who is a person falling within paragraph (2) of regulation 57.

(2)(a) Except where regulation 61(1)(d) or (e) applies, the period in the case of a person falling within paragraph 1(a) is the period which begins on the day on which that paragraph first applies to that person and ends on the day before the day on which that person attains the age of 18 or the day at the end of a period of 8 weeks immediately following the day on which paragraph 1(a) first had effect in relation to him, whichever is the earlier; and this period may include any week in which regulation 7 of the Child Benefit (General) Regulations 1976 (circumstances in which a person who has ceased to receive full-time education is to continue to be treated as a child) also applies to that person;

(b) except where regulation 61(1)(d) or (e) applies, the period in the case of any person falling within paragraph 1(b) is the period beginning on the day after he was discharged, and ends on the last day of the period of 8 weeks beginning with the date on which the period began or on the day before the date on which that person attains the age of 18, whichever first occurs.

(3) In this regulation, "week" means any period of 7 consecutive days.

DEFINITIONS

"child benefit extension period"—see reg. 57(1).
"young person"—*ibid*.

GENERAL NOTE

This provision is similar to the former reg. 13A(4)(c) and (d) of the Income Support Regulations (now revoked). The effect, with reg. 58, is to exempt 16- and 17-year-olds from the ordinary lower age limit for income-based JSA (see s. 3(1)(f)(i) of the Jobseekers Act) if they leave local authority care and have to live away from their parents and any substitute (para. (1)(a)), or if they have been discharged from custody after the end of the child benefit extension period and one of the conditions in reg. 57(2) applies (para. (1)(b)). Except where reg. 61(1)(d) or (e) applies (see the note to reg. 59 above as to when these apply), the exemption lasts for eight weeks, or until the person reaches 18, if sooner (para. (2)). If the exemption is under para. (1)(a), any week in the child benefit extension period can count in the eight weeks (it is understood that this is the intended meaning, although para. (2)(a) refers to reg. 7, not reg. 7D, of the Child Benefit Regulations).

Note that there is no equivalent to the former reg. 13A(4)(a) (incapacity for work and training which is likely to end within 12 months). Such a young person could claim income support: see para. 7 of Sched. 1B to the Income Support Regulations.

It is important to remember that reg. 60 only gets the young person past the age condition for income-based JSA. All the other conditions of entitlement must be met (see the note to the definition of "young person" in reg. 57(1)).

See also reg. 61.

Other young persons in prescribed circumstances

61.—(1) For the period specified in relation to him in paragraph (2), this regulation applies to a young person—

(a) who is a person who is laid off or kept on short-time and is available for employment in accordance with section 6 and Chapter II of Part II read with regulation 64;

(b) who is a member of a couple and is treated as responsible for a child who is a member of his household;

(c) who falls within a prescribed category of persons for the purposes of section 124(1)(e) of the Benefits Act and who is not claiming income support;

(d) to whom section 3(1)(f)(ii) does not apply, who is a person falling within paragraph (2) of regulation 57, sub-paragraph (a) or (b) of paragraph (1) of regulation 60 or sub-paragraph (b) or (c) and who is unable to register with the Careers Service because of an emergency affecting the Careers Service and registers with the Employment Service in accordance with regulation 62(2);

(e) to whom section 3(1)(f)(ii) does not apply, who is a person falling within paragraph (2) of regulation 57, sub-paragraph (a) or (b) of paragraph (1) of regulation 60 or sub-paragraph (b) or (c) and who would suffer hardship because of the extra time it would take him to register with the Careers Service and registers with the Employment Service in accordance with regulation 62(3);

(f) who has accepted a firm offer of enlistment by one of the armed forces with a starting date not more than 8 weeks after the offer was made who was not in employment or training at the time of that offer and whose jobseeker's allowance has never been reduced in accordance with regulation 63 or section 19(5)(b) or (c) or section 19(6)(c) or (d) read with regulation 68 or rendered not payable in accordance with section 19(6)(a) or (b) read with Part V.

(2)(a) The period in the case of any person falling within paragraph (1)(a) is the period starting with the date on which he was laid off or first kept on short-time and ending on the date on which he ceases to be laid off or kept on short-time or the day before the day he attains the age of 18 or at the expiry of the 13 week period starting with the date of the lay off, or date he was first kept on short-time, whichever first occurs;

(b) except where paragraph (1)(d) or (e) applies, the period in the case of any person falling within paragraph (1)(b) or (c) is the period until the day before that person attains the age of 18 or until paragraph (1)(b) or (c) ceases to apply, whichever first occurs;

(c) the period in the case of any person falling within paragraph (1)(d) is the period starting with the date of registration with the Employment Service and ending on the day on which the person is next due to attend in accordance with regulation 23 or on the date on which the period calculated in accordance with regulation 59(2) or 60(2) or sub-paragraph (b) would have expired, whichever first occurs;

(d) the period in the case of any person falling within paragraph 1(e) is the period starting on the date of registration with the Employment Service and ending five days after that date or on the day after the day on which he registered with the Careers Service, or on the date on which the period calculated in accordance with regulation 59(2) or 60(2) or sub-paragraph (b) would have expired, whichever first occurs;

(e) the period in the case of any person falling within paragraph 1(f) is the period starting with the date of claim and ending with the day before the day on which he is due to enlist or the day before he attains the age of 18, whichever first occurs.

(3) In this regulation "week" means a period of 7 consecutive days.

Definitions

"the Benefits Act"—see Jobseekers Act, s.35(1).
"the Careers Service"—see reg. 57(1).

"child"—see Jobseekers Act, s. 35(1).
"couple"—see reg. 1(3).
"a person who is kept on short-time"—see reg. 4.
"a person who is laid off"—*ibid.*

GENERAL NOTE

This sets out additional circumstances in which a 16- or 17-year-old will be exempt from the lower age limit imposed by s. 3(1)(f)(i) of the Jobseekers Act. Para. (1) defines the categories covered and para. (2) the length of the exemption.

Para. (1) (a). A person who is laid off or on short-time working and who is available for work (see reg. 64) will be exempt for up to 13 weeks (para. (2)(a)).

Para. (1) (b). A person who is a member of a couple and responsible for a child (see regs. 77 and 78) is exempt until 18 (except where para. (1)(d) or (1(e) applies, see below) (para. (2)(b)).

Para. (1) (c). A person who falls within para. 4ZA of, and Sched. 1B to, the Income Support Regulations (which prescribe the categories of people entitled to income support under s. 124(1)(e) of the SSCBA), and who is not claiming income support, is exempt until 18 (except where para. (1)(d) or (e) applies, see below) (para. (2)(b)). As the age limit for income support is now 16 (see s. 124(1)(a) of the SSCBA, amended with effect from October 7, 1996), it will be better for most young people who come within Sched. 1B to claim income support so as to avoid the risk of being sanctioned for not complying with the JSA labour market conditions.

Para. (1) (d) and (e). These sub-paras. do not apply if a severe hardship direction has been made. Except for a young person who is laid off or on short-time (sub-para. (a)) or has accepted an offer to enlist in the armed forces in the next eight weeks (sub-para. (f)), a 16- or 17-year-old who is eligible for income-based JSA must register with the Careers Service for work and training (reg. 62). If such a person is unable to register with the Careers Service because of "an emergency affecting the Careers Service" (sub-para. (d)), or would suffer hardship because of the extra time it would take for him to register with the Careers Service (sub-para. (e)), and registers with the Employment Service instead, he will be exempt from the lower age limit for JSA under sub-para. (d) until he is next due to attend (para. (2)(c)) or under sub-para. (e) for up to five days (para. (2)(d)) (or until he ceases to be eligible for JSA under reg. 59 or 60 or reaches 18, if this is earlier).

Para. (1) (f). This applies to a person who has accepted an offer (made when he was not employed or in training) to enlist in the armed forces within the next eight weeks and who has never been sanctioned for a training-related "offence" or refusing a job opportunity or voluntary unemployment or losing a job through misconduct. The exemption lasts until he enlists (para. (2)(e)).

Note that reg. 61 only gets the young person past the age condition for income-based JSA. All the other conditions of entitlement must be met (see the note to the definition of "young person" in reg. 57(1)).

Registration

62.—(1) Except in the circumstances set out in paragraphs (2) and (3) a young person to whom section 3(1)(f)(ii) or (iii) applies other than one falling within regulation 61(1)(a) or (f), must register with the Careers Service for both employment and training.

(2) A young person who is unable to register with the Careers Service because of an emergency affecting the Careers Service such as a strike or fire must register with the Employment Service for both employment and training.

(3) A young person who would suffer hardship because of the extra time it would take him to register with the Careers Service must register with the Employment Service for both employment and training.

DEFINITIONS

"the Careers Service"—see reg. 57(1)
"employment"—see reg. 4.
"training"—see reg. 57(1).
"young person"—*ibid.*

Except for a young person who is laid off or on short-time, or who has never been sanctioned for a training-related "offence" or refusing a job opportunity or voluntary unemployment or losing a job through misconduct and has accepted an offer to enlist in the armed forces within the next eight weeks, a 16- or 17-year-old who is exempt from the lower age limit for income-based JSA has to register with the Careers Service for work and training (para. (1)). If such a young person is unable to register with the Careers Service because of an emergency, *e.g.* a strike or fire (para. (2)), or would suffer hardship because of the extra time it would take for him to register with the Careers Service (para. (3)) he has to register with the Employment Service instead. See the note to reg. 61(1)(d) and (e) above.

While paras. (2) or (3) apply, he will be deemed to have entered into a jobseeker's agreement (reg. 66(2)).

See also regs. 64 to 66.

Reduced payments under section 17

63.—(1) Except as provided in paragraph (3), the amount of an income-based jobseeker's allowance which would otherwise be payable to a young person shall be reduced by[¹, if he is a single person or a lone parent,] a sum equal to 40% of the amount applicable in his case by way of a personal allowance determined [¹ in accordance with paragraph 1(1) or 1(2) of Schedule 1 (as the case may be) or, if he is a member of a couple, a sum equal to 40% of the amount which would have been applicable in his case if he had been a single person determined in accordance with paragraph 1(1) of Schedule 1] for the period set out in paragraph (2) if

    (a) he was previously entitled to an income-based jobseeker's allowance and that entitlement ceased by virtue of the revocation of a direction under section 16 because he had failed to pursue an opportunity of obtaining training or rejected an offer of training;

    (b) his allowance has at any time in the past been reduced in accordance with this regulation or in accordance with regulation 68 because he has done an act or omission falling within section 19(5)(b) or (c) or rendered not payable in accordance with section 19(6)(a) or (b) read with Part V and he has—

        (i) failed to pursue an opportunity of obtaining training without showing good cause for doing so,

        (ii) rejected an offer of training without showing good cause for doing so or

        (iii) failed to complete a course of training and no certificate has been issued to him under subsection (4) of section 17 with respect to that failure;

    (c) he has—

        (i) done an act or omission falling within section 16(3)(b)(i) or (ii) and has not shown good cause for doing so or done an act or omission falling within section 19(5)(b)(i), (ii) or (iv) without good cause or done an act or omission falling within section 19(5)(b)(i), (ii), or (iv) for which he was regarded as having good cause in accordance with regulation 67(1) and

        (ii) after that act or omission failed to complete a course of training and no certificate has been issued to him under subsection (4) of section 17 with respect to that failure

    and at the time he did the act or omission falling within sub-paragraph (i) he was a new jobseeker;

    (d) he has—

        (i) failed to complete a course of training and no certificate has been issued to him under subsection (4) of section 17 with respect to that failure or done an act or omission falling within section 19(5)(b)(iii) without good cause or done an act or omission falling within section 19(5)(b)(iii) for which he was regarded as having good cause in accordance with regulation 67(1) and

  (ii) after that failure he has failed to complete a course of training and no certificate has been issued to him under subsection (4) of section 17 with respect to that failure and on the day before the day he first attended the course referred to in sub-paragraph (i) he was a new jobseeker; or

 (e) he has failed to complete a course of training and no certificate has been issued to him under subsection (4) of section 17 with respect to that failure and on the day before he first attended the course he was not a new jobseeker; or

 (f) he has failed to complete a course of training and no certificate has been issued to him under subsection (4) of section 17 with respect to that failure and he lost his place on the course through his misconduct.

(2) The period shall start with the date on which the first severe hardship direction is made under section 16 after the act or acts referred to in paragraph (a), (b), (c), (d), (e) or (f) of paragraph (1) have taken place and shall end fourteen days later.

(3) In the case of a young person who is pregnant or seriously ill who does an act falling within sub-paragraphs (a)-(f) of paragraph (1), the reduction shall be [¹ if he is a single person or a lone parent] of 20 per cent of the amount applicable in his case by way of a personal allowance [¹ determined in accordance with paragraph 1(1) or 1(2) of Schedule 1 (as the case may be) or, if he is a member of a couple, of 20 per cent of the amount which would have been applicable in his case if he had been a single person determined in accordance with paragraph 1(1) of Schedule 1].

(4) For the purposes of this regulation, "new jobseeker" means a young person who has not since first leaving full-time education been employed or self-employed for 16 or more hours per week or completed a course of training or failed to complete a course of training and no certificate has been issued to him to show good cause for that failure under subsection (4) of section 17 or done an act or omission falling within section 19(5)(b)(iii) without good cause or done an act or omission falling within section 19(5)(c).

(5) A reduction under paragraph (1) or (3) shall, if it is not a multiple of 5p, be rounded to the nearest such multiple or, if it is a multiple of 2.5p but not of 5p, to the next lower multiple of 5p.

<small>AMENDMENT</small>

1. Social Security and Child Support (Miscellaneous Amendments) Regulations 1997 (S.I. 1997 No. 827), reg. 2 (April 7, 1997).

<small>DEFINITIONS</small>

   "full-time education"—see reg. 57(1).
   "income-based jobseeker's allowance"—see Jobseekers Act, s. 1(4).
   "training"—see reg. 57(1).
   "young person"—*ibid.*

<small>GENERAL NOTE</small>

Paragraph (1)
   Section 20(2) of the Act provides that where a severe hardship direction is in force and the young person has without good cause failed to pursue an opportunity, or rejected an offer, of training or failed to complete a training course, a s. 19(5) sanction will not be applied. Instead, the circumstances in which income-based JSA payable under a severe hardship direction will be paid at a reduced

rate are set out in this regulation. The reduction is 40 per cent of the appropriate single person or lone parent personal allowance under para. 1 of Sched. 1, or 20 per cent if the young person is pregnant or seriously ill (not defined) (para. (3)), and lasts for two weeks (para. (2)). If the person is a member of a couple, the same reduction is applied as if he was a single claimant.

The effect of para. (1) is that in some cases, *e.g.* where the person was previously a "new jobseeker," the reduction will only be applied where it is a "second offence". The detailed rules provide for the reduction to be imposed if:

(i) a previous severe hardship direction was revoked because the person failed to pursue an opportunity, or rejected an offer, of training without good cause (sub-para (a)); or

(ii) at any time in the past the person's JSA has been subject to a reduction under this regulation, or reg. 68 for a training-related "offence" or stopped because of voluntary unemployment or losing a job through misconduct, and then without good cause he fails to pursue an opportunity, or rejects an offer, or fails to complete a course, of training (sub-para. (b)); or

(iii) while he was a new jobseeker (defined in para. (4)) he failed to pursue an opportunity, or rejected an offer, of training without good cause while a severe hardship direction was in force, or did not avail himself of, or failed to apply for or accept after having been notified of, or failed to attend, a place on a training scheme or employment programme either without good cause, or only with deemed good cause under reg. 67(1), and then fails without good cause to complete a course of training (sub-para. (c)); or

(iv) he has failed to complete a course of training without good cause while a severe hardship direction was in force, or given up a training scheme or employment programme place either without good cause or only with deemed good cause under reg. 67(1), and was a new jobseeker (defined in para. (4)) on the day before he started the course, and then fails to complete a course of training without good cause (sub-para. (d)); or

(v) he has failed to complete a course of training without good cause and was not a new jobseeker on the day before he started the course (sub-para. (e)); or

(vi) he has lost his training place through misconduct before finishing the course (sub-para. (f)).

The above is a summary of the very detailed rules in para. (1) but the reader is advised to check the text of the regulation where there is any doubt as to whether a particular sub-paragraph applies.

Paragraph (4)

A new jobseeker is a 16- or 17-year-old who since leaving full-time education (see reg. 57(1)) has not been employed or self-employed for 16 hours or more a week, or finished a training course, or failed to finish a training course without good cause or given up without good cause or lost through misconduct a training scheme or employment programme place.

Availability for employment

64.—(1) A young person is required to be available for employment in accordance with section 6 and Chapter II of Part II except as provided in paragraphs (2) and (3).

(2) A young person whose jobseeker's allowance has not been reduced in accordance with regulation 63 or in accordance with regulation 68 because he has done an act or omission falling within section 19(5)(b) or (c) or section 19(6)(c) or (d) or rendered not payable in accordance with section 19(6)(a) or (b) read with Part V and who does not fall within regulation 61(1)(a) or (f) may restrict his availability for employment to employment where suitable training is provided by the employer.

(3) A young person who places restrictions on the nature of employment for which he is available as permitted by paragraph (2) does not have to show that he has reasonable prospects of securing employment notwithstanding those restrictions.

DEFINITIONS

"employment"—see reg. 4.
"suitable training"—see reg. 57(1)

GENERAL NOTE

In order to be entitled to JSA, a young person has to be available for work under the normal rules (see s. 6 of the Jobseekers Act and regs. 5 to 17) (para. (1)). However, provided that he is not subject to a sanction under reg. 63 or under reg. 68 for a training-related "offence" or refusing a job opportunity or voluntary unemployment or losing a job through misconduct, a 16- or 17-year-old can restrict his availability to employment where the employer provides "suitable training" (para. (2)). See reg. 57(1) for the definition of suitable training. This does not apply to a young person who has been laid off or is on short-time working, or who has never been sanctioned for a training-related "offence" or refusing a job opportunity or voluntary unemployment or losing a job through misconduct and has accepted an offer to join the armed forces in the next eight weeks. Presumably this is because such a young person is only expected to be unemployed for a short time and so it would not be reasonable to require an employer to provide him with training. The young person does not have to show that he still has reasonable prospects of obtaining work (para. (3)). Note also reg. 67(2).

In addition, see regs. 62 and 65 to 66.

Active seeking

65.—(1) Subject to the following paragraphs, Section 7 and Chapter III of Part II shall have effect in relation to a young person as if "employment" included "training".

(2) Subject to paragraphs (4) and (5), in order to have the best prospects of securing employment or training a young person can be expected to have to take more than one step on one occasion in any week unless taking one step on one occasion is all that it is reasonable for that person to do in that week, and unless it is reasonable for him to take only one step on one occasion, he can be expected to have to take at least one step to seek training and one step to seek employment in that week.

(3) Subject to paragraph (4), steps which it is reasonable for a young person to be expected to have to take include, in addition to those set out in regulation 18(2)—

    (a) seeking training and

    (b) seeking full-time education.

(4) Paragraphs (1), (2) and (3) do not apply to a young person falling within regulation 61(1)(a) or (f).

(5) Paragraphs (1) and (2) do not apply to a young person who has had his jobseeker's allowance reduced in accordance with regulation 63 or regulation 68 because he has done an act or omission falling within section 19(5)(b) or (c) or Section 19(6)(c) or (d) or rendered not payable in accordance with section 19(6)(a) or (b) read with Part V but paragraph (3) does apply to such a young person.

(6) "Training" in section 7 and in this regulation means suitable training.

DEFINITIONS

"employment"—see reg. 4.
"full-time education"—see reg. 57(1).
"suitable training"—*ibid.*
"young person"—*ibid.*

GENERAL NOTE

The normal rules in relation to actively seeking work apply to young people (see s. 7 of the Jobseekers Act and regs. 18 to 22) but they must seek training (which means suitable training (para. (6)) as well as work (para. (1)). See reg. 57(1) for the definition of "suitable training". They are expected to take more than one step (see reg. 18(2)) each week, including at least one step to find work and one to find training, unless it is reasonable to take only one step that week (para. (2)). In the case of a young person, "steps" include, as well as those referred to in reg. 18(2), seeking training and seeking full-time education (para. (3)).

These special rules do not apply to a young person who is laid off or on short-time working or who has never been sanctioned for a training-related "offence" or refusing a job opportunity or voluntary unemployment or losing a job through misconduct and has accepted an offer to join the armed forces within the next eight weeks (para. (4)). Presumably this is because they are only expected to be unemployed for a short time and so it would not be reasonable to require them to seek training or education in that time, only work.

Para. (5) appears to provide that a young person whose JSA is subject to a sanction under reg. 63 or under reg. 68 for a training-related "offence" or refusing a job opportunity or voluntary unemployment or losing a job through misconduct is not required to seek training as well as work, since it states that paras. (1) and (2) do not apply to such a person. But this is followed by the somewhat contradictory statement that para. (3) does apply; that is, such a young person *is* required to seek training and full-time education. The policy intention apparently is that a 16- or 17-year-old who has been sanctioned should only be seeking training (and education) with a view to finding work and not as an end in itself.

See also regs. 62, 64, 65A and 66.

[¹Attendance, information and evidence

65A. A young person who does not fall within regulation 61(1)(a) or (f) shall, if the Secretary of State requires him to do so, provide, in addition to the declaration specified in regulation 24(6), a declaration to the effect that since making a claim for a jobseeker's allowance or since he last provided a declaration in accordance with this regulation he has been actively seeking suitable training to the extent necessary to give him his best prospects of securing suitable training save as he has otherwise notified the Secretary of State.]

AMENDMENT

1. Jobseeker's Allowance and Income Support (General) (Amendment) Regulations 1996 (S.I. 1996 No. 1517), reg. 12 (October 7, 1996).

DEFINITIONS

"suitable training"—see reg. 57(1).
"young person"—*ibid.*

GENERAL NOTE

This regulation provides that a 16- or 17-year-old may be required to declare that he has been actively seeking suitable training as well as work when he signs on. There is the usual exception from this rule for a young person who has been laid off or is on short-time working, or who has never been sanctioned for a training-related "offence" or refusing a job opportunity or voluntary unemployment or losing a job through misconduct and has accepted an offer to join the armed forces within the next eight weeks.

See also regs. 62, 64, 65 and 66.

The jobseeker's agreement

66.—(1) In a jobseeker's agreement with a young person, other than one falling within regulation 61(1)(a) or (f), the following information is required in addition to that prescribed in chapter V of Part II: a broad description of the circumstances in which the amount of the person's benefit may be reduced in accordance with section 17 and regulation 63, or may be rendered not payable in accordance with section 19 read with Part V or may be payable at a reduced rate in accordance with sections 19 and 20 and regulation 68.

(2) A young person is to be treated as having entered into a jobseeker's agreement and as having satisfied the condition mentioned in section 1(2)(b) as long as the circumstances set out in [¹regulation 62(2) or 62(3) apply.]

AMENDMENT

1. Jobseekers's Allowance (Amendment) Regulations 1996 (S.I. 1996 No. 1516), reg. 8 and Sched. (October 7, 1996).

DEFINITIONS

"jobseeker's agreement"—see Jobseekers Act, s. 9(1).
"young person"—see reg. 57(1).

GENERAL NOTE

See the notes to ss. 9 to 11 of the Jobseekers Act and regs. 31 to 45 for the rules relating to jobseeker's agreements.

Paragraph (1)
A 16- or 17-year-old has to enter into a jobseeker's agreement as a condition of receiving JSA in the normal way. But the agreement must contain additional information as to the sanctions that can be applied. There is the usual exception from this rule for a young person who has been laid off or is on short-time working, or who has never been sanctioned for a training-related "offence" or refusing a job opportunity or voluntary unemployment or losing a job through misconduct and has accepted an offer to join the armed forces within the next eight weeks.

Paragraph (2)
A young person will be deemed to have entered into a jobseeker's agreement while he has to register with the Employment Service for work and training instead of the Careers Service due to an emergency or because the extra time involved in registering with the Careers Service would cause him hardship.

Sanctions

67.—(1)Without prejudice to any other circumstances in which a person may be regarded as having good cause for any act or omission for the purposes of section 19(5)(b), and in addition to the circumstances listed in regulation 73, a young person is to be regarded as having good cause for any act or omission for the purposes of section 19(5)(b) where
   (a) this is the first occasion on which he has done an act or omission falling within section 19(5)(b) and he has not while claiming a jobseeker's allowance failed to pursue an opportunity of obtaining training without good cause or rejected an offer of training without good cause or failed to complete a course of training and no certificate has been issued to him under subsection (4) of section 17 with respect to that training; and
   (b) at the time he did the act or omission falling within section 19(5)(b)(i), (ii) or (iv) he was [¹ . . .] a new jobseeker or, in the case of an act or omission falling with section 19(5)(b)(iii), at the time he first attended the scheme or programme he was [¹ . . .] a new jobseeker.
   (2) Without prejudice to any other circumstances in which a person may be regarded as having good cause for any act or omission for the purposes of section 19(6)(c) or (d), a young person is to be regarded as having good cause for any act or omission for the purposes of section 19(6)(c) or (d) where the employer did not offer suitable training unless he falls within regulation 61(1)(a) or (f) or his jobseeker's allowance has been reduced in accordance with regulation 63 or in accordance with regulation 68 because he has done an act or omission falling within section 19(5)(b) or (c) or section 19(6)(c) or (d) or rendered not payable in accordance with section 19(6)(a) or (b) read with Part V.
   (3) For the purposes of this regulation, "new jobseeker" means a young person who has not since first leaving full-time education been employed or self-employed for 16 or more hours per week or completed a course of training or failed to complete a course of training and no certificate has been issued to

him to show good cause for that failure under subsection (4) of section 17 or done an act or omission falling within section 19(5)(b)(iii) without good cause or done an act or omission falling within section 19(5)(c).

AMENDMENT

1. Jobseeker's Allowance and Income Support (General) (Amendment) Regulations 1996 (S.I. 1996 No. 1517), reg. 13 (October 7, 1996).

DEFINITIONS

"full-time education"—see reg. 57(1).
"suitable training"—*ibid.*
"training"—*ibid.*
"young person"—*ibid.*

GENERAL NOTE

See the notes to s. 19 of the Jobseekers Act for the circumstances in which sanctions may be applied.

Paragraph (1)
The broad effect of paragraph (1) is to give a "new jobseeker" (see para. (3)) a second chance in certain circumstances where a sanction might otherwise be imposed. He will be deemed to have good cause for the purposes of s.19(5)(b) if this is the first time he has refused or given up, etc. a training scheme or employment programme opportunity.

Paragraph (2)
This provides that unless a young person has been sanctioned under reg. 63 or under reg. 68 for a training-related "offence" or refusing a job opportunity or voluntary unemployment or losing a job through misconduct, he will have good cause for failing to apply for or accept a notified job, or for not taking advantage of a reasonable opportunity of employment if the employer does not offer suitable training (defined in reg. 57(1)). There is the usual exception from this rule for a young person who has been laid off or is on short-time working, or who has never been sanctioned for a training-related "offence" or refusing a job opportunity or voluntary unemployment or losing a job through misconduct and has accepted an offer to join the armed forces within the next eight weeks. See also s. 64 which provides that a 16- or 17-year-old may limit his availability to employment where the employer provides suitable training.

Paragraph (3)
See the note to reg. 63(4).

Reduced amount of allowance

68.—(1) Subject to paragraphs (2) and (4), the amount of an income-based jobseeker's allowance which would otherwise be payable to a young person shall be reduced by [¹, if he is a single person or a lone parent,] a sum equal to 40% of the amount applicable in his case by way of a personal allowance determined [¹ in accordance with paragraph 1(1) or 1(2) of Schedule 1 (as the case may be) or, if he is a member of a couple, a sum equal to 40% of the amount which would have been applicable in his case if he had been a single person determined in accordance with paragraph 1(1) of Schedule 1] for a period of two weeks from the beginning of the first week after the adjudication officer's decision where the young person has done any act or omission falling within section 19(5) or within 19(6)(c) or (d), unless the young person reaches the age of 18 before that two week period expires, in which case the allowance shall be payable at the full rate applicable in his case from the date he reaches the age of 18.

(2) Subject to paragraph (4), in a case where the young person or any member of his family is pregnant or seriously ill the amount of an income-based job-

seeker's allowance which would otherwise be payable to the young person shall be reduced by [¹, if he is a single person or a lone parent,] a sum equal to 20% of the amount applicable in his case by way of a personal allowance determined [¹ in accordance with paragraph 1(1) or 1(2) of Schedule 1 (as the case may be) or, if he is a member of a couple, a sum equal to 20% of the amount which would have been applicable in his case if he had been a single person determined in accordance with paragraph 1(1) of Schedule 1] for a period of two weeks from the beginning of the first week after the adjudication officer's decision where the young person has done any act or omission falling within section 19(5) or within 19(6)(c) or (d), unless the young person reaches the age of 18 before that two week period expires, in which case the allowance shall be payable at the full rate applicable in his case from the date he reaches the age of 18.

(3) A reduction under paragraph (1) or (2) shall, if it is not a multiple of 5p, be rounded to the nearest such multiple or if it is a multiple of 2.5p but not of 5p, to the next lower multiple of 5p.

(4) If a young person's claim for an income-based jobseeker's allowance is terminated before the expiry of the period determined in accordance with paragraphs (1) and (2), and he makes a fresh claim for the allowance, it shall be payable to him at the reduced rate determined in accordance with paragraph (1) or (2) for the balance of the time remaining of that two weeks, unless the young person reaches the age of 18 before that two week period expires, in which case the allowance shall be payable at the full rate applicable in his case from the date he reaches the age of 18.

(5) An income-based jobseeker's allowance shall be payable to a young person at the full rate applicable in his case after the expiry of the two week period referred to in paragraphs (1) and (2).

AMENDMENT

1. Social Security and Child Support (Miscellaneous Amendments) Regulations 1997 (S.I. 1997 No. 827), reg. 3 (April 7, 1997).

DEFINITIONS

"adjudication officer"—see Jobseekers Act, s. 35(1).
"income-based jobseeker's allowance"—see Jobseekers Act, s. 1(4).
"young person"—see reg. 57(1).

GENERAL NOTE

See the notes to s. 19 of the Jobseekers Act as to the circumstances in which sanctions may be applied.

The rules as to the amount and duration of a benefit sanction are different from those for adults. A person aged 18 or over who is sanctioned will only be paid JSA (at a reduced rate) if he is in hardship; see regs. 140–146. If a young person is "sanctioned" under s. 19(5) or (6)(c) or (d), his income-based JSA will continue to be paid but at a reduced rate. (Note that this does not apply if the sanction is imposed under s. 19(6)(a) and (b); in such a case the young person will only qualify for JSA if he can show hardship.) The reduction is 40 per cent of the appropriate single person or lone parent personal allowance under para. 1 of Sched. 1, or 20 per cent if the young person or any member of the family is pregnant or seriously ill. If the person is a member of a couple the same reduction is applied as if he was a single claimant. It lasts for two weeks but will cease if the young person becomes 18 within that time. If the young person stops receiving JSA before the end of the two weeks but then claims JSA again, the reduction will be applied for the unexpired balance of the two-week period or until the person reaches 18.

PART V

SANCTIONS

Prescribed period for purposes of section 19(2)

69. The prescribed period for the purposes of section 19(2) shall begin on the first day of the week following the date on which a jobseeker's allowance is determined not to be payable to the claimant and shall be—

(a) 4 weeks, in any case in which

(i) a jobseeker's allowance is determined not to be payable to the claimant in circumstances falling within section 19(5), and

[¹(ii) either—

(aa) where the determination mentioned in (i) above does not relate to an employment programme specified in regulation 75(1)(a)(ii), or the training scheme specified in regulation 75(1)(b)(ii), on a previous occasion the jobseeker's allowance was determined not to be payable to him in circumstances falling within section 19(5), or

(bb) where the determination mentioned in (i) above relates to an employment programme specified in regulation 75(1)(a)(ii), or the training scheme specified in regulation 75(1)(b)(ii), on a previous occasion the jobseeker's allowance was determined not to be payable to him in circumstances falling within section 19(5) that relate to such a programme or scheme, and]

(iii) the first date on which the jobseeker's allowance was not payable to him on that previous occasion falls within the period of 12 months preceding the date of the determination mentioned in (i) above;

(b) 2 weeks, in any other case.

AMENDMENT

1. Social Security Amendment (New Deal) Regulations 1997 (S.I. 1997 No. 2863), reg. 6 (January 5, 1998).

DEFINITIONS

"claimant"—see Jobseekers Act, s. 35(1).
"employment programme"—see reg. 75(1)(a).
"training scheme"—see reg. 75(1)(b).
"week"—see reg. 75(3).

GENERAL NOTE

This sets the period of sanction for non-compliance with a jobseeker's direction or loss or refusal of a training scheme or employment programme place (see s. 19(2) and (5) of the Jobseekers Act). A sanction will start on the first day of the benefit week (defined in reg. 1(3)) following the decision to apply it and will be for two weeks. But it will last for four weeks if the decision to impose it is within 12 months of a previous fixed sanction (the 12 months runs from the start of the earlier sanction).

Note that from January 5, 1998, sub-para. (ii) distinguishes between previous fixed sanctions in connection with the New Deal options for 18–24 year-olds ("New Deal sanctions") (head (bb)) and those that relate to jobseeker's directions or other employment programme or training schemes (head (aa)). A New Deal sanction is one that is imposed for failing without good cause to apply for or accept a notified place on a New Deal employment programme or training scheme, or failing without good cause to attend the programme or scheme, or giving the place up without good cause or losing it through misconduct. (Such a sanction could also be imposed for neglecting without good cause to avail oneself of a reasonable opportunity of a place on a New Deal option (see s. 19(5)(b)(i)) but is less likely to apply given the way the New Deal is intended to operate (see the note to reg. 75)). All other sanctions, even if they are imposed while the claimant is on the New Deal, will not be treated as sanctions under the New Deal. Thus *any* sanction relating to a jobseeker's direction will not count under head (bb). If a claimant is sanctioned under the New Deal the sanction will only be for four weeks if he has had a previous New Deal sanction in the last 12 months (but note that if the claimant had been sanctioned under the Project Work pilot scheme within the last 12 months a first New Deal sanction could be for four weeks. Project Work was abolished in May 1998; for a discussion of the conditions in the JSA (Pilot Scheme) Regulations 1996 (S.I. 1996 No. 1307) for the imposition of a Project Work sanction see *CJSA 5600/1997*). Any other sanction will not be relevant, even if it was incurred within the last 12 months. However, the reverse is not the case. A New Deal sanction will affect the period of any other sanction imposed under s. 19(5) which is imposed within the succeeding 12 months (head (aa)). See the note to reg. 75 for a brief summary of the New Deal for 18–24 year-olds.

The claimant may be eligible for a hardship payment: see regs. 141(6) and 142(5). But note that only claimants who fall within a "vulnerable group" (see reg. 140(1)) are eligible for such payments where a New Deal sanction has been imposed. Other claimants will not be eligible for a hardship payment for any period of a New Deal sanction (see regs. 140(4A) and 140A)

See further the notes to s. 19(5).

Sanctions of discretionary length

70. In determining a period under section 19(3) an adjudication officer shall take into account all the circumstances of the case and, in particular, the following circumstances—

   (a) where the employment would have lasted less than 26 weeks, the length of time which it was likely to have lasted;
   (b) in a case falling within section 19(6)(a) in which the employer has indicated an intention to re-engage the claimant, the date when he is to be re-engaged;
   (c) where the claimant has left his employment voluntarily and the hours of work in that employment were 16 hours or less a week, the rate of pay and hours of work in the employment which he left; and
   (d) where the claimant left his employment voluntarily or has neglected to avail himself of a reasonable opportunity of employment, any mitigating circumstances of physical or mental stress connected with his employment.

DEFINITIONS

   "claimant"—see Jobseekers Act, s. 35(1).
   "employment"—see reg. 75(4).
   "week"—see reg. 75(2).

GENERAL NOTE

See the notes to s. 19(3) of the Jobseekers Act.

Voluntary redundancy

71.—(1) A claimant is to be treated as not having left his employment voluntarily—

   (a) where he has been dismissed by his employer by reason of redundancy after volunteering or agreeing to be so dismissed, [¹ . . .]
   (b) where he has left his employment on a date agreed with his employer without being dismissed, in pursuance of an agreement relating to voluntary redundancy, [¹ or
   (c) where he has been laid-off or kept on short-time to the extent specified in sub-section (1) of section 88 of the Employment Protection

(Consolidation) Act 1978, and has complied with the requirements of that section.]

(2) In paragraph (1) "redundancy" means one of the facts set out in paragraphs (a) and (b) of section 81(2) of the Employment Protection (Consolidation) Act 1978.

AMENDMENT

1. Jobseeker's Allowance (Amendment) Regulations 1996 (S.I. 1996 No. 1516), reg. 5 (October 7, 1996).

DEFINITIONS

"claimant"—see Jobseekers Act, s. 35(1).
"employment"—see reg. 75(4).

GENERAL NOTE

Section 19(7) of the Jobseekers Act allows a person to be deemed not to have left his employment voluntarily in prescribed circumstances. This regulation sets out the situations when this will apply. See further the notes to s. 19(7) in *Bonner, Non-Means-Tested Benefits: the Legislation.*

Good cause for the purposes of section 19(5)(a) and (6)(c) and (d)

72.—(1) This regulation shall have effect for the purposes of section 19 (circumstances in which a jobseeker's allowance is not payable).

(2) Subject to paragraph (3), in determining whether a person has good cause for any act or omission for the purposes of section 19(5)(a) and (6)(c) and (d) the matters which are to be taken into account shall include the following—

(a) any restrictions on availability which apply in the claimant's case in accordance with regulations 6, 7, 8 [², 13 and 17A], having regard to the extent of any disparity between those restrictions and the requirements of the vacancy in question;

(b) any condition or personal circumstance of that person which indicates that a particular employment or carrying out the jobseeker's direction would be likely to or did—
    (i) cause significant harm to his health; or
    (ii) subject him to excessive physical or mental stress;

(c) the fact that the failure to undertake a particular employment or to carry out the jobseeker's direction resulted from a religious or conscientious objection sincerely held;

(d) any caring responsibilities which would, or did, make it unreasonable for the person to undertake a particular employment or carry out the jobseeker's direction;

(e) the time it took, or would normally take, for the person to travel from his home to the place of the employment or to a place mentioned in the jobseeker's direction and back to his home by a route and means appropriate to his circumstances and to the employment or to the carrying out of the jobseeker's direction;

(f) the expenses which were, or would be, necessarily and exclusively incurred by the person for the purposes of the employment or of carrying out the jobseeker's direction, together with any expenses of travelling to and from the place of the employment or a place mentioned in the jobseeker's direction by a route and means appropriate to his circumstances, if those expenses did, or would, represent an unreasonably high proportion of—

(i) in the case of employment, the remuneration which it is reasonable to expect that he would derive from that employment; or

(ii) in any other case, the income which he received, or would receive, while carrying out the jobseeker's direction.

(3) For the purposes of paragraph (2)(f), in considering whether expenses did, or would, represent an unreasonably high proportion of remuneration or income, the principle shall apply that the greater the level of remuneration or income the higher the proportion thereof which it is reasonable should be represented by expenses.

[²(3A) Without prejudice to any other circumstances in which a person may be regarded as having good cause for any act or omission for the purposes of section 19(6)(c) and (d), a person to whom regulation 17A(2) applies, in respect of whom an employment officer has determined that he may undertake a qualifying course, and who is undertaking such a course as a full-time student, is to be regarded as having good cause for any act or omission for the purposes of section 19(6)(c) and (d) where—

(a) the act or omission took place within a period of 4 weeks before the end of his qualifying course or of his examinations; or

(b) the employment consists of employment for which he is not required to be available in accordance with regulation 17A(3)(c) unless it is permanent full-time employment.

(3B) In paragraph (3A)(b), "full-time employment" means remunerative work as defined in regulation 51(1)(a).]

(4) Where a person has undergone training for a particular kind of employment for a period of not less than 2 months, he is to be regarded for a period of 4 weeks beginning with the day on which the training ends as having good cause for any act or omission for the purposes of section 19(5)(a) and (6)(c) and (d), for—

(a) refusing or failing to apply for, or refusing to accept, employment of any other kind when offered to him;

(b) neglecting to avail himself of a reasonable opportunity of employment of any other kind;

(c) refusing or failing to carry out a jobseeker's direction given to him with a view to assisting him to find employment of any other kind.

(5) A person is to be regarded as having good cause for any act or omission for the purposes of section 19(5)(a) and (6)(c) and (d) if, and to the extent that, the reason for that act or omission—

(a) results from restrictions on availability which apply in the claimant's case for the period permitted in accordance with regulations 16 and 17;

(b) results from the fact that the claimant is, in accordance with regulation 5(1) to (3) and (5), excepted from any requirement to be able to take up employment immediately, or is, in accordance with regulation 5(4), excepted from any requirement to be able to take up employment at a time when he is not available;

(c) [¹ ...]

[¹ (5A) A person is to be regarded as having good cause for any act or omission for the purposes of section 19(6)(c) and (d) if—

(a) in a case where it has been agreed that the claimant may restrict his hours of availability to less than 24 hours a week, the employment in question is for less than 16 hours a week; or

(b) in a case not falling within sub-paragraph (a), the employment is for less than 24 hours a week.]

(6) Subject to paragraphs (8) and (9), a person is not to be regarded as having good cause for any act or omission for the purposes of section 19(5)(a) and (6)(c) and (d) if, and to the extent that, the reason for that act or omission relates to—

(a) Subject to paragraph (7), his income or outgoings or the income or out-goings of any other member of his household, or the income or outgoings which he or any other member of his household would have if he were to become employed or to carry out the jobseeker's direction, or did have whilst carrying out the jobseeker's direction, but for the purposes of this sub-paragraph a person's outgoings shall not include any expenses taken into account under paragraph (2)(f);

(b) the time it took, or would normally take, for the person to travel from his home to the place of the employment, or a place mentioned in the jobseeker's direction, and back to his home where that time was or is normally less than one hour either way by a route and means appropriate to his circumstances and to the employment, or to the carrying out of the jobseeker's direction, unless, in view of the health of the person or any caring responsibilities of his, that time was or is unreasonable.

(7) Paragraph (6)(a) shall not apply—

(a) where the claimant has agreed a restriction on the level of remuneration he was prepared to accept under regulations 13(3) and 16; or

(b) the employment is remunerated only by commission.

(8) A person shall be regarded for the purposes of section 19(6)(d) as having good cause for neglecting to avail himself of an opportunity of employment unless the situation is a qualifying former employment of that person.

(9) For the purposes of paragraph (8) a situation is a qualifying former employment of any person if—

(a) it is employment with an employer for whom he has previously worked or with an employer who has succeeded that employer; and

(b) not more than 12 months have elapsed between—

(i) the date when he last worked for that employer and

(ii) the date when the question under section 19(6)(d) arose or, as the case may be, arises, and

(c) the terms and conditions of employment in the situation are not less favourable than those in the situation which he held when he last worked for that employer.

AMENDMENTS

1. Social Security (Miscellaneous Amendments) Regulations 1997 (S.I. 1997 No. 454), reg. 2(6) (April 7, 1997).

2. Social Security Amendment (New Deal) Regulations 1998 (S.I. 1998 No. 1274), reg. 7 (June 1, 1998).

DEFINITIONS

"caring responsibilities—see reg. 4.
"claimant"—see Jobseekers Act, s. 35(1).
"employment"—see reg. 75(4).
"employment officer"—see reg. 4.
"examination"—*ibid.*
"full-time student"—see reg. 1(3).
"qualifying course"—see regs. 4, 17A(7).
"week"—see reg. 75(2) and (3).

GENERAL NOTE

This regulation is concerned with good cause for the purposes of s. 19(5)(a) (non-compliance with a jobseeker's direction), (6)(c) (refusal or failure to apply for or accept a notified job) and (6)(d) (claimant's neglect to avail himself of a reasonable opportunity of employment). See the notes to s. 19(5) and (6). In addition, note s. 19(9) of the Jobseekers Act which states that, except where regulations otherwise provide (in this regard see paras. (2)(f), (5)(a), (7) and (9)(c)), the rate of pay is to be disregarded where good cause is in issue (but see the note to s.19(9) for the effect of the national minimum wage legislation on this rule). However, subject to this regulation and s. 19(9), the existing case law on good cause will continue to be relevant when considering questions of good cause under s. 19(5)(a), (6)(c) and (d). In *Crewe v. Social Security Commissioner* [1982] 2 All E.R. 745, 751 Slade L.J. suggested that good cause meant "reasonable cause" and involved a lower burden than showing "just cause", which required the balancing of individual interests against the interests of all the contributors to the National Insurance Fund. For detailed discussion of the extensive case law on good cause, see *Bonner, Non-Means-Tested Benefits: the Legislation.* Note also s. 20(1) of the Act which allows a claimant to refuse a job that is vacant because of a trade dispute.

This provision does three things. First, para. (2) lists a number of factors to be taken into account (the list is not exhaustive) when considering whether a claimant has good cause under s. 19(5)(a), (6)(c) or (d). Secondly, circumstances that will constitute good cause for these purposes are set out in paras. (4) and (5); see in addition paras. (3A) and (5A) which applies for the purposes of s. 19(6)(c) and (d) only and paras. (8) and (9) which relate to s. 19(6)(d) only. Thirdly, subject to paras. (8) and (9), para. (6) specifies factors that are not good cause for the purposes of s. 19(5)(a), (6)(c) and (d).

Paragraph (2)

This sets out some of the factors to be taken into account when considering whether a claimant had good cause for not complying with a jobseeker's direction under s. 19(5)(a), refusing or failing to apply for or accept a notified job under s. 19(6)(c) or neglecting to avail himself of a reasonable opportunity of employment under s. 19(6)(d). Other circumstances not listed may be relevant and these factors are not accorded any particular priority.

Sub-para. (a). Where the claimant has been allowed to place restrictions on his availability, the extent to which the requirements of the job on offer conflict with those restrictions has to be considered.

Sub-para. (b). If a particular job or complying with the jobseeker's direction, having regard to the claimant's condition or personal circumstances, is likely to "cause significant harm to his health" or "subject him to excessive physical or mental stress", this has to be taken into account. If this has happened in the past this will obviously be relevant (para. (b) uses the words "is likely to or did"). The *Adjudication Officer's Guide* states that medical evidence is not always necessary and gives as an example of good cause a claimant with asthma being required to work in a dusty atmosphere (see paras. 39469–76).

Sub-para. (c). This allows for a claimant's religious or conscientious objections to be given weight.

Sub-para. (d). Any caring responsibilities (defined in reg. 4) which make it unreasonable for the claimant to do the job or comply with the jobseeker's direction have to be considered.

Sub-para. (e). Travelling time (either normal or actual) "by a route and means appropriate to [the claimant's] circumstances and to the employment or to the carrying out of the jobseeker's direction" may be relevant. But this sub-paragraph has to be read in conjunction with para. (6)(b) which provides that travelling time (either normal or actual) of less than one hour each way does not constitute good cause unless the time taken is unreasonable in view of the claimant's health or caring responsibilities (defined in reg. 4). Thus if normal travelling time exceeds one hour each way the *Adjudication Officer's Guide* accepts that the claimant will usually have good cause, unless it would be reasonable to expect him to spend longer travelling, *e.g.* due to the limits he has placed on his availability or because he lives in a remote location (see para. 39498).

Sub-para. (f). If expenses "necessarily and exclusively incurred … for the purposes of the employment or of carrying out the jobseeker's direction" together with any travel expenses amount to an unreasonably high proportion of the claimant's expected pay (or income while carrying out the direction) this has to be taken into account. The greater a claimant's pay, the more he will be expected to spend on expenses (para. (3)). Note that the reference is not to expenses incurred *in the performance* of the employment, etc., (*cf.* reg. 98(1)(e)) but to those incurred for the purposes of the employment. This may mean that expenses to enable the claimant to carry out the employment (*e.g.* child care expenses) could be considered, although this is not the view taken in the *Adjudication Officer's Guide* (see paras. 39506 and 39686). See the note to reg. 35(1)(f) of the Income Support Regulations.

Paragraph (3A)

This provides that a claimant who is treated as available for employment under reg. 17A while attending a full-time employment related course will have automatic good cause for the purposes of s.19(6)(c) or (d) in the following situations. The first is where the act or omission took place in the four weeks before the end of his course or examinations (sub-para. (a)). The second is if the employment was not a full-time (*i.e.* 16 hours or more (para. (3B)) permanent job or was not casual work for which the claimant has to be available during course vacations (see reg. 17A(3)(c)) (sub-para. (b)).

Paragraphs (4) and (5)
These paragraphs specify the circumstances which will automatically constitute good cause for the purposes of s. 19(5)(a), (6)(c) and (d). See also paras. (3A) and (5A) which applies for the purposes of s. 19(6)(c) and (d) only and para. (8) which concerns good cause in relation to s. 19(6)(d) only.
The effect of para. (4) is that if a claimant has undertaken training of not less than two months for a particular kind of work he will not have to apply for or accept, etc., any other kind of work for a period of four weeks starting from the day the training ends. Note that training is not defined for the purposes of para. (4) and so is not restricted to training schemes provided or funded by the government but will include, for example, training that the claimant has paid for himself (see *AOG*, para. 39414).
Para. (5)(a) covers claimants during their permitted period and those who are laid off or on short time (see the notes to regs. 16 and 17). They will have good cause for not applying for or accepting employment etc., that does not accord with their permitted restrictions. Para. (5)(b) does the same for claimants who are not required to be immediately available under reg. 5(1)–(3) (carers, voluntary workers, those providing a service and those working less than 16 hours a week who are required to give notice) and for those who have been allowed to restrict their availability to certain times under regs. 7, 13 and 17.

Paragraph (5A)
This provides that a claimant will have automatic good cause for the purposes of s. 19(6)(c) or (d) if he refuses work of less than 24 hours a week, or less than 16 hours a week if he has been allowed to restrict his availability to less than 24 hours a week. (On the meaning of "week" in para. (5A) see reg. 75(2) and (3)). It is not necessary for the number of hours to be the specific reason for refusing the job. Thus even if the reason for the refusal of a job for less than 24/16 hours a week is, *e.g.* the hourly rate of pay, the claimant will still be able to rely on para. (5A). However, note that para. (5A) does not apply for the purposes of s. 19(5)(a) (jobseeker's directions (contrast para. (5)). Whether or not jobseeker's directions requiring claimants to apply for jobs of less than 24/16 hours a week will in fact be issued remains to be seen. The policy intention, apparently, is to retain the flexibility to issue such job descriptions, with a view to encouraging people back into full-time employment through the experience of part-time work. See para. 39651 of the *Adjudication Officer's Guide* which takes the view that a claimant will not have good cause just because the work the direction was aimed at was for less than 24/16 hours a week. But it does seem somewhat of a nonsense for an employment officer to be able to direct a person to apply for such a job when he is statutorily deemed to have good cause for refusing to do so.

Paragraphs (6) and (7)
Under para. (6)(a) a claimant will not have good cause for not complying with a jobseeker's direction or refusing or failing to apply for or accept a notified job, if the reason is the amount (or the amount if he were to take the job/carry out the direction) of his income or outgoings, or those of any member of his household. This rule also applies for the purposes of s.19(6)(d) (neglecting to avail himself of a reasonable job opportunity) but only if the job counts as a "qualifying former employment" (see paras. (8) and (9)). On membership of the same household see the notes to SSCBA, s. 137(1) under "*married couple*". The reference to the income and outgoings of other members of the claimant's household thus extends the scope of this provision beyond the members of the claimant's family (in the social security sense) to include, *e.g.* an adult non-dependant provided he is a member of the claimant's household. It should also be noted that para. (6)(a) refers to a claimant's (or any member of his household's) "income", not just his rate of pay from the employment in question.
But the following constraints on the ambit of this provision should be noted. First, see para. (2)(f) under which unreasonably high employment costs, combined with any travel expenses, are a factor in considering good cause. Secondly, para. (7) specifically provides that para. (6)(a) does not apply if the claimant has been allowed to place restrictions on his rate of pay under reg. 13(3) (physical or mental condition) or reg. 16 (permitted period), or where the employment pays commission only. Thus a claimant may be able to show good cause for not applying for or accepting a notified job, etc., in these circumstances. But in addition a claimant may also have good cause if he has been allowed to restrict the rate of pay he will accept under reg. 8 (reasonable prospects of finding

employment) (see para. (2)(a)). (Note that under reg. 9 any restriction that a claimant is allowed to place on the rate of pay he will accept is limited to six months, but see the note to reg. 13(3).) Thirdly, note the effect of the national minimum wage legislation (see the note to s.19(9) of the Jobseekers Act). Fourthly, a claimant's (or his household's) outgoings (or income) may also be relevant when considering other parts of para. (2), *e.g.* his personal circumstances under para. (2)(b) or possibly his caring responsibilities under para. (2)(d).

Under para. (6)(b), travelling time (either normal or actual) of less than one hour each way will not constitute good cause, unless the time taken is unreasonable in view of the claimant's health or caring responsibilities (defined in reg. 4). See the note to para. (2)(e) above. Again, sub-para. (b) does not apply in the case of neglect to avail under s. 19(6)(d) unless the employment on offer is a "qualifying former employment" (see paras. (8) and (9)).

Paragraphs (8) and (9)

These paragraphs restrict the operation of s. 19(6)(d) by providing that any claimant will automatically have good cause unless the employment opportunity of which he has neglected to avail himself is a "qualifying former employment". Employment counts as a qualifying former employment if the claimant worked for that employer (or his predecessor) within the last 12 months and the terms and conditions on offer are not less favourable than those of the previous job. The effect of this rule is that the main policing of the refusal of work will take place under s. 19(6)(c), a prerequisite of which is that the claimant has been notified of the job by an employment officer.

Good cause for the purposes of section 19(5)(b)

73.—(1) This regulation shall have effect for the purposes of section 19 (circumstances in which a jobseeker's allowance is not payable).

(2) Without prejudice to any other circumstances in which a person may be regarded as having good cause for any act or omission for the purposes of section 19(5)(b), a person is to be regarded as having good cause for any act or omission for those purposes if, and to the extent that, the act or omission is attributable to any of the following circumstances—

  (a) the claimant in question was suffering from some disease or bodily or mental disablement on account of which—

    (i) he was not able to attend the relevant training scheme or employment programme in question;

    (ii) his attendance would have put at risk his health; or

    (iii) his attendance would have put at risk the health of other persons;

  (b) the claimant's failure to participate in the training scheme or employment programme resulted from a religious or conscientious objection sincerely held;

  (c) the time it took, or would normally have taken, for the claimant to travel from his home to the training scheme or employment programme and back to his home by a route and means appropriate to his circumstances and to the scheme or programme exceeded, or would normally have exceeded, one hour in either direction or, where no appropriate training scheme or employment programme is available within one hour of his home, such greater time as is necessary in the particular circumstances of the nearest appropriate scheme or programme;

  (d) the claimant had caring responsibilities and—

    (i) no close relative of the person he cared for and no other member of that person's household was available to care for him; and

    (ii) in the circumstances of the case it was not practical for the claimant to make other arrangements for the care of that person;

  (e) the claimant was attending court as a party to any proceedings, or as a witness or as a juror;

   (f) the claimant was arranging or attending the funeral of a close relative or close friend;

  (g) the claimant was engaged in—
      (i) the manning or launching of a lifeboat; or
     (ii) the performance of duty as a part-time member of a fire brigade;

  (h) the claimant was required to deal with some domestic emergency; or

   (i) the claimant was engaged during an emergency in duties for the benefit of others;

  [¹(j) the claimant gave up a place on a training scheme or an employment programme and if he had continued to participate in it he would have, or would have been likely to have, put his health and safety at risk.]

[²(2A) Without prejudice to any other circumstances in which a person may be regarded as having good cause for any act or omission for the purposes of section 19(5)(b), a person is to be regarded as having good cause for any act or omission for those purposes if—

  (a) the act or omission relates to an employment programme specified in regulation 75(1)(a)(ii) or the training scheme specified in regulation 75(1)(b)(ii), and

  (b) he had not, prior to that act or omission, been given or sent a notice in writing by an employment officer referring to the employment programme or training scheme in question ("the specified programme") and advising him that if any of the circumstances mentioned in section 19(5)(b) arise in his case in relation to the specified programme his jobseeker's allowance could cease to be payable or could be payable at a lower rate.]

[³(2B) Without prejudice to any other circumstances in which a person may be regarded as having good cause for any act or omission for the purposes of section 19(5)(b), a person to whom regulation 17A(2) applies, in respect of whom an employment officer has determined that he may undertake a qualifying course, and who is undertaking such a course as a full-time student, is to be regarded as having good cause for any act or omission—

  (a) for the purposes of section 19(5)(b) where the act or omission was in relation to an employment programme and he was, or would have been, required to attend the employment programme at a time which would have prevented him from attending the qualifying course;

  (b) for the purposes of section 19(5)(b)(iii) and (iv) where—
      (i) the act or omission was in relation to a qualifying course undertaken by him and occurred less than 4 weeks after the first day of the period of study;
     (ii) the act or omission was in relation to a qualifying course undertaken by him and was due to his lack of ability; or
    (iii) the act or omission was in relation to a qualifying course undertaken by him which was not suitable for him;]

(3) For the purposes of paragraph (2)(i),

  (a) a person is engaged in duties for the benefit of others while—
      (i) providing assistance to any person whose life may be endangered or who may be exposed to the risk of serious bodily injury or whose health may be seriously impaired;
     (ii) protecting property of substantial value from imminent risk of serious damage or destruction; or
    (iii) assisting in measures being taken to prevent a serious threat to the health of the people;

as a member of a group of persons organised wholly or partly for the purpose of providing such assistance or, as the case may be, protection;

  (b) events which may give rise to an emergency include—

(i) a fire, flood or an explosion;
(ii) a natural catastrophe;
(iii) a railway or other transport accident;
(iv) a cave or mountain accident;
(v) an accident at sea;
(vi) a person being reported missing and the organisation of a search for that person.

[³(4) For the purposes of paragraph (2B)(b)(iii), a qualifying course is suitable for a person if it is suitable for him in vocationally relevant respects, namely his personal capacity, aptitude, his preference, the level of qualification aimed at, duration of the course and proportion of time, if any, which the person has spent on the training in relation to the length of the course.]

AMENDMENTS

1. Jobseeker's Allowance (Amendment) Regulations 1996 (S.I. 1996 No. 1516), reg. 6 (October 7, 1996).
2. Social Security Amendment (New Deal) Regulations 1997 (S.I. 1997 No. 2863), reg. 7 (January 5, 1998).
3. Social Security Amendment (New Deal) Regulations 1998 (S.I. 1998 No. 1274), reg. 8 (June 1, 1998).

DEFINITIONS

"caring responsibilities"—see reg. 4.
"claimant"—see Jobseekers Act, s. 35(1).
"close relative"—see reg. 4.
"employment officer"—see reg. 4.
"employment programme"—see reg. 75(1)(a).
"full-time student"—see reg. 1(3).
"period of study"—see reg. 4.
"part-time member of a fire brigade"—*ibid.*
"qualifying course"—*ibid*, reg. 17A(7).
"training scheme"—see reg. 75(1)(b).
"week"—see reg. 75(2).

GENERAL NOTE

Section 19(5)(b) (together with s. 19(2)) of the Jobseekers Act provides for sanctions (of two or four weeks, see reg. 69) to be imposed where without good cause a claimant neglects to avail himself of, gives up or fails to attend a training scheme or employment programme place or refuses or fails to apply for or accept such a place that has been notified to him by an employment officer. See further the notes to s. 19(5)(b). This regulation is concerned with good cause for the purposes of s.19(5)(b).

Reg. 75 defines "employment programme" and "training scheme" for the purposes of s.19 and Part V. A new form of reg. 75 was introduced on January 5, 1998 as a consequence of the "New Deal" for 18–24 year-olds (see the note to reg. 75 for a brief summary of the New Deal). This distinguishes between the employment programmes and the training scheme for this age group under the New Deal (see reg. 75(1)(a)(ii) and (b)(ii)) and other employment programmes and training schemes. Note also the separate provision in reg. 75(1)(b)(iii), introduced on June 1, 1998, which concerns claimants aged 25 or over who are being treated as available for work under reg. 17A while attending a full-time employment-related course (see the notes to reg. 17A).

Para. (2A) contains an additional ground for exemption from sanction that applies in relation to the New Deal options only. It provides that if the claimant has not previously had written notification referring to the New Deal programme or scheme in question which warned him that his JSA could stop or be reduced if he failed to attend or gave up etc. the programme or scheme, this will automatically constitute good cause for the purposes of s. 19(5)(b).

Para. (2B) only relates to claimants aged 25 or over who are treated as available for employment under reg. 17A while attending a full-time employment-related course. It applies in addition to any other circumstances that may constitute good cause. Under sub-para. (a) a claimant will have automatic good cause for the purposes of s.19(5)(b) if he has been required to attend an employment programme at a time which would prevent him from attending his course (presumably he can still be required to attend such a programme which does not conflict with his course). In addition, he will be exempt from sanction if he fails to attend or gives up the course within four weeks of it starting because of lack of ability or because the course was not "suitable" (see para. (4)) for him (sub-para. (b)).

Para. (2) (which applies to *all* employment programmes and training schemes covered by reg. 75) lists a number of circumstances that will amount to good cause for the purposes of s. 19(5)(b), but this is expressly stated to be without prejudice to any other circumstances that could ground good cause. One example of good cause given by the *Adjudication Officer's Guide* is where the claimant is studying part-time to increase his chances of obtaining a job (see para. 39811).

Most of the categories are self-explanatory and only a few comments are necessary.

Sub-para. (c) If the actual, or normal, travelling time by appropriate means to and from the training scheme or employment programme was, or is, over an hour in either direction the exemption from sanction will apply. But if there is no appropriate training scheme or employment programme available within one hour's travelling time from the claimant's home, he will be expected to travel for "such greater time as is necessary".

Sub-para. (d) See the notes to SSCBA, s. 137(1) under *"married couple"* for membership of a household.

Sub-para. (h) Domestic emergency is not defined.

Sub-para. (i) The restrictive conditions of this exemption are set out in para. (3). The list in para. (3)(b) is not exhaustive (and see *CU 113/1991*).

Person of prescribed description for the purpose of section 20(3)

74.—(1) Subject to paragraph (2), a person shall be of a prescribed description for the purposes of section 20(3) (exemption from non-payment of jobseeker's allowance) and shall not fall within section 19(6)(b) or (d) if he has neither worked in employed earner's employment, nor has been a self-employed earner, not been a full-time student nor been in relevant education, during the period of 13 weeks preceding the day of the commencement of the employment.

(2) For the purposes of paragraph (1), a person shall not be regarded as having—

(a) worked in employed earner's employment; or

(b) been a self-employed earner; or

(c) been a full-time student or been in relevant education;

by reason only of any engagement in an activity referred to in paragraph (3) or by his attendance for a period of up to 14 days at a work camp.

(3) The activities referred to in this paragraph are—

(a) the manning or launching of a lifeboat; or

(b) the performance of duty as a part-time member of a fire brigade.

(4) A trial period in section 20(3) means a period of 8 weeks beginning with the commencement of the fifth week of the employment in question and ending at the end of the twelfth week of that employment and for the purposes of this definition in determining the time at which the fifth week of the employment in question commences or at which the twelfth week of that employment ends, any week in which a person has not worked in the employment for at least 16 hours shall be disregarded.

DEFINITIONS

"employed earner"—see reg. 3, SSCBA, s. 2(1)(a), reg. 75(4).
"employment"—see reg. 75(4).
"full-time student"—see reg. 1(3).
"part-time member of a fire brigade"—see reg. 4.
"relevant education"—see Jobseekers Act, s. 35(2), reg. 54.
"self-employed earner"—see reg. 1(3), SSCBA, s. 2(1)(b).
"week"—see reg. 75(2).
"work camp—see reg. 4.

See the note to s. 20(3) of the Jobseekers Act.

[¹ Person in receipt of a training allowance

74A.—(1) An income-based jobseeker's allowance shall be payable to a claimant even though section 19 prevents payment of a jobseeker's allowance to him where the claimant is in receipt of a training allowance and is not receiving training falling within paragraph (2) of regulation 170 but the jobseeker's allowance shall be payable only if and for so long as he satisfies the conditions of entitlement to an income-based jobseeker's allowance other than those which he is not required to meet by virtue of regulation 170.

(2) An income-based jobseeker's allowance which is payable to a claimant in accordance with this regulation shall be payable to him at the full rate applicable in his case.]

AMENDMENT

1. Jobseeker's Allowance (Amendment) Regulations 1996 (S.I. 1996 No. 1516), reg. 7 (October 7, 1996).

DEFINITIONS

"claimant"—see Jobseekers Act, s. 35(1).
"income-based jobseeker's allowance"—*ibid.*, s. 1(4).
"training allowance"—see reg. 1(3).

GENERAL NOTE

This regulation allows income-based JSA to be paid even though a sanction under s. 19 has been imposed if the claimant is getting a training allowance but is not doing Work Based Training for Young People (which has replaced Youth Training and other training provision focused on 16/17 year olds). See reg. 170 which exempts such a claimant from having to satisfy the labour market conditions.

[¹Interpretation

75.—(1) For the purposes of section 19 and of this Part:
(a) "an employment programme" means—
  (i) any one of the following programmes of advice, guidance or job search assistance provided in pursuance of arrangements made by the Secretary of State under section 2 of the Employment and Training Act 1973, known as—
  (aa) Jobplan Workshop, being a programme of up to one week to provide advice and guidance on jobs, training and employment opportunity;
  (bb) [⁷. . .]
  (cc) [⁴. . .]
  (dd) [⁷. . .]
  (ee) [⁵Programme Centre Workshop, being a programme of up to 29 hours' attendance over a period not exceeding 28 days, and consisting of a series of individual modules providing job search advice and guidance, motivational assistance and assistance in the preparation of a curriculum vitae; and]
  (ii) any one of the following programmes, provided in pursuance of arrangements made by or on behalf of the Secretary of State under section 2 of the Employment and Training Act 1973 and for which

only persons who are aged 18 years or over and less than 26 years immediately prior to entry may be eligible, known as—

[³(aa) the Employment Option of the New Deal, being a programme which lasts for any individual for up to 26 weeks and which includes for that individual—

(i) employed earner's employment, training and support; or

(ii) assistance in pursuing self-employed earner's employment;]

(bb) the Voluntary Sector Option of the New Deal, being a programme which lasts for any individual for up to six months and which includes for that individual employed earner's employment or a work placement combined in either case with training, support and job search;

(cc) the Environment Task Force Option of the New Deal, being a programme which lasts for any individual for up to six months and which includes for that individual employed earner's employment or a work placement combined in either case with training, support and job search.

(b) "a training scheme" means—

(i) a scheme for training for which persons aged less than 18 years are eligible and for which persons aged 18 years or over and less than 25 years may be eligible, provided in England and Wales directly or indirectly by a Training and Enterprise Council [⁶, or a Chamber of Commerce, Training and Enterprise, under its contractual arrangement with the Secretary of State] and, in Scotland, directly or indirectly by a Local Enterprise Company pursuant to its arrangement with, as the case may be, Scottish Enterprise or Highlands and Islands Enterprise (whether that arrangement is known as an Operating Contract or by any other name); [². . .]

(ii) the scheme, provided in pursuance of arrangements made by or on behalf of the Secretary of State under section 2 of the Employment and Training Act 1973 and for which only persons who are aged 18 years or over and less than 26 years immediately prior to entry may be eligible, known as the Full-Time Education and Training Option of the New Deal, being a scheme which lasts for any individual for up to one year and which includes for that individual some or all of the following, namely education, training, work experience and support in job search [²skills; and]

[²(iii) for the purposes of section 19(5)(b)(iii) and (iv) and section 19(5)(c), in relation to a person who has been treated as available for employment to any extent under regulation 17A(3), the qualifying course in respect of which he has been so treated.]

(2) In section 19, except subsection (2), and in this Part, except regulation 69 and the first occasion on which the word occurs in regulation 72(5A)(a), "week" means any period of 7 consecutive days.

(3) In section 19(2), regulation 69 and the first occasion on which the word occurs in regulation 72(5A)(a), "week" means benefit week.

(4) In section 19, except subsection (9), and in this Part, "employment" means employed earner's employment other than such employment in which a person is employed whilst participating in an employment programme falling within paragraph (1)(a)(ii); and "employed earner" shall be construed accordingly.

(5) In section 19(9), "employment" means employed earner's employment.]

AMENDMENTS

1. Social Security Amendment (New Deal) Regulations 1997 (S.I. 1997 No. 2863), reg. 8 (January 5, 1998).

2. Social Security Amendment (New Deal) Regulations 1998 (S.I. 1998 No. 1274), reg. 9 (June 1, 1998).

3. Social Security (Miscellaneous Amendments) (No. 4) Regulations 1998 (S.I. 1998 No. 1174), reg. 3(2) (June 1, 1998).

4. Jobseeker's Allowance (Amendment) (No. 2) Regulations 1998 (S.I. 1998 No. 1698), reg. 3(a) (August 4, 1998).

5. Jobseeker's Allowance (Amendment) (No. 2) Regulations 1998 (S.I. 1998 No. 1698), reg. 3(b) (August 4, 1998).

6. Jobseeker's Allowance (Amendment) (No. 2) Regulations 1998 (S.I. 1998 No. 1698), reg. 4 (August 4, 1998).

7. Jobseeker's Allowance (Amendment) (No. 2) Regulations 1998 (S.I. 1998 No. 1698), reg. 3(c) (December 1, 1998).

DEFINITIONS

"benefit week"—see reg. 1(3).
"employed earner"—see reg. 3.
"qualifying course"—see reg. 4.

GENERAL NOTE

Paragraph (1)

Para. (1) defines "employment programme" and "training scheme" for the purposes of s. 19 of the Jobseekers Act and regs. 69 to 74A. See the notes to s. 19(5) of the Jobseekers Act for discussion of the "offences" in relation to such programmes and schemes that can lead to sanction. The form of this regulation in force from January 5, 1998 distinguishes between the three employment programmes and one training scheme that make up the "New Deal options" for 18–24 year-olds (see para. (1)(a)(ii) and (b)(ii)) and other employment programmes (listed in para. (1)(a)(i)) and training schemes (para. (1)(b)(i)). See below for a brief summary of the New Deal for 18–24 year-olds. Note also the separate provision in para. (1)(b)(iii), introduced on June 1, 1998, which concerns claimants aged 25 or over who are being treated as available for work under reg. 17A while attending a full-time employment-related course (see the notes to reg. 17A).

"Training scheme" in para. (1)(b)(i) means Work Based Training for Young People (in Scotland "Skillseekers") which is the new name for training focused on 16/17 year-olds (replacing Youth Training, Modern Apprenticeships, National Traineeships and other provision). Employment programmes and training schemes change from time to time. See the deletion of sub-heads (bb), (cc) and (dd) and the new form of sub-head (ee) in para. (1)(a)(i) which reflect the changes in the employment programmes that have been made. "Programme Centre Workshop" (see the new form of sub-head (ee)) has replaced Workwise (in Scotland, Worklink) and Restart course, 1-2-1 and Jobfinder have been replaced by Jobfinder Plus, which will similarly consist of a series of interviews. Attendance at Jobfinder Plus interviews is apparently to be enforced by means of the provisions in regs. 23 to 30 of the JSA Regulations, rather than by including it in this regulation. The employment programmes that are listed in para. (1)(a)(i) (together with the New Deal options and Work Based Training for Young People) are the programmes and schemes that are for the time being "compulsory" for the purposes of s. 19 (although note that in some areas of the country a claimant could in the past also have been sanctioned for refusing without good cause to take part in a pilot scheme called Project Work; Project Work was abolished in May 1998. For a discussion of the conditions in the JSA (Pilot Scheme) Regulations 1996 (S.I. 1996 No. 1307) for the imposition of a Project Work sanction see *CJSA 5600/1997*). Under para. (1)(b)(iii), note that a claimant aged 25 or over cannot be required to go on a qualifying course. However, if he is treated as available for employment under reg. 17A while attending such a course, he can be sanctioned for failing to attend, or giving up, the course without good cause, or losing his place through misconduct. In addition, it is also possible for an employment officer to issue a jobseeker's direction requiring the claimant to attend a "non-compulsory" programme; if the claimant failed to attend without good cause he could be liable to sanction under s. 19(5)(a). For further details of employment programmes and training schemes see CPAG's *Welfare Benefits Handbook* (1999/2000 ed.) and for updated information see CPAG's *Welfare Rights Bulletin*.

The basic sanction for refusing, or failing to attend, etc., a New Deal option is the same as that for the other prescribed employment programmes and training schemes (*i.e.* a fixed period of two weeks, or four weeks for a further offence within 12 months: see reg. 69). But a four-week New Deal sanction will only be imposed if it is incurred within 12 months of a previous New Deal sanction (although note that a first New Deal sanction could have been for four weeks if the claimant had been sanctioned under the Project Work pilot scheme within the last 12 months); in addition the eligibility for hardship payments is more limited in the case of New Deal sanctions (see regs. 140(4A) and 140A). See further the notes to reg. 69.

The New Deal
The "New Deal" for young people aged 18–24 who have claimed jobseeker's allowance for six months or more is a major component of the Government's Welfare to Work programme. It was introduced in a number of "pathfinder areas" of the country on January 5, 1998 and on a national basis on April 6, 1998. A number of other New Deal programmes are in the process of being implemented: for lone parents, the long-term unemployed and disabled people. (The provision in reg. 17A to enable claimants aged 25 or over to attend a full-time employment-related course while continuing to receive JSA is one of the measures that are designed to help the long-term unemployed.) For further information on these initiatives see CPAG's *Welfare Benefits Handbook* (1999/2000 ed.) and for updated information see CPAG's *Welfare Rights Bulletin.*
Although the New Deal for young people is aimed at 18–24 year-olds, a person who becomes 25 after entering the New Deal will be required to continue to take part (hence the reference in para. (1)(a)(ii) and (b)(ii) to those aged 18 or over and under 26). A claimant will be required to join the New Deal if he is aged 18 to 24 and has been claiming JSA for at least six months (this includes claimants who only get credits). In addition, some young people who are in "special needs groups") *e.g.* those who have literacy problems, or are disabled) can choose to enter the New Deal before they have claimed JSA for six months. If the claimant stops claiming JSA while he is on the New Deal, he will be required to rejoin if if he reclaims JSA within 13 weeks.
The New Deal starts with a "Gateway" period which lasts up to four months. During this period the claimant will receive extra help to find work, including access to careers advice and other forms of guidance, and also assistance with selecting the New Deal option that is appropriate for him. If the claimant is finding it difficult to choose an option he can be offered a "taster" (an opportunity to sample an option for a short time; see reg. 19(1)(r) (treated as actively seeking work) if the taster lasts more than three days in any benefit week). A New Deal Action Plan will be drawn up and any necessary changes made to the claimant's jobseeker's agreement in order to bring that into line with the Action Plan. The emphasis in the Employment Service Guidance is on encouraging claimants to take up opportunities voluntarily but clearly jobseeker's directions can be used if the claimant refuses to co-operate. In addition, if the claimant refuses to attend interviews in connection with the New Deal his entitlement to JSA can cease under reg. 25. During the Gateway period JSA will continue to be paid (as long as the claimant satisfies the conditions of entitlement for it).
The clear purpose of the Gateway period is to get a claimant back into work. However, if the claimant is still on JSA at the end of the period he will be referred to one of the four New Deal options. These are:

● *The Employment Option (sub-para. (a)(ii)(aa)).* Since June 1, 1998 this has been broadened to include a programme of training and support with a view to pursuing self-employment.

Employed earner route
This is a job with an employer for up to 26 weeks which includes at least one day a week in education or training leading to an approved qualification. The employer receives a subsidy of up to £60 per week and up to £750 towards the cost of the training. The claimant is employed by the employer and receives a wage which must be at least as much as the subsidy. But note the effect of para. (4) in relation to sanctions.
Because the claimant will be an employee he will be eligible for family credit, disability working allowance (to be replaced by working families tax credit and disabled person's tax credit respectively from October 5, 1999, see the 1999 Supplement to this book for further details) or, in certain areas of the country, earnings top-up; a back to work bonus or child maintenance bonus may also be payable. (This is on the assumption that the claimant is working at least 16 hours a week (or in the case of a partner who is on the New Deal 24 hours a week) which will normally be the case. However, if a claimant is working less than 16 hours a week, for example because of caring responsibilities or disability, he will not be in remunerative work). If a person receives assistance with childcare costs while on this option, any reimbursement of such expenses will not count as income (see para. 14(d) of Sched. 7).
In addition note the amendments to para. 13 of Sched. 2 to these Regulations and para. 14 of Sched. 3 to the Income Support Regulations introduced on January 5, 1998 which are intended to ensure (*inter alia*) that time spent on the New Deal counts towards any linking or waiting period for housing costs. See also the new sub-para. (4A) inserted into para. 4 of both these Schedules.

This has the effect of treating as part of the "relevant period" any time that a claimant or his partner spends on a New Deal employment programme as a result of which he (or his partner) is in remunerative work or has an income that is too high to qualify for income-based JSA/income support (or earnings that are too high to qualify for contribution-based JSA). See the notes to para. 4(4A) of Sched. 3 to the Income Support Regulations.

● *Self-employment route.* During the Gateway period a claimant who is interested in self-employment will receive advice and information about starting and running a business and be helped to draw up a business plan. JSA will continue to be paid (as long as the claimant satisfies the conditions of entitlement for it). This means, for example, that the claimant must continue to be available for work but note reg. 19(1)(r). This treats a claimant as actively seeking work in any week during which he is on one of the listed schemes with a view to establishing himself in self-employment. It can apply for up to eight weeks during a single period of continuous entitlement to JSA and starts with the week in which the claimant is accepted onto the scheme.

Once on the self-employment route of the Employment option a person will continue to receive support and guidance for a period of 26 weeks, while he gains experience of working in his own business (referred to as "test-trading"). He will also be required to undertake training leading to an approved qualification in this period. While on this option he will receive a training allowance plus a grant of £400 paid in instalments over the six months of the option (*i.e.* £15.38 per week). The grant is disregarded as income (see para. 60 of Sched. 7); it is also ignored as capital but only for 52 weeks from the date of receipt (see para. 45 of Sched. 8). For the equivalent disregards for the purposes of income support, family credit and disability working allowance, see para. 62 of Sched. 9 and para. 50 of Sched. 10 to the Income Support Regulations and para. 59 of Sched. 2 and para. 52 of Sched. 3 to the Family Credit Regulations and para. 57 of Sched. 3 and para. 51 of Sched. 4 to the Disability Working Allowance Regulations. The training allowance is equivalent to JSA, or to JSA less 10p if the person was getting income-based JSA immediately before starting on this option. In the latter case this will enable him to receive 10p income-based JSA, thus providing a passport to other benefits such as housing benefit and council tax benefit. In addition, the person may be eligible for assistance with childcare costs (any such reimbursement of childcare expenses will be ignored as income: para. 14(d) of Sched. 7).

While a person is receiving (or entitled to receive) a training allowance, he will be deemed not to be employed but will be treated as participating in training under s.2 of the Employment and Training Act 1973 (see art. 2(3) of the New Deal (Miscellaneous Provisions) Order 1998 (S.I. 1998 No. 217) as amended by the New Deal (Miscellaneous Provisions) (Amendment) Order 1998 (S.I. 1998 No. 1425)). He will be treated as not in remunerative work because he is being paid a training allowance (see reg. 53(b) and reg. 6(d) of the Income Support Regulations). He will also be exempt from the requirements of being available for and actively seeking work and having a jobseeker's agreement because he is in receipt of a training allowance (see reg. 170(1)).

Any gross receipts from trading while on the self-employment route of the Employment option will be taken into account in accordance with regs. 102A to 102D. The normal rules for the treatment of income do not apply (see reg. 88A). Gross receipts from trading while on this option will be paid into a special account in the names of the person on the option and the option provider. See the definition of "special account" in reg. 102A. The person will apparently not be allowed to withdraw any money from this account for his personal use while he remains on the self-employment route (the intention being to prevent any profit from the "test-trading" affecting his benefit/training allowance). See the note to reg. 102C as to how the money in the account will be taken into account if a claim for JSA or income support is made after the person finishes this option.

● *The Voluntary Sector Option (sub-para. (a)(ii)(bb)).* This is a work placement with a voluntary sector employer for up to 26 weeks which also will include at least one day a week's education or training leading to an approved qualification.

● *The Environment Task Force Option (sub-para. (a)(ii)(cc)).* This is similar to the Voluntary Sector option but in this case the work placement is in an environment task force. Again training or education for one day a week (or the equivalent) will be included.

While on the Voluntary Sector or the Environment Task Force option the claimant either receives an allowance equal to his JSA entitlement plus a grant of £400 paid in instalments over the six months of the option, or is paid a wage by the employer. If a wage is paid the employer receives a contribution of £43 per week and a £400 grant; the wage paid to the claimant must be at least the equivalent of this amount. If the claimant is an employee, he will be eligible for family credit, etc. (see under "*The Employment Option*" above). Note also the effect of para. (4).

The claimant can choose to be paid an allowance rather than a wage (if one is offered); clearly which is more advantageous will depend on the claimant's circumstances (*e.g.* whether he has a mortgage). If the claimant is paid an allowance he will be treated as being in training under s. 2 of the Employment and Training Act 1973 (see the New Deal (Miscellaneous Provisions) Order 1998 (S.I. 1998 No. 217), art. 2, as substituted by the New Deal (Miscellaneous Provisions) (Amendment) Order 1998 (S.I. 1998 No. 1425)). He will be deemed not to be in remunerative work (reg. 53(b) and reg. 6(d) of the Income Support Regulations). His training allowance will be equivalent to JSA, or to JSA less than 10p if he was getting income-based JSA immediately before starting the option, thus enabling him to receive 10p income-based JSA and providing a passport to other benefits such as housing benefit or council tax benefit. In addition he will be reimbursed travel costs (other than the first £4 per week) and may be eligible for assistance with childcare costs (up to £12 a day for the first child and £20 a day for two children or more; the conditions for this are similar to those for a childcare costs disregard for family credit). Any reimbursement of childcare expenses will be disregarded (see para. 14(d) of Sched. 7). The £400 grant is also ignored as income (Sched. 7, para. 60), and as capital (Sched. 8, para. 45; note that the disregard in para. 45 only applies for 52 weeks from the date of receipt). The claimant will also be exempt from the requirements of being available for and actively seek work and having a jobseeker's agreement because he is in receipt of a training allowance (see reg. 170(1)).

● *Full Time Education and Training Option (sub-para. (b)(ii)).* Under this option the person will receive full-time education or training for up to one year. The aim is to enable the person to reach National Vocational Qualification or Scottish Vocational Qualification level 2 or the equivalent, with a view to improving his employment prospects. In exceptional circumstances education or training aiming at a higher level qualification may be considered where this could result in immediate employment.

A claimant on this option will receive a training allowance plus 10p income-based JSA (see above under *"The Environment Task Force Option"*), together with payment of travel costs and possible help with further expenses such as the costs of living away from home or childcare costs from a Discretionary Fund operated by the Employment Service.

Note that while on this option a person will not count as in relevant education (see reg. 54(5)) nor as a full-time student (a person in receipt of a training allowance is excluded from the definition of "full-time student": see reg. 1(3)).

The intention is that wherever possible the claimant should choose which option he wishes to take part in. However, it may be that not all the options are available in a particular area or for that particular claimant; in addition the Full-Time Education and Training option may not be appropriate because the claimant already has NVQ, SVQ or an equivalent qualification. If at the end of the Gateway period the claimant has not accepted a place on an option he will be required to take up a place selected for him by the Employment Service. Once the claimant has accepted, or been mandatorily referred to, a place on an option, he will be notified in writing confirming the details of the place and advising him that benefit may be affected if he fails to attend, or gives up, the place without good cause or loses it through misconduct.

If the claimant finishes the option and has not found a job and so reclaims JSA, there will be a "follow through" support period of 13 weeks during which he will be given "intensive help" to find employment.

Paragraph (4)

The effect of this paragraph is that the claimant will not count as in employment for the purposes of s. 19 and this Part of the regulations, even if he has employed status while he is on any of the New Deal options in para. (1)(a)(ii). This means that if the claimant does leave his place on the option voluntarily or loses it through misconduct he will be subject to a fixed sanction under s. 19(5)(b) or (c), not the discretionary sanctions under s. 19(6)(a) or (b).

PART VI

MEMBERSHIP OF THE FAMILY

Persons of a prescribed description

76.—(1) Subject to paragraph (2), a person of a prescribed description for the purposes of the definition of "family" in section 35(1) of the Act is a person aged 16 or over but under 19 who is treated as a child for the purposes of section 142 of the Benefits Act (meaning of child), and in these Regulations, except in Part IV, such a person is referred to as a "young person".

(2) Paragraph (1) shall not apply to a person who is—

(a) on a course of advanced education;

(b) entitled to a jobseeker's allowance or would, but for section 3(1)(d) of the Act (provision against dual entitlement) be so entitled; or

(c) entitled to income support or would, but for section 134(2) of the Benefits Act (exclusion from benefit) be so entitled.

DEFINITIONS

"the Act"—see reg. 1(3).
"course of advanced education"—*ibid.*

GENERAL NOTE

This regulation is very similar to reg. 14 of the Income Support Regulations, except that para. (2) contains an additional exception that the person must not be entitled to income support in their own right (sub-para. (c)), as well as not receiving advanced education (sub-para. (a)) or entitled to JSA in their own right (sub-para. (b)). Note that para. (1) expressly provides that this definition of "young person" does not apply for the purposes of Part IV (entitlement of 16- and 17-year-olds to JSA).

For the circumstances in which a person aged 16 to 18 is treated as a child for child benefit purposes see regs. 5, 6, 7, 7A, 7C and 7D of the Child Benefit (General) Regulations 1976 in *Bonner, Non-Means Tested Benefits: The Legislation*, and the notes to reg. 54.

Circumstances in which a person is to be treated as responsible or not responsible for another

77.—(1) Subject to the following provisions of this regulation, a person is to be treated for the purposes of the Act as responsible for a child or young person for whom he is receiving child benefit.

(2) In a case where a child ("the first child") is in receipt of child benefit in respect of another child ("the second child"), the person treated as responsible for the first child in accordance with the provisions of this regulation shall also be treated as responsible for the second child.

(3) In the case of a child or young person in respect of whom no person is receiving child benefit, the person who shall be treated as responsible for that child or young person shall be—

(a) except where sub-paragraph (b) applies, the person with whom the child or young person usually lives; or

(b) where only one claim for child benefit has been made in respect of the child or young person, the person who made that claim.

(4) Where regulation 78(7) (circumstances in which a person is to be treated as being or not being a member of the household) applies in respect of a child or young person, that child or young person shall be treated as the responsibility of the claimant for that part of the week for which he is under that regulation treated as being a member of the claimant's household.

(5) Except where paragraph (4) applies, a child or young person shall be treated as the responsibility of only one person in any benefit week and any person other than the one treated as responsible for the child or young person under this regulation shall be treated as not so responsible.

DEFINITIONS

"the Act"—see reg. 1(3).
"benefit week"—*ibid.*
"child"—see Jobseekers Act, s. 35(1).
"claimant"—*ibid.*

"week"—*ibid.*
"young person"—see reg. 76.

GENERAL NOTE

The definition of family in s. 35(1) of the Jobseekers Act refers to a person being responsible for a child or young person (on which see reg. 76). This provision mirrors that in reg. 15 of the Income Support Regulations and makes the test of responsibility for a child or young person receipt of child benefit. See the notes to reg. 15.

Circumstances in which a person is to be treated as being or not being a member of the household

78.—(1) Subject to paragraphs (2) to (5), the claimant and any partner and, where the claimant or his partner is treated as responsible under regulation 77 (circumstances in which a person is to be treated as responsible or not responsible for another) for a child or young person, that child or young person and any child of that child or young person shall be treated for the purposes of the Act as members of the same household notwithstanding that any of them is temporarily living away from the other members of his family.

(2) Paragraph (1) shall not apply to a person who is living away from the other members of his family where—

(a) that person does not intend to resume living with the other members of his family; or

(b) his absence from the other members of his family is likely to exceed 52 weeks, unless there are exceptional circumstances (for example the person is in hospital or otherwise has no control over the length of his absence), and the absence is unlikely to be substantially more than 52 weeks.

(3) Paragraph (1) shall not apply in respect of any member of a couple or of a polygamous marriage where—

(a) one, both or all of them are patients detained in a hospital provided under section 4 of the National Health Service Act 1977 (special hospitals) or section 90(1) of the Mental Health (Scotland) Act 1984 (provision of hospitals for patients requiring special security); or

[²(b) one, both or all of them are—

(i) detained in custody pending trial or sentence upon conviction or under a sentence imposed by a court; or

(ii) on temporary release in accordance with the provisions of the Prison Act 1952 or rules made under section 39(6) of the Prisons (Scotland) Act 1989]

(c) the claimant is abroad and does not satisfy the conditions of regulation 50 (persons absent from Great Britain); or

(d) one of them is permanently in residential accommodation or a residential care home or a nursing home.

(4) A child or young person shall not be treated as a member of the claimant's household where he is—

(a) placed with the claimant or his partner by a local authority under section 23(2)(a) of the Children Act 1989 or by a voluntary organisation under section 59(1)(a) of that Act; or

(b) placed with the claimant or his partner prior to adoption; or

(c) in accordance with a relevant Scottish enactment, boarded out with the claimant or his partner, whether or not with a view to adoption; or

(d) placed for adoption with the claimant or his partner pursuant to a decision under the Adoption Agencies Regulations 1983 or the Adoption Agencies (Scotland) Regulations 1984.

(5) Subject to paragraphs (6) and (7), paragraph (1) shall not apply to a child or young person who is not living with the claimant and who—

(a) in a case which does not fall within sub-paragraph (b), has been continuously absent from Great Britain for a period of more than four weeks commencing—

    (i) where he went abroad before the date of the claim for a jobseeker's allowance, with that date;

    (ii) in any other case, on the day which immediately follows the day on which he went abroad; or

(b) where ['regulation 50(5)] or paragraph 11 or 13 of Schedule 5 (temporary absence abroad for the treatment of a child or young person) applies, has been continuously absent from Great Britain for a period of more than 8 weeks, that period of 8 weeks commencing—

    (i) where he went abroad before the date of the claim for a jobseeker's allowance, on the date of that claim;

    (ii) in any other case, on the day which immediately follows the day on which he went abroad; or

(c) has been an in-patient or in accommodation provided under any of the provisions referred to in any of sub-paragraphs (a) to (c) of the definition of residential accommodation in regulation 85 for a continuous period of more than 12 weeks commencing—

    (i) where he became an in-patient or, as the case may be, entered that accommodation before the date of the claim for a jobseeker's allowance, with that date; or

    (ii) in any other case, with the date on which he became an in-patient or entered that accommodation,

and, in either case, has not been in regular contact with either the claimant or any member of the claimant's household; or

(d) is being looked after by a local authority under a relevant enactment; or

(e) has been placed with a person other than the claimant prior to adoption; or

(f) is in the care of a local authority under a relevant Scottish enactment; or

(g) has been boarded out under a relevant Scottish enactment with a person other than the claimant prior to adoption; or

(h) has been placed for adoption pursuant to a decision under the Adoption Agencies Regulations 1983 or the Adoption Agencies (Scotland) Regulations 1984; or

(i) is detained in custody pending trial or sentence upon conviction or under a sentence imposed by a court.

(6) In the case of a person who was entitled to income support immediately before his entitlement to a jobseeker's allowance commenced, sub-paragraphs (a), (b) and (c) of paragraph (5) ['shall] each have effect as if head (i) was omitted.

(7) A child or young person to whom any of the circumstances mentioned in ['sub-paragraphs (d), (f) or (i)] of paragraph (5) applies shall be treated as being a member of the claimant's household only for that part of any benefit week where that child or young person lives with the claimant.

(8) Where a child or young person for the purposes of attending the educational establishment at which he is receiving relevant education is living with the claimant or his partner and neither one is treated as responsible for that child or young person that child or young person shall be treated as being a member of the household of the person treated as responsible for him and shall not be treated as a member of the claimant's household.

(9) In this regulation—

(a) "relevant enactment" means the Army Act 1955, the Social Work

(Scotland) Act 1968, the Matrimonial Causes Act 1973, the Adoption (Scotland) Act 1978, the Family Law Act 1986 and the Children Act 1989;

(b) ''relevant Scottish enactment'' means the Army Act 1955, the Air Force Act 1955, the Naval Discipline Act 1957, the Adoption Act 1958, the Matrimonial Proceedings Children Act 1958, the Children Act 1958, the Social Work (Scotland) Act 1968, the Family Law Reform Act 1969, the Children and Young Persons Act 1969, the Matrimonial Causes Act 1973, the Guardianship Act 1973, the Children Act 1975, the Domestic Proceedings and Magistrates' Courts Act 1978, the Adoption (Scotland) Act 1978, the Child Care Act 1980, and the Foster Children Act 1980;

(c) ''voluntary organisation'' has the meaning assigned to it in the Children Act 1989 or, in Scotland, the Social Work (Scotland) Act 1968.

AMENDMENTS

1. Jobseeker's Allowance (Amendment) Regulations 1996 (S.I. 1996 No. 1516), reg. 20 and Sched. (October 7, 1996).

2. Jobseeker's Allowance and Income Support (General) (Amendment) Regulations 1996 (S.I. 1996 No. 1517), reg. 18 (October 7, 1996).

DEFINITIONS

''the Act''—see reg. 1(3).
''claimant''—see Jobseekers Act, s. 35(1).
''child''—*ibid*.
''couple''—see reg. 1(3).
''date of claim''—*ibid*
''family''—see Jobseekers Act, s. 35(1).
''nursing home''—see reg. 1(3).
''partner''—*ibid*.
''polygamous marriage''—*ibid*.
''residential accommodation''—*ibid*.
''residential care home''—*ibid*.
''young person''—see reg. 76.

GENERAL NOTE

This regulation is very similar to reg. 16 of the Income Support Regulations. Unlike the Income Support Regulations, the JSA Regulations make separate reference to the Scottish legislation in the case of provisions that were amended in the Income Support Regulations as a consequence of the Children Act 1989 (see para. (4)(c), para. (5)(f) and (g) and (9)(b)).

See the notes to reg. 16 of the Income Support Regulations.

PART VII

AMOUNTS

Income-based jobseeker's allowance

82. Regulations 83 to 87 apply in the case of an income-based jobseeker's allowance.

Applicable amounts

83. Except in the case of a claimant to whom regulation 84, 85 or 86 or Part X (applicable amounts in other cases and urgent cases) applies, a claimant's weekly applicable amount shall be the aggregate of such of the following amounts as may apply in his case—

(a) an amount in respect of himself or if he is a member of a couple, an amount in respect of both of them, determined in accordance with sub-paragraph (1), (2) or (3), as the case may be, of paragraph 1 of Schedule 1;

(b) an amount determined in accordance with paragraph 2 of Schedule 1 in respect of any child or young person who is a member of his family, excluding a child or young person whose capital, if calculated in accordance with Part VIII in like manner as for the claimant would exceed £3,000, but including a child whose capital falls to be treated as income in accordance with regulation 106(1) (modification in respect of children and young persons);

(c) an amount in respect of himself, or where the claimant is a member of a family, an amount in respect of any member of the family aged 16 or over determined in accordance with paragraph 3 of Schedule 1 (residential allowance);

(d) where he is a member of a family of which at least one member is a child or young person, an amount determined in accordance with Part II of Schedule 1 (family premium);

(e) the amount of any premiums which may be applicable to him, determined in accordance with Parts III and IV of Schedule 1 (premiums); and

(f) any amounts determined in accordance with Schedule 2 (housing costs) which may be applicable to him in respect of mortgage interest payments or such other housing costs as are prescribed in that Schedule.

DEFINITIONS

"child"—see Jobseekers Act, s. 35(1).
"claimant"—*ibid.*
"couple"—see reg. 1(3).
"family"—see Jobseekers Act, s. 35(1).
"young person"—see reg. 76.

GENERAL NOTE

This provision only applies to income-based JSA (reg. 82).

Income-based JSA uses the same formula as income support for calculating the amount of a claimant's benefit, that is, by setting his "applicable amount" against his income. Reg. 83 sets out the categories which go towards the total applicable amount which are the same as those in reg. 17 of the Income Support Regulations. See the notes to reg. 17. There is no equivalent to reg. 17(1)(f) and (g) and (2) to (7) which contain various transitional protection provisions. But note the rules for "transitional supplement" to income-based JSA in reg. 87 which preserve the effect of these and other income support transitional protection provisions for JSA claimants who would have been covered by them had they been entitled to claim income support after October 6, 1996 (for claimants entitled to a special transitional addition or transitional addition under the Income Support (Transitional) Regulations before October 7, 1996, see para. (1) of reg. 87).

As with income support there are special rules for particular categories, see regs. 84 to 86.

Polygamous marriages

84.—(1) Except in the case of a claimant to whom regulation 83, 85 or 86 (applicable amounts in special cases and for those in residential care and nursing homes) or Part X or paragraph (2) applies, where a claimant is a member of a polygamous marriage his weekly applicable amount shall be the aggregate of such of the following amounts as may apply in his case—

(a) the highest amount applicable to him and one of his partners determined in accordance with sub-paragraph (3) of paragraph 1 of Schedule 1 as if he and that partner were a couple;

(b) an amount equal to the difference between the amounts specified in ['sub-paragraphs (3)(e)] and (1)(e) of paragraph 1 of Schedule 1 in respect of each of his other partners;

(c) an amount determined in accordance with paragraph 2 of Schedule 1 (applicable amounts) in respect of any child or young person for whom he or a partner of his is responsible and who is a member of the same household except a child or young person whose capital, if calculated in accordance with Part VIII in like manner as for the claimant, would exceed £3,000, but including a child whose capital falls to be treated as income in accordance with regulation 106(1) (modification in respect of children and young persons);

(d) an amount, whether in respect of the claimant or any member of his household aged 16 or over, determined in accordance with paragraph 3 of Schedule 1 (residential allowance);

(e) if he or another partner of the polygamous marriage is responsible for a child or young person who is a member of the same household, the amount specified in Part II of Schedule 1 (family premium);

(f) the amount of any premiums which may be applicable to him determined in accordance with Parts III and IV of Schedule 1 (premiums); and

(g) any amounts determined in accordance with Schedule 2 (housing costs) which may be applicable to him in respect of mortgage interest payments or such other housing costs as are prescribed in that Schedule.

(2) In the case of a partner who is aged less than 18 the amount which applies in respect of that partner shall be Nil unless that partner—

(a) is treated as responsible for a child; or

(b) is a person who, had he not been a member of a polygamous marriage, would have qualified for a jobseeker's allowance by virtue of section 3(1)(f)(ii) or section 3(1)(f)(iii) and the regulations made thereunder (jobseeker's allowance for persons aged 16 or 17).

AMENDMENT

1. Jobseeker's Allowance (Amendment) Regulations 1996 (S.I. 1996 No. 1516), reg. 20 and Sched. (October 7, 1996).

DEFINITIONS

"child"—see Jobseekers Act, s. 35(1).
"claimant"—*ibid.*
"couple"—see reg. 1(3).
"family"—see Jobseekers Act, s. 35(1).
"young person"—see reg. 76.

GENERAL NOTE

Reg. 84 contains the special rules for polygamous marriages, but not for other kinds of relationships. There the ordinary living together as husband and wife rule in s. 35(1) of the Jobseekers Act applies.

This provision only applies to income-based JSA (reg. 82).

Special cases

85.—(1) In the case of a person to whom any paragraph in column (1) of Schedule 5 applies (applicable amounts in special cases) the amount included in the claimant's weekly applicable amount in respect of him shall be the amount prescribed in the corresponding paragraph in column (2) of that Schedule but excluding an amount for a child or young person whose [⁴capital, if calculated] in accordance with Part VIII in like manner as for the claimant, would exceed £3,000, but including an amount for a child or young person whose capital falls to be treated as income in accordance with regulation 106(1) (modification in respect of children and young persons).

(2) Except where the amount prescribed in Schedule 5 in respect of a person to whom paragraph (1) applies includes an amount applicable under regulation 83(e) or 84(1)(f) a person to whom paragraph (1) applies shall be treated as not falling within the conditions specified in paragraph 15 of Schedule 1 (severe disability premium).

(3) In Schedule 5, for the purposes of paragraphs 1, 2 and 17 (persons in residential care or nursing homes who become patients), where a person has been a patient for two or more distinct periods separated by one or more intervals each not exceeding 28 days, he shall be treated as having been a patient continuously for a period equal in duration to the total of those distinct periods.

(4) [³Subject to paragraph (4A),] in this regulation and Schedule 5—
"person from abroad" means a person, who—

    (a) has a limited leave as defined in section 33(1) of the Immigration Act 1971 (hereinafter referred to as "the 1971 Act") to enter or remain in the United Kingdom which was given in accordance with any provision of the immigration rules (as defined in that section) which refers to there being, or to there needing to be, no recourse to public funds or to there being no charge on public funds during that limited leave; but this sub-paragraph shall not apply to a person who is a national of a Member State, a state which is a signatory to the European Convention on Social and Medical Assistance (done in Paris on [²11th December 1953) or a state] which is a signatory to the Council of Europe Social Charter (signed in Turin on 18th October 1961), unless, in the case of a national of a state which is a signatory of that European Convention, he has made an application for the conditions of his leave to remain in the United Kingdom to be varied, and that application has not been determined or an appeal from that application is pending under Part II of the 1971 Act (appeals); or

    (b) having a limited leave (as defined in section 33(1) of the 1971 Act) to enter or remain in the United Kingdom, has remained without further leave under that Act beyond the time limited by the leave; or

    (c) is the subject of a deportation order being an order under section 5(1) of the 1971 Act (deportation) requiring him to leave and prohibiting him from entering the United Kingdom; or

    (d) is adjudged by the immigration authorities to be an illegal entrant (as defined in section 33(1) of the 1971 Act) who has not subsequently been given leave under that Act to enter or remain in the United Kingdom; or

    (e) has been allowed temporary admission to the United Kingdom by virtue of paragraph 21 of Schedule 2 to the 1971 Act; or

    (f) has been allowed temporary admission to the United Kingdom by the Secretary of State outside any provision of the 1971 Act; or

    (g) has not had his immigration status determined by the Secretary of State; or

    (h) is a national of a Member State and is required by the Secretary of State to leave the United Kingdom; [¹or

    (i) has been given leave to enter, or remain in, the United Kingdom by the Secretary of State upon an undertaking given by another person or persons in writing in pursuance of immigration rules within the meaning of the Immigration Act 1971, to be responsible for his maintenance and accommodation; and he has not been resident in the United Kingdom for a period of at least 5 years beginning from the date of entry or the date on which the undertaking was given in respect of him, whichever date is the later; or

(j) while he is a person to whom any of the definitions in sub-paragraphs (a) to (i) applies in his case, submits a claim to the Secretary of State, which is not finally determined, for asylum under the Convention;

and for the purposes of this definition "the immigration authorities" means an adjudicator, an immigration officer or an immigration appeal tribunal appointed for the purposes of the Immigration Act 1971 and in addition means the Secretary of State.]

"person from abroad" also means a claimant who is not habitually resident in the United Kingdom, [¹ the Channel Islands, the Isle of Man or the Republic of Ireland,] but for this purpose, no claimant shall be treated as not habitually resident in the United Kingdom who is—

(a) a worker for the purposes of Council Regulation (EEC) No. 1612/68 or (EEC) No. 1251/70 or a person with a right to reside in the United Kingdom pursuant to Council Directive No. 68/360/EEC or No. 73/148/EEC; or

(b) a refugee within the definition of Article 1 of the Convention relating to the Status of Refugees done at Geneva on 28th July 1951, as extended by Article 1(2) of the Protocol relating to the Status of Refugees done at New York on 31st January 1967; or

(c) a person who has been granted exceptional leave [⁶to enter the United Kingdom by an immigration officer within the meaning of the Immigration Act 1971, or] to remain in the United Kingdom by the Secretary of State;

"patient" means a person (other than a prisoner) who is regarded as receiving free in-patient treatment within the meaning of the Social Security (Hospital In-Patients) Regulations 1975;

"prisoner" means a person who—

(a) is detained in custody pending trial or sentence upon conviction or under a sentence imposed by a court; or

(b) is on temporary release in accordance with the provisions of the Prison Act 1952 or the Prisons (Scotland) Act 1989,

other than a person [⁵who is detained in hospital under the provisions of the Mental Health Act 1983, or, in Scotland, under the provisions of the Mental Health (Scotland) Act 1984 or the Criminal Procedure (Scotland) Act 1995;]

"residential accommodation" means, subject to the following provisions of this regulation, accommodation provided by a local authority in a home owned or managed by that or another local authority—

(a) under sections 21 to 24 of the National Assistance Act 1948 (provision of accommodation); or

(b) in Scotland, under section 13B or 59 of the Social Work (Scotland) Act 1968 (provision of residential and other establishments); or

(c) under section 7 of the Mental Health (Scotland) Act 1984 (functions of local authorities),

where the accommodation is provided for a person whose stay in that accommodation has become other than temporary.

[³ (4A) In paragraph (4) "person from abroad" does not include any person in Great Britain who left the territory of Montserrat after 1st November 1995 because of the effect on that territory of a volcanic eruption.

(5) A person shall continue to be treated as being in residential accommodation within the meaning of paragraph (4) if—

(a) he is in, or only temporarily absent from, such residential accommoda-

701

tion, and the same accommodation subsequently becomes a residential care home for so long as he remains in that accommodation; or

(b) on 31st March 1993 he was in, or only temporarily absent from, accommodation of a kind mentioned in regulation 21(3B) to (3E) of the Income Support Regulations.]

(6) A person who would, but for this paragraph, be in residential accommodation within the meaning of paragraph (4) shall be treated as not being in residential accommodation where—

(a) he is under the age of 18 and in the care of a local authority under Part II or III of the Social Work (Scotland) Act 1968 (promotion of social welfare of children in need of care); or

(b) except where he is a person to whom paragraph (5)(b) applies, he is in accommodation where—

　(i) no cooked or prepared food is made available to him in consequence solely of his paying the charge for the accommodation or any other charge which he is required to pay as a condition of occupying the accommodation, or both of those charges, or

　(ii) such food is actually made available for his consumption on payment of a further charge or charges.

AMENDMENTS

1. Jobseeker's Allowance (Amendment) Regulations 1996 (S.I. 1996 No. 1516), reg. 10(1) (October 7, 1996).

2. Jobseeker's Allowance (Amendment) Regulations 1996 (S.I. 1996 No. 1516), reg. 20 and Sched. (October 7, 1996).

3. Social Security and Child Support (Jobseeker's Allowance) (Miscellaneous Amendments) Regulations 1996 (S.I. 1996 No. 2538), reg. 2(7) (October 28, 1996).

4. Social Security (Miscellaneous Amendments) Regulations 1997 (S.I. 1997 No. 454), reg. 2(10) (April 7, 1997).

5. Social Security (Miscellaneous Amendments) Regulations 1998 (S.I. 1998 No. 563), reg. 8(1) and (2)(d) (April 6, 1998).

6. Social Security (Miscellaneous Amendments) Regulations 1998 (S.I. 1998 No. 563), reg. 18(3) and (4)(d) (April 6, 1998).

DEFINITIONS

"child"—see Jobseekers Act, s. 35(1).
"claimant"—*ibid.*
"Income Support Regulations"—see reg. 1(3).
"nursing home"—*ibid.*
"residential care home"—*ibid.*
"young person"—see reg. 76.

GENERAL NOTE

This regulation only applies to income-based JSA (reg. 82).

Applicable amounts in special cases are to be as prescribed in Sched. 5.

This provision is similar to reg. 21 of the Income Support Regulations. See the notes to that regulation.

Applicable amounts for persons in residential care and nursing homes

86.—(1) Where a person has a preserved right and either—

(a) lives in a residential care or nursing home; or

(b) is a member of a family and he and the members of his family live in such a home,

his weekly applicable amount shall, except in a case to which regulation 85 (special cases) applies, be calculated in accordance with Schedule 4.

(2) A person has a preserved right for the purposes of this regulation if he satisfies the requirements for a preserved right under regulation 19 of and Schedule 4 to the Income Support Regulations.

(3) In Schedule 4, "temporary absence" means—

(a) in the case of a person who has a preserved right and to whom regulation 19(2) of the Income Support Regulations applies, 52 weeks; and

(b) in any other case, 13 weeks.

(4) In Schedule 4 the expressions "mental disorder", "mental handicap", "drug or alcohol dependence" and "disablement" have the same meanings as those expressions have for the purposes of the Registered Homes Act 1984 and Regulations made thereunder.

(5) Notwithstanding the foregoing paragraphs of this regulation, where—

(a) a person has been registered under the Registered Homes Act 1984 in respect of premises which have been carried on as a residential care home or, as the case may be, a nursing home, and that person has ceased to carry on such a home; and

(b) an application for registration under that Act has been made by another person and that application has not been determined or abandoned,

the applicable amount of a person resident in those premises shall be determined under Schedule 4 as if the most recent registration under the Registered Homes Act 1984 in respect of those premises continued until the day on which the application is determined or abandoned.

DEFINITIONS

"family"—see Jobseekers Act, s. 35(1).
"Income Support Regulations"—see reg. 1(3).
"nursing home"—*ibid.*
"residential care home"—*ibid.*

GENERAL NOTE

This regulation and Sched. 4 provide for the applicable amounts of residents in residential care or nursing homes who satisfy the rules for a preserved right under reg. 19 of the Income Support Regulations. See the notes to reg. 19 for those who qualify for a preserved right.

This regulation only applies to income-based JSA (reg. 82).

Transitional supplement to income-based jobseeker's allowance

87.—(1) In the case of a person who, before 7th October 1996 was entitled to a special transitional addition or transitional addition in accordance with the Income Support (Transitional) Regulations 1987, the amount of any income-based jobseeker's allowance payable to him shall be increased by an amount equal to those additions, but the increase shall continue to be payable only for so long as the claimant continues to satisfy the requirements imposed in those Regulations for payment of the addition.

(2) A claimant's weekly applicable amount shall include an amount (the "protected sum") equal to any protected sum which would have been applicable in his case under regulation 17(1)(g) or 18(1)(h) of, and Schedules 3A and 3B to, the Income Support Regulations had he been entitled to income support and not a jobseeker's allowance.

(3) In the case of any person who had he been entitled to income support and not a jobseeker's allowance, would in any week have had a higher applicable amount, in accordance with regulation 17(2) to (6A) of the Income Support Regulations, than the amount applicable to him in accordance with regulation 82 or, as the case may be, 83 then that amount shall be substituted for the applicable amount determined under that regulation.

(4) Paragraph (5) applies to a person who, had he been entitled to income support and not a jobseeker's allowance, would have been a person to whom any of the following transitional or savings provisions would have applied—
- (a) the Income Support (General) Amendment No.3 Regulations 1993 ("the 1993 Regulations"), regulation 4;
- (b) the Income-related Benefits Schemes (Miscellaneous Amendments) Regulations 1995 ("the 1995 Regulations"), regulation 28.

(5) Where this paragraph applies, the amount of housing costs applicable in the particular case shall be determined as if, in Schedule 2—
- (a) in a case to which regulation 4(1) of the 1993 Regulations would have applied, paragraph 10(4) to (9) was omitted;
- (b) in a case to which regulation 4(4) of the 1993 Regulations would have applied, in [¹paragraph 10(4)] for the reference to £100,000 there was substituted a reference to £150,000; and
- (c) in a case to which the 1995 Regulations apply, in [¹paragraph 10(4)] for the reference to £100,000 there was substituted a reference to £125,000.

(6) In determining for the purposes of this regulation whether, if the claimant were entitled to income support—
- (a) an amount would be applicable;
- (b) an amount would be payable; or
- (c) if an amount was payable, the rate at which it would be payable,

any requirement that the person be entitled to income support, or to income support for any period of time, shall be treated as if the reference to income support included also a reference to an income-based jobseeker's allowance.

(7) [²For the purposes of applying paragraph (1), regulation 2A of the Income Support (Transitional) Regulations, and for the purposes of paragraph (6), regulation 3A of the Income Support Regulations shall have effect in accordance with the following sub-paragraphs—]
- (a) as if in paragraph (1)(a), after the words "permitted period", there was included the words "subject to paragraph 2A"; and
- (b) with the addition after paragraph (1) of the following paragraphs—

"(2A) Subject to paragraph (2B) where the claimant or his partner has ceased to be engaged in remunerative work, the permitted period shall be 8 weeks if—
- (a) a jobseeker's allowance [²is not payable] to the claimant in the circumstances mentioned in section 19(6)(a) or (b) of the Jobseekers Act 1995 (employment left voluntarily or lost through misconduct); or
- (b) the claimant or his partner has ceased to be engaged in that work within 4 weeks of beginning it; or
- (c) at any time during the period of 13 weeks immediately preceding the beginning of that work, the person who has ceased to be engaged in it—
  - (i) was engaged in remunerative work; or
  - (ii) was in relevant education; or
  - (iii) was a student.

(2B) [¹Paragraph (2A)(b) or (2A)(c)] shall not apply in the case of a person who, by virtue of regulation 74 of the Jobseeker's Allowance Regulations 1996, is a person to whom section 19(6)(b) of the Jobseekers Act 1995 does not apply.

(2C) In this regulation, "remunerative work" means remunerative work for the purposes of the Jobseekers Act 1995."

AMENDMENTS

1. Jobseeker's Allowance (Amendment) Regulations 1996 (S.I. 1996 No. 1516), reg. 20 and Sched. (October 7, 1996).
2. Jobseeker's Allowance and Income Support (General) (Amendment) Regulations 1996 (S.I. 1996 No. 1517), reg. 20 (October 7, 1996).

DEFINITIONS

"claimant"—see Jobseekers Act, s. 35(1)
"Income Support Regulations"—*ibid.*
"remunerative work"—see reg. 51(1).

GENERAL NOTE

This provision only applies to income-based JSA (reg. 82).

Paras. (2) to (5) preserve the effect of various income support transitional protection provisions for JSA claimants who would have been covered by them had they been entitled to claim income support after October 6, 1996. Para. (1) concerns those who were entitled to a special transitional addition or transitional addition under the Income Support (Transitional) Regulations before October 7, 1996. For the regulations referred to in para. (4) see p. 493 and p. 496. The effect of those regulations is explained in the notes to para. 11((4)–(11) of Sched. 3 to the Income Support Regulations.

[¹ Minimum amount of a jobseeker's allowance

87A. Where the amount of a jobseeker's allowance is less than 10 pence week that allowance shall not be payable.]

AMENDMENT

1. Jobseeker's Allowance and Income Support (General) (Amendment) Regulations 1996 (S.I. 1996 No. 1517), reg. 21 (October 7, 1996).

PART VIII

INCOME AND CAPITAL

Chapter I

General

Calculation of income and capital of members of claimant's family and of a polygamous marriage

88.—(1) Subject to paragraphs (2) and (3) and to regulation 106 (modifications in respect of children and young persons), the income and capital of a claimant's partner and the income of a child or young person which by virtue of section 13(2) is to be treated as the income and capital of the claimant, shall be calculated in accordance with the following provisions of this Part in like manner as for the claimant; and any reference to the "claimant" shall, except where the context otherwise requires, be construed, for the purposes of this Part, as if it were a reference to his partner or that child or young person.

(2) Regulations 99(2) and 101(2), so far as they relate to paragraphs 1 to 13 and 19 of Schedule 6 (earnings to be disregarded) and regulation 104(1) (capital treated as income) shall not apply to a child or young person.

(3) Where at least one member of a couple is aged less than 18 and the applicable amount of the couple falls to be determined under [¹paragraph 1(3)(b), (c), (g) or (h)] of Schedule 1 (applicable amounts), the income of the claimant's partner shall not be treated as the income of the claimant to the extent that—

(a) in the case of a couple where both members are aged less than 18, the amount specified in paragraph 1(3)(a) of that Schedule exceeds the amount specified in paragraph 1(3)(c) of that Schedule; and

(b) in the case of a couple where only one member is aged less than 18, the amount specified in paragraph 1(3)(e) of that Schedule exceeds the amount which applies in that case which is specified in [¹paragraph 1(3)(g) or (h)] of that Schedule.

(4) Subject to paragraph (5), where a claimant is married polygamously to two or more members of his household—

(a) the claimant shall be treated as possessing capital and income belonging to each such member and the income of any child or young person who is one of that member's family; and

(b) the income and capital of that member or, as the case may be, the income of that child or young person shall be calculated in accordance with the following provisions of this Part in like manner as for the claimant or, as the case may be, as for any child or young person who is a member of his family.

(5) Where a member of a polygamous marriage is a partner aged less than 18 and the amount which applies in respect of him under regulation 84(2) (polygamous marriages) is nil, the claimant shall not be treated as possessing the income of that partner to the extent that an amount in respect of him would have been included in the applicable amount if he had fallen within the circumstances set out in regulation 84(2)(a) or (b).

AMENDMENT

1. Jobseeker's Allowance (Amendment) Regulations 1996 (S.I. 1996 No. 1516), reg. 20 and Sched. (October 7, 1996).

DEFINITIONS

"child"—see Jobseekers Act, s. 35(1).
"claimant"—*ibid.*
"family"—*ibid.*
"partner"—see reg. 1(3).
"polygamous marriage"—*ibid.*
"young person"—see reg. 76.

GENERAL NOTE

This regulation contains the basic rule on aggregation of resources which is the same as that in reg. 23 of the Income Support Regulations. The income and capital of the claimant's partner is treated as the claimant's, but only the income of a child or young person is aggregated with the claimant's (confirmed in reg. 109). If a child or young person has capital over £3,000 there is no personal allowance for that child (reg. 83(b) and any income of the child is not aggregated (reg. 106(5)).

See the notes to reg. 23.

The aggregation rule is primarily relevant to income-based JSA (although reg. 88 applies to both contribution and income-based JSA), since for contribution-based JSA only the *claimant's* earnings and pension payments are taken into account (see s. 2(1)(c) and 4(1) of the Jobseekers Act and regs. 56(2), 80(2) and 81 in *Bonner, Non-Means-Tested Benefits: the Legislation*).

[¹Income of participants in the self-employment route of the Employment Option of the New Deal

88A. Chapters II, III, IV, V, VII and VIII of this Part and regulations 131 to 136, 138 and 139 shall not apply to any income which is to be calculated in accordance with Chapter IVA of this Part (participants in the self-employment route of the Employment Option of the New Deal).]

AMENDMENT

1. Social Security (Miscellaneous Amendments) (No 4) Regulations 1998 (S.I. 1998 No. 1174), reg. 3(3) (June 1, 1998).

GENERAL NOTE

Regulation 88A takes any gross receipts from trading while on the self-employment route of the Employment option of the New Deal for 18 to 24-year-olds out of the categories of earnings, self-employed earnings and income other than earnings. The rules for liable relative payments, payments of child support maintenance and student income (except reg. 137) also do not apply. Any such receipts may only be taken into account in accordance with regs. 102A to 102D.

Liable relative payments

89.—Regulations 94 to 106, 108 to 115 and Chapter IX of this Part shall not apply to any payment which is to be calculated in accordance with Chapter VII thereof (liable relatives).

GENERAL NOTE

See reg. 25 of the Income Support Regulations.

Child support

90.—Regulations 94, 96, 97, 103 and 105 and Chapters VII and IX of this Part shall not apply to any payment which is to be calculated in accordance with Chapter VIII of this Part (child support).

GENERAL NOTE

Reg. 90 is to the same effect as reg. 25A of the Income Support Regulations and takes payments of child support maintenance, paid under an assessment carried out in accordance with the Child Support Acts 1991 to 1995, out of the categories of income other than earnings and of liable relative payments. (Reg. 90 also provides that the provisions relating to full-time students in Chapter IX do not apply to child support maintenance payments; there is no reference to such income support provisions in reg. 25A). Child support maintenance payments are only to be taken into account for the purposes of JSA in accordance with regs. 125 to 129 (which are similar to regs. 60A to 60E of the Income Support Regulations).

Calculation of income and capital of full-time students

91.—The provisions of Chapters II to VI of this Part (income and capital) shall have effect in relation to full-time students and their partners subject to the modifications set out in Chapter IX thereof (full-time students).

DEFINITIONS

"full-time student"—see reg. 1(3)
"partner"—*ibid.*

GENERAL NOTE

See reg. 26 of the Income Support Regulations.

Rounding of fractions

92.—Where any calculation under this Part results in a fraction of a penny that fraction shall, if it would be to the claimant's advantage, be treated as a penny, otherwise it shall be disregarded.

Chapter II

Income

Calculation of income

93.—(1) For the purposes of section 3(1) (the income-based conditions) the income of a claimant shall be calculated on a weekly basis—
(a) by determining in accordance with this Part, other than Chapter VI, the weekly amount of his income; and
(b) by adding to that amount the weekly income calculated under regulation 116 (calculation of tariff income from capital).
(2) For the purposes of paragraph (1) "income" includes capital treated as income under regulation 104 and income which a claimant is treated as possessing under regulation 105 (notional income).

DEFINITION

"claimant"—see Jobseekers Act, s. 35(1).

GENERAL NOTE

This confirms that for the purposes of income-based JSA all resources which come under the description of income, including resources specifically treated as earnings or income, are to be taken into account in the income calculation.

Calculation of earnings derived from employed earner's employment and income other than earnings

94.—(1) Earnings derived from employment as an employed earner and income which does not consist of earnings shall be taken into account over a period determined in accordance with the following paragraphs and at a weekly amount determined in accordance with regulation 97 (calculation of weekly amount of income).
(2) Subject to the following provisions of this regulation, the period over which a payment is to be taken into account shall be—
(a) in a case where it is payable in respect of a period, a period equal to the length of that period;
(b) in any other case, a period equal to such number of weeks as is equal to the number obtained (and any fraction shall be treated as a corresponding fraction of a week) by dividing the net earnings, or in the case of income which does not consist of earnings, the amount of that income less any amount paid by way of tax on that income which is disregarded under paragraph 1 of Schedule 7 (sums to be disregarded in the calculation of income other than earnings), by the amount of jobseeker's allowance which would be payable had the payment not been made plus an amount equal to the total of the sums which would fall to be disregarded from that payment under Schedule 6 (sums to be disregarded in the calculation of earnings) or, as the case may be, any paragraph of Schedule 7 other than paragraph 1 of that Schedule, as is appropriate in the claimant's case, and that period shall begin on the date on which the payment is treated as paid under regulation 96.
[¹(2A) The period over which a Career Development Loan, which is paid pursuant to section 2 of the Employment and Training Act 1973, shall be taken into account shall be the period of education and training intended to be supported by that loan.

(2B) Where grant income as defined in Chapter IX of this Part has been paid to a person who ceases to be a full-time student before the end of the period in respect of which that income is payable and, as a consequence, the whole or part of that income falls to be repaid by that person, that income shall be taken into account over the period beginning on the date on which that income is treated as paid under regulation 96 and ending—

    (a) on the date on which repayment is made in full; or

[²(aa) where the grant is paid in instalments, on the day before the next instalment would have been paid had the claimant remained a student; or]

    (b) on the last date of the academic term or vacation during which that person ceased to be a full-time student,

whichever shall first occur.]

(3) Where earnings not of the same kind are derived from the same source and the periods in respect of which those earnings would, but for this paragraph, fall to be taken into account—

    (a) overlap, wholly or partly, those earnings shall be taken into account over a period equal to the aggregate length of those periods;

    (b) and that period shall begin with the earliest date on which any part of those earnings would otherwise be treated as paid under regulation 96 (date on which income is treated as paid).

(4) In a case to which paragraph (3) applies, earnings under regulation 98 (earnings of employed earners) shall be taken into account in the following order of priority—

    (a) earnings normally derived from the employment;

    (b) any compensation payment;

    (c) any holiday pay.

(5) Where earnings to which regulation 98(1)(b) or (c) (earnings of employed earners) applies are paid in respect of part of a day, those earnings shall be taken into account over a period equal to a day.

(6) Subject to paragraph (7), the period over which a compensation payment is to be taken into account shall be the period beginning on the date on which the payment is treated as paid under regulation 96 (date on which income is treated as paid) and ending—

    (a) subject to sub-paragraph (b), where the person who made the payment represents that it, or part of it, was paid in lieu of notice of termination of employment or on account of the early termination of a contract of employment for a term certain, on the expiry date;

    (b) in a case where the person who made the payment represents that it, or part of it, was paid in lieu of consultation under section 188 of the Trade Union and Labour Relations (Consolidation) Act 1992, on the later of—

        (i) the date on which the consultation period under that section would have ended;

        (ii) in a case where sub-paragraph (a) also applies, the expiry date; or

        (iii) the standard date;

    (c) in any other case, on the standard date.

(7) The maximum length of time over which a compensation payment may be taken into account under paragraph (6) is 52 weeks from the date on which the payment is treated as paid under regulation 96.

(8) In this regulation—

    (a) ''compensation payment'' means any payment to which paragraph (3) of regulation 98 (earnings of employed earners) applies;

    (b) ''the expiry date'' means in relation to the termination of a person's employment—

        (i) the date on which the period of notice applicable to the person was due to expire, or would have expired had it not been waived; and for this purpose ''period of notice'' means the period of notice of termination of employment to which a person is entitled by statute or by contract, whichever is the longer, or, if he is not entitled to such notice, the period of notice which is customary in the employment in question; or

    (ii) subject to paragraph (9), where the person who made the payment represents that the period in respect of which that payment is made is longer than the period of notice referred to in head (i) above, the date on which that longer period is due to expire; or

    (iii) where the person had a contract of employment for a term certain, the date on which it was due to expire;

  (c) "the standard date" means the earlier of—

    (i) the expiry date; and

    (ii) the last day of the period determined by dividing the amount of the compensation payment by the maximum weekly amount which, on the date on which the payment is treated as paid under regulation 96, is specified in paragraph 8(1)(c) of Schedule 14 to the Employment Protection (Consolidation) Act 1978, and treating the result (less any fraction of a whole number) as a number of weeks.

  (9) For the purposes of paragraph (8), if it appears to the adjudication officer in a case to which sub-paragraph (b)(ii) of that paragraph applies that, having regard to the amount of the compensation payment and the level of remuneration normally received by the claimant when he was engaged in the employment in respect of which the compensation payment was made, it is unreasonable to take the payment into account until the date specified in that sub-paragraph, the expiry date shall be the date specified in paragraph (8)(b)(i).

  (10) For the purposes of this regulation the claimant's earnings and income which does not consist of earnings shall be calculated in accordance with Chapters III and V respectively of this Part.

AMENDMENTS

  1. Income-related Benefits and Jobseeker's Allowance (Miscellaneous Amendments) Regulations 1997 (S.I. 1997 No. 65), reg. 5(2) (April 7, 1997).

  2. Social Security (Miscellaneous Amendments) Regulations 1998 (S.I. 1998 No. 563), reg. 12 (April 6, 1998).

DEFINITIONS

  "adjudication officer"—see Jobseekers Act, s. 35(1).
  "claimant"—*ibid*, reg. 88(1)
  "earnings"—see reg. 1(3).
  "employed earner"—see reg. 3, SSCBA, s. 2(1)(a).
  "full-time student"—see reg. 1(3).
  "grant income"—see reg. 130.

GENERAL NOTE

  On paras. (1) to (5) see the notes to reg. 29(1) to (4A) of the Income Support Regulations. Under paras. (3) and (4) note the differences between the disregards in paras. 1 to 3 of Sched. 8 to the Income Support Regulations and paras. 1 to 4 of Sched. 6 to the JSA Regulations (see the notes to Sched. 6), and the differences between reg. 35 of the Income Support Regulations and reg. 98 of the JSA Regulations (see the notes to reg. 98).

  Note the effect of reg. 52(3) where a person who was in remunerative work receives holiday pay which counts as earnings (see reg. 98(1)(c)).

Paragraphs (6) to (9)
  These provisions define the length of the period for which a "compensation payment" (defined in reg. 98(3)) is to be taken into account. If the person receiving the payment was in remunerative work (see reg. 51) he will be treated as in remunerative work for the period covered by the payment

(see reg. 52(3)). There is no equivalent to reg. 29(4C) of the Income Support Regulations so it seems that a compensation payment made on the termination of part-time employment will be taken into account as earnings for the period covered by the payment.

See *CJSA 5529/1997* in which the effect of para. (6) was that the period to which the claimant's compensation payment was to be attributed ended before it started. On October 1, 1996 the claimant agreed with her employer that her employment would end on December 31, 1996 by way of voluntary redundancy. She was to receive a payment of £41,500 on January 4, 1997, which would not include any sum in lieu of notice. She claimed JSA with effect from January 1, 1997. The Commissioner states that the period for which the compensation period was to be taken into account under para. (6) ended on the "standard date". Under para. (8)(c) the standard date was the earlier of the "expiry date" and what might be termed the "apportionment date". The expiry date in this case was no later than December 31, 1996 because the claimant was entitled to 12 weeks (or three months') notice and the agreement for redundancy had been made on October 1, 1996 (see para. (8)(b)(i)). The result was that there was no period in respect of which the compensation payment was to be taken into account and thus no period during which she was to be treated as in remunerative work after December 31, 1996.

Calculation of earnings of self-employed earners

95.—(1) Except where paragraph (2) applies, where a claimant's income consists of earnings from employment as a self-employed earner the weekly amount of his earnings shall be determined by reference to his average weekly earnings from that employment—

    (a) over a period of one year; or

    (b) where the claimant has recently become engaged in that employment or there has been a change which is likely to affect the normal pattern of business, over such other period as may, in any particular case, enable the weekly amount of his earnings to be determined more accurately.

(2) Where the claimant's earnings consist of royalties or sums paid periodically for or in respect of any copyright those earnings shall be taken into account over a period equal to such number of weeks as is equal to the number obtained (and any fraction shall be treated as a corresponding fraction of a week) by dividing the earnings by the amount of jobseeker's allowance which would be payable had the payment not been made plus an amount equal to the total of the sums which would fall to be disregarded from the payment under Schedule 6 (earnings to be disregarded) as is appropriate in the claimant's case.

(3) For the purposes of this regulation the claimant's earnings shall be calculated in accordance with Chapter IV of this Part.

DEFINITIONS

    "claimant"—see Jobseekers Act, s. 35(1), reg. 88(1).
    "earnings"—see reg. 1(3).
    "self-employed earner"—*ibid.* SSCBA, s. 2(1)(b).

GENERAL NOTE

    See the notes to reg. 30 of the Income Support Regulations.

    Note the more general exception to the rule in para. (1)(a) that is hidden in reg. 101(11) which allows the amount of any item of income or expenditure to be calculated over a different period if that will produce a more accurate figure.

Date on which income is treated as paid

96.—(1) Except where paragraph (2) applies, a payment of income to which regulation 94 (calculation of earnings derived from employed earner's employment and income other than earnings) applies shall be treated as paid—

    (a) in the case of a payment which is due to be paid before the first benefit week pursuant to the claim, on the date on which it is due to be paid;

(b) in any other case, on the first day of the benefit week in which it is due to be paid or the first succeeding benefit week in which it is practicable to take it into account.

(2) Income support, maternity allowance, short-term or long-term incapacity benefit, severe disablement allowance or jobseeker's allowance shall be treated as paid on the day of the benefit week in respect of which it is payable.

DEFINITION

"benefit week"—see reg. 1(3)

GENERAL NOTE

See the notes to reg. 31 of the Income Support Regulations.

Calculation of weekly amount of income

97.—(1) For the purposes of regulation 94 (calculation of earnings derived from employed earner's employment and income other than earnings), subject to paragraphs (2) to [²(7)], where the period in respect of which a payment is made—
(a) does not exceed a week, the weekly amount shall be the amount of that payment;
(b) exceeds a week, the weekly amount shall be determined—
    (i) in a case where that period is a month, by multiplying the amount of the payment by 12 and dividing the product by 52;
    (ii) in a case where that period is three months, by multiplying the amount of the payment by 4 and dividing the product by 52;
    (iii) in a case where that period is a year by dividing the amount of the payment by 52;
    (iv) in any other case by multiplying the amount of the payment by 7 and dividing the product by the number equal to the number of days in the period in respect of which it is made.

(2) Where a payment for a period not exceeding a week is treated under regulation 96(1)(a) (date on which income is treated as paid) as paid before the first benefit week and a part is to be taken into account for some days only in that week ("the relevant days"), the amount to be taken into account for the relevant days shall be calculated by multiplying the amount of the payment by the number equal to the number of relevant days and dividing the product by the number of days in the period in respect of which it is made.

(3) Where a payment is in respect of a period equal to or in excess of a week and a part thereof is to be taken into account for some days only in a benefit week ("the relevant days"), the amount to be taken into account for the relevant days shall, except where paragraph (4) applies, be calculated by multiplying the amount of the payment by the number equal to the number of relevant days and dividing the product by the number of days in the period in respect of which it is made.

(4) In the case of a payment of—
(a) maternity allowance, short-term or long-term incapacity benefit or severe disablement allowance, the amount to be taken into account for the relevant days shall be the amount of benefit payable in respect of those days;
(b) jobseeker's allowance or income support, the amount to be taken into account for the relevant days shall be calculated by multiplying the weekly amount of the benefit by the number of relevant days and dividing the product by seven.

(5) Except in the case of a payment which it has not been practicable to treat under regulation 96(1)(b) as paid on the first day of the benefit week in which

it is due to be paid, where a payment of income from a particular source is or has been paid regularly and that payment falls to be taken into account in the same benefit week as a payment of the same kind and from the same source, the amount of that income to be taken into account in any one benefit week shall not exceed the weekly amount determined under paragraph (1)(a) or (b), as the case may be, of the payment which under regulation 96(1)(b) (date on which income is treated as paid) is treated as paid first.

(6) Where the amount of the claimant's income fluctuates and has changed more than once, or a claimant's regular pattern of work is such that he does not work every week, the foregoing paragraphs may be modified so that the weekly amount of his income is determined by reference to his average weekly income—

   (a) if there is a recognisable cycle of work, over a period of one complete cycle (including, where the cycle involves periods in which the claimant does no work, those periods but disregarding any other absences);

   (b) in any other case, over a period of five weeks or such other period as may, in the particular case, enable the claimant's average weekly income to be determined more accurately.

[¹(7) Where income is taken into account under paragraph (2B) of regulation 94 over the period specified in that paragraph, the amount of that income to be taken into account in respect of any week in that period shall be an amount equal to the amount of that income which would have been taken into account under regulation 131 had the person to whom that income was paid not ceased to be a full-time student.]

AMENDMENTS

1. Income-related Benefits and Jobseeker's Allowance (Miscellaneous Amendments) Regulations 1997 (S.I. 1997 No. 65), reg. 6(2) (April 7, 1997).
2. Social Security (Miscellaneous Amendments) Regulations 1997 (S.I. 1997 No. 454), reg. 2(11) (April 7, 1997).

DEFINITIONS

   "benefit week"—see reg. 1(3).
   "claimant"—see Jobseekers Act, s. 35(1), reg. 88(1).
   "full-time student"—see reg. 1(3).

GENERAL NOTE

   See the notes to reg. 32 of the Income Support Regulations. In relation to para. (5), the JSA disregards corresponding to the income support disregards referred to in those notes are in Sched. 6, para. 13, Sched. 7, para. 39, Sched. 6, para. 16 and Sched. 7 para. 37.
   Note that there is no equivalent of reg. 32(7) as the JSA rules for the treatment of compensation payments made on the termination of part-time employment are different from those under the income support scheme (see reg. 98((1)(b) and (3) and the note to reg. 94(6) to (9)).
   On calculation of entitlement to income-based JSA for part-weeks, see reg. 150.

Chapter III

Employed Earners

Earnings of employed earners

   98.—(1) Subject to paragraphs (2) and (3), "earnings" means in the case of employment as an employed earner, any remuneration or profit derived from that employment and includes—

   (a) any bonus or commission;

(b) any compensation payment;

(c) any holiday pay except any payable more than four weeks after the termination or interruption of employment but this exception shall not apply
to a person who is, or would be, prevented from being entitled to a
jobseeker's allowance by section 14 (trade disputes);

(d) any payment by way of a retainer;

(e) any payment made by the claimant's employer in respect of expenses
not wholly, exclusively and necessarily incurred in the performance of
the duties of the employment, including any payment made by the claimant's employer in respect of—

   (i) travelling expenses incurred by the claimant between his home and
place of employment;

   (ii) expenses incurred by the claimant under arrangements made for the
care of a member of his family owing to the claimant's absence
from home;

[¹(f) any payment or award of compensation made under section 68(2), 69,
71(2)(a), 77 or 79 of the Employment Protection (Consolidation) Act
1978 (remedies for unfair dismissal and compensation);

(ff) any payment or remuneration made under section 12, 19 or 47 of the
Employment Protection (Consolidation) Act 1978 (guaranteed payments,
remuneration whilst suspended from work on medical or maternity
grounds);]

(g) any award of compensation made under section 156, 157, 161 to 166,
189 or 192 of the Trade Union and Labour Relations (Consolidation) Act
1992 (compensation for unfair dismissal or redundancy on grounds of
involvement in trade union activities, and protective awards).

(2) "Earnings" shall not include—

(a) any payment in kind;

(b) any periodic sum paid to a claimant on account of the termination of his
employment by reason of redundancy;

(c) any remuneration paid by or on behalf of an employer to the claimant
in respect of a period throughout which the claimant is on maternity
leave or is absent form work because he is ill;

(d) any payment in respect of expenses wholly, exclusively and necessarily
incurred in the performance of the duties of the employment;

(e) any occupational pension;

(f) any redundancy payment within the meaning of section 81(1) of the
Employment Protection (Consolidation) Act 1978;

[²(g) any lump sum payment made under the Iron and Steel Re-adaptation
Benefits Scheme].

(3) In this regulation "compensation payment" means any payment made in
respect of the termination of employment other than—

(a) any remuneration or emolument (whether in money or in kind) which
accrued in the period before the termination;

(b) any holiday pay;

(c) any payment specified in paragraphs (1)(f)[,¹(ff),] or (g) or (2);

(d) any refund of contributions to which that person was entitled under an
occupational pension scheme.

AMENDMENTS

1. Jobseeker's Allowance and Income Support (General) (Amendment) Regulations 1996 (S.I.
1996 No. 1517), reg. 22 (October 7, 1996).
2. Social Security (Miscellaneous Amendments) Regulations 1997 (S.I. 1997 No. 454), reg. 2(12)
(April 7, 1997).

DEFINITIONS

"claimant"—see Jobseekers Act, s.35(1), reg. 88(1).
"employed earner"—see reg. 3, SSCBA, s. 2(1)(a).
"family"—see Jobseekers Act, s. 35(1).
"maternity leave"—see reg. 1(3).
"occupational pension"—*ibid.*

GENERAL NOTE

Reg. 98 applies to earnings from employment as an employed earner. It is similar to reg. 35 of the Income Support Regulations but there are some differences which are referred to below. Otherwise see the notes to reg. 35.

Like reg. 35(1), para. (1) first provides a general definition of earnings from employment as an employee—any remuneration or profit derived from that employment—and then deems certain payments to be earnings. Para. (2) provides a number of exceptions and Sched. 6 lists items which would otherwise count as earnings which are to be disregarded.

Paragraph (1)

Note that the particular categories that are deemed to be earnings are the same as for income support, except that there is no equivalent of reg. 35(1)(b), (c) and (i); instead sub-para. (b) refers to "any compensation payment" (defined in para. (3)). In addition, sub-paras. (f), (ff) and (g) slightly expand on the list of awards of compensation or pay made by an industrial tribunal and other payments under the employment protection legislation that are specifically deemed to count as earnings (compare reg. 35(1)(g) and (h)). For guarantee payments under income support, see the note to reg. 35(1)(e).

The categories of earnings that can lead to complete disentitlement to JSA under reg. 52(3) are those in sub-paras. (b) and (c) (compensation payments, but note the exclusions from the definition in para. (3), and holiday pay). Holiday pay outside the period in sub-para. (c) is capital (reg. 110(3)).

See the notes to reg. 35(1) for further discussion.

Paragraph (2)

Sub-paras. (b) and (f) contain two additions to the list of payments that do not count as earnings, which otherwise are the same as for income support. Sub-para. (b) in fact contains the same provision that in the Income Support Regulations is expressed as an exception to reg. 35(1)(b). But by placing it within the first part of the para. (2) list the JSA rules make it clear that such periodic redundancy payments although not earnings will count as income (see below). Sub-para. (f) expressly states that statutory redundancy payments are not earnings, nor are lump sum payments under the Iron and Steel Re-adaptation Benefits Scheme (sub-para. (g)).

Note that although the payments listed in para. (2)(a) to (e) are deemed not to be earnings they do count as other income (reg. 103(6)). However, income in kind is disregarded (Sched. 7, para. 22) and so are payments of necessary expenses (Sched. 7, para. 3). There is no provision for the disregard of the payments in sub-paras. (b), (c) and (e). Under sub-paras. (f) and (g) statutory redundancy payments and lump sum payments under the Iron and Steel Re-adaptation Benefits Scheme will count as capital.

See the notes to reg. 35(2) for further discussion.

Paragraph (3)

This provision is different from reg. 35(3) (see also reg. 35(1)(i) and (1A)) of the Income Support Regulations but is based on the previous unemployment benefit rule. It provides a broad definition of a "compensation payment" as "any payment made in respect of the termination of employment" but then lists those payments which are not to count as compensation payments. If a payment is a compensation payment it counts as earnings under para. (1)(b) and can lead to complete disentitlement to JSA in accordance with reg. 52(3) for the period covered by the payment (see reg. 94(6) to (9) and note *CJSA 5529/1997* referred to in the note to reg. 94(6) to (9)).

Calculation of net earnings of employed earners

99.—(1) For the purposes of regulation 94 (calculation of earnings of employed earners) the earnings of a claimant derived from employment as an employed earner to be taken into account shall, subject to paragraph (2), be his net earnings.

(2) Subject to paragraph (3), there shall be disregarded from a claimant's net earnings, any sum, where applicable, specified in paragraphs 1 to 16 and 19 of Schedule 6.

(3) [*Omitted as not relating to income-based jobseeker's allowance.*]

(4) For the purposes of paragraph (1) net earnings shall be calculated by taking into account the gross earnings of the claimant from that employment less—

    (a) any amount deducted from those earnings by way of—
        (i) income tax;
        (ii) primary Class 1 contributions payable under the Benefits Act; and
    (b) one-half of any sum paid by the claimant in respect of a pay period by way of a contribution towards an occupational or personal pension scheme.

DEFINITIONS

    "the Benefits Act"—see Jobseekers Act, s.35(1).
    "claimant"—*ibid.*, reg. 88(1).
    "employed earner"—see reg. 3, SSCBA, s. 2(1)(a).
    "occupational pension scheme"—see Jobseekers Act, s. 35(1).
    "pay period"—see reg. 1(3).
    "personal pension scheme"—see Jobseekers Act, s. 35(1).

GENERAL NOTE

    See the notes to reg. 36 of the Income Support Regulations.
    One of the issues discussed in those notes is the decision of the ECJ in *Cresswell v. Chief Adjudication Officer, Jackson v. Chief Adjudication Officer* [1992] E.C.R. I-4737, which held that income support did not come within E.C. Directive 79/7 or E.C. Directive 76/207. The position of income-based JSA would however seem to be different. Income-based JSA is clearly directly concerned with one of the risks in Article 3(1) of Directive 79/7, namely unemployment. Furthermore, Directive 76/207 may also be applicable. Further challenges against discriminatory aspects of income-based JSA, such as the lack of a child care costs disregard for part-time earnings, may therefore be possible. But note the final result of the *Meyers* case also referred to in the note to s. 36.

Chapter IV

Self-Employed Earners

Earnings of self-employed earners

100.—(1) Subject to paragraph (2), "earnings", in the case of employment as a self-employed earner, means the gross receipts of the employment and shall include any allowance paid under any scheme referred to in regulation 19(1)(r) (circumstances in which a person is to be treated as actively seeking employment: schemes for assisting persons to become self-employed earners) to the claimant for the purpose of assisting him in carrying on his business.

(2) "Earnings" shall not include—

    (a) where a claimant is involved in providing board and lodging accommodation for which a charge is payable, any payment by way of such a charge;

    (b) any payment to which paragraph 27 or 28 of Schedule 7 refers (payments in respect of a person accommodated with the claimant under an arrangement made by a local authority or voluntary organisation, and payments made to the claimant by a health authority, local authority or voluntary organisation in respect of persons temporarily in the claimant's care).

DEFINITIONS

"board and lodging accommodation"—see reg. 1(3)
"claimant"—see Jobseekers Act, s. 35(1), reg. 88(1).
"employment"—see reg. 3.
"self-employed earner"—see reg. 1(3), SSCBA, s. 2(1)(b).
"voluntary organisation"—see reg. 1(3).

GENERAL NOTE

See the notes to reg. 37 of the Income Support Regulations.

The payments in para. (2)(a) count as income under reg. 103(6) but subject to disregards. Para. (2)(b) applies to payments to foster-parents and to people for providing temporary care in their home. These payments are disregarded as income other than earnings under paras. 27 and 28 of Sched. 7. Para. (2)(b) ensures that they are not treated as earnings. See also reg. 53(f).

Calculation of net profit of self-employed earners

101.—(1) For the purposes of regulation 95 (calculation of earnings of self-employed earners), the earnings of a claimant to be taken into account shall be—

(a) in the case of a self-employed earner who is engaged in employment on his own account, the net profit derived from that employment;

(b) in the case of a self-employed earner whose employment is carried on in partnership, or is that of a share fisherman within the meaning of regulation 156, his share of the net profit derived from that employment less—

(i) an amount in respect of income tax and of social security contributions payable under the Benefits Act calculated in accordance with regulation 102 (deduction of tax and contributions for self-employed earners); and

(ii) one half of any premium paid in the period that is relevant under regulation 95 in respect of a personal pension scheme.

(2) Subject to paragraph (3), there shall be disregarded from a claimant's net profit any sum, where applicable, specified in paragraphs 1 to 16 of Schedule 6.

(3) For the purposes of calculating the amount to be deducted in respect of earnings under regulation 80 (contribution-based jobseeker's allowance: deductions in respect of earnings) the disregards in paragraphs 5 to 8 and 11 of Schedule 6 shall not apply.

(4) For the purposes of paragraph (1)(a) the net profit of the employment shall, except where paragraph (10) applies, be calculated by taking into account the earnings of the employment over the period determined under regulation 95 (calculation of earnings of self-employed earners) less—

(a) subject to paragraphs (6) to (8), any expenses wholly and exclusively defrayed in that period for the purposes of that employment;

(b) an amount in respect of—

(i) income tax; and

(ii) social security contributions payable under the Benefits Act, calculated in accordance with regulation 102 (deductions of tax and contributions for self-employed earners); and

(c) one-half of any premium paid in the period that is relevant under regulation 95 in respect of a personal pension scheme.

(5) For the purposes of paragraph (1)(b), the net profit of the employment shall be calculated by taking into account the earnings of the employment over the period determined under regulation 95 less, subject to paragraphs (6) to (8), any expenses wholly and exclusively defrayed in that period for the purposes of that employment.

(6) Subject to paragraph (7), no deduction shall be made under paragraph (4)(a) or (5) in respect of—
   (a) any capital expenditure;
   (b) the depreciation of any capital asset;
   (c) any sum employed or intended to be employed in the setting up or expansion of the employment;
   (d) any loss incurred before the beginning of the period determined under regulation 95;
   (e) the repayment of capital on any loan taken out for the purposes of the employment;
   (f) any expenses incurred in providing business entertainment.
(7) A deduction shall be made under paragraph (4)(a) or (5) in respect of the repayment of capital on any loan used for—
   (a) the replacement in the course of business of equipment or machinery; and
   (b) the repair of an existing business asset except to the extent that any sum is payable under an insurance policy for its repair.
(8) An adjudication officer shall refuse to make a deduction under paragraph (4)(a) or (5) in respect of any expenses where he is not satisfied that the expense has been defrayed or, having regard to the nature of the expense and its amount, that it has been reasonably incurred.
(9) For the avoidance of doubt—
   (a) a deduction shall not be made under paragraph (4)(a) or (5) in respect of any sum unless it has been expended for the purposes of the business;
   (b) a deduction shall be made thereunder in respect of—
      (i) the excess of any VAT paid over VAT received in the period determined under regulation 95;
      (ii) any income expended in the repair of an existing asset except to the extent that any sum is payable under an insurance policy for its repair;
      (iii) any payment of interest on a loan taken out for the purposes of the employment.
(10) Where a claimant is engaged in employment as a child-minder the net profit of the employment shall be one-third of the earnings of that employment, less—
   (a) an amount in respect of—
      (i) income tax; and
      (ii) social security contributions payable under the Benefits Act, calculated in accordance with regulation 102 (deductions of tax and contributions for self-employed earners); and
   (b) one half of any premium paid in the period that is relevant under regulation 95 in respect of a personal pension scheme.
(11) Notwithstanding regulation 95 and the foregoing paragraphs, an adjudication officer may assess any item of a claimant's income or expenditure over a period other than that determined under regulation 95 such as may, in the particular case, enable the weekly amount of that item of income or expenditure to be determined more accurately.
(12) For the avoidance of doubt where a claimant is engaged in employment as a self-employed earner and he is engaged in one or more other employments as a self-employed or employed earner, any loss incurred in any one of his employments shall not be offset against his earnings in any other of his employments.

DEFINITIONS

"the Benefits Act"—see Jobseekers Act, s.35(1).
"claimant"—*ibid.*, reg. 88(1).

"earnings"—see reg. 1(3), reg. 100.
"employment"—see reg. 3.
"personal pension scheme"—see Jobseekers Act, s. 35(1).
"self-employed earner"—see reg. 1(3), SSCBA, s. 2(1)(b).

GENERAL NOTE

See the notes to reg. 38 of the Income Support Regulations.

Deduction of tax and contributions for self-employed earners

102.—(1) The amount to be deducted in respect of income tax under regulation 101(1)(b)(i), (4)(b)(i) or (10)(a)(i) (calculation of net profit of self-employed earners) shall be calculated on the basis of the amount of chargeable income and as if that income were assessable to income tax at the lower rate or, as the case may be, the lower rate and the basic rate of tax less only the personal relief to which the claimant is entitled under sections 257(1), 257A(1) and 259 of the Income and Corporation Taxes Act 1988 (personal reliefs) as is appropriate to his circumstances; but, if the period determined under regulation 95 is less than a year, the earnings to which the lower rate of tax is to be applied and the amount of the personal relief deductible under this paragraph shall be calculated on a pro rata basis.

(2) The amount to be deducted in respect of social security contributions under regulation 101(1)(b)(i), (4)(b)(ii) or (10)(a)(ii) shall be the total of—
(a) the amount of Class 2 contributions payable under section 11(1) or, as the case may be, 11(3) of the Benefits Act at the rate applicable at the date of claim except where the claimant's chargeable income is less than the amount specified in section 11(4) of that Act (small earnings exception) for the tax year in which the date of claim falls; but if the period determined under regulation 95 is less than a year, the amount specified for that tax year shall be reduced pro rata; and
(b) the amount of Class 4 contributions (if any) which would be payable under section 15 of that Act (Class 4 contributions recoverable under the Income Tax Acts) at the percentage rate applicable at the date of claim on so much of the chargeable income as exceeds the lower limit but does not exceed the upper limit of profits and gains applicable for the tax year in which the date of claim falls; but if the period determined under regulation 95 is less than a year, those limits shall be reduced pro rata.

(3) In this regulation "chargeable income" means—
(a) except where sub-paragraph (b) applies, the earnings derived from the employment less any expenses deducted under paragraph (4)(a) or, as the case may be, (5), of regulation 101;
(b) in the case of employment as a child minder, one-third of the earnings of that employment.

DEFINITIONS

"the Benefits Act"—see Jobseekers Act, s.35(1).
"claimant"—*ibid.*, reg. 88(1).
"date of claim"—see reg. 1(3).
"earnings"—*ibid.*, reg. 100.
"lower rate"—see reg. 1(3).

GENERAL NOTE

See the notes to reg. 39 of the Income Support Regulations.

[¹Chapter IVA

Participants in the self-employment route of the Employment Option of the New Deal

Interpretation

102A. In this Chapter—
"self-employment route" means that part of the Employment Option of the New Deal which is specified in regulation 75(1)(a)(ii)(aa)(ii);
"special account" means, where a person was carrying on a commercial activity in respect of which assistance was received under the self-employment route, the account into which the gross receipts from that activity were payable during the period in respect of which such assistance was received.]

AMENDMENT

1. Social Security (Miscellaneous Amendments) (No. 4) Regulations 1998 (S.I. 1998 No. 1174), reg. 3(4) (June 1, 1998).

GENERAL NOTE

For a brief summary of the self-employment route of the New Deal see the note to reg. 75(1)(a)(ii)(aa).

[¹Treatment of gross receipts of participants in the self-employment route of the Employment Option of the New Deal

102B. The gross receipts of a commercial activity carried on by a person in respect of which assistance is received under the self-employment route, shall be taken into account in accordance with the following provisions of this Chapter.]

AMENDMENT

1. Social Security (Miscellaneous Amendments) (No. 4) Regulations 1998 (S.I. 1998 No. 1174), reg. 3(4) (June 1, 1998).

DEFINITION

"self-employment route"—see reg. 102A

[¹Calculation of income of participants in the self-employment route of the Employment Option of the New Deal

102C.—(1) The income of a person who has received assistance under the self-employment route shall be calculated by taking into account the whole of the monies in the special account at the end of the last day upon which such assistance was received and deducting from those monies—
(a) an amount in respect of income tax calculated in accordance with regulation 102D (deduction in respect of tax for participants in the self-employment route of the Employment Option of the New Deal); and
(b) any sum to which paragraph (4) refers.
(2) Income calculated pursuant to paragraph (1) shall be apportioned equally over a period which starts on the date the income is treated as paid under paragraph (3) and is equal in length to the period beginning with the day upon which assistance was first received under the self-employment route and ending on the last day upon which such assistance was received.

(3) Income calculated pursuant to paragraph (1) shall be treated as paid—

(a) in the case where it is due to be paid before the first benefit week in respect of which the participant or his partner first claims a jobseeker's allowance following the last day upon which assistance was received under the self-employment route, on the day in the week in which it is due to be paid which corresponds to the first day of the benefit week;

(b) in any other case, on the first day of the benefit week in which it is due to be paid.

(4) This paragraph refers, where applicable in each benefit week in respect of which income calculated pursuant to paragraph (1) is taken into account pursuant to paragraphs (2) and (3), to the sums which would have been disregarded under paragraphs 5 to 8, 11 and 12 of Schedule 6 had the income been earnings.]

AMENDMENT

1. Social Security (Miscellaneous Amendments) (No. 4) Regulations 1998 (S.I. 1998 No. 1174), reg. 3(4) (June 1, 1998).

DEFINITIONS

"benefit week"—see reg. 1(3).
"self-employment route"—see reg. 102A
"special account"—*ibid.*
"week"—see reg. 1(3).

GENERAL NOTE

This regulation, together with reg. 102D, applies to the income from "test-trading" of people who have taken part in the self-employment route of the New Deal for 18 to 24-year-olds. For a brief summary of this part of the Employment Option of the New Deal see the note to reg. 75(1)(a)(ii)(aa). See also reg. 88A which takes any gross receipts from trading while on the self-employment route out of the categories of earnings, self-employed earnings and income other than earnings. The rules for liable relative payments, payments of child support maintenance and student income (except reg. 137) also do not apply. Any such receipts may only be taken into account in accordance with regs. 102A to 102D.

There are several issues raised by reg. 102C that need clarifying. The intention seems to be that, after deducting an amount for income tax in accordance with reg. 102D and applying the relevant earnings disregard under paras. 5 to 8, 11 or 12 of Sched. 6 in each benefit week that would have been applicable if the income had been earnings, the balance of the money in the person's "special account" (defined in reg. 102A) at the end of the day on which he ceases to receive "assistance" (not defined) under the self-employment route is to be spread over a period equal in length to the period that the person received such assistance. The period starts on the date that the income is treated as paid under para. (3). Under para. (3)(a), if the income is due to be paid before the first benefit week pursuant to the claimant's (or his partner's) first JSA claim after assistance under the self-employment route finishes, it is treated as paid on the day that corresponds to the first day of the benefit week. In any other case it is treated as paid on the first day of the benefit week in which it is due (para. (3)(b)).

But when is this income due to be paid and what or who determines this? According to the guidance to AOs (AM(AOG)82), it is due to be paid on the day after (i) the person leaves the self-employment route of the Employment Option if he is not entitled to JSA or income support immediately after leaving the self-employment route; or (ii) his entitlement to JSA or income support ends if that entitlement stops within 13 weeks of the day after he left the self-employment route; or (iii) the expiry of 13 weeks starting on the day after he left the self-employment route if he is entitled to JSA or income support throughout that period. These rules are presumably part of the terms of this New Deal option, since such provisions do not appear in the JSA (or Income Support) Regulations themselves. The 13 weeks "period of grace" in (iii) may perhaps be related to the fact that according to Employment Service guidance a person can continue to receive assistance in connection with trying to establish himself in self-employment for a further 13 weeks after his participation in the self-employment route ends. Presumably the intention is that any profit from his "test-trading" should not affect his benefit entitlement until after that period.

Note also that para. (1) refers to "the whole of the monies" in the person's special account but reg. 102B refers to the "gross receipts" of the activity carried on while on the self-employment route. The normal rules for the calculation of earnings of self-employed earners (see regs. 100 to 102) do not apply (see reg. 88A), although presumably the caselaw on the meaning of "gross receipts" for self-employed earners will be relevant (see the notes to reg. 37 of the Income Support Regulations). However, certain sums are ignored in calculating the person's income in his "special account". Thus any payment to him from this account (whether before or after he leaves the self-employment route) will disregarded if it is (i) to meet expenses wholly and necessarily incurred in his business while on the self-employment route; or (ii) used, or intended to be used, to make repayments on a loan taken out for the purposes of that business (see para. 62 of Sched. 7). See also para. 11(3) and (4) of Sched. 8, which disregard any assets of the business while the person is participating in the self-employment route and, if the person later ceases to be engaged in that business, for a period which is reasonable to allow them to be disposed of. In addition, any capital acquired for the purposes of the business is ignored for 52 weeks from the date of receipt (para. 47 of Sched. 8).

See also regs. 23A and 39A to 39D of, and para. 64 of Sched. 9 and paras. 6(3) and (4) and 52 of Sched. 10 to, the Income Support Regulations which introduce similar provisions for the treatment of income from "test-trading" while on the self-employment route when the person or his partner claims income support. If family credit or disability working allowance is claimed, there are similar income and capital disregards to those in the JSA Regulations in relation to a business undertaken while on the self-employment route (see para. 61 of Sched. 2 and paras. 6(3) and (4) and 54 of Sched. 3 to the Family Credit Regulations and para. 59 of Sched. 3 and paras. 6(3) and (4) and 53 of Sched. 4 to the Disability Working Allowance Regulations). However, the gross receipts of the business carried on while on the self-employment route that are or were payable into the person's special account will count as capital for the purposes of any family credit or disability working allowance claim (see reg. 31(7) of the Family Credit Regulations and 34(7) of the Disability Working Allowance Regulations). For housing benefit and council tax benefit, the rules are similar to those for family credit.

[¹Deduction in respect of tax for participants in the self-employment route of the Employment Option of the New Deal

102D.—(1) The amount to be deducted in respect of income tax under regulation 102C(1)(a) (calculation of income of participants in the self-employment route of the Employment Option of the New Deal) in respect of the period determined under regulation 102C(2) shall be calculated as if—

    (a) the chargeable income is the only income chargeable to tax;

    (b) the personal reliefs which are applicable to the person receiving assistance under the self-employment route by virtue of section 257(1), 257A(1) and 259 of the Income and Corporation Taxes Act 1988 (personal reliefs) are allowable against that income; and

    (c) the rate at which the chargeable income less the personal relief is assessable to income tax is the lower rate of tax or, as the case may be, the lower rate and the basic rate of tax.

(2) For the purpose of paragraph (1), the lower rate of tax to be applied and the amount of the personal relief deductible shall, where the period determined under regulation 102C(2) is less than a year, be calculated on a pro rata basis.

(3) In this regulation, "chargeable income" means the monies in the special account at the end of the last day upon which assistance was received under the self-employment route.]

AMENDMENT

1. Social Security (Miscellaneous Amendments) (No. 4) Regulations 1998 (S.I. 1998 No. 1174), reg. 3(4) (June 1, 1998).

DEFINITIONS

    "lower rate"—see reg. 1(3).
    "self-employment route"—see reg. 102A.
    "special account"—*ibid.*

GENERAL NOTE

See the note to reg. 102C above.

Chapter V

Other Income

Calculation of income other than earnings

103.—(1) For the purposes of regulation 94 (calculation of income other than earnings) the income of a claimant which does not consist of earnings to be taken into account shall, subject to the following provisions of this regulation, be his gross income and any capital treated as income under regulations 104 and 106 (capital treated as income and modifications in respect of children and young persons).

(2) There shall be disregarded from the calculation of a claimant's gross income under paragraph (1) any sum, where applicable, specified in Schedule 7.

(3) Where the payment of any benefit under the Act or under the Benefits Act is subject to any deduction by way of recovery, the amount to be taken into account under paragraph (1) shall be the gross amount to which the beneficiary is entitled.

(4) Where the claimant is in receipt of payments under the earnings top-up scheme operated by the Secretary of State for Social Security, and those payments are subject to any deduction by way of recovery, the amount to be taken into account under paragraph (1) shall be the amount that the claimant would have received but for that deduction.

(5) Where a loan is made to a person pursuant to arrangements made under section 1 of the Education (Student Loans) Act 1990 or article 3 of the Education (Student Loans) (Northern Ireland) Order 1990 and that person ceases to be a student before the end of the academic year in respect of which the loan is payable or, as the case may be, before the end of his course, a sum equal to the weekly amount apportionable under paragraph (2) of regulation 136 (treatment of student loans) shall be taken into account under paragraph (1) for each [³ benefit week], in the period over which the loan fell to be apportioned, following the date on which that person ceases to be a student; but in determining the weekly amount apportionable under paragraph (2) of regulation 136 so much of that paragraph as provides for a disregard shall not have effect.

[²(5A) In the case of income to which regulation 94(2B) applies (calculation of income of former full-time students), the amount of income to be taken into account for the purposes of paragraph (1) shall be the amount of that income calculated in accordance with regulation 97(7) and on the basis that none of that income has been repaid.]

(6) For the avoidance of doubt there shall be included as income to be taken into account under paragraph (1) any payment to which regulations 98(2) [¹(a) to (e)] or 100(2) (payments not earnings) applies.

AMENDMENTS

1. Jobseeker's Allowance and Income Support (General) (Amendment) Regulations 1996 (S.I. 1996 No. 1517), reg. 23 (October 7, 1996).
2. Income-related Benefits and Jobseeker's Allowance (Miscellaneous Amendments) Regulations 1997 (S.I. 1997 No. 65), reg. 7(2) (April 7, 1997).
3. Social Security (Miscellaneous Amendments) Regulations 1997 (S.I. 1997 No. 454), reg. 2(13) (April 7, 1997).

DEFINITIONS

"the Act"—see reg. 1(3).
"the Benefits Act"—see Jobseekers Act, s. 35(1).
"benefit week"—see reg. 1(3).
"claimant"—see Jobseekers Act, s. 35(1), reg. 88(1).
"earnings"—see reg. 1(3).
"the Earnings Top-up Scheme"—*ibid.*
"full-time student"—*ibid.*

GENERAL NOTE

On paras. (1) to (3) and (5) to (6), see the notes to reg. 40 of the Income Support Regulations.

Para. (4) provides that if deductions are being made from payments of earnings top-up, the gross amount of the payments is used in the calculation of JSA. Earnings top-up is a new benefit, designed to assist people in low-paid work who do not have dependent children, which was introduced on a pilot basis for three years in eight areas of the country in October 1996. Such a provision is not needed in the Income Support Regulations because reg. 40(3) will apply (see reg. 2(4) of the Income Support Regulations).

Capital treated as income

104.—(1) Any capital payable by instalments which are outstanding on the first day in respect of which an income-based jobseeker's allowance is payable, or, in the case of a review, the date of that review, shall, if the aggregate of the instalments outstanding and the amount of the claimant's capital otherwise calculated in accordance with Chapter VI of this Part exceeds £8,000 [¹or, in a case where regulation 107(b) applies, £16,000], be treated as income.

(2) Any payment received under an annuity shall be treated as income.

(3) In the case of a person who is, or would be, prevented from being entitled to a jobseeker's allowance by section 14 (trade disputes), any payment under section 17 or 24 of the Children Act 1989 or, as the case may be, section 12, 24 or 26 of the Social Work (Scotland) Act 1968 (local authorities' duty to promote welfare of children and powers to grant financial assistance to persons in, or formerly in, their care) shall be treated as income.

(4) Any earnings to the extent that they are not a payment of income shall be treated as income.

[²(5) Any Career Development Loan paid pursuant to section 2 of the Employment and Training Act 1973 shall be treated as income.]

AMENDMENTS

1. Income-related Benefits and Jobseeker's Allowance (Miscellaneous Amendments) Regulations 1997 (S.I. 1997 No. 65), reg. 3(2) (April 7, 1997).
2. Income-related Benefits and Jobseeker's Allowance (Miscellaneous Amendments) Regulations 1997 (S.I. 1997 No. 65), reg. 3(3) (April 7, 1997).

DEFINITION

"claimant"—see Jobseekers Act, s. 35(1), reg. 88(1).

GENERAL NOTE

See the notes to reg. 41 of the Income Support Regulations.

Notional income

105.—(1) A claimant shall be treated as possessing income of which he has deprived himself for the purpose of securing entitlement to a jobseeker's allowance or increasing the amount of that allowance, or for the purpose of securing entitlement to, or increasing the amount of, income support.

(2) Except in the case of—

(a) a discretionary trust;

(b) a trust derived from a payment made in consequence of a personal injury;

[¹(c) child benefit to which paragraph (2A) refers;]

(d) family credit or disability working allowance;

(e) a jobseeker's allowance;

(f) payments under the earnings top-up scheme operated by the Secretary of State for Social Security;

(g) a personal pension scheme where the claimant is aged under 60; [²or

(h) any sum to which paragraph 42(a) or 43(a) of Schedule 8 (disregard of compensation for personal injuries which is administered by the Court) refers]; [⁵or

(i) rehabilitation allowance made under section 2 of the Employment and Training Act 1973],

income which would become available to the claimant upon application being made but which has not been acquired by him shall be treated as possessed by him but only from the date on which it could be expected to be acquired were an application made.

[¹(2A) This paragraph refers to child benefit payable in accordance with regulation 2(1)(a)(ii) of the Child Benefit and Social Security (Fixing and Adjustment of Rates) Regulations 1976 (weekly rate for only, elder or eldest child of a lone parent) but only to the extent that it exceeds the amount specified in regulation 2(1)(a)(i) of those Regulations.]

(3) Where a person, aged not less than 60, is a member of, or a person deriving entitlement to a pension under, a personal pension scheme, and—

(a) in the case of a personal pension scheme other than one referred to in sub-paragraph (b), he fails to purchase an annuity with the funds available in that scheme where—

(i) he defers, in whole or in part, the payment of any income which would have been payable to him by his pension fund holder;

(ii) he fails to take any necessary action to secure that the whole or part of any income which would be payable to him by his pension fund holder upon his applying for it, is so paid; or

(iii) income withdrawal is not available to him under that scheme; or

(b) in the case of a contract or trust scheme approved under Chapter III of Part XIV of the Income and Corporation Taxes Act 1988, he fails to purchase an annuity with the funds available under that contract or scheme,

the amount of any income foregone shall be treated as possessed by him, but only from the date on which it could be expected to be acquired were an application for it to be made.

(4) The amount of any income foregone in a case to which either head (i) or (ii) of paragraph (3)(a) applies shall be the maximum amount of income which may be withdrawn from the fund and shall be determined by the adjudication officer who shall take account of information provided by the pension fund holder in accordance with regulation 7(5) of the Social Security (Claims and Payments) Regulations 1987.

(5) The amount of any income foregone in a case to which either head (iii) of paragraph (3)(a), or paragraph (3)(b) applies shall be the income that the claimant could have received without purchasing an annuity had the fund held under the relevant personal pension scheme been held under a personal pension scheme where income withdrawal was available and shall be determined in the manner specified in paragraph (4).

(6) Subject to paragraph (7), any income which is due to be paid to the

claimant but has not been paid to him, shall be treated as possessed by the claimant.

(7) Paragraph (6) shall not apply to—

(a) any amount to which paragraph (8) or (9) applies;

(b) a payment to which section 74(2) or (3) of the Administration Act applies (abatement of prescribed payments from public funds which are not made before the prescribed date, and abatement from prescribed benefits where maintenance not paid); and

(c) a payment from a discretionary trust, or a trust derived from a payment made in consequence of a personal injury.

(8) This paragraph applies to an amount which is due to be paid to the claimant under an occupational pension scheme but which is not paid because the trustees or managers of the scheme have suspended or ceased payment due to an insufficiency of resources.

(9) This paragraph applies to any amount by which a payment made to the claimant from an occupational pension scheme falls short of the payment to which he was due under the scheme where the shortfall arises because the trustees or managers of the scheme have insufficient resources available to them to meet in full the scheme's liabilities.

(10) [⁶Any payment of income, other than a payment of income specified in paragraph (10A)], made—

(a) to a third party in respect of a single claimant or in respect of a single claimant or in respect of a member of the family shall be treated—

(i) in a case where that payment is derived from a payment of any benefit under the Act or under the Benefits Act, a war disablement pension or war widows pension, as possessed by that single claimant, if it would normally be paid to him, or as possessed by that member of the family, if it would normally be paid to that member;

(ii) in any other case, as possessed by that single claimant or by that member of the family to the extent that it is used for the food, ordinary clothing or footwear, household fuel, rent for which housing benefit is payable, or any housing costs to the extent that they are met under regulation 83(f) or 84(1)(g), of that single claimant or, as the case may be, of any member of the family, or is used for any council tax or water charges for which that claimant or member is liable;

(b) to a single claimant or a member of the family in respect of a third party (but not in respect of another member of the family) shall be treated as possessed by that single claimant or, as the case may be, that member of the family to the extent that it is kept or used by him or used by or on behalf of any member of the family;

but, except where sub-paragraph (a)(i) applies and in the case of a person who is, or would be, prevented from being entitled to a jobseeker's allowance by section 14 (trade disputes), this paragraph shall not apply to any payment in kind.

[⁶(10A) Paragraph (10) shall not apply in respect of a payment of income made—

(a) under the Macfarlane Trust, the Macfarlane (Special Payments) Trust, the Macfarlane (Special Payments) (No. 2) Trust, the Fund, the Eileen Trust or the Independent Living Funds;

(b) pursuant to section 19(1)(a) of the Coal Industry Act 1994 (concessionary coal); or

(c) pursuant to section 2 of the Employment and Training Act 1973 in respect of a person's participation—

(i) in an employment programme specified in regulation 75(1)(a)(ii);

(ii) in a training scheme specified in regulation 75(1)(b)(ii); or

(iii) in a qualifying course within the meaning specified in regulation 17A(7).]

(11) Where the claimant lives in a residential care home or a nursing home, or is temporarily absent from such a home, any payment made by a person other than the claimant or a member of his family in respect of some or all of the cost of maintaining the claimant or a member of his family in that home shall be treated as possessed by the claimant or by that member of his family.

(12) Where a claimant's earnings are not ascertainable at the time of the determination of the claim or of any subsequent review the adjudication officer shall treat the claimant as possessing such earnings as is reasonable in the circumstances of the case having regard to the number of hours worked and the earnings paid for comparable employment in the area.

(13) Where—

(a) a claimant performs a service for another person; and

(b) that person makes no payment of earnings or pays less than that paid for a comparable employment in the area,

the adjudication officer shall treat the claimant as possessing such earnings (if any) as is reasonable for that employment unless the claimant satisfies him that the means of that person are insufficient for him to pay or to pay more for the service; but this paragraph shall not apply to a claimant who is engaged by a charitable or voluntary organisation or is a volunteer if the adjudication officer is satisfied in any of those cases that it is reasonable for him to provide his services free of charge [⁴or in a case where the service is performed in connection with the claimant's participation in an employment or training programme in accordance with regulation 19(1)(q)].

(14) Where a claimant is treated as possessing any income under any of paragraphs (1) to (11) the foregoing provisions of this Part shall apply for the purposes of calculating the amount of that income as if a payment had actually been made and as if it were actual income which he does possess.

(15) Where a claimant is treated as possessing any earnings under paragraphs (12) or (13) the foregoing provisions of this Part shall apply for the purposes of calculating the amount of those earnings as if a payment had actually been made and as if they were actual earnings which he does possess, except that paragraph (4) of regulation 99 (calculation of net earnings of employed earners) shall not apply and his net earnings shall be calculated by taking into account the earnings which he is treated as possessing, less—

(a) an amount in respect of income tax equivalent to an amount calculated by applying to those earnings the lower rate or, as the case may be, the lower rate and the basic rate of tax in the year of assessment less only the personal relief to which the claimant is entitled under sections 257(1), 257A(1) and 259 of the Income and Corporation Taxes Act 1988 (personal reliefs) as is appropriate to his circumstances; but, if the period over which those earnings are to be taken into account is less than a year, the earnings to which the lower rate of tax is to be applied and the amount of the personal relief deductible under this paragraph shall be calculated on a pro rata basis;

(b) where the weekly amount of those earnings equals or exceeds the lower earnings limit, an amount representing primary Class 1 contributions under the Benefits Act, calculated by applying to those earnings the initial and main primary percentages in accordance with section 8(1)(a) and (b) of that Act; and

(c) one-half of any sum payable by the claimant in respect of a pay period by way of a contribution towards an occupational or personal pension scheme.

(16) In this regulation—

"ordinary clothing or footwear" means clothing or footwear for normal daily use, but does not include school uniforms, or clothing or footwear used solely for sporting activities;

"pension fund holder" means with respect to a personal pension scheme the trustees, managers or scheme administrators, as the case may be, of the scheme concerned;

"resources" has the same meaning as in section 181 of the Pension Schemes Act 1993.

AMENDMENTS

1. Child Benefit, Child Support and Social Security (Miscellaneous Amendments) Regulations 1996 (S.I. 1996 No. 1803), reg. 42 (April 7, 1997).

2. Income-related Benefits and Jobseeker's Allowance (Amendment) (No. 2) Regulations 1997 (S.I. 1997 No. 2197), reg. 6 (October 6, 1997).

3. Income-related Benefits and Jobseeker's Allowance (Amendment) (No. 2) Regulations 1997 (S.I. 1997 No. 2197), reg. 7(3) and (4)(f) (October 6, 1997).

4. Social Security Amendment (New Deal) Regulations 1997 (S.I. 1997 No. 2863), reg. 9 (January 5, 1998).

5. Social Security (Miscellaneous Amendments) Regulations 1998 (S.I. 1998 No. 563), reg. 6(1) and (2)(f) (April 6, 1998).

6. Social Security Amendment (New Deal) (No. 2) Regulations 1998 (S.I. 1998 No. 2117), reg. 2(1) (September 24, 1998).

DEFINITIONS

"the Act"—see reg. 1(3).
"the Benefits Act"—see Jobseekers Act, s. 35(1).
"claimant"—*ibid.*, reg. 88(1).
"earnings"—see reg. 1(3).
"the Earnings Top-Up Scheme"—*ibid.*
"family"—Jobseekers Act, s. 35(1).
"lower rate"—see reg. 1(3).
"occupational pension scheme"—see Jobseekers Act, s. 35(1).
"pay period"—see reg. 1(3).
"personal pension scheme"—see Jobseekers Act, s. 35(1).
"single claimant"—see reg. 1(3).
"the Eileen Trust"—*ibid.*
"the Fund"—*ibid.*
"the Independent Living Funds"—*ibid.*
"the Macfarlane (Special Payments) Trust"—*ibid.*
"the Macfarlane (Special Payments) (No. 2) Trust"—*ibid.*
"the Macfarlane Trust"—*ibid.*
"voluntary organisation"—*ibid.*
"war disablement pension"—*ibid.*
"war widow's pension"—*ibid.*
"water charges"—*ibid.*
"year of assessment"—*ibid.*

GENERAL NOTE

See the notes to reg. 42 of the Income Support Regulations.

Note that under para. (1) if a person has deprived himself of income he will be caught by this rule if the purpose of the deprivation was to secure entitlement to or increase the amount of jobseeker's allowance *or income support*. This avoids the question that might otherwise have arisen on a claimant transferring from income support to jobseeker's allowance whether a deprivation which had only been for the purposes of income support could be caught by para. (1).

Modifications in respect of children and young persons

106.—(1) Any capital of a child or young person payable by instalments which are outstanding on the first day in respect of which an income-based jobseeker's allowance is payable or, in the case of a review, the date of that review, shall, if the aggregate of the instalments outstanding and the amount of that child or young person's other capital calculated in accordance with Chapter VI of this Part in like manner as for the claimant would exceed £3,000, be treated as income.

(2) In the case of a child or young person who is residing at an educational establishment at which he is receiving relevant education—

(a) any payment made to the educational establishment, in respect of that child's or young person's maintenance, by or on behalf of a person who is not a member of the family or by a member of the family out of funds contributed for that purpose by a person who is not a member of the family, shall be treated as income of that child or young person but it shall only be taken into account over periods during which that child or young person is present at that educational establishment; and

(b) if a payment has been so made, for any period in a benefit week in term-time during which that child or young person returns home, he shall be treated as possessing an amount of income in that week calculated by multiplying the amount of personal allowance and disabled child premium, if any, applicable in respect of that child or young person by the number equal to the number of days in that week in which he was present at his educational establishment and dividing the product by seven; but this sub-paragraph shall not apply where the educational establishment is provided under section 8 of the Education Act 1944 (duty of local authority to secure primary and secondary schools) by a local education authority or where the payment is made under section 49 or 50 of the Education (Scotland) Act 1980 (power of education authority to assist persons).

(3) Where a child or young person—

(a) is resident at an educational establishment and he is wholly or partly maintained at that establishment by a local education authority under section 8 of the Education Act 1944; or

(b) is maintained at an educational establishment under section 49 or 50 of the Education (Scotland) Act 1980, he shall for each day he is present at that establishment be treated as possessing an amount of income equal to the sum obtained by dividing the amount of personal allowance and disabled child premium, if any, applicable in respect of him by seven.

(4) Where the income of a child or young person who is a member of the claimant's family calculated in accordance with Chapter I to V of this Part exceeds the amount of the personal allowance and disabled child premium, if any, applicable in respect of that child or young person, the excess shall not be treated as the income of the claimant.

(5) Where the capital of a child or young person if calculated in accordance with Chapter VI of this Part in like manner as for the claimant, except as provided in paragraph (1), would exceed £3,000, any income of that child or young person shall not be treated as the income of the claimant.

(6) In calculating the net earnings or net profit of a child or young person there shall be disregarded (in addition to any sum which falls to be disregarded under paragraphs 14 to 16), any sum specified in paragraphs 17 and 18 of Schedule 6 (earnings to be disregarded).

(7) Any income of a child or young person which is to be disregarded under Schedule 7 (income other than earnings to be disregarded) shall be disregarded in such manner as to produce the result most favourable to the claimant.

(8) Where a child or young person is treated as possessing any income under paragraphs (2) or (3) the foregoing provisions of this Part shall apply for the purposes of calculating that income as if a payment had actually been made and as if it were actual income which he does possess.

(9) For the purposes of this regulation, a child or young person shall not be

treated as present at his educational establishment on any day if on that day he spends the night with the claimant or a member of his household.

DEFINITIONS

"child"—see Jobseekers Act, s. 35(1).
"claimant"—*ibid.*, reg. 88(1).
"family"—see Jobseekers Act, s. 35(1).
"young person"—see reg. 76.

GENERAL NOTE

See the notes to reg. 44 of the Income Support Regulations.

Chapter VI

Capital

Capital limit

[¹**107.** For the purposes of section 13(1) (no entitlement to an income-based jobseeker's allowance if capital exceeds a prescribed amount)—
   (a) except where paragraph (b) applies, the prescribed amount is £8,000;
   (b) in the case to which regulation 116(1B) applies, the prescribed amount is £16,000.]

AMENDMENT

1. Jobseeker's Allowance (Amendment) Regulations 1996 (S.I. 1996 No. 1516), reg. 11 (October 7, 1996).

DEFINITION

"claimant"—see Jobseekers Act, s. 35(1), reg. 88(1).

GENERAL NOTE

Under s. 13(1) of the Jobseekers Act there is no entitlement to income-based JSA if the claimant's capital exceeds the prescribed amount. The limit is the same as it is for income support; that is, for most claimants it is £8,000 (para. (a)), but it is £16,000 for claimants living permanently in residential care or nursing homes (including those with preserved rights), residential accommodation or Polish resettlement homes (para. (b)). The capital of a claimant's partner is aggregated with the claimant's (reg. 88(1)), but not that of children and young persons (reg. 109).
   See the notes to reg. 45 of the Income Support Regulations.

Calculation of capital

108.—(1) Subject to paragraph (2), the capital of a claimant to be taken into account shall be the whole of his capital calculated in accordance with this Part and any income treated as capital under regulation 110.
   (2) There shall be disregarded from the calculation of a claimant's capital under paragraph (1) any capital, where applicable, specified in Schedule 8.

DEFINITION

"claimant"—see Jobseekers Act, s. 35(1), reg. 88(1).

GENERAL NOTE

See the notes to reg. 46 of the Income Support Regulations.

Disregard of capital of child or young person

109. The capital of a child or young person who is a member of the claimant's family shall not be treated as capital of the claimant.

DEFINITIONS

"child"—see Jobseekers Act, s. 35(1).
"claimant"—*ibid.*, reg. 88(1).
"family"—see Jobseekers Act, s. 35(1)
"young person"—see reg 76.

GENERAL NOTE

This is the same rule as for income support (see reg. 47 of the Income Support Regulations). The capital of a child or young person is not aggregated with the claimant's. But if that person's capital is over £3,000 there is no personal allowance for that person (reg. 83(b)) and any income is not aggregated with the claimant's (reg. 106(5)).

Income treated as capital

110.—(1) Any bounty derived from employment to which paragraph 9 of Schedule 6 applies and paid at intervals of at least one year shall be treated as capital.

(2) Except in the case of an amount to which section 15(2)(c)(i) (refund of tax in trade dispute cases) applies, any amount by way of a refund of income tax deducted from profits or emoluments chargeable to income tax under Schedule D or E shall be treated as capital.

(3) Any holiday pay which is not earnings under regulation 98(1)(c) (earnings of employed earners) shall be treated as capital.

(4) Except any income derived from capital disregarded under paragraphs 1, 2, 4 to 8, 11 or 17 of Schedule 8, any income derived from capital shall be treated as capital but only from the date it is normally due to be credited to the claimant's account.

(5) Subject to paragraph (6), in the case of employment as an employed earner, any advance of earnings or any loan made by the claimant's employer shall be treated as capital.

(6) Paragraph (5) shall not apply to a person who is, or would be, prevented from being entitled to a jobseeker's allowance by section 14 (trade disputes).

(7) Any payment under section 30 of the Prison Act 1952 (payments for discharged prisoners) or allowance under section 17 of the Prisons (Scotland) Act 1989 (allowances to prisoners on discharge) shall be treated as capital.

(8) Any payment made by a local authority which represents arrears of payments under paragraph 15 of Schedule 1 to the Children Act 1989 (power of a local authority to make contributions to a person with whom a child lives as a result of a residence order) or under section 50 of the Children Act 1975 (contributions to a custodian towards the cost of accommodation and maintenance of a child) [¹or any payment, made by an authority, as defined in Article 2 of the Children Order, which represents arrears of payments under Article 15

of, and paragraph 17 of Schedule 1 to, that Order (contribution by an authority to child's maintenance),] shall be treated as capital.

(9) Any charitable or voluntary payment which is not made or not due to be made at regular intervals, other than one to which paragraph (10) applies, shall be treated as capital.

(10) This paragraph applies to a payment—

(a) which is made to a person who is, or would be, prevented from being entitled to a jobseeker's allowance by section 14 (trade disputes);

(b) to which regulation 106(2) (modifications in respect of children and young persons) applies; or

(c) which is made under the Macfarlane Trust, the Macfarlane (Special Payments) Trust, the Macfarlane (Special Payments) (No.2) Trust, the Fund, the Eileen Trust or the Independent Living Funds.

AMENDMENT

1. Social Security (Miscellaneous Amendments) Regulations 1998 (S.I. 1998 No. 563), reg. 14(2) (April 6, 1998).

DEFINITIONS

"child"—see Jobseekers Act, s. 35(1).
"the Children Order"—see reg. 1(3).
"claimant"—Jobseekers Act, s.35(1), reg. 88(1).
"earnings"—see reg. 1(3).
"employed earner"—see reg. 3, SSCBA, s. 2(1)(a).
"family"—see Jobseekers Act, s. 35(1).
"the Eileen Trust"—see reg. 1(3).
"the Fund"—*ibid.*
"the Independent Living Funds"—*ibid.*
"the Macfarlane (Special Payments) Trust"—*ibid.*
"the MacFarlane (Special Payments) (No. 2) Trust"—*ibid.*
"the Macfarlane Trust"—*ibid.*

GENERAL NOTE

See the notes to reg. 48 of the Income Support Regulations. Most of the categories deemed to be capital are self-explanatory. They are then disregarded as income (Sched. 7, para. 34).

There is no equivalent to reg. 48(11) of the Income Support Regulations because the JSA rules for the treatment of "compensation payments" (defined in reg. 98(3)) made on the termination of employment differ from those of income support (see the notes to regs. 98(3) and 94(6) to (9)).

Calculation of capital in the United Kingdom

111. Capital which a claimant possesses in the United Kingdom shall be calculated—

(a) except in a case to which sub-paragraph (b) applies, at its current market or surrender value, less—

(i) where there would be expenses attributable to sale, 10 per cent; and

(ii) the amount of any incumbrance secured on it;

(b) in the case of a National Savings Certificate—

(i) if purchased from an issue the sale of which ceased before 1st July last preceding the first day on which an income-based jobseeker's allowance is payable or, in the case of a review, the date of that review, at the price which it would have realised on that 1st July had it been purchased on the last day of that issue;

(ii) in any other case, at its purchase price.

DEFINITION

"claimant"—see Jobseekers Act, s. 35(1), reg. 88(1).

GENERAL NOTE

See the notes to reg. 49 of the Income Support Regulations.

Calculation of capital outside the United Kingdom

112. Capital which a claimant possesses in a country outside the United Kingdom shall be calculated—
  (a) in a case in which there is no prohibition in that country against the transfer to the United Kingdom of an amount equal to its current market or surrender value in that country, at that value;
  (b) in a case where there is such a prohibition, at the price which it would realise if sold in the United Kingdom to a willing buyer,
less, where there would be expenses attributable to sale, 10 per cent. and the amount of any incumbrance secured on it.

DEFINITION

"claimant"—see Jobseekers Act, s. 35(1), reg. 88(1).

GENERAL NOTE

See the note to reg. 50 of the Income Support Regulations.

Notional capital

113.—(1) A claimant shall be treated as possessing capital of which he has deprived himself for the purpose of securing entitlement to a jobseeker's allowance or increasing the amount of that allowance, or for the purpose of securing entitlement to or increasing the amount of income support, except—
  (a) where that capital is derived from a payment made in consequence of a personal injury and is placed on trust for the benefit of the claimant; or
  (b) to the extent that the capital he is treated as possessing is reduced in accordance with regulation 114 (diminishing notional capital rule); [¹or
  (c) any sum to which paragraph 42(a) or 43(a) of Schedule 8 (disregard of compensation for personal injuries which is administered by the Court) refers].
  (2) Except in the case of—
  (a) a discretionary trust;
  (b) a trust derived from a payment made in consequence of a personal injury;
  (c) any loan which would be obtainable only if secured against capital disregarded under Schedule 8; or
  (d) a personal pension scheme; [¹or
  (e) any sum to which paragraph 42(a) or 43(a) of Schedule 8 (disregard of compensation for personal injuries which is administered by the Court) refers],
any capital which would become available to the claimant upon application being made but which has not been acquired by him shall be treated as possessed by him but only from the date on which it could be expected to be acquired were an application made.
  (3) [³Any payment of capital, other than a payment of capital specified in paragraph (3A)], made—

  (a) to a third party in respect of a single claimant or in respect of a member of the family shall be treated—
      (i) in a case where that payment is derived from a payment of any benefit under the Act or under the Benefits Act, a war disablement pension or war widow's pension, as possessed by that single claimant, if it would normally be paid to him, or as possessed by that member of the family, if it would normally be paid to that member;
      (ii) in any other case, as possessed by that single claimant or by that member of the family to the extent that it is used for the food, ordinary clothing or footwear, household fuel, rent for which housing benefit is payable, or any housing costs to the extent that they are met under regulation 83(f) or 84(1)(g) or accommodation charge to the extent that it is met under regulation 86 (persons in residential care or nursing homes), of that single claimant or, as the case may be, of any member of the family, or is used for any council tax or water charges for which that claimant or member is liable;
  (b) to a single claimant or a member of the family in respect of a third party (but not in respect of another member of the family) shall be treated as possessed by that single claimant or, as the case may be, that member of the family to the extent that it is kept or used by him or by or on behalf of any member of the family.

[³(3A) Paragraph (3) shall not apply in respect of a payment of capital made—
  (a) under the Macfarlane Trust, the Macfarlane (Special Payments) Trust, the Macfarlane (Special Payments) (No. 2) Trust, the Fund, the Eileen Trust or the Independent Living Funds; or
  (b) pursuant to section 2 of the Employment and Training Act 1973 in respect of a person's participation—
      (i) in an employment programme specified in regulation 75(1)(a)(ii);
      (ii) in a training scheme specified in regulation 75(1)(b)(ii); or
      (iii) in a qualifying course within the meaning specified in regulation 17A(7).]

(4) Where a claimant stands in relation to a company in a position analogous to that of a sole owner or a partner in the business of that company, he shall be treated as if he were such sole owner or partner and in such a case—
  (a) the value of his holding in that company shall, notwithstanding regulation 108 (calculation of capital), be disregarded; and
  (b) he shall, subject to paragraph (5), be treated as possessing an amount of capital equal to the value or, as the case may be, his share of the value of the capital of that company and the foregoing provisions of this Chapter shall apply for the purposes of calculating that amount as if it were actual capital which he does possess.

(5) For so long as the claimant undertakes activities in the course of the business of the company, the amount which he is treated as possessing under paragraph (4) shall be disregarded.

(6) Where a claimant is treated as possessing any capital under any of paragraphs (1) to (4) the foregoing provisions of this Chapter shall apply for the purposes of calculating the amount of that capital as if it were actual capital which he does possess.

(7) For the avoidance of doubt a claimant is to be treated as possessing capital under paragraph (1) only if the capital of which he has deprived himself is actual capital.

(8) In paragraph (3) the expression "ordinary clothing or footwear" means clothing or footwear for normal daily use, but does not include school uniforms, or clothing or footwear used solely for sporting activities.

AMENDMENTS

1. Income-related Benefits and Jobseeker's Allowance (Amendment) (No. 2) Regulations 1997 (S.I. 1997 No. 2197), reg. 6 (October 6, 1997).
2. Social Security Amendment (New Deal) Regulations 1997 (S.I. 1997 No. 2863), reg. 10 (January 5, 1998).
3. Social Security Amendment (New Deal) (No. 2) Regulations 1998 (S.I. 1998 No. 2117), reg. 3(1) (September 24, 1998).

DEFINITIONS

"the Act"—see reg. 1(3).
"the Benefits Act"—see Jobseekers Act, s. 35(1).
"claimant"—*ibid.*, reg. 88(1).
"family"—see Jobseekers Act, s. 35(1).
"personal pension scheme"—*ibid.*
"the Eileen Trust"—see reg. 1(3).
"the Fund"—*ibid.*
"the Independent Living Funds"—*ibid.*
"the Macfarlane (Special Payments) Trust"—*ibid.*
"the Macfarlane (Special Payments) (No. 2) Trust"—*ibid.*
"the Macfarlane Trust"—*ibid.*
"single claimant"—*ibid.*
"war disablement pension"—*ibid.*
"war widow's pension"—*ibid.*
"water charges"—*ibid.*

GENERAL NOTE

See the notes to reg. 51 of the Income Support Regulations.
Note that under para. (1) if a person has deprived himself of capital he will be caught by this rule if the purpose of the deprivation was to secure entitlement to or increase the amount of job-seeker's allowance *or income support*. This avoids the question that might otherwise have arisen on a claimant transfering from income support to jobseeker's allowance whether a deprivation which had only been for the purposes of income support could be caught by para. (1).

Diminishing notional capital rule

114.—(1) Where a claimant is treated as possessing capital under regulation 113(1) (notional capital), the amount which he is treated as possessing—
(a) in the case of a week that is subsequent to—
(i) the relevant week in respect of which the conditions set out in paragraph (2) are satisfied, or
(ii) a week which follows that relevant week and which satisfies those conditions,
shall be reduced by an amount determined under paragraph (2);
(b) in the case of a week in respect of which paragraph (1)(a) does not apply but where—
(i) that week is a week subsequent to the relevant week, and
(ii) that relevant week is a week in which the condition in paragraph (3) is satisfied,
shall be reduced by an amount determined under paragraph (3).
(2) This paragraph applies to a benefit week or part week where the claimant satisfies the conditions that—
(a) he is in receipt of a jobseeker's allowance; and
(b) but for regulation 113(1), he would have received an additional amount of jobseeker's allowance in that benefit week or, as the case may be, that part week;

and in such a case, the amount of the reduction for the purposes of paragraph (1)(a) shall be equal to that additional amount.

(3) Subject to paragraph (4), for the purposes of paragraph (1)(b) the condition is that the claimant would have been entitled to an income-based jobseeker's allowance in the relevant week but for regulation 113(1), and in such a case the amount of the reduction shall be equal to the aggregate of—

(a) the amount of jobseeker's allowance to which the claimant would have been entitled in the relevant week but for regulation 113(1); and for the purposes of this sub-paragraph if the relevant week is a part-week that amount shall be determined by dividing the amount of jobseeker's allowance to which he would have been entitled by the number equal to the number of days in the part-week and multiplying the quotient by 7;

(b) the amount of housing benefit (if any) equal to the difference between his maximum housing benefit and the amount (if any) of housing benefit which he is awarded in respect of the benefit week which includes the last day of the relevant week, and for this purpose "benefit week" has the same meaning as in regulation 2(1) of the Housing Benefit (General) Regulations 1987 (interpretation);

(c) the amount of council tax benefit (if any) equal to the difference between his maximum council tax benefit and the amount (if any) of council tax benefit which he is awarded in respect of the benefit week which includes the last day of the relevant week, and for this purpose "benefit week" has the same meaning as in regulation 2(1) of the Council Tax Benefit (General) Regulations 1992 (interpretation).

(4) The amount determined under paragraph (3) shall be re-determined under that paragraph if the claimant makes a further claim for a jobseeker's allowance and the conditions in paragraph (5) are satisfied, and in such a case—

(a) sub-paragraphs (a), (b) and (c) of paragraph (3) shall apply as if for the words "relevant week" there were substituted the words "relevant subsequent week"; and

(b) subject to paragraph (6), the amount as re-determined shall have effect from the first week following the relevant subsequent week in question.

(5) The conditions referred to in paragraph (4) are that—

(a) a further claim is made 26 or more weeks after—

   (i) the date on which the claimant made a claim for a jobseeker's allowance in respect of which he was first treated as possessing the capital in question under regulation 113(1); or

   (ii) in a case where there has been at least one re-determination in accordance with paragraph (4), the date on which he last made a claim for a jobseeker's allowance which resulted in the weekly amount being re-determined; or

   (iii) the date on which he last ceased to be in receipt of a jobseeker's allowance;

   whichever last occurred; and

(b) the claimant would have been entitled to a jobseeker's allowance but for regulation 113(1).

(6) The amount as re-determined pursuant to paragraph (4) shall not have effect if it is less than the amount which applied in that case immediately before the re-determination and in such a case the higher amount shall continue to have effect.

(7) For the purposes of this regulation—

(a) "part-week" has the same meaning as in regulation 150(3);

(b) "relevant week" means the benefit week or part-week in which the capital in question of which the claimant has deprived himself within the meaning of regulation 113(1)—

> (i) was first taken into account for the purposes of determining his entitlement to a jobseeker's allowance or income support; or
>
> (ii) was taken into account on a subsequent occasion for the purposes of determining or re-determining his entitlement to a jobseeker's allowance or income support on that subsequent occasion and that determination or re-determination resulted in his beginning to receive, or ceasing to receive, a jobseeker's allowance or income support;
>
> and where more than one benefit week or part-week is identified by reference to heads (i) and (ii) of this sub-paragraph, the later or latest such benefit week or part-week;
>
> (c) "relevant subsequent week" means the benefit week or part-week which includes the day on which the further claim or, if more than one further claim has been made, the last such claim was made.

DEFINITIONS

"benefit week"—see reg. 1(3).
"claimant"—see Jobseekers Act, s. 35(1), reg. 88(1).
"week"—see Jobseekers Act, s. 35(1).

GENERAL NOTE

See the notes to reg. 51A of the Income Support Regulations.

Capital jointly held

115. Except where a claimant possesses capital which is disregarded under regulation 113(4) (notional capital), where a claimant and one or more persons are beneficially entitled in possession to any capital asset, they shall be treated as if each of them were entitled in possession [¹to the whole beneficial interest therein in an equal share and the foregoing provisions of this Chapter shall apply for the purposes of calculating the amount of capital which the claimant is treated as possessing as if it were actual capital which the claimant does possess.]

AMENDMENT

1. Social Security Amendment (Capital) Regulations 1998 (S.I. 1998 No. 2250), reg. 2 (October 12, 1998).

DEFINITION

"claimant"—see Jobseekers Act, s. 35(1), reg. 88(1).

GENERAL NOTE

See the notes to reg. 52 of the Income Support Regulations.

Calculation of tariff income from capital

116.—(1) [¹Except in a case to which paragraph (1B) applies,] where the claimant's capital calculated in accordance with this Part exceeds £3,000 it shall be treated as equivalent to a weekly income of £1 for each complete £250 in excess of £3,000 but not exceeding £8,000.

[¹(1A) In the case of a claimant to whom paragraph (1B) applies and whose capital calculated in accordance with Chapter VI of Part VIII exceeds £10,000, it shall be treated as equivalent to a weekly income of £1 for each complete £250 in excess of £10,000 but not exceeding £16,000.

(1B) This paragraph applies where the claimant lives permanently in—

(a) a residential care or nursing home [² . . .] and that home [² . . .] provides board and personal care for the claimant by reason of his disablement, past or present dependence on alcohol or drugs or past or present mental disorder; or

(b) an establishment run by the Abbeyfield Society including all bodies corporate or incorporate which are affiliated to that Society; or

(c) accommodation provided under section 3 of, and Part II of the Schedule to, the Polish Resettlement Act 1947 (provision of accommodation in camps) where the claimant requires personal care [³by reason of old age, disablement, past or present dependence on alcohol or drugs, past or present mental disorder or a terminal illness and the care is provided in the home];

[²(d) residential accommodation.]

(1C) For the purpose of paragraph (1B), a claimant shall be treated as living permanently in such home or accommodation where he is absent—

(a) from a home or accommodation referred to in sub-paragraph [²(a), (b) or (d)] of paragraph (1B)—

(i) in the case of a claimant referred to in regulation 19(2) of the Income Support (General) Regulations 1987 for a period not exceeding 52 weeks, and

(ii) in any other case, for a period not exceeding 13 weeks;

(b) from accommodation referred to in sub-paragraph (c) of paragraph (1B), but intends, with the agreement of the manager of the accommodation, to return to the accommodation in due course.]

(2) Notwithstanding [¹paragraphs (1) and (1A)], where any part of the excess is not a complete £250 that part shall be treated as equivalent to a weekly income of £1.

(3) For the purposes of [¹paragraphs (1) and (1A)], capital includes any income treated as capital under regulations 110 and 124 (income treated as capital and liable relative payments treated as capital).

[¹(4) In its application to this regulation, the definition of "residential accommodation" in regulation 85(4) (special cases) shall have effect as if, after the words "subject to the following provisions of this regulation", there were inserted the words "(except paragraph (6))".]

AMENDMENTS

1. Jobseeker's Allowance (Amendment) Regulations 1996 (S.I. 1996 No. 1516), reg. 12 (October 7, 1996).

2. Income-related Benefits and Jobseeker's Allowance (Miscellaneous Amendments) Regulations 1997 (S.I. 1997 No. 65), reg. 8 (April 7, 1997).

3. Income-related Benefits and Jobseeker's Allowance (Amendment) (No. 2) Regulations 1997 (S.I. 1997 No. 2197), reg. 7(5) and (6)(b) (October 6, 1997).

DEFINITIONS

"claimant"—see Jobseekers Act, s. 35(1), reg. 88(1)
"nursing home"—see reg. 1(3).
"residential accommodation"—*ibid.*
"residential care home"—*ibid.*

GENERAL NOTE

See the notes to reg. 53 of the Income Support Regulations.

Chapter VII

Liable Relatives

Interpretation

117. In this Chapter, unless the context otherwise requires—
"claimant" includes a young claimant;
"liable relative" means—
  (a) a spouse or former spouse of a claimant or of a member of the claimant's family;
  (b) a parent of a young claimant or of a child or young person who is a member of a claimant's family;
  (c) a person who has not been adjudged to be the father of a young claimant or of a child or young person who is a member of a claimant's family, where that person is contributing to the maintenance of that young claimant, child or young person and by reason of that contribution he may reasonably be treated as the father of that young claimant, child or young person;
  (d) a person liable to maintain another person by virtue of section 78(6)(c) of the Administration Act where the latter is the claimant or a member of the claimant's family,
  and, in this definition, a reference to a child's, young person's or young claimant's parent includes any person in relation to whom the child, young person or young claimant was treated as a child or a member of the family;
"payment" means a periodical payment or any other payment made by or derived from a liable relative including, except in the case of a discretionary trust, any payment which would be so made or derived upon application being made by the claimant but which has not been acquired by him, but only from the date on which it could be expected to be acquired were an application made; but it does not include any payment—
  (a) arising as a consequence of a disposition of property made in contemplation of, or as a consequence of—
    (i) an agreement to separate; or
    (ii) any proceedings for judicial separation, divorce or nullity of marriage;
  (b) made after the death of the liable relative;
  (c) made by way of a gift but not in aggregate or otherwise exceeding £250 in the period of 52 weeks beginning with the date on which the payment, or if there is more than one such payment the first payment, is made; and in the case of a claimant who continues to be in receipt of an income-based jobseeker's allowance at the end of the period of 52 weeks, this provision shall continue to apply thereafter with the modification than any subsequent period of 52 weeks shall begin with the first day of the benefit week in which the first payment is made after the end of the previous period of 52 weeks;
  (d) to which regulation 106(2) applies (payments in respect of children and young persons who reside at an educational establisment);
  (e) made—
    (i) to a third party in respect of the claimant or a member of the claimant's family; or
    (ii) to the claimant or to a member of the claimant's family in respect of a third party,
    where having regard to the nature of the payment, the terms under

which it is made and its amount, it is unreasonable to take it into account;

  (f) in kind;

  (g) to or in respect of a child or young person who is to be treated as not being a member of the claimant's household under regulation 78;

  (h) which is not a periodical payment, to the extent that any amount of that payment—

    (i) has already been taken into account under this Part by virtue of a previous claim or determination; or

    (ii) has been recovered under section 74(1) of the Administration Act (prevention of duplication of payments) or is currently being recovered; or

    (iii) at the time the determination is made, has been used by the claimant except where he has deprived himself of that amount for the purpose of securing entitlement to a jobseeker's allowance or increasing the amount of that allowance;

"periodical payment" means—

  (a) a payment which is made or is due to be made at regular intervals in pursuance of a court order or agreement for maintenance;

  (b) in a case where the liable relative has established a pattern of making payments at regular intervals, any such payment;

  (c) any payment not exceeding the amount of jobseeker's allowance payable had that payment not been made;

  (d) any payment representing a commutation of payments to which sub-paragraph (a) or (b) of this definition applies whether made in arrears or in advance,

but does not include a payment due to be made before the benefit week in which the claimant first became entitled to an income-based jobseeker's allowance, which was not so made;

"young claimant" means a person aged 16 or over but under 19 who makes a claim for a jobseeker's allowance.

DEFINITIONS

"benefit week"—see reg. 1(3).
"child"—see Jobseekers Act, s. 35(1).
"claimant"—*ibid*, reg. 88(1).
"farmly"—see Jobseekers Act, s. 35(1).
"young person"—see reg. 76.

GENERAL NOTE

See the notes to reg. 54 of the Income Support Regulations.

Treatment of liable relative payments

118. Subject to regulation 119 and except where regulation 124(1) applies (liable relative payments to be treated as capital) a payment shall—

  (a) to the extent that it is not a payment of income, be treated as income;

  (b) be taken into account in accordance with the following provisions of this Chapter.

DEFINITION

"payment"—see reg. 117.

GENERAL NOTE

See the note to reg. 55 of the Income Support Regulations.

Disregard of payments treated as not relevant income

119. Where the Secretary of State treats any payment as not being relevant income for the purposes of section 74A of the Administration Act (payment of benefit where maintenance payments collected by Secretary of State), that payment shall be disregarded in calculating a claimant's income.

DEFINITIONS

"payment"—see reg. 117.
"relevant income"—see reg. 2(c), Social Security Benefits (Maintenance Payments and Consequential Amendments) Regulations 1996.

GENERAL NOTE

See reg. 55A of the Income Support Regulations and the note to s. 74A of the Administration Act. The Social Security Benefits (Maintenance Payments and Consequential Amendments) Regulations 1996 are on pp. 1442–1443.

Period over which periodical payments are to be taken into account

120.—(1) The period over which a periodical payment is to be taken into account shall be—
   (a) in a case where the payment is made at regular intervals, a period equal to the length of that interval;
   (b) in a case where the payment is due to be made at regular intervals but is not so made, such number of weeks as is equal to the number obtained (and any fraction shall be treated as a corresponding fraction of a week) by dividing the amount of that payment by the weekly amount of that periodical payment as calculated in accordance with regulation 122(4);
   (c) in any other case, a period equal to a week.
   (2) The period under paragraph (1) shall begin on the date on which the payment is treated as paid under regulation 123.

DEFINITION

"periodical payment"—see reg. 117.

GENERAL NOTE

See the note to reg. 56 of the Income Support Regulations.

Period over which payments other than periodical payments are to be taken into account

121.—(1) Subject to paragraph (2), the number of weeks over which a payment other than a periodical payment is to be taken into account shall be equal to the number (and any fraction shall be treated as a corresponding fraction of a week) obtained by dividing that payment by—
   (a) where the payment is in respect of the claimant or the claimant and any child or young person who is a member of the claimant's family, the aggregate of £2 and the amount of jobseeker's allowance which would be payable had the payment not been made;
   (b) where the payment is in respect of one, or more than one, child or young person who is a member of the family, the lesser of the amount (or the aggregate of the amounts) prescribed under Schedule 1, in respect of—
      (i) the personal allowance of the claimant and each such child or young person;

    (ii) any family [¹ . . .] premium;

    (iii) any disabled child premium in respect of such a child; and

    (iv) any carer premium but only if that premium is payable because the claimant is in receipt, or is treated as being in receipt, of invalid care allowance by reason of the fact that he is caring for such a child or young person who is severely disabled,

and the aggregate of £2 and the amount of jobseeker's allowance which would be payable had the payment not been made.

(2) Where a liable relative makes a periodical payment and any other payment concurrently and the weekly amount of that periodical payment, as calculated in accordance with regulation 122 (calculation of the weekly amount of a liable relative payment), is less than—.

    (a) in a case where the periodical payment is in respect of the claimant or the claimant and any child or young person who is a member of the claimant's family, the aggregate of £2 and the amount of jobseeker's allowance which would be payable had the payments not been made; or

    (b) in a case where the periodical payment is in respect of one or more than one child or young person who is a member of the family, the aggregate of the amounts prescribed in Schedule 1 in respect of each such child or young person and any family [¹ . . .] premium,

that other payment shall, subject to paragraph (3), be taken into account over a period of such number of weeks as is equal to the number obtained (and any fraction shall be treated as a corresponding fraction of a week) by dividing that payment by an amount equal to the extent of the difference between the amount referred to in sub-paragraph (a) or (b), as the case may be, and the weekly amount of the periodical payment.

(3) If—

    (a) the liable relative ceases to make periodical payments, the balance (if any) of the other payment shall be taken into account over the number of weeks equal to the number obtained (and any fraction shall be treated as a corresponding fraction of a week) by dividing that balance by the amount referred to in sub-paragraph (a) or (b), as the case may be, of paragraph (1);

    (b) the amount of any subsequent periodical payment varies, the balance (if any) of the other payment shall be taken into account over a period of such number of weeks as is equal to the number obtained (and any fraction shall be treated as a corresponding fraction of a week) by dividing that balance by an amount equal to the extent of the difference between the amount referred to in sub-paragraph (a) or (b), as the case may be, of paragraph (2), and the weekly amount of the subsequent periodical payment.

(4) The period under paragraph (1) or (2) shall begin on the date on which the payment is treated as paid under regulation 123, and under paragraph (3) shall begin on the first day of the benefit week in which the cessation or variation of the periodical payment occurred.

AMENDMENT

1. Child Benefit, Child Support and Social Security (Miscellaneous Amendments) Regulations 1996 (S.I. 1996 No. 1803), reg. 43 (April 7, 1997).

DEFINITIONS

    "child"—see Jobseekers Act, s. 35(1).
    "claimant"—*ibid.*, reg. 88(1).
    "family"—see Jobseekers Act, s. 35(1).
    "liable relative"—see reg. 117.

"payment"—*ibid.*
"periodical payment"—*ibid.*
"young person"—see reg. 76.

See the note to reg. 57 of the Income Support Regulations.

Calculation of the weekly amount of a liable relative payment

122.—(1) Where a periodical payment is made or is due to be made at intervals of one week, the weekly amount shall be the amount of that payment.

(2) Where a periodical payment is made or is due to be made at intervals greater than one week and those intervals are monthly, the weekly amount shall be determined by multiplying the amount of the payment by 12 and dividing the product by 52.

(3) Where a periodical payment is made or is due to be made at intervals and those intervals are neither weekly or monthly, the weekly amount shall be determined by dividing that payment by the number equal to the number of weeks (including any part of a week) in that interval.

(4) Where a payment is made and that payment represents a commutation of periodical payments whether in arrears or in advance, the weekly amount shall be the weekly amount of the individual periodical payments so commuted as calculated under paragraphs (1) to (3) as appropriate.

(5) The weekly amount of a payment to which regulation 121 applies (period over which payments other than periodical payments are to be taken into account) shall be equal to the amount of the divisor used in calculating the period over which the payment or, as the case may be, the balance is to be taken into account.

DEFINITIONS

"payment"—see reg. 117.
"periodical payment"—*ibid.*

GENERAL NOTE

See the note to reg. 58 of the Income Support Regulations.

Date on which a liable relative payment is to be treated as paid

123.—(1) A periodical payment is to be treated as paid—
- (a) in the case of a payment which is due to be made before the benefit week in which the claimant first became entitled to an income-based jobseeker's allowance, on the day in the week in which it is due to be paid which corresponds to the first day of the benefit week;
- (b) in any other case, on the first day of the benefit week in which it is due to be paid unless, having regard to the manner in which jobseeker's allowance is due to be paid in the particular case, it would be more practicable to treat it as paid on the first day of a subsequent benefit week.

(2) Subject to paragraph (3), any other payment shall be treated as paid—
- (a) in the case of a payment which is made before the benefit week in which the claimant first became entitled to an income-based jobseeker's allowance, on the day in the week in which it is paid which corresponds to the first day of the benefit week;
- (b) in any other case, on the first day of the benefit week in which it is paid

unless, having regard to the manner in which jobseeker's allowance is due to be paid in the particular case, it would be more practicable to treat it as paid on the first day of a subsequent benefit week.

(3) Any other payment paid on a date which falls within the period in respect of which a previous payment is taken into account, not being a periodical payment, is to be treated as paid on the first day following the end of that period.

DEFINITIONS

"benefit week"—see reg. 1(3).
"payment"—see reg. 117.
"periodical payment"—*ibid.*

GENERAL NOTE

See the notes to reg. 59 of the Income Support Regulations.

Liable relative payments to be treated as capital

124.—(1) Subject to paragraph (2), where a liable relative makes a periodical payment concurrently with any other payment, and the weekly amount of the periodical payment as calculated in accordance with regulation 122(1) to (4) (calculation of the weekly amount of a liable relative payment) is equal to or greater than the amount referred to in sub-paragraph (a) of regulation 121(2) (period over which payments other than periodical payments are to be taken into account), less the £2 referred to therein, or sub-paragraph (b) of that regulation, as the case may be, the other payment shall be treated as capital.

(2) If, in any case, the liable relative ceases to make periodical payments, the other payment to which paragraph (1) applies shall be taken into account under paragraph (1) of regulation 121 but, notwithstanding paragraph (4) thereof, the period over which the payment is to be taken into account shall begin on the first day of the benefit week following the last one in which a periodical payment was taken into account.

DEFINITIONS

"benefit week"—see reg. 1(3).
"liable relative"—see reg. 117.
"payment"—*ibid.*
"periodical payment"—*ibid.*

GENERAL NOTE

See the note to reg. 60 of the Income Support Regulations.

Chapter VIII

Child Support

Interpretation

125. In this Chapter—
"child support maintenance" means such periodical payments as are referred to in section 3(6) of the Child Support Act 1991;
"maintenance assessment" has the same meaning as in the Child Support Act 1991 by virtue of section 54 of that Act.

GENERAL NOTE

See the note to reg. 60A of the Income Support Regulations.

Treatment of child support maintenance

126. Subject to regulation 127, all payments of child support maintenance shall to the extent that they are not payments of income be treated as income and shall be taken into account on a weekly basis in accordance with the following provisions of this Chapter.

DEFINITIONS

"child support maintenance"—see reg. 125.
"payment"—see reg. 1(3).

GENERAL NOTE

See the note to reg. 60B of the Income Support Regulations.

Disregard of payments treated as not relevant income

127. Where the Secretary of State treats any payment of child support maintenance as not being relevant income for the purposes of section 74A of the Administration Act (payment of benefit where maintenance payments collected by Secretary of State), that payment shall be disregarded in calculating a claimant's income.

DEFINITIONS

"child support maintenance"—see reg. 125.
"payment"—see reg. 1(3).
"relevant income"—see reg. 2(c), Social Security Benefits (Maintenance Payments and Consequential Amendments) Regulations 1996.

GENERAL NOTE

See reg. 60E of the Income Support Regulations and the note to s. 74A of the Administration Act. The Social Security Benefits (Maintenance Payments and Consequential Amendments) Regulations 1996 are on pp. 1442–1443.

Calculation of the weekly amount of child support maintenance

128.—(1) The weekly amount of child support maintenance shall be calculated in accordance with the following provisions of this regulation.

(2) Where payments of child support maintenance are made weekly, the weekly amount shall be the amount of that payment.

(3) Where payments of child support maintenance are made monthly, the weekly amount shall be determined by multiplying the amount of the payment by 12 and dividing the product by 52.

(4) Where payments of child support are made at intervals and those intervals are not a week or a month, the weekly amount shall be determined by dividing that payment by the number equal to the number of weeks (including any part of a week) in that interval.

(5) Where a payment is made and that payment represents a commutation of child support maintenance, the weekly amount shall be the weekly amount of the individual child support maintenance payments so commuted as calculated in accordance with paragraphs (2) to (4) as appropriate.

(6) Paragraph (2), (3), or, as the case may be, (4) shall apply to any payments made at the intervals specified in that paragraph whether or not—
- (a) the amount paid is in accordance with the maintenance assessment; and
- (b) the intervals at which the payments are made are in accordance with the intervals specified by the Secretary of State under regulation 4 of the Child Support (Collection and Enforcement) Regulations 1992.

DEFINITIONS

"child support maintenance"—see reg. 125.
"maintenance assessment"—*ibid.*
"payment"—see reg. 1(3).

GENERAL NOTE

See the notes to reg. 60C of the Income Support Regulations.

Date on which child support maintenance is to be treated as paid

129.—(1) Subject to paragraph (2), a payment of child support maintenance is to be treated as paid—
- (a) [¹subject to sub-paragraph (aa),] in the case of a payment which is due to be made before the benefit week in which the claimant first became entitled to an income-based jobseeker's allowance, on the day in the week in which it is due to be paid which corresponds to the first day of the benefit week;
- [¹(aa) in the case of any amount of a payment which represents arrears of maintenance for a week prior to the benefit week in which the claimant first became entitled to an income-based jobseeker's allowance, on the day of the week in which it became due which corresponds to the first day of the benefit week;]
- (b) in any other case, on the first day of the benefit week in which it is due to be paid or the first day of the first succeeding benefit week in which it is practicable to take it into account.

[¹(2) Where a payment to which paragraph (1)(b) refers is made to the Secretary of State and then transmitted to the person entitled to receive it, the payment shall be treated as paid on the first day of the benefit week in which it is transmitted or, where it is not practicable to take it into account in that week, the first day of the first succeeding benefit week in which it is practicable to take the payment into account.]

AMENDMENT

1. Social Security and Child Support (Jobseeker's Allowance) (Miscellaneous Amendments) Regulations 1996 (S.I. 1996 No. 2538), reg. 2(8) (October 28, 1996).

DEFINITIONS

"benefit week"—see reg. 1(3).
"child support maintenance"—see reg. 125.

GENERAL NOTE

See the note to reg. 60D of the Income Support Regulations.

Chapter IX

Full-time Students

Interpretation

130. In this Chapter, unless the context otherwise requires—

"contribution" means any contribution in respect of the income [¹of a student or] of any other person which the Secretary of State or an education authority takes into account in ascertaining the amount of the student's grant, or any sums, which in determining the amount of a student's allowance or bursary in Scotland in terms of the Students' Allowances (Scotland) Regulations 1991 or the Education Authority (Bursaries) (Scotland) Regulations 1995, the Secretary of State or education authority takes into account being sums which the Secretary of State or the education authority consider that the holder of the allowance or bursary, the holder's parents and the holder's spouse can reasonably be expected to contribute towards the holder's expenses;

"covenant income" means the income payable to a student under a deed of covenant by a person whose income is, or is likely to be, taken into account in assessing the student's grant or award;

"education authority" means a government department, a local education authority as defined in section 114(1) of the Education Act 1944, a local education authority as defined in section 123 of the Local Government (Scotland) Act 1973, an education and library board established under article 3 of the Education and Libraries (Northern Ireland) Order 1986, any body which is a research council for the purposes of the Science and Technology Act 1965 or any analogous government department, authority, board or body, of the Channel Islands, Isle of Man or any other country outside Great Britain;

"grant" means any kind of educational grant or award and includes any scholarship, studentship, exhibition, allowance or bursary but does not include a payment derived from funds made available by the Secretary of State for the purpose of assisting students in financial difficulties under section 100 of the Education Act 1944, section 65 of the Further and Higher Education Act 1992 or section 73 of the Education (Scotland) Act 1980;

"grant income" means—

(a) any income by way of a grant;

(b) in the case of a student other than one to whom sub-paragraph (c) refers, any contribution that has been taken into account whether or not it has been paid;

(c) in the case of a student who satisfies the additional conditions for a disability premium in paragraph 14 of Schedule 1 (applicable amounts), any contribution which has been taken into account and which has been paid,

and any such contribution which is paid by way of a covenant shall be treated as part of the student's grant income;

"last day of the course" means the date on which the last day of the final academic term falls in respect of the course in which the student is enrolled;

"periods of experience" has the meaning prescribed in paragraph 1(1) of Schedule 5 to the Education (Mandatory Awards) Regulations 1995;

"standard maintenance grant" means—

(a) except where paragraph (b) or (c) applies, in the case of a student attending a course of study at the University of London or an establishment within the area comprising the City of London and the Metropolitan Police District, the amount specified for the time being in paragraph 2(2)(a) of Schedule 2 to the Education (Mandatory Awards) Regulations 1995 ("the 1995 regulations") for such a student;

(b) except where paragraph (c) applies, in the case of a student residing at his parents' home, the amount specified in paragraph 3(2) thereof;

(c) in the case of a student receiving an allowance or bursary under the Students' Allowance (Scotland) Regulations 1991 or the Education Authority (Bursaries) (Scotland) Regulations 1995, the amount of money specified as "standard maintenance allowance" for the relevant year appropriate for the student set out in the Guide to Undergraduate allowances issued by the Student Awards Agency for Scotland, or its nearest equivalent in the case of a bursary as set by the local education authority;

(d) in any other case, the amount specified in paragraph 2(2) of the 1995 regulations other than in sub-paragraph (a) or (b) thereof;

"student" means a full-time student;

"year", in relation to a course, means the period of 12 months beginning on 1st January, 1st April or 1st September according to whether the academic year of the course in question begins in the spring, the summer or the autumn respectively.

AMENDMENT

1. Social Security (Miscellaneous Amendments) Regulations 1998 (S.I. 1998 No. 563), reg. 4(1) and (2)(f) (April 6, 1998).

DEFINITION

"full-time student"—see reg. 1(3).

GENERAL NOTE

See the notes to reg. 61 of the Income Support Regulations.

Under JSA the definition of "student" refers over to the definition of "full-time student" in reg. 1(3). In that definition the cut off for a course funded by the FEFC is 16 or more "guided learning hours" (England and Wales) (note the different definition in Scotland), but for courses which are not so funded, whether or not a course is full-time will be determined by the facts in each case. The same definition of "student" applies under income support but is achieved by a different route, namely a combination of the definitions of "student" and "full-time course of study" in reg. 61 of the Income Support Regulations. Note also the definition of "full-time course of advanced education" in reg. 1(3) (for the income support provision, see reg. 61) for people who are under 19.

Calculation of grant income

131.—(1) The amount of a student's grant income to be taken into account shall, subject to paragraphs (2) and (3), be the whole of his grant income.

(2) There shall be disregarded from the amount of a student's grant income any payment—

(a) intended to meet tuition fees or examination fees;

(b) intended to meet additional expenditure incurred by a disabled student in respect of his attendance on a course;

(c) intended to meet additional expenditure connected with term time residential study away from the student's educational establishment;

(d) on account of the student maintaining a home at a place other than that at which he resides while attending his course but only to the extent that his rent is not met by housing benefit;

(e) on account of any other person but only if that person is residing outside the United Kingdom and there is no applicable amount in respect of him;

(f) intended to meet the cost of books and equipment [¹ . . .] or if not so intended an amount equal to [²£295] towards such costs;

(g) intended to meet travel expenses incurred as a result of his attendance on the course.

(3) Where in pursuance of an award a student is in receipt of a grant in respect of maintenance under regulation 17(1)(b) of the Education (Mandatory Awards) Regulations 1995, there shall be excluded from his grant income a sum equal to the amount from time to time specified in paragraph 7(4) of Schedule 2 to those Regulations, being the amount to be disregarded in respect of travel costs in the particular circumstances of his case.

(4) A student's grant income except any amount intended for the maintenance of dependants under Part III of Schedule 2 to the Education (Mandatory Awards) Regulations 1995 or otherwise, or intended for an older student under Part IV of that Schedule, shall be apportioned—

(a) subject to paragraph (6), in a case where it is attributable to the period of study, equally between the weeks in that period;

(b) in any other case, equally between the weeks in the period in respect of which it is payable.

(5) Any amount intended for the maintenance of dependants or for an older student under the provisions referred to in paragraph (4) shall be apportioned equally over a period of 52 weeks, or if there are 53 weeks (including part-weeks) in the year, 53.

(6) In the case of a student on a sandwich course, any periods of experience within the period of study shall be excluded and the student's grant income shall be apportioned equally between the remaining weeks in that period.

AMENDMENTS

1. Jobseeker's Allowance (Amendment) Regulations 1996 (S.I. 1996 No. 1516), reg. 20 and Sched. (October 7, 1996).

2. Social Security (Student Amounts Amendment) Regulations 1998 (S.I. 1998 No. 1379), reg. 2 (August 31, 1998, or if the student's period of study begins between August 1, and 30, 1998, the first day of the period).

DEFINITIONS

"grant income"—see reg. 130
"period of study"—see reg. 1(3).
"periods of experience"—see reg. 130.
"sandwich course"—see reg. 1(3).
"student"—see reg. 130, reg. 1(3).

GENERAL NOTE

See the notes to reg. 62 of the Income Support Regulations.

Calculation of covenant income where a contribution is assessed

132.—(1) Where a student is in receipt of income by way of a grant during a period of study and a contribution has been assessed, the amount of his covenant income to be taken into account for that period and any summer vacation immediately following shall be the whole amount of his covenant income less, subject to paragraph (3), the amount of the contribution.

(2) The weekly amount of the student's covenant income shall be determined—

(a) by dividing the amount of income which falls to be taken into account

749

under paragraph (1) by 52 or, if there are 53 benefit weeks (including part-weeks) in the year, 53; and
(b) by disregarding £5 from the resulting amount.
(3) For the purposes of paragraph (1), the contribution shall be treated as increased by the amount, if any, by which the amount excluded under regulation 131(2)(g) falls short of the amount for the time being specified in paragraph 7(4)(i) of Schedule 2 to the Education (Mandatory Awards) Regulations 1995 (travel expenditure).

DEFINITIONS

"benefit week"—see reg. 1(3).
"contribution"—see reg. 130.
"covenant income"—*ibid.*
"grant"—*ibid.*
"period of study"—see reg. 1(3).
"standard maintenance grant"—see reg. 130.
"student"—*ibid.*, reg. 1(3).

GENERAL NOTE

See the note to reg. 63 of the Income Support Regulations.

Covenant income where no grant income or no contribution is assessed

133.—(1) Where a student is not in receipt of income by way of a grant the amount of his covenant income shall be calculated as follows—
(a) any sums intended for any expenditure specified in regulation 131(2)(a) to (e), necessary as a result of his attendance on the course, shall be disregarded;
(b) any covenant income, up to the amount of the standard maintenance grant, which is not so disregarded, shall be apportioned equally between the weeks of the period of study and there shall be disregarded from the covenant income to be so apportioned the amount which would have been disregarded under regulation 131(2)(f) and (g) and (3) had the student been in receipt of the standard maintenance grant;
(c) the balance, if any, shall be divided by 52 or, if there are 53 benefit weeks (including part-weeks) in the year, 53 and treated as weekly income of which £5 shall be disregarded.
(2) Where a student is in receipt of income by way of a grant and no contribution has been assessed, the amount of his covenant income shall be calculated in accordance with paragraph (1), except that—
(a) the value of the standard maintenance grant shall be abated by the amount of his grant income less an amount equal to the amount of any sums disregarded under regulation 131(2)(a) to (e); and
(b) the amount to be disregarded under paragraph (1)(b) shall be abated by an amount equal to the amount of any sums disregarded under regulation 131(2)(f) and (g) and (3).

DEFINITIONS

"benefit week"—see reg.1(3).
"contribution"—see reg.130.
"covenant income"—*ibid.*
"grant income"—*ibid.*
"standard maintenance grant"—*ibid.*
"student"—*ibid.*, reg.1(3).

GENERAL NOTE

See the note to reg. 64 of the Income Support Regulations.

Relationship with amounts to be disregarded under Schedule 7

134. No part of a student's covenant income or grant income shall be disregarded under paragraph 15 of Schedule 7 (charitable and voluntary payments) and any other income to which sub-paragraph (1) of that paragraph applies shall be disregarded only to the extent that the amount disregarded under regulation 132(2)(b) (calculation of covenant income where a contribution is assessed) or, as the case may be, 133(1)(c) (covenant income where no grant income or no contribution is assessed) is less than £20.

DEFINITIONS

"covenant income"—see reg.130.
"grant income"—*ibid.*
"student"—*ibid.* reg.1(3).

GENERAL NOTE

See reg. 65 of the Income Support Regulations.

Other amounts to be disregarded

135.—(1) For the purposes of ascertaining income other than grant income, covenant income, and loans treated as income in accordance with regulation 136, any amounts intended for any expenditure specified in regulation 131(2) (calculation of grant income) necessary as a result of the student's attendance on the course shall be disregarded but only if, and to the extent that, the necessary expenditure exceeds or is likely to exceed the amount of the sums disregarded under regulation 131(2) and (3), 132(3) and 133(1)(a) or (b) (calculation of grant income and covenant income) on like expenditure.

(2) Where a claim is made in respect of any period in the normal summer vacation and any income is payable under a deed of covenant which commences or takes effect after the first day of that vacation, that income shall be disregarded.

DEFINITIONS

"covenant income"—see reg.130.
"grant income"—*ibid.*

GENERAL NOTE

See the note to reg. 66 of the Income Support Regulations.

Treatment of student loans

136.—(1) A loan which is made to a student pursuant to arrangements made under section 1 of the Education (Student Loans) Act 1990 or article 3 of the Education (Student Loans) (Northern Ireland) Order 1990 shall be treated as income.

(2) In calculating the weekly amount of the loan to be taken into account as income
   (a) except where sub-paragraph (b) applies, the loan shall be apportioned

equally between the weeks in the academic year in respect of which the loan is payable;

(b) in the case of a loan which is payable in respect of the final academic year of the course or if the course is of only one academic year's duration, in respect of that year, the loan shall be apportioned equally between the weeks in the period beginning with the start of the final academic year or, as the case may be, the single academic year and ending with the last day of the course,

and from the weekly amount so apportioned there shall be disregarded £10.

(3) For the purposes of this regulation a student shall be treated as possessing the maximum amount of any loan referred to in paragraph (1) which he will be able to acquire in respect of an academic year by taking reasonable steps to do so.

GENERAL NOTE

See the note to reg. 66A of the Income Support Regulations.

Disregard of contribution

137. Where the claimant or his partner is a student and, for the purposes of assessing a contribution to the student's grant, the other partner's income has been taken into account, an amount equal to that contribution shall be disregarded for the purposes of assessing that other partner's income.

DEFINITIONS

"claimant"—see Jobseekers Act, s.35(1), reg. 88(1).
"contribution"—see reg.130.
"grant"—*ibid*.
"partner"—see reg. 1(3).
"student"—see reg. 130. reg. 1(3).

GENERAL NOTE

See reg. 67 of the Income Support Regulations.

[¹Further disregard of student's income

137A. Where any part of a student's income has already been taken into account for the purposes of assessing his entitlement to a grant, the amount taken into account shall be disregarded in assessing that student's income.]

AMENDMENT

1. Social Security (Miscellaneous Amendments) Regulations 1998 (S.I. 1998 No. 563), reg. 4(3) and (4)(f) (April 6, 1998).

DEFINITIONS

"grant"—see reg. 130.
"student"—*ibid*.

Income treated as capital

138. Any amount by way of a refund of tax deducted from a student's income shall be treated as capital.

DEFINITION

"student"—see reg. 130, reg.1(3).

GENERAL NOTE

See reg. 68 of the Income Support Regulations.

Disregard of changes occurring during summer vacation

139. In calculating a student's income an adjudication officer shall disregard any change in the standard maintenance grant occurring in the recognised summer vacation appropriate to the student's course, if that vacation does not form part of his period of study, from the date on which the change occurred up to the end of that vacation.

DEFINITIONS

"period of study"—see reg.1(3).
"standard maintenance grant—see reg. 130.
"student"—*ibid.*, see reg.1(3).

GENERAL NOTE

See reg. 69 of the Income Support Regulations.

PART IX

HARDSHIP

GENERAL NOTE

This Part deals with the circumstances in which a hardship payment of JSA will be made. A hardship payment can only be paid if a s. 19 sanction has been imposed; or the claimant is waiting for a decision at the beginning of his claim as to whether he satisfies the labour market conditions in s. 1(2)(a) to (c) of the Jobseekers Act; or payment of JSA has been suspended because a question has arisen as to whether the claimant satisfies the labour market conditions; or, in the case of a claimant who is in a "vulnerable group' (see reg. 140(1)) only, an AO has decided that he does not satisfy the labour market conditions. Hardship payments are not available in any other circumstances.

See reg. 140 for the meaning of "hardship". Unless the claimant falls into a vulnerable group (see reg. 140(1)), no hardship payment will be made for the first two weeks, however severe the person's hardship. In addition, hardship payments are not available throughout the period of a "New Deal sanction" (see the notes to reg. 69), unless the claimant is in a vulnerable group (see regs. 140(4A) and 140A. If a hardship payment is made, it will be subject to a 40 per cent or 20 per cent reduction of the appropriate personal allowance for a single claimant (see reg. 145). While hardship payments are being paid the claimant must continue to satisfy the other conditions of entitlement for income-based JSA and in addition will be required to sign a declaration of hardship (see reg. 143).

See also the notes to s. 20(4) to (6) of the Jobseekers Act on hardship payments where a s. 19 sanction has been imposed.

Meaning of "person in hardship"

140.—(1) In this Part of these Regulations, a "person in hardship" means for the purposes of regulation 141 a claimant, other than a claimant to whom paragraph (3) or (4) applies, who—
    (a) is a single woman—
        (i) who is pregnant; and

    (ii) in respect of whom the adjudication officer is satisfied that, unless a jobseeker's allowance is paid to her, she will suffer hardship; or

(b) is a single person who is responsible for a young person, and the adjudication officer is satisfied that, unless a jobseeker's allowance is paid to the single person, the young person will suffer hardship; or

(c) is a member of a married or unmarried couple, where—
    (i) the woman is pregnant; and
    (ii) the adjudication officer is satisfied that, unless a jobseeker's allowance is paid, the woman will suffer hardship; or

(d) is a member of a polygamous marriage and—
    (i) one member of the marriage is pregnant; and
    (ii) the adjudication officer is satisfied that, unless a jobseeker's allowance is paid, that woman will suffer hardship; or

(e) is a member of a married or unmarried couple or of a polygamous marriage where
    (i) one or both members of the couple, or one or more members of the polygamous marriage, are responsible for a child or young person; and
    (ii) the adjudication officer is satisfied that, unless a jobseeker's allowance is paid, the child or young person will suffer hardship; or

(f) has an award of a jobseeker's allowance which includes or would, if a claim for a jobseeker's allowance from him were to succeed have included, in his applicable amount a disability premium and—
    (i) where the person has an award, a jobseeker's allowance is not payable either because it is suspended or because section 19 (circumstances in which a jobseeker's allowance is not payable) applies in his case; and
    (ii) the adjudication officer is satisfied that, unless a jobseeker's allowance is paid, the person who would satisfy the conditions of entitlement to that premium would suffer hardship; or

(g) suffers, or whose partner suffers from a chronic medical condition which results in functional capacity being limited or restricted by physical impairment and the adjudication officer is satisfied that—
    (i) the suffering has already lasted, or is likely to last, for not less than 26 weeks; and
    (ii) unless a jobseeker's allowance is paid to the claimant the probability is that the health of the person suffering would, within 2 weeks of the adjudication officer making his decision, decline further than that of a normally healthy adult and that person would suffer hardship; or

(h) does, or whose partner does, or in the case of a claimant who is married to more than one person under a law which permits polygamy, at least one of those persons do, devote a considerable portion of each week to caring for another person who—
    (i) is in receipt of an attendance allowance or the care component of disability living allowance at one of the two higher rates prescribed under [²section 72(4)] of the Benefits Act; or
    (ii) has claimed either attendance allowance or disability living allowance, but only for so long as the claim has not been determined, or for, 26 weeks from the date of claiming, [¹whichever is the earlier; or
    (iii) has claimed either attendance allowance or disability living allowance and has an award of either attendance allowance or the care component of disability living allowance at one of the two higher rates prescribed under section 72(4) of the Benefits Act for a period commencing after the date on which that claim was made,]

and the adjudication officer is satisfied, after taking account of the factors set out in [²paragraph (5)] in so far as they are appropriate to the particular circumstances of the case, that the person providing the care will not be able to continue doing so unless a jobseeker's allowance is paid to the claimant; or

(i) is a person or is the partner of a person to whom section 16 applies by virtue of a direction issued by the Secretary of State, except where the person to whom the direction applies does not satisfy the requirements of section 1(2)(a) to (c); or

(j) is a person—
    (i) to whom section 3(1)(f)(iii) (persons under the age of 18) applies, or is the partner of such a person; and
    (ii) in respect of whom the adjudication officer is satisfied that the person will, unless a jobseeker's allowance is paid, suffer hardship.

(2) Except in a case to which paragraph (3) [² . . .] [⁴or (4A)] applies a "person in hardship" means for the purposes of regulation 142, a claimant where the adjudication officer is satisfied that he or his partner will suffer hardship unless a jobseeker's allowance is paid to him.

(3) In paragraphs (1) and (2) a "person in hardship" does not include a claimant who is entitled, or whose partner is entitled, to income support or [³ a claimant or a partner of a claimant] who falls within a category of persons prescribed for the purpose of section 124(1)(e) of the Benefits Act.

(4) Paragraph (1)(h) shall not apply in a case where the person being cared for resides in a residential care home or nursing home.

[⁴(4A) In paragraph (2), a "person in hardship" does not include a claimant to whom section 19(5)(b) or (c) applies by virtue of any act or omission relating to an employment programme specified in regulation 75(1)(a)(ii) or to the training scheme specified in regulation 75(1)(b)(ii).]

(5) Factors which, for the purposes of paragraphs (1) and (2), an adjudication officer is to take into account in determining whether a person will suffer hardship are—

(a) the presence in the claimant's family of a person who satisfies the requirements for a disability premium specified in paragraphs 13 and 14 of Schedule 1 [¹or for a disabled child premium specified in paragraph 16 of that Schedule;]

(b) the resources which, without a jobseeker's allowance, are likely to be available to the claimant's family, the amount by which these resources fall short of the amount applicable in his case in accordance with regulation 145 (applicable amount in hardship cases), the amount of any resources which may be available to members of the claimant's family from any person in the claimant's household who is not a member of his family, and the length of time for which those factors are likely to persist;

(c) whether there is a substantial risk that essential items, including food, clothing, heating and accommodation, will cease to be available to the claimant or to a member of the claimant's family, or will be available at considerably reduced levels and the length of time those factors are likely to persist.

AMENDMENTS

1. Jobseeker's Allowance (Amendment) Regulations 1996 (S.I. 1996 No. 1516), reg. 13 (October 7, 1996).

2. Jobseeker's Allowance (Amendment) Regulations 1996 (S.I. 1996 No. 1516), reg. 20 and Sched. (October 7, 1996).

3. Jobseeker's Allowance and Income Support (General) (Amendment) Regulations 1996 (S.I. 1996 No. 1517), reg. 25 (October 7, 1996).

4. Social Security Amendment (New Deal) Regulations 1997 (S.I. 1997 No. 2863), reg. 11 (January 5, 1998).

DEFINITIONS

"attendance allowance"—see reg. 1(3).
"child"—see Jobseekers Act, s. 35(1).
"claimant"—*ibid.*
"disability living allowance"—see reg. 1(3).
"married couple"—see Jobseekers Act, s. 35(1).
"partner"—see reg. 1(3).
"polygamous marriage"—*ibid.*
"unmarried couple"—see Jobseekers Act, s. 35(1).
"week"—see reg. 1(3).
"young person"—see reg. 76.

GENERAL NOTE

Paragraph (1)
This lists those claimants who are eligible for hardship payments without any waiting period (the "vulnerable groups"). Note the exclusion in para. (3) of claimants who (or whose partners) are in a category who can claim income support (claimants who, or whose partners, are entitled to income support would in any event be excluded from JSA under s. 3(1)(b) or (c) of the Jobseekers Act).
The categories are:
 (i) a single claimant who is pregnant whom the AO accepts will suffer hardship if no payment is made (sub-para. (a));
 (ii) a member of a couple, or of a polygamous marriage, where the/a woman is pregnant and the AO accepts that the woman will suffer hardship if no payment is made (sub-paras. (c) and (d));
 (iii) a member of a couple, or of a polygamous marriage, who is/are responsible (see reg. 77) for a child or young person (see reg. 76) and the AO accepts that the child or young person will suffer hardship if no payment is made (sub-para. (e));
 (iv) a single claimant who is responsible (see reg. 77) for a *young person* (*i.e.* a 16- to 18-year-old, see reg. 76) and the AO accepts that the young person will suffer hardship if no payment is made (sub-para. (b)). (Note that single people who are responsible for a *child* are not included as they are eligible for income support under Sched. 1B to the Income Support Regulations and see para. (3); it would normally be better for such a person to claim income support);
 (v) people eligible for a disability premium in their income-based JSA and the AO accepts that the person who qualifies for the disability premium would suffer hardship if no payment is made (sub-para. (f)). In contrast to the other sub-paragraphs, sub-para. (f) refers to a person who "has an award of" JSA which includes a disability premium (or whose claim, if successful, would include a disability premium). The intention would seem to be that this category does not apply if the reason for the non-payment of JSA is that the claimant has failed to satisfy the labour market conditions (in such a case the person would not have an award of JSA and see head (i)). But if such a person having failed to satisfy the labour market conditions then makes a further claim for JSA, arguably he falls within sub-para. (f) because he has made a claim for JSA which were it to succeed would include a disability premium.
 (vi) a claimant who, or whose partner, has a chronic medical condition resulting in his functional capacity being restricted by physical impairment which has lasted, or is likely to last, for at least 26 weeks and the AO accepts that in the next two weeks the person's health is likely to "decline further than that of a normally healthy adult" and that that person will suffer hardship if no payment is made (sub-para. (g)). If such a person is incapable of work he will be eligible for income support and so will not qualify for a hardship payment (see para. (3)).
 (vii) a claimant who, or whose partner, "devotes a considerable portion of each week" to caring for someone (not in a residential care or nursing home, see para. (4)) who is in receipt of, or (in certain circumstances) has claimed attendance allowance, or the higher or middle rate care component of disability living allowance and the AO accepts that the person will not be able to continue caring if no payment is made (sub-para. (h)). The *Adjudication Officer's Guide* suggests that "considerable portion" means a "large or significant part" (para.

40110). (Note: a person in this situation may well be eligible for income support, see paras. 4 to 6 of Sched. 1B to the Income Support Regulations);
- (viii) a claimant who, or whose partner, is under 18, the subject of a severe hardship direction and who satisfies the labour market conditions (sub-para. (i));
- (ix) a claimant who, or whose partner, is under 18, but eligible for JSA and the AO accepts that that person will suffer hardship if no payment is made (sub-para. (j)). (*Note*: a 16- or 17-year-old who is being sanctioned for an "offence" under s. 19(5) or s. 19(6)(c) or (d) of the Jobseekers Act will automatically be paid a reduced rate of JSA and will not need to rely on this provision: see reg. 68.)

See para. (5) for the factors the AO must consider when deciding whether a person will suffer hardship.

Note the requirement under reg. 143 for the claimant to sign a written declaration as to why he will suffer hardship if no payment is made.

Paragraph (2)

If a person does not come within one of the categories listed in para. (1) he will only be entitled to a hardship payment after two weeks (reg. 142(2), (4) and (5)) and if the AO accepts that he or his partner will suffer hardship if no payment is made. Note the exclusions in paras. (3) and (4A). As regards para. (3), claimants who, or whose partners, are entitled to income support would in any event be excluded from JSA under s. 3(1)(b) or (c) of the Jobseekers Act. Para. (4A) excludes claimants who are subject to "New Deal sanctions" (see the note to para. (4A) and reg. 140A). See para. (5) for the factors the AO must consider when deciding whether hardship will occur and reg. 143 for the declaration the claimant will be required to sign.

Paragraph (4A)

The effect of this paragraph is to prevent a claimant who is not in a vulnerable group from having access to hardship payments throughout the period of a "New Deal sanction" (even one of four weeks duration). Note reg. 140A(2) and (3) where the claimant was already receiving hardship payments when the New Deal sanction was imposed. A New Deal sanction is one that is imposed for an offence under s. 19(5)(b) or (c) of the Jobseekers Act in relation to a place on one of the New Deal options. See further the notes to reg. 69. For a brief summary of the New Deal for 18–24 year-olds see the notes to reg. 75.

Paragraph (5)

This lists factors that the AO must consider when deciding whether a person will suffer hardship. The list is not exhaustive and the AO should consider all the circumstances of the claimant and his family (if any) (*Adjudication Officer's Guide*, paras. 40156 and 40160). "Hardship" is not defined. The *Adjudication Officer's Guide* suggests that it means "severe suffering or privation", and that "privation means a lack of the necessities of life" (para. 40155).

The factors that the AO must consider are whether a member of the claimant's family qualifies for a disability or a disabled child premium (sub-para. (a)); other available resources, including those which may be available to the claimant's family from anyone else in the claimant's household (sub-para. (b)); and whether there is a "substantial risk" that the claimant or a member of his family will go without essential items such as food, clothing, heating and accommodation, or that they will be available at "considerably reduced" levels, and if so, for how long (sub-para. (c)).

Sub-para. (a) is straightforward. Under sub-para. (b) the AO has to take into account other resources that are likely to be available to the claimant or his family. Thus income and capital that is normally disregarded (*e.g..* disability living allowance) will be taken into account under sub-para. (b). But note that para. 40180 of the *Adjudication Officer's Guide* considers that JSA paid for an earlier period should not be taken into account. (Note that if the AO does decide that the person is in hardship the normal income and capital rules will be applied when calculating the amount of a hardship payment; unlike urgent cases payments there are no special rules for the calculation of income and capital. However, the payment will be reduced by 40 or 20 per cent of the appropriate personal allowance for a single person of the claimant's age: see reg. 145.) In addition, if there are any non-dependents (for example, a grown-up son or daughter) living in the claimant's household, any contribution that they might be expected to make will be considered. But the resources have to be available to the claimant. So, for example, if a payment from a pension fund will only be available in four weeks' time, or savings can only be cashed after a period of notice has been given, a hardship payment can be made until these resources become available (see paras. 40185 to 40195 of *AOG*). Moreover, money that might be obtainable from credit facilities (*e.g.* a credit card or overdraft) should not be taken into account as such facilities are not resources but only increase the claimant's indebtedness (see para. 40196 of *AOG*). The AO also has to consider the length of time for which any other resources are likely to be available. Clearly the longer the period of time that JSA will not be payable (*e.g.* if a sanction of several weeks or months' duration has been imposed) the more likely it is that hardship will occur. Sub-para. (c) gives examples of essential items that the AO should take into account but this does not exclude consideration of other items that may be essential to the particular claimant or a member of his family.

If the claimant is not in hardship when the claim is first made but the AO decides that hardship will be established by a later date, see reg. 13 of the Claims and Payments Regulations under which hardship payments can be awarded from that later date, provided this is within three months of the date of claim.

[¹Period when a person is not a person in hardship

140A.—(1) A claimant who is not a person in hardship by virtue of regulation 140(4A) shall not be a person in hardship throughout the period of—
    (a) 4 weeks in a case to which regulation 69(a) applies; or
    (b) 2 weeks in any other case,
beginning on the day from which the decision that section 19(5)(b) or (c) applies by virtue of an act or omission specified in regulation 140(4A)("the New Deal decision"), has effect by virtue of regulation 69 or, as the case may be, by virtue of regulation 56A(6) of the Social Security (Adjudication) Regulations 1995.

(2) Where a claimant who is not a person in hardship by virtue of regulation 140(4A) was a person in hardship for the purposes of regulation 142 immediately before the commencement of the period referred to in paragraph (1), that claimant shall, subject to paragraph (3), again become a person in hardship for the purposes of regulation 142 on the day following the expiration of that period.

(3) A claimant to whom paragraph (2) applies shall not again become a person in hardship for the purposes of regulation 142 if—
    (a) the day following the day the period referred to in paragraph (1) expires is a day within a period in respect of which a subsequent New Deal decision applies by virtue of paragraph (1); or
    (b) on the day following the expiry of the period referred to in paragraph (1), he is not a person in hardship for the purposes of regulation 142.]

AMENDMENT

1. Social Security Amendment (New Deal) Regulations 1997 (S.I. 1997 No. 2863), reg. 12 (January 5, 1998).

DEFINITION

"claimant"—see Jobseekers Act, s. 35(1).

GENERAL NOTE

Para. (1) confirms that a claimant who is not in a vulnerable group (see reg. 140(1)) and who has incurred a New Deal sanction (see the notes to reg. 69) of either two or four weeks' duration will not have access to hardship payments during the period of that sanction. See also reg. 140(4A). This will be the case even if the claimant might otherwise have been considered to be a person in hardship *i.e.* because this had been accepted in connection with a non-New Deal sanction to which he was already subject. The intention is that in those circumstances the New Deal sanction will take precedence. However, in such a case, once the New Deal sanction expires, the claimant will again become eligible for hardship payments, unless another New Deal sanction immediately takes effect, or he is not a person in hardship for the purposes of reg. 142 (*e.g.* because the previous non-New Deal sanction has expired) (paras. (2) and (3)).

Circumstances in which an income-based jobseeker's allowance is payable to a person in hardship

141.—(1) This regulation applies to persons in hardship within the meaning of regulation 140(1), and is subject to the provisions of regulations 143 and 144.

(2) Subject to paragraph (3) a person in hardship [¹, other than a person to whom regulation 46(1) (waiting days) applies, shall be treated as entitled to an income-based jobseeker's allowance for the period beginning with the 4th day of the jobseeking period or,] if later, from the day he first becomes a person in hardship and ending on the day before the claim is determined where [²the sole reason for the delay] in determining the claim is that a question arises as to whether the claimant satisfies any of the conditions of entitlement specified in section 1(2)(a) to (c) [²provided he satisfies the conditions of entitlement specified in paragraph (d)(ii) of subsection (2) of section 1.]

(3) A person in hardship to whom paragraph (2) applies may be treated as entitled to an income-based jobseeker's allowance for a period after the date [¹ . . .] referred to in that paragraph [¹which is applicable in his case] but before the date the statement mentioned in regulation 143(1) is furnished where the adjudication officer is satisfied that the claimant suffered hardship because of a lack of resources during that period.

(4) A person in hardship, except where the person has been treated as not available for employment in accordance with regulations under section 6(4) of the Act shall, subject to the conditions specified in regulation 143 (conditions for hardship payments), be entitled to an income-based jobseeker's allowance without satisfying the requirements of section 1(2)(a) to (c) of the Act provided he satisfies the other conditions of entitlement to that benefit.

(5) An income-based jobseeker's allowance shall be payable to a person in hardship even though payment to him of a jobseeker's allowance has been suspended in accordance with regulation 37 of the Claims and Payments Regulations on the ground that a doubt has arisen as to whether he satisfies the requirements of section 1(2)(a) to (c), but the allowance shall be payable only if and for so long as the claimant satisfies the other conditions of entitlement to an income-based jobseeker's allowance.

(6) An income-based jobseeker's allowance shall be payable to a person in hardship even though section 19 (circumstances in which a jobseeker's allowance is not payable) prevents payment of a jobseeker's allowance to him but the allowance shall be payable only if and for so long as he satisfies the conditions of entitlement to an income-based jobseeker's allowance.

AMENDMENTS

1. Jobseeker's Allowance and Income Support (General) (Amendment) Regulations 1996 (S.I. 1996 No. 1517), reg. 26 (October 7, 1996).
2. Social Security and Child Support (Jobseeker's Allowance) (Miscellaneous Amendments) Regulations 1996 (S.I. 1996 No. 2538), reg. 2(9) (October 28, 1996).

DEFINITIONS

"claimant"—see Jobseekers Act, s. 35(1).
"entitled"—*ibid.*

GENERAL NOTE

The circumstances in which hardship payments can be made are set out in this regulation for claimants who can be paid immediately and in reg. 142 for claimants who have to wait two weeks. No payment will be made under this regulation or reg. 142 unless the claimant has signed the declaration required by reg. 143 (but note para. (3) below) and provided information about the person in hardship (see reg. 144).

Para. (2) applies where a question arises as to whether the claimant satisfies the labour market conditions in s. 1(2)(a)–(c) of the Jobseekers Act (availability for work, signing a jobseeker's agreement, actively seeking work) when a claim is made. This has to be the only reason for the delay in deciding the claim; hardship payments will not be available if the delay is for some other reason (*e.g.* because there is a question whether the person has too much capital or income). If hardship is established a payment will be made until the claim is decided, except for the first three waiting days (see para. 4 of Sched. 1 to the Jobseekers Act and reg. 46) if these apply. The claimant must continue to satisfy the other conditions of entitlement for income-based JSA in s. 3 of the Jobseekers Act. A payment under para. (2) may also be made for the period before the claimant has completed a reg. 143 declaration if the AO accepts that he suffered hardship because of "a lack of resources" during that period (para. (3)). Once the AO has decided the claim this paragraph no longer applies but the claimant may be eligible for hardship payments under para. (4).

Para. (4) covers a person who is not entitled to JSA because an AO has decided that he does not satisfy the labour market conditions in s. 1(2)(a) to (c) of the Jobseekers Act. But it does not apply if the person is treated as not available for work under reg. 15 (full-time students, prisoners on temporary release, women in receipt of maternity pay or allowance, people treated as not available at the start of a claim). The person must be in hardship and continue to satisfy the other conditions of entitlement for income-based JSA. Hardship payments can start from the date of the AO's decision and continue for as long as the person remains in hardship. There is no requirement that the claimant has appealed against the AO's decision. Note that there is no equivalent of this provision in reg. 142 (persons eligible for hardship payments after waiting period).

Para. (5) applies where payment of a person's JSA has been suspended because a question has arisen as to whether he satisfies the labour market conditions. The person must be in hardship and continue to satisfy the other conditions of entitlement for income-based JSA. Hardship payments can be made until the suspension is lifted or the AO decides that the claimant does not satisfy the labour market conditions. If the decision goes against the claimant he may be eligible for hardship payments under para. (4).

Under para. (6) a person can be paid hardship payments if a s. 19 sanction has been applied, provided that he is in hardship and that he continues to satisfy the other conditions of entitlement for income-based JSA (including the labour market conditions). Payments under para. (6) can last as long as the sanction lasts.

See reg. 145 for the amount of a hardship payment.

Further circumstances in which an income-based jobseeker's allowance is payable to a person in hardship

142.—(1) This regulation applies to a person in hardship who falls within paragraph (2) but not paragraph (1) of regulation 140 and is subject to the provisions of regulations 143 and 144.

(2) A person in hardship shall be treated as entitled to an income-based job-seeker's allowance for a period commencing on whichever is the later of—

[¹(a) the 15th day following the date of claim disregarding any waiting days; or]

(b) [¹ . . .]

(c) the day the claimant complies with the requirements of regulation 143, and ending on the day before the claim is determined where [¹the sole reason for the delay] in determining the claim is that a question arises as to whether the claimant satisfies any of the conditions of entitlement specified in section 1(2)(a) to (c) [¹provided he satisfies the conditions of entitlement specified in paragraph (d)(ii) of subsection (2) of section 1.]

(3) An income-based jobseeker's allowance shall be payable subject to paragraph (4) to a person in hardship even though payment to him of a jobseeker's allowance has been suspended in accordance with regulations made by virtue of section 5(1)(n) of the Administration Act (suspension of benefit) on the ground that a doubt has arisen as to whether he satisfies the requirements of section 1(2)(a) to (c) but the allowance shall be payable only if and for so long as the claimant satisfies the other conditions of entitlement to an income-based jobseeker's allowance.

(4) An income-based jobseeker's allowance shall not be payable in respect of the first 14 days of the period of suspension.

(5) An income-based jobseeker's allowance shall be payable to a person in hardship even though section 19 (circumstances in which a jobseeker's allow-

INCOME RELATED BENEFITS: THE LEGISLATION

SUPPLEMENT

COMMENTARY BY PENNY WOOD, MARK ROWLAND AND NICK WIKELEY

- New content structure
- New added commentary for specialists by Mark Rowland and Nick Wikeley
- Working families tax credit
- Disabled person's tax credit
- Major changes to decision-making and appeals as a result of the 1998 Social Security Act
- Updating of legislation relating to means-tested benefits and notes on the relevant Commissioner and court decisions

1999

Sweet & Maxwell

QTY	TITLE	PRICE	POSTAGE	TOTAL
	INCOME RELATED BENEFITS: THE LEGISLATION SUPPLEMENT 1999	£18.00		

POSTAGE AND PACKING IS FREE WITHIN THE UK. OVERSEAS: Airmail £15.00 for the first item, then £5.00 for each additional item.

MY PERSONAL DETAILS ARE:

Title: _____

First names: _____

Surname: _____

Job title: _____

MY FIRM/ORGANISATION DETAILS ARE:

Name: _____

Address: _____

Town: _____

County: _____

Postcode: _____

Country: _____

DX address: _____

Telephone: _____

Fax: _____

E-mail address: _____

I WOULD LIKE TO PAY:

Using my Sweet & Maxwell Account:
_____

Please charge my credit card:

☐ AMEX ☐ Visa

☐ Mastercard ☐ Diners Club

Expiry Date: _____

Card No.: _____

Or

☐ I enclose a cheque payable to Sweet & Maxwell Ltd

☐ Please supply on 28 days approval
(Orders over £40.00 in Europe only)

EU MEMBER STATES: CAT, TVA, MWST, IVA, BTW, FPA, MOMS will be charged to your order if applicable

Please state your number: _____

Signature: _____

Date: _____

Your order is not valid unless signed

Sweet & Maxwell

ance is not payable) prevents payment of a jobseeker's allowance to him, but the allowance—

    (a) shall not be payable under this paragraph in respect of the first 14 days of the period to which section 19 applies; and

    (b) shall be payable thereafter only where the conditions of entitlement to an income-based jobseeker's allowance are satisfied.

AMENDMENT

1. Social Security and Child Support (Jobseeker's Allowance) (Miscellaneous Amendments) Regulations 1996 (S.I. 1996 No. 2538), reg. 2(10) (October 28, 1996).

DEFINITION

"claimant"—see Jobseekers Act, s. 35(1).

GENERAL NOTE

See the notes to reg. 141. This regulation applies to claimants who do not come within any of the categories listed in reg. 140(1) and so have to wait for two weeks before any hardship payments can be made. Note that a claimant who does not come within reg. 140(1) and who has incurred a New Deal sanction (see the notes to reg. 69) will not have access to hardship payments during the period of that sanction (even if it is for four weeks) (see regs. 140(4A) and 140A).

The circumstances in which hardship payments can be made under this regulation are similar to those in reg. 141 (the differences are noted below), *except* that there is no provision for payment to claimants who have failed to satisfy the labour market conditions in s. 1(2)(a) to (c) (compare reg. 141(4)); there is only provision in para. (2) for payment where a question arises when a claim is made as to whether a claimant satisfies the labour market conditions and in para. (3) where a claimant's benefit has been suspended because of doubt as to whether these conditions are satisfied. Once an AO has decided that the person does not satisfy the labour market conditions he will not be eligible for hardship payments if he is not in a "vulnerable group". This is the case even if the claimant is appealing against the AO's decision. Such a person may be eligible for a crisis loan from the social fund but this will be limited to expenses which result from a disaster or items required for cooking or heating (including fireguards) for 14 days from the first day of the benefit week following the disallowance decision, or the day of the decision if it is made on the first day of a benefit week (Social Fund Direction 17(b) and (f)); the person's partner can apply for a crisis loan for living expenses: see Direction 18(2).

Paras. (3) and (5) correspond to paras. (5) and (6) in reg. 141, except that in each case a hardship payment under this regulation is not payable for the first two weeks (see para. (4) and para. (5)(a)). Para. (2) is the equivalent of reg. 141(2) except that under this regulation a hardship payment can only be made from the 15th day after the date of claim, or the 18th day if the "waiting days" apply (see para. 4 of Sched. 1 to the Jobseekers Act and reg. 46) or from the day the claimant makes the declaration required by reg. 143, whichever is the later. There is thus no discretion in the case of hardship payments under para. (2) of this regulation to make any payment for the period before a reg. 143 declaration is signed (compare para. (3) of reg. 141).

Conditions for hardship payments

143.—(1) A jobseeker's allowance shall not be payable in accordance with regulation 141 or, as the case may be, 142, except where the claimant has—

    (a) furnished on a form approved for the purpose by the Secretary of State or in such other form as he may in any particular case approve a statement of the circumstances he relies upon to establish entitlement under regulation 141 or as the case may be regulation 142; and

    (b) signed the statement.

(2) The completed and signed form shall be delivered by the claimant to such office as the Secretary of State may specify.

DEFINITION

"claimant"—see Jobseekers Act, s. 35(1).

Provision of information

144. For the purposes of [¹section 20(5) of and] paragraph 10(3) of Schedule 1 to the Act, a claimant shall provide to the Secretary of State information as to the circumstances of the person alleged to be in hardship.

AMENDMENT

1. Jobseeker's Allowance (Amendment) Regulations 1996 (S.I. 1996 No. 1516), reg. 14 (October 7, 1996).

DEFINITION

"claimant"—see Jobseekers Act, s. 35(1).

Applicable amount in hardship cases

145.—[¹(1) The weekly applicable amount of a person to whom an income-based jobseeker's allowance is payable in accordance with this Part of these Regulations shall be reduced by a sum equivalent to 40% or, in a case where the claimant or any other member of his family is either pregnant or is seriously ill, 20% of the following amount—]

  (a) where he is a single claimant aged less than 18 or a member of a couple or a polygamous marriage where all the members, in either case, are less than 18, the amount specified in paragraph 1(1)(a), (b) or (c), as the case may be, of Schedule 1 (applicable amounts);

  (b) where he is a single claimant aged not less than 18 but less than 25 or a member of a couple or polygamous marriage where one member is aged not less than 18 but less than 25 and the other member or, in the case of a polygamous marriage each other member, is a person under 18 who is not eligible for an income-based jobseeker's allowance under section 3(1)(f)(iii) or is not subject to a direction under section 16, the amount specified in paragraph 1(1)(d) of Schedule 1;

  (c) where he is a single claimant aged not less than 25 or a member of a couple or a polygamous marriage (other than a member of a couple or polygamous marriage to whom sub-paragraph (b) [²applies]) at least one of whom is aged not less than 18, the amount specified in paragraph 1(1)(e) of Schedule 1.

  (2) [¹. . .]

  (3) A reduction under paragraph (1) or (2) shall, if it is not a multiple of 5p, be rounded to the nearest such multiple or, if it is a multiple of 2.5p but not of 5p, to the next lower multiple of 5p.

AMENDMENTS

1. Jobseeker's Allowance (Amendment) Regulations 1996 (S.I. 1996 No. 1516), reg. 15 (October 7, 1996).
2. Jobseeker's Allowance and Income Support (General) (Amendment) Regulations 1996 (S.I. 1996 No. 1517), reg. 28 (October 7, 1996).

DEFINITIONS

"claimant"—see Jobseekers Act, s. 35(1).
"couple"—see reg. 1(3).

"polygamous marriage"—*ibid.*
"single claimant"—*ibid.*

<small>GENERAL NOTE</small>

Hardship payments of JSA are paid at a reduced rate. The reduction in benefit is 40 per cent of the appropriate personal allowance for a single claimant of that age, or 20 per cent if a member of the claimant's family is pregnant or seriously ill (not defined).

Payments made on account of suspended benefit

146.—(1) This regulation applies to a person to whom—
(a) payments of a jobseeker's allowance have been suspended in accordance with regulations made under section 5(1)(n) of the Administration Act;
(b) an income-based jobseeker's allowance is paid under regulation 141 or 142.
(2) In the case of a person to whom—
(a) this regulation applies; and
(b) payments in respect of the benefit suspended fall to be made,
any benefit paid or payable by virtue of regulation 141(5) or 142(3) shall be treated as having been paid on account of the suspended benefit and only the balance of the suspended benefit (if any) shall be payable.

<small>GENERAL NOTE</small>

This provides that hardship payments made while payment of a claimant's JSA was suspended will be taken into account if it is later decided that the suspension should be lifted, and only the balance of the benefit owing will be paid. In other cases (*e.g.* where hardship payments have been made because of a delay in deciding the claim for JSA) offsetting will be applied under the normal rules (see reg. 5 of the Payments on Account, Overpayments and Recovery Regulations).

PART X

URGENT CASES

Urgent cases

147.—(1) In a case to which this regulation applies, a claimant's weekly applicable amount and his income and capital shall be calculated for the purposes of an income-based jobseeker's allowance in accordance with the following provisions of this Part.
(2) This regulation applies in accordance with the following provisions to—
(a) a claimant to whom paragraph (3) (certain persons from abroad) applies;
(b) a claimant to whom paragraph (6) (certain persons whose income is not readily available to them) applies.
[¹(3) This paragraph applies to a person from abroad within the meaning of regulation 85(4) (special cases) who—
(a) is an asylum seeker; and
(b) holds a work permit or has written authorisation from the Secretary of State permitting him to work in the United Kingdom.
(4) For the purposes of this regulation, a person—
(a) is an asylum seeker when he submits on his arrival (other than on his re-entry) in the United Kingdom from a country outside the Common Travel Area, a claim for asylum to the Secretary of State that it would be contrary to the United Kingdom's obligations under the Convention

for him to be removed from, or required to leave, the United Kingdom and that claim is recorded by the Secretary of State as having been made; or

(b) becomes, while present in Great Britain, an asylum seeker when—

    (i) the Secretary of State makes a declaration to the effect that the country of which he is a national is subject to such a fundamental change in circumstances that he would not normally order the return of a person to that country; and

    (ii) he submits, within a period of 3 months from the day that declaration was made, a claim for asylum to the Secretary of State under the Convention relating to the Status of Refugees; and

    (iii) his claim for asylum under that Convention is recorded by the Secretary of State as having been made; and

(c) ceases to be an asylum seeker—

    (i) in the case of a claim for asylum which, on or after 5th February 1996, is recorded by the Secretary of State as having been determined (other than on appeal) or abandoned, on the date on which it is so recorded; or

    (ii) in the case of a claim for asylum which is recorded as determined before 5th February 1996 and in respect of which there is either an appeal pending on 5th February 1996 or an appeal is made within the time limits specified in rule 5 of the Asylum Appeals (Procedure) Rules 1993, on the date on which that appeal is determined.

(5) In this Regulation—

"the Common Travel Area" means the United Kingdom, the Channel Islands, the Isle of Man and the Republic of Ireland collectively;

"the Convention" means the Convention relating to the Status of Refugees done at Geneva on 28th July 1951 and the Protocol to that Convention;

"work permit" has the meaning it bears in the Immigration Act 1971 by virtue of section 33(1) of that Act.]

(6) This paragraph shall only apply to a person who is treated as possessing income by virtue of regulation 105(6) and (7) (notional income) where the income he is treated as possessing is not readily available to him; and—

(a) the amount of jobseeker's allowance payable to him otherwise than under this Part is less than the amount of a jobseeker's allowance payable to him under this Part; and

(b) the adjudication officer is satisfied that, unless the provisions of this Part are applied to the claimant, the claimant or his family will suffer hardship.

AMENDMENT

1. Jobseeker's Allowance (Amendment) Regulations 1996 (S.I. 1996 No. 1516), reg. 10(2) (October 7, 1996).

DEFINITIONS

"claimant"—see Jobseekers Act, s. 35(1).
"income-based jobseeker's allowance—see Jobseekers Act, s. 1(4).

GENERAL NOTE

There are only two categories who can qualify for urgent cases payments of income-based JSA: claimants who are treated as possessing income which is due but has not been paid and certain asylum seekers who have a work permit or written permission from the Secretary of State to work.

An asylum seeker can apply to the Home Office for permission to work after six months. However, in most circumstances it will be better for the person to claim urgent cases payments of income support rather than income-based JSA so as to avoid the risk of being sanctioned for not complying with the JSA labour market conditions.

See the notes to reg. 70 of the Income Support Regulations for further discussion of this provision. Apart from the additional requirement in para. (3)(b) (and the definition of ''work permit'' in para. (5)), paras (3)–(6) are broadly the same as paras. (3)(b) and (3A)–(4) of reg. 70.

Applicable amount in urgent cases

148.—(1) For the purposes of calculating any entitlement to an income-based jobseeker's allowance under this Part—

(a) except in a case to which sub-paragraph (b), (c) or (d) applies, a claimant's weekly applicable amount shall be the aggregate of—

    (i) 90 per cent. of the amount applicable (reduced where appropriate in accordance with regulation 145 (applicable amount in hardship cases)) in respect of himself or, if he is a member of a couple or of a polygamous marriage, of the amount applicable in respect of both of them under paragraph 1(1), (2) or (3) of Schedule 1 or, as the case may be, the amount applicable in respect of them under regulation 84 (polygamous marriages);

    (ii) the amount applicable under paragraph 2 of Schedule 1 in respect of any child or young person who is a member of his family except a child or young person whose capital, if calculated in accordance with Part VIII in like manner as for the claimant, except as provided in regulation 106(1) (modifications in respect of children and young persons), would exceed £3,000;

    (iii) the amount, if applicable, specified in Part II or III of Schedule 1 (premiums);

    (iv) any amounts applicable under regulation 83(f) or, as the case may be, 84(1)(g) (housing costs);

    (v) the amount, if applicable, specified in paragraph 3 of Schedule 1; and

    (vi) the amount of any protected sum which may be applicable to him in accordance with regulation 87(2);

(b) where the claimant is a resident in a residential care home or a nursing home and has a preserved right, his weekly applicable amount shall be the aggregate of—

    (i) 90 per cent, of the amout of the allowance for personal expenses prescribed in paragraph 11(a) of Schedule 4 (applicable amounts of persons in residential care and nursing homes), or, if he is a member of a couple or of a polygamous marriage, of the amount applicable in respect of both or all of them; and where regulation 145 (applicable amount in hardship cases) applies, the reference in this head to 90 per cent. of the amount so reduced shall be construed as a reference to 90 per cent. of the relevant amount under that regulation reduced by the percentage specified in paragraph (1) or (2), as the case may be, of that regulation;

    (ii) the amount applicable under paragraph 11(b) to (e) of Schedule 4 in respect of any child or young person who is a member of his family except a child or young person whose capital, if calculated in accordance with Part VIII in like manner as for the claimant, except as provided in regulation 106(1) (modifications in respect of children and young persons), would exceed £3,000;

    (iii) the amount in respect of the weekly charge for his accommodation calculated in accordance with regulation 86 and Schedule 4 except

any amount in respect of a child or young person who is a member
of the family and whose capital, if calculated in accordance with
Part VIII in like manner as for the claimant, except as provided in
regulation 106(1) (modifications in respect of children and young
persons), would exceed £3,000;

(c) where the claimant is resident in residential accommodation, his weekly
applicable amount shall be the aggregate of—

   (i) 98 per cent. of the amount referred to in column (2) of paragraph
   15(1)(a) to (c) and (e) of Schedule 5 (applicable amounts in special
   cases) applicable to him;

   (ii) the amount applicable under column (2) of paragraph 15(1)(d) of
   Schedule 5, in respect of any child or young person who is a
   member of the family, except a child or young person whose capital,
   if calculated in accordance with Part VIII in like manner as for the
   claimant, except as provided in regulation 106(1) (modifications in
   respect of children and young persons), would exceed £3,000;

(d) except where sub-paragraph (b) or (c) applies, in the case of a person to
whom any paragraph, other than paragraph 14 in column (1) of Schedule
5 (special cases) applies, the amount shall be 90 per cent. of the amount
applicable in column 2 of that Schedule in respect of the claimant and
partner (if any), plus, if applicable—

   (i) any amount in respect of a child or young person who is a member
   of the family except a child or young person whose capital, if calculated in accordance with Part VIII in like manner as for the claimant,
   except as provided in regulation 106(1) (modifications in respect of
   children and young persons), would exceed £3,000;

   (ii) any premium under Part II or III of Schedule 1; and

   (iii) any amounts applicable under regulation 83(f) or, as the case may
   be, 84(1)(g); and

   (iv) the amount of the protected sum which may be applicable to him in
   accordance with regulation 87(2).

(2) Where the calculation of a claimant's applicable amount under this regulation results in a fraction of a penny that fraction shall be treated as a penny.

DEFINITIONS

   "child"—see Jobseekers Act, s. 35(1).
   "claimant"—*ibid.*
   "couple"—see reg. 1(3).
   "family"—see Jobseekers Act, s. 35(1).
   "nursing home"—see reg. 1(3).
   "polygamous marriage"—*ibid.*
   "residential accomodation"—*ibid.*
   "residential care home"—*ibid.*
   "young person"—see reg. 76.

GENERAL NOTE

See reg. 71 of the Income Support Regulations.

Assessment of income and capital in urgent cases

149.—(1) The claimant's income shall be calculated in accordance with Part
VIII subject to the following modifications—

[²(a) any income other than—
   (i) a payment of income or income in kind made under the Macfarlane Trust, the Macfarlane (Special Payments) Trust, the Macfarlane (Special Payments) (No.2) Trust, the Fund, the Eileen Trust or the Independent Living Funds; or
   (ii) income to which paragraph 6, 8 (but only to the extent that a concessionary payment would be due under that paragraph for any non-payment of jobseeker's allowance under regulation 147 of these Regulations or of income support under regulation 70 of the Income Support Regulations (urgent cases)), 33, 41(2), (3) or (4) or 42 of Schedule 7 (disregard of income other than earnings) applies, possessed or treated as possessed by him, shall be taken into account in full notwithstanding any provision in that Part disregarding the whole or any part of that income;]
   (b) any income to which regulation 116 (calculation of tariff income from capital) applies shall be disregarded;
   (c) income treated as capital by virtue of regulation 110(1), (2), (3) and (9) (income treated as capital) shall be taken into account as income;
   (d) in a case to which paragraph (2)(b) of regulation 147 (urgent cases) applies, any income to which regulation 105(6) and (7) (notional income) applies shall be disregarded.

(2)The claimant's capital calculated in accordance with Part VIII, but including any capital referred to in paragraphs 3 and, to the extent that such assets as are referred to in paragraph 11 consist of liquid assets, 11 and, except to the extent that the arrears referred to in paragraph 12 [¹ consist] of arrears of housing benefit payable under Part VII of the Benefits Act or Part II of the Social Security and Housing Benefits Act 1982 [²or any arrears of benefit due under regulation 147 of these Regulations or regulation 70 of the Income Support Regulations (urgent cases)], 12, 14(b), 24 and 32 of Schedule 8 (capital to be disregarded) shall be taken into account in full and the amount of a job-seeker's allowance which would, but for this paragraph be payable under this regulation, shall be payable only to the extent that it exceeds the amount of that capital.

AMENDMENTS

1. Jobseeker's Allowance (Amendment) Regulations 1996 (S.I. 1996 No. 1516), reg. 20 and Sched. (October 7, 1996).
2. Social Security (Miscellaneous Amendments) Regulations 1998 (S.I. 1998 No. 563), reg. 19(2) (April 6, 1998).

DEFINITIONS

"the Benefits Act"—see Jobseekers Act, s.35(1).
"claimant"—*ibid.*
"concessionary payment"—see reg. 1(3).
"the Eileen Trust"—*ibid.*
"the Fund"—*ibid.*
"the Independent Living Funds"—*ibid.*
"the Macfarlane (Special Payments) Trust"—*ibid.*
"the Macfarlane (Special Payments) (No. 2) Trust"—*ibid.*
"the Macfarlane Trust"—*ibid.*

GENERAL NOTE

See the note to reg. 72 of the Income Support Regulations. But note the slightly different treatment of income and capital for the purpose of urgent cases payments under income support.

767

PART XI

PART-WEEKS

Amount of a jobseeker's allowance payable

150.—(1) Subject to the following provisions of this Part, the amount payable by way of an income-based jobseeker's allowance in respect of part-week shall be calculated by applying the formula—

(a) where the claimant has no income—

$$\frac{N \times A}{7}; \text{ or}$$

(b) where the claimant has an income—

$$\frac{(N \times (A-I))}{(7)} - B,$$

where—

> A is the claimant's weekly applicable amount in the relevant week;
> B is the amount of any jobseeker's allowance, income support, maternity allowance, incapacity benefit or severe disablement allowance payable to any member of the claimant's family other than the claimant in respect of any day in the part-week;
> I is the claimant's weekly income in the relevant week less B;
> N is the number of days in the part-week.

(2) [*Omitted as not relating to income-based jobseeker's allowance.*]

(3) In this Part—

"part-week" means an entitlement to a jobseeker's allowance in respect of any period of less than a week;

"relevant week" means the period of 7 days determined in accordance with regulation 152.

DEFINITION

"claimant"—see Jobseekers Act, s. 35(1).

Amount of a jobseeker's allowance payable where a person is in a residential care or nursing home

151.—(1) Subject to regulations 153 and 154 in the case of a claimant—

(a) or whom regulation 86 (applicable amounts for persons in residential care or nursing homes) applies, and

(b) for whom the weekly charge for the accommodation is due to be paid during a part-week to which regulation 152(1) applies,

the amount of a jobseeker's allowance payable shall be—

> (i) where the claimant has no income, A; or
> (ii) where the claimant has income, calculated in accordance with the formula (A-I)-B,

where "A", "B" and "I" have the values set out in regulation 150(1).

(2) In a case to which paragraph (1) applies, the claimant's weekly applicable amount shall be—

(a) where the weekly charge for the accommodation includes all meals, the aggregate of the following amounts—

> (i) the weekly charge for the accommodation determined in accordance with paragraph 1(1)(a) of Schedule 4; and
> (ii) the amount calculated in accordance with the formula—

$$\frac{(N \times P)}{7} + \frac{(N \times H)}{7};$$

(b) where the weekly charge for the accommodation does not include all meals, the aggregate of the following amounts—
  (i) the weekly charge for the accommodation determined in accordance with paragraph 1(1)(a) of Schedule 4 less M; and
  (ii) the amount calculated in accordance with the formula—

$$\frac{(N \times M)}{7} + \frac{(N \times P)}{7} + \frac{(N \times H)}{7}.$$

(3) In paragraph 2—

"H" means the weekly amount determined in accordance with paragraph 1(1)(c) of Schedule 4;

"M" means the amount of the increase for meals calculated on a weekly basis in accordance with paragraph 2 of Schedule 4;

"P" means the weekly amount for personal expenses determined in accordance with paragraph 11 of Schedule 4;

[¹"N" is the number of days in the part-week.]

AMENDMENT

1. Jobseeker's Allowance (Amendment) Regulations 1996 (S.I. 1996 No. 1516), reg. 16 (October 7, 1996).

DEFINITIONS

"claimant"—see Jobseekers Act, s. 35(1).
"nursing home"—see reg. 1(3).
"residential care home"—*ibid.*

Relevant week

152.—(1) Where the part-week—
(a) is the whole period for which a jobseeker's allowance is payable or occurs at the beginning of an award, the relevant week is the period of 7 days ending on the last day of that part-week; or
(b) occurs at the end of an award, the relevant week is the period of 7 days beginning on the first day of the part-week; or
(c) occurs because a jobseeker's allowance is not payable for any period in accordance with section 19 of the Act (circumstances in which a jobseeker's allowance is not payable), the relevant week is the 7 days ending immediately before the start of the next benefit week to commence for that claimant.

(2) Where a person has an award of a jobseeker's allowance and his benefit week changes, for the purpose of calculating the amounts of a jobseeker's allowance payable for the part-week beginning on the day after his last complete benefit week before the change and ending immediately before the change, the relevant week is the period of 7 days beginning on the day after the last complete benefit week.

DEFINITION

"benefit week"—see reg. 1(3).

Modification in the calculation of income

153. For the purposes of regulation 150 (amount of jobseeker's allowance payable for part-weeks) a claimant's income and, in determining the amount payable by way of an income-based jobseeker's allowance, the income of any person which the claimant is treated as possessing under section 12(4) or regulation 88(4), shall be calculated in accordance with Parts VIII, and, where applicable, IX and X subject to the following changes—

(a) any income which is due to be paid in the relevant week shall be treated as paid on the first day of that week;

(b) in determining the amount payable by way of an income-based jobseeker's allowance, any jobseeker's allowance, income support, maternity allowance, incapacity benefit or severe disablement allowance under the Benefits Act payable in the relevant week but not in respect of any day in the part-week shall be disregarded;

(c) in determining the amount payable by way of a contribution-based jobseeker's allowance, any widow's benefit, invalid care allowance, training allowance or any increase in disablement pension payable in accordance with Part I of Schedule 7 to the Benefits Act (Unemployment Supplement) which is payable in the relevant week but not in respect of any day in the part-week shall be disregarded;

(d) where the part-week occurs at the end of the claim, any income or any change in the amount of income of the same kind which is first payable within the relevant week but not on any day in the part-week shall be disregarded;

(e) where the part-week occurs immediately after a period in which a person was treated as engaged in remunerative work under regulation 52 (persons treated as engaged in remunerative work) any earnings which are taken into account for the purposes of determining that period shall be disregarded;

(f) where only part of the weekly amount of income is taken into account in the relevant week, the balance shall be disregarded.

DEFINITIONS

"the Benefits Act"—see Jobseekers Act, s.35(1).
"claimant"—*ibid.*

Reduction in certain cases

154. The reduction to be made in accordance with Part IX (Hardship) in respect of an income based jobseeker's allowance shall be an amount equal to one seventh of the reduction which would be made under that Part for a week multiplied by the number of days in the part-week.

Modification of section 15(2) of the Act

155. In its application to an income-based jobseeker's allowance payable for a part-week, section 15(2)(d) shall have effect subject to the following modification—

"(d) any payment by way of an income-based jobseeker's allowance for that period or any part of it which apart from this paragraph would be made to the claimant—

(i) shall not be made, if the amount of an income-based jobseeker's allowance which would be payable for a period of less than a week is equal to or less than the proportion of the prescribed sum appropriate to the number of days in the part-week;

(ii) shall be at a rate equal to the difference between the amount which would be payable for a period of less than a week and the prescribed sum where that amount would be more than the prescribed sum.''

PART XIII

MISCELLANEOUS

Recovery of Maintenance

Recovery orders

169.—(1) Where an award of income-based jobseeker's allowance has been made to a person (''the claimant''), the Secretary of State may apply to the court for a recovery order against the claimant's spouse (''the liable person'').

(2) On making a recovery order the court may order the liable person to pay such amount at such intervals as it considers appropriate, having regard to all the circumstances of the liable person and in particular his income.

(3) Except in Scotland, a recovery order shall be treated for all purposes as if it were a maintenance order within the meaning of section 150(1) of the Magistrates Courts Act 1980.

(4) Where a recovery order requires the liable person to make payments to the Secretary of State, the Secretary of State may, by giving notice in writing to the court which made the order, the liable person, and the claimant, transfer to the claimant the right to receive payments under the order and to exercise the relevant rights in relation to the order.

(5) In this regulation—

the expressions ''the court'' and ''recovery order'' have the same meanings as in section 23 of the Act; and

''the relevant rights'' means, in relation to a recovery order, the right to bring any proceedings, take any steps or do any other thing under or in relation to the order.

DEFINITION

''claimant''—see Jobseekers Act, s. 35(1).

GENERAL NOTE

See the note to s. 23 of the Jobseekers Act.

Training Allowance

Persons in receipt of a training allowance

170.—(1) A person who is in receipt of a training allowance and who is not receiving training falling within paragraph (2) may be entitled to an income-based jobseeker's allowance without—

(a) being available for employment;

(b) having entered into a jobseeker's agreement; or

(c) actively seeking employment.

(2) Training falls within this paragraph if it is training for which persons aged under 18 are eligible and for which persons aged 18 to 24 may be eligible provided in England and Wales directly or indirectly by a Training and Enter-

prise Council [¹, or a Chamber of Commerce, Training and Enterprise, under its contractual arrangement with the Secretary of State] and, in Scotland, directly or indirectly by a Local Enterprise Company pursuant to its arrangement with, as the case may be, Scottish Enterprise or Highlands and Islands Enterprise (whether that arrangement is known as an Operating Contract or by any other name).

AMENDMENT

1. Jobseeker's Allowance (Amendment) (No. 2) Regulations 1998 (S.I. 1998 No. 1698), reg. 5 (August 4, 1998).

DEFINITIONS

"employment"—see reg. 4.
"training allowance"—see reg. 1(3).

Trade Disputes

Trade disputes: exemptions from section 15 of the Act

171. Section 15(2) (trade disputes: effect on other claimants) shall not apply to a claimant during any period where—
  (a) a member of the claimant's family is, or would be, prevented by section 14 from being entitled to a jobseeker's allowance; and
  (b) that member is—
    (i) a child or young person; or
    (ii) [¹incapable of work] or within the maternity period, and for this purpose "the maternity period" means the period commencing at the beginning of the 6th week before the expected week of confinement and ending at the end of the 7th week after the week in which confinement takes place.

AMENDMENT

1. Jobseeker's Allowance (Amendment) Regulations 1996 (S.I. 1996 No. 1516), reg. 20 and Sched. (October 7, 1996).

DEFINITIONS

"child"—see Jobseekers Act, s. 35(1).
"claimant"—*ibid.*
"family"—*ibid.*
"trade dispute"—*ibid.*
"young person"—see reg. 76.

GENERAL NOTE

See the note to s. 15 of the Jobseekers Act.

Trade disputes: prescribed sum

172. The prescribed sum for the purposes of section 15(2)(d) is [¹£27.50].

AMENDMENT

1. Social Security Benefits Up-rating Order 1999 (S.I. 1999 No. 264), art. 25 (April 12, 1999).

SCHEDULE 1   **Regulations 83 and 84(1)**

APPLICABLE AMOUNTS

[⁹PART I

Personal Allowances

1. The weekly amounts specified in column (2) below in respect of each person or couple specified in column (1) shall be the weekly amounts specified for the purposes of regulations 83 and 84(1) (applicable amounts and polygamous marriages).

(1)	(2)
Person or Couple	*Amount*
(1) Single claimant aged—	
(a) except where head (b) or (c) of this sub-paragraph applies, less than 18;	1. (a) £30.95
(b) less than 18 who falls within paragraph (2) of regulation 57 and who—	(b) £40.70
(i) is a person to whom regulation 59, 60 or 61 applies [¹. . .]; or	
(ii) is the subject of a direction under section 16;	
(c) less than 18 who satisfies the condition in paragraph 13(a) of Part 3;	(c) £40.70
(d) not less than 18 but less than 25;	(d) £40.70
(e) not less than 25.	(e) £51.40
(2) Lone parent aged—	
(a) except where head (b) or (c) of this sub-paragraph applies, less than 18;	2. (a) £30.95
(b) less than 18 who falls within paragraph (2) of regulation 57 and who—	(b) £40.70
(i) is a person to whom regulation 59, 60 or 61 applies [¹. . .]; or	
(ii) is the subject of a direction under section 16;	
(c) less than 18 who satisfies the condition in paragraph 13(a) [²of Part 3];	(c) £40.70
(d) not less than 18.	(d) £51.40
(3) Couple—	
(a) where both members are aged less than 18 and—	3. (a) £61.35
(i) at least one of them is treated as responsible for a child; or	
(ii) had they not been members of a couple, each would have been a person to whom regulation 59, 60 or 61 (circumstances in which a person aged 16 or 17 is eligible for a jobseeker's allowance) applied or	
(iii) had they not been members of a couple, the claimant would have been a person to whom regulation 59, 60 or 61 (circumstances in which a person aged 16 or 17 is eligible for a jobseeker's allowance) applied and his partner satisfies the requirements for entitlement to income support other than the requirement to make a claim for it; or	
[¹(iv) they are married and one member of the couple is a person to whom regulation 59, 60 or 61 applies and the other member is registered in accordance with regulation 62; or	

(1)	(2)
Person or Couple	*Amount*
(iva) they are married and each member of the couple is a person to whom regulation 59, 60 or 61 applies; or]	
(v) there is a direction under section 16 (jobseeker's allowance in cases of severe hardship) in respect of each member; or	
(vi) there is a direction under section 16 in respect of one of them and the other is a person to whom regulation 59, 60 or 61 applies [¹. . .]; or	
(vii) there is a direction under section 16 in respect of one of them and the other satisfies requirements for entitlement to income support other than the requirement to make a claim for it;	
(b) where both members are aged less than 18 and sub-paragraph (3)(a) does not apply but one member of the couple falls within paragraph (2) of regulation 57 and either—	(b) £40.70
(i) is a person to whom regulation 59, 60 or 61 applies [¹. . .]; or	
(ii) is the subject of a direction under section 16 of the Act;	
(c) where both members are aged less than 18 and neither head (a) nor (b) of sub-paragraph (3) applies but one member of the couple—	(c) £30.95
(i) is a person to whom regulation 59, 60 or 61 applies [¹. . .]; or	
(ii) is the subject of a direction under section 16;	
(d) where both members are aged less than 18 and none of heads (a), (b) or (c) of sub-paragraph (3) apply but one member of the couple is a person who satisfies the requirements of paragraph 13(a);	(d) £40.70
(e) where both members are aged not less than 18;	(e) £80.65
(f) where one member is aged not less than 18 and the other member is a person under 18 who—	(f) £80.65
(i) is a person to whom regulation 59, 60 or 61 applies [¹. . .]; or	
(ii) is the subject of a direction under section 16; and	
(iii) satisfies requirements for entitlement to income support other than the requirement to make a claim for it;	
(g) where one member is aged not less than 18 but less than 25 and the other member is a person under 18—	(g) £40.70
(i) to whom none of the regulations 59 to 61 applies; or	
(ii) who is not the subject of a direction under section 16; and	
(iii) does not satisfy requirements for entitlement to income support disregarding the requirement to make a claim for it;	
(h) where one member is aged not less than 25 and the other member is a person under 18—	(h) £51.40
(i) to whom none of the regulations 59 to 61 applies; or	
(ii) is not the subject of a direction under section 16; and	
(iii) does not satisfy requirements for entitlement to income support disregarding the requirement to make a claim for it.	

2. [⁵—(1)] The weekly amounts specified in column (2) below in respect of each person specified in column (1) shall[⁵, for the relevant period specified in column (1),] be the weekly amounts specified for the purposes of regulations 83(b) and 84(1)(c).

(1)	(2)
Child or Young Person	*Amount*
[⁵Person in respect of the period—	
(a) beginning on that person's date of birth and ending on the day preceding the first Monday in September following that person's eleventh birthday;	(a) £20.20
(b) beginning on the first Monday in September following that person's eleventh birthday and ending on the day preceding the first Monday in September following that person's sixteenth birthday;	(b) £25.90
(c) beginning on the first Monday in September following that person's sixteenth birthday and ending on the day preceding that person's nineteenth birthday.]	(c) £30.95

[⁵(2) In column (1) of the table in paragraph (1), "the first Monday in September" means the Monday which first occurs in the month of September in any year.]

3.—(1) The weekly amount for the purposes of regulations 83(c) and 84(1)(d) (residential allowance) in respect of a person who satisfies the conditions specified in sub-paragraph (2) shall be—

  (a) except in a case to which head (b) applies, £59.40; and

  (b) where the home in which the person resides is situated within the area described in Schedule 3 (the Greater London area), £66.10.]

(2) Subject to sub-paragraphs (3), (4) and (5), the conditions are—

  (a) the person resides in a residential care home or a nursing home or is regarded pursuant to sub-paragraph (5) as residing in such a home;

  (b) the person both requires personal care [⁶by reason of old age, disablement, past or present dependence on alcohol or drugs, past or present mental disorder or a terminal illness and the care is provided in the home];

  (c) he does not have a preserved right;

  (d) he is aged 16 or over;

  (e) both the person's accommodation and such meals (if any) as are provided for him are provided on a commercial basis; and

  (f) no part of the weekly charge for accommodation is met by housing benefit.

(3) For the purposes of sub-paragraph (2), but subject to sub-paragraph (4), a person resides in a residential care home where the home in which he resides—

  (a) is registered under Part I of the Registered Homes Act 1984 or is deemed to be so registered by virtue of section 2(3) of the Registered Homes (Amendment) Act 1991 (registration of small homes where application for registration not determined);

  (b) is managed or provided by a body incorporated by Royal Charter or constituted by Act of Parliament (other than a social services authority) and provides both board and personal care for the claimant; or

  (c) is in Scotland and is registered under section 61 of the Social Work (Scotland) Act 1968 or is an establishment provided by a housing association registered with Scottish Homes established by the Housing (Scotland) Act 1988 which provides care equivalent to that given in residential accommodation provided under Part IV of the Social Work (Scotland) Act 1968;

and a person resides in a nursing home where the home in which he resides is such a home within the meaning of regulation 1(3).

(4) A person shall not be regarded as residing in a nursing home for the purposes of sub-paragraph (2) where the home in which he resides is a hospice, and for this purpose "hospice" means a nursing home which—

  (a) if situate in England or Wales, is registered under Part II of the Registered Homes Act 1984, or

    (b) if situate in Scotland, is exempted from the operation of the Nursing Homes Registration (Scotland) Act 1938 by virtue of section 6 of that Act,
and whose primary function is to provide palliative care for persons resident there who are suffering from a progressive disease in its final stages.

    (5) For the purposes of sub-paragraph (2)(a), where a person's principal place of residence is a residential care home or a nursing home, and he is temporarily absent from that home, he shall be regarded as continuing to reside at that home—

    (a) where he is absent because he is a patient, for the first six weeks of any such period of absence, and for this purpose—

      (i) "patient" has the meaning it has in Schedule 5 by virtue of regulation 85, and

      (ii) periods of absence separated by not more than 28 days shall be treated as a single period of absence equal in duration to all those periods; and

    (b) for the first three weeks of any other period of absence.

    (6) Where—

    (a) a person has been registered under the Registered Homes Act 1984 in respect of premises which have been carried on as a residential care home or, as the case may be, a nursing home, and that person has ceased to carry on such a home; and

    (b) an application for registration under that Act has been made by another person and that application has not been determined or abandoned,
then any question arising for determination under this paragraph shall be determined as if the most recent registration under that Act in respect of those premises continued until the day on which the application is determined or abandoned.

PART II

Family Premium

    4. [7—(1)] The weekly amount for the purposes of regulations 83(d) and 84(1)(e) in respect of a family of which at least one member is a child or young person shall be
[4—(a) where the claimant is a lone parent [7to whom the conditions in both sub-paragraphs (2) and (3) apply] and no premium is applicable under paragraph 10, [7. . .] 12 or 13, £15.75;

    (b) in any other case,] [10£13.90].

    [7(2) The first condition for the purposes of sub-paragraph (1)(a) is that the claimant—

    (a) was both a lone parent and entitled to an income-based jobseeker's allowance on 5th April 1998; or

    (b) does not come within head (a) above but—

      (i) was both a lone parent and entitled to an income-based jobseeker's allowance on any day during the period of 12 weeks ending on 5th April 1998;

      (ii) was both a lone parent and entitled to an income-based jobseeker's allowance on any day during the period of 12 weeks commencing on 6th April 1998; and

      (iii) the last day in respect of which (i) above applied was no more than 12 weeks before the first day in respect of which (ii) above applied.

    (3) The second condition for the purposes of sub-paragraph (1)(a) is that as from the appropriate date specified in sub-paragraph (4), the claimant has continued, subject to sub-paragraph (5), to be both a lone parent and entitled to an income-based jobseeker's allowance.

    (4) The appropriate date for the purposes of sub-paragraph (3) is—

    (a) in a case to which sub-paragraph (2)(a) applies, 6th April 1998;

    (b) in a case to which sub-paragraph (2)(b) applies, the first day in respect of which sub-paragraph 2(b)(ii) applied.

    (5) For the purposes of sub-paragraph (3), where the claimant has ceased, for any period of 12 weeks or less, to be—

(a) a lone parent; or

(b) entitled to an income-based jobseeker's allowance; or

(c) both a lone parent and entitled to an income-based jobseeker's allowance,

the claimant shall be treated, on again becoming both a lone parent and entitled to an income-based jobseeker's allowance, as having continued to be both a lone parent and entitled to an income-based jobseeker's allowance throughout that period.

(6) In determining whether the conditions in sub-paragraphs (2) and (3) apply, entitlement to income support shall be treated as entitlement to an income-based jobseeker's allowance for the purposes of any requirement that a person is entitled to an income-based jobseeker's allowance.]

PART III

Premiums

5. Except as provided in paragraph 6, the weekly premiums specified in Part IV of this Schedule shall for the purposes of regulations 83(e) and 84(1)(f), be applicable to a claimant who satisfies the condition specified in [⁴ paragraphs 10] to 17 in respect of that premium.

6. Subject to paragraph 7, where a claimant satisfies the conditions in respect of more than one premium in this Part of this Schedule, only one premium shall be applicable to him and, if they are different amounts, the higher or highest amount shall apply.

7.—(1) The severe disability premium to which paragraph 15 applies may be applicable in addition to any other premium which may apply under this Schedule.

(2) The disabled child premium to which paragraph 16 applies may be applicable in addition to any other premium which may apply under this Schedule.

(3) The carer premium to which paragraph 17 applies may be applicable in addition to any other premium which may apply under this Schedule.

8.—(1) Subject to sub-paragraph (2) for the purposes of this Part of this Schedule, once a premium is applicable to a claimant under this Part, a person shall be treated as being in receipt of any benefit—

(a) in the case of a benefit to which the Social Security (Overlapping Benefits) Regulations 1979 applies, for any period during which, apart from the provisions of those Regulations, he would be in receipt of that benefit; and

[³(b) for any period spent by a claimant in undertaking a course of training or instruction provided or approved by the Secretary of State for Education and Employment under section 2 of the Employment and Training Act 1973, or by Scottish Enterprise or Highlands and Islands Enterprise under section 2 of the Enterprise and New Towns (Scotland) Act 1990 or for any period during which he is in receipt of a training allowance.]

(2) For the purposes of the carer premium under paragraph 17, a person shall be treated as being in receipt of invalid care allowance by virtue of sub-paragraph (1)(a) only if and for so long as the person in respect of whose care the allowance has been claimed remains in receipt of attendance allowance, or the care component of disability living allowance at the highest or middle rate prescribed in accordance with section 72(3) of the Benefits Act.

Lone parent premium

9. [⁴ . . .]

Pensioner premium for persons over 60

10. The condition is that the claimant—

(a) is a single claimant or lone parent who has attained the age of 60; or

(b) has attained the age of 60 and has a partner; or

(c) has a partner and the partner has attained the age of 60 but not the age of 75.

Pensioner premium where claimant's partner has attained the age of 75

11. The condition is that the claimant has a partner who has attained the age of 75 but not the age of 80.

Higher pensioner premium

12.—(1) The condition is that—

(a) the claimant is a single claimant or lone parent who has attained the age of 60 and either—

    (i) satisfies one of the additional conditions specified in paragraph 14(1)(a), (c), (e), (f) or (h); or

    (ii) was entitled to either income support or income-based jobseeker's allowance and the disability premium was applicable to him in respect of a benefit week within 8 weeks of his 60th birthday and he has, subject to sub-paragraph (2), remained continuously entitled to one of those benefits since attaining that age; or

(b) the claimant has a partner and—

    (i) the partner has attained the age of 80; or

    (ii) the partner has attained the age of 60 but not the age of 80, and the additional conditions specified in paragraph 14 are satisfied in respect of him; or

(c) the claimant—

    (i) has attained the age of 60;

    [³(ii) satisfies the requirements of either sub-head (i) or (ii) of paragraph 12(1)(a); and]

    (iii) has a partner.

(2) For the purposes of this paragraph and paragraph 14—

(a) once the higher pensioner premium is applicable to a claimant, if he then ceases, for a period of eight weeks or less, to be entitled to either income support or income-based jobseeker's allowance, he shall, on becoming re-entitled to either of those benefits, thereafter be treated as having been continuously entitled thereto;

(b) in so far as sub-paragraphs (1)(a)(ii) and (1)(c)(ii) are concerned, if a claimant ceases to be entitled to either income support or an income-based jobseeker's allowance for a period not exceeding eight weeks which includes his 60th birthday, he shall, on becoming re-entitled to either of those benefits, thereafter be treated as having been continuously entitled thereto.

[⁸(3) In this paragraph where a claimant's partner is a welfare to work beneficiary, sub-paragraphs (1)(a)(ii) and (2)(b) shall apply to him as if for the words "8 weeks" there were substituted the words "52 weeks".]

Disability premium

13. The condition is that the claimant—

(a) is a single claimant or lone parent who has not attained the age of 60 and satisfies any one of the additional conditions specified in paragraph 14(1)(a), (c), (e), (f) or (h); or

(b) has not attained the age of 60, has a partner and the claimant satisfies any one of the additional conditions specified in paragraph 14(1)(a), (c), (e), (f) or (h); or

(c) has a partner and the partner has not attained the age of 60 and also satisfies any one of the additional conditions specified in paragraph 14.

Additional conditions for higher pensioner and disability premium

14.—(1) The additional conditions specified in this paragraph are that—

(a) the claimant or, as the case may be, his partner, is in receipt of either disability working allowance or mobility supplement;

(b) the claimant's partner is in receipt of severe disablement allowance;

(c) the claimant or, as the case may be, his partner, is in receipt of attendance allowance or disability living allowance or is a person whose disability living allowance is payable, in whole or in part, to another in accordance with regulation 44 of the Claims and Payments Regulations (payment of disability living allowance on behalf of third party);

(d) the claimant's partner is in receipt of long-term incapacity benefit or is a person to whom section 30B(4) of the Benefits Act (long term rate of incapacity benefit payable to those who are terminally ill) applies;

(e) the claimant or, as the case may be, his partner, has an invalid carriage or other vehicle provided to him by the Secretary of State under section 5(2)(a) of and Schedule 2 to the National Health Service Act 1977 or under section 46 of the National Health Service (Scotland) Act 1978 or provided by the Department of Health and Social Services for Northern Ireland under article 30(1) of the Health and Personal Social Services (Northern Ireland) Order 1972, or receives payments by way of grant from the Secretary of State under paragraph 2 of Schedule 2 to the Act of 1977 (additional provisions as to vehicles) or, in Scotland, under section 46 of the Act of 1978;

(f) the claimant or, as the case may be, his partner, is a person who is entitled to the mobility component of disability living allowance but to whom the component is not payable in accordance with regulation 42 of the Claims and Payments Regulations (cases where disability living allowance not payable);

(g) the claimant's partner was either—

(i) in receipt of long term incapacity benefit under section 30A(5) of the Benefits Act immediately before attaining pensionable age and he is still alive; or

(ii) entitled to attendance allowance or disability living allowance but payment of that benefit was suspended in accordance with regulations under section 113(2) of the Benefits Act or otherwise abated as a consequence of [²the partner] becoming a patient within the meaning of regulation 85(4) (special cases),

and in either case the higher pensioner premium or disability premium had been applicable to the claimant or his partner;

(h) the claimant or, as the case may be, his partner, is registered as blind in a register compiled by a local authority under section 29 of the National Assistance Act 1948 (welfare services), or, in Scotland, has been certified as blind and in consequence is registered as blind in a register maintained by or on behalf of a regional or islands council.

(2) For the purposes of sub-paragraph (1)(h), a person who has ceased to be registered as blind on regaining his eyesight shall nevertheless be treated as blind and as satisfying the additional condition set out in that sub-paragraph for a period of 28 weeks following the date on which he ceased to be so registered.

Severe disability premium

15.—(1) In the case of a single claimant, a lone parent or a claimant who is treated as having no partner in consequence of sub-paragraph (3), the condition is that—

(a) he is in receipt of attendance allowance or the care component of disability living allowance at the highest or middle rate prescribed in accordance with section 72(3) of the Benefits Act; and

(b) subject to sub-paragraph (4), there are no non-dependants aged 18 or over normally residing with him or with whom he is normally residing; and

(c) an invalid care allowance under section 70 of the Benefits Act is not in payment to anyone engaged in caring for him.

(2) Where the claimant has a partner, the condition is that—

(a) the claimant is in receipt of attendance allowance or the care component of disability living allowance at the highest or middle rate prescribed in accordance with section 72(3) of the Benefits Act (the "qualifying benefit"); and

(b) the partner is also in receipt of a qualifying benefit, or if he is a member of a polygamous marriage, all the partners of that marriage are in receipt of a qualifying benefit; and

(c) subject to sub-paragraph (4), there is no non-dependant aged 18 or over normally residing with him or with whom he is normally residing; and

(d) either—

    (i) an invalid care allowance under section 70 of the Benefits Act is not in payment to anyone engaged in caring for either member of the couple or all the members of the polygamous marriage; or

    (ii) a person is engaged in caring for one member (but not both members) of the couple, or one or more but not all members of the polygamous marriage, and in consequence is in receipt of an invalid care allowance under section 70 of the Benefits Act.

(3) Where the claimant has a partner who does not satisfy the condition in sub-paragraph (2)(b), and that partner is blind or treated as blind within the meaning of paragraph 14(1)(h) and (2), that partner shall be treated for the purposes of sub-paragraph (2) as if he were not a partner of the claimant.

(4) The following persons shall not be regarded as a non-dependant for the purposes of sub-paragraphs (1)(b) and (2)(c)—

(a) a person in receipt of attendance allowance or the care component of disability living allowance at the highest or middle rate prescribed in accordance with section 72(3) of the Benefits Act;

(b) subject to sub-paragraph (6), a person who joins the claimant's household for the first time in order to care for the claimant or his partner and immediately before so joining the claimant or his partner satisfied the condition in sub-paragraph (1) or, as the case may be, (2);

(c) a person who is blind or treated as blind within the meaning of paragraph 14(1)(h) and (2).

(5) For the purposes of sub-paragraph (2), a person shall be treated as being in receipt of—

(a) attendance allowance, or the care component of disability living allowance at the highest or middle rate prescribed in accordance with section 72(3) of the Benefits Act if he would, but for his being a patient for a period exceeding 28 days, be so in receipt;

(b) invalid care allowance if he would, but for the person for whom he was caring being a patient in hospital for a period exceeding 28 days, be so in receipt.

(6) Sub-paragraph (4)(b) shall apply only for the first 12 weeks following the date on which the person to whom that provision applies first joins the claimant's household.

(7) For the purposes of sub-paragraph (1)(c) and (2)(d), no account shall be taken of an award of invalid care allowance to the extent that payment of such an award is back-dated for a period before the date on which the award is made.

(8) A person shall be treated as satisfying this condition if he would have satisfied the condition specified for a severe disability premium in income support in paragraph 13 of Schedule 2 to the Income Support Regulations by virtue only of regulations 4 to 6 of the Income Support (General) Amendment (No. 6) Regulations 1991 (savings provisions in relation to severe disability premium) and for the purposes of determining whether in the particular case regulation 4 of those Regulations had ceased to apply in accordance with regulation 5(2)(a) of those Regulations, a person who is entitled to an income-based jobseeker's allowance shall be treated as entitled to income support.

Disabled child premium

16. The condition is that a child or young person for whom the claimant or a partner of his is responsible and who is a member of the claimant's household—

(a) has no capital or capital which, if calculated in accordance with Part VIII in like manner as for the claimant, except as provided in regulation 106(1) (modifications in respect of children and young persons), would not exceed £3,000; and

(b) is in receipt of disability living allowance or is no longer in receipt of that allowance because he is a patient provided that the child or young person continues to be a member of the family; or

(c) is blind or treated as blind within the meaning of paragraph 14(1)(h) and (2).

Carer premium

17.—(1) Subject to sub-paragraphs (3) and (4), the condition is that the claimant or his partner is, or both of them are, in receipt of invalid care allowance under section 70 of the Benefits Act.

(2) The claimant, his partner, or both of them, as the case may be, shall be treated for the purposes of sub-paragraph (1) as being in receipt of an invalid care allowance where—

(a) either or both of them would be in receipt of such an allowance but for any provision of the Social Security (Overlapping Benefits) Regulations 1979; and

(b) the claim for that allowance was made on or after 1st October 1990; and

(c) the person or persons in respect of whose care the allowance has been claimed remains or remain in receipt of attendance allowance or the care component of disability living allowance at the highest or middle rate prescribed in accordance with section 72(3) of the Benefits Act.

(3) Where a carer premium is awarded but the person in respect of whom it has been awarded either ceases to be in receipt of, or ceases to be treated as being in receipt of, invalid care allowance, the condition for the award of the premium shall be treated as satisfied for a period of eight weeks from the date on which that person ceased to be in receipt of, or ceased to be treated as being in receipt of, invalid care allowance.

(4) Where a person who has been receiving, or who has been treated as receiving invalid care allowance ceases to be in receipt of, or ceases to be treated as being in receipt of, that allowance and makes a claim for income-based jobseeker's allowance, the condition for the award of the carer premium shall be treated as satisfied for a period of eight weeks from the date the person ceased to be in receipt of, or ceased to be treated as being in receipt of, invalid care allowance.

Persons in receipt of concessionary payments

18. For the purpose of determining whether a premium is applicable to a person under paragraphs 14 to 17, any concessionary payment made to compensate that person for the non-payment of any benefit mentioned in those paragraphs shall be treated as if it were a payment of that benefit.

Person in receipt of benefit

19. For the purposes of this Part of this Schedule, a person shall be regarded as being in receipt of any benefit if, and only if, it is paid in respect of him and shall be so regarded only for any period in respect of which that benefit is paid.

[¹¹ PART IV

Weekly Amounts of Premiums Specified in Part III

Premium	Amount
20.—(1) [⁴. . .]	(1) [⁴. . .]
(2) Pensioner premium for persons aged over 60—	
(a) where the claimant satisfies the condition in paragraph 10(a);	(2) (a) £23.60.
(b) where the claimant satisfies the condition in paragraph 10(b).	(b) £35.95.
(c) where the claimant satisfies the condition in paragraph 10(c).	(c) £35.95.
(3) Pensioner premium for claimants whose partner has attained the age of 75 where the claimant satisfies the condition in paragraph 11;	(3) £39.20.
(4) Higher Pensioner Premium—	
(a) where the claimant satisfies the condition in paragraph 12(1)(a);	(4) (a) £30.85.
(b) where the claimant satisfies the condition in paragraph 12(1)(b) or (c).	(b) £44.65.
(5) Disability Premium—	
(a) where the claimant satisfies the condition in paragraph 13(a);	(5) (a) £21.90.
(b) where the claimant satisfies the condition in paragraph 13(b) or (c).	(b) £31.25.
(6) Severe Disability Premium—	
(a) where the claimant satisfies the condition in paragraph 15(1);	(6) (a) £39.75.
(b) where the claimant satisfies the condition in paragraph 15(2)—	(b)
(i) if there is someone in receipt of an invalid care allowance or [²if any partner of the claimant] satisfies that condition by virtue of paragraph 15(5);	(i) £39.75
(ii) if no-one is in receipt of such an allowance.	(ii) £79.50.
(7) Disabled Child Premium.	(7) £21.90 in respect of each child or young person in respect of whom the conditions specified in paragraph 16 are satisfied.
(8) Carer Premium.	(8) £13.95 in respect of each person who satisfied the condition specified in paragraph 17.]

PART V

Rounding of Fractions

21. Where an income-based jobseeker's allowance is awarded for a period which is not a complete benefit week and the applicable amount in respect of that period results in an amount which includes a fraction of one penny that fraction shall be treated as one penny.

AMENDMENTS

1. Jobseeker's Allowance (Amendment) Regulations 1996 (S.I. 1996 No. 1516), reg. 18 (October 7, 1996).
2. Jobseeker's Allowance (Amendment) Regulations 1996 (S.I. 1996 No. 1516), reg. 20 and Sched. (October 7, 1996).
3. Social Security and Child Support (Jobseeker's Allowance) (Miscellaneous Amendments) Regulations 1996 (S.I. 1996 No. 2538), reg. 2(11) (October 28, 1996).
4. Child Benefit, Child Support and Social Security (Miscellaneous Amendments) Regulations 1996 (S.I. 1996 No. 1803), reg. 44 (April 7, 1997).
5. Income-related Benefits and Jobseeker's Allowance (Personal Allowances for Children and Young Persons) (Amendment) Regulations 1996 (S.I. 1996 No. 2545), reg. 2 (April 7, 1997).
6. Income-related Benefits and Jobseeker's Allowance (Amendment) (No. 2) Regulations 1997 (S.I. 1997 No. 2197), reg. 7(5) and (6)(b) (October 6, 1997).
7. Social Security Amendment (Lone Parents) Regulations 1998 (S.I. 1998 No. 766), reg. 14 (April 6, 1998).
8. Social Security (Welfare to Work) Regulations 1998 (S.I. 1998 No. 2231), reg. 14(3) (October 5, 1998).
9. Social Security Benefits Up-rating Order 1999 (S.I. 1999 No. 264), art. 24(3) and Sched. 13 (April 12, 1999).
10. Social Security Benefits Up-rating Order 1999 (S.I. 1999 No. 264), art. 24(4)(b) (April 12, 1999).
11. Social Security Benefits Up-rating Order 1999 (S.I. 1999 No. 264), art. 24(5) and Sched. 14 (April 12, 1999).

DEFINITIONS

"attendance allowance"—see reg. 1(3).
"the Benefits Act"—see Jobseekers Act, s.35(1).
"child"—*ibid*.
"claimant"—*ibid*.
"couple"—see reg. 1(3).
"disability living allowance"—*ibid*.
"disability working allowance"—*ibid*.
"family"—see Jobseeker Act, s. 35(1).
"invalid carriage or other vehicle"—see reg. 1(3).
"lone parent"—*ibid*.
"mobility supplement"—*ibid*.
"non-dependent"—see reg. 2.
"nursing home"—see reg. 1(3).
"partner"—*ibid*.
"polygamous marriage"—*ibid*.
"preserved right"—*ibid*.
"residential care home"—*ibid*.
"single claimant"—*ibid*.
"welfare to work beneficiary"—*ibid*.
"young person"—see reg. 76.

GENERAL NOTE

Here the details of the personal allowances and premiums for income-based JSA are set out. They follow a similar pattern to those for income support. But there are some differences. These are in relation to the qualifying conditions for the different rates of personal allowance paid where one or both members of a couple are under 18 (see para. 1(3)) and the conditions for the pensioner and disability premiums.

See the notes to Sched. 2 to the Income Support Regulations for discussion of the personal allowances and premiums where the rules are the same for JSA and income support. The note below just refers to the main differences.

Paragraph 1

The conditions for the lower and higher rate of personal allowance for 16- or 17-year-olds who are single or lone parents match those that applied under income support before October 7, 1996 (see the 1996 edition of this book). Similarly JSA, like income support, is paid at a lower rate for single people who are under 25.

But in relation to couples there are some additional categories so that para. 1(3) is even more complex than the pre-October 7, 1996 form of para. 1(3) of Sched. 2 to the Income Support Regulations. See heads (a)(iii), (a)(vii), (f)(iii), (g)(iii) and (h)(iii) where the fact that the other member of the couple would or would not be eligible for income support is an additional means of the couple qualifying or not qualifying for a higher rate. (Should the "and" at the end of head (f)(ii) not be an "or"?) Note also the new categories in heads (a)(iv) and (d).

Paragraph 2

New age bands apply for dependent children and young persons from April 7, 1997 (see further the notes to para. 2 of Sched. 2 to the Income Support Regulations). Note the transitional protection in reg. 10(1) and (2) of the Income-related Benefits and Jobseeker's Allowance (Personal Allowance for Children and Young Persons) (Amendment) Regulations 1996 (p. 502) in relation to children and young persons who reached 11, 16 or 18 before April 7, 1997; it is not necessary for income-based JSA to have been in payment on the relevant birthday.

Paragraph 4

On the abolition of the lone parent premium, and the changes to the family premium introduced in April 1997 and April 1998, see the note to para. 3 of Sched. 2 to the Income Support Regulations. Under sub-para. (6) entitlement to income support counts as entitlement to income-based JSA for the purpose of satisfying the conditions in sub-paras. (2) and (3). Similarly, entitlement to income-based JSA counts as entitlement to income support for the purposes of meeting the conditions in para. 3(2) and (3) of Sched. 2 to the Income Support Regulation (see para. 3(6) of those Regulations). A lone parent can thus move from income support to income-based JSA (or vice versa) (including a period of no more than 12 weeks when there is no entitlement to either benefit) and the higher rate of the family premium will still be applicable as long as the other conditions in sub-paras. (2) and (3) continue to be satisfied.

Paragraphs 10 and 11

The conditions for qualifying for a pensioner premium (for the rates see para. 20; the premiums are paid at the same rate as the pensioner premiums for income support) differ from the income support rules to reflect the fact that the claimant must be under pensionable age to be entitled to JSA (s. 1(2)(h) of the Jobseekers Act). For the premium under para. 10 to be payable the claimant must be 60 or over, or have a partner aged 60–74. If his partner is aged 75–79 the claimant will qualify for the premium under para. 11.

Paragraphs 12 to 14

Similarly, the rules for the higher pensioner and disability premiums differ from those for income support to reflect the fact that to be entitled to JSA the claimant has to be capable of work (s. 1(2)(f) of the Jobseekers Act). Thus severe disablement allowance and long-term incapacity benefit (or short-term incapacity benefit at the higher rate payable to people who are terminally ill) remain qualifying benefits for the purpose of these premiums but only where it is the claimant's partner that receives them (see para. 14(1)(b) and (d)). See also para. 14(1)(g) (and note the differences from para. 12(1)(c) of the Income Support Regulations). In addition, there is (obviously) no equivalent to para. 12(1)(b) of Sched 2 to the Income Support Regulations (claimant incapable of work for at least 52 weeks or 28 weeks in the case of terminal illness).

Paragraph 15

Note the saving provision in sub-para. (8). Regs. 4 to 6 of the Income Support (General) Amendment (No. 6) Regulations 1991 are on pp. 488–491.

SCHEDULE 2   **Regulations 83(f)**
and 84(1)(g)

HOUSING COSTS

Housing costs

1.—(1) Subject to the following provisions of this Schedule, the housing costs applicable to a claimant are those costs—

(a) which he or, where he is a member of a family, he or any member of that family is, in accordance with paragraph 2, liable to meet in respect of the dwelling occupied as the home which he or any other member of his family is treated as occupying; and

(b) which qualify under paragraphs 14 to 16.

(2) In this Schedule—

"housing costs" means those costs to which sub-paragraph (1) refers;

"existing housing costs" means housing costs arising under an agreement entered into before 2nd October 1995, or under an agreement entered into after 1st October 1995 ("the new agreement")—

(a) which replaces an existing agreement between the same parties in respect of the same property; and

(b) where the existing agreement was entered into before 2nd October 1995; and

(c) which is for a loan of the same amount as or less than the amount of the loan under the agreement it replaces, and for the purpose of determining the amount of the loan under the new agreement, any sum payable to arrange the new agreement and included in the loan shall be disregarded;

"new housing costs" means housing costs arising under an agreement entered into after 1st October 1995 other than an agreement referred to in the definition of "existing housing costs";

"standard rate" means the rate for the time being specified in paragraph 11.

(3) For the purposes of this Schedule a disabled person is a person—

(a) in respect of whom a disability premium, a disabled child premium, a pensioner premium where the claimant's partner has attained the age of 75 or a higher pensioner premium is included in his applicable amount or the applicable amount of a person living with him; or

(b) who, had he in fact been entitled to a jobseeker's allowance or to income support, would have had included in his applicable amount a disability premium, a disabled child premium, a pensioner premium where the claimant's partner has attained the age of 75 or a higher pensioner premium; or

(c) who satisfies the requirements of paragraph 9A of Schedule 2 to the Income Support [¹Regulations] (pensioner premium for person aged 75 or over).

(4) For the purposes of sub-paragraph (3), a person shall not cease to be a disabled person on account of his being disqualified for receiving benefit or treated as capable of work by virtue of the operation of section 171E of the Benefits Act (incapacity for work, disqualification etc.).

[⁵Previous entitlement to income support

1A.—(1) Where a claimant or his partner was in receipt of or was treated as being in receipt of income support not more than 12 weeks before one of them becomes entitled to income-based jobseeker's allowance or, where the claimant or his partner is a person to whom paragraph 13(2) or (10) (linking rules) refers, not more than 26 weeks before becoming so entitled and—

(a) the applicable amount for income support included an amount in respect of housing costs under paragraph 15 or 16 of Schedule 3 to the Income Support Regulations; and

(b) the circumstances affecting the calculation of those housing costs remain unchanged since the last calculation of those costs,

the applicable amount in respect of housing costs for income-based jobseeker's allowance shall be the applicable amount in respect of those costs current when entitlement to income support was last determined.

(2) Where, in the period since housing costs were last calculated for income support, there has been a change of circumstances, other than a reduction in the amount of an outstanding loan, which increases or reduces those costs, the amount to be met under

this Schedule shall, for the purposes of the claim for income-based jobseeker's allowance, be recalculated so as to take account of that change.]

Circumstances in which a person is liable to meet housing costs

2.—(1) A person is liable to meet housing costs where—
(a) the liability falls upon him or his partner but not where the liability is to a member of the same household as the person on whom the liability falls;
(b) because the person liable to meet the housing costs ['is not meeting them], the claimant has to meet those costs in order to continue to live in the dwelling occupied as the home and it is reasonable in all the circumstances to treat the claimant as liable to meet those costs;
(c) he in practice shares the housing costs with other members of the household none of whom are close relatives either of the claimant or his partner, and
   (i) one or more of those members is liable to meet those costs, and
   (ii) it is reasonable in the circumstances to treat him as sharing responsibility.
(2) Where any one or more, but not all, members of the claimant's family are affected by a trade dispute, the housing costs shall be treated as wholly the responsibility of those members of the family not so affected.

Circumstances in which a person is to be treated as occupying a dwelling as his home

3.—(1) Subject to the following provisions of this paragraph, a person shall be treated as occupying as his home the dwelling normally occupied as his home by himself or, if he is a member of a family, by himself and his family and he shall not be treated as occupying any other dwelling as his home.
(2) In determining whether a dwelling is the dwelling normally occupied as the claimant's home for the purposes of sub-paragraph (1) regard shall be had to any other dwelling occupied by the claimant or by him and his family whether or not that other dwelling is in Great Britain.
(3) Subject to sub-paragraph (4), where a single claimant or a lone parent is a full-time student or is on a training course and is liable to make payments (including payments of mortgage interest or, in Scotland, payments under heritable securities or, in either case, analogous payments) in respect of either (but not both) the dwelling which he occupies for the purpose of attending his course of study or his training course or, as the case may be, the dwelling which he occupies when not attending his course, he shall be treated as occupying as his home the dwelling in respect of which he is liable to make payments.
(4) A full-time student shall not be treated as occupying a dwelling as his home for any week of absence from it, other than an absence occasioned by the need to enter hospital for treatment, outside the period of study, if the main purpose of his occupation during the period of study would be to facilitate attendance on his course.
(5) Where a claimant has been required to move into temporary accommodation by reason of essential repairs being carried out to the dwelling normally occupied as his home and he is liable to make payments (including payments of mortgage interest or, in Scotland, payments under heritable securities or, in either case, analogous payments) in respect of either (but not both) the dwelling normally occupied or the temporary accommodation, he shall be treated as occupying as his home the dwelling in respect of which he is liable to make those payments.
(6) Where a person is liable to make payments in respect of two (but not more than two) dwellings, he shall be treated as occupying both dwellings as his home only—
(a) where he has left and remains absent from the former dwelling occupied as the home through fear of violence in that dwelling or by a former member of his family and it is reasonable that housing costs should be met in respect of both his former dwelling and his present dwelling occupied as the home; or
(b) in the case of a couple or a member of a polygamous marriage where a partner is

a full-time student or is on a training course and it is unavoidable that he or they should occupy two separate dwellings and reasonable that housing costs should be met in respect of both dwellings; or

(c) in the case where a person has moved into a new dwelling occupied as the home, except where sub-paragraph (5) applies, for a period not exceeding four benefit weeks if his liability to make payments in respect of two dwellings is unavoidable.

(7) Where—

(a) a person has moved into a dwelling and was liable to make payments in respect of that dwelling before moving in; and

(b) he had claimed a jobseeker's allowance before moving in and either that claim has not yet been determined or it has been determined but an amount has not been included under this Schedule and if the claim has been refused a further claim has been made within four weeks of the date on which the claimant moved into the new dwelling occupied as the home; and

(c) the delay in moving into the dwelling in respect of which there was liability to make payments before moving in was reasonable and—

    (i) that delay was necessary in order to adapt the dwelling to meet the disablement needs of the claimant or any member of his family; or

    (ii) the move was delayed pending the outcome of an application under Part VIII of the Benefits Act for a social fund payment to meet a need arising out of the move or in connection with setting up the home in the dwelling and either a member of the claimant's family is aged five or under or the claimant's applicable amount includes a premium under paragraph 10, 11, 12, 13, 15 or 16 of Schedule 1; or

    (iii) the person became liable to make payments in respect of the dwelling while he was a patient or was in residential accommodation,

he shall be treated as occupying the dwelling as his home for any period not exceeding four weeks immediately prior to the date on which he moved into the dwelling and in respect of which he was liable to make payments.

(8) This sub-paragraph applies to a person who enters residential accommodation—

(a) for the purpose of ascertaining whether the accommodation suits his needs; and

(b) with the intention of returning to the dwelling which he normally occupies as his home should, in the event, the residential accommodation prove not to suit his needs,

and while in the accommodation, the part of the dwelling which he normally occupies as his home is not let, or as the case may be, sub-let to another person.

(9) A person to whom sub-paragraph (8) applies shall be treated as occupying the dwelling he normally occupies as his home during any period (commencing with the day he enters the accommodation) not exceeding 13 weeks in which the person is resident in the accommodation, but only in so far as the total absence from the dwelling does not exceed 52 weeks.

(10) A person, other than a person to whom sub-paragraph (11) applies, shall be treated as occupying a dwelling as his home throughout any period of absence not exceeding 13 weeks, if, and only if—

(a) he intends to return to occupy the dwelling as his home; and

(b) the part of the dwelling normally occupied by him has not been let or, as the case may be, sub-let to another person; and

(c) the period of absence is unlikely to exceed 13 weeks.

(11) This sub-paragraph applies to a person whose absence from the dwelling he normally occupies as his home is temporary and—

(a) he intends to return to occupy the dwelling as his home; and

(b) while the part of the dwelling which is normally occupied by him has not been let or, as the case may be, sub-let; and

(c) he is—

    (i) required, as a condition of bail, to reside in a hostel approved under section 27(1) of the Probation Service Act 1993, or

    (ii) resident in a hospital or similar institution as a patient and is treated under regulation 55 as capable of work, or

    (iii) undergoing or, as the case may be, his partner or his dependent child is undergoing, in the United Kingdom or elsewhere, medical treatment, or medically approved convalescence, in accommodation other than residential accommodation, or

    (iv) following, in the United Kingdom or elsewhere, a training course, or

    (v) undertaking medically approved care of a person residing in the United Kingdom or elsewhere, or

    (vi) undertaking the care of a child whose parent or guardian is temporarily absent from the dwelling normally occupied by that parent or guardian for the purpose of receiving medically approved care or medical treatment, or

    (vii) a person who is, whether in the United Kingdom or elsewhere, receiving medically approved care provided in accommodation other than residential accommodation, or

    (viii) a full-time student to whom sub-paragraph (3) or (6)(b) does not apply, or

    (ix) a person other than a person to whom sub-paragraph (8) applies, who is receiving care provided in residential accommodation, or

    (x) a person to whom sub-paragraph (6)(a) does not apply and who has left the dwelling he occupies as his home through fear of violence in that dwelling or by a person who was formerly a member of [¹ his] family, and

(d) the period of his absence is unlikely to exceed a period of 52 weeks or, in exceptional circumstances, is unlikely substantially to exceed that period.

(12) A person to whom sub-paragraph (11) applies is to be treated as occupying the dwelling he normally occupies as his home during any period of absence not exceeding 52 weeks beginning with the first day of that absence.

(13) In this paragraph—

(a) "medically approved" means certified by a registered medical practitioner;

(b) "patient" means a person who is undergoing medical or other treatment as an in-patient in a hospital or similar institution;

(c) "residential accommodation" means accommodation—

    (i) provided under sections 21 to 24 and 26 of the National Assistance Act 1948 (provision of accommodation); or

    (ii) provided under sections 13B and 59 of the Social Work (Scotland) Act 1968 (provision of residential and other establishments) where board is available to the claimant; or

    (iii) which is a residential care home within the meaning of that expression in regulation 1(3) other than sub-paragraph (b) of that definition; or

    (iv) which is a nursing home;

(d) "training course" means such a course of training or institution provided wholly or partly by or on behalf of or in pursuance of arrangements made with, or approved by or on behalf of, Scottish Enterprise, Highlands and Islands Enterprise, a government department or the Secretary of State.

Housing costs not met

4.—(1) No amount may be met under the provisions of this Schedule—

(a) in respect of housing benefit expenditure; or

(b) where the claimant is in accommodation which is a residential care home or a nursing home except where he is in such accommodation during a temporary absence from the dwelling he occupies as his home and in so far as they relate to temporary absences, the provisions of paragraph 3(8) to (12) apply to him during that absence.

(2) Subject to the following provisions of this paragraph, loans which, apart from this paragraph, qualify under paragraph 14 shall not so qualify where the loan was incurred during the relevant period and was incurred—

    (a) after 7th October 1996, or

    (b) after 2nd May 1994 and the housing costs applicable to that loan were not met in income support by virtue of the former paragraph 5A of Schedule 3 to the Income Support Regulations or paragraph 4(2)(a) of that Schedule in any one or more of the 26 weeks [³preceding] 7th October 1996, or

    (c) subject to sub-paragraph (3), in the 26 weeks preceding 7th October 1996 by a person—

        (i) who was not at that time entitled to income support; and

        (ii) who becomes, or whose partner becomes entitled to a jobseeker's allowance after 6th October 1996 and that entitlement is within 26 weeks of an earlier entitlement to income support for the claimant or his partner.

    (3) Sub-paragraph (2)(c) shall not apply in respect of a loan where the claimant has interest payments on that loan met without restrictions under an award of income support in respect of a period commencing before 7th October 1996.

    (4) The "relevant period" for the purposes of this paragraph is any period during which the person to whom the loan was made—

    (a) is entitled to a jobseeker's allowance, or

    (b) is living as a member of a family one of whom is entitled to a jobseeker's allowance,

together with any linked period, that is to say a period falling between two such periods of entitlement to a jobseeker's allowance, separated by not more than 26 weeks.

    [⁶(4A) For the purposes of sub-paragraph (4), a person shall be treated as entitled to a jobseeker's allowance during any period when he or his partner was not so entitled because—

    (a) that person or his partner was participating in an employment programme specified in regulation 75(1)(a)(ii); and

    (b) in consequence of such participation that person, or his partner, was engaged in remunerative work or failed to satisfy the condition specified either in section 2(1)(c) or in section 3(1)(a).]

    (5) For the purposes of sub-paragraph (4)—

    (a) any week in the period of 26 weeks ending on 7th October 1996 on which there arose an entitlement to income support shall be taken into account in determining when the relevant period commences; and

    (b) two or more periods of entitlement and any intervening linked periods shall together form a single relevant period.

    (6) Where the loan to which sub-paragraph (2) refers has been applied—

    (a) for paying off an earlier loan, and that earlier loan qualified under paragraph 14 [²during the relevant period]; or

  [²(b) to finance the purchase of a property where an earlier loan, which qualified under paragraphs 14 and 15 during the relevant period in respect of another property, is paid off (in whole or in part) with monies received from the sale of that property;]

then the amount of the loan to which sub-paragraph (2) applies is the amount (if any) by which the new loan exceeds the earlier loan.

    (7) Notwithstanding the preceding provisions of this paragraph, housing costs shall be met in any case where a claimant satisfies any of the conditions specified in sub-paragraphs (8) to (11) below, but—

    (a) those costs shall be subject to any additional limitations imposed by the sub paragraph; and

    (b) where the claimant satisfies the conditions in more than one of these sub-paragraphs, only one sub-paragraph shall apply in his case and the one that applies shall be the one most favourable to him.

    (8) The conditions specified in this sub-paragraph are that—

    (a) during the relevant period the claimant or a member of his family acquires an interest ("the relevant interest") in a dwelling which he then occupies or continues to occupy as his home; and

(b) in the week preceding the week in which the relevant interest was acquired, housing benefit was payable to the claimant or a member of his family;

so however that the amount to be met by way of housing costs shall initially not exceed the aggregate of—

　　(i) the housing benefit payable in the week mentioned at sub-paragraph (8)(b); and

　　(ii) any amount included in the applicable amount of the claimant or a member of his family in accordance with regulation 83(f) or 84(1)(g) in that week;

and shall be increased subsequently only to the extent that it is necessary to take account of any increase, arising after the date of the acquisition, in the standard rate or in any housing costs which qualify under paragraph 16 (other housing costs).

(9) The condition specified in this sub-paragraph is that the loan was taken out, or an existing loan increased, to acquire alternative accommodation more suited to the special needs of a disabled person than the accommodation which was occupied before the acquisition by the claimant.

(10) The conditions specified in this sub-paragraph are that—

(a) the loan commitment increased in consequence of the disposal of the dwelling occupied as the home and the acquisition of an alternative such dwelling; and

(b) the change of dwelling was made solely by reason of the need to provide separate sleeping accommodation for children of different sexes aged 10 or over who belong to the same family as the claimant.

(11) The conditions specified in this sub-paragraph are that—

(a) during the relevant period the claimant or a member of his family acquires an interest (''the relevant interest'') in a dwelling which he then occupies as his home; and

(b) in the week preceding the week in which the relevant interest was acquired, the applicable amount of the claimant or a member of his family included an amount determined by reference to paragraph 16 and did not include any amount specified in paragraph 14 or paragraph 15;

so however that the amount to be met by way of housing costs shall initially not exceed the amount so determined, and shall be increased subsequently only to the extent that it is necessary to take account of any increase, arising after the date of acquisition, in the standard rate or in any housing costs which qualify under paragraph 16 (other housing costs).

(12) The following provisions of this Schedule shall have effect subject to the provisions of this paragraph.

Apportionment of housing costs

5.—(1) Where the dwelling occupied as the home is a composite hereditament and—

(a) before 1st April 1990 for the purposes of section 48(5) of the General Rate Act 1967 (reduction of rates on dwellings), it appeared to a rating authority or it was determined in pursuance of sub-section (6) of section 48 of that Act that the hereditament, including the dwelling occupied as the home, was a mixed hereditament and that only a proportion of the rateable value of the hereditament was attributable to use for the purpose of a private dwelling; or

(b) in Scotland, before 1st April 1989 an assessor acting pursuant to section 45(1) of the Water (Scotland) Act 1980 (provision as to valuation roll) has apportioned the net annual value of the premises including the dwelling occupied as the home between the part occupied as a dwelling and the remainder,

the amounts applicable under this Schedule shall be such proportion of the amounts applicable in respect of the hereditament or premises as a whole as is equal to the proportion of the rateable value of the hereditament attributable to the part of the hereditament used for the purposes of a private tenancy or, in Scotland, the proportion of the net annual value of the premises apportioned to the part occupied as a dwelling house.

(2) Subject to sub-paragraph (1) and the following provisions of this paragraph, where the dwelling occupied as the home is a composite hereditament, the amount applicable under this Schedule shall be the relevant fraction of the amount which would otherwise be applicable under this Schedule in respect of the dwelling occupied as the home.

(3) For the purposes of sub-paragraph (2), the relevant fraction shall be obtained in accordance with the formula—

$$\frac{A}{A + B}$$

where—

"A" is the current market value of the claimant's interest in that part of the composite hereditament which is domestic property within the meaning of section 66 of the Act of 1988;

"B" is the current market value of the claimant's interest in that part of the composite hereditament which is not domestic property within that section.

(4) In this paragraph—

"composite hereditament" means—

(a) as respects England and Wales, any hereditament which is shown as a composite hereditament in a local non-domestic rating list;

(b) as respects Scotland, any lands and heritages entered in the valuation roll which are part residential subjects within the meaning of section 26(1) of the Act of 1987;

"local non-domestic rating list" means a list compiled and maintained under section 41(1) of the Act of 1988;

"the Act of 1987" means the Abolition of Domestic Rates Etc. (Scotland) Act 1987;

"the Act of 1988" means the Local Government Finance Act 1988.

(5) Where responsibility for expenditure which relates to housing costs met under this Schedule is shared, the amounts applicable shall be calculated by reference to the appropriate proportion of that expenditure for which the claimant is responsible.

Existing housing costs

6.—(1) Subject to the provisions of this Schedule the existing housing costs to be met in any particular case are—

(a) where the claimant has been entitled to a jobseeker's allowance for a continuous period of 26 weeks or more, the aggregate of—

(i) an amount determined in the manner set out in paragraph 9 by applying the standard rate to the eligible capital for the time being owing in connection with a loan which qualifies under paragraph 14 or 15; and

(ii) an amount equal to any payments which qualify under paragraph 16(1)(a) to (c);

(b) where the claimant has been entitled to a jobseeker's allowance for a continuous period of not less than 8 weeks but less than 26 weeks, an amount which is half the amount which would fall to be met by applying the provisions of sub-paragraph (a);

(c) in any other case, nil.

(2) For the purposes of sub-paragraph (1) [⁵and subject to sub-paragraph (3)], the eligible capital for the time being owing shall be determined on the date the existing housing costs are first met and thereafter on each anniversary of that date.

[⁵(3) Where a claimant or his partner ceases to be in receipt of or treated as being in receipt of income support and one of them becomes entitled to income-based jobseeker's allowance in a case to which paragraph 1A applies, the eligible capital for the time being owing shall be recalculated on each anniversary of the date on which the housing costs were first met for whichever of the benefits concerned the claimant or his partner was first entitled.]

New housing costs

7.—(1) Subject to the provisions of this Schedule, the new housing costs to be met in any particular case are—
   (a) where the claimant has been entitled to a jobseeker's allowance for a continuous period of 39 weeks or more, an amount—
      (i) determined in the manner set out in paragraph 9 by applying the standard rate to the eligible capital for the time being owing in connection with a loan which qualifies under paragraph 14 or 15; and
      (ii) equal to any payments which qualify under paragraph 16(1)(a) to (c);
   (b) in any other case, nil.
   (2) For the purposes of sub-paragraph (1) [⁵and subject to sub-paragraph (2A)], the eligible capital for the time being owing shall be determined on the date the new housing costs are first met and thereafter on each anniversary of that date.
   [⁵(2A) Where a claimant or his partner ceases to be in receipt of or treated as being in receipt of income support and one of them becomes entitled to income-based jobseeker's allowance in a case to which paragraph 1A applies, the eligible capital for the time being owing shall be recalculated on each anniversary of the date on which the housing costs were first met for whichever of the benefits concerned the claimant or his partner was first entitled.]
   (3) This sub-paragraph applies to a claimant who at the time the claim is made has been refused payments under a policy of insurance on the grounds that—
   (a) the claim under the policy is the outcome of a pre-existing medical condition which, under the terms of the policy, does not give rise to any payment by the insurer; or
   (b) he was infected by the Human Immunodeficiency Virus,
and the policy was taken out to insure against the risk of being unable to maintain repayments on a loan which is secured by a mortgage or a charge over land, or (in Scotland) by a heritable security.
   (4) This sub-paragraph applies subject to [¹sub-paragraph (7)] where a person claims a jobseeker's allowance because of—
   (a) the death of a partner; or
   (b) being abandoned by his partner,
and where the person's family includes a child.
   (5) This sub-paragraph applies to a person who at the time the claim is made is engaged in caring for a person who falls within any of the circumstances specified in [¹heads (i) to (iv) of sub-paragraph (c)] of paragraph (3) of regulation 51 (remunerative work).
   (6) In the case of a claimant to whom sub-paragraph (3), (4) or (5) applies, any new housing costs shall be met as though they were existing housing costs and paragraph 6 applied to them.
   (7) Sub-paragraph (4) shall cease to apply to a person who subsequently becomes one of a couple.

General exclusions from paragraphs 6 and 7

8.—(1) Paragraphs 6 and 7 shall not apply where—
   (a) the claimant or his partner is aged 60 or over;
   (b) the housing costs are payments—

(i) under a co-ownership agreement;

(ii) under or relating to a tenancy or licence of a Crown tenant; or

(iii) where the dwelling occupied as the home is a tent, in respect of the tent and the site on which it stands.

(2) In a case falling within sub-paragraph (1), the housing costs to be met are—

(a) where head (a) of sub-paragraph (1) applies, an amount—

(i) determined in the manner set out in paragraph 9 by applying the standard rate to the eligible capital for the time being owing in connection with a loan which qualifies under paragraph 14 or 15; and

(ii) equal to the payments which qualify under paragraph 16;

(b) where head (b) of sub-paragraph (1) applies, an amount equal to the payments which qualify under paragraph 16(1)(d) to (f).

The calculation for loans

9.—(1) The weekly amount of existing housing costs or, as the case may be, new housing costs to be met under this Schedule in respect of a loan which qualifies under paragraph 14 or 15 shall be calculated by applying the formula—

$$\frac{A \times B \times C}{52}$$

where—

A = the amount of the loan which qualifies under paragraph 14 or 15;

B = the standard rate for the time being specified in respect of that loan under paragraph 11;

C = the difference between 100 per cent. and the applicable percentage of income tax within the meaning of section 369(1A) of the Income and Corporation Taxes Act 1988 (mortgage interest payable under deduction of tax) for the year of assessment in which the payment of interest becomes due.

(2) Where section 369 of the Income and Corporation Taxes Act 1988 does not apply to the interest on a loan or a part of a loan, the formula applied in sub-paragraph (1) shall have effect as if C had a value of 1.

General provisions applying to new and existing housing costs

10.—(1) Where a person enters into a new agreement in respect of a dwelling and an agreement entered into before 2nd October 1995 ("the earlier agreement") continues in force independently of the new agreement, then—

(a) the housing costs applicable to the new agreement shall be calculated by reference to the provisions of paragraph 7 (new housing costs);

(b) the housing costs applicable to the earlier agreement shall be calculated by reference to the [¹provisions] of paragraph 6 (existing housing costs);

and the resulting amounts shall be aggregated.

(2) Sub-paragraph (1) does not apply in the case of a claimant to whom paragraph 8 applies.

(3) Where for the time being a loan exceeds, or in a case where more than one loan is to be taken into account, the aggregate of those loans exceeds the appropriate amount specified in sub-paragraph (4), then the amount of the loan or, as the case may be, the aggregate amount of those loans, shall for the purposes of this Schedule, be the appropriate amount.

(4) Subject to the following provisions of this paragraph, the appropriate amount is £100,000.

(5) Where a person is treated under paragraph 3(6) (payments in respect of two dwellings) as occupying two dwellings as his home, then the restrictions imposed by sub-paragraph (3) shall be applied separately to the loans for each dwelling.

(6) In a case to which paragraph 5 (apportionment of housing costs) applies, the appropriate amount for the purposes of sub-paragraph (3) shall be the lower of—
  (a) a sum determined by applying the formula—
    $P \times Q$,
    where—
      P = the relevant fraction for the purposes of paragraph 5, and
      Q = the amount or, as the case may be, the aggregate amount for the time being of any loan or loans which qualify under this Schedule; or
  (b) the sum for the time being specified in sub-paragraph (4).

(7) In a case to which paragraph 14(3) or 15(3) (loans which qualify in part only) applies, the appropriate amount for the purposes of sub-paragraph (3) shall be the lower of—
  (a) a sum representing for the time being the part of the loan applied for the purposes specified in paragraph 14(1) or (as the case may be) paragraph 15(1); or
  (b) the sum for the time being specified in sub-paragraph (4).

(8) In the case of any loan to which paragraph 15(2)(k) (loan taken out and used for the purpose of adapting a dwelling for the special needs of a disabled person) applies the whole of the loan, to the extent that it remains unpaid, shall be disregarded in determining whether the amount for the time being specified in sub-paragraph (4) is exceeded.

(9) Where in any case the amount for the time being specified for the purposes of sub-paragraph (4) is exceeded and there are two or more loans to be taken into account under either or both [¹paragraphs 14 and 15], then the amount of eligible interest in respect of each of those loans to the extent that the loans remain outstanding shall be determined as if each loan had been reduced to a sum equal to the qualifying portion of that loan.

(10) For the purposes of sub-paragraph (9), the qualifying portion of a loan shall be determined by applying the following formula—

$$R \times \frac{S}{T}$$

  where—
  R = the amount for the time being specified for the purposes of sub-paragraph (4);
  S = the amount of the outstanding loan to be taken into account;
  T = the aggregate of all outstanding loans to be taken into account under paragraphs 14 and 15.

The standard rate

11.—(1) The standard rate is the rate of interest applicable to a loan which qualifies under this Schedule and—
  [²(a) except where sub-paragraph (2) applies shall be the rate specified in paragraph 12(1)(a) of Schedule 3 to the Income Support Regulations; or]
  (b) where sub-paragraph (2) applies, shall equal the actual rate of interest charged on the loan on the day the housing costs first fall to be met.

(2) This sub-paragraph applies where the actual rate of interest charged on the loan which qualifies under this Schedule is less than 5 per cent. per annum on the day the housing costs first fall to be met and ceases to apply when the actual rate of interest on that loan is 5 per cent. per annum or higher.

(3) Where in a case to which sub-paragraph (2) applies, the actual rate of interest on the loan rises to 5 per cent. per annum or higher, the standard rate applicable on that loan shall be determined in accordance with sub-paragraph (1)(a).

Excessive housing costs

12.—(1) Housing costs which, apart from this paragraph, fall to be met under this Schedule shall be met only to the extent specified in sub-paragraph (3) where—

(a) the dwelling occupied as the home, excluding any part which is let, is larger than is required by the claimant and his family and any child or young person to whom regulation 78(4) applies (foster children) and any other non-dependants having regard, in particular, to suitable alternative accommodation occupied by a household of the same size; or

(b) the immediate area in which the dwelling occupied as the home is located is more expensive than other areas in which suitable alternative accommodation exists; or

(c) the outgoings of the dwelling occupied as the home which are met under paragraphs 14 to 16 are higher than the outgoings of suitable alternative accommodation in the area.

(2) For the purposes of heads (a) to (c) of sub-paragraph (1), no regard shall be had to the capital value of the dwelling occupied as the home.

(3) Subject to the following provisions of this paragraph, the amount of the loan which falls to be met shall be restricted and the excess over the amounts which the claimant would need to obtain suitable alternative accommodation shall not be allowed.

(4) Where, having regard to the relevant factors, it is not reasonable to expect the claimant and his family to seek alternative cheaper accommodation, no restriction shall be made under sub-paragraph (3).

(5) In sub-paragraph (4) "the relevant factors" are—

(a) the availability of suitable accommodation and the level of housing costs in the area; and

(b) the circumstances of the family including in particular the age and state of health of its members, the employment prospects of the claimant and, where a change in accommodation is likely to result in a change of school, the effect on the education of any child or young person who is a member of his family, or any child or young person who is not treated as part of his family by virtue of regulation 78(4) (foster children).

(6) Where sub-paragraph (4) does not apply and the claimant (or other member of the family) was able to meet the financial commitments for the dwelling occupied as the home when these were entered into, no restriction shall be made under this paragraph during the first 26 weeks of any period of entitlement to a jobseeker's allowance nor during the next 26 weeks if and so long as the claimant uses his best endeavours to obtain cheaper accommodation or, as the case may be, no restriction shall be made under this paragraph on review during the 26 weeks from the date of the review nor during the next 26 weeks if and so long as the claimant uses his best endeavours.

(7) For the purposes of calculating any period of 26 weeks referred to in sub-paragraph (6), and for those purposes only, a person shall be treated as entitled to a jobseeker's allowance for any period of 12 weeks or less in respect of which he was not in receipt of a jobseeker's allowance and which fell immediately between periods in respect of which he was in receipt thereof.

(8) Any period in respect of which—

(a) a jobseeker's allowance was paid to a person, and

(b) it was subsequently determined on appeal or review that he was not entitled to a jobseeker's allowance for that period,

shall be treated for the purposes of sub-paragraph (7) as a period in respect of which he was not in receipt of a jobseeker's allowance.

(9) Heads (c) to (f) of sub-paragraph (1) of paragraph 13 shall apply to sub-paragraph (7) as they apply to paragraphs 6 and 7 but with the modification that the words "Subject to sub-paragraph (2)" are omitted and as if references to "the claimant" were references to the person mentioned in sub-paragraph (7).

Linking rule

13.—(1) Subject to sub-paragraph (2) for the [¹purposes] of this Schedule—
(a) a person shall be treated as being in receipt of a jobseeker's allowance during the following periods—
    (i) any period in respect of which it was subsequently held, on appeal or review, that he was so entitled to a jobseeker's allowance; and
    (ii) any period of 12 weeks or less in respect of which he was not in receipt of a jobseeker's allowance and which fell immediately between periods in respect of which
        [²(aa) he was, or was treated as being, in receipt of a jobseeker's allowance,
        (bb) he was treated as entitled to a jobseeker's allowance for the purposes of sub-paragraphs (5), (6) and (7), or
        (cc) (i) above applies;]
(b) a person shall be treated as not being in receipt of a jobseeker's allowance during any period other than a period to which (a)(ii) above applies in respect of which it is subsequently held on appeal or review that he was not so entitled;
(c) where—
    (i) the claimant was a member of a couple or a polygamous marriage; and
    (ii) his partner was, in respect of a past period, in receipt of a jobseeker's allowance for himself and the claimant; and
    (iii) the claimant is no longer a member of that couple or polygamous marriage; and
    (iv) the claimant made his claim for a jobseeker's allowance within twelve weeks of ceasing to be a member of that couple or polygamous marriage,
he shall be treated as having been in receipt of a jobseeker's allowance for the same period as his former partner had been or had been treated, for the purposes of this Schedule, as having been;
(d) where the claimant's partner's applicable amount was determined in accordance with paragraph 1(1) (single claimant) or paragraph 1(2) (lone parent) of Schedule 1 (applicable amounts) in respect of a past period, provided that the claim was made within twelve weeks of the claimant and his partner becoming one of a couple or polygamous marriage, the claimant shall be treated as having been in receipt of a jobseeker's allowance for the same period as his partner had been or had been treated, for the purposes of this Schedule, as having been;
(e) where the claimant is a member of a couple or a polygamous marriage and his partner was, in respect of a past period, in receipt of a jobseeker's allowance for himself and the claimant, and the claimant has begun to receive a jobseeker's allowance as a result of an election by the members of the couple or polygamous marriage, he shall be treated as having been in receipt of a jobseeker's allowance for the same period as his partner had been or had been treated, for the purposes of this Schedule, as having been;
[⁶(ee) where the claimant—
    (i) is a member of a couple or a polygamous marriage and the claimant's partner was, immediately before the participation by any member of that couple or polygamous marriage in an employment programme specified in regulation 75(1)(a)(ii), in receipt of income-based jobseeker's allowance and his applicable amount included an amount for the couple or for the partners of the polygamous marriage; and
    (ii) has, immediately after that participation in that programme, begun to receive income-based jobseeker's allowance as a result of an election under regulation 4(3B) of the Claims and Payments Regulations by the members of the couple or polygamous marriage,
the claimant shall be treated as having been in receipt of a jobseeker's allowance

for the same period as his partner had been or had been treated, for the purposes of this Schedule, as having been;]

(f) where—
>   (i) the claimant was a member of a family of a person (not being a former partner) entitled to a jobseeker's allowance and at least one other member of that family was a child or young person; and
>   (ii) the claimant becomes a member of another family which includes that child or young person; and
>   (iii) the claimant made his claim for a jobseeker's allowance within 12 weeks of the date on which the person entitled to a jobseeker's allowance mentioned in head (i) above ceased to be so entitled,
>
> the claimant shall be treated as being in receipt of a jobseeker's allowance for the same period as that person had been or had been treated, for the purposes of this Schedule, as having been.

(2) Where a claimant, with the care of a child, has ceased to be in receipt of a jobseeker's allowance in consequence of the payment of child support maintenance under the Child Support Act 1991 and immediately before ceasing to be so in receipt an amount determined in accordance with paragraph 6(1)(a)(i) or paragraph 7(1)(a)(i) was applicable to him, then—

(a) if the child support maintenance assessment concerned is terminated or replaced on review by a lower assessment in consequence of the coming into force on or after 18th April 1995 of regulations made under the Child Support Act 1991; or

(b) where the child support maintenance assessment concerned is an interim maintenance assessment and, in circumstances other than those referred to in head (a), it is terminated or replaced after termination by another interim maintenance assessment or by a maintenance assessment made in accordance with Part I of Schedule 1 to the Child Support Act 1991, in either case of a lower amount than the assessment concerned,

sub-paragraph (1)(a)(ii) shall apply to him as if for the words "any period of 12 weeks or less" there were substituted the words "any period of 26 weeks or less".

[⁴ (3) For the purposes of this Schedule, where a claimant has ceased to be entitled to a jobseeker's allowance because he or his partner is participating in arrangements for training made under section 2 of the Employment and Training Act 1973 or attending a course at an employment rehabilitation centre established under that section, he shall be treated as if he had been in receipt of a jobseeker's allowance for the period during which he or his partner was participating in such a course.]

[⁶ (3A) For the purposes of this Schedule, a claimant who has ceased to be entitled to a jobseeker's allowance because—

(a) that claimant or his partner was participating in an employment programme specified in regulation 75(1)(a)(ii), and

(b) in consequence of such participation the claimant or his partner was engaged in renumerative work or failed to satisfy the condition specified either in section 2(1)(c) or in section 3(1)(a),

shall be treated as if he had been in receipt of a jobseeker's allowance for the period during which he or his partner was participating in that programme.]

(4) Where, for the purposes of sub-paragraphs [⁶(1), (3) and (3A)], a person is treated as being in receipt of a jobseeker's allowance, for a certain period, he shall be treated as being entitled to a jobseeker's allowance for the same period.

(5) For the purposes of this Schedule, sub-paragraph (6) applies where a person is not entitled to an income-based jobseeker's allowance by reason only that he has—

(a) capital exceeding £8,000; or

(b) income exceeding the applicable amount which applies in his case; or

[³ (bb) a personal rate of contribution-based jobseeker's allowance that is equal to, or exceeds, the applicable amount in his case; or]

(c) both capital exceeding £8,000 and income exceeding the applicable amount which applies in his case.

(6) A person to whom sub-paragraph (5) applies shall be treated as entitled to a jobseeker's allowance throughout any period of not more than 39 weeks which comprises only days—

    (a) on which he is entitled to a contribution-based jobseeker's allowance, statutory sick pay or incapacity benefit; or

    (b) on which he is, although not entitled to any of the benefits mentioned in head (a) above, entitled to be credited with earnings equal to the lower earnings limit for the time being in force in accordance with [⁹regulation 8A or 8B of the Social Security (Credits) Regulations 1975].

(7) Subject to sub-paragraph (8), a person to whom sub-paragraph (5) applies and who is either a person to whom regulation 13(4) applies (persons with caring responsibilities) or a lone parent shall, for the purposes of this Schedule, be treated as entitled to a jobseeker's allowance throughout any period of not more than 39 weeks following the refusal of a claim for a jobseeker's allowance made by or on behalf of that person.

(8) Sub-paragraph (7) shall not apply in relation to a person mentioned in that sub-paragraph who, during the period referred to in that sub-paragraph—

    (a) is engaged in, or is treated as engaged in, remunerative work or whose partner is engaged in, or is treated as engaged in, remunerative work;

    (b) is treated as not available for employment by virtue of regulation 15(a) (circumstances in which students are not treated as available for employment);

    (c) is temporarily absent from Great Britain, other than in the circumstances specified in regulation 50 (temporary absence from Great Britain).

(9) In a case where—

    (a) sub-paragraphs (6) and (7) apply solely by virtue of sub-paragraph (5)(b), and

    (b) the claimant's income includes payments under a policy taken out to insure against the risk that the policy holder is unable to meet any loan or payment which qualifies under paragraphs 14 to 16,

sub-paragraphs (6) and (7) shall have effect as if for the words "throughout any period of not more than 39 weeks" there are substituted the words "throughout any period that payments are made in accordance with the terms of the policy".

(10) This sub-paragraph applies—

    (a) to a person who claims a jobseeker's allowance, or in respect of whom a jobseeker's allowance is claimed, and who—

        (i) received payments under a policy of insurance taken out to insure against loss of employment, and those payments are exhausted; and

        (ii) had a previous award of a jobseeker's allowance where the applicable amount included an amount by way of housing costs; and

    (b) where the period in respect of which the previous award of jobseeker's allowance was payable ended not more than 26 weeks before the date the claim was made.

(11) Where sub-paragraph (10) applies, in determining—

    (a) for the purposes of paragraph 6(1) whether a person has been entitled to a jobseeker's allowance for a continuous period of 26 weeks or more; or

    (b) for the purposes of paragraph 7(1) whether a claimant has been entitled to a jobseeker's allowance for a continuous period of 39 weeks or more,

any week falling between the date of the termination of the previous award and the date of the new claim shall be ignored.

[⁸(12) Where the claimant's partner to whom this paragraph applies is a welfare to work beneficiary, sub-paragraphs (1)(a)(ii), (1)(d) and (1)(f)(iii) shall apply to him as if for the words "twelve weeks" there were substituted the words "52 weeks".]

Loans on residential property

14.—(1) A loan qualifies under this paragraph where the loan was taken out to defray monies applied for any of the following purposes—

(a) acquiring an interest in the dwelling occupied as the home; or

(b) paying off another loan to the extent that the other loan would have qualified under head (a) above had the loan not been paid off.

(2) For the purposes of this paragraph, references to a loan include also a reference to money borrowed under a hire purchase agreement for any purpose specified in heads (a) and (b) of sub-paragraph (1) above.

(3) Where a loan is applied only in part for the purposes specified in heads (a) and (b) of sub-paragraph (1), only that portion of the loan which is applied for that purpose shall qualify under this paragraph.

Loans for repairs and improvements to the dwelling occupied as the home

15.—(1) A loan qualifies under this paragraph where the loan was taken out, with or without security, for the purpose of—

(a) carrying out repairs and improvements to the dwelling occupied as the home;

(b) paying any service charge imposed to meet the cost of repairs and improvements to the dwelling occupied as the home;

(c) paying off another loan to the extent that the other loan would have qualified under head (a) or (b) of this sub-paragraph had the loan not been paid off,

and the loan was used for that purpose, or is used for that purpose within 6 months of the date of receipt or such further period as may be reasonable in the particular circumstances of the case.

(2) In sub-paragraph (1) "repairs and improvements" means any of the following measures undertaken with a view to maintaining the fitness of the dwelling for human habitation or, where the dwelling forms part of a building, any part of the building containing that dwelling—

(a) provision of a fixed bath, shower, wash basin, sink or lavatory, and necessary associated plumbing, including the provision of hot water not connected to a central heating system;

(b) repairs to existing heating system;

(c) damp proof measures;

(d) provision of ventilation and natural lighting;

(e) provision of drainage facilities;

(f) provision of facilities for preparing and cooking food;

(g) provision of insulation of the dwelling occupied as the home;

(h) provision of electric lighting and sockets;

(i) provision of storage facilities for fuel or refuse;

(j) repairs of unsafe structural defects;

(k) adapting a dwelling for the special needs of a disabled person; or

(l) provision of separate sleeping accommodation for children of different sexes aged 10 or over who are part of the same family as the claimant.

(3) Where a loan is applied only in part for the purposes specified in sub-paragraph (1), only that portion of the loan which is applied for that purpose shall qualify under this paragraph.

Other housing costs

16.—(1) Subject to the deduction specified in sub-paragraph (2) and the reductions applicable in sub-paragraph (5), there shall be met under this paragraph the amounts, calculated on a weekly basis, in respect of the following housing costs—

(a) payments by way of rent or ground rent relating to a long tenancy and, in Scotland, payments by way of feu duty;

(b) service charges;

(c) payments by way of the rentcharge within the meaning of section 1 of the Rentcharges Act 1977;

   (d) payments under a co-ownership scheme;

   (e) payments under or relating to a tenancy or licence of a Crown tenant;

   (f) where the dwelling occupied as the home is a tent, payments in respect of the tent and the site on which it stands.

(2) Subject to sub-paragraph (3), the deductions to be made from the weekly amounts to be met under this paragraph are—

   (a) where the costs are inclusive of any of the items mentioned in paragraph 5(2) of Schedule 1 to the Housing Benefit (General) Regulations 1987 (payment in respect of fuel charges), the deductions prescribed in that paragraph unless the claimant provides evidence on which the actual or approximate amount of the service charge for fuel may be estimated, in which case the estimated amount;

   (b) where the costs are inclusive of ineligible service charges within the meaning of paragraph 1 of Schedule 1 to the Housing Benefit (General) Regulations 1987 (ineligible service charges) the amounts attributable to those ineligible service charges or where that amount is not separated from or separately identified within the housing costs to be met under this paragraph, such part of the payments made in respect of those housing costs which are fairly attributable to the provision of those ineligible services having regard to the costs of comparable services;

   (c) any amount for repairs and improvements, and for this purpose the expression "repairs and improvements" has the same meaning it has in paragraph 15(2).

(3) Where arrangements are made for the housing costs, which are met under this paragraph and which are normally paid for a period of 52 weeks, to be paid instead for a period of 53 weeks, or to be paid irregularly, or so that no such costs are payable or collected in certain periods, or so that the costs for different periods in the year are of different amounts, the weekly amount shall be the amount payable for the year divided by 52.

(4) Where the claimant or a member of his family—

   (a) pays for reasonable repairs or redecoration to be carried out to the dwelling they occupy; and

   (b) that work was not the responsibility of the claimant or any member of his family; and

   (c) in consequence of that work being done, the costs which are normally met under this paragraph are waived,

then those costs shall, for a period not exceeding 8 weeks, be treated as payable.

(5) Where in England and Wales an amount calculated on a weekly basis in respect of housing costs specified in sub-paragraph (1)(e) (Crown tenants) includes water charges, that amount shall be reduced—

   (a) where the amount payable in respect of water charges is known, by that amount;

   (b) in any other case, by the amount which would be the likely weekly water charge had the property not been occupied by a Crown tenant.

Non-dependant deductions

17.—(1) Subject to the following provisions of this paragraph, the following deductions from the amount to be met under the preceding paragraphs of this Schedule in respect of housing costs shall be made—

   [⁷(a) in respect of a non-dependant aged 18 or over who is engaged in any remunerative work, [¹⁰£46.35];]

   (b) in respect of a non-dependant aged 18 or over to whom head (a) does not apply, [¹⁰£7.20].

(2) In the case of a non-dependant aged 18 or over to whom sub-paragraph (1)(a) applies because he is in remunerative work, where the claimant satisfies the adjudication officer that the non-dependant's gross weekly income is—

(a) less than [¹⁰£80.00], the deduction to be made under this paragraph shall be the deduction specified in sub-paragraph (1)(b);

(b) not less than [¹⁰£80.00], but less than [¹⁰ £118.00], the deduction to be made under this paragraph shall be [¹⁰£16.50];

(c) not less than [¹⁰£118.00] but less than [¹⁰£155.00], the deduction to be made under this paragraph shall be [¹⁰£22.65];

[⁷(d) not less than [¹⁰£155.00] but less than [¹⁰£204.00], the deduction to be made under this paragraph shall be [¹⁰£37.10];

(e) not less than [¹⁰£204.00] but less than [¹⁰£255.00], the deduction to be made under this paragraph shall be [¹⁰£42.25]].

(3) Only one deduction shall be made under this paragraph in respect of a couple or, as the case may be, the members of a polygamous marriage, and where, but for this sub-paragraph, the amount that would fall to be deducted in respect of one member of a couple or polygamous marriage is higher than the amount (if any) that would fall to be deducted in respect of the other, or any other member, the higher amount shall be deducted.

(4) In applying the provisions of sub-paragraph (2) in the case of a couple or, as the case may be, a polygamous marriage, regard shall be had, for the purpose of sub-paragraph (2), to the couple's or, as the case may be, all the members of the polygamous marriage's, joint weekly income.

(5) Where a person is a non-dependant in respect of more than one joint occupier of a dwelling (except where the joint occupiers are a couple or members of a polygamous marriage), the deduction in respect of that non-dependant shall be apportioned between the joint occupiers (the amount so apportioned being rounded to the nearest penny) having regard to the number of joint occupiers and the proportion of the housing costs in respect of the dwelling occupied as the home payable by each of them.

(6) No deduction shall be made in respect of any non-dependants occupying the dwelling occupied as the home of the claimant, if the claimant or any partner of his is—

(a) blind or treated as blind within the meaning of paragraph 14(1)(h) and (2) of Schedule 1 (additional condition for the higher pensioner and disability premiums); or

(b) receiving in respect of himself either—

(i) an attendance allowance, or

(ii) the care component of the disability living allowance.

(7) No deduction shall be made in respect of a non-dependant—

(a) if, although he resides with the claimant, it appears to the adjudication officer that the dwelling occupied as his home is normally elsewhere; or

[²(b) if he is in receipt of [³a training allowance paid in connection with a Youth Training Scheme established under section 2 of the Employment and Training Act 1973 or section 2 of the Enterprise and New Towns (Scotland) Act 1990; or]]

(c) if he is a full-time student during a period of study or, if he is not in remunerative work, during a recognised summer vacation appropriate to his course; or

(d) if he is aged under 25 and in receipt of [⁴an income-based jobseeker's allowance] or income support; or

(e) in respect of whom a deduction in the calculation of a rent rebate or allowance falls to be made under regulation 63 of the Housing Benefit (General) Regulations 1987 (non-dependant deductions); or

(f) to whom, but for paragraph (5) of regulation 2 (definition of non-dependant) paragraph (4) of that regulation would apply; or

(g) if he is not residing with the claimant because he has been a patient for a period in excess of six weeks, or is a prisoner, and for these purposes—

(i) "patient" and "prisoner" respectively have the meanings given in regulation 85(4) (special cases), and

(ii) the period of six weeks shall be calculated by reference to paragraph (2) of that regulation as if that paragraph applied in his case.

(8) In the case of a non-dependant to whom sub-paragraph (2) applies because he is in remunerative work, there shall be disregarded from his gross income—

(a) any attendance allowance or disability living allowance received by him;

(b) any payment made under the Macfarlane Trust, the Macfarlane (Special Payments) Trust, the Macfarlane (Special Payments) (No.2) Trust, the Fund, the Eileen Trust or the Independent Living Funds which, had his income fallen to be calculated under regulation 103 (calculation of income other than earnings), would have been disregarded under paragraph 22 of Schedule 7 (income in kind); and

(c) any payment which, had his income fallen to be calculated under regulation 103 would have been disregarded under paragraph 41 of Schedule 7 (payments made under certain trusts and certain other payments).

Continuity with income support

18.—(1) For the purpose of providing continuity between income support and a jobseeker's allowance—

(a) any housing costs which would, had the claimant been entitled to income support, have been existing housing costs and not new housing costs shall, notwithstanding the preceding provisions of this Schedule, be treated as existing housing costs, and any qualifications or limitations which would have applied to those costs had the award been an award of income support shall likewise apply to the costs in so far as they are met in jobseeker's allowance;

(b) had the award of a jobseeker's allowance been an award of income support and the housing costs which would then have been met would have included an additional amount met in accordance with paragraph 7 of Schedule 3 to the Income Support Regulations (add back), an amount equal to that additional amount shall be added to the housing costs to be met under this Schedule, but that amount shall be subject to the same qualifications and limitations as it would have been had the award been of income support; and

(c) for the purposes of any linking rule [²or for determining whether any qualifying or other period is satisfied], any reference to a jobseeker's allowance in this Schedule shall be taken also to include a reference to income support.

(2) Any loan which, had the claimant been entitled to income support and not a jobseeker's allowance, would have been a qualifying loan for the purposes of Schedule 3 to the Income Support Regulations by virtue of regulation 3 of the Income Support (General) Amendment and Transitional Regulations 1995 shall be treated also as a qualifying loan for the purposes of paragraph 14 or 15, as the case may be, of this Schedule; and for the purpose of determining whether a claimant would satisfy the provision of regulation 3(2) of those Regulations, a person in receipt of an income-based jobseeker's allowance shall be treated as being in receipt of income support.

Rounding of Fractions

19. Where any calculation made under this Schedule results in a fraction of a penny, that fraction shall be treated as a penny.

AMENDMENTS

1. Jobseeker's Allowance (Amendment) Regulations 1996 (S.I. 1996 No. 1516), reg. 20 and Sched. (October 7, 1996).
2. Jobseeker's Allowance and Income Support (General) (Amendment) Regulations 1996 (S.I. 1996 No. 1517), reg. 29 (October 7, 1996).
3. Social Security and Child Support (Jobseeker's Allowance) (Miscellaneous Amendments) Regulations 1996 (S.I. 1996 No. 2538), reg. 2(12) (October 28, 1996).
4. Social Security and Child Support (Miscellaneous Amendments) Regulations 1997 (S.I. 1997 No. 827), reg. 4 (April 7, 1997).

5. Social Security (Miscellaneous Amendments) (No. 4) Regulations 1997 (S.I. 1997 No. 2305), reg. 3 (October 22, 1997).

6. Social Security Amendment (New Deal) Regulations 1997 (S.I. 1997 No. 2863), reg. 13 (January 5, 1998).

7. Social Security (Non-Dependant Deductions) Regulations 1996 (S.I. 1996 No. 2518), reg. 4 (April 6, 1998).

8. Social Security (Welfare to Work) Regulations 1998 (S.I. 1998 No. 2231), reg. 14(4) (October 5, 1998).

9. Social Security Benefits (Miscellaneous Amendments) Regulations 1999 (S.I. 1999 No. 714), reg. 2(2) (April 5, 1999).

10. Social Security Benefits Up-rating Order 1999 (S.I. 1999 No. 264), art. 24(6) (April 12, 1999).

DEFINITIONS

"attendance allowance"—see reg. 1(3).
"the Benefits Act"—see Jobseekers Act, s.35(1).
"benefit week"—see reg. 1(3).
"claimant"—see Jobseekers Act, s. 35(1).
"close relative"—see reg. 1(3).
"couple"—*ibid.*
"course of study"—*ibid.*
"co-ownership scheme"—*ibid.*
"Crown tenant"—*ibid.*
"disability living allowance"—*ibid.*
"dwelling occupied as the home"—*ibid.*
"the Eileen Trust"—*ibid.*
"family"—see Jobseekers Act, s. 35(1).
"the Fund"—see reg. 1(3).
"housing benefit expenditure"—*ibid.*
"the Independent Living Funds"—*ibid.*
"lone parent"—*ibid.*
"the Macfarlane (Special Payments) Trust"—*ibid.*
"the Macfarlane (Special Payments) (No. 2) Trust"—*ibid.*
"the Macfarlane Trust"—*ibid.*
"non-dependant"—see reg. 2.
"nursing home"—see reg. 1(3).
"partner"—*ibid.*
"period of study"—*ibid.*
"polygamous marriage"—*ibid.*
"remunerative work"—see reg. 51(1).
"residential care home"—see reg. 1(3).
"single claimant"—*ibid.*
"student"—see reg. 130, reg. 1(3).
"training allowance"—see reg. 1(3).
"water charges"—*ibid.*
"welfare to work beneficiary"—*ibid.*
"year of assessment"—*ibid.*

GENERAL NOTE

Most of this Schedule is very similar to Sched. 3 to the Income Support Regulations, subject to some minor differences in the wording. See the notes to Sched. 3. There are a few differences which reflect the fact that a claimant must satisfy the labour market conditions in order to be entitled to JSA. Thus there is no equivalent of para. 8(2)(b) of Sched. 3 in para. 7 (new housing costs); see also the differences in para. 3(11)(c)(i) and (ii) (person treated as occupying his home during temporary absences of up to 52 weeks). Note also in para. 13 (linking rules) the additional category (from October 28, 1996) in sub-para. (5)(bb): person who is not entitled to income-based JSA because his contribution-based JSA equals or exceeds his applicable amount for income-based JSA; and that a carer in sub-para. (7) is defined by reference to reg. 13(4) (person with caring responsibilities, see reg. 4 for the definition of "caring responsibilities") rather than being restricted to a person who cares for someone receiving attendance allowance or disability living allowance, etc.

Note that in relation to, for example, satisfying the waiting periods for housing costs, periods during which hardship payments are being made will count, since hardship payments are payments of JSA. In addition, periods when a claimant is sanctioned will count towards the waiting periods, since entitlement to JSA continues during the sanction, even though JSA is not paid. This will be so whether or not a hardship payment is made. But "waiting days" at the beginning of a JSA claim are not days of entitlement.

The transitional protection provisions in Sched. 3 to the Income Support Regulations have been omitted, but note the effect of para. 18(1)(b). Para 18 is important for claimants transferring from income support to jobseeker's allowance. For the equivalent of para. 18(1)(c) where the transfer is the other way round, see reg. 32 of the Income Support (General) (Jobseeker's Allowance Consequential Amendments) Regulations 1996 (p. 500)). See p. 497 for reg. 3 of the Income Support (General) Amendment and Transitional Regulations 1995 referred to in para. 18(2) and see the note to para. 7 of Sched. 3. Note also the further transitional provisions in reg. 87(4) to (6).

SCHEDULE 3   **Schedule 1,**

paragraph 3(1)(b)

THE GREATER LONDON AREA

The area described in this Schedule comprises—

(a)   the Boroughs of

Barking and Dagenham	Hillingdon
Barnet	Hounslow
Bexley	Islington
Brent	Kensington and Chelsea
Bromley	Kingston-upon-Thames
Camden	Lambeth
City of Westminster	Lewisham
Croydon	Merton
Ealing	Newham
Enfield	Redbridge
Greenwich	Richmond-upon-Thames
Hackney	Southwark
Hammersmith & Fulham	Sutton
Haringay	Tower Hamlets
Harrow	Waltham Forest
Havering	Wandsworth;

(b) the City of London, the Inner Temple and the Middle Temple;

(c) in the County of Essex that part of the district of Epping Forest which comprises the parishes of Chigwell and Waltham Holy Cross;

(d) in the County of Hertfordshire, that part of the Borough of Broxbourne which lies south of Cheshunt Park, including Slipe Lane, and that part of the district of Hertsmere which comprises the former parishes of Elstree, Ridge, Shenley and South Mimms;

(e) in the County of Surrey, the Borough of Spelthorne and that part of the Borough of Elmbridge which was formerly administered by the [¹old] Esher District Council.

AMENDMENT

1. Social Security (Miscellaneous Amendments) Regulations 1997 (S.I. 1997 No. 454), reg. 2(14) (April 7, 1997).

SCHEDULE 4   **Regulation 86**

APPLICABLE AMOUNTS OF PERSONS IN RESIDENTIAL CARE AND NURSING HOMES

1.—(1) Subject to sub-paragraph (2), the weekly applicable amount of a claimant to whom regulation 86 applies shall be the aggregate of—

(a) subject to paragraph 3, the weekly charge for the accommodation, including all meals and services, provided for him or, if he is a member of a family, for him and his family increased, where appropriate, in accordance with paragraph 2 but, except in a case to which paragraph 10 applies, subject to the maximum determined in accordance with paragraph 4; and

(b) a weekly amount for personal expenses for him and, if he is a member of a family, for each member of his family determined in accordance with paragraph 11; and

(c) where he is only temporarily in such accommodation any amount applicable under regulation 83(f) or 84(1)(g) (housing costs) in respect of the dwelling normally occupied as the home; and

(d) any amount applicable in accordance with regulation 87(3).

(2) No amount shall be included in respect of any child or young person who is a member of the claimant's family if the capital of that child or young person calculated in accordance with Part VIII in like manner as for the claimant, except where otherwise provided, would exceed £3,000.

2.—(1) Where, in addition to the weekly charge for accommodation, a separate charge is made for the provision of heating, attention in connection with bodily functions, supervision, extra baths, laundry or a special diet needed for a medical reason, the weekly charge for the purpose of paragraph 1(1)(a) shall be increased by the amount of that charge.

(2) Where the weekly charge for the accommodation does not include the provision of all meals, it shall for the purpose of paragraph 1(1)(a), be increased in respect of the claimant or, if he is a member of a family, in respect of each member of his family by the following amount:

(a) if the meals can be purchased within the residential care or nursing home, the amount equal to the actual cost of the meals, calculated on a weekly basis; or

(b) if the meals cannot be so purchased, the amount calculated on a weekly basis—

  (i) for breakfast, at a daily rate of £1.10;

  (ii) for a midday meal, at a daily rate of £1.55; and

  (iii) for an evening meal, at a daily rate of £1.55;

except that, if some or all of the meals are normally provided free of charge or at a reduced rate, the amount shall be reduced to take account of the lower charge or reduction.

3. Where any part of the weekly charge for the accommodation is met by housing benefit, an amount equal to the part so met shall be deducted from the amount calculated in accordance with paragraph 1(1)(a).

4.—(1) Subject to paragraph 10 the maximum referred to in paragraph 1(1)(a) shall be—

(a) in the case of a single claimant, the appropriate amount in respect of that claimant specified in or determined in accordance with paragraphs 5 to 9;

(b) in the case of a claimant who is a member of a family the aggregate of the following amounts—

  (i) in respect of the claimant, the appropriate amount in respect of him specified in or determined in accordance with paragraphs 5 to 9;

     (ii) in respect of each member of his family who lives in the home aged under 11, $1\frac{1}{2}$ times the amount specified in paragraph 2(a) of Schedule 1;

     (iii) in respect of each member of his family aged not less than 11 who lives in the home, an amount which would be the appropriate amount specified in or determined in accordance with paragraphs 5 to 9 if the other member were the claimant.

(2) The maximum amount in respect of a member of the family aged under 11 calculated in the manner referred to in sub-paragraph (1)(b)(i) shall be rounded to the nearest multiple of 5p by treating an odd amount of 2.5p or more as 5p and by disregarding an odd amount of less than 2.5p.

Residential care homes

[²**5.** Subject to paragraphs 7 to 9, where the accommodation provided for the claimant is a residential care home for persons in need of personal care by virtue of—

(a) past or present mental disorder but excluding mental handicap, the appropriate amount shall be £230.00 per week;

(b) past or present drug or alcohol dependence, the appropriate amount shall be £230.00 per week;

(c) mental handicap, the appropriate amount shall be £262.00 per week;

(d) physical disablement, the appropriate amount shall be £298.00 per week;

(e) any condition not falling within sub-paragraphs (a) to (d) above, the appropriate amount shall be £218.00 per week.]

Nursing homes

[²**6.** Subject to paragraphs 7 to 9, where the accommodation provided for the claimant is a nursing home for persons in need of personal care by virtue of—

(a) past or present mental disorder but excluding mental handicap, the appropriate amount shall be £326.00 per week;

(b) mental handicap, the appropriate amount shall be £332.00 per week;

(c) past or present drug or alcohol dependence, the appropriate amount shall be £326.00 per week;

(d) physical disablement, the appropriate amount shall be £367.00 per week;

(e) terminal illness, the appropriate amount shall be £325.00 per week;

(f) any condition not falling with sub-paragraphs (a) to (e), the appropriate amount shall be £325.00 per week.]

7. The appropriate amount applicable to a claimant in a residential care home or nursing home shall, subject to paragraph 8, be determined—

(a) where the home is a residential care home registered under Part I of the Registered Homes Act 1984, by reference to the particulars recorded in the register kept by the relevant registration authority for the purposes of that Act; or

(b) where the home is a residential care home not so registered or a nursing home, by reference to the type of care which, taking into account the facilities and accommodation provided, the home is providing to the claimant.

8.—(1) Where more than one amount would otherwise be applicable, in accordance with paragraph 7, to a claimant in a residential care home or a nursing home, the appropriate amount in any case shall be determined in accordance with the following sub-paragraphs.

(2) Where the home is a residential care home registered under Part I of the Registered Homes Act 1984 and where the personal care that the claimant is receiving corresponds to the care received by a category of residents for whom the register indicates that the home provides accommodation, the appropriate amount shall be the amount, in paragraph 5, as is consistent with that personal care.

(3) Where the home is a residential care home which is so registered but where the personal care that the claimant is receiving does not correspond to the care received by

a category of residents for whom the register indicates that the home provides accommodation, the appropriate amount [¹shall be the lesser or least amount] in paragraph 5, as is consistent with those categories.

(4) In any case not falling within sub-paragraph (2) or (3), the appropriate amount shall be whichever amount of the amounts applicable in accordance with paragraph 5, 6, or 7 is, having regard to the types of personal care that the home provides, most consistent with personal care being received by the claimant in that accommodation.

[²9.—(1) Where the accommodation provided for the claimant is a residential care home or a nursing home which is, in either case, situated in the Greater London area and the actual charge for that accommodation exceeds the appropriate amount in his case by virtue of the preceding paragraphs of this Schedule, the amount shall be increased by any excess up to—

    (a) in the case of a residential care home, £45.00;

    (b) in the case of a nursing home, £50.00.]

(2) In sub-paragraph (1), the "Greater London area" means all those areas specified in Schedule 3.

Circumstances in which the maximum is not to apply

10.—(1) Where a claimant who satisfies the conditions in sub-paragraph (2) has been able to meet the charges referred to in paragraphs 1 and 2 without recourse to a jobseeker's allowance, income support or supplementary benefit, the maximum determined in accordance with paragraph 4 shall not apply for the period of 13 weeks or, if alternative accommodation is found earlier, such lesser period following the date of claim except to the extent that the claimant is able to meet out of income disregarded for the purposes of Part VIII the balance of the actual charge over the maximum.

(2) The conditions for the purposes of sub-paragraph (1) are that—

    (a) the claimant has lived in the same accommodation for more than 12 months; and

    (b) he was able to afford the charges in respect of that accommodation when he took up residence; and

    (c) having regard to the availability of suitable alternative accommodation and to the circumstances mentioned in paragraph 12(5)(b) of Schedule 2 (housing costs), it is reasonable that the maximum should not apply in order to allow him time to find alternative accommodation; and

    (d) he is not a person who is being accommodated—

        (i) by a housing authority under Part III of the Housing Act 1985 (housing the homeless), or

        (ii) by a local authority under section 20 of the Children Act 1989 (provision for accommodation for children: general) or, in Scotland, section 12 of the Social Work (Scotland) Act 1968 (general welfare); and

    (e) he is seeking alternative accommodation and intends to leave his present accommodation once alternative accommodation is found.

(3) Where—

    (a) the claimant was a resident in a residential care home or nursing home immediately before 29th April 1985 and has continued after that date to be resident in the same accommodation, apart from any period of temporary absence; and

    (b) immediately before that date, the actual charge for the claimant's accommodation was being met either wholly or partly out of the claimants resources, or, wholly or partly out of other resources which can no longer be made available for this purpose; and

    (c) since that date the local authority have not at any time accepted responsibility for the making of arrangements for the provision of such accommodation for the claimant; and

    (d) the adjudication officer is satisfied that, unless this provision applies in the claimant's case, he will suffer exceptional hardship, the maximum amount shall be the rate specified in sub-paragraph (4) if that rate exceeds the maximum which, but for this sub-paragraph, would be determined under paragraph 4.

(4) For the purposes of sub-paragraph (3) the rate is either—

(a) the actual weekly charge for the accommodation immediately before 29th April 1985 plus £10; or

(b) the aggregate of the following amounts—

    (i) the amount estimated under regulation 9(6) of the Supplementary Benefit (Requirements) Regulations 1983 as then in force as the reasonable weekly charge for the area immediately before that date;

    (ii) £26.15; and

    (iii) if the claimant was entitled at that date to attendance allowance under [¹section 64] of the Benefits Act at the higher rate £28.60 or, as the case may be, at the lower rate, £19.10,

whichever is the lower amount.

Personal allowances

[²**11.** The allowance for personal expenses for the claimant and each member of his family referred to in paragraph 1(1)(b) shall be—

(a) for the claimant £14.75, and if he has a partner, for his partner, £14.75;

(b) for a young person aged 18, £14.75;

(c) for a young person aged under 18 but over 16, £10.25;

(d) for a child aged under 16 but over 11, £8.85;

(e) for a child aged under 11, £6.05.]

AMENDMENTS

1. Jobseeker's Allowance (Amendment) Regulations 1996 (S.I. 1996 No. 1516), reg. 20 and Sched. (October 7, 1996).
2. Social Security Benefits Up-rating Order 1999 (S.I. 1999 No. 264), art. 24(7) and Sched. 15 (April 12, 1999).

DEFINITIONS

"attendance allowance"—see reg. 1(3).
"the Benefits Act"—see Jobseekers Act, s.35(1).
"benefit week"—see reg. 1(3).
"child"—see Jobseekers Act, s. 35(1).
"claimant"—see reg. 1(3).
"date of claim"—see reg. 1(3).
"disability living allowance"—*ibid.*
"disablement"—see reg. 86(4).
"drug or alcohol dependence"—*ibid.*
"family"—see Jobseekers Act, s. 35(1).
"mental disorder"—see reg. 86(4).
"mental handicap"—*ibid.*
"nursing home"—see reg. 1(3).
"partner"—*ibid.*
"relevant enactment"—*ibid.*
"residential care home"—*ibid.*
"single claimant"—*ibid.*
"temporary absence"—see reg. 86(3).
"young person"—see reg. 76.

GENERAL NOTE

See the notes to Part I of Sched. 4 to the Income Support Regulations. This Schedule is similar to Part I of Sched. 4, except that there are some adjustments in the wording in particular due to the fact that a person is only entitled to jobseeker's allowance if he is below pensionable age.

SCHEDULE 5   **Regulation 85**

APPLICABLE AMOUNTS IN SPECIAL CASES

Column (1)	Column (2)
[[6]**Person other than claimant who is a patient**	
1. Subject to paragraphs [[1]2, 15 and 17], a person who has been a patient for more than 6 weeks and who is— (a) a member of a couple and the other member is the claimant, or (b) a member of a polygamous marriage and the claimant is a member of the marriage but not a patient.	**1.** (a) the applicable amount for a couple under regulation 83 reduced by £13.35; (b) the applicable amount under regulation 84 (polygamous marriages) reduced by £13.35 in respect of each member who is a patient.
2. (a) A claimant who is not a patient and who is a member of a family of which another member is a child or young person who has been a patient for a period of more than 12 weeks; or (b) where the person is a member of a family and paragraph 1 applies to him and another member of the family who is a child or young person has been a patient for a period of more than 12 weeks.	**2.** (a) The amount applicable to him under [[1]regulation 83 or 84] except that the amount applicable under [[1]regulation 83(b) or 84(1)(c)] in respect of the child or young person referred to in Column (1) of this paragraph shall be £13.35 instead of an amount determined in accordance with paragraph 2 of Schedule 1; or (b) the amount applicable to him under paragraph 1 except that the amount applicable under regulation 83(b) or 84(1)(c) in respect of the child or young person referred to in Column (1) of this paragraph shall be £13.35 instead of an amount determined in accordance with paragraph 2 of Schedule 1.]
Claimants Without Accommodation **3.** A claimant who is without accommodation.	**3.** The amount applicable to him under regulation 83(a) (personal allowance) only.
Members of Religious Orders **4.** A claimant who is a member of and fully maintained by a religious order.	**4.** Nil

Specified Cases of Temporarily Separated Couples
5. A claimant who is a member of a couple and who is temporarily separated from his partner, where—
(a) one member of the couple is—
  (i) not a patient but is resident in a nursing home, or
  (ii) resident in a residential care home, or
  (iii) resident in premises used for the rehabilition of alcoholics or drug addicts, or
  (iv) resident in accommodation provided under section 3 of and Part II of the Schedule to, the Polish Resettlement Act 1947 (provision of accommodation in camps),
  (v) or participating in arrangements for training made under section 2 of
	5. Either—
	
	(a) the amount applicable to him as a member of a couple under regulation 83; or

Column (1)	Column (2)
the Employment and Training Act 1973, or section 2 of the Enterprise and New Towns (Scotland) Act 1990 or participating in an employment rehabilitation programme established under that section of the Act of 1973, where the course requires him to live away from the dwelling occupied as the home, or	
(vi) in a probation or bail hostel approved for the purpose by the Secretary of State, and	
(b) the other member of the couple is—	(b) the aggregate of his applicable amount and that of his partner assessed under the provisions of these Regulations as if each of them were a single claimant, or a lone parent.
(i) living in the dwelling occupied as the home, or	
(ii) a patient, or	
(iii) in residential accommodation, or	
(iv) resident in a residential care home or nursing home	whichever is the greater.

Polygamous Marriages where one or more partners are temporarily separated

6. A claimant who is a member of a polygamous marriage and who is temporarily separated from a partner of his, where one of them is living in the home while the other member is—

6. Either—

(a) not a patient but is resident in a nursing home; or

(a) the amount applicable to the members of the polygamous marriage under regulation 84; or

(b) resident in a residential care home; or

(c) resident in premises used for the rehabilitation of alcoholics or drug addicts; or

(b) the aggregate of the amount applicable for the members of the polygamous marriage who remain in the home under regulation 84 and the amount applicable in respect of those members not in the home calculated as if each of them were a single claimant, or a lone parent,

(d) attending a course of training or instruction provided or approved by the Secretary of State where the course requires him to live away from home; or

(e) in a probation or bail hostel approved for the purpose by the Secretary of State.

whichever is the greater.

[⁶Single claimants temporarily in local authority accommodation

7. A single claimant who is temporarily in accommodation provided by a local authority of a kind specified in the definition of residential accommodation in regulation 85 (special cases).

7. £66.75 of which £14.75 is for personal expenses plus any amounts applicable under regulation 83(f) and 87(2) and (3).]

[⁶Couples and members of polygamous marriages where one member is or all are temporarily in local authority accommodation

8.—(1) A claimant who is a member of a couple and temporarily separated from his partner where one of them is living in the home while the other is in accommodation provided by a local authority of a kind specified in the definition of residential accommodation in regulation 85 (special cases).

8.—(1) The aggregate of the amount applicable for the member who remains in the home calculated as if he were a single claimant under regulation 83, 85 or 86 and in respect of the other member £66.75 of which £14.75 is for personal expenses.

Column (1)	Column (2)
(2) A claimant who is a member of a polygamous marriage and who is temporarily separated from a partner of his where one is, or some are, living in the home while one is, or some are, in accommodation referred to in sub-paragraph (1).	(2) The aggregate of the amount applicable, for the members of the polygamous marriage who remain in the home, under regulation 84 and in respect of each member not in the home £66.75 of which £14.75 is for personal expenses.
(3) A claimant who is a member of a couple or a member of a polygamous marriage where both members of that couple or all the members of that marriage are in accommodation referred to in sub-paragraph (1).	(3) For each member of that couple or marriage £66.75 of which £14.75 is for personal expenses plus, if appropriate, the amount applicable under regulation 83(f), [¹84(1)(g)] and 87(2) and (3).
Lone parents who are in residential accommodation temporarily **9.** A claimant who is a lone parent who has entered residential accommodation temporarily.	**9.** £66.75 of which £14.75 is for personal expenses, plus— (a) in respect of each child or young person who is a member of his family, the amount in respect of him prescribed in paragraph 2(a), (b), (c) or (d) of Schedule 1 or under this Schedule as appropriate; and (b) any amount which would be applicable to the claimant if he were not temporarily living away from the dwelling occupied as his home, under [⁴regulation 83(d) or (f)] or under regulation 87(2) or (3).]
Couples where one member is absent from the United Kingdom **10.** Subject to paragraph 11, a claimant who is a member of a couple and whose partner is temporarily absent from the United Kingdom.	**10.** For the first four weeks of that absence, the amount applicable to them as a couple under regulation 83 or 86 as the case may be and thereafter the amount applicable to the claimant in Great Britain under regulation 83 or 86 as the case may be as if the claimant were a single claimant or, as the case may be, a lone parent.
Couple or member of couple taking child or young person abroad for treatment **11.**—(1) A claimant who is a member of a couple where either— (a) he or his partner is, or (b) both he and his partner are absent from [¹United Kingdom] in the circumstances specified in sub-paragraph (2), (2) For the purpose of sub-paragraph (1), the specified circumstances are— (a) the claimant is absent from the United Kingdom but is treated as [⁵available for and actively seeking] employment in accordance with regulations 14(1) and 19(1); (b) the claimant's partner is absent from the United Kingdom and regulation 50(5) would have applied to him if he had claimed a jobseeker's allowance.	**11.** For the first 8 weeks of that absence, the amount applicable to the claimant under regulation 83 or 86, as the case may be, and, thereafter, if the claimant is in Great Britain the amount applicable to him under regulation 83 or 86, as the case may be, as if the claimant were a single claimant, or, as the case may be, a lone parent

Column (1)	Column (2)

Polygamous marriages where any member is abroad
12. Subject to paragraph 13 a claimant who is a member of a polygamous marriage where—
  (a) he or one of his partners is, or
  (b) he and one or more of his partners are, or
  (c) two or more of his partners are, temporarily absent from the United Kingdom.
	12. For the first four weeks of that absence, the amount applicable to the claimant under regulations 84 to 87, as the case may be, and thereafter, if the claimant is in Great Britain the amount applicable to him under regulations 84 to 87, as the case may be, as if any member of the polygamous marriage not in the United Kingdom were not a member of the marriage.

Polygamous marriage: taking child or young person abroad for treatment
13.—(1) A claimant who is a member of a polygamous marriage where—
  (a) he or one of his partners is,
  (b) he and one of his partners are, or
  [¹(c) two or more of his partners are, absent from the United Kingdom in the circumstances specified in sub-paragraph (2).]
 	
  (2) For the purposes of sub-paragraph (1) the specified circumstances are—
  (a) in respect of the claimant,
  [³. . .] he is absent from the United Kingdom but is treated as available for and actively seeking employment in accordance with regulations 14(1) and 19(1); or
  [³(b)] one or more of the members of the polygamous marriage is absent from the United Kingdom and regulation 50(5) would have applied to the absent partner [¹if he had claimed a jobseeker's allowance.]
	13. For the first 8 weeks of that absence, the amount applicable to the claimant under regulations 84 to 87, as the case may be, and thereafter, if the claimant is in Great Britain the amount applicable to him under regulations 84 to 87, as the case may be, as if any member of the polygamous marriage not in the United Kingdom were not a member of the marriage.

Persons from Abroad
14. Except in relation to a person from abroad to whom regulation 147 applies (urgent cases)—
  (a) a person from abroad who is a single claimant or lone parent
  (b) a member of a couple—
    (i) where the claimant is not a person from abroad but his partner is such a person, whether or not regulation 147 applies to that partner;
 	
    (ii) where the claimant is a person from abroad but his partner is not such a person;
    (iii) where the claimant and his partner are both persons from abroad;
  (c) where regulation 84 (polygamous marriages) applies and—
    (i) the claimant is not a person from abroad but one or more but not all of
	14. (a) Nil.
	
	(b)(i) the amount applicable in respect of him only under regulation 83(a) plus in respect of any child or young person who is a member of his family and who is not a person from abroad, any amounts which may be applicable to him under regulation 83(b), (d) or (e) plus the amount applicable to him under regulation 83[¹. . .](f) and 87(2) or (3) or, as the case may be, regulation 85 or 86;
	(ii) nil;
	
	(iii) nil;
	
	(c)(i) the amounts determined in accordance with that regulation or regulation 85 or 86 in respect of the claimant and any partners of his and

Column (1)	Column (2)
his partners are persons from abroad;	any child or young person for whom he or any partner is treated as responsible, who are not persons from abroad;
(ii) the claimant is a person from abroad, whether or not one or more of his partners are persons from abroad;	(ii) nil;
(iii) the claimant and all his partners are persons from abroad;	(iii) nil;
(d) where any amount is applicable to the claimant under regulation 83(e) because of Part III of Schedule 1 because he or his partner satisfies the conditions prescribed therein and he or his partner as the person so satisfying the condition is a person from abroad.	(d) no amount shall be applicable under regulation, [¹83(e)] because of Part III of Schedule 1.
[⁶Persons in residential accommodation	
15.—(1) Subject to sub-paragraph (2), a person in or only temporarily absent from residential accommodation who is—	**15.**—(1) Any amount applicable under regulation 87(2) and (3), plus—
(a) a single claimant;	(a) £66.75 of which £14.75 is for personal expenses;
(b) a lone parent;	(b) the amount specified in sub-paragraph (a) of [¹this] column;
(c) one of a couple;	(c) twice the amount specified in sub-paragraph (a) of this column;
(d) a child or young person;	(d) the appropriate amount in respect of him prescribed in paragraph 2 of Schedule 1 (applicable amounts);
(e) a member of a polygamous marriage.	(e) the amount specified in sub-paragraph (a) of this column multiplied by the number of members of the polygamous marriage in or only temporarily absent from that accommodation.
(2) A single claimant who has become a patient and whose residential accommodation was provided by and managed by a local authority.	(2) Any amount applicable under regulation 87(2) and (3), plus £14.75.]
Persons temporarily absent from a hostel, residential care or nursing home	
16. Where a person is temporarily absent from accommodation for which he is liable to pay a retaining fee, and but for his temporary absence from that accommodation his applicable amount would be calculated in accordance with regulation 86 (applicable amounts for persons in residential care and nursing homes), and	**16.** The amount otherwise applicable to him under these Regulations may be increased to take account of the retaining fee by an amount not exceeding 80 per cent of the applicable amount referred to in paragraph 1(1)(a) of Schedule 4 (applicable amounts of persons in residential care or nursing homes) and any such increase shall not be for a continuous period of more than 52 weeks;
(a) he is a person in accommodation provided by a local authority of a kind specified in the definition of residential accommodation in regulation 85(4) (special cases) and paragraph 15 does not apply to him by reason only that his stay in that accommodation has not become other than temporary; or	
(b) he is a person to whom paragraph 1 or 2 (person other than claimant who is a patient) applies.	

Column (1)	Column (2)
[6**Persons in residential care or nursing homes who become patients** **17.** A claimant to whom regulation 86 (persons in residential care or nursing homes) applies immediately before he or a member of his family became a patient where— (a) he has been a patient for not more than 2 weeks or any member of his family has been a patient for not more than six weeks and the claimant—	17.(a)
(i) continues to be liable to meet the weekly charge for the accommodation without reduction in respect of himself or that member of his family who is a patient;	(i) the amount which would be applicable under regulation 86 as if the claimant or the member of the family who is a patient were resident in the accommodation to which regulation 86 applies;
(ii) continues to be liable to meet the weekly charge for the accommodation but at a reduced rate;	(ii) the amount which would be applicable under regulation 86 having taken into account the reduced charge, as if the claimant or the member of the family who is a patient were resident in the accommodation to which regulation 86 applies;
(iii) is a single claimant who has been a patient for not more than 2 weeks and is likely to return to the accommodation, but has ceased to be liable to meet the weekly charge for that accommodation; or	(iii) the amount applicable to him (if any) under paragraph 2(2) of Schedule 4 (meal allowances) plus the amount in respect of him as an allowance for personal expenses under paragraph 11 of Schedule 4 as if he were residing in the accommodation to which regulation 86 applies plus any amount applicable under regulation 87(3);
(iv) is a single claimant who has been a patient for not more than 2 weeks and who ceases to be liable to meet the weekly charge for the accommodation, and who is unlikely to return to the accommodation;	(iv) the amount which would be applicable to him under regulation 83;
(b) the claimant is one of a couple or polygamous marriage and either— [2(i) the claimant is not a patient and the other member of the couple or one or more members of the marriage has been a patient for a period of more than 6 weeks; or	(b) Where— (i) the members of the family not patients remain in the accommodation, the amount applicable to the family as if regulation 86 having taken into account any reduction in charge, continued to apply to all the members of the family except that in respect of the member of the couple or polygamous marriage who has been a patient for more than six weeks no amount shall be applicable in respect of him under paragraph 2(2) of Schedule 4 and for the amount in respect of the allowance for personal expenses prescribed by paragraph 11 of Schedule 4 there shall be substituted the amount of £16.70;
(ii) the claimant is a patient but has not been a patient for more than 2 weeks and the other member of the couple	(ii) one or more children or young persons are also patients and have been so for more than 12 weeks, in

Column (1)	Column (2)
or one or more members of the marriage has been a patient for more than 6 weeks;]	respect of those children and young persons and the member of the couple ['or polygamous] marriage remaining in the accommodation the amount specified in column (2) of sub-paragraph (b)(i) save that the child or young person who has been a patient for more than 12 weeks shall be disregarded as a member of the family in assessing the amount applicable under regulation 86 and in respect of each such child or young person there shall be added the amount of £13.35;
(c) a child or young person who has been a patient for a period of more than 12 weeks.	(c) the amount applicable under regulation 85 as if that child or young person was not a member of the family plus an amount of £13.35 in respect of that child or young person.]

Rounding of fractions

18. Where any calculation under this Schedule or as a result of a jobseeker's allowance being awarded for a period less than one complete benefit week results in a fraction of a penny that fraction shall be treated as a penny.

AMENDMENTS

1. Jobseeker's Allowance (Amendment) Regulations 1996 (S.I. 1996 No. 1516), reg. 20 and Sched. (October 7, 1996).
2. Jobseeker's Allowance and Income Support (General) (Amendment) Regulations 1996 (S.I. 1996 No. 1517), reg. 30 (October 7, 1996).
3. Social Security and Child Support (Jobseeker's Allowance) (Miscellaneous Amendments) Regulations 1996 (S.I. 1996 No. 2538), reg. 2(13) (October 28, 1996).
4. Child Benefit, Child Support and Social Security (Miscellaneous Amendments) Regulations 1996 (S.I. 1996 No. 1803), reg. 45 (April 7, 1997).
5. Social Security (Miscellaneous Amendments) Regulations 1997 (S.I. 1997 No. 454), reg. 2(15) (April 7, 1997).
6. Social Security Benefits Up-rating Order 1999 (S.I. 1999 No. 264), art. 24(8) and Sched. 16 (April 12, 1999).

DEFINITIONS

"child"—see Jobseekers Act, s. 35(1).
"claimant"—*ibid.*
"couple"—see reg. 1(3).
"family"—see Jobseekers Act, s. 35(1).
"lone parent"—see reg. 1(3).
"nursing home"—*ibid.*
"partner"—*ibid.*
"patient"—see reg. 85(4).
"person from abroad"—*ibid.*
"polygamous marriage"—see reg. 1(3).
"prisoner"—see reg. 85(4).
"relative"—see reg. 1(3).
"residential accommodation"—*ibid.*
"residential care home"—*ibid.*

"single claimant"—*ibid.*
"young person"—see reg. 76.

GENERAL NOTE

See the note to reg. 85.
There are some differences between this Schedule and Sched. 7 to the Income Support Regulations, mainly due to the different conditions of entitlement for JSA (see, for example paras. 1 and 2).

SCHEDULE 6   **Regulations 99(2), 101(2) and 106(6)**

SUMS TO BE DISREGARDED IN THE CALCULATION OF EARNINGS

1. In the case of a claimant who has been engaged in remunerative work as an employed earner or, had the employment been in Great Britain, would have been so engaged—
(a) any earnings paid or due to be paid in respect of that employment which has terminated—
  (i) by way of retirement but only if on retirement he is entitled to a retirement pension under the Benefits Act, or would be so entitled if he satisfied the contribution conditions;
  (ii) otherwise than by retirement except earnings to which [²regulation 98(1)(b), (c), (d), (f)[³, (ff)] and (g)] applies (earnings of employed earners);
(b) where—
  (i) the employment has not been terminated, but
  (ii) the claimant is not engaged in remunerative work,
any earnings in respect of that employment except earnings to which regulation 98(1)(c) and (d) applies; but this sub-paragraph shall not apply where the claimant has been suspended from his employment.

2. In the case of a claimant who, before the date of claim—
(a) has been engaged in part-time employment as an employed earner or, where the employment has been outside Great Britain, would have been so engaged had the employment been in Great Britain, and
(b) has ceased to be engaged in that employment, whether or not that employment has terminated,
any earnings in respect of that employment except earnings to which regulation 98(1)(b), (c), (d), (f)[³, (ff)] or (g) applies; but this paragraph shall not apply where the claimant has been suspended from his employment.

3. Any payment to which regulation 98(1)(f) applies—
(a) which is due to be paid more than 52 weeks after the date of termination of the employment in respect of which the payment is made; or
(b) which is a compensatory award within the meaning of section 72(1)(b) of the Employment Protection (Consolidation) Act 1978 for so long as such an award remains unpaid and the employer is insolvent within the meaning of section 127 of that Act.

4. In the case of a claimant who has been engaged in remunerative work or part-time employment as a self-employed earner or, had the employment been in Great Britain, would have been so engaged and who has ceased to be so employed, from the date of the cessation of his employment any earnings derived from that employment except earnings to which regulation 95(2) (royalties etc.) applies.

5.—(1) In a case to which this paragraph applies, £15; but notwithstanding regulation 88 (calculation of income and capital of members of claimant's family and of a polygamous marriage), if this paragraph applies to a claimant it shall not apply to his partner except where, and to the extent that, the earnings of the claimant which are to be disregarded under this paragraph are less than £15.

816

(2) This paragraph applies where the claimant's applicable amount includes, or but for his being an in-patient or in accommodation in a residential care home or nursing home or in residential accommodation would include, an amount by way of a disability premium under Schedule 1 (applicable amounts).

(3) This paragraph applies where—

(a) the claimant is a member of a couple, and—

    (i) his applicable amount would include an amount by way of the disability premium under Schedule 1 but for the higher pensioner premium under that Schedule being applicable; or

    (ii) had he not been an in-patient or in accommodation in a residential care home or nursing home or in residential accommodation his applicable amount would include the higher pensioner premium under that Schedule and had that been the case he would also satisfy the condition in (i) above; and

(b) he or his partner is under the age of 60 and at least one is engaged in part-time employment.

(4) This paragraph applies where—

(a) the claimant's applicable amount includes, or but for his being an in-patient or in accommodation in a residential care home or nursing home or in residential accommodation would include, an amount by way of the higher pensioner premium under Schedule 1; and

(b) the claimant or, if he is a member of a couple, either he or his partner has attained the age of 60; and

(c) immediately before attaining that age he or, as the case may be, he or his partner was engaged in part-time employment and the claimant was entitled by virtue of sub-paragraph (2) or (3) to a disregard of £15; and

(d) he or, as the case may be, he or his partner has continued in part-time employment.

(5) This paragraph applies where—

(a) the claimant is a member of a couple and—

    (i) his applicable amount would include an amount by way of the disability premium under Schedule 1 but for the pensioner premium where the claimant's partner has attained the age of 75 being applicable under that Schedule; or

    (ii) had he not been an in-patient or in accommodation in a residential care home or nursing home or in residential accommodation his applicable amount would include the pensioner premium where the claimant's partner has attained the age of 75 under that Schedule; and had that been the case he would also satisfy the condition in (i) above; and

(b) the claimant is under the age of 60 and his partner has attained the age of 75 but is under the age of 80 and at least one member of the couple is engaged in part-time employment.

(6) This paragraph applies where—

(a) the claimant is a member of a couple and has attained the age of 60 and his partner has attained the age of 75 but is under the age of 80; and

(b) immediately before the claimant attained the age of 60 either member of the couple was engaged in part-time employment and the claimant was entitled by virtue of sub-paragraph (5) to a disregard of £15; and

(c) either he or his partner has continued in part-time employment.

(7) For the purposes of this paragraph—

(a) except where head (b) or (c) applies, no account shall be taken of any period not exceeding eight consecutive weeks occurring—

    (i) on or after the date on which the claimant or, if he is a member of a couple, he or his partner attained the age of 60 during which either was or both were not engaged in part-time employment or the claimant was not entitled to a jobseeker's allowance or income support; or

    (ii) immediately after the date on which the claimant or his partner ceased to participate in arrangements for training made under section 2 of the Employment and Training Act 1973 or section 2 of the Enterprise and New Towns (Scotland) Act 1990 or to participate in an employment rehabilitation programme established under that section of the 1973 Act;

(b) in a case where the claimant has ceased to be entitled to a jobseeker's allowance or income support because he, or if he is a member of a couple, he or his partner becomes engaged in remunerative work, no account shall be taken of any period, during which he was not entitled to a jobseeker's allowance or income support, not exceeding the permitted period, occurring on or after the date on which the claimant or, as the case may be, his partner attained the age of 60;

(c) no account shall be taken of any period occurring on or after the date on which the claimant or, if he is a member of a couple, he or his partner attained the age of 60 during which the claimant was not entitled to a jobseeker's allowance or income support because he or his partner was participating in arrangements for training made under section 2 of the Employment and Training Act 1973 or section 2 of the Enterprise and New Towns (Scotland) Act 1990 or participating in an employment rehabilitation programme established under that section of the 1973 Act;

[⁵**6.** In a case where the claimant is a lone parent and paragraph 5 does not apply, £15.]

7.—(1) In a case to which neither paragraph 5 or 6 applies to the claimant, and subject to sub-paragraph (2), where the claimant's applicable amount includes an amount by way of the carer premium under Schedule 1 (applicable amounts), £15 of the earnings of the person who is, or at any time in the preceding eight weeks was, in receipt of invalid care allowance or treated in accordance with paragraph 17(2) of that Schedule as being in receipt of invalid care allowance.

(2) Where the carer premium is awarded in respect of the claimant and of any partner of his, their earnings shall for the purposes of this paragraph be aggregated, but the amount to be disregarded in accordance with sub-paragraph (1) shall not exceed £15 of the aggregated amount.

8. Where the carer premium is awarded in respect of a claimant who is a member of a couple and whose earnings are less than £15, but is not awarded in respect of the other member of the couple, and that other member is engaged in an employment—

(a) specified in paragraph 9(1), so much of the other member's earnings as would not when aggregated with the amount disregarded under paragraph 7 exceed £15;

(b) other than one specified in paragraph 9(1), so much of the other member's earnings from such other employment up to £5 as would not when aggregated with the amount disregarded under paragraph 7 exceed £15.

9.—(1) In a case to which none of paragraphs 5 to 8 applies to the claimant, £15 of earnings derived from one or more employments as—

(a) a part-time member of a fire brigade maintained in pursuance of the Fire Services Acts 1947 to 1959;

(b) an auxiliary coastguard in respect of coast rescue activities;

(c) a person engaged part-time in the manning or launching of a lifeboat;

(d) a member of any territorial or reserve force prescribed in Part I of Schedule 3 to the Social Security (Contributions) Regulations 1979;

but, notwithstanding regulation 88 (calculation of income and capital of members of claimant's family and of a polygamous marriage), if this paragraph applies to a claimant it shall not apply to his partner except to the extent specified in sub-paragraph (2).

(2) If the claimant's partner is engaged in employment—

(a) specified in sub-paragraph (1), so much of his earnings as would not in aggregate with the amount of the claimant's earnings disregarded under this paragraph exceed £15;

(b) other than one specified in sub-paragraph (1), so much of his earnings from that employment up to £5 as would not in aggregate with the claimant's earnings disregarded under this paragraph exceed £15.

10. Where the claimant is engaged in one or more employments specified in paragraph

9(1) but his earnings derived from such employments are less than £15 in any week and he is also engaged in any other part-time employment, so much of his earnings from that other employment up to £5 as would not in aggregate with the amount of his earnings disregarded under paragraph 9 exceed £15.

11. Where the claimant is a member of a couple [¹ . . .]—

(a) in a case to which none of paragraphs 5 to 10 applies, £10; but, notwithstanding regulation 88 (calculation of income and capital of members of a claimant's family and of a polygamous marriage), if this paragraph applies to a claimant it shall not apply to his partner except where, and to the extent that, the earnings of the claimant which are to be disregarded under this sub-paragraph are less than £10;

(b) in a case to which one or more of paragraphs 5 to 10 applies and the total amount disregarded under those paragraphs is less than £10, so much of the claimant's earnings as would not in aggregate with the amount disregarded under paragraphs 5 to 10 exceed £10.

12. In a case to which none of paragraphs 5 to 11 applies to the claimant, £5.

13. Notwithstanding the foregoing provisions of this Schedule, where two or more payments of the same kind and from the same source are to be taken into account in the same benefit week, because it has not been practicable to treat the payments under regulation 96(1)(b) (date on which income treated as paid) as paid on the first day of the benefit week in which they were due to be paid, there shall be disregarded from each payment the sum that would have been disregarded if the payment had been taken into account on the date on which it was due to be paid.

14. Any earnings derived from employment which are payable in a country outside the United Kingdom for such period during which there is a prohibition against the transfer to the United Kingdom of those earnings.

15. Where a payment of earnings is made in a currency other than sterling, any banking charge or commission payable in converting that payment into sterling.

16. Any earnings which are due to be paid before the date of claim and which would otherwise fall to be taken into account in the same benefit week as a payment of the same kind and from the same source.

17. Any earnings of a child or young person except earnings to which paragraph 18 applies.

18. In the case of earnings of a child or young person who although not receiving full-time education for the purposes of section 142 of the Benefits Act (meaning of "child") is nonetheless treated for the purposes of these Regulations as receiving relevant education and who is engaged in remunerative work—

(a) if an amount by way of a disabled child premium under Schedule 1 (applicable amounts) is, or but for his accommodation in a residential care home or nursing home would be, included in the calculation of his applicable amount and his earning capacity is not, by reason of his disability, less than 75 per cent. of that which he would, but for that disability, normally be expected to earn, £15;

(b) in any other case, £5.

19. In the case of a claimant who—

(a) has been engaged in employment as a member of any territorial or reserve force prescribed in Part I of Schedule 3 to the Social Security (Contributions) Regulations 1979; and

(b) by reason of that employment has failed to satisfy any of the conditions of entitlement to a jobseeker's allowance, other than the condition in section 2(1)(c) (prescribed amount of earnings) or section 3(1)(a) (income not in excess of applicable amount),

any earnings from that employment paid in respect of the period in which the claimant was not entitled to a jobseeker's allowance.

20. In this Schedule "part-time employment" means employment in which the person is not to be treated as engaged in remunerative work under regulation 52 or 53 (persons treated as engaged, or not engaged, in remunerative work).

21. In paragraph 5(7)(b) "permitted period" means a period determined in accordance with regulation 3A of the Income Support Regulations, as it has effect by virtue of regulation 87(7) of these Regulations.

AMENDMENTS

1. Jobseeker's Allowance (Amendment) Regulations 1996 (S.I. 1996 No. 1516), reg. 19 (October 7, 1996).
2. Jobseeker's Allowance (Amendment) Regulations 1996 (S.I. 1996 No. 1516), reg. 20 and Sched. (October 7, 1996).
3. Jobseeker's Allowance and Income Support (General) (Amendment) Regulations 1996 (S.I. 1996 No. 1517), reg. 31 (October 7, 1996).
4. Child Benefit, Child Support and Social Security (Miscellaneous Amendments) Regulations 1996 (S.I. 1996 No. 1803), reg. 46 (April 7, 1997).
5. Social Security Amendment (Lone Parents) Regulations 1998 (S.I. 1998 No. 766), reg. 15 (April 6, 1998).

DEFINITIONS

"the Benefits Act"—see Jobseekers Act, s.35(1).
"benefit week"—see reg. 1(3)
"child"—see Jobseekers Act, s. 35(1)
"claimant"—*ibid.*, reg. 88(1).
"couple"—see reg. 1(3).
"date of claim"—*ibid.*
"employment"—see reg.3
"employed earner"—see reg. 3, SSCBA, s. 2(1)(a).
"Great Britain"—see Jobseekers Act, s. 35(1).
"family"—*ibid.*
"nursing home"—see reg. 1(3).
"partner"—*ibid.*
"polygamous marriage"—*ibid.*
"remunerative work"—*ibid*, reg. 51(1).
"residential accommodation"—see reg. 1(3).
"residential care home"—*ibid.*
"self employed earner"—*ibid.*, SSCSA, s. 2(1)(b).
"young person"—*ibid.*, reg. 76

GENERAL NOTE

Paras. 1 to 16 and 19 apply to adults. Paras. 17 and 18 apply to children and young persons. Paras. 1 to 13 and 19 do not apply to children or young persons (reg. 88(2)).

The disregards in this Schedule are similar to those in Schedule 8 to the Income Support Regulations but there are some differences which are referred to below. See the notes to Sched. 8.

Note that where the claimant is a member of a couple, unless the £15 disregard in paras. 5 to 10 applies (para. 6 cannot in fact apply as it only applies to lone parents) the earnings disregard is £10 (para. 11). Since October 7, 1996 this has also been the case for income support (replacing the previous £15 earnings disregard for long-term unemployed couples aged less than 60). For a single claimant the earnings disregard is £5 (unless the £15 disregard in paras. 5 to 10 applies) (para. 12).

There are some differences in the wording of para. 5 due to the fact that for a person to be entitled to JSA he must be under pensionable age (s. 1(2)(h) of the Jobseekers Act). But the main difference from the income support provisions is the treatment of earnings where part-time employment has stopped (para. 2) and the new disregard in para. 3.

Paragraph 1

As with income support the disregard in para. 1 is crucial to entitlement following the termination of remunerative work. The effect of sub-para. (a)(ii) is that final payments of wages are disregarded. This means that entitlement can begin immediately, unless a compensation payment is made (reg. 98(1)(b)) or holiday pay (reg. 98(1)(c)) is due. If either of these payments are made, reg. 52(3) treats the claimant as in remunerative work for the number of weeks covered by the payments (reg. 94(2) and (6) to (9)). Note the other earnings that are not disregarded under sub-para. (a)(ii) and see the notes to para. 1 of Sched 8.

Paragraph 2

See the notes to para. 2 of Sched. 8 to the Income Support Regulations. Under JSA the disregard is not more extensive where the claimant's part-time work (see para. 20) has stopped before the claim. The same disregard applies as in the case of termination of full-time employment under para. 1(a)(ii) (but in the case of part-time work it is not necessary for the employment to have ended). Para. 2 does not apply if the claimant has been suspended. If the part-time work ends while the claimant is claiming JSA, payments will be taken into account as earnings in the usual way.

Paragraph 3

Under JSA, any payment for compensation for unfair dismissal under ss. 68(2), 69, 71(2)(a), 77 or 79 of the Employment Protection (Consolidation) Act 1978 (the references need to be updated to the Employment Rights Act 1996) is disregarded if it is due to be paid more than 52 weeks after the end of the employment to which it relates (sub-para. (a)). In addition, any unpaid compensatory award under s. 72(1)(b) of the 1978 Act where the employer is insolvent is also disregarded (sub-para. (b)).

SCHEDULE 7 **Regulation 103(2)**

SUMS TO BE DISREGARDED IN THE CALCULATION OF INCOME OTHER THAN EARNINGS

1. Any amount paid by way of tax on income which is taken into account under regulation 103 (calculation of income other than earnings).

2. Any payment in respect of any expenses incurred by a claimant who is—

(a) engaged by a charitable or voluntary organisation; or

(b) a volunteer,

if he otherwise derives no remuneration or profit from the employment and is not to be treated as possessing any earnings under regulation 105(13) (notional income).

3. In the case of employment as an employed earner, any payment in respect of expenses wholly, exclusively and necessarily incurred in the performance of the duties of the employment.

4. In the case of a payment of statutory sick pay or statutory maternity pay or any remuneration paid by or on behalf of an employer to the claimant who for the time being is unable to work due to illness or maternity—

(a) any amount deducted by way of primary Class 1 contributions under the Benefits Act;

(b) one-half of any sum paid by the claimant by way of a contribution towards an occupational or personal pension scheme.

5. In the case of the payment of statutory sick pay or statutory maternity pay under Parts XI or XII of the Social Security Contributions and Benefits (Northern Ireland) Act 1992—

(a) any amount deducted by way of primary Class 1 contributions under that Act;

(b) one-half of any sum paid by way of a contribution towards an occupational or personal pension scheme.

6. Any housing benefit.

7. The mobility component of disability living allowance, or any mobility allowance accrued under the repealed section 37A of the Social Security Act 1975.

8. Any concessionary payment made to compensate for the non-payment of—

(a) any payment specified in paragraph 7 or 10;

(b) a jobseeker's allowance or income support.

9. Any mobility supplement or any payment intended to compensate for the non-payment of such a supplement.

10. Any attendance allowance or the care component of disability living allowance, but, where the claimant's applicable amount falls to be calculated in accordance with Schedule 4, only to the extent that it exceeds the amount for the time being specified as the higher rate of attendance allowance for the purposes of section 64(3) of the Benefits

Act or, as the case may be, the highest rate of the care component of disability living allowance for the purposes of section 72(4)(a) of that Act.

11. Any payment to the claimant as holder of the Victoria Cross or George Cross or any analogous payment.

12. Any sum in respect of a course of study attended by a child or young person payable by virtue of regulations made under section 81 of the Education Act 1944 (assistance by means of scholarships and otherwise), or by virtue of section 2(1) of the Education Act 1962 (awards for courses of further education) or section 49 of the Education (Scotland) Act 1980 (power to assist persons to take advantage of educational facilities) [⁵or section 12(2)(c) of the Further and Higher Education (Scotland) Act 1992 (provision of financial assistance to students)].

13. In the case of a claimant to whom regulation 11 (part-time students) applies, any sums intended for any expenditure specified in paragraph (2) of regulation 131 (calculation of grant income) necessary as a result of his attendance on his course.

14. In the case of a claimant participating in arrangements for training made under section 2 of the Employment and Training Act 1973 or section 2 of the Enterprise and New Towns (Scotland) Act 1990, or in an employment rehabilitation programme established under that section of the 1973 Act—

(a) any travelling expenses reimbursed to the claimant;

(b) any living away from home allowance under section 2(2)(d) of the 1973 Act or section 2(4)(c) of the 1990 Act but only to the extent that rent payable in respect of accommodation not normally occupied by him as his home is not met by housing benefit;

(c) any training premium,

[⁶(d) any child care expenses reimbursed to the claimant in respect of his participation in an employment programme specified in regulation 75(1)(a)(ii) or in a training scheme specified in regulation 75(1)(b)(ii),]

but this paragraph, except in so far as it relates to a payment under sub-paragraph (a), [⁶(b), (c) or (d)], does not apply to any part of any allowance under section 2(2)(d) of the 1973 Act or section 2(4)(c) of the 1990 Act.

15.—(1) Subject to sub-paragraph (3) and paragraphs 38, 39 and 41, £20 of any charitable payment or of any voluntary payment made or due to be made at regular intervals, except any payment to which sub-paragraph (2) or paragraph 16 applies.

(2) Subject to sub-paragraphs (3) and (6) and paragraph 41, any charitable payment or voluntary payment made or due to be made at regular intervals which is intended and used for an item other than food, ordinary clothing or footwear, household fuel, rent for which housing benefit is payable, any housing costs to the extent that they are met under regulation 83(f) or 84(1)(g) (housing costs) or any accommodation charges to the extent that they are met under regulation 86 (persons in residential care or nursing homes), of a single claimant or, as the case may be, of the claimant or any other member of his family, or is used for any council tax or water charges for which that claimant or member is liable.

(3) Sub-paragraphs (1) and (2) shall not apply—

(a) to a payment which is made by a person for the maintenance of any member of his family or of his former partner or of his children;

(b) to a payment made—

(i) to a person who is, or would be, prevented from being entitled to a jobseeker's allowance by section 14 (trade disputes); or

(ii) to a member of the family of such a person where the payment is made by virtue of that person's involvement in the trade dispute.

(4) For the purposes of sub-paragraph (1) where a number of charitable or voluntary payments fall to be taken into account in any one week they shall be treated as though they were one such payment.

(5) For the purposes of sub-paragraph (2) the expression "ordinary clothing or footwear" means clothing or footwear for normal daily use, but does not include school uniforms, or clothing or footwear used solely for sporting activities.

(6) Sub-paragraph (2) shall apply to a claimant in a residential care home or nursing home only if his applicable amount falls to be calculated in accordance with regulation 86.

16.—(1) Subject to the following provisions of this paragraph, in the case of a claimant placed in a residential care home or nursing home by a local authority under section 26 of the National Assistance Act 1948, sections 13A, 13B and 59(2)(c) of the Social Work (Scotland) Act 1968 or section 7 of the Mental Health (Scotland) Act 1984 any charitable payment or voluntary payment made or due to be made at regular intervals.

(2) This paragraph shall apply only where—
- (a) the claimant was placed in the residential care or nursing home by the local authority because the home was the preferred choice of the claimant, and
- (b) the cost of the accommodation was in excess of what the authority would normally expect to pay having regard to the needs of the claimant assessed in accordance with section 47 of the National Health Service and Community Care Act 1990.

(3) This paragraph shall not apply in the case of a person whose applicable amounts falls to be calculated under regulation 86 (persons in residential care or nursing homes with preserved rights).

(4) The amount to be disregarded under sub-paragraph (1) shall not exceed the difference between the actual cost of the accommodation provided by the local authority and the cost the authority would normally incur for a person with the particular needs of the claimant.

[²**16A.**—(1) Subject to sub-paragraphs (2) and (3), where a claimant—
- (a) is a person to whom Schedule 4 (applicable amounts of persons in residential care and nursing homes) or paragraph 16 or 17 of Schedule 5 (applicable amounts in special cases) applies;
- (b) is not residing with his spouse; and
- (c) has at least 50 per cent. of any occupational pension of his[³, or of any income from a personal pension scheme of his,] being paid to, or in respect of, his spouse for that spouse's maintenance,

an amount equal to 50 per cent. of the pension[³, pensions or income] concerned.

[³(2) Where a claimant is entitled to pensions or income referred to in sub-paragraph (1) from more than one source, all such pensions and income to which he is entitled shall be aggregated for the purposes of that sub-paragraph.]

(3) This paragraph shall not have effect in respect of that part of any [³pension or income referred to in sub-paragraph (1)] to which a spouse is legally entitled whether under a court order or not.]

17. Subject to paragraphs 38 and 39, £10 of any of the following, namely—
- (a) a war disablement pension or war widow's pension or a payment made to compensate for the non-payment of such a pension, except in so far as such a pension or payment falls to be disregarded under paragraphs 9 or 10;
- (b) a pension paid by the government of a country outside Great Britain which is either—
    - (i) analogous to a war disablement pension; or
    - (ii) analogous to a war widow's pension;
- (c) a pension paid under any special provision made by the law of the Federal Republic of Germany or any part of it or of the Republic of Austria, to victims of National Socialist persecution.

18. Where a claimant receives income under an annuity purchased with a loan which satisfies the following conditions—
- (a) that the loan was made as part of a scheme under which not less than 90 per cent. of the proceeds of the loan were applied to the purchase by the person to whom it was made of an annuity ending with his life or with the life of the survivor of two or more persons (in this paragraph referred to as "the annuitants") who include the person to whom the loan was made;
- (b) that the interest on the loan is payable by the person to whom it was made or by one of the annuitants;

(c) that at the time the loan was made the person to whom it was made or each of the annuitants had attained the age of 65;

(d) that the loan was secured on a dwelling in Great Britain and the person to whom the loan was made or one of the annuitants owns an estate or interest in that dwelling; and

(e) that the person to whom the loan was made or one of the annuitants occupies the accommodation on which it was secured as his home at the time the interest is paid,

the amount, calculated on a weekly basis equal to—

(i) where, or in so far as, section 369 of the Income and Corporation Taxes Act 1988 (mortgage interest payable under deduction of tax) applies to the payments of interest on the loan, the interest which is payable after deduction of a sum equal to income tax on such payments at the applicable percentage of income tax within the meaning of section 369(1A) of that Act;

(ii) in any other case the interest which is payable on the loan without deduction of such a sum.

19. Any payment made to the claimant by a person who normally resides with the claimant, which is a contribution towards that person's living and accommodation costs, except where that person is residing with the claimant in circumstances to which paragraph 20 or 21 refers.

20. Where the claimant occupies a dwelling as his home and the dwelling is also occupied by another person and there is a contractual liability to make payments to the claimant in respect of the occupation of the dwelling by that person or a member of his family—

(a) £4 of the aggregate of any payments made in respect of any one week in respect of the occupation of the dwelling by that person or a member of his family, or by that person and a member of his family; and

(b) a further £9.25, where the aggregate of any such payments is inclusive of an amount for heating.

21. Where the claimant occupies a dwelling as his home and he provides in that dwelling board and lodging accommodation, an amount, in respect of each person for whom such accommodation is provided for the whole or any part of a week, equal to—

(a) where the aggregate of any payments made in respect of any one week in respect of such accommodation provided to such person does not exceed £20, 100% of such payments; or

(b) where the aggregate of any such payments exceeds £20, £20 and 50% of the excess over £20.

22.—(1) Subject to sub-paragraph (2), except where regulation 105(10)(a)(i) (notional income) applies or in the case of a payment made—

(a) to a person who is, or would be, prevented from being entitled to a jobseeker's allowance by section 14 (trade disputes); or

(b) to a member of the family of such a person where the payment is made by virtue of that person's involvement in the trade dispute,

any income in kind.

(2) The exceptions under sub-paragraph (1) shall not apply where the income in kind is received from the Macfarlane Trust, the Macfarlane (Special Payments) Trust, the Macfarlane (Special Payments) (No.2) Trust, the Fund, the Eileen Trust or the Independent Living Funds.

23.—(1) Any income derived from capital to which the claimant is, or is treated under regulation 115 (capital jointly held) as, beneficially entitled but, subject to sub-paragraph (2), not income [¹ derived] from capital disregarded under paragraph 1, 2, 4 to 8, 11 or 17 of Schedule 8.

(2) Income derived from capital disregarded under paragraph 2 or 4 to 8 of Schedule 8 but only to the extent of—

(a) any mortgage repayments made in respect of the dwelling or premises in the period during which that income accrued; or

(b) any council tax or water charges which the claimant is liable to pay in respect of the dwelling or premises and which are paid in the period during which that income accrued.

(3) The definition of "water charges" in regulation 1(3) shall apply to sub-paragraph (2) with the omission of the words "in so far as such charges are in respect of the dwelling which a person occupies as his home".

24. Any income which is payable in a country outside the United Kingdom for such period during which there is prohibition against the transfer to the United Kingdom of that income.

25. Where a payment of income is made in a currency other than sterling, any banking charge or commission payable in converting that payment into sterling.

26.—(1) Any payment made to the claimant in respect of a child or young person who is a member of his family—

(a) in accordance with regulations made pursuant to section 57A of the Adoption Act 1976 (permitted allowances) or with a scheme approved by the Secretary of State under section 51 of the Adoption (Scotland) Act 1978 (schemes for payment of allowances to adopters);

(b) which is a payment made by a local authority in pursuance of section 50 of the Children Act 1975 (contributions to a custodian towards the cost of the accommodation and maintenance of a child);

(c) which is a payment made by a local authority in pursuance of section 15(1) of, and paragraph 15 of Schedule 1 to, the Children Act 1989 (local authority contribution to a child's maintenance where the child is living with a person as a result of a residence order);

[⁷(d) which is a payment made by an authority, as defined in Article 2 of the Children Order, in pursuance of Article 15 of, and paragraph 17 of Schedule 1 to, that Order (contribution by an authority to child's maintenance);]

to the extent specified in sub-paragraph (2).

(2) In the case of a child or young person—

(a) to whom regulation 106(5) (capital in excess of £3,000) applies, the whole payment;

(b) to whom that regulation does not apply, so much of the weekly amount of the payment as exceeds the applicable amount in respect of that child or young person and where applicable to him any amount by way of a disabled child premium.

27. Any payment made by a local authority to the claimant with whom a person is accommodated by virtue of arrangements made under section 23(2)(a) of the Children Act 1989 (provision of accommodation and maintenance for a child whom they are looking after) or, as the case may be, section 21 of the Social Work (Scotland) Act 1968 or by a voluntary organisation under section 59(1)(a) of the 1989 Act (provision of accommodation by voluntary organisations) or by a care authority under regulation 9 of the Boarding Out and Fostering of Children (Scotland) Regulations 1985 (provision of accommodation and maintenance for children in care).

28. [⁸Any payment made to the claimant or his partner for a person ("the person concerned"), who is not normally a member of the claimant's household but is temporarily in his care, by—

(a) a health authority;

(b) a local authority;

(c) a voluntary organisation; or

(d) the person concerned pursuant to section 26(3A) of the National Assistance Act 1948.]

29. Except in the case of a person who is, or would be, prevented from being entitled to a jobseeker's allowance by section 14 (trade disputes), any payment made by a local authority in accordance with section 17 or 24 of the Children Act 1989 or, as the case may be, section 12, 24 or 26 of the Social Work (Scotland) Act 1968 (local authorities' duty to promote welfare of children and powers to grant financial assistance to persons in, or formerly in, their care).

30.—(1) Subject to sub-paragraph (2), any payment received under an insurance policy, taken out to insure against the risk of being unable to maintain repayments on a loan which qualifies under paragraph 14 or 15 of Schedule 2 (housing costs in respect of loans to acquire an interest in the dwelling, or for repairs and improvements to the dwelling, occupied as the home) and used to meet such repayments, to the extent that it does not exceed the aggregate of—

   (a) the amount, calculated on a weekly basis, of any interest on that loan which is in excess of the amount met in accordance with Schedule 2 (housing costs);

   (b) the amount of any payment, calculated on a weekly basis, due on the loan attributable to the repayment of capital; and

   (c) any amount due by way of premiums on—

      (i) that policy, or

      (ii) an insurance policy taken out to insure against loss or damage to any building or part of a building which is occupied by the claimant as his home.

(2) This paragraph shall not apply to any payment which is treated as possessed by the claimant by virtue of regulation 105(10)(a)(ii) (notional income).

31.—(1) Except where paragraph 30 [¹⁰or 31A] applies, and subject to sub-paragraph (2), any payment made to the claimant which is intended to be used and is used as a contribution towards—

   (a) any payment due on a loan if secured on the dwelling occupied as the home which does not qualify under Schedule 2 (housing costs);

   (b) any interest payment or charge which qualifies in accordance with paragraphs 14 to 16 of Schedule 2 to the extent that the payment or charge is not met;

   (c) any payment due on a loan which qualifies under paragraph 14 or 15 of Schedule 2 attributable to the payment of capital;

   (d) any amount due by way of premiums on—

      (i) an insurance policy taken out to insure against the risk of being unable to make the payments referred to in (a) to (c) above, or

      (ii) an insurance policy taken out to insure against loss or damage to any building or part of a building which is occupied by the claimant as his home;

   (e) his rent in respect of the dwelling occupied by him as his home but only to the extent that it is not met by housing benefit; or his accommodation charge but only to the extent that the actual charge increased, where appropriate, in accordance with paragraph 2 of Schedule 4 exceeds the amount determined in accordance with regulation 86 (residential care and nursing homes) or the amount payable by a local authority in accordance with Part III of the National Assistance Act 1948.

(2) This paragraph shall not apply to any payment which is treated as possessed by the claimant by virtue of regulation 105(10)(a)(ii) (notional income).

[¹⁰**31A.**—(1) Subject to sub-paragraph (2), any payment received under an insurance policy, other than an insurance policy referred to in paragraph 30, taken out to insure against the risk of being unable to maintain repayments under a regulated agreement as defined for the purposes of the Consumer Credit Act 1974 or under a hire-purchase agreement or a conditional sale agreement as defined for the purposes of Part III of the Hire-Purchase Act 1964.

(2) A payment referred to in sub-paragraph (1) shall only be disregarded to the extent that the payment received under that policy does not exceed the amounts, calculated on a weekly basis, which are used to—

   (a) maintain the repayment referred to in sub-paragraph (1); and

   (b) meet any amount due by way of premiums on that policy.]

32.—(1) Subject to sub-paragraphs (2) and (3), in the case of a claimant in a residential care home or nursing home, any payment, whether or not the payment is charitable or voluntary but not a payment to which paragraph 16 applies, made to the claimant which is intended to be used and is used to meet the cost of maintaining the claimant in that home.

(2) This paragraph shall not apply to a claimant for whom accommodation in a residential care home or nursing home is provided by a local authority under section 26 of the

National Assistance Act 1948 or section 59 of the Social Work (Scotland) Act 1968, or whose applicable amount falls to be calculated in accordance with regulation 86.

(3) The amount to be disregarded under this paragraph shall not exceed the difference between—

(a) the claimant's applicable amount less any of the amounts referred to in paragraph 11 of Schedule 4 (personal allowances) which would be applicable to the claimant if his applicable amount fell to be calculated in accordance with that Schedule, and

(b) the weekly charge for the accommodation.

33. Any social fund payment made pursuant to Part VIII of the Benefits Act.

34. Any payment of income which under regulation 110 (income treated as capital) is to be treated as capital.

35. Any payment under Part X of the Benefits Act (pensioner's Christmas bonus).

36. In the case of a person who is, or would be, prevented from being entitled to a jobseeker's allowance by section 14 (trade disputes), any payment up to the amount of the prescribed sum within the meaning of section 15(2)(d) made by a trade union.

37. Any payment which is due to be paid before the date of claim which would otherwise fall to be taken into account in the same benefit week as a payment of the same kind and from the same source.

38. The total of a claimant's income or, if he is a member of a family, the family's income and the income of any person which he is treated as possessing under regulation 88(4) (calculation of income and capital of members of claimant's family and of a polygamous marriage) to be disregarded under regulations 132(2)(b) and 133(1)(c) (calculation of covenant income where a contribution assessed), regulation 136(2) (treatment of student loans) and paragraphs 15(1) and 17 shall in no case exceed £20 per [⁴benefit week].

39. Notwithstanding paragraph 38, where two or more payments of the same kind and from the same source are to be taken into account in the same benefit week, there shall be disregarded from each payment the sum which would otherwise fall to be disregarded under this Schedule; but this paragraph shall only apply in the case of a payment which it has not been practicable to treat under regulation 96(1)(b) (date on which income treated as paid) as paid on the first day of the benefit week in which it is due to be paid.

40. Any resettlement benefit which is paid to the claimant by virtue of regulation 3 of the Social Security (Hospital In-Patients) Amendment (No.2) Regulations 1987.

41.—(1) Any payment made under the Macfarlane Trust, the Macfarlane (Special Payments) Trust, the Macfarlane (Special Payments) (No.2) Trust, the Fund, the Eileen Trust ("the Trusts") or the Independent Living Funds.

(2) Any payment by or on behalf of a person who is suffering or who suffered from haemophilia or who is or was a qualifying person, which derives from a payment made under any of the Trusts to which sub-paragraph (1) refers and which is made to or for the benefit of—

(a) that person's partner or former partner from whom he is not, or where that person has died was not, estranged or divorced;

(b) any child or young person who is a member of that person's family or who was such a member and who is a member of the claimant's family.

(3) Any payment by or on behalf of the partner or former partner of a person who is suffering or who suffered from haemophilia or who is or was a qualifying person, provided that the partner or former partner and that person are not, or if either of them has died were not, estranged or divorced, which derives from a payment made under any of the Trusts to which sub-paragraph (1) refers and which is made to or for the benefit of—

(a) the person who is suffering from haemophilia or who is a qualifying person;

(b) any child or young person who is a member of that person's family or who was such a member and who is a member of the claimant's family.

(4) Any payment by a person who is suffering from haemophilia or who is a qualifying person, which derives from the payment under any of the Trusts to which sub-paragraph (1) refers, where

(a) that person has no partner or former partner from whom he is not estranged or divorced, nor any child or young person who is or had been a member of that person's family; and

(b) the payment is made either—

    (i) to that person's parent or step-parent, or

    (ii) where that person at the date of the payment is a child, a young person or a student who has not completed his full-time education, and had no parent or step-parent, to his guardian,

but only for a period from the date of the payment until the end of two years from that person's death.

(5) Any payment out of the estate of a person who suffered from haemophilia or who was a qualifying person, which derives from a payment under any of the Trusts to which sub-paragraph (1) refers, where—

(a) that person at the date of his death (the relevant date) had no partner or former partner from whom he was not estranged or divorced, nor any child or young person who was or had been a member of his family; and

(b) the payment is made either—

    (i) to that person's parent or step-parent, or

    (ii) where that person at the relevant date was a child, a young person or a student who had not completed his full-time education, and had no parent or step-parent, to his guardian,

but only for a period of two years from the relevant date.

(6) In the case of a person to whom or for whose benefit a payment referred to in this paragraph is made, any income which derives from any payment of income or capital made under or deriving from any of the Trusts.

42. Any payment made by the Secretary of State to compensate for the loss (in whole or in part) of entitlement to housing benefit.

43. Any payment made to a juror or a witness in respect of attendance at a court other than compensation for loss of earnings or for the loss of a benefit payable under the Act or the Benefits Act.

44. Any community charge benefit.

45. Any payment in consequence of a reduction of a personal community charge pursuant to regulations under section 13A of the Local Government Finance Act 1988 or section 9A of the Abolition of Domestic Rates Etc. (Scotland) Act 1987 (reduction of liability for personal community charges) or reduction of council tax under section 13 or, as the case may be, section 80 of the Local Government Finance Act 1992 (reduction of liability for council tax).

46. Any special war widows payment made under—

(a) the Naval and Marine Pay and Pensions (Special War Widows Payment) Order 1990 made under section 3 of the Naval and Marine Pay and Pensions Act 1865;

(b) the Royal Warrant dated 19th February 1990 amending the Schedule to the Army Pensions Warrant 1977;

(c) the Queen's Order dated 26th February 1990 made under section 2 of the Air Force (Constitution) Act 1917;

(d) the Home Guard War Widows Special Payments Regulations 1990 made under section 151 of the Reserve Forces Act 1980;

(e) the Orders dated 19th February 1990 amending Orders made on 12th December 1980 concerning the Ulster Defence Regiment, made in each case under section 140 of the Reserve Forces Act 1980;

and any analogous payment made by the Secretary of State for Defence to any person who is not a person entitled under the provisions mentioned in sub-paragraphs (a) to (e) of this paragraph.

47.—(1) Any payment or repayment made—

(a) as respects England and Wales, under regulation 3, 5 or 8 of the National Health Service (Travelling Expenses and Remission of Charges) Regulations 1988 (travelling expenses and health service supplies);

(b) as respects Scotland, under regulation 3, 5 or 8 of the National Health Service (Travelling Expenses and Remission of Charges) (Scotland) Regulations 1988 (travelling expenses and health service supplies).

(2) Any payment or repayment made by the Secretary of State for Health, the Secretary of State for Scotland or the Secretary of State for Wales which is analogous to a payment or repayment mentioned in sub-paragraph (1).

48. Any payment made under regulation 9 to 11 or 13 of the Welfare Food Regulations 1988 (payments made in place of milk tokens or the supply of vitamins).

49. Any payment made either by the Secretary of State for the Home Department or by the Secretary of State for Scotland under a scheme established to assist relatives and other persons to visit persons in custody.

50. Any payment (other than a training allowance) made, whether by the Secretary of State or by any other person, under the Disabled Persons (Employment) Act 1944 or in accordance with arrangements made under section 2 of the Employment and Training Act 1973, to assist disabled persons to obtain or retain employment despite their disability.

51. Any council tax benefit.

52. Where the claimant is in receipt of any benefit under Parts II, III or V of the Benefits Act, any increase in the rate of that benefit arising under Part IV (increases for dependants) or section 106(a) (unemployability supplement) of that Act where the dependant in respect of whom the increase is paid is not a member of the claimant's family.

53. Any supplementary pension under article 29(1A) of the Naval, Military and Air Forces etc. (Disablement and Death) Service Pensions Order 1983 (pensions to widows).

54. In the case of a pension awarded at the supplementary rate under article 27(3) of the Personal Injuries (Civilians) Scheme 1983 (pensions to widows), the sum specified in paragraph 1(c) of Schedule 4 to that Scheme.

55.—(1) Any payment which is—

(a) made under any of the Dispensing Instruments to a widow of a person—
  (i) whose death was attributable to service in a capacity analogous to service as a member of the armed forces of the Crown; and
  (ii) whose service in such capacity terminated before 31st March 1973; and
(b) equal to the amount specified in article 29(1A) of the Naval, Military and Air Forces etc. (Disablement and Death) Service Pensions Order 1983 (pensions to widows).

(2) In this paragraph "the Dispensing Instruments" means the Order in Council of 19th December 1881, the Royal Warrant of 27th October 1884 and the Order by His Majesty of 14th January 1922 (exceptional grants of pay, non-effective pay and allowances).

[³**56.** Any payment made under the Community Care (Direct Payments) Act 1996 or under section 12B of the Social Work (Scotland) Act 1968.

57.—(1) Subject to paragraph 58, any Career Development Loan paid to the claimant pursuant to section 2 of the Employment and Training Act 1973 except to the extent that the loan has been applied for and paid in respect of living expenses for the period of education and training supported by that loan and those expenses relate to any one or more of the items specified in sub-paragraph (2).

(2) The items specified for the purposes of sub-paragraph (1) are food, ordinary clothing or footwear, household fuel, rent for which housing benefit is payable, or any housing costs to the extent that they are met under regulation 83(f) or 84(1)(g) (housing costs) or any accommodation charges to the extent that they are met under regulation 86 (persons in residential care or nursing homes), of the claimant or, where the claimant is a member of a family, any other member of his family, or any council tax or water charges for which that claimant or member is liable.

(3) For the purposes of this paragraph, "ordinary clothing and footwear" means clothing or footwear for normal daily use, but does not include school uniforms, or clothing and footwear used solely for sporting activities.

58. Any Career Development Loan paid to the claimant pursuant to section 2 of the

Employment and Training Act 1973 where the period of education and training supported by that loan has been completed.

59.—(1) Any payment specified in sub-paragraph (2) to a claimant who was formerly a full-time student and who has completed the course in respect of which those payments were made.

(2) The payments specified for the purposes of sub-paragraph (1) are—

(a) any grant income and covenant income as defined for the purposes of Chapter IX of Part VIII;

(b) any loan made pursuant to arrangements made under section 1 of the Education (Student Loans) Act 1990 or article 3 of the Education (Student Loans) (Northern Ireland) Order 1990.]

[¹¹**60.** Any mandatory top-up payment made to a person pursuant to section 2 of the Employment and Training Act 1973 in respect of that person's participation in an employment programme specified in—

(a) regulation 75(1)(a)(ii)(aa)(ii) (self-employment route of the Employment Option of the New Deal);

(b) regulation 75(1)(a)(ii)(bb) (Voluntary Sector Option of the New Deal); or

(c) regulation 75(1)(a)(ii)(cc) (Environment Task Force Option of the New Deal).]

[⁶**61.** Any discretionary payment to meet, or to help to meet, special needs, made to a person pursuant to section 2 of the Employment and Training Act 1973 in respect of that person's participation in the Full-Time Education and Training Option of the New Deal as specified in regulation 75(1)(b)(ii).]

[¹²**62.**—(1) Subject to sub-paragraph (2), in the case of a person who is receiving, or who has received, assistance under an employment programme specified in regulation 75(1)(a)(ii)(aa)(ii) (self-employment route of the Employment Option of the New Deal), any payment to that person—

(a) to meet expenses wholly and necessarily incurred whilst carrying on the commercial activity;

(b) which is used or intended to be used to maintain repayments on a loan taken out by that person for the purpose of establishing or carrying on the commercial activity,

in respect of which such assistance is or was received.

(2) Sub-paragraph (1) shall apply only in respect of payments which are paid to that person from the special account as defined for the purposes of Chapter IVA of Part VIII.]

[¹³**63.**—(1) Subject to sub-paragraph (2), any discretionary payment made pursuant to section 2 of the Employment and Training Act 1973 to meet, or help meet, special needs of a person who is undertaking a qualifying course within the meaning specified in regulation 17A(7).

(2) No amount shall be disregarded pursuant to sub-paragraph (1) in respect of travel expenses incurred as a result of the student's attendance on the course where an amount in respect of those expenses has already been disregarded pursuant to regulation 135(1) (student's income to be disregarded).]

[¹⁴**64.** Any payment which falls to be treated as notional income made under paragraph (11) of regulation 105 above (payments made in respect of a person in a residential care or nursing home).]

AMENDMENTS

1. Jobseeker's Allowance (Amendment) Regulations 1996 (S.I. 1996 No. 1516), reg. 20 and Sched. (October 7, 1996).

2. Jobseeker's Allowance and Income Support (General) (Amendment) Regulations 1996 (S.I. 1996 No. 1517), reg. 32 (October 7, 1996).

3. Income-related Benefits and Jobseeker's Allowance (Miscellaneous Amendments) Regulations 1997 (S.I. 1997 No. 65), reg. 2(4) (April 7, 1997).

4. Social Security (Miscellaneous Amendments) Regulations 1997 (S.I. 1997 No. 454), reg. 2(16) (April 7, 1997).

5. Income-related Benefits and Jobseeker's Allowance (Amendment) (No. 2) Regulations 1997 (S.I. 1997 No. 2197), reg. 7(7) and (8)(f) (October 6, 1997).

6. Social Security Amendment (New Deal) Regulations 1997 (S.I. 1997 No. 2863), reg. 14 (January 5, 1998).

7. Social Security (Miscellaneous Amendments) Regulations 1998 (S.I. 1998 No. 563), reg. 7(1) and (2)(e) (April 6, 1998).

8. Social Security (Miscellaneous Amendments) Regulations 1998 (S.I. 1998 No. 563), reg. 7(3) and (4)(f) (April 6, 1998).

9. Social Security (Miscellaneous Amendments) Regulations 1998 (S.I. 1998 No. 563), reg. 13(2) (April 6, 1998).

10. Social Security (Miscellaneous Amendments) (No. 3) Regulations 1998 (S.I. 1998 No. 1173), reg. 5 (June 1, 1998).

11. Social Security (Miscellaneous Amendments) (No. 4) Regulations 1998 (S.I. 1998 No. 1174), reg. 4(a) (June 1, 1998).

12. Social Security (Miscellaneous Amendments) (No. 4) Regulations 1998 (S.I. 1998 No. 1174), reg. 4(b) (June 1, 1998).

13. Social Security Amendment (New Deal) (No. 2) Regulations 1998 (S.I. 1998 No. 2117), reg. 4(1) (September 24, 1998).

14. Social Security Amendment (New Deal) (No. 2) Regulations 1998 (S.I. 1998 No. 2117), reg. 6(1) (September 24, 1998).

DEFINITIONS

"attendance allowance"—see reg. 1(3).
"the Benefits Act"—see Jobseekers Act, s. 35(1).
"benefit week"—see reg. 1(3).
"board and lodging accommodation"—*ibid.*
"child"—see Jobseekers Act, s. 35(1).
"the Children Order"—see reg. 1(3).
"claimant"—see Jobseekers Act, s.35(1), reg. 88(1).
"concessionary payment"—see reg. 1(3).
"course of study"—*ibid.*
"disability living allowance"—*ibid.*
"dwelling occupied as the home"—*ibid.*
"employed earner"—see reg. 3, SSCBA, s. 2(1)(a).
"family"—see Jobseekers Act, s. 35(1).
"mobility supplement"—see reg. 1(3).
"nursing home"—*ibid.*
"occupational pension scheme"—see Jobseekers Act, s. 35(1).
"partner"—see reg. 1(3).
"payment"—*ibid.*
"personal pension scheme"—see Jobseekers Act, s. 35(1).
"qualifying person"—see reg. 1(3).
"residential care home"—*ibid.*
"the Eileen Trust"—*ibid.*
"the Fund"—*ibid.*
"the Independent Living Funds"—*ibid.*
"the Macfarlane (Special Payments) Trust"—*ibid.*
"the Macfarlane (Special Payments) (No. 2) Trust"—*ibid.*
"the Macfarlane Trust"—*ibid.*
"training allowance"—*ibid.*
"voluntary organisation"—*ibid.*
"war disablement pension"—*ibid.*
"war widow's pension"—*ibid.*
"young person"—see reg. 76.

GENERAL NOTE

The disregards in Sched. 7 are the same as those in Sched. 9 to the Income Support Regulations (with minor adjustments in the wording). See the notes to Sched. 9. The only paragraphs in Sched. 9 that have not been reproduced in Sched. 7 are paras. 41 and 42 which related to compensation payments made as a consequence of the 1988 benefit changes and so are not relevant. In addition, there is no equivalent to para. 57 of Sched. 9 (backdated payments under reg. 21ZA of the Income Support Regulations), but the disregard in para. 12 of Sched. 8 should apply to such payments.

Note para. 60 under which the grant of £400 (spread over six months) that is paid to a person who is getting a training allowance rather than a wage when taking part in either the Voluntary Sector or the Environment Task Force options of the New Deal, or who is on the self-employment route of the Employment Option, is disregarded. Similarly any discretionary payments to a participant on the Full-Time Education and Training option to cover exceptional costs are ignored (para. 61), as are payments for childcare costs to a person taking part in any New Deal option (para. 14(d)). These disregards are necessary so that the person's entitlement to benefit is not affected. For a brief summary of the New Deal for 18–24 year-olds see the notes to reg. 75. On para. 62, see the note to reg. 102C. Para. 63 disregards any discretionary payments to cover special needs made to a claimant aged 25 or over who is treated as available for employment under reg. 17A while attending a full-time employment-related course. Para. 64 is in fact the previous para. 63 re-numbered.

SCHEDULE 8   **Regulation 108(2)**

CAPITAL TO BE DISREGARDED

1. The dwelling occupied as the home but, notwithstanding regulation 88, (calculation of income and capital of members of claimant's family and of a polygamous marriage), only one dwelling shall be disregarded under this paragraph.

2. Any premises acquired for occupation by the claimant which he intends to occupy as his home within 26 weeks of the date of acquisition or such longer period as is reasonable in the circumstances to enable the claimant to obtain possession and commence occupation of the premises.

3. Any sum directly attributable to the proceeds of sale of any premises formerly occupied by the claimant as his home which is to be used for the purchase of other premises intended for such occupation within 26 weeks of the date of sale, or such longer period as is reasonable in the circumstances to enable the claimant to complete the purchase.

4. Any premises occupied in whole or in part by—
(a) a partner or relative of a single claimant or of any member of the family as his home where that person is aged 60 or over or is incapacitated;
(b) the former partner of a claimant as his home; but this provision shall not apply where the former partner is a person from whom the claimant is estranged or divorced.

5. Where a claimant has ceased to occupy what was formerly the dwelling occupied as the home following his estrangement or divorce from his former partner, that dwelling for a period of 26 weeks from the date on which he ceased to occupy that dwelling.

6. Any premises where the claimant is taking reasonable steps to dispose of those premises, for a period of 26 weeks from the date on which he first took such steps, or such longer period as is reasonable in the circumstances to enable him to dispose of those premises.

7. Any premises which the claimant intends to occupy as his home, and in respect of which he is taking steps to obtain possession and has sought legal advice or has commenced legal proceedings with a view to obtaining possession, for a period of 26 weeks from the date on which he first sought such advice or first commenced such proceedings, whichever is earlier, or such longer period as is reasonable in the circumstances to enable him to obtain possession and commence occupation of those premises.

8. Any premises which the claimant intends to occupy as his home to which essential repairs or alterations are required in order to render them fit for such occupation, for a period of 26 weeks from the date on which the claimant first takes steps to effect those repairs or alterations, or such longer period as is reasonable in the circumstances to enable those repairs or alterations to be carried out and the claimant to commence occupation of the premises.

9. Any grant made to the claimant in accordance with a scheme made under section

129 of the Housing Act 1988 or section 66 of the Housing (Scotland) Act 1988 (schemes for payments to assist local housing authority and local authority tenants to obtain other accommodation) which is to be used—

    (a) to purchase premises intended for occupation as his home; or

    (b) to carry out repairs or alterations which are required to render premises fit for occupation as his home,

for a period of 26 weeks from the date on which he received such a grant or such longer period as is reasonable in the circumstances to enable the purchase, repairs or alterations to be completed and the claimant to commence occupation of those premises as his home.

10. Any future interest in property of any kind, other than land or premises in respect of which the claimant has granted a subsisting lease or tenancy, including sub-leases or sub-tenancies.

11.—(1) The assets of any business owned in whole or in part by the claimant and for the purposes of which he is engaged as a self-employed earner or, if he has ceased to be so engaged, for such period as may be reasonable in the circumstances to allow for disposal of any such asset.

(2) The assets of any business owned in whole or in part by the claimant where—

    (a) he is not engaged as a self-employed earner in that business by reason of some disease or bodily or mental disablement; but

    (b) he intends to become engaged (or, as the case may be, re-engaged) as a self-employed earner in that business as soon as he recovers or is able to become engaged or re-engaged in that business,

for a period of 26 weeks from the date on which the claim for a jobseeker's allowance is made, or is treated as made, or if it is unreasonable to expect him to become engaged or re-engaged in that business within that period, for such longer period as is reasonable in the circumstances to enable him to become so engaged or re-engaged.

[⁴(3) In the case of a person who is receiving assistance under an employment programme specified in regulation 75(1)(a)(ii)(aa)(ii) (self-employment route of the Employment Option of the New Deal), the assets acquired by that person for the purpose of establishing or carrying on the commercial activity in respect of which such assistance is being received.

(4) In the case of a person who has ceased carrying on the commercial activity in respect of which assistance was received as specified in sub-paragraph (3), the assets relating to that activity for such period as may be reasonable in the circumstances to allow for disposal of any such asset.]

12. Any arrears of, or any concessionary payment made to compensate for arrears due to the non-payment of—

    (a) any payment specified in paragraph 7, 9 or 10 of Schedule 7 (other income to be disregarded);

    (b) a jobseeker's allowance or an income-related benefit under Part VII of the Benefits Act;

[¹(c) any allowance paid by the Secretary of State under the Earnings Top-up Scheme,] but only for a period of 52 weeks from the date of receipt of the arrears or the concessionary payment.

13. Any sum—

    (a) paid to the claimant in consequence of damage to, or loss of, the home or any personal possession and intended for its repair or replacement; or

    (b) acquired by the claimant (whether as a loan or otherwise) on the express condition that it is to be used for effecting essential repairs or improvements to the home,

and which is to be used for the intended purpose, for a period of 26 weeks from the date on which it was so paid or acquired or such longer period as is reasonable in the circumstances to enable the claimant to effect the repairs, replacement or improvements.

14. Any sum—

    (a) deposited with a housing association as defined in section 1(1) of the Housing Associations Act 1985 as a condition of occupying the home;

    (b) which was so deposited and which is to be used for the purchase of another home, for the period of 26 weeks or such longer period as is reasonable in the circumstances to complete the purchase.

15. Any personal possessions except those which have or had been acquired by the claimant with the intention of reducing his capital in order to secure entitlement to a jobseeker's allowance or to income support or to increase the amount of those benefits.

16. The value of the right to receive any income under an annuity and the surrender value (if any) of such an annuity.

17. Where the funds of a trust are derived from a payment made in consequence of any personal injury to the claimant, the value of the trust fund and the value of the right to receive any payment under that trust.

18. The value of the right to receive any income under a life interest or from a liferent.

19. The value of the right to receive any income which is disregarded under paragraph 14 of Schedule 6 or paragraph 24 of Schedule 7 (earnings or other income payable in a country outside the United Kingdom).

20. The surrender value of any policy of life insurance.

21. Where any payment of capital falls to be made by instalments, the value of the right to receive any outstanding instalments.

22. Except in the case of a person who is, or would be prevented from being entitled to a jobseeker's allowance by section 14 (trade disputes), any payment made by a local authority in accordance with section 17 or 24 of the Children Act 1989 or, as the case may be, section 12, 24 or 26 of the Social Work (Scotland) Act 1968 (local authorities' duty to promote welfare of children and powers to grant financial assistance to persons in, or formerly in, their care).

23. Any social fund payment made pursuant to Part VIII of the Benefits Act.

24. Any refund of tax which falls to be deducted under section 369 of the Income and Corporation Taxes Act 1988 (deductions of tax from certain loan interest) on a payment of relevant loan interest for the purpose of acquiring an interest in the home or carrying out repairs or improvements in the home.

25. Any capital which under regulation 104, 106(1) or 136 (capital treated as income, modifications in respect of children and young persons and treatment of student loans) is to be treated as income.

26. Where a payment of capital is made in a currency other than sterling, any banking charge or commission payable in converting that payment into sterling.

27.—(1) Any payment made under the Macfarlane Trust, the Macfarlane (Special Payments) Trust, the Macfarlane (Special Payments) (No. 2) Trust, the Fund, the Eileen Trust ("the Trusts") or the Independent Living Funds.

(2) Any payment by or on behalf of a person who is suffering or who suffered from haemophilia or who is or was a qualifying person, which derives from a payment made under any of the Trusts to which sub-paragraph (1) refers and which is made to or for the benefit of—

    (a) that person's partner or former partner from whom he is not, or where that person had died was not, estranged or divorced;

    (b) any child or young person who is a member of that person's family or who was such a member and who is a member of the claimant's family.

(3) Any payment by or on behalf of the partner or former partner of a person who is suffering or who suffered from haemophilia or who is or was a qualifying person, provided that the partner or former partner and that person are not, or if either of them has died were not, estranged or divorced, which derives from a payment made under any of the Trusts to which sub-paragraph (1) refers and which is made to or for the benefit of

    (a) the person who is suffering from haemophilia or who is a qualifying person;

    (b) any child or young person who is a member of that person's family or who was such a member and who is a member of the claimant's family.

(4) Any payment by a person who is suffering from haemophilia or who is a qualifying person, which derives from a payment made under any of the Trusts to which sub-paragraph (1) refers, where—

    (a) that person has no partner or former partner from whom he is not estranged or divorced, nor any child or young person who is or had been a member of that person's family; and

(b) the payment is made either—

    (i) to that person's parent or step-parent, or

    (ii) where that person at the date of payment is a child, a young person or a student who has not completed his full-time education, and has no parent or step-parent, to his guardian,

but only for a period from the date of the payment until the end of two years from that person's death.

(5) Any payment out of the estate of a person who suffered from haemophilia or who was a qualifying person, which derives from a payment made under any of the Trusts to which sub-paragraph (1) refers, where—

(a) that person at the date of his death (the relevant date) had no partner or former partner from whom he was not estranged or divorced, nor any child or young person who was or had been a member of his family; and

(b) the payment is made either—

    (i) to that person's parent or step-parent, or

    (ii) where that person at the relevant date was a child, a young person or a student who had not completed his full-time education, and had no parent or step-parent, to his guardian,

but only for a period of two years from the relevant date.

(6) In the case of a person to whom or for whose benefit a payment referred to in this paragraph is made, any capital resource which derives from any payment of income or capital made under or deriving from any of the Trusts.

28. The value of the right to receive an occupational or personal pension.

29. The value of any funds held under a personal pension scheme.

30. The value of the right to receive any rent except where the claimant has a reversionary interest in the property in respect of which rent is due.

31. Any payment in kind made by a charity or under the Macfarlane Trust, the Macfarlane (Special Payments) Trust, the Macfarlane (Special Payments) (No. 2) Trust, the Fund, the Eileen Trust or the Independent Living Funds.

32. £200 of any payment or, if the payment is less than £200, the whole of any payment made under section 2 of the Employment and Training Act 1973 or section 2 of the Enterprise and New Towns (Scotland) Act 1990, as a training bonus to a person participating in arrangements for training.

33. Any payment made by the Secretary of State to compensate for the loss (in whole or in part) of entitlement to housing benefit.

34. Any payment made to a juror or a witness in respect of attendance at a court other than compensation for loss of earnings or for the loss of a benefit payable under the Act or under the Benefits Act.

35. Any payment in consequence of a reduction of a personal community charge pursuant to regulations under section 13A of the Local Government Finance Act 1988 or section 9A of the Abolition of Domestic Rates Etc. (Scotland) Act 1987 (reduction of liability for personal community charge) or reduction of council tax under section 13 or, as the case may be, section 80 of the Local Government Finance Act 1992 (reduction of liability for council tax), but only for a period of 52 weeks from the date of the receipt of the payment.

36.—(1) Any payment or repayment made—

(a) as respects England and Wales, under regulations 3, 5 or 8 of the National Health Service (Travelling Expenses and Remission of Charges) Regulations 1988 (travelling expenses and health service supplies);

(b) as respects Scotland, under regulation 3, 5 or 8 of the National Health Service (Travelling Expenses and Remission of Charges) (Scotland) Regulations 1988 (travelling expenses and health service supplies),

but only for a period of 52 weeks from the date of receipt of the payment or repayment.

(2) Any payment or repayment made by the Secretary of State for Health, the Secretary

of State for Scotland or the Secretary of State for Wales which is analogous to a payment or repayment mentioned in sub-paragraph (1); but only for a period of 52 weeks from the date of receipt of the payment or repayment.

37. Any payment made under regulation 9 to 11 or 13 of the Welfare Food Regulations 1988 (payments made in place of milk tokens or the supply of vitamins), but only for a period of 52 weeks from the date of receipt of the payment.

38. Any payment made either by the Secretary of State for the Home Department or by the Secretary of State for Scotland under a scheme established to assist relatives and other persons to visit persons in custody, but only for a period of 52 weeks from the date of receipt of the payment.

39. Any arrears of special war widows payment which is disregarded under paragraph 46 of Schedule 7 (sums to be disregarded in the calculation of income other than earnings) or of any amount which is disregarded under paragraph 53, 54 or 55 of that Schedule, but only for a period of 52 weeks from the date of receipt of the arrears.

40. Any payment (other than a training allowance, or a training bonus under section 2 of the Employment and Training Act 1973) made, whether by the Secretary of State or by any other person, under the Disabled Persons (Employment) Act 1944 or in accordance with arrangements made under section 2 of the Employment and Training Act 1973, to assist disabled persons to obtain or retain employment despite their disability.

41. Any payment made by a local authority under section 3 of the Disabled Persons (Employment) Act 1958 to homeworkers assisted under the Blind Homeworkers Scheme.

42. Any sum of capital administered on behalf of a person [². . .] by the High Court under the provisions of Order 80 of the Rules of the Supreme Court, the County Court under Order 10 of the County Court Rules 1981, or the Court of Protection where such sum derives from—

    (a) an award of damages for a personal injury to that person; or

    (b) compensation for the death of one or both parents [²where the person concerned is under the age of 18].

43. Any sum of capital administered on behalf of a person [². . .] in accordance with an order made under Rule 43.15 of the Act of Sederunt (Rules of the Court of Session 1994) 1994 or under Rule 131 of the Act of Sederunt (Rules of the Court, consolidation and amendment) 1965, or under Rule 36.14 of the Ordinary Cause Rules 1993 or under Rule 128 of the Ordinary Cause Rules, where such sum derives from—

    (a) an award of damages for a personal injury to that person; or

    (b) compensation for the death of one or both parents [²where the person concerned is under the age of 18].

44. Any payment to the claimant as holder of the Victoria Cross or George Cross.

[⁵**45.** Any mandatory top-up payment made to a person pursuant to section 2 of the Employment and Training Act 1973 in respect of that person's participation in an employment programme specified in—

    (a) regulation 75(1)(a)(ii)(aa)(ii) (self-employment route of the Employment Option of the New Deal);

    (b) regulation 75(1)(a)(ii)(bb) (Voluntary Sector Option of the New Deal); or

    (c) regulation 75(1)(a)(ii)(cc) (Enviromental Task Force Option of the New Deal), but only for a period of 52 weeks from the date of receipt of the payment.]

[³**46.** Any discretionary payment to meet, or to help to meet, special needs made to a person pursuant to section 2 of the Employment and Training Act 1973 in respect of that person's participation in the Full-Time Education and Training Option of the New Deal as specified in regulation 75(1)(b)(ii) but only for a period of 52 weeks from the date of receipt of the payment.]

[⁶**47.** In the case of a person who is receiving, or who has received, assistance under an employment programme specified in regulation 75(1)(a)(ii)(aa)(ii) (self-employment route of the Employment Option of the New Deal), any sum of capital which is acquired by that person for the purpose of establishing or carrying on the commercial activity in respect of which such assistance is or was received but only for a period of 52 weeks from the date on which that sum was acquired.]

[⁷**48.** Any discretionary payment made pursuant to section 2 of the Employment and Training Act 1973 to meet, or help meet, special needs of a person who is undertaking a qualifying course within the meaning specified in regulation 17A(7) but only for the period of 52 weeks from the date of receipt of that payment.]

AMENDMENTS

1. Social Security and Child Support (Jobseeker's Allowance) (Miscellaneous Amendments) Regulations 1996 (S.I. 1996 No. 2538), reg. 2(14) (October 28, 1996).
2. Income-related Benefits and Jobseeker's Allowance (Amendment) (No. 2) Regulations 1997 (S.I. 1997 No. 2197), reg. 7(9) and (10)(f) (October 6, 1997).
3. Social Security Amendment (New Deal) Regulations 1997 (S.I. 1997 No. 2863), reg. 15 (January 5, 1998).
4. Social Security (Miscellaneous Amendments) (No. 4) Regulations 1998 (S.I. 1998 No. 1174), reg. 5(a) (June 1, 1998).
5. Social Security (Miscellaneous Amendments) (No. 4) Regulations 1998 (S.I. 1998 No. 1174), reg. 5(b) (June 1, 1998).
6. Social Security (Miscellaneous Amendments) (No. 4) Regulations 1998 (S.I. 1998 No. 1174), reg. 5(c) (June 1, 1998).
7. Social Security Amendment (New Deal) (No. 2) Regulations 1998 (S.I. 1998 No. 2117), reg. 5(1) (September 24, 1998).

DEFINITIONS

"the Benefits Act"—see Jobseekers Act, s. 35(1).
"child"—*ibid.*
"claimant"—*ibid.*, reg. 88(1).
"concessionary payment"—see reg. 1(3).
"dwelling occupied as the home"—*ibid.*
"the Eileen Trust"—*ibid.*
"the Earnings Top-up Scheme"—*ibid.*
"family"—see Jobseekers Act, s. 35(1).
"the Fund"—see reg. 1(3).
"the Independent Living Funds"—*ibid.*
"the Macfarlane (Special Payments) Trust"—*ibid.*
"the Macfarlane (Special Payments) (No. 2) Trust"—*ibid.*
"the Macfarlane Trust"—*ibid.*
"occupational pension"—*ibid.*
"partner"—*ibid.*
"payment"—*ibid.*
"personal pension scheme"—see Jobseekers Act, s. 35(1).
"policy of life insurance"—see reg. 1(3).
"qualifying person"—*ibid.*
"relative"—*ibid.*
"self-employed earner"—*ibid.*, SSCBA, s. 2(1))b).
"training allowance"—see reg. 1(3).
"young person"—see reg. 76.

GENERAL NOTE

The disregards in Sched. 8 are the same as those in Sched. 10 to the Income Support Regulations (subject to some reordering and minor adjustments in the wording). See the notes to Sched. 10.
Paras. 32 and 33 of Sched. 10 have not been reproduced in Sched. 8 as they are no longer relevant. There is also no equivalent of paras 47 to 49 of Sched. 10, but see para. 12 of this Schedule.
Note that in para. 15 the disregard of the value of personal possessions does not apply if they have been acquired in order to reduce capital so as to gain jobseeker's allowance *or income support.* This avoids the question that might otherwise have arisen on a claimant transfering from income support to jobseeker's allowance whether if the acquisition had only been for the purposes of income support the disregard in para. 15 applies.
On paras 45, 46 and 48 see the note to paras 60, 61 and 63 of Sched. 7. But note that if these payments count as capital the disregard only applies for 52 weeks from the date of receipt. On paras. 11(3) and (4) and 47, see the note to reg. 102C.

Jobseeker's Allowance (Transitional Provisions) Regulations 1996

(S.I. 1996 No. 2567)

Made by the Secretary of State under ss. 35(1), 36(2) to (5) and 40 of the Jobseekers Act 1995

GENERAL NOTE

These regulations replaced the Jobseeker's Allowance (Transitional Provisions) Regulations 1995 (S.I. 1995 No. 3276) with effect from November 4, 1996. See the 1996 Supplement to this book for the 1995 Regulations.

Citation, commencement and interpretation

1.—(1) These Regulations may be cited as the Jobseeker's Allowance (Transitional Provisions) Regulations 1996 and shall come into force on 4th November 1996.

(2) In these Regulations—

"the Act" means the Jobseekers Act 1995;

"benefit week"—

(a) where the benefit is income support, has the meaning it has in the Income Support Regulations by virtue of regulation 2(1) of those Regulations;

(b) where the benefit is unemployment benefit, means a period of 7 days ending on the day corresponding to the particular day specified in a written notice last given him by the Secretary of State for the purpose of claiming unemployment benefit;

(c) where the benefit is a jobseeker's allowance, has the same meaning it has in the Jobseeker's Allowance Regulations by virtue of regulation 1(3) of those Regulations;

"Claims and Payments Regulations" means the Social Security (Claims and Payments) Regulations 1987;

"day of unemployment" means a day which would, for the purposes of section

25A of the Benefits Act as in force on 6th October 1996, be treated as a
day of unemployment;

"the Income Support Regulations" means the Income Support (General) Regulations 1987;

"the Jobseeker's Allowance Regulations" means the Jobseeker's Allowance
Regulations 1996;

"jobseeking period" has the meaning specified in regulation 2;

"period of interruption of employment" in relation to unemployment benefit
has the same meaning in these Regulations as it had in the Benefits
Act by virtue of section 25A of that Act as in force on 6th October
1996;

"the relevant day" means—

    (a) in relation to income support, 6th October 1996; and

    (b) in relation to unemployment benefit—

        (i) except in a case to which head (ii) applies, 5th October 1996; or

        (ii) where in any particular case 6th October 1996 is a day of unem-
ployment, that day;

"training" means training for which a training allowance is payable;

"training allowance" means an allowance (whether by way of periodical grants
or otherwise) payable—

    (a) out of public funds by a Government department or by or on behalf
of the Secretary of State for Education and Employment, Scottish
Enterprise or Highlands and Islands Enterprise; and

    (b) to a person for his maintenance or in respect of a member of his
family; and

    (c) for the period, or part of the period, during which he is following a
course of training or instruction provided by, or in pursuance of
arrangements made with, that department or approved by or on
behalf of the Secretary of State for Education and Employment,
Scottish Enterprise or Highlands and Islands Enterprise,

but it does not include an allowance paid by any Government department
to or in respect of a person by reason of the fact that he is following a
course of full-time education, other than under arrangements made under
section 2 of the Employment and Training Act 1973, or section 2 of
the Enterprise and New Towns (Scotland) Act 1990 or is training as a
teacher;

"transitionally protected period" means the period specified in regulation 10;

"the Unemployment Benefit Regulations" means the Social Security
(Unemployment, Sickness and Invalidity Benefit) Regulations 1983.

(3) In these Regulations, unless the context otherwise requires a reference—

(a) to a numbered section is to the section of the Act bearing that number;

(b) to a numbered regulation is to the regulation in these Regulations bearing
that number;

(c) in a regulation to a numbered paragraph is to the paragraph in that regulation bearing that number;

(d) in a paragraph to a lettered or numbered sub-paragraph is to the sub-
paragraph in that paragraph bearing that letter or number.

(4) For the avoidance of doubt, a person complies with any requirement or
provision of these Regulations if he is treated as complying with that requirement or provision.

Jobseeking period

2.—(1) For the purposes of these Regulations, but subject to the following
provisions of this regulation, the "jobseeking period" means any period

throughout which the claimant satisfies or is treated as satisfying the conditions specified in paragraphs (a) to (c) and (e) to (i) of subsection (2) of section 1 (conditions of entitlement to a jobseeker's allowance).

(2) Any period in which—

(a) a claimant does not satisfy any of the requirements in section 1(2)(a) to (c); and

(b) a jobseeker's allowance is payable to him on the grounds that the adjudication officer is satisfied that unless a jobseeker's allowance is paid to the claimant he or a member of his family will suffer hardship,

shall, for the purposes of paragraph (1), be treated as a period in which the claimant satisfies the conditions specified in paragraphs (a) to (c) of subsection (2) of section 1.

(3) Any period in which a claimant is entitled to a jobseeker's allowance in accordance with regulation 13(3) shall, for the purposes of paragraph (1), be treated as a period in which the claimant satisfies the conditions specified in paragraphs (a) to (c) and (e) to (i) of subsection (2) of section 1.

(4) The following periods shall not be, or be part of, a jobseeking period—

(a) any period in respect of which no claim for a jobseeker's allowance has been made or treated as made;

(b) such period as falls before the day on which a claim for a jobseeker's allowance is made or is treated as made or, where good cause is shown for a claim outside the prescribed time for claiming, before the earliest date in respect of which good cause is shown;

(c) where a claim for a jobseeker's allowance has been made or treated as made but no entitlement to benefit arises in respect of a period before the date of claim by virtue of section 1(2) of the Administration Act (limits for backdating entitlement), that period;

(d) where—

(i) a claimant satisfies the conditions specified in paragraphs (a) to (c) and (e) to (i) of subsection (2) of section 1; and

(ii) entitlement to a jobseeker's allowance ceases on the ground that the claimant failed to comply with requirements imposed by regulations made under section 8(1) (attendance, information and evidence),

the period beginning with the date in respect of which, in accordance with any such regulations, entitlement ceases and ending with the day before the date in respect of which the claimant again becomes entitled to a jobseeker's allowance; or

(e) any week in which a claimant is not entitled to a jobseeker's allowance in accordance with section 14 (trade disputes).

Linking periods

3.—(1) For the purposes of these Regulations, two or more jobseeking periods shall be treated as one jobseeking period where they are separated by a period comprising only—

(a) any period of not more than 12 weeks;

(b) a linked period;

(c) any period of not more than 12 weeks falling between—

(i) any two linked periods; or

(ii) a jobseeking period and a linked period;

(d) a period in respect of which the claimant is summoned to jury service and is required to attend court.

(2) Linked periods for the purposes of these Regulations are any of the following periods—

(a) to the extent specified in ['paragraph (5)], any period throughout which the claimant is entitled to an invalid care allowance under section 70 of the Benefits Act;

(b) any period throughout which the claimant is incapable of work, or is treated as incapable of work, in accordance with Part XIIA of the Benefits Act;

(c) any period throughout which the claimant was entitled to a maternity allowance under section 35 of the Benefits Act;

(d) any period throughout which the claimant was engaged in training;

(e) a period which includes 6th October 1996 during which the claimant attends court in response to a summons for jury service and which was immediately preceded by a period of entitlement to unemployment benefit.

(3) For the purpose of paragraph (4) a day of unemployment shall form part of a period of interruption of employment if a jobseeking period begins within 6 days of that day.

(4) Any period of interruption of employment which ends within 8 weeks of the commencement of a jobseeking period as described in regulation 2(1) shall be treated, for the purposes of this regulation, as a jobseeking period.

(5) A period of entitlement to an invalid care allowance shall be a linked period only where it enables the claimant to satisfy contribution conditions for entitlement to a contribution-based jobseeker's allowance which he would otherwise be unable to satisfy.

AMENDMENT

1. Social Security (Miscellaneous Amendments) Regulations 1997 (S.I. 1997 No. 454), reg. 4(2) (March 21, 1997).

Termination and cancellation of awards of income support

4.—(1) An award of income support current in the benefit week which includes the relevant day ("the current benefit week") shall terminate immediately before the beginning of the benefit week which follows the current benefit week—

(a) where—
  (i) the person entitled was required to satisfy the provisions of section 124(1)(d)(i) of the Benefits Act (available for and actively seeking employment) as in force on the relevant day; and
  (ii) but for any provision of the Act and these Regulations, the award would have continued beyond the current benefit week; or

(b) where the person—
  (i) is not required, in accordance with regulation 8 of, and Schedule 1 to, the Income Support Regulations to be available for employment; and
  (ii) is not a person to whom regulation 8 of the Claims and Payments Regulations (attendance in person) applies; and
  (iii) does in fact make himself available for and actively seek employment and declares himself to be so.

(2) An award of income support to a person commencing on a date after the current benefit week, shall be cancelled where the person's entitlement was dependent upon his satisfying the requirements of section 124(1)(d)(i) of the Benefits Act (available for and actively seeking employment) as in force on the relevant day.

Transition from unemployment benefit to a jobseeker's allowance

5.—(1) Paragraph (2) shall apply in the case of a person to whom unemployment benefit was payable in respect of the relevant day.

(2) In a case where, in accordance with a notice issued to him under regulation 19 of, and paragraph 1 of Schedule 5 to, the Claims and Payments Regulations, a person claims unemployment benefit—

(a) on or after 7th October 1996 but before 13th October 1996 and in consequence of that claim unemployment benefit is awarded, that award shall have effect as—

(i) an award of unemployment benefit until the end of the benefit week that includes the relevant day; and

(ii) thereafter as an award of a jobseeker's allowance until such date as the claimant fails to satisfy, or in respect of which he ceases to be treated as satisfying, any condition of entitlement to a jobseeker's allowance that applies in his case;

(b) on a day falling on or after 14th October 1996 but before 20th October 1996 and in consequence of that claim unemployment benefit is awarded, that award shall have effect as—

(i) an award of unemployment benefit for the first benefit week falling within the period of the claim; and

(ii) thereafter as an award of a jobseeker's allowance until such date as the claimant fails to satisfy, or in respect of which he ceases to be treated as satisfying, any condition of entitlement to a jobseeker's allowance which applies in his case.

(3) An award of unemployment benefit—

(a) made in accordance with regulation 17(2)(b) of the Claims and Payments Regulations; or

(b) which is made on or after 7th October 1996 for a period commencing before 7th October 1996,

and which extends beyond the benefit week which includes the relevant day shall terminate at the end of that benefit week.

(4) In the case of a person to whom paragraph (2) or (3) applies, his entitlement to unemployment benefit in the benefit week which includes the relevant day shall be determined as if the provisions of the Benefits Act, the Administration Act and the Regulations made under those Acts relating to unemployment benefit had continued in force in his case until the end of that benefit week and as if the Act did not apply to him in that benefit week.

(5) A person who is treated as making a claim for a jobseeker's allowance under this regulation shall, if he satisfies the conditions of entitlement to unemployment benefit in force on 6th October 1996, but subject to the provisions of these Regulations, be treated as satisfying the requirements of sections 1 and 2.

Transition from unemployment benefit to a jobseeker's allowance: further provisions

6.—(1) A person who has an award of unemployment benefit, or unemployment benefit and income support, for the benefit week that includes the 7th October 1996, but to whom unemployment benefit is not payable in respect of the relevant day shall—

(a) be treated as having an award of a jobseeker's allowance from the first day of the benefit week after the benefit week that includes the relevant day until such date as he fails to satisfy, or ceases to be treated as satisfying, any condition of entitlement to a jobseeker's allowance that applies in his case; and

(b) be treated as satisfying the requirements of section 1(2)(b) (jobseeker's agreement) until the day he actually enters into a jobseeker's agreement in accordance with section 9(1) or until, in a case where a proposed jobseeker's agreement is referred to an adjudication officer for him to determine, the day the adjudication officer gives a direction in accordance with section 9(7).

(2) For the purposes of paragraph (1), a person who is disqualified for receiving unemployment benefit in accordance with section 28 of the Benefits Act as in force on 6th October 1996 for the benefit week that includes 7th October 1996 shall be treated as having an award of unemployment benefit for that week.

(3) A person who, in respect of his claim for unemployment benefit, or unemployment benefit and income support, has restricted the hours he is available for work to 40 hours or more a week, shall be treated as having recorded his pattern of availability in the jobseeker's agreement he is treated as having entered into under paragraph (1)(b).

Jobseeker's allowance to replace income support and unemployment benefit

7.—(1) Subject to the following provisions of this regulation, a person who is paid benefit in respect of the relevant day in accordance with an award of income support or unemployment benefit, or income support and unemployment benefit, and the award is terminated in accordance with the preceding provisions of these Regulations shall be treated as having been awarded a jobseeker's allowance for a period commencing on the first day of the next benefit week to begin for that claimant on or after 7th October 1996 and continuing until such date as he fails to satisfy, or in respect of which he ceases to be treated as satisfying, any condition of entitlement to a jobseeker's allowance, except in relation to a contribution-based jobseeker's allowance, those specified in sections 1(2)(e) and 2(1)(c), which applies in his case.

(2) A person whose award of income support is cancelled in accordance with regulation 4(2) shall be treated as having been awarded an income-based jobseeker's allowance as from the date the award of income support would have taken effect and continuing until such date as he fails to satisfy, or in respect of which he ceases to be treated as satisfying, any condition of entitlement to a jobseeker's allowance which applies in his case.

(3) A person—
- (a) to whom unemployment benefit was payable in respect of the relevant day; and
- (b) to whom unemployment benefit was not payable in respect of either 6th or 7th April 1996; and
- (c) who had on the relevant day been entitled to unemployment benefit for 156 days or more (including the relevant day) in the period of interruption of employment which included the relevant day,

shall not be treated as entitled to a contribution-based jobseeker's allowance in accordance with paragraph (1) nor as having an award of a jobseeker's allowance in accordance with regulation 5(2).

Claims for entitlement to a jobseeker's allowance

8.—(1) The following provisions of this regulation shall apply in the case of a person who is treated as having an award of a jobseeker's allowance in accordance with regulation 5 or 7.

(2) A person to whom regulation 5 or 7 applies shall be treated as having satisfied the condition mentioned in section 1(2)(b) (jobseeker's agreement) for so long as the award is in force or, if earlier, until the day he actually enters into such an agreement in accordance with section 9(1) or until, in a case where a proposed jobseeker's agreement is referred to an adjudication officer for him

to determine, the day the adjudication officer gives a direction in accordance with section 9(7).

(3) A person who, in respect of his claim for income support or unemployment benefit, or income support and unemployment benefit, has restricted the hours he is available for work to 40 hours or more a week shall be treated as having recorded his pattern of availability in the jobseeker's agreement he is treated as having entered into under paragraph (2).

(4) In the case of a person to whom unemployment benefit was payable in respect of either 6th or 7th April 1996 and where the period of interruption of employment that was current on that date was also current on the relevant day—

(a) section 5(1) shall have effect as if the reference to 182 days was a reference to 312 days [²but only in so far as this sub-paragraph has effect in the case of any person in respect of any date falling before 1st December 1997]; and

(b) in any benefit week commencing on or after 7th October 1996, Sunday or such other day of the week which before that date was, in the claimant's case, substituted for Sunday in accordance with regulation 4 of the Unemployment Benefit Regulations as in force on 6th October 1996 shall be disregarded solely for the purpose of determining whether in the aggregate a person has been entitled to a contribution-based jobseeker's allowance for 312 days.

(5) In the case of a person to whom unemployment benefit was not payable in respect of either 6th or 7th April 1996—

(a) section 5(1) shall have effect as if the reference to 182 days was a reference to 156 days; and

(b) in any benefit week commencing on or after 7th October 1996, Sunday or such other day of the week which before that date was, in the claimant's case, substituted for Sunday in accordance with regulation 4 of the Unemployment Benefit Regulations as in force on 6th October 1996 shall be disregarded solely for the purpose of determining whether in the aggregate a person has been entitled to a contribution-based jobseeker's allowance for 156 days.

(6) Any day of unemployment which fell within a period of interruption of employment current on the relevant day shall be treated as a day of entitlement to a contribution-based jobseeker's allowance for the purpose of determining whether the 182 days mentioned in section 5(1), or 312 days in a case to which [¹paragraph (4)] applies [¹ or 156 days in a case to which paragraph (5) applies], has been exceeded.

(7) In the case of a person who on the relevant day—

(a) was summoned for jury service and unemployment benefit was payable to him in respect of the day immediately preceding the day on which he was required to serve as a juror; or

(b) was taking part in training and unemployment benefit or income support was, or both were, payable to him in respect of the day immediately preceding the day in respect of which that training began; and

(c) would, but for being summoned for jury service or taking part in training, have been available for and actively seeking employment,

he shall be treated for the purposes of these Regulations as if—

(i) on the relevant day, he had an award of unemployment benefit if he had such an award immediately before the jury service or, as the case may be, the training began; or

(ii) on the relevant day, he had an award of income support if he had such an award before the training began; and

(iii) the award he was treated as having was terminated in accordance with paragraph (1) or, as the case may be, paragraph (2) of regulation 4.

(8) Where a person to whom paragraph (7) applies had been entitled to an increase in his unemployment benefit in respect of an adult dependant and that increase was payable to him immediately preceding the day on which he was required to serve as a juror or the day training began, he shall be treated for the purposes of these Regulations as if that increase was payable to him in respect of the relevant day.

(9) In the case of a person to whom the requirements of one or more of sub-paragraphs (a), (b) or (c) of paragraph (7) apply on either 6th or 7th April 1996, regulation 7 shall apply in his case as if he had in fact been in receipt of unemployment benefit for one of those days.

(10) In the case of a person who on the relevant day—

(a) was summoned for jury service and was required to serve as a juror; and

(b) was entitled to income support; and

(c) would but for being summoned for jury service have been available for and actively seeking employment,

and where income support was payable to him in respect of the day immediately preceding the day on which he was required to serve as a juror, his award of income support shall end at the end of the benefit week which includes the last day in respect of which he was summoned for jury service and regulation 7 shall apply in his case as if paragraph (1) referred to that benefit week and not the benefit week which commenced on or after 7th October 1996.

AMENDMENTS

1. Social Security (Miscellaneous Amendments) Regulations 1997 (S.I. 1997 No. 454), reg. 4(3) (March 21, 1997).

2. Jobseeker's Allowance (Amendment) (No. 2) Regulations 1997 (S.I. 1997 No. 2677), reg. 3 (December 1, 1997).

Further provisions applying to a continuing entitlement to a jobseeker's allowance

9.—(1) A person's continuing entitlement to a jobseeker's allowance shall be subject to the following provisions of this regulation where an award of jobseeker's allowance-

(a) is made on a claim treated as made for that benefit in accordance with regulation 5; or

(b) has effect in accordance with regulation 7.

(2) A claimant is required to satisfy—

(a) the conditions of entitlement set out in section 1(2)(a) to (c) on a weekly basis; and

(b) the other conditions for entitlement to a contribution-based jobseeker's allowance other than those specified in sections 1(2)(e) and 2(1)(c), for each day of the week except Sunday or, where in a particular case another day was substituted for Sunday under regulation 4 of the Unemployment Benefit Regulations as in force on 6th October 1996, except that day of the week.

(3) Paragraph (4) applies—

(a) as from the first day in the benefit week which in a particular case immediately follows the benefit week which includes 6th April 1997 except in the case of a person whose transitionally protected period ended before that date; or

845

(b) as from the first day in an award of a jobseeker's allowance where the claimant satisfied the requirements of section 2 and where—
>   (i) that day forms part of a jobseeking period separated by more than 8 weeks but less than 12 weeks from the last day of the transitionally protected period, or where there is no such day, the relevant day if unemployment benefit was payable in respect of that day; [¹or]
>   (ii) that day [¹ is after the last day of the transitionally protected period and] forms part of a jobseeking period which is separated by not more than 12 weeks from a period of interruption of employment [¹...]
>   (iii) [¹...].

(4) Where this paragraph applies the number of days which are to be aggregated for the purposes of section 5(1) shall be determined in accordance with the formula—

$$(A + B) \times \frac{7}{6}$$

where—
>   A = the number of days entitlement to unemployment benefit in any period of interruption of employment to which paragraph (3) refers;
>   B = the number of days entitlement to a contribution-based jobseeker's allowance falling within the transitionally protected period.

(5) Any fraction produced by applying the formula set out in paragraph (4) shall be disregarded.

(6) Paragraphs (4) and (5) shall apply to a claimant to whom a jobseeker's allowance is awarded other than in accordance with regulation 5 or 7 where—
>   (a) the first day of that award forms part of a jobseeking period which is separated by not more than 12 weeks from a period of interruption of employment; or
>   (b) the tax years which in accordance with section 2 are to be satisfied for entitlement to a contribution-based jobseeker's allowance to arise are the same tax years as those by reference to which entitlement to unemployment benefit arose on a claim made by the claimant in respect of a day before 7th October 1996.

AMENDMENT

1. Social Security (Miscellaneous Amendments) Regulations 1997 (S.I. 1997 No. 454), reg. 4(4) (March 21, 1997).

Transitionally protected period

10.—(1) The transitionally protected period commences in the case of any particular claimant on the first day in the benefit week which commences in his case on or after 7th October 1996 and applies to a claimant—
>   (a) who was awarded a jobseeker's allowance on a claim treated as made under regulation 5(2); or
>   (b) whose award of unemployment benefit terminated in accordance with regulation 5(3).

(2) The transitionally protected period ends in the case of any particular claimant on the last day in the benefit week which includes 6th April 1997 or, if earlier, on the termination of any period of entitlement to a contribution-based jobseeker's allowance which does not link, in accordance with this regulation, with any subsequent period of entitlement to a contribution-based jobseeker's allowance.

(3) For the purposes of determining whether in any particular case the trans-

itionally protected period has ended, periods of entitlement to a contribution-based jobseeker's allowance—

(a) separated by not more than 8 weeks shall link;

(b) separated by more than 8 weeks shall not link,

and in determining whether any particular periods of entitlement link, any period which is for the purposes of regulation 3(2) a linked period shall be disregarded.

(4) Where a person—

(a) is entitled to a jobseeker's allowance and that entitlement falls within the transitionally protected period;

(b) satisfies the requirements of section 2 but not those of section 3; and

(c) unemployment benefit was payable in respect of the relevant day and the benefit included an increase for an adult dependant,

that dependency increase shall be payable as an addition to the person's contribution-based jobseeker's allowance but only for so long as he continues to satisfy the conditions of entitlement to the dependency increase which applied on that day, and the provisions of Part III of the Social Security (Dependency) Regulations 1977 and Part III of the Social Security (Hospital In-Patients) Regulations 1975 as they apply to unemployment benefit as in force on 6th October 1996 shall apply to it.

(5) Where a person had not attained the age of 55 on the relevant day then for any week falling within the transitionally protected period in which he has still not attained that age section 30 of the Benefits Act shall apply in his case as if it had not been repealed, and the deductions prescribed under section 4(1)(b) in so far as they relate to pension payments shall not be made.

(6) In the case of a person who, on the relevant day—

(a) had attained pensionable age; and

(b) to whom unemployment benefit was payable in accordance with an award made by virtue of section 25(2)(b) or (c) of the Benefits Act,

his continuing entitlement to a contribution-based jobseeker's allowance shall be determined in the transitionally protected period as if those provisions of the Benefits Act continued to apply in his case and the requirement of section 1(2)(h) did not apply, but subject to section 5(1) and regulation 9 (further provisions applying to a continuing entitlement to a jobseeker's allowance).

(7) In the transitionally protected period, where the weekly amount payable in accordance with section 4(1)(a) is less than the amount of unemployment benefit payable in the claimant's case for the benefit week which includes the relevant day or which would have been payable in that week, but for any adjustments made in that week, in accordance with paragraph 1 of [¹ Part I of] Schedule 4 to the Benefits Act, the age-related amount applicable in that case shall be an amount equal to the amount formerly payable by way of unemployment benefit under that provision.

(8) In paragraph (7) the reference to the amount of unemployment benefit includes a reference to the amount of unemployment benefit which would have been payable had not the claimant been summoned as a juror or been undergoing training.

(9) Where a person is entitled to an income-based jobseeker's allowance, an amount equal to any dependency increase payable to him in accordance with section 82 of the Benefits Act in respect of an adult dependant for the relevant day who does not reside with him, or any dependency increase payable to him in accordance with section 80(2)(a) of the Benefits Act in respect of the relevant day in respect of a child who does not reside with him, shall be—

(a) included in the applicable amount of the person; and

(b) disregarded in determining the amount of the person's income,

but only for so long as he continues to satisfy the conditions of entitlement to the dependency increase which applied on that day, or until the end of the benefit week which for him includes 7th April 1997, whichever is the earlier.

(10) In a case where unemployment benefit was payable in respect of the relevant day and the benefit included an increase for an adult dependant, continuing entitlement to the benefit and the increase shall be determined as if the provisions of regulation 14(1)(b) of the Social Security (Overlapping Benefits) Regulations 1979 continued to apply, notwithstanding that those provisions have ceased to have effect.

(11) In the transitionally protected period, the provisions of regulation 14(2) of the Social Security (Overlapping Benefits) Regulations 1979 shall continue to apply in order to adjust the amount of unemployment benefit payable to a claimant for part of a week, notwithstanding that those provisions have ceased to have effect.

AMENDMENT

1. Social Security (Miscellaneous Amendments) Regulations 1997 (S.I. 1997 No. 454), reg. 4(5) (March 21, 1997).

Saving provisions

11.—(1) During the transitionally protected period—
(a) regulation 3(3), (4A), (4B), (5) and (6) of the Social Security Benefit (Computation of Earnings) Regulations 1978 as in force on 6th October 1996 shall continue to apply for the purposes of calculating or estimating a person's earnings in determining his entitlement to a contribution-based jobseeker's allowance; and
(b) regulation 4 of the Unemployment Benefit Regulations as in force on 6th October 1996 shall continue to apply for the purpose of determining whether a day of the week substituted for Sunday shall be disregarded in calculating a person's aggregate entitlement to a contribution-based jobseeker's allowance.

Jurors entitled to income support on the relevant day

12.—(1) This regulation applies to a person who in the benefit week which includes the relevant day was a juror and—
(a) was entitled to income support without satisfying the requirement that he be available for employment in that week by virtue of regulation 8(1) of, and paragraph 17 of Schedule 1 to, the Income Support Regulations;
(b) immediately before commencing his duties as a juror was entitled to income support where the applicable amount was reduced in accordance with regulation 21A or 22 of the Income Support Regulations; and
(c) before the benefit week which includes 6th April 1997, he ceases to be a juror.
(2) When the person to whom paragraph (1) applies ceases to be a juror—
(a) his award of income support shall terminate at the end of the benefit week in which he ceases to be a juror; and
(b) he shall be treated as having been awarded an income-based jobseeker's allowance for a period commencing on the first day of the benefit week which follows the benefit week in which his award of income support is terminated.
(3) Where an amount prescribed in accordance with section 4(5) which is applicable in the case of a person treated as having been awarded an income-based jobseeker's allowance under paragraph (2)(b) is less than the amount which was applicable for the purpose of his award of income support under Schedule 2, or, as the case may be, Schedule 7 to the Income Support Regulations, reduced in accordance with regulation 21A or 22 of those Regulations,

in the last benefit week to which his applicable amount was subject to such a reduction, then the higher amount which was applicable in the award of income support shall also be applicable for the purposes of determining the amount of income-based jobseeker's allowance payable in his case.

(4) An award having effect in accordance with this regulation shall continue until such date as the claimant fails to satisfy, or in respect of which he ceases to be treated as satisfying, any condition of entitlement which applies in his case, or if earlier, until the end of the benefit week which includes 6th April 1997.

Earnings during the transitionally protected period

13.—(1) During the transitionally protected period, a person's entitlement to a contribution-based jobseeker's allowance shall be subject to the conditions set out in this regulation.

(2) A person's entitlement to a contribution-based jobseeker's allowance in any week is subject to the condition that, on each day in that week he continues to satisfy the requirements of regulation 7(1)(g)(i) and (iii) and (o) of the Unemployment Benefit Regulations as in force on 6th October 1996, except on a day on which regulation 9 of those Regulations would have applied to him, notwithstanding that those provisions have ceased to have effect but as if the references to regulations 10, 11 and 12 were omitted and as if regulation 7(5B) continued to apply.

(3) Regulation 7(1)(g)(i) and (iii) and (o) of the Unemployment Benefit Regulations shall apply as if the reference to "unemployment benefit" was a reference to a contribution-based jobseeker's allowance, and as if for references to "day of unemployment" there were substituted references to a day on which a person satisfies the conditions of entitlement to a jobseeker's allowance specified in sections 1(2)(a) to (c) and (f) to (i) and 2(1)(a), (b) and (d).

(4) Where a person has one or more days in any week on which he fails to satisfy the conditions of paragraph (2)—

(a) he may nonetheless qualify for a contribution-based jobseeker's allowance on the other days in that week except Sunday or the day which in his case was substituted for Sunday in accordance with regulation 4 of the Unemployment Benefit Regulations as in force on 6th October 1996; and

(b) except where sub-paragraph (c) applies, the amount of the contribution-based jobseeker's allowance payable to him in that week shall be reduced by an amount equal to one-sixth of the weekly amount for each day in that week on which he fails to satisfy those requirements; or

(c) no contribution-based jobseeker's allowance shall be payable to him in that week where, had regulation 7(1)(o) of the Unemployment Benefit Regulations (weekly earnings in excess of lower earnings limit) as in force on 6th October 1996 applied in his case, no unemployment benefit would have been payable for that week.

(5) Where a person has one or more days in a week on which he fails to satisfy the conditions specified in paragraph (2) and in consequence of which a jobseeker's allowance is not payable, those days shall not be treated as days of entitlement to a contribution-based jobseeker's allowance for the purposes of section 5(1).

Earnings generally

14.—(1) In the transitionally protected period, the amount of a person's earnings shall, for the purpose of determining a person's entitlement to an amount of a contribution-based jobseeker's allowance, be calculated or estimated in accordance with section 3 of the Benefits Act and regulations 2 to 4 of the Social Security Benefit (Computation of Earnings) Regulations 1978.

(2) In any case where—

(a) the amount of a person's earnings are determined in accordance with provisions which applied before 7th October 1996 (''the old rules''); and

(b) the person's earnings subsequently fall to be determined in accordance with the provisions of the Act and the regulations made thereunder (''the new rules''),

any earnings determined in accordance with the old rules shall be disregarded for the purposes of the new rules.

Part-time students

15.—(1) This regulation applies to a person (referred to in this regulation as a ''participant'') to whom regulation 5 or 7 applies and who on 31st July 1996 was entitled to income support or unemployment benefit.

(2) In the case of a participant who on 31st July 1996 was treated as available for employment in accordance with regulation 9(1)(c) of the Income Support Regulations, he shall continue to be treated as available for employment for the purposes of a jobseeker's allowance, notwithstanding any regulation to the contrary, for so long as he continues to satisfy—

(a) the requirements of regulation 9(1)(c) of the Income Support Regulations as in force on 31st July 1996; and

(b) the provisions of paragraph (4).

(3) A participant who on 31st July 1996—

(a) although attending a course of study within the meaning of regulation 7(3)(c) of the Unemployment Benefit Regulations was not a student for the purposes of regulation 7(1)(m) of those Regulations; or

(b) although attending a course of study was not a student for the purposes of regulation 10 of the Income Support Regulations,

shall be treated for the purposes of any regulations relating to a jobseeker's allowance as if he was a part-time student within the meaning of those regulations for so long as he continues—

(i) to attend the course of study referred to in sub-paragraph (a) or (b); and

(ii) to satisfy the provisions of paragraph (4).

(4) The provisions of this paragraph are that—

(a) the participant continues to follow the course of study or, as the case may be, the course of education, training or instruction, which he was following on 31st July 1996; and

(b) his award of a jobseeker's allowance which arose in accordance with regulation 5 or on a claim treated as made under regulation 7 has not terminated and for the purpose of determining whether the award has terminated any period which is a linked period under regulation 3 shall be disregarded and two awards separated by a linking period shall be treated as a single award.

Claimants subject to disqualification or reduction in benefit

16.—(1) In the case of a person who on the relevant day was disqualified for receiving unemployment benefit in accordance with section 28 of the Benefits Act for a period which would not, but for the replacement of unemployment benefit with a jobseeker's allowance, have expired on that day, the award of a contribution-based jobseeker's allowance which arises under regulation 6 (Transition from Unemployment Benefit to a Jobseeker's Allowance: further provisions) shall not be payable for the balance of that period.

(2) A period of disqualification for receiving unemployment benefit as referred to in paragraph (1) shall be treated as a period during which a contribution-based jobseeker's allowance was not payable to the claimant under section 19 and days during that period shall be treated as days of entitlement to a contribution-based jobseeker's allowance for the purposes of section 5(1).

(3) In the case of a person who on the relevant day was entitled to income support at a rate reduced in accordance with regulation 21A or 22 of the Income Support Regulations, any award of an income-based jobseeker's allowance which has effect in accordance with regulation 7 shall be payable at the rate appropriate under section 4(3), reduced by a sum equal to the amount by which the income support had been reduced and only the balance (if any) shall be payable.

(4) In the case of a person who on the relevant day had an award of income support and whose weekly applicable amount was reduced after the relevant day in accordance with regulation 21A of the Income Support Regulations—

(a) any award of an income-based jobseeker's allowance shall be reduced by a sum equal to an amount by which the weekly applicable amount would have been reduced; and

(b) any denial of a jobseeker's allowance in accordance with section 19 of the Act in respect of the period during which the weekly applicable amount would have been reduced shall be disregarded.

(5) The reduction mentioned in paragraph (3) or (4) shall end—

(a) in a case where the claimant was disqualified for receiving unemployment benefit and paragraph (1) applies, on the day after the day the balance of the period mentioned in that paragraph ends;

(b) where a claim for unemployment benefit by the claimant, or a question which arose in connection with his award of unemployment benefit, had not been determined on the relevant day, on the day that claim or question is determined in the claimant's favour;

(c) except in a case which has already ended in accordance with sub-paragraph (a) or (b), on whichever day is the earlier of—

(i) the date the award of an income-based jobseeker's allowance terminates; or

(ii) the benefit week which included 6th April 1997.

(6) In the case of a person to whom a jobseeker's allowance is not payable in accordance with section 19 or paragraph (1) for a period ending before or during the benefit week which includes 6th April 1997—

(a) where the period during which a jobseeker's allowance was not payable ends during a benefit week, any award of an income-based jobseeker's allowance under section 20(4) or paragraph (3) shall end on the last day of the previous benefit week;

(b) where the period during which a jobseeker's allowance was not payable ends on the last day of a benefit week, any award of an income-based jobseeker's allowance under section 20(4) or paragraph (3) shall end on that day.

(7) For the purpose of determining in accordance with paragraph (5)(c)(i) whether an award has terminated, periods of entitlement to an income-based jobseeker's allowance-

(a) separated by not more than 8 weeks shall link;

(b) separated by more than 8 weeks shall not link,

and in determining whether any particular periods of entitlement link, any period which is for the purposes of regulation 3(2) a linked period shall be disregarded.

Treatment of contribution-based jobseeker's allowance as earnings

17.—(1) In the transitionally protected period, a payment of a contribution-based jobseeker's allowance which falls to be taken into account in determining the income of any person shall be treated as if it was payable on a daily basis for six days per week.

(2) Paragraph (1) shall apply only in a case where the contribution-based jobseeker's allowance is payable to a person who was entitled to unemployment benefit in the benefit week which included the relevant day.

(3) The days of the week in respect of which the payment is treated as made shall be the same days as those in respect of which unemployment benefit was paid in the benefit week which included in the relevant day.

(4) The amount payable in respect of each of the 6 days shall be calculated—

    (a) except where sub-paragraph (b) applies, by dividing the total benefit payable for the week by 6; or

    (b) where payment is made for a part-week by dividing the total benefit payable by the number of days in the part-week and assigning no amount to the remaining days.

Questions not immediately ascertainable

18.—(1) During the transitionally protected period, where on consideration of a claim or question relating to a jobseeker's allowance it appears to an adjudication officer that the claimant's entitlement to, or the rate or amount of, that benefit depends on the determination of—

    (a) a question as to the amount of housing costs to be included in the claimant's applicable amount, and the adjudication officer is satisfied that not all the housing costs can be immediately ascertained, he shall proceed to determine the claim or question on the assumption that the housing costs to be included in the claimant's applicable amount are those which are immediately ascertainable;

    (b) a question as to whether the conditions specified in section 1(2) other than sub-paragraph (d)(i), or a question as to whether the conditions specified in section 2, other than those specified in sub-section (1)(c) or (d), are satisfied, and the adjudication officer is satisfied that the answer to one of those questions cannot be immediately ascertained, he shall proceed to determine the claim on the assumption that the answers to either question are those which are immediately ascertainable;

    (c) any of the questions mentioned in paragraph (2), and he is satisfied that the questions cannot be immediately determined, he shall proceed to determine the claim or question on the assumption that the determination of that question will be adverse to the claimant.

(2) The questions referred to in paragraph (1)(c) are—

    (a) whether section 19 (circumstances in which a jobseeker's allowance is not payable) applies for any period;

    (b) whether in relation to any claimant the applicable amount includes an amount by way of a severe disability premium by virtue of regulation 17(1)(d) or 18(1)(e) of, and paragraph 13 of Schedule 2 to, the Income Support Regulations (applicable amounts).

(3) A determination relating to a jobseeker's allowance made in accordance with the foregoing provisions of this regulation shall be reviewed where it is necessary to give effect to any determination on a question to which those provisions apply.

Claims for a jobseeker's allowance

19.—(1) Claims made on or after 7th October 1996 for a jobseeker's allowance may be treated by the Secretary of State as a claim in addition to, or as a claim for unemployment benefit or income support or both for a period before 7th October 1996.

(2) A claim treated as made for unemployment benefit or income support in accordance with paragraph (1) shall be treated as made on the day the claim for a jobseeker's allowance was made.

Attendance

20. For the purposes of these Regulations, a direction to attend an unemployment benefit office or to attend an office for the purposes of furnishing information or evidence under regulation 8(1) or (2) of the Claims and Payments Regulations in respect of a claim for income support or unemployment benefit and a written notice to attend an interview as referred to in regulation 7(1)(i) of the Unemployment Benefit Regulations shall continue to apply and both the direction and the written notice shall be treated as a notice under regulation 23 of the Jobseeker's Allowance Regulations.

Evidence and information

21.—(1) In the period commencing on 7th October 1996 and ending on 20th October 1996, the requirement to provide information or evidence on or by a particular date under regulation 7(1) or 32(1) of the Claims and Payments Regulations shall continue to apply and shall be treated as a requirement to provide a signed declaration under regulation 24(6) of the Jobseeker's Allowance Regulations on the day specified by the Secretary of State in accordance with regulation 24(10) of those Regulations.

(2) Where a claimant has complied with regulation 7(1) or 32(1) of the Claims and Payments Regulations during the period commencing on 30th September 1996 and ending on 13th October 1996 for the purpose of claiming income support or unemployment benefit, information provided under those provisions shall be treated as satisfying the requirements of regulation 24(6) of the Jobseeker's Allowance Regulations.

(3) During the period commencing on 30th September 1996 and ending on 27th October 1996 for the purposes of regulation 26 of the Jobseeker's Allowance Regulations, the reference to a claimant providing information or evidence which shows that he continues to be entitled to a jobseeker's allowance shall include a reference to the requirement to comply with regulation 7(1) or 32(1) of the Claims and Payments Regulations for the purpose of claiming income support or unemployment benefit, and the reference to the day after he last attended in compliance with a notice under regulation 23 of the Jobseeker's Allowance Regulations shall include a reference to the first day of his award of a jobseeker's allowance.

Revocations

22. These Regulations revoke the Jobseeker's Allowance (Transitional Provisions) Regulations 1995, the Jobseeker's Allowance (Transitional Provisions) (Amendment) Regulations 1996, regulation 2 of the Social Security and Child Support (Jobseeker's Allowance) (Transitional Provisions) (Amendment) Regulations 1996, regulation 2 of the Social Security (Jobseeker's Allowance and Payments on account) (Miscellaneous Amendments) Regulations 1996 and regulation 3 of the Social Security and Child Support (Jobseeker's Allowance) (Miscellaneous Amendments) Regulations 1996.

PART IV

FAMILY CREDIT

Family Credit (General) Regulations 1987

(S.I. 1987 No. 1973)

Made by the Secretary of State under ss.20(1), (5)(c), (6), (10), (11) and (12), 21(3) and (6)(a), 22(1) and (5) to (9), 51(1)(h) and 84(1) of the Social Security Act 1986 and ss.104(5) and 166(1) to (3A) of the Social Security Act 1975.

44. Disregard of tax refund
45. Disregard of changes occurring during summer vacation

GENERAL NOTE

The family credit scheme was described as "the jewel in the crown" of the April 1988 social security reforms. Some £200 million p.a. over and above what was spent on family income supplement (FIS) was allowed in the family credit estimates. In November 1998, approximately 790,000 families were on family credit receiving an average of £60.61 p.w.

Although there are superficial similarities between FIS and family credit, the differences are important. First, the calculations are made on net income, rather than gross. This eases the worst of the poverty trap problems. Second, the maximum family credit is paid at all levels of income up to the applicable amount (reg. 47). Third, if income is above that level the maximum family credit is reduced by 70p for every £1 of excess, rather than by 50p. Fourth, an £8000/£3000 capital rule is applied (regs. 28 and 36). Fifth, the definition of full-time work was changed to 24 hours per week (reg. 4), rather than 30 for most claimants.

One of the most important subsequent changes was a further reduction in the qualifying hours to 16 per week in April 1992. At the same time, there was a slight easing in the way in which the test is applied. The combination brought more claimants within family credit rather than income support.

In April 1992 a disregard of the first £15 of maintenance was introduced and there were further changes in April 1993 to accommodate the child support system.

Since October 1994, certain family credit claimants have been able to offset child care costs of up to £40 per week (increased to £60 from April 1996 and to £100 from June 1998 where the claimant has more than one child) against their earnings. This also applies to disability working allowance (and housing and council tax benefit), but not income support or income-based JSA. Although this is an important change in principle the scope of the disregard is still limited (see the notes to regs. 13 and 13A).

As part of the Government's emphasis on increasing in-work benefits (at the expense of out-of-work benefits), from July 1995 the maximum credit for family credit has been increased by £10 and (now £11.05 from April 1999) for those who work 30 hours or more a week. The same applies to disability working allowance. There is provision in the Housing Benefit and Council Tax Benefit

Regulations to ensure that this gain is not lost by decreased housing/council tax benefit. (Note also the provisions first introduced in April 1996 that enable certain people who were previously in receipt of income support or income-based JSA to be paid their existing rate of housing benefit and council tax benefit for four weeks after taking up work.) The government also undertook that from April 1996 most new family credit claims would be dealt with within five days. Moreover, in October 1996 a new benefit, earnings top-up, was introduced on a pilot basis in eight areas of the country. Its purpose is to assist people in low-paid work who do *not* have dependent children but otherwise it is broadly similar to family credit. Couples and single people, aged 18 and over but under 65, who work 16 hours a week or more may be eligible. Benefit is paid at a lower rate in four areas and at a higher rate in the other four, which is intended to test its effectiveness at different levels of assistance. The pilot scheme will run for three years.

More negatively, a further change is that from July 1996 a family credit award will cease when the only remaining young person (see reg. 6) in the family leaves full-time education, rather than payment continuing for the normal 26 weeks. Note also that since October 7, 1997 the credit for a child does not increase until the first Tuesday in September after their 11th or 16th birthday and there is no longer an increase at the age of 18. For the transitional protection for a child or young person who reached the relevant age before October 7, 1997 see reg. 10(3) and (4) of the Income-related Benefits and Jobseeker's Allowance (Personal Allowances for Children and Young Persons) (Amendment) Regulations 1996 (p. 968). There is a parallel change to the child care costs disregard in reg. 13A (see the notes to that regulation).

Note that family credit is to be replaced by working families tax credit from October 5, 1999. See the 1999 Supplement to this book for details of the new scheme.

PART I

GENERAL

Citation and commencement

1. These Regulations may be cited as the Family Credit (General) Regulations 1987, and shall come into force on 11th April 1988.

Interpretation

2.—(1) In these Regulations, unless the context otherwise requires—
"the Act" means the Social Security Act 1986;
[6"assessment period" means, in the case of an employed earner, a period determined in accordance with [13regulation 14 or, as the case may be, 14A] and, in the case of a self-employed earner, a period determined in accordance with regulation 15;]
[17"the benefit Acts" means the Contributions and Benefits Act and the Job-seekers Act 1995;]
[19"the Children Order" means the Children (Northern Ireland) Order 1995;]
"claim" means a claim for family credit;
"claimant" means a person claiming family credit;
"close relative" means a parent, parent-in-law, son, son-in-law, daughter, daughter-in-law, step-parent, step-son, step-daughter, brother, sister, or the spouse of any of the preceding persons or, if that person is one of an unmarried couple, the other member of that couple;
[9"community charge benefit" means community charge benefits under Part VII of the Contributions and Benefits Act 1992 as originally enacted;]
"concessionary payment" means a payment made under arrangements made by the Secretary of State with the consent of the Treasury which is charged either to the National Insurance Fund or to a Departmental Expenditure Vote to which payments of benefit under the Act, the

Social Security Act or the Child Benefit Act 1975 [SSCBA] are charged;

[⁹"the Contributions and Benefits Act" means the Social Security Contributions and Benefits Act 1992;]

[¹⁴"Crown property" means property held by Her Majesty in right of the Crown or by a government department or which is held in trust for Her Majesty for the purposes of a government department, except (in the case of an interest held by Her Majesty in right of the Crown) where the interest is under the management of the Crown Estate Commissioners;]

"date of claim" means the date on which the claimant makes, or is treated as making, a claim for family credit;

[¹³"director" means a director of a company, and for this purpose "company" means a company within the meaning of section 735(1) of the Companies Act 1985 or a body corporate to which, by virtue of section 718 of that Act, any provision of that Act applies;]

[⁵"disability living allowance" means a disability living allowance under section 372A of the Social Security Act [SSCBA, s.71];

"disability working allowance" means a disability working allowance under section 20 of the Act [SSCBA, s.129];]

"earnings" has the meaning prescribed in regulation 19 or, as the case may be, 21;

[¹⁸"earnings top-up" means the allowance paid by the Secretary of State under the Earnings Top-up Scheme;]

[¹⁸"the Earnings Top-up Scheme" means the Earnings Top-up Scheme 1996;]

"employed earner" shall be construed in accordance with section 2(1)(a) of the Social Security Act [SSCBA, s.2(1)(a)];

[¹⁴"lone parent" means a person who has no partner and who is responsible for, and a member of the same household as, a child or young person;]

[⁸"lower rate" where it relates to rates of tax has the same meaning as in the Income and Corporation Taxes Act 1988 by virtue of section 832(1) of that Act;]

[¹²"maternity leave" means a period during which a woman is absent from work because she is pregnant or has given birth to a child, and at the end of which she has a right to return to work either under the terms of her contract of employment or under Part III of the Employment Protection (Consolidation) Act 1978;]

[⁵"mobility allowance" means an allowance under section 37A of the Social Security Act;

"mobility supplement" means any supplement under article 26A of the Naval, Military and Air Forces etc. (Disablement and Death) Service Pensions Order 1983 including such a supplement by virtue of any other scheme or order or under article 25A of the Personal Injuries (Civilians) Scheme 1983;

"net earnings" means such earnings as are calculated in accordance with regulation 20;

"net profit" means such profit as is calculated in accordance with regulation 22;

"occupational pension" means any pension or other periodical payment under an occupational pension scheme but does not include any discretionary payment out of a fund established for relieving hardship in particular cases;

"partner" means, where a claimant—

(a) is a member of a married or unmarried couple, the other member of that couple,

(b) is married polygamously to two or more members of the same household, any such member;

[⁶"pay period" has the meaning given in regulation 14(7)(b);]

"payment" includes a part of a payment;

[¹⁶"pension fund holder" means with respect to a personal pension scheme or retirement annuity contract, the trustees, managers or scheme administrators, as the case may be, of the scheme or contract concerned;]

[¹²"personal pension scheme" has the same meaning as in [¹⁶section 1 of the Pension Schemes Act 1993] and, in the case of a self-employed earner, includes a scheme approved by the Inland Revenue under Chapter IV of Part XIV of the Income and Corporation Taxes Act 1988;]

"policy of life insurance" means any instrument by which the payment of money is assured on death (except death by accident only) or the happening of any contingency dependent on human life, or any instrument evidencing a contract which is subject to payment of premiums for a term dependent on human life;

[⁷"qualifying person" means a person in respect of whom payment has been made from the Fund [¹¹ or the Eileen Trust];]

[¹⁶"retirement annuity contract" means a contract or trust scheme approved under Chapter III of Part XIV of the Income and Corporation Taxes Act 1988;]

"self-employed earner" shall be construed in accordance with section 2(1)(b) of the Social Security Act [SSCBA, s.2(1)(b)];

"Social Security Act" means the Social Security Act 1975;

"student" has the meaning prescribed in regulation 37;

[¹¹"the Eileen Trust" means the charitable trust of that name established on 29th March 1993 out of funds provided by the Secretary of State for the benefit of persons eligible for payment in accordance with its provisions;]

[⁷"the Fund" means moneys made available from time to time by the Secretary of State for the benefit of persons eligible for payment in accordance with the provisions of a scheme established by him on 24th April 1992 or, in Scotland, on 10th April 1992;]

[¹⁰"the Independent Living (Extension) Fund" means the Trust of that name established by a deed dated 25th February 1993 and made between the Secretary of State for Social Security of the one part and Robin Glover Wendt and John Fletcher Shepherd of the other part;]

[²"the Independent Living Fund" means the charitable trust established out of funds provided by the Secretary of State for the purpose of providing financial assistance to those persons incapacitated by or otherwise suffering from very severe disablement who are in need of such assistance to enable them to live independently;]

[¹⁰"the Independent Living (1993) Fund" means the Trust of that name established by a deed dated 25th February 1993 and made between the Secretary of State for Social Security of the one part and Robin Glover Wendt and John Fletcher Shepherd of the other part;]

[¹⁰"the Independent Living Funds" means the Independent Living Fund, the Independent Living (Extension) Fund and the Independent Living (1993) Fund;]

[³"the Macfarlane (Special Payments) Trust" means the trust of that name, established on 29th January 1990 partly out of funds provided by the Secretary of State, for the benefit of certain persons suffering from haemophilia;]

[⁴"the Macfarlane (Special Payments) (No. 2) Trust" means the trust of that name, established on 3rd May 1991 partly out of funds provided by the Secretary of State, for the benefit of certain persons suffering from haemophilia and other beneficiaries;]

[¹"the Macfarlane Trust" means the charitable trust, established partly out of funds provided by the Secretary of State to the Haemophilia Society, for the relief of poverty or distress among those suffering from haemophilia;]

[⁶"training allowance" means an allowance (whether by way of periodical grants or otherwise) payable—

(a) out of public funds by a Government department or by or on behalf of the Secretary of State, Scottish Enterprise or Highlands and Islands Enterprise;

(b) to a person for his maintenance or in respect of a member of his family; and

(c) for the period, or part of the period, during which he is following a course of training or instruction provided by, or in pursuance of arrangements made with, that department or approved by that department in relation to him or so provided or approved by or on behalf of the Secretary of State, Scottish Enterprise or Highlands and Islands Enterprise,

but it does not include an allowance paid by any Government department to or in respect of a person by reason of the fact that he is following a course of full-time education, other than arrangements made under section 2 of the Employment and Training Act 1973, or is training as a teacher;]

[¹⁵"voluntary organisation" means a body, other than a public or local authority, the activities of which are carried on otherwise than for profit;]

[⁹"water charges" means—

(a) as respects England and Wales, any water and sewerage charges under Chapter I of Part V of the Water Industry Act 1991;

(b) as respects Scotland, any water and sewerage charges under Schedule 11 to the Local Government Finance Act 1992;]

"week" means a period of seven days beginning with midnight between Saturday and Sunday;

"week of claim" means the week which includes the date of claim;

"year of assessment" has the same meaning prescribed in section 526(5) of the Income and Corporation Taxes Act 1970;

"young person" has the meaning prescribed in regulation 6.

(2) Unless the context otherwise requires, any reference in these Regulations to a numbered regulation, Part or Schedule is a reference to the regulation, Part or Schedule bearing that number in these Regulations and any reference in a regulation or Schedule to a numbered paragraph is a reference to the paragraph in that regulation or Schedule bearing that number.

AMENDMENTS

1. Family Credit (General) Amendment Regulations 1988 (S.I. 1988 No. 660), reg. 2 (April 11, 1988).

2. Family Credit and Income Support (General) Amendment Regulations 1988 (S.I. 1988 No. 999), reg. 2 (June 9, 1988).

3. Income-related Benefits Schemes Amendment Regulations 1990 (S.I. 1990 No. 127), reg. 2 (January 31, 1990).

4. Income-related Benefits Schemes and Social Security (Recoupment) Amendment Regulations 1991 (S.I. 1991 No. 1175), reg. 5 (May 11, 1991).

5. Disability Living Allowance and Disability Working Allowance (Consequential Provisions) Regulations 1991 (S.I. 1991 No. 2742), reg. 13(2) (April 6, 1992).

6. Family Credit (General) Amendment Regulations 1992 (S.I. 1992 No. 573), reg. 2 (April 7, 1992).

7. Income-related Benefits Schemes and Social Security (Recoupment) Amendment Regulations 1992 (S.I. 1992 No. 1101), reg. 6 (May 7, 1992).

8. Income-related Benefits Schemes (Miscellaneous Amendments) (No. 3) Regulations 1992 (S.I. 1992 No. 2155), reg. 4 (October 5, 1992).

9. Income-related Benefits Schemes (Miscellaneous Amendments) Regulations 1993 (S.I. 1993 No. 315), reg. 10 (April 13, 1993).

10. Social Security Benefits (Miscellaneous Amendments) (No. 2) Regulations 1993 (S.I. 1993 No. 963), reg. 3(2) (April 22, 1993).

11. Income-related Benefits Schemes and Social Security (Recoupment Amendment Regulations 1993 (S.I. 1993 No. 1249), reg. 2(2) (May 14, 1993).

12. Income-related Benefits Schemes (Miscellaneous Amendments) (No. 4) Regulations 1993 (S.I. 1993 No. 2119), reg. 25 (October 5, 1993).

13. Income-related Benefits Schemes (Miscellaneous Amendments) Regulations 1994 (S.I. 1994 No. 527), reg. 10 (April 12, 1994).

14. Income-related Benefits Schemes (Miscellaneous Amendments) (No. 4) Regulations 1994 (S.I. 1994 No. 1924), reg. 4(2) (October 4, 1994).

15. Income-related Benefits Schemes (Miscellaneous Amendments) Regulations 1995 (S.I. 1995 No. 516), reg. 10 (April 11, 1995).

16. Income-related Benefits Schemes and Social Security (Claims and Payments) (Miscellaneous Amendments) Regulations 1995 (S.I. 1995 No. 2303), reg. 4(2) (October 3, 1995).

17. Social Security and Child Support (Jobseeker's Allowance) (Consequential Amendments) Regulations 1996 (S.I. 1996 No. 1345), reg. 8(2) (October 7, 1996).

18. Income-related Benefits Schemes and Social Fund (Miscellaneous Amendments) Regulations 1996 (S.I. 1996 No. 1944), reg. 13 and Sched., para. 1 (October 7, 1996).

19. Social Security (Miscellaneous Amendments) Regulations 1998 (S.I. 1998 No. 563), reg. 5(1) and (2)(c) (April 7, 1998).

DEFINITION

"occupational pension scheme"—see PSA, s.1.

GENERAL NOTE

"*date of claim.*" See the Claims and Payments Regulations, reg. 6.

"*the Earnings Top-up Scheme*". See the note at the beginning of these Regulations.

"*employed earner.*" The meaning in s.2(1)(a) of the Contributions and Benefits Act (1975 Act, s.2(1)(a)) is "a person who is gainfully employed in Great Britain either under a contract of service, or in an office (including elective office) with emoluments chargeable to income tax under Schedule E."

"*partner.*" See the notes to s.137(1) of the Contributions and Benefits Act for "married couple" and "unmarried couple."

"*personal pension scheme*". See the notes to reg. 2(1) of the Income Support Regulations.

"*self-employed earner.*" The meaning in s.2(1)(b) of the Contributions and Benefits Act (1975 Act, s.2(1)(b)) is "a person who is gainfully employed in Great Britain otherwise than in employed earner's employment (whether or not he is also employed in such employment)."

"*year of assessment.*" The meaning in s.526(5) of the Income and Corporation Taxes Act 1970 (s.832(1) of the consolidating 1988 Act) is "with reference to any tax year, the year for which such tax was granted by any Act granting income tax." A tax year is the 12 months beginning with April 6 in any year.

[¹Disapplication of section 1(1A) of the Administration Act

2A. Section 1(1A) of the Administration Act (requirement to state national insurance number) shall not apply—

(a) to a child or young person in respect of whom family credit is claimed;

(b) to any claim for family credit made or treated as made before 9th February 1998;

(c) to a partner in respect of whom a claim for family credit is made or treated as made before 5th October 1998.]

AMENDMENT

1. Social Security (National Insurance Number Information: Exemption) Regulations 1997 (S.I. 1997 No. 2676), reg. 6 (December 1, 1997).

DEFINITIONS

"child"—see SSCBA, s. 137(1).
"partner"—see reg. 2(1).
"young person"—see reg. 6.

GENERAL NOTE

See the notes to s. 1(1A)–(1C) of the Administration Act and reg. 2A of the Income Support Regulations. Note that in the case of family credit (and disability working allowance) the requirement to have, or apply for, a national insurance number as a condition of entitlement to benefit does not apply to any claim made, or treated as made, before February 9, 1998 (para. (b)). Like income support, a partner is exempt where the claim is made or treated as made before October 5, 1998 (para. (c)).

PART II

PRESENCE IN GREAT BRITAIN AND REMUNERATIVE WORK

Circumstances in which a person is treated as being or as not being in Great Britain

3.—(1) A person shall be treated as being in Great Britain if, on the date of claim—

(a) he is present and ordinarily resident in Great Britain; and
[²(aa) subject to paragraph (1A), his right to reside or remain in Great Britain is not subject to any limitation or condition, and]
(b) his partner, if any, is ordinarily resident in the United Kingdom; and
(c) his earnings or the earnings of his partner, if any, derive at least in part from remunerative work in the United Kingdom; and
(d) his earnings do not wholly derive from remunerative work outside the United Kingdom nor do the earnings of his partner, if any.

[²(1A) For the purposes of paragraph (1)(aa), a person's right to reside or remain in Great Britain is not to be treated as if it were subject to a limitation or condition if—

(a) he is a person recorded by the Secretary of State as a refugee within the definition in Article 1 of the Convention relating to the Status of Refugees done at Geneva on 28th July 1951, as extended by Article 1(2) of the Protocol relating to the Status of Refugees done at New York on 31st January 1967;
(b) he is a person who has been granted exceptional leave outside the provisions of the immigration rules within the meaning of the Immigration Act 1971;
    [³(i) to enter the United Kingdom by an immigration officer appointed for the purposes of the Immigration Act 1971; or
    (ii) to remain in the United Kingdom by the Secretary of State];
(c) he is a national, or a member of the family of a national, of a State contracting party to the Agreement on the European Economic Area signed at Oporto on 2nd May 1992 as adjusted by the Protocol signed at Brussels on 17th March 1993; or
(d) he is a person who is—
    (i) lawfully working in Great Britain and is a national of a State with which the Community has concluded an Agreement under article 238 of the Treaty establishing the European Community providing, in the field of social security, for the equal treatment of workers who are nationals of the signatory State and their families, or

(ii) a member of the family of, and living with, such a person.]
(2) A person shall be treated as not being in Great Britain during any period for which he, or his partner, is entitled to be paid family credit [¹or disability working allowance] under the law of Northern Ireland.

AMENDMENTS

1. Disability Living Allowance and Disability Working Allowance (Consequential Provisions) Regulations 1991 (S.I. 1991 No. 2742), reg. 13(3) (April 6, 1992).
2. Social Security (Persons from Abroad) Miscellaneous Amendments Regulations 1996 (S.I. 1996 No. 30), reg. 6 (February 5, 1996).
3. Social Security (Miscellaneous Amendments) Regulations 1998 (S.I. 1998 No. 563), reg. 18(1) and (2)(c) (April 7, 1998).

DEFINITIONS

"date of claim"—see reg. 2(1).
"disability working allowance"—*ibid.*
"earnings"—*ibid.*
"family"—see SSCBA, s.137(1).
"partner"—see reg. 2(1).

GENERAL NOTE

The requirement for the claimant to be in Great Britain at the date of claim appears in s.128(1) of the Contributions and Benefits Act (1986 Act, s.20(5)). See the notes to s. 128(1) for the compatibility of the rule with EC Regulation 1408/71. By s.137(2) (1986 Act, s.20(12)(a)) regulations may provide for circumstances in which a person is to be treated as being or not being in Great Britain.

Paragraph (1)
The form of this provision is peculiar. It sets out a composite sufficient condition for treating a person as being in Great Britain. But because the opening phrase is "if," not "if and only if" (or even "only if"), it appears to remain open to a person to show actual presence in Great Britain on a straightforward factual basis. However, in *R(FC) 2/93* the Commissioner has specifically rejected this view, because it would involve giving no meaning to para. (1)(a). He holds that para. (1) prescribes exhaustively the circumstances in which a person is to be treated as present in Great Britain, so that if the circumstances fall outside para. (1) the person is to be treated as not present. Then para. (2) applies to people who would otherwise come within para. (1). Although the drafting is unsatisfactory, *R(FC) 2/93* must be followed by SSATs. And now see sub-para. (aa) and para. (1A).
Sub-paras. (a) and (b). The phrase "ordinarily resident" was considered in *R(M) 1/85*, where the Commissioner adopted the approach of Lord Scarman in *R. v. Barnet London Borough Council, ex parte Shah* [1983] 2 A. C. 309, that the words must be given their natural and ordinary meaning unless there is something in the statute to indicate otherwise. The ordinary meaning is that the person must be habitually and normally resident apart from temporary or occasional absences. The word "habitually" imports that the residence has been adopted voluntarily and for settled purposes as part of the regular order of his life for the time being, although not necessarily with the intention of remaining indefinitely or for more than a limited period. This may be slightly wider than the approach adopted in *R(P) 1/78* and *R(F) 1/62* (see *CA 35/1992*). Residence which is unlawful cannot be ordinary residence. See also the notes to the additional definition of "person from abroad" introduced into reg. 21(3) of the Income Support Regulations from August 1, 1994 on the meaning of "habitual residence".
The presence of the claimant is a matter of fact. The claimant's partner need not be present in Great Britain, but for para. (1) to apply must be ordinarily resident in the United Kingdom (on which see above). Note that if a claimant's spouse is not a member of the same household as the claimant the spouse does not come within the definition of "partner" in reg. 2(1) (*CFC 11/1992*).
Sub-para. (aa). See the note to para. (1A).
Sub-paras. (c) and (d). Remunerative work is defined in reg. 4. Either the claimant or the partner must work for at least 16 hours a week in the United Kingdom (which includes Northern Ireland as well as Great Britain (Interpretation Act 1978, Sched.1)). But if either the claimant or partner

derives all their income from remunerative work outside the United Kingdom, then under sub-para. (d) the deeming provision cannot operate.

Paragraph (1A)

From February 5, 1996 a new requirement has been introduced that the claimant's right to be in Great Britain must not be subject to any limitation or condition (sub-para. (aa)); an example would be if the claimant has been granted leave to remain for six months as a visitor. The same applies to disability working allowance (and most other non-contributory benefits). But the rule does not apply if the claimant has been recognised as a refugee or granted exceptional leave to enter or remain (sub-paras. (a) and (b)), or is, or is a member of the family of, an EEA national (see the notes to reg. 21(3) of the Income Support Regulations) (sub-para. (c)), or is lawfully working in Great Britain and is a national of a country with which the E.C. has an agreement providing for equal treatment in social security (or is a member of the family of, and living with, such a person) (sub-para. (d)). Such agreements have been signed with Algeria, Morocco, Slovenia and Tunisia. "Lawfully" presumably means that the person does not have any restriction on taking employment here.

Reg. 3 only has to be satisfied at the date of claim so the new test can only apply to family credit claims made after February 4, 1996. And note the transitional protection for claimants receiving family credit before February 5, 1996 in reg. 12(3) of the Social Security (Persons From Abroad) Miscellaneous Amendments Regulations 1996 (p. 967). This provides that their entitlement continues until it is reviewed under s. 25 of the Administration Act (s. 30 of that Act also referred to in reg. 12(3) does not apply to family credit). There are only limited grounds on which a family credit award can be reviewed (see s. 128(3) of the Contributions and Benefits Act and regs. 49 to 51A). Moreover, a review is not necessary to bring a family credit award to an end, since an award expires by effluxion of time after six months. There is no reference in reg. 12(3) to an award of family credit coming to an end (or indeed to an award of family credit). Reg. 12(3) only refers to "a person [who] is receiving . . . family credit . . ." whose entitlement is reviewed under s. 25. Thus the effect of reg. 12(3) seemed to be to allow existing claimants who would otherwise be affected by the new test in para. (1A) to continue to be entitled to family credit (not only in relation to their current award but also on the basis of subsequent renewal claims) unless and until there were grounds for review of their family credit entitlement.

But in *CFC 1580/1997* the Commissioner holds that the transitional protection in reg. 12(3) did not apply to repeat claims. The AO had submitted that reg. 12(3) continued entitlement for a person receiving family credit when the 1996 Regulations came into effect, and that on a literal construction that entitlement ended when her current award of benefit expired. However, this was rejected by the Commissioner who pointed out that reg. 12(3) was not drafted in terms of the claimant's entitlement surviving the coming into force of the 1996 Regulations but in terms of the Family Credit Regulations having effect in their unamended form (subject to the claimant's entitlement being reviewed). Nevertheless, in his view the reference to review in reg. 12(3) was significant and indicated that the transitional protection was only to continue until the claimant's case was looked at again. He considered it inconceivable that it was intended that transitional protection would be lost on a review but not when an award came to an end.

Sedley J. reached the opposite conclusion in *R. v. Adjudication Officer, ex parte B*, High Court, June 19, 1998 (which concerned a renewal claim for disability living allowance but the same principles will apply to family credit). He did not consider it appropriate to introduce words or impute intention to overcome what he regarded as the clear effect of reg. 12(3), *i.e.*, that for a claimant receiving one of the listed benefits immediately before February 5, 1996 the regulations governing entitlement to that benefit continued to operate as if the 1996 Regulations had not been made. However, his decision was overturned on appeal (*R. v. Chief Adjudication Officer, ex parte B, The Times*, December 23, 1998). The Court of Appeal, by a majority, took the view that the wording and context of reg. 12(3) indicated that the draftsman was only looking at awards of benefit that were current on February 5, 1996. It would be uncharacteristic of transitional protection to extend such protection to an entitlement that was not yet in existence, *i.e.* one based on a new (albeit repeat) claim made after the coming into force of the 1996 Regulations. Peter Gibson L.J. agreed with *CFC 1580/1997* that it would indeed be surprising if the transitional protection was lost on a review but not on a repeat claim.

Paragraph (2)

If either the claimant or the partner is entitled to family credit or disability working allowance in Northern Ireland, the claimant is to be treated as not present in Great Britain.

[¹Remunerative work

4.—(1) For the purposes of Part II of the Act [SSCBA, Part VII] as it applies to family credit, and subject to paragraph (3), a person shall be treated as engaged in remunerative work where—

(a) the work he undertakes is for not less than 16 hours per week;

(b) the work is done for payment or in expectation of payment; and

(c) he is employed at the date of claim and satisfies the requirements of paragraph (5).

(2) A person who does not satisfy all the requirements of sub-paragraphs (a) to (c) of paragraph (1) shall not be treated as engaged in remunerative work.

[³(3) A person who otherwise satisfies all the requirements of paragraph (1) shall not be treated as engaged in remunerative work insofar as—

(a) he is engaged by a charitable or voluntary organisation or is a volunteer, where the only payment received by him or due to be paid to him is a payment which is to be disregarded under regulation 24(2) and paragraph 2 of Schedule 2 (sums to be disregarded in the calculation of income other than earnings);

(b) he is engaged in caring for a person in respect of whom he receives payments to which paragraph 24 of Schedule 2 refers; or

(c) he is engaged on a scheme for which a training allowance is being paid.]

(4) [⁴Subject to paragraph (4A),] in determining for the purposes of sub-paragraph (a) of paragraph (1) whether the work a person undertakes is for not less than 16 hours per week—

(a) there shall be included in the calculation any time allowed for meals or refreshment but only where the person is, or expects to be, paid earnings in respect of that time; and

(b) if he is a person to whom regulation 14(5) (normal weekly earnings of employed earners) applies, the hours worked shall be calculated by reference to the average number of hours which his employer expects him to work in a week; or

(c) where paragraph (b) does not apply and—

(i) a recognised cycle of working has been established at the date of claim, the hours worked shall be calculated by reference to the average number of hours worked in a week over the period of one complete cycle (including where the cycle involves periods in which the person does not normally work, those periods, but disregarding any other absences); or

(ii) no recognised cycle of working has been established at the date of claim, the hours worked shall be calculated by reference to—

(aa) the average number of hours worked over the five weeks immediately preceding the week of claim, or such other longer time preceding that week as may, in the particular case, enable the person's weekly average hours of work to be determined more accurately; or

(bb) where he is a self-employed earner and he has worked for less than 5 weeks at the date of claim [⁵or he has, in the five weeks immediately preceding the week of claim, increased the number of hours that he works from below 16 hours to 16 hours or more per week,] the average number of hours he expects to work in a week.

[⁴(4A) Where for the purpose of paragraph (4)(c)(i), a person's recognised cycle of work at a school, other educational establishment or other place of employment is one year and includes periods of school holidays or similar vacations during which he does not work, those periods and any other periods not forming part of such holidays or vacations during which he is not required to work shall be disregarded in establishing the average hours for which he is engaged in work.]

(5) Subject to paragraph (6), the requirements of this paragraph are that the person—

    (a) worked not less than 16 hours in either—

        (i) the week of claim; or

        (ii) either of the two weeks immediately preceding the week of claim; or

    (b) is expected by his employer to work or, where he is a self-employed earner he expects to work, not less than 16 hours in the week next following the week of claim; or

    (c) cannot satisfy the requirements of either sub-paragraph (a) or (b) above and at the date of claim he is absent from work by reason of a recognised, customary or other holiday but he is expected by his employer to work, or where he is a self-employed earner he expects to work, not less than 16 hours in the week following his return to work from that holiday,

and for the purposes of calculating the number of hours worked, sub-paragraph (a) of paragraph (4) shall apply to this paragraph as it applies to sub-paragraph (a) of paragraph (1).

[²(6) For the purposes of paragraph (5)—

    (a) work which a person does only qualifies if—

        (i) it is the work he normally does, and

        (ii) it is likely to last for a period of 5 weeks or more beginning with the week of claim; and

    (b) a person shall be treated as not on a recognised, customary or other holiday on any day on which the person is on maternity leave or is absent from work because he is ill.]

(7) Where a person is treated as engaged in remunerative work in accordance with the above paragraphs, he shall also be treated as normally engaged in remunerative work.]

[³(8)[⁴. . . .]]

AMENDMENTS

    1. Family Credit (General) Amendment Regulations 1992 (S.I. 1992 No. 573), reg. 3 (April 7, 1992).

    2. Income-related Benefits Schemes (Miscellaneous Amendments) (No. 4) Regulations 1993 (S.I. 1993 No. 2119), reg. 26 (October 5, 1993).

    3. Income-related Benefits Schemes (Miscellaneous Amendments) (No. 5) Regulations 1994 (S.I. 1994 No. 2139), reg. 11 (October 4, 1994).

    4. Income-related Benefits Schemes (Miscellaneous Amendments) Regulations 1995 (S.I. 1995 No. 516), reg. 11 (April 11, 1995).

    5. Family Credit and Disability Working Allowance (General) Amendment Regulations 1997 (S.I. 1997 No. 806), reg. 2 (October 7, 1997).

DEFINITIONS

    "the Act"—see reg. 2(1).
    "claim"—*ibid.*
    "date of claim"—*ibid.*
    "maternity leave"—*ibid.*
    "training allowance"—*ibid.*
    "voluntary organisation"—*ibid.*
    "week"—*ibid.*
    "week of claim"—*ibid.*

GENERAL NOTE

    Under s.128(1)(b) of the Contributions and Benefits Act (1986 Act, s.20(5)(b)) it is a condition of entitlement that at the date of claim either the claimant or her partner (if any) is engaged and normally engaged in remunerative work. Reg. 4 now provides an exhaustive test of whether this condition is satisfied. In April 1992 the test was somewhat simplified and definitely clarified in its compression into one regulation. It was previously very confusingly split between regs. 4 and 5. The family credit regulation is now very close to that adopted for disability working allowance. In the past there has been an attempt (not by any means successful) to maintain a uniform test for income support and family credit, so that if a claimant or a partner did not qualify as in remunerative work for family credit purposes, she should not be excluded from income support as being in remunerative work. However, the income support provisions have not been reformed as the family credit provisions have been and there seems now to be even more scope for different decisions between the two benefits (and now income-based JSA). Moreover, this approach was further abandoned in October 1996 when the limit for remunerative work for a partner for the purposes of income support/income-based JSA was increased to 24 hours a week. There is now the possibility of a partner qualifying for family credit (or in certain areas of the country, earnings top-up if they are a couple without children) while the claimant is claiming income support/income-based JSA. But any award of family credit (or earnings top-up) will be taken into account in full as income and could therefore have the effect of "floating the claimant off" income support/income-based JSA (income support/income-based JSA is ignored as income for family credit: see para. 3 of Sched. 2, and is also disregarded under the earnings top-up rules). In such a situation a couple may well have to calculate whether they stand to gain or lose by claiming family credit, bearing in mind the loss of passported benefits such as free school meals, etc. Family credit does not count as notional income for the purposes of income support/income-based JSA, nor does earnings top-up (reg. 42(2)(e) and (h) of the Income Support Regulations and reg. 105(2)(d) and (f) of the JSA Regulations). Note also reg. 6(27) and (28) of the Claims and Payments Regulations, the effect of which is to allow a 14-day period of grace where claims for family credit or disability working allowance are made when income support or income-based JSA should have been claimed instead because of the remunerative work rules, and vice versa.

Para. (1) breaks down the question of remunerative work into three conditions, all of which must be satisfied. If any one of them is not met, then the person is deemed not to be in remunerative work (para. (2)). The three conditions are that:

(a) the work is for at least 16 hours per week;

(b) the work is remunerative; and

(c) there has been or will be 16 hours work in a specified week.

Even if all three conditions are met, a volunteer or a person working for a charity or voluntary organisation who receives only expenses is excluded under para. (3)(a). (A volunteer is someone who without any legal obligation performs a service for another person without expectation of payment (*R(IS) 12/92*)). So also from October 4, 1994, is a person being paid by a health or local authority or voluntary organisation for providing temporary care in their home (para. (3)(b)), and a person in receipt of a training allowance (para. (3)(c)). *CDWA 1/1992* had held that a trainee on a YTS scheme was in remunerative work for the purposes of disability working allowance and the same principle would have applied to family credit. However, sub-para. (c) now specifically excludes this possibility.

The following notes deal with each of the three conditions in turn, rather than proceed paragraph by paragraph.

Work for at least 16 hours per week

First, note that the test is not in terms of employment, but in terms of work, which is a broader concept. See, in particular, *R(FC) 2/90* and *CFC 7/1989*, discussed in the notes to reg. 5 of the Income Support (General) Regulations. *R(FIS) 1/86* suggests that a student is engaged in "work," but will normally be knocked out by the fact that the work is not remunerative. Note the exclusions in para. (3).

Para. 50381 of the *Adjudication Officer's Guide* states that the total hours can be made up from more than one job.

Second, note that the concept of "activities in the course of work" has disappeared from the regulations. The terms are simply "work" or "working." There will be difficult questions deciding what sort of activities count as work. The only help in the regulation itself is that meal or refreshment breaks count only if they are paid (para. (4)(a)). Presumably, "working" means actually being at work, as undertaking activities in the course of work did (*R(FIS) 2/81, R(FIS) 2/82* and *R(FIS) 1/85*). See *CFC 588/1995* in which a traffic warden who was suspended on full pay was not "working" for the purposes of her family credit claim, even though she remained liable to be recalled to her duties at any time.

It is clear that the focus is on the hours actually worked, rather than the hours specified in any contract. The approach of *R(FC) 1/92*, that in each case it must be asked what time is necessarily spent carrying out activities in the course of the work, may be helpful. It was suggested there that in some jobs (*e.g.* teaching or in the health service) it may not be practicable to work to precise time limits. In *R(FC) 1/92*, the claimant worked as an ambulance transport clerk and gave evidence that she regularly had to stay on after hours because of delays. In other cases, it may be shown that preparation outside contractual hours is necessary. For the self-employed, the test will be the hours of activity essential to the undertaking (see *R(FIS) 6/85*). However, in some cases the activity need not be very active, *e.g.* keeping a shop or workshop open to the public. See the notes to reg. 5 of the Income Support (General) Regulations.

Para. (4) defines how hours of work are to be calculated for the 16 hour test under para. (1)(a). The effect is that in most cases it is the period before the date of claim which has to be looked at. The first exception is under sub-para. (b). Where a person has only recently started or resumed work as an employed earner, within the limits supplied by reg. 14(5), the number of hours which the employer expects the person to work are taken. See sub-para. (c)(ii)(bb) below for a similar effect for the self-employed (see below).

Outside sub-para. (b), the calculation is to be made under sub-para. (c), which now clearly covers all cases. If a recognised cycle of working has been established as at the date of claim, then an average must be taken over one complete cycle (head (i)). Whether a cycle has been established and its length is a matter of judgment for the AO or the SSAT. It is not clear that the word "recognised" adds anything to the provision, even if it means something different from "recognisable," the word in the old regulation. Does a "cycle" imply some fluctuation in hours or of periods of work and no work? It is arguable that it does, so that someone who works absolutely regular hours would not come within head (i). However, this is not the view taken by the *Adjudication Officer's Guide* (see para. 50412). Periods of no work which are built into the cycle are included in the averaging (although now see para. (4A)), but not other absences. *R(IS) 15/94* held that in the case of a school receptionist the school holidays were periods of no work. Her contract of employment continued during the holidays but she was not paid, except for the occasional day's work that she was asked to do. The Commissioner disagreed with *CIS 261/1990* (unstarred) which suggested that school holidays counted as other absences to be excluded in the averaging (see the note to reg. 5(1) of the Income Support Regulations). He held that the claimant's recognisable cycle was a yearly one. *R(IS) 7/96* further held that where a school ancillary worker was paid for 44 weeks each year but only required to work during term time (38 weeks), it was the total number of hours she actually worked (20 hours × 38 weeks) that had to be averaged over the one year cycle. The approach of *R(IS) 15/94* and *R(IS) 7/96* produced a lower weekly figure which could assist a claimant in qualifying for income support, but caused difficulty for certain family credit claimants. The policy intention apparently was that benefit entitlement should be based on the average hours worked during term time and so para. (4A) has been introduced. This provides that if a person has an annual cycle of work which includes periods of no work, for example, school holidays, such periods are ignored in averaging hours of work. A similar rule has been introduced for income support (and now JSA) and disability working allowance (and housing benefit and council tax benefit). The new rule will benefit those claiming family credit and disability working allowance but will work to the disadvantage of income support and JSA claimants. It should be noted that para. (4A) only applies where the recognised cycle is a year. This may not always be the case, for example, if a person has a separate contract of employment for each period of work. See the notes to reg. 5 of the Income Support (General) Regulations, and in particular the discussion under the heading "*Term-time only workers*".

If no recognised cycle has been established, the calculation in most cases is under head (ii)(aa). The basic rule is to take an average over the five weeks before the week of claim. If it will enable the person's average weekly hours of work to be determined more accurately, a longer period before the week of claim may be used. But it must positively be shown that the result is more accurate than that produced by the normal rule (*R(FIS) 1/81* and *R(FIS) 2/83*). It is not enough that the AO does not like the result of applying the normal rule.

Head (ii)(bb) deals with a self-employed person who has worked for less than five weeks at the date of claim, and so has not had time to establish a cycle of working. The October 1997 amendment to sub-head (bb) means that this provision will also apply where a self-employed person has increased his hours of work to 16 or more hours a week in the five weeks immediately before the date of claim. If the hours worked have been uniform, this is not a cycle. If they fluctuate, there has not been time to see if there is a pattern. The test is then the average number of hours the person expects to work. This must turn mainly on what the person declares his expectations to be. There is no requirement for the expectations to be reasonable, but there will be a point at which something is so unrealistic that an adjudicating authority can conclude that it cannot truly be part of a person's expectations.

Remunerative work

The condition laid down in para. (1)(b) is not elaborated any further in the regulation. See above and the notes to reg. 5 of the Income Support Regulations.

16 hours work in specified weeks

The condition in para. (1)(c) is in fact quite complex. The first part is that the person must be employed at the date of claim. This appears to mean that there must be an employment situation in existence. It does not require the person actually to be working. The second part is to satisfy the requirements of para. (5). Here, the major test is of 16 hours work in a specified week, but para. (6)(a) applies extra tests of normality.

The weeks in which the 16-hour test can be satisfied are the week of claim (sub-para. (a)(i)), either of the two weeks before the week of claim (sub-para. (a)(ii)), the week following the week of claim, on the basis of what is expected (sub-para. (b)) or the week following an absence on holiday, again on the basis of what is expected (sub-para. (c)). Sub-paras. (b) and (c) were new in April 1992, and remove the difficulties exposed in decisions such as *CFC 1/1989* and *R(FC) 2/91*, where the claimant happened to have holiday absences in the then crucial weeks although it was absolutely clear that she normally worked the required number of hours. There could also be problems where someone started work and immediately claimed family credit. The new flexibility is wholly welcome. But note that sub-para. (c) only applies where the claimant's absence from work at the date of claim is by reason of a recognised, customary or other holiday. In *CFC 15/1992* the Commissioner holds that "or other holiday" can mean a day that is a non-working day by agreement between employers and workers and that this could include maternity leave. Para. (6)(b) now specifically provides that in the case of absence through sickness or maternity leave a person is not treated as on holiday. A claimant in this situation will have to claim income support for the period not worked. The definition of maternity leave in reg. 2(1) means that a woman counts as on maternity leave only if she has either a statutory or a contractual right to return to work. See also *CFC 588/ 1995* above where a claimant has been suspended from her employment.

Work cannot count towards the 16 hours in one of the specified weeks if it is not the work which the person normally does and it is not likely to last for five weeks or more from (and including) the week of claim. There was a test of normality for family income supplement. "Normal" was said to have its ordinary everyday meaning (*R(FIS) 2/83*). In *R(FIS) 6/83* the claimant was working full-time as a temporary porter at the date of claim. This was in the summer following the end of a three-year degree course. He had the offer of a place on a further degree course starting the next term, but had not decided whether or not to take it up. The Commissioner holds that on the appropriate time-scale, the claimant was not normally engaged in full-time work. Since the award of benefit was for 52 weeks, something like the situation at the date of claim needed to be expected to prevail for 52 weeks. In *R(FIS) 1/84* the claimant was on a four-year "sandwich" degree course, as part of which he had a job from May to September 1982. The Commissioner holds that the SSAT was entitled to take account of the fact that the claimant was primarily a student and of the length of an award in excluding the claimant. Although the same general principle will apply to family credit, the fact that the normal length of an award is 26 weeks (Contributions and Benefits Act, s.128(3); 1986 Act, s.20(6)) changes the context. But the fact that a person is primarily a student, or that a job is known to be coming to an end in the near future, will still be relevant.

The requirement that the work is likely to continue for at least five weeks from the week of claim then seems merely to provide a short cut in some cases. If the work is likely to end within five weeks it will not be normal, but it is easier to strike it out under para. (6)(a)(ii). However, work which is likely to last for more than five weeks is not necessarily normal. Para. (6)(a)(ii) does not impose a limit on the operation of para. (5)(c) because the counting is from the week of claim, not from the week of expected return from holiday.

It is the rule about normality which is the major cause of claimants being excluded from both income support (and now income-based JSA) and family credit. If the claimant counts as in remunerative work in any week, there cannot be entitlement to income support/income-based JSA in that week (Contributions and Benefits Act, s. 124(1)(c); Jobseekers Act, s. 1(2)(e)). But if the work is not normal there will not be entitlement to family credit either.

[¹Further provision as to remunerative work

4A.—Whether, for the purposes of regulation 46(1)(aa) (determination of appropriate maximum family credit) and paragraph 1A of Schedule 4, the work a person undertakes is for not less than 30 hours per week shall be determined in accordance with regulation 4(1)(b), (3), (4) and (4A) except that for the words "16 hours" in paragraph (4) there shall be substituted the words "30 hours".]

AMENDMENT

1. Income-related Benefits Schemes (Miscellaneous Amendments) (No. 2) Regulations 1995 (S.I. 1995 No. 1339), reg. 6 (July 18, 1995).

GENERAL NOTE

See the note to reg. 46(1).

Engagement in remunerative work and normal engagement

5. [¹ . . .]

AMENDMENT

1. Family Credit (General) Amendment Regulations 1992 (S.I. 1992 No. 573), reg. 3 (April 7, 1992).

PART III

MEMBERSHIP OF A FAMILY

Persons of a prescribed description

6.—(1) Subject to paragraph (2), a person of a prescribed description for the purposes of section 20(5)(c) [SSCBA, s.128(1)(d)] (entitlement) and section 20(11) of the Act [SSCBA, s.137(1)] (definition of the family) as it applies to family credit is a person aged 16 or over but under 19 who is receiving full-time education within section 2(1)(b) of the Child Benefit Act 1975 [SSCBA, s.142(1)(b)] (meaning of child), and in these Regulations such a person is referred to as "a young person."

[¹(2) Paragraph (1) shall not apply to a person—

(a) who is entitled to income support or would, but for section 20(9) of the Act [SSCBA, s.134(2)] (provision against dual entitlement of members of family), be so entitled;

[²(aa) who is entitled to income-based jobseeker's allowance or would, but for section 3(1)(d) of the Jobseekers Act 1995 (provision against dual entitlement of members of family), be so entitled;]

(b) who is receiving advanced education within the meaning of regulation 1(2) of the Child Benefit (General) Regulations 1976; or

(c) who has ceased to receive full-time education but is to continue to be treated as a child by virtue of regulation 7 of the Child Benefit (General) Regulations 1976.]

AMENDMENTS

1. Family Credit (General) Amendment Regulations 1992 (S.I. 1992 No. 574), reg. 4 (April 10, 1992).
2. Social Security and Child Support (Jobseeker's Allowance) (Consequential Amendments) Regulations 1996 (S.I. 1996 No. 1345), reg. 8(3) (October 7, 1996).

DEFINITION

"the Act"—see reg. 2(1).

GENERAL NOTE

Para. (1) is very similar to, although not identical with, reg. 14(1) of the Income Support (General) Regulations. Reg. 14 refers to a person who is treated as a child for the purposes of s.142 of the Contributions and Benefits Act (Child Benefit Act 1975, s.2). Reg. 6 refers to a person who is receiving full-time education within s.142(1)(b) (Child Benefit Act 1975, s.2(1)(b)). *CFC 21/1990* shows that this difference is significant where a person has just left school. In the period up to the next "terminal date" the person is treated under reg. 7 of the Child Benefit (General) Regulations as a child. This brings the person within reg. 14 of the Income Support Regulations, but not within reg. 6(1), because the person is not treated as still in full-time education. See the notes to reg. 14 of the Income Support Regulations for further details. In both cases, the person is called a "young person."

The operation of para. (2) is to much the same effect as reg. 14(2) of the Income Support Regulations (although there is no equivalent of sub-para. (aa) in reg. 14(2)). Sub-para. (c), excluding school-leavers until the terminal date, seems unnecessary, for such people are not receiving full-time education within s.142(1)(b) of the Contributions and Benefits Act (Child Benefit Act 1975, s.2(1)(b)). And see *CFC 21/1990*. But it marks a difference from the income support rule. Such school-leavers count as young persons under reg. 14, as do people until the end of the child benefit extension period. Neither category is a young person for family credit purposes.

Note that from July 2, 1996 a family credit award will terminate when the only remaining young person in a claimant's family leaves full-time education (rather than continue to the end of the 26 weeks). See reg. 49A and the note to that regulation.

Circumstances in which a person is to be treated as responsible or not responsible for another

7.—(1) Subject to the following provisions of this regulation, a person shall be treated as responsible for a child or young person who is normally living with him.

(2) Where a child or young person spends equal amounts of time in different households, or where there is a question as to which household he is living in, the child or young person shall be treated for the purposes of paragraph (1) as normally living with—

(a) the person who is receiving child benefit in respect of him; or

(b) if there is no such person—

  (i) where only one claim for child benefit has been made in respect of him, the person who made that claim, or

  (ii) in any other case the person who has the primary responsibility for him.

(3) For the purposes of these Regulations a child or young person shall be treated as the responsibility of only one person during the period of an award and any person other than the one treated as responsible for the child or young person under the foregoing paragraphs shall be treated as not so responsible.

DEFINITIONS

"child"—see 1986 Act, s.20(11) (SSCBA. s.137(1)).
"young person"—see reg. 2(1), reg. 6.

GENERAL NOTE

Under s.128(1)(d) of the Contributions and Benefits Act (1986 Act, s.20(5)(c)) it is a condition that one of the adults in the family is responsible for a child or young person who is a member of the same household. Reg. 8 deals with membership of the household. Reg. 7 deals with responsibility. The effect of para. (3) is that paras. (1) and (2) provide an exhaustive test of responsibility.

Para. (1) starts by making the test whether the child or young person is normally living with the adult. This exact test is a new one, although the phrase "living with" is used in the child benefit legislation (see, in particular *R(F) 2/79* and *R(F) 2/81*). *CFC 1537/1995* decides that a child "normally lives with" a person if he spends more time with that person than anyone else. This was the construction that made sense of para. (2). Para. (2) made provision for cases where a child spent equal amounts of time in different households and where there was doubt as to which household a child was living in because there was no established pattern. But para. (2) only applied in cases of real doubt; if there was simply a factual dispute this was not enough to bring para. (2) into play. The Commissioner also comments on the point made in previous editions of this book about the sloppy use of language in para. (2) (*e.g.* the reference to living in a household, when the question is of normally living with a particular person). In his view, "household" is simply used as a collective noun to describe the adults and child living together. But he does accept that a consequence is that there is no means of deciding (if this is necessary) which of the various people in the household is to be treated as responsible for the child.

If para. (2) applies, there is then a series of tests. The first is receipt of child benefit, whose rules include methods of establishing priorities between claimants. If no-one is receiving child benefit then if only one person has claimed child benefit, that person has priority. If there have been no claims or more than one, the final test is who has "primary responsibility." Until October 4, 1993, this concept also appeared in reg. 15 of the Income Support (General) Regulations. "Responsibility" has no special meaning in the legislation and so must be determined according to the ordinary everyday meaning of the word.

It would seem that under reg. 7 responsibility or the normality of living may be judged on an overall basis over a period. This is different from the income support provision, where the test of responsibility has to be applied week by week (*CIS 49/1991* and *Whelan v. Chief Adjudication Officer, The Independent*, November 14, 1994).

Para. (3) secures that a child or young person, once attached to an adult, is only to be treated as the responsibility of that person for the duration of a family credit award. Also if a person meets the tests of paras. (1) and (3), no-one else can allege that they are responsible for the child for the purposes of family credit. But see the notes to reg. 15(4) of the Income Support Regulations where another person is claiming income support (and now income-based JSA).

Membership of the same household

8.—(1) Except in a case to which paragraph (2) applies, where a claimant or any partner is treated as responsible for a child or young person by virtue of regulation 7 (circumstances where a person is treated as responsible or not responsible for another), that child or young person and any child of that child or young person shall be treated as a member of the claimant's household.

(2) A child or young person shall not be treated as a member of the claimant's household in any case where the child or young person—

(a) is a patient or in residential accommodation on account of physical or mental handicap or physical or mental illness and has been so accommodated for the 12 weeks immediately before the date of claim and is no longer in regular contact with the claimant or any member of the claimant's household; or

[¹(b) has been placed with the claimant or his partner prior to adoption; or

(c) has been placed with the claimant or his partner by a local authority under section 23(2)(a) of the Children Act 1989 or by a voluntary organisation under section 59(1)(a) of that Act; or]

(d) has been placed for adoption with the claimant or his partner pursuant to a decision under the Adoption Agencies Regulations 1983 or the Adoption Agencies (Scotland) Regulations 1984; or

(e) is detained in custody under a sentence imposed by a court.

(3) In this regulation—

(a) "patient" means a person (other than a person who is serving a sentence imposed by a court in a prison or youth custody institution) who is regarded as receiving free in-patient treatment within the meaning of the Social Security (Hospital In-Patients) Regulations 1975.

(b) [¹. . .];

(c) "residential accommodation" means accommodation for a person whose

stay in the accommodation has become other than temporary which is provided under—
- (i) sections 21 to 24 and 26 of the National Assistance Act 1948; or
- (ii) section 21(1) of, and paragraph 1 or 2 of Schedule 8 to, the National Health Service Act 1977 (prevention, care and after-care) or, in Scotland, for the purposes of section 27 of the National Health Services (Scotland) Act 1947 (prevention of illness and after-care) or under section 59 of the Social Work (Scotland) Act 1968 (provision of residential and other establishments) or under section 7 of the Mental Health (Scotland) Act 1984 (functions of local authorities).

AMENDMENT

1. Family Credit (General) Amendment Regulations 1992 (S.I. 1992 No. 573), Sched., para. 2 (April 7, 1992).

DEFINITIONS

"child"—see 1986 Act, s.20(11) (SSCBA, s.137(1)).
"claimant"—see reg. 2(1).
"date of claim"—*ibid.*
"partner"—*ibid.*
"voluntary organisation"—*ibid.*
"young person"—*ibid.*, reg. 6.

GENERAL NOTE

Paragraph (1)
The general rule is that if an adult is treated as responsible for a child or young person under reg. 7 the child or young person is to be treated as a member of the adult's household.

Paragraph (2)
This provision supplies exceptions to the general rule. It is necessary because there are circumstances in which entitlement to child benefit can continue, sometimes for a specified number of weeks, despite the absence of the child.
The previous form (see the 1991 edition) of sub-paras. (b) and (c) remains in force in Scotland. The new form was introduced on April 7, 1992, as a consequence of the Children Act 1989.

Paragraph (3)
This supplies the necessary definitions. See the notes to reg. 21(3) of the Income Support (General) Regulations for "patient."
The definition of "relevant enactment" previously contained in sub-para. (b) remains in force in Scotland (see the 1991 edition). It was no longer necessary for England and Wales because of the new form of para. (2)(c), introduced as a consequence of the Children Act 1989. Now see the Children (Scotland) Act 1995.

Circumstances in which a person is to be treated as being no longer a member of the same household

9.—[²(1) Subject to the following provisions of this regulation, where the claimant and any partner of his are living apart from each other they shall be treated as members of the same household unless they do not intend to resume living together.]

(2) Where one of the members of a married or unmarried couple is a hospital [¹patient] or [¹detained in custody] he shall not be treated, on this account, as ceasing to be a member of the same household as his partner—
- (a) unless he has been [¹a patient] in a hospital for 52 weeks or more; or
- (b) unless he is a patient detained in a hospital provided under section 4 of

the National Health Service Act 1977 (special hospitals) or section 90(1) of the Mental Health (Scotland) Act 1984 (provision of hospitals for patients requiring special security); or

(c) unless he is [¹detained in custody whilst] serving a sentence of 52 weeks or more imposed by a court,

but shall be treated as not being a member of the same household as his partner wherever the conditions in sub-paragraphs (a), (b) or (c) are fulfilled.

[¹(3) In this regulation ''patient'' has the same meaning as in regulation 8(3)(a) (membership of the same household).]

AMENDMENTS

1. Family Credit (General) Amendment Regulations 1988 (S.I. 1988 No. 660), reg. 3 (April 11, 1988).
2. Income-related Benefits Schemes (Miscellaneous Amendments) (No. 4) Regulations 1993 (S.I. 1993 No. 2119), reg. 27 (October 5, 1993).

DEFINITIONS

''partner''—see reg. 2(1).
''married couple''—see 1986 Act, s.20(11) (SSCBA, s.137(1)).
''unmarried couple''—*ibid.*

GENERAL NOTE

A single parent or a couple can be entitled to family credit, and the basic calculation of benefit is the same.

The old form of reg. 9 (up to October 5, 1993) only dealt with some specific cases in which a couple no longer counted as members of the same household. Para. (1) now contains a more general rule that a claimant and her partner are deemed to be members of the same household, notwithstanding that they are living apart unless they do not intend to resume living together. (On intention see *CIS 508/1992* and *CIS 484/1993* in the notes to para. 3 of Sched. 3 to the Income Support Regulations and on the effect of the placing of the word ''not'' see *CIS 13805/1996* in the notes to reg. 16(2) of the Income Support Regulations.) There are exceptions in para. (2). This brings the family credit provision more in line with the test in reg. 16(1) and (2) of the Income Support Regulations but there are differences. For family credit purposes, unless the couple do not intend to resume living together, the deeming applies whether or not the absence is temporary, or likely to last more than 52 weeks (unless para. (2) applies). However, for the reasons given in the notes to reg. 16(1), para. (1) cannot subvert the general meaning of household (see the notes to s. 137(1) of the Contributions and Benefits Act and *CIS 671/1992*). Para. (1) must only mean that because a couple are living apart this does not in itself mean that membership of the same household ceases.

In addition, for para. (1) to operate, it is necessary for there to be a finding that the couple previously lived as members of the same household. The Commissioner in *CIS 508/1992* seems to have accepted that the home in which the couple previously lived need not have been in this country. But how this applies to the current test of living apart from the other partner is not entirely clear.

Membership of the same household is crucial in deciding whether a particular adult's income or capital is to be treated as the claimant's. It is also relevant to the question whether a claimant satisfies the residence test in reg. 3. So, for example, in the case of a couple where one partner has come to this country ahead of the other, para. (1) may mean that the claimant is not entitled to family credit if her partner is not ordinarily resident in the U.K., or has earnings all of which derive from work outside the U.K. See the notes to reg. 3 on the meaning of ''ordinarily resident''.

Paragraph (2)

A partner ceases to be a member of the household if he has been a hospital in-patient (see reg. 8(3)(a)) for at least 52 weeks, is detained in a special hospital, or is serving a prison or youth custody sentence of at least 52 weeks. Until in-patients have clocked up 52 weeks, they are still to be treated as members of the household, as are prisoners with sentences under 52 weeks.

Part IV

Income and Capital

Chapter I

General

Calculation of income and capital of members of claimant's family and of a polygamous marriage

10.—(1) The income and capital of a claimant's partner and, subject to regulation 27 (modifications in respect of children and young persons), the income of a child or young person, which by virtue of section 22(5) of the Act [SSCBA, s.136(1)] is to be treated as income and capital of the claimant, shall be calculated or estimated in accordance with the following provisions of this Part in like manner as for the claimant; and any reference to the "claimant" shall, except where the context otherwise requires, be construed, for the purposes of this Part, as if it were a reference to his partner or that child or young person.

(2) Where a claimant or the partner of a claimant is married polygamously to two or more members of the same household—

(a) the claimant shall be treated as possessing capital and income belonging to each such member and the income of any child or young person who is one of that member's family; and

(b) the income and capital of that member or, as the case may be, the income of that child or young person shall be calculated in accordance with the following provisions of this Part in like manner as for the claimant or, as the case may be, as for any child or young person who is a member of his family.

Definitions

"the Act"—see reg. 2(1).
"child"—see 1986 Act, s.20(11) (SSCBA, s.137(1)).
"claimant"—see reg. 2(1).
"family"—see 1986 Act, s.20(11) (SSCBA, s.137(1)).
"partner"—see reg. 2(1).
"young person"—*ibid.*, reg. 6.

General Note

The income and capital of married and unmarried couples (see Contributions and Benefits Act, s.137(1); 1986 Act, s.20(11)) are to be put together and treated as the claimant's (normally the woman: Claims and Payments Regulations, reg. 4(2)). Although s.136(1) (1986 Act, s.22(5)) and this regulation require the income and capital of a child or young person also to be treated as the claimant's, reg. 27, in conjunction with reg. 46(4) and (5), contains special rules for this situation, and under para. 2 of Sched. 1 the earnings of a child or young person are to be disregarded completely.

Note that para. (2) only applies to polygamous marriages, not to polygamous relationships generally.

Calculation of income and capital of students

11. The provisions of Chapters II to VI of this Part (income and capital) shall have effect in relation to students and their partners subject to the modifications set out in Chapter VII thereof (students).

DEFINITIONS

"partner"—see reg. 2(1).
"student"—*ibid.*

[¹Rounding of fractions

12. Where any calculation under this Part results in a fraction of a penny that fraction shall, if it would be to the claimants' advantage, be treated as a penny, otherwise it shall be disregarded.]

AMENDMENT

1. Family Credit (General) Amendment Regulations 1988 (S.I. 1988 No. 660), reg. 4 (April 11, 1988).

Chapter II

Normal Weekly Income

Calculation of income on a weekly basis

13.—(1) For the purposes of section 20(5) of the Act [SSCBA, s.128(1)] (conditions of entitlement to family credit), the income of a claimant shall be calculated on a weekly basis—

(a) by ascertaining in accordance with this Chapter and Chapter V of this Part (other income) the amount of his normal weekly income; [²...]

(b) by adding to that amount the weekly income calculated under regulation 36 (calculation of tariff income from capital); [²and]

[²(c) by then deducting any relevant child care charges to which regulation 13A (treatment of child care charges) applies from any earnings which form part of the normal weekly income, up to a maximum deduction in respect of the claimant's family of [³whichever of the sums specified in paragraph (1A) below applies in his case].]

[⁴(1A) The maximum deduction to which paragraph (1)(c) above refers shall be—

(a) where the claimant's family includes only one child in respect of whom relevant child care charges are paid, £60 per week;

(b) where the claimant's family includes more than one child in respect of whom relevant child care charges are paid, £100 per week.]

[¹(2) For the purposes of paragraph (1) "income" includes capital treated as income under regulation 25 (capital treated as income) and income which a claimant is treated as possessing under regulation 26 (notional income).]

AMENDMENTS

1. Family Credit (General) Amendment Regulations 1991 (S.I. 1991 No. 1520), reg. 3 (October 8, 1991).
2. Income-related Benefits Schemes (Miscellaneous Amendments) (No. 4) Regulations 1994 (S.I. 1994 No. 1924), reg. 4(3) (October 4, 1994).
3. Income-related Benefits (Miscellaneous Amendments) Regulations 1997 (S.I. 1997 No. 2793), reg. 2(1) and (2)(c) (June 2, 1998).
4. Income-related Benefits (Miscellaneous Amendments) Regulations 1997 (S.I. 1997 No. 2793), reg. 2(3) (June 2, 1998).

DEFINITIONS

"the Act"—see reg. 2(1).

"claimant"—*ibid.*, reg. 10(1).
"earnings"—see reg. 2(1).
"family"—see 1986 Act, s.20(11) (SSCBA, s. 137(1)).
"relevant child care charges"—see reg. 13A.

GENERAL NOTE

A claimant's income means hers and her partner's plus any income of a child or young person which counts (regs. 10(1) and 27). The categories are earnings of employed earners, earnings of directors, self-employed earnings, other income (including that mentioned in para. (2)) and the tariff income from capital (reg. 36). Regs. 14, 14A, 15 and 16 respectively start the chain of regulations for calculating each of the first four categories of income.

Para. (1)(c) and reg. 13A provide for the childcare disregard that was introduced for family credit from October 4, 1994. The disregard remains limited in scope as only certain claimants and types of childcare are covered, but the ceiling for the charges that can be deducted became a little more realistic when it was increased to £60 in April 1996. However, until June 1998 the limit was the same, regardless of the number of children in the family. From June 2, 1998 the ceiling remains at £60 for one child, but has been raised to £100 where the claimant has more than one child for whom she is paying qualifying childcare costs. Note also that from June 1998 the disregard is available if the award of benefit begins before the first Tuesday in September following the child's 12th (not 11th) birthday. The disregard also applies to disability working allowance (and housing and council tax benefit), but not income support or income-based JSA. Before income support was introduced in April 1988, the full cost of childcare (and other work-related expenses such as fares) could be offset against earnings when calculating entitlement to supplementary benefit.

Sub-para. (c) contains the basic rule and most of the detail is in reg. 13A. "Relevant child care charges" (defined in reg. 13A(2)) up to a maximum of £60 (increased from £40 in April 1996) a week for one child, from June 2, 1998, £100 if the claimant has more than one child for whom she is paying eligible childcare charges, can be offset against earnings. Because of the taper in the family credit calculation, the maximum increase in family credit that will be payable where the £60 disregard applies is £42 (£70 in the case of the £100 disregard). Since the recommended rates for full-time childcare with a registered childminder range from £60 to £90 per week per child, the alowance will continue to be only a contribution towards childcare costs in many cases.

Note that there will be changes to the rules for the treatment of child care costs when family credit is replaced by working families tax credit on October 5, 1999. See the 1999 Supplement to this book for details.

[¹Treatment of child care charges

13A.—(1) This regulation applies where a claimant is incurring [⁵or in the case of a claimant to whom paragraph (6A) applies, will incur] relevant child care charges and—

(a) is a lone parent and is engaged in remunerative work;

(b) is a member of a couple both of whom are engaged in remunerative work; or

(c) is a member of a couple where one member is engaged in remunerative work and the other member is incapacitated.

(2) In this regulation—

"local authority" means, in relation to England and Wales, the council of a county or district, a metropolitan district, a London Borough, the Common Council of the City of London or the Council of the Isles of Scilly or, in relation to Scotland, a regional, islands or district council;

"relevant child care charges" means the charges paid by the claimant for care provided for any child of the claimant's family [³ in respect of the period beginning on that child's date of birth and ending on the day preceding the first Tuesday in September following that child's [⁴ twelfth birthday]], other than charges paid in respect of the child's compulsory education, [² or charges paid by a claimant to a partner or by a partner to a claimant in respect of any child for whom either or any of them is responsible in accordance with regulation 7 (circumstances in which a person is to be treated as responsible or not responsible for another),] where the care is provided—

(a) by persons registered under section 71 of the Children Act 1989 (registration of child minders and persons providing day care for young children);

(b) for children [³ in respect of the period beginning on their eighth birthday and ending on the day preceding the first Tuesday in September following their [⁴ twelfth birthday]], out of school hours, by a school on school premises or by a local authority; or

(c) by a child care scheme operating on Crown property where registration under section 71 of the Children Act 1989 is not required, [² or

(d) in schools or establishments which are exempted from registration under section 71 of the Children Act 1989 by virtue of section 71(16) of and paragraph 3 or 4 of Schedule 9 to that Act,

and shall be calculated on a weekly basis in accordance with paragraphs (3) to (6) [⁵or, in the case of a claimant to whom paragraph (6A) applies, with paragraphs (6B) and (6C)];

"school term-time" means the school term-time applicable to the child for whom care is provided.

[³(2A) In paragraph (2)—

(a) the age of a child referred to in that paragraph shall be determined by reference to the age of the child at the date on which the period under section 128(3) of the Contributions and Benefits Act (period of award) begins;

(b) "the first Tuesday in September" means the Tuesday which first occurs in the month of September in any year.]

[⁵(c) in the definition of "relevant child care charges" the words "charges paid" shall be taken to include charges which will be incurred and to which paragraph (6A) applies.]

(3) Subject to paragraphs (4) to (6), relevant child care charges shall be calculated in accordance with the formula—

$$\frac{X + Y}{52}$$

where—

X is the average weekly charge paid for child care in the most recent 4 complete weeks which fall in school term-time in respect of the child or children concerned, multiplied by 39; and

Y is the average weekly charge paid for child care in the most recent 2 complete weeks which fall out of school term-time in respect of that child or those children, multiplied by 13.

(4) Subject to paragraph (5), where child care charges are being incurred in respect of a child who does not yet attend school, the relevant child care charges shall mean the average weekly charge paid for care provided in respect of that child in the most recent 4 complete weeks.

(5) Where in any case the charges in respect of child care are paid monthly, the average weekly charge for the purposes of paragraph (3) shall be established—

(a) where the charges are for a fixed monthly amount, by multiplying that amount by 12 and dividing the product by 52;

(b) where the charges are for variable monthly amounts, by aggregating the charges for the previous 12 months and dividing the total by 52.

(6) In a case where there is no information or insufficient information for establishing the average weekly charge paid for child care in accordance with paragraphs (3) to (5). the average weekly charge for care shall be estimated in accordance with information provided by the child minder or person providing

the care or, if such information is not available, in accordance with information provided by the claimant.

[⁵(6A) Where a claimant—

(a) has entered into an agreement for the provision of child care; and

(b) will incur under that agreement relevant child care charges in respect of child care during the period of the family credit award,

the weekly charge for child care shall be calculated in accordance with paragraphs (6B) and (6C), based upon a written estimate of the relevant future charges provided by the claimant and child minder or other child care provider.

(6B) Subject to paragraph (6C), relevant child care charges which fall under paragraph (6A) shall be calculated in accordance with formula—

$$\frac{X + Y}{52}$$

where—

X is the weekly estimate provided by the child minder or other child care provider for child care in those weeks which will fall in school term-time in respect of the child or children concerned, multiplied by 39; and

Y is the weekly estimate provided by the child minder or other child care provider for child care in those weeks which will fall out of school term-time in respect of the child or children concerned, multiplied by 13.

(6C) Where relevant child care charges fall under paragraph (6A) and they are in respect of a child who does not attend school, the relevant child care charges shall mean the weekly estimate provided by the child minder or other child care provider multiplied by the number of weeks during the period of the family credit award in which relevant child care charges will be paid, divided by 26.]

(7) For the purposes of paragraph (1)(c) the other member of a couple is incapacitated where—

(a) either council tax benefit or housing benefit is payable under Part VII of the Contributions and Benefits Act to the other member or his partner and the applicable amount of the person entitled to the benefit includes—

(i) a disability premium; or

(ii) a higher pensioner premium by virtue of the satisfaction of—

(aa) in the case of council tax benefit, paragraph 11(2)(b) of Schedule 1 to the Council Tax Benefit (General) Regulations 1992;

(bb) in the case of housing benefit, paragraph 10(2)(b) of Schedule 2 to the Housing Benefit (General) Regulations 1987,

on account of the other member's incapacity; [²or either regulation 13A(1)(c) of the Council Tax Benefit (General) Regulations 1992 (treatment of child care charges) or, as the case may be, regulation 21A(1)(c) of the Housing Benefit (General) Regulations 1987 (treatment of child care charges) applies in that person's case;]

(b) there is payable in respect of him one or more of the following pensions or allowances—

(i) invalidity pension under section 33, 40 or 41 of the Contributions and Benefits Act;

(ii) attendance allowance under section 64 of that Act;

(iii) severe disablement allowance under section 68 of that Act;

(iv) disability living allowance under section 71 of that Act;

(v) increase of disablement pension under section 104 of that Act;

(vi) a pension increase under a war pension scheme or an industrial injuries scheme which is analogous to an allowance or increase of disablement pension under head (ii), (iv) or (v) above;

(c) a pension or allowance to which head (ii), (iv), (v) or (vi) of sub-paragraph (b) above refers, was payable on account of his incapacity but has ceased to be payable in consequence of his becoming a patient within

the meaning of regulation 8(3)(a) (membership of the same household);
- (d) sub-paragraph (b) or (c) would apply to him if the legislative provisions referred to in those sub-paragraphs were provisions under any corresponding enactment having effect in Northern Ireland; or
- (e) he has an invalid carriage or other vehicle provided to him by the Secretary of State under section 5(2)(a) of and Schedule 2 to the National Health Service Act 1977 or under section 46 of the National Health Service (Scotland) Act 1978 or provided by the Department of Health and Social Services for Northern Ireland under Article 30(1) of the Health and Personal Social Services (Northern Ireland) Order 1972.]

AMENDMENTS

1. Income-related Benefits Schemes (Miscellaneous Amendments) (No. 4) Regulations 1994 (S.I. 1994 No. 1924), reg. 4(4) (October 4, 1994).
2. Income-related Benefits Schemes (Miscellaneous Amendments) Regulations 1995 (S.I. 1995 No. 516), reg. 12 (April 11, 1995).
3. Income-related Benefits and Jobseeker's Allowance (Personal Allowances for Children and Young Persons) (Amendment) Regulations 1996 (S.I. 1996 No. 2545), reg. 4 (October 7, 1997).
4. Income-related Benefits (Miscellaneous Amendments) Regulations 1997 (S.I. 1997 No. 2793), reg. 2(4) and (5)(c) (June 2, 1998).
5. Social Security Benefits (Miscellaneous Amendments) Regulations 1999 (S.I. 1999 No. 714), reg. 4 (April 6, 1999).

DEFINITIONS

"claimant"—see reg. 2(1), reg. 10(1).
"Contributions and Benefits Act"—see reg. 2(1).
"Crown property"—*ibid.*
"lone parent"—*ibid.*
"partner"—*ibid.*

GENERAL NOTE

To qualify for the disregard in reg. 13(1)(c) the claimant must be a lone parent or a member of a couple where both partners are working full-time (16 hours or more a week), or where one is working full-time and the other is incapacitated (para. (1)). A person counts as incapacitated if (i) they are in receipt of any of the following (or its Northern Ireland equivalent): (a) short-term (higher rate) or long-term incapacity benefit (under s. 13(2)(b) of the Social Security (Incapacity for Work) Act 1994 any reference in primary or secondary legislation to invalidity benefit or invalidity pension is treated as a reference to higher rate short-term incapacity benefit or long-term incapacity benefit from April 13, 1995) or severe disablement allowance, or (b) attendance allowance, disability living allowance or constant attendance allowance (or an equivalent to any of the last three under a war pension or industrial injuries scheme), or they would be but for the fact that they are in hospital; or (ii) they have an invalid carriage or similar vehicle; or (iii) housing benefit or council tax benefit is payable which includes on account of that person's incapacity a disability premium, a higher pensioner premium or a child care costs disregard (para. (7)).

Para. (2) specifies the types of child care costs that are eligible. From June 2, 1998 the disregard applies to charges (but not charges made by one member of a couple to the other) paid for care of children if the award of benefit begins before the first Tuesday in September following the child's twelfth birthday. The care has to be provided by a registered childminder or nursery/playscheme (sub-para. (a)), or in schools (charges for compulsory education are excluded) or other establishments (*e.g.* hospitals or children's homes) exempt from registration under the Children Act 1989 (sub-para. (d)), or, for children aged eight up to the first Tuesday in September after their 12th birthday, out of school hours by a school on school premises or by a local authority (sub-para. (b)). In addition, child care schemes run on Crown property also qualify (sub-para. (c)).

Paras. (3) to (6) provide the method for calculating the weekly amount of deductible child care costs. The formula in para. (3) applies where the child attends school and is intended to take account of the fact that child care costs are likely to vary considerably between term-time (defined in para. (2)) and holiday periods. For pre-school children the average weekly charge for the most recent four full weeks is taken (para. (4)). But in any case where the charges are paid monthly, para. (5) applies.

If there is no, or insufficient, information to calculate the child care costs under these rules (such as when child care has only recently been arranged), an estimate will be made based on information from the person providing care or, if that is not available, the claimant (para. (6)). The April 1999 amendments allow child care charges that will be incurred during the period of the family credit award, even if these are not payable at the date of claim, to be taken into account (see paras. (6A) to (6C)).

Until October 4, 1994 family credit did not permit the offsetting of child care expenses against earnings. In *CFC 19/1990 (Meyers)*, to be reported as *R(FC) 2/98*, the claimant argued that this indirectly discriminated against women in breach of EC Directive 76/207, which prohibits discrimination on the grounds of sex as regards access to employment, vocational training and promotion, and working conditions. It was contended that the inability to deduct child care costs created a barrier to equal access to employment, which particularly affected lone parents, nine out of 10 of whom are women. The question whether family credit came within the scope of Directive 76/207 was referred to the ECJ by the Commissioner. On July 13, 1995 the ECJ (*Meyers v. Adjudication Officer*, Case C-116/94 [1995] All E.R.(E.C.) 705) held that it did. The court confirmed that a benefits scheme could not be excluded from the scope of Directive 76/207 simply because it was part of a national social security system (see *Jackson and Cresswell v. Chief Adjudication Officer*, Joined Cases C-63/91 and C-64/91 [1992] E.C.R. I-4737). Family credit was only awarded if the claimant or her partner was in remunerative work. Its purpose was to keep low paid workers in employment and to ensure that families were not worse off in work than they would be if they were not working. Thus family credit was about access to employment. The U.K. Government had argued that family credit was not concerned with access to employment because it was awarded to people who were already employed. But access to employment did not only involve the conditions existing before the work commenced. The prospect of receiving family credit also encouraged a person to accept low paid work. In addition the Court concluded that since family credit was necessarily linked to an employment relationship it constituted a working condition within Art. 5 of the Directive. Working conditions were not confined to those laid down in the contract of employment or applied by the employer.

The case then went back to the Commissioner for him to consider whether the family credit scheme did indirectly discriminate against women and, if so, whether this was objectively justifiable.

The Commissioner accepted that the evidence put forward by the claimant showed that the absence of a child care costs disregard did have a disparate impact on women. However, as regards the issue of objective justification, it was clear that the U.K. Government had a broad discretion in relation to social and employment policy (see the decisions of the ECJ in *Nolte v. Landesversicherungsanstalt Hannover* [1996] I.R.L.R. 225, *Megner and Scheffel v. Innungskrankenkasse Vordertpfalz* [1996] I.R.L.R.] 236, *Y.M. Posthuma-Van Damme v. Bestuur van de Bedrijfsvereniging voor Detailhandel and anr* (Case C 280/94, February 1, 1996) and *C.B. Lapperre v. Bestuurscommissie Beroepszaken in de Provincie Zuid-Holland* (Case C 08/94, February 8, 1996). The family credit scheme did recognise that lone parents might have special needs (the adult credit was the same for single parents and couples, and one parent benefit was disregarded). Moreover, the Commissioner accepted the evidence put forward by the AO that when the family credit scheme was devised the cost of child care did not appear to be a significant factor in deterring lone parents from taking up employment and that the introduction of family credit had resulted in large numbers of families, including one parent families, being better off in work. He therefore concluded that having regard to the Government's wide margin of discretion, the chosen design of the family credit scheme reflected its aims and was appropriate and necessary to achieve those aims (see *R. v. Secretary of State for Employment, ex parte Seymour-Smith* [1995] I.C.R. 889). Thus the test of objective justification was satisfied and accordingly the family credit scheme was compatible with Directive 76/207. Leave to appeal to the Court of Appeal against this decision was granted by the Commissioner but the appeal was not pursued because of legal costs.

[¹Normal weekly earnings of employed earners

14.—(1) Where a claimant's income consists of earnings from employment as an employed earner, [²except where those earnings arise from employment as a director,] his normal weekly earnings shall, subject to paragraphs (3) to (6), be determined [⁵by taking account of his earnings from that employment which are received in the assessment period relevant to his case, whether the amount so received was earned in respect of that period or not, and in accordance with the following provisions of this regulation.]

(2) A claimant's assessment period, subject to [³paragraphs (2A) to (6)], shall be, in respect of a claimant whose pay period is—

[³(a) a week—

    (i) except where head (ii) applies, a period of 6 consecutive weeks immediately preceding the week of claim; or

    (ii) where the adjudication officer has insufficient information for the claimant's normal weekly earnings to be determined in accordance with head (i), a period of 6 consecutive weeks ending with the week before the week immediately preceding the week of claim;

[⁴(aa) a fortnight,—

    (i) except where head (ii) applies, a period of three consecutive fortnights immediately preceding the week of claim; or

    (ii) where the adjudication officer has insufficient information for the claimant's normal weekly earnings to be determined in accordance with head (i), a period of three consecutive fortnights ending with the fortnight before the week immediately preceeding the week of claim;]]

(b) four weeks or a month, a period of 12 consecutive weeks or, as the case may be, 3 consecutive months, immediately preceding the week of claim;

(c) any period of less than one month (a shorter period), other than one to which sub-paragraph (a) or (b) refers, 6 consecutive shorter periods immediately preceding the week of claim;

(d) any period of more than one month (a longer period), a period of one year ending immediately before the week of claim.

[³(2A) Where an adjudication officer considers, on the basis of available evidence, that the claimant has elected to work fewer hours than he would otherwise have worked in the whole or part of the assessment period referred to in paragraph (2) with the result that, but for this paragraph, he would secure entitlement or increased entitlement to family credit, the adjudication officer may determine the claimant's normal weekly earnings by [⁵taking account of his earnings received] during the period equal to, and ending immediately before, the period determined in accordance with paragraph (2), unless the claimant satisfies him that the reason for reducing his hours of work was otherwise than to secure such an entitlement or increased entitlement.]

(3) Where during a claimant's assessment period his earnings are reduced because of his involvement in a trade dispute at his place of employment, that assessment period shall be varied in that—

(a) any pay period during which his earnings are so reduced shall be omitted from it; and

(b) subject to sub-paragraph (c), his assessment period shall commence one pay period earlier (the extra period) for each period so omitted;

(c) where any extra period under sub-paragraph (b) is one in which his earnings are reduced because of his involvement in a trade dispute at his place of employment, that extra period shall also be omitted from his assessment period and his assesssment period shall commence one pay period earlier, for each extra period so omitted,

but so that his assessment period remains a period equal in length to the assessment period which would otherwise apply in his case under paragraph (2) but as if the words "consecutive" and "immediately" were omitted from that paragraph on each occasion where they appear.

(4) Where a claimant's earnings, whether during his assessment period or not, include a bonus or commission which is paid within 52 weeks preceding the week of claim and that bonus or commission is paid separately from his other earnings or is paid in respect of a period longer than the pay period relating to the other earnings with which it is paid, his normal weekly earnings shall be

treated as including an amount in respect of that bonus or commission calculated in accordance with regulation 20A (calculation of bonus or commission).

(5) Where at the date if claim—
  (a) the claimant—
    (i) has been in his employment, or
    (ii) after a continuous period of interruption exceeding four weeks, has resumed his employment, or
    (iii) has changed the number of hours for which he is contracted to work; and
  (b) the period of his employment or the period since he resumed his employment or the period since the change in the number of hours took place, as the case may be, is less than the assessment period in paragraph (2) appropriate in his case,

his normal weekly earnings shall be determined in accordance with paragraph (6).

(6) In a case to which this paragraph applies, the Secretary of State shall require the claimant's employer to furnish him with an estimate of the claimant's likely earnings for the pay period for which he is or will normally be paid and the claimant's normal weekly earnings shall be determined by [⁵taking account of] that estimate.

(7) For the purposes of this regulation—
  (a) the claimant's earnings shall be calculated in accordance with Chapter III of this Part;
  (b) "pay period" means the period in respect of which a claimant is, or expects to be [³normally] paid by his employer, being a week, a fortnight, four weeks, a month or other shorter or longer period, as the case may be.]

AMENDMENTS

1. Family Credit (General) Amendment Regulations 1992 (S.I. 1992 No. 573), reg. 4 (April 7, 1992).
2. Income-related Benefits Schemes (Miscellaneous Amendments) Regulations 1944 (S.I. 1994 No. 527), reg. 11 (April 12, 1994).
3. Income-related Benefits Schemes (Miscellaneous Amendments) (No. 5) Regulations 1994 (S.I. 1994 No. 2139), reg. 12 (October 4, 1994).
4. Income-related Benefits Schemes (Miscellaneous Amendments) Regulations 1996 (S.I. 1996 No. 462), reg. 7 (April 9, 1996).
5. Disability Working Allowance and Family Credit (General) Amendment Regulations 1996 (S.I. 1996 No. 3137), reg. 3(2) (January 7, 1997).

DEFINITIONS

"claim"—see reg. 2(1).
"claimant"—*ibid*, reg.10(1).
"director"—see reg. 2(1).
"earnings"—see reg. 2(1), reg. 19.
"employed earner"—see reg. 2(1).
"trade dispute"—see 1986 Act, s.84(1).
"week"—see reg. 2(1).
"week of claim"—*ibid*.

GENERAL NOTE

Paras. (1) and (2) supply the general rule for defining the period over which earnings from employment are averaged. There are separate rules for earnings of directors in reg. 14A.

Para. (3) deals with trade disputes. Para. (4) deals with payments of bonus or commission. Paras. (5) and (6) deal with employees who have just started or resumed employment. The calculation of "earnings" is dealt with in regs. 19 and 20. Although "the claimant" is referred to throughout, this word includes any member of the family whose earnings are taken into account (reg. 10(1)).

Paragraphs (1) and (2)

These provisions, in conjunction with the new (from April 1992) reg. 20(5), produce a much simplified method of calculating the earnings of employees. This should enable decisions to be taken more quickly and reliably, but at the cost of a certain amount of rough justice (see below).

The normal assessment period, over which the earnings of an employee received in that time (whether or not they are earned in that period) are taken, is set in para. (2) according to the length of the person's pay period. The pay period is the period in respect of which the person is, or expects to be, normally paid by the employer (para. (7)(b)). In the standard cases of payment by the week or month, the assessment period is the six consecutive weeks (sub-para. (a)(i)) or the three consecutive months (sub-para. (b)) before the week of claim. The assessment period is fixed and there is no longer any discretion to use a shorter or longer period. The new form of sub-para. (a) from October 1994 removes, in the case of a weekly paid person, the previous very limited flexibility whereby six consecutive weeks out of the seven before the week of the claim were taken. Now the six weeks which end one week before the week of claim can only be used where all the earnings information is not available (sub-para. (a)(ii)). A rule along similar lines for those who are fortnightly paid is in sub-para. (aa). Before April 1992, there was a power to exclude weeks from the assessment period under reg. 17 where earnings in a week were irregular or unusual. This power has been removed and reg. 17 now only applies to the self-employed. Instead there is a relatively mechanical formula under reg. 20(5) under which abnormal weeks are to be excluded.

The potential for unfairness in these rules has been increased by the January 1997 amendments to para. (1) and reg. 20(1). The purpose of these amendments is to reverse the effect of *CFC 6910/ 1995*, to be reported as *R(FC) 1/98*. In that case the claimant's husband's pay for the last week of his six week assessment period included two weeks' advanced holiday pay. The Commissioner held that the holiday pay was not to be taken into account as part of his earnings during the assessment period. Holiday pay was to be treated as earned in respect of the period over which the holiday was taken. It was not derived from employment in the pay period in which it was received. The Commissioner pointed out that para. (1) had been amended in April 1994 to require that a person's normal weekly earnings be determined by reference to his earnings *received* in the assessment period. But there had been no corresponding amendment to reg. 20 which governed the calculation of net earnings (see para. (7) (a)). *CSFC 7/1994* had decided that under reg. 20 only earnings *earnt* during the assessment period were to be taken into account. In the Commissioner's view the April 1994 amendment had not affected the decision in *CSFC 7/1994* so the position remained that under reg. 20 payments of earnings received within an assessment period in respect of a pay period outside it were not to be taken into account in the calculation of net earnings. But as a result of the January 1997 amendments holiday pay (or *e.g.* overtime pay) will be taken into account when it is received, irrespective of the period in which it was earnt. This rule, taken together with the current rigidity of the assessment period and the very limited formula in reg. 20(5) for excluding abnormal weeks, has the potential to substantially reduce a claimant's family credit award if any unusual payments are received during the assessment period. The timing of a family credit claim in these circumstances may thus be of crucial importance.

Paragraph (2A)

If an AO thinks that a claimant has chosen to work less hours in her normal assessment period, he can take the preceding assessment period, unless the claimant proves (on the balance of probabilities) that securing entitlement to, or increasing the amount of, family credit was not the reason for the reduction in hours. The rule is discretionary and will require the AO to form a judgment on a number of questions. According to the DSS, this provision is designed to deal with a small number of cases of blatant manipulation of the benefit rules; it is not proposed that AOs should normally seek this information.

Paragraph (3)

If the person's earnings are reduced because of his involvement in a trade dispute at his place of employment, then the assessment period is shifted backwards so that it contains no pay periods affected by such a reduction, while remaining the same length. There is no definition of "trade dispute" specifically for the purposes of family credit, although no doubt the meaning in s.27(3)(b) of the Contributions and Benefits Act (1975 Act, s.19(2)(b)) would be adopted. There is no requirement that there should be a stoppage of work, so that a reduction in wages due to a work-to-rule or overtime ban will be covered. But there may in some cases be difficult questions about what amounts to involvement in a trade dispute.

Paragraph (4)

Where a bonus or commission is paid separately from normal remuneration or for a longer pay period a special rule applies. The amount calculated in reg. 20A is included in the claimant's normal weekly earnings and the actual payment is excluded (reg. 20(3)(c)).

Paragraphs (5) and (6).

These provisions apply where a person has recently started work or resumed work after a gap of at least four weeks or changed his contractual hours. Then if the period from that event to the date of claim is less than the appropriate assessment period in para. (2), the special rule in para. (6) applies. There is no discretion to apply this rule or not. If the time condition is met, para. (6) must be applied. This requires the employer to estimate the person's likely earnings, which must then be taken as the normal earnings.

[¹Normal weekly earnings of directors

14A.—(1) Subject to paragraph (2) and regulation 17 (periods to be disregarded), where a claimant's income includes earnings from employment as a director, his normal weekly earnings from that employment shall be determined [²by taking account of his earnings from that employment received in the year immediately preceding the week of claim, whether the amount so received was earned in respect of that period or not.]

(2) Where at the date of claim the claimant has been in employment as a director for less than a year, his normal weekly earnings from that employment shall be [²determined by taking account of his earnings from that employment received in the period that he has been in that employment] and by reference to an estimate of the earnings likely to be received in the remainder of the first year of the employment.]

AMENDMENTS

1. Income-related Benefits Schemes (Miscellaneous Amendments) Regulations 1994 (S.I. 1994 No. 527), reg. 12 (April 12, 1994).
2. Disability Working Allowance and Family Credit (General) Amendment Regulations 1996 (S.I. 1996 No. 3137), reg. 3(3) (January 7, 1997).

DEFINITIONS

"claimant"—see reg. 2(1), reg. 10(1).
"date of claim"—see reg. 2(1).
"director"—*ibid.*
"earnings"—*ibid.* reg. 19.
"week of claim"—see reg. 2(1).

GENERAL NOTE

This regulation contains separate rules for the assessment period over which earnings as a director are to be taken. This is one year before the week of claim (para. (1)). Weeks in which no work is done and no pay is received are disregarded (reg. 17(b)). If the claimant has been employed as a director for less than a year at the date of claim the earnings received so far from the employment are taken together with an estimate of the likely earnings over the remainder of the 52 weeks (para. (2)). This brings directors more in line with the self-employed.

On the amendments introduced on January 7, 1997, see *CFC 6910/1995*, to be reported as *R(FC) 1/98*, in the notes to reg. 14(1) and (2).

Normal weekly earnings of self-employed earners

15.—(1) Subject to regulation 17 (periods to be disregarded), where a claimant's income consists of earnings from employment as a self-employed earner, his normal weekly earnings shall be determined, subject to paragraph (2), by reference to his weekly earnings from that employment—

[²(a) except where a sub-paragraph (aa) or (b) applies, over a period of 6 consecutive complete months up to and including the second last complete month immediately preceding the date of claim; or

(aa) except where sub-paragraph (b) applies, where the claimant provides in respect of the employment a statement of his earnings and expenses for the six consecutive complete months up to and including the last complete month immediately preceding the date of claim, over that period of six months; or]

[¹(b) where the claimant provides in respect of the employment a profit and loss account and, where appropriate, a trading account or a balance sheet or both, and the profit and loss account is in respect of a period of at least six months but not exceeding 15 months and that period terminates within the 12 months preceding the date of claim, over that period; or]

(c) over such other period of weeks [³or months] preceding the week in which [¹ the date of claims falls] as may, in any particular case, enable his normal weekly earnings to be determined more accurately.

[¹(1A) In paragraph (1)(b)

(a) "balance sheet" means a statement of the financial position of the employment disclosing its assets, liabilities and capital at the end of the period in question;

(b) "profit and loss account" means a financial statement showing the net profit or loss of the employment for the period in question; and

(c) "trading account" means a financial statement showing the revenue from sales, the cost of those sales and the gross profit arising during the period in question.]

[²(2) Subject to regulation 17, in a case where the claimant has been in employment as a self-employed earner for less than 7 complete months, his normal weekly earnings shall be determined over a period of 6 consecutive complete months commencing with the first complete month after the claimant began that employment, and that determination shall be based on either—

(a) where the claimant provides in relation to that employment a statement of his earnings and expenses for the complete months up to and including the last complete month immediately preceding the date of claim, the earnings he received in those months, or

(b) where no such statement is provided, any earnings he received in the period up to and including the second last complete month immediately preceding the date of claim,

together with an estimate of the earnings likely to be received in the balance of the 6 month period.].

(3) For the purposes of this regulation, the claimant's earnings shall be calculated in accordance with Chapter IV of this Part.

[²(4) In this regulation a "complete month" begins on the first day of the month and ends on the last day of the month.]

AMENDMENTS

1. Family Credit (General) Amendment No. 4 Regulations 1988 (S.I. 1988 No. 1970), reg. 3 (December 5, 1988).

2. Income-related Benefits Schemes (Miscellaneous Amendments) Regulations 1994 (S.I. 1994 No. 527), reg. 13 (April 12, 1994).

3. Income-related Benefits Schemes (Miscellaneous Amendments) (No. 5) Regulations 1994 (S.I. 1994 No. 2139), reg. 13 (October 4, 1994).

DEFINITIONS

"claim"—see reg. 2(1).
"claimant"—*ibid.*, reg. 6.
"date of claim"—see reg. 2(1).

"earnings"—see reg. 2(1), reg. 21.
"self-employed earnings"—see reg. 2(1).
"week"—*ibid.*

GENERAL NOTE

Paragraph (1)
The new form of this provision applies where the person has been in self-employment for at least seven calendar (see para. (4)) months (see para. (2)). The basic rule is now contained in sub-para. (b). If the claimant provides accounts for a period between six and 15 months ending in the year before the date of claim these are taken. If these are not produced but the claimant provides a statement of earnings and expenses for the six calendar months before the date of claim this is taken (sub-para. (aa)). If this is not provided the claimant's earnings over the six calendar months which end one calendar month before the date of claim are taken (sub-para. (a)). Alternatively, sub-para. (c) allows another past period to be chosen, if it produces a more accurate determination of normal earnings.

In *CFC 5/1993* the claimant's husband ran a shoe shop. Her claim for family credit made in June 1991, was originally assessed on the basis of the pre-April 1994 form of para. (a) and refused as the earnings figure was too high. By the SSAT hearing accounts for the years to August 1990, and August 1991, were available. The SSAT decided that family credit was not payable even on the lower earnings figure produced by the accounts. The Commissioner holds that sub-para. (c) provides an alternative to either sub-para (a) or (b) (now (a), (aa) or (b)). To apply sub-para. (c) an adjudicating authority must be satisfied that there is an alternative period the use of which will (not might) enable normal weekly earnings at the date of claim to be determined more accurately. The alternative period does not have to be a 26-week period. Evidence in the accounts for the year to August 1991, as to the pattern of the claimant's husband's expenditure on stock, did suggest that an alternative period under sub-para. (c) should be used. Although the period covered by the accounts for the year to August 1991 could not be used under sub-para. (b) because it ended after the date of claim, evidence contained in those accounts could be considered in deciding whether an alternative period should be adopted under sub-para. (c). Another example in which sub-para. (c) was applied is *CFC 836/1995*. The claimant's husband ran a post office and shop in the same premises. In calculating any family credit entitlement, his earnings as an employed earner (from carrying out the office of sub-postmaster, see *R(FC) 1/93*) and his self-employed earnings from the shop had to be taken into account. The AO had originally assessed the earnings from the shop under sub-para. (a), but by the time the claimant asked for a review of the initial decision on the claim a profit and loss account had become available. However, the Commissioner decides that sub-para. (c) should be applied. The profit and loss account was a combined account for the post office and the shop (and did not allocate the operational expenses between the two) and the period it covered ended about six months before the claim. Where, as in this case, there was a somewhat artificial division of the overall business into two employments, and a period immediately before the claim (three months under reg. 14(2)(b)) had to be looked at in relation to the employed earnings, some comparable period should be looked at in assessing the earnings from the self-employment. Thus the assessment was to be carried out under sub-para. (c) using the figures that were available for the 26 weeks before the week of claim.

See also *CFC 19/1993*, *CFC 10/1993* and *R(FC) 1/96* on the valuation of opening and closing stock where earnings are assessed under sub-para. (b) in the notes to reg. 22(3A).

Note also the effect of reg. 17, under which weeks in which no activities are carried out are excluded from the period by reference to which earnings are calculated.

Paragraph (1A)
Simply provides definitions for para. (1)(b).

Paragraph (2)
If the person has been in self-employment for less than seven calendar months the assessment period is six calendar months starting from the beginning of the first complete month of the person's self-employment. Either the claimant can produce a statement of earnings and expenses for the calendar months before the date of claim, or earnings actually received up to the beginning of the last calendar month before the date of claim are taken. To this is added an estimate of the likely earnings over the remainder of the six-month period. Until October 1992 reference to other evidence which would enable normal weekly earnings to be estimated more accurately was allowed. The Commissioner in *CFC 14/1991* held that that allowed a SSAT on an appeal to take into account the claimant's actual earnings since the date of claim. The

removal of the power to consider such evidence from the old form of para. (2) was intended to reverse the effect of *CFC 14/1991*. It now appears that a SSAT must consider what could have been estimated as future earnings on the information which was available at the date of claim, even if that estimate turns out to have been mistaken. But the SSAT must consider what would be a realistic and proper estimate on that information. It is not obliged to accept the claimant's, or anyone else's, estimate.

The useful FIS power to make an award for less than the usual period in cases of doubt has gone (see *R(FIS) 1/82* for an example).

Reg. 17 may operate to exclude certain weeks from the assessment period.

Normal weekly income other than earnings

16.—(1) Subject to [²paragraphs (2) and (2A)], [³where a claimant's normal weekly income does not consist of earnings, or includes income that does not consist of earnings, that income] shall be determined by reference to his weekly income over a period of 26 weeks immediately preceding [¹the week in which the date of claim falls] or over such period immediately preceding [¹that week] as may, in any particular case, enable his weekly income to be determined more accurately.

(2) Where a claimant's income consists of any payments made by a person, whether under a court order or not, for the maintenance of any member of [²the claimant's family], and those payments are made or due to be made at regular intervals, his normal weekly income shall[², except where paragraph (2A) applies,] be determined—

    (a) if before the date of claim those payments are made at regular intervals [³and of regular amounts], by reference to the normal weekly amount;

    (b) if they are not so made, by reference to the average of such payments received in the 13 weeks immediately preceding the week in which [¹the date of claim falls].

[²(2A) Where a claimant's income consists of child support maintenance, his normal weekly income in respect of that maintenance shall be determined—

    (a) if before the date of claim those maintenance payments are made at regular intervals [³and of regular amounts], by reference to the normal weekly amount;

    (b) if they are not so made, [³except in a case to which sub-paragraph (*c*) applies,] by reference to the average of such payments received in the 13 weeks immediately preceding the week in which the date of claim falls,

    [³(c) where the maintenance assessment has been notified to the claimant under regulation 10 of the Child Support (Maintenance Assessment Procedure) Regulations 1992 during the 13 weeks immediately preceding the week of claim, by reference to the average of such payments, calculated on a weekly basis, received in the interim period,]

and if the resulting sum exceeds the amount of child maintenance due under the maintenance assessment, the normal weekly income shall be the amount due under the maintenance assessment.]

(3) For the purposes of this regulation, income other than earnings shall be calculated in accordance with Chapter V of this Part.

    [²(4) In this regulation—

    (a) "child support maintenance" means such periodical payments as are referred to in section 3(6) of the Child Support Act 1991;

    (b) "maintenance assessment" has the same meaning as in the Child Support Act 1991 by virtue of section 54 of that Act.]

    [³(c) "the interim period" means the week in which the date of notification of the maintenance assessment falls and the subsequent period up to and including the week immediately preceding the week of claim.]

AMENDMENTS

1. Family Credit (General) Amendment No. 4 Regulations 1988 (S.I. 1988 No. 1970), reg. 4 (December 5, 1988).
2. Income-related Benefits Schemes (Miscellaneous Amendments) Regulations 1993 (S.I. 1993 No. 315), reg. 11 (April 13, 1993).
3. Income-related Benefits Schemes (Miscellaneous Amendments) (No. 4) Regulations 1993 (S.I. 1993 No. 2119), reg. 28 (October 5, 1993).

DEFINITIONS

"claim"—see reg. 2(1).
"claimant"—*ibid.*, reg. 10(1).
"date of claim"—see reg. 2(1).
"earnings"—*ibid.*, reg. 19.
"family"—see 1986 Act, s.20(11) (SSCBA, s.137(1)).
"payment"—see reg. 2(1).
"week"—*ibid.*

GENERAL NOTE

Note that reg. 16 is not subject to reg. 17.

Paragraph (1)
This provision deals with income which is not earnings and is not maintenance (see para. (2)). See Chapter V for what falls into this category. The general rule is to take the 26 weeks before the week in which the date of claim falls. Another period may be taken, if it produces a more accurate determination.

Paragraph (2)
This provision applies a special rule to payments of maintenance, apart from payments assessed under the Child Support Acts 1991–1995 (for which, see para. (2A)). "Maintenance" is not defined, and it seems that it is not restricted to payments from liable relatives as defined in s.78(6) of the Administration Act (1986 Act, s.26).
The first £15 per week of any maintenance payments made by a former partner of the claimant or her current partner or by an absent parent of a child or young person is disregarded (Sched. 2, para. 47, in effect from April 7, 1992).
If payments of maintenance are made to the claimant or another member of her family (reg. 10(1)) of regular amounts and at regular intervals, then the normal weekly amount (calculated under reg. 18) is taken. Otherwise the receipts in the 13 weeks before the week of claim are averaged. It is the date of receipt by the claimant that counts, not the court or the DSS where maintenance is paid to them. They were not acting as the claimant's agent in these circumstances (*CFC 48/1993*).
Any payments not either made or due to be made at regular intervals count as capital (reg. 31(6)).

Paragraph (2A)
"Child support maintenance" is defined in para. (4) to cover payments required by an assessment under the Child Support Acts 1991–1995. The weekly amount is to be calculated as under para. (2), except that if the claimant has only been notified of the maintenance assessment in the 13 weeks before the week of the family credit claim, just the payments received from the week of the notification are averaged. But the amount due under the assessment supplies a maximum. If an absent parent pays more than required by the assessment (for instance, if a payment includes arrears) the excess does not affect the claimant's family credit entitlement.
The first £15 of whatever amount is calculated is disregarded under para. 47 of Sched. 2.

Periods to be disregarded

[¹17. For the purposes of ascertaining a claimant's normal weekly earnings there shall be disregarded—
    (a) where the claimant is a self-employed earner, any week or period of

weeks in his assessment period during which no activities have been carried out for the purposes of the business;

(b) where the claimant is a director, any week or period of weeks in his assessment period during which he has done no work and in respect of which he has received no earnings; and

his normal weekly earnings shall be determined by reference to his earnings in the remainder of that period (the reduced period) and in these Regulations any reference to an assessment period shall in its application to such a case be construed as a reference to that reduced period.]

AMENDMENT

1. Income-related Benefits Schemes (Miscellaneous Amendments) Regulations 1994 (S.I. 1994 No. 527), reg. 14 (April 12, 1994).

DEFINITIONS

"assessment period"—see reg. 2(1), reg. 15.
"claimant"—*ibid*., reg. 10(1).
"director"—see reg. 2(1).
"earnings"—*ibid*.
"self-employed earner"—*ibid*.
"week"—*ibid*.

GENERAL NOTE

Reg. 17 modifies the period used for calculation of earnings from self-employment under reg. 15 and as a director under reg. 14A. With the amendment of regs. 14 and 20 from April 1992 no extra provision is needed for employed earners.

Para. (a). This requires weeks in which the person did not carry out any activities for the purpose of the self-employment to be disregarded. The concept of activities in the course of work is no longer part of reg. 4, which since April 1992 simply refers to hours of work. No doubt the approach put forward in *R(FIS) 6/85* would be applicable. It was held there that activities were not limited to those which could be charged to a particular client, but extended to activities, like preparation and planning, which were essential to the self-employment. Only weeks (*i.e.* Sunday to Saturday) in which no activities at all are carried out can be excluded under reg. 17. The obvious examples are periods of holiday or incapacity.

Para. (b). Weeks in which the person has not worked as a director and for which he has not been paid are disregarded.

Calculation of weekly amount of income

18. [⁴—(1) For the purposes of regulation 14 (normal weekly earnings of employed earners) and 16 (normal weekly income other than earnings), where the claimant's pay period or, as the case may be, the period in respect of which a payment is made—]

(a) does not exceed a week, the weekly amount shall be the amount of that payment;

(b) exceeds a week, the weekly amount shall be determined—

    (i) in a case where that period is a month, by multiplying the amount of the payment by 12 and dividing the product by 52;

    (ii) in a case where that period is 3 months, by multiplying the amount of the payment by 4 and dividing the product by 52;

    (iii) in a case where that period is a year, by dividing the amount of the payment by 52;

    (iv) in any other case, by multiplying the amount of the payment by 7 and dividing the product by the number equal to the number of days in the period in respect of which it is made.

[²(2) For the purposes of regulation 15 (normal weekly earnings of self-employed earners) the weekly amount of earnings of a claimant shall be determined—

[³(a) except where sub-paragraph (b) applies, by multiplying by 7 his earnings—

    (i) received in the assessment period, or

    (ii) estimated for the assessment period, or

    (iii) both received in and estimated for that period,

as the case may be, and dividing the product by the number equal to the number of days in that period;]

  (b) in a case where regulation 15(1)(b) applies, by multiplying his earnings relevant to the assessment period (whether or not received in that period) by 7 and dividing the product by the number equal to the number of days in that period.]

[³(3) For the purposes of regulation 14A (normal weekly earnings of directors) the weekly amount of earnings of a claimant shall be determined by dividing his earnings—

    (i) received in the assessment period, or

    (ii) estimated for the assessment period, or

    (iii) both received in and estimated for that period,

as the case may be, by the number equal to the number of weeks in that period.]

AMENDMENTS

1. Family Credit (General) Amendment No. 3 Regulations 1988 (S.I. 1988 No. 1438), reg. 4 (September 12, 1988).

2. Family Credit (General) Amendment No. 4 Regulations 1988 (S.I. 1988 No. 1970), reg. 5 (December 5, 1988).

3. Income-related Benefits Schemes (Miscellaneous Amendments) Regulations 1994 (S.I. 1994 No. 527), reg. 15 (April 12, 1994).

4. Disability Working Allowance and Family Credit (General) Amendment Regulations 1996 (S.I. 1996 No. 3137), reg. 3(4) (January 7, 1997).

DEFINITIONS

    "assessment period"—see reg. 2(1).
    "claimant"—*ibid.*
    "director"—*ibid.*
    "pay period"—*ibid.*
    "payment"—*ibid.*
    "week"—*ibid.*

GENERAL NOTE

    See notes to reg. 32(1) of the Income Support (General) Regulations, except for paras. (2) and (3).

Chapter III

Employed Earners

Earnings of employed earners

    19.—(1) Subject to paragraph (2), "earnings" means in the case of employment as an employed earner, any remuneration or profit derived from that employment and includes—

  (a) any bonus or commission;

  (b) any holiday pay except any payable more than 4 weeks after termination of the employment;

(c) any payment by way of a retainer;

(d) any payment made by the claimant's employer in respect of any expenses not wholly, exclusively and necessarily incurred in the performance of the duties of the employment, including any payment made by the claimant's employer in respect of—

   (i) travelling expenses incurred by the claimant between his home and place of employment;

   (ii) expenses incurred by the claimant under arrangements made for the care of a member of his family owing to the claimant's absence from home;

(e) any award of compensation made under section 68(2) or 71(2)(a) of the Employment Protection (Consolidation) Act 1978 (remedies and compensation for unfair dismissal);

(f) any such sum as is referred to in section 18(2) of the Social Security (Miscellaneous Provisions) Act 1977 (certain sums to be earnings for social security purposes);

[¹(g) any statutory sick pay under Part I of the Social Security and Housing Benefits Act 1982 [SSCBA, Part XI];

(h) any statutory sick pay under Part II of the Social Security (Northern Ireland) Order 1982.]

(2) Earnings shall not include—

(a) subject to paragraph (3), any payment in kind;

(b) any payment in respect of expenses wholly, exclusively and necessarily incurred in the performance of the duties of the employment;

(c) any occupational pension;

[²(d) any statutory maternity pay or a corresponding benefit under any enactment having effect in Northern Ireland.]

(3) Where living accommodation is provided for a claimant by reason of his employment, the claimant shall be treated as being in receipt of weekly earnings of an amount equal to—

(a) where no charge is made in respect of the provision of that accommodation, £12;

(b) where a charge is made and that weekly charge is less than £12, the amount of the difference,

except that where the claimant satisfies the adjudication officer that the weekly value to him of the provision of that accommodation is an amount less than the amount in sub-paragraph (a) or (b), as the case may be, he shall be treated as being in receipt of that lesser value.

AMENDMENTS

1. Family Credit (General) Amendment Regulations 1992 (S.I. 1992 No. 573), reg. 6 (April 7, 1992).

2. Income-related Benefits Schemes (Miscellaneous Amendments) Regulations 1993 (S.I. 1993 No. 315), reg. 12 (April 13, 1993).

DEFINITIONS

"the Act"—see reg. 2(1).
"claimant"—*ibid.*, reg. 10(1).
"employed earner"—see reg. 2(1).
"family"—see 1986 Act, s.20(11) (SSCBA, s.137(1)).
"occupational pension"—see reg. 2(1).
"payment"—*ibid.*
"week"—*ibid.*

GENERAL NOTE

Paragraph (1)

See the notes to reg. 35(1) of the Income Support (General) Regulations for most categories of earnings. There are some differences. Categories in those Regulations which do not appear here are payments in lieu of remuneration and in lieu of notice. Presumably they are excluded as not relating to actual work, but will, as payments of income, fall into reg. 24. Holiday pay is counted subject to slightly different conditions. Sub-paras. (g) and (h) specifically including statutory sick pay (but not, from April 1992, statutory maternity pay) do not appear in the Income Support Regulations. Statutory maternity pay is from April 1993 expressly excluded from the category of earnings by para. (2)(d). Sched. 2, paras. 27 and 31 provide that statutory maternity pay and maternity allowance are disregarded as income.

Note the disregarded categories set out in Sched. 1 (reg. 20(2)), and that notional earnings under reg. 26 may be included.

Paragraph (2)

Payments in kind (see the notes to reg. 35(2) of the Income Support (General) Regulations) are excluded from earnings, except where living accommodation is provided under para. (3). See the notes to reg. 35 for necessary expenses and occupational pensions.

In some earlier editions it has been asserted rather loosely that the rule on expenses effectively legislates the decision in *Parsons v. Hogg* [1985] 2 All E.R. 897 (*R(FIS) 4/85*). It is certainly the case that the part of the Commissioner's decision in *R(FIS) 4/85* which was not challenged in the Court of Appeal is confirmed by para. (1)(d) and (2)(b), *i.e.* payments from the employer which are simply reimbursement of necessary, etc. expenses do not count as earnings, but reimbursement of expenses outside that category (including for child care) does count. However, the major issue in the Court of Appeal in *Parsons v. Hogg* was whether expenses necessarily incurred by the employee were to be deducted in calculating the claimant's gross earnings. It was held that sums which the claimant necessarily had to spend to secure those earnings should be deducted for FIS purposes. Child care expenses did not fall into that category (*R(FIS) 2/88*). See the notes to reg. 20 on the application of the principle of *Parsons v. Hogg* to the meaning of "gross earnings" in reg. 20(3). See also regs. 13(1)(c) and 13A for the limited disregard for child care expenses introduced from October 4, 1994. In *CFC 19/1990 (Meyers)*, to be reported as *R(FC) 2/98*, the claimant contended that the previous inability to offset child care costs against earnings indirectly discriminated against women contrary to E.C. Directive 76/207 (see further the notes to reg. 13A).

The intention seems to be that reg. 19 should apply to payments from the employer, while reg. 20(3) deals with which expenditure by the employee can be deducted. However, the decision in *CFC 2/1989* raised the possibility that such payments by the employee should be excluded from the calculation of gross earnings under reg. 19(2)(b). The Commissioner in fact held that the payments in question (for child care expenses) did not fall into the necessary, etc., category (following *R(FIS) 2/88*). But if they had done so it was apparently not disputed that the exclusion under reg. 19(2)(b) would follow. That provision does not say "payments by the employer," so that it can be argued that it also covers payments by the employee. But in the context of reg. 19 as a whole this seems unlikely. Para. (1) is expressly subject to para. (2) and lists a variety of payments made by the employer to the employee. Para. (2)(a) and (c) clearly refer to forms of payment made by the employer. The context suggests that para. (2)(b) refers only to payments by the employer in respect of necessary etc. expenses rather than the ordinary remuneration for work done, and not to expenditure by the employee. The Commissioner's decision in *R(FC) 1/90* rejects the view expressed in *CFC 2/1989* and is to be preferred. See also *R(IS) 16/93* and *CIS 77/1993*. However, the effect of this construction is mitigated by the application of the principle of *Parsons v. Hogg* to the meaning of "gross earnings" in reg. 20(3) (see the notes to reg. 20).

The categories excluded as earnings under para. (2) are income under reg. 24 (reg. 24(5)), but note the disregards in paras. 20, 27, 31 and 32 of Sched. 2.

Paragraph (3)

In *R(FC) 2/90* both the claimant and her husband worked for the Salvation Army and were provided with free accommodation. Only one sum of £12 was to be assumed as part of their earnings, even if they had two separate employments. They only had one house provided. In *R(FC) 1/94* the claimant's husband was a vicar who until April 1990, was provided with accommodation free of rent and rates. After that date they became liable to pay the community charge, which, they argued, should be deducted from the £12 as the value of the free accommodation had decreased. It is held that para. (3) imposes a mandatory sum to be assumed as income where free accommodation is provided (subject to the proviso). The proviso did not permit the deduction of community charge liability.

Calculation of net earnings of employed earners

20.—[¹(1) For the purposes of regulation 14 (normal weekly earnings of employed earners) the earnings of a claimant to be taken into account shall be his average weekly net [⁶earnings and] where an estimate of earnings has been made in his case, as estimated, and those weekly net earnings shall be determined in accordance with the following paragraphs.]

(2) There shall be disregarded from a claimant's net earnings, any sum, where applicable, specified in Schedule 1.

(3) [¹A claimant's net earnings shall, except where paragraph (4) applies, be calculated by taking into account his gross earnings from that employment] [⁶. . .], less—

    (a) any amount deducted from those earnings by way of—
        (i) income tax;
        (ii) primary Class 1 contributions under the Social Security Act [SSCBA]; and
    (b) one-half of any sum paid by the claimant [⁵in respect of a pay period] by way of a contribution towards an occupational or personal pension scheme; [¹and
    (c) the net amount of bonus or commission (if any) which is paid separately from his other earnings or is paid in respect of a period longer than the pay period relating to the other earnings with which it is paid and that net amount shall be the gross amount of that bonus or commission after deducting from it sums calculated in accordance with paragraphs (a) to (c) of regulation 20A (calculation of bonus or commission).]

(4) Where the earnings of a claimant are [¹estimated under paragraph (6)] of regulation 14 (normal weekly earnings of employed earners), his net earnings shall be calculated by taking into account those earnings over [²the period in respect of which the estimate is made], less—

    (a) an amount in respect of income tax equivalent to an amount calculated by applying to those earnings [²the lower rate or, as the case may be, the lower rate and the basic rate of tax] in the year of assessment in which the claim was made less only the personal relief to which the claimant is entitled under sections 8(1) and (2) and 14(1)(a) and (2) of the Income and Corporation Taxes Act 1970 (personal relief) as is appropriate to his circumstances; but, if the assessment period is less than a year, [²the earnings to which the lower rate [⁴ . . .] of tax is to be applied and] the amount of the personal relief deductible under this sub-paragraph shall be calculated on a pro rata basis;
    [³(b) where the weekly amount of those earnings equals or exceeds the lower earnings limit, an amount representing primary Class 1 contributions under the Contributions and Benefits Act, calculated by applying to those earnings the initial and main primary percentages applicable at the date of claim in accordance with section 8(1)(a) and (b) of that Act; and]
    [⁵(c) one half of any sum which would be payable by the claimant by way of a contribution towards an occupational or personal pension scheme, if the earnings so estimated were actual earnings.]

[¹(5) When a claimant's net earnings have been calculated in accordance with paragraph (3), his average net earnings have in respect of his pay period shall be calculated as follows—

    (a) the net earnings in each of the pay periods in his assessment period shall be aggregated, that total shall then be divided by the number of pay periods in his assessment period and the resulting amount shall be the average net earnings for his pay period;

(b) where in respect of any pay period, a claimant's net earnings are twenty per cent. or more higher, or twenty per cent. or more lower, than his average net earnings, those net earnings and that pay period shall be omitted, his assessment period shall be reduced accordingly and his average net earnings shall, subject to sub-paragraph (c), be re-calculated in accordance with sub-paragraph (a);

(c) where the operation of sub-paragraph (b) results in no pay period remaining in a claimant's assessment period there shall be omitted from the assessment period any pay period in which no earnings are received or in which the net earnings received are for a period longer than his normal pay period and his average net earnings shall be re-calculated in accordance with sub-paragraph (a);

(d) where the operation of sub-paragraph (c) results in no pay periods remaining, paragraph (6) of regulation 14 (normal weekly earnings of employed earners) and paragraph (4) of this regulation shall apply in his case.

(6) Where a claimant's average net earnings for his pay period have been calculated in accordance with paragraph (5) and his pay period is—

(a) a week, a fortnight or four weeks, his average net earnings for his pay period shall be divided by the number of weeks in that period;

(b) a month, his average net earnings shall be multiplied by 12, the resulting product divided by 52;

(c) any shorter or longer period than those referred to in sub-paragraphs (a) and (b), his average net earnings for his pay period shall be multiplied by seven and the product divided by the number equal to the number of days in his pay period,

and the resulting amount shall be his average weekly net earnings.]

AMENDMENTS

1. Family Credit (General) Amendment Regulations 1992 (S.I. 1992 No. 573), reg. 7 (April 7, 1992).

2. Income-related Benefits Schemes (Miscellaneous Amendments) (No. 3) Regulations 1992 (S.I. 1992 No. 2155), reg. 6 (October 5, 1992).

3. Income-related Benefits Schemes (Miscellaneous Amendments) Regulations 1994 (S.I. 1994 No. 527), reg. 16 (April 12, 1994).

4. Income-related Benefits Schemes (Miscellaneous Amendments) (No. 5) Regulations 1994 (S.I. 1994 No. 2139), reg. 14 (October 4, 1994).

5. Income-related Benefits Schemes (Miscellaneous Amendments) (No. 5) Regulations 1994 (S.I. 1994 No. 2139), reg. 15 (October 4, 1994).

6. Disability Working Allowance and Family Credit (General) Amendment Regulations 1996 (S.I. 1996 No. 3137), reg. 3(5) (January 7, 1997).

DEFINITIONS

"assessment period"—see reg. 2(1), reg. 14.
"claimant"—see reg. 2(1), reg. 10(1).
"earnings"—see reg. 2(1).
"employed earner"—*ibid.*
"lower rate"—*ibid.*
"occupational pension scheme"—see 1986 Act, s.84(1) (PSA, s.1).
"pay period"—see reg. 2(1), reg. 14(7)(b).
"personal pension scheme"—see reg. 2(1).
"Social Security Act"—*ibid.*
"year of assessment"—*ibid.*

GENERAL NOTE

One of the main differences between family credit and FIS is that for family credit net, rather than gross, earnings are used for calculating benefit. Para. (1) expresses this rule, and requires that what is to be taken into account are average weekly net earnings. On the effect of the January 1997 amendment to para. (1) see *CFC 6910/1995*, to be reported as *R(FC) 1/98*, in the notes to reg. 14(1) and (2).

Para. (2) incorporates a limited number of disregards, set out in Sched. 1. Payments which are disregarded under this provision cannot be counted as income other than earnings under reg. 24. This is because the payments do not cease to be "earnings" and reg. 24 only applies to income which does not consist of earnings.

Para. (3) sets out how net earnings are to be calculated from gross earnings. The basic process is as in reg. 36(3) of the Income Support (General) Regulations. See the notes to that provision, where there is discussion of the decision in *R(FC) 1/90*, which applies the principle of *Parsons v. Hogg* (see notes to reg. 19(2)) to the meaning of "gross earnings" in para. (3). *R(IS) 16/93* has now expressly decided that the principle of *Parsons v. Hogg* applies to reg. 36 of the Income Support Regulations. See also *CFC 836/1995* in the notes to reg. 38(11) of the Income Support Regulations. The result is that expenditure by the employee which had to be incurred in order to secure the earnings should first be deducted, before the deductions expressly listed in para. (3) are made. Para. (4) is necessary to estimate the deductions in a case where future earnings are estimated under reg. 14(6).

Paragraphs (5) and (6)

Para. (5) takes the process on from the identification of net earnings for each pay period under para. (3). The first step under sub-para. (a) is to put together all the net earnings in the pay periods in the assessment period and produce the average net earnings for those pay periods. Then under sub-para. (b) the net earnings for each pay period must be inspected. If the figure for any pay period is 20 per cent. or more higher or lower than the average net earnings, that pay period is excluded and a new figure of average net earnings is calculated using the net earnings from the remaining pay periods. If the result of sub-para. (b) would be that no pay period at all would remain, then sub-para. (c) applies instead. Only pay periods in which no earnings are received or in which the earnings received are for a longer period than the pay period are excluded before the new average is calculated. If the result of sub-para. (c) would be that no pay periods at all would remain, sub-para. (d) applies and an estimate by the employer under reg. 14(6) must be accepted.

This mechanical process removes all issues of judgment. It should allow for quick and accurate calculations, although the result may be rather crude in some cases.

Finally, para. (6) converts the average net earnings for the pay period into the average weekly net earnings.

[¹Calculation of net earnings of directors

20ZA.—(1) For the purposes of regulation 14A (normal weekly earnings of directors) the earnings of a claimant to be taken into account shall be his net earnings [³. . .] and those net earnings shall be determined in accordance with the following paragraphs.

(2) There shall be disregarded from a claimant's net earnings any sum, where applicable, specified in Schedule 1.

(3) A claimant's net earnings shall, except where paragraph (4) applies, be calculated by taking into account his gross earnings from that employment, less—

    (a) any amount deducted from those earnings by way of—
        (i) income tax;
        (ii) primary Class 1 contributions under the Contributions and Benefits Act; and
    (b) one-half of any sum paid by the claimant [²in respect of a pay period] by way of a contribution towards an occupational or personal pension scheme.

(4) Where some or all of the claimant's earnings are estimated under regulation 14A(2), those net earnings shall be calculated by taking into account the estimated gross earnings, less—

    (a) an amount representing income tax, calculated by applying to those ear-

899

nings the lower rate or, as the case may be, the lower rate and the basic rate of income tax in the year of assessment in which the claim was made, taking into account the personal relief to which the claimant would be entitled under sections 257(1), 257A(1) and 259 of the Income and Corporation Taxes Act 1988 (personal relief); except that if the period in respect of which the estimate is made is less than a year, [²the earnings to which the lower rate of tax is to be applied] and the amount of the personal relief allowable under this sub-paragraph shall be reduced pro-rata;

(b) where the weekly amount of those earnings equals or exceeds the lower earnings limit, an amount representing primary Class 1 contributions under the Contributions and Benefits Act, calculated by applying to those earnings the initial and main primary percentages applicable at the date of claim in accordance with section 8(1)(a) and (b) of that Act; and

(c) one-half of any sum which would be payable by the claimant by way of a contribution towards an occupational or personal pension scheme[², if the earnings so estimated were actual earnings].]

AMENDMENTS

1. Income-related Benefits Schemes (Micellanous Amendments) Regulations 1994 (S.I. 1994 No. 527), reg. 17 (April 12, 1994).
2. Income-related Benefits Schemes (Miscellaneous Amendments) (No. 5) Regulations 1994 (S.I. 1994 No. 2139), reg. 16 (October 4, 1994).
3. Disability Working Allowance and Family Credit (General) Amendment Regulations 1996 (S.I. 1996 No. 3137), reg. 3(6) (January 7, 1997).

DEFINITIONS

"assessment period"—see reg. 2(1), reg. 14A.
"claimant"—see reg. 2(1), reg. 10(1).
"director"—see reg. 2(1)
"earnings"—*ibid.*
"lower rate"—*ibid.*
"occupational pension scheme"—see 1986 Act, s.84(1) (PSA, s.1).
"pay period"—see reg.2(1), reg. 14(7)(b).
"personal pension scheme"—see reg. 2(1).
"year of assessment"—*ibid.*

GENERAL NOTE

The earnings to be taken into account under reg. 14A are the earnings as a director less income tax, social security contributions, half of any contribution to an occupational or personal pension and any applicable disregards in Sched. 1. If any of the earnings are estimated, the tax, social security contributions and pension contributions will be assessed notionally.

On the effect of the January 1997 amendment to para. (1) see *CFC 6910/1995*, to be reported as *R(FC) 1/98*, in the notes to reg. 14(1) and (2).

[¹Calculation of bonus or commission

20A. Where a claimant's earnings include a bonus or commission to which [²paragraph (4)] of regulation 14 (normal weekly earnings of employed earners) applies that part of his earnings shall be calculated by aggregating any payments of bonus or commission and [³deducting from it—]

(a) an amount in respect of income tax equivalent to an amount calculated by applying to that part of the earnings the basic rate of tax in the year of assessment in which the claim is made; and

[⁴(b) an amount representing primary Class 1 contributions under the Contributions and Benefits Act, calculated by applying to that part of the earnings the main primary percentage applicable at the date of claim; and]

(c) one-half of any sum payable by the claimant in respect of that part of the earnings by way of a contribution towards an occupational pension [³scheme;

and dividing the resulting sum by 52.]]

AMENDMENTS

1. Family Credit (General) Amendment Regulations 1990 (S.I. 1990, No. 574), reg. 8 (April 10, 1990).
2. Family Credit (General) Amendment Regulations 1992 (S.I. 1992 No. 573), reg. 8 (April 7, 1992).
3. Income-related Benefits Schemes (Miscellaneous Amendments) (No. 3) Regulations 1992 (S.I. 1992 No. 2155), reg. 7 (October 5, 1992).
4. Income-related Benefits Schemes (Miscellaneous Amendments) Regulations 1994 (S.I. 1994 No. 527), reg. 18 (April 12, 1994).

DEFINITIONS

"claimant"—see reg. 2(1).
"occupational pension scheme"—see 1986 Act, s.84(1) (PSA, s.1).
"Social Security Act"—see reg. 2(1).
"year of assessment"—*ibid.*

GENERAL NOTE

The effect of reg. 14(4) is that any bonus or commission separate from ordinary earnings which is paid in the 52 weeks before the week of claim is to be brought into the calculation of earnings. Under reg. 20A the aggregate of such payments is divided by 52 to reach a weekly figure. The standard deductions are to be made under paras. (a) to (c) before doing the division. But there seems to be no scope for a *Parsons v. Hogg* deduction (see notes to reg. 20) and paras. (a) and (c) are defective in not referring to the lower rate of income tax (applicable from April 1992) or to contributions to personal pension schemes.

See reg. 20(3)(c) for the exclusion of the actual payment of such bonus or commission from the calculations.

Chapter IV

Self-employed earners

Earnings of self-employed earners

21.—(1) Subject to [³ paragraphs (2) and (3)], "earnings", in the case of employment as a self-employed earner, means the gross receipts of the employment and shall include any allowance paid under section 2 of the Employment and Training Act 1973 [²or section 2 of the Enterprise and New Towns (Scotland) Act 1990] to the claimant for the purpose of assisting him in carrying on his business unless at the date of claim the allowance has been terminated.

(2) Where a claimant is employed in providing board and lodging accommodation for which a charge is payable, any income consisting of payments of such a charge shall only be taken into account under this Chapter as earnings if it forms a major part of the total of the claimant's weekly income less any sums disregarded under Schedule 2 [¹other than under paragraph 40 of that Schedule.]

[³(3) "Earnings" shall not include any payments to which paragraph 24 of Schedule 2 refers (sums to be disregarded in the calculation of income other than earnings).]

AMENDMENTS

1. Family Credit (General) Amendment Regulations 1990 (S.I. 1990 No. 574), reg. 9 (April 10, 1990).
2. Enterprise (Scotland) Consequential Amendments Order 1991 (S.I. 1991 No. 387), art. 2 (April 1, 1991).
3. Income-related Benefits Schemes (Miscellaneous Amendments) (No. 5) Regulations 1994 (S.I. 1994 No. 2139), reg. 17 (October 4, 1994).

DEFINITIONS

"claimant"—see reg. 2(1), reg. 10(1).
"date of claim"—see reg. 2(1).
"payment"—*ibid.*
"self-employed earner"—*ibid.*

GENERAL NOTE

Paragraph (1)
The starting point in the calculations for the self-employed is the amount of the gross receipts, although reg. 22 immediately shifts to net profits. The receipts are to include any Business Start-up Allowance (previously enterprise allowance) paid to the person unless the allowance has been terminated at the date of claim. This appears to mean that even though such an allowance has been paid in most of the 26-week period under reg. 15(1), it should not count in the calculation if it has ended by the date of claim (which is not necessarily the same as the date on which the claim is received). The timing of a claim may thus be crucial.
See the notes to reg. 37(1) of the Income Support (General) Regulations for discussion of the general meaning of "gross receipts" and in particular the vexed question of capital receipts, now comprehensively resolved by *CFC 3/1992*.

Paragraph (2)
The income from taking boarders does not count as earnings from self-employment unless it forms "a major part" of the family's income which is not disregarded under Sched. 2 (apart from the provision on income from boarders). "A major part" presumably means more than 50 per cent. A person is "employed" in providing board and lodging providing that he is occupied in doing so. It does not have to be by way of business (*CIS 55/1989*). For "charge", see the notes to the definition of "board and lodging accommodation" in reg. 2(1) of the Income Support (General) Regulations.
If the income does not count under para. (2), see reg. 24.

Paragraph (3)
This applies to payments to people for providing temporary care in their home. These payments are disregarded as income other than earnings under para. 24 of Sched. 2. Para. (3) ensures that they are not treated as earnings.

Calculation of net profit of self-employed earners

22.—(1) For the purposes of regulation 15 (normal weekly earnings of self-employed earners), the earnings of a claimant to be taken into account shall be—

   (a) in the case of a self-employed earner who is engaged in employment on his own account, the net profit derived from that employment;

   (b) in the case of a self-employed earner whose employment is carried on in partnership or is that of a share fisherman within the meaning of the Social Security (Mariners' Benefits) Regulations 1975, his share of the net profit derived from that employment less—

      (i) an amount in respect of income tax and social security contributions payable under the Social Security Act [SSCBA] calculated in accordance with regulation 23 (deduction of tax and contributions for self-employed earners); and

      (ii) [³one half of the amount in respect of any qualifying premium calcu-
lated in accordance with paragraph (13)].

(2) There shall be disregarded from a claimant's net profit any sum, where
applicable, specified in Schedule 1.

(3) For the purposes of paragraph (1)(a) the net profit of the employment shall,
except where paragraph [¹(3A),] (9) or (10) applies, be calculated by taking into
account the earnings of the employment [¹received in the assessment period],
less—

(a) subject to paragraphs (5) to (7), any expenses wholly and exclusively
defrayed in that period for the purposes of that employment;

(b) an amount in respect of—
    (i) income tax; and
    (ii) social security contributions payable under the Social Security Act
[SSCBA], calculated in accordance with regulation 23 (deduction
of tax and contributions for self-employed earners); and

(c) [³one half of the amount in respect of any qualifying premium calculated
in accordance with paragraph (13)].

[³(3A) For the purposes of paragraph (1)(a), in a case where the assessment
period is determined under regulation 15(1)(b), the net profit of the employment
shall, except where paragraph (9) applies, be calculated by taking into account
the earnings of the employment relevant to that period (whether or not received
in that period), less—

(a) subject to paragraphs (5) to (7), any expenses relevant to that period
(whether or not defrayed in that period) and which were wholly and
exclusively incurred for the purposes of that employment;

(b) an amount in respect of—
    (i) income tax; and
    (ii) social security contributions payable under the Social Security Act
[SSCBA], calculated in accordance with regulation 23; and

(c) [³one half of the amount in respect of any qualifying premium calculated
in accordance with paragraph (13)].]

(4) For the purposes of paragraph (1)(b) the net profit of the employment
shall, except where paragraph [¹(4A), (9) or] (10) applies, be calculated by
taking into account the earnings of the employment [¹received in the assessment
period] less, subject to paragraphs (5) to (7), any expenses wholly and exclusively defrayed in that period for the purposes of that employment.

[¹(4A) For the purposes of paragraph (1)(b), in a case where the assessment
period is determined under regulation 15(1)(b) the net profit of the employment
shall, except where paragraph (9) applies, be calculated by taking into account
the earnings of the employment relevant to that period (whether or not received
in that period) less, subject to paragraphs (5) to (7), any expenses relevant to
that period (whether or not defrayed in that period) and which were wholly and
exclusively incurred for the purposes of that employment.]

(5) Subject to paragraph (6), no deduction shall be made under [¹para-
graphs (3)(a), (3A)(a), (4) or (4A), as the case may be,] in respect of—

(a) any capital expenditure;

(b) the depreciation of any capital asset;

(c) any sum employed, or intended to be employed, in the setting up or
expansion of the employment;

(d) any loss incurred before the beginning of the assessment period;

(e) the repayment of capital on any loan taken out for the purposes of the
employment;

(f) any expenses incurred in providing business entertainment.

(6) A deduction shall be made under [¹paragraphs (3)(a), (3A)(a), (4) or (4A),
as the case may be,] in respect of the repayment of capital on any loan used
for—

(a) the replacement in the course of business of equipment or machinery; and

(b) the repair of an existing business asset except to the extent that any sum is payable under an insurance policy for its repair.

(7) An adjudication officer shall refuse to make a deduction in respect of any expenses under ['paragraphs (3)(a), (3A)(a), (4) or (4A), as the case may be,] where he is not satisfied that the expense has been defrayed or given the nature and the amount of the expense that it has been reasonably incurred.

(8) For the avoidance of doubt—

(a) a deduction shall not be made under ['paragraphs (3)(a), (3A)(a), (4) or (4A), as the case may be,] in respect of any sum unless it has been expended for the purposes of the business;

(b) a deduction shall be made thereunder in respect of—

(i) the excess of any VAT paid over VAT received in the assessment period;

(ii) any income expended in the repair of an existing business asset except to the extent that any sum is payable under an insurance policy for its repair;

(iii) any payment of interest on a loan taken out for the purposes of the employment.

(9) Where a claimant is engaged in employment as a child minder the net profit of the employment to be taken into account shall be one-third of the earnings of that employment, less—

(a) an amount in respect of—

(i) income tax; and

(ii) social security contributions payable under the Social Security Act [SSCBA],

calculated in accordance with regulation 23 (deduction of tax and contributions for self-employed earners); and

(b) [³one half of the amount in respect of any qualifying premium calculated in accordance with paragraph (13)].

[¹(10) Where regulation 15(2) (normal weekly earnings of self-employed earners) applies—

(a) for the purposes of paragraph (1)(a), the net profit derived from the employment shall be calculated by taking into account the claimant's estimated and, where appropriate, actual earnings from the employment less the amount of the deductions likely to be made and, where appropriate, made under sub-paragraphs (a) to (c) of paragraph (3); or

(b) for the purposes of paragraph (1)(b), his share of the net profit of the employment shall be calculated by taking into account the claimant's estimated and, where appropriate, his share of the actual earnings from the employment less the amount of his share of the expenses likely to be deducted and, where appropriate, deducted under paragraph (4); or

(c) in the case of employment as a child-minder, the net profit of the employment shall be calculated by taking into account one-third of the claimant's estimated earnings and, where appropriate, actual earnings from the employment less the amount of the deductions likely to be made and, where appropriate made under sub-paragraphs (a) and (b) of paragraph (9).]

(11) For the avoidance of doubt where a claimant is engaged in employment as a self-employed earner and he is also engaged in one or more other employments as a self-employed or employed earner any loss incurred in any one of his employments shall not be offset against his earnings in any other of his employments.

[²(12) [³In this regulation—

(a) "qualifying premium" means any premium which at the date of claim is payable periodically in respect of a retirement annuity contract or a personal pension scheme;

(b)] [⁴. . .]]

[³(13) The amount in respect of any qualifying premium shall be calculated by multiplying the daily amount of the qualifying premium by the number equal to the number of days in the assessment period; and for the purposes of this regulation the daily amount of the qualifying premium shall be determined—

(a) where the qualifying premium is payable monthly, by multiplying the amount of the qualifying premium by 12 and dividing the product by 365;

(b) in any other case, by dividing the amount of the qualifying premium by the number equal to the number of days in the period to which the qualifying premium relates.]

AMENDMENTS

1. Family Credit (General) Amendment No. 4 Regulations 1988 (S.I. 1988 No. 1970), reg. 6 (December 5, 1988).

2. Income-related Benefits Schemes (Miscellaneous Amendments) (No.4) Regulations 1993 (S.I. 1993 No. 2119), reg. 59 (October 3, 1993).

3. Income-related Benefits Schemes (Miscellaneous Amendments) Regulations 1994 (S.I. 1994 No. 527) reg. 19 (April 12, 1994).

4. Income-related Benefits Schemes and Social Security (Claims and Payments) (Miscellaneous Amendments) Regulations 1995 (S.I. 1995 No. 2303), reg. 4(3) (October 3, 1995).

DEFINITIONS

"assessment period"—see reg. 2(1), reg. 15.
"claimant"—see reg. 2(1), reg. 10(1).
"earnings"—see reg. 2(1).
"employed earner"—*ibid.*
"retirement annuity contract"—*ibid.*
"self-employed earner"—*ibid.*
"Social Security Act"—*ibid.*

GENERAL NOTE

See the notes to reg. 38(1) to (9) and (11) of the Income Support (General) Regulations for the substance of this provision. Para. (10) here deals with estimated earnings. The main differences otherwise are in the cross-references and the provision in paras. (3A) and (4A) for the assessment period identified in reg. 15(1)(b).

Paragraphs (3A) and (4A).

CFC 19/1993 decides that in calculating the net profit of a business under para. (3A) it is necessary to take account of the opening and closing stock. The claimant had produced a profit and loss account and the claim was assessed on the basis of reg. 15(1)(b). It was argued on behalf of the AO that "expenses" in para. (3A) was confined to purchases during the year. The Commissioner rejects that approach. In order to produce sales stock had to be consumed. Stock constituted an expense deductible under para. (3A). Such stock comprised both the opening stock and purchases during the year less the closing stock. In taking this view the Commissioner differs from that taken in *C2/89* (a decision of the Chief Commissioner of Northern Ireland) which has been followed by some Commissioners in England (see *CFC 22/1989* and *CFC 19/1992*). The Commissioner in *CFC 10/1993* declines to follow *CFC 19/1993*. In his view regs. 21(1) and 22(7) make clear that only earnings actually received and expenses actually defrayed may be taken into account. The Commissioner observes that for tax purposes there are clearly strong arguments for taking a long-term view and making the notional adjustments to income and expenditure involved in taking into account stock valuation. But in his view it is consistent with the purposes of a social security scheme that only money actually received or actually expended should be taken into account. The Commissioner also points out that variations in stock valuation will not always operate in a claimant's favour. The issue was also considered in *R(FC) 1/96*. The Commissioner follows *CFC 19/1993*, pointing to the use of the phrase "whether or not received in that period" in reg. 22(3A) in relation to earnings and a similar wording as regards expenses. Thus there was nothing in the family credit scheme to indicate that normal accountancy procedures should not be applied. The definition of "trading account" in reg. 15(1A)(c) which referred to "the cost of *those* sales" also supported this conclusion. Reg. 22(3A) was to be contrasted with the position where accounts were not supplied when a strictly cash basis was applied by reg. 22(3). While this conflict of view between the Commissioners continues, SSATs faced with an appeal on this issue will have to decide which approach they prefer, but the current weight of authority seems to be in favour of taking account of opening and closing stock.

Deduction of tax and contributions for self-employed earners

23.—(1) The amount to be deducted in respect of income tax under regulation 22(1)(b)(i), (3)(b)(i)[², (3A)(b)(i)] or (9)(a)(i) (calculation of net profit of self-employed earners) shall be calculated on the basis of the amount of chargeable income, and as if that income were assessable to income tax at [³the lower rate or, as the case may be, the lower rate and the basic rate of tax] in the year of assessment in which the claim was made, less only the personal relief to which the claimant is entitled under sections 8(1) and (2) and 14(1)(a) and (2) of the Income and Corporation Taxes Act 1970 (personal relief) as is appropriate to his circumstances; but, if the assessment period is less than a year [³the earnings to which the lower rate [⁴ . . .] of tax is to be applied and] the amount of the personal relief deductible under this paragraph shall be calculated on a pro rata basis.

(2) The amount to be deducted in respect of social security contributions under regulation 22(1)(b)(i), (3)(b)(ii)[², (3A)(b)(ii)] or (9)(a)(ii) shall be [⁵. . .]—

[¹(a) [⁵an amount in respect of Class 2 contributions calculated by multiplying the weekly rate of such contributions applicable at the date of claim by virtue of section 11(1) or, as the case may be, (3) of the Contributions and Benefits Act by the number of days in the assessment period and dividing the product by 7,] except where the claimant's chargeable income is less than the amount specified in [⁵ section 11(4)] of that Act (small earnings exception) for the tax year in which the date of claim falls; but if the assessment period is less than a year, the amount specified for that tax year shall be calculated on a pro rata basis; and

(b) the amount of Class 4 contributions (if any) which would be payable under [⁵ section 15(3)] of that Act (Class 4 contributions) at the percentage rate applicable at the date of claim on so much of the chargeable income as exceeds the lower limit but does not exceed the upper limit of profits and gains applicable for the tax year in which the date of claim falls; if the assessment period is less than a year, those limits shall be calculated on a pro rata basis.]

[²(3) In this regulation "chargeable income" means—

(a) except where sub-paragraph (b) or (c) applies, the earnings derived from the employment, less any expenses deducted under paragraph (3)(a), (3A)(a), (4) or (4A), as the case may be, of regulation 22;

(b) except where sub-paragraph (c)(iii) applies, in the case of employment as a child minder one-third of the earnings of that employment; or

(c) where regulation 15(2) applies (normal weekly earnings of self-employed earners)

　(i) in the case of a self-employed earner who is engaged in employment on his own account, the claimant's estimated and, where appropriate, actual earnings from the employment less the amount of the deductions likely to be made and, where appropriate, made under sub-paragraph (a) of paragraph (3) of regulation 22;

　(ii) in the case of a self-employed earner whose employment is carried on in partnership or is that of a share fisherman within the meaning of the Social Security (Mariners' Benefits) Regulations 1975, the claimant's estimated and, where appropriate, his share of the actual earnings from the employment less the amount of his share of the expenses likely to be deducted and, where appropriate, deducted under paragraph (4) of regulation 22;

(iii) in the case of employment as a child minder, one-third of the claimant's estimated and, where appropriate, actual earnings from that employment.]

AMENDMENTS

1. Family Credit (General) Amendment Regulations 1988 (S.I. 1988 No. 660), reg. 7 (April 11, 1988).

2. Family Credit (General) Amendment No. 4 Regulations 1988 (S.I. 1988 No. 1970), reg. 7 (December 5, 1988).

3. Income-related Benefits Schemes (Miscellaneous Amendments) (No.3) Regulations 1992 (S.I. 1992 No. 2155), reg. 8 (October 5, 1992).

4. Income-related Benefits Schemes (Miscellaneous Amendments) (No. 5) Regulations 1994 (S.I. 1994 No. 2139), reg. 14 (October 4, 1994).

5. Disability Working Allowance and Family Credit (General) Amendment Regulations 1996 (S.I. 1996 No. 3137), reg. 3(7) (January 7, 1997).

DEFINITIONS

"assessment period"—see reg. 2(1), reg. 15.
"claim"—see reg. 2(1).
"claimant"—*ibid.*, reg. 10(1).
"earnings"—see reg. 2(1).
"self-employed earner"—*ibid.*
"Social Security Act"—*ibid.*
"year of assessment"—*ibid.*

GENERAL NOTE

Paragraph (1)
Since the actual income tax to be paid by the self-employed may take some time to calculate (and is normally not payable until the tax year after that in which the profits are made) this provision supplies a simple rule to be applied immediately. The lower, or lower and basic rate (as appropriate) of income tax for the tax year, in which the claim is made is applied, less the personal relief for a year or part of a year.

Paragraph (2)
The appropriate amounts of Class 2 (flat-rate) and Class 4 (profit-related) social security contributions for the period over which earnings are averaged are to be deducted.

Paragraph (3)
This paragraph defines the earnings on which the deductions for tax and social security contributions are to be calculated.

Chapter V

Other Income

Calculation of income other than earnings

24.—(1) For the purposes of regulation 16 (normal weekly income other than earnings), the income of a claimant which does not consist of earnings to be taken into account shall, subject to paragraphs [²(2) to (4A)], be his gross income and any capital treated as income under [⁴regulations 25 and 27 (capital treated as income and modifications in respect of children and young persons).]

(2) There shall be disregarded from the calculation of a claimant's gross income under paragraph (1), any sum, where applicable, specified in Schedule 2.

(3) [¹. . .]

(4) Where the payment of any benefit under the benefit Acts is subject to any deduction by way of recovery the amount to be taken into account under paragraph (1) shall be the gross amount payable.

[²(4A) Where a loan is made to a person pursuant to arrangements made under section 1 of the Education (Student Loans) Act 1990 [³or Article 3 of the Education (Student Loans) (Northern Ireland) Order 1990] and that person ceases to be a student before the end of the academic year in respect of which the loan is payable or, as the case may be, before the end of his course, a sum equal to the weekly amount apportionable under paragraph (2) of regulation 42A shall be taken into account under paragraph (1) for each week, in the period over which the loan fell to be apportioned, following the date on which that person ceases to be a student; but in determining the weekly amount apportionable under paragraph (2) of regulation 42A so much of that paragraph as provides for a disregard shall not have effect.]

(5) For the avoidance of doubt there shall be included as income to be taken into account under paragraph (1) any payment to which regulation 19(2) applies (payments not earnings).

AMENDMENTS

1. Family Credit (General) Amendment Regulations 1990 (S.I. 1990 No. 574), reg. 10 (April 10, 1990).

2. Social Security Benefits (Student Loans and Miscellaneous Amendments) Regulations 1990 (S.I. 1990 No. 1549), reg. 3(2) (September 1, 1990).

3. Family Credit (General) Amendment Regulations 1991 (S.I. 1991 No. 1520), reg. 4 (August 6, 1991).

4. Income-related Benefits Schemes (Miscellaneous Amendments) (No. 4) Regulations 1993 (S.I. 1993 No. 2119), reg. 30 (October 5, 1993).

DEFINITIONS

"the benefit Acts"—see reg. 2(1).
"claimant"—see reg. 2(1), reg. 10(1).
"earnings"—see reg. 2(1).

GENERAL NOTE

Paragraph (1)

Income which is not earnings comes into this category. It specifically includes capital treated as income under reg. 25 and reg. 27 (capital payable by instalments), and must also include the tariff income from capital between £3,000 and £8,000 under reg. 36. Perhaps the main category covered will be social security benefits which are not disregarded under Sched. 2 (in particular, child benefit is disregarded). The intention seems to be that income from boarders which does not count as earnings from self-employment under reg. 21(2) should count here, but after the revocation of para. (3) it is not clear that this works. It is not income other than earnings. The income to be taken into account is the gross amount, *i.e.* without any deductions. See the notes to reg. 40(1) of the Income Support Regulations.

Note the disregard of the first £15 of maintenance payments under reg. 16(2) and (2A) (Sched. 2, para. 47).

Paragraph (2)

There is a long list of disregards in Sched. 2.

Paragraph (4)

If a social security benefit is to be taken into account any deduction by way of recovery (*e.g.* of an overpayment or of a social fund loan) is ignored. The gross amount is taken.

Paragraph (5)

Payments which are excluded from the category of earnings by reg. 19(2) count as income, but see the disregard of payments in kind (para. 20), statutory maternity pay (para. 27) and payments for necessary, etc., expenses (para. 32) in Sched. 2. Earnings which are disregarded under Sched. 1 do not count as income because they remain "earnings" and reg. 24 only applies to income which does not consist of earnings.

Capital treated as income

25.—(1) Any capital payable by instalments which are outstanding at the date of the claim shall, if the aggregate of the instalments outstanding and the amount of the claimant's capital otherwise calculated in accordance with Chapter VI of this Part exceeds [¹£8,000], be treated as income.

(2) Any payment received under an annuity shall be treated as income.

[²(3) Any Career Development Loan paid pursuant to section 2 of the Employment and Training Act 1973 shall be treated as income.]

AMENDMENTS

1. Income-related Benefits (Miscellaneous Amendments) Regulations 1990 (S.I. 1990 No. 671), reg. 3 (April 9, 1990).
2. Income-related Benefits and Jobseeker's Allowance (Miscellaneous Amendments) Regulations 1997 (S.I. 1997 No. 65), reg. 3(3) (April 8, 1997).

DEFINITIONS

"claimant"—see reg. 2(1), reg. 10(1).
"date of claim"—see reg. 2(1).

GENERAL NOTE

Paragraph (1)

The value of the right to receive any outstanding instalments of capital to be paid by instalments is disregarded under para. 17 of Sched. 3 as a capital asset. Generally, each instalment, when it is paid, is added to the person's capital. However, if the person's existing capital plus the amount of any outstanding instalments comes to more than £8,000, this provision applies. The sensible result would then be that each instalment received when para. (1) applied would be treated as income. However, this is not what para. (1) says. It appears to require all of the capital payable by instalments to be treated as income, but there is no clue how this might be done. Perhaps the sensible result is the only possible outcome. See reg. 27(1) for payments to a child or young person.

See *Lillystone v. SBC* [1982] 3 F.L.R. 52 for an example of a capital sum payable by instalments.

Paragraph (2)

The value of the right to receive income under an annuity is disregarded as a capital asset under para. 12 of Sched. 3.

Paragraph (3)

See the note to reg. 41(6) of the Income Support Regulations and para. 58 of Sched. 2 for the disregard that is applied to such loans.

Notional income

26.—(1) A claimant shall be treated as possessing income of which he has deprived himself for the purpose of securing entitlement to family credit or increasing the amount of that benefit.

(2) [¹⁶Except in the case of—

    (a) a discretionary trust;

    (b) a trust derived from a payment made in consequence of a personal injury; or

    (c) a personal pension scheme or retirement annuity contract where the claimant is aged under 60,] [[17] or

    (d) any sum to which paragraph 46(a) or 47(a) of Schedule 3 (disregard of compensation for personal injuries which is administered by the Court) refers,] [[21] or

    (e) rehabilitation allowance made under section 2 of the Employment and Training Act 1973]

any income which would become available to the claimant upon application being made, but which has not been acquired by him, shall be treated as possessed by the claimant.

    [[16](2A) Where a person, aged not less than 60, is a member of, or a person deriving entitlement to a pension under, a personal pension scheme, or is a party to, or a person deriving entitlement to a pension under, a retirement annuity contract, and—

    (a) in the case of a personal pension scheme, he fails to purchase an annuity with the funds available in that scheme where—

        (i) he defers, in whole or in part, the payment of any income which would have been payable to him by his pension fund holder;

        (ii) he fails to take any necessary action to secure that the whole of any income which would be payable to him by his pension fund holder upon his applying for it, is so paid; or

        (iii) income withdrawal is not available to him under that scheme; or

    (b) in the case of a retirement annuity contract, he fails to purchase an annuity with the funds available under that contract,

the amount of any income foregone shall be treated as possessed by him, but only from the date on which it could be expected to be acquired were an application for it to be made.

    (2B) The amount of any income foregone in a case to which either head (2A)(a)(i) or (ii) applies shall be the maximum amount of income which may be withdrawn from the fund and shall be determined by the adjudication officer who shall take account of information provided by the pension fund holder in accordance with regulation 7(5) of the Social Security (Claims and Payments) Regulations 1987.

    (2C) The amount of any income foregone in a case to which either head (2A)(a)(iii) or sub-paragraph (2A)(b) applies shall be the income that the claimant could have received without purchasing an annuity had the funds held under the relevant personal pension scheme or retirement annuity contract been held under a personal pension scheme where income withdrawal was available and shall be determined in the manner specified in paragraph (2B).]

    (3) [[22]Any payment of income, other than a payment of income specified in paragraph (3A)], made—

    [[3](a) to a third party in respect of a member of [[4]the family] (but not a member of the third party's family) shall be treated as possessed by that member of the family to the extent that it is used for his food, ordinary clothing or footwear, household fuel [[7]. . .] or housing costs [[7]or is used for any personal community [[10]charge,] collective community charge contribution [[10]or council tax] for which that member is liable]; and in this sub-paragraph the expression "ordinary clothing or foot-wear" means clothing or footwear for normal daily use, but does not include school uniforms, or clothing or footwear used solely for sporting activities;]

    (b) to a member of the family in respect of a third party (but not in respect of another member of that family) shall be treated as possessed by that member to the extent that it is kept him or used by or on behalf of any member of the family.

[²²(3A) Paragraph (3) shall not apply in respect of a payment of income made—

(a) under the Macfarlane Trust, the Macfarlane (Special Payments) Trust, the Macfarlane (Special Payments) (No. 2) Trust, the Fund, the Eileen Trust or the Independent Living Funds;

(b) pursuant to section 19(1)(a) of the Coal Industry Act 1994 (concessionary coal); or

(c) pursuant to section 2 of the Employment and Training Act 1973 in respect of a person's participation—

    (i) in an employment programme specified in regulation 75(1)(a)(ii) of the Jobseeker's Allowance Regulations 1996;

    (ii) in a training scheme specified in regulation 75(1)(b)(ii) of those Regulations; or

    (iii) in a qualifying course within the meaning specified in regulation 17A(7) of those Regulations.]

(4) Where—

(a) a claimant performs a service for another person; and

(b) that person makes no payment of earnings or pays less than that paid for a comparable employment in the area; and

(c) the adjudication officer is satisfied that the means of that person are sufficient for him to pay or to pay more for the service,

the adjudication officer shall treat the claimant as possessing such earnings (if any) as is reasonable for that employment; but this paragraph shall not apply to a claimant who is engaged by a charitable or [¹⁵voluntary organisation] or is a volunteer if the adjudication officer is satisfied [¹⁵in any of those cases] that it is reasonable for him to provide his services free of charge [²⁰ or in a case where the service is performed in connection with the claimant's participation in an employment or training programme in accordance with regulation 19(1)(q) of the Jobseeker's Allowance Regulations 1996].

(5) Where a claimant is treated as possessing any income under any of paragraphs (1) to (3), the foregoing provisions of this Part shall apply for the purposes of calculating the amount of that income as if a payment had actually been made and as if it were actual income which he does possess.

(6) Where a claimant is treated as possessing any earnings under paragraph (4), the foregoing provisions of this Part shall apply for the purposes of calculating the amount of those earnings as if a payment had actually been made and as if they were actual earnings which he does possess, except that paragraph (3) of regulation 20 (calculation of net earnings of employed earners) shall not apply and his net earnings shall be calculated by taking into account those earnings which he is treated as possessing, less—

(a) an amount in respect of income tax equivalent to an amount calculated by applying to those earnings [⁹the lower rate or, as the case may be, the lower rate and the basic rate of tax] in the year of assessment in which the claim was made less only the personal relief to which the claimant is entitled under sections 8(1) and (2) and 14(1)(a) and (2) of the Income and Corporation Taxes Act 1970 (personal relief) as is appropriate to his circumstances; but, if the assessment period is less than a year, [⁹the earnings to which the lower rate [¹⁴. . .] of tax is to be applied and] the amount of the personal relief deductible under this subparagraph shall be calculated on a pro rata basis;

[¹³(b) where the weekly amount of those earnings equals or exceeds the lower earnings limit, an amount representing primary Class 1 contributions under the Contributions and Benefits Act, calculated by applying to those

earnings the initial and main primary percentages applicable at the date of claim in accordance with section 8(1)(a) and (b) of that Act; and]
(c) one-half of any sum payable by the claimant by way of a contribution towards an occupational or personal pension scheme.

AMENDMENTS

1. Family Credit (General) Amendment Regulations 1988 (S.I. 1988 No. 660), reg. 8 (April 11, 1988).
2. Family Credit and Income Support (General) Amendment Regulations 1988 (S.I. 1988 No. 999), reg. 3 (June 9, 1988).
3. Family Credit (General) Amendment No. 3 Regulations 1988 (S.I. 1988 No. 1438), reg. 5 (September 12, 1988).
4. Family Credit (General) Amendment No. 4 Regulations 1988 (S.I. 1988 No. 1970), reg. 8 (December 5, 1988).
5. Income-related Benefits Schemes Amendment Regulations 1990 (S.I. 1990 No. 127), reg. 2 (January 31, 1990).
6. Income-related Benefits Schemes and Social Security (Recoupment) Amendment Regulations 1991 (S.I. 1991 No. 1175), reg. 3 (May 11, 1991).
7. Family Credit (General) Amendment Regulations 1991 (S.I. 1991 No. 1520), reg. 5 (October 8, 1991).
8. Income-related Benefits Schemes and Social Security (Recoupment) Amendment Regulations 1992 (S.I. 1992 No. 1101), reg. 4(3) (May 7, 1992).
9. Income-related Benefits Schemes (Miscellaneous Amendments) (No. 3) Regulations 1992 (S.I. 1992 No. 2155), reg. 9 (October 5, 1992).
10. Income-related Benefits Schemes (Miscellaneous Amendments) Regulations 1993 (S.I. 1993 No. 315), Sched., para. 7 (April 1, 1993).
11. Social Security Benefits (Miscellaneous Amendments) (No. 2) Regulations 1993 (S.I. 1993 No. 963), reg. 3(3) (April 22, 1993).
12. Income-related Benefits Schemes and Social Security (Recoupment) Amendment Regulations 1993 (S.I. 1993 No. 1249), reg. 2(3) (May 14, 1993).
13. Income-related Benefits Schemes (Miscellaneous Amendments) Regulations 1994 (S.I. 1994 No. 527), reg. 20 (April 12, 1994).
14. Income-related Benefits Schemes (Miscellaneous Amendments) (No. 5) Regulations 1994 (S.I. 1994 No. 2139), reg. 14 (October 4, 1994).
15. Income-related Benefits Schemes (Miscellaneous Amendments) Regulations 1995 (S.I. 1995 No. 516), reg. 13 (April 11, 1995).
16. Income-related Benefits Schemes and Social Security (Claims and Payments) (Miscellaneous Amendments) Regulations 1995 (S.I. 1995 No. 2303), reg. 4(4) (October 3, 1995).
17. Income-related Benefits and Jobseeker's Allowance (Amendment) (No. 2) Regulations 1997 (S.I. 1997 No. 2197), reg. 3 (October 7, 1997).
18. Income-related Benefits and Jobseeker's Allowance (Amendment) (No. 2) Regulations 1997 (S.I. 1997 No. 2197), reg. 7(3) and (4)(c) (October 7, 1997).
19. Social Security Amendment (New Deal) Regulations 1997 (S.I. 1997 No. 2863), reg. 17(1) and (2)(c) (January 5, 1998).
20. Social Security Amendment (New Deal) Regulations 1997 (S.I. 1997 No. 2863), reg. 17(3) and (4)(c) (January 5, 1998).
21. Social Security (Miscellaneous Amendments) Regulations 1998 (S.I. 1998 No. 563), reg. 6(1) and (2)(c) (April 7, 1998).
22. Social Security Amendment (New Deal) (No. 2) Regulations 1998 (S.I. 1998 No. 2117), reg. 2(3) (September 24, 1998).

DEFINITIONS

"assessment period"—see reg. 2(1).
"claimant"—*ibid.*, reg. 10(1).
"earnings"—see reg. 2(1).
"family"—see 1986 Act, s.20(11) (SSCBA, s.137(1)).
"occupational pension scheme"—see 1986 Act, s.84(1) (PSA, s.1).
"payment"—see reg. 2(1).
"pension fund holder"—*ibid.*

"personal pension scheme"—*ibid.*
"retirement annuity contract"—*ibid.*
"the Eileen Trust"—see reg. 2(1).
"the Fund"—*ibid.*
"the Independent Living Funds"—*ibid.*
"the Macfarlane (Special Payments) Trust"—*ibid.*
"the Macfarlane (Special Payments) (No. 2) Trust"—*ibid.*
"the Macfarlane Trust"—*ibid.*
"voluntary organisation"—*ibid.*
"year of assessment"—*ibid.*

GENERAL NOTE

Paragraph (1)
See the notes to reg. 42(1) of the Income Support (General) Regulations. However, this provision only applies if the purpose is to gain entitlement to family credit. The approach of *R(IS) 14/93* suggests that if the purpose is to gain entitlement to, for example income support or family income supplement, this provision cannot apply.

Paragraph (2)
See the notes to reg. 42(2)–(2C) of the Income Support (General) Regulations for when income would become available upon application. Here the only exceptions are discretionary trusts, trusts of payments of compensation for personal injury, personal pension schemes and retirement annuity contracts where the person is aged under 60, funds held in court that derive from damages for personal injury and a rehabilitation allowance under s. 2 of the Employment and Training Act 1973. On paras. (2A)–(2C), see the notes to reg. 42(2)–(2C).

Paragraphs (3) and (3A)
See the notes to reg. 42(4) and (4ZA) of the Income Support (General) Regulations for the general tests. There are slight differences only.
In *CFC 13585/1996* the claimant's husband, from whom she was separated, was paying the mortgage payments on her home. They were joint owners of the property. The AO contended that the entire amount of these payments should be regarded as her notional income under para. (3)(a). However, the Commissioner holds that this only applied to one half of the payments. Although the claimant and her husband were jointly and severally liable to the lender for the repayment of the mortgage, as between themselves they were each only responsible for repaying one half. Thus the claimant was to be treated as possessing income equal to half the mortgage payments, subject to a disregard of £15 per week under para. 47 of Sched. 2 (maintenance disregard).

Paragraph (4)
See the notes to reg. 42(6) of the Income Support (General) Regulations. Sub-para. (c) of this paragraph is not separated out in reg. 42(6), with the effect that the burden of proof is different. In reg. 42(6), if the other conditions are met, the provision applies unless the claimant satisfies the AO that the person's means are insufficient to pay the going rate. Here, the AO must be satisfied that the person's means are sufficient before para. (4) can apply.

Paragraphs (5) and (6)
Notional income and earnings are to be treated as actual income and earnings, including the appropriate deductions to reach a figure of net earnings.

Modifications in respect of children and young persons

27.—(1) Any capital of a child or young person payable by instalments which are outstanding at the date of claim shall, if the aggregate of the instalments outstanding and the amount of that child's or young person's other capital calculated in accordance with Chapter VI of this Part in like manner as for the claimant, [². . .], would exceed £3,000, be treated as income.

(2) Where the income of a child or young person, other than income consisting of payments of maintenance whether under a court order or not, calculated in accordance with [²Chapters I to V] of this Part exceeds the sum specified as a credit for that child or young person in Schedule 4 and regulation 46(5)

(sum for child or young person who has income in excess to be nil) applies, that income shall not be treated as income of the claimant.

(3) Where the capital of a child or young person, if calculated in accordance with Chapter VI of this Part in like manner as for the claimant, [²except as provided in paragraph (1)], would exceed £3,000, any income of that child or young person[¹, other than income consisting of any payment of maintenance whether under a court order or not] shall not be treated as income of the claimant.

(4) Any income of a child or young person which is to be disregarded under Schedule 2 shall be disregarded in such manner as to produce the result most favourable to the claimant.

AMENDMENTS

1. Income-related Benefits Schemes (Miscellaneous Amendments) Regulations 1993 (S.I. 1993 No. 315), reg. 13 (April 13, 1993).
2. Income-related Benefits Schemes (Miscellaneous Amendments) (No. 4) Regulations 1993 (S.I. 1993 No. 2119), reg. 31 (October 5, 1993).

DEFINITIONS

"child"—see 1986 Act, s.20(11) (SSCBA, s.137(1)).
"claimant"—see reg. 2(1), reg. 10(1).
"date of claim"—see reg. 2(1).
"payment"—*ibid.*
"young person"—*ibid.*, reg. 6.

GENERAL NOTE

There are important modifications where children or young persons in the family have capital or income. Note that the earnings of a child or young person are disregarded under para. 2 of Sched. 1.

Paragraph (1)
See reg. 25(1) for the general treatment of capital payable by instalments. If the payment is to a child or young person, the rule comes in at £3,000.

Paragraph (2)
If the income of a child or young person exceeds the amount of the credit for a person of that age specified in Sched. 4, then under reg. 46(5) the credit for that person is nil. As compensation, the child's or young person's income is not treated as the claimant's. It is as if the child or young person had been taken out of the family. See also the effect of para. (3).

Paragraph (3)
If the capital of a child or young person exceeds £3,000, then under reg. 46(4) the credit for that person is nil. Any capital of a child or young person is not in any circumstances treated as the claimant's (reg. 30). This paragraph means that any income of the child or young person, other than maintenance, is ignored when reg. 46(4) applies.

Paragraph (4)
Self-explanatory.

Chapter VI

Capital

Capital limit

28. For the purposes of section 22(6) of the Act [SSCBA, s.134(1)] as it applies to family credit (no entitlement to benefit if capital exceeds prescribed amount), the prescribed amount is [¹£8,000].

AMENDMENT

1. Income-related Benefits (Miscellaneous Amendments) Regulations 1990 (S.I. 1990 No. 671), reg. 3 (April 9, 1990).

DEFINITION

"the Act"—see reg. 2(1).

GENERAL NOTE

There was no capital limit for FIS. The introduction of a limit for family credit in s.22(6) of the 1986 Act (now s.134(1) of the Contributions and Benefits Act) was an important reform. Reg. 28 adopts the same ordinary limit as for income support, raised from £6,000 to £8,000 in April 1990. (From April 1996 the income support limit has been raised to £16,000 for claimants in residential care: see reg. 45 of the Income Support Regulations.) The limit applies to all the capital of the family which is treated as the claimant's under reg. 10(1). Capital belonging to children and young persons is disregarded under reg. 30, but see the effect on the entitlement through reg. 46(4).

See reg. 29 for the calculation of capital.

Calculation of capital

29.—(1) For the purposes of Part II of the Act [SSCBA, Part VII] as it applies to family credit, the capital of a claimant to be taken into account shall, subject to paragraph (2), be the whole of his capital calculated in accordance with this Part and any income treated as capital under regulation 31 (income treated as capital).

(2) There shall be disregarded from the calculation of a claimant's capital under paragraph (1) any capital, where applicable, specified in Schedule 3.

DEFINITIONS

"the Act"—see reg. 2(1).
"claimant"—*ibid.*, reg. 10(1).

GENERAL NOTE

The main point here, apart from confirming the effect of reg. 31, is to provide for the capital specified in Sched. 3 to be disregarded.

Disregard of capital of child or young person

30. The capital of a child or young person who is a member of the claimant's family shall not be treated as capital of the claimant.

DEFINITIONS

"child"—see 1986 Act, s.20(11) (SSCBA, s.137(1)).
"claimant"—see reg. 2(1), reg. 10(1).
"family"—see 1986 Act, s.20(11) (SSCBA, s.137(1)).
"young person"—see reg. 2(1), reg. 6.

GENERAL NOTE

Where the claimant's family includes a child or young person, any capital belonging to the child or young person is not treated as the claimant's, and so does not count towards the £8,000 limit. If an individual child or young person has capital of more than £3,000, no credit is allowed for that person (reg. 46(4)).

Income treated as capital

31.—(1) Any amount by way of a refund of income tax deducted from profits or emoluments chargeable to income tax under Schedule D or E shall be treated as capital.

(2) Any holiday pay which is not earnings under regulation 19(1)(b) (earnings of employed earners) shall be treated as capital.

[²(3) Any charitable or voluntary payment which is not made or is not due to be made at regular intervals, other than a payment which is made under the Macfarlane Trust, the Macfarlane (Special Payments) Trust, the Macfarlane (Special Payments) (No. 2) Trust[³, the Fund][⁵, the Eileen Trust] or [⁴the Independent Living Funds] shall be treated as capital.]

(4) Except any income derived from capital disregarded under paragraph 1, 2, 4, 6[¹, 13 or 26 to 30] of Schedule 3, any income derived from capital shall be treated as capital but only from the date it is normally due to be credited to the claimant's account.

(5) In the case of employment as an employed earner, any advance of earnings or any loan made by the claimant's employer shall be treated as capital.

(6) Any maintenance payment other than one to which regulation 16(2) [⁶or (2A)](normal weekly income other than earnings) applies shall be treated as capital.

[⁷(7) There shall be treated as capital the gross receipts of any commercial activity carried on by a person in respect of which assistance is received under an employment programme specified in regulation 75(1)(a)(ii)(aa)(ii) of the Job-seeker's Allowance Regulations 1996 (self-employment route of the Employment Option of the New Deal), but only in so far as those receipts were payable into a special account (as defined for the purposes of Chapter IVA of Part VIII of those Regulations) during the period in which that person was receiving such assistance.]

AMENDMENTS

1. Family Credit (General) Amendment No. 4 Regulations 1988 (S.I. 1988 No. 1970), reg. 9 (December 5, 1988).

2. Income-related Benefits Schemes and Social Security (Recoupment) Amendment Regulations 1991 (S.I. 1991 No. 1175), reg. 3 (May 11, 1991).

3. Income-related Benefits Schemes and Social Security (Recoupment) Amendment Regulations 1992 (S.I. 1992 No. 1101). reg. 6 (May 7, 1992).

4. Social Security Benefits (Miscellaneous Amendments) (No. 2) Regulations 1993 (S.I. 1993 No. 963), reg. 3(3) (April 22, 1993).

5. Income-related Benefits Schemes and Social Security (Recoupment) Amendment Regulations 1993 (S.I. 1993 No. 1249), reg. 2(3) (May 14, 1993).

6. Income-related Benefits Schemes (Miscellaneous Amendments) (No. 5) Regulations 1994 (S.I. 1994 No. 2139), reg. 18 (October 4, 1994).

7. Social Security (Miscellaneous Amendments) (No. 4) Regulations 1998 (S.I. 1998 No. 1174), reg. 7(1) and (2)(c) (June 1, 1998).

DEFINITIONS

"claimant"—see reg. 2(1), reg. 10(1).
"earnings"—see reg. 2(1).
"employed earner"—*ibid.*
"the Eileen Trust"—*ibid.*
"the Fund"—*ibid.*
"the Independent Living Funds"—*ibid.*
"the Macfarlane (Special Payments) Trust"—*ibid.*
"the Macfarlane (Special Payments) (No. 2) Trust"—*ibid.*
"the Macfarlane Trust"—*ibid.*

GENERAL NOTE

If income is treated as capital under this regulation, it is to be disregarded as income (Sched. 2, para. 26).

Paragraph (1)
Refunds of income tax under Schedule E (PAYE) or Schedule D are capital.

Paragraph (2)
Holiday pay payable more than four weeks after the termination of employment is capital.

Paragraph (3)
Charitable or voluntary payments which are due to be made at regular intervals will be income (subject to the disregard in para. 13 of Sched. 2). See the notes to para. 15 of Sched. 9 to the Income Support (General) Regulations. If the payment is not made, or not due to be made, at regular intervals it is capital. There is an exception for payments from the government-funded trusts for haemophiliacs, non–haemophiliacs and the severely disabled. Note that paras. 46 and 47 of Sched. 3 have not been added to the list of excepted cases. See further the notes to reg. 48(4) of the Income Support Regulations.

Paragraph (4)
The general rule is that the income derived from capital is treated as capital from the date on which it increases the existing balance. The exceptions are premises, the capital value of which is disregarded, plus business assets and trust funds derived from compensation for personal injury.

Paragraph (5)
Any advance of earnings or loan made by an employer to an employee is capital.

Paragraph (6)
Reg. 16(2) deals with maintenance payments (rather vaguely defined) which are made or due to be made at regular intervals. If the payments are neither made nor due to be made at regular intervals, they count as capital when they arrive. There is obvious scope for benefit planning here (compared to the rigidity of the income support rules).
Para. (6) has been amended from October 1994 to take account of child support maintenance under the Child Support Acts 1991–1995, which falls under reg. 16(2A) and not reg. 16(2).

Paragraph (7)
See the note to reg. 102C of the JSA Regulations. For a brief summary of the self-employment route of the Employment option of the New Deal for 18 to 24-year-olds see the note to reg. 75(1) of the JSA Regulations.

Calculation of capital in the United Kingdom

32. Capital which a claimant possesses in the United Kingdom shall be calculated—
   (a) except in a case to which sub-paragraph (b) applies, at its current market or surrender value less—
      (i) where there would be expenses attributable to sale, 10 per cent.; and
      (ii) the amount of any incumbrance secured on it;
   (b) in the case of a National Savings Certificate—
      (i) if purchased from an issue the sale of which ceased before 1st July last preceding the date of claim, at the price which it would have realised on that 1st July had it been purchased on the last day of that issue;
      (ii) in any other case, at its purchase price.

DEFINITION

"claimant"—see reg. 2(1), reg. 10(1).

See the notes to reg. 49 of the Income Support (General) Regulations.

Calculation of capital outside the United Kingdom

33. Capital which a claimant possesses in a country outside the United Kingdom shall be calculated—
- (a) in a case where there is no prohibition in that country against the transfer to the United Kingdom of an amount equal to its current market or surrender value in that country, at that value;
- (b) in a case where there is such a prohibition, at the price which it would realise if sold in the United Kingdom to a willing buyer,

less, where there would be expenses attributable to sale, 10 per cent. and the amount of any incumbrance secured on it.

DEFINITION

"claimant"—see reg. 2(1), reg. 10(1).

GENERAL NOTE

See the notes to reg. 50 of the Income Support (General) Regulations.

Notional capital

34.—(1) A claimant shall be treated as possessing capital of which he has deprived himself for the purpose of securing entitlement to family credit or increasing the amount of that benefit [⁶except—
- (a) where that capital is derived from a payment made in consequence of any personal injury and is placed on trust for the benefit of the claimant; or
- (b) to the extent that the capital which he is treated as possessing is reduced in accordance with regulation 34A (diminishing notional capital rule)] [¹⁴ or
- (c) any sum to which paragraph 46(a) or 47(a) of Schedule 3 (disregard of compensation for personal injuries which is administered by the Court) refers].
- (2) Except in the case of a—
- (a) a discretionary trust;
- (b) a trust derived from a payment made in consequence of a personal injury; or
- (c) any loan which would be obtainable only if secured against capital disregarded under Schedule 3, [¹³ or
- (d) a personal pension scheme or retirement annuity contract] [¹⁴ or
- (e) any sum to which paragraph 46(a) or 47(a) of Schedule 3 (disregard of compensation for personal injuries which is administered by the Court) refers,]

any capital which would become available to the claimant upon application being made but which has not been acquired by him shall be treated as possessed by him.

(3) [¹⁶Any payment of capital, other than a payment of capital specified in paragraph (3A)], made
- [³(a) to a third party in respect of a member of [⁴the family] (but not a member of the third party's family) shall be treated as possessed by that member of the family to the extent that it is used for his food, ordinary clothing or footwear, household fuel [⁸. . .] or housing costs [⁸or is used for any personal community [¹⁰charge,] collective community charge contribu-

918

tion [¹⁰or council tax] for which that member is liable]; and in this sub-paragraph the expression "ordinary clothing or footwear" means clothing or footwear for normal daily use, but does not include school uniforms, or clothing or footwear used solely for sporting activities;]

(b) to a member of the family in respect of a third party (but not in respect of another member of the family) shall be treated as possessed by that member to the extent that it is kept by him or used on behalf of any member of the family.

[¹⁶(3A) Paragraph (3) shall not apply in respect of a payment of capital made—

(a) under the Macfarlane Trust, the Macfarlane (Special Payments) Trust, the Macfarlane (Special Payments) (No. 2) Trust, the Fund, the Eileen Trust or the Independent Living Funds;

(b) pursuant to section 2 of the Employment and Training Act 1973 in respect of a person's participation—
   (i) in an employment programme specified in regulation 75(1)(a)(ii) of the Jobseeker's Allowance Regulations 1996;
   (ii) in a training scheme specified in regulation 75(1)(b)(ii) of those Regulations; or
   (iii) in a qualifying course within the meaning specified in regulation 17A(7) of those Regulations.]

(4) Where a claimant stands in relation to a company in a position analogous to that of a sole owner or partner in the business of that company, he shall be treated as if he were such sole owner or partner and in such a case—

(a) the value of his holding in that company shall, notwithstanding regulation 29 (calculation of capital) be disregarded; and

(b) he shall, subject to paragraph (5), be treated as possessing an amount of capital equal to the value or, as the case may be, his share of the value of the capital of that company and the foregoing provisions of this Chapter shall apply for the purposes of calculating that amount as if it were actual capital which he does possess.

(5) For so long as the claimant undertakes activities in the course of the business of the company, the amount which he is treated as possessing under paragraph (4) shall be disregarded.

(6) Where a claimant is treated as possessing capital under any of paragraphs (1) to (4) the foregoing provisions of this Chapter shall apply for the purposes of calculating its amount as if it were actual capital which he does possess.

[¹(7) For the avoidance of doubt a claimant is to be treated as possessing capital under paragraph (1) only if the capital of which he has deprived himself is actual capital.]

AMENDMENTS

1. Family Credit (General) Amendment Regulations 1988 (S.I. 1988 No. 660), reg. 9 (April 11, 1988).

2. Family Credit and Income Support (General) Amendment Regulations 1988 (S.I. 1988 No. 999), reg. 3 (June 9, 1988).

3. Family Credit (General) Amendment No. 3 Regulations 1988 (S.I. 1988 No. 1438), reg. 5 (September 12, 1988).

4. Family Credit (General) Amendment No. 4 Regulations 1988 (S.I. 1988 No. 1970), reg. 10 (December 5, 1988).

5. Income-related Benefits Schemes Amendment Regulations 1990 (S.I. 1990 No. 127), reg. 2 (January 31, 1990).

6. Family Credit (General) Amendment No. 2 Regulations 1990 (S.I. 1990 No. 1774), reg. 3 (October 2, 1990).

7. Income-related Benefits Schemes and Social Security (Recoupment) Amendment Regulations 1991 (S.I. 1991 No. 1175), reg. 3 (May 11, 1991).

8. Family Credit (General) Amendment Regulations 1991 (S.I. 1991 No. 1520), reg. 5 (October 8, 1991).

9. Income-related Benefits Schemes and Social Security (Recoupment) Amendment Regulations 1992 (S.I. 1992 No. 1101), reg. 6 (May 7, 1992).

10. Income-related Benefits Schemes (Miscellaneous Amendments) Regulations 1993 (S.I. 1993 No. 315), Sched., para. 8 (April 1, 1993).

11. Social Security Benefits (Miscellaneous Amendments) (No. 2) Regulations 1993 (S.I. 1993 No. 963), reg. 3(3) (April 22, 1993).

12. Income-related Benefits Schemes and Social Security (Recoupment) Amendment Regulations 1993 (S.I. 1993 No. 1249), reg. 2(3) (May 14, 1993).

13. Income-related Benefits Schemes and Social Security (Claims and Payments) (Miscellaneous Amendments) Regulations 1995 (S.I. 1995 No. 2303), reg. 4(5) (October 3, 1995).

14. Income-related Benefits and Jobseeker's Allowance (Amendment) (No. 2) Regulations 1997 (S.I. 1997 No. 2197), reg. 3 (October 7, 1997).

15. Social Security Amendment (New Deal) Regulations 1997 (S.I. 1997 No. 2863), reg. 17(5) and (6)(c) (January 5, 1998).

16. Social Security Amendment (New Deal) (No. 2) Regulations 1998 (S.I. 1998 No. 2117), reg. 3(2) and (3)(b) (September 24, 1998).

DEFINITIONS

"claimant"—see reg. 2(1), reg. 10(1).
"family"—see 1986 Act, s.20(11) (SSCBA, s.137(1)).
"personal pension scheme"—see reg. 2(1).
"retirement annuity contract"—*ibid.*
"the Eileen Trust"—*ibid.*
"the Fund"—*ibid.*
"the Independent Living Funds"—*ibid.*
"the Macfarlane (Special Payments) Trust"—*ibid.*
"the Macfarlane (Special Payments) (No. 2) Trust"—*ibid.*
"the Macfarlane Trust"—*ibid.*

GENERAL NOTE

Paragraph (1)
See the notes to reg. 51(1) of the Income Support (General) Regulations. Note, however, that this paragraph only applies where the purpose is to gain entitlement to family credit. The approach of *R(IS) 14/93* suggests that if the purpose is to gain entitlement to, for example income support or family income supplement, the family credit rule cannot apply. The effect of para. (7) is to confirm that para. (1) only operates if the person has deprived himself of actual capital.

Paragraph (2)
See the notes to reg. 51(2) of the Income Support (General) Regulations. There are slight differences in wording.

Paragraphs (3) and (3A)
See the notes to reg. 51(3) and (3A) of the Income Support (General) Regulations and the differences in sub-para. (a).

Paragraphs (4) to (6)
See the notes to reg. 51(4) to (6) of the Income Support (General) Regulations.

[¹Diminishing notional capital rule

34A.—(1) Where a claimant is treated as possessing capital under regulation 34(1) (notional capital), the amount which he is treated as possessing—
   (a) in the case of a benefit week which is subsequent to—
      (i) the relevant week in respect of which the conditions set out in paragraph (2) are satisfied, or
      (ii) a week which follows that relevant week and which satisfies those conditions,

shall be reduced by an amount determined under paragraph (3);
  (b) in the case of a benefit week in respect of which paragraph (1)(a) does not apply but where—
      (i) that week is a week subsequent to the relevant week, and
      (ii) that relevant week is a week in which the condition in paragraph (4) is satisfied,
    shall be reduced by the amount determined under paragraph (4).
  (2) This paragraph applies to a benefit week where the claimant satisfies the conditions that—
  (a) he is entitled to family credit; and
  (b) but for regulation 34(1), he would have been entitled to an additional amount of family credit in that benefit week.
  (3) In a case to which paragraph (2) applies, the amount of the reduction for the purposes of paragraph (1)(a) shall be equal to the aggregate of—
  (a) the additional amount of family credit to which the claimant would have been entitled; and
[²(b) if the claimant would, but for regulation 43(1) of the Housing Benefit (General) Regulations 1987 (notional capital), have been entitled to housing benefit or to an additional amount of housing benefit in respect of the benefit week in which the date of the last claim for family credit falls, the amount (if any) which is equal to—
      (i) in a case where no housing benefit is payable, the amount to which he would have been entitled, or
      (ii) in any other case, the amount equal to the additional amount of housing benefit to which he would have been entitled; and
  (c) if the claimant would, but for regulation 33(1) of the Community Charge Benefits (General) Regulations 1989 (notional capital) have been entitled to community charge benefit or to an additional amount of community charge benefit in respect of the benefit week in which the date of the last claim for family credit falls, the amount (if any) which is equal to—
      (i) in a case where no community charge benefit is payable, the amount to which he would have been entitled, or
      (ii) in any other case, the amount equal to the additional amount of community charge benefit to which he would have been entitled[³; and
  (d) if the claimant would, but for regulation 34(1) of the Council Tax Benefit (General) Regulations 1992 (notional capital), have been entitled to council tax benefit or to an additional amount of council tax benefit in respect of the benefit week in which the date of the last claim for family credit falls, the amount (if any) which is equal to—
      (i) in a case where no council tax benefit is payable, the amount to which he would have been entitled, or
      (ii) in any other case, the amount equal to the additional amount of council tax to which he would have been entitled.]]
  (4) Subject to paragraph (5), for the purposes of paragraph (1)(b) the condition is that the claimant would have been entitled to family credit in the relevant week, but for regulation 34(1) and in such a case the amount shall be equal to the aggregate of—
  (a) the amount of family credit to which the claimant would have been entitled in the relevant week but for regulation 34(1);
[²(b) if the claimant would, but for regulation 43(1) of the Housing Benefit (General) Regulations 1987 have been entitled to housing benefit or to an additional amount of housing benefit in respect of the benefit week in which the first day of the relevant week falls, the amount (if any) which is equal to—

      (i) in a case where no housing benefit is payable, the amount to which he would have been entitled, or

      (ii) in any other case, the amount equal to the additional amount of housing benefit to which he would have been entitled; and

  (c) if the claimant would, but for regulation 33(1) of the Community Charge Benefits (General) Regulations 1989 have been entitled to community charge benefit or to an additional amount of community charge benefit in respect of the benefit week in which the first day of the relevant week falls, the amount (if any) which is equal to—

      (i) in a case where no community charge benefit is payable, the amount to which he would have been entitled, or

      (ii) in any other case, the amount equal to the additional amount of community charge benefit to which he would have been entitled[3; and

  (d) if the claimant would, but for regulation 34(1) of the Council Tax Benefit (General) Regulations 1992 (notional capital), have been entitled to council tax benefit or to an additional amount of council tax benefit in respect of the benefit week in which the first day of the relevant week falls, the amount (if any) which is equal to—

      (i) in a case where no council tax benefit is payable, the amount to which he would have been entitled, or

      (ii) in any other case, the amount equal to the additional amount of council tax to which he would have been entitled.]]

(5) The amount determined under paragraph (4) shall be re-determined under that paragraph if the claimant makes a further claim for family credit and the conditions in paragraph (6) are satisfied, and in such a case—

  (a) sub-paragraphs (a), (b) and (c) of paragraph (4) shall apply as if for the words "relevant week" there were substituted the words "relevant subsequent week"; and

  (b) subject to paragraph (7), the amount as re-determined shall have effect from the first week following the relevant subsequent week in question.

(6) The conditions are that—

  (a) a further claim is made 22 or more weeks after—

      (i) the first day of the relevant week;

      (ii) in a case where there has been at least one re-determination in accordance with paragraph (5), the first day of the relevant subsequent week which last occurred;

    whichever last occurred; and

  (b) the claimant would have been entitled to family credit but for regulation 34(1).

(7) The amount as re-determined pursuant to paragraph (5) shall not have effect if it is less than the amount which applied in that case immediately before the re-determination and in such a case the higher amount shall continue to have effect.

(8) For the purpose of this regulation—

  (a) "benefit week" has the meaning prescribed in regulations 16 (date of entitlement under an award) and 27 (family credit) of the Social Security (Claims and Payments) Regulations 1987 except where it appears in paragraphs [3(3)(b), (c) and (d) and (4)(b), (c) and (d)] where it has the meaning prescribed in regulation 2(1) of the Housing Benefit (General) Regulations [31987 (interpretation),] regulation 2(1) of the Community Charge Benefits (General) Regulations 1989 (interpretation) [3or regulation 2(1) of the Council Tax Benefit (General) Regulations 1992 (interpretation)] as the case may be;

  (b) "relevant week" means the benefit week in which the capital in question

of which the claimant has deprived himself within the meaning of regulation 34(1)—
  (i) was for the first time taken into account for the purpose of determining his entitlement to family credit; or
  (ii) was taken into account on a subsequent occasion for that purpose other than in respect of either a benefit week to which paragraph (2) applies or a further claim to which paragraph (5) applies;
  and, where more than one benefit week is identified by reference to heads (i) and (ii) of this sub-paragraph, the later or latest such benefit week;
  (c) ''relevant subsequent week'' means the benefit week in which any award of family credit in respect of the further claim referred to in paragraph (6)(a) would, but for regulation 34(1), have commenced, but it shall not be earlier than the twenty-seventh week after the week in which the existing amount took effect.]

AMENDMENTS

  1. Family Credit (General) Amendment No. 2 Regulations 1990 (S.I. 1990 No. 1774), reg. 3 (October 2, 1990).
  2. Family Credit (General) Amendment Regulations 1991 (S.I. 1991 No. 1520), reg. 6 (October 8, 1991).
  3. Income-related Benefits Schemes (Miscellaneous Amendments) Regulations 1993 (S.I. 1993 No. 315), Sched., para. 9 (April 1, 1993).

DEFINITION

  ''claimant''—see regs. 2(1), 10(1).

GENERAL NOTE

  See reg. 51A of the Income Support (General) Regulations.

Capital jointly held

35. Except where a claimant possesses capital which is disregarded under regulation 34(4) (notional capital), where a claimant and one or more persons are beneficially entitled in possession to any capital asset they shall be treated as if each of them were entitled in possession [¹to the whole beneficial interest therein in an equal share and the foregoing provisions of this Chapter shall apply for the purposes of calculating the amount of capital which the claimant is treated as possessing as if it were actual capital which the claimant does possess.]

AMENDMENT

  1. Social Security Amendment (Capital) Regulations 1998 (S.I. 1998 No. 2250), reg. 2 (October 12, 1998).

DEFINITION

  ''claimant''—see reg. 2(1), reg. 10(1).

GENERAL NOTE

  See the notes to reg. 52 of the Income Support (General) Regulations.

Calculation of tariff income from capital

36.—(1) Where the claimant's capital calculated in accordance with this Chapter exceeds £3,000, it shall be treated as equivalent to a weekly income of £1 for each complete £250 in excess of £3,000 but not exceeding [¹£8,000].

(2) Notwithstanding paragraph (1), where any part of the excess is not a complete £250 that part shall be treated as equivalent to a weekly income of £1.

(3) For the purposes of paragraph (1), capital includes any income treated as capital under regulation 31 (income treated as capital).

AMENDMENT

1. Income-related Benefits (Miscellaneous Amendments) Regulations 1990 (S.I. 1990 No. 671), reg. 3 (April 9, 1990).

DEFINITION

"claimant"—see reg. 2(1), reg. 10(1).

GENERAL NOTE

The treatment of capital between £3,000 and £8,000 is the same as for income support (but note the increase in the income support lower limit for claimants in residential care from April 1996: see reg. 53 of the Income Support Regulations). Each complete £250 between those levels is treated as producing a weekly income of £1. If the capital does not divide exactly into £250 chunks anything left over is treated as producing £1 a week. Thus if the claimant's capital is exactly £8,000 the tariff income is £20 a week. If the claimant's capital is £4,001, the tariff income is £5 a week.

Para. (3) merely confirms the effect of reg. 31. Notional capital must also count although not expressly mentioned.

Note reg. 30 on the capital of children and young persons.

Chapter VII

Students

Interpretation

37. In this Chapter, unless the context otherwise requires—
"a course of advanced education" means—
- (a) a full-time course leading to a postgraduate degree or comparable qualification, a first degree or comparable qualification, a diploma of higher education, a higher national diploma, [⁴a higher national diploma or higher national certificate of either the Business & [⁵Technology] Education Council] or the Scottish Vocational Education Council or a teaching qualification; or
- (b) any other full-time course which is a course of a standard above ordinary national diploma, [⁴a national diploma or national certificate of either the Business & [⁵Technology] Education Council or the Scottish Vocational Education Council], a general certificate of education (advanced level), a Scottish certificate of education [⁴(higher level)] or a Scottish certificate of sixth year studies;

"contribution" means any contribution in respect of the income [⁷ of a student or] of any other person which a Minister of the Crown or an education authority takes into account in assessing the amount of the student's grant and by which that amount is, as a consequence, reduced;

"course of study" means any full-time course of study or sandwich course whether or not a grant is made for attending it;

"covenant income" means the gross income payable to a student under a Deed of Covenant by a person whose income is, or is likely to be, taken into account in assessing the student's grant or award;

"education authority" means a government department, a local education authority as defined in section 114(1) of the Education Act 1944 (interpretation), an education authority as defined in section 135(1) of the Education (Scotland) Act 1980 (interpretation), an education and library board established under Article 3 of the Education and Libraries (Northern Ireland) Order 1986, any body which is a research council for the purposes of the Science and Technology Act 1965 or any analogous government department, authority, board or body, of the Channel Islands, Isle of Man or any other country outside Great Britain;

"grant" means any kind of educational grant or award and includes any scholarship, studentship, exhibition, allowance or bursary [¹but does not include a payment derived from funds made available by the Secretary of State for the purpose of assisting students in financial difficulties under section 100 of the Education Act 1944, sections 131 and 132 of the Education Reform Act 1988 or section 73 of the Education (Scotland) Act 1980];

"grant income" means—

    (a) any income by way of a grant;

    (b) any contribution which has been assessed whether or not it has been paid,

and any such contribution which is paid by way of a covenant shall be treated as part of the student's grant income;

[²"last day of the course" means the date on which the last day of the final academic term falls in respect of the course in which the student is enrolled;]

"period of study" means—

    (a) in the case of a course of study for one year or less, the period beginning with the start of the course to the end,

    (b) in the case of a course of study for more than one year, in the first or, as the case may be, any subsequent year of the course, the period beginning with the start of the course or, as the case may be, that year's start and ending with either—

        (i) the day before the start of the next year of the course in a case where the student's grant is assessed at a rate appropriate to his studying throughout the year, or, if he does not have a grant, where it would have been assessed at such a rate had he had one; or

        (ii) in any other case the day before the start of the normal summer vacation appropriate to his course;

    [²(c) in the final year of a course of study of more than one year, the period beginning with that year's start and ending with the last day of the course;]

"periods of experience" has the meaning prescribed in paragraph 1(1) of Schedule 5 to the Education (Mandatory Awards) Regulations 1987;

"sandwich course" has the meaning prescribed in paragraph 1(1) of Schedule 5 to the Education (Mandatory Awards) Regulations 1987;

"standard maintenance grant" means—

    (a) except where paragraph (b) applies, in the case of a student attending a course of study at the University of London or an establishment within the area comprising the City of London and the Metropolitan Police District, the amount specified for the time being in paragraph 2(2)(a) of Schedule 2 to the Education (Mandatory Awards) Regulations 1987 for such a student; and

    (b) in the case of a student residing at his parents' home, the amount specified in paragraph 3(2) thereof;

    (c) in any other case; the amount specified in paragraph 2(2) other than in sub-paragraph (a) or (b) thereof.

[³''student'' means a person, other than a person in receipt of a training allowance, who is aged less than 19 and attending a full-time course of advanced education or, as the case may be, who is aged 19 or over and attending a full-time course of study] at an educational establishment; and for the purposes of this definition—

    (a) a person who has started on such a course shall be treated as attending it [⁶. . .] until [²the last day of the course] or such earlier date as he abandons it or is dismissed from it;

    (b) a person on a sandwich course shall be treated as attending a full-time course of advanced education or, as the case may be, of study;

''year'' in relation to a course, means the period of 12 months beginning on 1st January, 1st April or 1st September according to whether the academic year of the course in question begins in the spring, the summer or the autumn respectively.

AMENDMENTS

1. Social Security Benefits (Student Loans and Miscellaneous Amendments) Regulations 1990 (S.I. 1990 No. 1549), reg. 2(3) (September 1, 1990).

2. Family Credit (General) Amendment Regulations 1991 (S.I. 1991 No. 1520), reg. 7 (August 6, 1991).

3. Family Credit (General) Amendment Regulations 1992 (S.I. 1992 No. 573), reg. 9 (April 7, 1992).

4. Income-related Benefits Schemes (Miscellaneous Amendments) (No. 3) Regulations 1992 (S.I. 1992 No. 2155), reg. 10 (October 5, 1992).

5. Income-related Benefits Schemes (Miscellaneous Amendments) (No. 4) Regulations 1993 (S.I. 1993 No. 2119), reg. 32 (October 5, 1993).

6. Social Security Benefits (Miscellaneous Amendments) Regulations 1995 (S.I. 1995 No. 1742), reg. 2 (August 1, 1995).

7. Social Security (Miscellaneous Amendments) Regulations 1998 (S.I. 1998 No. 563), reg. 4(1) and (2)(c) (April 7, 1998).

GENERAL NOTE

See the notes to reg. 61 of the Income Support (General) Regulations, but note that the definitions in reg. 37 were not amended in line with the amendments made in October 1996 to various definitions in reg. 61. One of the main effects of those amendments was to provide a cut-off of 16 or more ''guided learning hours'' for full-time courses funded by the FEFC (England and Wales) (note the differences in Scotland), although not for courses which are not so funded.

There are also a few other differences in the definitions. There is a definition of ''course of study'' here, which is in reg. 2(1) of the Income Support Regulations. The definition of ''grant income'' here does not have any special provision for single parents or disabled students. The definition of ''student'' here can extend to a person over pensionable age!

Calculation of grant income

38.—(1) The amount of a student's grant income to be taken into account shall, subject to [²paragraphs (2) and (2A)], be the whole of his grant income.

    (2) There shall be disregarded from a student's grant income any payment—

    (a) intended to meet tuition fees or examination fees;

    (b) [³. . .]

    (c) intended to meet additional expenditure incurred by a disabled student in respect of his attendance on a course;

    (d) intended to meet additional expenditure connected with term time residential study away from the student's educational establishment;

   (e) on account of the student maintaining a home at a place other than that at which he resides during his course;

   (f) intended to meet the cost of books and equipment [³. . .] or, if not so intended, an amount equal to [⁴£295] towards such costs;

   (g) intended to meet travel expenses incurred as a result of his attendance on the course.

[²(2A) Where in pursuance of an award a student is in receipt of a grant in respect of maintenance under regulation 17(b) of the Education (Mandatory Awards) Regulations 1991, there shall be excluded from his grant income a sum equal to the amount specified in paragraph 7(4) of Schedule 2 to those Regulations, being the amount to be disregarded in respect of travel costs in the particular circumstances of his case.]

   (3) A student's grant income[¹, except any amount intended for the maintenance of dependants under [²Part 3 of Schedule 2 to the Education (Mandatory Awards) Regulations 1991] or intended for an older student under Part 4 of that Schedule,] shall be apportioned—

   (a) subject to paragraph (4), in a case where it is attributable to the period of study, equally between the weeks in that period;

   (b) in any other case, equally between the weeks in the period in respect of which it is payable.

   [¹(3A) Any amount intended for the maintenance of dependants or for an older student under the provisions referred to in paragraph (3) shall be apportioned equally over a period of 52 weeks commencing with the week in which the period of study begins.]

   (4) In the case of a student on a sandwich course, any periods of experience within the period of study shall be excluded and the student's grant income shall be apportioned equally between the remaining weeks in that period.

AMENDMENTS

   1. Family Credit (General) Amendment Regulations 1988 (S.I. 1988 No. 660), reg. 10 (April 11, 1988).

   2. Family Credit (General) Amendment Regulations 1992 (S.I. 1992 No. 573), reg. 10 (April 7, 1992).

   3. Income-related Benefits Schemes and Social Fund (Miscellaneous Amendments) Regulations 1996 (S.I. 1996 No. 1944), reg. 4(2) (October 8, 1996).

   4. Social Security (Student Amounts Amendment) Regulations 1998 (S.I. 1998 No. 1379), reg. 2 (September 1, 1998 or, where a student's period of study begins between August 1 and 31, 1998, the first Tuesday of that period).

DEFINITIONS

   "grant income"—see reg. 37.
   "payment"—see reg. 2(1).
   "period of study"—see reg. 37.
   "periods of experience"—*ibid.*
   "sandwich course"—*ibid.*
   "student"—*ibid.*
   "week"—see reg. 2(1).

GENERAL NOTE

   See the notes to reg. 62 of the Income Support (General) Regulations. There is one less disregard in para. (2) here (payments for dependants outside the United Kingdom).

   Para. (2)(e) is more comprehensive than the income support counterpart, having no reference to housing benefit.

Calculation of covenant income where a contribution is assessed

39.—(1) Where a student is in receipt of income by way of a grant during a period of study and a contribution has been assessed, the amount of his covenant income to be taken into account shall be the whole amount of his covenant income less, subject to paragraph (3), the amount of the contribution.

(2) The weekly amount of the student's covenant income shall be determined—
   (a) by dividing the amount of income which fails to be taken into account under paragraph (1) by 52; and
   (b) by disregarding from the resulting amount, £5.

(3) For the purposes of paragraph (1), the contribution shall be treated as increased by the amount, if any, by which the amount excluded under ['regulation 38(2)(g) (calculation of grant income) falls short of the amount specified in paragraph 7(4)(i) of Schedule 2 to the Education (Mandatory Awards) Regulations 1991 (travel expenditure).]

AMENDMENT

1. Family Credit (General) Amendment Regulations 1992 (S.I. 1992 No. 573), reg. 11 (April 7, 1992).

DEFINITIONS

   "contribution"—see reg. 37.
   "covenant income"—*ibid.*
   "grant"—*ibid.*
   "student"—*ibid.*

GENERAL NOTE

See the notes to reg. 63 of the Income Support (General) Regulations. The differences are that this provision makes no reference to the period over which the covenant income is to be taken into account and that the annual amount is simply divided by 52 to reach the weekly figure.

Covenant income where no grant income or no contribution is assessed

40.—(1) Where a student is not in receipt of income by way of a grant the amount of his covenant income shall be calculated as follows—
   (a) any sums intended for any expenditure specified in regulation 38(2)(a) to (e) (calculation of grant income), necessary as a result of his attendance on the course, shall be disregarded;
   (b) any covenant income, up to the amount of the standard maintenance grant, which is not so disregarded, shall be apportioned equally between the weeks of the period of study and there shall be disregarded from the covenant income to be so apportioned the amount which would have been disregarded under ['regulation 38(2)(f) and (g) and (2A)] had the student been in receipt of the standard maintenance grant; and
   (c) the balance, if any, shall be divided by 52 and treated as weekly income of which £5 shall be disregarded.

(2) Where a student is in receipt of income by way of a grant and no contribution has been assessed, the amount of his covenant income shall be calculated in accordance with sub-paragraphs (a) to (c) of paragraph (1), except that—

(a) the value of the standard maintenance grant shall be abated by the amount of his grant income less an amount equal to the amount of any sums disregarded under regulation 38(2)(a) to (e); and

(b) the amount to be disregarded under paragraph (1)(b) shall be abated by an amount equal to the amount of any sums disregarded under ['regulation 38(2)(f) and (g) and (2A)].

AMENDMENT

1. Family Credit (General) Amendment Regulations 1992 (S.I. 1992 No. 573), reg. 12 (April 7, 1992).

DEFINITIONS

"covenant income"—see reg. 37.
"grant"—*ibid.*
"grant income"—*ibid.*
"period of study"—*ibid.*
"standard maintenance grant"—*ibid.*
"student"—*ibid.*
"week"—see reg. 2(1).

GENERAL NOTE

See the notes to reg. 64 of the Income Support (General) Regulations. There is a difference in that the annual amount is simply divided by 52 to reach the weekly figure.

Relationship with amounts to be disregarded under Schedule 2

41. No part of a student's covenant income or grant income shall be disregarded under paragraph 13 of Schedule 2 and any ['other income to which sub-paragraph (1) of that paragraph applies shall be disregarded thereunder only to the extent that] the amount disregarded under regulation 39(2)(b) (calculation of covenant income where a contribution is assessed) or, as the case may be, 40(1)(c) (covenant income where no grant income or no contribution is assessed) is less than [²£20].

AMENDMENTS

1. Family Credit (General) Amendment Regulations 1990 (S.I. 1990 No. 574), reg. 13 (April 10, 1990).
2. Income-related Benefits Schemes (Miscellaneous Amendments) Regulations 1996 (S.I. 1996 No. 462), reg. 8 (April 9, 1996).

DEFINITIONS

"covenant income"—see reg. 37.
"grant income"—*ibid.*
"student"—*ibid.*

GENERAL NOTE

See the notes to reg. 65 of the Income Support (General) Regulations. Para. 13 of Sched. 2 deals with charitable or voluntary payments.

Other amounts to be disregarded

42. For the purposes of ascertaining income ['other than grant income, covenant income and loans treated as income in accordance with regulation 42A], any amounts intended for any expenditure specified in regulation 38(2) (calculation of grant income) necessary as a result of his attendance on the course shall be disregarded but only if, and to the extent that, the necessary expenditure exceeds or is likely to exceed the amount of the sums disregarded under regulation 38(2) [¹and (2A)], 39(3) and 40(1)(a) or (b) (calculation of grant income and covenant income) on like expenditure.

AMENDMENT

1. Income-related Benefits Schemes (Miscellaneous Amendments) Regulations 1994 (S.I. 1994 No. 527), reg. 21 (April 12, 1994).

DEFINITIONS

"covenant income"—see reg. 37.
"grant income"—*ibid.*

GENERAL NOTE

See the notes to reg. 66(1) of the Income Support (General) Regulations.

[¹Treatment of student loans

42A.—(1) A loan which is made to a student pursuant to arrangements made under section 1 of the Education (Student Loans) Act 1990 [²or Article 3 of the Education (Student Loans) (Northern Ireland) Order 1990] shall be treated as income.

(2) In calculating the weekly amount of the loan to be taken into account as income—

  (a) except where sub-paragraph (b) applies, the loan shall be apportioned equally between the weeks in the academic year in respect of which the loan is payable;

  (b) in the case of a loan which is payable in respect of the final academic year of the course or if the course is only of one academic year's duration, in respect of that year the loan shall be apportioned equally between the weeks in the period beginning with the start of the final academic year or, as the case may be, the single academic year and ending with [²the last day of the course],

and from the weekly amount so apportioned there shall be disregarded £10.

[³(3) For the purposes of this regulation a student shall be treated as possessing the maximum amount of any loan referred to in paragraph (1) which he will be able to acquire in respect of an academic year by taking reasonable steps to do so.]]

AMENDMENTS

1. Social Security Benefits (Student Loans and Miscellaneous Amendments) Regulations 1990 (S.I. 1990 No. 1549), reg. 3(5) (September 1, 1990).
2. Family Credit (General) Amendment Regulations 1991 (S.I. 1991 No. 1520), reg. 9 (August 6, 1991).
3. Income-related Benefits Schemes (Miscellaneous Amendments) Regulations 1996 (S.I. 1996 No. 462), reg. 9 (April 9, 1996).

GENERAL NOTE

See the notes to reg. 66A of the Income Support (General) Regulations.

Disregard of contribution

43. Where the claimant or his partner is a student and [¹, for the purposes of assessing a contribution to the student's grant, the other partner's income has been taken into account, an amount equal to that contribution shall be disregarded for the purposes of assessing that other partner's income.]

AMENDMENT

1. Income-related Benefits Schemes (Miscellaneous Amendments) Regulations 1996 (S.I. 1996 No. 462), reg. 10 (April 9, 1996).

DEFINITIONS

"claimant"—see reg. 2(1), reg. 10(1).
"contribution"—see reg. 37.
"grant"—*ibid.*
"partner"—see reg. 2(1).
"student"—see reg. 37.

[¹Further disregard of student's income

43A. Where any part of a student's income has already been taken into account for the purposes of assessing his entitlement to a grant, the amount taken into account shall be disregarded in assessing that student's income.]

AMENDMENT

1. Social Security (Miscellaneous Amendments) Regulations 1998 (S.I. 1998 No. 563), reg. 4(3) and (4)(c) (April 7, 1998).

DEFINITIONS

"grant"—see reg. 37.
"student"—*ibid.*

Disregard of tax refund

44. Any amount by way of a refund of tax deducted from a student's covenant income shall be disregarded in calculating the student's income or capital.

DEFINITIONS

"covenant income"—see reg. 37.
"student"—*ibid.*

GENERAL NOTE

Because "covenant income" covers the gross amount payable under the covenant (reg. 37) it is necessary to disregard any refund to the student of tax deducted by the payer.

Disregard of changes occurring during summer vacation

45. In calculating a student's income there shall be disregarded any change in the standard maintenance grant occurring in the recognised summer vacation appropriate to the student's course, if that vacation does not form part of his period of study, from the date on which the change occurred to the end of that vacation.

DEFINITIONS

"period of study"—see reg. 37.

"standard maintenance grant"—*ibid.*
"student"—*ibid.*

GENERAL NOTE

See the notes to reg. 69 of the Income Support (General) Regulations. The differences in drafting do not seem to affect the substance.

PART V

CONDITIONS OF ENTITLEMENT

Determination of maximum family credit

46.—(1) Subject to [¹paragraphs (2) to (7)] of this regulation, the appropriate maximum family credit shall be the aggregate of the following credits—
  (a) in respect of a claimant or, if he is a member of a married or unmarried couple, in respect of the couple, the credit specified in column (2) of Schedule 4 against paragraph 1 (adult);
[⁴(aa) in respect of a lone parent who works, or a claimant who is a member of a married or unmarried couple either or both of whom work, for not less than 30 hours per week, the credit specified in column (2) of Schedule 4 against paragraph 1A;]
  (b) in respect of any child or young person for whom the claimant or his partner is treated as responsible by virtue of regulation 7 (circumstances in which a person is treated as responsible, or not responsible, for another), the credit specified in column (2) of Schedule 4 [⁵ in respect of the period specified in either paragraph 2 or 3 of column (1) as appropriate to] the child or young person concerned [⁵ and in those paragraphs, "the first Tuesday in September" means the Tuesday which first occurs in the month of September in any year].
  (2) Where a claimant or, as the case may be, the partner of a claimant is married polygamously to two or more members of the same household, the maximum amount shall include, in respect of every such member but the first, an additional credit which [⁵ equals the credit specified in column (2) of Schedule 4 against paragraph 3 in column (1).]
  (3) For the purposes of paragraph (2), a person shall not be treated as a member of the same household as someone to whom he is married polygamously if he would not be so treated in the case of a monogamous marriage.
  (4) Where the capital of a child or young person, if calculated in accordance with Part IV (income and capital) in like manner as for the claimant, [²except as provided in regulation 27(1) (modifications in respect of children and young persons)], would exceed £3,000, the credit in respect of that child or young person shall be nil.
  (5) Where the income of a child or young person, other than income consisting of payments of maintenance whether under a court order or not, calculated in accordance with Part IV, exceeds the amount specified for that child or young person in Schedule 4, the credit in respect of that child or young person shall be nil.
  (6) Where a child or young person is, for the purposes of regulation 8(2)(a) (membership of the same household), a patient or in residential accommodation on account of physical or mental handicap or physical or mental illness and has

been so accommodated for the 52 weeks immediately before the date of claim, the credit in respect of that child or young person shall be nil.

[¹(7) For the purposes of this regulation the amount of any credit and the [⁵period during which that amount is appropriate in respect] of any child or young person shall be determined by reference to the credit specified in Schedule 4 and the [⁵relevant period which includes] the date on which the period under [³section 128(3) of the Contributions and Benefits Act] (period of award) begins.]

AMENDMENTS

1. Family Credit (General) Amendment Regulations 1988 (S.I. 1988 No. 660), reg. 11 (April 11, 1988).
2. Income-related Benefits Schemes (Miscellaneous Amendments) (No. 4) Regulations 1993 (S.I. 1993 No. 2119), reg. 33 (October 5, 1993).
3. Income-related Benefits Schemes (Miscellaneous Amendments) Regulations 1995 (S.I. 1995 No. 516), reg. 14 (April 11, 1995).
4. Income-related Benefits Schemes (Miscellaneous Amendments) (No. 2) Regulations 1995 (S.I. 1995 No. 1339), reg. 7 (July 18, 1995).
5. Income-related Benefits and Jobseeker's Allowance (Personal Allowances for Children and Young Persons) (Amendment) Regulations 1996 (S.I. 1996 No. 2545), reg. 5 (October 7, 1997).

DEFINITIONS

"child"—see 1986 Act, s.20(11) (SSCBA, s.137(1)).
"claimant"—see reg. 2(1).
"lone parent"—*ibid.*
"partner"—*ibid.*
"young person"—*ibid.*, reg. 6.

GENERAL NOTE

The determination of the maximum family credit is the essential starting point in the calculation of benefit. If the family's income is not more than the applicable amount specified in reg. 47, the maximum family credit is payable (Contributions and Benefits Act, s.128(2)(a); 1986 Act, s.21(2)). If the income is above that amount, the maximum family credit is to be reduced at the rate specified in reg. 48 (Contributions and Benefits Act, s.128(2)(b); 1986 Act, s.21(3)).

Paragraph (1)

The maximum family credit is made up of an adult credit (the same for a single person or a couple), plus the appropriate amount for children and young persons for whom an adult is responsible, plus from July 1995 an additional credit under sub-para. (aa) where a lone parent or either or both partners in a couple are working 30 hours or more a week. The amounts are specified in Sched. 4. The credit under sub-para. (aa) was initially £10 (now increased to £11.05 in April 1999). See also reg. 4A on calculating the 30 hours. A corresponding disregard of the equivalent amount of family credit for claimants entitled to the credit under sub-para. (aa) has been introduced into the Housing Benefit and Council Tax Benefit Regulations so that the additional benefit is not clawed back.

See paras. (4)–(7) for details relating to children. The effect of para. (7) is that the amount of the credit is set according to the ages of children and the amounts specified as at the beginning of the award. See reg. 16(1A) and (1B) of the Claims and Payments Regulations.

From October 7, 1997 the credit for a child does not increase until the first Tuesday in September after their 11th or 16th birthday and there is no longer an increase at the age of 18 (see the new paras. 2 and 3 in col. 1 of Sched. 4). There are the same amendments to disability working allowance; similar changes were made to income support and income-based JSA on April 7, 1997 (see the notes to para. 2 of Sched. 2 to the Income Support Regulations). The new age bands only apply if a dependent child or young person becomes 11, 16 or 18 on or after October 7, 1997. See the transitional protection in reg. 10(3) and (4) of the Income-related Benefits and Jobseeker's Allowance (Personal Allowances for Children and Young Persons) (Amendment) Regulations 1996 (p. 968) for those reaching 11, 16 or 18 before that date; note that it is not necessary for family credit to have been in payment on the relevant birthday. See also reg. 13A for the changes that have been made to the period for which a childcare costs disregard can apply.

Paragraph (2)
In the case of polygamous marriages (but not other polygamous relationships) extra members of the family beyond the first two qualify for extra credits.

Paragraph (4)
If the capital belonging to a child or young person exceeds £3,000, no credit is allowed for that person. The capital of a child or young person is not treated as the claimant's (reg. 30), so that it does not count against the usual £8,000 or £3,000 limits. Nor does that person's income count (reg. 27(3)).

Paragraph (5)
If a child's or young person's income (apart from maintenance payments) exceeds the credit for that person, no credit is allowed. That person's income is then not treated as the claimant's for calculating the entitlement of the family in general (reg. 27(2)). Maintenance payments, even if paid directly to the child, are treated as income of the claimant.

Paragraph (6)
This provision is necessary because of the odd definition of the children for whom a credit is allowed in para. (1). In order to qualify for family credit an adult must have at least one child or young person who is a member of the same household (Contributions and Benefits Act, s.128(1)(d); 1986 Act, s.20(5)). But, providing that this qualification is met, para. (1) appears to allow a credit for any child or young person for whom the adult is responsible, even though that person is not a member of the household. The test of responsibility under reg. 7 is whether the child "normally lives" with the adult, referring to who gets child benefit in cases of doubt. Thus, para. (6) specifically excludes children in these circumstances, where, if there is still contact by parents, the child would be normally living with the parent, and part of the household.

Paragraph (7)
See para. (1).

[²Applicable amount of family credit

47.—(1) The applicable amount] for the purposes of section 20(5)(a) of the Act [SSCBA, s.128(1)(a)] (conditions of entitlement to family credit) shall be [³£80.65] per week.

[¹(2) For the purposes of section 20(5A) of the Act [SSCBA, s.128(2)] (date on which applicable amount is to be determined) the prescribed date is the date on which the period under section 20(6) of the Act [SSCBA, s.128(3)] (period of the award) begins.]

AMENDMENTS

1. Family Credit (General) Amendment Regulations 1988 (S.I. 1988 No. 660), reg. 12 (April 11, 1988).
2. Income-related Benefits Schemes (Miscellaneous Amendments) (No. 3) Regulations 1992 (S.I. 1992 No. 2155), reg. 11 (October 5, 1992).
3. Social Security Benefits Up-rating Order 1999 (S.I. 1999 No. 264), art. 16(c) (April 13, 1999).

DEFINITION

"the Act"—see reg. 2(1).

GENERAL NOTE

See the note to reg. 46 for the calculation of benefit (and s.128(2) of the Contributions and Benefits Act; 1986 Act, s.21(2) and (3)). The applicable amount prescribed at the beginning of the period of award controls the calculation.

Entitlement to family credit where income exceeds the applicable amount

48. The prescribed percentage for the purpose of section 21(3) of the Act [SSCBA, s.128(2)(b)] (percentage of excess of income over applicable amount which is deducted from maximum family credit) shall be 70 per cent.

DEFINITION

"the Act"—see reg. 2(1).

GENERAL NOTE

Where the income exceeds the applicable amount the maximum family credit is reduced by 70 per cent. of the excess. The taper of 70 per cent. is higher than that of 50 per cent. for FIS, but since the calculation is based on net earnings, cumulative effective tax rates of more than 100 per cent. will be avoided.

PART VI

CHANGES OF CIRCUMSTANCES

Death of claimant

49.—(1) Except as provided in paragraph (2), an award of family credit shall cease to have effect upon the death of the claimant.

(2) Where a claimant dies and is survived by a partner who was the claimant's partner at the date of claim, an award of family credit made in the claimant's favour shall have effect for its unexpired period as if originally made in favour of the partner.

DEFINITIONS

"claimant"—see reg. 2(1).
"partner"—*ibid.*

GENERAL NOTE

Death of a single claimant terminates an award, but if one partner dies, an award of family credit continues to be paid to the surviving partner.

[¹Young person leaving full-time education

49A.—(1) Subject to paragraph (3), where an award of family credit is payable and the claimant or his partner are responsible, or are treated as being responsible for the purposes of regulation 7 (circumstances in which a person is to be treated as responsible or not responsible for another), for a young person and that young person—

    (a) is, for the purpose of that award, a person of a prescribed description under section 128(1)(d) of the Contributions and Benefits Act; and

    (b) ceases, or has ceased, to receive full-time education,

that cessation shall be a change of circumstances affecting the award, the award shall be reviewed and the award shall cease with effect from the date specified in paragraph (2).

(2) The date specified for the purposes of paragraph (1) shall be—

    (a) 2nd July 1996 where the young person ceased to receive full-time education as from a date before that date; or

(b) the date upon which the young person attains the age of 16 or ceases to receive full-time education, whichever is the later.

(3) Paragraph (1) shall not apply where a young person referred to in that paragraph is a member of the same household as one or more children or, as the case may be, young persons who are receiving full-time education and for whom the claimant or his partner are responsible or are treated as responsible for the purposes of regulation 7.

(4) For the purposes of paragraphs (1) and (2), "young person" includes a young person who attains the age of 19—

(a) during the period between the date of claim and the date from which the claimant is awarded family credit; or

(b) during the period an award of family credit is payable.

(5) In this regulation, "full-time education" means full-time education, either by attendance at a recognised educational establishment as defined in section 147(1) of the Contributions and Benefits Act or otherwise, if such education is recognised by the Secretary of State pursuant to section 142(2) of that Act, but is not a course of advanced education for the purpose of Chapter VII of Part IV (income and capital of students).]

AMENDMENT

1. Family Credit (General) Amendment Regulations 1996 (S.I. 1996 No. 1418), reg. 2 (July 2, 1996).

DEFINITIONS

"claimant"—see reg. 2(1).
"partner"—*ibid.*
"young person"*ibid.*, reg. 6.

GENERAL NOTE

This regulation provides (contrary to the normal rule that a family credit award is not affected by a change of circumstances during the period of the award, SSCBA s.128(3)) that from July 2, 1996 a family credit award will terminate on the date that the last or only young person in the family becomes 16 or leaves full-time non-advanced education (see para. (5)), whichever is the later. For the Social Security Advisory Committee's report on the change see Cm. 3297/1996. The Committee's primary recommendation was that entitlement to family credit should not cease until the child benefit terminal date, or until child benefit was withdrawn due to the young person starting work or training, if earlier. But this was rejected by the government on the basis that for a young person to be treated as a dependant for the purposes of family credit he must be in full-time education (see reg. 6(1)). There is no doubt that this change will cause hardship in some cases. The justification for focusing on this change of circumstances as a reason for the immediate cessation of a family credit award while continuing to disregard other changes that occur during the currency of an award seems only to be one of cost.

Prevention of duplication of awards of family credit and income support

50. Where provision is made for the same child or young person in awards for overlapping periods, the first being an award of family credit and the second an award of [¹family credit, income support [², income-based jobseeker's allowance] or disability working allowance], and at the start of the period of overlap that child or young person is no longer a member of the household of the claimant under the first award, the first award shall terminate with effect from the start of the period of overlap.

AMENDMENTS

1. Disability Living Allowance and Disability Working Allowance (Consequential Provisions) Regulations 1991 (S.I. 1991 No. 2742), reg. 13(4) (April 6, 1992).
2. Social Security and Child Support (Jobseeker's Allowance) (Consequential Amendments) Regulations 1996 (S.I. 1996 No. 1345), reg. 8(4) (October 7, 1996).

DEFINITIONS

"child"—see 1986 Act, s.20(11) (SSCBA, s.137(1)).
"claimant"—see reg. 2(1).
"disability working allowance"—*ibid*.
"young person"—*ibid*., reg. 6.

[¹Overlapping awards

51.—(1) An award of family credit (the new award) which is made in consequence of a claim in respect of a period beginning before the commencement of an existing award of family credit (the existing award) and which overlaps with the period of the existing award, shall be treated as a relevant change of circumstances affecting the existing award and the existing award shall be reviewed and shall terminate with effect from the date on which the decision of the adjudication officer making the new award is notified to the claimant.

(2) An award of disability working allowance which is made in consequence of a claim in respect of a period beginning [² on or] before the commencement of an existing award of family credit (the existing award) and which overlaps with the period of the existing award, shall be treated as a change of circumstances affecting the existing award and the existing award shall be reviewed and shall terminate with effect from the date on which the decision of the adjudication officer awarding disability working allowance is notified to the claimant.]

AMENDMENTS

1. Income-related Benefits Schemes (Miscellaneous Amendments) (No. 5) Regulations 1994 (S.I. 1994 No. 2139), reg. 19 (October 4, 1994).
2. Income-related Benefits Schemes and Social Fund (Miscellaneous Amendments) Regulations 1996 (S.I. 1996 No. 1944), reg. 4(3) (October 8, 1996).

DEFINITIONS

"claimant"—see reg. 2(1).
"disability working allowance"—*ibid*.

GENERAL NOTE

The previous form of reg. 51 applied only where an overlapping award of family credit was made on review or appeal. The new form covers any award of family credit or disability working allowance made for an earlier and overlapping period (*e.g.* where the claimant has made a late claim for the earlier period). It also makes it clear that the original award will end on the date that the claimant is notified of the new award.

[¹Reduced benefit direction

51A.—(1) The following occurrences shall be changes of circumstances which affect an award of family credit and the rate at which it is payable—
    (a) a reduced benefit direction given by a child support officer under section 46(5) of the Child Support Act 1991;

(b) the cessation or cancellation of a reduced benefit direction under Part IX of the maintenance regulations;

(c) the suspension of a reduced benefit direction under regulation 48(1) of the maintenance regulations;

(d) the removal of a suspension imposed under paragraph (1) of regulation 48 of the maintenance regulations in accordance with paragraph (3) of that regulation.

(2) In this regulation—

(a) "child support officer" means a person appointed in accordance with section 13 of the Child Support Act 1991;

(b) "the maintenance regulations" means the Child Support (Maintenance Assessment Procedure) Regulations 1992.]

AMENDMENT

1. Income-related Benefits Schemes (Miscellaneous Amendments) Regulations 1993 (S.I. 1993 No. 315), reg. 14 (April 13, 1993).

GENERAL NOTE

Where a parent with care of a child who claims family credit (as well as income support, income-based JSA or disability working allowance) fails to authorise the Secretary of State to take action against the absent parent under the Child Support Act 1991 (s.6(1)) or to give the information required to trace the absent parent (s.6(9)) the child support officer may make a reduced benefit direction against the parent with care under s.46(5) of the 1991 Act. The amount of the reduction is specified in reg. 36 of the Child Support (Maintenance Assessment Procedure) Regulations 1992; directions given on or after October 7, 1996 are at the rate of 40 per cent of the income support personal allowance for a single claimant aged not less than 25 and will last for three years. The direction can be given effect to at the beginning of a family credit award. Reg. 51A allows the amount of an existing award to be altered when a direction becomes effective or when some change affecting the reduction happens.

[¹PART VII

ENTITLEMENT TO FAMILY CREDIT AND DISABILITY WORKING ALLOWANCE

Prescribed circumstances for entitlement to family credit

52. For the purposes of section 20(5)(bb) of the Act [SSCBA, s.128(1)(c)] (prescribed circumstances) where a claimant or a member of his family is entitled to disability working allowance, he is entitled to family credit, if—

(a) at the date of the claim for family credit the award of disability working allowance for him or a member of his family will expire within 42 days; and

(b) the claimant is or would otherwise be entitled to family credit by virtue of these Regulations; and

(c) the claim for family credit is made in respect of a period which commences immediately after the expiry of the award of disability working allowance.]

AMENDMENT

1. Disability Working Allowance (General) Regulations 1991 (S.I. 1991 No. 2887), reg. 58 (April 7, 1992).

DEFINITIONS

"the Act"—see reg. 2(1).
"claimant"—*ibid.*
"date of claim"—*ibid.*
"disability working allowance"—*ibid.*
"family"—see 1986 Act, s.20(11) (SSCBA, s.137(1)).

GENERAL NOTE

The general rule, under s.128(1) of the Contributions and Benefits Act (1986 Act, s.20(5)), is that the conditions of entitlement to family credit, including not being entitled to disability working allowance, must be satisfied at the date of claim. This provision allows a claim for family credit in advance of the expiry of an award of disability working allowance to succeed from the end of that award.

SCHEDULES

SCHEDULE 1   Regulations 20(2) and 22(2)

SUMS TO BE DISREGARDED IN THE CALCULATION OF EARNINGS

1. Any earnings derived from employment which are payable in a country outside the United Kingdom where there is a prohibition against the transfer to the United Kingdom of those earnings.
2. Any earnings of a child or young person.
3. Where a payment of earnings is made in a currency other than sterling, any banking charge or commission payable in converting that payment to sterling.

DEFINITIONS

"child"—see 1986 Act, s.20(11) (SSCBA, s.137(1)).
"earnings"—see reg. 2(1).
"young person"—*ibid.*, reg. 6.

GENERAL NOTE

The most important of these disregards is that in para. 2. Earnings of children and young persons are disregarded in all circumstances.

SCHEDULE 2   Regulation 24(2)

SUMS TO BE DISREGARDED IN THE CALCULATION OF INCOME OTHER THAN EARNINGS

1. Any amount paid by way of tax on income which is taken into account under regulation 24 (calculation of income other than earnings).
2. Any payment in respect of any expenses incurred by a claimant who is—
(a) engaged by a charitable or [25voluntary organisation]; or
(b) a volunteer,
if he otherwise derives no remuneration or profit from the employment and is not to be treated as possessing any earnings under regulation 26(4) (notional income).
3. Any housing benefit [31, income-based jobseeker's allowance] or income support.

939

4. Any mobility allowance[¹², disability living allowance or disability working allowance.]

5. Any concessionary payment made to compensate for the non-payment of—

(a) any payment specified paragraph 4 or 7;

(b) income support [³¹ or income-based jobseeker's allowance].

6. Any mobility supplement or any payment intended to compensate for the non-payment of such a supplement.

7. Any payment which is—

(a) an attendance allowance under section 35 of the Social Security Act [SSCBA, s.64];

(b) an increase of disablement pension under sections 61 or 63 of that Act [SSCBA, s.104 or 105];

(c) a payment made under regulations made in exercise of the power conferred by section 159(3)(b) of that Act [SSCBA, Sched. 8, para. 7(2)(b)];

(d) an increase of allowance payable in respect of constant attendance under section 5 of the Industrial Injuries and Diseases (Old Cases) Act 1975;

(e) payable by virtue of articles 14, 15, 16, 43 or 44 of the Personal Injuries (Civilians) Scheme 1983 or any analogous payment; or

(f) a payment based on need for attendance which is paid as part of a war disablement pension.

8. Any payment to the claimant as holder of the Victoria Cross or of the George Cross or any analogous payment.

9. Any sum in respect of a course of study attended by a child or young person payable by virtue of regulations made under section 81 of the Education Act 1944 (assistance by means of scholarship or otherwise), or by virtue of section 2(1) of the Education Act 1962 (awards for courses of further education) or section 49 of the Education (Scotland) Act 1980 (power to assist persons to take advantage of educational facilities) [³⁵or section 12(2)(c) of the Further and Higher Education (Scotland) Act 1992 (provision of financial assistance to students)].

10. In the case of a student, any sums intended for any expenditure specified in paragraph (2) of regulation 38 (calculation of grant income) necessary as a result of his attendance on his course.

[¹**11.** In the case of a claimant participating in arrangements for training made under section 2 of the Employment and Training Act 1973 [⁹or section 2 of the Enterprise and New Towns (Scotland) Act 1990] or attending a course at an employment rehabilitation centre established under that section [⁹of the 1973 Act]—

(a) any travelling expenses reimbursed to the claimant; and

(b) any living away from home allowance under section 2(2)(d) [⁹of the 1973 Act or section 2(4)(c) of the 1990 Act];

(c) any training premium,

[³⁶(d) any child care expenses reimbursed to the claimant in respect of his participation in an employment programme specified in regulation 75(1)(a)(ii) of the Jobseeker's Allowance Regulations 1996 or in a training scheme specified in regulation 75(1)(b)(ii) of those Regulations,]

but this paragraph, except in so far as it relates to a payment under sub-paragraph (a), [³⁶(b), (c) or (d)], does not apply to any part of any allowance under section 2(2)(d) [⁹of the 1973 Act or section 2(4)(c) of the 1990 Act].]

[²⁶**12.** Any Jobmatch Allowance payable pursuant to arrangements made under section 2(1) of the Employment and Training Act 1973 where the payments will cease by the date on which the period under section 128(3) of the Contributions and Benefits Act (period of award) is to begin.]

[⁶**13.**—(1) Except where sub-paragraph (2) applies and subject to sub-paragraph (3) and paragraphs 29 and 34, [²⁹£20] of any charitable payment or of any voluntary payment made or due to be made at regular intervals.

(2) Subject to sub-paragraph (3) and paragraph 34, any charitable payment or voluntary payment made or due to be made at regular intervals which is intended and used for an

item other than food, ordinary clothing or footwear, household fuel, community charge, [¹¹or housing costs of any member of the family or is used for any personal community [¹⁸charge,] collective community charge contribution [¹⁸or council tax] for which any member of the family is liable].

[¹³(3) Sub-paragraphs (1) and (2) shall not apply to a payment which is made or due to be made by—

(a) a former partner of the claimant, or a former partner of any member of the claimant's family; or

(b) the parent of a child or young person where that child or young person is a member of the claimant's family.]

(4) For the purposes of sub-paragraph (1) where a number of charitable or voluntary payments fall to be taken into account they shall be treated as though they were one such payment.

(5) For the purposes of sub-paragraph (2) the expression "ordinary clothing or footwear" means clothing or footwear for normal daily use, but does not include school uniforms, or clothing or footwear used solely for sporting activities.]

[²⁷**14.** Subject to paragraph 29, £10 of any of the following, namely—

(a) a war disablement pension (except in so far as such a pension falls to be disregarded under paragraph 6 or 7);

(b) a war widow's pension;

(c) a pension payable to a person as a widow under the Naval, Military and Air Forces Etc. (Disablement and Death) Service Pensions Order 1983 insofar as that Order is made under the Naval and Marine Pay and Pensions Act 1865 [²⁸or the Pensions and Yeomanry Pay Act 1884], or is made only under section 12(1) of the Social Security (Miscellaneous Provisions) Act 1977 and any power of Her Majesty otherwise than under an enactment to make provision about pensions for or in respect of persons who have been disabled or have died in consequence of service as members of the armed forces of the Crown;

(d) a payment made to compensate for the non-payment of such a pension as is mentioned in any of the preceding sub-paragraphs;

(e) a pension paid by the government of a country outside Great Britain which is analogous to any of the pensions mentioned in sub-paragraphs (a) to (c) above;

(f) a pension paid to victims of National Socialist persecution under any special provision made by the law of the Federal Republic of Germany, or any part of it, or of the Republic of Austria.]

15. Any child benefit under Part I of the Child Benefit Act 1975 [SSCBA, Part IX].

16.—(1) Any income derived from capital to which the claimant is, or is treated under regulation 35 (capital jointly held) as, beneficially entitled but, but subject to sub-paragraph (2), not income derived from capital disregarded under paragraph 1, 2, 4, [²13or 26 to 30] of Schedule 3.

(2) Income derived from capital disregarded under paragraph 2[², 4 or 26 to 30] of Schedule 3 but [¹⁹only to the extent of—

(a) any mortgage repayments made in respect of the dwelling or premises in the period during which that income accrued; or

(b) any council tax or water charges which the claimant is liable to pay in respect of the dwelling or premises and which are paid in the period during which that income accrued.]

17. Where a person receives income under an annuity purchased with a loan which satisfies the following conditions—

(a) that the loan was made as part of a scheme under which not less than 90 per cent. of the proceeds of the loan were applied to the purchase by the person to whom it was made of an annuity ending with his life or with the life of the survivor of two or more persons (in this paragraph referred to as "the annuitants") who include the person to whom the loan was made;

(b) that the interest on the loan is payable by the person to whom it was made or by one of the annuitants;

(c) that at the time the loan was made the person to whom it was made or each of the annuitants had attained the age of 65;

(d) that the loan was secured on a dwelling in Great Britain and the person to whom the loan was made or one of the annuitants owns an estate or interest in that dwelling; and

(e) that the person to whom the loan was made or one of the annuitants occupies the dwelling on which it was secured as his home at the time the interest is paid,

the amount, calculated on a weekly basis equal to—

    [²⁴(i) where, or in so far as, section 369 of the Income and Corporation Taxes Act 1988 (mortgage interest payable under deduction of tax) applies to the payments of interest on the loan, the interest which is payable after deduction of a sum equal to income tax on such payments at the applicable percentage of income tax within the meaning of section 369(1A) of that Act;]

    (ii) in any other case the interest which is payable on the loan without deduction of such a sum.

[²⁵**18.** Any payment made to the claimant by a person who normally resides with the claimant, which is a contribution towards that person's living and accommodation costs, except where that person is residing with the claimant in circumstances to which paragraph 19 or 40 or regulation 21(2) (earnings of self-employed earners) refers.]

[²³**19.** Where the claimant occupies a dwelling as his home and the dwelling is also occupied by [²⁵another person], and there is a contractual liability to make payments to the claimant in respect of the occupation of the dwelling by that person or a member of his family—

(a) £4 of the aggregate of any payments made in respect of any one week in respect of the occupation of the dwelling by that person or a member of his family, or by that person and a member of his family; and

(b) a further [³⁰£9.25], where the aggregate of any such payments is inclusive of an amount for heating.]

20. Any income in kind.

21. Any income which is payable in a country outside the United Kingdom where there is a prohibition against the transfer to the United Kingdom of that income.

22.—(1) Any payment made to the claimant in respect of a child or young person who is a member of his family—

[¹⁶(a) in accordance with regulations made pursuant to section 57A of the Adoption Act 1976 (permitted allowances) or with a scheme approved by the Secretary of State under section 51 of the Adoption (Scotland) Act 1978 (schemes for payments of allowances to adopters);

(b) which is a payment made by a local authority in pursuance of section 15(1) of, and paragraph 15 of Schedule 1 to, the Children Act 1989 (local authority contribution to a child's maintenance where the child is living with a person as a result of a residence order),]

[³⁸(c) which is a payment made by an authority, as defined in Article 2 of the Children Order, in pursuance of Article 15 of, and paragraph 17 of Schedule 1 to, that Order (contribution by an authority to child's maintenance);]

to the extent specified in sub-paragraph (2).

(2) In the case of a child or young person—

(a) to whom regulation [³⁴27] applies (capital in excess of £3,000), the whole amount;

(b) to whom that regulation does not apply, so much of the weekly amount of the payment as exceeds the credit in respect of that child or young person under Schedule 4.

[¹⁶**23.** Any payment made by a local authority to the claimant with whom a person is accommodated by virtue of arrangements made under section 23(2)(a) of the Children Act 1989 or, as the case may be, section 21 of the Social Work (Scotland) Act 1968 or by a voluntary organisation under section 59(1)(a) of the 1989 Act or by a care authority under regulation 9 of the Boarding Out and Fostering of Children (Scotland) Regulations

1985 (provision of accommodation and maintenance for children by local authorities and voluntary organisations).]

24. [³⁹Any payment made to the claimant or his partner for a person ("the person concerned"), who is not normally a member of the claimant's household but is temporarily in his care, by—

(a) a health authority;

(b) a local authority;

(c) a voluntary organisation; or

(d) the person concerned pursuant to section 26(3A) of the National Assistance Act 1948.]

[¹⁶**25.** Any payment made by a local authority in accordance with section 17 or 24 of the Children Act 1989 or, as the case may be, section 12, 24 or 26 of the Social Work (Scotland) Act 1968 (provision of services for children and their families and advice and assistance to certain children).]

[⁴⁰**25A.**—(1) Subject to sub-paragraph (2), any payment received under an insurance policy taken out to insure against the risk of being unable to maintain repayments—

(a) on a loan which is secured on the dwelling which the claimant occupies as his home; or

(b) under a regulated agreement as defined for the purposes of the Consumer Credit Act 1974 or under a hire-purchase agreement or a conditional sale agreement as defined for the purposes of Part III of the Hire-Purchase Act 1964.

(2) A payment referred to in sub-paragraph (1) shall only be disregarded to the extent that the payment received under that policy does not exceed the amounts, calculated on a weekly basis, which are used to—

(a) maintain the repayment referred to in sub-paragraph (1)(a) or, as the case may be, (b); and

(b) meet any amount due by way of premiums on—

　　(i) that policy; or

　　(ii) in a case to which sub-paragraph (1)(a) applies, an insurance policy taken out to insure against loss or damage to any building or part of a building which is occupied by the claimant as his home and which is required as a condition of the loan referred to in sub-paragraph (1)(a).]

26. Any payment of income which under regulation 31 (income treated as capital) is to be treated as capital.

[¹⁵**27.** Any maternity allowance under section 22 of the Social Security Act [SSCBA, s.35] or statutory maternity pay under Part V of the Act [SSCBA, Part XII].]

28. Any payment under paragraph 2 of Schedule 6 to the Act [SSCBA, s.148] (pensioners Christmas bonus).

29. The total of a claimant's income or, if he is a member of a family, the family's income and the income of any person which he is treated as possessing under regulation 10(2) (calculation of income and capital of members of claimant's family and of a polygamous marriage) to be disregarded under regulation 39(2)(b) (calculation of covenant income where a contribution assessed)[⁷, regulation 42A(2) (treatment of student loans)] and paragraphs [⁶13(1)] and 14, shall in no case exceed [²⁹£20] per week.

30. Where a payment of income is made in a currency other than sterling, any banking charge or commission payable in converting that payment into sterling.

[¹⁵**31.** Any maternity allowance under section 22 of the Social Security (Northern Ireland) Act 1975 or statutory maternity pay under Part VI of the Social Security (Northern Ireland) Order 1986.]

[¹**32.** Any payment in respect of expenses to which regulation 19(2) (earnings of employed earners) applies.

33. Any resettlement benefit which is paid to the claimant by virtue of regulation 3 to the Social Security (Hospital In-Patients) Amendment (No. 2) Regulations 1987 (transitional provisions)].

[⁹**34.**—(1) Any payment made under the Macfarlane Trust, the Macfarlane (Special

Payments) Trust, the Macfarlane (Special Payments) (No. 2) Trust ("the Trusts"), [16the Fund][21, the Eileen Trust] or [20the Independent Living Funds].

(2) Any payment by or on behalf of a person who is suffering or who suffered from haemophilia [17or who is or was a qualifying person], which derives from a payment made under any of the Trusts to which sub-paragraph (1) refers and which is made to or for the benefit of—

(a) that person's partner or former partner from whom he is not, or where that person has died was not, estranged or divorced;

(b) any child who is a member of that person's family or who was such a member and who is a member of the claimant's family; or

(c) any young person who is a member of that person's family or who was such a member and who is a member of the claimant's family.

(3) Any payment by or on behalf of the partner or former partner of a person who is suffering or who suffered from haemophilia [17or who is or was a qualifying person] provided that the partner or former partner and that person are not, or if either of them has died were not, estranged or divorced, which derives from a payment made under any of the Trusts to which sub-paragraph (1) refers and which is made to or for the benefit of—

(a) the person who is suffering from haemophilia [17or who is a qualifying person];

(b) any child who is a member of that person's family or who was such a member and who is a member of the claimant's family; or

(c) any young person who is a member of that person's family or who was such a member and who is a member of the claimant's family.

(4) Any payment by a person who is suffering from haemophilia [17or who is a qualifying person], which derives from a payment under any of the Trusts to which sub-paragraph (1) refers, where—

(a) that person has no partner or former partner from whom he is not estranged or divorced, nor any child or young person who is or had been a member of that person's family; and

(b) the payment is made either—
   (i) to that person's parent or step-parent, or
   (ii) where that person at the date of the payment is a child, a young person or a student who has not completed his full-time education and has no parent or step-parent, to his guardian,

but only for a period from the date of the payment until the end of two years from that person's death.

(5) Any payment out of the estate of a person who suffered from haemophilia [17or who was a qualifying person], which derives from a payment under any of the Trusts to which sub-paragraph (1) refers, where—

(a) that person at the date of his death (the relevant date) had no partner or former partner from whom he was not estranged or divorced, nor any child or young person who was or had been a member of his family; and

(b) the payment is made either—
   (i) to that person's parent or step-parent, or
   (ii) where that person at the relevant date was a child, a young person or a student who had not completed his full-time education and had no parent or step-parent, to his guardian,

but only for a period of two years from the relevant date.

(6) In the case of a person to whom or for whose benefit a payment referred to in this paragraph is made, any income which derives from any payment of income or capital made under or deriving from any of the Trusts.]

[17(7) For the purposes of sub-paragraphs (2) to (6), any reference to the Trusts shall be construed as including a reference to the Fund [21and the Eileen Trust].]

[235. Any payment made by the Secretary of State to compensate for the loss (in whole or in part) of entitlement to housing benefit.]

[336. Any payment made by the Secretary of State to compensate a person who was

944

entitled to supplementary benefit in respect of a period ending immediately before 11th April 1988 but who did not become entitled to income support in respect of a period beginning with that day.

37. Any payment made by the Secretary of State to compensate for the loss of housing benefit supplement under regulation 19 of the Supplementary Benefit (Requirements) Regulations 1983.

38. Any payment made to a juror or witness in respect of attendance at court other than compensation for loss of earnings or for the loss of a benefit payable under the benefit Acts.

39. [[18...].]

[[23**40.** Where the claimant occupies a dwelling as his home and he provides in that dwelling board and lodging accommodation, an amount, in respect of each person for whom such accommodation is provided for the whole or any part of a week, equal to—

(a) where the aggregate of any payments made in respect of any one week in respect of such accommodation provided to such person does not exceed £20.00, 100 per cent of such payments; or

(b) where the aggregate of any such payments exceeds £20.00, £20.00 and 50 per cent of the excess over £20.00.]

[[5**41.** Any community charge benefit.

42. Any payment in consequence of a reduction of a personal community charge pursuant to regulations under section 13A of the Local Government Finance Act 1988 or section 9A of the Abolition of Domestic Rates Etc (Scotland) Act 1987 (reduction of liability for personal community charge) [[18; or reduction of council tax under section 13 or, as the case may be, section 80 of the Local Government Finance Act 1992 (reduction of liability for council tax).]

43. Any special war widows payment made under—

(a) the Naval and Marine Pay and Pensions (Special War Widows Payment) Order 1990 made under section 3 of the Naval and Marine Pay and Pensions Act 1865;

(b) the Royal Warrant dated 19th February 1990 amending the Schedule to the Army Pensions Warrant 1977;

(c) the Queen's Order dated 26th February 1990 made under section 2 of the Air Force (Constitution) Act 1917;

(d) the Home Guard War Widows Special Payments Regulations 1990 made under section 151 of the Reserve Forces Act 1980;

(e) the Orders dated 19th February 1990 amending Orders made on 12th December 1980 concerning the Ulster Defence Regiment made in each case under section 140 of the Reserve Forces Act 1980;

and any analogous payment by the Secretary of State for Defence to any person who is not a person entitled under the provisions mentioned in sub-paragraphs (a) to (e) of this paragraph.]

[[8**44.**—(1) Any payment or repayment made—

(a) as respects England and Wales, under regulation 3, 5 or 8 of the National Health Service (Travelling Expenses and Remission of Charges) Regulations 1988 (travelling expenses and health service supplies);

(b) as respects Scotland, under regulation 3, 5 or 8 of the National Health Service (Travelling Expenses and Remission of Charges) (Scotland) Regulations 1988 (travelling expenses and health service supplies).

(2) Any payment or repayment made by the Secretary of State for Health, the Secretary of State for Scotland or the Secretary of State for Wales which is analogous to a payment or repayment mentioned in sub-paragraph (1).

45. Any payment made under regulation 9 to 11 or 13 of the Welfare Food Regulations 1988 (payments made in place of milk tokens or the supply of vitamins).

46. Any payment made either by the Secretary of State for the Home Department or by the Secretary of State for Scotland under a scheme established to assist relatives and other persons to visit persons in custody.]

[¹³**47.**—(1) £15 of any payment of maintenance, whether under a court order or not which is made or due to be made by—

(a) the claimant's former partner, or the claimant's partner's former partner; or

(b) the parent of a child or young person where that child or young person is a member of the claimant's family except where that parent is the claimant or the claimant's partner.

(2) For the purposes of sub-paragraph (1), where more than one maintenance payment falls to be taken into account in any week, all such payments shall be aggregated and treated as if they were a single payment.]

[¹⁵**48.** Any payment (other than a training allowance) made, whether by the Secretary of State or any other person, under the Disabled Persons (Employment) Act 1944 or in accordance with arrangements made under section 2 of the Employment and Training Act 1973 to assist disabled persons to obtain or retain employment despite their disability.]

[¹⁹**49.** Any council tax benefit.

50. Any guardian's allowance.]

[²³**51.** Where the claimant is in receipt of any benefit under Parts II, III or V of the Contributions and Benefits Act [²⁶or pension under the Naval, Military and Air Forces Etc. (Disablement and Death) Service Pensions Order 1983], any increase in the rate of that benefit arising under Part IV (increases for dependants) or section 106(a) (unemployability supplement) of that Act [²⁶or the rate of that pension under that Order] where the dependant in respect of whom the increase is paid is not a member of the claimant's family.]

[²⁴**52.** Any supplementary pension under article 29(1A) of the Naval, Military and Air Forces etc. (Disablement and Death) Service Pensions Order 1983 (pensions to widows).

53. In the case of a pension awarded at the supplementary rate under article 27(3) of the Personal Injuries (Civilians) Scheme 1983 (pensions to widows), the sum specified in paragraph (1)(c) of Schedule 4 to that Scheme.

54.—(1) Any payment which is—

(a) made under any of the Dispensing Instruments to a widow of a person—
   (i) whose death was attributable to service in a capacity analogous to service as a member of the armed forces of the Crown; and
   (ii) whose service in such capacity terminated before 31st March 1973; and

(b) equal to the amount specified in article 29(1A) of the Naval, Military and Air Forces etc. (Disablement and Death) Service Pensions Order 1983 (pensions to widows).

(2) In this paragraph "the Dispensing Instruments" means the Order in Council of 19th December 1881, the Royal Warrant of 27th October 1884 and the Order by His Majesty of 14th January 1922 (exceptional grants of pay, non-effective pay and allowances).]

[²⁵**55.** Any payment made by the Secretary of State to compensate for a reduction in a maintenance assessment made under the Child Support Act 1991.]

[³²**56.** Any payment made by the Secretary of State under the Earnings Top-up Scheme.]

[³³**57.** Any payment made under the Community Care (Direct Payments) Act 1996 or under section 12B of the Social Work (Scotland) Act 1968.

58.—(1) Any Career Development Loan paid to the claimant pursuant to section 2 of the Employment and Training Act 1973 except to the extent that the loan has been applied for and paid in respect of living expenses for the period of education and training supported by that loan and those expenses relate to any one or more of the items specified in sub-paragraph (2).

(2) The items specified for the purposes of sub-paragraph (1) are food, ordinary clothing or footwear, household fuel or housing costs of any member of the family or any personal community charge, collective community charge contribution or any council tax for which any member of the family is liable.

(3) For the purposes of this paragraph, "ordinary clothing and footwear" means cloth-

ing or footwear for normal daily use, but does not include school uniforms, or clothing and footwear used solely for sporting activities.]

[[41]**59.** Any mandatory top-up payment made to a person pursuant to section 2 of the Employment and Training Act 1973 in respect of that person's participation in an employment programme specified in—

(a) regulation 75(1)(a)(ii)(aa)(ii) of the Jobseeker's Allowance Regulations 1996 (self-employment route of the Employment Option of the New Deal);

(b) regulation 75(1)(a)(ii)(bb) of those Regulations (Voluntary Sector Option of the New Deal; or

(c) regulation 75(1)(a)(ii)(cc) of those Regulations (Environment Task Force Option of the New Deal).]

[[37]**60.** Any discretionary payment to meet, or to help meet, special needs made to a person pursuant to section 2 of the Employment and Training Act 1973 in respect of that person's participation in the Full-Time Education and Training Option of the New Deal as specified in regulation 75(1)(b)(ii) of the Jobseeker's Allowance Regulations 1996.]

[[42]**61.**—(1) Subject to sub-paragraph (2), in respect of a person who is receiving, or who has received, assistance under an employment programme specified in regulation 75(1)(a)(ii)(aa)(ii) of the Jobseeker's Allowance Regulations 1996 (self employment route of the Employment Option of the New Deal), any payment to that person—

(a) to meet expenses wholly and necessarily incurred whilst carrying on the commercial activity;

(b) which is used or intended to be used to maintain repayments on a loan taken out by that person for the purpose of establishing or carrying on the commercial activity,

in respect of which such assistance is or was received.

(2) Sub-paragraph (1) shall apply only in respect of payments which are paid to that person from the special account as defined for the purposes of Chapter IVA of Part VIII of the Jobseeker's Allowance Regulations 1996.]

[[43]**62.**—(1) Subject to sub-paragraph (2), any discretionary payment made pursuant to section 2 of the Employment and Training Act 1973 to meet, or help meet, special needs of a person who is undertaking a qualifying course within the meaning specified in regulation 17A(7) of the Jobseeker's Allowance Regulations 1996.

(2) No amount shall be disregarded pursuant to sub-paragraph (1) in respect of travel expenses incurred as a result of the student's attendance on the course where an amount in respect of those expenses has already been disregarded pursuant to regulation 42 (student's income to be disregarded).]

AMENDMENTS

1. Family Credit (General) Amendment Regulations 1988 (S.I. 1988 No. 660), reg. 13 (April 11, 1988).

2. Family Credit (General) Amendment No. 3 Regulations 1988 (S.I. 1988 No. 1438), reg. 8 (September 12, 1988).

3. Family Credit (General) Amendment No. 4 Regulations 1988 (S.I. 1988 No. 1970), reg. 11 (December 5, 1988).

4. Family Credit and Income Support (General) Amendment Regulations 1989 (S.I. 1989 No. 1034), reg. 3 (July 10, 1989).

5. Family Credit (General) Amendment Regulations 1990 (S.I. 1990 No. 574), reg. 14(f) (April 3, 1990).

6. Family Credit (General) Amendment Regulations 1990 (S.I. 1990 No. 574), reg. 14(a) to (e) (April 10, 1990).

7. Income-related Benefits Amendment Regulations 1990 (S.I. 1990 No. 1657), reg. 3(2) (September 1, 1990).

8. Family Credit (General) Amendment No. 2 Regulations 1990 (S.I. 1990 No. 1774), reg. 4 (October 2, 1990).

9. Enterprise (Scotland) Consequential Amendments Order 1991 (S.I. 1991 No. 387), arts. 2 and 12 (April, 1991).

10. Income-related Benefits Schemes and Social Security (Recoupment) Amendment Regulations 1991 (S.I. 1991 No. 1175), reg. 3 (May 11, 1991).

11. Family Credit (General) Amendment Regulations 1991 (S.I. 1991 No. 1520), reg. 10 (October 8, 1991).

12. Disability Living Allowance and Disability Working Allowance (Consequential Provisions) Regulations 1991 (S.I. 1991 No. 2742), reg. 13(5) (April 6, 1992).

13. Income-related Benefits Schemes (Miscellaneous Provisions) Amendment Regulations 1991 (S.I. 1991 No. 2695), reg. 3 (April 7, 1992).

14. Social Security Benefits Up-rating (No. 2) Order 1991 (S.I. 1991 No. 2910), art. 12 (April 7, 1992).

15. Family Credit (General) Amendment Regulations 1992 (S.I. 1992 No. 573), reg. 13 (April 7, 1992).

16. Family Credit (General) Amendment Regulations 1992 (S.I. 1992 No. 573), Sched., para. 3 (April 7, 1992).

17. Income-related Benefits Schemes and Social Security (Recoupment) Amendment Regulations 1992 (S.I. 1992 No. 1101), reg. 4(6) (May 7, 1992).

18. Income-related Benefits Schemes (Miscellaneous Amendments) Regulations 1993 (S.I. 1993 No. 315), Sched., para. 10 (April 1, 1993).

19. Income-related Benefits Schemes (Miscellaneous Amendments) Regulations 1993 (S.I. 1993 No. 315), reg. 15 (April 13, 1993).

20. Social Security Benefits (Miscellaneous Amendments) (No. 2) Regulations 1993 (S.I. 1993 No. 963), reg. 3(3) (April 22, 1993).

21. Income-related Benefits Schemes and Social Security (Recoupment) Amendment Regulations 1993 (S.I. 1993 No. 1249), reg. 2(4) (May 14, 1993).

22. Income-related Benefits Schemes (Miscellaneous Amendments) (No. 4) Regulations 1993 (S.I. 1993 No. 2119), reg. 34 (October 5, 1993).

23. Income-related Benefits Schemes (Miscellaneous Amendments) Regulations 1994 (S.I. 1994 No. 527), reg. 22 (April 12, 1994).

24. Income-related Benefits Schemes (Miscellaneous Amendments) (No. 5) Regulations 1994 (S.I. 1994 No. 2139), reg. 20 (October 4, 1994).

25. Income-related Benefits Schemes (Miscellaneous Amendments) Regulations 1995 (S.I. 1995 No. 516), reg. 15 (April 11, 1995).

26. Income-related Benefits Schemes and Social Security (Claims and Payments) (Miscellaneous Amendments) Regulations 1995 (S.I. 1995 No. 2303), reg. 4(7) (October 3, 1995).

27. Income-related Benefits Schemes Amendment (No. 2) Regulations 1995 (S.I. 1995 No. 2792), reg. 4 (October 28, 1995).

28. Income-related Benefits Schemes (Widows' etc. Pensions Disregards) Amendment Regulations 1995 (S.I. 1995 No. 3282), reg. 2 (December 20, 1995).

29. Income-related Benefits Schemes (Miscellaneous Amendments) Regulations 1996 (S.I. 1996 No. 462), reg. 8 (April 9, 1996).

30. Social Security Benefits Up-rating Order 1996 (S.I. 1996 No. 599), art. 16(e) (April 9, 1996).

31. Social Security and Child Support (Jobseeker's Allowance) (Consequential Amendments) Regulations 1996 (S.I. 1996 No. 1345), reg. 8(5) (October 7, 1996).

32. Income-related Benefits Schemes and Social Fund (Miscellaneous Amendments) Regulations 1996 (S.I. 1996 No. 1944), reg. 13 and Sched., para. 5 (October 7, 1996).

33. Income-related Benefits and Jobseeker's Allowance (Miscellaneous Amendments) Regulations 1997 (S.I. 1997 No. 65), reg. 2(5) and (6) (April 8, 1997).

34. Income-related Benefits and Jobseeker's Allowance (Miscellaneous Amendments) Regulations 1997 (S.I. 1997 No. 65), reg. 2(7) (April 8, 1997).

35. Income-related Benefits and Jobseeker's Allowance (Amendment) (No. 2) Regulations 1997 (S.I. 1997 No. 2197), reg. 7(7) and (8)(c) (October 7, 1997),

36. Social Security Amendment (New Deal) Regulations 1997 (S.I. 1997 No. 2863), reg. 17(7) and (8)(c) (January 5, 1998).

37. Social Security Amendment (New Deal) Regulations 1997 (S.I. 1997 No. 2863), reg. 17(9) and (10)(c) (January 5, 1998).

38. Social Security (Miscellaneous Amendments) Regulations 1998 (S.I. 1998 No. 563), reg. 7(1) and (2)(c) (April 7, 1998).

39. Social Security (Miscellaneous Amendments) Regulations 1998 (S.I. 1998 No. 563), reg. 7(3) and (4)(c) (April 7, 1998).

40. Social Security (Miscellaneous Amendments) (No. 3) Regulations 1998 (S.I. 1998 No. 1173), reg. 3 (June 2, 1998).

41. Social Security (Miscellaneous Amendments) (No. 4) Regulations 1998 (S.I. 1998 No. 1174), reg. 7(3) and (4)(c) (June 1, 1998).

42. Social Security (Miscellaneous Amendments) (No. 4) Regulations 1998 (S.I. 1998 No. 1174), reg. 7(5) and (6)(c) (June 1, 1998).

43. Social Security Amendment (New Deal) (No. 2) Regulations 1998 (S.I. 1998 No. 2117), reg. 4(3) (September 24, 1998).

DEFINITIONS

    "the Act"—see reg. 2(1).
    "the benefit Acts"—*ibid.*
    "child"—see 1986 Act, s.20(11) (SSCBA, s.137(1)).
    "the Children Order"—see reg. 2(1).
    "claimant"—*ibid.*
    "disability living allowance"—*ibid.*
    "disability working allowance"—*ibid.*
    "dwelling"—see 1986 Act, s.84(1) (SSCBA, s.137(1)).
    "the Earnings Top-up Scheme"—see reg. 2(1).
    "family"—see 1986 Act, s.20(11) (SSCBA, s.137(1)).
    "local authority"—see 1986 Act, s.84(1).
    "mobility allowance"—see reg. 2(1).
    "mobility supplement"—*ibid.*
    "payment"—*ibid.*
    "student"—*ibid.* reg. 37.
    "the Eileen Trust"—see reg. 2(1).
    "the Fund"—*ibid.*
    "the Independent Living Funds"—*ibid.*
    "the Macfarlane (Special Payments) Trust"—*ibid.*
    "the Macfarlane (Special Payments) (No. 2) Trust"—*ibid.*
    "the Macfarlane Trust"—*ibid.*
    "voluntary organisation"—*ibid.*
    "year of assessment"—see reg. 2(1).
    "young person"—*ibid.*, reg. 6.

GENERAL NOTE

Many of these disregarded categories of income coincide with those listed in Sched. 9 to the Income Support (General) Regulations (Sched. 9 (IS)), apart from necessary differences in cross-references.

Paragraphs 1 and 2
See paras. 1 and 2 of Sched. 9 (IS).

Paragraph 3
Any payments of income support, income-based JSA or housing benefit are ignored.

Paragraphs 4–6
See paras. 6–8 of Sched. 9 (IS).

Paragraph 7
Attendance allowance and analogous payments are disregarded.

Paragraphs 8–11
See paras. 10–13 of Sched. 9 (IS).

Paragraph 13
The substance is the same as para. 15 of Sched. 9 (IS). Para. 29 limits the total disregard under paras. 13(1) and 14 and reg. 39(2)(b). Para. 34 covers payments from certain trusts.

Paragraph 14
See para. 16 of Sched. 9 (IS). The £10 disregard under sub-para. (a) only applies if the payment is not fully disregarded under paras. 6 or 7.

Paragraph 15

Child benefit (including one parent benefit) is disregarded in the calculation of family credit. This is an important difference from income support.

Paragraph 16

The general rule is that income from capital is disregarded as income. It can then add to the total of capital under reg. 31(4). The exceptions cover the income from certain categories of disregarded capital, mainly premises whose value is ignored. Under sub-para. (2) income from premises whose capital value is disregarded is itself disregarded in so far as it is put towards mortgage repayments, council tax or water charges for those premises. See the notes to para. 22 of Sched. 9(IS).

Note that paras. 46 and 47 of Sched. 3 (funds held in court that derive from damages for personal injury) have not been added to the exceptions in sub-para. (1), although this list does include trusts of personal injury compensation (disregarded under para. 13 of Sched. 3). See further the notes to reg. 48(4) of the Income Support Regulations.

Paragraphs 17–19

See paras. 17–19 of Sched. 9 (IS).

Paragraph 20

All forms of income in kind are disregarded. The general rule is the same for earnings from employment (reg. 19(2)(a)) but these are then treated as income under reg. 24(5) before being disregarded under this provision.

Paragraph 21

See para. 23 of Sched. 9 (IS).

Paragraphs 22–25

See paras. 25–28 of Sched. 9 (IS). Note that there is no special rule for trade disputes in para. 25 as there is in the equivalent income support provision.

Paragraph 25A

On the disregard in sub-para. (1)(b), see the note to para. 30ZA of Sched. 9 (IS). Sub-para. (1)(a) applies to payments received under a policy taken out to insure against failure to make payments on a loan secured on the claimant's home. There is no requirement that the loan was in connection with the purchase of the home. (For the equivalent income support/income-based JSA provisions, see paras 29 and 30 of Sched. 9 (IS) and paras 30 and 31 of Sched. 7(JSA)). Note that the disregard in sub-para. (1)(a) only covers the amount of the repayments due, plus any premium on the policy and on any policy against loss or damage to the claimant's home that was a condition of the loan. Any excess counts as income (sub-para. (2)).

Paragraph 26

This provision confirms that income treated as capital under reg. 31 cannot also count as income.

Paragraph 27

Statutory maternity pay and the maternity allowance is disregarded as income other than earnings. Statutory sick pay is no longer (from April 1992) disregarded under this provision, and is treated as earnings from employment under reg. 19(1)(g). Statutory maternity pay is now (April 1993) expressly deemed not to be earnings (reg. 19(2)(d)).

Paragraph 28

See para. 33 of Sched. 9 (IS).

Paragraph 29

This provision limits the total disregard under paras. 13(1) and 14 and regs. 39(2)(b) and 42A(2) to £20 per week.

Paragraph 30

See para. 24 of Sched. 9 (IS).

Paragraph 31
This applies the same rule as in para. 27 to payments under the Northern Ireland legislation.

Paragraph 32
A payment of necessary expenses by an employer to an employee is disregarded as income. It is excluded from earnings by reg. 19(2).

Paragraphs 33 and 34
See paras. 38 and 39 of Sched. 9 (IS).

Paragraphs 35–38
See paras. 40–43 of Sched. 9 (IS).

Paragraph 40
See para. 20 of Sched. 9 (IS).

Paragraphs 41–46
See paras. 45–50 of Sched. 9 (IS).

Paragraph 47
The important disregard of the first £15 of any maintenance payments was a forerunner of the more radical reforms to the system of child support brought into operation in April 1993. "Maintenance" is not defined, but the payment must come from one of the people identified in sub-paras. (a) and (b). It will include payments due under an assessment of child support maintenance.

Maintenance payments count as income other than earnings, to be calculated under reg. 16(2) or (2A).

Paragraphs 48 and 49
See paras. 51 and 52 of Sched. 9 (IS). Any payment of council tax benefit is disregarded.

Paragraph 50
Payments of guardian's allowance are disregarded.

Paragraph 51
See para. 53 of Sched. 9 (IS).

Paragraphs 52–54
See para. 43 and the notes to paras. 54 to 56 of Sched. 9 (IS).

Paragraphs 57–58
See the notes to paras. 58 and 59 of Sched. 9 (IS).

Paragraphs 59–61
See the notes to paras 62 to 64 of Sched. 9 (IS).

Paragraph 62
See the note to para. 63 of Sched. 7 (JSA).

SCHEDULE 3   **Regulation 29(2)**

CAPITAL TO BE DISREGARDED

1. The dwelling, together with any garage, garden and outbuildings, normally occupied by the claimant as his home including any premises not so occupied which it is impracticable or unreasonable to sell separately, in particular, in Scotland, any croft land on which

951

the dwelling is situated; but, notwithstanding regulation 10 (calculation of income and capital of members of claimant's family and of a polygamous marriage), only one dwelling shall be disregarded under this paragraph.

2. Any premises acquired for occupation by the claimant which he intends to occupy [³as his home] within 26 weeks of the date of acquisition or such longer period as is reasonable in the circumstances to enable the claimant to obtain possession and commence occupation of the premises.

3. Any sum directly attributable to the proceeds of sale of any premises formerly occupied by the claimant as his home which is to be used for the purchase of other premises intended for such occupation within 26 weeks of the date of sale or such longer period as is reasonable in the circumstances to enable the claimant to complete the purchase.

4. Any premises occupied in whole or in part by a partner or relative (that is to say any close relative, grandparent, grandchild, uncle, aunt, nephew or niece) of any member of the family, [³as his home] where that person is aged 60 or over or has been incapacitated for a continuous period of at least 13 weeks immediately preceding the date of the claim.

[²⁴**5.** Any future interest in property of any kind, other than land or premises in respect of which the claimant has granted a subsisting lease or tenancy, including sub-leases or sub-tenancies.]

6.—[¹⁰(1)] The assets of any business owned in whole or in part by the claimant and for the purposes of which he is engaged as a self-employed earner or, if he has ceased to be so engaged, for such period as may be reasonable in the circumstances to allow for disposal of any such asset.

[¹⁰(2) The assets of any business owned in whole or in part by the claimant where—

(a) he has ceased to be engaged as a self-employed earner in that business by reason of some disease or bodily or mental disablement; and

(b) he intends to become re-engaged as a self-employed earner in that business as soon as he recovers or is able to be re-engaged in that business;

for a period of 26 weeks from the date on which the claimant last ceased to be engaged in that business, or, if it is unreasonable to expect him to become re-engaged in that business within that period, for such longer period as is reasonable in the circumstances to enable him to become so re-engaged.]

[³²(3) In the case of a person who is receiving assistance under an employment programme specified in regulation 75(1)(a)(ii)(aa)(ii) of the Jobseeker's Allowance Regulations 1996 (self-employment route of the Employment Option of the New Deal), the assets acquired by that person for the purpose of establishing or carrying on the commercial activity in respect of which such assistance is being received.

(4) In the case of a person who has ceased carrying on the commerical activity in respect of which assistance was received as specified in sub-paragraph (3), the assets relating to that activity for such period as may be reasonable in the circumstances to allow for disposal of any such asset.]

7. Any sum attributable to the proceeds of sale of any asset of such a business which is re-invested or to be re-invested in the business within 13 weeks of the date of sale or such longer period as may be reasonable to allow for the re-investment.

8. Any arrears of, or any concessionary payment made to compensate for arrears due to non-payment of—

(a) any payment specified in paragraphs 4, 6, or 7 of Schedule 2;

(b) an income-related benefit [²⁶or income-based jobseeker's allowance,] or supplementary benefit under the Supplementary Benefits Act 1976, family income supplement under the Family Income Supplements Act 1970 or housing benefit under Part II of the Social Security and Housing Benefits Act 1982,

[²⁷(c) any earnings top-up,]

but only for a period of 52 weeks from the date of the receipt of the arrears or of the concessionary payment.

9. Any sum—

(a) paid to the claimant in consequence of damage to, or loss of, the home or any personal possession and intended for its repair or replacement; or

(b) acquired by the claimant (whether as a loan or otherwise) on the express condition that it is to be used for effecting essential repairs or improvements to the home,

which is to be used for the intended purpose, for a period of 26 weeks from the date on which it was so paid or acquired or such longer period as is reasonable in the circumstances to enable the claimant to effect the repairs, replacement or improvements.

10. Any sum—

(a) deposited with a housing association as defined in section 1(1) of the Housing Associations Act 1985 or section 338(1) of the Housing (Scotland) Act 1987 as a condition of occupying the home;

(b) which was so deposited and which is to be used for the purchase of another home, for the period of 26 weeks or such longer period as may be reasonable in the circumstances to complete the purchase.

11. Any personal possessions except those which have been acquired by the claimant with the intention of reducing his capital in order to secure entitlement to family credit or to increase the amount of that benefit.

12. The value of the right to receive any income under an annuity or the surrender value (if any) of such an annuity.

[¹⁰**13.** Where the funds of a trust are derived from a payment made in consequence of any personal injury to the claimant, the value of the trust fund and the value of the right to receive any payment under that trust.]

14. The value of the right to receive any income under a life interest or from a liferent.

15. The value of the right to receive any income which is disregarded under paragraph 1 of Schedule 1 or 21 of Schedule 2.

16. The surrender value of any policy of life insurance.

17. Where any payment of capital falls to be made by instalments, the value of the right to receive any outstanding instalments.

[¹⁵**18.** Any payment made by a local authority in accordance with section 17 or 24 of the Children Act 1989 or, as the case may be, section 12, 24 or 26 of the Social Work (Scotland) Act 1968 (provision of services for children and their families and advice and assistance to certain children).]

[¹⁴**19.** Any social fund payment made pursuant to Part III of the Act [SSCBA, Part VIII].]

20. Any refund of tax which falls to be deducted under section 26 of the Finance Act 1982 (deductions of tax from certain loan interest) on a payment of relevant loan interest for the purpose of acquiring an interest in the home or carrying out repairs or improvements to the home.

[²¹**21.**—Any capital which by virtue of regulations 25 (capital treated as income), 27(1) (modifications in respect of children and young persons) or 42A (treatment of student loans) is to be treated as income.]

22. Where a payment of capital is made in a currency other than sterling, any banking charge or commission payable in converting that payment to sterling.

[¹²**23.**—(1) Any payment made under the Macfarlane Trust, the Macfarlane (Special Payments) Trust, the Macfarlane (Special Payments) (No. 2) Trust ("the Trusts"), [¹⁶the Fund] [²⁰, the Eileen Trust] or [¹⁸the Independent Living Funds].

(2) Any payment by or on behalf of a person who is suffering or who suffered from haemophilia [⁶or who is or was a qualifying person], which derives from a payment made under any of the Trusts to which sub-paragraph (1) refers and which is made to or for the benefit of—

(a) that person's partner or former partner from whom he is not, or where that person has died was not, estranged or divorced;

(b) any child who is a member of that person's family or who was such a member and who is a member of the claimant's family; or

(c) any young person who is a member of that person's family or who was such a member and who is a member of the claimant's family.

(3) Any payment by or on behalf of the partner or former partner of a person who is suffering or who suffered from haemophilia [¹⁶or who is or was a qualifying person] provided that the partner or former partner and that person are not, or if either of them has died were not, estranged or divorced, which derives from a payment made under any of the Trusts to which sub-paragraph (1) refers and which is made to or for the benefit of—

(a) the person who is suffering from haemophilia [¹⁶or who is a qualifying person];

(b) any child who is a member of that person's family or who was such a member and who is a member of the claimant's family; or

(c) any young person who is a member of that person's family or who was such a member and who is a member of the claimant's family.

(4) Any payment by a person who is suffering from haemophilia [¹⁶or who is a qualifying person], which derives from a payment under any of the Trusts to which sub-paragraph (1) refers, where—

(a) that person has no partner or former partner from whom he is not estranged or divorced, nor any child or young person who is or had been a member of that person's family; and

(b) the payment is made either—

    (i) to that person's parent or step-parent, or

    (ii) where that person at the date of the payment is a child, a young person or a student who has not completed his full-time education and has no parent or step-parent, to his guardian,

but only for a period from the date of the payment until of end of two years from that person's death.

(5) Any payment out of the estate of a person who suffered from haemophilia [¹⁶or who was a qualifying person], which derives from a payment under any of the Trusts to which sub-paragraph (1) refers, where—

(a) that person at the date of his death (the relevant date) had no partner or former partner from whom he was not estranged or divorced, nor any child or young person who was or had been a member of his family; and

(b) the payment is made either—

    (i) to that person's parent or step-parent, or

    (ii) where that person at the relevant date was a child, a young person or a student who had not completed his full-time education and had no parent or step-parent, to his guardian.

but only for a period of two years from the relevant date.

(6) In the case of a person to whom or for whose benefit a payment referred to in this paragraph is made, any capital resource which derives from any payment of income or capital made under or deriving from any of the Trusts.]

[¹⁶(7) For the purposes of sub-paragraphs (2) to (6), any reference to the Trusts shall be construed as including a reference to the Fund [²⁰and the Eileen Trust].]

[¹24. The value of the right to receive an occupational [¹³or personal] pension.

[²⁴24A. The value of any funds held under a personal pension scheme or retirement annuity contract.]

25. The value of the right to receive any rent [²⁴except where the claimant has a reversionary interest in the property in respect of which rent is due.]]

[²26.—(1) Where a claimant has ceased to occupy what was formerly the dwelling occupied as the home following his estrangement or divorce from his former partner, that dwelling for a period of 26 weeks from the date on which he ceased to occupy that dwelling.

(2) In this paragraph "dwelling" includes any garage, garden and out-buildings which were formerly occupied by the claimant as his home and any premises not so occupied which it is impracticable or unreasonable to sell separately, in particular, in Scotland, any croft land on which the dwelling is situated.

27. Any premises where the claimant is taking reasonable steps to dispose of those

premises, for a period of 26 weeks from the date on which he first took such steps, or such longer period as is reasonable in the circumstances to enable him to dispose of those premises.]

[⁴**28.** Any premises which the claimant intends to occupy as his home, and in respect of which he is taking steps to obtain possession and has sought legal advice, or has commenced legal proceedings, with a view to obtaining possession, for a period of 26 weeks from the date on which he first sought such advice or first commenced such proceedings whichever is the earlier, or such longer period as is reasonable in the circumstances to enable him to obtain possession and commence occupation of those premises.]

[²**29.** Any premises which the claimant intends to occupy as his home to which essential repairs or alterations are required in order to render them fit for such occupation, for a period of 26 weeks from the date on which the claimant first takes steps to effect those repairs or alterations, or such longer period as is reasonable in the circumstances to enable those repairs or alterations to be carried out and the claimant to commence occupation of the premises.

30. Any premises occupied in whole or in part by the former partner of a claimant as his home; but this provision shall not apply where the former partner is a person from whom the claimant is estranged or divorced.]

[³**31.** Any payment in kind made by a charity [⁶or under the Macfarlane (Special Payments) Trust][¹⁶or, the Macfarlane (Special Payments) (No. 2) Trust [¹⁹, the Fund or the Independent Living (1993) Fund]].

32. [²¹£200 of any payment, or, if the payment is less than £200, the whole of any payment] made under section 2 of the Employment and Training Act 1973 (functions of the Secretary of State) [¹¹or under section 2 of the Enterprise and New Towns (Scotland) Act 1990] as a training bonus to a person participating in arrangements for training made under [¹¹either of those sections] [⁴but only for a period of 52 weeks from the date of the receipt of that payment.]

33. Any payment made by the Secretary of State to compensate for the loss (in the whole or in part) of entitlement to housing benefit.]

[⁴**34.** Any payment made by the Secretary of State to compensate a person who was entitled to supplementary benefit in respect of a period ending immediately before 11th April 1988 but who did not become entitled to income support in respect of a period beginning with that day.

35. Any payment made by the Secretary of State to compensate for the loss of housing benefit supplement under regulation 19 of the Supplementary Benefit (Requirements) Regulations 1983.

36. Any payment made to a juror or witness in respect of attendance at court other than compensation for loss of earnings or for the loss of a benefit payable under the benefit Acts.

37. [¹⁷ . .].]

[⁷**38.** Any payment in consequence of a reduction of a personal community charge pursuant to regulations under section 13A of the Local Government Finance Act 1988 or section 9A of the Abolition of Domestic Rates Etc (Scotland) Act 1987 (reduction of liability for personal community charge) [¹⁷or reduction of council tax under section 13 or, as the case may be, section 80 of the local Government Finance Act 1992 (reduction of liability for council tax),] but only for a period of 52 weeks from the date of receipt of the payment.]

[⁸**39.** Any grant made to the claimant in accordance with a scheme made under section 129 of the Housing Act 1988 or section 66 of the Housing (Scotland) Act 1988 (schemes for payments to assist local housing authority and local authority tenants to obtain other accommodation) which is to be used—

(a) to purchase premises intended for occupation as his home; or
(b) to carry out repairs or alterations which are required to render premises fit for occupation as his home.

for a period of 26 weeks from the date on which he received such a grant or such longer period as is reasonable in the circumstances to enable the purchase, repairs or alterations to be completed and the claimant to commence occupation of those premises as his home.]

[¹⁰·**40.**—(1) Any payment or repayment made—

    (a) as respects England and Wales, under regulation 3, 5 or 8 of the National Health Service (Travelling Expenses and Remission of Charges) Regulations 1988 (travelling expenses and health service supplies);

    (b) as respects Scotland, under regulation 3, 5 or 8 of the National Health Service (Travelling Expenses and Remission of Charges) (Scotland) Regulations 1988 (travelling expenses and health service supplies);

but only for a period of 52 weeks from the date of receipt of the payment orrepayment.

(2) Any payment or repayment made by the Secretary of State for Health, the Secretary of State for Scotland or the Secretary of State for Wales which is analogous to a payment or repayment mentioned in sub-paragraph (1); but only for a period of 52 weeks from the date of receipt of the payment or repayment.

41. Any payment made under regulation 9 to 11 or 13 of the Welfare Food Regulations 1988 (payments made in place of milk tokens or the supply of vitamins), but only for a period of 52 weeks from the date of receipt of the payment.

42. Any payment made either by the Secretary of State for the Home Department by the Secretary of State for Scotland under a scheme established to assist relatives and other persons to visit persons in custody, but only for a period of 52 weeks from the date of receipt of the payment.

43. Any arrears of special war widows payment which is disregarded under paragraph 43 of Schedule 2 (sums to be disregarded in the calculation of income other than earnings) [²²or any amount which is disregarded under paragraph 52, 53 or 54 of that Schedule], but only for a period of 52 weeks from the date of receipt of the arrears.]

[¹⁴**44.** Any payment (other than a training allowance or training bonus under section 2 of the Employment and Training Act 1973) made, whether by the Secretary of State or any other person, under the Disabled Persons (Employment) Act 1944 or in accordance with arrangements made under section 2 of the Employment and Training Act 1973 to assist disabled persons to obtain or retain employment despite their disability.

45. Any payment made by a local authority under section 3 of the Disabled Persons (Employment) Act 1958 to homeworkers assisted under the Blind Homeworkers' Scheme.]

[²²**46.** Any sum of capital administered on behalf of a person [³⁰ . . .] by the High Court under the provisions of Order 80 of the Rules of the Supreme Court, the County Court under Order 10 of the County Court Rules 1981, or the Court of Protection, where such sum derives from—

    (a) an award of damages for a personal injury to that person; or

    (b) compensation for the death of one or both parents [³⁰where the person concerned is under the age of 18].

47. Any sum of capital administered on behalf of a person [³⁰ . . .] in accordance with an order made under rule 43.15 of the Act of Sederunt (Rules of the Court of Session 1994) 1994 or under rule 131 of the Act of Sederunt (Rules of the Court, consolidation and amendment) 1965, or under rule 36.14 of the Ordinary Cause Rules 1993, or under rule 128 of the Ordinary Cause Rules, where such sum derives from—

    (a) an award of damages for a personal injury to that person; or

    (b) compensation for the death of one or both parents [³⁰where the person concerned is under the age of 18].]

[²³**48.** Any payment made by the Secretary of State to compensate for a reduction in a maintenance assessment made under the Child Support Act 1991, but only for a period of 52 weeks from the date of receipt of that payment.]

[²⁵**49.** Any payment to the claimant as holder of the Victoria Cross or George Cross.]

[²⁶**50.** The amount of any back to work bonus payable by way of a jobseeker's allowance or income support in accordance with section 26 of the Jobseekers Act 1995, or a corresponding payment under article 28 of the Jobseekers (Northern Ireland) Order 1995, but only for a period of 52 weeks from the date of receipt.]

[²⁸ [²⁹**51.**] The amount of any child maintenance bonus payable by way of a jobseeker's allowance or income support in accordance with section 10 of the Child Support Act 1995, or a corresponding payment under Article 4 of the Child Support (Northern Ireland) Order 1995, but only for a period of 52 weeks from the date of receipt.]

[³³**52.** Any mandatory top-up payment made to a person pursuant to section 2 of the Employment and Training Act 1973 in respect of that person's participation in an employment programme specified in—

(a) regulation 75(1)(a)(ii)(aa)(ii) of the Jobseeker's Allowance Regulations 1996 (self-employment route of the Employment Option of the New Deal);

(b) regulation 75(1)(a)(ii)(bb) of those Regulations (Voluntary Sector Option of the New Deal); or

(c) regulation 75(1)(a)(ii)(cc) of those Regulations (Environment Task Force Option of the New Deal),

but only for a period of 52 weeks from the date of receipt of the payment.]

[³¹**53.** Any discretionary payment to meet, or to help meet, special needs made to a person pursuant to section 2 of the Employment and Training Act 1973 in respect of that person's participation in the Full-Time Education and Training Option of the New Deal as specified in regulation 75(1)(b)(ii) of the Jobseeker's Allowance Regulations 1996 but only for a period of 52 weeks from the date of receipt of the payment.]

[³⁴**54.** In the case of a person who is receiving, or who has received, assistance under an employment programme specified in regulation 75(1)(a)(ii)(aa)(ii) of the Jobseeker's Allowance Regulations 1996 (self-employment route of the Employment Option of the New Deal), any sum of capital which is acquired by that person for the purpose of establishing or carrying on the commercial activity in respect of which such assistance is or was received but only for a period of 52 weeks from the date on which that sum was acquired.]

[³⁵**55.** Any discretionary payment made pursuant to section 2 of the Employment and Training Act 1973 to meet, or help meet, special needs of a person who is undertaking a qualifying course within the meaning specified in regulation 17A(7) of the Jobseeker's Allowance Regulations 1996 but only for the period of 52 weeks from the date of receipt of that payment.]

AMENDMENTS

1. Family Credit (General) Amendment Regulations 1988 (S.I. 1988 No. 660), reg. 14 (April 11, 1988).

2. Family Credit (General) Amendment No. 2 Regulations 1988 (S.I. 1988 No. 908), reg. 2 (May 30, 1988).

3. Family Credit (General) Amendment No. 3 Regulations 1988 (S.I. 1988 No. 1438), reg. 9 (September 12, 1988).

4. Family Credit (General) Amendment No. 4 Regulations 1988 (S.I. 1988 No. 1970), reg. 12 (December 5, 1988).

5. Family Credit and Income Support (General) Amendment Regulations 1989 (S.I. 1989 No. 1034), reg. 3 (July 10, 1989).

6. Income-related Benefits Schemes Amendment Regulations 1990 (S.I. 1990 No. 127), reg. 2 (January 31, 1990).

7. Family Credit (General) Amendment Regulations 1990 (S.I. 1990 No. 574), reg. 15(a) (April 3, 1990).

8. Family Credit (General) Amendment Regulations 1990 (S.I. 1990 No. 574), reg. 15(b) (April 10, 1990).

9. Social Security Benefits (Student Loans and Miscellaneous Amendments) Regulations 1990 (S.I. 1990 No. 1549), reg. 3(6) (September 1, 1990).

10. Family Credit (General) Amendment No. 2 Regulations 1990 (S.I. 1990 No. 1774), reg. 5 (October 2, 1990).

11. Enterprise (Scotland) Consequential Amendments Order (S.I. 1991 No. 387), arts. 2 and 12 (April 1, 1991).

12. Income-related Benefits Schemes and Social Security (Recoupment) Amendment Regulations 1991 (S.I. 1991 No. 1175), reg. 3 (May 11, 1991).

13. Family Credit (General) Amendment Regulations 1991 (S.I. 1991 No. 1520), reg. 11 (October 8, 1991).

14. Family Credit (General) Amendment Regulations 1992 (S.I. 1992 No. 573), reg. 14 (April 7, 1992).

15. Family Credit (General) Amendment Regulations 1992 (S.I. 1992 No. 573), Sched. para. 4 (April 7, 1992).

16. Income-related Benefits Schemes and Social Security (Recoupment) Amendment Regulations 1992 (S.I. 1992 No. 1101), reg. 4(7) (May 7, 1992).

17. Income-related Benefits Schemes (Miscellaneous Amendments) Regulations 1993 (S.I. 1993 No. 315), Sched., para. 11 (April 1, 1993).

18. Social Security Benefits (Miscellaneous Amendments) (No. 2) Regulations 1993 (S.I. 1993 No. 963), reg. 3(3) (April 22, 1993).

19. Social Security Benefits (Miscellaneous Amendments) (No. 2) Regulations 1993 (S.I. 1993 No. 963), reg. 3(5) (April 22, 1993).

20. Income-related Benefits Schemes and Social Security (Recoupment) Amendment Regulations 1993 (S.I. 1993 No. 1249), reg. 2(5) (May 14, 1993).

21. Income-related Benefits Schemes (Miscellaneous Amendments) (No. 4) Regulations 1993 (S.I. 1993 No. 2119), reg. 35 (October 5, 1993).

22. Income-related Benefits Schemes (Miscellaneous Amendments) (No. 5) Regulations 1994 (S.I. 1994 No. 2139), reg. 21 (October 4, 1994).

23. Income-related Benefits Schemes (Miscellaneous Amendments) Regulations 1995 (S.I. 1995 No. 516), reg. 16 (April 11, 1995).

24. Income-related Benefits Schemes and Social Security (Claims and Payments) (Miscellaneous Amendments) Regulations 1995 (S.I. 1995 No. 2303), reg. 4(8) (October 3, 1995).

25. Income-related Benefits Schemes (Miscellaneous Amendments) Regulations 1996 (S.I. 1996 No. 462), reg. 11(3) (April 9, 1996).

26. Social Security and Child Support (Jobseeker's Allowance) (Consequential Amendments) Regulations 1996 (S.I. 1996 No. 1345), reg. 8(6) (October 7, 1996).

27. Income-related Benefits Schemes and Social Fund (Miscellaneous Amendments) Regulations 1996 (S.I. 1996 No. 1944), reg. 13 and Sched., para. 7 (October 7, 1996).

28. Social Security (Child Maintenance Bonus) Regulations 1996 (S.I. 1996 No. 3195), reg. 15 (April 7, 1997).

29. Social Security (Miscellaneous Amendments) Regulations 1997 (S.I. 1997 No. 454), reg. 8(9) (April 6, 1997).

30. Income-related Benefits and Jobseeker's Allowance (Amendment) (No. 2) Regulations 1997 (S.I. 1997 No. 2197), reg. 7(9) and (10)(c) (October 7, 1997).

31. Social Security Amendment (New Deal) Regulations 1997 (S.I. 1997 No. 2863), reg. 17(11) and (12)(c) (January 5, 1998).

32. Social Security (Miscellaneous Amendments) (No. 4) Regulations 1998 (S.I. 1998 No. 1174), reg. 7(7) and (8)(c) (June 1, 1998).

33. Social Security (Miscellaneous Amendments) (No. 4) Regulations 1998 (S.I. 1998 No. 1174), reg. 7(9) and (10)(c) (June 1, 1998).

34. Social Security (Miscellaneous Amendments) (No. 4) Regulations 1998 (S.I. 1998 No. 1174), reg. 7(11) and (12)(c) (June 1, 1998).

35. Social Security Amendment (New Deal) (No. 2) Regulations 1998 (S.I. 1998 No. 2117), reg. 5(2) and (3)(b) (September 24, 1998).

DEFINITIONS

"the benefit Acts"—see reg. 2(1).
"claimant"—*ibid.*, reg. 10(1).
"close relative"—see reg. 2(1).
"date of claim"—*ibid.*
"dwelling"—see 1986 Act, s.84(1) (SSCBA, s.137(1)).
"earnings top-up"—see reg. 2(1).
"family"—see 1986 Act, s.20(11) (SSCBA, s.137(1)).
"occupational pension"—see reg. 2(1)
"partner"—*ibid.*
"personal pension scheme"—*ibid.*
"policy of life insurance"—*ibid.*
"retirement annuity contract"—*ibid.*
"the Eileen Trust"—*ibid.*

"the Fund"—*ibid.*
"the Independent Living Funds"—*ibid.*
"the Independent Living (1993) Fund"—*ibid.*
"Macfarlane (Special Payments) Trust"—*ibid.*
"Macfarlane (Special Payments) (No. 2) Trust"—*ibid.*
"the Macfarlane Trust"—*ibid.*

GENERAL NOTE

Many of these categories of disregarded capital are the same in substance (there are occasional differences in cross references) as in Sched. 10 of the Income Support (General) Regulations (Sched. 10 (IS)). More substantial differences are noted.

Paragraphs 1–3
See paras. 1–3 of Sched. 10 (IS).

Paragraph 4
This is almost identical to para. 4 of Sched. 10 (IS), with the spelling out of the meaning of "relative," defined in reg. 2(1) of the Income Support (General) Regulations. But there is no requirement in Sched. 10 (IS) that the person has been incapacitated for at least 13 weeks.

Paragraphs 5 and 6
See paras. 5 and 6 of Sched. 10 (IS).

Paragraph 7
The proceeds of sale of a business asset, which are to be re-invested in the business, are disregarded. This provision has no equivalent in Sched. 10 (IS).

Paragraphs 8–10
See paras. 7–9 of Sched. 10 (IS).

Paragraph 11
The basic rule here is the same as that in para. 10 of Sched. 10 (IS), but in order for the value of personal possessions to count the intention in buying them must have been to reduce capital to gain entitlement to family credit. If the intention was to gain entitlement to, for example income support or family income supplement, para. 11 will not apply.

Paragraph 13
See para. 12 of Sched. 10 (IS).

Paragraphs 14–25
See paras. 13–24 of Sched. 10 (IS).

Paragraphs 26–29
See paras. 25–28 of Sched. 10 (IS).

Paragraph 30
See para. 4(b) of Sched. 10 (IS).

Paragraphs 31–36
See paras. 29–34 of Sched. 10 (IS).

Paragraphs 38 and 39
See paras. 36 and 37 of Sched. 10 (IS).

Paragraphs 40–43
See paras. 38–41 of Sched. 10 (IS).

Paragraphs 44 and 45
See paras. 42 and 43 of Sched. 10 (IS).

Family Credit (General) Regulations 1987

Paragraphs 46 and 47
See paras. 44 and 45 of Sched. 10 (IS).

Paragraph 49
See para. 46 of Sched. 10 (IS).

Paragraphs 52–54
See the note to paras. 50 to 52 of Sched. 10 (IS).

Paragraph 55
See the note to para. 48 of Sched. 8 (JSA).

SCHEDULE 4   **Regulation 46**

DETERMINATION OF MAXIMUM FAMILY CREDIT: ADULT, CHILD AND YOUNG PERSON CREDITS

Column (1)	Column (2)
Adult, child, young person	*Amount of Credit*
1. Adult	[⁴£49.80].
[¹**1A.** In the case of an adult or adults to whom regulation 46(1)(aa) applies.	[⁴£11.05]].
[²**2.** Person in respect of the period—	
(a) beginning on that person's date of birth and ending on the day preceding the first Tuesday in September following that person's eleventh birthday;	(a) [⁴£15.15];
(b) beginning on the first Tuesday in September following that person's eleventh birthday and ending on the day preceding the first Tuesday in September following that person's sixteenth birthday.	(*b*) [⁴£20.90].
3. Person in respect of the period beginning on the first Tuesday in September following that person's sixteenth birthday and ending on the day preceding that person's nineteenth birthday.]	[³[⁴£25.95]].

AMENDMENTS

1. Income-related Benefits Schemes (Miscellaneous Amendments) (No. 2) Regulations 1995 (S.I. 1995 No. 1339), reg. 8 (July 18, 1995).
2. Income-related Benefits and Jobseeker's Allowance (Personal Allowances for Children and Young Persons) (Amendment) Regulations 1996 (S.I. 1996 No. 2545), reg. 6 (October 7, 1997).
3. Family Credit and Disability Working Allowance (General) Amendment Regulations 1997 (S.I. 1997 No. 806), reg. 3 (October 7, 1997).
4. Social Security Benefits Up-rating Order 1999 (S.I. 1999 No. 264), art. 16(d) and Sched. 2 (April 13, 1999).

DEFINITIONS

"child"—see 1986 Act, s.20(11) (SSCBA, s.137(1)).
"young person"—see reg. 2(1), reg. 6

GENERAL NOTE

See the notes to reg. 46.

(S.I. 1987 No. 1974)

Family Credit (Transitional) Regulations 1987

(S.I. 1987 No. 1974)

Made by the Secretary of State under ss.84(1) and 89(1) of the Social Security Act 1986.

ARRANGEMENT OF REGULATIONS

Citation and commencement

1. These Regulations may be cited as the Family Credit (Transitional) Regulations 1987 and shall come into force on 1st January 1988.

Interpretation

2.—(1) In these Regulations, unless the context otherwise requires—
"the Act" means the Social Security Act 1986;
"appropriate office" means an office of the Department of Health and Social Security;
"child" has the same meaning as in Part II of the Act [SSCBA, Part VII];
"family" has the same meaning as in Part II of the Act [SSCBA, Part VII];
"family income supplement" means benefit under the Family Income Supplements Act 1970;
"married or unmarried couple" has the same meaning as in Part II of the Act [SSCBA, Part VII];
"renewal claim" means a claim for family income supplement which is so described in regulation 3(2) of the Family Income Supplements (General) Regulations 1980;
"young person" means a person aged 16 or over but under 19 who is receiving full-time education within section 2(1)(b) of the Child Benefit Act 1975 [SSCBA, s.142(1)(b)].
(2) Unless the context otherwise requires, any reference in these Regulations to a numbered regulation is a reference to the regulation bearing that number in these Regulations, and any reference in a regulation to a numbered paragraph is a reference to the paragraph bearing that number in that regulation.

Claims for family credit treated as made on 11th April 1988

3.—(1) A written claim for family credit which is delivered or sent to an appropriate office on or after 1st March 1988 and received on or before 11th April 1988 shall be treated as made on 11th April 1988.
(2) Where family income supplement is payable to a person under an award for a period which includes 5th April 1988 and does not exceed 51 weeks it shall not be a condition of entitlement to family credit for a period beginning

11th April 1988 that the person makes a claim for such benefit and a claim, in such a case, for family credit shall be treated as made on 11th April 1988.

(3) Where a claim for family income supplement is made on or after 1st March 1988 but on or before 5th April 1988, but no award of that benefit is made, that claim shall, if the Secretary of State in his discretion so determines, be treated as including a claim for family credit made on 11th April 1988.

(4) Where, after 5th April 1988, a claim is made for family income supplement which is neither a renewal claim nor a claim in respect of a period before 11th April 1988 it shall be treated as a claim for family credit which shall be treated as made on 11th April 1988 if received at an appropriate office on or before that date but otherwise on the date on which it is received at such an office.

(5) In a case to which paragraph (2), (3) or (4) applies, where the claim for family income supplement was made by a married or unmarried couple, the claim for family credit shall be treated as made by the woman except that the claim shall be treated as made by the man if the Secretary of State is satisfied, in that case, as that it would be reasonable so to treat it.

(6) A claim which is treated as made on 11th April 1988 by virtue of the provisions of this regulation may nevertheless be determined at any earlier date on which the conditions for treating it as made on 11th April 1988 are satisfied; and any such claim shall be determined in accordance with the Act and Regulations made under that Act as if those provisions were in force.

DEFINITIONS

"appropriate office"—see reg. 2(1).
"family income supplement"—*ibid.*
"married couple"—*ibid.*, 1986 Act, s.20(11) (SSCBA, s.137(1)).
"renewal claim"—see reg. 2(1), General Regulations, reg. 3(2).
"unmarried couple"—see reg. 2(1), 1986 Act, s.20(11) (SSCBA, s.137(1)).

GENERAL NOTE

Paragraph (1)
Claims for family credit could be made from March 1, 1988. If received before April 12, 1988, they were treated as made on April 11, 1988. See para. (6) and regs. 4 and 7.

Paragraph (2)
Any awards of FIS starting after March 24, 1987, were adjusted so as to expire before April 11, 1988, instead of running for the usual 52 weeks. Where such an award includes April 5, 1988, and has not been for a full 52 weeks, it is assumed that a family credit award on such a claim will be for the balance of 52 weeks from the beginning of the last FIS award (reg. 9(1)). See reg. 6.

Paragraph (3)
An unsuccessful FIS claim made after February 29, 1988, may be treated as a family credit claim made on April 11, 1988, at the discretion of the Secretary of State. See reg. 6.

Paragraph (4)
A fresh claim for FIS made after April 5, 1988, is to be treated as a family credit claim.

Paragraph (5)
A family credit claim usually has to be made by the woman (Claims and Payments Regulations, reg. 4(2)). Para. (5) allows this condition to be treated as met where a FIS claim is treated as a family credit claim.

Paragraph (6)
This provision allows decisions to be made in advance of April 11, 1988. This was necessary to secure continuity of payments, the printing of order books, etc.

Claims for family credit treated as including renewal claims for family income supplement

4. Where a claim for family credit is treated as made on 11th April 1988 by virtue of regulation 3(1) (claim received before 11th April 1988) and a renewal claim could properly have been made on the date when the claim for family credit was received at an appropriate office, such a renewal claim shall be treated as so made.

DEFINITIONS

"appropriate office"—see reg. 2(1).
"renewal claim"—*ibid.*, General Regulations, reg. 3(2).

Claims for family income supplement to be determined first

5. Where, before 11th April 1988, a person makes a claim for family credit and also claims family income supplement in respect of a period before 11th April 1988, the determination of the claim for family credit shall be postponed or, if it has already been determined, shall be of no effect until, and may be reviewed when, the claim for family income supplement has been determined.

DEFINITION

"family income supplement"—see reg. 2(1).

Determination of circumstances where family credit replaces, or arises out of a claim for, family income supplement

6.—(1) Subject to paragraphs (2) and (3), in a case to which regulation 3(2) or (3) applies (family credit treated as claimed on 11th April 1988 where family income supplement awarded or claimed) the provisions of [¹section 20(5)] of the Act [SSCBA, s.128(1)] (conditions of entitlement to family credit) shall be modified to the extent that entitlement to family credit shall be determined upon the assumption that the circumstances of the family (but not the ages of its members except where a young person attains the age of 19 on or before 11th April 1988) are the same on 11th April 1988 as they were at the date of the claim for family income supplement.

(2) In a case to which regulation 3(2) or (3) applies, the weekly earnings of the claimant and, if he is a member of a married or unmarried couple, those of the other member shall be calculated by deducting from the weekly earnings as calculated for the purpose of assessing entitlement to family income supplement—

(a) an amount in respect of income tax equivalent to an amount calculated by applying the basic rate of tax for the tax year 1987/88 to those earnings, less only the personal relief, appropriate to a week, to which the claimant is entitled under sections 8(1) and (2) and 14(1)(a) and (2) of the Income and Corporation Taxes Act 1970 (personal and additional relief); and

(b) an amount in respect of primary Class I contributions under the Social Security Act 1975 [SSCBA, Part I] equivalent to an amount calculated by applying the appropriate percentage rate specified in section 4(6B) of that Act [SSCBA, s.8(2)] in respect of the tax year 1987/88 to those earnings.

(3) In a case to which regulation 3(2) or (3) applies the weekly income of a claimant and, if he is a member of a married or unmarried couple, that of the other member of the couple, other than earnings to which paragraph (2) applies,

963

shall be calculated by deducting from the gross weekly income as calculated for the purpose of assessing entitlement to family income supplement the sums, where applicable, specified in Schedule 2 to the Family Credit (General) Regulations 1987 (income other than earnings to be disregarded).

AMENDMENT

1. Family Credit (Transitional) Amendment Regulation 1988 (S.I. 1988 No. 239), reg. 2 (February 20, 1988).

DEFINITIONS

"the Act"—see reg. 2(1).
"family"—*ibid.*, 1986 Act, s.20(11) (SSCBA, s.137(1)).
"family income supplement"—see reg. 2(1).
"married couple"—*ibid.*, 1986 Act, s.20(11) (SSCBA, s.137(1)).
"unmarried couple"—see reg. 2(1), 1986 Act, s.20(11) (SSCBA, s.137(1)).
"young person"—see reg. 2(1).

GENERAL NOTE

Paragraph (1)
Where reg. 3(2) or (3) applies, the family credit claim is to be determined as if the number and ages of the children on April 11, 1988, are the same as they were at the date of the FIS claim. The one exception is where a young person has reached 19, and so ceases to qualify for a credit. The family's income at the date of this FIS claim is also taken. In the case of a reg. 3(2) claim the family credit award will only be for the balance of 52 weeks from the date of the FIS award (reg. 9(1)).

Paragraph (2)
In a case falling under para. (1), the gross earnings for FIS are converted to net earnings.

Paragraph (3)
The disregarded categories of income in Sched. 2 to the Family Credit (General) Regulations apply to cases falling under para. (1).

Determination of circumstances where family credit is claimed before 11th April 1988

7. In a case to which regulation 3(1) applies (claim received before 11th April 1988), [¹sections 20(5) and 22(6)] of the Act [SSCBA, ss.128(1) and 134(1)] (conditions of entitlement to family credit) shall be modified to the extent that the circumstances of the family (but not the ages of its members) shall be determined as at the date when the claim is received at an appropriate office.

AMENDMENT

1. Family Credit (Transitional) Amendment Regulations 1988 (S.I. 1988 No. 239), reg. 2 (February 20, 1988).

DEFINITIONS

"the Act"—see reg. 2(1).
"the family"—*ibid.*, 1986 Act, s.20(11) (SSCBA, s.137(1)).

GENERAL NOTE

Where an advance claim for family credit was made before April 11, 1988, it was to be determined on the circumstances as at the date on which the claim was actually received, but of course according to family credit rules (since the claim was treated as made on April 11, 1988).

Entitlement to family credit following entitlement to family income supplement

8.—(1) Where a claim for family credit is treated as made on 11th April 1988, by virtue of regulation 3(2) (pre-existing entitlement to family income supplement) and all the conditions of entitlement to family credit as modified by regulation 6 (determination of circumstances where family credit replaces family income supplement), are satisfied, including the capital conditions in section 22(6) of the Act [SSCBA, s.134(1)] and the income conditions in section 20(5)(a) of the Act [SSCBA, s.128(1)(a)], family credit shall be awarded at the rate at which family income supplement was payable on 5th April 1988, together with an additional £2.55 per week for each child or young person included in the family for which family income supplement was payable on 5th April 1988, except where such a rate would be lower than the rate at which family credit would otherwise be payable.

(2) Where a claim for family credit is treated as made on 11th April 88, by virtue of regulation 3(2), and, apart from the income conditions in section 20(5)(a) of the Act [SSCBA, s.128(1)(b)], all the conditions of entitlement to family credit as modified by regulation 6, including the capital conditions in section 22(6) of the Act [SSCBA, s.134(1)], are satisfied, family credit shall be awarded at the rate at which family income supplement was payable on 5th April 1988, together with an additional £2.55 per week for each child or young person included in the family for which family income supplement was payable on 5th April 1988.

(3) In the case of an award of family credit on a claim treated as made on 11th April 1988 by virtue of regulation 3(1) or (2), in respect of a person for whom family income supplement was payable on 5th April 1988, the first day of the award (namely 11th April 1988) shall be treated as a week for the purpose of calculating—

    (a) the amount payable; and

    (b) the number of weeks for which family credit should be payable under section 20(6) of the Act [SSCBA, s.128(3)] (period for which family credit payable), as modified by regulation 3 (initial periods of family credit).

DEFINITIONS

    "the Act"—see reg. 2(1).
    "child"—*ibid.*, 1986 Act, s.20(11) (SSCBA, s.137(1)).
    "family"—*ibid.*
    "family income supplement"—see reg. 2(1).
    "young person"—*ibid.*

GENERAL NOTE

    Reg. 8 contains the transitional protection for families entitled to FIS immediately before the start of family credit.

Paragraph (1)
    This provision applies where the claimant met the £6,000 capital rule and also qualifies for family credit on income grounds, and any other conditions. If the amount of FIS payable on April 5, 1988, plus £2.55 for each child or young person in the family (to take account of the loss of entitlement to free school meals and milk), exceeded the amount of family credit calculated in the ordinary way, family credit was to be paid at the higher rate. This protection only applied to the initial claim treated as made on April 11, 1988, by virtue of reg. 3(2) and thus expired when that award (limited by reg. 9(1)) expired.

Paragraph (2)

This provision applied when the conditions of para. (1) were met except that on the income tests there was no entitlement on family credit. Family credit was paid at the FIS rate for April 5, 1988, plus £2.55 for each child or young person.

Initial periods of family credit

9.—(1) In the case of an award of family credit on a claim treated as made on 11th April 1988 by virtue of regulation 3(2) (pre-existing entitlement to family income supplement), section 20(6) of the Act [SSCBA, s.128(3)] shall be modified by substituting for the words "for a period of 26 weeks or such other period as may be prescribed, beginning with the week in which the claim is made or is treated as made" the words "for a period beginning with the week in which a claim for it is made or is treated as made and ending 52 weeks after the start of the most recent award of family income supplement, or on such earlier date as the Secretary of State shall in any case decide, and".

(2) In the case of an award of family credit on any claim made or treated as made before 5th October 1988, except an award to which paragraph (1) applies, section 20(6) of the Act [SSCBA, s.128(3)] shall be modified by substituting for the words "for a period of 26 weeks or such other period as may be prescribed" the words "for such period of at least 14 weeks but not more than 39 weeks, as the Secretary of State shall in any case decide".

DEFINITIONS

"the Act"—see reg. 2(1).
"family income supplement"—*ibid.*

GENERAL NOTE

Paragraph (1)

On a claim under reg. 3(2) an award of family credit was to be for the balance of 52 weeks from the beginning of the last FIS award. Subsequent awards will be for 26 weeks, unless para. (2) applies.

Paragraph (2)

In the case of any family credit claim before October 5, 1988, the Secretary of State has power to depart from the normal 26 week award, within limits of 14 and 39 weeks. This will enable the expiry of awards to be staggered, so that there is not a disproportionate burden of administrative work at one point in the year. This provision is not limited to claimants moving from FIS to family credit (*CFC 13/1989*).

Family Credit (Transitional) Regulations 1992

(S.I. 1992 No. 573)

[*In force, April 7, 1992*]

Extension of award period

15.—(1) In the case of an award of family credit on any claim to which paragraph (4) of regulation 13 of the Social Security (Claims and Payments) Regulations 1987 applies (advance claims and awards), for the purposes of section 20(6) of the Social Security Act 1986 [SSCBA, s.128(3)] the prescribed period shall be determined in accordance with paragraph (2) of this regulation.

(2) For the purposes of determining the prescribed period the Secretary of

State shall assign a number to the claim in question (the claim number), and where that claim number—

   (a) is exactly divisible by 13, the prescribed period shall be 27 weeks;

   (b) is not exactly divisible by 13, the remainder shall be multiplied by 13 and the prescribed period shall be the number of weeks equal to the sum of the resulting product plus 27.]

GENERAL NOTE

Reg. 13(4) of the Claims and Payments Regulations allows for advance claims for family credit immediately before the change in the minimum qualifying hours from 24 to 16 on April 7, 1992, by claimants who did not previously meet that qualification. This provision secures that all the awards made on such claims do not run out on the same date and thus impose an impracticable administrative burden. Awards are intended to be for a randomly chosen period between 27 and 39 weeks, but para. (2)(b) appears to allow a period of up to 183 weeks!

Social Security (Persons from Abroad) Miscellaneous Amendments Regulations 1996

(S.I. 1996 No. 30)

Made by the Secretary of State under ss.64(1), 68(4)(c)(i), 70(4), 71(6), 123(1), 124(1), 128(1), 129(1), 130(1) and (2), 131(1) and (3), 135, 137(1) and (2)(a) and (i) and 175(1) and (3) to (5) of the Social Security Contributions and Benefits Act 1992 and s.5(1)(r) of the Social Security Administration Act 1992

[In force February 5, 1996]

Saving

12.—(3) Where, before the coming into force of these Regulations, a person is receiving attendance allowance, disability living allowance, disability working allowance, family credit, invalid care allowance or severe disablement allowance under, as the case may be, the Attendance Allowance Regulations, Disability Living Allowance Regulations, Disability Working Allowance Regulations, Family Credit Regulations, Invalid Care Allowance Regulations or Severe Disablement Allowance Regulations, those Regulations shall, until such time as his entitlement to that benefit is reviewed under section 25 or 30 of the Social Security Administration Act 1992, have effect as if regulation 2, 4, 5, 6, 9 or 11, as the case may be, of these Regulations had not been made.

GENERAL NOTE

See the notes to reg. 3 of the Family Credit Regulations.

Income-related Benefits and Jobseeker's Allowance (Personal Allowances for Children and Young Persons) (Amendment) Regulations 1996

(S.I. 1996 No. 2545)

Made by the Secretary of State under ss.128(1)(a)(i) and (5), 129(1)(c)(i) and (8), 135(1), 136(3) and (4), 137(1) and 175(1), (3) and (4) of the Social Security Contributions and Benefits Act 1992 and ss.4(5), 35(1) and 36(1), (2) and (4) of the Jobseekers Act 1995

[In force October 7, 1997]

Transitional provisions

10.—(3) Where, in any particular case, the appropriate maximum family credit or, as the case may be, the appropriate maximum disability working allowance includes a credit or allowance in respect of one or more children or young persons who are, as at 6th October 1997, aged 11, 16 or 18, the Family Credit Regulations or, as the case may be, the Disability Working Allowance Regulations shall have effect, for the period specified in paragraph (4) below, as if regulations 5 and 6 or, as the case may be, 8 and 9 of these Regulations ['or regulation 3 or 4 of the Family Credit and Disability Working Allowance (General) Amendment Regulations 1997] had not been made.

(4) The period specified for the purposes of paragraph (3) above shall be, in relation to each particular child or young person referred to in that paragraph, the period beginning on 7th October 1997 and ending—

(a) where that child or young person is aged 11 or 16 as at 6th October 1997, on 31st August 1998;

(b) where that young person is aged 18 as at 6th October 1997, on the day preceding the day that young person ceases to be a person of a prescribed description for the purposes of regulation 6 of the Family Credit Regulations or, as the case may be, regulation 8 of the Disability Working Allowance Regulations.

AMENDMENT

1. Family Credit and Disability Working Allowance (General) Amendment Regulations 1997 (S.I. 1997 No. 806), reg. 5(3) (October 7, 1997).

GENERAL NOTE

See the notes to reg 46 of the Family Credit Regulations. Reg. 46 of and Sched. 4 to the Family Credit Regulations were amended by regs. 5 and 6 of these Regulations on October 7, 1997.

The credit for a young person aged not less than 18 but less than 19 years in sub-para. (b) of the previous form of para. 3 of Sched. 4 was increased to £35.55 from April 7, 1998 (Social Security Benefits Up-rating Order 1998 (S.I. 1998 No. 470), art. 16(2)). The weekly amounts in paras. 2(b) and 3(a) were also increased and were the same as the amounts in paras. 2(b) and 3 of the new form of Sched. 4.

PART V

DISABILITY WORKING ALLOWANCE

Disability Working Allowance (General) Regulations 1991

(S.I. 1991 No. 2887)

Made by the Secretary of State under ss.20(1), (5)(bb), (6A)(d), (6C) to (6F), (11) and (12), 21(3B) and (6)(aa), 22(1) and (5) to (9), 27B(2) and (4) and 84(1) of the Social Security Act 1986 and s.166(1) to (3A) of the Social Security Act 1975.

GENERAL NOTE

For many years one of the biggest gaps in the British social security system has been that there was no provision for partial capacity for work. A person was either incapable of any work he could reasonably be expected to do, and so entitled to incapacity benefits, or he was not incapable. There was no special recognition of a lesser reduction in working and earning ability. This was one of the weaknesses identified in the Social Security Advisory Committee's special report, *Benefits for Dis-*

abled People: a Strategy for Change (1988). The Government's White Paper, *The Way Ahead: Benefits for Disabled People* (1990, Cm. 917) proposed a new benefit along the lines of family credit, but restricted to disabled people and not limited to people with children. Disability working allowance is the result.

Even with the shift in the minimum hours to 16 a week for the income-related benefits generally, disabled people who can only do a little work will still be excluded. The need to satisfy the criterion of entitlement to some other incapacity or disability benefit under s.129(2)–(2B) of the Contributions and Benefits Act, will also exclude some claimants who are partially capable of work. The initial estimates were that about 50,000 claimants would benefit from disability working allowance, so that it is designed to be a limited scheme.

If a person has the choice of claiming family credit or disability working allowance, they will generally be better off on disability working allowance, because it is usually paid at a higher rate and will entitle the person to a disability or higher pensioner premium for housing benefit/council tax benefit. In addition, a disabled child's allowance has been introduced for disability working allowance (but not for family credit) from April 11, 1995. However, in the past disability working allowance did not operate as a passport to schemes like those for exemption from prescription charges and dental and optician's charges. This has been remedied from April 1995, but only for recipients of disability working allowance who have capital of £8,000 or less (the capital limit for disability working allowance is £16,000).

Since October 1994, certain disability working allowance claimants have been able to offset child care costs of up to £40 per week (increased to £60 from April 1996 and to £100 from June 1998 where the claimant has more than one child) against their earnings. This also applies to family credit (and housing and council tax benefit) but not income support or income-based JSA. Although this is an important change in principle, the scope of the disregard is quite limited (see regs. 15 and 15A and the notes to regs. 13 and 13A of the Family Credit Regulations). In addition, from July 1995 an additional allowance of £10 (now £11.05 from April 1999) has been included in the disability working allowance calculation for those who work 30 hours or more a week. The same applies to family credit.

Note also that since October 7, 1997 the allowance for a child does not increase until the first Tuesday in September after their 11th or 16th birthday and there is no longer an increase at the age of 18. For the transitional protection for a child or young person who reached the relevant age before October 7, 1997 see reg. 10(3) and (4) of the Income-related Benefits and Jobseeker's Allowance (Personal Allowances for Children and Young Persons) (Amendment) Regulations 1996 (p. 1055). There is a parallel change to the child care costs disregard in reg. 15A (see the notes to regulation 13A of the Family Credit Regulations).

Note that disability working allowance is to be replaced by disabled person's tax credit from October 5, 1999. See the 1999 Supplement to this book for details of the new scheme.

Part I

General

Citation and commencement

1. These Regulations may be cited as the Disability Working Allowance (General) Regulations 1991, and shall come into force on 7th April 1992.

Interpretation

2.—(1) In these Regulations, unless the context otherwise requires—
"the Act" means the Social Security Act 1986;
"assessment period" means such period as is prescribed in regulations 16 to 19 over which income falls to be calculated;
"attendance allowance" means—
    (a) an attendance allowance under section 35 of the Social Security Act [SSCBA, s.64];

(b) an increase of disablement pension under section 61 or 63 of that Act [SSCBA, ss.104 or 105];

(c) a payment under regulations made in exercise of the power conferred by section 159(3)(b) of that Act [SSCBA, Sched. 8, para. 7(2)(b)];

(d) an increase of an allowance which is payable in respect of constant attendance under section 5 of the Industrial Injuries and Diseases (Old Cases) Act 1975;

(e) a payment by virtue of article 14, 15, 16, 43 or 44 of the Personal Injuries (Civilians) Scheme 1983 or any analogous payment; or

(f) any payment based on need for attendance which is paid as part of a war disablement pension;

[¹⁰"the benefit Acts" means the Contributions and Benefits Act and the Jobseekers Act 1995;]

[¹³"the Children Order" means the Children (Northern Ireland) Order 1995;]

"claim" means a claim for disability working allowance;

"claimant" means a person claiming disability working allowance;

"close relative" means a parent, parent-in-law, son, son-in-law, daughter, daughter-in-law, step-parent, step-son, step-daughter, brother, sister, or the spouse of any of the preceding persons or, if that person is one of an unmarried couple, the other member of that couple;

[³"community charge benefit" means community charge benefits under Part VII of the Contributions and Benefits Act as originally enacted;]

"concessionary payment" means a payment made under arrangements made by the Secretary of State with the consent of the Treasury which is charged either to the National Insurance Fund or to a Departmental Expenditure Vote to which payments of benefit under the Act, the Social Security Act or the Child Benefit Act 1975 are charged;

[³"the Contributions and Benefits Act" means the Social Security Contributions and Benefits Act 1992;]

[⁷"Crown property" means property held by Her Majesty in right of the Crown or by a government department or which is held in trust for Her Majesty for the purposes of a government department, except (in the case of an interest held by Her Majesty in right of the Crown) where the interest is under the management of the Crown Estate Commissioners;]

"date of claim" means the date on which the claimant makes, or is treated as making, a claim for disability working allowance;

"earnings" has the meaning prescribed in regulation 21 or, as the case may be, 24;

[¹¹"earnings top-up" means the allowance paid by the Secretary of State under the Earnings Top-up Scheme;]

[¹¹"the Earnings Top-up Scheme" means the Earnings Top-up Scheme 1996;]

"employed earner" shall be construed in accordance with section 2(1)(a) of the Social Security Act [SSCBA, s.2(1)(a)];

"lone parent" means a person who has no partner and who is responsible for, and a member of the same household as, a child or young person;

[²"lower rate" where it relates to rates of tax has the same meaning as in the Income and Corporation Taxes Act 1988 by virtue of section 832(1) of that Act;]

[⁶"maternity leave" means a period during which a woman is absent from work because she is pregnant or has given birth to a child, and at the end of which she has a right to return to work either under the terms of her contract of employment or under Part III of the Employment Protection (Consolidation) Act 1978;]

"mobility allowance" means an allowance under section 37A of the Social Security Act;

"mobility supplement" means any supplement under article 26A of the Naval, Military and Air Forces etc. (Disablement and Death) Service Pensions Order 1983 including such a supplement by virtue of any other scheme or order or under Article 25A of the Personal Injuries (Civilians) Scheme 1983;

"net earnings" means such earnings as are calculated in accordance with regulation 22;

"net profit" means such profit as is calculated in accordance with regulation 25;

"occupational pension" means any pension or other periodical payment under an occupational pension scheme but does not include any discretionary payment out of a fund established for relieving hardship in particular cases;

"partner" means, where a claimant—
(a) is a member of a married or unmarried couple, the other member of that couple,
(b) is married polygamously to two or more members of the same household, any such member;

"payment" includes a part of a payment,

[¹²"pay period" means the period in respect of which a claimant is, or expects to be normally paid by his employer, being a week, a fortnight, four weeks, a month or other shorter or longer period, as the case may be:]

[⁹"pension fund holder" means with respect to a personal pension scheme or retirement annuity contract, the trustees, managers or scheme administrators, as the case may be, of the scheme or contract concerned;]

[⁶"personal pension scheme" has the same meaning as in [⁹section 1 of the Pension Schemes Act 1993] and, in the case of a self-employed earner, includes a scheme approved by the Inland Revenue under Chapter IV of Part XIV of the Income and Corporation Taxes Act 1988;]

"policy of life insurance" means any instrument by which the payment of money is assured on death (except death by accident only) or the happening of any contingency dependent on human life, or any instrument evidencing a contract which is subject to payment of premiums for a term dependent on human life;

[¹"qualifying person" means a person in respect of whom payment has been made from the Fund [⁵or the Eileen Trust];]

[⁹"retirement annuity contract" means a contract or trust scheme approved under Chapter III of Part XIV of the Income and Corporation Taxes Act 1988;]

"self-employed earner" shall be construed in accordance with section 2(1)(b) of the Social Security Act [SSCBA, s.2(1)(b)];

"single claimant" means a claimant who has neither a partner nor is a lone parent;

"Social Security Act" means the Social Security Act 1975;

"student" has the meaning prescribed in regulation 41;

[⁵"the Eileen Trust" means the charitable trust of that name established on 29th March 1993 out of funds provided by the Secretary of State for the benefit of persons eligible for payment in accordance with its provisions;]

[¹"the Fund" means moneys made available from time to time by the Secretary of State for the benefit of persons eligible for payment in accordance with the provisions of a scheme established by him on 24th April 1992 or, in Scotland, on 10th April 1992;]

[⁴"the Independent Living (Extension) Fund" means the Trust of that name established by a deed dated 25th February 1993 and made between the Secretary of State for Social Security of the one part and Robin Glover Wendt and John Fletcher Shepherd of the other part;]

"the Independent Living Fund" means the charitable trust established out of funds provided by the Secretary of State for the purpose of providing financial assistance to those persons incapacitated by or otherwise suffering from very severe disablement who are in need such assistance to enable them to live independently;

[4"the Independent Living (1993) Fund" means the Trust of that name established by a deed dated 25th February 1993 and made between the Secretary of State for Social Security of the one part and Robin Glover Wendt and John Fletcher Shepherd of the other part;]

[4"the Independent Living Funds" means the Independent Living Fund, the Independent Living (Extension) Fund and the Independent Living (1993) Fund;]

"the Macfarlane (Special Payments) Trust" means the trust of that name, established on 29th January 1990 partly out of funds provided by the Secretary of State, for the benefit of certain persons suffering from haemophilia;

"the Macfarlane (Special Payments) (No. 2) Trust" means the trust of that name, established on 3rd May 1991 partly out of funds provided by the Secretary of State, for the benefit of certain persons suffering from haemophilia and other beneficiaries;

"the Macfarlane Trust" means the charitable trust, established partly out of funds provided by the Secretary of State to the Haemophilia Society, for the relief of poverty or distress among those suffering from haemophilia;

[2"training allowance" means an allowance (whether by way of periodical grants or otherwise) payable—

(a) out of public funds by a Government department or by or on behalf of the Secretary of State, Scottish Enterprise or Highlands and Islands Enterprise;

(b) to a person for his maintenance or in respect of a member of his family; and

(c) for the period, or part of the period, during which he is following a course of training or instruction provided by, or in pursuance of arrangements made with, that department or approved by that department in relation to him or so provided or approved by or on behalf of the Secretary of State, Scottish Enterprise or Highlands and Islands Enterprise, but it does not include an allowance paid by any Government department to or in respect of a person by reason of the fact that he is following a course of full-time education, other than an allowance paid pursuant to arrangements made under section 2 of the Employment and Training Act 1973, or is training as a teacher;]

[8"voluntary organisation" means a body, other than a public or local authority, the activities of which are carried on otherwise than for profit;]

[3"water charges" means—

(a) as respects England and Wales, any water and sewerage charges under chapter I of Part V of the Water Industry Act 1991;

(b) as respects Scotland, any water and sewerage charges under Schedule 11 to the Local Government Finance Act 1992;]

"week" means a period of seven days beginning with Sunday;

"week of claim" means the week which includes the date of claim;

"year of assessment" has the same meaning prescribed in section 832(1) of the Income and Corporation Taxes Act 1988;

"young person" has the meaning prescribed in regulation 8.

(2) Unless the context otherwise requires, any reference in these Regulations to a numbered regulation, Part or Schedule is a reference to the regulation, Part or Schedule bearing that number in these Regulations and any reference in a

regulation or Schedule to a numbered paragraph is a reference to the paragraph in that regulation or Schedule bearing that number.

AMENDMENTS

1. Income-related Benefits Schemes and Social Security (Recoupment) Amendment Regulations 1992 (S.I. 1992 No. 1101), reg. 6(2) (May 7, 1992).
2. Income-related Benefits Schemes (Miscellaneous Amendments) (No. 3) Regulations 1992 (S.I. 1992 No. 2155), reg. 2 (October 5, 1992).
3. Income-related Benefits Schemes (Miscellaneous Amendments) Regulations 1993 (S.I. 1993 No. 315), reg. 16 (April 13, 1993).
4. Social Security Benefits (Miscellaneous Amendments) (No.2) Regulations 1993 (S.I. 1993 No. 963), reg. 6(2) (April 22, 1993).
5. Income-related Benefits Schemes and Social Security (Recoupment) Amendment Regulations 1993 (S.I. 1993 No. 1249), reg. 5(2) (May 14, 1993).
6. Income-related Benefits Schemes (Miscellaneous Amendments) (No.4) Regulations 1993 (S.I. 1993 No. 2119), reg. 36 (October 5, 1993).
7. Income-related Benefits Schemes (Miscellaneous Amendments) (No. 4) Regulations 1994 (S.I. 1994 No. 1924), reg. 3(2) (October 4, 1994).
8. Income-related Benefits Schemes (Miscellaneous Amendments) Regulations 1995 (S.I. 1995 No. 516), reg. 2 (April 11, 1995).
9. Income-related Benefits Schemes and Social Security (Claims and Payments) (Miscellaneous Amendments) Regulations 1995 (S.I. 1995 No. 2303), reg. 3(2) (October 3, 1995).
10. Social Security and Child Support (Jobseeker's Allowance) (Consequential Amendments) Regulations 1996 (S.I. 1996 No. 1345), reg. 7(2) (October 7, 1996).
11. Income-related Benefits Schemes and Social Fund (Miscellaneous Amendments) Regulations 1996 (S.I. 1996 No. 1944), reg. 13 and Sched., para. 1 (October 7, 1996).
12. Disability Working Allowance and Family Credit (General) Amendment Regulations 1996 (S.I. 1996 No. 3137), reg. 2(2) (January 7, 1997).
13. Social Security (Miscellaneous Amendments) Regulations 1998 (S.I. 1998 No. 563), reg. 5(1) and (2)(b) (April 7, 1998).

DEFINITIONS

"married couple"—see 1986 Act, s.84(1) (SSCBA, s.137(1)).
"occupational pension scheme"—see 1986 Act, s.84(1) (PSA, s.1).
"unmarried couple"—see 1986 Act, s.84(1) (SSCBA, s.137(1)).

GENERAL NOTE

"*the Act.*" The amendments inserted into the Social Security Act 1986 on entitlement to disability working allowance with effect from April 7, 1992, by the Disability Living Allowance and Disability Working Allowance Act 1991 are (from July 1, 1992) consolidated into s.129 of the Contributions and Benefits Act and the Administration Act. This is the form which appears in this book. See the Preface for how cross-referencing is done.
"*date of claim.*" See the Claims and Payments Regulations, reg. 6.
"*employed earner.*" The meaning in s.2(1)(a) of the Social Security Act 1975 (SSCBA, s.2(1)(a)) is "a person who is gainfully employed in Great Britain either under a contract of service, or in an office (including elective office) with emoluments chargeable to income tax under Schedule E."
"*lone parent.*" See regs. 9 to 11 for responsibility and membership of the household.
"*occupational pension.*" An "occupational pension scheme" is defined in s.84(1) of the 1986 Act as having the same meaning as in s.66(1) of the Social Security Pensions Act 1975. This definition is not carried over into the Contributions and Benefits Act, but is now in s.1 of the Pension Schemes Act 1993.
"*partner*" See the notes to s.137(1) of the Contributions and Benefits Act for "married couple" and "unmarried couple."
"*self-employed earner.*" The meaning in s.2(1)(b) of the Social Security Act 1975 (SSCBA, s.2(1)(b)) is "a person who is gainfully employed in Great Britain otherwise than in employed earner's employment (whether or not he is also employed in such employment)."
"*year of assessment.*" The meaning in s.832(1) of the Income and Corporation Taxes Act 1988

is "with reference to any tax year, the year for which such tax was granted by any Act granting income tax." A tax year is the 12 months beginning with April 6 in any year.

[¹Disapplication of section 1(1A) of the Administration Act

2A. Section 1(1A) of the Administration Act (requirement to state national insurance number) shall not apply—
  (a) to a child or young person in respect of whom disability working allowance is claimed;
  (b) to any claim for disability working allowance made or treated as made before 9th February 1998;
  (c) to a partner in respect of whom a claim for disability working allowance is made or treated as made before 5th October 1998.]

AMENDMENT

1. Social Security (National Insurance Number Information: Exemption) Regulations 1997 (S.I. 1997 No. 2676), reg. 5 (December 1, 1997).

DEFINITIONS

"child"—see SSCBA, s. 137(1).
"partner"—see reg. 2(1).
"young person"—see reg. 8.

GENERAL NOTE

See the notes to s. 1(1A)–(1C) of the Administration Act and reg. 2A of the Family Credit Regulations.

PART II

DISABILITY TEST

Person at a disadvantage in getting a job

3.—(1) A person has a disability which puts him at a disadvantage in getting a job where—
  (a) in respect of an initial claim one or more of the paragraphs in Parts I, II or III of Schedule 1 apply to him;
  (b) In respect of a repeat claim one or more of the paragraphs in Part I or II of Schedule 1 apply to him.
  (2) In this regulation and in regulation 4, the expressions "initial claim" and "repeat claim" the same meanings as in section 27B of the Act [SSAA, s.11].

GENERAL NOTE

See s.129(1)(b) and (3) of the Contributions and Benefits Act (1986 Act, s.20(6A)(b) and (6C)). A person is only to be treated as having a disability which puts him at a disadvantage in getting a job in the circumstances specified in Sched. 1. Different conditions apply to initial claims and to repeat claims. On an initial claim, the claimant's declaration that he has such a disability is conclusive (Administration Act, s.11(2); 1986 Act, s.27B(2)) subject to the exceptions in reg. 4.

The question whether a person satisfies this condition is a "disability question" which on appeal can never be determined by a SSAT, but has to go to a DAT (Adjudication Regulations, reg. 27).

Declaration by claimant

4. On an initial claim, a declaration by the claimant that he has a physical or mental disability which puts him at a disadvantage in getting a job is not conclusive that for the purposes of section 20(6A)(b) of the Act [SSCBA, s.129(1)(b)] he has a disability, where—
- (a) the claim itself contains contrary indications, or
- (b) the adjudication officer has before him other evidence which contradicts that declaration.

DEFINITIONS

"the Act"—see reg. 2(1).
"claim"—*ibid.*
"claimant"—*ibid.*

GENERAL NOTE

See Administration Act, s.11(2) (1986 Act, s.27B(2)). The "claim" here presumably means the information and evidence, including the self-assessments, entered on the claim form by or on behalf of the claimant. It is a matter of judgment how strong a contrary indication is required before the claimant's declaration is not treated as conclusive.

PART III

PRESENCE IN GREAT BRITAIN AND REMUNERATIVE WORK

Circumstances in which a person is treated as being or as not being in Great Britain

5.—(1) A person shall be treated as being in Great Britain if, on the date of claim—
- (a) he is present and ordinarily resident in Great Britain; and
- [¹(aa) subject to paragraph (1A), his right to reside or remain in Great Britain is not subject to any limitation or condition; and]
- (b) his partner, if any, is ordinarily resident in the United Kingdom; and
- (c) his earnings or the earnings of his partner, if any, derive at least in part from remunerative work in the United Kingdom; and
- (d) his earnings do not wholly derive from remunerative work outside the United Kingdom nor do the earnings of his partner, if any.

[¹(1A) For the purposes of paragraph (1)(aa), a person's right to reside or remain in Great Britain is not to be treated as if it were subject to a limitation or condition if—
- (a) he is a person recorded by the Secretary of State as a refugee within the definition in Article 1 of the Convention relating to the Status of Refugees done at Geneva on 28th July 1951, as extended by Article 1(2) of the Protocol relating to the Status of Refugees done at New York on 31st January 1967;
- (b) he is a person who has been granted exceptional leave outside the provisions of the immigration rules within the meaning of the Immigration Act 1971
    - [²(i) to enter the United Kingdom by an immigration officer appointed for the purposes of the Immigration Act 1971; or

(ii) to remain in the United Kingdom by the Secretary of State];
(c) he is a national, or a member of the family of a national, of a State contracting party to the Agreement on the European Economic Area signed at Oporto on 2nd May 1992 as adjusted by the Protocol signed at Brussels on 17th March 1993; or
(d) he is a person who is—
(i) lawfully working in Great Britain and is a national of a State with which the Community has concluded an Agreement under article 238 of the Treaty establishing the European Community providing, in the field of social security, for the equal treatment of workers who are nationals of the signatory State and their families, or
(ii) a member of the family of, and living with, such a person.]

(2) A person shall be treated as not being in Great Britain during any period for which he, or his partner, is entitled to be paid disability working allowance or family credit under the law of Northern Ireland.

AMENDMENTS

1. Social Security (Persons from Abroad) Miscellaneous Amendments Regulations 1996 (S.I. 1996 No. 30), reg. 5 (February 5, 1996).
2. Social Security (Miscellaneous Amendments) Regulations 1998 (S.I. 1998 No. 563), reg. 18(1) and (2)(b) (April 7, 1998).

DEFINITIONS

"claim"—see reg. 2(1).
"date of claim"—*ibid.*
"family"—see SSCBA, s.137(1).
"partner"—see reg. 2(1).

GENERAL NOTE

The requirement for the claimant to be in Great Britain at the date of claim appears in s.129(1) of the Contributions and Benefits Act (1986 Act, s.20(6A)). By s.137(2)(a) (1986 Act, s.20(12)(a)) regulations may provide for circumstances in which a person is to be treated as being or not being in Great Britain. See the notes to reg. 3 of the Family Credit (General) Regulations.

Remunerative work

6.—(1) [¹For the purposes of Part VII of the Social Security Contributions and Benefits Act 1992 as it applies to disability working allowance and subject to paragraph (3), a person shall be treated as engaged in remunerative work] where—
(a) the work he undertakes is for not less than 16 hours per week;
(b) the work is done for payment or in expectation of payment; and
(c) he is employed at the date of claim and satisfies the requirements of paragraph (5).

(2) A person who does not satisfy all the requirements of sub-paragraphs (a) to (c) of paragraph (1) shall not be treated as engaged [¹. . .] in remunerative work.

[³(3) A person who otherwise satisfies all the requirements of paragraph (1) shall not be treated as engaged in remunerative work in so far as—
(a) he is engaged by a charitable or voluntary organisation or is a volunteer, where the only payment received by him or due to be paid to him is a payment which is to be disregarded under regulation 27(2) and paragraph 2 of Schedule 3 (sums to be disregarded in the calculation of income other than earnings);

(b) he is engaged in caring for a person in respect of whom he receives payments to which paragraph 24 of Schedule 3 refers; or

(c) he is engaged on a scheme for which a training allowance is being paid.]

(4) [⁴Subject to paragraph (4A),] in determining for the purposes of sub-paragraph (a) of paragraph (1) whether a person has undertaken work of not less than 16 hours per week—

(a) there shall be included in the calculation any time allowed—
  (i) for meals or refreshment; or
  (ii) for visits to a hospital, clinic or other establishment for the purpose only of treating or monitoring the person's disability,
  but only where the person is, or expects to be, paid earnings in respect of that time; and

(b) where at the date of claim the claimant has within the previous 5 weeks—
  (i) started a new job;
  (ii) resumed work after a break of at least 13 weeks; or
  (iii) changed his hours,
  the hours worked shall be calculated by reference to the number of hours, or where these are expected to fluctuate, the average number of hours, which he is expected to work in a week; or

(c) where none of heads (i) to (iii) of [¹this paragraph] apply, and
  (i) a recognised cycle of working has been established at the date of claim, the hours worked shall be calculated by reference to the average number of hours worked in a week over the period of one complete cycle (including where the cycle involves periods in which the person does not work, those periods, but disregarding any other absences); or
  (ii) no recognised cycle of working has been established at that date, the hours worked shall be calculated by reference to the average number of hours worked over the 5 weeks immediately preceding the week in which the claim is made, or such other length of time preceding that week as may, in the particular case, enable the person's weekly average hours of work to be determined more accurately.

[⁴(4A) Where for the purpose of paragraph (4)(c)(i), a person's recognised cycle of work at a school, other educational establishment or other place of employment is one year and includes periods of school holidays or similar vacations during which he does not work, those periods and any other periods not forming part of such holidays or vacations during which he is not required to work shall be disregarded in establishing the average hours for which he is engaged in work.]

(5) Subject to paragraph (6), the requirements of this paragraph are that the person—

(a) worked not less than 16 hours in either—
  (i) the week of claim; or
  (ii) either of the two weeks immediately preceding the week of claim; or

(b) is expected by his employer to work [¹or, where he is a self-employed earner he expects to work,] not less than 16 hours in the week next following the week of claim; or

(c) cannot satisfy the requirements of sub-paragraph (a) or (b) above at the date of claim because he is or will be absent from work by reason of a recognised, customary or other holiday but he is expected by his employer to work [¹or, where he is a self-employed earner he expects to work,] not less than 16 hours in the week following his return to work, and for the purposes of calculating the number of hours worked, sub-paragraph (a) of paragraph (4) shall apply to this paragraph as it applies to sub-paragraph (a) of paragraph (1).

[²(6) For the purposes of paragraph (5)—
  (a) work which a person does only qualifies if—
      (i) it is the work which he normally does, and
      (ii) it is likely to last for a period of 5 weeks or more beginning with the week in which the claim is made; and
  (b) a person shall be treated as not on a recognised, customary or other holiday on any day on which the person is on maternity leave or is absent from work because he is ill.]

[¹(7) Where a person is treated as engaged in remunerative work in accordance with the above paragraphs, he shall also be treated as normally engaged in remunerative work.]

[³(8) [⁴. . .]]

AMENDMENTS

1. Income-related Benefits Schemes (Miscellaneous Amendments) (No. 3) Regulations 1992 (S.I. 1992 No. 2155), Sched., para. 2 (October 5, 1992).
2. Income-related Benefits Schemes (Miscellaneous Amendments) (No. 4) Regulations 1993 (S.I. 1993 No. 2119), reg. 37 (October 5, 1993).
3. Income-related Benefits Schemes (Miscellaneous Amendments) (No. 5) Regulations 1994 (S.I. 1994 No. 2139), reg. 2 (October 4, 1994).
4. Income-related Benefits Schemes (Miscellaneous Amendments) Regulations 1995 (S.I. 1995 No. 516), reg. 3 (April 11, 1995).

DEFINITIONS

    "the Act"—see reg. 2(1).
    "claim" —*ibid.*
    "claimant"—*ibid.*
    "maternity leave"—*ibid.*
    "self-employed earner"—*ibid.*
    "training allowance"—*ibid.*
    "voluntary organisation"—*ibid.*
    "week"—*ibid.*
    "week of claim"—*ibid.*

GENERAL NOTE

See the notes to reg. 4 of the Family Credit (General) Regulations. The October 1992 amendments bring the form of reg. 6 into line with that of reg. 4.

Para. (3)(c) was introduced to reverse the effect of *CDWA 1/1992* which had decided that a claimant who was a trainee on a YTS scheme was in remunerative work. At that time there was no provision in the Disability Working Allowance Regulations (or the Family Credit Regulations) corresponding to reg. 6(d) of the Income Support Regulations. For family credit, now see reg. 4(3)(c) of the Family Credit Regulations.

[¹Further provision as to remunerative work

6A. Whether, for the purposes of regulation 51(1)(bb) (determination of appropriate maximum disability working allowance) and paragraph 2A of Schedule 5, the work a person undertakes is for not less than 30 hours per week shall be determined in accordance with regulation 6(1)(b), (3), (4) and (4A) except that for the words "16 hours" in paragraph (4) there shall be substituted the words "30 hours".]

AMENDMENT

1. Income-related Benefits Schemes (Miscellaneous Amendments) (No. 2) Regulations 1995 (S.I. 1995 No. 1339), reg. 3 (July 18, 1995).

See reg. 4A of the Family Credit Regulations.

Income-related benefits

7. For the purposes of subsection (6E) of section 20 of the Act [SSCBA, s.129(4)] the prescribed circumstances are that the person's weekly applicable amount included a higher pensioner or disability premium in respect of him, determined—

    (a) [¹in the case of] income support, in accordance with paragraphs 10(1)(b) [³, 10(2)(b)] or 11, and 12 of Part III of Schedule 2 to the Income Support (General) Regulations 1987 (applicable amounts);

[⁴(aa) in the case of income-based jobseeker's allowance, in accordance with paragraphs 12(1)(a), (b)(ii) or (c) or 13, and 14 of Schedule 1 to the Jobseeker's Allowance Regulations 1996 (applicable amounts).]

    (b) in the case of housing benefit, in accordance with paragraphs 10(1)(b) [³, 10(2)(b)] or 11, and 12 of Part III of Schedule 2 to the Housing Benefit (General) Regulations 1987 (applicable amounts);

    (c) in the case of community charge benefit, in accordance with paragraphs 11 or 12, and 13 of Part III of Schedule 1 to the Community Charge Benefits (General) Regulations 1989 (applicable amounts); [².. .]

[²(ca) in the case of council tax benefit, in accordance with paragraphs [³11(1)(b), 11(2)(b)] or 12, and 13 of Part III of Schedule 1 to the Council Tax Benefit (General) Regulations 1992; or]

    (d) in accordance with any provision equivalent to one of those specified in [¹paragraphs [²(a) to (ca)]] above and having effect in Northern Ireland.

1. Income-related Benefits Schemes (Miscellaneous Amendments) (No. 3) Regulations 1992 (S.I. 1992 No. 2155), Sched., para. 3 (October 5, 1992).
2. Income-related Benefits Schemes (Miscellaneous Amendments) Regulations 1993 (S.I. 1993 No. 315), Sched., para. 12 (April 1, 1993).
3. Income-related Benefits Schemes (Miscellaneous Amendments) Regulations 1995 (S.I. 1995 No. 516), reg. 4 (April 11, 1995).
4. Social Security and Child Support (Jobseeker's Allowance) (Consequential Amendments) Regulations 1996 (S.I. 1996 No. 1345), reg. 7(3) (October 7, 1996).

"the Act"—see reg. 2(1).

See the notes to s. 129 of the Contributions and Benefits Act.

[¹Definition of "training for work"

7A. For the purposes of section 129(2A) of the Contributions and Benefits Act (which provides that a period of training for work may count towards the period of qualification for disability working allowance) "training for work" also includes any training received on a course which a person attends for 16 hours or more a week, the primary purpose of which is the teaching of occupational or vocational skills.]

AMENDMENT

1. Disability Working Allowance and Income Support (General) Amendment Regulations 1995 (S.I. 1995 No. 482), reg. 2 (April 13, 1995).

GENERAL NOTE

See the notes to s. 129(2A) of the Contributions and Benefits Act.

[¹Days to be disregarded

7B.—(1) For the purposes of section 129(2B)(c) of the Contributions and Benefits Act (days to be disregarded in determining a period of training for work) there shall be disregarded any day on which the claimant was—
  (a) on holiday;
  (b) attending court as a justice of the peace, a party to any proceedings, a witness or a juror;
  (c) suffering from some disease or bodily or mental disablement as a result of which he was unable to attend training for work, or his attendance would have put at risk the health of other persons;
  (d) unable to participate in training for work because—
    (i) he was looking after a child because the person who usually looked after that child was unable to do so;
    (ii) he was looking after a member of his family who was ill;
    (iii) he was required to deal with some domestic emergency; or
    (iv) he was arranging or attending the funeral of his partner or a relative; or
  (e) authorised by the training provider to be absent from training for work.
  (2) For the purposes of paragraph (1)(d)(iv), "relative" means close relative, grandparent, grandchild, uncle, aunt, nephew or niece.]

AMENDMENT

1. Disability Working Allowance and Income Support (General) Amendment Regulations 1995 (S.I. 1995 No. 482), reg. 2 (April 13, 1995).

DEFINITION

"child"—see SSCBA, s. 137(1).
"claimant"—see reg. 2(1).
"close relative"—*ibid.*
"partner"—*ibid.*

GENERAL NOTE

See the notes to s. 129(2B) of the Contributions and Benefits Act.

PART IV

MEMBERSHIP OF A FAMILY

Persons of a prescribed description

8.—(1) Subject to paragraph (2), a person of a prescribed description for the purposes of section 20(11) of the Act [SSCBA, s.137(1)] (meaning of the family) as it applies to disability working allowance is a person aged 16 or over but under 19 who is receiving full-time education within section 2(1)(b) of the

Child Benefit Act 1975 (meaning of child), and in these Regulations such a person is referred to as "a young person".

(2) Paragraph (1) shall not apply to a person—

   (a) who is entitled to income support or would, but for section 20(9) of the Act [SSCBA, s.134(2)] (provision against dual entitlement of members of family), be so entitled;

[¹(aa) who is entitled to income-based jobseeker's allowance or would, but for section 3(1)(d) of the Jobseekers Act 1995 (provision against dual entitlement of members of family), be so entitled;]

   (b) who is receiving advanced education within the meaning of regulation 1(2) of the Child Benefit (General) Regulations 1976; or

   (c) who has ceased to receive full-time education but is to continue to be treated as a child by virtue of regulation 7 of the Child Benefit (General) Regulations 1976.

AMENDMENT

1. Social Security and Child Support (Jobseeker's Allowance) (Consequential Amendments) Regulations 1996 (S.I. 1996 No. 1345), reg. 7(4) (October 7, 1996).

DEFINITION

"the Act"—see reg. 2(1).

GENERAL NOTE

See the notes to reg. 6 of the Family Credit (General) Regulations.

Circumstances in which a person is to be treated as responsible or not responsible for another

9.—(1) Subject to the following provisions of this regulation, a person shall be treated as responsible for a child or young person who is normally living with him.

(2) Where a child or young person spends equal amounts of time in different households, or where there is a question as to which household he is living in, the child or young person shall be treated for the purposes of paragraph (1) as normally living with—

   (a) the person who is receiving child benefit in respect of him; or

   (b) if there is no such person—

      (i) where only one claim for child benefit has been made in respect of him, the person who made that claim, or

      (ii) in any other case the person who has the primary responsibility for him.

(3) For the purposes of these Regulations a child or young person shall be treated as the responsibility of only one person during the period of an award and any person other than the one treated as responsible for the child or young person under the foregoing paragraphs shall be treated as not so responsible.

DEFINITIONS

"child"—see 1986 Act, s.20(11) (SSCBA, s.137(1)).
"young person"—see reg. 2(1), reg. 8.

GENERAL NOTE

See the notes to reg. 7 of the Family Credit (General) Regulations.

Membership of the same household

10.—(1) Except in a case to which paragraph (2) applies, where a claimant or any partner is treated as responsible for a child or young person by virtue of regulation 9 (circumstances where a person is treated as responsible or not responsible for another), that child or young person and any child of that child or young person shall be treated as a member of the claimant's household.

(2) A child or young person shall not be treated as a member of the claimant's household in any case where the child or young person—

(a) is a patient or in residential accommodation on account of physical or mental handicap or physical or mental illness and has been so accommodated for the 12 weeks immediately before the date of claim and is no longer in regular contact with the claimant or any member of the claimant's household; or

(b) is in a foster placement, or in Scotland boarded out, with the claimant or his partner prior to adoption; or

(c) is in a foster placement, or in Scotland boarded out, with the claimant or his partner under a relevant enactment; or

(d) has been placed for adoption with the claimant or his partner pursuant to a decision under the Adoption Agencies Regulations 1983 or the Adoption Agencies (Scotland) Regulations 1984; or

(e) is detained in custody under a sentence imposed by a court.

(3) In this regulation—

(a) "patient" means a person (other than a person who is serving a sentence imposed by a court in a prison or youth custody institution) who is regarded as receiving free in-patient treatment within the meaning of the Social Security (Hospital In-Patients) Regulations 1975;

(b) "relevant enactment" means the Army Act 1955, the Air Force Act 1955, the Naval Discipline Act 1957, the Adoption Act 1958, the Matrimonial Proceedings (Children) Act 1958, the Social Work (Scotland) Act 1968, the Family Law Reform Act 1969, the Children and Young Persons Act 1969, the Matrimonial Causes Act 1973, the Guardianship Act 1973, the Children Act 1975, the Adoption Act 1976, the Domestic Proceedings and Magistrates' Courts Act 1978, the Adoption (Scotland) Act 1978, the Child Care Act 1980 and the Children Act 1989;

(c) "residential accommodation" means accommodation for a person whose stay in the accommodation has become other than temporary which is provided under—

(i) sections 21 to 24 and 26 of the National Assistance Act 1948 (provision of accommodation); or

(ii) section 21(1) of, and paragraph 1 or 2 of Schedule 8 to, the National Health Service Act 1977 (prevention, care and after-care) or, in Scotland, for the purposes of section 27 of the National Health Services (Scotland) Act 1947 (prevention of illness and after-care) or under section 59 of the Social Work (Scotland) Act 1968 (provision of residential and other establishments) or under section 7 of the Mental Health (Scotland) Act 1984 (functions of local authorities).

DEFINITIONS

"child"—see 1986 Act, s.20(11) (SSCBA, s.137(1)).
"claimant"—see reg. 2(1).
"date of claim"—*ibid.*
"partner"—*ibid.*
"young person"—*ibid.*, reg. 8.

GENERAL NOTE

See the notes to reg. 8 of the Family Credit (General) Regulations. Reg. 10 has not been updated to take account of the implementation of the Children Act 1989.

Circumstances in which a person is to be treated as being no longer a member of the same household

11.—[¹(1) Subject to the following provisions of this regulation, where the claimant and any partner of his are living apart from each other they shall be treated as members of the same household unless they do not intend to resume living together.]

(2) Where one of the members of a married or unmarried couple is a hospital patient or detained in custody he shall not be treated, on this account, as ceasing to be a member of the same household as his partner—

(a) unless he has been a patient in a hospital for 52 weeks or more; or

(b) unless he is a patient detained in a hospital provided under section 4 of the National Health Service Act 1977 (special hospitals) or section 90(1) of the Mental Health (Scotland) Act 1984 (provision of hospitals for patients requiring special security); or

(c) unless he is detained in custody whilst serving a sentence of 52 weeks or more imposed by a court,

but shall be treated as not being a member of the same household as his partner wherever the conditions in sub-paragraphs (a), (b) or (c) are fulfilled.

(3) In this regulation "patient" has the same meaning as in regulation 10(3)(a) (membership of the same household).

AMENDMENT

1. Income-related Benefits Schemes (Miscellanous Amendments) (No. 4) Regulations 1993 (S.I. 1993 No. 2119), reg. 38 (October 5, 1993).

DEFINITIONS

"partner"—see reg. 2(1).
"married couple"—see 1986 Act, s.20(11) (SSCBA, s.137(1)).
"unmarried couple"—*ibid.*

GENERAL NOTE

See the notes to reg. 9 of the Family Credit (General) Regulations.

PART V

INCOME AND CAPITAL

Chapter I

General

Calculation of income and capital of members of claimant's family and of a polygamous marriage

12.—(1) The income and capital of a claimant's partner and, subject to regulation 30 (modifications in respect of children and young persons), the income of a child or young person, which by virtue of section 22(5) of the Act [SSCBA, s.136(1)] is to be treated as income and capital of the claimant, shall be calculated or estimated in accordance with the following provisions of this Part in like manner as for the claimant; and any reference to the "claimant" shall, except where the context otherwise requires, be construed, for the purposes of this Part, as if it were a reference to his partner or that child or young person.

(2) Where a claimant or the partner of a claimant is married polygamously to two or more members of the same household—

  (a) the claimant shall be treated as possessing capital and income belonging to each such member and the income of any child or young person who is one of that member's family; and

  (b) the income and capital of that member or, as the case may be, the income of that child or young person shall be calculated in accordance with the following provisions of this Part in like manner as for the claimant or, as the case may be, as for any child or young person who is a member of his family.

DEFINITIONS

  "the Act"—see reg. 2(1).
  "child"—see 1986 Act, s.20(11) (SSCBA, s.137(1)).
  "claimant"—see reg. 2(1).
  "family"—see 1986 Act, s.20(11) (SSCBA, s.137(1)).
  "partner"—see reg. 2(1).
  "young person"—*ibid.*, reg. 8.

GENERAL NOTE

  See the notes to reg. 10 of the Family Credit (General) Regulations.

Calculation of income and capital of students

13. The provisions of Chapters II to VI of this Part (income and capital) shall have effect in relation to students and their partners subject to the modifications set out in Chapter VII thereof (students).

DEFINITIONS

  "partner"—see reg. 2(1).
  "student"—*ibid.*, reg. 41.

Rounding of fractions

14. Where any calculation under this Part results in a fraction of a penny that fraction shall, if it would be to the claimant's advantage, be treated as a penny, otherwise it shall be disregarded.

Chapter II

Normal Weekly Income

Calculation of income on a weekly basis

15.—(1) For the purposes of section 20(6A) of the Act [SSCBA, s.129(1)] (conditions of entitlement to disability working allowance), the income of a claimant shall be calculated on a weekly basis—

   (a) by ascertaining in accordance with this Chapter and Chapter V of this Part (other income) the amount of his normal weekly income; [¹. . .]

   (b) by adding to that amount the weekly income calculated under regulation 40 (calculation of tariff income from capital) [and

[¹(c) by then deducting any relevant child care charges to which regulation 15A (treatment of child care charges) applies from any earnings which form part of the normal weekly income, up to a maximum deduction in respect of the claimant's family of [²whichever of the sums specified in paragraph (1A) below applies in his case] per week.]

[³(1A) The maximum deduction to which paragraph (1)(c) above refers shall be—

   (a) where the claimant's family includes only one child in respect of whom relevant child care charges are paid, £60 per week;

   (b) where the claimant's family includes more than one child in respect of whom relevant child care charges are paid, £100 per week.]

(2) For the purposes of paragraph (1) "income" includes capital treated as income under regulation 28 (capital treated as income) and income which a claimant is treated as possessing under regulation 29 (notional income).

<small>AMENDMENTS</small>

   1. Income-related Benefits Schemes (Miscellaneous Amendments) (No. 4) Regulations 1994 (S.I. 1994 No. 1924), reg. 3(3) (October 4, 1994).

   2. Income-related Benefits (Miscellaneous Amendments) Regulations 1997 (S.I. 1997 No. 2793), reg. 2(1) and (2)(b) (June 2, 1998).

   3. Income-related Benefits (Miscellaneous Amendments) Regulations 1997 (S.I. 1997 No. 2793), reg. 2(3) (June 2, 1998).

<small>DEFINITIONS</small>

   "the Act"—see reg. 2(1).
   "claimant"—*ibid.*, reg. 12(1).
   "earnings"—see reg. 2(1).
   "family"—see 1986 Act, s.20(11) (SSCBA, s.137(1)).
   "relevant child care charges"—see reg. 15A.

<small>GENERAL NOTE</small>

   See the notes to reg. 13 of the Family Credit (General) Regulations.

   Note that there will be changes to the rules for the treatment of child care costs when disability working allowance is replaced by disabled person's tax credit on October 5, 1999. See the 1999 Supplement to this book for details.

[¹Treatment of child care charges

   15A.—(1) This regulation applies where a claimant is incurring; [⁵or in the case of a claimant to whom paragraph (6A) applies, will incur] relevant child care charges and—

   (a) is a lone parent and is engaged in remunerative work;

   (b) is a member of a couple both of whom are engaged in remunerative work; or

   (c) is a member of a couple where one member is engaged in remunerative work and the other member is incapacitated.

   (2) In this regulation—

"local authority" means, in relation to England and Wales, the council of a county or district, a metropolitan district, a London Borough, the Common Council of the City of London or the Council of the Isles of Scilly or, in relation to Scotland, a regional, islands or district council;

"relevant child care charges" means the charges paid by the claimant for care provided for any child of the claimant's family [³ in respect of the period beginning on that child's date of birth and ending on the day preceding the first Tuesday in September following that child's [⁴twelfth birthday]], other than charges paid in respect of the child's compulsory education, [²or charges paid by a claimant to a partner or by a partner to a claimant in respect of any child for whom either or any of them is responsible in accordance with regulation 9 (circumstances in which a person is to be treated as responsible or not responsible for another),] where the care is provided—

(a) by persons registered under section 71 of the Children Act 1989 (registration of child minders and persons providing day care for young children);

(b) for children [³in respect of the period beginning on their eighth birthday and ending on the day preceding the first Tuesday in September following their [⁴twelfth birthday]], out of school hours, by a school on school premises or by a local authority; or

(c) by a child care scheme operating on Crown property where registration under section 71 of the Children Act 1989 is not required, [²or

(d) in schools or establishments which are exempted from registration under section 71 of the Children Act 1989 by virtue of section 71(16) of and paragraph 3 or 4 of Schedule 9 to that Act,]

and shall be calculated on a weekly basis in accordance with paragraphs (3) to (6) [⁵or, in the case of a claimant to whom paragraph (6A) applies, with paragraphs (6B) and (6C)];

"school term-time" means the school term-time applicable to the child for whom care is provided.

[³(2A) In paragraph (2)—

(a) the age of a child referred to in that paragraph shall be determined by reference to the age of the child at the date on which the period under section 129(6) of the Contributions and Benefits Act (period of award) begins;

(b) "the first Tuesday in September" means the Tuesday which first occurs in the month of September in any year.]

[⁵(c) in the definition of "relevant child care charges" the words "charges paid" shall be taken to include charges which will be incurred and to which paragraph (6A) applies.]

(3) Subject to paragraphs (4) to (6), relevant child care charges shall be calculated in accordance with the formula—

$$\frac{X + Y}{52}$$

where—

X is the average weekly charge paid for child care in the most recent 4 complete weeks which fall in school term-time in respect of the child or children concerned, multiplied by 39; and

Y is the average weekly charge paid for child care in the most recent 2 complete weeks which fall out of school term-time in respect of that child or those children, multiplied by 13.

(4) Subject to paragraph (5), where child care charges are being incurred in respect of a child who does not yet attend school, the relevant child care charges

shall mean the average weekly charge paid for care provided in respect of that child in the most recent 4 complete weeks.

(5) Where in any case the charges in respect of child care are paid monthly, the average weekly charge for the purposes of paragraph (3) shall be established—

(a) where the charges are for a fixed monthly amount, by multiplying that amount by 12 and dividing the product by 52;

(b) where the charges are for variable monthly amounts, by aggregating the charges for the previous 12 months and dividing the total by 52.

(6) In a case where there is no information or insufficient information for establishing the average weekly charge paid for child care in accordance with paragraphs (3) to (5), the average weekly charge for care shall be estimated in accordance with information provided by the child minder or person providing the care or, if such information is not available, in accordance with information provided by the claimant.

[⁵(6A) Where a claimant—

(a) has entered into an agreement for the provision of child care; and

(b) will under that agreement incur relevant child care charges in respect of child care during the period of the disability working allowance award, the weekly charge for child care shall be calculated in accordance with paragraphs (6B) and (6C), based upon a written estimate of the relevant future charges provided by the claimant and child minder or other child care provider.

(6B) Subject to paragraph (6C), relevant child care charges which fall under paragraph (6A) shall be calculated in accordance with the formula—

$$\frac{X + Y}{52}$$

where—

X is the weekly estimate provided by the child minder or other child care provider for child care in those weeks which will fall in school term-time in respect of the child or children concerned, multiplied by 39; and

Y is the weekly estimate provided by the child minder or other child care provider for child care in those weeks which will fall out of school term-time in respect of the child or children concerned, multiplied by 13.

(6C) Where relevant child care charges fall under paragraph (6A) and they are in respect of a child who does not attend achool, the relevant child care charges shall mean the weekly estimate provided by the child minder or other child care provider multiplied by the number of weeks during the period of the disability working allowance award in which relevant child care charges will be paid, divided by 26.]

(7) For the purposes of paragraph (1)(c) the other member of a couple is incapacitated where—

(a) either council tax benefit or housing benefit is payable under Part VII of the Contributions and Benefits Act to the other member or his partner and the applicable amount of the person entitled to the benefit includes—

(i) a disability premium; or

(ii) a higher pensioner premium by virtue of the satisfaction of—

(aa) in the case of council tax benefit, paragraph 11(2)(b) of Schedule 1 to the Council Tax Benefit (General) Regulations 1992;

(bb) in the case of housing benefit, paragraph 10(2)(b) of Schedule 2 to the Housing Benefit (General) Regulations 1987,

on account of the other member's incapacity; [²or either regulation 13A(1)(c) of the Council Tax Benefit (General) Regulations 1992 (treatment of child care charges) or, as the case may be, regulation 21A(1)(c) of the Housing Benefit (General) Regulations 1987 (treatment of child care charges) applies in that person's case;]

(b) there is payable in respect of him one or more of the following pensions or allowances—
   (i) invalidity pension under section 33, 40 or 41 of the Contributions and Benefits Act 1992;
   (ii) attendance allowance under section 64 of that Act;
   (iii) severe disablement allowance under section 68 of that Act;
   (iv) disability living allowance under section 71 of that Act;
   (v) increase of disablement pension under section 104 of that Act;
   (vi) a pension increase under a war pension scheme or an industrial injuries scheme which is analogous to an allowance or increase of disablement pension under head (ii), (iv) or (v) above;
(c) a pension or allowance to which head (ii), (iv), (v) or (vi) of sub-paragraph (b) above refers was payable on account of his incapacity but has ceased to be payable in consequence of his becoming a patient within the meaning of regulation 10(3)(a) (membership of the same household);
(d) sub-paragraph (b) or (c) above would apply to him if the legislative provisions referred to in those sub-paragraphs were provisions under any corresponding enactment having effect in Northern Ireland; or
(e) he has an invalid carriage or other vehicle provided to him by the Secretary of State under section 5(2)(a) of and Schedule 2 to the National Health Service Act 1977 or under section 46 of the National Health Service (Scotland) Act 1978 or provided by the Department of Health and Social Services for Northern Ireland under Article 30(1) of the Health and Personal Social Services (Northern Ireland) Order 1972.]

AMENDMENTS

1. Income-related Benefits Schemes (Miscellaneous Amendments) (No. 4) Regulations 1994 (S.I. 1994 No. 1924), reg. 3(4) (October 4, 1994).
2. Income-related Benefits Schemes (Miscellaneous Amendments) Regulations 1995 (S.I. 1995 No. 516), reg. 5 (April 11, 1995).
3. Income-related Benefits and Jobseeker's Allowance (Personal Allowances for Children and Young Persons) (Amendment) Regulations 1996 (S.I. 1996 No. 2545), reg. 7 (October 7, 1997).
4. Income-related Benefits (Miscellaneous Amendments) Regulations 1997 (S.I. 1997 No. 2793), reg. 2(4) (June 2, 1998).
5. Social Security Benefits (Miscellaneous Amendments) Regulations 1999 (S.I. 1999 No. 714), reg. 5 (April 6, 1999).

DEFINITIONS

"claimant"—see reg. 2(1).
"Contributions and Benefits Act"—*ibid.*
"Crown property"—*ibid.*
"lone parent"—*ibid.*
"partner"—*ibid.*

GENERAL NOTE

See the notes to reg. 13A of the Family Credit (General) Regulations.

Normal weekly earnings of employed earners

16.—(1) Subject to regulation 19, where the claimant's income consists of earnings from employment as an employed earner, his normal weekly earnings shall be determined [²by taking account of his earnings from that employment which are received in the assessment period relevant to his case, whether the amount so received was earned in respect of that period or not, and in accordance with the following provisions of this regulation.]

(2) Subject to paragraph (7), where the claimant is paid weekly, his normal weekly earnings shall be determined by [²taking account of] his earnings over 5 consecutive weeks in the 6 weeks immediately preceding the week in which the date of claims falls.

(3) Subject to paragraph (7), where at the date of claim there is a trade dispute or period of short-time working at the claimant's place of employment, then his normal weekly earnings shall be determined by [²taking account of] his earnings over the 5 weeks immediately preceding the start of that dispute or period of short-time working.

(4) Subject to paragraph (7), where the claimant is paid monthly, his normal weekly earnings shall be determined by [²taking account of] his earnings—

(a) over a period of 2 months immediately preceding the week in which the date of claim falls; or

(b) where, at the date of claim, there is a trade dispute or a period of short-time working at his place of employment, over a period of 2 months immediately preceding the date of the start of that dispute or period of short-time working.

(5) Subject to paragraph (7), whether or not paragraph (2), (3) or (4) applies, where a claimant's earnings fluctuate or are not likely to represent his weekly earnings, his normal weekly earnings shall be determined by [²taking account of] his weekly earnings over such other period preceding the week in which the date of claim falls as may, in any particular case, enable his normal weekly earnings to be determined more accurately.

(6) Where a claimant's earnings include a bonus or commission which is paid within 52 weeks preceding the week in which the date of claim falls, and the bonus or commission is paid separately or relates to a period longer than a period relating to the other earnings with which it is paid, his normal weekly earnings shall be treated as including an amount calculated in accordance with regulation 23 (calculation of bonus or commission).

(7) Where at the date of claim—

(a) the claimant—

(i) has been in his employment; or

(ii) after a continuous period of interruption exceeding 13 weeks, has resumed his employment; or

(iii) has changed the number of hours for which he is contracted to work; and

(b) the period of his employment or the period since he resumed his employment or the period since the change in the number of hours took place, as the case may be, [¹is less than the assessment period in paragraphs (2) to (5) appropriate in his case],

his normal weekly earnings shall be determined in accordance with paragraph (8).

(8) In a case to which this paragraph applies, the Secretary of State shall require the claimant's employer to furnish an estimate of the claimant's average likely earnings for the period for which he will normally be paid and the claimant's normal weekly earnings shall be determined by [²taking account of] that estimate.

(9) For the purposes of this regulation—

(a) the claimant's earnings shall be calculated in accordance with Chapter III of this Part;

(b) "a period of short-time working" means a continuous period not exceeding 13 weeks during which the claimant is not required by his employer to be available to work the full number of hours normal in his case under the terms of his employment.

AMENDMENTS

1. Income-related Benefits Schemes and Social Fund (Miscellaneous Amendments) Regulations 1996 (S.I. 1996 No. 1944), reg. 3(2) (October 8, 1996).
2. Disability Working Allowance and Family Credit (General) Amendment Regulations 1996 (S.I. 1996 No. 3137), reg. 2(3) (January 7, 1997).

DEFINITIONS

"claim"—see reg. 2(1).
"claimant"—*ibid.*, reg. 12(1).
"earnings"—see reg. 2(1), reg. 21.
"employed earner" see reg. 2(1).
"trade dispute"—see 1986 Act, s.84(1).
"week"—see reg. 2(1).

GENERAL NOTE

Although the test of hours of remunerative work under reg. 6 is the same as the April 1992 family credit test, the method of calculation of earnings for employees is not in line with the April 1992 form of reg. 14 of the Family Credit (General) Regulations. Instead, a slightly refined version of the pre-April 1992 family credit test is used (for which, see p. 307 of the 1991 edition).

Paras. (2) to (4) supply the general rules for defining the period over which the earnings of weekly paid and monthly paid employees are to be calculated. There appears to be no provision for those paid regularly at different intervals. Para. (5) provides a general power to use a different period to produce a more accurate figure. Para. (6) deals with bonuses and commission. Paras. (7) and (8) contain special rules where the person has recently started work or changed contractual hours. Reg. 19 allows certain weeks within the period fixed under reg. 16 to be discarded from the calculation.

Regs. 21 to 23 define what counts as earnings.

Paragraphs (2) and (3)

Normally, for weekly paid employees, earnings are to be calculated over five consecutive weeks (*i.e.* Sunday to Saturday) in the six weeks immediately before the week of claim. The effect is that either the first or the last of the six weeks can be discarded, presumably whichever is more favourable to the claimant. A different period can be taken under the conditions of para. (5) and weeks within the period discarded under reg. 19.

If, at the date of claim, there is a trade dispute or a period of short-time working (defined in para. (9)) at the person's place of employment, the six weeks immediately before the beginning of that interruption must be taken (para. (3)). It is not necessary that there should be a stoppage of work, merely a trade dispute (presumably as defined in s.27 of the Contributions and Benefits Act). Thus a work-to-rule or overtime ban at the person's own place of employment (also defined in s.27) will affect the choice of period. Para. (3) is only triggered by the circumstances at the date of claim. If earnings in the weeks which would otherwise form the period of assessment are affected by a dispute or period of short-time working which has finished by the date of claim, then para. (5) or (7) or reg. 19 might need consideration.

Paragraph (4)

The period of assessment for the monthly paid is set in the same way as under paras. (2) and (3), except that the standard period is the two months immediately preceding the week of claim.

Paragraph (5)

Where a person's earnings fluctuate or are not likely to represent his weekly earnings a different period from that produced by paras. (2) to (4) may be taken. Para. (5) may cover employees paid otherwise than by the week or month, but not, it seems, if there is absolutely regular payment. The equivalent family credit provision had caused considerable difficulties and its simplification in April 1992 was overdue. Those difficulties remain for disability working allowance.

The two conditions are alternative. On fluctuation, the immediate problem is over what period fluctuation is to be considered. Arguably, if there is no fluctuation within the period fixed by paras. (2) to (4) there is no warrant for choosing another period. On the second condition, there seems to be a circular process required. In order to determine that earnings in the period fixed by paras. (2) to (4) are not likely to represent the person's weekly earnings, a standard of normality or usualness has to be set up, but no basis is provided for that standard. Only when the condition is satisfied can the authorities look at a different period for a more accurate figure. However, despite the logical difficulties, a similar process was approved for family income supplement purposes by the Court of Appeal in *Lowe v. Adjudication Officer* [1985] 2 All E.R. 903 (*R(FIS) 2/85*) and the Commissioner in *R(FIS) 1/87*. In *Lowe* the claimant was on strike. In *R(FIS) 1/87* the claimant was on maternity leave. It was found that during the periods affected by these events, the claimant, if asked what her/his normal earnings were, would have replied that normally they were X, but at present they were less because of the strike/maternity leave. Perhaps this is the only sort of test which can be used, which will now have to be applied in a context of a 26 week award, rather than the 52 weeks of family income supplement. There is a very large element of judgment involved.

Once one of the conditions is satisfied, another period should be chosen only if it will enable normal weekly earnings to be more accurately determined. Thus there is a burden on the AO to show that some other period will produce a more accurate figure than the basic five weeks or two months (see *R(FIS) 1/81* and *R(FIS) 2/83*).

Paragraph (6)
There is a special rule for payments of bonus or commission paid separately from other earnings or in relation to different periods. See regs. 19(a)(ii) and 23.

Paragraphs (7) and (8)
There is a special rule where a person has been in his employment for less than nine weeks. Then the earnings figure is to be based on estimates from the employer of average likely earnings. The same rule applies to resumption of employment after an interruption of more than 13 weeks or to a change in contractual hours. What counts as an interruption is far from clear. It clearly does not require the contract of employment to be terminated. Could it cover any period of non-working, such as absences for sickness, pregnancy, personal reasons, strikes, holidays, etc.?

Normal weekly earnings of self-employed earners

17.—(1) Subject to regulation 19 (periods to be disregarded), where a claimant's income consists of earnings from employment as a self-employed earner, his normal weekly earnings shall be determined, subject to paragraph (2), by reference to his weekly earnings from that employment—
   (a) except where sub-paragraph (b) applies, over a period of 26 weeks immediately preceding the week in which the date of claim falls; or
   (b) where the claimant provides in respect of the employment a profit and loss account and, where appropriate, a trading account or a balance sheet or both, and the profit and loss account is in respect of a period of at least 6 months but not exceeding 15 months and that period terminates within the 12 months preceding the date of claim, over that period; or
   (c) over such other period of weeks [¹or months] preceding the week in which the date of claims falls as may, in any particular case, enable his normal weekly earnings to be determined more accurately.
   (2) In paragraph (1)(b)—
   (a) "balance sheet" means a statement of the financial position of the employment disclosing its assets, liabilities and capital at the end of the period in question;
   (b) "profit and loss account" means a financial statement showing the net profit or loss of the employment for the period in question; and
   (c) "trading account" means a financial statement showing the revenue from sales, the cost of those sales and the gross profit arising during the period in question.
   (3) Subject to regulation 19, where the claimant has been in employment as a self-employed earner for less than the period specified in paragraph (1)(a) his normal weekly earnings shall be determined by reference to an estimate of his likely weekly earnings over the 26 weeks next following the date of claim.
   (4) For the purposes of this regulation, the claimant's earnings shall be calculated in accordance with Chapter IV of this Part.

AMENDMENT

1. Income-related Benefits Schemes (Miscellaneous Amendments) (No. 5) Regulations 1994 (S.I. 1994 No. 2139), reg. 3 (October 4, 1994.)

DEFINITIONS

> "claim"—see reg. 2(1).
> "claimant"—*ibid.*, reg. 8.
> "earnings"—see reg. 2(1), reg. 24.
> "self-employed earner"—see reg. 2(1).
> "week"—*ibid.*

GENERAL NOTE

See the notes to reg. 15 of the Family Credit (General) Regulations, although para. (3) is a simplification of reg. 15(2).

Normal weekly income other than earnings

18.—(1) Subject to [¹paragraphs (2) and (2A)], [²where a claimant's normal weekly income does not consist of earnings, or includes income that does not consist of earnings, that income] shall be determined by [³taking account of] his weekly income over a period of 26 weeks immediately preceding the week in which the date of claim falls or over such period immediately preceding that week as may, in any particular case, enable his normal weekly income to be determined more accurately.

(2) Where a claimant's income consists of any payments made by a person, whether under a court order or not, for the maintenance of any member of [¹the claimant's family], and those payments are made or due to be made at regular intervals, his normal weekly income shall [¹, except where paragraph (2A) applies,] be determined—

    (a) if before the date of claim those payments are made at regular intervals [²and of regular amounts], by [³taking account of] the normal weekly amount;

    (b) if they are not so made, by [³taking account of] the average of such payments received in the 13 weeks immediately preceding the week in which the date of claim falls.

[¹(2A) Where a claimant's income consists of child support maintenance, his normal weekly income in respect of that maintenance shall be determined—

    (a) if before the date of claim those maintenance payments are made at regular intervals [²and of regular amounts], by [³taking account of] the normal weekly amount;

    (b) if they are not so made, [²except in a case to which sub-paragraph (c) applies], by [³taking account of] the average of such payments received in the 13 weeks immediately preceding the week in which the date of claim falls,

    [²(c) where the maintenance assessment has been notified to the claimant under regulation 10 of the Child Support (Maintenance Assessment Procedure) Regulations 1992 during the 13 weeks immediately preceding the week of claim, by [³taking account of] the average of such payments, calculated on a weekly basis, received in the interim period,]

and if the resulting sum exceeds the amount of child support maintenance due under the maintenance assessment, the normal weekly income shall be the amount due under the maintenance assessment.]

(3) For the purposes of this regulation, income other than earnings shall be calculated in accordance with Chapter V of this Part.

[¹(4) In this regulation—
(a) "child support maintenance" means such periodical payments as are referred to in section 3(6) of the Child Support Act 1991;
(b) "maintenance assessment" has the same meaning as in the Child Support Act 1991 by virtue of section 54 of that Act];
[²(c) "the interim period" means the week in which the date of notification of the maintenance assessment falls and the subsequent period up to and including the week immediately preceding the week of claim.]

AMENDMENTS

1. Income-related Benefits Schemes (Miscellaneous Amendments) Regulations 1993 (S.I. 1993 No. 315), reg. 17 (April 13, 1993).
2. Income-related Benefits Schemes (Miscellaneous Amendments) (No. 4) Regulations 1993 (S.I. 1993 No. 2119), reg. 39 (October 5, 1993).
3. Disability Working Allowance and Family Credit (General) Amendment Regulations 1996 (S.I. 1996 No. 3137), reg. 2(4) (January 7, 1997).

DEFINITIONS

"claim"—see reg. 2(1).
"claimant"—*ibid.*, reg. 12(1).
"date of claim"—see reg. 2(1).
"earnings"—*ibid.*, regs. 21 and 24.
"family"—see 1986 Act, s.20(11) (SSCBA, s.137(1)).
"payment"—see reg. 2(1).
"week"—*ibid.*

GENERAL NOTE

See the notes to reg. 16 of the Family Credit (General) Regulations.

Periods to be disregarded

19. For the purposes of ascertaining a claimant's normal weekly earnings there shall be disregarded—
(a) for the purposes of regulation 16(1) (normal weekly earnings of employed earners), in the case of an employed earner—
(i) any period in the assessment period where the earnings of the claimant are irregular or unusual;
(ii) any period in the assessment period in which a bonus or commission to which regulation 16(6) applies is paid where that bonus or commission is in respect of a period longer than the period relating to the other earnings with which it is paid.
(b) in the case of a self-employed earner, any week or period of weeks in the assessment period during which no activities have been carried out for the purposes of the business,
and his normal weekly earnings shall be determined by reference to his weekly earnings in the remainder of that period and in such a case any reference in these Regulations to a claimant's assessment period shall be construed as a reference to the latter period.

DEFINITIONS

"assessment period"—see reg. 2(1).
"claimant"—*ibid.*, reg. 12(1).
"earnings"—see reg. 2(1).
"employed earner"—*ibid.*

"self-employed earner"—*ibid.*
"week"—*ibid.*

GENERAL NOTE

Paragraph (a)
Para. (a) allows modification of the period of assessment established for an employee by reg. 16. It requires particular weeks to be discarded from that period. Sub-para. (i) applies to weeks in which earnings are "irregular or unusual." This is a very vague test. The meaning of "irregular" is particularly obscure when other provisions deal with fluctuating earnings. It is an issue of judgment when earnings are far enough away from the norm to be "unusual." There appears to be no necessity for any identifiable special factor to have caused the unusualness, but no doubt weeks in which, say, large tax refunds or accrued holiday pay are paid, or large deductions are made would be excluded. For family credit from April 1992, the regulations require any week in which the earnings deviate from the average by at least 20 per cent to be discarded (Family Credit (General) Regulations, reg. 20).

Sub-para. (ii) covers bonus and commission payments under reg. 16(6).

Paragraph (b)
See reg. 17 of the Family Credit Regulations.

Calculation of weekly amount of income

20. [¹—(1) For the purposes of regulations 16 (normal weekly earnings of employed earners) and 18 (normal weekly income other than earnings), where the claimant's pay period or, as the case may be, the period in respect of which a payment is made—]
  (a) does not exceed a week, the weekly amount shall be the amount of that payment;
  (b) exceeds a week, the weekly amount shall be determined—
      (i) in a case where that period is a month, by multiplying the amount of the payment by 12 and dividing the product by 52;
      (ii) in a case where that period is 3 months, by multiplying the amount of the payment by 4 and dividing the product by 52;
      (iii) in a case where that period is a year, by dividing the amount of the payment by 52;
      (iv) in any other case, by multiplying the amount of the payment by 7 and dividing the product by the number equal to the number of days in the period in respect of which it is made.
(2) For the purposes of regulation 17 (normal weekly earnings of self-employed earners) the weekly amount of earnings of a claimant shall be determined—
  (a) except where sub-paragraph (b) applies, by dividing his earnings received in the assessment period or, as the case may be, estimated for that period by the number equal to the number of weeks in that period;
  (b) in a case where regulation 17(1)(b) applies, by multiplying his earnings relevant to the assessment period (whether or not received in that period) by 7 and dividing the product by the number equal to the number of days in that period.

AMENDMENT

1. Disability Working Allowance and Family Credit (General) Amendment Regulations 1996 (S.I. 1996 No. 3137), reg. 2(5) (January 7, 1997).

"assessment period"—see reg. 2(1).
"claimant"—*ibid*.
"payment"—*ibid*.
"pay period"—*ibid*.
"week"—*ibid*.

GENERAL NOTE

See the notes to reg. 32(1) of the Income Support (General) Regulations, except for para. (2).

Chapter III

Employed Earners

Earnings of employed earners

21.—(1) Subject to paragraph (2), "earnings" means in the case of employment as an employed earner, any remuneration or profit derived from that employment and includes—

(a) any bonus or commission;

(b) any holiday pay except any payable more than 4 weeks after termination of the employment;

(c) any payment by way of a retainer;

(d) any payment made by the claimant's employer in respect of any expenses not wholly, exclusively and necessarily incurred in the performance of the duties of the employment, including any payment made by the claimant's employer in respect of—

(i) travelling expenses incurred by the claimant between his home and place of employment;

(ii) expenses incurred by the claimant under arrangements made for the care of a member of his family owing to the claimant's absence from home;

(e) any award of compensation made under section 68(2) or 71(2)(a) of the Employment Protection (Consolidation) Act 1978 (remedies and compensation for unfair dismissal);

(f) any such sum as is referred to in section 18(2) of the Social Security (Miscellaneous Provisions) Act 1977 (certain sums to be earnings for social security purposes);

(g) any statutory sick pay under Part I of the Social Security and Housing Benefits Act 1982 [SSCBA, Part XI];

(h) any statutory sick pay under Part II of the Social Security (Northern Ireland) Order 1982;

(i) any payment made by the claimant's employer in respect of any Community Charge [¹or council tax] to which the claimant is subject.

(2) Earnings shall not include—

(a) subject to paragraph (3), any payment in kind;

(b) any payment in respect of expenses wholly, exclusively and necessarily incurred in the performance of the duties of the employment;

(c) any occupational pension;

[²(d) any statutory maternity pay or a corresponding benefit under any enactment having effect in Northern Ireland.]

(3) Where living accommodation is provided for a claimant by reason of his employment, the claimant shall be treated as being in receipt of weekly earnings of an amount equal to—

(a) where no charge is made in respect of the provision of that accommodation, £12;

(b) where a charge is made and that weekly charge is less than £12, the amount of the difference,

except that where the claimant satisfies the adjudication officer that the weekly value to him of the provision of that accommodation is an amount less than the amount in sub-paragraph (a) or (b), as the case may be, he shall be treated as being in receipt of that lesser value.

AMENDMENTS

1. Income-related Benefits Schemes (Miscellaneous Amendments) Regulations 1993 (S.I. 1993 No. 315), Sched., para. 13 (April 1, 1993).

2. Income-related Benefits Schemes (Miscellaneous Amendments) Regulations 1993 (S.I. 1993 No. 315), reg. 18 (April 13, 1993).

DEFINITIONS

"the Act"—see reg. 2(1).
"claimant"—*ibid.*, reg. 12(1).
"employed earner"—see reg. 2(1).
"family"—see 1986 Act, s.20(11) (SSCBA, s.137(1)).
"occupational pension"—see reg. 2(1).
"payment"—*ibid.*
"week"—*ibid.*

GENERAL NOTE

See the notes to reg. 19 of the Family Credit (General) Regulations.

Calculation of net earnings of employed earners

22.—(1) For the purposes of regulation 16 (normal weekly earnings of employed earners), the earnings of a claimant derived or likely to be derived from employment as an employed earner to be taken into account shall, subject to paragraph (2), be his net earnings.

(2) There shall be disregarded from a claimant's net earnings, any sum, where applicable, specified in Schedule 2.

(3) For the purposes of paragraph (1), net earnings shall, except where paragraph (4) applies, be calculated by taking into account the gross earnings of the claimant from that employment over the assessment period, less—

(a) any amount deducted from those earnings by way of—
   (i) income tax;
   (ii) primary Class 1 contributions under the Social Security Act [SSCBA]; and

(b) one-half of any sum paid by the claimant [⁴in respect of a pay period] by way of a contribution towards an occupational or personal pension scheme.

(4) Where the earnings of a claimant are estimated under paragraph (8) of regulation 16 (normal weekly earnings of employed earners), his net earnings shall be calculated by taking into account those earnings over the assessment period, less—

(a) an amount in respect of income tax equivalent to an amount calculated by applying to those earnings [¹the lower rate of tax or, as the case may be, the lower rate and the basic rate of tax] in the year of assessment in which the claim was made less only the personal relief to which the claimant is entitled under sections 257(1), (6) and (7) and 259 of the Income and Corporation Taxes Act 1988 (personal relief) as is appropri-

1001

ate to his circumstances; but, if the assessment period is less than a year, ['the earnings to which the lower rate [³. . .] of tax is to be applied and] the amount of the personal relief deductible under this sub-paragraph shall be calculated on a pro rata basis;

[²(b) where the weekly amount of those earnings equals or exceeds the lower earnings limit, an amount representing primary Class 1 contributions under the Contributions and Benefits Act, calculated by applying to those earnings the initial and main primary percentages applicable at the date of claim in accordance with section 8(1)(a) and (b) of that Act; and]

[⁴(c) one half of any sum which would be payable by the claimant by way of a contribution towards an occupational or personal pension scheme, if the earnings so estimated were actual earnings.]

AMENDMENTS

1. Income-related Benefits Schemes (Miscellaneous Amendments) (No. 3) Regulations 1992 (S.I. 1992 No. 2155), Sched., para. 4 (October 5, 1992).
2. Income-related Benefits Schemes (Miscellaneous Amendments) Regulations 1994 (S.I. 1994 No. 527), reg. 23 (April 12, 1994).
3. Income-related Benefits Schemes (Miscellaneous Amendments) (No. 5) Regulations 1994 (S.I. 1994 No. 2139), reg. 4 (October 4, 1994).
4. Income-related Benefits Schemes (Miscellaneous Amendments) (No. 5) Regulations 1994 (S.I. 1994 No. 2139), reg. 5 (October 4, 1994).

DEFINITIONS

"assessment period"—see reg. 2(1).
"claimant"—*ibid.*, reg. 12(1).
"date of claim"—see reg. 2(1).
"earnings"—*ibid.*
"employed earner"—*ibid.*
"lower rate"—*ibid.*
"occupational pension scheme"—see 1986 Act, s.84(1) (PSA, s.1).
"pay period"—see reg. 2(1).
"personal pension scheme"—*ibid.*
"Social Security Act"—*ibid.*
"year of assessment"—*ibid.*

GENERAL NOTE

See the notes to reg. 20 of the Family Credit (General) Regulations.

Calculation of bonus or commission

23. Where a claimant's earnings include a bonus or commission to which paragraph (6) of regulation 16 (normal weekly earnings of employed earners) applies that part of his earnings shall be calculated by aggregating any payments of bonus or commission and ['deducting from it—]

(a) an amount in respect of income tax equivalent to an amount calculated by applying to that part of the earnings the basic rate of tax in the year of assessment in which the claim is made; and

[²(b) an amount representing primary Class 1 contributions under the Contributions and Benefits Act, calculated by applying to that part of the earnings the main primary percentage applicable at the date of claim; and]

(c) one-half of any sum payable by the claimant in respect of that part of the earnings by way of a contribution towards an occupational or personal pension ['scheme;

and dividing the resulting sum by 52.]

AMENDMENTS

1. Income-related Benefits Schemes (Miscellaneous Amendments) (No. 3) Regulations 1992 (S.I. 1992 No. 2155), Sched., para. 5 (October 5, 1992).
2. Income-related Benefits Schemes (Miscellaneous Amendments) Regulations 1994 (S.I. 1994 No. 527), reg. 24 (April 12, 1994).

DEFINITIONS

"claimant"—see reg. 2(1).
"date of claim"—*ibid.*
"occupational pension scheme"—see 1986 Act, s.84(1) (PSA, s.1).
"personal pension scheme"—see reg. 2(1).
"Social Security Act"—*ibid.*
"year of assessment"—*ibid.*

GENERAL NOTE

See the notes to reg. 20A of the Family Credit (General) Regulations. Reg. 23(c) applies to contributions to personal pension schemes as well as to occupational pension schemes.

Chapter IV

Self-Employed Earners

Earnings of self-employed earners

24.—(1) Subject to [¹paragraphs (2) and (3)], "earnings", in the case of employment as a self-employed earner, means the gross receipts of the employment and shall include any allowance paid under section 2 of the Employment and Training Act 1973 or section 2 of the Enterprise and New Towns (Scotland) Act 1990 to the claimant for the purpose of assisting him in carrying on his business unless at the date of claim the allowance has been terminated.

(2) Where a claimant is employed in providing board and lodging accommodation for which a charge is payable, any income consisting of payments of such a charge shall only be taken into account under this Chapter as earnings if it forms a major part of the total of the claimant's weekly income less any sums disregarded under Schedule 3 other than under paragraph 38 of that Schedule.

[¹(3) "Earnings" shall not include any payments to which paragraph 24 of Schedule 3 refers (sums to be disregarded in the calculation of income other than earnings).]

AMENDMENT

1. Income-related Benefits Schemes (Miscellaneous Amendments) (No. 5) Regulations 1994 (S.I. 1994 No. 2139), reg. 6 (October 4, 1994).

DEFINITIONS

"claimant"—see reg. 2(1), reg. 12(1).
"date of claim"—see reg. 2(1).
"payment"—*ibid.*
"self-employed earner"—*ibid.*

See the notes to reg. 21 of the Family Credit (General) Regulations.

Calculation of net profit of self-employed earners

25.—(1) For the purposes of regulation 17 (normal weekly earnings of self-employed earners), the earnings of a claimant to be taken into account shall be—
- (a) in the case of a self-employed earner who is engaged in employment on his own account, the net profit derived from that employment;
- (b) in the case of a self-employed earner whose employment is carried on in partnership or is that of a share fisherman within the meaning of the Social Security (Mariners' Benefits) Regulations 1975, his share of the net profit derived from that employment less—
    - (i) an amount in respect of income tax and social security contributions payable under the Social Security Act [SSCBA] calculated in accordance with [¹regulation 26] (deduction of tax and contributions for self-employed earners); and
    - (ii) [³one half of the amount in respect of any qualifying premium calculated in accordance with paragraph (15)].

(2) There shall be disregarded from a claimant's net profit any sum, where applicable, specified in Schedule 2.

(3) For the purposes of paragraph (1)(a) the net profit of the employment shall, except where paragraph (4), (11) or (12) applies, be calculated by taking into account the earnings of the employment received in the assessment period, less—
- (a) subject to paragraphs (7) to (9), any expenses wholly and exclusively defrayed in that period for the purposes of that employment;
- (b) an amount in respect of—
    - (i) income tax; and
    - (ii) social security contributions payable under the Social Security Act [SSCBA], calculated in accordance with regulation 26 (deduction of tax and contributions for self-employed earners); and
- (c) [³one half of the amount in respect of any qualifying premium calculated in accordance with paragraph (15)].

(4) For the purposes of paragraph (1)(a), in a case where the assessment period is determined under regulation 17(1)(b), the net profit of the employment shall, except where paragraph (11) applies, be calculated by taking into account the earnings of the employment relevant to that period (whether or not received in that period), less—
- (a) [¹subject to paragraphs (7) to (10)], any expenses relevant to that period (whether or not defrayed in that period) and which were wholly and exclusively incurred for the purposes of that employment;
- (b) an amount in respect of—
    - (i) income tax; and
    - (ii) social security contributions payable under the Social Security Act [SSCBA], calculated in accordance with regulation 26; and
- (c) [³one half of the amount in respect of any qualifying premium calculated in accordance with paragraph (15)].

(5) For the purposes of [¹paragraph] (1)(b) the net profit of the employment shall, except where [¹paragraph] (6), (11) or (12) applies, be calculated by taking into account the earnings of the employment received in the assessment period less, subject to paragraphs (7) to (9), any expenses wholly and exclusively defrayed in that period for the purposes of that employment.

(6) For the purposes of paragraph (1)(b), in a case where the assessment

period is determined [¹under regulation 17(1)(b) (normal weekly earnings of self-employed earners)], the net profit of the employment shall, except where paragraph (11) applies, be calculated by taking into account the earnings of the employment relevant to that period (whether or not received in that period) less, subject to paragraphs (7) to (9), any expenses relevant to that period (whether or not defrayed in that period) and which were wholly and exclusively incurred for the purposes of that employment.

(7) Subject to paragraph (8), no deduction shall be made under paragraphs (3)(a), (4)(a), (5) or (6), as the case may be, in respect of—
  (a) any capital expenditure;
  (b) the depreciation of any capital asset;
  (c) any sum employed, or intended to be employed, in the setting up or expansion of the employment;
  (d) any loss incurred before the beginning of the assessment period;
  (e) the repayment of capital on any loan taken out for the purposes of the employment;
  (f) any expenses incurred in providing business entertainment.

(8) A deduction shall be made under paragraphs (3)(a), (4)(a), (5) or (6), as the case may be, in respect of the repayment of capital on any loan used for—
  (a) the replacement in the course of business of equipment or machinery; and
  (b) the repair of an existing business asset except to the extent that any sum is payable under an insurance policy for its repair.

(9) An adjudication officer shall refuse to make a deduction in respect of any expenses under paragraphs (3)(a), (4)(a), (5) or (6), as the case may be, where he is not satisfied that the expense has been defrayed or given the nature and the amount of the expense that it has been reasonably incurred.

(10) For the avoidance of doubt—
  (a) a deduction shall not be made under paragraphs (3)(a), (4)(b), (5) or (6), as the case may be, in respect of any sum unless it has been expended for the purposes of the business;
  (b) a deduction shall be made thereunder in respect of—
    (i) the excess of any VAT paid over VAT received in the assessment period;
    (ii) any income expended in the repair of an existing business asset except to the extent that any sum is payable under an insurance policy for its repair;
    (iii) any payment of interest on a loan taken out for the purposes of the employment.

(11) Where a claimant is engaged in employment as a child-minder the net profit of the employment to be taken into account shall be one-third of the earnings of that employment, less—
  (a) an amount in respect of—
    (i) income tax; and
    (ii) social security contributions payable under the Social Security Act [SSCBA], calculated in accordance with regulation 26 (deduction of tax and contributions for self-employed earners); and
  (b) [³one half of the amount in respect of any qualifying premium calculated in accordance with paragraph (15)].

(12) Where regulation 17(3) (normal weekly earnings of self-employed earners) applies—
  (a) for the purposes of paragraph (1)(a), the net profit derived from the employment shall be calculated by taking into account the claimant's estimated and, where appropriate, actual earnings from the employment less the amount of the deductions likely to be made and, where appropriate, made under sub-paragraphs (a) to (c) of paragraph (3); or

(b) for the purposes of paragraph (1)(b), his share of the net profit of the employment shall be calculated by taking into account the claimant's estimated and, where appropriate, his share of the actual earnings from the employment less the amount of his share of the expenses likely to be deducted and, where appropriate, deducted under paragraph (5); or

(c) in the case of employment as a child-minder, the net profit of the employment shall be calculated by taking into account one-third of the claimant's estimated earnings and, where appropriate, actual earnings from the employment less the amount of the deductions likely to be made and, where appropriate, made under sub-paragraphs (a) and (b) of paragraph (11).

(13) For the avoidance of doubt where a claimant is engaged in employment as a self-employed earner and he is also engaged in one or more other employments as a self-employed or employed earner any loss incurred in any one of his employments shall not be offset against his earnings in any other of his employments.

[²(14) [³In this regulation—

(a) "qualifying premium" means any premium which at the date of claim is payable periodically in respect of a retirement annuity contract or a personal pension scheme;

(b)] [⁴. . .]]

[³(15) The amount in respect of any qualifying premium shall be calculated by multiplying the daily amount of the qualifying premium by the number equal to the number of days in the assessment period; and for the purposes of this regulation the daily amount of the qualifying premium shall be determined—

(a) where the qualifying premium is payable monthly, by multiplying the amount of the qualifying premium by 12 and dividing the product by 365;

(b) in any other case, by dividing the amount of the qualifying premium by the number equal to the number of days in the period to which the qualifying premium relates.]

Amendments

1. Income-related Benefits Schemes (Miscellaneous Amendments) (No. 3) Regulations 1992 (S.I. 1992 No. 2155), Sched., para. 6 (October 5, 1992).

2. Income-related Benefits Schemes (Miscellaneous Amendments) (No. 4) Regulations 1993 (S.I. 1993 No. 2119), reg. 40 (October 5, 1993).

3. Income-related Benefits Schemes (Miscellaneous Amendments) Regulations 1994 (S.I. 1994 No. 527), reg. 25 (April 12, 1994).

4. Income-related Benefits Schemes and Social Security (Claims and Payments) (Miscellaneous Amendments) Regulations 1995 (S.I. 1995 No. 2303), reg. 3(3) (October 3, 1995).

Definitions

"assessment period"—see reg. 2(1).
"claimant"—*ibid.*, reg. 12(1).
"earnings"—see reg. 2(1).
"employed earner"—*ibid.*
"retirement annuity contract"—*ibid.*
"self-employed earner"—*ibid.*
"Social Security Act"—*ibid.*

General Note

See the notes to reg. 22 of the Family Credit (General) Regulations.

Deduction of tax and contributions for self-employed earners

26.—(1)The amount to be deducted in respect of income tax under regulation 25(1)(b)(i), (3)(b)(i), (4)(b)(i) or (11)(a)(i) (calculation of net profit of self-employed earners) shall be calculated on the basis of the amount of chargeable income, and as if that income were assessable to income tax at [¹the lower rate or, as the case may be the basic rate of tax] in the year of assessment in which the claim was made, less only the personal relief to which the claimant is entitled under [¹sections 257(1), (6) and (7) and 259] of the Income and Corporation Taxes Act 1988 (personal relief) as is appropriate to his circumstances; but, if the assessment period is less than a year [¹the earnings to which the lower rate [². . .] of tax is to be applied and] the amount of the personal relief deductible under this paragraph shall be calculated on a pro rata basis.

(2) The amount to be deducted in respect of social security contributions under regulation 25(1)(b)(i), (3)(b)(ii) (4)(b)(ii) or (11)(a)(ii) shall be the total of—

(a) the amount of Class 2 contributions payable under section 7(1) or, as the case may be, (4) of the Social Security Act [SSCBA, s.11(1) and (3)] at the rate applicable at the date of claim except where the claimant's chargeable income is less than the amount specified in section 7(5) of that Act [SSCBA, s.11(4)] (small earnings exception) for the tax year in which the date of claim falls; but if the assessment period is less than a year, the amount specified for that tax year shall be calculated on a pro rata basis; and

(b) the amount of Class 4 contributions (if any) which would be payable under section 9(2) of that Act [SSCBA, s.15(1)] (Class 4 contributions) at the percentage rate applicable at the date of claim on so much of the chargeable income as exceeds the lower limit but does not exceed the upper limit of profits and gains applicable for the tax year in which the date of claim falls; but, if the assessment period is less than a year, those limits shall be calculated on a pro rata basis.]

(3) In this regulation ''chargeable income'' means—

(a) except where sub-paragraph (b) or (c) applies, the earnings derived from the employment, less any expenses deducted under paragraph (3)(a), (4)(a), (5) or (6), as the case may be, of regulation 25;

(b) except where sub-paragraph (c)(iii) applies, in the case of employment as a child minder one-third of the earnings of that employment; or

(c) where regulation 17(3) applies (normal weekly earnings of self-employed earners)—

(i) in the case of a self-employed earner who is engaged in employment on his own account, the claimant's estimated and, where appropriate, actual earnings from the employment less the amount of the deductions likely to be made and, where appropriate, made under sub-paragraph (a) of paragraph (3) of regulation 25;

(ii) in the case of a self-employed earner whose employment is carried on in partnership or is that of a share fisherman within the meaning of the Social Security (Mariners' Benefits) Regulations 1975, the claimant's estimated and, where appropriate, his share of the actual earnings from the employment less the amount of his share of the expenses likely to be deducted and, where appropriate, deducted [¹under paragraph (5)] of regulation 25;

(iii) in the case of employment as a child minder, one-third of the claimant's estimated and, where appropriate, actual earnings from that employment.

AMENDMENTS

1. Income-related Benefits Schemes (Miscellaneous Amendments) (No. 3) Regulations 1992 (S.I. 1992 No. 2155), Sched., para. 7 (October 5, 1992).
2. Income-related Benefits Schemes (Miscellaneous Amendments) (No. 5) Regulations 1994 (S.I. 1994 No. 2139), reg. 4 (October 4, 1994).

DEFINITIONS

"assessment period"—see reg. 2(1).
"claim"—*ibid.*
"claimant"—*ibid.*, reg. 12(1).
"date of claim"—see reg. 2(1).
"lower rate"—*ibid.*
"earnings"—*ibid.*
"self-employed earner"—*ibid.*
"Social Security Act"—*ibid.*
"year of assessment"—*ibid.*

GENERAL NOTE

See the notes to reg. 23 of the Family Credit (General) Regulations.

Chapter V

Other Income

Calculation of income other than earnings

27.—(1) For the purposes of regulation 18 (normal weekly income other than earnings), the income of a claimant which does not consist of earnings to be taken into account shall, subject to paragraphs to (2) to (5), be his gross income and any capital treated as income under [[1] regulations 28 and 30 (capital treated as income and modifications in respect of children and young persons).]

(2) There shall be disregarded from the calculation of a claimant's gross income under paragraph (1), any sum, where applicable, specified in Schedule 3.

(3) Where the payment of any benefit under the benefit Acts is subject to any deduction by way of recovery the amount to be taken into account under paragraph (1) shall be the gross amount payable.

(4) Any payment to which regulation 21(2) applies (payments not earnings) shall be taken into account as income for the purpose of paragraph (1).

(5) Where a loan is made to a person pursuant to arrangements made under section 1 of the Education (Student Loans) Act 1990 or Article 3 of the Education (Student Loans) (Northern Ireland) Order 1990 and that person ceases to be a student before the end of the academic year in respect of which the loan is payable or, as the case may be, before the end of his course, a sum equal to the weekly amount apportionable under paragraph (2) of regulation 47 shall be taken into account under paragraph (1) for each week, in the period over which the loan fell to be apportioned, following the date on which that person ceases to be a student; but in determining the weekly amount apportionable under paragraph (2) of regulation 47 so much of that paragraph as provides for a disregard shall not have effect.

AMENDMENT

1. Income-related Benefits Schemes (Miscellaneous Amendments) (No. 4) Regulations 1993 (S.I. 1993 No. 2119), reg. 41 (October 5, 1993).

DEFINITIONS

"the benefit Acts"—see reg. 2(1).
"claimant—see reg. 2(1), reg. 12(1).
"earnings"—see reg. 2(1).

See the notes to reg. 24 of the Family Credit (General) Regulations.

Capital treated as income

28.—(1) Any capital payable by instalments which are outstanding at the date of the claim shall, if the aggregate of the instalments outstanding and the amount of the claimant's capital otherwise calculated in accordance with Chapter VI of this Part exceeds £16,000, be treated as income.

(2) Any payment received under an annuity shall be treated as income.

[¹(3) Any Career Development Loan paid pursuant to section 2 of the Employment and Training Act 1973 shall be treated as income.]

AMENDMENT

1. Income-related Benefits and Jobseeker's Allowance (Miscellaneous Amendments) Regulations 1997 (S.I. 1997 No. 65), reg. 3(3) (April 8, 1997).

DEFINITIONS

"claimant"—see reg. 2(1), reg. 12(1).
"date of claim"—see reg. 2(1).

GENERAL NOTE

Paragraph (1)
See the notes to reg. 25 of the Family Credit (General) Regulations, with the substitution of £16,000 for £8,000 as the capital limit.

Paragraph (3)
See the note to reg. 41(6) of the Income Support Regulations and para. 56 of Sched. 3 for the disregard that is applied to such loans.

Notional income

29.—(1) A claimant shall be treated as possessing income of which he has deprived himself for the purpose of securing entitlement to disability working allowance or increasing the amount of that benefit.

(2) [⁹Except in the case of—

(a) a discretionary trust;

(b) a trust derived from a payment made in consequence of a personal injury; or

(c) a personal pension scheme or retirement annuity contract where the claimant is aged under 60,] [¹⁰ or

(d) any sum to which paragraph 45(a) or 46(a) of Schedule 4 (disregard of compensation for personal injuries which is administered by the Court) refers,] [¹⁴or

(e) rehabilitation allowance made under section 2 of the Employment and Training Act 1973]

any income which would become available to the claimant upon application being made, but which has not been acquired by him, shall be treated as possessed by the claimant.

[⁹(2A) Where a person, aged not less than 60, is a member of, or a person deriving entitlement to a pension under, a personal pension scheme, or is a party to, or a person deriving entitlement to a pension under, a retirement annuity contract, and—

(a) in the case of a personal pension scheme, he fails to purchase an annuity with the funds available in that scheme where—

    (i) he defers, in whole or in part, the payment of any income which
        would have been payable to him by his pension fund holder;

    (ii) he fails to take any necessary action to secure that the whole of any
        income which would be payable to him by his pension fund holder
        upon his applying for it, is so paid; or

    (iii) income withdrawal is not available to him under that scheme; or

  (b) in the case of a retirement annuity contract, he fails to purchase an annu-
     ity with the funds available under that contract,

the amount of any income foregone shall be treated as possessed by him, but
only from the date on which it could be expected to be required were an application for it to be made.

  (2B) The amount of any income foregone in a case to which either head
(2A)(a)(i) or (ii) applies shall be the maximum amount of income which may
be withdrawn from the fund and shall be determined by the adjudication officer
who shall take account of information provided by the pension fund holder in
accordance with regulation 7(5) of the Social Security (Claims and Payments)
Regulations 1987 (evidence and information).

  (2C) The amount of any income foregone in a case to which either head
(2A)(a)(iii) or sub-paragraph (2A)(b) applies shall be the income that the claimant could have received without purchasing an annuity had the funds held under
the relevant personal pension scheme or retirement annuity contract been held
under a personal pension scheme where income withdrawal was available and
shall be determined in the manner specified in paragraph (2B).]

  (3) [¹⁵Any payment of income, other than a payment of income specified in
paragraph (3A)], made—

  (a) to a third party in respect of a single claimant or member of the family
     (but not a member of the third party's family) shall be treated as pos-
     sessed by [¹that single claimant or] that member of the family to the
     extent that it is used for his food, ordinary clothing or footwear, house-
     hold fuel, or housing costs or is used for any personal community
     [³charge,] collective community charge contribution [³or council tax] for
     which that member is liable; and in this subparagraph the expression
     "ordinary clothing or footwear" means clothing or footwear for normal
     daily use, but does not include school uniforms, or clothing or footwear
     used solely for sporting activities;

[²(b) to a single claimant or a member of the family in respect of a single
     claimant or a third party (but not in respect of another member of the
     family) shall be treated as possessed by that single claimant or, as the
     case may be, that member of the family to the extent that it is kept or
     used by him or used by or on behalf of any member of the family.]

  [¹⁵(3A) Paragraph (3) shall not apply in respect of a payment of income
made—

  (a) under the Macfarlane Trust, the Macfarlane (Special Payments) Trust,
     the Macfarlane (Special Payments) (No. 2) Trust, the Fund, the Eileen
     Trust or the Independent Living Funds;

  (b) pursuant to section 19(1)(a) of the Coal Industry Act 1994 (concessionary
     coal); or

  (c) pursuant to section 2 of the Employment and Training Act 1973 in
     respect of a person's participation—

    (i) in an employment programme specified in regulation 75(1)(a)(ii) of
        the Jobseeker's Allowance Regulations 1996;

    (ii) in a training scheme specified in regulation 75(1)(b)(ii) of those
        Regulations; or

    (iii) in a qualifying course within the meaning specified in regulation
        17A(7) of those Regulations.]

  (4) Where—

(a) a claimant performs a service for another person; and
(b) that person makes no payment of earnings or pays less than that paid for a comparable employment in the area;

the adjudication officer shall treat the claimant as possessing such earnings (if any) as is reasonable for that employment unless the claimant satisfies him that the means of that person are insufficient for him to pay or to pay more for the service, but this paragraph shall not apply to a claimant who is engaged by a charitable or [⁸voluntary organisation] or is a volunteer if the adjudication officer is satisfied [⁸in any of those cases] that it is reasonable for him to provide his services free of charge [¹³or in a case where the service is performed in connection with the claimant's participation in an employment or training programme in accordance with regulation 19(1)(q) of the Jobseeker's Allowance Regulations 1996].

(5) Where a claimant is treated as possessing any income under any of paragraphs (1) to (3), the foregoing provisions of this Part shall apply for the purposes of calculating the amount of that income as if a payment had actually been made and as if it were actual income which he does possess.

(6) Where a claimant is treated as possessing any earnings under paragraph (4), the foregoing provisions of this Part shall apply for the purposes of calculating the amount of those earnings as if a payment had actually been made and as if they were actual earnings which he does possess, except that paragraph (3) of regulation 22 (calculation of net earnings of employed earners) shall not apply and his net earnings shall be calculated by taking into account those earnings which he is treated as possessing, less—

(a) an amount in respect of income tax equivalent to an amount calculated by applying to those earnings [²the lower rate or, as the case may be, the lower rate and the basic rate of tax] in the year of assessment in which the claim was made less only the personal relief to which the claimant is entitled under sections 257(1), (6) and (7) and 259 of the Income and Corporation Taxes Act 1988 (personal relief) as is appropriate to his circumstances; but, if the assessment period is less than a year, [²the earnings to which the lower rate [⁷. . .] of tax is to be applied and] the amount of the personal relief deductible under this sub-paragraph shall be calculated on a pro rata basis;

[⁶(b) where the weekly amount of those earnings equals or exceeds the lower earnings limit, an amount representing primary Class 1 contributions under the Contributions and Benefits Act, calculated by applying to those earnings the initial and main primary percentages applicable at the date of claim in accordance with section 8(1)(a) and (b) of that Act; and]

(c) one-half of any sum payable by the claimant by way of a contribution towards an occupational or personal pension scheme.

AMENDMENTS

1. Income-related Benefits Schemes and Social Security (Recoupment) Amendment Regulations 1992 (S.I. 1992 No. 1101), reg. 3(3) (May 7, 1992).

2. Income-related Benefits Schemes (Miscellaneous Amendments) (No. 3) Regulations 1992 (S.I. 1992 No. 2155), Sched., para. 8 (October 5, 1992).

3. Income-related Benefits Schemes (Miscellaneous Amendments) Regulations 1993 (S.I. 1993 No. 315), Sched., para. 14 (April, 1993).

4. Social Security Benefits (Miscellaneous Amendments) (No. 2) Regulations 1993 (S.I. 1993 No. 963), reg. 6(3) (April 22, 1993).

5. Income-related Benefits Schemes and Social Security (Recoupment) Amendment Regulations 1993 (S.I. 1993 No. 1249), reg. 5(3) (May 14, 1993).

6. Income-related Benefits Schemes (Miscellaneous Amendments) Regulations 1994 (S.I. 1994 No. 527), reg. 26 (April 12, 1994).

7. Income-related Benefits Schemes (Miscellaneous Amendments) (No. 5) Regulations 1994 (S.I. 1994 No. 2139), reg. 4 (October 4, 1994).

8. Income-related Benefits Schemes (Miscellaneous Amendments) Regulations 1995 (S.I. 1995 No. 516), reg. 6 (April 11, 1995).

9. Income-related Benefits Schemes and Social Security (Claims and Payments) (Miscellaneous Amendments) Regulations 1995 (S.I. 1995 No. 2303), reg. 3(4) (October 3, 1995).

10. Income-related Benefits and Jobseeker's Allowance (Amendment) (No. 2) Regulations 1997 (S.I. 1997 No. 2197), reg. 2 (October 7, 1997).

11. Income-related Benefits and Jobseeker's Allowance (Amendment) (No. 2) Regulations 1997 (S.I. 1997 No. 2197), reg. 7(3) and (4)(b) (October 7, 1997).

12. Social Security Amendment (New Deal) Regulations 1997 (S.I. 1997 No. 2863), reg. 17(1) and (2)(b) (January 5, 1998).

13. Social Security Amendment (New Deal) Regulations 1997 (S.I. 1997 No. 2863), reg. 17(3) and (4)(b) (January 5, 1998).

14. Social Security (Miscellaneous Amendments) Regulations 1998 (S.I. 1998 No. 563), reg. 6(1) and (2)(b) (April 7, 1998).

15. Social Security Amendment (New Deal) (No. 2) Regulations 1998 (S.I. 1998 No. 2117), reg. 2(3) (September 24, 1998).

DEFINITIONS

"assessment period"—see reg. 2(1).
"claimant"—*ibid*, reg. 12(1).
"earnings"—see reg. 2(1).
"family"—see 1986 Act, s.20(11) (SSCBA, s.137(1)).
"lower rate"—see reg. 2(1).
"occupational pension scheme"—see 1986 Act, s.84(1) (PSA, s.1).
"payment"—see reg. 2(1).
"pension fund holder"—*ibid*.
"personal pension scheme"—*ibid*.
"retirement annuity contract"—*ibid*.
"single claimant"—see reg. 2(1).
"Social Security Act"—*ibid*.
"the Eileen Trust"—*ibid*.
"the Fund"—*ibid*.
"the Independent Living Funds"—*ibid*.
"the Macfarlane (Special Payments) Trust"—*ibid*.
"the Macfarlane (Special Payments)(No. 2) Trust"—*ibid*.
"the Macfarlane Trust"—*ibid*.
"voluntary organisation"—*ibid*.
"year of assessment"—*ibid*.

GENERAL NOTE

See, in general, the notes to reg. 26 of the Family Credit (General) Regulations.

Paragraph (1)
It is only income which the claimant deprives himself of for the purpose of entitlement to disability working allowance which he is to be treated as possessing under this provision. If the purpose is solely to secure entitlement to some other benefit, para. (1) cannot apply. See the notes to reg. 51(1) of the Income Support (General) Regulations (at the end of the section on *Purpose*) for discussion of the problem of deprivations occurring before a benefit comes into effect.

Paragraph (4)
This provision adopts the formula, with its different balance of burden of proof, of reg. 42(6) of the Income Support (General) Regulations, rather than reg. 26(4) of the Family Credit Regulations.

Modifications in respect of children and young persons

30.—(1) Any capital of a child or young person payable by instalments which are outstanding at the date of claim shall, if the aggregate of the instalments outstanding and the amount of that child's or young person's other capital calcu-

1012

lated in accordance with Chapter VI of this Part in like manner as for the claimant, [² . . .], would exceed £3,000, be treated as income.

(2) Where the income of a child or young person, other than income consisting of payments of maintenance whether under a court order or not, calculated in accordance with [²Chapters I to V] of this Part exceeds the sum specified as an allowance for that child or young person in Schedule 5 and regulation 51(5) (sum for child or young person who has income in excess to be nil) applies, that income shall not be treated as income of the claimant.

(3) Where the capital of a child or young person, if calculated in accordance with Chapter VI of this Part in like manner as for the claimant, [²except as provided in paragraph 1], would exceed £3,000, any income of that child or young person[¹, other than income consisting of any payment of maintenance whether under a court order or not,] shall not be treated as income of the claimant.

(4) Any income of a child or young person which is to be disregarded under Schedule 3 shall be disregarded in such manner as to produce the result most favourable to the claimant.

AMENDMENTS

1. Income-related Benefits Schemes (Miscellaneous Amendments) Regulations 1993 (S.I. 1993 No. 315), reg. 19 (April 13, 1993).
2. Income-related Benefits Schemes (Miscellaneous Amendments) (No. 4) Regulations 1993 (S.I. 1993 No. 2119), reg. 42 (October 5, 1993).

DEFINITIONS

"child"—see 1986 Act, s.20(11) (SSCBA, s.137(1)).
"claimant"—see reg. 2(1), reg. 12(1).
"date of claim"—see reg. 2(1).
"payment"—*ibid.*
"young person"—*ibid.*, reg. 8.

GENERAL NOTE

See the notes to reg. 27 of the Family Credit (General) Regulations.

Chapter VI

Capital

Capital limit

31. For the purposes of section 22(6) of the Act [SSCBA, s.134(1)] as it applies to disability working allowance (no entitlement to benefit if capital exceeds prescribed amount), the prescribed amount is £16,000.

DEFINITION

"the Act"—see reg. 2(1).

GENERAL NOTE

See the notes to reg. 28 of the Family Credit (General) Regulations. One of the most significant differences in the structure of assessment adopted for disability working allowance, as compared to family credit, is that the Government was persuaded to make the capital limit £16,000, rather than £8,000. The thinking of the SSAC, one of the main proponents of the change, was that the disabled have different needs to the non-disabled population and may have to pay out sums for special equipment, adaptations or services. Therefore, they may need a larger reserve of capital.

Calculation of capital

32.—(1) For the purposes of Part II of the Act [SSCBA, Part VI] as it applies to disability working allowance, the capital of a claimant to be taken into account shall, subject to paragraph (2), be the whole of his capital calculated in accordance with this Part and any income treated as capital [¹under regulation 34] (income treated as capital).

(2) There shall be disregarded from the calculation of a claimant's capital under paragraph (1) any capital, where applicable, specified in Schedule 4.

AMENDMENT

1. Income-related Benefits Schemes (Miscellaneous Amendments) (No. 3) Regulations 1992 (S.I. 1992 No. 2155), Sched., para. 9 (October 5, 1992).

DEFINITIONS

"the Act"—see reg. 2(1).
"claimant"—*ibid.*, reg. 12(1).

GENERAL NOTE

See the notes to reg. 29 of the Family Credit (General) Regulations.

Disregard of capital of child or young person

33. The capital of a child or young person who is a member of the claimant's family shall not be treated as capital of the claimant.

DEFINITIONS

"child"—see 1986 Act, s.20(11) (SSCBA, s.137(1)).
"claimant"—see reg. 2(1), reg. 12(1).
"family"—see 1986 Act, s.20(11) (SSCBA, s.137(1)).
"young person"—see reg. 2(1), reg. 8.

GENERAL NOTE

See the notes to reg. 30 of the Family Credit (General) Regulations.

Income treated as capital

34.—(1) Any amount by way of a refund of income tax deducted from profits or emoluments chargeable to income tax under Schedule D or E shall be treated as capital.

(2) Any holiday pay which is not earnings under regulation 21(1)(b) earnings of employed earners) shall be treated as capital.

(3) Any charitable or voluntary payment which is not made or is not due to be made at regular intervals, other than a payment which is made under the Macfarlane Trust, the Macfarlane (Special Payments) Trust, the Macfarlane (Special Payments) (No. 2) Trust[¹, the Fund] [³, the Eileen Trust] or [²the Independent Living Funds] shall be treated as capital.

(4) Except any income derived from capital disregarded under paragraph 1, 2, 4, 6, 13 or 26 to 30 of Schedule 4, any income derived from capital shall be treated as capital but only from the date it is normally due to be credited to the claimant's account.

(5) In the case of employment as an employed earner, any advance of earnings or any loan made by the claimant's employer shall be treated as capital.

(6) Any maintenance payment other than one to which regulation 18(2) [⁴or (2A)] (normal weekly income other than earnings) applies shall be treated as capital.

[⁵(7) There shall be treated as capital the gross receipts of any commercial activity carried on by a person in respect of which assistance is received under an employment programme specified in regulation 75(1)(a)(ii)(aa)(ii) of the Job-seeker's Allowance Regulations 1996 (self-employment route of the Employ-ment Option of the New Deal), but only in so far as those receipts were payable into a special account (as defined for the purposes of Chapter IVA of Part VIII of those Regulations) during the period in which that person was receiving such assistance.]

AMENDMENTS

1. Income-related Benefits Schemes and Social Security (Recoupment) Amendment Regulations 1992 (S.I. 1992 No. 1101), reg. 3(4) (May 7, 1992).
2. Social Security Benefits (Miscellaneous Amendments) (No. 2) Regulations 1993 (S.I. 1993 No. 963), reg. 6(3) (April 22, 1993).
3. Income-related Benefits Schemes and Social Security (Recoupment) Amendment Regulations 1993 (S.I. 1993 No. 1249), reg. 5(3) (May 14, 1993).
4. Income-related Benefits Schemes (Miscellaneous Amendments) (No. 5) Regulations 1994 (S.I. 1994 No. 2139), reg. 7 (October 4, 1994).
5. Social Security (Miscellaneous Amendments) (No. 4) Regulations 1998 (S.I. 1998 No. 1174), reg. 7(1) and (2)(b) (June 1, 1998).

DEFINITIONS

"claimant"—see reg. 2(1), reg. 12(1).
"earnings"—see reg. 2(1).
"employed earner"—*ibid.*
"payment"—*ibid.*
"the Eileen Trust"—*ibid.*
"the Fund"—*ibid.*
"the Independent Living Funds"—*ibid.*
"the Macfarlane (Special Payments) Trust"—*ibid.*
"the Macfarlane (Special Payments) (No. 2) Trust"—*ibid.*
"the Macfarlane Trust"—*ibid.*

GENERAL NOTE

See the notes to reg. 31 of the Family Credit (General) Regulations.

Calculation of capital in the United Kingdom

35. Capital which a claimant possesses in the United Kingdom shall be calculated—
(a) except in a case to which [¹paragraph] (b) applies, at its current market or surrender value less—
    (i) where there would be expenses attributable to sale, 10 per cent; and
    (ii) the amount of any incumbrance secured on it;
(b) in the case of a National Savings Certificate—
    (i) if purchased from an issue the sale of which ceased before 1st July last preceding the date of claim, at the price which it would have realised on that 1st July had it been purchased on the last day of that issue;
    (ii) in any other case, at its purchase price.

AMENDMENT

1. Income-related Benefits Schemes (Miscellaneous Amendments) (No. 3) Regulations 1992 (S.I. 1992 No. 2155), Sched., para.10 (October 5, 1992).

DEFINITIONS

"claimant"—see reg. 2(1), reg. 12(1).
"date of claim"—see reg. 2(1).

GENERAL NOTE

See the notes to reg. 49 of the Income Support (General) Regulations.

Calculation of capital outside the United Kingdom

36. Capital which a claimant possesses in a country outside the United Kingdom shall be calculated—
  (a) in a case where there is no prohibition in that country against the transfer to the United Kingdom of an amount equal to its current market or surrender value in that country, at that value;
  (b) in a case where there is such a prohibition, at the price which it would realise if sold in the United Kingdom to a willing buyer,
less, where there would be expenses attributable to sale, 10 per cent and the amount of any incumbrance secured on it.

DEFINITION

"claimant"—see reg. 2(1), reg. 12(1).

GENERAL NOTE

See the notes to reg. 50 of the Income Support (General) Regulations.

Notional capital

37.—(1) [². . .] A claimant shall be treated as possessing capital of which he has deprived himself for the purpose of securing entitlement to disability working allowance or increasing the amount of that benefit except—
  (a) where that capital is derived from a payment made in consequence of any personal injury and is placed on trust for the benefit of the claimant; or
  (b) to the extent that the capital which he is treated as possessing is reduced in accordance with regulation 38 (diminishing notional capital rule) [⁷ or
  (c) any sum to which paragraph 45(a) or 46(a) of Schedule 4 (disregard of compensation for personal injuries which is administered by the Court) refers].
  (2) Except in the case of—
  (a) a discretionary trust;
  (b) a trust derived from a payment made in consequence of a personal injury; or
  (c) any loan which would be obtainable only if secured against capital disregarded under Schedule 4, [⁶ or
  (d) a personal pension scheme or retirement annuity contract,] [⁷ or
  (e) any sum to which paragraph 45(a) or 46(a) of Schedule 4 (disregard of compensation for personal injuries which is administered by the Court) refers,]
any capital which would become available to the claimant upon application

being made but which has not been acquired by him shall be treated as possessed by him.

(3) [⁹Any payment of capital, other than a payment of capital specified in paragraph (3A)], made—

(a) to a third party in respect of a single claimant or a member of the family (but not a member of the third party's family) shall be treated as possessed by that single claimant or member of the family to the extent that it is used for his food, ordinary clothing or footwear, household fuel, or housing costs or is used for any personal community [³charge,] collective community charge contribution [³or council tax] for which that member is liable; and in this sub-paragraph the expression "ordinary clothing or footwear" means clothing or footwear for normal daily use, but does not include school uniforms, or clothing or footwear used solely for sporting activities;

(b) to a single claimant or a member of the family in respect of a third party (but not in respect of another member of the family) shall be treated as possessed by that single claimant or member to the extent that it is kept by him or used on behalf of any member of the family.

[⁹(3A) Paragraph (3) shall not apply in respect of a payment of capital made—

(a) under the Macfarlane Trust, the Macfarlane (Special Payments) Trust, the Macfarlane (Special Payments) (No. 2) Trust, the Fund, the Eileen Trust or the Independent Living Funds;

(b) pursuant to section 2 of the Employment and Training Act 1973 in respect of a person's participation—

(i) in an employment programme specified in regulation 75(1)(a)(ii) of the Jobseeker's Allowance Regulations 1996;

(ii) in a training scheme specified in regulation 75(1)(b)(ii) of those Regulations; or

(iii) in a qualifying course within the meaning specified in regulation 17A(7) of those Regulations.]

(4) Where a claimant stands in relation to a company in a position analogous to that of a sole owner or partner in the business of that company, he shall be treated as if he were such sole owner or partner and in such a case—

(a) the value of his holding in that company shall, notwithstanding regulation 32 (calculation of capital), be disregarded; and

(b) he shall, subject to paragraph (5), be treated as possessing an amount of capital equal to the value or, as the case may be, his share of the value of the capital of that company and the foregoing provisions of this Chapter shall apply for the purposes of calculating that amount as if it were actual capital which he does possess.

(5) For so long as the claimant undertakes activities in the course of the business of the company, the amount which he is treated as possessing under paragraph (4) shall be disregarded.

(6) Where a claimant is treated as possessing capital under any of paragraphs (1) to (4) the foregoing provisions of this Chapter shall apply for the purposes of calculating its amount as if it were actual capital which he does possess.

(7) For the avoidance of doubt a claimant is to be treated as possessing capital under paragraph (1) only if the capital of which he has deprived himself is actual capital and not capital which he is treated as possessing under regulation 39.

AMENDMENTS

1. Income-related Benefits Schemes and Social Security (Recoupment) Amendment Regulations 1992 (S.I. 1992 No. 1101), reg. 6 (May 7, 1992).

2. Income-related Benefits Schemes (Miscellaneous Amendments) (No. 3) Regulations 1992 (S.I. 1992 No. 2155), Sched., para. 11 (October 5, 1992).

3. Income-related Benefits Schemes (Miscellaneous Amendments) Regulations 1993 (S.I. 1993 No. 315), Sched., para. 15 (April 1, 1993).

4. Social Security Benefits (Miscellaneous Amendments) (No. 2) Regulations 1993 (S.I. 1993 No. 963), reg. 6(3) (April 22, 1993).

5. Income-related Benefits Schemes and Social Security (Recoupment) Amendment Regulations 1993 (S.I. 1993 No. 1249), reg. 5(3) (May 14, 1993).

6. Income-related Benefits Schemes and Social Security (Claims and Payments) (Miscellaneous Amendments) Regulations 1995 (S.I. 1995 No. 2303), reg. 3(5) (October 3, 1995).

7. Income-related Benefits and Jobseeker's Allowance (Amendment) (No. 2) Regulations 1997 (S.I. 1997 No. 2197), reg. 2 (October 7, 1997).

8. Social Security Amendment (New Deal) Regulations 1997 (S.I. 1997 No. 2863), reg. 17(5) and (6)(b) (January 5, 1998).

9. Social Security Amendment (New Deal) (No. 2) Regulations 1998 (S.I. 1998 No. 2117), reg. 3(2) and (3)(a) (September 24, 1998).

DEFINITIONS

"claimant"—see reg. 2(1), reg. 12(1).
"family"—see 1986 Act, s.20(11) (SSCBA, s.137(1)).
"personal pension scheme"—see reg. 2(1).
"retirement annuity contract"—*ibid.*
"single claimant"—*ibid.*
"the Eileen Trust"—*ibid.*
"the Fund"—*ibid.*
"the Independent Living Funds"—see reg. 2(1).
"the Macfarlane (Special Payments) Trust"—*ibid.*
"the Macfarlane (Special Payments) (No. 2) Trust"—*ibid.*
"the Macfarlane Trust"—*ibid.*

GENERAL NOTE

Paragraph (1)
See the notes to reg. 51(1) of the Income Support (General) Regulations. Note, however, that this paragraph only applies where the purpose is to gain entitlement to or to increase the amount of disability working allowance. If the purpose is solely to gain entitlement to some other benefit the disability working allowance rule is not triggered. The effect of para. (7) is to confirm that para. (1) only operates if the person has deprived himself of actual capital. It further confirms that a deemed share in jointly held capital (reg. 39) does not count as actual capital for this purpose.

Paragraph (2)
See the notes to reg. 51(2) of the Income Support (General) Regulations. There are slight differences in wording.

Paragraphs (3) and (3A)
See the notes to reg. 51(3) and (3A) of the Income Support (General) Regulations and the differences in sub-para. (a).

Paragraphs (4)–(6)
See the notes to reg. 51(4) to (6) of the Income Support (General) Regulations.

Diminishing notional capital rule

38.—(1) Where a claimant is treated as possessing capital under regulation 37(1) (notional capital), the amount which he is treated as possessing—
  (a) in the case of a benefit week which is subsequent to—
      (i) the relevant week in respect of which the conditions set out in paragraph (2) are satisfied; or
      (ii) a week which follows that relevant week and which satisfies those conditions, shall be reduced by an amount determined under paragraph (3);

1018

  (b) in the case of a benefit week in respect of which paragraph (1)(a) does not apply but where—
      (i) that week is a week subsequent to the relevant week; and
     (ii) that relevant week is a week in which the condition in paragraph (4) is satisfied, shall be reduced by the amount determined under paragraph (4).

  (2) This paragraph applies to a benefit week where the claimant satisfies the conditions that—
  (a) he is entitled to disability working allowance; and
  (b) but for regulation 37, he would have been entitled to an additional amount of disability working allowance in that benefit week.

  (3) In a case to which paragraph (2) applies, the amount of the reduction for the purposes of paragraph (1)(a) shall be equal to the aggregate of—
  (a) the additional amount of disability working allowance to which the claimant would have been entitled; and
  (b) if the claimant would, but for regulation 43(1) of the Housing Benefit (General) Regulations 1987 (notional capital), have been entitled to housing benefit or to an additional amount of housing benefit in respect of the benefit week in which the date of the last claim for disability working allowance falls, the amount (if any) which is equal to—
      (i) in a case where no housing benefit is payable, the amount to which he would have been entitled, or
     (ii) in any other case, the amount equal to the additional amount of housing benefit to which he would have been entitled; and
  (c) if the claimant would, but for regulation 33(1) of the Community Charge Benefits (General) Regulations 1989 (notional capital) have been entitled to community charge benefit or to an additional amount of community charge benefit in respect of the benefit week in which the date of the last claim for disability working allowance falls, the amount (if any) which is equal to—
      (i) in a case where no community charge benefit is payable, the amount to which he would have been entitled, or
     (ii) in any other case, the amount equal to the additional amount of community charge benefit to which he would have been [¹entitled; and
  (d) if the claimant would, but for regulation 34(1) of the Council Tax Benefit (General) Regulations 1992 (notional capital), have been entitled to council tax benefit or to an additional amount of council tax benefit in respect of the benefit week in which the date of the last claim for disability working allowance falls, the amount (if any) which is equal to—
      (i) in a case where no council tax benefit is payable, the amount to which he would have been entitled, or
     (ii) in any other case, the amount equal to the additional amount of council tax benefit to which he would have been entitled.]

  (4) Subject to paragraph (5), for the purposes of paragraph (1)(b) the condition is that the claimant would have been entitled to disability working allowance in the relevant week, but for regulation 37(1) and in such a case the amount shall be equal to the aggregate of—
  (a) the amount of disability working allowance to which the claimant would have been entitled in the relevant week but for regulation 37(1);
  (b) if the claimant would, but for regulation 43(1) of the Housing Benefit (General) Regulations 1987 (notional capital), have been entitled to housing benefit or to an additional amount of housing benefit in respect of the benefit week in which the first day of the relevant week falls, the amount (if any) which is equal to—

    (i) in a case where no housing benefit is payable, the amount to which he would have been entitled, or

    (ii) in any other case, the amount equal to the additional amount of housing benefit to which he would have been entitled; and

(c) if the claimant would, but for regulation 33(1) of the Community Charge Benefits (General) Regulations 1989 (notional capital) have been entitled to community charge benefit or to an additional amount of community charge benefit in respect of the benefit week in which the first day of the relevant week falls, the amount (if any) which is equal to—

    (i) in a case where no community charge benefit is payable, the amount to which he would have been entitled, or

    (ii) in any other case, the amount equal to the additional amount of community charge benefit to which he would have been ['entitled; and

(d) if the claimant would, but for regulation 34(1) of the Council Tax Benefit (General) Regulations 1992 (notional capital), have been entitled to council tax benefit or to an additional amount of council tax benefit in respect of the benefit week in which the first day of the relevant week falls, the amount (if any) which is equal to—

    (i) in a case where no council tax benefit is payable, the amount to which he would have been entitled, or

    (ii) in any other case, the amount equal to the additional amount of council tax benefit to which he would have been entitled.]

(5) The amount determined under paragraph (4) shall be re-determined under that paragraph if the claimant makes a further claim for disability working allowance and the conditions in paragraph (6) are satisfied, and in such a case—

(a) sub-paragraphs (a), (b) and (c) of paragraph (4) shall apply as if for the words "relevant week" there were substituted the words "relevant subsequent week",

(b) subject to paragraph (7), the amount as re-determined shall have effect from the first week following the relevant subsequent week in question.

(6) The conditions are that—

(a) a further claim is made 20 or more weeks after—

    (i) the first day of the relevant week;

    (ii) in a case where there has been at least one re-determination in accordance with paragraph (5), the first day of the relevant subsequent week which last occurred;

    whichever last occurred; and

(b) the claimant would have been entitled to disability working allowance but for regulation 37(1).

(7) The amount as re-determined pursuant to paragraph (5) shall not have effect if it is less than the amount which applied in that case immediately before the re-determination and in such a case the higher amount shall continue to have effect.

(8) For the purpose of this regulation—

(a) "benefit week" has the meaning prescribed in regulations 16 (date of entitlement under an award) and 27 (family credit and disability working allowance) of the Social Security (Claims and Payments) Regulations 1987 except where it appears in paragraphs ['(3)(b), (c) and (d) and (4)(b), (c) and (d)] where it has the meaning prescribed in regulation 2(1) of the Housing Benefit (General) Regulations ['1987 (interpretation),] regulation 2(1) of the Community Charge Benefits (General) Regulations 1989 (interpretation) ['or regulation 2(1) of the Council Tax Benefit (General) Regulations 1992 (interpretation)] as the case may be;

(b) "relevant week" means the benefit week in which the capital in question of which the claimant has deprived himself within the meaning of regulation 37(1)—

  (i) was for the first time taken into account for the purpose of determining his entitlement to disability working allowance; or

  (ii) was taken into account on a subsequent occasion for that purpose other than in respect of either a benefit week to which paragraph (2) applies or a further claim to which paragraph (5) applies;

and, where more than one benefit week is identified by reference to heads (i) and (ii) of this sub-paragraph, the later or latest such benefit week;

(c) "relevant subsequent week" means the benefit week in which any award of disability working allowance in respect of the further claim referred to in paragraph (6)(a) would, but for regulation 37(1), have commenced, but it shall not be earlier than the twenty-seventh week after the week in which the existing amount took effect.

AMENDMENT

1. Income-related Benefits Schemes (Miscellaneous Amendments) Regulations 1993 (S.I. 1993 No. 315), Sched., para. 16 (April 1, 1993).

DEFINITION

"claimant"—see regs. 2(1), 12(1).

GENERAL NOTE

See reg. 51A of the Income Support (General) Regulations.

Capital jointly held

39. Except where a claimant possesses capital which is disregarded under regulation 37(4) (notional capital), where a claimant and one or more persons are beneficially entitled in possession to any capital asset they shall be treated as if each of them were entitled in possession ['to the whole beneficial interest therein in an equal share and the foregoing provisions of this Chapter shall apply for the purposes of calculating the amount of capital which the claimant is treated as possessing as if it were actual capital which the claimant does possess].

AMENDMENT

1. Social Security Amendment (Capital) Regulations 1998 (S.I. 1998 No. 2250), reg. 2 (October 12, 1998).

DEFINITION

"claimant"—see reg. 2(1), reg. 12(1).

GENERAL NOTE

See the notes to reg. 52 of the Income Support (General) Regulations.

Calculation of tariff income from capital

40.—(1) Where the claimant's capital calculated in accordance with this Chapter exceeds £3,000, it shall be treated as equivalent to a weekly income of £1 for each complete £250 in excess of £3,000 but not exceeding £16,000.

(2) Notwithstanding paragraph (1), where any part of the excess is not a

complete £250 that part shall be treated as equivalent to a weekly income of £1.

(3) For the purposes of paragraph (1), capital includes any income treated as capital under regulation 34 (income treated as capital).

DEFINITION

"claimant"—see reg. 2(1), reg. 12(1).

GENERAL NOTE

The treatment of capital over £3,000 is the same as for family credit, except that the tariff income is derived from capital up to £16,000. Each complete £250 between those levels is treated as producing a weekly income of £1. If the capital does not divide exactly into £250 chunks anything left over is treated as producing £1 a week. Thus if the claimant's capital is exactly £16,000 the tariff income is £40 a week. If the claimant's capital is £4,001, the tariff income is £5 a week.

Para. (3) merely confirms the effect of reg. 34. Notional capital must also count although not expressly mentioned.

Note reg. 33 on the capital of children and young persons.

Chapter VII

Students

Interpretation

41. In this Chapter, unless the context otherwise requires—
"a course of advanced education" means—
   (a) a full-time course leading to a postgraduate degree or comparable qualification, a first degree or comparable qualification, a diploma of higher education, a higher national diploma, ['a higher national diploma or higher national certificate of either the Business & [²Technology] Education Council] or the Scottish Vocational Education tion Council or a teaching qualification; or
   (b) any other full-time course which is a course of a standard above ordinary national diploma, ['a national diploma or national certificate of either the Business & [²Technology] Education Council or the Scottish Vocational Education Council], a general certificate of education (advanced level), a Scottish certificate of education ['(higher level)] or a Scottish certificate of sixth year studies;
"contribution" means any contribution in respect of the income [⁴of a student or] of any other person which a Minister of the Crown or an education authority takes into account in assessing the amount of the student's grant and by which that amount is, as a consequence, reduced;
"course of study" means any full-time course of study or sandwich course whether or not a grant is made for attending it;
"covenant income" means the gross income payable to a student under a Deed of Covenant by a person whose income is, or is likely to be, taken into account in assessing the student's grant or award;
"education authority" means a government department, a local education authority as defined in section 114(1) of the Education Act 1944 (interpretation), an education authority as defined in section 135(1) of the Education (Scotland) Act 1980 (interpretation), an education and library board established under Article 3 of the Education and Libraries (Northern Ireland) Order 1986, any body which is a research council for the purposes of the Science and Technology Act 1965 or any analogous government department, authority, board or body, of the Channel Islands, Isle of Man or any other country outside Great Britain;

"grant" means any kind of educational grant or award and includes any scholarship, studentship, exhibition, allowance or bursary but does not include a payment derived from funds made available by the Secretary of State for the purpose of assisting students in financial difficulties under section 100 of the Education Act 1944, sections 131 and 132 of the Education Reform Act 1988 or section 73 of the Education (Scotland) Act 1980;

"grant income" means—

(a) any income by way of a grant;

(b) any contribution which has been assessed whether or not it has been paid,

and any such contribution which is paid by way of a covenant shall be treated as part of the student's grant income;

"last day of the course" means the date on which the last day of the final academic term falls in respect of the course in which the student is enrolled;

"period of study" means—

(a) in the case of a course of study for one year or less, the period beginning with the start of the course and ending with the last day of the course;

(b) in the case of a course of study for more than one year, in the first or, as the case may be, any subsequent year of the course, the period beginning with the start of the course or, as the case may be, that year's start and ending with either—

(i) the day before the start of the next year of the course in a case where the student's grant is assessed at a rate appropriate to his studying throughout the year, or, if he does not have a grant, where it would have been assessed at such a rate had he had one; or

(ii) in any other case the day before the start of normal summer vacation appropriate to his course;

(c) in the final year of a course of study of more than one year, the period beginning with that year's start and ending with the last day of the course;

"periods of experience" has the meaning prescribed in paragraph 1(1) of Schedule 5 to the Education (Mandatory Awards) Regulations 1991;

"sandwich course" has the meaning prescribed in paragraph 1(1) of Schedule 5 to the Education (Mandatory Awards) Regulations 1991;

"standard maintenance grant" means—

(a) except where paragraph (b) applies, in the case of a student attending a course of study at the University of London or an establishment within the area comprising the City of London and the Metropolitan Police District, the amount specified for the time being in paragraph 2(2)(a) of Schedule 2 to the Education (Mandatory Awards) Regulations 1991 for such a student; and

(b) in the case of a student residing at his parent's home, the amount specified in paragraph 3(2) thereof; and

(c) in any other case, the amount specified in paragraph 2(2) other than in sub-paragraph (a) or (b) thereof;

[¹"student" means a person,other than a person in receipt of a training allowance, who is aged less than 19 and attending a full-time course of advanced education or, as the case may be, who is aged 19 or over and attending a full-time course of study] at an educational establishment; and for the purposes of this definition—

(a) a person who has started on such a course shall be treated as

attending it [³. . .] until the last day of the course or such earlier date as he abandons it or is dismissed from it;
  (b) a person on a sandwich course shall be treated as attending a full-time course of advanced education or, as the case may be, of study;
"year" in relation to a course, means the period of 12 months beginning on 1st January, 1st April or 1st September according to whether the academic year of the course in question begins in the spring, the summer or the autumn respectively.

AMENDMENTS

1. Income-related Benefits Schemes (Miscellaneous Amendments) (No. 3) Regulations 1992 (S.I. 1992 No. 2155), Sched., para.12 (October 5, 1992).
2. Income-related Benefits Schemes (Miscellaneous Amendments) (No. 4) Regulations 1993 (S.I. 1993 No. 2119), reg. 43 (October 5, 1993).
3. Social Security Benefits (Miscellaneous Amendments) Regulations 1995 (S.I. 1995 No. 1742), reg. 2 (August 1, 1995).
4. Social Security (Miscellaneous Amendments) Regulations 1998 (S.I. 1998 No. 563), reg. 4(1) and (2)(b) (April 7, 1998).

DEFINITION

"training allowance"—see reg. 2(1).

GENERAL NOTE

See the notes to reg. 37 of the Family Credit (General) Regulations.

Calculation of grant income

42.—(1) The amount of a student's grant income to be taken into account shall, subject to [¹paragraphs (2) and (2A)], be the whole of his grant income.
  (2) There shall be disregarded from a student's grant income any payment—
  (a) intended to meet tuition fees or examination fees;
  (b) intended to meet additional expenditure incurred by a disabled student in respect of his attendance on a course;
  (c) intended to meet additional expenditure connected with term time residential study away from the student's educational establishment;
  (d) on account of the student maintaining a home at a place other than that at which he resides during his course;
  (e) intended to meet the cost of books and equipment or, if not so intended, an amount equal to [²£295];
  (f) intended to meet travel expenses incurred as a result of his attendance on the course.
  [¹(2A) Where in pursuance of an award a student is in receipt of a grant in respect of maintenance under regulation 17(b) of the Education (Mandatory Awards) Regulations 1991 (payments), there shall be excluded from his grant income a sum equal to the amount specified in paragraph 7(4) of Schedule 2 to those Regulations (disregard of travel costs), being the amount to be disregarded in respect of travel costs in the particular circumstances of his case.]
  (3) A student's grant income, except any amount intended for the maintenance of dependants under Part 3 of Schedule 2 to the Education (Mandatory Awards) Regulations 1991 or intended for an older student under Part 4 of that Schedule, shall be apportioned—
  (a) subject to paragraph (5), in a case where it is attributable to the period of study, equally between the weeks in that period;
  (b) in any other case, equally between the weeks in the period in respect of which it is payable.

(4) Any amount intended for maintenance of dependants or for an older student under the provisions referred to in paragraph (3) shall be apportioned equally over a period of 52 weeks commencing with the week in which the period of study begins.

(5) In the case of a student on a sandwich course, any periods of experience within the period of study shall be excluded and the student's grant income shall be apportioned equally between the remaining weeks in that period.

AMENDMENTS

1. Income-related Benefits Schemes (Miscellaneous Amendments) (No. 3) Regulations 1992 (S.I. 1992 No. 2155), Sched., para. 13 (October 5, 1992).
2. Social Security (Student Amounts Amendment) Regulations 1998 (S.I. 1998 No. 1379), reg. 2 (September 1, 1998, or, where the student's period of study begins between August 1 and 31, 1998, the first Tuesday of that period).

DEFINITIONS

"grant income"—see reg. 41.
"payment"—see reg. 2(1).
"period of study"—see reg. 41.
"periods of experience"—*ibid.*
"sandwich course"—*ibid.*
"student"—*ibid.*
"week"—see reg. 2(1).

GENERAL NOTE

See the notes to reg. 38 of the Family Credit (General) Regulations.

Calculation of covenant income where a contribution is assessed

43.—(1) Where a student is in receipt of income by way of a grant during a period of study and a contribution has been assessed, the amount of his covenant income to be taken into account shall be the whole amount of his covenant income less, subject to paragraph (3), the amount of the contribution.

(2) The weekly amount of the student's covenant income shall be determined—
  (a) by dividing the amount of income which falls to be taken into account under paragraph (1) by 52; and
  (b) by disregarding from the resulting amount, £5.

(3) For the purposes of paragraph (1), the contribution shall be treated as increased by the amount, if any, by which the amount excluded under ['regulation 42(2)(f) (calculation of grant income) falls short of the amount specified in paragraph 7(4)(i) of Schedule 2 to the Education (Mandatory Awards) Regulations 1991 (travel expenditure)].

AMENDMENT

1. Income-related Benefits Schemes (Miscellaneous Amendments) (No. 3) Regulations 1992 (S.I. 1992 No. 2155), Sched., para. 14 (October 5, 1992).

DEFINITIONS

"contribution"—see reg. 41.
"covenant income"—*ibid.*
"grant"—*ibid.*
"standard maintenance grant"—*ibid.*
"student"—*ibid.*

GENERAL NOTE

See the notes to reg. 39 of the Family Credit (General) Regulations.

Covenant income where no grant income or no contribution is assessed

44.—(1) Where a student is not in receipt of income by way of a grant the amount of his covenant income shall be calculated as follows—

 (a) any sums intended for any expenditure specified in regulation 42(2)(a) to (d) (calculation of grant income), necessary as a result of his attendance on the course, shall be disregarded;

 (b) any covenant income, up to the amount of the standard maintenance grant, which is not so disregarded, shall be apportioned equally between the weeks of the period of study and there shall be disregarded from the covenant income to be so apportioned the amount which would have been disregarded ['under regulation 42(2)(e) and (f) and (2A)] had the student been in receipt of the standard maintenance grant; and

 (c) the balance, if any, shall be divided by 52 and treated as weekly income of which shall be disregarded.

(2) Where a student is in receipt of income by way of a grant and no contribution has been assessed, the amount of his covenant income shall be calculated in accordance with sub-paragraphs (a) to (c) of paragraph (1), except that—

 (a) the value of the standard maintenance grant shall be abated by the amount of his grant income less an amount equal to the amount of any sums disregarded under regulation 42(2)(a) to (d); and

 (b) the amount to be disregarded under paragraph (1)(b) shall be abated by an amount equal to the amount of any sums disregarded ['under regulation 42(2)(e) and (f) and (2A)].

AMENDMENT

1. Income-related Benefits Schemes (Miscellaneous Amendments) (No. 3) Regulations 1992 (S.I. 1992 No. 2155), Sched., para. 15 (October 5, 1992).

DEFINITIONS

 "covenant income"—see reg. 41.
 "grant"—*ibid.*
 "grant income"—*ibid.*
 "period of study"—*ibid.*
 "standard maintenance grant"—*ibid.*
 "student"—*ibid.*
 "week"—see reg. 2(1).

GENERAL NOTE

See the notes to reg. 40 of the Family Credit (General) Regulations.

Relationship with amounts to be disregarded under Schedule 2

45. No part of a student's covenant income or grant income shall be disregarded under paragraph 12 of Schedule 3 and any other income to which sub-paragraph (1) of that paragraph applies shall be disregarded thereunder only to the extent that the amount disregarded under regulation 43(2)(b) (calculation of covenant income where a contribution is assessed) or, as the case may be, 44(1)(c) (covenant income where no grant income or no contribution is assessed) is less than ['£20].

AMENDMENT

1. Income-related Benefits Schemes (Miscellaneous Amendments) Regulations 1996 (S.I. 1996 No. 462), reg. 8 (April 9, 1996).

DEFINITIONS

"covenant income"—see reg. 41.
"grant income"—*ibid.*
"student"—*ibid.*

GENERAL NOTE

See the notes to reg. 41 of the Family Credit (General) Regulations.

Other amounts to be disregarded

46. For the purposes of ascertaining income [¹other than grant income, covenant income and loans treated as income in accordance with regulation 47], any amounts intended for any expenditure specified in regulation 42(2) (calculation of grant income) necessary as a result of his attendance on the course shall be disregarded but only if, and to the extent that, the necessary expenditure exceeds or is likely to exceed the amount of the sums disregarded under regulation 42(2) [¹and (2A)], 43(3) and 44(1)(a) or (b) (calculation of grant income and covenant income) on like expenditure.

AMENDMENT

1. Income-related Benefits Schemes (Miscellaneous Amendents) Regulations 1994 (S.I. 1994 No. 527), reg. 27 (April 12, 1994).

DEFINITIONS

"covenant income"—see reg. 41.
"grant income"—*ibid.*

GENERAL NOTE

See the notes to reg. 42 of the Family Credit (General) Regulations.

Treatment of student loans

47.—(1) A loan which is made to a student pursuant to arrangements made under section 1 of the Education (Student Loans) Act 1990 or Article 3 of the Education (Student Loans) (Northern Ireland) Order 1990 shall be treated as income—

(2) In calculating the weekly amount of the loan to be taken into account as income—

(a) except where sub-paragraph (b) applies, the loan shall be apportioned equally between the weeks in the academic year in respect of which the loan is payable;

(b) in the case of a loan which is payable in respect of the final academic year of the course or if the course is only of one academic year's duration, in respect of that year the loan shall be apportioned equally between the weeks in the period beginning with the start of the final academic year or, as the case may be, the single academic year and ending with the last day of the course,

and from the weekly amount so apportioned there shall be disregarded £10.

[¹(3) For the purposes of this regulation a student shall be treated as possessing the maximum amount of any loan referred to in paragraph (1) which he will be able to acquire in respect of an academic year by taking reasonable steps to do so.]

AMENDMENT

1. Income-related Benefits Schemes (Miscellaneous Amendments) Regulations 1996 (S.I. 1996 No. 462), reg. 9 (April 9, 1996).

GENERAL NOTE

See the notes to reg. 66A of the Income Support (General) Regulations.

Disregard of contribution

48. Where the claimant or his partner is a student and [¹, for the purposes of assessing a contribution to the student's grant, the other partner's income has been taken into account, an amount equal to that contribution shall be disregarded for the purposes of assessing that other partner's income.]

AMENDMENT

1. Income-related Benefits Schemes (Miscellaneous Amendments) Regulations 1996 (S.I. 1996 No. 462), reg. 10 (April 9, 1996).

DEFINITIONS

"claimant"—see reg. 2(1), reg. 12(1).
"contribution"—see reg. 41.
"grant"—*ibid.*
"partner"—see reg. 2(1).
"student"—see reg. 41.

[¹**Further disregard of student's income**

48A. Where any part of a student's income has already been taken into account for the purposes of assessing his entitlement to a grant, the amount taken into account shall be disregarded in assessing that student's income.]

AMENDMENT

1. Social Security (Miscellaneous Amendments) Regulations 1998 (S.I. 1998 No, 563), reg. 4(3) and (4)(b) (April 7, 1998).

DEFINITIONS

"grant"—see reg. 41.
"student"—*ibid.*

Disregard of tax refund

49. Any amount by way of a refund of tax deducted from a student's covenant income shall be disregarded in calculating the student's income or capital.

DEFINITIONS

"covenant income"—see reg. 41.
"student"—*ibid.*

GENERAL NOTE

See the notes to reg. 44 of the Family Credit (General) Regulations.

Disregard of changes occurring during summer vacation

50. In calculating a student's income there shall be disregarded any change in the standard maintenance grant occurring in the recognised summer vacation appropriate to the student's course, if that vacation does not form part of his period of study[¹,] from the date on which the change occurred to the end of that vacation.

AMENDMENT

1. Income-related Benefits Schemes (Miscellaneous Amendments) (No. 3) Regulations 1992 (S.I. 1992 No. 2155), Sched., para. 16 (October 5, 1992).

DEFINITIONS

"period of study"—see reg. 41.
"standard maintenance grant"—*ibid.*
"student"—*ibid.*

GENERAL NOTE

See the notes to reg. 69 of the Income Support (General) Regulations. The differences in drafting do not seem to affect the substance.

PART VI

CALCULATION OF ENTITLEMENT

Determination of appropriate maximum disability working allowance

51.—(1) Subject to paragraphs (2) to (7), the appropriate maximum disability working allowance shall be the aggregate of the following allowances—
  (a) in respect of a single claimant, the allowance specified in column (2) of Schedule 5 at paragraph 1;
  (b) in respect of a claimant who is a member of a married or unmarried couple, or who is a lone parent who is treated as responsible for a child or young person by virtue of regulation 9 (circumstances in which a person is treated as responsible or not responsible for another), the allowance specified in column (2) of Schedule 5 at paragraph 2;
[⁵(bb) in respect of a claimant who is—
      (i) a single claimant or lone parent who works, or
      (ii) a member of a married or unmarried couple either or both of whom work,
    for not less than 30 hours per week, the allowance specified in column (2) of Schedule 5 at paragraph 2A]
  (c) in respect of any child or young person for whom the claimant or his partner is treated as responsible by virtue of regulation 9 (circumstances in which a person is treated as responsible or not responsible for another), the allowance specified in column (2) of Schedule 5 [⁶in respect of the period specified in either paragraph 3 or 4 of column (1) as appropriate to] the child or young person concerned [⁶and in those paragraphs, "the first Tuesday in September" means the Tuesday which first occurs in the month of September in any year]
  [³(d) in respect of any child or young person to whom paragraph (1A) applies, the allowance specified in paragraph 5 of column (2) of Schedule 5.

(1A) This paragraph applies to a child or young person for whom the claimant or his partner is responsible and who is a member of the claimant's household, and—

(a) in respect of whom disability living allowance is payable, or has ceased to be payable solely because he is a patient; or

(b) who is registered as blind in a register compiled by a local authority under section 29 of the National Assistance Act 1948 (welfare services) or, in Scotland, has been certified as blind and in consequence he is registered as blind in a register maintained by or on behalf of a regional or islands council; or

(c) who ceased to be registered as blind in such a register within the 28 weeks immediately preceding the date of claim.

(1B) For the purposes of paragraph (1A)(a), "patient" has the same meaning it has in regulation 10.]

(2) Where a claimant or, as the case may be, the partner of a claimant is married polygamously to two or more members of the same household, the maximum amount shall include, in respect of every such member but the first, an additional allowance which [⁶equals the allowance specified in column (2) of Schedule 5 against paragraph 4 in column (1).]

(3) For the purposes of paragraph (2), a person shall not be treated as a member of the same household as someone to whom he is married polygamously if he would not be so treated in the case of a monogamous marriage.

(4) Where the capital of a child or young person, if calculated in accordance with Part V (income and capital) in like manner as for the claimant, [²except as provided in regulation 30(1) (modifications in respect of children and young persons)], would exceed £3,000, the allowance in respect of that child or young person shall be nil.

(5) Where the weekly income of a child or young person, other than income consisting of payments of maintenance whether under a court order or not, calculated [¹in accordance with Part V], exceeds the amount specified for that child or young person in Schedule 5, the allowance in respect of that child or young person shall be nil.

(6) Where a child or young person is, for the purposes of regulation 10(2)(a) (membership of the same household), a patient or in residential accommodation on account of physical or mental handicap or physical or mental illness and has been so accommodated for the 52 weeks immediately before the date of claim, the allowance in respect of that child or young person shall be nil.

(7) For the purposes of this regulation the amount of any disability working allowance and the [⁶period during which that amount is appropriate in respect] of any child or young person shall be determined by reference to the allowance specified in Schedule 5 and the [⁶relevant period which includes] the date on which the period under [⁴section 129(6) of the Contributions and Benefits Act] (period of award) begins.

AMENDMENTS

1. Income-related Benefits Schemes (Miscellaneous Amendments) (No. 3) Regulations 1992 (S.I. 1992 No. 2155), Sched., para. 17 (October 5, 1992).

2. Income-related Benefits Schemes (Miscellaneous Amendments) (No. 4) Regulations 1993 (S.I. 1993 No. 2119), reg. 44 (October 5, 1993).

3. Disability Working Allowance and Income Support (General) Amendment Regulations 1995 (S.I. 1995 No. 482), reg. 3 (April 11, 1995).

4. Income-related Benefits Schemes (Miscellaneous Amendments) Regulations 1995 (S.I. 1995 No. 516), reg. 7 (April 11, 1995).

5. Income-related Benefits Schemes (Miscellaneous Amendments) (No. 2) Regulations 1995 (S.I. 1995 No. 1339), reg. 4 (July 18, 1995).

6. Income-related Benefits and Jobseeker's Allowance (Personal Allowances for Children and Young Persons) (Amendment) Regulations 1996 (S.I. 1996 No. 2545), reg. 8 (October 7, 1997).

DEFINITIONS

"child"—see 1986 Act, s.20(11) (SSCBA, s.137(1)).
"claimant"—see reg. 2(1).
"lone parent"—*ibid.*
"married couple"—see 1986 Act, s.84(1) (SSCBA, s.137(1)).
"partner"—see reg. 2(1).
"single claimant"—*ibid.*
"unmarried couple"—see 1986 Act, s.84(1) (SSCBA, s.137(1)).
"young person"—see reg. 2(1), reg. 8.

GENERAL NOTE

The determination of the maximum disability working allowance is the essential starting point in the calculation of benefit, just as it is for family credit. If the claimant's income is not more than the applicable amount specified in reg. 52, the maximum allowance is payable (Contributions and Benefits Act, s.129(5)(a); 1986 Act, s.21(3A)). If the income is above that amount, the maximum allowance is to be reduced at the rate specified in reg. 53 (Contributions and Benefits Act, s.129(5)(b); 1986 Act, s.21(3B)) The rate is 70 per cent, the same as for family credit.

Paragraph (1)
The structure for fixing the maximum disability working allowance is slightly different from family credit, because there is no requirement that the claimant should have a child in the household. Thus a maximum allowance for a single claimant has to be specified under sub-para. (a). Under sub-para. (b) there is the same maximum for a lone parent or a couple. To the allowance fixed under sub-para. (a) or (b) is added the appropriate amount for children and young persons for whom an adult is responsible under sub-para. (c) and, if applicable, sub-para. (d). Sub-para. (d) introduces a disabled child's allowance from April 11, 1995. The conditions for this are in para. (1A) and are similar to those for a disabled child premium in income support. See paras. (4) to (7) below for further rules for the allowances for children. In addition, from July 1995 sub-para. (bb) provides for an extra allowance of £10 (now increased to £11.05 from April 1999, see para. (2A) of Sched. 5) where the claimant or partner (if any) or both are working 30 hours or more a week. See also reg. 6A on calculating the 30 hours. A corresponding disregard of the equivalent amount of disability working allowance for claimants entitled to this allowance has been introduced into the Housing Benefit and Council Tax Benefit Regulations so that the additional benefit is not clawed back.
The amounts are specified in Sched. 5. The amount for a couple or lone parent is higher than the maximum family credit by the amount of the income support disability premium. It is not clear how the amount for a single claimant was calculated. The amounts for children under sub-para. (c) are the same as for family credit. The amount for a disabled child under sub-para. (d) is the same as the income support disabled child premium.
The effect of para. (7) is that the amount of the allowance is set according to the ages of children and the amounts specified as at the beginning of the award. See reg. 16(1A) and (1B) of the Claims and Payments Regulations.
From October 7, 1997 the allowance for a child does not increase until the first Tuesday in September after their 11th or 16th birthday and there is no longer an increase at the age of 18 (see the new paras. 3 and 4 in col. 1 of Sched. 5). There are the same amendments to family credit; similar changes were made to income support and income-based JSA on April 7, 1997 (see the notes to para. 2 of Sched. 2 to the Income Support Regulations). The new age bands only apply if a dependent child or young person becomes 11, 16 or 18 on or after October 7, 1997. See the transitional protection in reg. 10(3) and (4) of the Income-related Benefits and Jobseeker's Allowance (Personal Allowances for Children and Young Persons) (Amendment) Regulations 1996 (p. 1055) for these reaching 11, 16 or 18 before that date; note that it is not necessary for disability working allowance to have been in payment on the relevant birthday. See also reg. 15A for the changes that have been made to the period for which a childcare costs disregard can apply.

Paragraphs (2)–(6)
See the notes to reg. 46 of the Family Credit (General) Regulations.

[¹Applicable amount of disability working allowance

52.—(1) The applicable amount] for the purposes of section 20(6A) of the

Act [SSCBA, s.129(1)] (conditions of entitlement to disability working allowance) shall, in the case of a claimant who is—
  (a) single, be [²£60.50] per week;
  (b) a member of a married or unmarried couple, or a lone parent, be [²£80.65] per week.

(2) For the purposes of section 20(6D) of the Act [SSCBA, s.129(1)(c)] (date on which applicable amount is to be determined) the prescribed date is the date on which the period under section 20(6F) of the Act [SSCBA, s.129(6)] (period of the award) begins.

AMENDMENTS

1. Income-related Benefits Schemes (Miscellaneous Amendments) (No. 3) Regulations 1992 (S.I. 1992 No. 2155), Sched., para. 18 (October 5, 1992).
2. Social Security Benefits Up-rating Order 1999 (S.I. 1999 No. 264), art. 17(c) (April 13, 1999).

DEFINITIONS

"the Act"—see reg. 2(1).
"claimant"—*ibid.*
"lone parent"—*ibid.*
"married couple"—see 1986 Act, s.84(1) (SSCBA, s.137(1)).
"single claimant"—see reg.2(1).
"unmarried couple"—see 1986 Act, s.84(1) (SSCBA, s.137(1)).

GENERAL NOTE

See the note to reg. 51 for the calculation of benefit (and s.129(5) of the Contribution and Benefits Act; 1986 Act, s.21(3A) and (3B)). The applicable amount prescribed at the beginning of the period of an award controls the calculation.

The applicable amount for couples and lone parents is the same as for family credit, the equivalent of the income support rate for couples both over 18. The applicable amount for single claimants has no equivalent in family credit. It is now above the income support figure for a single claimant aged 25 or over, having been increased as part of the changes associated with the introduction of incapacity benefit in April 1995.

Entitlement to disability working allowance where income exceeds the applicable amount

53. The prescribed percentage for the purpose of section 21 (3B) of the Act [SSCBA, s.129(5)(b)] (percentage of excess of income over applicable amount which is deducted from maximum disability working allowance) shall be 70 per cent.

DEFINITION

"the Act"—see reg. 2(1).

GENERAL NOTE

Where the income exceeds the applicable amount the maximum disability working allowance is reduced by 70 per cent of the excess, just as for family credit.

PART VII

CHANGES OF CIRCUMSTANCES

Death of claimant

54.—(1) Except as provided in paragraph (2), an award of disability working allowance shall cease to have effect upon the death of the claimant.

(2) Where a claimant dies and is survived by a partner who was the claimant's partner at the date of claim, an award of disability working allowance made in the claimant's favour shall have effect for its unexpired period as if originally made in favour of the partner.

DEFINITIONS

"claimant"—see reg. 2(1).
"date of claim"—*ibid.*
"partner"—*ibid.*

GENERAL NOTE

See the notes to reg. 49 of the Family Credit (General) Regulations.

Prevention of duplication of awards of family credit, disability working allowance and income support

55. Where provision is made for the same child or young person in awards for overlapping periods, the first being an award of disability working allowance and the second an award of disability working allowance, family credit [¹, income-based jobseeker's allowance] or income support, and at the start of the period of overlap that child or young person is no longer a member of the household of the claimant under the first award, the first award shall terminate with effect from the start of the period of overlap.

AMENDMENT

1. Social Security and Child Support (Jobseeker's Allowance) (Consequential Amendments) Regulations 1996 (S.I. 1996 No. 1345), reg. 7(5) (October 7, 1996).

DEFINITIONS

"child"—see 1986 Act, s.20(11) (SSCBA, s.137(1)).
"claimant"—see reg. 2(1).
"young person"—*ibid.*, reg. 8.

[¹Overlapping awards

56.—(1) An award of disability working allowance (the new award) which is made in consequence of a claim in respect of a period beginning before the commencement of an existing award of disability working allowance (the existing award) and which overlaps with the period of the existing award, shall be treated as a relevant change of circumstances affecting the existing award and the existing award shall be reviewed and shall terminate with effect from the date on which the decision of the adjudication officer making the new award is notified to the claimant.

(2) An award of family credit which is made in consequence of a claim in respect of a period beginning [² on or] before the commencement of an existing award of disability working allowance (the existing award) and which overlaps with the period of the existing award, shall be treated as a change of circumstances affecting the existing award and the existing award shall be reviewed and shall terminate with effect from the date on which the decision of the adjudication officer awarding family credit is notified to the claimant.]

AMENDMENTS

1. Income-related Benefits Schemes (Miscellaneous Amendments) (No. 5) Regulations 1994 (S.I. 1994 No. 2139), reg. 8 (October 4, 1994).

2. Income-related Benefits Schemes and Social Fund (Miscellaneous Amendments) Regulations 1996 (S.I. 1996 No. 1944), reg. 3(3) (October 8, 1996).

DEFINITION

"claimant"—see reg. 2(1).

GENERAL NOTE

See the note to reg. 51 of the Family Credit Regulations.

[¹Reduced benefit direction

56A.—(1) The following occurrences shall be changes of circumstances which affect an award of disability working allowance and the rate at which it is payable—
  (a) a reduced benefit direction given by a child support officer under section 46(5) of the Child Support Act 1991;
  (b) the cessation or cancellation of a reduced benefit direction under Part IX of the maintenance regulations;
  (c) the suspension of a reduced benefit direction under regulation 48(1) of the maintenance regulations;
  (d) the removal of a suspension imposed under paragraph (1) of regulation 48 of the maintenance regulations in accordance with paragraph (3) of that regulation.
  (2) In this regulation—
  (a) "child support officer" means a person appointed in accordance with section 13 of the Child Support Act 1991;
  (b) "the maintenance regulations" means the Child Support (Maintenance Assessment Procedure) Regulations 1992]

AMENDMENT

1. Income-related Benefits Schemes (Miscellaneous Amendments) Regulations 1993 (S.I. 1993 No. 315), reg. 20 (April 13, 1993).

GENERAL NOTE

See the note to reg. 51A of the Family Credit (General) Regulations. The application of reduced benefit directions under the Child Support Act 1991 to disability working allowance is required by reg. 34 of the Child Support (Maintenance Assessment Procedure) Regulations 1992.

PART VIII

ENTITLEMENT TO FAMILY CREDIT AND DISABILITY WORKING ALLOWANCE

Prescribed circumstances for entitlement to disability working allowance

57. For the purposes of section 20(6A)(d) of the Act [SSCBA, s.129(1)(d)] (prescribed circumstances) where a claimant or a member of his family is entitled to family credit, he is entitled to disability working allowance, if—
  (a) at the date of the claim for disability working allowance the award of family credit for him or a member of his family will expire within 28 days; and
  (b) the claimant is or would be otherwise entitled to disability working allowance by virtue of these Regulations; and

(c) the claim for disability working allowance is made in respect of a period which commences immediately after the expiry of the award of family credit.

DEFINITIONS

"the Act"—see reg. 2(1).
"claimant"—*ibid.*
"date of claim"—*ibid.*
"family"—see 1986 Act, s.84(1) (SSCBA, s.137(1)).

SCHEDULES

SCHEDULE 1   **Regulation 3**

DISABILITY WHICH PUTS A PERSON AT A DISADVANTAGE IN GETTING A JOB

PART I

1. When standing he cannot keep his balance unless he continually holds onto something.

2. Using any crutches, walking frame, walking stick, prosthesis or similar walking aid which he habitually uses, he cannot walk a continuous distance of 100 metres along level ground without stopping or without suffering severe pain.

3. He can use neither of his hands behind his back as in the process of putting on a jacket or of tucking a shirt into trousers.

4. He can extend neither of his arms in front of him so as to shake hands with another person without difficulty.

5. He can put neither of his hands up to his head without difficulty so as to put on a hat.

6. Due to lack of manual dexterity he cannot [¹, with one hand, pick up] a coin which is not more than $2\frac{1}{2}$ centimetres in diameter.

7. He is not able to use his hands or arms to pick up a full jug of 1 litre capacity and pour from it into a cup, without difficulty.

8. He can turn neither of his hands sideways through 180°.

9. He is registered as blind or registered as partially sighted in a register compiled by a local authority under section 29(4)(g) of the National Assistance Act 1948 (welfare services) or, in Scotland, has been certified as blind or as partially sighted and in consequence registered as blind or partially sighted in a register maintained by or on behalf of a regional or island council.

10. He cannot see to read 16 point print at a distance greater than 20 centimetres, if appropriate, wearing the glasses he normally uses.

11. He cannot hear a telephone ring when he is in the same room as the telephone, if appropriate, using a hearing aid he normally uses.

12. In a quiet room he has difficulty in hearing what someone talking in a loud voice at a distance of 2 metres says, if appropriate, using a hearing aid he normally uses.

13. People who know him well have difficulty in understanding what he says.

14. When a person he knows well speaks to him, he has difficulty in understanding what that person says.

15. At least once a year during waking hours he is in a coma or has a fit in which he loses consciousness.

16. He has a mental illness for which he receives regular treatment under the supervision of a medically qualified person.

17. Due to mental disability he is often confused or forgetful.

18. He cannot do the simplest addition and subtraction.

19. Due to mental disability he strikes people or damages property or is unable to form normal social relationships.

20. He cannot normally sustain an 8 hour working day or a 5 day working week due to a medical condition or intermittent or continuous severe pain.

PART II

21. Subject to paragraph 24, there is payable to him—

(a) the highest or middle rate of the care component of disability living allowance.

(b) the higher rate of the mobility component of disability living allowance.

(c) an attendance allowance under section 35 of the Social Security Act [SSCBA, s.64],

(d) disablement benefit where the extent of the disablement is assessed at not less than 80 per cent. in accordance with section 57 of and Schedule 8 to the Social Security Act [SSCBA, s.103, Sched. 6],

(e) a war pension in respect of which the degree of disablement is certified at not less than 80 per cent; and for the purposes of this sub-paragraph ''war pension'' means a war pension in accordance with section 25(4) of the Social Security Act 1989.

(f) mobility supplement, or

(g) a benefit corresponding to a benefit mentioned in sub-paragraphs (a)-(f), under any enactment having effect in Northern Ireland.

22. Subject to paragraph 24, for one or more of the 56 days immediately preceding the date when the initial claim for disability working allowance was made or treated as made, there was payable to him severe disablement allowance or a corresponding benefit under any enactment having effect in Northern Ireland.

23. Subject to paragraph 24, he has an invalid carriage or other vehicle provided by the Secretary of State under section 5(2)(a) of the National Health Service Act 1977 and Schedule 2 to that Act or under section 46 of the National Health Service (Scotland) Act 1978 or provided under Article 30(1) of the Health and Personal Social Services (Northern Ireland) Order 1972.

24. Paragraphs 21 to 23 are subject to the condition that no evidence is before the adjudication officer which gives him reasonable grounds for believing that in respect of an initial claim, none of the paragraphs in Part I or Part III of this Schedule apply to the claimant and in respect of a repeat claim, none of the paragraphs in Part I apply to the claimant.

PART III

25. As a result of an illness or accident he is undergoing a period of habilitation or rehabilitation.

AMENDMENT

1. Income-related Benefits Schemes and Social Security (Claims and Payments) (Miscellaneous Amendments) Regulations 1995 (S.I. 1995 No. 2303), reg. 3(7) (October 3, 1995).

DEFINITIONS

"claimant"—see reg. 2(1).
"the Social Security Act"—*ibid.*

GENERAL NOTE

See the notes to reg. 3 for the application of these tests to initial and repeat claims. For discussion of the substance of Sched.1, see Rowland, *Medical and Disability Appeal Tribunals: the Legislation* and note *CDWA 3123/1997*. The claimant in that case had no thumb on his left hand and the terminal joint of his right thumb was missing. He maintained that he was only able to pick up a coin of 2.5 centimetres in diameter by pushing it across a surface and catching it in his hand. The Commissioner holds that the tests in Schedule 1 were to be performed in the normal way and not by employing some unusual or awkward manoeuvre. The normal way of picking up coins with one hand was to use the pinch grip between the thumb and fingers. An ability to pick up with the fingers alone was irrelevant because that ability did not demonstrate the presence or absence of the pinch grip. The Commissioner also confirmed that para. 6 would be satisfied if the claimant could not pick up a coin of the prescribed size with one hand even if he could with the other. The position was different under para. 7 since there the question was whether the claimant could perform the pouring task using both hands and both arms together. But any realistic difficulty, however slight, in carrying out that task would satisfy the test in para. 7.

SCHEDULE 2   Regulations 19(2) and 21(2)

Sums to be Disregarded in the Calculation of Earnings

1. Any earnings derived from employment which are payable in a country outside the United Kingdom where there is a prohibition against the transfer to the United Kingdom of those earnings.

2. Any earnings of a child or young person.

3. Where a payment of earnings is made in a currency other than sterling, any banking charge or commission payable in converting that payment to sterling.

Definitions

"child"—see 1986 Act, s.20(11) (SSCBA, s.137(1)).
"earnings"—see reg. 2(1).
"young person"—*ibid.*, reg. 8.

General Note

The most important of these disregards is that in para. 2. Earnings of children and young persons are disregarded in all circumstances.

SCHEDULE 3   Regulation 27(2)

Sums to be Disregarded in the Calculation of Income other than Earnings

1. Any amount paid by way of tax on income which is taken into account under regulation 27 (calculation of income other than earnings).

2. Any payment in respect of any expenses incurred by a claimant who is—
(a) engaged by a charitable or [⁹voluntary organisation]; or
(b) a volunteer,
if he otherwise derives no remuneration or profit from the employment and is not to be treated as possessing any earnings under regulation 29(4) (notional income).

3. Any housing benefit [¹⁵, income-based jobseeker's allowance] or income support.

4. Any mobility allowance or disability living allowance.

5. Any concessionary payment made to compensate for the non-payment of—
(a) any payment specified in paragraph 4 or 7;
(b) income support [¹⁵ or income-based jobseeker's allowance].

6. Any mobility supplement or any payment intended to compensate for the non-payment of such a supplement.

7. Any attendance allowance.

8. Any payment to the claimant as holder of the Victoria Cross or of the George Cross or any analogous payment.

9. Any sum in respect of a course of study attended by a child or young person payable by virtue of regulations made under section 81 of the Education Act 1944 (assistance by means of scholarship or otherwise), or by virtue of section 2(1) of the Education Act 1962 (awards for courses of further education) or section 49 of the Education (Scotland) Act 1980 (power to assist persons to take advantage of educational facilities) [¹⁸or section 12(2)(c) of the Further and Higher Education (Scotland) Act 1992 (provision of financial assistance to students)].

10. In the case of a student, any sums intended for any expenditure specified in paragraph (2) of regulation 42 (calculation of grant income) necessary as a result of his attendance on his course.

11. In the case of a claimant participating in arrangements for training made under section 2 of the Employment and Training Act 1973 or section 2 of the Enterprise and New Towns (Scotland) Act 1990 or attending a course at an employment rehabilitation centre established under section 2 of the 1973 Act—

(a) any travelling expenses reimbursed to the claimant;

(b) any living away from home allowance under section 2(2)(d) of the 1973 Act or section 2(4)(c) of the 1990 Act;

(c) any training premium,

[¹⁹(d) any child care expenses reimbursed to the claimant in respect of his participation in an employment programme specified in regulation 75(1)(a)(ii) of the Jobseeker's Allowance Regulations 1996 or in a training scheme specified in regulation 75(1)(b)(ii) of those Regulations,]

but this paragraph, except insofar as it relates to a payment under sub-paragraph (a), [¹⁹(b), (c) or (d)], does not apply to any part of any allowance under section 2(2)(d) of the 1973 Act or section 2(4)(c) of the 1990 Act.

[¹⁰**11A.** Any Jobmatch Allowance payable pursuant to arrangements made under section 2(1) of the Employment and Training Act 1973 where the payments will cease by the date on which the period under section 129(6) of the Contributions and Benefits Act 1992 (period of award) is to begin.]

12.—(1) Except where sub-paragraph (2) applies and subject to sub-paragraph (3) and paragraphs 29 and 33, [¹³£20] of any charitable payment or of any voluntary payment made or due to be made at regular intervals.

(2) Subject to sub-paragraph (3) and paragraph 33, any charitable payment or voluntary payment made or due to be made at regular intervals which is intended and used for an item other than food, ordinary clothing or footwear, household fuel, or housing costs of any member of the family, or is used for any personal community [²charge,] collective community charge contribution [² or council tax] for which any member of the family is liable.

(3) Sub-paragraphs (1) and (2) shall not apply to a payment which is made or due to be made by—

(a) a former partner of the claimant, or former parent of any member of the claimant's family; or

(b) the parent of a child or young person is a member of the claimant's family's.

(4) For the purposes of sub-paragraph (1) where a number of charitable or voluntary payments may fall to be taken into account they shall be treated as though they were one such payment.

(5) For the purposes of sub-paragraph (2) the expression "ordinary clothing or footwear" means clothing or footwear for normal daily use, but does not include school uniforms, or clothing or footwear used solely for sporting activities.

13.—(1) Where the claimant or his partner is treated as responsible for a child or young person by virtue of regulation 9 (circumstances in which a person is to be treated as responsible or not responsible for another), £15 of any payment of maintenance, whether under a court order or not, which is made or due to be made by—

(a) the claimant's former partner, or the claimant's partner's former partner; or

(b) the parent of a child or young person where that child or young person is a member of the claimant's family except where that parent is the claimant or the claimant's partner.

(2) For the purposes of sub-paragraph (1) where more than one maintenance payment falls to be taken into account in any week, all such payments shall be aggregated and treated as if they were a single payment.

[¹¹**14.** Subject to paragraph 29, £10 of any of the following, namely—

(a) a war disablement pension (except insofar as such a pension falls to be disregarded under paragraph [¹²6 or 7]);

(b) a war widow's pension;

(c) a pension payable to a person as a widow under the Naval, Military and Air Forces Etc. (Disablement and Death) Service Pensions Order 1983 in so far as that Order is made under the Naval and Marine Pay and Pensions Act 1865 [¹²or the Pensions and Yeomanry Pay Act 1884], or is made only under section 12(1) of the Social Security (Miscellaneous Provisions) Act 1977 and any power of Her Majesty otherwise than under an enactment to make provision about pensions for or in respect of persons who have been disabled or have died in consequence of service as members of the armed forces of the Crown;

(d) a payment made to compensate for the non-payment of such a pension as is mentioned in any of the preceding sub-paragraphs;

(e) a pension paid by the goverment of a country outside Great Britain which is analogous to any of the pensions mentioned in sub-paragraphs (a) to (c) above;

(f) a pension paid to victims of National Socialist persecution under any special provision made by the law of the Federal Republic of Germany, or any part of it, or of the Republic of Austria.]

15. Any child benefit under Part I of the Child Benefit Act 1975 [SSCBA, Part IX].

16.—(1) Any income derived from capital to which the claimant is, or is treated under regulation 39 (capital jointly held) as, beneficially entitled but, but subject to sub-paragraph (2), not income derived from capital disregarded under paragraph 1, 2, 4, 13 or 26 to 30 of Schedule 4.

(2) Income derived from capital disregarded under paragraph 2, 4 or 26 to 30 of Schedule 4 but [³only to the extent of—

(a) any mortgage repayments made in respect of the dwelling or premises in the period during which that income accrued; or

(b) any council tax or water charges which the claimant is liable to pay in respect of the dwelling or premises and which are paid in the period during which that income accrued.]

17. Where a person receives income under an annuity purchased with a loan which satisfies the following conditions—

(a) that the loan was made as part of a scheme under which not less than 90 per cent of the proceeds of the loan were applied to the purchase by the person to whom it was made of an annuity ending with his life or with the life of the survivor of two or more persons (in this paragraph referred to as "the annuitants") who include the person to whom the loan was made;

(b) that the interest on the loan is payable by the person to whom it was made or by one of the annuitants;

(c) that at the time the loan was made the person to whom it was made or each of the annuitants had attained the age of 65;

(d) that the loan was secured on a dwelling in Great Britain and the person to whom the loan was made or one of the annuitants owns an estate or interest in that dwelling; and

(e) that the person to whom the loan was made or one of the annuitants occupies the dwelling on which it was secured as his home at the time the interest is paid,

the amount, calculated on a weekly basis equal to—

[⁸(i) where, or in so far as, section 369 of the Income and Corporation Taxes Act 1988 (mortgage interest payable under deduction of tax) applies to the payments of interest on the loan, the interest which is payable after deduction of a sum equal to income tax on such payments at the applicable percentage of income tax within the meaning of section 369(1A) of that Act;]

    (ii) in any other case the interest which is payable on the loan without deduction of such a sum.

[⁹**18.** Any payment made to the claimant by a person who normally resides with the claimant, which is a contribution towards that person's living and accommodation costs, except where that person is residing with the claimant in circumstances to which paragraph 19 or 38 or regulation 24(2) (earnings of self-employed earners) refers.]

[⁷**19.** Where the claimant occupies a dwelling as his home and the dwelling is also occupied by [⁹ another person], and there is a contractual liability to make payments to the claimant in respect of the occupation of the dwelling by that person or a member of his family—

    (a) £4 of the aggregate of any payments made in respect of any one week in respect of the occupation of the dwelling by that person or a member of his family, or by that person and a member of his family; and

    (b) a further [¹⁴£9.25], where the aggregate of any such payments is inclusive of an amount for heating.]

20. Any income in kind.

21. Any income which is payable in a country outside the United Kingdom where there is a prohibition against the transfer to the United Kingdom of that income.

22.—(1) Any payment made to the claimant in respect of a child or young person who is a member of his family—

    (a) in accordance with a scheme approved by the Secretary of State under section 57A of the Adoption Act 1976, or as the case may be, section 51 of the Adoption (Scotland) Act 1978 (schemes for payments of allowances to adopters);

    (b) which is a payment made by a local authority in pursuance of paragraph 15(1) of Schedule 1 to the Children Act 1989 (local authority contributions to a custodian to child's maintenance),

[²¹(c) which is a payment made by an authority, as defined in Article 2 of the Children Order, in pursuance of Article 15 of, and paragraph 17 of Schedule 1 to, that Order (contribution by an authority to child's maintenance);]

to the extent specified in sub-paragraph (2).

    (2) In the case of a child or young person—

    (a) to whom regulation 30 applies (capital in excess of £3,000), the whole payment;

    (b) to whom that regulation does not apply, so much of the weekly amount of the payment as exceeds the allowance in respect of that child or young person under Schedule 5.

23. Any payment made by a local authority to the claimant with whom a person is accommodated and maintained by virtue of arrangements made under section 23(2)(a) of the Children Act 1989 or, as the case may be, section 21 of the Social Work (Scotland) Act 1968 or by a voluntary organisation under section 59(1)(a) of the Children Act 1989 or by a care authority under regulation 9 of the Boarding Out and Fostering of Children (Scotland) Regulations 1985 (provision of accommodation and maintenance for children by local authorities and voluntary organisations).

24. [²²Any payment made to the claimant or his partner for a person ("the person concerned"), who is not normally a member of the claimant's household but is temporarily in his care, by—

    (a) a health authority;

    (b) a local authority;

    (c) a voluntary organisation; or

    (d) the person concerned pursuant to section 26(3A) of the National Assistance Act 1948].

25. Any payment made by a local authority under section 17 or 24 of the Children Act 1989 or, as the case may be, section 12, 24 or 26 of the Social Work (Scotland)

Act 1968 (provision of services for children and their families and advice and assistance to certain children).

[²³**25A.**—(1) Subject to sub-paragraph (2), any payment received under an insurance policy taken out to insure against the risk of being unable to maintain repayments—

(a) on a loan which is secured on the dwelling which the claimant occupies as his home; or

(b) under a regulated agreement as defined for the purposes of the Consumer Credit Act 1974 or under a hire-purchase agreement or a conditional sale agreement as defined for the purposes of Part III of the Hire-Purchase Act 1964.

(2) A payment referred to in sub-paragraph (1) shall only be disregarded to the extent that the payment received under that policy does not exceed the amounts, calculated on a weekly basis, which are used to—

(a) maintain the repayments referred to in sub-paragraph (1)(a) or, as the case may be, (b); and

(b) meet any amount due by way of premiums on—

(i) that policy; or

(ii) in a case to which sub-paragraph (1)(a) applies, an insurance policy taken out to insure against loss or damage to any building or part of a building which is occupied by the claimant as his home and which is required as a condition of the loan referred to in sub-paragraph (1)(a).]

26. Any payment of income which under regulation 34 (income treated as capital) is to be treated as capital.

27. Any statutory maternity pay under Part V of the Act [SSCBA, Part XII] or maternity allowance under section 22 of the Social Security Act [SSCBA, s.35].

28. Any payment under paragraph 2 of Schedule 6 to the Act [SSCBA, s.148] (pensioners Christmas bonus).

29. The total of a claimant's income or, if he is a member of a family, the family's income and the income of any person which he is treated as possessing under regulation 12(2) (calculation of income and capital of members of claimant's family and of a polygamous marriage) to be disregarded under regulation 43(2)(b) (calculation of covenant income where a contribution is assessed), regulation 44(1)(c) (covenant income where no grant income or no contribution is assessed), regulation 47(2) (treatment of student loans) and paragraphs 12(1) and 14, shall in no case exceed [¹³£20] per week.

30. Where a payment of income is made in a currency other than sterling, any banking charge or commission payable in converting that payment into sterling.

31. Any statutory maternity pay under Part VI of the Social Security (Northern Ireland) Order 1986 or maternity allowance under section 22 of the Social Security (Northern Ireland) Act 1975.

32. Any payment in respect of expenses to which regulation 21(2) (earnings of employed earners) applies.

33.—(1) Any payment made under the Macfarlane Trust, the Macfarlane (Special Payments) Trust, the Macfarlane (Special Payments) (No.2) Trust ("the Trusts"), [¹the Fund][⁵, the Eileen Trust] or [⁴, the Independent Living Funds].

(2) Any payment by or on behalf of a person who suffered or is suffering from haemophilia [¹or who is or was a qualifying person], or by or on behalf of his partner or former partner from whom he is not, or, where either that person or his former partner has died, was not, estranged or divorced, which derives from a payment under any of the Trusts to which sub-paragraph (1) refers and which is made to or for the benefit of—

(a) that person or that person's partner or former partner to whom this sub-paragraph refers;

(b) any child who is a member of that person's family or who was such a member and who is a member of the claimant's family; or

(c) any young person who is a member of that person's family or who was such a member and who is a member of the claimant's family.

(3) Any payment by a person who is suffering from haemophilia [¹or who is a qualify-

ing person], which derives from a payment under any of the Trusts to which sub-paragraph (1) refers, where—

    (a) that person has no partner or former partner from whom he is not estranged or divorced, nor any child or young person who is or had been a member of that person's family; and

    (b) the payment is made either—

        (i) to that person's parent or step-parent, or

        (ii) where that person at the date of the payment is a child, a young person or a student who has not completed his full-time education and has no parent or step-parent, to his guardian,

but only for a period from the date of the payment until the end of two years from that person's death.

(4) Any payment out of the estate of a person who suffered from haemophilia ['or who was a qualifying person], which derives from a payment under any of the Trusts to which sub-paragraph (1) refers, where—

    (a) that person at the date of his death (the relevant date) had no partner or former partner from whom he was not estranged or divorced, nor any child or young person who was or had been a member of his family; and

    (b) the payment is made either—

        (i) to that person's parent or step-parent, or

        (ii) where that person at the relevant date was a child, a young person or a student who had not completed his full education and had no parent or step-parent, to his guardian,

but only for a period of 2 years from the relevant date.

(5) In the case of a person to whom or for whose benefit a payment under sub-paragraph (1), (2), (3) or (4) is made, any income which derives from any payment of income or capital made under or deriving from any of the Trusts.

['(6) For the purposes of sub-paragraphs (2) to (5), any reference to the Trusts shall be construed as including a reference to the Fund [⁵ and the Eileen Trust].]

34. Any payment made by the Secretary of State to compensate for the loss (in whole or in part) of entitlement to housing benefit.

35. Any payment made by the Secretary of State to compensate a person who was entitled to supplementary benefit in respect of a period ending immediately before 11th April 1988 but who did not become entitled to income support in respect of a period beginning with that day.

36. Any payment made by the Secretary of State to compensate for the loss of housing benefit supplement under regulation 19 of the Supplementary Benefit (Requirements) Regulations 1983.

37. Any payment made to a juror or witness in respect of attendance at court other than compensation for loss of earnings or for the loss of a benefit payable under the benefit Acts.

[⁷**38.** Where the claimant occupies a dwelling as his home and he provides in that dwelling board and lodging accommodation, an amount, in respect of each person for whom such accommodation is provided for the whole or any part of a week, equal to—

    (a) where the aggregate of any payments made in respect of any one week in respect of such accommodation provided to such person does not exceed £20.00, 100 per cent of such payments; or

    (b) where the aggregate of any such payments exceeds £20.00, £20.00 and 50 per cent of the excess over £20.00.]

39. Any community charge benefit.

40. Any payment in consequence of a reduction of a personal community charge pursuant to regulations under section 13A of the Local Government Finance Act 1988 or section 9A of the Abolition of Domestic Rates Etc. (Scotland) Act 1987 (reduction of liability for personal community charge) [²or reduction of council tax under section 13 or, as the case may be, section 80 of the Local Government Finance Act 1992 (reduction of liability for council tax).]

41. Any special war widows payment made under—

(a) the Naval and Marine Pay and Pensions (Special War Widows Payment) Order 1990 made under section 3 of the Naval and Marine Pay and Pensions Act 1865;

(b) the Royal Warrant dated 19th February 1990 amending the Schedule to the Army Pensions Warrant 1977;

(c) the Queen's Order dated 26th February 1990 made under section 2 of the Air Force (Constitution) Act 1917;

(d) the Home Guard War Widows Special Payments Regulations 1990 made under section 151 of the Reserve Forces Act 1980;

(e) the Orders dated 19th February 1990 amending Orders made on 12th December 1980 concerning the Ulster Defence Regiment made in each case under section 140 of the Reserve Forces Act 1980;

and any analogous payment by the Secretary of State for Defence to any person who is not a person entitled under the provisions mentioned in sub-paragraphs (a) to (e) of this paragraph.

42.—(1) Any payment or repayment made—

(a) as respects England and Wales, under regulation 3, 5 or 8 of the National Health Service (Travelling Expenses and Remission of Charges) Regulations 1988 (travelling expenses and health service supplies);

(b) as respects Scotland, under regulation 3, 5 or 8 of the National Health Service (Travelling Expenses and Remission of Charges) (Scotland) Regulations 1988 (travelling expenses and health service supplies).

(2) Any payment or repayment made by the Secretary of State for Health, the Secretary of State for Scotland or the Secretary of State for Wales which is analogous to a payment or repayment mentioned in sub-paragraph (1).

43. Any payment made under regulation 9 to 11 or 13 of the Welfare Food Regulations 1988 (payments made in place of milk tokens or the supply of vitamins).

44. Any payment made either by the Secretary of State for the Home Department or by the Secretary of State for Scotland under a scheme established to assist relatives and other persons to visit persons in custody.

45. Any payment made, whether by the Secretary of State or any other person, under the Disabled Persons Employment Act 1944 or in accordance with arrangements made under section 2 of the Employment and Training Act 1973 to assist disabled persons to obtain or retain employment despite their disability.

46. Any family credit.

[³**47.** Any council tax benefit.

48. Any guardian's allowance.]

[⁷**49.** Where the claimant is in receipt of any benefit under Part II, III or V of the Contributions and Benefits Act, [¹⁰or pension under the Naval, Military and Air Forces Etc. (Disablement and Death) Service Pensions Order 1983], any increase in the rate of that benefit arising under Part IV (increases for dependants) or section 106(a) (unemployability supplement) of that Act [¹⁰or the rate of that pension under that Order] where the dependant in respect of whom the increase is paid is not a member of the claimant's family.]

[⁸**50.** Any supplementary pension under article 29(1A) of the Naval, Military and Air Forces etc. (Disablement and Death) Service Pensions Order 1983 (pensions to widows).

51. In the case of a pension awarded at the supplementary rate under article 27(3) of the Personal Injuries (Civilians) Scheme 1983 (pensions to widows), the sum specified in paragraph 1(c) of Schedule 4 to that Scheme.

52.—(1) Any payment which is—

(a) made under any of the Dispensing Instruments to a widow of a person—

(i) whose death was attributable to service in a capacity analogous to service as a member of the armed forces of the Crown; and

1043

    (ii) whose service in such capacity terminated before 31st March 1973; and
- (b) equal to the amount specified in article 29(1A) of the Naval, Military and Air Forces etc. (Disablement and Death) Service Pensions Order 1983 (pensions to widows).

(2) In this paragraph "the Dispensing Instruments" means the Order in Council of 19th December 1881, the Royal Warrant of 27th October 1884 and the Order by His Majesty of 14th January 1922 (exceptional grants of pay, non-effective pay and allowances).]

[⁹53. Any payment made by the Secretary of State to compensate for a reduction in a maintenance assessment made under the Child Support Act 1991.]

[¹⁶ 54. Any payment made by the Secretary of State under the Earnings Top-up Scheme.]

[¹⁷ 55. Any payment made under the Community Care (Direct Payments) Act 1996 or under section 12B of the Social Work (Scotland) Act 1968.

56.—(1) Any Career Development Loan paid to the claimant pursuant to section 2 of the Employment and Training Act 1973 except to the extent that the loan has been applied for and paid in respect of living expenses for the period of education and training supported by that loan and those expenses relate to any one or more of the items specified in sub-paragraph (2).

(2) The items specified for the purposes of sub-paragraph (1) are food, ordinary clothing or footwear, household fuel or housing costs of any member of the family or any personal community charge, collective community charge contribution or any council tax for which any member of the family is liable.

(3) For the purposes of this paragraph, "ordinary clothing and footwear" means clothing or footwear for normal daily use, but does not include school uniforms, or clothing and footwear used solely for sporting activities.]

[²⁴57. Any mandatory top-up payment made to a person pursuant to section 2 of the Employment and Training Act 1973 in respect of that person's participation in an employment programme specified in—
- (a) regulation 75(1)(a)(ii)(aa)(ii) of the Jobseeker's Allowance Regulations 1996 (self-employment route of the Employment Option of the New Deal);
- (b) regulation 75(1)(a)(ii)(bb) of those Regulations (Voluntary Sector Option of the New Deal); or
- (c) regulation 75(1)(a)(ii)(cc) of those Regulations (Environment Task Force Option of the New Deal).]

[²⁰58. Any discretionary payment to meet, or to help meet, special needs made to a person pursuant to section 2 of the Employment and Training Act 1973 in respect of that person's participation in the Full-Time Education and Training Option of the New Deal as specified in regulation 75(1)(b)(ii) of the Jobseeker's Allowance Regulations 1996.]

[²⁵59.—(1) Subject to sub-paragraph (2), in respect of a person who is receiving, or who has received, assistance under an employment programme specified in regulation 75(1)(a)(ii)(aa)(ii) of the Jobseeker's Allowance Regulations 1996 (self-employment route of the Employment Option of the New Deal), any payment to that person—
- (a) to meet expenses wholly and necessarily incurred whilst carrying on the commercial activity;
- (b) which is used or intended to be used to maintain repayments on a loan taken out by that person for the purpose of establishing or carrying on the commercial activity,

in respect of which such assistance is or was received.

(2) Sub-paragraph (1) shall apply only in respect of payments which are paid to that person from the special account as defined for the purposes of Chapter IVA of Part VIII of the Jobseeker's Allowance Regulations 1996.]

[²⁶60.—(1) Subject to sub-paragraph (2), any discretionary payment made pursuant to section 2 of the Employment and Training Act 1973 to meet, or help meet, special needs of a person who is undertaking a qualifying course within the meaning specified in regulation 17A(7) of the Jobseeker's Allowance Regulations 1996.

(2) No amount shall be disregarded pursuant to sub-paragraph (1) in respect of travel expenses incurred as a result of the student's attendance on the course where an amount in respect of those expenses has already been disregarded pursuant to regulation 46 (student's income to be disregarded).]

AMENDMENTS

1. Income-related Benefits Schemes and Social Security (Recoupment) Amendment Regulations 1992 (S.I. 1992 No. 1101), reg. 3(6) (May 7, 1992).
2. Income-related Benefits Schemes (Miscellaneous Amendments) Regulations 1993 (S.I. 1993 No. 315), Sched., para. 17 (April 1, 1993).
3. Income-related Benefits Schemes (Miscellaneous Amendments) Regulations 1993 (S.I. 1993 No. 315), reg. 21 (council tax and council tax benefit: April 1, 1993; otherwise: April 13, 1993).
4. Social Security Benefits (Miscellaneous Amendments) (No. 2) Regulations 1993 (S.I. 1993 No. 963), reg. 6(3) (April 22, 1993).
5. Income-related Benefits Schemes and Social Security (Recoupment) Amendment Regulations 1993 (S.I. 1993 No. 1249), reg. 5(4) (May 14, 1993).
6. Income-related Benefits Schemes (Miscellaneous Amendments) (No. 4) Regulations 1993 (S.I. 1993 No. 2119), reg. 45 (October 5, 1993).
7. Income-related Benefits Schemes (Miscellaneous Amendments) Regulations 1994 (S.I. 1994 No. 527), reg. 28 (April 12, 1994).
8. Income-related Benefits Schemes (Miscellaneous Amendments) (No. 5) Regulations 1994 (S.I. 1994 No. 2139), reg. 9 (October 4, 1994).
9. Income-related Benefits Schemes (Miscellaneous Amendments) Regulations 1995 (S.I. 1995 No. 516), reg. 8 (April 11, 1995).
10. Income-related Benefits Schemes and Social Security (Claims and Payments) (Miscellaneous Amendments) Regulations 1995 (S.I. 1995 No. 2303), reg. 3(8) (October 3, 1995).
11. Income-related Benefits Schemes Amendment (No. 2) Regulations 1995 (S.I. 1995 No. 2792), reg. 3 (October 28, 1995).
12. Income-related Benefits Schemes (Widows' etc. Pensions Disregards) Amendment Regulations 1995 (S.I. 1995 No. 3282), reg. 3 (December 20, 1995).
13. Income-related Benefits Schemes (Miscellaneous Amendments) Regulations 1996 (S.I. 1996 No. 462), reg. 8 (April 9, 1996).
14. Social Security Benefits Up-rating Order 1996 (S.I. 1996 No. 599), art. 17(e) (April 9, 1996).
15. Social Security and Child Support (Jobseeker's Allowance) (Consequential Amendments) Regulations 1996 (S.I. 1996 No. 1345), reg. 7(6) (October 7, 1996).
16. Income-related Benefits Schemes and Social Fund (Miscellaneous Amendments) Regulations 1996 (S.I. 1996 No. 1944), reg. 13 and Sched., para. 5 (October 7, 1996).
17. Income-related Benefits and Jobseeker's Allowance (Miscellaneous Amendments) Regulations 1997 (S.I. 1997 No. 65), reg. 2(5) and (6) (April 8, 1997).
18. Income-related Benefits and Jobseeker's Allowance (Amendment) (No. 2) Regulations 1997 (S.I. 1997 No. 2197), reg. 7(7) and (8)(b) (October 7, 1997).
19. Social Security Amendment (New Deal) Regulations 1997 (S.I. 1997 No. 2863), reg. 17(7) and (8)(b) (January 5, 1998).
20. Social Security Amendment (New Deal) Regulations 1997 (S.I. 1997 No. 2863), reg. 17(9) and (10)(b) (January 5, 1998).
21. Social Security (Miscellaneous Amendments) Regulations 1998 (S.I. 1998 No. 563), reg. 7(1) and (2)(b) (April 7, 1998).
22. Social Security (Miscellaneous Amendments) Regulations 1998 (S.I. 1998 No. 563), reg. 7(3) and (4)(b) (April 7, 1998).
23. Social Security (Miscellaneous Amendments) (No. 3) Regulations 1998 (S.I. 1998 No. 1173), reg. 3 (June 2, 1998).
24. Social Security (Miscellaneous Amendments) (No. 4) Regulations 1998 (S.I. 1998 No. 1174), reg. 7(3) and (4)(b) (June 1, 1998).
25. Social Security (Miscellaneous Amendments) (No. 4) Regulations 1998 (S.I. 1998 No. 1174), reg. 7(5) and (6)(b) (June 1, 1998).
26. Social Security Amendment (New Deal) (No. 2) Regulations 1998 (S.I. 1998 No. 2117), reg. 4(2) (September 24, 1998).

DEFINITIONS

"the Act"—see reg. 2(1).
"attendance allowance"—*ibid.*

"the benefit Acts"—*ibid.*
"child"—see 1986 Act, s.84(1) (SSCBA, s.137(1)).
"the Children Order"—see reg. 2(1).
"claimant"—*ibid.*
"dwelling"—see 1986 Act, s.84(1) (SSCBA, s.137(1)).
"the Earnings Top-up Scheme—see reg. 2(1).
"family"—see 1986 Act, s.20(11) (SSCBA, s.137(1)).
"local authority"—see 1986 Act, s.84(1).
"mobility allowance"—see reg. 2(1).
"mobility supplement"—*ibid.*
"payment"—*ibid.*
"qualifying person"—*ibid.*
"Social Security Act"—*ibid.*
"student"—*ibid.*,reg. 41.
"the Eileen Trust"—*ibid.*
"the Fund"—see reg. 2(1).
"the Independent Living Funds"—*ibid.*
"the Macfarlane (Special Payments) Trust"—*ibid.*
"the Macfarlane (Special Payments)(No.2) Trust"—*ibid.*
"the Macfarlane Trust"—*ibid.*
"voluntary organisation"—*ibid.*
"year of assessment"—see reg. 2(1).
"young person"—*ibid.*, reg. 8.

GENERAL NOTE

See the notes to Sched. 2 to the Family Credit (General) Regulations, with the necessary differences in cross-references. Para. 46 is an addition.

SCHEDULE 4   **Regulation 32(2)**

CAPITAL TO BE DISREGARDED

1. The dwelling, together with any garage, garden and outbuildings, normally occupied by the claimant as his home including any premises not so occupied which it is impracticable or unreasonable to sell separately, in particular, in Scotland, any croft land on which the dwelling is situated; but, notwithstanding regulation 12 (calculation of income and capital of members of claimant's family and of a polygamous marriage), only one dwelling shall be disregarded under this paragraph.

2. Any premises acquired for occupation by the claimant which he intends to occupy as his home within 26 weeks of the date of acquisition or such longer period as is reasonable in the circumstances to enable the claimant to obtain possession and commence occupation of the premises.

3. Any sum directly attributable to the proceeds of sale of any premises formerly occupied by the claimant as his home which is to be used for the purchase of other premises intended for such occupation within 26 weeks of the date of sale or such longer period as is reasonable in the circumstances to enable the claimant to complete the purchase.

4. Any premises occupied in whole or in part by a partner or relative (that is to say any close relative, grandparent, grandchild, uncle, aunt, nephew or niece) of any member of the family as his home, where that person is aged 60 or over or has been incapacitated for a continuous period of at least 13 weeks immediately preceding the date of the claim.

[⁹**5.** Any future interest in property of any kind, other than land or premises in respect of which the claimant has granted a subsisting lease or tenancy, including sub-leases or subtenancies.]

6.—(1) The assets of any business owned in whole or in part by the claimant and for the purposes of which he is engaged as a self-employed earner or, if he has ceased to be so engaged, for such period as may be reasonable in the circumstances to allow for disposal of any such asset.

(2) The assets of any business owned in whole or in part by the claimant where—

(a) he has ceased to be engaged as a self-employed earner in that business by reason of some disease or bodily or mental disablement; and

(b) he intends to become re-engaged as a self-employed earner in that business as soon as he recovers or is able to be re-engaged in that business,

for a period of 26 weeks from the date on which the claimant last ceased to be engaged in that business, or, if it is unreasonable to expect him to become re-engaged in that business within that period, for such longer period as is reasonable in the circumstances to enable him to become so re-engaged.

[[17](3) In the case of a person who is receiving assistance under an employment programme specified in regulation 75(1)(a)(ii)(aa)(ii) of the Jobseeker's Allowance Regulations 1996 (self-employment route of the Employment Option of the New Deal), the assets acquired by that person for the purpose of establishing or carrying on the commercial activity in respect of which such assistance is being received.

(4) In the case of a person who has ceased carrying on the commercial activity in respect of which assistance was received as specified in sub-paragraph (3), the assets relating to that activity for such period as may be reasonable in the circumstances to allow for disposal of any such asset.]

7. Any sum attributable to the proceeds of sale of any asset of such a business which is re-invested or to be re-invested in the business within 13 weeks of the date of sale or such longer period as may be reasonable to allow for the re-investment.

8. Any arrears of, or any concessionary payment made to compensate for arrears due to non-payment of—

(a) any payment specified in paragraphs 4, 6, or 7 of Schedule 3;

(b) an income-related benefit [[11]or income-based jobseeker's allowance,] or supplementary benefit under the Supplementary Benefits Act 1976, family income supplement under the Family Income Supplements Act 1970 or housing benefit under Part II of the Social Security and Housing Benefits Act 1982,

[[12](c) any earnings top-up,]

but only for a period of 52 weeks from the date of the receipt of the arrears or of the concessionary payment.

9. Any sum—

(a) paid to the claimant in consequence of damage to, or loss of, the home or any personal possession and intended for its repair or replacement; or

(b) acquired by the claimant (whether as a loan or otherwise) on the express condition that it is to be used for effecting essential repairs or improvements to the home,

which is to be used for the intended purpose, for a period of 26 weeks from the date on which it was so paid or acquired or such longer period as is reasonable in the circumstances to enable the claimant to effect the repairs, replacement or improvements.

10. Any sum—

(a) deposited with a housing association as defined in section 1(1) of the Housing Associations Act 1985 or section 338(1) of the Housing (Scotland) Act 1987 as a condition of occupying the home;

(b) which was so deposited and which is to be used for the purchase of another home, for the period of 26 weeks or such longer period as may be reasonable in the circumstances to complete the purchase.

11. Any personal possessions except those which have been acquired by the claimant with the intention of reducing his capital in order to secure entitlement to disability working allowance or to increase the amount of that benefit.

12. The value of the right to receive any income under an annuity or the surrender value (if any) of such an annuity.

13. Where the funds of a trust are derived from a payment made in consequence of any personal injury to the claimant, the value of the trust fund and the value of the right to receive any payment under that trust.

14. The value of the right to receive any income under a life interest or from a liferent.

15. The value of the right to receive any income which is disregarded under paragraph 1 of Schedule 2 or 21 of Schedule 3.

16. The surrender value of any policy of life insurance.

17. Where any payment of capital falls to be made by instalments, the value of the right to receive any outstanding instalments.

18. Any payment made by a local authority under [²section 17 or 24] of the Children Act 1989 or, as the case may be, section 12, 24 or 26 of the Social Work (Scotland) Act 1968 (provision of services for children and their families and advice and assistance for certain children).

19. Any social fund payment under Part III of the Act [SSCBA, Part VIII].

20. Any refund of tax which falls to be deducted under section 26 of the Finance Act 1982 (deductions of tax from certain loan interest) on a payment of relevant loan interest for the purpose of acquiring an interest in the home or carrying out repairs or improvements to the home.

21. Any capital which by virtue of regulations 28 (capital treated as income)[⁶, 30(1) (modifications in respect of children and young persons)] or 47 (treatment of student loans) is to be treated as income.

22. Where a payment of capital is made in a currency other than sterling, any banking charge or commission payable in converting that payment to sterling.

23.—(1) Any payment made under the Macfarlane Trust, the Macfarlane (Special Payments) Trust, the Macfarlane (Special Payments) (No. 2) Trust ("the Trusts"), [¹the Fund][⁵, the Eileen Trust] or [³the Independent Living Funds].

(2) Any payment by or on behalf of a person who suffered or who is suffering from haemophilia [¹or who is or was a qualifying person], or by or on behalf of his partner or former partner from whom he is not or, where either that person or his former partner has died, was not estranged or divorced, which derives from a payment made under any of the Trusts to which sub-paragraph (1) refers and which is made to or for the benefit of—

(a) that person or that person's partner or former partner to whom this sub-paragraph refers;

(b) any child who is a member of that person's family or who was such a member and who is a member of the claimant's family; or

(c) any young person who is a member of that person's family or who was such a member and who is a member of the claimant's family.

(3) Any payment by a person who is suffering from haemophilia [¹or who is a qualifying person], which derives from a payment under any of the Trusts to which sub-paragraph (1) refers, where—

(a) that person has no partner or former partner from whom he is not estranged or divorced, nor any child or young person who is or had been a member of that person's family; and

(b) the payment is made either—

(i) to that person's parent or step-parent; or

(ii) where that person at the date of the payment is a child, a young person or a student who has not completed his full-time education and has no parent or step-parent, to his guardian,

but only for a period from the date of the payment until the end of two years from that person's death.

(4) Any payment out of the estate of a person who suffered from haemophilia [¹or who was a qualifying person], which derives from a payment under any of the Trusts to which sub-paragraph (1) refers, where—

(a) that person at the date of his death (the relevant date) had no partner or former partner from whom he was not estranged or divorced, nor any child or young person who was or had been a member of his family; and

(b) the payment is made either—

(i) to that person's parent or step-parent, or

(ii) where that person at the relevant date was a child, a young person or a student who had not completed his education and had no parent or step-parent, to his guardian,

but only for a period of 2 years from the relevant date.

(5) In the case of a person to whom or for whose benefit a payment under sub-paragraph (1), (2), (3) or (4) is made, any capital resource which derives from any payment of income or capital made under or deriving from any of the Trusts.

[¹(6) For the purposes of sub-paragraphs (2) to (5), any reference to the Trusts shall be construed as including a reference to the Fund [⁵and the Eileen Trust].]

24. The value of the right to receive an occupational or personal pension.

[⁹**24A.** The value of any funds held under a personal pension scheme or retirement annuity contract.]

25. The value of the right to receive any rent [⁹except where the claimant has a reversionary interest in the property in respect of which rent is due.]

26.—(1) Where a claimant has ceased to occupy what was formerly the dwelling occupied as the home following his estrangement or divorce from his former partner, that dwelling for a period of 26 weeks from the date on which he ceased to occupy that dwelling.

(2) In this paragraph "dwelling" includes any garage, garden and outbuildings which were formerly occupied by the claimant as his home and any premises not so occupied which it is impracticable or unreasonable to sell separately, in particular, in Scotland, any croft land on which the dwelling is situated.

27. Any premises where the claimant is taking reasonable steps to dispose of those premises, for a period of 26 weeks from the date on which he first took such steps, or such longer period as is reasonable in the circumstances to enable him to dispose of those premises.

28. Any premises which the claimant intends to occupy as his home, and in respect of which he is taking steps to obtain possession and has sought legal advice, or has commenced legal proceedings, with a view to obtaining possession, for a period of 26 weeks from the date on which he first sought such advice or first commenced such proceedings whichever is the earlier, or such longer period as is reasonable in the circumstances to enable him to obtain possession and commence occupation of those premises.

29. Any premises which the claimant intends to occupy as his home to which essential repairs or alterations are required in order to render them fit for such occupation, for a period of 26 weeks from the date on which the claimant first takes steps to effect those repairs or alterations, or such longer period as is reasonable in the circumstances to enable those repairs or alterations to be carried out and the claimant to commence occupation of the premises.

30. Any premises occupied in whole or in part by the former partner of a claimant as his home; but this provision shall not apply where the former partner is a person from whom the claimant is estranged or divorced.

31. Any payment in kind made by a charity or under the Macfarlane (Special Payments) Trust[¹, the Macfarlane (Special Payments) (No. 2) Trust[⁴, the Fund or the independent Living (1993) Fund]].

32. [⁶£200 of any payment, or, if the payment is less than £200, the whole of any payment] made under section 2 of the Employment and Training Act 1973 (functions of the Secretary of State) or section 2 of the Enterprise and New Towns (Scotland) Act 1990 as a training bonus to a person participating in arrangements for training made under either of those sections but only for a period of 52 weeks from the date of the receipt of that payment.

33. Any payment made by the Secretary of State to compensate for the loss (in the whole or in part) of entitlement to housing benefit.

34. Any payment made by the Secretary of State to compensate a person who was entitled to supplementary benefit in respect of a period ending immediately before 11th April 1988 but who did not become entitled to income support in respect of a period beginning with that day.

35. Any payment made by the Secretary of State to compensate for the loss of housing benefit supplement under regulation 19 of the Supplementary Benefit (Requirements) Regulations 1983.

36. Any payment made to a juror or witness in respect of attendance at court other than compensation for loss of earnings or for the loss of a benefit payable under the benefit Acts.

37. Any payment in consequence of a reduction of a personal community charge pursuant to regulations under section 13A of the Local Government Finance Act 1988 or section 9A of the Abolition of Domestic Rates Etc (Scotland) Act 1987 (reduction of liability for personal community charge) [²or reduction of council tax under section 13 or, as the case may be, section 80 of the Local Government Finance Act 1992 (reduction of liability for council tax),] but only for a period of 52 weeks from the date of receipt of the payment.

38. Any grant made to the claimant in accordance with a scheme made under section 129 of the Housing Act 1988 or section 66 of the Housing (Scotland) Act 1988 (schemes for payments to assist local housing authority and local authority tenants to obtain other accommodation) which is to be used—

  (a) to purchase premises intended for occupation as his home; or

  (b) to carry out repairs or alterations which are required to render premises fit for occupation as his home,

for a period of 26 weeks from the date on which he received such a grant or such longer period as is reasonable in the circumstances to enable the purchase, repairs or alterations to be completed and the claimant to commence occupation of those premises as his home.

39.—Any payment or repayment made—

  (a) as respects England and Wales, under regulation 3, 5 or 8 of the National Health Service (Travelling Expenses and Remission of Charges) Regulations 1988 (travelling expenses and health service supplies);

  (b) as respects Scotland, under regulation 3, 5 or 8 of the National Health Service (Travelling Expenses and Remission of Charges) (Scotland) 1988 (travelling expenses and health service supplies);

but only for a period of 52 weeks from the date of receipt of the payment or repayment.

(2) Any payment or repayment made by the Secretary of State for Health, the Secretary of State for Scotland or the Secretary of State for Wales which is analogous to a payment or repayment mentioned in sub-paragraph (1); but only for a period of 52 weeks from the date of receipt of the payment or repayment.

40. Any payment made under regulations 9 to 11 or 13 of the Welfare Food Regulations 1988 (payments made in place of milk tokens or the supply of vitamins), but only for a period of 52 weeks from the date of receipt of the payment.

41. Any payment made either by the Secretary of State for the Home Department or by the Secretary of State for Scotland under a scheme established to assist relatives and other persons to visit persons in custody, but only for a period of 52 weeks from the date of receipt of the payment.

42. Any arrears of special war widows payment which is disregarded under paragraph 41 of Schedule 3 (sums to be disregarded in the calculation of income other than earnings) [⁷ or of any amount which is disregarded under paragraph 50, 51 or 52 of that Schedule], but only for a period of 52 weeks from the date of receipt of the arrears.

43. Any payment made, whether by the Secretary of State or any other person, under the Disabled Persons Employment Act 1944 or in accordance with arrangements made under section 2 of the Employment and Training Act 1973 to assist disabled persons to obtain or retain employment despite their disability.

44. Any payment made by a local authority under section 3 of the Disabled (Employment) Act 1958 to homeworkers assisted under the Blind Homeworkers' Scheme.

[⁷**45.** Any sum of capital administered on behalf of a person [¹⁵ . . .] by the High Court under the provisions of Order 80 of the Rules of the Supreme Court, the County Court under Order 10 of the County Court Rules 1981, or the Court of Protection, where such sum derives from—

(a) an award of damages for a personal injury to that person; or

(b) compensation for the death of one or both parents [[15]where the person concerned is under the age of 18].

46. Any sum of capital administered on behalf of a person [[15] . . .] in accordance with an order made under Rule 43.15 of the Act of Sederunt (Rules of the Court of Session 1994) 1994, or under Rule 131 of the Act of Sederunt (Rules of the Court, consolidation and amendment) 1965, or under Rule 36.14 of the Ordinary Cause Rules 1993, or under Rule 128 of the Ordinary Cause Rules, where such sum derives from—

(a) an award of damages for a personal injury to that person; or

(b) compensation for the death of one or both parents [[15]where the person concerned is under the age of 18].

[[8]**47.** Any payment made by the Secretary of State to compensate for a reduction in a maintenance assessment made under the Child Support Act 1991, but only for a period of 52 weeks from the date of receipt of that payment.]

[[10]**48.** Any payment to the claimant as holder of the Victoria Cross or George Cross.]

[[11]**49.** The amount of any back to work bonus payable by way of a jobseeker's allowance or income support in accordance with section 26 of the Jobseekers Act 1995, or a corresponding payment under article 28 of the Jobseekers (Northern Ireland) Order 1995, but only for a period of 52 weeks from the date of receipt.]

[[13] [[14]**50.**] The amount of any child maintenance bonus payable by way of a jobseeker's allowance or income support in accordance with section 10 of the Child Support Act 1995, or a corresponding payment under Article 4 of the Child Support (Northern Ireland) Order 1995, but only for a period of 52 weeks from the date of receipt.]

[[18]**51.** Any mandatory top-up payment made to a person pursuant to section 2 of the Employment and Training Act 1973 in respect of that person's participation in an employment programme specified in—

(a) regulation 75(1)(a)(ii)(aa)(ii) of the Jobseeker's Allowance Regulations 1996 (self-employment route of the Employment Option of the New Deal);

(b) regulation 75(1)(a)(ii)(bb) of those Regulations (Voluntary Sector Option of the New Deal); or

(c) regulation 75(1)(a)(ii)(cc) of those Regulations (Environment Task Force Option of the New Deal),

but only for a period of 52 weeks from the date of receipt of the payment.]

[[16]**52.** Any discretionary payment to meet, or to help meet, special needs made to a person pursuant to section 2 of the Employment and Training Act 1973 in respect of that person's participation in the Full-Time Education and Training Option of the New Deal as specified in regulation 75(1)(b)(ii) of the Jobseeker's Allowance Regulations 1996 but only for a period of 52 weeks from the date of receipt of the payment.]

[[19]**53.** In the case of a person who is receiving, or who has received, assistance under an employment programme specified in regulation 75(1)(a)(ii)(aa)(ii) of the Jobseeker's Allowance Regulations 1996 (self-employment route of the Employment Option of the New Deal), any sum of capital which is acquired by that person for the purpose of establishing or carrying on the commercial activity in respect of which such assistance is or was received but only for a period of 52 weeks from the date on which that sum was acquired.]

[[20]**54.** Any discretionary payment made pursuant to section 2 of the Employment and Training Act 1973 to meet, or help meet, special needs of a person who is undertaking a qualifying course within the meaning specified in regulation 17A(7) of the Jobseeker's Allowance Regulations 1996 but only for the period of 52 weeks from the date of receipt of that payment.]

Amendments

1. Income-related Benefits Schemes and Social Security (Recoupment) Amendment Regulations 1992 (S.I. 1992 No. 1101), reg. 3(7) (May 7, 1992).

2. Income-related Benefits Schemes (Miscellaneous Amendments) Regulations 1993 (S.I. 1993 No. 315), Sched., para. 18 (April 1, 1993).

3. Social Security Benefits (Miscellaneous Amendments) (No. 2) Regulations 1993 (S.I. 1993 No. 963), reg. 6(3) (April 22, 1993).

4. Social Security Benefits (Miscellaneous Amendments) (No. 2) Regulations 1993 (S.I. 1993 No. 963), reg. 6(5) (April 22, 1993).

5. Income-related Benefits Schemes and Social Security (Recoupment) Amendment Regulations 1993 (S.I. 1993 No. 1249), reg. 5(5) (May 14, 1993).

6. Income-related Benefits Schemes (Miscellaneous Amendments) (No. 4) Regulations 1993 (S.I. 1993 No. 2119), reg. 46 (October 5, 1993).

7. Income-related Benefits Schemes (Miscellaneous Amendments) (No. 5) Regulations 1994 (S.I. 1994 No. 2139), reg. 10 (October 4, 1994).

8. Income-related Benefits Schemes (Miscellaneous Amendments) Regulations 1995 (S.I. 1995 No. 516), reg. 9 (April 11, 1995).

9. Income-related Benefits Schemes and Social Security (Claims and Payments) (Miscellaneous Amendments) Regulations 1995 (S.I. 1995 No. 2303), reg. 3(9) (October 3, 1995).

10. Income-related Benefits Schemes (Miscellaneous Amendments) Regulations 1996 (S.I. 1996 No. 462), reg. 11(2) (April 9, 1996).

11. Social Security and Child Support (Jobseeker's Allowance) (Consequential Amendments) Regulations 1996 (S.I. 1996 No. 1345), reg. 7(7) (October 7, 1996).

12. Income-related Benefits Schemes and Social Fund (Miscellaneous Amendments) Regulations 1996 (S.I. 1996 No. 1944), reg. 13 and Sched., para. 7 (October 7, 1996).

13. Social Security (Child Maintenance Bonus) Regulations 1996 (S.I. 1996 No. 3195), reg. 15 (April 7, 1997).

14. Social Security (Miscellaneous Amendments) Regulations 1997 (S.I. 1997 No. 454), reg. 8(9) (April 6, 1997).

15. Income-related Benefits and Jobseeker's Allowance (Amendment) (No. 2) Regulations 1997 (S.I. 1997 No. 2197), reg. 7(9) and (10)(b) (October 7, 1997).

16. Social Security Amendment (New Deal) Regulations 1997 (S.I. 1997 No. 2863), reg. 17(11) and (12)(b) (January 5, 1998).

17. Social Security (Miscellaneous Amendments) (No. 4) Regulations 1998 (S.I. 1998 No. 1174), reg. 7(7) and (8)(b) (June 1, 1998).

18. Social Security (Miscellaneous Amendments) (No. 4) Regulations 1998 (S.I. 1998 No. 1174), reg. 7(9) and (10)(b) (June 1, 1998).

19. Social Security (Miscellaneous Amendments) (No. 4) Regulations 1998 (S.I. 1998 No. 1174), reg. 7(11) and (12)(b) (June 1, 1998).

20. Social Security Amendment (New Deal) (No. 2) Regulations 1998 (S.I. 1998 No. 2117), reg. 5(2) and (3)(a) (September 24, 1998).

DEFINITIONS

"the Act"—see reg. 2(1).
"the benefit Acts"—*ibid.*
"claimant"—see reg. 2(1), reg. 12(1).
"close relative"—see reg. 2(1).
"date of claim"—*ibid.*
"dwelling"—see 1986 Act, s.84(1) (SSCBA, s.137(1)).
"earnings top-up"—see reg. 2(1).
"family"—see 1986 Act, s.20(11) (SSCBA, s.137(1)).
"occupational pension"—see reg. 2(1).
"partner"—*ibid.*
"personal pension scheme "—*ibid.*
"policy of life insurance"—*ibid.*
"qualifying person"—*ibid.*
"retirement annuity contract"—*ibid.*
"self-employed earner"—*ibid.*
"the Eileen Trust"—*ibid.*
"the Fund"—*ibid.*
"the Independent Living Funds"—*ibid.*
"the Independent Living (1993) Fund"—*ibid.*
"the Macfarlane (Special Payments) Trust"—*ibid.*

"the Macfarlane (Special Payments) (No. 2) Trust"—*ibid.*
"the Macfarlane Trust"—*ibid.*

GENERAL NOTE

See the notes to Sched. 3 to the Family Credit (General) Regulations, with the necessary changes in cross-references. There are some simplifications in the form of these provisions, *e.g.* para. 33.

SCHEDULE 5   **Regulations 51**

DETERMINATION OF APPROPRIATE MAXIMUM DISABILITY WORKING ALLOWANCE

Column (1)	Column (2)
Claimant, child, young person	*Amount of allowance*
1. Single claimant.	**1.** [⁵£51.80].
2. Claimant who is a member of a married or unmarried couple, or is a lone parent.	**2.** [⁵£81.05].
[²**2A.** In the case of a claimant to whom regulation 51(1)(bb) applies.	**2A.** [⁵£11.05]].
[³**3.** Persons in respect of the period— (a) beginning on that person's date of birth and ending on the day preceding the first Tuesday in September following that person's eleventh birthday; (b) beginning on the first Tuesday in September following that person's eleventh birthday and ending on the day preceding the first Tuesday in September following that person's sixteenth birthday.	**3.** (a) [⁵£15.15]; (b) [⁵£20.90];
4. Person in respect of the period beginning on the first Tuesday in September following that person's sixteenth birthday and ending on the day preceding that person's nineteenth birthday.]	[⁴**4.** [⁵£25.95]];
[¹**5.** Child or young person to whom regulation 51(1A) applies (disabled child or young person).	**5.** [⁵£21.90]].

AMENDMENTS

1. Disability Working Allowance and Income Support (General) Amendment Regulations 1995 (S.I. 1995 No. 482), reg. 4 (April 11, 1995).
2. Income-related Benefits Schemes (Miscellaneous Amendments) (No. 2) Regulations 1995 (S.I. 1995 No. 1339), reg. 5 (July 18, 1995).
3. Income-related Benefits and Jobseeker's Allowance (Personal Allowances for Children and Young Persons) (Amendment) Regulations 1996 (S.I. 1996 No. 2545), reg. 9 (October 7, 1997).
4. Family Credit and Disability Working Allowance (General) Amendment Regulations 1997 (S.I. 1997 No. 806), reg. 4 (October 7, 1997).
5. Social Security Benefits Up-rating Order 1999 (S.I. 1999 No. 264), art. 17(d) and Sched. 3 (April 13, 1999).

DEFINITIONS

"child"—see 1986 Act, s.20(11) (SSCBA, s.137(1)).
"claimant"—see reg. 2(1).
"lone parent"—*ibid.*
"married couple"—see 1986 Act, s.20(11) (SSCBA, s.137(1)).
"single claimant"—see reg. 2(1).

"unmarried couple"—see 1986 Act, s.20(11) (SSCBA, s.137(1)).
"young person"—see reg. 2(1), reg. 8.

GENERAL NOTE

See the notes to reg. 51.

Disability Working Allowance and Income Support (General) Amendment Regulations 1995

(S.I. 1995 No. 482)

Made by the Secretary of State under ss. 124(1)(d)(i) and (3), 129(2B)(b) and (c) and (8), 135(1), 137(1) and 175(1), (3) and (4) of the Social Security Contributions and Benefits Act 1992 and s. 12(1) of the Social Security (Incapacity for Work) Act 1994

[In force April 13, 1995]

Transitional provisions with respect to the Disability Working Allowance Regulations

18.—(1) Where invalidity pension was payable to the claimant for one or more of the 56 days immediately preceding the date on which the claim for disability working allowance was made or was treated as made, the payments shall be treated for the purposes of section 129(2)(a)(i) of the Contributions and Benefits Act as payments of long-term incapacity benefit.

(2) Any day on which a claimant was entitled to invalidity pension under sections 33, 40 or 41 of the Contributions and Benefits Act as in force on 12th April 1995 shall be treated for the purposes of section 129(2A)(b) of the Contributions and Benefits Act as a day on which he was entitled to long-term incapacity benefit.

GENERAL NOTE

See the notes to s. 129(2) and (2A) of the Contributions and Benefits Act.

Social Security (Persons From Abroad) Miscellaneous Amendments Regulations 1996

(S.I. 1996 No. 30)

Made by the Secretary of State under ss.64(1), 68(4)(c)(i), 70(4), 71(6), 123(1), 124(1), 128(1), 129(1), 130(1) and (2), 131(1) and (3), 135, 137(1) and (2)(a) and (i) and 175(1) and (3) to (5) of the Social Security Contributions and Benefits Act 1992 and s.5(1)(r) of the Social Security Administration Act 1992

[In force February 5, 1996]

Saving

12.—(3) Where, before the coming into force of these Regulations, a person is receiving attendance allowance, disability living allowance, disability working allowance, family credit, invalid care allowance or severe disablement allowance under, as the case may be, the Attendance Allowance Regulations, Disability Living Allowance Regulations, Disability Working Allowance Regulations, Family Credit Regulations, Invalid Care Allowance Regulations or Severe Disablement Allowance Regulations, those Regulations shall, until such time as his entitlement to that benefit is reviewed under section 25 or 30 of the Social Security Administration Act 1992, have effect as if regulation 2, 4, 5, 6, 9 or 11, as the case may be, of these Regulations had not been made.

GENERAL NOTE

See the notes to reg. 3 of the Family Credit Regulations.

Income-related Benefits and Jobseeker's Allowance (Personal Allowances for Children and Young Persons) (Amendment) Regulations 1996

(S.I. 1996 No. 2545)

Made by the Secretary of State under ss. 128(1)(a)(i) and (5), 129(1)(c)(i) and (8), 135(1), 136(3) and (4), 137(1) and 175(1), (3) and (4) of the Social Security Contributions and Benefits Act 1992 and ss. 4(5), 35(1) and 36(1), (2) and (4) of the Jobseekers Act 1995.

[In force October 7, 1997]

Transitional provisions

10.—(3) Where, in any particular case, the appropriate maximum family credit or, as the case may be, the appropriate maximum disability working allowance includes a credit or allowance in respect of one or more children or young persons who are, as at 6th October 1997, aged 11, 16 or 18, the Family Credit Regulations or, as the case may be, the Disability Working Allowance Regulations shall have effect, for the period specified in paragraph (4) below, as if regulations 5 and 6 or, as the case may be, 8 and 9 of these Regulations ['or regulation 3 or 4 of the Family Credit and Disability Working Allowance (General) Amendment Regulations 1997] had not been made.

(4) The period specified for the purposes of paragraph (3) above shall be, in relation to each particular child or young person referred to in that paragraph, the period beginning on 7th October 1997 and ending—
  (a) where that child or young person is aged 11 or 16 as at 6th October 1997, on 31st August 1998;
  (b) where that young person is aged 18 as at 6th October 1997, on the day preceding the day that young person ceases to be a person of a prescribed description for the purposes of regulation 6 of the Family Credit Regulations or, as the case may be, regulation 8 of the Disability Working Allowance Regulations.

AMENDMENT

1. Family Credit and Disability Working Allowance (General) Amendment Regulations 1997 (S.I. 1997 No. 806), reg. 5(3) (October 7, 1997).

GENERAL NOTE

See the notes to reg. 46 of the Family Credit Regulations. Reg. 51 of and Sched. 5 to the Disability Working Allowance Regulations were amended by regs. 8 and 9 of these Regulations on October 7, 1997.

The weekly amount for a young person aged not less than 18 but less than 19 years in sub-para. (b) of the previous form of para. 4 of Sched. 5 was increased to £35.55 from October 7, 1997 (Social Security Benefits Up-rating Order 1998 (S.I. 1998 No. 470), art. 17(2)). The weekly amounts in paras. 3(b) and 4(a) were also increased and were the same as the amounts in paras. 3(b) and 4 of the new form of Sched. 5.

PART VI

THE SOCIAL FUND

Social Fund Cold Weather Payments (General) Regulations 1988

(S.I. 1988 No. 1724)

Made by the Secretary of State under ss.32(2A) and 84(1) of the Social Security Act 1986 and s.166(1) to (3A) of the Social Security Act 1975.

GENERAL NOTE

The cold weather payments scheme has been in operation since April 1988, but has undergone several changes in that time. The most significant has been that taking effect in November 1991. It stemmed from a general review announced in February 1991, when the temperature conditions were deemed to be triggered for the whole country for two weeks and the weekly amount of the payment was increased from £5 to £6.

Since s.138(2) of the Contributions and Benefits Act (1986 Act. s.32(2A)) provides the merest framework, the changes were made by amendment of these Regulations. There are three main changes from November 1991. First, no separate claim needs to be, or can be, made for a cold weather payment. Entitlement simply depends on a person being in the right category of income support (or, from November 4, 1996, income-based JSA) recipient and on the temperature conditions being triggered for the area in which he lives. Second, the temperature conditions can be triggered by a forecast, rather than waiting for a week of cold weather to have happened. Thus payments can potentially be made at the time that expenditure is needed, not after the event.

Third, the system of attaching areas to weather stations has been revised. It is now based on postcode districts, rather than DSS Local Office areas (which no longer exist under the Benefits Agency) or local government areas. The system can be more discriminating, but some weather stations still cover areas a long way away, and there have been complaints about bizarre differences in treatment within towns and cities. The increase in the number of weather stations from 55 to 70 in November 1996 (now further increased to 72 from November 1997) was intended to assist in improving the sensitivity of the scheme.

It appears that a decision to make a payment will be made by an AO, but since no claim is possible there will be no notification to a person that a payment will not be made. If a person does not receive a payment to which he thinks he is entitled, it appears that he will have to request a negative AO's decision before there is something to appeal against.

Citation, commencement and interpretation

1.—(1) These regulations may be cited as the Social Fund Cold Weather Payments (General) Regulations 1988 and shall come into force on 7th November 1988.

(2) In these Regulations, unless the context otherwise requires—

"the Act" means the Social Security Act 1986;

"the General Regulations" means the Income Support (General) Regulations 1987;

[4"the Meteorological Office" means the Meteorological Office of the Ministry of Defence;]

"child" has the meaning assigned to it by section 20(11) of the Act [SSCBA, s.137(1)];

[2"claimant" means a person who is claiming or has claimed income support;]

"family" has the meaning assigned to it by section 20(11) of the Act [SSCBA, s.137(1)] and for the purposes of these Regulations includes persons who are members of a polygamous marriage;

[2"forecast" means a weather forecast produced by the Meteorological Office [4. . .] and supplied to the Department of Social Security on a daily basis

[⁴ between 1st November in any year and 31st March in the following year,] which provides the expected average mean daily temperature for a period of 7 consecutive days;

"forecasted period of cold weather" means a period of 7 consecutive days, during which the average of the mean daily temperature for that period is forecasted to be equal to or below 0 degrees celsius; and for the purposes of this definition where a day forms part of a forecasted period of cold weather it shall not form part of any other such forecasted period;]

"home" means the dwelling, together with any garage, garden and outbuildings normally occupied by the claimant as his home, including any premises not so occupied which it is impracticable or unreasonable to sell separately in particular, in Scotland, any croft land on which the dwelling is situated;

[⁴"income-based jobseeker's allowance" has the same meaning in these Regulations as it has in the Jobseekers Act 1995 by virtue of section 1(4) of that Act;]

"income support" means income support under Part II of the Act [SSCBA, Part VII] and includes transitional addition, personal expenses addition and special transitional addition as defined in the Income Support (Transitional) Regulations 1987;

"married couple" means a man and a woman who are married to each other and are members of the same household;]

"mean daily temperature" means, in respect of a day, the average of the maximum temperature and minimum temperature recorded at a station for that day;

[²"overlap period" means any period of a day or days, where a day forms part of a recorded period of cold weather and also forms part of a forecasted period of cold weather;]

[¹"partner" means one of a married or unmarried couple or a member of a polygamous relationship;] [². . .]

"polygamous marriage" means any marriage during the subsistence of which a party to it is married to more than one person and the ceremony of marriage took place under the law of a country which permits polygamy;

[⁴"postcode district" means a Post Office postcode district [⁵except in the case of any postcode district which is identified with an alpha suffix which shall, for the purposes of these Regulations, be treated as if it forms part of a postcode district which is identified without that suffix]];

"recorded period of cold weather" means a period of 7 consecutive days, during which the average of the mean daily temperature recorded for that period was equal to or below 0 degrees celsius; and for the purposes of this definition where a day forms part of a recorded period of cold weather it shall not form part of any other such recorded period;

[⁴. . .]

[⁴"station" means a station accredited by the Meteorological Office at which a period of cold weather may be forecasted or recorded for the purposes of these Regulations;]

[¹"unmarried couple" means a man and a woman who are not married to each other but are living together as husband and wife.]

[¹(2A) For the purposes of these Regulations, a person shall be treated as a member of a polygamous relationship where, but for the fact that the relationship includes more than two persons, he would be one of a married or unmarried couple.]

(3) In these Regulations, unless the context otherwise requires, a reference to a numbered regulation is to the regulation in these Regulations bearing that

number and a reference in a regulation to a numbered paragraph or sub-paragraph is to the paragraph or sub-paragraph in that regulation bearing that number.

AMENDMENTS

1. Social Fund (Miscellaneous Amendments) Regulations 1990 (S.I. 1990 No. 580), reg. 3 (April 9, 1990).
2. Social Fund Cold Weather Payments (General) Amendment No. 2 Regulations 1991 (S.I. 1991 No. 2238), reg. 2 (November 1, 1991).
3. Social Fund Cold Weather Payments (General) Amendment (No. 2) Regulations 1992 (S.I. 1992 No. 2448), reg. 2 (November 1, 1992).
4. Social Fund Cold Weather Payments (General) Amendment Regulations 1996 (S.I. 1996 No. 2544), reg. 2 (November 4, 1996).
5. Social Fund Cold Weather Payments (General) Amendment Regulations 1997 (S.I. 1997 No. 2311), reg. 2 (November 1, 1997).

GENERAL NOTE

"*home.*" See the notes to reg. 2(1) of the Income Support (General) Regulations under "dwelling occupied as the home".

"*forecasted period of cold weather.*" The original definition of a "period of cold weather" required it to run from a Monday to a Sunday. Since the test of the average of the mean daily temperature (*i.e.* the average of maximum and minimum temperature for each day) for the seven days being below 0 degrees Celsius is a tough one, to have required also that the weather conformed to calendar weeks would have made the operation of the regulation excessively arbitrary. Thus, any consecutive seven days over which the average temperature test is met will do.

The departure in November 1991 is to include a period where the temperature is forecasted to meet the test. See reg. 2 for the interrelationship with periods where the temperature test is actually met. If a day falls into a forecasted period of cold weather it cannot count in any other forecasted period, but it can be part of a recorded period of cold weather (see the definition of "overlap period").

In the cold weather payments scheme under the Supplementary Benefit (Single Payments) Regulations the crucial average temperature was 1.5 degrees celsius, rather than 0 degrees celsius.

"*recorded period of cold weather.*" See the notes on a forecasted period and the definition of "overlap period."

"*unmarried couple.*" and "*married couple.*" See notes to s.137(1) of the Contributions and Benefits Act (1986 Act, s.20(11)).

[¹Prescribed description of persons

1A. The description of persons prescribed as persons to whom a payment may be made out of the Social Fund to meet expenses for heating under section 32(2A) of the Act [SSCBA, s.138(2)] is claimants who have been awarded income support [³ or income-based jobseeker's allowance] in respect of at least one day during the recorded or the forecasted period of cold weather specified in regulation 2(1)(a) and either—
  (i) whose applicable amount includes one or more of the premiums specified in paragraphs 9 to 14 of Part III of Schedule 2 to the General Regulations [², but does not include the allowance specified in paragraph 2A of that Schedule (residential allowances)]; or
[³(ia) whose applicable amount includes one or more of the premiums specified in paragraphs 10 to 16 of Part III of Schedule 1 to the Jobseeker's Allowance Regulations 1996 but does not include the allowance specified in paragraph 3 of that Schedule (residential allowances); or]
  (ii) whose family includes a member aged less than 5.]

AMENDMENTS

1. Social Fund Cold Weather Payments (General) Amendment No. 3 Regulations 1991 (S.I. 1991 No. 2448), reg. 2 (November 1, 1991).

2. Social Fund Cold Weather Payments (General) Amendment Regulations 1993 (S.I. 1993 No. 2450), reg. 2 (November 1, 1993).

3. Social Fund Cold Weather Payments (General) Amendment Regulations 1996 (S.I. 1996 No. 2544), reg. 3 (November 4, 1996).

DEFINITIONS

"the Act"—see reg 1(2).
"the General Regulations"—*ibid.*
"claimant"—*ibid.*
"family"—*ibid.*
"forecasted period of cold weather"—*ibid.*
"income-based jobseeker's allowance"—*ibid.*
"income support"—*ibid.*
"recorded period of cold weather"—*ibid.*

GENERAL NOTE

Only claimants who have been awarded income support or income-based JSA for at least one day in a period of cold weather (forecasted or recorded) can qualify for a payment. Merely having underlying entitlement to income support or income-based JSA will not do. However, only certain claimants meet the conditions prescribed by reg. 1A. The claimant's income support or income-based JSA must include one of the pensioner or disability premiums (but from November 1, 1993, claimants who live in a residential care or nursing home and do not have a preserved right do not qualify), or there must be a child under five in the household. Since no claim for a cold weather payment is possible, the AO will identify qualifying claimants and make a payment automatically.

[¹Prescribed circumstances

2.—(1) The prescribed circumstances in which a payment may be made out of the social fund to meet expenses for heating under section 32(2A) of the Act [SSCBA, s.138(2)] are—
   (a) subject to paragraphs [⁵(1A), (1B),] (3), (4) and (5)—
         (i) there is a recorded period of cold weather at a station [³identi-fied] in column (1) of Schedule 1 to these Regulations [⁴. . .]; or
         (ii) there is a forecasted period of cold weather at a station [³identified] in column (1) of Schedule 1 to these Regulations; [⁵ and]
         [⁴(iii) [⁵. . .]
   (b) the home of the claimant is, or by virtue of paragraph (2)(b) is treated as, situated in a postcode district in respect of which the station mentioned in sub-paragraph (a)(i) or, as the case may be, (a)(ii) is the designated station.]
   (c) [². . .]
[⁵(1A) For the purposes of paragraph (1)(a)(i),where a station identified in column (1) of Schedule 1 to these Regulations (in this paragraph and in para-graph (1B) referred to as "the primary station") is unable to provide temper-ature information in respect of a particular day, the mean daily temperature on that day—
   (a) at the alternative station for that primary station specified in column (2) of Schedule 2 to these Regulations; or
   (b) where there is no such alternative station specified, at the nearest station to that primary station able to provide temperature information in respect of that day,
shall be used to determine whether or not there is a recorded period of cold weather at the relevant primary station.

(1B) For the purposes of paragraph (1)(a)(ii), where the Meteorological Office is unable to produce a forecast in respect of a particular period at a primary station, any forecast produced in respect of that period—

(a) at the alternative station for that primary station specified in column (2) of Schedule 2 to these Regulations; or

(b) where there is no such alternative station specified, at the nearest station to that primary station able to provide temperature information for that period,

shall be used to determine whether or not there is a forecasted period of cold weather at the relevant primary station.]

(2) For the purposes of this regulation—

(a) the station [³identified] in column (1) of Schedule 1 to these Regulations is the designated station for the [⁴postcode districts] [³identified] in the corresponding paragraph in column (2) of that Schedule;

(b) where the home of the claimant is not situated within a [⁴postcode district] [³[⁴. . .] identified] in column (2) of that Schedule, it shall be treated as situated within the [⁴postcode district] [⁴. . .] nearest to it [³identified] in that column.

(3) Subject to paragraphs (4) and (5) where a recorded period of cold weather is joined by an overlap period to a forecasted period of cold weather a payment under paragraph (1) may only be made in respect of the forecasted period of cold weather.

(4) Where—

(a) there is a continuous period of forecasted periods of cold weather, each of which is linked by an overlap period; and

(b) the total number of recorded periods of cold weather during that continuous period is greater than the total number of forecasted periods of cold weather,

a payment in respect of the last recorded period of cold weather may also be made under paragraph (1).

(5) Where—

(a) a claimant [²falls within the description of persons prescribed in Regulation 1A and] satisfies the prescribed circumstances for a payment under paragraph (1) above in respect of a recorded period of cold weather; and

(b) a payment in respect of the recorded period of cold weather does not fall to be made by virtue of paragraph (4); and

(c) the claimant does not [²fall within the description of persons prescribed in Regulation 1A] above in respect of the forecasted period of cold weather which is linked to the recorded period of cold weather by an overlap period,

a payment in respect of that recorded period of cold weather may also be made under paragraph (1).

AMENDMENTS

1. Social Fund Cold Weather Payments (General) Amendments No. 2 Regulations 1991 (S.I. 1991 No. 2238) reg. 3 (November 1, 1991).

2. Social Fund Cold Weather Payments (General) Amendment No. 3 Regulations 1991 (S.I. 1991 No. 2448), reg. 3 (November 1, 1991).

3. Social Fund Cold Weather Payments (General) Amendment (No. 2) Regulations 1992 (S.I. 1992 No. 2448), reg. 3 (November 1, 1992).

4. Social Fund Cold Weather Payments (General) Amendment Regulations 1996 (S.I. 1996 No. 2544), reg. 4 (November 4, 1996).

5. Social Fund Cold Weather Payments (General) Amendment Regulations 1997 (S.I. 1997 No. 2311), reg. 3 (November 1, 1997).

DEFINITIONS

"the Act"—see reg. 1(2).
"the General Regulations"—*ibid.*
"claimant"—*ibid.*
"family"—*ibid.*
"forecasted period of cold weather"—*ibid.*
"home"—*ibid.*
"income support"—*ibid.*
"overlap period"—*ibid.*
"postcode district"—*ibid.*
"recorded period of cold weather"—*ibid.*
"station"—*ibid.*

GENERAL NOTE

Section 138(2) of the Contributions and Benefits Act (1986 Act, s.32(2A)) allows any circumstances to be prescribed. Reg. 1A prescribes the categories of income support or income-based JSA recipients who can qualify.

The qualifications under reg. 2 have become rather more complex in November 1991. Under para. (1)(a) and (b), a period of cold weather (*i.e.* seven consecutive days) must be either recorded or forecast at the weather station relevant to the claimant's home. If a period of cold weather is forecast, but the forecast turns out to be wrong and there are not seven consecutive days of the necessary temperature actually recorded, the situation is simple. Only the forecast period is relevant. Things become more complicated where there is a recorded period of cold weather which coincides wholly or partly with the forecasted period. While an individual day can only count as part of one recorded period of cold weather or one forecasted period of cold weather (see the definitions in reg. 1(2)), it can be part of both a recorded and a forecasted period. There is then an overlap period, again defined in reg. 1(2). Since the aim is, if possible, to make the payment before the extra heating is required, the general rule, under para. (3), is that payment is to be made only for the forecasted period. However, that rule would lead to unfairness if, for instance, recorded periods of cold weather come at the beginning and end of a continuous series, with forecasted periods only starting towards the end of the first recorded period and finishing towards the start of the last recorded period. In such circumstances, payments can be made for an extra recorded period over the number of forecasted periods (para. (4)). Also, if the claimant does not qualify under reg. 1A for any day of the forecasted period, but does qualify for a day of the recorded period, then a payment can be made for the recorded period (para. (5)).

Prescribed amount

3. [¹. . .] The amount of the payment in respect of each period of cold weather shall be [²£8.50].

AMENDMENTS

1. Social Fund Cold Weather Payments (General) Amendment No. 2 Regulations 1991 (S.I. 1991 No. 2238), reg. 4 (November 1, 1991).
2. Social Fund Cold Weather Payments (General) Amendment Regulations 1995 (S.I. 1995 No. 2620) reg. 2 (November 1, 1995).

GENERAL NOTE

The fixed payment is £8.50 for each week which counts under regs. 1A and 2. The amount had been fixed at £5 from 1988, until it was increased to £6 in February 1991, at the same time as the temperature condition was deemed to have been triggered for the whole country for two weeks. It was increased to £7 in November 1994 and became £8.50 in November 1995.

Effect and calculation of capital

4. [¹. . .]

AMENDMENT

1. Social Fund Cold Weather Payments (General) Amendment No. 2 Regulations 1991 (S.I. 1991 No. 2238), reg. 5 (November 1, 1991).

GENERAL NOTE

There is now no capital limit for cold weather payments.

SCHEDULES

[¹SCHEDULE 1   Regulation 2(1)(a) and (2)

IDENTIFICATION OF STATIONS AND POSTCODE DISTRICTS

Column (1)	Column (2)
Meteorological Office Station	*Postcode districts*
1. ABBOTSINCH (Glasgow Airport)	G1–5, G11–15, G20–23, G31–34, G40–46, G51–53, G60–62, G64–G69, G71–78, G81–84. KA1–26, KA28–30. ML1–5. PA1–27, PA30, PA32.
2. ABERPORTH	SA35–48, SA64–65. SY20, SY23–25.
3. ANDREWSFIELD	AL1–10. CB10–11. CM1–9, CM11–24. CO9. RM14–20. SG1–2, SG9–14.
4. AULTBEA	IV21–22, IV26, IV40, IV52–54.
5. AVIEMORE	AB31, AB33, AB34, AB36–37. PH18–26.
6. BEDFORD	LU1–7. MK1–19, MK40–46. NN1–16, NN29. PE19. SG3–7, SG15–19.
7. BINGLEY	BB4, BB8–12, BB18. BD1–24. DE4, DE45. HD1–8. HX1–7. LS21, LS29. OL3, OL12–15. S32–33, S36. SK12, SK17, SK22–23. ST13.
8. BOLTSHOPE PARK	DH8. DL8, DL11–13. NE19, NE44, NE47–48.

Column (1)	Column (2)
Meteorological Office Station	*Postcode districts*
9. BOSCOMBE DOWN	BA12. SP1–5, SP7, SP9.
10. BOULMER	NE22, NE24, NE61–71. TD15.
11. BRACKNELL, BEAUFORT PARK	GU1–4, GU9–25. GU46–47. HP1–16, HP23. RG1–2, RG4–10, RG12, RG14, RG17–31, RG40–42, RG45. SL0–9. SP10–11.
12. BRAEMAR	AB35.
13. BRIZE NORTON	CV36. GL54–56. HP17–22, HP27. OX1–18, OX20, OX33, OX44. SN7.
14. CAPEL CURIG	LL20–21, LL23–25, LL41.
15. CARDINHAM (Bodmin)	PL13–17, PL22–35. TR2, TR9.
16. CARLISLE	CA1–11, CA16–17. LA6–10, LA22–23. NE49.
17. CHIVENOR	EX22–23, EX31–34, EX39.
18. COLESHILL	B1–21, B23–38, B40, B42–50, B60–80, B90–98. CV1–12, CV21–23, CV31–35, CV37. DY1–14. LE10. WS1–15. WV1–16.
19. COLTISHALL	NR1–35.
20. CROSBY	BB1–3, BB5–7. CH1–8. FY1–8. L1–49, L60–66. LL11–14. PR1–9. SY14. WA1–6, WA10–12. WN1–8.
21. CULDROSE	TR1, TR3–6, TR10–20, TR26–27.
22. DUMFRIES, DRUNGANS	DG1–2, DG5–7, DG11–12, DG16.
23. DUNKESWELL AERODROME	DT6–8. EX1–15. TA21. TQ1–6, TQ9–14.

Column (1)	Column (2)
Meteorological Office Station	*Postcode districts*
24. DYCE (Aberdeen Airport)	AB10–16, AB21–25, AB30, AB32, AB39, AB41–43, AB51–54. DD8–11.
25. ESKDALEMUIR	DG3–4, DG10, DG13–14. EH46. ML12. TD1–4, TD6–10.
26. ESKMEALS	CA12–15, CA18–28. LA1–5, LA11–21.
27. FLYING DALES	TS13. YO11–18, YO21–22, YO25.
28. GREAT MALVERN	GL1–6, GL10–20, GL50–53. HR1–9. NP5. SY8. WR1–15.
29. HEATHROW	BR1–8. CR0, CR2–8. DA1–2, DA4–8, DA14–18. E1–18. EC1–4. EN1–11. HA0–9. IG1–11. KT1–24. N1–22. NW1–11. RM1–13. SE1–28. SM1–7. SW1–20. TW1–20. UB1–10. W1–14. WC1–2. WD1–7.
30. HERSTMONCEUX, WEST END	BN7–8, BN20–24, BN26–27. TN21, TN31–40.
31. HURN (Bournemouth Airport)	BH1–25, BH31. DT1–2, DT11. SP6.
32. KINLOSS	AB38, AB44–45, AB55–56. IV1–2, IV5, IV7–20, IV30–32, IV36.
33. KIRKWALL	KW15–17.
34. LEEDS	HG1–5. LS1–20, LS22–28. S1–14, S17–18, S20–21, S35, S60–66, S70–75. WF1–17.

1067

Column (1)	Column (2)
Meteorological Office Station	*Postcode districts*
35. LERWICK	ZE1–3.
36. LEUCHARS	DD1–7.
	KY1–2, KY4–10,
	KY14–16.
	PH1–2, PH7,
	PH12–14.
37. LINTON ON OUSE	DL1–7, DL9–10.
	TS1–12, TS14–26.
	YO7–8, YO10, YO19, YO23–24,
	YO26, YO30–32, YO41–43, YO51,
	YO60–62.
38. LISCOMBE	EX16–21, EX35–38.
	PL19–20.
	TA22, TA24.
39. LOCH GLASCARNOCH	IV3–4, IV6,
	IV23–24.
40. LUSA	IV47–49, IV51, IV55–56.
41. LYNEHAM	BA1–3, BA11,
	BA13–15.
	GL7–9.
	SN1–6, SN8–16.
42. MACHRIHANISH	KA27.
	PA28–29, PA31,
	PA34, PA37,
	PA41–49, PA60–76.
	PH36, PH38–41.
43. MANSTON	CT1–21.
	CM0.
	DA3, DA9–13.
	ME1–13.
	SS0–17.
	TN23–26, TN28–30.
44. MARHAM	IP24–28.
	PE12–14, PE30–38.
45. NEWCASTLE	DH1–7, DH9.
	DL14–17.
	NE1–13, NE15–18,
	NE20–21, NE23,
	NE25–43, NE45–46.
	SR1–8.
	TS27–29.
46. NOTTINGHAM	CV13.
	DE1–3, DE5–7,
	DE11–15, DE21–24,
	DE55–56, DE65,
	DE72–75.
	LE1–9, LE11–14,
	LE16–18, LE65,
	LE67.
	NG1–22, NG25, NG31–34.
	S25–26, S40–45,
	S80–81.
	ST10, ST14.
47. PEMBREY SANDS	SA1–18, SA31–34,
	SA61–63, SA66–73.
48. PLYMOUTH	PL1–12, PL18, PL21.
	TQ7–8.
49. PORTLAND	DT3–5.

Column (1)	Column (2)
Meteorological Office Station	*Postcode districts*
50. REDHILL	BN5–6, BN44. GU5–8, GU26–33, GU35. ME14–20. RHI–20 TN1–20, TN22, TN27.
51. RHYL	LL15–19, LL22, LL26–32.
52. RINGWAY (Manchester Airport)	BL0–9. CW1–12. M1–9, M11–35, M38, M40–41, M43–46, M90. OL1–2, OL4–11, OL16. SK1–11, SK13–16. WA7–9, WA13–16.
53. SALSBURGH	ML6–11. EH43–45.
54. SCILLY, ST MARY	TR21–25.
55. SENNYBRIDGE	CF37–48, CF81–82. LD1–8. NP2–4, NP7–8. SA19–20. SY7, SY9–11, SY15–19, SY21–22.
56. SHAWBURY	ST1–9, ST11–12, ST15–21. SY1–6, SY12–13. TF1–13.
57. SOUTHAMPTON	GU34. SO14–24, SO30–32, SO40–43, SO45, SO50–53.
58. ST. ATHAN	BS1–11, BS13–16, BS20–24, BS29, BS30–32, BS34–37, BS39–41, BS48–49. CF1–5, CF31–36, CF61–64, CF71–72, CF83. NP1, NP6, NP9, NP44.
59. ST. CATHERINE'S POINT	PO30, PO38–41.
60. ST. MAWGAN	TR7–8.
61. STORNOWAY AIRPORT	HS1–9.
62. THORNEY ISLAND	BN1–3, BN9–18, BN25, BN41–43, BN45. PO1–22, PO31–37.
63. TIREE	IV41–46. PA77–78. PH42–44.
64. TULLOCH BRIDGE	PA33, PA35–36, PA38–40. PH8–11, PH15–17, PH30–35, PH37.
65. TURNHOUSE (Edinburgh Airport)	EH1–42, EH47–49, EH51–55. FK1–21. G63. KY3, KY11–13. PH3–6. TD5, TD11–14.

Column (1)	Column (2)
Meteorological Office Station	*Postcode districts*
66. VALLEY	LL33–40, LL42–49, LL51–78.
67. WADDINGTON	DN1–22, DN31–41.
	HU1–20.
	LN1–13.
	NG23–24.
	PE10–11, PE20–25.
68. WATTISHAM	CB9.
	CO1–8, CO10–16.
	IP1–23, IP29–33.
69. WEST FREUGH	DG8–9.
70. WICK AIRPORT	IV25, IV27–28.
	KW1–3, KW5–14.
71. WITTERING	CB1–8.
	LE15.
	NN17–18.
	PE1–9, PE15–18.
	SG8.
72. YEOVILTON	BA4–10, BA16,
	BA20–22.
	BS25–28.
	DT9–10.
	SP8.
	TA1–20, TA23.]

AMENDMENT

1. Social Fund Cold Weather Payments (General) Amendment Regulations 1998 (S.I. 1998 No. 2455), reg. 2 and Sched. 1 (November 1, 1998).

DEFINITIONS

''Meteorological Office''—see reg. 1(2).
''postcode district''—*ibid.*.
''station''—*ibid.*

[¹SCHEDULE 2   **Regulation 2(1A)(a) and (1B)(a)**

SPECIFIED ALTERNATIVE STATIONS

Column (1)	Column (2)
Meteorological Office Station	*Specified Alternative Station*
Abbotsinch (Glasgow Airport)	Bishopton
Andrewsfield	Wattisham
Coleshill	Church Lawford
Kinloss	Lossiemouth
Portland	Isle of Portland
Redhill	Kenley Airfield
St. Athan	Cardiff Weather Centre
Turnhouse	Salsburgh]

AMENDMENT

1. Social Fund Cold Weather Payments (General) Amendment Regulations 1998 (S.I. 1998 No. 2455), reg. 3 and Sched. 2 (November 1, 1998).

DEFINITIONS

"Meteorological Office"—see reg. 1(2).
"station"—*ibid.*

Social Fund Winter Fuel Payment Regulations 1998

(S.I. 1998 No. 19)

Made by the Secretary of State under ss. 138(2) and (4) and 175(1), (3) and (4) of the Social Security Contributions and Benefits Act 1992 and ss. 5(1)(i), 59(1) and (2)(c) and 189(1) and (3) to (5) of, and para. 4 of Sched. 3 to, the Social Security Administration Act 1992.

GENERAL NOTE

In November 1997 the Government announced that all pensioner households would receive a one-off payment in the winter of 1998 (and another in 1999) towards their fuel bills. These payments would be in addition to any cold weather payments which might be awarded under the Social Fund Cold Weather Payments Regulations. As is the case under those Regulations no separate claim needs to be made for a winter fuel payment. Entitlement simply depended on the person being an eligible pensioner on at least one day in the week commencing on January 5, 1998. The payment is at a higher rate (£50) for pensioners who are getting income support or income-based JSA. The Government stated that it intended to make the 1998 payments to pensioners in receipt of income support or income-based JSA before the end of January 1998 and to other eligible pensioners by the end of March 1998.

The original regulations concerned the payment for 1998. The conditions for the 1999 payment are very similar.

It has been announced that the scheme will be continued for the winter of 1999/2000 when the payment for people in receipt of income support will be increased from £50 to £100.

Citation, commencement and interpretation

1.—(1) These Regulations may be cited as the Social Fund Winter Fuel Payment Regulations 1998 and shall come into force on 16th January 1998.

(2) In these Regulations—

"the Administration Act" means the Social Security Administration Act 1992;

['. . .]

"the Contributions and Benefits Act" means the Social Security Contributions and Benefits Act 1992;

"graduated retirement benefit" means the benefit to which section 62 of the Contributions and Benefits Act applies;

"income-based jobseeker's allowance" has the same meaning in these Regulations as it has in the Jobseekers Act 1995 by virtue of section 1(4) of that Act;

"the Income Support Regulations" means the Income Support (General) Regulations 1987;

['"industrial injuries benefit" means a benefit of that name to which Part V of the Contributions and Benefits Act refers];

"the Jobseeker's Allowance Regulations" means the Jobseeker's Allowance Regulations 1996;

"married couple" means a man and woman who are married to each other and are members of the same household;

"partner" means where a person—

(a) is a member of a married or an unmarried couple living in the same household, the other member of that couple;

(b) is married polygamously to two or more members of his household, any such member living in the same household;

"the qualifying week" means the week beginning on ['9th November 1998];

"retirement pension" for the purposes of regulation 2(6) means a retirement pension to which Parts II and III of the Contributions and Benefits Act refer;

"unmarried couple" means a man and woman who are not married to each other but are living together as husband and wife;

"winter fuel payment" means a payment made under these Regulations out of the social fund, to meet expenses for heating pursuant to section 138(2) of the Contributions and Benefits Act;

['"workmen's compensation and industrial diseases benefit" means the payments and allowances to which section 111 of, and Schedule 8 to, the Contributions and Benefits Act refer].

(3) Whether in any case a person is or is not to be treated as being a member of a household is to be determined in accordance with regulation 16 of the Income Support Regulations.

(4) In these Regulations, unless the context otherwise requires, a reference—

(a) to a numbered regulation is to the regulation in these Regulations bearing that number;

(b) in a regulation to a numbered paragraph is to the paragraph in that regulation bearing that number.

AMENDMENT

1. Social Fund Winter Fuel Payment Amendment Regulations 1998 (S.I. 1998 No. 1910), reg. 2(a) (November 20, 1998).

GENERAL NOTE

"*married couple*" and "*unmarried couple*". See the notes to s. 137(1) of the Contributions and Benefits Act.

Prescribed description of persons

2.—(1) Subject to regulation 3, a winter fuel payment shall be paid to persons who come within either of the categories specified in paragraph (2) or (5) below.

(2) Except in the case of a person to whom paragraph (3) applies, the first category comprises persons to whom in respect of any day in the qualifying week—

(a) income support is payable and whose applicable amount includes one or more of the premiums specified in paragraphs 9, 9A or 10 of Schedule 2 to the Income Support Regulations; or

(b) income-based jobseeker's allowance is payable and whose applicable amount includes one or more of the premiums specified in paragraphs 10 to 12 of Schedule 1 to the Jobseeker's Allowance Regulations.

(3) Subject to paragraph (4), persons to whom income support or income-based jobseeker's allowance is payable and whose applicable amount includes the allowance specified in paragraph 2A of Schedule 2 to the Income Support Regulations or paragraph 3 of Schedule 1 to the Jobseeker's Allowance Regulations (residential allowance) as the case may be, shall not be entitled to a winter fuel payment.

(4) Paragraph (3) shall not have effect in the case of a person or his partner whose applicable amount includes a residential allowance while temporarily residing in accommodation to which—

 (a) paragraph 9(a)(i) or (ii) of column (1) in Schedule 7 to the Income Support Regulations refers and that person's partner is a person to whom paragraph 9(b)(i) or (ii) applies;

 (b) paragraph 5(a)(i) or (ii) of column (1) in Schedule 5 to the Jobseeker's Allowance Regulations refers and that person's partner is a person to whom paragraph 5(b)(i) or (ii) applies;

 (c) paragraph 10(a) or (b) of column (1) in Schedule 7 to the Income Support Regulations refers or, as the case may be, paragraph 6(a) or (b) of column (1) in Schedule 5 to the Jobseeker's Allowance Regulations, applies.

(5) Except in the case of a person to whom paragraph (3) applies or is excluded by virtue of paragraph (7), the second category comprises persons who, in respect of any day falling within the qualifying week, are ordinarily resident in Great Britain and who fall within any of the classes of persons to which paragraph (6) refers.

(6) The classes of persons to which this paragraph refers are men aged 65 or over and women aged 60 or over to whom any of the following benefits or pensions is payable in respect of a period which includes a day in the qualifying week—

 (a) attendance allowance, [¹. . .], disability living allowance, incapacity benefit, [¹industrial injuries benefit], invalid care allowance [¹severe disablement allowance or workmen's compensation and industrial diseases benefit] under the Contributions and Benefits Act;

 (b) income-based jobseeker's allowance, where the claimant's applicable amount is determined in accordance with paragraph 3 of Schedule 5 to the Jobseeker's Allowance Regulations;

 (c) income support, where the claimant's applicable amount is determined in accordance with paragraph 6 of Schedule 7 to the Income Support Regulations;

 (d) retirement pension or graduated retirement benefit;

 (e) [¹. . .]

 (f) war disablement pension, war widow's pension or temporary allowance to widows of severely disabled war pensioners under the Naval, Military and Air Forces Etc. (Disablement and Death) Service Pensions Order 1983 or payable by virtue of any Scheme made under—

  (i) the Personal Injuries (Emergency Provisions) Act 1939;

  (ii) the Pensions (Navy, Army, Air Force and Mercantile Marine) Act 1939;

  (iii) the Polish Resettlement Act 1947; or

  (iv) the Reserve Forces Act 1980; and

 (g) widowed mother's allowance or a widow's pension under section 37 or 38 of the Contributions and Benefits Act.

(7) Except in the case of persons to whom paragraph (8) refers, the persons excluded by this paragraph are—

 (a) persons and the partners of persons to whom paragraph (2) applies;

 (b) hospital in-patients to whom regulation 6 of the Social Security (Hospital In-Patients) Regulations 1975 (adjustment of personal benefit after 52 weeks in hospital) applies;

[²(bb) persons to whom regulation 12B(10) of the Social Security (Disability Living Allowance) Regulations 1991 (persons in receipt of the mobility component of disability living allowance while undergoing medical or other treatment in a hospital or other institution) refers and who have been receiving free hospital in-patient treatment for more than 52 weeks;]

  (c) persons to whom income support or income-based jobseeker's allowance is payable by virtue of—

      (i) regulation 19 of the Income Support Regulations or regulation 86 of the Jobseeker's Allowance Regulations (persons in residential care and nursing homes); or

     (ii) regulation 21 of the Income Support Regulations or regulation 85 of the Jobseeker's Allowance Regulations and either—

        (aa) paragraph 13 of Schedule 7 to the Income Support Regulations or paragraph 15 of Schedule 5 to the Jobseeker's Allowance Regulations (persons in residential accommodation); or

        (bb) paragraph 13A or 13B of Schedule 7 to the Income Support Regulations (Polish resettlement);

  (d) persons in respect of whom a deduction is being made by the Secretary of State from an award under the Naval, Military and Air Forces Etc. (Disablement and Death) Service Pensions Order 1983 or the Personal Injuries (Civilians) Scheme 1983 or under any other Scheme made under any of the Acts specified in paragraph (6)(f), where such persons have been maintained in a hospital or similar institution for a continuous period exceeding 52 weeks.

(8) Paragraph (7)(c)(ii)(aa) shall not have effect to exclude persons from entitlement to a winter fuel payment where the person concerned is temporarily in local authority accommodation under paragraph 10B(1) or (2) of Schedule 7 to the Income Support Regulations.

AMENDMENTS

1. Social Fund Winter Fuel Payment Amendment Regulations 1998 (S.I. 1998 No. 1910), reg. 2(b) (November 20, 1998).
2. Social Fund Winter Fuel Payment Amendment Regulations 1998 (S.I. 1998 No. 1910), reg. 2(c) (November 20, 1998).

DEFINITIONS

"constant attendance allowance"—see reg. 1(2).
"the Contributions and Benefits Act"—*ibid.*
"graduated retirement benefit"—*ibid.*
"income-based jobseeker's allowance"—*ibid.*
"the Income Support Regulations"—*ibid.*
"industrial death benefit"—*ibid.*
"the Jobseeker's Allowance Regulations"—*ibid.*
"partner"—*ibid.*
"the qualifying week"—*ibid.*
"retirement pension"—*ibid.*
"winter fuel payment"—*ibid.*

GENERAL NOTE

This regulation sets out who will be paid a winter fuel payment. There are two main categories, which in turn determines the amount of the payment (see reg. 3). First, claimants to whom income support or income-based JSA, which included one of the pensioner premiums, was payable for at least one day in the week beginning on November 9, 1998 qualify (para. (2)). (The qualifying week for the 1997/98 payment was January 5, 1998: see the definition of "qualifying week" in the 1998 edition of this book.) But those who live in a residential care or nursing home and whose income support or income-based JSA includes a residential allowance are not eligible (para. (3)), unless they are a couple, one member of which is temporarily in a residential care or nursing home while the other is living at home or is in hospital (para. (4)).

Note that claimants in receipt of income support/income-based JSA who live in residential care or nursing homes, residential accommodation or a Polish resettlement home are generally also excluded from a para. (5) payment, except those covered by para. (8) (see below).

Under para. (5) the second category who qualify for a payment are men over the age of 64 and women over the age of 59 who were ordinarily resident in Great Britain, and receiving any of the benefits in para. (6) on at least one day in the week beginning on November 9, 1998. But a para. (5) payment will not be made if the person has been in hospital for more than 52 weeks, is receiving income support or income-based JSA and lives in (i) a residential care or nursing home or (ii) residential accommodation (unless the person is only temporarily in such accommodation and his partner is at home (para. (8)) or (iii) a Polish resettlement home, has an award under specified legislation from which a deduction is being made because the person has been in hospital, etc. for more than 52 weeks, or either he or his partner qualify for a payment under para. (2) (paras. (5) and (7)).

Note that income support, income-based JSA or one of the other qualifying benefits must be *payable* on at least one day in the week beginning on November 9, 1998; mere underlying entitlement will not do. But note reg. 3(4).

Since no claim for a winter fuel payment is necessary, the AO will identify qualifying claimants and make a payment automatically.

Prescribed amount

3.—(1) Subject to paragraphs (2) to (4), winter fuel payments shall be of the following amounts—
(a) in the case of a person to whom regulation 2(2) applies, £50;
(b) in the case of a person to whom regulation 2(5) applies—
   (i) who is living in a household where there is no other person in that household who is entitled to a payment under this regulation, £20;
   (ii) who is [¹without accommodation], £20; or
   (iii) in every other case, £10.

(2) Where a person falls within both of the categories of persons to which regulation 2(2) or (5) refers, payment shall be made under paragraph (1)(a) only.

(3) Subject to paragraph (4), where a person falls within more than one class of person to which regulation 2(6) refers only one payment shall be made under paragraph (1)(b).

(4) Where a person who has received a payment under paragraph (1)(b) is subsequently awarded income support or income-based jobseeker's allowance in respect of [²any day in] the qualifying week, he shall be paid the difference between the amount he and his partner, if any, have already received and the amount to which paragraph (1)(a) refers.

AMENDMENTS

1. Social Fund Winter Fuel Payment Amendment Regulations 1998 (S.I. 1998 No. 1910), reg. 2(d) (November 20, 1998).
2. Social Fund Winter Fuel Payment Amendment Regulations 1998 (S.I. 1998 No. 1910), reg. 2(e) (November 20, 1998).

DEFINITIONS

"income-based jobseeker's allowance"—see reg. 1(2).
"partner"—*ibid.*
"the qualifying week"—*ibid.*
"winter fuel payment"—*ibid.*

GENERAL NOTE

In the case of a person who qualifies under reg. 2(2), the amount of a winter fuel payment is £50 (para. (1)(a)); if only reg. 2(5) applies, the amount of the payment is £20 if no other person in the household (see reg. 1(3)) is eligible for a winter fuel payment, or the person is of no fixed abode, and £10 in any other case (para. (1)(b)). Only one payment will be made even if a person qualifies under both reg. 2(2) and (5), or more than one sub-paragraph of reg. 2(6) applies (paras. (2) and (3)). If payment at the lower rate only has been made and the person is subsequently awarded income support or income-based JSA for the week beginning November 9, 1998, the payment (including that received by any partner) will be made up to £50 (para. (4)).

Official records

4.—(1) Subject to paragraph (2), official records held by the Secretary of State as to a person's circumstances shall be sufficient evidence thereof for the purpose of deciding his entitlement to a winter fuel payment and its amount.

(2) Paragraph (1) shall not apply so as to exclude a review of the decision under section 25 of the Administration Act or the consideration on that review of fresh evidence.

DEFINITION

"winter fuel payment"—see reg. 1(2).

GENERAL NOTE

As is the case for cold weather payments, no separate claim needs to be made for a winter fuel payment, as entitlement will be decided on the basis of information already held by the Benefits Agency (para. (1)). But the effect of para. (2) is to confirm that decisions under these Regulations will be made by an AO and thus will be susceptible to appeal as well as review under s. 25 of the Administration Act. A person who receives a lower rate payment but considers that he is entitled to a higher rate should be in no difficulty as he will have been notified of the decision in his case. Presumably a person who does not receive any payment when he thinks that he is entitled to one, will have to request a negative AO's decision before there is something to seek review of and/or appeal against.

Social Fund Maternity and Funeral Expenses (General) Regulations 1987

(S.I. 1987 No. 481)

Made by the Secretary of State under the Social Security Act 1986, ss. 32(2)(a), 84(1) and 89(1), and the Supplementary Benefits Act 1976, ss. 3, 4 and 34.

ARRANGEMENT OF REGULATIONS

PART I

GENERAL

PART I

GENERAL

Citation and commencement

1. These regulations may be cited as the Social Fund Maternity and Funeral Expenses (General) Regulations 1987 and shall come into force on 6th April 1987.

Revocation

2. The Social Fund Maternity and Funeral Expenses (General) Regulations 1986 are hereby revoked.

Interpretation

3.—(1) In these regulations unless the context otherwise requires—
[¹"the Act" means the Social Security Act 1986;]
[⁷"the Income Support Regulations" means the Income Support (General) Regulations 1987;]
[⁷"the Jobseeker's Allowance Regulations" means the Jobseeker's Allowance Regulations 1996;]
[⁹"absent parent" means a parent of a child who has died where—
    (a) that parent was not living in the same household with the child at the date of that child's death; and
    (b) that child had his home, at the date of death, with a person who was responsible for that child for the purposes of Part IX of the Social Security Contributions and Benefits Act 1992;]
"child" means a person under the age of 16 [³or a young person within the meaning of regulation 14 of the Income Support [⁷Regulations or, as the case may be, of regulation 76 of the Jobseeker's Allowance Regulations];]

"claimant" means a person claiming a social fund payment in respect of maternity or funeral expenses;

[[6]"close relative" means a parent, parent-in-law, son, son-in-law, daughter, daughter-in-law, step-parent, step-son, step-son-in-law, step-daughter, step-daughter-in-law, brother, brother-in-law, sister or sister-in-law;]

"confinement" means labour resulting in the issue of a living child, or labour after [[4]24 weeks] of pregnancy resulting in the issue of a child whether alive or dead;

"family" means—

    (a) a married or unmarried couple and any children who are members of the same household and for whom one of the couple is or both are responsible;

    (b) a person who is not a member of a married or unmarried couple and any children who are members of the same household and for whom that person is responsible;

    (c) persons who are members of the same household and between whom there is a polygamous relationship and any children who are members of the same household and for whom a member of the polygamous relationship is responsible;

[[1]. . .]

"funeral" means a burial or a cremation;

"funeral payment" is to be construed in accordance with regulation 7;

[[8]"immediate family member" means a parent, son or daughter;]

[[7]"income-based jobseeker's allowance" has the same meaning in these Regulations as it has in the Jobseekers Act 1995 by virtue of section 1(4) of that Act;]

[[1]. . .]

"married couple" means a man and a woman who are married to each other and are members of the same household;

"maternity payment" is to be construed in accordance with regulation 5;

[[6]"partner" means where a person—

    (a) is a member of a married or unmarried couple, the other member of that couple;

    (b) is married polygamously to two or more members of his household, any such member;]

"occupational pension scheme" has the same meaning as in the Social Security Pensions Act 1975;

[[8] "prescribed time for claiming" means the appropriate period during which a maternity payment or, as the case may be, a funeral payment, may be claimed pursuant to regulation 19 of, and Schedule 4 to, the Social Security (Claims and Payments) Regulations 1987;]

[[1]"person affected by a trade dispute" means a person—

    (a) to whom section 23 of the Act [SSCBA, s.126] applies; or

    (b) to whom that section would apply if a claim to income support were made by or in respect of him;]

[[5]"responsible person" is to be construed in accordance with regulation [[8]7(1)(a)];]

[[1]. . .]

[[4]"still-born child" has the same meaning as in section 12 of the Births and Deaths Registration Act 1926 and section 56(1) of the Registrations of Births, Deaths and Marriages (Scotland) Act 1965 as they are amended by section 1 of the Still-birth (Definition) Act 1992;]

"unmarried couple" means a man and a woman who are not married to each other but are living together as husband and wife.

[[8](1A) For the purposes of Part III of these Regulations, persons are to be treated as members of the same household where those persons—

(a) are married to each other and are living in the same residential accommodation, residential care home or nursing home as defined for the purposes of the Income Support Regulations or, as the case may be, of the Jobseeker's Allowance Regulations; or

(b) were partners immediately before either or both or any or all of those persons moved permanently into such accommodation or home as is referred to in sub-paragraph (a) above.

and that person is or, as the case may be, those persons are resident in such accommodation or home at the date of death of the person in respect of whom a funeral payment is claimed.]

[¹(2) For the purposes of these Regulations, two persons are to be treated as not being members of the same household in the circumstances set out in regulation 16(2) and (3) [⁷(a) to (d)] of the Income Support [⁷Regulations or, as the case may be, in regulation 78(2) and (3)(a) to (c) of the Jobseeker's Allowance Regulations].]

(3) For the purposes of these Regulations, a person shall be treated as a member of a polygamous relationship where, but for the fact that the relationship includes more than two persons, he would be one of a married or unmarried couple.

(4) In these Regulations, unless the context otherwise requires, any reference to a numbered regulation is a reference to the regulation bearing that number in these regulations and any reference in a regulation to a numbered paragraph is a reference to the paragraph of that regulation bearing that number.

AMENDMENTS

1. Social Fund Maternity and Funeral Expenses (General) Amendment Regulations 1988 (S.I. 1988 No. 36), reg. 2 (April 11, 1988).

2. Social Fund Maternity and Funeral Expenses (General) Amendment Regulations 1989 (S.I. 1989 No. 379), reg. 2 (April 1, 1989).

3. Social Fund (Miscellaneous Amendments) Regulations 1990 (S.I. 1990 No. 580), reg. 5 (April 9, 1990).

4. Social Fund Maternity and Funeral Expenses (General) Amendment Regulations 1992 (S.I. 1992 No. 2149), reg. 2 (October 1, 1992).

5. Social Fund Maternity and Funeral Expenses (General) Amendment Regulations 1994 (S.I. 1994 No. 506), reg. 2 (April 1, 1994).

6. Social Fund Maternity and Funeral Expenses (General) Amendment Regulations 1995 (S.I. 1995 No. 1229), reg. 2 (June 5, 1995).

7. Social Fund Maternity and Funeral Expenses (General) Amendment Regulations 1996 (S.I. 1996 No. 1443), reg. 2 (October 7, 1996).

8. Social Security (Social Fund and Claims and Payments) (Miscellaneous Amendments) Regulations 1997 (S.I. 1997 No. 792), reg. 2 (April 7, 1997).

9. Social Fund Maternity and Funeral Expenses (General) Amendment Regulations 1997 (S.I. 1997 No. 2538), reg. 3 (November 17, 1997).

GENERAL NOTE

Paragraph (1)

"*close relative.*" See the note to "close relative" in reg. 2(1) of the Income Support Regulations.

"*confinement.*" Note that a payment can be made for a stillbirth only if it occurs after the 24th week of the pregnancy (reduced from 28 weeks in October 1992).

"*family.*" Note that the definition differs slightly from that in s.137(1) of the Contributions and Benefits Act (1986 Act, s.20(11)), which applies for the purposes of income support, family credit and disability working allowance and s. 35(1) of the Jobseekers Act, which applies for the purpose of income-based JSA. So far as married and unmarried couples go, the approach is the same (see the notes to s.137(1)). Para. (2) goes further than the income support/income-based JSA rules by deeming members of a couple not to be members of the same household in these circumstances. Para. (2) does not cover the circumstances in which people are treated as members of the same household (but see para. (1A) where people are in residential care), so that presumably the general law on when membership of a household endures through a temporary absence will apply (see *England v. Secretary of State for Social Services* [1982] 3 F.L.R. 222; *Taylor v. Supplementary Benefit Officer (R(FIS) 5/85)*; *Santos v. Santos* [1972] 2 All E.R. 246). See the note to para. (1A).

Until the amendment in April 1990 the definition of "child" meant that beyond the age of 15 a child could not be part of the family although continuing in secondary education and not entitled to income support in her own right. Thus some 16–18-year-old mothers were excluded from maternity payments. The reference to young persons, as defined in reg. 14 of the Income Support (General) Regulations, or, from October 1996, reg. 76 of the JSA Regulations, remedies this.

"funeral." The old form of the Single Payments Regulations on funerals left it unclear whether "funeral" meant the ceremonies or religious services which accompany burial or cremation, or simply "burial." *R(SB)23/86* held that, in that context, it meant the latter. The present definition does make it clear it is the burial or cremation which is covered, rather than any accompanying or religious services.

"prescribed time for claiming". Claims for a maternity payment may be made from the beginning of the 11th week before the expected week of confinement until three months after the actual date of confinement, or the date of the adoption order in the case of an adopted child, or the date of the parental order under s. 30 of the Human Fertilisation and Embryology Act 1990 in the case of a child by a surrogate mother (reg. 19 and para. 8 of Sched. 4 to the Claims and Payments Regulations). The time limit for a funeral payment claim is three months from the date of the funeral (Sched. 4, para. 9). From April 7, 1997 there is no longer any provision allowing claims to be made outside these time limits. But note that where at the date of claim the claimant has claimed, but not yet been awarded, a qualifying benefit and so the claim for a maternity or funeral payment is refused, if a further claim is made within three months of the qualifying benefit being awarded, it will be treated as made on the date of the original claim, or the date the qualifying benefit was awarded, whichever is later (reg. 6(24) and (25) of the Claims and Payments Regulations).

"still-born child." The definition referred to is "a child which has issued forth from its mother after the twenty-fourth week of pregnancy and which did not at any time after being completely expelled from its mother draw breath or show any other signs of life."

Paragraph (1A)

The purpose of this paragraph (see also the amendment to para. (2) deleting the reference to reg. 16(3)(e) of the Income Support Regulations) is to enable a surviving partner in a home to qualify as "the responsible person" for the purposes of a funeral payment where one or both of them lives or lived in residential care. Sub-para. (a) will apply, *inter alia*, where a couple marry whilst in residential care; under this sub-paragraph they must be living in the same residential care or nursing home or residential accommodation. Otherwise sub-para. (b) requires them to have been a married or unmarried couple before one or both of them moved permanently into residential care.

Provision against double payment

4.—(1) Subject to paragraph (2), no maternity payment shall be made under these Regulations if such a payment has already been made in respect of the child in question.

(2) Notwithstanding that a maternity payment has been made to the natural mother of a child or to one of her family, a second such payment may, subject to the following provisions of these Regulations, be made to the adoptive parents of the child in question [¹ or to persons who have been granted an order in respect of the child in question pursuant to section 30 of the Human Fertilisation and Embryology Act 1990 (parental orders)].

(3) [²Except in a case to which paragraph (4) applies,] no funeral payment shall be made under these Regulations if such a payment has already been made in respect of the funeral expenses in question [¹or in respect of any [²further] funeral expenses arising from the death of the same person].

[²(4) Notwithstanding paragraph (3), a further funeral payment may be made under these Regulations in respect of any funeral expenses arising from the death of a person in respect of which such a payment has already been made where—

  (a) the decision pursuant to which the funeral payment was awarded has been reviewed; and

(b) the amount of the award as revised on that review, together with the amount of the funeral payment already paid in respect of the death of that person, does not exceed the amount of any funeral payment which may be awarded pursuant to regulation 7A(2).]

AMENDMENTS

1. Social Security (Social Fund and Claims and Payments) (Miscellaneous Amendments) Regulations 1997 (S.I. 1997 No. 792), reg. 3 (April 7, 1997).
2. Social Fund Maternity and Funeral Expenses (General) Amendment Regulations 1997 (S.I. 1997 No. 2538), reg. 4 (November 17, 1997).

DEFINITIONS

"child"—see reg. 3(1).
"family"—*ibid.*
"funeral payment"—*ibid.*
"maternity payment"—*ibid.*

GENERAL NOTE

Paras. (1) and (3) contain rules preventing double payments in the case of maternity and funeral payments respectively. Where a funeral payment was for less than the maximum, para. (4) is intended to allow an additional payment to be made on review, subject to the limit on funeral expenses in reg. 7A(2) (the words "the amount of the award as revised on that review" in sub-para. (b) presumably refer to the additional, and not the total, award).

Only a lawful payment bars another payment (*CG 30/1990*). So where the first payment was made to the partner of the maternity grant claimant (who was the income support claimant) and not to her, this did not prevent her receiving a payment.

Paragraph (2) provides an exception in the case of maternity payments as it allows the adoptive parents of a child, or those who have been granted a parental order of a child by a surrogate mother, to receive a payment although a payment has already been made for the natural mother. *CIS 13389/ 1996* decides that a person only qualifies as an adoptive parent if he has acquired parental responsibility by means of a court order (see the definition of "adoption order" in s. 12(1) of the Adoption Act 1976). The claimant had made an agreement with the child's mother under s. 4(1)(b) of the Children Act 1989 which conferred parental responsibility on him. However, this was not, and did not purport to be, an order (court orders for parental responsibility were dealt with under s. 4(1)(a)) and so the claimant had not acquired parental responsibility by means of adoption. Since a maternity payment had already been made to the child's mother, para. (1) barred a payment to the claimant.

PART II

PAYMENTS FOR MATERNITY EXPENSES

Entitlement

5.—(1) Subject to regulation 6 and Parts IV and V of these Regulations, a payment to meet maternity expenses (referred to in these regulations as a "maternity payment") shall be made only where—
[¹(a) the claimant or the claimant's partner has, in respect of the date of the claim for a maternity payment, been awarded either income support [⁴income-based jobseeker's allowance,] [², family credit or disability working allowance]; and]
(b) either—
(i) the claimant or, if the claimant is a member of a family, one of the family is pregnant or has given birth to a child [³or still-born child]; or

      (ii) the claimant or the claimant's partner or both of them have adopted a child not exceeding the age of twelve months at the date of the claim; [⁵or]

    [⁵(iii) the claimant and the claimant's spouse have been granted an order in respect of a child pursuant to section 30 of the Human Fertilisation and Embryology Act 1990 (parental orders); and]

  (c) the claim is made within the [⁵prescribed time for claiming a maternity payment].

[³(2) Subject to Part IV of these Regulations, the amount of a maternity payment shall be—

  (a) where the claim is made before confinement, £100 in respect of each expected child;

  (b) where the claim is made after confinement, £100 in respect of each child, including any still-born child;

  (c) where the claim is made after a child has already been adopted, £100 in respect of that child.]

[⁵(d) where the claim is made after an order referred to in paragraph (1)(b) (iii) has already been granted in respect of a child, £100 in respect of that child.]

AMENDMENTS

1. Social Fund Maternity and Funeral Expenses (General) Amendment Regulations 1988 (S.I. 1988 No. 36), reg. 3 (April 11, 1988).

2. Disability Living Allowance and Disability Working Allowance (Consequential Provisions) Regulations 1991 (S.I. 1991 No. 2742), reg. 10 (April 6, 1992).

3. Social Fund Maternity and Funeral Expenses (General) Amendment Regulations 1992 (S.I. 1992 No. 2149), reg. 3 (October 1, 1992).

4. Social Fund Maternity and Funeral Expenses (General) Amendment Regulations 1996 (S.I. 1996 No. 1443), reg. 3 (October 7, 1996).

5. Social Security (Social Fund and Claims and Payments) (Miscellaneous Amendments) Regulations 1997 (S.I. 1997 No. 792), reg. 4 (April 7, 1997).

DEFINITIONS

    "child"—see reg. 3(1).
    "claimant"—*ibid.*
    "confinement"—*ibid.*
    "family"—*ibid.*
    "partner"—*ibid.*
    "prescribed time for claiming"—*ibid.*
    "still-born child"—*ibid.*

GENERAL NOTE

Paragraph (1)

The three conditions specified must all be satisfied for a payment to be made but no needs have to be proved beyond them. Under sub-para. (a) either the person claiming the maternity payment or that person's partner must have been awarded income support, income-based JSA, family credit or disability working allowance. The original form of this regulation referred to the claimant being "in receipt" of benefit, which probably meant "entitled to receive benefit" (*R(SB)12/87*). Now the crucial matter is an award, rather than the actual payment of benefit. Although para. (a) talks of the claimant having been awarded benefit, an award which is made after the date of the claim for a maternity payment (*e.g.* following an appeal or a review) will presumably do, provided that it covers the date of claim. The original form of reg. 5 also left unclear the exact date on which this condition had to be satisfied. This is now fixed as the date of claim.

Under sub-para. (b), the issues will normally be simple ones of fact. The October 1992 amendments to reg. 3 and this regulation mean that a payment can be made when a child is still-born after a confinement of at least 24 weeks. Note that while a payment can be made in advance of the actual birth of a child to a member of the family, in the case of an adoption or surrogacy one can only be made after the event. See the definition of "family" in reg. 3(1) and the notes to s.137(1) of the Contributions and Benefits Act (1986 Act, s.20(11)).

Under sub-para. (c), the period within which the claim has to be made begins 11 weeks before the first day of the expected week of confinement and ends three months after the actual date of confinement (or the date of the adoption order, in the case of an adopted baby, or the date of the parental order in the case of a child by a surrogate mother) (Claims and Payments Regulations, Sched. 4, para. 8). From April 7, 1997 there is no longer any provision allowing claims to be made outside this time limit. But note that under reg. 6(24) and (25) of the Claims and Payments Regulations, where at the date of claim the claimant has claimed, but not yet been awarded, a qualifying benefit and so the claim for a maternity payment is refused, if a further claim is made within three months of the qualifying benefit being awarded, it will be treated as made on the date of the original claim, or the date the qualifying benefit was awarded, whichever is later.

The other major rule of eligibility is imposed by Part IV of the Regulations, which applies a £500 or £1,000 capital rule (like that for single payments). Part V contains transitional provisions.

Paragraph (2)

The amount of the payment is (from April 1990) £100 per child, having been at £85 for two years, which will not go very far. Note the effect of the £500 and £1,000 capital rule (reg. 9). Although para. (2) is not expressly made subject to Part V, reg. 12(4) secured that any maternity grant awarded (before its abolition on April 6, 1987) in respect of the same confinement was to be deducted from what would otherwise have been awarded.

Persons affected by a trade dispute

6. Where the claimant or the claimant's partner is a person affected by a trade dispute, a maternity payment shall be made only if—

(a) in the case where the claimant or the claimant's partner is in receipt of [¹income support], [³or income-based jobseeker's allowance] the trade dispute has, at the date of the claim for that payment, continued for not less than six weeks; or

(b) in the case where the claimant or the claimant's partner is in receipt of [¹family credit], the claim in respect of which [¹family credit] was awarded was made before the beginning of the trade dispute[²; or

(c) in the case where the claimant or the claimant's partner is in receipt of disability working allowance, the claim in respect of which disability working allowance was awarded was made before the beginning of the trade dispute.]

AMENDMENTS

1. Social Fund Maternity and Funeral Expenses (General) Amendment Regulations 1988 (S.I. 1988 No. 36) reg. 4 (April 11, 1988).

2. Disability Living Allowance and Disability Working Allowance (Consequential Provisions) Regulations 1991 (S.I. 1991 No. 2742), reg. 10 (April 6, 1992).

3. Social Fund Maternity and Funeral Expenses (General) Amendment Regulations 1996 (S.I. 1996 No. 1443), reg. 4 (October 7, 1996).

DEFINITIONS

"claimant"—see reg. 3(1).
"maternity payment"—*ibid.*
"partner"—*ibid.*
"person affected by a trade dispute"—*ibid.*

GENERAL NOTE

Para. (a) took over a similar rule which used to be in the Supplementary Benefit (Trade Disputes and Recovery from Earnings) Regulations, but the excluding period is reduced from 11 weeks to six weeks. The crucial date is that of the claim for the maternity payment. It may sometimes be difficult to tell when a trade dispute started, since the dispute is to be distinguished from the stoppage of work due to it. See reg. 3(1) for "person affected by a trade dispute."

Paras. (b) and (c) only exclude payments where the claim for family credit or disability working allowance was made after the beginning of the trade dispute.

PART III

PAYMENTS FOR FUNERAL EXPENSES

[¹Entitlement

7.—(1) Subject to the following provisions of this regulation, regulation 8 and to Parts IV and V of these Regulations, a social fund payment (referred to in these Regulations as a "funeral payment") to meet funeral expenses shall be made only where—

    (a) the claimant or his partner (in this Part of these Regulations referred to as "the responsible person"), at the date of the claim for a funeral payment—

        (i) has an award of income support, income-based jobseeker's allowance, family credit, disability working allowance, housing benefit or council tax benefit where, in the case of council tax benefit, that benefit is awarded by virtue of the claimant or his partner having fulfilled the conditions of entitlement specified in section 131(3) to (5) of the Social Security Contributions and Benefits Act 1992 (certain conditions for entitlement to council tax benefit); or

        (ii) is a person to whom (by virtue of sub-section (7) of section 131 of that Act) sub-section (6) of that section applies where, on a claim for council tax benefit, the conditions of entitlement specified in section 131(3) and (6) for an award of an alternative maximum council tax benefit are fulfilled;

  [²(b) the funeral takes place—

        (i) in a case where the responsible person is a person to whom paragraph (1A) applies, in an EEA State;

        (ii) in any other case, in the United Kingdom,

    and for the purposes of this sub-paragraph, "EEA State" means a State which is a contracting party to the Agreement on the European Economic Area signed at Oporto on 2nd May 1992 as adjusted by the Protocol signed at Brussels on 17th March 1993;]

    (c) the deceased was ordinarily resident in the United Kingdom at the date of his death;

    (d) the claim is made within the prescribed time for claiming a funeral payment; and

    (e) the claimant or his partner accepts responsibility for those expenses and—

        (i) the responsible person was the partner of the deceased at the date of death; or

      [²(ii) in a case where the deceased was—

        (aa) a child and there is no absent parent or there is an absent parent who, or whose partner, had an award of a benefit to which sub-paragraph (a) above refers current as at the date of death, the responsible person was the person or the partner of the person responsible for that child for the purposes of Part IX of the Social Security Contributions and Benefits Act 1992 as at the date of death; or (bb) a still-born child, the responsible person was a parent of that still-born child or the partner of a parent of that still-born child as at the date when the child was still-born; or

(iii) in a case where the deceased had no partner and (ii) above does not apply, the responsible person was, subject to paragraphs (3) and (4), an immediate family member of the deceased and it is reasonable for the responsible person to accept responsibility for those expenses; or

(iv) in a case where the deceased had no partner and (ii) and (iii) above do not apply, the responsible person was, subject to paragraphs (3) and (4), either—

(aa) a close relative of the deceased; or

(bb) a close friend of the deceased,

and it is reasonable for the responsible person to accept responsibility for those expenses.

(1A) This paragraph applies to a person who is—

(a) a worker for the purposes of Council Regulation (EEC) No. 1612/68 or (EEC) No. 1251/70;

(b) a member of the family of a worker for the purposes of Council Regulation (EEC) No. 1612/68;

(c) in the case of a worker who has died, a member of the family of that worker for the purposes of Council Regulation (EEC) No. 1251/70; or

(d) a person with a right to reside in the United Kingdom pursuant to Council Directive No. 68/360/EEC or No. 73/148/EEC.]

(2) For the purposes of paragraph (1)(e)(iii) and (iv), the deceased shall be treated as having had no partner where the deceased had a partner at the date of death and—

(a) no claim for funeral expenses is made by the partner in respect of the death of the deceased; and

(b) that partner dies before the date upon which the deceased's funeral takes place.

(3) [²Subject to paragraph (4), the responsible person shall not be entitled to a funeral payment where he is an immediate family member, a close relative or a close friend of the deceased and—]

(a) there are one or more immediate family members of the deceased (not including any immediate family members who were children at the date of death of the deceased);

(b) neither those immediate family members nor their partners have been awarded a benefit to which paragraph (1)(a) refers; and

(c) any of the immediate family members to which sub-paragraph (b) above refers was not estranged from the deceased at the date of his death.

(4) Paragraph (3) shall not apply to disentitle the responsible person from a funeral payment where the immediate family member to whom that paragraph applies is—

(a) a person who is aged less than 19 and who is attending a full-time course of advanced education as defined in regulation 61 of the Income Support Regulations or, as the case may be, a person aged 19 or over but under pensionable age who is attending a full-time course of study at an educational establishment;

(b) a member of, and fully maintained by, a religious order;

(c) being detained in a prison, remand centre or youth custody institution and either that immediate family member or his partner had been awarded a benefit to which paragraph (1)(a) refers immediately before that immediate family member was so detained; or

(d) a person who is regarded as receiving free in-patient treatment within the meaning of the Social Security (Hospital In-Patients) Regulations

1975 or, as the case may be, the Social Security (Hospital In-Patients) Regulations (Northern Ireland) 1975 and either that immediate family member or his partner had been awarded a benefit to which paragraph (1)(a) refers immediately before that immediate family member was first regarded as receiving such treatment.

(5) In a case to which paragraph (1)(e)(iii) or (iv) applies, whether it is reasonable for a person to accept responsibility for meeting the expenses of a funeral shall be determined by the nature and extent of that person's contact with the deceased.

(6) Except in a case where paragraph (7) applies, in a case where the deceased had one or more close relatives and the responsible person is a person to whom paragraph (1)(e)(iii) or (iv) applies, if on comparing the nature and extent of any close relative's contact with the deceased and the nature and extent of the responsible person's contact with the deceased, any such close relative was—

(a) in closer contact with the deceased than the responsible person; or
(b) in equally close contact with the deceased and neither that close relative nor his partner, if he has one, has been awarded a benefit to which paragraph (1)(a) refers; or
(c) in equally close contact with the deceased and possesses, together with his partner, if he has one, more capital than the responsible person and his partner and that capital exceeds,
  (i) where the close relative or his partner is aged 60 or over, £1,000; or
  (ii) where the close relative and his partner, if he has one, are both aged under 60, £500,

the responsible person shall not be entitled to a funeral payment under these Regulations in respect of those expenses.

(7) Paragraph (6) shall not apply where the close relative who was in closer contact with the deceased than the responsible person or, as the case may be, was in equally close contact with the deceased—

(a) was a child at the date of death; and
(b) was the only close relative (not being a child) to whom any of sub-paragraphs (a) to (c) of paragraph (6) applies.]

AMENDMENTS

1. Social Security (Social Fund and Claims and Payments) (Miscellaneous Amendments) Regulations 1997 (S.I. 1997 No. 792), reg. 5 (April 7, 1997).
2. Social Fund Maternity and Funeral Expenses (General) Amendment Regulations 1997 (S.I. 1997 No. 2538), reg. 5 (November 17, 1997).

DEFINITIONS

"absent parent"—see reg. 3(1).
"child"—*ibid*.
"claimant"—*ibid*.
"close relative"—*ibid*.
"funeral"—*ibid*.
"immediate family member"—*ibid*.
"partner"—*ibid*.
"prescribed time for claiming"—*ibid*.
"still-born child"—*ibid*.

GENERAL NOTE

This provision replaced both the contributory death grant, which had stood at £30 for many years, and reg. 8 of the Supplementary Benefit (Single Payments) Regulations. In its original form it provided effectively the same level of payment as under the Single Payments Regulations, but under wider conditions.

However, on June 5, 1995, a ceiling was imposed on the amount that can be awarded for a funeral payment. At the same time, a new priority order was introduced for deciding who was to be treated as "the responsible person", and the financial test that is applied where the deceased has more than one surviving close relative was tightened up. There was transitional protection for claims for funeral expenses in respect of a death before June 5, 1995 where the funeral took place by September 5, 1995. In such a case the former rules applied (see the 1995 edition of this book). Further minor adjustments were made in October 1996 (see the 1996 Supplement to this book for these changes). But this was rapidly followed by another major overhaul of the funeral payments scheme, as a result of which the new form of reg. 7 and the new reg. 7A were introduced on April 7, 1997. See also the changes to reg. 8 made at the same time.

The Social Security Advisory Committee's main recommendation in response to these proposed changes was that rather than seeking to tighten the criteria for entitlement to a payment still further, a new approach to help with funeral costs, possibly involving some form of insurance, needed to be considered. They referred to the evidence presented to them (largely anecdotal) that there was a growing problem of the system failing to meet the costs of a simple funeral. In a highly critical report (Cm. 3585) their main conclusion was that the new rules on eligibility added such complexity that it was doubtful whether they were understandable or workable. They considered that the proposals were "unreasonably intrusive" and that particularly those aspects concerning absent parents and the "immediate family" test appeared "to embody a narrow and inflexible view of family responsibilities which ignores the diversity of present day society and would . . . create inequity as well as delaying payments still further, while investigations are made into the relationships of deceased people". However, with one or two minor exceptions, SSAC's strongly voiced concerns were ignored by the Government. There is transitional protection for claims in respect of a death before April 7, 1997 where the funeral takes place by July 7, 1997 (see Social Security (Social Fund and Claims and Payments) (Miscellaneous Amendments) Regulations 1997, reg. 9 on p. 1100). In such a case the former rules will apply (see the 1996 edition of this book, together with the 1996 Supplement).

Reg. 7 deals with entitlement; reg. 7A defines the amount of the payment. Note also the deductions that will be made from any award under reg. 8 and that entitlement is subject to the £500 or £1,000 capital rule in reg. 9.

Paragraph (1)

All five conditions specified must be satisfied.

Note that the definition of funeral in reg. 3(1) avoids the problems of interpretation revealed in *R(SB) 23/86*. It is the cost of a burial or a cremation which is covered, rather than the accompanying ceremonies.

Sub-para. (a). An award of housing benefit or council tax benefit to either the claimant or his partner will do, as well as an award of income support, income-based JSA, family credit or disability working allowance. The award must be in respect of the date of claim for the funeral payment. See the notes to reg. 5(1) and note *CIS 2059/1995*. In that case the claimant's claim for a funeral payment had been rejected on the ground that he was not entitled to income support. However, the consequence of the Commissioner allowing his appeal against the decision refusing income support was that the basis for the rejection of his claim for a funeral payment had gone. Thus the tribunal's decision on that appeal, although sound when it was given, had become erroneous and it too had to be set aside.

On head (ii), para. 2005 of the *Social Fund Maternity and Funeral Payments Guide* now states that if alternative maximum council tax benefit (usually known as second adult rebate) is the qualifying benefit, it is the person in respect of whom the second adult rebate has been awarded (*i.e.* the non-householder) who can qualify for a funeral payment, not the householder who receives the council tax benefit (see also para. 44116 of the *Adjudication Officer's Guide*). Although the wording of head (ii) is not entirely clear, this approach is logical, since it is the circumstances of the non-householder, not the householder, that warrant the rebate.

Sub-para. (b). The previous form of sub-para. (b) required the funeral, *i.e.* the burial or cremation, to take place in the U.K. (*i.e.* Great Britain and Northern Ireland: Interpretation Act 1978, Sched. 1). A new form has finally been introduced following the ECJ's judgment in *O'Flynn v. Adjudication Officer*, Case C-237/94, [1996] All E.R. (E.C.) 541. The new rule applies to claims for funeral payments made, or treated as made, after November 16, 1997 (reg. 2 of the amending regulations). However, the effect of the ECJ's judgment is to produce a similar result in respect of claims for funeral payments made before that date, since clearly the old form of sub-para. (b) has to be read subject to that judgment.

Mr O'Flynn was an Irish national resident in the U.K. His son died in the U.K. but the burial took place in Ireland. The ECJ held that the rule that the funeral must take place in the U.K.

indirectly discriminated against nationals of other Member States and so was in breach of Art. 7(2) of EC Regulation 1612/68 (social and tax advantages). Migrant workers were more likely to have to arrange for burial in another Member State in view of the links which members of such a family generally maintained with their country of origin. As regards the cost of a funeral in another Member State, there was nothing to prevent the U.K. from limiting the amount of the payment to the normal cost of a funeral in the U.K. The cost of transporting the coffin to a place distant from the deceased's home was not covered in any event. When the case returned to a Commissioner he held that not only had the ECJ decided that the rule was discriminatory but also that it was not objectively justified. Accordingly the rule was to be disapplied and the claimant was entitled to a funeral payment (*CIS 51/1990*, to be reported as *R(IS) 4/98*). The amount claimed in that case was limited to the costs incurred within the U.K. However, the Commissioner did raise the issue of the costs of transporting a body to another Member State for burial or cremation and the costs of the funeral there. He considered that in relation to transport costs, the approach to be adopted was the same as that taken in *R(IS) 11/91* to transport within the U.K. (note in particular para. 9 of *R(IS) 11/91* as regards transport costs under what is now reg. 7A(2)(e)); as regards the funeral costs, in his view expenses incurred in the other Member State had to be dealt with in the same way as if the funeral had taken place in a part of the U.K. distant from the deceased's home. The Commissioner expressed no opinion on the question of travel costs for the responsible person but note the new reg. 7A(2)(f) in force from November 17, 1997. In considering any claim for a funeral in another Member State, adjudicating authorities will of course have to bear in mind the particular form of reg. 7 (or 7A) in force at the time of the claim; note that the DSS accepts that the effect of *R(IS) 4/98* should be applied without any restriction (*e.g.* under s. 69 of the Administration Act).

The new sub-para. (b) provides that the funeral can take place in any EEA state if the "responsible person" (see sub-para. (a)) is a worker for the purposes of EC Regulations 1612/68 or 1251/70, a member of the family of a worker for the purposes of Regulation 1612/68, a member of the family of a worker who has died and to whom Regulation 1251/70 applied, or a person who has a right to reside in the U.K. under EC Directives 68/360 or 73/148; otherwise it must take place in the U.K. The EEA states are the EU member states (Austria, Belgium, Denmark, Finland, France, Germany, Greece, Republic of Ireland, Italy, Luxembourg, the Netherlands, Portugal, Spain, Sweden and the U.K.) plus Iceland, Liechtenstein and Norway. See the notes to the additional definition of "person from abroad" in reg. 21(3) of the Income Support Regulations for discussion of the meaning of "worker" and who has a right to reside under these Directives. Under Art. 10 of Regulation 1612/68 the members of the family of a worker include his spouse, his, or his spouse's, children, grandchildren, great grandchildren, etc. who are either under 21 or dependent, parents, parents-in-law, grandparents, grandparents-in-law, etc. if they are dependent, and any other member who is dependent or who was living with the worker before he came to the U.K. The same definition applies for the purposes of Regulation 1251/70 (see Art. 1 of that Regulation).

Note also that reg. 7A(2)(f) no longer restricts eligible travel expenses to those within the U.K.

The argument that the rule in sub-para. (b) is unlawful under the Race Relations Act 1976 was rejected in *R. v. Secretary of State for Social Security, ex parte Nessa, The Times*, November 15, 1994. Section 75 of the 1976 Act states that the Act applies to acts done by, *inter alia*, ministers, as it applies to acts done by a private person. But Auld J. holds that acts of a governmental nature, such as the making of regulations, were not subject to the control of the 1976 Act as they were not acts of a kind that could be done by a private person.

Sub-para. (c). This is a new rule from April 7, 1997. The deceased must be ordinarily resident in the U.K. at the date of his death. On the meaning of "ordinary residence" see the notes to reg. 3(1) of the Family Credit Regulations. The requirement is one of ordinary residence, not presence, so, for example, a claim can be made in respect of a U.K. resident who dies while on holiday abroad for the cost of the funeral in the U.K. (although the cost of transporting the body back to the U.K. would not be covered, except possibly under sub-para. (g) of reg. 7A(2)).

Sub-para. (d). The time limit is specified in para. 9 of Sched. 4 to the Claims and Payments Regulations as three months from the date of the funeral. From April 7, 1997 there is no longer any provision allowing claims to be made outside this time limit (see the new form of reg. 19 of the Claims and Payments Regulations). Thus if the circumstances in *CIS 4931/1995* were repeated (claimant who did not qualify for income support until four months after his wife's funeral because only half his mortgage interest was included in his applicable amount until that date was held to have good cause for a late claim for a funeral payment), there would be no entitlement. See the 1996 edition for further details of *CIS 4931/1995*. But note that under reg. 6(24) and (25) of the Claims and Payments Regulations, where a claim for a qualifying benefit has been made but not yet determined when the claim for a funeral payment is made and so the claim is refused, if a further claim is made within three months of the qualifying benefit being awarded, it will be treated as made on the date of the original claim for a funeral payment, or the date the qualifying benefit was awarded, whichever is later.

Paragraph (1)(e) and paragraphs (2) to (7).

Paragraph (1)(e) introduced major new restrictions on eligibility for a funeral payment by imposing a stricter priority order for deciding who is to be treated as the "responsible person". (See reg. 9 of the Social Security (Social Fund and Claims and Payments) (Miscellaneous Amendments) Regulations 1997 (p. 1100) for the transitional protection for claims in respect of deaths before April 7, 1997 where the funeral takes place by July 7, 1997.) The November 1997 amendments to sub-para. (e) have mainly tidied up the wording in order to clarify the policy intention.

It is first necessary for the claimant or partner to have accepted responsibility (see below) for the costs of the funeral. Then, unless the deceased is a child or still-born child (see below), the person must have been the deceased's partner at the date of death (head (i)), or, if the deceased had no partner, an "immediate family member" (*i.e.* parent, son or daughter, see reg. 3(1)) (head (iii)), or, if there is no immediate family member, another close relative (defined in reg. 3(1)) or a close friend (head (iv)). Thus an ex-partner (or someone who is no longer treated as a partner), or the surviving partner in a gay couple (or a relative who is not a close relative) will have to qualify under the category of close friend. According to para. 44162 of the *Adjudication Officer's Guide*, in considering whether a person was a close friend of the deceased, the depth of the relationship will be more important than its duration. Para. (2) makes specific provision for some very limited circumstances in which the deceased will be treated as having no partner.

Where heads (iii) or (iv) apply, it must be reasonable for the person to accept responsibility for the funeral expenses, which is to be decided by considering the nature and extent of that person's contact with the deceased (para. (5)). *CIS 12783/1996* (to be reported as *R(IS) 3/98*) holds that in deciding this question, regard should be had to the person's relationship with the deceased as a whole and not just during the period immediately preceding the date of death. The claimant had claimed a funeral payment in respect of his late father whom he had not seen for 24 years. He was the only close relative. The Commissioner decides that the lack of contact over the last 24 years did not automatically erase the contact they had had in the preceding 30 years. It was not unreasonable for a son to wish to pay his last respects to his father whatever the reasons for their estrangement. See also *CIS 13120/196* (claimant divorced from the deceased only two weeks before his death after 40 years of marriage), a decision on the form of reg. 7(1)(b)(iii) as in force up to June 5, 1995 (although the actual result would be different on the current form of reg. 7). The fact that it is reasonable for one person to assume responsibility for the cost of a funeral does not mean that it is not reasonable for someone else to do so (*CIS 13120/196*).

But even if it is reasonable for the person to accept responsibility for the cost of the funeral, the intention is that the person will not be entitled to a funeral payment if there are any immediate family members (other than those who were children (*i.e.* under 19 and receiving relevant education (reg. 3(1)) at the date of death) who or whose partners, have not been awarded a qualifying benefit, unless they were estranged from the deceased or one of the limited exceptions in para. (4) applies (para. (3)). "Estrangement" has "connotations of emotional disharmony" (*R(SB) 2/87*) and may exist even though financial support is being provided. But the wording of para. (3) is not particularly clear; for example, read literally para. (3)(b) could mean that if *any* such immediate family member has been awarded a qualifying benefit, para. (3) will not apply. *CIS 2288/1998*, however, confirms that read as a whole the meaning of para. (3) was clear. A person was not entitled to a funeral payment if there was at least one other immediate family member who was not estranged from the deceased and neither that member nor the member's partner was in receipt of a qualifying benefit. A further point had arisen in *CIS 1218/1998*. The claimant in that case had applied for a funeral payment in respect of his late mother. His sister was not in receipt of a qualifying benefit. The SSAT decided that para. (3)(b) referred to both the claimant and his sister and since he was in receipt of a qualifying benefit the disentitlement imposed by para. (3) did not apply. The AO appealed, contending that if the tribunal's interpretation was correct, no claim would ever be caught by para. (3) since it was a requirement under para. (1)(a) that the responsible person be in receipt of a qualifying benefit. In addition, there would be no need to exempt from the operation of para. (3) those immediate family members listed in para. (4). The Commissioner agreed; in his view the immediate family members referred to in sub-paras. (a) and (b) did not include the responsible person.

Under para. (4), an immediate family member who is a student under 19 doing a full-time course of advanced education, or 19 or over but under pensionable age doing any full-time course; or a member of, and maintained by, a religious order; or in prison, remand centre or youth custody or receiving free in-patient treatment and who (or whose partner) was in receipt of a qualifying benefit immediately before he went into prison, etc., or hospital, will not disqualify the claimant from a funeral payment.

If the deceased was a child, the person entitled to a funeral payment will be the person (or his partner) responsible for the child at the date of death, unless there is an absent parent (defined in reg. 3(1)) who (or whose partner) was not receiving a qualifying benefit at the date of death (head (ii)(aa)). In that case (or if there is no parent/person (including any partner) responsible for the child) entitlement to a funeral payment will be decided in accordance with heads (iii) and (iv) and the additional rules in paras (2)–(7). A person is responsible for a child if he is counted as such for the purposes of child benefit.

In the case of a still born child, the rules have been simplified from November 17, 1997 so that a parent (or partner) will qualify for a funeral payment, whether or not there is an absent parent (head (ii)(bb)).

As SSAC commented, these rules could have the effect of placing responsibility for a funeral on a relative who is not prepared to accept it and moreover which cannot be enforced. This may cause particular difficulties, for example, in the case of a deceased child depending on the state of relations between the parent with care and the absent parent. In addition, the "immediate family test" will make it difficult to claim a funeral payment where a parent, son or daughter of the deceased is living outside the U.K., as they will not be entitled to a U.K. means-tested benefit, and thus this rule may disadvantage ethnic minorities. Moreover, although the surviving partner in a gay couple can qualify for a funeral payment under the category of close friend, the immediate family test may well prevent this in many cases. SSAC recommended that where "interdependence" (shared household with shared expenses) could be shown, such a claimant should be given the same priority as if he or she were the partner (in the social security sense) of the deceased, but in common with most of their other recommendations this was not accepted.

In addition to the above rules, if the responsible person is an immediate family member, another close relative or a close friend, and the deceased had one or more close relatives, the nature and extent of their contact with the deceased will be compared (para. (6)). This is a separate test from deciding whether it is reasonable for the person to have accepted responsibility for the funeral costs (see para. (5)), as confirmed in *CIS 12783/1996* (to be reported as *R(IS) 3/98*). If any close relative had closer contact the responsible person will not be entitled to a funeral payment (para. (6)(a)). If the contact was equally close, a payment will also be refused if the close relative (or their partner) is either not getting a qualifying benefit (see para. (6)(b)) or has more capital than the responsible person, and that capital exceeds £1,000 if the close relative or partner is 60 or over, or £500 if both are under 60 (para. (6)(c)). This rule does not apply if the close relative was a child (defined in reg. 3(1)) at the date of death (para. (7)). Close contact will be a question of fact in each case. It should be noted that the test involves having regard to the nature as well as the extent of the contact. Thus this will bring in issues of quality as well as quantity. See *CIS 8485/1995* which states that when considering the question of contact with the deceased tribunals should adopt a broad brush, commonsense approach. The amount of time spent with the deceased is only one factor, and the nature of the contact should be judged not just by visits, letters etc but also by the quality of the contact. So if the claimant's half-brother's unpredictable nature had affected his relationship with his late mother, that should have been taken into account in assessing the nature of his contact with her. The guidance given to AOs by the *Adjudication Officer's Guide* is that the "AO should consider the overall nature and extent of the contact with the deceased given the circumstances of the individual. For example, domestic or work responsibilities may prevent a close relative from keeping in regular contact with the deceased but the nature of the contact may be equally as close as a close friend who visited every day." The guidance suggests that factors to be considered include the nature of the relationship, frequency of contact, type of contact, domestic or caring assistance given to the deceased, social outings and holidays, domestic or work responsibilities and estrangements or arguments with the deceased (paras, 44181–2).

"Accepts responsibility" for the funeral costs

As regards acceptance of responsibility for the expenses, the decision in *CSB 488/1982*, that the fact that someone else makes the arrangements does not mean that the claimant has not taken responsibility for the costs, remains applicable. The *Social Fund Maternity and Funeral Payments Guide* has now been amended (see paras. 2109–2113) so that it no longer implies that the test is who is responsible for arranging the funeral. It may be that if the person making the arrangements enters into a direct contractual relationship with an undertaker (rather than as agent for the claimant) that person has taken responsibility for the costs. But it is not necessary for the funeral account to be in the claimant's (or partner's) name. In *CIS 12344/1996* the claimant's son made the funeral arrangements; his mother was unable to do so because of her age and the sudden death of her husband. The bill was in his name and he paid it before the claim for a social fund funeral payment was made. It is held that the son had been acting as agent for his mother and the fact that the account was addressed to him did not detract from this. The claimant had accepted responsibility for the funeral costs. In *CIS 975/1997* the Commissioner retracts his statement in *CIS 12344/1996* that it was necessary for the undertakers to know of the agency. The concept of the "undisclosed principal" in the law of agency allowed an agency to exist even where this was not disclosed to the third party, provided that the agent had in fact had authority beforehand. But if there was no agency at the time the funeral debt was incurred, it was not open to a person to intervene later and claim to be legally responsible for the debt (although depending on the circumstances a novation may achieve that result, see below).

Such an agency situation should be distinguished from a novation, or transfer, of the contract as occurred in *CIS 85/1991* (which was to have been reported as *R(IS) 9/93* but has been withdrawn from reporting). The Commissioner follows *CSB 423/1989* in holding that if another person has initially made a contract with the undertakers the claimant may assume liability for the funeral costs by a novation of the contract under which the claimant assumes the other person's liability and the undertakers release the other person from his liability. The novation requires the consent of all three parties, but no consideration or further payment is necessary. Providing that the claimant comes within one of the heads of what is now in sub-para. (e) and has assumed responsibility for the costs before the AO's decision is made (or possibly before the claim is made) the condition is satisfied. Often, arrangements will be made without thinking about the legal niceties, and a commonsense view should be taken.

[¹Amount of funeral payment

7A.—(1) Subject to paragraphs (4) and (5), regulation 8 and Part IV of these Regulations, the amount of a funeral payment shall be an amount sufficient to meet any of the costs which fall to be met or have been met by the claimant or his partner or a person acting on their behalf and which are specified in paragraph (2), inclusive of any available discount on those costs allowed by the funeral director or by any other person who arranges the funeral.

(2) The costs which may be met for the purposes of paragraph (1) are—

(a) except where sub-paragraph (b) applies, in the case of a burial—
  (i) the necessary costs of purchasing a new burial plot for the deceased, together with an exclusive right of burial in that plot;
  (ii) the necessary costs of the burial;

(b) in the case of a cremation—
  (i) the necessary costs of the cremation, including medical references;
  (ii) the cost of any necessary registered medical practitioner's certificates;
  (iii) the fee payable for the removal of any device as defined for the purposes of the Active Implantable Medical Devices Regulations 1992 save that where that removal is carried out by a person who is not a registered medical practitioner, no more than £20 shall be met in respect of that fee;

(c) the cost of obtaining any documentation, production of which is necessary in order to release any assets of the deceased which may be deducted from a funeral payment pursuant to regulation 8;

(d) where the deceased died at home or away from home and it is necessary to transport the deceased within the United Kingdom in excess of 50 miles to the funeral director's premises or to the place of rest, the reasonable cost of transport in excess of 50 miles;

[²(e) where transport is provided by a vehicle for the coffin and bearers and by one additional vehicle, from the funeral director's premises or the place of rest to the funeral and—
  (i) the distance travelled, in the case of a funeral which consists of a burial where no costs have been incurred under sub-paragraph (a)(i) above, exceeds 50 miles; or
  (ii) the distance travelled, in the case of any other funeral, necessarily exceeds 50 miles,

subject to paragraph (4A), the reasonable cost of the transport provided, other than the cost in respect of the first 50 miles of the distance travelled;
  (f) subject to paragraph (4B), the necessary cost of one return journey for the responsible person, either for the purpose of making arrangements for, or for attendance at, the funeral;]
  (g) any other funeral expenses which shall not exceed £600 in any case.
  [²(3) All references in paragraph (2)(d) and (e) to 50 miles shall be construed as applying to—
  (a) in a case to which paragraph (2)(d) applies, the combined distance from the funeral director's premises or the deceased's place of rest to the place of death and of the return journey;
  (b) in a case to which paragraph (2)(e) applies, the combined distance from the funeral director's premises or the deceased's place of rest to the funeral and of the return journey.]
  (4) The cost of items and services which may be met under paragraph (2) (a), (d) and (e) shall not be taken to include any element in the cost of those items and services which relates to a requirement of the deceased's religious faith.
  [²(4A) Costs shall only be met pursuant to head (i) of sub-paragraph (e) of paragraph (2) to the extent that the cost incurred under that head, together with the cost incurred under paragraph (2)(a)(ii), does not exceed the costs which would have been incurred under paragraph (2)(a)(i) and (ii) and, where appropriate, (e)(ii) if it had been necessary to purchase a new burial plot for the deceased with an exclusive right of burial in that plot.
  (4B) Costs shall only be met pursuant to sub-paragraph (f) of paragraph (2) to the extent that those costs do not exceed the costs which would have been incurred in respect of a return journey from the home of the responsible person to the location where the necessary costs of the burial or, as the case may be, cremation, would have been incurred pursuant to paragraph (2)(a) or, as the case may be, (b).]
  (5) Where items and services have been provided on the death of the deceased under a pre-paid funeral plan or under any analogous arrangement—
  (a) no funeral payment shall be made in respect of items or services referred to in paragraph (2) which have been provided under such a plan or arrangement; and
  (b) paragraph (2)(g) shall have effect in relation to that particular claim as if for the sum "£600", there were substituted the sum "£100".]

AMENDMENTS

  1. Social Security (Social Fund and Claims and Payments) (Miscellaneous Amendments) Regulations 1997 (S.I. 1997 No. 792), reg. 5 (April 7, 1997).
  2. Social Fund Maternity and Funeral Expenses (General) Amendment Regulations 1997 (S.I. 1997 No. 2538), reg. 6 (November 17, 1997).

DEFINITIONS

  "claimant"—see reg. 3(1).
  "funeral"—*ibid.*

GENERAL NOTE

  This regulation contains the limits on eligible funeral costs. (See reg. 9 of the Social Security (Social Fund and Claims and Payments) (Miscellaneous Amendments) Regulations 1997 (p. 1100) for the transitional protection for claims in respect of deaths before April 7, 1997 where the funeral takes place by July 7, 1997. See also the note to s. 138(1)(a) of the Contributions and Benefits Act.) Note that a funeral payment will be made even if the costs have already been met by the claimant, his partner, or a person acting on their behalf.

A payment can be made for the expenses that are listed in para. (2)(a) to (f) (except for those that have been met by a pre-paid funeral plan or similar arrangement (para. (5)(a)), together with up to £600 for other funeral expenses, or £100 if some of the funeral costs have been met under a pre-paid funeral plan or similar arrangement (paras (2)(g) and (5)(b)). Any element in the burial or transport costs that relates to a requirement of the deceased's religious faith will not be met (para. (4)). See *CSIS 42/1996*, a decision on the previous form of reg. 7, which held that a vigil is a requirement of the Roman Catholic faith.

CIS 16192/1996 decided that under the previous form of reg. 7 the cost of *either* a cremation *or* a burial was allowed but not both (see reg. 7(4)(a) and (b) in the 1996 edition of this book). Thus the cost of the interment of the deceased's ashes following a cremation was not covered, since the disposal of the ashes was not part of the cremation process. The Commissioner in *CIS 12838/1996* took the same view, despite the fact that the former reg. 7(4)(a) referred to interment rather than burial; although it was common to speak of the interment (rather than a burial) of the ashes, he concluded that in the context of reg. 7(4) interment meant burial without there having been a cremation. Para. (2)(a) has removed this confusion by referring to burial rather than interment; moreover, unlike the former reg. 7(4)(a), it excludes cases where sub-para. (b) applies.

The expenses to be covered by para. (2)(g) are not specified but will include items such as a funeral director's fees, church fees or flowers. But there is no definition of funeral expenses and so any expense that is a funeral expense should be allowed. In addition, there is nothing to prevent para. (2)(g) being used to pay for the cost of items or services in paras (2)(a) to (f) that have not been fully met or to cover the cost of a religious requirement.

It will be noted that some of sub-paragraphs (a) to (f) in para. (2) contain an express limitation to "reasonable" costs and some do not (in others the word "necessary" is used). On a previous form of this provision *R(IS) 14/92* considered that the word "reasonable" should be read into the listed categories even where it was not expressed. But in *CIS 6818/1995* the Commissioner concluded that what was said about reasonableness in *R(IS) 14/92* was not an essential part of the decision. He expressed the view (which was also not necessary to *his* decision) that each sub-paragraph in what was then reg. 7(2) contained its own complete test and that there was no room for any further conditions to be implied. In view of the quite specific nature of the items or services covered by para. (2)(a)–(f) it is suggested that the approach of *CIS 6818/1995* is to be preferred. Under para. (2)(g) there is no limit on the funeral expenses that are to be met, other than the £600 (or £100) ceiling.

R(IS) 11/91 decided that the deceased's "home" (see para. (2)(d)) was the accommodation where he normally lived prior to his death, as opposed to his "home town". *CIS 14261/1996* considered the meaning of "necessary costs of a new or re-opened grave" in what was then reg. 7(4)(a) (now see para. (2)(a)). The Commissioner decides that the word "necessary" implied that any expense over that which was properly required was to be excluded. However, its effect was not to require the purchase of the cheapest possible plot without regard to any other consideration. Account should be taken of the proximity to the deceased's residence while he was alive and of the deceased's religion, so that, for example a person of the Greek Orthodox faith was entitled to be buried in an area set aside for people of that faith.

Para. (2)d) and (e) allow certain transport costs for distances (*i.e.* the combined distance of the outward and return journey (para. (3)), in excess of 50 miles to be met. The previous form of para. (2)(e)(ii) (now sub-para. (e)(i)) did not appear to allow *any* award where the costs of transport and burial in an existing plot (*i.e.* usually away from where the deceased lived) exceeded the purchase and burial costs of a new plot, plus any necessary transport costs (*i.e.* the costs of burying locally). The effect of the new para. (4A) and para. (2)(e)(i) is that such costs will be met up to the level of the local burial costs.

Para. (2)(f) covers one return journey for the responsible person for arranging the funeral or attending it. The November 17, 1997 form of sub-para. (f) (introduced following the ECJ's judgment in *O'Flynn*, see the notes to reg. 7(1)(b)) no longer restricts the journey to one within the U.K. However, para. (4B) limits the costs that will be met to those of a return journey from the responsible person's home to the place where the funeral costs would have been incurred (although the drafting is not entirely clear, it is understood that the intention is to restrict payment of travel costs to those that would have been incurred if the funeral had taken place in the U.K.). Note that sub-para. (f) now only covers necessary travel expenses; the previous form referred to "reasonable" expenses. *CIS 16957/1996* decides that although sub-para. (f) refers to a "return journey" it did also apply where the claimant only undertook a single journey (her husband had died away from home and she had travelled home to attend the funeral). Others who are relatives of the deceased may be eligible for a community care grant for the cost of travel to and from a funeral in the United Kingdom (see Social Fund direction 4(b)(ii)). The applicant must be a member of a family containing a claimant in receipt of income support or income-based JSA.

From the amount calculated under reg. 7A must be deducted the amounts listed in reg. 8. These do not include the value of the deceased's estate, but by virtue of s. 78(4) of the Administration Act any funeral payment from the social fund is a first charge on the estate.

The £500 or £1,000 capital rule will also be applied (reg. 9). Reg. 9(3)(c) secures that if the amount of capital as at the date of claim has been reduced by a payment towards the expenses of the funeral in question, the amount of the payment is to be added back. If the funeral costs have not been paid at the date of claim any funeral payment is to be made direct to the creditor (Claims and Payments Regulations, reg. 35(2)).

Deductions from an award of a funeral payment

8.[⁴—(1) Subject to paragraph (2),] there shall be deducted from the amount of any award which would, but for this regulation, be made under regulation 7 the following amounts:—

(a) the amount of any assets of the deceased which are available to the [¹responsible person] (on application or otherwise) or any other member of his family without probate or letters of administration [³or in Scotland, confirmation,] having been granted;

(b) the amount of any lump sum due to the [¹responsible person] or any other member of his family on the death of the deceased by virtue of any insurance policy, occupational pension scheme, or burial club or any analogous arrangement;

(c) the amount of any contribution [⁴towards funeral expenses] which has been received by the [¹responsible person] or any other member of his family from a charity or a relative of his or of the deceased[⁴ . . .];

(d) the amount of any funeral grant, made out of public funds, in respect of the death of a person who was entitled to a war disablement pension.

[⁴(e) in relation to a pre-paid funeral plan or any analogous arrangement—

    (i) where the plan or arrangement had not been paid for in full prior to the death of the deceased, the amount of any sum payable under that plan or arrangement in order to meet the deceased's funeral expenses;

    (ii) where the plan or arrangement had been paid for in full prior to the death of the deceased, the amount of any allowance paid under that plan or arrangement in respect of funeral expenses.

(2) The amount of any payment made under the Macfarlane Trust, the Macfarlane (Special Payment) Trust, the Macfarlane (Special Payments) (No. 2) Trust, the Fund or the Eileen Trust shall be disregarded from any deduction made under this regulation and for the purpose of this paragraph, "the Macfarlane Trust", "the Macfarlane (Special Payments) Trust", "the Macfarlane (Special Payments) (No. 2) Trust", "the Fund" and "the Eileen Trust" shall have the same meaning as in regulation 2(1) of the Income Support Regulations.]

AMENDMENTS

1. Social Fund Maternity and Funeral Expenses (General) Amendment Regulations 1994 (S.I. 1994 No. 506), reg. 4 (April 1, 1994).

2. Social Fund Maternity and Funeral Expenses (General) Amendment Regulations 1995 (S.I. 1995 No. 1229), reg. 4 (June 5, 1995).

3. Social Fund Maternity and Funeral Expenses (General) Amendment Regulations 1996 (S.I. 1996 No. 1443), reg. 6 (October 7, 1996).

4. Social Security (Social Fund and Claims and Payments) (Miscellaneous Amendments) Regulations 1997 (S.I. 1997 No. 792), reg. 6 (April 7, 1997).

DEFINITIONS

"family"—see reg. 3(1).

"occupational pension scheme"—see 1986 Act, s.84(1) (PSA, s.1).
"responsible person"—see reg. 3(1).

GENERAL NOTE

Paragraph (1)
The amounts specified are to be deducted from the amount calculated under reg. 7A, it would appear before the £500 or £1000 capital rule is applied. Note the exception in para. (2).

Sub-para. (a). Under the Administration of Estates (Small Payments) Act 1965 certain sums can be distributed from the estate to beneficiaries without a grant of probate or letters of administration. The current limit is £5,000. In addition many statutes regulating Post Office and building society accounts, savings certificates, etc., (but not, after privatisation, Trustee Savings Bank accounts) allow payment to be made after the owner's death. There is a similar power for most social security benefits. For details, see Parry & Clark, *The Law of Succession* (8th ed.), pp. 165–7, and *Halsbury's Laws of England* (4th ed.), Vol. 17, para. 970. One problem is that these provisions are generally merely permissive, so that payment cannot be demanded as of right. In *R(IS) 14/91* the Commissioner indicates that in straightforward cases it may be concluded that such an amount is available on application. However, the circumstances (*e.g.* some dispute between next of kin of equal status) may point to the opposite conclusion. *R(IS) 14/91* also decides that evidence of availability of assets from the date of death up to the date of the AO's decision is relevant. Thus where the claim was made on the date of death, a sum of £1300 in the deceased's building society account was available, although the claimant did not obtain the money until a week later. Nor was that conclusion defeated by the fact that before the AO's decision the claimant had distributed or spent most of the money. Funeral expenses are a first charge on the estate *(R(SB) 18/84)*. If there are liquid assets in the estate, these may be immediately available for funeral expenses regardless of other debts. In *R(IS) 12/93* arrears of attendance allowance for the deceased were paid to the claimant as next-of-kin. The Commissioner holds that the arrears were available. Since they exceeded the cost of the funeral, no award was made.

Sub-para. (b). For this paragraph to apply the amount must be due to the claimant or a member of his family (defined in reg. 3(1)). Due must mean legally due. Sometimes such a member will have a clear legal entitlement under an insurance policy or a pension scheme. Sometimes trustees may have a discretion as to who should be paid a lump sum. In these circumstances no amount can be legally due until the trustees have exercised that discretion.

Sub-para. (c). This paragraph only applies to sums which have actually been received, presumably at the date of claim, since that is the date specified in reg. 7(1), although *R(IS) 14/91* casts doubt on this. Only payments towards funeral expenses from charities or from relatives of the deceased or the claimant's family count. Payments from anyone else do not count, except to the extent that they may increase the claimant's capital. From April 7, 1997, any relevant payments are taken into account in full. But if a contribution is for expenses which are not funeral expenses (*e.g.* clothing to wear to the funeral), it is not included under para. (c).

CIS 450/1995 decides that a genuine loan from a relative that is legally recoverable is not a "contribution" and is not caught by sub-para. (c).

Sub-para. (d). This paragraph is straightforward.

Sub-para. (e). Any amount payable under a pre-paid funeral plan or similar arrangement will be deducted.

Paragraph (2)
No deduction is to be made for payments received from these trusts.

PART IV

EFFECT OF CAPITAL

Effect of capital

9.—[²(1) Where—
(a) a claimant or a claimant's partner is aged 60 or over and the claimant has capital which is in excess of £1,000; or

(b) the claimant is or, if he has a partner, both he and his partner are aged under 60 and the claimant has capital which is in excess of £500,

a maternity payment or funeral payment which, but for this regulation, would be payable shall be payable only if, and to the extent that, the amount of the payment is more than the excess.]

[¹(2) For the purposes of paragraph (1)—

    (a) any capital possessed by any person whose capital is for the purposes of entitlement to income support [⁵or, as the case may be, to income-based jobseeker's allowance], treated as that of the claimant by virtue of section 22(5) of the Social Security Act 1986 [SSCBA, s.136(1)] or the provisions of regulation 23(3) of the Income Support [⁴Regulations or, as the case may be, of regulation 88(4) of the Jobseeker's Allowance Regulations] (calculation of income and capital) shall be treated as that of the claimant;

    (b) subject to paragraph (3), the claimant's capital shall be calculated in the same manner as his capital is calculated under the Income Support [⁴Regulations or, as the case may be, under the Jobseeker's Allowance Regulations] for the purposes of determining his entitlement to income support [⁴or, as the case may be, income-based jobseeker's allowance].

(3) For the purposes of paragraph (1)—

    (a) any sum acquired by the claimant (whether as a loan or otherwise) on the express condition that it is to be used to meet the funeral expenses in respect of which the claim is made shall be disregarded;

    (b) in the case of a claim for a maternity payment or a funeral payment which is made within 12 months of the death of the husband of the claimant, any lump sum payable to that claimant as a widow by virtue of section 24 of the Social Security Act 1975 [SSCBA, s.36] shall be disregarded;

    (c) the amount of any payment out of capital, other than capital disregarded under sub-paragraphs (a) and (b) above or under [⁴regulation 46(2) or 47] of, and Schedule 10 to, the Income Support [⁴Regulations or, as the case may be, under regulation 108(2) or 109 of, and Schedule 8 to, the Jobseeker's Allowance Regulations] (capital disregards), which has already been made towards the funeral expenses (whether or not the expenses are within the scope of [³regulation [⁵7A(2)]]), shall be added back to that capital as if the payment had not been made.]

<small>AMENDMENTS</small>

1. Social Fund Maternity and Funeral Expenses (General) Amendment Regulations 1989 (S.I. 1989 No. 379), reg. 4 (April 1, 1989).

2. Social Fund (Miscellaneous Amendments) Regulations 1990 (S.I. 1990 No. 580), reg. 7 (April 9, 1990).

3. Social Fund Maternity and Funeral Expenses (General) Amendment Regulations 1995 (S.I. 1995 No. 1229), reg. 4 (June 5, 1995).

4. Social Fund Maternity and Funeral Expenses (General) Amendment Regulations 1996 (S.I. 1996 No. 1443), reg. 7 (October 7, 1996).

5. Social Security (Social Fund and Claims and Payments) (Miscellaneous Amendments) Regulations 1997 (S.I. 1997 No. 792), reg. 7 (April 7, 1997).

<small>DEFINITIONS</small>

    "the Act"—see reg. 3(1).
    "claimant"—*ibid.*
    "funeral payment"—*ibid.*
    "maternity payment"—*ibid.*

<small>GENERAL NOTE</small>

Paragraph (1)
    Any excess of the claimant's capital over £500, or £1,000 if either the claimant or his partner is aged

over 59, is to be set against the amount of a payment calculated under Part II or III. This may wipe out the entitlement, or if the initial amount of the payment is higher than the excess the difference is paid.

Reg. 9 does not specify the date at which capital is to be calculated. It was clear under the Single Payments Regulations that the date of claim was the crucial date. It is possible that for social fund purposes changes in capital up to the date of decision are relevant, and this seems to be in line with the approach in *R(IS) 14/91* (see note to reg. 8(1)(a)). The Commissioner there did point out that reg. 8 is not concerned with entitlement, but with deductions from an award. Thus it can still be argued that the capital test should be applied at the date fixed in reg. 5(1)(a) and 7(1)(a), *i.e.* the date of claim. But not all the elements of entitlement can necessarily be identified at that date (see reg. 7(1)(b)), so that the question remains open.

Paragraph (2)

Because a social fund payment is not income support, the income support/income-based JSA capital rules have to be specifically incorporated.

Sub-para. (a). Section 136(1) of the Contributions and Benefits Act (1986 Act, s.22(5)) provides that the capital of all members of the claimant's family (as defined in s.137(1); 1986 Act, s.20(11)) counts as the claimant's. (The sub-paragraph has not been updated to include a reference to s. 13(2) of the Jobseekers Act 1995.) But see the immediate effect of sub-para. (b) below. Reg. 23(3) of the Income Support (General) Regulations and reg. 88(4) of the JSA Regulations deal with polygamous marriages (but not other polygamous relationships).

Sub-para. (b). This sub-paragraph makes clear that capital is to be calculated in the same way as for income support/income-based JSA, subject to the special rules set out in para. (3). Thus an adjudicating authority will have to consider, for example, whether money in a bank account is capital or merely income (see the note to reg. 23 of the Income Support Regulations) and, if it counts as capital, whether any of the disregards in Sched. 10 apply (*CIS 12838/1996*). There may be some difficulties in directly applying some of the income support/income-based JSA rules. For instance, if a claimant gives away money so as to get below the £500 or £1000 capital rule, he would not seem to be fixed with notional capital of the amount given away under reg. 51(1) of the Income Support (General) Regulations (reg. 113(1) JSA Regulations). Those regulations only apply where the person's purpose is to secure or increase entitlement to income support (or income-based JSA or income support in the case of JSA). A social fund payment is not income support/income-based JSA. Equally, if a claimant spends capital on personal possessions so as to get below the limit, the disregard of the value of personal possessions in para. 10 of Sched. 10 to the Income Support (General) Regulations/para. 15 of Sched. 8 to the JSA Regulations (incorporated by reg. 9(2)(b) above) still applies.

Note that there is no general requirement under the income support/income-based JSA rules that capital should be available before it is taken into account. Availability may sometimes be a factor in assessing market value.

Paragraph (3)

These are special rules for social fund payments, where the income support/income-based JSA rules do not necessarily apply.

Sub-para. (a). Sums acquired by the claimant in these circumstances would probably not be part of the claimant's capital anyway (see *Barclays Bank Ltd. v. Quistclose Investments Ltd.* [1970] A.C. 567; *R(SB) 53/83; R(SB) 1/85; R(SB) 12/86*).

Sub-para. (b). A payment under s.36 of the Contributions and Benefits Act (1975 Act, s.24) is known as a widow's payment. It is a contributory benefit of £1,000 paid to widows, intended to help with immediate "bereavement associated" expenses. It is to be disregarded for a year from the date of the husband's death, in the case of both funeral and maternity payments.

Sub-para. (c). This provision applies only to funeral payments. If (presumably before the date of claim) capital which is not disregarded under sub-paras. (a) or (b) or Sched. 10 to the Income Support (General) Regulations/Sched. 8 to the JSA Regulations has been used for funeral expenses, then the amount used is to be added back into the claimant's capital. A payment for funeral expenses which fall outside reg. 7A(2) is caught by this provision, but not a payment for expenses which are not truly funeral expenses (*e.g.* obituary notices).

Assessment of capital

10. [¹. . .]

AMENDMENT

1. Social Fund Maternity and Funeral Expenses (General) Amendment Regulations 1989 (S.I. 1989 No. 379), reg. 5 (April 15, 1989).

PART V

TRANSITIONAL PROVISIONS

Interpretation of Parts V and VI

11. In this Part and Part VI of these Regulations—
"the Single Payments Regulations" means the Supplementary Benefit (Single Payments) Regulations 1981;
"the Trade Dispute Regulations" means the Supplementary Benefit (Trade Disputes and Recovery from Earnings) Regulations 1980;
"the Urgent Cases Regulations" means the Supplementary Benefit (Urgent Cases) Regulations 1981.

Transitional arrangements—maternity payments

12.—(1) Subject to paragraph (2), no maternity payment shall be made in the case where the confinement or adoption occurred before 6th April 1987.

(2) Subject to paragraph (3), a maternity payment may be made, so long as the claimant satisfies the conditions of Part II of these Regulations, in respect of a confinement or adoption which occurred on or after 9th March 1987 but only if the claimant or his partner was or would have been, had a claim been made, entitled to supplementary benefit for any period including 9th March 1987 or beginning after that date which falls before the coming into operation of these Regulations.

(3) No maternity payment shall be made in a case where, in respect of the same confinement or adoption, the claimant or his partner has received or is entitled to a single payment of supplementary benefit by virtue of regulation 7 of the Single Payments Regulations or an additional requirement was applicable by virtue of regulation 7 of the Trade Disputes Regulations.

(4) The amount of a maternity payment shall be reduced by the amount of an award, in respect of the same confinement, of a maternity grant under section 21 of the Social Security Act 1975.

DEFINITIONS

"claimant"—see reg. 3(1).
"confinement"—*ibid.*
"maternity payment"—*ibid.*
"partner"—*ibid.*
"Single Payments Regulations"—see reg. 11.
"Trade Disputes Regulations"—*ibid.*

GENERAL NOTE

The general rule, under para. (1), is that maternity payments can only be made for births or adoptions after April 5, 1987. Up to that date reg. 7 of the Single Payments Regulations was still in operation. However, the crucial date under those regulations is the date of claim, so that if a claim was not made before April 6, 1987, no payment for maternity expenses under reg. 7 can be paid. Therefore, if no single payment has been made (para. (3)) a social fund payment can be made for births or adoptions occurring after March 8, 1987 (para. (2)). The ordinary conditions of regs. 4 and 5 must be met, and in addition the claimant or his partner must have satisfied the conditions for entitlement to supplementary benefit for some time between March 9 and April 5, 1987, inclusive.

Note that para. (3) provides a general exclusion when there has already been a single payment or trade dispute payment for the same birth or adoption. Similarly, under para. (4) if there has been an award of maternity grant the £25 is to be deducted from any social fund payment.

Transitional payments—funeral payments

13.—(1) Subject to paragraph (2) no funeral payment shall be made where the deceased died before 6th April 1987.

1098

(2) Subject to paragraph (3) a funeral payment may be made, so long as the claimant satisfies the conditions of regulation 6, where the deceased died on or after 9th March 1987 but only if the claimant or his partner was or would have been, had a claim been made, entitled to supplementary benefit for any period including 9th March 1987 or beginning after that date which falls before the coming into operation of these Regulations.

(3) No funeral payment shall be made in the case where, in respect of the same funeral, the claimant or his partner has received or is entitled to a single payment of supplementary benefit by virtue of regulation 8 of the Single Payments Regulations or an additional requirement was applicable by virtue of regulation 7A of the Trade Disputes Regulations.

(4) The amount of a funeral payment shall be reduced by the amount of an award, in respect of the same funeral, of a death grant under section 32 of the Social Security Act 1975 unless that grant has been spent on any item in respect of which a funeral payment would otherwise have been made.

DEFINITIONS

"claimant"—see reg. 3(1).
"funeral"—*ibid.*
"funeral payment"—*ibid.*
"partner"—*ibid.*
"Single Payments Regulations"—see reg. 11.
"Trade Disputes Regulations"—*ibid.*

GENERAL NOTE

The general rule, under para. (1), is that funeral payments can only be made for deaths occurring after April 5, 1987. Up to that date, reg. 8 of the Single Payments Regulations was still in operation. But the crucial thing under those regulations is the date of claim and if no claim had been made before April 6, 1987, no single payment could be awarded. Therefore, providing that no single payment or trade dispute payment has been made (para. (3)) a social fund payment can be made for deaths after March 8, 1987. The ordinary conditions of reg. 6 must be met, and in addition the claimant or his partner must for some period between March 9 and April 5, 1987, inclusive, have satisfied the conditions for entitlement to supplementary benefit.

Para. (3) provides a general exception from entitlement. Under para. (4) the amount of a social fund payment is to be reduced by the amount of any death grant awarded, unless the grant has been spent on an item covered by reg. 6(2). Presumably in this case, a social fund payment will not be made for that item because the person will not have taken responsibility for that item.

PART VI

CONSEQUENTIAL AMENDMENTS

14., 15., and **16**. [*Omitted*]

Social Fund Maternity and Funeral Expenses (General) Amendment Regulations 1995

(S.I. 1995 No. 1229)

Made by the Secretary of State under ss.138(1) and (4) and 175(1), (3) and (4) of the Social Security Contributions and Benefits Act 1992

[In force June 5, 1995]

Transitional provision with respect to deaths occurring before 5th June 1995

5. Where, in respect of a death which occurs before 5th June 1995, a claim is made by the responsible person for funeral expenses from the social fund in respect of a funeral which takes place on or before 5th September 1995, regulations 2 to 4 of these Regulations shall not have effect with respect to that claim.

<small>GENERAL NOTE</small>

See the notes to reg. 7 of the Social Fund Maternity and Funeral Expenses (General) Regulations. Regs, 7, 8 and 9 were amended by regs. 2–4 of these Regulations on June 5, 1995.

Social Fund Maternity and Funeral Expenses (General) Amendment Regulations 1996

(S.I. 1996 No. 1443)

Made by the Secretary of State of State under ss. 138(1)(a) and (4) and 175(1), (3) and (4) of the Social Security Contributions and Benefits Act 1992.

[In force October 7, 1996].

Transitional provision

8. Regulations 2(3) and (4), 5(3) to (7) and 6 of these Regulations shall not have effect with respect to any claim for a funeral payment made before 7th October 1996.

<small>GENERAL NOTE</small>

The regulations referred to in this provision effected amendments to regs. 3, 7 and 8 of the Social Fund Maternity and Funeral Expenses (General) Regulations on October 7, 1996.

Social Security (Social Fund and Claims and Payments) (Miscellaneous Amendments) Regulations 1997

(S.I. 1997 No. 792)

Made by the Secretary of State under ss. 138(1)(a) and (4) and 175(1), (3) and (4) of the Social Security Contributions and Benefits Act 1992 and sections 5(1)(a), 189(1), (3) and (4) and 191 of the Social Security Administration Act 1992.

[In force April 7, 1997].

Transitional provision

9. Where, in respect of a death which occurs before 7th April 1997, a claim is made for funeral expenses from the social fund in respect of a funeral which takes place on or before 7th July 1997, regulations 2, 3(b), 5, 6 and 7 of these Regulations shall not have effect with respect to that claim.

<small>GENERAL NOTE</small>

See the notes to regs. 7, 7A and 8 of the Social Fund Maternity and Funeral Expenses (General) Regulations. Regs. 3, 4(3), 8 and 9 of those Regulations were amended and new regs. 7 and 7A were inserted by regs. 2, 3(b), 5, 6 and 7 of these Regulations on April 7, 1997.

Social Fund (Application for Review) Regulations 1988

(S.I. 1988 No. 34)

Made by the Secretary of State under the Social Security Act 1986, ss.34(1) and (3) and 84(1).

GENERAL NOTE

These regulations prescribe the procedure for applying for a review in cases in which decisions on the social fund are taken by social fund officers rather than AOs. Thus they apply to budgeting loans, crisis loans and community care grants, but not to maternity or funeral payments or payments for exceptionally cold weather.

Citation, commencement and interpretation

1.—(1) These Regulations may be cited as the Social Fund (Application for review) Regulations 1988 and shall come into force on 11th April 1988.

(2) Any reference in regulation 2 of these Regulations to a numbered paragraph is a reference to the paragraph in that regulation bearing that number.

Manner of making application for review or further review and time limits

2.—(1) Any application for—

(a) a review of any determination made by a social fund officer;

(b) a further review by a social fund inspector of a determination of a social fund officer which has been reviewed,

shall be in writing and shall be made within the time specified in paragraph (2) by sending or delivering it to an office of the Department of Social Security.

(2) The time specified for the purposes of paragraph (1) is—

(a) in the case of an application to which paragraph (1)(a) applies, 28 days from the date on which the determination to which that application relates was issued;

(b) in the case of an application to which paragraph (1)(b) applies, 28 days from the date on which the determination on review was issued.

(3) The time specified in paragraph (2) may be extended for special reasons, even though the time so specified may already have expired, by the social fund officer or, as the case may be, the social fund inspector.

(4) The application for review or, as the case may be, further review shall contain particulars of the specific grounds on which it is made and shall be signed by the person making the application.

(5) Where it appears to the social fund officer or, as the case may be, the social fund inspector that a person has submitted an application which is incomplete in that it contains insufficient particulars to enable any material question to be determined, he may request that person to furnish within a specified time such further particulars as may be reasonably required to complete the application; and if the person does so the application shall be treated as having been made within the time specified in paragraph (2) or, as the case may be, extended under paragraph (3).

[¹(6) Where an application is to be made on behalf of a person to whom the determination relates, that person shall signify in writing his consent to the application being made on his behalf unless the person making the application is a person appointed by the Secretary of State under regulation 33(1) of the

Social Security (Claims and Payments) Regulations 1987 to act on behalf of the person to whom the determination relates.]

(7) For the purposes of paragraph (2) the date on which a determination or a determination on review is issued is the date on which notice of that determination was given or sent to the applicant for review or further review, and, if sent by post to the applicant's last known or notified address, that notice shall be treated for the purposes of this regulation as having been sent on the day that it was posted.

AMENDMENT

1. Social Fund (Miscellaneous Amendments) Regulations 1990 (S.I. 1990 No. 580), reg. 2 (April 9, 1990).

GENERAL NOTE

R. v. Social Fund Officer ex p. Hewson (High Court, June 22, 1995) concerned an application for review of a social fund officer's decision under s. 66(1)(b) of the Administration Act. It clarifies that special reasons for extending the 28-day time limit in para. (2)(a) only have to be shown for the purposes of a review under s. 66(1)(a). They are not required for a review under s. 66(1)(b). Further, although direction 31 of the Social Fund Directions applies to reviews under s. 66(1)(b), reviews under this provision are not restricted to the grounds laid down in direction 31.

Social Fund (Applications) Regulations 1988

(S.I. 1988 No. 524)

Citation, commencement and interpretation

1.—(1) These Regulations may be cited as the Social Fund (Applications) Regulations 1988 and shall come into force on 11th April 1988.

(2) In these Regulations, unless the context otherwise requires—
"the Act" means the Social Security Act 1986;
"appropriate office" means an office of the Department of Social Security.

Form and manner in which an application is to be made

2.—(1) Every application for a payment out of the social fund under section 32(2)(b) of the Act [SSCBA, s.138(1)(b)] payment to meet needs other than in prescribed circumstances) shall be made in writing, on a form approved by the Secretary of State and completed in accordance with the instructions on that form, or in such other manner, being in writing, as the Secretary of State may accept as sufficient in the circumstances of any particular case.

(2) Forms of application shall be supplied, without charge, by such persons as the Secretary of State may appoint or authorise for that purpose.

(3) Every application shall be delivered or sent to an appropriate office.

(4) Where an application is to be made on behalf of a person, that person shall signify in writing his consent to the application being made on his behalf unless the person making the application is a person appointed by the Secretary of State under regulation 33(1) of the Social Security (Claims and Payments) Regulations 1987 to act on the beneficiary's behalf.

(5) Where it appears to the Secretary of State that an application which has been submitted is incomplete in that—
(a) the form approved has been used but it has not been completed in accordance with the instructions given on that form, the Secretary of State may

return the form to the person making the application for proper completion by him; or

(b) it contains insufficient particulars to enable any material question to be determined, the Secretary of State may request that person to furnish in writing or by attendance at the appropriate office such further particulars as may reasonably be required to complete the application.

['Time at which an application is to be treated as made

3. The time at which an application to which regulation 2 above applies is to be treated as made shall be—

(a) in the case of an application which meets the requirements of regulation 2(1), the date on which it is received in an appropriate office;

(b) in the case of an application which does not meet the requirements of regulation 2(1), but where the person complies with the requirements of the Secretary of State pursuant to regulation 2(5), the date on which the application was received in an appropriate office in the first instance.]

AMENDMENT

1. Social Fund (Miscellaneous Provisions) Regulations 1990 (S.I. 1990 No. 1788), reg. 4 (September 24, 1990).

Social Fund (Miscellaneous Provisions) Regulations 1990

(S.I. 1990 No. 1788)

Citation, commencement and interpretation

1.—(1) These Regulations may be cited as the Social Fund (Micellaneous Provisions) Regulations 1990 and shall come into force on 24th September 1990.

(2) In these Regulations, "the Act" means the Social Security Act 1986.

Condition to be satisfied before payment of a social fund award

2.—(1) Before a payment of an award out of the social fund under section 32(2)(b) of the Act [SSCBA, s. 138(1)(b)] (payment to meet needs other than in prescribed circumstances) is made for a category of need which is specified in directions given by the Secretary of State to be repayable, the person by or on behalf of whom the application was made shall notify the Secretary of State in writing of his agreement to the terms and conditions of which he has been notified by the Secretary of State in accordance with subsection (4A) of section 33 of the Act [SSCBA, s. 139(4)] within 14 days of the date on which that notification was issued to that person.

(2) The time specified in paragraph (1) above may be extended by the Secretary of State for special reasons, even though the time so specified may already have expired.

Circumstances in which an award is to be extinguished

3. An award of a payment out of the social fund under section 32(2)(b) of the Act [SSCBA, s.138(1)(b)] shall be extinguished where—

(a) the person by or on behalf of whom the application was made fails to satisfy the condition in regulation 2(1) above, within the time there specified or as extended under regulation 2(2), as the case may be; or

(b) the payment has been made to the person by or on behalf of whom the application was made or to a third party but the person or the third party, as the case may be, has failed to present for payment the instrument of payment within 12 months of its issue.

Social Fund (Recovery by Deductions from Benefits) Regulations 1988

(S.I. 1988 No. 35)

Made by the Secretary of State under the Social Security Act 1986, ss. 33(6) and 84(1).

Citation and commencement

1. These Regulations may be cited as the Social Fund (Recovery by Deductions from Benefits) Regulations 1988 and shall come into force on 11th April 1988.

Interpretation

2. In these Regulations "the principal Act" means the Social Security Act 1975.

Benefits from which an award from the social fund may be recovered

3. The following benefits are prescribed for the purposes of section 33(6) of the Social Security Act 1986 [SSAA, s.78(2)] as benefits from which an award from the social fund may be recovered by deduction—

- (a) income support[³, other than a back to work bonus payable by way of income support or jobseeker's allowance in pursuance of section 26 of the Jobseekers Act 1995;]
- (b) family credit;
- [³(c) a jobseeker's allowance other than a back to work bonus payable by way of income support or jobseeker's allowance in pursuance of section 26 of the Jobseekers Act 1995;];
- [²(d) incapacity benefit under section 86A of the Social Security Contributions and Benefits Act 1992;]
- (e) [². . .];
- (f) [². . .];
- (g) maternity allowance under section 22(1) of the principal Act [SSCBA, s.34];
- (h) widowed mother's allowance under section 25(1) and (2) of the principal Act [SSCBA, s.37];
- (i) widow's pension under section 26(1) of the principal Act [SSCBA, s.38];
- (j) retirement pension (Categories A and B) under sections 28(1) and 29(1) of the principal Act [SSCBA, ss.44 and 49];
- (k) severe disablement allowance under section 36 of the principal Act [SSCBA, s.68];
- (l) invalid care allowance under section 37 of the principal Act [SSCBA, s.70];
- (m) retirement pension (Categories C and D) under section 39(1) of the principal Act [SSCBA, s.78];
- (n) age addition under section 40(1) and (2) of the principal Act [SSCBA, s.79];
- (o) increases to [³. . .] [²incapacity benefit] and Category A, B and C retirement pension under section 41(1) of the principal Act [SSCBA, s.80];

(p) increases to [³. . .] [²short-term incapacity benefit] and maternity allowance under section 44(1) and (2) of the principal Act [SSCBA, s.82];

(q) increases to Category A and Category C retirement pension or to [²long-
term incapacity benefit] under section 45(2) of the principal Act [SSCBA,
s.83];

(r) increases to Category A retirement pension under section 45A(1) of the
principal Act [SSCBA, s.84];

(s) increases to Category A and Category C retirement pension and [²long-
term incapacity benefit] under section 46(2) of the principal Act [SSCBA,
s.85];

(t) increase to [²long-term incapacity benefit] under section 47(1) of the principal Act [SSCBA, s.86];

(u) increases to severe disablement allowance and invalid care allowance
payable under section 49(a) and (b) of the principal Act [SSCBA, s.90];

(v) disablement benefit under section 57(1) of the principal Act [SSCBA,
s.103];

(w) reduced earnings allowance under section 59A(1) of the principal Act
[SSCBA, s.106];

(x) industrial death benefit under section 67 to 70 to the principal Act
[SSCBA, s. 106];

(y) additions to Category A and Category B retirement pension under sections 6 to 10 of, and Schedule 1 to, the Social Security Pensions Act
1975;

(z) additional pension payable as widows benefit under sections 6 and 13 of
the Social Security Pensions Act 1975;

(aa) [². . .];

(bb) [². . .];

(cc) graduated retirement benefit under sections 36 and 37 of the National
Insurance Act 1965;

[¹(dd) disability working allowance under section 20 of the Social Security Act
1986 [SSCBA, s.129].]

AMENDMENTS

1. Disability Living Allowance and Disability Working Allowance (Consequential Provisions)
Regulations 1991 (S.I. 1991 No. 2742), reg. 14 (April 6, 1992).
2. Social Security (Incapacity Benefit) (Consequential and Transitional Amendments and Savings)
Regulations 1995 (S.I. 1995 No. 829), reg. 20 (April 13, 1995).
3. Income-related Benefits Schemes and Social Fund (Miscellaneous Amendments) Regulations
1996 (S.I. 1996 No. 1944), reg. 9 (October 7, 1996).

GENERAL NOTE

See the notes to s. 78(2) of the Administration Act.
The October 1996 amendments to paras. (a) and (c) were made as a consequence of the introduction of JSA. JSA is prescribed as a benefit from which deduction for recovery of a social fund loan
may be made (para. (c)) but no such deduction may be made from a back to work bonus payable
by way of either income support or JSA (paras. (a) and (c)), nor from a child maintenance bonus
(see reg. 4).

[¹[² Social Security (Child Maintenance Bonus)]

4. In regulation 3 above, income support and a jobseeker's allowance do not
include any sum payable by way of child maintenance bonus in accordance with
section 10 of the Child Support Act 1995 and the Child Maintenance Bonus
Regulations 1996.]

AMENDMENTS

1. Social Security (Child Maintenance Bonus) Regulations 1996 (S.I. 1996 No. 3195), reg. 16(4) (April 7, 1997).
2. Social Security (Miscellaneous Amendments) Regulations 1997 (S.I. 1997 No. 454), reg. 8(10) (April 6, 1997).

Social Fund Directions

Directions issued by the Secretary of State for Social Security under sections 138(1)(b), 140(1A), 140(2), 140(3) and 140(4) of the Social Security Contributions and Benefits Act 1992 and sections 66(7), 66(7A) (as inserted by paragraph 7(e) of Schedule 6 to the Social Security Act 1998), 66(8)(a) and (b) and 168(5) of the Social Security Administration Act 1992.

ARRANGEMENT OF DIRECTIONS

GENERAL

BUDGETING LOANS

CRISIS LOANS

COMMUNITY CARE GRANTS

REVIEWS

THE BUDGET

OVERPAYMENTS

COMMUNITY CARE GRANTS AND CRISIS LOAN APPLICATIONS

Social Fund Directions

BUDGETING LOAN PRIORITISATION AND AWARDS

remain in the community rather than enter institutional or residential accommodation in which he will receive care; or
- (iii) ease exceptional pressures on the applicant and his family; or
- (iv) allow the applicant or his partner to care for a prisoner or young offender on release on temporary licence under rule 6 of the Prison Rules 1964 or, in Scotland, on temporary release under Part XIV of the Prisons and Young Offenders Institutions (Scotland) Rules 1994; or
- (v) help the applicant to set up home in the community as a part of a planned resettlement programme following a period during which he has been without a settled way of life; or
- (b) by assisting an applicant and one or more members of his family, or any of those persons, with expenses of travel including any reasonable charges for overnight accommodation within the United Kingdom in order to—
  - (i) visit someone who is ill; or
  - (ii) attend a relative's funeral; or
  - (iii) ease a domestic crisis; or
  - (iv) visit a child who is with the other parent pending a court decision; or
  - (v) move to suitable accommodation.

4A. [*Deleted with effect from November 27, 1991*]

Grants and loans

5. Any award within direction 2 or 3 shall include a determination that it is repayable; an award within direction 2 is referred to in these directions as a budgeting loan and an award within direction 3 is referred to as a crisis loan.

6. Any award within direction 4 shall not include a determination that it is repayable; an award within direction 4 is referred to in these directions as a community care grant.

6A. [*Deleted with effect from November 27, 1991*]

Repeat applications

7. (1) A social fund officer shall not determine an application for a crisis loan or grant from the social fund made within 26 weeks of a previous application for a crisis loan or grant for the same item or service for which a payment has already been awarded or refused, unless there has been a relevant change in the applicant's circumstances.

(2) A social fund officer shall not determine an application for a crisis loan or grant from the social fund made within 26 weeks of a previous application for a budgeting loan for the same item or service for which a payment has already been awarded or refused under the directions and guidance which had been in force as at 4 April 1999, unless there has been a relevant change in the applicant's circumstances.

BUDGETING LOANS

Eligibility

8. (1) A social fund payment under direction 2 shall only be awarded to an applicant if, at the date of the determination of the application—
- (a) he is in receipt of a qualifying benefit, which, for the purposes of this direction means either
  - (i) income support; or
  - (ii) income-based jobseeker's allowance; and

(b) neither he nor his partner is disentitled from receiving a jobseeker's allowance pursuant to section 14 of the Jobseekers Act 1995 (trade disputes) nor would they be so disentitled if otherwise entitled to that allowance; and

(c) for each week of the 26 weeks immediately preceding the date of determination of the application, he has been in receipt of a qualifying benefit or the partner of a person in receipt of a qualifying benefit.

(2) For the purpose of paragraph (1)(c), where the applicant or, as the case may be, his partner, has been in receipt of a qualifying benefit for two or more periods, the last of which includes the date of the determination of the application and those periods are separated by an interval of not more than 28 days, those periods, or the later of those periods and that interval, may be treated as a continuous period of receipt of a qualifying benefit.

(3) For the purposes of paragraphs (1)(c) and (2), where an applicant or, as the case may be, his partner has been in receipt of income-based jobseeker's allowance, the period of three waiting days prescribed by regulation 46(2) of the Jobseeker's Allowance Regulations 1996 shall not be treated as a period of receipt of a qualifying benefit.

Effect of capital

9. (1) Where—

(a) the applicant, or his partner, is aged 60 or over and the total capital resources of the applicant and his partner exceed £1000; or

(b) the applicant is, or if he has a partner, both are aged under 60 and the total capital resources of the applicant and his partner exceed £500

any budgeting loan which would but for this direction be awarded shall be awarded only if, and to the extent that, the amount of the award is more than the excess.

(2) Subject to paragraph (4) in this direction, "total capital resources" shall be calculated in accordance with—

(a) where the applicant or his partner is in receipt of income support, Chapter VI (capital) of Part V of, and Schedule 10 to, the Income Support (General) Regulations 1987

(b) where the applicant or his partner is in receipt of income-based jobseeker's allowance, Chapter VI (capital) of Part VII of, and Schedule 8 to, the Jobseeker's Allowance Regulations 1996.

(3) In this direction, any payment made to the applicant or to his partner under the Social Security (Back to Work Bonus) (No. 2) Regulations 1996 shall be treated as capital.

(4) There shall be disregarded from the total capital resources for the purposes of paragraph (2)—

(a) any payments made from the Family Fund to the applicant or to his partner or children.

Maximum and minimum amounts

10. The minimum amount that may be awarded as a budgeting loan is £30. The maximum that may be awarded as a budgeting loan is the difference between any sum already repayable to the social fund by the applicant and his partner and £1000.

11. No budgeting loan may be awarded in excess of the amount which the applicant is likely to be able to repay.

12. [*Deleted with effect from April 5, 1999*].

13. [*Direction 13 has been deleted. It required applications to be made in writing on the approved form (unless the Secretary of State allowed otherwise).*

This is now provided for in the Social Fund (Applications) Regulations 1988 (S.I. 1988 No. 524).]

CRISIS LOANS

Eligibility

14. A social fund payment under direction 3 shall only be awarded to an applicant if at the date when the application is determined;
   (a) he is aged 16 or over; and
   (b) he is without sufficient resources to meet the immediate short-term needs of himself or his family, or both himself and his family.

15. A crisis loan may not be awarded in respect of a person who is—
   (a) a resident in accommodation to which Part III of the National Assistance Act 1948 or Part IV of the Social Work (Scotland) Act 1968 applies, or in a nursing home or residential care home or a hospital in-patient, unless it is planned that the person will be discharged within the following two weeks; or
   (b) a prisoner or person who is lawfully detained or is on release on temporary licence under rule 6 of the Prison Rules 1964 or, in Scotland, on temporary release under Part XIV of the Prisons and Young Offenders Institutions (Scotland) Rules 1994; or
   (c) a person who is a member of and fully maintained by a religious order; or
   (d) a person who is (or would be) treated as—
      (i) a person in full time relevant education for the purpose of income support; or
      (ii) a person receiving relevant education for the purpose of income-based jobseeker's allowance

   and, as a result, falls into a category whereby he is not (or would not be) entitled to income support or income-based jobseeker's allowance.

16. Where the applicant is:
   (a) a full time student except where he is in receipt of either income support or income-based jobseeker's allowance; or
   (b) a person who is (or would be) treated as a person from abroad for the purposes of either income support or, as the case may be income-based jobseeker's allowance and, as a result, falls into a category whereby s/he is not (or would not be) entitled to income support or income-based jobseeker's allowance

a social fund payment under direction 3 shall only be awarded in order to alleviate the consequences of a disaster.

17. *Trade Disputes*
   (a) Where the applicant or his partner:
      (i) is disentitled from receiving a jobseeker's allowance pursuant to section 14 of the Jobseekers Act 1995 (referred to in this direction as 'the Act') or would be so disentitled if otherwise entitled to that allowance; or
      (ii) is in receipt of a reduced rate of jobseeker's allowance pursuant to section 15 of the Act (trade disputes—effect on other claimants)

the expenses for which a crisis loan may be awarded are limited to those specified in (f) until the date when the applicant is no longer disentitled from receiving jobseeker's allowance under section 14 of the Act or until the date when the applicant is no longer in receipt of a reduced rate jobseeker's allowance under section 15 of the Act.

   Disallowances
   (b) Subject to paragraph (e), where an applicant's claim for jobseeker's

1110

allowance has been disallowed under section 1(2)(a) to (c) of the Act (conditions of entitlement to jobseeker's allowance), the expenses for which a crisis loan may be awarded are limited to those specified in (f) for 14 days starting on the first day of the benefit week immediately following the disallowance decision, or the benefit week commencement date if the disallowance decision is made on that day.

Sanctions

(c) Subject to paragraph (e) and except in a case to which paragraph (d) applies, where jobseeker's allowance is not payable to an applicant on the basis that one or more of the circumstances specified in section 19(5) or (6) of the Act applies to him, the expenses for which a crisis loan may be awarded are limited to those specified in (f) for 14 days starting on the first day of benefit week immediately following the end of the period during which jobseeker's allowance was not payable.

New Deal Sanctions

(d) Subject to paragraph (e), where it is determined that a jobseeker's allowance is not payable to the applicant on the basis that either or both of section 19(5)(b) or (c) of the Act apply in relation to an employment programme specified in regulation 75(1)(a)(ii) of the Jobseeker's Allowance Regulations 1996 or in relation to a training scheme specified in regulation 75(1)(b)(ii) of those Regulations, the expenses for which a crisis loan may be awarded are limited to those specified in (f) throughout the period when he is not a person in hardship pursuant to regulation 140A(1) of those Regulations.

(e) Paragraphs (b) (c) and (d) shall not apply where the applicant is in receipt of income-based jobseeker's allowance by virtue of his being a 'person in hardship' as defined in regulation 140(1) of the Jobseeker's Allowance Regulations 1996.

(f) The specified expenses are—
    (i) expenses which are the consequence of a disaster; and
    (ii) expenses, outside (i), in respect of items required for the purpose only of cooking or space heating (including fireguards).

Maximum awards

18. (1) The maximum amount that may be awarded as a crisis loan in respect of living expenses for applicants, other than people whose income-based jobseeker's allowance is reduced by virtue of regulation 145 of the Jobseeker's Allowance Regulations 1996 (hardship cases), is the aggregate of—

(a) an amount equal to 75% of the appropriate income support personal allowance, or, as the case may be, income-based jobseeker's allowance personal allowance, for the applicant and any partner; and

(b) for each child, an amount equal to the income support personal allowance at the rate applicable to children before the first Monday in September following their 11th birthday, or, as the case may be, an amount equal to the income-based jobseeker's allowance personal allowance at the rate applicable to children before the first Monday in September following their 11th birthday;

but must not in any case exceed the difference between any sum already repayable to the social fund by the applicant and his partner and £1000.

(2) The maximum amount that may be awarded by way of a crisis loan in respect of living expenses to the partner of an applicant specified in paragraphs (b) and (c) of direction 17 is an amount equal to 75% of the applicable amount specified in paragraphs 1(1)(a) to (e) of Schedule 1 to the Jobseeker's Allowance Regulations 1996 as is applicable to the partner, but must not in any case exceed

any sum already repayable to the social fund by the partner and/or the applicant and £1000.

19. [*Direction 19 has been deleted*]

20. The maximum amount that may be awarded as a crisis loan in respect of living expenses for applicants whose income-based jobseeker's allowance is reduced by virtue of regulation 145 (hardship cases) of the Jobseeker's Allowance Regulations 1996 is—

   (a) the aggregate of—
      (i) an amount equal to 75% of the appropriate income-based jobseeker's allowance personal allowance for the applicant and any partner; and
      (ii) for each child, an amount equal to the income-based jobseeker's allowance personal allowance at the rate applicable to children before the first Monday in September following their 11th birthday; or
   (b) the income-based jobseeker's allowance applicable amount payable in such circumstances

whichever is the lower, but must not in any case exceed the difference between any sum already repayable to the social fund by the applicant and his partner and £1000.

21. The maximum amount which may be awarded in respect of any item or service which is within direction 3 (crisis loans) is the lesser of—

   (a) in the case of an existing item, the cost of repair; or
   (b) the reasonable costs of replacing an existing item, or purchasing a new item or service (including delivery and installation),

but the amount must not in any case exceed the difference between any sum already repayable to the social fund by the applicant and his partner and £1000.

22. No crisis loan may be awarded in excess of the amount which the applicant is likely to be able to repay.

Exclusions

23.—(1) A crisis loan may not be awarded in respect of

   (a) any of the following:
      (i) any need which occurs outside the United Kingdom;
      (ii) an educational or training need including clothing and tools;
      (iii) distinctive school uniform or sports clothes of any description for use at school or equipment of any description to be used at school;
      (iv) travelling expenses to or from school;
      (v) school meals taken during school holidays by children who are entitled to free school meals;
      (vi) expenses in connection with court (legal) proceedings (including a community service order) such as legal fees, court fees, fines, costs, damages, subsistence or travelling expenses (other than a crisis loan for emergency travelling expenses where an applicant is stranded away from home);
      (vii) removal or storage charges where an applicant is rehoused following the imposition of a compulsory purchase order, or a redevelopment or closing order, or a compulsory exchange of tenancies, or pursuant to a housing authority's statutory duty to the homeless under Part VII of the Housing Act 1996 or Part II of the Housing (Scotland) Act 1987;
      (viii) domestic assistance and respite care;
      (ix) any repair to property of any body mentioned in section 80(1) of the Housing Act 1985 or section 61(2)(a) of the Housing (Scotland) Act 1987 and, in the case of Scotland, any repair to property of any housing trust in existence on 13 November 1953;

(x) a medical, surgical, optical, aural or dental item or service;

(xi) work related expenses;

(xii) debts to government departments;

(xiii) investments *or*

(b) in respect of any expense which is excluded by direction 17.

(2) In addition to the expenses excluded by paragraph (1), a crisis loan may not be awarded for any expenses in respect of any of the following items—

(a) costs of purchasing, renting or installing a telephone and of any call charges;

(b) mobility needs;

(c) holidays;

(d) a television or radio, or licence, aerial or rental charges for a television or radio;

(e) garaging, parking, purchase, and running costs of any motor vehicle except where payment is being considered for emergency travelling expenses;

(f) housing costs, including repairs and improvements to the dwelling occupied as the home including any garage, garden and outbuildings, and including deposits to secure accommodation, mortgage payments, water rates, sewerage rates, service charges, rent and analogous charges for accommodation, other than:

(i) payments for intermittent housing costs not met by housing benefit, income support or income-based jobseeker's allowance or for which direct payments cannot be implemented such as the cost of emptying cess pits or septic tanks; or

(ii) rent in advance which is payable to secure fresh accommodation where the landlord is not a local authority; or

(iii) charges for board and lodging accommodation and residential charges for hostels, but not deposits, whether included in the total charge or not; or

(iv) minor repairs and improvements;

(g) council tax, council water charges, arrears of community charge, collective community charge contributions or community water charges.

24. [*Direction 24 has been deleted*]

COMMUNITY CARE GRANTS

Eligibility

25.—(1) For the purposes of this direction, a qualifying benefit is, either—

(a) income support; or

(b) income-based jobseeker's allowance.

(2) A social fund payment under direction 4 shall only be awarded to an applicant if:

(a) subject to sub-paragraph (b) of this paragraph, the application is treated as made on a date upon which the applicant is in receipt of a qualifying benefit; or

(b) in a case where the conditions set out in direction 4(a)(i) are satisfied at the date the application is treated as made, and it is planned that the applicant will be discharged within six weeks and is likely to receive a qualifying benefit upon discharge.

(3) For the purposes of direction 4(a)(ii) to (iv) and direction 4(b), the applicant shall not be deemed to be in receipt of income-based jobseeker's allowance

where the application is made on one of the three waiting days prescribed by regulation 46(2) of the Jobseeker's Allowance Regulations 1996.

26. Where the applicant, or his partner, is disentitled from receiving a jobseeker's allowance pursuant to section 14 of the Jobseekers Act 1995 (trade disputes) or would be so disentitled if otherwise entitled to that allowance, or is in receipt of reduced rate income-based jobseeker's allowance pursuant to section 15 of the Jobseekers Act 1995 (trade disputes—effect on other claimants) a community care grant may not be awarded except in respect of travelling expenses within the United Kingdom in the following situations—

    (a) if the visit is made by a partner or dependant who is not affected by the trade dispute, an award may be made in respect of travelling expenses for

        (i) a visit to a patient who is a close relative or who was prior to his admission to hospital or similar institution a member of the same household; or

        (ii) a visit to a person who is a close relative or who was prior to his illness a member of the same household as the visitor and is critically ill but not in hospital or similar institution;

    (b) if the visit is made by a person who is affected by the trade dispute, an award may be made in respect of travelling expenses for

        (i) a visit to a partner in hospital or similar institution; or

        (ii) a visit to a dependant in hospital or similar institution, if the person affected by the trade dispute has no partner living with him who would be eligible for an award within paragraph (a) of this direction, or the partner is also in hospital or similar institution; or

        (iii) a visit to a critically ill close relative or member of the household of the person affected by the trade dispute, whether or not he is in hospital or similar institution.

Effect of capital

27.—(1) Where—

    (a) the applicant, or his partner, is aged 60 or over and the total capital resources of the applicant and his partner exceed £1000; or

    (b) the applicant is, or if he has a partner both are aged under 60 and the total capital resources of the applicant and his partner exceed £500

any community care grant which would but for this direction be awarded shall be awarded only if, and to the extent that, the amount of the award is more than the excess.

(2) In this direction "total capital resources" shall be calculated in accordance with—

    (a) where the applicant or his partner is in receipt of income support, Chapter VI (capital) of Part V of, and Schedule 10 to, the Income Support (General) Regulations 1987, except that any payments made from the Family Fund to the applicant or to his partner or children shall be disregarded;

    (b) where the applicant or his partner is in receipt of income-based jobseeker's allowance, Chapter VI (capital) of Part VIII of, and Schedule 8 to, the Jobseeker's Allowance Regulations 1996, except that any payments made from the Family Fund to the applicant or to his partner or children shall be disregarded.

(3) In this direction, any payment made to the applicant or to his partner under the Social Security (Back to Work Bonus) (No. 2) Regulations 1996 shall be treated as capital.

Minimum awards

28.—

    (a) Subject to paragraph (b) below, the minimum amount that may be awarded as a community care grant under direction 4(a) is £30, but no award shall be made under direction 4(a) where the value of an item of expense which would otherwise qualify for an award, or in the case of more than one such item their aggregate value, amounts to less than £30.

(b) Paragraph (a) shall not apply in respect of awards made for either daily living expenses or travelling expenses.

Exclusions

29. A community care grant may not be awarded in respect of any expenses which are excluded by direction 23(1)(a)(i)–(xiii) nor in respect of—

(a) costs of purchasing, renting or installing a telephone and of any call charges;

(b) any expenses which the local authority has a statutory duty to meet;

(c) costs of fuel consumption and any associated standing charges;

(d) housing costs, including repairs and improvements to the dwelling occupied as the home, including any garage, garden and outbuildings, and including deposits to secure accommodation, mortgage payments, water rates, sewerage rates, service charges, rent, and all other charges for accommodation, whether or not such charges include payment for meals and/or services other than:

   (i) minor repairs and improvements; or

   (ii) charges for accommodation applied for under direction 4(b);

(e) council tax, council water charges, arrears of community charge, collective community charge contributions or community water charges.

(f) any daily living expenses such as food and groceries, except:

   (i) where such expenses are incurred in caring for a prisoner or young offender on release on temporary licence under rule 6 of the Prison Rules 1964, or, in Scotland, on temporary release under Part XIV of the Prisons and Young Offenders Institutions (Scotland) Rules 1994; or

   (ii) where a crisis loan cannot be awarded for such expenses because the maximum amount referred to in direction 18 has already been reached.

29A. [*Direction 29A has been deleted with effect from November 27, 1991*]

29B. [*Direction 29B has been deleted with effect from November 27, 1991*]

29C. [*Direction 29C has been deleted with effect from November 27, 1991*]

30. [*Direction 30 has been deleted*]

REVIEWS

Circumstances in which a determination is to be reviewed

31. (1) A determination made by a social fund officer relating to a community care grant or a crisis loan must be reviewed where it appears that the determination concerned—

(a) was based on a mistake as to the law or the directions;

(b) was given in ignorance of, or was based on a mistake as to, some material fact; or

(c) there has been any relevant change of circumstances since the decision was given.

(2) A determination made by a social fund officer relating to a budgeting loan must be reviewed where it appears that the determination concerned—

(a) was based on a mistake as to the law or the directions; or

(b) was given in ignorance of, or was based on a mistake as to, some material fact; or

(c) there has been any relevant change of circumstance with regard to:
    — both the state of the relevant allocation and local guidance by the Area Social Fund Officer as to the maximum amount available to each budgeting loan applicant; and
    — the likelihood of repayment and the time within which repayment is likely

(3) Reviews referred to in paragraphs (1) and (2) above shall be undertaken by a social fund officer (who may be the social fund officer who made the original determination), or by a social fund review officer appointed for the purpose of carrying out social fund reviews.

(4) A social fund officer or social fund review officer to whom paragraph (3) above refers shall, in Directions 32 to 39 be referred to as the reviewing officer.

Manner in which a review is to be conducted

32. (1) In reviewing a community care grant determination the reviewing officer having first considered the matters specified in Direction 39(1), must have full regard to:

(a) all the circumstances which existed at the time the original determination was made;

(b) any new evidence which has since been produced; and

(c) any relevant change of circumstances.

(2) In reviewing a budgeting loan determination the reviewing officer having first considered the matters specified in Direction 39(2), must, have full regard to:

(a) the applicant's personal circumstances as they existed at the time the original determination was made;

(b) the material facts confirming the applicant's personal circumstances which existed at the time the original determination was made

(c) any new evidence, supporting the material facts which confirm the applicant's personal circumstances existing at the time the original determination was made and which has since been produced

(d) both the state of the relevant allocation and local guidance issued by the Area Social Fund Officer as to the maximum amount available to each budgeting loan applicant

(e) the likelihood of repayment and the time within which repayment is likely

(3) For the purposes of paragraph (2)(a) to (c) above, the reviewing officer shall have regard to those of the applicant's personal circumstances which are both applicable to him and which are specified in directions issued by the Secretary of State pursuant to section 140(1A) of the Social Security Contributions and Benefits Act 1992.

(4) For the purpose of paragraph (2)(d) and (e) above, the reviewing officer shall take into account any relevant change of circumstance which has occurred in the period commencing on the date of the original determination and ending on the day on which the reviewing officer makes his determination.

33. (1) If a reviewing officer is minded not to revise the determination wholly in the applicant's favour, the applicant must, subject to paragraphs (2) and (3), be given the opportunity of being interviewed in person, accompanied by a relative, friend or representative if he wishes, by the reviewing officer before a determination is made.

(2) The applicant may, notwithstanding paragraph (1), be given the opportunity of taking part in a telephone interview with the reviewing officer before a determination is made where—

(a) it is not practicable for the applicant to be interviewed in person; or

(b) the applicant has agreed both to forego the opportunity of being interviewed in person and to take part in a telephone interview.

(3) Circumstances in which the applicant may, subject to paragraph (4), not be given the opportunity of being interviewed in person by the reviewing officer before a determination is made are where:

(a) the applicant is not in receipt and not likely to be in receipt of the relevant qualifying benefit as defined for the purposes of Direction 8 or, as the case may be, 25; or

(b) the original award was a partial award or a partial award can be made on review.

(4) Notwithstanding paragraph (3) above, an applicant to whom that paragraph applies may, before a determination is made, be given the opportunity of being interviewed in person by the reviewing officer or of taking part in a telephone interview where—

(a) the applicant has requested an interview; or

(b) the reviewing officer has determined that it would be appropriate to conduct an interview in the applicant's case.

34. (1) If an applicant is interviewed in person by the reviewing officer he must be given:

(a) an explanation of the reasons for the determination complained of;

(b) an opportunity to make any representations, including the provision of additional evidence, in relation to his application.

(2) If a telephone interview is conducted with the applicant, he must be given:

(a) an explanation of the reasons for the determination;

(b) an opportunity to make any representations in relation to his application.

35. (1) If an applicant is interviewed in person the reviewing officer must make a written record of any representations made at the interview by the applicant in relation to his case, and this must be agreed with the applicant.

(2) If the reviewing officer conducts a telephone interview with the applicant, the reviewing officer must make a written record of any representations made by the applicant in relation to his case during the interview, and this must be agreed with the applicant. A copy of an accurate account of the interview must be sent to the applicant together with any decision issued in accordance with Direction 36(2).

36. (1) Where the applicant either declines or fails to attend an interview offered in accordance with Direction 33(1); or (4) or declines a telephone interview offered in accordance with Direction 33(2) or (4), the reviewing officer having decided whether or not to revise the determination concerned, shall inform the applicant of his decision in writing. The reviewing officer shall also inform him of his right to apply for a further review of that decision by a social fund inspector. The decision letter must also mention that the applicant had either declined, or failed to attend, an interview, whichever is appropriate.

(2) Where an applicant attends an interview offered in accordance with Direction 33 (1) or (4) or takes part in a telephone interview offered in accordance with Direction 33(2) or (4), the reviewing officer, having decided whether or not to revise the determination concerned, shall inform the applicant of his decision in writing. The reviewing officer shall also inform him of his right to apply for a further review of that decision by a social fund inspector.

37. If an applicant indicates in writing that he does not wish to proceed with his application the reviewing officer should take no further action unless satisfied that he should conduct a review in accordance with direction 31 (circumstances in which a determination is to be reviewed).

38. A social fund review officer shall consider carefully any cases referred by the social fund inspector for redetermination. He should take into account any reasons given by the social fund inspector in reaching his decision to refer the matter to him, remedy any defects drawn attention to by the social fund inspector and note that he has done so when determining the case afresh.

39. (1) In reviewing a community care grant or crisis loan determination the reviewing officer must have full regard initially to:

(a) whether the SFO applied the law correctly in arriving at his decision. In particular:
— that the decision is sustainable on the evidence;
— that the SFO took all relevant considerations into account and did not take irrelevant considerations into account;
— that the SFO interpreted the law—including Secretary of State directions—correctly;

(b) whether the SFO acted fairly and exercised his discretion to arrive at a conclusion that was reasonable in the circumstances—*i.e.* a decision that a reasonable SFO could have reached;

(c) whether the required procedural steps have been followed; that the applicant had sufficient opportunity to put his case; and there has been no bias.

(2) In reviewing a budgeting loan determination the reviewing officer must have full regard initially to:

(a) whether the SFO applied the law correctly in arriving at his decision. In particular:
— that the decision is sustainable on the evidence;
— that the SFO took all relevant considerations into account and did not take irrelevant considerations into account;
— that the SFO interpreted the law—including Secretary of State directions—correctly;

(b) whether the SFO should have exercised his discretion in relation to the maximum amounts specified in local guidance as available to budgeting loan applicants;

(c) whether the required procedural steps have been followed; that the applicant had sufficient opportunity to put his case; and there has been no bias.

THE BUDGET

40.—
(a) SFOs shall determine budgeting loan applications by taking account of the maximum amount specified in ASFO guidance as available to each applicant so as to enable them effectively to control and manage the amounts allocated to them throughout the period of the allocation, and

(b) Social fund officers shall control and manage the relevant amounts allocated to them so that throughout the period of the allocation they can give priority to high priority needs in circumstances so specified for the purposes of making community care grants and crisis loan payments.

41. The Area social fund officer shall:
(a) make a plan of the level of expenditure for the relevant social fund officers throughout the period of the allocation; and

(b) issue guidance which specifies the levels of priority which may be met from the allocations for grants under direction 4 and crisis loans under direction 3;

(c) profile budgeting loan expenditure to ensure that, as far as possible, the maximum amount specified in the ASFO guidance as available to each budgeting loan applicant may be maintained throughout the period of the allocation;

(d) issue guidance which will specify the maximum amount available to each budgeting loan applicant which is to be taken into account by SFOs when determining whether a budgeting loan should be awarded and if so, the amount of that award, pursuant to direction 53;

(e) on at least one occasion during every month monitor and review the plan made under paragraph (a) the profile of budgeting loan expenditure under paragraph (c) and the guidance under paragraphs (b) and (d); and

(f) revise the plan, profile and guidance as is necessary to ensure the planned level of expenditure is not exceeded for the period of the allocation.

42. A social fund officer or group of social fund officers shall not in the period of the allocation make an award—

(a) in accordance with direction 2 (budgeting loans) or direction 3 (crisis loans) which in the aggregate with other awards in accordance with those directions in that period exceeds the allocation to that social fund officer or group of social fund officers in that period; or

(b) in accordance with direction 4 (community care grants) which in the aggregate with other awards in accordance with that direction in the period exceeds the allocation to that social fund officer or group of social fund officers in that period.

Overpayments—misrepresentation etc

43. If any question arises as to whether, in consequence of a misrepresentation or failure to disclose any material fact by any person who applied for a discretionary social fund payment, an amount of a community care grant, budgeting loan or crisis loan has been overpaid and is recoverable:

(a) the determination may be reviewed by a social fund officer;

(b) the questions which shall be determined on that review are whether any misrepresentation or failure to disclose a material fact has occurred and if so, whether any and if so, what amount(s) has been overpaid and is recoverable in consequence of the misrepresentation or failure to disclose.

Action following the SFO's overpayment determination

44. (1) Where following a review under direction 43, the social fund officer has determined that a person has obtained a community care grant, budgeting loan or crisis loan in consequence of a misrepresentation or failure to disclose any material fact and as a result of that misrepresentation or failure, an amount has been overpaid and is recoverable, he shall notify the person in writing of his determination.

(2) The written notification referred to in paragraph (1) above shall advise the person that if he does not agree with the determination made under direction 43, he must so notify the social fund officer within the time specified in the social fund officer's written notification, whereupon that determination will be reviewed by another social fund officer (referred to in this direction and in directions 45 to 48 as the "social fund overpayments review officer").

(3) Where the person to whom the determination made under direction 43 relates, informs the social fund officer that he does not agree with that determination, the social fund officer must pass all the papers relevant to that determination to a social fund overpayments review officer, who will freshly determine the question referred to in direction 43 (making a written record of his

determination) and that determination will supersede that of the social fund officer.

Manner in which a review of an overpayment determination is to be conducted

45. In reviewing an overpayment determination pursuant to direction 44, the social fund overpayments review officer must have full regard initially to:
  (a) whether the SFO applied the law correctly in arriving at his decision. In particular:
      — that the overpayment determination is sustainable on the evidence;
      — that the SFO interpreted the law—including Secretary of State directions—correctly.
  (b) whether the required procedural steps have been followed; that the applicant has had sufficient opportunity to put his case; and there has been no bias.

46. Having first considered the matters specified in direction 45, the social fund overpayments review officer in reviewing the overpayment determination concerned must have full regard to:
  (a) the material facts and circumstances of any misrepresentation or failure to disclose;
  (b) any new evidence which has since been produced; and
  (c) whether any, and if so what, amount is recoverable as a consequence of the misrepresentation or failure to disclose any material fact.

47. The social fund overpayments review officer, after determining whether any, and if so what, amount is recoverable shall inform the applicant of his decision in writing and shall also inform him of his right to apply for a further review of that decision by a social fund inspector.

48. A social fund overpayments review officer shall consider carefully any case referred by a social fund inspector for redetermination. He shall take into account any reasons given by the social fund inspector in reaching his decision to refer the matter to him, remedy any defects drawn attention to by the social fund inspector and note that he has done so when determining the case afresh.

Applications for crisis loans and community care grants

49. (1) Where the applicant for a crisis loan the social fund officer may determine the application as an application for a grant, provided there is no application for a crisis loan, or for a grant, to meet the same need which is being considered by a social fund officer, or by a social fund inspector, as at the date of determination.

(2) Where the applicant applies for a grant the social fund officer may determine the application as an application for a crisis loan, provided there is no application for a crisis loan, or for a grant, to meet the same need which is being considered by a social fund officer, or by a social fund inspector, as at the date of determination.

BUDGETING LOAN PRIORITISATION AND AWARDS

Personal circumstances under the initial test

50. (1) In determining whether to make an award of a budgeting loan to the applicant or the amount to be awarded, the social fund officer shall have regard to the following personal circumstances of the applicant:
  (a) subject to paragraphs (2) and (3) below, the period of time in respect of

which the applicant has, at the date of the determination of the application, continuously been in receipt of a qualifying benefit, or was the partner of a person receiving a qualifying benefit;

   (b) the number of persons who are members of the applicant's household at the date of the determination;

(2) For the purposes of paragraph (1)(a) above, the applicant or, as the case may be, his partner, shall be treated as having been in receipt of a qualifying benefit during any period of 28 days or less:

   (a) in respect of which neither of them was in receipt of such a benefit; and

   (b) which falls immediately between periods in respect of which either of them was in receipt of such a benefit.

(3) For the purpose of para (1)(a) above, the social fund officer shall not have regard to any period in respect of which the applicant or his partner was in receipt of a qualifying benefit which is more than three years prior to the date of determination.

(4) For the purpose of paragraph (1)(b) above, a person shall be treated as being, or not being, a member of the applicant's household at the date of the determination in accordance with regulation 16 of the Income Support (General) Regulations 1987 or, as the case may be, in accordance with regulation 78 of the Jobseeker's Allowance Regulations 1996.

(5) In this direction, "qualifying benefit" shall have the same meaning as in direction 8(1)(a).

Personal circumstances under the wider test

51. (1) Where, having regard to the applicant's personal circumstances as specified in direction 50(1)(a) and (b), no budgeting loan may be awarded, the social fund officer shall determine whether to make an award of a budgeting loan, and the amount of that award, by having regard instead to the personal circumstances specified in direction 50(1)(a) and (b), those personal circumstances as are specified in sub-paragraphs (a) to (c) below, and also to the provisions of paragraph 1A(a) to (c) below:

   (a) subject to paragraphs (2), (3) and (4) below, any period in respect of which the applicant was in receipt of Family Credit, Housing Benefit or Council Tax Benefit (the "secondary benefits"), or was the partner of a person receiving a secondary benefit, which ended no more than 28 days before the date upon which he was first in receipt of a qualifying benefit as determined for the purposes of direction 50(1)(a); and

   (b) all persons who share the applicant's private residence but are not members of the same household as defined by regulation 16 of the Income Support (General) Regulations 1987 or, as the case may be, regulation 78 of the Jobseeker's Allowance Regulations 1996 at the date of the determination and who are either in receipt of a qualifying benefit or are the partner or dependant of those persons; and

   (c) where the applicant or his partner is pregnant, any unborn child who is likely to become a member of the applicant's household.

(1A) Where:

   (a) the applicant has outstanding debt arising from a previous budgeting loan awarded on a date when the applicant had a partner and/or dependants; and

   (b) at the date of determination of the current budgeting loan application, the applicant's applicable amount for the purposes of his entitlement to income support or to income-based jobseeker's allowance, does not include any amount in respect of that partner or dependants; and

   (c) the current application for a budgeting loan has been made as a consequence of the applicant's separation from that partner and/or dependants;

that budgeting loan shall be disregarded for the purposes of calculating the applicant's existing debt in accordance with direction 53(3)(b).

(2) For the purpose of paragraph (1)(a) above, the social fund officer shall not have regard to any period in respect of which the applicant or his partner was in receipt of a secondary benefit which is more than three years prior to the date of the determination.

(3) For the purposes of paragraph (1)(a) and subject to paragraph 4 below, where the applicant or his partner was in receipt of two or more secondary benefits during the period specified in paragraph (2) above, either simultaneously or concurrently, the social fund officer shall have regard to the secondary benefit which the applicant or, as the case may be, his partner had been in receipt of for the longest continuous period.

(4) For the purposes of paragraph (1)(a) above, any period of 28 days or less in respect of which the applicant or, as the case may be, his partner, has not been in receipt of any secondary benefit shall be disregarded but only where that period separates two periods in respect of which the applicant or, as the case may be, his partner, was in receipt of the same secondary benefit.

(5) For the purpose of para (1)(b) above, a person shall be treated as being, or not being, a member of the applicant's household at the date of the determination in accordance with regulation 16 of the Income Support (General) Regulations 1987 or, as the case may be, in accordance with regulation 78 of the Jobseeker's Allowance Regulations 1996.

(6) In this direction, ''qualifying benefit'' shall have the same meaning as in direction 8(1)(a).

Weightings for personal circumstances

52. (1) The priority of a budgeting loan application shall first be determined by the applicant's particular circumstances under each of the personal circumstances as specified in direction 50, and the weighting given to each of those personal circumstances in the following sub-paragraphs:

(a) in relation to the period in respect of which the applicant or, as the case may be, his partner, has at the date of determination been continuously in receipt of a qualifying benefit as defined in direction 8(1)(a):
  (i) where that period is equal to, or exceeds, the maximum period specified in direction 50(3), the weighting value shall be one and a half times the minimum period of 26 weeks specified in direction 8(1)(c);
  (ii) where the period exceeds 26 weeks but is less than the maximum period specified in direction 50(3), the proportion of the weighting value specified in sub-paragraph (i) above to be attributed shall be the proportion of the difference between the minimum and maximum periods represented by that period.

(b) where the applicant has a partner, the second adult in the household shall be treated as having a weighting value of one third of the applicant;

(c) where there are children aged 18 and under in the applicant's household:
  (i) the first child shall be treated as having a weighting value of two thirds of the applicant;
  (ii) the second child and any subsequent children shall be treated as having a weighting value of one third of the applicant.

(2) Where, taking into account the weighting values specified in paragraph (1) above, the applicant's personal circumstances as specified in direction 50(1)(a) and (b) preclude the award of a budgeting loan, the priority of the application shall instead be determined by the applicant's personal circum-

stances as specified in direction 51(1), the weightings given to each of those circumstances in paragraph (1)(a) to (c) above, and to the following sub-paragraphs:

    (a) in relation to the period of time in which the applicant or, as the case may be, his partner, has at the date of determination been continuously in receipt of a secondary benefit as defined in direction 51(1)(a):

        (i) where that period is equal to, or exceeds, the maximum period specified in direction 51(2), the weighting value shall be one and a half times the minimum period of time in receipt of a qualifying benefit, as specified in direction 8(1)(c), of 26 weeks;

        (ii) where that period exceeds 26 weeks but is less than the maximum period specified in direction 51(2), the proportionate weighting value shall be equivalent to that in paragraph 1(a)(ii) above.

    (b) where there are persons in the same private residence as the applicant to whom direction 51(1)(b) applies at the date of the determination and who are either in receipt of a qualifying benefit or are the partner or dependant of those persons (the "secondary family"):

        (i) any adult in the secondary family shall be treated as having a weighting value of one-third of the applicant;

        (ii) where the applicant has a dependant child(ren) and there are also children in the secondary family, the first and subsequent children in the secondary family shall be treated as having a weighting value of one-third of the applicant; but

        (iii) where the applicant has no dependent children but there are children in the secondary family, the first child therein shall be treated as having a weighting value of two-thirds of the applicant, and the second or any subsequent children, one-third.

(3) For the purposes of paragraphs (1) and (2) of this direction, weighting values shall be determined on the basis that the weighting value to be attached—

    (a) to a period of continuous receipt of a qualifying benefit of exactly 26 weeks; and

    (b) to a household containing only the applicant,

shall, in both cases, be 1.

(4) The applicant's circumstances as specified in direction 50(1)(a) and (b) and direction 51(1)(a) to (c) as weighted by paragraphs (1) and (2) above, shall determine each applicant's relative priority, by:

    (a) providing that identical personal circumstances will always result in identical weightings, and therefore identical priority levels; and

    (b) ensuring that the differential in priority between two different sets of personal circumstances will always remain constant; and

    (c) ensuring that the differential in priority will be reflected in the limit on the maximum amount of budgeting loan each applicant can borrow, as contained in guidance issued by the Area Social Fund Officer under direction 41.

What to award

53. (1) The applicant's priority will first be determined in accordance with the applicant's personal circumstances as specified in direction 50(a) and (b), and the weighting values applying to those personal circumstances as specified in direction 52(1)(a) to (c).

(2) The social fund officer will then determine the maximum amount of budgeting loan the applicant may borrow appropriate to those personal circumstances by reference to direction 40 and the guidance of his Area Social Fund Officer (the "maximum amount").

(3) Subject to paragraphs (4) to (6) below and to directions 9 to 11, the

amount of the award shall be determined in accordance with the following sub-paragraphs:
- (a) where the applicant has no existing budgeting loan debt, the maximum loan which could be awarded shall be the maximum amount, so that:
  - (i) where the amount applied for is equal to or below the maximum amount, the applicant shall be awarded that amount;
  - (ii) where the amount applied for exceeds the maximum amount, the amount of the applicant's award shall be restricted to the maximum amount;
- (b) where the applicant has existing budgeting loan debt, the total of the existing and proposed debt must not exceed the maximum amount, so that:
  - (i) where the amount applied for would result in the total of existing and proposed debt being equal to or below the maximum amount, the applicant shall be awarded the amount applied for;
  - (ii) where the amount applied for would result in the total of proposed and existing debt exceeding the maximum amount, the amount of the applicant's award shall be restricted to the amount which results in the total of the applicant's existing and proposed debt being equal to the maximum amount,

and for the purpose of this paragraph, "proposed debt" means the total of the existing debt and the amount applied for.

(4) No award will be made where, having applied paragraphs (3)(a) and (b) above a budgeting loan could not be awarded or could be awarded but only for less than £30, and the applicant has not declared personal circumstances as specified in direction 51(1)(a) to (c), or satisfies the provisions of direction 51(1A).

(5) Where having applied paragraphs (3)(a) and (b) above a budgeting loan could not be awarded or could only be awarded for less than £30, and the applicant has declared personal circumstances as specified in direction 51(a) to (c), or the applicant satisfies the provisions of direction 51(1A), or both, the application shall be determined on the basis of such weighting values applied to those personal circumstances as specified in direction 52(2), before determining the amount of the award in accordance with paragraph (3) above, and (6) below.

(6) No award shall be made where, having applied paragraph (5) above a budgeting loan cannot be awarded on the basis of paragraphs (3)(a) and (b) above, or could only be be awarded for less than £30.

GENERAL NOTE

These directions relate to social fund payments under s.138(1)(b) of the Contributions and Benefits Act (1986 Act, s.32(2)(b)), where decisions are made by social fund officers (SFOs), not AOs, and there is therefore no right of appeal to a SSAT. (Note that under the Social Security Act 1998 SFOs will be replaced by "appropriate officers" who will take decisions on behalf of the Secretary of State (see s.36 of the 1998 Act). The separate system of social fund reviews will continue (see s.38 of the Act). The changes are due to take effect for the Social Fund on November 29, 1999.) Section 140(2) of the Contributions and Benefits Act (1986 Act, s.33(10)) requires a SFO to determine questions in accordance with general directions issued by the Secretary of State. A SFO must also take account of general guidance issued by the Secretary of State. See *R v. Social Fund Inspector ex parte Taylor, The Times*, January 20, 1998 in the notes to s. 140(1) of the Contributions and Benefits Act. Both guidance and directions are contained in the *Social Fund Guide*, a new form of which was issued in May 1999.

Several aspects of these directions have come under challenge in judicial review cases. The most general challenge was raised in *R. v. Social Fund Officer and Secretary of State for Social Services, ex p. Stitt*, where it was argued that the 1986 Act did not give the Secretary of State power to make directions restricting the categories of need which could be considered for payments out of the Fund. This would have resulted in the striking down of directions 12, 17, 23 and 29. An associated case which would have directly raised the issue of whether the Secretary of State had power to make directions restricting the categories of persons eligible for payments was discontinued following the death of the applicant. However, the Divisional Court (*The Times*, February 23, 1990; *The Independent*, February 23, 1990) held that there was power to make directions which can reasonably be regarded as necessary for the proper control and management of the Social Fund.

The Court of Appeal (*The Times*, July 4, 1990) agreed that there was power to make the directions, but suggested that the power was free of the control and management restriction. Leave to appeal to the House of Lords was refused. In *R. v. Secretary of State for Social Security, ex parte Healey* and the associated actions *Ellison and Stitt II* (*The Times*, December 31, 1991) the Court of Appeal re-affirms this approach. See the notes to s.138(1)(b) of the Contributions and Benefits Act (1986 Act, s.32(2)(b)).

R. v. Social Fund Inspector, ex parte Sherwin, The Times, February 23, 1990; *The Independent*, February 23, 1990, raised a question on the interpretation of direction 4(a)(i) on community care grants. The application was for a grant to set up home in a local authority tenancy granted to someone in a homeless persons' hostel. The application was refused because the applicant had not been in the hostel for the three months laid down in the guidance in what was then the *Social Fund Manual*. The Divisional Court held that the direction should be interpreted in a common sense way and not with a technicality which would conflict with the obvious policy of the direction. Thus, looking at direction 4(a)(i) along with direction 4(a)(ii), the word "re-establish" should not be interpreted strictly and not too much weight given to the three month period.

In the *Healey* case (see above) the same common sense approach, to give effect to the obvious intent of the directions, was commended. But the Court of Appeal in fact construes direction 4 rather strictly. Mr Healey was single. He moved from a psychiatric hospital to residential care, sharing a house which had permanent staff. It was unlikely that he would be able to live more independently. He claimed a community care grant of £150 for new clothes. The refusal of the grant was upheld on the ground that he did not come under either direction 4(a)(i) or (iii). In order to re-establish himself in the community the person must be actually or imminently in the community following a stay in care. A move in that direction is not enough. The Court of Appeal did not need to deal with the conclusion of the Divisional Court below that a grant could not ease exceptional pressures on Mr Healey and his family, because he did not have a family.

The question of re-establisment in the community was also an issue in *R. v. Social Fund Inspector, ex parte Ahmed Mohammed* (*The Times*, November 25, 1992). The applicant was a single woman who had been living in a refugee camp in Somalia before coming to the U.K. and applying for asylum. She was initially placed in temporary accommodation and then allocated a flat. She applied for a community care grant of £500 to furnish the flat. The refusal of the application was confirmed by the SFI on the ground that she could not re-establish herself in the community in the U.K. because she had not previously lived in that community. Brooke J. upholds that decision, considering the ordinary meaning of "re-establish" and the normal territorial application of a U.K. statute.

In another case heard at the same time, *R. v. Social Fund Inspector, ex parte Ali*, Brooke J. considered the circumstances in which the provision of an item would ease exceptional pressures on a family (direction 4(a)(iii)). The applicant lived with his wife and five children in a damp flat. All the children were in poor health (one with a heart condition). Three were under five. The application was for a community care grant for a replacement refrigerator. The SFI accepted that the family was under exceptional stress, but considered that provision of a refrigerator would not ease the particular pressure. She accepted that shopping for food every day would be more inconvenient than being able to store food and medicine but not more expensive. Brooke J. decides that that approach was flawed in that the SFI should have looked at the totality of the family's needs and considered the possibility that an adult would not be able to shop every day (for instance if children were ill). On the evidence the only reasonable conclusion was that it would make managing the large family easier if it was not necessary to shop every day, so that direction 4(a)(iii) was satisfied. But the authorities would then have to consider priorities and the budget.

In *R. v. Secretary of State for Social Security, ex parte Smith, The Times*, April 22, 1991, the exclusion of housing costs in direction 29(d) was in issue. The claim was for a grant to buy a caravan. The Divisional Court holds that housing costs are the costs of a person's accommodation and that there should be no distinction between movable and immovable accommodation.

R. v. Social Fund Inspector and Secretary of State for Social Security, ex parte Roberts, The Times, February 23, 1990; *The Independent*, February 23, 1990, raised the nature of the review process, and the role of the budget, which was not then covered in the directions. The existing guidance to SFOs was struck down as it was expressed not in the language of guidance, but of direction. The result was that SFOs were obliged to do no more than have regard to the budget under s.33(9) (Contributions and Benefits Act, s.140(1)). In September 1990, the Secretary of State issued directions 40 to 42, requiring SFOs to keep to local budgets. The *Roberts* case was directed particularly to review by the SFI, on which see below, but may have implications for reviews by the SFO. See also *R. v. Social Fund Inspector, ex parte Ledicott* in the notes to the Directions to Social Fund Inspectors.

R v. Social Fund Inspector, ex parte Connick [1994] C.O.D. 75 concerned an application for a community care grant to buy incontinence pads. Hidden J. decides that the exclusion of a medical item in directions 12(j) and 29 does not cover items in ordinary use. He holds that directions 12(j) and 29 in directing that a community care grant "may not be awarded" for a medical, etc., item or service were mandatory and permitted no discretion. However, the SFI had applied the wrong test in deciding that since the pads would not be needed unless there was a medical problem they were a medical item. Items are not medical items just because the need for them arises from a medical condition. That conclusion is in line with Commissioners' decisions *R(SB) 23/87* and *CSB 1482/85* on the slightly different provision in reg. 6(2)(n) of the Supplementary Benefits (Single Payments) Regulations, to which Hidden J. referred.

In *R v. Social Fund Inspector ex parte Ibrahim* [1994] C.O.D. 260 Turner J. holds that in interpreting direction 4(a)(i) the question to be asked was whether the accommodation (in that case a hostel for single women) was set up to provide institutional or residential care, rather than did the applicant receive such care. The guidance was then amended to put more emphasis on examining in each case the actual care a particular applicant is receiving.

In *R v. Social Fund Inspector ex p. Tuckwood* (High Court, April 27, 1995) the SFI had decided that an application for a community care grant for repairs of a central heating system was excluded by direction 29 because the repairs fell within what was then para. 8(3)(h) of Sched. 3 to the Income Support Regulations. It was argued by the claimant that "provision" in para. 8(3)(h) did not cover repairs of an existing system but meant initial provision of heating. That interpretation was supported by the use of "provision" in contrast to "improvements" in several of the heads in para. 8(3). However, the argument was rejected by Popplewell J. who held that "provision" was not restricted to the first installation and did cover repairs to or replacement of an existing boiler. Repairs to a central heating system constituted a measure undertaken with a view to improving fitness for occupation (as required by para. 8(3)) and so the social fund inspector's decision had been correct.

Directions 8(1)(a) and 25(1) require an applicant to be "in receipt of" either income support or income-based JSA. In *R. v. Social Fund Inspector and another, ex parte Davey* (October 19, 1998, HC, unreported), Moses J. held that this meant that the applicant had to be the income support/income-based JSA claimant (*not* a member of his family). Further, if a review removed entitlement to benefit retrospectively, this resulted in the applicant not being in receipt of income support/income-based JSA at the date of the social fund application.

Note that from September 1995 the review process at local level has been changed so that there is now only one tier of review. A claimant can then ask for a further review by a social fund inspector.

On repayment of social fund loans by deductions from benefits, see the notes to s.78(2) of the Administration Act.

DIRECTIONS TO SOCIAL FUND INSPECTORS

The Directions issued by the Secretary of State for Social Security under sections 138(1)(b), 140(2) and 140(3) of the Social Security Contributions and Benefits Act 1992 and sections 66(7) and 66(8)(a) and (b) of the Social Security Administration Act 1992 to the Social Fund Inspectors.

Role of Social Fund Inspectors

1. In reviewing a determination a social fund inspector must have full regard initially to:
  (a) whether the SFO applied the law correctly in arriving at his decision on review. In particular:
    — that the decision is sustainable on the evidence;
    — that the SFO took all relevant considerations into account and did not take irrelevant considerations into account;
    — that the SFO interpreted the law including Secretary of State directions correctly;
  (b) whether the SFO acted fairly and exercised his discretion to arrive at a conclusion that was reasonable in the circumstances—*i.e.* a decision that a reasonable SFO could have reached;

(c) whether the required procedural steps have been followed; that the applicant had sufficient opportunity to put his case; and there has been no bias.

Social Fund Inspectors reviews

2. If in reviewing a determination initially, a social fund inspector is satisfied that the decision was reached correctly, having regard to the factors in direction 1, the social fund inspector in reviewing the determination thereafter must have full regard to
  (a) all the circumstances, including the state of the budget and local priorities, that existed at the time the original decision was made;
  (b) any new evidence which has since been produced; and
  (c) any relevant changes of circumstances.

Social Fund Inspectors reviews—budgeting loan determinations

3. In reviewing a budgeting loan determination a social fund inspector must have full regard initially to:
  (a) whether the SFO applied the law correctly in arriving at his decision. In particular:
    — that the decision is sustainable on the evidence;
    — that the SFO took all relevant considerations into account and did not take irrelevant considerations into account;
    — that the SFO interpreted the law—including Secretary of State directions—correctly;
  (b) whether the SFO exercised his discretion in relation to the maximum amounts specified in local guidance as available to budgeting loan applicants
  (c) whether the required procedural steps have been followed; that the applicant had sufficient opportunity to put his case; and there has been no bias.

4. (1) If in reviewing a budgeting loan determination initially, a social fund inspector is satisfied that the decision was reached correctly, having regard to the factors in direction 3, the social fund inspector in reviewing the determination thereafter must, have full regard to
  (a) the applicant's personal circumstances as they existed at the time the original determination was made;
  (b) the material facts confirming the applicant's personal circumstances which existed at the time the original determination was made;
  (c) any new evidence supporting the material facts which confirm the applicant's personal circumstances existing at the time the original determination was made and which has since been produced.
  (d) both the state of the relevant allocation and local guidance issued by the Area Social Fund Officer as to the maximum amount available to each budgeting loan applicant; and
  (e) the likelihood of repayment and time within which repayment is likely

(2) For the purposes of paragraph (1(a) to (c)) above, the social fund inspector shall have regard to those of the applicant's personal circumstances which are applicable to him and which are specified in directions issued by the Secretary of State pursuant to section 140(1A) of the Social Security Contributions and Benefits Act 1992.

(3) For the purpose of paragraph (1)(d) and (e) above, the Social Fund Inspector shall take into account any relevant change of circumstance which has occurred in the period commencing on the date of the original determination and ending on the day on which the Social Fund Inspector makes his determination.

Social Fund Inspectors reviews—Overpayments

5. In reviewing an overpayment determination a social fund inspector must have full regard initially to:

  (a) whether the SFO applied the law correctly in arriving at his decision. In particular:

      — that the overpayment determination is sustainable on the evidence;

      — that the SFO interpreted the law—including Secretary of State directions—correctly.

  (b) whether the required procedural steps have been followed; that the applicant has had sufficient opportunity to put his case; and there has been no bias.

6. If in reviewing an overpayment determination initially, a social fund inspector is satisfied that the overpayment determination was both legally sustainable and made in accordance with the correct procedure, having regard to the factors set out in direction 5, the social fund inspector in reviewing the overpayment determination thereafter must have full regard to:

  (a) the material facts and circumstances of misrepresentation or failure to disclose;

  (b) any new evidence which has since been produced; and

  (c) whether any, and if so what, amount is recoverable as a consequence of the misrepresentaiton of failure to disclose any material fact.

GENERAL NOTE

In the *Roberts* and *Ellison* cases (see above), it was held first that the Secretary of State had power under s.34 of the 1986 Act, now s.66 of the Administration Act, to make directions limiting the scope of review and second that the directions actually made required a two-stage process. The first stage involved an investigation similar to that carried out on judicial review. The second stage goes beyond that in requiring the examination of new evidence and changes of circumstances, but does not involve a complete rehearing. In *R. v. Social Fund Inspector, ex parte Ledicott, The Times*, May 24, 1995, Sedley J. holds that a SFI conducting a review should apply the law as in force at the date of her decision, not the law as it stood at the date of the SFO's decision that is the subject of the review. In his view, direction 2 which permitted the SFI, *inter alia*, to take account of any relevant change of circumstances (which would include a change in the law) was within the terms of s. 66(4) of the Administration Act. Sedley J. did not consider that this interpretation involved any retrospectivity, but if it did, the wording of s. 66(4) was wide enough to provide a statutory licence for any retrospectivity that existed.

PART VII

ADJUDICATION AND ADMINISTRATION

Social Security Administration Act 1992

(1992 c. 5)

PART III

OVERPAYMENTS AND ADJUSTMENTS OF BENEFIT

Misrepresentation, etc.

PART V

INCOME SUPPORT AND THE DUTY TO MAINTAIN

Social Security Administration Act 1992

PART VII

PROVISION OF INFORMATION

The Registration Service

PART I

CLAIMS FOR AND PAYMENTS AND GENERAL ADMINISTRATION OF BENEFIT

Necessity of claim

Entitlement to benefit dependent on claim

1.—(1) Except in such cases as may be prescribed, and subject to the following provisions of this section and to section 3 below, no person shall be entitled to any benefit unless, in addition to any other conditions relating to that benefit being satisfied—

(a) he makes a claim for it in the manner, and within the time, prescribed in relation to that benefit by regulations under this Part of this Act; or

(b) he is treated by virtue of such regulations as making a claim for it.

[² (1A) No person whose entitlement to any benefit depends on his making a claim shall be entitled to the benefit unless subsection (1B) below is satisfied in relation both to the person making the claim and to any other person in respect of whom he is claiming benefit.

(1B) This subsection is satisfied in relation to a person if—

(a) the claim is accompanied by—

(i) a statement of the person's national insurance number and information or evidence establishing that that number has been allocated to the person; or

(ii) information or evidence enabling the national insurance number that has been allocated to the person to be ascertained; or

(b) the person makes an application for a national insurance number to be allocated to him which is accompanied by information or evidence enabling such a number to be so allocated.

(1C) Regulations may make provision disapplying subsection (1A) above in the case of—

(a) prescribed benefits;

(b) prescribed descriptions of persons making claims; or

(c) prescribed descriptions of persons in respect of whom benefit is claimed, or in other prescribed circumstances.]

(2) Where under subsection (1) above a person is required to make a claim or to be treated as making a claim for a benefit in order to be entitled to it—

(a) if the benefit is a widow's payment, she shall not be entitled to it in respect of a death occurring more than 12 months before the date on which the claim is made or treated as made; and

(b) if the benefit is any other benefit except disablement benefit or reduced earnings allowance, the person shall not be entitled to it in respect of any period more than 12 months before that date,

except as provided by section 3 below.

(3) [*Omitted as applying only to attendance allowance and disability living allowance*]

(4) In this section and in section 2 below "benefit" means—

(a) benefit as defined in section 122 of the Contributions and Benefits Act;
[¹(aa) a jobseeker's allowance;] and
(b) any income-related benefit.

(5) This section (which corresponds to section 165A of the 1975 Act, as it had effect immediately before this Act came into force) applies to claims made on or after 1st October 1990 or treated by virtue of regulations under that section or this section as having been made on or after that date.

(6) Schedule 1 to this Act shall have effect in relation to other claims.

DERIVATION

Social Security Act 1975, s.165A.

AMENDMENTS

1. Jobseekers Act 1995, Sched. 2, para. 38 (October 7, 1996).
2. Social Security Administration (Fraud) Act 1997, s.19 (December 1, 1997).

DEFINITIONS

"the 1975 Act"—see s.191.
"claim"—*ibid.*
"disablement benefit"—*ibid.*
"the Contributions and Benefits Act"—*ibid.*
"income-related benefit"—*ibid.*
"prescribe"—*ibid.*

GENERAL NOTE

Subsection (1)
The general rule is that there cannot be entitlement to benefit unless a claim is made for it. Section 1 applies to JSA and to income-related benefits, *i.e.* including income support, family credit and disability working allowance, but excluding supplementary benefit or FIS or payments from the social fund (subs. (4)). "Benefit" as defined in s.122 of the Contributions and Benefits Act does not include income-related benefits. Section 1 applies to claims made on or after October 1, 1990. Sched. 1 deals with earlier claims.

See reg. 3 of the Claims and Payments Regulations for the circumstances in which no claim is necessary for JSA.

The introduction of the predecessor of s.1 was precipitated by the decision of the House of Lords in *Insurance Officer v. McCaffrey* [1984] 1 W.L.R. 1353 that (subject to an express provision to the contrary) a person was entitled to benefit if he met the conditions of entitlement even though he had not made a claim for that benefit. Claiming went to payability, not entitlement. This was contrary to the long-standing assumption of the DSS and was corrected with effect from September 2, 1985.

Section 3, which is excluded from the operation of s.1, deals with late claims for widow's benefits where the death of the spouse is difficult to establish.

Subsection (1A)–(1C)
These provisions were inserted by s.19 of the Social Security Administration (Fraud) Act 1997 and came into force on December 1, 1997. The effect of subss. (1A) and (1B) is to impose an additional condition of entitlement to benefit where subs. (1)(a) applies (*i.e.* in the normal case). A claimant will not be entitled to benefit unless when making a claim he provides a national insurance (NI) number, together with information or evidence to show that it is his, or provides evidence or information to enable his NI number to be traced, or applies for a NI number and provides sufficient information or evidence for one to be allocated to him. This requirement for an NI number applies to both the claimant and any person for whom he is claiming, except in prescribed circumstances (subs. (1C)). See reg. 2A of the Income Support Regulations, the Jobseeker's Allowance Regulations, the Family Credit Regulations and the Disability Working Allowance Regulations respectively, for who is exempt and note the different dates from which this requirement bites for these benefits.

Subsection (2)

This provision imposes an overall limit of 12 months to the entitlement to benefit before the date of claim. Not all benefits are caught by subs.(1) and there is a further exclusion in para. (b). Reg. 19 of and Sched. 4 to the Claims and Payments Regulations impose the ordinary time-limits for claiming and since April 1997 allow the limits in the cases of income support, JSA, family credit and disability working allowance to be extended for a maximum of three months only in tightly defined circumstances. The test of good cause has been abandoned. Where there is such an extension, the claim is then treated as made on the first day of the period for which the claim is allowed to relate (reg. 6(3)). Although the drafting is not at all clear, the reference in subs.(2) to the 12-month limit from the date on which the claim is made or is treated as made seems to make the limit start from the date fixed by reg. 6(3). However, reg. 19(4) prevents an extension of the time-limit for the benefits covered by reg. 6(3) leading to entitlement earlier than three months before the actual date of claim. But the restriction seems to stem from that regulation and not from s.1(2), or the earlier forms set out in Sched. 1.

Note that from April 1997 the time limit for claiming social fund maternity and funeral payments is three months (Claims and Payments Regulations, reg. 19(1) and Sched. 4, paras. 8 and 9) and there is no longer any provision allowing claims for these payments to be made outside this time limit.

Retrospective effect of provisions making entitlement to benefit dependent on claim

2.—(1) This section applies where a claim for benefit is made or treated as made at any time on or after 2nd September 1985 (the date on which section 165A of the 1975 Act (general provision as to necessity of claim for entitlement to benefit), as originally enacted, came into force) in respect of a period the whole or any part of which falls on or after that date.

(2) Where this section applies, any question arising as to—

(a) whether the claimant is or was at any time (whether before, on or after 2nd September 1985) entitled to the benefit in question, or to any other benefit on which his entitlement to that benefit depends; or

(b) in a case where the claimant's entitlement to the benefit depends on the entitlement of another person to a benefit, whether that other person is or was so entitled,

shall be determined as if the relevant claim enactment and any regulations made under or referred to in that enactment had also been in force, with any necessary modifications, at all times relevant for the purpose of determining the entitlement of the claimant, and, where applicable, of the other person, to the benefit or benefits in question (including the entitlement of any person to any benefit on which that entitlement depends, and so on).

(3) In this section "the relevant claim enactment" means section 1 above as it has effect in relation to the claim referred to in subsection (1) above.

(4) In any case where—

(a) a claim for benefit was made or treated as made (whether before, on or after 2nd September 1985, and whether by the same claimant as the claim referred to in subsection (1) above or not), and benefit was awarded on that claim, in respect of a period falling wholly or partly before that date; but

(b) that award would not have been made had the current requirements applied in relation to claims for benefit, whenever made, in respect of periods before that date; and

(c) entitlement to the benefit claimed as mentioned in subsection (1) above depends on whether the claimant or some other person was previously entitled or treated as entitled to that or some other benefit,

then, in determining whether the conditions of entitlement to the benefit so claimed are satisfied, the person to whom benefit was awarded as mentioned in paragraphs (a) and (b) above shall be taken to have been entitled to the benefit so awarded, notwithstanding anything in subsection (2) above.

(5) In subsection (4) above "the current requirements" means—

(a) the relevant claim enactment, and any regulations made or treated as made under that enactment, or referred to in it, as in force at the time of the claim referred to in subsection (1) above, with any necessary modifications; and

(b) subsection (1) (with the omission of the words following "at any time") and subsections (2) and (3) above.

DERIVATION

Social Security Act 1975, s.165B.

DEFINITIONS

"the 1975 Act"—s.191.
"benefit"—see s.1(1).
"claim"—see s.191.
"claimant"—*ibid.*

GENERAL NOTE

There are a number of benefits where entitlement can depend on whether a person was entitled to a benefit at some earlier date (*e.g.* on reaching pensionable age). While the predecessor of s.1 clearly governed such questions from September 2, 1985, onwards, it was arguable that in relation to earlier dates the *McCaffrey* principle (see note to s.1(1) above) had to be applied. *R(S) 2/91* decided that that argument was correct. The predecessor of s.2 was inserted by the Social Security Act 1990 to reverse the effect of that decision and to do so retrospectively back to September 2, 1985.

The form of s.2 is complex and the retrospective effects are difficult to work out. It only applies to claims made or treated as made on or after September 2, 1985 (subs.(1)). Thus very late appeals or very long good causes for late claim might not be affected. Then on any such claim if a question of entitlement at any other date arises (including dates before September 2, 1985) that question is to be decided according to the principle of s.1 as it was in force at the relevant time (subs.(2)). The only exception to this is that if for any period benefit has been awarded following a claim, that beneficiary is to be treated as entitled to that benefit even though under the current requirements he would not be (subs.(4)).

Claims and payments regulations

Regulations about claims for and payments of benefit

5.—(1) Regulations may provide—

(a) for requiring a claim for a benefit to which this section applies to be made by such person, in such manner and within such time as may be prescribed;

(b) for treating such a claim made in such circumstances as may be prescribed as having been made at such date earlier or later than that at which it is made as may be prescribed;

(c) for permitting such a claim to be made, or treated as if made, for a period wholly or partly after the date on which it is made;

(d) for permitting an award on such a claim to be made for such a period subject to the condition that the claimant satisfies the requirements for entitlement when benefit becomes payable under the award;

(e) for a review of any such award if those requirements are found not to have been satisfied;

(f) for the disallowance on any ground of a person's claim for a benefit to which this section applies to be treated as a disallowance of any further claim by that person for that benefit until the grounds of the original disallowance have ceased to exist;

(g) for enabling one person to act for another in relation to a claim for a benefit to which this section applies and for enabling such a claim to be made and proceeded with in the name of a person who has died;

(h) for requiring any information or evidence needed for the determination of such a claim or of any question arising in connection with such a claim to be furnished by such person as may be prescribed in accordance with the regulations;

(i) for the person to whom, time when and manner in which a benefit to which this section applies is to be paid and for the information and evidence to be furnished in connection with the payment of such a benefit;

(j) for notice to be given of any change of circumstances affecting the continuance of entitlement to such a benefit or payment of such a benefit;

(k) for the day on which entitlement to such a benefit is to begin or end;

(l) for calculating the amounts of such a benefit according to a prescribed scale or otherwise adjusting them so as to avoid fractional amounts or facilitate computation;

(m) for extinguishing the right to payment of such a benefit if payment is not obtained within such period, not being less than 12 months, as may be prescribed from the date on which the right is treated under the regulations as having arisen;

(n) for suspending payment, in whole or in part, where it appears to the Secretary of State that a question arises whether—
    (i) the conditions for entitlement are or were fulfilled;
    (ii) an award ought to be revised;
    (iii) an appeal ought to be brought against an award;

[²(nn) for suspending payment, in whole or in part, where an appeal is pending against the decision given in a different case by a social security appeal tribunal, a Commissioner or a court, and it appears to the Secretary of State that if the appeal were to be determined in a particular way an issue would arise whether the award in the case itself ought to be revised;]

(o) for withholding payments of a benefit to which this section applies in prescribed circumstances and for subsequently making withheld payments in prescribed circumstances;

(p) for the circumstances and manner in which payments of such a benefit may be made to another person on behalf of the beneficiary for any purpose, which may be to discharge, in whole or in part, an obligation of the beneficiary or any other person;

(q) for the payment or distribution of such a benefit to or among persons claiming to be entitled on the death of any person and for dispensing with strict proof of their title;

(r) for the making of a payment on account of such a benefit—
    (i) where no claim has been made and it is impracticable for one to be made immediately;
    (ii) where a claim has been made and it is impracticable for the claim or an appeal, reference, review or application relating to it to be immediately determined;
    (iii) where an award has been made but it is impracticable to pay the whole immediately.

(2) This section applies to the following benefits—

(a) benefits as defined in section 122 of the Contributions and Benefits Act;

[¹(aa) a jobseeker's allowance;]

(b) income support;

(c) family credit;

(d) disability working allowance;

(e) housing benefit;

(f) any social fund payments such as are mentioned in section 138(1)(a) a or 2) of the Contributions and Benefits Act;

(g) child benefit; and

(h) Christmas bonus.

(3), (4) & (5) [*Omitted as not applying to income-related benefits, except housing benefit.*]

Subss. (1) and (2): Social Security Act 1986, s.51(1) and (2).

AMENDMENTS

1. Jobseekers Act 1995, Sched. 2, para. 39 (October 7, 1996).
2. Social Security Act 1998, Sched. 6, para. 5(1) (May 21, 1998). This amendment applies from May 21, 1998 until s.21(2)(d) of the 1998 Act comes into force.

DEFINITIONS

"the Contributions and Benefits Act"—see s.191.
"prescribed"—*ibid.*

Community charge benefits, etc.

Relationship between community charge benefits and other benefits

7.—(1) Regulations may provide for a claim for one relevant benefit to be treated, either in the alternative or in addition, as a claim for any other relevant benefit that may be prescribed.

(2) Regulations may provide for treating a payment made or right conferred by virtue of regulations—

(a) under section 5(1)(r) above; or

(b) under section 6(1)(r) to (t) above,

as made or conferred on account of any relevant benefit that is subsequently awarded or paid.

(3) For the purposes of subsections (1) and (2) above relevant benefits are—

(a) any benefit to which section 5 above applies; and

(b) [¹council tax benefit].

DERIVATION

Social Security Act 1986, s.51B.

AMENDMENT

1. Local Government Finance Act 1992, Sched. 9, para. 13 (April 1, 1993).

DEFINITIONS

"claim"—see s.191.
"prescribed"—*ibid.*

GENERAL NOTE

Subsection (1)
See Claims and Payments Regulations, Sched. 1.

Subsection (2)
See the Social Security (Payments on account, Overpayments and Recovery) Regulations, regs.
5 to 8.

Disability working allowance

Initial claims and repeat claims

11.—(1) In this section—

"initial claim" means a claim for a disability working allowance made by a person—

    (a) to whom it has not previously been payable; or

    (b) to whom it has not been payable during the period of 2 years immediately preceding the date on which the claim is made or is treated as made; and

"repeat claim" means any other claim for a disability working allowance.

(2) On an initial claim a declaration by a claimant that he has a physical or mental disability which puts him at a disadvantage in getting a job is conclusive, except in such circumstances as may be prescribed, that for the purposes of section 129(1)(b) of the Contributions and Benefits Act he has such a disability (in accordance with regulations under section 129(3) of that Act).

(3) If—

    (a) a repeat claim is made or treated as made not later than the end of the period of 8 weeks commencing with the last day of the claimant's previous award; and

    (b) on the claim which resulted in that award he qualified under section 129(2) of the Contributions and Benefits Act by virtue—

        (i) of paragraph (a) of that subsection; or

        (ii) of there being payable to him a benefit under an enactment having effect in Northern Ireland and corresponding to a benefit mentioned in that paragraph,

he shall be treated on the repeat claim as if he still so qualified.

DERIVATION

Social Security Act 1986, s.27B(1) to (3).

DEFINITION

"the Contributions and Benefits Act"—see s.191.

GENERAL NOTE

Section 11 supplies some special rules under which some parts of the qualifications for disability working allowance are deemed to be satisfied.

Subsection (1)
An initial claim is one made by a person who has never been entitled to disability working allowance or whose last week of entitlement was more than two years before the date of claim. Any other claim is a repeat claim.

Subsection (2)
On an initial claim a claimant's declaration, on the elaborate self-assessment claim form, that he has a disability which puts him at a disadvantage in getting a job is conclusive. This general rule does not apply if the claim itself contains indications to the contrary or the AO has before him evidence pointing to the contrary (Disability Working Allowance (General) Regulations, reg. 4).

Subsection (3)
This provision applies to claimants who have been awarded disability working allowance on the

basis that they were entitled to higher rate short-term incapacity benefit, long-term incapacity benefit (or invalidity benefit: reg. 18(1) of the Disability Working Allowance and Income Support (General) Amendment Regulations 1995, p. 1054), severe disablement allowance or income support, housing benefit or council tax benefit with the disability premium or pensioner premium for disability or any Northern Ireland equivalent (see Contributions and Benefits Act, s.129(2)(a) and (4) and Disability Working Allowance Regulations, reg. 7). When such an award expires and the repeat claim is made within eight weeks, the claimant is deemed to satisfy the requirement. Thus if a claimant initially qualifies on this ground and continues to satisfy the other conditions of entitlement, awards may continue indefinitely.

The social fund

Necessity of application for certain payments

12.—(1) A social fund payment such as is mentioned in section 138(1)(b) of the Contributions and Benefits Act may be awarded to a person only if an application for such a payment has been made by him or on his behalf in such form and manner as may be prescribed.

(2) The Secretary of State may by regulations—

(a) make provision with respect to the time at which an application for such a social fund payment is to be treated as made;

(b) prescribe conditions that must be satisfied before any determination in connection with such an application may be made or any award of such a payment may be paid;

(c) prescribe circumstances in which such an award becomes extinguished.

DERIVATION

Social Security Act 1986, s.33(1) and (13).

DEFINITIONS

"the Contributions and Benefits Act"—see s.191.
"prescribed"—*ibid.*

GENERAL NOTE

Subsection (1)
This provision applies to the "ordinary" social fund, not to funeral or maternity payments or cold weather payments. See the Social Fund (Applications) Regulations.

Subsection (2)
See the Social Fund (Miscellaneous Provisions) Regulations.

[¹*Payments in respect of mortgage interest etc.*

Payment out of benefit of sums in respect of mortgage interest etc.

15A.—(1) This section applies in relation to cases where—

(a) mortgage interest is payable to a qualifying lender by a person ("the borrower") who is entitled, or whose partner, former partner or qualifying associate is entitled, to income support [²or an income-based jobseeker's allowance]; and

(b) a sum in respect of that mortgage interest is or was brought into account in determining the applicable amount for the purposes of income support [² or an income-based jobseeker's allowance] in the case of the borrower or the partner, former partner or qualifying associate;

and any reference in this section to "the relevant beneficiary" is a reference to the person whose applicable amount for the purposes of income support [²or an income-based jobseeker's allowance] is or was determined as mentioned in paragraph (b) above.

(2) Without prejudice to paragraphs (i) and (p) of section 5(1) above, regulations may, in relation to cases where this section applies, make provision—

(a) requiring that, in prescribed circumstances, a prescribed part of any relevant benefits to which the relevant beneficiary is entitled shall be paid by the Secretary of State directly to the qualifying lender and applied by that lender towards the discharge of the liability in respect of the mortgage interest;

(b) for the expenses of the Secretary of State in administering the making of payments under the regulations to be defrayed, in whole or in part, at the expense of qualifying lenders, whether by requiring them to pay prescribed fees or by deducting and retaining a prescribed part of the payments that would otherwise be made to them under the regulations or by such other method as may be prescribed;

(c) for requiring a qualifying lender, in a case where by virtue of paragraph (b) above the amount of the payment made to him under the regulations is less than it would otherwise have been, to credit against the liability in respect of the mortgage interest (in addition to the payment actually made) an amount equal to the difference between—

    (i) the payment that would have been so made, apart from paragraph (b) above; and

    (ii) the payment actually made;

and, in any such case, for treating the amount so credited as properly paid on account of benefit due to the relevant beneficiary;

(d) for enabling a body which, or person who, would otherwise be a qualifying lender to elect not to be regarded as such for the purposes of this section, other than this paragraph;

(e) for the recovery from any body or person—

    (i) of any sums paid to that body or person by way of payment under the regulations that ought not to have been so paid; or

    (ii) of any fees or other sums due from that body or person by virtue of paragraph (b) above;

(f) for cases where the same person is the borrower in relation to mortgage interest payable in respect of two or more different loans; and

(g) for any person of a prescribed class or description who would otherwise be regarded for the purposes of this section as the borrower in relation to any mortgage interest not to be so regarded, except for the purposes of this paragraph;

but the Secretary of State shall not make any regulations under paragraph (b) above unless he has consulted with such organisations representing qualifying lenders likely to be affected by the regulations as he considers appropriate.

(3) The bodies and persons who are "qualifying lenders" for the purposes of this section are—

(a) any authorised institution, within the meaning of the Banking Act 1987, to which section 67 of that Act applies (companies and partnerships which may describe themselves as banks etc),

(b) any building society incorporated under the Building Societies Act 1986,

(c) any body or person carrying on insurance business, within the meaning of the Insurance Companies Act 1982,

(d) any county council, district council, islands council or London Borough Council,

(e) the common Council of the City of London,

(f) the Council of the Isles of Scilly,

(g) any new town corporation,

and such bodies or persons not falling within the above paragraphs as may be prescribed.

(4) In this section—

"mortgage interest" means interest on a loan which is secured by a mortgage of or charge over land, or (in Scotland) by a heritable security, and which has been taken out to defray money applied for any of the following purposes, that is to say—

    (a) acquiring any residential land which was intended, at the time of the acquisition, for occupation by the borrower as his home;

    (b) carrying out repairs or improvements to any residential land which was intended, at the time of taking out the loan, for occupation by the borrower as his home;

    (c) paying off another loan; or

    (d) any prescribed purpose not falling within paragraphs (a) to (c) above;

but interest shall be regarded as mortgage interest by virtue of paragraph (c) above only to the extent that interest on that other loan would have been regarded as mortgage interest for the purposes of this section had the loan not been paid off;

"partner" means—

    (a) any person to whom the borrower is married and who is a member of the same household as the borrower; or

    (b) any person to whom the borrower is not married but who lives together with the borrower as husband and wife, otherwise than in prescribed circumstances;

and "former partner" means a person who has at some time been, but no longer is, the borrower's partner;

"qualifying associate", in relation to the borrower, means a person who, for the purposes of income support [²or an income-based jobseeker's allowance], falls to be treated by regulations under Part VII of the Contributions and Benefits Act [² or (as the case may be) under the Jobseekers Act 1995,] as responsible for so much of the expenditure which relates to housing costs (within the meaning of those regulations) as consists of any of the mortgage interest payable by the borrower, and who falls to be so treated because—

    (a) the borrower is not meeting those costs, so that the person has to meet them if he is to continue to live in the dwelling occupied as his home; and

    (b) the person is one whom it is reasonable, in the circumstances, to treat as liable to meet those costs;

"relevant benefits" means such of the following benefits as may be prescribed, namely—

    (a) benefits, as defined in section 122 of the Contributions and Benefits Act;

    [²(aa) a jobseeker's allowance;]

    (b) income support;

"residential land" means any land which consists of or includes a dwelling.

(5) For the purposes of this section, regulations may make provision—

    (a) as to circumstances in which residential land is or is not to be treated as intended for occupation by the borrower as his home; or

    (b) as to circumstances in which persons are to be treated as being or not being members of the same household.]

AMENDMENTS

1. Social Security (Mortgage Interest Payments) Act 1992, s.1(12) and Sched., para. 1 (July 1,

1992; the equivalent amendment to the Social Security Act 1986 came into force on March 16, 1992).

2. Jobseekers Act 1995, Sched. 2, para. 40 (October 7, 1996).

DEFINITION

"Contributions and Benefits Act"—see s.191.

GENERAL NOTE

Section 15A authorises the regulations which set out the meat of the scheme for direct payment to lenders of the element of housing costs in income support, and from October 7, 1996, income-based JSA, to cover mortgage interest and supplies some basic definitions. The main provisions are in Sched. 9A to the Claims and Payments Regulations.

Emergency payments

Emergency payments by local authorities and other bodies

16.—(1) The Secretary of State may make arrangements—

(a) with a local authority to which this section applies; or

(b) with any other body,

for the making on his behalf by members of the staff of any such authority or body of payments on account of benefits to which section 5 above applies in circumstances corresponding to those in which the Secretary of State himself has the power to make such payments under subsection (1)(r) of that section; and a local authority to which this section applies shall have power to enter into any such arrangements.

(2) A payment under any such arrangements shall be treated for the purposes of any Act of Parliament or instrument made under an Act of Parliament as if it had been made by the Secretary of State.

(3) The Secretary of State shall repay a local authority or other body such amount as he determines to be the reasonable administrative expenses incurred by the authority or body in making payments in accordance with arrangements under this subsection.

(4) The local authorities to which this section applies are—

(a) a local authority as defined in section 270(1) of the Local Government Act 1972, other than a parish or community council;

(b) the Common Council of the City of London; and

(c) a local authority as defined in section 235(1) of the Local Government (Scotland) Act 1973.

DERIVATION

Social Security Act 1988, s.8.

PART II

ADJUDICATION

GENERAL NOTE

The entirety of Part II of the Social Security Administration Act 1992 is to be repealed by the Social Security Act 1998 in order to give effect to the policy proposals outlined in the Government's Consultation Paper, *Improving Decision Making and Appeals in Social Security*, Cm 3328. The theme of the proposals is to modernise the administration of the social security system. The emphasis

is placed on simplifying organisational structures, defining responsibilities and streamlining procedures. The Consultation Paper points to 13 different types of decision-maker involved in the determination of claims to benefit. In particular, the split between AOs' and Secretary of State's decisions
is criticised for causing confusion for both Departmental staff and claimants, especially where one
individual officer is simply acting in different capacities. The lack of a right of appeal from Secretary
of State decisions creates further anomalies.

The proliferation of decision-makers at the appeals level is also seen as inflexible and cumbersome. The distinctive jurisdictions of Social Security Appeal Tribunals, Disability Appeal Tribunals,
Medical Appeal Tribunals, Child Support Appeal Tribunals and Vaccine Damage Tribunals are felt
to impose rigid, categorical boundaries. The rectification of manifest errors in tribunal decisions
requires a ponderous trek to the Commissioners.

The remedial measures, however, go far beyond those necessary to tackle complexity and delay.
Greater managerial control is the order of the day. Thus, the division between AO's and Secretary
of State's decisions is resolved by abolishing AO's and having all decisions on and in relation to
claims taken in the name of the Secretary of State. In this way, the prerogative of AO's to "act
independently of Agency Managers, Chief Executives and Ministers when making decisions", which
is evidently treated by the Consultation Paper as a problem, is bluntly terminated. Similarly to
disappear are the Chief Adjudication Officer, who is responsible for monitoring and promoting
standards of administrative decision-making, and the Central Adjudication Service, which serve as
a source of relatively policy-free guidance on the interpretation and application of the law. At the
appeals level, the clock is turned back 15 years, to before the days of the Independent Tribunal
Service (and its precursor, the Office of the President of Social Security Appeal Tribunals). The
administration of the appeals system is to revert to the Department through the mechanism of an
appeals agency headed by a Chief Executive accountable to the Minister. The ITS as such will be
replaced by The Appeals Service—a dualistic body comprising the appeals agency and a judicial
arm headed by a President.

The transition from the old administrative and tribunal arrangements to the new is to be phased
in benefit by benefit during the course of 1999. The timetable is set out in the General Note at the
beginning of the Social Security (Adjudication) Regulations 1995. A series of commencement orders
will set out the transitional and savings provisions on each conversion date. See the 1999 Supplement
to this book for further details.

However, the intended simplification of responsibility for decision-making fragments with the
introduction of the Social Security Contributions (Transfer of Functions, etc.) Act 1999, which
moves responsibility for deciding most of the contribution questions vested in the Secretary of State
by s.17 Social Security Administration Act 1992 to the Board of Inland Revenue with corresponding
rights of appeal to the tax appeal Commissioners.

Adjudication by adjudication officers

Claims and questions to be submitted to adjudication officer

20.—(1) Subject to section 54 below, there shall be submitted forthwith to an
adjudication officer for determination in accordance with this Part of this
Act—
  (a) any claim for a benefit to which this section applies;
  (b) subject to subsection (2) below, any question arising in connection with
      a claim for, or award of, such a benefit; [².. .]
[¹(c) any question whether, if he otherwise had a right to it, a person would
      be disqualified under or by virtue of any provision of the Contributions
      and Benefits Act for receiving a benefit to which this section applies] [²;
      and
  (d) any question whether a jobseeker's allowance is not payable to a person
      by virtue of section 19 of the Jobseekers Act 1995.]
  (2) Subsection (1) above does not apply to any question which [²—
  (a) may be determined by an adjudication officer under section 9(6) or 10(5)
      of the Jobseekers Act 1995; or
  (b)] falls to be determined otherwise than by an adjudication officer.
  (3) [³. . .]
  (4) If—

(a) a person submits a question relating to the age, marriage or death of any person; and

(b) it appears to the adjudication officer that the question may arise if the person who has submitted it to him submits a claim to a benefit to which this section applies,

the adjudication officer may determine the question.

(5) Different aspects of the same claim or question may be submitted to different adjudication officers; and for that purpose this section and the other provisions of this Part of this Act with respect to the determination of claims and questions shall apply with any necessary modifications.

(6) This section applies to the following benefits—

(a) benefits as defined in section 122 of the Contributions and Benefits Act;

[²(aa) a jobseeker's allowance;]

(b) income support;

(c) family credit;

(d) disability working allowance;

(e) any social fund payment such as is mentioned in section 138(1)(a) or (2) of the Contributions and Benefits Act;

(f) child benefit;

(g) [³. . .]

(h) [³. . .]

DERIVATION

Social Security Act 1975, s.98.

AMENDMENTS

1. Social Security (Incapacity for Work) Act 1994, Sched. 1, para. 46 (April 13, 1995).

2. Jobseekers Act 1995, Sched. 2, para. 42 (October 7, 1996).

3. Modified by Social Security Contributions, etc. (Decisions and Appeals—Transitional Modifications) Regulations 1999 (S.I. 1999 No. 978), reg. 2 and Sched., until Chapter II of Part I of the Social Security Act 1998 (social security decisions and appeals) is wholly in force (April 1, 1999).

DEFINITION

"the Contributions and Benefits Act"—see s.191.

GENERAL NOTE

Subsection (1)

See subs. (6) for the benefits to which this section applies.

In *R. v. Secretary of State for Social Services, ex parte CPAG and others* [1990] 2 Q.B. 540, the Court of Appeal decided that the duty to submit a claim "forthwith" does not arise until the DSS is in possession of the basic information necessary to determine the claim. The obligation on the claimant under reg. 7(1) of the Claims and Payments Regulations to supply such evidence etc. as the Secretary of State requires is relevant to this stage of the claim (*R(IS) 4/93*). However, once the basic information is there, the *CPAG* case holds that any need for verification does not justify delay in submitting the claim to the AO. It would then be for the AO to make enquiries, if he considered that verification was necessary.

In *R(SB) 29/84* the Tribunal of Commissioners (by a majority) held that the question whether payment had actually been made following an award (*i.e.* what should happen following an allegedly lost giro) was not a "question relating to supplementary benefit" (Supplementary Benefits Act 1976, s.2(1)), and therefore was not a matter for an AO or SSAT. Any remedy was to be pursued through the courts. *R(IS) 7/91* holds, after an exhaustive review of the legislation, that the result is the same under the predecessor of subs. (1)(b). The question whether the Secretary of State has implemented an award of benefit is not a question in connection with an award of benefit.

Subsection (2)
Under para. (a), where an employment officer refers questions about a proposed jobseeker's agreement, or a proposed variation, to an AO, the resulting decision is not given under ss.20 and 21.

Subsection (6)
Under para. (e) s.20 applies to funeral and maternity payments and cold weather payments from the social fund.

Decision of adjudication officer

21.—(1) An adjudication officer to whom a claim or question is submitted under section 20 above (other than a claim which under section 30(12) or (13) or 35(7) below falls to be treated as an application for a review) shall take it into consideration and, so far as practicable, dispose of it, in accordance with this section, and with procedure regulations under section 59 below, within 14 days of its submission to him.

(2) Subject to subsection (3) and section 37 below, the adjudication officer may decide a claim or question himself or refer it to a social security appeal tribunal.

(3) The adjudication officer must decide a claim for or a question relating to attendance allowance, a disability living allowance or a disability working allowance himself.

(4) [².. .]

(5) [² Notice] in writing of the reference shall be given to the claimant.

(6) Where—

(a) a case has been referred to a social security appeal tribunal ("the tribunal"); and

(b) the claimant makes a further claim which raises the same or similar questions; and

(c) that further claim is referred to the tribunal by the adjudication officer, then the tribunal may proceed to determine the further claim whether or not notice of its reference has been given to the claimant under subsection [².. .] (5) above.

[¹(7) Where at any time a claim for a benefit to which section 20 above applies is decided by an adjudication officer or by a social security appeal tribunal on a reference by such an officer—

(a) the claim shall not be regarded as subsisting after that time; and

(b) accordingly, the claimant shall not (without making a further claim) be entitled to the benefit on the basis of circumstances not obtaining at that time.]

DERIVATION

Social Security Act 1975, s.99.

AMENDMENTS

1. Social Security Act 1998, Sched. 6, para. 2 (May 21, 1998). This amendment applies from May 21, 1998 until s.8(2) of the 1998 Act comes into force.
2. Modified by Social Security Contributions, etc. (Decisions and Appeals—Transitional Modifications) Regulations 1999 (S.I. 1999 No. 978), reg. 2 and Sched., until Chapter II of Part I of the Social Security Act 1998 (social security decisions and appeals) is wholly in force (April 1, 1999).

GENERAL NOTE

Note that under the Social Security Act 1998 the functions presently exercised by AOs will be transferred to the Secretary of State. There will no longer be a statutory reference to dealing with a claim within 14 days. See the 1999 Supplement to this book for further details.

Subsection (1)

The general rule is that the AO should make a decision within 14 days, once the claim or question is submitted to him under s.20. In *R. v. Secretary of State for Social Services, ex parte CPAG and others* [1990] 2 Q. B. 540, the Court of Appeal upheld Schiemann J.'s decision that there was no breach of the predecessor of subs. (1) if a heavy work load prevented an AO from disposing of the claim or question within the 14 days. It was clear that the Act intended that claims should be dealt with expeditiously, but this was merely one factor which the Secretary of State had to consider in exercising his discretion as to the number of AOs to appoint. He was under no duty to appoint enough AOs to deal with all claims within 14 days.

It also appears that the need to obtain verification of information may make it not practicable to reach a decision within 14 days. *R(SB) 29/83* mentions the obligation of a claimant under the equivalent of reg. 7 of the Claims and Payments Regulations to provide such evidence, information, etc., as required by the Secretary of State as being relevant to practicability. But the supplementary benefit provision on adjudication made the AO's duty expressly subject to the equivalent of reg. 7. Section 21(1) is significantly different, as pointed out in *R(IS) 4/93*. Once a claim or question has been referred to the AO, the question of whether reg. 7 is satisfied is irrelevant to the issue of entitlement. The principle stated in *R(SB) 29/83*, that after a reasonable length of time, even if further information is not forthcoming, the AO must make a decision on the evidence available to him, still holds. Then, if the decision is adverse, the claimant has something to appeal against and the adequacy of the information before the AO can be dealt with by the SSAT applying the appropriate burden of proof (*R(IS) 4/93*).

Note that there is no longer a power for the Secretary of State to deem a claim to have been withdrawn if the information required under reg. 7 is not produced.

It has been held that an AO does not "discharge responsibilities of a judicial nature" (Glidewell L.J. in *Jones v. Department of Employment* [1988] 1 All E. R. 725, 733), but clearly the AO's administrative decisions must be reached in a judicial manner. The investigatory functions, most recently emphasised in the *CPAG* case, do not extend to a duty to investigate the claimant's entire financial situation on a review *(Duggan v. Chief Adjudication Officer, The Times*, December 19, 1988; *R(SB) 13/89*).

The Court of Appeal in *Chief Adjudication Officer v. Foster* [1992] Q.B. 31, [1991] 3 All E.R. 846 decided that the AO (as well as social security appeal tribunals and Commissioners) must reach decisions on the basis that all regulations are validly made, on the ground that only the High Court or the Court of Appeal has the jurisdiction to declare regulations *ultra vires*. The House of Lords (*Foster v. Chief Adjudication Officer* [1993] A. C. 754, [1993] 1 All E.R. 705) disagreed and held that Social Security Commissioners have undoubted jurisdiction, in the course of deciding issues within their statutory powers, to determine whether regulations have been validly made or not. See the notes to s.23 for more details. Lord Bridge accepts that "if the Commissioner can base his decision in any case on the invalidity of some provision in regulations made under the Act, it must follow that appeal tribunals and adjudication officers can do likewise." He rejects the arguments which persuaded the Court of Appeal to the contrary. These were that it cannot have been intended that officials of the level and qualifications of AOs should have the power to question the validity of regulations made by the Secretary of State particularly when the Secretary of State cannot be a party to proceedings before an appeal tribunal. Lord Bridge suggests that in any case where there was a challenge to the *vires* of a regulation an AO would use the power in subs. (2) to refer the claim to a SSAT, where the views of the Secretary of State could in practice be put through the AO.

An AO cannot be bound by any assurance given by an employee of the DSS about a claimant's entitlement, but must come to a proper decision on the law applicable to the case. Even if a claimant had relied on a statement from or on behalf of an AO, this requirement to carry out the statutory duty prevents an estoppel arising (*R(SB) 14/88, R(SB) 14/89* and Woolf L.J. refusing leave to appeal in *R(SB) 4/91*). This has recently been confirmed in *CIS 101/1994* and *CF 1015/1995* (to be reported as *R(F) 3/96*).

The claims excluded from the operation of subs. (1) by the words in brackets are certain claims for disability living allowance or disability working allowance. Under ss.30(12) and 35(7), if an award of either of those benefits has been made for a period, a further claim made within that period is treated as an application to review the existing award. Under s.30(13), where an AO's decision is not to award one of those benefits or attendance allowance, any further claim made during the period prescribed for applying for a review of that decision on any ground (*i.e.* three months: Adjudication Regulations, reg. 25) is treated as an application for review.

Subsection (2)

The AO no longer has express power to decide questions in any particular way. The power to

1149

make references to the SSAT in supplementary benefit and FIS cases was new in 1984. The procedure is used sparingly in income support and family credit cases, but is sometimes invoked where
there is a conflict of evidence which the AO feels unable to resolve. According to Lord Bridge in
Foster v. Chief Adjudication Officer [1993] A.C. 754, [1993] 1 All E.R. 705 it should be used if
the validity of any regulations is challenged before the AO. The effect of subs. (3) is that such
references cannot be made in disability working allowance cases. Section 37 is concerned with the
reference of special questions to authorities other than the AO.

Subsection (3)

In these cases the AO must determine the claim or question himself, and so cannot refer a matter
to a SSAT. This is no doubt because the process of appeal for these benefits must start with a
review by another AO before there can be an appeal to the SSAT.

Subsection (5)

Subs. (5) does not prescribe any particular period in advance of the hearing for the written notice
of a reference to be given. The Tribunal of Commissioners in *R(S) 5/86* decides that whatever is
a reasonable time in the circumstances is the test. The same decision holds that the requirement
that the reference is to be in writing cannot be waived by the claimant. Note the exception introduced
by subs. (6) which has been in operation since April 1990.

Subsection (6)

Once a case has been properly referred to a SSAT under subs. (2) a further claim raising similar
questions may be referred to the SSAT for decision without notice in writing being given to the
claimant. It is obviously desirable that notice that the SSAT is to be asked to deal with the further
claim should be given to the claimant if possible.

Subsection (7)

This subsection, inserted by Sched. 6 to the Social Security Act 1998 with effect from May 21,
1998, is one of the transitional provisions that will apply until the new system of decision-making
and adjudication under the 1998 Act comes fully into operation. It applies to decisions made on or
after May 21, 1998. The consequence will be that if a claimant is not entitled at the date of the
AO's decision but does qualify at some later date he will have to make a further claim in order to
establish entitlement. It will not be possible to review the decision refusing the claim on the basis
of change of circumstances as the claim will no longer subsist after the AO's decision is made. A
claimant, for example, who has been found not to be habitually resident, or who is seeking to claim
benefit on the ground of incapacity for work, or whose capital has increased above the prescribed
limit (or the limit for tariff income: for income support see reg. 53 of the Income Support
Regulations), will therefore have to submit a fresh claim (or claims) as time elapses (and appeal
as necessary), in order for any possible changes in his circumstances to be considered. This seems
likely to lead to an unsatisfactory proliferation of claims in some cases. See also the new subs. (8),
inserted into s.22 with effect from May 21, 1998, under which a tribunal can only take account of
the circumstances existing at the date of the AO's decision.

Although subs. (7) does not expressly state that it only applies where the decision is to refuse the
claim, this would seem to be the only sensible interpretation. Where an award is made on a claim
for income support or income-based JSA this will generally continue to be for an indefinite period
(see reg. 17 of the Claims and Payments Regulations). Thus the effect of subs. (7) would primarily
seem to be to bolster up the "*not* down to the date of decision" approach introduced by s. 22(8)
and to confirm existing caselaw which holds that a decision refusing a claim cannot be *reviewed* on
the ground of a subsequent change of circumstances (see *R(A)2/81*, *CIS 767/1994* and *CDLA 15961/
1996*).

Subs. (7) will apply to decisions that are made on or after May 21, 1998 (the date Sched. 6 to
the 1998 Act came into force). However, s.22(8) (under which a tribunal can only take account of
the circumstances existing at the date of the AO's decision) applies to appeals lodged on or after
May 21, 1998 (see the note to s.22(8)). This could work unfairly in relation to a claimant who
appeals after May 20, 1998 against an AO's decision made before May 21. The tribunal hearing the
appeal will only be able to deal with the position as at the date of the AO's decision. But at the
time that decision was made, the claimant, on the basis of the law as it then stood, was entitled to
rely on the fact that the tribunal would consider the matter down to the date of the hearing and that
therefore there was no need for him to make a fresh claim if the circumstances changed. It may be
argued that s.22(8) thus has retrospective effect in some cases. However, the presumption against
retrospectivity does not apply where a contrary intention is indicated (Intrepretation Act 1978, s.
16(1)(c)). The specific statement in para. 3 of Sched. 6 that s.22(8) applies to appeals brought after

the passing of the Act and the wording of subs. (7) ("at any time") would seem to evidence such a contrary intention.

See also the note to s.22(8).

Appeals from adjudication officers—general

Appeal to social security appeal tribunal

22.—(1) Subject to subsection (3) below, where the adjudication officer has decided a claim or question other than a claim or question relating to an attendance allowance, a disability living allowance or a disability working [²allowance, the claimant shall have the right to appeal to a social security appeal tribunal.]

(2) A person with a right of appeal under this section shall be given such notice of a decision falling within subsection (1) above and of that right as may be prescribed.

(3) No appeal lies under this section where—

(a) in connection with the decision of the adjudication officer there has arisen any question which under or by virtue of this Act [² or Part II of the Social Security Contributions (Transfer of Functions, etc.) Act 1999] falls to be determined otherwise than by an adjudication officer; and

(b) the question has been determined; and

(c) the adjudication officer certifies that the decision on that question is the sole ground of his decision.

(4) Regulations may make provision as to the manner in which, and the time within which, appeals are to be brought.

(5) Where an adjudication officer has determined that any amount, other than an amount—

(a) of an attendance allowance;

(b) of a disability living allowance;

(c) of a disability working allowance;

(d) [². . .]

(e) [². . .]

is recoverable under or by virtue of section 71 or 74 below, any person from whom he has determined that it is recoverable shall have the same right of appeal to a social security appeal tribunal as a claimant.

(6) [*Omitted as only applying to industrial injuries benefits*]

(7) Subsection (2) above shall apply to a person with a right of appeal under subsection (5) or (6) above as it applies to a claimant.

[¹(8) In deciding an appeal under this section, a social security appeal tribunal shall not take into account any circumstances not obtaining at the time when the decision appealed against was made.]

DERIVATION

Social Security Act 1975, s.100.

AMENDMENTS

1. Social Security Act 1998, Sched. 6, para. 3(1) (May 21, 1998). This amendment applies from May 21, 1998 until s.12(8)(b) of the 1998 Act comes into force.

2. Modified by Social Security Contributions, etc. (Decisions and Appeals—Transitional Modifications) Regulations 1999 (S.I. 1999 No. 978), reg. 2 and Sched., until Chapter II of Part I of the Social Security Act 1998 (social security decisions and appeals) is wholly in force (April 1, 1999).

GENERAL NOTE

Note that under the provisions of the Social Security Act 1998 appealable decisions of the Secretary of State (see s.12(1) and Sched. 3) will go to a (unified) appeal tribunal.

Subsection (1)
There is a general right of appeal for a claimant against any decision of an AO on any claim or question. Note that under subs. (5) a person from whom an overpayment of most benefits has been determined to be recoverable has the same right of appeal as a claimant. Subsection (1) does not cover disability working allowance. See ss.30 to 33.

Subsection (2)
See the Adjudication Regulations, particularly regs. 18 and 55.

Subsection (3)
This procedure is unlikely to affect appeals on income-related benefits.

Subsection (4)
See reg. 3 and Sched. 2 to the Adjudication Regulations.

Subsection (5)
A person from whom it is determined that an overpayment of most benefits is recoverable has a right to appeal against the AO's decision to that effect. This applies to overpayments under s.71 (misrepresentation or failure to disclose) and s.74 (duplication of income support and other payments). A person falling within subs. (5) must be given notice of the decision and the right of appeal (subss. (7) and (2)).
The benefits listed in paras. (a) to (e) are excluded from the operation of subs. (5). See s.32(9) for rights of appeal against decisions on the recoverability of disability working allowance.

Subsection (8)
This subsection, inserted by Sched. 6 to the Social Security Act 1998 with effect from May 21, 1998, is one of the transitional provisions that will apply until the new system of decision-making and adjudication under the 1998 Act comes fully into operation. It applies in relation to appeals brought on or after May 21, 1998. It abolishes a tribunal's duty to deal with the appeal down to the date of its decision (see further the notes to reg. 17(1) of the Claims and Payments Regulations). A tribunal will no longer be able to take account of changes of circumstances that have occurred since the AO's decision was made. This is particularly likely to be an issue in appeals involving habitual residence, incapacity for work, fluctuating capital, etc. See also the new subs. (7) inserted into s.21 with effect from May 21, 1998. Note President's Circular No. 15, which helpfully points out that *evidence* that comes into existence after the AO's decision is made will not necessarily be irrelevant.
Para. 3 of Sched. 6 which inserted subs. (8) states that it applies to appeals " brought after the passing of this Act". (Sched. 6 itself came into force on Royal Assent.) Presumably an appeal is "brought" on the day that it is lodged, *i.e.* received in a local office (regs. 1(3)(a) and 3 of, and para. 4 of Sched. 2 to, the Adjudication Regulations). The Act was passed (*i.e.* received the Royal Assent) on May 21, 1998. Although an Act (or a provision of an Act) speaks from the beginning of the day of its commencement (Interpretation Act, s.4), it was arguable that since para. 3 of Sched. 6 did not refer to appeals brought "*on or* after the date of the passing of this Act" but simply to appeals brought "after the passing of this Act", this meant that subs. (8) only applied to appeals lodged after the day that event happened (*i.e.* from May 22 onwards). This was the approach originally taken in this book. However, further research unearthed the case of *Tomlinson v. Bullock* [1879] 4 Q.B.D. 230 which concerned an Act dealing with applications for affiliation orders. It was held that a child was born "after the passing of this Act" if it was born at any time on August 10, 1872, which was the day on which the Act, which came into immediate operation, received the Royal assent. It therefore seems that subs. (8) will apply to appeals received *on or after* May 21, 1998.
See also the note to s.21(7) above where the AO's decision was made before May 21, 1998 but the appeal was lodged on or after that date.
Note that subs. (8) has no effect on the period of any award made by a tribunal hearing an appeal lodged on or after May 21, 1998. Any such award of income support or income-based JSA will normally be for an indefinite period (see reg. 17 of the Claims and Payments Regulations and the notes to that regulation).

Note also that a tribunal hearing an appeal made before May 21, 1998 will still be required to consider any changes in circumstances down to the date of its hearing (see the notes to reg. 17(1) of the Claims and Payments Regulations).

Appeal from social security appeal tribunal to Commissioner

23.—(1) Subject to the provisions of this section, an appeal lies to a Commissioner from any decision of a social security appeal tribunal under section 22 above on the ground that the decision of the tribunal was erroneous in point of law.

(2) *[Omitted as only applying to statutory sick pay and statutory maternity pay]*

(3) In any other case an appeal lies under this section at the instance of any of the following—

(a) an adjudication officer;

(b) the claimant;

(c) in any of the cases mentioned in subsection (5) below, a trade union; and

(d) a person from whom it is determined that any amount is recoverable under section 71(1) or 74 below.

(4) *[Omitted as only applying to industrial injuries benefits]*

(5) The following are the cases in which an appeal lies at the instance of a trade union—

(a) where the claimant is a member of the union at the time of the appeal and was so immediately before the question at issue arose;

(b) where that question in any way relates to a deceased person who was a member of the union at the time of his death;

(c) *[Omitted as only applying to industrial injuries benefits]*

(6) Subsections (2), (3) and (5) above, as they apply to a trade union, apply also to any other association which exists to promote the interests and welfare of its members.

[¹(6A) If each of the principal parties to the appeal expresses the view that the decision appealed against was erroneous in point of law, the Commissioner may set aside the decision and refer the case to a tribunal with directions for its determination.

In this subsection "principal parties" means—

(a) in a case relating to statutory sick pay or statutory maternity pay, the persons mentioned in subsection (2)(a), (b) and (c) above;

(b) in any other case—

(i) the persons mentioned in subsection (3)(a) and (b) above; and

(ii) where applicable, the person mentioned in subsection (3)(d) and such a person as is first mentioned in subsection (4) of that section.]

(7) Where the Commissioner holds that the decision was erroneous in point of law, he shall set it aside and—

(a) he shall have the power—

(i) to give the decision which he considers the tribunal should have given, if he can do so without making fresh or further findings of fact; or

(ii) if he considers it expedient, to make such findings and to give such decision as he considers appropriate in the light of them; and

(b) in any other case he shall refer the case to a tribunal with directions for its determination.

(8) Subject to any direction of the Commissioner, the tribunal on a reference under [¹ subsection (6A) or (7)(b) above] shall consist of persons who were not members of the tribunal which gave the erroneous decision.

(9) No appeal lies under this section without the leave—

(a) of the person who was the chairman of the tribunal when the decision

was given or, in a prescribed case, the leave of some other chairman; or
(b) subject to and in accordance with regulations, of a Commissioner.
(10) Regulations may make provision as to the manner in which, and the
time within which, appeals are to be brought and applications made for leave
to appeal.

DERIVATION

Social Security Act 1975, s.101.

AMENDMENT

1. Social Security Act 1998, Sched. 6, para. 4(1) (May 21, 1998). This amendment applies from
May 21, 1998 until s.14(7) of the 1998 Act comes into force.

DEFINITIONS

"Commissioner"—see s.191.
"prescribed"—*ibid.*

GENERAL NOTE

Subsection (1)

There may only be an appeal from a decision under s.22 to the Commissioner on the ground
that the SSAT made an error of law. See s.34 for disability working allowance cases. Note also the
requirement under subs. (9) for leave to appeal to be given by the SSAT chairman (or a substitute) or
a Commissioner.

There are conflicting Commissioners' decisions about whether there is an appealable decision
where a SSAT adjourns the hearing of an appeal. In *CSIS 118/1990* the SSAT had determined that
a recoverable overpayment had been made, but adjourned the question of the amount of the overpayment. The Commissioner holds that an appeal was possible in relation to the issues which the SSAT
had decided, declining to follow the decision of the Tribunal of Commissioners in *CA 126/1989*
because that decision did not mention *R. v. Medical Appeal Tribunal (Midland Region), ex parte
Carrarini* [1966] 1 W.L.R. 883 or *CSU 14/1964*. However, in *CSB 83/1991* the Commissioner
followed *CA 126/1989*, holding that the *Carrarini* case was not in point because there the tribunal's
decision was to refuse to adjourn. He held that there is only a right of appeal from a final decision
of a SSAT, which finally disposes of the issues before it. In *CIS 628/1992* where the SSAT had
failed to deal with all the issues arising on an appeal, it is held that there was no decision within
the meaning of s.23 against which an appeal could be made. The Commissioner declines to follow
CSIS 118/1990, holding that s.20(5) does not authorise the division of a claim or question into parts
so that a decision dealing with some parts and adjourning others may be appealed to the Commissioner. See the notes to reg. 23 of the Adjudication Regulations for the guidance given in *CIS 628/
1992* as to how to proceed in such a case. See also *CIS 451/1992* in the notes to reg. 25. But
in *CSIS 110/1991* the Commissioner follows *CSIS 118/1990*. He points out that the Tribunal of
Commissioners in *CA 126/1989* did not refer to decisions such as *Re Yates Settlement Trusts* [1954]
1 All E.R. 619, in which the Court of Appeal held that an order to adjourn was a judicial act and
could be the subject of appeal (while indicating that it would be slow to interfere with such an
order). He did not consider *Bland v. Chief Supplementary Benefit Officer* (see the note to s.24),
which the Commissioner in *CSB 83/1991* had regarded as supporting *CA 126/1989*, to derogate
from the principle in *Yates*. Morever, as *CSU 14/1964* had stated, a decision to adjourn might in
some instances amount to a denial of justice. *CIS 260/1993* follows *CA 126/1989*, *CSB 83/1991*
and *CIS 628/1992* (although the Commissioner states that if he was dealing with an appeal emanating
from Scotland he would follow *CSIS 118/1990* and *CSIS 110/1991*). Previous editions of this book
have suggested that in the current state of the authorities, tribunals should follow *CA 126/1989,
CSB 83/1991* and *CIS 628/1992*, but clearly clarification of the position is needed.

But where a SSAT decides that there has been a recoverable overpayment and remits the calculation of the amount to the AO, subject to reference back in case of disagreement, that is a sufficiently
complete decision for the purposes of s.23 (*R(SB) 15/87, CSB 83/1991, Riches v. Social Security
Commissioner* (Court of Session, May 4, 1993 and *CIS 628/1992*). In this situation the only matter
remaining is that of quantification, the tribunal having determined the issues of legal principle. *CIS
501/1993* holds that a SSAT's decision to refer a question to the ECJ for a preliminary ruling is a
final decision and so appealable to the Commissioner.

CIS 749/1991 and *CS 159/1991* deal with a similar point but in relation to a Commissioner's decision. In *CIS 749/1991* the Commissioner who initially heard the appeal held that the claimant was entitled to housing costs in respect of a loan for a loft conversion; he went on to state that in the event of disagreement as to the arrears due or the implementation of the decision the matter was to be referred to him for determination. There was a dispute as what parts of the loan were allowable, but unfortunately the Commissioner died before the matter could be determined. The Commissioner who then dealt with the case held that "referred to me" meant "referred to me in my office as a duly appointed Social Security Commissioner", with the result that he could deal with the outstanding question in the case. Further, the decision that had been given by the first Commissioner was a final decision, in the sense that an appeal could have been brought against it; what had happened was that a further decision was necessary because the outstanding matter could not be resolved by agreement. This was different from the situation where an appeal had been adjourned part-heard, in which case a different Commissioner would have had to hold a complete rehearing. But he was bound by the first Commissioner's decision, as that Commissioner would have been if he had been able to deal with the outstanding issue. To the extent that *CIS 442/1992* suggested that there had to be an entire rehearing before a different Commissioner he declined to follow it.

In *CS 159/1991* the Commissioner had allowed the claimant's appeal against refusal of invalidity benefit and directed that if there was a dispute as to the sum owing after the offsetting of the unemployment benefit that the claimant had received against the arrears of invalidity benefit due, the matter was to be referred to him for determination. The claimant did not agree the calculation, but sadly the Commissioner (the same Commissioner as in *CIS 749/1991*) died before the hearing could be restored. The Commissioner to whom this case was referred (who was the Commissioner in *CIS 442/1992*) holds that if the decision had been incomplete he would have had to decide the whole appeal afresh. However, the first Commissioner's decision was not incomplete as he had determined the entire subject matter of the appeal. The correct calculation of the benefit due was not before the first Commissioner and he did not have jurisdiction on this question. This was not a case where the subject matter of the appeal involved the actual calculation. The second Commissioner in *CS 159/1991* disagrees with the approach taken in *CIS 749/1991*. In his view, the question of the meaning of "referred to *me*" only arose if the first Commissioner's decision was incomplete because decisions could not be split into parts. The approach of *CIS 749/1991* is certainly less cumbersome in practice, since if the disputed items of the claimant's housing costs had not been dealt with in this way, presumably it would have been necessary either for the AO to issue a formal determination, with a fresh right of appeal, or for the first Commissioner's decision to be set aside.

CDWA1/1992 holds that a Commissioner does have power, even after he has given his decision, to inquire into a complaint that the decision has not been properly implemented. The Commissioner can give a supplemental decision. The supplemental decision cannot subtract from, or vary, the original decision; it can only supplement it. In fact, the Commissioner in *CDWA1/1992* decides that his decision had been fully implemented by the award of disability working allowance for 26 weeks and that the question of any subsequent award was not within his jurisdiction.

There are a number of other parts of the Commissioners' jurisdiction where appeal is on a point of law only and the well established tests have been taken over here. In *R(SB) 6/81* the most accurate and concise summary is said to be that set out in *R(A) 1/72*. This holds that a decision would be wrong in law if:
  (i) it contained a false proposition of law on its face;
  (ii) it was supported by no evidence; or
  (iii) the facts found were such that no person acting judicially and properly instructed as to the relevant law could have come to the determination in question.
CSB 29/81 refers to *R(I) 14/75*, which sets out the three heads quoted above and adds:
  (iv) breach of the requirements of natural justice; and
  (v) failure to state adequate reasons.
The formula of five headings is adopted in *R(SB) 11/83* (although by reference to decisions of the courts rather than the Commissioners) and is now clearly accepted. A retrospective change in the law can render a decision, which was correct at the time it was made, erroneous in law so that it may be appealed, or reviewed under s.25(2) if made by an AO (*R(F) 1/95*). (Such a change can also amount to a change of circumstances: see *Chief Adjudication Officer v. McKiernon*, Court of Appeal, July 8, 1993, in the notes to s.25.)

In addition, a failure to provide an adequate (*CIS 12032/1996* and *CDLA 16902/1996*) or a legible (*CIB 3013/1997* and *CDLA 4110/1997*) record of the tribunal's proceedings, including a proper note of the evidence given (*CIS 12032/1996* and *CDLA 16902/1996*), will be an error of law. Note also *CDLA 1389/1997*. See reg. 23(4) of the Adjudication Regulations and the notes to that paragraph.

The result of the House of Lord's decision in *Foster v. Chief Adjudication Officer* [1993] A.C.

754, [1993] 1 All E.R. 705 is that it is an error of law under head (i) for a SSAT to rely on a regulation which has not been validly made, even though it has not been declared to be *ultra vires* in judicial review proceedings. This result was found to be desirable because it avoids the duplication of proceedings that would have been caused by forcing parties into separate judicial review actions to test validity and because the courts will have the benefit of the Commissioners' expert views on the question of validity if an appeal is taken beyond the Commissioners.

Having disposed of the objections to AOs and SSATs having the power to determine the validity of regulations (see the notes to s.21(1)), Lord Bridge was left with three objections to giving the words "erroneous in point of law" their ordinary meaning in the context of the Commissioners' jurisdiction. The first was that the same words were used in the part of the legislation dealing with adjudication by the Secretary of State and it could not have been intended to give the Secretary of State power to decide whether he had acted *ultra vires* or not. Lord Bridge shows that in fact such a power is necessary. The second objection was that the Commissioners have no power to declare regulations *ultra vires*. Lord Bridge holds that the absence of that power does not throw any light on the Commissioners' power to determine incidentally to a decision on an appeal that a regulation is *ultra vires*. The third objection was more constitutional, that if the Commissioners have jurisdiction to question the *vires* of a regulation then that jurisdiction must embrace challenges on the basis of irrationality or unreasonableness as well as illegality. Lord Bridge avoided the issue by saying that the challenge in *Foster* was solely on the basis of illegality—that the regulations were not within the scope of the enabling power—and that there was no doubt of the Commissioners' jurisdiction on illegality.

This approach leaves two uncertainties: first what is the power of the ordinary courts to strike down regulations which have been approved by Parliament on the ground of irrationality; and second whether there is any difference between the courts' powers and those of the Commissioners. On the first question, Lord Bridge suggests that while Lord Jauncey in *City of Edinburgh District Council v. Secretary of State for Scotland* (1985) S.L.T. 551 held that a statutory instrument considered by Parliament could only be held to be *ultra vires* if it was patently defective, *i.e.* where it was not authorised by the enabling statute or the required procedure was not followed, the House of Lords in *R. v. Secretary of State for the Environment, ex parte Nottinghamshire County Council* [1986] A.C. 240 left open possible exceptions from the rule that the courts may not strike down statutory instruments on the ground of irrationality. He says that the *Foster* case did not provide the occasion to decide whether those exceptions should exist. The view was expressed in previous editions that Lord Scarman's speech in the *Nottinghamshire* case appears to limit the exceptions where there has been Parliamentary approval of the instrument or decision under challenge, to situations where there has been bad faith or misconduct by the Minister concerned, in the form of misleading Parliament. That is a very limited exception. But see *O'Connor* below. It is unfortunate that the House of Lords has left doubt about its existence or scope. It certainly made no reference to it in deciding that the October 1989 amendment to the definition of non-dependant in reg. 3 was not open to challenge for irrationality.

The second uncertainty is raised by what Lord Bridge says after referring to the possible exceptions to Lord Jauncey's approach in the *City of Edinburgh* case:

> "But I have no doubt that the Social Security Commissioners have good pragmatic reasons not to take it on themselves to identify any such exceptional case, but to leave that to the higher courts, who, as Lord Jauncey pointed out, have never yet done so in any reported case."

This seems to suggest that the Commissioners should refuse to consider any challenges to regulations on the ground of irrationality (which are bound to be made given the uncertainties left by *Foster*). However, that approach would deprive the higher courts of the benefits of the Commissioners' expert views on the issue. Lord Bridge's reference to "pragmatic reasons" also suggests that the Commissioners' legal jurisdiction is co-extensive with that of the ordinary courts (whatever that is).

In *CIS 391/1992* (which was to be reported as *R(IS) 5/98* but now will be *R(IS) 26/95*) a Tribunal of Commissioners had to decide how to exercise that jurisdiction. The Tribunal holds that *Foster* clearly states that the Commissioners do have jurisdiction to consider whether a regulation is invalid on the ground of irrationality. It was submitted by the *amicus curiae* in the case that Lord Bridge's approach could be taken to mean that Commissioners should not be astute to find secondary legislation irrational. The Tribunal appear to have taken this on board in stating that this jurisdiction should only be exercised where a determination whether or not a regulation is valid is necessary to the determination of the issue which arises and if a serious issue of irrationality arises. However, the Commissioners were able to reject the argument for irrationality by deciding that in the circumstances of the case the Secretary of State could not be said to have taken leave of his senses (*cf.* Lord Diplock in *Council of Civil Service Unions v. Minister for the Civil Service* [1985] A.C. 374 at 410, quoted in *CIS 250/1992*) in making reg. 52 of the Income Support

Regulations in the terms in which he did. The question of whether the *Nottinghamshire* conditions were met therefore did not arise.

In *CIS 14141/1996*, the Commissioner held that *CIS 391/1992* should not be read as detracting from the need for the *Nottinghamshire* conditions to be met before a Commissioner could find a regulation which had been subject to Parliamentary scrutiny invalid on the ground of irrationality. The case concerned the effect of para. 5A of Sched. 3 to the Income Support Regulations in the form in which it was introduced on May 2, 1994 and in force until October 1995. Para. 5A provided a general rule that the interest on loans taken out after May 2, 1994 (or an increase of an existing loan) was not to be met as a housing cost. There was an exception from that rule where the loan was to pay for certain essential repairs and improvements. As the Commissioner held that para. 5A had to be interpreted, that exception was confined to claimants who already had some loan interest met as a housing cost and was denied to claimants who did not have any existing loan interest to be met. Despite agreeing that the result was absurd and unfair, the Commissioner felt unable to say that no Secretary of State in his senses could have made the regulation in that way, and, in the light of Lord Bridge's warning in *Foster*, did not find the provision invalid. However, he would have found the *Nottinghamshire* conditions satisfied, as Parliament had been misled by the Secretary of State's statement under s.174(2) of the Administration Act 1992 about the extent to which he had given effect to the recommendations of the Social Security Advisory Committee in framing the regulations inserting para. 5A. The statement asserted that there was a general exception for essential repairs and improvements, without the distinction between categories of claimants.

But note that in *O'Connor v. Chief Adjudication Officer and another, The Times*, March 11, 1999, CA Auld L.J., who gave the leading judgment for the majority, states that the test on irrationality was the normal *Wednesbury* one, *i.e.* was the regulation at issue outside the range of reasonable options open to the Secretary of State given the terms of the empowering provisions? The Commissioner in that case seemed to have taken the view that where the Secretary of State's regulation-making power was subject to parliamentary scrutiny, irrationality could only be found if the Secretary of State had misled or deceived Parliament or had otherwise acted in bath faith. That was too narrow a view. It was also wrong to deduce from dicta in the *Nottinghamshire* case (that the Secretary of State "must have taken leave of his senses") or from Lord Bridge's reference to "manifest absurdity" in *R. v. Secretary of State for the Environment, ex parte Hammersmith LBC* [1991] A.C. 521, HL that there was a notion of "extreme" irrationality. However, in the case of subsidiary legislation subject to parliamentary scrutiny, there was a heavy evidential burden to establish irrationality of a regulation where this might owe much to political, social and economic considerations in the primary legislation. The fact that a regulation might produce hardship in individual cases did not make it irrational (see *R. v. Social Fund Inspector, ex parte Healey and others* [1991] 4 Admin. L.R. 713, CA). Auld J. also held that there was no basis in that case for the "modified" human rights application of the *Wednesbury* principle indicated by the Court of Appeal in *R. v. Minister of Defence, ex parte Smith* [1996] Q.B. 517. Although the claimant had sought to rely on the right to education set out in Art. 2 of the First Protocol to the European Convention on Human Rights, Art. 2 was not applicable in the circumstances.

If Commissioners have the jurisdiction to find regulations invalid on the ground of irrationality, so must SSATs and AOs.

In determining whether there is an error of law under head (ii) it is necessary to look at all the evidence presented to the tribunal, not only that recorded in the findings of fact or the chairman's notes of evidence. It is only if a decision cannot be supported looking at the totality of the evidence presented that an error of law is committed (*CSB 15/82, R(SB) 16/82, R(S) 1/88*). If an item of evidence was not before the SSAT, it cannot in itself be an error of law not to have considered it (*R(S) 1/88*). The Commissioners have held that they are not restricted to looking at the formal SSAT documents but may consider any reliable account of what evidence was presented (*CSB 34/81, R(SB) 10/82, R(SB) 18/83*). However, the approach to such accounts is somewhat cautious. The Commissioner in *R(SB) 10/82* suggested an over-elaborate procedure for producing an account agreed between the parties to be referred to the SSAT chairman. That view is rejected in *R(M) 1/89*. The Tribunal of Commissioners there holds that it is a matter for the Commissioner's discretion what evidence about the proceedings to admit.

See the notes to reg. 2 of the Adjudication Regulations for the requirements of natural justice and the notes to reg. 23 for adequate reasons.

Subsections (2)–(6)

These provisions define the parties who may make an appeal from a SSAT and deal with trade unions and other organisations.

This subsection, inserted by Sched. 6 to the Social Security Act 1998 with effect from May 21, 1998, is one of the transitional provisions that will apply until the new system of decision-making and adjudication under the 1998 Act comes fully into operation. It applies from May 21, 1998. A Commissioner will have discretion (the provision is not mandatory) to set aside a tribunal's decision and refer it back to a differently constituted (unless the Commissioner otherwise directs: (subs. (8)) tribunal if the "principal parties" (as defined) believe the decision is wrong in law. See subs. (7) for the Commissioner's existing powers where *he* considers the decision to be wrong in law. Presumably a Commissioner will not exercise his discretion under subs. (6A) if he does not think the tribunal's decision is erroneous. However, the provision should at least allow a speeding-up of the appeal process where a tribunal have clearly fallen into error.

See the Practice Memorandum issued by the Chief Commissioner on August 11, 1998 for appeals lodged on or after August 17, 1998. Note also the Note on Procedure in Schedule 6 cases issued by the Chief Commissioner on August 6, 1998.

Note that s.13(1) of the 1998 Act (when in force) will accelerate the process of rectifying erroneous tribunal decisions still further by providing that, where an appeal is made to the tribunal chairman for leave to appeal to the Commissioner, the chairman may, if he considers the decision erroneous in law, set the decision aside and refer the case for redetermination by the original tribunal or by a differently constituted tribunal. More controversially, s.13(3) provides that the chairman *shall* set aside the decision if each of the principal parties to the appeal expresses the view that the decision is erroneous in law. The chairman is not to be afforded the discretion given to the Commissioner in such circumstances to decline to set aside.

Subsection (7)
This important provision on the powers of the Commissioner seems oddly placed in the middle of s.23. (From May 21, 1998, see also subs. (6A)). The Commissioner's powers in supplementary benefit and FIS cases were until April 6, 1987 contained in reg. 27 of the 1984 Adjudication Regulations. Under those provisions if the Commissioner found an error of law he had to send the appeal back to a SSAT unless it was expedient for him to give the decision which the SSAT should have given. If sufficient facts had not been found by the SSAT (a common situation when the SSAT has gone wrong in law) the Commissioner could not give the decision which the SSAT should have given. There was some criticism of this procedure, which could be ponderous and time-consuming.

Para. (a)(i) confirms the power of the Commissioner to give the decision the SSAT should have given where no further findings of fact are necessary. Para. (a)(ii) gives the power (new in 1987) for the Commissioner, when he considers it expedient, to make fresh or further findings of fact and then to give a decision in the light of those findings. The power has been used by Commissioners in a large number of appeals, including *R(SB) 11/88* and *CSB 176/1987*. In the first decision, the Commissioner held that the power existed from April 6, 1987, and that it did not matter that the SSAT decision was before that date. In the second, the Commissioner called for quite a lot of new evidence, although there was no real dispute over the facts. A Commissioner is more likely to send factual disputes back to a SSAT, although practice varies. The power is most often used where the SSAT has failed to make express findings on matters which are not in dispute or on which the result of the existing evidence is clear. There may be some difficulty if a Commissioner is making a decision partly on his own assessment of evidence and partly on the SSAT's assessment of evidence which the Commissioner has not seen.

If para. (a) does not apply, then under para. (b) the case must be referred to a SSAT with directions. These have normally included a direction that no members of the original SSAT should be on the new one, as is now expressly required by subs. (8) unless the Commissioner directs otherwise. See *CIS 749/1991* and *CS 159/1991* above.

Subsection (9)
A party who wishes to appeal from a SSAT decision must get leave either from the chairman of the SSAT (or a substitute under reg. 24(4) of the Adjudication Regulations) or a Commissioner. Reg. 24 deals with the procedure for applying for leave to the chairman, and the time limit is three months from the date on which a full statement of the SSAT's decision is given or sent to the applicant (Adjudication Regulations, Sched. 2, para. 7). If the chairman refuses leave, a party has 1 month (previously 42 days) to apply to a Commissioner for leave (Social Security Commissioners (Procedure) Regulations 1999, reg. 9(2)). A Commissioner may deal with late applications if, for special reasons, he thinks fit (reg. 9(3) and (4)).

On the question of whether a Commissioner has jurisdiction to hear an appeal from a SSAT if the appellant has not obtained a full statement of the tribunal's decision, see *CIS 3299/1997* and *CIB 4189/1997* in the notes to reg. 24 of the Adjudication Regulations.

A mere assertion of a mistake of law is not enough for leave to be granted. There must be some material in the case indicating that there is a sensible argument in support *(R(SB) 1/81)*. There is, in the nature of things, not much further guidance given to chairmen about whether to give leave or not. The most helpful statement is in para. 30 of *R(S) 4/82*. The Commissioners stress that the chairman's discretion is unfettered providing that it is exercised in a judicial manner, but say that chairmen should bear in mind that the object of requiring leave to be given is to restrict appeals to those which are neither hopeless nor frivolous and raise a serious issue. If the conduct of the tribunal's proceedings is seriously in question, leave should be given, but if the allegations are general, with no supporting detail, leave should be refused. The party always has another chance by applying to the Commissioner for leave.

It is suggested that if the grounds put forward by the claimant or the AO do not contain any allegations of error of law (either expressly or by obvious implication) then the SSAT chairman should refuse leave to appeal. In particular, if the complaint is that the SSAT should have made a different decision on the facts, or that there is some new or different evidence which was not put to the SSAT *(R(S) 1/88)*, that is not good enough. It is suggested that normally the chairman should not give leave simply because, on looking beyond the application, he considers that there might be some error of law in the SSAT's decision, such as inadequate findings of fact or reasons. That is something which is better dealt with by a Commissioner if the claimant or the AO makes a further application for leave to appeal.

If the Commissioner refuses leave to appeal that is not a decision within the meaning of s.24 below (Social Security Act 1980, s.14) and so cannot be appealed to the Court of Appeal *(Bland v. CSBO* [1983] 1 All E. R. 537, *R(SB) 12/83, Kuganathan v. Chief Adjudication Officer, The Times,* March 1, 1995). There is no right of appeal from a refusal of leave by a chairman. The only right of appeal is from a decision of a SSAT.

Subsection (10)

See the Adjudication Regulations, regs. 3 and 24 and Sched. 2, and the Social Security Commissioners Procedure Regulations 1987 (S.I. 1987 No. 214). On late appeals see the notes to reg. 3(3) to (3E) of the Adjudication Regulations. *CIS 550/1993* holds that service by courier is not service by post within reg. 30(3) of the Social Security Commissioners Procedure Regulations.

Under the new system for decision-making and appeals being brought in by the Social Security Act 1998 time limits for appeals and applications are to be standardised at one month.

An appeal to the Court of Appeal in *CIS 39/1993* raised a point on the construction of regs. 15(2) and 29(1)(b) of the Commissioners Procedure Regulations. The claimant's request for an oral hearing of his appeal to the Commissioner had been refused by a Nominated Officer. It was contended that only the power to *grant* an oral hearing could be delegated to a Nominated Officer, whereas the power to *refuse* an oral hearing had to be exercised by a Commissioner. However the Court of Appeal decided that a Nominated Officer does have the power to refuse, as well as grant, an oral hearing *(Fiore v. Adjudication Officer,* June 20, 1995).

Appeal from Commissioners on point of law

24.—(1) Subject to subsections (2) and (3) below, an appeal on a question of law shall lie to the appropriate court from any decision of a Commissioner [¹or given in consequence of a reference under section 112(4) of the 1975 Act (which enabled a medical appeal tribunal to refer a question of law to a Commissioner)].

(2) No appeal under this section shall lie from a decision except—

  (a) with the leave of the Commissioner who gave the decision or, in a prescribed case, with the leave of a Commissioner selected in accordance with regulations; or

  (b) if he refuses leave, with the leave of the appropriate court.

(3) An application for leave under this section in respect of a Commissioner's decision may only be made by—

  (a) a person who, before the proceedings before the Commissioner were begun, was entitled to appeal to the Commissioner from the decision to which the Commissioner's decision relates;

  (b) any other person who was a party to the proceedings in which the first decision mentioned in paragraph (a) was given;

  (c) the Secretary of State, in a case where he is not entitled to apply for leave by virtue of paragraph (a) or (b) above;

(d) any other person who is authorised by regulations to apply for leave; and regulations may make provision with respect to the manner in which and the time within which applications must be made to a Commissioner for leave under this section and with respect to the procedure for dealing with such applications.

(4) On an application to a Commissioner for leave under this section it shall be the duty of the Commissioner to specify as the appropriate court—

    (a) the Court of Appeal if it appears to him that the relevant place is in England or Wales;

    (b) the Court of Session if it appears to him that the relevant place is in Scotland; and

    (c) the Court of Appeal in Northern Ireland if it appears to him that the relevant place is in Northern Ireland,

except that if it appears to him, having regard to the circumstances of the case and in particular to the convenience of the persons who may be parties to the proposed appeal, that he should specify a different court mentioned in paragraphs (a) to (c) above as the appropriate court, it shall be his duty to specify that court as the appropriate court.

(5) In this section—

    "the appropriate court", except in subsection (4) above, means the court specified in pursuance of that subsection;

    "the relevant place", in relation to an application for leave to appeal from a decision of a Commissioner, means the premises where the authority whose decision was the subject of the Commissioner's decision usually exercises its functions.

[[1](5A) In relation to a decision of a Commissioner which was given in consequence of a reference under section 112(4) of the 1975 Act subsections (3) and (5) of this section shall have effect with such modifications as may be prescribed by regulations.]

(6) The powers to make regulations conferred by this section shall be exercisable by the Lord Chancellor.

DERIVATION

Social Security Act 1980, s.14.

AMENDMENT

1. Social Security (Consequential Provisions) Act 1992, Sched. 4, paras. 1 and 12 (until the repeal of s.14(7) of the Social Security Act 1980 in Sched. 9 to the Social Security Act 1989 comes into force).

DEFINITIONS

    "the Commissioner"—see s.191.
    "prescribed"—*ibid.*

GENERAL NOTE

This section provides for an appeal on a point of law to the Court of Appeal, Court of Session or Court of Appeal in Northern Ireland, as appropriate, from a decision of a Commissioner, with the leave of a Commissioner or the court. See the Social Security Commissioners (Procedure) Regulations 1999 (S.I. 1999 No. 1495) (in force from June 1, 1999).

For the procedure applicable in Scotland, see Books of Sederunt, Rules of Court, rules 290 and 293B (inserted by S.I. 1980 No. 1745 (s.151)).

A decision of a Commissioner to grant or refuse leave to appeal to the Commissioner is not a "decision" from which an appeal may lie under this section (*Bland v. Chief Supplementary Benefit Officer* [1983] 1 All E.R. 537, *Kuganathan v. Chief Adjudication Officer, The Times*, March 1, 1995).

See also the notes to s. 23(1) on the question of when there is a final decision.

In *CIS 16992/1996, CIS 2809/1997* and *CFC 1580/1997* the Commissioner discusses the extent to which Commissioners are bound by decisions of the High Court (or in Scotland, the Outer House of the Court of Session). He concludes that a Commissioner is not bound by a decision of a single judge of the High Court on a substantive point of social security law (although he should follow the decision unless he was convinced that it was wrong), because such a decision arose out of a co-ordinate, and not a supervisory, jurisdiction. But decisions given by a single judge in exercise of the High Court's supervisory jurisdiction in respect of Commissioners clearly were binding. So too was a decision of a Divisional Court (except perhaps one concerning a pre-1978 supplementary benefit case—see *R(SB) 52/83*) for much the same reasons that a single Commissioner was bound by a Tribunal of Commissioners (see *R(I) 12/75*). A Tribunal of Commissioners would not normally be bound by a decision of a Divisional Court (see *R(SB) 52/83*).

Reviews—general

Review of decisions

25.—(1) Subject to the following provisions of this section, any decision under this Act of an adjudication officer, a social security appeal tribunal or a Commissioner (other than a decision relating to an attendance allowance, a disability living allowance or a disability working allowance) may be reviewed at any time by an adjudication officer or, on a reference by an adjudication officer, by a social security appeal tribunal, if—

(a) the officer or tribunal is satisfied that the decision was given in ignorance of, or was based on a mistake as to, some material fact; or

(b) there has been any relevant change of circumstances since the decision was given; or

(c) it is anticipated that a relevant change of circumstances will so occur; or

(d) the decision was based on a decision of a question which under or by virtue of this Act falls to be determined otherwise than by an adjudication officer, and the decision of that question is revised; or

(e) the decision falls to be reviewed under section [¹6(6) or 7(7) of the Job-seekers Act 1995].

(2) Any decision of an adjudication officer (other than a decision relating to an attendance allowance, a disability living allowance or a disability working allowance) may be reviewed, upon the ground that it was erroneous in point of law, by an adjudication officer or, on a reference from an adjudication officer, by a social security appeal tribunal.

(3) Regulations may provide that a decision may not be reviewed on the ground mentioned in subsection (1)(a) above unless the officer or tribunal is satisfied as mentioned in that paragraph by fresh evidence.

(4) In their application to family credit, subsection (1)(b) and (c) above shall have effect subject to section 128(3) of the Contributions and Benefits Act (change of circumstances not to affect award or rate during specified period).

(5) Where a decision is reviewed on the ground mentioned in subsection (1)(c) above, the decision given on the review—

(a) shall take effect on the day prescribed for that purpose by reference to the date on which the relevant change of circumstances is expected to occur; and

(b) shall be reviewed again if the relevant change of circumstances either does not occur or occurs otherwise than on that date.

DERIVATION

Subs. (1): Social Security Act 1975, s.104(1).
Subs. (2): 1975 Act, s.104(1A).
Subs. (3): 1975 Act, s.104(1).
Subs. (4): Social Security Act 1986, s.52(8).

Social Security Administration Act 1992

Subs. (5): 1975 Act, s.104(1ZA).

AMENDMENT

1. Jobseekers Act 1995, Sched. 2, para. 43 (October 7, 1996).

DEFINITIONS

"Commissioner"—see s.191.
"the Contributions and Benefits Act"—*ibid.*
"prescribed"—*ibid.*

GENERAL NOTE

Note that under the Social Security Act 1998 there wil be a two-fold system of reconsideration, labelled "revision" and "supersession". See the 1999 Supplement to this book for details.

Section 25 does not apply to disability working allowance. See ss.30 to 35 for reviews and appeals in that benefit.

Subsection (1)
Any decision to which s.25 applies may be reviewed by an AO on one of the five grounds set out in paras. (a) to (e). According to the Tribunal of Commissioners in *CSIS 137/1994*, the process of review involves both reconsidering the relevant aspects of a claimant's case and making any necessary redetermination. It is not restricted to just one part of this process, as sometimes suggested (see, *e.g. R(S) 3/94* and *CDLA 1715/1995*). Where, as is normally the case for income support, an award is for an indefinite period (Claims and Payments Regulations, reg. 17(1)), any alteration to that award must be by way of review and revision. The principle flows from the fundamental rule in s.60 of the Administration Act (1975 Act, s.117(1)) that a decision on a claim, for whatever period covered by the decision, is final, subject to the processes of appeal or review under s.25 (see *CSSB 544/1989* and the Common Appendix to the group of decisions including *CSSB 281/1989*). Even if the award is for a definite period, any alteration of that award within that period is subject to the same limitation.
There are a number of potential exceptions to this general principle. In the past one has been thought to be created by reg. 17(4) of the Claims and Payments Regulations, which has been used as the basis for submissions that awards made for days after the date of claim may be terminated whenever the claimant ceases to satisfy the conditions of entitlement. But see the notes to reg. 17(4) for the limitations of this provision, and in particular *CSIS 137/1994*, to be reported as *R(IS) 2/98*, in which a Tribunal of Commissioners declines to follow *R(S) 5/89* and holds that reg. 17(4) does not provide a separate basis for conducting reviews. Another is that ss.159 to 160A below provide for most alterations in rates of income support and income-based JSA and some prescribed figures to take effect automatically without the need for a decision by an AO. Where some kind of transitional addition is in payment, review by an AO under reg. 63(3) of the Adjudication Regulations is necessary. Some powers of review in income support cases are given directly by reg. 63(4) and paras. (5) to (10) of reg. 63 and reg. 64 set out circumstances in which review under s. 25(1) is not to take place. See reg. 63A for income-based JSA. However, outside these circumstances s.25(1) provides the general rule.
It is clearly established (see, *e.g. CSB 376/1983* applying *R(I) 1/71* and *CI 11/77*) that the onus lies on the person wanting the review to establish both facts justifying the review and the correctness of the subsequent revised decision. That will be the normal situation, but if the other party wishes the decision to be revised in some other way, the onus will be on that party (*CIS 247/1991*). Thus if, as in *CSB 376/1983*, the AO withdraws benefit on a change of circumstances when there is insufficient information to work out benefit, he has to justify the decision on the balance of probabilities. He cannot simply rely on the claimant not having proved his right to benefit. The same approach is taken in *CIS 1/1988*. If it is the claimant requesting the review (*e.g.* by raising the question whether a previous decision denying benefit should be revised: *R(SB) 9/84*), then the onus is on him. Although s.26(1) mentions an application in writing to the AO, a request for review may be oral or even implied (*CSB 336/1987*). *CIS 30/1993* confirms that a failure to identify a ground for review will be an error of law, even if there clearly was a relevant change of circumstances which could provide grounds for review. The SSAT (and the AO) had to be clear about the nature of the decision being made, because of the importance of the correct placing of the burden of proof.

1162

See also *R(IS) 2/96* and *CSIS 60/1994* in the notes to s. 71(5) which hold that computer print-outs are insufficient to establish that a valid review has been carried out.

A number of Commissioners' decisions have illuminated the general area of review through a detailed examination of review in supplementary benefit cases. The individual decisions are noted in the 1991 Supplement. The most general point is that in principle it is for the party seeking a review to identify the decision which he wishes to have reviewed (*CSSB 540/1989* and *CIS 77/1992*). Only once that is done can any potential grounds for review be properly identified. However, if, as was often the case, the claimant was not properly notified of the exact terms of an AO's decision (see Adjudication Regulations, reg. 63, now reg. 55), due allowances must be made (*CSSB 470/1989*). If what is being put forward is a change of circumstances after the date of the decision, it will not be so important to establish the grounds of the original decision.

Secondly, doubt is cast on the proposition in *R(A) 2/90* that once one ground of review of a determination is established the whole determination is open to reconsideration (*CSSB 238/1989*). Even if this were right about an attendance allowance decision, the Commissioner holds that it does not apply to supplementary benefit decisions. Supplementary benefit awards (and, it would seem by analogy, income support awards) are made up of a continuing award of benefit co-existing with a series of review adjustments to particular elements of the award (*CSSB 238/1989* and the Common Appendix to the group of decisions including *CSSB 281/1989*). Thus where there are grounds for review of one element this does not in itself allow review of any other elements. And if one element is revised on review, that does not affect the existence of the underlying continuing award or the other elements of it, unless a separate ground of review exists in relation to those other elements. That approach is applied to income support in *CIS 77/1992* and *CIS 303/1992* (to be reported as *R(IS) 15/93*). In *CIS 303/1992*, in distinction to *CIS 77/1992*, a separate ground of review was put forward before the SSAT and should have been dealt with under s.36. Previous decisions appearing to suggest that a decision on review completely supersedes the decision reviewed are shown to be limited to decisions which are different in nature to supplementary benefit decisions and are indivisible, such as decisions that an overpayment is recoverable (*CSB 64/1986* and *R(SB) 15/87*) or attendance allowance cases where the review is in effect the first stage of an appeal (*R(A) 5/89*). See also *R(SB) 1/82* and *R(P) 1/82*. And see *CAO v. Eggleton and Others* (the appeal from *CIS 566/1991* and *CIS 788/1991*) below.

Perhaps the most controversial and difficult part of these decisions is the proposition that a request for review must be directed at the last operative decision dealing with the element of which review is sought (Common Appendix to group of decisions including *CSSB 281/1989*, as explained and expanded in *CSSB 238/1989* and *CSSB 544/1989*). If there has been a series of review decisions on that element, the chain must be traced backwards, at each decision asking whether grounds for review of the immediately preceding decision exist. However, the basis for this proposition has not yet been clearly established, and its application could cause considerable problems for claimants and for the DSS. For instance, if an old award is discovered to have been based on a misrepresentation of a material fact, must the AO trace a chain of review back to the relevant decision in order to carry out the review and revision which is a necessary basis of a decision on recoverability of the overpayment? *R(IS) 11/93* holds, without discussing any of the decisions cited above, that any supplementary benefit decision is open to review. *CIS 566/1991* dealt with the effect on the original decision of an AO's refusal to revise on review and *CIS 788/1991* with the effect where there had been a partial revision on review. In both cases the claimants had applied for a review of their income support so as to include a severe disability premium (following *CIS 180/1989*) and then obtained leave to bring a late appeal against the original decision awarding income support in April 1988. In *CIS 566/1991* the claimant's application for review was not made until August 1990, and the AO refused to revise the original decision because of s.104(7) and (8) of the Social Security Act 1975, now s.69 of the Administration Act. The AO argued that a late appeal could not be admitted because the original decision awarding benefit in April 1988 had been replaced by the review decision. This was rejected by the Commissioner who held that a decision refusing to revise did not alter the previous decision (applying para. 13 of *CSSB 540/1989*). In *CIS 788/1991* the AO had revised the original decision but limited payment of arrears to 12 months before the request for review under reg. 69, (now reg. 63) of the Ajudication Regulations. The Commissioner held that where a decision had only been partially revised the original decision was not superseded (see *CSSB 238/1989* and *R(P) 1/82*).

Both decisions were appealed. In *Chief Adjudication Officer v. Eggleton and Others* (March 17, 1995) (to be reported as *R(IS) 23/95*) the Court of Appeal dismissed the appeals. The Court holds that in *Eggleton* (and all the other cases except *James* (*CIS 788/1991*)) there had in fact been no review. Such evidence as there was (for example, specimen letters to the claimants following the request for a review) demonstrated a refusal to review (because of s. 69) rather than a review. But where there had been a review, as in *James*, the question of whether an original decision lapsed or was superseded when it was reviewed depended on the nature and the extent of the review. If the whole of the original decision was revised from the date on which it was made, there was nothing left of it and it therefore could not be appealed. But if it was only varied in part, or from a particular date, for example because revision was precluded after a certain date, the original decision subsided, save as affected by the review, and was thus susceptible to appeal (or late appeal: see the notes to reg. 3(3) of the Adjudication Regulations on late appeals). Similarly, where the power to revise was limited by s. 69, the original decision remained operative for the period prior to review. The Court disagreed with the opposite conclusion reached by the Court of Appeal in Northern Ireland in *Thompson v. DHSS* (September 8, 1993, unreported). The Court rejected the CAO's submission that the implication of s. 29 (review following appeal) was that decisions are superseded upon review. Moreover, it was noteworthy that there was no equivalent in the adjudication scheme for income support to s. 32(1). If it had been intended that an award on review replaced the award the subject of the review in the case of income support, a similar express provision to s. 32(1) would have been expected. The Court referred to *R(A) 5/89*, among other decisions, but pointed out that there were important differences between the adjudication schemes for income support and the benefits covered by ss. 30–35. The Court did not consider that there was any inconsistency between the reasoning in *R(A) 5/89* and its own conclusion.

The lack of distinction in the Court's judgment, at least in places, between review and revision on review is not very helpful. But the tenor of the judgment is clear. Where a review does not lead to revision, the effect is that the original decision remains in existence. But see below for discussion of the effect of what is now reg. 63 of the Adjudication Regulations.

Paragraphs (a) to (c)
These paragraphs cover the grounds of ignorance of or mistake as to a material fact and relevant change of circumstances. Past editions have distinguished the two as follows. Mistake or ignorance presupposes that the material fact existed at the date of the decision which someone wishes to review *(CIS 650/1991)*. Relevant change of circumstances requires that a material fact has changed since the date of that decision. But in *CSIS 83/1994* the Commissioner declines to follow *CIS 650/1991*. The facts in *CIS 650/1991* and *CSIS 83/1994* were virtually identical. The claimant in *CSIS 83/1994* had been in receipt of income support since 1991. He was awarded disability living allowance in September 1993, some 18 months after he first claimed it. When he asked for his income support to be reviewed to include a severe disability premium, the premium was only backdated for 12 months (see reg. 69, now reg. 63, of the Adjudication Regulations). The Commissioner decides that subs. (1)(a) grounds of review did exist and that reg. 64A(2)(c) (now reg. 57(2)(c)) applied to lift the 12-month limit under reg. 69. The adjudication officer's decision was made in ignorance of a material fact (the claimant's entitlement to disability living allowance from April 1992) which could not have been known until the decision awarding disability living allowance had been made. It did not matter that the fact did not "exist" at the time of the adjudication officer's original decision, since the concept of a fact was not restricted to a matter that already existed but could extend to factual consequence that occurred in the future (in this case entitlement to disability living allowance, once awarded, from the date of claim). Moreover, there was no reason for restricting this to the inevitable effects of facts already in existence, or known to exist. The Commissioner in effect seems to be saying that a decision may be reviewed under subs. (1)(a) if it *becomes* one given in ignorance of a material fact (in *CSIS 83/1994* the claim for disability living allowance was made some four months after income support was first awarded). A number of other Commissioners' decisions (e.g. *CSSB 16/1994* and *CM 936/1995*) declined to follow *CSIS 83/1994*, and on June 19, 1997 the Court of Session allowed the AO's appeal against this decision (*Chief Adjudication Officer v. Coombe*). The Court held that it was not possible for the AO to be ignorant of a fact that did not exist at the time of his decision. *R(1S) 14/94* contains a view to the same effect as *CSIS 83/1994*, but as that was a matter of assumption rather than argument it need not be followed. (See the note to reg. 57(2)(c) for further discussion on the backdating of a severe disability premium in these circumstances.)

For review under any of paras. (a) to (c) it is necessary to identify what is a material fact. The Commissioners have drawn a distinction between material facts and conclusions of fact (*e.g.* that a person is incapable of work, or is cohabiting). In *R(1) 3/75* (applied in *R(S) 4/86*) it is held that review is not allowed if the AO is simply satisfied that a mistaken inference was drawn from the evidence. He must go further and prove "that the inference might not have been drawn, or that a different inference might have been drawn, if the determining authority had not been ignorant of some specific fact of which it could have been aware, or had not been mistaken as to some specific fact which it took into consideration." This principle was also applied in *R(A) 2/81*. The Court of Appeal in *Saker v. Secretary of State for Social Services (R(1) 2/88)* has expressly decided that for a fact to be material it is not necessary that knowledge of it would have altered the decision. It is enough that the fact is one that would have called for serious consideration by the authority which made the decision and might well have affected its decision.

In *R(A) 2/90*, the Commissioner applied this approach to the question of when a change of circumstances is relevant. This throws doubt on decisions such as *R(I) 56/54* and *R(A) 4/81*, where it is said that the change of circumstances must make the original decision cease to be correct. This test may be too stringent, given the authority of *Saker*, but a reported decision would clarify this important area. *R(I) 56/54* has recently been applied in *CDLA 1715/1995*. It is accepted that merely obtaining a different medical opinion is not a change of circumstances, although it may be evidence of an underlying change *(R(S) 6/78, R(S) 4/86)*. A change in the law may amount to a change of circumstances *(R(A) 4/81* and *R(SB) 4/92)*, even if it operates retrospectively *(R(G) 3/58* and *Chief Adjudication Officer v. McKiernon*, CA, appendix to *R(I) 2/94)*, from the date of the change. The *McKiernon* case means that a retrospective change of law constitutes grounds for reviewing a decision of an AO, SSAT or Commissioner, even though the decision was correct given the law at the time it was made. Some other changes of circumstances, for instance a decision that a claimant has been entitled to another benefit from some past date, may also have a retrospective effect. However, the Court of Appeal in *McKiernon* considered that a court judgment declaring the law to be different from what had previously been supposed was probably not a relevant change of circumstances.

It is not clear quite how subs. (2) allowing review where a decision was erroneous in law affects the principles noted above. If a wrong inference is drawn from correct primary facts because the wrong legal test is applied, that is clearly an error of law. If no person properly directing himself as to the law could have drawn that inference from those primary facts, then that will be an error of law *(cf. R(A) 1/72, R(I) 14/75)*. But if the AO simply changes his mind about an "inference of fact" there has been no error of law. A retrospective change in the law will enable review under subs. (2) *(R(F) 1/95)*.

CIS 767/1994 confirms that a change of circumstances that is not operative until after the end of the period covered by a decision (in that case a decision disallowing benefit) is not a relevant change of circumstances. The claimant had been refused income support on the ground that his income exceeded his applicable amount in July 1991. Following the April 1992 uprating of benefit rates the claimant might have been entitled to income support but he did not make another claim for income support until June 1993. In July 1993 the claimant asked for the award of income support made in July 1993 to be backdated. The question arose as to whether that request could be treated as an application for review of the decision refusing income support in July 1991. It is held that since a disallowance of benefit will not, unless it expressly covers some definite period, be effective beyond the date it is made, the change in circumstances in April 1992 could not be relevant to the July 1991 decision.

Paragraph (d)

This paragraph applies where the income support etc. decision was based on a decision made by someone other than the AO, typically the Secretary of State. If that other decision is revised, the income support, etc., decision is to be reviewed and revised in line with it.

Paragraph (e)

These provisions of the Jobseekers Act deal with availability and actively seeking work in JSA.

Benefit payable on review

Regs. 63 and 63A of the Adjudication Regulations, as amended in April 1997, prevent any revision on review from making benefit payable or increasing the amount of income support or income-based JSA payable more than one month before the request for review. The predecessors of these provisions were originally introduced in response to the confirmation in *R(SB) 9/84* that the existing regulations did not impose any time limit on the review of decisions denying benefit or single payments. However, they are subject to reg. 57 (formerly reg. 64A, which from August 31, 1991, replaced the controversial reg. 72), allowing the one month limit to be lifted in deserving cases. *CSSB 470/1989* and *R(SB) 4/92* held that a SSAT should consider whether there are grounds for review of an identified decision and, if so, whether that decision should be revised, and from what date, before considering regs. 69 to 71 (now regs. 63 and 65 to 67) and reg. 72 or 64A (now reg. 57), particularly if the SSAT's decision is to alter past entitlement in some way. It may be that in exceptional cases, where it is plain that there can be no practical advantage to the claimant from a review and revision if the conditions of reg. 72 or 64A (now reg. 57) are not satisfied, for a SSAT to deal only with that point if it is adverse to the claimant *(CSB 56/1992)*. But as explained in *CIS*

714/1991, in the great majority of cases it is necessary first to identify any grounds for review and revision and it is desirable in all cases for SSATs to follow the logical chain of the regulations. It should be remembered that reg. 63 only prevents revision so as to make more benefit payable. It is possible that a claimant may derive a practical advantage from a revision of a decision to the effect that he is entitled to benefit or increased benefit, even if that benefit or increased benefit is not payable (*e.g.* a decision that a claimant was entitled to more supplementary benefit could affect his income support by means of a higher transitional addition). The Court of Appeal in *CAO v. Eggleton and Others* (see above) considered that where revision was precluded the original decision remained in existence (*i.e.* that any review was of no effect). But the Court did not expressly deal with the point that what is now reg. 63 only prevents revision so as to make more benefit payable.

See the more specific provisions limiting review for other income-related benefits in regs. 65 (family credit), 66 (DWA) and 67 (social fund) of the Adjudication Regulations.

Subsection (2)

Note that only AO decisions may be reviewed on the ground of error of law, not decisions of SSATs or the Commissioners. Otherwise the provisions on appeals would be undermined. See the notes to s.23 for "error of law". Review on this ground in income support and income-based JSA cases is subject to the restrictions of regs. 63 and 63A of the Adjudication Regulations, with the exemptions in reg. 57, and s.69. See notes to s.69 and in particular *Chief Adjudication Officer and Another v. Bate* [1996] 1 W.L.R. 814, [1996] 2 All E.R. 790, HL, discussed at the end of the notes.

This provision was first extended to "national insurance" benefits on April 23, 1984. *R(P) 1/85* decides that a decision relating to one of those benefits made before that date may subsequently be reviewed, but may not be revised. That was a case where the revision would have removed a claimant's entitlement, so that the principle probably does not apply where the revision would lead to entitlement or increased entitlement to benefit. However, a power to review supplementary benefit decisions for error of law existed from the beginning of the scheme (and appears also to have existed for national assistance). The principle of *R(P) 1/85* is therefore not a bar to review and revision of supplementary benefit and national assistance decisions for error of law. But see the notes to reg. 49 of the Claims and Payments Regulations.

Subsection (3)

No regulations have yet been made prescribing circumstances in which fresh evidence is required to trigger review.

Subsection (4)

Awards of family credit, which are normally made for a fixed period of 26 weeks, may not generally be reviewed on the ground of an actual or anticipated change of circumstances (see s.128(3) of the Contributions and Benefits Act).

Subsection (5)

There are special rules where there is review in advance of an anticipated change of circumstances under subs. (1)(c). The decision on review takes effect on the date identified by para. 7 of Sched. 7 to the Claims and Payments Regulations. There must be a further review if the change does not happen at all, or on a different date.

Procedure for reviews

26.—(1) A question may be raised with a view to a review under section 25 above by means of an application in writing to an adjudication officer, stating the grounds of the application.

(2) On receipt of any such application, the adjudication officer shall proceed to deal with or refer any question arising on it in accordance with sections 21 to 23 above.

(3) Regulations may provide for enabling, or requiring, in prescribed circumstances, a review under section 25 above notwithstanding that no application for a review has been made under subsection (1) above.

Derivation

Social Security Act 1975, s.104(2) to (3A).

Subsection (1)

Although this provides a useful procedure, it is not compulsory (*CSB 336/1987*). On general principle review should occur at any time if the AO is satisfied that the conditions are met, wherever the evidence comes from. But doubt was cast on this conclusion by the introduction of the predecessor of subs. (3) in 1987, after the time relevant to *CSB 336/1987*. In the Common Appendix to the group of decisions including *CSSB 281/1989*, the Commissioner suggests that the duty is on the Secretary of State to submit in writing to the AO any requests for review received, in whatever form, from claimants.

CSSB 290/1997 holds that notwithstanding the absence of any express restriction in subs. (1) as to who may apply for a review, the claimant, as executrix of her late husband, had no locus to apply for a review of his supplementary benefit claim because there was no debt due to the deceased at the date of his death. The right to seek a review "died with the claimant", unless it could be demonstrated that the social security "debt" was established at the date of death.

Subsection (3)

This power is only doubtfully necessary (see notes to subs. (1)).

Reviews under s.25—supplementary

27.—(1) Regulations—
  (a) may prescribe what are, or are not, relevant changes of circumstances for the purposes of section 25 above; and
  (b) may make provision restricting the payment of any benefit, or any increase of benefit, to which a person would, but for this subsection, be entitled by reason of review in respect of any period before or after the review (whether that period falls wholly or partly before or after the making of the regulations).
  (2) [*Omitted as not applying to income-related benefits*]

DEFINITION

Social Security Act 1975, s.104(5).

DEFINITION

"prescribe"—see s.191.

GENERAL NOTE

On para. (a), see regs. 51 and 51A of the Family Credit (General) Regulations, regs. 56 and 56A of the Disability Working Allowance (General) Regulations and reg. 63(5) to (10) and reg. 64 of the Adjudication Regulations. On para. (b) see regs. 63 and 63A and 65 to 67 of the Adjudication Regulations.

Appeals following reviews or refusals to review

28. A decision given on a review under section 25 above, and a refusal to review a decision under that section, shall be subject to appeal in like manner as an original decision, and sections 21 to 23 above shall, with the necessary modifications, apply in relation to a decision given on such a review as they apply to the original decision of a question.

DERIVATION

Social Security Act 1975, s.104(4).

GENERAL NOTE

The ordinary rights to appeal arise from a revised decision given on review or a refusal to review. This can be a useful way of getting round the time limits on appealing from an AO's decision (although the severe restrictions on payment of arrears on review in the April 1997 amendments to the Adjudication Regulations and the effect of s. 69 have reduced the potential benefits sharply). A request to review the decision will, if it does not produce all that the claimant wants, generate a fresh right of appeal.

In *CIS 354/1994* the claimant's housing costs had been restricted under what was then para. 10(4) (now see para. 13) of Sched. 3 to the Income Support Regulations. He appealed against an AO's decision on review amending the calculation of his housing costs. It is held that the AO's review decision implied a continuance of the restriction and so opened up all the questions involved in the calculation of the claimant's housing costs, including whether the restriction had been properly imposed initially.

Review after claimant appeals

29. Where a claimant has appealed against a decision of an adjudication officer and the decision is reviewed by an adjudication officer under section 25 above—

    (a) if the adjudication officer considers that the decision which he has made on the review is the same as the decision that would have been made on the appeal had every ground of the claimant's appeal succeeded, then the appeal shall lapse; but

    (b) in any other case, the review shall be of no effect and the appeal shall proceed accordingly.

DERIVATION

Social Security Act 1975, s.104(3B).

GENERAL NOTE

The predecessor of this provision made an important change in the relationship between review and appeals. Previously, it was established, at least in relation to some types of decision, that if a decision was reviewed it ceased to exist, being replaced by the decision made on review *(R(SB) 1/82, R(SB) 15/87)*. The effect was that any appeal already lodged against the original decision would "lapse," because there was nothing left for the appeal to bite on *(R(A) 5/89*, which contains an authoritative review of all the earlier decisions). It is now clear from *CSSB 238/1989* that this only applies to decisions which are in their nature indivisible, like decisions that an overpayment is recoverable *(R(SB) 15/87)* or attendance allowance decisions reviewed in what is effectively the first stage of the appeal process *(R(A) 5/89)*. In other cases, a review of one element of a decision leaves the rest of it intact *(R(P) 1/82*, para. 3). Commissioners had in any event been able to get round the inconvenient effects of this principle in some circumstances, by treating the appeal as against the revised decision although no notice of appeal had been given *(R(SB) 15/87)*. The suggestion in *R(SB) 1/82*, that if an appeal had been lodged a decision should not be reviewed unless the revised decision gave the claimant everything that could have been obtained in the appeal, was only patchily applied.

Now, for reviews after April 5, 1990, if there is an appeal pending from an AO decision, a review is only of effect if the AO considers that the revised decision is the same as would have been made if every ground of the claimant's appeal had succeeded. In this case, but no other, the appeal lapses. This effect turns on the AO's opinion, but, as a matter of general principle, if the claimant disputes that the revised decision is the same as if every ground of the appeal had succeeded, the issue ought to go to the SSAT in the original appeal, although the amendment to what was reg. 24(1) (now reg. 22(1)) of the Adjudication Regulations suggests otherwise. Note that the grounds set out in the claimant's appeal are the crucial elements, not further arguments which might be raised against the AO's decision (see reg. 3(5) of the Adjudication Regulations).

Note also that s.29 only applies to reviews of AO decisions, not to reviews of SSAT or Commissioners' decisions.

This provision will change under the new system for decision-making and appeals. The test for whether an appeal lapses will become whether the revised decision is more advantageous to the appellant (reg. 30 of the Social Security and Child Support (Decisions and Appeals) Regulations 1999 (S.I. 1999 No. 991). See the 1999 Supplement to this book for further details.

Attendance allowance, disability living allowance and disability working allowance

Reviews of decisions of adjudication officers

30.—(1) On an application under this section made within the prescribed period, a decision of an adjudication officer under section 21 above which relates to an attendance allowance, a disability living allowance or a disability working allowance may be reviewed on any ground subject, in the case of disability working allowance, to section 129(6) of the Contributions and Benefits Act.

(2) to (4) [*Omitted as not applying to disability working allowance*]

(5) On an application under this section made after the end of the prescribed period, a decision of an adjudication officer under section 21 above which relates to a disability working allowance may be reviewed if—

(a) the adjudication officer is satisfied that the decision was given in ignorance of, or was based on a mistake as to, some material fact; or

(b) subject to section 129(6) of the Contributions and Benefits Act, there has been any prescribed change of circumstances since the decision was given; or

(c) the decision was erroneous in point of law; or

(d) the decision was to make an award for a period wholly or partly after the date on which the claim was made or treated as made but subject to a condition being fulfilled and that condition has not been fulfilled,

but regulations may provide that a decision may not be reviewed on the ground mentioned in paragraph (a) above unless the officer is satisfied as mentioned in that paragraph by fresh evidence.

(6) The claimant shall be given such notification as may be prescribed of a decision which may be reviewed under this section and of his right to a review under subsection (1) above.

(7) A question may be raised with a view to a review under this section by means of an application made in writing to an adjudication officer stating the grounds of the application and supplying such information and evidence as may be prescribed.

[¹ (7A) The Secretary of State may undertake investigations to obtain information and evidence for the purposes of making applications under subsection (7) above.]

(8) Regulations—

(a) may provide for enabling, or requiring, in prescribed circumstances, a review under this section notwithstanding that no application under subsection (7) above has been made; and

(b) if they do so provide, shall specify under which provision of this section a review carried out by virtue of any such regulations falls.

(9) Reviews under this section shall be carried out by adjudication officers.

(10) Different aspects of any question which arises on such a review may be dealt with by different adjudication officers; and for this purpose this section and the other provisions of this Part of this Act which relate to reviews under this section shall apply with any necessary modifications.

(11) If a review is under subsection (1) above, the officer who took the decision under review shall not deal with any question which arises on the review.

(12) [*Omitted as not applying to disability working allowance*]

(13) Where—

(a) a claim for an attendance allowance, a disability living allowance or a disability working allowance in respect of a person has been refused; and

   (b) a further claim for the same allowance is made in respect of him within the period prescribed under subsection (1) above,

the further claim shall be treated as an application for a review under that subsection.

DERIVATION

   Subs. (1): Social Security Act 1975, s.100A(1).
   Subs. (5): 1975 Act, s.100A(2) and (3).
   Subss. (6) to (13): 1975 Act, s.100A(5) to (12).

AMENDMENT

   1. Social Security Administration (Fraud) Act 1997, s. 17(1) (July 1, 1997).

DEFINITIONS

   "the Contributions and Benefits Act"—see s.191.
   "prescribed"—*ibid.*

GENERAL NOTE

   Note that under the Social Security Act 1998 the rules relating to reviews of disability living allowance, attendance allowance and disability working allowance will be harmonised with other benefits, although special provisions will apply to the effective date of revision and supersession.

   Section 30 deals with two types of review in disability working allowance cases. The first, under subs. (1), is review as the first stage of appeal against the initial AO's decision. The second, under subs. (5), is the "ordinary" review, but on slightly more restricted grounds than provided in s.25(1).

Subsection (1)
   There is no provision in the legislation for an appeal from the initial decision of an AO under s.21 on a disability working allowance claim. Therefore, a claimant dissatisfied with the initial decision must apply for a review under this provision. The application must be made within the prescribed period. *i.e.* three months from the date on which notice of the AO's decision was given (Adjudication Regulations, reg. 25). It seems that because review can only be considered "on an application under this section," the claimant must make an application and it must, under subs. (7), be made in writing to an AO. Although the words of subs. (7) are merely permissive, the words of subs. (1) seem to produce a different result to those of s.26(1). This is unfortunate, because review on specified grounds under subs. (5) is not available until after the end of the prescribed period unless there has already been a review under subs. (1). If, for instance, an AO notices just after an initial decision has been issued to the claimant that there has been an error of law, it appears that the decision cannot be reviewed unless the AO invites the claimant to apply for a review. Possibly an application could be made to the AO by a person acting on behalf of the Secretary of State.
   Once an application has been made, review may be on any ground. This obviously covers mistake or ignorance of material facts as at the date of the decision or an error of law. But it can also cover a difference of opinion as to what conclusion to draw from the material facts, and changes of circumstances after the date of the decision. However, note that if the AO has made an award of disability working allowance, there can be no review on the basis of a change of circumstances (Contributions and Benefits Act, s. 129(6)). It also used to be the case that if the AO's initial decision was not to make an award, any revised decision on review under subs. (1) could only take effect from the date of the application for review (see the previous form of reg. 66(1) of the Adjudication Regulations in the 1996 edition of this book). This rule seemed completely wrong if review is the first stage of the appeal process and it reveals that the decision has been mistaken from the outset, but was clearly set out in the regulations. But it now only applies if after a decision refusing an award, a claimant makes a new *claim* during the prescribed period. See subs. (13) which treats such a claim as an application for review under subs. (1). See the notes to reg. 66(1) for more details.

The review is to be carried out by a different AO to the AO who made the initial decision (subss. (9) and (11)). The claimant has a right of appeal to a tribunal under s.33(1).

Subsection (5)

See the notes to subs. (1) for the argument that the opening words of this subsection mean that an application in writing to the AO is necessary before review can be considered. The argument that an application can be made on behalf of the Secretary of State is much stronger here, otherwise there would be no way of reviewing an award wrongly made to a claimant.

Normally an application under subs. (5) has to be made after the end of the prescribed period of three months from the date on which notice of the AO's initial decision was given (Adjudication Regulations, reg. 25(1)). But if there has been a decision on review under subs. (1), whether favourable or unfavourable to the claimant, then an application under subs. (5) can be made at any time to review that decision (s.31(1)).

See the notes to s.25(1)(a) and (b) and (2) for review under paras. (a), (b), and (c). Section 129(6) of the Contributions and Benefits Act prevents review of an award of disability working allowance, or of the level of benefit, on the ground of change of circumstances, except where regulations prescribe otherwise. No regulations have been made requiring fresh evidence to be produced for para. (a), but see reg. 66(2) of the Adjudication Regulations.

Para. (d) is roughly equivalent to reg. 17(4) of the Claims and Payments Regulations, which appears to apply a condition to awards of benefit including disability working allowance, but clearly para. (d) creates an independent ground of review.

If a person is dissatisfied with a refusal to review or a decision on review, then there must be an application for a further review under the conditions of subs. (1) before there can be an appeal to a tribunal (s.31(2)).

Subsection (6)

Separate provision needs to be made for requiring notice of initial disability working allowance decisions and the right to apply for review under subs. (1) because of the exclusion in s.22(1).

Subsection (7)

This subsection only says that review "may" be started by an application in writing to an AO, but the wording of subss. (1) and (5) seems to require there to be such an application. In the ordinary case the application will be made by the claimant, but if circumstances showing that a ground for review has arisen come to the DSS's attention a person acting on behalf of the Secretary of State should make an application to the AO. Otherwise, there is no way of reviewing a decision based on a misrepresentation or failure to disclose material facts by the claimant. The principle should hold where the review would be in favour of the claimant.

No regulations have been made specifying any particular information or evidence to be supplied with the application.

Subsection (8)

No regulations have been made under subs. (8).

Subsections (9) to (11)

Applications for review must be decided initially by an AO. There is no power for the AO to refer a question to a tribunal (*cf.* s.21(3)).

Where the review is under subs. (1) the AO who carries out the review must be a different person from the AO who made the initial decision.

Subsection (13)

If an AO's decision is to refuse the claim and another claim is made within the prescribed period (three months from the date of notice of the AO's decision: Adjudication Regulations, reg. 25(1)), the claim is to be treated as an application for review under subs. (1). The first claim is then to be treated as having been made on the date of the second claim (Claims and Payments Regulations, reg. 6(11)). In any case any award made on the review could only take effect from that date (Adjudication Regulations, reg. 66(1)).

Further reviews

31.—(1) Subsections (2), (4) and (5) of section 30 above shall apply to a decision on a review under subsection (1) of that section as they apply to a decision of an adjudication officer under section 21 above but as if the words "made after the end of the prescribed period" were omitted from each subsection.

(2) Subsections (1), (2), (4) and (5) of section 30 above shall apply—

   (a) to a decision on a review under subsection (2), (4) or (5) of that section; and

   (b) to a refusal to review a decision under subsection (2), (4) or (5) of that section,

as they apply to a decision of an adjudication officer under section 21 above.

(3) The claimant shall be given such notification as may be prescribed—

   (a) of a decision on a review under section 30 above;

   (b) if the review was under section 30(1), of his right of appeal under section 33 below; and

   (c) if it was under section 30(2), (4) or (5), of his right to a further review under section 30(1).

DERIVATION

Social Security Act 1975, s.100B.

DEFINITION

"prescribed"—see s.191.

GENERAL NOTE

Subsection (1)
A decision on a review under s.30(1) may be reviewed as if it was an initial decision by an AO, but with no need to wait the prescribed three months.

Subsection (2)
If a person wishes to challenge a refusal to review under s.30(5) (s.30(2) and (4) only apply to disability living allowance and attendance allowance), there must first be an application for further review under s.30(1) before there can be an appeal to a tribunal.

Subsection (3)
Notice must be given to the claimant of all decisions on review under s.30 (which must include a refusal to review under s.30(5)) and of the appropriate rights of appeal or further review (Adjudication Regulations, reg. 18(1)). Separate provision is necessary because of the exclusion in s.22(1).

Reviews of decisions as to attendance allowance, disability living allowance or disability working allowance—supplementary

32.—(1) An award of an attendance allowance, a disability living allowance or a disability working allowance on a review under section 30 above replaces any award which was the subject of the review.

(2)–(6) [*Omitted as not applying to disability working allowance*]

(7) Where a claimant has appealed against a decision of an adjudication officer under section 33 below and the decision is reviewed again under section 30(2), (4) or (5) above by an adjudication officer, then—

   (a) if the adjudication officer considers that the decision which he has made on the review is the same as the decision that would have been made on the appeal had every ground of the appeal succeeded, then the appeal shall lapse; but

   (b) in any other case, the review shall be of no effect and the appeal shall proceed accordingly.

(8) Regulations may make provision restricting the payment of any benefit, or any increase of benefit, to which a person would, but for this subsection, be

entitled by reason of a review in respect of any period before or after the review (whether that period falls wholly or partly before or after the making of the regulations).

(9) Where an adjudication officer has determined that any amount paid by way of an attendance allowance, a disability living allowance or a disability working allowance is recoverable under or by virtue of section 71 below, any person from whom he has determined that it is recoverable shall have the same right of review under section 30 above as a claimant.

(10) This Act and the Contributions and Benefits Act shall have effect in relation to a review by virtue of subsection (9) above as if any reference to the claimant were a reference to a person from whom the adjudication officer has determined that the amount in question is recoverable.

DERIVATION

Subs. (1): Social Security Act 1975, s.100C(1).
Subss. (6) to (10): 1975 Act, s.100C(6) to (10).

DEFINITIONS

"the Contributions and Benefits Act"—see s.191.
"prescribed"—*ibid.*

GENERAL NOTE

Subsection (1)
Note the changes to reg. 66(1) of the Adjudication Regulations made on April 8, 1997 as to the date from which a replacement award of disability working allowance on review can take effect.

Subsection (7)
See notes to s.29.

Subsection (8)
See reg. 66(2) of the Adjudication Regulations.

Subsections (9) and (10)
Where an AO has decided that an overpayment of disability working allowance has been made and is recoverable under s.71, the review and appeal process is the same as for an initial claim.

Appeals following reviews

33.—(1) Where an adjudication officer has given a decision on a review under section 30(1) above, the claimant or such other person as may be prescribed may appeal—

  (a) in prescribed cases, to a disability appeal tribunal; and

  (b) in any other case, to a social security appeal tribunal.

(2) Regulations may make provision as to the manner in which, and the time within which, appeals are to be brought.

(3) An award on an appeal under this section replaces any award which was the subject of the appeal.

(4)–(6) [*Omitted as not applying to disability working allowance*]

[¹(7) The tribunal shall not take into account any circumstances not obtaining at the time when the decision appealed against was made.]

DERIVATION

Social Security Act 1975, s.100D.

AMENDMENT

1. Social Security Act 1998, Sched. 6, para. 3(2) (May 21, 1998). This amendment applies from May 21, 1998 until s.12(8)(b) of the 1998 Act comes into force.

DEFINITION

"prescribed"—see s.191.

GENERAL NOTE

Subsection (1)
Where there has been a second tier review under s.30(1) following an initial decision on disability working allowance by an AO the claimant may appeal to a tribunal. The effect of paras. (a) and (b) seems to be that if appeal to a disability appeal tribunal (DAT) is possible, that is where the appeal must go. It is only where appeal to the DAT is not possible that the appeal goes to the SSAT. Reg. 27(1) of the Adjudication Regulations prescribes that the claimant may appeal to the DAT where either a disability question or both a disability question and any other question relating to disability working allowance arises. A disability question for this purpose is whether a person has a physical or mental disability which puts him at a disadvantage in getting a job (Contributions and Benefits Act, s.129(1)(b) and Sched. 1 to the Disability Working Allowance (General) Regulations). Thus a SSAT may never consider a disability question, since if such a question first arises in the course of an appeal properly made to a SSAT, the SSAT cannot deal with it (s.36(2)). But a DAT has to consider all the conditions of entitlement to disability working allowance if a disability question arises along with other matters.
The merger of SSATs and DATS into unified appeal tribunals under the Social Security Act 1998 should obviate these jurisdictional questions (see the note to s.40).

Subsection (2)
See Sched. 2 to the Adjudication Regulations.

Subsection (7)
This subsection, inserted by Sched. 6 to the Social Security Act 1998 with effect from May 21, 1998, is one of the transitional provisions that will apply until the new system of decision-making and adjudication under the 1998 Act comes into operation. It applies in relation to appeals brought on or after May 21, 1998. See the notes to s.22(8) and President's Circular No. 15.

Appeal from social security appeal tribunals or disability appeal tribunals to Commissioners and appeals from Commissioners

34.—(1) Subject to the provisions of this section, an appeal lies to a Commissioner from any decision of a social security appeal tribunal or disability appeal tribunal under section 33 above on the ground that the decision of the tribunal was erroneous in point of law.
(2) An appeal lies under this section at the instance of any of the following—
(a) an adjudication officer;
(b) the claimant;
(c) a trade union—
 (i) where the claimant is a member of the union at the time of the appeal and was so immediately before the question at issue arose;
 (ii) where that question in any way relates to a deceased person who was a member of the union at the time of his death; and
(d) a person from whom it is determined that any amount is recoverable under section 71(1) below.
(3) Subsection (2) above, as it applies to a trade union, applies also to any other association which exists to promote the interests and welfare of its members.
(4) Subsections [¹(6A) to (10) of section 23] above have effect for the purposes of this section as they have effect for the purposes of that section.

(5) Section 24 above applies to a decision of a Commissioner under this section as it applies to a decision of a Commissioner under section 23 above.

DERIVATION

Subss. (1) to (3): Social Security Act 1975, s.101(1) to (4).

AMENDMENT

1. Social Security Act 1998, Sched. 6, para. 4(2) (May 21, 1998). This amendment applies from May 21, 1998 until s.14(7) of the 1998 Act comes into force.

DEFINITION

"Commissioner"—see s.191.

GENERAL NOTE

Subsection (1)
See notes to s.23(1).

Subsections (2) and (3)
See notes to s.23(3), (5) and (6).

Subsection (4)
See notes to s.23(6A) to (10).

Subsection (5)
See notes to s.24. Subs. (5) is probably redundant as s.24 was finally drafted.

Reviews of decisions on appeal

35.—(1) and (2) [*Omitted as not relating to disability working allowance*]
(3) Any decision under this Act of a social security appeal tribunal, a disability appeal tribunal or a Commissioner which relates to a disability working allowance may be reviewed at any time by an adjudication officer if—
  (a) he is satisfied that the decision was given in ignorance of, or was based on a mistake as to, some material fact; or
  (b) subject to section 129(7) of the Contributions and Benefits Act, there has been any prescribed change of circumstances since the decision was given; or
  (c) the decision was to make an award for a period wholly or partly after the date on which the claim was made or treated as made but subject to a condition being fulfilled and that condition has not been fulfilled,
but regulations may provide that a decision may not be reviewed on the ground mentioned in paragraph (a) above unless the officer is satisfied as mentioned in that paragraph by fresh evidence.
(4) A question may be raised with a view to a review under this section by means of an application made in writing to an adjudication officer stating the grounds of the application and supplying such information and evidence as may be prescribed.
(5) Regulations may provide for enabling or requiring, in prescribed circumstances, a review under this section notwithstanding that no application for a review has been made under subsection (4) above.
(6) Reviews under this section shall be carried out by adjudication officers.
(7) [*Omitted as not applying to disability working allowance*]
(8) Subsections (1), (2), (4) and (5) of section 30 above shall apply—
  (a) to a decision on a review under this section; and

(b) to a refusal to review a decision such as is mentioned in subsection (1) above,

as they apply to a decision of an adjudication officer under section 21 above.

(9) The person whose claim was the subject of the appeal the decision on which has been reviewed under this section shall be given such notification as may be prescribed—

(a) of the decision on the review; and

(b) of his right to a further review under section 30(1) above.

(10) Regulations may make provision restricting the payment of any benefit, or any increase of benefit, to which a person would, but for this subsection, be entitled by reason of a review in respect of any period before or after the review (whether that period falls wholly or partly before or after the making of the regulations).

(11) [*Omitted as not applying to disability working allowance*]

(12) Section 30(10) above and section 32(1) to (5) above shall apply in relation to a review under this section as they apply to a review under section 30 above.

DERIVATION

Subss. (3) and (4): Social Security Act 1975, s.104A(1) to (3).
Subs. (5): 1975 Act, s.104(3A).
Subs. (6): 1975 Act, s.104A(4).
Subss. (8) and (9): 1975 Act, s.104A(6) and (7).
Subs. (10): 1975 Act, s.104(5)(b).
Subs. (11): 1975 Act, s.104(1ZA).
Subs. (12): 1975 Act, s.104A(8).

DEFINITIONS

"Commissioner"—see s.191.
"the Contributions and Benefits Act"—*ibid.*
"prescribed"—*ibid.*

GENERAL NOTE

Subsection (3)

See the notes to s.30(5). A decision of a SSAT, a DAT or a Commissioner cannot be reviewed as being erroneous in point of law, otherwise the appeal process would be subverted. To make sense, the reference in para. (b) should be to s.129(6) of the Contributions and Benefits Act. See regs. 56 and 56A of the Disability Working Allowance (General) Regulations.

Note that review under subs. (3) does not have to be "on an application made under this section." Therefore it seems that an application under subs. (4) is just one way of raising the question of review and that an AO can carry out a review without an application having been made.

Subsections (4) and (5)

See notes to s.26(1) and (3). No regulations have been made under this subsection prescribing any information to be provided.

Subsection (8)

If the claimant is dissatisfied with the decision on a review under this section he must apply for a further review under s.30(1) before he can appeal to a tribunal.

Questions first arising on appeal

Questions first arising on appeal

36.—(1) Where a question which but for this section would fall to be determined by an adjudication officer first arises in the course of an appeal to a social security appeal tribunal, a disability appeal tribunal or a Commissioner, the tribunal, subject to subsection (2) below, or the Commissioner may, if they or he think fit, proceed to determine the question notwithstanding that it has not been considered by an adjudication officer.

(2) A social security appeal tribunal may not determine a question by virtue of subsection (1) above if an appeal in relation to such a question would have lain to a disability appeal tribunal.

DERIVATION

Social Security Act 1975, s.102.

DEFINITION

"Commissioner"—see s.191.

GENERAL NOTE

Subsection (1)

A provision in similar terms to this had existed for some time for benefits falling directly under the 1975 Act. The extension to social fund, supplementary benefit and FIS cases raised problems. Before April 6, 1987, the SSAT's powers in supplementary benefit and FIS cases were defined in reg. 71 of the 1984 Adjudication Regulations. In a number of decisions (see the notes to reg. 71(2) in the 1986 edition of this book for details) the Commissioners held that the SSAT could only deal with matters "within the purview of the original claim" *(R(SB) 9/81)*. While there was only one claim for the whole of weekly supplementary benefit, there were separate claims for each item for which a single payment was claimed *(R(SB) 42/83)*. Thus, on an appeal from a refusal of a single payment the SSAT could not make a decision about the rate of weekly benefit, unless exceptionally the original claim could be said to cover both a single payment claim and a request to review weekly benefit. Several decisions commented that there was nothing in the supplementary benefit legislation corresponding to s.102 of the 1975 Act *(R(SB) 1/82, R(SB) 14/82, R(SB) 42/83)*.

Section 36 then replaced s.102 of the 1975 Act and does apply in income support, income-based JSA, family credit and disability working allowance cases. What is its effect? It might at first sight appear to allow a SSAT or Commissioner to go outside the purview of the original claim, although there is little scope for this under the new regulations. However, s.36 only applies to questions which arise in the course of an appeal. This does not mean in the course of the hearing of the appeal *(CS 101/1986)*. The question must be connected with whatever question is properly before the SSAT in the appeal. In *CIS 807/1992* the claimant asked for a review of her supplementary benefit entitlement. The AO never made a decision on this application but the matter reached a SSAT as the claimant had appealed against another decision in connection with her income support. The SSAT assumed jurisdiction in reliance on s.102(1) of the Social Security Act 1975 (now s.36(1)). The Commissioner holds that the question of the claimant's entitlement to additional supplementary benefit had not first arisen "in the course of an appeal" but in connection with a request for a review. There was no appeal in the course of which it could first arise as there had been no initial adjudication. The SSAT's decision was made without authority and was of no effect. The Commissioner also states that "considered" in subs. (1) means "fully considered". As the AO had not reached a decision on the claimant's request for a review of her supplementary benefit he had not "considered" it within subs. (1). *CS 104/1987* confirms that s.36 can only be invoked where the question *first* arises in the course of an appeal. Thus if an AO has decided a question, from which decision no appeal has been made, the SSAT cannot deal with that question under s.36 as it does not first arise in the course of the appeal. The suggestion in *CS 101/1986* that the section could be used where a question might have been referred to the SSAT, but was not, must then be restricted to cases where the AO has not made a decision on that question.

But there is growing support for giving a wide scope to s.36. In two recent decisions Commissioners have held that SSATs should consider issues of review beyond the scope of the original application. In *R(IS) 11/93* review was sought from 1979. Before the SSAT the period from 1973 was raised and dealt with. That was held to be proper. In *CIS 303/1992* (to be reported as *R(IS) 15/93*) a review of housing costs for mortgage interest by the AO was in issue. Before the SSAT the claimant argued that her housing costs should no longer be restricted. It was held that the SSAT was wrong to refuse to consider that point. See also *CSB 1272/1989* (notes to s.71(5)).

In addition, there are two controls. First, the SSAT has a discretion to decide the new question. It may consider the argument that when the only appeal from the SSAT is on the ground of error of law, the claimant may be deprived of a stage in the appeal process if the SSAT, rather than the AO, makes an initial decision. But in *CIS 21/1993* the Commissioner says that where the new question is clearly tied to the matter in front of the tribunal, it should determine it under subs. (1), or ensure that the AO will consider it. The Commissioner states: ''this is an inquisitorial jurisdiction and it is full of procedural pitfalls. Claimants cannot be expected to take the right points and s.36 exists to introduce some flexibility in the interests of justice''. Second, the principles of natural justice would require that a SSAT should not make a decision on a new point if all parties have not had a fair opportunity of dealing with it *(R(F) 1/72)*.

The power under s.36 applies to Commissioners as well as SSATs.

Subsection (2)

If a SSAT is hearing a disability working allowance appeal and a question arises for the first time about whether the claimant satisfies the condition in s.129(1)(b) of the Contributions and Benefits Act (physical or mental disability which puts the claimant at a disadvantage in getting a job), then the SSAT cannot deal with that question. If there is such a disability question (with or without some other point in dispute) when an appeal is made, the whole appeal goes to the DAT (s.33(1) and Adjudication Regulations, reg. 27). But it appears that if an appeal has properly gone to the SSAT before the disability question first arises, then the SSAT should continue to deal with the questions raised in the original appeal. By definition, the disability question must have been decided by the AO under s.30(1) in the claimant's favour, otherwise the appeal would already be before the DAT. If something comes to light in the SSAT appeal which casts doubt on that, but the SSAT determines all the other questions in the claimant's favour, there is a difficult question on the SSAT's proper course of action. Should it make an award of disability working allowance, and leave the AO to review that award under s.35(3), or simply determine the questions before it and leave the AO to review the disability question? On balance, the first alternative seems more in line with the scheme of the legislation.

Reference of special questions

Reference of special questions

37.—(1) Subject to subsection (2) below—
  (a) if on consideration of any claim or question an adjudication officer is of opinion that there arises any question which under or by virtue of this Act falls to be determined otherwise than by an adjudication officer, he shall refer the question for such determination; and
  (b) if on consideration of any claim or question a social security appeal tribunal or Commissioner is of opinion that any such question arises, the tribunal or Commissioner shall direct it to be referred by an adjudication officer for such determination.
(2) The person or tribunal making or directing the reference shall then deal with any other question as if the referred question had not arisen.
(3) The adjudication officer, tribunal or Commissioner may—
  (a) postpone the reference of, or dealing with, any question until other questions have been determined;
  (b) in cases where the determination of any question disposes of a claim or any part of it, make an award or decide that an award cannot be made, as to the claim or that part of it, without referring or dealing with, or before the determination of, any other question.

DERIVATION

Social Security Act 1975, s.103.

Adjudication officers and the Chief Adjudication Officer

Adjudication officers

38.—(1) Adjudication officers shall be appointed by the Secretary of State, subject to the consent of the Treasury as to number, and may include—

(a) officers of the Department of Employment appointed with the concurrence of the Secretary of State in charge of that Department; or

(b) officers of the Northern Ireland Department appointed with the concurrence of that Department.

(2) An adjudication officer may be appointed to perform all the functions of adjudication officers under any enactment or such functions of such officers as may be specified in his instrument of appointment.

DERIVATION

Social Security Act 1975, s.97(1) and (1A).

DEFINITION

"the Northern Ireland Department"—see s.191.

GENERAL NOTE

Note that under the Social Security Act 1998 the functions exercised by AOs will in future be exercised by the Secretary of State. See the 1999 Supplement to this book for further details.

Subsection (1)
The Secretary of State is not obliged to appoint enough AOs to dispose of all claims submitted to them within 14 days under s.21(1) (*R. v. Secretary of State for Social Services, ex parte CPAG* [1990] 2 Q.B. 540).

Subsection (2)
The current instrument of appointment was signed on behalf of the Secretary of State on March 25, 1996, and is reproduced as Appendix 1 to Part 01 of the *Adjudication Officer's Guide*. It directs that all persons appointed shall carry out all the functions of AOs. In practice, most AOs will deal with only a limited number of benefits, but will formally have the power to carry out any AO function.

See reg. 56 of the Adjudication Regulations for the consequences of the limited practical range of expertise of individual AOs.

The Chief Adjudication Officer

39.—(1) The Secretary of State shall appoint a Chief Adjudication Officer.

(2) It shall be the duty of the Chief Adjudication Officer to advice adjudication officers on the performance of their functions under this or any other Act.

(3) The Chief Adjudication Officer shall keep under review the operation of the system of adjudication by adjudication officers and matters connected with the operation of that system.

(4) The Chief Adjudication Officer shall report annually in writing to the Secretary of State on the standards of adjudication and the Secretary of State shall publish his report.

DERIVATION

Social Security Act 1975, s.97(IB) to (IE).

GENERAL NOTE

The Chief Adjudication Officer combines the functions of the former Chief Insurance Officer and the Chief Supplementary Benefit Officer. But his advisory duties were given statutory expression for the first time in 1984. The duty to report publicly on standards of adjudication was also new. The CAO's first report was published in 1986. This and the subsequent annual reports contain much interesting and critical material. The more recent reports contain fascinating material on the relationship of the adjudication system with the Benefits Agency.

The office of the Chief Adjudication Officer disappears under the provisions of the Social Security

Act 1998. The responsibility for reporting on standards of adjudication is partly inherited by the President of Appeal Tribunals, who is required by Sched. 1, para. 10 to the Act to provide to the Secretary of State an annual report based on the cases coming before the tribunals on the standards achieved by the Secretary of State in the making of decisions against which an appeal lies. The Secretary of State is required to publish the President's report.

Social security appeal tribunals

Panels for appointment to social security appeal tribunals

40.—(1) The President shall constitute for the whole of Great Britain, to act for such areas as he thinks fit and be composed of such persons as he thinks fit to appoint, panels of persons to act as members of social security appeal tribunals.

(2) The panel for an area shall be composed of persons appearing to the President to have knowledge or experience of conditions in the area and to be representative of persons living or working in the area.

(3) Before appointing members of a panel, the President shall take into consideration any recommendations from such organisations or persons as he considers appropriate.

(4) The members of the panels shall hold office for such period as the President may direct, but the President may at any time terminate the appointment of any member of a panel.

DERIVATION

Social Security Act 1975, Sched. 10, para. 1(1) to (6).

DEFINITION

"President"—see s.191.

GENERAL NOTE

The President of Social Security Appeal Tribunals etc. is to appoint members to a national panel and assign them to particular areas.

There is now one panel of members. The temporary survival after April 1984 of the two panels left over from the old supplementary benefit appeal tribunals and national insurance local tribunals, conceded in order to get the Health and Social Services and Social Security Adjudications Act 1983 through Parliament before the 1983 General Election, came to an end on September 26, 1984. This was in fulfilment of the Government's original intention.

The test for appointment under subs. (2) is a dual one. The member must have knowledge or experience of conditions in the area to which the appointment applies and be representative of persons living or working in the area. The first part seems to be a watered down version of the old SBAT test for "Secretary of State's" members, omitting the requirement of knowledge or experience of the problems of people living on low incomes. This requirement was presumably thought inappropriate to the wider jurisdiction of the SSAT, but it is a pity that it should be lost altogether. It is far from clear what the "representative" test requires. The intention apparently is that the range of organisations consulted about membership under subs. (3) should be widened out from Trade Councils, Chambers of Commerce, etc., to include groups representing ethnic minorities, the disabled, one-parent families, etc. This is laudable in an attempt to secure a balanced panel, although of course it does not secure any specific balance on an individual tribunal. However, the member does not have to be nominated by an organisation. The test is not of a representative in that sense. The test is whether a person is representative of the local population. Individuals who do not belong to groups or organisations are also eligible, and may have much to offer.

Social Security Act 1998
The Social Security Act 1998 introduces major changes in the constitution and composition of appeal tribunals. The principal changes include:

(a) The existing 5 jurisdictions that make up the Independent Tribunal Service (ITS), namely SSATs, DATs, MATs, CSATs and VDTs will be replaced by a single unified appeal tribunal;

(b) Members of the unified appeal tribunal will be drawn from a panel appointed by the Lord Chancellor. The President loses his power of appointment;

(c) Lay membership of tribunals disappears. Membership of the Appeals Panel will be restricted to legally qualified, medically qualified or disability qualified members. The requisite qualifications are set out in Sched. 3 to the Social Security and Child Support (Decisions and Appeals) Regulations 1999 (S.I. 1999 No. 991). (There is also provision for the appointment of financial experts in relation to child support appeals);

(d) The number of members required to constitute an appeal tribunal will vary according to the benefit under appeal. In the case of income-related social security benefits, the appeal will typically be heard by a legally qualified member sitting alone. In the case of appeals involving the all work test the tribunal will comprise a legally qualified member and a medically qualified member. The role of the medical assessor in such appeals will disappear;

(e) ITS will be replaced by a new hybrid body consisting of an executive agency (the Appeals Agency) headed by a Chief Executive accountable to the Secretary of State and a non-departmental public body (the "judicial wing") headed by a President. Responsibility for and control of the administration of the appeals system accordingly moves away from the President to the Secretary of State. This, in effect, represents a reversion to the pre-1984 position when the Department ran the appeals system and invited such criticism of the lack of independence that it led to the creation of ITS;

(f) The procedural rules governing the administration of appeals will be substantially revised. Among the more significant procedural changes to be introduced by the 1998 Act and the 1999 Regulations are a standardisation of time-limits (one month for appeals and applications and 14 days for directions, with tight controls over extensions); increased devolution of decision-making powers from chairmen to clerks (the latter, of course, being Secretary of State officers); increased striking-out powers for failure to prosecute an appeal; the concept of "misconceived appeals" which lack a reasonable prospect of success and may be summarily dismissed; tribunal powers to summon witnesses, to require evidence on oath and to require a claimant in disability or incapacity related cases to undergo a medical examination; a power for the Secretary of State to stay appeals involving issues that arise on appeal in other cases.

The transition from old-style tribunals to the unified appeal tribunal will be phased in benefit by benefit during the course of 1999. The timetable is set out in the General Note to the Social Security (Adjudication) Regulations 1995. So, for example, on the appointed day for income support (namely November 29, 1999) the jurisdiction of the SSAT to hear and determine income support appeals expires and such appeals will be heard instead by an appeal tribunal. The transitional and savings provisions will be set out in a series of commencement orders. However, the President of ITS has taken advantage of the transitional powers conferred by Sched. 6 to the 1998 Act to modify the composition of SSATs from earlier dates (see the notes to s.41).

Constitution of social security appeal tribunals

41.—(1) A social security appeal tribunal shall consist of a chairman [² sitting either alone or with one or two other persons].

(2) [²Any members other than the chairman] shall be drawn from the appropriate panel constituted under section 40 above.

(3) The President shall nominate the chairman.

(4) The President may nominate as chairman—

(a) himself;

(b) one of the full-time chairmen appointed under section 51(1) below; or

(c) a person drawn from the panel appointed by the Lord Chancellor or, as the case may be, the Lord President of the Court of Session under [¹section 6 of the Tribunals and Inquiries Act 1992].

(5) No person shall be appointed chairman of a tribunal under subsection (4)(*c*) above unless he has a 5 year general qualification or he is an advocate or solicitor in Scotland of at least 5 years' standing.

[²(6) Where the appeal tribunal hearing a case consists of more than one member it shall, if practicable, include at least one member who is of the same sex as the claimant.]

(7) Schedule 2 to this Act shall have effect for supplementing this section.

DERIVATION

Subss. (1) to (5): Social Security Act 1975, s.97(2) to (2E).
Subs. (6): 1975 Act, Sched. 10, para. 1(6).
Subs. (7): 1975 Act, s.97(4).

AMENDMENTS

1. Tribunals and Inquiries Act 1992, Sched. 3, para. 36 (October 1, 1992).
2. Social Security Act 1998, Sched. 6, para. 1 (May 21, 1998). This amendment applies from May 21, 1998 until s.7 of the 1998 Act, in so far as it relates to appeals under s.12 of the Act, comes into force.

DEFINITIONS

"5 year general qualification"—see s.191.
"President"—*ibid.*

GENERAL NOTE

Subsection (1)
Note the amendments to this subsection and subs. (2) that have been made by Sched. 6 to the Social Security Act 1998 with effect from May 21, 1998. See also the substituted subs. (6).

In exercise of the transitional powers conferred by Sched. 6 to the Social Security Act 1998 the President has issued a series of directives (Circulars) that dilute the former general requirements in s.41 that a SSAT shall consist of a chairman and two members. The directives allow the tribunal to be validly constituted by a chairman sitting alone. The consent of the claimant is not required to these modifications. The gender criterion in s.41(6) will only apply where the tribunal consists of more than one person. The operative dates in the directives are:

May 21, 1998	A chairman sitting alone may deal with setting aside applications and "paper determinations". A chairman may also proceed alone to hear an appeal where one or both members cancel or fail to arrive and replacements cannot be arranged (President's Circular No. 14).
September 28, 1998	A chairman sitting alone may deal with applications for correction of decisions and appeals involving the all work test (though the presence of a medical assessor is also required in such appeals) (President's Circular No. 16).
October 1, 1999	All appeals heard by a SSAT (prior to conversion to the new unified appeal tribunal) may be dealt with by a chairman sitting alone (President's Circular No. 17).

On the question of chairmen sitting alone, the comments of the Employment Appeal Tribunal in *Sogbetun v. London Borough of Hackney* [1998] I.R.L.R. 676 may be of interest.

Subsection (2)
There is now one panel for each area from which members of a particular tribunal are chosen. The old division between the Trades Council members and the Secretary of State's members on supplementary benefit appeal tribunals and between employers' and employees' representatives on national insurance local tribunals has gone. There is no longer any guarantee of having a member from any particular background on any individual tribunal. Members need no longer be summoned in turn to sit on tribunals. See s.40 for appointment to the panel of members.

Subsection (4)

The panel referred to in para. (c) is of the ordinary part-time chairmen of SSATs, appointed by the Lord Chancellor (or the Lord President in Scotland). The President assigns chairmen to act in particular areas.

See s.51 for regional and other full-time chairmen.

Subsection (5)

Since 1984 part-time chairmen have had to have professional legal qualifications. This was a controversial provision, which required the discarding of some highly experienced and knowledgeable supplementary benefit appeal tribunal chairmen. However, it was probably inevitable in view of the excessive legalisation of the supplementary benefit system detailed in past editions of this book. What remains controversial is the requirement of professional legal qualifications (which, to put it kindly, do not guarantee any knowledge of, or interest in, social security law), rather than some other evidence of legal skills (*e.g.* a law degree).

From January 1, 1991, the nature of the required professional legal qualification in England and Wales has changed, following the reforms embodied in the Courts and Legal Services Act 1990. A person has a general qualification under s.71 of that Act if he has a right of audience, granted by an authorised body, in relation to any class of proceedings in the Supreme Court or all proceedings in county courts or magistrates' courts. To meet tests of having had a qualification for a particular length of time a person must currently hold the qualification and have held it for the required number of years, not necessarily consecutive (s.71(5)). There are transitional provisions under which solicitors and barristers admitted or called before 1991 are deemed to have been granted the appropriate right of audience.

Subsection (6)

This provision has been amended by Sched. 6 to the Social Security Act 1998 with effect from May 21, 1998. Sched. 6 contains the transitional provisions that will apply until the new system of decision-making and adjudication under the 1998 Act comes into operation.

The Commissioner in *R(SB) 2/88* holds that practicability imposes quite a strict requirement. The provision is mandatory, and if the SSAT does not have a member of the same sex as the claimant it must be shown that it was not practicable to do otherwise. This cannot be presumed. The chairman should ask the clerk about the circumstances, and endorse the record of decision (ITS/RP) accordingly. If non-practicability cannot be proved, the SSAT's decision will be in error of law even though the claimant consents to the hearing continuing. However, the Commissioner in *CS 99/1993* holds that a claimant may consent to a tribunal proceeding. He points out that even where a procedural rule is expressed in mandatory terms it can be waived by the party for whose benefit it exists (unless it is a matter where there is a wider public interest in compliance with the rule). In *CSB 36/1992* the Commissioner set aside the SSAT's decision as it appeared as though subs. (6) had just been overlooked. If it is not practicable to have a member of the same sex as the claimant it might be appropriate to offer the claimant an adjournment.

The President and full-time chairmen of tribunals

The President of social security appeal tribunals, medical appeal tribunals and disability appeal tribunals and regional chairmen and other full-time chairmen.

51.—(1) The Lord Chancellor may, after consultation with the Lord Advocate, appoint—

(a) a President of social security appeal tribunals, medical appeal tribunals and disability appeal tribunals; and

(b) regional and other full-time chairmen of such tribunals.

(2) A person is qualified to be appointed President if he has a 10 year general qualification or he is an advocate or solicitor in Scotland of at least 10 years' standing.

(3) A person is qualified to be appointed a full-time chairman if he has a 5 year general qualification or he is an advocate or solicitor in Scotland of at least 5 years' standing.

(4) Schedule 2 to this Act shall have effect for supplementing this section.

DERIVATION

Social Security Act 1975, Sched. 10, para. 1A(1) to (3).

DEFINITIONS

"5 year general qualification"—see s.191.
"10 year general qualification"—*ibid.*

GENERAL NOTE

On the Social Security Act 1998 changes see the note to s.40.

One of the major innovations in the reform of tribunals in 1984 was the appointment of a President who took over the appointment of SSAT members and clerks as well as the training of chairmen and members. In effect, the administration of SSATs was removed from the DSS into the hands of an entirely independent agency. The reality of this independence has largely been secured, but still depends on the resources allowed to the President by the Treasury. The DSS, as the "sponsoring" Department, has a direct influence on the availability of resources. The President has added DATs, CSATs (see para. 1 of Sched. 3 to the Child Support Act 1991) and Vaccine Damage Tribunals to his remit.

The first incumbent, Judge H. J. Byrt, took up his post towards the end of 1983 and completed his initial term of office in 1988. He was replaced by Judge Derek Holden in February 1990, who served until August 1992, and was followed by Judge Anthony Thorpe and then Judge Keith Bassingthwaighte. The current President is Judge Michael Harris.

Regional chairmen are responsible for the deployment and support of judicial resources. The number of full-time chairmen appointed has increased from 7 to over 50. Initially full-time chairmen acted mainly as "troubleshooters", being called upon to hear unusually complex cases or to clear backlogs. The full-time chairman has evolved into a "district chairman", responsible for case management and support of part-time chairmen and members in a defined area. Hearing the more complicated cases, however, continues to be the main task.

The Social Security Act 1998 effaces all reference to regional chairmen and full-time chairmen, using simply the undifferentiated title of "legally qualified member of the appeals panel." Nevertheless, the Lord Chancellor, who is responsible for making these appointments, has indicated that the roles will continue.

Social Security Commissioners

Appointment of Commissioners

52.—(1) Her Majesty may from time to time appoint, from among persons who have a 10 year general qualification or advocates or solicitors in Scotland of at least 10 years' standing—

(a) a Chief Social Security Commissioner; and

(b) such number of other Social Security Commissioners, as Her Majesty thinks fit.

(2) If the Lord Chancellor considers that, in order to facilitate the disposal of the business of Social Security Commissioners, he should make an appointment in pursuance of this subsection, he may appoint—

(a) a person who has a 10 year general qualification; or

(b) an advocate or solicitor in Scotland of at least 10 years' standing; or

(c) a member of the bar of Northern Ireland or solicitor of the Supreme Court of Northern Ireland of at least 10 years' standing, to be a Social Security Commissioner (but to be known as a deputy Commissioner) for such period or on such occasions as the Lord Chancellor thinks fit.

(3) When the Lord Chancellor proposes to exercise the power conferred on him by subsection (2) above, it shall be his duty to consult the Lord Advocate with respect to the proposal.

(4) Schedule 2 to this Act shall have effect for supplementing this section.

DERIVATION

Subs. (1): Social Security Act 1975, s.97(3).
Subss. (2) and (3): Social Security Act 1980, s.13(5) and (6).

DEFINITION

"10 year general qualification"—see s.191.

References by authorities

Power of adjudicating authorities to refer matters to experts

53.—(1) An authority to which this section applies may refer any question of special difficulty arising for decision by the authority to one or more experts for examination and report.

(2) The authorities to which this section applies are—
  (a) an adjudication officer;
  (b) an adjudicating medical practitioner, or two or more such practitioners acting together;
  (c) a specially qualified adjudicating medical practitioner appointed by virtue of section 62 below, or two or more such practitioners acting together;
  (d) a social security appeal tribunal;
  (e) a disability appeal tribunal;
  (f) a medical appeal tribunal;
  (g) a Commissioner;
  (h) the Secretary of State.

(3) Regulations may prescribe cases in which a Commissioner shall not exercise the power conferred by subsection (1) above.

(4) In this section "expert" means a person appearing to the authority to have knowledge or experience which would be relevant in determining the question of special difficulty.

DERIVATION

Social Security Act 1975, s.115A.

DEFINITIONS

"Commissioner"—see s.191.
"prescribed"—*ibid.*

GENERAL NOTE

This general power may be useful to SSATs in exceptional circumstances, perhaps being more relevant to AOs or MATs and DATs. The question must be of special difficulty and needs to be carefully specified. The power should not be used to get the SSAT off the hook of coming to a decision on conflicting evidence.

Under the provisions of the Social Security Act 1998 the functions of the authorities at paras. (a), (b) and (c) are transferred to the Secretary of State, while the tribunals at paras. (d), (e) and (f) become merged in the unified appeal tribunal. The unified appeal tribunal will be restricted to assistance from experts who are members of the appeals panel (Social Security Act 1998, s.7(4) and (5)), but see the note to s.56.

Claims relating to attendance allowance, disability living allowance and disability working allowance

54.—(1) Before a claim for an attendance allowance, a disability living allowance or a disability working allowance or any question relating to such an allowance is submitted to an adjudication officer under section 20 above the Secretary of State may refer the person in respect of whom the claim is made or the question is raised to a medical practitioner for such examination and report as appears to him to be necessary—

(a) for the purpose of providing the adjudication officer with information for use in determining the claim or question; or

(b) for the purpose of general monitoring of claims for attendance allowances, disability living allowances and disability working allowances.

(2) An adjudication officer may refer—

(a) a person in respect of whom such a claim is made or such a question is raised;

(b) a person [¹ in respect of whom an application for a review under section 30 or 35 above has been made or is treated as having been made,]

to a medical practitioner for such examination and report as appears to the adjudication officer to be needed to enable him to reach a decision on the claim or question or the matter under review.

(3) [*Omitted as not applying to disability working allowance*]

(4) An adjudication officer may refer for advice any case relating to disability working allowance to such a medical practitioner.

(5) and (6) [*Omitted as not applying to disability working allowance*]

(7) A medical practitioner who is an officer of the Secretary of State and to whom a question relating to disability working allowance is referred under section 53 above may obtain information about it from another medical practitioner.

(8) Where—

(a) the Secretary of State has exercised the power conferred on him by subsection (1) above or an adjudication officer has exercised the power conferred on him by subsection (2) above; and

(b) the medical practitioner requests the person referred to him to attend for or submit himself to medical examination; but

(c) he fails without good cause to do so,

the adjudication officer shall decide the claim or question or matter under review against him.

DERIVATION

Social Security Act 1975, s.115C.

AMENDMENT

1. Social Security Administration (Fraud) Act 1997, Sched. 1, para. 2 (July 1, 1997).

The powers contained in this section will in disability working allowance cases mainly be used in relation to the disability question under s.129(1)(b) of the Contributions and Benefits Act, which is not a concern of the SSAT.

Determination of questions of special difficulty

Assessors

56.—(1) Where it appears to an authority to which this section applies that a matter before the authority involves a question of fact of special difficulty, then, unless regulations otherwise provide, the authority may direct that in dealing with that matter they shall have the assistance of one or more assessors.

(2) The authorities to which this section applies are—

(a) two or more adjudicating medical practitioners acting together;

(b) two or more specially qualified adjudicating medical practitioners, appointed by virtue of section 62 below, acting together;

(c) a social security appeal tribunal;

(d) a disability appeal tribunal;

(e) a medical appeal tribunal;

(f) a Commissioner;

(g) the Secretary of State.

DERIVATION

Social Security Act 1975, s.115B.

GENERAL NOTE

Presumably the principles laid down in *R(I) 14/51* in relation to earlier legislation will continue to apply. The assessor's role is to assist the authority to understand the factual issues and to evaluate the evidence. He does not himself give evidence and so cannot be questioned by the parties to the proceedings. His advice should be summarised and the parties given the opportunity to comment on it. *CS 175/1992* holds that a medically qualified member of a SSAT was not performing an analogous role to that of a medical assessor when putting her expert interpretation on the evidence presented to the tribunal. An assessor is not entitled to be present while the decision is being made (regs. 2(2) and 4(6) of the Adjudication Regulations) whereas clearly a member is, and indeed, must be.

The express power of a tribunal to appoint an assessor disappears under the Social Security Act 1998 but it is arguable that there may be an inherent power for a tribunal to appoint assessors in appropriate cases.

Tribunal of three Commissioners

57.—(1) If it appears to the Chief Social Security Commissioner (or, in the case of his inability to act, to such other of the Commissioners as he may have nominated to act for the purpose) that an appeal falling to be heard by one of the Commissioners involves a question of law of special difficulty, he may direct that the appeal be dealt with, not by that Commissioner alone, but by a Tribunal consisting of any 3 of the Commissioners.

(2) If the decision of the Tribunal is not unanimous, the decision of the majority shall be the decision of the Tribunal.

DERIVATION

Social Security Act 1975, s.116.

GENERAL NOTE

Under the legislation in force before April 1984 there was no express power for the Chief Commissioner to convene a Tribunal of Commissioners in supplementary benefit or FIS cases. The power was found by implication (*R(FIS) 1/82*). It is often invoked where individual Commissioners have reached conflicting decisions. Individual Commissioners are bound to follow a decision of a Tribunal of Commissioners, unless there are compelling reasons to the contrary (*R(I) 12/75* and *CM 44/1991*, to be reported as *R(M)2/94*). A Tribunal of Commissioners may depart from a previous Tribunal decision if satisfied that it was wrong (*R(U) 4/88*).

With the expansion in the number of Commissioners it can no longer be guaranteed that the approach adopted by the three Commissioners on a Tribunal will be accepted by the Commissioners as a whole. In recent years, a number of Tribunal decisions have been left unreported. This may be because of lack of support by the Commissioners as a whole, but it is impossible from the outside to tell. A SSAT must follow a Tribunal's decision, whether reported or unreported, in preference to a decision of an individual Commissioner. Possibly, if an individual Commissioner finds compelling reasons for departing from an unreported Tribunal decision, a SSAT would be entitled to follow the individual Commissioner.

Regulations

Regulations as to the determination of questions and matters arising out of, or pending, reviews and appeals

58.—(1) Subject to the provisions of this Act, provision may be made by regulations for the determination—

(a) by the Secretary of State; or

(b) by a person or tribunal appointed in accordance with the regulations,

of any question arising under or in connection with the Contributions and Benefits Act [¹, the Jobseekers Act 1995] or the former legislation, including a claim for benefit.

(2) In this section "the former legislation" means the National Insurance Acts 1965 to 1974 and the National Insurance (Industrial Injuries) Acts 1965 to 1974 and the 1975 Act and Part II of the 1986 Act.

(3) Regulations under subsection (1) above may modify, add to or exclude any provisions of this Part of this Act, so far as relating to any questions to which the regulations relate.

(4)–(8) [*Omitted as not applying to SSATs*]

DERIVATION

Social Security Act 1975, s.114(1) and (2).

AMENDMENT

1. Jobseekers Act 1995, Sched. 2, para. 44 (October 7, 1996).

DEFINITIONS

"the 1975 Act"—see s.191.
"the 1986 Act"—*ibid.*
"the Contributions and Benefits Act"—*ibid.*

Procedure

59.—(1) Regulations (in this section referred to as "procedure regulations") may make any such provision as is specified in Schedule 3 to this Act.

(2) Procedure regulations may deal differently with claims and questions relating to—

(a) benefit under Parts II to IV of the Contributions and Benefits Act;

(b) industrial injuries benefit;

(c) each of the other benefits to which section 20 above applies.

(3)–(5) [*Omitted as not applying to SSATs*]

(6) It is hereby declared—

(a) that the power to prescribe procedure includes power to make provision as to the representation of one person, at any hearing of a case, by another person whether having professional qualifications or not; and

(b) that the power to provide for the manner in which questions arising for determination by the Secretary of State are to be raised includes power to make provision with respect to the formulation of any such questions, whether, arising on a reference under section 117 below or otherwise.

(7) Except so far as it may be applied in relation to England and Wales by procedure regulations, the Arbitration Act 1950 shall not apply to any proceedings under this Part of this Act.

DERIVATION

Social Security Act 1975, ss.115(1) to (3), and (6) to (7).

DEFINITIONS

"the Contributions and Benefits Act"—see s.191.
"industrial injuries benefit"—*ibid.*

GENERAL NOTE

See Sched. 3 and the Adjudication Regulations.

Finality of decisions

60.—(1) Subject to the provisions of this Part of this Act, the decision of any claim or question in accordance with the foregoing provisions of this Part of this Act shall be final; and subject to the provisions of any regulations under section 58 above, the decision of any claim or question in accordance with those regulations shall be final.

(2) Subsection (1) above shall not make any finding of fact or other determination embodied in or necessary to a decision, or on which it is based, conclusive for the purpose of any further decision.

(3)–(5) [*Omitted as not applying to income-related benefits*]

DERIVATION

Social Security Act 1975, s.117(1) and (2).

GENERAL NOTE

Jones v. Department of Employment [1988] 1 All E.R. 725 decides that an AO cannot be sued for negligently making a decision, partly because of the effect of the predecessor of s.60. The principle of finality is fundamental to the system of social security adjudication. It means that once a decision is made on a claim or question, it can only be altered within the period covered by the decision when a power to do so is expressly granted by the legislation, as on appeal or review. See reg. 17 of the Claims and Payments Regulation for the period covered by a claim and an award. Disallowance of a claim for an open-ended period operates down to the date of the decision (*R(S) 14/81*).

Although decisions are final, under subs. (2) findings of fact or other determinations are not conclusive for the purpose of any further decision. It used to be the case that decisions of the insurance officer on certain questions were conclusive for supplementary benefit purposes. This issue is now covered by regs. 56 and 56A of the Adjudication Regulations. The issue is only really a live one before a tribunal, and here it is clear from regs. 56 and 56A that, although an AO must first make a decision on a relevant question, the SSAT can deal with both income support or JSA and the contributory or non-contributory benefit questions together.

Subs. (2) also confirms that on a fresh claim, issues of fact and law are for decision afresh. For instance, if an income support claim is rejected on the ground that a claimant has notional capital under the deprivation rule, a claim a month or a week later cannot be rejected simply by reference to the earlier decision.

Regulations about supplementary matters relating to determinations

61.—(1) Regulations may make provision as respects matters arising—
  (a) pending the determination under this Act (whether in the first instance or on an appeal or reference, and whether originally or on review)—
    (i) of any claim for benefit to which this section applies; or
    (ii) of any question affecting any person's right to such benefit or its receipt; or
    (iii) of any person's liability for contributions [2. . .]; or
  (b) out of the revision on appeal or review of any decision under this Act on any such claim or question.
(2) Without prejudice to the generality of subsection (1) above, regulations thereunder may include provision as to the date from which any decision on a review is to have effect or to be deemed to have had effect.
(3) [*Omitted as not applying to income-related benefits*]
(4) This section applies—
  (a) to benefit as defined in section 122 of the Contributions and Benefits Act;
[1(aa) to a jobseeker's allowance;]
  (b) to child benefit;
  (c) to statutory sick pay;
  (d) to statutory maternity pay;
  (e) to income support;
  (f) to family credit;
  (g) to disability working allowance; and
  (h) to any social fund payments such as are mentioned in section 138(1)(a) or (2) of the Contributions and Benefits Act.

DERIVATION

Social Security Act 1975, s.119(3) and (4)(a).

AMENDMENTS

1. Jobseekers Act 1995, Sched. 2, para. 45 (October 7, 1996).
2. Social Security Administration (Fraud) Act 1997, s. 22 and Sched. 2 (July 1, 1997).

DEFINITION

"the Contributions and Benefits Act"—see s.191.

GENERAL NOTE

See the Adjudication Regulations and the Claims and Payments Regulations.

[1*Incapacity for work*

Adjudication: incapacity for work

61A.—(1) The following provisions apply in relation to the determination, for any purpose for which the provisions of Part XIIA of the Contributions and Benefits Act apply, whether a person—

(a) is, or is to be treated as, capable or incapable of work, or

(b) falls to be disqualified for any period in accordance with regulations under section 171E of that Act,

and to the determination for any such purpose of such other related questions as may be prescribed.

(2) Provision may be made by regulations for a determination made for one such purpose to be treated as conclusive for another such purpose.

Regulations may in particular provide that a determination that a person is disqualified for any period in accordance with regulations under section 171E of the Contributions and Benefits Act shall have effect for such purposes as may be prescribed as a determination that he is to be treated as capable of work for that period, and *vice versa.*

(3) Provision may be made by regulations for questions of such descriptions as may be prescribed to be determined by an adjudication officer, notwithstanding that other questions fall to be determined by another authority.

(4) Provision may be made by regulations—

(a) requiring a social security appeal tribunal to sit with one or more medical assessors in such classes of case as may be prescribed, and

(b) as to the constitution of panels of medical practitioners to act as medical assessors in such cases;

and regulations under this subsection may confer on the President, or such other person as may be prescribed, such functions as may be prescribed.]

AMENDMENT

1. Social Security (Incapacity for Work) Act 1994, s. 6(2) (April 13, 1995).

DEFINITION

"the Contributions and Benefits Act"—see s. 191.

GENERAL NOTE

For the details of the new rules for deciding incapacity for work see *Bonner, Non-Means Tested Benefits: the Legislation.* See also the notes to para. 7 of Sched. 1B to the Income Support Regulations for a brief summary. The framework is in Part XIIA of the Contributions and Benefits Act (s.171A-G) and this section; the main detail of the new rules is mostly in the Social Security (Incapacity for Work) (General) Regulations 1995 (S.I. 1995 No. 311).

Subsection (2)

See reg. 19 of the Incapacity for Work (General) Regulations on the first part, and reg. 18 on the second. Note that under the new system for decision-making and appeals coming into force for income support on November 29, 1999 (and for incapacity benefit on September 6, 1999) regs. 19–22 of the Incapacity for Work Regulations will be revoked. For the new form of reg. 19 see reg. 10 of the Social Security and Child Support (Decisions and Appeals) Regulations 1999 (S.I. 1999 No. 991).

See also *CIB 16092/1996* and *CIB 90/1997* in which the Commissioner conducts an extensive analysis of the nature of an AO's decision under reg. 19 of the Incapacity for Work Regulations where this arises in the context of a decision on "incapacity credits". He stresses the importance of identifying the "lead" AO's decision that the claimant is incapable of work. This should be clearly recorded as such in the AO's decision. In addition, a decision that is based on the conclusive effect of another decision under reg. 19 should also clearly record that fact. On an appeal, any other purpose for which the decision under appeal has had a conclusive effect should be brought to the tribunal's attention, "so that it can be ascertained that the claimant has not been disadvantaged by any obscurities of procedure". The Commissioner also suggests that any related appeals should, if possible, be heard together. See further the notes to para. 7 of Sched. 1B to the Income Support Regulations.

Subsection (3)

See reg. 20 of the Incapacity for Work (General) Regulations. Note *CIB 17622/1996* and *CIS 17615/1996* in which the Commissioner confirms that reg. 20 clearly confers jurisdiction on an AO to determine a question whether a claimant is incapable of work for the purpose of "credits" and that s.22 is sufficiently broad to permit an appeal to be brought against an AO's decision under reg. 20. And see *CIB 16092/1996* and *CIB 90/1997* in the note to subs. (2).

Note that reg. 20 will be revoked when the new system for decision-making and appeals comes into force. See the note to subs. (2) above.

Subsection (4)

Reg. 21 of the Incapacity for Work (General) Regulations provides that a SSAT must sit with a medical assessor in any case that involves consideration of whether the claimant satisfies the "all work test". For details of this test and when it applies, see *Bonner, Non-Means Tested Benefits: the Legislation*. Whether an assessor is required will be a matter for the chairman under reg. 2(1)(a) of the Adjudication Regulations; if one is required, but not present, the hearing will have to be postponed and relisted with an assessor present. See reg. 5(2) of the Adjudication Regulations which gives a chairman power to postpone a hearing without any application being made.

Presumably the case law on s. 56 (power to appoint assessors in cases of special difficulty) will apply; see the notes to s. 56. An assessor is not a member of the tribunal and should enter and leave the room with the parties. An assessor should not participate in any appeal in which he has knowledge of the appellant. The role of the assessor is to give impartial advice to the tribunal; the parties must be given the opportunity to comment on anything he says, but cannot cross-examine him. He should not ask questions himself except through the chairman, and may not physically examine the claimant (*R(I) 14/51*).

The medical assessor is not there to give his opinion as to the claimant's capacity for work, or whether any particular "descriptor" applies (see the Schedule to the Social Security (Incapacity for Work) (General) Regulations 1995 (S.I. 1995 No 311) for the "descriptors" involved in the new "all work test"). But an assessor will be provided with a copy of the tribunal papers and shown any documents presented during the hearing. So it seems that the assessor's role in an appeal involving the all work test will be to assist the tribunal to understand and evaluate the evidence, by, for example, explaining medical terms, or the significance of, or side-effects of, any medication, or the likely consequences of any condition. He may also suggest that further medical evidence needs to be obtained. But the decision as to whether the particular claimant satisfies the test remains that of the tribunal alone. Note that this approach to the role of the medical assessor has been confirmed by *CSIB 101/1996* and *CSIB 72/1996* (see the notes to para. 7 of Sched. 1B to the Income Support Regulations). See also *CSIB 172/1997* in which the Commissioner considered that there was no objection in itself to the medical assessor and the presenting officer sharing a room.

Note that under the new system for decision-making and appeals coming into force for income support on November 29, 1999 (and for incapacity benefit on September 6, 1999) regs. 19–22 of the Incapacity for Work Regulations will be revoked. Appeals about incapacity for work will be heard by a two-person tribunal consisting of a chairman and a doctor; there will no longer be a medical assessor sitting with the tribunal in all work test cases.

Social fund officers and inspectors and the social fund Commissioner

Social fund officers

64.—(1) The Secretary of State shall appoint officers, to be known as "social fund officers", for the purpose of performing functions in relation to payments out of the social fund such as are mentioned in section 138(1)(b) of the Contributions and Benefits Act.

(2) A social fund officer may be appointed to perform all the functions of social fund officers or such functions of such officers as may be specified in his instrument of appointment.

(3) The Secretary of State may nominate for an area a social fund officer who shall issue general guidance to the other social fund officers in the area about such matters relating to the social fund as the Secretary of State may specify.

DERIVATION

Social Security Act 1986, s.32(8) to (10).

DEFINITION

"the Contributions and Benefits Act"—see s.191.

GENERAL NOTE

Subsection (3)
See s.140(5) of the Contributions and Benefits Act and s.66(9) below for the status of guidance issued by area social fund officers.
Note that under the Social Security Act 1998 social fund officers will be replaced by "appropriate officers" who will take decisions on behalf of the Secretary of State (see s.36 of the 1998 Act).

The social fund Commissioner and inspectors

65.—(1) There shall continue to be an officer, to be known as "the social fund Commissioner" (in this section referred to as "the Commissioner").

(2) The Commissioner shall be appointed by the Secretary of State.

(3) The Commissioner—

(a) shall appoint such social fund inspectors; and

(b) may appoint such officers and staff for himself and for social fund inspectors,

as he thinks fit, but with the consent of the Secretary of State and the Treasury as to numbers.

(4) Appointments under subsection (3) above shall be made from persons made available to the Commissioner by the Secretary of State.

(5) It shall be the duty of the Commissioner—

(a) to monitor the quality of decisions of social fund inspectors and give them such advice and assistance as he thinks fit to improve the standard of their decisions;

(b) to arrange such training of social fund inspectors as he considers appropriate; and

(c) to carry out such other functions in connection with the work of social fund inspectors as the Secretary of State may direct.

(6) The Commissioner shall report annually in writing to the Secretary of State on the standards of reviews by social fund inspectors and the Secretary of State shall publish his report.

DERIVATION

Social Security Act 1986, s.35.

GENERAL NOTE

The Annual Reports of the Social Fund Commissioner contain much interesting material. Inspectors have been recruited from outside and inside the DSS and have established an independence of operation.

Reviews

66.—(1) A social fund officer—

(a) shall review a determination made under the Contributions and Benefits Act by himself or some other social fund officer, if an application for review is made within such time and in such form and manner as may be prescribed by or on behalf of the person who applied for the payment to which the determination relates; and

[¹(aa) may review such a determination on the ground that the person who applied for the payment to which the determination relates misrepresented, or failed to disclose, any material fact; and]
(b) may review such a determination in such other circumstances as he thinks fit;

and may exercise on a review any power exercisable by an officer under Part VIII of the Contributions and Benefits Act.

(2) The power to review a determination conferred on a social fund officer by subsection (1) above includes power to review a determination made by a social fund officer on a previous review.

(3) On an application made by or on behalf of the person to whom a determination relates within such time and in such form and manner as may be prescribed a determination of a social fund officer which has been reviewed shall be further reviewed by a social fund inspector.

(4) On a review a social fund inspector shall have the following powers—
(a) power to confirm the determination made by the social fund officer;
(b) power to make any determination which a social fund officer could have made;
(c) power to refer the matter to a social fund officer for determination.

(5) A social fund inspector may review a determination under subsection (3) above made by himself or by some other social fund inspector.

[¹(5A) In making a determination on a review a social fund officer or a social fund inspector need not consider—
(a) in the case of a determination on a review under subsection (1)(a) above, any issue that is not raised by the application;
(b) in the case of a determination on a review under subsection (1)(aa) above, any issue that is not raised by the material fact;
(c) in the case of a determination on a review under subsection (1)(b) above, any issue that did not cause him to carry out the review.

(6) In determining a question on a review under subsection (1)(a) or (b) above a social fund officer or social fund inspector shall, subject to subsection (7) below, have regard to whichever of the following are applicable, namely—
(a) all the circumstances of the case and, in particular, the criteria specified in paragraphs (a) to (e) of subsection (1) of section 140 of the Contributions and Benefits Act;
(b) the criteria mentioned in paragraphs (a) and (b) of subsection (1A) of that section; and
(c) the criterion specified in directions issued by the Secretary of State under that subsection and the criteria mentioned in paragraph (b) of that subsection.]

(7) An officer or inspector shall determine any question on a review [¹under subsection (1)(a) or (b) above] in accordance with any general directions issued by the Secretary of State under section 140(2) of the Contributions and Benefits Act and any general directions issued by him with regard to reviews and in determining any such question shall take account of any general guidance issued by him under that subsection or with regard to reviews.

[¹(7A) In making a determination on a review under subsection (1)(aa) above a social fund officer or a social fund inspector shall—
(a) act in accordance with any general directions issued by the Secretary of State; and
(b) take account of any general guidance issued by the Secretary of State.

(7B) Any reference in subsection (5A), (6), (7) or (7A) above to a determination on a review under a particular provision of subsection (1) above shall be construed, in relation to a social fund inspector, as a reference to a determination on a further review of a determination which has been reviewed under that provision.]

(8) Directions under this section may specify—
(a) the circumstances in which a determination is to be reviewed; and
(b) the manner in which a review is to be conducted.

(9) In reviewing a question under [¹subsection (1)(a) or (b) above] a social fund officer shall take account (subject to any directions or guidance issued by the Secretary of State under this section) of any guidance issued by the social fund officer nominated for his area under section 64(3) above.

(10) A social fund inspector reviewing a determination [¹which has been reviewed under subsection (1)(a) or (b) above] shall be under the same duties in relation to such guidance as the social fund officer or inspector who made the determination.

DERIVATION

Subss.(1) to (8): Social Security Act 1986, s.34.
Subss.(9) and (10): 1986 Act, s.32(11) and (12).

AMENDMENT

1. Social Security Act 1998, Sched. 6, para. 7 (May 21, 1998).

DEFINITION

"the Contributions and Benefits Act"—see s.191.

GENERAL NOTE

Note the various amendments that have been made to this section by para. 7 of Sched. 6 to the Social Security Act 1998 with effect from May 21, 1998. These amendments apply until s.38 of the Act is brought into force.

Subsections (1) and (3)
See the Social Fund (Application for Review) Regulations 1988 and *R. v. Social Fund Officer, ex p. Hewson* (High Court, June 22, 1995) referred to in the note to reg. 2.

Subsection (4)
See *R. v. Social Fund Inspector, ex p. Ledicott, The Times.* May 24, 1995, in the note to Directions to Social Fund Inspectors (p. 1128).

Subsections (7) and (8)
See directions 31 to 42 and 45 of the Secretary of State's directions to SFOs and the directions to SFIs, together with the notes to those directions.

Restrictions on entitlement to benefit following erroneous decision

Restrictions on entitlement to benefit in certain cases of error

68.—(1) This section applies where—
(a) on the determination, whenever made, of a Commissioner or the court (the "relevant determination"), a decision made by an adjudicating authority is or was found to have been erroneous in point of law; and
(b) after both—
   (i) 13th July 1990 (the date of the coming into force of section 165D of the 1975 Act, the provision of that Act corresponding to this section); and
   (ii) the date of the relevant determination,
a claim which falls, or which would apart from this section fall, to be decided in accordance with the relevant determination is made or treated under section 7(1) above as made by any person for any benefit.

(2) Where this section applies, any question which arises on, or on the review of a decision which is referable to, the claim mentioned in subsection (1)(b) above and which relates to the entitlement of the claimant or any other person to any benefit—

(a) in respect of a period before the relevant date; or

(b) in the case of a widow's payment, in respect of a death occurring before that date,

shall be determined as if the decision referred to in subsection (1)(a) above had been found by the Commissioner or court in question not to have been erroneous in point of law.

(3) In determining whether a person is entitled to benefit in a case where—

(a) his entitlement depends on his having been entitled to the same or some other benefit before attaining a particular age; and

(b) he attained that age—

(i) before both the date of the relevant determination and the date of the claim referred to in subsection (1)(b) above, but

(ii) not before the earliest day in respect of which benefit could, apart from this section, have been awarded on that claim,

subsection (2) above shall be disregarded for the purpose only of determining the question whether he was entitled as mentioned in paragraph (a) above.

(4) In this section—

"adjudicating authority" means—

(a) an adjudication officer or, where the original decision was given on a reference under section 21(2) or 25(1) above, a social security appeal tribunal, a disability appeal tribunal or a medical appeal tribunal;

(b) any of the following former bodies or officers, that is to say, the National Assistance Board, the Supplementary Benefits Commission, the Attendance Allowance Board, a benefit officer, an insurance officer or a supplement officer; or

(c) any of the officers who, or tribunals or other bodies which, in Northern Ireland correspond to those mentioned in paragraph (a) or (b) above;

"benefit" means—

(a) benefit as defined in section 122 of the Contributions and Benefits Act;

[¹(aa) a jobseeker's allowance;] and

(b) any income-related benefit;

"the court" means the High Court, the Court of Appeal, the Court of Session, the High Court or Court of Appeal in Northern Ireland, the House of Lords or the Court of Justice of the European Community;

"the relevant date" means whichever is the latest of—

(a) the date of the relevant determination;

(b) the date which falls 12 months before the date on which the claim referred to in subsection (1)(b) above is made or treated under section 7(1) above as made; and

(c) the earliest date in respect of which the claimant would, apart from this section, be entitled on that claim to the benefit in question.

(5) For the purpose of this section—

(a) any reference in this section to entitlement to benefit includes a reference to entitlement—

(i) to any increase in the rate of a benefit; or

(ii) to a benefit, or increase of benefit, at a particular rate; and

(b) any reference to a decision which is "referable to" a claim is a reference to—

(i) a decision on the claim,

(ii) a decision on a review of the decision on the claim, or

(iii) a decision on a subsequent review of the decision on the review, and so on.

(6) The date of the relevant determination shall, in prescribed cases, be determined for the purposes of this section in accordance with any regulations made for that purpose.

DERIVATION

Social Security Act 1975, s.165D.

AMENDMENT

1. Jobseekers Act 1995, Sched. 2, para. 46 (October 7, 1996).

DEFINITIONS

"the 1975 Act"—see s.191.
"Commissioner"—*ibid.*
"the Contributions and Benefits Act"—*ibid.*
"income-related benefit"—*ibid.*

GENERAL NOTE

See the notes to s.69 below for the general background and effect of ss. 68 and 69, and for discussion of the definitions in s.68(4).

Section 68 can only apply when a claim is actually made after the date of some Commissioner's or court decision which finds the DSS view of the law to be wrong. Then, in so far as the claim can be treated as for a period before the date of claim and the claimant would otherwise be entitled to benefit, entitlement for any period before the "relevant date" is to be determined as if the decision had gone the other way (subs. (2)). The "relevant date" is either the date of the decision or 12 months before the actual date of claim, if later (subs. (4), paras.(a) and (b) of the definition). Para. (c) of the definition merely seems to confirm what would be the case anyway.

There is a small exception in subs. (3) where payment of benefit is not in issue, but merely establishing an entitlement to a benefit at a particular age.

CS 184/1994 confirms that the House of Lords' judgment in *Chief Adjudication Officer v. Bate* applies equally to s. 68, as it does to s. 69. Thus tribunals did have to apply the "anti-test case" rule in relation to claims, even when exercising their appellate jurisdiction (as opposed to deciding a reference by an AO).

Determination of questions on review following erroneous decisions

69.—(1) Subsection (2) below applies in any case where—

(a) on the determination, whenever made, of a Commissioner or the court (the "relevant determination"), a decision made by an adjudicating authority is or was found to have been erroneous in point of law; and

(b) in consequence of that determination, any other decision—

(i) which was made before the date of that determination; and

(ii) which is referable to a claim made or treated as made by any person for any benefit,

falls (or would, apart from subsection (2) below, fall) to be revised on a review carried out under section 25(2) above on or after 13th July 1990 (the date of the passing of the Social Security Act 1990, which added to the 1975 Act sections 104(7) to (10), corresponding to this section) or on a review under section 30 above on the ground that the decision under review was erroneous in point of law.

[¹(1A) Where the review under section 25(2) or 30 above was carried out on an application under section 26(1) or (as the case may be) section 30, it is immaterial for the purposes of subsection (1) above whether the application was made before or after the date of the relevant determination.]

(2) Where this subsection applies, any question arising on the review referred to in subsection (1)(b) above, or on any subsequent review of a decision which is referable to the same claim, as to any person's entitlement to, or right to payment of, any benefit—

    (a) in respect of any period before the date of the relevant determination; or

    (b) in the case of widow's payment, in respect of a death occurring before the date,

shall be determined as if the decision referred to in subsection (1)(a) above had been found by the Commissioner or court in question not to have been erroneous in point of law.

(3) In determining whether a person is entitled to benefit in a case where his entitlement depends on his having been entitled to the same or some other benefit before attaining a particular age, subsection (2) above shall be disregarded for the purpose only of determining the question whether he was so entitled before attaining that age.

(4) For the purposes of this section—

    (a) "adjudicating authority" and "the court" have the same meaning as they have in section 68 above;

    (b) any reference to—

        (i) a person's entitlement to benefit; or

        (ii) a decision which is referable to a claim, shall be constructed in accordance with subsection (5) of that section; and

    (c) the date of the relevant determination shall, in prescribed cases, be determined in accordance with any regulations made under subsection (6) of that section.

DERIVATION

Social Security Act 1975, s.104(7) to (10).

AMENDMENT

1. Social Security Act 1998, Sched. 6, para. 6 (May 21, 1998). This amendment applies from May 21, 1998 until s.27 of the 1998 Act come into force.

DEFINITIONS

"the 1975 Act"—see s.191.
"Commissioner"—*ibid.*

GENERAL NOTE

The predecessor of s.69 formed a package with the predecessor of s.68 on claims when they were introduced in 1990. The aim is that where an established interpretation of the law is overturned by a decision of a Social Security Commissioner or a higher court, effect can only be given to the new interpretation for other claimants on review or a fresh claim with effect from the date of that decision (the decision is referred to below as the J decision and the date as the J Day).

Background

The general rule on claims for benefit is that there can be no entitlement for a period more than 12 months before the actual date of claim, however good the reasons for delay in claiming (s.1(2); 1975 Act, s.165A(2)). None of the exceptions to the general rule applies to income-related benefits. At the time of the introduction of the new package in 1990, if a possible entitlement was revealed by a J decision and the person had not previously claimed, the 12-month limit on past entitlement would apply. Now, from April 1997 the limit has been reduced to three months (see reg. 19 of the Claims and Payments Regulations).

If the person had already had a decision on a claim and applied for a review of that decision based on the new interpretation, again there was in 1990 a general limit of 12 months before the date of the request for review (Adjudication Regulations, regs. 59, 63 and 65 to 67 as they then were). However, there was until August 31, 1991, an exemption from this limit under reg. 72(1) of the 1986 Adjudication Regulations where, among other things, the decision to be reviewed was erroneous by reason of a mistake made by an adjudication officer (AO). Acting on a mistaken view of the law could obviously come within reg. 72(1) (*R(SB) 10/91* and *CIS 11/1991*), so that a revision on review triggered by the J decision could go back to the date of the original decision. Alarm about this effect led to the insertion of reg. 72(2) into the 1986 Regulations from September 1, 1987, which provided that reg. 72 should not apply where review was on the ground that the original decision was erroneous in law by reason of the J decision. The result was that in such cases the normal 12 month limit applied. The argument that the original decision was not erroneous by reason of the J decision, but was simply revealed to have been erroneous all along was rejected in *R(SB) 11/89*. (Note that the general limit has from April 1997 been reduced to one month).

In an investigation by the Parliamentary Commissioner for Administration (the Ombudsman) into the decision of the Secretary of State about how extensively to trawl back for past entitlements following a Commissioner's decision on the offsetting of payments of occupational pension against dependency additions to invalidity benefit, the Ombudsman raised the effect of reg. 72(2) of the 1986 Adjudication Regulations (Case No. C191/88, Fourth Report of the PCA for 1989–90). He was concerned that the longer the delay in identifying a claimant's case as requiring review the more benefit was lost, because of the absolute time limit recently reintroduced. He was not convinced that this effect was brought to Ministers' attention. In the course of responding to that point the DSS said that it would introduce a common start date for entitlement on review in such cases, but gave no indication of what sort of date would be chosen. The new provisions introduced by the Social Security Act 1990 were said to be in fulfilment of this undertaking. See HL *Hansard*, May 21, 1990, Vol. 519, cols. 684–6 (Lord Henley).

Reg. 72 of the 1986 Adjudication Regulations was replaced with effect from August 31, 1991 by reg. 64A (now reg. 57 of the 1995 Regulations), which also allows the general limit on review to be lifted, but uses a more restricted approach to errors of law. See the notes to that regulation.

The new provisions

The new provisions came into force on July 13, 1990.

There are a number of important definitions. The first is of a J decision, or in the statutory words "a relevant determination." It is "a determination, whenever made, of a Commissioner or the court ... [whereby] a decision made by an adjudicating authority is or was found to have been erroneous in point of law" (s.68(1)(a) and s.69(1)(a)).

An "adjudicating authority" was originally defined to cover an AO or any of his legislative predecessors, a SSAT, a MAT, the Attendance Allowance Board, the Supplementary Benefits Commission or the National Assistance Board. The DAT was added in April 1991. However, the form of words in the 1992 Act (s.68(4)) has introduced a significant change. Tribunals are only included where the original decision was given on a reference by the AO to a SSAT under s.21(2) or 25(1). There was no condition of this kind in the pre-July 1992 legislation. The change is not covered by a Law Commission recommendation (see the Report on the consolidation of certain enactments relating to Social Security: Law Com. No. 203). Therefore, it must have been considered to come within the corrections and minor improvements which can properly be authorised by s.2 of the Consolidation of Enactments (Procedure) Act 1949. The Joint Committee on Consolidation Bills (HL Paper 23–I, HC Paper 141–I, Session 1991–2) gave their opinion that this was so (although they also considered that the Administration Act and the Contributions and Benefits Act represented "pure consolidation" of the existing law), so that presumably the new form has to be accepted.

"The court" includes everything above the Commissioner (s.68(4)). Then if any decision made before J Day would otherwise fall to be revised on review for error of law carried out on or after July 13, 1990, "in consequence of that determination" (s.69(1)(b)), entitlement before J Day is to be determined as if the adjudicating authority's decision had been found not to be erroneous in point of law (s.69(2)). In addition, reg. 64B (now reg. 58) of the Adjudication Regulations requires the revised decision on review to take effect only from J Day. This important change is operative from March 9, 1992. Alternatively, if a new claim is made after J Day, entitlement before that date is to be decided on the same assumption (s.68(2)).

The aim of the provisions is clear—a common start date for revising other claimants' entitlements when an appeal overturns the previously accepted DSS interpretation of the law. The main political argument against their introduction was that the start date was placed unacceptably and unfairly late at J Day. (The possibility of bringing a late appeal by which claimants could still obtain unlimited arrears remained, but now note the new (from February 28, 1996) limits on bringing late appeals in reg. 3(3)–(3E) of the Adjudication Regulations; see the notes to reg. 3(3)–(3E).) While reg. 72(2) of the 1986 Adjudication Regulations still existed there was only a common start date when the review took place within 12 months of J Day. For reviews which take place after reg. 64A (now reg. 57) had taken over, the 12-month or one-month limit will only be lifted if the J Decision shows that the previous interpretation involved errors of law of particular kinds (see reg. 57(3)). But the form of the new provisions, both before and after July 1, 1992, raised more fundamental problems.

See the 1995 edition for discussion of these problems. However, as a result of the House of Lords' judgment delivered on May 16, 1996 in *Chief Adjudication Officer and Another v. Bate* (see below), it is clear that these provisions are to be given a broad interpretation and are of wide effect.

Before dealing with that decision a few points should be made. First, note that the provisions only apply where a claim is made or a review is requested or, if there was no request, is carried out, after J Day (*CDLA 577/1994*; in this connection see also *CIS 11/1991* in the notes to reg. 72(2) of the 1986 Adjudication Regulations). If the effect of the J decision is an issue in adjudicating on a claim or request for review made before that date, then ss. 68 and 69 do not apply at all. That conclusion follows from the express words of s.68(1)(b)(ii) in the case of claims. In the case of reviews, it follows from an interpretation of s.69(1)(b) to be consistent with s.68(1)(b), which was accepted in *CDLA 577/1994* as also producing a fair result. *CDLA 577/1994* was upheld by the Court of Appeal (by a majority) in *Chief Adjucation Officer and Another v. Woods* (December 12, 1997) (to be reported as *R(DLA)5/98*). The CAO was to have appealed to the House of Lords but the petition for leave to appeal has been withdrawn. It may be that this is because of subs. (1A), inserted by para. 6 of Sched. 6 to the Social Security Act 1998 with effect from May 21, 1998. Subs. (1A) is intended to reverse the decision in *Woods*. It provides that the rule is s.69 will apply regardless of whether the application for review was made before or after the J decision. (Note also *CIS 8074/1995* which holds that s.69 did not apply to the decision in *CDLA 577/1994* itself.)

Secondly, s. 69(1)(b) only applies where the decision falls to be revised on review "in consequence of" the J decision. There must be a clear connection between the grounds for review in other cases and the J decision. Thus, if the J decision does not decide a new point but simply applies existing principles the rule in s. 69(2) should not be applied. In *CFC 2298/1995* it was decided that the consent order of the Court of Appeal in *Kostanczuk v. Chief Adjudication Officer* (August 21, 1992, appeal from *CFC 4/1991*), given without argument or reasons by a registrar, was not a "relevant determination" of a court. Even if it was, since the directions given in the order were not binding on anyone other than the parties to *CFC 4/1991* and the SSAT concerned, review could not follow "in consequence" of the order.

Thirdly, and linked to this, is the problem of identifying which of a series of decisions ought to count as the J decision. The question is which decision is it in consequence of that decisions on other claimants' claims fall to be revised on review as erroneous in point of law. AOs commonly do not carry out such reviews if a single Commissioner's decision goes against the DSS view, especially if an appeal is being taken to the Court of Appeal. If the Court of Appeal then confirms the Commissioner's decision, the J Day ought to be the date of the Commissioner's decision. But if there are a series of equally authoritative decisions which one establishes the J Day? It ought to be the earliest one. If the decision which therefore is to be reviewed and revised as erroneous in point of law was made after this J Day, the review based on the effect of the J decision is free of the rule in s. 69(2). The condition in subs. (1)(b)(i) is not met. See *CFC 2298/1995*.

Fourthly, it must be remembered that s.69 only applies to reviews carried out on the ground of error of law. If the claimant is able to rely on some other ground of review, such as ignorance of or mistake as to a material fact, the provision does not apply. This is the case, even though it might not have been realised that the facts were material until the J decision said so (*CDLA 12045/1996*). The Commissioner in *CDLA 12045/1996* confirms the view he expressed on this issue in *CDLA 577/1994* (para. 15) (note that the Court of Appeal in *Woods* did not comment on this aspect of the Commissioner's decision). And see *CSA 4/1995* (below). This point would not seem to be affected by the new subs. (1A) (discussed above).

Fifthly, in relation to disability working allowance (and disability living allowance and attendance allowance), note *CSA 4/1995*. For these benefits a claimant can only appeal to a tribunal after there has been a second tier review under s.30(1). The Commissioner holds that in hearing an appeal against an adverse review decision under s.30(1), the tribunal was not carrying out a review but conducting a complete rehearing of all the issues in the case. In any event, even if the tribunal was carrying out a review, it was a review under s.30(1), whereas s.69(1)(b) only applied to reviews under s.30(2)(d) (error of law). It was irrelevant that a s.30(1) review could encompass errors of law as well. The AO appealed against this decision to the Court of Session but the appeal was withdrawn. The AO apparently accepted that the Commissioner's decision could not be challenged in the light of the Court of Appeal's decision in *Woods* (see *Welfare Rights Bulletin* 148, p. 19).

Finally, the provisions may well be ineffective in relation to rulings on the effect of European Community law by the European Court of Justice (see the definition of "court" in s.68(4)) and by British courts. For the British legislature to remove a person's entitlement based on such a ruling would be a breach of the obligation in EC law to provide an adequate remedy. See *Von Colson* [1984] E.C.R. 1891. In *Johnson v. Chief Adjudication Officer (No. 2)* C-410/92, [1994] E.C.R. I-5483, the ECJ held that the 12 month limit on arrears of benefit (now in s.1(2); since April 1997 the limit is three months: see reg. 19(4) Claims and Payments Regulations) could be applied even where a claim was based on the direct effect of EC Directive 79/7 (equal treatment for men and women in matters of social security) and the Directive had not been properly transposed into United Kingdom law within the prescribed period. However, it is difficult to reconcile this judgment with that of the ECJ in *Emmott v. Minister for Social Welfare* [1991] E.C.R. I-4269, where the ECJ had disapplied a national rule on the limitation period for instituting judicial review proceedings. Although the ECJ drew a distinction between time limits on bringing proceedings at all and time limits on payments of arrears, what was at stake in *Emmott* and *Johnson* was in fact the same – payment of benefit for a past period. It is suggested that s.69 would seem to fall on the *Emmott* side of the line rather than the *Johnson* side, since the effect of s.69 may be the denial of any benefit (or virtually any benefit), particularly if amending regulations are speedily introduced. Although this point is touched on by the House of Lords in *Bate*, Lord Slynn simply states that his interpretation of the provisions is not incompatible with European Community law, without giving any reasons for this conclusion. Thus, there remains room for argument on this question in a case where the point directly arises.

The House of Lords' decision in "Bate"

In *Chief Adjudication Officer and Another v. Bate* [1996] 1 W.L.R. 814, [1996] 2 All E.R. 790, the House of Lords unanimously upheld the DSS's interpretation of these provisions, allowing the CAO's appeal against the Court of Appeal's decision. See the 1995 edition for a summary of the Court of Appeal's decision (the appeal from *CIS 787/1991*).

Lord Slynn, delivering the only substantive judgment, stated that s.104(7) (s.69(1)) applied where in Case B the Commissioner or the court decided that an adjudicating authority had made a decision in that case which was erroneous in law and a decision in an earlier case, Case A, had been based on the same error of law, so that but for s.104(8) (s.69(2)) the earlier decision would fall to be revised on review for error of law. The effect of subs. (8) (s.69(2)) was that on a review of Case A the Commissioner's or court's determination was to be taken as being that the decision was not erroneous in law in respect of any period before the date of the determination. The intention was to exclude claims for benefit for the period prior to the determination in Case B. This meant that for that period the decision in Case A was to be treated as correct at all stages of the process of review. The process remained one of review whether the reconsideration was being undertaken by the adjudication officer or at appellate level. The reference in subs. (8) (s.69(2)) to "any subsequent review of a decision which is referable to the same claim" was wide enough to include decisions by a higher authority. The object of s.104(7) and (8) (s.69(1) and (2)) was not simply to allow review to begin at the appellate level for which leave was required as the Court of Appeal had thought.

Lord Slynn rejected the contention that the effect of subs. (8) (s.69(2)) was limited to cases where a previous binding interpretation had been reversed. He also dismissed arguments based on the word "found", holding that "found" in subs. (7)(a) (s.69(1)(a)) was used "in the general sense of declared" and that it was not appropriate to "draw a legalistic distinction between "found" for facts and "held" for law in this context. The approach of the Commissioner, who had held that the provision applied where a Commissioner or court indirectly found an AO's decision wrong in law, was correct.

Lord Slynn acknowledged that s.104(7) and (8) (s.69(1) and (2)) had introduced a substantial change in the law. But in a revealing comment which seems to underlie the House of Lords' whole approach, he stated:

"The provisions allowing for decisions to be re-opened on review (which go back in one form or another to the Supplementary Benefit (General) Regulations 1966 (S.I. 1966 No. 1065)) are in a sense a concession since, contrary to the practice in the courts, they allow cases closed by, for example, the decision of an Adjudication Officer to be re-opened before an Adjudication Officer or, on a reference by him, by a Social Security Appeal Tribunal. It is, therefore, perhaps not surprising that some limit was introduced in the Regulations to the retrospective effect of subsequent decisions on the law."

The effect of the House of Lords' judgment is fairly clear. Subject to any further arguments that are brought forward in the future, where these provisions apply, claimants will only be able to benefit from decisions in other cases from the date of the J decision. But note the points made above as to when these provisions will not operate. In *CDLA 577/1994* the Commissioner expressly found that *Bate* did not affect the conclusion that s.69 does not apply to reviews requested before J day (note however the new subs. (1A)).

One other issue is whether the effect of s.69(1) and (2) in relation to the period before the J day is that there is to be no review, or a review but no revision, of decisions on other claimants' entitlement. The Court of Appeal in *Bate* seems (at least in places) to take the former view, although the point is not dealt with explicitly (nor is it dealt with by the House of Lords). In *Chief Adjudication Officer v. Eggleton and Others*, (March 17, 1995) the Court of Appeal found on the evidence that no reviews had been carried out where s.69 had been applied to the period at issue. Stuart-Smith L.J. did not consider that an AO "has to go through the farcical process of actually conducting a review and then deciding that he cannot revise the decision because of s.104(7) and (8) (s.69(1) and (2)). He may equally well refuse to review the decision at all". That case also decides that the extent of the revision on review determines how much of the original decision remains in existence. See the notes to s.25. Note also the effect of reg. 58 of the Adjudication Regulations.

Correction of errors

Regulations as to correction of errors and setting aside of decisions

70.—(1) Regulations may make provision with respect to—
  (a) the correction of accidental errors in any decision or record of a decision given with respect to a claim or question arising under or in connection with any relevant enactment by a body or person authorised to decide the claim or question; and
  (b) the setting aside of any such decision in a case where it appears just to set the decision aside on the ground that—
      (i) a document relating to the proceedings in which the decision was given was not sent to, or was not received at an appropriate time by, a party to the proceedings or a party's representative or was not received at an appropriate time by the body or person who gave the decision; or
      (ii) a party to the proceedings or a party's representative was not present at a hearing related to the proceedings.

(2) Nothing in subsection (1) above shall be construed as derogating from any power to correct errors or set aside decisions which is exercisable apart from regulations made by virtue of that subsection.

(3) In this section "relevant enactment" means any enactment contained in—
  (a) the National Insurance Acts 1965 to 1974;
  (b) the National Insurance (Industrial Injuries) Acts 1965 to 1974;
  (c) the Industrial Injuries and Diseases (Old Cases) Acts 1967 to 1974;
  (d) the Social Security Act 1973;
  (e) the Social Security Acts 1975 to 1991;
  (f) the Old Cases Act;
  (g) the Child Benefit Act 1975;
  (h) the Family Income Supplements Act 1970;
  (i) the Supplementary Benefits Act 1976; [¹. . .]
  (j) the Contributions and Benefits Act [¹; or
  (k) the Jobseekers Act 1995.]

DERIVATION

National Insurance Act 1974, s.6(1) and (3).

AMENDMENT

1. Jobseekers Act 1995, Sched. 2, para 47 (October 7, 1996).

"the Contributions and Benefits Act"—see s.191.
"the Old Cases Act"—*ibid.*

GENERAL NOTE

See regs. 9 to 11 of the Adjudication Regulations. The form of subs. (1)(b), which reproduces the earlier legislation, only authorises reg. 10(1)(a) and (b). Reg. 10(1)(c) ("the interests of justice so require") is made under para. 2 of Sched. 3 *(R(U) 3/89)*.

PART III

OVERPAYMENTS AND ADJUSTMENTS OF BENEFIT

Misrepresentation, etc.

Overpayments—general

71.—(1) Where it is determined that, whether fraudulently or otherwise, any person has misrepresented, or failed to disclose, any material fact and in consequence of the misrepresentation or failure—

(a) a payment has been made in respect of a benefit to which this section applies; or

(b) any sum recoverable by or on behalf of the Secretary of State in connection with any such payment has not been recovered,

the Secretary of State shall be entitled to recover the amount of any payment which he would not have made or any sum which he would have received but for the misrepresentation or failure to disclose.

[¹ (2) Where any such determination as is referred to in subsection (1) above is made, the person making the determination shall—

(a) determine whether any, and if so what, amount is recoverable under that subsection by the Secretary of State, and

(b) specify the period during which that amount was paid to the person concerned.]

(3) An amount recoverable under subsection (1) above is in all cases recoverable from the person who misrepresented the fact or failed to disclose it.

(4) In relation to cases where payments of a benefit to which this section applies have been credited to a bank account or other account under arrangements made with the agreement of the beneficiary or a person acting for him, circumstances may be prescribed in which the Secretary of State is to be entitled to recover any amount paid in excess of entitlement; but any such regulations shall not apply in relation to any payment unless before he agreed to the arrangements such notice of the effect of the regulations as may be prescribed was given in such manner as may be prescribed to the beneficiary or to a person acting for him.

(5) Except where regulations otherwise provide, an amount shall not be recoverable under [¹. . .] regulations under subsection (4) above unless—

(a) the determination in pursuance of which it was paid has been reversed or varied on an appeal or revised on a review; and

(b) it has been determined on the appeal or review that the amount is so recoverable.

[¹(5A) Except where regulations otherwise provide, an amount shall not be recoverable under subsection (1) above unless the determination in pursuance

1203

of which it was paid has been reversed or varied on an appeal or revised on a review.]

(6) Regulations may provide—

(a) that amounts recoverable under subsection (1) above or regulations under subsection (4) above shall be calculated or estimated in such manner or on such basis as may be prescribed;

(b) for treating any amount paid to any person under an award which is subsequently determined was not payable—

(i) as properly paid; or

(ii) as paid on account of a payment which it is determined should be or should have been made, and for reducing or withholding any arrears payable by virtue of the subsequent determination;

(c) for treating any amount paid to one person in respect of another as properly paid for any period for which it is not payable in cases where in consequence of a subsequent determination—

(i) the other person is himself entitled to a payment for that period; or

(ii) a third person is entitled in priority to the payee to a payment for that period in respect of the other person,

and for reducing or withholding any arrears payable for that period by virtue of the subsequent determination.

(7) Circumstances may be prescribed in which a payment on account made by virtue of section 5(1)(r) above may be recovered to the extent that it exceeds entitlement.

(8) Where any amount paid is recoverable under—

(a) subsection (1) above;

(b) regulations under subsection (4) or (7) above; or

(c) section 74 below,

it may, without prejudice to any other method of recovery, be recovered by deduction from prescribed benefits.

(9) Where any amount paid in respect of a married or unmarried couple is recoverable as mentioned in subsection (8) above, it may, without prejudice to any other method of recovery, be recovered, in such circumstances as may be prescribed, by deduction from prescribed benefits payable to either of them.

(10) Any amount recoverable under the provisions mentioned in subsection (8) above—

(a) if the person from whom it is recoverable resides in England and Wales and the county court so orders, shall be recoverable by execution issued from the county court or otherwise as if it were payable under an order of that court; and

(b) if he resides in Scotland, shall be enforced in like manner as an extract registered decree arbitral bearing a warrant for execution issued by the sheriff court of any sheriffdom in Scotland.

[² (10A) Where—

(a) a jobseeker's allowance is payable to a person from whom any amount is recoverable as mentioned in subsection (8) above; and

(b) that person is subject to a bankruptcy order,

a sum deducted from that benefit under that subsection shall not be treated as income of his for the purposes of the Insolvency Act 1986.

(10B) Where—

(a) a jobseeker's allowance is payable to a person from whom any amount is recoverable as mentioned in subsection (8) above; and

(b) the estate of that person is sequestrated,

a sum deducted from that benefit under that subsection shall not be treated as income of his for the purposes of the Bankruptcy (Scotland) Act 1985.]

(11) This section applies to the following benefits—

(a) benefits as defined in section 122 of the Contributions and Benefits Act;

[³(aa) subject to section 71A below, a jobseeker's allowance;]
  (b) [⁴ . . .] income support;
  (c) family credit:
  (d) disability working allowance;
  (e) any social fund payments such as are mentioned in section 138(1)(a) or (2) of the Contributions and Benefits Act; and
  (f) child benefit.

DERIVATION

Social Security Act 1986, s.53.

AMENDMENTS

1. Social Security (Overpayments) Act 1996, s.1 (July 24, 1996).
2. Jobseekers Act 1995, s. 32(1) (October 7, 1996).
3. Jobseekers Act 1995, Sched. 2, para. 48 (October 7, 1996).
4. Jobseekers Act 1995, Sched. 3 (October 7, 1996).

DEFINITIONS

"the Contributions and Benefits Act"—see s.191.
"married couple"—see Contributions and Benefits Act, s.137.
"prescribed"—see s.191.
"unmarried couple"—see Contributions and Benefits Act, s.137.

GENERAL NOTE

The predecessor of s.71 (s.53 of the 1986 Act) was intended to produce a common rule on overpayments across all social security benefits. Since the new rule was based on the old supplementary benefit rule (Supplementary Benefits Act 1976, s.20), many of the existing principles developed in Commissioners' decisions will continue to be relevant.

In *Plewa v. Chief Adjudication Officer* [1995] A.C. 249, [1994] 3 All E.R. 323, the question was whether s. 53 had retrospective effect, so as to apply to all determinations of overpayments as part of reviews carried out on or after April 6, 1987 (when the section came into force), regardless of when the overpayment occurred. The Court of Appeal in *Secretary of State for Social Security v. Tunnicliffe* [1991] 2 All E.R. 712 had held that it did (see the 1994 edition for details of this decision). Section 53 replaced s. 119 of the Social Security Act 1975 (which applied to overpayments of non-means tested benefits) and s. 20 of the 1976 Act. Although the requirements of s. 53 and s. 20 were very similar, there were substantial differences from s. 119. It was pointed out to the House of Lords in *Plewa* that under s. 53 third parties who misrepresented or failed to disclose a material fact (however innocently) could be required to make a repayment, even though they personally never received any benefit, whereas this was not possible in the case of s. 119 (although it was under s. 20). This point had not been put to the Court of Appeal in *Tunnicliffe*. Lord Woolf, who delivered the main judgment in *Plewa*, considered that it might have materially affected the Court's decision if it had. He accepted that s. 53 was therefore "creating an entirely new obligation" to which the common law presumption against statutes having retrospective effect (see Lord Brightman in *Yew Bon Tew v. Kenderaan Bas Mara* [1983] 1 A.C. 553 at p. 558) applied "with full effect". In addition, Lord Woolf would have given more weight than the Court of Appeal did in *Tunnicliffe* to the possible unfairness to claimants if s. 53 had retrospective effect, because of the removal of the defence of due care and diligence. He also held that although there was no transitional provision, this did not mean that some overpayments would be irrecoverable. The effect of s. 16 of the Interpretation Act 1978 was to enable the Secretary of State still to recover under s. 119 or s. 20 if prior to April 6, 1987 a claimant would have been liable to repay under those sections.

This judgment will obviously have most impact on the recovery of overpayments of non-means tested benefits made before April 6, 1987 because of the differences between the test in s. 119 and s. 53. The test in s. 20 was very similar to that in s. 53 (although there was no equivalent of what is now s. 71(5) and (5A)). However, a SSAT dealing with any overpayment of supplementary benefit which occurred before April 6, 1987 must apply s. 20 to that payment (see *CSSB 6/1995*). In addition, it must apply s. 20 to any part of the overpayment occurring after April 5, 1987 that was a consequence of a misrepresentation or failure to disclose a material fact made before that date (see Lord Woolf's summary of the effect of the judgment in *Plewa* [1995] A.C. 249 at 260.) Section 53 (now s. 71) only applies where both the overpayment occurred, and the misrepresentation or failure to disclose was made, on or after April 6, 1987 (*CIS 332/1993*).

It does not matter how far back the overpayments occurred. The time limits of the Limitation Act 1980 have no application to proceedings before the adjudicating authorities and do not start to run until there has been a determination under s.71 or one of its predecessors giving the Secretary of State the right of recovery (*R(SB) 5/91, R(A) 2/86* and *CIS 26/1994*).

The question of recovery itself lies solely within the jurisdiction of the Secretary of State (*R(SB) 5/91*). A SSAT cannot stipulate in its decision that recovery is not to be carried out, although if it finds there are mitigating circumstances, it could request the Secretary of State to consider not pursuing recovery. However in *CIS 37/1994*, by the time the claimant's appeal reached the Commissioner, the Compensation Recovery Unit had already effected recovery from his damages award of any benefit that might have been overpaid to the claimant. In view of the law's general prohibition against double recovery, the Commissioner directs the new SSAT to indicate, if they did find that there had been a recoverable overpayment, that the Secretary of State had no further right of recovery against the claimant. See also *CIS 683/1994* where the Commissioner accepts that if a compensation order had been made in favour of the DSS by a magistrates court under s.35 of the Powers of Criminal Courts Act 1973, the amount to be recovered under s.71 would be reduced by the payments made under the order.

Social Security (Overpayments) Act 1996

Before considering the rules on recovery of overpayments, note the important conditions imposed by subss. (2), (5) and (5A), as amended with effect from July 24, 1996 by the Social Security (Overpayments) Act 1996. Prior to July 24, 1996 the rule was that an overpayment determination could only be made in the course of a review of the decision or decisions awarding benefit (or on an appeal from such a decision). See *CIS 451/1995* in the notes to the 1996 edition (although note *CSIS 174/1996* which expresses a contrary view to that taken in *CIS 451/1995*). (This applies from April 6, 1990 when s.53 of the 1986 Act was amended by the Social Security Act 1989: see further P. Stagg, "*The Social Security (Overpayments) Act 1996*" (1997) 4 J.S.S.L. 155–171.) However, that rule is no longer supported by subs. (2). A SSAT must be satisfied that a valid review and revision has taken place before considering the rest of s.71 (subs. (5A), but it does not now matter that the adjudication officer's overpayment decision was given separately from the review decision. See the notes to subs. (5A) for the condition of a prior review.

There may be some difficulties in determining precisely the cases to which the new form of s.71 applies. Section 1(5) of the Social Security (Overpayments) Act 1996 provides that the amendments apply where a determination under s.71(1) is made after July 24, 1996 and that "the date of the occurrence of any other event is immaterial". The position seems clear at the level of the AO. It does not matter that the overpayment was incurred or that the review decision was made before July 25, 1996. The AO may make a determination under subs. (1) and (2). The difficulties arise where before July 25, 1996, the AO makes an overpayment decision separately from the review decision, which would fall foul of the principle of *CIS 451/1995*, and there is an appeal to a SSAT. It can be argued that as the appeal is a complete rehearing, the SSAT, if it makes its decision after July 24, 1996, must apply the new form of s.71 even though the adjudication officer's decision was ineffective under the old form. The question is whether the terms of s.1(5) of the 1996 Act are clear enough to have that retrospective effect. If they are, they would presumably also affect the situation where a SSAT's decision made before July 25, 1996 is set aside by a Commissioner and the appeal is reheard by a new SSAT.

It was suggested in the 1997 edition of this book that s.1(5) did not achieve this result. This approach has been confirmed by a Commissioner in *CSIS 174/1996* (although it was not necessary to the decision in that case). In his view, the 1996 Act only applied to overpayment determinations made after it came into force. The determination referred to in s.1(5) meant one made by an AO and did not include that of a tribunal rehearing the matter on appeal. This has been followed in *CSIS 160/1996*. However, the Commissioner in *CSIS 174/1996* did go on to say that it might still be open to an AO to make a new determination under the current form of s.71. The same view is taken by the Commissioner in *CIS 595/1997*. The Commissioner in that case gave reasons for refusing leave to appeal. He states that even if he had held the overpayment decision in that case to be void, an AO would be able to make a new decision to the same effect by reviewing the relevant review decision for error of law and dealing with the recoverability of the overpayment within the new review. This was because the original review decision was erroneous because it has not considered at the same time whether any amount of benefit was recoverable. (But as there is no *requirement* on the AO to decide that an overpayment is recoverable (he may simply decide that the decision awarding benefit is to be reviewed), it seems questionable that the *review* decision itself is erroneous in these circumstances. If there are no grounds for review of the original review decision then a review of that decision will be invalid. See also *CSIS 160/1996*.)

But in *CIS 12791/1996* (see also *CIS 13520/1996*) and *CIS 1055/1997* other Commissioners take the view that a tribunal can rectify the position. In *CIS 12791/1996* the Commissioner states that one course of action in this situation was for the Commissioner (or tribunal) to declare the AO's decision void and of no effect. The AO could then make a new overpayment decision relying on the current form of s.71 and s.1(5) of the 1996 Act. However, he also considered that it was open to the tribunal to make a new overpayment decision in exercise of the power in s.36. This seems doubtful since the question of whether there is a recoverable overpayment has not first arisen in the course of the appeal, since this is the very issue under appeal (see further the notes to s.36).

In *CIS 1055/1997* the Commissioner considered that s.1(5) meant that a separate overpayment decision could be validly made after July 24, 1996, whatever the date of the review decision, and that "determination" in s.1(5) was not restricted to decisions made by AOs but included decisions made on appeal. See the references in s.71 to determinations being made on appeal. (It should, however, be pointed out that the reference in subs (5A) to determinations being varied on appeal relates to the decision under which benefit was originally paid, not to the overpayment decision; moreover subs. (2) no longer refers to determinations being made on appeal at all.) The Commissioner in *CIS 1055/1997* took the view the express words of s.1(5) precluded reliance on any general presumption against retrospective legislation.

However, it does seem that s.1(5) is intended to provide some protection, however limited. Its final words make it clear that, for example, the misrepresentation or failure to disclose, or the review, can pre-date the 1996 Act. But s.1(5) also expressly states that this does not apply to the overpayment determination itself. It is therefore suggested that s.1(5) should be interpreted as meaning that the current form of s.71 applies where the *initial* determination that an overpayment is recoverable is made after July 24, 1996, since any other construction renders s.1(5) virtually meaningless.

For further discussion of the effect of the 1996 Act see *Stagg, op. cit.*

Note also the point made in *CIS 13520/1996* but a tribunal should require sight of the separate review decision in order to ascertain its terms. *CSIS 174/1996* emphasises that it is highly desirable for the original of the decision (or decisions) under appeal to be produced before a SSAT; the Commissioner did not consider the recital of the decision on the form AT2 sufficient, since this was not always an accurate record of the actual decision. See further the notes to subs. (5A).

Subsection (1)

This expresses the general rule on recovery of overpayments. There is no provision for the recovery of administrative costs, and if payments are made which go beyond what has been awarded by an AO recovery is a matter for the civil law (see *CSB 830/1985* on the old s.20). Note the condition imposed by subss. (2), (5) and (5A): see the note to subs. (5A).

For the right of recovery to exist, a person must have misrepresented or failed to disclose a material fact. Then it must be shown that a payment of benefit, or non-recovery, was a consequence of the misrepresentation or failure to disclose. Finally the amount recoverable and the period to which it relates must be determined. *R(SB) 2/92* decides that the words "whether fraudulently or otherwise" do not impose any further condition of there having been some kind of dishonesty. This decision was upheld by the Court of Appeal in *Page v. Chief Adjudication Officer* (*The Times*, July 4, 1991, and appendix to *R(SB) 2/92*). The Court of Appeal holds that the plain meaning of the words is "whether fraudulently or not."

It was clearly established under the old s.20 that the burden of proof of all issues lay on the AO (*R(SB) 34/83*). The same will apply to s.71. It was also established that if an initial decision is based on a failure to disclose (or misrepresentation), it is open to a SSAT to base its decision on misrepresentation (or failure to disclose), provided that the claimant has had a fair opportunity of dealing with that new point (*R(SB) 40/84*).

AOs' submissions to SSATS in overpayment cases frequently quote the six tests propounded in *R(SB) 54/83* for recovery on the ground of failure to disclose: (i) failure to disclose (ii) where disclosure could reasonably be expected (iii) of a material fact (iv) by a person who knew that fact (v) as a consequence of which expenditure was incurred (vi) by the Secretary of State who seeks to recover it. In *R(IS)17/95* the Commissioner states that it is not necessary for a tribunal expressly to deal with all six tests in every case. Where there was, for example, no doubt as to the claimant's knowledge of the material fact (the claimant's contention was that *he* had informed the DSS of the changes in his mortgage interest rate), the tribunal's failure to make an express finding on that point did not vitiate their decision. The six tests were of great assistance in identifying the salient points that arose in any case, but they should be applied intelligently by AOs and SSATS.

Material fact

Section 71 only applies where there has been a misrepresentation of or a failure to disclose a material fact. There is often a concentration on the circumstances of a failure to disclose or a misrepresentation and the significance of whether something is a material fact or not is forgotten. There are three main limitations imposed.

First, matters of law are not covered. It is established for purposes of review that a mistake of law is not a mistake of material fact *(R(G) 18/52)*. Entitlement to benefit is a conclusion of law based on findings of fact. This has now been expressly stated by Evans L.J. in *Jones and Sharples v. Chief Adjudication Officer* [1993] 1 All E.R. 225. He holds that the representation "I am entitled to the above sum" at the end of the standard order book declaration is one of law, not fact, and so cannot ground recovery under s.53 (now s.71) (although he accepted that it could include 'a representation of the limited facts, such as that 'I, the person claiming, am the person to whom the award was made, or to whom the order book was sent' "). The other two judges (Stuart-Smith L.J. and Dillon L.J.) did not have to deal with this question in view of their interpretation of the second part of this declaration (see below). Thus Evans L.J.'s conclusion that a representation of entitlement to benefit is one of law is the most authoritative statement so far on the point, and SSATs should draw a distinction between matters of material fact and law. *CS 102/1993* has now expressly decided that "I am entitled to the above sum" in this context is a representation of law, although the Commissioner did go on to decide that by signing the order book, a claimant could make a representation of fact that he believed that there was a current award in his favour (see below). But this is not followed in *CIS 309/1994*. The Commissioner disagrees that a claimant's *belief* as to his entitlement is a material fact. What a claimant believed or did not believe was not material since payment of benefit did not depend on a claimant's belief. The Commissioner was also not inclined to accept that a representation as to entitlement did include some further representation as to "background facts" of the kind suggested by Evans L.J. and in *CS 102/1993*.

Secondly, in the context of the powers to review contained in s.25(1), the Commissioners have drawn a distinction between material facts and conclusions of fact, or inferences from primary fact *(R(I) 3/75, R(A) 2/81* and *R(S) 4/86*, discussed in the note to s.25). The same principle should apply here, so that only misrepresentations or failures to disclose primary facts can found recovery under s.71. So a representation that the claimant was incapable of work would not be enough in itself, unless it contained by necessary implication a representation that the claimant's underlying condition had not changed.

The third requirement is that the fact in issue is a *material* fact. In the context of review, the Court of Appeal in *Saker v. Secretary of State for Social Services (R(I) 2/88)* has decided that for a fact to be material it is not necessary that knowledge of it would have altered the decision. It is enough that the fact is one which would have called for serious consideration by the authority which made the decision and which might well have affected the decision. No doubt the same interpretation should be given to "material fact" here, as was effectively done in *CSB 1006/1985*, but since it is only benefit which would not have been paid but for the misrepresentation or failure to disclose which can be recovered under s.71, it is necessary that knowledge of the material fact would have altered the decision awarding benefit. This is confirmed by the definition posited by the Commissioner in *CS 16448/1996*, namely that a material fact is one "which, if known and properly acted on, would have prevented all or part of the overpayment which is the subject of the decision under s. 71". In *R(SB) 2/91* a student was alleged to have failed to disclose that his course was full-time. The Commissioner held that since a student's own opinion of whether the course was full-time was irrelevant (the objective classification of the course being the issue) disclosure was not reasonably to be expected. Although the Commissioner does not expressly say that the student's opinion was not a material fact, the points he makes about the relevant information having to be gathered from the institution at which the claimant was studying lead inevitably to that conclusion. See also *CIS 309/1994* above.

There is, however, an extra complication in s.71 cases. When considering review, only facts material to the question of entitlement are relevant. Under s.71 facts material to the payment of benefit are also relevant. So if a claimant wrongly declares that he has correctly reported any fact which could affect the amount of his payment, this does not seem to be a misrepresentation of a material fact in the review sense. But following the Court of Appeal's decision in *Jones and Sharples v. Chief Adjudication Officer* [1993] 1 All E.R. 225 there will have been a misrepresentation of a material fact for the purposes of s.71. See below under *Misrepresentation*.

Note also that the test for the purposes of s.71 is whether the fact in question would affect the decision on the authority of which payment was made to the claimant. This applies even if the award of benefit had been wrongly made and the fact was not material to the claimant's (lack of) entitlement *(CF 3532/1997)*. In *CF 3532/1997* the claimant was employed by the NAAFI in Germany. The AO had taken the view that, through a combination of E.C. Regulation 1408/71 and the

Anglo-German Convention on Social Security, the claimant was entitled to U.K. child benefit for his children, who were resident in Germany, so long as he remained in his employment with the NAAFI. The Commissioner, however, holds that because he became ordinarily resident in Germany before his children were born, the Convention then ceased to provide for him to be subject to U.K. legislation and he was never entitled to child benefit. The claimant was made redundant by the NAAFI in March 1994 but did not inform the Child Benefit Centre until May 1995. The Commissioner concludes that in relation to the overpayment after March 1994 his loss of employment was a material fact because it was material to the operative decision on the authority of which benefit had been paid, even if not material to his underlying entitlement. The loss of employment was not turned into a non-material fact because the AO's decision was wrong for another, more fundamental, reason.

Misrepresentation

The meaning of misrepresentation is fairly clear. It requires an actual statement to have been made which is untrue *(CSB 1006/1985)*. The statement of material fact may be oral or written, or in some circumstances may arise from conduct, *e.g.* cashing a giro-cheque. But in this last case there must be some positive conduct from which a statement can be implied, rather than a failure to act. An example where this principle worked in the claimant's favour is *R(SB) 18/85*. The claimant had signed a statement of his resources which omitted his Army pension, but he had produced his pension book to the officer who had filled in the form. The Commissioner holds that the circumstances surrounding the completion of a form must be looked at in deciding what has been represented. If the claimant had qualified the written form by saying that the Army pension should be taken into account, the writing could only be taken into account subject to that qualification. The same result would follow if he had indicated by his actions (*e.g.* producing the pension book) that the pension should be taken into account.

In *CS 102/1993* notification of an AO's review decision that he was no longer entitled to invalidity benefit was sent to the claimant on March 13, 1992 and he was asked to return his order book. The claimant cashed the order for 11 to 17 March on March 17 and the DSS received the order book on March 18. The AO decided that the claimant had been overpaid £72.12p, which was recoverable on the grounds of misrepresentation. The Commissioner holds that the representation "I am entitled to the above sum" at the end of the standard order book declaration is one of law. However, by his conduct in signing the order book, a claimant could make a representation of fact that he believed that there was a current award in his favour (see *CSB 249/1989*). Following *Jones* (see below) there would be a misrepresentation of fact if he did not believe this. However, in *CIS 309/1994* it is doubted whether these sorts of representations can be implied by the signing of an order and whether the claimant's belief or otherwise in entitlement is a *material* fact. The Commissioner in *CS 102/1993* also holds that even though the payment was made after the award had been reviewed it was still a payment "in respect of a benefit" for the purposes of s. 53(1)(a) (now s. 71(1)(a)). Further, although it had not been determined on the review that the amount was recoverable (because at the time the invalidity benefit was reviewed there had not yet been an overpayment) and so s. 53(4)(b) (now s. 71(5)(b)) had not been complied with, the Commissioner finds that this was a case where reg. 12 of the Payments Regulations could apply. The circumstances of the overpayment did not provide a basis for a further review and revision of the invalidity benefit award and so reg. 12 applied.

Even where there is a straightforward written statement its precise terms must be considered. In *CSB 1006/1985* the declaration on the B1 form (since changed) signed by the claimant was "as far as I know the information on this form is true and complete." Although a capital resource was omitted from the form, there was no misrepresentation because the claimant honestly believed that the resource was not available to him. The same declaration had been signed by Mr Sharples in *Jones and Sharples v. Chief Adjudication Officer* [1993] 1 All E.R. 225. On his claim form for supplementary benefit Mr Sharples had ticked the "No" box in answer to the question about whether any member of the assessment unit had any life insurance or endowment policies. Unknown to him his partner had inherited a number of policies, of sufficient value that there was no entitlement to supplementary benefit. The Court of Appeal unanimously held that the signed declaration qualified the answers on the rest of the B1 form and there had been no misrepresentation. This decision will apply to other forms where there is a general declaration at the end. But everything will depend on the drafting of the particular form and the wording of the particular declaration.

The declaration at issue in Mr Jones's case was that signed by him when cashing his income support order book. It was the standard order book declaration which reads "I declare that I have read and understand all the instructions in this order book, that I have correctly reported any facts which could affect the amount of my payment and that I am entitled to the above sum". An overpayment had occurred because, due to the proper procedure not being followed, Mr Jones's income support had not taken account of his receipt of unemployment benefit. Mr Jones had stated when claiming income support that he had applied for unemployment benefit, but he did not report its subsequent award. Recovery was sought on the ground of misrepresentation. Evans L.J., dissenting, accepted the submission made on behalf of Mr Jones that the declaration in the order book contained no representation as to any material fact. A material fact for the purposes of s.53 (now s.71) is one relevant to the calculation of benefit. Whether or not Mr Jones had *reported* material facts was not itself a material fact. His declaration did not make any statement or misrepresentation as to the material facts themselves. The representation "I am entitled to the above sum" was one of law, not fact. Mr Jones's appeal was, however, dismissed by the majority of the Court of Appeal. Stuart-Smith L.J. held that the statement that "I have correctly reported any facts which could affect the amount of my benefit" was a statement of a material fact because unless the statement was true Mr Jones was not entitled to the amount of benefit received. Therefore there was a misrepresentation of a material fact within s.53 (now s.71). Dillon L.J. simply held that since the declaration was incorrect, the overpayment was recoverable. But the reasoning of the majority is deficient and does not answer Evans L.J.'s cogent analysis. What leads to non-entitlement is the existence of the facts which affect the amount of benefit, not whether those facts have been disclosed or not. Nevertheless, the majority's approach has to be applied by SSATs and Commissioners.

It must be noted, however, that Stuart-Smith L.J. and Dillon L.J. qualified the declaration by implying the words "known to me" after "correctly reported any facts". Dillon L.J. stated that the "representation must be limited, as a matter both of common sense and law, to a representation that [the claimant] has disclosed or reported all material facts known to him, since he cannot sensibly be expected to represent that he has disclosed all material facts that are not known to him". Dillon L.J. concluded reluctantly that it could not be further limited to disclosure of facts that could reasonably be expected. (*CSB 790/1988*, which decided to the contrary, should therefore not be followed.) The claimant does not have to know that the fact is material (*CIS 695/1992*). Thus, signing the standard order book declaration will only amount to a misrepresentation if all the material facts known to the claimant have not been disclosed. Therefore, the AO will have to show that the claimant did know the fact, that it was a material fact, and not, for example, an inference from primary facts (see under *Material Fact* above) and that it has not been disclosed.

In *CP 34/1993*, however, the Commissioner held that the claimant's knowledge of the material fact when signing the standard order book declaration was irrelevant. In his view the statements of Stuart-Smith L.J. and Dillon L.J. in *Jones* were *obiter* (*i.e.* not necessary to the decision) and ran contrary to authority that knowledge is not material as far as innocent misrepresentation is concerned (see, for example, *Page v. CAO* above). He therefore declined to follow them. But, as is stated in *CIS 695/1992*, the Court of Appeal's approach in *Jones* is not in conflict with *Page*. What the Court of Appeal was referring to in *Jones* was not the nature of misrepresentation, but the nature of the declaration at issue. The majority's statements in *Jones* were concerned with what exactly the alleged misrepresentation consisted of, rather than whether, once a misrepresentation had been established, the claimant's innocence was of any relevance. Moreover, although technically *obiter*, the majority's statements in *Jones* are important to their decision. See also *CIS 674/1994* where the Commissioner points out that the majority's construction of the declaration was their answer to the point made by Evans L.J., that to construe the declaration as a representation of material fact was to convert all *failures* to disclose into misrepresentations. If this conversion also included other non-disclosures as well it would substantially increase the Secretary of State's right to recover overpaid benefit. The majority's construction of the standard declaration was their (partial) answer to this concern.

This issue has now been resolved by the Court of Appeal in *Franklin v. Chief Adjudication Officer, The Times*, December 29, 1995 (the appeal from *CIS 145/1994* which had followed *CP 34/1993*). The Court held that the order book declaration was to be construed in the way it had been construed by Stuart-Smith L.J. and Dillon L.J. in *Jones*. Accordingly there had been no misrepresentation when the claimant signed the order book because she did not know that her mortgage interest rate had reduced. Staughton L.J., in response to the CAO's point that the Court had not inserted words such as "as far as I know" in the declaration at issue in *Sheriff* (see below), stated that this was because that was not a case where an attempt was being made to convert non-disclosure into misrepresentation. The declaration in *Sheriff* was in a different form and was that the information given on the claim form was "correct and complete". The Court also dealt briefly with the argument that if the order book declaration had meant that there could be a misrepresentation even if the claimant was unaware of the fact she had failed to report, this was outside the powers of the Secretary of State. Staughton L.J. stated that it was s.71 alone which regulated the consequences of misrepresentation and non-disclosure (if reg. 32 of the Claims and Payments Regulations did purport to do this it was not authorised by the Act: see s.5(i) and (j) of the Administration Act). He continued, "It is not open to the Secretary of State to provide—as the declaration seeks to provide—that non-disclosure shall count as misrepresentation and therefore attract a sanction which is not available in the case of non-disclosure under section 71 of the Act.''

A further limitation on the ambit of the representation made by signing the declaration on a payable order is suggested (*obiter*) by the Commissioner in *CG 662/1998, CG 1567/1998* and *CG 2112/1998*. In those cases, an indefinite award of invalid care allowance had been made to the claimant in respect of caring for a person who had been awarded disability living allowance for a fixed period. The claimant did not report the non-renewal of the disability living allowance award (contrary to the instruction at the back of his order book) and an overpayment of invalid care allowance occurred. The Commissioner decides on the basis of the majority decision in *Jones* that by signing the order book declaration the claimant had misrepresented that he had correctly reported any fact that could affect the amount of benefit payable. The relevant fact was the ending of the award of disability living allowance *and* its non-replacement. However, he went on to suggest that the representation made by signing the declaration was limited not only to facts known to the claimant (see *Jones*) but also to facts that had not already been reported on the signatory's behalf or otherwise. But this was subject to the conditions set out in para. 29 of *R(SB) 15/87*, namely that ''(a) the information was given to the relevant benefit office; (b) the claimant was aware that the information had been so given; and (c) in the circumstances it was reasonable for the claimant to believe that it was unnecessary for him to take any action himself''. In his view these conditions had to be strictly applied. Thus, on the facts of these cases, while the existence of *accurate* information in the computer system might be enough to satisfy (a) (it was accepted that the ICA Unit both knew that disability living allowance had been awarded for a fixed term and had the means of knowing (through the Benefits Agency's computer records) that a renewal claim had not been successful to the required extent), (b) was not satisfied because the claimant could not have known, at the time he signed the order book, whether or not the information was accurate. In addition, (c) was not met because the Benefits Agency was perfectly entitled to ask the claimant to report facts as a means of checking the accuracy of information held on computer and the fact that the Agency apparently did not use the computer at all in these circumstances did not make it reasonable for the claimant not to follow the instruction in the order book. The view expressed by the Commissioner is *obiter* and did not assist the claimant in this case but might apply on other facts. For example, if the claimant could show that he knew that the appropriate benefit office had the correct information, it might well be reasonable for him to take no further action, depending on the particular circumstances of the case.

On the interpretation of the order book declaration, note also *CIS 583/1994*. The claimant had continued to cash her order book after starting a job for $17\frac{1}{2}$ hours a week. She stated that she had telephoned the DSS before starting work and had been told that her income support would be unaffected if she worked for these hours. The Commissioner said ''I do not think that a claimant can be sensibly read as assuring the Department that he or she has reported to it as 'facts which could affect the amount of my payment' facts which have not been reported because the Department has said that they could *not* affect the amount of the payment. The scope of what is included in the claimant's declaration about 'facts which could affect the amount of my payment' must fall to be interpreted in the context of what the claimant has been given to understand by the Department about the information it requires.'' He stated that this could apply even if the advice from the local office went against the general guidance in the back of the order book but in that case clear evidence would be needed of the specific advice given.

CIS 372/1994 concerned the representations the claimant made on form UB24 each time he signed on at the UBO. The Commissioner decided that these related to his claim for unemployment benefit. Although in para. 4 of the declaration on Form UB24 the claimant acknowledges a duty to report matters relevant to a claim for income support, this could not be construed as a declaration that the claimant *had* reported all material facts to the DSS. Thus it did not constitute a misrepresentation for the purposes of his income support claim.

There have been other cases where the unqualified nature of a declaration has worked against the claimant, for example, *R(SB) 9/86*. There the claimant regularly signed declarations that his circumstances had not changed although (unknown to him) his wife's earnings had gone up. The Commissioner says that the claimant should have added something like ''not to my knowledge'' to his declaration. This may not be necessary to avoid recovery in the future if words such as those implied by the Court of Appeal in *Jones* and *Franklin* were also held to qualify other similar declarations. However, it will all depend on the wording of the declaration. In *Jones* and *Franklin* the Court of Appeal accepted that a claimant could only report the facts known to him/her. This may not be applicable in relation to other declarations, for example, if the claimant signs a declaration that the answers on the form are correct and complete. In *CIS 674/1994* the Commissioner construes the standard declaration at the end of the income support claim form, ''I declare that the information I have given on this form is correct and complete'' to mean that the claimant was guaranteeing the accuracy of his answers to specific questions (see *Joel v. Law Union and Crown Insurance Co.* [1908] 2 K.B. 863 concerning similar declarations on insurance forms). Thus lack of knowledge on his part was no bar to recovery if any answers were wrong. It is not known what would happen if a claimant tried adding to, or crossing out some of, a declaration on an order book or form.

R(SB) 9/85 illustrates that a wholly innocent misrepresentation may trigger recovery. The section applies whether the person acts "fraudulently or otherwise" (see *Page v. Chief Adjudication Officer*, above). In *R(SB) 9/85* the rule that the absence of knowledge of the facts which make the statement untrue is irrelevant is justified on the ground that misrepresentation is based on positive and deliberate action. Similarly, the reasonableness of any belief that a fact was not material is irrelevant (*R(SB) 18/85*). In *R(SB) 3/90* it was suggested that a future case might have to determine whether mental incapacity could prevent there being a misrepresentation at all. On the facts, where the claimant was at the crucial time recovering from a nervous breakdown and treatment including ECT and drugs, there was a misrepresentation, but it was wholly innocent. Subsequent cases have accepted that mental incapacity could prevent there being a misrepresentation. In *CSB 1093/1989* the Commissioner applied the common law principles relating to *non est factum*, a defence that a document signed by a person was not his deed, and suggests that the necessary degree of understanding required to say that the person's mind went with his pen varies according to the nature of the transaction involved. In the social security context, if a claimant has signed a benefit order, the question would be whether he appreciates that the document was a benefit order which was to be cashed. This confines the effect of mental incapacity within quite narrow limits. Expert medical evidence of the claimant's mental capacity at the time would be particularly relevant. In *CIS 545/ 1992* the Commissioner's approach was broader. He rejected the argument that the doctrine of *non est factum* was relevant, since it could only apply in a contractual context and a claim for benefit was not a contract. However, he held that as the claimant lacked the power of reasoning necessary for her to be negligent in the legal sense she was mentally incapable of making a misrepresentation. The Commissioner went on to state that in the case of a claimant who was subject to an order of the Court of Protection there should be a presumption that he or she was personally incapable of making any valid representation with regard to entitlement to benefit, and that a heavy onus would rest upon anyone seeking to rebut that presumption. The decision contains a useful discussion of the effect of Court of Protection orders. The Commissioner points out that the Court has extensive and exclusive powers over all aspects of a person's property and affairs, which, until a receiver is appointed, are exercised by the Court. Thus, until he was appointed receiver the claimant's son had no legal responsibilities *vis-á-vis* his mother, and indeed, no right to take any action on her behalf. After his appointment the son had disclosed the claimant's capital when he became aware of the need to do so and therefore no liability attached to him. The CAO appealed against this decision to the Court of Appeal, which in *Chief Adjudication Officer v. Sherriff, The Times*, May 10, 1995, allowed the appeal. The Court rejected the argument that the claimant had to know that a representation was being made. If she need have no knowledge of the material fact being misrepresented, there was no reason why she had to know that a representation was being made. If the claimant had the capacity to make a claim, she had the capacity to make a representation. Although the nursing home had filled in the claim form on the claimant's behalf, she had signed the form herself. She had thus made any representations it contained her own. If the claimant was mentally incapable of understanding that she was making a representation, she also lacked the necessary mental capacity to make a claim. If that had been the case, since it was a necessary condition of entitlement to benefit that a valid claim had been made, the income support that had been paid would be recoverable not under s. 53(1) (now subs. (1)) but on the ordinary principles of restitution. In *Sherriff* the Court of Appeal viewed the claim and the misrepresentation as indivisible and considered that the question of whether the claimant was capable of making a representation was answered by whether she had the capacity to make a claim. But what if the representation is not made on the claim form but elsewhere?

See also *CSB 218/1991* where the Commissioner holds that a claimant who was senile and did not understand her actions, but for whom no representative had been appointed for benefit purposes could not escape the consequences of the misrepresentation that she had made on the claim form.

Note also *CIS 222/1991* under "*Causation*" below.

Failure to disclose

A failure to disclose is a much more troublesome concept, and there is a good deal of confusing case-law. An essential background is that reg. 32 of the Claims and Payments Regulations imposes a duty on claimants entitled to benefit to notify the Secretary of State in writing of any change of circumstance specified in the notice of determination or order book or any other change which the person might reasonably be expected to know might affect the right to benefit. However, there is not a straightforward link with s.71. For example, recovery may be pursued against any person who fails to disclose or misrepresents a material fact (see, *e.g. R(SB) 21/82* (spouse) and *R(SB) 28/83* (receiver of a mentally infirm person's estate)). Such persons may not be covered by reg. 32. Secondly, the right of recovery only arises under the conditions of s.71. (See *Franklin* above.) If an order book required a claimant to notify the Secretary of State of a fact which was not material, a failure to do so would not trigger s.71. See above for what amounts to a material fact. Although reg. 32 requires notification in writing it has long been settled that an oral disclosure is as effective as one in writing for the purposes of s.71 *(CSB 688/1982* and *R(SB) 40/84).*

What does disclosure mean? In *R(SB) 15/87* a Tribunal of Commissioners holds, adopting an opinion in an Australian case, that it is a statement of a fact so as to reveal that which so far as the discloser knows was previously unknown to the person to whom the statement is made. This is in line with the ordinary everyday meaning of "disclose." Once disclosure has been made to a particular person there can be no question of there being an obligation to repeat that disclosure to the same person. The question of to whom disclosure is to be made is considered below.

The Act uses the words "fails to disclose," not "does not disclose." Therefore it is necessary to consider what amounts to such a failure. In *CSB 53/1981* (a decision of a Tribunal of Commissioners, but not reported) the statement of Diplock J. in *R. v. Medical Appeal Tribunal (North Midland Region), ex p. Hubble* [1958] 2 Q. B. 228, 242, was applied to the old section 20. "'Non-disclosure' in the context of the subsection, where it is coupled with misrepresentation, means a failure to disclose a fact known to the person who does not disclose it . . . It is innocent if the person failing to disclose the fact does not appreciate its materiality, fraudulent if he does." In *CSB 53/1981,* the claimant had either overlooked or failed to appreciate the relevance of £1000 of premium bonds, so was innocent, but had still failed to disclose. This approach gives the impression that if a fact is material and is known to the person, no other factors are relevant. It is certainly the case that knowledge of the fact is an essential requirement. Where the person is the owner of an asset and has once known of its existence, he will normally be fixed with that knowledge even if he later forgets about it *(R(SB) 21/82,* para. 20(4)). However, in some cases a person may not be mentally capable of knowing that he continues to possess the asset. This was so in *R(SB) 28/83,* where the Commissioner says that it must be shown that the person either knew or with reasonable diligence ought to have known that he possessed the assets. In *R(SB) 40/84* there was a possibility that, in view of her advanced age, the claimant had never known that her superannuation had been increased. Similar arguments can be applied, for instance, to the addition of interest to Building Society accounts. Knowledge of this process can normally be assumed if a person knows of the account, but depending on the medical evidence, may not exist in some circumstances. *R(A) 1/95* holds that mental capacity is only relevant to the question whether or not the claimant knew the material fact. It is not relevant to the claimant's ability to understand the materiality of the fact (see below). However, the Commissioner in *CIS 12032/1996* considers that *R(A) 1/95* goes too far. In his view the authorities indicated that a person's mental state could be relevant but only where it rendered the claimant wholly incapable of appreciating the need to disclose the material fact of which he knew.

If the person from whom recovery is sought is not the owner of the asset, it seems that there is less room for assumptions and that knowledge of its existence must be proved *(R(SB) 21/82,* para. 20(4)). This is expanded in *CIS 734/1992* where the Commissioner distinguishes between the standard of the duty to disclose of a receiver and an appointee. In the case of a receiver appointed by the Court of Protection, since he has precise information as to the assets, constructive knowledge (*i.e.* what a person ought to know) is enough. However, as far as an appointee is concerned, it is necessary to show that he actually had sufficient knowledge of the material fact.

Once it is proved that the person has sufficient knowledge of a material fact, there must still be something which amounts to a "failure." In para. 4(2) of *R(SB) 21/82* the Commissioner says that this "necessarily imports the concept of some breach of obligation, moral or legal—*i.e.* the non-disclosure must have occurred in circumstances in which, at lowest, disclosure by the person in question was reasonably to be expected." This statement has been accepted in many decisions, including *R(SB) 28/83, R(SB) 54/83* and *R(SB) 15/87,* but does not provide a simple solution to problems when it is also clear that an innocent failure to disclose can trigger the right to recover. In *CSB 1006/1985* it is suggested that the statement does not apply at all where non-disclosure by the claimant himself of an asset of his own is being considered. This is probably going too far, but it is necessary to attempt to spell out some limitations. First, the test is an objective one *(CF 26/1990).* It must depend on what a reasonable person in the position of the person from whom recovery is sought, with that person's knowledge, would have done. Thus, in general the fact that, as in *CSB 1006/1985,* the claimant did not consider that an asset was relevant, would be irrelevant. A reasonable person would not take that view. See also *R(A) 1/95* and *CIS 757/1994:* the question whether disclosure was reasonably to be expected had to be determined without regard to the mental capacity of the claimant. But if, say, a DSS official had expressly assured the claimant that an undoubtedly material fact did not need to be disclosed, this surely would create a situation in which disclosure was not reasonably to be expected. This would be in line with the result of *R(SB) 3/81* where a course of conduct which had evolved over several years between the DSS and the claimant concerning the handing over of P60s was held to have affected the claimant's obligation.

A slight extension is shown in *CSB 727/1987*, where it is held that the terms of a DSS form and the answers given by the claimant are relevant to whether a later disclosure is reasonably to be expected. The claim for supplementary benefit was made soon after the birth of the claimant's child. On the claim form she said that she was owed family allowance and had applied for child benefit and one parent benefit. Supplementary benefit was awarded without any deduction for child benefit or one parent benefit. The claimant's child benefit and one parent benefit order book was sent to her on December 17, 1984. She did not notify the local supplementary benefit office until February 24, 1986, and in the meantime supplementary benefit was paid without taking account of the income from child benefit and one parent benefit. Most SSATs would have regarded this as an open and shut case of failure to disclose, but the Commissioner holds that in these circumstances disclosure was not reasonably to be expected. The claimant had given detailed answers about her claims and made it clear that she regarded child benefit and one parent benefit as due to her. She might then expect not to have to report their actual receipt. Although her supplementary benefit did not go down, she might well have thought that such benefits did not affect the amount of supplementary benefit. The questions on the claim form could easily have led her to think that her answers were all the information the DSS required unless they expressly asked for more. Nor did the instructions in the supplementary benefit order book alter the situation, since they concerned reporting income or benefit not already reported to the Issuing Office. The claimant could justifiably think that she had already reported the benefits. The decision must depend on its particular facts, and some of the Commissioner's assumptions might not have held up under close examination of the claimant's actual knowledge, but it does indicate the necessity to consider what is reasonably to be expected in a broad context.

The general principle has been applied in a number of unreported decisions. In *CSB 677/1986* a supplementary benefit claimant was also in receipt of sickness benefit, both being administered in the same local office. He received a notification from the local office that he had progressed from sickness benefit to invalidity benefit (paid at a higher rate). The claimant did not inform the supplementary benefit section, but the Commissioner held that he could not reasonably be expected to inform the office which had informed him, especially if the notes in his order book turned out to refer simply to the "issuing office." In *CSB 1246/1986* it was held that there was no obligation to disclose the annual up-rating of unemployment benefit, since this was public knowledge. *CSB 790/1988* takes the same line as *CSB 677/1986* on whether, when an order book instructs a claimant to report changes to "the issuing office," a claimant would reasonably expect to have to report to one part of an integrated local office receipt of benefit from another part.

In *CIS 627/1995*, the claimant stated on her claim form that she received a Canadian pension and that the sterling equivalent varied with fluctuations in the exchange rate. The DSS asked her what the last monthly payment was in sterling. Her income support was calculated on that amount. The Commissioner held that there was no failure to disclose in her not sending to the DSS statements of subsequent sterling values.

Precise proof of what instructions were included in the order book actually issued to the claimant was crucial in *CP 20/1990*. An increase of benefit for the claimant's wife was improperly awarded, then excluded from payment by an administrative procedure, but allegedly actually paid to the claimant. The Commissioner says that in an ordinary case where proper awards are made, a photocopy of the Departmental record of the award and the issue of order books, together with a specimen of the order books current at the time will suffice to show the instructions given in the book about disclosure. But here it could not be assumed that the appropriate order book with the appropriate instructions had been issued.

CSB 510/1987 decided that advice from the claimant's solicitor and barrister that she did not need to tell the Department about an increase in her children's maintenance payments could make disclosure not reasonably expected.

In *CS 130/1992* the Commissioner suggests that disclosure of an intention to start work, if the intention was sufficiently settled so that an AO could reasonably review an award on the basis of it, may suffice, even if the actual start of work is not disclosed. See also *CS 234/1994*, where the Commissioner states that if the claimant was not informed that further disclosure (of the actual start of work) was required, she was entitled to assume that adequate disclosure had been made.

In *R(SB) 2/91* the Commissioner held that a claimant could not reasonably be expected to disclose a matter which was irrelevant to the question on which entitlement depended. However, it is expecting too much for a claimant to assess whether a matter is relevant or not, and this case would have been better dealt with on the basis that what was not disclosed was not a material fact (see above).

If one is concerned with disclosure by the claimant of someone else's asset (*e.g.* in *R(SB) 54/83*, the fact that the claimant's wife was working), the *R(SB) 21/82* test may be useful in marginal cases. Its most direct application will be, as in *R(SB) 21/82* itself, in deciding whether some person other than the claimant is under an obligation to disclose. *R(SB) 28/83* is a further example. Since the receiver of the mentally infirm claimant knew of his assets and knew or ought to have known that he was receiving supplementary benefit, he came under an obligation to disclose.

The next issue is to whom must disclosure be made. The leading decision is now *R(SB) 15/87*. Since the concern under the old s.20 was with breaches of the obligation to disclose which had the consequence that the Secretary of State incurred expenditure, it was held that the obligation was to disclose to a member or members of staff of an office of the Department handling the transaction giving rise to the expenditure. Although the wording of s.71 is somewhat different, it is thought that the obligation would be similar, relating to the office handling the claim giving rise to the payment of benefit alleged to have been overpaid. The Tribunal rejects the argument that disclosure to any member of the staff of the Department or to anyone in the "integrated office" in which the claimant was claiming would do. It is accepted that the claimant cannot be expected to identify the precise person dealing with his claim, but the Tribunal is then rather vague about how the obligation is to be fulfilled. They say it is best fulfilled by disclosure to the local office either on a claim form or making sufficient reference to the claim for the information to be referred to the proper person. If this is done, then there can be no further duty to disclose that matter. In the case of a claimant who is required to be available for work and thus has to deliver his claim form to the unemployment benefit office (UBO), disclosure on a claim form delivered there fulfils the duty. The Tribunal also accepts the decision in *R(SB) 54/83* that if an officer in another office accepts information in circumstances which make it reasonable for the claimant to think that the information will be passed on to the proper local office the duty is fulfilled. It holds that it is only in this kind of situation that there is a continuing duty of disclosure, as suggested in para. 18 of *R(SB) 54/83*. If the claimant should subsequently have realised that the information had not reached the proper person then a further obligation to disclose to the proper person would arise. The Tribunal expressly leaves open the question whether the claimant must actually know that the information has not got through.

Although the decision in *R(SB) 15/87* clears up a number of points, it does still leave some uncertainties. The major one is in what circumstances disclosure to the UBO might fulfil the claimant's obligation. It was suggested in *R(SB) 54/83* that in the case of a claimant who is required to declare his availability for work at, and is paid through, the UBO, the UBO is the agent of the supplementary benefit office, so that notice to the UBO would be imputed to the supplementary benefit office (and now the office dealing with income support). The Commissioner did not have to decide the point, but the issue was exhaustively discussed by a Tribunal of Commissioners in *R(SB) 36/84* and *CSB 397/1983*. There is an identical appendix in both decisions setting out in detail the arrangements between the DHSS and the Department of Employment (DE), who administer UBOs. The preliminary conclusion is that having regard to the past 40 years' arrangements, in particular those under which payment to claimants required to register or be available for work is made on the instructions of the UBO, there is an agency relationship. The decisions were not directly to do with recovery of overpayments, but the result in this context would be as suggested in *R(SB) 54/83*, regardless of the fact that the two Departments are otherwise independent. Some earlier decisions like *CSB 14/1982* must now be rejected as being based on mistaken assumptions about the independence of Departments (although it is clear that the principle can only apply in the special case of claimants paid through the UBO). However, the point has been treated as one of fact for each SSAT, rather than a matter on which a definite legal answer has been given (*R(SB) 10/85*).

The Tribunal of Commissioners in *R(SB) 15/87* certainly does not expressly reject the agency argument. Some doubt is raised because the Tribunal mention several ways of fulfilling the duty of disclosure, including delivering a claim form to the UBO, without mentioning the general agency argument. There is an obscure passage (para. 30) on causation (see below) which refers to para. 6549 of the *S Manual*. This does not seem to be relevant, but para. 6548 said that claimants who were required to be available were required to declare their earnings at the UBO. This reinforces the agency argument, but the context in the Tribunal's decision is of a situation where the claimant is said to have failed to disclose. In *R(SB) 2/91* it was accepted by the representative of the Chief Adjudication Officer that the DE were the agents of the DHSS for the purposes of the payment of supplementary benefit, so that information given to the UBO constituted information given to the supplementary benefit section of the DHSS. This view was approved by the Commissioner. The weight of the decisions is clearly that the DE now acts as the agent of the DSS in cases in which income support is paid through the UBO, so that in those cases disclosure to the UBO is disclosure to the office dealing with the claim, and there can be no question of a continuing duty to disclose.

In *CSB 699/1986* the Commissioner considers the circumstances in which, once disclosure has been made, there is no further obligation to disclose "the same matter." He suggests that the "same matter" is not restricted to one-off events, but could extend to a continuing state of affairs, such as the receipt of another benefit. But a transition from sickness to invalidity benefit would be a different matter. Similarly, disclosure on the claim form on a previous claim for the same benefit does not lift the duty to disclose on a fresh claim (*R(SB) 3/90*).

R(SB) 15/87 also deals with the question of by whom disclosure can be made in order to fulfil the claimant's obligation. One daughter, for whom the claimant had received benefit as a dependant, had made a claim in her own right for supplementary benefit at the same office. In respect of another child who started a YTS course, the child benefit book had been surrendered to the contributory benefits section of the same office by the claimant's wife. The Tribunal holds that neither of these actions was sufficient disclosure in relation to the claimant's entitlement to benefit for the children. Disclosure can be made by a third party on behalf of the claimant. but if this is done in the course of a separate transaction, the information must be given to the relevant benefit office and the claimant must know that it has been done and reasonably believe that it is unnecessary for him to take any action himself. In *Riches v. Social Security Commissioner* (Court of Session, May 4, 1993), it was accepted that it was reasonable for the claimant to assume that his wife had disclosed that he was getting invalidity benefit for her when she herself claimed sickness benefit, as she had done this in past claims. However, there was a continuing duty to disclose in these circumstances, and the claimant should have taken further steps when there was no follow-up action by the DSS. See also *CIS 14025/1996*.

CSB 347/1983 (approved in *R(SB) 10/85*) holds that while an AO might discharge his initial burden of proof by showing that there is no official record of a change of circumstances, thus leaving it for the claimant to prove on a balance of probabilities that he had made a disclosure, this only applies if a proper foundation is laid by evidence (not mere assertion) as to the instructions for recording information and how these are in practice carried out. The distinction between evidence and assertion is strongly supported in *CSB 1195/1984*. The claimant said that she had told two visiting officers that she was receiving unemployment benefit, but there was no official record of such a statement. The Commissioner stresses that what the claimant says about her own acts is evidence, while what a presenting officer says is not evidence unless backed up by personal knowledge of the facts. He says that the new SSAT should call the two visiting officers to give evidence. If they failed to appear without adequate excuse, the weight of the assertions alleged to have been made by them would be reduced to little or nothing. In *CSB 615/1985* it is stressed that there is no rule that only documentary evidence is admissible or that oral evidence requires corroboration.

Causation

It must be shown by the AO that any overpayment resulted from the misrepresentation or failure to disclose. In *R(SB) 3/81* the SBAT simply failed to look at the issue. In *R(SB) 21/82* the Commissioner holds that the right to recovery arises "only on a clearly stipulated causal basis." In that case the claimant's wife had made declarations in 1969 and 1971, but made no more until after the claimant's death in 1979. It was not clear how far any overpayment of benefit was in consequence of those earlier declarations when there were many intervening declarations by the claimant. See also *CIS 395/1992*. In that case the claimant, who had been living in a woman's aid refuge, returned to live with her husband. She gave him her income support order book to send back to the local office as she thought he was now claiming for the family. Her order book was subsequently cashed. The Commissioner holds that if the husband had cashed the orders without her knowledge, the payments made were not in consequence of her failure to disclose that she had left the refuge. The effective cause of the overpayment was the husband's theft of the order book, not the claimant's failure to disclose.

It is clear that if a claimant has disclosed a material fact to the relevant office in relation to the relevant claim there can be no recovery of subsequent benefit based on a failure to disclose that fact. This was decided in *CSB 688/1982* and *CSB 347/1983*, and confirmed in *R(SB) 15/87*. On principle, it would seem that proper disclosure would rob a subsequent misrepresentation of any causative effect. This appeared to be the result in *CSB 688/1982*, where the claimant orally disclosed to an officer that he had a mine-worker's pension. The officer omitted this from the statement which the claimant then signed as a true and complete statement of his circumstances. The Commissioner holds that the disclosure was fatal to the right of recovery. Although this had been put only on the ground of failure to disclose, the Commissioner felt able to make the decision that the overpayment was not recoverable. Since there had obviously been a misrepresentation, it looked as though the Commissioner must have considered that it could have no legal effect. However, in the very similar case of *R(SB) 18/85* the same Commissioner concentrates on the misrepresentation (see above) and makes no mention of the causation issue. It may be that since the appeal had to be sent back to the SBAT for proper findings of fact, the decision should be regarded as neutral on the causation issue. Whether disclosure does rob a subsequent misrepresentation of causative effect would seem to depend to some extent on the circumstances. In *R(SB) 3/90* the basic principle that if a misrepresentation induces a person to act it is irrelevant that the person had a means of verifying the information was applied. But the disclosure relied on in that case was in an earlier claim. During the currency of one claim the principle of *R(SB) 15/87* would undermine that approach where the means of verification stems from the claimant's disclosure. In *CSB 108/1992* the claimant argued that the fact that he had been advised in 1965/66 that he did not have to disclose his war pension absolved him from any charge of misrepresentation despite the fact that between then and 1985 when the DSS found out about the pension he had made at least 43 written misrepresentations. The Commissioner holds that that advice meant that there had been no contemporaneous misrepresentation, but that it did not assist the claimant in relation to subsequent statements. Clearly the length of time involved in this case (was it reasonable for the claimant to assume that something he was told in 1965 remained valid in 1985?) was a relevant factor. However, in *CS 130/1992* the Commissioner takes the view that contemporaneity may not be essential in all circumstances. A claimant can rely on prior qualification of a misrepresentation if the earlier disclosure was in sufficiently clear terms that the claimant could reasonably believe that it had not been overlooked.

Breakdown of DSS procedures and AO error

One of the most controversial issues is the effect of the breakdown of procedures within the DSS for notifying the income support office that a person has been awarded some other benefit (see, *e.g., Income Support Guide*, Other Benefits Vol. 2, paras. 4010–4049 for the child benefit procedure). The argument is that even though a claimant may have failed to disclose receipt of the other benefit the operative cause of the overpayment is the failure of the administrative procedure to get notice of entitlement to the other benefit from the other section concerned to the income support office. This argument has been rejected in a number of Commissioner's decisions, most recently in *CSB 64/1986* and *R(SB) 3/90*. The question asked there is, would the Secretary of State have avoided the relevant expenditure if the claimant had not failed to disclose the relevant material fact? If the answer is "yes," then the failure is the cause of the expenditure. The DSS procedure is in that sense a back-up one. The validity of this approach is confirmed by the Court of Appeal in *Duggan v. Chief Adjudication Officer (R(SB) 13/89)*. The claimant had failed to disclose his wife's unemployment benefit, but argued that on a review the AO should have investigated the full financial situation. It is held that if one cause of the overpayment was the failure to disclose, the overpayment is recoverable. The new wording in s.71, describing the amount recoverable as any payment which the Secretary of State would not have made but for the misrepresentation or failure to disclose, reinforces this conclusion.

However, it is vital to note that the principles just set out only apply when the other section of the DSS fails to inform the income support section. It is different if the information is received, but the income support section fails to act on it. The Tribunal of Commissioners in *R(SB) 15/87* recognise that if the DSS procedure works it may break the causal link between the claimant's failure and the overpayment. This is now explicitly dealt with in *CIS 159/1990*, where the Child Benefit Centre informed the local office dealing with the income support claim of the issue of an order book with an increased amount of child benefit, plus some arrears. The claimant did not report the arrival of the order book. The Commissioner holds that the overpayment was not in consequence of the failure to disclose, because the local office already knew of the material fact. The principle has been applied by a Commissioner to circumstances in which he was satisfied that the same officer in a particular local office would have dealt with both the claimant's and his wife's claim (*CS 11700/1996*). See also *CSIS 7/1994*, in which the local income support office had been notified of the award of family credit by the Family Credit Unit, although this had not been reported by the claimant. It was held that the cause of the overpayment was the local office's failure to act on the information, rather than the claimant's failure to disclose it.

CSIS 7/1994 is doubted in *CG 662/1998*, *CG 1567/1998* and *CG 2112/1998* on the basis of *Duggan* and *CF 3532/1997*. But it is suggested that the point of distinction in *CSIS 7/1994* and other similar cases, namely that the local office was in possession of the relevant information but failed to act on it, remains valid and that *CG 662/1998*, *CG 1567/1998* and *CG 2112/1998* and *CF 3532/1997* can be distinguished on their facts.

In *CF 3532/1997* the issues was since the claimant should never have been awarded child benefit while he was employed by the NAAFI in Germany, did his failure to disclose the fact that he was no longer employed by the NAAFI cause (at least in part) the overpayment in respect of the period after his employment ceased? The Commissioner accepted that it could be argued that as it would not make any difference to his lack of entitlement, the loss of that employment was not a material fact. He concluded, however, that the loss of employment with the NAAFI was material to the decision under which child benefit was paid and thus the failure to disclose was *a* cause of the overpayment.

In *CG 662/1998*, *CG 1567/1998* and *CG 2112/1998* the claimant who was getting invalid care allowance did not report that the person for whom he was caring was no longer in receipt of disability living allowance. The issue was whether the overpayment of invalid care allowance was recoverable, given that the ICA Unit both knew that disability living allowance had been awarded for a fixed term and had the means of knowing (through the Benefits Agency's computer records) that a renewal claim had not been successful to the required extent. The Commissioner accepts that there would be cases where the Benefits Agency had failed to act on the basis of information in their possession and would be unable to show that they would have reacted differently to the same information being supplied by the claimant. But in his view the question was whether the reporting of the material fact by the claimant could actually have prevented the overpayment, even when account was taken of the Agency's failing. He considered that the claimant's failure to reporrt was *a* cause of the overpayment and applying *Duggan* this was sufficient to ground recovery.

It is suggested that neither of these cases are on all fours with the siutation in *CSIS 7/1994* and similar cases. In *CF 3532/1997* the overpayment was due (in part) to the AO's misunderstanding of the law; the question of a failure to act on information did not arise. The facts in *CG 662/1998*, *CG 1567/1998* and *CG 2112/1998* are much closer to those in *CSIS 7/1994* but it is suggested that they can still be distinguished. In *CG 662/1998*, *CG 1567/1998* and *CG 2112/1998* the evidence was that there was no mechanism in place at that time to ensure that records were checked when an award of attendance allowance or disability living allowance was due to expire in order to see whether a renewal claim had been made and had been sufficiently successful. Instead the ICA Unit relied upon claimants to inform them. This was therefore not a case of the Benefits Agency failing to act on information in its possession, rather of the Agency failing to obtain information and choosing to rely on claimants to provide that information, which the Commissioner accepted they were entitled to do (although he doubted the wisdom of this approach when modern technology provided a "fairly simple and reasonably reliable additional source of information").

The scope of *Duggan* where there has been error or neglect by the AO is also discussed in *CIS 2447/1998*. The claimant had stated on her income support claim form in November 1993 that her partner was not working. In October 1995 it came to light that he had always been in full-time work. The claimant's income support award had been reviewed in March 1994 following the birth of her son. It was argued that any overpayment after that review resulted not from the misrepresentation on the claim form but from the AO's negligence. This was because the AO had failed to identify any basis for the claimant's continued entitlement to income support after that time. She was no longer exempted from the condition of being available for work on the ground of pregnancy and she was not a single parent. The SSAT rejected this argument, holding that the circumstances were not distinguishable from those in *Duggan*. The Commissioner, however, holds that the tribunal had misinterpreted the effect of *Duggan*. The Court of Appeal's decision in that case was closely related to its particular facts. It had not lain down a general rule that, whatever the extent or nature of the error by an AO, it did not remove the causative effect of some earlier failure to disclose or misrepresentation by a claimant. All the circumstances of the case had to be looked at. For example, if in the present case the claimant had later told the income support office that she had won £10,000 and the AO had mistakenly determined that that did not affect entitlement to income support, the continued payment of benefit could not be said to have as even one of its causes the initial misrepresentation that her partner was not in full-time work. However, the actual facts of this case did not fall into that category. The information that her baby had been born would not on its own have inevitably led to the conclusion that entitlement to income support should cease. Even though para. 9 of Sched. 1 to the Income Support Regulations as then in force would have ceased to apply to the claimant seven weeks after the birth of her baby, her entitlement to income support would only have stopped if no other paragraph of Sched. 1 applied, or if she had failed to make herself available for work. The AO's failure to investigate was thus an additional, but not the sole, cause of the overpayment and not such as to break the causative link between the misrepresentation and the subsequent payment of income support. As he had pointed out in *CF 3532/1997*, adjudicating authorities had no power to apportion responsibility for overpayments as between a number of causes. But this was a matter that the Secretary of State could take into account when deciding whether to enforce recovery of the full amount of the overpayment.

An example of where error by the AO did exonerate the claimant is *CIS 222/1991*. In that case the Commissioner holds that if the claimant's answers on the claim form were plainly inconsistent and ambiguous this put the AO on notice to investigate the position. If this was not done, any overpayment was not recoverable as it was due to error on the part of the Department rather than a misrepresentation by the claimant. The distinction between this and the other cases discussed above would seem to be that the information that should have triggered investigation by the AO was given on the claim form and yet the AO choose to make an award without resolving those contradictions.

Note that if income support is paid while a claimant is waiting for a decision on entitlement for another benefit and arrears of the other benefit are paid for this period, any excess income support cannot be recovered under this section, since it does not result from a failure to disclose. But s.74 and the Payments Regulations will operate to allow the excess to be deducted from the arrears of the other benefit or recovered from the recipient.

Couples claiming as single people

The situation dealt with in *CIS 13742/1996* is a particular illustration of the fact that the overpayment has to result from the misrepresentation or failure to disclose. The claimant and her partner (who were now separated) had each claimed benefit as single people while they were living together as husband and wife (and thus had been paid more benefit in total than they would have been entitled to if they had claimed as a couple). The AO decided that the total amount of the overpayment was recoverable from the claimant. However the Commissioner holds that that was incorrect. Any overpayment to the partner was not due to any action or failure to act on the part of the claimant but due to the fact that he had held himself out as a single person. Thus the claimant was not the cause of any overpayment to her partner and as a result recovery of any such overpayment could not be sought from her. But had the claimant herself been overpaid benefit? From November 21, 1983 the claimant could have claimed benefit in respect of herself and her family (up to November 21, 1983 the claim could only have been made by her partner). Thus if the claimant could show that such a claim would have been successful (the onus being on her to show that offsetting under reg. 13(b)(ii) of the Payments Regulations applied), there would be no question of an overpayment because she would have received less benefit than she was entitled to. If, however, she could not have qualified as the claimant for the family, she would be liable to repay *all* the benefit that she had received in the relevant period. The Commissioner did, however, comment that in his view it would be inequitable for the Secretary of State to require her to repay more than the amount of the actual excess benefit paid.

The question of recovery of an overpayment from one member of a couple where both had been claiming income support separately was also considered in *CIS 619/1997*. The Commissioner agrees with *CIS 13742/1996* that unless there had been a reivew of the decision awarding benefit to the other member of the couple (in this case the husband), the overpayment, and any offset against it under reg. 13(b)(ii), could only be considered in connection with the claimant's own claim. It was therefore incumbent on the tribunal to ascertain the position on the husband's claim (which they had not done).

Amount of overpayment

The calculation of the amount to be recovered has given considerable problems in the past. Subs. (6)(a) below allows regulations to be made on this issue. Regs. 13 and 14 of the Payments Regulations are relevant.

The starting point is the amount of benefit which would not have been paid but for the misrepresentation or failure to disclose. This is in line with the approach set out in *R(SB) 20/84* and *R(SB) 10/85* of looking at what the revised decision would be when the full facts are known. Normally there is no difficulty in determining the amount of benefit which was actually paid, but there may be exceptional cases, like *CP 20/1990*, where evidence of the amounts of payment, rather than a second-hand description, is required. See also *CIS 13148/1996* which points out that a computer printout of payments made is *prima facie* evidence of payment (although not strictly of receipt), but may be displaced by other evidence of non-payment.

A controversial question under the pre-April 1987 law was how far it was possible to take account of underpayments of benefit against the overpayment. Reg. 13(b) of the Payments Regulations provides that from the gross amount of the overpayment is to be deducted any additional amount of income support which should have been awarded on the basis of the claim as originally presented or with the addition of the facts misrepresented or not disclosed. This allows a somewhat more extensive set-off than under the old law (for which, see *R(SB) 20/84, R(SB) 10/85* and *R(SB) 11/86*). *CSIS 8/1995* holds that reg. 13 makes it mandatory for an AO to consider the question of a possible underpayment of income support when calculating an overpayment. (But this does not by virtue of reg. 31 of the Payments Regulations extend to supplementary benefit unless the overpayment involves supplementary benefit.) The AO does not need to state expressly that he has considered reg. 13, provided there is a reference to it in the legislation stated to have been taken into consideration. If the AO has not considered reg. 13, a tribunal may remedy this deficiency. A SSAT must deal with the question of any offset before it reaches a decision on the recoverability of an overpayment. It cannot decide that an overpayment is recoverable and then refer the question of any offset back to the AO (*CSG 357/1997*).

R(IS) 5/92 confirms that the reg. 13(b) deduction is not limited to the period after the beginning of the overpayment, but can go back to the date of claim. In addition, *CSIS 8/1995* points out that the overpayment may relate to an entirely different benefit (see the definition of "benefit" in reg. 1(2) of the Payments Regulations). Again, there need be no connection between the respective periods. But the examination of the additional amount which would have been payable must be based on the claim as originally presented, or with the addition of the material facts misrepresented or not disclosed. For an example see *CIS 13742/1996* in the notes under the heading "Causation" above. Thus, if, for instance, evidence suggesting that a premium should have been allowed is produced for the first time once an overpayment has been determined by an AO, the amount of that premium is not to be offset against the gross amount of the overpayment (confirming the result of *CSB 615/1985*). In that case, any arrears must be obtained through the ordinary process of review under s.25, and subject to the then 12 (now one) month limit imposed by reg. 69 of the Adjudication Regulations. If the award of benefit has been reviewed, *e.g.* to include a premium, but the arrears have not yet been paid when the overpayment is determined, there can be an offset under regs. 5(2), Case 1, and 13(a). Any other offset under reg. 5 is to be deducted, but no other deduction for underpayments is to be made. In *R(IS) 5/92* the Commissioner construes "claim as presented" in reg. 13(b)(i) as including facts that would be discovered by "any reasonable enquiry . . . prompted by the claim form". This is applied in *CIS 137/1992* to require the AO to consider reg. 8(3) of the Income Support Regulations (income support on hardship grounds) where it has been decided that neither para. 5 nor 6 of Sched. 1 apply to the claimant but she does not make herself available for work. The Commissioner states that there is always the possibility of hardship where a person is left on an income below the level of reduced income support; the fact that her claim form did not reveal that she would suffer hardship if no benefit was paid was thus not material. *CIS 137/1992* further points out that reg. 13 is concerned with deductions from an overpayment and so only comes into play after the overpayment has been calculated. The review which results in a decision as to the amount of benefit that ought to have been paid is therefore to be carried out without any fetter being imposed by reg. 13.

Another problem now dealt with by regulations arises when the misrepresentation or failure to disclose is of capital resources. If it emerged that a claimant who had been in receipt of income support or family credit for a few years throughout had capital of £1 over the limit, it would be most unfair to require repayment of the whole amount of benefit. If the capital had been properly taken into account, so that benefit was not initially awarded, the capital would have immediately been reduced below the limit in order to provide for living expenses. So the Commissioners applied the "diminishing capital" principle (*CSB 53/1981, CSBO v. Leary*, appendix to *R(SB) 6/85, R(SB) 15/85*). The position is now governed by reg. 14 of the Payments Regulations. This provides for the reduction of the figure of capital resources at quarterly intervals from the beginning of the overpayment period by the amount overpaid in income support or family credit in the previous quarter. No other reduction of the actual amount of capital resources is allowed (reg. 14(2)). Under the Commissioners' approach the notional reduction had to be made week by week. It will be considerably easier to make the calculation at 13 week intervals, but the tendency will be for smaller reductions of the overpayment to be produced.

It is for the AO to prove the existence and amount of capital taken into account in calculating an overpayment (*R(SB) 21/82*). Here, sums had suddenly appeared in Building Society accounts and there was no evidence where they had come from. The Commissioner commends the adoption of a lower figure of overpayment rather than a higher one based on the assumption that the capital assets had not been possessed before any evidence existed about them. The Commissioner in *R(SB) 34/83* agrees strongly on the burden of proof, but points out that if the person concerned was alive and failed to give any proper explanation of the origin of such sums, adverse inferences could be drawn against him, enabling the AO to discharge his burden of proof. He goes on to hold that the estate of a deceased person should be in the same position. Therefore, a heavy responsibility devolved on the executor to make every reasonable enquiry as to the origin of the money. But if after such efforts there was no evidence where the money came from the burden of proof on the AO would not have been discharged.

It is essential that on an appeal a SSAT should clearly state the amount which is recoverable, and state how that amount is calculated (*R(SB) 9/85*). If there is no dispute about the amount of the overpayment a SSAT may not need to describe the calculation (*CSB 218/1991*). If the SSAT cannot make the calculation at the time of their initial decision they can refer the matter back to the AO for recalculation on the basis determined by the SSAT, but only if the decision expressly allows the matter to be referred back to the SSAT if agreement cannot be reached on the recalculation (*R(SB) 11/86, R(SB) 15/87*). The suggestion in *CSB 83/1991* that this valuable practice is invalidated by subs. (2) is rightly rejected in *CIS 442/1992*. That decision also suggests that if there is a reference back to the SSAT, and the members of the new tribunal are not the same as those who sat on the tribunal which made the main decision, the whole matter, including the question of liability, must be reconsidered. The basis for this suggestion seems dubious. Such a decision is a final decision of the SSAT, and there seems to be no doubt that there can be an appeal to the Commissioner under s.23(1) from such a decision (see the notes to s.23(1) for further discussion).

One reason why SSATs must be careful to specify the amount recoverable is that often differing amounts are calculated by the AO after his initial decision. If this is done there was before April 1990 no bar to this operating as a review and revision of the initial decision. The initial decision, being on a single indivisible question, would thus be replaced and any appeal lodged against it would lapse. However, appeals in these circumstances were commonly continued as though they had not lapsed. In *CSB 64/1986*, where the claimant's representative insisted that the appeal was against the initial decision, the Commissioner held that the SSAT's decision was given without authority as the appeal had lapsed. In *R(SB) 15/87*, the appeal was treated as against the revised decision, although no notice of appeal against that decision had been given. The Tribunal of Commissioners holds that in this case the failure to comply with the procedural requirements, did not make the SSAT's proceedings a nullity. There had been substantial compliance with the requirements, there was no public interest in strict compliance and the claimant would be prejudiced if the procedural failure was not ignored, since the time for appealing against the revised decision had expired. The predecessor of s.29 of the Administration Act provided from April 1990 that once an appeal has been lodged, a review is to be of no effect unless it gives the claimant everything that the claimant could possibly obtain in the appeal, so that if there is merely a revision of the amount of an overpayment the appeal against the original decision continues in being.

Subsection (2)

See the notes to subs. (5A).

Subsection (3)

This provision confirms that amounts are recoverable from the person who made the misrepresentation or failed to make disclosure. Presumably the principle that after the person's death the overpayment is recoverable from his estate (*Secretary of State for Social Services v. Solly* [1974] 3 All E.R. 922, *R(SB) 21/82, R(SB) 28/83*) is not affected. See *CSSB 6/1995*. Note that the time limit of the Limitation Act 1980 does not begin to run until there is a determination of an overpayment by an AO which gives the Secretary of State the right of recovery (*R(SB) 5/91, R(A) 2/86*). See also *CIS 26/1994* at the beginning of this note.

CIS 332/1993 decides that if an appointee signs a misrepresentation in the capacity of appointee, there can only be recovery from the claimant and not from her personally. Any misrepresentation or failure to disclose by the appointee acting in that capacity was attributable to the claimant and so any resulting overpayment was recoverable from the claimant (*R(SB) 28/83*). Thus, if in this situation it was as if the claimant had personally misrepresented or failed to disclose the material fact, it could not at the same time be said that the appointee had personally misrepresented or failed to disclose the fact. When a person was acting in the capacity of an appointee she was not a third party in the sense that had been considered by the House of Lords in *Plewa*, but her acts and omissions were those of the claimant's. The situation would of course be different if the appointee had been acting in a personal capacity. The Commissioner declined to follow *CIS 734/1992* which held that where the appointment was made because of the claimant's mental incapacity, any failure to disclose by the appointee could not be imputed to the claimant and so the overpayment was recoverable only from the appointee personally. See also *CIS 649/1993*.

In *CIS 12022/1996* another Commissioner has held that *CIS 332/1993* was wrongly decided and that when subs. (3) refers to overpayments being recoverable from the person who misrepresented or failed to disclose a material fact it simply means what it says. A failure to disclose by an appointee could lead to recovery from the claimant, but it could also lead to recovery from the appointee personally, in the same way as, when an employee or an agent commits a tort, action can be taken against both the employer or principal and against the employee or agent personally. In effect, the Commissioner held that an appointee should be in no different position from any other third party who acts on behalf of a claimant. SSATs may therefore have to weigh up the merits of the opposing arguments in deciding which decision to follow. Neither outcome is free from difficulty. Reference to the reported decisions *R(SB) 21/82* and *R(SB) 28/83*, relied on in *CIS 12022/1996*, does not in fact resolve the question of whether appointees (or receivers appointed by the Court of Protection) are in any special position.

Similar problems can arise where claimants have executed enduring powers of attorney and subsequently become incapable of managing their affairs. Further Commissioners' decisions are expected, which it is hoped will resolve at least some of the difficulties.

Subsections (4) and (5)

Subsection (4) applies where benefit is paid by automatic credit transfer directly into a bank or other account. See reg. 21 of the Claims and Payments Regulations for payment and reg. 11 of the Payments Regulations for recovery of overpayments. Subsection (5) imposes the additional conditions that, where an overpayment is recoverable under reg. 11 of the Payments Regulations, not only must the decision awarding the benefit in question have been revised on review (or reversed on appeal), but the decision that the overpayment is recoverable must be made "on the appeal or review". This may mean something different from "in the course of the appeal or review" (the interpretation of which phrase in *CIS 451/1995* led to the passing of the Social Security (Overpayments) Act 1996), but it is not clear just how the condition now differs from that under subs. (5A). It may be that, following *CSSB 316/1989* (see note to subs. (5A) below), separate decisions can be given on review and on recoverability.

Subsection (5A)

This provision applies to decisions under subs. (1), and not to decisions under the Payments Regulations, made after July 24, 1996 (see the beginning of this note for the temporal effect of the Social Security (Overpayments) Act 1996). In conjunction with the substituted form of subs. (2), it has the effect that it is no longer necessary for the overpayment decision to be made as part of and at the same time as the relevant review decision. See the notes to s.71(5) in the 1996 edition for *CIS 451/1995*, which confirmed that result on the pre-July 24, 1996 legislation. It is now only necessary that the decision under which the benefit alleged to have been overpaid was awarded has been revised on review or varied on appeal.

However, regulations may provide otherwise, and must be taken as having done so. Reg. 12 of the Payments Regulations provides that s.53(4) of the Social Security Act 1986 does not apply in the circumstances it prescribes. On the consolidation into the Social Security Administration Act 1992, that reference became, under s.2(4) of the Social Security (Consequential Provisions) Act 1992, a reference to s.71(5). Now that the 1996 Act has split the previous subs. (5) into two, reg. 12 must be taken as referring to both subss. (5) and (5A). The circumstances prescribed in reg. 12 are that the fact and circumstances of the misrepresentation or non-disclosure do not provide a basis for reviewing and revising the initial decision. This formulation is rather obscure, but it seems to mean that if the conditions for review and revision do not exist there can still be a determination that an overpayment is recoverable. See *CS 102/1993* in the note to misrepresentation above for an example of where reg. 12 applied. But if the conditions for review and revision do exist then the determination of the recoverable overpayment must be made following a review decision or not at all (see also subs. (2)). *R(SB) 7/91* has now decided that this is so. See also *CIS 35/1990* (para. 11) and *CSB 1272/1989* (para. 10).

A number of decisions have held that (outside reg. 12) it is an essential pre-condition of an overpayment determination that there should be proof of a valid revision of entitlement on review. See *CSSB 105/1989*, followed in *CIS 179/1990* and *CIS 360/1990*. The principle is accepted in *CSSB 316/1989*, where the Commissioner also deals with the requirement in what is now subs. (5A) that the overpayment determination must be made "on the appeal or review." He says "[the] earliest possible correction of a continuing award which has been found to be incorrect is obviously desirable and I accept that an effective decision for the purposes of section 53(1), (1A) and (4) can be made notwithstanding that grounds of review and revisal of the award for the past and the future, which must of course be appropriate, are established at a date prior to the making of the decision establishing the detail of the overpayment." (See also *CSIS 174/1996* which disagrees more explicitly with *CIS 451/1995* that under the pre-July 24, 1996 legislation the overpayment decision had to be made at the same time as the review decision.)

In *CSIS 64/1992* the Commissioner regards it as essential that the review decision be produced in any recovery case in order to show, not just that subs. (5A) has been complied with, but also that the review itself has been properly carried out under s.25 (including taking account of any awards that should have been made in the claimant's favour), and that reg. 20 (now reg. 18) of the Adjudication Regulations has been complied with. See also *CIS 13520/1996* in which the Commissioner points out the need for the tribunal to have sight of the review decision in order to ascertain its precise terms. Now that separate review and overpayment decisions are permitted, it will be particularly pertinent for a tribunal hearing an appeal against the overpayment decision to see the original of the review decision in order to check the validity and the terms of that decision. *CSIS 174/1996* further emphasises that the original of decisions should be produced, rather than their effect simply being recited (sometimes inaccurately) on the form AT2. In *CSIS 78/1993*, to be reported as *R(IS) 2/96*, the Commissioner did not consider that proof of a proper prior review was established by production of largely unintelligible computer print outs, which did not show the actual terms of the review, nor that this had been communicated to the claimant. *CSIS 60/1994* also stresses the inadequacy of computer print outs as proof of review. Presumably it might be possible for the individual adjudication officer concerned to give oral evidence as to the review. If no evidence of a review is put before a tribunal, it is obliged to enquire into this. If it does not do so, the fact that a review decision could have been produced will not vitiate this error (*CSIS 62/1991*).

There remains some uncertainty about what a SSAT should do if faced with an overpayment decision when there has not been a valid revision of entitlement on review. In *CSSB 105/1989, CSSB 316/1989* and *CSSB 540/1989*, the Commissioner suggests that the SSAT should simply determine that no valid AO's decision on the overpayment has been made. In *R(SB) 7/91* the Commissioner holds that the SSAT should determine that the AO's decision is of no force or effect. However, this seems to leave the possibility of an AO's reviewing the defective AO's decision for error of law under s.25(2) of the Administration Act (suggested in *CSSB 105/1989*) or of the AO starting the overpayment procedure all over again by a valid revision of entitlement on review. A SSAT's decision in this form does not decide that an overpayment can never be recovered. It secures that the proper process must be applied. But the final result may be the same and the claimant has to appeal yet again to challenge it. It may therefore be asked why the SSAT should not follow the general principle put forward in *CSSB 540/1989* that on appeal a SSAT can correct a defective review decision. In *CSB 1272/1989* the Commissioner, in an effort to avoid the expense and delay of starting the whole process again, suggests that where in overpayments cases the AO has omitted to carry out a review, the SSAT should make good the omission using its power under s.36 of the Administration Act (1975 Act, s.102) to determine questions first arising in the course of the appeal. This approach seems rather dubious, since the review question seems to be part and parcel of the overpayment question already before the AO and the SSAT, and not one which first arises in the course of the appeal. In addition, none of the decisions mentioned earlier are cited in *CSB 1272/1989*. For these reasons the Commissioner in *CSIS 64/1992* did not consider that in overpayment cases a tribunal could itself conduct the review and in *CSIS 78/1993*, to be reported as *R(IS) 2/96*, he states that the review certainly should not be carried out at Commissioner level. The position thus remains somewhat unresolved until some authoritative decision emerges from the Commissioners. But at the moment the weight of authority would seem to be in favour of a SSAT determining that no valid overpayment decision has been made. This is the approach taken in *CIS 312/1992*. There is in any case a difficulty in "correcting" an AO's decision where no review decision at all has been made. There may however be exceptional circumstances, for instance where a SSAT is clear that an overpayment would not be recoverable under s.71, where a SSAT should deal with the review issue (*cf. CSB 274/1990*).

The most recent Commissioner's decision, *CSG 2/1996*, deals with the, perhaps more common, situation where a valid review decision was in fact made by an AO, but was not produced to a SSAT, which consequently determined that the AO had failed to establish any entitlement to recover the alleged overpayment. The AO then purported to carry out a fresh review of the awarding decision, incorporating a decision that the resulting overpayment was recoverable. A second SSAT confirmed the AO's decision on the basis that the first review decision, which had been produced, was a nullity. The Commissioner held that the second SSAT was wrong to adopt that basis. The first SSAT had not decided that the review decision was a nullity. It had merely decided that the AO had not discharged the onus of proving that there had been a review. The AO's decision before the second SSAT was therefore of no effect.

CSG 2/1996 illustrates the important distinction between a case where there has been no review at all or no valid review and a case where it is simply that an AO has failed to prove to a SSAT that a review has taken place. In the first case, it seems that an AO may carry out a proper review with a following overpayment decision. In the second case, the AO cannot make a fresh review decision (unless there is some ground for reviewing the existing review decision). Before the coming into operation of the Social Security (Overpayments) Act 1996, that would have left the AO unable to make another overpayment decision. However, it seems that now there is no reason why the AO cannot rely on the existing review decision to make a fresh overpayment decision after a SSAT has decided that the previous overpayment decision was of no effect because no review decision had been proved.

If there is no doubt that the AO has carried out a proper review and revision, it is not an error of law for the SSAT not to mention the issue, although it is better if it does (*CSIS 62/1991*).

The point made in *CF 3532/1997* should also be noted. An overpayment of child benefit was made because the AO wrongly believed the claimant to be entitled to child benefit while employed by the NAAFI in Germany. The claimant was then made redundant by the NAAFI but did not report this fact until over a year later. It is held that the overpayment after the cessation of his employment was recoverable on the ground of failure to disclose a material fact. His loss of employment was material to the operative decision on the authority of which benefit had been paid, even if not material to his underlying entitlement. The Commissioner states that it also did not matter that the proper ground for review was not related to the material fact whose misrepresentation or failure to disclose was a cause of the overpayment. It was sufficient that there had been a revision on review which covered at least the period of the alleged overpayment and that from some date the overpayment was a result of a misrepresentation or failure to disclose. In that case the proper ground for review was error of law, not change of circumstances, because the change of circumstances was not relevant to the claimant's entitlement to child benefit.

Subsection (6)

The Payments Regulations have been made under these powers.

Subsection (7)

See Part II of the Payments Regulations.

Subsection (8)

The benefits from which deductions may be made are prescribed by reg. 15 of the Payments Regulations. They include most social security benefits. Limits to the weekly amounts which may be deducted from income support and family credit are set by reg. 16. Reg. 20(2) of the 1987 Payments Regulations provides that subs. (8) also applies to amounts recoverable under any enactment repealed by the 1986 Act or regulation revoked by the 1987 Regulations. The Divisional Court in *R. v. Secretary of State for Social Services, ex p. Britnell, The Times*, January 27, 1989, decided that reg. 20(2) did not offend the rule of construction against retrospection. Its effect was merely to provide an additional method of recovery where there was no dispute that a liability to repay existed. In the Court of Appeal (*The Times*, February 16, 1990) and the House of Lords ([1991]1 W.L.R. 198, [1991] 2 All E.R. 726), the point on retrospection was not argued and reg. 20(2) was found to have been validly made under s.89(1) of the 1986 Act.

See the notes to s.78 for the effect of a claimant's bankruptcy or sequestration.

Subsection (9)

See reg. 17 of the Payments Regulations.

[¹Overpayments out of social fund

71ZA.—(1) Subject to subsection (2) below, section 71 above shall apply in relation to social fund payments to which this section applies as it applies in relation to payments made in respect of benefits to which that section applies.

[²(2) Section 71 above as it so applies shall have effect as if the following provisions were omitted, namely—

(a) in paragraph (a) of subsection (5) and subsection (5A), the words "reversed or varied on an appeal or";

(b) in paragraph (b) of subsection (5), the words "appeal or"; and

(c) subsections (7), (10A) and (10B).]

(3) This section applies to social fund payments such as are mentioned in section 138(1)(b) of the Contributions and Benefits Act.]

AMENDMENTS

1. Social Security Act 1998, s. 75(1) (October 5, 1998).
2. Note that until ss. 9, 10 and 38 of the 1998 Act come into force, subs. (2) is substituted by para. 8 of Sched. 6 to the Act.

GENERAL NOTE

Section 75(2) of the Social Security Act 1998 provides that s. 71ZA applies to social fund overpayment decisions made on or after October 5, 1998.

[¹*Jobseekers's allowance*

Recovery of jobseeker's allowance: severe hardship cases

71A.—(1) Where—

(a) a severe hardship direction is revoked; and

(b) it is determined by an adjudication officer that—

    (i) whether fraudulently or otherwise, any person has misrepresented, or failed to disclose, any material fact; and

    (ii) in consequence of the failure or misrepresentation, payment of a jobseeker's allowance has been made during the relevant period to the person to whom the direction related,

an adjudication officer may determine that the Secretary of State is entitled to recover the amount of the payment.

(2) In this section—

"severe hardship direction" means a direction given under section 16 of the Jobseekers Act 1995; and

"the relevant period" means—

    (a) if the revocation is under section 16(3)(a) of that Act, the period begining with the date of the change of circumstances and ending with the date of the revocation; and

    (b) if the revocation is under section 16(3)(b) or (c) of that Act, the period during which the direction was in force.

(3) Where a severe hardship direction is revoked, the Secretary of State may certify whether there has been misrepresentation of a material fact or failure to disclose a material fact.

(4) If the Secretary of State certifies that there has been such misrepresentation or failure to disclose, he may certify—

    (a) who made the misrepresentation or failed to make the disclosure; and

    (b) whether or not a payment of jobseeker's allowance has been made in consequence of the misrepresentation or failure.

(5) If the Secretary of State certifies that a payment has been made, he may certify the period during which a jobseeker's allowance would not have been paid but for the misrepresentation or failure to disclose.

(6) A certificate under this section shall be conclusive as to any matter certified.

(7) Subsections (3) and (6) to (10) of section 71 above apply to a jobseeker's allowance recoverable under subsection (1) above as they apply to a jobseeker's allowance recoverable under section 71(1) above.

(8) The other provisions of section 71 above do not apply to a jobseeker's allowance recoverable under subsection (1) above.]

AMENDMENT

1. Jobseekers Act 1995, s. 18 (October 7, 1996).

GENERAL NOTE

Section 16 of the Jobseekers Act 1995 enables the Secretary of State to direct that a person under the age of 18 is to qualify for JSA in order to avoid severe hardship. The direction may be revoked on the ground of change of circumstances (s.16(3)(a)) or on the ground that the young person has failed to pursue an opportunity, or rejected an offer, of training without good cause (s.16(3)(b)) or on the ground that mistake as to or ignorance of a material fact led to the determination that severe hardship would result if JSA was not paid (s.16(3)(c)). A special provision is needed for recovery in cases of misrepresentation or failure to disclose because the revocation of the direction is not a review which can found action under s.71 and it appears that it does not enable the decision on entitlement to JSA to be reviewed for any period before the date of the revocation. Although the determination is made by the AO under subs. (1), the Secretary of State's certificate is conclusive on almost every issue (subs. (3) to (6)). The provisions of s.71 about the mechanics of recovery apply.

Special provision as to recovery of income support

72.—[¹...]

AMENDMENT

1. Repealed by Jobseekers Act 1995, Sched. 3 (October 7, 1996).

Adjustments of benefits

Income support and other payments

74.—(1) Where—
  (a) a payment by way of prescribed income is made after the date which is the prescribed date in relation to the payment; and
  (b) it is determined that an amount which has been paid by way of income support [¹or an income-based jobseeker's allowance] would not have been paid if the payment had been made on the prescribed date,
the Secretary of State shall be entitled to recover that amount from the person to whom it was paid.
  (2) Where—
  (a) a prescribed payment which apart from this subsection falls to be made from public funds in the United Kingdom or under the law of any other member State is not made on or before the date which is the prescribed date in relation to the payment; and
  (b) it is determined that an amount ("the relevant amount") has been paid by way of income support [¹or an income-based jobseeker's allowance] that would not have been paid if the payment mentioned in paragraph (a) above had been made on the prescribed date,
then—
      (i) in the case of a payment from public funds in the United Kingdom, the authority responsible for making it may abate it by the relevant amount; and
      (ii) in the case of any other payment, the Secretary of State shall be entitled to receive the relevant amount out of the payment.
  (3) Where—
  (a) a person (in this subsection referred to as A) is entitled to any prescribed benefit for any period in respect of another person (in this subsection referred to as B); and
  (b) either—
      (i) B has received income support [¹or an income-based jobseeker's allowance] for that period; or
      (ii) B was, during that period, a member of the same family as some person other than A who received income support [¹or an income-based jobseeker's allowance] for that period; and
  (c) the amount of the income support [¹or an income-based jobseeker's allowance] has been determined on the basis that A has not made payments for the maintenance of B at a rate equal to or exceeding the amount of the prescribed benefit,
the amount of the prescribed benefit may, at the discretion of the authority administering it, be abated by the amount by which the amounts paid by way of income support [¹or an income-based jobseeker's allowance] exceed what it is determined that they would have been had A, at the time the amount of the income support [¹or an income-based jobseeker's allowance] was determined,

been making payments for the maintenance of B at a rate equal to the amount of the prescribed benefit.

(4) Where an amount could have been recovered by abatement by virtue of subsection (2) or (3) above but has not been so recovered, the Secretary of State may recover it otherwise than by way of abatement—

(a) in the case of an amount which could have been recovered by virtue of subsection (2) above, from the person to whom it was paid; and

(b) in the case of an amount which could have been recovered by virtue of subsection (3) above, from the person to whom the prescribed benefit in question was paid.

(5) Where a payment is made in a currency other than sterling, its value in sterling shall be determined for the purposes of this section in accordance with regulations.

DERIVATION

Social Security Act 1986, s.27.

AMENDMENT

1. Jobseekers Act 1995, Sched. 2, para. 50 (October 7, 1996).

DEFINITION

"prescribed"—see s.191.

GENERAL NOTE

Most of this section was originally, in substance, s.12 of the Supplementary Benefits Act 1976. There are changes in form from the old s.12, but the overall aim is the same, to prevent a claimant from getting a double payment when other sources of income are not paid on time. This is an important provision, which is often overlooked. It now extends to income-based JSA as well as to income support.

Subsection (1)

Prescribed income is defined in reg. 7(1) of the Social Security (Payments on account, Overpayments and Recovery) Regulations 1988 ("the Payments Regulations") as any income which is to be taken into account under Part V of the Income Support (General) Regulations or Part VIII of the Jobseeker's Allowance Regulations. The prescribed date under reg. 7(2) is, in general, the first day of the period to which that income relates. If as a result of that income being paid after the prescribed date, more income support or income-based JSA is paid than would have been paid if the income had been paid on the prescribed date, the excess may be recovered. Note that the right to recover is absolute and does not depend on lack of care on the claimant's part, or on the effect of this section having been pointed out. That approach is confirmed in *CIS 625/1991*, where the Commissioner rejected the argument that there had to be an investigation of what an AO would in practice have done if the income had been paid on time. An example would be where a claimant has not been paid part-time earnings when they were due and as a result has been paid income support on the basis of having no earnings. Once the arrears of wages are received, the excess benefit would be recoverable. Late payment of most social security benefits is covered in subss. (2) and (4), but can also come within subs. (1). For instance, if a claim is made for child benefit and while a decision is awaited income support is paid without any deduction for the amount of the expected child benefit, then if arrears of child benefit are eventually paid in full (*i.e.* the abatement procedure of subs. (2) does not work) the "excess" income support for the period covered by the arrears is recoverable under subs. (1) or (4).

It is essential that the dates on which prescribed income was due to be paid and on what dates due payments would have affected income support entitlement should be determined *(R(SB) 28/85* and *CIS 625/1991)*.

Subsection (2)

Prescribed payments are listed in reg. 8(1) of the Payments Regulations and include most social security benefits, training allowances and social security benefits from other E.C. countries. As under subs. (1), a claimant is not to keep excess income support or income-based JSA resulting from late payment of one of the prescribed payments. However, the primary mechanism here where the payment is due from public funds in the U.K. is for the arrears due to be abated (*i.e.* reduced) by the amount of the excess income support or JSA (subs. (2)(a) and (i)). Note that the abatement may be applied to benefits due to another member of the claimant's family (*e.g.* retirement pension due to the wife of the income support claimant in *CSB 383/1988*). If this mechanism breaks down and the arrears are paid in full, then under subs. (1) or (4) the Secretary of State can recover the excess from the income support or JSA recipient.

In *R(IS) 14/94* the claimant's income support included a severe disability premium (SDP). Her daughter was later awarded invalid care allowance (ICA) for caring for the claimant and arrears for March 1989 to July 1990 were paid. The AO reviewed the decision awarding the claimant an SDP from March 1989 to July 1990 on the ground that it was made in ignorance of a material fact, and decided that the resulting overpayment was recoverable from the claimant under s.27 of the Social Security Act 1986 (now s.74). The Commissioner held that the arrears of ICA could have been abated under s.27(2) (now s.74(2)), despite the fact that the daughter was not a member of the claimant's family for the purposes of income support. An SDP would not have been paid if the award of ICA had been known. The Commissioner also rejected the argument that ICA was not "in payment" until July 1990 and so the condition in para. 13(2)(a)(iii) of Sched. 2 to the Income Support Regulations was satisfied. "In payment" did not mean timeously in payment. Since the power of abatement had not been exercised, the overpaid income support could be recovered under s.27(4) (now s.74(4)) from the claimant as the person to whom it had been paid. The claimant was granted leave to appeal against the Commissioner's decision by the Court of Appeal. However, the appeal was not proceeded with as the Secretary of State issued internal guidance stating that where a carer receives arrears of ICA and an SDP has been in payment to the person cared for, no recovery should be sought of the consequent overpayment of income support. The Commissioner's interpretation was therefore not tested before the Court of Appeal. However, if through the operation of s.74 a person who is entitled to benefit can be deprived of it because an overpayment of income support has been made to some other independent person, this seems arbitrary and unfair. The position has now been remedied in relation to SDP and arrears of ICA by the introduction of para. 13(3ZA) of Sched. 2 to the Income Support Regulations. See the notes to para. 13. This should avoid any question of an overpayment of an SDP by reason of a backdated award of ICA. One other point should be made. The Commissioner in *R(IS) 14/94* accepted that the claimant's income support was properly reviewed on the ground of ignorance of a material fact. It was suggested in the 1995 edition that the correct ground would seem to have been change of circumstances. The basis of this was that it was difficult to see how an AO could be said to have been ignorant of a fact which did not exist at the date of the decision (see *CIS 650/1991*). Although *CSIS 83/1994* did decide that it did not matter that the fact did not "exist" at the time of the AO's original decision, this was overturned by the Court of Session (see the notes to s. 25(1)(a) to (c) of the Administration Act).

In the case of other payments (which will normally be benefits due from other E.C. countries) recovery is the primary mechanism (subs. (2)(ii)). If the payment is routed through the DSS, as was the case for the arrears of a German invalidity pension in *R(SB) 3/91* (see also *R(SB) 1/91* and *CIS 501/1993*), a deduction can be made before the arrears are paid over to the claimant. Although reg. 8(1)(g) of the Payments Regulations makes a reference to E.C. Regulation 1408/71, the s.74 procedure is not limited to benefits obtained by virtue of the Regulation. See also *CIS 12082/1996* in which the DSS had requested that payment be made to them by the Italian authorities of the arrears of the claimant's Italian retirement pension. The DSS relied on Art. 111 of E.C. Regulation 574/72. The Commissioner decides that Art. 111 did not apply but that this did not prevent the application of subs. (2). The Italian authorities had chosen to remit the arrears to the DSS and this then allowed the Secretary of State to recover the supplementary benefit and income support that had been overpaid to the claimant out of the arrears. The procedure followed in this case was not precluded by Art. 111 and there was nothing in Regulation 574/72 (or E.C. Regulation 1408/91) that prevented the application of subs. (2) in these circumstances.

Once again, the operation of the provision is automatic. Any undertaking by the claimant to repay seems superfluous. However, the Secretary of State might choose not to enforce his right to recovery.

Under s.71(8)(c), amounts may be recovered by deduction from most benefits.

Subsection (3)

Prescribed benefits are listed in reg. 9 of the Payments Regulations. They are benefits, like child benefit, which can be claimed if a person (A) is contributing to the support of another person (B) at at least the rate of the benefit. If income support or income-based JSA has been paid for B on the basis that this contribution was not paid, the prescribed benefit may be abated by the amount of the excess income support or JSA. If the abatement mechanism breaks down, the Secretary of State may recover the excess under subs. (4). Under s.71(8))(c), amounts may be recovered by deduction from most benefits.

Subsection (4)
See notes to subss. (2) & (3).

Subsection (5)
R(SB) 28/85 had revealed problems in valuing a payment of arrears in a foreign currency which might cover quite a long period during which exchange rates varied. This provision authorises regulations to be made to deal with the conversion. See reg. 10 of the Payments Regulations, which appears to require the actual net amount received to be taken into account, reversing the effect of *R(SB) 28/85.*

[¹Payment of benefit where maintenance payments collected by Secretary of State

74A.—(1) This section applies where—
 (a) a person (''the claimant'') is entitled to a benefit to which this section applies;
 (b) the Secretary of State is collecting periodical payments of child or spousal maintenance made in respect of the claimant or a member of the claimant's family; and
 (c) the inclusion of any such periodical payment in the claimant's relevant income would, apart from this section, have the effect of reducing the amount of the benefit to which the claimant is entitled.

(2) The Secretary of State may, to such extent as he considers appropriate, treat any such periodical payment as not being relevant income for the purposes of calculating the amount of benefit to which the claimant is entitled.

(3) The Secretary of State may, to the extent that any periodical payment collected by him is treated as not being relevant income for those purposes, retain the whole or any part of that payment.

(4) Any sum retained by the Secretary of State under subsection (3) shall be paid by him into the Consolidated Fund.

(5) In this section—
''child'' means a person under the age of 16;
''child maintenance'', ''spousal maintenance'' and ''relevant income'' have such meaning as may be prescribed;
''family'' means—
 (a) a married or unmarried couple;
 (b) a married or unmarried couple and a member of the same household for whom one of them is, or both are, responsible and who is a child or a person of a prescribed description;
 (c) except in prescribed circumstances, a person who is not a member of a married or unmarried couple and a member of the same household for whom that person is responsible and who is a child or a person of a prescribed description;
''married couple'' means a man and woman who are married to each other and are members of the same household; and
''unmarried couple'' means a man and woman who are not married to each other but are living together as husband and wife otherwise than in prescribed circumstances.

(6) For the purposes of this section, the Secretary of State may by regulations make provision as to the circumstances in which—
 (a) persons are to be treated as being or not being members of the same household;
 (b) one person is to be treated as responsible or not responsible for another.

(7) The benefits to which this section applies are income support, an income-based jobseeker's allowance and such other benefits (if any) as may be prescribed.]

AMENDMENT

1. Child Support Act 1995, s.25 (October 1, 1995).

GENERAL NOTE

See reg. 2 of the Social Security Benefits (Maintenance Payments and Consequential Amendments) Regulations 1996 for definitions of "child maintenance", "spousal maintenance" and "relevant income" and regs. 3 to 5 for other points of interpretation.

Where maintenance payments are being collected on behalf of an income support or income-based JSA claimant or any member of the family, s.74A provides for part or the whole of those payments to be retained by the Secretary of State, in which case they will be disregarded for the purpose of calculating the claimant's benefit. See regs. 55A and 60E of the Income Support Regulations and regs. 119 and 127 of the Jobseeker's Allowance Regulations.

Social fund awards

Recovery of social fund awards

78.—(1) A social fund award which is repayable shall be recoverable by the Secretary of State.

(2) Without prejudice to any other method of recovery, the Secretary of State may recover an award by deduction from prescribed benefits.

(3) The Secretary of State may recover an award—
  (a) from the person to or for the benefit of whom it was made;
  (b) where that person is a member of a married or unmarried couple, from the other member of the couple;
  (c) from a person who is liable to maintain the person by or on behalf of whom the application for the award was made or any person in relation to whose needs the award was made.

[¹ (3A) Where—
  (a) a jobseeker's allowance is payable to a person from whom an award is recoverable under subsection (3) above; and
  (b) that person is subject to a bankruptcy order,
a sum deducted from that benefit under subsection (2) above shall not be treated as income of his for the purposes of the Insolvency Act 1986.

(3B) Where—
  (a) a jobseeker's allowance is payable to a person from whom an award is recoverable under subsection (3) above; and
  (b) the estate of that person is sequestrated,
a sum deducted from that benefit under subsection (2) above shall not be treated as income of his for the purposes of the Bankruptcy (Scotland) Act 1985.]

(4) Payments to meet funeral expenses may in all cases be recovered, as if they were funeral expenses, out of the estate of the deceased, and (subject to section 71 above) by no other means.

(5) In this section—
  "married couple" means a man and woman who are married to each other and are members of the same household;
  "unmarried couple" means a man and a woman who are not married to each other but are living together as husband and wife otherwise than in circumstances prescribed under section 132 of the Contributions and Benefits Act.

(6) For the purposes of this section—

(a) a man shall be liable to maintain his wife and any children of whom he is the father; and

(b) a woman shall be liable to maintain her husband and any children of whom she is the mother;

(c) a person shall be liable to maintain another person throughout any period in respect of which the first-mentioned person has, on or after 23rd May 1980 (the date of the passing of the Social Security Act 1980) and either alone or jointly with a further person, given an undertaking in writing in pursuance of immigration rules within the meaning of the Immigration Act 1971 to be responsible for the maintenance and accommodation of the other person; and

(d) "child" includes a person who has attained the age of 16 but not the age of 19 and in respect of whom either parent, or some person acting in place of either parent, is receiving income support [² or an income-based jobseeker's allowance].

(7) Any reference in subsection (6) above to children of whom the man or the woman is the father or mother shall be construed in accordance with section 1 of the Family Law Reform Act 1987.

(8) Subsection (7) above does not apply in Scotland, and in the application of subsection (6) above to Scotland any reference to children of whom the man or the woman is the father or the mother shall be construed as a reference to any such children whether or not their parents have ever been married to one another.

(9) A document bearing a certificate which—

(a) is signed by a person authorised in that behalf by the Secretary of State; and

(b) states that the document apart from the certificate is, or is a copy of, such an undertaking as is mentioned in subsection (6)(c) above,

shall be conclusive of the undertaking in question for the purposes of this section; and a certificate purporting to be so signed shall be deemed to be so signed until the contrary is proved.

DERIVATION

Subss. (1) to (3): Social Security Act 1986, s.33(5) to (7).
Subs. (4): 1986 Act, s.32(4).
Subs. (5): 1986 Act, s.33(12).
Subss. (6) to (9): 1986 Act, ss.26(3) to (6) and 33(8).

AMENDMENTS

1. Jobseekers Act 1995, s.32(2) (October 7, 1996).
2. Jobseekers Act 1995, Sched. 2, para. 51 (October 7, 1996).

DEFINITION

"prescribed"—see s.191.

GENERAL NOTE

Subsections (1) to (3)
These provisions give the framework for recovery of social fund loans. See the Social Fund (Recovery by Deductions from Benefits) Regulations 1988.

Income support and JSA are prescribed benefits for the purposes of subs. (2) (reg. 3(a) and (c) of the Social Fund (Recovery by Deductions from Benefits) Regulations). In *Mulvey v. Secretary of State for Social Security* (March 13, 1997), the House of Lords held that where deductions were being made from benefit under subs. (2) when the claimant was sequestrated (the Scottish equivalent of a declaration of bankruptcy), the Secretary of State was entitled to continue to make the deductions. If that were not so, the gross benefit would become payable to the claimant, who would thus gain an immediate financial advantage from sequestration, a result which Parliament could not have intended.

> "Prior to sequestration the [claimant] had no right to receive by way of income support more than her gross entitlement under deduction of such sum as had been notified to her by the [Secretary of State] prior to payment of the award by the [Secretary of State]. This was the result of the statutory scheme and she could not have demanded more. The [Secretary of State's] continued exercise of a statutory power of deduction after sequestration was unrelated thereto and was not calculated to obtain a benefit for him at the expense of other creditors. The only person who had any realistic interest in the deductions was the [claimant] from which it follows that the [Secretary of State] was not seeking to exercise any right against the permanent trustee." (Lord Jauncey)

The view of the Inner House of the Court of Session was thus approved. See the notes in the 1996 edition for the earlier decisions in *Mulvey*.

English bankruptcy law is not the same as Scottish sequestration law. However, in *R. v. Secretary of State for Social Security, ex p. Taylor and Chapman, The Times*, February 5, 1996, Keene J. reached the same conclusion as the Inner House in *Mulvey* in relation to the effect of s.285(3) of the Insolvency Act 1986 in these circumstances. The deductions in *Chapman* were not being made under subs. (2) but from the claimant's retirement pension under s.71(8) in order to recover an overpayment of income support, but it was accepted that the position was the same in both cases. Keene J. rejected a submission by the Secretary of State that the operation of s.285(3) was precluded in this situation, but held that it did not prevent the deductions under subs. (2) and s.71(8) being made. The Secretary of State was not seeking to go against "the property of the bankrupt" within the terms of s.285(3) as the claimants' entitlement under the 1992 Act was to the net amount of benefit. In *Mulvey* (above) Lord Jauncey said this about the contrary argument:

> "Even more bizarre would be the situation where overpayments obtained by fraud were being recovered by deduction from benefits. On sequestration the fraudster would immediately receive the gross benefit. It is difficult to believe that Parliament can have intended such a result."

Note that s.32 of the Jobseekers Act 1995 amends both ss. 78 and 71 to provide that amounts deducted under subs. (2) or s.71(8) from JSA payable to a bankrupt person are not to be treated as income for the purposes of the Insolvency Act 1986 and the Bankruptcy (Scotland) Act 1985 (in effect giving preference to the DSS over other creditors, although the House of Lords in *Mulvey* rejected such a comparison).

Subsection (4)

Subs. (4) contains an important provision for the recovery of any payment for funeral expenses out of the estate of the deceased. Reg. 8 of the Social Fund Maternity and Funeral Expenses (General) Regulations lists sums to be deducted in calculating the amount of a funeral payment. These include assets of the deceased which are available before probate or letters of administration have been granted. The old reg. 8(3)(a) of the Single Payments Regulations required the deduction of the value of the deceased's estate, but since it might take some time for the estate to become available, the provision in subs. (4) is preferable.

The funeral payment is to be recovered as if it was funeral expenses. Funeral expenses are a first charge on the estate, in priority to anything else (see *R(SB) 18/84*, paras. 8 and 10, for the law in England and Scotland). *CIS 616/1990* decides that the right to recover is given to the Secretary of State. The AO (and the SSAT) has no role in subs. (4).

The only other method of recovery is under s.71, which applies generally where there has been misrepresentation or a failure to disclose and does depend on a review of entitlement by an AO, followed by a determination of an overpayment.

Subsections (6) to (9)

See the notes to s.105.

Northern Ireland payments

Recovery of Northern Ireland payments

79. Without prejudice to any other method of recovery—

(a) amounts recoverable under any enactment or instrument having effect in Northern Ireland and corresponding to an enactment or instrument mentioned in section 71(8) above shall be recoverable by deduction from benefits prescribed under that subsection;

(b) amounts recoverable under any enactment having effect in Northern Ireland and corresponding to section 75 above shall be recoverable by deduction from benefits prescribed under subsection (4) of that section; and

(c) awards recoverable under Part III of the Northern Ireland Administration Act shall be recoverable by deduction from benefits prescribed under subsection (2) of section 78 above and subsection (3) of that section shall have effect in relation to such awards as it has effect in relation to such awards out of the social fund under this Act.

DERIVATION

Para. (a): Social Security Act 1986, s.53(7A).
Para. (b): 1986 Act, s.29(8).
Para. (c): 1986 Act, s.33(8A).

DEFINITIONS

"the Northern Ireland Administration Act"—see s.191.
"prescribed"—*ibid*.

PART V

INCOME SUPPORT AND THE DUTY TO MAINTAIN

Failure to maintain—general

105.—(1) If—
(a) any person persistently refuses or neglects to maintain himself or any person whom he is liable to maintain; and
(b) in consequence of his refusal or neglect income support [¹or an income-based jobseeker's allowance] is paid to or in respect of him or such a person,
he shall be guilty of an offence and liable on summary conviction to imprisonment for a term not exceeding 3 months or to a fine of an amount not exceeding level 4 on the standard scale or to both.

(2) For the purposes of subsection (1) above a person shall not be taken to refuse or neglect to maintain himself or any other person by reason only of anything done or omitted in furtherance of a trade dispute.

(3) [¹Subject to sub-section (4) below,] subsections (6) to (9) of section 78 above shall have effect for the purposes of this Part of this Act as they have effect for the purposes of that section.

[¹(4) For the purposes of this section, in its application to an income-based jobseeker's allowance, a person is liable to maintain another if that other person is his or her spouse.]

DERIVATION

Social Security Act 1986, s.26.

AMENDMENT

1. Jobseekers Act 1995, Sched. 2, para. 53 (October 7, 1996).

Subsection (1)

The criminal offence created by subs. (1) of refusing or neglecting to maintain oneself is at first sight rather extraordinary, but it is only committed if as a consequence income support or income-based JSA is paid. Prosecution is very much a last resort after the ordinary sanctions against voluntary unemployment have been used. In 1984/5 there were none (NACRO, *Enforcement of the Law Relating to Social Security*, para. 8.6). Prosecution of those who refuse or neglect to maintain others is more common.

Liability to maintain

Under subs. (3), liability to maintain another person for the purposes of Part V is tested, except in relation to income-based JSA, according to s.78(6) to (9). Both men and women are liable to maintain their spouses and children. This liability remains in force despite the enactment of the Child Support Act 1991, with the result that the DSS retains its power to enforce that liability under ss.106 to 108. But although this power remains, in practice the DSS does not enforce the liability to maintain children now that the Child Support Agency has acquired this role. Note also that since April 5, 1993, the courts have not had power to make new orders for maintenance for children (s. 8(3) Child Support Act 1991). Under subs. (4) the only liability to maintain which is relevant to s.105 for the purposes of income-based JSA is the liability of one spouse to maintain the other.

The definition of child goes beyond the usual meaning in s.137 of the Contributions and Benefits Act of a person under 16 to include those under 19 who count as a dependant in someone else's income support entitlement (s.78(6)(d)). The effect of the reference in s.78(4) to s.1 of the Family Law Reform Act 1987 is that in determining whether a person is the father or mother of a child it is irrelevant whether the person was married to the other parent at the time of the birth or not. If a married couple divorce, their liability to maintain each other ceases for the purposes of Part V, but the obligation to maintain their children remains. This then is the remnant of the old family means-test that used to extend much wider until the Poor Law was finally "abolished" by the National Assistance Act 1948. For the enforcement of this liability, see ss.106 to 108, and for a criminal offence, subs. (1).

Section 78(6)(c) was new in 1980. In *R. v. W. London SBAT, ex p. Clarke* [1975] 1 W.L.R. 1396, SB7, the court had held that the sponsor of an immigrant was under no obligation to maintain the immigrant for supplementary benefit purposes. This position is now reversed, and s.78(9) provides for conclusive certificates of an undertaking to maintain to be produced. The liability to maintain is enforced under s.106. The SBC policy struck down in *Clarke*'s case had deemed the immigrant to be receiving the support from his sponsor even where it was not forthcoming. This is not now the case. It is only a resource when actually received.

Recovery of expenditure on benefit from person liable for maintenance

106.—(1) Subject to the following provisions of this section, if income support is claimed by or in respect of a person whom another person is liable to maintain or paid to or in respect of such a person, the Secretary of State may make a complaint against the liable person to a magistrates' court for an order under this section.

(2) On the hearing of a complaint under this section the court shall have regard to all the circumstances and, in particular, to the income of the liable person, and may order him to pay such sum, weekly or otherwise, as it may consider appropriate, except that in a case falling within section 78(6)(c) above that sum shall not include any amount which is not attributable to income support (whether paid before or after the making of the order).

(3) In determining whether to order any payments to be made in respect of income support for any period before the complaint was made, or the amount of any such payments, the court shall disregard any amount by which the liable person's income exceeds the income which was his during that period.

(4) Any payments ordered to be made under this section shall be made—

(a) to the Secretary of State in so far as they are attributable to any income support (whether paid before or after the making of the order);

(b) to the person claiming income support or (if different) the dependant; or

(c) to such other person as appears to the court expedient in the interests of the dependant.

(5) An order under this section shall be enforceable as a magistrates' court maintenance order within the meaning of section 150(1) of the Magistrates' Court Act 1980.

(6) In the application of this section to Scotland, subsection (5) above shall be omitted and for the references to a complaint and to a magistrates' court there shall be substituted respectively references to an application and to the sheriff.

(7) On an application under subsection (1) above a court in Scotland may make a finding as to the parentage of a child for the purpose of establishing whether a person is, for the purposes of section 105 above and this section, liable to maintain him.

DERIVATION

Social Security Act 1986, s.24.

DEFINITION

"child"—see ss.105(3) and 78(b).

GENERAL NOTE

This section gives the DSS an independent right to enforce the liability to maintain in s.78(6), which now covers both spouses and children, by an order in the magistrates' court, providing that income support has been claimed or paid for the person sought to be maintained.

Children

From April 1993 the Child Support Act 1991 has introduced an entirely new system of determining and enforcing the liability of parents to maintain children, through the Child Support Agency. This book does not deal with that system, for which, see Jacobs and Douglas, *Child Support Legislation.* But the DSS's rights under s.106 remain in force not only between spouses, but also as between parents and children. It is not clear in what circumstances action against a parent may be taken under s.106 rather than through the Child Support Agency. The DSS have said that they do not intend to use the s. 106 power in relation to children, and this seems to be implicit in the Income Support Special Circumstances Guide, paras. 6000–6014. The Child Support Agency phased in applications for child support maintenance for income support claimants. It was originally intended that all income support claimants would have been required to apply under s. 6 of the Child Support Act 1991 by April 1996; however, there have been some delays in taking on cases. Despite the delays, claimants receiving maintenance under a court order or an arrangement with liable relative officers were given priority by the Child Support Agency and so there should no longer be any cases where maintenance for dependent children is still being dealt with by the Benefits Agency. Benefit may only be reduced for failure to comply with obligations under s. 6, not for failure to co-operate in relation to the liability to maintain in s. 78(6). Note also that since April 5, 1993, the courts have not had the power to make new orders for maintenance for children (s. 8(3) Child Support Act 1991).

Spouses

The usual procedure was last described in detail in Chapter 13 of the *Supplementary Benefits Handbook* (1984 ed.) and will presumably continue to apply, since it was repeated in essence in the DSS *Guide to Income Support*, although there were some administrative changes. The current Income Support Guide does not contain the liable relative procedure. This apparently is now in an internal guide called "Residual Liable Relatives and Proceedings Guide". The most common situation is where a breakdown of marriage leads to separation or divorce and the woman claims income support. The same procedures can apply if it is the man who claims benefit. If there has already been a divorce then there is no liability to maintain between the ex-spouses. If there has merely been a separation then the wife is entitled to benefit as a single person, but there will be an investigation of the circumstances to ensure that the separation is genuine. If the husband is already paying maintenance under a court order or the wife has taken proceedings herself which are reasonably advanced, no approach to the husband will be made by the DSS. Otherwise, the wife will be asked for information about the whereabouts of the liable relative (although producing the information cannot be made a condition of receiving benefit) and he will be contacted as soon as possible. The husband is asked to pay as much as he can, if possible enough to remove the need for income support to be paid to the wife and any children.

In deciding what level of payment is acceptable on a voluntary basis, it is understood that the following formula is used as a starting point. The income support personal allowances and premiums for the man are taken, plus rent, or mortgage payments, council tax and 15 per cent of his net wage. If the man has a new partner, two calculations are done—one as if the man was single and the other using joint incomes. The lower figure is then taken. The excess over this amount is regarded as available to be used as maintenance. But this is only a basis for discussion and payment of a lesser sum may be agreed, particularly if there are other essential expenses. Clearly there is scope for negotiation here. Thus if the man himself is receiving income support he would not be expected to pay anything.

If the husband is unwilling to make a payment voluntarily, although the DSS believe that he has sufficient income, then legal proceedings may be considered. The first step will be to see if the wife will take action. The official policy is that the wife will merely be advised on the advantages of taking proceedings herself (that she may get enough maintenance to lift her off benefit and that an order for maintenance will continue if she ceases to be entitled to income support, as by working full-time). The first advantage is likely to be real in only a small minority of cases and the force of the second has been reduced by the introduction of the procedure in s.107(3) to (14). The choice should be left entirely to the woman. A wife may of course take proceedings herself even though the DSS have accepted voluntary payments from the husband.

The courts have refused to adopt the ''liable relative formula'' in private proceedings by wives or ex-wives (*Shallow v. Shallow* [1979] Fam. 1) and will only have regard to the man's subsistence level. By this they mean the ordinary scale rates of benefit plus housing costs. A more realistic approach may have been presaged by *Allen v. Allen* [1986] 2 F.L.R. 265, where the Court of Appeal used the long-term scale rate (now disappeared) as a yardstick. In *Delaney v. Delaney* [1990] 2 F.L.R. 457, the Court of Appeal accepted the principle that where the man had insufficient resources after taking account of his reasonable commitments to a new family to maintain his former wife and family properly, a maintenance order should not financially cripple him where the wife is entitled to social security benefits. But no calculation of the man's income support level was made.

If the wife does not take proceedings, then the DSS may. The court is to have regard to all the circumstances, in particular the husband's resources, and may order him to pay whatever sum is appropriate (subs. (2)). Presumably, the same principles will govern the amount of an order as in a private application. There were some new provisions in s.107(1) in cases where the order included amounts for children, but it is not at all clear how these interacted with the general test of appropriateness under subs. (2). Note that since April 5, 1993 the courts have not had the power to make new orders for maintenance for children (s. 8(3) Child Support Act 1991). The wife's adultery or desertion or other conduct is only a factor to be taken into account, not a bar to any order. Nor is the existence of a separation agreement under which the wife agrees not to claim maintenance a bar (*National Assistance Board v. Parkes* [1955] 2 Q.B. 506). Although *Hulley v. Thompson* [1981] 1 W.L.R. 159 concerned only the liability to maintain children, because there had been a divorce, it showed that not even a consent order under which the man transferred the matrimonial home to his ex-wife and she agreed to receive no maintenance for herself or the children, barred the statutory liability to maintain the children. However, it seems that the existence of the order could be taken into account in deciding what amount it is appropriate for the man to pay.

Proceedings by the DSS are relatively rare. In 1979 there were only 431 (SBC Annual Report for 1979 (Cmnd. 8033), para. 8.30).

Recovery of expenditure on income support: additional amounts and transfer of orders

107.—(1) In any case where—
  (a) the claim for income support referred to in section 106(1) above is or was made by the parent of one or more children in respect of both himself and those children; and
  (b) the other parent is liable to maintain those children but, by virtue of not being the claimant's husband or wife, is not liable to maintain the claimant,
the sum which the court may order that other parent to pay under subsection

(2) of that section may include an amount, determined in accordance with regulations, in respect of any income support paid to or for the claimant by virtue of such provisions as may be prescribed.

(2) Where the sum which a court orders a person to pay under section 106 above includes by virtue of subsection (1) above an amount (in this section referred to as a "personal allowance element") in respect of income support by virtue of paragraph 1(2) of Schedule 2 to the Income Support (General) Regulations 1987 (personal allowance for lone parent) the order shall separately identify the amount of the personal allowance element.

(3) In any case where—

(a) there is in force an order under subsection (2) of section 106 above made against a person ("the liable parent") who is the parent of one or more children, in respect of the other parent or the children; and

(b) payments under the order fall to be made to the Secretary of State by virtue of subsection (4)(a) of that section; and

(c) that other parent ("the dependent parent") ceases to claim income support,

the Secretary of State may, by giving notice in writing to the court which made the order and to the liable parent and the dependent parent, transfer to the dependent parent the right to receive the payments under the order, exclusive of any personal allowance element, and to exercise the relevant rights in relation to the order, except so far as relating to that element.

(4) Notice under subsection (3) above shall not be given (and if purportedly given, shall be of no effect) at a time when there is in force a maintenance order made against the liable parent—

(a) in favour of the dependent parent or one or more of the children; or

(b) in favour of some other person for the benefit of the dependent parent or one or more of the children;

and if such a maintenance order is made at any time after notice under that subsection has been given, the order under section 106(2) above shall cease to have effect.

(5) In any case where—

(a) notice is given to a magistrates' court under subsection (3) above,

(b) payments under the order are required to be made by any method of payment falling within section 59(6) of the Magistrates' Courts Act 1980 (standing order, etc.), and

(c) the clerk to the justices for the petty sessions area for which the court is acting decides that payment by that method is no longer possible,

the clerk shall amend the order to provide that payments under the order shall be made by the liable parent to the clerk.

(6) Except as provided by subsections (8) and (12) below, where the Secretary of State gives notice under subsection (3) above, he shall cease to be entitled—

(a) to receive any payment under the order in respect of any personal allowance element; or

(b) to exercise the relevant rights, so far as relating to any such element,

notwithstanding that the dependent parent does not become entitled to receive any payment in respect of that element or to exercise the relevant rights so far as so relating.

(7) If, in a case where the Secretary of State gives notice under subsection (3) above, a payment under the order is or has been made to him wholly or partly in respect of the whole or any part of the period beginning with the day on which the transfer takes effect and ending with the day on which the notice under subsection (3) above is given to the liable parent, the Secretary of State shall—

    (a) repay to or for the liable parent so much of the payment as is referable to any personal allowance element in respect of that period or, as the case may be, the part of it in question; and

    (b) pay to or for the dependent parent so much of any remaining balance of the payment as is referable to that period or part;

and a payment under paragraph (b) above shall be taken to discharge, to that extent, the liability of the liable parent to the dependent parent under the order in respect of that period or part.

    (8) If, in a case where the Secretary of State has given notice under subsection (3) above, the dependent parent makes a further claim for income support, then—

    (a) the Secretary of State may, by giving a further notice in writing to the court which made the order and to the liable parent and the dependent parent, transfer back from the dependent parent to himself the right to receive the payments and to exercise the relevant rights; and

    (b) that transfer shall revive the Secretary of State's right to receive payment under the order in respect of any personal allowance element and to exercise the relevant rights so far as relating to any such element.

    (9) Subject to subsections (10) and (11) below, in any case where—

    (a) notice is given to a magistrates' court under subsection (8) above, and

    (b) the method of payment under the order which subsists immediately before the day on which the transfer under subsection (8) above takes effect differs from the method of payment which subsisted immediately before the day on which the transfer under subsection (3) above (or, as the case may be, the last such transfer) took effect,

the clerk to the justices for the petty sessions area for which the court is acting shall amend the order by reinstating the method of payment under the order which subsisted immediately before the day on which the transfer under subsection (3) above (or, as the case may be, the last such transfer) took effect.

    (10) The clerk shall not amend the order under subsection (9) above if the Secretary of State gives notice in writing to the clerk, on or before the day on which notice under subsection (8) above is given, that the method of payment under the order which subsists immediately before the day on which the transfer under subsection (8) above takes effect is to continue.

    (11) In any case where—

    (a) notice is given to a magistrates' court under subsection (8) above,

    (b) the method of payment under the order which subsisted immediately before the day on which the transfer under subsection (3) above (or, if there has been more than one such transfer, the last such transfer) took effect was any method of payment falling within section 59(6) of the Magistrates' Courts Act 1980 (standing order, etc.), and

    (c) the clerk decides that payment by that method is no longer possible,

the clerk shall amend the order to provide that payments under the order shall be made by the liable parent to the clerk.

    (12) A transfer under subsection (3) or (8) above does not transfer or otherwise affect the right of any person—

    (a) to receive a payment which fell due to him at a time before the transfer took effect; or

    (b) to exercise the relevant rights in relation to any such payment;

and, where notice is given under subsection (3), subsection (6) above does not deprive the Secretary of State of his right to receive such a payment in respect of any personal allowance element or to exercise the relevant rights in relation to such a payment.

    (13) For the purposes of this section—

    (a) a transfer under subsection (3) above takes effect on the day on which the dependent parent ceases to be in receipt of income support in con-sequence of the cessation referred to in paragraph (c) of that subsection, and

(b) a transfer under subsection (8) above takes effect on—

(i) the first day in respect of which the dependent parent receives income support after the transfer under subsection (3) above took effect, or

(ii) such later day as may be specified for the purpose in the notice under subsection (8).

irrespective of the day on which notice under the subsection in question is given.

(14) Any notice required to be given to the liable parent under subsection (3) or (8) above shall be taken to have been given if it has been sent to his last known address.

(15) In this section—

"child" means a person under the age of 16, notwithstanding section 78(6)(d) above;

"court" shall be construed in accordance with section 106 above;

"maintenance order"—

(a) in England and Wales, means—

(i) any order for the making of periodical payments or for the pay-ment of a lump sum which is, or has at any time been, a mainten-ance order within the meaning of the Attachment of Earnings Act 1971;

(ii) any order under Part III of the Matrimonial and Family Proceed-ings Act 1984 (overseas divorce) for the making of periodical payments or for the payment of a lump sum;

(b) in Scotland, has the meaning given by section 106 of the Debtors (Scotland) Act 1987, but disgarding paragraph (h) (alimentary bond or agreement);

"the relevant rights", in relation to an order under section 106(2) above, means the right to bring any proceedings, take any steps or do any other thing under or in relation to the order which the Secretary of State could have brought, taken or done apart from any transfer under this section.

DERIVATION

Social Security Act 1986, s.24A, as amended by the Maintenance Enforcement Act 1991, s.9, with effect from April 1, 1992 (Maintenance Enforcement Act 1991 (Commencement) (No. 2) Order 1992 (S.I. 1992 No. 455)).

GENERAL NOTE

The predecessors of this section and s.108 formed one of the central strategic objectives of the Social Security Act 1990 (HC *Hansard*, April 3, 1990, Vol. 170, col. 1137 (Tony Newton); HL *Hansard*, April 20, 1990, Vol. 518, col. 234 (Lord Henley)), but were only introduced at the Report stage in the Commons. They therefore received relatively little Parliamentary discussion due to the operation of the guillotine. The Government carried out a general review of the maintenance system, based on a survey of work in U.K. courts and DSS offices and study of overseas systems, and produced radical proposals in *Children Come First* (Cm. 1264), now embodied in the Child Support Act 1991 from April 1993. But action had already been taken to tighten up the assessment of an absent parent's ability to pay maintenance for his family on income support. The new provisions were regarded as desirable in the short term to improve the effectiveness of the present system, pending the more radical reform (HC *Hansard*, March 28, Vol. 170, col. 566). However, ss.107 and 108 remain in force despite the implementation of the Child Support Act.

Section 107 contains two elements. The first relates to the situation where a lone parent is receiv-ing income support, but the absent parent of the child(ren) is not liable to maintain the parent under s.78(6) because the parents are not or are no longer married. Where the DSS seeks its own order against the absent parent, courts are empowered to take into account income support relating to the lone parent in calculating the amount to be paid for the child(ren) and the DSS may of course take this into account in negotiating voluntary agreements. The second is to allow a DSS order to be transferred to the lone parent when that person comes off income support, rather than the lone parent having to obtain a separate private maintenance order. Note that since April 5, 1993, the courts have not had the power to make new orders for maintenance for children (s.8(3) Child Support Act 1991).

Subsections (1) and (2)

These provisions comprise the first element identified above. They apply when both of conditions (a) and (b) in subs. (1) are satisfied. Under para. (a), s.106 gives the DSS power to obtain an order against a person who is liable to maintain a claimant of income support or a person included in the family for claiming purposes. Section 78(6) defines liability to maintain for this purpose. There is a liability to maintain a spouse and any children. Under s.78(6)(d) "child" includes a person aged 16 to 18 (inclusive) who is still a member of the claimant's family for income support purposes (*e.g.* because still in full-time education). However, s.107(15) provides that for the purposes of s.107 "child" is restricted to a person under the age of 16. Thus, lone parent claimants whose children are all over 15 will fall outside this provision. Under para. (b), the absent parent must not be married to the lone parent, so that the obligation to maintain under s.78(6) is only in respect of the child(ren). If both these conditions are met, a court may include whatever amount the regulations determine in respect of the income support paid for the lone parent. The Income Support (Liable Relatives) Regulations specify in general the children's personal allowances, family premium, lone parent premium (now the higher rate of family premium), disabled child premium and the carer premium in respect of care for a child.

The intention was said to be that the regulation-making power "will be used to specify that once having looked at the allowances and premiums that are paid because there are children, the court should also have regard to the income support personal allowance paid for the mother" (HC *Hansard*, March 28, 1990, Vol. 170, col. 567). The Liable Relatives Regulations provide that if the liable parent has the means to pay in addition to the amounts already specified, a court order may include some or all of the dependent parent's personal allowance.

It was said that in a private maintenance order for children the court could take account of the parent's care costs and that social security law was thus being brought into line with family law. However, there was nothing as specific as s.107 in family law. The existing power of the court on orders sought by the DSS was already wide and it is not clear how much real difference the new powers made. Under s.106(2) the court may order payment of such sum as it may consider appropriate. The assumption seems to be that not only could the personal allowance for a child under 16 be considered under this provision, but also the family premium (paid to all claimants with a child or young person (16–18) in the family) and the additional lone parent premium (now the higher rate of family premium). If such amounts can be considered under the existing law (and they might be considered to reflect the care costs of the lone parent) there seems no reason why the court could not also consider some part of the parent's personal allowance if that was considered "appropriate." However, s. 107(1) and the Liable Relatives Regulations make the position clear, which should be an advantage.

It is notable that the court retains a discretion as to what amounts to consider and that the overriding factor under s.106(2) is what is appropriate. Under para. 1 of Sched. 2 to the Income Support (General) Regulations 1987 the personal allowance for a lone parent aged under 18 or over 24 is the same as for a single person with no dependants. There is only a difference (currently £10.50 p.w.) for those aged 18 to 24.

Subs. (2) provides that if the lone parent's personal allowance under Sched. 2 is covered by the order, this element must be separately identified. This has no bearing on subs. (1), but is relevant to the procedure set up by subss. (3) to (14).

Subsections (3) to (15)

These provisions contain the once-important procedure allowing the transfer of a DSS order to the lone parent on coming off income support. The conditions for transfer under subs. (3) are that in such a case (remembering that "child" is defined to cover only those under 16 (subs. (15)) the Secretary of State gives notice to the court which made the order and to both the parents. Then the right to enforce or apply for variation of the order (apart from any personal allowance element identified under subs. (2)) is transferred to the lone parent (known as "the dependent parent"). Thus, the personal allowance element, which is of no net benefit to the lone parent while she is on income support, is removed at the point when its value would actually be felt by the lone parent. The DSS can no longer enforce the personal allowance element of the order (subs. (6)). Under subs.

(13)(a) the transfer takes effect on the day on which the dependent parent ceases to receive income support in consequence of ceasing to claim. This is a peculiar way of putting things. If the dependent parent's circumstances change (*e.g.* her capital goes over the cut-off limit or she starts full-time work) her entitlement to income support may be terminated on review by the AO under s.25. She may well then choose not to claim income support again, as it would be a useless exercise. The dependent parent could with some strain be said to cease to claim income support and so to satisfy subs. (3)(c), but the cessation of receipt of income support is not in consequence of the cessation of claiming but of the review and revision by the AO.

Subs. (3) is not to apply if a private maintenance order (see subs. (15) for definition) is in existence, and if the dependent parent obtains one after a transfer the right to enforce the DSS order disappears (subs. (4)).

If, after a transfer, the dependent parent makes another claim for income support (presumably only while still having children under 16), the Secretary of State may by giving notice to all parties re-transfer to the DSS the right to enforce the order and revive the personal allowance element on the dependent parent becoming entitled to income support (subss. (8) and (13)(b)). Presumably, the revival of the personal allowance element depends on the conditions of subss. (1) and (2) being met at the date of revival.

Reduction of expenditure on income support: certain maintenance orders to be enforceable by the Secretary of State

108.—(1) This section applies where—

(a) a person ("the claimant") who is the parent of one or more children is in receipt of income support either in respect of those children or in respect of both himself and those children; and

(b) there is in force a maintenance order made against the other parent ("the liable person")—

    (i) in favour of the claimant or one or more of the children, or

    (ii) in favour of some other person for the benefit of the claimant or one or more of the children,

and in this section "the primary recipient" means the person in whose favour that maintenance order was made.

(2) If, in a case where this section applies, the liable person fails to comply with any of the terms of the maintenance order—

(a) the Secretary of State may bring any proceedings or take any other steps to enforce the order that could have been brought or taken by or on behalf of the primary recipient; and

(b) any court before which proceedings are brought by the Secretary of State by virtue of paragraph (a) above shall have the same powers in connection with those proceedings as it would have had if they had been brought by the primary recipient.

(3) The Secretary of State's powers under this section are exercisable at his discretion and whether or not the primary recipient or any other person consents to their exercise; but any sums recovered by virtue of this section shall be payable to or for the primary recipient, as if the proceedings or steps in question had been brought or taken by him or on his behalf.

(4) The powers conferred on the Secretary of State by subsection (2)(a) above include power—

(a) to apply for the registration of the maintenance order under—

    (i) section 17 of the Maintenance Orders Act 1950;

    (ii) section 2 of the Maintenance Orders Act 1958; or

    (iii) the Civil Jurisdiction and Judgments Act 1982; and

(b) to make an application under section 2 of the Maintenance Orders (Reciprocal Enforcement) Act 1972 (application for enforcement in reciprocating country).

(5) Where this section applies, the prescribed person shall in prescribed circumstances give the Secretary of State notice of any application—

(a) to alter, vary, suspend, discharge, revoke, revive, or enforce the maintenance order in question; or

(b) to remit arrears under that maintenance order;

and the Secretary of State shall be entitled to appear and be heard on the
application.

(6) Where, by virtue of this section, the Secretary of State commences any
proceedings to enforce a maintenance order, he shall, in relation to those proceedings, be treated for the purposes of any enactment or instrument relating
to maintenance orders as if he were a person entitled to payment under the
maintenance order in question (but shall not thereby become entitled to any
such payment).

(7) Where, in any proceedings under this section in England and Wales, the
court makes an order for the whole or any part of the arrears due under the
maintenance order in question to be paid as a lump sum, the Secretary of State
shall inform the Legal Aid Board of the amount of that lump sum if he knows—

(a) that the primary recipient either—

  (i) received legal aid under the Legal Aid Act 1974 in connection with
  the proceedings in which the maintenance order was made, or

  (ii) was an assisted party, within the meaning of the Legal Aid Act
  1988, in those proceedings; and

(b) that a sum remains unpaid on account of the contribution required of the
primary recipient—

  (i) under section 9 of the Legal Aid Act 1974 in respect of those proceedings, or

  (ii) under section 16 of the Legal Aid Act 1988 in respect of the costs of
  his being represented under Part IV of that Act in those proceedings,

  as the case may be.

(8) In this section "maintenance order" has the same meaning as it has in
section 107 above but does not include any such order for the payment of a
lump sum.

DERIVATION

Social Security Act 1986, s.24B.

GENERAL NOTE

Section 108 enables the DSS to enforce certain private maintenance orders in favour of lone
parent claimants of income support. Only lone parents are covered by subs. (1)(a), and not mere
separated or divorced spouses, but the maintenance order may be in favour either of the parent or
the child(ren) or both. The Secretary of State may at his discretion and without the consent of the
lone parent take steps (including those specified in subs. (5)) to enforce the order as if he were the
person entitled to payment under the order (subss. (2), (3) and (6)). But any sums recovered are
payable to the primary recipient under the order (subss. (3) and (6)). Under subs. (5) regulations
may specify who has to inform the DSS of applications to vary, suspend etc the private order or
to remit arrears. Reg. 3 of the Income Support (Liable Relatives) Regulations specifies various court
officials. The Secretary of State is given the right to be heard on any such application, but has no
power to make such an application, *e.g.* to increase the amount of an order. This is because subs.
(2) only operates when there is a failure to comply with the terms (*i.e.* the existing terms) of the
order.

Subs. (7) requires the Secretary of State to inform the Legal Aid Board when a lump sum
of arrears is to be paid when the Board might be able to recover a contribution out of the lump
sum.

Overall s.108 is a powerful weapon for the DSS to enforce the payment of maintenance orders.
If the lone parent has her own order, which is not being paid, income support will make up the
shortfall. There is thus no great incentive for the lone parent to go through all the hassle of enforcement, and there may be other circumstances making her reluctant to take action. The DSS will have
no such inhibitions.

The Secretary of State predicted that the amount of maintenance recovered by the DSS in respect of lone parents on income support would rise to about £260 million in 1990–91, having gone up from £155 million in 1988–89 to £180 million in 1989–90 (HC *Hansard*, March 28, 1990, Vol. 170, col. 571). The predicted increase was partly based on the provisions now contained in ss.107 and 108 and partly on giving greater priority and resources to such work, with changes in the administrative guidance. These changes are to point up the need to stress to lone parents on benefits the advantages of reflecting the absent parent's proper responsibilities in the maintenance arrangements from the outset and also to indicate that the "normal expectation" should be that a lone parent will co-operate in establishing where responsibility lies. It is, however, recognised that there may be circumstances in which lone parents will not wish to name the father of a child. The White paper, *Children Come First*, proposed reductions in the lone parent's benefit if she declines without good cause to take maintenance proceedings. The Child Support Act 1991 imposes such an obligation only in relation to applications under the Act.

Diversion of arrested earnings to Secretary of State—Scotland

109.—(1) Where in Scotland a creditor who is enforcing a maintenance order or alimentary bond or agreement by a current maintenance arrestment or a conjoined arrestment order is in receipt of income support, the creditor may in writing authorise the Secretary of State to receive any sums payable under the arrestment or order until the creditor ceases to be in receipt of income support or in writing withdraws the authorisation, whichever occurs first.

(2) On the intimation by the Secretary of State—

(a) to the employer operating the current maintenance arrestment; or

(b) to the sheriff clerk operating the conjoined arrestment order;

of an authorisation under subsection (1) above, the employer or sheriff clerk shall, until notified by the Secretary of State that the authorisation has ceased to have effect, pay to the Secretary of State any sums which would otherwise be payable under the arrestment or order to the creditor.

DERIVATION

Social Security Act 1986, s.25A.

PART VII

PROVISION OF INFORMATION

The Registration Service

Provisions relating to age, death and marriage

124.—(1) Regulations made by the Registrar General under section 20 of the Registration Service Act 1953 or section 54 of the Registration of Births, Deaths and Marriages (Scotland) Act 1965 may provide for the furnishing by superintendent registrars and registrars, subject to the payment of such fee as may be prescribed by the regulations, of such information for the purposes—

(a) of the provisions of the Contributions and Benefits Act to which this section applies;

[[1](aa) of the provisions of Parts I and II of the Jobseekers Act 1995;] and

(b) the provisions of this Act so far as they have effect in relation to matters arising under those provisions,

including copies or extracts from the registers in their custody, as may be so prescribed.

(2) This section applies to the following provisions of the Contributions and Benefits Act—

(a) Parts I to VI except section 108;

(b) Part VII, so far as it relates to income support and family credit;

(c) Part VIII, so far as it relates to any social fund payment such as is mentioned in section 138(1)(a) or (2);

(d) Part IX;

(e) Part XI; and

(f) Part XII.

(3) Where the age, marriage or death of a person is required to be ascertained or proved for the purposes mentioned in subsection (1) above, any person—

(a) on presenting to the custodian of the register under the enactments relating to the registration of births, marriages and deaths, in which particulars of the birth, marriage or death (as the case may be) of the first-mentioned person are entered, a duly completed requisition in writing in that behalf; and

(b) on payment of a fee of £1.50 in England and Wales and £4 in Scotland,

shall be entitled to obtain a copy, certified under the hand of the custodian, of the entry of those particulars.

(4) Requisitions for the purposes of subsection (3) above shall be in such form and contain such particulars as may from time to time be specified by the Registrar General, and suitable forms of requisition shall, on request, be supplied without charge by superintendent registrars and registrars.

(5) In this section—

(a) as it applies to England and Wales—

"Registrar General" means the Registrar General for England and Wales; and

"superintendent registrar" and "registrar" mean a superintendent registrar or, as the case may be, registrar for the purposes of the enactments relating to the registration of births, deaths and marriages; and

(b) as it applies to Scotland—

"Registrar General" means the Registrar General of Births, Deaths and Marriages for Scotland;

"registrar" means a district registrar, senior registrar or assistant registrar for the purposes of the enactment relating to the registration of births, deaths and marriages in Scotland.

DERIVATION

Social Security Act 1975, s.160.

AMENDMENT

1. Jobseekers Act 1995, Sched. 2, para. 59 (October 7, 1996).

DEFINITIONS

"the Contributions and Benefits Act"—see s.191.
"prescribed"—*ibid*.

Regulations as to notifications of deaths

125.—(1) Regulations [³made with the concurrence of the Inland Revenue] may provide that it shall be the duty of any of the following persons—

(a) the Registrar General for England and Wales;

(b) the Registrar General of Births, Deaths and Marriages for Scotland;

(c) each registrar of births and deaths,

to furnish the Secretary of State, [³or the Inland Revenue, for the purposes of their respective functions] under the Contributions and Benefits Act [¹, the

Jobseekers Act 1995] [²the Social Security (Recovery of Benefits) Act 1997] and this Act and the functions of the Northern Ireland Department under any Northern Ireland legislation corresponding to [¹any of those Acts], with the prescribed particulars of such deaths as may be prescribed.

(2) The regulations may make provision as to the manner in which and the times at which the particulars are to be furnished.

DERIVATION

Social Security Act 1986, s.60.

AMENDMENTS

1. Jobseekers Act 1995, Sched. 2, para. 60 (October 7, 1996).
2. Social Security (Recovery of Benefits) Act 1997, s. 33 and Sched. 3, para. 5 (October 6, 1997).
3. Social Security Contributions (Transfer of Functions, etc.) Act 1999, s.1(1) and Sched. 1, para. 25 (April 1, 1999).

DEFINITIONS

"the Contributions and Benefits Act"—see s.191.
"the Northern Ireland Department"—*ibid.*
"prescribed"—*ibid.*

Personal representatives—income support and supplementary benefit

Personal representatives to give information about the estate of a deceased person who was in receipt of income support or supplementary benefit

126.—(1) The personal representatives of a person who was in receipt of income support [¹, an income-based jobseeker's allowance] or supplementary benefit at any time before his death shall provide the Secretary of State with such information as he may require relating to the assets and liabilities of that person's estate.

(2) If the personal representatives fail to supply any information within 28 days of being required to do so under subsection (1) above, then—
  (a) the appropriate court may, on the application of the Secretary of State, make an order directing them to supply that information within such time as may be specified in the order; and
  (b) any such order may provide that all costs (or, in Scotland, expenses) of and incidental to the application shall be borne personally by any of the personal representatives.

(3) In this section "the appropriate court" means—
  (a) in England and Wales, a county court;
  (b) in Scotland, the sheriff;
and any application to the sheriff under this section shall be made by summary application.

DERIVATION

Social Security Act 1986, s.27A.

AMENDMENT

1. Jobseekers Act 1995, Sched. 2, para. 61 (October 7, 1996).

GENERAL NOTE

Under s.71(3) an overpayment which would have been recoverable from a person is recoverable from that person's estate (*Secretary of State for Social Services v. Solly* [1974] 3 All E.R. 922, *CSSB 6/1995*). Section 126 provides a specific obligation for the estate to provide information about the assets in it. However, s.126 only applies to the estates of income support, income-based JSA or supplementary benefit claimants. It does not apply to family credit, FIS, disability working allowance, housing benefit or council tax benefit claimants, all of whom can be overpaid by concealing capital. Nor does it apply to anyone other than a recipient of income support, JSA or supplementary benefit. Sometimes a person other than a recipient may become liable to recovery by making a misrepresentation or failing to disclose a material fact (*R(SB) 21/82* and *R(SB) 28/83*). See the note to s.71(3).

Maintenance proceedings

Furnishing of addresses for maintenance proceedings, etc.

133. The Secretary of State may incur expenses for the purpose of furnishing the address at which a man or woman is recorded by him as residing, where the address is required for the purpose of taking or carrying on legal proceedings to obtain or enforce an order for the making by the man or woman of payments—
  (a) for the maintenance of the man's wife or former wife, or the woman's husband or former husband; or
  (b) for the maintenance or education of any person as being the son or daughter of the man or his wife or former wife, or of the woman or her husband or former husband.

DERIVATION

Social Security Act 1975, s.161(1).

PART XI

COMPUTATION OF BENEFITS

Effect of alteration in the component rates of income support

159.—(1) Subject to such exceptions and conditions as may be prescribed, where—
  (a) an award of income support is in force in favour of any person ("the recipient"); and
  (b) there is an alteration in any of the relevant amounts, that is to say—
        (i) any of the component rates of income support;
        (ii) any of the other sums specified in regulations under Part VII of the Contributions and Benefits Act; or
        (iii) the recipient's benefit income; and
  (c) the alteration affects the computation of the amount of income support to which the recipient is entitled,
then subsection (2) or (3) below (as the case may be) shall have effect.
  (2) Where, in consequence of the alteration in question, the recipient becomes entitled to an increased or reduced amount of income support ("the new amount"), then, as from the commencing date, the amount of income support payable to or for the recipient under the award shall be the new amount, without any further decision of an adjudication officer, and the award shall have effect accordingly.
  (3) Where, notwithstanding the alteration in question, the recipient continues on and after the commencing date to be entitled to the same amount of income support as before, the award shall continue in force accordingly.

(4) In any case where—

(a) there is an alteration in any of the relevant amounts; and

(b) before the commencing date (but after that date is fixed) an award of income support is made in favour of a person,

the award either may provide for income support to be paid as from the commencing date, in which case the amount shall be determined by reference to the relevant amounts which will be in force on that date, or may provide for an amount determined by reference to the amounts in force at the date of the award.

(5) In this section—

"alteration" means—

(a) in relation to—

(i) the component rates of income support; or

(ii) any other sums specified in regulations under Part VII of the Contributions and Benefits Act,

their alteration by or under any enactment whether or not contained in that Part; and

(b) in relation to a person's benefit income, the alteration of any of the sums referred to in section 150 above—

(i) by any enactment; or

(ii) by an order under section 150 or 152 above,

to the extent that any such alteration affects the amount of his benefit income;

"benefit income", in relation to any person, means so much of his income as consists of—

(a) benefit under the Contributions and Benefits Act, other than income support; or

(b) a war disablement pension or war widow's pension;

"the commencing date" in relation to an alteration, means the date on which the alteration comes into force in the case of the person in question;

"component rate", in relation to income support, means the amount of—

(a) the sum referred to in section 126(5)(b)(i) and (ii) of the Contributions and Benefits Act; or

(b) any of the sums specified in regulations under section 135(1) of that Act; and

"relevant amounts" has the meaning given by subsection (1)(b) above.

DERIVATION

Social Security Act 1986, s.64A.

DEFINITIONS

"the Contributions and Benefits Act"—see s.191.
"war disablement pension"—*ibid.*
"war widow's pension"—*ibid.*

GENERAL NOTE

The general rule under s.159 is that if there is an alteration in the prescribed figures for personal allowances, premiums, the relevant sum (*i.e.* assumed "strike pay" in trade dispute cases), or any social security benefits which count as income for income support purposes (subss.(1) and (5)), then any consequent change in the amount of income support which is payable takes effect automatically without the need for a decision by an AO (subs. (2)). Thus no right of appeal arises against the change in the amount, although the claimant can always request a review of the decision awarding benefit, as altered under s.159. The former power to review an award of income support in such circumstances was removed by the amendment to what was reg. 69(3) (now reg. 63(2)) of the

Adjudication Regulations, except where some kind of transitional addition is in payment. In this latter case, there must be a review under reg. 63(3) to give effect to the change.

[¹Effect of alteration of rates of a jobseeker's allowance

159A.—(1) This section applies where—
(a) an award of a jobseeker's allowance is in force in favour of any person (''the recipient''); and
(b) an alteration—
    (i) in any component of the allowance, or
    (ii) in the recipient's benefit income,
affects the amount of the jobseeker's allowance to which he is entitled.

(2) Subsection (3) applies where, as a result of the alteration, the amount of the jobseeker's allowance to which the recipient is entitled is increased or reduced.

(3) As from the commencing date, the amount of the jobseeker's allowance payable to or for the recipient under the award shall be the increased or reduced amount, without any further decision of an adjudication officer; and the award shall have effect accordingly.

(4) In any case where—
(a) there is an alteration of a kind mentioned in subsection (1)(b); and
(b) before the commencing date (but after that date is fixed) an award of a jobseeker's allowance is made in favour of a person,
the award may provide for the jobseeker's allowance to be paid as from the commencing date, in which case the amount of the jobseeker's allowance shall be determined by reference to the components applicable on that date, or may provide for an amount determined by reference to the components applicable at the date of the award.

(5) In this section—
''alteration'' means—
    (a) in relation to any component of a jobseeker's allowance, its alteration by or under any enactment; and
    (b) in relation to a person's benefit income, the alteration of any of the sums referred to in section 150 above by any enactment or by an order under section 150 above, to the extent that any such alteration affects the amount of the recipient's benefit income;
''benefit income'', in relation to a recipient, means so much of his income as consists of—
    (a) benefit under the Contributions and Benefits Act; or
    (b) a war disablement pension or war widow's pension;
''the commencing date'' in relation to an alteration, means the date on which the alteration comes into force in relation to the recipient;
''component'', in relation to a jobseeker's allowance, means any of the sums specified in regulations under the Jobseekers Act 1995 which are relevant in calculating the amount payable by way of a jobseeker's allowance.]

AMENDMENT

1. Jobseekers Act 1995, s.24 (October 7, 1996).

DEFINITIONS

''the Contributions and Benefit Act''—see s.191.
''war disablement pension''—*ibid.*
''war widow's pension—*ibid.*

GENERAL NOTE

This section has the same effect for income-based JSA as s.159 does for income support.

Implementation of increases in income support due to attainment of particular ages

160.—(1) This section applies where—
(a) an award of income support is in force in favour of a person ("the recipient"); and
(b) there is a component which becomes applicable, or applicable at a particular rate, in his case if he or some other person attains a particular age.

(2) If, in a case where this section applies, the recipient or other person attains the particular age referred to in paragraph (b) of subsection (1) above and, in consequence—
(a) the component in question becomes applicable, or applicable at a particular rate, in the recipient's case (whether or not some other component ceases, for the same reason, to be applicable, or applicable at a particular rate, in his case; and
(b) after taking account of any such cessation, the recipient becomes entitled to an increased amount of income support,
then, except as provided by subsection (3) below, as from the day on which he becomes so entitled, the amount of income support payable to or for him under the award shall be that increased amount, without any further decision of an adjudication officer, and the award shall have effect accordingly.

(3) Subsection (2) above does not apply in any case where, in consequence of the recipient or other person attaining the age in question, some question arises in relation to the recipient's entitlement to any benefit under the Contributions and Benefits Act, other than—
(a) the question whether the component concerned, or any other component, becomes or ceases to be applicable, or applicable at a particular rate, in his case; and
(b) the question whether, in consequence, the amount of his income support falls to be varied.

(4) In this section "component", in relation to a person and his income support, means any of the sums specified in regulations under section 135(1) of the Contributions and Benefits Act.

DERIVATION

Social Security Act 1986, s.64B.

DEFINITION

"the Contributions and Benefits Act"—see s.191.

GENERAL NOTE

Section 160 extends the process begun by s.159 of taking routine adjustments in the amount of income support out of the ordinary mechanism of review by an AO under s.25.

[¹ Implementation of increases in income-based jobseeker's allowance due to attainment of particular ages

160A.—(1) This section applies where—
(a) an award of an income-based jobseeker's allowance is in force in favour of a person ("the recipient"); and

(b) a component has become applicable, or applicable at a particular rate, because he or some other person has reached a particular age ("the qualifying age")

(2) If, as a result of the recipient or other person reaching the qualifying age, the recipient becomes entitled to an income-based jobseeker's allowance of an increased amount, the amount payable to or for him under the award shall, as from the day on which he becomes so entitled, be that increased amount, without any further decision of an adjudication officer; and the award shall have effect accordingly.

(3) Subsection (2) above does not apply where, in consequence of the recipient or other person reaching the qualifying age, a question arises in relation to the recipient's entitlement to—

(a) a benefit under the Contributions and Benefits Act; or

(b) a jobseeker's allowance.

(4) Subsection (3)(b) above does not apply to the question—

(a) whether the component concerned, or any other component, becomes or ceases to be applicable, or applicable at a particular rate, in the recipient's case; and

(b) whether, in consequence, the amount of his income-based jobseeker's allowance falls to be varied.

(5) In this section "component", in relation to a recipient and his jobseeker's allowance, means any of the amounts determined in accordance with regulations made under section 4(5) of the Jobseekers Act 1995.]

AMENDMENT

1. Jobseekers Act 1995, s.25 (October 7, 1996).

DEFINITION

"the Contributions and Benefits Act"—see s.191.

GENERAL NOTE

See s.160.

PART XII

FINANCE

The social fund

167.—(1) The fund known as the social fund shall continue in being by that name.

(2) The social fund shall continue to be maintained under the control and management of the Secretary of State and payments out of it shall be made by him.

(3) The Secretary of State shall make payments into the social fund of such amounts, at such times and in such manner as he may with the approval of the Treasury determine.

(4) Accounts of the social fund shall be prepared in such form, and in such manner and at such times, as the Treasury may direct, and the Comptroller and Auditor General shall examine and certify every such account and shall lay copies of it, together with his report, before Parliament.

(5) The Secretary of State shall prepare an annual report on the social fund.

(6) A copy of every such report shall be laid before each House of Parliament.

DERIVATION

Subs.(1): Social Security Act 1986, s.32(1).
Subss. (2) to (6): 1986 Act, s.32(5) to (7B).

Allocations from social fund

168.—(1) The Secretary of State shall allocate amounts for payments from the social fund such as are mentioned in section 138(1)(b) of the Contributions and Benefits Act in a financial year.

(2) The Secretary of State may specify the amounts either as sums of money or by reference to money falling into the social fund on repayment or partial repayment of loans, or partly in the former and partly in the latter manner.

(3) Allocations—
(a) may be for payments by a particular social fund officer or group of social fund officers;
(b) may be for different amounts for different purposes;
(c) may be made at such time or times as the Secretary of State considers appropriate; and
(d) may be in addition to any other allocation to the same officer or group of officers or for the same purpose.

(4) The Secretary of State may at any time re-allocate amounts previously allocated, and subsections (2) and (3) above shall have effect in relation to a re-allocation as they have effect in relation to an allocation.

(5) The Secretary of State may give general directions to social fund officers or groups of social fund officers, or to any class of social fund officers, with respect to the control and management by social fund officers or groups of social fund officers of the amounts allocated to them under this section.

DERIVATION

Social Security Act 1986, s.32(8A) to (8E).

DEFINITION

"the Contributions and Benefits Act"—see s.191.

GENERAL NOTE

See the notes to the social fund directions.

Adjustments between social fund and other sources of finance

169.—(1) There shall be made—
(a) out of the social fund into the Consolidated Fund or the National Insurance Fund;
(b) into the social fund out of money provided by Parliament or the National Insurance Fund,
such payments by way of adjustment as the Secretary of State determines (in accordance with any directions of the Treasury) to be appropriate in consequence of any enactment or regulations relating to the repayment or offsetting of a benefit or other payment under the Contributions and Benefits Act.

(2) Where in any other circumstances payments fall to be made by way of adjustment—

    (a) out of the social fund into the Consolidated Fund or the National Insurance Fund; or

    (b) into the social fund out of money provided by Parliament or the National Insurance Fund,

then, in such cases or classes of cases as may be specified by the Secretary of State by order, the amount of the payments to be made shall be taken to be such, and payments on account of it shall be be made at such times and in such manner, as may be determined by the Secretary of State in accordance with any direction given by the Treasury.

DERIVATION

    Social Security Act 1986, s.85(11) and (12).

DEFINITION

    "the Contributions and Benefits Act"—see s.191.

PART XV

MISCELLANEOUS

National insurance numbers

[¹Requirement to apply for national insurance number

182C.—(1) Regulations may make provision requiring a person to apply for a national insurance number to be allocated to him.

    [²(1A) Regulations under subsection (1) above may require the application to be made to the Secretary of State or to the Inland Revenue.]

    (2) An application required by regulations under subsection (1) above shall be accompanied by information or evidence enabling such a number to be allocated.]

AMENDMENTS

    1. Social Security Administration (Fraud) Act 1997, Sched. 1, para. 9 (July 1, 1997).
    2. Social Security Contributions (Transfer of Functions, etc.) Act 1999, s.1(1) and Sched. 1, para. 31 (April 1, 1999).

GENERAL NOTE

    See subss. (1A)–(1C) of s. 1, inserted by s. 19 of the Social Security Administration (Fraud) Act, which make having, or applying for, a national insurance number a condition of entitlement to benefit in most cases.

Supplementary benefit etc.

Applications of provisions of Act to supplementary benefit etc.

186. Schedule 10 to this Act shall have effect for the purposes of making provision in relation to the benefits there mentioned.

Miscellaneous

Certain benefit to be inalienable

187.—(1) Subject to the provisions of this Act, every assignment of or charge on—

    (a) benefit as defined in section 122 of the Contributions and Benefits Act;

[¹(aa) a jobseeker's allowance;]

    (b) any income-related benefit; or

    (c) child benefit,

and every agreement to assign or charge such benefit shall be void; and, on the bankruptcy of a beneficiary, such benefit shall not pass to any trustee or other person acting on behalf of his creditors.

(2) In the application of subsection (1) above to Scotland—

    (a) the reference to assignment of benefit shall be read as a reference to assignation, "assign" being construed accordingly;

    (b) the reference to a beneficiary's bankruptcy shall be read as a reference to the sequestration of his estate or the appointment on his estate of a judicial factor under section 41 of the Solicitors (Scotland) Act 1980.

(3) In calculating for the purposes of section 5 of the Debtors Act 1869 or section 4 of the Civil Imprisonment (Scotland) Act 1882 the means of any beneficiary, no account shall be taken of any increase of disablement benefit in respect of a child or of industrial death benefit.

DERIVATION

    Social Security Act 1975, s.87.

AMENDMENT

    1. Jobseekers Act 1995, Sched. 2, para. 72 (October 7, 1996).

DEFINITIONS

    "the Contributions and Benefits Act"—see s.191.
    "income-related benefit"—*ibid.*

GENERAL NOTE

    The House of Lords in *Mulvey v. Secretary of State for Social Security* (March 13, 1997) dealt with the part of s.187(1) providing that, on bankruptcy or sequestration of a beneficiary, benefit does not pass to the trustee in bankruptcy. It held that the purpose was "to make clear beyond peradventure that the permanent trustee [the Scottish equivalent of the trusteee in bankruptcy] could have no interest in any entitlement of a debtor to receive any of the social security benefits to which it applied" (Lord Jauncey). The Secretary of State's obligation to make payment of benefit is owed to the beneficiary and cannot be owed to the trustee in bankruptcy or permanent trustee. See the notes to s.78(2) for the situation where deductions are being made from benefit for the repayment of social fund loans or the recovery of overpayments.

PART XVI

GENERAL

Supplementary

Interpretation—general

191. In this Act, unless the context otherwise requires—
"the 1975 Act" means the Social Security Act 1975;
"the 1986 Act" means the Social Security Act 1986;

"benefit" means benefit under the Contributions and Benefits Act [²and includes a jobseeker's allowance];

[*Omitted definitions not applying to the benefits in this book*]

"Commissioner" means the Chief Social Security Commissioner or any other Social Security Commissioner and includes a tribunal of 3 Commissioners constituted under section 57 above;

[*Omitted definition not applying to the benefits in this book*]

"the Consequential Provisions Act" means the Social Security (Consequential Provisions) Act 1992;

[³"contribution" means a contribution under Part I of the Contributions and Benefits Act;]

[²"contribution-based jobseeker's allowance" has the same meaning as in the Jobseekers Act 1995;]

[*Omitted definition not applying to the benefits in this book*]

"the Contributions and Benefits Act" means the Social Security Contributions and Benefits Act 1992;

"disablement benefit" is to be construed in accordance with section 94(2)(a) of the Contributions and Benefits Act;

"the disablement questions" is to be construed in accordance with section 45 above;

"dwelling" means any residential accommodation, whether or not consisting of the whole or part of a building, and whether or not comprising separate and self-contained premises;

"5 year general qualification" is to be construed in accordance with section 71 of the Courts and Legal Services Act 1991;

[*Omitted definitions not applying to the benefits in this book*]

[²"income-based jobseeker's allowance" has the same meaning as in the Jobseekers Act 1995;]

"income-related benefit" means—
- (a) income support;
- (b) family credit;
- (c) disability working allowance;
- (d) housing benefit; and
- [¹(e) council tax benefit];

"industrial injuries benefits" means benefit under Part V of the Contributions and Benefits Act, other than under Schedule 8;

[⁴ "Inland Revenue" means the Commissioners of Inland Revenue;]

[*Omitted definitions not applying benefits in this book*]

"local authority" means—
- (a) in relation to England and Wales, the council of a district or London borough, the Common Council of the City of London or the Council of the Isles of Scilly; and
- (b) in relation to Scotland, an islands or district council;

[*Omitted definitions not applying to the benefits in this book*]

"the Northern Ireland Department" means the Department of Health and Social Services for Northern Ireland [³but in section 122 and sections 122B to 122E also includes the Department of the Environment for Northern Ireland;]

"the Northern Ireland Administration Act" means the Social Security (Northern Ireland) Administration Act 1992;

"occupational pension scheme" has the same meaning as in section 66(1) of the Social Security Pensions Act 1975;

"the Old Cases Act" means the Industrial Injuries and Diseases (Old Cases) Act 1975;

[*Omitted definition not applying to the benefits in this book*]

"the Pensions Act" means the Social Security Pensions Act 1975;

"personal pension scheme" has the meaning assigned to it by section 84(1) of the 1986 Act;

"prescribe" means prescribe by regulations;

"President" means the President of social security appeal tribunals, disability appeal tribunals and medical appeal tribunals;

[Omitted definitions not applying to the benefits in this book]

"10 year general qualification" is to be construed in accordance with section 71 of the Courts and Legal Services Act 1991.

[Omitted definition not applying to the benefits in this book]

DERIVATION

Social Security Act 1975, Sched. 20 and Social Security Act 1986, s.84(1).

AMENDMENTS

1. Local Government Finance Act 1992, Sched. 9, para. 25 (April 1, 1993).
2. Jobseekers Act 1995, Sched. 2, para. 73 (October 7, 1996).
3. Social Security Administration (Fraud) Act 1997, Sched. 1, para. 12 (July 1, 1997).
4. Social Security Contributions (Transfer of Functions, etc.) Act 1999, s.1(1) and Sched. 1, para. 32 (April 1, 1999).

Short title, commencement and extent

192.—(1) This Act may be cited as the Social Security Administration Act 1992.

(2) This Act is to be read, where appropriate, with the Contributions and Benefits Act and the Consequential Provisions Act.

(3) The enactments consolidated by this Act are repealed, in consequence of the consolidation, by the Consequential Provisions Act.

(4) Except as provided in Schedule 4 to the Consequential Provisions Act, this Act shall come into force on 1st July 1992.

(5) The following provisions extend to Northern Ireland—

section 24;

[¹. . .]

section 170 (with Schedule 5);

section 177 (with Schedule 8); and

this section.

(6) Except as provided by this section, this Act does not extend to Northern Ireland.

AMENDMENT

1. Social Security (Recovery of Benefits) Act 1997, s. 33 and Sched. 3, para. 13 (October 6, 1997).

DEFINITIONS

"the Consequential Provisions Act"—see s.191.

"the Contributions and Benefits Act"—*ibid.*

SCHEDULES

SCHEDULE 1   Section 1(6)

Claims for Benefit made or Treated as made before 1st October 1990

Claims made or treated as made on or after 2nd September 1985 and before 1st October 1986

1. Section 1 above shall have effect in relation to a claim made or treated as made on or after 2nd September 1985 and before 1st October 1986 as if the following subsections were substituted for subsections (1) to (3)—

"(1) Except in such cases as may be prescribed, no person shall be entitled to any benefit unless, in addition to any other conditions relating to that benefit being satisfied—
  (a) he makes a claim for it—
    (i) in the prescribed manner; and
    (ii) subject to subsection (2) below, within the prescribed time; or
  (b) by virtue of a provision of Chapter VI of Part II of the 1975 Act or of regulations made under such a provision he would have been treated as making a claim for it.

(2) Regulations shall provide for extending, subject to any prescribed conditions, the time within which a claim may be made in cases where it is not made within the prescribed time but good cause is shown for the delay.

(3) Notwithstanding any regulations made under this section, no person shall be entitled to any benefit (except disablement benefit or industrial death benefit) in respect of any period more than 12 months before the date on which the claim is made."

Claims made or treated as made on or after 1st October 1986 and before 6th April 1987

2. Section 1 above shall have effect in relation to a claim made or treated as made on or after 1st October 1986 and before 6th April 1987 as if the subsections set out in paragraph 1 above were substituted for subsections (1) to (3) but with the insertion in subsection (3) of the words ", reduced earnings allowance" after the words "disablement benefit".

Claims made or treated as made on or after 6th April 1987 and before 21st July 1989

3. Section 1 above shall have effect in relation to a claim made or treated as made on or after 6th April 1987 and before 21st July 1989, as if—
  (a) the following subsection were substituted for subsection (1)—
"(1) Except in such cases as may be prescribed, no person shall be entitled to any benefit unless, in addition to any other conditions relating to that benefit being satisfied—
  (a) he makes a claim for it in the prescribed manner and within the prescribed time; or
  (b) by virtue of regulations made under section 51 of the 1986 Act he would have been treated as making a claim for it."; and
  (b) there were omitted—
    (i) from subsection (2), the words "except as provided by section 3 below"; and
    (ii) subsection (3).

Claims made or treated as made on or after 21st July 1989 and before 13th July 1990

4. Section 1 above shall have effect in relation to a claim made or treated as made on or after 21st July 1989 and before 13th July 1990 as if there were omitted—

(a) from subsection (1), the words "and subject to the following provisions of this section and to section 3 below";

(b) from subsection (2), the words "except as provided by section 3 below"; and

(c) subsection (3).

Claims made or treated as made on or after 13th July 1990 and before 1st October 1990

5. Section 1 above shall have effect in relation to a claim made or treated as made on or after 13th July 1990 and before 1st October 1990 as if there were omitted—

(a) from subsection (1), the words "the following provisions of this section and to"; and

(b) subsection (3).

<small>DEFINITIONS</small>

"disablement benefit"—see s.191.
"prescribe"—*ibid.*

SCHEDULE 2   Sections 41, 43 and 50 to 52

COMMISSIONERS, TRIBUNALS ETC.—SUPPLEMENTARY PROVISIONS

Tenure of offices

1.—(1) Subject to the following provisions of this paragraph, the President and the regional and other full-time chairmen of social security appeal tribunals, medical appeal tribunals and disability appeal tribunals shall hold and vacate office in accordance with the terms of their appointment.

(2) Commissioners, the President and the full-time chairmen shall vacate their offices [¹on the day on which they attain the age of 70, but subject to section 26(4) to (6) of the Judicial Pensions and Retirement Act 1993 (power to authorise continuance in office up to the age of 75).]

(3) [². . .]

(4) A Commissioner, the President and a full-time chairman may be removed from office by the Lord Chancellor on the ground of incapacity or misbehaviour.

(5) Where the Lord Chancellor proposes to exercise a power conferred on him by sub-paragraph [³. . .] (4) above, it shall be his duty to consult the Lord Advocate with respect to the proposal.

(6) Nothing in sub-paragraph (2) [³. . .] above or in section 13 or 32 of the Judicial Pensions Act 1981 (which relate to pensions for Commissioners) shall apply to a person by virtue of his appointment in pursuance of section 52(2) above.

(7) Nothing in sub-paragraph [³. . .] (4) above applies to a Commissioner appointed before 23rd May 1980.

Remuneration etc. for President and Chairmen

2. [⁴—(1)] The Secretary of State may pay, or make such payments towards the provision of, such remuneration, pensions, allowances or gratuities to or in respect of the President and full-time chairmen as, with the consent of the Treasury, he may determine.

[⁴(2) Sub-paragraph (1) above, so far as relating to pensions, allowances and gratuities, shall not have effect in relation to persons to whom Part I of the Judicial Pensions and Retirement Act 1993 applies, except to the extent provided by or under that Act.]

Officers and staff

3. The President may appoint such officers and staff as he thinks fit—
(a) for himself;
(b) for the regional and other full-time chairmen;
(c) for social security appeal tribunals;
(d) for disability appeal tribunals; and
(e) for medical appeal tribunals,
with the consent of the Secretary of State and the Treasury as to numbers and as to remuneration and other terms and conditions of service.

Clerks to social security appeal tribunals and disability appeal tribunals

4.—(1) The President shall assign clerks to service the social security appeal tribunal for each area and the disability appeal tribunal for each area.
(2) The duty of summoning members of a panel to serve on such a tribunal shall be performed by the clerk to the tribunal.

Miscellaneous administrative duties of President

5. It shall be the duty of the President—
(a) to arrange—
  (i) such meetings of chairmen and members of social security appeal tribunals, chairmen and members of disability appeal tribunals and chairmen and members of medical appeal tribunals;
  (ii) such training for such chairmen and members, as he considers appropriate; and
(b) to secure that such works of reference relating to social security law as he considers appropriate are available for the use of chairmen and members of social security appeal tribunals, disability appeal tribunals and medical appeal tribunals.

Remuneration etc.

6. The Lord Chancellor shall pay to a Commissioner such salary or other remuneration, and such expenses incurred in connection with the work of a Commissioner or any tribunal presided over by a Commissioner, as may be determined by the Treasury.
7.—(1) The Secretary of State may pay—
(a) to any person specified in sub-paragraph (2) below, such remuneration and such travelling and other allowances;
(b) to any person specified in sub-paragraph (3) below, such travelling and other allowances; and
(c) subject to sub-paragraph (4) below, such other expenses in connection with the work of any person, tribunal or inquiry appointed or constituted under any provision of this Act,
as the Secretary of State with the consent of the Treasury may determine.
(2) The persons mentioned in sub-paragraph (1)(a) above are—
(a) any person (other than a Commissioner) appointed under this Act to determine questions or as a member of, or assessor to, a social security appeal tribunal, a disability appeal tribunal or a medical appeal tribunal; and
[⁵(aa) a person appointed as medical assessor to a social security appeal tribunal under regulations under section 61A(4) above; and]
(b) a medical officer appointed under regulations under section 62 above.
(3) The persons mentioned in sub-paragraph (1)(b) above are—
(a) any person required to attend at any proceedings or inquiry under this Act; and
(b) any person required under this Act (whether for the purposes of this Act or

otherwise) to attend for or to submit themselves to medical or other examination or treatment.

(4) Expenses are not payable under sub-paragraph (1)(c) above in connection with the work—

(a) of a tribunal presided over by a Commissioner; or

(b) of a social fund officer, a social fund inspector or the social fund Commissioner.

(5) In this paragraph references to travelling and other allowances include references to compensation for loss of remunerative time but such compensation shall not be paid to any person in respect of any time during which he is in receipt of remuneration under this paragraph.

Certificates of decisions

8. A document bearing a certificate which—

(a) is signed by a person authorised in that behalf by the Secretary of State; and

(b) states that the document, apart from the certificate, is a record of a decision—

    (i) of a Commissioner;

    (ii) of a social security appeal tribunal;

    (iii) of a disability appeal tribunal; or

    (iv) of an adjudication officer,

shall be conclusive evidence of the decision; and a certificate purporting to be so signed shall be deemed to be so signed unless the contrary is proved.

DERIVATION

Para. 1: Social Security Act 1975, Sched. 10, para. 1A and Social Security Act 1980, s.13.
Paras. 2 and 3: 1975 Act, Sched. 10, para. 1A(10) and (11).
Paras. 4 and 5: 1975 Act, Sched. 10, paras. 1B to 1D and Sched. 10A, para. 11.
Para. 6: 1975 Act, Sched. 10, para. 4.
Para. 7: 1975 Act, Sched. 10, para. 3 and Sched. 10A, para. 11.
Para. 8: Social Security Act 1980, s.17.

AMENDMENTS

1. Judicial Pensions and Retirement Act 1993, Sched. 6, para. 21(2) (March 31, 1995).
2. Judicial Pensions and Retirement Act 1993, Sched. 6, para. 21(3) and Sched. 9 (March 31, 1995).
3. Judicial Pensions and Retirement Act 1993, Sched. 6, para. 21 and Sched. 9 (March 31, 1995).
4. Judicial Pensions and Retirement Act 1993, Sched. 8, para. 23 (March 31, 1995).
5. Social Security (Incapacity for Work) Act 1994, Sched. 1, para. 53 (April 13, 1995).

DEFINITIONS

"Commissioner"—see s.191.
"President"—*ibid.*

GENERAL NOTE

Paragraph 4

Of the President's detailed powers and duties, the duty to assign the clerk to SSATs and DATs (but, oddly, not to MATs) under para. 4 is particularly important, especially in view of the extended responsibilities given in reg. 3(5) to (6C) of the Adjudication Regulations. The fact that SBAT clerks were in the past DHSS employees had long been a source of criticism, although their role had become less prominent as SBATs themselves became stronger. The President's own regional offices have now been established for some years. Clerks work from these offices as part of the President's own staff and the independence of this system has been clearly established. The President also appoints clerks for CSATs (see para. 6 of Sched. 3 to the Child Support Act 1991).

See the note to s.40 concerning the position under the new system for decision-making and appeals introduced by the Social Security Act 1998.

Paragraph 5
The President's powers to arrange training and to provide materials are unlimited, but he is constrained by the budget allowed to him for these purposes.

SCHEDULE 3 Section 59

REGULATIONS AS TO PROCEDURE

Interpretation

1. In this Schedule "competent tribunal" means—
(a) a Commissioner;
(b) a social security appeal tribunal;
(c) a disability appeal tribunal;
(d) a medical appeal tribunal;
(e) an adjudicating medical practitioner.

Provision which may be made

2. Provision prescribing the procedure to be followed in connection with the consideration and determination of claims and questions by the Secretary of State, an adjudication officer and a competent tribunal, or in connection with the withdrawal of a claim.

3. Provision as to the striking out of proceedings for want of prosecution.

4. Provision as to the form which is to be used for any document, the evidence which is to be required and the circumstances in which any official record or certificate is to be sufficient or conclusive evidence.

5. Provision as to the time to be allowed—
(a) for producing any evidence; or
(b) for making an appeal.

6. Provision as to the manner in which, and the time within which, a question may be raised with a view to its decision by the Secretary of State under Part II of this Act or with a view to the review of a decision under that Part.

7. Provision for summoning persons to attend and give evidence or produce documents and for authorising the administration of oaths to witnesses.

8. Provision for authorising a competent tribunal consisting of two or more members to proceed with any case, with the consent of the claimant, in the absence of any member.

9. Provision for giving the chairman or acting chairman of a competent tribunal consisting of two or more members a second or casting vote where the number of members present is an even number.

10. Provision empowering the chairman of a social security appeal tribunal, a disability appeal tribunal or a medical tribunal to give directions for the disposal of any purported appeal which he is satisfied that the tribunal does not have jurisdiction to entertain.

11. Provision for the non-disclosure to a person of the particulars of any medical advice or medical evidence given or submitted for the purposes of a determination.

12. Provision for requiring or authorising the Secretary of State to hold, or to appoint a person to hold, an inquiry in connection with the consideration of any question by the Secretary of State.

DERIVATION

Social Security Act 1975, Sched. 13.

SCHEDULE 10 **Section 186**

SUPPLEMENTARY BENEFIT ETC.

Interpretation

1. In this Schedule—
"the former National Insurance Acts" means the National Insurance Act 1946 and the National Insurance Act 1965; and
"the former Industrial Injuries Acts" means the National Insurance (Industrial Injuries) Act 1946 and the National Insurance (Industrial Injuries) Act 1965.

Claims and payments

2.—(1) Section 5 above shall have effect in relation to the benefits specified in sub-paragraph (2) below as it has effect in relation to the benefits to which it applies by virtue of subsection (2).
(2) The benefits mentioned in sub-paragraph (1) above are benefits under—
(a) the former National Insurance Acts;
(b) the former Industrial Injuries Acts;
(c) the National Assistance Act 1948;
(d) the Supplementary Benefit Act 1966;
(e) the Supplementary Benefits Act 1976;
(f) the Family Income Supplements Act 1970.

Adjudication

3.—(1) Sections 20 to 29, 36 to 43, 51 to 61 and section 124 above shall have effect for the purposes of the benefits specified in paragraph 2(2) above as they have effect for the purposes of benefit within the meaning of section 122 of the Contributions and Benefits Act other than attendance allowance, disability living allowance and disability working allowance.
(2) Procedure regulations made under section 59 above by virtue of sub-paragraph (1) may make different provision in relation to each of the benefits specified in paragraph 2(2) above.

Overpayments etc.

4.—(1) Section 71 above shall have effect for the purposes of the benefits specified in paragraph 2(2) above as it has effect in relation to the benefits to which it applies by virtue of subsection (11).
(2) Section 74 above shall have effect in relation to supplementary benefit as it has effect in relation to income support.
(3) The reference to housing benefit in section 75 above includes a reference to housing benefits under Part II of the Social Security and Housing Benefits Act 1982.

Inspection

5. Section 110 above shall have effect as if it also applied to—
(a) the Supplementary Benefits Act 1976,
(b) the Family Income Supplements Act 1970.

1261

Legal proceedings

6. Section 116 above shall have effect as if any reference to that Act in that section included—

(a) the National Assistance Act 1948;

(b) the Supplementary Benefit Act 1966;

(c) the Supplementary Benefits Act 1976;

(d) the Family Income Supplements Act 1970.

DERIVATION

Social Security Act 1986, Sched. 7.

DEFINITION

"the Contributions and Benefits Act"—see s.191.

Social Security (Consequential Provisions) Act 1992

(1992 c. 6)

ARRANGEMENT OF SECTIONS

Meaning of "the consolidating Acts"

1. In this Act—

"the consolidating Acts" means the Social Security Contributions and Benefits Act 1992 ("the Contributions and Benefits Act"), the Social Security Administration Act 1992 ("the Administration Act") and, so far as it reproduces the effect of the repealed enactments, this Act; and

"the repealed enactments" means the enactments repealed by this Act.

Continuity of the law

2.—(1) The substitution of the consolidating Acts for the repealed enactments does not affect the continuity of the law.

(2) Anything done or having effect as if done under or for the purposes of a provision of the repealed enactments has effect, if it could have been done under or for the purposes of the corresponding provision of the consolidating Acts, as if done under or for the purposes of that provision.

(3) Any reference, whether express or implied, in the consolidating Acts or any other enactment, instrument or document to a provision of the consolidating Acts shall, so far as the context permits, be construed as including, in relation to the times, circumstances and purposes in relation to which the corresponding

provision of the repealed enactments has effect, a reference to that corresponding provision.

(4) Any reference, whether express or implied, in any enactment, instrument or document to a provision of the repealed enactments shall be construed, so far as is required for continuing its effect, as including a reference to the corresponding provision of the consolidating Acts.

DEFINITIONS

    "the consolidating Acts"—see s.1.
    "the repealed enactments"—*ibid.*

GENERAL NOTE

    These provisions spell out what would anyway be the effect under the Interpretation Act 1978. For the practical purposes of this book, the most important provision is subs. (4). Any reference in a regulation to a section of the repealed legislation is to be construed as including a reference to the corresponding section of the Administration Act or the Contributions and Benefits Act. These updated references are included in square brackets in the appropriate places in the regulations.

Repeals

3.—(1) The enactments mentioned in Schedule 1 to this Act are repealed to the extent specified in the third column of that Schedule.

(2) Those repeals include, in addition to repeals consequential on the consolidation of provisions in the consolidating Acts, repeals in accordance with the Recommendations of the Law Commission and the Scottish Law Commission, of section 30(6)(b) of the Social Security Act 1975, paragraphs 2 to 8 of Schedule 9 to that Act, paragraph 2(1) of Schedule 10 to that Act and section 10 of the Social Security Act 1988.

(3) The repeals have effect subject to any relevant savings in Schedule 3 to this Act.

DEFINITION

    "the consolidating Acts"—see s.1.

Consequential amendments

4. The enactments mentioned in Schedule 2 to this Act shall have effect with the amendments there specified (being amendments consequential on the consolidating Acts).

DEFINITION

    "the consolidating Acts"—see s.1.

Transitional provisions and savings

5.—(1) The transitional provisions and savings in Schedule 3 to this Act shall have effect.

(2) Nothing in that Schedule affects the general operation of section 16 of the Interpretation Act 1978 (general savings implied on repeal) or of the previous provisions of this Act.

GENERAL NOTE

The effect of s.16 of the Interpretation Act 1978 is that regulations validly made under the repealed legislation continue to be treated as validly made after the consolidating legislation has taken over. (*Cottingham v. Chief Adjudication Officer* and *Geary v. Chief Adjudication Officer*, December 2, 1992, CA).

Transitory modifications

6. The transitory modifications in Schedule 4 to this Act shall have effect.

Short title, commencement and extent

7.—(1) This Act may be cited as the Social Security (Consequential Provisions) Act 1992.

(2) This Act shall come into force on 1st July 1992.

(3) Section 2 above and this section extend to Northern Ireland.

(4) Subject to subsection (5) below, where any enactment repealed or amended by this Act extends to any part of the United Kingdom, the repeal or enactment extends to that part.

(5) The repeals—

(a) of provisions of sections 10, 13 and 14 of the Social Security Act 1980 and Part II of Schedule 3 to that Act;

(b) of enactments amending those provisions;

(c) of paragraph 2 of Schedule 1 to the Capital Allowances Act 1990; and

(d) of section 17(8) and (9) of the Social Security Act 1990,

do not extend to Northern Ireland.

(6) Section 6 above and Schedule 4 to this Act extend to Northern Ireland in so far as they give effect to transitory modifications of provisions of the consolidating Acts which so extend.

(7) Except as provided by this section, this Act does not extend to Northern Ireland.

(8) Section 4 above extends to the Isle of Man so far as it relates to paragraphs 52 and 3 of Schedule 2 to this Act.

DEFINITION

"the consolidating Acts"—see s.1

SCHEDULE

SCHEDULE 3   **Section 5**

TRANSITIONAL PROVISIONS AND SAVINGS (INCLUDING SOME TRANSITIONAL PROVISIONS RETAINED FROM PREVIOUS ACTS)

Part I

General and Miscellaneous

Questions relating to contributions and benefits

1.—(1) A question other than a question arising under any of sections 1 to 3 of the Administration Act—

(a) whether a person is entitled to benefit in respect of a time before 1st July 1992;

(b) whether a person is liable to pay contributions in respect of such a time,

and any other question not arising under any of those sections with respect to benefit or contributions in respect of such a time is to be determined, subject to section 68 of the Administration Act, in accordance with provisions in force or deemed to be in force at that time.

(2) Subject to sub-paragraph (1) above, the consolidating Acts apply to matters arising before their commencement as to matters arising after it.

General saving for old savings

2. The repeal by this Act of an enactment previously repealed subject to savings (whether or not in the repealing enactment) does not affect the continued operation of those savings.

Documents referring to repealed enactments

3. Any document made, served or issued after this Act comes into force which contains a reference to any of the repealed enactments shall be construed, except so far as a contrary intention appears, as referring or, as the context may require, including a reference to the corresponding provision of the consolidating Acts.

Provisions relating to the coming into force of other provisions

4. The repeal by this Act of a provision providing for or relating to the coming into force of a provision reproduced in the consolidating Acts does not affect the operation of the first provision, in so far as it remains capable of having effect, in relation to the enactment reproducing the second provision.

Continuing powers to make transitional etc. regulations

5. Where immediately before 1st July 1992 the Secretary of State has power under any provision of the Social Security Acts 1975 to 1991 not reproduced in the consolidating Acts by regulations to make provision or savings in preparation for or in connection with the coming into force of a provision repealed by this Act but reproduced in the consolidating Acts, the power shall be construed as having effect in relation to the provision reproducing the repealed provision.

6. The repeal by this Act of a power by regulations to make provision or savings in preparation for or in connection with the coming into force of a provision reproduced in the consolidating Acts does not affect the power, in so far as it remains capable of having effect, in relation to the enactment reproducing the second provision.

Provisions contained in enactments by virtue of orders or regulations

7.—(1) Without prejudice to any express provision in the consolidating Acts, where this Act repeals any provision contained in any enactment by virtue of any order or regulations and the provision is reproduced in the consolidating Acts, the Secretary of State shall have the like power to make orders or regulations repealing or amending the provision of the consolidating Acts which reproduces the effect of the repealed provision as he had in relation to that provision.

(2) Sub-paragraph (1) above applies to a repealed provision which was amended by Schedule 7 to the Social Security Act 1989 as it applies to a provision not so amended.

Amending orders made after passing of Act

8. An order which is made under any of the repealed enactments after the passing of this Act and which amends any of the repealed enactments shall have the effect also of making a corresponding amendment of the consolidating Acts.

DEFINITIONS

"the Administration Act"—see s.1.
"the consolidating Acts"—*ibid.*
"the repealed enactments"—*ibid.*

Social Security Act 1998

(1998 c. 14)

PART I

DECISIONS AND APPEALS

Use of computers

2.—(1) Any decision, determination or assessment falling to be made or certificate falling to be issued by the Secretary of State under or by virtue of a relevant enactment, or in relation to a war pension, may be made or issued not only by an officer of his acting under his authority but also—
  (a) by a computer for whose operation such an officer is responsible; and
  (b) in the case of a decision, determination or assessment that may be made or a certificate that may be issued by a person providing services to the Secretary of State, by a computer for whose operation such a person is responsible.
  (2) In this section "relevant enactment" means any enactment contained in—
  [¹(a) Chapter II of this Part;]
  (b) the Social Security Contributions and Benefits Act 1992 ("the Contributions and Benefits Act");
  (c) the Administration Act;
  (d) the Child Support Act;
  (e) the Social Security (Incapacity for Work) Act 1994;
  (f) the Jobseekers Act 1995 ("the Jobseekers Act");
  (g) the Child Support Act 1995; or
  (h) the Social Security (Recovery of Benefits) Act 1997.
  (3) In this section and section 3 below "war pension" has the same meaning as in section 25 of the Social Security Act 1989 (establishment and functions of war pensions committees).

AMENDMENT

1. Subs. (2)(a) is not yet in force.

GENERAL NOTE

Section 2 (except subs. (2)(a)) came into force on September 8, 1998 (Social Security Act 1998 (Commencement No. 1) Order 1998 (S.I. 1998 No. 2209), art. 2(a) and Part 1).

Part IV

MISCELLANEOUS AND SUPPLEMENTAL

Pilot schemes

77.—(1) Any regulations to which this subsection applies may be made so as to have effect for a specified period not exceeding 12 months.

(2) Any regulations which, by virtue of subsection (1) above, are to have effect for a limited period are referred to in this section as ''a pilot scheme''.

(3) A pilot scheme may provide that its provisions are to apply only in relation to—

(a) one or more specified areas or localities;

(b) one or more specified classes of person;

(c) persons selected—

    (i) by reference to prescribed criteria; or

    (ii) on a sampling basis.

(4) A pilot scheme may make consequential or transitional provision with respect to the cessation of the scheme on the expiry of the specified period.

(5) A pilot scheme (''the previous scheme'') may be replaced by a further pilot scheme making the same, or similar, provision (apart from the specified period) to that made by the previous scheme.

(6) In so far as a pilot scheme would, apart from this subsection, have the effect of—

(a) treating as capable of work any person who would not otherwise be so treated; or

(b) reducing the total amount of benefit that would otherwise be payable to any person,

it shall not apply in relation to that person.

(7) Subsection (1) above applies to—

(a) regulations made under section 171D of the Contributions and Benefits Act (incapacity for work: persons treated as incapable of work); and

(b) in so far as they are consequential on or supplementary to any such regulations, regulations made under any of the provisions mentioned in subsection (8) below.

(8) The provisions are—

(a) subsection (5)(a) of section 22 of the Contributions and Benefits Act (earnings factors);

(b) section 30C of that Act (incapacity benefit);

(c) sections 68 and 69 of that Act (severe disablement allowance);

(d) subsection (1)(e) of section 124 of that Act (income support) and, so far as relating to income support, subsection (1) of section 135 of that Act (the applicable amount);

(e) Part XIIA of that Act (incapacity for work);

(f) section 61A of the Administration Act and section 31 above (incapacity for work).

(9) A statutory instrument containing (whether alone or with other provisions) a pilot scheme shall not be made unless a draft of the instrument has been laid before Parliament and approved by a resolution of each House of Parliament.

GENERAL NOTE

This section came into force on the commencement of the Act, *i.e.* May 21, 1998.

Regulations and orders

79.—(1) Subject to subsection (2) below and paragraph 6 of Schedule 4 to this Act, regulations under this Act shall be made by the Secretary of State.

(2) Regulations with respect to proceedings before the Commissioners (whether for the determination of any matter or for leave to appeal to or from the Commissioners) shall be made by the Lord Chancellor; and where the Lord Chancellor proposes to make regulations under this Act it shall be his duty to consult the Lord Advocate with respect to the proposal.

(3) Powers under this Act to make regulations or orders are exercisable by statutory instrument.

(4) Any power conferred by this Act to make regulations or orders may be exercised—

(a) either in relation to all cases to which the power extends, or in relation to those cases subject to specified exceptions, or in relation to any specified cases or classes of case;

(b) so as to make, as respects the cases in relation to which it is exercised—

    (i) the full provision to which the power extends or any less provision (whether by way of exception or otherwise);

    (ii) the same provision for all cases in relation to which the power is exercised, or different provision for different cases or different classes of case or diffferent provision as respects the same case or class of case for different purposes of this Act;

    (iii) any such provision either unconditionally or subject to any specified condition;

and where such a power is expressed to be exercisable for alternative purposes it may be exercised in relation to the same case for any or all of those purposes.

(5) Powers to make regulations for the purposes of any one provision of this Act are without prejudice to powers to make regulations for the purposes of any other provision.

(6) Without prejudice to any specific provision in this Act, a power conferred by this Act to make regulations includes power to make thereby such incidental, supplementary, consequential or transitional provision as appears to the authority making the regulations to be expedient for the purposes of those regulations.

(7) Without prejudice to any specific provisions in this Act, a power conferred by any provision of this Act to make regulations includes power to provide for a person to exercise a discretion in dealing with any matter.

(8) Any power conferred by this Act to make regulations relating to housing benefit or council tax benefit shall include power to make different provision for different areas or different authorities.

(9) In this section "Commissioner" has the the same meaning as in Chapter II of Part I.

GENERAL NOTE

This section came into force on the commencement of the Act, *i.e.* May 21, 1998.

Parliamentary control of regulations

80.—(1) Subject to the provisions of this section, a statutory instrument containing (whether alone or with other provisions) regulations under—

(a) section 7, 12(2) or 72 above; or

(b) paragraph 12 of Schedule 1, paragraph 9 of Schedule 2 or paragraph 2 of Schedule 5 to this Act, shall not be made unless a draft of the instrument has been laid before Parliament and been approved by a resolution of each House of Parliament.

(2) A statutory instrument—

(a) which contains (whether alone or with other provisions) regulations made under this Act by the Secretary of State; and

(b) which is not subject to any requirement that a draft of the instrument be laid before and approved by resolution of each House of Parliament,

shall be subject to annulment in pursuance of a resolution of either House of Parliament.

(3) A statutory instrument—

(a) which contains (whether alone or with other provisions) regulations made under this Act by the Lord Chancellor; and

(b) which is not subject to any requirement that a draft of the instrument be laid before and approved by a resolution of each House of Parliament,

shall be subject to annulment in pursuance of a resolution of either House of Parliament.

GENERAL NOTE

This section came into force on the commencement of the Act, *i.e.* May 21, 1998.

Transitory provisions

83. Schedule 6 to this Act (which contains transitory provisions) shall have effect.

GENERAL NOTE

Schedule 6 came into force on the commencement of the Act, *i.e.* May 21, 1998. It contains a number of important "transitory provisions" that have effect until the corresponding provisions in the 1998 Act are brought into force. These provisions have been incorporated into the text of the legislation reproduced in this book.

Interpretation: general

84. In this Act—

"the Administration Act" means the Social Security Administration Act 1992.

"the Child Support Act" means the Child Support Act 1991;

"the Contributions and Benefits Act" means the Social Security Contributions and Benefits Act 1992;

"the Jobseekers Act" means the Jobseekers Act 1995;

"the Vaccine Damage Payments Act" means the Vaccine Damage Payments Act 1979;

"prescribe" means prescribe by regulations.

GENERAL NOTE

This section came into force on the commencement of the Act, *i.e.* May 21, 1998.

Short title, commencement and extent

87.—(1) This Act may be cited as the Social Security Act 1998.

(2) This Act, except—

(a) sections 66, 69, 72 and 77 to 85, this section and Schedule 6 to this Act; and

(b) subsection (1) of section 50 so far as relating to a sum which is chargeable to tax by virtue of section 313 of the Income and Corporation Taxes Act 1988, and subsections (2) to (4) of that section,

shall come into force on such day as may be appointed by order made by the Secretary of State; and different days may be appointed for different provisions and for different purposes.

(3) An order under subsection (2) above may make such savings, or such transitional or consequential provision, as the Secretary of State considers necessary or expedient—

(a) in preparation for or in connection with the coming into force of any provision of the Act; or

(b) in connection with the operation of any enactment repealed or amended by a provision of this Act during any period when the repeal or amendment is not wholly in force.

(4) This Act, except—

(a) section 2 so far as relating to war pensions;

(b) sections 3, 15, 45 to 47, 59, 78 and 85 and this section; and

(c) section 86 and Schedules 7 and 8 so far as relating to enactments which extend to Northern Ireland,

does not extend to Northern Ireland.

(5) The following provisions of the Act extend to the Isle of Man, namely—

(a) in section 4, subsections (1)(c) and (2)(c);

(b) sections 6 and 7 and Schedule 1 so far as relating to appeals under the Vaccine Damage Payments Act;

(c) sections 45 to 47 and this section;

(d) paragraphs 5 to 10 of Schedule 7 and section 86(1) so far as relating to those paragraphs; and

(e) section 86(2) and Schedule 8 so far as relating to the Vaccine Damage Payments Act.

GENERAL NOTE

This section came into force on the commencement of the Act, *i.e.* May 21, 1998.

Social Security (Adjudication) Regulations 1995

(S.I. 1995 No. 1801)

Made by the Secretary of State under the powers in the Social Security Administration Act set out in Sched. 1.

ARRANGEMENT OF REGULATIONS

PART I

GENERAL

PART II

COMMON PROVISIONS

PART III

ADJUDICATING AUTHORITIES

SECTION B—ADJUDICATION OFFICERS

SECTION C—APPEAL TRIBUNALS

SECTION D—DISABILITY ADJUDICATION

PART IV

PROVISIONS RELATING TO PARTICULAR BENEFITS OR PROCEDURES

SECTION B—INCOME SUPPORT

SECTION C—REVIEW OF DECISIONS

PART V

TRANSITIONAL PROVISIONS AND REVOCATIONS

SCHEDULE

These regulations revoke the Social Security (Adjudication) Regulations 1986 and re-enact their provisions taking account of the consolidation effected by the Social Security Contributions and Benefits Act 1992 and the Social Security Administration Act 1992 and the changes made by the Social Security (Incapacity for Work) Act 1994. They came into force on August 10, 1995.

Sched. 4 is not set out. The major revocation is of the 1986 Regulations.

These regulations do not cover proceedings before the Social Security Commissioners, which are subject to the Social Security Commissioners (Procedure) Regulations 1987. A new form of these regulations (S.I. 1999 No. 1495 replacing S.I. 1987 No. 214) came into force on June 1, 1999.

Substantial changes to the system of decision-making and appeals in relation to social security benefits follow in the wake of the Social Security Act 1998. The stated policy intention is to improve the processes for decisions and appeals, providing a less complex, more accurate and cost-effective system for making and changing decisions. The chosen measures include simplifying the arrangements for first-tier decision-making by having all decisions taken in the name of the Secretary of State (instead of variously by the Secretary of State, adjudication officers, child support officers, etc), placing greater responsibility on the claimant to provide the evidence on which the claim is to be assessed and improving the scope for decisions to be rectified promptly. Correspondingly, at the appeals level, the diversity of jurisdictions (SSATs, DATs, MATs etc) will be replaced by a single unified appeal tribunal, appellants will be expected to comply with more stringent conditions for launching and pursuing their appeals and speedier redress of flawed tribunal decisions will be available.

To give effect to these measures the 1995 Regulations will be replaced by the Social Security and Child Support (Decisions and Appeals) Regulations 1999 (S.I. 1999 No. 991). The transition to the new arrangements is being phased, each stage being marked by the transfer of one or more categories of social security benefit, with child support being transferred first. The timetable is:—

June 1, 1999:	Child Support
July 5, 1999:	Disablement Benefit
	Reduced Earnings Allowance
	Retirement Allowance
	Child Benefit & Guardians Allowance
September 6, 1999:	Incapacity Benefit
	Severe Disablement Allowance
	Retirement Benefit
	Widows Benefit
	Maternity Allowance
October 5, 1999:	Family Credit
	Disability Working Allowance
October 18, 1999:	Jobseeker's Allowance
	Disability Living Allowance
	Attendance Allowance
	Invalid Care Allowance
November 29, 1999:	All other benefits, including:—
	Income Support and social fund payments

On and from each transition date all claims or pending appeals in relation to the particular benefit converted on that date will be dealt with under the new arrangements. A series of commencement orders will give effect to the transitional measures.

PART I

GENERAL

Citation, commencement and interpretation

1.—(1) These Regulations may be cited as the Social Security (Adjudication) Regulations 1995 and shall come into force on 10th August 1995.

(2) In these Regulations, unless the context otherwise requires—

[¹ "the Acts" means the Social Security Contributions and Benefits Act 1992, the Social Security Administration Act 1992 and the Jobseekers Act 1995;]

"the Administration Act" means the Social Security Administration Act 1992;

"adjudicating authority" means, as the case may be, an adjudicating medical practitioner, the Chief or any other adjudication officer, an appeal tribunal, a medical appeal tribunal, a disability appeal tribunal, a medical board or a special medical board;

"adjudicating medical authority" has the meaning assigned to it by regulation 34;

"adjudicating medical practitioner" means a medical practitioner appointed in accordance with section 49(1) of the Administration Act;

"adjudication officer" means an officer appointed in accordance with section 38(1) of the Administration Act;

"appeal tribunal" means a social security appeal tribunal constituted in accordance with section 41(1) to (5) of the Administration Act;

"Chief Adjudication Officer" means the Chief Adjudication Officer appointed under section 39(1) of the Administration Act;

"claimant" means a person who has claimed benefit under the Acts (including, in relation to an award or decision, a beneficiary under the award or a person affected by the decision) or from whom benefit is alleged to be recoverable, and in relation to statutory maternity pay includes both the employee alleged to be entitled to and the employer alleged to be liable to pay such pay;

[²"clerk to the tribunal" means, as the case may be, a clerk to a social security appeal tribunal, a clerk to a disability appeal tribunal or a clerk to a medical appeal tribunal appointed in accordance with section 41, 43, or 50 of and paragraph 3 of Schedule 2 to, the Administration Act, or a person acting as the clerk to a medical board or a special medical board constituted in accordance with these Regulations;]

"Commissioner" means the Chief or any other Social Security Commissioner appointed in accordance with section 52(1) of the Administration Act and includes a Tribunal of 3 such Commissioners constituted in accordance with section 57 of that Act;

"the Contributions and Benefits Act" means the Social Security Contributions and Benefits Act 1992;

"disability appeal tribunal" means a tribunal constituted in accordance with section 43 of the Administration Act;

"disability question" has the meaning assigned by regulation 27(2);

[³"full statement of the tribunal's decision" means the statement referred to in regulations 23(3A), 29(6A) and 38(5A);]

"full-time chairman" means a regional or other full-time chairman of appeal tribunals, medical appeal tribunals and disability appeal tribunals appointed under section 51 of the Administration Act;

"income support" means income support under Part VII of the Contributions and Benefits Act and includes personal expenses addition, special transitional addition and transitional addition as defined in the Income Support (Transitional) Regulations 1987;

"Income Support Regulations" means the Income Support (General) Regulations 1987;

"inquiry" means an inquiry held pursuant to section 17(4) of the Administration Act;

[¹"the Jobseekers Act" means the Jobseekers Act 1995;

"the Jobseeker's Allowance Regulations" means the Jobseeker's Allowance Regulations 1996;]

"local office" means an office of the Department of Social Security, an office of the Department for Education and Employment or the office of the Chief Adjudication Officer,

"medical appeal tribunal" means a tribunal constituted in accordance with section 50 of the Administration Act;

"medical board" and "special medical board" have the meanings assigned to the by regulation 34;

"party to the proceedings" means—

(a) the claimant;

(b) in proceedings before an appeal tribunal or a disability appeal tribunal, the adjudication officer;

(c) in proceedings relating to the determination of a question included in section 17(1) of the Administration Act, any person interested within the meaning of regulation 12;

(d) in any other proceedings, the adjudication officer and the Secretary of State except in proceedings in which the adjudication officer or the Secretary of State is the adjudicating authority;

(e) any other person appearing to the Secretary of State, the adjudicating authority or, in the case of a tribunal or board, its chairman or in relation to an inquiry, the person appointed to hold the inquiry, to be interested in the proceedings;

"the Prescribed Diseases Regulations" means the Social Security (Industrial Injuries) (Prescribed Diseases) Regulations 1985;

"President" means the President of social security appeal tribunals, medical appeal tribunals and disability appeal tribunals appointed under section 51(1) of the Administration Act;

"proceedings" means proceedings on a claim, application, appeal or reference to which these Regulations apply;

"specially qualified adjudicating medical practitioner" means a specially qualified adjudicating medical practitioner appointed by virtue of section 62 of the Administration Act; and

"the Supplementary Benefits Act" means the Supplementary Benefits Act 1976.

(3) Where, by any provision of the Acts or of these Regulations—

(a) any notice or other document is required to be given or sent to any office, that notice or document shall be treated as having been so given or sent on the day that it is received in that office; and

(b) any notice or other document is required to be given or sent to any person, that notice or document shall, if sent by post to that person's last known or notified address, be treated as having been given or sent on the day that it was posted.

(4) Unless the context otherwise requires, any reference in these Regulations to a numbered or lettered Part, section, regulation or Schedule is a reference to the Part, Section, regulation or Schedule bearing that number or letter in these Regulations and any reference in a regulation to a numbered paragraph is a reference to the paragraph of that regulation bearing that number.

(5) Unless otherwise provided, where by these Regulations any power is conferred on a chairman of an appeal tribunal, a medical appeal tribunal or a disability appeal tribunal then—

(a) if the power is to be exercised at the hearing of an appeal or application, it shall be exercised by the chairman of the tribunal hearing the appeal or application; and

(b) otherwise, it shall be exercised by a person who is eligible to be nominated to act as a chairman of an appeal tribunal under section 41 of the Administration Act.

AMENDMENTS

1. Social Security (Adjudication) Amendment Regulations 1996 (S.I. 1996 No. 1518), reg. 2(2) (October 7, 1996).
2. Social Security (Adjudication) and Child Support Amendment (No. 2) Regulations 1996 (S.I. 1996 No. 2450), reg. 2 (October 21, 1996).
3. Social Security (Adjudication) and Commissioners Procedure and Child Support Commissioners (Procedure) Amendment Regulations 1997 (S.I. 1997 No. 955), reg. 2 (April 28, 1997).

GENERAL NOTE

"Party to the proceedings"
Note, under head (b), that the reference is to *the* AO. This probably refers to the AO who made the decision under appeal, although it might possibly extend to any AO currently concerned with the case. Such an AO would presumably fall within head (e) anyway. But the AO who made the original decision must remain a party to the proceedings.

Paragraph (3)
There had been doubt about the meaning of what was then reg. 1(5) of the 1984 Adjudication Regulations but the position was made clear by the 1986 form. Where a notice is to be sent to an office, typically a DSS local office, it is deemed to have been sent on the day that it is received at that office. There will normally be a date of receipt stamped on such a document. Particularly cogent evidence, such as direct evidence of delivery by hand on an earlier date, would be required to displace the effect of such a stamp.
Where notice is to be given to a person and it is sent by post, then it is deemed to have been given on the day of posting. Service by courier is not service by post (*CIS 550/1993*). Again, there will normally be an official record of the date of posting, although perhaps claimants should be advised to keep all envelopes from the DSS for the postmark! The wording of sub-para. (b) was brought into line with that of sub-para. (a), removing speculation about the possible difference in effect (see p. 337 of 1989 edition). Posting to the person's last notified (presumably notified to the body giving the notice) address will do. *R(SB) 55/83* held on a similar form of words to that in sub-para. (b) that proof that a notice had not arrived did not defeat the operation of the deeming. Nor was it a breach of natural justice for the tribunal to have heard the appeal in the absence of the claimant when it later transpired that he had had no notice of the hearing. His remedy was to apply for the tribunal decision to be set aside (see now reg. 10). Whenever a claimant complains of not having been notified of a hearing the matter should be referred forthwith to a SSAT under this procedure (*R(SB) 19/83*).

PART II

COMMON PROVISIONS

Procedure in connection with determinations; and right to representation

2.—(1) Subject to the provisions of the Administration Act and of these Regulations—
(a) the procedure in connection with the consideration and determination of any claim or question to which these Regulations relate shall be such as the Secretary of State, the adjudicating authority or the person holding the inquiry, as the case may be, shall determine; so however that in the case of a tribunal or board, the procedure shall be such as the chairman shall determine;
[¹(aa) the chairman of a tribunal or board may give directions requiring any party to the proceedings to comply with any provision of these Regulations and may further at any stage of the proceedings either of his own motion or on a written application made to the clerk to the tribunal by any party to the proceedings give such directions as he may consider

necessary or desirable for the just, effective and efficient conduct of the proceedings and may direct any party to provide such further particulars or to produce such documents as may reasonably be required;

(ab) where under these Regulations the clerk to the tribunal is authorised to take steps in relation to the procedure of the tribunal or board, he may give directions requiring any party to the proceedings to comply with any provision of these Regulations;]

(b) any person who by virtue of the provisions of these Regulations has the right to be heard at a hearing or an inquiry may be accompanied and may be represented by another person whether having professional qualifications or not and, for the purposes of the proceedings at any such hearing or inquiry, any such representative shall have all the rights and powers to which the person whom he represents is entitled under the Administration Act and these Regulations.

(2) For the purpose of arriving at its decision an appeal tribunal, a medical board, a special medical board, a medical appeal tribunal or a disability appeal tribunal, as the case may be, shall, and for the purpose of discussing any question of procedure may, notwithstanding anything contained in these Regulations, order all persons not being members of the tribunal or board, other than the person acting as clerk to the tribunal or board, to withdraw from the sitting of tribunal or board, except that,

(a) a member of the Council on Tribunals or of the Scottish Committee of the Council and the President and any full-time chairman; and

(b) with the leave of the chairman of the tribunal or board, and if no person having the right to be heard objects, any person mentioned in regulation 4(6)(b) and (d) (except a person undergoing training as an adjudication officer or as an adjudicating medical practitioner),

may remain present at any such sitting.

(3) Noting in these Regulations shall prevent a member of the Council on Tribunals or of the Scottish Committee of the Council from being present at a hearing before an appeal tribunal, a medical appeal tribunal or a disability appeal tribunal or at any inquiry, in his capacity as such, notwithstanding that the hearing or inquiry is not in public.

AMENDMENT

1. Social Security (Adjudication) and Child Support Amendment (No. 2) Regulations 1996 (S.I. 1996 No. 2450), reg. 3 (October 21, 1996).

DEFINITIONS

"the Acts"—see reg. 1(2).
"adjudicating authority"—*ibid.*
"appeal tribunal"—*ibid.*
"clerk to the tribunal"—*ibid.*
"disability appeal tribunal"—*ibid.*
"full-time chairman"—*ibid.*
"inquiry"—*ibid.*
"medical appeal tribunal"—*ibid.*
"medical board"—see reg. 34.
"President"—see reg. 1(2).
"proceedings"—*ibid.*
"special medical board"—see reg. 34.

GENERAL NOTE

Paragraph (1)(a)
   Although the adjudicating authority is given discretion to decide matters of procedure, the rules

laid down in the rest of these regulations must be followed (see in particular regs. 4 to 6). In the case of a SSAT a distinction has to be drawn between matters of substance, which are for the tribunal as a whole to decide, and matters of procedure, which are for the chairman.

Natural justice

In addition, the principles of natural justice must be followed. These principles can be summed up rather crudely by saying that both parties to an appeal must be given a fair hearing by an unbiased tribunal.

Bias

So far as bias goes, the *Guide to procedure* (2nd ed.), para. 50, probably sets out the position accurately (see *R. v. Gough* [1993] 2 All E.R. 724, HL). If any member of the SSAT finds that he is personally acquainted with the appellant or has some other contact with him which might give the appearance of bias, he should not take part in the hearing. *CIS 6/1989* holds that the fact that the chairman had heard a previous appeal by the claimant does not constitute a breach of the rules of natural justice. If it is the chairman who is affected, then the appeal must be heard by a different tribunal. If it is a member who is affected, it is possible for the hearing to proceed in his absence under reg. 22(2). Where there is this strong connection the member should not take part even though the appellant and the presenting officer wish the hearing to proceed. They might think differently after knowing the outcome. If there is a remoter connection (and it is in the chairman's discretion where to draw the line) it would be enough for that to be declared at the beginning of the hearing and for the member to take part in the absence of any objection. Acquaintance with a representative is assumed not to give rise to any natural justice problems. Nonetheless, the tribunal should avoid giving any impression of partiality towards one side or the other. In particular, the arrangement of the furniture in the tribunal room should put the presenting officer in the same position as the appellant and/or any representative (*Guide to procedure* (2nd ed.), para. 48). This usually means facing the tribunal at the other side of a table. The presenting officer should not creep round the corner leaving the appellant alone facing the tribunal. The presence in the appeal papers of decisions by previous tribunals is not a breach of natural justice (*CS 176/1990*). CSDLA 855/1997 holds that there had been a breach of the rules of natural justice where the medical member of a DAT was a member of the same practice as the examining medical practitioner (EMP) whose report was before the tribunal.

A rather peculiar situation was dealt with in *CSB 226/1981*. The appellant arrived late at the SBAT after her appeal had been determined in her absence. The SBAT re-heard the case fully and comprehensively, but determined against the appellant, as they had the first time. The Commissioner held this to be a breach of natural justice in that there may have been an appearance of injustice. The appellant could easily have thought that the members of the SBAT had already made up their minds against her. An impression strengthened by the fact that the decision form LT 235 appeared to be the one completed first time round, simply altered to record the appellant as present rather than not present. She should have been offered a rehearing by a differently constituted tribunal. But the Commissioner does point out that the situation would have been different if the claimant had consented to a rehearing by the same tribunal. She should have been offered the option of having her appeal reheard by a differently constituted tribunal, or asked whether she was willing to have a rehearing by the same tribunal. (Since the first ''decision'' had not yet been promulgated, it could be revoked or varied informally (see *R(I) 14/74*, para. 14).) Clearly if the claimant does consent to a fresh hearing by the same tribunal the appeal must be completely re-heard and a separate record of proceedings completed.

Another example of when a rehearing by a differently constituted tribunal may need to be offered is if in the course of a hearing a tribunal member says something which might indicate that his mind is already made up (although the indication of a preliminary view may be an acceptable way of saving time).

Inquisitorial jurisdiction

It is clear that the SSAT, like other social security tribunals, is inquisitorial (*R(SB) 2/83, R(IS) 12/91* and *Page v. Chief Adjudication Officer*, appendix to *R(SB) 2/92*). Its object is to reach the correct entitlement for the appellant, which should also be the object of the AO. The SSAT is not refereeing a game between two sides in the traditional manner of the courts. As it has most recently been put in *R(IS) 5/93*, with copious supporting authority, the SSAT's ''investigatory function has as its object the ascertainment of the truth and is not restricted as in ordinary litigation where there are proceedings between parties, to accepting or rejecting the respective contentions of the claimant on the one hand and of the adjudication officer on the other.''

This means that it is the duty of the SSAT to consider any point which could be made in favour of the claimant (*R(SB) 2/83*, para. 10; *R(SB) 30/84*, para. 5). It is not clear how far the Commissioners extend this principle to matters of fact. In *R(SB) 2/83* they say that the SSAT is not expected to question the facts presented, especially if agreed by the appellant. On the other hand a factual point may be so obvious that it ought to be considered even though it was not put forward by the appellant. But since the primary duty is on the appellant to make out his case a decision will only be struck down for failure to identify such a factual point in the most clear-cut circumstances. This appears to leave it open to a SSAT (although not obligatory) to explore factual issues, to go behind general statements and to investigate matters that a non-expert might not realise were relevant. Such an approach would not amount to bias and a breach of the principles of natural justice. However, by the same token an appellant must expect his assertions to be tested by questioning from the SSAT and this does not amount to bias against him (see *R(S) 4/82*). The tribunal should also consider any points not put forward by the AO but it may be that the investigation need not be as elaborate, for the presenting officer can be expected to understand the point and to indicate whether the AO relies on it or not. See *CIS 451/1995* in the notes to s.71(5) of the Administration Act which holds that if on an appeal against a review decision, the AO chose not to raise the question of recoverability of an overpayment, the tribunal was not obliged, and had no power, to consider this question. However, if the AO makes a concession on a point of fact or law, that does not, in consequence of the inquisitorial nature of the jurisdiction, prevent the AO from relying on the point later (*R(IS) 14/93*.)

Fair hearing

The second element of natural justice is that each party must be given a fair opportunity to state his case. This is largely covered by the specific provisions of reg. 4(2) and (5), but some other points can be covered here. It is not necessarily a breach of the rules of natural justice to proceed in the absence of the claimant, but may be in some circumstances (see notes to reg. 4(3) and *R(SB) 23/82*). It is an important principle that each party should know what is the evidence against him and have a fair opportunity of countering it. So in *R(SB) 18/83* the presenting officer had put in evidence only one of a number of letters written by the claimant's accountants to the DSS. Since these letters were about the matter in dispute this was inconsistent with the objectivity expected of presenting officers and meant that the SBAT's decision was in breach of the rules of natural justice (*R. v. Leyland Justices, ex p. Hawthorne* [1979] Q.B. 283). If a new piece of evidence is produced for the first time before the SSAT, or an entirely new point of substance, it may be necessary for the hearing to be adjourned, to give the other party a fair opportunity of dealing with it (*Guide to procedure* (2nd ed.), paras. 61 and 65). In *CCS 6/1995* the appellant produced a lengthy written submission at the beginning of the hearing. The chairman declined to read it on the ground that it was not reasonable to expect the tribunal, presenting officer or the other party to be able to assimilate it just before the hearing. The Commissioner decides that it was a breach of the rules of natural justice not to offer an adjournment in these circumstances. An adjournment may also be necessary if a concession on some point is withdrawn, or questioned by a SSAT. Presenting officers are instructed to ask for an adjournment if an unreported Commissioner's decision is relied on for the first time at the hearing, often arguing that the AO who made the decision will not have had the opportunity to see the decision. Here, matters are not so clear-cut and, though an adjournment may be appropriate, the question should be whether the presenting officer has a fair opportunity to deal with the point rather than whether the original AO can consider it. (See also *CSIB 848/1997*.) Similarly, although SSAT members may use their own knowledge of the locality, etc., any information should be disclosed to both parties during the hearing (*Guide to procedure* (2nd ed.), para. 62). There is a thin line between using local knowledge and experience in the evaluation of evidence (perfectly proper) and relying on information which the parties should have the opportunity of commenting on. This approach is affirmed by the Commissioner in *CS 142/1991*, to be reported as *R(S) 1/94*, where a SSAT's decision was struck down because it was based on a member's experience of the kind of work done in Remploy workshops, which had not been mentioned during the hearing. But *CS 175/1992*, where one of the members was a doctor, fell on the other side of the line. The Commissioner holds that the member was merely putting her expert interpretation on the evidence given to the tribunal. There was no need for a member's opinion to be communicated in advance of the decision unless, for example, it raised a new issue. It would have been preferable if the member's medical qualifications had been mentioned at the beginning of the hearing (or when she was asking questions), but a failure to do so was not a breach of the rules of natural justice. The Commissioner also rejects the argument that she was performing a role analogous to that of an assessor (see the notes to s.56 of the Administration Act). If a SSAT is presented with new written evidence the proceedings should stop while this is read, since the tribunal must be seen to be giving the case its undivided attention (see *R. v. Marylebone Magistrates Court ex p. Joseph, The Independent*, April 30, 1993).

The Commissioners have taken into account the practicalities of tribunal arrangements and premises. In *CSB 453/1983* one of the claimant's complaints was that when he and his solicitor entered the tribunal room they found the presenting officer already there. The Commissioner says that decisions have been set aside on this ground alone. The presenting officer should leave the room even if on the previous appeal the claimant was not there. If this is not done for some reason, only an immediate explanation could ensure that justice was seen to be done. The mere fact that a presenting officer has been in the tribunal room on an earlier appeal with no appellant present appears to require no explanation (*CIS 6/1989*). In *CSB 483/1982* the presenting officer entered the tribunal room before the hearing to leave his hat and bag and to pass the time of day. The Commissioner stresses that the claimant must not feel that his case is being discussed behind his back, but the nature of the accommodation may make it necessary for the presenting officer to go into the room. Here, since the door was left open there was no breach of natural justice. If it had been closed there would have been! More recently *R(IS)15/94* has reinforced the importance of one party to an appeal, *e.g.* the presenting officer, not being in the presence of the tribunal before the other, even in a case where the presenting officer has been engaged in earlier cases. The correct course must be for the presenting officer to leave the tribunal room at the end of each hearing and not to enter it again until the next case is called.

Even if the presenting officer is not seen to enter the tribunal room, there may be a problem, as in *CIS 50/1990*. The claimant's father was representing her. The appeal was scheduled for 10 a.m., but the father was not brought by the clerk from the waiting room to the tribunal room until after 10.10 a.m. When they arrived, the door to the tribunal room was wide open and the presenting officer was waiting just outside. The Commissioner holds that these circumstances could cause a reasonable person to fear that justice might not fully have been done. The father might have thought that the presenting officer could have talked to the tribunal or overheard their preliminary discussions. The Commissioner rightly stresses that the door to the tribunal room should be kept closed until the appeal begins and that the claimant and/or representative and the presenting officer should be brought in together. Tribunals must be sensitive to appearances when many claimants and representatives are unfamiliar with the tribunal's custom and practice.

Paragraph (1)(aa)

This provision covers two matters: the giving of directions to comply with the Adjudication Regulations and giving directions for the conduct of the proceedings or for other purposes.

At first sight there seems little point in empowering a SSAT chairman to give directions that some provision of the Regulations must be complied with by a party to the proceedings. But the point emerges when the sanctions for failure to comply with directions under paragraph (1)(aa) are examined. They are in regs. 4(2A) and 7(1). Under reg. 4(2A) one of the circumstances in which a chairman may give notice for the determination of an appeal forthwith (whatever that means) is where a party to the proceedings has failed to comply with a direction under para. (1)(aa) requiring information. Under reg. 7(1) one of the reasons for which a chairman can strike out an application or an appeal is the failure to comply with a direction given under para. (1)(aa). Thus, the giving of a direction can get over the problem that a requirement of the Regulations with no sanction for non-compliance may be said to be merely directory (see *CDLA 12125/1996*), so that a failure to comply does not invalidate the proceedings.

The same sanctions apply to a failure to comply with directions of the second sort. This covers directions for any party to provide further particulars or produce documents, but only in either case when reasonably required, and directions for the just, effective and efficient conduct of the proceedings. The latter category appears rather sweeping, as the chairman need only consider it desirable or necessary to give the directions. But they must be for the just, efficient *and* (not *or*) effective conduct of the proceedings. Cumulatively, those conditions are quite hard to satisfy.

If a party objects that any directions fall outside the powers given by para. (1)(aa), that could be raised under the procedures in reg. 4(2A) and reg. 7(2). But ultimately it would seem that a legal test could only be by way of judicial review.

Paragraph (1)(ab)

This provision is very unfortunately worded when it gives an unprecedented power to the clerk to a tribunal. The opening words suggest that it applies only to the matters in relation to which the clerk is authorised to take steps in the tribunal procedure. For instance, under reg. 3(6) the clerk can direct an appellant to provide the particulars required under reg. 3(5); under reg. 5(1) the clerk can grant or refuse requests for postponement of hearings; and under reg. 22(1) and (1A) the clerk is to direct every party to the proceedings to give notification of whether that party wishes an oral hearing to be held. However, the later words of para. (1)(ab) suggest that the clerk may give directions requiring compliance with any provision of the Regulations. It would be contrary to principle to allow such a wide power to a clerk merely because an appeal is at a stage where the clerk has to carry out some administrative task. It is suggested that the power must be restricted to the matters where a clerk is given a specific responsibility under the Regulations.

Paragraph (1)(b)

The issue of representation has a long and intricate history. Immediately before the November 1980 reforms the position was that an interested person had the right to be accompanied and represented by not more than two persons. The present provision has no limit of numbers. Thus, since under the Interpretation Act 1978, s.6(c), the singular includes the plural unless the context otherwise requires, it seems clear that there is no limit under this paragraph to the number of representatives or companions. The limit comes from the power of the chairman to control procedure under para. (1)(a). He can clearly determine what is an improper number of extra people at the hearing (compare the approach of the Divisional Court to "McKenzie friends" in *R. v. Leicester City Justices, ex p. Barrow* [1991] 2 All E.R. 437). There is no direct right of appeal from his decision (*CSB 103/1984*). The *Guide to procedure* (2nd ed.), para. 38(1) now makes it clear that the number of representatives permitted is a matter for the chairman.

The presenting officer's powers appear to stem from this provision as a representative of the AO who made the decision under appeal.

Paragraph (2)

Here the main powers and duties are given to the tribunal, etc., not to the chairman. The effect is that a member of the Council on Tribunals, the President or a full-time chairman (not acting as chairman of the particular tribunal) is entitled to remain with the tribunal when they are discussing their decision. Trainee chairmen, members or clerks (reg. 4(6)(b)) may remain, but not trainee AOs (reg. 2(2)(b)) or a person supervising training of clerks or AOs (reg. 4(6)(c)). Anyone else may stay only if no party to the proceedings (regs. 4(5) and 1(2)), or their representative (reg. 2(1)(b)) objects. For a person to be in this category, the positive consent of all parties to the proceedings who are present is required (reg. 4(6)(d)). In practice this will mean the claimant and/or representative and the presenting officer representing the AO. But the chairman (no longer the tribunal) has to give leave, and it should be made clear that the person plays no part in making the decision. Although a party to the proceedings may not object to the clerk remaining in the room, it is open to the tribunal to require him to leave. This might conceivably be necessary to ensure natural justice, *e.g.* if the clerk has taken an over-active part in the hearing.

Paragraph (3)

This allows a member of the Council on Tribunals to remain during an oral hearing, even though it is in private. It should logically go in reg. 4(6).

Manner of making applications, appeals or references; and time limits

3.—(1) Any application, appeal or reference mentioned in column (1) of Schedule 2 shall be in writing [²and, in the case of an appeal, shall be on a form approved by the Secretary of State] and shall be made or given by sending or delivering it to the appropriate office within the specified time.

(2) In this regulation—

  (a) "the appropriate office" means the office specified in column (2) of Schedule 2 opposite the description of the relevant application, appeal or reference listed in column (1); and

  (b) "the specified time" means the time specified in column (3) of that Schedule opposite the description of the relevant application, appeal or reference so listed.

[²(3) The time specified by this regulation and Schedule 2 for the making of any application, appeal or reference (except an application to the chairman of an appeal tribunal, a medical appeal tribunal or a disability appeal tribunal for leave to appeal to a Commissioner) may be extended, even though the time so specified may already have expired—

  (a) in the case of an application or reference, for special reasons;

  (b) in the case of an appeal, provided the conditions set out in paragraphs (3A) to (3E) are satisfied;

and any application for an extension of time under this paragraph shall be made to and determined by the person or body to whom the application, appeal or reference is sought to be made or, in the case of a tribunal or board, its chairman.]

[[1](3A) Where the time specified for the making of an appeal has already expired, an application for an extension of time for making an appeal shall not be granted unless the applicant has satisfied the person considering the application that—

    (a) if the application is granted there are reasonable prospects that such an appeal will be successful; and

    (b) it is in the interests of justice that the application be granted.

(3B) For the purposes of paragraph (3A) it shall not be considered to be in the interests of justice to grant an application unless the person considering the application is satisfied that—

    (a) special reasons exist, which are wholly exceptional and which relate to the history or facts of the case; and

    (b) such special reasons have existed throughout the period beginning with the day following the expiration of the time specified by Schedule 2 for the making of an appeal and ending with the day on which the application for an extension of time is made; and

    (c) such special reasons manifestly constitute a reasonable excuse of compelling weight for the applicant's failure to make an appeal within the time specified.

(3C) In determining whether there are special reasons for granting an application for an extension of time for making an appeal under paragraph (3) the person considering the application shall have regard to the principle that the greater the amount of time that has elapsed between the expiration of the time specified for the making of the appeal and the making of the application for an extension of time, the more cogent should be the special reasons on which the application is based.

(3D) In determining whether facts consitute special reasons for granting an application for an extension of time for making an appeal under paragraph (3) no account shall be taken of the following—

    (a) that the applicant or anyone acting for him or advising him was unaware of or misunderstood the law applicable to his case (including ignorance or misunderstanding of any time limits imposed by Schedule 2);

    (b) that a Commissioner or a court has taken a different view of the law from that previously understand and applied.

(3E) Notwithstanding paragraph (3), no appeal may in any event be brought later than 6 years after the beginning of the period specified in column (3) of Schedule 2.]

(4) An application under paragraph (3) for an extension of time which has been refused may not be renewed.

[[2](5) Any application, appeal or reference under these Regulations shall contain the following particulars—

    (a) in the case of an appeal, the date of the notification of the decision against which the appeal is made, the claim or question under the Acts to which the decision relates, and a summary of the arguments relied on by the person making the appeal to support his contention that the decision was wrong;

    (b) in the case of an application under paragraph (3) for an extension of time in which to appeal, in relation to the appeal which it is proposed to bring, the particulars required under sub-paragraph (a) together with particulars of the special reasons on which the application is based:

    (c) in the case of any other application or any reference, the grounds on which it is made or given.

(5A) Where an appeal is not made on the form approved for the time being, but is made in writing and contains all the particulars required under paragraph (5), the chairman of the tribunal may treat that appeal as duly made.

(6) Where it appears—

(a) to the chairman of a tribunal or board or the clerk to the tribunal that an application, appeal or reference which is made to him or to the tribunal or board; or

(b) to the Secretary of State or an adjudication officer that an application or reference which is made to him,

does not contain the particulars required under paragraph (5), he may direct the person making the application, appeal or reference to provide such particulars.

(6A) Where further particulars are required under paragraph (6), the chairman of the tribunal or board, the clerk to the tribunal, the Secretary of State or the adjudication officer, as the case may be, may extend the time specified by this regulation and Schedule 2 for making the application, appeal or reference by a period of not more than 14 days.

(6B) Where further particulars are required under paragraph (6), in the case of an appeal they shall be sent or delivered to the clerk to the tribunal within such period as the chairman or the clerk to the tribunal may direct.

(6C) The date of an appeal shall be the date on which all the particulars required under paragraph (5) are received by the clerk to the tribunal.]

(7) A chairman of an appeal tribunal, a medical appeal tribunal or a disability appeal tribunal may give directions for the disposal of any purported appeal where he is satisfied that the tribunal does not have jurisdiction to entertain the appeal.

[¹(8) In the case of an application under paragraph (3) for an extension of time for making an appeal, the person who determines that application shall record his decision in writing together with a statement of the reasons for the decision.

(9) As soon as practicable after the decision has been made it shall be communicated to the applicant and to every other party to the proceedings and if within 3 months of such communication being sent the applicant or any other party to the proceedings so requests in writing, a copy of the record referred to in paragraph (8) shall be supplied to him.]

AMENDMENTS

1. Social Security (Adjudication) and Child Support Amendment Regulations 1996 (S.I. 1996 No. 182), reg. 2(2) (February 28, 1996).

2. Social Security (Adjudication) and Child Support Amendment (No. 2) Regulations 1996 (S.I. 1996 No. 2450), reg. 4 (October 21, 1996).

DEFINITIONS

"the Acts"—see reg. 1(2).
"adjudication officer"—*ibid.*
"appeal tribunal"—*ibid.*
"clerk to the tribunal"—*ibid.*
"Commissioner"—*ibid.*
"disability appeal tribunal"—*ibid.*
"medical appeal tribunal"—*ibid.*

GENERAL NOTE

Paragraphs (1) and (2)

These provisions provide first the requirement that any applications, appeals and references must be made in writing, and that appeals must be made on a form approved by the Secretary of State. But note that under para. (5A) a chairman may accept a written appeal not on the approved form if it contains the particulars required by para. (5). Presumably the approved form will contain questions directed to those particulars. The general requirement of writing seems likely to be mandatory.

The second object is to apply the time-limits set out in Sched. 2. Since there is specific provision for the extension of time in limited circumstances in paras. (3) to (3E), the effect of failing to meet a time-limit, as extended or not, must be to prevent the matter in question going any further.

Paragraphs (3) to (3E)
These paragraphs deal with the extension of time-limits.

Late appeals
From February 28, 1996, the scope for making a late appeal to a tribunal has been considerably reduced (see paras. (3A) to (3E)). (Note that there was no parallel amendment to the provisions in the Social Security Commissioners Procedure Regulations 1987 (S.I. 1987 No. 214) dealing with late appeals and applications to a Commissioner: see below.) The justification given to the Council on Tribunals for the new rules was the desire to give legislative effect to some of the existing case law in view of the granting of late appeals against some very old decisions. The new rules, however, are very prescriptive and taken as a whole go far beyond existing case law principles. They substantially restrict the exercise of judicial discretion in certain circumstances and are thus much stricter than in other jurisdictions (*e.g.* in the Court of Appeal where the question whether to extend time for appealing is left to the general discretion of the Court).

If the time limit for appealing has expired, it can now only be extended (subject to an absolute limit of six years from the date the decision in question was notified to the claimant (para. (3E)) if the appeal has reasonable prospects of success and it is in the interests of justice to grant leave (para. (3A)).

"Interests of justice" is defined in para. (3B) to require that "special reasons", which for this purpose has a particular restricted meaning, must have existed throughout the period from the expiry of the relevant time limit to the day the application for an extension of time was made. The "special reasons" must be "wholly exceptional", relate to the history or facts of the case, and "manifestly constitute a reasonable excuse of compelling weight" for the claimant's failure to appeal in time (para. (3B)). In addition, no account is to be taken of the fact that the claimant or his adviser was ignorant of, or misunderstood, the relevant law (including the time limit for appeal—does this mean that if an appeal is late due to an adviser's *negligence*, this can be taken into consideration?) (para. (3D)(a)). (Contrast the long-standing test for "good cause" which involved considering the reasonableness of the ignorance, etc.: see the notes to reg. 19(2) of the Claims and Payments Regulations in the 1996 edition.) But sub-para. (a) should not include the situation where a claimant (or his adviser) has been given incorrect information, *e.g.* by the DSS, since that is not a case of a misunderstanding but of misadvice. The fact that a Commissioner or court has taken a different view of the law from that previously applied also has to be ignored (para. (3D)(b)). This is clearly aimed at preventing the mechanism of late appeal being used to get round the "anti-test-case" rules (see s.69 of the Administration Act). However, this provision may well be ineffective in relation to rulings by the European Court of Justice if it amounts to breach of the obligation in E.C. law to provide an adequate remedy (see *Von Colson* [1984] E.C.R. 1891 and *Emmott* below). Finally para. (3C) provides that in deciding whether there are special reasons the length of the delay is relevant.

Claimants seeking to bring late appeals would thus be well advised to set out their "special reasons" in detail, as well as why they think the appeal is likely to succeed (see para. (3A)(a)). (Note also para. (5)(b) which requires a summary of the arguments in support of the appeal itself to be stated.) Subject to the restrictions in paras. (3B) and (3D), the existing case law on the meaning of "special reasons" will still be relevant (see below).

Note the new requirement under para. (8) for reasons to be given for the granting or refusal of leave to bring a late appeal. But the statement of reasons will not be automatically sent out; the claimant (or any other party) must request it within three months of being sent the decision (para. (9)).

Late applications
The time limit for applications may still simply be extended for "special reasons". However, the three months for applying to a tribunal chairman for leave to appeal to a Commissioner cannot be extended. This is because if a party misses the limit the Commissioner has power to deal with a late application (Social Security Commissioners Procedure Regulations 1987, reg. 3(2)) if special reasons are shown (from June 1, 1999 see reg. 9(3) and (4) of the 1999 Regulations). "Special reasons" clearly has a wider meaning here (and in relation to late appeals and applications to a Commissioner) than in the context of late appeals to a tribunal (see above).

In *CU 12/1994* (which concerned a similar provision in reg. 7(2) of the Social Security Commissioners Procedure Regulations 1987) the Commissioner states that "special reasons" meant that something more than mere non-prejudice to the other party or the fact that the period of delay was only short had to be shown. There has to be something unusual in the history or facts of the case (*R(SB) 1/95* and *CSB 123/1993*). But the words are wide and allow almost anything to be brought forward for consideration (*R. v. Social Security Appeal Tribunal, ex p. O'Hara*, Divisional Court, July 13, 1994). The special reasons need not relate to the delay as such, but can be found in the surrounding circumstances, such as the applicant's health and personal circumstances (*R(I) 5/91*, following *R(U) 8/68* and *R(M) 1/87*, and *ex p. O'Hara*). The merits of the case can be considered (*R(M) 1/87*, following *R. v. Secretary of State for the Home Department, ex p. Mehta* [1975] 2 All E.R. 1084 and *CU 12/1994*). The fact that the decision in question is clearly wrong can be a factor. However, in *R(S) 8/85* the Commissioner held that an "alteration" in the law by a subsequent decision of a superior court was not *of itself* a ground for a substantial extension of time. Clearly all the circumstances have to be considered (see *Re Wigfall* [1919] 1 Ch. 52 and *Re Berkeley* [1945] 1 Ch. 1 referred to in *R(S) 8/85*). In *CIS 147/1995* the Commissioner considered that the question was whether it was just in all the circumstances to extend time, and that a different view of the law *was* a factor, although not a conclusive one. The relevant factors were essentially the same as those taken into account in late appeals to the Court of Appeal (length of, and reasons for, the delay, the chances of the appeal succeeding and the degree of prejudice to the potential respondent: see the notes to Ord. 59, r.4 of the Rules of the Supreme Court). See also *ex p. O'Hara* in which the Divisional Court expressed surprise that in view of the claimant's disability her application to bring a late appeal (based on *CIS 180/89*: see notes to reg. 3(2B)–(2C) of the Income Support Regulations) had been refused, although the Court did not find that it was perverse or unreasonable in the *Wednesbury* ([1948] 1 K.B. 223) sense and so did not grant her application for judicial review.

Other points on late appeals

If the case involves European law (for example, the claimant is alleging that the U.K. Government is in breach of its obligations under E.C. Directive 79/7 on equal treatment for men and women in matters of social security) time limits for bringing proceedings cannot be used to defeat the claim (*Emmott v. Minister for Social Welfare* [1991] E.C.R. 1–4569). The proper approach would normally be for the chairman to extend the time limit in these cases. The ECJ's reasoning in *Emmott* was based on whether the law was certain. The ECJ concluded that, so long as a directive had not been properly translated into national law, individuals were unable to ascertain the full extent of their rights. Only when that had happened could there be said to be the legal certainty which had to exist if individuals were to assert their rights.

Chief Adjudication Officer v. Eggleton and Others (to be reported as *R(IS) 23/95*) (see the notes to s. 25 of the Administration Act) confirms that where a decision has been reviewed, the original decision remains in existence except as affected by the revision on review. Thus a late appeal against the original decision may still be admitted.

R(SB) 1/95 holds that if no valid extension of time has been granted, jurisdiction cannot be conferred on the tribunal by agreement of the parties. In *R(SB) 1/95* the Commissioner also considered that reg. 3(5) of the 1986 Regulations meant that an application for a late appeal was invalid unless it identified the date of the AO's decision against which it was sought to appeal. That seemed to go beyond the requirements of para. (5)(a) as they were at the time, which were only that sufficient particulars were given to enable the decision under appeal to be identified. However the form of para. (5) in force from October 1996 requires that both appeals and applications for an extension of time state the date of notification of the decision appealed against.

In *R(IS) 5/94* the claimant's appeal was withdrawn at the hearing with the leave of the chairman. He subsequently obtained leave to bring a late appeal. The SSAT declined to hear the appeal on the ground of lack of jurisdiction. The Commissioner holds that the principle of *res judicata* (that once a matter has been adjudicated on by a competent authority another authority of the same level cannot readjudicate on the matter) did not apply. Where an appeal is withdrawn with the leave of the chairman or the AO's agreement there has been no decision by a tribunal and there is nothing to prevent a new appeal being made. It would be different if the first appeal had been dismissed by a SSAT.

Paragraph (4)

This paragraph prevents a party from having more than one bite at the cherry in requesting an extension of time. Since there is no appeal from a decision not to extend a time limit, this is a serious matter, although sometimes another application or appeal can be made. *CIS 93/1992* holds that the decision of a chairman is subject to reconsideration by the same chairman, particularly if new matters are brought to his attention. The only other method of challenge would be by way of judicial review.

Paragraphs (5) to (6C)

These provisions have been significantly tightened up with effect from October 21, 1996. They now prescribe in more detail the particulars which have to be given when making an appeal, application or reference and the consequences of a failure to do so.

Para. (5) specifies the particulars that must be given in each case. For appeals to tribunals (under sub-para. (a)), the appellant must identify the date of notification of the decision appealed against and the claim or question to which that decision relates, and give a summary of the arguments on which the decision is said to be wrong. All of these requirements may cause problems for claimants. If the letter informing the claimant of the decision has been kept, the date of notification can easily be identified. It should not be a requirement that the claim or question is identified in a technically perfect way, if enough detail is given for the right decision (possibly out of several given together) to be identified. Similarly, the summary of the arguments to be relied on, especially as they have to be formulated within a tight time-limit and limited reasons may have been given by an AO, cannot be expected to be of any sophistication. Under sub-para. (b), where there is an application for an extension of time to appeal to a tribunal, the same particulars as under sub-para. (a) must be given (often they will have already been given because the application and the appeal are made together) plus particulars of the special reasons put forward for an extension of time. For any other application (e.g. for the setting aside of a tribunal's decision) or reference (to a tribunal by an AO) "grounds" must be given. This probably requires something less than a reasoned statement (see *R. v. Secretary of State for Social Services, ex parte Loveday, The Times*, February 18, 1983, and appendix to *R(M) 5/86)*.

Under para. (6), the decision whether or not the particulars required by para. (5) have been given, belongs, in the case of a tribunal, to either a chairman or a clerk to the tribunal. There is no express provision about how decisions should be distributed between chairmen and clerks. It seems quite inappropriate, and contrary to accepted principles of judicial responsibility, for clerks to take decisions of such sensitivity and seriousness. However, like it or not, para. (6), as well as paras. (6A) and (6B), gives the power to clerks. It is to be hoped that they will be instructed to make decisions under these provisions only in manifestly obvious cases. Current ITS practice is in fact that a clerk may decide that the appeal does contain sufficient particulars to be admitted as valid but, if unable to decide that point in the claimant's favour, the clerk should refer the question to the chairman. Where the appeal initially lacks sufficient particulars, the chairman or clerk "may" direct the person concerned to provide them. In view of the apparent consequences under para. (6C) of the required particulars not being received, "may" should be interpreted as "shall." The directions should specify the time within which the particulars are to be sent (para. (6B). When directions are given, the chairman or clerk can also extend the relevant time-limit by up to 14 days. This may be necessary if the timing is close to the normal limit.

The main sanction for a failure to comply with directions to produce particulars in the case of an appeal, either by a failure to reply or by providing particulars which are still inadequate, appears as a result of para. (6C) to be that no appeal will have been made within the time-limit. The appeal accordingly cannot proceed. In practice the chairman will issue a ruling that the appeal cannot be admitted because it has not been duly made. It is unclear whether the issue of this ruling purports to be in exercise of the power contained in para. (7).

In the case of applications or references, the main sanction would seem to be striking out under reg. 7.

Paragraph (7)

Before April 1990 if an appeal was expressed to be made to the SSAT, a rejection of the appeal on the ground that it was outside the SSAT's jurisdiction could only properly be made by the whole tribunal. This was a cumbersome procedure, which was often ignored in practice, for instance in relation to decisions by social fund officers where the applicant purported to appeal to the SSAT. Para. (7) carries out the power to make regulations given by para. 7A of Sched. 13 to the 1975 Act (now para. 10 of Sched. 3 to the Administration Act). Although the wording of para. (7) could be more explicit, presumably the power to give directions for the "disposal" of an appeal covers the appeal's rejection or termination. The power may be exercised by any chairman of a SSAT, including a regional or full-time chairman. Note that there is no power for a chairman to give directions for the disposal of a reference to the SSAT, rather than an appeal (*R(I) 3/92*).

Since there is no appeal from such a ruling by a chairman, the scope of para. (7) has not been directly considered by the Commissioners. However, in *CI 78/1990* the issue was whether a Medical Appeal Tribunal (MAT 3) had jurisdiction to hear an appeal where a decision by MAT 1 had been set aside by MAT 2 acting beyond its powers. The Commissioner says that it would be "wholly inappropriate for a tribunal chairman to exercise that power (which is obviously suitable for misconceived or misdirected appeals) in a case where the lack of jurisdiction was considered to arise in the circumstances under consideration in this reference. It would be manifestly unsatisfactory for a tribunal chairman in effect to hold a setting aside determination invalid in a ruling made at his own hand, which would not be subject to appeal and which could be challenged only by judicial review." Similarly, in *CSB 1182/1989* the Commissioner expresses some doubt about what para. (7) empowers chairmen to do.

Paragraphs (8) and (9)
    See the notes to paras. (3) to (3E) under the heading "*late appeals*".

Oral hearings and inquiries

4.—(1) This regulation applies to any oral hearing of an application, appeal or reference and to any inquiry.

(2) ['Except where paragraph (2C) applies, not less than 7 days notice] beginning with the day on which the notice is given and ending on the day before the hearing of the case or, as the case may be, the inquiry is to take place) of the time and place of any oral hearing before an adjudicating authority or of an inquiry shall be given to every party to the proceedings, and if such notice has not been given to a person to whom it should have been given under the provisions of this paragraph the hearing or inquiry may proceed only with the consent of that person.

['(2A) The chairman of an appeal tribunal, a medical appeal tribunal or a disability appeal tribunal may give notice for the determination forthwith, in accordance with the provisions of these Regulations, of an appeal notwithstanding that a party to the proceedings has failed to indicate his availability for a hearing or to provide all the information which may have been requested, if the chairman is satisfied that such party—
    (a) has failed to comply with a direction regarding his availability or requiring information under regulation 2(1)(aa) or (ab); and
    (b) has not given any explanation for his failure to comply with such a direction;
provided that the chairman is satisfied that the tribunal has sufficient particulars in order for the appeal to be determined.

(2B) The chairman of an appeal tribunal, a medical appeal tribunal or a disability appeal tribunal may give notice for the determination forthwith, in accordance with the provisions of these Regulations, of an appeal which he believes has no reasonable prospect of success.

(2C) Any party to the proceedings may waive his right to receive not less than 7 days notice of the time and place of any oral hearing as specified in paragraph (2).]

(3) If a party to the proceedings to whom notice has been given under paragraph (2) ['fails to appear] at the hearing or inquiry the adjudicating authority or the person holding the inquiry may, having regard to all the circumstances including any explanation offered for the absence ['and where applicable the circumstances set out in sub-paragraphs (a) or (b) of paragraph (2A), proceed with the hearing or inquiry] notwithstanding his absence, or give such directions with a view to the determination of the case or conduct of the inquiry as it or he may think proper.

['(3A) If a party to the proceedings has waived his right to be given notice under paragraph (2C) the adjudicating authority or the person holding the inquiry or hearing may proceed with the hearing or inquiry notwithstanding his absence.]

(4) Any oral hearing before an adjudicating authority and any inquiry shall be in public except where (in the case of an oral hearing) the claimant requests

a private hearing or (in any case) the chairman or the person holding the inquiry is satisfied that intimate personal or financial circumstances may have to be disclosed or that considerations of public security are involved, in which case the hearing or inquiry shall be in private.

(5) At any oral hearing or inquiry any party to the proceedings shall be entitled to be present and be heard.

(6) The following persons shall also be entitled to be present at an oral hearing (whether or not it is otherwise in private) but shall take no part in the proceedings—

(a) the President and any full-time chairman;

(b) any person undergoing training as a chairman or other member of an appeal tribunal, a medical appeal tribunal or a disability appeal tribunal or as a clerk to any such tribunal, or as an adjudication officer or an adjudicating medical practitioner;

(c) any person acting on behalf of the President, the Chief Adjudication Officer or the Secretary of State in the training or supervision of clerks to appeal tribunals, medical appeal tribunals or disability appeal tribunals or of adjudication officers or officers of the Secretary of State or in the monitoring of standards of adjudication by adjudication officers; and

(d) with the leave of the chairman of the tribunal or board, as the case may be, and the consent of every party to the proceedings actually present, any other person.

(7) At any inquiry (whether or not it is otherwise in private) the following persons shall be entitled to be present but shall take no part in the proceedings—

(a) any person undergoing training as an officer of the Secretary of State; and

(b) any person acting on behalf of the Secretary of State in the training or supervision of officers of the Secretary of State; and

(c) with the leave of the person holding the inquiry and the consent of all parties to the proceedings actually present, any other person.

(8) Nothing in paragraph (6) affects the rights of any person mentioned in sub-paragraphs (a) and (b) of that paragraph at any oral hearing where he is sitting as a member of the tribunal or acting as its clerk, and nothing in this regulation prevents the presence at an oral hearing or an inquiry of any witness.

(9) Any person entitled to be heard at an oral hearing or inquiry may address the adjudicating authority or person holding the inquiry, may give evidence, may call witnesses and may put questions directly to any other person called as a witness.

AMENDMENT

1. Social Security (Adjudication) and Child Support Amendment (No. 2) Regulations 1996 (S.I. 1996 No. 2450), reg. 5 (October 21, 1996).

DEFINITIONS

"adjudicating authority"—see reg. 1(2).
"adjudicating medical practitioner"—*ibid.*
"adjudication officer"—*ibid.*
"appeal tribunal"—*ibid.*
"Chief Adjudication Officer"—*ibid.*
"disability appeal tribunal"—*ibid.*
"full-time chairman"—*ibid.*
"inquiry"—*ibid.*
"medical appeal tribunal"—*ibid.*

"party to the proceedings"—*ibid.*
"President"—*ibid.*
"proceedings"—*ibid.*

GENERAL NOTE

The arrangement of paragraphs is as follows
(1) General
(2) Notice of hearings
(2A) Notice for determination forthwith
(2B) Notice for determination forthwith
(2C) Waiver of right to notice
(3) Powers if party fails to appear
(3A) Powers if party fails to appear
(4) Public or private hearing
(5) Parties entitled to be present
(6) Persons entitled to attend private hearing
(7) Persons entitled to attend private inquiry
(8) Presence of members, clerk or witness
(9) Rights of parties at hearing

Paragraph (2)

Reg. 1(3) deems the date on which notice is given to be the date of posting of the notice, providing that it is sent to the person's last known or notified (to ITS) address. From October 21, 1996, the requirement to give reasonable notice has been removed and the minimum period of notice has been reduced from 10 days to seven. The Chief Executive of ITS has decided that it is good practice to continue to give at least 10 days' notice where possible and it is hoped that longer notice will continue to be given in order to aid the smooth arrangement of hearings. In addition, the need for preparation by tribunal members must be considered. The reduction in the minimum to seven days may result in more attention being given to the precise calculation of the period. The language of para. (1) remains ambiguous, apart from the express provision that the period of notice must end on the day before the hearing. The use of the word "notice" would usually lead to the position that the date of giving notice is excluded from the period concerned. However, when a relevant period is defined as beginning on a particular date, that date is usually included in the period (*Trow v. Ind Coope (West Midlands) Ltd* [1967] 2 Q.B. 899, applied in *CIS 550/1993*). This latter rule, which accords with ITS practice, is probably controlling. If so, for a hearing on the 10th of a month, notice would have to be posted to the parties no later than the 3rd of the month.

The requirement of a minimum period of seven days' notice does not apply in relation to any party who has under para. (2C) waived the right to receive not less than seven days'notice. This will allow appeals to be listed at the last moment, with the claimant's consent, if slots become unexpectedly available. It seems to be assumed in para. (3A) that a party can waive the right to be given any notice at all, but that cannot be right if the party still wishes there to be an oral hearing (see reg. 22(1)). The more natural reading of para. (2C) is that it allows a party merely to waive the right to receive no less than seven days' notice.

The notice must be given to all parties to the proceedings. This phrase is defined in reg. 1(2) and covers, as well as the claimant, any person appearing to be interested in the proceedings. See the notes to reg. 1(2). It is not the general practice to inform anyone other than the AO and the claimant (and any representative). There is likely only to be a problem if it is said that a decision should be set aside under reg. 10 on the ground that a document was not sent to an interested person. Reg. 4(2) no longer requires copies of the documents provided for a tribunal to be sent to the claimant, but the principle of natural justice that a person should know the case he has to meet certainly does require it.

If a person who has not received the required notice and who has not made a waiver under para. (2C) positively consents to the hearing going on nevertheless, then it may do so. If the claimant or his representative is present, there is little problem. If neither is present, *R(SB) 19/83* decides that the tribunal must ask the clerk if the claimant has been properly notified. The date of the return of the form (AT 6) formerly sent with the appeal papers used to settle the matter. The Commissioner holds that the hearing should be adjourned if due notification cannot be shown, preferably by evidence of the date of posting and a copy of the AT6.

A national procedure for the listing of appeals was introduced for appeals lodged from September 1, 1992. This has now been changed following the October 1996 amendments. The current procedure is as follows. As soon as notification of the appeal is received by ITS, a leaflet is sent to the claimant giving details of the appeal process and advice about getting help from a representative. Also sent at the same time is a letter (GAPS 11/97) asking the claimant to complete and return within 14 days an enquiry form (together with a pre-paid reply envelope). The purpose of the enquiry form is to establish whether the claimant wants an oral hearing of his appeal, and if he does, whether there are any dates or times to avoid. It also asks the claimant whether he is willing to have his appeal heard by two people if one of the members cannot attend. The claimant is asked to return the enquiry form within 14 days of the date on the GAPS 11/97 letter (this is longer than the minimum prescribed in reg. 22(1A), but not much longer). The GAPS 11/97 letter states that if the claimant does not return the enquiry form within 14 days it will be assumed that the claimant wants his appeal decided on the papers. But in practice the claimant can still ask for an oral hearing up to the date of the hearing (see the notes to reg. 22(1) to (1C)).

If the claimant opts for an oral hearing the AT2 submission will not now be sent to the claimant (and any representative) as soon as it is received from the AO. It will be sent only when the date of the hearing has been set, together with a GAPS 140/97 letter which gives details of when and where the hearing will be held. Clearly if the AT2 submission is not sent out until this stage it will mean that the claimant (and/or any representative) only has limited time to prepare for the appeal hearing. It is understood that in some regions at least the intention is to give several weeks' notice of the hearing date whenever possible. This will obviously lessen the problem to some degree, but if insufficient notice is given this is only likely to lead to an increase in the number of requests for postponements.

If the claimant decides that he wishes his appeal to be dealt with on the papers, he (and any representative) *will* be sent the AT2 submission as soon as ITS receives it from the AO, together with a letter (GAPS 90/97). The GAPS 90/97 asks the claimant to send in any further information within 14 days and to contact the ITS if he needs longer to do this. It may well be that having seen the AT2 submission the claimant will change his mind and decide to ask for an oral hearing (indeed, as pointed out in the notes to reg. 22(1) to (1C), it may be difficult for him to decide whether or not to go for an oral hearing until this point).

Clearly one result of these changes to the listing procedures is a vast increase in the number of paper hearings. It is now the practice to have whole sittings devoted to papers hearings only. An unwelcome development in relation to these sittings is that the papers are not sent out to the members in advance. This must inevitably diminish the input they can make. And now members will increasingly not be involved in these sittings at all: see President's Circular No. 14.

Another consequence is that the striking-out procedure under reg. 7 will no longer be employed simply because the claimant does not reply to the letter asking whether or not he wants to attend an oral hearing (see the 1996 edition of this book for criticism of the use of this procedure in this context). But although this is an improvement in that there will now at least be a consideration of the claimant's appeal on the papers the criticism of the philosophy of the listing procedure remains. A claimant has a right to appeal to a SSAT. The emphasis in the past has been on enabling a claimant to present his case as fully as possible. The statement of a presumption that the claimant does not wish to have an oral hearing of his appeal unless he replies within 14 days could give the impression that the claimant is imposing a burden on the appeal process which he must justify. While recognising that the non-attendance of claimants at hearings was a considerable problem, the new procedure in September 1992 was seen as an inappropriate response. This criticism remains. The recent changes are a further step in the wrong direction. For example, although it is possible for a claimant to change his mind and decide that after all he does want an oral hearing (and this possibility is briefly referred to in the leaflet sent out by ITS when the claimant's appeal is first received), there is a danger that many claimants will not realise that this option remains. But it should not be forgotten that a chairman does have power to order an oral hearing (see reg. 22(1C)) if he considers that one is required to enable the tribunal to reach a decision.

From April 1999 the above arrangements change as follows. Notice of appeal is still required to be lodged or sent by the claimant to the local office issuing the decision that is to be challenged. But, instead of that office immediately forwarding the notice of appeal to ITS for registration, the notice is retained within the Benefits Agency until the AO has drafted the appeal submission. The Benefits Agency then sends ITS both the notice and appeal submission and simultaneously issues to the claimant a copy of the submission and the enquiry form that formerly was the responsibility of ITS to issue. The claimant then has 14 days within which to submit the completed enquiry form to ITS. The advantages claimed for these changes are that the claimant should have sight of the appeal submission much earlier and that it will be easier to pinpoint where, between the Benefits Agency and ITS, responsibility lies for delays in the appeals process.

See President's Circular No. 4 on domiciliary hearings (p. 1453).

Paragraph (2A) and (2B)

These two paragraphs empower a chairman to give a direction for the "determination forthwith" of an appeal. "Forthwith" does not seem here to mean immediately, but rather that the appeal might be moved towards the head of the queue for listing out of its former place. That is because notice has to be given, presumably to all the parties to the proceedings, and there is nothing in paras. (2A) or (2B) to exempt cases in which a notice for determination forthwith is given from the provisions about giving notice of a hearing.

Under para. (2A), a chairman may act if three conditions are met. A party to the proceeding must have failed to comply with a "direction regarding his availability" (presumably this means a chairman's direction under reg. 2(1)(a) or (aa) that the party say when he is able to attend a hearing, or a direction by a chairman or clerk under reg. 2(1)(aa) or (ab); note that the GAPS 11/97 letter sent to claimants on receipt of their appeal (see the notes to para. (2) above) "directs" the claimant to reply within 14 days stating whether he wants an oral hearing). The party must have not given *any* explanation of the failure to comply with the direction (even an inadequate or daft explanation apparently removes the power to act under para. (2A)). Finally, the chairman must be satisfied that the tribunal has sufficient particulars in order for the appeal to be determined. This last condition can easily be satisfied if the view is taken that an appeal should be determined against a party who has the burden of proving an issue and puts no evidence forward in support. If the three conditions are satisfied, the expedited listing can be ordered although a party has not given information about availability to attend a hearing or other information which has been requested. See para. (3) for the effect of the meeting of the conditions in sub-paras. (a) and (b) when the party concerned does not attend the hearing.

Under para. (2B), a chairman who believes that an appeal (*N.B.* and not any other form of proceedings) has no reasonable prospect of success may give notice for the determination forthwith of the appeal. Chairmen will be reluctant to use this power except in the very clearest of cases, as experience shows that appeals which appear hopeless can sometimes take on a completely different aspect when fresh information emerges at a hearing.

Paragraph (2C)

See notes to para. (2).

Paragraph (3)

This provision clearly gives the SSAT discretion to hear an appeal although the appellant does not attend and is not represented. If he expressly asks for an adjournment for some good reason or gives a reason for not being able to attend on a particular date, then it may well be a breach of the rules of natural justice to proceed in the appellant's absence. Thus in *CS 1939/1995* the Commissioner set aside a decision made when the claimant had telephoned to say that he could not attend because of an allergic reaction to a bee-sting. See notes to reg. 5 for more on adjournments. Of course, an appellant is not entitled to string out the process indefinitely (especially if recovery of an overpayment is being sought by the DSS).

If the appellant has requested an oral hearing but does not turn up, the SSAT's discretion is more open. In the first case, given that the appellant will have been given notice of the date of the hearing, a decision by a SSAT to proceed in the appellant's absence would be hard to challenge. If the hearing has been listed following a chairman's direction under para. (2A) for determination forthwith of the appeal, the fact that the party concerned had failed to comply with a direction mentioned in para. (2A)(a) or give any explanation for the failure to comply may be taken into account. If the party has, since the giving of the direction, remedied either of those deficiencies, that must also of course be taken into account as part of "all the circumstances". In the second case, the official guidance to SSATs is that when a claimant has said that he will attend the hearing but does not do so, the hearing should normally proceed in his absence. But no form or reply-paid envelope is sent to the appellant with the notice of the date of the hearing on which the appellant can say that he is unable to attend on the particular date. He must make a positive effort to contact ITS. In the necessary consideration of all relevant circumstances before deciding whether to proceed in the appellant's absence it is suggested that little weight should be given to the official guidance. Since a SSAT is an inquisitorial body, the central issue must be a balance of the ability of the SSAT to make the necessary findings of fact without evidence from the appellant against the principle that the appellant need only be given a fair opportunity to attend.

In *R(SB) 23/83* the Commissioner holds that SSATs should always enquire if the appellant has stated that he wishes to be present and would have set aside a decision if there was evidence that the SSAT acted in ignorance of such a statement. See para. 42 of the *Guide to procedure* (2nd ed.).

CSB 582/1987, followed in *CSB 383/1988*, holds that para. (3) does not give a SSAT an automatic authority to proceed if the AO or the presenting officer is not present. The AO is not just a party to the proceedings, but is in the position of *amicus curiae*, with a duty to present the facts and law objectively (see Diplock L.J. in *R. v. Deputy Industrial Injuries Commissioner, ex p. Moore* [1965] 1 Q.B. 456 and *Ward v. SSAT* 1995 S.C.L.R. 1134). If the AO is not present or represented (though this has become the norm), there is a danger that the SSAT will not be properly informed about the facts and the law. If, as in *CSB 582/1987*, there is an implied request from the claimant for an adjournment so that questions can be put to the presenting officer, it is a breach of natural justice for the SSAT not to grant the adjournment.

In *CIS 853/1995* and *CI 11449/1995* no presenting officer attended the hearings, apparently because of staffing difficulties. In both cases the tribunals decided the appeals in favour of the claimants. The AO then appealed to the Commissioner. In *CIS 853/1995* the claimant argued that, not having attended the hearing, the AO should not be entitled to appeal. The Commissioner expressed considerable sympathy with this argument, stressing the essential role of the presenting officer, but was forced to reject it. The tribunal had clearly erred in law and, exercising an inquisitorial jurisdiction, the Commissioner had to give effect to that conclusion. A similar result was reached by the same Commissioner in *CI 11449/1995*, where it was said that the tribunal could not be blamed for proceeding in the absence of the presenting officer when the claimant had not asked for an adjournment. Tribunals should consider the point made in that decision, that if a presenting officer had been present at the hearing, to make the adjudication officer's legal case fully, the delay, inconvenience and expense of an appeal to the Commissioner might have been avoided.

A party to the proceedings may apply to have a SSAT decision set aside on the ground that he or his representative was not present at a hearing (reg. 10; note reg. 10(1A)). If the proceedings have been struck out under reg. 7 they can be reinstated within 3 months under reg. 7(3), but from October 1996 only on one highly restricted ground.

Paragraph (3A)
    See notes to para. (2).

Paragraph (4)
    Before April 1984 all SBAT hearings were in private. NILT hearings were open to the public. The effect of this rule is that a claimant (or his representative: reg. 2(1)(b)) can insist on a private hearing. Secondly, if intimate personal or financial circumstances may have to be disclosed, the hearing is to be private. This would cover many income support appeals to a SSAT, although this could hardly have been the intention. But see para. (6)(d). The third category, public security, will rarely arise.

Paragraph (5)
    This provision does little more than spell out what is implicit in the notion of an oral hearing. Note that in the definition of "party to the proceedings" the reference is to "the adjudication officer." This appears to mean the AO who made the decision or reference. If the presenting officer is a different person he has the rights of a representative under reg. 2(1)(b).

Paragraph (6)
    The rights of a person entitled to be heard are set out in para. (9).
    These people may be present during a private hearing. For the deliberations of the tribunal, see reg. 2(2). The only DSS employees entitled to remain are those listed in sub-para. (c). Under sub-para. (d) anyone may be admitted with the leave of the chairman, although any party to the proceedings (or a representative: reg. 2(1)(b)) who is actually present has a veto.

Paragraph (7)
    Deals with inquiries.

Paragraph (8)
    Confirms that these people are entitled to take part in the proceedings despite para. (6). The provision about witnesses is presumably also directed at para. (4). Because it only provides that reg. 4 is not to prevent the presence of a witness, it does not inhibit the chairman's power under reg. 2(1) to exclude witnesses from the hearing except when giving evidence.

Paragraph (9)
    The rights set out here would probably be secured anyway by the rules of natural justice. But these elements are not in the chairman's discretion; they must be followed. So, for instance, a party has the right to put questions directly to any witness, not merely to put them through the chairman. However, the chairman has a discretion as to the limits of these rights. Thus he can determine that

a party has had a sufficient opportunity of addressing the tribunal, or that evidence is irrelevant (see below). If he gets it wrong in a way which prejudices a full and fair hearing, this will be an error of law (*R(SB) 1/81, R(SB) 6/82*).

Either party may call witnesses to give evidence. It is for the chairman to decide if they should be allowed in to the tribunal room from the start of the hearing, or only admitted at the point at which they are to give evidence (*Guide to procedure* (2nd ed.), para. 60). Usually the informality of the proceedings is such that a representative or person accompanying the claimant in practice gives evidence as a witness without any clear demarcation line, but there may be circumstances in which the importance of evidence being independent means that the witness should not hear what goes on before he gives evidence. A SSAT is not bound by the rules of evidence applied in courts, so that hearsay evidence (*i.e.* the witness is not giving evidence of his direct knowledge, but of someone else's knowledge) can be admitted. However, before admitting it the SSAT must "carefully weigh up its probative value, bearing in mind that the original maker of the statement is not present at the hearing to be questioned on what he actually saw" (*R(SB) 5/82*, and see *Guide to procedure* (2nd ed.), para. 57). But any evidence which has any probative value must be listened to before it is given its appropriate weight, regardless of whether it is hearsay or not (*R(IS) 5/93*, drawing on *R. v. Deputy Industrial Injuries Commissioner, ex p Moore* [1965] 1 Q.B. 456 and *Miller v. Minister of Housing and Local Government* [1968] 1 W.L.R. 992). Often the evidence presented by the AO to a SSAT will be hearsay, such as written reports from visiting officers or copies of records made by unidentified officers. If hearsay evidence is directly challenged it may sometimes be necessary to adjourn to enable a person who can give direct evidence to attend a hearing. A related point was dealt with in *CIS 143/1994*. The claimant was in receipt of invalidity benefit and income support. It was alleged that he was working. Identification evidence from two employees was given to the tribunal hearing his appeal against the overpayment of invalidity benefit in February 1992. The employees did not attend the hearing of the income support appeal which was adjourned three times. On the third occasion the tribunal requested that they be *subpoenaed*, following an allegation that they had been threatened. Subsequently, a tribunal dismissed the appeal, adopting the findings of the February 1992 tribunal on identification. The Commissioner decides that before accepting those findings, the tribunal should have pressed for the *subpoenas* to be issued, or inquired why they had not been issued, or if they had, why the witnesses had not attended (note that the tribunal itself possesses no power of subpoena).

Although the rules say nothing about the admission of documents and written evidence, clearly these are valuable. Indeed, the Commissioners have insisted that since the presenting officer is not a witness, a mere statement by him is not evidence unless supported by some elementary statement from the source of the fact it is desired to submit (*CSB 13/82* [1982] J.S.W.L. 383, *CSB 420/1981* [1983] J.S.W.L. 375, *CSB 728/1984*). In *CSB 517/1982*, the Commissioner expressed disquiet at the refutation of the claimant's expert medical evidence by the statement in the papers that medical advice to the SBO was to the contrary. He held that the claimant was entitled to "chapter and verse" of any evidence relied on. This general approach to statements from presenting officers is confirmed by the Tribunal of Commissioners in *R(SB) 8/84*. There has more recently been a particularly strong statement in *R(SB) 10/86*. However, in *CS 16448/96* the Commissioner makes the point that in the tribunal context roles are often not clear cut. In his view there was no reason in principle why a presenting officer could not give evidence, albeit that it would be hearsay if he was relaying statements made by another. The issue was the weight to be accorded to such evidence; if it was possible to produce the original source but this had not been done, a tribunal might choose to give little or no weight to the evidence. The Commissioner considered that the same reasoning applied to statements by representatives. It is suggested that there is not necessarily a conflict between these decisions; the distinction to be drawn would seem to be that between a presenting officer's *submission* (*i.e.* argument) and *statements* made by him in the course of that submission that are based on his own knowledge or evidence from others. The tribunal's main task, however, will be deciding the value to be given to such evidence, particularly in the case of hearsay evidence. See also *CU 47/1993* where the SSAT erred in not asking to see the notes that the claimant stated he had made of his conversations with the UBO.

There is, however, no requirement that evidence from the claimant or anyone else must be corroborated (*R(I) 2/51*). But as *CIB 5794/1997* points out, this does not absolve a tribunal from the need to weigh up all the evidence, including any uncorroborated evidence, as a whole. Corroboration, like hearsay, goes to the weight to be given to the evidence in question.

A representative has all the rights of an interested person, but someone merely accompanying the claimant does not (reg. 2(1)(b)). If a tribunal is aware of a fundamental misconception on the part of a representative it should disabuse him of his erroneous view (see *Dennis v. United Kingdom Central Council for Nursing, Midwifery, and Health Visiting, The Times*, April 2, 1993).

Postponement and adjournment

5.—[¹(1) Where a person to whom notice of an oral hearing or inquiry has been given wishes to request a postponement of that hearing or inquiry—
  (a) in the case of an oral hearing by an adjudicating authority, he shall do so in writing to the clerk to the tribunal stating his reasons for the request, and the clerk to the tribunal may grant or refuse the request as he thinks fit or may pass the request to the chairman, who may grant or refuse the request as he thinks fit;
  (b) in the case of an inquiry, he shall do so in writing to the person appointed to hold the inquiry stating his reasons for the request, and the person appointed may grant or refuse the request as he thinks fit.]
  (2) A chairman [¹or the clerk to the tribunal] may of his own motion at any time before the beginning of the hearing postpone the hearing.
  (3) An oral hearing or an inquiry may be adjourned by the adjudicating authority or, as the case may be, the person appointed to hold the inquiry at any time on the application of any party to the proceedings or of its or his own motion.

AMENDMENT

1. Social Security (Adjudication) and Child Support Amendment (No. 2) Regulations 1996 (S.I. 1996 No. 2450), reg. 6 (October 21, 1996).

DEFINITIONS

"adjudicating authority"—see reg. 1(2)
"clerk to the tribunal"—*ibid.*
"inquiry"—*ibid.*
"party to the proceedings"—*ibid.*

GENERAL NOTE

Paragraphs (1) and (2)
Para. (1) provides that a party to the proceedings who wishes to have a hearing which has been fixed postponed is to apply in writing to the clerk to the tribunal giving reasons. The clerk may grant or refuse the request or pass it to a tribunal chairman. Any cases which involve any degree of exercise of judicial discretion should be passed to a chairman. It may be of value for clerks to be able to deal with cases where there has been some administrative or clerical error. Para. (2), giving a general power to postpone to clerks and chairmen, allows, amongst other things, telephone requests to be dealt with. If a request for a postponement is refused by a clerk, there is no express provision for reconsideration by a chairman on request. But on an analogy with *CIS 93/1992* (see notes to reg. 3(4)), it may be that whoever has refused a request can reconsider it on request, especially if new matters are put forward. A clerk could then decide to pass the request to a chairman.
  If a request for a postponement has been refused, there remains the general power under para. (3) for an adjudicating authority (which in the case of a tribunal means the whole tribunal and not just the chairman) to adjourn. *CDLA 3680/1997* holds that where there has been an unsuccessful application for a postponement, the tribunal should consider whether there should be an adjournment (unless of course the party who made the postponement application was content for the hearing to proceed). This could not be done unless the tribunal was aware of the ground(s) of the postponement request. The Commissioner therefore set aside the tribunal's decision on the basis that a relevant document (*i.e.* the postponement request) was not before the tribunal.

Paragraph (3)
If there has not been a postponement by a clerk or chairman, under paras. (1) or (2), any adjournment (except maybe short adjournments which may be part of the chairman's power to control procedure) must be agreed by the tribunal as a whole. There are many occasions when an adjournment is appropriate. Apart from cases where the claimant fails to appear (see reg. 4(3)), another situation is where a new point of substance, either of law or fact, is raised in the course of the hearing. Here, the test must be whether both parties or their representatives have had a fair opportun-

ity of dealing with the point. If a tribunal considers that further evidence, or the presence of a particular witness, is necessary in order to reach a proper decision then an adjournment should be considered. One factor to be weighed up is the likelihood that the evidence can be produced. Another is whether one party could have been expected to have produced the evidence earlier. In *R(SB) 10/86*, where the presenting officer asserted that beds were available at a particular shop at a particular price, but could produce no supporting evidence, the Commissioner said that if "the adjudication officer comes to the hearing unprepared to support his statement by evidence they [the SSAT] must either decide the appeal on the basis that the facts are unproved or adjourn to give the officer an opportunity of proving them. And where the claimant has been kept waiting they should hesitate to permit a further long wait." The undesirability of subjecting the claimant to delay and possibly a new hearing by a completely differently constituted tribunal is mentioned in the helpful discussion in paras. 65 and 66 of the *Guide to procedure* (2nd ed.).

See further Neville Harris, "Adjournments in social security tribunals", (1996) 3 J.S.S.L. 11. Note also *Ward v. SSAT* 1995 S.C.L.R. 1134 in the notes to reg. 10.

In *R(SB) 2/88* the Commissioner suggests that if the SSAT does not contain a member of the same sex as the claimant, as required if practicable by s.41(6) of the Administration Act, an adjournment should be offered to the claimant. See the notes to s.41(6).

It is suggested in *CS 1939/1995* that although it is always desirable for a tribunal to indicate briefly on the record of proceedings why a request for an adjournment has been refused (in that case the request was because the claimant could not attend having been stung by a bee), there is no legal requirement to do so. That is said to be because reg. 23(2) only applies to "decisions", not to rulings of this kind. However, where a specific request for an adjournment has been made, such a separation seems artificial.

Under the changes to the listing procedure introduced in October 1996, if a claimant replies on the enquiry form that he wishes to have an oral hearing, notice of the date of the hearing will be given. The enquiry form indicates that once an oral hearing has been arranged, a postponement will only be granted if unexpected circumstances have occurred. Advice has been given, in some regions at least, that if a claimant who has said that he will attend does not do so on the date fixed, the hearing should normally proceed in his absence. It is suggested that a decision to proceed in the claimant's absence can only properly be made after considering all the relevant circumstances and how far it is possible to determine the issues in the appeal without the claimant's evidence. Simply to follow advice from a regional or full-time chairman is a failure to act in a judicial manner. There is no form or pre-paid envelope sent with the notice of the date of the hearing on which a claimant can reply that he cannot attend on that date. The claimant must therefore take the initiative to bring any difficulties to the tribunal's notice.

Note President's Circular No. 1 on adjournments (p. 1447) and Circular No. 9 (p. 1455). The approach of Circular No. 9 to the question of adjournments pending the result of a "test case" is quite different from that in ITS President's Practice Direction No. 3 which was withdrawn on June 1, 1995. First, the Circular states that appeals will often not be listed until the decision in the test case is known, although if this happens claimants will be informed of their right to insist that their appeal be heard. Secondly, it states that when considering whether to grant an adjournment tribunals should bear in mind that: (1) if the appeal succeeds the Secretary of State will usually suspend payment of benefit pending further appeal (see reg. 37 of the Claims and Payments Regulations); and (2) "all benefit routes are not closed" to the claimant as a result of the delay in hearing the appeal (para. 5). But particularly where the appeal concerns a decision refusing income support (*e.g.* if the person has failed the habitual residence test) it is difficult to see what those other avenues are. There is no longer any access to interim payments in these circumstances (see reg. 2(1A) of the Payments Regulations) and a crisis fund from the social fund will not be available if the person is unlikely to have the means to repay it. Moreover, a tribunal should not assume in advance that the Secretary of State will exercise his discretion to suspend payment of an award, since he may be persuaded, *e.g.* on grounds of hardship, not to do so. It is suggested that a tribunal should at the most only take into account the possibility that the Secretary of State might suspend payment. (Note that reg. 37A of the Claims and Payments Regulations, in fact declared *ultra vires* in *R. v. Secretary of State for Social Security, ex parte Sutherland* (November 7, 1996), does not apply to tribunal awards). The issue before the tribunal is the claimant's *entitlement* to the benefit in question; issues as to *payment* are not within the tribunal's jurisdiction. There may often be sound reasons for determining the claimant's entitlement without any further delay (particularly in view of the length of time the decision in the test case may take to resolve).

A SSAT's decision to adjourn having been told by the AO that the Secretary of State would suspend payment of any award pending the appeal to the Court of Appeal in *CIS 472/1994* (see the notes to reg. 21(3)(h) of the Income Support Regulations) was challenged in *R. v. Oxford SSAT, ex p. Wolke* (High Court, April 30, 1996, unreported). It was contended that the tribunal could not be certain that the Secretary of State would suspend payment and to adjourn for what could be a lengthy period flew in the face of the fact that income support was intended to meet present needs. Popplewell J. considered that the point was of academic interest because he had dealt with the substantive issue and in his view no question of principle was involved. But he did comment that a pending appeal of a "lookalike" case to the Court of Appeal was a factor that a tribunal should take into account, as was the point that the Secretary of State *might* (the tribunal would be wrong to assume that he would) suspend payment. But there were other factors the tribunal should consider. The Court of Appeal (June 18, 1996) refused leave to pursue the point as they agreed that it was academic. However, Phillips L.J. did comment that they were "by no means convinced that the SSAT had acted appropriately in adjourning Ms Wolke's appeal . . .". Thus the point is unresolved and a tribunal should, as the Circular advises, makes its decision in the light of all the available information. However, there can be real difficulties for all concerned if large numbers of cases are stacked up, having been decided by tribunals, which can only be disposed of after the decision in the test case by the Commissioners (see the thousands of *Bate* cases).

See also *CIS 383/1997* which deals with the situation where a tribunal was not told of a postponement application.

Withdrawal of applications, appeals and references

6.—(1) A person who has made an application to the chairman of the tribunal for leave to appeal to a Commissioner against a decision of an appeal tribunal, a medical appeal tribunal or a disability appeal tribunal may withdraw his application at any time before it is determined by giving written notice of intention to withdraw to the chairman.

(2) Any appeal to an adjudicating authority made under the Administration Act or these Regulations may be withdrawn by the person who made the appeal—

[¹(a) before the hearing begins, provided that, in the case of a tribunal or board, the clerk to the tribunal has not received any notice under paragraph (2A), by giving written notice of intention to withdraw to the adjudicating authority to whom the appeal was made and with the consent in writing of any other party to the proceedings other than—

    (i) in a case which originated in a decision of an adjudication officer, an adjudication officer;

    (ii) in any other case, the Secretary of State; or]

(b) after the hearing has begun, with the leave of the adjudicating authority or, in the case of a tribunal or board, its chairman, at any time before the determination is made.

[¹(2A) An appeal to a tribunal or board shall not be withdrawn under subparagraph (a) of paragraph (2) if the clerk to the tribunal has previously received notice opposing a withdrawal of such appeal from—

(a) in a case which orginated in a decision of an adjudication officer, an adjudication officer; or

(b) in any other case, the Secretary of State.]

(3) A reference by an adjudication officer to an appeal tribunal under section 21(2) of the Administration Act or to a medical board under regulation 45(3) or to a medical appeal tribunal under section 46(3) of the Administration Act may be withdrawn by him at any time before the reference is determined by giving written notice of intention to withdraw to the adjudicating authority to whom the reference was made, but in the case of a reference under section 46(3) of the Administration Act made at the instance of the Secretary of State only with his consent.

(4) An application under regulation 13 for a decision of the Secretary of State on any question may, with his leave, be withdrawn at any time before the decision is given.

AMENDMENT

1. Social Security (Adjudication) and Child Support Amendment (No. 2) Regulations 1996 (S.I. 1996 No. 2450), reg. 7 (October 21, 1996).

DEFINITIONS

"the Acts"—see reg. 1(2).
"adjudicating authority"—*ibid.*
"adjudication officer"—*ibid.*
"appeal tribunal"—*ibid.*
"clerk to the tribunal"—*ibid.*
"Commissioner"—*ibid.*
"disability appeal tribunal"—*ibid.*
"medical appeal tribunal"—*ibid.*
"medical board"—see reg. 34.
"party to the proceedings"—see reg. 1(2).

GENERAL NOTE

Paragraph (1)
An application for leave to appeal may be withdrawn at any time before a determination is given.

Paragraphs (2) and (2A)
It might be questioned why a claimant's withdrawal of an appeal should not be automatically effective, as is a withdrawal of a claim before it is determined. The answer is that there is a public interest in ensuring that the correct entitlement is applied to the claimant, whether that leaves him worse or better off than under the original decision. So a claimant should not automatically be allowed to withdraw an appeal.

Sub-para. (a) applies before a hearing begins. It is not clear exactly when a hearing begins, but the crucial point appears to be when the tribunal as a body begins its formal consideration of the appeal. This would mean that para. (2) was in line with the pre-April 1984 NILT practice, rather than that in the SBAT. It is also assumed that if there has been an adjourned hearing, then any subsequent withdrawal must be dealt with under sub-para. (b), but even this is not certain (see reg. 22(3)). Note that under sub-para. (a) the appellant's written notice of intention must be given to the adjudicating authority. There is no particular form in which a withdrawal needs to be expressed. The enquiry form issued to the claimant invites him to indicate whether he wishes to continue with the appeal. Note that there has been a change in the conditions from October 1996. Up till then, the withdrawal of the claimant's appeal was effective if an AO and any other party to the proceedings consented. As suggested in the notes in earlier editions, it was arguable that the consent was required of the specific AO who made the decision under appeal, who would be a party to the proceedings under the definition in reg. 1(2). Now the general condition of the consent of *an* AO has gone. If an AO has given the clerk to the tribunal a notice opposing the withdrawal, the effect of para. (2A) is that the claimant's appeal cannot be withdrawn under para. (2)(a). If such a notice has not been given, then consent is only required from a party to the proceedings other than, where the case originated in an AO's decision, an AO. This form of words is not absolutely clear, but seems to exclude an argument that the consent is needed of the specific AO who made the decision under appeal.

Where an AO has given the clerk a notice of opposition under para. (2A), so that there cannot be a withdrawal under para. (2)(a), the claimant's application to withdraw the appeal would have to be considered by the tribunal chairman under para. (2)(b) once the hearing has begun, unless the claimant has changed his mind.

Under sub-para. (b), when the hearing has begun, the matter is for the chairman, bearing in mind the public interest noted above, and the probable lack of expertise of the claimant. There is no requirement that the claimant's wish to withdraw should be in writing, and the consent or otherwise of any other parties is irrelevant, although a chairman may wish to ascertain the presenting officer's opinion.

Reg. 6 is silent about whether a withdrawn appeal can be "reinstated", in contrast to reg. 26(3) of the Social Security Commissioners (Procedure) Regulations 1999 (which leaves the question to the discretion of a Commissioner). *R(IS) 5/94* decides that providing that any necessary leave to appeal out of time has been granted, a fresh appeal may be brought against an AO's decision, even though an earlier appeal against the same decision has been withdrawn under reg. 6. Where the chairman or an AO has agreed a withdrawal under para. (2) there has been no decision by a tribunal and so the principle of *res judicata* (that once a matter has been adjudicated on by a competent authority another authority of the same level cannot readjudicate on the matter) does not apply. It would be different if the first appeal had been dismissed by a SSAT.

(S.I. 1995 No. 1801, reg. 7)

Striking-out of proceedings for want of prosecution

7.—(1) The chairman of an appeal tribunal, a medical appeal tribunal or a disability appeal tribunal may, subject to paragraph (2), on the application of any party to the proceedings or of his own motion, strike out any application, appeal or reference for want of prosecution including the failure of the appellant to comply with a direction given by the chairman [¹or the clerk to the tribunal] under [¹ regulation 2(1)(aa) or (ab)].

[¹(1A) Where the chairman decides not to strike out an appeal under paragraph (1) he shall consider whether the appeal should be determined forthwith in accordance with these Regulations.

(1B) Where the chairman decides that an appeal should not be determined forthwith under paragraph (1A) he shall consider whether he should make further directions with a view to expediting the hearing of the appeal.]

(2) The chairman shall not make an order under paragraph (1) before a notice has been sent to the person against whom it is proposed that any such order should be made giving him a reasonable opportunity to show cause why such an order should not be made.

[¹(2A) Paragraph (2) shall not apply where the address of the person against whom it is proposed that an order under paragraph (1) should be made is unknown to the chairman or to the clerk to the tribunal and cannot be ascertained by reasonable enquiry.]

(3) The chairman of an appeal tribunal, a medical appeal tribunal or a disability appeal tribunal may, on application by the party concerned, made not later than [¹3 months] beginning with the date of the order made under paragraph (1), give leave to reinstate any application, appeal or reference which has been struck out in accordance with paragraph (1)[¹, if he is satisfied that the party concerned did not receive a notice under paragraph (2) and that the conditions in paragraph (2A) were not met].

AMENDMENT

1. Social Security (Adjudication) and Child Support Amendment (No. 2) Regulations 1996 (S.I. 1996 No. 2450), reg. 8 (October 21, 1996).

DEFINITIONS

"appeal tribunal"—see reg. 1(2).
"clerk to the tribunal"—*ibid.*
"disability appeal tribunal"—*ibid.*
"medical appeal tribunal"—*ibid.*
"party to the proceedings"—*ibid.*

GENERAL NOTE

This power to strike out applications, appeals and references for want of prosecution, *i.e.* failure to proceed at an acceptable rate, was introduced in April 1987. There is some doubt whether reg. 7 of the 1986 Regulations was validly made, as argued in earlier editions. However, there seems no doubt about that in relation to the 1995 Regulations.

Reg. 7 appears to give the chairman of a SSAT an unfettered discretion to strike out an application, appeal or reference for want of prosecution, *i.e.* failure to proceed at an acceptable rate, whenever the circumstances appear appropriate. However, the Court of Appeal in *Executors of Evans v. Metropolitan Police Authority* [1992] I.R.L.R. 570 held that it was inconceivable that a provision in similar terms in the Industrial Tribunal (Rules of Procedure) Regulations 1980 and 1985 gave an unfettered power. Rather, the principles laid down by the House of Lords in *Birkett v. James* [1978] A.C. 297 in relation to ordinary civil actions were applied, subject only to such adaptation as was required by the differences between industrial tribunal proceedings and actions in the ordinary courts. Although there are differences between industrial tribunal proceedings and SSAT proceedings, it seems clear that the *Birkett v. James* principles apply with the necessary adaptations. The industrial

1297

tribunal procedure does not contain the possibility of reinstating a struck-out appeal, as in reg. 7(3), but does have a right of appeal against the striking-out order, which does not exist when a SSAT chairman makes an order. The powers are more or less equally draconian, although the amendment to para. (3) from October 1996 significantly reduces the possibility of reinstating an appeal to a SSAT.

In *Birkett v. James* Lord Diplock held that the power to strike out for want of prosecution should be exercised only where the court is satisfied:

"either (1) that the default has been intentional and contumelious, *e.g.* disobedience to a peremptory order of the court or conduct amounting to an abuse of the process of the court; or (2) (a) that there has been inordinate and inexcusable delay on the part of the plaintiff or his lawyers, and (b) that such delay will give rise to a substantial risk that it is not possible to have a fair trial of the issues in the action or is such as is likely to cause or to have caused serious prejudice to the defendants either as between themselves and the plaintiff or between each other or between them and a third party."

Under head (1), a peremptory order is one expressly requiring specified action by the plaintiff by a specified date. In the SSAT context some orders made under powers in the Adjudication Regulations could be peremptory in form, *e.g.* a chairman's direction under reg. 3(6) or possibly a direction given by a SSAT on an adjournment. However, the more extensive powers given to chairmen under reg. 2(1)(aa) and to tribunal clerks under reg. 2(1)(ab) to give directions to comply with provisions of the Regulations are obviously designed with reg. 7 in mind. See the notes to reg. 2 for the scope of those powers. The failure to comply with directions under those provisions is expressly caught by reg. 7(1), whether or not there would otherwise be said to have been a want of prosecution by the claimant.

Under head (2), the degree of delay that might be unjustifiable in the SSAT context is debatable, but there must also be either some substantial risk to the ability of the SSAT to deal with the appeal fairly or some degree of prejudice to the DSS from the delay.

In all cases SSAT chairmen should think carefully before exercising the power under reg. 7(1), especially if there has been no application for striking-out from any party to the proceedings. Even if there has been a want of prosecution in the *Birkett v. James* sense or a failure to comply with a direction under reg. 2(1)(aa) or (ab), the chairman has a discretion which must be exercised judicially in the light of all the circumstances. This is now emphasised by two of the changes made in October 1996. The first is the amendment to para. (3) restricting the possibility of reinstating a struck-out appeal to very limited circumstances. The second is the insertion of paras. (1A) and (1B), pointing out alternative avenues—directing determination of the appeal forthwith (see reg. 4(2A) and (2B)) or making further directions with a view to expediting the appeal (see reg. 2(1)(aa)). Although in form these alternatives are to be considered only after the chairman has decided not to strike out under para. (1), their existence is clearly to be taken into account in the exercise of the discretion under para. (1). It will often be preferable and secure greater finality for a substantive decision on the appeal to be made.

There is also an uncertainty as to the identity of the person "against whom" an order is made (who must under para. (2) be given an opportunity to show cause why an order should not be made). An appeal to a tribunal can only be made by a claimant, who will be the relevant person in such cases. But a reference can only be made by an AO (Administration Act, s.21(2): 1975 Act, s.99(2)). Presumably the person against whom an order would be made is the AO, but the claimant might be prejudiced by the failure of the tribunal to make a decision. Applications, *e.g.* for leave to appeal, may be made by any party.

Para. (2A) may provide a method of clearing appeals off the books where the claimant's current address cannot reasonably be ascertained which is welcome administratively. In such circumstances a notice giving the claimant opportunity to show cause why there should not be a striking-out need not be sent.

The change introduced into para. (3) has altered the entire nature of reg. 7. Before October 1996, the person identified in para. (2) could apply within 12 months to have any matter which had been struck out reinstated. The chairman then had an unfettered discretion whether or not to give leave for reinstatement. Now not only must the application be made within three months, but leave can be given on one ground only. That is the highly restricted ground that the person concerned did not receive a notice under para. (2) and the condition in para. (2A) did not apply. The wording of para. (3) indicates that the deeming of reg. 1(3) (notice deemed to be given on date of posting to last known or notified address) is not relevant and that the question is whether or not the person did actually receive the notice. Any other reason, however meritorious, cannot lead to reinstatement. This makes the striking-out of an appeal a much more final and serious matter. However, the reasoning of *R(IS) 5/94* (see notes to reg. 6), would seem to apply here. If an appeal has been struck out, there has been no decision on it by a tribunal, so that the claimant can make a fresh appeal against the same decision. The difficulty will be obtaining leave to appeal outside the ordinary time-limit (see reg. 3(3) to (4)).

Non-disclosure of medical evidence

8.—(1) Where, in connection with the consideration and determination of any claim or question there is before an adjudicating authority medical advice or medical evidence relating to a person which has not been disclosed to him and in the opinion of the adjudicating authority or, in the case of a tribunal or board, its chairman, the disclosure to that person of that advice or evidence would be harmful to his health, such advice or evidence shall not be required to be disclosed to that person.

(2) Evidence such as is mentioned in paragraph (1) shall not be disclosed to any person acting for or representing the person to whom it relates or, in a case where a claim for benefit is made by reference to the disability of a person other than the claimant and the evidence relates to that other person, shall not be disclosed to the claimant or any person acting for or representing him, unless the adjudicating authority, or in the case of a tribunal or board, its chairman, is satisfied that it is in the interests of the person to whom the evidence relates to do so.

(3) An adjudicating authority shall not be precluded from taking into account for the purposes of the determination evidence which has not been disclosed to a person under the provisions of paragraph (1) or (2).

(4) In this regulation ''adjudicating authority'' includes the Secretary of State in a case involving a question which is for determination by him.

DEFINITION

''adjudicating authority''—see reg. 1(2).

GENERAL NOTE

The use and operation of this provision was considered in *CSDLA 5/1995*. In connection with a renewal claim for attendance allowance on behalf of her daughter, the claimant's current G.P. submitted a medical report indicating that the true problem might be that the claimant herself suffered from Munchausen By Proxy Syndrome. As a consequence of advice from a Benefits Agency medical officer that this report could cause ''considerable difficulty and distress'', it was not disclosed to the claimant. When she later obtained representation it was still not disclosed.

The Commissioner states that this provision must be operated with caution (see *R(A) 4/89*). Disclosure could only be refused if the harm to health would be substantial (which was a very different test from that of ''would cause considerable difficulty and distress''), and if the claimant was told that evidence was not being disclosed. The regulation also had to be applied in a manner consistent with the principles of natural justice. Thus the claimant should at least have been given an indication of the gist of the evidence against her so that she had a proper opportunity to put forward her case. Moreover, cases in which there should not be disclosure to a responsible representative would be extremely rare. In addition the decision not to disclose was an ongoing one and so needed to be reconsidered at various stages in the appeal as the circumstances could change.

If undisclosed evidence was taken into account by a tribunal in reaching its decision, this had to be stated openly (para. 05156 of the *Adjudication Officers' Guide* was too wide and invited a breach of reg. 25 (now reg. 23)). Moreover, if the undisclosed evidence had not been taken into account, this should also be clearly stated, since otherwise it would probably be assumed that it had so that any appeal would necessarily be allowed.

Correction of accidental errors in decisions

9.—(1) Subject to regulation 11 (provisions common to regulations 9 and 10) accidental errors in any decision or record of a decision may at any time be corrected by the adjudicating authority who gave the decision or by an authority of like status.

(2) A correction made to, or to the record of, a decision shall be deemed to be part of the decision or of that record and written notice of it shall be given as soon as practicable to every party to the proceedings.

"adjudicating authority"—see reg. 1(2).
"party to the proceedings"—*ibid.*

GENERAL NOTE

Only accidental errors, such as slips of the pen or arithmetical errors or such like, can be corrected through this procedure (*CM 209/1987, CM 264/1993* and *CSI 57/1993*). It cannot be used for afterthoughts or corrections of failures to deal with particular points. Also, although it is the duty of the chairman of a SSAT to record the tribunal's decision (reg. 23(2)), it is the whole tribunal which has to correct any errors. It used to be the case that another SSAT could correct errors only if it was impracticable or would cause undue delay to reconvene the original tribunal. From April 1987 an authority of like status could make the correction in any case. It remains preferable that the original people, who will know best what they intended, should carry out the procedure.

See President's Circular No. 10 (p. 1457), issued following *CSSB 76/1993*, which had held that a correction under reg. 9 can only be carried out by a sitting tribunal and not by the former practice of postal consultation of the members of the tribunal which made the decision. The Circular stresses the importance of, wherever possible, securing that the tribunal which decides whether or not the correction should be made has the same chairman as the tribunal which made the decision. Unfortunately, the Circular makes no reference to the importance or desirability of having the same wing-members and seems, wrongly, to assume that another authority of like status will be involved only where the chairman is different.

Note that from September 28, 1998, corrections may be dealt with by the chairman alone (see President's Circular No. 16 (p. 1464)). Presumably the guidance in President's Circular No. 10 that wherever possible the correction should be put to the original chairman will still apply.

It was held in *CSB 226/1981* that a "decision" does not exist until a copy of the written record is sent to the interested parties. Therefore up to that point the chairman of a SSAT may make corrections and additions (providing that these represent the reasoning of the tribunal as a whole) without invoking the procedure of reg. 9 (and see reg. 11(4)). This view is supported by the decision of the Tribunal of Commissioners in *CI 141/1987*. This indicates that an oral decision announced at the end of a hearing can be withdrawn or amended before it is promulgated in writing, within the limits of a judicial discretion. However, in *Gutzmore v. Wardly, The Times*, March 4, 1993, the Court of Appeal decides that inconsistency between the oral and written decision of an industrial tribunal required there to be a rehearing in the circumstances of that case. There seems to be less room for the application of these decisions in view of the summary decision procedure. See the notes to reg. 23(3).

If a tribunal's handwritten record of decision is inaccurately typed and issued, the procedure of reg. 9 need not be involved. The chairman will not have seen or approved the typed version. An accurate copy will be prepared without formality (President's Circular No. 10, para. 6).

There can be no appeal from the determination to make a correction (reg. 11(3)) but time for appealing or applying for leave to appeal does not start to run until notice of the correction is given (regs. 11(2) and 1(3)). See *CSI 57/1993* in the notes to reg. 10(1) for the position where a tribunal has exceeded the power of correction under reg. 9.

Setting aside decisions on certain grounds

10.—(1) Subject to regulation 11 (provisions common to regulations 9 and 10), on an application made by a party to the proceedings, a decision may be set aside by the adjudicating authority who gave the decision or by an authority of like status in a case where it appears just to set the decision aside on the ground that—

(a) a document relating to the proceedings in which the decision was given was not sent to, or was not received at an appropriate time by, a party to the proceedings or the party's representative or was not received at an appropriate time by the adjudicating authority who gave the decision; or

(b) a party to the proceedings in which the decision was given or the party's representative was not present at a hearing or inquiry relating to the proceedings; or

(c) the interests of justice so require.

[¹(1A) In determining whether it is just to set aside a decision on the ground set out in paragraph (1)(b), the adjudicating authority shall determine whether the party making the application gave notice that he wished an oral hearing to be held, and if that party did not give such notice the adjudicating authority shall not set the decision aside unless it is satisfied that the interests of justice manifestly so require.]

(2) An application under this regulation shall be made in accordance with regulation 3 and Schedule 2.

(3) Where an application to set aside a decision is entertained under paragraph (1), every party to the proceedings shall be sent a copy of the application and shall be afforded a reasonable opportunity of making representations on it before the application is determined.

(4) Notice in writing of a determination on an application to set aside a decision shall be given to every party to the proceedings as soon as may be practicable and the notice shall contain a statement giving the reasons for the determination.

(5) For the purposes of determining under these Regulations an application to set aside a decision there shall be disregarded regulation 1(3)(b) and any provision in any enactment or instrument to the effect that any notice or other document required or authorised to be given or sent to any person shall be deemed to have been given or sent if it was sent by post to that person's last known or notified address.

AMENDMENT

1. Social Security (Adjudication) and Child Support Amendment (No. 2) Regulations 1996 (S.I. 1996 No. 2450), reg. 9 (October 21, 1996).

DEFINITIONS

"adjudicating authority"—see reg. 1(2).
"party to the proceedings"—*ibid.*

GENERAL NOTE

Paragraphs (1) and (1A)

Grounds for setting aside

An application to have a decision set aside may be made by any party to the proceedings (see notes to reg. 1(2)). Under reg. 3(5) the application must specify the grounds on which it is made, and so presumably must refer in some way to at least one of conditions (a), (b) or (c). The validity of para. (c) is accepted in *R(U) 3/89*. Under (a) the deeming provisions of reg. 1(3) and the Interpretation Act 1978 do not apply (para. (5)), so the question is whether documents did actually arrive at the right time. The standard case is where notice of a hearing was never received by the claimant or a representative, but the non-receipt of a letter or document from the claimant to the tribunal would equally satisfy (a). Under (b) absence from a hearing for whatever reason will do, except where the claimant has not requested an oral hearing (para. (1A)). In that case there can be a setting aside on ground (b) only if the interests of justice manifestly so require. In cases under ground (b) where an oral hearing was requested, *R(S) 12/81* decides that when a claimant has not attended the hearing it is irrelevant what evidence he might have given or whether it would have been likely to affect the decision. The question is whether the circumstances of his absence make it just to set the decision aside. For the overriding question in all cases is that of justice.

Condition (c) cannot take away from any rights given by (a) and (b), but allows any deserving case to be considered. (Note President's Circular No. 6, p. 1454.) However, it can only apply to procedural matters, otherwise the right of appeal to the Commissioner and the finality of SSAT decisions, subject to appeal or review, would be undermined (but see *CM 278/1993*). In *R(S) 3/89* it is said (in relation to the equivalent provision in the Social Security Commissioners Procedure Regulations) that the provision is confined to cases where there have been obvious mistakes or procedural mishaps. In *R(U) 3/89* the Commissioner confines its scope to procedural irregularities, not least because the legislation authorising the making of this regulation deals only with procedure. In *R(SB) 4/90* the Commissioner who decided *R(S) 3/89* holds that he was wrong to mention obvious mistakes, and that the more limited approach of *R(U) 3/89* is right. In *R(SB) 4/90* a crucial regulation was not mentioned in an AO's submission to the "original" SSAT and was ignored in their decision. The AO applied for the decision to be set aside and another SSAT did so under para.(c). A subsequent SSAT heard the appeal and correctly decided against the claimant. On appeal, the Commissioner held that the subsequent SSAT's decision was a nullity because it was purporting to decide a question which had already been decided by the original SSAT, whose decision had not been validly set aside. The setting aside SSAT had no power to act as they did and therefore its determination was declared to be a nullity. Although there is no direct appeal from a determination to set aside (reg. 11(3)) this does not prevent the Commissioner from considering whether the subsequent SSAT had jurisdiction. *R(SB) 1/92* confirms that a failure by a party to produce sufficient evidence to satisfy a SSAT is not a procedural irregularity. SSAT 1 decided that an alleged overpayment was not recoverable, despite written statements from two witnesses that the claimant's wife was known to them as working under another name. The AO applied to have the decision set aside "in the interests of natural justice" (!) to enable the two witnesses to give oral evidence to a new SSAT. SSAT 2 did set aside the first decision and SSAT 3 decided the appeal against the claimant. The Commissioner holds that SSAT 3 had no jurisdiction to hear the appeal since SSAT 1's decision had not validly been set aside.

In *Ward v. SSAT* 1995 S.C.L.R. 1134 the AO had requested a postponement of the hearing as no presenting officer was available but this had been refused. The SSAT allowed the appeal. The record of proceedings simply noted the fact that no presenting officer was present. The AO applied for the decision to be set aside on the grounds that there was no evidence that the SSAT had considered whether it was appropriate to proceed with the hearing in the absence of a presenting officer and, in the AO's opinion, the SSAT would have reached a different decision if the presenting officer had been there. SSAT 2 set aside the decision, giving their reasons as, "The AO's representative was not present. Interests of justice to set aside for procedural irregularity". Lord Coulsfield granted the claimant's application for judicial review. The power to set aside was not to be used as a substitute for an appeal and its exercise was confined to cases where there has been a readily identifiable error or mishap (see *R(U) 3/89*, *R(S) 3/89* and *CI 79/1990*). There was no positive evidence that SSAT 1 had failed to consider the effect of the absence of the presenting officer and the argument that SSAT 1 had a duty to consider this which it had failed to carry out was one that could only properly be considered on an appeal. As regards the second part of SSAT 2's reasoning, the presenting officer's absence was not a procedural irregularity in itself. The presenting officer's role was not that of a party adverse to the claimant but more an *amicus curiae* (see Diplock L.J. in *R. v. Deputy Industrial Injuries Commissioner, ex p. Moore* [1965] 1 Q.B. 456). Even if the claimant had requested the officer's presence (as in *CSB 582/1987*) or there was a possibility that the tribunal had not had some essential information due to the absence of a presenting officer, the proper course would have been that of appeal, not setting aside. Although the basis of Lord Coulsfield's decision could be criticised in view of the terms of para. (1)(b), the important point of principle is that reg. 10 should only by used in cases of real procedural irregularity, as also stressed by the Tribunal of Commissioners in *CI 79/1990*.

Power to examine validity of intervening determinations and decisions

In *R(SB) 4/90* and *R(SB) 1/92*, the determination of the invalidity of the setting aside determination was made by a Commissioner. *R(G) 2/93* holds that in similar circumstances SSAT 3 would have jurisdiction even though SSAT 2 had no power to set aside the decision of SSAT 1. This was because the Commissioner, as confirmed by the House of Lords in *Foster v. Chief Adjudication Officer* [1993] A.C. 754; [1993] 1 All E.R. 705, has no judicial review powers to make declarations of invalidity. It is true that in *R(SB) 4/90* the Commissioner did purport to declare the decision of SSAT 2 (which was not under appeal to him) a nullity, but that may not have been necessary to his decision. The Commissioner in *R(G) 2/93* does not deal with *R(SB) 1/92* or *CI 78/1990* (see below), where the point is made that in order to determine whether SSAT 3 has jurisdiction it may be necessary incidentally to determine that SSAT 2 did not have jurisdiction. This can be done without purporting to declare as a general matter that the decision of SSAT 2 was a nullity. However, the existence of so many conflicting decisions meant that the central question could not be regarded as finally resolved. But now see *CI 79/1990* below.

If it is concluded that a Commissioner may set aside a decision by SSAT 3 in these circumstances, the question arises of what a tribunal in the position of SSAT 3 should do. *CI 78/1990* decides that if a setting aside determination is plainly invalid on its face, a subsequent tribunal may determine that it has no jurisdiction to hear the appeal. *R(SB) 1/92* accepts this principle. In general, an intervening setting aside determination should be accepted at face value by SSAT 3 and any detailed investigation should be left to the Commissioner. A SSAT requires a very clear case to impugn a determination of a body of equal status. However, there remains some difference of opinion about what amounts to plain invalidity on the face of a setting aside determination. On the facts of *R(SB) 1/92*, the Commissioner considered that SSAT 2's determination was not plainly invalid on its face, so that SSAT 3 was right to hear the appeal. He gives as examples of plain invalidity, SSAT 2 not being properly constituted or notice of the application to set aside not having been given to all parties. In *CI 78/1990* the defect in the SSAT's proceedings was of a similar kind to that in *R(SB) 1/92*, but the Commissioner did not specifically say that the invalidity was not plain. It is clearly not satisfactory if SSAT 3 has to hear an appeal after a plainly defective setting aside by SSAT 2 and leave the claimant to the long delays and inconvenience of a further appeal to the Commissioner. Nor can SSAT 3 avoid impugning a determination of a body of equivalent status. If it accepts a plainly defective setting aside by SSAT 2, it has impugned a perfectly valid decision by SSAT 1.

The issue of the extent of the power of SSATs and Commissioners to examine the validity of intervening decisions and determinations has now been comprehensively examined by a Tribunal of Commissioners in *CI 79/1990*. The facts were that the claimant's appeal was dismissed by SSAT 1. He applied for the decision to be set aside, but SSAT 2 refused that application. He then applied for leave to appeal. In the light of information in that application, the chairman (who had chaired both SSAT 1 and 2) decided that the application to set aside should be reconsidered. SSAT 3 (with an entirely different membership) then set aside the decision of SSAT 1 and SSAT 4 allowed the claimant's appeal. The AO appealed, contending that SSAT 4 was not entitled to hear the appeal, since SSAT 2 had refused the application to set aside and there was no provision for this to be reversed.

The central question was whether the Tribunal of Commissioners had to accept that as a result of SSAT 3's determination SSAT 1's decision had ceased to exist, or could they in the course of establishing whether SSAT 4 had jurisdiction, examine whether SSAT 3's determination was effective to set aside SSAT 1's decision?

The Tribunal agreed with *R(G) 2/93* to the extent that it was clear (see *Foster*) that Commissioners do not have power to make declarations as to the validity of decisions or determinations not under appeal to them. Thus para. 17 of *R(SB) 4/90* was too wide. However, that did not mean that SSATs and Commissioners, in the course of determining whether an appeal tribunal had jurisdiction to hear an appeal, could not determine whether an intervening appeal tribunal's setting aside determination had been effective or not. To that extent the Tribunal agreed with *R(SB) 4/90*, *CI 78/1990* and *R(SB) 1/92*. But Commissioners and appeal tribunals could only consider whether the earlier appeal tribunal had jurisdiction in the narrow sense (see Lord Reid in *Anisminic v. Foreign Compensation Commission* [1967] 2 A.C. 147 at p. 171) of being able to enter into consideration of the matter before it. If the intervening appeal tribunal had made an error *within* jurisdiction, *e.g.* set aside a decision on grounds outside para. (1), that did not allow the validity of its decision or determination to be examined. Thus *R(SB) 4/90*, *CI 78/1990* and *R(SB) 1/92* were wrong in adopting a wider approach.

The essential elements to establish jurisdiction in a setting aside case were: a valid application by a prescribed person which had not already been determined (the Tribunal did not decide the question of whether it was possible to reconsider an application to set aside) and a properly constituted appeal tribunal which made the determination. (*Note*: reg. 22(2) does not apply to setting aside determinations). Failure to send a copy of the application to set aside to other parties to the proceedings (as required by para. (3)) did not deprive the appeal tribunal of jurisdiction (although this was a mandatory requirement, see the note to para. (3)).

Applying this to the circumstances in this case, the result was that SSAT 1's decision and SSAT 2's determination were made within jurisdiction; SSAT 3's determination was made without jurisdiction because the claimant's application to set aside had already been determined by SSAT 2 acting within jurisdiction. (The claimant's application for leave to appeal was not a request for reconsideration of his setting aside application, and the chairman had no authority to treat it as such or reconsider the determination of SSAT 2 himself.) Therefore SSAT 4 had no jurisdiction. SSAT 4 should have investigated whether it had jurisdiction. Although SSAT 4's decision was invalid it had sufficient legal existence to be susceptible to appeal (*Calvin v. Carr* [1980] A.C. 574, applied in para. 6 of *R(S) 13/81*). The consequence was that the claimant's application for leave to appeal against the decision of SSAT 1 remained outstanding and should be dealt with as quickly as possible.

CI 79/1990 is followed in *CIS 373/1994*. See also *CSI 57/1993* which applies *CI 79/1990* to a correction outside a tribunal's powers under reg. 9.

CI 78/1990 also decides that only "decisions" can be set aside under what is now reg. 10. Since a setting aside ruling, although made by the whole tribunal, is a "determination," reg. 10 cannot be used to set aside a setting aside determination. There is a clear distinction in the language within reg. 10, which does not necessarily hold in other contexts. It may be possible for a tribunal to reconsider a refusal to set aside (by analogy with *CIS 93/1992*, see the notes to reg. 3(4)) if further information is provided. This question was referred to, but not decided by, the Tribunal of Commissioners in *CI 79/1990*.

Who may set aside

The setting aside is to be done by the adjudicating authority which gave the original decision, or one of like status (but note President's Circular No. 6 if the setting aside application is based on complaints about the conduct of the tribunal, an assessor or a member of the ITS staff). So in the case of a SSAT, this requires all three members of the tribunal, not just the chairman (*R(G) 1/81*). But now see President's Circular No. 14 (p. 1461). There is no restriction on the circumstances in which another, rather than the original, authority may set aside the decision. Since an "adjudicating authority" includes an AO, this procedure may, in exceptional circumstances, provide a useful alternative to a review of the AO's decision. But the limitation to procedural irregularities must be carefully observed.

In some cases, an oral hearing of the application may be made necessary by the principles of natural justice (*CU 270/1986*), but there is no general right to such a hearing (*CSB 172/1990*).

An AO may apply to have a SSAT decision set aside although the claimant objects (*R(SB) 31/85*).

Paragraph (2)

Under para. 11 of Sched. 2 an application to have a decision set aside must be made within three months beginning with the date on which notice of the decision was given to the applicant. See reg. 1(3) for calculating the limit. The time limit may be extended for special reasons under reg. 3(3). The application must state grounds (reg. 3(5)) and further particulars can be required (reg. 3(6)).

Paragraph (3)

Every person interested in the decision must be sent a copy of the application. This particularly includes AOs in the case of a SSAT decision. The importance of their representations was stressed in *R(S) 12/81*. The former practice of IOs in disclaiming their opportunity to make representations was disapproved of. It also appears from *R(S) 12/81* that although the word "representations" suggests something written, an oral hearing may be appropriate. The Commissioners there disapproved of the method of informal postal circulation used.

In *CS 453/1993* the Commissioner decides that the equivalent provision in the Social Security Commissioners Procedure Regulations 1987 (reg. 25(3)) did not require him to obtain the Secretary of State's representation on an application to set aside a refusal of leave to appeal. In that case the Secretary of State had had no previous involvement and the application to set aside was without merit. But the Tribunal of Commissioners in *CI 79/1990* holds that para. (3) is mandatory and that it would be an error of law for an appeal tribunal to determine a setting aside application without being satisfied that a copy of the application had been sent to all parties. Moreover, although it was not a statutory requirement, the Tribunal considered that the principles of natural justice required that where another party did make representations a copy had to be sent to the applicant who had to be given an opportunity to reply.

Paragraph (4)

Notice of the determination (*N.B.* it is not a "decision") with reasons is to be given. There is no appeal from the determination (reg. 11(3)), but a party could apply for judicial review (*Bland v. CSBO* [1983] 1 All E. R. 537, *R(SB) 12/83*) and the validity (but not the merits) of the determination can be raised in a subsequent SSAT hearing (see *R(SB) 4/90*, *R(SB) 1/92*, *CI 78/1990* and *CI 79/1990*, discussed in the note to para. (1)).

Paragraph (5)
Excludes the operation of reg. 1(3) and s.7 of the Interpretation Act 1978.

Provisions common to regulations 9 and 10

11.—(1) In regulations 9 and 10 "adjudicating authority" includes the Secretary of State.

(2) In calculating any time specified in Schedule 2 there shall be disregarded any day falling before the day on which notice was given of a correction of a decision or the record thereof pursuant to regulation 9 or on which notice is given of a determination that a decision shall not be set aside following an application made under regulation 10, as the case may be.

(3) There shall be no appeal against a correction made under regulation 9 or a refusal to make such a correction or against a determination given under regulation 10.

(4) Nothing in this Part shall be construed as derogating from any power to correct errors or set aside decisions which is exercisable apart from these Regulations.

GENERAL NOTE

Most of these provisions are mentioned at the appropriate point in the notes to regs. 9 and 10. The time for appealing or applying for leave to appeal runs from the date of notice of a correction or that a decision is not to be set aside (para. (2)).

PART III

ADJUDICATING AUTHORITIES

SECTION B—ADJUDICATION OFFICERS

Notification of decisions

18.—(1) Subject to paragraph (2) and regulation 55, the decision of an adjudication officer on any claim or question and the reasons for it shall be notified in writing to the claimant who shall at the same time be informed—

(a) in the case of a decision of an adjudication officer—
    (i) under section 21 of the Administration Act relating to attendance allowance, disability living allowance or disability working allowance, or
    (ii) on a review under section 30(2) or (4) or section 35 of the Administration Act,
of his right to a review under section 30(1) of that Act;

(b) in the case of a decision of an adjudication officer under section 30(1) of that Act, of his right of appeal—
    (i) to a disability appeal tribunal where the appeal relates to the determination of a disability question, and
    (ii) to an appeal tribunal in any other case;

(c) in all other cases, of his right of appeal to an appeal tribunal under section 22 of that Act.

(2) Paragraph (1) does not apply in relation to a decision (other than a decision given on review) awarding benefit for a period which begins immediately after a period in respect of which the claimant had been awarded benefit of the same kind and at the same rate as that awarded by the first-mentioned decision.

"adjudication officer"—see reg. 1(2).
"appeal tribunal"—*ibid.*
"disability appeal tribunal"—*ibid.*
"disability question"—*ibid.*
"claimant"—*ibid.*

GENERAL NOTE

For the purposes of this book, reg. 18 applies to decisions on family credit, disability working allowance and social fund maternity, funeral and cold weather payments. Income support and JSA decisions are dealt with by reg. 55.

For all cases within reg. 18, there is an obligation under para. (1) on the AO to notify the claimant of the precise terms of any decision and the reasons for it. Then for family credit and social fund cases, the right of appeal direct to a SSAT must be mentioned under para. (1)(c). Since for disability working allowance a claimant must first apply for a review of the AO's initial decision, before having the right of appeal to a SSAT or DAT against the AO's decision given on review, the provisions of para. (1)(a) and (b) are more complex. If a disability question arises, whether alone or along with other issues, the appeal must be to a DAT (Administration Act, s.33(1) (1975 Act, s.100D(1)) and reg. 27. Only if no disability question arises does the appeal go to a SSAT.

SECTION C—APPEAL TRIBUNALS

Oral hearing of appeals and references

22.—[¹(1) Where an appeal or reference is made to an appeal tribunal, the clerk to the tribunal shall direct every party to the proceedings to notify him if that party wishes an oral hearing of that appeal or reference to be held.

(1A) A notification under paragraph (1) shall be in writing and shall be made within 10 days of receipt of the direction from the clerk to the tribunal or within such other period as the clerk to the tribunal or the chairman of the tribunal may direct.

(1B) Where the clerk to the tribunal receives notification in accordance with paragraph (1A) the appeal tribunal shall hold an oral hearing.

(1C) The chairman of an appeal tribunal may of his own motion require an oral hearing to be held if he is satisfied that such a hearing is necessary to enable the tribunal to reach a decision.]

(2) Any case may with the consent of the claimant or his representative, but not otherwise, be proceeded with in the absence of any one member other than the chairman.

(3) Where an oral hearing is adjourned and at the hearing after the adjournment the tribunal is differently constituted, otherwise than through the operation on that occasion of paragraph (2), the proceedings at that hearing shall by by way of a complete rehearing of the case.

(4) Paragraphs (3) and (4) of regulation 21 apply to an appeal tribunal as they apply to an adjudication officer, except that a tribunal shall, instead of referring a question in accordance with paragraph (3)(a) of that regulation, direct it to be so referred by an adjudication officer.

AMENDMENT

1. Social Security (Adjudication) and Child Support Amendment (No. 2) Regulations 1996 (S.I. 1996 No. 2450), reg. 10 (October 21, 1996).

DEFINITIONS

"adjudication officer"—see reg. 1(2).
"appeal tribunal"—*ibid.*

"clerk to the tribunal"—*ibid.*
"claimant"—*ibid.*

GENERAL NOTE

Paragraph (1) to (1C)

These controversial provisions introduce the possibility of "paper determinations". In the past around 30% of appellants have not attended the oral hearing of their appeal. The success rate of such appellants has also been lower than that of those who do attend, particularly if they are represented. There will be no need to give notice of when the determination is to take place, as reg. 4 only applies to oral hearings. The new system therefore offers administrative flexibility and savings.

Para. (1) requires the clerk to a tribunal to direct every party to an appeal or a reference to give notification if that party wants there to be an oral hearing. Only if there is notification from at least one party in accordance with para. (1A) must there be an oral hearing (para. (1B)). Para. (1A) requires the notification to be made in writing within 10 days of receipt of the clerk's direction. That limit can be altered, apparently up or down, by a clerk or a tribunal chairman (see below). The fact that a chairman can direct that the period be other than 10 days seems to show that such an extension can be made after a notification is received. Finally, under para. (1C) a chairman may require an oral hearing when that is necessary to enable the tribunal to reach a decision.

That is a very broad framework and a great deal will depend on how these provisions are operated in practice. For instance, para. (1) does not define at what stage in the proceedings the clerk is to send the direction requiring notification. Some appellants, especially those who are represented by an advice agency of some kind, may well state in the appeal itself that an oral hearing is required. If so, there is no point in going through the process under paras. (1) and (1A), which could then be regarded as merely directory. If no such statement is made, it would be unfair to send the direction immediately on receipt of the appeal, because at that stage the claimant cannot make a sensible judgment about whether an oral hearing is needed. That can only be done after the Benefits Agency has completed its review process, the AO has prepared the written submission to the tribunal and the claimant knows the case against him. He can then think about whether he wishes to obtain or present written evidence of his own and whether he wishes there to be an oral hearing. The listing procedures in operation since April 1999 (see the note to reg. 4(2)) seem to have taken this into account.

The information given to claimants about the options will be very important. The documents sent about hearings in the recent past have been encouraging towards attendance, stressing that the tribunal wants to hear the claimant's side of their case in their own words. That indeed is at the heart of the tribunal system: a recognition that many claimants are more comfortable in explaining things face-to-face (even though a tribunal hearing is still often seen as an ordeal) and that the peculiarities and difficulties of individual circumstances often do not fit the standard questions and boxes of official forms. The tribunal hearing may be the first time that anyone with any real knowledge of the legal position has talked to the claimant. It can of course be said that the new provisions allow claimants who see those advantages to claim them as of right. But everything will depend on how matters are presented when the choice has to be made. There is evidence that many claimants misunderstand the nature of the AO's written submission and think that it is a preliminary judgment against them. Great sensitivity will have to be shown by ITS in implementing the changes if one of the central strengths of the tribunal system (which after all is there to protect the interests of claimants) is not to be undermined.

The 10-day limit under para. (1A) will be difficult to enforce. It runs from the date of receipt of the direction by the party to the proceedings. The deeming rules in reg. 1(2) and in s.7 of the Interpretation Act 1978 about treating notices as sent on the date of posting do not seem to apply. Clerks or chairmen might be well-advised to define the period for reply under para. (1A) in terms of a period running from the date of sending the direction. The GAPS 11/97 letter does in fact give 14 days from the date the letter is sent. For further details of how the listing procedure is being operated in practice, see the notes to reg. 4(2).

The power under para. (1C) for a chairman to order an oral hearing may be able to make up for the strict limits of the other provisions. The power may be exercised at any time. Thus an order could be made as a preliminary matter or at a paper determination, if issues emerge which require an oral hearing. It must be remembered that there will be no presenting officer representing the AO at a paper determination and the tribunal will not be able to examine the claimant's DSS file. It seems to follow that if at any time up to the making of a paper determination a claimant makes a request for an oral hearing of the appeal, that request should be put to a chairman for consideration. See *CIB 3899/1997* in which the Commissioner states that if a substantial new point emerges at a paper hearing the case will cease to be suitable for such a hearing. The parties should at least be given the opportunity of dealing with the point in written submissions and of requesting an oral hearing in the changed circumstances.

There is no longer any express exception for the operation of s.29 of the Administration Act on the lapsing of appeals if a review by an AO gives the claimant everything which could have been obtained in the appeal. But if the appeal has lapsed under s.29, and at least if there is no dispute by the claimant, there is nothing on which a tribunal can make any kind of determination.

If the claimant dies after lodging an appeal, a SSAT cannot hear the appeal unless there is a personal representative appointed under a grant of probate or letters of administration or an appointee appointed by the Secretary of State under reg. 30 of the Claims and Payments Regulations (*R(SB) 8/88*). Once such an appointment is made, it has retrospective effect and the appeal can continue (*R(SB) 5/90, R(A) 1/92* and *CIS 379/1992*). The same applies if the claimant dies before an AO makes a decision on the claim (*CIS 379/1992*). See also the notes to reg. 33 of the Claims and Payments Regulations.

Paragraph (2)

A hearing may proceed in the absence of one member of the SSAT, other than the chairman, only with the consent of the claimant. Other parties, including the AO, have no say in the matter. But the claimant's representative is given express power to consent on his behalf (reg. 2(1)(b)). Mere absence of objection will not do. If the claimant or a representative attends the hearing there will be no problem. If the claimant has returned the enquiry form, there is a question on it asking "If one of the members cannot attend for any reason. . . are you still willing to have your appeal heard by two people . . .?" If the claimant does not send the enquiry form back having answered "Yes" to this question and he does not have an authorised representative at the hearing the SSAT hearing cannot proceed. But now see the amendments to s.41 of the Administration Act, introduced by para. 1 of Sched. 6 to the Social Security Act 1998 with effect from May 21, 1998. See President's Circular No. 14 on these changes in relation to SSATs.

Where a member is missing, the chairman has a casting vote (reg. 23(1)). The suggestion that unless this was explained to a claimant before his consent was given, a hearing might be in breach of natural justice was rejected in *CSB 389/1982*. But the Commissioner says that it is desirable that this explanation should be given before the final consent is obtained.

Paragraph (3)

The effect of this provision is that on an adjournment a SSAT cannot bind in any way the second tribunal, if its members are not exactly the same. The Tribunal of Commissioners in *R(U) 3/88* has settled some controversy on what a "complete rehearing" requires. The new SSAT is wholly unfettered by what happened at the previous hearing, so that the hearing starts afresh. Everything that requires to be established must be established, even if established before. But it is not compulsory that all oral evidence given at the previous hearing be repeated. The written record or part of it (*e.g.* a witness's statement) may be treated by the parties as an agreed statement of facts. If either party wishes a witness to be further examined, every effort should be made to secure the witness's attendance. Equally, it is open to either party to develop new points or produce new evidence. The excessively strict view of *CS 427/1984* is rejected. *CIS 740/1993* endorses the point in *R2/88 (IVB)* (a decision of a Northern Ireland Commissioner) that it should be recorded in the notes of evidence that a complete rehearing took place.

The difficulties involved in such a rehearing lead the Tribunal in *R(U) 3/88* to make a number of further suggestions. The first is that every effort should be made to avoid a change in the composition of the SSAT. In practice this will require a SSAT, on adjourning, to direct that the next hearing be before an identically constituted tribunal. In this case there need not be a complete rehearing. The second suggestion is that if the SSAT is not identically constituted then no member of the previous SSAT should sit on the new one. Otherwise there is a danger that one member has knowledge of evidence not shared by the other members. This suggestion seems not to have been adopted in practice. The danger is lessened if the nature of a rehearing is kept clearly in mind.

Paragraph (4)

Reg. 21 is about the reference of special questions in child benefit cases to the Secretary of State.

Decisions of appeal tribunals

23.—(1) The decision of the majority of the appeal tribunal shall be the decision of the tribunal but, where the tribunal consists of an even number, the chairman shall have a second or casting vote.

[²(2) Every decision of an appeal tribunal shall be recorded in summary by the chairman in such written form of decision notice as shall have been approved by the President, and such decision notice shall be signed by the chairman.

(3) As soon as may be practicable after a case has been decided by an appeal tribunal, a copy of the decision notice made in accordance with paragraph (2) shall be sent or given to every party to the proceedings who shall also be informed of—

(a) his right under paragraph (3C); and

(b) the conditions governing appeals to a Commissioner.

(3A) A statement of the reasons for the tribunal's decision and of its findings on questions of fact material thereto may be given—

(a) orally at the hearing; or

(b) in writing at such later date as the chairman may determine.

(3B) Where the statement referred to in paragraph (3A) is given orally, it shall be recorded in such medium as the chairman may determine.

(3C) A copy of the statement referred to in paragraph (3A) shall be supplied to the parties to the proceedings if requested by any of them within 21 days after the decision notice has been sent or given, and if the statement is one to which sub-paragraph (a) of that paragraph applies, that copy shall be supplied in such medium as the chairman may direct.

(3D) If a decision is not unanimous, the statement referred to in paragraph (3A) shall record that one of the members dissented and the reasons given by him for dissenting.]

[¹(4) A record of the proceedings at the hearing shall be made by the chairman in such medium as he may direct and preserved by the clerk to the tribunal for 18 months, and a copy of such record [². . .] shall be supplied to the parties if requested by any of them within that period.]

AMENDMENTS

1. Social Security (Adjudication) and Child Support Amendment Regulations 1996 (S.I. 1996 No. 182), reg. 2(3) (February 28, 1996).

2. Social Security (Adjudication) and Child Support Amendment (No. 2) Regulations 1996 (S.I. 1996 No. 2450), reg. 11 (October 21, 1996).

DEFINITIONS

"adjudication officer"—see reg. 1(2).

"appeal tribunal"—*ibid.*

"Commissioner"—*ibid.*

"party to the proceedings"—*ibid.*

GENERAL NOTE

Paragraph (1)

Normally a simple majority will suffice. The chairman's vote has no extra value unless a member is missing. The reasons for any dissent must be recorded (para. (2)(c)). The references to "the tribunal" emphasise that no other person should take any part in the decision or the deliberations leading up to it. The Commissioner in *R(SB) 13/83* stresses that the tribunal and the clerk should not do anything that would suggest to the claimant that the clerk was participating in the decision-making.

The SSAT seems not to have any express powers in income-related benefit cases. On general principle, and by analogy with the previous practice in non-means tested benefit cases, the SSAT must reach and express a decision on the matter under appeal, as the AO does initially. This will be particularly important where it differs from the AO's decision (*R(SB) 20/82*). It cannot simply say "appeal allowed" or something similar. But the decision does not need to be quantified in pounds and pence. This can be left to the AO, particularly in cases where complicated calculations etc., might be necessary, providing that it is made clear that in the event of any dispute the appeal can be restored to the tribunal for final determination (*R(SB) 16/83*). See the notes to para. (2)

below and the decisions referred to in the notes to s.23(1) of the Administration Act on the meaning of "decision". Although the SSAT no longer has the express power simply to confirm the AO's decision, and so ought to set out the decision in full, a decision in the old form might be acceptable providing that it was absolutely clear what decision was being confirmed (see *R(SB) 9/85*, especially on the situation where the AO's decision has been revised). *CS 99/1993* suggests that where a SSAT does not allow an appeal and the AO's decision is quite long, it is better for the tribunal to say simply "the appeal is dismissed", or "the AO's decision is confirmed", thereby preserving the terms of the original decision, rather than record an incomplete decision. In that case, although the SSAT's reasons made it clear that it recognised that it was dealing with a review decision, the decision recorded in box 3 on form AT3 did not do so.

Every decision must be recorded. *CSB 635/1982* confirms that if a specific request is made for an adjournment the tribunal is bound to record its decision on that request. But *CS 1939/1995* suggests that while it is desirable for brief reasons for the refusal of an adjournment to be recorded, this is not obligatory, as para. (2) applies only to "decisions". Where a specific request has been made, a distinction between rulings preceding the decision and the decision itself seems artificial. It is implied here that the tribunal must make a decision on every matter in issue in the appeal or reference. In *R(SB) 6/81* the tribunal failed to record any conclusion at all on the claimant's appeal for clothes for himself, as opposed to his wife, and so breached this rule. *CIS 628/1992* decides that where the SSAT has failed to deal with all the issues arising on an appeal there is no decision within the meaning of s.23(1) of the Administration Act. The SSAT had purported to refer to an AO substantive matters going beyond questions of calculation or quantification. The Commissioner gives the following guidance to AOs and SSATs in this situation. The AO should not determine the outstanding issues, even with the consent of the claimant, but the appeal should be placed before the tribunal again. If it is not practicable to re-constitute the same tribunal, none of its members should sit on the tribunal for the resumed hearing. If the tribunal is not identically constituted, there must be a complete rehearing (within the guidelines given in para.7 of *R(U) 3/88*). If it is the same tribunal, evidence given at the earlier hearing need not be given again, but the tribunal will not be bound by any finding of fact or any conclusion reached at the previous hearing. If the SSAT is minded to differ from any finding of fact or conclusion it previously reached, it must ensure that the parties have a fair opportunity to deal with this. In *CIS 451/1992* the SSAT chose to deal with a preliminary point only and gave leave to appeal on that issue. The Commissioner refers to the House of Lords' criticism in *Tilling v. Whiteman* [1980] A.C. 1 of such a practice, and their Lordships' suggestion that it should be confined to cases where the facts are complicated and the legal issues short, or to exceptional cases.

There was a huge weight of authority that a SSAT should deal with the position from the date of claim down to the date of its decision (see the 1998 edition of this book for discussion of the decisions). But note that in relation to appeals brought on or after May 21, 1998, a tribunal will only be able to consider the position up to the date of the AO's decision (see the new subs. (8) inserted into s.22 of the Administration Act by para. 3 of Sched. 6 to the Social Security Act 1998). Thus a claimant will have to submit a fresh claim (or claims) as time elapses (and appeal as necessary), in order for any changes in his circumstances to be considered. See President's Circular No. 15 (p. 1462) which helpfully points out that this does not necessarily render irrelevant evidence which comes into existence after the AO's decision. A tribunal will still be able to take this into account if it throws further light on circumstances that did obtain at the time of the decision. And note that s.22(8) has no effect on the period of any award made by a tribunal hearing an appeal lodged on or after May 21, 1998. Any such award of income support or income-based JSA will normally be for an indefinite period (see reg. 17 of the Claims and Payments Regulations).

Paragraphs (2) and (3)

The obligation to complete the record of the SSAT's decision, either in summary form under para. (2) or a full statement of reasons, is on the chairman, rather than the tribunal as a whole. This would seem to allow a chairman to complete the record after the decisions have been made, in the absence of the other members. However, it must remain the chairman's duty to ensure that the record represents the corporate view of all three members (*CSSB 1/1982*, approved in *R(SB) 13/83*). It would be at least polite for a chairman to ask the other members' permission to complete the record in their absence.

The Commissioners have consistently held that it is only permissible for the record to be made by the clerk at the chairman's specific direction (*CSSB 1/1982*, approved in *R(SB) 13/83*; *CSB 226/1981*). While there is nothing in the regulations to prevent a chairman from asking a clerk for drafting suggestions, it is clear that such a practice would be frowned on and is now virtually unknown.

From October 1996 there has been an important distinction between the summary of the decision under para. (2), which must be provided to each party to the proceedings in every case (para. (3)), and the full statement of reasons and findings under para. (3A), which need only be given on request or as the chairman thinks fit. The particular significance of the distinction is that, following the amendment to reg. 24 of the Adjudication Regulations and reg. 4 of the Social Security Commissioners Procedure Regulations 1987 with effect from April 28, 1997, any application for leave to appeal from a tribunal's decision to the Commissioners must have annexed to it a copy of the full statement of the decision under para. (3A). See the notes to reg. 24 for that requirement, and the notes to paras. (3A) and (3C) below for the circumstances in which the full statement may or must be provided.

Para. 7 of President's Circular No. 2 (amended in November 1997) (p. 1449) explains that the President has approved a decision form for use in each form of tribunal. It is to be legibly handwritten by the chairman so that a carbon copy can be handed to the parties who are present at the end of the proceedings. The decision should be recorded in sufficient detail to enable immediate payment of benefit, if the claimant has been successful. The President advises that the summary of the reasons is intended to be a two or three sentence explanation of the reasons for success or failure.

When the summary is given to the parties who are present, or sent to those who are not, information must be given about the right to request a full statement of the decision under para. (3C) and about the conditions governing appeals to the Commissioner. It is to be hoped that information will also be given about the chairman's discretion under para. (3A)(b).

In the past the regulations did not say anything about the recording of the evidence presented. The Commissioners had held that it was obligatory for the chairman to make a note of evidence, either on form ITS/RP or on a document which would accompany it (see most recently *CSSB 212/1987*, confirming that failure to record a note of evidence, if there was any dispute, was an error of law; see further the note to para. (4) below). See para. 59 of the *Guide to procedure* (2nd ed.). If the clerk takes notes or lists documents produced and these are used by the tribunal, they should be available to the parties. It is wrong for the clerk's notes to be put forward as the chairman's, but it is proper for him to endorse them as in accordance with his recollection (*R(SB) 13/83*). But para. (4) now imposes a statutory duty on the chairman to keep a record of the proceedings and removes the requirement to automatic issue with the record of proceedings. See below.

Paragraphs (3A) to (3C)

These new provisions contain the conditions under which, from October 1996, a full statement of a decision, with findings of fact and reasons, is to be provided.

The interrelationship of the paragraphs raises some difficulties. Under para. (3A)(a), the chairman may give the full statement orally at the hearing, in which case it will be tape-recorded there and then (para. (3B) and President's Circular No. 2, para. 14). Under para. (3A)(b) the statement may be given in writing at such later date as the chairman determines. This clearly covers the situation where the chairman decides at the time that the tribunal makes its determination that a full decision is appropriate. However, it also covers the situation where at that time the chairman considers the summary under para. (2) to be sufficient, but later is requested to provide a full statement. A party to the proceedings may require the chairman to provide a copy of the full statement by making a request within 21 days after the summary decision was given or sent. However, if a request is made after the end of that 21-day period, it must be referred to the chairman, who has a discretion under para. (3A)(b) to give a full statement, a copy of which may be supplied to the parties to the proceedings. It is clearly implied that, if a chairman decides from the outset to give a full statement of the decision, a copy of the statement should be supplied to the parties no matter how long after the hearing the statement is produced. There is no reason why the result should be different if the chairman exercises the discretion to provide a full statement at a later date. The effect of para. (3C) is then seen to be that a chairman is bound to provide a full statement, a copy of which can be supplied to the parties, when the conditions of para. (3C) are met. But if those conditions are not met, the chairman must consider all the circumstances and exercise a judicial discretion whether or not to give a full statement under para. (3A)(b). It is still a matter of great concern that the 21-day period under para. (3C) is so short and that it cannot be extended however good any reasons for delay are, but the existence of the more general discretion will allow a chairman to do justice.

However, if a chairman's oral statement of reasons at the hearing has been recorded under para. (3A)(a) and (3B), it seems that a copy may only be provided under the conditions of para. (3C). That will have to be an accurate transcription of the oral statement. The chairman cannot have any discretion in those circumstances to provide any alternative statement of findings and reasons.

There will obviously be practical difficulties for chairmen if they are attempting some time after the hearing to produce a full statement of the findings of fact and reasons for the decision made by the tribunal as a body of three persons. They have been provided with judicial notebooks in which to keep a personal record of those present at the hearing and the essential elements of the reasoning behind the decision (see President's Circular No. 2, para. 17). The difficulty of reconstructing the reasoning after a lapse of time should not in itself justify declining to exercise the discretion to provide a full statement of the decision. It remains to be seen whether the policy adopted will have any overall advantage over the previous requirement for the provision of findings and reasons in all cases or an alternative of requiring chairmen to record a full statement in all cases, but only supplying copies to the parties on request. Note that there is no power for another chairman to write the full statement, although it might be possible for another member of the tribunal to do so (*CIS 2132/ 1998*). The Commissioner in *CIS 2132/1998* holds that the chairman's power to produce a full statement continues even after his appointment ceases and it was not acceptable for the regional chairman to produce a full statement in his stead.

It will be a matter for the chairman's discretion when the circumstances make it desirable for a full statement of findings and reasons to be given without any request from a party. If there are complicated issues of law or disputes of evidence to be resolved, that will point towards giving a full statement automatically. Such matters cannot confidently be dealt with after a lapse of time. It is suggested below, in the note to para. (3D), that if the decision is a majority one, that a full statement will almost always be necessary.

See *CIS 3299/1997* and *CIB 4189/1997*, *CSI 591/1998* and *CDLA 4278/1998* discussed in the note to reg. 24(1) for the position in relation to applications for leave to appeal to a Commissioner where there is no full statement. Note also *CIB 5065/1997* in which the Commissioner expresses the desirability of treating an application for a full statement as an application also for the record of proceedings (the same view is taken in *CIS 3299/1997* and *CIB 4189/1997*).

Where a full statement of the decision is given, the general standard of adequacy of findings of fact and reasons established by the authorities before October 1996 should continue to apply. In *R(SB) 6/81* and *R(SB) 11/82* the general test of the adequacy of reasons set out in *R(A) 1/72* was adopted. There is a requirement "to do more than only state the conclusion, and for the determining authority to state that on the evidence the authority is not satisfied that the statutory conditions are met, does no more than this . . . the minimum requirement must at least be that the claimant, looking at the decision should be able to discern on the face of it reasons why the evidence failed to satisfy the authority." This test was expressly adopted in, *e.g. R(SB) 6/81* and *R(SB) 11/82*, and implicitly adopted in many more decisions. Most of the specific instances of failure to state adequate reasons mentioned below are merely elaborations of the basic principle that both parties should be able to see why the decision was made.

It is now clear that a failure to state adequate reasons is in itself an error of law. Some decisions adopted the formulation in *Crake v. SBC, Butterworth v. SBC* [1982] 1 All E.R. 498 that there was an error of law only when the reasons were so inadequate as to indicate that the tribunal had failed to direct their minds to the proper questions or evidence. However, the Commissioners have later (particularly in *R(SB) 11/82* and *R(SB) 11/83*) distinguished *Crake* as resting on the pre-November 1980 law and held that any failure to give proper reasons is a denial of justice and thus an error of law. The Tribunal of Commissioners in *R(SB) 26/83* confirmed that a failure either to find material facts or to state adequate reasons is in itself an error of law.

Findings of fact

There are a great many Commissioners' decisions holding that tribunals have failed to make adequate findings of fact. For if the tribunal gets its legal approach wrong or does not get to grips with the legal complexities this is almost bound to be reflected in a failure to make findings on the right issues. A good example is *R(SB) 5/82*. But although there is agreement about the general test (see above) there is some difference of approach in applying that test. On the one side are decisions like *R(SB) 5/81*, indicating that a record of reasons or findings in the detail or style of a reasoned court judgment is not expected and that so long as findings of fact are clear, there need not be a detailed enumeration, and *CSB 568/1981*, where a statement that the statutory conditions were not met was in the circumstances enough to make it clear that the presenting officer's argument on the facts was accepted. On the other hand are decisions like *R(SB) 23/82* indicating that findings of primary facts must be made, not simply secondary findings reflecting the terms of regulations and *R(SB) 18/83* indicating that findings have to be made on all submissions put to the tribunal. So far as there is any trend it is probably towards requiring more detailed findings of fact, but perhaps the key is in this statement in *R(SB) 5/81*. "It is not possible to lay down a general rule for recording findings and reasons since that depends on the nature of the evidence and of the case before them [the tribunal]."

What is clear is that conclusions of fact must be recorded, not merely what was said about the issue *(R(SB) 42/84)*. The SSAT must state whether evidence recorded is accepted or rejected *(R(SB) 8/84*, para. 25). It seems to be accepted that this can be done by reference to other documents, providing the result is unambiguous and clear (see *Guide to procedure* (2nd ed.), para. 75). The Commissioners have frequently warned that a mere adoption of the facts as set out in box 5 of form AT2 (the AO's written submission to the SSAT) is unlikely to be sufficient. In *R(IS) 4/93* it is said that it is acceptable for a SSAT to make findings of fact solely by reference to the summary of facts on form AT2 only where what are incorporated are conclusions of fact, rather than mere contentions or statements of evidence, and where findings on all relevant matters are made. To record in box 2 of the form AT3 (findings of fact) "As Box 1" (*CIS 685/1992*), or "The basic facts are set out in the first paragraph of Box 1" (*R(IS) 9/94*), did not constitute findings of fact as it was not possible to tell what parts of the claimant's evidence and the presenting officer's submissions were accepted. The change introduced by para. (4) from February 28, 1996 may mean (at least for some tribunals) an increase in the length of the findings of fact, since it will no longer be possible to adopt the accepted evidence in the record of proceedings as findings of fact (unless of course the chairman directs that that record is sent out with the decision: see the note to para. (4)).

There is no rule that the claimant's evidence always has to be corroborated, *e.g.* by medical evidence *(R(S) 2/51*, applied in the instructive decision in *R(SB) 33/85*). CSB 615/1985* reminds tribunals that oral evidence is as admissible as documentary evidence and does not necessarily require corroboration.

Reasons for decisions

There is a rather similar difference of approach to the level of detail required in the giving of reasons. Many cases clearly fail the test by merely stating a conclusion. A good example is *R(SB) 31/83:* "The tribunal faced with conflicting evidence decided that the benefit officer had correctly applied Resources Regulation 4(1)." But in more complex cases, there is on the one hand the approach of *R(SB) 5/81* and *CSB 568/1981* that detailed reference to all regulations concerned is not necessary so long as it appears that the tribunal have not misinterpreted them. On the other hand is the approach of *CSB 26/1981* indicating that particularly in single payments cases regulations relied on should be identified down to paragraphs and sub-paragraphs, and *CSB 32/1981* indicating that a complicated inter-relationship between two sets of regulations had to be dealt with. Once again the key is probably that it all depends on the circumstances and that the test is whether the losing party is left in the dark as to why he lost *(R(A) 2/81*). A tribunal is not required to deal with every regulation which does not assist the claimant if those regulations were never in contention *(CSB 1291/1985)*. Where a specific contention put forward by or on behalf of the claimant is rejected, reasons should be given *(R(I) 18/61)*. That will often entail explaining why the claimant's evidence has been rejected or why some other evidence is preferred, if that is the case.

Under the regulations in operation before October 1996, there were sometimes problems in determining whether a sufficiently authenticated copy of the tribunal's decision and reasons existed. See the discussion in the note to reg. 23(3) in the 1996 edition, plus *CDLA 616/1995*, which explains that a document may be authenticated in other ways than by a signature. The problems only mattered if there was some dispute as to the authentic text. There should be no difficulty under the current form of reg. 23. The summary decision only exists in the handwritten form signed by the chairman. It is that which appears to constitute the tribunal's decision. There is no express requirement that the chairman's statement of findings and reasons be signed. Because of the circumstances in which it will be produced and a copy (which can include a fully typed-out copy with no manual signature: *CSB 830/1985*) supplied to the parties, there should be few if any circumstances in which the authenticity of the text is in doubt.

The time for applying for leave to appeal from a tribunal's decision runs from the date on which a full statement of the tribunal's decision is given or sent to the applicant (Sched. 2, paras. 7 and 9).

Paragraph (3D)

If a decision is not unanimous, the chairman's statement under para. (3A) must record that one member dissented from the majority decision and what reasons were given by that member for dissenting. It will therefore continue to be an error of law for a chairman to fail to do this. It would seem that the only realistic way for a chairman to carry out the duty is by determining at the time that the tribunal reaches its decision to give a full statement of findings and reasons.

Paragraph (4)

This now provides statutory confirmation of the chairman's duty to make a note of the proceedings (see above). The real change is that the notes of evidence will no longer be automatically sent out to the parties. They will be kept for 18 months (which period seems to run from the date of the hearing). If any party requests a copy within that time, then one will be sent to all the parties. Clearly a claimant (or an AO) wishing to pursue an appeal to the Commissioner will need to obtain a copy, so one effect of this rule could be to further increase the delays involved in such appeals.

However, there seems to be no reason why the request for the record of the proceedings to be supplied cannot be made at the hearing. See also the detailed guidance in President's Circular No. 2 (p. 1449). Note that para. 2 of the Circular points out that para. (4) does not prevent the chairman from deciding that a note of the proceedings should be issued in a particular case, *e.g.* where an appeal is likely. Another example would be where a hearing is adjourned after evidence has been given or submissions made, so that that record is available for the use of the tribunal and the parties at the next hearing.

In *CDLA 16902/1996* the Commissioner commented on the practice of not automatically sending out the tribunal's notes of evidence to the parties as follows:

"A proper record of the tribunal's proceedings, from which it can be seen that the claimant's case has been given its due consideration and from which the result can be understood, is a requirement of the general law that does not depend on the terms of subordinate legislation: *cf. R(A) 1/72.* Save perhaps where the whole case depends on a simple point of law and no facts are in issue, this requiremnt is not met without a proper record of the eivdence taken, from which it can be seen how the tribunal's findings and conclusions are related to what was placed before them: *R(SB) 8/84* para. 25, *CSSB 212/87* para. 3''.

In addition see *CIS 12032/1996* which also confirms that lack of an adequate record will be an error of law. *CIB 3013/1997* and *CDLA 4110/1997* both hold that failure to provide a *legible* record of the tribunal's proceedings will also be an error of law. Note also *CDLA 1389/1997.*

Application for leave to appeal to a Commissioner from an appeal tribunal

24.—[[1](1) Subject to the following provisions of this regulation, an application to the chairman of an appeal tribunal for leave to appeal to a Commissioner from a decision of an appeal tribunal shall—

(a) be made in accordance with regulation 3 and Schedule 2; and

(b) have annexed to it a copy of the full statement of the tribunal's decision.]

(2) Where an application in writing for leave to appeal is made by an adjudication officer the clerk to the tribunal shall, as soon as may be practicable, send a copy of the application to every other party to the proceedings.

(3) The decision of the chairman on an application for leave to appeal [[1]. . .] shall be recorded in writing and a copy shall be sent to every party to the proceedings.

(4) Where in any case it is impracticable, or it would be likely to cause undue delay for an application for leave to appeal against a decision of an appeal tribunal to be determined by the person who was the chairman of that tribunal, that application shall be determined by any other person qualified under section 41(4) of the Administration Act to act as a chairman of appeal tribunals.

AMENDMENT

1. Social Security (Adjudication) and Commissioners Procedure and Child Support Commissioners (Procedure) Amendment Regulations 1997 (S.I. 1997 No. 955), reg. 3 (April 28, 1997).

DEFINITIONS

"adjudication officer"—see reg. 1(2).
"appeal tribunal"—*ibid.*
"clerk to the tribunal"—*ibid.*
"Commissioner"—*ibid.*
"full statement of the tribunal's decision"—*ibid.*
"party to the proceedings"—*ibid.*

GENERAL NOTE

Paragraph (1)
Under s.23(9) of the Administration Act (1975 Act, s.101(5A)) an appeal lies from SSATs only with the leave of the chairman or a Commissioner, regardless of the nature of the decision. An application can no longer be made orally at the tribunal hearing after the decision has been

announced. In accordance with reg. 3 and Sched. 2 it must be in writing and be delivered to the office of the tribunal clerk. That must be done within the specified time, *i.e.* three months beginning with the date on which a copy of the full statement of the tribunal's decision under reg. 23(3A) is given or sent to the applicant. There is the additional condition in para. (1)(b) that the application must have annexed to it a copy of the full statement. If that condition did not exist, it might have been argued that in any case a valid application could not be made before the beginning of the specified time. However, the specified time might just set the end date within which an application can be made. The additional condition appears to make it a mandatory requirement that a full statement of the tribunal's findings and reasons should have been provided. This would be a serious impediment to the right to appeal in cases where the chairman does not provide a statement without a request being made if parties are restricted to 21 days from the giving of the summary decision notice under reg. 23(2). There would have been a drastic reduction in the time-limit for applying for leave to appeal by the back-door. However, it is shown in the notes to reg. 23(3) to (3C) that a chairman may be requested outside the 21-day limit to provide a full statement of the tribunal's decision and that the chairman must then exercise a judicial discretion whether or not to provide a full statement. If the chairman does so, the time for applying for leave to appeal runs from the date that it is given or sent to the applicant. Thus, the result of the amendments has been to open up the possibility of an application for leave to appeal being made to a chairman much longer after the date of the tribunal decision.

There is no appeal from a chairman's refusal of leave to appeal (*Bland v. CSBO* [1993] 1 All E.R. 537, *R(SB) 12/83*), but in this case the disappointed party may apply to the Commissioner for leave to appeal under s.23(9)(b) of the Administration Act (1975 Act, s.101(5A)(b)). This is now to be done within 1 month (previously 42 days) Commissioners (Procedure) Regulations 1999, reg. 9(2)). *CIS 550/1993* holds that in computing the time limit, the day of notification of the refusal of leave is not to be counted. The same principle applies to reg. 13(1) of the Commissioners (Procedure) Regulations, which requires notice of appeal to be served within 1 month of the notification of grant of leave. If the time limit for applying to the chairman is missed a party may still go straight to a Commissioner with his application, which may be accepted for special reasons. It is a condition of making an application to the Commissioner that a copy of the full statement of the tribunal's decision is annexed to the application (Commissioners (Procedure) Regulations, reg. 10(2)).

In *CIS 3299/1997* and *CIB 4189/1997* the Commissioner considers the position under the 1987 Commissioners Procedure Regulations where no full statement has been obtained. He holds that in such a case a chairman of a SSAT has no jurisdiction to consider an application for leave to appeal to a Commissioner. This was because the lack of a full statement meant that the specified time for appealing (see para. 7 of Sched. 2) had never started to run. But a Commissioner could consider an application under reg. 3(2) of the 1987 Commissioners' Procedure Regulations (failure to apply to chairman for leave within specified time). There was nothing in reg. 3(2) to suggest that it was only applicable in the case of late applications and it therefore enabled the institution of appeals, notwithstanding that the period for appealing had not in fact commenced. (The Commissioner clearly considered that the procedural requirement in reg. 4(1) of the 1987 Commissioners Procedure Regulations for a copy of the full statement to be annexed to the leave application could be waived). However, the Commissioner acknowledged that, in the absence of a full statement, the scope for finding that the tribunal's decision was erroneous in law would be constrained. The Commissioner also considered whether an application for leave to appeal should be taken to imply a request for a full statement of the tribunal's decision if one had not already been issued. He concludes that it would certainly be preferable if all applications for leave were treated as requests for full statements. Moreover, a request for a full statement should also be treated as a request for a copy of the record of proceedings (the same view is expressed in *CIB 5065/1997*).

This decision is not followed in *CSI 591/1998*. In that case the AO had applied for a full statement but it had not been forthcoming. The Commissioner states that as the full statement had not been issued the time for applying for leave to appeal had not started to run. He disagreed that reg. 3(2) of the 1987 Commissioners' Procedure Regulations permitted an application for leave to appeal to the Commissioner in these circumstances. In his view reg. 3(2) clearly implied that there had to have been a lost opportunity through lateness to apply to a chairman for leave to appeal. Following this decision the Commissioner who decided *CIS 3299/1997* and *CIB 4189/1997* has again considered this issue. In *CDLA 4278/1998* he states that he agrees with *CSI 591/1998* that there could not be a failure to apply to a chairman for leave to appeal within the specified period when it was still possible to make an application within that period. Thus when there was an existing request for a full statement that had not been rejected the applicant had to pursue that request and could not abandon it. In the light of *CSI 591/1998* he considered that in all but exceptional cases a claimant should apply to a chairman for a full statement before applying to a Commissioner for leave to appeal, even if the request was out of time. But that situation was to be distinguished from a case where a request for a full statement had been refused. In this case ITS had lost the claimant's file and it was clear that no full statement would be forthcoming.

Note that these decisions will not apply to reg. 9 of the 1999 Commissioners (Procedure) Regulations.

In *R(S) 4/82* a Tribunal of Commissioners holds that the chairman's discretion whether or not to grant leave is unfettered, providing that he exercises it in a judicial manner. But they draw attention to the object of the legislation (in NILT cases then only requiring leave if the tribunal had been unanimous) to restrict appeals to those which are neither hopeless nor frivolous and raise a serious issue. If the conduct of the tribunal proceedings is seriously in question, leave should he given. But if the complaint is in general terms only, leave should be refused. There is alwavs another bite of the cherry before the Commissioner. See further the notes to s.23(9) of the Administration Act.

Usually, the application goes to the person who chaired the SSAT, but there is provision under para. (4) for other chairmen to deal with it.

Paragraph (2)

Para. (2) requires the clerk to a tribunal to send a copy of an application for leave to appeal by an AO to every other party to the proceedings. *CDLA 12125/1996* decides that this requirement is merely directory, not mandatory. The clerk's failure to comply with the same requirement in reg. 32(2) did not invalidate the chairman's grant of leave or the subsequent appeal. It was held that the legislative intention was that, if the requirement is not carried out, the application should remain valid. The primary purpose of para. (2) was not to give the claimant an opportunity to make representations to the chairman against leave being granted to the AO, but to warn the claimant that the application has been made and that any award made by the tribunal is at risk. There is an examination of recent caselaw on the common situation where legislation imposes a requirement, but does not specify the consequences of non-compliance, and the distinction between mandatory and directory requirements. The failure to comply with a mandatory requirement will invalidate anything that purports to follow on. The failure to comply with a directory requirement will not.

Paragraph (4)

Where it is impracticable or would cause undue delay to go to the original chairman, the application can go to any chairman.

SECTION D—DISABILITY ADJUDICATION

Prescribed period

25.—(1) Subject to paragraph (2), the prescribed period for the purposes of section 30(1), (2) and (4) of the Administration Act shall be three months beginning with the date on which notice in writing of the decision of an adjudication officer under section 21 of that Act was given to the claimant.

(2) Where a claimant submits an application for review under section 30(1) of the Administration Act by post which would have arrived in a local office in the ordinary course of the post within the period prescribed by paragraph (1) but is delayed by postal disruption caused by industrial action whether within the postal service or elsewhere, that period shall expire on the day the application is received in the local office if that day does not fall within the period prescribed by paragraph (1).

DEFINITIONS

"adjudication officer"—see reg. 1(2).
"claimant"—*ibid.*
"local office"—*ibid.*

GENERAL NOTE

The three-month period prescribed in reg. 25 provides the limit within which the application for review on any ground of an AO's initial decision (in effect, the first stage of appeal) must be made, and beyond which review on the usual grounds is available.

See reg. 1(3) for the general rule about the dates when notices are to be treated as given to claimants and applications etc are to be treated as made. Para. (2) allows an extension to the three months where an application is delayed by industrial action. There is no other provision for extending the three months for special reasons or good cause. Therefore, it is particularly important for claimants and advisers to keep the time-limit in mind. Under reg. 26, applications must be made to local offices.

See the notes to s.30 of the Administration Act for the question of when an application for review is necessary.

Manner of making applications for review under section 30(1) of the Administration Act

26. An application for a review of a decision of an adjudication officer under section 30(1), (2) and (4) of the Administration Act shall be made to a local office.

DEFINITIONS

"adjudication officer"—see reg. 1(2).
"local office"—*ibid.*

Appeal to a disability appeal tribunal

27.—(1) The claimant may appeal to a disability appeal tribunal from a decision of an adjudication officer under section 30(1) of the Administration Act in any case in which there arises—
 (a) a disability question; or
 (b) both a disability question and any other question relating to attendance allowance, disability living allowance or disability working allowance.
 (2) In this regulation "disability question" means a question as to—
 (a) whether the claimant satisfies the conditions for entitlement to—
  (i)–(iii) [*Omitted as not applying to disability working allowance*]
  (iv) a disability working allowance specified in section 129(1)(b) of the Contributions and Benefits Act;
 (b)–(d) [*Omitted as not applying to disability working allowance*]

DEFINITIONS

"adjudication officer"—see reg. 1(2).
"claimant"—*ibid.*
"disability appeal tribunal"—*ibid.*
"disability question"—*ibid.*

GENERAL NOTE

This provision is made under s.33(1) of the Administration Act. Although it uses the word "may," in fact it does not give the claimant any choice about what kind of tribunal to appeal to. Under s.33(1)(a), the claimant may appeal to a DAT in prescribed cases. It is only in another case that there can be an appeal to a SSAT. Thus, if the regulations allow an appeal to a DAT, appeal to a SSAT is excluded.

The "disability question" under para. (2)(a)(iv) is whether the claimant has a physical or mental disability which puts him at a disadvantage in getting a job. If this is the only ground for not awarding the claimant disability working allowance, then the appeal must be to a DAT, which is particularly qualified to decide that question. In these circumstances, the AO may not have made a calculation of the claimant's weekly income to determine the level of the potential entitlement. If the DAT decides the disability question in the claimant's favour, it would seem that it ought to go on and determine all the questions necessary to decide whether the claimant is entitled to disability working allowance and, if so, of what amount. If a DAT refers any calculation back to the AO it should be on the basis that the appeal is to be returned to the DAT for final decision if there is not agreement about the result.

Although it appears odd that a DAT, rather than a SSAT, should determine the non-disability questions, this is expressly required by para. (1)(b) where an appeal raises both a disability question and some other question. The appeal on all questions must go to a DAT.

If in the course of an appeal before a SSAT a disability question arises for the first time, the SSAT may not determine that question under the powers of s.36 of the Administration Act (1975 Act, s.102). It is rather hard to envisage how this could happen, because by definition the disability question must originally have been determined in the claimant's favour for the appeal to have gone to the SSAT. See the notes to s.36 for more discussion.

Persons who may appeal to disability appeal tribunals and appeal tribunals

28. A person purporting to act on behalf of a person who is terminally ill as defined in section 66(2) of the Contributions and Benefits Act, whether or not that other person is acting with his knowledge or authority, may appeal to a disability appeal tribunal or an appeal tribunal, as appropriate, in accordance with section 33(1) of the Administration Act in any case where the ground of appeal is that that person is or was at any time terminally ill.

DEFINITIONS

"appeal tribunal"—see reg. 1(2).
"disability appeal tribunal"—*ibid.*

GENERAL NOTE

Under s.33(1) of the Administration Act appeals to tribunals must be made by the claimant or other prescribed persons. This provision is the only prescription. It cannot apply to disability working allowance, because being terminally ill is not a relevant ground of appeal. Therefore, for disability working allowance the appeal must be made by the claimant (or an official appointee) personally and not by some other person or group, unless expressly authorised by the claimant.

PART IV

PROVISIONS RELATING TO PARTICULAR BENEFITS OR PROCEDURES

[¹SECTION B—INCOME SUPPORT AND JOBSEEKER'S ALLOWANCE

Notification of decisions in income support and jobseeker's allowance cases

55.—(1) Subject to paragraphs (2) to (4), where an adjudication officer has given a decision on any claim or question relating to income support or jobseeker's allowance, the claimant shall be notified in writing of the effect of that decision and he shall at the same time be notified of his right to request a statement of the reasons for the decision and of his right of appeal to an appeal tribunal.

(2) Where, under arrangements made by the Secretary of State either throughout or in any part of Great Britain, income support is payable together with another benefit under the Contributions and Benefits Act, notice of the aggregate amount so payable shall be notice for the purpose of paragraph (1).

(3) Written notice shall not be required of a determination awarding benefit which is implemented by a cash payment if in all the circumstances it would be impracticable to do so.

(4) Written notice shall not be required of a determination terminating entitlement to income support or jobseeker's allowance if the reason for the termination is already known to the claimant or it is otherwise reasonable in the circumstances not to give such notice.

(5) So far as may be practicable, and subject to paragraph (6), where a claimant is notified of a decision under paragraph (1) or (2) the Secretary of State shall also give or send him a written notice of assessment showing—

(a) the total amounts of the personal allowances, family premium, other premiums and housing costs determined under Part IV of the Income Support Regulations or, as the case may be, Part VII of the Jobseeker's Allowance Regulations as are appropriate in his case; and

(b) the income taken into account; and

(c) any personal expenses addition, special transitional addition and transitional addition payable under the Income Support (Transitional) Regulations 1987, any transitional supplement payable under regulation 87 of the Jobseeker's Allowance Regulations and any transitional allowance payable by virtue of regulations made under section 40(2) of the Jobseekers Act.

(6) Paragraph (5) shall not apply to any determination—

(a) that income support or income-based jobseeker's allowance is not payable for any reason other than that the claimant's income exceeds the applicable amount;

(b) made on review under paragraph (3) of regulation 63 or paragraph (4) of regulation 63A, or, where the Secretary of State considers a written notice of assessment unnecessary, under any other provision of those regulations;

(c) in respect of a claimant to whom section 127 of the Contributions and Benefits Act (return to work after trade dispute) applies.

(7) If, within the time limited by regulation 3 and Schedule 2 for the bringing of an appeal against an adjudication officer's decision, the claimant requests a statement of the reasons for that decision he shall be given such a statement in writing and shall again be informed of his right of appeal.]

AMENDMENT

1. Social Security (Adjudication) Amendment Regulations 1996 (S.I. 1996 No. 1518), reg. 2 (October 7, 1996).

DEFINITIONS

"adjudication officer"—see reg. 1(2).
"appeal tribunal"—*ibid.*
"claimant"—*ibid.*
"income support"—*ibid.*
"Jobseekers Act"—*ibid.*
"Jobseeker's Allowance Regulations"—*ibid.*

GENERAL NOTE

Paragraph (1)
Paras. (2), (3) and (4) supply exceptions to the general obligation to provide a written statement of the effect of a decision. The right to a statement of reasons is under para. (7). A notice of assessment, showing how benefit is worked out (normally on a form A14) is dealt with in paras. (5) and (6).

The obligation under para. (1) is no longer to provide the actual and complete terms of the decision in writing to the claimant, as had been decided in the Common Appendix to *CSSB 281/1989* and associated decisions and *CSSB 540/1989*. The implication of the former requirement was that the AO ought to have recorded all decisions in writing. The Commissioner in the Common Appendix shows graphically how the former requirement was not met in the past, especially in supplementary benefit cases, where decisions often had to be "reconstructed" from ticks on forms and such-like evidence of what was done. Similar reconstruction is not unknown in the present. This is particulary troublesome in review cases, where the terms of and reasons for the decision of which review is sought are vital. See *CSIS 78/1993*, to be reported as *R(IS) 2/96*, and *CSIS 60/1994* in the notes to s.71(5) of the Administration Act.

However, from October 1996 the requirement in income support and JSA has been weakened to giving notice of "the effect of" a decision, rather than giving the actual and complete terms. No-one knows quite what level of detail will suffice. The change is hardly an incentive towards proper record-keeping.

The obligation applies to review decisions as well as initial decisions on a claim (subject to the exception in para. (4)). It is not uncommon for an AO to terminate or alter an award without referring to any grounds for review. If such a decision comes before a SSAT, it may normally correct the deficiency by dealing with the grounds of review itself (*CSSB 540/1989*).

Paragraph (2)
Presumably a statement of the aggregate amount must still be accompanied by notification of the right to request reasons and the right of appeal.

Paragraphs (3) and (4)
The circumstances in which, under para. (4), it is reasonable not to give written notice of the termination of entitlement must be severely limited. It looks as though the obligation to notify the claimant of his right to receive reasons and the right of appeal disappears along with the obligation to give written notice (to which it is attached in para. (1)), although it is to be hoped that in practice the information is given.

Paragraph (5)
The general rule is that if a written notice has to be given under paras. (1) and (2) a notice showing the assessment of the claimant's applicable amount and the income taken into account (A14) must be given. The exceptions are listed in para. (6).

However, the overall obligation is subject to the condition of practicability. It is not clear whether shortage of staff would be relevant to this issue.

Paragraph (6)
A notice of assessment need not be given in the following circumstances:
  (a) where entitlement is denied on any ground except that income exceeds the applicable amount;
  (b) where there is a review of a continuing entitlement and the Secretary of State considers a notice unnecessary (it would be a nuisance to have to produce a new notice every time the amount of benefit went up or down or in the unusual case where an AO has to make a review decision to give effect to a change in the prescribed rate of benefit; and
  (c) where the claimant is entitled for the first 15 days of return to work after a trade dispute.

Paragraph (7)
This is an important provision. It is often said that a proportion of appeals are really about getting a proper explanation of the decision and that once this is provided in the appeal papers the claimant is satisfied. It is to be hoped that this provision would enable that process to take place without the time and expense involved in starting the appeal process. It can only achieve this if the statements of reasons are both full and understandable.

The procedure may also be another way of getting a decision looked at again, without invoking the appeal process. The search for reasons may reveal mistakes in the original decision, which the AO should then correct by review.

Under para. 4 of Sched. 2, a claimant has three months from the date on which notice of the AO's decision was given to appeal. The request for reasons must be made within this period, which can be extended (reg. 3(3)). Until April 1987, the time for appealing ran from the date on which a statement of reasons was given. But when the normal period for appealing was extended from 28 days to three months, this concession was considered unnecessary. But a long delay in producing a statement of reasons might well influence a chairman to extend the period for appealing.

[¹ **Income support and social fund questions not immediately determinable**

56.—(1) Where on consideration of a claim or question relating to income support or to payment of maternity expenses from the social fund under Part

VIII of the Contributions and Benefits Act it appears to an adjudication officer that the claimant's entitlement to, or the rate or amount of, such benefit depends on the determination of—

  (a) the question as to what housing costs are to be included in the claimant's applicable amount by virtue of regulation 17(1)(e) or 18(1)(f) of, and Schedule 3 to, the Income Support Regulations (applicable amounts) and the adjudication officer is satisfied that not all of those housing costs can be immediately determined, he shall proceed to determine the claim or question on the assumption that the housing costs to be included in the claimant's applicable amount are those that can be immediately determined;

  (b) any of the questions mentioned in paragraph (3), and he is satisfied that the question cannot be immediately determined, he shall proceed to determine the claim or question on the assumption that the determination of the question so mentioned will be adverse to the claimant.

(2) Without prejudice to the power of an adjudication officer to refer any claim or question to an appeal tribunal under section 21(2) of the Administration Act and notwithstanding the provisions of section 22 of that Act, on an appeal to an appeal tribunal in any case where the adjudication officer has applied the provisions of paragraph (1) in relation to any of the questions mentioned or referred to in that paragraph, the tribunal shall not determine any such question until it has been determined by an adjudication officer.

(3) The questions referred to in sub-paragraph (1)(b) are—

  (a) whether in relation to any person the applicable amount falls to be reduced or disregarded to any extent by virtue of section 126(3) of the Contributions and Benefits Act (persons affected by trade disputes);

  (b) whether for the purposes of regulation 12 of the Income Support Regulations (relevant education) a person is by virtue of that regulation to be treated as receiving relevant education:

  (c) whether in relation to any claimant the applicable amount includes severe disability premium by virtue of regulation 17(1)(d) or 18(1)(e) of, and paragraph 13 of Schedule 2 to, the Income Support Regulations.]

AMENDMENT

1. Social Security (Adjudication) Amendment Regulations 1996 (S.I. 1996 No. 1518), reg. 2 (October 7, 1996).

DEFINITIONS

"adjudication officer"—see reg. 1(2).
"appeal tribunal"—*ibid.*
"claimant"—*ibid.*
"income support"—*ibid.*

GENERAL NOTE

The substance of this important provision has been in place since 1984.

The procedure has the effect that all decisions are made by an AO exercising a social fund or income support jurisdiction. The AO merely has the power to defer making a final decision. The result is that on an appeal to a SSAT, which must be against the social fund or income support decision, once all the questions are determined, all the issues are before the SSAT, including the correctness of the answers to all of the questions (*R(SB) 22/85*, para. 21(2)).

Paragraph (1)
Where one of the questions listed in para. (3) arises before the AO on a social fund or income support claim he has a choice of courses. He may decide that he can determine the question himself immediately. He may consider that the answer is clear, there may be an existing decision on, *e.g.*, child benefit or JSA which he decides to adopt, or he may informally consult another AO specialising in child benefit

or JSA. Whatever the reason, if the question is decided immediately, reg. 56 does not apply. There has been an ordinary adjudication with the ordinary rights of appeal. Note also that reg. 56 does not apply at all in some circumstances where the income support decision depends on the decision on another benefit. The main example was the reduction in benefit under reg. 22(4)(c)(i) and (ii) of the Income Support (General) Regulations (reg. 22 was revoked on October 7, 1996).

If the AO decides that he cannot immediately determine a question listed in para. (3), then paras. (1)(b) and (2) do come into play. Under para. (1)(b) the claimant's entitlement must be determined on the assumption that the question will be answered adversely to him. This means adversely from the income support point of view (*R(SB) 22/82*). Para. (2) deals with the effect on appeals. Once again, even if the question is passed on to another AO for decision, that AO, even if purporting to decide the question as part of his child benefit or JSA jurisdiction, will do so under the income support or social fund jurisdiction. The proper procedure, no doubt, is for the income support AO to make the determination after a delay for consulting the other AO. If the eventual determination of the question is adverse to the claimant, the interim treatment of his entitlement is confirmed, although he has a right of appeal. If the eventual determination is favourable to the claimant, the initial decision on entitlement must be reviewed under reg. 63(4)(b).

Para. (1)(a) concerns cases where the claimant's full housing costs cannot be immediately determined.

If the AO is proceeding under reg. 56 the claimant should be told this expressly, at the latest at the time of any appeal (*R(IS) 6/91*). The claimant is entitled to know what rights of appeal he has.

Paragraph (2)

Where an AO has made his decision on an assumption under para. (1), a SSAT is not to decide any such question until that question has been decided by an AO. In practice it seems that when an AO makes such an initial decision and there is an appeal on the question whose decision is delayed, the AO will not prepare his submissions and send the papers on to the SSAT clerk until both decisions have been made. Then the SSAT has jurisdiction to deal with both decisions together and the reasons for both will be given on the tribunal papers (*R(SB) 22/85*).

This leaves the situation where the AO makes some mistake, or perhaps bases his decision on a ground which is rejected by the SSAT on appeal, and one of these questions arises for the first time before the SSAT. The SSAT is not prevented from dealing with the question by para. (2) because there will not have been a decision under para. (1). There is nothing in the regulations to give the SSAT power to refer the question to an AO. Thus the SSAT has jurisdiction to decide the question which is relevant to income support or social fund entitlement. This conclusion is reinforced by the fact that s.36 of the Administration Act (1975 Act, s.102) allowing a SSAT to determine questions first arising in the course of an appeal, applies to income support and social fund cases. The control must come from the principles of natural justice. If a new issue, particularly one turning on legislation with which the presenting officer is not familiar, is raised at a hearing, then the presenting officer may legitimately request an adjournment in order to be able to deal with the issue. The same would apply if the claimant or his representative were to be unexpectedly asked to deal with a new issue.

Paragraph (3)

The precision of the references to other regulations in para. (3) must be carefully noted. See the notes to those regulations. See reg. 56A for the questions which are relevant in JSA cases.

[¹Jobseeker's allowance questions not immediately determinable

56A.—(1) Where on consideration of a claim or question relating to jobseeker's allowance it appears to an adjudication officer that the claimant's entitlement to, or the rate or amount of, that allowance depends on the determination of any of the questions mentioned in paragraph (2), and he is satisfied that the question cannot be immediately determined, he shall proceed to determine the claim or question on the assumption that the determination of the question so mentioned will be adverse to the claimant.

(2) The questions referred to in paragraph (1) are—
  (a) whether in relation to any person the applicable amount falls to be reduced or disregarded to any extent by virtue of section 15 of the Jobseekers Act (persons affected by trade disputes);
  (b) whether for the purposes of regulation 54(2) to (4) of the Jobseeker's

Allowance Regulations (relevant education) a person is by virtue of that regulation to be treated as receiving relevant education.

(3) Where—

(a) a person has made a claim for a jobseeker's allowance; and

(b) the adjudication officer is satisfied that the claimant satisfies the requirements for entitlement to a jobseeker's allowance specified in sections 1(2) and 2 or 3 of the Jobseekers Act; but

(c) the adjudication officer is unable to determine for the time being a question arising under section 19 of that Act,

then the adjudication officer shall, pending the determination of that question, determine the claim on the assumption that section 19 does not restrict payment of benefit.

(4) Without prejudice to the power of the adjudication officer to refer any claim or question to an appeal tribunal under section 21(2) of the Administration Act and notwithstanding the provisions of section 22 of that Act, on an appeal to an appeal tribunal in any case where the adjudication officer has applied the provisions of paragraphs (1) or (3) in relation to any of the questions mentioned or referred to in those paragraphs, the tribunal shall not determine any such question until it has been determined by an adjudication officer.

(5) A determination made pursuant to paragraph (3) shall be reviewed by an adjudication officer or, on a reference by him, by an appeal tribunal, where it is necessary to give effect to a determination given on a question arising under section 19 of the Jobseekers Act.

(6) A determination on review undertaken in consequence of a decision on a question arising under section 19 of the Jobseekers Act shall have effect—

(a) except where sub-paragraph (b) applies, from the day immediately following the end of the benefit week in which the determination was made; or

(b) where in accordance with regulation 26A(1) of the Social Security (Claims and Payments) Regulations 1987 a jobseeker's allowance is paid otherwise than fortnightly in arrears, and notwithstanding the provisions of regulation 69 of the Jobseeker's Allowance Regulations, from the day immediately following the end of the last benefit week in respect of which a jobseeker's allowance was paid.

(7) Where in consequence of the determination of any question arising under section 19 of the Jobseekers Act, a jobseeker's allowance is not payable, the period in respect of which it is not payable shall begin on the date the revised determination takes effect.

(8) In this regulation "benefit week" has the same meaning as in regulation 1(3) of the Jobseeker's Allowance Regulations.]

AMENDMENT

1. Social Security (Adjudication) Amendment Regulations 1996 (S.I. 1996 No. 1518), reg. 2 (October 7, 1996).

DEFINITIONS

"adjudication officer"—see reg. 1(2).
"appeal tribunal"—*ibid*
"claimant"—*ibid*.
"Jobseekers Act"—*ibid*.
"Jobseeker's Allowance Regulations"—*ibid*.

GENERAL NOTE

This regulation does two things. First, it provides a similar procedure to that under reg. 56 for JSA. Note that there is no equivalent to reg. 56(3)(c) in para. (2). Secondly, it extends that procedure to the situation where an AO is unable to decide immediately whether a benefit sanction under s.19 of the Jobseekers Act should be imposed. But in this case the claim is to be determined on the assumption that the question will be answered in the claimant's favour (para. (3)). Paras. (5) to (7) apply where it is subsequently decided that a sanction should be imposed.

[¹Termination of awards of income support or jobseeker's allowance where alternative benefit is claimed

56B.—(1) This regulation applies in a case where an award of income support or jobseeker's allowance ("the existing benefit") exists in favour of a person and, if that award did not exist and a claim was made by that person or his partner for jobseeker's allowance or, as the case may be, income support ("the alternative benefit"), an award of the alternative benefit would be made on that claim.

(2) In a case to which this regulation applies, if, but only if, a claim for the alternative benefit is made an adjudication officer may bring to an end the award of the existing benefit if he is satisfied that an award of the alternative benefit will be made on that claim.

(3) Where, under paragraph (2), an adjudication officer brings an award of the existing benefit to an end he shall do so with effect from the day immediately preceding the first day on which the award of the alternative benefit has effect.

(4) Where an award of jobseeker's allowance is made in accordance with the provisions of this regulation, paragraph 4 of Schedule 1 to the Jobseekers Act (waiting days) shall not apply.]

Amendment

1. Social Security (Adjudication) Amendment Regulations 1996 (S.I. 1996 No. 1518), reg. 2 (October 7, 1996).

Definitions

"adjudication officer"—see reg. 1(2).
"income support"—*ibid*
"Jobseekers Act"—*ibid*.

General Note

This provides for a claimant's existing award of JSA to be brought to an end if he or his partner is awarded income support and vice versa. Note para. (4) in relation to waiting days for JSA.

SECTION C—REVIEW OF DECISIONS

Date from which revised decision has effect on a review

57.—(1) In the case of a review to which either paragraph (2) or paragraph (3) applies, the decision given shall have effect from the date from which the decision being reviewed had effect or from such earlier date as the authority giving the decision being reviewed could have awarded benefit had that authority taken account of the evidence mentioned in paragraph (2) or not overlooked or misconstrued some provision or determination as mentioned in paragraph (3).

(2) This paragraph applies to a review under sections 25(1)(a), [¹30(2)(a), (4) and (5)(a), and 35(1)(a) and (3)(a)] of the Administration Act (review for error of fact) of any decision, whether that decision was made before or after the coming into force of this regulation, where the reviewing authority, that is to say the adjudication officer or, as the case may be, the appeal tribunal, is satisfied that—

(a) the evidence upon which it is relying to revise the decision under review is specific evidence which the authority which was then determining the claim or question had before it at the time of making the decision under review and which was directly relevant to the determination of that claim or question but which that authority failed to take into account; or

(b) the evidence upon which it is relying to revise the decision under review is a document or other record containing such evidence which at the time of making the submission to the authority which was then to determine the claim or question, the officer of the Department of Social Security, the Department for Education and Employment, the former Department of Employment or the former Department of Health and Social Security who made the submission had in his possession but failed to submit; or

(c) the evidence upon which it is relying to revise the decision under review did not exist and could not have been obtained at that time, but was produced to an officer of one of those Departments or to the authority which made that decision as soon as reasonably practicable after it became available to the claimant.

(3) This paragraph applies to a review under sections 25(2) and 30(2)(d) [¹and (5)(c)] of the Administration Act (review for error of law) of any decision, whether that decision was made before or after the coming into force of this regulation, where the adjudication officer or, as the case may be, the appeal tribunal, is satisfied that the adjudication officer, in giving the decision under review, overlooked or misconstrued either—

(a) some provision in an Act of Parliament or in any Order or Regulations; or

(b) a determination of the Commissioner or the court, which, had he taken it properly into account, would have resulted in a higher award of benefit or, where no award was made, an award of benefit.

(4) The following provisions of this Section, including regulation 63, are subject to the provisions of this regulation.

(5) In this regulation "court" has the same meaning as it has in section 68 of the Administration Act.

AMENDMENT

1. Social Security (Miscellaneous Amendments) (No. 2) Regulations 1997 (S.I. 1997 No. 793), reg. 9 (April 7, 1997).

GENERAL NOTE

The predecessor of this provision replaced reg. 72 of the 1986 Regulations (see p. 1341), with the same effect of lifting the normal 12-month (now one month) limit to backdating on a review, from August 31, 1991. On general principle, the new conditions applied to reviews requested or, if not requested, carried out from that date, while the old rules applied to reviews before that date (*R(SB) 26/83, R(SB) 48/83* and *CIS 11/1991*). However, this was expressly confirmed by reg. 3 of the 1991 amending Regulations (S.I. 1991 No. 1950, now revoked by Sched. 4 to these regulations), which provided that the new rules did not apply to reviews pursuant to applications for review made before August 31, 1991.

The date of the coming into force of the amendment was itself a matter of some controversy. The first amending Regulations were made on August 19, 1991, and were due to come into force on September 11, 1991. The Government became concerned at the prospect of mass applications for review being submitted before September 11. On August 30, without notice, the No. 2 amending Regulations were made, coming into force the next day and thus cutting off the possibility of new applications being made to which reg. 72 would apply.

There had been difficulties in the interpretation of reg. 72. The Government was concerned that it was being exploited by applications for review of every decision made on a claim from a person's 16th birthday. The DSS proposed an amendment which would have simply prevented arrears of supplementary benefit or national assistance being awarded in a review decision. This provoked considerable opposition and the Social Security Advisory Committee rejected it in principle (see Cm. 1607 for their report, which also describes the background). The SSAC's suggestion was that if it was thought that reg. 72 was being used in wider circumstances than those originally intended, the solution was to define the conditions which merited the payment of arrears more closely. This, as set out in the Secretary of State's statement in Cm. 1607, is what was done.

If either para. (2) or para. (3) applies, what is now the one-month limit on payment of benefit following review in regs. 63, 63A and 67 (as well as reg. 59 on most social security benefits) does not apply. The decision (which must mean the revised decision on review) then has effect either from the date on which the decision under review took effect or from an earlier date from which benefit could have been awarded in that decision. There may be some difficulties if the decision being reviewed is itself a refusal to review or a revised decision given on review. The powers on review which existed at that time would then seem to control how far back entitlement could have gone from that decision. The interaction with the principles set out in the Common Appendix to *CSSB 281/1989*, etc., *CSSB 238/1989* and *CSSB 544/ 1989* will require careful working out. See also *Chief Adjudication Officer v. Eggleton and Others*, Court of Appeal, March 17, 1995 (to be reported as *R(IS) 23/95*) (effect on decision of no, or only partial, revision on review) in the notes to s. 25 of the Administration Act.

Paras. (2) and (3) helpfully provide expressly that they apply whether the decision under review was made before or after August 10, 1995.

Paragraph (2)

This provision covers cases where review is on the ground that the decision was made in ignorance of or under a mistake as to some material fact. Note that it does not cover reviews on the ground of change of circumstances. The one-month limit is lifted if one of the three alternative conditions is satisfied. These are carefully drawn, although there are still several areas of uncertainty.

Under sub-para. (a) the authority making the decision under review (*i.e.* the AO, a SSAT or a Commissioner giving the decision the SSAT should have given) must have failed to take into account specific evidence which was before it at the time. It is not clear what "specific" evidence is. The underlying intention is no doubt that a claimant should point to some particular piece of evidence which was ignored, rather than make generalised assertions that circumstances could not have been taken into account, but the degree of specification needed is obscure. There are also difficulties in talking about evidence, not about the material fact of which it is evidence. The structure might make sense where there is a clear distinction between the AO making a decision on the basis of evidence submitted and officers acting for the Secretary of State in gathering evidence. However, the practice in supplementary benefit and national assistance was for such a distinction often to be blurred. A visiting officer who went to see the claimant's home circumstances might also be the AO who made the decision. Is what the AO saw with his own eyes specific evidence which was before him? The specific evidence must also be "directly relevant" to the decision under review. The test of whether a fact is material is whether it would have called for serious consideration, not that it would necessarily have led to a different decision if it had been known (*Saker v. Secretary of State for Social Services, R(I) 2/88*). Does the "directly relevant" test require that the evidence would definitely have led to a different decision? The precise words suggest not, so that the reviewing authority, once the conditions for review are met, can draw different inferences and conclusions from the same primary facts. Sub-para. (a) only applies when the evidence in question was before the AO, not when the evidence should have been before the AO, but was not (*CIS 14342/1996*).

Under sub-para. (b) the evidence on which review is based must have been in the possession of an officer of the DSS/DHSS or the Department of Employment, but not been submitted to the AO, SSAT or Commissioner. The same difficulty as noted in relation to sub-para. (a), the blurring of roles in the administration of supplementary benefit and national assistance, will appear here. The evidence of the material fact must also be embodied in some document or record which an officer failed to submit. It is hard to see how the evidence can be a document containing such evidence, but the above seems to be the most sensible construction. Sub-para. (b) only applies when the evidence was in the possession of the officer who submitted the case to the AO, It does not apply where the evidence is in the possession of some other officer within the Benefits Agency or the Department of Employment (*CIS 14342/1996*, followed in *CIS 14465/1996*). That is so even if the other officer, under interdepartmental procedures, ought to have sent the evidence on, but failed to do so.

Finally, under sub-para. (c) the evidence of the material fact must have not existed at the time of the decision under review. *CIS 650/1991* decided that the material fact must have existed at the time for there to be ignorance or a mistake as to it. (Note that the appeal against *CSIS 83/1994* which held that it did not matter that the fact did not already "exist" at the time of the adjudication officer's original decision was allowed: see below.) There is a second condition that evidence of that fact could not have been obtained at the time. This is intended to be a tough test: it is not a question of reasonableness but of possibility. If these two hurdles are crossed, it must be shown that the evidence was produced to the DSS, Department of Employment or the AO as soon as reasonably practicable after it became available to the claimant. The test is not when it comes to the claimant's knowledge, but when it becomes available to him. If the evidence is in the hands of an adviser or representative, is it available to the claimant?

It is understood that the DSS apparently accepted that sub-para. (c) could apply where an income support decision was reviewed (to award, for example, a severe disability premium) following an award of attendance allowance or disability living allowance that was backdated for more than 12 months. The basis of this was that the AO had made a mistake as to fact (the AO believed that the claimant was not entitled to this benefit when in fact he was) when he made the income support decision. In this situation the DSS said that full arrears could be paid. But what if the start of the entitlement to disability living allowance, when it was ultimately awarded, was later than the date of the original income support decision. This was the situation in *CSIS 83/1994*. The claimant had been in receipt of income support since 1991. He claimed disability living allowance (middle rate) in April 1992 but the decision to award it was not made until September 1993. The claimant then asked for his income support to be reviewed to include a severe disability premium from April 1992. The Commissioner held that para. (c) did apply to lift the then 12-month limit under reg. 69 (now reg. 63), so that the claimant was entitled to payment of the severe disability premium from April 1992. But this was overturned by the Court of Session on appeal (*Chief Adjudication Officer v Coombe*, June 19, 1997). See the note to s. 25(1)(a) to (c) of the Administration Act for further discussion of *CSIS 83/1994*. Furthermore, *CSIS 80/1995* has since rejected an argument that the effect of para. 14B of Sched. 2 to the Income Support Regulations is to deem a person to be in receipt of the relevant benefit for any period that it is paid, with the result that an award of the relevant qualifying benefit can be deemed to be in existence at the date of the income support decision. As a consequence of this decision, it is understood that the DSS no longer considers that sub-para. (c) can apply in these circumstances. See also *CIS 12447/1996* which adopts the same approach as that taken in *CSIS 80/1995*.

However, for reviews carried out on or after April 7, 1997, this particular problem has been removed by para. (1A) of reg. 63 and 63A respectively. See the notes to reg. 63(1A) and note *CIS 12447/1996*. But reg. 63(1A) and reg. 63A(1A) do not deal with the problem of a person who is not *entitled* to income support or JSA until the qualifying benefit is awarded. The later award of a qualifying benefit does not mean that the decision refusing income support or JSA was made in ignorance of a material fact (*CAO v. Coombe, CSIS 80/1995*) and a refusal of a claim cannot be reviewed on the ground of a subsequent change of circumstances (see *R(A) 2/81* and *CIS 767/1994*). This is despite the wording of para. (1A) of reg. 63/63A which clearly indicates an intention that para. (1A) should apply where income support/JSA is *awarded* as well as increased. Although the person could make a fresh claim for income support or JSA once the qualifying benefit has been awarded, any possible backdating of the claim would be restricted to a maximum of three months (see reg. 19 of the Claims and Payments Regulations). It is understood that the DSS is adopting a policy of "stockpiling" claims for income support or JSA in these circumstances, *i.e.* not making a decision on the income support/JSA claim until the qualifying benefit is awarded. But this does not seem to be a very satisfactory solution, certainly in the long term. See further *Welfare Rights Bulletin 144* (June 1998). Note, however, *CIS 902/1998* which makes the point that *CIS 767/1994* was concerned with a change of circumstances that occurred *after* the decision refusing the claim or terminating entitlement. If the change of circumstances was retrospective in effect so that it became operative in the period *before* that decision (*e.g.* because the claimant's award of disability living allowance had been reinstated), there would be grounds for review of the decision terminating entitlement to income support (although in the circumstances of that case this did not assist the claimant because of the provisions concerning arrears on review in force at that time).

The alternative tests in sub-paras. (a), (b) and (c) certainly define clearly deserving cases, but only time will tell whether the lines have been drawn too strictly.

If review is sought going back a long way, it is quite likely that documents relating to the original decision will have been destroyed under the DSS's arrangements for clearing storage space. In those circumstances, no presumptions can be drawn about the contents of the destroyed documents (*R(IS) 11/92*). A claimant may then well be unable to show that the conditions of paras. (a) or (b) have been satisfied. *R(IS) 11/92* shows that *The Ophelia* [1916] 2 A.C. 206 merely applied the established rules of evidence to the effect that if a person destroys documents with the intention of destroying evidence, then in any litigation concerning that person the contents of the destroyed documents are presumed to have gone against that person's case. Para. 7 of *CSB 1288/1985* gave a mistaken view of the effect of *The Ophelia*.

Paragraph (3)

This provision covers cases of review for error of law. Only AO's decisions may be reviewed under this power, not decisions of a SSAT or Commissioner. The error of law must be of one of the two kinds specified.

The first (sub-para. (a)) is overlooking or misconstruing some provision in an Act of Parliament, Order or Regulations. By definition, the provision must be in force at the relevant time (or there would not be an error of law) and in existence at the date of the decision (so that retrospective legislation does not count). However, it does not matter for these purposes (where the hurdle of s.69 of the Administration Act must already have been overcome) that the misconstruction is revealed as such by a decision of the courts or the Commissioner which comes after the date of the decision under review. Note that European Community legislation, even though directly effective in English law, is not directly referred to. But if a decision was reviewed as given in error of European Community law which was part of English law that same law would require an adequate remedy to be provided.

The second kind of error of law (sub-para. (b)) is overlooking or misconstruing a determination of the Commissioner or the court. The court means the High Court, the Court of Appeal, the Scottish and Northern Irish equivalents, the House of Lords and the European Court of Justice (para. (5) and Administration Act, s.68(4); 1975 Act, s.165D(4)). By definition, the determination which is overlooked or misconstrued must have been made before the date of the decision under review. Since under the Interpretation Act the singular includes the plural unless the context requires otherwise, misconstruing the combined effect of a number of decisions would seem to fall within para. (3). As under sub-para. (a), it does not matter that it is a Commissioner's or court decision after the decision under review which reveals that some earlier Commissioner's or court decision has been misconstrued or overlooked. It must nevertheless be shown that if the effect of the decision or decisions had been properly taken into account the decision under review would have been more favourable to the claimant.

Review of decisions in cases to which section 69(1) of the Administration Act applies

58. In any case to which section 69(1) of the Administration Act applies, the decision given on review shall have effect from the date of the relevant determination within the meaning of that subsection whether the decision which is being reviewed was made before, on or after 9th March 1992.

GENERAL NOTE

Section 69(1) of the Administration Act deals with the effect of "test cases" on reviews of entitlements in the cases of other claimants, and lays down the legal basis on which entitlement before the date of the test case (*i.e.* the "relevant determination") must be decided. The effect of reg. 58 seems to make that result academic, by only allowing a review to have effect from the date of the test case. This makes it all the more important to establish exactly what cases s.69(1) applies to. Note *Chief Adjudication Officer v. Eggleton and Others* (Court of Appeal, March 17, 1995) (to be reported as *R(IS) 23/95*) on the effect on decisions where there is no, or only partial, revision on review (see the notes to s. 25 of the Administration Act). As to when s. 69(1) applies, see *Chief Adjudication Officer and Another v. Bate* [1996] 1 W.L.R. 814, [1996] 2 All E.R. 790, HL in the notes to s. 69 and the discussion in those notes.

Review in income support cases

63.—(1) Except in a case to which regulation 57(2) or (3) or regulation 58 applies, [³and subject to paragraph (1A),] a determination on a claim or question relating to income support shall not be revised on review under section 25 of the Administration Act so as to make income support payable or to increase the amount of income support payable in respect of—

(a) any period which falls more than [³one month] before the date on which the review was requested or, where no request is made, the date of the review; or

(b) any past period which falls within the period of [³one month] mentioned in sub-paragraph (a) above and has been followed by termination or interruption of entitlement to income support and—

    (i) the total amount of the increase would be £5 or less, or

(ii) the grounds for review are a material fact or relevant change of circumstances of which the claimant was aware but of which he previously failed to furnish information to the Secretary of State [⁴or

(c) in a case to which paragraph (1B) applies, any period which falls more than 8 weeks before the date on which the review was requested or, where no request is made, the date of the review.]

[³(1A) A determination on a claim or question relating to income support may be revised on a review so as to make income support payable, or to increase the claimant's applicable amount under Part IV of the Income Support Regulations, or to increase the amount of income support payable, in respect of a period which falls more than one month before the date the review was requested, or, where no request is made, the date of the review, (''the one-month period'') where—

[⁴(a) the reason for the revised determination is that the claimant or a member of his family has become entitled to another benefit, or to an increase in the rate of another benefit, and

(b) that other benefit or increase is awarded in respect of a period before the one-month period.

(1B) This paragraph applies where—

(a) on a review it is determined that there is to be included in the claimant's applicable amount an amount in respect of a loan which qualifies under paragraph 15 or 16 of Schedule 3 to the Income Support Regulations; and

(b) the determination could not have been made earlier because information necessary to make the determination, requested otherwise than in accordance with paragraph 10(3)(b) of Schedule 9A to the Social Security (Claims and Payments) Regulations 1987 (annual requests for information), had not been supplied to the Secretary of State by the lender.]

(2) Section 159 of the Administration Act (which relates to the effect of alterations in the component rates of income support) shall not apply to any award of income support in force in favour of a person where there is applicable to that person—

(a) any amount determined in accordance with regulation 17(2) to (7) of the Income Support Regulations; or

(b) any protected sum determined in accordance with Schedule 3A or 3B of those Regulations; or

(c) any transitional addition, personal expenses addition or special transitional addition applicable under Part II of the Income Support (Transitional) Regulations 1987 (transitional protection).

(3) Where section 159 of the Administration Act does not apply to an award of income support by virtue of paragraph (2), that award may be reviewed by an adjudication officer or, on a reference by him, by an appeal tribunal for the sole purpose of givine effect to any change made by an order under section 150 of the Administration Act.

(4) A determination relating to income support made by an adjudicating authority or a Commissioner shall be reviewed by an adjudication officer or, on a reference by him, by an appeal tribunal where this is necessary to give effect to—

(a) [¹. . .]

(b) a determination given on a question to which regulation 56 applies; or

(c) a change of circumstances to which regulation 14 (reduction and termination of transitional and personal expenses addition) and regulation 15 (special transitional addition) of the Income Support (Transitional) Regulations 1987 apply.

(5) Where a claimant in receipt of income support, other than a claimant to

whom Part II of Schedule 4 to the Income Support Regulations applies, lives in a nursing home or residential care home and he is absent from the home for a period of less than one week, that absence shall not be treated as a relevant change of circumstances for the purposes of section 25(1)(b) and (c) of the Administration Act.

(6) In paragraph (5), "nursing home" and "residential care home" have the same meanings as they have in regulation 19 of the Income Support Regulations.

[²(7) [⁵Subject to regulation 63B (further provision on reviews of income support cases and jobseeker's allowance cases) and,] where a claimant is in receipt of income support and his applicable amount includes an amount determined in accordance with Schedule 3 to the Income Support Regulations (housing costs), and there is a reduction in the amount of eligible capital owing in connection with a loan which qualifies under paragraph 15 or 16 of that Schedule, a determination on a review undertaken as a result of that reduction shall have effect—

(a) on the first anniversary of the date on which the claimant's housing costs were first met under that Schedule; or

(b) where the reduction in eligible capital occurred after the first anniversary of the date referred to in sub-paragraph (a), on the next anniversary of that date following the date of the reduction.

(8) Where a claimant is in receipt of income support and payments made to that claimant which fall within paragraph 29 or 30(1)(a) to (c) of Schedule 9 to the Income Support Regulations have been disregarded in relation to the determination or review of the claim, and there is a change in the amount of interest payable—

(a) on a loan qualifying under paragraph 15 of 16 or Schedule 3 to those Regulations to which those payments relate; or

(b) on a loan not so qualifying which is secured on the dwelling occupied as the home to which those payments relate,

any determination on a review undertaken as a result of that change in the amount of interest payable shall have effect on whichever of the dates referred to in paragraph (9) is appropriate in the claimant's case.

(9) The date on which a determination on a review has effect for the purposes of paragraph (8) is—

(a) the date when the claimant's housing costs are first met under paragraph 6(1)(a), 8(1)(a) or 9(2)(a) of Schedule 3 to the Income Support Regulations; or

(b) where the change in the amount of interest payable occurred after the date referred to in sub-paragraph (a), on the date of the next alteration in the standard rate following the date of that change.

(10) In paragraph (9), "standard rate" has the same meaning as it has in paragraph 1(2) of Schedule 3 to the Income Support Regulations.]

AMENDMENTS

1. Social Security (Adjudication) Amendment Regulations 1996 (S.I. 1996 No. 1518), reg. 2(5) (October 7, 1996).

2. Social Security (Claims and Payments and Adjudication) Amendment Regulations 1996 (S.I. 1996 No. 2306), reg. 8 (October 7, 1996).

3. Social Security (Miscellaneous Amendments) (No. 2) Regulations 1997 (S.I. 1997 No. 793), reg. 13 (April 7, 1997).

4. Social Security (Claims and Payments and Adjudication) Amendment No. 2 Regulations 1997 (S.I. 1997 No. 2290), reg. 3 (October 13, 1997).

5. Social Security (Miscellaneous Amendments) (No. 4) Regulations 1997 (S.I. 1997 No. 2305), reg. 4(a) (October 22, 1997).

(S.I. 1995 No. 1801, reg. 63)

"adjudicating authority"—see reg. 1(2).
"adjudication officer"—*ibid.*
"appeal tribunal"—*ibid.*
"Commissioner"—*ibid.*
"income support"—*ibid.*

General Note

Paras. (1) and (2) impose limits or qualifications on the power to review decisions under s.25 of the Administration Act. But the power granted by reg. 57 to award benefit free of these limitations in cases of official error or newly discovered evidence must be carefully noted. Paras. (2) and (3) concern the effect of s.159 of the Administration Act. Paras. (3) and (4) allow review to take place outside s.25 in some circumstances.

There has been a drastic change in April 1997 to reduce the normal limit under reg. 63 from 12 months to one month, at an estimated saving in relation to income support reviews of £50 million in 1997/98 (see Memorandum to the Social Security Advisory Committee in Cm. 3586). The concern was said to be to align the rules on reviews with the rules on the backdating of claims. This was largely on the basis that a claimant could be expected to report a change of circumstances in the same way as a person could be expected to make a claim. But the restriction in reg. 63 applies to reviews on all grounds and not just to reviews on the ground of change of circumstances. The exceptions from the limit in cases of review on the ground of error of fact or law are the severely limited ones in reg. 57. The Social Security Advisory Committee advised that the rules should remain as they were, but the Government's view was that a substantial degreee of complexity required alignment into a simple rule. This is another example of simplification by removing entitlements.

Paragraph (1)

Sub-paras. (a) and (b) make it crystal clear that in ordinary cases (*i.e.* outside those covered by reg. 57) a revision on review under s.25 of the Administration Act (but not the rest of reg. 63) cannot make weekly benefit payable, or increase the amount of benefit, more than one month before the date review was requested, or the date of review if no request was made. But note the important exception in para. (1A). See also the slight exception in sub-para. (c).

Logically, reg. 63 should only be considered once it has been determined that there are grounds for review of an identified decision which would, apart from reg. 63, lead to review (*CSSB 470/1989* and *R(SB) 4/92*). Then reg. 63 prevents the revision having effect on the payability of benefit for any period prior to the one-month limit. A revision of entitlement, without payment, may still be of advantage to the claimant. For instance, if supplementary benefit entitlement immediately before April 11, 1988, is revised on review, that may have an effect on the claimant's income support transitional addition. That is because reg. 9 of the Income Support (Transitional) Regulations 1987 defines a person's total benefit income in their last week of supplementary benefit in terms of entitlement, not payment or payability. That is one reason why the Commissioner's view expressed in *CSB 56/1992*, that a SSAT need not consider the issues of review and revision if it is plain that because of what were then regs. 69 and 72 or 64A (now regs. 63 and 57) the claimant can gain no practical advantage from the review, must be treated with caution (see *CIS 714/1991*). It also promotes clarity of thought for a SSAT to follow the logical chain of the regulations. Clearly, if a decision is to make benefit payable on review within the one-month limit the issues of review and revision must be fully dealt with. Note that *CIS 788/1991* held that where a decision has only been partially revised on review because of the 12-months limit in reg. 69 (now reg. 63), the review is restricted to the period covered by the revisal. Thus a late appeal can be admitted against the original decision that remains in existence for any prior period. This decision has been confirmed by the Court of Appeal in *Chief Adjudication Officer v. Eggleton and Others* (March 17, 1995) (to be reported as *R(IS) 23/95*). See the notes to s.25 of the Administration Act.

Presumably the question of what in sub-para. (b) is meant by "failing" to furnish information will be decided on the same basis as the meaning of "failure to disclose" in s.71 of the Administration Act (1986 Act, s.53) (see extensive notes to that section).

If reg. 63 limits the amount of benefit payable on review, it must then be considered whether reg. 57 applies to lift the limit. (See reg. 72 of the 1986 Adjudication Regulations for reviews requested, or if not requested carried out, before August 31, 1991, but after April 5, 1987.)

A revision on review may remove or decrease entitlement for any past period, without time limit, providing it seems that the ground of review relied on existed in relation to the benefit in question

1331

at the time that it was paid *(R(P) 1/85)*. Then the question of the Secretary of State's right to recover an overpayment under s.71 is raised.

R(SB) 48/83 makes it clear that the AO's power to review decisions is fixed by the statutory provisions in force at the date review is requested. Similar limitations to those imposed by reg. 57 have applied since April 23, 1984. See *R(SB) 9/84* for discussion of the rule when it was contained in reg. 4 of the Supplementary Benefit (Determination of Questions) Regulations 1980.

Paragraph (1A)

This provision now deals expressly with the situation where an income support claimant, or a member of his family, receives an award, or higher rate, of some other benefit which leads to a review to increase the amount of income support entitlement, *e.g.* by qualifying the claimant for the disability premium or severe disability premium. The revised decision on the income support review may make the increase payable for any past period free of the one-month limit. It does not matter for this purpose that the proper ground of review is a change of relevant circumstances, thus avoiding the problem which *CSIS 83/1994* strove to get around. See *CIS 12447/1996* in which the Deputy Commissioner also points out that this provision does not appear to be limited to reviews of decisions made since para. (1A) was introduced.

For discussion of the continuing problem where the claimant is not *entitled* to income support until the qualifying benefit is awarded see the notes to reg. 57(2).

Paragraphs (2) and (3)

The normal rule under s.159 of the Administration Act is that alterations in the prescribed rates of benefit take effect automatically without any decision being given by an AO. Para. (2) preserves the review process where a transitional addition of some kind under the 1987 Transitional Regulations or the General Regulations is in payment. The right to review where s.159 does not apply is created independently by para. (3). Since the decision is to be made by an AO, there ought to be a right of appeal to a SSAT (possibly under s.22(1) of the Administration Act). But there is not the express provision which is made in ordinary cases of review by s.28 of the Administration Act, so that the position is not entirely clear.

Paragraph (4)

Sub-paras. (a) and (b) confirm that where an AO has made an income-support decision on the assumption that a decision on another question will be adverse to the claimant but that decision turns out to be favourable, then the income support decision is to be reviewed.

Paragraphs (5) and (6)

Claimants entitled to the special rates of income support for residents in residential care or nursing homes cannot have benefit reviewed for a change of circumstances on an absence of less than a week.

Paragraphs (7) to (10)

See the notes to para. 6 of Sched. 3 and paras. 29 and 30 of Sched. 9 to the Income Support Regulations.

[¹Review in jobseeker's allowance cases

63A.—(1) Except in a case to which regulation 57(2) or (3) or regulation 58 applies, and subject to [⁴paragraph (1A)], a determination on a claim or question relating to jobseeker's allowance shall not be revised on review under section 25 of the Administration Act so as to make jobseeker's allowance payable or to increase the amount of jobseeker's allowance payable in respect of—

    (a) [⁴...]

    (b) [⁴...] any period which falls more than [⁴one month] before the date on which the review was requested or, where no request is made, the date of the review; or

    (c) [⁴...] any past period which falls within the period of [⁴one month] mentioned in sub-paragraph (b) above and which has been followed by termination or interruption of entitlement to jobseeker's allowance and where—

        (i) the total amount of the increase would be £5 or less; or

(ii) the grounds for review are a material fact or relevant change of circumstances of which the claimant was aware but of which he previously failed to furnish information to the Secretary of State [⁵ or

(d) in a case to which paragraph (1B) applies, any period which falls more than 8 weeks before the date on which the review was requested or, where no request is made, the date of the review.]

[⁴(1A) A determination on a claim or question relating to jobseeker's allowance may be revised on a review so as to make jobseeker's allowance payable, or to increase the claimant's applicable amount under Part VII of the Jobseeker's Allowance Regulations, or to increase the amount of jobseeker's allowance payable, in respect of a period which falls more than one month before the date the review was requested, or, where no request is made, the date of the review, ("the one-month period") where—

[⁵(a) the reason for the revised determination is that the claimant or a member of his family has become entitled to another benefit, or to an increase in the rate of another benefit, and

(b) that other benefit or increase is awarded in respect of a period before the one-month period.

(1B) This paragraph applies where—

(a) on a review it is determined that there is to be included in the claimant's applicable amount an amount in respect of a loan which qualifies under paragraph 14 or 15 of Schedule 2 to the Jobseeker's Allowance Regulations; and

(b) the determination could not have been made earlier because information necessary to make the determination, requested otherwise than in accordance with paragraph 10(3)(b) of Schedule 9A to the Social Security (Claims and Payments) Regulations 1987 (annual requests for information), had not been supplied to the Secretary of State by the lender.]

(2) [⁴...]

(3) Section 159A of the Administration Act (which relates to the effect of alterations in the component rates of jobseeker's allowance) shall not apply to any award of jobseeker's allowance in force in favour of a person where there is applicable to that person any amount determined in accordance with regulation 87 of the Jobseeker's Allowance Regulations.

(4) Where section 159A of the Administration Act does not apply to an award of jobseeker's allowance by virtue of paragraph (3), that award may be reviewed by an adjudication officer or, on reference by him, by an appeal tribunal for the sole purpose of giving effect to any change made by an order under section 150 of the Administration Act.

(5) A determination relating to jobseeker's allowance made by an adjudicating authority or a Commissioner shall be reviewed by an adjudication officer or, on reference by him, by an appeal tribunal where this is necessary to give effect to—

(a) a determination given on a question to which regulation 56A applies; or

(b) a change of circumstances to which regulation 14 (reduction and termination of transitional and personal expenses addition) and regulation 15 (special transitional addition) of the Income Support (Transitional) Regulations 1987 apply by virtue of regulation 87(1) of the Jobseeker's Allowance Regulations.

(6) Where a claimant in receipt of a jobseeker's allowance lives in a nursing home or residential care home and he is absent from that home for a period of less than one week, that absence shall not be treated as a relevant change of circumstances for the purposes of section 25(1)(b) and (c) of the Administration Act.

(7) In paragraph (6), "nursing home" and "residential care home" have the

same meaning as they have in regulation 1(3) of the Jobseeker's Allowance Regulations.

(8) Where—

(a) it has been determined that the amount of a jobseeker's allowance payable to a young person is to be reduced under regulation 63 of the Jobseeker's Allowance Regulations because paragraphs (1)(b)(iii),(c),(d),(e) or (f) of that regulation (failed to complete a course of training and no certificate has been issued to him under subsection (4) of section 17 with respect to that failure) applied in his case; and

(b) that determination falls to be reviewed because the Secretary of State has subsequently issued a certificate under section 17(4) of the Jobseekers Act with respect to the failure in question,

the determination given on review shall have effect from the same date as the determination under review had effect.

[²(9) [⁶Subject to regulation 63B (further provision on reviews of income support cases and jobseeker's allowance cases) and,] [³except in a case to which paragraphs (13) to (15) apply, where] a claimant is in receipt of a jobseeker's allowance and his applicable amount includes an amount determined in accordance with Schedule 2 to the Jobseeker's Allowance Regulations (housing costs), and there is a reduction in the amount of eligible capital owing in connection with a loan which qualifies under paragraph 14 or 15 of that Schedule, a determination on a review undertaken as a result of that reduction shall have effect—

(a) on the first anniversary of the date on which the claimant's housing costs were first met under that Schedule; or

(b) where the reduction in eligible capital occurred after the first anniversary of the date referred to in sub-paragraph (a), on the next anniversary of that date following the date of the reduction.

(10) Where a claimant is in receipt of a jobseeker's allowance and payments made to that claimant which fall within paragraph 30 or 31(1)(a) to (c) of Schedule 7 to the Jobseeker's Allowance Regulations have been disregarded in relation to the determination or review of the claim, and there is a change in the amount of inerest payable—

(a) on a loan qualifying under paragraph 14 or 15 of Schedule 2 to those Regulations to which those payments relate; or

(b) on a loan not so qualifying which is secured on the dwelling occupied as the home to which those payments relate,

any determination on a review undertaken as a result of that change in the amount of interest payable shall have effect on whichever of the dates referred to in paragraph (11) is appropriate in the claimant's case.

(11) The date on which a determination on a review has effect for the purposes of paragraph (10) is—

(a) the date when the claimant's housing costs are first met under paragraph 6(1)(a), 7(1)(a) or 8(2)(a) of Schedule 2 to the Jobseeker's Allowance Regulations; or

(b) where the change in the amount of interest payable occurred after the date referred to in sub-paragraph (a), on the date of the next alteration in the standard rate following the date of that change.

(12) In paragraph (11), "standard rate" has the same meaning as it has in paragraph 1(2) of Schedule 2 to the Jobseeker's Allowance Regulations.]

[³(13) Paragraph (14) applies in the case of a claimant who is treated as having been awarded a jobseeker's allowance by virtue of regulation 7 of the Jobseeker's Allowance (Transitional Provisions) Regulations 1996 (jobseeker's allowance to replace income support and unemployment benefit), was paid benefit in accordance with an award of income support in respect of 6th October 1996 and whose applicable amount includes an amount determined in accordance with Schedule 3 to the Income Support (General) Regulations 1987 (housing costs).

(14) In a case to which this paragraph applies, a determination on a review undertaken as a result of a reduction in the amount of eligible capital owing in connection with a loan which qualifies under paragraph 15 or 16 of Schedule 3 to the Income Support (General) Regulations 1987 shall have effect on the first and each subsequent anniversary of the date on which the claimant's housing costs were first met under that Schedule unless that anniversary date falls on or after 7th October but precedes 8th November 1996 in which case paragraph (15) shall apply.

(15) In a case to which this paragraph applies a determination on a review shall have effect on 8th November 1996 and thereafter on the first and each subsequent anniversary of the date on which the claimant's housing costs were first met under Schedule 3 to the Income Support (General) Regulations 1987.]]

AMENDMENTS

1. Social Security (Adjudication) Amendment Regulations 1996 (S.I. 1996 No. 1518), reg. 2 (October 7, 1996).
2. Social Security (Claims and Payments and Adjudication) Amendment Regulations 1996 (S.I. 1996 No. 2306), reg. 9 (October 7, 1996).
3. Social Security (Adjudication) Amendment (No. 2) Regulations 1996 (S.I. 1996 No. 2659), reg. 2 (November 8, 1996).
4. Social Security (Miscellaneous Amendments) (No. 2) Regulations 1997 (S.I. 1997 No. 793), reg. 14 (April 7. 1997).
5. Social Security (Claims and Payments and Adjudication) Amendment No. 2 Regulations 1997 (S.I. 1997 No. 2290), reg. 4 (October 13, 1997).
6. Social Security (Miscellaneous Amendments) (No. 4) Regulations 1997 (S.I. 1997 No. 2305), reg. 4(b) (October 22, 1997).

DEFINITIONS

"adjudicating authority"—see reg. 1(2).
"adjudication officer"—*ibid.*
"the Administration Act"—*ibid.*
"appeal tribunal"—*ibid.*
"claimant"—*ibid.*
"Commissioner"—*ibid.*
"income support"—*ibid.*
"the Jobseeker's Allowance Regulations"—*ibid.*

GENERAL NOTE

Reg. 63A makes essentially the same provision for reviews of JSA decisions as reg. 63 makes for reviews of income support decisions. The extra provisions which do not have an equivalent in reg. 63 are paras. (13) to (15). These deal with the dates of reviews for reductions in eligible loan capital where claimants had been in receipt of income support on October 6, 1996.

[¹Further provision on reviews in income support cases and jobseeker's allowance cases—

63B. Where, in any case to which regulation 63(7) or 63A(9) applies (reviews of housing costs on the anniversaries of the date on which a claimant's mortgage interest costs are first met for income support or jobseeker's allowance), a claimant has been continuously in receipt of or treated as having been continuously in receipt of income support or jobseeker's allowance, or one of those benefits followed by the other, and he or his partner continues to receive either benefit, the anniversary to which those paragraphs refer shall be the anniversary of the earliest date on which benefit (whether income support or jobseeker's allowance) in respect of those mortgage interest costs became payable.]

AMENDMENT

1. Social Security (Miscellaneous Amendments) (No. 4) Regulations 1997 (S.I. 1997 No. 2305), reg. 4(c) (October 22, 1997).

Repayment of student loan not a change of circumstances

64. The repayment of a loan to which regulation 66A of the Income Support Regulations[¹, regulation 136 of the Jobseeker's Allowance Regulations] or regulation 42A of the Family Credit (General) Regulations 1987 (treatment of student loans) applies shall not be treated as a relevant change of circumstances for the purposes of section 25(1)(b) and (c) of the Administration Act.

AMENDMENT

1. Social Security (Adjudication) Amendment Regulations 1996 (S.I. 1996 No. 1518), reg. 2(7) (October 7, 1996).

DEFINITIONS

"the Administration Act"—see reg. 1(2).
"Income Support Regulations"—*ibid.*
"the Jobseeker's Allowance Regulations"—*ibid.*

Review in family credit cases

65. Where a review under section 25(1)(a) of the Administration Act of a decision relating to family credit arises from a disclosure of a material fact of which the person who claimed family credit was, or could reasonably have been expected to be, aware but of which he previously failed to furnish information to the Secretary of State, then if that review would result in either a new award of family credit or an increase in the amount of family credit payable, such new award or increase shall not be payable in respect of any period earlier than [¹one month] before the date on which which that person first furnished that information.

AMENDMENT

1. Social Security (Miscellaneous Amendments) (No. 2) Regulations 1997 (S.I. 1997 No. 793), reg. 15 (April 7, 1997).

DEFINITION

"the Administration Act"—see reg. 1(2).

GENERAL NOTE

Reg. 65 is not made subject to reg. 57, it seems because the limits it imposes on review for error of fact in family credit cases are within what would be allowed by reg. 57. There is no limit on how far back a review on the ground of error of law may go in family credit cases (*CFC 2298/1995*).

A review on the ground of ignorance of or mistake as to some material fact is normally without limit. But if it results from the disclosure of a fact which the claimant knew or could reasonably have been expected to know, but which had not been disclosed to the DSS, no extra benefit can be paid for a period earlier than one month before the date of disclosure.

Review in disability working allowance cases

66.—[²(1) Where a claim for disability working allowance has been refused and a further claim for disability working allowance is made within the period prescribed under section 30(1) of the Administration Act and is accordingly treated

1336

as an application for review in accordance with section 30(13) of that Act, then if that further claim results in an award of disability working allowance, the decision on review shall have effect from the date on which the further claim is made.]

(2) Where a review under section 30(1) or (5)(a) or section 35(3)(a) of the Administration Act of a decision relating to disability working allowance arises from a disclosure of a material fact of which the person who claimed disability working allowance was, or could reasonably have been expected to be, aware but of which he previously failed to furnish information to the Secretary of State, then if that review would result in either a new award of disability working allowance or an increase in the amount of disability working allowance payable, the decision on review shall not have effect in respect of any period earlier than [¹one month] before the date on which that person first furnished that information.

AMENDMENTS

1. Social Security (Miscellaneous Amendments) (No. 2) Regulations 1997 (S.I. 1997 No. 793), reg. 16 (April 7, 1997).
2. Income-related Benefits and Jobseeker's Allowance (Miscellaneous Amendments) Regulations 1997 (S.I. 1997 No. 65), reg. 16 (April 8, 1997).

DEFINITION

"the Administration Act"—see reg. 1(2).

GENERAL NOTE

Paragraph (1)
This provision used to contain a special rule for the review which is the first stage of appeal in disability working allowance that applied in all cases (see the 1996 edition of this book for the form of reg. 66(1) in force before April 8, 1997). But it now only applies if the AO's initial decision was to refuse to make an award of disability working allowance and a further *claim* is made within three months. Such a claim is treated as an application for review (Administration Act, s. 30(13)). Para. (1) provides that any award following this deemed review can only take effect from the date the further claim was made. Para. (1) no longer applies to applications for *review* under s. 30(1) which if successful can now take effect from the date of the original claim (if appropriate). But for the rule to apply at all still seems unfair if, for example, the initial AO made a clear mistake. It is not clear why a distinction has been drawn between actual and deemed applications for review in these circumstances.
If the initial AO's decision is to make an award of disability working allowance, so that the application for review is about the amount or duration of the award, para. (1) does not apply. The general principle that the review should operate from the beginning of the award will operate.

Paragraph (2)
This is the equivalent of reg. 65 on family credit. It will rarely apply to review under s.30(1) of the Administration Act. An application for such a review has to be made within three months of notification of the initial AO's decision.

Review in social fund maternity, funeral or heating expenses cases

67. Except in a case to which regulation 57(2) or (3) or regulation 58 applies, a determination on a claim or question relating to maternity or funeral expenses [¹. . .] out of the social fund under Part VIII of the Contributions and Benefits Act [¹. . .] shall not be revised on review under sections 25 to 29 and 69 of the Administration Act so as to make such expenses payable or to increase the amount of such expenses payable in respect of a determination of a claim for such expenses [¹where the application for review was made more than one month after the expiry of the time for claiming the payment in respect of the expenses under Schedule 4 to the Social Security (Claims and Payments) Regulations 1987.]

1. Social Security (Miscellaneous Amendments) (No. 2) Regulations 1997 (S.I. 1997 No. 793), reg. 17 (April 7, 1997).

DEFINITION

"the Contributions and Benefits Act"—see reg. 1(2).

GENERAL NOTE

The normal limit on review leading to an extra payment is one month before the date on which review is requested. If entitlement to social fund payments is to be determined as at the date of claim. then review on the ground of change of circumstances will not be possible, but this point remains to be settled. Note the exemptions from the one-month limit in cases of official error or newly discovered evidence (reg. 57).

PART V

TRANSITIONAL PROVISIONS AND REVOCATIONS

Transitional provisions

68.—(1) The Social Security (Adjudication) Regulations 1986 as originally made, shall continue to apply to the adjudication of any claim or question under the National Assistance Act 1948 or the Supplementary Benefit Act 1966 as they apply to a corresponding claim or question under the Supplementary Benefits Act 1976 and to the adjudication of any claim or question under the Supplementary Benefits Act 1976 as if the present Regulations had not been made.

(2) Anything done, begun or deemed to be done or begun under the Social Security (Adjudication) Regulations 1986 shall be deemed to have been done or continued under the corresponding provisions of these Regulations.

(3) So much of any document as refers expressly or by implication to any regulation revoked by these Regulations shall, if and so far as the context permits, for the purposes of these Regulations be treated as referring to the corresponding provision of these Regulations.

(4) Nothing in paragraphs (2) and (3) shall be taken as affecting the general application of the rules for the construction of Acts of Parliament contained in sections 15 to 17 of the Interpretation Act 1978 (repealing enactments) with regard to the effect of revocations.

(5) Without prejudice to the powers conferred on the Lord Chancellor or the Lord President of the Court of Session by section 6 of the Tribunals and Inquiries Act 1992 or on the Secretary of State or the President by Part II of and Schedule 2 to the Administration Act, any person who, immediately before the coming into force of section 25 of and Schedule 8 to the Health and Social Services and Social Security Adjudication Act 1983, held a subsisting appointment as—

    (a) a members of any of the panels of persons constituted under the said section 6 from which were selected chairman of National Insurance Local Tribunals (constituted under section 97(2) of the Social Security Act 1975) or, as the case may be, of Supplementary Benefit Appeal Tribunals (constituted under Schedule 4 to the Supplementary Benefits Act) shall be deemed to have been appointed to the panel from which chairmen of appeal tribunals are selected for a period corresponding to that of his subsisting appointment;

    (b) a member of either of the tribunal membership panels mentioned in section 97(2)(a) of the Social Security Act 1975 and paragraph 1(a) of Schedule 4 to the Supplementary Benefits Act (representing employers and earners other than employed earners) shall be deemed to have been appointed to the panel constituted by the President under paragraph 1(4) of Schedule 10 to the 1975 Act for a period corresponding to that of his subsisting appointment;

(c) a member of either of the tribunal membership panels mentioned in section 97(2)(b) of the Social Security Act 1975 and paragraph 1(b) of Schedule 4 to the Supplementary Benefits Act (respresenting employed earners) shall be deemed to have been appointed to the panel constituted by the President under paragraph 1(3) of Schedule 10 to the 1975 Act for a period corresponding to that of his subsisting appointment;

(d) a clerk to any National Insurance Local Tribunal or Supplementary Benefit Appeal Tribunal shall be deemed to have been assigned by the President as a clerk to the appeal tribunal for the area in question;

(e) a member of a pneumoconiosis medical panel (under regulation 49 of the Social Security (Industrial Injuries) (Prescribed Diseases) Regulations 1980) shall be deemed to have been appointed as a specially qualified adjudicating medical practitioner.

DEFINITIONS

''appeal tribunal''—see reg. 1(2).
''President''—*ibid.*
''specially qualified adjudicating medical practitioner''—*ibid.*

Revocations

69. The Regulations set out in column (1) of Schedule 4 are revoked to the extent mentioned in column (3) of that Schedule.

GENERAL NOTE

Sched. 4 is not set below. The major revocation is of the 1986 Regulations.

SCHEDULES

SCHEDULE 2   Regulation 3

TIME LIMITS FOR MAKING APPLICATIONS, APPEALS OR
REFERENCES

Column (1) *Application, appeal or reference*	Column (2) *Appropriate Office*	Column (3) *Specified time*
4. Appeal to an appeal tribunal from a decision of an adjudication officer (section 22(1) of the Administration Act.)	A local office.	3 months beginning with the date when notice of the decision was given to the appellant.
5. Appeal to a disability appeal tribunal from a decision on review of an adjudication officer under section 30(1) of the Administration Act.	A local office.	3 months beginning with the date when notice in writing of the decision was given to the appellant.

Column (1) *Application, appeal or* *reference*	Column (2) *Appropriate Office*	Column (3) *Specified time*
6. Appeal to an appeal tribunal from a decision on a review of an adjudication officer under section 30(1) of the Administration Act.	A local office.	3 months beginning with the date when notice in writing of the decision was given to the appellant.
7. Application to the chairman for leave to appeal to a Commissioner from the decision of an appeal tribunal (regulation 24(1)).	The office of the clerk to the appeal tribunal.	3 months beginning with the date when [²a copy of the full statement of the tribunal's decision was given or sent to the applicant].
9. Application to the chairman for leave to appeal to a Commissioner from the decision of a disability appeal tribunal (regulation 32(1)).	The office of the clerk to the disability appeal tribunal.	3 months beginning with the date when [²a copy of the full statement of the tribunal's decision was given or sent to the applicant].
11. Application to an adjudicating authority to set aside decision (regulation 10(2)).	A local office of the Department of Social Security or, in the case of unemployment benefit [¹or jobseeker's allowance], either at such an office or at a local office of the Department for Education and Employment or, in any case, at the office of the authority who gave the decision.	3 months beginning with the date when notice in writing of the decision was given to the applicant.

AMENDMENTS

1. Social Security (Adjudication) Amendment Regulations 1996 (S.I. 1996 No. 1518), reg. 2(8) (October 7, 1996).
2. Social Security (Adjudication) and Commissioners Procedure and Child Support Commissioners (Procedure) Amendment Regulations 1997 (S.I. 1997 No. 955), reg. 6 (April 28, 1997).

DEFINITIONS

"adjudicating authority"—see reg. 1(2).
"adjudication officer"—*ibid.*
"appeal tribunal"—*ibid.*
"Commissioner"—*ibid.*
"full statement of the tribunal's decision"—*ibid.*
"local office"—*ibid.*

GENERAL NOTE

See notes to reg. 1(3) for the dates on which notices, etc., are deemed to have been given. See the notes to the regulations referred to for further information on rights of appeal. The period for making the applications and appeals mentioned in Sched. 2 has the day on which the relevant notice is given as its first day (*Trow v. Ind Coope (West Midlands) Ltd.* [1967] 2 Q.B. 899 referred to in *CIS 550/1993*). Thus if notice of an AO's decision is given on January 10, 1997, an appeal to a SSAT must be made no later than April 9, 1997.

Note that the full statement of the tribunal's decision can be given quite a long time after the date of the hearing. See reg. 3(3) to (3E) as to when the time limits can be extended.

Social Security (Adjudication) Regulations 1986

(S.I. 1986 No. 2218)

Made by the Secretary of State under the Social Security Act 1986, ss.52(4), 89(1) and Sched. 7, the Health and Social Services and Social Security Adjudications Act 1983, Sched. 8, and various other provisions set out in Sched. 1.

[*Reg. 72 below is revoked with effect from August 31, 1991: see General Note*]

Exemption from limitations on payments of arrears of benefit

72.—[¹(1) Subject to paragraph (2),] nothing in this section shall operate so as to limit the amount of benefit or additional benefit that may be awarded on a review of a decision if the adjudicating authority making the review is satisfied either—

(a) that the decision under review was erroneous by reason only of a mistake made, or something done or omitted to be done by an officer of the [²Department of Social Security] or of the Department of Employment acting as such, or by an adjudicating authority or the clerk or other officer of such an authority, and that the claimant and anyone acting for him neither caused nor materially contributed to that mistake, act or omission; or

(b) that where the grounds for review are that the decision was given in ignorance of or was based on a mistake as to a material fact, those grounds are established by evidence which was not before the adjudicating authority which gave the decision; that the claimant and anyone acting for him could not reasonably have produced that evidence to the authority at or before the time the decision was given, and that it has been produced as soon as reasonably practicable.

[¹(2) This regulation shall not apply to a review of a decision by an adjudication officer or, on a reference by an adjudication officer, by an appeal tribunal, where the ground for review is that the decision was erroneous in point of law by virtue of a determination by a Commissioner, the High Court, the Court of Appeal, the Court of Session, the House of Lords or the Court of Justice of the European Communities given subsequent to the decision.]

AMENDMENTS

1. Social Security (Adjudication) Amendment Regulations 1987 (S.I. 1987 No. 1424), reg. 2 (September 1, 1987).
2. Transfer of Functions (Health and Social Security) Order 1988 (S.I. 1988 No. 1843), art. 3(4) (November 28, 1988).
Revocation: Social Security (Adjudication) Amendment (No. 2) Regulations 1991 (S.I. 1991 No. 1950), reg. 2(5) (August 31, 1991).

GENERAL NOTE

Although reg. 72 has been revoked, the text and the notes are being retained because there may still be outstanding applications and appeals to which it applies. Reg. 3 of the Social Security (Adjudication) Amendment (No. 2) Regulations 1991 confirmed that reg. 72 continued to apply to applications for review made before August 31, 1991. (The 1991 Regulations were revoked by the 1995 Adjudication Regulations (Sched. 4)).

Paragraph (1)
The provision gave a very welcome power from April 6, 1987 to allow arrears of benefit to be

1341

paid free of the limits otherwise imposed in Section D of Part IV of the 1986 Regulations in cases where the claimant was clearly not to blame for the mistaken decision. Formerly, there had been quite a bit of criticism of the imbalance between the power of the Secretary of State to recover past overpayments of benefit without limit of time and the power to pay arrears representing past underpayments. It is particularly significant that the power to make awards was given to the adjudicating authority making the review, not to the Secretary of State. If an AO refused to review a decision and on appeal a SSAT did review and revise the decision the same power under reg. 72 was available to the SSAT.

In *CSB 1153/1989*, the Commissioner, disagreeing with *CSB 271/1990* and *CSB 433/1989*, held that reg. 72 lifts the limits on entitlements to arrears of benefit in reviews requested or, if not requested, carried out from April 6, 1987, onwards. It did not matter that any mistake by an AO leading to an erroneous decision was made before the regulation came into force. The Commissioner held that this does not offend the presumption against retrospectivity because it does not adversely affect any rights of the claimant. And to take the opposite view would mean that reg. 72 would have had no practical effect until 12 months after it came into force. *CSB 1153/1989* is in accord with the general principle described in *R(SB) 48/83*, that the powers available on a review are those given by the review legislation at the date of the review, and has settled the issue. It is true that in *R(P) 1/85* it was held that while s.104(1A) of the 1975 Act (now s.25(2) of the Administration Act) on review for error of law could be used to review AOs' decisions made before it came into force in relation to "national insurance" benefits (April 23, 1984) it did not allow the revision of entitlement before that date. However, that was a case where the revision would have been to remove entitlement under an award of benefit. The Commissioner held that s.104(1A) should not operate retrospectively to remove an accrued entitlement. That objection does not exist where the effect of revision on review would be to create a new entitlement or to increase the amount of benefit. Although there would be a retrospective effect on the liabilities of the DSS, it is arguable that it is not an unfair one when, by definition, the original decision was made under an error of law.

CSB 112/1993 decides that reg. 72 could apply to an application for review made in 1991 even though the review application concerned the same issue (higher rate heating addition) which had been the subject of a review in 1985. At that time backdating on review was limited to 52 weeks under reg. 87 of the Social Security (Adjudication) Regulation 1984. The claimant had appealed to a tribunal in 1985 which had upheld the AO's decision on backdating. The Commissioner holds that the principle of *res judicata* (that once a matter has been adjudicated on by a competent authority another authority of the same level cannot readjudicate on the matter) did not apply in relation to the matters before the 1992 tribunal. The 1985 tribunal had had no opportunity to consider the factual issues raised by reg. 72, since, of course, the regulation was not in force at that time. Thus the claimant was entitled to have these questions considered. Nor did s. 60 of the Administration Act mean that the 1985 tribunal's decision was final in relation to the issues raised by the claimant's 1991 application.

Reg. 72 only needed to be considered once it had been determined that reg. 69 or 71 of the 1986 Regulations (see the 1995 edition of this book) limited the payment of benefit following a revision of a decision on review. It was desirable that in all cases a SSAT should follow through this logical sequence (*CIS 714/1991*). A SSAT must certainly deal with all the issues if its decision is to make some benefit payable on the review (*CSSB 470/1989*). It may be that if it is plain that the claimant cannot satisfy the conditions of reg. 72 and cannot then derive any practical benefit from the review, a SSAT need only deal with reg. 72 (*CSB 56/1992*). But even then it must be determined what grounds of review have been established in order to tell whether reg. 72(1)(b) might apply or not.

The lifting of the time limit on payment of benefit for past periods occurred only when either sub-para. (a) or (b) was satisfied. The conditions are quite complex and must all be met.

Under both sub-paragraphs the claimant will need to establish the circumstances of the decision under review in order to meet the conditions. If the DSS has destroyed the documents relating to that decision in the course of its normal "weeding" procedure, the claimant may be left with a gap in the evidence. Arguments have been made that the principle of *The Ophelia* [1916] 2 A.C. 206, as explained in *CSB 1288/1985*, was that the contents of the destroyed documents should be presumed to go against the interests of the DSS and in favour of the claimant. *R(IS) 11/92* decides that that strong presumption does not arise in such circumstances. It only arises when documents are destroyed with the intention to destroy evidence.

Sub-para. (a). Under this head the decision must be wrong solely because of official error or omission, either of a DSS or DE employee or of an adjudicating authority or clerk. In *R(SB) 10/91*, the Commissioner says that the regulation applies only to "clear mistakes of fact or law in relation to an actual issue in a given case at a time when the officer of the relevant Department, etc., was actively required by his duties under the social security legislation to arrive at a decision or take some administrative act. It certainly does not impose a general duty on the officers etc. of the Department of their own accord constantly to keep all cases under review in order to see whether or not any particular exempting regulation might apply.'' *R(SB) 2/93* holds that visiting officers should not be taken to be under a duty to interogate claimants as to every conceivable circumstance which might affect supplementary benefit. ''Mistakes'' are limited to clear and obvious mistakes on the facts disclosed or which the office had reason to believe were relevant. So where the claimant had said that he hoped to obtain work in the near future, it was not an error or omission for the visiting officer not to enquire about his health. *CIS 11/1991* confirms that an error of law can amount to a mistake under sub-para. (a).

R(P) 1/92 holds that a failure to take account of a future contingency, in that case the likelihood of the claimant being divorced, and to advise the claimant on the effect which this would have on her benefit situation cannot render the AO's decision erroneous. The error must lie in the decision itself.

Any erroneous decision could not be solely due to an official mistake if the claimant had caused or materially contributed to the mistake, so that the end of the paragraph is really spelling out the implication of the first part. Here the claimant's obligation under reg. 32 of the Claims and Payments Regulations to notify the Secretary of State of changes of circumstances which he might reasonably be expected to know might affect his right to benefit must be relevant. See the discussion of causation in the notes to s.71 of the Administration Act.

Sub-para. (b). Here evidence must have come to light which was not before the adjudicating authority when the original decision was made. Secondly, neither the claimant nor anyone acting on his behalf must have been able reasonably to have produced that evidence before that original decision was made. The question of what factors can be taken into account in deciding the issue of reasonableness here will be a difficult one. The test seems to be related to the particular claimant concerned, rather than some hypothetical reasonable claimant. Thirdly, the evidence must have been produced (who to?) as soon as reasonably practicable. Thus any unnecessary delay may prejudice the right to arrears although the mistake in the original decision was not the claimant's fault.

Paragraph (2)

The intention of this addition to the original form of reg. 72 was to contain the knock-on effect of test cases which are decided against the DSS. If it applies, it means that the ordinary 12 month rule of reg. 69 of the 1986 Regulations defines the extent of arrears payable on review (although extra-statutory payments may be considered). It was argued in the 1988 edition that the scope of para. (2) is limited in the following way. If a decision of a Commissioner or a court shows that an accepted interpretation of a regulation is wrong, that decision merely reveals what the law has been all along. Decisions made on the mistaken interpretation are not erroneous in law by virtue of the appeal decision. They are erroneous because they got the law wrong. Where para. (2) will apply is in the situation where decisions are made according to one appeal decision, which is then overruled by a more authoritative decision. However, in *R(SB) 11/89* a Tribunal of Commissioners rejected such limitations. Decisions had been made based on regulations later declared *ultra vires* by the Court of Appeal in the *Cotton* case. The Tribunal would have applied para. (2) in these circumstances. Although it was not necessary for them actually to do so, this is an authoritative expression of view within the social security system, despite its constitutional weakness. The Commissioner in *CIS 11/1991* holds that the ruling in *R(SB) 11/89* only applies when the request for review is made after the decision of the Commissioner or court which reveals the AO's error of law. Since the powers on review are determined as at the date of the request for review, and that is the start of the 12 month limit in reg. 69, the claimant should not be prejudiced by the chance that a Commissioner or court decision confirming his, rather than the AO's, view of the law emerges after his request. This analysis of reg. 72(2) seems cogent. *R(IS) 10/92* confirms that the application of reg. 72(2) is not confined to the situation where a claimant has asked for a review because he knew of a relevant Commissioner's decision. The grounds for review are not limited to those put forward by the claimant; the determining factor is what in fact are the grounds for review.

It has been argued that para. (2) does not cover a SSAT hearing an appeal from an AO's revised decision on review or refusal to review. The words of para. (2) only mention a SSAT dealing with a reference by an AO, where the AO has not made a decision, but the argument is misconceived. The legislation does not define the powers of SSATs. Section 104(1) and (1A) of the 1975 Act (Administration Act, s.25(1) and (2)) equally only refers to a SSAT dealing with a reference, yet a right of appeal to a SSAT from an AO is expressly provided in s.104(4). The SSAT on such an appeal must have the power to make a decision. On principle, that power must be to do what an AO could do in the circumstances. The SSAT must equally be subject to the restrictions of reg. 72(2).

Social Security (Adjudication) and Child Support Amendment (No.2) Regulations 1996

(S.I. 1996 No. 2450)

Made by the Secretary of State under ss. 21(2) and (3), 51 and 52 of the Child Support Act 1991 and ss. 22(2), 22(4), 33(2), 46(2), 59(1), 189 and 191 of, and paras. 2–5 of Sched. 3 to, the Social Security Administration Act 1992.

[In force October 21, 1996]

Saving provision

22. In a case where an appeal, application or reference was made before the date on which these Regulations come into force, regulations 3, 7(3), 22, 29(1) and 38(1) of the Adjudication Regulations and regulations 3, 6(3), and 11(1) of the Appeal Regulations shall apply as if these Regulations had not been made.

Social Security (Claims and Payments) Regulations 1987

(S.I. 1987 No. 1968)

Made by the Secretary of State under ss.165a and 166(2) of the Social Security Act 1975, s.6(1) of the Child Benefit Act 1975 and ss.21(7), 51(1)(a) to (s), 54(1) and 84(1) of the Social Security Act 1986.

REGULATIONS REPRODUCED

PART I

GENERAL

PART II

CLAIMS

Part III

Payments

20. Time and manner of payment: general provisions
20A. Payment on presentation of an instrument for benefit payment
21. Direct credit transfer
26. Income support
26A. Jobseeker's allowance
27. Family credit and disability working allowance
28. Fractional amounts of benefit
29. Payments to a person under age 18
30. Payments on death
32. Information to be given when obtaining payment of benefit

Part IV

Third Parties

33. Persons unable to act
34. Payment to another person on the beneficiary's behalf
34A. Deductions of mortgage interest which shall be made from benefit and paid to qualifying lenders
35. Deductions which may be made from benefit and paid to third parties
35A. Transitional provisions for persons in hostels or certain residential accommodation
36. Payment to a partner as an alternative payee

Part V

Suspension and Extinguishment

37. Suspension in individual cases
37A. Suspension in identical cases
37AA. Withholding of benefit in prescribed circumstances
37AB. Payment of withheld benefit
37B. Witholding payment of arrears of benefit
38. Extinguishment of right to payment of sums by way of benefit where payment is not obtained within the prescribed period

Part VII

Miscellaneous

47. Instruments of payment, etc. and instruments for benefit payment
48. Revocations
49. Savings

Schedules

1. Part I—Benefit claimed and other benefit which may be treated as if claimed in addition or in the alternative
4. Part I—Prescribed times for claiming benefit
7. Manner and time of payment, effective date of change of circumstances and commencement of entitlement in income support cases
9. Deductions from benefit and direct payment to third parties
9A. Deductions of mortgage interest from benefit and payment to qualifying lenders

Citation and commencement

1. These Regulations may be cited as the Social Security (Claims and Payments) Regulations 1987 and shall come into operation on 11th April 1988.

Interpretation

2.—(1) In these Regulations, unless the context otherwise requires—

"adjudicating authority" means any person or body with responsibility under the Social Security Acts 1975 to 1986 [SSAA], and regulations made thereunder, for the determination of claims for benefit and questions arising in connection with a claim for, or award of, or disqualification for receiving benefits;

"appropriate office" means an office of the [²Department of Social Security] or [¹⁰the Department for Education and Employment];

[¹¹"claim for asylum" has the same meaning as in the Asylum and Immigration Appeals Act 1993;]

"claim for benefit" includes—

    (a) an application for a declaration that an accident was an industrial accident;

    (b) [³. . .]

    (c) an application for the review of an award or a decision for the purpose of obtaining any increase of benefit [⁶in respect of a child or adult dependant under the Social Security Act 1975 or an increase in disablement benefit under section 60 (special hardship), 61 (constant attendance), 62 (hospital treatment allowance) or 63 (exceptionally severe disablement) of the Social Security Act 1975], but does not include any other application for the review of an award or a decision;

[⁸"instrument for benefit payment" means an instrument issued by the Secretary of State under regulation 20A on the presentation of which benefit due to a beneficiary shall be paid in accordance with the arrangements set out in that regulation;]

[¹⁰"the Jobseekers Act" means the Jobseekers Act 1995;

"jobseeker's allowance" means an allowance payable under Part I of the Jobseekers Act;

"the Jobseeker's Allowance Regulations" means the Jobseeker's Allowance Regulations 1996;]

"long-term benefits" means any retirement pension, a widowed mother's allowance, a widow's pension, attendance allowance, [⁵disability living allowance], invalid care allowance, guardian's allowance, any pension or allowance for industrial injury or disease and any increase in any such benefit;

"married couple" means a man and a woman who are married to each other and are members of the same household;

"partner" means one of a married or unmarried couple; [⁴. . .]

[⁹"pension fund holder" means with respect to a personal pension scheme or retirement annuity contract, the trustees, managers or scheme administrators, as the case may be, of the scheme or contract concerned;]

[⁹"personal pension scheme" has the same meaning as in section 1 of the Pension Schemes Act 1993 in respect of employed earners and in the case of self-employed earners, includes a scheme approved by the Board of Inland Revenue under Chapter IV of Part XIV of the Income and Corporation Taxes Act 1988;]

[[11]"refugee" means a person recorded by the Secretary of State as a refugee within the definition in Article 1 of the Convention relating to the Status of Refugees done at Geneva on 28th July 1951 as extended by Article 1(2) of the Protocol relating to the Status of Refugees done at New York on 31st January 1967;]

[[9]"retirement annuity contract" means a contract or trust scheme approved under Chapter III of Part XIV of the Income and Corporation Taxes Act 1988;]

"unmarried couple" means a man and a woman who are not married to each other but are living together as husband and wife otherwise than in prescribed circumstances; and

"week" means a period of 7 days beginning with midnight between Saturday and Sunday.

(2) Unless the context otherwise requires, any reference in these Regulations to—

(a) a numbered regulation, Part or Schedule is a reference to the regulation, Part or Schedule bearing that number in these Regulations and any reference in a regulation to a numbered paragraph is a reference to the paragraph of that regulation having that number;

(b) a benefit includes any benefit under the Social Security Act 1975 [SSCBA], child benefit under Part I of the Child Benefit Act 1975, income support[[7], family credit and disability working allowance under the Social Security Act 1986 [SSCBA] and any social fund payments such as are mentioned in section 32(2)(a) [[1]and section 32(2A)] of that Act [SSCBA, s.138(1)(a) and (2)] [[10]and a jobseeker's allowance under Part I of the Jobseekers Act].

[[10](2A) References in regulations 20, 21 (except paragraphs (3) and (3A)), 29, 30, 32 to 34, 37 (except paragraph (1A)), 37A, 37AA (except paragraph (3)), 37AB, 37B, 38 and 47 to "benefit", "income support" or "a jobseeker's allowance", include a reference to a back to work bonus which, by virtue of regulation 25 of the Social Security (Back to Work Bonus) Regulations 1996, is to be treated as payable as income support or, as the case may be, as a jobseeker's allowance.]

(3) For the purposes of the provisions of these Regulations relating to the making of claims every increase of benefit under the Social Security Act 1975 [SSCBA] shall be treated as a separate benefit [[12]. . .].

AMENDMENTS

1. Social Security (Common Provisions) Miscellaneous Amendment Regulations 1988 (S.I. 1988 No. 1725), reg. 3 (November 7, 1988).

2. Transfer of Functions (Health and Social Security) Order 1988 (S.I. 1988 No. 1843), art. 3(4) (November 28, 1988).

3. Social Security (Medical Evidence, Claims and Payments) Amendment Regulations 1989 (S.I. 1989 No. 1686), reg. 3 (October 9, 1989).

4. Social Security (Miscellaneous Provisions) Amendment Regulations 1991 (S.I. 1991 No. 2284), reg. 5 (November 1, 1991).

5. Social Security (Claims and Payments) Amendment Regulations 1991 (S.I. 1991 No. 2741), reg. 2(a) (February 3, 1992).

6. Social Security (Miscellaneous Provisions) Amendment Regulations 1992 (S.I. 1992 No. 247), reg. 9 (March 9, 1992).

7. Social Security (Claims and Payments) Amendment Regulations 1991 (S.I. 1991 No. 2741), reg. 2(b) (March 10, 1992).

8. Social Security (Claims and Payments) Amendment (No. 4) Regulations 1994 (S.I. 1994 No. 3196), reg. 2 (January 10, 1995).

9. Income-related Benefits Schemes and Social Security (Claims and Payments) (Miscellaneous Amendments) Regulations 1995 (S.I. 1995 No. 2303), reg. 10(2) (October 2, 1995).

10. Social Security (Claims and Payments) (Jobseeker's Allowance Consequential Amendments) Regulations 1996 (S.I. 1996 No. 1460), reg. 2(2) (October 7, 1996).

11. Income Support and Social Security (Claims and Payments) (Miscellaneous Amendments) Regulations 1996 (S.I. 1996 No. 2431), reg. 7(a) (October 15, 1996).

12. Child Benefit, Child Support and Social Security (Miscellaeous Amendments) Regulations 1996 (S.I. 1996 No. 1803), reg. 18 (April 7, 1997).

General Note

"claim for benefit." Under sub-para. (c) a claim includes, for the purposes of these Regulations, an application for review for the purpose of securing any increase of benefit. The March 1992 amendment restricts the scope of this provision to applications for review to obtain increases for spouses or dependants or the listed industrial injury "benefits" which are (or were, since special hardship allowance and hospital treatment allowance have ceased to exist) technically not separate benefits, but increases of disablement benefit. In *CIS 515/1990*, the Commissioner took the view that the pre-amendment form of the definition applied to any application for review which requested an increase in the amount of any benefit. The subsequent amendment cannot affect the authority of this decision before the date of the amendment, but para. (3) makes it dubious.

See the notes to s.137(1) of the Contributions and Benefits Act for "married couple" and "unmarried couple."

PART II

Claims

Claims not required for entitlement to benefit in certain cases

3. It shall not be a condition of entitlement to benefit that a claim be made for it in the following cases:—
  (a) to (f) [*Omitted as not relating to income-related benefits*]
  [¹(g) in the case of a jobseeker's allowance where—
      (i) that allowance has previously been claimed and an award made;
      (ii) the Secretary of State has directed under regulation 37(1A) that payment under that award be suspended for a definite or indefinite period on the ground that a question arises whether the conditions for entitlement to that allowance are or were fulfilled or the award ought to be revised;
      (iii) subsequently that suspension expires or is cancelled in respect of a part only of the period for which it has been in force;
      (iv) it is then determined that the award should be revised to the effect that there was no entitlement to the allowance in respect of all or any part of the period between the start of the period over which the award has been suspended and the date when the suspension expires or is cancelled; and
      (v) there are no other circumstances which cast doubt on the claimant's entitlement.]

Amendment

1. Social Security (Claims and Payments) (Jobseeker's Allowance Consequential Amendments) Regulations 1996 (S.I. 1996 No. 1460), reg. 2(3) (October 7, 1996).

Definition

"jobseeker's allowance"—see reg. 2(1).

Making a claim for benefit

4.—(1) Every claim for benefit [⁷other than a claim for income support or jobseeker's allowance] shall be made in writing on a form approved by the Secretary of State [³for the purpose of the benefit for which the claim is made], or in such other manner, being in writing, as the Secretary of State may accept as sufficient in the circumstances of any particular case.

[⁷ (1A) In the case of a claim for income support or jobseeker's allowance, the claim shall—

(a) be made in writing on a form approved by the Secretary of State for the purpose of the benefit for which the claim is made;

(b) unless any of the reasons specified in paragraph (1B) applies, be made in accordance with the instructions on the form; and

(c) unless any of the reasons specified in paragraph (1B) applies, include such information and evidence as the form may require in connection with the claim.

(1B) The reasons referred to in paragraph (1A) are—

(a) (i) the person making the claim is unable to complete the form in accordance with the instructions or to obtain the information or evidence it requires because he has a physical, learning, mental or communication difficulty; and

(ii) it is not reasonably practicable for the claimant to obtain assistance from another person to complete the form or obtain the information or evidence;

or

(b) the information or evidence required by the form does not exist;

or

(c) the information or evidence required by the form can only be obtained at serious risk of physical or mental harm to the claimant, and it is not reasonably practicable for the claimant to obtain the information or evidence by other means;

or

(d) the information or evidence required by the form can only be obtained from a third party, and it is not reasonably practicable for the claimant to obtain such information or evidence from such third party;

or

(e) the Secretary of State is of the opinion that the person making the claim has provided sufficient information or evidence to show that he is not entitled to the benefit for which the claim is made, and that it would be inappropriate to require the form to be completed or further information or evidence to be supplied.

(1C) If a person making a claim is unable to complete the claim form or supply the evidence or information it requires because one of the reasons specified in sub-paragraphs (a) to (d) of paragraph (1B) applies, he may so notify an appropriate office by whatever means.]

(2) In the case of a claim for family credit, where a married or unmarried couple is included in the family, the claim shall be made by the woman, unless the Secretary of State is satisfied that it would be reasonable to accept a claim by the man.

(3) [⁵Subject to paragraph (3C),] in the case of a married or unmarried couple, a claim for income support shall be made by whichever partner they agree should so claim or, in default of agreement, by such one of them as the Secretary of State shall in his discretion determine.

[²(3A) In the case of a married or unmarried couple where both partners satisfy the conditions set out in Section 20(6A) of the Social Security Act 1986 [SSCBA, s.129(1)], a claim for disability working allowance shall be made by whichever partner they agree should so claim, or in default of agreement, by such one of them as the Secretary of State shall determine.]

[⁴(3B) For the purposes of income-based jobseeker's allowance—

(a) in the case of a married or unmarried couple, a claim shall be made by whichever partner they agree should so claim or, in default of agreement, by such one of them as the Secretary of State shall in his discretion determine;

(b) where there is no entitlement to contribution-based jobseeker's allowance on a claim made by one partner and the other partner wishes to claim income-based jobseeker's allowance, the claim made by that other partner shall be treated as having been made on the date on which the first partner made his claim; and

(c) where entitlement to income-based jobseeker's allowance arises on the expiry of entitlement to contribution-based jobseeker's allowance consequent on a claim made by one partner and the other partner then makes a claim—

(i) the claim of the first partner shall be terminated; and

(ii) the claim of the second partner shall be treated as having been made on the day after the entitlement to contribution-based jobseeker's allowance expired.]

[⁵(3C) In the case of a claim for income support for a period to which regulation 21ZA(2) of the Income Support (General) Regulations 1987 (treatment of refugees) refers, the claim shall be made by the refugee or in the case of a married or unmarried couple both of whom are refugees, by either of them.]

(4) Where one of a married or unmarried couple is entitled to income support under an award and, with his agreement, his partner claims income support that entitlement shall terminate on the day before that claim is made or treated as made.

[⁶(5) Where a person who wishes to make a claim for benefit and who has not been supplied with an approved form of claim notifies an appropriate office (by whatever means) of his intention to make a claim, he shall be supplied, without charge, with such form of claim by such person as the Secretary of State may appoint or authorise for that purpose.]

[⁴(6) A person wishing to make a claim for benefit shall—

(a) if it is a claim for a jobseeker's allowance, unless the Secretary of State otherwise directs, attend in person at an appropriate office or such other place, and at such time, as the Secretary of State may specify in his case in a notice under regulation 23 of the Jobseeker's Allowance Regulations;

(b) if it is a claim for any other benefit, deliver or send the claim to an appropriate office.]

(7) If a claim [⁷other than a claim for income support or jobseeker's allowance,] is defective at the date when it is received or has been made in writing but not on the form approved for the time being, the Secretary of State may refer the claim to the person making it or, as the case may be, supply him with the approved form, and if the form is received properly completed within one month, or such longer period as the Secretary of State may consider reasonable, from the date on which it is so referred or supplied, the Secretary of State shall treat the claim as if it has been duly made in the first instance.

[⁷ (7A) In the case of a claim for income support or jobseeker's allowance, if a defective claim is received, the Secretary of State shall advise the person making the claim of the defect and of the relevant provisions of regulation 6(1A) or 6(4A) relating to the date of claim.

(8) A claim, other than a claim for income support or jobseeker's allowance, which is made on the form approved for the time being is, for the purposes of these Regulations, properly completed if completed in accordance with the instructions on the form and defective if not so completed.

(9) In the case of a claim for income support or jobseeker's allowance, a properly completed claim is a claim which meets the requirements of paragraph (1A) and a defective claim is a claim which does not meet those requirements.]

AMENDMENTS

1. Social Security (Miscellaneous Provisions) Amendment Regulations 1990 (S.I. 1990 No. 2208), reg. 8 (December 5, 1990).
2. Social Security (Claims and Payments) Amendment Regulations 1991 (S.I. 1991 No. 2741), reg. 3 (February 3, 1992).
3. Social Security (Miscellaneous Provisions) Amendment Regulations 1992 (S.I. 1992 No. 247), reg. 10 (March 9, 1992).
4. Social Security (Claims and Payments) (Jobseeker's Allowance Consequential Amendments) Regulations 1996 (S.I. 1996 No. 1460), reg. 2(4) (October 7, 1996).
5. Income Support and Social Security (Claims and Payments) (Miscellaneous Amendments) Regulations 1996 (S.I. 1996 No. 2431), reg. 7(b) (October 15, 1996).
6. Social Security (Miscellaneous Amendments) (No. 2) Regulations 1997 (S.I. 1997 No. 793), reg. 2(4) (April 7, 1997).
7. Social Security (Miscellaneous Amendments) (No. 2) Regulations 1997 (S.I. 1997 No. 793), reg. 2 (October 6, 1997).

DEFINITIONS

"appropriate office"—see reg. 2(1).
"benefit"—see reg. 2(2).
"claim for benefit"—see reg. 2(1).
"jobseeker's allowance"—*ibid.*
"married couple"—*ibid.*
"partner"—*ibid.*
"refugee"—*ibid.*
"unmarried couple"—*ibid.*

GENERAL NOTE

Paragraph (1)
Note that from October 6, 1997, para. (1) no longer applies to claims for income support and JSA, for which see paras. (1A) to (1C).
For other benefits covered by this book, para. (1) provides that claims must be made in writing, normally on an official form, although the Secretary of State may accept some other kind of written claim. In such a case, under para. (7), the Secretary of State may require the claimant to fill in the proper form. If this is done in the proper time the claim is treated as duly made in the first instance. It no longer seems possible for an oral claim to be accepted. However, see reg. 6(1)(aa) for the position when a claimant contacts an office with a view to making a claim. Note also reg. 19(6), under which the Secretary of State still has the power to extend the time for claiming by up to a month if it is considered that to do so would be consistent with the proper administration of benefit. But the discretion is no longer open-ended and one of the circumstances in reg. 19(7) must apply. If the claim is properly made within the month, it is treated under reg. 6(3) as made at the beginning of the period specified by the Secretary of State under reg. 19(6) (which normally will be equal to the time taken to return the claim form). The procedure provided for in reg. 19(6) and (7) also applies to income support and JSA, whereas reg. 6(1)(aa) does not apply to claims for those benefits where the first notification of an intention to claim was received after October 5, 1997. But for income support and JSA claims after that date, see reg. 6(1A) and (4A)–(4AB).
Note also *R(SB) 9/84* where a Tribunal of Commissioners holds that where a claim has been determined, the Secretary of State must be deemed, in the absence of any challenge at the time, to have accepted that the claim was made in sufficient manner. See the notes to reg. 33. See also *CDLA 15961/1996* in which the Commissioner set aside the tribunal's decision because they had failed to consider whether they should refer to the Secretary of State the question whether the claimant's application for review should be treated as a claim under para. (1).

Paragraphs (1A) to (1C)
These new provisions, together with the new reg. 6(1A) and (4A) to (4AB), introduce the so-called "onus of proof" changes for claims for income support and JSA from October 6, 1997. The aim

is to place more responsibility on claimants for these benefits to provide information and evidence to support their claim (see the DSS's Memorandum to the Social Security Advisory Committee (SSAC) annexed to the Committee's report (Cm. 3586) on the proposals). SSAC supported this principle but considered that it was "premature to introduce penalties for failure to provide information when it is more likely that the current problems lie more with the forms and procedures than with dilatory or obstructive claimants". As the Committee pointed out, the current claim forms are lengthy, complex and difficult for many people to understand, and moreover in the past told claimants not to delay sending in the claim form even if they had not got all the required information. Furthermore, since income support and income-based JSA are basic subsistence benefits, claimants have every incentive to cooperate in providing all the information needed to get an early payment. Thus SSAC's main recommendation was that the claim forms and guidance to claimants should first be revised and tested "before introducing new penalties, which together with the proposed changes to backdating rules [see reg. 19], will only serve to complicate the social security system and penalise the most disadvantaged claimants". But this recommendation was rejected by the Government, although the final form of the regulations did take limited account of some of SSAC's other recommendations.

Under the new rules, in order for a claim for income support or JSA to be validly made, it must be in writing on a properly completed approved form (there is no longer any provision for the Secretary of State to accept any other kind of written claim) and all the information and evidence required by the form must have been provided (para. (1A)). However, the requirement to complete the form fully or to provide the required evidence does not apply in the circumstances set out in para. (1B). The list in para. (1B) is exhaustive and there is no category of analogous circumstances. If any of sub-paras. (a) to (d) of para. (1B) do apply, the person can inform an appropriate office (defined in reg. 2(1)) "by whatever means" (*e.g.* verbally or through a third party) (para. (1C)). Note that the obligation to provide information and evidence only relates to that required by the claim form; if a claim is accepted as validly made it will still be open to the Benefits Agency to seek further information if this is required in order to decide the claim, but this will not alter the date of claim.

See reg. 6(1A) for the date of claim for an income support claim and reg. 6(4A)–(4AB) for the date of claim for JSA claims (and note the differences).

Thus the major effect of these new rules is that there is now a requirement to produce the specified information and evidence *before* a claim is treated as having been made (although see reg. 6(1A) and (4A)–(4AB) for the date of claim). Whether the necessary evidence has been produced or whether a claimant is exempt under para. (1B) will therefore be a decision for the Secretary of State, *i.e.* there will be no right of appeal to a tribunal in cases of dispute. SSAC's proposal that the decision as to whether a person is exempt from the claiming requirements should be for an AO was not accepted by the Government. But note *R(SB) 9/84(T)* which holds that where a claim has been determined, the Secretary of State must be deemed, in the absence of any challenge at the time, to have accepted that the claim was made in sufficient manner. See the notes to reg. 33.

Note also s. 1(1A) of the Administration Act, under which claimants will not be entitled to benefit unless they satisfy requirements relating to the provision of national insurance numbers.

Paragraph (2)

In family credit cases, if a couple is involved, the claim must normally be made by the woman. The Secretary of State has discretion to accept a claim from the man.

Paragraph (3)

In income support cases, where a couple is involved, either partner can be the claimant, except in the case of a refugee under para. (3C). The exceptionally complex rules of reg. 1A of the Supplementary Benefit (Aggregation) Regulations, incorporating the "nominated breadwinner" scheme, were abandoned. There is now free choice. If the couple cannot jointly agree who should claim, the Secretary of State is to break the tie. There are still some differences in entitlement according to which partner is the claimant, particularly since only the claimant is required to be available for work. In addition, head (b) of para. 12(1) of Sched. 2 to the Income Support Regulations (disability and higher pensioner premium) can only be satisfied by the claimant. But there is now no long-term rate and the full-time employment of either partner excludes entitlement to income support. See reg. 7(2). Under the Income Support (Transitional) Regulations transitional protection is lost if the claimant for the couple changes. *CIS 8/1990* and *CIS 375/1990* challenged this rule on the grounds that it was indirectly discriminatory against women (since in 98 per cent. of couples (at that time) the man was the claimant). Following the ECJ's decision in the *Cresswell* case that income support is not covered by E.C. Directive 79/7 on equal treatment for men and women in social security (see the notes to reg. 36 of the Income Support Regulations), the claimants could not rely on

European law. The Commissioner also rejects a submission that the Sex Discrimination Act 1975 prevented the discriminatory effect of regs. 2 and 10 of the Transitional Regulations. Para. (4) below deals with changes of partner.

Paragraph (3A)

Normally a claim for disability working allowance must be made by the person who is disabled and in remunerative work. Under para. (3A), if both partners in a couple satisfy the conditions of entitlement, they may choose which one of them is to claim. If they cannot choose, the Secretary of State makes the decision.

Paragraph (3B)

Sub-para. (a) applies the normal income support rule for couples to income-based JSA. Sub-paras. (b) and (c) make provision about the deemed date of the claim for income-based JSA by one partner when a claim for contribution-based JSA by the other partner fails or entitlement comes to an end.

Paragraph (3C)

Where one of a couple is a refugee, the claim for income support must be made by that partner. If both are refugees, there is a free choice.

Paragraph (4)

If there is a change of claimant within a couple in the middle of a continuing income support claim, the claims are not to overlap. The change is a matter of a new claim for benefit, not review as it was for supplementary benefit *(R(SB) 1/93)*. In *CSIS 66/1992* the Commissioner rejects the argument that para. (4) combined with s.20(9) of the Social Security Act 1986 (SSCBA s.134(2)) meant that a change of claimant could not be backdated. If the claimant could show good cause for her delay in claiming, regs. 19(2) and 6(3) enabled her claim to be backdated to the date from which she had good cause (subject to the then 12-month limit in reg. 19(4)). Duplication of payment could be avoided by the AO reviewing the claimant's husband's entitlement for any past period in respect of which the claimant was held to be entitled to benefit and applying reg. 5(1) and (2), Case 1, of the Payments Regulations. By becoming the claimant the wife qualified for a disability premium. There is a specific provision in para. 19 of Sched. 7 to the Income Support Regulations for arrears of a disability premium in these circumstances.

Paragraph (6)

The claim, except in the case of JSA, must be delivered or sent to the appropriate office. In *CS 175/1988* the claimant took a claim form to the local office. The counter-clerk told him to get his employer to correct a mistake and he took it away. The Commissioner holds that a claim was not made on that date, because it was not lodged, but merely shown to the clerk for advice. This distinction is unrealistic.

In *CSIS 48/1992* the Commissioner considered the effect of para. (6) in the light of s.7 and s.23 of the Interpretation Act 1978. He concludes that the effect of these provisions is that a claim for a social security benefit is a document authorised by an Act to be served by post, which is presumed to have been delivered in the ordinary course of post unless this is proved not to have been the case. The SSAT should therefore have considered whether it accepted that the claim had been posted, and, if so, whether the presumption of delivery had been rebutted by the AO. *CSIS 48/1992* has been followed in *CIS 759/1992*.

For JSA, a claimant wishing to make an initial claim must normally go in person to the nearest Job Centre to obtain a claim pack from the new jobseeker receptionist. An appointment will then be made for the claimant to return, usually within five days, for a new jobseeker interview. This is all part of the concept of "active signing". The claim will be treated as made on the date of the first attendance, if it is received properly completed within a month (reg. 6(1)(aa) and (4A)).

Paragraphs (7) and (8)

Para. (7), which does not apply to claims for income support or JSA (for which see para. (7A)), deals with written claims not made on the proper form (for which, see para. (1)), and situations where the proper form is not completed according to the instructions (see para. 8)). The Secretary of State may simply treat this as an ineffective attempt to claim, but also has power to refer the form back to the claimant. Then there is one month (extendable by the Secretary of State) to complete the form properly, in which case the claim is treated as made on the date of the original attempt to claim (see reg. 6(1)(b)). Note also *R(SB) 9/84*; see the note to para. (1).

Paragraphs (7A) and (9)

If a claim for income support or JSA is defective (on which see para. (9)), the Secretary of State will simply advise the claimant of the defect and of the rules in reg. 6(1A) (for income support claims) or reg. 6(4A) (for JSA claims) as appropriate. It will then be up to the claimant to comply with those provisions if he is in a position to do so.

Amendment and withdrawal of claim

5.—(1) A person who has made a claim may amend it at any time by notice in writing received in an appropriate office before a determination has been made on the claim, and any claim so amended may be treated as if it had been so amended in the first instance.

(2) A person who has made a claim may withdraw it at any time before a determination has been made on it, by notice to an appropriate office, and any such notice of withdrawal shall have effect when it is received.

Definition

"appropriate office"—see reg. 2(1).

Date of claim

6.—(1) [³Subject to the following provisions of this regulation] the date on which a claim is made shall be—

(a) in the case of a claim which meets the requirements of regulation 4(1), the date on which it is received in an appropriate office;

[¹²(aa) in the case of a claim for—

family credit;

disability working allowance;

jobseeker's allowance if first notification is received before 6th October 1997; or

income support if first notification is received before 6th October 1997;

which meets the requirements of regulation 4(1) and which is received in an appropriate office within one month of first notification in accordance with regulation 4(5), whichever is the later of—

(i) the date on which that notification is received; and

(ii) the first date on which that claim could have been made in accordance with these Regulations;]

(b) in the case of a claim which does not meet the requirements of regulation 4(1) but which is treated, under regulation 4(7) as having been duly made, the date on which the claim was received in an appropriate office in the first instance.

[¹³ (1A) In the case of a claim for income support—

(a) subject to the following sub-paragraphs, the date on which a claim is made shall be the date on which a properly completed claim is received in an appropriate office or the first day in respect of which the claim is made if later;

(b) where a properly completed claim is received in an appropriate office within one month of first notification of intention to make that claim, the date of claim shall be the date on which that notification is deemed to be made or the first day in respect of which the claim is made if later;

(c) a notification of intention to make a claim will be deemed to be made on the date when an appropriate office receives—

(i) a notification in accordance with regulation 4(5); or

(ii) a defective claim.]

(2) [¹...]

[¹(3) In the case of a claim for income support, family credit[⁷, disability working allowance] [¹²or jobseeker's allowance][⁵. . .], where the time for claiming is extended under regulation 19 the claim shall be treated as made on the first day of the period in respect of which the claim is, by reason of the operation of that regulation, timeously made.

(4) Paragraph (3) shall not apply when the time for claiming income support[⁷, family credit[¹⁰, disability working allowance or jobseeker's allowance]] has been extended under regulation 19 and the failure to claim within the prescribed time for the purposes of that regulation is for the reason only that the claim has been sent by post.]

[¹³(4A) Where a person notifies the Secretary of State (by whatever means) that he wishes to claim a jobseeker's allowance—

(a) if he is required to attend under regulation 4(6)(a)—

    (i) if he subsequently attends for the purpose of making a claim for that benefit at the time and place specified by the Secretary of State and complies with the requirements of paragraph (4AA), the claim shall be treated as made on whichever is the later of first notification of intention to make that claim and the first day in respect of which the claim is made;

    (ii) if, without good cause, he fails to attend for the purpose of making a claim for that benefit at either the time or place so specified, or does not comply with the requirements of paragraph (4AA), the claim shall be treated as made on the first day on which he does attend at that place and does provide a properly completed claim;

(b) if under regulation 4(6)(a) the Secretary of State directs that he is not required to attend—

    (i) subject to the following sub-paragraph, the date on which the claim is made shall be the date on which a properly completed claim is received in an appropriate office or the first day in respect of which the claim is made if later;

    (ii) where a properly completed claim is received in an appropriate office within one month of first notification of intention to make that claim, the date of claim shall be the date of that notification.

(4AA) Unless the Secretary of State otherwise directs, a properly completed claim shall be provided at or before the time when the person making the claim for a jobseeker's allowance is required to attend for the purpose of making a claim.

(4AB) The Secretary of State may direct that the time for providing a properly completed claim may be extended to a date no later than the date one month after the date of first notification of intention to make that claim.]

(4B) Where a person's entitlement to a jobseeker's allowance has ceased in any of the circumstances specified in regulation 25(1)(a), (b) or (c) of the Jobseeker's Allowance Regulations (entitlement ceasing on a failure to comply) and—

(a) where he had normally been required to attend in person, he shows that the failure to comply which caused the cessation of his previous entitlement was due to any of the circumstances mentioned in regulation 30(c) or (d) of those Regulations, and no later than the day immediately following the date when those circumstances cease to apply he makes a further claim for jobseeker's allowance; or

(b) where he had not normally been required to attend in person, he shows that he did not receive the notice to attend and he immediately makes a further claim for jobseeker's allowance,

that further claim shall be treated as having been made on the day following that cessation of entitlement.

(4C) Where a person's entitlement to a jobseeker's allowance ceases in the circumstances specified in regulation 25(1)(b) of the Jobseeker's Allowance Regulations (failure to attend at time specified) and that person makes a further claim for that allowance on the day on which he failed to attend at the time specified, that claim shall be treated as having been made on the following day.]

[¹¹(4D) In the case of a claim for income support to which regulation 4(3C) (claim by refugee) refers, the claim shall be treated as made—

    (a) in the case of a claimant who made a claim for asylum upon arrival in the United Kingdom, on the date on which his claim for asylum was first refused by the Secretary of State; or

    (b) in the case of a claimant whose claim for asylum was made other than on arrival in the United Kingdom, on the date of that claim for asylum.]

[²(5) Where a person submits a claim for attendance allowance [⁶or disability living allowance or a request under paragraph (8)] by post and the arrival of that [⁶claim or request] at an appropriate office is delayed by postal disruption caused by industrial action, whether within the postal service or elsewhere, the [⁶claim or request] shall be treated as received on the day on which it would have been received if it had been delivered in the ordinary course of post.]

[³(6) Where—

    (a) on or after 9th April 1990 a person satisfies the capital condition in section 22(6) of the Social Security Act 1986 [SSCBA, s.134(1)] for income support and he would not have satisfied that condition had the amount prescribed under regulation 45 of the Income Support (General) Regulation 1987 been £6,000; and

    (b) a claim for that benefit is received from him in an appropriate office not later than 27th May 1990;

the claim shall be treated as made on the date [⁴not later than 5th December 1990] determined in accordance with paragraph (7).

(7) For the purpose of paragraph (6), where—

    (a) the claimant satisfies the other conditions of entitlement to income support on the date on which he satisfies the capital condition, the date shall be the date on which he satisfies that condition;

    (b) the claimant does not satisfy the other conditions of entitlement to income support on the date on which he satisfies the capital condition, the date shall be the date on which he satisfies the conditions of entitlement to that benefit.]

[⁶(8) [⁸Subject to paragraph (8A),] where—

    (a) a request is received in an appropriate office for a claim form for disability living allowance or attendance allowance; and

    (b) in response to the request a claim form for disability living allowance or attendance is issued from an appropriate office; and

    (c) within the time specified the claim form properly completed is received in an appropriate office,

the date on which the claim is made shall be the date which the request was received in the appropriate office.

[⁸(8A) Where, in a case which would otherwise fall within paragraph (8), it is not possible to determine the date when the request for a claim form was received in an appropriate office because of a failure to record that date, the claim shall be treated as having been made on the date 6 weeks before the date on which the properly completed claim form is received in an appropriate office.]

(9) [⁹In paragraph (8) and (8A)]—

"a claim form" means a form approved by the Secretary of State under regulation 4(1); "properly completed" has the meaning assigned by regulation 4(8);

"the time specified" means 6 weeks from the date on which the request was received or such longer period as the Secretary of State may consider reasonable.]

[⁷(10) Where a person starts a job on a Monday or Tuesday in any week and he makes a claim for disability working allowance in that week the claim shall be treated as made on the Tuesday of that week.

(11) Where a claim for disability working allowance in respect of a person has been refused and a further claim for the same allowance is made in respect of him within the period prescribed under section 100A(1) of the Social Security Act 1975 [SSAA, s.30(1)] and that further claim has been treated as an application for review in accordance with section 100A(12) of that Act [SSAA, s.30(13)] then the original claim shall be treated as made on the date on which the further claim is made or treated as made.]

[¹²(12) Subject to paragraph (14), where a person has claimed disability working allowance and that claim ("the original claim") has been refused, and a further claim is made in the circumstances specified in paragraph (13), that further claim shall be treated as made—

(a) on the date of the original claim; or

(b) on the first date in respect of which the qualifying benefit was payable, whichever is the later.

(13) The circumstances referred to in paragraph (12) are that—

(a) the original claim was refused on the ground that the claimant did not qualify under section 129(2) of the Contributions and Benefits Act;

(b) at the date of the original claim the claimant had made a claim for a qualifying benefit and that claim had not been determined;

(c) after the original claim had been determined, the claim for the qualifying benefit was determined in the claimant's favour; and

(d) the further claim for disability working allowance was made within three months of the date that claim for the qualifying benefit was determined.

(14) Paragraph (12) shall not apply in a case where the further claim for disability working allowance is made within the period prescribed under section 30(1) of the Social Security Administration Act 1992, and is accordingly treated as an application for a review under section 30(13) of that Act.

(15) In paragraphs (12) and (13) "qualifying benefit" means any of the benefits referred to in section 129(2) of the Contributions and Benefits Act.

(16)–(23) [*Omitted as not applying to income-related benefits*].

(24) Where a person has claimed a social fund payment in respect of maternity or funeral expenses and that claim ("the original claim") has been refused, and a further claim is made in the circumstances specified in paragraph (25), that further claim shall be treated as made—

(a) on the date of the original claim; or

(b) on the first date in respect of which the qualifying benefit was awarded, whichever is the later.

(25) The circumstances referred to in paragraph (24) are that—

(a) the original claim was refused on the ground that the claimant had not been awarded a qualifying benefit;

(b) at the date of the original claim the claimant had made a claim for a qualifying benefit and that claim had not been determined;

(c) after the original claim had been determined, the claim for the qualifying benefit was determined in the claimant's favour; and

(d) the further claim for a social fund payment was made within three months of the date that the claim for the qualifying benefit was determined.

(26) In paragraphs (24) and (25) "qualifying benefit" means—

(a) in the case of a claim for a social fund payment in respect of maternity expenses, any benefit referred to in regulation 5(1)(a) of the Social Fund Maternity and Funeral Expenses (General) Regulations 1987;

(b) in the case of a claim for a social fund payment in respect of funeral expenses, any benefit referred to in regulation 7(1)(a) of those Regulations.

(27) Where a claim is made for family credit or disability working allowance, and—

(a) the claimant had previously made a claim for income support or jobseeker's allowance ("the original claim");

(b) the original claim was refused on the ground that the claimant or his partner was in remunerative work; and

(c) the claim for family credit or disability working allowance was made within 14 days of the date that the original claim was determined,

that claim shall be treated as made on the date of the original claim, or, if the claimant so requests, on a later date specified by the claimant.

(28) Where a claim is made for income support or jobseeker's allowance, and—

(a) the claimant had previously made a claim for family credit or disability working allowance ("the original claim");

(b) the original claim was refused on the ground that the claimant or his partner was not in remunerative work; and

(c) the claim for income support or jobseeker's allowance was made within 14 days of the date that the original claim was determined,

that claim shall be treated as made on the date of the original claim, or, if the claimant so requests, on a later date specified by the claimant.]

AMENDMENTS

1. Social Security (Claims and Payments) Amendment Regulations 1988 (S.I. 1988 No. 522), reg. 2 (April 11, 1988).

2. Social Security (Medical Evidence, Claims and Payments) Amendment Regulations 1989 (S.I. 1989 No. 1686), reg. 4 (October 9, 1989).

3. Social Security (Claims and Payments) Amendment Regulations 1990 (S.I. 1990 No. 725), reg. 2 (April 9, 1990).

4. Social Security (Miscellaneous Provisions) Amendment Regulations (S.I. 1990 No. 2208), reg. 9 (December 5, 1990).

5. Social Security (Miscellaneous Provisions) Amendment Regulations 1991 (S.I. 1991 No. 2284), reg. 6 (November 1, 1991).

6. Social Security (Claims and Payments) Amendment Regulations 1991 (S.I. 1991 No. 2741), reg. 4 (February 3, 1992).

7. Social Security (Claims and Payments) Amendment Regulations 1991 (S.I. 1991 No. 2741), reg. 4 (March 10, 1992).

8. Social Security (Claims and Payments) Amendment (No. 3) Regulations 1993 (S.I. 1993 No. 2113), reg. 3 (September 27, 1993).

9. Social Security (Claims and Payments) Amendment Regulations 1994 (S.I. 1994 No. 2319), reg. 2 (October 3, 1994).

10. Social Security (Claims and Payments) (Jobseeker's Allowance Consequential Amendments) Regulations 1996 (S.I. 1996 No. 1460), reg. 2(5) (October 7, 1996).

11. Income Support and Social Security (Claims and Payments) (Miscellaneous Amendments) Regulations 1996 (S.I. 1996 No. 2431), reg. 7(c) (October 15, 1996).

12. Social Security (Miscellaneous Amendments) (No. 2) Regulations 1997 (S.I. 1997 No. 793), reg. 3 (April 7, 1997).

13. Social Security (Miscellaneous Amendments) (No. 2) Regulations 1997 (S.I. 1997 No. 793), reg. 3(3) and (5) (October 6, 1997).

DEFINITIONS

"appropriate office"—see reg. 2(1).
"claim for asylum"—*ibid.*
"claim for benefit"—*ibid.*
"jobseeker's allowance"—*ibid.*

"refugee"—*ibid.*
"week"—*ibid.*

GENERAL NOTE

Paragraph (1)
A properly completed claim on the proper form is made on the date that it is received in a benefit office. See *CS 175/1988*, discussed in the notes to reg. 4(6). If a claim is treated as properly made under reg. 4(7), it is made on the date when the original attempt to claim was received.

There are now many complications around this basic rule in sub-paras (a) and (b), following the introduction of JSA and the severe restriction on the backdating of claims under reg. 19 from April 1997. These appear in sub-para. (aa) and the later provisions in reg. 6.

The main addition is under sub-para. (aa). In claims for family credit or disability working allowance or, up to October 5, 1997, income support or JSA, providing that the claimant is supplied with a claim form on notifying an office of the intention to claim, there is automatically a period of a month for the properly completed claim form to be returned. The claim is then treated as having been made on the earliest appropriate date back to the date of notificaton. For income support and JSA claims after October 5, 1997, see para. (1A) and (4A)–(4AB) respectively.

R(SB) 8/89 holds that if the DSS puts it out of its power to receive a claim, as by closing its office and arranging with the Post Office not to deliver mail, *e.g.* on a Saturday, then if that day is the day on which the claim would have been delivered, it is the date of claim. It can be said that by making the arrangement with the Post Office the DSS constitute the Post Office bailees of the mail (see *Hodgson v. Armstrong* [1967] Q.B. 299 and *Lang v. Devon General Limited* [1987] I.C.R. 4). The Commissioner does not deal expressly with the situation where the office is closed, but there is no arrangement about the mail, *e.g.* if an office is closed on a Saturday and the Saturday and Monday mail is all stamped with the Monday date in the office. Here, principle would suggest that if it can be shown that in the normal course of the post delivery would have been on the Saturday, then the Saturday is the date of receipt and the date of claim. If a claimant proves a delivery by hand when the office is closed, the date of delivery is the date of receipt.

See *CSIS 48/1992* in the notes to reg. 4(6) on the presumption of delivery for claims sent by post.

Paragraph (1A)
This provides that the date of claim for an income support claim will be the date a properly completed claim (*i.e.* one that complies with reg. 4(1A) (reg. 4(9)) is received (or the first day claimed for, if later). But if such a claim is received within one month of the date that the person first contacted the Benefits Agency with a view to making a claim, or a previous defective claim (*i.e.* one that does not comply with reg. 4(1A)), the date of claim will be the date of that initial contact or defective claim (or the first day claimed for, if later). Thus if more than a month elapses before the claimant complies with the requirements of reg. 4(1A), the date of claim will be the date of that compliance (unless the rules on backdating apply: see reg. 19(4) to (7)). See further the note to reg. 4(1A) to (1C).

Paragraph (3)
For these benefits, if the time for claiming is extended under reg. 19, the claim is treated as made at the beginning of the period for which the claim is deemed to be in time. Initial claims for family credit and disability working allowance and claims for income support and JSA have to be made on the first day of the period claimed for (Sched. 4, paras. 6, 7 and 11).

Paragraph (4)
The interaction of this provision with others is far from clear (at least to me). It does not look as though it can apply directly in a case where the Secretary of State has extended the time for claiming by up to a month under reg. 19(6). If the claim is not actually made (*i.e.* received: para. (1)) within the extended period, the claim is not timeously made and para. (3) above does not apply anyway. Postal delay is not a circumstance listed in reg. 19(5) (replacing the old good cause rule), but may be relevant to the reasonableness of the delay in claiming. See also reg. 19(7).

Paragraphs (4A) to (4AB)
In the case of JSA, if the person attends the JobCentre for the purpose of making a claim when required to do so and provides a properly completed claim (*i.e.* with all the necessary information: see reg. 4(1A) and (9)), the date of claim will be the date the person first contacted the JobCentre (or the first day claimed for, if later) (para. (4)(a)(i) and (4AA)). Note the *discretion* to extend the

time for delivery of a properly completed claim form under para. (4AB); unlike income support (and JSA postal signers) the month's allowance to return the fully completed claim form is not automatic. Note also para. (4A)(a)(ii) which provides that if the person fails to comply with these requirements without good cause the date of claim will be the date that he does comply. Thus if the person does have good cause for not so complying, presumably para. (4A)(a)(i) will apply when he does attend and does provide a fully completed claim form (and note the discretion in relation to the claim form under para. (4AB)). For claimants who are not required to attend the JobCentre in person (*i.e.* who are allowed to apply by post), their claim will be treated as made on the day they first contacted the JobCentre with a view to making a claim (or on the first day claimed for, if later) if a properly completed claim is received within one month, or the date the properly completed claim is received if more than one month has elapsed (para. (4A)(b)). See further the note to reg. 4(1A) to (1C)).

Paragraphs (4B) and (4C)

These paragraphs deal with certain cases where entitlement to JSA has ceased because of a failure to attend the Job Centre or to provide a signed declaration of availability and active search for employment, so that a new claim is necessary.

Paragraph (4D)

These are special rules for claims by refugees.

Paragraphs (6) and (7)

These provisions create a special rule on the increase of the capital limit for income support to £8,000. Where, from April 9, 1990, a claimant has capital of more than £6,000 but not more than £8,000, a claim made before May 28, 1990, can be back-dated to the date on which all the conditions of entitlement are satisfied.

Paragraph (10)

Where a claimant starts work on a Monday or Tuesday and makes a claim for disability working allowance at any time in that week (*i.e.* Sunday to Saturday), the claim is treated as made on the Tuesday. Disability working allowance benefit weeks begin on Tuesdays (reg. 16(3)(b)).

Paragraph (11)

In these circumstances, where a further claim for disability working allowance is treated as an application for review under s.30(1) of the Administration Act (1975 Act, s.100A(1)), any award on that review can only have effect from the date of the further claim (Adjudication Regulations, reg. 66(1)). Treating the original claim as having been made at the same date seems to require that all the conditions of entitlement in s.129(1) of the Contributions and Benefits Act (1986 Act, s.20(6A)) must be satisfied at that date. Even if the original AO's decision was clearly wrong it seems that benefit cannot be awarded for the intervening dates.

Paragraphs (12) to (15)

Where a claim for disability working allowance is disallowed on the ground that a qualifying benefit is not payable, although a claim for that benefit has been made, and later the qualifying benefit is awarded, a fresh claim for disability working allowance made within three months of the award of the qualifying benefit is to be treated as made on the date of the original claim (or the date from which the qualifying benefit is awarded, if later). This rule is made necessary by the restrictions from April 1997 on the backdating of claims under reg. 19 and on the effect of reviews.

Paragraphs (24) to (26)

These provisions apply a similar rule to that in paras (12) to (15) to claims for maternity or funeral payments under the social fund.

Paragraphs (27) and (28)

These paragraphs apply where a claim for income support or JSA is disallowed on the ground that the claimant or any partner is in remunerative work (para. (27)) or a claim for family credit or disability working allowance is disallowed on the ground that the claimant and any partner is *not* in remunerative work (para. (28)). Providing that a claim for the right benefit is made within 14 days of the disallowance, it is treated as made on the date of the original claim.

Evidence and information

7.—(1) [³Subject to paragraph (7),] every person who makes a claim for bene-fit shall furnish such certificates, documents, information and evidence in con-nection with the claim, or any question arising out of it, as may be required by the Secretary of State and shall do so within one month of being required to do so or such longer period as the Secretary of State may consider reasonable.

(2) [³Subject to paragraph (7),] where a benefit may be claimed by either of two partners or where entitlement to or the amount of any benefit is or may be affected by the circumstances of a partner, the Secretary of State may require the partner other than the claimant to certify in writing whether he agrees to the claimant making the claim or, as the case may be, that he confirms the informa-tion given about his circumstances.

(3) In the case of a claim for family credit [¹or disability working allowance], the employer of the claimant or, as the case may be, of the partner shall furnish such certificates, documents, information and evidence in connection with the claim or any question arising out of it as may be required by the Secretary of State.

[²(4) In the case of a person who is claiming disability working allowance, family credit[³, income support or jobseeker's allowance], where that person or any partner is aged not less than 60 and is a member of, or a person deriving entitlement to a pension under, a personal pension scheme, or is a party to, or a person deriving entitlement to a pension under, a retirement annuity contract, he shall where the Secretary of State so requires furnish the following information—

    (a) the name and address of the pension fund holder;

    (b) such other information including any reference or policy number as is needed to enable the personal pension scheme or retirement annuity con-tract to be identified.

(5) Where the pension fund holder receives from the Secretary of State a request for details concerning the personal pension scheme or retirement annuity contract relating to a person or any partner to whom paragraph (4) refers, the pension fund holder shall provide the Secretary of State with any information to which paragraph (6) refers.

(6) The information to which this paragraph refers is—

    (a) where the purchase of an annuity under a personal pension scheme has been deferred, the amount of any income which is being withdrawn from the personal pension scheme;

    (b) in the case of—

        (i) a personal pension scheme where income withdrawal is available, the maximum amount of income which may be withdrawn from the scheme; or

        (ii) a personal pension scheme where income withdrawal is not avail-able, or a retirement annuity contract, the maximum amount of income which might be withdrawn from the fund if the fund were held under a personal pension scheme where income withdrawal was available,

calculated by or on behalf of the pension fund holder by means of tables pre-pared from time to time by the Government Actuary which are appropriate for this purpose.]

[³(7) Paragraphs (1) and (2) do not apply in the case of jobseeker's allowance.]

AMENDMENTS

1. Social Security (Claims and Payments) Amendment Regulations 1991 (S.I. 1991 No. 2741), reg. 5 (March 10, 1992).

2. Income-related Benefits Schemes and Social Security (Claims and Payments) (Miscellaneous Amendments) Regulations 1995 (S.I. 1995 No. 2303), reg. 10(3) (October 2, 1995).

3. Social Security (Claims and Payments) (Jobseeker's Allowance Consequential Amendments) Regulations 1996 (S.I. 1996 No. 1460), reg. 2(6) (October 7, 1996).

DEFINITIONS

"benefit"—see reg. 2(2).
"claim for benefit"—see reg. 2(1).
"jobseeker's allowance"—*ibid.*
"partner"—*ibid.*
"pension fund holder"—*ibid.*
"personal pension scheme"—*ibid.*
"retirement annuity contract"—*ibid.*

GENERAL NOTE

Paragraph (1)
This obligation does not arise until a valid claim has been made (*CSB 841/1986*). A failure to produce the information required may mean that a claim does not have to be submitted "forthwith" to the AO (Administration Act, s.20; 1975 Act, s.98). There is no direct sanction for a failure to comply with the requirement. The old supplementary benefit rule allowing a claim to be deemed to have been withdrawn has not been translated into the present Claims and Payments Regulations. After a lapse of a reasonable time, the Secretary of State should refer the claim to the AO to make a decision on the evidence available (*R(SB) 29/83*). If there is a significant gap in the evidence the claimant is likely not to have proved his entitlement on the balance of probabilities. Reg. 7 is only relevant to s.20 of the Administration Act. Once the claim has been referred to the AO the question of whether reg. 7 is satisfied or not is not directly relevant (*R(IS) 4/93*).
See reg. 32 for the continuing obligations of beneficiaries.
Para. (1) does not apply to JSA. See reg. 24 of the Jobseeker's Allowance Regulations for JSA obligations.

Paragraphs (4) to (6)
See reg. 42(2A)–(2C) of the Income Support Regulations and the note to those paragraphs, and reg. 105(3) to (5) of the Jobseeker's Allowance Regulations.

Attendance in person

8.—(1)[¹. . .]
(2) Every person who makes a claim for benefit [¹(other than a jobseeker's allowance)] shall attend at such office or place and on such days and at such times as the Secretary of State may direct, for the purpose of furnishing certificates, documents, information and evidence under regulation 7, if reasonably so required by the Secretary of State.

AMENDMENT

1. Social Security (Claims and Payments) (Jobseeker's Allowance Consequential Amendments) Regulations 1996 (S.I. 1996 No. 1460), reg. 2(7) (October 7, 1996).

DEFINITIONS

"benefit"—see reg. 2(2).
"claim for benefit"—see reg. 2(1).

GENERAL NOTE

There seems now to be no direct sanction for a failure to comply with reg. 8(2) in relation to benefits other than JSA. For JSA obligations, see reg. 23 of the Jobseeker's Allowance Regulations and reg. 37AA(3) of these Regulations.

Interchange with claims for other benefits

9.—(1) Where it appears that a person who has made a claim for benefit specified in column (1) of Part I of Schedule 1 may be entitled to the benefit specified opposite it in column (2) of that Part, any such claim may be treated by the Secretary of State as a claim alternatively, or in addition, to the benefit specified opposite to it in that column.

(2)–(7) [*Omitted as not applying to income-related benefits*]

DEFINITIONS

"benefit"—see reg. 2(2).
"claim for benefit"—see reg. 2(1).

GENERAL NOTE

See Sched. 1.

In *R. v. Secretary of State for Social Security, ex parte Cullen* and *Secretary of State for Social Security v. Nelson* (*The Times*, May 16, 1997), the Court of Appeal confirmed the decision of Harrison J. in *Cullen* (November 16, 1996) and reversed the decision of the Commissioner in *Nelson* (*CA 171/1993*). In both cases, unsuccessful claims for supplementary benefit had been made prior to April 11, 1988. At that time, the 1979 Claims and Payments regulations allowed the Secretary of State to treat a claim for supplementary benefit as in the alternative a claim for attendance allowance. The 1987 Claims and Payments Regulations, which came into effect on April 11, 1988, contained no such power. In 1991 (Cullen) and 1993 (Nelson) claims for attendance allowance were made and it was sought to have the supplementary benefit claims treated as claims for attendance allowance. The Court of Appeal held that the Secretary of State had no power to do so, so that the Commissioner in *CA 171/1993* was wrong to refer the question to the Secretary of State for determination. Once the 1979 Regulations were revoked, the Secretary of State could no longer exercise a power which no longer existed. As the Secretary of State had only had a discretion under the 1979 Regulations whether or not to treat a supplementary benefit claim as in the alternative a claim for attendance allowance, the claimants had no accrued rights which were preserved on the revocation of the 1979 Regulations under s. 16 of the Interpretation Act 1978.

Advance claims and awards

13.—(1) Where, although a person does not satisfy the requirements for entitlement to benefit on the date on which a claim is made, the adjudicating authority is of the opinion that unless there is a change of circumstances he will satisfy those requirements for a period beginning on a day ("the relevant day") not more than 3 months after the date on which the claim is made, then that authority may—

(a) treat the claim as if made for a period beginning with the relevant day; and

(b) award benefit accordingly, subject to the condition that the person satisfies the requirements for entitlement when benefit becomes payable under the award.

(2) An award under paragraph (1)(b) shall be reviewed by the adjudicating authority if the requirements for entitlement are found not to have been satisfied on the relevant day.

(3) [⁵Subject to paragraph (4), paragraphs (1) and (2) do not] apply to any claim for maternity allowance, attendance allowance, [²disability living allowance], retirement pension or increase, family credit [⁴disability working allowance], or any claim within regulation 11(1)(a) or (b).

[¹(4) Paragraphs (1) and (2) of this regulation shall apply to a claim for family credit made—

    (a) on or after 10th March 1992 and before 7th April 1992;

    (b) in respect of a period beginning on or after 7th April 1992; and

    (c) by a person who, if he is a member of a married or unmarried couple, he or the other member of the couple, is engaged and normally engaged in remunerative work for not less than 16 but less than 24 hours a week on the date the claim is made.

    (5) In paragraph (4)(c) "remunerative work" and "engaged and normally engaged in remunerative work" shall be construed in accordance with regulations 4 and 5 respectively of the Family Credit (General) Regulations 1987 [³save that in their application to paragraph 4(c) those regulations shall be read as though for the words "not less than 24 hours" there were substituted the words "not less than 16 hours but less than 24 hours"].]

    [⁵(6) Where a person claims family credit or disability working allowance but does not satisfy the requirements for entitlement to that benefit on the date on which the claim is made, and the adjudicating authority is of the opinion that he will satisfy those requirements for a period beginning on a day not more than 3 days after the date on which the claim is made, the adjudicating authority may treat the claim as if made for a period beginning with that day, and award benefit accordingly.]

AMENDMENTS

    1. Social Security (Miscellaneous Provisions) Amendment Regulations 1991 (S.I. 1991 No. 2284), reg. 7 (November 1, 1991).
    2. Social Security (Claims and Payments) Amendment Regulations 1991 (S.I. 1991 No. 2741), reg. 6(a) (February 3, 1992).
    3. Social Security (Miscellaneous Provisions) Amendment Regulations 1992 (S.I. 1992 No. 247), reg. 13 (March 9, 1992).
    4. Social Security (Claims and Payments) Amendment Regulations 1991 (S.I. 1991 No. 2741), reg. 6(b) (March 10, 1992).
    5. Social Security (Claims and Payments) Amendment Regulations 1994 (S.I. 1994 No. 2319), reg. 3 (October 3, 1994).

DEFINITIONS

    "adjudicating authority"—see reg. 2(1).
    "benefit"—see reg. 2(2).
    "married couple"—see reg. 2(1).
    "unmarried couple"—*ibid.*

GENERAL NOTE

    Paras. (1) and (2) contain a useful power in income support and social fund maternity and funeral expenses cases, to make awards in advance, subject to review if circumstances change. Para. (1) gives a wide discretion (*CIS 459/1994*).
    The general rule in para. (3) is that the power in paras. (1) and (2) does not apply to family credit, but para. (4) allowed advance claims immediately in advance of the change in the number of qualifying hours from 24 to 16 in April 1992. See also para. (6).
    The power in paras. (1) and (2) does not apply to disability working allowance (para. (3)), but see reg. 13B for claims in advance of the start of the scheme, and para. (6).
    From October 1994, para. (6) allows family credit and disability working allowance claims to be made up to three days in advance.

[¹Advance claim for and award of disability working allowance

    13B.—(1) Where a person makes a claim for disability working allowance on or after 10th March 1992 and before 7th April 1992 the adjudicating authority may—

(a) treat the claim as if it were made for a period beginning on 7th April 1992; and

(b) An award benefit accordingly, subject to the condition that the person satisfies the requirements for entitlement on 7th April 1992.

(2) An award under paragraph (1)(b) shall be reviewed by the adjudicating authority if the requirements for entitlement are found not to have been satisfied on 7th April 1992.]

AMENDMENT

1. Social Security (Claims and Payments) Amendment Regulations 1991 (S.I. 1991 No. 2741), reg. 7(2) (March 10, 1992).

DEFINITION

"adjudicating authority"—see reg. 2(1).

GENERAL NOTE

This allowed an advance claim in the few weeks immediately before the start of the scheme on April 7, 1992.

Cold weather payments

15A. [¹ . . .]

AMENDMENT

1. Social Security (Miscellaneous Provisions) Amendment Regulations 1991 (S.I. 1991 No. 2284), reg. 8 (November 1, 1991).

GENERAL NOTE

Claims for cold weather payments are no longer necessary or possible.

Date of entitlement under an award for the purpose of payability of benefit and effective date of change of rate

16.—(1) For the purpose only of determining the day from which benefit is to become payable, where a benefit other than one of those specified in paragraph (4) is awarded for a period of a week, or weeks, and the earliest date on which entitlement would otherwise commence is not the first day of a benefit week, entitlement shall begin on the first day of the benefit week next following.

[¹(1A) Where a claim for family credit is made in accordance with paragraph 7(a) [²or (aa)] of Schedule 4 for a period following the expiration of an existing award of family credit [²or disability working allowance], entitlement shall begin on the day after the expiration of that award.

(1B) Where a claim for family credit [²or disability working allowance] is made on or after the date when an up-rating order is made under section 63(2) of the Social Security Act 1986 [SSAA, s.150], but before the date when that order comes into force, and—

(a) an award cannot be made on that claim as at the date it is made but could have been made if that order were then in force, and

(b) the period beginning with the date of claim and ending immediately before the date when the order came into force does not exceed 28 days, entitlement shall begin from the date the up-rating order comes into force.]

[²(1C) Where a claim for disability working allowance is made in accordance with paragraph 11(a) or (b) of Schedule 4 for a period following the expiration

of an existing award of disability working allowance or family credit, entitlement shall begin on the day after the expiration of that award.]

(2) Where there is a change in the rate of any benefit to which paragraph (1)
applies the change, if it would otherwise take effect on a day which is not the
appropriate pay day for that benefit, shall take effect from the appropriate pay
day next following.

[¹(3) For the purposes of this regulation the first day of the benefit week—
  (a) in the case of child benefit is Monday,
  (b) in the case of family credit [²or disability working allowance] is Tuesday,
       and
  (c) in any other case is the day of the week on which the benefit is payable
       in accordance with regulation 22 (long-term benefits).]

(4) The benefits specified for exclusion from the scope of paragraph (1) are
[⁴jobseeker's allowance], [³incapacity benefit], maternity allowance, [¹. . .],
severe disablement allowance, income support [¹. . .] and any increase of those
benefits.

AMENDMENTS

   1. Social Security (Claims and Payments) Amendment Regulations 1988 (S.I. 1988 No. 522),
reg. 3 (April 11, 1988).
   2. Social Security (Claims and Payments) Amendment Regulations 1991 (S.I. 1991 No. 2741),
reg. 9 (March 10, 1992).
   3. Social Security (Claims and Payments) Amendment (No. 2) Regulations 1994 (S.I. 1994 No.
2943), reg. 6 (April 13, 1995).
   4. Social Security (Claims and Payments) (Jobseeker's Allowance Consequential Amendments)
Regulations 1996 (S.I. 1996 No. 1460), reg. 2(9) (October 7, 1996).

DEFINITIONS

   "benefit"—see reg. 2(2).
   "jobseeker's allowance"—see reg. 2(1).
   "week"—*ibid.*

GENERAL NOTE

   Reg. 16 does not apply to income support (para. (4)). See Sched. 7 for the income support rules.
Reg. 16 is inappropriate for social fund payments. It does apply to family credit and disability
working allowance. Para. (1) supplies the normal rule for the beginning of entitlement, *i.e.* the first
day of the benefit week beginning on the date of claim or in the following six days. Note that under
para. (3) and reg. 27 the family credit and disability working allowance pay-day is a Tuesday, and
it is paid in arrears. Paras.(1A) to (1C) provide for awards of family credit or disability working
allowance which follow on from an award of family credit or disability working allowance to begin
on the day after the end of the previous award.

Duration of awards

   17.—(1) Subject to the provisions of this regulation and of section [¹37ZA(3)
of the Social Security Act 1975 (disability living allowance) and section] 20(6)
[²and (6F)] of the Social Security Act 1986 (family credit [²and disability
working allowance]) [SSCBA, ss. 71(3), 128(3) and 129(6)] a claim for benefit
shall be treated as made for an indefinite period and any award of benefit on
that claim shall be made for an indefinite period.

   [³(1A) Where an award of income support or an income-based jobseeker's
allowance is made in respect of a married or unmarried couple and one member
of the couple is, at the date of claim, a person to whom section 126 of the
Contributions and Benefits Act or, as the case may be, section 14 of the Jobseekers Act applies, the award of benefit shall cease when the person to whom

section 126 or, as the case may be, section 14 applies returns to work with the same employer.]

(2) [³. . .]

(3) If[³. . .] it would be inappropriate to treat a claim as made and to make an award for an indefinite period (for example where a relevant change of circumstances is reasonably to be expected in the near future) the claim shall be treated as made and the award shall be for a definite period which is appropriate in the circumstances.

(4) In any case where benefit is awarded in respect of days subsequent to the date of claim the award shall be subject to the condition that the claimant satisfies the requirements for entitlement; and where those requirements are not satisfied the award shall be reviewed.

(5) The provisions of Schedule 2 shall have effect in relation to claims for [³jobseeker's allowance] made during periods connected with public holidays.

AMENDMENTS

1. Social Security (Claims and Payments) Amendment Regulations 1991 (S.I. 1991 No. 2741), reg. 10 (February 3, 1992).
2. Social Security (Claims and Payments) Amendment Regulations 1991 (S.I. 1991 No. 2741), reg. 10 (March 10, 1992).
3. Social Security (Claims and Payments) (Jobseeker's Allowance Consequential Amendments) Regulations 1996 (S.I. 1996 No. 1460), reg. 2(10) (October 7, 1996).

DEFINITIONS

"benefit"—see reg. 2(2).
"claim for benefit"—see reg. 2(1).
"jobseeker's allowance"—*ibid.*
"the Jobseekers Act"—*ibid.*

GENERAL NOTE

Paragraph (1)
A claim for income support or income-based JSA is generally to be treated as for an indefinite period, and an award is for an indefinite period. The presumption in para. (1) is a strong one (*R(IS) 8/95*), discussed in the note to para. (3)). Any subsequent change in or removal of entitlement must be by way of review under s.25 of the Administration Act (1975 Act, s.104). See *CIS 620/1990*. An exception is provided in para. (2). Family credit and disability working allowance is payable for a period of 26 weeks and is not affected by change of circumstances (Contributions and Benefits Act, ss.128(3) and 129(6); 1986 Act, ss.20(6) and (6A)). The running of a claim is not automatically terminated by the submission of a new claim, although this will be the case if an undisputed award is made on the new claim (para. 11 of *R(S) 1/83*, applied in *CIS 181/1993*, to be reported as *R(IS) 5/95*, and *CIS 82/1993*). See also *CIS 701/1993*. *CS 12476/1996* states that this applies whether the new claim is decided favourably *or* adversely to the claimant. This is based on *CM 91A/1993*, but would seem to go beyond what was said by the Tribunal of Commissioners in *R(S) 1/83*. An express withdrawal or termination will end a claim, for example, if the claimant "signs off" on starting work (*CIS 240/1992*). But a failure to sign on does not indicate that the claim has terminated (*CIS 563/1991*).

Note *CSIS 28/1992* and *CSIS 40/1992* (to be reported as *R(IS) 17/94*) in which a Tribunal of Commissioners holds that a SSAT should deal with the position from the date of claim down to the date of its decision, preferring the approach of another Tribunal of Commissioners in *CIS 391/1992* and *CIS 417/1992* (to be reported as *R(IS) 5/98*) to that of *CIS 649/1992*, where the Commissioner decided that an adjudicating authority should only consider the position as at the date from which benefit is sought. *CIS 649/1992* is also inconsistent with, for example, *CIS 654/1991* (to be reported as *R(IS) 3/93*), *CIS 30/1993*, *CIS 181/1993*, *R(IS) 8/95*, *CIS 563/1991* and *CIS 11481/1995*. In *CIB 14430/1996*, *CIS 12015/1996* and *CS 12054/1996* another Tribunal of Commissioners has recently confirmed that the down to the date of hearing principle applies not only in relation to an appeal against a refusal of an original claim but also one concerning a decision on review. See further the notes to reg. 23(2) of the Adjudication Regulations.

But note that in relation to appeals brought on or after May 21, 1998, a tribunal will only be able to consider the position up to the date of the AO's decision (see the new subs. (8) inserted into s.22 of the Administration Act by para. 3 of Sched. 6 to the Social Security Act 1998; note also the new subs. (7) of s.21, inserted by para. 2 of Sched. 6 to the 1998 Act). Thus a claimant will have to submit a fresh claim (or claims) as time elapses (and appeal as necessary), in order for any changes in his circumstances to be considered. See President's Circular No. 15 which helpfully points out that this does not necessarily render irrelevant evidence which comes into existence after the AO's decision. A tribunal will still be able to take this into account if it throws further light on circumstances that did obtain at the time of the decision.

Note that s.22(8) of the Administration Act has no effect on the period of any award made by a tribunal hearing an appeal lodged on or after May 21, 1998. Any such award of income support or income-based JSA will continue to be normally for an indefinite period (subject to the termination of the running of the claim, see above), unless an award for a definite period is appropriate (see para. (3)).

Paragraph (1A)

An award of income support or income-based JSA for a couple, where at the date of claim one partner was caught by the trade dispute rule (Contributions and Benefits Act, s. 126; Jobseekers Act 1995, s. 14), ends when that partner returns to work with the same employer. It appears that a fresh claim for income support has to be made under s. 127 of the Contributions and Benefits Act for the first 15 days back at work.

Paragraph (3)

If an award of income support or income-based JSA for an indefinite period is inappropriate then an award can be made for a definite period. The discretion to determine what is or is not appropriate should be exercised in an informed, reasonable and practical manner (*CIS 83/1990*). In *R(IS) 8/95*, the Commissioner states that what is appropriate or inappropriate has to be determined in the light of all the circumstances and the relevant legislative provisions. The claimant normally worked a 37 hour week but went onto a period of short time, working one week on and one week off. There was a possibility that he might be called in on non-working weeks. The claimant therefore argued that his claim should be considered on a week by week basis and that he was entitled to income support in the weeks off. The Commissioner, however, holds that in deciding whether the claimant was engaged in remunerative work under reg. 5 of the Income Support (General) Regulations, the question whether his hours of work fluctuated had to be looked at over a period which was longer than a week because the aim was to decide the hours worked in a week. This indicated that the claim was to be treated as made for an indefinite period, rather than a definite period, or series of definite periods. Although a claim may be limited to certain weeks that did not prevent an adjudicating authority from treating it as made for an indefinite period. However, the fact that an adjudicating authority could deal with a claim down to the date of its decision must mean that it could make an award limited to only some of the weeks in that period. As regards weeks after the date of the adjudicating authority's decision, clearly an award for an indefinite period could be made under reg. 17(1). However, the Commissioner considered that an award for a definite period, or periods, in the future could only be made for periods defined by particular dates.

Para. (3) refers as an example of when a definite award might be appropriate to a case where a change of circumstances is reasonably expected in the near future. Examples might be that a person is about to start a job or become a student. However. there may be other situations in which an award for an indefinite period is inappropriate, as illustrated by *R(S) 1/92*. In that case the Commissioner holds that the fact that the time was approaching when the claimant's incapacity to work would have to be tested against a wider field of employment could justify the making of an award for a definite period, although no change in the claimant's medical condition was anticipated.

An award is to be presumed to be for an indefinite period unless it is expressly made for a definite period. Even if the award is expressly made for a definite period, on appeal the SSAT may investigate whether the AO has shown that an indefinite award was inappropriate (see *R(IS) 8/95* above).

Para. (3) can obviously apply to an initial claim, when entitlement begins on the date of claim (Sched. 7, para. 6(2A)) and continues for the appropriate period. It was held in relation to the corresponding supplementary benefit provision that an indefinite award could be reviewed and replaced by a definite award when the end of entitlement was foreseeable (*CSB 1053/1986*). However, it appears that such a procedure is not now possible under para. (3) where the initial claim and award were made for an indefinite period. If at some later date the end of entitlement becomes foreseeable, that is no ground for treating the claim as having been made for a definite period, which is the first stage of making an award for a definite period. It seems that the proper procedure in these circumstances is either to wait until the event occurs and then review the award on a change of circumstances (Administration Act, s.25(1)(b); 1975 Act, s.104(1)(b)) or review the award in advance on an anticipated change of circumstances (s.25(1)(c); s.104(1)).

See Sched. 7, para. 7 for the date from which a revised decision on a change of circumstances is to take effect.

Paragraph (4)

This provision will apply to virtually every income support, income-based JSA, family credit and disability working allowance award, for it covers all cases where benefit is awarded for days subsequent to the date of claim. Initial claims for income support, JSA, family credit and disability working allowance have to be made on the first day of the period claimed for (Sched. 4, paras. 1, 6, 7 and 11). The predecessor of para. (4) applied to sickness and invalidity benefits and para. (4) has been used most commonly in that context. However, its use in income support cases has been approved in *R(IS) 20/93* and *CIS 620/1990*.

Para. (4) apparently requires an award to be reviewed whenever the claimant does not satisfy the requirements for entitlement. In *R(S) 5/89* a Tribunal of Commissioners held that a similar, but not identical, power in relation to sickness and invalidity benefit in reg. 11 of the 1979 Claims and Payments Regulations was independent of s.104 of the 1975 Act (now s.25 of the Administration Act). They put the burden of showing that the claimant had ceased to satisfy the requirements for entitlement on the AO. *R(S) 3/90* expressly holds that the burden of proving the conditions for a review under para. (4) is on the AO. This was a matter that was often overlooked by AOs and SSATs. As the Commissioner stresses in *CIS 620/1990*, this is a matter of substance and not a technicality.

The scope of para. (4) thus seemed to be very sweeping because the ground for review had wrapped up in it the conclusion that the award of benefit be revised so as to terminate entitlement. The AO needs no warrant to consider whether para. (4) applies other than his own opinion that the claimant does not satisfy the conditions for entitlement (*R(S) 3/94*).

However, in *CSIS 137/1994* (to be reported as *R(IS) 2/98*) another Tribunal of Commissioners declines to follow *R(S) 5/89*. They hold that para. (4) does not provide a separate and independent jurisdiction for conducting reviews but acts as a trigger for the operation of the normal review procedures. The Commissioners point out that para. (4) does not set up a separate review machinery. In their view there was no need for an independent system since ss. 25, 30 and 31 already covered all the relevant situations where a review would be required. Moreover, if para. (4) did provide a separate review procedure, this could by-pass ss. 30–35 of the Administration Act and leave a claimant in disability cases without any right of appeal to a tribunal at all, since neither s. 22 nor s. 33 would apply. Thus the purpose of para. (4) was to make mandatory a review of a continuing (or future) award under the normal review powers, if the requirements on which the award was based were no longer (or not) satisfied. This meant, for instance, that if a review had been correctly conducted under the power, *e.g.*, in s. 25(1)(b) (relevant change of circumstances), the fact that the AO had only referred to para. (4) as the authority for the review did not invalidate it. It also followed that there was no special rule against retrospective review applying to cases within para. (4) (contrary to the view expressed in, *e.g. CIS 413/1992* and *CSIS 92/1994*).

This approach to para. (4) is cogently argued and it is suggested that it should be followed in preference to *R(S) 5/89* (which in any event dealt with a differently worded regulation made under a different power: see the notes to para. (4) in the 1995 edition). The argument that para. (4) was *ultra vires* (the authority for making the provision presumably being what is now s. 5(1)(d) and (e) of the Administration Act) was not pursued before the Tribunal in *R(IS) 2/98* (rightly in their view).

The Commissioners also held that para. (4) operated at any point when the "requirements for entitlement" to the benefit concerned were not, or were no longer, satisfied (following *R(S) 3/94* which rejected the argument that para. (4) only allowed review where a claimant did not satisfy the requirements at the *outset* of an award). In addition, it applied whenever *any* of the requirements ceased to be met, whether the whole award was to be terminated or just a component of it revised (see *CSIS 92/1994*). The Tribunal disagreed with *CIS 627A/1992, CIS 251/1993, CIS 45/1994* and *CIS 856/1994* (see the 1995 edition for details of these decisions) that para. (4) was restricted to cases where entitlement to benefit was to be extinguished.

In income support cases the question of the scope and effect of para. (4) has most recently arisen where an AO has decided that a claimant is no longer entitled to income support on the ground of incapacity for work. (See the 1995 edition for the various decisions which led to the Tribunal of Commissioners being appointed in *R(IS) 2/98* to determine this issue.) The Commissioners in *R(IS) 2/98* set out how a SSAT should approach disputed review decisions in such cases. An AO's decision should not be held invalid solely on the basis that the only reference is to para. (4), without considering whether grounds for review have in fact arisen. If a review has not been properly carried out, the tribunal should decide whether they have sufficient information to carry out the review themselves. They should also, as far as possible, conduct any later review that may be needed down to the date of their decision.

The Tribunal in *R(IS) 2/98* also confirmed that a decision that a person was not incapable of work did not itself trigger the operation of para. (4) because incapacity was not at that time a condition of entitlement for income support (see *CSIS 99/1994* and *CIS 783/1994* in the notes to para. 5 of Sched. 1 to the Income Support Regulations in the 1996 edition of this book as to the effect at that time of such a decision on a claimant's right to income support). However, if entitlement to the disability premium was involved, para. (4) required a review as soon as the conditions for this ceased to be met.

The effect of *R(IS) 2/98* is thus that the AO will have to establish grounds for review under s. 25 (see the notes to s. 25). A different medical opinion is not a change of circumstances, although it may be evidence of an underlying change if there is other evidence of this, *e.g.* if a person has resumed work or has recovered (*R(S) 6/78, R(S) 4/86*). This is confirmed in *R(IS) 2/98*. The Commissioners approved the approach of *CIS 856/1994* that, although not a relevant change in itself, an up-to-date medical report may nevertheless disclose new facts that would constitute a change of circumstances. Another relevant change could be if the time had come to apply a different test to ascertain a claimant's capacity for work (see *CIS 251/1993*). However, grounds for review will not be shown on a second or subsequent application of the "all work test" (see the notes to para. 7 of Sched. 1B to the Income Support Regulations) by the AO simply scoring the claimant at less than 15 points (*CIS 3899/1997*). The Commissioner states that a comparison with the evidence which led to the previous decision was necessary and therefore AOs and tribunals would need to have available and take into consideration the evidence relating to the previous application of the all work test to see whether grounds for review had been made out. The Commissioner in *CIS 3899/1997* also confirms that where there had been an AO's decision that the claimant satisfies the all work test, a subsequent decision that the claimant was not incapable of work could only take effect if there had been a reivew of the earlier decision (see further *CIB 16092/1996 and CIB 90/1997* in the notes to para. 7 of Sched. 1B to the Income Support Regulations).

[¹Time for claiming benefit

19.—(1) Subject to the following provisions of this regulation, the prescribed time for claiming any benefit specified in column (1) of Schedule 4 is the appropriate time specified opposite that benefit in column (2) of that Schedule.

(2) The prescribed time for claiming the benefits specified in paragraph (3) is three months beginning with any day on which, apart from satisfying the condition of making a claim, the claimant is entitled to the benefit concerned.

(3) The benefits to which paragraph (2) applies are—

(a) child benefit;

(b) guardian's allowance;

(c) graduated retirement benefit;

(d) invalid care allowance;

(e) maternity allowance;

(f) retirement pension of any category;

(g) widow's benefit;

(h) except in a case to which section 3(3) of the Social Security Administration Act 1992 applies (late claims for widowhood benefits where death is difficult to establish), any increase in any benefit (other than income support or jobseeker's allowance) in respect of a child or adult dependant.

(4) Subject to paragraph (8), in the case of a claim for income support, jobseeker's allowance, family credit or disability working allowance, where the claim is not made within the time specified for that benefit in Schedule 4, the prescribed time for claiming the benefit shall be extended, subject to a maximum extension of three months, to the date on which the claim is made, where—

(a) any of the circumstances specified in paragraph (5) applies or has applied to the claimant; and

(b) as a result of that circumstance or those circumstances the claimant could not reasonably have been expected to make the claim earlier.

(5) The circumstances referred to in paragraph (4) are—

(a) the claimant has difficulty communicating because—

(i) he has learning, language or literacy difficulties; or

(ii) he is deaf or blind,

and it was not reasonably practicable for the claimant to obtain assistance from another person to make his claim;

(b) except in the case of a claim for jobseeker's allowance, the claimant was ill or disabled, and it was not reasonably practicable for the claimant to obtain assistance from another person to make his claim;

(c) the claimant was caring for a person who is ill or disabled, and it was not reasonably practicable for the claimant to obtain assistance from another person to make his claim;

(d) the claimant was given information by an officer of the Department of Social Security or of the Department for Education and Employment which led the claimant to believe that a claim for benefit would not succeed;

(e) the claimant was given written advice by a solicitor or other professional adviser, a medical practitioner, a local authority, or a person working in a Citizens Advice Bureau or a similar advice agency, which led the claimant to believe that a claim for benefit would not succeed;

(f) the claimant or his partner was given written information about his income or capital by his employer or former employer, or by a bank or building society, which led the claimant to believe that a claim for benefit would not succeed;

(g) the claimant was required to deal with a domestic emergency affecting him and it was not reasonably practicable for him to obtain assistance from another person to make his claim; or

(h) the claimant was prevented by adverse weather conditions from attending the appropriate office.

(6) In the case of a claim for income support, jobseeker's allowance, family credit or disability working allowance, where—

(a) the claim is not made within the time specified for that benefit in Schedule 4, but is made within one month of the expiry of that time; and

(b) the Secretary of State considers that to do so would be consistent with the proper administration of benefit,

the Secretary of State may direct that the prescribed time for claiming shall be extended by such period as he considers appropriate, subject to a maximum of one month, where any of the circumstances specified in paragraph (7) applies.

(7) The circumstances referred to in paragraph (6) are—

(a) the appropriate office where the claimant would be expected to make a claim was closed and alternative arrangements were not available;

(b) the claimant was unable to attend the appropriate office due to difficulties with his normal mode of transport and there was no reasonable alternative available;

(c) there were adverse postal conditions;

(d) the claimant was previously in receipt of another benefit, and notification of expiry of entitlement to that benefit was not sent to the claimant before the date that his entitlement expired;

(e) in the case of a claim for family credit, the claimant had previously been entitled to income support or jobseeker's allowance ("the previous benefit"), and the claim for family credit was made within one month of expiry of entitlement to the previous benefit;

(f) except in the case of a claim for family credit or disability working allowance, the claimant had ceased to be a member of a married or unmarried couple within the period of one month before the claim was made; [² . . .]

(g) during the period of one month before the claim was made a close relative of the claimant had died, and for this purpose "close relative" means partner, parent, son, daughter, brother or [² sister; or]

[²(h) in the case of a claim for disability working allowance, the claimant had previously been entitled to income support, jobseeker's allowance, incapacity benefit or severe disablement allowance ("the previous benefit"), and the claim for disability working allowance was made within one month of expiry of entitlement to the previous benefit.]

(8) This regulation shall not have effect with respect to a claim to which regulation 21ZA(2) of the Income Support (General) Regulations 1987 (treatment of refugees) applies.]

AMENDMENTS

1. Social Security (Miscellaneous Amendments) (No. 2) Regulations 1997 (S.I. 1997 No. 793), reg. 6 (April 7, 1997).
2. Social Security (Claims and Payments and Adjudication) Amendment No. 2 Regulations 1997 (S.I. 1997 No. 2290), reg. 6 (October 13, 1997).

DEFINITIONS

"appropriate office"—see reg. 2(1).
"jobseeker's allowance"—*ibid.*
"married couple"—*ibid.*
"partner"—*ibid.*
"unmarried couple"—*ibid.*

GENERAL NOTE

Paragraph (1)
The prescribed time for claiming the income-related benefits dealt with in this book are set out in Sched. 4. For income support, JSA and new claims for family credit and disability working allowance, the prescribed time is the first day of the period in respect of which the claim is made. In view of the changes made to the rules on the backdating of claims, discussed below, claimants may need to be very careful in defining the period for which they wish to claim. Note that if a claimant signs an ordinary income support claim form, which contains no question asking from what date benefit is claimed, the claim will be interpreted as a claim for an indefinite period from the date on which the claim is made. If the claimant wishes to claim for a past period, that must be stated expressly (*R(SB) 9/84*). Note *CIS 2057/1998* in which the Commissioner accepted that by putting the words "disabled—aged 16" on her claim form the claimant had indicated an intention to claim income support from her sixteenth birthday. If, before a decision is made on an ordinary claim, the claimant indicates a wish to claim for a past period, that can operate as an amendment of the original claim taking effect on the original date. But if, after there has been a decision on the claim, the claimant indicates such a wish (as often happens when the original claim has been successful), it is generally assumed that that can only be treated as a fresh claim on the date on which it was made and that any question of backdating under reg. 19(4) has to be assessed according to that date of claim.

Paragraphs (2) and (3)
The prescribed time for claiming the benefits listed in para. (3), none of which fall within the scope of this book, is three months beginning with any day of potential entitlement. The contrast between this formulation of normal backdating and the technique adopted for income-related benefits may be important.

Paragraphs (4) and (5)
From April 1997 the time-honoured test of good cause for backdating claims, for most, but not all, benefits subject to a 12-month limit under s. 1(2) of the Administration Act, has been abolished. The new test for income support, JSA, family credit and disability working allowance is, by comparison, severely limited in two ways. First, the limit of backdating is fixed at three months rather than 12. Secondly, the flexibility of the good cause test has been replaced by a limited list of circumstances which must exist before a claim can be backdated. In the Memorandum to the Social Security Advisory

Committee (SSAC) on the amending regulations (in Cm. 3586) it is estimated that the change in the rules will result in a saving of £22 million in 1997/98 and similar savings in future years.

The thinking behind the change is set out in the Government's response to the SSAC's recommendation that the backdating rules, subject to the good cause test, should remain as they stand:

"The Government does not accept this proposal or the Committee's view that the backdating rules are already substantially aligned. As the Department's memorandum to the Committee states, there are now ten different rules for backdating claims and six for backdating reviews. The Government believes that this degree of complexity stands in the way of more efficient administration and can be confusing for both the Department's staff and customers. The current provisions on whether a claimant has good cause for making a late claim are particularly complex and time consuming to apply since they require consideration of a substantial body of caselaw when deciding whether to award backdating. The objective of the changes to the backdating rules is to improve administrative efficiency. The Committee's recommendation would not support this objective."

"Administrative efficiency" includes assisting in the aim of "developing a single, streamlined computer system" (para. 3 of the Memorandum to the SSAC).

Although it is common to speak of the backdating of claims, it is vital to appreciate that the technique of para. (4) is to extend the time for claiming for a past period forward from the first day of that period. There is an immediate problem in the working of the three-month limit. If on May 31, 1997 a claim is made for income support for the period from February 1, 1997 to May 30 1997, it appears that the time for claiming for the whole period cannot be extended under para. (4) because that would go beyond the three-month limit. It does not matter that one of the listed circumstances has made it reasonable for the claim not to be made earlier. The claim could be amended before it is adjudicated on, so as to make it a claim from March 1, 1997. Then there could be an extension. It would therefore be good practice for AOs, if dealing with a claim which inevitably breaks the three-month limit, not to decide the claim, but to invite the claimant to amend the period claimed for. It remains to be seen if that practice will be adopted. An alternative approach could be for an AO to treat a claim for an extension that exceeds three months as being for the maximum period that is permitted, *i.e.*, three months. It seems likely that most claimants, if asked, would say that they would prefer this approach, if the alternative was the total rejection of their claim for an extension.

If an adverse decision is made by an AO, it was suggested in the 1997 edition that the problem could not be cured by a SSAT. But the consequences of this seem likely to cause such unfairness that an alternative suggestion is now put forward. Although reg. 5(1) only expressly provides for a claim to be amended before a determination on it has been made, it does not explicitly state that a claim may not be amended after a determination has been made. Thus if such an amendment is made before, or at, the appeal hearing, it is suggested that a tribunal would be able to deal with the claim for an extension, as amended. Since the tribunal is conducting a complete rehearing of all the issues under appeal, it may also wish to consider whether to treat the claim as simply being a claim for the maximum period allowed for an extension, whatever period was initially requested by the claimant. It certainly does seem doubtful that the intention was that only claims made for extensions of three months or less could be considered under para. (4).

There are two questions to be answered before there can be an extension under para. (4). The first is that one of the circumstances listed in para. (5) has applied to the claimant. There is no condition that the circumstance must have applied throughout the period claimed for or continues to apply at the date of claim. Such consideration may come in under the second question, which is whether as a result of the circumstance or a combination of them, the claimant could not reasonably have been expected to make the claim earlier. Thus, if a claimant who has been affected by a listed circumstance, such as illness, delays unreasonably after the circumstance ceases to exist, the claim for extension of time will fail on the second question. Such a claim could also fail if there has been unreasonable delay at some earlier stage, before one of the listed circumstances intervenes.

Under the first question, in para. (4)(a), at least one of the circumstances listed in para. (5) must at some time have applied or currently apply to the claimant. The list in para. (5) is exhaustive and there is no category of analogous circumstances to deal with meritorious cases which were not foreseen by the draftsman.

At this point, no detailed analysis is attempted of the eight sub-paragraphs of para. (5), as no doubt authority on them will soon arise (see below for the first Commissioners' decisions that are now emerging). Adjudicating authorities must consider the actual words of para. (5). A few points may be noted. Ignorance of one's rights or of the procedure for claiming, whether reasonable or otherwise, does not feature in para. (5). Several sub-paragraphs refer to the question of whether it is reasonably practicable for the claimant to obtain assistance from some other person. While practicability might point one to physical feasibility, the addition of reasonableness requires a judgment to be made about the individual circumstances. If one person is physically available to assist the claimant and that person is reasonably ignorant of the claimant's rights or the need to make any inquiry, is that relevant? Is there a difference between the giving of information (see sub-para. (d) on official information) and giving advice (see sub-para. (e) on advice from advisers)? If a claimant genuinely believes as a result of information received from an officer of the DSS that a claim for benefit would not succeed, but that belief is unreasonably drawn from the information given, is the case nonetheless within sub–para. (d)? Is the information in a leaflet given by an officer of the DSS? Enough has been said to show that the new test will be a fertile source of misunderstanding, dispute and troublesome administration.

See the notes to reg. 25 of the JSA Regulations where the claimant is appealing against a decision not to backdate a fresh claim for JSA made after a previous claim has been "closed" on the grounds that the claimant has failed to sign on.

Interpretation of para. (5)

A very common problem is the gap in benefit that often occurs when a claimant transfers from JSA to income support because he has become incapable of work. It was thus perhaps predictable that the first Commissioners' decisions on the new rules for the backdating of income support claims would stem from this issue. In *CIS 610/1998* the claimant, who had been claiming JSA, took a Med 3 issued by his G.P. to the Benefits Agency. There was a queue so he approached the security guard. The guard advised him that he did not have to fill in any forms, took his medical certificate and wrote his N.I. number in a logging-in book. A week later he received an incapacity benefit claim form in the post, which he filled in and took to the Benefits Agency. While in the queue he was advised by another claimant that he should complete an income support claim form as well. He checked this advice when he reached the counter and then submitted an income support claim form with his incapacity benefit claim form. The AO refused to backdate his claim for income support. The Commissioner considered both para. (5)(b) and (d). On sub-para. (d), he holds that on the facts of this case the security guard constituted an "officer of the Department", and that because of what he was told by the guard the claimant may have been under the impression that he did not need to make another claim in connection with his transfer from JSA to income support and that in that sense any new claim would not succeed ("claim" in sub-para. (d) referred to the new claim(s) that the person was being advised about). On sub-para. (b), the Commissioner states that the tribunal should have investigated the nature of the claimant's illness and whether this prevented him from queuing. The Commissioner also drew attention to the powers of the Secretary of State to treat the claim as validly made under regs. 4(1) and (7) and 19(6).

See also *CIS 1721/1998* in which the claimant was given an incapacity benefit claim form when she went to the Job Centre with a medical certificate after fracturing her wrist. Two weeks later her claim for incapacity benefit was refused and she was advised to claim income support. The AO refused to backdate her income support claim. The Commissioner accepts that the implication of the advice to claim incapacity benefit was that the claimant would be entitled to that benefit and not income support. He considered that this was a reasonable belief on her part (incapacity benefit, if payable, would have exceeded her income support applicable amount). The Commissioner also took account of reg. 4(5). The official to whom she produced her medical certificate should have supplied her with an income support claim form. A failure to supply such a form would also have led to a belief that there was no entitlement to income support. *CIS 3749/1998* expands on this point. The Commissioner states that in his view claimants were entitled by reason of reg. 4(5) to assume that they had been given the right forms for the benefits they requested, and if they were not, sub-para. (d) clearly should be considered. The claimant in that case had been receiving income-based JSA, so there was at least a reasonable possibility that a claim for incapacity benefit would fail for lack of contributions. The Commissioner also drew attention to the fact that a failure to provide the right form brought reg. 4(7A) into effect, which would give the Secretary of State a discretion to accept a late claim.

On "not reasonably practicable for the claimant to obtain assistance from another person to make his claim" (see para. (5)(a), (b), (c) and (g)), note *CIS 2057/1998*. The Commissioner points out that the question is whether it is reasonably practicable for the claimant to seek assistance from another person to make the claim, not whether it is reasonably practicable for another person to take the initiative in offering assistance. The claimant in that case had learning difficulties. She made a claim for income support which was awarded. Later her mother requested on her behalf that benefit be backdated to her sixteenth birthday (no-one had been appointed to act on behalf of the claimant). The tribunal took the view that the claimant had a supportive family who should have taken the initiative in finding out about her benefit entitlement. However, the Commissioner considered that she came within para. (5)(a)(i).

CJSA 1136/1998 considers the requirement in sub-para. (e) that the advice must be in writing.

The claimant had been dismissed and was advised by his trade union official not to claim any benefit until the reasons for his dismissal had been investigated through his employers' appeal procedure. This advice was confirmed in writing in a letter produced for the tribunal hearing in January 1998. The Commissioner states that the reason sub-para. (e) required the advice to be in writing was to avoid any doubt or argument as to the contents of that advice. If before the decision made by the AO or tribunal, the advice was confirmed in writing, these difficulties were avoided and the advice then amounted to written advice for the purposes of sub-para. (e). But note effect of s.22(8) Administration Act for appeals lodged on or after May 21, 1998.

Paragraphs (6) and (7)

For income support, JSA, family credit and disability working allowance claims, the Secretary of State retains the existing power to extend the time for claiming by up to a month if it is considered that to do so would be consistent with the proper administration of benefit. The difference is that the discretion is no longer an open-ended one. One of the circumstances set out in para. (7) must apply. Once again, the list is exhaustive and has no category of analogous circumstances. It by no means covers the circumstances in which the Secretary of State would formerly use the discretion, but see reg. 6(1)(aa) and (1A) for the automatic allowance of a month to return claim forms; note, however, that in the case of JSA the month's extension is discretionary (see reg. 6(4AB)), unless the claimant is a postal signer when it is automatic if a properly completed claim is received within a month (see reg. 6(4A)(b)(ii)). No doubt the principle of *CSIS 61/1992* still applies, that in every case where a claim is made outside the limit specified in Sched. 4, the Secretary of State should consider the use of the discretion under para. (6) before the claim is referred to an AO for decision.

PART III

PAYMENTS

Time and manner of payment: general provision

20. Subject to the provisions of [¹regulations 20A to 27], benefit shall be paid in accordance with an award as soon as is reasonably practicable after the award has been made, by means of an instrument of payment or by such other means as appears to the Secretary of State to be appropriate in the circumstances of any particular case.

AMENDMENTS

1. Social Security (Claims and Payments) Amendment (No. 4) Regulations 1994 (S.I. 1994 No. 3196), reg. 3 (January 10, 1995).

DEFINITION

"benefit"—see reg. 2(2).

[¹Payment on presentation of an instrument for benefit payment

20A.—(1) Where it appears to the Secretary of State to be appropriate in any class of case, benefit due to a beneficiary falling within such a class shall be paid on presentation of an instrument for benefit payment in accordance with the arrangements set out in this regulation.

[²(2) Where a beneficiary falls within a class mentioned in paragraph (1) the Secretary of State shall issue an instrument for benefit payment to whichever one or more of the following persons seems to him to be appropriate in the circumstances of the case—

    (a) that beneficiary;

    (b) in England and Wales, the receiver appointed by the Court of Protection with power to receive benefit on behalf of that claimant;

(c) in Scotland, the tutor, curator or other guardian acting or appointed in terms of law to administer the estate of that beneficiary;

(d) the person appointed by the Secretary of State under regulation 33 to act on behalf of that beneficiary;

(e) subject to paragraph (4A), the person authorised by that beneficiary to act on his behalf;

(f) the person to whom benefit is to be paid on that beneficiary's behalf further to a direction by the Secretary of State under regulation 34; and

(g) the alternative payee under regulation 36.]

(3) Instruments for benefit payment shall be in such form as the Secretary of State may from time to time approve.

(4) Benefit shall not be paid under this regulation other than to—

(a) a person to whom an instrument for benefit payment has been issued in accordance with paragraph (2); or

(b) [²Subject to paragraph (4A),] a person not falling within sub-paragraph (a) who has been authorised by a beneficiary to whom an instrument for benefit payment has been issued to act on his behalf.

[²(4A) A person authorised by the beneficiary to act on his behalf under paragraph (2)(e) must be so authorised in respect of all benefits, payment of which may be obtained by means of that instrument for benefit payment.]

(5) The Secretary of State shall provide the paying agent with information as to the amount of benefit, if any, due to the beneficiary where the paying agent uses the instrument for benefit payment to request that information.

[²(5A) When an instrument for benefit payment is presented for payment the Secretary of State may require the person presenting that instrument to accept payment—

(a) if the instrument is presented—

(i) for the purpose of obtaining payment of any benefit to which the person presenting it is entitled in his own right; or

(ii) by a person such as is mentioned in paragraph (2)(b), (c), (d), (e) or (f) for the purpose of obtaining payment of any benefit to which the person in respect of whom the appointment, authorisation or, as the case may be, direction mentioned in those provisions relate is so entitled,

of all monies then due in respect of such benefits; or

(b) if the instrument is presented for the purpose of obtaining payment of any benefit which that person is entitled to receive by virtue of regulation 36 (payment to a partner as alternative payee), of all monies then due in respect of such benefits,

payment of which may be obtained by means of that instrument.]

(6) Where a paying agent pays benefit in accordance with this regulation, the person receiving it shall sign a receipt in a form approved by the Secretary of State and such signature shall be sufficient discharge to the Secretary of State for any sum so paid.

(7) In this regulation, "paying agent" means a person authorised by the Secretary of State to make payments of benefit in accordance with the arrangements for payment set out in this regulation.]

AMENDMENTS

1. Social Security (Claims and Payments) Amendment (No. 4) Regulations 1994 (S.I. 1994 No. 3196), reg. 4 (January 10, 1995).

2. Social Security (Claims and Payments Etc.) Amendment Regulations 1996 (S.I. 1996 No. 672), reg. 2(2) (April 4, 1996).

"instrument for benefit payment"—see reg. 2(1).
"benefit"—see reg. 2(2).

GENERAL NOTE

This regulation and the amendments to regs. 27 and 47 have been introduced as a consequence of the Government's plans eventually to replace benefit order books by social security payment cards.

Direct credit transfer

21.—(1) Subject to the provisions of this regulation, [¹benefit [⁵. . .]] may, on the application of the person claiming, or entitled to it, and with the consent of the Secretary of State, be paid by way of automated [¹. . .] credit transfer into a bank or other account—
- (a) in the name of the person entitled to benefit, or his spouse [³or partner],
- ‧ or a person acting on his behalf, or
- (b) in the joint names of the person entitled to benefit and his spouse [³or partner], or the person entitled to benefit and a person acting on his behalf.

(2) An application for benefit to be paid in accordance with paragraph (1)—
- (a) shall be in writing on a form approved for the purpose by the Secretary of State or in such other manner, being in writing, as he may accept as sufficient in the circumstances, and
- (b) shall contain a statement or be accompanied by a written statement made by the applicant declaring that he has read and understood the conditions applicable to payment of benefit in accordance with this regulation

(3) [²Subject to paragraph (3A)] benefit shall be paid in accordance with paragraph (1) within seven days of the last day of each successive period of entitlement as may be provided in the application.

[²(3A) Income Support shall be paid in accordance with paragraph (1) within 7 days of the time determined for the payment of income support in accordance with Schedule 7.]

(4) In respect of benefit which is the subject of an arrangement for payment under this regulation, the Secretary of State may make a particular payment by credit transfer otherwise than is provided by paragraph (3) [²or (3A)] if it appears to him appropriate to do so for the purpose of—
- (a) paying any arrears of benefit, or
- (b) making a payment in respect of a terminal period of an award or for any similar purpose.

(5) The arrangement for benefit to be payable in accordance with this regulation may be terminated—
- (a) by the person entitled to benefit or a person acting on his behalf by notice in writing delivered or sent to an appropriate office or
- (b) by the Secretary of State if the arrangement seems to him to be no longer appropriate to the circumstances of the particular case.

(6) [⁵. . .]

AMENDMENTS

1. Social Security (Miscellaneous Provisions) Amendment Regulations 1992 (S.I. 1992 No. 247), reg. 15 (March 9, 1992).
2. Social Security (Claims and Payments) Amendment (No. 2) Regulations 1993 (S.I. 1993 No. 1113), reg. 2 (May 12, 1993).
3. Social Security (Claims and Payments) Amendment Regulations 1994 (S.I. 1994 No. 2319), reg. 4 (October 3, 1994).

4. Social Security (Claims and Payments) Amendment (No. 2) Regulations 1994 (S.I. 1994 No. 2943), reg. 8 (April 13, 1995).

5. Social Security (Claims and Payments Etc.) Amendment Regulations 1996 (S.I. 1996 No. 672), reg. 2(3) (April 4, 1996).

DEFINITION

"appropriate office"—see reg. 2(1).
"partner"—*ibid.*.

GENERAL NOTE

Until May 12, 1993, it was not possible for income support to be paid by direct credit transfer.

Income support

26.—(1) [³Subject to regulation 21 (direct credit transfer), Schedule 7] shall have effect for determining the manner in and time at which income support is to be paid, the day when any change of circumstances affecting entitlement is to have effect and the day when entitlement to income support is to begin.

(2) Where income support paid by means of a book of serial orders is increased [²or reduced] on review by an amount which, with any previous such increase [²or reduction], is less than 50 pence per week, the Secretary of State may defer payment of that increase [²or disregard the reduction] until not later than either—

    (a) the termination of entitlement; or

    (b) the expiration of the period of one week from the date specified for
        payment in the last order in that book of serial orders,
whichever is the earlier.

[²(3) Where income support is payable to a beneficiary by means of a book of serial orders and a payment to a third party under Schedule 9 is increased on review so that the amount of income support payable to the beneficiary is reduced by an amount which with any previous reduction is less than 50 pence per week, the Secretary of State may make the payment to the third party and disregard the reduction in respect of the beneficiary for the period to which the book relates.]

(4) Where the entitlement to income support is less than 10 pence or, in the case of a beneficiary to whom [¹section 23(a)] of the Social Security Act 1986 [SSCBA, s.126] applies, £5, that amount shall not be payable unless the claimant is also entitled to payment of any other benefit with which income support [²may be paid] under arrangements made by the Secretary of State.

AMENDMENTS

1. Social Security (Claims and Payments) Amendment Regulations 1988 (S.I. 1988 No. 522), reg. 6 (April 11, 1988).

2. Social Security (Claims and Payments and Payments on account, Overpayments and Recovery) Amendment Regulations 1989 (S.I. 1989 No. 136), reg. 2 (February 27, 1989).

3. Social Security (Claims and Payments) Amendment (No. 2) Regulations 1993 (S.I. 1993) (No. 1113), reg. 3 (May 12, 1993).

[¹Jobseeker's allowance

26A.—(1) Subject to the following provisions of this regulation, jobseeker's allowance shall be paid fortnightly in arrears unless in any particular case or class of case the Secretary of State arranges otherwise.

(2) The provisions of paragraph 2A of Schedule 7 (payment of income support at times of office closure) shall apply for the purposes of payment of a jobseek-

er's allowance as they apply for the purposes of payment of income support, except that in sub-paragraph (1)(b) of that paragraph the reference to an office of the Department of Social Security or associated office shall be read as a reference to an office of the Department for Education and Employment.

(3) Where the amount of a jobseeker's allowance is less than £1.00 a week the Secretary of State may direct that it shall be paid at such intervals, not exceeding 13 weeks, as may be specified in the direction.

(4) Subject to paragraphs (5) to (8), where an award of jobseeker's allowance is revised on the ground that there has been, or there is expected to be, a relevant change of circumstances, the revised award shall have effect from the first day of the benefit week (as defined in regulation 1(3) of the Jobseeker's Allowance Regulations) in which that relevant change of circumstances ocurred or is expected to occur.

(5) Where the relevant change of circumstances giving rise to the revised award is that—

(a) entitlement to jobseeker's allowance ends, or is expected to end, for a reason other than that the claimant no longer satisfies the provisions of section 3(1)(a) of the Jobseekers Act; or

(b) a child or young person who is normally in the care of a local authority or who is detained in custody lives, or is expected to live, with the claimant for a part only of a benefit week; or

(c) the claimant or his partner enters, or is expected to enter, a nursing home or residential care home for a period of no more than 8 weeks; or

(d) the partner of the claimant or a member of his family ceases, or is expected to cease, to be a hospital in-patient for a period of less than a week,

the revised award shall have effect on the date that the relevant change of circumstances occurs or is expected to occur.

(6) Where the relevant change of circumstances giving rise to a revised award is any of those specified in paragraph (5), and, in consequence of those circumstances ceasing to apply, the award is again revised, the award, as again revised, shall have effect on the date that those circumstances ceased to apply.

(7) Where, under the provisions of regulation 96 [² or 102C(3)] of the Jobseeker's Allowance Regulations, income is treated as paid on a certain date and that payment gives rise, or is expected to give rise, to a relevant change of circumstances resulting in a revised award, that revised award shall have effect on that date.

(8) Where a relevant change of circumstances occurs which results, or is expected to result, in a reduced award of jobseeker's allowance then, if the Secretary of State is of the opinion that it will be impracticable to give effect to that revised award in accordance with the other provisions of this regulation, the revised award shall have effect on the first day of the benefit week following that in which the relevant change of circumstances occurs.]

AMENDMENTS

1. Social Security (Claims and Payments) (Jobseeker's Allowance Consequential Amendments) Regulations 1996 (S.I. 1996 No. 1460), reg. 2(14) (October 7, 1996).

2. Social Security (Miscellaneous Amendments) (No. 4) Regulations 1998 (S.I. 1998 No. 1174), reg. 8(3)(a) (June 1, 1998).

DEFINITIONS

"jobseeker's allowance"—see reg. 2(1).
"the Jobseeker's Allowance Regulations"—*ibid.*
"partner"—*ibid.*
"week"—*ibid.*

[¹Family credit and disability working allowance

27.—(1) Subject to regulation 21 [²and paragraph (1A)], family credit and disability working allowance shall be payable in respect of any benefit week on the Tuesday next following the end of that week by means of a book of serial orders [³or on presentation of an instrument for benefit payment] unless in any case the Secretary of State arranges otherwise.

[²(1A) Subject to paragraph (2), where an amount of family credit or disability working allowance becomes payable which is at a weekly rate of not more than £4.00, that amount shall, if the Secretary of State so directs, be payable as soon as practicable by means of a single payment; except that if that amount represents an increase in the amount of either of those benefits which has previously been paid in respect of the same period, this paragraph shall apply only if that previous payment was made by means of a single payment.]

(2) Where the entitlement to family credit or disability working allowance is less than 50 pence a week that amount shall not be payable.

AMENDMENTS

1. Social Security (Claims and Payments) Amendment Regulations 1991 (S.I. 1991 No. 2741), reg. 14 (April 6, 1992).
2. Social Security (Claims and Payments) Amendment (No. 3) Regulations 1993 (S.I. 1993 No. 2113), reg. 3 (October 25, 1993).
3. Social Security (Claims and Payments) Amendment (No. 4) Regulations 1994 (S.I. 1994 No. 3196), reg. 7 (January 10, 1995).

GENERAL NOTE

From October 25, 1993, family credit and disability working allowance of £4 or less a week can be paid in a lump sum at the beginning of an award. If the award of £4 or less is an increase of a previous award for the same period, it will only be paid in a lump sum if the previous award was so paid. The stated purpose of this provision is to recognise the costs (including childcare costs) of starting work.

Fractional amounts of benefit

28. Where the amount of any benefit payable would, but for this regulation, include a fraction of a penny, that fraction shall be disregarded if it is less than half a penny and shall otherwise be treated as a penny.

DEFINITION

"benefit"—see reg. 2(2).

[¹Payments to persons under age 18

29. Where benefit is paid to a person under the age of 18 (whether on his own behalf or on behalf of another) the receipt of that person shall be a sufficient discharge to the Secretary of State.]

AMENDMENT

1. Social Security (Claims and Payments Etc.) Amendment Regulations 1996 (S.I. 1996 No. 672), reg. 2(4) (April 4, 1996).

DEFINITION

"benefit"—see reg. 2(2).

Payments on death

30.—(1) On the death of a person who has made a claim for benefit, the Secretary of State may appoint such person as he may think fit to proceed with the claim.

(2) Subject to paragraph (4), any sum payable by way of benefit which is payable under an award on a claim proceeded with under paragraph (1) may be paid or distributed by the Secretary of State to or amongst persons over the age of 16 claiming as personal representatives, legatees, next of kin, or creditors of the deceased (or, where the deceased was illegitimate, to or amongst other persons over the age of 16), and the provisions of regulation 38 (extinguishment of right) shall apply to any such payment or distribution; and—

  (a) the receipt of any such person shall be a good discharge to the Secretary of State for any sum so paid; and

  (b) where the Secretary of State is satisfied that any such sum or part thereof is needed for the benefit of any person under the age of 16, he may obtain a good discharge therefor by paying the sum or part thereof to a person over that age who satisfies the Secretary of State that he will apply the sum so paid for the benefit of the person under the age of 16.

(3) Subject to paragraph (2), any sum payable by way of benefit to the deceased, payment of which he had not obtained at the date of his death, may, unless the right thereto was already extinguished at that date, be paid or distributed to or amongst such persons as are mentioned in paragraph (2), and regulation 38 shall apply to any such payment or distribution, except that, for the purpose of that regulation, the period of 12 months shall be calculated from the date on which the right to payment of any sum is treated as having arisen in relation to any such person and not from the date on which that right is treated as having arisen in relation to the deceased.

(4) Paragraphs (2) and (3) shall not apply in any case unless written application for the payment of any such sum is made to the Secretary of State within 12 months from the date of the deceased's death or within such longer period as the Secretary of State may allow in any particular case.

(5), (6), (6A), (6B) & (7) [*Omitted as not relating to income-related benefits*]

(8) The Secretary of State may dispense with strict proof of the title of any person claiming in accordance with the provisions of this regulation.

(9) In paragraph (2) "next of kin" means—

  (a) in England and Wales, the persons who would take beneficially on an intestacy; and

  (b) in Scotland, the persons entitled to the moveable estate of the deceased on intestacy.

DEFINITION

   "benefit"—see reg. 2(2).

GENERAL NOTE

   See *CIS 642/1994* in the notes to reg. 33 and the notes to reg. 22(1) of the Adjudication Regulations.

Information to be given when obtaining payment of benefit

32.—(1) [³Except in the case of a jobseeker's allowance,] every beneficiary and every person by whom or on whose behalf sums payable by way of benefit are receivable shall furnish in such manner and at such times as the Secretary of State may determine such certificates and other documents and such information or facts affecting the right to benefit or to its receipt as the Secretary of

State may require (either as a condition on which any sum or sums shall be receivable or otherwise), and in particular shall notify the Secretary of State of any change of circumstances which he might reasonably be expected to know might affect the right to benefit, or to its receipt, as soon as reasonably practicable after its occurrence, by giving notice in writing [¹(unless the Secretary of State determines in any particular case to accept notice given otherwise than in writing)] of any such change to the appropriate office.

(2) Where any sum is receivable on account of an increase of benefit in respect of an adult dependant, the Secretary of State may require the beneficiary to furnish a declaration signed by such dependant confirming the particulars respecting him, which have been given by the claimant.

[²(3) In the case of a person who is claiming income support [³or a jobseeker's allowance], where that person or any partner is aged not less than 60 and is a member of, or a person deriving entitlement to a pension under, a personal pension scheme, or is a party to, or a person deriving entitlement to a pension under, a retirement annuity contract, he shall where the Secretary of State so requires furnish the following information—

(a) the name and address of the pension fund holder;

(b) such other information including any reference or policy number as is needed to enable the personal pension scheme or retirement annuity contract to be identified.

(4) Where the pension fund holder receives from the Secretary of State a request for details concerning a personal pension scheme or retirement annuity contract relating to a person or any partner to whom paragraph (3) refers, the pension fund holder shall provide the Secretary of State with any information to which paragraph (5) refers.

(5) The information to which this paragraph refers is—

(a) where the purchase of an annuity under a personal pension scheme has been deferred, the amount of any income which is being withdrawn from the personal pension scheme;

(b) in the case of—

(i) a personal pension scheme where income withdrawal is available, the maximum amount of income which may be withdrawn from the scheme; or

(ii) a personal pension scheme where income withdrawal is not available, or a retirement annuity contract, the maximum amount of income which might be withdrawn from the fund if the fund were held under a personal pension scheme where income withdrawal was available,

calculated by or on behalf of the pension fund holder by means of tables prepared from time to time by the Government Actuary which are appropriate for this purpose.]

AMENDMENTS

1. Social Security (Miscellaneous Provisions) Amendment (No. 2) Regulations 1992 (S.I. 1992 No. 2595), reg. 4 (November 16, 1992).

2. Income-related Benefits Schemes and Social Security (Claims and Payments) (Miscellaneous Amendments) Regulations 1995 (S.I. 1995 No. 2303), reg. 10(4) (October 2, 1995).

3. Social Security (Claims and Payments) (Jobseeker's Allowance Consequential Amendments) Regulations 1996 (S.I. 1996 No. 1460), reg. 2(16) (October 7, 1996).

DEFINITIONS

"appropriate office"—see reg. 2(1).
"beneficiary"—see Social Security Act 1975, Sched. 20.
"benefit"—see reg. 2(2).

"jobseeker's allowance—see reg. 2(1).
"pension fund holder"—*ibid.*
"personal pension scheme"—*ibid.*
"retirement annuity contract"—*ibid.*

GENERAL NOTE

Paragraph (1)

Notes in order books and on notices of determination require claimants to inform the DSS of various changes of circumstances, and there is also a general duty to report changes of circumstances which the claimant might reasonably be expected to know might affect entitlement. This obligation can be relevant to the recoverability of an overpayment under s.71 of the Administration Act (Social Security Act 1986, s.53). Although reg. 32 requires notice generally to be given in writing, the Secretary of State can now accept notification otherwise than in writing. Oral disclosures have always counted as disclosure under s.71 (*R(SB) 40/84*). See reg. 24 of the Jobseeker's Allowance Regulations, in particular para. (7), for the obligations in JSA cases.

See reg. 37AA(1) for the withholding of benefit if para. (1) is not complied with and reg. 37AB for payment of benefit that has been withheld.

Paragraphs (3) to (5)

See reg. 42(2A)–(2C) of the Income Support Regulations and the note to those paragraphs and reg. 105(3) to (5) of the Jobseeker's Allowance Regulations.

PART IV

THIRD PARTIES

Persons unable to act

33.—(1) Where—

(a) a person is, or is alleged to be, entitled to benefit, whether or not a claim for benefit has been made by him or on his behalf; and
(b) that person is unable for the time being to act; and either
(c) no receiver has been appointed by the Court of Protection with power to claim, or as the case may be, receive benefit on his behalf; or
(d) in Scotland, his estate is not being administered by any tutor, curator or other guardian acting or appointed in terms of law,

the Secretary of State may, upon written application made to him by a person who, if a natural person, is over the age of 18, appoint that person to exercise, on behalf of the person who is unable to act, any right to which that person may be entitled and to receive and deal on his behalf with any sums payable to him.

(2) Where the Secretary of State has made an appointment under paragraph (1)—

(a) he may at any time revoke it;
(b) the person appointed may resign his office after having given one month's notice in writing to the Secretary of State of his intention to do so;
(c) any such appointment shall terminate when the Secretary of State is notified that a receiver or other person to whom paragraph (1)(c) or (d) applies has been appointed.

(3) Anything required by these regulations to be done by or to any person who is for the time being unable to act may be done by or to the receiver, tutor, curator or other guardian, if any, or by or to the person appointed under this regulation or regulation 43 [¹(disability living allowance for a child)] and the

receipt of any person so appointed shall be a good discharge to the Secretary of State for any sum paid.

AMENDMENT

1. Social Security (Claims and Payments) Amendment Regulations 1991 (S.I. 1991 No. 2741), reg. 16 (February 3, 1992).

DEFINITIONS

"benefit"—see reg. 2(2).
"claim for benefit"—see reg. 2(1).

GENERAL NOTE

Even if no appointment has been made, a claim made by a person unable to act, or by an "unauthorised person" on their behalf, is still valid (*CIS 812/1992*, applying para. 8 of *R(SB) 9/84* where a Tribunal of Commissioners holds that in the absence of any challenge at the time the Secretary of State must be deemed to have accepted that the claim was made in sufficient manner). In *Walsh v. CAO* (Consent Order, January 19, 1995) the Court of Appeal also applied *R(SB) 9/84* when setting aside *CIS 638/1991* in which the Commissioner had held that a claim made on behalf of a person unable to act by a person who had not been formally appointed was a nullity.

Note that any subsequent appointment has retrospective effect (*R(SB) 5/90*).

In *CIS 642/1994* the claimant's husband was her appointee under reg. 33. She died before the SSAT hearing. The Commissioner holds that the tribunal decision was a nullity because there had been no appointment under reg. 30 (deceased persons). Appointments under reg. 30 were a distinct and different form of appointment from reg. 33 appointments. He dissents from para. 8 of *R(SB) 9/84* and repeats his view (see *CIS 638/1991*) that it is open to AOs and tribunals (and Commissioners) to determine that a claim is a nullity in cases where a person is unable to act and there has been no valid appointment. This is out of step with the current weight of authority. See also the notes to reg. 22(1) of the Adjudication Regulations.

CIS 812/1992 also confirms that, in relation to the pre-April 1997 form of the rules for backdating claims, if there has been no appointment it is only necessary to decide whether the claimant has good cause for a late claim; it is not necessary to consider the reasonableness of the failure to claim of a person who has been acting informally on his behalf. The Commissioner declines to follow paras. 12 and 13 of *R(IS) 5/91* since this could not be reconciled with paras. 9 and 10 of *R(SB) 9/84* (which was a Tribunal of Commissioners' decision). See also *CSB 168/1993* which takes a similar view and contains a useful summary of the authorities on this issue.

Under the current form of reg. 19(5) the test is also of the claimant's personal circumstances, if there is no appointee, but those circumstances sometimes expressly include whether there is anyone who could help the claimant.

Payment to another person on the beneficiary's behalf

34. The Secretary of State may direct that benefit shall be paid, wholly or in part, to [¹another natural person] on the beneficiary's behalf if such a direction as to payment appears to the Secretary of State to be necessary for protecting the interests of the beneficiary, or any child or dependant in respect of whom benefit is payable.

AMENDMENT

1. Social Security (Miscellaneous Provisions) Amendment (No. 2) Regulations 1992 (S.I. 1992 No. 2595), reg. 5 (January 4, 1993).

DEFINITIONS

"beneficiary"—see Social Security Act 1975, Sched. 20.
"benefit"—see reg. 2(2).
"child"—see 1986 Act, s 20(11).

[¹Deductions of mortgage interest which shall be made from benefit and paid to qualifying lenders

34A.—(1) In relation to cases to which section 51C(1) of the Social Security Act 1986 [SSAA, s.15A(1)] (payment out of benefit of sums in respect of mortgage interest etc.) applies and in the circumstances specified in Schedule 9A, such part of any relevant benefits to which a relevant beneficiary is entitled as may be specified in that Schedule shall be paid by the Secretary of State directly to the qualifying lender and shall be applied by that lender towards the discharge of the liability in respect of that mortgage interest.

(2) The provisions of Schedule 9A shall have effect in relation to mortgage interest payments.]

AMENDMENT

1. Social Security (Claims and Payments) Amendment Regulations 1992 (S.I. 1992 No. 1026), reg. 3 (May 25, 1992).

DEFINITIONS

"qualifying lender"—see Administration Act, s.15A(3).
"relevant beneficiary"—see Administration Act, s.15A(1).
"relevant benefits"—see Administration Act, s.15A(4).

[¹[³Deductions which may be made from benefit and paid to third parties

35.—(1) Except as provided for in regulation 34A and Schedule 9A, deductions] may be made from benefit and direct payments may be made to third parties on behalf of a beneficiary in accordance with the provisions of Schedule 9.

(2) Where a social fund payment for maternity or funeral expenses [²or expenses for heating which appear to the Secretary of State to have been or to be likely to be incurred in cold weather] is made, wholly or in part, in respect of a debt which is, or will be, due to a third person, the instrument of payment may be, and in the case of funeral expenses shall be, made payable to that person and it may, in any case, be delivered or sent to that person as a direct payment.]

AMENDMENTS

1. Social Security (Claims and Payments) Amendment Regulations 1988 (S.I. 1988 No. 522, reg. 7 (April 11, 1988).
2. Social Security (Common Provisions) Miscellaneous Amendment Regulations 1988 (S.I. 1988 No. 1725), reg. 3, (November 7, 1988).
3. Social Security (Claims and Payments) Amendment Regulations 1992 (S.I. 1992 No. 1026), reg. 4 (May 25, 1992).

DEFINITIONS

"beneficiary"—see Social Security Act 1975, Sched. 20.
"benefit"—see reg. 2(2).

[¹Transitional provisions for persons in hostels or certain residential accommodation

35A.—(1) In this regulation—
"benefit week" has the same meaning as it has in Schedule 7, paragraph 4;
"specified benefit" has the same meaning as it has in Schedule 9, paragraph 1; and

"Schedule 3B" means Schedule 3B to the Income Support (General) Regulations 1987.

(2) Expressions used in this regulation and in Schedule 3B have, unless the context otherwise requires, the same meanings in this regulation as they have in that Schedule.

(3) Where—

(a) immediately before the coming into force of Schedule 3B a beneficiary was in, or temporarily absent from, a hostel and a payment in respect of his accommodation charges was, or would but for that absence have been, made for the first week to a third party under—

(i) Schedule 9, paragraph 4 (miscellaneous accommodation costs), or

(ii) regulation 34 (payment to another person on the beneficiary's behalf); and

(b) the beneficiary is entitled to eligible housing benefit for the period mentioned in sub-paragraph (b) of the expression "eligible housing benefit"; and

(c) the beneficiary continues to reside in the same hostel,

the adjudicating authority shall in a case to which paragraph (6) applies determine that an amount of specified benefit shall, subject to paragraphs (8) and (9), be paid to that third party.

(4) Where a beneficiary is in, or is temporarily absent from, accommodation which—

(a) was a hostel before the March benefit week; and

(b) in the second week is residential accommodation within the meaning of regulation 21 of the Income Support (General) Regulations 1987,

paragraph (3) shall apply as if sub-paragraph (b) was omitted and as if the reference to paragraph (6) was a reference to paragraph (7).

(5) An amount of specified benefit shall not be paid to a third party under paragraph (3), as applied by paragraph (4), where the beneficiary—

(a) is in residential accommodation in the benefit week which commences in the period of 7 consecutive days beginning on 9th October 1989, but

(b) is a person to whom a protected sum is not applicable in accordance with paragraph 3(3) of Schedule 3B.

(6) This paragraph applies in a case where—

(a) the amount of the eligible housing benefit referred to in paragraph (3)(b) is less than

(b) the amount of the direct payment or the payment under regulation 34 in respect of the first week or the amount which would have been payable but for the temporary absence of the beneficiary in the first week;

and where this paragraph applies the amount of the specified benefit determined in accordance with paragraph (3) shall be the difference between the amounts specified in sub-paragraphs (a) and (b).

(7) This paragraph applies where the applicable amount which was appropriate to the beneficiary by way of personal expenses in the first week is less than the total applicable amount appropriate to the beneficiary in the second week; and where this paragraph applies the amount of the specified benefit determined in accordance with paragraph (3) as applied by paragraph (4) shall be the difference between those two amounts.

(8) Where immediately before the coming into force of Schedule 3B a beneficiary was temporarily absent from a hostel and the charge levied on him during that period of absence was less than the full charge for the accommodation, an amount of specified benefit shall not be paid to the third party in respect of the period for which less than the full charge was levied but shall be paid when the full charge is levied.

(9) Specified benefit shall not be paid to a third party in accordance with this regulation unless the amount of the beneficiary's award of the specified benefit

is not less than the total of the amount otherwise authorised to be so paid under this regulation plus 10 pence.

(10) For the purposes of paragraph (3)(c) residence shall be regarded as continuous where the only absences occurred during the permitted period and for this purpose ''permitted period'' has the same meaning as it has in regulation 3A of the Income Support (General) Regulations 1987.

(11) This regulation shall cease to apply, where a beneficiary's benefit week in the week commencing 2nd April 1990—

      (i) begins on that day, on the day immediately following 8th April 1990;

      (ii) begins on a day other than that day, on the day immediately following the last day in his benefit week.]

AMENDMENT

1. Social Security (Medical Evidence, Claims and Payments) Amendment Regulations 1989 (S.I. 1989 No. 1686), reg. 6 (October 9, 1989).

DEFINITIONS

    ''adjudicating authority''—see reg. 2(1).
    ''beneficiary''—see Social Security Act 1975, Sched. 20.
    ''eligible housing benefit''—see Income Support (General) Regulations, Sched. 3B, para. 1(1).
    ''first week''—*ibid*.
    ''hostel''—*ibid*.
    ''March benefit week''—*ibid*.
    ''second week''—*ibid*.

Payment to a partner as an alternative payee

36. Where one of a married or unmarried couple residing together is entitled to child benefit or family credit the Secretary of State may make arrangements whereby that benefit, as well as being payable to the person entitled to it, may, in the alternative, be paid to that person's partner on behalf of the person entitled.

DEFINITIONS

    ''married couple''—see reg. 2(1).
    ''partner''—*ibid*.
    ''unmarried couple''—*ibid*.

PART V

SUSPENSION AND EXTINGUISHMENT

[¹ Suspension in individual cases

37.—(1) [³Subject to paragraph (1A),] where it appears to the Secretary of State that a question arises whether—

    (a) the conditions for entitlement are or were fulfilled;

    (b) an award ought to be revised; or

    (c) subject to paragraph (2), an appeal ought to be brought against an award, the Secretary of State may direct that payment of benefit under an award be suspended, in whole or in part, pending the determination of that question on review, appeal or reference.

[³(1A) Where, in the case of a person who is in receipt of a jobseeker's allowance, it appears to the Secretary of State that a question arises whether that person is or was available for employment or whether he is or was actively seeking employment, payment of benefit shall be suspended until such time as that question has been determined.]

(2) Where it appears to the Secretary of State that a question arises under paragraph (1)(c), he may only give directions that payment of benefit under the award be suspended [²within the relevant period]

(3) A suspension of benefit under paragraph (1)(c) shall cease unless, [²within the relevant period], the claimant is given notice in writing that either an appeal or an application or petition for leave to appeal, whichever is appropriate, has been made against that decision.

(4) Where the claimant has been given notice [²within the relevant period] that either an appeal or an application or petition for leave to appeal has been made, the suspension may continue until the appeal or the application or the petition and any subsequent appeal have been determined.

[²(5) For the purposes of this regulation—

[⁴(a) "relevant period" means the period of 3 months beginning with the date on which notice in writing of the decision in question and of the reasons for it is received by the adjudication officer; and]

   (b) a claimant is to be treated as having been given the notice required by paragraph (3) on the date that it is posted to him at his last known address.]]

AMENDMENTS

1. Social Security (Miscellaneous Provisions) Amendment Regulations 1992 (S.I. 1992 No. 247), reg. 16 (March 9, 1992).

2. Social Security (Claims and Payments) Amendment (No. 3) Regulations 1993 (SI 1993 No. 2113), reg. 3(6) (September 27, 1993).

3. Social Security (Claims and Payments) (Jobseeker's Allowance Consequential Amendments) Regulations 1996 (S.I. 1996 No. 1460), reg. 2(17) (October 7, 1996).

4. Social Security (Claims and Payments and Adjudication) Amendment Regulations 1996 (S.I. 1996 No. 2306), reg. 4 (October 7, 1996).

DEFINITION

"benefit"—see reg. 2(2).
"jobseeker's allowance"—see reg. 2(1).

GENERAL NOTE

This regulation and regs. 37A and 37B represent a recasting and an intended clarification of the previous reg. 37. Unfortunately, they do not fully succeed in this second aim (although the latest form (from September 27, 1993) of reg. 37A certainly makes more sense) mainly because of the need to keep to the powers conferred by s.51(1)(p) of the Social Security Act 1986 (now s.5(1)(n) of the Administration Act). Indeed, the new reg. 37A has been declared *ultra vires* by Laws J. in *R. v. Secretary of State for Social Security, ex parte Sutherland* (November 7, 1996). The new reg. 37(1) deals with broadly two situations. The first, under para. (1)(a) and (b), is where there is a question whether the conditions of entitlement for a claimant are satisfied or whether an award ought to be revised. The second, under para. (1)(c), concerns awards made on appeal. In both cases, all matters are for the Secretary of State to determine, so that no appeal lies to a SSAT or a Commissioner against any determination. Challenge through judicial review would be possible. As the Secretary of State is given a discretion ("may"), the circumstances of each individual case must be considered. Para. (1A) contains a specific duty to suspend payment in some JSA cases.

Paragraphs (1)(a) and (b)

By definition an award of benefit has been made, by an AO, by a SSAT or by a Commissioner or a court giving the decision which a SSAT should have given. Therefore, the award may be altered only by review or appeal. If the Secretary of State considers that there is a question whether the conditions of entitlement are satisfied at any date from the beginning of the award or whether the award should be revised, he may direct that payment under the award is to be suspended. Presumably, a question whether a ground for review exists involves the question whether the award ought to be revised. The direction may then continue until a review is carried out. If the outcome of the review is not to revise the award of benefit, arrears will be paid. If the outcome is to revise the award, no overpayment will have been incurred.

Note that a decision of a SSAT or a Commissioner may be reviewed by an AO on the grounds of mistake or ignorance of a material fact or a relevant change of circumstances (Administration Act, s.25(1); 1975 Act, s.104(1)).

There is some doubt whether para. (1)(a) can apply when the question over the fulfilment of the conditions of entitlement arises in the context of whether to appeal against a decision, since that is specifically dealt with in para. (1)(c). However, because of the uncertainties surrounding para. (1)(c), para (1)(a) may have to be considered.

See reg. 37B for questions about whether overpayments of benefit are recoverable.

Paragraph (1)(c)

Since an AO cannot appeal against an AO's decision, this provision applies to awards made by decisions of a SSAT or a Commissioner exercising the power in s.23(7)(a) of the Administration Act (1975 Act s.101(5)(a)). On appeal from the Commissioner, the Court of Appeal or the Court of Session has all the authority of the Commissioner (Supreme Court Act 1981, s.15(2)). Therefore, the courts can make an award in the same circumstances in which the Commissioner can, but a confirmation by the Court of Appeal of an award made by the Commissioner would not seem itself to be an award. In that latter situation, para (1)(c) does not apply directly to a question whether to appeal to the House of Lords against a decision of the Court of Appeal or the Court of Session. If the Secretary of State considers that an appeal ought to be made against a decision making an award, then providing he gives the direction within the period specified in para. (5)(a), he may suspend payment of the award (para. (2)). The period in para. (5)(a) is now three months beginning with the date of receipt of the full decision by the AO in all cases. Before October 1996 the relevant period was one month in the case of appeals to the Social Security Commissioner. Within this period, the claimant must be given written notice that the appeal process has been started, otherwise the suspension ends (para. (3)). But para. (3) does not invalidate an appeal if the notice is not given within a month (*CSB 72/1992*).

However, the question of how long the suspension can last is left very obscure. Para. (1) on its own makes little sense. The question in sub-para. (c) is "whether . . . an appeal ought to be brought against an award." Para. (1) gives power to suspend payment of benefit "pending the determination of that question." The question whether an appeal ought to be brought is determined by an appeal being started, but this is not a determination "on review, appeal or reference." Para. (1) either does not make sense or would terminate the suspension when the appeal is started, which is clearly not the intention of the rest of the regulation. Therefore, one has to look to para. (4), which provides that if the notice referred to in para. (3) has been given, the suspension may continue until the appeal or the application or petition for leave to appeal and any subsequent appeal have been determined. The order of these phrases follows the order in which the various ways of starting an appeal are set out. This starts with a direct appeal, which is not usually possible. Usually, leave to appeal is necessary. So the next in order are applications or petitions for leave to appeal. If leave is granted, then an appeal can be made and determined. The really obscure point is whether "any subsequent appeal" refers only to the appeal for which leave was given or whether it can refer to further appeals.

Take an example of a SSAT decision awarding benefit, contrary to the AO's view of the law. The AO applies for leave to appeal and the Secretary of State decides to suspend payment of the SSAT's award under para. (1)(c). Leave to appeal is granted. On the appeal the Commissioner upholds the SSAT's decision. The AO applies for and is granted leave to appeal to the Court of Appeal. Under para. (4), the suspension of payment can clearly continue up to the date of the Commissioner's decision. But is that the determination of any subsequent appeal following the application for leave, or can the initial suspension continue until the determination of the appeal to the Court of Appeal, or even a further appeal to the House of Lords? There is certainly a good argument that the words of the regulation are not clear enough to produce this adverse effect on the claimant. Then it would appear that para. (1)(c) cannot be applied afresh to the Commissioner's decision (or to the upholding of that decision by the Court of Appeal) because that decision was not an award of benefit. On the other hand, it can be argued that the plain words simply refer to appeals which follow after the award.

If the restrictive argument put above is correct then the Secretary of State might have to rely on the general power of suspension under para. (1)(a). But it is certainly arguable that para. (1)(a) is not appropriate where the question of suspension arises in the context of an appeal, since otherwise there would be no need for para. (1)(c).

It is certainly unfortunate that the considerable efforts to achieve clarity seem to have missed their mark. Nor is there likely to be any authoritative clarification because the issues never get before the Commissioners, being entirely matters for the Secretary of State. See by way of example *Carrigan v. Secretary of State for Social Security and Others* (Court of Session, March 14, 1997). By the time the claimant's application for judicial review of the decision to suspend payment pending an appeal to the Commissioner was heard, the SSAT's decision in his case had been shown to be in error of law as a consequence of the House of Lords' decision in *Bate*. The application for judicial review was therefore refused on the basis that the matter was academic.

See *R. v. Secretary of State for Social Services, ex p. Sherwin* (High Court, February 16, 1996) in the notes to reg. 37A.

Paragraph (1A)

This provision applies where the claimant has been awarded JSA and the Secretary of State considers that a question arises as to the claimant's availability for employment and active search for employment. If so, the Secretary of State is then under a duty ("shall") to suspend payment of JSA until the question is resolved. The existence of hardship is therefore irrelevant, in contrast to the position under para. (1) (although the claimant may qualify for hardship payments of JSA: see Part IX of the JSA Regulations). Section 5(1)(n) of the Administration Act appears to allow regulations to impose a duty to suspend payment.

Paragraph (5)

This provision makes the start of the three-month period relevant under paras. (2) to (4) the date of actual receipt of written notice of the decision and the reasons for it by the AO. Presumably this means the full statement of the tribunal's decision under reg. 23 of the Adjudication Regulations. However, para. (5) has not been amended to bring it into line with the changes in the Adjudication Regulations from October 1996 and April 1997. The reference to the AO presumably means the AO who made the decision under appeal, or it may extend to any AO currently concerned with the appeal. But the claimant is deemed to have received the notice under para. (3) on the day it is posted to him (para. (5)(b)).

[¹Suspension in identical cases

37A. Where—
- (a) an appeal is pending against the decision given in a case ("the primary case") by a Commissioner or a court; and
- (b) it appears to the Secretary of State that if the appeal were to be determined in a particular way an issue would arise whether the award in another case ("the secondary case") ought to be revised,

the Secretary of State may direct that payment of benefit under the award in the secondary case be suspended, in whole or in part, for as long as the appeal against the decision given in the primary case is pending.]

AMENDMENT

1. Social Security (Claims and Payments) Amendment Regulations 1998 (S.I. 1998 No. 1381), reg. 2 (June 30, 1998).

DEFINITION

"benefit"—see reg. 2(2).

GENERAL NOTE

The intended aim of reg. 37A is to authorise suspension of payment of other claimants' benefit while an appeal in the "primary case" is brought. The current form of reg. 37A was made under the new para. (nn) inserted into s.5(1) of the Administration Act by para. 5(1) of Sched. 6 to the Social Security Act 1998 with effect from May 21, 1998. The previous form of reg. 37A was declared *ultra vires* in *R. v. Secretary of State for Social Security, ex parte Sutherland*, November 6, 1996.

The argument accepted in *Sutherland* was as follows. Section 5(1)(n)(ii) allows regulations to provide for suspending payment of benefit where it appears to the Secretary of State that a question arises whether an award ought to be revised. That means that it must appear to the Secretary of State that a *present* question exists. The use of the phrase "question arising" in s.20(1)(b) of the Administration Act (on questions to be submitted forthwith to the AO) necessarily refers to present questions and s. 5(1)(n) must be construed in the same sense. However, reg. 37A purported to allow the Secretary of State to suspend payment where there was no present question, but a question would arise in the future if the primary case were decided one way rather than the other. Therefore, s. 5(1)(n)(ii) did not authorise the making of reg. 37A. It was no answer that it would have been sensible or desirable for primary legislation to give such authorisation. In fact, it had not.

Sutherland overtook more limited points on the scope of reg. 37A, but two earlier decisions remain of interest. In *Mulgrew v. Secretary of State for Social Security* (Outer House of the Court of Session, November 30, 1995) the DSS conceded that reg. 37A could not be used where the award had been made by a tribunal. This would also be the case if the award was made by a Commissioner or court (giving the decision that the tribunal should have given). That was because only AO's decisions may be reviewed for error of law.

In *R. v. Secretary of State for Social Security, ex. p. Sherwin*, (High Court, February 6, 1996) it was argued that the creation of the Benefits Agency meant that decisions to suspend payment of benefit under regs. 37 and 37A could not be regarded as being taken by the Secretary of State within the limits of *Carltona Ltd v. Commissioner of Works* {1943] 2 All E.R. 560 (which was concerned with the conditions for the delegation of decision-making by ministers). However, it was held that a decision taken by a person of suitable seniority in the Benefits Agency was a decision taken under the authority of the Secretary of State (applying the approach of Lord Griffiths in *R. v. Secretary of State for Home Department, ex p. Oladehine* [1991] 1 A.C. 254). Leave to appeal against this decision was refused by the Court of Appeal. It has since been accepted by the DSS in *Mackenzie and Laughlin v. Secretary of State for Social Security* (Outer House of the Court of Session, May 17, 1996) that "suitable seniority" means higher executive officer level. Another argument in *Sherwin* was that the Benefits Agency's letter indicated that *all* awards of benefit in "lookalike" cases were being suspended. The Secretary of State had a discretion to suspend payment but it seemed that he had adopted a blanket policy which it was submitted was unlawful. But the Court accepted that the evidence showed that a discretion had been exercised. Clearly in deciding whether to suspend payment, account should be taken of individual circumstances (*e.g.* whether hardship will result from the suspension).

[¹Withholding of benefit in prescribed circumstances

37AA.—(1) Where a person who is in receipt of benefit fails to comply with the provisions of regulation 32(1), in so far as they relate to documents, information or facts required by the Secretary of State, that benefit may be withheld, in whole or in part, from a date not earlier than 28 days after the date on which the requirement is imposed.

(2) Where the Secretary of State is satisfied that the last known address of a person who is in receipt of benefit is not the address at which that person is residing or that a serious doubt exists as to whether that person is residing at that address, that benefit may be withheld from the date on which the Secretary of State is so satisfied or such later date as he may determine.

[²(3) Where a person who is in receipt of a jobseeker's allowance—

(a) has previously attended in compliance with a notice under regulation 23 of the Jobseeker's Allowance Regulations (attendance) but subsequently fails to attend in compliance with such a notice, benefit may be withheld from a date not earlier than the day following the last day on which he did attend in compliance with such a notice;

(b) is a person who has not previously been required to attend in compliance with such a notice, is served with such a notice but fails to attend in compliance with it, benefit may be withheld from the day following the last day in respect of which the last payment of benefit was made to him;

(c) is a person who has made a claim but who has not yet received any payment in respect of that claim and who fails to attend in compliance with such a notice, benefit may be withheld from the date of that claim.

(3A) Where a person who is in receipt of a jobseeker's allowance—

(a) has previously provided a signed declaration as referred to in regulation 24(6) of the Jobseeker's Allowance Regulations but subsequently fails to provide such a declaration in accordance with regulation 24(10) of those Regulations, benefit may be withheld from a date not earlier than the day following the last day on which he provided such a declaration;

(b) is a person who has not previously been required to provide such a declaration, is required to do so in accordance with regulation 24(10) of those Regulations, but fails to do so, benefit may be withheld from the day following the last day in respect of which the last payment of benefit was made to him;

(c) is a person who has made a claim but who has not yet received any payment in respect of that claim and who fails to provide such a declaration when required to do so under regulation 24(10) of those Regulations, benefit may be withheld from the date of that claim.]

(4) Where a person—

(a) claims any benefit, and entitlement to that benefit depends on his being incapable of work during the period to which his claim relates; or

[³(b) claims income support, and qualifies for income support by virtue of paragraph 7 of Schedule 1B to the Income Support (General) Regulations 1987,]

and that person fails to provide evidence of incapacity in accordance with regulation 2 of the Social Security (Medical Evidence) Regulations 1976 (evidence of incapacity for work), that benefit may be withheld from the date from which he has ceased to comply with the requirements of that regulation, or as soon as practicable thereafter.]

AMENDMENTS

1. Social Security (Claims and Payments) Amendment Regulations 1994 (S.I. 1994 No. 2319), reg. 6 (October 3, 1994).

2. Social Security (Claims and Payments) (Jobseeker's Allowance Consequential Amendments) Regulations 1996 (S.I. 1996 No. 1460), reg. 2(18) (October 7, 1996).

3. Social Security (Claims and Payments and Adjudication) Amendment Regulations 1996 (S.I. 1996 No. 2306), reg. 5 (October 7, 1996).

DEFINITIONS

"benefit"—see reg. 2(2).
"jobseeker's allowance"—see reg. 2(1)
"the Jobseeker's Allowance Regulations"—*ibid.*

[¹Payment of withheld benefit

37AB.—(1)   Subject to paragraph (2), where the circumstances in which any benefit that has been withheld under the provisions of regulation 37AA no longer exist, and—

(a) the Secretary of State is satisfied that no question arises in connection with the award of that benefit, payments of that benefit shall be made;

(b) a question arises in connection with the award of that benefit and that question has been determined, payments of benefit that the beneficiary is entitled to in accordance with that determination shall be made.

(2) Subject to paragraph (3)—

(a) a payment of any sum by way of benefit shall not be made under paragraph (1) after the expiration of a period of 12 months from the date the right to that payment arose;

(b) where a person from whom benefit has been withheld satisfies the adjudicating authority that there was good cause for his failure to act from a day within the period specified in sub-paragraph (a) and continuing after the expiration of that period, the period specified in that sub-paragraph shall be extended to the date on which the adjudicating authority is so satisfied, or the date on which good cause ceases, whichever is the earlier.

(3) For the purposes of paragraph (2), the following periods shall be disregarded—

(a) any period during which the Secretary of State possesses information which is sufficient—

    (i) to enable him to be satisfied that no question arises in connection with the award of that benefit, or

    (ii) to enable him to decide that a question does arise in connection with the award of that benefit;

(b) in a case where a question in connection with the award of the benefit arises, the period commencing on the date the question is submitted to an adjudication officer and ending on the date that question is finally determined.]

AMENDMENT

1. Social Security (Claims and Payments) Amendment Regulations 1994 (S.I. 1994 No. 2319), reg. 6 (October 3, 1994).

DEFINITION

"benefit"—see reg. 2(2).

['Witholding payment of arrears of benefit

37B. Where it appears to the Secretary of State that a question has arisen whether any amount paid or payable to a person by way of, or in connection with a claim for, benefit is recoverable under section 27 or 53 of the Social Security Act 1986 [SSAA, ss.74 and 71], or regulations made under either section, he may direct that any payment of arrears of benefit to that person shall be suspended, in whole or in part, pending determination of that question.]

AMENDMENT

1. Social Security (Miscellaneous Provisions) Amendment Regulations 1992 (S.I. 1992 No. 247), reg. 16 (March 9, 1992).

DEFINITION

"benefit"—see reg. 2(2).

GENERAL NOTE

It does not seem to be necessary that the arrears of benefit withheld under this regulation relate to the same period, or even the same benefit, as that to which the potential overpayment relates.

Extinguishment of right to payment of sums by way of benefit where payment is not obtained within the prescribed period

38.—(1) ['Subject to paragraph (2A), the right to payment of any sum by way of benefit shall be extinguished] where payment of that sum is not obtained within the period of 12 months from the date on which the right is to be treated as having arisen; and for the purposes of this regulation the right shall be treated as having arisen—

   (a) in relation to any such sum contained in an instrument of payment which has been given or sent to the person to whom it is payable, or to a place approved by the Secretary of State for collection by him (whether or not received or collected as the case may be)—

      (i) on the date of the said instrument of payment, or

      (ii) if a further instrument of payment has been so given or sent as a replacement, on the date of the last such instrument of payment;

[³(aa) in relation to any such sum which is payable by means of an instrument for benefit payment, on the first date when payment of that benefit could be obtained by that means;]

   (b) in relation to any such sum to which sub-paragraph (a) does not apply, where notice is given (whether orally or in writing) or is sent that the sum contained in the notice is ready for collection on the date of the notice or, if more than one such notice is given or sent, the date of the first such notice;

   (c) in relation to any such sum to which [³none of (a), (aa) or (b) apply], on such date as the Secretary of State determines.

(2) The giving or sending of an instrument of payment under paragraph (1)(a), or of a notice under paragraph (1)(b), shall be effective for the purposes of that paragraph, even where the sum contained in that instrument, or notice, is more or less than the sum which the person concerned has the right to receive.

[¹(2A) Where a question arises whether the right to payment of any sum by way of benefit has been extinguished by the operation of this regulation and the adjudicating authority is satisfied that—

   (a) the Secretary of State has first received written notice requesting payment of that sum after the expiration of 12 months; and

   (b) from a day within that period of 12 months and continuing until the day the written notice was given, there was good cause for not giving the notice; and

[²(c) the Secretary of State has certified either—

      (i) that no instrument of payment has been given or sent to the person to whom it is payable and that no payment has been made under the provisions of regulation 21 (automated credit transfer); or

      (ii) that such instrument has been produced to him and that no further instrument has been issued as a replacement,]

the period of 12 months shall be extended to the date on which the adjudicating authority decides that question, and this regulation shall accordingly apply as though the right to payment had arisen on that date.]

(3) For the purposes of paragraph (1) the date of an instrument of payment is the date of issue of that instrument or, if the instrument specifies a date which is the earliest date on which payment can be obtained on the instrument and which is later than the date of issue, that date.

(4) This regulation shall apply to a person authorised or appointed to act on behalf of a beneficiary as it applies to a beneficiary.

(5) [*Omitted as not applying to income-related benefits*]

AMENDMENTS

1. Social Security (Medical Evidence, Claims and Payments) Amendment Regulations 1989 (S.I. 1989 No. 1686), reg. 7 (October 9, 1989).

2. Social Security (Claims and Payments) Amendment (No. 3) Regulations 1993 (S.I. 1993 No. 2113), reg. 3(8) (September 27, 1993).

3. Social Security (Claims and Payments Etc.) Amendment Regulations 1996 (S.I. 1996 No. 672), reg. 2(5) (April 4, 1996).

DEFINITIONS

"beneficiary"—see Social Security Act 1975, Sched. 20.
"benefit"—see reg. 2(2).
"instrument for benefit payment"—see reg. 2(1).

GENERAL NOTE

See *R(A) 2/93* on the pre-October 1989 form of reg. 38.
The new form applies to decisions extinguishing the right from October 9, 1989, onwards (*R/(P) 3/93*). The claimant only has to produce the instrument of payment under para. (2A)(c) if one was issued to him.

PART VII

MISCELLANEOUS

[¹Instruments of payment, etc and instruments for benefit payment

47.—(1) Instruments of payment, books of serial orders and instruments for benefit payment issued by the Secretary of State shall remain his property.

(2) Any person having an instrument of payment or book of serial orders shall, on ceasing to be entitled to the benefit to which such instrument or book relates, or when so required by the Secretary of State, deliver it to the Secretary of State or such other person as he may direct.

(3) Any person having an instrument for benefit payment shall, when so required by the Secretary of State, deliver it to the Secretary of State or such other person as he may direct.]

AMENDMENT

1. Social Security (Claims and Payments) Amendment (No. 4) Regulations 1994 (S.I. 1994 No. 3196), reg. 8 (January 10, 1995).

DEFINITIONS

"instrument for benefit payment"—see reg. 2(1).
"benefit"—see reg. 2(2).

Revocations

48. The regulations specified in column (1) of Schedule 10 to these regulations are hereby revoked to the extent mentioned in column (2) of that Schedule, in exercise of the powers specified in column (3).

Savings

49. [¹ . . .]

AMENDMENT

1. Social Security (Miscellaneous Provisions) Amendment (No. 2) Regulations 1992 (S.I. 1992 No. 2595), reg. 6 (November 16, 1992).

GENERAL NOTE

Reg. 49 maintained in force regulations about claims and reviews relating to supplementary benefit and family income support. See *CIS 465/1991*. Because its terms led to the mistaken impression that the substantive terms of the schemes survived the repeal of the Supplementary Benefits Act 1976 and the Family Income Supplements Act 1970 by the Social Security Act 1986, reg. 49 has been revoked from November 16, 1992. See *R(SB) 1/94*. It is not immediately apparent that reg. 49 was necessary in order to allow claims to be made for supplementary benefit for periods prior to April 11, 1988, and reviews of entitlement for such periods to be carried out. Therefore its revocation may have no effect on such matters. See Sched. 10 to the Administration Act. However, *CSB 168/1993* is to the contrary.

In *CIS 12016/1996* a Commissioner, after a detailed review of the legal issues, concluded that from November 16, 1992, it has been impossible for an effective claim to be made for supplementary benefit. This was in spite of the powerful argument that an underlying entitlement to supplementary benefit for a period before April 11, 1988, and the right to pursue a remedy in respect of that entitlement could be preserved by s. 16(1) of the Interpretation Act 1978 on the revocation of the supplementary benefit legislation. The reason was that any remedy protected would be under reg. 3(1) of the Supplementary Benefit (Claims and Payments) Regulations 1981, which required a claim for weekly supplementary benefit to be made in writing on a form approved by the Secretary of State or in such other manner as the Secretary of State accepted as sufficient. In *CIS 12016/1996*, the claim was made in a letter in July 1993. By that date, the Secretary of State had no power to accept the manner of claim as sufficient, because the 1981 Regulations no longer existed. Since the Secretary of State's power was discretionary, the claimant had no accrued right which could be preserved by s. 16(1). It had been held in *R. v. Secretary of State for Social Security, ex parte Cullen* (November 21, 1996), now confirmed by the Court of Appeal (*The Times*, May 16, 1997, and see the notes to reg. 9) that the hope of having a discretion to treat a claim for supplementary benefit as in the alternative a claim for attendance allowance was not preserved by s.16(1) as an accrued right. The same had to apply to the power to accept claims as made in sufficient manner.

Note also *CIS 7009/1995* which confirms that it was not possible to make a late claim for National Assistance after the start of the supplementary benefit scheme on November 24, 1966. There were no savings provisions to enable claims for National Assistance to succeed after that date (see *CSB 61/1995*).

SCHEDULES

SCHEDULE 1   **Regulation 9(1)**

PART I

BENEFIT CLAIMED AND OTHER BENEFIT WHICH MAY BE TREATED AS IF CLAIMED IN ADDITION OR IN THE ALTERNATIVE

Column (1)	Column (2)
Benefit Claimed	*Alternative Benefit*
Income support	Supplementary benefit, or an invalid care allowance.
[¹Disability working allowance	Family credit.
Family credit	Disability working allowance.]

AMENDMENT

1. Social Security (Claims and Payments) Amendment Regulations 1991 (S.I. 1991 No. 2741), reg. 25 (March 10, 1992).

SCHEDULE 4   **Regulation 19(1)**

PART I

PRESCRIBED TIMES FOR CLAIMING BENEFIT

Column (1)	Column (2)	
Description of benefit	*Prescribed time for claiming benefit*	
1. [⁴Jobseeker's allowance.		The first day of the period in respect of which the claim is made.
6. Income support.		The first day of the period in respect of which the claim is made.]
7. Family credit.	(a)	Where family credit has previously been claimed and awarded the period beginning 28 days before and ending 14 days after the last day of that award;
	[³(aa)	where disability working allowance has previously been claimed and awarded the period beginning 42 days before and ending 14 days after the last day of that award of disability working allowance;]
	(b)	subject to [³(a) and (aa)], the first day of the period in respect of which the claim is made.
	[¹(c)	where a claim for family credit is treated as if made for a period beginning with the relevant day by virtue of regulation 13 of these Regulations, the period beginning on 10th March 1992 and ending on 6th April 1992.]
8. Social fund payment in respect of maternity expenses.		[⁶The period beginning 11 weeks before the first day of the expected week of confinement and ending 3 months after—
	(a)	the actual date of confinement; or
	(b)	in the case of an adopted child, the date of the adoption order; or
	(c)	in the case of a child in respect of whom an order has been granted pursuant to section 30 of the Human Fertilisation and Embryology Act, the date of that Order.]
9. Social fund payment in respect of funeral expenses.		[⁵The period beginning with the date of the death and ending 3 months after the date of the funeral]
9A. [². . .]		
[³**11.** Disability working allowance.	(a)	Where disability working allowance has previously been claimed and awarded the period beginning 42 days before and ending 14 days after the last day of that award;
	(b)	where family credit has previously been claimed and awarded the period beginning 28 days before and ending 14 days after the last day of that award of family credit;
	(c)	subject to (c) and (b), the first day of the period in respect of which the claim is made;
	(d)	where a claim for disability working allowance is made by virtue of regulation 13B(1), the period beginning on 10th March 1992 and ending on 6th April 1992.]

For the purposes of this Schedule—

"actual date of confinement" means the date of the issue of the child or, if the woman is confined of twins or a greater number of children, the date of the issue of the last of them; and

"confinement" means labour resulting in the issue of a living child, or labour after 28 weeks of pregnancy resulting in the issue of a child whether alive or dead.

AMENDMENTS

1. Social Security (Miscellaneous Provisions) Amendment Regulations 1991 (S.I. 1991 No. 2284), reg. 10 (November 1, 1991).
2. Social Security (Miscellaneous Provisions) Amendment Regulations 1991 (S.I. 1991 No. 2284), reg. 11 (November 1, 1991).
3. Social Security (Claims and Payments) Amendment Regulations 1991 (S.I. 1991 No. 2741), reg. 26 (March 10, 1992).
4. Social Security (Claims and Payments) (Jobseeker's Allowance Consequential Amendments) Regulations 1996 (S.I. 1996 No. 1460), reg. 2(22) (October 7, 1996).
5. Social Security (Claims and Payments and Adjudication) Amendment Regulations 1996 (S.I. 1996 No. 2306), reg. 6 (October 7, 1996).
6. Social Security (Social Fund and Claims and Payments) (Miscellaneous Amendments) Regulations 1997 (S.I. 1997 No. 792), reg. 8 (April 7, 1997)

SCHEDULE 7   **Regulation 26**

MANNER AND TIME OF PAYMENT, EFFECTIVE DATE OF CHANGE OF CIRCUMSTANCES AND COMMENCEMENT OF ENTITLEMENT IN INCOME SUPPORT CASES

Manner of payment

1. Except as otherwise provided in these Regulations income support shall be paid in arrears in accordance with the award by means of an instrument of payment [⁸or an instrument for benefit payment].

Time of payment

2. Income support shall be paid in advance where the claimant is—
(a) in receipt of retirement pension; or
(b) over pensionable age and not in receipt of [⁹. . .] [⁷incapacity benefit or severe disablement allowance and is not a person to whom section 126 of the Social Security Contributions and Benefits Act 1992 (trade disputes) applies] unless he was in receipt of income support immediately before the trade dispute began; or
(c) in receipt of widow's benefit and is not registering or required to register as available for work or providing or required to provide medical evidence of incapacity for work; or
(d) a person to whom [¹section 23(a)] of the Social Security Act 1986 [SSCBA, s.127] applies, but only for the period of 15 days mentioned in that subsection.
[²**2A.**—(1) For the purposes of this paragraph—
(a) "public holiday" means, as the case may be, Christmas Day, Good Friday or a Bank Holiday under the Banking and Financial Dealings Act 1971 or in Scotland local holidays, and

1398

(b) "office closure" means a period during which an office of the Department of Social Security or associated office is closed in connection with a public holiday.

(2) Where income support is normally paid in arrears and the day on which the benefit is payable by reason of paragraph 3 is affected by office closure it may for that benefit week be paid wholly in advance or partly in advance and partly in arrears and on such a day as the Secretary of State may direct.

(3) Where under this paragraph income support is paid either in advance or partly in advance and partly in arrears it shall for any other purposes be treated as if it was paid in arrears.]

[³3.—(1) Subject to [⁷sub-paragraph (1A) and to] any direction given by the Secretary of State in accordance with sub-paragraph (2), income support in respect of any benefit week shall, if the beneficiary is entitled to a relevant social security benefit or would be so entitled but for failure to satisfy the contribution conditions or had not exhausted his entitlement, be paid on the day and at the intervals appropriate to payment of that benefit.

[⁷(1A) Subject to sub-paragraph (2), where income support is paid to a person on the grounds of incapacity for work, that entitlement commenced on or after 13th April 1995, and no relevant social security benefit is paid to that person, the income support shall be paid fortnightly in arrears.]

(2) The Secretary of State may direct that income support in respect of any benefit week shall be paid at such intervals and on such days as he may in any particular case or class of case determine.

3A.—(1) Income support for any part-week shall be paid in accordance with an award on such day as the Secretary of State may in any particular case direct.

(2) In this paragraph, "part-week" has the same meaning as it has in Part VII of the Income Support (General) Regulations 1987.]

4. [¹In this Schedule]—
"benefit week" means, if the beneficiary is entitled to a relevant social security benefit or would be so entitled but for failure to satisfy the contribution conditions or had not exhausted his entitlement, the week corresponding to the week in respect of which that benefit is paid, and in any other case a period of 7 days beginning or ending with such day as the Secretary of State may direct;

[¹"Income Support Regulations" means the Income Support (General) Regulations 1987;] and

"relevant social security benefit" means [⁹. . .] [⁷incapacity benefit], severe disablement allowance, retirement pension or widow's benefit.

Payment of small amounts of income support

5. Where the amount of income support is less than £1.00 a week the Secretary of State may direct that it shall be paid at such intervals as may be specified not exceeding 13 weeks.

Commencement of entitlement to income support

6.—(1) Subject to sub-paragraphs (3) and (4), in a case where income support is payable in arrears entitlement shall commence on the date of claim.

(2) [¹Subject to sub-paragraphs (2A) and (3)], in a case where, under paragraph 2, income support is payable in advance entitlement shall commence on the date of claim if that day is a day for payment of income support as determined under paragraph 3 but otherwise on the first such day after the date of claim.

[¹(2A) Where income support is awarded under regulation 17(3) for a definite period which is not a benefit week or a multiple of such a week entitlement shall commence on the date of claim.

(3) In a case where regulation 13 applies, entitlement shall commence on the day

which is the relevant day for the purposes of that regulation [⁵except where income support is paid in advance, when entitlement shall commence on the relevant day, if that day is a day for payment as determined under paragraph 3 but otherwise on the first day for payment after the relevant day].]

(4) [¹. . .]

[⁹(5) If a claim is made by a claimant within 3 days of the date on which he became resident in a resettlement place provided pursuant to section 30 of the Jobseekers Act or at a centre providing facilities for the rehabilitation of alcoholics or drug addicts, and the claimant is so resident for the purposes of that rehabilitation, then the claim shall be treated as having been made on the day the claimant became so resident.]

(6) Where, in consequence of a further claim for income support such as is mentioned in sub-paragraph 4(7) of Schedule 3 to the Income Support (General) Regulations 1987, a claimant is treated as occupying a dwelling as his home for a period before moving in, that further claim shall be treated as having been made on the date from which he is treated as so occupying the dwelling or the date of the claim made before he moved in to the dwelling and referred to in that subparagraph, whichever is the later.

[⁴Date when change of circumstances is to take effect

7.—(1) Subject to the following sub-paragraphs, where the amount of income support payable under an award is changed because of a change of circumstances that change shall have effect—

> (i) where income support is paid in arrears, from the first day of the benefit week in which the change occurs or is expected to occur; or
>
> (ii) where income support is paid in advance, from the date of the relevant change of circumstances, or the day on which the relevant change of circumstances is expected to occur, if either of those days is the first day of the benefit week and otherwise from the next following such day, and

for the purposes of this paragraph any period of residence in temporary accommodation pursuant to arrangements for training under section 2 of the Employment and Training Act 1973 [⁵or section 2 of the Enterprise and New Towns (Scotland) Act 1990] for a period which is expected to last for seven days or less shall not be regarded as a change of circumstances.]

(2) In the cases set out in sub-paragraph (3) the decision given on review shall have effect on the day on which the relevant change of circumstances occurs or is expected to occur.

(3) The cases referred in sub-paragraph (2) are where—

(a) income support is paid in arrears and entitlement ends, or is expected to end, for a reason other than that the claimant no longer satisfies the provisions of section 20(3)(b) of the Social Security Act 1986 [SSCBA, s.124(1)(b)];

(b) a child or young person referred to in regulation 16(6) of the Income Support Regulations (child in care of a local authority or detained in custody) lives, or is expected to live, with the claimant for part only of the benefit week;

(c) a claimant or his partner (as defined in regulation 2(1) of the Income Support Regulations) enters, or is expected to enter, a nursing home or a residential care home (as defined in regulation 19(3) of those Regulations) or residential accommodation (as defined in regulation 21(3)(a) to (d) of those Regulations) for a period of not more than 8 weeks;

(d) a person referred to in paragraphs 1, 2, 3 or 18 of Schedule 7 to the Income Support Regulations either—

> (i) ceases, or is expected to cease, to be a patient, or

      (ii) a member of his family ceases, or is expected to cease, to be a patient, in either case for a period of less than a week;

[⁶(dd) a person referred to in paragraph 8 of Schedule 7 to the Income Support Regulations either—

      (i) ceases to be a prisoner, or.

      (ii) becomes a prisoner;]

  (e) a person to whom section 23 of the Social Security Act 1986 [SSCBA, s.126] (trade disputes) applies either—

      (i) becomes incapable of work by reason of disease or bodily or mental disablement, or

      (ii) enters the maternity period (as defined in section 23(2) of that Act) or the day is known on which that person is expected to enter the maternity period;

  (f) during the currency of a claim the claimant makes a claim for a relevant social security benefit—

      (i) the result of which is that his benefit week changes; or

      (ii) under regulation 13 and an award of that benefit on the relevant day for the purposes of that regulation means that his benefit week is expected to change.

(4) Where income is treated as paid on a particular day under regulation 31(1)(b) or (2) [¹⁰ or 39C(3)] of the Income Support Regulations (date on which income is treated as paid) any relevant change of circumstances which occurs, or is expected to occur, resulting from that payment shall have effect on the day on which it was treated as paid.

(5) Where the relevant change of circumstances requires, or is expected to require, a reduction in the amount of income support then, if the Secretary of State certifies that it will be impracticable to give effect to that reduction from the day prescribed in the preceding sub-paragraphs, except where (3)(f) or (4) apply, the change shall have effect either from the first day of the following benefit week or, where the relevant change of circumstances is expected to occur, from the first day of the benefit week following that in which that change of circumstances is expected to occur.

(6) Where in the cases set out in sub-paragraphs (b), (c), (d), (e) and (f) of paragraph (3) the review has been carried out under section 104(1)(b) of the Social Security Act 1975 and the circumstances which have caused the award to be revised cease to apply and the award is reviewed and revised again that second change of circumstances shall take effect from the date of the second change.

AMENDMENTS

1. Social Security (Claims and Payments) Amendment Regulations 1988 (S.I. 1988 No. 522), reg. 10 (April 11, 1988).

2. Social Security (Claims and Payments and Payments on account, Overpayments and Recovery) Amendment Regulations 1989 (S.I. 1989 No. 136), reg. 2(b) (February 27, 1989).

3. Social Security (Medical Evidence, Claims and Payments) Amendment Regulations 1989 (S.I. 1989 No. 1686), reg. 8 (October 9, 1989).

4. Social Security (Miscellaneous Provisions) Amendment Regulations 1990 (S.I. 1990 No. 2208), reg. 15 (December 5, 1990).

5. Enterprise (Scotland) Consequential Amendments Order 1991 (S.I. 1991 No. 387), art. 2 and Sched. (April 1, 1991).

6. Social Security (Miscellaneous Provisions) Amendment Regulations 1992 (S.I. 1992 No. 247), reg. 17 (March 9, 1992).

7. Social Security (Claims and Payments) Amendment (No. 2) Regulations 1994 (S.I. 1994 No. 2943), reg. 14 (April 13, 1995).

8. Social Security (Claims and Payments Etc.) Amendment Regulations 1996 (S.I. 1996 No. 672), reg. 2(6) (April 4, 1996).

9. Social Security (Claims and Payments) (Jobseeker's Allowance Consequential Amendments) Regulations 1996 (S.I. 1996 No. 1460), reg. 2(24) (October 7, 1996).

10. Social Security (Miscellaneous Amendments) (No. 4) Regulations 1998 (S.I. 1998 No. 1174), reg. 8(3)(b) (June 1, 1998).

Social Security (Claims and Payments) Regulations 1987

GENERAL NOTE

Paragraph 1

One of the most significant changes from supplementary benefit is encapsulated in this provision. The general rule is that income support is paid in arrears, rather than in advance. This is perhaps a further step in the integration of means-tested benefits (where the approach in the past has been to make the benefit available at the time of need) with other kinds of benefit. Exceptions to the general rule are in paras. 2 and 2A. The day of payment is dealt with in paras. 3 to 4.

If a claimant is without resources until the first payment of income support at the end of the first benefit week then there may be eligibility for a crisis loan under the social fund. Any resources actually available or which could be obtained in time to meet the need must be considered. A crisis loan may be made for living expenses (see Social Fund Directions 18–20).

On the changeover to income support from April 11, 1988, a special transitional payment of income support was to be paid after that date to bridge the gap from supplementary benefit paid in advance to income support paid in arrears (Income Support (Transitional) Regulations, reg. 7).

Paragraph 2

These categories of claimant are paid income support in advance. Apart from pensioners and most widows, those returning to work after a trade dispute are covered.

Paragraphs 3 and 4

Where a claimant meets the conditions of entitlement for one of the benefits listed as a "relevant social security benefit," the income support benefit week, pay-day and interval of payment is the same as for that benefit. Thus, those incapable of work are paid fortnightly in arrears (reg. 24(1)), although under reg. 24 the Secretary of State can arrange payment of incapacity benefit at other intervals (*e.g.* weekly), in which case income support follows suit. Otherwise the benefit week is to be defined by the Secretary of State. Income support paid for a definite period under reg. 17(3) need not be in terms of benefit weeks. Para. 3A provides that payments for part-weeks may be made as the Secretary of State directs.

Paragraph 6

The general rule for income support paid in arrears is that entitlement begins on the date of claim. The first payment on the pay day at the end of the first benefit week (or the second benefit week in the case of the unemployed) can thus be precisely calculated to include the right number of days. Payments can then continue on a weekly basis.

If income support is paid in advance, then, as for supplementary benefit, entitlement begins on the next pay day following the claim or coinciding with the date of claim.

Where the award is for a definite period under reg. 17(3) entitlement begins with the date of claim (sub-para. (2A)). Sub-para. (3) deals with the special case of advance awards. Sub-paras. (5) and (6) cover other special cases.

Paragraph 7

This provision deals with the date on which a review on the ground of a change of circumstances (Administration Act, s.25(1)(b); 1975 Act, s.104(1)(b)) or an anticipated change of circumstances (Administration Act, s.25(1)(c); 1975 Act, s.104(1)(bb)) takes effect. The review legislation does not specify the date on which a revised decision on review is to take effect.

Although sub-para. (1) refers to the amount of income support payable being changed, it is apparent from the rest of para. 7 that changes which result in entitlement to income support being entirely removed are equally covered. Sub-para. (1) establishes two general rules, which are subject to exceptions in sub-paras. (2) to (6).

The general rule where benefit is paid in arrears is that the change of circumstances is to take effect from the first day of the benefit week (defined in para. 4) in which it occurs, or is expected to occur (sub-para. (1)(i)). Where benefit is paid in advance the change takes effect from the first day of the benefit week which starts on the date of the change or in the next six days (sub-para. (1)(ii)). Sub-para. (3) lists cases in which the change of circumstances takes effect on the date of the change. The most important is (a), which covers the ending of entitlement (other than on capital grounds) where benefit is being paid in arrears. Sub-para. (4) deals with changes in most payments of income. Sub-para. (5) provides a general exception allowing the effect of a change to be deferred to the next benefit week following the normal day, if the Secretary of State certifies that it would be impracticable to follow the normal rule.

SCHEDULE 9   **Regulation 35**

DEDUCTIONS FROM BENEFIT AND DIRECT PAYMENT TO THIRD PARTIES

Interpretation

1. [²⁰—(1)] In this Schedule—

[¹¹"the Community Charges Regulations" means the Community Charges (Deductions from Income Support (No. 2) Regulations 1990;

"the Community Charges (Scotland) Regulations" means the Community Charges (Deductions from Income Support) (Scotland) Regulations 1989;]

[²¹"contribution-based jobseeker's allowance" means any contribution-based jobseeker's allowance which does not fall within the definition of "specified benefit";]

"family" in the case of a claimant who is not a member of a family means that claimant;

[¹¹"the Fines Regulations" means the Fines (Deductions from Income Support) Regulations 1992;]

[⁶"5 per cent of the personal allowance for the single claimant aged not less than 25" means where the percentage is not a multiple of 5 pence the sum obtained by rounding that 5 per cent to the next higher such multiple;

"hostel" means a building other than a residential care home or nursing home within the meaning of regulation 19(3) of the Income Support Regulations or residential accommodation within the meaning of regulation 21(3) of those Regulations—

  (a) in which there is provided for persons generally, or for a class of persons. accommodation, otherwise than in separate and self-contained premises, and either board or facilities of a kind set out in paragraph 4A(1)(d) below adequate to the needs of those persons and—

  (b) which is—

    (i) managed by or owned by a housing association registered with the Housing Corporation established by the Housing Act 1964; or

    (ii) managed or owned by a housing association registered with Scottish Homes established by the Housing (Scotland) Act 1988; or

    (iii) operated other than on a commercial basis and in respect of which funds are provided wholly or in part by a government department or a local authority; or

    (iv) managed by a voluntary organisation or charity and provides care, support or supervision with a view to assisting those persons to be rehabilitated or resettled within the community.

  (c) In sub-paragraph (iv) above, "voluntary organisation" shall mean a body the activities of which are carried out otherwise than for profit, but shall not include any public or local authority;

"housing authority" means a local authority, a new town corporation, Scottish Homes or the Rural Development Board for Rural Wales;]

"the Housing Benefit Regulations" means the Housing Benefit (General) Regulations 1987;

[²⁰"housing costs" means any housing costs met under—

  (a) Schedule 3 to the Income Support Regulations but—

    (i) excludes costs under paragraph 17(1)(f) of that Schedule (tents and tent sites); and

    (ii) includes costs under paragraphs 17(1)(a) (ground rent and feu duty) and 17(1)(c) (rentcharges) of that Schedule but only when they are paid with costs under paragraph 17(1)(b) of that Schedule (service charges); or

  (b) Schedule 2 to the Jobseeker's Allowance Regulations but—

  (i) excludes costs under paragraph 16(1)(f) of that Schedule (tents and tent sites); and

  (ii) includes costs under paragraphs 16(1)(a) (ground rent and feu duty) and 16(1)(c) (rentcharges) of that Schedule but only when they are paid with costs under paragraph 16(1)(b) of that Schedule (service charges);]

[² "income support" means income support under Part II of the Social Security Act 1986 [SSCBA, Part VII] and includes transitional addition, personal expenses addition and special transitional addition as defined in the Income Support (Transitional) Regulations 1987;]

"the Income Support Regulations" means the Income Support (General) Regulations 1987;

"miscellaneous accommodation costs" has the meaning assigned by paragraph 4(1);

[²⁰ "mortgage payment" means the aggregate of any payments which fall to be met under—

 (a) Schedule 3 to the Income Support Regulations in accordance with paragraphs 6 to 10 of that Schedule (housing costs to be met in income support) on a loan which qualifies under paragraph 15 or 16 of that Schedule, but less any amount deducted under paragraph 18 of that Schedule (non-dependant deductions); or

 (b) Schedule 2 to the Jobseeker's Allowance Regulations in accordance with paragraphs 6 to 9 of that Schedule (housing costs to be met in jobseeker's allowance) on a loan which qualifies under paragraph 14 or 15 of that Schedule, but less any amount deducted under paragraph 17 of that Schedule (non-dependant deductions),

 as the case may be.]

"personal allowance for a single claimant aged not less than 25 years" means the amount specified in [⁶ paragraph 1(1)(e)] of column 2 of Schedule 2 to the Income Support Regulations [²⁰ or, as the case may be, paragraph 1(1)(e) of Schedule 1 to the Jobseeker's Allowance Regulations];

[² . . .]

"rent" has the meaning assigned to it in the Housing Benefit Regulations and, for the purposes of this Schedule

 (a) includes any water charges which are paid with or as part of the rent;

 (b) where in any particular case a claimant's rent includes elements which would not otherwise fall to be treated as rent, references to rent shall include those elements; and

 (c) references to "rent" include references to part only of the rent; and

[¹⁷ "specified benefit" means—

 (a) in respect of any period during which benefit is paid by means of an instrument of payment, income support either alone or together with any [²⁰ . . .] incapacity benefit, retirement pension or severe disablement allowance which is paid by means of the same instrument of payment; and

 (b) in respect of any period during which benefit is paid by means of an instrument for benefit payment, income support and, where paid concurrently with income support, [²⁰ . . .] incapacity benefit, retirement pension or severe disablement allowance; [²⁰ and

 (c) subject to sub-paragraph (2), jobseeker's allowance;]

[²³ but does not include any sum payable by way of child maintenance bonus in accordance with section 10 of the Child Support Act 1995) and the [²⁴ Social Security (Child Maintenance Bonus)] Regulations 1996;]]

[⁸ "water charges" means charges for water or sewerage under Chapter I of Part V of the Water Industry Act 1991;]

[⁶ "water undertaker" means a company which has been appointed under section 11(1) of the Water Act 1989 to be the water or sewerage undertaker for any area in England and Wales.]

[20(2) For the purposes of the definition of "specified benefit" in sub-paragraph (1), "jobseeker's allowance" means—

    (a) income-based jobseeker's allowance; and

    (b) in a case where, if there was no entitlement to contribution-based jobseeker's allowance, there would be entitlement to income-based jobseeker's allowance at the same rate, contribution-based jobseeker's allowance.]

General

2.—(1) The specified benefit may be paid direct to a third party in accordance with the following provisions of this Schedule in discharge of a liability of the beneficiary or his partner to that third party in respect of—

    (a) housing costs;

    (b) miscellaneous accommodation costs;

[6(bb) hostel payments;]

    (c) service charges for fuel, and rent not falling within head (a) above;

    (d) fuel costs; [10. . .]

    (e) water charges; [10and

    (f) payments in place of payments of child support maintenance under section 43(1) of the Child Support Act 1991 and regulation 28 of the Child Support (Maintenance Assessments and Special Cases) Regulations 1992.]

(2) No payment to a third party may be made under this Schedule under the amount of the beneficiary's award of the specified benefit is not less than the total of the amount otherwise authorised to be so paid under this Schedule plus 10 pence.

(3) A payment to be made to a third party under this Schedule shall be made, at such intervals as the Secretary of State may direct, on behalf of and in discharge (in whole or in part) of the obligation of the beneficiary or, as the case may be, of his partner, in respect of which the payment is made.

Housing costs

3.—(1) Subject to [7sub-paragraphs (4) to (6)] and paragraph 8, where a beneficiary who has been awarded the specified benefit or his partner is in debt for any item of housing costs which continues to be applicable to the beneficiary in the determination of his applicable amount, the adjudicating authority may, if in its opinion it would be in the interests of the family to do so, determine that the amount of the award of the specified benefit ("the amount deductible") calculated in accordance with the following sub-paragraphs shall be paid in accordance with sub-paragraph 2(3).

(2) [7Subject to sub-paragraphs (2A) and (3)], the amount deductible shall be such weekly aggregate of the following as is appropriate:—

    (a) in respect of any debt to which sub-paragraph (1) applies, or where the debt owed is in respect of an amount which includes more than one item of housing costs, a weekly amount equal to 5 per cent. of the personal allowance for a single claimant aged not less than 25 [1. . .] for such period as it is necessary to discharge the debt, so however that in aggregate the weekly amount calculated under this sub-paragraph shall not exceed 3 times that 5 per cent;

    (b) for each such debt—

        (i) in respect of mortgage payments, the weekly amount of the mortgage payment in that case; and

        (ii) for any other housing item, the actual weekly cost necessary in respect of continuing needs for the relevant items,

and the adjudicating authority may direct that, when the debt is discharged, the amount determined under sub-paragraph (b) shall be the amount deductible.

[⁷(2A) Where a payment falls to be made to a third party in accordance with this Schedule, and—

(a) more than one item of housing costs falls to be taken into account in determining the beneficiary's applicable amount; and

(b) in accordance with [¹⁶paragraph 4(8) or (11) or] [¹⁵paragraph 18] of Schedule 3 to the Income Support Regulations [²⁰or, as the case may be, paragraph 4(8) or (11) or paragraph 17 of Schedule 2 to the Jobseeker's Allowance Regulations] an amount is not allowed or a deduction falls to be made from the amount to be met by way of housing costs,

then in calculating the amount deductible, the weekly aggregate amount ascertained in accordance with sub-paragraph (2) shall be reduced by an amount determined by applying the formula—

$$C \times \frac{B}{A}$$

where—

A = housing costs;

B = the item of housing costs which falls to be paid to a third party under this Schedule;

C = the sum which is not allowed or falls to be deducted in accordance with [¹⁵paragraph 4(8) or (11) or paragraph 18] of Schedule 3 to the Income Support Regulations. [²⁰or, as the case may be, paragraph 4(8) or (11) or paragraph 17 of Schedule 2 to the Jobseeker's Allowance Regulations]]

(3) Where the aggregate amount calculated under sub-paragraph (2) is such that paragraph 2(2) would operate to prevent any payment under this paragraph being made that aggregate amount shall be adjusted so that 10 pence of the award is payable to the beneficiary.

(4) Sub-paragraph (1) shall not apply to any debt which is either—

(a) in respect of mortgage payments and the beneficiary or his partner has in the preceding 12 weeks paid sums equal to [⁸or greater than] 8 week's mortgage payments due in that period; or

(b) for any other item of housing costs and is less than half the annual amount due to be paid by the beneficiary or his partner in respect of that item,

unless, in either case, in the opinion of the adjudicating authority it is in the overriding interests of the family that paragraph (1) should apply.

[⁷(5) No amount shall be paid pursuant to this paragraph in respect of mortgage interest in any case where a specified part of relevant benefits—

(a) is required to be paid directly to a qualifying lender under regulation 34A and Schedule 9A; or

(b) would have been required to be paid to a body which, or a person who, would otherwise have been a qualifying lender but for an election given under paragraph 9 of Schedule 9A not to be regarded as such.

(6) In sub-paragraph (5), "specified part" and "relevant benefits" have the meanings given to them in paragraph 1 of Schedule 9A.]

Miscellaneous accommodation costs

[⁹**4.**—(1) Where an award of income support [²⁰or jobseeker's allowance]—

(a) is made to a person in a residential care home or nursing home as defined in regulation 19(3) of the Income Support Regulations [²⁰or, as the case may be, regulation 1(3) of the Jobseeker's Allowance Regulations], or

(b) includes an amount under Schedule 4 (persons in residential care and nursing homes) or paragraph 13 (residential accommodation) or 13A (Polish resettlement) of Schedule 7 to the Income Support Regulations [²⁰or, as the case may be, Schedule 4 (applicable amounts of persons in residential care and nursing homes) or paragraph 15 of Schedule 5 (persons in residential accommodation) to the Jobseeker's Allowance Regulations], (hereafter in this paragraph referred to as "miscellaneous accommodation costs")] the adjudicating authority may determine that an amount of the specified benefit shall be paid direct to the person or body to whom the charges in respect of that accommodation are payable, but, except in a case to which paragraph [⁶13A] [⁴. . .] of Schedule 7 to the Income Support Regulations apply or where the accommodation is [²run by a voluntary organisation either for purposes similar to the purposes for which resettlement units are provided] or which provides facilities for alcoholics or drug addicts, only if the adjudicating authority is satisfied that the beneficiary has failed to budget for the charges and that it is in the interests of the family.

(2) [²Subject to sub-paragraph (3), in relation to miscellaneous accommodation costs the amount] of any payment of income support [²⁰or jobseeker's allowance] to a third party determined [²under sub-paragraph (1)] shall be—

(a) the amount of the award under paragraph 1(1)(a) of Schedule 4 to the Income Support Regulations excluding any increase under paragraph 2(2) of that Schedule [²⁰or, as the case may be, the amount of the award under paragraph 1(1)(a) of Schedule 4 to the Jobseeker's Allowance Regulations excluding any increase under paragraph 2(2) of that Schedule]; or

[⁹(aa) an amount equal to the amount of any payment the beneficiary is liable to make to the local authority under section 22 of the National Assistance Act 1948;]

[¹²(ab) in a case where the beneficiary does not have a preserved right within the meaning of regulation 19 of the Income Support Regulations and is not liable to make a payment to a local authority under section 22 of the National Assistance Act 1948 an amount equal to the amount of the award of income support [²⁰or jobseeker's allowance] payable to the claimant but excluding an amount, if any, which when added to any other income of the beneficiary (as determined in accordance with regulation 28 of the Income Support Regulations [²⁰or, as the case may be, regulation 93 of the Jobseeker's Allowance Regulations]) will equal the aggregate of the amounts—

(i) prescribed by paragraph 13 of Schedule 4 to the Income Support Regulations [²⁰or, as the case may be, paragraph 11 of Schedule 4 to the Jobseeker's Allowance Regulations]; and

(ii) where the charge for the accommodation does not include the provision of all meals, an amount calculated under paragraph 2(2)(b) of [²⁰whichever of those Schedules is applicable].]

(b) [⁴. . .]

(c) the amount of the award [²under paragraph 13(1)(a), (b), (c), or (e)], [⁴or, as the case may be, 14] of Schedule 7 to [²⁰the Income Support Regulations or, as the case may be, under paragraph 15(1)(a), (b), (c) or (e) of Schedule 5 to the Jobseeker's Allowance Regulations] excluding the amount allowed by those paragraphs in respect of personal expenses,

as the case may be.

[²[²⁰(3) In relation to miscellaneous accommodation costs—

(a) where an award of income support is calculated in accordance with Part VII of the Income Support Regulations (calculation of income support for part-weeks) the amount of any payment of income support to a third party determined under sub-paragraph (1) shall be—

(i) where the amount is calculated under regulation 73(1) of the Income Support Regulations, an amount calculated in accordance with sub-paragraph (2)(a) or,as the case may be, (c) above, divided by 7 and multiplied by the number of days in the part-week; or

(ii) where the amount is calculated under regulation 73(2) of those Regulations, an amount calculated in accordance with regulation 73(4)(a)(i) or (b)(i) as the case may be; or

(b) where an award of jobseeker's allowance is calculated in accordance with Part XI of the Jobseeker's Allowance Regulations (part-weeks) the amount of any payment of jobseeker's allowance to a third party determined under sub-paragraph (1) shall be—

    (i) where the amount is calculated under regulation 150(1) of the Jobseeker's Allowance Regulations, an amount calculated in accordance with sub-paragraph (2)(a) or, as the case may be, (c) above, divided by 7 and multiplied by the number of days in the part-week; or

    (ii) where the amount is calculated under regulation 151(1) of those Regulations, an amount calculated in accordance with regulation 151(2)(a)(i) or (b)(i) as the case may be,

and no payment shall be made to a third party under this sub-paragraph where the Secretary of State certifies it would be impracticable to do so in that particular case.]

(4) Where the amount calculated under sub-paragraph (2) or (3) is such that paragraph 2(2) would operate to prevent any payment under this paragraph being made the amount shall be adjusted so that 10 pence of the award is payable to the beneficiary.]

[⁶Hostel payments

4A.—(1) This paragraph applies to a beneficiary if—

(a) he has been awarded specified benefit; and

(b) he or his partner has claimed housing benefit in the form of a rent rebate or rent allowance; and

(c) he or his partner is resident in a hostel; and

(d) the charge for that hostel includes a payment, whether direct or indirect, for one or more of the following services—

    (i) water;

    (ii) a service charge for fuel;

    (iii) meals;

    (iv) laundry;

    (v) cleaning (other than communal areas).

(2) Subject to sub-paragraph (3) below, where a beneficiary [⁸. . .] has been awarded specified benefit the adjudicating authority may determine that an amount of specified benefit shall be paid to the person or body to whom the charges referred to in sub-paragraph (1)(d) above are or would be payable.

(3) The amount of any payment to a third party under this paragraph shall be either—

(a) the aggregate of the amounts determined by a housing authority in accordance with the provisions specified in sub-paragraph (4); or

(b) if no amount has been determined under paragraph (a) of this sub-paragraph, an amount which the adjudicating authority estimates to be the amount which is likely to be so determined.

(4) The provisions referred to in sub-paragraph (3)(a) above are regulation 10(6) of, and paragraphs 1(a)(ii) and (iv), [⁸1A, 2, 3 and either 5(1)(b) or 5(2) or 5(2A)] of Schedule 1 to, the Housing Benefit Regulations.

(5) Sub-paragraph (2) above shall not apply to a deduction in respect of a service charge for fuel if that charge is one such as is mentioned in paragraph 5(5) of Schedule 1 to the Housing Benefit Regulations (variable service charges for fuel) unless the adjudicating authority is satisfied on the evidence available at the date of the determination that the amount of the charge does not normally alter more than twice in any one year.

[²⁰(6) Where—

(a) an award of income support is calculated in accordance with regulation 73(1) of the Income Support Regulations (calculation of income support for part-weeks); or

(b) an award of jobseeker's allowance is calculated in accordance with regulation 150(1) of the Jobseeker's Allowance Regulations (amount of a jobseeker's allowance payable),

the amount of any payment of income support or, as the case may be, jobseeker's allowance payable to a third party determined under sub-paragraph (2) above shall be an amount calculated in accordance with sub-paragraph (3)(a) or (b) above divided by 7 and multiplied by the number of days in the part-week, and no payment shall be made to a third party under this sub-paragraph where the Secretary of State certifies that it would be impracticable to do so in that particular case.]]

Service charges for fuel, and rent not falling within paragraph 2(1)(a)

5.—(1) Subject to paragraph 8, this paragraph applies to a beneficiary if—
(a) he has been awarded the specified benefit; and
(b) he or his partner is entitled to housing benefit in the form of a rent rebate or rent allowance; and
(c) he or his partner has arrears of rent which equal or exceed four times the full weekly rent payable and—
   (i) there are arrears of rent in respect of at least 8 weeks and the landlord has requested the Secretary of State to make payments in accordance with this paragraph; or
   (ii) there are arrears of rent in respect of less than 8 weeks and in the opinion of the adjudicating authority it is in the overriding interests of the family that payments shall be made in accordance with this paragraph.
(2) For the purposes of sub-paragraph (1) arrears of rent do not include—
(a) the 20 per cent of eligible rates excluded from a rent allowance under regulation 61 of the Housing Benefit Regulations (maximum housing benefit); or
(b) any amount falls to be deducted when assessing a person's rent rebate or rent allowance under regulation 63 of those Regulations (non-dependants).
(3) Subject to sub-paragraph (4), the adjudicating authority shall determine that a weekly amount of the specified benefit awarded to the beneficiary shall be paid to his or his partner's landlord if—
(a) he or his partner is entitled to housing benefit and in calculating that benefit a deduction is made under regulation 10(3) of the Housing Benefit Regulations in respect of either or both of water charges or service charges for fuel; and
(b) the amount of the beneficiary's award is not less than the amount of the deduction, and the amount to be paid shall be equal to the amount of the deduction.
(4) Sub-paragraph (3) shall not apply to a deduction in respect of a service charge for fuel if that charge is one such as is mentioned in paragraph 5(5) of Schedule 1 to the Housing Benefit Regulations (variable service charges for fuel) unless the adjudicating authority is satisfied on the evidence available at the date of the determination that the amount of the charge does not normally alter more than twice in any one year.
[[20](5) A determination under this paragraph shall not be made without the consent of the beneficiary if the aggregate amount calculated in accordance with sub-paragraphs (3) and (6) exceeds a sum equal to 25 per cent of the applicable amount for the family as is awarded under—
(a) in the case of income support, sub-paragraphs (a) to (d) of regulation 17(1) (applicable amounts) or sub-paragraphs (a) to (e) of regulation 18(1) (polygamous marriages) of the Income Support Regulations; or
(b) in the case of jobseeker's allowance, paragraphs (a) to (e) of regulation 83 (applicable amounts) or sub-paragraphs (a) to (f) of regulation 84(1) (polygamous marriages) of the Jobseeker's Allowance Regulations.]
(6) In a case to which sub-paragraph (1) applies the adjudicating authority may determine that a weekly amount of the specified benefit awarded to that beneficiary equal to 5 per cent. of the personal allowance for a single claimant aged not less than 25 [6. . .] shall be paid to his landlord until the debt is discharged.
[[8](7) Immediately after the discharge of any arrears of rent to which sub-paragraph (1) applies and in respect of which a determination has been made under sub-paragraph (6) the adjudicating authority may, if satisfied that it would be in the interests of the family to do so, direct that an amount, equal to the amount by which the eligible rent is to be

reduced by virtue of regulation 10(3) of the Housing Benefit Regulations in respect of charges for water or service charges for fuel or both, shall be deductible.]

Fuel costs

6.—(1) Subject to sub-paragraph (6) and paragraph 8, where a beneficiary who has been awarded the specified benefit or his partner is in debt for any item of mains gas or mains electricity [[13]including any charges for the reconnection of gas or disconnection or reconnection of electricity] (''fuel item'') to an amount not less than the rate of personal allowance for a single claimant aged not less than 25 and continues to require that fuel, the adjudicating authority, if in its opinion it would be in the interests of the family to do so, may determine that the amount of the award of the specified benefit (''the amount deductible'') calculated in accordance with the following paragraphs shall be paid to the person or body to whom payment is due in accordance with paragraph 2(3).

(2) The amount deductible shall, in respect of any fuel item, be such weekly aggregate of the following as is appropriate:—

[[6](a) in respect of each debt to which sub-paragraph (1) applies (''the original debt''), a weekly amount equal to 5 per cent of the personal allowance for a person aged not less than 25 for such period as is necessary to discharge the original debt, but the aggregate of the amounts, calculated under this paragraph shall not exceed twice 5 per cent of the personal allowance for a single claimant aged not less than 25;]

(b) except where current consumption is paid for by other means (for example pre-payment meter), an amount equal to the estimated average weekly cost necessary to meet the continuing needs for that fuel item, varied, where appropriate, in accordance with sub-paragraph (4)(a).

(3) [[6]. . .]

(4) Where an amount is being paid direct to a person or body on behalf of the beneficiary or his partner in accordance with a determination under sub-paragraph (1) and that determination falls to be reviewed—

(a) where since the date of that determination the average weekly cost estimated for the purpose of sub-paragraph (2)(b) has either exceeded or proved insufficient to meet the actual cost of continuing consumption so that in respect of the continuing needs for that fuel item the beneficiary or his partner is in credit or, as the case may be, a further debt has accrued, the adjudicating authority may determine that the weekly amount calculated under that paragraph shall, for a period of 26 weeks [[8]or such longer period as may be reasonable in the circumstances of the case], be adjusted so as to take account of that credit or further debt;

(b) where an original debt in respect of any fuel item has been discharged the adjudicating authority may determine that the amount deductible in respect of that fuel item shall be the amount determined under sub-paragraph (2)(b).

(5) [[6]. . .]

[[20](6) Subject to paragraph 8, a determination under this paragraph shall not be made without the consent of the beneficiary if the aggregate amount calculated in accordance with sub-paragraph (2) exceeds a sum equal to 25 per cent of the applicable amount for the family as is awarded under—

(a) in the case of income support, sub-paragraphs (a) to (d) of regulation 17(1) (applicable amounts) or sub-paragraphs (a) to (e) of regulation 18(1) (polygamous marriages) of the Income Support Regulations; or

(b) in the case of a jobseeker's allowance, paragraphs (a) to (e) of regulation 83 (applicable amounts) or sub-paragraphs (a) to (f) of regulation 84(1) (polygamous marriages) of the Jobseeker's Allowance Regulations.]

(7) [[6]. . .]

[⁶**Water charges**

7.—(1) This paragraph does not apply where water charges are paid with rent; and in this paragraph "original debt" means the debt to which sub-paragraph (2) applies, [¹³including any disconnection or reconnection charges and any other costs (including legal costs) arising out of that debt].

(2) Where a beneficiary or his partner is liable, whether directly or indirectly, for water charges and is in debt for those charges, the adjudicating authority may determine, subject to paragraph 8, that a weekly amount of the specified benefit shall be paid either to a water undertaker to whom that debt is owed, or to the person or body authorised to collect water charges for that undertaker, [⁸but only if the authority is satisfied that the beneficiary or his partner has failed to budget for those charges, and that it would be in the interests of the family to make the determination.]

(3) Where water charges are determined by means of a water meter, the weekly amount to be paid under sub-paragraph (2) shall be the aggregate of—

    (a) in respect of the original debt, an amount equal to 5 per cent of the personal allowance for a single claimant aged not less than 25 years; and

    (b) the amount which the adjudicating authority estimates to be the average weekly cost necessary to meet the continuing need for water consumption.

(4) Where the sum estimated in accordance with sub-paragraph (3)(b) proves to be greater or less than the average weekly cost necessary to meet continuing need for water consumption so that a beneficiary or his partner accrues a credit, or as the case may be a further debt, the adjudicating authority may determine that the sum so estimated shall be adjusted for a period of 26 weeks [⁸or such longer period as may be reasonable in the circumstances of the case] to take account of that credit or further debt.

(5) Where water charges are determined other than by means of a water meter the weekly amount to be paid under sub-paragraph (2) shall be the aggregate of—

    (a) the amount referred to in sub-paragraph (3)(a); and

    (b) an amount equal to the weekly cost necessary to meet the continuing need for water consumption.

(6) Where the original debt in respect of water charges is discharged, the adjudicating authority may direct that the amount deductible shall be—

    (a) where water charges are determined by means of a water meter, the amount determined under sub-paragraph (3)(b) taking into account any adjustment that may have been made in accordance with sub-paragraph (4); and

    (b) in any other case, the amount determined under sub-paragraph (5)(b).

(7) Where the beneficiary or his partner is in debt to two water undertakers—

    (a) only one weekly amount under sub-paragraph (3)(a) or (5)(a) shall be deducted; and

    (b) a deduction in respect of an original debt for sewerage shall only be made after the whole debt in respect of an original debt for water has been paid; and

    (c) deductions in respect of continuing charges for both water and for sewerage may be made at the same time.

[²⁰(8) Subject to paragraph 8 (maximum amount of payments to third parties), a determination under this paragraph shall not be made without the consent of the beneficiary if the aggregate amount calculated in accordance with sub-paragraphs (3), (4), (5) and (6) exceeds a sum equal to 25 per cent of the applicable amount for the family as is awarded under—

    (a) in the case of income support, sub-paragraphs (a) to (d) of regulation 17(1) (applicable amounts) or sub-paragraphs (a) to (e) of regulation 18(1) (polygamous marriages) of the Income Support Regulations; or

    (b) in the case of jobseeker's allowance, paragraphs (a) to (e) of regulation 83 (applicable amounts) or sub-paragraphs (a) to (f) of regulation 84(1) (polygamous marriages) of the Jobseeker's Allowance Regulations.]]

[¹⁰Payments in place of payments of child support maintenance

7A.—[¹²(1) Subject to paragraph (2), where a child support officer (within the meaning of section 13 of the Child Support Act 1991) has determined that section 43 of that Act and regulation 28 of the Child Support (Maintenance Assessments and Special Cases) Regulations 1992 (contribution to maintenance by deduction from benefit) apply in relation to a beneficiary or his partner, the adjudicating authority shall (subject to paragraph 8), if it is satisfied that there is sufficient specified benefit in payment, determine that a weekly amount of that benefit shall be deducted by the Secretary of State for transmission to the person or persons entitled to it.]

(2) Not more than one deduction shall be made under [¹²sub-paragraph (1)] in any one benefit week as defined in paragraph 4 of Schedule 7.

(3) [¹⁸Subject to sub-paragraph (4),] the amount of specified benefit to be paid under this paragraph shall be the amount prescribed by regulation 28(2) of the Child Support (Maintenance Assessments and Special Cases) Regulations 1992 for the purposes of section 43(2)(a) of the Child Support Act 1991 [¹⁸. . .].]

[¹⁸(4) Where, apart from the provisions of this sub-paragraph, the provisions of paragraphs 8(1) and 9 would result in the maximum aggregate amount payable equalling 2 times 5 per cent of the personal allowance for a single claimant aged not less than 25 years, the amount of specified benefit to be paid under this paragraph shall be one half of the amount specified in sub-paragraph (3).]

[²¹Arrears of child support maintenance

7B.—(1) Where a beneficiary is entitled to contribution-based jobseeker's allowance and an arrears notice has been served on the beneficiary, the Secretary of State may request in writing that an amount in respect of arrears of child support maintenance be deducted from the beneficiary's jobseeker's allowance.

(2) Where a request is made in accordance with sub-paragraph (1), the adjudicating authority shall determine that an amount in respect of the arrears of child support maintenance shall be deducted from the beneficiary's jobseeker's allowance for transmission to the person entitled to it.

(3) Subject to sub-paragraphs (4) and (5), the amount to be deducted under sub-paragraph (2) shall be the weekly amount requested by the Secretary of State, subject to a maximum of one-third of the age-related amount applicable to the beneficiary under section 4(1)(a) of the Jobseekers Act.

(4) No deduction shall be made under this paragraph where a deduction is being made from the beneficiary's contribution-based jobseeker's allowance under the Community Charges Regulations, the Community Charges (Scotland) Regulations, the Fines Regulations or the Council Tax Regulations.

(5) Where the sum that would otherwise fall to be deducted under this paragraph includes a fraction of a penny, the sum to be deducted shall be rounded down to the next whole penny.

(6) In this paragraph—

"arrears notice" means a notice served in accordance with regulation 2(2) of the Child Support (Arrears, Interest and Adjustment of Maintenance Assessments) Regulations 1992; and

"child support maintenance" means such periodical payments as are referred to in section 3(6) of the Child Support Act 1991.]

Maximum amount of payments to third parties

8.—(1) The maximum aggregate amount payable under [¹⁹paragraphs] 3(2)(a), 5(6), 6(2)(a)[⁶, 7(3)(a)[¹¹, 7(5)(a) and 7A]] [²². . .] [¹¹, and [¹³regulation 7 of the Council Tax Regulations] and regulation 6 of the Fines Regulations] shall not exceed an amount equal

1412

to 3 times 5 per cent. of the personal allowance for a single claimant aged not less than 25 years.

(2) The maximum [⁵aggregate] amount payable under [⁶paragraphs 3(2)(a), 5, 6 and 7] shall not without the consent of the beneficiary, exceed a sum equal to 25 per cent. of so much of the applicable amount for the family as is awarded under—

[²⁰(a) in the case of income support, sub-paragraphs (a) to (d) of regulation 17(1) (applicable amounts) or sub-paragraphs (a) to (e) of regulation 18(1) (polygamous marriages) of the Income Support Regulations; or

(b) in the case of a jobseeker's allowance, paragraphs (a) to (e) of regulation 83 (applicable amounts) or sub-paragraphs (a) to (f) of regulation 84(1) (polygamous marriages) of the Jobseeker's Allowance Regulations.]

(3) [²²...]

Priority as between certain debts

[¹¹**9.**—(1)(A) Where in any one week—

(a) more than one of the paragraphs 3 to 7A are applicable to the beneficiary; or

(b) one or more of those paragraphs are applicable to the beneficiary and one or more of the following provisions, namely, [²²...] regulation 2 of the Community Charges Regulations, regulation 2 of the Community Charges (Scotland) Regulations, regulation 6 of the Fines Regulations and regulation 7 of the Council Tax Regulations also applies; and

(c) the amount of the specified benefit which may be made to third parties is insufficient to meet the whole of the liabilities for which provision is made;

the order of priorities specified in sub-paragraph (1)(B) shall apply.

(1)(B) The order of priorities which shall apply in sub-paragraph (1)(A) is—

(za) [²²...]

(a) any liability mentioned in paragraph 3 (housing costs);

(b) any liability mentioned in paragraph 5 (service charges for fuel and rent not falling within paragraph 2(1)(a));

(c) any liability mentioned in paragraph 6 (fuel costs);

(d) any liability mentioned in paragraph 7 (water charges);

(e) any liability mentioned in regulation 2 of the Community Charges Regulations (deductions from income support), regulation 2 of the Community Charges (Scotland) Regulations (deductions from income support) or any liability mentioned in regulation 7 of the Council Tax Regulations (deductions from debtor's income support);

(f) any liability mentioned in regulation 6 of the Fines Regulations (deductions from offenders income support);

(g) any liability mentioned in paragraph 7A (payments in place of payments of child support maintenance).]

(2) As between liability for items of housing costs liabilities in respect of mortgage payments shall have priority over all other items.

(3) As between liabilities for items of gas or electricity the adjudicating authority shall give priority to whichever liability it considers it would, having regard to the circumstances and to any requests of the beneficiary, be appropriate to discharge.

(4) [⁶...]

Amendments

1. Social Security (Claims and Payments) Amendment Regulations 1988 (S.I. 1988 No. 522), reg. 11 (April 11, 1988).

2. Social Security (Claims and Payments and Payments on account, Overpayments and Recovery) Amendment Regulations 1989 (S.I. 1989 No. 136), reg. 2(7) (February 27, 1989).

3. Social Security (Claims and Payments and Payments on account, Overpayments and Recovery) Amendment Regulations 1989 (S.I. 1989 No. 136), reg. 2(7) (April 10, 1989).

4. Social Security (Medical Evidence, Claims and Payments) Amendment Regulations 1989 (S.I. No. 1686), reg. 9 (October 9, 1989).

5. Social Security (Miscellaneous Provisions) Amendment Regulations 1990 (S.I. 1990 No. 2208), reg. 16 (December 5, 1990).

6. Social Security (Miscellaneous Provisions) Amendment Regulations 1991 (S.I. 1991 No. 2284), regs. 12 to 20 (November 1, 1991).

7. Social Security (Claims and Payments) Amendment Regulations 1992 (S.I. 1992 No. 1026), reg. 5 (May 25, 1992).

8. Social Security (Miscellaneous Provisions) Amendment (No. 2) Regulations 1992 (S.I. 1992 No. 2595), reg. 8 (November 16, 1992).

9. Social Security Benefits (Amendments Consequential Upon the Introduction of Community Care) Regulations 1992 (S.I. 1992 No. 3147), Sched. 1, para. 8 (April 1, 1993).

10. Social Security (Claims and Payments) Amendment Regulations 1993 (S.I. 1993 No. 478), reg. 2 (April 1, 1993).

11. Deductions from Income Support (Miscellaneous Amendment) Regulations 1993 (S.I. 1993 No. 495), reg. 2 (April 1, 1993).

12. Social Security (Claims and Payments) Amendment (No. 3) Regulations 1993 (S.I. 1993 No. 2113), reg. 3 (September 27, 1993).

13. Social Security (Claims and Payments) Amendment Regulations 1994 (S.I. 1994 No. 2319), reg. 7 (October 3, 1994).

14. Social Security (Claims and Payments) Amendment (No. 2) Regulations 1994 (S.I. 1994 No. 2943), reg. 15 (April 13, 1995).

15. Social Security (Income Support and Claims and Payments) Amendment Regulations 1995 (S.I. 1995 No. 1613), reg. 3 and Sched. 2 (October 2, 1995).

16. Social Security (Income Support, Claims and Payments and Adjudication) Amendment Regulations 1995 (S.I. 1995 No. 2927), reg. 3 (December 12, 1995).

17. Social Security (Claims and Payments Etc.) Amendment Regulations 1996 (S.I. 1996 No. 672), reg. 2(7) (April 4, 1996).

18. Child Support (Maintenance Assessments and Special Cases) and Social Security (Claims and Payments) Amendment Regulations 1996 (S.I. 1996 No. 481), reg. 5 (April 8, 1996).

19. Child Support (Maintenance Assessments and Special Cases) and Social Security (Claims and Payments) Amendment Regulations 1996 (S.I. 1996 No. 481), reg. 6 (April 8, 1996).

20. Social Security (Claims and Payments) (Jobseeker's Allowance Consequential Amendments) Regulations 1996 (S.I. 1996 No. 1460), reg. 2(26) (October 7, 1996).

21. Social Security (Jobseeker's Allowance Consequential Amendments) (Deductions) Regulations 1996 (S.I. 1996 No. 2344), reg. 25 (October 7, 1996).

22. Social Security and Child Support (Miscellaneous Amendments) Regulations 1997 (S.I. 1997 No. 827), reg. 7(2) (April 7, 1997).

23. Social Security (Child Maintenance Bonus) Regulations 1996 (S.I. 1996 No. 3195), reg. 16(2) (April 7, 1997).

24. Social Security (Miscellaneous Amendments) Regulations 1997 (S.I. 1997 No. 454), reg. 8(10) (April 6, 1997).

DEFINITIONS

"adjudicating authority"—see reg. 2(1).
"beneficiary"—see Social Security Act 1975, Sched. 20.
"family"—see 1986 Act, s.20(11) (SSCBA, s.137(1)).
"instrument for benefit payment"—see reg. 2(1).
"jobseeker's allowance"—*ibid.*
"partner"—*ibid.*
"qualifying lender"—see Administration Act, s.15A(3).

Note that these references are only to phrases defined outside Sched. 9 itself. See para. 1 for definitions special to Sched. 9.

GENERAL NOTE

The provisions for part of weekly benefit to be diverted direct to a third party are of great importance in determining the actual weekly incomes of claimants. There have been changes in the provisions on fuel and water charges and Sched. 9A now deals specifically with payments of mortgage interest.

On deductions in respect of rent arrears under para. 5(6), *R(IS) 14/95* holds that the arrears must be proved, at least where these are disputed. In addition, the existence of an arguable counterclaim in possession proceedings is a matter that an adjudicating authority might properly take into account in deciding whether to exercise the discretionary power to make deductions under para. 5(6).

[¹SCHEDULE 9A

DEDUCTIONS OF MORTGAGE INTEREST FROM BENEFIT AND PAYMENT TO QUALIFYING LENDERS

Interpretation

1. In this Schedule—

[⁹. . .]

"Income Support Regulations" means the Income Support (General) Regulations 1987;

[⁷"relevant benefits" means—

(a) in respect of any period during which benefit is paid by means of an instrument of payment, income support either alone or together with any [⁸. . .] incapacity benefit, retirement pension or severe disablement allowance which is paid by means of the same instrument of payment; and

(b) in respect of any period during which benefit is paid by means of an instrument for benefit payment, income support and, where paid concurrently with income support, [⁸. . .] incapacity benefit, retirement pension or severe disablement allowance; [⁸and

(c) income-based jobseeker's allowance;]

[¹⁰but does not include any sum payable by way of child maintenance bonus in accordance with section 10 of the Child Support Act 1995 and the [¹¹Social Security (Child Maintenance Bonus)] Regulations 1996;]]

"specified part" shall be construed in accordance with paragraph 3.

Specified circumstances

[⁵**2.** The circumstances referred to in regulation 34A are that—

[⁸(a) the amount to be met under Schedule 3 to the Income Support Regulations or, as the case may be, Schedule 2 to the Jobseeker's Allowance Regulations is determined by reference to the standard rate (whether at the full rate or a lesser rate) and, in the case of income support, to any amount payable in accordance with paragraph 7 of Schedule 3 to the Income Support Regulations;] and

(b) the relevant benefits to which a relevant beneficiary is entitled are payable in respect of a period of 7 days or a multiple of such a period.]

Specified part of relevant benefit

3. [⁵(1) Subject to the following provisions of this paragraph, the part of any relevant benefits which, as determined by the adjudicating authority in accordance with regulation 34A, shall be paid by the Secretary of State directly to the qualifying lender ("the specified part") is[⁸, in the case of income support,] a sum equal to the amount of mortgage interest to be met in accordance with paragraphs 6 and 8 to 10 of Schedule 3 to the Income Support Regulations (housing costs) together with an amount (if any) determined under paragraph 7 of that Schedule (transitional protection) [⁸or, in the case of jobseeker's allowance, a sum equal to the amount of mortgage interest to be met in accordance with paragraphs 6 to 9 of Schedule 2 to the Jobseeker's Allowance Regulations].]

(2) [⁵. . .]

(3) Where, in determining a relevant beneficiary's applicable amount for the purposes of income support [⁸or income-based jobseeker's allowance]—

(a) a sum in respect of housing costs is brought into account in addition to a sum in respect of mortgage interest; and

(b) in accordance with [⁵paragraph 4(8) or (11) or paragraph 18] of Schedule 3 to the Income Support Regulations [⁸or, as the case may be, paragraph 4(8) or (11) or paragraph 17 of Schedule 2 to the Jobseeker's Allowance Regulations] an amount is not allowed or a deduction falls to be made from the amount to be met under [⁸either of those Schedules],

then the specified part referred to in sub-paragraph (1) of this paragraph is the mortgage interest minus a sum calculated by applying the formula—

$$C \times \frac{B}{A}$$

[⁵where—

A = housing costs within the meaning of paragraph 1 of Schedule 3 to the Income Support Regulations [⁸or, as the case may be, paragraph 1 of Schedule 2 to the Jobseeker's Allowance Regulations];

B = the housing costs to be met in accordance with paragraphs 6 and 8 to 10 of Schedule 3 to the Income Support Regulations (housing costs) together with an amount (if any) determined under paragraph 7 of that Schedule (transitional protection) [⁸or, as the case may be, paragraphs 6 to 9 of Schedule 2 to the Jobseeker's Allowance Regulations]; and

C = the sum which is not allowed or falls to be deducted in accordance with paragraph 18 of Schedule 3 to the Income Support Regulations [⁸or, as the case may be, paragraph 4(8) or (11) or paragraph 17 of Schedule 2 to the Jobseeker's Allowance Regulations].]

(4) Where a payment is being made under a policy of insurance taken out by a beneficiary to insure against the risk of his being unable to maintain repayments of mortgage interest to a qualifying lender, then the amount of any relevant benefits payable to that lender shall be reduced by a sum equivalent to so much of the amount payable under the policy of insurance as represents payments in respect of mortgage interest.

(5) [⁹. . .]

(6) [⁹. . .]

(7) [⁵. . .]

(8) Where the amount of any relevant benefits to which a relevant beneficiary is entitled is less than the sum which would, but for this sub-paragraph, have been the specified part, then the specified part shall be the amount of any relevant benefits to which the relevant beneficiary is entitled less 10p.

Direct payment: more than one loan

4.—(1) This paragraph applies where the borrower is liable to pay mortgage interest in respect of two or more different loans.

[⁵(2) Subject to the following provisions of this paragraph, the Secretary of State shall pay to the qualifying lender or, if there is more than one qualifying lender, to each qualifying lender—

(a) a sum equal to the mortgage interest determined by reference to paragraph 12 of Schedule 3 to the Income Support Regulations [⁸or, as the case may be, paragraph 11 of Schedule 2 to the Jobseeker's Allowance Regulations] (standard rate) in respect of each loan made by that lender, plus

(b) any amount payable in accordance with paragraph 7 of Schedule 3 to the Income

Support Regulations (transitional protection) attributable to the particular loan; [⁹...]

(c) any additional amount attributable to a particular loan which may, under paragraph 3(5), have been taken into account in calculating the specified part.]

(3) If, by virtue of deductions made under either paragraph 3(2) or 3(3), the specified part is less than the amount payable by the borrower in respect of mortgage interest, then the sum payable under sub-paragraph (2)(a) shall be minus such proportion of the sum subtracted under those sub-paragraphs as is attributable to the particular loan.

(4) Paragraph 3(4) shall apply to reduce the amount payable to a qualifying lender mentioned in sub-paragraph (2) above as it applies to reduce the amount of any relevant benefits payable to a qualifying lender under paragraph 3.

(5) Where the specified part is the part referred to in paragraph 3(8), the Secretary of State shall pay the specified part directly to the qualifying lenders to whom mortgage interest is payable by the borrower in order of the priority of mortgages or (in Scotland) in accordance with the preference in ranking of heritable securities.

Relevant benefits

5.—[⁷...]

Time and manner of payments

6. Payments to qualifying lenders under regulation 34A and this Schedule shall be made in arrears at intervals of 4 weeks.

Fees payable by qualifying lenders

7. For the purposes of defraying the expenses of the Secretary of State in administering the making of payments under regulation 34A and this Schedule a qualifying lender shall pay to the Secretary of State a fee of [¹³£0.60] in respect of each payment made under regulation 34A and this Schedule.

Qualifying lenders

8. The following bodies and persons shall be qualifying lenders—
(a) the Housing Corporation;
(b) Housing for Wales;
(c) Scottish Homes;
(d) the Development Board for Rural Wales; and
(e) any body incorporated under the Companies Act 1985 whose main objects include the making of loans secured by a mortgage of or a charge over land or (in Scotland) by a heritable security.

Election not to be regarded as a qualifying lender

9.—(1) A body which, or a person who, would otherwise be a qualifying lender may elect not to be regarded as such for the purposes of these Regulations by giving notice of election under this paragraph to the Secretary of State in accordance with sub-paragraphs (2) and (3).

(2) Subject to sub-paragraph (3), notice of election shall be given in writing—
(a) in the case of the financial year 1992 to 1993, before 23rd May 1992 and shall take effect on that date; and
(b) in the case of any other financial year, before 1st February in the preceding year and shall take effect on 1st April following the giving of the notice.

(3) A body which, or a person who, becomes a qualifying lender during a financial year and who wishes to elect not to be regarded as such for the purposes of these Regula-

tions shall give notice of election in writing within a period of six weeks from the date on which the person or body becomes a qualifying lender.

(4) Regulation 34A shall not apply to a body which, or a person who, becomes a qualifying lender during a financial year for a period of six weeks from the date on which the person or body became a qualifying lender unless, either before the start of that period or at any time during that period, the person or body notifies the Secretary of State in writing that this sub-paragraph should not apply.

(5) A body which, or a person who, has made an election under this paragraph may revoke that election by giving notice in writing to the Secretary of State before 1st February in any financial year and the revocation shall take effect on the 1st April following the giving of the notice.

(6) Where a notice under this paragraph is sent by post it shall be treated as having been given on the day it was posted.

Provision of information

10.—(1) A qualifying lender shall provide the Secretary of State with information relating to—

(a) the mortgage interest payable by a borrower;
(b) the amount of the loan;
(c) the purpose for which the loan is made;
(d) the amount outstanding on the loan on which the mortgage interest is payable;
(e) any change in the amount of interest payable by the borrower;

at the times specified in sub-paragraphs (2) and (3).

(2) [¹²Subject to sub-paragraph (4),] the information referred to in heads (a), (b), (c) and (d) of sub-paragraph (1) shall be provided at the request of the Secretary of State when a claim for income support [⁸or income-based jobseeker's allowance] is made and a sum in respect of mortgage interest is to be brought into account in determining the applicable amount.

(3) [¹²Subject to sub-paragraph (4),] the information referred to in heads (d) and (e) of sub-paragraph (1) shall be provided at the request of the Secretary of State—

(a) when a claim for income support [⁸or income-based jobseeker's allowance] ceases to be paid to a relevant beneficiary; and
(b) once every 12 months notwithstanding that, in relation to head (d), the information may already have been provided during the period of 12 months preceding the date of the Secretary of State's request.

[¹²(4) Where a claimant or his partner is a person to whom either paragraph 1A of Schedule 3 to the Income Support (General) Regulations 1987 (housing costs) or paragraph 1A of Schedule 2 to the Jobseeker's Allowance Regulations 1996 (housing costs) refers, the information to which sub-paragraphs (2) and (3)(b) refer shall be provided at the request of the Secretary of State on the anniversary of the date on which the housing costs in respect of mortgage interest were first brought into account in determining the applicable amount of the person concerned.]

Recovery of sums wrongly paid

11.—(1) Where sums have been paid to a qualifying lender under regulation 34A which ought not to have been paid for one or both of the reasons mentioned in sub-paragraph (2) of this paragraph, the qualifying lender shall, at the request of the Secretary of State, repay the sum overpaid.

(2) The reasons referred to in sub-paragraph (1) of this paragraph are—
(a) that—
(i) the rate at which the borrower pays mortgage interest has been reduced [⁵or the rate specified in paragraph 12 of Schedule 3 to the Income Support Regulations [⁸or, as the case may be, paragraph 11 of Schedule 2 to the

Jobseeker's Allowance Regulations] (standard rate) has been reduced] or the amount outstanding on the loan has been reduced, and

(ii) as a result of this reduction the applicable amount of the relevant beneficiary has also been reduced, but

(iii) no corresponding reduction was made to the specified part; or

(b) subject to paragraph (3), that the relevant beneficiary has ceased to be entitled to any relevant benefits.

(3) A qualifying lender shall only repay sums which ought not to have been paid for the reason mentioned in sub-paragraph (2)(b) of this paragraph if the Secretary of State has requested that lender to repay the sums within a period of 4 weeks starting with the last day on which the relevant beneficiary was entitled to any relevant benefits.]

AMENDMENTS

1. Social Security (Claims and Payments) Amendment Regulations 1992 (S.I. 1992 No. 1026), reg. 6 and Sched. (May 25, 1992).
2. Social Security (Claims and Payments) Amendment (No. 3) Regulations 1993 (S.I. 1993 No. 2113), reg. 3 (September 27, 1993).
3. Social Security (Claims and Payments) Amendment (No. 3) Regulations 1994 (S.I. 1994 No. 2944), reg. 2 (April 1, 1995).
4. Social Security (Claims and Payments) Amendment (No. 2) Regulations 1994 (S.I. 1994 No. 2943), reg. 16 (April 13, 1995).
5. Social Security (Income Support and Claims and Payments) Amendment Regulations 1995 (S.I. 1995 No. 1613), reg. 3 and Sched. 2 (October 2, 1995).
6. Social Security (Claims and Payments) Amendment (No. 2) Regulations 1996 (S.I. 1996 No. 2988), reg. 2 (April 1, 1997).
7. Social Security (Claims and Payments Etc.) Amendment Regulations 1996 (S.I. 1996 No. 672), reg. 2(8) (April 4, 1996).
8. Social Security (Claims and Payments) (Jobseeker's Allowance Consequential Amendments) Regulations 1996 (S.I. 1996 No. 1460), reg. 2(27) (October 7, 1996).
9. Social Security and Child Support (Miscellaneous Amendments) Regulations 1997 (S.I. 1997 No. 827), reg. 7(3) (April 7, 1997).
10. Social Security (Child Maintenance Bonus) Regulations 1996 (S.I. 1996 No. 3195), reg. 16(2) (April 7, 1997).
11. Social Security (Miscellaneous Amendments) Regulations 1997 (S.I. 1997 No. 454), reg. 8(10) (April 6, 1997).
12. Social Security (Miscellaneous Amendments) (No. 4) Regulations 1997 (S.I. 1997 No. 2305), reg. 5 (October 22, 1997).
13. Social Security (Claims and Payments) Amendment (No. 2) Regulations 1998 (S.I. 1998 No. 3039), reg. 2 (April 1, 1999).

DEFINITIONS

"instrument for benefit payment"—see reg. 2(1).
"jobseeker's allowance"—*ibid.*
"mortgage interest"—see Administration Act, s.15A(4).
"qualifying lender"—see Administration Act, s.15A(3).
"relevant beneficiary"—see Administration Act, s.15A(1).

GENERAL NOTE

Para. 11 only authorises recovery of overpaid interest in the circumstances specified in sub-paras. (2) and (3).

In previous editions of this book it was suggested that it was not clear who decides that the interest has been overpaid, and that it was certainly arguable that this is the type of decision that should be made by an AO. *CIS 288/1994* and *CSIS 98/1994* hold that any decision regarding the recovery of any overpayment of mortgage interest from a qualifying lender is a matter for the Secretary of State, not the AO. The mortgage interest payment provisions are outside the scope of s.71 of the Administration Act (*CSIS 98/1994*). But in *CIS 5206/1995* the Commissioner reaches the opposite conclusion. He points out that under s.20 of the Administration Act all questions arising on claims or awards of benefit are to be determined by AOs, unless reserved to the Secretary of State (or other bodies). The question of whether the Secretary of State was *entitled* to recover a payment under para. 11 (which required consideration of whether the conditions in para. 11(2) were satisifed and also required calculation of the amount of the overpayment) was not reserved by para. 11 (or any other provision) to the Secretary of State. It therefore fell to be determined by an AO. Once it had been detemined that an overpayment was recoverable, the Secretary of State then had the discretion as to whether to request the lender to repay the sum to him. The process of adjudication was thus the same as that under s.71 of the Act, even though the circumstances in which recovery could be sought were different. Furthermore, where any question of recovery under para. 11 arose, the claimant's award must first be reviewed and revised under s.25 (as had been accepted by the Court of Appeal in *Golding*, see below). If not, the Secretary of State would be bound to pay any overpayment recovered from the lender to the claimant, since the money recovered represented part of the benefit due to the claimant. There is thus a conflict between these decisions but *CIS 5206/ 1995* is cogently argued and it is suggested that it is to be preferred.

Note also that under para. 3(1) the amount that will be paid to the qualifying lender by the Secretary of State under reg. 34A (the ''specified part'') is defined by reference to the amount of mortgage interest met in the income support or JSA assessment. Thus, if the claimant disputes the amount that has been awarded for mortgage interest, or maintains that there are no grounds for reviewing the amount of an existing award, he will have a right of appeal to a SSAT in the normal way.

In *R. v. Secretary of State for Social Security, ex p. Golding, The Times*, March 15, 1996, there had been an overpayment of mortgage interest because the claimant's interest rate had reduced. Recovery of the overpayment was implemented by withholding current payments due to the claimant's building society. Brooke J. accepted the claimant's contention that the effect of sub-para. (2)(iii) was that the Secretary of State could only recover an overpayment where an AO had decided under sub-para. (2)(ii) that a claimant's applicable amount should be reduced but the amount paid to the lender had not changed. Thus the Secretary of State could not recover the overpayment from the lender under para. 11 in respect of the period before the AO's decision. Para. 11 only applied to overpayments made after that decision (*i.e.* as a result of the decision not being implemented). The result of this decision would have been that in effect recovery of any overpayment would be governed by s.71 of the Administration Act (since it would normally be the period between the reduction in the interest rate and the AO's review decision that would be in issue, assuming the AO's decision was implemented promptly).

The Court of Appeal on July 1, 1996 reversed Brooke J.'s decision. It was held that in sub-para. (2)(ii), the applicable amount means the amount as determined by the adjudication officer's assessment current at the date when the question is asked. Thus, once there had been a review with retrospective effect of Mr Golding's entitlement to take account of the reduction in interest rates, there was a reduction for that retrospective period in his applicable amount, so that sub-para. (2) (ii) was met. Sub-para. (2)(iii) was also met, because the ''specified part'' actually paid to the lender in that past period could not be reduced. Therefore the overpayment was repayable by the lender. The Court of Appeal rejected Mr Golding's argument that the condition in sub-para. (1) that the sums ''ought not to have been paid'' was not met, because the sums were paid under the current adjudication officer's assessment. The provisions were to be interpreted so as to be consistent with the clear statutory intention of dealing with the built-in problem under the direct payment scheme of annual retrospective notification of interest rate changes under para. 10. Note the circumstances in which there can be no review on a reduction in interest rates where the claimant's liability remains constant (Adjudication Regulations, reg. 63(7)).

The Court of Appeal did express concern over the method of recovery adopted by the Secretary of State, who had not asked the lender to repay the overpayment, but had made deductions from the amounts of mortgage interest currently being paid direct to the lender. The concern was that that might put the claimant into arrears. The Secretary of State accepted that he could only use the set-off method if it did not adversely affect the position of the claimant. The Court of Appeal considered that that would only be so if each deduction was accompanied in the lender's accounting system by a corresponding credit to the claimant's interest account. The DSS has apparently carried out a review of the arrangements for recovery of overpayments from lenders.

It should be noted that para. 11 only applies where the overpayment has occurred for the reasons specified in sub-para. (2) and not, for example, where it is due to an incorrect amount of capital being taken into account.

Until April 1997, deductions could be made from a claimant's benefit in respect of mortgage interest arrears under para. 3(5) (the April 1996 rate was £2.40). This is no longer possible if the lender is covered by the mortgage payments direct scheme. *CIS 15146/1996* holds that it was for the AO to decide whether such deductions were to be made and that a decision to alter the amount of a deduction had to be made by way of review, as this was not one of the up-rating changes which took effect auto-matically under s.159 of the Act without the need for a review decision. Furthermore, it was necessary to investigate whether there were in fact mortgage arrears, as the existence of arrears had to be proved in order to justify the deduction (see *R(IS) 14/95* which had adopted the same approach in relation to deductions under para. 5 of Sched. 9). AOs and SSATs were not limited to determining whether there was sufficient income support in payment to sustain the direct payment.

Social Security (Income Support and Claims and Payments) Amendment Regulations 1995

(S.I. 1995 No. 1613)

Made by the Secretary of State under ss.135(1), 136(5)(b), 137(1) and 175(1) and (3) to (5) of the Social Security Contributions and Benefits Act 1992 and ss.5(1)(p), 15A(2), 189(1) and (4) and 191 of the Social Security Administration Act 1992.

[In force October 2, 1995]

SCHEDULE 2

4. In a case where, on 1st October 1995, a claimant's housing costs were limited to 50 per cent of the eligible interest in accordance with paragraph 7(1)(b)(ii) of Schedule 3 to the Income Support Regulations as then in force, then for so long as that paragraph would have continued to apply to him had it remained in force, the provisions of Sched-ule 9 shall apply to him as if the amendments made to it by paragraphs 2 and 3 above had not been made.

GENERAL NOTE

This saving provision concerns the amendments to paras. 1 and 3(2A) of Sched. 9 to the Claims and Payments Regulations made by paras. 2 and 3 of Sched. 2 to these Regulations on October 2, 1995.

Social Security (Payments on Account, Overpayments and Recovery) Regulations 1987

(S.I. 1987 No. 491)

Made by the Secretary of State under the Social Security Act 1986, ss.27, 51(1)(t), 84(1) and 89.

Transitional provisions

20.—(1) *[Revoked by the 1988 Regulations].*

(2) Section 53(7) and (9) [SSAA, s.71(8) and (10)] (recovery by deductions from benefit and recovery through the county court or sheriff court) and Part VII of these regulations (the process of recovery) shall apply to any amount recoverable or repayable under any enactment repealed by the Act or any regula-tions revoked by these regulations as if it were an amount recoverable under section 53(1) [SSAA, s.71(1)].

(3) Section 53(9) [SSAA, s.71(10)] shall apply to any amount which was, or would have been, recoverable through the county court or sheriff court under enactments repealed by the Act as if it was an amount recoverable under section 53(1) [SSAA, s.71(1)].

General Note

These provisions are specifically continued in force (along with reg. 19 and the Schedule thereto—not reproduced) beyond the general revocation of the 1987 Regulations on April 6, 1988, by reg. 31(1) of the 1988 Regulations. "The Act" is the 1986 Act.

Social Security (Payments on Account, Overpayments and Recovery) Regulations 1988

(S.I. 1988 No. 664)

Made by the Secretary of State under the Social Security Act 1986, ss.23(8), 27, 51(1)(t), (u), 53, 83(1), 84(1) and 89.

Arrangement of Regulations

PART I

GENERAL

Citation, commencement and interpretation

1.—(1) These regulations may be cited as the Social Security (Payments on account, Overpayments and Recovery) Regulations 1988 and shall come into force on 6th April 1988.

(2) In these Regulations, unless the context otherwise requires—

"the Act" means the Social Security Act 1986;

"adjudicating authority" means, as the case may be, the Chief or any other adjudication officer, a social security appeal tribunal, [²a disability appeal tribunal] the Chief or any other Social Security Commissioner or a Tribunal of Commissioners;

"benefit" means [⁴a jobseeker's allowance and] any benefit under the Social Security Act 1975 [SSCBA, Parts II to V], child benefit, family credit, income support and [¹any social fund payment under sections 32(2)(a) and 32(2A) of the Act [SSCBA, s.138(1)(a) and (2)] [³and any incapacity benefit under sections 30A(1) and (5) of the Contributions and Benefits Act]];

"child benefit" means benefit under Part I of the Child Benefit Act 1975 [SSCBA, Part IX];

"the Claims and Payments Regulations" means the Social Security (Claims and Payments) Regulations 1987;

[³"the Contributions and Benefits Act" means the Social Security Contributions and Benefits Act 1992;]
[²"disability living allowance" means a disability living allowance under section 37ZA of the Social Security Act 1975 [SSCBA, s.71];
"disability working allowance" means a disability working allowance under section 20 of the Act [SSCBA, s.129];]
"family credit" means family credit under Part II of the Act [SSCBA, Part VII];
"guardian's allowance" means an allowance under section 38 of the Social Security Act 1975 [SSCBA, s.77];
"income support" means income support under Part II of the Act [SSCBA, Part VII] and includes personal expenses addition, special transitional addition and transitional addition as defined in the Income Support (Transitional) Regulations 1987;
"Income Support Regulations" means the Income Support (General) Regulations 1987;
[⁴"Jobseeker's Allowance Regulations" means the Jobseeker's Allowance Regulations 1996;]
"severe disablement allowance" means an allowance under section 36 of the Social Security Act 1975 [SSCBA, s.68].
(3) Unless the context otherwise requires, any reference in these regulations to a numbered Part or regulation is a reference to the Part or regulation bearing that number in these Regulations and any reference in a regulation to a numbered paragraph is a reference to the paragraph of that regulation bearing that number.

AMENDMENTS

1. Social Security (Claims and Payments and Payments on account, Overpayments and Recovery) Amendment Regulations 1989 (S.I. 1989 No. 136), reg. 3 (February 27, 1989).
2. Disability Living Allowance and Disability Working Allowance (Consequential Provisions) Regulations 1991 (S.I. 1991 No. 2742), reg. 15 (April 6, 1992).
3. Social Security (Incapacity Benefit) (Consequential and Transitional Amendments and Savings) Regulations 1995 (S.I. 1995 No. 829), reg. 21(2) (April 13, 1995).
4. Social Security and Child Support (Jobseeker's Allowance) (Consequential Amendments) Regulations 1996 (S.I. 1996 No. 1345), reg. 23(2) (October 7, 1996).

PART II

INTERIM PAYMENTS

Making of interim payments

2.—(1) [³Subject to paragraph (1A),] the Secretary of State may, in his discretion, make an interim payment, that is to say a payment on account of any benefit to which it appears to him that a person is or may be entitled, in the following circumstances—
 (a) a claim for that benefit has not been made in accordance with the Claims and Payments Regulations and it is impracticable for such a claim to be made immediately; or
 (b) a claim for that benefit has been so made, but it is impracticable for it or a reference, review, application or appeal which relates to it to be determined immediately; or
 (c) an award of that benefit has been made but it is impracticable for the

beneficiary to be paid immediately, except by means of an interim payment.

[³(1A) Paragraph (1) shall not apply pending the determination of an appeal unless the Secretary of State is of the opinion that there is entitlement to benefit.]

(2) [¹Subject to paragraph (3)] on or before the making of an interim payment the recipient shall be given notice in writing of his liability under this Part to have it brought into account and to repay any overpayment.

(3) [*Omitted as only applying to disability living allowance*]

[²(4) Where an interim payment of income support is made because a payment to which the recipient is entitled by way of child support maintenance under the Child Support Act 1991, or periodical payments under a maintenance agreement within the meaning of section 9(1) of that Act or under a maintenance order within the meaning of section 107(15) of the Social Security Administration Act 1992, has not been made, the requirement in paragraph (2) of this regulation to give notice shall be omitted.]

AMENDMENTS

1. Disability Living Allowance and Disability Working Allowance (Consequential Provisions) Regulations 1991 (S.I. 1991 No. 2742), reg. 15 (April 6, 1992).
2. Social Security (Payments on account, Overpayments and Recovery) Amendment Regulations 1993 (S.I. 1993 No. 650), reg. 2 (April 5, 1993).
3. Social Security (Persons From Abroad) Miscellaneous Amendments Regulations 1996 (S.I. 1996 No. 30), reg. 10 (February 5, 1996).

GENERAL NOTE

Interim payments are made at the discretion of the Secretary of State. Thus there is no right of appeal and any refusal can only be challenged (other than by making further representations) by judicial review. The test under para. (1) is not whether it is "clear" that the person will qualify for a particular benefit, but whether it appears to the Secretary of State that he "is or may be entitled" to that benefit (*R. v. Secretary of State for Social Security, ex parte Sarwar, Getachew and Urbanek*, High Court, April 11, 1995). Thus the Secretary of State can decide to make interim payments even where entitlement to, for example, income support is not certain. Interim payments are recoverable if the person is subsequently found not to be entitled to the benefit claimed (see reg. 4).

The introduction of an habitual residence rule for income support from August 1, 1994 (see the additional definition of "person from abroad" in reg. 21(3) of the Income Support Regulations) focussed fresh attention on this regulation. Most claimants who fail the test were not eligible for urgent cases payments under reg. 70(3) of the Income Support Regulations, even before the February 1996 changes, and so face a delay of what can be several months until their appeal is heard without any benefit. This led to many claimants asking for interim payments pending the hearing of their appeals which in a few cases at least were paid. But this in turn precipitated the introduction of para. (1A).

Under para. (1A), in force from February 5, 1996, an interim payment will not be made if an appeal is pending unless the Secretary of State considers that there *is* entitlement to benefit. (See *R. v. Secretary of State for Social Security ex parte Grant* (High Court, July 31, 1997.)) This change is apparently to restore the original policy intention that interim payments could be made where entitlement was clear but the amount of benefit due was not (para. 46 of the DSS Explanatory Memorandum to the Social Security Advisory Committee (Cm.3062/1996)). But the wording of para. (1)(b) and the first part of reg. 4(3)(ii) somewhat belies this. Moreover, if the case involves a point of E.C. law (as, *e.g.* an appeal concerning the habitual residence test may do), para. (1A) could be in breach of E.C. law in so far as it prevents the Secretary of State from having the power to grant interim relief (see *Factortame Ltd and others v. Secretary of State for Transport (No. 2)* [1991] 1 A.C. 603, [1991] 1 All E.R. 70).

In a ruling made in the appeal *CDLA 913/1994*, the Commissioner held that he had no jurisdiction to order interim payment of benefit where a question had been referred to the European Court of Justice (ECJ) for a preliminary ruling. The case in which the question arose was concerned with entitlement, not payment, and to make such an order would go beyond what was required by Community law. The Commissioner left it open whether there was jurisdiction to make an interim or provisional award of benefit in such circumstances, since he was satisfied that, even if such a power exists, he would not exercise his discretion to make an award.

That ruling was challenged by way of judicial review. In *R. v. Social Security Commisioner, ex parte Snares*, March 24, 1997, Popplewell J. rejected the challenge. He decided that the exercise of discretion by the Commissioner could not be impugned. Unfortunately, however, Popplewell J. did not adopt the distinction made by the Commissioner between an award of entitlement and an order for payment and tended to run the two issues together. If it had been necessary to the determination, he would have regarded the question of the interim remedies available pending a ruling by the ECJ as not *acte claire* and would have made a further reference to the ECJ.

Bringing interim payments into account

[¹**3.** Where it is practicable to do so and, where notice is required to be given under regulation 2(2), such notice has been given—
  (a) any interim payment, other than an interim payment made in the circumstances mentioned in regulation 2(4),—
      (i) which was made in anticipation of an award of benefit shall be offset by the adjudicating authority in reduction of the benefit to be awarded; and
      (ii) whether or not made in anticipation of an award, which is not offset under sub-paragraph (i) shall be deducted by the Secretary of State from—
          (a) the sum payable under the award of benefit on account of which the interim payment was made; or
          (b) any sum payable under any subsequent award of the same benefit to the same person; and
  (b) any interim payment made in the circumstances mentioned in regulation 2(4) shall be offset by the Secretary of State against any sum received by him in respect of arrears of child support maintenance payable to the person to whom the interim payment was made.]

Amendment

1. Social Security (Payments on account, Overpayments and Recovery) Amendment Regulations 1993 (S.I. 1993 No. 650), reg. 2 (April 5, 1993).

Recovery of overpaid interim payments

4.—(1) Where the adjudicating authority has determined that an interim payment has been overpaid in circumstances which fall within paragraph (3) and [¹where notice is required to be given under regulation 2(2), such notice has been given], that authority shall determine the amount of the overpayment.

(2) The amount of the overpayment shall be recoverable by the Secretary of State, by the same procedures and subject to the same conditions as if it were recoverable under section 53(1) of the Act [SSAA, s.71(1)].

(3) The circumstances in which an interim payment may be determined to have been overpaid are as follows:—
  (a) an interim payment has been made under regulation 2(1)(a) or (b) but—
      (i) the recipient has failed to make a claim in accordance with the Claims and Payments Regulations as soon as practicable, or has made a claim which is either defective or is not made on the form approved for the time being by the Secretary of State and the Secretary of State has not treated the claim as duly made under regulation 4(7) of the Claims and Payments Regulations; or
      (ii) it has been determined that there is no entitlement on the claim, or that the entitlement is less than the amount of the interim payment or that benefit is not payable; or

      (iii) the claim has been withdrawn under regulation 5(2) of the Claims and Payments Regulations; or

  (b) an interim payment has been made under regulation 2(1)(c) which exceeds the entitlement under the award of benefit on account of which the interim payment was made[¹; or

  (c) an interim payment of income support has been made under regulation 2(1)(b) in the circumstances mentioned in regulation 2(4).]

  (4) For the purposes of this regulation a claim is defective if it is made on the form approved for the time being by the Secretary of State but is not completed in accordance with the instructions on the form.

AMENDMENT

1. Social Security (Payments on account, Overpayments and Recovery) Amendment Regulations 1993 (S.I. 1993 No. 650), reg. 2 (April 5, 1993).

PART III

OFFSETTING

Offsetting prior payment against subsequent award

  5.—(1) Subject to regulation 6 (exception from offset of recoverable overpayment), any sum paid in respect of a period covered by a subsequent determination in any of the cases set out in paragraph (2) shall be offset against arrears of entitlement under the subsequent determination and, except to the extent that the sum exceeds the arrears, shall be treated as properly paid on account of them.

  (2) Paragraph (1) applies in the following cases—

Case 1: Payment under an award which is revised, reversed or varied

Where a person has been paid a sum by way of benefit under an award which is subsequently varied on appeal or revised on a review.

Case 2: Award or payment of benefit in lieu

Where a person has been paid a sum by way of benefit under the original award and it is subsequently determined, on review or appeal, that another benefit should be awarded or is payable in lieu of the first.

Case 3: Child benefit and severe disablement allowance

Where either—

  (a) a person has been awarded and paid child benefit for a period in respect of which severe disablement allowance is subsequently determined to be payable to the child concerned; or

  (b) severe disablement allowance is awarded and paid for a period in respect of which child benefit is subsequently awarded to someone else, the child concerned in the subsequent determination being the beneficiary of the original award.

Case 4: Increase of benefit for dependant

Where a person has been paid a sum by way of an increase in respect of a dependent person under the original award and it is subsequently determined that that other person is entitled to benefit for that period, or that a third person is entitled to the increase for that period in priority to the beneficiary of the original award.

Case 5: Increase of benefit for partner

Where a person has been paid a sum by way of an increase in respect of a partner (as defined in regulation 2 of the Income Support Regulations) and it is subsequently determined that that other person is entitled to benefit for that period.

(3) Where an amount has been deducted under regulation 13(b) (sums to be deducted in calculating recoverable amounts) an equivalent sum shall be offset against any arrears of entitlement of that person under a subsequent award of income support[¹, or income-based jobseeker's allowance] for the period to which the deducted amount relates.

(4) Where child benefit which has been paid under an award in favour of a person (the original beneficiary) is subsequently awarded to someone else for any week, the benefit shall nevertheless be treated as properly paid if it was received by someone other than the original beneficiary, who—

 (a) either had the child living with him or was contributing towards the cost of providing for the child at a weekly rate which was not less than the weekly rate under the original award, and

 (b) could have been entitled to child benefit in respect of that child for that week had a claim been made in time.

(5) Any amount which is treated, under paragraph (4), as properly paid shall be deducted from the amount payable to the beneficiary under the subsequent award.

AMENDMENT

1. Social Security and Child Support (Jobseeker's Allowance) (Consequential Amendments) Regulations 1996 (S.I. 1996 No. 1345), reg. 23(5) and (6) (October 7, 1996).

Exception from offset of recoverable overpayment

6. No amount may be offset under regulation 5(1) which has been determined to be a recoverable overpayment for the purposes of section 53(1) of the Act [SSAA, s.71(1)].

PART IV

PREVENTION OF DUPLICATION OF PAYMENTS

Duplication and prescribed income

7.—[¹(1) For the purposes of section 74(1) of the Social Security Administration Act 1992 (income support [³and income-based jobseeker's allowance] and other payments), a person's prescribed income is—

 (a) income required to be taken into account in accordance with Part V of the Income Support Regulations [³or, as the case may be, Part VIII of the Jobseeker's Allowance Regulations], except for the income specified in sub-paragraph (b); and]

 [²(b) income which, if it were actually paid, would be required to be taken into account in accordance with Chapter VIIA of Part V of the Income Support Regulations [³or, as the case may be, Chapter VIII of Part VIII of the Jobseeker's Allowance Regulations] (child support maintenance); but only in so far as it relates to the period beginning with the effective date of the maintenance assessment under which it is payable, as determined in accordance with regulation 30 of the Child Support (Maintenance Assessment Procedure) Regulations 1992, and ending with the first day which is a day specified by the Secretary of State under regulation 4(1) of the Child Support (Collection and Enforcement) Regu-

lations 1992 as being a day on which payment of child support maintenance under that maintenance assessment is due.]

(2) The prescribed date in relation to any payment of income prescribed by
['paragraph (1)(a)] is—

(a) where it is made in respect of a specific day or period, that day or the
first day of the period;

(b) where it is not so made, the day or the first day of the period to which
it is fairly attributable.

[²(3) Subject to paragraph (4), the prescribed date in relation to any payment
of income prescribed by paragraph (1)(b) is the last day of the maintenance
period, determined in accordance with regulation 33 of the Child Support
(Maintenance Assessment Procedure) Regulations 1992, to which it relates.

(4) Where the period referred to in paragraph (1)(b) does not consist of a
number of complete maintenance periods the prescribed date in relation to
income prescribed by that sub-paragraph which relates to any part of that period
which is not a complete maintenance period is the last day of that period.]

AMENDMENTS

1. Social Security (Payments on account, Overpayments and Recovery) Amendment Regulations
1993 (S.I. 1993 No. 650), reg. 2, as amended by reg. 4 of the Social Security (Miscellaneous
Provisions) Amendment Regulations 1993 (S.I. 1993 No. 846) (April 5, 1993).

2. Social Security (Payments on account, Overpayments and Recovery) Amendment Regulations
1993 (S.I. 1993 No. 650), reg. 2, as amended by reg. 4 of the Social Security (Miscellaneous
Provisions) Amendment Regulations 1993 (S.I. 1993 No. 846) (April 19, 1993).

3. Social Security and Child Support (Jobseeker's Allowance) (Consequential Amendments)
Regulations 1996 (S.I. 1996 No. 1345), reg. 23(3) (October 7, 1996).

GENERAL NOTE

See the notes to s.74(1) of the Administration Act.

Under s.54 of the Child Support Act 1991 "maintenance assessment" means an assessment of
maintenance made under that Act, including, except where regulations prescribe otherwise, an
interim assessment. Under reg. 30 of the Child Support (Maintenance Assessment Procedure) Regulations 1992, the effective date of a new assessment is usually, when the application was made by
the person with care of the child, the date on which a maintenance enquiry form was sent to the
absent parent or, where the application was made by the absent parent, the date on which an effective
maintenance form was received by the Secretary of State. Arrears will inevitably accrue while the
assessment is being made. In the meantime income support or income-based JSA can be paid in
full to the parent with care. When the arrears are paid, the amount of "overpaid" income support
or JSA is recoverable under s.74(1) of the Administration Act.

See the notes to reg. 60C of the Income Support (General) Regulations for the interaction with
payments of other arrears of child support maintenance, which are excluded from the operation of
s.74(1). Note also s.74A of the Administration Act and regs. 55A and 60E of the Income Support
Regulations and regs. 119 and 127 of the Jobseeker's Allowance Regulations.

Duplication and prescribed payments

8.—(1) For the purposes of section 27(2) of the Act [SSAA, s.74(2)] (recovery
of amount of benefit awarded because prescribed payment not made on prescribed date), the payment of any of the following is a prescribed payment:—

(a) any benefit under the Social Security Act 1975 [SSCBA, Parts II to V]
other than any grant or gratuity or a widow's payment;

(b) any child benefit;

(c) any family credit;

(d) any war disablement pension or war widow's pension which is not in the
form of a gratuity and any payment which the Secretary of State accepts
as analogous to any such pension;

(e) any allowance paid under the Job Release Act 1977;

(f) any allowance payable by or on behalf of [²Scottish Enterprise Highlands and Islands Enterprise or] [¹the Secretary of State] to or in respect of a person for his maintenance for any period during which he is following a course of training or instruction provided or approved by [²Scottish Enterprise Highlands and Islands Enterprise or] [¹the Secretary of State]

(g) any payment of benefit under the legislation of any member State other than the United Kingdom concerning the branches of social security mentioned in Article 4(1) of Regulation (EEC) No. 1408/71 on the application of social security schemes to employed persons, to self-employed persons and to members of their families moving within the Community, whether or not the benefit has been acquired by virtue of the provisions of that Regulation;

[³(h) any disability working allowance.]

(2) The prescribed date, in relation to any payment prescribed by paragraph (1) is the date by which receipt of or entitlement to that benefit would have to be notified to the Secretary of State if it were to be taken into account in determining, whether on review or otherwise, the amount of or entitlement to income support [⁴, or income-based jobseeker's allowance].

AMENDMENTS

1. Employment Act 1989, Sched. 5, paras. 1 and 4 (November 16, 1989).
2. Enterprise (Scotland) Consequential Amendments Order 1991 (S.I. 1991 No. 387), art. 14 (April 1, 1991).
3. Disability Living Allowance and Disability Working Allowance (Consequential Provisions) Regulations 1991 (S.I. 1991 No. 2742), reg. 15 (April 6, 1992).
4. Social Security and Child Support (Jobseeker's Allowance) (Consequential Amendments) Regulations 1996 (S.I. 1996 No. 1345), reg. 23(5) and (6) (October 7, 1996).

GENERAL NOTE

See the notes to s.74(2) of the Administration Act.

Duplication and maintenance payments

9. For the purposes of section 27(3) of the Act [SSAA, s.74(3)] (recovery of amount of benefit awarded because maintenance payments not made), the following benefits are prescribed:—

(a) child benefit;
(b) increase for dependants of any benefit under the Social Security Act 1975 [SSCBA, Parts II to V];
(c) child's special allowance under section 31 of the Social Security Act 1975 [SSCBA, s.56]; and
(d) guardian's allowance.

GENERAL NOTE

See the notes to s.74(3) of the Administration Act.

Conversion of payments made in a foreign currency

10. Where a payment of income prescribed by regulation 7(1), or a payment prescribed by regulation 8(1), is made in a currency other than sterling, its value in sterling, for the purposes of section 27 of the Act [SSAA, s.74] and this Part, shall be determined, after conversion by the Bank of England, or by [¹any institution which is authorised under the Banking Act 1987], as the net sterling sum into which it is converted, after any banking charge or commission on the transaction has been deducted.

AMENDMENT

1. Social Security (Payments on account, Overpayments and Recovery) Amendment Regulations 1988 (S.I. 1988 No. 688), reg. 2(2) (April 11, 1988).

PART V

DIRECT CREDIT TRANSFER OVERPAYMENTS

Recovery of overpayments by automated or other direct credit transfer

11.—(1) Where it is determined by the adjudicating authority that a payment in excess of entitlement has been credited to a bank or other account under an arrangement for automated or other direct credit transfer made in accordance with regulation 21 of the Claims and Payments Regulations and that the conditions prescribed by paragraph (2) are satisfied, the excess, or the specified part of it to which the Secretary of State's certificate relates, shall be recoverable under this regulation.

(2) The prescribed conditions for recoverability under paragraph (1) are as follows—

(a) the Secretary of State has certified that the payment in excess of entitlement, or a specified part of it, is materially due to the arrangements for payments to be made by automated or other direct credit transfer; and

(b) notice of the effect which this regulation would have, in the event of an overpayment, was given in writing to the beneficiary, or to a person acting for him, before he agreed to the arrangement.

(3) Where the arrangement was agreed to before April 6, 1987 the condition prescribed by paragraph (2)(b) need not be satisfied in any case where the application for benefit to be paid by automated or other direct credit transfer contained a statement, or was accompanied by a written statement made by the applicant, which complied with the provisions of regulation 16A(3)(b) and (8) of the Social Security (Claims and Payments) Regulations 1979 or, as the case may be, regulation 7(2)(b) and (6) of the Child Benefit (Claims and Payments) Regulations 1984.

PART VI

REVISION OF DETERMINATION AND CALCULATION OF AMOUNT RECOVERABLE

Circumstances in which determination need not be revised

12. Section 53(4) of the Act [SSAA, s.71(5)] (recoverability dependent on reversal, variation or revision of determination) shall not apply where the fact and circumstances of the misrepresentation or non-disclosure do not provide a basis for reviewing and revising the determination under which payment was made.

GENERAL NOTE

See the notes to s.71(5A) of the Administration Act.

Sums to be deducted in calculating recoverable amounts

13. In calculating the amounts recoverable under section 53(1) of the Act [SSAA, s.71(1)] or regulation 11, where there has been an overpayment of benefit, the adjudicating authority shall deduct—
  (a) any amount which has been offset under Part III;
  (b) any additional amount of income support[¹, or income-based jobseeker's allowance] which was not payable under the original, or any other, determination, but which should have been determined to be payable—
    (i) on the basis of the claim as presented to the adjudicating authority, or
    (ii) on the basis of the claim as it would have appeared had the misrepresentation or non-disclosure been remedied before the determination;
but no other deduction shall be made in respect of any other entitlement to benefit which may be, or might have been, determined to exist.

AMENDMENT

1. Social Security and Child Support (Jobseeker's Allowance) (Consequential Amendments) Regulations 1996 (S.I. 1996 No. 1345), reg. 23(5) and (6) (October 7, 1996).

GENERAL NOTE

See the notes to s.71(1) and (2) of the Administration Act, under the heading *Amount of overpayment*.

Quarterly diminution of capital resources

14.—(1) For the purposes of section 53(1) of the Act [SSAA, s.71(1)], where income support[², or income-based jobseeker's allowance][¹, family credit or disability working allowance] has been overpaid in consequence of a misrepresentation as to the capital a claimant possesses or a failure to disclose its existence, the adjudicating authority shall treat that capital as having been reduced at the end of each quarter from the start of the overpayment period by the amount overpaid by way of income support[², or income-based jobseeker's allowance] [¹, family credit or disability working allowance] within that quarter.
  (2) Capital shall not be treated as reduced over any period other than a quarter or in circumstances other than those for which paragraph (1) provides.
  (3) In this regulation—
"a quarter" means a period of 13 weeks starting with the first day on which the overpayment period began and ending on the 90th consecutive day thereafter.
"overpayment period" is a period during which income support [³or an income-based jobseeker's allowance,] [¹family credit or disability working allowance] is overpaid in consequence of a misrepresentation as to capital or a failure to disclose its existence.

AMENDMENTS

1. Disability Living Allowance and Disability Working Allowance (Consequential Provisions) Regulations 1991 (S.I. 1991 No. 2742), reg. 15 (April 6, 1992).
2. Social Security and Child Support (Jobseeker's Allowance) (Consequential Amendments) Regulations 1996 (S.I. 1996 No. 1345), reg. 23(5) and (6) (October 7, 1996).
3. Social Security (Jobseeker's Allowance and Payments on Account) (Miscellaneous Amendments) Regulations 1996 (S.I. 1996 No. 2519), reg. 3(2) (October 7, 1996).

General Note

See the notes to s.71(1) and (2) of the Administration Act, under the heading *Amount of overpayment.*

Part VII

The Process of Recovery

Recovery by deduction from benefits

15.—(1) Subject to regulation 16, where any amount is recoverable under sections 27 or 53(1) of the Act [SSAA, ss.74 or 71(1)], or under these Regulations, that amount shall be recoverable by the Secretary of State from any of the benefits prescribed by the next paragraph, to which the person from whom ['the amount is determined] to be recoverable is entitled.

(2) The following benefits are prescribed for the purposes of this regulation—

(a) subject to paragraphs (1) and (2) of regulation 16, any benefit under the Social Security Act 1975 [SSCBA, Parts II to V];

(b) subject to paragraphs (1) and (2) of regulation 16, any child benefit;

(c) any family credit;

(d) subject to regulation 16, any income support, [⁴or a jobseeker's allowance].

[²(e) any disability working allowance.]

[³(f) any incapacity benefit.]

Amendments

1. Social Security (Payments on account, Overpayments and Recovery) Amendment Regulations 1988 (S.I. 1988 No. 688), reg. 2(3) (April 11, 1988).

2. Disability Living Allowance and Disability Working Allowance (Consequential Provisions) Regulations 1991 (S.I. 1991 No. 2742), reg. 15 (April 6, 1992).

3. Social Security (Incapacity Benefit) (Consequential and Transitional Amendments and Savings) Regulations 1995 (S.I. 1995 No. 829), reg. 21(3) (April 13, 1995).

4. Social Security (Jobseeker's Allowance and Payments on Account) (Miscellaneous Amendments) Regulations 1996 (S.I. 1996 No. 2519), reg. 3(3) (October 7, 1996).

Limitations on deductions from prescribed benefits

16.—(1) Deductions may not be made from entitlement to the benefits prescribed by paragraph (2) except as a means of recovering an overpayment of the benefit from which the deduction is to be made.

(2) The benefits ['prescribed] for the purposes of paragraph (1) are guardian's allowance, [². . .] and child benefit.

(3) Regulation 15 shall apply without limitation to any payment of arrears of benefit other than any arrears caused by the operation of regulation 37(1) of the Claims and Payments Regulations (suspension of payments).

(4) Regulation 15 shall apply to the amount of [⁵benefit] to which a person is presently entitled only to the extent that there may, subject to paragraphs 8 and 9 of Schedule 9 to the Claims and Payments Regulations, be recovered in respect of any one benefit week—

(a) in a case to which paragraph (5) applies, not more than the amount there specified; and

(b) in any other case, 3 times 5 per cent of the personal allowance for a single claimant aged not less than 25, that 5 per cent being, where it is not a multiple of 5 pence, rounded to the next higher such multiple.

[⁶(4A) Paragraph (4) shall apply to the following benefits—
   (a) income support;
   (b) an income-based jobseeker's allowance;
   (c) where, if there was no entitlement to a contribution-based jobseeker's allowance, there would be entitlement to an income-based jobseeker's allowance at the same rate, a contribution-based jobseeker's allowance.]

   (5) Where the person responsible for the misrepresentation of or failure to disclose a material fact has, by reason thereof, been found guilty of an offence under section 55 of the Act [SSAA, s.112] or under any other enactment, or has made a written statement after caution in admission of deception or fraud for the purpose of obtaining benefit, the amount mentioned in paragraph (4)(a) shall be 4 times 5 per cent. of the personal allowance for a single claimant aged not less than 25, that 5 per cent being, where it is not a multiple of 10 pence, rounded to the nearest such multiple or, if it is a multiple of 5 pence but not of 10 pence, the next higher multiple of 10 pence.

   [⁶(5A) Regulation 15 shall apply to an amount of a contribution-based jobseeker's allowance, other than a contribution-based jobseeker's allowance to which paragraph (4) applies in accordance with paragraph (4A)(c), to which a person is presently entitled only to the extent that there may, subject to paragraphs 8 and 9 of Schedule 9 to the Claims and Payments Regulations be recovered in respect of any one benefit week a sum equal to one third of the age-related amount applicable to the claimant under section 4(1)(a) of the Jobseekers Act 1995.

   (5B) For the purposes of paragraph (5A) where the sum that would otherwise fall to be deducted includes a fraction of a penny, the sum to be deducted shall be rounded down to the nearest whole penny.]

   (6) [⁵Where—
   (a) in the calculation of the income of a person to whom income support is payable, the amount of earnings or other income falling to be taken into account is reduced by paragraphs 4 to 9 of Schedule 8 to the Income Support Regulations (sums to be disregarded in the calculation of earnings) or paragraphs 15 and 16 of Schedule 9 to those Regulations (sums to be disregarded in the calculation of income other than earnings); or
   (b) in the calculation of the income of a person to whom income-based jobseeker's allowance is payable, the amount of earnings or other income falling to be taken into account is reduced by paragraphs 5 to 12 of Schedule 6 to the Jobseeker's Allowance Regulations (sums to be disregarded in the calculation of earnings) or paragraphs 15 and 17 of Schedule 7 to those Regulations (sums to be disregarded in the calculation of income other than earnings),
the weekly amount] applicable under paragraph (4) may be increased by not more than half the amount of the reduction, and any increase under this paragraph has priority over any increase which would, but for this paragraph, be made under paragraph 6(5) of Schedule 9 to the Claims and Payments Regulations.

   (7) Regulation 15 shall not be applied to a specified benefit so as to reduce the benefit in any one benefit week to less than 10 pence.

   (8) In this regulation—
"benefit week" means the week corresponding to the week in respect of which the benefit is paid;
"personal allowance for a single claimant aged not less than 25" means the amount specified in paragraph 1(1)(c) of column 2 of Schedule 2 to the Income Support Regulations [⁵or, in the case of a person who is entitled to income-based jobseeker's allowance, the amount for the time being

specified in paragraph 1(1)(e) of column (2) of Schedule 1 to the Job-seeker's Allowance Regulations;]

[⁴"specified benefit" means—

(a) in respect of any period during which benefit is paid by means of an instrument of payment, [⁶a jobseeker's allowance, or] income support either alone or together with any [⁵. . .] [⁶. . .] incapacity benefit, retirement pension or severe disablement allowance which is paid by means of the same instrument of payment; and

(b) in respect of any period during which benefit is paid by means of an instrument for benefit payment, [⁶a jobseeker's allowance] income support and, where paid concurrently with income support, [⁵. . .] [⁶. . .] incapacity benefit, retirement pension or severe disablement allowance [⁶. . .];

[⁷but does not include any sum payable by way of child maintenance bonus in accordance with section 10 of the Child Support Act 1995 and the [⁸Social Security (Child Maintenance Bonus)] Regulations 1996;]]

"written statement after caution" means—

    (i) in England and Wales, a written statement made in accordance with the Police and Criminal Evidence Act 1984 (Codes of Practice) (No. 1) Order 1985, or, before that Order came into operation, the Judges Rules;

    (ii) in Scotland, a written statement duly witnessed by two persons.

AMENDMENTS

1. Social Security (Payments on account, Overpayments and Recovery) Amendment Regulations 1988 (S.I. 1988 No. 688), reg. 2(4) (April 11, 1988).

2. Disability Living Allowance and Disability Working Allowance (Consequential Provisions) Regulations 1991 (S.I. 1991 No. 2742), reg. 15 (April 6, 1992).

3. Social Security (Incapacity Benefit) (Consequential and Transitional Amendments and Savings) Regulations 1995 (S.I. 1995 No. 829), reg. 21(4) (April 13, 1995).

4. Social Security (Claims and Payments Etc.) Amendment Regulations 1996 (S.I. 1996 No. 672), reg. 4 (April 4, 1996).

5. Social Security and Child Support (Jobseeker's Allowance) (Consequential Amendments) Regulations 1996 (S.I. 1996 No. 1345), reg. 23(4) (October 7, 1996).

6. Social Security (Jobseeker's Allowance and Payments on Account) (Miscellaneous Amendments) Regulations 1996 (S.I. 1996 No. 2519), reg. 3(4) (October 7, 1996).

7. Social Security (Child Maintenance Bonus) Regulations 1996 (S.I. 1996 No. 3195), reg. 16(3) (April 7, 1997).

8. Social Security (Miscellaneous Amendments) Regulations 1997 (S.I. 1997 No. 454), reg. 8(10) (April 6, 1997).

Recovery from couples

17. In the case of an overpayment of income support[², or income-based jobseeker's allowance] [¹, family credit or disability working allowance] to one of a married or unmarried couple, the amount recoverable by deduction, in accordance with regulation 15, may be recovered by deduction from income support [², or income-based jobseeker's allowance] [¹, family credit or disability working allowance] payable to either of them, provided that the two of them are a married or unmarried couple at the date of the deduction.

AMENDMENTS

1. Disability Living Allowance and Disability Working Allowance (Consequential Provisions) Regulations 1991 (S.I. 1991 No. 2742), reg. 15 (April 6, 1992).

2. Social Security and Child Support (Jobseeker's Allowance) (Consequential Amendments) Regulations 1996 (S.I. 1996 No. 1345), reg. 23(5) and (6) (October 7, 1996).

PART VIII

RECOVERY BY DEDUCTIONS FROM EARNINGS FOLLOWING TRADE DISPUTE

Recovery by deductions from earnings

18.—(1) Any sum paid to a person on an award of income support made to him by virtue of section 23(8) of the Act [SSCBA, s.127] (effect of return to work after a trade dispute) shall be recoverable from him in accordance with this Part of these Regulations.

(2) In this Part, unless the context otherwise requires—

"available earnings" means the earnings, including any remuneration paid by or on behalf of an employer to an employee who is for the time being unable to work owing to sickness, which remain payable to a claimant on any pay-day after deduction by his employer of all amounts lawfully deductible by the employer otherwise than by virtue of a deduction notice;

"claimant" means a person to whom an award is made by virtue of section 23(8) of the Act [SSCBA, s.127];

"deduction notice" means a notice under regulation 20 or 25; "employment" means employment (including employment which has been suspended but not terminated) in remunerative work, and related expressions shall be construed accordingly;

"pay-day" means an occasion on which earnings are paid to a claimant;

"protected earnings" means protected earnings as determined by an adjudicating authority, in accordance with regulation 19(2), under regulation 19(1)(a) or 24;

"recoverable amount" means the amount (determined in accordance with regulation 20(3) or (5) or regulation 25(2)(a)) by reference to which deductions are to be made by an employer from a claimant's earnings by virtue of a deduction notice;

"repaid by the claimant" means paid by the claimant directly to the Secretary of State by way of repayment of income support otherwise recoverable under this Part of these Regulations.

(3) Any notice or other document required or authorised to be given or sent to any person under the provisions of this Part shall be deemed to have been given or sent if it was sent by post to that person in accordance with paragraph (6) of regulation 27 where that regulation applies and, in any other case, at his ordinary or last known address or in the case of an employer at the last place of business where the claimant to which it relates is employed, and if so sent to have been given or sent on the day on which it was posted.

Award and protected earnings

19.—(1) Where an adjudicating authority determines that a person claiming income support is entitled by virtue of section 23(8) of the Act [SSCBA, s.127] (effect of return to work after a trade dispute) and makes an award to him accordingly he shall determine the claimant's protected earnings (that is to say the amount below which his actual earnings must not be reduced by any deduction made under this Part).

(2) The adjudicating authority shall include in his decision—

(a) the amount of income support awarded together with a statement that the claimant is a person entitled by virtue of section 23(8) of the Act [SSCBA, s.127] and that accordingly any sum paid to him on that award will be recoverable from him as provided in this Part;

(b) the amount of the claimant's protected earnings, and

(c) a statement of the claimant's duty under regulation 28 (duty to give notice of cessation or resumption of employment).

[¹(3) The protected earnings of the claimant shall be the sum determined by—

    (a) taking the sum specified in paragraph (4),

    (b) adding the sum specified in paragraph (5), and

    (c) subtracting from the result any child benefit which falls to be taken into account in calculating his income for the purposes of Part V of the Income Support Regulations.]

(4) The sum referred to in paragraph (3)(a) shall be the aggregate of the amounts calculated under regulation 17(a) to (d), 18(a) to (e), 20 or 21, as the case may be, of the Income Support Regulations.

(5) The sum referred to in paragraph (3)(b) shall be £27 except where the sum referred to in paragraph (3)(a) includes an amount calculated under regulation 20 in which case the sum shall be £8.00.

AMENDMENT

1. Social Security (Payments on account, Overpayments and Recovery) Amendment Regulations 1988 (S.I. 1988 No. 688), reg. 2(5) (April 11, 1988).

Service and contents of deduction notices

20.—(1) Where the amount of income support has not already been repaid by the claimant, the Secretary of State shall serve a deduction notice on the employer of the claimant.

(2) A deduction notice shall contain the following particulars—

    (a) particulars enabling the employer to identify the claimant;

    (b) the recoverable amount;

    (c) the claimant's protected earnings as specified in the notification of award.

(3) Subject to paragraph (5) the recoverable amount shall be—

    (a) the amount specified in the decision as having been awarded to the claimant by way of income support; reduced by

    (b) the amount (if any) which has been repaid by the claimant before the date of the deduction notice.

(4) If a further award relating to the claimant is made the Secretary of State shall cancel the deduction notice (giving written notice of the cancellation to the employer and the claimant) and serve on the employer a further deduction notice.

(5) The recoverable amount to be specified in the further deduction notice shall be the sum of—

    (a) the amount determined by applying paragraph (3) to the further award; and

    (b) the recoverable amount specified in the cancelled deduction notice less any part of that amount which before the date of the further notice has already been deducted by virtue of the cancelled notice or repaid by the claimant.

Period for which deduction notice has effect

21.—(1) A deduction notice shall come into force when it is served on the employer of the claimant to whom it relates and shall cease to have effect as soon as any of the following conditions is fulfilled—

    (a) the notice is cancelled by virtue of regulation 20(4) or paragraph (2) of this regulation;

(b) the claimant ceases to be in the employment of the person on whom the notice was served;

(c) the aggregate of—
    (i) any part of the recoverable amount repaid by the claimant on or after the date of the deduction notice, and
    (ii) the total amount deducted by virtue of the notice,
reaches the recoverable amount;

(d) there has elapsed a period of 26 weeks beginning with the date of the notice.

(2) The Secretary of State may at any time give a direction in writing cancelling a deduction notice and—

(a) he shall cause a copy of the direction to be served on the employer concerned and on the claimant;

(b) the direction shall take effect when a copy of it is served on the employer concerned.

Effect of deduction notice

22.—(1) Where a deduction notice is in force the following provisions of this regulation shall apply as regards any relevant pay-day.

(2) Where a claimant's earnings include any bonus, commission or other similar payment which is paid other than on a day on which the remainder of his earnings is paid, then in order to calculate his available earnings for the purposes of this regulation any such bonus, commission or other similar payment shall be treated as being paid to him on the next day of payment of the remainder of his earnings instead of on the day of actual payment.

(3) If on a relevant pay-day a claimant's available earnings—

(a) do not exceed his protected earnings by at least £1, no deduction shall be made;

(b) do exceed his protected earnings by at least £1, his employer shall deduct from the claimant's available earnings one half of the excess over his protected earnings,

so however that where earnings are paid other than weekly the amount of the protected earnings and the figure of £1 shall be adjusted accordingly, in particular—

(c) where earnings are paid monthly, they shall for this purpose be treated as paid every five weeks (and the protected earnings and the figure of £1 accordingly multiplied by five);

(d) where earnings are paid daily, the protected earnings and the figure of £1 shall be divided by five,

and if, in any case to which sub-paragraph (c) or (d) does not apply, there is doubt as to the adjustment to be made this shall be determined by the Secretary of State on the application of the employer or the claimant.

(4) Where on a relevant pay-day earnings are payable to the claimant in respect of more than one pay-day the amount of the protected earnings and the figure of £1 referred to in the preceding paragraph, adjusted where appropriate in accordance with the provisions of that paragraph, shall be multiplied by the number of pay-days to which the earnings relate.

(5) Notwithstanding anything in paragraph (3)—

(a) the employer shall not make a deduction on a relevant pay-day if the claimant satisfies him that up to that day he has not obtained payment of the income support to which the deduction notice relates;

(b) the employer shall not on any relevant pay-day deduct from the claimant's earnings by virtue of the deduction notice an amount greater than the excess of the recoverable amount over the aggregate of all such amounts as, in relation to that notice, are mentioned in regulation 21(1)(c)(i) and (ii); and

(c) where the amount of any deduction which by this regulation the employer is required to make would otherwise include a fraction of 1p, that amount shall be reduced by that fraction.

(6) For the purpose of this regulation "relevant pay-day" means any pay-day beginning with—

(a) the first pay-day falling after the expiration of the period of one month from the date on which the deduction notice comes into force; or

(b) if the employer so chooses, any earlier pay-day after the notice has come into force.

Increase of amount of award on appeal or review

23. If the amount of the award is increased, whether on appeal or on review by an adjudicating authority, this Part shall have effect as if on the date on which the amount of the award was increased—

(a) the amount of the increase was the recoverable amount; and

(b) the claimant's protected earnings were the earnings subsequently reviewed under regulation 24.

Review of determination of protected earnings

24.—(1) A determination of a claimant's protected earnings, whether made under [¹regulation 19(1)] or under this regulation, may be reviewed by an adjudicating authority if he is satisfied that it was based on a mistake as to the law or was made in ignorance of, or was based on a mistake as to, some material fact.

(2) Where the claimant's protected earnings are reviewed under paragraph (1) the Secretary of State shall give the employer written notice varying the deduction notice by substituting for the amount of the protected earnings as there specified (or as previously reviewed under this regulation) the amount of the protected earnings determined on review.

(3) Variation of a deduction notice under paragraph (2) shall take effect either from the end of the period of 10 working days beginning with the day on which notice of the variation is given to the employer or, if the employer so chooses, at any earlier time after notice is given.

AMENDMENT

1. Social Security (Payments on account, Overpayments and Recovery) Amendment Regulations 1988 (S.I. 1988 No. 688), reg. 2(6) (April 11, 1988).

Power to serve further deduction notice on resumption of employment

25.—(1) Where a deduction notice has ceased to have effect by reason of the claimant ceasing to be in the employment of the person on whom the notice was served, the Secretary of State may, if he thinks fit, serve a further deduction notice on any person by whom the claimant is for the time being employed.

(2) Notwithstanding anything in the foregoing provisions of these Regulations, in any such deduction notice—

(a) the recoverable amount shall be equal to the recoverable amount as specified in the previous deduction notice less the aggregate of—

(i) the total of any amounts required to be deducted by virtue of that notice, and

      (ii) any additional part of that recoverable amount repaid by the claimant on or after the date of that notice,

or, where this regulation applies in respect of more than one such previous notice, the aggregate of the amounts as so calculated in respect of each such notice;

  (b) the amount specified as the claimant's protected earnings shall be the same as that so specified in the last deduction notice relating to him which was previously in force or as subsequently reviewed under regulation 24.

Right of Secretary of State to recover direct from claimant

26. Where the Secretary of State has received a notification of award and it is at any time not practicable for him, by means of a deduction notice, to effect recovery of the recoverable amount or of so much of that amount as remains to be recovered from the claimant, the amount which remains to be recovered shall, by virtue of this regulation, be recoverable from the claimant by the Secretary of State.

Duties and liabilities of employers

27.—(1) An employer shall keep a record of the available earnings of each claimant who is an employee in respect of whom a deduction notice is in force and of the payments which he makes in pursuance of the notice.

(2) A record of every deduction made by an employer under a deduction notice on any pay-day shall be given or sent by him to the Secretary of State, together with payment of the amount deduced, by not later than the 19th day of the following month.

(3) Where by reason only of the circumstances mentioned in regulation 22(5)(a) the employer makes no deduction from a claimant's weekly earnings on any pay-day he shall within 10 working days after that pay-day give notice of that fact to the Secretary of State.

(4) Where a deduction notice is cancelled by virtue of regulation 20(4) or 21(2) or ceases to have effect by virtue of regulation 21(1) the employer shall within 10 working days after the date on which the notice is cancelled or, as the case may be, ceases to have effect—

  (a) return the notice to the Secretary of State and, where regulation 21(1) applies, give notice of the reason for its return;

  (b) give notice, in relation to each relevant pay-day (as defined in regulation 22(6)), of the available earnings of the claimant and of any deduction made from those earnings.

(5) If on any pay-day to which regulation 22(3)(b) applies the employer makes no deduction from a claimant's available earnings, or makes a smaller deduction than he was thereby required to make, and in consequence any amount is not deducted while the deduction notice, or any further notice which under regulation 20(4) cancels that notice, has effect—

  (a) the amount which is not deducted shall, without prejudice to any other method of recovery from the claimant or otherwise, be recoverable from the employer by the Secretary of State; and

  (b) any amount so recovered shall, for the purposes of these Regulations, be deemed to have been repaid by the claimant.

(6) All records and notices to which this regulation applies shall given or sent to the Secretary of State, on a form approved by him, at such office of the ['Department of Social Security] as he may direct.

AMENDMENT

1. Transfer of Functions (Health and Social Security) Order 1988 (S.I. 1988 No. 1843), art. 3(4) (November 28, 1988).

Claimants to give notice of cessation or resumption of employment

28.—(1) Where a claimant ceases to be in the employment of a person on whom a deduction notice relating to him has been duly served knowing that the full amount of the recoverable amount has not been deducted from his earnings or otherwise recovered by the Secretary of State, he shall give notice within 10 working days to the Secretary of State of his address and of the date of such cessation of employment.

(2) Where on or after such cessation the claimant resumes employment (whether with the same or some other employer) he shall within 10 working days give notice to the Secretary of State of the name of the employer and of the address of his place of employment.

Failure to notify

29. If a person fails to comply with any requirement under regulation 27 or 28 to give notice of any matter to the Secretary of State he shall be guilty of an offence and liable on summary conviction to a fine not exceeding—

(a) for any one offence, level 3 on the standard scale; or
(b) for an offence of continuing any such contravention, £40 for each day on which it is so continued.

PART IX

REVOCATION, TRANSITIONAL PROVISIONS AND SAVINGS

Revocation

30. Subject to regulation 31(3), the Social Security (Payments on account, Overpayments and Recovery) Regulations 1987 are hereby revoked except for regulations 19 and the Schedule thereto and 20(2) and (3) which shall continue in force.

Transitional provisions and savings

31.—(1) These Regulations shall apply to any question relating to the repayment or recoverability of family income supplement and supplementary benefit as though the definition of ''benefit'' in regulation 1(2) included references to both those benefits and as though any reference in Part VIII to income support was a reference to income support and supplementary benefit.

(2) Anything done or begun under the Social Security (Payments on account, Overpayments and Recovery) Regulations 1987 or Part IV of the Supplementary Benefit (Trade Disputes and Recovery from Earnings) Regulations 1980 shall be deemed to have been done or, as the case may be, continued under the corresponding provisions of these Regulations.

(3) Where this regulation applies—

(a) regulation 3(b)(ii) shall have effect as though for the words ''the same benefit'' there were substituted the words ''income support'' if the interim payment was of supplementary benefit and ''family credit'' if the interim payment was of family income supplement;

(b) regulation 13(b) shall have effect as though for the words "income support" there were substituted the words "supplementary benefit".

(4) In this Part—

"family income supplement" means benefit under the Family Income Supplements Act 1970;

"supplementary benefit" means benefit under Part I of the Supplementary Benefits Act 1976.

Social Security Benefits (Maintenance Payments and Consequential Amendments) Regulations 1996

(S.I. 1996 No. 940)

Made by the Secretary of State under ss. 74A(5) and (6), 189(1) and (3)–(5) and 191 of the Social Security Administration Act 1992 and ss. 136(5)(b), 137(1) and 175(1)–(4) of the Social Security Contributions and Benefits Act 1992

[In force April 19, 1996]

Interpretation for the purposes of section 74A of the Act

2. In section 74A of the Act (payment of benefit where maintenance payments collected by Secretary of State)—

(a) "child maintenance" means any payment towards the maintenance of a child or young person, including payments made—

(i) under a court order;

(ii) under a maintenance assessment made under the Child Support Act 1991;

(iii) under an agreement for maintenance; or

(iv) voluntarily,

and for this purpose a "young person" is a person referred to in regulation 3 of these Regulations (persons of a prescribed description);

(b) "spousal maintenance" means any payment made by a person towards the maintenance of that person's spouse, including payments made—

(i) under a court order;

(ii) under an agreement for maintenance; or

(iii) voluntarily;

(c) "relevant income" means—

(i) any income which is taken into account under Part V of the Income Support Regulations for the purposes of calculating the amount of income support to which the claimant is entitled; or

(ii) any income which is taken into account under Part VIII of the Jobseeker's Allowance Regulations for the purposes of calculating the amount of jobseeker's allowance to which the claimant is entitled.

Persons of a prescribed description

3. For the purposes of the definition of "family" in section 74A(5) of the Act, a person of a prescribed description is any person who—

(a) is referred to as a "young person" in the Income Support Regulations by virtue of regulation 14 of those Regulations; or

(b) is referred to as a ''young person'' in the Jobseeker's Allowance Regulations by virtue of regulation 76 of those Regulations.

Circumstances in which a person is to be treated as responsible for another

4. A person shall be treated as responsible for another for the purposes of section 74A of the Act if he is treated as responsible for that other person under either regulation 15 of the Income Support Regulations or regulation 77 of the Jobseeker's Allowance Regulations.

Circumstances in which persons are to be treated as being members of the same household

5. Persons shall be treated as members of the same household for the purposes of section 74A of the Act if they are treated as members of the same household under either regulation 16 of the Income Support Regulations or regulation 78 of the Jobseeker's Allowance Regulations.

GENERAL NOTE

See the notes to s.74A of the Administration Act.

PART VIII

PRESIDENT'S CIRCULARS

INDEX

GENERAL NOTE

In October 1995 the then President of ITS, Judge Bassingthwaighte, withdrew the ITS President's Practice Directions. He issued instead a number of President's Circulars, which are intended "to provide guidance and advice to tribunals in some complex or contentious areas", but not "to restrict or to remove . . . individual judicial discretion". A set of the Circulars is available at each tribunal venue. Further Circulars have been issued by the current President (see Circular No. 14 onwards).

President's Circular No. 1

ADJOURNMENTS

Generally

1. Tribunals have the power to adjourn hearings, either of their own motion or upon application of a party and it will often be necessary for the tribunal, in the interests of justice, to exercise that power.

2. Tribunals should, however, remind themselves that the unnecessary adjournment of a hearing should always be avoided; the consequent delay can cause hardship or distress to a party, and can waste valuable public resources which could be more efficiently and properly used.

3. Tribunals will wish, therefore, to articulate very carefully the reason for an adjournment before initiating or agreeing to that action, and to be sure, in those cases where the seeking or obtaining of additional evidence [medical or otherwise] is the reason for the adjournment, that that additional evidence is likely to assist the tribunal in its deliberations and is relevant to the issue to be decided.

4. I regard it as good practice in the fulfilment of the judicial role to articulate the reason for the adjournment in the written decision, and I would hope that tribunal chairmen would follow that practice. An entry reading simply "adjourned for additional evidence", I would not regard as meeting that criterion of good judicial practice. A form now exists [ITS/ADJ] which is to be used on every occasion when a tribunal adjourns a hearing and which is to be handed to the parties who are present before the tribunal or sent within 2 days of the hearing to any absent party.

Where the tribunal accepts that it needs further evidence

5. The tribunal's judicial task is to determine an appeal before it, on the basis of its assessment of the evidence produced, its findings of fact following such assessment and its application of the relevant law to those findings. Experience shows that in the normal course of events the evidence produced is such as to enable the tribunal properly to complete this task without an adjournment for the purpose of producing further evidence.

6. However, there may be circumstances where the available evidence is insufficient so that it is in the interests of justice for the tribunal to exercise its discretion to adjourn.

7. It is important for the adjournment decision to record who should supply any further evidence i.e. the appellant, his representative or the AO and by when it should be supplied; it is also important to impose a timescale for the case to be relisted. The direction should always make it clear whether the case is to be listed before the same or a differently constituted tribunal. The reservation of cases to the same tribunal should only be done in exceptional circumstances i.e. where substantial oral evidence has been taken or complex legal argument is under consideration.

8. If the tribunal is exercising its power under Section 53 of the Social Security Administration Act 1992 so that the ITS is required to take some action that exercise of power should be expressly indicated on the form ITS [ADJ] and attention should be drawn to the need for the ITS administration to take relevant action and to the form which that action should take.

9. Where the tribunal adjourns for the ITS to obtain a medical report it is important that the report is obtained expeditiously, so that the matter can be relisted without unnecessary delay. There is, therefore, a need to publicise the ways in which the tribunal's decision to adjourn to obtain a medical report may be formulated in such a way as to minimise any such delay.

10. As a first step the form ITS/ADJ on which the chairman records the tribunal's decision to adjourn, should clearly summarise the reasons why the tribunal considered that it should adjourn and why it considered that the ITS should obtain a medical report. Form ITS/FME1 should be contemporaneously completed in all such cases. The purpose of the form is to specify the kind of report being sought, from whom, whether it requires fresh examination or review of existing medical records, what aspects of the claimed benefit it addresses and to what questions such as diagnosis or treatment, it should be directed. This information is essential to enable the formulation of a proper request for a medical report.

11. It is the chairman's responsibility to complete ITS/FME1, which should be done in the hearing room and in the presence of any party who has attended the hearing so that a medical member of the tribunal or the medical assessor can advise upon its content. The use of form DAT 32 is now discontinued.

Further consideration

12. Tribunals should always remind themselves that where benefit has been withdrawn upon review, the burden of providing that that action was justified, upon the balance of probabilities, lies upon the AO. Where the tribunal is of the opinion that the AO should have sought medical or other evidence to put before the tribunal in order to discharge that burden, but has failed to do so without good cause, the tribunal will always want to ask itself [albeit recognising that they exercise an inquisitorial jurisdiction] whether the tribunal should expend resources in and cause further delay by seeking evidence which the AO should have obtained in order to support the review decision. The preferable course may be either to adjourn to enable the AO to seek the necessary evidence within a specified timescale [if a just decision cannot be reached without that evidence and if the PO can offer an acceptable explanation for the failure to produce it] or to decide the case by reference to the facts before the tribunal and the applicable burden of proof.

13. A similar problem may arise where an appellant, on first application for the benefit, appeals against the disallowance, produces no medical evidence yet suggests that it is available and that the tribunal should seek it. It may also occur that, during the course of the hearing, the tribunal identifies a need for additional medical evidence. Tribunals should remind themselves that in these cases the burden of proof lies with the appellant [also on the balance of probabilities] and that they should then consider the extent to which public resources should be expended if what is then proposed is the seeking of evidence which, strictly, the appellant should have sought and produced before the hearing. That consideration may not be appropriate where the tribunal itself identifies the need for further evidence. In deciding whether or not to adjourn and, if so, for what purpose, tribunals should, while reminding themselves that they exercise an inquisitorial jurisdiction, consider the likely availability of the suggested evidence within a reasonable timescale, its relevance to the issues before the tribunal and [where appropriate] the appellant's reasons for not providing that evidence to the tribunal. If the tribunal decides to adjourn for evidence to be obtained, the adjournment decision should make it clear whether the ITS or the appellant is to obtain the evidence and should impose realistic timescales for evidence provision and relisting of the hearing.

14. The practical directions for the obtaining of medical reports and other medical evidence are contained in President's Circular No. 13.

June 1997

President's Circular No. 2

RECORDING AND NOTIFYING TRIBUNAL PROCEEDINGS AND DECISIONS: FORM AND CONTENT

Record of proceedings

1. In this area amendments occurred by virtue of the Social Security [Adjudication] and Child Support Amendment Regulations 1996 which came into force on 28 February 1996. As a result of those regulations, chairmen should keep a written record of evidence [both oral and written], submissions and the progress of the hearing [a "record of proceedings"] on form ITS[RP]; that record will be kept for 18 months and supplied in its handwritten form to any party to the proceedings who requests them.

2. Chairmen are reminded that the presence of the regulation does not mean that the record of proceedings should never be issued. It is a chairman's decision whether to do so and he/she might consider it prudent [and a saving of administrative resources] to request that a copy of that record be supplied in particularly contentious cases where an appeal—and a request for a copy of the record of proceedings—is likely. If that is done, the full decision [see paragraph 12 below] should record that a copy of the manuscript note of proceedings on form ITS[RP] is attached.

Oral notification

3. Whenever an appellant or his/her representative attends a tribunal hearing, I regard it as good judicial practice and in the interests of the appellant for a tribunal chairman orally to announce the result at the conclusion of the hearing, unless there are compelling reasons to the contrary. This applies whatever the nature of the tribunal's decision.

4. The following are examples of "compelling reasons":—
   a. An appellant/representative does not or cannot wait to hear the decision.
   b. An appellant/representative cannot hear or understand the decision.
   c. There is reason to believe that, if told the decision, a party will become distressed or distraught.
   d. There is reason to believe that a party will become violent to himself or another, or to property, if told the decision at the conclusion of the hearing.
   e. The decision is too complex to explain to a party without causing undue confusion or anxiety.

5. The chairman should normally use non-technical ordinary language to indicate the decision and its effect, and should explain the procedures for written notification.

Written notification

6. As a result of further Adjudication Regulation changes following the enactment of Statutory Instrument 1996 No. 2450, new written decision procedures come into effect on and from 21 October 1996. The new procedures apply to SSATs, MATs, DATs and CSATs but not to VDTs. The Adjudication Regulations provided, inter alia, for the introduction of decision notices on the day of the hearing and for statements of the tribunal's findings of fact and reasons for its decision to be provided later, either on request or of a chairman's own motion. In this Circular, the latter document is referred to, for convenience, as a "full decision".

7. Decision Notices. A decision notice is a form which the regulation gives me the power to approve. I have approved a form of decision notice for use in each jurisdiction to be known respectively as ITS[DN][SSAT], [CSAT] etc.; only that form as drafted has my approval under the Adjudication Regulations. That printed form should not be amended nor should anything [other than an AWT schedule] be attached to it. The decision notice is to be legibly handwritten by the chairman; the tribunal clerk will hand a copy of the carbonised decision notice to the parties as they leave the hearing. They will, either at the same time or earlier, have been advised in writing of their right to appeal and to apply for a record of proceedings and a full decision, but tribunal chairmen may want specifically to enquire of the parties whether they want a full decision, since the earlier such a request is notified, the less the effort expended in producing it.

The decision notice dispenses with the need for separate forms AT3A or DAT28A [the use of which has been discontinued].

8. Decision notices must be written and issued in every case and at the hearing where the decision has been announced. If the decision has not been announced or following determination of a case in the absence of a party or by consideration of the papers alone, the decision notice should be written by the chairman on the day of the hearing and sent by the clerk to any party who was not present at the hearing on the next working day following the hearing. The decision notice will record the decision of the tribunal [in sufficient detail, where an appellant is successful, to enable immediate payment of benefit] and will provide for inclusion of a summary of the tribunal's reasons for that decision [see paragraph 9, below].

9. Where there has been no request for a full decision at the hearing and the chairman does not intend to issue one, the decision notice will contain a summary of the tribunal's reasons for its decision: that summary is not intended to be an exhaustive recital of the tribunal's process of reasoning but to be a two or three sentence explanation of the reasons for success or failure. For example, in an IB case, the relevant paragraph could read "After examining all the claimed and relevant descriptor areas, we were satisfied that the appellant could not be awarded sufficient points to reach the AWT threshold of 15" or "After examining all the claimed and relevant descriptor areas, the appellant satisfied the AWT as a result of our award of points with reference to the following physical functions i.e. walking [7 points], standing [7 points] and hearing [8 points]." Where a full decision is to be issued or where an extempore decision has been given and taped, the relevant paragraph of the decision notice could read "A written document, which includes the reasons for our decision, will be issued to the parties later" or "The reasons for our decision were explained to the parties at the hearing."

10. There are three decision notices for use in DATs: the ITS/DN/DAT/REF, the ITS/DN/DAT/DLA/AW and the ITS/DN/DAT/AA/AW, the first recording a refusal for both DLA and AA, the second an award of DLA and the third an award of AA. In those cases where the award of both care and mobility components of DLA are in issue, but the tribunal awards one and not the other, chairmen should be aware that **both** DLA decision notices should be issued and that on the award notice the box marked "linked Decision" should be ticked.

11. It is always for a chairman to decide whether only a decision notice, or a decision notice and full decision, needs to be issued in any particular case. He/she should always consider very carefully to what extent the decision notice alone is appropriate for the case which the tribunal has just decided, bearing in mind the area and scope of dispute, and the likelihood of appeal.

12. There may be some cases which are so straightforward that, even if requested to provide a full decision, the chairman will not be able to add anything to what is contained in the decision notice. Where that is the case, the decision notice should clearly state on its face that it "includes the full statement of the reasons for the tribunal's decision and of its findings on questions of fact material thereto to which Regulation 23[3A] of the Social Security [Adjudication] Regulations 1995 refers".

13. Full Decisions. A chairman will need to prepare a decision which contains "the reasons for the tribunal's decision and its findings on questions of fact material thereto" only if he/she decides to do so or if a party, either at the hearing or within 21 days of issue of a decision notice, so requests. Chairmen will note that the full decision incorporates, by specific reference therein, the terms of the decision notice already issued.

14. If a chairman wishes to give a full decision at the hearing, the regulations provide that he/she may choose to deliver an extempore decision which can be tape-recorded. If a chairman chooses that option and if a request is made for a transcript of that record, it will be typed and sent to the chairman for signature. **It will not be possible for the chairman to correct or alter the typed transcript, except in the case of typing errors**.

15. If a chairman decides upon, or a party requests, preparation of a full decision at the hearing, I would expect it to be ordinarily available within 14 days of the hearing. Chairmen may use any of the currently approved methods for preparation of that decision and should ensure that that decision is provided to the ITS office concerned within 3 working days. The chairman should ensure, whenever a clerk is not present in the tribunal room to appreciate that a full decision will be issued, that the clerk is so advised; the intention to issue a full decision should also be apparent from the face of the decision notice [see paragraph 9. above].

16. If a party requests preparation of a full decision within 21 days of the issue of the decision notice, the chairman concerned must be notified of that request within 3 days of its receipt in ITS offices and he/she must be sent, within that same timescale, a copy of the tribunal papers [and of any additional written evidence received thereat], of the record of proceedings, of the decision notice and of the written request for the full decision. Chairmen should aim to provide that full decision to the ITS office within 3 working days of receipt of the request. I consider that a chairman may, at his/her discretion, agree to issue a full decision even though the request is made outside the 21 day period. If such a request is made, but refused, I do not, however, consider that a chairman is obliged to give reasons for that decision.

17. Chairmen will no doubt wish to keep some personal record of the identities of those present at the hearing and of the rationale of decisions and closed session discussion against the possibility that a full decision may be later requested. For that reason, judicial notebooks have been acquired and will be available to all chairmen. They are personal records to be kept by chairmen and are *not* to be deposited in ITS offices for safekeeping; it should be noted that it is my opinion that these notebooks will not contain formal records, the production of which I would expect to be compellable either by parties or by the appellate jurisdictions.

18. I regret that ITS resources cannot be used for the precautionary recording of full decisions simply in case one should later be requested. Clerks have, therefore, been advised to decline the use of ITS recording equipment unless it is indicated in the decision notice that a full decision will be issued or the chairman, having initially decided not to issue a full decision, changes his/her mind on the day of the hearing and so advises the clerk. If chairmen wish to do so on their own equipment, that is a matter for them but it would obviously assist if it was ensured that that equipment is compatible with that in use in ITS offices.

19. The issue of a decision notice does not affect rights of appeal against the tribunal's decision. Time limits for appeal now run from the date of issue of the full decision.

November 1997

President's Circular No. 3

NO SMOKING POLICY

1. For the health and comfort of all who use tribunal hearing rooms, there shall be no smoking in these rooms whether or not a hearing is in progress.

2. Chairmen and members should accept it as their personal responsibility to ensure compliance with the rule. Observance of this rule is a condition of continued appointment to the tribunals operated by the Independent Tribunal Service.

3. Administrative arrangements already ensure that appropriate notices are posted to discourage smoking in all parts of tribunal suites.

President's Circular No. 4

DOMICILIARY HEARINGS

1. Tribunals have the power to hold a hearing at a claimant's home in appropriate cases: they are known as domiciliary visits [DVs]. A tribunal is never under a legal obligation to hold such a hearing.

2. Administrative staff of the ITS are not to arrange a DV before the tribunal has convened to hear the case, unless the President, a regional or any full-time chairman has so instructed. That instruction will generally not be given unless it is obvious that there are no other reasonable means of ensuring that a just decision is made by the tribunal, taking into account the principles of natural justice.

3. A tribunal or chairman should always give very careful consideration to the facts before ordering a DV. In particular, consider whether:—

(a) there is already sufficient evidence on which to allow an appeal in full,

(b) sufficient evidence to reach a just decision can reasonably be obtained in some other way, including those indicated in paragraph 4 below, and

(c) there is any other reasonable way to obtain the attendance of the parties, including those indicated in paragraph 5 below.

4. "Other ways of obtaining evidence" include:—

(a) requesting the attendance of a family member, a carer or some other witness who could give the evidence that could be given by the parties;

(b) requesting written or recorded evidence from the parties, a carer or some other witness;

(c) referring a question of special difficulty to an expert [including a general practitioner] for report under section 53 of the Social Security Administration Act 1993;

(d) the exercise of the power of the chairman to give such directions as he may consider necessary or desirable for just, effective and efficient conduct of the proceedings under Regulation 2[1][aa] of S.I. 1996 No. 2450.

5. "Other ways of obtaining the attendance of the parties" include:—

(a) providing a taxi or a private hire car to bring the parties from home to the tribunal hearing, and

(b) arranging for the parties to be brought from home to the usual venue by St John's Ambulance or similar suitable vehicle.

6. In deciding whether to adjourn and order a DV, a tribunal, in particular, should also take into account:—

(a) that members of the tribunal may have disabilities which would cause difficulties in arranging a DV, and

(b) that it may often be preferable to adjourn for another hearing at the usual venue, rather than to arrange an unnecessary DV.

7. There may be occasions when only the obtaining of a General Practitioner's report will enable a tribunal or chairman to make an informed decision. Provided that unacceptable delay will not be occasioned by such a request, such a report may be requested before a tribunal or chairman makes the decision.

June 1997

President's Circular No. 5

[Withdrawn March 1996]

President's Circular No. 6

SETTING-ASIDE APPLICATIONS: CONDUCT OF TRIBUNAL CHAIRMEN/MEMBERS/ASSESSORS/ITS STAFF

1. Regulations provide that a tribunal may set aside the decision of its own or of another tribunal where it is just to do so on the grounds that:—
  (a) a relevant document was not sent or received at the appropriate time by a party [or a representative] or by the adjudicating authority who gave the decision,
  (b) a party [or a representative] was not present, or
  (c) the interests of justice so require.
The latter ground has been interpreted to relate only to procedural irregularities, since to do otherwise would undermine the right of appeal to a Commissioner and the finality of tribunal decisions [subject to appeal or review].

2. The tribunal must firstly decide and make appropriate findings of fact, in respect of sub-para a, b or c above. Then, if one [or more] section is satisfied, the tribunal should consider whether it is *just* to set aside the earlier decision on that ground. The tribunal has discretion; a useful test to be applied in all setting aside decisions is *whether any party had reasonable grounds to believe that there has or may have been unfair prejudice as a result of what occurred.*

3. Tribunals will be very familiar with the operation of the regulation in routine cases. This circular also draws to your attention the issues which arise where the basis of the setting-aside application is an allegation concerning the conduct of a tribunal chairman/member/assessor or other member of ITS staff on the day of the hearing.

4. A different tribunal should always deal with such a case; it will have no way of knowing whether the complaint is true, misconceived or malicious. Such allegations are easy to make and it would be unfortunate if it ever became the case that, whenever such allegations were made, the application was automatically granted, since it would encourage the making of false allegations where an appellant had lost his/her earlier appeal.

5. Whenever a complaint about the conduct of tribunal personnel or staff on the day of the hearing forms the basis for a setting aside application, the tribunal should firstly decide, in the event that the complaint should be correct, whether what is complained of amounts to a procedural irregularity, such that it is just to set aside the previous decision.

6. If the tribunal decides that the complaint could properly lead to the decision being set aside, the tribunal should adjourn the application to enable responses to be sought from the appropriate tribunal personnel in accordance with President's Instruction No. 10 and for the application to be heard by a different tribunal.

7. If the tribunal decides that, even if correct, the complaint could not properly lead to the decision being set aside, it should so record in its decision rejecting the application.

President's Circular No. 7

TRIBUNALS' USE OF "LIBERTY TO RESTORE"

1. The order "Liberty to restore" is a common one in civil jurisdictions: it has not had extensive use in ITS tribunals but it is appropriate to give guidance about its use.

2. There is a proper use of the order where a hearing is adjourned sine die, when no relisting action is anticipated unless a party so requests. Its use in these circumstances will be rare in the ITS jurisdictions.

3. Tribunals should beware of too-ready use of the order in other circumstances. It can be a proper order, but tribunals should be aware:—

    (a) that it is good judicial practice to specify when making the order for what purpose the hearing may be restored,

    (b) that it is good judicial practice to use the order only when, for some specified reason, part of the original hearing remains unsettled, and

    (c) that it is never good judicial practice to use the order when the result of it, consciously or otherwise, is the avoidance of otherwise proper review or appeal procedures.

4. Where a tribunal uses the order [other than as envisaged in para 2 above], it will have embarked upon the hearing, yet will have decided that, for some reason, its order is incomplete. It will have decided not to adjourn. In consequence, where a tribunal has given liberty to restore in such circumstances it is appropriate for the *same tribunal* to consider the restored issue[s] in the light of the evidence which it has already heard.

5. A tribunal making such an order should therefore give appropriate instructions to the listing officer, so that the file may be marked accordingly.

President's Circular No. 8

[Withdrawn February 1996]

President's Circular No. 9

ACTION IN MULTIPLE CASES WHERE THE DECISION OF A COMMISSIONER OR OF A SUPERIOR COURT IS AWAITED

1. Where these cases are concerned, [which are referred to generically as "appeal dependent cases"] it is always necessary to consider the best way of dealing with them. On many occasions, I will agree that it is desirable that they should not be listed for hearing until the decision in the lead case is known.

2. Where that action has been taken, appellants and their representatives will have been informed of the reason for that action in the terms of the specimen letter attached, and will also have been informed of their right to require a case to be listed despite my direction to the contrary.

3. Such cases may, therefore, come before a tribunal. If that occurs, tribunals will have before them a copy of the ITS letter to the appellant/representative and of any additional information, giving the full context of the case and its likely progress through the appellate levels beyond the ITS. It will then be necessary for the tribunal to decide whether to hear the case or to adjourn it, pending resolution of the relevant issue[s].

4. Tribunals should ensure that they are in possession of all such additional information before making a decision. They must make that decision judicially on the facts before them, having considered the submissions of the presenting officer and/or the appellant and his/her representative.

5. Tribunals should bear in mind that, although delay will occur if there is an adjournment:—

    a. a successful appellant [if the case had been heard] is likely to have gained little, since the Secretary of State may well appeal the tribunal's decision, which will permit the suspension of payment of any awarded benefit in such disputed circumstances, and

    b. all benefit routes are not closed to an appellant who alleges that he/she suffers financial hardship as a result of the delay in resolution of the appeal.

6. It sometimes occurs that a party or representative before the tribunal will allege that "there is a lead case pending", although the tribunal has no information before it of the type mentioned in the preceding paragraphs. Tribunals should be wary of acting upon unsubstantiated suggestion and should, unless compelling detail is provided and if there is sufficient information and evidence before it, decide the case according to the existing law.

June 1997

SPECIMEN LETTER

Dear

Important information about your appeal

1. I am writing about your appeal against *[here describe the nature of the appeal]*.

2. Your appeal, with many others, involves a difficult point of law. *[Here describe the legal issue]*. Consequently, *[here describe who has appealed, to which court and the time frame for appeal]*. Until then, therefore, the law is not clear or settled.

3. If your case was to come before a tribunal and be decided in your favour, I understand that the Adjudication Officer is likely to appeal that decision to the Commissioners. Any advantage you may have gained as a result of the decision could then be lost, since, pending the appeal in your case being decided by the Commissioner, the Secretary of State has, by law, the power to suspend payment of any benefit awarded by the tribunal. In view of that, and of the number of similar cases, a great deal of time and energy could be wasted with little positive outcome for any of the parties. For this reason, we consider that it is in the interests of all concerned not to hear your case—or that of any of the other similar placed appellants—until this period of uncertainty is resolved by the decision of the *[here insert identity of appeal court]*. You have my assurance that your appeal will then be dealt with urgently.

4. I appreciate that this letter may come as a disappointment to you. However, I hope that you will accept our concern about delays which arise when difficult questions have to be resolved in the Courts.

5. I will keep you informed from time to time about how the lead appeal is progressing. However, it may be some months before I have any new information to report. You should be aware that if you disagree with the decision not to list your case for hearing for the present, you can request the Independent Tribunal Service [ITS] to list it for hearing. If you do, I am informed that the department's representative is likely to apply for an adjournment; if that is granted by the tribunal, it means that resources have been used which could have been applied to the determination of other cases not affected by pending legislation. I hope, therefore, that you will agree that the decision taken is in the best interests of all concerned.

6. It may also help you to know that not all benefit routes are closed to you while the legal issue is going through the Courts. You should contact your local office of the Benefits Agency for advice or seek that advice from representative sources, such as the Citizens' Advice Bureau or a local welfare rights' organisation. The Secretary of State does also have the discretion to decide not to suspend any benefit which may be awarded by a tribunal if hardship is caused by that suspension. You may, therefore, use that argument if you ask for your case to be listed, despite this letter, and if the Department's representative seeks to persuade the tribunal to adjourn your application. You should realise, however, that the discretion has only been exercised in severe cases in the recent past.

7. I am sending a copy of this letter to major representatives' organisations, although not necessarily to individual representatives. Any enquiries should be addressed to this office.

Yours sincerely,

President's Circular No. 10

CORRECTING ACCIDENTAL ERRORS IN TRIBUNAL DECISIONS

1. Regulation 9 of the Social Security (Adjudication) Regulations 1995 permits the above procedure to be carried out by the original tribunal or by a tribunal of like status.

2. Commissioner's decision CSSB/76/93 requires that procedure to be effected by a sitting tribunal and indicates that it should not be done by postal confirmation, as previously occurred.

3. Wherever possible, correction of a decision should be put to a tribunal which is chaired by the chairman of the original tribunal, since he/she will have prepared the relevant decision.

4. If, for any reason, unacceptable delay will occur in seeking a correction decision from a tribunal chaired by the original chairman, a differently constituted tribunal of like status may be asked to make that decision after the reaction of the original chairman has been obtained, either in writing or by telephone. His/her comment should be put before the correcting tribunal and it is within the judicial discretion of that tribunal to decide whether it feels competent to make the suggested, or any, correction to the original decision.

5. If, for any reason, the reaction of the original chairman cannot be obtained without unacceptable delay, a correction decision may be sought from any differently constituted tribunal of like status without the original chairman's comment. If that occurs, it is within the judicial discretion of the latter tribunal to decide whether it feels competent to make the suggested, or any, correction to the original decision.

6. A failure accurately and correctly to type a chairman's handwritten decision is not an error in the tribunal's decision requiring correction under regulation 9. In that case a correctly typed copy of the decision can be prepared and made available to the parties without formality.

7. In this Circular "unacceptable delay" means a delay of more than one calendar month.

September 1996

President's Circular No. 12

REFERENCES TO THE COURT OF JUSTICE OF THE EUROPEAN COMMUNITIES [ECJ]

1. Chairmen will all be aware that, in cases where appropriate guidance is sought, tribunals are empowered to make a direct reference to the European Court of Justice [ECJ].

2. Guidance in the procedures to be followed and about occasions on which such a reference may be appropriate is contained in the attached note, which has been issued by the ECJ.

3. The decision whether to make a reference to the ECJ must be a matter for an individual tribunal to decide. However, chairmen may consider it advisable to discuss whether a reference would be appropriate with me, or with their regional chairman, before making that decision.

4. The fact that such a reference has been made should always be notified to my office, together with a copy of all supporting and relevant papers.

November 1996

COURT OF JUSTICE OF THE EUROPEAN COMMUNITIES

Note for guidance on references by national courts for preliminary rulings

The development of the Community legal order is largely the result of cooperation between the Court of Justice of the European Community and national courts and tribunals through the preliminary ruling procedure under Article 177 of the EC Treaty and the corresponding provisions of the ECSC and Euratom Treaties.[1]

In order to make this cooperation more effective, and so enable the Court of Justice better to meet the requirements of national courts by providing helpful answers to preliminary questions, this Note for Guidance is addressed to all interested parties, in particular to all national courts and tribunals.

It must be emphasised that the Note is for guidance only and has no binding or interpretative effect in relation to the provisions governing the preliminary ruling procedure. It merely contains practical information which, in the light of experience in applying the preliminary ruling procedure, may help to prevent the kind of difficulties which the Court has sometimes encountered.

1. Any court or tribunal of a Member State may ask the Court of Justice to interpret a rule of Community law, whether contained in the Treaties or in acts of secondary law, if it consider that this is necessary for it to give judgment in a case pending before it.

Courts or tribunals against whose decisions there is no judicial remedy under national law must refer questions of interpretation arising before them to the Court of Justice, unless the Court has already ruled on the point or unless the correct application of the rule of Community law is obvious.[2]

2. The Court of Justice has jurisdiction to rule on the validity of acts of the Community institutions. National courts or tribunals may reject a plea challenging the validity of such an act. But where a national court (even one whose decision is still subject to appeal) intends to question the validity of a Community act, it must refer that question to the Court of Justice.[3]

Where, however, a national court or tribunal has serious doubts about the validity of a Community act on which a national measure is based, it may, in exceptional cases, temporarily suspend application of the latter measure or grant other interim relief with respect to it. It must then refer the question of validity to the Court of Justice, stating the reasons for which it considers that the Community act is not valid.[4]

3. Questions referred for a preliminary ruling must be limited to the interpretation or validity of a provision of Community law, since the Court of Justice does not have jurisdiction to interpret national law or assess its validity. It is for the referring court or tribunal to apply the relevant rule of Community law in the specific case pending before it.

4. The order of the national court or tribunal referring a question to the Court of Justice for a preliminary ruling may be in any form allowed by national procedural law. Reference of a question or questions to the Court of Justice generally involves stay of the national proceedings until the Court has given its ruling, but the decision to stay proceedings is one which it is for the national court alone to take in accordance with its own national law.

5. The order for reference containing the question or questions referred to the Court will have to be translated by the Court's translators into the other official languages of the Community. Questions concerning the interpretation or validity of Community law are frequently of general interest and the Member States and Community institutions are entitled to submit observations. It is therefore desirable that the reference should be drafted as clearly and precisely as possible.

6. The order for reference should contain a statement of reasons which is succinct but sufficiently complete to give the Court, and those to whom it must be notified (the Member States, the Commission and in certain cases the Council and the European Parliament), a clear understanding of the factual and legal context of the main proceedings.[5]

In particular, it should include:
— a statement of the facts which are essential to a full understanding of the legal significance of the main proceedings;
— an exposition of the national law which may be applicable;
— a statement of the reasons which have prompted the national court to refer the question or questions to the Court of Justice; and
— where appropriate, a summary of the arguments of the parties.

The aim should be to put the Court of Justice in a position to give the national court an answer which will be of assistance to it.

The order for reference should also be accompanied by copies of any documents needed for a proper understanding of the case, especially the text of the applicable national provisions. However, as the case-file or documents annexed to the order for reference are not always translated in full into the other official languages of the Community, the national court should ensure that the order for reference itself includes all the relevant information.

7. A national court or tribunal may refer a question to the Court of Justice as soon as it finds that a ruling on the point or points of interpretation or validity is necessary to enable it to give judgment. It must be stressed, however, that it is not for the Court of Justice to decide issues of fact or to resolve disputes as to the interpretation of application of rules of national law. It is therefore desirable that a decision to refer should not be taken until the national proceedings have reached a stage where the national court is able to define, if only as a working hypothesis, the factual and legal context of the question; on any view, the administration of justice is likely to be best served if the reference is not made until both sides have been heard.[6]

8. The order for reference and the relevant documents should be sent by the national court directly to the Court of Justice, by registered post, addressed to:

The Registry,
Court of Justice of the European Communities
L-2925 Luxembourg
Telephone (352) 43031

The Court Registry will remain in contact with the national court until judgment is given, and will send copies of the various documents (written obvservations, Report for the Hearing, opinion of the Advocate General). The Court will also send its judgment to the national court. The Court would appreciate being informed about the application of its judgment in the national proceedings and being sent a copy of the national court's final decision.

9. Proceedings for a preliminary ruling before the Court of Justice are free of charge. The Court does not rule on costs.

1. A preliminary ruling procedure is also provided for by protocols to several conventions concluded by the Member States, in particular the Brussels Convention on Jurisdiction and the Enforcement of Judgments in Civil and Commercial Matters.

2. Judgment in Case 283/81 *CILFIT v. Ministry of Health* [1982] E.C.R. 3415.

3. Judgment in Case 314/85 *Foto-Frost v. Hauptzollamt Lübeck-Ost* [1987] E.C.R. 4199.

4. Judgments in Joined Cases C-143/88 and C-92/89 *Zuckerfabrik Soest* [1991] E.C.R. I-415 and in Case C-465/93 *Atlanta Fruchthandelsgesellschaft* [1995] E.C.R. I-3761.

5. Judgment in Joined Cases C-320/90, C-321/90 and C-322/90 *Telemarsicabruzzo* [1993] E.C.R. I-393.

6. Judgment in Case 70/77 *Simmenthal v Amministrazione delle Finanze dello Stato* [1978] E.C.R. 1453.

President's Circular No. 13

THE OBTAINING OF FURTHER MEDICAL EVIDENCE
[ALL JURISDICTIONS]
BY ORDER OF THE TRIBUNAL

1. The ITS has now introduced new procedures where a tribunal decides that the ITS should obtain further medical evidence following an adjournment of an appeal. Requests for medical reports will be actioned by the ITS administrative staff [not BAMS/DBC as was previously the case] and issued direct to the medical profession. Requests for Examining Medical Practitioner [EMP] reports in DATs and Hospital Case Notes' [HCNs] extracts in MATs will, in the future, be processed by the ITS administration via a medical services' contract with the private sector [these requests are still currently being processed via BAMS until the new contract is in place, however administrative staff will prepare the request before issuing to BAMS/DBC].

2. Further changes are as follows:—
  a. Form DAT 32—this is now obsolete,
  b. Introduction of form ITS/FME 1—this form should be used in all jurisdictions when FME is required in the form of:—
      Examining Medical Practitioner [EMP] reports
      GP factual reports
      Hospital factual reports
      Consultant reports
      Any other specialist reports, for example, school reports, and
  c. It is the chairman's responsibility to complete the ITS/FME1, which should be done in the hearing room and in the presence of any party who has attended the hearing so that the medical member/assessor of the tribunal can advise upon the content of the questions to be addressed.

3. Tribunals should remind themselves, in the interests of a prompt resolution of an appeal, that GP factual and EMP reports can usually be received within 4 weeks, whereas other reports can often take several months to obtain.

4. Referrals back to BAMS for the All Work Test [AWT] [IB cases only]. AWT referrals should continue to be requested in the usual way on the ITS/

DN/ADJ. Administrative staff will continue to forward these requests to the originating Benefit Agency [BA] office as is currently the case.

5. X-rays [MAT cases only]. Form MAT 5 series should continue to be used and requests issued directly to the owner of the x-rays. Requests for new x-rays will also continue to be processed in the usual way.

6. Hospital Case Notes [MAT cases only]. Sight of the original case notes can be requested where needed but tribunals should always consider very carefully whether those notes are needed. It is the case that notes of treatment at the time of injury will not always be helpful. MATs are often concerned not with the treatment of the injury but with the resultant disablement, which they have to assess. If production of HCNs is considered relevant, wherever possible an extract of HCNs should be requested, as suggested in my memorandum of 1 April 1997 [a copy of which is attached to this Circular]. These requests should be made on the ITS/DN/ADJ. Another alternative to sight of the HCNs is the hospital factual report, see paragraph 2b. above.

June 1997

President's Circular No. 14

THE SOCIAL SECURITY ACT 1998—SOCIAL SECURITY APPEAL
TRIBUNAL [SSAT] COMPOSITION

1. The Act came into force on 21 May 1998.

2. It amended Section 41 of the Social Security Administration Act 1992 so that it reads:—

(1) A Social Security Appeal Tribunal shall consist of a chairman **sitting either alone or with one or two other persons**.

Subsections (2) and (6) have also been amended but only consequential upon the amendment above.

No other changes have been made either to Section 41 or to the regulations which relate to tribunal composition. That includes the same sex provision and the need to obtain consent to a reduction in numbers [though both provisions will have to be considered in the light of the amendment].

3. The following guidelines are designed to ensure that there is uniformity across the ITS.

4. Unless and until I issue guidelines to the contrary, a SSAT should comprise, as now, a legally qualified chairman and two lay members, with the three exceptions covered in paragraphs 5–7 below.

5. SETTING ASIDES: As from the date when the Act was passed, applications to set aside pursuant to Regulation 10 of the Social Security [Adjudication] Regulations 1995 [whether considered on the written representations of the parties or orally] may be heard by a full-time legally qualified chairman sitting alone.

6. PAPER DETERMINATIONS: As from the date when the Act was passed, but only where the parties have been given advance notice of this legislative change, appeals which are determined on the written representations of both parties may be determined by a legally qualified chairman sitting alone.

7. REPLACEMENT SIDE MEMBERS NOT AVAILABLE: As from the date when the Act was passed, where a tribunal comprising a legally qualified chairman and two members has been summoned to hear an oral appeal, the hearing may proceed in the absence of one or two lay members provided:—

a. advance notice of legislative change has been given to the appellant,

    b. one or both lay members cancel in advance or fail to arrive on the day, and

    c. all reasonable efforts to find a replacement[s] have been unsuccessful [the clerk will certify to that effect].

8. Where an appellant has not been notified of the legislative change and a lay member is not available, the existing "incomplete" tribunal provisions will apply [i.e. consent of the appellant to proceed]. The clerk's certificate will indicate whether an appellant has been notified of the legislative change.

9. Please note that in Incapacity Benefit cases a medical assessor is still necessary in both oral and written appeals.

10. A copy of the relevant parts of Schedule 6 is appended to this Circu-

lar.**May 1998**

Annex to President's Circular No. 14

THE RELEVANT PARTS OF SCHEDULE 6 OF THE SOCIAL SECURITY ACT 1998

SCHEDULE 6

TRANSITORY PROVISIONS

CONSTITUTION OF APPEAL TRIBUNALS

1. *In relation to any time before the commencement of section 7 of this Act so far as it related to appeals under section 12 of this Act, section 41 of the Administration Act [constitution of social security appeal tribunals] shall have effect as if—*

    (a) in subsection (1), for the words "and two other persons" there were substituted the words "sitting either alone or with one or two other persons".

    (b) in subsection (2), for the words "The members other than the chairman" there were substituted the words "Any members other than the chairman";

    (c) for subsection (6) there were substituted the following subsection—

        "(6) Where the appeal tribunal hearing a case consists of more than one member it shall, if practicable, include at least one member who is of the same sex as the claimant."

President's Circular No. 15

THE SOCIAL SECURITY ACT 1998—"DOWN TO THE DATE OF DECISION"

1. The Act came into force on 21 May 1998.

2. Schedule 6 contains a group of transitory provisions which forbids some of our tribunals from considering circumstances which may have arisen after the decision appealed against was made. They are as follows:—

Claims no longer subsisting after decisions made

2. In relation to any time before the commencement of section 8(2) of this Act, section 21 of the Administration Act [decision of adjudication officer] shall have effect as if after subsection [6] there were inserted the following subsection—

"(7) Where at any time a claim for a benefit to which section 20 above applies is decided by an adjudication officer or by a social security appeal tribunal on a reference by such an officer—

    (a) the claim shall not be regarded as subsisting after that time; and

    (b) accordingly, the claimant shall not [without making a further claim] be entitled to the benefit on the basis of circumstances not obtaining at that time."

Appeals to tribunals

3(1) In relation to appeals brought after the passing of this Act and any time before the commencement of section 12(8)(b) of this Act, section 22 of the Administration Act [appeal to social security appeal tribunal] shall have effect as if after subsection (7) there were inserted the following subsection—

"(8) In deciding an appeal under this section, a social security appeal tribunal shall not take into account any circumstances not obtaining at the time when the decision appealed against was made."

3(2) In relation to such appeals and any such time, section 33 of that Act [appeal following reviews] shall have effect as if after subsection (6) there were inserted the following subsection—

"(7) The tribunal shall not take into account any circumstances not obtaining at the time when the decision appealed against was made."

Child support: appeals to tribunals

9. In relation to appeals brought after the passing of this Act and any time before the commencement of section 42 of this Act, section 20 the Child Support Act (appeals) shall have effect as if after subsection (4) there were inserted the following subsection—

"(5) In deciding an appeal under this section, the tribunal shall not take into account any circumstances not obtaining at the time when the decision appealed against was made."

3. These provisions apply to decisions made [paragraph 2] and appeals brought [paragraphs 3 and 9] after the passing of the Act.

4. The amendments are substantially in the same form:

"In deciding an appeal under this section, the tribunal shall not take into account any circumstances not obtaining at the time when the decision appealed against was made."

5. This is a mandatory requirement. There is no discretion.

6. "Circumstances not obtaining at the time when the decision ... was made." The amendments do not necessarily render irrelevant evidence which comes into existence after the decision. For example, a post decision medical report may well throw light on circumstances obtaining at the time of the decision. Always ask the question: was this circumstance obtaining at the time when the decision appealed against was made?

July 1998

President's Circular No. 16

THE SOCIAL SECURITY ACT 1998—SOCIAL SECURITY APPEAL TRIBUNAL [SSAT] COMPOSITION

1. This Circular should be read together with Circular No. 14.

2. In addition to the exceptions set out in paragraphs 5, 6 and 7 of that Circular, the following exceptions shall apply.

3. CORRECTIONS: As from 28 September 1998 corrections of accidental errors pursuant to Regulation 9 of the Social Security [Adjudication] Regulations 1995 may be heard by a legally qualified chairman sitting alone.

4. APPEALS INVOLVING THE ALL WORK TEST: As from 2 November 1998 appeals which involve a question as to whether a person satisfies the all work test may be determined by a legally qualified chairman sitting alone.

5. Regulation 21 of the Social Security [Incapacity for Work] [General] Regulations 1995 [which requires a tribunal to sit with a medical assessor in such cases] continues to apply.

September 1998

President's Circular No. 17

THE SOCIAL SECURITY ACT 1998—SOCIAL SECURITY APPEAL TRIBUNAL [SSAT] COMPOSITION

1. This Circular should be read together with President's Circulars No. 14 and No. 16 (which introduced changes to the composition of Social Security Appeal Tribunals).

2. As from 1 October 1999 all appeals heard by a SSAT (including those covered by President's Circulars No. 14 and No. 16) may be determined by a legally qualified chairman sitting alone.

May 1999

Practice Memorandum

SCHEDULE 6 OF THE SOCIAL SECURITY ACT 1998, WHICH AMENDS SECTIONS 23, 34 AND 48 OF THE SOCIAL SECURITY ADMINISTRATION ACT 1992

The 1992 Act has been amended by inserting into sections 23, 34 and 48 the words—

"(6A) If each of the principal parties to the appeal expresses the view that the decision appealed against was erroneous in point of law, the Commissioner may set aside the decision and remit the case to a tribunal with directions for its determination."

This Schedule of the Act has already been implemented.

The introduction of this amendment is intended to expedite the determination of some supported appeals and to ensure that the matter is returned to the tribunal below as early as possible. It will be necessary before this procedure can be followed that each party to the appeal—

(a) Expresses the view that the decision was erroneous in point of law.

(b) The Commissioner in his/her discretion is prepared to set the decision aside.

This Practice Memorandum is designed to assist parties in making full use of the amendment to the 1992 Act. The following practice is proposed—

1. In all new appeals, lodged on or after 17 August 1998 the Commissioner will consider using the new procedure if the appeal is supported. It will be open to a claimant to invite the Commissioner to deal with the matter under the provisions of Schedule 6.

2. The adjudication officer or Secretary of State in his submission in reply to the grounds will indicate that he expresses the view that the decision is erroneous in point of law, and invite the Commissioner to deal with the matter under the provisions of Schedule 6.

3. It is essential when the adjudication officer/Secretary of State supports an appeal and invite the Commissioner to adopt the procedure under Schedule 6 that the submission gives some indication of the error of law, a simple statement—

(1) Insufficient findings of fact.
(2) The conflict between the evidence is unresolved.
(3) The claimant is left guessing as to the conclusions reached by the tribunal.

will be unhelpful unless in short from the adjudication officer/Secretary of State indicate specifically the facts and matters relied upon.

There will, of course, be appeals where the adjudication officer/Secretary of State can adopt the grounds of appeal.

4. Appeals currently dealt with under Regulation 22(2) of the Social Security Commissioners Procedure Regulations 1987 will usually be suitable for disposal under Schedule 6.

5. The attention of both parties to an appeal is drawn to the language of Schedule 6 which gives a discretion to the Commissioner, the discretion is one that will be exercised judically.

In suitable appeals the Commissioner may initiate the procedure.

6. Schedule 6 provides that a Commissioner must give directions to the tribunal below on the remission of the appeal. It is open to the adjudication officer/ Secretary of State and the claimant to suggest an appropriate direction or directions.

7. The claimant when receiving the submission of the adjudication officer/ Secretary of State may if he is in broad agreement indicate that he has nothing to add and invite the Commissioner to deal with the matter under Schedule 6 and remit the appeal.

In Scotland in cases under the Schedule this step may be omitted as a pilot measure in advance of the bringing into force of the permanent provision under section 14(7) of the Social Security Act 1998.

8. It is not considered that Schedule 6 will usually be appropriate for appeals by the adjudication officer and Secretary of State.

9. This Practice Memorandum is issued on behalf of the Social Security Commissioners in England, Wales and Scotland, and its proper use will ensure the expedited return of the appeal to the tribunal.

Kenneth Machin QC
Chief Commissioner

11 August, 1998

Procedure in Schedule 6 Cases

This procedural note is not part of the Practice Memorandum.

Consideration for determination under Schedule 6 will arise when—

1. Leave to appeal has been granted by the chairman of the Social Security Tribunal or the Commissioner.

2. There will be a number of cases where the claimant may suggest that it is suitable for determination under Schedule 6, when lodging the appeal.

3. In appeals the adjudication officer/Secretary of State will before the Commissioner considers the application of Schedule 6—
   (a) Support the appeal.
   (b) Express the view that the decision is erroneous in point of law and say why.
   (c) Invite the Commissioner to determine the matter under the provisions of Schedule 6.

4. The claimant will see a copy of the adjudication officer/Secretary of State's submission and he will be able if he wishes to invited the Commissioner to determine the matter under the provisions of Schedule 6. It is likely in such cases that the claimant will have nothing to add in his reply.

In Scotland in cases under the Schedule this step may be omitted as a pilot measure in advance of the bringing into force of the permanent provision under section 14(7) of the Social Security Act 1998.

5. The Commissioner may in these circumstances—
   (a) Set aside the decision of the tribunal under appeal.
   (b) Remit the matter to the tribunal below.
   (c) Issue a direction which may be very short to the tribunal.

6. In a case where at any stage the Commissioner does not exercise his/her discretion under Schedule 6 further directions may be issued and the appeal will proceed in the normal way.

7. Schedule 6 can only be used for appeals where the matter must be sent back to the tribunal below.

8. It is anticipated that some existing supported appeals which are in the Commissioner's Office may be suitable for determination under Schedule 6. In such cases both parties will receive a communication from this Office prior to any determination.

Kenneth Machin QC
Chief Commissioner

11 August, 1998

INDEX

Index

1480

Index

Index